The Norton Anthology
of World Masterpieces

FIFTH EDITION

VOLUME 2

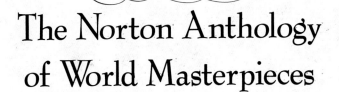

The Norton Anthology
of World Masterpieces

FIFTH EDITION

Maynard Mack, *General Editor*

Bernard M. W. Knox

John C. McGalliard

P. M. Pasinetti

Howard E. Hugo

Patricia Meyer Spacks

René Wellek

Kenneth Douglas

Sarah Lawall

VOLUME 2
Literature of Western Culture since the Renaissance

W · W · NORTON & COMPANY · *New York* · *London*

The text of this book is composed in Electra, with display type set in Bernhard
Modern. Composition by Vail-Ballou. Manufacturing by R. R. Donnelley. Book
design by Antonina Krass.

Library of Congress Cataloging in Publication Data
Main entry under title:

The Norton anthology of world masterpieces.

Includes indexes.
Contents: v. 1. Literature of Western culture through the Renaissance—
v. 2. Literature of Western culture since the Renaissance.
1. Literature Collections.   I. Mack, Maynard, 1909–
PN6014.N66   1985   808.8   84-18882
ISBN 0-393-95430-7 (v. 2)
ISBN 0-393-95434-X (pbk. : v. 2)

W. W. Norton & Company, Inc., 500 Fifth Avenue, New York, N.Y. 10110
W. W. Norton & Company Ltd., 37 Great Russell Street, London WC1B 3NU

2 3 4 5 6 7 8 9 0

Marcel Proust: "Swann's Way: Overture" from REMEMBRANCE OF THINGS PAST, Volume
    One, by Marcel Proust, translated by C. K. Scott Moncrieff and Terence Kilmartin. Trans-
    lation copyright © 1981 by Random House, Inc., and Chatto & Windus. Reprinted by
    permission of Random House, Inc., and Chatto & Windus.
Jean Racine: "Phaedra" from JEAN RACINE: FIVE PLAYS, translated by Kenneth Muir. Copy-
    right © 1960 by Kenneth Muir. Reprinted by permission of Hill and Wang, a division of
    Farrar, Straus and Giroux, Inc.
Jean Renoir: "Grand Illusion." Scenario, adaptation, and dialogue by Charles Spaak and Jean
    Renoir. English translation copyright © 1968 by Lorimer Publishing Limited. All rights
    reserved including the right of reproduction in whole or in part in any form.
Rainer Maria Rilke: "Archaic Torso of Apollo," "The First Elegy," and "The Ninth Elegy" from
    THE SELECTED POETRY OF RAINER MARIA RILKE, edited and translated by Ste-
    phen Mitchell. Copyright © 1982 by Steven Mitchell. Reprinted by permission of Random
    House, Inc.
Allain Robbe-Grillet: "The Secret Room" from SNAPSHOTS. Reproduced by kind permission
    of Grove Press, Inc., the author, and John Calder Publishers, Ltd. Copyright © 1962 by Les
    Editions de Minuit; 1968 by Grove Press, Inc.
Jean-Jacques Rousseau: "Confessions." Reprinted by permission of J. M. Dent and Sons, Ltd.
    (Everyman's Library).
Alexander Solzhenitsyn: "Matryona's Home," translated by H. T. Willetts. First published in May
    1963 issue of ENCOUNTER. Reprinted by permission. All rights reserved.
Wole Soyinka: "The Lion and the Jewel" from COLLECTED PLAYS 2 by Wole Soyinka (1974).
    © Wole Soyinka 1963. Reprinted by permission of Oxford University Press.
Wallace Stevens: "Sunday Morning," "Peter Quince at the Clavier," "Anecdote of the Jar," "The
    Emperor of Ice-Cream," copyright 1923 and renewed 1951 by Wallace Stevens. "The Idea
    of Order at Key West," copyright 1936 by Wallace Stevens and renewed 1964 by Holly
    Stevens. "The Man on the Dump," copyright 1942 by Wallace Stevens and renewed 1970
    by Holly Stevens. Reprinted from THE COLLECTED POEMS OF WALLACE STE-
    VENS, by permission of Alfred A. Knopf, Inc.
Jonathan Swift: "A Modest Proposal," reprinted by permission of Basil Blackwell Publishers, Oxford,
    England.
Leo Tolstoy: "The Death of Ivan Ilyich" from THE DEATH OF IVAN ILYICH AND OTHER
    STORIES by Leo Tolstoy, translated by Louise and Aylmer Maude (1935). Reprinted by
    permission of Oxford University Press.
Voltaire: From Voltaire, CANDIDE or Optimism. A Norton Critical Edition, translated and
    edited by Robert M. Adams, by permission of W. W. Norton & Company, Inc. Copyright
    © 1966 by W. W. Norton & Company, Inc.
Virginia Woolf: "An Unwritten Novel" from A HAUNTED HOUSE by Virginia Woolf, copy-
    right 1944, 1972 by Harcourt Brace Jovanovich, Inc. Reprinted by permission of the pub-
    lisher, the author's Literary Estate, and the Hogarth Press.
William Butler Yeats: "Leda and the Swan" and "Among School Children," copyright 1928 by
    Macmillan Publishing Co., Inc., renewed 1956 by Georgie Yeats. "Byzantium," copyright
    1933 by Macmillan Publishing Co., Inc., renewed 1961 by Bertha Georgie Yeats. "When
    You Are Old," copyright 1956 by Macmillan Publishing Co., Inc. Reprinted with permission
    of Macmillan Publishing Company, Michael Yeats, and Macmillan London Limited from
    COLLECTED POEMS by William Butler Yeats.

Contents

Masterpieces of the Nineteenth Century: Realism, Naturalism, and the New Poetry

Masterpieces of the Twentieth Century: Varieties of Modernism

Masterpieces of the Twentieth Century: Contemporary Explorations

GABRIEL GARCÍA MÁRQUEZ (1928–   )

WOLE SOYINKA (1934–   )

Preface
To The Fifth Edition

The Fifth Edition of the *Norton Anthology of World Masterpieces* is a new book throughout.

Every selection has been carefully reconsidered, both for its intrinsic interest to today's students and for its contribution to their understanding of the author and period from which it comes, as well as its representation of the ever-broadening cultural tradition that in these latter years of the twentieth century we all share.

Introductions and notes have been extensively revised—in many cases entirely rewritten—to bring them into line with the best critical scholarship of the 1980s, but also, and most particularly, to guarantee their clarity and attractiveness for current student readers. In the same interest, introductions to individual selections now appear as headnotes, placed immediately before the work to which they refer, and all suggested lists of supplementary reading have been annotated to help students find their way about. Both volumes of the anthology, it is hardly necessary to add, have been entirely redesigned and reset to produce a work rich in content but easy for student and teacher to handle and read.

The same principles have determined our Fifth Edition selections. On the advice of our users, a few have been dropped, some have been expanded or curtailed, many have been added. Our representation of the Ancient World now contains, for instance, the *Odyssey*—complete—in the sensitive translation of Robert Fitzgerald. It also contains the three plays of Aeschylus's great trilogy, the *Oresteia*, in a new translation by Robert Fagles, greeted by reviewers generally as a triumph. To Fagles we have also turned for the most faithful as well as most readable renderings of *Oedipus the King* and *Antigone* that this century has yet produced. Other vitalizing changes for the Ancient World include a liberal selection from Ovid's *Metamorphoses* in a rollicking English by Rolfe Humphries that admirably suits the witty genius of that Roman poet; and a shift, for our selections from the *Aeneid*, to the new Robert Fitzgerald version that we have been awaiting for some time. Though Virgil is the most difficult of all Latin poets to translate, this version comes closer than any other to catching the authentic Virgilian tone.

Improvements no less striking appear throughout the book. One of the most notable is the result of our success in obtaining the use of John Ciardi's hitherto unavailable translation of Dante. Acceptable English versions of the *Divine Comedy* abound, and we have in the past printed more than one of them ourselves. But for reading pleasure, and for the indispensable sense that what one is reading is not a treatise but a great poem, Ciardi easily tops all. We are proud to be permitted to offer here a work of such distinction.

With almost equal pride, we call attention to our inclusion of Madame de la Fayette's *The Princess of Clèves* among our selections from the early literature of the Enlightenment. This is a pioneering psychological novel of great depth and subtlety, genuinely a world masterpiece, and by English readers too little known. By college students, in particular, a more sensitive appreciation of the struggles, oppressions, and aspirations of the lives of women may be had from such imaginative explorations as are found in *The Princess of Clèves*, *Madame Bovary*, and *Hedda Gabler* than from any number of theoretical treatises. It is by imagination, not argument, that empathy is learned.

Equally inspired enlargements in this edition, we believe, are the four brilliant short pieces in the medieval section bringing to vivid life the fortitude and laughter of the Celtic and Nordic peoples; the addition to the Enlightenment period of selections from Samuel Johnson's *The History of Rasselas, Prince of Abyssinia*, providing a fascinating counterpoint not only with Voltaire's *Candide*, published the same year, but with the *Confessions* of Rousseau; the generous space allotted in this edition to the poetry of Baudelaire, again a dramatic opening into aspects of nineteenth-century thought and feeling that do not become explicit, though often implicit, in the plays and narratives of the time; and—a particularly valuable accession from this point of view—Frederick Douglass's autobiographical narrative of his life as a slave. This work has the double virtue of being a factual account of kinds of experience not met with in our other nineteenth-century offerings and at the same time a serious work of art, thoughtfully and skilfully shaped by a master hand.

As the foregoing statements will, we hope, make clear, the Norton Anthology of World Literature has never aspired to be either a grab-bag or an encyclopaedia. It is a teaching instrument. From its first edition in 1956, it has been a carefully planned whole, each of its parts designed and executed by a recognized authority in that field, but changing steadily with the times and with the needs and preferences of the hundreds of teachers who year after year have insisted on nothing but the best for their students, and, by generously pooling their classroom experiences with ours, have guided us in our efforts to deliver it. Like the syllabus of every sound multiple-division course, the anthology offers more than any class can master in a single year, in order to leave options for the individual teacher and provide supplementary outside reading (often not available in the college library in sufficient copies) for those who wish it. On the other hand, we have been careful not to overwhelm the student new to world literature with masses of material unrelated except by their appearance between the same covers.

We have equally taken pains to make our selections from any given period or culture truly representative. We include both Shakespeare's *Hamlet* and Marlowe's *The Tragedy of Dr. Faustus* in our Renaissance section, for example, because these two plays sum up the complex sensibility of that era more fully than any other two works now extant, and at the same time have an unmatched pertinence for us. Today's students, growing up in a nuclear world they never made and burdened with a life-or-death imperative to "set it right," identify more readily with Shakespeare's young prince, similarly burdened and like them a university student, than with any other character in literature. Nor are they unmindful of that Faustian thrust to power in humankind which helps create the threat of annihilation we all face and which is so richly and unforgettably depicted from differing perspectives in Marlowe's play and Goethe's dramatic poem. On the same grounds, and also because we intend this book to be an effective teaching instrument offering many interconnections, we include not merely the magical and folktale side of Greek literature, represented in the *Odyssey*, but the fiercely realist and "heroic" side represented by that greatest of epic poems, the *Iliad*, without which such later works as Milton's *Paradise Lost* and Pope's *Rape of the Lock* cannot be understood. For the *Iliad* in this fifth edition, however, our own experience as well as consultation with our users has dictated a return to the translation of Richmond Lattimore, which, deprived though it is of a certain "nobility" by the informalization of twentieth century English, can nevertheless flash into electric moments:

> Honor then the gods, Achilleus, and take pity upon me
> remembering your father, yet I am still more pitiful;
> I have gone through what no other mortal on earth has gone through;
> I put my lips to the hands of the man who has killed my children.

Nowhere, we believe, is our determination to do full justice to the complexities of a given period while at the same time opening new horizons to class discussion more apparent than in our treatment in this fifth edition of the literature of our own century. Here we offer for the first time a movie script, Jean Renoir's *Grand Illusion*, from which one of the greatest films of our time (some think the very greatest) was made. With or without the picture produced from it, it is a fascinating text for close study, an exercise not only for the visual imagination but for the moral sense. We offer also in this section (as with Douglass's slave narrative earlier) some important windows opening on experiences and ways of life which are not part of the cultural tradition students brought up on the American continent usually know best: Yukio Mishima's grim but brilliant "Patriotism," R. K. Narayan's "Emden," and Wole Soyinka's hilarious yet poignant *The Lion and the Jewel*.

Other authors new to the anthology in this edition are Samuel Beckett (*Endgame*), Doris Lessing ("To Room Nineteen"), Gabriel García Márquez ("Death Constant Beyond Love"), and Alain Robbe-Grillet ("The Secret Room"). Authors restored from earlier editions by popular request are Ralph Ellison ("King of the Bingo Game"), Federico García Lorca ("Lament for [the Matador] Ignacio Sanchez Mejias"), Rainer Maria Rilke (*Duino Elegies*, 1 and 10, and "Archaic Torso of Apollo"), and Alexander Solzhenitsyn ("Matryona's Home"). Needless to say, in making these additions we have not scanted the earlier great innovators like Proust in fiction, without whom the course of the twentieth-century novel is unintelligible, Pirandello and Brecht in drama, or Yeats and Eliot in modern verse.

To clarify further the development of twentieth-century literature, we have made what we believe will be for most students a helpful division between works that a by now fairly wide consensus agrees are the characteristic products of "Modernism," i.e., the shift from nineteenth-century values and techniques, and works which so far are less assimilable to any generally recognized cultural pattern—"Contemporary Explorations," we have called them for want of a better name. Among these, we suspect, lie the seeds of the future, including the gradual enlargement of what we have customarily called world literature to a literature genuinely worldwide in scope. In the meantime, as Dryden said of Chaucer, here is "God's plenty."

It is a pleasure to welcome to our group with this edition Patricia Meyer Spacks, Professor of English at Yale University, and to re-welcome Sarah Lawall, Professor of Comparative Literature at the Amherst campus of the University of Massachusetts. Users of these volumes whose special interests draw them to works of the Enlightenment and Romanticism, or to those of our own century, will quickly understand our pride in their company.

THE EDITORS

Masterpieces of the Enlightenment

"I wonder if it is not better to try to correct and moderate men's passions than to try to suppress them altogether." The sentence, from Jean-Baptiste Molière's 1669 preface to his biting comedy about religious hypocrisy, *Tartuffe*, captures something of the anxiety and the optimism of a period for which subsequent generations have found no adequate single designation. "The Neo-Classic Period," "The Age of Reason," "The Enlightenment": such labels suggest, accurately enough, that thinkers between (roughly) 1660 and 1770 emphasized the powers of the mind and turned to the Roman past for models. But these terms do not convey the awareness of limitation expressed in Molière's sentence, an awareness as typical of the historical period to which the sentence belongs as is the expressed aspiration toward correctness and moderation. The effort to correct and moderate the passions might prove less foolhardy than the effort to suppress them, but both endeavors would involve human nature's struggle with itself, a struggle necessarily perpetual. "On life's vast ocean diversely we sail, / Reason the card, but Passion is the gale," Alexander Pope's *Essay on Man* (1733) pointed out. One could hope to steer with reason as guide only by remembering the omnipresence of passion as impetus. Eighteenth-century thinkers analyzed, and eighteenth-century imaginative writers dramatized intricate interchanges and conflicts between these aspects of our selves.

The drama of reason and passion played itself out in society, the system of association human beings had devised partly to control passion and institutionalize reason. Structured on the basis of a rigid class system, the traditional social order began to face incipient challenges in the eighteenth century as new commerce generated new wealth, whose possessors felt entitled to claim their own share of social power. The threat to established hierarchies extended even to kings. Thomas Hobbes, in *Leviathan* (1651), had argued for the secular origins of the social contract. Kings arise, he said, not by divine ordinance but out of human need; they exist to prevent what would otherwise be a war of all on all. Monarchs still presided over European nations in the eighteenth century, but with less security than before. The English had executed their ruler in 1642; the French would perform another royal decapitation before the end of the eighteenth century. The mortality of kings had become a political fact, a fact implying the conceivable instability of the social order over which kings presided.

A sense of the contingencies of the human condition impinged on many minds in a world where men and women no longer automatically assumed God's benign supervision of human affairs or the primacy of their own Christian obligations. The fierce strife between Protestants and Catholics lapsed into relative quiescence by the end of the seventeenth century, but the Protestant English deposed their king in 1688 because of his marriage to a Catholic princess and their fear of a Catholic dynasty; and in France Louis XIV in 1685 revoked the Edict of Nantes, which had granted religious toleration to Protestants. The overt English struggle of Cavaliers and Puritans ended with the restoration of Charles II to the throne in 1660. Religious differences now became translated into divisions of social class and of political conviction—divisions no less powerful for lacking the claim of supernatural authority. To England, the eighteenth century brought two unsuccessful but bitterly divisive rebellions on behalf of the deposed Stuart succession, as well as the cataclysmic American Revolution. In France, the century ended in revolution. Throughout the eighteenth century, wars erupted over succession to European thrones and over nationalistic claims, although no fighting took place on such a scale as that of the devastating Thirty Years' War (1618–1648). On the whole, divisions within nations in France and England assumed greater importance than those between nations.

Philosophers now turned their attention to defining the possibilities and limitations of the human position in the material universe. "I think, therefore I am," René Descartes pronounced, declaring the mind the source of individual being. But this idea proved less reassuring than it initially seemed. Subsequent philosophers, exploring the concept's implications, realized the possibility of the mind's isolation in its own constructions. Perhaps, Wilhelm Leibnitz suggested, no real communication can take place between one consciousness and another. Possibly, according to David Hume, the idea of individual identity itself derives from the mind's efforts to manufacture continuity out of discontinuous memories. Philosophers pointed out the impossibility of knowing for sure even the reality of the external world: the only certainty is that we think it exists. If contemplating the nature of human reason thus led philosophic skeptics to restrict severely the area of what we can know with certainty, other contemplations induced other thinkers to insist on the existence, beyond men, of an entirely rational physical and moral universe. Sir Isaac Newton's demonstrations of the order of natural law greatly encouraged this line of thought. The fullness and complexity of the perceived physical world testified, as many wrote, to the sublime rationality of a divine plan. The Planner, however, did not necessarily supervise the day-to-day operations of His arrangements; He might rather, as a popular analogy had it, resemble the watchmaker who winds the watch and leaves it running.

Deism, evoking a depersonalized deity, insisted on the logicality of the universe and encouraged the separation of ethics from religion. Ethics, too, could be understood as a matter of reason. "He that thinks reasonably must think morally," Samuel Johnson observed, echoing the noble horses Jonathan Swift had imagined in the fourth book of *Gulliver's Travels*. But such statements expressed wish more than perception. Awareness of the passions continued to haunt thinkers yearning for rationality. Swift's Houyhnhnms, creatures of his imagination, might achieve flawless rationality, with accompanying wisdom and benevolence, but actual human beings could only dream of such an ideal, while experiencing—as men and women have always experienced—the confusion of conflicting impulses often at war with the dictates of reason.

Although the social, economic, and political organizations in which the thinkers of this period participated hardly resemble our own, the questions they raised about the human condition have plagued the Western mind ever since. Though we no longer locate the solution to all problems in an unattainable ideal of "reason," we too struggle to find the limits of certainty, have problems of identity and isolation, and recognize the impossibility of altogether controlling internal forces now identified as "the unconscious" rather than "the passions." But we confront such issues largely from the position of isolated individuals. In the late seventeenth and early eighteenth centuries, in England and on the Continent, the sense of obligation to society had far more power than it possesses today. Society provided the standards and the instruments of control that might help to counter the tumult of individual impulse.

SOCIETY

"Society," in this period, designates both a powerful idea and an omnipresent fact of experience. Prerevolutionary French society, like English society in the same period, depended upon clear hierarchical structures. The literature of both countries issued from a small cultural elite, writing for others of their kind and assuming the rightness of their own knowledge of how people should feel and behave.

For the English and French upper classes, as for the ancient Romans they admired, public life mattered more than private. At one level, the "public" designated the realms of government and diplomacy: occupations allowing and encouraging oratory, frequent travel, negotiation, the exercise of political and economic power. In this sense, the public world belonged entirely to men, who determined the course of government, defined the limits of the important, enforced their sense of the fitness of things. By another definition, "public" might refer to the life of formal social intercourse. In France, such social life took place often in "salons," gatherings to engage in intellectual as well as frivolous conversation. Women typically presided over these salons, thus declaring both their intellectual authority and their capacity to combine high thought with high style. Until rather late in the eighteenth century, on the other hand, England allowed women no such commanding position; there, men controlled intellectual as well as political discourse. The male voice, accordingly, dominated English literature until the development of the novel provided new opportunities for women writers and for the articulation of domestic values.

Both the larger and the more limited "public" spheres depended on well-defined codes of behavior. The discrepancy between the forms of self-presentation dictated by these codes and the operations such forms might disguise—a specific form of the reason-passion conflict—provides one of the insistent themes of French and English literature in the century beginning around 1660. Molière, examining religious sham; Mme. de La Fayette, considering the dilemma of a woman whose sense of propriety wars with her desire; Swift, lashing the English for institutionalized hypocrisy; Pope, calling attention to ambiguities inherent in sexual mores; Voltaire and Johnson, sending naive fictional protagonists to encounter the world's inconsistencies of profession and practice—such writers call attention to the deceptiveness and the possible misuses of social norms, as well as to their necessity. None suggests that the codes themselves are at fault. If people lived up to what they profess, the world would be a better place; ideally, they would modify not their standards of behavior but their tendency to hide behind them.

We in the twentieth century have become accustomed to the notion of the sacredness of the individual, encouraged to believe in the high value of expressiveness, originality, specialness. Eighteenth-century writers, on the other hand, assumed the superior importance of the social group and of shared opinion. "Expressiveness," in their view, should provide an instrument for articulating the will of the community, not the eccentric desires of individuals. The mad astronomer in *Rasselas*, who as a result of isolation develops an exaggerated sense of his own power, epitomizes the danger of allowing oneself to believe too readily in the self's specialness. Society implies subordination: not only class hierarchy, but individual submission to the good of the group.

French writers of imaginative literature often used domestic situations as ways to examine larger problems. Marriage, an institution at once social and personal, provides a useful image for human relationship as social and emotional fact. The developing eighteenth-century novel, in England and France alike, would assume marriage as the normal goal for men and women; Molière, Racine, and de La Fayette, writing before the turn of the century, examine economic, psychological, moral, and social implications of specific imagined marriages. The sexual alliances of rulers, Racine's subject in *Phaedra*, have literal consequences far beyond the individuals involved. Molière evokes a private family to suggest how professed sentiment can obscure the operations of ambition; de La Fayette depicts intricate social and emotional pressures impinging on men and women of good will. All three understand marriage as social microcosm, a society in miniature, not merely as a structure for fulfillment of personal desire.

In England, writers in genres other than the novel typically focus their attention on a broader panorama. Pope, Swift, and Johnson, like Voltaire satirists of the human scene, consider varied operations of social law and pressure. In *The Rape of the Lock*, Pope uses a card party to epitomize social structures; Swift imagines idealized forms of social institutions ranging from marriage to parliament, contrasting the ideals with evocations of their actual English counterparts; or he fantasizes the horrifying consequences of venture capitalism in the processing of infants for food; Johnson's world tourists and Voltaire's witness and participate in a vast range of sobering experience. In general women fill subordinate roles in the harsh social environments evoked by these satiric works. Dr. Johnson praised Shakespeare because he did not make love the only spring of action; other passions, Johnson suggested, more powerfully motivate human activity. As the evoked social scene widens, erotic love plays a less important part and the position of women becomes increasingly insignificant: women's sphere is the home, and home life matters less than does public life. It is perhaps not irrelevant to note that no work in this section describes or evokes children. Only in adulthood do people assume social responsibility; only then do they provide interesting substance for social commentary.

NATURE

Society establishes one locus of reality for eighteenth-century thinkers, although they understand it as a human construct. Nature comprises another assumed measure of the real. The meanings of the word *nature* vary greatly in eighteenth-century usage, but two large senses are most relevant to the works here included: nature as the inherent order of things, including the physical universe, hence evidence of the deity's plan; and nature meaning specifically *human* nature.

Despite their pervasive awareness of natural contingency (vividly dramatized by Voltaire among others, in his account of the disastrous Lisbon earthquake), writers of this period locate their sense of permanence particularly in the idea of nature. Pope's *Essay on Man* comprises one of the most extensive—as well as intensive—examinations of the concept of natural order and its implications. Emphasizing the inadequacy of human reason, the poem insistently reminds the reader of limitation. We cannot hope to grasp the arrangement of the universe, Pope tells us; how can a part comprehend the whole? Human pride in reason only obscures from its possessors the great truths of a universal structure as flawlessly articulated in every detail as the stellar systems Newton and others had revealed. Contemplation of nature can both humble and exalt its practitioner, teaching the insufficiency of human powers in comparison with divine, but also reminding human beings that they inhabit a wondrous universe in which all functions precisely as it should.

The notion of a permanent, divinely ordained natural order offers a good deal of comfort to those aware of flaws in actual social arrangements. It embodies an ideal of harmony, of order in variety, which, although it cannot be fully grasped by human intelligence, can yet provide a model for social complexities. It posits a *system*, a structure of relationships that at some theoretical level necessarily makes sense; thus it provides an assumed substructure of rationality for all experience of irrationality. It supplies a means of valuing all appearances of the natural world: every flower, every minnow, has meaning beyond itself, as part of the great pattern. The ardency with which the period's thinkers cling to belief in such a pattern suggests once more a pervasive anxiety about what human reason could not do. Human beings create a vision of something at once sublimely reasonable and beyond reason's grasp to reassure themselves that the limits of the rational need not coincide with the limits of the human.

The permanence of the conceptual natural order corresponds to that of human nature, as conceived in the eighteenth century. Human nature, it was generally believed, remains in all times and places the same. Thus Racine could re-present a fable from Greek tragedy, using classical setting and characters, with complete assurance that his imagining of Phaedra's conflict and suffering would speak to his contemporaries without falsifying the classical original. Despite social divergencies, fundamental aspects of personality do in fact remain constant: all people hope and fear, feel envy and lust, possess the capacity to reason. All suffer loss, all face death. Thinkers of the Enlightenment emphasized these common aspects of humanity far more than they considered cultural divergencies. Readers and writers alike could draw on this conviction about universality. It provided a test of excellence: if an author's imagining of character failed to conform to what eighteenth-century readers understood as human nature, a work might be securely judged inadequate. Conversely, the idea of a constant human nature held out the hope of longevity for writers who successfully evoked it. Moral philosophers could define human obligation and possibility in the conviction that they too wrote for all time; ethical standards would never change. Like the vision of order in the physical universe, the notion of constancy in human nature provided bedrock for an increasingly secularized society.

CONVENTION AND AUTHORITY

Eighteenth-century society, like all societies, operated, and its literary figures wrote, on the basis of established conventions. Manners are social conventions: agreed upon systems of behavior declared appropriate for specific situations. Guides to manners proliferated in the eighteenth century, expressing a widespread sense that commitment to decorum helped to preserve society's important standards. Literary conventions—agreed upon systems of verbal behavior—served comparable purposes in another sphere. Like established codes of manners, such conventions declare continuity between present and past.

The literary conventions of the past, like outmoded manners or styles of dress, may strike the twentieth-century reader as antiquated and artificial. A woman who curtseyed in a modern living room, a man who appeared in a wig, would seem to us ridiculous, even insane; but of course a young woman in blue jeans would affect our predecessors as equally perverse. The plaintive lyrics of current country music, say, are governed by highly restrictive conventions which affect their hearers as "natural" only because they are so familiar. Eighteenth-century writers had at their disposal an established set of conventions for every traditional literary genre. As the repetitive rhythms of the country ballad tell listeners what to expect, these literary conventions provided readers with clues about the kind of experience they could anticipate in a given poem or play.

Underlying all specific conventions was the classical assumption that literature existed to delight and to instruct its readers. The various genres represented in this volume embody such belief in literature's dual function. Stage comedy and tragedy, the early novel, satire in prose and verse, didactic poetry, the philosophic tale: each form developed its own set of devices for involving audiences and readers in situations requiring moral choice, as well as for creating pleasure. The insistence in drama on unity of time and place (stage action occupying no more time than its representation, with no change of scene) exemplifies one such set, intended to facilitate in audiences the kind of belief encouraging maximum emotional and moral effect. The elevated diction of the *Essay on Man* ("Mark how it mounts, to Man's imperial race, / From the green myriads in the peopled grass"), like the mannered but less dignified language of *The Rape of the Lock* ("Here thou, great Anna! whom three realms obey, / Does sometimes counsel take—and sometimes tea"), the two-dimensional characters of Johnson's and Voltaire's tales: such (to us) unfamiliar aspects of these texts provide signals about authorial intention and about anticipated reader response.

One dominant convention of twentieth-century poetry and prose is something we call "realism." In fiction, verse, and drama, writers often attempt to convey the literal feel of experience, the shape in which events actually occur in the world, the way people really talk. Racine, Pope, Voltaire pursued no such goal. Despite their concern with permanent patterns of thought and feeling, they employed deliberate and obvious forms of artifice as modes of emphasis and of indirection. The rapidity with which de La Fayette summarizes crucial events (as when her heroine's mother reports some thirty years of court history in two or three pages), like the sonorous verse in which Racine's characters reflect on their passions ("I hate my life, abominate my lust; / Longing by death to rescue my good name / And hide my black love from the light of day"), embodies a form of stylization. Artistic transformation of life, the period's writers believed, involves the imposition of formal order on the endless flux of event and feeling. The formalities of this literature constitute part of its meaning: its statement that what experience shows as unstable, art makes stable.

Reliance on convention as a mode of control expressed an aspect of the period's constant effort toward elusive stability. The classical past, for many, provided an emblem of that stability, a standard of permanence. But some felt a problem inherent in the high valuing of the past, a problem dramatized by the so-called quarrel of Ancients and Moderns in England and in France. At stake in this controversy was the value of permanence as against the value of change. Proponents of the Ancients believed that the giants of Greece and Rome had not only established standards applicable to all subsequent accomplishment but provided models of achievement never to be excelled. Homer wrote the first great epics; subsequent endeavors in the same genre could only imitate him. Innovation came when it came by making the old new, as Pope makes a woman's dressing for conquest new by comparing it to the arming of Achilles. Moderns who valued originality for its own sake, who multiplied worthless publications, who claimed significance for what time had not tested thereby testified to their own inadequacies and their foolish pride.

Those proud to be Moderns, on the other hand, held that men (possibly even women) standing on the shoulders of the Ancients could see farther than their predecessors. The new conceivably exceeded in value the old; one might discover flaws even in revered figures of the classic past. Not everything had yet been accomplished; fresh possibilities remained always potential. This view, of course, corresponds to one widely current since the eighteenth century, but it did not triumph easily: many powerful thinkers of the late seventeenth and early eighteenth century adhered to the more conservative position.

Also at issue in this debate was the question of authority. What position should one assume who hoped to write and be read? Did authority reside only in tradition? If so, one must write in classical forms, rely on classical allusions. Until late in the eighteenth century, virtually all important writers attempted to ally themselves with the authority of tradition, declaring themselves part of a community extending through time as well as space. The problems of authority became particularly important in connection with satire, a popular Enlightenment form. Satire involves criticism of vice and folly; Molière, Pope, Swift, Voltaire, Johnson at least on occasion wrote in the satiric mode. To establish the right to criticize fellow men and women, the satirist must establish a rhetorical ascendancy such as the pulpit gives the priest—an ascendancy most readily obtained by at least implicit alliance with literary and moral tradition. The satirist, like the moral philosopher, cannot afford to seem idiosyncratic when prescribing and condemning the behavior of others. The fact that satire flourished so richly in this period suggests another version of the central conflict between reason and passion, the forces of stability and of instability. In its heightened description of the world (people eating babies, young women initiating epic battles over the loss of a lock of hair), satire calls attention to the powerful presence of the irrational, opposing to that presence the clarity of the satirist's own claim to reason and tradition. As it chastises human beings for their eruptions of passion, urging resistance and control, satire reminds its readers of the universality of the irrational as well as of opposition to it. The effort "to correct and moderate men's [and women's] passions," that great theme of the Enlightenment, can equally generate hope or despair: opposed moods richly expressed throughout this period.

FURTHER READING

Useful books on the enlightenment include, for English background, H. Nicolson, *The Age of Reason: The Eighteenth Century* (1960), and, for an opposed view, D. Greene, *The Age of Exuberance: Backgrounds to Eighteenth-Century English Literature* (1970). For the intellectual and social situation in France, L. Crocker, *An Age of Crisis: Man and World in Eighteenth-Century French Thought* (1959), and L. Gossman, *French Society and Culture: Background for Eighteenth-Century Literature* (1972). An excellent treatment of the period's literature in England is M. Price, *To the Palace of Wisdom: Studies in Order and Energy from Dryden to Blake* (1964).

JEAN-BAPTISTE POQUELIN MOLIÈRE
1622–1673

Son of a prosperous Paris merchant, Molière (originally named Poquelin) devoted his entire adult life to the creation of stage illusion, as playwright and as actor. At about the age of twenty-five, he joined a company of traveling players established by the Béjart family; with them he toured the provinces for about twelve years. In 1658 the company was ordered to perform for Louis XIV in Paris; a year later, Molière's first great success, *The High-Brow Ladies (Les Précieuses ridicules)*, was produced. The theatrical company to which he belonged, patronized by the king, became increasingly successful, developing finally (1680) into the Comédie Française. In 1662, Molière married Armande Béjart. He died a few hours after performing in the lead role of his own play, *The Imaginary Invalid*.

Molière wrote both broad farce and comedies of character, in which he caricatured some form of vice or folly by embodying it in a single figure. His targets included the miser, the aspiring but vulgar middle class, female wouldbe intellectuals, the hypochondriac, and, in *Tartuffe*, the religious hypocrite.

In *Tartuffe* (1664), as in his other plays, Molière employs classic comic devices of plot and character—here, a foolish, stubborn father blocking the course of young love; an impudent servant commenting on her superiors' actions; a happy ending involving a marriage facilitated by implausible means. He uses such devices, however, often to comment on his own immediate social scene, imagining how universal patterns play themselves out in a specific historical context. *Tartuffe* had contemporary relevance so transparent that the Catholic Church forced the king to ban it, although Molière managed to have it published and produced once more by 1669.

The play's emotional energy derives not from the simple discrepancy of man and mask in Tartuffe ("Is not a face quite different from a mask?" inquires the normative character Cléante, who has no trouble making such distinctions) but from the struggle for erotic, psychic, and economic power in which people employ their masks. One can readily imagine modern equivalents for the stresses and strains within Orgon's family. Orgon, an aging man with grown children, seeks ways to preserve control. His mother, Mme. Pernelle, encourages his efforts, thus fostering her illusion that *she* still runs things. Orgon identifies his own interests with those of the hypocritical Tartuffe, toward whom he plays a benevolent role. Because Tartuffe fulsomely hails him as benefactor, Orgon feels utterly powerful in relation to his fawning dependent. When he orders his passive daughter Marianne to marry Tartuffe, he reveals his vision of complete domestic autocracy. Tartuffe's lust, one of those passions forever eluding human mastery, disturbs Orgon's arrangements; in the end, the will of the offstage king orders everything, as though a benevolent god had intervened.

To make Tartuffe a specifically religious hypocrite is an act of inventive daring. Orgon, like his mother, conceals from himself his will to power by verbally subordinating himself to that divinity which Tartuffe too invokes.

Although one may readily accept Molière's defense of his intentions (not to mock faith but to attack its misuse), it is not hard to see why the play might trouble religious authorities. Molière suggests how readily religious faith lends itself to misuse, how high-sounding pieties allow men and women to evade self-examination and immediate responsibilities. Tartuffe deceives others by his grandiosities of mortification ("Hang up my hair shirt") and charity; he encourages his victims in their own grandiosities. Orgon can indulge a fantasy of self-subordination (remarking of Tartuffe, "He guides our lives") at the same time that he furthers his more hidden desire for power. Religion offers ready justification for a course manifestly destructive as well as self-seeking.

Cléante, before he meets Tartuffe, claims (accurately) to understand him by his effects on others. Throughout the play, Cléante speaks in the voice of wisdom, counseling moderation, common sense, and self-control, calling attention to folly. More important, he emphasizes how the issues Molière examines in this comedy relate to dominant late seventeenth-century themes.

> Ah, Brother, man's a strangely fashioned creature
> Who seldom is content to follow Nature,
> But recklessly pursues his inclination
> Beyond the narrow bounds of moderation,
> And often, by transgressing Reason's laws,
> Perverts a lofty aim or noble cause.

To follow Nature means to act appropriately to the human situation in the created universe. Humankind occupies a middle position, between beasts and angels; such aspirations as Orgon's desire to control his daughter completely, or his apparent wish to submit himself absolutely to Tartuffe's claim of heavenly wisdom, imply a hope to surpass limitations inherent in the human condition. As Cléante's observations suggest, "to follow Nature," given the rationality of the universe, implies adherence to "Reason's laws." All transgression involves failure to submit to reason's dictates. Molière, with his stylized comic plot, makes that point as insistently as does Racine, who depicts grand passions and cataclysmic effects from them.

Although Cléante understands and can enunciate the principles of proper conduct, his wisdom has no direct effect on the play's action. In spite of the fact that the comedy suggests a social world in which women exist in utter subordination to fathers and husbands, in the plot two women bring about the clarifications that unmask the villain. The virtuous wife Elmire, object of Tartuffe's lust, and the articulate servant girl Dorine confront the immediate situation with pragmatic inventiveness. Dorine goads others to response; Elmire encourages Tartuffe to play out his sexual fantasies before a hidden audience. Both women have a clear sense of right and wrong, although they express it in less resounding terms than does Cléante. Their concrete insistence on facing what's really going on, cutting through all obfuscation, rescues the men from entanglement in their own abstract formulations.

The women's clarifications, however, do not resolve the comedy's dilemmas. Suddenly the context shifts: economic terms replace erotic ones. It is as though Tartuffe were only playing in his attempt to seduce Elmire; now we get to what really matters: money. For all his claims of disinterestedness, Tartuffe has managed to get control of his dupe's property. Control of property, the action gradually reveals, amounts to power over life itself: prison threatens Orgon, and the prospect of expulsion from their home menaces him and his family alike. Only the convenient and ostentatious artifice of royal intervention rescues the victims and punishes their betrayer.

Comedies conventionally end in the restoration of order, declaring that good inevitably triumphs; rationality renews itself despite the temporary deviations of the foolish and the vicious. At the end of *Tartuffe*, Orgon and his mother have been chastened by revelation of their favorite's depravity; Mariane has been allowed to marry her lover; Tartuffe has been judged; the king's power and justice have reasserted themselves and been acknowledged. In the organization of family and nation (metaphorically a larger family), order reassumes dominion. Yet the arbitrary intervention of the king leaves a disturbing emotional residue. The play has demonstrated that Tartuffe's corrupt will to power (as opposed to Orgon's merely foolish will) can ruthlessly aggrandize itself. Money speaks, in Orgon's society as in ours; possession of wealth implies total control over others. Only a kind of miracle can save Orgon. The miracle occurs, given the benign world of comedy, but the play reminds its readers of the extreme precariousness with which reason finally triumphs, even given the presence of such reasonable people as Cléante and Elmire. Tartuffe's monstrous lust, for women, money, power, genuinely endangers the social structure. *Tartuffe* enforces recognition of the constant threats to rationality, of how much we have at stake in trying to use reason as principle of action.

K. Mantzius, *Molière* (1908), provides a good biographical introduction to Molière. Useful critical studies include J. D. Hubert, *Molière and the Comedy of Intellect* (1962), and L. Gossman, *Men and Masks: A Study of Molière* (1963).

Tartuffe[1]

Preface

Here is a comedy that has excited a good deal of discussion and that has been under attack for a long time; and the persons who are mocked by it have made it plain that they are more powerful in France than all whom my plays have satirized up to this time. Noblemen, ladies of fashion, cuckolds, and doctors all kindly consented to their presentation, which they themselves seemed to enjoy along with everyone else; but hypocrites do not understand banter: they became angry at once, and found it strange that I was bold enough to represent their actions and to care to describe a profession shared by so many good men. This is a crime for which they cannot forgive me, and they have taken up arms against my comedy in a terrible rage. They were careful not to attack it at the point that had wounded them: they are too crafty for that and too clever to reveal their true character. In

---

1. Translated by Richard Wilbur. The first version of *Tartuffe* was performed in 1664 and the second in 1667. When a second edition of the third version was printed in June 1669, Molière added his three petitions to Louis XIV; they follow the preface.

keeping with their lofty custom, they have used the cause of God to mask their private interests; and *Tartuffe*, they say, is a play that offends piety: it is filled with abominations from beginning to end, and nowhere is there a line that does not deserve to be burned. Every syllable is wicked, the very gestures are criminal, and the slightest glance, turn of the head, or step from right to left conceals mysteries that they are able to explain to my disadvantage. In vain did I submit the play to the criticism of my friends and the scrutiny of the public: all the corrections I could make, the judgment of the king and queen who saw the play,[2] the approval of great princes and ministers of state who honored it with their presence, the opinion of good men who found it worthwhile, all this did not help. They will not let go of their prey, and every day of the week they have pious zealots abusing me in public and damning me out of charity.

I would care very little about all they might say except that their devices make enemies of men whom I respect and gain the support of genuinely good men, whose faith they know and who, because of the warmth of their piety, readily accept the impressions that others present to them. And it is this which forces me to defend myself. Especially to the truly devout do I wish to vindicate my play, and I beg of them with all my heart not to condemn it before seeing it, to rid themselves of preconceptions, and not aid the cause of men dishonored by their actions.

If one takes the trouble to examine my comedy in good faith, he will surely see that my intentions are innocent throughout, and tend in no way to make fun of what men revere; that I have presented the subject with all the precautions that its delicacy imposes; and that I have used all the art and skill that I could to distinguish clearly the character of the hypocrite from that of the truly devout man. For that purpose I used two whole acts to prepare the appearance of my scoundrel. Never is there a moment's doubt about his character; he is known at once from the qualities I have given him; and from one end of the play to the other, he does not say a word, he does not perform an action which does not depict to the audience the character of a wicked man, and which does not bring out in sharp relief the character of the truly good man which I oppose to it.

I know full well that by way of reply, these gentlemen try to insinuate that it is not the role of the theater to speak of these matters; but with their permission, I ask them on what do they base this fine doctrine. It is a proposition they advance as no more than a supposition, for which they offer not a shred of proof; and surely it would not be difficult to show them that comedy, for the ancients, had its origin in religion and constituted a part of its ceremonies; that our neighbors, the Spaniards, have hardly a single holiday celebration in which a comedy is not a part; and that even here in France, it owes its birth to the efforts of a religious brotherhood who still own the Hôtel de Bourgogne, where the most important mystery plays of our faith were presented;[3] that you can still find comedies printed in gothic letters under the name of a learned doctor of the Sorbonne;[4] and without

2. Louis XIV was married to Marie Thérèse of Austria.   3. A reference to the *Confrérie de la Passion et Résurrection de Notre-Seigneur* (the Fraternity of the Passion and Resurrection of Our Saviour), founded in 1402. The Hôtel de Bourgogne was a rival theater of Molière.   4. Probably Maître Jehán Michel, a medical doctor who wrote mystery plays.

going so far, in our own day the religious dramas of Pierre Corneille[5] have been performed to the admiration of all France.

If the function of comedy is to correct men's vices, I do not see why any should be exempt. Such a condition in our society would be much more dangerous than the thing itself; and we have seen that the theater is admirably suited to provide correction. The most forceful lines of a serious moral statement are usually less powerful than those of satire; and nothing will reform most men better than the depiction of their faults. It is a vigorous blow to vices to expose them to public laughter. Criticism is taken lightly, buy men will not tolerate satire. They are quite willing to be mean, but they never like to be ridiculed.

I have been attacked for having placed words of piety in the mouth of my impostor. Could I avoid doing so in order to represent properly the character of a hypocrite? It seemed to me sufficient to reveal the criminal motives which make him speak as he does, and I have eliminated all ceremonial phrases, which nonetheless he would not have been found using incorrectly. Yet some say that in the fourth act he sets forth a vicious morality; but is not this a morality which everyone has heard again and again? Does my comedy say anything new here? And is there any fear that ideas so thoroughly detested by everyone can make an impression on men's minds; that I make them dangerous by presenting them in the theater; that they acquire authority from the lips of a scoundrel? There is not the slightest suggestion of any of this; and one must either approve the comedy of *Tartuffe* or condemn all comedies in general.

This has indeed been done in a furious way for some time now, and never was the theater so much abused.[6] I cannot deny that there were Church Fathers who condemned comedy; but neither will it be denied me that there were some who looked on it somewhat more favorably. Thus authority, on which censure is supposed to depend, is destroyed by this disagreement; and the only conclusion that can be drawn from this difference of opinion among men enlightened by the same wisdom is that they viewed comedy in different ways, and that some considered it in its purity, while others regarded it in its corruption and confused it with all those wretched performances which have been rightly called performances of filth.

And in fact, since we should talk about things rather than words, and since most misunderstanding comes from including contrary notions in the same word, we need only to remove the veil of ambiguity and look at comedy in itself to see if it warrants condemnation. It will surely be recognized that as it is nothing more than a clever poem which corrects men's faults by means of agreeable lessons, it cannot be condemned without injustice. And if we listened to the voice of ancient times on this matter, it would tell us that its most famous philosophers have praised comedy—they who professed so austere a wisdom and who ceaselessly denounced the vices of their times. It would tell us that Aristotle spent his evenings at the theater[7] and took the

---

5. Pierre Corneille (1606–1684) and Racine were France's two greatest writers of classic tragedy. The two dramas Molière doubtlessly had in mind were *Polyeucte* (1643) and *Théodore, vierge et martyre* (1645). 6. Molière had in mind Nicole's two attacks on the theater: *Visionnaries* (1666) and *Traité de Comédie*, the Prince de Conti's *Traité de Comédie* (1666). 7. A reference to Aristotle's *Poetics* (composed between 335 and 322 B.C., the year of his death).

trouble to reduce the art of making comedies to rules. It would tell us that some of its greatest and most honored men took pride in writing comedies themselves;[8] and that others did not disdain to recite them in public; that Greece expressed its admiration for this art by means of handsome prizes and magnificent theaters to honor it; and finally, that in Rome this same art also received extraordinary honors; I do not speak of Rome run riot under the license of the emperors, but of disciplined Rome, governed by the wisdom of the consuls, and in the age of the full vigor of Roman dignity.

I admit that there have been times when comedy became corrupt. And what do men not corrupt every day? There is nothing so innocent that men cannot turn it to crime; nothing so beneficial that its values cannot be reversed; nothing so good in itself that it cannot be put to bad uses. Medical knowledge benefits mankind and is revered as one of our most wonderful possessions; and yet there was a time when it fell into discredit, and was often used to poison men. Philosophy is a gift of Heaven; it has been given to us to bring us to the knowledge of a God by contemplating the wonders of nature; and yet we know that often it has been turned away from its function and has been used openly in support of impiety. Even the holiest of things are not immune from human corruption, and every day we see scoundrels who use and abuse piety, and wickedly make it serve the greatest of crimes. But this does not prevent one from making the necessary distinctions. We do not confuse in the same false inference the goodness of things that are corrupted with the wickedness of the corrupt. The function of an art is always distinguished from its misuse; and as medicine is not forbidden because it was banned in Rome,[9] nor philosophy because it was publicly condemned in Athens,[1] we should not suppress comedy simply because it has been condemned at certain times. This censure was justified then for reasons which no longer apply today; it was limited to what was then seen; and we should not seize on these limits, apply them more rigidly than is necessary, and include in our condemnation the innocent along with the guilty. The comedy that this censure attacked is in no way the comedy that we want to defend. We must be careful not to confuse the one with the other. There may be two persons whose morals may be completely different. They may have no resemblance to one another except in their names, and it would be a terrible injustice to want to condemn Olympia, who is a good woman, because there is also an Olympia who is lewd. Such procedures would make for great confusion everywhere. Everything under the sun would be condemned; now since this rigor is not applied to the countless instances of abuse we see every day, the same should hold for comedy, and those plays should be approved in which instruction and virtue reign supreme.

I know there are some so delicate that they cannot tolerate a comedy, who say that the most decent are the most dangerous, that the passions they present are all the more moving because they are virtuous, and that men's feelings are stirred by these presentations. I do not see what great crime it is

---

8. The Roman consul and general responsible for the final destruction of Carthage in 146 B.C., Scipio Africanus Minor (ca. 185–129 B.C.), collaborated with the writer of comedies, Terence (Publius Terentius Afer, ca. 195 or 185–ca. 159 B.C.).   9. Pliny the Elder says that the Romans expelled their doctors at the same time that the Greeks did theirs.   1. An allusion to Socrates' condemnation to death.

to be affected by the sight of a generous passion; and this utter insensitivity to which they would lead us is indeed a high degree of virtue! I wonder if so great a perfection resides within the strength of human nature, and I wonder if it is not better to try to correct and moderate men's passions than to try to suppress them altogether. I grant that there are places better to visit than the theater; and if we want to condemn every single thing that does not bear directly on God and our salvation, it is right that comedy be included, and I should willingly grant that it be condemned along with everything else. But if we admit, as is in fact true, that the exercise of piety will permit interruptions, and that men need amusement, I maintain that there is none more innocent than comedy. I have dwelled too long on this matter. Let me finish with the words of a great prince on the comedy, *Tartuffe*.[2]

Eight days after it had been banned, a play called *Scaramouche the Hermit*[3] was performed before the court; and the king, on his way out, said to this great prince: "I should really like to know why the persons who make so much noise about Molière's comedy do not say a word about *Scaramouche*." To which the prince replied, "It is because the comedy of *Scaramouche* makes fun of Heaven and religion, which these gentlemen do not care about at all, but that of Molière makes fun of *them*, and that is what they cannot bear."

THE AUTHOR

First Petition[4]

(PRESENTED TO THE KING ON THE COMEDY OF TARTUFFE)

Sire,

As the duty of comedy is to correct men by amusing them, I believed that in my occupation I could do nothing better than attack the vices of my age by making them ridiculous; and as hypocrisy is undoubtedly one of the most common, most improper, and most dangerous, I thought, Sire, that I would perform a service for all good men of your kingdom if I wrote a comedy which denounced hypocrites and placed in proper view all of the contrived poses of these incredibly virtuous men, all of the concealed villainies of these counterfeit believers who would trap others with a fraudulent piety and a pretended virtue.

I have written this comedy, Sire, with all the care and caution that the delicacy of the subject demands; and so as to maintain all the

---

2. One of Molière's benefactors who liked the play was the Prince de Condé; de Condé had *Tartuffe* read to him and also privately performed for him.   3. A troupe of Italian comedians had just performed the licentious farce, where a hermit dressed as a monk makes love to a married woman, announcing that *questo e per mortificar la carne* ("this is to mortify the flesh").   4. The first of the three *petitions* or *placets* to Louis XIV concerning the play. On May 12, 1664, *Tartuffe*—or at least the first three acts roughly as they now stand—was performed at Versailles. A cabal unfavorable to Molière, including the Archbishop of Paris, Hardouin de Péréfixe, Queen-Mother Anne of Austria, certain influential courtiers, and the Brotherhood or Company of the Holy Sacrament (formed in 1627 to enforce morality), arranged that the play be banned and Molière censured.

more properly the admiration and respect due to truly devout men, I have delineated my character as sharply as I could; I have left no room for doubt; I have removed all that might confuse good with evil, and have used for this painting only the specific colors and essential lines that make one instantly recognize a true and brazen hypocrite.

Nevertheless, all my precautions have been to no avail. Others have taken advantage of the delicacy of your feelings on religious matters, and they have been able to deceive you on the only side of your character which lies open to deception: your respect for holy things. By underhanded means, the Tartuffes have skillfully gained Your Majesty's favor, and the models have succeeded in eliminating the copy, no matter how innocent it may have been and no matter what resemblance was found between them.

Although the suppression of this work was a serious blow for me, my misfortune was nonetheless softened by the way in which Your Majesty explained his attitude on the matter; and I believed, Sire, that Your Majesty removed any cause I had for complaint, as you were kind enough to declare that you found nothing in this comedy that you would forbid me to present in public.

Yet, despite this glorious declaration of the greatest and most enlightened king in the world, despite the approval of the Papal Legate[5] and of most of our churchmen, all of whom, at private readings of my work, agreed with the views of Your Majesty, despite all this, a book has appeared by a certain priest[6] which boldly contradicts all of these noble judgments. Your Majesty expressed himself in vain, and the Papal Legate and churchmen gave their opinion to no avail: sight unseen, my comedy is diabolical, and so is my brain; I am a devil garbed in flesh and disguised as a man,[7] a libertine, a disbeliever who deserves a punishment that will set an example. It is not enough that fire expiate my crime in public, for that would be letting me off too easily: the generous piety of this good man will not stop there; he will not allow me to find any mercy in the sight of God; he demands that I be damned, and that will settle the matter.

This book, Sire, was presented to Your Majesty; and I am sure that you see for yourself how unpleasant it is for me to be exposed daily to the insults of these gentlemen, what harm these abuses will do my reputation if they must be tolerated, and finally, how important it is for me to clear myself of these false charges and let the public know that my comedy is nothing more than what they want it to be. I will not ask, Sire, for what I need for the sake of my reputation and the innocence of my work: enlightened kings such as

---

5. Cardinal Legate Chigi, nephew to Pope Alexander VII, heard a reading of *Tartuffe* at Fontainebleau on August 4, 1664.   6. Pierre Roullé, the curate of St. Barthélémy, who wrote a scathing attack on the play and sent his book to the king.   7. Molière took some of these phrases from Roullé.

you do not need to be told what is wished of them; like God, they see what we need and know better than we what they should give us. It is enough for me to place my interests in Your Majesty's hands, and I respectfully await whatever you may care to command.

(*August, 1664*)

Second Petition[8]

Sire,

It is bold indeed for me to ask a favor of a great monarch in the midst of his glorious victories; but in my present situation, Sire, where will I find protection anywhere but where I seek it, and to whom can I appeal against the authority of the power that crushes me,[9] if not to the source of power and authority, the just dispenser of absolute law, the sovereign judge and master of all?

My comedy, Sire, has not enjoyed the kindnesses of Your Majesty. All to no avail, I produced it under the title of *The Hypocrite* and disguised the principal character as a man of the world; in vain I gave him a little hat, long hair, a wide collar, a sword, and lace clothing,[1] softened the action and carefully eliminated all that I thought might provide even the shadow of grounds for discontent on the part of the famous models of the portrait I wished to present; nothing did any good. The conspiracy of opposition revived even at mere conjecture of what the play would be like. They found a way of persuading those who in all other matters plainly insist that they are not to be deceived. No sooner did my comedy appear than it was struck down by the very power which should impose respect; and all that I could do to save myself from the fury of this tempest was to say that Your Majesty had given me permission to present the play and I did not think it was necessary to ask this permission of others, since only Your Majesty could have refused it.

I have no doubt, Sire, that the men whom I depict in my comedy will employ every means possible to influence Your Majesty, and will use, as they have used already, those truly good men who are all the more easily deceived because they judge of others by themselves.[2] They know how to display all of their aims in the most favorable light; yet, no matter how pious they may seem, it is surely not

---

8. On August 5, 1667, *Tartuffe* was performed at the Palais-Royal. The opposition—headed by the First President of Parliament—brought in the police, and the play was stopped. Since Louis was campaigning in Flanders, friends of Molière brought the second *placet* to Lille. Louis had always been favorable toward the playwright; in August, 1665, Molière's company, the *Troupe de Monsieur* (nominally sponsored by Louis's brother Philippe, Duc d'Orléans) had become the *Troupe du Roi*.   9. President de Lanvignon, in charge of the Paris police.   1. There is evidence that in 1664 Tartuffe played his role dressed in a cassock, thus allying him more directly to the clergy.   2. Molière apparently did not know that de Lanvignon had been affiliated with the Company of the Holy Sacrament for the previous ten years.

the interests of God which stir them; they have proven this often enough in the comedies they have allowed to be performed hundreds of times without making the least objection. Those plays attacked only piety and religion, for which they care very little; but this play attacks and makes fun of them, and that is what they cannot bear. They will never forgive me for unmasking their hypocrisy in the eyes of everyone. And I am sure that they will not neglect to tell Your Majesty that people are shocked by my comedy. But the simple truth, Sire, is that all Paris is shocked only by its ban, that the most scrupulous persons have found its presentation worthwhile, and men are astounded that individuals of such known integrity should show so great a deference to people whom everyone should abominate and who are so clearly opposed to the true piety which they profess.

I respectfully await the judgment that Your Majesty will deign to pronounce; but it's certain, Sire, that I need not think of writing comedies if the Tartuffes are triumphant, if they thereby seize the right to persecute me more than ever, and find fault with even the most innocent lines that flow from my pen.

Let your goodness, Sire, give me protection against their envenomed rage, and allow me, at your return from so glorious a campaign, to relieve Your Majesty from the fatigue of his conquests, give him innocent pleasures after such noble accomplishments, and make the monarch laugh who makes all Europe tremble!

(*August, 1667*)

Third Petition

(PRESENTED TO THE KING)

Sire,

A very honest doctor[3] whose patient I have the honor to be, promises and will legally contract to make me live another thirty years if I can obtain a favor for him from Your Majesty. I told him of his promise that I do not deserve so much, and that I should be glad to help him if he will merely agree not to kill me. This favor, Sire, is a post of canon at your royal chapel of Vincennes, made vacant by death.

May I dare to ask for this favor from Your Majesty on the very day of the glorious resurrection of *Tartuffe*, brought back to life by your goodness? By this first favor I have been reconciled with the devout, and the second will reconcile me with the doctors.[4] Undoubtedly this would be too much grace for me at one time, but perhaps it

---

3. A physician friend, M. de Mauvillain, who helped Molière with some of the medical details of *Le Malade imaginaire*.   4. Doctors are ridiculed to varying degrees in earlier plays of Molière: *Dom Juan*, *L'Amour médecin*, and *Le Médecin malgré lui*.

would not be too much for Your Majesty, and I await your answer
to my petition with respectful hope.
   (February, 1669)

Characters[5]

MADAME PERNELLE, *Orgon's mother*
ORGON, *Elmire's husband*
ELMIRE, *Orgon's wife*
DAMIS, *Orgon's son, Elmire's stepson*
MARIANE, *Orgon's daughter, Elmire's stepdaughter, in love with*
      Valère
VALERE, *in love with Mariane*
CLEANTE, *Orgon's brother-in-law*
TARTUFFE, *a hypocrite*
DORINE, *Mariane's lady's-maid*
M. LOYAL, *a bailiff*
A POLICE OFFICER
FLIPOTE, *Mme Pernelle's maid*
The SCENE *throughout: Orgon's house in Paris*

Act I

SCENE 1. *Madame Pernelle and Flipote, her maid, Elmire,*
         Mariane, Dorine, Damis, Cléante

MADAME PERNELLE. Come, come, Flipote; it's time I left this place.
ELMIRE. I can't keep up, you walk at such a pace.
MADAME PERNELLE. Don't trouble, child; no need to show me out.
   It's not your manners I'm concerned about.
ELMIRE. We merely pay you the respect we owe.   5
   But, Mother, why this hurry? Must you go?
MADAME PERNELLE. I must. This house appals me. No one in it
   Will pay attention for a single minute.
   I offer good advice, but you won't hear it.
   Children, I take my leave much vexed in spirit.   10
   You all break in and chatter on and on.
   It's like a madhouse[6] with the keeper gone.
DORINE. If . . .
MADAME PERNELLE. Girl, you talk too much, and I'm afraid

---

5. The name Tartuffe has been traced back to an older word associated with liar or charlatan:
truffer, "to deceive" or "to cheat." Then there was also the Italian actor, Tartufo, physically
deformed and truffle-shaped. Most of the other names are typical of this genre of court-comedy
and possess rather elegant connotations of pastoral and *bergerie*.   Dorine would be a *demoiselle
de compagne* and not a mere maid; that is, a female companion to Mariane of roughly the same
social status. This in part accounts for the liberties she takes in conversation with Orgon, Madame
Pernelle, and others. Her name is short for Théodorine.   6. In the original, *la cour du roi
Pétaud*, the Court of King Pétaud where all are masters; a house of misrule.

You're far too saucy for a lady's-maid.
You push in everywhere and have your say.   15
DAMIS. But . . .
MADAME PERNELLE. You, boy, grow more foolish every day.
  To think my grandson should be such a dunce!
  I've said a hundred times, if I've said it once,
  That if you keep the course on which you've started,
  You'll leave your worthy father broken-hearted.   20
MARIANE. I think . . .
MADAME PERNELLE.   And you, his sister, seem so pure,
  So shy, so innocent, and so demure.
  But you know what they say about still waters.
  I pity parents with secretive daughters.
ELMIRE. Now, Mother . . .   25
MADAME PERNELLE.   And as for you, child, let me add
  That your behavior is extremely bad,
  And a poor example for these children, too.
  Their dear, dead mother did far better than you.
  You're much too free with money, and I'm distressed
  To see you so elaborately dressed.   30
  When it's one's husband that one aims to please,
  One has no need of costly fripperies.
CLEANTE. Oh, Madam, really . . .
MADAME PERNELLE.   You are her brother, Sir,
  And I respect and love you; yet if I were
  My son, this lady's good and pious spouse,   35
  I wouldn't make you welcome in my house.
  You're full of worldly counsels which, I fear,
  Aren't suitable for decent folk to hear.
  I've spoken bluntly, Sir; but it behooves us
  Not to mince words when righteous fervor moves us.   40
DAMIS. Your man Tartuffe is full of holy speeches . . .
MADAME PERNELLE. And practises precisely what he preaches.
  He's a fine man, and should be listened to.
  I will not hear him mocked by fools like you.
DAMIS. Good God! Do you expect me to submit   45
  To the tyranny of that carping hypocrite?
  Must we forgo all joys and satisfactions
  Because that bigot censures all our actions?
DORINE. To hear him talk—and he talks all the time—
  There's nothing one can do that's not a crime.   50
  He rails at everything, your dear Tartuffe.
MADAME PERNELLE. Whatever he reproves deserves reproof.
  He's out to save your souls, and all of you

Must love him, as my son would have you do.

DAMIS. Ah no, Grandmother, I could never take 55
To such a rascal, even for my father's sake.
That's how I feel, and I shall not dissemble.
His every action makes me seethe and tremble,
With helpless anger, and I have no doubt
That he and I will shortly have it out. 60

DORINE. Surely it is a shame and a disgrace
To see this man usurp the master's place—
To see this beggar who, when first he came,
Had not a shoe or shoestring to his name
So far forget himself that he behaves 65
As if the house were his, and we his slaves.

MADAME PERNELLE. Well, mark my words, your souls would fare far better
If you obeyed his precepts to the letter.

DORINE. You see him as a saint. I'm far less awed;
In fact, I see right through him. He's a fraud. 70

MADAME PERNELLE. Nonsense!

DORINE.   His man Laurent's the same, or worse;
I'd not trust either with a penny purse.

MADAME PERNELLE. I can't say what his servant's morals may be;
His own great goodness I can guarantee.
You all regard him with distaste and fear 75
Because he tells you what you're loath to hear,
Condemns your sins, points out your moral flaws,
And humbly strives to further Heaven's cause.

DORINE. If sin is all that bothers him, why is it
He's so upset when folk drop in to visit? 80
Is Heaven so outraged by a social call
That he must prophesy against us all?
I'll tell you what I think: if you ask me,
He's jealous of my mistress' company.

MADAME PERNELLE. Rubbish! [*To* ELMIRE] He's not alone, child, in complaining 85
Of all of your promiscuous entertaining.
Why, the whole neighborhood's upset, I know,
By all these carriages that come and go,
With crowds of guests parading in and out
And noisy servants loitering about. 90
In all of this, I'm sure there's nothing vicious;
But why give people cause to be suspicious?

CLEANTE. They need no cause; they'll talk in any case.
Madam, this world would be a joyless place

If, fearing what malicious tongues might say,   95
We locked our doors and turned our friends away.
And even if one did so dreary a thing,
D' you think those tongues would cease their chattering?
One can't fight slander; it's a losing battle;
Let us instead ignore their tittle-tattle.   100
Let's strive to live by conscience' clear decrees,
And let the gossips gossip as they please.
DORINE.. If there is talk against us, I know the source:
   It's Daphne and her little husband, of course.
   Those who have greatest cause for guilt and shame   105
   Are quickest to besmirch a neighbor's name.
   When there's a chance for libel, they never miss it;
   When something can be made to seem illicit
   They're off at once to spread the joyous news,
   Adding to fact what fantasies they choose.   110
   By talking up their neighbor's indiscretions
   They seek to camouflage their own transgressions,
   Hoping that others' innocent affairs
   Will lend a hue of innocence to theirs,
   Or that their own black guilt will come to seem   115
   Part of a general shady color-scheme.
MADAME PERNELLE. All this is quite irrelevant. I doubt
   That anyone's more virtuous and devout
   Than dear Orante; and I'm informed that she
   Condemns your mode of life most vehemently.   120
DORINE. Oh, yes, she's strict, devout, and has no taint
   Of worldliness; in short, she seems a saint.
   But it was time which taught her that disguise;
   So long as her attractions could enthrall,
   She flounced and flirted and enjoyed it all,   125
   But now that they're no longer what they were
   She quits a world which fast is quitting her,
   And wears a veil of virtue to conceal
   Her bankrupt beauty and her lost appeal.   130
   That's what becomes of old coquettes today:
   Distressed when all their lovers fall away,
   They see no recourse but to play the prude,
   And so confer a style on solitude.
   Thereafter, they're severe with everyone,   135
   Condemning all our actions, pardoning none,
   And claiming to be pure, austere, and zealous
   When, if the truth were known, they're merely jealous,
   And cannot bear to see another know
   The pleasures time has forced them to forgo.   140

MADAME PERNELLE. [*Initially to* ELMIRE] That sort of talk[7] is what
    you like to hear;
  Therefore you'd have us all keep still, my dear,
  While Madam rattles on the livelong day.
  Nevertheless, I mean to have my say.
  I tell you that you're blest to have Tartuffe   145
  Dwelling, as my son's guest, beneath this roof;
  That Heaven has sent him to forestall its wrath
  By leading you, once more, to the true path;
  That all he reprehends is reprehensible,
  And that you'd better heed him, and be sensible.   150
  These visits, balls, and parties in which you revel
  Are nothing but inventions of the Devil.
  One never hears a word that's edifying:
  Nothing but chaff and foolishness and lying,
  As well as vicious gossip in which one's neighbor   155
  Is cut to bits with épée, foil, and saber.
  People of sense are driven half-insane
  At such affairs, where noise and folly reign
  And reputations perish thick and fast.
  As a wise preacher said on Sunday last,   160
  Parties are Towers of Babylon,[8] because
  The guests all babble on with never a pause;
  And then he told a story which, I think . . .
    [*To* CLEANTE] I heard that laugh, Sir, and I saw that wink!
  Go find your silly friends and laugh some more!   165
  Enough; I'm going; don't show me to the door.
  I leave this household much dismayed and vexed;
  I cannot say when I shall see you next.
    [*Slapping* FLIPOTE] Wake up, don't stand there gaping into space!
  I'll slap some sense into that stupid face.   170
  Move, move, you slut.

SCENE 2. *Cléante, Dorine*

CLEANTE.   I think I'll stay behind;
  I want no further pieces of her mind.
  How that old lady . . .
DORINE.   Oh, what wouldn't she say
  If she could hear you speak of her that way!
  She'd thank you for the *lady,* but I'm sure   5
  She'd find the *old* a little premature.
CLEANTE. My, what a scene she made, and what a din!

---

7. In the original, a reference to a collection of novels about chivalry found in *La Bibliothèque
bleue (The Blue Library).* written for children.   8. I.e., Tower of Babel. Mme. Pernelle's mala-
propism is the cause of Cléante's laughter.

And how this man Tartuffe has taken her in!
DORINE. Yes, but her son is even worse deceived;
    His folly must be seen to be believed.   10
    In the late troubles,[9] he played an able part
    And served his king with wise and loyal heart,
    But he's quite lost his senses since he fell
    Beneath Tartuffe's infatuating spell.
    He calls him brother, and loves him as his life,   15
    Preferring him to mother, child, or wife.
    In him and him alone will he confide;
    He's made him his confessor and his guide;
    He pets and pampers him with love more tender
    Than any pretty maiden could engender,   20
    Gives him the place of honor when they dine,
    Delights to see him gorging like a swine,
    Stuffs him with dainties till his guts distend,
    And when he belches, cries "God bless you, friend!"
    In short, he's mad; he worships him; he dotes;   25
    His deeds he marvels at, his words, he quotes,
    Thinking each act a miracle, each word
    Oracular as those that Moses heard.
    Tartuffe, much pleased to find so easy a victim,
    Has in a hundred ways beguiled and tricked him,   30
    Milked him of money, and with his permission
    Established here a sort of Inquisition.
    Even Laurent, his lackey, dares to give
    Us arrogant advice on how to live;
    He sermonizes us in thundering tones   35
    And confiscates our ribbons and colognes.
    Last week he tore a kerchief into pieces
    Because he found it pressed in a *Life of Jesus:*
    He said it was a sin to juxtapose
    Unholy vanities and holy prose.   40

    SCENE 3. *Elmire, Mariane, Damis, Cléante, Dorine*

ELMIRE. [*To* CLEANTE] You did well not to follow; she stood in the
    door
    And said *verbatim* all she'd said before.
    I saw my husband coming. I think I'd best
    Go upstairs now, and take a little rest.
CLEANTE. I'll wait and greet him here; then I must go.   5

9. A series of political disturbances during the minority of Louis XIV. Specifically these consisted
of the *Fronde* ("opposition") of the Parlement (1648–1649) and the *Fronde* of the Princes (1650–
1653). Orgon is depicted as supporting Louis XIV in these outbreaks and their resolution.

I've really only time to say hello.
DAMIS. Sound him about my sister's wedding, please.
I think Tartuffe's against it, and that he's
Been urging Father to withdraw his blessing.
As you well know, I'd find that most distressing. 10
Unless my sister and Valère can marry,
My hopes to wed *his* sister will miscarry.
And I'm determined . . .
DORINE.   He's coming.

SCENE 4. *Orgon, Cléante, Dorine*

ORGON.   Ah, Brother, good-day.
CLEANTE. Well, welcome back, I'm sorry I can't stay.
How was the country? Blooming, I trust, and green?
ORGON. Excuse me, Brother; just one moment.
    [*To* DORINE]   Dorine . . .
    [*To* CLEANTE] To put my mind at rest, I always learn 5
The household news the moment I return.
    [*To* DORINE] Has all been well, these two days I've been gone?
How are the family? What's been going on?
DORINE. Your wife, two days ago, had a bad fever,
And a fierce headache which refused to leave her. 10
ORGON. Ah. And Tartuffe?
DORINE.   Tartuffe? Why, he's round and red.
Bursting with health, and excellently fed.
ORGON. Poor fellow!
DORINE.   That night, the mistress was unable
To take a single bite at the dinner-table.
Her headache-pains, she said, were simply hellish. 15
ORGON. Ah. And Tartuffe?
DORINE.   He ate his meal with relish,
And zealously devoured in her presence
A leg of mutton and a brace of pheasants.
ORGON. Poor fellow!
DORINE.   Well, the pains continued strong,
And so she tossed and tossed the whole night long, 20
Now icy-cold, now burning like a flame.
We sat beside her bed till morning came.
ORGON. Ah. And Tartuffe?
DORINE.   Why, having eaten, he rose
And sought his room, already in a doze,
Got into his warm bed, and snored away 25
In perfect peace until the break of day.
ORGON. Poor fellow!

DORINE.   After much ado, we talked her
   Into dispatching someone for the doctor.
   He bled her, and the fever quickly fell.
ORGON. Ah. And Tartuffe?
DORINE.   He bore it very well.   30
   To keep his cheerfulness at any cost,
   And make up for the blood Madame had lost,
   He drank, at lunch, four beakers full of port.
ORGON. Poor fellow.
DORINE.   Both are doing well, in short.
   I'll go and tell Madame that you've expressed   35
   Keen sympathy and anxious interest.

SCENE 5. *Orgon, Cléante*

CLEANTE. That girl was laughing in your face, and though
   I've no wish to offend you, even so
   I'm bound to say that she had some excuse.
   How can you possibly be such a goose?
   Are you so dazed by this man's hocus-pocus   5
   That all the world, save him, is out of focus?
   You've given him clothing, shelter, food, and care;
   Why must you also . . .
ORGON.   Brother, stop right there.
   You do not know the man of whom you speak.
CLEANTE. I grant you that. But my judgment's not so weak   10
   That I can't tell, by his effect on others . . .
ORGON. Ah, when you meet him, you two will be like brothers!
   There's been no loftier soul since time began.
   He is a man who . . . a man who . . . an excellent man.
   To keep his precepts is to be reborn,   15
   And view this dunghill of a world with scorn.
   Yes, thanks to him I'm a changed man indeed.
   Under his tutelage my soul's been freed
   From earthly loves, and every human tie:
   My mother, children, brother, and wife could die,   20
   And I'd not feel a single moment's pain.
CLEANTE. That's a fine sentiment, Brother; most humane.
ORGON. Oh, had you seen Tartuffe as I first knew him,
   Your heart, like mine, would have surrendered to him.
   He used to come into our church each day   25
   And humbly kneel nearby, and start to pray.
   He'd draw the eyes of everybody there
   By the deep fervor of his heartfelt prayer;
   He'd sigh and weep, and sometimes with a sound
   Of rapture he would bend and kiss the ground;   30

And when I rose to go, he'd run before
To offer me holy-water at the door.
His serving-man, no less devout than he,
Informed me of his master's poverty;
I gave him gifts, but in his humbleness   35
He'd beg me every time to give him less.
"Oh, that's too much," he'd cry, "too much by twice!
I don't deserve it. The half, Sir, would suffice."
And when I wouldn't take it back, he'd share
Half of it with the poor, right then and there.   40
At length, Heaven prompted me to take him in
To dwell with us, and free our souls from sin.
He guides our lives, and to protect my honor
Stays by my wife, and keeps an eye upon her;
He tells me whom she sees, and all she does,   45
And seems more jealous than I ever was!
And how austere he is! Why, he can detect
A moral sin where you would least suspect;
In smallest trifles, he's extremely strict.
Last week, his conscience was severely pricked   50
Because, while praying, he had caught a flea
And killed it, so he felt, too wrathfully. [1]

CLEANTE. Good God, man! Have you lost your common sense—
    Or is this all some joke at my expense?
    How can you stand there and in all sobriety . . .   55
ORGON. Brother, your language savors of impiety.
    Too much free-thinking's made your faith unsteady,
    And as I've warned you many times already,
    'Twill get you into trouble before you're through.
CLEANTE. So I've been told before by dupes like you: 60
    Being blind, you'd have all others blind as well;
    The clear-eyed man you call an infidel,
    And he who sees through humbug and pretense
    Is charged, by you, with want of reverence.
    Spare me your warnings, Brother; I have no fear   65
    Of speaking out, for you and Heaven to hear,
    Against affected zeal and pious knavery.
    There's true and false in piety, as in bravery,
    And just as those whose courage shines the most
    In battle, are the least inclined to boast,   70
    So those whose hearts are truly pure and lowly
    Don't make a flashy show of being holy.

1. In the *Golden Legend* (*Legenda santorum*), a popular collection of the lives of the saints written in the thirteenth century, it is said of St. Marcarius the Elder (d. 390) that he dwelt naked in the desert for six months, a penance he felt appropriate for having killed a flea.

There's a vast difference, so it seems to me,
Between true piety and hypocrisy:
How do you fail to see it, may I ask?   75
Is not a face quite different from a mask?
Cannot sincerity and cunning art,
Reality and semblance, be told apart?
Are scarecrows just like men, and do you hold
That a false coin is just as good as gold?   80
Ah, Brother, man's a strangely fashioned creature
Who seldom is content to follow Nature,
But recklessly pursues his inclination
Beyond the narrow bounds of moderation,
And often, by transgressing Reason's laws,   85
Perverts a lofty aim or noble cause.
A passing observation, but it applies.
ORGON. I see, dear Brother, that you're profoundly wise;
    You harbor all the insight of the age.
    You are our one clear mind, our only sage,   90
    The era's oracle, its Cato[2] too,
    And all mankind are fools compared to you.
CLEANTE. Brother, I don't pretend to be a sage,
    Nor have I all the wisdom of the age.
    There's just one insight I would dare to claim: 95
    I know that true and false are not the same;
    And just as there is nothing I more revere
    Than a soul whose faith is steadfast and sincere,
    Nothing that I more cherish and admire
    Than honest zeal and true religious fire,   100
    So there is nothing that I find more base
    Than specious piety's dishonest face—
    Than these bold mountebanks, these histrios
    Whose impious mummeries and hollow shows
    Exploit our love of Heaven, and make a jest   105
    Of all that men think holiest and best;
    These calculating souls who offer prayers
    Not to their Maker, but as public wares,
    And seek to buy respect and reputation
    With lifted eyes and sighs of exaltation;   110
    These charlatans, I say, whose pilgrim souls
    Proceed, by way of Heaven, toward earthly goals,
    Who weep and pray and swindle and extort,
    Who preach the monkish life, but haunt the court,
    Who make their zeal the partner of their vice—   115

---

2. Roman statesman (95 B.C.–46 B.C.) with an enduring reputation for honesty and incorrupti-
bility.

Such men are vengeful, sly, and cold as ice,
And when there is an enemy to defame
They cloak their spite in fair religion's name,
Their private spleen and malice being made
To seem a high and virtuous crusade,   120
Until, to mankind's reverent applause,
They crucify their foe in Heaven's cause.
Such knaves are all too common; yet, for the wise,
True piety isn't hard to recognize,
And, happily, these present times provide us   125
With bright examples to instruct and guide us.
Consider Ariston and Périandre;
Look at Oronte, Alcidamas, Clitandre;[3]
Their virtue is acknowledged; who could doubt it?
But you won't hear them beat the drum about it.   130
They're never ostentatious, never vain,
And their religion's moderate and humane;
It's not their way to criticize and chide:
They think censoriousness a mark of pride,
And therefore, letting others preach and rave,   135
They show, by deeds, how Christians should behave.
They think no evil of their fellow man,
But judge of him as kindly as they can.
They don't intrigue and wangle and conspire;
To lead a good life is their one desire;   140
The sinner wakes no rancorous hate in them;
It is the sin alone which they condemn;
Nor do they try to show a fiercer zeal
For Heaven's cause than Heaven itself could feel.
These men I honor, these men I advocate   145
As models for us all to emulate.
Your man is not their sort at all, I fear:
And, while your praise of him is quite sincere,
I think that you've been dreadfully deluded.
ORGON. Now then, dear Brother, is your speech concluded?   150
CLEANTE. Why, yes.
ORGON.   Your servant, Sir.   [*He turns to go.*]
CLEANTE.   No, Brother; wait.
    There's one more matter. You agreed of late
    That young Valère might have your daughter's hand.
ORGON. I did.
CLEANTE.   And set the date, I understand.
ORGON. Quite so.

3. Vaguely Greek and Roman names derived from the elegant literature of the day; not names of actual persons.

CLEANTE.   You've now postponed it; is that true?   155
ORGON. No doubt.
CLEANTE.   The match no longer pleases you?
ORGON. Who knows?
CLEANTE.   D'you mean to go back on your word?
ORGON. I won't say that.
CLEANTE.   Has anything occurred
    Which might entitle you to break your pledge?
ORGON. Perhaps.
CLEANTE.   Why must you hem, and haw, and hedge?
    The boy asked me to sound you in this affair . . .   160
ORGON. It's been a pleasure.
CLEANTE.   But what shall I tell Valère?
ORGON. Whatever you like.
CLEANTE.   But what have you decided?
    What are your plans?
ORGON.   I plan, Sir, to be guided
    By Heaven's will.
CLEANTE.   Come, Brother, don't talk rot.   165
    You've given Valère your word; will you keep it, or not?
ORGON. Good day.
CLEANTE.   This looks like poor Valère's undoing;
    I'll go and warn him that there's trouble brewing.

Act II

SCENE 1. *Orgon, Mariane*

ORGON. Mariane.
MARIANE.   Yes, Father?
ORGON.   A word with you; come here.
MARIANE. What are you looking for?
ORGON. [*Peering into a small closet*] Eavesdroppers, dear.
    I'm making sure we shan't be overheard.
    Someone in there could catch our every word.
    Ah, good, we're safe. Now, Mariane, my child,   5
    You're a sweet girl who's tractable and mild,
    Whom I hold dear, and think most highly of.
MARIANE. I'm deeply grateful, Father, for your love.
ORGON. That's well said, Daughter; and you can repay me
    If, in all things, you'll cheerfully obey me.   10
MARIANE. To please you, Sir, is what delights me best.
ORGON. Good, good. Now, what d'you think of Tartuffe, our guest?
MARIANE. I, Sir?
ORGON.   Yes. Weigh your answer; think it through.
MARIANE. Oh, dear. I'll say whatever you wish me to.

ORGON. That's wisely said, my Daughter. Say of him, then,   15
  That he's the very worthiest of men,
  And that you're fond of him, and would rejoice
  In being his wife, if that should be my choice.
  Well?
MARIANE. What?
ORGON.   What's that?
MARIANE.   I . . .
ORGON.   Well?
MARIANE.   Forgive me, pray.
ORGON. Did you not hear me?
MARIANE.   Of *whom,* Sir, must I say   20
  That I am fond of him, and would rejoice
  In being his wife, if that should be your choice?
ORGON. Why, of Tartuffe.
MARIANE.   But, Father, that's false, you know.
  Why would you have me say what isn't so?
ORGON. Because I am resolved it shall be true.   25
  That it's my wish should be enough for you.
MARIANE. You can't mean, Father . . .
ORGON.   Yes, Tartuffe shall be
  Allied by marriage[4] to this family,
  And he's to be your husband, is that clear?
  It's a father's privilege . . .

SCENE 2. *Dorine, Orgon, Mariane*

ORGON. [*To* DORINE]   What are you doing in here?
  Is curiosity so fierce a passion
  With you, that you must eavesdrop in this fashion?
DORINE. There's lately been a rumor going about—
  Based on some hunch or chance remark, no doubt—   5
  That you mean Mariane to wed Tartuffe.
  I've laughed it off, of course, as just a spoof.
ORGON. You find it so incredible?
DORINE.   Yes, I do.
  I won't accept that story, even from you.
ORGON. Well, you'll believe it when the thing is done.   10
DORINE. Yes, yes, of course. Go on and have your fun.
ORGON. I've never been more serious in my life.
DORINE. Ha!
ORGON.   Daughter, I mean it; you're to be his wife.

4. This assertion is important and more than a mere device in the plot of the play. The second *placet* or petition insists that Tartuffe be costumed as a layman, and Orgon's plan for him to marry again asserts Tartuffe's position in the laity. In the 1664 version of the play Tartuffe had been dressed in a cassock suggestive of the priesthood, and Molière was now anxious to avoid any suggestion of this kind.

DORINE. No, don't believe your father; it's all a hoax.

ORGON. See here, young woman . . .

DORINE.   Come, Sir, no more jokes;
   You can't fool us.   15

OREGON.   How dare you talk that way?

DORINE. All right, then: we believe you, sad to say.
   But how a man like you, who looks so wise
   And wears a moustache of such splendid size,
   Can be so foolish as to . . .

ORGON.   Silence, please!   20
   My girl, you take too many liberties.
   I'm master here, as you must not forget.

DORINE. Do let's discuss this calmly; don't be upset.
   You can't be serious, Sir, about this plan.
   What should that bigot want with Mariane?   25
   Praying and fasting ought to keep him busy.
   And then, in terms of wealth and rank, what is he?
   Why should a man of property like you
   Pick out a beggar son-in-law?

ORGON.   That will do.
   Speak of his poverty with reverence.   30
   His is a pure and saintly indigence
   Which far transcends all worldly pride and pelf.
   He lost his fortune, as he says himself,
   Because he cared for Heaven alone, and so
   Was careless of his interests here below.   35
   I mean to get him out of his present straits
   And help him to recover his estates—
   Which, in his part of the world, have no small fame.
   Poor though he is, he's a gentleman just the same.

DORINE. Yes, so he tells us; and, Sir, it seems to me   40
   Such pride goes very ill with piety.
   A man whose spirit spurns this dungy earth
   Ought not to brag of lands and noble birth;
   Such worldly arrogance will hardly square
   With meek devotion and the life of prayer.   45
   . . . But this approach, I see, has drawn a blank;
   Let's speak, then, of his person, not his rank.
   Doesn't it seem to you a trifle grim
   To give a girl like her to a man like him?
   When two are so ill-suited, can't you see   50
   What the sad consequence is bound to be?
   A young girl's virtue is imperilled, Sir,
   When such a marriage is imposed on her;
   For if one's bridegroom isn't to one's taste,

It's hardly an inducement to be chaste,   55
And many a man with horns upon his brow
Has made his wife the thing that she is now.
It's hard to be a faithful wife, in short,
To certain husbands of a certain sort,
And he who gives his daughter to a man she hates   60
Must answer for her sins at Heaven's gates.
Think, Sir, before you play so risky a role.
ORGON. This servant-girl presumes to save my soul!
DORINE. You would do well to ponder what I've said.
ORGON. Daughter, we'll disregard this dunderhead.   65
Just trust your father's judgment. Oh, I'm aware
That I once promised you to young Valère;
But now I hear he gambles, which greatly shocks me;
What's more, I've doubts about his orthodoxy.
His visits to church, I note, are very few.   70
DORINE. Would you have him go at the same hours as you,
And kneel nearby, to be sure of being seen?
ORGON. I can dispense with such remarks, Dorine.
[*To* MARIANE] Tartuffe, however, is sure of Heaven's blessing.
And that's the only treasure worth possessing.   75
This match will bring you joys beyond all measure;
Your cup will overflow with every pleasure;
You two will interchange your faithful loves
Like two sweet cherubs, or two turtle-doves.
No harsh word shall be heard, no frown be seen,   80
And he shall make you happy as a queen.
DORINE. And she'll make him a cuckold, just wait and see.
ORGON. What language!
DORINE.   Oh, he's a man of destiny;
He's *made* for horns, and what the stars demand
Your daughter's virtue surely can't withstand.   85
ORGON. Don't interrupt me further. Why can't you learn
That certain things are none of your concern?
DORINE. It's for your own sake that I interfere.
    [*She repeatedly interrupts* ORGON *just as he is turning to speak
    to his daughter.*]
ORGON. Most kind of you. Now, hold your tongue, d'you hear?
DORINE. If I didn't love you . . .
ORGON.   Spare me your affection.
DORINE. I'll love you, Sir, in spite of your objection.   90
ORGON. Blast!
DORINE.   I can't bear, Sir, for your honor's sake,
To let you make this ludicrous mistake.
ORGON. You mean to go on talking?

DORINE.   If I didn't protest
This sinful marriage, my conscience couldn't rest.   95
ORGON. If you don't hold your tongue, you little shrew . . .
DORINE. What, lost your temper? A pious man like you?
ORGON. Yes! Yes! You talk and talk. I'm maddened by it.
Once and for all, I tell you to be quiet.
DORINE. Well, I'll be quiet. But I'll be thinking hard.   100
ORGON. Think all you like, but you had better guard
That saucy tongue of yours, or I'll . . .
          [*Turning back to* MARIANE]   Now, child,
I've weighed this matter fully.
DORINE. [*Aside*]   It drives me wild
That I can't speak.
          [ORGON *turns his head, and she is silent.*]
OREGON.   Tartuffe is no young dandy,
But, still, his person . . .
DORINE. [*Aside*]   Is as sweet as candy.
ORGON. Is such that, even if you shouldn't care
For his other merits . . .
          [*He turns and stands facing* DORINE, *arms crossed.*]
DORINE. [*Aside*]   They'll make a lovely pair.
If I were she, no man would marry me
Against my inclination, and go scot-free.
He'd learn, before the wedding-day was over,   110
How readily a wife can find a lover.
ORGON. [*To* DORINE] It seems you treat my orders as a joke.
DORINE. Why, what's the matter? 'Twas not to you I spoke.
ORGON. What *were* you doing?
DORINE.   Talking to myself, that's all.
ORGON. Ah! [*Aside*] One more bit of impudence and gall,   115
And I shall give her a good slap in the face.
          [*He puts himself in position to slap her;* DORINE, *whenever he
          glances at her, stands immobile and silent.*]
Daughter, you shall accept, and with good grace,
The husband I've selected . . . Your wedding-day . . .
          [*To* DORINE] Why don't you talk to yourself?
DORINE.   I've nothing to say.
ORGON. Come, just one word.
DORINE.   No thank you, Sir. I pass.
ORGON. Come, speak; I'm waiting.   120
DORINE.   I'd not be such an ass.
ORGON. [*Turning to* MARIANE] In short, dear Daughter, I mean to be
obeyed,
And you must bow to the sound choice I've made.
DORINE. [*moving away*] I'd not wed such a monster, even in jest.

[ORGON *attempts to slap her, but misses.*]

ORGON. Daughter, that maid of yours is a thorough pest;   125
    She makes me sinfully annoyed and nettled.
    I can't speak further; my nerves are too unsettled.
    She's so upset me by her insolent talk,
    I'll calm myself by going for a walk.

SCENE 3. *Dorine, Mariane*

DORINE. [*Returning*] Well, have you lost your tongue, girl? Must I play
    Your part, and say the lines you ought to say?
    Faced with a fate so hideous and absurd,
    Can you not utter one dissenting word?
MARIANE. What good would it do? A father's power is great.   5
DORINE. Resist him now, or it will be too late.
MARIANE. But . . .
DORINE.   Tell him one cannot love at a father's whim;
    That you shall marry for yourself, not him;
    That since it's you who are to be the bride,
    It's you, not he, who must be satisfied;   10
    And that if his Tartuffe is so sublime,
    He's free to marry him at any time.
MARIANE. I've bowed so long to Father's strict control,
    I couldn't oppose him now, to save my soul.   15
DORINE. Come, come, Mariane. Do listen to reason, won't you?
    Valère has asked your hand. Do you love him, or don't you?
MARIANE. Oh, how unjust of you! What can you mean
    By asking such a question, dear Dorine?
    You know the depth of my affection for him;
    I've told you a hundred times how I adore him.   20
DORINE. I don't believe in everything I hear;
    Who knows if your professions were sincere?
MARIANE. They were, Dorine, and you do me wrong to doubt it;
    Heaven knows that I've been all too frank about it.
DORINE. You love him, then?
MARIANE.   Oh, more than I can express.
DORINE. And he, I take it, cares for you no less?   25
MARIANE. I think so.
DORINE.   And you both, with equal fire,
    Burn to be married?
MARIANE.   That is our one desire.
DORINE. What of Tartuffe, then? What of your father's plan?
MARIANE. I'll kill myself, if I'm forced to wed that man.   30
DORINE. I hadn't thought of that recourse. How splendid!

Just die, and all your troubles will be ended!
A fine solution. Oh, it maddens me
To hear you talk in that self-pitying key.
MARIANE. Dorine, how harsh you are! It's most unfair.   35
You have no sympathy for my despair.
DORINE. I've none at all for people who talk drivel
And, faced with difficulties, whine and snivel.
MARIANE. No doubt I'm timid, but it would be wrong . . .
DORINE. True love requires a heart that's firm and strong.   40
MARIANE. I'm strong in my affection for Valère,
But coping with my father is his affair.
DORINE. But if your father's brain has grown so cracked
Over his dear Tartuffle that he can retract
His blessing, though your wedding-day was named,   45
It's surely not Valère who's to be blamed.
MARIANE. If I defied my father, as you suggest,
Would it not seem unmaidenly, at best?
Shall I defend my love at the expense
Of brazenness and disobedience?   50
Shall I parade my heart's desires, and flaunt . . .
DORINE. No, I ask nothing of you. Clearly you want
To be Madame Tartuffe, and I feel bound
Not to oppose a wish so very sound.
What right have I to criticize the match?   55
Indeed, my dear, the man's a brilliant catch.
Monsieur Tartuffe! Now, there's a man of weight!
Yes, yes, Monsieur Tartuffe, I'm bound to state,
Is quite a person; that's not to be denied;
'Twill be no little thing to be his bride.   60
The world already rings with his renown;
He's a great noble—in his native town;
His ears are red, he has a pink complexion,
And all in all, he'll suit you to perfection.
MARIANE. Dear God!
DORINE.   Oh, how triumphant you will feel
At having caught a husband so ideal!   65
MARIANE. Oh, do stop teasing, and use your cleverness
To get me out of this appalling mess.
Advise me, and I'll do whatever you say.
DORINE. Ah, no, a dutiful daughter must obey   70
Her father, even if he weds her to an ape.
You've a bright future; why struggle to escape?
Tartuffe will take you back where his family lives,
To a small town aswarm with relatives—
Uncles and cousins whom you'll be charmed to meet.   75

You'll be received at once by the elite,
Calling upon the bailiff's wife,[5] no less—
Even, perhaps, upon the mayoress,[6]
Who'll sit you down in the *best* kitchen chair.[7]
Then, once a year, you'll dance at the village fair   80
To the drone of bagpipes—two of them, in fact—
And see a puppet-show, or an animal act.[8]
Your husband . . .

MARIANE.   Oh, you turn my blood to ice!
Stop torturing me, and give me your advice.

DORINE. [*Threatening to go*] Your servant, Madam.

MARIANE.   Dorine, I beg
of you . . .   85

DORINE. No, you deserve it; this marriage must go through.

MARIANE. Dorine!

DORINE.   No.

MARIANE.   Not Tartuffe! You know I think him . . .

DORINE. Tartuffe's your cup of tea, and you shall drink him.

MARIANE. I've always told you everything, and relied . . .

DORINE. No. You deserve to be tartuffified.   90

MARIANE. Well, since you mock me and refuse to care,
I'll henceforth seek my solace in despair:
Despair shall be my counsellor and friend,
And help me bring my sorrows to an end. [*She starts to leave.*]

DORINE. There now, come back; my anger has subsided.   95
You do deserve some pity, I've decided.

MARIANE. Dorine, if Father makes me undergo
This dreadful martyrdom, I'll die, I know.

DORINE. Don't fret; it won't be difficult to discover
Some plan of action . . . But here's Valère, your lover.   100

SCENE 4. *Valère, Mariane, Dorine*

VALERE. Madam, I've just received some wondrous news
Regarding which I'd like to hear your views.

MARIANE. What news?

VALERE.   You're marrying Tartuffe.

MARIANE.   I find
That Father does have such a match in mind.

VALERE. Your father, Madam . . .

MARIANE.   . . . has just this minute said

---

5. A high-ranking official in the judiciary, not simply a sheriff's deputy as today.   6. The wife
of a tax collector (*élu*), an important official controlling imports, elected by the Estates General.
7. In elegant society of Molière's day, there was a hierarchy of seats and the use of each was
determined by rank. The seats descended from *fauteuils, chaises, perroquets, tabourets,* to *pliants.*
Thus Mariane would get the lowest seat in the room.   8. In the original, *fagotin,* literally a
monkey dressed up in a man's clothing.

That it's Tartuffe he wishes me to wed.   5
VALERE. Can he be serious?
MARIANE.   Oh, indeed he can;
    He's clearly set his heart upon the plan.
VALERE. And what position do you propose to take,
    Madam?
MARIANE. Why—I don't know.
VALRIE.   For heaven's sake—   10
    You don't know?
MARIANE.   No.
VALERE.   Well, well!
MARIANE.   Advise me, do.
VALERE. Marry the man. That's my advice to you.
MARIANE. That's your advice?
VALERE.   Yes.
MARIANE.   Truly?
VALERE.   Oh, absolutely.
    You couldn't choose more wisely, more astutely.
MARIANE. Thanks for this counsel; I'll follow it, of course.   15
VALERE. Do, do; I'm sure 'twill cost you no remorse.
MARIANE. To give it didn't cause your heart to break.
VALERE. I gave it, Madam, only for your sake.
MARIANE. And it's for your sake that I take it, Sir.
DORINE. [*Withdrawing to the rear of the stage*]
    Let's see which fool will prove the stubborner.   20
VALERE. So! I am nothing to you, and it was flat
    Deception when you . . .
MARIANE.   Please, enough of that.
    You've told me plainly that I should agree
    To wed the man my father's chosen for me,
    And since you've deigned to counsel me so wisely,   25
    I promise, Sir, to do as you advise me.
VALERE. Ah, no, 'twas not by me that you were swayed.
    No, your decision was already made;
    Though now, to save appearances, you protest
    That you're betraying me at my behest.   30
MARIANE. Just as you say.
VALERE.   Quite so. And I now see
    That you were never truly in love with me.
MARIANE. Alas, you're free to think so if you choose.
VALERE. I choose to think so, and here's a bit of news:
    You've spurned my hand, but I know where to turn   35
    For kinder treatment, as you shall quickly learn.
MARIANE. I'm sure you do. Your noble qualities
    Inspire affection . . .

VALERE.   Forget my qualities, please.
  They don't inspire you overmuch, I find.
  But there's another lady I have in mind   40
  Whose sweet and generous nature will not scorn
  To compensate me for the loss I've borne.
MARIANE. I'm no great loss, and I'm sure that you'll transfer
  Your heart quite painlessly from me to her.
VALERE. I'll do my best to take it in my stride.   45
  The pain I feel at being cast aside
  Time and forgetfulness may put an end to.
  Or if I can't forget, I shall pretend to.
  No self-respecting person is expected
  To go on loving once he's been rejected.   50
MARIANE. Now, that's a fine, high-minded sentiment.
VALERE. One to which any sane man would assent.
  Would you prefer it if I pined away
  In hopeless passion till my dying day?
  Am I to yield you to a rival's arms   55
  And not console myself with other charms?
MARIANE. Go then; console yourself; don't hesitate.
  I wish you to; indeed, I cannot wait.
VALERE. You wish me to?
MARIANE.   Yes.
VALERE.   That's the final straw.
  Madam, farewell. Your wish shall be my law.   60
  [*He starts to leave, and then returns: this repeatedly.*]
MARIANE. Splendid.
VALERE. [*Coming back again*] This breach, remember, is of your
  making;
  It's you who've driven me to the step I'm taking.
MARIANE. Of course.
VALERE. [*Coming back again*] Remember, too, that I am merely
  Following your example.
MARIANE.   I see that clearly.
VALERE. Enough. I'll go and do your bidding, then.   65
MARIANE. Good.
VALERE. [*Coming back again*] You shall never see my face again.
MARIANE. Excellent.
VALERE. [*Walking to the door, then turning about*]
                Yes?
MARIANE.   What?
VALERE.   What's that? What did you say?
MARIANE. Nothing. You're dreaming.
VALERE.   Ah. Well, I'm on my way.
  Farewell, Madame.   [*He moves slowly away.*]

MARIANE.   Farewell.

DORINE. [*To* MARIANE]   If you ask me,
   Both of you are as mad as mad can be.   70
   Do stop this nonsense, now. I've only let you
   Squabble so long to see where it would get you.
   Whoa there, Monsieur Valère!
     [*She goes and seizes* VALERE *by the arm; he makes a great show
     of resistance.*]

VALERE.   What's this, Dorine?

DORINE. Come here.

VALERE.   No, no, my heart's too full of spleen.
   Don't hold me back; her wish must be obeyed.   75

DORINE. Stop!

VALERE.   It's too late now; my decision's made.

DORINE. Oh, pooh!

MARIANE. [*Aside*] He hates the sight of me, that's plain.
   I'll go, and so deliver him from pain.

DORINE. [*Leaving* VALERE, *running after* MARIANE]
   And now *you* run away! Come back.

MARIANE.   No, no
   Nothing you say will keep me here. Let go!   80

VALERE. [*Aside*] She cannot bear my presence, I perceive.
   To spare her further torment, I shall leave.

DORINE. [*Leaving* MARIANE, *running after* VALERE]
   Again! You'll not escape, Sir; don't you try it.
   Come here, you two. Stop fussing and be quiet.
     [*She takes* VALERE *by the hand, then* MARIANE, *and draws them
     together.*]

VALERE. [*To* DORINE] What do you want of me?   85

MARIANE. [*To* DORINE] What is the point of this?

DORINE. We're going to have a little armistice.
   [*To* VALERE] Now, weren't you silly to get so overheated?

VALERE. Didn't you see how badly I was treated?

DORINE. [*To* MARIANE] Aren't you a simpleton, to have lost your
   head?

MARIANE. Didn't you hear the hateful things he said?   90

DORINE. [*To* VALERE] You're both great fools. Her sole desire, Val-
   ère,
   Is to be yours in marriage. To that I'll swear.
   [*To* MARIANE] He loves you only, and he wants no wife
   But you, Mariane. On that I'll stake my life.   95

MARIANE. [*To* VALERE] Then why you advised me so, I cannot see.

VALERE. [*To* MARIANE] On such a question, why ask advice of *me*?

DORINE. Oh, you're impossible. Give me your hands, you two.
   [*To* VALERE] Yours first.

VALERE. [*Giving* DORINE *his hand*] But why?
DORINE. [*To* MARIANE]   And now a hand from
    you.
MARIANE. [*Also giving* DORINE *her hand*]
    What are you doing?
DORINE.   There: a perfect fit.   100
    You suit each other better than you'll admit.
        [VALERE *and* MARIANE *hold hands for some time without look-
        ing at each other.*]
VALERE. [*Turning toward* MARIANE]
    Ah, come, don't be so haughty. Give a man
    A look of kindness, won't you, Mariane?
        [MARIANE *turns toward* VALERE *and smiles.*]
DORINE. I tell you, lovers are completely mad!
VALERE. [*To* MARIANE] Now come, confess that you were very bad 105
    To hurt my feelings as you did just now.
    I have a just complaint, you must allow.
MARIANE. *You* must allow that you were most unpleasant . . .
DORINE. Let's table that discussion for the present;
    Your father has a plan which must be stopped.   110
MARIANE. Advise us, then; what means must we adopt?
DORINE. We'll use all manner of means, and all at once.
    [*To* MARIANE] Your father's addled; he's acting like a dunce.
    Therefore you'd better humor the old fossil.
    Pretend to yield to him, be sweet and docile,   115
    And then postpone, as often as necessary,
    The day on which you have agreed to marry.
    You'll thus gain time, and time will turn the trick.
    Sometimes, for instance, you'll be taken sick,
    And that will seem good reason for delay;   120
    Or some bad omen will make you change the day—
    You'll dream of muddy water, or you'll pass
    A dead man's hearse, or break a looking-glass.
    If all else fails, no man can marry you
    Unless you take his ring and say "I do."   125
    But now, let's separate. If they should find
    Us talking here, our plot might be divined.
    [*To* VALERE] Go to your friends, and tell them what's occurred,
    And have them urge her father to keep his word.
    Meanwhile, we'll stir her brother into action,   130
    And get Elmire,[9] as well, to join our faction.
    Good-bye.

9. Orgon's second wife.

VALÈRE. [*To* MARIANE] Though each of us will do his best,
  It's your true heart on which my hopes shall rest.
MARIANE. [*To* VALÈRE] Regardless of what Father may decide,
  None but Valère shall claim me as his bride.   135
VALÈRE. Oh, how those words content me! Come what will . . .
DORINE. Oh, lovers, lovers! Their tongues are never still.
  Be off, now.
VALÈRE. [*Turning to go, then turning back.*]
           One last word . . .
DORINE.   No time to chat:
  You leave by this door; and *you* leave by that.
    [DORINE *pushes them, by the shoulders, toward opposing doors.*]

Act III

SCENE 1. *Damis, Dorine*

DAMIS. May lightning strike me even as I speak,
  May all men call me cowardly and weak,
  If any fear or scruple holds me back
  From settling things, at once, with that great quack!
DORINE. Now, don't give way to violent emotion.   5
  Your father's merely talked about this notion,
  And words and deeds are far from being one.
  Much that is talked about is never done.
DAMIS. No, I must stop that scoundrel's machinations;
  I'll go and tell him off; I'm out of patience.   10
DORINE. Do calm down and be practical. I had rather
  My mistress dealt with him—and with your father.
  She has some influence with Tartuffe, I've noted.
  He hangs upon her words, seems most devoted,
  And may, indeed, be smitten by her charm.   15
  Pray Heaven it's true! 'Twould do our cause no harm.
  She sent for him, just now, to sound him out
  On this affair you're so incensed about;
  She'll find out where he stands, and tell him, too,
  What dreadful strife and trouble will ensue   20
  If he lends countenance to your father's plan.
  I couldn't get in to see him, but his man
  Says that he's almost finished with his prayers.
  Go, now. I'll catch him when he comes downstairs.
DAMIS. I want to hear this conference, and I will.   25
DORINE. No, they must be alone.
DAMIS.   Oh, I'll keep still.

DORINE. Not you. I know your temper. You'd start a brawl,
  And shout and stamp your foot and spoil it all.
  Go on.
DAMIS.   I won't; I have a perfect right . . .   30
DORINE. Lord, you're a nuisance! He's coming; get out of sight.
  [DAMIS *conceals himself in a closet at the rear of the stage.*]

SCENE 2. *Tartuffe, Dorine*

TARTUFFE. [*Observing* DORINE, *and calling to his manservant off-
  stage*] Hang up my hair-shirt, put my scourge in place,
  And pray, Laurent, for Heaven's perpetual grace.
  I'm going to the prison now, to share
  My last few coins with the poor wretches there.
DORINE. [*Aside*] Dear God, what affectation! What a fake!   5
TARTUFFE. You wished to see me?
DORINE.   Yes . . .
TARTUFFE. [*Taking a handkerchief from his pocket*]
                                      For mercy's sake,
  Please take this handkerchief, before you speak.
DORINE. What?
TARTUFFE.   Cover that bosom,[1] girl. The flesh is weak.
  And unclean thoughts are difficult to control.
  Such sights as that can undermine the soul.   10
DORINE. Your soul, it seems, has very poor defenses,
  And flesh makes quite an impact on your senses.
  It's strange that you're so easily excited;
  My own desires are not so soon ignited,
  And if I saw you naked as a beast,   15
  Not all your hide would tempt me in the least.
TARTUFFE. Girl, speak more modestly; unless you do,
  I shall be forced to take my leave of you.
DORINE. Oh, no, it's I who must be on my way;
  I've just one little message to convey.   20
  Madame is coming down, and begs you, Sir,
  To wait and have a word or two with her.
TARTUFFE. Gladly.
DORINE. [*Aside*]   *That* had a softening effect!
  I think my guess about him was correct.
TARTUFFE. Will she be long?
DORINE.   No: that's her step I hear.   25
  Ah, here she is, and I shall disappear.

1. The Brotherhood of the Holy Sacrament practiced almsgiving to prisoners and kept a careful,
censorious check on female wearing apparel if they deemed it lascivious. Thus, Molière's audience would have identified Tartuffe as sympathetic—hypocritically—to the aims of the organization.

SCENE 3. *Elmire, Tartuffe*

TARTUFFE. May Heaven, whose infinite goodness we adore,
  Preserve your body and soul forevermore,
  And bless your days, and answer thus the plea
  Of one who is its humblest votary.
ELMIRE. I thank you for that pious wish. But please,   5
  Do take a chair and let's be more at ease.
    [*They sit down.*]
TARTUFFE. I trust that you are once more well and strong?
ELMIRE. Oh, yes: the fever didn't last for long.
TARTUFFE. My prayers are too unworthy, I am sure,
  To have gained from Heaven this most gracious cure;   10
  But lately, Madam, my every supplication
  Has had for object your recuperation.
ELMIRE. You shouldn't have troubled so. I don't deserve it.
TARTUFFE. Your health is priceless, Madam, and to preserve it
  I'd gladly give my own, in all sincerity.   15
ELMIRE. Sir, you outdo us all in Christian charity.
  You've been most kind. I count myself your debtor.
TARTUFFE. 'Twas nothing, Madam. I long to serve you better.
ELMIRE. There's a private matter I'm anxious to discuss.
  I'm glad there's no one here to hinder us.   20
TARTUFFE. I too am glad; it floods my heart with bliss
  To find myself alone with you like this.
  For just this chance I've prayed with all my power—
  But prayed in vain, until this happy hour.
ELMIRE. This won't take long, Sir, and I hope you'll be   25
  Entirely frank and unconstrained with me.
TARTUFFE. Indeed, there's nothing I had rather do
  Than bare my inmost heart and soul to you.
  First, let me say that what remarks I've made
  About the constant visits you are paid   30
  Were prompted not by any mean emotion,
  But rather by a pure and deep devotion,
  A fervent zeal . . .
ELMIRE.   No need for explanation.
  Your sole concern, I'm sure, was my salvation.
TARTUFFE. [*Taking* ELMIRE'S *hand and pressing her fingertips*]
  Quite so; and such great fervor do I feel . . .   35
ELMIRE. Ooh! Please! You're pinching!
TARTUFFE.   'Twas from excess of zeal.
  I never meant to cause you pain, I swear.
  I'd rather . . .   [*He places his hand on* ELMIRE'S *knee.*]

ELMIRE.   What can your hand be doing there?
TARTUFFE. Feeling your gown: what soft, fine-woven stuff!
ELMIRE. Please, I'm extremely ticklish. That's enough.   40
    [*She draws her chair away;* TARTUFFE *pulls his after her.*]
TARTUFFE. [*Fondling the lace collar of her gown*]
   My, my, what lovely lacework on your dress!
   The workmanship's miraculous, no less.
   I've not seen anything to equal it.
ELMIRE. Yes, quite. But let's talk business for a bit.
   They say my husband means to break his word   45
   And give his daughter to you, Sir. Had you heard?
TARTUFFE. He did once mention it. But I confess
   I dream of quite a different happiness.
   It's elsewhere, Madam, that my eyes discern
   The promise of that bliss for which I yearn.   50
ELMIRE. I see: you care for nothing here below.
TARTUFFE. Ah, well—my heart's not made of stone, you know.
ELMIRE. All your desires mount heavenward, I'm sure,
   In scorn of all that's earthly and impure.
TARTUFFE. A love of heavenly beauty does not preclude   55
   A proper love for earthly pulchritude;
   Our senses are quite rightly captivated
   By perfect works our Maker has created.
   Some glory clings to all that Heaven has made;
   In you, all Heaven's marvels are displayed.   60
   On that fair face, such beauties have been lavished,
   The eyes are dazzled and the heart is ravished;
   How could I look on you, O flawless creature,
   And not adore the Author of all Nature,
   Feeling a love both passionate and pure   65
   For you, his triumph of self-portraiture?
   At first, I trembled lest that love should be
   A subtle snare that Hell had laid for me;
   I vowed to flee the sight of you, eschewing
   A rapture that might prove my soul's undoing;   70
   But soon, fair being, I became aware
   That my deep passion could be made to square
   With rectitude, and with my bounden duty,
   I thereupon surrendered to your beauty.
   It is, I know, presumptuous on my part   75
   To bring you this poor offering of my heart,
   And it is not my merit, Heaven knows,
   But your compassion on which my hopes repose.
   You are my peace, my solace, my salvation;

On you depends my bliss—or desolation;   80
  I bide your judgment and, as you think best,
  I shall be either miserable or blest.
ELMIRE. Your declaration is most gallant, Sir,
  But don't you think it's out of character?
  You'd have done better to restrain your passion   85
  And think before you spoke in such a fashion.
  It ill becomes a pious man like you . . .
TARTUFFE. I may be pious, but I'm human too:
  With your celestial charms before his eyes,
  A man has not the power to be wise.   90
  I know such words sound strangely, coming from me,
  But I'm no angel, nor was meant to be,
  And if you blame my passion, you must needs
  Reproach as well the charms on which it feeds.
  Your loveliness I had no sooner seen   95
  Than you became my soul's unrivalled queen;
  Before your seraph glance, divinely sweet,
  My heart's defenses crumbled in defeat,
  And nothing fasting, prayer, or tears might do
  Could stay my spirit from adoring you.   100
  My eyes, my sighs have told you in the past
  What now my lips make bold to say at last,
  And if, in your great goodness, you will deign
  To look upon your slave, and ease his pain,—
  If, in compassion for my soul's distress,   105
  You'll stoop to comfort my unworthiness,
  I'll raise to you, in thanks for that sweet manna,
  An endless hymn, an infinite hosanna.
  With me, of course, there need be no anxiety,
  No fear of scandal or of notoriety.   110
  These young court gallants, whom all the ladies fancy,
  Are vain in speech, in action rash and chancy;
  When they succeed in love, the world soon knows it;
  No favor's granted them but they disclose it
  And by the looseness of their tongues profane   115
  The very altar where their hearts have lain.
  Men of my sort, however, love discreetly,
  And one may trust our reticence completely.
  My keen concern for my good name insures
  The absolute security of yours;   120
  In short, I offer you, my dear Elmire,
  Love without scandal, pleasure without fear.
ELMIRE. I've heard your well-turned speeches to the end,
  And what you urge I clearly apprehend.

Aren't you afraid that I may take a notion   125
To tell my husband of your warm devotion,
And that, supposing he were duly told,
His feelings toward you might grow rather cold?

TARTUFFE. I know, dear lady, that your exceeding charity
Will lead your heart to pardon my temerity;   130
That you'll excuse my violent affection
As human weakness, human imperfection;
And that—O fairest!— you will bear in mind
That I'm but flesh and blood, and am not blind.

ELMIRE. Some women might do otherwise, perhaps,   135
But I shall be discreet about your lapse;
I'll tell my husband nothing of what's occurred
If, in return, you'll give your solemn word
To advocate as forcefully as you can
The marriage of Valère and Mariane,   140
Renouncing all desire to dispossess
Another of his rightful happiness,
And . . .

SCENE 4. *Damis, Elmire, Tartuffe*

DAMIS. [*Emerging from the closet where he has been hiding*]
            No! We'll not hush up this vile affair;
I heard it all inside that closet there,
Where Heaven, in order to confound the pride
Of this great rascal, prompted me to hide.
Ah, now I have my long-awaited chance   5
To punish his deceit and arrogance,
And give my father clear and shocking proof
Of the black character of his dear Tartuffe.

ELMIRE. Ah no, Damis; I'll be content if he
Will study to deserve my leniency.   10
I've promised silence—don't make me break my word;
To make a scandal would be too absurd.
Good wives laugh off such trifles, and forget them;
Why should they tell their husbands, and upset them?

DAMIS. You have your reasons for taking such a course,   15
And I have reasons, too, of equal force.
To spare him now would be insanely wrong.
I've swallowed my just wrath for far too long
And watched this insolent bigot bringing strife
And bitterness into our family life.   20
Too long he's meddled in my father's affairs,
Thwarting my marriage-hopes, and poor Valère's.
It's high time that my father was undeceived,

And now I've proof that can't be disbelieved—
Proof that was furnished me by Heaven above. 25
It's too good not to take advantage of.
This is my chance, and I deserve to lose it
If, for one moment, I hesitate to use it.
ELMIRE. Damis . . .
DAMIS.   No, I must do what I think right.
   Madam, my heart is bursting with delight, 30
   And, say whatever you will, I'll not consent
   To lose the sweet revenge on which I'm bent.
   I'll settle matters without more ado;
   And here, most opportunely, is my cue.[2]

SCENE 5. *Orgon, Damis, Tartuffe, Elmire*

DAMIS. Father, I'm glad you've joined us. Let us advise you
   Of some fresh news which doubtless will surprise you.
   You've just now been repaid with interest
   For all your loving-kindness to our guest.
   He's proved his warm and grateful feelings toward you; 5
   It's with a pair of horns he would reward you.
   Yes, I surprised him with your wife, and heard
   His whole adulterous offer, every word.
   She, with her all too gentle disposition,
   Would not have told you of his proposition; 10
   But I shall not make terms with brazen lechery,
   And feel that not to tell you would be treachery.
ELMIRE. And I hold that one's husband's peace of mind
   Should not be spoilt by tattle of this kind.
   One's honor doesn't require it: to be proficient 15
   In keeping men at bay is quite sufficient.
   These are my sentiments, and I wish, Damis,
   That you had heeded me and held your peace.

SCENE 6. *Orgon, Damis, Tartuffe*

ORGON. Can it be true, this dreadful thing I hear?
TARTUFFE. Yes, Brother, I'm a wicked man, I fear:
   A wretched sinner, all depraved and twisted,
   The greatest villain that has ever existed.
   My life's one heap of crimes, which grows each minute; 5
   There's naught but foulness and corruption in it;
   And I perceive that Heaven, outraged by me,

---

2. In the original stage directions, Tartuffe now reads silently from his breviary—in the Roman Catholic Church, the book containing the Divine Office for each day, which those in holy orders are required to recite.

Has chosen this occasion to mortify me.
Charge me with any deed you wish to name;
I'll not defend myself, but take the blame.   10
Believe what you are told, and drive Tartuffe
Like some base criminal from beneath your roof;
Yes, drive me hence, and with a parting curse:
I shan't protest, for I deserve far worse.

ORGON. [*To* DAMIS] Ah, you deceitful boy, how dare you try   15
    To stain his purity with so foul a lie?

DAMIS. What! Are you taken in by such a fluff?
    Did you not hear . . . ?

ORGON.   Enough, you rogue, enough!

TARTUFFE. Ah, Brother, let him speak: you're being unjust.
    Believe his story; the boy deserves your trust.   20
    Why, after all, should you have faith in me?
    How can you know what I might do, or be?
    Is it on my good actions that you base
    Your favor? Do you trust my pious face?
    Ah, no, don't be deceived by hollow shows;   25
    I'm far, alas, from being what men suppose;
    Though the world takes me for a man of worth,
    I'm truly the most worthless man on earth.
            [*To* DAMIS]
    Yes, my dear son, speak out now: call me the chief
    Of sinners, a wretch, a murderer, a thief;   30
    Load me with all the names men most abhor;
    I'll not complain; I've earned them all, and more;
    I'll kneel here while you pour them on my head
    As a just punishment for the life I've led.

ORGON. [*To* TARTUFFE] This is too much, dear Brother.
    [*To* DAMIS]   Have you no heart?

DAMIS. Are you so hoodwinked by this rascal's art . . . ?   35

ORGON. Be still, you monster.
    [*To* TARTUFFE]   Brother, I pray you, rise.
    [*To* DAMIS] Villain!

DAMIS.   But . . .

ORGON.   Silence!

DAMIS.   Can't you realize . . . ?

ORGON. Just one word more, and I'll tear you limb from limb.

TARTUFFE. In God's name, Brother, don't be harsh with him.   40
    I'd rather far be tortured at the stake
    Than see him bear one scratch for my poor sake.

ORGON.]*To* DAMIS] Ingrate!

TARTUFFE.   If I must beg you, on bended knee,

To pardon him . . .

ORGON. [*Falling to his knees, addressing* TARTUFFE]
                    Such goodness cannot be!
[*To* DAMIS] Now, *there's* true charity!

DAMIS.   What, you . . . ?

ORGON.   Villain, be still!   45
I know your motives; I know you wish him ill:
Yes, all of you—wife, children, servants, all—
Conspire against him and desire his fall,
Employing every shameful trick you can
To alienate me from this saintly man.   50
Ah, but the more you seek to drive him away,
The more I'll do to keep him. Without delay,
I'll spite this household and confound its pride
By giving him my daughter as his bride.

DAMIS. You're going to force her to accept his hand?   55

ORGON. Yes, and this very night, d'you understand?
I shall defy you all, and make it clear
That I'm the one who gives the orders here.
Come, wretch, kneel down and clasp his blessed feet,
And ask his pardon for your black deceit.   60

DAMIS. I ask that swindler's pardon? Why, I'd rather . . .

ORGON. So! You insult him, and defy your father!
A stick! A stick! [*To* TARTUFFE.] No, no—release me, do.
[*To* DAMIS.] Out of my house this minute! Be off with you,
And never dare set foot in it again.   65

DAMIS. Well, I shall go, but . . .

ORGON.   Well, go quickly, then.
I disinherit you; an empty purse
Is all you'll get from me—except my curse!

SCENE 7. *Orgon, Tartuffe*

ORGON. How he blasphemed your goodness! What a son!

TARTUFFE. Forgive him, Lord, as I've already done.
[*To* ORGON] You can't know how it hurts when someone tries
To blacken me in my dear brother's eyes.

ORGON. Ahh!

TARTUFFE.   The mere thought of such ingratitude   5
Plunges my soul into so dark a mood . . .
Such horror grips my heart . . . I gasp for breath,
And cannot speak, and feel myself near death.

ORGON. [*He runs, in tears, to the door through which he has just
driven his son.*]
You blackguard! Why did I spare you? Why did I not
Break you in little pieces on the spot?   10

Compose yourself, and don't be hurt, dear friend.
TARTUFFE. These scenes, these dreadful quarrels, have got to end.
    I've much upset your household, and I perceive
    That the best thing will be for me to leave.
ORGON. What are you saying!
TARTUFFE.   They're all against me here;
    They'd have you think me false and insincere.   15
ORGON. Ah, what of that? Have I ceased believing in you?
TARTUFFE. Their adverse talk will certainly continue,
    And charges which you now repudiate
    You may find credible at a later date.   20
ORGON. No, Brother, never.
TARTUFFE.   Brother, a wife can sway
    Her husband's mind in many a subtle way.
ORGON. No, no.
TARTUFFE.   To leave at once is the solution;
    Thus only can I end their persecution.
ORGON. No, no, I'll not allow it; you shall remain.   25
TARTUFFE. Ah, well; 'twill mean much martyrdom and pain,
    But if you wish it . . .
ORGON.   Ah!
TARTUFFE.   Enough; so be it.
    But one thing must be settled, as I see it.
    For your dear honor, and for our friendship's sake,
    There's one precaution I feel bound to take.   30
    I shall avoid your wife, and keep away . . .
ORGON. No, you shall not, whatever they may say.
    It pleases me to vex them, and for spite
    I'd have them see you with her day and night.
    What's more, I'm going to drive them to despair   35
    By making you my only son and heir;
    This very day, I'll give to you alone
    Clear deed and title to everything I own.
    A dear, good friend and son-in-law-to-be
    Is more than wife, or child, or kin to me.   40
    Will you accept my offer, dearest son?
TARTUFFE. In all things, let the will of Heaven be done.
ORGON. Poor fellow! Come, we'll go draw up the deed.
    Then let them burst with disappointed greed!

Act IV

SCENE 1. *Cléante, Tartuffe*

CLEANTE. Yes, all the town's discussing it, and truly,
    Their comments do not flatter you unduly.

I'm glad we've met, Sir, and I'll give my view
Of this sad matter in a word or two.
As for who's guilty, that I shan't discuss; 5
Let's say it was Damis who caused the fuss;
Assuming, then, that you have been ill-used
By young Damis, and groundlessly accused,
Ought not a Christian to forgive, and ought
He not to stifle every vengeful thought? 10
Should you stand by and watch a father make
His only son an exile for your sake?
Again I tell you frankly, be advised:
The whole town, high and low, is scandalized;
This quarrel must be mended, and my advice is 15
Not to push matters to a further crisis.
No, sacrifice your wrath to God above,
And help Damis regain his father's love.

TARTUFFE. Alas, for my part I should take great joy
In doing so. I've nothing against the boy. 20
I pardon all, I harbor no resentment;
To serve him would afford me much contentment.
But Heaven's interest will not have it so:
If he comes back, then I shall have to go.
After his conduct—so extreme, so vicious— 25
Our further intercourse would look suspicious.
God knows what people would think! Why, they'd describe
My goodness to him as a sort of bribe;
They'd say that out of guilt I made pretense
Of loving-kindness and benevolence— 30
That, fearing my accuser's tongue, I strove
To buy his silence with a show of love.

CLEANTE. Your reasoning is badly warped and stretched,
And these excuses, Sir, are most far-fetched.
Why put yourself in charge of Heaven's cause? 35
Does Heaven need our help to enforce its laws?
Leave vengeance to the Lord, Sir; while we live,
Our duty's not to punish, but forgive;
And what the Lord commands, we should obey
Without regard to what the world may say. 40
What! Shall the fear of being misunderstood
Prevent our doing what is right and good?
No, no: let's simply do what Heaven ordains,
And let no other thoughts perplex our brains.

TARTUFFE. Again, Sir, let me say that I've forgiven 45
Damis, and thus obeyed the laws of Heaven;
But I am not commanded by the Bible

To live with one who smears my name with libel.
CLEANTE. Were you commanded, Sir, to indulge the whim
  Of poor Orgon, and to encourage him   50
  In suddenly transferring to your name
  A large estate to which you have no claim?
TARTUFFE. 'Twould never occur to those who know me best
  To think I acted from self-interest.
  The treasures of this world I quite despise;   55
  Their specious glitter does not charm my eyes;
  And if I have resigned myself to taking
  The gift which my dear Brother insists on making,
  I do so only, as he well understands,
  Lest so much wealth fall into wicked hands,   60
  Lest those to whom it might descend in time
  Turn it to purposes of sin and crime,
  And not, as I shall do, make use of it
  For Heaven's glory and mankind's benefit.
CLEANTE. Forget these trumped-up fears. Your argument   65
  Is one the rightful heir might well resent;
  It *is* a moral burden to inherit
  Such wealth, but give Damis a chance to bear it.
  And would it not be worse to be accused
  Of swindling, than to see that wealth misused?   70
  I'm shocked that you allowed Orgon to broach
  This matter, and that you feel no self-reproach;
  Does true religion teach that lawful heirs
  May freely be deprived of what is theirs?
  And if the Lord has told you in your heart   75
  That you and young Damis must dwell apart,
  Would it not be the decent thing to beat
  A generous and honorable retreat,
  Rather than let the son of the house be sent,
  For your convenience, into banishment?   80
  Sir, if you wish to prove the honesty
  Of your intentions . . .
TARTUFFE.   Sir, it is a half past three.
  I've certain pious duties to attend to,
  And hope my prompt departure won't offend you.
CLEANTE. [*Alone*] Damn.

SCENE 2. *Elmire, Mariane, Cléante, Dorine*

DORINE. Stay, Sir, and help Mariane, for Heaven's sake!
  She's suffering so, I fear her heart will break.
  Her father's plan to marry her off tonight
  Has put the poor child in a desperate plight.

I hear him coming. Let's stand together, now,   5
And see if we can't change his mind, somehow,
About this match we all deplore and fear.

SCENE 3. *Orgon, Elmire, Mariane, Cléante, Dorine*

ORGON. Hah! Glad to find you all assembled here.
   [*To* MARIANE] This contract, child, contains your happiness,
   And what it says I think your heart can guess.
MARIANE. [*Falling to her knees*]
   Sir, by that Heaven which sees me here distressed,
   And by whatever else can move your breast,   5
   Do not employ a father's power, I pray you,
   To crush my heart and force it to obey you,
   Nor by your harsh commands oppress me so
   That I'll begrudge the duty which I owe—
   And do not so embitter and enslave me   10
   That I shall hate the very life you gave me.
   If my sweet hopes must perish, if you refuse
   To give me to the one I've dared to choose,
   Spare me at least—I beg you, I implore—
   The pain of wedding one whom I abhor;   15
   And do not, by a heartless use of force,
   Drive me to contemplate some desperate course.
ORGON. [*Feeling himself touched by her*]
   Be firm, my soul. No human weakness, now.
MARIANE. I don't resent your love for him. Allow
   Your heart free rein, Sir; give him your property,   20
   And if that's not enough, take mine from me;
   He's welcome to my money; take it, do,
   But don't, I pray, include my person too.
   Spare me, I beg you; and let me end the tale
   Of my sad days behind a convent veil.   25
ORGON. A convent! Hah! When crossed in their amours,
   All lovesick girls have the same thought as yours.
   Get up! The more you loathe the man, and dread him,
   The more ennobling it will be to wed him.
   Marry Tartuffe, and mortify your flesh!   30
   Enough; don't start that whimpering afresh.
DORINE. But why . . . ?
ORGON.   Be still, there. Speak when you're spoken to.
   Not one more bit of impudence out of you.
CLEANTE. If I may offer a word of counsel here . . .
ORGON. Brother, in counselling you have no peer;   35
   All your advice is forceful, sound, and clever;
   I don't propose to follow it, however.

ELMIRE. [*To* ORGON] I am amazed, and don't know what to say;
   Your blindness simply takes my breath away.
   You are indeed bewitched, to take no warning   40
   From our account of what occurred this morning.
ORGON. Madam, I know a few plain facts, and one
   Is that you're partial to my rascal son;
   Hence, when he sought to make Tartuffe the victim
   Of a base lie, you dared not contradict him.   45
   Ah, but you underplayed your part, my pet;
   You should have looked more angry, more upset.
ELMIRE. When men make overtures, must we reply
   With righteous anger and a battle-cry?
   Must we turn back their amorous advances   50
   With sharp reproaches and with fiery glances?
   Myself, I find such offers merely amusing,
   And make no scenes and fusses in refusing;
   My taste is for good-natured rectitude,
   And I dislike the savage sort of prude   55
   Who guards her virtue with her teeth and claws,
   And tears men's eyes out for the slightest cause:
   The Lord preserve me from such honor as that,
   Which bites and scratches like an alley-cat!
   I've found that a polite and cool rebuff   60
   Discourages a lover quite enough.
ORGON. I know the facts, and I shall not be shaken.
ELMIRE. I marvel at your power to be mistaken.
   Would it, I wonder, carry weight with you
   If I could *show* you that our tale was true?   65
ORGON. Show me?
ELMIRE.   Yes.
ORGON.   Rot.
ELMIRE.   Come, what if I found a way
   To make you see the facts as plain as day?
ORGON. Nonsense.
ELMIRE.   Do answer me; don't be absurd.
   I'm not now asking you to trust our word.
   Suppose that from some hiding-place in here   70
   You learned the whole sad truth by eye and ear—
   What would you say of your good friend, after that?
ORGON. Why, I'd say . . . nothing, by Jehoshaphat!
   It can't be true.
ELMIRE.   You've been too long deceived,
   I'm quite tired of being disbelieved.   75
   Come now: let's put my statements to the test,
   And you shall see the truth made manifest.

ORGON. I'll take that challenge. Now do your uttermost.
   We'll see how you make good your empty boast.
ELMIRE. [*To* DORINE] Send him to me.
DORINE.   He's crafty; it may be hard
   To catch the cunning scoundrel off his guard.   80
ELMIRE. No, amorous men are gullible. Their conceit
   So blinds them that they're never hard to cheat.
   Have him come down. [*To* CLEANTE & MARIANE] Please leave us,
   for a bit.

SCENE 4. *Elmire, Orgon*

ELMIRE. Pull up this table, and get under it.
ORGON. What?
ELMIRE.   It's essential that you be well-hidden.
ORGON. Why there?
ELMIRE.   Oh, Heavens! Just do as you are bidden.
   I have my plans; we'll soon see how they fare.
   Under the table, now; and once you're there,   5
   Take care that you are neither seen nor heard.
ORGON. Well, I'll indulge you, since I gave my word
   To see you through this infantile charade.
ELMIRE. Once it is over, you'll be glad we played.
   [*To her husband, who is now under the table*]
   I'm going to act quite strangely, now, and you   10
   Must not be shocked at anything I do.
   Whatever I may say, you must excuse
   As part of that deceit I'm forced to use.
   I shall employ sweet speeches in the task
   Of making that impostor drop his mask;   15
   I'll give encouragement to his bold desires,
   And furnish fuel to his amorous fires.
   Since it's for your sake, and for his destruction,
   That I shall seem to yield to his seduction,
   I'll gladly stop whenever you decide.   20
   That all your doubts are fully satisfied.
   I'll count on you, as soon as you have seen
   What sort of man he is, to intervene,
   And not expose me to his odious lust
   One moment longer than you feel you must.   25
   Remember: you're to save me from my plight
   Whenever . . . He's coming! Hush! Keep out of sight!

SCENE 5. *Tartuffe, Elmire, Orgon*

TARTUFFE. You wish to have a word with me, I'm told.
ELMIRE. Yes, I've a little secret to unfold.

Before I speak, however, it would be wise
To close that door, and look about for spies.
  [TARTUFFE *goes to the door, closes it, and returns.*]
The very last thing that must happen now   5
Is a repetition of this morning's row.
I've never been so badly caught off guard.
Oh, how I feared for you! You saw how hard
I tried to make that troublesome Damis
Control his dreadful temper, and hold his peace.   10
In my confusion, I didn't have the sense
Simply to contradict his evidence;
But as it happened, that was for the best,
And all has worked out in our interest.
This storm has only bettered your position;   15
My husband doesn't have the least suspicion,
And now, in mockery of those who do,
He bids me be continually with you.
And that is why, quite fearless of reproof,
I now can be alone with my Tartuffe,   20
And why my heart—perhaps too quick to yield—
Feels free to let its passion be revealed.
TARTUFFE. Madam, your words confuse me. Not long ago,
  You spoke in quite a different style, you know.
ELMIRE. Ah, Sir, if that refusal made you smart,   25
  It's little that you know of woman's heart,
  Or what that heart is trying to convey
  When it resists in such a feeble way!
  Always, at first, our modesty prevents
  The frank avowal of tender sentiments: 30
  However high the passion which inflames us,
  Still, to confess its power somehow shames us.
  Thus we reluct, at first, yet in a tone
  Which tells you that our heart is overthrown,
  That what our lips deny, our pulse confesses,   35
  And that, in time, all noes will turn to yesses.
  I fear my words are all too frank and free,
  And a poor proof of woman's modesty;
  But since I'm started, tell me, if you will—
  Would I have tried to make Damis be still,   40
  Would I have listened, calm and unoffended,
  Until your lengthy offer of love was ended,
  And been so very mild in my reaction,
  Had your sweet words not given me satisfaction?
  And when I tried to force you to undo   45
  The marriage-plans my husband has in view,

What did my urgent pleading signify
If not that I admired you, and that I
Deplored the thought that someone else might own
Part of a heart I wished for mine alone?   50
TARTUFFE. Madam, no happiness is so complete
    As when, from lips we love, come words so sweet;
    Their nectar floods my every sense, and drains
    In honeyed rivulets through all my veins.
    To please you is my joy, my only goal;   55
    Your love is the restorer of my soul;
    And yet I must beg leave, now, to confess
    Some lingering doubts as to my happiness.
    Might this not be a trick? Might not the catch
    Be that you wish me to break off the match   60
    With Mariane, and so have feigned to love me?
    I shan't quite trust your fond opinion of me
    Until the feelings you've expressed so sweetly
    Are demonstrated somewhat more concretely,
    And you have shown, by certain kind concessions,   65
    That I may put my faith in your professions
ELMIRE. [*She coughs, to warn her husband.*] Why be in such a hurry?
    Must my heart
    Exhaust its bounty at the very start?
    To make that sweet admission cost me dear,
    But you'll not be content, it would appear,   70
    Unless my store of favors is disbursed
    To the last farthing, and at the very first.
TARTUFFE. The less we merit, the less we dare to hope,
    And with our doubts, mere words can never cope.
    We trust no promised bliss till we receive it;   75
    Not till a joy is ours can we believe it.
    I, who so little merit your esteem,
    Can't credit this fulfillment of my dream,
    And shan't believe it, Madam, until I savor
    Some palpable assurance of your favor.   80
ELMIRE. My, how tyrannical your love can be,
    And how it flusters and perplexes me!
    How furiously you take one's heart in hand,
    And make your every wish a fierce command!
    Come, must you hound and harry me to death?   85
    Will you not give me time to catch my breath?
    Can it be right to press me with such force,
    Give me no quarter, show me no remorse,
    And take advantage, by your stern insistence,
    Of the fond feelings which weaken my resistance?   90

TARTUFFE. Well, if you look with favor upon my love,
    Why, then, begrudge me some clear proof thereof?
ELMIRE. But how can I consent without offense
    To Heaven, toward which you feel such reverence?
TARTUFFE. If Heaven is all that holds you back, don't worry.   95
    I can remove that hindrance in a hurry.
    Nothing of that sort need obstruct our path.
ELMIRE. Must one not be afraid of Heaven's wrath?
TARTUFFE. Madam, forget such fears, and be my pupil,
    And I shall teach you how to conquer scruple.   100
    Some joys, it's true, are wrong in Heaven's eyes;
    Yet Heaven is not averse to compromise;
    There is a science, lately formulated,
    Whereby one's conscience may be liberated,[3]
    And any wrongful act you care to mention   105
    May be redeemed by purity of intention.
    I'll teach you, Madam, the secrets of that science;
    Meanwhile, just place on me your full reliance.
    Assuage my keen desires, and feel no dread:
    The sin, if any, shall be on my head.   110
        [ELMIRE *coughs, this time more loudly.*]
    You've a bad cough.
ELMIRE.   Yes, yes, It's bad indeed.
TARTUFFE. [*Producing a little paper bag*]
    A bit of licorice may be what you need.
ELMIRE. No, I've a stubborn cold, it seems. I'm sure it
    Will take much more than licorice to cure it.
TARTUFFE. How aggravating.
ELMIRE.   Oh, more than I can say.   115
TARTUFFE. If you're still troubled, think of things this way:
    No one shall know our joys, save us alone,
    And there's no evil till the act is known;
    It's scandal, Madam, which makes it an offense,
    And it's no sin to sin in confidence.   120
ELMIRE. [*Having coughed once more*]
    Well, clearly I must do as you require,
    And yield to your importunate desire.
    It is apparent, now, that nothing less
    Will satisfy you, and so I acquiesce.
    To go so far is much against my will;   125
    I'm vexed that it should come to this; but still,
    Since you are so determined on it, since you
    Will not allow mere language to convince you,

---

3. Molière appended his own footnote to this line: "It is a scoundrel who speaks."

And since you ask for concrete evidence, I
See nothing for it, now, but to comply.   130
If this is sinful, if I'm wrong to do it,
So much the worse for him who drove me to it.
The fault can surely not be charged to me.
TARTUFFE. Madam, the fault is mine, if fault there be,
And . . .
ELMIRE.   Open the door a little, and peek out;   135
I wouldn't want my husband poking about.
TARTUFFE. Why worry about the man? Each day he grows
More gullible; one can lead him by the nose.
To find us here would fill him with delight,
And if he saw the worst, he'd doubt his sight.   140
ELMIRE. Nevertheless, do step out for a minute
Into the hall, and see that no one's in it.

SCENE 6. *Orgon, Elmire*

ORGON. [*Coming out from under the table*]
That man's a perfect monster, I must admit!
I'm simply stunned. I can't get over it.
ELMIRE. What, coming out so soon? How premature!
Get back in hiding, and wait until you're sure.
Stay till the end, and be convinced completely;   5
We mustn't stop till things are proved concretely.
ORGON. Hell never harbored anything so vicious!
ELMIRE. Tut, don't be hasty. Try to be judicious.
Wait, and be certain that there's no mistake.
No jumping to conclusions, for Heaven's sake!   10
    [*She places* ORGON *behind her, as* TARTUFFE *re-enters.*]

SCENE 7. *Tartuffe, Elmire, Orgon*

TARTUFFE. [*Not seeing* ORGON]
Madam, all things have worked out to perfection;
I've given the neighboring rooms a full inspection;
No one's about; and now I may at last . . .
ORGON. [*Intercepting him*] Hold on, my passionate fellow, not so
fast!
I should advise a little more restraint.   5
Well, so you thought you'd fool me, my dear saint!
How soon you wearied of the saintly life—
Wedding my daughter, and coveting my wife!
I've long suspected you, and had a feeling
That soon I'd catch you at your double-dealing.   10
Just now, you've given me evidence galore;
It's quite enough; I have no wish for more.

ELMIRE. [*To* TARTUFFE] I'm sorry to have treated you so slyly,
   But circumstances forced me to be wily.
TARTUFFE. Brother, you can't think . . .
ORGON.   No more talk from you;
   Just leave this household, without more ado.   15
TARTUFFE. What I intended . . .
ORGON.   That seems fairly clear.
   Spare me your falsehoods and get out of here.
TARTUFFE. No, I'm the master, and you're the one to go!
   This house belongs to me, I'll have you know,   20
   And I shall show you that you can't hurt *me*
   By this contemptible conspiracy,
   That those who cross me know not what they do,
   And that I've means to expose and punish you,
   Avenge offended Heaven, and make you grieve   25
   That ever you dared order me to leave.

SCENE 8. *Elmire, Orgon*

ELMIRE. What was the point of all that angry chatter?
ORGON. Dear God, I'm worried. This is no laughing matter.
ELMIRE. How so?
ORGON.   I fear I understood his drift.
   I'm much disturbed about that deed of gift.
ELMIRE. You gave him . . . ?
ORGON.   Yes, it's all been drawn and signed.
   But one thing more is weighing on my mind.   5
ELMIRE. What's that?
ORGON.   I'll tell you; but first let's see if there's
   A certain strong-box in his room upstairs.

Act V

SCENE 1. *Orgon, Cléante*

CLEANTE. Where are you going so fast?
ORGON.   God knows!
CLEANTE.   Then wait;
   Let's have a conference, and deliberate
   On how this situation's to be met.
ORGON. That strong-box has me utterly upset;
   This is the worst of many, many shocks.   5
CLEANTE. Is there some fearful mystery in that box?
ORGON. My poor friend Argas brought that box to me
   With his own hands, in utmost secrecy;
   'Twas on the very morning of his flight.

It's full of papers which, if they came to light,   10
Would ruin him—or such is my impression.
CLEANTE. Then why did you let it out of your possession?
ORGON. Those papers vexed my conscience, and it seemed best
    To ask the counsel of my pious guest.
    The cunning scoundrel got me to agree   15
    To leave the strong-box in his custody,
    So that, in case of an investigation,
    I could employ a slight equivocation
    And swear I didn't have it, and thereby,
    At no expense to conscience, tell a lie.   20
CLEANTE. It looks to me as if you're out on a limb.
    Trusting him with that box, and offering him
    That deed of gift, were actions of a kind
    Which scarcely indicate a prudent mind.
    With two such weapons, he has the upper hand,   25
    And since you're vulnerable, as matters stand,
    You erred once more in bringing him to bay.
    You should have acted in some subtler way.
ORGON. Just think of it: behind that fervent face,
    A heart so wicked, and a soul so base!   30
    I took him in, a hungry beggar, and then . . .
    Enough, by God! I'm through with pious men:
    Henceforth I'll hate the whole false brotherhood,
    And persecute them worse than Satan could.
CLEANTE. Ah, there you go—extravagant as ever!   35
    Why can you not be rational? You never
    Manage to take the middle course, it seems,
    But jump, instead, between absurd extremes.
    You've recognized your recent grave mistake
    In falling victim to a pious fake;   40
    Now, to correct that error, must you embrace
    An even greater error in its place,
    And judge our worthy neighbors as a whole
    By what you've learned of one corrupted soul?
    Come, just because one rascal made you swallow   45
    A show of zeal which turned out to be hollow,
    Shall you conclude that all men are deceivers,
    And that, today, there are no true believers?
    Let atheists make that foolish inference;
    Learn to distinguish virtue from pretense,   50
    Be cautious in bestowing admiration,
    And cultivate a sober moderation.
    Don't humor fraud, but also don't asperse
    True piety; the latter fault is worse,

And it is best to err, if err one must,   55
As you have done, upon the side of trust.

SCÈNE 2. *Damis, Orgon, Cléante*

DAMIS. Father, I hear that scoundrel's uttered threats
  Against you; that he pridefully forgets
  How, in his need, he was befriended by you,
  And means to use your gifts to crucify you.
ORGON. It's true, my boy. I'm too distressed for tears.   5
DAMIS. Leave it to me, Sir; let me trim his ears.
  Faced with such insolence, we must not waver.
  I shall rejoice in doing you the favor
  Of cutting short his life, and your distress.
CLEANTE. What a display of young hotheadedness!   10
  Do learn to moderate your fits of rage.
  In this just kingdom, this enlightened age,
  One does not settle things by violence.

SCÈNE 3. *Madame Pernelle, Mariane, Elmire, Dorine, Damis, Orgon, Cléante*

MADAME PERNELLE. I hear strange tales of very strange events.
ORGON. Yes, strange events which these two eyes beheld.
  The man's ingratitude is unparalleled.
  I save a wretched pauper from starvation,
  House him, and treat him like a blood relation,   5
  Shower him every day with my largesse,
  Give him my daughter, and all that I possess;
  And meanwhile the unconscionable knave
  Tries to induce my wife to misbehave;
  And not content with such extreme rascality,   10
  Now threatens me with my own liberality,
  And aims, by taking base advantage of
  The gifts I gave him out of Christian love,
  To drive me from my house, a ruined man,
  And make me end a pauper, as he began.   15
DORINE. Poor fellow!
MADAME PERNELLE. No, my son, I'll never bring
  Myself to think him guilty of such a thing.
ORGON. How's that?
MADAME PERNELLE. The righteous always were maligned.
ORGON. Speak clearly, Mother. Say what's on your mind.
MADAME PERNELLE. I mean that I can smell a rat, my dear.
  You know how everybody hates him, here.   20
ORGON. That has no bearing on the case at all.
MADAME PERNELLE. I told you a hundred times, when you were small,

That virtue in this world is hated ever;
Malicious men may die, but malice never.   25

ORGON. No doubt that's true, but how does it apply?

MADAME PERNELLE. They've turned you against him by a clever lie.

ORGON. I've told you, I was there and saw it done.

MADAME PERNELLE. Ah, slanderers will stop at nothing, Son.

ORGON. Mother, I'll lose my temper . . . For the last time,   30
I tell you I was witness to the crime.

MADAME PERNELLE. The tongues of spite are busy night and noon,
And to their venom no man is immune.

ORGON. You're talking nonsense. Can't you realize
I saw it; saw it; saw it with my eyes?   35
Saw, do you understand me? Must I shout it
Into your ears before you'll cease to doubt it?

MADAME PERNELLE. Appearances can deceive, my son. Dear me,
We cannot always judge by what we see.

ORGON. Drat! Drat!

MADAME PERNELLE. One often interprets things awry;   40
Good can seem evil to a suspicious eye.

ORGON. Was I to see his pawing at Elmire
As an act of charity?

MADAME PERNELLE.   Till his guilt is clear,
A man deserves the benefit of the doubt.
You should have waited, to see how things turned out.   45

ORGON. Great God in Heaven, what more proof did I need?
Was I to sit there, watching, until he'd . . .
You drive me to the brink of impropriety.

MADAME PERNELLE. No, no, a man of such surpassing piety
Could not do such a thing. You cannot shake me.   50
I don't believe it, and you shall not make me.

ORGON. You vex me so that, if you weren't my mother,
I'd say to you . . . some dreadful thing or other.

DORINE. It's your turn now, Sir, not to be listened to;
You'd not trust us, and now she won't trust you.   55

CLEANTE. My friends, we're wasting time which should be spent
In facing up to our predicament.
I fear that scoundrel's threats weren't made in sport.

DAMIS. Do you think he'd have the nerve to go to court?

ELMIRE. I'm sure he won't: they'd find it all too crude   60
A case of swindling and ingratitude.

CLEANTE. Don't be too sure. He won't be at a loss
To give his claims a high and righteous gloss;
And clever rogues with far less valid cause
Have trapped their victims in a web of laws.   65

I say again that to antagonize
A man so strongly armed was most unwise.
ORGON. I know it; but the man's appalling cheek
Outraged me so, I couldn't control my pique.
CLEANTE. I wish to Heaven that we could devise   70
Some truce between you, or some compromise.
ELMIRE. If I had known what cards he held, I'd not
Have roused his anger by my little plot.
ORGON. [*To* DORINE, *as* M. LOYAL *enters*] What is that fellow looking
for? Who is he?
Go talk to him—and tell him that I'm busy.   75

SCENE 4. *Monsieur Loyal, Madame Pernelle, Orgon, Damis,*
Mariane, Dorine, Elmire, Cléante

MONSIEUR LOYAL. Good day, dear sister. Kindly let me see
Your master.
DORINE.   He's involved with company,
And cannot be distrubed just now, I fear.
MONSIEUR LOYAL. I hate to intrude; but what has brought me here
Will not disturb your master, in any event.   5
Indeed, my news will make him most content.
DORINE. Your name?
MONSIEUR LOYAL.   Just say that I bring greetings from
Monsieur Tartuffe, on whose behalf I've come.
DORINE. [*To* ORGON] Sir, he's a very gracious man, and bears
A message from Tartuffe, which, he declares,   10
Will make you most content.
CLEANTE.   Upon my word,
I think this man had best be seen, and heard.
ORGON. Perhaps he has some settlement to suggest.
How shall I treat him? What manner would be best?
CLEANTE. Control your anger, and if he should mention   15
Some fair adjustment, give him your full attention.
MONSIEUR LOYAL. Good health to you, good Sir. May Heaven con-
found
Your enemies, and may your joys abound.
ORGON. [*Aside, to* CLEANTE] A gentle salutation: it confirms
My guess that he is here to offer terms.   20
MONSIEUR LOYAL. I've always held your family most dear;
I served your father, Sir, for many a year.
ORGON. Sir, I must ask your pardon; to my shame,
I cannot now recall your face or name.
MONSIEUR LOYAL. Loyal's my name; I come from Normandy,   25

And I'm a bailiff, in all modesty.
For forty years, praise God, it's been my boast
To serve with honor in that vital post,
And I am here, Sir, if you will permit
The liberty, to serve you with this writ . . .   30
ORGON. To—*what?*
MONSIEUR LOYAL.   Now, please, Sir, let us have no friction:
It's nothing but an order of eviction.
You are to move your goods and family out
And make way for new occupants, without
Deferment or delay, and give the keys . . .   35
ORGON. I? Leave this house?
MONSIEUR LOYAL.   Why yes, Sir, if you please.
This house, Sir, from the cellar to the roof,
Belongs now to the good Monsieur Tartuffe,
And he is lord and master of your estate
By virtue of a deed of present date,   40
Drawn in due form, with clearest legal phrasing . . .
DAMIS. Your insolence is utterly amazing!
MONSIEUR LOYAL. Young man, my business here is not with you
But with your wise and temperate father, who,
Like every worthy citizen, stands in awe   45
Of justice, and would never obstruct the law.
ORGON. But . . .
MONSIEUR LOYAL. Not for a million, Sir, would you rebel
Against authority; I know that well.
You'll not make trouble, Sir, or interfere
With the execution of my duties here.   50
DAMIS. Someone may execute a smart tattoo
On that black jacket[4] of yours, before you're through.
MONSIEUR LOYAL. Sir, bid your son be silent. I'd much regret
Having to mention such a nasty threat
Of violence, in writing my report.   55
DORINE. [*Aside*] This man Loyal's a most disloyal sort!
MONSIEUR LOYAL. I love all men of upright character,
And when I agreed to serve these papers, Sir,
It was your feelings that I had in mind.
I couldn't bear to see the case assigned   60
To someone else, who might esteem you less
And so subject you to unpleasantness.
ORGON. What's more unpleasant than telling a man to leave
His house and home?

---

4. In the original, *justaucorps à longues basques*, a close-fitting, long black coat with skirts, the customary dress of a bailiff.

MONSIEUR LOYAL.   You'd like a short reprieve?
  If you desire it, Sir, I shall not press you,   65
  But wait until tomorrow to dispossess you.
  Splendid. I'll come and spend the night here, then,
  Most quietly, with half a score of men.
  For form's sake, you might bring me, just before
  You go to bed, the keys to the front door.   70
  My men, I promise, will be on their best
  Behavior, and will not disturb your rest.
  But bright and early, Sir, you must be quick
  And move out all your furniture, every stick:
  The men I've chosen are both young and strong,   75
  And with their help it shouldn't take you long.
  In short, I'll make things pleasant and convenient,
  And since I'm being so extremely lenient,
  Please show me, Sir, a like consideration,
  And give me your entire cooperation.   80
ORGON. [*Aside*] I may be all but bankrupt, but I vow
  I'd give a hundred louis, here and now,
  Just for the pleasure of landing one good clout
  Right on the end of that complacent snout.
CLEANTE. Careful; don't make things worse.
DAMIS.   My bootsole itches
  To give that beggar a good kick in the breeches.   85
DORINE. Monsieur Loyal, I'd love to hear the whack
  Of a stout stick across your fine broad back.
MONSIEUR LOYAL. Take care: a woman too may go to jail if
  She uses threatening language to a bailiff.   90
CLEANTE. Enough, enough, Sir. This must not go on.
  Give me that paper, please, and then begone.
MONSIEUR LOYAL. Well, *au revoir*. God give you all good cheer!
ORGON. May God confound you, and him who sent you here!

  SCENE 5. *Orgon, Cléante, Mariane, Elmire, Madame Pernelle,*
               Dorine, Damis

ORGON. Now, Mother, was I right or not? This writ
  Should change your notion of Tartuffe a bit.
  Do you perceive his villainy at last?
MADAME PERNELLE. I'm thunderstruck. I'm utterly aghast.
DORINE. Oh, come, be fair. You mustn't take offense   5
  At this new proof of his benevolence.
  He's acting out of selfless love, I know.
  Material things enslave the soul, and so
  He kindly has arranged your liberation

From all that might endanger your salvation.   10
ORGON. Will you not ever hold your tongue, you dunce?
CLEANTE. Come, you must take some action, and at once.
ELMIRE. Go tell the world of the low trick he's tried.
   The deed of gift is surely nullified
   By such behavior, and public rage will not   15
   Permit the wretch to carry out his plot.

SCENE 6. *Valère, Orgon, Cléante, Elmire, Mariane, Madame*
              Pernelle, Damis, Dorine

VALERE. Sir, though I hate to bring you more bad news,
   Such is the danger that I cannot choose.
   A friend who is extremely close to me
   And knows my interest in your family
   Has, for my sake, presumed to violate   5
   The secrecy that's due to things of state,
   And sends me word that you are in a plight
   From which your one salvation lies in flight.
   That scoundrel who's imposed upon you so
   Denounced you to the King an hour ago   10
   And, as supporting evidence, displayed
   The strong-box of a certain renegade
   Whose secret papers, so he testified,
   You had disloyally agreed to hide.
   I don't know just what charges may be pressed,   15
   But there's a warrant out for your arrest;
   Tartuffe has been instructed, furthermore,
   To guide the arresting officer to your door.
CLEANTE. He's clearly done this to facilitate
   His seizure of your house and your estate.   20
ORGON. That man, I must say, is a vicious beast!
VALERE. You can't afford to delay, Sir, in the least.
   My carriage is outside, to take you hence;
   This thousand louis should cover all expense.
   Let's lose no time, or you shall be undone;   25
   The sole defense, in this case, is to run.
   I shall go with you all the way, and place you
   In a safe refuge to which they'll never trace you.
ORGON. Alas, dear boy, I wish that I could show you
   My gratitude for everything I owe you.   30
   But now is not the time; I pray the Lord
   That I may live to give you your reward.
   Farewell, my dears; be careful . . .

CLEANTE. Brother, hurry.
We shall take care of things; you needn't worry.

SCENE 7. *The Officer, Tartuffe, Valère, Orgon, Elmire, Mariane,*
Madame Pernelle, Dorine, Cléante, Damis

TARTUFFE. Gently, Sir, gently; stay right where you are.
No need for haste; your lodging isn't far.
You're off to prison, by order of the Prince.
ORGON. This is the crowning blow, you wretch; and since
It means my total ruin and defeat,   5
Your villainy is now at last complete.
TARTUFFE. You needn't try to provoke me; it's no use.
Those who serve Heaven must expect abuse.
CLEANTE. You are indeed most patient, sweet, and blameless.
DORINE. How he exploits the name of Heaven! It's shameless.   10
TARTUFFE. Your taunts and mockeries are all for naught;
To do my duty is my only thought.
MARIANE. Your love of duty is most meritorious,
And what you've done is little short of glorious.
TARTUFFE. All deeds are glorious, Madam, which obey   15
The sovereign prince who sent me here today.
ORGON. I rescued you when you were destitute;
Have you forgotten that, you thankless brute?
TARTUFFE. No, no, I well remember everything;
But my first duty is to serve my King.   20
That obligation is so paramount
That other claims, beside it, do not count;
And for it I would sacrifice my wife,
My family, my friend, or my own life.
ELMIRE. Hypocrite!
DORING.   All that we most revere, he uses   25
To cloak his plots and camouflage his ruses.
CLEANTE. If it is true that you are animated
By pure and loyal zeal, as you have stated,
Why was this zeal not roused until you'd sought
To make Orgon a cuckold, and been caught?   30
Why weren't you moved to give your evidence
Until your outraged host had driven you hence?
I shan't say that the gift of all his treasure
Ought to have damped your zeal in any measure;
But if he is a traitor, as you declare,   35
How could you condescend to be his heir?
TARTUFFE. [*To the* OFFICER] Sir, spare me all this clamor; it's grow-
ing shrill.

Please carry out your orders, if you will.
OFFICER.[5] Yes, I've delayed too long, Sir. Thank you kindly.
    You're just the proper person to remind me.   40
    Come, you are off to join the other boarders
    In the King's prison, according to his orders.
TARTUFFE. Who? I, Sir?
OFFICER.   Yes.
TARTUFFE.   To prison? This can't be true!
OFFICER. I owe an explanation, but not to you.
    [*To* ORGON] Sir, all is well; rest easy, and be grateful.   45
    We serve a Prince to whom all sham is hateful,
    A Prince who sees into our inmost hearts,
    And can't be fooled by any trickster's arts.
    His royal soul, though generous and human,
    Views all things with discernment and acumen;   50
    His sovereign reason is not lightly swayed,
    And all his judgments are discreetly weighed.
    He honors righteous men of every kind,
    And yet his zeal for virtue is not blind,
    Nor does his love of piety numb his wits   55
    And make him tolerant of hypocrites.
    'Twas hardly likely that this man could cozen
    A King who's foiled such liars by the dozen.
    With one keen glance, the King perceived the whole
    Perverseness and corruption of his soul,   60
    And thus high Heaven's justice was displayed:
    Betraying you, the rogue stood self-betrayed.
    The King soon recognized Tartuffe as one
    Notorious by another name, who'd done
    So many vicious crimes that one could fill   65
    Ten volumes with them, and be writing still.
    But to be brief: our sovereign was appalled
    By this man's treachery toward you, which he called
    The last, worst villainy of a vile career,
    And bade me follow the imposter here   70
    To see how gross his impudence could be,
    And force him to restore your property.
    Your private papers, by the King's command,
    I hereby seize and give into your hand.
    The King, by royal order, invalidates   75
    The deed which gave this rascal your estates,
    And pardons, furthermore, your grave offense
    In harboring an exile's documents.

5. In the original, *un exempt*. He would actually have been a gentleman from the king's personal
bodyguard with the rank of lieutenant-colonel or "master of the camp."

By these decrees, our Prince rewards you for
Your loyal deeds in the late civil war,[6]   80
And shows how heartfelt is his satisfaction
In recompensing any worthy action,
How much he prizes merit, and how he makes
More of men's virtues than of their mistakes.
DORINE. Heaven be praised!
MADAME PERNELLE.   I breathe again, at last.   85
ELMIRE. We're safe.
MARIANE.   I can't believe the danger's past.
ORGON. [*To* TARTUFFE]. Well, traitor, now you see . . .
CLEANTE. Ah, brother, please,
   Let's not descend to such indignities.
   Leave the poor wretch to his unhappy fate,
   And don't say anything to aggravate   90
   His present woes; but rather hope that he
   Will soon embrace an honest piety,
   And mend his ways, and by a true repentance
   Move our just King to moderate his sentence.
   Meanwhile, go kneel before your sovereign's throne   95
   And thank him for the mercies he has shown.
ORGON. Well said: let's go at once and, gladly kneeling,
   Express the gratitude which all are feeling.
   Then, when that first great duty has been done,
   We'll turn with pleasure to a second one,   100
   And give Valère, whose love has proven so true,
   The wedded happiness which is his due.

MARIE DE LA VERGNE DE LA FAYETTE
1634–1693

The Princess of Clèves, Mme. de La Fayette's masterpiece, is generally agreed
to be the first important French novel. Out of the psychological situation of
a woman who rejects romantic love, it generates fiction of compelling
interest.

   Its author had an unusual career. At the age of twenty-two, Marie de la
Vergne married the Comte de La Fayette, who thereupon took her to one
of his estates in rural Auvergne. The young woman, born in Paris, had
always lived in the metropolis, where her mother and her stepfather (her
father had died when she was sixteen) frequented intellectual circles on the
fringe of the court. Until 1659, Mme. de La Fayette remained in the country,
bearing and raising two sons; then she returned alone to Paris, where she

6. A reference to Orgon's role in supporting the king during the Fronde.

handled some of her husband's business affairs, became hostess of an important literary salon whose frequenters included Madame de Sévigné and the Duc de La Rochefoucauld, and developed friendships with important figures at court. She wrote five novels and *Memoirs of the French Court for the Years 1688 and 1689*, a historical work reporting both such public events as the English revolution that deposed James II and the private affairs of figures more or less directly connected with important happenings. She outlived her husband by thirteen years.

The Princess of Clèves, first published (anonymously) in 1678, won instantaneous popular success. Set in the sixteenth-century French court, it incorporated the names and on occasion the histories of real people; even the Prince of Clèves, in this novel the heroine's husband, once actually lived (d. 1564). (In reality he never married.) Its immediate interest, however, and its lasting appeal depend not on its historical allusions but on its psychological profundity. At a time when virtually all French fiction took the form of long, fanciful romances, it inaugurated a new novelistic tradition of concern with character and narrative economy.

The single event in *The Princess of Clèves* that most intensely interested de La Fayette's contemporaries involved the heroine's confession to her husband of her interest in another man. The princess acknowledges her attraction to the Duke of Nemours not to justify it but to ask for help in combating it. She wishes to remain a faithful wife, although many around her at court happily conduct adulterous love affairs; she yearns to retreat to the country in order to avoid constant anguishing temptation. Her husband finds this confession as astonishing as de La Fayette's readers did; her would-be lover, who overhears it, is equally amazed. The remarkable action calls attention to the princess's overwhelming desire to keep her integrity as a person, which her desire to love would destroy. At no time does she deviate significantly from her yearning after virtue.

The novelist provides a psychological history of her heroine's devotion to goodness, reporting the young woman's early relation to her mother and that mother's undeviating insistence on the importance of female chastity and fidelity. When the mother dies, the orphaned daughter incorporates more strongly than ever the doctrines her parent has taught. Her acceptance of such standards appears a form of repression: she feels no erotic passion for her devoted husband, and the narrative provides no reason to expect her to develop capacity for such feeling. When a handsome, brave, courteous, intelligent, kind, witty aristocrat falls in love with her, when the princess realizes that she now feels that passion she has never experienced, the stage is set for a conventional conflict of love and duty. The novel renders exactly this conflict; but in ways far from conventional.

The Princess of Clèves is not, as it may seem, only a story of female self-abnegation. It is relevant to remember that the princess's lover for his beloved's sake gives up his chance to marry the Queen of England, a bit of *male* abnegation, and an indication of the female protagonist's emotional power. The heroine suppresses erotic impulse—or, at any rate, such impulse's expression—but she allows herself gratification compatible with her goodness: the satisfaction of the dominance she achieves by her steady withholding of response. She does not consciously experience her situation as one of mastery; the reader, however, may realize her innocent force.

The twentieth-century reader, like de La Fayette's contemporaries, finds him or herself caught up in knotty problems of psychological interpretation. Is the princess honorable or needlessly cruel in confessing to her husband? Does she behave like a child or like a mature woman? Does she reject her lover at last out of virtue or (as she herself suggests) from fear of his eventual infidelity? Does she consolidate or yield her power by this rejection? Does she choose happiness or misery in committing herself to celibate widowhood?

The reader's problem of understanding and interpreting the protagonist duplicates the situation of characters within the fiction. In the confined social and political world here depicted, shifting sexual alliances often prefigure movements of power. Royal marriages dictate national policy; royal love affairs may have equally potent effects; the sexual arrangements of those near the throne imply political consequences. Hence the effort to understand people's sexual behavior involves, by extension, matters of public importance. For the princess herself, however, love remains an intensely personal matter, despite her full awareness of how personal meanings can enlarge themselves. The princess thinks about her virtue, her commitments, her feelings. And she thinks about how to protect those feelings from the knowledge of the avid watchers and interpreters who compose her society.

Everyone watches everyone else in the court of Henri II, where "what appears is seldom the truth." For the princess and the duke, looking at one another, in the flesh or in some form of representation, is their most fulfilling erotic activity. The duke steals a miniature of his beloved, who watches him doing so. The princess, alone in her pavilion, gazes at a painted battle scene including a depiction of the duke. Outside her window, the duke, himself unseen, watches her looking at his picture. At the edge of the park, another watcher, sent by the princess's husband, seeks to comprehend the duke's activities. This third watcher represents the social world constantly impinging on individual desire; the duke's watching, like the princess's contemplation of his image, epitomizes desire. Similarly, in a late episode (after the prince's death), the duke watches the princess from a distant window. She in turn watches his window from her own apartment, her erotic imagination aroused by the idea that her lover seeks opportunity merely to look at her. But she can allow herself no satisfaction beyond this attenuated variety. As she says proudly in her final interview with the duke, "You have seen that my feelings did not guide my actions."

The court's obsessive watching generates an atmosphere of tension. Every appearance provides matter for speculation: the colors a nobleman wears in a tournament, a letter falling out of someone's pocket, the degree of splendor with which a lady dresses for a ball. Often watchers make mistakes, which then become part of the dense social texture enveloping everyone. The princess would like to remove herself from the arena of watchers, but proper social behavior demands participation, as object or as subject.

The woman at the novel's center of interest and of power initiates little action. She provides an interesting contrast with Racine's Phaedra, also cen-

tral to an imaginative work, a woman torn by passion and forever acting to
disastrous effect. The Princess of Clèves, more passive, only allows herself
to be loved. The prince, her husband, feels intense passion for her; she keeps
it alive by never reciprocating it; he dies partly of grief over her imagined
infidelity. The duke who loves her wins her acknowledged love in return,
but she will not marry him after her husband dies: withholding herself, she
cannot become vulnerable to the possible diminution of his passion. Her
beauty has the greater power over observers because she refuses to bestow it.

The princess's withholding, although she gains power from it, derives
from no desire for power. On the contrary, it declares a woman's experience
of powerlessness. Her mother's urging of chastity insists on love's dangers;
she explains "how insincere men are, how false and deceitful." In a society
where "love was always mixed with politics, and politics with love," where
"ambition and gallantry were the sole occupation of the court," the princess's self-protection is only sensible. Although The Princess of Clèves, like
other works of its period, endorses the principle of controlling passion by
reason, it also reveals the costs of such control. And it suggests awareness
that actual, as opposed to ideal, social orders reflect the shape of individual
passion more clearly than they declare the organizing force of reason.

The array of characters in the opening pages of The Princess of Clèves may
seem forbidding; it is difficult for modern readers to keep them straight or to
remember their connections with one another. In fact, the novel provides
necessary information as it goes along, and one need not know historical
facts to enjoy the fictional arrangement of them. A preliminary summary of
the situation and characters specified in the first section may, however, be
helpful. Henri II of France (1519–1559), known as a patron of the arts and
as a brave soldier, heads the court. The queen, Catherine de Médicis (1529–
1589), has less social and political power than does the king's long-time
mistress, Diane de Poitiers, Duchess of Valentinois (1499–1566). Also politically important is the woman usually referred to as "Madame," the king's
sister, Marguerite (1525–1574). The two dominant factions at court are headed
by the Duke of Montmorency, Constable of France (1492–1567), member
of an enormously powerful family, and François de Lorraine, Chevalier of
Guise (d. 1562). Various marital alliances link the families of these persons
with the Duchess of Valentinois, to whose patronage all aspire.

The title character, the princess, and her mother are entirely fictional,
but they are said to belong to the family of another historical character, the
powerful François de Vendôme, Vidame of Chartres (1522–1560). Both the
prince whom the protagonist marries, and Jacques de Savoie, Duke of Nemours (1531–1585), whom she loves, actually existed.

The most important historical facts to keep in mind are the rivalry between
the Duchess of Valentinois and the Queen, and between the Montmorency
and Guise families. The court intrigues reported in the novel mainly stem
from these oppositions.

Little has been written in English about Mme. de La Fayette. The best
general introduction is S. Haig's biographical and critical study, Madame
de Lafayette (1970). M. Turnell's The Novel in France (1950) contains a
short treatment of The Princess of Clèves.

The Princess of Clèves[1]

Part I

There never was in France so brilliant a display of magnificence and gallantry as during the last years of the reign of Henri II. This monarch was gallant, handsome, and susceptible; although his love for Diane de Poitiers, Duchess of Valentinois, had lasted twenty years, its ardor had not diminished, as his conduct testified.

He was remarkably skilful in physical exercises, and devoted much attention to them; every day was filled with hunting and tennis, dancing, running at the ring, and sports of that kind. The favorite colors and the initials of Madame de Valentinois were to be seen everywhere, and she herself used to appear dressed as richly as Mademoiselle de la Marck, her granddaughter, who was then about to be married.

The fact that the queen was there, accounted for her presence. This princess, although she had passed her first youth, was still beautiful; she was fond of splendor, magnificence, and pleasure. The king had married her while still Duke of Orléans, in the lifetime of his elder brother, the dauphin, who afterward died at Tournon, mourned as a worthy heir to the position of Francis I, his father.

The queen's ambition made her like to reign. She seemed indifferent to the king's attachment to the Duchess of Valentinois, and never betrayed any jealousy; but she was so skilled a dissembler that it was hard to discover her real feelings, and she was compelled by policy to keep the duchess near her if she wanted to see anything of the king. As for him, he liked the society of women, even of those with whom he was not at all in love. He was with the queen every day at her audience,[2] when all the most attractive lords and ladies were sure to appear.

At no court had there ever been gathered together so many lovely women and brave men. It seemed as if Nature had made an effort to show her highest beauty in the greatest lords and ladies. Madame Elisabeth of France, afterwards queen of Spain, began to show her wonderful intelligence and that unrivalled beauty which was so fatal to her. Mary Stuart, the queen of Scotland, who had just married the dauphin and was called the crown princess, or dauphiness, was faultless in mind and body. She had been brought up at the French court and had acquired all its polish; she was endowed by Nature with so strong a love for the softer graces that in spite of her youth she admired and understood them perfectly. Her mother-in-law, the queen, and Madame, the king's sister, were also fond of poetry, of

1. Translated by Thomas Sergeant Perry.   2. A formal gathering.

comedy, and of music. The interest which King Francis I had felt in poetry and letters still prevailed in France and since the king, his son, was devoted to physical exercise, pleasures of all sorts were to be found at the court. But what rendered the court especially fine and majestic was the great number of princes and lords of exceptional merit; those I am about to name were, in their different ways, the ornament and the admiration of their age.

The King of Navarre inspired universal respect by his exalted rank and his royal bearing. He excelled in the art of war; but the Duke of Guise had shown himself so strong a rival that he had often laid aside his command to enter the duke's service as a private soldier in the most dangerous battles. This duke had manifested such admirable bravery with such remarkable success that he was an object of envy to every great commander. He had many conspicuous qualities besides his personal courage,—he possessed a vast and profound intelligence, a noble, lofty mind, and equal capacity for war and affairs. His brother, the Cardinal of Lorraine, was born with an unbridled ambition, and had acquired vast learning; this he turned to his profit by using it in defence of Catholicism, which had begun to be attacked. The Chevalier de Guise, afterwards known as the Grand Prior, was loved by all; he was handsome, witty, clever, and his courage was renowned throughout Europe. The short, ill-favored body of the Prince of Condé held a great and haughty soul, and an intelligence that endeared him to even the most beautiful women. The Duke of Nevers, famous for his military prowess and his important services to the state, though somewhat advanced in years was adored by all the court. He had three handsome sons,—the second, known as the Prince of Clèves, was worthy to bear that proud title; he was brave and grand, and was withal endowed with a prudence rare in the young. The Vidame[3] of Chartres, a scion of the old house of Vendôme, a name not despised by princes of the blood, had won equal triumphs in war and gallantry; he was handsome, attractive, brave, hardy, generous; all his good qualities were distinct and striking,—in short, he was the only man fit to be compared, if such comparison be possible, with the Duke of Nemours. This nobleman was a masterpiece of Nature; the least of his fascinations was his extreme beauty; he was the handsomest man in the world. What made him superior to every one else was his unrivalled courage and a charm manifested in his mind, his expression, and his actions, such as no other showed. He possessed a certain playfulness that was equally attractive to men and women; he was unusually skilful in physical exercises; and he dressed in a way that every one tried in vain to imitate; moreover, his bearing was such that all eyes followed him whenever he appeared. There

---

3. The title *vidame* designated the lay representative of a Bishop and the commander of the Bishop's troops.

was no lady in the court who would not have been flattered by his
attentions; few of those to whom he had devoted himself could boast
of having resisted him; and even many in whom he had shown no
interest made very clear their affection for him. He was so gentle and
courteous that he could not refuse some attentions to those who tried
to please him,—hence he had many mistresses; but it was hard to
say whom he really loved. He was often to be seen with the dauphiness; her beauty, her gentleness, her desire to please every one, and
the especial regard she showed for this prince, made some imagine
that he dared to raise his eyes to her. The Guises, whose niece she
was, had acquired influence and position by her marriage; they aspired
to an equality with the princes of the blood and to a share of the
power exercised by the Constable of Montmorency. It was to the
constable[4] that the king confided the greater part of the cares of state,
while he treated the Duke of Guise and the Marshal of Saint-André
as his favorites. But those attached to his person by favor or position
could only keep their place by submitting to the Duchess of Valentinois, who, although no longer young or beautiful, ruled him so
despotically that she may be said to have been the mistress of his
person and of the state.

The king had always loved the constable, and at the beginning of
his reign had summoned him from the exile into which he had been
sent by Francis I. The court was divided between the Guises and the
constable, who was the favorite of the princes of the blood. Both
parties had always struggled for the favor of the Duchess of Valentinois. The Duke of Aumale, brother of the Duke of Guise, had married one of her daughters. The constable aspired to the same alliance,
not satisfied with having married his eldest son to Madame Diane, a
daughter of the king by a lady of Piedmont who entered a convent
after the birth of her child. The promises which Monsieur de Montmorency had made to Mademoiselle de Piennes, one of the queen's
maids-of-honor, had proved a serious obstacle to this match; and
although the king had removed it with extreme patience and kindness, the constable still felt insecure until he had won over the Duchess
of Valentinois and had separated her from the Guises, whose greatness had begun to alarm her. She had delayed in every way in her
power the marriage between the dauphin and the Queen of Scotland; this young queen's beauty and intelligence, and the position
given to the Guises by this marriage, were very odious to her. She
especially detested the Cardinal of Lorraine, who had addressed her
in bitter, even contemptuous terms. She saw that he was intriguing
with the queen; hence the constable found her ready to join forces
with him by bringing about the marriage of Mademoiselle de la Marck,

4. The title of *constable* at this time designated the highest ranking official of the court.

her granddaughter, to Monsieur d'Anville, his second son, who succeeded to his post in the reign of Charles IX. The constable did not
expect that Monsieur d'Anville would have any objections to this
marriage, as had been the case with Monsieur de Montmorency; but
though the reasons were more hidden, the difficulties were no less
obstinate. Monsieur d'Anville was desperately in love with the crown
princess; and although his passion was hopeless, he could not persuade himself to contract other ties. The Marshal of Saint-André was
almost the only courtier who had taken sides with neither faction; he
was one of the favorites, but this position he held simply by his own
merits. Ever since he had been the dauphin, the king had been
attached to this nobleman, and later had made him marshal of France,
at an age when men are satisfied with lesser honors. His advance
gave him a distinction which he maintained by his personal worth
and charm, by a costly table and rich surroundings, and by more
splendor than any private individual had yet displayed. The king's
generosity warranted this sumptuousness. There was no limit to this
monarch's generosity to those he loved. He did not possess every
great quality, but he had many, and among them the love of war
and a good knowledge of it. This accounted for his many successes;
and if we except the battle of St. Quentin, his reign was an unbroken
series of victories. He had won the battle of Renty in person, Piedmont had been conquered, the English had been driven from France,
and the Emperor Charles V had seen his good fortune desert him
before the city of Metz,[5] which he had besieged in vain with all the
forces of the Empire and of Spain. Nevertheless, since the defeat of
St. Quentin had diminished our hope of conquest, and fortune seemed
to favor one king as much as the other, they were gradually led to
favor peace.

    The Dowager Duchess of Lorraine had begun to lead the way to
a cessation of hostilities at the time of the dauphin's marriage, and
ever since then there had been secret negotiations. At last Cercamp,
in the Province of Artois, was chosen as the place of meeting. The
Cardinal of Lorraine, the constable, and the Marshal of Saint-André
appeared in behalf of the King of France; the Duke of Alva and the
Prince of Orange in behalf of Philip II. The Duke and Duchess of
Lorraine were the mediators. The leading articles were the marriage
of Madame Elisabeth of France to Don Carlos, Infanta of Spain,
and that of Madame, the king's sister, with Monsieur de Savoie.

    Meanwhile the king remained on the frontier, and there heard of
the death of Mary, queen of England. He sent the Count of Randan

---

5. Henri II had continued the struggle of his father, Francis I, against Charles V, leader of the
Holy Roman Empire, for supremacy in Europe and particularly for control in Italy. The battles
here alluded to belong to that struggle. At Saint-Quentin the French armies were defeated in
1557; the French drove the English from Calais in 1558; Metz was captured in 1552.

to Elizabeth to congratulate her on ascending the throne. She was very glad to receive him, because her rights were so insecure that it was of great service to her to have them acknowledged by the king. The count found her well informed about the interests of France and the capabilities of those who composed the court, but especially familiar with the reputation of the Duke of Nemours. She spoke of this nobleman so often and with such warmth that when Monsieur de Randan returned and recounted his journey to the king, he told him that there was nothing to which Monsieur de Nemours could not aspire, and that she would be capable of marrying him. That very evening the king spoke to this nobleman, and made Monsieur de Randan repeat to him his conversation with Elizabeth, urging him to essay this great fortune. At first Monsieur de Nemours thought that the king was jesting; but when he saw his mistake he said,—

"At any rate, sire, if I undertake a fantastic enterprise under the advice and in behalf of your Majesty, I beg of you to keep it secret until success shall justify me before the public, and to guard me from appearing vain enough to suppose that a queen who has never seen me should wish to marry me from love."

The king promised to speak of the plan to no one but the constable, and agreed that secrecy was essential for its success. Monsieur de Randan advised Monsieur de Nemours to visit England as a simple traveller; but the latter could not make up his mind to do this. He sent Lignerolles, an intelligent young man, one of his favorites, to ascertain the queen's feeling and to try to open the matter. Meanwhile he went to see the Duke of Savoy, who was then at Brussels with the King of Spain. The death of Mary of England[6] raised great obstacles to any treaty of peace; the commission broke up at the end of November, and the king returned to Paris.

At that moment there appeared at court a young lady to whom all eyes were turned, and we may well believe that she was possessed of faultless beauty, since she aroused admiration where all were well accustomed to the sight of handsome women. Of the same family as the Vidame of Chartres, she was one of the greatest heiresses in France. Her father had died young, leaving her under the charge of his wife, Madame de Chartres, whose kindness, virtue, and worth were beyond praise. After her husband's death she had withdrawn from court for many years; during this period she had devoted herself to the education of her daughter, not merely cultivating her mind and her beauty, but also seeking to inspire her with the love of virtue and to make her attractive. Most mothers imagine that it is enough never to speak of gallantry to their daughters to guard them from it forever. Madame de Chartres was of a very different opinion; she

6. Mary Tudor (1516–1558), "Bloody Mary," wife of Philip II of Spain.

often drew pictures of love to her daughter, showing her its fascinations, in order to give her a better understanding of its perils. She
told her how insincere men are, how false and deceitful; she described
the domestic miseries which illicit love-affairs entail, and, on the
other hand, pictured to her the peaceful happiness of a virtuous
woman's life, as well as the distinction and elevation which virtue
gives to a woman of rank and beauty. She taught her, too, how hard
it was to preserve this virtue without extreme care, and without that
one sure means of securing a wife's happiness, which is to love her
husband and to be loved by him.

This heiress was, then, one of the greatest matches in France, and
although she was very young, many propositions of marriage had
been made to her. Madame de Chartres, who was extremely proud,
found almost nothing worthy of her daughter, and the girl being in
her sixteenth year, she was anxious to take her to court. The Vidame
went to welcome her on her arrival, and was much struck by the
marvellous beauty of Mademoiselle de Chartres,—and with good
reason: her delicate complexion and her blond hair gave her a unique
brilliancy; her features were regular, and her face and person were
full of grace and charm.

The day after her arrival she went to match some precious stones
at the house of an Italian who dealt in them. He had come from
Florence with the queen, and had grown so rich by his business that
his house seemed that of some great nobleman rather than of a merchant. The Prince of Clèves happened to come in while she was
there; he was so struck by her beauty that he could not conceal his
surprise, and Mademoiselle de Chartres could not keep from blushing when she saw his astonishment: she succeeded, however, in
regaining her composure without paying any further attention to the
prince than civility required for a man of his evident importance.
Monsieur de Clèves gazed at her admiringly, wondering who this
beauty was whom he did not know. He perceived from her bearing
and her suite[7] that she must be a lady of high rank. She was so young
that he thought she must be unmarried; but since she had not her
mother with her, and the Italian, who did not know her, addressed
her as "madame," he was in great doubt, and stared at her with
continual surprise. He saw that his glances embarrassed her, unlike
most young women, who always take pleasure in seeing the effect of
their beauty; it even seemed to him that his presence made her anxious to go away, and in fact she left very soon. Monsieur de Clèves
consoled himself for her departure with the hope of finding out who
she was, and was much disappointed to learn that no one knew. He
was so struck by her beauty and evident modesty that from that moment

---

7. Group of attendants or servants.

he conceived for her the greatest love and esteem. That evening he called on Madame, the king's sister.

This princess was held in high esteem on account of her influence with the king, her brother; and this influence was so great that when the king made peace he consented to restore Piedmont to enable her to marry Monsieur de Savoie. Although she had always meant to marry, she had determined to give her hand to none but a sovereign, and had for that reason refused the King of Navarre when he was Duke of Vendôme, and had always felt an interest in Monsieur de Savoie after seeing him at Nice on the occasion of the interview between Francis I and Pope Paul III.[8] Since she possessed great intelligence and a fine taste, she drew pleasant persons about her, and at certain hours the whole court used to visit her.

Thither Monsieur de Clèves went, as was his habit. He was so full of the wit and beauty of Mademoiselle de Chartres that he could speak of nothing else; he talked freely of his adventure, and set no limit to his praise of the young woman he had seen but did not know. Madame said to him that there was no such person as he described, and that if there were, every one would have known about her. Madame de Dampierre, her lady-in-waiting and a friend of Madame de Chartres, when she heard the conversation moved near the princess and said to her in a low voice that doubtless it was Mademoiselle de Chartres whom Monsieur de Clèves had seen. Madame turned towards him and said that if he would return the next day, she would show him this beauty who had so impressed him. Mademoiselle de Chartres made her appearance the next day. The queen received her with every imaginable attention, and she was greeted with such admiration by every one that she heard around her nothing but praise. This she received with such noble modesty that she seemed not to hear it, or at least not to be affected by it. Then she visited the apartments of Madame, the king's sister. The princess, after praising her beauty, told her the surprise she had given to Monsieur de Clèves. A moment after, that person appeared.

"Come," she said to him, "see if I have not kept my word, and if, when I point out Mademoiselle de Chartres to you, I do not show you the beauty you sought; at any rate, thank me for telling her how much you already admire her."

Monsieur de Clèves was filled with joy to find that this young woman whom he had found so attractive was of a rank proportionate to her beauty. He went up to her and asked her to remember that he had been the first to admire her, and that without knowing her he had felt all the respect and esteem that were her due.

The Chevalier de Guise, his friend, and he left the house together.

8. The meeting took place in 1538; the Pope helped to arrange a ten-year truce between France and the Empire.

At first they praised Mademoiselle de Chartres without stint; then they found that they were praising her too much, and both stopped saying what they thought of her: but they were compelled to talk about her on the following days wherever they met. This new beauty was for a long time the general subject of conversation. The queen praised her warmly and showed an extraordinary regard for her; the dauphiness made her one of her favorites, and begged Madame de Chartres to bring her to see her very often; the daughters of the king invited her to all their entertainments,—in short, she was loved and admired by the whole court, except by Madame de Valentinois. It was not that this new beauty gave her any uneasiness,—her long experience had made her sure of the king,—but she so hated the Vidame of Chartres, whom she had desired to ally with herself by the marriage of one of her daughters, while he had joined the queen's party, that she could not look with favor on any one who bore his name and seemed to enjoy his friendship.

The Prince of Clèves fell passionately in love with Mademoiselle de Chartres, and was eager to marry her; but he feared lest the pride of Madame de Chartres should prevent her from giving her daughter to a man who was not the eldest of his family. Yet this family was so distinguished, and the Count of Eu, who was the head of the house, had just married a woman so near to royalty, that it was timidity rather than any true reason that inspired the fear of Monsieur de Clèves. He had many rivals; the Chevalier de Guise seemed to him the most formidable, on account of his birth, his ability, and the brilliant position of his family. This prince had fallen in love with Mademoiselle de Chartres the first day he saw her; he had noticed the passion of Monsieur de Clèves just as the latter had noticed his. Though the two men were friends, the separation which resulted from this rivalry gave them no chance to explain themselves, and their friendship cooled without their having courage to come to an understanding. The good fortune of Monsieur de Clèves in being the first to see Mademoiselle de Chartres seemed to him a happy omen, and to promise him some advantage over his rivals; but he foresaw serious obstacles on the part of the Duke of Nevers, his father. This duke was bound to the Duchess of Valentinois by many ties; she was an enemy of the Vidame, and this was reason enough to prevent the Duke of Nevers from consenting that his son should think of that nobleman's niece.

Madame de Chartres, who had already taken such pains to fill her daughter with a love of virtue, did not remit them in this place where they were still so necessary, and bad examples were so frequent. Ambition and gallantry were the sole occupation of the court, busying men and women alike. There were so many interests and so many different intrigues in which women took part that love was always mingled with politics, and politics with love. No one was calm or indifferent; every one sought to rise, to please, to serve, or to injure; no one was weary or idle, every one was taken up with pleasure or intrigue. The ladies had their special interest in the queen, in the crown princess, in the Queen of Navarre, in Madame the king's sister, or in the Duchess of Valentinois, according to their inclinations, their sense of right, or their humor. Those who had passed their first youth and assumed an austere virtue, were devoted to the queen; those who were younger and sought pleasure and gallantry, paid their court to the crown princess. The Queen of Navarre had her favorites; she was young, and had much influence over her husband the king,[9] who was allied with the constable, and hence highly esteemed. Madame the king's sister still preserved some of her beauty, and gathered several ladies about herself. The Duchess of Valentinois was sought by all those whom she deigned to regard; but the women she liked were few, and with the exception of those who enjoyed her intimacy and confidence, and whose disposition bore some likeness to her own, she received only on the days when she assumed to hold a court like the queen.

All these different cliques were separated by rivalry and envy. Then, too, the women who belonged to each one of them were also jealous of one another, either about their chances of advancement, or about their lovers; often their interests were complicated by other pettier, but no less important questions. Hence there was in this court a sort of well-ordered agitation, which rendered it very charming, but also very dangerous, for a young woman. Madame de Chartres saw this peril, and thought only of protecting her daughter from it. She besought her, not as a mother, but as a friend, to confide to her all the sweet speeches that might be made to her, and promised her aid in all those matters which so often embarrass the young.

The Chevalier de Guise made his feelings for Mademoiselle de Chartres and his intentions so manifest that every one could see them; yet he well knew the very grave difficulties that stood in his way. He was aware that he was not a desirable match, because his fortune was too small for his rank. He knew, too, that his brothers would disapprove of his marrying, through fear of the loss of position which sometimes befalls great families through the marriage of younger sons. The Cardinal of Lorraine soon proved to him that his fears were well grounded, for he denounced the chevalier's love for Mademoiselle de Chartres very warmly, though he concealed his true reasons. The cardinal nourished a hatred for the Vidame, which was hidden at the time, and only broke out later. He would have preferred to see his brother ally himself with any other family than that

9. Antoine de Bourbon, King of Navarre (1518–1562), father of Henri IV of France.

of the Vidame, and gave such public expression to his dislike that
Madame de Chartres was plainly offended. She took great pains to
show that the Cardinal of Lorraine had no cause for fear, and that
she herself never contemplated the match. The Vidame adopted the
same course, and with a better understanding of the cardinal's objection, because he knew the underlying reason.

The Prince of Clèves had concealed his passion quite as little as
had the Chevalier de Guise. The Duke of Nevers was sorry to hear
of this attachment, but thought that his son would forget it at a word
from him; great was his surprise when he found him determined to
marry Mademoiselle de Chartres. He opposed this determination
with a warmth so ill concealed that the whole court soon had wind
of it, and it came to the knowledge of her mother. She had never
doubted that Monsieur de Nevers would regard this match as an
advantageous one for his son, and was much surprised that both the
house of Clèves and that of Guise dreaded the alliance instead of
desiring it. She was so chagrined that she sought to marry her daughter to some one who could raise her above those who fancied themselves superior to her; and after carefully going over the ground, pitched
on the prince dauphin, the son of the Duke of Montpensier. He was
of the right age to marry, and held the highest position at court.
Since Madame de Chartres was a very clever woman, and was aided
by the Vidame, who at that time had great influence, while her
daughter was in every way a good match, she played her cards so
cleverly and successfully that Monsieur de Montpensier appeared to
desire the marriage, and it seemed as if nothing could stand in its
way.

The Vidame, though aware of Monsieur d'Anville's devotion to
the crown princess, still thought that he might make use of the influence which she had over him to induce him to speak well of Mademoiselle de Chartres to the king and to the Prince of Montpensier,
whose intimate friend he was. He mentioned this to the princess,
who took up the matter eagerly, since it promised advancement to a
young woman of whom she had become very fond. This she told the
Vidame, assuring him that though she knew she should offend her
uncle, the Cardinal of Lorraine, this would be no objection, because
she had good grounds for disliking him, since he every day furthered
the queen's interests in opposition to her own.

Persons in love are always glad of any excuse for talking about the
object of their affection. As soon as the Vidame had gone, the crown
princess ordered Châtelart, the favorite of Monsieur d'Anville and
the confidant of his love for her, to tell him to be at the queen's
reception that evening. Châtelart received this command with great
delight. He belonged to a good family of Dauphiné, but his merit
and intelligence had raised him to a higher place than his birth war-

ranted. He was received and treated with kindness by all the great lords at the court, and the favor of the family of Montmorency had attached him especially to Monsieur d'Anville. He was handsome and skilled in all physical exercises; he sang agreeably, wrote verses, and had a gallant, ardent nature, which so attracted Monsieur d'Anville that he made him a confidant of his love for the crown princess. The confidence brought him into the society of that lady, and thus began that unhappy passion, which robbed him of his reason and finally cost him his life.

Monsieur d'Anville did not fail to make his appearance that evening in the queen's drawing-room; he was pleased that the dauphiness had chosen him to aid her, and he promised faithfully to obey her commands. But Madame de Valentinois had heard of the contemplated marriage and had laid her plans to thwart it; she had been so successful in arousing the king's opposition that when Monsieur d'Anville spoke of it, he showed his disapproval, and commanded him to apprise the Prince of Montpensier of it. It is easy to imagine the feelings of Madame de Chartres at the failure of a plan she had so much desired, especially when her ill-success gave so great an advantage to her enemies and did so much harm to her daughter.

The crown princess kindly expressed to Mademoiselle de Chartres her regrets at not being able to further her interests. "You see," she said, "I have but very little power; I am so detested by the queen and the Duchess of Valentinois that they or their attendants always oppose everything I desire. Still," she added, "I have always tried to please them, and they hate me only on account of my mother, who used to fill them with uneasiness and jealousy. The king had been in love with her before he loved Madame de Valentinois, and in his early married life, before he had any children, though he loved this duchess, he seemed bent on dissolving that marriage to marry the queen my mother. Madame de Valentinois dreaded the woman he had loved so well, lest her wit and beauty should diminish her own power, and entered into an alliance with the constable, who was also opposed to the king's marrying a sister of the Guises. They won over the late king; and though he hated the Duchess of Valentinois as much as he loved the queen, he joined with them in preventing the king from dissolving his marriage. In order to make this impossible, they arranged my mother's marriage with the King of Scotland, whose first wife had been Madame Magdeleine, the king's sister,—this they did because it was the first thing that offered; though they broke the promises that had been made to the King of England, who was deeply in love with her. In fact, this matter nearly caused a falling out between the two kings. Henry VIII could not be consoled for not marrying my mother; and whenever any other French princess was proposed to him, he used to say that she would never take the place of the one they had taken from him. It is true that my mother was a perfect beauty, and it is remarkable that when she was the widow of a duke of Longueville, three kings should have wanted to marry her. It was her misfortune to be married to the least important of them all, and to be sent to a kingdom where she has found nothing but unhappiness. I am told that I am like her; I dread the same sad fate, and whatever happiness seems to be awaiting me, I doubt if I ever enjoy it."

Mademoiselle de Chartres assured the crown princess that these gloomy presentiments were so fantastic that they could not long disturb her, and that she ought not to doubt that her good fortune would give the lie to her fears.

Henceforth no one dared to think of Mademoiselle de Chartres, through fear of displeasing the king or of not succeeding in winning a young woman who had aspired to a prince of the blood. None of these considerations moved Monsieur de Clèves. The death of his father, the Duke of Nevers, which happened at that time, left him free to follow his own inclinations, and as soon as the period of mourning had passed, he thought of nothing but marrying Mademoiselle de Chartres. He was glad to make his proposal at a time when circumstances had driven away all rivals and when he felt almost sure that she would not refuse him. What dimmed his joy was the fear of not being agreeable to her; and he would have preferred the happiness of pleasing her to the certainty of marrying her when she did not love him.

The Chevalier de Guise had somewhat aroused his jealousy; but since this was inspired more by his rival's merits than by the conduct of Mademoiselle de Chartres, he thought of nothing but ascertaining whether by good fortune she would approve of his designs. He met her only at the queen's rooms or in company, yet he managed to speak to her of his intentions and hopes in the most respectful way; he begged her to let him know how she felt towards him, and told her that his feelings for her were such that he should be forever unhappy if she obeyed her mother only from a sense of duty.

Mademoiselle de Chartres, having a very noble heart, was really grateful to the Prince of Clèves for what he did. This gratitude lent to her answer a certain gentleness, which was quite sufficient to feed the hope of a man as much in love as he was, and he counted on attaining at least a part of what he desired.

Mademoiselle repeated this conversation to her mother, who said that Monsieur de Clèves was of such high birth, possessed so many fine qualities, and seemed so discreet for a man of his age, that if she inclined to marry him she would herself gladly give her consent. Mademoiselle de Chartres replied that she had noticed the same fine qualities, and that she would rather marry him than any one else, but that she had no special love for him.

The next day the prince had his offer formally made to Madame de Chartres; she accepted it, being willing to give her daughter a husband she did not love. The marriage settlement was drawn up, the king was told of it, and the marriage became known to every one.

Monsieur de Clèves was very happy, although not perfectly satisfied; it gave him much pain to see that what Mademoiselle de Chartres felt for him was only esteem and gratitude, and he could not flatter himself that she nourished any warmer feeling; for had she done so, she would have readily shown it in their closer intimacy. Within a few days he complained to her of this.

"Is it possible," he said, "that I may not be happy in my marriage? Yet assuredly I am not happy. You have a sort of kindly feeling for me which cannot satisfy me; you are not impatient, uneasy, or grieved: you are as indifferent to my love as if this were given to your purse, and not to your charms."

"You do wrong to complain," she replied. "I do not know what more you can ask; it seems to me that you have no right to demand anything more."

"It is true," he said, "that you have a certain air with which I should be satisfied if there were anything behind it; but instead of your being restrained by a sense of propriety, it is a sense of propriety which inspires your actions. I do not touch your feelings or your heart; my presence causes you neither pleasure nor pain."

"You cannot doubt," she made answer, "that I am glad to see you, and I blush so often when I do see you that you may be sure that the sight of you affects me."

"I am not deceived by your blushes," he urged; "they come from modesty, and not from any thrill of your heart, and I do not exaggerate their importance."

Mademoiselle de Chartres did not know what to answer; these distinctions were outside of her experience. Monsieur de Clèves saw only too well how far removed she was from feeling for him as he should have liked, when he saw that she had no idea of what that feeling was.

The Chevalier de Guise returned from a journey a few days before the wedding. He had seen so many insurmountable obstacles in the way of his marrying Mademoiselle de Chartres that he knew he had no chance of success; yet he was evidently distressed at seeing her become the wife of another. This grief did not extinguish his passion, and he remained quite as much in love as before. Mademoiselle de Chartres had not been ignorant of his devotion. On his return he let her know that she was the cause of the deep gloom that marked his face; and he had so much merit and charm that it was almost impossible to make him unhappy without regretting it. Hence she was depressed; but this pity went no further, and she told her mother how much pain this prince's love caused her.

Madame de Chartres admired her daughter's frankness, and with good reason, for it could not be fuller or simpler; she regretted, how-ever, that her heart was not touched, especially when she saw that the prince had not affected it any more than the others. Hence she took great pains to attach her to her future husband, and to impress upon her what she owed him for the interest he had taken in her before he knew who she was, and for the proof he had given of his love in choosing her at a time when no one else ventured to think of her.

The marriage ceremony took place at the Louvre,[1] and in the evening the king and queen, with all the court, supped at the house of Madame de Chartres, who received them with great splendor. The Chevalier de Guise did not venture to make himself conspicu-ous by staying away, but his dejection was evident.

Monsieur de Clèves did not find that Mademoiselle de Chartres had altered her feelings when she changed her name. His position as her husband gave him greater privileges, but no different place in her heart. Though he had married her, he did not cease to be her lover,[2] because there was always left something for him to desire; and though she lived on the best of terms with him, he was not yet perfectly happy. He preserved for her a violent and restless passion, which marred his joy. Jealousy had no part in it, for never had a husband been further from feeling it, or a wife from inspiring it. Yet she was exposed to all the temptations of the court, visiting the queen and the king's sister every day. All the young and fashionable men met her at her own house and at that of her brother-in-law, the Duke of Nevers, whose doors were always open; but she always had an air that inspired respect, and seemed so remote from gallantry that the Marshal of Saint-André, though bold and protected by the king's favor, was touched by her beauty without venturing to show it except by delicate attentions. There were many others who felt as did the marshal; and Madame de Chartres added to her daughter's natural modesty such a keen sense of propriety that she made her seem like a woman to be sighed for in vain.

The Duchess of Lorraine, while trying to bring about peace, had also tried to arrange the marriage of her son, the Duke of Lorraine, and had succeeded; he was to marry Madame Claude of France, the king's second daughter. The wedding had been settled for the month of February.

Meanwhile the Duke of Nemours had remained at Brussels, com-pletely taken up with his plans for England. He was always sending and receiving messengers. His hopes grew from day to day, and at last Lignerolles told him that it was time for him to appear and finish in person what had been so well begun. He received this news with

---

1. At this time, a royal residence.   2. I.e., he continued to love her.

all the satisfaction that an ambitious man can feel at seeing himself
raised to a throne simply through his reputation. He had gradually
grown so accustomed to the contemplation of this great piece of good
fortune that whereas at first he had regarded it as an impossibility,
all difficulties had vanished, and he foresaw no obstacles.

He at once despatched to Paris orders for a magnificent outfit, that
he might make his appearance in England with a splendor proportionate to his designs, and also hastened to court to be present at the
wedding of the Duke of Lorraine. He arrived the day before the
formal betrothal, and that same evening went to report to the king
the condition of affairs and to receive his advice and commands about
his future conduct. Thence he went to pay his respects to the queens.
Madame de Clèves was not there, so that she did not see him, and
was not even aware of his arrival. She had heard every one speak of
this prince as the handsomest and most agreeable man at court, and
Madame the Dauphiness had spoken of him so often and in such
terms that she felt some curiosity to see him.

Madame de Clèves spent the day of the betrothal at home dressing
herself for the ball in the evening at the Louvre. When she made
her appearance, her beauty and the splendor of her dress aroused
general admiration. The ball opened, and while she was dancing
with Monsieur de Guise, there was a certain commotion at the door
of the ballroom, as if some one were entering for whom way was
being made. Madame de Clèves finished her dance, and while she
was looking about for another partner, the king called out to her to
take the gentleman who had just arrived. She turned, and saw a
man, who she thought must be Monsieur de Nemours, stepping
over some seats to reach the place where the dancing was going on.
No one ever saw this prince for the first time without amazement;
and this evening he was more striking than ever in the rich attire
which set off his natural beauty to such great advantage; and it was
also hard to see Madame de Clèves for the first time without astonishment.

Monsieur de Nemours was so amazed by her beauty that when he
drew near her and bowed to her he could not conceal his wonder
and delight. When they began their dance, a murmur of admiration
ran through the ball-room. The king and the queens remembered
that the pair had never met, and saw how strange it was that they
should be dancing together without being acquainted. They summoned them when they had finished the set, and without giving
them a chance to speak to any one, asked if each would not like to
know who the other was, and whether either had any idea.

"As for me, Madame," said Monsieur de Nemours, "I have no
doubts; but since Madame de Clèves has not the same reasons for
guessing who I am that I have for recognizing her, I must beg your

Majesty to be good enough to tell her my name."

"I fancy," said the dauphiness, "that she knows it as well as you know hers."

"I assure you, Madame," said Madame de Clèves, who seemed a little embarrassed, "that I cannot guess so well as you think."

"You can guess very well," replied the dauphiness, "and you are very kind to Monsieur de Nemours in your unwillingness to acknowledge that you recognize him without ever having seen him before."

The queen interrupted the conversation, that the ball might go on, and Monsieur de Nemours danced with the dauphiness. This lady was a perfect beauty, and had always appeared to be one in the eyes of Monsieur de Nemours before he went to Flanders; but all that evening he admired no one but Madame de Clèves.

The Chevalier de Guise, who never ceased worshipping her, was standing near, and this incident caused him evident pain. He regarded it as a sure sign that fate meant that Monsieur de Nemours should fall in love with Madame de Clèves; and whether it was that he saw something in her face, or that jealousy sharpened his fears, he believed that she had been moved by the sight of this prince, and he could not keep from telling her that Monsieur de Nemours was very fortunate in making her acquaintance in such a gallant and unusual way.

Madame de Clèves went home so full of what had happened at the ball that though it was very late, she went to her mother's room to tell her about it; and she praised Monsieur de Nemours with a certain air that made Madame de Chartres entertain the same suspicion as the Chevalier de Guise.

The next day the wedding took place; Madame de Clèves there saw the Duke of Nemours, and was even more struck by his admirable grace and dignity than before.

On succeeding days she met him at the drawing-room of the dauphiness, saw him playing tennis with the king and riding at the ring, and heard him talk; and she always found him so superior to every one else, and so much outshining all in conversation wherever he might be, by the grace of his person and the charm of his wit, that he soon made a deep impression on her heart.

Then, too, the desire to please made the Duke of Nemours, who was already deeply interested, more charming than ever; and since they met often, and found each other more attractive than any one else at court, they naturally experienced great delight in being together.

The Duchess of Valentinois took part in all the merry-making, and the king showed her all the interest and attention that he had done when first in love with her. Madame de Clèves, who was then of an age at which it is usual to believe that no woman can ever be

loved after she is twenty-five years old, regarded with great amazement the king's attachment to this duchess, who was a grandmother
and had just married[3] her granddaughter. She often spoke of it to
Madame de Chartres. "Is it possible," she asked, "that the king has
been in love so long? How could he get interested in a woman much
older than himself, and who had been his father's mistress, as well
as that of a great many other men, as I have heard?"

"It is true," was the answer, "that neither merit nor fidelity inspired
the king's passion, or has kept it alive. And this is something which
is scarcely to be excused; for had this woman had youth and beauty
as well as rank, had she loved no one else, had she loved the king
with untiring constancy, for himself alone, and not solely for his
wealth and position, and had she used her power for worthy objects
such as the king desired, it would have been easy to admire his great
devotion to her. If," Madame de Chartres went on, "I were not afraid
that you would say of me what is always said of women of my age,
that we like to talk about old times, I would tell you the beginning
of the king's love for this duchess; and many things that happened at
the court of the late king bear much resemblance to what is now
going on."

"So far from accusing you of repeating old stories," said Madame
de Clèves, "I regret that you have told me so little about the present,
and that you have not taught me the different interests and intrigues
of the court. I am so ignorant of them that a few days ago I thought
the constable was on the best of terms with the queen."

"You were very far from the truth," replied Madame de Chartres.
"The queen hates the constable, and if she ever gets any power he
will learn it very quickly. She knows that he has often told the king
that of all his children it is only his bastards who look like him."

"I should never have imagined this hatred," interrupted Madame
de Clèves, "after seeing the zeal with which the queen wrote to the
constable when he was in prison, the joy she manifested at his return,
and the familiarity of her address as regards him."

"If you judge from appearances here," replied Madame de Chartres,
"you will be often mistaken; what appears is seldom the truth.

"But to return to Madame de Valentinois: you know her name is
Diane de Poitiers. She is of illustrious family, being descended from
the old dukes of Aquitaine; her grandmother was a natural daughter
of Louis XI,—in short, there is no common blood in her veins.
Saint-Vallier, her father, was implicated in the affair of the Constable of Bourbon, of which you have heard, was condemned to be
beheaded, and was led to the scaffold. His daughter, who was
remarkably beautiful, and had already pleased the late king, man-

3. Married off.

aged, I don't know how, to save her father's life. His pardon was granted him when he was expecting the mortal stroke; but fear had so possessed him that he did not recover consciousness, but died a few days later. His daughter made her appearance at court as the king's mistress. His journey to Italy and his imprisonment interrupted this passion. When he returned from Spain and Madame Régente went to meet him at Bayonne, she had with her all her young women, among whom was Mademoiselle de Pisseleu, afterwards Duchess of Estampes. The king fell in love with her, though she was inferior in birth, beauty, and intelligence to Madame de Valentinois: the only advantage she had was that she was younger. I have often heard her say that she was born on the day that Diane de Potiers was married; but that remark was more malicious than truthful, for I am much mistaken if the Duchess of Valentinois did not marry Monsieur de Brézé, grand seneschal of Normandy, at the same time that the king fell in love with Madame d'Estampes. Never was there fiercer hatred than existed between those two women. The Duchess of Valentinois could not forgive Madame d'Estampes for depriving her of the title of the king's mistress. Madame d'Estampes was madly jealous of Madame de Valentinois because the king maintained his relations with her. This king was never rigorously faithful to his mistresses; there was always one who had the title and the honors, but the ladies of what was called the little band shared his attentions. The death of his oldest son, it was supposed by poison, at Tournon, was a great blow to him. He had much less love for his second son, the present king, who was in every way far less to his taste, and whom he even regarded as lacking courage and spirit. He was lamenting this one day to Madame de Valentinois, whereupon she said she would like to make him fall in love with her, that he might become livelier and more agreeable. She succeeded, as you know. This love has lasted more than twenty years, without being dimmed by time or circumstances.

"At first the late king objected to it,—whether because he was still enough in love with Madame de Valentinois to feel jealous, or because he was influenced by Madame d'Estampes, who was in despair when the dauphin became attached to her enemy, is uncertain; however that may be, he viewed this passion with an anger and a disapproval that were apparent every day. His son feared neither his wrath nor his hate; and since nothing could induce him to abate or to conceal his attachment, the king was forced to endure it as best he could. His son's opposition to his wishes estranged him still more, and attached him more closely to the Duke of Orléans, his third son. This prince was handsome, energetic, ambitious, of a somewhat tempestuous nature, which needed to be controlled, but who in time would become a really fine man.

"The elder son's rank as dauphin and the father's preference for the Duke of Orléans inspired a rivalry between them which amounted to hatred. This rivalry had begun in their childhood, and lasted until the death of the latter. When the emperor entered French territory[4] he gave his whole preference to the Duke of Orléans. This so pained the dauphin that when the emperor was at Chantilly he tried to compel the constable to arrest him, without waiting for the king's orders; but the constable refused. Afterward the king blamed him for not following his son's advice; and this had a good deal to do with his leaving the court.

"The division between the two brothers induced the Duchess of Estampes to rely on the Duke of Orléans for protection against the influence which Madame de Valentinois had over the king. In this she succeeded; the duke, without falling in love with her, was as warm in defence of her interests as was the dauphin in defence of those of Madame de Valentinois. Hence there were two cabals in the court such as you can imagine; but the intrigues were not limited to two women's quarrels.

"The emperor, who had maintained his friendship for the Duke of Orléans, had frequently offered him the duchy of Milan. In the subsequent negotiations about peace, he raised hopes in the breast of the duke that he would give him the seventeen provinces[5] and his daughter's hand. The dauphin, however, desired neither peace nor this marriage. He made use of the constable, whom he had always loved, to convince the king how important it was not to give to his successor a brother so powerful as would be the Duke of Orléans in alliance with the emperor and governing the seventeen provinces. The constable agreed the more heartily with the dauphin's views because he also opposed those of Madame d'Estampes, who was his avowed enemy, and ardently desired that the power of the Duke of Orléans should be increased.

"At that time the dauphin was in command of the king's army in Champagne, and had reduced that of the emperor to such extremities that it would have utterly perished had not the Duchess of Estampes, fearing that too great success would prevent our granting peace and consenting to the marriage, secretly sent word to the enemy to surprise Epernay and Château-Thierry, which were full of supplies. This they did, and thereby saved their whole army.

"This duchess did not long profit by her treason. Soon afterward the Duke of Orléans died at Farmoutier of some contagious disease. He loved one of the most beautiful women of the court, and was beloved by her. I shall not tell you who it was, because her life since

4. Despite the enmity between France and the Empire, Charles V was allowed to cross France in 1539 on his way to put down a revolt in the Netherlands.   5. The Spanish Netherlands, which included most of modern Belgium and Holland.

that time has been most decorous; and she has tried so hard to have her affection for the prince forgotten that she deserves to have her reputation left untarnished. It so happened that she heard of her husband's death on the same day that she heard of that of Monsieur d'Orléans; consequently she was able to conceal her real grief without an effort.

"The king did not long survive his son's decease,—he died two years later. He urged the dauphin to make use of the services of the Cardinal of Tournon and of the Amiral d'Annebauld, without saying a word about the constable, who at that time was banished to Chantilly. Nevertheless, the first thing the present king did after his father's death was to call the constable back and intrust him with the management of affairs.

"Madame d'Estampes was sent away, and became the victim of all the ill-treatment she might have expected from an all-powerful enemy. The Duchess of Valentinois took full vengeance on this duchess and on all who had displeased her. Her power over the king seemed the greater because it had not appeared while he was dauphin. During the twelve years of his reign she has been in everything absolute mistress. She disposes of places and controls affairs of every sort; she secured the dismissal of the Cardinal of Tournon, of the Chancelier Olivier, and of Villeroy. Those who have endeavored to open the king's eyes to her conduct have been ruined for their pains. The Count of Taix, commander-in-chief of the artillery, who did not like her, could not keep from talking about her love affairs, and especially about one with the Count of Brissac, of whom the king was already very jealous. Yet she managed so well that the Count of Taix was disgraced and deprived of his position; and impossible as it may sound, he was succeeded by the Count of Brissac, whom she afterward made a marshal of France. Still, the king's jealousy became so violent that he could not endure having this marshal remain at court; but though usually jealousy is a hot and violent passion, it is modified and tempered in him by his extreme respect for his mistress, so that the only means he ventured to use to rid himself of his rival was by intrusting to him the government of Piedmont. There he has spent several years; last winter, however, he returned, under the pretext of asking for men and supplies for the army under his command. Possibly the desire of seeing Madame de Valentinois and dread of being forgotten had something to do with this journey. The king received him very coldly. The Guises, who do not like him, did not dare betray their feelings, on account of Madame de Valentinois, so they made use of the Vidame, his open enemy, to prevent his getting any of the things he wanted. It was not hard to injure him. The king hated him, and was made uneasy by his presence; consequently he was obliged to go back without getting any advantage from his journey,—unless, possibly, he had rekindled in the heart of Madame de Valentinois feelings which absence had nearly extinguished. The king has had many other grounds for jealousy, but either he has not known them, or he has not dared to complain.

"I am not sure, my dear," added Madame de Chartres, "that you may not think I have told you more than you cared to hear."

"Not at all," answered Madame de Clèves; "and if I were not afraid of tiring you, I should ask you many more questions."

Monsieur de Nemours' love for Madame de Clèves was at first so violent that he lost all interest in those he had formerly loved, and with whom he had kept up relations during his absence. He not merely did not seek any excuses for deserting them, he would not even listen to their complaints or reply to their reproaches. The dauphiness, for whom he had nourished very warm feelings, was soon forgotten by the side of Madame de Clèves. His impatience for his journey to England began to abate, and he ceased to hasten his preparations for departure. He often visited the crown princess, because Madame de Clèves was frequently in her apartments, and he was not unwilling to give some justification to the widespread suspicions about his feelings for the dauphiness. Madame de Clèves seemed to him so rare a prize that he decided to conceal all signs of his love rather than let it be generally known. He never spoke of it even to his intimate friend the Vidame de Chartres, to whom he usually confided everything. He was so cautious and discreet that no one suspected his love for Madame de Clèves except the Chevalier de Guise; and the lady herself would scarcely have perceived it had not her own interest in him made her watch him very closely, so that she became sure of it.

Madame de Clèves did not find herself so disposed to tell her mother what she thought of this prince's feelings as had been the case with her other lovers; and without definitely deciding on reserve, she yet never spoke of the subject. But Madame de Chartres soon perceived this, as well as her daughter's interest in him. This knowledge gave her distinct pain, for she well understood how dangerous it was for Madame de Clèves to be loved by a man like Monsieur de Nemours, especially when she was already disposed to admire him. An incident that happened a few days later confirmed her suspicions of this liking.

The Marshal of Saint-André, who was always on the look-out for opportunities to display his magnificence, made a pretext of desiring to show his house, which had just been finished, and invited the king to do him the honor of supping there with the queens. The marshal was also glad to be able to show to Madame de Clèves his lavish splendor.

A few days before the one of the supper, the dauphin, whose health was delicate, had been ailing and had seen no one. His wife, the crown princess, had spent the whole day with him, and toward evening, as he felt better, he received all the persons of quality who were in his ante-chamber. The crown princess went to her own apartment, where she found Madame de Clèves and a few other ladies with whom she was most intimate.

Since it was already late, and the crown princess was not dressed, she did not go to the queen, but sent word she could not come; she then had her jewels brought, to decide what she should wear at the Marshal of Saint-André's ball, and to give some, according to a promise she had made, to Madame de Clèves. While they were thus occupied, the Prince of Condé, whose rank gave him free admission everywhere, entered. The crown princess said to him that he doubtless came from her husband, and asked what was going on in his apartments.

"They are having a discussion, Madame, with Monsieur de Nemours," he answered. "He defends the side he has taken so eagerly that he must have a personal interest in it. I fancy he has a mistress who makes him uneasy when she goes to a ball, for he maintains that it makes a lover unhappy to see the woman he loves at such a place."

"What!" said the dauphiness, "Monsieur de Nemours does not want his mistress to go to a ball? I thought husbands might object, but I never supposed that lovers could have such a feeling."

"Monsieur de Nemours," replied the Prince of Condé, "declares that a ball is most distressing to lovers, whether they are loved or not. He says if their love is returned, they have the pain of being loved less for several days; that there is not a woman in the world who is not prevented from thinking of her lover by the demands of her toilet,[6] which entirely engrosses her attention; that women dress for every one as well as for those they love; that when they are at the ball they are anxious to please all who look at them; that when they are proud of their beauty, they feel a pleasure in which the lover plays but a small part. He says, too, that one who sighs in vain suffers even more when he sees his mistress at an entertainment; that the more she is admired by the public, the more one suffers at not being loved, through fear lest her beauty should kindle some love happier than his own; finally, that there is no pain so keen as seeing one's mistress at a ball, except knowing that she is there while absent one's self."

Madame de Clèves, though pretending not to hear what the Prince of Condé was saying, listened attentively. She readily understood her share in the opinion expressed by Monsieur de Nemours, especially when he spoke of his grief at not being at the ball with his mistress,

6. The process of dressing.

because he was not to be at that given by the Marshal of Saint-André, being ordered by the king to go to meet the Duke of Ferrara.

The crown princess laughed with the Prince of Condé, and expressed her disapproval of the views of Monsieur de Nemours. "There is only one condition, Madame," said the prince, "on which Monsieur de Nemours is willing that his mistress should go to a ball, and that is that he himself should give her permission. He said that last year when he gave a ball to your Majesty, he thought that his mistress did him a great favor in coming to it, though she seemed to be there only as one of your suite; that it is always a kindness to a lover to take part in any entertainment that he gives; and that it is also agreeable to a lover to have his mistress see him the host of the whole court and doing the honors fittingly."

"Monsieur de Nemours did well," said the dauphiness, with a smile, "to let his mistress go to that ball; for so many women claimed that position that if they had not come, there would have been scarcely any one there."

As soon as the Prince of Condé had begun to speak of what Monsieur de Nemours thought of the ball, Madame de Clèves was very anxious not to go to that of the Marshal of Saint-André. She readily agreed that it was not fitting for a woman to go to the house of a man who was in love with her, and she was glad to have so good a reason for doing a kindness to Monsieur de Nemours. Nevertheless, she took away the jewels which the crown princess had given her; that evening, however, when she showed them to her mother, she told her that she did not mean to wear them, that the Marshal of Saint-André had made his love for her so manifest that she felt sure he meant to have it thought that she was to have some part in the entertainment he was to give to the king, and that under the pretext of doing honor to the king he would pay her attentions which might perhaps prove embarrassing.

Madame de Chartres argued for some time against her daughter's decision, which she thought singular, but at last yielded, and told her she must pretend to be ill, in order to have a good excuse for not going, because her real reasons would not be approved and should not be suspected. Madame de Clèves gladly consented to stay at home for a few days, in order not to meet Monsieur de Nemours, who left without having the pleasure of knowing that she was not going to the ball.

The duke returned the day after the ball, and heard that she had not been there; but inasmuch as he did not know that his talk with the dauphin had been repeated to her, he was far from thinking that he was fortunate enough to be the cause of her absence.

The next day, when Monsieur de Nemours was calling on the queen and talking with the dauphiness, Madame de Chartres and

Madame de Clèves happened to come in and approached this princess. Madame de Clèves was not in full dress, as if she were not very
well, though her countenance belied her attire.

"You look so well," said the crown princess, "that I can scarcely
believe that you have been ill. I fancy that the Prince of Condé,
when he told you what Monsieur de Nemours thought about the
ball, convinced you that you would do a kindness to the Marshal of
Saint-André by going to his ball, and that that was the reason you
stayed away."

Madame de Clèves blushed at the dauphiness's accurate guess which
she thus expressed before Monsieur de Nemours.

Madame de Chartres saw at once why her daughter did not go to
the ball, and in order to throw Monsieur de Nemours off the track,
she at once addressed the dauphiness with an air of sincerity. "I
assure you, Madame," she said, "that your Majesty pays an honor to
my daughter which she does not deserve. She was really ill; but I am
sure that if I had not forbidden it, she would have accompanied you,
unfit as she was, to have the pleasure of seeing the wonderful entertainment last evening."

The dauphiness believed what Madame de Chartres said, and
Monsieur de Nemours was vexed to see how probable her story was;
nevertheless the confusion of Madame de Clèves made him suspect
that the dauphiness's conjecture was not without some foundation
in fact. At first Madame de Clèves had been annoyed because Monsieur de Nemours had reason to suppose that it was he who had kept
her from going to the ball, and then she felt regret that her mother
had entirely removed the grounds for this supposition.

Although the attempt to make peace at Cercamp had failed, negotiations still continued, and matters had assumed such a shape that
toward the end of February a meeting was held at Câteau-Cambrésis.[7] The same commissioners had assembled there, and the
departure of the Marshal of Saint-André freed Monsieur de Nemours from a rival who was more to be dreaded on account of his close
observation of all those who approached Madame de Clèves than
from any real success of his own.

Madame de Chartres did not wish to let her daughter see that she
knew her feeling for this prince, lest she should make her suspicious
of the advice she wanted to give her. One day she began to talk about
him. She spoke of him in warm terms, but craftily praised his discretion in being unable to fall really in love and in seeking only pleasure, not a serious attachment, in his relations with women. "To be
sure," she went on, "he has been suspected of a great passion for the

7. Negotiations were beginning toward a peace treaty between France and the Empire. The death
of Queen Mary of England ended the preliminary meetings which had begun at Cercamp in
1558; the next year they resumed and ended with the treaty of Câteau-Cambrésis.

dauphiness; I notice that he visits her very often, and I advise you to avoid talking with him as much as possible, especially in private, because you are on such terms with the crown princess that people would say that you were their confidant, and you know how disagreeable that would be. I think that if the report continues, you would do well to see less of the crown princess, that you may not be connected with love-affairs of that sort."

Madame de Clèves had never heard Monsieur de Nemours and the dauphiness talked about, and was much surprised by what her mother said. She was so sure that she had misunderstood the prince's feelings for her that she changed color. Madame de Chartres noticed this, but company coming in at that moment, Madame de Clèves went home and locked herself up in her room.

It is impossible to express her grief when her mother's words opened her eyes to the interest she took in Monsieur de Nemours; she had never dared to acknowledge it to herself. Then she saw that her feelings for him were what Monsieur de Clèves had so often supplicated, and she felt the mortification of having them for another than a husband who so well deserved them. She felt hurt and embarrassed, fearing that Monsieur de Nemours might have used her as a pretext for seeing the dauphiness; and this thought decided her to tell Madame de Chartres what she had hitherto kept secret.

The next morning she went to her mother to carry out this decision; but Madame de Chartres was a little feverish, and did not care to talk with her. The illness seemed so slight, however, that Madame de Clèves called on the dauphiness after dinner, and found her in her room with two or three ladies with whom she was on intimate terms.

"We were talking about Monsieur de Nemours," said the queen when she saw her, "and were surprised to see how much he is changed since his return from Brussels; before he went, he had an infinite number of mistresses, and it was a positive disadvantage to him, because he used to be kind both to those who were worthy and to those who were not. Since his return, however, he will have nothing to do with any of them. There has never been such a change. His spirits, moreover, seem to be affected, as he is much less cheerful than usual."

Madame de Clèves made no answer; she thought with a sense of shame that she would have taken all that they said about the change in him for a proof of his passion if she had not been undeceived. She was somewhat vexed with the dauphiness for trying to explain and for expressing surprise at something of which she must know the real reason better than any one else. She could not keep from showing her annoyance, and when the other ladies withdrew, she went up to the crown princess and said in a low voice,—

"Is it for my benefit that you have just spoken, and do you want to hide from me that you are the cause of the altered conduct of Monsieur de Nemours?"

"You are unjust," said the crown princess; "you know that I never keep anything from you. It is true that before he went to Brussels, Monsieur de Nemours meant to have me understand that he did not hate me; but since his return he seems to have forgotten all about it, and I confess that I am a little curious about the reason of this change. I shall probably find it out," she went on, "as the Vidame de Chartres, his intimate friend, is in love with a young woman over whom I have some power, and I shall know from her what has made this change."

The dauphiness spoke with an air that carried conviction to Madame de Clèves, who found herself calmer and happier than she had been before. When she went back to her mother, she found her much worse than when she had left her. She was more feverish, and for some days it seemed as if she were going to be really ill. Madame de Clèves was in great distress, and did not leave her mother's room. Monsieur de Clèves spent nearly all his time there too, both to comfort his wife and to have the pleasure of seeing her: his love had not lessened.

Monsieur de Nemours, who had always been one of his friends, had not neglected him since his return from Brussels. During the illness of Madame de Chartres he found it possible to see Madame de Clèves very often, under pretence of calling on her husband or of stopping to take him to walk. He even sought him at hours when he knew he was not in; then he would say that he would wait for him, and used to stay in the ante-chamber of Madame de Chartres, where were assembled many persons of quality. Madame de Clèves would often look in, and although she was in great anxiety, she seemed no less beautiful to Monsieur de Nemours. He showed her how much he sympathized with her distress, and soon convinced her that it was not with the dauphiness that he was in love.

She could not keep from being embarrassed, and yet delighted to see him; but when he was out of her sight and she remembered that this pleasure was the beginning of an unhappy passion, she felt she almost hated him, so much did the idea of guilty love pain her.

Madame de Chartres rapidly grew worse, and soon her life was despaired of; she heard the doctors' opinion of her danger with a courage proportionate to her virtue and piety. After they had left her, she dismissed all who were present, and sent for Madame de Clèves.

"We have to part, my daughter," she said, holding out her hand; "and the peril in which you are and the need you have of me, double my pain in leaving you. You have an affection for Monsieur de Nemours; I do not ask you to confess it, as I am no longer able to make use of your sincerity in order to guide you. It is long since I perceived this affection, but I have been averse to speaking to you about it, lest you should become aware of it yourself. Now you know it only too well. You are on the edge of a precipice: a great effort, a violent struggle, alone can save you. Think of what you owe your husband, think of what you owe yourself, and remember that you are in danger of losing that reputation which you have acquired and which I have so ardently desired for you. Take strength and courage, my daughter: withdraw from the court; compel your husband to take you away. Do not be afraid of making a difficult decision. Terrible as it may appear at first, it will in the end be pleasanter than the consequences of a love-affair. If any other reasons than virtue and duty can persuade you to what I wish, let me say that if anything is capable of destroying the happiness I hope for in another world, it would be seeing you fall like so many women; but if this misfortune must come to you, I welcome death that I may not see it."

Madame de Clèves' tears fell on her mother's hand, which she held clasped in her own, and Madame de Chartres saw that she was moved. "Good-by, my daughter," she said; "let us put an end to a conversation which moves us both too deeply, and remember, if you can, all I have just said to you."

With these words she turned away and bade her daughter call her women, without hearing or saying more. Madame de Clèves left her mother's room in a state that may be imagined, and Madame de Chartres thought of nothing but preparing herself for death. She lingered two days more, but refused again to see her daughter,—the only person she loved.

Madame de Clèves was in sore distress; her husband never left her side, and as soon as Madame de Chartres had died, he took her into the country, to get her away from a place which continually renewed her grief, which was intense. Although her love and gratitude to her mother counted for a great deal, the need she felt of her support against Monsieur de Nemours made the blow even more painful. She lamented being left to herself when she had her emotions so little under control, and when she so needed some one to pity her and give her strength. Her husband's kindness made her wish more than ever to be always true to him. She showed him more affection and kindliness than she had ever done before, and she wanted him always by her side; for it seemed to her that her attachment to him would prove a defence against Monsieur de Nemours.

This prince went to visit Monsieur de Clèves in the country, and did his best to see Madame de Clèves; but she declined to receive him, knowing that she could not fail to find him charming. More-over, she resolutely determined to avoid every occasion of meeting him, so far as she was able.

Monsieur de Clèves repaired[8] to Paris to pay his respects at court, promising his wife to return the next day; but he did not return till the day after.·

"I expected you all day yesterday," Madame de Clèves said to him when he arrived, "and I ought to find fault with you for not returning when you promised. You know that if I could feel a new sorrow in the state I am in, it would be at the death of Madame de Tournon, of which I heard this morning. I should have been distressed by it even if I had not known her. It is always painful when a young and beautiful woman like her dies after an illness of only two days, and much more so when it is one of the persons I liked best in the world, and who seemed as modest as she was worthy."

"I was sorry not to return yesterday," answered Monsieur de Clèves; "but it was so imperatively necessary that I should console an unhappy man that I could not possibly leave him. As for Madame de Tournon, I advise you not to be too profoundly distressed, if you mourn her as an upright woman who deserved your esteem."

"You surprise me," said Madame de Clèves, "as I have often heard you say that there was no woman at court whom you esteemed more highly."

"That is true," he answered; "but women are incomprehensible, and the more I see of them, the happier I feel that I have married you, and I cannot be sufficiently grateful for my good fortune."

"You think better of me than I deserve," exclaimed Madame de Clèves, with a sigh, "and it is much too soon to think me worthy of you. But tell me, please, what has undeceived you about Madame de Tournon."

"I have long been undeceived in regard to her," he replied, "and have long known that she loved the Count of Sancerre, to whom she held out hopes that she would marry him."

"I can scarcely believe," interrupted Madame de Clèves, "that Madame de Tournon, after the extraordinary reluctance to matrimony which she showed after she became a widow, and after her public assertions that she would never marry again, should have given Sancerre any hopes."

"If she had given them only to him," replied Monsieur de Clèves, "there would be little occasion for surprise; but what is astounding is that she also gave them to Estouteville at the same time, and I will tell you the whole story."

Part II

"You know," Monsieur de Clèves continued, "what good friends Sancerre and I are; yet when, about two years ago, he fell in love

---

8. Went.

with Madame de Tournon, he took great pains to conceal it from me, as well as from every one else, and I was far from suspecting it. Madame de Tournon appeared still inconsolable for her husband's death, and was still living in the most absolute retirement. Sancerre's sister was almost the only person she saw, and it was at her house that the count fell in love with her.

"One evening when there was to be a play at the Louvre, and while they were waiting for the king and Madame de Valentinois in order to begin, word was brought that she was ill and that the king would not come. Every one guessed that the duchess's illness was some quarrel with the king. We knew how jealous he had been of the Marshal of Brissac during his stay at court; but the marshal had gone back to Piedmont a few days before, and we could not imagine the cause of this falling-out.

"While I was talking about it with Sancerre, Monsieur d'Anville came into the hall and whispered to me that the king was in a state of distress and anger most piteous to see; that when he and Madame de Valentinois were reconciled a few days before, after their quarrels about the Marshal of Brissac, the king had given her a ring and asked her to wear it. While she was dressing for the play, he had noticed its absence, and had asked her the reason. She seemed surprised to miss it, and asked her women for it; but they, unfortunately, perhaps because they had not been put on their guard, said that it was some four or five days since they had seen it.

" 'That exactly corresponded with the date of the Marshal of Brissac's departure,' Monsieur d'Anville went on; 'and the king is convinced that she gave him the ring when she bade him good-by. This thought has so aroused all his jealousy, which was by no means wholly extinguished, that, contrary to his usual custom, he flew into a rage and reproached her bitterly. He has gone back to his room in great distress, whether because he thinks that Madame de Valentinois has given away his ring, or because he fears that he has displeased her by his wrath, I do not know.'

"As soon as Monsieur d'Anville had finished, I went up to Sancerre to tell him the news, assuring him that it was a secret that had just been told me, and was to go no farther.

"The next morning I called rather early on my sister-in-law, and found Madame de Tournon there. She did not like Madame de Valentinois, and knew very well that my sister-in-law also had no reason for being fond of her. Sancerre had seen her when he left the play, and had told her about the king's quarrel with the duchess; this she had come to repeat to my sister-in-law, either not knowing or not remembering that it was I who had told her lover.

"When I came in, my sister-in-law said to Madame de Tournon that I could be trusted with what she had just told her, and without waiting for permission she repeated to me word for word everything I had told Sancerre the previous evening. You will understand my surprise. I looked at Madame de Tournon, who seemed embarrassed, and her embarrassment aroused my suspicions. I had mentioned the matter to no one but Sancerre, who had left me after the play, without saying where he was going; but I remembered hearing him praise Madame de Tournon very warmly. All these things opened my eyes, and I soon decided that there was a love-affair between them, and that he had seen her after he left me.

"I was so annoyed to find that he kept the matter secret from me that I said a good many things that made it clear to Madame de Tournon that she had been imprudent; as I handed her to her carriage, I assured her that I envied the happiness of the person who had informed her of the falling-out of the king and Madame de Valentinois.

"At once I went to see Sancerre; I reproached him, and said that I knew of his passion for Madame de Tournon, but I did not say how I had found it out. He felt obliged to make a complete confession. I then told him how it was I had discovered his secret, and he told me all about the affair; he said that inasmuch as he was a younger son, and far from having any claims to such an honor, she was yet determined to marry him. No one could be more surprised than I was. I urged Sancerre to hasten his marriage, and told him that he would be justified in fearing anything from a woman who was so full of craft that she could play so false a part before the public. He said in reply that her grief had been sincere, but that it had yielded before her affection for him, and that she could not suddenly make this great change manifest. He brought up many other things in her defence, which showed me clearly how much in love he was; he assured me that he would persuade her to let me know all about the passion he had for her, since it was she who had let out the secret,—and in fact he compelled her to consent, though with much difficulty, and I was from that time fully admitted to their confidence.

"I have never seen a woman so honorable and agreeable toward her lover; yet I was always pained by her affectation of grief. Sancerre was so much in love, and so well satisfied with the way she treated him, that he was almost afraid to urge their marriage, lest she should think that he was moved thereto by interest rather than passion. Still, he often talked to her about it, and she seemed to have decided to marry him; she even began to leave her retirement and to reappear in the world,—she used to come to my sister-in-law's at the time when part of the court used to be there. Sancerre came very seldom; but those who were there every evening and met her often, found her very charming.

"Shortly after she began to come out again into society, Sancerre

imagined that he detected some coolness in her love for him. He
spoke to me about it several times without rousing any anxiety in me
by his complaints; but when at length he told me that instead of
hastening, she seemed to be postponing their marriage, I began to
think that he had good grounds for uneasiness. I said that even if
Madame de Tournon's passion should lessen after lasting for two
years, he ought not to be surprised; that even if it did not lessen, and
though it should not be strong enough to persuade her to marry him,
he ought not to complain; since their marriage would injure her
much in the eyes of the public, not only because he was not a very
good match for her, but because it would affect her reputation: hence
that all he could reasonably desire was that she should not deceive
him and feed him with false hopes. I also said that if she had not the
courage to marry him, or if she should confess that she loved some
one else, he ought not to be angry or complain, but preserve his
esteem and gratitude for her.

" 'I give you the advice,' I said to him, 'which I should take myself;
for I am so touched by sincerity that I believe that if my mistress, or
my wife, were to confess that any one pleased her, I should be distressed without being angered, and should lay aside the character of
lover or husband to advise and sympathize with her.' "

At these words Madame de Clèves blushed, finding a certain likeness to her own condition which surprised her and distressed her for
some time.

"Sancerre spoke to Madame de Tournon," Monsieur de Clèves
went on, "telling her everything I had advised; but she reassured him
with such tact and seemed so pained by his suspicions that she entirely
dispelled them. Nevertheless she postponed their marriage until after
a long journey which he was about to make; but her conduct was so
discreet up to the time of his departure, and she seemed so grieved
at parting with him, that I, as well as he, believed that she truly loved
him. He went away about three months ago. During his absence I
saw Madame de Tournon very seldom; you have taken up all my
time, and I only knew that Sancerre was to return soon.

"The day before yesterday, on my arrival in Paris, I heard that she
was dead. I at once sent to his house to find out if they had heard
from him, and was told that he had arrived the day before,—the very
day of Madame de Tournon's death. I went at once to see him,
knowing very well in what a state I should find him; but his agony
far exceeded what I had imagined. Never have I seen such deep and
tender grief. As soon as he saw me, he embraced me, bursting into
tears. 'I shall never see her again,' he said, 'I shall never see her
again; she is dead! I was not worthy of her; but I shall soon follow
her.'

"After that he was silent; then from time to time he repeated: 'She

is dead, and I shall never see her again!' Thereupon he would again
burst into tears, and seemed out of his head. He told me he had
received but few letters from her while away, but that this did not
surprise him, because he well knew her aversion to running any risk
in writing letters. He had no doubt that she would have married him
on his return; and he looked upon her as the most amiable and
faithful woman who had ever lived; he believed that she loved him
tenderly, and that he had lost her at the moment when he made sure
of winning her forever. These thoughts plunged him into the deepest
distress, by which he was wholly overcome, and I confess that I was
deeply moved.

"Nevertheless, I was obliged to leave him to go to the king, but I
promised to return soon. This I did; but imagine my surprise when
I found that he was in an entirely different mood. He was pacing up
and down his room with a wild face, and he stopped as if he were
beside himself and said: 'Come, come! see the most desperate man
in the world; I am ten thousand times unhappier than I was before,
and what I have just heard of Madame de Tournon is worse than her
death.'

"I thought that his grief had crazed him, for I could imagine nothing more terrible than the death of a loved mistress who returns one's
love. I told him that so long as his grief had been within bounds I
had understood and sympathized with it; but that I should cease to
pity him if he gave way to despair and lost his mind. 'I wish I could
lose it, and my life too,' he exclaimed. 'Madame de Tournon was
unfaithful to me; and I ascertained her infidelity and treachery the
day after I heard of her death, at a time when my soul was filled with
the deepest grief and the tenderest love that were ever felt,—at a time
when my heart was filled with the thought of her as the most perfect
creature that had ever lived, and the most generous to me. I find
that I was mistaken in her, and that she does not deserve my tears;
nevertheless, I have the same grief from her death as if she had been
faithful to me, and I suffer from her infidelity as if she were not dead.
Had I known of her changed feeling before she died, I should have
been wild with wrath and jealousy, and should have been in some
way hardened against the blow of her death; but now I can get no
consolation from it or hate her.'

"You may judge of my surprise at what Sancerre told me; I asked
him how he found this out. He told me that the moment I had left
his room, Estouteville, an intimate friend of his, though he knew
nothing of his love for Madame de Tournon, had come to see him;
that as soon as he had sat down, he burst into tears and said he
begged his pardon for not having told him before what he was about
to say; that he had come to open his heart to him; and that he saw

before him a man utterly crushed by the death of Madame de Tour-non.

" 'That name,' said Sancerre, 'surprised me so that my first impulse was to tell him that I was much more distressed than he; but I was unable to speak a word. He went on and told me that he had been in love with her for six months; that he had always meant to tell me, but she had forbidden it so firmly that he had not dared to disobey her; that almost ever since he fell in love with her she had taken a tender interest in him; that he only visited her secretly; that he had had the pleasure of consoling her for the loss of her husband; and, finally, that he was on the point of marrying her at the time of her death, but that this marriage, which would have been one of love, would have appeared to be one of duty and obedience, because she had won over her father to command this marriage, in order that there should not be any great change in her conduct, which had indicated an unwillingness to contract a second marriage.

" 'While Estouteville was speaking,' Sancerre went on, 'I fully believed him, because what he said seemed likely, and the time he had mentioned as that when he fell in love with Madame de Tour-non coincided with that of her altered treatment of me. But a moment after, I thought him a liar, or at least out of his senses, and I was ready to tell him so. I thought, however, I would first make sure; hence I began to question him and to show that I had my doubts. At last I was so persistent in the search of my unhappiness that he asked if I knew Madame de Tournon's handwriting, and placed on my bed four of her letters and her portrait. My brother happened to come in at that moment. Estouteville's face was so stained with tears that he had to go away in order not to be seen in that state; he told me that he would come back that evening to get the things he left. I sent my brother away, pretending that I was not feeling well, being impatient to read the letters, and still hoping to find something which would convince me that Estouteville was mistaken. But, alas, what did I not find! What tenderness, what protestations, what promises to marry him, what letters! She had never written me any like them. So,' he went on, 'I suffer at the same time grief for her death and for her faithlessness,—two misfortunes which have often been compared, but have never been felt at the same time by one person. I confess, to my shame, that I feel much more keenly her death than her change; I cannot find her guilty enough to deserve to die. If she were still alive, I should have the pleasure of reproaching her, of avenging myself by showing her how great was her injustice. But I shall never see her again.' He repeated, 'I shall never see her again,—that is the bitterest blow of all; I would gladly give up my life for hers. What a wish! If she were to return, she would live for Estouteville. How happy I was yesterday!' he exclaimed, 'how happy I was then! I was the most sorely distressed man in the world; but my distress was in the order of nature, and I drew some comfort from the thought that I could never be consoled. To-day all my feelings are false ones; I pay to the pretended love she felt for me the same tribute that I thought due to a real affection. I can neither hate nor love her memory; I am incapable of consolation or of grief. At least,' he said, turning suddenly toward me, 'let me, I beg of you, never see Estouteville again; his very name fills me with horror. I know very well that I have no rason to blame him; it is my own fault for concealing from him my love for Madame de Tournon: if he had known of it, he would perhaps have never cared for her, and she would not have been unfaithful to me. He came to see me to confide his grief; I really pity him. Yes, and with good reason,' he exclaimed; 'he loved Madame de Tournon and was loved by her. He will never see her again; yet I feel that I cannot keep from hating him. Once more, I beg of you never to let me see him again.'

"Thereupon Sancerre burst again into tears, mourning Madame de Tournon, saying to her the tenderest things imaginable; thence he changed to hatred, complaints, reproaches, and denunciations of her conduct. When I saw him in this desperate state I knew that I should need some aid in calming him, so I sent for his brother, whom I had just left with the king. I went out to speak to him in the hall before he came in, and I told him what a state Sancerre was in. We gave orders that he was not to see Estouteville, and spent a good part of the night trying to persuade him to listen to reason. This morning I found him in still deeper distress; his brother is staying with him, and I have returned to you."

"No one could be more surprised than I am," said Madame de Clèves, "for I thought Madame de Tournon incapable of both love and deception."

"Address and dissimulation,"[9] answered Monsieur de Clèves, "could not go further. Notice that when Sancerre thought she had changed toward him, she really had, and had begun to love Estouteville. She told her new lover that he consoled her for her husband's death, and that it was he who was the cause of her returning to society; while it seemed to Sancerre that it was because we had decided that she should no longer appear to be in such deep affliction. She was able to persuade Estouteville to conceal their relations, and to seem obliged to marry him by her father's orders, as if it were the result of her care for her reputation,—and this in order to abandon Sancerre without leaving him ground for complaint. I must go back," continued Monsieur de Clèves, "to see this unhappy man, and I think you had

9. Skill and tact.

better return to Paris. It is time for you to see company and to begin
to receive the number of visits that await you."

Madame de Clèves gave her consent, and they returned the next
day. She found herself more tranquil about Monsieur de Nemours
than she had been; Madame de Chartres' dying words and her deep
grief had for a time dulled her feelings, and she thought they had
entirely changed.

The evening of Madame de Clèves' arrival the dauphiness came
to see her, and after expressing her sympathy with her affliction, said
that in order to drive away her sad thoughts she would tell her everything that had taken place at court during her absence, and narrated
many incidents. "But what I most want to tell you," she added, "is
that it is certain that Monsieur de Nemours is passionately in love,
and that his most intimate friends are not only not in his confidence,
but they can't even guess whom it is whom he loves. Yet this love is
strong enough to make him neglect, or rather give up, the hope of a
crown."

The dauphiness then told Madame de Clèves the whole plan about
England. "I heard what I have just told you," she went on, "from
Monsieur d'Anville; and he said to me this morning that the king
sent last evening for Monsieur de Nemours, after reading some letters from Lignerolles, who is anxious to return, and had written to
the king that he was unable to explain to the Queen of England
Monsieur de Nemours' delay; that she is beginning to be offended;
and that although she has given no positive answer, she had said
enough to warrant him in starting. The king read this letter to Monsieur de Nemours, who instead of talking seriously, as he had done
in the beginning, only laughed and joked about Lignerolles' hopes.
He said that the whole of Europe would blame his imprudence if he
were to presume to go to England as a claimant for the queen's hand
without being assured of success. 'It seems to me too,' he went on,
'that I should not choose the present time for my journey, when the
King of Spain is doing his best to marry her.[1] In a love-affair he
would not be a very formidable rival; but I think that in a question
of marrying, your Majesty would not advise me to try my chances
against him.' 'I do advise you so in the present circumstances,'
answered the king. 'But you have no occasion to fear him. I know
that he has other thoughts, and even if he had not, Queen Mary was
too unhappy under the Spanish yoke for one to believe that her sister
wishes to assume it, or would let herself be dazzled by the splendor
of so many united crowns.' 'If she does not let herself be dazzled by
them,' went on Monsieur de Nemours, 'probably she will wish to
marry for love; she has loved Lord Courtenay for several years. Queen

---

1. At the death of his wife, Mary Tudor, in 1558, Philip II of Spain (1527–1598) considered
marrying her sister, Elizabeth of England.

Mary also loved him, and she would have married him, with the consent of the whole of England, had she not known that the youth and beauty of her sister Elizabeth attracted him more than the desire of reigning. Your Majesty knows that her violent jealousy caused her to throw them both into prison, then to exile Lord Courtenay, and finally decided her to marry the King of Spain. I believe that Elizabeth, now that she is on the throne, will soon recall this lord and thus choose a man she has loved, who is very attractive, and who has suffered so much for her, rather than another whom she has never seen.' 'I should agree with you,' replied the king, 'if Courtenay were still living; but some days ago I heard that he had died at Padua, where he was living in banishment. I see very well,' he added, as he left Monsieur de Nemours, 'that it will be necessary to celebrate your marriage as we should celebrate the dauphin's, by sending ambassadors to marry the Queen of England by procuration.'

"Monsieur d'Anville and the Vidame, who were present while the king was talking with Monsieur de Nemours, are convinced that it is this great passion which has dissuaded him from this plan. The Vidame, who is more intimate than any one with him, said to Madame de Martigues that the prince is changed beyond recognition; and what amazes him still more is that he never finds him engaged or absent, so that he supposes he never meets the woman he loves; and what is so surprising, is to see Monsieur de Nemours in love with a woman who does not return his passion."

All this story that the dauphiness told her was as poison to Madame de Clèves. It was impossible for her not to feel sure that she was the woman whose name was unknown; and she was overwhelmed with gratitude and tenderness when she learned from one who had the best means of knowing that this prince, who had already aroused her interest, hid his passion from every one, and for love of her gave up his chances of a crown. It is impossible to describe her agitation. If the dauphiness had observed her with any care, she would at once have seen that the story she had just repeated was by no means without interest to her; but having no suspicion of the truth, she went on without noticing her. "Monsieur d'Anville," she added, "who, as I said, told me all this, thinks that I know more about it than he does, and he has so high an opinion of my charms that he is convinced that I am the only person who can make such a great change in Monsieur de Nemours."

Madame de Clèves was agitated by this last remark of the crown princess, though not in the same way as a few moments before. "I should readily agree with Monsieur d'Anville," she replied, "and it is certainly probable, Madame, that no one but a princess like you could make him indifferent to the Queen of England."

"I should at once acknowledge it," said the dauphiness, "if I knew

that was the case, and I should know if it were true. Love-affairs of
that sort do not escape the notice of those who inspire them; they are
the first to perceive them. Monsieur de Nemours has never paid me
any but the most insignificant attentions; but there is nevertheless so
great a difference between his way with me and his present conduct
that I can assure you I am not the cause of the indifference he shows
for the crown of England.

"I forget everything while I am with you," she went on, "and it
had slipped my mind that I must go to see Madame Elisabeth.[2] You
know that peace is nearly concluded, but what you don't know is
that the King of Spain would not agree to a single article except on
the condition that he, instead of the prince Don Carlos, his son,
should marry this princess. The king had great difficulty in agreeing
to this; at last he yielded, and has gone to tell Madame. I fancy she
will be inconsolable; it certainly cannot be pleasant to marry a man
of the age and temper of the King of Spain, especially for her, who,
in all the pride of youth and beauty, expected to marry a young
prince for whom she has a fancy, though she has never seen him. I
don't know whether the king will find her as docile as he wishes, and
he has asked me to go to see her; for he knows that she is fond of me,
and imagines that I have some influence over her. I shall then make
a very different visit, for I must go to congratulate Madame, the
king's sister. Everything is arranged for her marriage with Monsieur
de Savoie, and he will be here shortly. Never was a person of the age
of that princess so glad to marry. The court will be finer and larger
than it has ever been, and in spite of your afflictions you must come
and help us show the foreigners that we have some famous beauties
here."

Then the dauphiness left Madame de Clèves, and the next day
Madame Elisabeth's marriage was known to every one. A few days
later the king and the queens called on Madame de Clèves. Monsieur de Nemours, who had awaited her return with extreme impatience, and was very desirous of speaking to her alone, put off his
call until every one should have left and it was unlikely that others
would come in. His plan was successful, and he arrived just as the
latest visitors were taking their departure.

The princess was still lying down;[3] it was warm, and the sight of
Monsieur de Nemours gave her face an additional color, which did
not lessen her beauty. He sat down opposite her with the timidity
and shyness that real passion gives. It was some time before he spoke;
Madame de Clèves was equally confused, so that they kept a long
silence. At last Monsieur de Nemours took courage, and expressed

---

2. Elizabeth of France (1545–1568), daughter of Henri II. Philip indeed married her; despite the
fact that she was "inconsolable" about the idea, she was in fact happy with him.   3. It was
common at this period for women to receive visitors in their bedrooms.

his sympathy with her grief. Madame de Clèves, who was glad to
keep the conversation on this safe topic, spoke for some time about
the loss she had experienced; and finally she said that when time
should have dimmed the intensity of her grief, it would still leave a
deep and lasting impression, and that her whole nature had been
changed by it.

"Great afflictions and violent passions," replied Monsieur de
Nemours, "do greatly alter people; as for me, I am entirely changed
since I returned from Flanders. Many persons have noticed this
alteration, and even the dauphiness spoke of it last evening."

"It is true," said Madame de Clèves, "that she has noticed it, and
I think I have heard her say something about it."

"I am not sorry, Madame," Monsieur de Nemours continued,
"that she perceived it, but I should prefer that she should not be the
only one to notice it. There are persons to whom one does not dare
to give any other marks of the love one feels for them than those
which do not affect them in any but an indirect way; and since one
does not dare to show one's love, one would at least desire that they
should see that one wishes not to be loved by any one else. One
would like to have them know that there is no beauty, of whatever
rank, whom one would not regard with indifference, and that there
is no crown which one would wish to buy at the price of never seeing
them. Women generally judge the love one has for them," he went
on, "by the pains one takes to please them and to pursue them; but
that is an easy matter, provided they are charming. What is difficult
is not to yield to the pleasure of pursuing them—it is to avoid them,
from fear of showing to the public or to them one's feelings; and the
most distinctive mark of a true attachment is to become entirely different from what one was, to be indifferent to ambition or pleasure
after having devoted one's whole life to one or the other."

Madame de Clèves readily understood the reference to her in these
words. It seemed to her that she ought to answer them and express
her disapproval; it also seemed to her that she ought not to listen to
them or show that she took his remarks to herself: she believed that
she ought to speak, and also that she ought to say nothing. The
remarks of Monsieur de Nemours pleased and offended her equally;
she saw in them a confirmation of what the crown princess had made
her think,—she found them full of gallantry and respect, but also
bold and only too clear. Her interest in the prince caused an agitation which she could not control. The vaguest words of a man one
likes produce more emotion than the open declarations of a man
one does not like. Hence she sat without saying a word, and Monsieur de Nemours noticed her silence, which would have seemed to
him a happy omen, if the arrival of Monsieur de Clèves had not put
an end to the talk and to his visit.

The Prince de Clèves had come to tell his wife the latest news about Sancerre; but she had no great curiosity about the rest of that affair. She was so interested in what had just happened that she could hardly hide her inattention. When she was able to think it all over, she perceived that she had been mistaken when she fancied that she had become indifferent to Monsieur de Nemours. His words had made all the impression he could desire, and had thoroughly convinced her of his passion. His actions harmonized too well with his words for her to have any further doubts on the subject. She did not any longer indulge in the hope of not loving him; she merely determined to give him no further sign of it. This was a difficult undertaking,—how difficult she knew already. She was aware that her only chance of success lay in avoiding the prince, and her mourning enabled her to live in retirement; she made it a pretext for not going to places where she might meet him. She was in great dejection; her mother's death appeared to be the cause, and she sought no other.

Monsieur de Nemours was in despair at not seeing her oftener; and knowing that he should not meet her at any assembly or entertainment at which the whole court was present, he could not make up his mind to go to them; he pretended a great interest in hunting, and made up hunting-parties on the days of the queens' assemblies. For a long time a slight indisposition served as a pretext for staying at home, and thus escaping going to places where he knew that Madame de Clèves would not be.

Monsieur de Clèves was ailing at nearly the same time, and Madame de Clèves never left his room during his illness; but when he was better and began to see company, and among others Monsieur de Nemours, who, under the pretext of being still weak, used to spend a good part of every day with him, she determined not to stay there. Nevertheless, she could not make up her mind to leave during his first visits; it was so long since she had seen him that she was anxious to meet him again. He too managed to make her listen to him, by what seemed like general talk; though she understood, from its reference to what he had said in his previous visit to her, that he went hunting to get an opportunity for meditation, and that he stayed away from the assemblies because she was not there.

At last Madame de Clèves put into execution her decision to leave her husband's room when the duke should be there, though she found it a difficult task: Monsieur de Nemours observed that she avoided him, and was much pained.

Monsieur de Clèves did not at first notice his wife's conduct; but at last he saw that she was unwilling to stay in his room when company was present. He spoke to her about it, and she replied that she did not think it quite proper that she should meet every evening all the young men of the court. She begged him to let her lead a more retired life than she had done before, because the presence of her mother, who was renowned for her virtue, had authorized many things impossible for a woman of her age.

Monsieur de Clèves, who was generally kind and pleasant to his wife, was not so on this occasion; he told her he was averse to any change in her conduct. She was tempted to tell him that there was a report that Monsieur de Nemours was in love with her; but she did not feel able to mention his name. She was also ashamed to assign a false reason, and to hide the truth from a man who had so good an opinion of her.

A few days later, the king happened to be with the queen when she was receiving, and the company was talking about horoscopes and predictions. Opinions were divided about the credence that ought to be given to them. The queen was inclined to believe in them; she maintained that after so many predictions had come true, it was impossible to doubt the exactness of this science. Others again held that the small number of lucky hits out of the numerous predictions that were made, proved that they were merely the result of chance.

"In former times," said the king, "I was very curious about the future; but I was told so much that was false or improbable that I became convinced that we can know nothing certain. A few years ago a famous astrologer came here. Every one went to see him, I as well as the rest, but without saying who I was; and I carried with me Monsieur de Guise and D'Escars, sending them into the room in front of me. Nevertheless the astrologer addressed me first, as if he thought I was their master; perhaps he knew me, although he said something to me which seemed to show that he did not know who I was. He prophesied that I should be killed in a duel; then he told Monsieur de Guise that he would be killed from behind, and D'Escars that he would have his skull broken by a kick from a horse. Monsieur de Guise was almost angry at hearing this,—as if he were accused of running away; D'Escars was no more pleased at learning that he was going to perish by such an unfortunate accident,—so that we all left the astrologer in extreme discontent. I have no idea what will happen to Monsieur de Guise or to D'Escars, but it is very unlikely that I shall be killed in a duel. The King of Spain and I have just made peace; and even if we had not, I doubt if we should resort to a personal combat, and it seems unlikely that I should challenge him, as my father challenged Charles V."

After the king had mentioned the unhappy end which had been foretold him, those who had supported astrology gave up and agreed that it was unworthy of belief. "For my part," said Monsieur de Nemours, "I am the last man in the world to place any confidence in it"; and turning to Madame de Clèves, near whom he was, he said in a low voice: "I was told that I should be made happy by the kindness of the woman for whom I should have the most violent and the most respectful passion. You may judge, Madame, whether I ought to believe in predictions."

The dauphiness, who fancied, from what Monsieur de Nemours had said aloud, that he was mentioning some absurd prophecy that had been made about him, asked him what he was saying to Madame de Clèves. He would have been embarrassed by this question if he had had less presence of mind; but he answered without hesitation: "I was saying, Madame, that it had been predicted about me that I should rise to a lofty position to which I should not even dare to aspire."

"If that is the only prediction that has been made about you," replied the dauphiness, smiling, and thinking of the English scheme, "I do not advise you to denounce astrology; you might find good reasons for supporting it."

Madame de Clèves understood what the crown princess referred to; but she also understood that the happiness of which Monsieur de Nemours spoke, was not that of being king of England.

As it was some time since her mother's death, Madame de Clèves had to appear again in society and to resume her visits at court. She met Monsieur de Nemours at the dauphiness's and at her own house, whither he often came with young nobles of his own age, in order not to be talked about; but she never saw him without an agitation which he readily perceived.

In spite of the care she took to escape his glances and to talk less with him than with others, certain things inadvertently escaped her which convinced this prince that she was not indifferent to him. A less observant man than he would not, perhaps, have noticed them; but so many women had been in love with him that it was hard for him not to know when he was loved. He perceived that the Chevalier de Guise was his rival, and that prince knew that Monsieur de Nemours was his. He was the only man at court who would have discovered this truth; his interest had rendered him more clear-sighted than the others. The knowledge they had of each other's feelings so embittered their relations that although there was no open breach, they were opposed in everything. In running at the ring[4] and in all the amusements in which the king took part they were always on different sides, and their rivalry was too intense to be hidden.

The English scheme often recurred to Madame de Clèves, and she felt that Monsieur de Nemours would not be able to withstand the king's advice and Lignerolles' urging. She noticed with pain that this last had not yet returned, and she awaited him with impatience. If she had followed his movements, she would have learned the con-

---

4. In a court game, men mounted on horseback competed to carry away a suspended metal ring on the point of a lance.

dition of that matter; but the same feeling that inspired her curiosity compelled her to conceal it, and she contented herself with making inquiries about the beauty, intelligence, and character of Queen Elizabeth. A portrait of her was carried to the palace, and she found Elizabeth more beautiful than was pleasant to her, and she could not refrain from saying that it must flatter her.

"I don't think so," replied the dauphiness, who was present. "Elizabeth has a great reputation as a beauty and as the possessor of a mind far above the common, and I know that all my life she has been held up to me as an example. She ought to be attractive if she is like Anne Boleyn, her mother. Never was there a more amiable woman or one more charming both in appearance and disposition. I have been told that her face was exceptionally vivacious, and that she in no way resembled most English beauties."

"It seems to me," said Madame de Clèves, "that I have heard that she was born in France."

"Those who think so," replied the crown princess, "are in error, and I will tell you her history in a few words. She was born of a good English family. Henry VIII had been in love with her sister and her mother, and it had even been suspected that she was his daughter. She came here with the sister of Henry VII, who married Louis XII. This young and gallant princess found it very hard to leave the court of France after her husband's death; but Anne Boleyn, who shared her mistress's feelings, decided to stay. The late king was in love with her, and she remained as maid of honor to Queen Claude. This queen died, and Madame Marguerite, the king's sister, the Duchess of Alençon, since then Queen of Navarre, whose stories you have seen, added Anne to her suite; it was from her that this queen received her inclination toward the new religion. Then Anne returned to England, where she delighted every one. She had French manners, which please all nations; she sang well, and danced charmingly. She was made a lady in waiting to Queen Catherine of Aragon, and King Henry VIII fell desperately in love with her.

"Cardinal Wolsey, his favorite and prime minister, desired to be made pope; and being dissatisfied with the emperor for not supporting his claims, he resolved to avenge himself by allying the king his master with France. He suggested to Henry VIII that his marriage with the emperor's aunt was null and void, and proposed to him to marry the Duchess of Alençon, whose husband had just died. Anne Boleyn, being an ambitious woman, looked on this divorce as a possible step to the throne. She began to instile into the King of England the principles of Lutheranism, and persuaded the late king to urge at Rome Henry's divorce, in the hope of his marriage with Madame d'Alençon. Cardinal Wolsey contrived to be sent to France on other pretexts to arrange this affair; but his master would not consent to have the proposition made, and sent orders to Calais that this marriage was not to be mentioned.

"On his return from France, Cardinal Wolsey was received with honors equal to those paid to the king himself; never did a favorite display such haughtiness and vanity. He arranged an interview between the two kings, which took place at Boulogne. Francis I offered his hand to Henry VIII, who was unwilling to take it; they treated each other with great splendor, each giving the other clothes like those he himself wore. I remember having heard that those the late king sent to the King of England were of crimson satin trimmed with pearls and diamonds arranged in triangles, the cloak of white velvet embroidered with gold. After spending a few days at Boulogne, they went to Calais. Anne Boleyn was quartered in the house with Henry VIII in the queen's suite, and Francis I made her the same presents and paid her the same honors as if she had been a queen herself. At last, after being in love with her for nine years, Henry married her, without waiting for the annulment of his first marriage, which he had long been asking of Rome. The pope at once excommunicated him; this so enraged Henry that he declared himself the head of the Church, and carried all England into the unhappy change of religion in which you now see it.

"Anne Boleyn did not long enjoy her grandeur, for one day, when she thought her position assured by the death of Catherine of Aragon, she happened to be present with all the court when the Viscount Rochford, her brother, was running at the ring. The king was suddenly overwhelmed by such an access of jealousy that he instantly left the spot, hastened to London, and gave orders for the arrest of the queen, the Viscount Rochford, and many others whom he believed to be the queen's lovers or confidants. Although this jealousy seemed the work of a moment, it had for some time been instigated by the Viscountess Rochford, who could not endure her husband's intimacy with the queen, and represented it to the king as criminal intimacy; consequently he, being already in love with Jane Seymour, thought only of getting rid of Anne Boleyn. In less than three weeks he succeeded in having the queen and her brother brought to trial and beheaded, and he married Jane Seymour. He had afterward several wives, whom he either divorced or put to death, among others Catherine Howard, who had been the confidante of the Viscountess of Rochford, and was beheaded with her. Hence she was punished for the crimes with which she had blackened Anne Boleyn, and Henry VIII, having reached a monstrous size, died."

All the ladies present thanked the dauphiness for teaching them so much about the English court, and among others Madame de Clèves, who could not refrain from asking more questions about Queen Elizabeth.

The dauphiness had miniatures painted of all the beauties of the court to send to the queen her mother. The day when that of Madame de Clèves was receiving the last touches the crown princess came to spend the afternoon with her. Monsieur de Nemours was also there, for he neglected no opportunity of seeing Madame de Clèves, although he never seemed to court her society. She was so beautiful that day that he would surely have fallen in love with her then if he had not done so already; but he did not dare to sit with his eyes fixed on her, while she feared lest he should show too plainly the pleasure he found in looking at her.

The crown princess asked Monsieur de Clèves for a miniature he had of his wife, to compare it with the one that was painting. All who were there expressed their opinion of both, and Madame de Clèves asked the painter to make a little correction in the hair of the old one. The artist took the miniature out of its case, and after working on it, set it down on the table.

For a long time Monsieur de Nemours had been desiring to have a portrait of Madame de Clèves. When he saw this one, though it belonged to her husband, whom he tenderly loved, he could not resist the temptation to steal it; he thought that among the many persons present he should not be suspected.

The dauphiness was seated on the bed, speaking low to Madame de Clèves, who was standing in front of her. One of the curtains was only partly closed, and Madame de Clèves was able to see Monsieur de Nemours, whose back was against the table at the foot of the bed, without turning his head pick up something from this table. She at once guessed that it was her portrait, and she was so embarrassed that the crown princess noticed she was not listening to her, and asked her what she was looking at. At these words Monsieur de Nemours turned round and met Madame de Clèves' eyes fastened on him; he felt sure that she must have seen what he had just done.

Madame de Clèves was greatly embarrassed. Her reason bade her ask for her portrait; but if she asked for it openly, she would announce to every one the prince's feelings for her, and by asking for it privately, she would give him an opportunity to speak to her of his love, so that at last she judged it better to let him keep it,—and she was very glad to be able to grant him a favor without his knowing that she did it of her own choice. Monsieur de Nemours, who observed her embarrassment and guessed its cause, came up to her and said in a low voice: "If you saw what I ventured to do, be good enough, Madame, to let me suppose that you know nothing about it; I do not dare to ask anything more." Then he went away, without waiting for an answer.

The dauphiness, accompanied by all her ladies, went out for a walk. Monsieur de Nemours locked himself up in his own room, being unable to contain his joy at having in his possession a portrait of Madame de Clèves. He felt all the happiness that love can give. He loved the most charming woman of the court, and felt that in spite of herself she loved him; he saw in everything she did the agitation and embarrassment which love evokes in the innocence of early youth.

That evening every one looked carefully for the portrait; when they found the case, no one supposed that it had been stolen, but that it had been dropped somewhere. Monsieur de Clèves was distressed at its loss, and after hunting for it in vain, told his wife, but evidently in jest, that she doubtless had some mysterious lover to whom she had given the portrait, or who had stolen it, for no one but a lover would care for the portrait without the case.

Although these words were not said seriously, they made a deep impression on the mind of Madame de Clèves and filled her with remorse. She thought of the violence of her love for Monsieur de Nemours, and perceived that she could not control either her words or her face. She reflected that Lignerolles had returned, and that the English scheme had no terrors for her; that she had no longer grounds for suspecting the dauphiness; and finally, that, as she was without further defence, her only safety was in flight. Since, however, she knew she could not go away, she saw that she was in a most perilous condition, and ready to fall into what she judged to be the greatest possible misfortune,—namely, betraying to Monsieur de Nemours the interest she felt in him. She recalled everything her mother had said to her on her death-bed, and her advice to try everything rather than enter upon a love-affair. She remembered what her husband had said about her sincerity when he was speaking about Madame de Tournon, and it seemed to her that it was her duty to confess her passion for Monsieur de Nemours. She pondered over this for a long time; then she was astonished that the thought occurred to her: she deemed it madness, and fell back into the agony of indecision.

Part III

When peace was signed,[5] Madame Elisabeth, though with great repugnance, determined to obey her father the king. The Duke of Alva had been deputed to marry her in the name of the Catholic king, and he was expected to arrive shortly. The Duke of Savoy was also expected; he was to marry Madame the king's sister, and the two weddings were to take place at the same time. The king thought of nothing but making these events illustrious by entertainments at which

5. The peace treaty of Câteau-Cambrésis (April, 1559).

he could display all the brilliancy and splendor of his court. It was
suggested that plays and ballets should be sumptuously set upon the
stage; but the king thought that too meagre a form of entertainment,
and desired something more magnificent. He determined to have a
tournament at which the foreigners might enter, and to admit the
populace as spectators. All the princes and young noblemen gladly
furthered the king's plan, and especially the Duke of Ferrara, Monsieur de Guise, and Monsieur de Nemours, who surpassed all others
in exercises of this sort. The king chose them to be, with himself,
the four champions of the tournament.

It was announced throughout the whole kingdom that a tournament would be opened in the city of Paris on the fifteenth day of
June by His Very Christian Majesty and by the Prince Alphonso of
Este Duke of Ferrara, Francis of Lorraine Duke of Guise, and James
of Savoy Duke of Nemours, who were ready to meet all comers. The
first combat was to be on horseback, with four antagonists, with four
assaults with the lance, and one for the ladies; the second combat
with swords, either singly or in couples, as should be determined;
the third combat on foot, three assaults with the pike, and six with
the sword. The champions were to supply the lances, swords, and
pikes, from which the assailants might choose their weapons. Any
one striking a horse in the attack was to be put out of the ranks.
There would be four masters of the camp who should have command, and those of the assailants who should be most successful
would receive a prize, of a value to be determined by the judges. All
the assailants, French or foreign, were to be obliged to come and
touch one or more of the shields hanging by the steps at the end of
the lists; there they would find an officer to receive and enroll them
according to their rank and the shields they had touched. The assailants were to have a gentleman bring their shields with their arms, to
be hung by the steps three days before the beginning of the tournament, otherwise they would not be received without the permission
of the champions.

A great field was made ready near the Bastille, extending from the
castle of Tournelles, across the Rue St. Antoine, to the royal mews.
On each side scaffolding was raised, with rows of seats and covered
boxes and galleries, fine to look upon, and capable of holding a vast
number of spectators. All the princes and lords were thinking of nothing
but their preparations to make a magnificent appearance, and were
busily occupied in working some device into their initials or mottoes
that should flatter the woman they loved.

A few days before the Duke of Alva's arrival the king went to play
tennis with Monsieur de Nemours, the Chevalier de Guise, and the
Vidame of Chartres. The queens went with their suites, and Madame de Clèves among the others, to watch the game. After it was

over, and they were leaving the court, Châtelart went up to the dauphiness and told her that he had just found a love-letter that had fallen from Monsieur de Nemours' pocket. The crown princess, who was always curious about everything that concerned that prince, told Châtelart to give it to her; she took it, and followed the queen her mother-in-law, who was going with the king to see the preparations for the tournament. After they had been there some time the king sent for some horses which he had recently bought. Though they had not been broken, he wanted to mount them, and he also had them saddled for the gentlemen with him. The king and Monsieur de Nemours got on the most fiery ones, and they tried to spring at one another. Monsieur de Nemours, fearful of injuring the king, backed his horse suddenly against a post with such violence that he was dismounted. The attendants ran up to him and thought he was seriously injured; Madame de Clèves thought him more hurt than did the others. Her interest in him inspired an agitation which she did not think of concealing; she went up to him with the queens, and her color was so changed that a man less interested than the Chevalier de Guise would have noticed it. He remarked it at once, and gave much more attention to the condition of Madame de Clèves than to that of Monsieur de Nemours. This prince was so stunned by the fall that his head had to be supported by those about him. When he came to himself, the first person he saw was Madame de Clèves; he read on her face all the pity she felt, and his expression showed that he was grateful. He then thanked the queens for their kindness, and apologized for appearing before them in such a state. The king ordered him to go home and lie down.

After Madame had recovered from her fright she began to recall the way she had betrayed it. The Chevalier de Guise did not leave her long to enjoy the hope that no one had observed it. As he gave her his hand to lead her from the field, he said: "I am more to be pitied, Madame, than Monsieur de Nemours. Pardon me if I abandon the profound reserve which I have always shown in regard to you, and if I betray the keen grief I feel at what I have just seen; it is the first time that I have been bold enough to speak to you, and it will be the last. Death, or at any rate an eternal separation, will remove me from a place where I cannot live, now that I have lost the sad consolation of believing that all those who dare to look upon you are as unhappy as I."

Madame de Clèves answered with a few disjointed words, as if she did not understand what the Chevalier de Guise meant. At any other time she would have been offended at his speaking of his feelings for her; but at that moment she thought only of her pain at perceiving that he had detected her own for Monsieur de Nemours. The Chevalier de Guise was so overwhelmed and pained by this discovery that

he at once resolved never to think of winning Madame de Clèves'
love; but the abandonment of a design which had seemed so difficult
and glorious required one of equal moment to take its place, hence
he thought of going to take Rhodes,[6]—a plan he had already meditated. When he died, in the flower of his youth, just when he had
acquired a reputation as one of the greatest princes of his century,
his only regret was that he had not been able to carry out that noble
project, which seemed on the point of accomplishment.

Madame de Clèves at once went to the queen, with her mind
intent on what had just happened. Monsieur de Nemours came there
soon afterward, in magnificent attire, as if he had forgotten what had
just happened. He appeared even gayer than usual, and his delight
at what he thought he had seen added to his content. Every one was
surprised to see him, and asked him how he felt, except Madame de
Clèves, who remained by the fire-place, as if she did not see him.
The king came out of his room, and observing him there, called him
to ask about his mishap. As Monsieur de Nemours passed by Madame de Clèves, he said in a low voice: "I have received to-day, Madame, tokens of your pity, but not those I most deserve." Madame de
Clèves had suspected that the prince had noticed her emotion at his
accident, and his words showed her that she was not mistaken. She
was deeply pained to see that she could not control her emotions,
and had even made them manifest to the Chevalier de Guise. It
distressed her, too, to perceive that Monsieur de Nemours had read
them; but this distress was tempered by a certain pleasure.

The dauphiness, who was impatient to know what was in the letter
that Châtelart had given her, went up to Madame de Clèves. "Read
this letter," she said; "it is addressed to Monsieur de Nemours, and
apparently is from that mistress for whom he has left all the others.
If you cannot read it now, keep it; come to me this evening and give
it back to me, and tell me whether you know the handwriting." With
these words the crown princess turned away from Madame de Clèves,
leaving her so astonished and agitated that she could scarcely move.
Her emotion and impatience were so great that she could not stay
longer with the queen, and she went home, though it was much
earlier than her usual hour of leaving. Her hands, in which she held
the letter, trembled; her thoughts were all confused, and she felt an
unendurable pain such as she had never known. As soon as she was
safe in her room she opened the letter, and read as follows:—

"I love you too much to let you think that the change you see in
me is the result of my fickleness; I want you to know that the real

---

6. The Turks had recaptured the island of Rhodes from the Christians in 1523. François de
Lorraine, Chevalier de Guise, in fact later led an expedition there. He was killed at the battle of
Dreux in the religious wars against the Huguenots in 1563, at the age of 29.

cause is your infidelity. You are surprised that I say your 'infidelity';
you have concealed it so craftily, and I have taken such pains to hide
from you my knowledge of it, that you are naturally astonished that
I should have detected it. I am myself surprised that I have been able
to keep it from you. Never was there any grief like mine; I imagined
that you felt for me a violent passion. I did not conceal what I felt
for you, and at the time when I let you see it, I learned that you were
deceiving me, that you loved another, and, according to all appearances, were sacrificing me to a new mistress. I knew it the day of the
running at the ring, and that is why I was not there. I pretended to
be ill, in order to conceal my emotion; but I really became so, for
my body could not stand the intense agitation. When I began to get
better, I pretended to be still suffering, in order to have an excuse for
not seeing or writing to you; I wanted time to decide how I should
act toward you. Twenty times at least I formed and changed my
decision; but at last I judged you unworthy to see my grief, and I
determined to hide it from you. I wished to wound your pride by
letting you see my love for you fade away. I thought thus to diminish
the price of the sacrifice you made of it; I did not wish you to have
the pleasure of showing how much I loved you in order to appear
more amiable. I resolved to write to you indifferent, dull letters, to
suggest to the woman to whom you gave them that you were loved
less. I did not wish her to have the pleasure of learning that I knew
of her triumph over me, or to add to her triumph by my despair and
reproaches. I thought I could not punish you sufficiently by breaking
with you, and that I should inflict but a slight pain if I ceased to love
you when you had ceased to love me. I thought you must love me,
if you were to know the pang of not being loved, which tormented
me so sorely. I thought that if anything could rekindle the feelings
you had had for me, it was by showing that my own were changed,
but to show this by pretending to hide it from you, as if I had not
strength to tell you. I decided on this; but how hard it was to do so,
and when I saw you, how almost impossible to carry it out! Hundreds
of times I was ready to spoil all with my reproaches and tears. The
state of my health helped me to conceal my emotion and distress.
Afterward I was borne up by the pleasure of dissimulating to you as
you dissimulated to me; nevertheless I did myself such violence to
tell you and to write to you that I loved you, that you saw sooner
than I had intended that I had not meant to let you see that my
feelings were altered. You were wounded, and complained to me. I
tried to reassure you, but in such an artificial way that you were more
convinced than ever that I did not love you. At last I succeeded in
what I had meant to do. The capriciousness of your heart made you
turn again toward me when you saw me leaving you. I have tasted
all the joy of vengeance; it has seemed to me that you loved me better

than ever, and I have shown you that I did not love you. I have had reason to believe that you had entirely abandoned her for whom you had left me. I have also had grounds for supposing that you never spoke to her of me. But your return and your desertion have not been able to make good your fickleness; your heart has been divided between me and another; you have deceived me: that is enough to deprive me of the pleasure of being loved by you as I thought I deserved, and to fix me in the resolution that I had formed never to see you again, which so surprises you."

Madame de Clèves read and re-read this letter several times without understanding it; all that she made out was that Monsieur de Nemours did not love her as she had thought, and that he loved other women, whom he deceived as he did her. This was a grievous blow to a woman of her character, who was deeply in love, and had just shown this to a man whom she deemed unworthy, in sight of another whom she maltreated for love of his rival. Never was sorrow more bitter! It seemed to her that what had happened that day gave it a special sting, and that if Monsieur de Nemours had not had reason to suppose that she loved him, she would not care whether he had loved another woman. But she deceived herself; the pang she found so unendurable was that of jealousy, with all its hideous accompaniments. This letter showed her that Monsieur de Nemours had had a love affair for some time. She thought that it attested the writer's cleverness and worth, and she seemed a woman who deserved to be loved. She appeared to have more courage than herself, and she envied her the strength of character she showed in concealing her feelings from Monsieur de Nemours. The end of the letter showed that the woman thought herself still loved; she imagined that his constant discretion, which had so touched her, was perhaps only the effect of his love for the other, whom he feared to offend. In a word, all her thoughts only fed her grief and despair. How often she thought of herself; how often of her mother's counsels! How bitterly she regretted that she had not withdrawn from the world, in spite of Monsieur de Clèves, or that she had not followed her plan of confessing to him her feeling for Monsieur de Nemours! She judged that she would have done better to tell everything to a husband whose generosity she knew, and who would be interested in keeping her secret, than to betray it to a man unworthy of it, who was moved to love of her by no other feeling than pride or vanity. In a word, she deemed every evil that could befall her, every misery to which she might be reduced, insignificant by the side of letting Monsieur de Nemours see that she loved him, and knowing that he loved another woman. Her only consolation was that henceforth she need have no fear of herself, and that she was entirely cured of her love for him.

She gave no thought to the dauphiness's command to come to her that evening; she went to bed and pretended to be indisposed, so that when Monsieur de Clèves came back from seeing the king, he was told that she was asleep. But she was far from enjoying the calmness that induces sleep. She spent the night in self-reproach and in reading over the letter.

Madame de Clèves was not the only person whose rest was disturbed by this letter. The Vidame of Chartres, who had lost it, not Monsieur de Nemours, was very uneasy about it. He had spent the evening with Monsieur de Guise, who had given a grand supper to his brother-in-law, the Duke of Ferrara, and all the young men of the court. It so happened that during the supper the conversation turned to bright letters, and the Vidame said he had in his pocket the brightest letter that ever was written. He was asked to show it to them, but he refused. Monsieur de Nemours thereupon declared that he had never had it, and was only boasting. The Vidame replied that he tempted him to commit an indiscretion, but he would not show the letter, though he would read a few passages that would prove that few men ever received one like it. At the same time he felt for the letter, but could not find it; he sought everywhere in vain. They laughed at his discomfiture, but he seemed so uneasy that they soon stopped talking about it. He left before the others, hastening home to see if he had left the missing letter there. While he was still hunting for it, a first *valet de chambre*[7] of the queen came to tell him that the Vicomtesse d'Uzès thought it well to let him know that they were talking at the queen's apartment about a love-letter he had dropped from his pocket while he was playing tennis; that they had repeated a good deal that was in the letter; that the queen had expressed a strong desire to see it; that she had asked one of her gentlemen-in-waiting for it; but he had answered that he had given it to Châtelart.

The *valet de chambre* said many other things to the Vidame which only added to his distress. He went out at once to see a gentleman who was a great friend of Châtelart; he made him get out of bed, although it was very late, to go and ask for the letter, without telling him who wanted it or who had written it. Châtelart, who was confident that it had been written to Monsieur de Nemours, and that he was in love with the dauphiness, felt sure that he knew who had asked for it. He replied, with malicious joy, that he had handed the letter to the dauphiness. The gentleman brought this answer back to the Vidame of Chartres; it gave him only fresh uneasiness. After long hesitation about what he should do, he decided that Monsieur de Nemours was the only man who could aid him.

The Vidame thereupon went to the house of the duke, and entered his bedroom at about daybreak. The prince was sleeping calmly; what

7. A personal manservant.

he had seen that day of Madame de Clèves gave him only agreeable thoughts. He was much surprised when he was awakened by the Vidame, and he asked him whether this had been done out of revenge for what he had said at the supper. The Vidame's countenance showed that he had come on some serious matter. "I have come," he said, "to confide to you the most important event of my life. I know very well that you have no cause to be grateful, because I do this at a moment when I need your aid; but I know that I should have sunk in your esteem if without being compelled by necessity I had told you what I am about to say. Some time yesterday I dropped the letter of which I was speaking last evening; it is of extreme importance that no one should know that it was written to me. It has been seen by a number of persons who were at the tennis-court when I dropped it. Now, you were there too, and I beg of you to say that it was you who lost it."

"You must suppose that I am not in love with any woman," answered Monsieur de Nemours, smiling, "to make such a proposition to me, and to imagine that there is no one with whom I might fall out if I let it be thought that I receive letters of that sort."

"I beg you," said the Vidame, "to listen to me seriously. If you have a mistress, as I do not doubt, though I have no idea who she is, it will be easy for you to explain yourself, and I will tell you how to do it. Even if you do not have an explanation with her, your falling-out will last but a few moments; whereas I by this mischance bring dishonor to a woman who has loved me passionately, and is one of the most estimable women in the world; and moreover, from another quarter I bring upon myself an implacable hatred, which will certainly cost me my fortune, and may cost me something more."

"I do not understand what you tell me," replied Monsieur de Nemours; "but you imply that the current rumors about the interest a great princess takes in you are not entirely without foundation."

"They are not," exclaimed the Vidame; "but would to God they were! In that case I should not be in my present trouble. But I must tell you what has happened, to give you an idea of what I have to fear.

"Ever since I have been at court, the queen has always treated me with much distinction and amiability, and I have reason to believe that she has had a kindly feeling for me; yet there was nothing marked about it, and I had never dreamed of other feelings toward me than those of respect. I was even much in love with Madame de Themines; the sight of her is enough to prove that a man can have a great deal of love for her when she loves him,—and she loved me. Nearly two years ago, when the court was at Fontainebleau, I happened to talk with the queen two or three times when very few people were there. It seemed to me that I pleased her, and that she was interested in all that I said. One day especially we were talking about confidence. I said I did not confide wholly in any one; that one always repented absolute unreserve sooner or later; and that I knew a number of things of which I had never spoken to any one. The queen said that she thought better of me for that; that she had not found any one in France who had any reserve; and that this had troubled her greatly, because it had prevented her confiding in any one; that one must have somebody to talk to, especially persons of her rank. The following days she several times resumed the same conversation, and told me many tolerably secret things that were happening. At last it seemed to me that she wanted to test my reserve, and that she wished to intrust me with some of her own secrets. This thought attached me to her; I was flattered by the distinction, and I paid her my court with more assiduity than usual. One evening, when the king and all the ladies had gone out to ride in the forest, she remained at home, because she did not feel well, and I stayed with her. She went down to the edge of the pond and let go of the equerry's hand, to walk more freely. After she had made a few turns, she came near me and bade me follow her. 'I want to speak to you,' she said, 'and you will see from what I wish to say that I am a friend of yours.' Then she stopped and gazed at me intently. 'You are in love,' she went on, 'and because you do not confide in any one, you think that your love is now known; but it is known even to the persons interested. You are watched; it is known where you see your mistress: a plan has been made to surprise you. I do not know who she is, I do not ask you; I only wish to save you from the misfortunes into which you may fall.' Observe, please, the snare the queen set for me, and how difficult it was to escape it. She wanted to find out whether I was in love; and by not asking with whom, and by showing that her sole intention was to aid me, she prevented my thinking that she was speaking to me from curiosity or with premeditation.

"Nevertheless, in the face of all appearances I made out the truth. I was in love with Madame de Themines; but though she loved me, I was not fortunate enough to meet her in any private place where we could be surprised, hence I saw that it was not she whom the queen meant. I knew too that I had a love-affair with a woman less beautiful and less severe than Madame de Themines, and it was not impossible that the place where I used to meet her had been discovered; but since I took but little interest in her, it was easy for me to escape from perils of that sort by ceasing to see her. Hence I decided to confess nothing to the queen, but to assure her that I had long since given up the desire to win the love of such women as might smile on me, because I deemed them unworthy of an honorable man's devotion, and it would take women far above them to fascinate me. 'You are not frank,' replied the queen; 'I know the opposite of what you say. The way in which I speak to you binds you to conceal nothing from me. I want you to be one of my friends,' she went on; 'but when I give you that place, I must know all your ties. Consider whether you care to purchase it at the price of informing me; I give you two days to think it over. But be careful what you say to me at the expiration of that time, and remember that if I find out afterward that you have deceived me, I shall never pardon you so long as I live.' Thereupon the queen left me, without awaiting my reply.

"You may well imagine that I was much impressed by what she had just said. The two days she had given me for consideration did not seem to me too long. I perceived that she wished to know whether I was in love, and hoped that I was not. I saw the importance of the decision I was about to make. My vanity was not a little flattered by a love-affair with a queen, and a queen who was still so charming. To be sure, I love Madame de Themines, and although I was unfaithful to her in a way with that other woman I mentioned, I could not make up my mind to break with her. I also saw the danger to which I exposed myself in deceiving the queen, and how hard it would be to deceive her; yet I could not decide to refuse what fortune offered me, and I determined to risk the consequences of my evil conduct. I broke with that woman with whom my relations might be discovered, and I hoped to conceal those I had with Madame de Themines.

"At the expiration of the two days that the queen had granted me, as I was entering a room where all her ladies were assembled, she said to me aloud, with a seriousness that surprised me,—

" 'Have you thought over that matter of which I spoke to you, and do you know the truth about it?'

" 'Yes, Madame,' I replied, 'and it is as I told your Majesty.'

" 'Come this evening at the hour that I shall write to you, and I will give you the rest of my orders.'

"I made a deep bow, without answering, and did not fail to appear at the hour set. I found her in the gallery with her secretary and some of her ladies. As soon as she saw me, she came up to me and led me to the other end of the gallery.

" 'Well!' she said, 'is it after due reflection that you have nothing to say to me, and does not my treatment of you deserve that you should speak to me frankly?'

" 'It is because I am frank with you, Madame,' I replied, 'that I have nothing to tell you; and I swear to your Majesty, with all the respect I owe you, that I am not in love with any lady of the court.'

" 'I am willing to believe it,' resumed the queen, 'because I wish to; and I wish it because I desire that you should be unreservedly attached to me; and I could not possibly be satisfied with your friendship if you were in love. One may trust those who are, but it is impossible to have confidence in their secrecy. They are too inattentive and have too many distractions; their mistress is their main interest,—and that would not suit the way in which I want you to be attached to me. Remember, it is on account of your oath that you are free that I choose you for the recipient of my confidence. Remember that I wish yours without reserve, that I want you to have no friend, man or woman, except such as shall be agreeable to me, and that you will give up every aim except pleasing me. I shall not let harm come to your fortune,—I shall look after that more zealously than you do; and whatever I do for you, I shall consider myself more than paid if I find that you are to me what I hope. I choose you in order to confide in you all my anxieties, and to help me endure them. You will see that they are not light. To all appearance I suffer no pain from the king's attachment to Madame de Valentinois; but I can scarcely bear it. She controls the king; she is false to him; she despises me; all my people are devoted to her. My daughter-in-law, the crown princess, is vain of her beauty and of her uncle's power, and pays no respect to me. The Constable of Montmorency is master of the king and of the kingdom; he hates me, and has given me tokens of his hatred which I can never forget. The Marshal of Saint-André is an audacious young favorite, who treats me no better than do the others. The full list of my sufferings would arouse your compassion. Hitherto I have not dared to trust any one; I do put confidence in you: act in such a way that I shall not repent of it, and be my sole consolation.'

"The queen's eyes filled with tears as she said these last words, and I was on the point of throwing myself at her feet, so deeply was I moved by the kindness she showed me. Since that day she has had perfect confidence in me; she never takes a step without talking it over with me, and my alliance with her still lasts.

Part IV

"Still, though much taken up by my new intimacy with the queen, I was bound to Madame de Themines by a feeling which I could not overcome. It seemed to me that her love for me was waning; and although if I had been wise I should have taken advantage of this change I saw in her to try to forget her, as it was, my love for her redoubled, and I managed so ill that the queen in time learned something about this attachment. Persons of her nation[8] are always inclined to jealousy, and possibly her feelings toward me were warmer

8. Italy.

than she herself supposed. But at last the report that I was in love gave her such distress and grief that I very often felt sure that I had wholly lost her favor. I reassured her by my attentions, submissiveness, and by many false oaths; but I could not have long deceived her if Madame de Themines' altered demeanor had not at last set me free in spite of myself. She made me see that she loved me no longer, and I was so sure of this that I felt compelled to cease persecuting her with my attentions. Some time after, she wrote me the letter that I have lost. That told me that she knew about my relations with the other woman I mentioned, and that this was the reason of the change. Since, then, there was no one to divide my attentions, the queen was tolerably satisfied with me; but inasmuch as my feeling for her was not of a sort to render me incapable of another attachment, and it is impossible for a man to control his heart by force of will, I fell in love with Madame de Martigues, in whom I had been much interested before, when she was a Villemontais[9] and maid-of-honor to the dauphiness. I had reason for believing that she did not hate me, and that she was pleased with my discreet conduct, although she did not understand all its reasons. The queen has no suspicions about this affair, but there is another which torments her a great deal. Since Madame de Martigues is always with the crown princess, I go there oftener than usual. The queen has taken it into her head that it is with this princess that I am in love. The dauphiness's rank, which is equal to her own, and her advantages of youth and beauty, inspire a jealousy which amounts to madness, and she cannot conceal her hatred of her daughter-in-law. The Cardinal of Lorraine, who seems to me to have been for a long time an aspirant for the queen's good graces, and who sees me occupying a place that he would like to fill, under the pretence of bringing about a reconciliation between her and the crown princess is looking into the causes of their dissension. I do not doubt that he has found out the real cause of the queen's bitterness, and I fancy that he has done me many an evil turn, though without showing his hand. That is the state of affairs now. Judge then what will be the effect of the letter I lost when I was unfortunate enough to put it into my pocket to return it to Madame de Themines. If the queen sees this letter, she will know that I have deceived her, and that at almost the same time when I was false to her on account of Madame de Themines, I was false to Madame de Themines on account of another woman. Judge then what sort of an opinion she will have of me, and whether she will ever believe me again. If she does not see this letter, what shall I say to her? She knows that it has been in the dauphiness's hands;

9. I.e., before her marriage: *Villemontais* was her maiden name.

she will think that Châtelart recognized that princess's handwriting, and that the letter is from her; she will imagine that she is perhaps the woman whose jealousy is mentioned,—in a word, there is nothing which she may not think, and there is nothing I may not fear from her thoughts. Add to this that I am sincerely interested in Madame de Martigues, that the crown princess will certainly show her this letter, and that she will believe it was written very recently. So I shall be embroiled both with the woman I love best in the world and with the woman from whom I have most to fear. Consider now whether I am not justified in begging you to say that the letter is yours and in asking you as a favor to try to get it from the dauphiness."

"It is very plain," said Monsieur de Nemours, "that one could hardly be in more serious perplexity than you are; and you must confess that you got into it by your own fault. I have been accused of being a faithless lover and of carrying on several love-affairs at the same time; but I am nothing by the side of you, for I should never have dreamed of doing what you have done. Could you suppose it possible to keep on good terms with Madame de Themines when you formed your alliance with the queen; and did you hope to become intimate with the queen and yet succeed deceiving her? She is an Italian and a queen, and hence suspicious, jealous, and haughty. When your good luck rather than your good conduct got you out of one entanglement, you got into a new one, and imagined that here, amid the whole court, you could love Madame de Martigues without out the queen's knowing anything about it. You could not have been too careful to rid her of the mortification of having taken the first steps. She has a violent passion for you. You are too discreet to say so, and I am too discreet to ask any questions; but she loves you, she distrusts you, and the facts justify her."

"Is it for you to overwhelm me with reproaches?" interrupted the Vidame. "Ought not your experience to make you indulgent to my faults? Still, I am willing to confess that I did wrong; but consider, I beg of you, how to get me out of my present complications. It seems to me that you must see the crown princess as soon as she is up, and ask her for the letter as if it were yours."

"I have already told you," replied Monsieur de Nemours, "that this is a somewhat extraordinary request, and one that, the circumstances being what they are, I do not find very easy to grant. Then, too, if the letter was seen to fall from your pocket, how can I convince them that it fell from mine?"

"I thought I had said that they told the dauphiness that it was from yours that it fell."

"What!" said Monsieur de Nemours with some asperity, for he

saw at once that this mistake might complicate matters with Madame de Clèves. "So the dauphiness has been told that I dropped this letter?"

"Yes," answered the Vidame; "that is what they told her,—and the mistake arose in this way: there were several of the queen's gentlemen in one of the rooms by the tennis-court where our clothes were hanging, and when we sent for them the letter dropped; these gentlemen took it up and read it aloud. Some thought it was written to you; others, that it was written to me. Châtelart, who took it, and from whom I have just tried to get it, said he had given it to the crown princess as a letter of yours; those who mentioned it to the queen unfortunately said it was mine,—so you can easily do what I wish, and get me out of this terrible complication."

Monsieur de Nemours had always been very fond of the Vidame of Chartres, and his relationship to Madame de Clèves rendered him still dearer. Nevertheless, he could not make up his mind to run the risk of her hearing of this letter as something in which he was concerned. He began to meditate profoundly, and the Vidame, guessing the nature of his thoughts, said: "I really believe you are afraid of falling out with your mistress; and I should be inclined to think that it is about the dauphiness that you are anxious, were it not that your freedom from any jealousy of Monsieur d'Anville forbids the thought. But however that may be, you must not sacrifice your peace of mind to mine, and I will make it possible for you to prove to the woman you love that this letter was written to me, and not to you. Here is a note from Madame d'Amboise; she is a friend of Madame de Themines, and to her she has confided all her feelings about me. In this note she asks me for her friend's letter,—the one I lost. My name is on the note, and its contents prove beyond the possibility of doubt that the letter she asks for is the one that has been picked up. I intrust this note to you, and I am willing that you should show it to your mistress in order to clear yourself. I beg of you not to lose a moment, but to go to the dauphiness this morning."

Monsieur de Nemours gave his promise to the Vidame of Chartres and took Madame d'Amboise's note. But his intention was not to see the crown princess; he thought he had something more urgent to do. He felt sure that she had already spoken about this letter to Madame de Clèves, and he could not endure that a woman he loved so much should have any reason for thinking that he was attached to any other.

He went to her house as soon as he thought she might be awake, and sent up word that he would not ask to have the honor at such an extraordinary hour if it were not on very important business. Madame de Clèves was not yet up; she was much embittered and agitated by the gloomy thoughts that had tormented her all night. She was extremely surprised when she heard that Monsieur de Nemours wanted to see her. Grieved as she was, she did not hesitate to send him word that she was ill, and unable to see him.

He was not pained by this refusal; an act of coolness at a time when she might be jealous was no unfavorable omen. He went to Monsieur de Clèves' apartments and told him that he had just called on his wife; that he was very sorry he could not see her, because he wished to speak to her of a matter of importance in which the Vidame of Chartres was interested. In a few words he told Monsieur de Clèves how serious the matter was, and Monsieur de Clèves took him at once to his wife's room. Nothing but the darkness enabled her to hide her agitation and surprise at seeing Monsieur de Nemours brought into her room by her husband. Monsieur de Clèves said that there was some question about a letter, and the Vidame's interests required her aid; he added that Monsieur de Nemours would tell her what was to be done, and that he should go to the king, who had just sent for him.

Monsieur de Nemours was left alone with Madame de Clèves,— which was exactly what he wanted. "I have come, Madame," he began, "to ask you if the dauphiness has not spoken to you about a letter which Châtelart gave her."

"She said something about it to me," answered Madame de Clèves; "but I don't understand how this letter concerns my uncle, and I am able to assure you that his name is not mentioned in it."

"True, Madame," Monsieur de Nemours went on, "his name is not mentioned; nevertheless, it was written to him, and it is of the utmost importance to him that you should get it out of her hands."

"I fail to understand," said Madame de Clèves, "how it concerns him that this letter should not be seen, and why it should be asked for in his name."

"If you will kindly listen to me," said Monsieur de Nemours, "I will speedily explain the matter to you, and you will soon see that the Vidame is so implicated that I should not have said anything about it even to the Prince of Clèves if I had not needed his assistance in order to have the honor of seeing you."

"I think that all that you might take the trouble to say to me would be useless," replied Madame de Clèves, somewhat tartly; "and it is much better that you should go to the crown princess and tell her frankly your interest in this letter, since it has been said that it belongs to you."

The vexation that Monsieur de Nemours saw in Madame de Clèves gave him the keenest pleasure he had yet known, and fully consoled him for his impatience to explain himself. "I do not know, Mad-

ame," he began, "what may have been said to the dauphiness; but
this letter does not concern me personally, and it was written to the
Vidame."

"That I believe," replied Madame de Clèves; "but the dauphiness
has been told the contrary, and it will not seem to her likely that the
Vidame's letters should fall out of your pockets. That is why, unless
you have some good reason for concealing the truth from her, I
advise you to confess it to her."

"I have nothing to confess to her," he went on; "the letter is none
of mine, and if there is any one I wish to convince of this, it is not
the crown princess. But, Madame, since the Vidame's fate is at stake,
permit me to tell you some things which you will find quite worth
listening to."

The silence of Madame de Clèves showed that she was willing to
listen, and Monsieur de Nemours repeated in as few words as possible what the Vidame had told him. Although this might well have
surprised, or at least interested, her, Madame de Clèves listened with
such marked indifference that she seemed to doubt it or to find it
unworthy of her attention. She maintained this indifference until
Monsieur de Nemours mentioned Madame d'Amboise's note to the
Vidame of Chartres, which was the proof of all he had just been
saying. Since Madame de Clèves knew that she was a friend of Madame de Themines, it seemed to her possible that Monsieur de Nemours had been speaking the truth, and she began to think that possibly
the letter in question had not been written to him. This thought
suddenly dispelled her indifference. The prince read her the note,
which exonerated him completely, and then handed it to her for
examination, telling her that perhaps she knew the handwriting; she
was compelled to take it and to read the address, and indeed every
word, in order to make sure that the letter asked for was the one in
her possession. Monsieur de Nemours said everything he could think
of to convince her; and since a pleasant truth is readily believed, he
succeeded in proving to Madame de Clèves that he had no part
whatsoever in the letter.

Then she began to reflect on the Vidame's troubles and danger,
to blame his evil conduct, and to desire means to aid him. She was
surprised at the queen's behavior; she confessed to Monsieur de
Nemours that the letter was in her possession,—in a word, so soon
as she thought him innocent, she interested herself at once with the
utmost cordiality in the very things that at first left her perfectly indifferent. They agreed that it was not necessary to return the letter to
the crown princess, lest she should show it to Madame de Martigues,
who knew Madame de Themines' handwriting, and would at once
have guessed, from her interest in the Vidame, that the letter had
been written to him. They also thought that it was better not to

confide to the dauphiness the part concerning her mother-in-law, the queen. Madame de Clèves, under the pretext of her concern for her uncle's affairs, gladly promised to keep every secret that Monsieur de Nemours might intrust to her.

This prince would have talked with her about other things than the Vidame's affairs, and would have taken advantage of this opportunity to speak to her with greater freedom than he had ever done, were it not that word was brought to Madame de Clèves that the dauphiness had sent for her; Monsieur de Nemours consequently was obliged to withdraw. He went to see the Vidame, to tell him that after leaving him he had thought it better to see his niece, Madame de Clèves, than to go straight to the dauphiness. He brought forward many good arguments in support of what he had done and to make success seem probable.

Meanwhile Madame de Clèves dressed in all haste to go to the crown princess. She had scarcely entered the room when the dauphiness called her to her, and said in a low voice,—

"I have been waiting two hours for you, and never had more difficulty in concealing the truth than I have had this morning. The queen has heard about the letter I gave you yesterday, and thinks it was the Vidame of Chartres who dropped it; you know she takes a good deal of interest in him. She wanted to see the letter, and sent to ask Châtelart for it; he told her he had given it to me, and then they came to ask me for it, under the pretext that it was a very bright letter, which the queen was anxious to see. I did not dare say that you had it; I feared she would think that it had been placed in your hands because the Vidame is your uncle, and that there was some understanding between you and me. It has already occurred to me that she did not like his seeing me often; so I said the letter was in the pocket of the clothes I wore yesterday, and that those who had the key of the room in which they were locked had gone out. So give me the letter at once, that I may send it to her; and let me look at it before I send it, to see if I know the handwriting."

Madame de Clèves was even more embarrassed than she had expected. "I don't know, Madame," she answered, "what you will do; for Monsieur de Clèves, to whom I had given it, gave it back to Monsieur de Nemours, who came this morning to get him to ask you to return it to him. Monsieur de Clèves was imprudent enough to say that it was in his possession, and weak enough to yield to Monsieur de Nemours' entreaties and to give it to him."

"You have put me in the greatest possible embarrassment," said the dauphiness, "and you did very wrong to return the letter to Monsieur de Nemours; since I gave it you, you ought not to have returned it without my permission. What can I say to the queen, and what will she think? She will believe, and on good grounds, that this letter concerns me, and that there is something between the Vidame and me. She will never believe that the letter belongs to Monsieur de Nemours."

"I am extremely sorry," answered Madame de Clèves, "for the trouble I have caused,—I see just how great it is; but it is Monsieur de Clèves' fault, not mine."

"It is yours," retorted the dauphiness, "because you gave him the letter. There is not another woman in the world who would confide to her husband everything she knows."

"I acknowledge that I was wrong, Madame," said Madame de Clèves; "but think rather of repairing than of discussing my fault."

"Don't you remember pretty well what was in the letter?" asked the crown princess.

"Yes, Madame," was the reply; "I remember it, for I read it over more than once."

"In that case, you must go at once and write it in a disguised hand. This copy I will send to the queen. She will not show it to any one who has seen the original; and even if she should, I shall always maintain that it was the one that Châtelart gave me, and he will not dare to deny it."

Madame de Clèves agreed to this plan, and all the more readily because she thought she would send for Monsieur de Nemours to let her have the letter again, in order to copy it word for word, and so far as possible imitate the handwriting; in this way she thought the queen could not fail to be deceived. As soon as she got home she told her husband about the dauphiness's embarrassment, and begged him to send for Monsieur de Nemours; this was done, and he came at once. Madame de Clèves repeated to him what she had just told her husband, and asked him for the letter. Monsieur de Nemours replied that he had already given it back to the Vidame de Chartres, who was so glad to see it again and to be out of danger that he had at once sent it to Madame de Themines. Madame de Clèves was in new trouble; but at last, after discussing the matter together, they determined to write the letter from memory. They locked themselves up to work, left word at the door that no one was to be let in, and sent off Monsieur de Nemours' servants. This appearance of mystery and of confidence was far from unpleasant to this prince, and even to Madame de Clèves. The presence of her husband and the thought that she was furthering the Vidame's interests almost calmed her scruples. She felt only the pleasure of seeing Monsieur de Nemours; it was a fuller and purer joy than any she had ever felt, and it inspired her with a liveliness and ease that Monsieur de Nemours had never seen in her, and his love for her was only deepened. Since he had never before had such pleasant moments, his own spirits rose, and when Madame de Clèves wanted to recall the letter and to write, he, instead of aiding her seriously, did nothing but interrupt her with idle jests. Madame de Clèves was quite as merry; so that they had been long shut up together, and twice word had come from the dauphiness urging Madame de Clèves to make haste, before half the letter was written.

Monsieur de Nemours was only too happy to prolong so pleasant a visit, and forgot his friend's interests. Madame de Clèves was amusing herself, and forgot those of her uncle. At last, at four o'clock, the letter was hardly finished, and the handwriting was so unlike that of the original that it was impossible that the queen should not at once detect the truth; and she was not deceived by it. Although they did their best to convince her that the letter was written to Monsieur de Nemours, she remained convinced, not only that it was addressed to the Vidame de Chartres, but that the dauphiness had something to do with it, and that there was some understanding between him and her. This thought so intensified her hatred of this princess that she never forgave her, and persecuted her till she drove her from France.

As for the Vidame of Chartres, he was ruined so far as she was concerned; and whether it was that the Cardinal of Lorraine had already acquired an ascendency over her, or that the affair of this letter, in which she saw that she had been deceived, opened her eyes to the other deceptions of which the Vidame had been guilty, it is certain that he could never bring about a satisfactory reconciliation. Their intimacy was at an end, and she accomplished his ruin afterward at the time of the conspiracy of Amboise,[1] in which he was implicated.

After the letter had been sent to the crown princess, Monsieur de Clèves and Monsieur de Nemours went away. Madame de Clèves was left alone; and as soon as she was deprived of the presence of the man she loved, she seemed to awaken from a dream. She thought with surprise of the difference between her state of mind the previous evening and that she then felt; she pictured the coldness and harshness she had shown to Monsieur de Nemours so long as she had supposed that Madame de Themines' letter had been written to him, and the tranquillity and happiness that had succeeded them when he had proved to her that this letter in no way concerned him. When she recalled that the day before she had reproached herself, as if it were a crime, for having shown an interest that mere compassion had called forth, and that by her harshness she had betrayed a feeling of jealousy,—a certain proof of affection,—she scarcely recognized herself. When she thought further that Monsieur de Nemours saw that she was aware of his love; when he saw that, in spite of this, she treated him with perfect cordiality in her husband's presence,—indeed

1. A conspiracy (1560) led by Louis de Bourbon, Prince of Condé, and the Huguenot party in an effort to destroy the influence of the Guises over King Francis II. The plot failed.

that she had treated him with more kindness than ever before, that she was the cause of her husband's sending for him, and that they had just passed an afternoon together privately,—she saw that there was an understanding between herself and Monsieur de Nemours; that she was deceiving a husband who deserved to be deceived less than any husband in the world; and she was ashamed to appear so unworthy of esteem even before the eyes of her lover. But what pained her more than all the rest was the memory of the state in which she had passed the night, and the acute grief she had suffered from the thought that Monsieur de Nemours loved another and that she had been deceived.

Up to that time she had not known the stings of mistrust and jealousy; her only thought had been to keep from loving Monsieur de Nemours, and she had not yet begun to fear that he loved another. Although the suspicions that this letter had aroused were wholly removed, they opened her eyes to the danger of being deceived, and gave her impressions of mistrust and jealousy such as she had never felt before. She was astounded that she had never yet thought how improbable it was that a man like Monsieur de Nemours, who had always treated women with such fickleness, should be capable of a sincere and lasting attachment. She thought it almost impossible that she could ever be satisfied with his love. "But if I could be," she asked herself, "what could I do with it? Do I wish it? Could I return it? Do I wish to begin a love-affair? Do I wish to fail in my duty to Monsieur de Clèves? Do I wish to expose myself to the cruel repentance and mortal anguish that are inseparable from love? I am overwhelmed by an affection which carries me away in spite of myself; all my resolutions are vain; I thought yesterday what I think to-day, and I act to-day in direct contradiction to my resolutions of yesterday. I must tear myself away from the society of Monsieur de Nemours; I must go to the country, strange as the trip may seem; and if Monsieur de Clèves persists in opposing it, or in demanding my reasons, perhaps I shall do him and myself the wrong of telling them to him." She held firm to this resolution, and spent the evening at home, instead of going to find out from the dauphiness what had become of the Vidame's pretended letter.

When Monsieur de Clèves came home she told him she wanted to go into the country; that she was not feeling well, and needed a change of air. Monsieur de Clèves, who felt sure from her appearance that there was nothing serious ailed her, at first laughed at the proposed trip, and told her that she forgot the approaching marriages of the princesses and the tournament, and that she would not have time enough to make her preparations for appearing in due splendor alongside the other ladies. Her husband's arguments did not move her; she begged him, when he went to Compiègne with the king, to let her go to Coulommiers,[2]—a country-house they were building at a day's journey from Paris. Monsieur de Clèves gave his consent; so she went off with the intention of not returning at once, and the king left for a short stay at Compiègne.

Monsieur de Nemours felt very bad at not seeing Madame de Clèves again after the pleasant afternoon he had spent with her, which had so fired his hopes. His impatience to meet her once more left him no peace; so that when the king returned to Paris he determined to make a visit to his sister, the Duchess of Mercœur, who lived in the country not far from Coulommiers. He proposed to the Vidame to go with him; the latter gladly consented, to the delight of Monsieur de Nemours, who hoped to make sure of seeing Madame de Clèves by calling in company with the Vidame.

Madame de Mercœur was delighted to see them, and at once began to devise plans for their amusement. While they were deer-hunting, Monsieur de Nemours lost his way in the forest; and when he asked what road he should take, he was told that he was near Coulommiers. When he heard this word, "Coulommiers," he at once, without thinking, without forming any plan, dashed off in that direction. He got once more into the forest, and followed such paths as seemed to him to lead to the castle. These paths led to a summer-house, which consisted of a large room with two closets,[3] one opening on a flower-garden separated from the forest by a fence, and the other opening on one of the walks of the park. He entered the summer-house, and was about to stop and admire it, when he saw Monsieur and Madame de Clèves coming along the path, followed by a number of servants. Surprised at seeing Monsieur de Clèves, whom he had left with the king, his first impulse was to hide. He entered the closet near the flower-garden, with the intention of escaping by a door opening into the forest; but when he saw Madame de Clèves and her husband sitting in the summer-house, while their servants stayed in the park, whence they could not reach him without coming by Monsieur and Madame de Clèves, he could not resist the temptation to watch her, or overcome his curiosity to listen to her conversation with her husband, of whom he was more jealous than of any of his rivals.

He heard Monsieur de Clèves say to his wife: "But why don't you wish to return to Paris? What can keep you in the country? For some time you have had a taste for solitude which surprises me and pains me, because it keeps us apart. I find you in even lower spirits than usual, and I am afraid something distresses you."

"I have nothing on my mind," she answered, with some embarrassment; "but the bustle of a court is so great, and our house is

2. About 25 miles east of Paris.   3. Small private rooms for reading or meditation.

always so thronged, that it is impossible for mind and body not to be tired and to need rest."

"Rest," he answered, "is not needed by persons of your age. Neither at home nor at court do you get tired, and I should be rather inclined to fear that you are glad to get away from me."

"If you thought that, you would do me great injustice," she replied, with ever-growing embarrassment; "but I beg of you to leave me here. If you could stay too I should be very glad, provided you would stay alone, and did not care for the throng of people who almost never leave you."

"Ah, Madame," exclaimed Monsieur de Clèves, "your air and your words show me that you have reasons for wishing to be alone which I don't know, and which I beg of you to tell me."

For a long time the prince besought her to tell him the reason, but in vain; and after she had refused in a way that only redoubled his curiosity, she stood for a time silent, with eyes cast down; then, raising her eyes to his, she said suddenly,—

"Don't compel me to confess something which I have often meant to tell you, but had not the strength. Only remember that prudence does not require that a woman of my age, who is mistress of her actions, should remain exposed to the temptations of the court."

"What is it you suggest, Madame?" exclaimed Monsieur de Clèves. "I should not dare to say, for fear of offending you."

Madame de Clèves did not answer, and her silence confirming her husband's suspicions, he went on,—

"You are silent, and your silence tells me I am not mistaken."

"Well, sir," she answered, falling on her knees, "I am going to make you a confession such as no woman has ever made to her husband; the innocence of my actions and of my intentions gives me strength to do so. It is true that I have reasons for keeping aloof from the court, and I wish to avoid the perils that sometimes beset women of my age. I have never given the slightest sign of weakness, and I should never fear displaying any, if you would leave me free to withdraw from court, or if Madame de Chartres still lived to guide my actions. Whatever the dangers of the course I take, I pursue it with pleasure, in order to keep myself worthy of you. I beg your pardon a thousand times if my feelings offend you; at any rate I shall never offend you by my actions. Remember that to do what I am now doing requires more friendship and esteem for a husband than any one has ever had. Guide me, take pity on me, love me, if you can."

All the time she was speaking, Monsieur de Clèves sat with his head in his hands; he was really beside himself, and did not once think of lifting his wife up. But when she had finished, and he looked down and saw her, her face wet with tears, and yet so beautiful, he thought he should die of grief. He kissed her, and helped her to her feet.

"Do you, Madame, take pity on me," he said, "for I deserve it; and excuse me if in the first moments of a grief so poignant as mine I do not respond as I should to your appeal. You seem to me worthier of esteem and admiration than any woman that ever lived; but I also regard myself as the unhappiest of men. The first moment that I saw you, I was filled with love of you; neither your indifference to me nor the fact that you are my wife has cooled it: it still lives. I have never been able to make you love me, and I see that you fear you love another. And who, Madame, is the happy man that inspires this fear? Since when has he charmed you? What has he done to please you? What was the road he took to your heart? I found some consolation for not having touched it in the thought that it was beyond any one's reach; but another has succeeded where I have failed. I have all the jealousy of a husband and of a lover; but it is impossible to suffer as a husband after what you have told me. Your noble conduct makes me feel perfectly secure, and even consoles me as a lover. Your confidence and your sincerity are infinitely dear to me; you think well enough of me not to suppose that I shall take any unfair advantage of this confession. You are right, Madame,—I shall not; and I shall not love you less. You make me happy by the greatest proof of fidelity that a woman ever gave her husband; but, Madame, go on and tell me who it is you are trying to avoid."

"I entreat you, do not ask me," she replied; "I have determined not to tell you, and I think that the more prudent course."

"Have no fear, Madame," said Monsieur de Clèves; "I know the world too well to suppose that respect for a husband ever prevents men falling in love with his wife. He ought to hate those who do so, but without complaining; so once more, Madame, I beg of you to tell me what I want to know."

"You would urge me in vain," she answered; "I have strength enough to keep back what I think I ought not to say. My avowal is not the result of weakness, and it requires more courage to confess this truth than to undertake to hide it."

Monsieur de Nemours lost not a single word of this conversation, and Madame de Clèves' last remark made him quite as jealous as it made her husband. He was himself so desperately in love with her that he supposed every one else was just as much so. It was true in fact that he had many rivals, but he imagined even more than there were; and he began to wonder whom Madame de Clèves could mean. He had often believed that she did not dislike him, and he had formed this opinion from things which now seemed so slight that he could not imagine he had kindled a love so intense that it called for this desperate remedy. He was almost beside himself with excitement, and could not forgive Monsieur de Clèves for not insisting on knowing the name his wife was hiding.

Monsieur de Clèves, however, was doing his best to find it out, and after he had entreated her in vain, she said: "It seems to me that you ought to be satisfied with my sincerity; do not ask me anything more, and do not give me reason to repent what I have just done. Content yourself with the assurance I give you that no one of my actions has betrayed my feelings, and that not a word has ever been said to me at which I could take offence."

"Ah, Madame," Monsieur de Clèves suddenly exclaimed, "I cannot believe you! I remember your embarrassment the day your portrait was lost. You gave it away, Madame,—you gave away that portrait which was so dear to me, and belonged to me so legitimately. You could not hide your feelings; it is known that you are in love: your virtue has so far preserved you from the rest."

"Is it possible," the princess burst forth, "that you could suspect any misrepresentation in a confession like mine, which there was no ground for my making? Believe what I say: I purchase at a high price the confidence that I ask of you. I beg of you, believe that I did not give away the portrait; it is true that I saw it taken, but I did not wish to show that I saw it, lest I should be exposed to hearing things which no one had yet dared to say."

"How then did you see his love?" asked Monsieur de Clèves. "What marks of love were given to you?"

"Spare me the mortification," was her answer, "of repeating all the details which I am ashamed to have noticed, and have only convinced me of my weakness."

"You are right, Madame," he said, "I am unjust. Deny me when I shall ask such things, but do not be angry if I ask them."

At this moment some of the servants who were without, came to tell Monsieur de Clèves that a gentleman had come with a command from the king that he should be in Paris that evening. Monsieur de Clèves was obliged to leave at once, and he could say to his wife nothing except that he begged her to return the next day, and besought her to believe that though he was sorely distressed, he felt for her an affection and esteem which ought to satisfy her.

When he had gone, and Madame de Clèves was alone and began to think of what she had done, she was so amazed that she could scarcely believe it true. She thought that she had wholly alienated her husband's love and esteem, and had thrown herself into an abyss from which escape was impossible. She asked herself why she had done this perilous thing, and saw that she had stumbled into it without intention. The strangeness of such a confession, for which she knew no precedent, showed her all her danger.

But when she began to think that this remedy, violent as it was, was the only one that could protect her against Monsieur de Nemours, she felt that she could not regret it, and that she had not gone too far. She spent the whole night in uncertainty, anxiety, and fear; but at last she grew calm. She felt a vague satisfaction in having given this proof of fidelity to a husband who so well deserved it, who had such affection and esteem for her, and who had just shown these by the way in which he had received her avowal.

Meanwhile Monsieur de Nemours had left the place where he had overheard a conversation which touched him keenly, and had hastened into the forest. What Madame de Clèves had said about the portrait gave him new life, by showing him that it was he whom she did not hate. He first gave himself up to this joy; but it was not of long duration, for he reflected that the same thing which showed him that he had touched the heart of Madame de Clèves, ought to convince him that he would never receive any token of it, and that it was impossible to gain any influence over a woman who resorted to so strange a remedy. He felt, nevertheless, great pleasure in having brought her to this extremity. He felt a certain pride in making himself loved by a woman so different from all others of her sex,—in a word, he felt a hundred times happier and unhappier. Night came upon him in the forest, and he had great difficulty in finding the way back to Madame de Mercœur's. He reached there at daybreak. He found it very hard to explain what had delayed him, but he made the best excuses he could, and returned to Paris that same day with the Vidame.

Monsieur de Nemours was so full of his passion and so surprised by what he had heard that he committed a very common imprudence,—that of speaking in general terms of his own feelings and of describing his own adventures under borrowed names. On his way back he turned the conversation to love: he spoke of the pleasure of being in love with a worthy woman; he mentioned the singular effects of this passion; and, finally, not being able to keep to himself his astonishment at what Madame de Clèves had done, he told the whole story to the Vidame, without naming her and without saying that he had any part in it. But he manifested such warmth and admiration that the Vidame at once suspected that the story concerned the prince himself. He urged him strongly to acknowledge this; he said that he had long known that he nourished a violent passion, and that it was wrong not to trust in a man who had confided to him the secret of his life. Monsieur de Nemours was too much in love to acknowledge his love; he had always hidden it from the Vidame, though he loved him better than any man at court. He answered that one of his friends had told him this adventure, and had made him promise not to speak of it, and he besought him to keep his secret. The Vidame promised not to speak of it; nevertheless, Monsieur de Nemours repented having told him.

Meanwhile, Monsieur de Clèves had gone to the king, his heart sick with a mortal wound. Never had a husband felt warmer love or higher respect for his wife. What he had heard had not lessened his respect, but this had assumed a new form. His most earnest desire was to know who had succeeded in pleasing her. Monsieur de Nemours was the first to occur to him, as the most fascinating man at court, and the Chevalier de Guise and the Marshal of Saint-André as two men who had tried to please her and had paid her much attention; so that he decided it must be one of these three. He reached the Louvre, and the king took him into his study to tell him that he had chosen him to carry Madame to Spain; that he had thought that the prince would discharge this duty better than any one; and that no one would do so much credit to France as Madame de Clèves. Monsieur de Clèves accepted this appointment with due respect, and even looked upon it as something that would remove his wife from court without attracting any attention; but the date of their departure was still too remote to relieve his present embarrassment. He wrote at once to Madame de Clèves to tell her what the king had said, and added that he was very anxious that she should come to Paris. She returned in obedience to his request, and when they met, each found the other in the deepest gloom.

Monsieur de Clèves addressed her in the most honorable terms, and seemed well worthy of the confidence she had placed in him.

"I have no uneasiness about your conduct," he said; "you have more strength and virtue than you think. It is not dread of the future that distresses me; I am only distressed at seeing that you have for another feelings that I have not been able to inspire in you."

"I do not know how to answer you," she said; "I am ready to die with shame when I speak to you. Spare me, I beg of you, these painful conversations. Regulate my conduct; let me see no one,— that is all I ask; but permit me never to speak of a thing which makes me seem so little worthy of you, and which I regard as so unworthy of me."

"You are right, Madame," he answered; "I abuse your gentleness and your confidence. But do you too take some pity on the state into which you have cast me, and remember that whatever you have told me, you conceal from me a name which excites an unendurable curiosity. Still, I do not ask you to gratify it; but I must say that I believe the man I must envy to be the Marshal of Saint-André, the Duke of Nemours, or the Chevalier de Guise."

"I shall not answer," she said, blushing, "and I shall give you no occasion for lessening or strengthening your suspicions; but if you try to find out by watching me, you will surely make me so embarrassed that every one will notice it. In Heaven's name," she went on, "invent some illness, that I may see no one!"

"No, Madame," he replied, "it would soon be found that it was not real; and moreover I want to place my confidence in you alone,—that is the course my heart recommends, and my reason too. In your present mood, by leaving you free, I protect you by a closer guard than I could persuade myself to set about you."

Monsieur de Clèves was right; the confidence he showed in his wife proved a stronger protection against Monsieur de Nemours and inspired her to make austerer resolutions than any form of constraint could have done. She went to the Louvre and visited the dauphiness as usual; but she avoided Monsieur de Nemours with so much care that she took away nearly all his happiness at thinking that she loved him. He saw nothing in her actions which did not prove the contrary. He was almost ready to believe that what he had heard was a dream, so unlikely did it appear. The only thing that assured him that he was not mistaken was the extreme sadness of Madame de Clèves, in spite of all her efforts to conceal it. Possibly kind words and glances would not have so fanned Monsieur de Nemours' love as did this austere conduct.

One evening, when Monsieur and Madame de Clèves were with the queen, some one said that it was reported that the king was going to name another nobleman of the court to accompany Madame to Spain. Monsieur de Clèves fixed his eyes on his wife when the speaker added that it would be either the Chevalier de Guise or the Marshal of Saint-André. He noticed that she showed no agitation at either of these names, or at the mention of their joining the party. This led him to think that it was neither of these that she dreaded to see; and wishing to determine the matter, he went to the room where the king was. After a short absence he returned to his wife and whispered to her that he had just learned that it would be Monsieur de Nemours who would go with them to Spain.

The name of Monsieur de Nemours and the thought of seeing him every day during a long journey, in her husband's presence, so agitated Madame de Clèves that she could not conceal it, and wishing to assign other reasons, she answered,—

"The choice of that gentleman will be very disagreeable for you; he will divide all the honors, and I think you ought to try to have some one else appointed."

"It is not love of glory, Madame," said Monsieur de Clèves, "that makes you dread that Monsieur de Nemours should come with me. Your regret springs from another cause. This regret tells me what another woman would have told by her delight. But do not be alarmed; what I have just told you is not true: I made it up to make sure of a thing which I had only too long inclined to believe." With these words he went away, not wishing by his presence to add to his wife's evident embarrassment.

At that moment Monsieur de Nemours entered, and at once noticed Madame de Clèves' condition. He went up to her, and said in a low voice that he respected her too much to ask what made her so thoughtful. His voice aroused her from her revery; and looking at him, without hearing what he said, full of her own thoughts and fearful that her husband would see him by her side, she said: "In Heaven's name, leave me alone!"

"Alas! Madame," he replied, "I leave you only too much alone. Of what can you complain? I do not dare to speak to you, or even to look at you; I never come near you without trembling. How have I brought such a remark on myself, and why do you make me seem to have something to do with the depression in which I find you?"

Madame de Clèves deeply regretted that she had given Monsieur de Nemours an opportunity to speak to her more frankly than he had ever done. She left him without giving him any answer, and went home in a state of agitation such as she had never known. Her husband soon noticed this; he perceived that she was afraid lest he should speak to her about what had just happened. He followed her into her room and said to her,—

"Do not try to avoid me, Madame; I shall say nothing that could displease you. I beg your pardon for surprising you as I did; I am sufficiently punished by what I learned. Monsieur de Nemours was the man whom I most feared. I see your danger: control yourself for your own sake, and, if possible, for mine. I do not ask this as your husband, but as a man, all of whose happiness you make, and who feels for you a tenderer and stronger love than he whom your heart prefers." Monsieur de Clèves nearly broke down at these last words, which he could hardly utter. His wife was much moved, and bursting into tears, she embraced him with a gentleness and a sorrow that almost brought him to the same condition. They remained for some time perfectly silent, and separated without having strength to utter a word.

The preparations for Madame Elisabeth's marriage was completed, and the Duke of Alva[4] arrived for the ceremony. He was received with all the pomp and formality that the occasion required. The king sent the Prince of Condé, the Cardinals of Lorraine and Guise, the Dukes of Lorraine, Ferrara, Aumale, Bouillon, Guise, and Nemours to meet him. They were accompanied by many gentlemen and a great number of pages wearing their liveries. The king himself received the Duke of Alva at the first door of the Louvre

---

4. He acted as a stand-in for Philip II at the marriage.

with two hundred gentlemen in waiting, with the constable at their head. As the duke drew near the king, he wished to embrace his knees;[5] but the king prevented him, and made him walk by his side to call on the queen and on Madame Elisabeth, to whom the Duke of Alva brought a magnificent present from his master. He then called on Madame Marguerite, the king's sister, to convey to her the compliments of Monsieur de Savoie, and to assure her that he would arrive in a few days. There were large receptions at the Louvre, to show the Duke of Alva and the Prince of Orange, who accompanied him, the beauties of the court.

Madame de Clèves did not dare to stay away, much as she desired it, through fear of displeasing her husband, who gave her special orders to go. What made him even more determined was the absence of Monsieur de Nemours. He had gone to meet Monsieur de Savoie, and after that prince's arrival he was obliged to be with him almost all the time, to help him in his preparations for the wedding ceremonies; hence Madame de Clèves did not meet him so often as usual, and she was able to enjoy a little peace.

The Vidame of Chartres had not forgotten the talk he had had with Monsieur de Nemours. He had made up his mind that the adventure this prince had told him was his own, and he watched him so closely that perhaps he would have made out the truth, had not the arrival of the Duke of Alva and of Monsieur de Savoie so changed and busied the court that he had no further opportunity. His desire for more information, or, rather, the natural tendency to tell all one knows to the woman one loves, make him mention to Madame de Martigues the extraordinary conduct of the woman who had confessed to her husband the love she felt for another man. He assured her that it was Monsieur de Nemours who had inspired this violent passion, and he besought her to aid him in observing this prince. Madame de Martigues was greatly interested in what the Vidame had told her, and her curiosity about the dauphiness's relations with Monsieur de Nemours made her more anxious than ever to get to the bottom of the affair.

A few days before the one set for the wedding the crown princess gave a supper to her father-in-law the king and the Duchess of Valentinois. Madame de Clèves, who was delayed in dressing, started for the Louvre a little later than usual, and on her way met a gentleman coming from the dauphiness to fetch her. When she entered the room the crown princess called out to her from the bed on which she was lying that she had been waiting for her with the utmost impatience.

5. An act of homage.

"I fancy, Madame," she replied, "that I have no cause to be grateful to you for this impatience; it is doubtless for some other reason that you were eager to see me."

"You are right," said the dauphiness; "but, nevertheless, you ought to be obliged to me, for I am going to tell you something that I am sure you will be very glad to hear."

Madame de Clèves knelt down by the side of the bed in such a way that, fortunately for her, her face was in the dark. "You know," said the crown princess, "how anxious we have been to find out the cause of the change in the Duke of Nemours; I think I have found out, and it is something that will surprise you. He is desperately in love with one of the most beautiful women of the court, and the lady returns his love."

These words, which Madame de Clèves could not take to herself, because she thought that no one knew of her love for this prince, gave her a pang that may be easily imagined.

"I see nothing in that," she replied, "which is surprising for a man of his age and appearance."

"But that," resumed the dauphiness, "is not the surprising part; what is amazing is the fact that this woman who loves Monsieur de Nemours has never given him any token of it, and that her fear that she may not always be able to control her passion has caused her to confess it to her husband to persuade him to take her away from court. And it is Monsieur de Nemours himself who is the authority for what I say."

If Madame de Clèves had been grieved at first by thinking that the affair in no way concerned her, these last words of the dauphiness filled her with despair, since they made it sure that it did concern her only too deeply. She could make no reply, but remained with her head resting on the bed while the dauphiness went on talking, too much taken up with what she was saying to notice her embarrassment. When Madame de Clèves had recovered some of her self-control, she answered,—

"This does not sound like a very probable story, and I wonder who told it to you."

"It was Madame de Martigues, who heard it from the Vidame. You know he is her lover; he told it to her as a secret, as he heard it from the Duke of Nemours. It is true that the Duke of Nemours did not mention the lady's name and did not even acknowledge that it was he who was loved; but the Vidame de Chartres has no doubt about that."

As the dauphiness pronounced these last words, some one drew near the bed. Madame de Clèves was turned away so that she could not see who it was; but she knew when the dauphiness exclaimed, with an air of surprise and amusement, "There he is himself, and I am going to ask how much truth there is in it."

Madame de Clèves knew that it must be the Duke of Nemours, and so it was. Without turning toward him, she leaned over to the crown princess and whispered to her to be careful not to say a word about this adventure, that he had told it to the Vidame in confidence, and that this would very possibly set them by the ears. The dauphiness answered laughingly that she was absurdly prudent, and turned toward Monsieur de Nemours. He was arrayed for the evening entertainment, and addressed her with all his usual grace.

"I believe, Madame," he began, "that I can think, without impertinence, that you were talking about me when I came in, that you wanted to ask me something, and that Madame de Clèves objected."

"You are right," replied the dauphiness; "but I shall not be as obliging to her as I usually am. I want to know whether a story I have heard is true, and whether you are the man who is in love with and is loved by a lady of the court who carefully conceals her passion from you and has confessed it to her husband."

Madame de Clèves' agitation and embarrassment cannot be conceived, and she would have welcomed death as an escape from her sufferings; but Monsieur de Nemours was even more embarrassed, if that is possible. This statement from the lips of the dauphiness, who, he had reason to believe, did not hate him, in the presence of Madame de Clèves, whom he loved better than any woman at court, and who also loved him, so overwhelmed him that he could not control his face. The embarrassment into which his blunder had plunged Madame de Clèves, and the thought of the good reason he gave her to hate him, made it impossible for him to answer. The dauphiness, noticing his intense confusion, said to Madame de Clèves: "Look at him, look at him, and see whether this is not his own story!"

Meanwhile Monsieur de Nemours, recovering from his first agitation, and recognizing the importance of escaping from this dangerous complication, suddenly recovered his presence of mind and regained his composure.

"I must acknowledge, Madame," he said, "that no one could be more surprised and distressed than I am by the Vidame de Chartres' treachery in repeating the adventure of one of my friends which I told to him in confidence. I might easily revenge myself," he went on, smiling in a way that almost dispelled the dauphiness's suspicions; "since he has confided to me matters of considerable importance. But I fail to understand why you do me the honor of implicating me in this affair. The Vidame cannot say that it concerns me, because I told him the very opposite. It may do very well to represent me as a man in love; but it will hardly do to represent me as a man who is loved,—which, Madame, is what you do."

Monsieur de Nemours was very glad to say something to the dauphiness which had some connection with his appearance in former times, in order to divert her thoughts. She caught his meaning; but without referring to these last words of his, she continued to harp on his evident confusion.

"I was embarrassed, Madame," he replied, "out of zeal for my friend and from fear of the reproaches he would be justified in making to me for repeating a thing dearer to him than life. Nevertheless, he only told me half, and did not mention the name of the woman he loves. I simply know that he is more in love and more to be pitied than any man in the world."

"Do you find him so worthy of pity," asked the crown princess, "because he is loved?"

"Are you sure that he is?" he answered; "and do you think that a woman who felt a real love would confide it to her husband? This woman, I am sure, knows nothing about love, and has mistaken for it a faint feeling of gratitude for his devotion to her. My friend cannot nourish any hope; but, wretched as he is, he has at least the consolation of having made her fearful of loving him, and he would not change his fate for that of any man in the world."

"Your friend's love is easily satisfied," said the crown princess, "and I begin to think that you can't be talking about yourself; I am inclined to agree with Madame de Clèves, who maintains that there can be no truth in the whole story."

"I don't think there can be," said Madame de Clèves, who had not yet said a word; "and if it were true, how could it become known? It is extremely unlikely that a woman capable of such an extraordinary thing would have the weakness to tell of it. Evidently a husband would not think of doing such a thing, unless he were a husband very unworthy of the confidence that was placed in him."

Monsieur de Nemours, who saw that Madame de Clèves' suspicions had fallen on her husband, was very glad to strengthen them; he knew that he was his strongest rival.

"Jealousy," he replied, "and the desire to find out more than he had been told, may induce a husband to commit a great many indiscretions."

Madame de Clèves was at the end of her strength; and being unable to carry on the conversation further, she was about to say that she did not feel well, when, fortunately for her, the Duchess of Valentinois came in to tell the dauphiness that the king would arrive very soon. The crown princess accordingly went into her room to dress; whereupon Monsieur de Nemours came up to Madame de Clèves as she was about to follow her, and said,—

"Madame, I would give my life to speak to you a moment; but of all the important things I should have to say to you, nothing seems to me more important than to beg you to believe that if I have said anything which might seem to refer to the dauphiness, I have done so for reasons which do not concern her."

Madame de Clèves pretended not to hear him, but moved away without looking at him and joined the suite of the king, who had just come in. There being a great crowd present, her foot caught in her dress, and she made a misstep; she took advantage of this excuse to leave a place where she had no strength to stay longer, and went away pretending that she could not stand.

Monsieur de Clèves went to the Louvre, and being surprised not to see his wife, he was told of the accident that had just happened to her. He left at once, to find out how she was; he found her in bed, and she told him that she was but slightly hurt. When he had been with her for some time he saw that she was exceedingly sad; this surprised him, and he asked her, "What is the matter? You seem to suffer in some other way than that you have told me."

"I could not be in greater distress than I am," she answered. "What use did you make of the extraordinary, I might say foolish, confidence I had in you? Was I not worthy of secrecy on your part? And even if I was unworthy of it, did not your own interest urge it? Was it necessary that your curiosity to know a name which I ought not to tell you, could force you to confide in any one else in order to discover it? Nothing but curiosity could have led you to commit such an imprudence. The consequences have been most disastrous; the story is known, and has just been told to me, without any notion that I was the person most concerned."

"What do you say, Madame?" he replied. "You accuse me of having repeated what passed between us, and you tell me the story is known! I shall not defend myself from the charge of repeating it; you can't believe it, and you must have taken to yourself something said about some other woman."

"Oh, sir," she said, "in the whole world there is not another case like mine; there is not another woman capable of doing what I have done! Chance could not make any one invent it; no one has ever imagined it,—the very thought never entered any one's mind but mine. The dauphiness has just told me the whole story; she heard it from the Vidame of Chartres, and he had it from Monsieur de Nemours."

"Monsieur de Nemours!" exclaimed Monsieur de Clèves, with a gesture expressive of the wildest despair. "What, Monsieur de Nemours knows that you love him and that I know it!"

"You always want to fix on Monsieur de Nemours rather than any one else," she replied; "I told you that I should never say anything about your suspicions. I cannot say whether Monsieur de Nemours knows my share in this affair, or the part you assign to him; but he told it to the Vidame de Chartres, saying that he had it from one of his friends, who did not give the name of the woman. This friend of Monsieur de Nemours must be one of your friends, and you must have told the story to him in an effort to get some information."

"Is there a friend in the world," he exclaimed, "to whom any one would make a confidence of that sort? And would any one try to confirm his suspicions by telling another what one would wish to hide from one's self? Consider rather to whom you have spoken. It is more likely that the secret got out from you than from me. You could not endure your misery alone, and you sought solace in making a confidant of some friend who has played you false."

"Do not torment me further," she burst forth, "and do not be so cruel as to charge me with a fault which you have committed. Could you suspect me of that? And because I was capable of speaking to you, am I capable of speaking of it to any one else?"

His wife's confession had so convinced Monsieur de Clèves of her frankness, and she so warmly denied having mentioned the incident to any one, that Monsieur de Clèves did not know what to think. For his own part, he was sure that he had repeated nothing; it was something nobody could have guessed: it was known, and it must have become known through one of them. But what caused the liveliest grief was the knowledge that this secret was in somebody's hands, and apparently would be soon divulged.

Madame de Clèves' thoughts were nearly the same; she held it equally impossible that her husband should have spoken and should not have spoken. What Monsieur de Nemours had said, that curiosity might make a husband indiscreet, seemed to apply so well to just the state of mind in which Monsieur de Clèves was, that she could not think it was a mere strange coincidence; and this probability compelled her to believe that Monsieur de Clèves had abused her confidence in him. They were both so busy with their thoughts that they for a long time did not speak, and when they broke the silence, it was but to repeat what they had already said very often, and they felt farther apart than they had ever been.

It is easy to picture the way they passed the night. Monsieur de Clèves' constancy had been nearly worn out by his effort to endure the unhappiness of seeing his wife, whom he adored, touched with love for another man. His courage was wellnigh exhausted; he even doubted whether this was an opportunity to make use of it, in a matter in which his pride and honor were so sorely wounded. He no longer knew what to think of his wife; he could not decide what course of action he should urge her to take nor how he should himself act; on all sides he saw nothing but precipices and steep abysses. At last, after long distress and uncertainty, reflecting that he should soon have to go to Spain, he made up his mind to do nothing that should confirm any one's suspicions or knowledge of his unhappy condition. He went to Madame de Clèves and told her that it was not worth while to discuss which of them had betrayed their secret, but that it was very important to prove that the story that had been told was a mere invention in no way referring to her; that it depended on her to convince Monsieur de Nemours and the rest of this; that she had only to treat him with the severity and coldness which she ought to have for a man who made love to her, and that in this way she would soon dispel the notion that she had any interest in him. Hence, he argued, there was no need of her distressing herself about what he might have thought, because if henceforth she should betray no weakness, his opinion would necessarily change; and above all, he urged upon her the necessity of going to the palace and into the world as much as usual.

When he had finished, Monsieur de Clèves left his wife without awaiting her answer. She thought what he had said very reasonable, and her indignation against Monsieur de Nemours made her think it would be very easy to carry it out; but she found it very hard to appear at all the wedding festivities with a calm face and an easy mind. Nevertheless, since she had been selected to carry the train of the dauphiness's dress,—a special honor to her alone of all the princesses,—she could not decline it without exciting much attention and wonder. Hence she resolved to make a great effort to control herself; but the rest of the day she devoted to preparations and to indulging the feelings that harassed her. She shut herself up alone in her room. What most distressed her was to have grounds for complaint against Monsieur de Nemours, with no chance of excusing him. She felt sure that he had told the story to the Vidame,—this he had acknowledged; and she felt sure too, from the way in which he spoke of it, that he knew that she was implicated. What excuse could be found for so great a piece of imprudence, and what had become of the prince's discretion, that had once so touched her? "He was discreet," she said to herself, "so long as he thought himself unhappy; but the mere thought of happiness, vague as it was, put an end to his discretion. He could not imagine that he was loved without wishing it to be known. He has said everything he could say. I have not confessed that it was he whom I loved; he suspected it, and showed his suspicions. If he had been sure of it, he would have done the same thing. I did wrong to think that there ever was a man capable of concealing what flattered his vanity. Yet it is for this man, whom I thought so different from other men, that I find myself in the same plight as other women whom I so little resemble. I have lost the love and esteem of a husband who ought to make me happy; soon every one will look upon me as a woman possessed by a mad and violent passion. The man for whom I feel it is no longer ignorant of it, and it is to escape just these evils that I have imperilled all my peace of mind, and even my life." These sad reflections were followed by a torrent of tears; but whatever the grief by which she felt herself overwhelmed, she knew that she could have endured it if she had been satisfied with Monsieur de Nemours.

This prince's state of mind was no more tranquil. His imprudence in unbosoming himself to the Vidame of Chartres, and the cruel results of this imprudence, caused him great pain. He could not without intense mortification recall Madame de Clèves' agitation and embarrassment. He could not forgive himself for having spoken about that affair in terms which, though courteous in themselves, must have seemed coarse and impolite, since they had implied to Madame de Clèves that he knew that she was the woman who was deeply in love, and with him. All that he could wish was a conversation with her; but he thought this more to be dreaded than desired. "What should I have to say to her?" he exclaimed. "Should I once more undertake to tell her what I have already made too clear to her? Shall I let her see that I know she loves me,—I, who have never dared to tell her that I loved her? Shall I begin by speaking to her openly of my passion, in order to appear like a man emboldened by hope? Can I think merely of going near her, and should I dare to embarrass her by my presence? How could I justify myself? I have no excuse, I am unworthy to appear before Madame de Clèves, and I do not venture to hope that she will ever look at me again. By my own fault, I have given her a better protection against me than any she sought, and sought perhaps in vain. By my imprudence I have lost the happiness and pride of being loved by the most charming and estimable woman in the world. If I had lost this happiness without her suffering, without having inflicted on her a bitter blow, that would be some consolation; and at this moment I feel more keenly the harm I have done her than I did when I was in her presence."

Monsieur de Nemours long tortured himself with these thoughts. The desire to see Madame de Clèves perpetually haunted him, and he began to look about for means of communicating with her. He thought of writing to her; but he considered, after his blunder, and in view of her character, that the best thing he could do would be to show his profound respect, and by silence and evident distress to make it clear that he did not dare to meet her, and to wait until time, chance, or her own interest in him should work in his favor. He resolved also to forbear from reproaching the Vidame of Chartres for his treachery, lest he should confirm his suspicions.

The betrothal of Madame Elisabeth, which was to take place on the morrow, and the wedding, which was to be celebrated on the following day, so occupied the court that Madame de Clèves and Monsieur de Nemours had no difficulty in concealing their grief and annoyance from the public. The dauphiness referred only lightly to their talk with Monsieur de Nemours, and Monsieur de Clèves took pains not to say anything more to his wife about what had happened, so that soon she found herself more at ease than she had supposed possible.

The betrothal was celebrated at the Louvre; and after the banquet and the ball, the whole royal household went to the bishop's palace to pass the night, as was the custom. The next morning the Duke of Alva, who always dressed very simply, put on a coat of cloth of gold, mingled with red, yellow, and black, and all covered with precious stones; on his head he wore a crown. The Prince of Orange, arrayed in equal splendor, came with his servants, and all the Spaniards with theirs, to fetch the Duke of Alva from the Villeroy mansion, where he was staying; and they started, walking four abreast, for the bishop's palace. As soon as they arrived, they went in due order to the church. The king conducted Madame Elisabeth, who also wore a crown; her dress was held by Mesdemoiselles de Montpensier and De Longueville; then came the queen, but not wearing a crown; after her came the dauphiness, the king's sister, Madame de Lorraine, and the Queen of Navarre, with princesses holding their trains. The queens and princesses had all their maids-of-honor magnificently dressed in the same colors that they themselves wore, so that the maids-of-honor could be at once distinguished by the colors of their dresses. They ascended the platform set up in the church, and the wedding ceremony took place. Then they returned to dinner at the bishop's palace, and at about five left for the palace, to be present at the banquet to which the parliament, the sovereign courts,[6] and the city officials had been invited. The king, the queens, the princes, and princesses ate at the marble table in the great hall of the palace, the Duke of Alva being seated near the new Queen of Spain. Below the steps of the marble table, on the king's right hand, was a table for the ambassadors, the archbishops, and the knights of the order,[7] and on the other side a table for the members of parliament.

The Duke of Guise, dressed in a robe of cloth of gold, was the king's major-domo, the Prince of Condé his head butler, the Duke of Nemours his cupbearer.[8] After the tables were removed, the ball began; it was interrupted by the ballets and by extraordinary shows; then it was renewed, until, after midnight, the king and all the court returned to the Louvre. Though Madame de Clèves was very much depressed, she yet appeared in the eyes of every one, and especially in those of Monsieur de Nemours, incomparably beautiful. He did not dare to speak to her, although the confusion of the ceremony

6. The Parliament of Paris was essentially a judicial body; the sovereign courts were legal courts of appeal.   7. The Order of the Knights of Malta, a military religious order which had led many battles against the Turks.   8. The positions of butler and cupbearer were honorific designations only for the duration of the ceremonies.

gave him many opportunities; but his demeanor was so dejected, and he showed such fear of approaching her, that she began to deem him less blameworthy, though he had not said a word in excuse of his conduct. His behavior was the same on the succeeding days, and continued to produce the same impression on Madame de Clèves.

At last the day of the tournament came. The queens betook themselves to the galleries and the raised seats set apart for them. The four champions appeared at the end of the lists, with a number of horses and servants, who formed the most magnificent spectacle ever seen in France.

The king's colors were plain black and white, which he always wore for the sake of Madame de Valentinois, who was a widow. The Duke of Ferrara and all his suite wore yellow and red. Monsieur de Guise appeared in pink and white: no one knew why he wore these colors; but it was remembered that they were those of a beautiful woman whom he had loved before she was married, and still loved, though he did not dare to show it. Monsieur de Nemours wore yellow and black,—why, no one knew. Madame de Clèves, however, had no difficulty in guessing: she remembered telling him one day that she liked yellow, and was sorry she was a blonde, because she could never wear that color. He believed that he could appear in it without indiscretion, because since Madame de Clèves never wore it, no one could suspect that it was hers.

Never was there seen greater skill than the four champions displayed. Although the king was the best horseman in the kingdom, it was hard to know to whom to give the palm.[9] Monsieur de Nemours showed a grace in all he did that inclined in his favor women less interested than Madame de Clèves. As soon as she saw him at the end of the lists she felt an unusual emotion, and every time he ran she could scarcely conceal her joy when he escaped without harm.

Toward evening, when all was nearly over, and the company on the point of withdrawing, the evil fate of the country made the king wish to break another lance. He ordered the Count of Montgomery, who was very skilful, to enter the lists. The count begged the king to excuse him, and made every apology he could think of; but the king, with some annoyance, sent him word that he insisted upon it. The queen sent a message to the king beseeching him not to run again, saying that he had done so well he ought to be satisfied, and that she entreated him to come to her. He answered that it was for love of her that he was going to run again, and entered the field. She sent Monsieur de Savoie to beg him again to come; but all was in vain. He started, the lances broke, and a splinter from that of the Count of Montgomery struck him in the eye and remained in it. He fell at

9. Award the victory. The palm was an ancient symbol of victory.

once to the ground. His equerries and Monsieur de Montgomery, one of the marshals of the field, ran up to him, and were alarmed to see him so severely wounded. The king was not alarmed; he said it was a slight matter, and that he forgave the count. It is easy to conceive the excitement and distress caused by this unhappy accident after a day devoted to merry-making. As soon as the king had been carried to his bed the surgeons examined his wound, which they found very serious. The constable at that moment recalled the prediction made to the king that he should be slain in single combat, and he had no doubt that the prophecy would come true.

As soon as the King of Spain, who was then in Brussels, heard of this accident, he sent his physician, a man of vast experience; but he thought the king's state desperate.

The court, thus distracted and torn by conflicting interests, was much excited on the eve of this great event; but all dissensions were quieted, and there seemed to be no other cause of anxiety than the king's health. The queens, the princes, and the princesses scarcely left his ante-chamber.

Madame de Clèves, knowing that she was compelled to be there and to meet Monsieur de Nemours, and that she could not hide from her husband the embarrassment that the sight of him would produce; knowing too that the mere presence of this prince would excuse him and overthrow all her plans,—decided to feign illness. The court was too busy to notice her conduct or to make out how much was true and how much feigned in her illness. Her husband alone could know the truth; but she was not sorry to have him know it, so she remained at home, thinking little of the great change that was impending, and perfectly free to indulge in her own reflections. Every one was with the king. Monsieur de Clèves came at certain hours to tell her the news. He treated her as he had always done, except that when they were alone his manner was a little colder and stiffer. He never spoke to her again about what had happened, and she lacked the strength and deemed it unwise to reopen the subject.

Monsieur de Nemours, who had expected to find a few moments to speak to Madame de Clèves, was much surprised and pained not to have even the pleasure of seeing her. The king grew so much worse that on the seventh day his physicians gave him up. He received the news of his approaching death with wonderful firmness, all the more admirable because he died by such an unfortunate accident, in the prime of life, full of happiness, adored by his subjects, and loved by a mistress whom he madly worshipped. The evening before his death he had Madame his sister married with Monsieur de Savoie, very quietly.

It is easy to conceive in what state was Madame de Valentinois. The queen did not permit her to see the king, and sent to her to ask

for the king's seals and for the crown jewels, which were in her keeping. The duchess asked if the king was dead; and when they told her
no, she said: "Then I have no master, and no one can compel me
to return what he intrusted to my hands."

As soon as he had died, at the castle of Tournelles, the Duke of
Ferrara, the Duke of Guise, and the Duke of Nemours conducted to
the Louvre the queen-dowager, the king,[1] and his wife the queen.
Monsieur de Nemours escorted the queen-dowager. Just as they were
starting, she drew back a little and told her daughter-in-law she was
to go first; but it was easy to see that there was more vexation than
politeness in this compliment.

Part V

The Cardinal of Lorraine had acquired complete ascendency over
the mind of the queen-dowager; the Vidame de Chartres had completely fallen from her good graces, but his love for Madame de
Martigues and his enjoyment of his freedom had prevented him from
suffering from this change as much as he might have done. During
the ten days of the king's illness the cardinal had had abundant leisure to form his plans and to persuade the queen to take measures in
conformity with his projects; hence as soon as the king was dead, the
queen ordered the constable to remain at the castle of Tournelles to
keep watch by the body of the late king and to take charge of the
customary ceremonies. This order kept him aloof from everything,
and prevented all action on his part. He sent a messenger to the king
of Navarre to summon him in all diligence, in order that they might
combine to oppose the promotion that evidently awaited the Guises.
The command of the army was given to the Duke of Guise; that of
the treasury to the Cardinal of Lorraine; the Duchess of Valentinois
was driven from the court; the Cardinal of Tournon, the avowed
enemy of the constable, was recalled, as well as the Chancelier Olivier, the open enemy of the Duchess of Valentinois, so that the
aspect of the court was completely changed. The Duke of Guise was
made equal to the princes of the blood, and allowed to carry the
king's mantle at the funeral; he and his brothers were placed high in
authority, not merely through the cardinal's influence over the queen,
but also because she believed that she could overthrow them if they
should offend her, while she would not be able to overthrow the
constable, who was supported by the princes of the blood.

After the funeral the constable went to the Louvre, but met with
a cold reception from the king. He desired to speak with the king in

1. The new king, Francis II, married to Mary Stuart, who became Mary, Queen of Scots after
her husband's death in 1560; the queen-dowager: the dead king's widow, Catherine de Médicis.

private; but the king called the Guises and told him in their presence
that he advised him to seek retirement, that the treasury and the
command of the army were already disposed of, and that whenever
he might need his counsels he should summon him. The queen-
dowager received him even more coldly than the king; she went so
far as to remind him of his insulting remark to the late king about
his children not looking like him. The King of Navarre arrived, and
was received no better. The Prince of Condé, who was less patient
than his brother, complained bitterly, but all in vain; he was exiled
from court under the pretext of sending him to Flanders to sign the
ratification of the treaty of peace.[2] The King of Navarre was shown
a forged letter of the King of Spain which accused him of making
attempts on his territory, and he was made to fear for his own possessions, and induced to return to his kingdom. The queen made
this easy for him by assigning to him the duty of escorting Madame
Elisabeth; she even obliged him to start before her, so that there was
no one left at court to oppose the power of the household of Guise.

   Although it was most unfortunate for Monsieur de Clèves that he
could not escort Madame Elisabeth, he still could not complain, in
view of the lofty rank of the man who was preferred; but the deprivation of the dignity was not what pained him, but rather that his
wife lost an opportunity of absenting herself from court without exciting
comment.

   A few days after the king's death it was decided that the court
should go to Rheims for the coronation. Madame de Clèves, who
had hitherto stayed at home under pretence of illness, begged her
husband to excuse her from accompanying the court, and to let her
go to Coulommiers to get strength from the change of air. He replied
that he would not ask her whether it was care for her health that
compelled her to give up the journey, but that he was willing she
should not take it. He readily consented to a plan he had already
decided on. High as was his opinion of his wife's virtue, he saw very
clearly that it was not well for her to be exposed longer to meeting a
man she loved.

   Monsieur de Nemours soon learned that Madame de Clèves was
not to accompany the court. He could not bear to think of leaving
without seeing her; and the day before he was to start he called on
her as late as he could, in order to find her alone. Fortune favored
him, and as he entered the courtyard he met Madame de Nevers and
Madame de Martigues coming out. They told him they had left her
alone. He went upstairs in a state of agitation that can only be compared with that of Madame de Clèves when his name was announced.
Her fear that he would mention his love; her apprehension lest she

---

2. Again, the Treaty of Cateau-Cambrésis, by which France gave up her claims in Italy.

should give him a favorable answer; the anxiety that this visit would give her husband; the difficulty of repeating or concealing everything that happened,—all crowded on her mind at once, and so embarrassed her that she determined to avoid the thing she desired most in the world. She sent one of her maids to Monsieur de Nemours, who was in the hall, to tell him that she was not feeling well, and much regretted that she could not have the honor of receiving him. It was a grievous blow to him that he could not see Madame de Clèves because she was unwilling to receive him. He was to leave the next day, and there was no chance of his meeting her. He had not spoken to her since their conversation at the crown princess's, and he had reason to believe that his mistake in speaking to the Vidame had shattered all his hopes; consequently, he went away in deep rejection.

As soon as Madame de Clèves had somewhat recovered from the agitation of the prince's threatened visit, all the arguments that had made her decline it vanished from her mind; she even thought she had made a mistake, and if she had dared, and there had still been time, she would have called him back.

Madame de Nevers and Madame de Martigues, after leaving her, went to the crown princess's and found Monsieur de Clèves there. The princess asked them where they had been. They said they had just come from Madame de Clèves', where they had spent the afternoon with a number of persons, and that they had left no one there except Monsieur de Nemours. These words, which they thought thoroughly insignificant, were quite the opposite for Monsieur de Clèves, although it must have been evident to him that Monsieur de Nemours could easily find opportunities to speak to his wife. Nevertheless, the thought that he was with her alone, and able to speak to her of his love, seemed to him at that moment such a new and unendurable thing that his jealousy flamed out with greater fury than ever. He was not able to stay longer with the dauphiness, but left, not knowing why he did so, or whether he meant to interrupt Monsieur de Nemours. As soon as he got home he looked to see if that gentleman was still there; and when he had the consolation of finding him gone, he rejoiced to think that he could not have stayed long. He fancied that perhaps it was not Monsieur de Nemours of whom he ought to be jealous; and although he did not really doubt it, he tried his best to do so: but so many things pointed in that direction that he could not long enjoy the happiness of uncertainty. He went straight to his wife's room, and after a little talk on indifferent matters, he could not refrain from asking her what she had done and whom she had seen. Observing that she did not mention Monsieur de Nemours, he asked her, trembling with excitement, if those were all she had seen, in order to give her an opportunity to mention him, and thus save him from the pain of thinking she was capable of deception. Since she had not seen him, she said nothing about him; whereupon Monsieur de Clèves, in a tone that betrayed his distress, asked:

"And Monsieur de Nemours, didn't you see him, or have you forgotten him?"

"I did not see him, in point of fact; I was not feeling well, and I sent my regrets by one of my maids."

"Then you were ill for him alone," he went on, "since you received everybody else? Why this difference for him? Why is he not the same to you as all the rest? Why should you dread meeting him? Why do you show him that you make use of the power his passion gives you over him? Would you dare to refuse to see him if you did not know that he is able to distinguish your severity from incivility? Why should you be severe to him? From a person in your position, Madame, everything is a favor except indifference."

"I never thought," answered Madame de Clèves, "that however suspicious you might be of Monsieur de Nemours, you would reproach me for not seeing him."

"I do, however," he went on, "and with good cause. Why do you decline to see him, if he has not said anything to you? But, Madame, he has spoken to you; had his silence been the only sign of his passion, it would have made no such deep impression. You have not been able to tell me the whole truth; you have even repented telling me the little you did, and you have not the strength to go on. I am more unhappy than I supposed,—I am the unhappiest of men. You are my wife, I love you devotedly, and I see you love another man! He is the most fascinating man at court, he sees you every day, he knows that you love him. And I," he exclaimed,—"I could bring myself to believe that you would overcome your passion for him! I must have lost my reason when I imagined such a thing possible."

"I don't know," replied Madame de Clèves, sadly, "whether you were wrong in judging such extraordinary conduct as mine so favorably; I don't feel sure that I was right in thinking that you would do me justice."

"Do not doubt it, Madame," said Monsieur de Clèves. "You were mistaken; you expected of me things quite as impossible as what I expected of you. How could you expect me to retain my self-control? Have you forgotten that I loved you madly and that I was your husband? Either case is enough to drive a man wild: what must it be when the two combine? And see what they do! I am torn by wild and uncertain feelings that I cannot control; I find myself no longer worthy of you,—you seem no more worthy of me. I adore you, and I hate you; I offend you, and I beg your pardon; I admire you, and I am ashamed of my admiration,—in a word, I have lost all my calmness, all my reason. I do not know how I have been able to live since you spoke with me at Coulommiers, and since the day when you learned from the dauphiness that your adventure was known. I cannot conjecture how it came out, or what passed between Monsieur de Nemours and you on this subject. You will never tell me, and I don't ask you to tell me; I beg of you only to remember that you have made me the unhappiest man in the world."

With those words Monsieur de Clèves left his wife's room, and went away the next morning without seeing her, although he wrote her a letter full of grief, consideration, and gentleness. She wrote him a touching answer, containing such assurances about her past and future conduct that, since they sprang from the truth and were her real feelings, the letter carried great weight with Monsieur de Clèves and calmed him somewhat. Moreover, since Monsieur de Nemours was also on his way to join the king, her husband had the consolation of knowing that he was separated from Madame de Clèves. Whenever she spoke with her husband, the love he showed her, the uprightness of his treatment of her, her own affection for him, and her sense of duty, made an impression on her heart which effaced all thought of Monsieur de Nemours. But this was only for a time; the remembrance of him soon returned with greater force than ever.

The first days after that prince had left, she scarcely noticed his absence; then it began to appear painful,—for since she began to love him, hardly a day had passed in which she had not either feared or hoped to see him; and it was to her a melancholy thought that chance could no longer make her meet him.

She went to Coulommiers, taking with her copies she had had made of the large pictures with which Madame de Valentinois had adorned her fine house at Anet.[3] All the memorable events of the king's reign were represented in these pictures. Among others was one of the Siege of Metz, with excellent likenesses of the principal officers, among whom was Monsieur de Nemours; and that was perhaps why Madame de Clèves cared for the pictures.

Madame de Martigues, having been unable to accompany the court, promised to spend a few days with her at Coulommiers. The queen's favor, which they both enjoyed, did not make them jealous or hostile; they were good friends, although they did not confide to each other everything. Madame de Clèves knew that Madame de Martigues loved the Vidame, but Madame de Martigues did not know that Madame de Clèves loved Monsieur de Nemours and was loved by him. The fact that she was a niece of the Vidame endeared her to Madame de Martigues; and Madame de Clèves was drawn

---

3. A château, about 40 miles east of Paris, built for her by Henri II.

toward her as a woman who, like herself, was in love, and with her lover's most intimate friend.

Madame de Martigues kept her promise, and went to Coulommiers. She found Madame de Clèves leading a most retired life,—indeed, she had sought absolute solitude, spending her evenings in the gardens, unaccompanied by her servants. She used to go into the summer-house where Monsieur de Nemours had overheard her talking with her husband, and enter the closet which opened on the garden. Her women and the servants would stay in the summer-house or in the other closet, coming to her only when they were called. Madame de Martigues had never seen Coulommiers; she was delighted with all the loveliness she found there, and especially with the comfort of this summer-house, in which she and Madame de Clèves spent every evening. Their solitude after dark, in the most beautiful place in the world, made easy prolonged talks between these two young women, who were both in love; and although they did not confide in each other, they delighted in talking together. Madame de Martigues would have been very sorry to leave Coulommiers if she had not been going to meet the Vidame; she went to Chambord, where was the whole court.

The new king was crowned at Rheims by the Cardinal of Lorraine, and the rest of the summer was to be spent at the castle of Chambord, then newly built. The queen manifested great pleasure at seeing Madame de Martigues again; and after giving expression to her joy, she asked after Madame de Clèves and what she was doing in the country. Monsieur de Nemours and Monsieur de Clèves were then with the queen. Madame de Martigues, who had been delighted with Coulommiers, described its beauty, and spoke at great length of the summer-house in the wood and of the pleasant evenings she had passed there with Madame de Clèves. Monsieur de Nemours, who was sufficiently familiar with the place to know what Madame de Martigues was talking about, thought that it might be possible to see Madame de Clèves there without being seen by her. He questioned Madame de Martigues, in order to get further information; and Monsieur de Clèves, who had kept his eyes on him while Madame de Martigues was talking, fancied that he detected his design. The questions that Monsieur de Nemours asked only strengthened his suspicions, so that he felt sure the duke intended to go to see his wife. He was right; this plan so attracted Monsieur de Nemours that after spending the night in devising plans to carry it into execution, the next morning he asked leave of the king to go to Paris on some pretext he had invented.

Monsieur de Clèves had no doubt about his reasons for going away, but he determined to seek information on his wife's conduct, and no longer to remain in cruel uncertainty. He desired to leave at the same time with Monsieur de Nemours, and from some place of concealment to discover what success he might have; but he feared lest their simultaneous absence might attract attention, or that Monsieur de Nemours might get wind of it and adopt other measures; so he determined to rely on one of the gentlemen in his suite, in whose fidelity and intelligence he felt confidence. He told him in what trouble he was, and what Madame de Clèves's virtue had been hitherto, and ordered him to follow in Monsieur de Nemours' footsteps, to watch him closely, and to see if he did not go to Coulommiers and enter the garden by night.

This gentleman, who was well suited for the duty, discharged it with the utmost exactness. He followed Monsieur de Nemours to a village half a league from Coulommiers, where the prince stopped, and the gentleman easily guessed that this was to await the approach of night. He did not think it well to wait there too, but passed through the village and made his way into the forest, to a spot which he thought Monsieur de Nemours would have to pass. He was not mistaken; as soon as night had fallen, he heard footsteps, and though it was dark, he easily recognized Monsieur de Nemours. He saw him walk about the garden as if to find out if he could hear some one, and to choose the most convenient spot for entering it. The palings were very high, and there were some beyond to bar the way, so that it was not easy to get in; nevertheless, Monsieur de Nemours succeeded. As soon as he had made his way into the garden, he had no difficulty in making out where Madame de Clèves was, as he saw many lights in the closet. All the windows were open; and creeping along the palings, he approached it with an emotion that can easily be imagined. He hid behind one of the long windows by which one entered the closet, to see what Madame de Clèves was doing. He saw that she was alone; she was so beautiful that he could scarcely control his rapture at the spectacle. It was warm, and her head and shoulders had no other covering than her loosely fastened hair. She was on a couch behind a table, on which were many baskets of ribbons; she was picking some out, and Monsieur de Nemours observed that they were of the same colors that he had worn in the tournament. He saw that she was fastening bows on a very peculiar stick that he had carried for some time and had given to his sister, from whom Madame de Clèves had taken it, without seeming to recognize it as belonging to Monsieur de Nemours. When she had finished her work with a grace and gentleness that reflected on her face the feelings that filled her heart, she took a light and drew near to a large table opposite the picture of the Siege of Metz, in which was the portrait of Monsieur de Nemours; then she sat down and gazed at this portrait with a rapt attention such as love alone could give.

It would be impossible to describe everything that Monsieur de Nemours felt at this moment. To see, in the deep night, in the most beautiful spot in the world, the woman he adored; to see her without her seeing him, busied with things that bore reference to him and to the hidden love she felt for him,—all that is something no other lover ever enjoyed or imagined.

Monsieur de Nemours was so entranced that he stood motionless, contemplating Madame de Clèves, without remembering that every moment was precious. When he had come to his senses again, he thought he ought to wait till she came into the garden before speaking to her; this he reflected would be safer, because then she would be farther from her maids. When, however, he saw that she remained in the closet, he decided to go in there. When he tried to do it, he was overwhelmed with agitation and with the fear of displeasing her. He could not bear the thought of seeing the face, just before so gentle, suddenly darken with anger and surprise.

He thought it madness, not his undertaking to see Madame de Clèves without being seen, but to think of showing himself; he saw everything that he had not before thought of. It seemed to him foolhardy to surprise at midnight a woman to whom he had never spoken of his love. He thought he had no right to assume that she would consent to listen to him, and he knew she would have good grounds for indignation at the danger to which he exposed her from the possible consequences of his acts. All his courage abandoned him, and more than once he was on the point of deciding that he would go back without seeing her. But he was so anxious to speak to her, and so encouraged by what he had seen, that he pushed on a few steps, though in such agitation that his scarf caught on the window and made a noise. Madame de Clèves turned her head; and whether it was that her mind was full of this prince, or that his face was actually in the light, she thought that she recognized him; and without hesitation or turning toward him, she rejoined her maids. She was so agitated that she had to trump up an excuse of not feeling well; and she said it also to attract their attention and thus give Monsieur de Nemours time to beat a retreat. After a little reflection she decided that she had been mistaken, and that the vision of Monsieur de Nemours was a mere illusion. She knew that he had been at Chambord, and she judged it extremely unlikely that he could have undertaken so perilous an enterprise; several times she was on the point of going back into the closet to see if there was any one in the garden. Perhaps she hoped as much as she feared to find Monsieur de Nemours there; but at last reason and prudence prevailed over every other feeling, and she decided that she should do better to stay where she was than to seek any further information. She was long in making up her mind to leave a place near which he might be, and it was almost morning when she returned to the castle.

Monsieur de Nemours stayed in the garden as long as he saw a light. He had not given up all hope of seeing Madame de Clèves again, although he was sure that she had recognized him and had only left in order to avoid him; but when he saw the servants locking the doors, he knew that he had no further chance. He retraced his steps, passing by the place where the friend of Monsieur de Clèves was in waiting. This gentleman followed him to the village, whence he had started in the evening. Monsieur de Nemours determined to spend the whole day there, in order to return to Coulommiers that night, to see if Madame de Clèves would be cruel enough to flee from him, or not to let him look at her. Although he was highly delighted to find that her mind was occupied with him, he was deeply pained to see her so instinctively taking flight.

Never was there a tenderer or intenser love than that which animated this prince. He strolled beneath the willows beside a little brook which ran behind the house in which he was concealed. He kept himself out of sight as much as possible, that no one might know of his presence. He gave himself up to the transports of love, and his heart was so full that he could not keep from shedding a few tears; but these were not of grief, they were tempered with all the sweetness that only love can give.

He recalled all Madame de Clèves' actions since he had fallen in love with her,—the honorable and modest severity with which she had treated him, although she loved him. "For she does indeed love me," he exclaimed; "she loves me,—I cannot doubt it. The most fervent protestations, the greatest favors, are no surer tokens than those I have received; and yet she treats me with the same austerity as if she hated me. I thought time would bring a change, but I can expect nothing more from it; I see her always on her guard against me and against herself. If she did not love me, I should try to please her; but I do please her, she loves me, and hides her love. What then am I to hope,—what change in my fate can I expect. What! the most charming woman in the world loves me, and I cannot enjoy the supreme happiness that comes from the first certainty of being loved, except in the agony of being ill-treated! Show, fair princess," he called aloud, "that you love me; show me that you really feel! If you will only once let me hear from you what your feelings are, I am willing that you should resume for ever the severity with which you overwhelm me. At least look at me with those eyes that I saw gazing at my portrait. Could you look at it with such gentleness, and then flee from me so cruelly? What do you fear? Why do you so dread my love? You love me, and you hide your love to no purpose; you have yourself given me tokens of it unawares. I know my good fortune: let me enjoy it, and cease making me unhappy. Is it possible that Madame de Clèves loves me, and I am still unhappy? How beautiful she was last night! How could I resist my longing to fling myself at her feet? Had I done so, I might have prevented her flight; my respectful bearing would have reassured her. But perhaps she did not recognize me,—I distress myself more than I should; and the sight of a man at such an extraordinary hour frightened her."

These thoughts haunted Monsieur de Nemours all day. He awaited the night with impatience, and when it had come he took once more the road to Coulommiers. The friend of Monsieur de Clèves, having assumed a disguise to avoid being recognized, followed him as he had done the previous evening, and saw him enter the same garden. Then Monsieur de Nemours perceived that Madame de Clèves was unwilling to run the risk of his trying to see her; every entrance was closed. He wandered in every direction to find some light, but his search was vain.

Madame de Clèves, suspecting that Monsieur de Nemours might come back, stayed in her own room; she feared lest strength to flee should be denied her, and she did not wish to risk the possibility of speaking to him in a manner that might contradict her previous conduct. Although Monsieur de Nemours had no hope of seeing her, he could not make up his mind to leave at once a place where she had been so often. He spent the whole night in the garden, finding some slight consolation in at least gazing on the same objects which she saw every day. The sun had risen before he thought of leaving; but at last the fear of being observed compelled him to go.

It was impossible for him to return without seeing Madame de Clèves; hence he went to see Madame de Mercœur, who was then living in her house not far from Coulommiers. She was extremely surprised at her brother's arrival. He invented some specious excuse for his journey, which completely deceived her, and at last managed so cleverly that she herself proposed their calling on Madame de Clèves. This plan they carried out that very day, and Monsieur de Nemours told his sister that he would leave her at Coulommiers to return with all speed to the king. He devised this plan of parting from her at Coulommiers in the hope that she would be the first to leave; in this way he imagined he could not fail to have an opportunity of speaking to Madame de Clèves.

When they reached Coulommiers, they found Madame de Clèves walking in a broad path along the edge of the flower-garden. The sight of Monsieur de Nemours embarrassed her not a little, and made her sure that it was he whom she had seen the previous night. This conviction filled her with anger that he should have been so bold and imprudent. He noticed with pain her evident coldness. The talk ran on insignificant subjects, and yet he succeeded in displaying so much wit and amiability, and so much admiration for Madame de Clèves, that he finally dispelled some of her coolness, in spite of her determination not to be appeased.

When he had got over his first timidity, he expressed great curiosity to see the summer-house in the wood; he described it as the most delightful spot in the world, and with so many details that Madame de Mercœur said he must have often seen it, to be so familiar with all its beauty.

"Still, I do not believe," answered Madame de Clèves, "that Monsieur de Nemours has ever been in it; it has been finished only a very short time."

"It is not long, either, since I was there," he retorted, looking at her; "and I do not know whether I ought not to be very glad that you have forgotten having seen me there."

Madame de Mercœur, who was busy looking at the garden, paid no attention to what her brother was saying. Madame de Clèves, blushing, and casting down her eyes so as not to see Monsieur de Nemours, said:

"I do not remember ever having seen you there, and if you ever have been there, it was without my knowledge."

"It is true, Madame," he said, "that I have been there without your permission, and I have spent there the most blissful and the most wretched moments of my life."

Madame de Clèves knew only too well what he meant; but she made no answer. She was thinking how she should keep Madame de Mercœur from going into the closet which contained the portrait of Monsieur de Nemours: this she did not want her to see. She succeeded so well that the time passed imperceptibly, and Madame de Mercœur spoke of leaving; but when Madame de Clèves noticed that Madame de Mercœur and her brother were not going away together, she saw the impending danger, and was as much embarrassed as she had been in Paris, and she decided on the same course. Her fear lest this visit should only confirm her husband's suspicions helped her to form this decision, and in order to prevent Monsieur de Nemours from being alone with her, she told Madame de Mercœur that she would accompany her to the edge of the forest, and ordered her carriage to follow her. This prince's grief at finding Madame de Clèves as austere as ever was so keen that he turned pale. Madame de Mercœur asked him if he was ill; but he looked at Madame de Clèves without being seen by any one, and let her see that he was suffering from nothing but despair. Nevertheless, he was compelled to let them go without daring to follow them; and after what he had said, he could not go back with his sister. He returned to Paris, and left it the next day.

Monsieur de Clèves' friend had watched him all the while. He also returned to Paris; and when he saw that Monsieur de Nemours had left for Chambord, he took the post in order to get there before him, and to make his report about his expedition. His master was awaiting his return to determine his life's unhappiness.

As soon as Monsieur de Clèves saw him, he read in his expression and his silence that he had brought only bad news. He remained for some time overwhelmed with grief, his head bowed, unable to speak; then he motioned to him to withdraw. "Go," he said; "I see what you have to tell me, but I am not strong enough to hear it."

"I have nothing to report," answered the gentleman, "from which it is possible to form an accurate judgment. It is true that Monsieur de Nemours entered the garden in the woods two nights running, and called at Coulommiers the next day with Madame de Mercœur."

"That is enough," replied Monsieur de Clèves, "that is enough"; and then, again motioning to him to leave, he added, "I have no need of further information."

The gentleman was forced to leave his master plunged in despair. Never, perhaps, has there been more poignant grief, and few men who possessed so much spirit and so affectionate a heart as Monsieur de Clèves have suffered the agony of discovering at the same time a wife's infidelity and the mortification of being deceived by a woman.

Monsieur de Clèves was overwhelmed by this grievous blow. That same night he was seized with a fever of such severity that at once his life was in peril. Word was sent to Madame de Clèves, and she went to him with all speed. He was worse when she reached him, and she noticed something cold and icy in his manner toward her that greatly surprised and pained her. He even seemed to be annoyed at the attention she paid him; but at last she thought this was perhaps a result of his illness.

As soon as Madame de Clèves had arrived at Blois, where the court was at that time, Monsieur de Nemours was filled with joy at knowing that she was in the same place as himself. He tried to see her, and called at the house every day, under pretext of inquiring after Monsieur de Clèves; but it was all in vain. She never left her husband's room, and was very anxious about him. Monsieur de Nemours regretted that she suffered so much; he readily saw how this grief would be likely to rekindle her love for Monsieur de Clèves, and how this affection would prove a dangerous foe to the love she bore in her heart. This feeling depressed him for some time; but the extreme seriousness of Monsieur de Clèves' illness soon gave him new hopes. He saw that Madame de Clèves would soon be free to follow her own wishes, and that in the future he might find lasting happiness. This thought filled him with almost painful rapture, and he banished it from his mind, lest he should be too miserable if his hopes were disappointed.

Meanwhile Monsieur de Clèves was almost given up. One of the last days of his illness, after he had passed a very bad night, he said, toward morning, that he would like to rest. Madame de Clèves alone stayed in his room. It seemed to her that, instead of resting, he was very uneasy; she went up to him and knelt down by his bed, with her face covered with tears. Monsieur de Clèves had made up his mind to say nothing about his grievance against her; but her attentions and her sorrow, which seemed genuine, and which he sometimes regarded as tokens of deceit and treachery, produced such conflicting and painful feelings that he could not repress them.

"You, Madame," he said, "are shedding a great many tears for a death of which you are the cause, and which cannot give you the sorrow which you display. I am no longer able to reproach you," he went on, in a voice weakened by illness and grief, "but I am dying of the cruel suffering you have inflicted on me. Was it necessary that so extraordinary an action as that of speaking to me as you did at Coulommiers should have so little result? Why confide to me your love for Monsieur de Nemours, if your virtue was not strong enough to resist it? I loved you so that I was glad to be deceived,—I confess it to my shame; I have since longed for the false tranquillity of which you robbed me. Why did you not leave me in the calm blindness in which so many husbands are happy? I should perhaps have never known that you loved Monsieur de Nemours. I am dying," he went on; "but bear it in mind that you make me welcome death, and that since you have robbed me of the love and esteem I felt for you, I dread living. What would life be to me, if I had to spend it with a woman I have loved so much and who has so cruelly deceived me, or if I had to live apart from her, after a scene of violence utterly repugnant to my disposition and to the love I bear you? My love for you, Madame, has been far deeper than you know; I have concealed the greater part of it, from fear of tormenting you or of lessening your esteem by a manner unbecoming to a husband; I really deserved your affection. I say it once more: I die without regret, since I could not win this, and now can no longer wish for it. Farewell, Madame. Some day you will mourn a man who had for you a true and lawful love. You will know the misery that overtakes women who fall into these entanglements, and you will learn the difference between being loved as I loved you, and being loved by men who, while protesting their love, seek only the honor of misleading you. But my death will leave you free, and you will be able to make Monsieur de Nemours happy without doing anything criminal. What do I care what may happen when I shall be no more? Must I be weak enough to look upon it?"

Madame de Clèves was so far from imagining that her husband could suspect her that she listened to him without understanding what he was saying, and supposing that he was blaming her interest in Monsieur de Nemours. At last, suddenly grasping his meaning, she exclaimed,—

"I a criminal! The very thought of it never entered my head. The severest virtue could command no different course of conduct than mine, and I have not done one thing of which I should not be glad to have you an eye-witness."

"Should you have been glad," asked Monsieur de Clèves, looking at her somewhat disdainfully, "to have had me for an eye-witness of the nights you spent with Monsieur de Nemours? Ah! Madame, am I speaking of you when I speak of a woman who has spent nights with a man?"

"No," she answered, "no; it is not of me that you are speaking,— I have never passed nights or moments with Monsieur de Nemours; he has never seen me in private; I have never had anything to do with him or listened to him, and I will swear—"

"Say no more," interrupted Monsieur de Clèves; "false oaths or a confession would give me equal pain."

Madame de Clèves could not answer; her tears and her grief choked her. At last, making a great effort, she said: "Look at me, at least; listen to me. If it concerned me alone, I should endure these reproaches; but it is your life that is at stake. Listen to me for your own sake; it is impossible that, with all the truth on my side, I should not convince you of my innocence."

"Would to God that you could convince me!" he exclaimed. "But what can you say to me? Was not Monsieur de Nemours at Coulommiers with his sister, and had he not passed the two previous nights with you in the garden in the forest?"

"If that is my crime," she replied, "I can clear myself easily. I don't ask you to believe me, but believe your servants: ask them if I was in the garden the evening Monsieur de Nemours came to Coulommiers, and if I didn't leave it the evening before, two hours earlier than usual."

She then told him how she had imagined she saw some one in the garden, and confessed that she had thought it was Monsieur de Nemours. She spoke with such earnestness, and the truth, even when improbable, carries such weight, that Monsieur de Clèves was almost convinced of her innocence.

"I do not know," he said, "whether I dare believe you; I am so near death that I do not want to see anything that might make me long to live. Your explanation comes too late; but it will always be a consolation to think that you are worthy of the esteem I have had for you. I beg of you to let me have the additional consolation of knowing that my memory will be dear to you, and that if it had depended on you, you would have had for me the feeling you have had for another."

He wanted to go on; but a sudden faintness made it impossible, and Madame de Clèves summoned the physicians. They found him almost lifeless. Nevertheless he lingered a few days longer, and at last died, having displayed admirable firmness.

Madame de Clèves was almost crazed by the intensity of her grief. The queen at once came to see her, and carried her to a convent, without her knowing whither she was going. Her sisters-in-law brought her to Paris before she was yet able to realize her afflictions. When she began to be strong enough to think about it, and saw what a husband she had lost, and reflected that she was the cause of his death by means of her love for another man, the horror she felt at herself and at Monsieur de Nemours cannot be described.

At first this prince did not venture to pay her any other attentions than such as etiquette required. He knew Madame de Clèves well enough to be sure that anything more marked would displease her; but what he learned later assured him that he would have to maintain this reserve for a long time. One of his equerries told him that Monsieur de Clèves's gentleman,[4] a friend of his, had told him, in his deep regret for the loss of his master, that Monsieur de Nemours's trip to Coulommiers was the cause of his death. Monsieur de Nemours was extremely surprised to hear this; but on thinking it over, he made out a part of the truth, and conjectured what would be the feelings of Madame de Clèves, and how she would detest him if she thought her husband's illness had been due to jealousy. He thought that the best thing would be not to have his name brought to her notice, and he regulated his conduct accordingly, painful as he found it.

The prince went to Paris, and could not refrain from calling on Madame de Clèves to ask how she was. He was informed that she saw no one, and had even given orders that she was not to be told who had inquired after her. Possibly these rigid orders were given solely on account of the prince, and to avoid hearing his name mentioned. But Monsieur de Nemours was too desperately in love to be able to live with absolutely no chance of seeing Madame de Clèves. He resolved to try every means, no matter how difficult, to escape from such an unendurable condition of affairs.

The princess's grief passed all bounds of reason. Her dying husband,—dying for her sake, and filled with such tender love for her,—was never absent from her mind; she continually recalled everything she owed him, and blamed herself for not having loved him,—as if

---

4. Attendant. *Equerries*: Personal attendants.

that were a thing that depended on her will. Her sole consolation was the thought that she mourned him as he deserved, and that for the rest of her life she would only do what he would have approved if he had lived.

She had often wondered how he knew that Monsieur de Nemours had come to Coulommiers; she did not suspect that the prince had spoken of it, and it even seemed to her that it was immaterial whether he had said anything about it, so thoroughly rid of her passion did she feel. Nevertheless, she was deeply distressed to think that he was the cause of her husband's death, and she remembered with sorrow the fear that had tormented Monsieur de Clèves on his deathbed lest she should marry him; but all these various sources of grief were lost in that over her husband's death, and the others sank into insignificance.

After many months had passed, she recovered from her violent grief, becoming sad and languid. Madame de Martigues made a visit to Paris, and saw her repeatedly during her stay there. She talked with her about the court and of all that had happened; and although Madame de Clèves seemed to take no interest, Madame de Martigues went on talking in order to divert her. She told her all about the Vidame, Monsieur de Guise, and all the other men of note.

"As for Monsieur de Nemours," she said, "I do not know whether his occupations have taken the place of gallantry, but he is less cheerful than he used to be; he shuns the society of women; he continually runs up to Paris, and I believe is here now."

Monsieur de Nemours's name surprised Madame de Clèves and made her blush; she changed the subject, and Madame de Martigues did not notice her confusion.

The next day, the princess, being anxious to find some occupation suitable for her condition, went to see a man living close by who worked in silk in a peculiar way, with the intention of undertaking something of the sort herself. After looking at what he had to show, her eyes fell on the door of a room in which she thought there were some more, and asked to have it opened. The man replied that he did not have the key, and that it was occupied by a man who came there sometimes to draw the fine houses and gardens to be seen from the windows. "He is the handsomest man in the world," he went on, "and does not seem obliged to support himself by his work. Whenever he comes here, I see him always looking at the houses and gardens, but I have never seen him at work."

Madame de Clèves listened with great attention; what Madame de Martigues had said about Monsieur de Nemours coming some times to Paris, as well as her vision of this handsome man who had taken quarters near her house, made her think of that prince, and suggested that he was trying to see her. This thought produced in her an agitation which she could not understand. She went to the windows to see on what they looked, and saw that it was on her garden and her own apartment; and when she was in her room she saw the same window to which she had been told that the stranger used to come. The conjecture that it was Monsieur de Nemours entirely altered the current of her thoughts; she no longer felt the sad tranquillity which she had begun to enjoy,—she was uneasy and agitated. At last, unable to endure her loneliness, she went out to take the air in a garden in the faubourgs,[5] where she expected to find solitude. At first she supposed no one was there; the place seemed deserted, and she strolled about for some little time.

After passing through a little thicket, she saw at the end of the path, in the most retired part of the garden, a sort of summer-house open on all sides, and she turned in that direction. When she had got near it, she saw a man lying on the benches who seemed sunk in deep thought, and she recognized Monsieur de Nemours. At the sight of him she stopped short; but her servants, who were following her, made some noise that aroused him. Without looking at them, he arose, to avoid their company, and turned into another path, bowing deeply, so that he was unable to see whom he was saluting.

Had Monsieur de Nemours known from whom he was running away, he would have eagerly retraced his steps; but as it was, he followed the path and went out by a sidegate, at which his carriage was waiting. This incident made a deep impression on Madame de Clèves' heart; all her love was suddenly rekindled with its former fervor. She went on and sat down in the place which Monsieur de Nemours had just left, and there she remained, completely overwhelmed. Her mind was full of this prince, more fascinating than any man in the world; loving her long with respect and constancy; giving up everything for her; respecting even her grief; trying to see her, without himself being seen; abandoning the court, where he was a favorite, to look upon the walls behind which she was immured, to come and muse in places where he could not hope to meet her,— in short, a man worthy to be loved for his love alone, and for whom she felt a passion so violent that she would have loved him even if he had not loved her, and one moreover of a lofty nature perfectly in harmony with her own. Duty and virtue could not restrain her emotions; every obstacle vanished; and of all her past she remembered nothing but her love for Monsieur de Nemours and his for her.

All these thoughts were new to the princess; she had been so lost in grief for her husband's death that she had given them no attention. With the sight of Monsieur de Nemours they all recurred to

5. Suburbs.

her. But when they came fastest, and she remembered that this same man whom now she thought of as able to marry her was the one she had loved during her husband's lifetime and was the cause of his death; that on his deathbed he had manifested his fear lest she should marry him,—her rigid virtue was so pained by the thought that it seemed to her quite as grievous a crime to marry Monsieur de Nemours as it had been to love him while her husband was living. She gave herself up to these reflections, which were so hostile to her happiness, and confirmed them by many arguments concerning her peace of mind and the evils she foresaw in case she married him. At last, after spending two hours there, she returned home, convinced that she ought to avoid the sight of him as a real obstacle to her duty.

But this conviction, the product of reason and virtue, did not control her heart, which remained attached to Monsieur de Nemours with a violence that reduced her to a most restless and pitiable state. That night was one of the unhappiest she had ever known. In the morning her first thought was to go to see if there was any one at the window which commanded her house; she looked out and saw Monsieur de Nemours. This surprised her, and she drew back so quickly that he felt sure she must have recognized him. This he had long wished might happen, since he had devised this method of seeing her; and when it seemed hopeless, he used to go and meditate in the garden where she had seen him.

Worn out at last by grief and uncertainty, the duke made up his mind to find some way of determining his fate. "Why should I wait?" he asked. "I have long known she loved me; she is free, and duty no longer stands in her way. Why should she force me to see her without being seen by her and with no chance to speak to her? Can love have so absolutely destroyed my reason and my boldness that I am not what I was when in love before? I was bound to respect Madame de Clèves' grief; but I have respected it too long, and I am giving her time to forget the affection she feels for me."

Thereupon he began to devise some way of seeing her. He fancied that there was no good reason for concealing his love from the Vidame of Chartres, and he resolved to speak to him and to confide to him his plans about his niece. The Vidame was then in Paris, like all the rest of the court, who had come to town to make their preparations for accompanying the king, who was to escort the Queen of Spain. Accordingly, Monsieur de Nemours called on the Vidame and frankly told him everything he had kept hidden until then, except Madame de Clèves' feelings, which he did not wish to appear to know.

The Vidame heard him with great pleasure, and answered that, with no knowledge of his feelings, he had often, since Madame de Clèves had become a widow, thought that she was the only woman worthy of him. Monsieur de Nemours besought his aid in getting a chance to address her, in order to find out her intentions.

The Vidame proposed taking him to call on her; but Monsieur de Nemours feared that she would not like this, because she did not yet see any one. They decided that the Vidame should invite her to come and see him on some pretext or other, and that Monsieur de Nemours should enter by a hidden staircase, in order not to be seen. This was carried out according to their plans. Madame de Clèves came; the Vidame went to receive her, and led her into a small room at the end of his apartment. Shortly after, Monsieur de Nemours came in, as if by chance. Madame de Clèves was much surprised to see him; she blushed, and tried to hide her blushes. The Vidame began to talk about unimportant subjects, and then went away, under the pretext of having some orders to give. He asked Madame de Clèves to do the honors in his place, and said he should return in a moment.

It would be impossible to express the feelings of Monsieur de Nemours and Madame de Clèves when they for the first time found themselves alone and free to talk. They remained for a long time without a word; then at last Monsieur de Nemours broke the silence. "Will you, Madame, forgive the Vidame," he said, "for having given me an opportunity to see you and to speak with you, which you have always cruelly denied me?"

"I ought not to forgive him," she replied, "for having forgotten my position and to what he exposes my reputation." As she uttered these words she started to leave; but Monsieur de Nemours delayed her, saying:

"Do not be alarmed, Madame; no one knows that I am here, and there is no danger. Listen to me, Madame,—if not through kindness, at least through love of yourself, and in order to protect yourself against the extravagances to which I shall certainly be led by an uncontrollable passion."

For the first time Madame de Clèves yielded to her tenderness for Monsieur de Nemours, and looking at him with eyes full of gentleness and charm, she said: "But what do you hope from the kindness that you ask of me? You would certainly regret obtaining it, and I should regret granting it. You deserve a happier fate than you have yet had, and can have in the future, unless you seek it elsewhere."

"I, Madame, find such happiness elsewhere! Is there any other happiness than winning your love? Although I have never spoken with you, I cannot think that you are ignorant of my affection, or that you do not know that it is truer and warmer than ever. How much it has been tried by events unknown to you, and how much by your severity!"

"Since you wish me to speak, and I decide it best," answered Madame de Clèves, sitting down, "I will do so, with a frankness that you will not always find in women. I shall not tell you that I have not noticed your attachment to me,—perhaps you could not believe me if I were to say so; I confess, then, not only that I have noticed it, but also just as you wished it to appear."

"And, Madame, if you have seen it," he interrupted, "is it possible that you have not been touched by it; and may I venture to ask if it has made no impression on your heart?"

"You should have judged of that from my conduct," she replied; "but I should be glad to know what you have thought of it."

"I should have to be in a happier condition to dare to tell you," he answered, "and my fate has too little relation with what I should say. All that I can tell you, Madame, is that you would not have confessed to Monsieur de Clèves what you concealed from me, and that you would have concealed from him what you would have let me see."

"How were you able to find out," she asked, blushing, "that I confessed anything to Monsieur de Clèves?"

"I heard it from your own lips, Madame," he replied; "but as an excuse for my boldness in listening to you, consider whether I misused what I had heard, whether my hopes were strengthened by it, whether I became bold enough to speak to you."

He began to tell her how he had heard her conversation with Monsieur de Clèves: but she interrupted him in the middle.

"Say no more," she said; "I now see how you came to know too much: that you did, was very plain to me at the dauphiness's when she had heard the story from those to whom you had told it."

Monsieur de Nemours then explained to her how that had happened.

"Do not apologize," she resumed; "I forgave you a long time ago, before you told me how it occurred. But since you have yourself heard from me what I had meant to keep a secret from you all my life, I confess that you have inspired me with emotions unknown before I saw you, and so unfamiliar to me that they filled me with a surprise which greatly added to the agitation they produced. I confess this with the less shame because I may now do it innocently, and you have seen that my feelings did not guide my actions."

"Do you believe, Madame," exclaimed Monsieur de Nemours, falling on his knees, "that I am not ready to die at your feet with joy and rapture?"

"I only tell you," she answered, smiling, "what you already know only too well."

"Ah! Madame," he said, "what a difference between finding something out by accident, and hearing it from you, and seeing that you wish me to know it."

"It is true," said she, "that I wish you to know it, and that I take pleasure in telling you. I am not certain that I do not tell it more from love of myself than from love of you; for certainly this avowal will have no consequences, and I shall follow the rigid rules that my condition imposes."

"You will not think of such a thing, Madame," replied Monsieur de Nemours; "you are bound by no further duty; you are free; and if I dared, I should even tell you that it depends on you so to act that your duty shall some day oblige you to preserve the feelings that you have for me."

"My duty," she replied, "forbids my ever thinking of any one, and of you last of all, for reasons unknown to you."

"Perhaps they are not, Madame," he pleaded; "but those are no true reasons. I have reason to believe that Monsieur de Clèves thought me happier than I was, and imagined that you approved of mad freaks of mine which my passion suggested without your knowledge."

"Let us not speak of that affair," she said. "I cannot bear the thought of it; it fills me with shame, and its consequences were too painful. It is only too likely that you are the cause of Monsieur de Clèves' death; the suspicions you aroused, your inconsiderate conduct, cost him his life as truly as if you had taken it with your own hands. Think of what I should do if you had come to such extremities and the same unhappy result had followed. I know very well this is not the same thing in the eyes of the world; but in mine there is no difference, for I know it was from you he got his death, and on account of me."

"Oh! Madame," interposed Monsieur de Nemours, "what phantom of duty do you oppose to my happiness? What! Madame, a vain and baseless fancy can prevent your making happy a man you do not hate, when he has conceived the hope of passing his life with you, his fate leading him to love you as the best woman in the world, finding in you every charming trait, incurring not your hatred, and seeing in you everything that best becomes a woman,—for, Madame, there is no other woman who combines what you do. Men who marry their mistresses who love them, tremble from fear lest they should renew their misconduct with others; but nothing of the sort is to be feared in you: you are only to be admired. Can I have foreseen such felicity only to find you raising obstacles? Ah! Madame, you forget that you chose me from other men,—or rather, you did not; you made a mistake, and I have flattered myself."

"You did not flatter yourself," she replied; "the reasons for my acting as I do would not, perhaps, seem to me so strong, had I not chosen you as you suspect,—and that is what makes me foresee unhappiness if I should take an interest in you."

"I have no answer," he said, "when you show me that you fear unhappiness; but I confess that, after all you have been good enough to say to me, I did not expect to be opposed by such a cruel argument." "It is so far from uncomplimentary to you," she answered, "that I shall even find it hard to tell it to you."

"Alas! Madame, what you can fear will flatter me too much after what you have just said to me?"

"I wish still to speak to you as frankly as I began," she explained, "and I want to dispense with all the reserve and formalities that I should respect in a first conversation; but I beg of you to listen to me without interruption.

"I think it but a slight reward for your affection that I should hide from you none of my feelings, but should let you see them exactly as they are. This probably will be the only time in my life that I shall take the liberty of letting you see them; nevertheless, I cannot confess to you without deep shame that the certainty of not being loved by you as I am, seems to me a horrible misfortune; that if there were not already insurmountable claims of duty, I doubt if I could make up my mind to risk this unhappiness. I know that you are free, as I am, and that we are so situated that the world would probably blame neither of us if we should marry; but do men keep their love in these permanent unions? Ought I to expect a miracle in my case, and can I run the risk of seeing this passion, which would be my only happiness, fade away? Monsieur de Clèves was perhaps the only man in the world capable of keeping his love after marriage. My fate forbade my enjoying this blessing. Perhaps, too, his love only survived because he found none in me. But I should not have the same way of preserving yours; I believe that the obstacles you have met have made you constant; those were enough to make you yearn to conquer them, and my involuntary actions,—things you learned by chance,—gave you enough hope to keep you interested."

"Oh! Madame," replied Monsieur de Nemours, "I can no longer maintain the silence you impose on me; you do me too much injustice, and you let me see how far you are from being prejudiced in my favor."

"I confess," she said, "that I may be moved by my emotions, but they cannot blind me; nothing can prevent my seeing that you are born with every disposition for gallantry, and with all the qualities proper to secure speedy success. You have already been in love several times,—you would be again very often. I should not make you happy; I should see you interested in another as you have been in me: this would inflict on me a mortal blow, and I should never feel sure that I should not be jealous. I have said too much to try to hide from you that you have already made me feel this passion, and that I suffered cruel tortures that evening when the queen gave me that letter from Madame de Themines which was said to be directed to you, and that the impression left on me is that jealousy is the greatest unhappiness in the world.

"Vanity or taste makes all women try to secure you; there are few whom you do not please,—my own experience teaches me that there are few whom you might not please. I should always imagine that you were loved and in love, and I should not be often wrong. Yet in this condition I could only suffer,—I should not dare to complain. One may make reproaches to a lover, but can a woman reproach her husband for ceasing to love her? If I could become hardened to that misfortune, could I become hardened to imagining that I saw Monsieur de Clèves charging you with his death, reproaching me for loving you, and showing the difference between his affection and yours? It is impossible to resist such arguments; I must remain in my present position and in my immovable determination never to leave it."

"But do you think you can, Madame?" exclaimed Monsieur de Nemours. "Do you think that your resolutions can hold out against a man who worships you and is fortunate enough to please you? It is harder than you think, Madame, to resist what pleases us and one who loves us. You have done it by an austere virtue which is almost without a precedent; but this virtue no longer conflicts with your emotions, and these I hope you will follow, in spite of yourself."

"I know that there is nothing harder than what I undertake; I mistrust my own strength, supported by all my arguments. What I think due to the memory of Monsieur de Clèves would be ineffectual, if it were not reinforced by my anxiety for my own peace of mind; and these arguments need to be strengthened by those of duty. But though I mistrust myself, I think I shall never overcome my scruples, and I do not hope to overcome my interest in you. It will make me unhappy, and I shall deny myself the pleasure of seeing you, whatever pain this may cost me. I am in a position which makes that a crime which at any other time would be permissible, and mere etiquette forbids that we should meet."

Monsieur de Nemours flung himself at her feet and gave expression to all the emotion that filled him. He manifested, by his words and tears, the liveliest and tenderest passion that heart ever felt. Madame de Clèves was not unmoved; and looking at Monsieur de Nemours with eyes heavy with tears, she exclaimed,—

"Why must I charge you with the death of Monsieur de Clèves? Why did I not learn to know you when I was free; or why did I not know you before I was married? Why does fate divide us by such an insuperable obstacle?"

"There is no obstacle," pleaded Monsieur de Nemours; "you alone thwart my happiness, you alone impose a law which virtue and reason could not impose."

"It is true," she replied, "that I make a great sacrifice to a duty which exists only in my imagination. Wait to see what time will do. Monsieur de Clèves has but just died, and that fatal event is too recent for me to judge clearly. Meanwhile you have the pleasure of having won the love of a woman who would never have loved had she not seen you; be sure that my feelings for you will never change and will always survive, whatever I do.

"Good by," she said. "This conversation fills me with shame. Repeat it to the Vidame; I give my consent,—nay, I beg of you to do so."

With these words she left the room, Monsieur de Nemours being unable to prevent her. She found the Vidame in the next room. He saw her so agitated that he did not dare to speak to her, and he handed her to her carriage without a word. He went back to Monsieur de Nemours, who was in such a whirl of joy, sadness, surprise, and admiration,—in short, so possessed by all the emotions that spring from a passion full of hope and dread,—that he seemed beside himself. It was long before the Vidame got any clear notion of what they had said; finally, however, he succeeded; and Monsieur de Chartres, without being the least in love, had no less admiration for the virtue, intelligence, and worth of Madame de Clèves than had Monsieur de Nemours himself. They tried to determine the prince's probable chances; and whatever the fears that love might arouse, the prince agreed with the Vidame that it was impossible that Madame de Clèves should persist in her resolutions. Nevertheless, they agreed to follow her orders, from fear lest, if the duke's love for her should become known, she should in some way bind herself, and would not change from fear of its being thought that she had loved him while her husband was living.

Monsieur de Nemours determined to join the king, as he could no longer stay away, and he made up his mind to start without even trying to see Madame de Clèves again. He begged the Vidame to speak to her. He told him a number of things to say to her, and suggested countless arguments with which to overcome her scruples. At last a good part of the night was gone before Monsieur de Nemours thought of leaving to seek repose.

Madame de Clèves was in no condition to find rest; it was for her such a new thing to lay aside the reserve which she had imposed upon herself, to permit a man to tell her that he loved her, to confess that she too was in love, that she did not recognize herself. She was amazed at what she had done, and repented it bitterly; she was also made happy by it,—she was completely upset by love and agitation. She went over once more the arguments in defence of her duty which stood in the way of her happiness; she lamented their strength, and regretted having stated them so strongly to Monsieur de Nemours. Although the thought of marrying him had occurred to her the moment she saw him again in the garden, it had not made so deep an impression on her as had her talk with him; and at moments she could scarcely believe that she would be unhappy if she should marry him. She would have liked to be able to say that she was wrong both in her scruples about the past and in her fears for the future. At other moments reason and duty convinced her of the opposite, and decided her not to marry again or ever to see Monsieur de Nemours; but this resolution was extremely repugnant to her when her heart was so much moved and had so recently seen the joys of love. At last, in order to allay her agitation, she thought it was not necessary for her to do herself the violence of forming a decision,—etiquette left her still much time for making up her mind; but she resolved to abide by her determination to have nothing to do with Monsieur de Nemours meanwhile.

The Vidame came to see her, and pleaded his friend's cause with all possible skill and earnestness; but he could not persuade her to modify her own conduct or that which she had imposed on Monsieur de Nemours. She told him that she did not mean to change her present condition, that she knew it would be hard for her to carry out this intention, but that she hoped she should be strong enough to do so. She showed him how firmly convinced she was that Monsieur de Nemours had caused her husband's death, and that she should do wrong in marrying him; so that the Vidame feared it would not be easy to convince her of the opposite. He did not confide to this prince what he thought, and when he reported his talk with her, he let him enjoy all the hope that reason can awaken in a man who is loved.

The next day they left to join the king. The Vidame, at the request of Monsieur de Nemours, wrote to Madame de Clèves, in order to speak of him; and in a second letter, which soon followed, Monsieur de Nemours added a few lines himself. But Madame de Clèves, who did not wish to infringe her rules, and who feared the perils of correspondence, told the Vidame that she should decline to receive his letters if he continued to write about Monsieur de Nemours; and this she said so earnestly that this prince himself begged his friend never to mention his name.

The court left to escort the Queen of Spain as far as Poitou. Madame de Clèves was left to herself during their absence, and the farther she was removed from Monsieur de Nemours and from anything that could remind her of him, the more she recalled the memory of Monsieur de Clèves, which she was bent on keeping ever present before her. Her reasons for not marrying Monsieur de Nemours seemed strong so far as her duty, and irrefutable so far as her tranquillity, was concerned. The fading of his love after marriage, and all the pangs of jealousy, which she regarded as certain, showed her the misery to which she would expose herself; but she saw too that she had assumed an impossible task in undertaking to resist the most fascinating of men, whom she loved and who loved her, in a matter which offended neither virtue nor propriety. She decided that only separation could give her strength; and this she felt that she needed, not merely to maintain her determination not to marry, but also to protect herself from the sight of Monsieur de Nemours. Hence she resolved to make a long journey during the time that etiquette forced her to spend in retirement. Some large estates that she owned in the Pyrénées seemed to her the best place she could choose. She started a few days before the court returned; and just before leaving, she wrote to the Vidame to beg that no one should inquire after her or write to her.

Monsieur de Nemours was as much afflicted by her absence as another man would have been by the death of the woman he loved. The thought of this long separation from Madame de Clèves was a constant source of suffering, especially after he had tasted the pleasure of meeting her and seeing that she loved him. He could do nothing but grieve, and his grief increased daily. Madame de Clèves, as a result of all her agitation, fell seriously ill after her arrival at her country place, and news of this reached the court. Monsieur de Nemours was inconsolable, and fell into the most unbounded despair. The Vidame had great difficulty in keeping him from letting his love be seen, as well as from following after her to find out how she was. The Vidame's relationship and intimacy served as a pretext for sending constant letters. At last word came that she had passed the turning point of her dangerous illness, but was still so weak that all were very anxious.

This long and near view of death enabled Madame de Clèves to judge mundane matters in a very different spirit from that of health. Her imminent peril taught her indifference to everything, and the length of her illness enforced this upon her. Yet when she had recovered, she found that she had not wholly forgotten Monsieur de Nemours; but she summoned to her aid every argument she could devise against marrying him. The conflict was a stern one; but at last she conquered what was left of this passion, which was already diminished by her reflections during her illness. The thought of death had revived her memory of Monsieur de Clèves; and this, harmonizing with her sense of duty, made a strong impression on her heart. The affections and ties of the world appeared to her as they appear to persons of enlarged views. Her health, which was still delicate, helped her to preserve those feelings; but knowing how circumstances affect the wisest resolutions, she was unwilling to run the risk of seeing her own altered, or of returning to the place where lived the man she had loved. Under the pretext of needing change of air, she withdrew to a religious house, without making known her determination to leave the court.

When Monsieur de Nemours heard of this, he at once saw what a decisive step it was, and feared that he had no more ground for hope. Yet the destruction of his hopes did not prevent his doing his utmost to bring about her return; he made the queen write to her, and even persuaded the Vidame to visit her: but it was all to no purpose. The Vidame saw her; she did not tell him that she had resolved upon this, but he decided that she would never return. At last Monsieur de Nemours went himself, under the pretext of going to the baths.[6] She was much moved and astonished when she heard that he had come. She sent him a message by one of her trusty companions that she begged him not to be surprised if she was unwilling to run the risk of seeing him again and of having the feelings she felt bound to maintain swept away by his presence; that she wanted him to know that having found her duty and her peace of mind unalterably opposed to her interest in him, everything else in the world seemed so indifferent that she had abandoned it entirely, had given all her thoughts to another life, and had no other feeling left but her desire to have him share the same sentiments.

Monsieur de Nemours thought he should die of grief in the presence of the woman who brought this message. He begged her twenty times to go back to Madame de Clèves, to entreat her to let him see her; but she told him that Madame de Clèves had forbidden her, not only to bring her any message from him, but even to repeat to her what he might say. At last he had to leave, as completely overwhelmed with grief as a man could be who had lost all hopes of ever seeing again a woman whom he loved with the most violent and the most natural passion possible. Yet he did not yield even then; he did everything he could to induce her to alter her decision. At last, when years had passed, time and separation allayed his grief and extinguished his passion. Madame de Clèves led such a life that it was evident she meant never to go into the world again; part of each year she spent in this religious house, and the other part at home, but in retirement, busied with severer tasks than those of the austerest convents. Her life, which was not long, furnished examples of the loftiest virtue.

6. At a resort or spa where bathing, usually in natural springs, is part of the medical treatment.

JEAN RACINE
1639–1699

Racine's capacity to communicate the full intensity of passion in tragedies marked by their formal decorum and their elevated tone gave him immediate and lasting fame among French dramatists. He brings to material adapted from classic texts an immediacy of psychological insight to which twentieth-century audiences readily respond.

Born into the family of a government official in the Valois district, eighty miles from Paris, Racine attended the College de Beauvais. Later (1655–1659), he studied in the Jansenist center of Port-Royal. (Jansenism, a strict Catholic movement emphasizing moral self-examination and severely controlled conduct, exercised a profound influence on Racine.) In 1660, encouraged by the poet Jean de la Fontaine, Racine came to Paris, where his early plays failed, driving him to a period of seclusion in Provence. When he returned to Paris in 1663, however, the court and the nobility patronized him, and he rapidly developed a reputation as a major playwright. In 1677 he left Paris and returned to Port-Royal, an environment appropriate to his increasing interest in religious thought. He married Catherine de Romanet, who bore him seven children, most of whom became nuns or priests. Remaining in the country, he wrote history, made short trips to Paris, and traveled as historiographer with Louis XIV's campaigns. Buried at Port-Royal, he was exhumed in 1711 and reburied next to Pascal at the church of St. Étienne-du-Mont in Paris.

Only one of Racine's twelve plays, an early comedy, deviated from the tragic mode. His first tragedies imitated the work of his contemporary, Pierre Corneille; later, he chose Biblical and classical models. *Phaedra* (1677) adapts, with new emphasis, the action of Euripides' *Hippolytus*, making the guilty woman rather than the relatively passive man the protagonist and using the highly charged sexual situation between the two to generate intense psychological drama. To twentieth-century readers, the play's most immediately obvious aspect may be its conventional formalities: long declamatory speeches, stylized exchanges in compressed half lines, the artificiality of conveying such complicated relationships and histories through the action of a single day. Such devices, however—which would have seemed as artificial to seventeenth-century audiences as they do to us, although more familiar—intensify the impact of the central characters' anguish and their desperate attempts to deal with it. If the play's surface is formal, its depths seethe with passion.

Passion, of course, is the subject of *Phaedra*. The conflict between reason and passion that preoccupied many thinkers in the late seventeenth and early eighteenth centuries here plays itself out with stark urgency. Passion triumphs, in *Phaedra*, over all principles of control, bringing death to the two central characters and misery to their survivors. As in Greek tragedy, although by rather different means, the reader feels not only the self-destructiveness of the human psyche but the pathos and the heroism of the doomed effort to transcend the limits of the given.

The play opens not with Phaedra herself but with Hippolytus, meditating about his heroic father, Theseus. Like Molière, Racine uses the family as microcosm of larger social orders, but the intense conflicts that throb beneath the surface in many real-life families here undergo no comic transformation. Hippolytus has his own problems, quite apart from Phaedra. Blessed and burdened with a larger-than-life father, he must choose whether to try to imitate that father or to seek other ways of being a man. "I sucked the pride which so amazes you / From an Amazonian mother," he tells his friend Theramenes, alluding to the "proud, disdainful sentiments" that have prevented him from feeling interest in any woman. But matters cannot remain so simple. Theseus has distinguished himself in two ways: by heroic womanizing (he leaves a trail of women behind him wherever he goes) and by heroic action, the conquering and destruction of monsters human and inhuman. As the play opens, Hippolytus acknowledges in himself the first incursions of love. No longer can his adolescent defense, his refusal of any resemblance to his father, serve him. When Theseus returns, Hippolytus will beg permission to seek his own heroism:

> Before
> You reached my present age, already
> More than one tyrant, more than one grim monster
> Had felt your mighty strength. . . .
> Suffer my courage to be used at last.

He wants, he says, even by death to "prove to all the world / I was your son." By the time he makes this plea, however, his innocent desire to prove his manhood, to declare his separateness from and worthiness of his father, has been overwhelmed by darker forces.

Phaedra's impulses are less innocent—less "natural," she suggests. In a poignant passage, she imagines Hippolytus and his youthful beloved, Aricia, expressing their love in a natural setting, themselves a part of the natural world. She understands her own sin as an internal revolution of feeling against control; she speaks of desperately seeking her "lost reason" in the entrails of sacrifices she makes to Venus, trying to avert her fate. Never does she excuse herself, never does she believe herself justified in loving the son of the man who kidnapped her into marriage. When Theseus is thought dead, Phaedra declares herself unworthy to rule a nation because she cannot rule herself. Yet such moral awareness fails to help her: knowing her sin, she continues to enact it, at least in feeling. The play evokes the full torment of such experience.

As for powerful Theseus, conqueror of women, defier of the supernatural, ally of Neptune—this kingly figure returns to find himself powerless at home. The son and wife who by social convention exist in utter subordination to him turn into enemies he has no capacity to master. First his wife's nurse tells him that his son has attempted to seduce Phaedra. The rivalry of sons and fathers lies deep: if sons fear they can never equal their fathers, fathers fear that the young necessarily overcome the old. Theseus believes the nurse's bare assertion, unsupported by substantial evidence. He banishes his son and invokes Neptune's power to destroy him. Then Aricia's hints lead him to suspect his wife, who confesses her own emotional sin while already on the verge of self-inflicted death. Theseus remains alone, bereft, his tyrannical impulse now devoid of domestic object. His own passions, too quickly fired—jealous possessiveness of his wife, jealous rivalry with his son—have deprived him of two beings he loved.

The play provides no villains. Phaedra, in other versions of the story a monster of lust, here becomes a woman struggling against her nature, as profoundly committed to standards of control as to the violent feelings that overthrow them. Hippolytus, in the process of self-discovery, at a delicate balance point of maturity, cannot protect himself against the alternations of closely linked love and hate in a woman whose passions, and whose self-awareness, far exceed his. Theseus, in the ignorance of success, fails in comprehension, not understanding himself, his wife, or his son. All three exemplify the pathos and the dignity of the human struggle to be human.

Phaedra dies with the word *purity* on her lips, seeking self-purification in death, the only course now possible to her. Hippolytus dies in the beauty of his youth, deprived of age's suffering and fulfillment. Theseus lives to try once more to rule adequately, perhaps chastened by suffering into greater awareness. The names of the Greek gods survive in this drama: Aphrodite torments Phaedra, Neptune serves Theseus' impetuous will. But the gods now function as projections of human passion: Phaedra's sexual lust, Theseus' lust for power. Phaedra's torment suggests a Christian effort at purification, a Christian ideal of self-denial. The drama, in Racine's handling of the ancient story, projects upon a giant screen conflicts all men and women undergo, the surge of feeling warring with the ideal of self-restraint. By concentrating the play of passions within a small family group and a confined space of time, while recalling connections between the characters' feelings and historical events that lie behind them; by giving Theseus and Phaedra heroic dignity and stature; by linking this family with the fate of nations, Racine forces his readers to feel the intensity and the large significance of feelings and happenings that might in other treatments seem merely sordid. He gives his characters timeless reality—speaking to his time, and to ours.

To translate Racine into English involves particularly difficult problems, since the French Alexandrine couplet, composed of twelve-syllable lines, does not adapt naturally to English verse. Kenneth Muir's version, in blank verse, sacrifices rhyme for the sake of easy movement but succeeds in approximating the high dignity of the original.

A useful biography of Racine is A. F. B. Clark, *Racine* (1939). G. Brereton, *Jean Racine: A Critical Biography* (1951), combines biography with literary criticism. Valuable critical insight is provided by O. de Mourgues, *Racine: Or, The Triumph of Relevance* (1967).

Phaedra[1]

Dramatis Personæ

THESEUS, *King of Athens*
PHAEDRA, *his wife*

1. Translated by Kenneth Muir.

HIPPOLYTUS, *son of Theseus and Antiope*
ARICIA, *Princess of the blood royal of Athens*
THERAMENES, *tutor to Hippolytus*
ŒNONE, *nurse and confidante of Phaedra*
ISMENE, *confidante of Aricia*
PANOPE, *woman of Phaedra's suite*
GUARDS

SCENE—*Troezen*

Act I

SCENE 1. *Hippolytus and Theramenes*

HIPPOLYTUS. It is decided, dear Theramenes.
  I'm leaving now, and cutting short my stay
  In pleasant Troezen. In my state of doubt
  I blush at my own sloth. Six months and more
  My father has been absent, yet I stay   5
  Still ignorant of his fate, not even knowing
  In what part of the world he hides his head.
THERAMENES. Where will you seek him then? I have already,
  My lord, to satisfy your natural fears,
  Crossed the Corinthian sea, and asked for Theseus   10
  Upon those distant shores where Acheron[2]
  Is lost among the dead. I went to Elidos
  And sailed from Tenaros upon the sea
  Where Icarus[3] once fell. By what new hope,
  Or in what lucky region will you find   15
  His footprints now? Who knows, indeed, who knows
  Whether it is the King your father's will,
  That we should try to probe the mystery
  Of his long absence? While we are afraid,
  Even for his life, that hero, unperturbed,   20
  Screening from us his latest love exploit,
  May just be waiting till a woman . . .
HIPPOLYTUS.   Stop,
  Dear Theramenes; respect the King
  Who has outgrown the headstrong faults of youth.   25
  No such unworthy obstacle detains him.
  Phaedra has conquered his inconstancy,
  And fears no rival now. In seeking him,

2. A river that flows into Hades; across it Charon ferried the dead.   3. Son of Daedalus. Escaping from Crete by means of wings made by his father, Icarus flew so high that the sun melted the wax holding his wings and he fell to his death.

I do my duty, and thereby escape
A place I dare not stay in.   30
THERAMENES.   Since when, my lord,
   Have you been frightened of the peaceful place
   You used to love in childhood? You once preferred it
   To the noisy pomp of Athens and the court.
   What danger, or rather, should I say, what grief   35
   Drives you away?
HIPPOLYTUS.   Alas, that happy time
   Is now no more. For everything has changed
   Since to these shores the gods despatched the Queen,
   The daughter of Minos and of Pasiphaë.[4]   40
THERAMENES. I know the cause indeed; for Phaedra here
   Vexes and wounds your sight—a dangerous
   Stepmother, who had scarce set eyes on you
   Ere she procured your exile. But her hatred
   Is either vanished, or at least relaxed.   45
   Besides, what perils can you undergo
   From a dying woman, one who seeks to die?
   Phaedra, who will not speak about her illness,
   Tired of herself and even of the sunshine,
   Is scarcely hatching plots against you.   50
HIPPOLYTUS.   No:
   Her vain hostility is not my fear.
   In leaving her, I flee another foe:
   I flee—I will admit it—young Aricia,
   Last of a fatal race that has conspired   55
   Against us.
THERAMENES. What? Do you yourself, my lord,
   Persecute her? The Pallantids' lovely sister[5]
   Was not involved in her treacherous brothers' plots.
   And should you hate her innocent charms?   60
HIPPOLYTUS.   If I
   Did hate her, I would not be fleeing.
THERAMENES.   My lord,
   May I explain your flight? Is it that you
   No longer are that proud Hippolytus,   65
   Relentless enemy of the laws of love,
   And of a yoke to which your father bowed
   So many times? Does Venus whom your pride

---

4. Phaedra was the daughter of King Minos of Crete and of Pasiphaë, sister to Circe. Enamored of a white bull sent by Poseidon, Pasiphaë consequently gave birth to the Minotaur, the Cretan monster later killed by Theseus. Phaedra was thus half-sister to the Minotaur.   5. The Pallantids were the fifty sons of Pallas, Pandion's second son. Aegeus, father of Theseus, was Pandion's adopted son. Theseus killed all the Pallantids because they threatened his kingship of Athens; their "lovely sister" is Aricia.

So long has slighted wish to justify
The amorous Theseus? While, like the rest of mortals,   70
You're forced to cense her altars? Are you in love,
My lord?
HIPPOLYTUS. What do you dare to ask, my friend?
You have known my heart since it began to beat,
And can you ask me to repudiate   75
My former proud, disdainful sentiments?
I sucked the pride which so amazes you
From an Amazonian mother;[6] and when I reached
A riper age, and knew myself, I gloried
In what I was. Then in your friendly zeal   80
You told me all my father's history.
My soul, attentive to your voice, was thrilled
To hear the tale of his heroic deeds—
Consoling mortals for Alcides' absence,[7]
By slaying monsters, putting brigands down,   85
Procrustes, Cercyon, Sciron, and Sinis,
The scattered bones of the giant of Epidaurus,
Crete reeking with the Minotaur's foul blood.
But when you told of deeds less glorious,
The way his faith was pledged a hundred times—   90
Helen of Sparta[8] stolen from her kin,
Salamis witness of Periboea's tears,
And many more, whose names he has forgotten,
Of credulous women by his love deceived:
Ariadne on her rocky isle   95
Telling her wrongs;[9] and Phaedra at the last,
Kidnapped, but under better auspices;
You know how listening to the sorry tale
I begged you cut it short, and would have been
Happy to blot out from my memory   100
The worser half of the tale. And shall I now
Be bound so ignominiously by the gods?
My base affections, unlike those of Theseus,
Can claim no heap of honors as excuse,
And so deserve more scorn. As I have slain   105
No monster yet, I have not earned the right
So to transgress; and if my pride must melt,

---

6. Hippolytus't mother was Antiope, sister of Hippolyta, queen of the Amazons.
7. Hercules.   8. Daughter of Zeus and Leda, later the wife of Menelaus of Sparta (and the
cause of the Trojan War). In her girlhood she was abducted by Theseus and Peirithous; her
brothers rescued her and brought her back home. Periboea, the mother of Ajax, was one of the
women Theseus seduced and abandoned.   9. Ariadne, Phaedra's sister, was abandoned by Theseus
on the island of Naxos after she rescued him from the Minotaur.

Should I have chosen for my conqueror
Aricia? Surely my wandering senses
Should have recalled that we are kept apart   110
By an eternal obstacle. My father
Holds her in reprobation, and forbids her
Ever to marry: of a guilty stem
He fears a shoot, and wishes to entomb
With her the memory of her brothers' name.   115
Under his tutelage until she dies,
Never for her shall Hymen's fires be lit.[1]
Should I support her rights against a father
Incensed against her, give example to
Temerity, and let my youth embark   120
Upon a wild sea? . . .

THERAMENES.   If your hour is come,
My lord, heaven cares not for our reasons. Theseus,
Wishing to shut your eyes, has opened them.
His hatred, rousing a rebellious flame,   125
Lends a new luster to his enemy.
But, after all, why fear an honest love?
If it is sweet, why should you not dare taste it?
Why will you trust a shy or sullen scruple?
Or fear to walk where Hercules once trod?   130
What spirits had not Venus tamed? And where
Would you be, you who fight against her, if
Antiope,[2] always to her laws opposed,
Had not with modest ardor burned for Theseus?
But why do you affect a haughty speech?   135
Confess that all is changed: and for some days
You're seen less often, proud and solitary,
Racing the chariot on the shore, or skilled
In the art of Neptune, making the wild steeds
Obedient to the bit. The forest echoes   140
Less often to our shouts. Your eyes are heavy,
Charged with a secret passion. There is no doubt:
You love, you burn; you perish from an illness
Which you conceal. And are you now in love
With charming Aricia?   145

HIPPOLYTUS.   Theramenes,
I'm setting off in quest of my lost father.

THERAMENES. Won't you see Phaedra, my lord, before you go?

HIPPOLYTUS. So I intend; and you may tell her so.

1. I.e., she will never marry: Hymen was the god of marriage.   2. As an Amazon, Hippolytus'
mother Antiope was committed to chastity.

I'll see her—since my duty thus ordains.   150
But what's the new misfortune which disturbs
Her dear Œnone?

SCENE 2. *Hippolytus, Theramenes, Œnone*

ŒNONE. Alas! my lord, what trouble
  Can equal mine? The Queen has nearly reached
  Her fatal term. In vain both night and day   155
  I've watched beside her. She's dying of a sickness
  She hides from me; and in her spirit reigns
  Continual disorder. Restless affliction
  Now drags her from her bed to see once more
  The light of day; and her deep grief demands   160
  That all should keep away. She's coming now.
HIPPOLYTUS. It is enough. I'll leave this place to her,
  And not offend her with my hated face.

SCENE 3. *Phaedra and Œnone*

PHAEDRA. Let's go no further, dear Œnone, stay.
  I've reached the limit of my strength; my eyes   165
  Are blinded by the daylight, and my knees
  Give way beneath me.
ŒNONE.   O all-powerful Gods,   [*She sits.*]
  May all our tears appease you!
PHAEDRA.   How these vain   170
  Adornments, how these veils, now weigh me down.
  What busy hand, in tying all these knots,
  Has taken care to gather on my brow
  This heavy load of hair? Now all afflicts me,
  Hurts me, and conspires to hurt me.
ŒNONE.   How   175
  Her wishes seem now to destroy each other!
  Madam, it was yourself, with your own hands,
  Who dressed and decked your hair, wishing to show
  Yourself, and see once more the light of day.   180
  But now you see it, ready to hide yourself,
  You hate the day you sought.
PHAEDRA.   O shining Sun,[3]
  Author of my sad race, thou of whom my mother
  Boasted herself the daughter, who blush perhaps   185
  At these my sufferings, I see you now
  For the last time.
ŒNONE.   What! have you not lost

---

3. Helios, the sun-god, was the father of Phaedra's mother Pasiphaë.

That cruel desire? And shall I see you still
Renouncing life and making of your death   190
The dreadful preparations?
PHAEDRA.   O that I were seated
  In the forest shade, where through a cloud of dust
  I could behold a chariot racing by!
ŒNONE. What, madam?   195
PHAEDRA.   Fool! Where am I? What have I said?
  Where have my wits been wandering? I have lost them.
  The gods have robbed me of them. I blush, Œnone.
  I let you see too much my shameful sorrows,
  And, spite of me, my eyes are filled with tears.   200
ŒNONE. If you must blush, blush rather at your silence
  Which but augments your griefs. Deaf to our pleading,
  Rebellious to our care, and without pity,
  Do you wish to end your days? What madness now
  Stops them in mid-career? What spell or poison   205
  Has drained their source? Three nights have come and gone
  Since sleep last entered in your eyes; three days
  Have chased the darkness since you took some food.
  What frightful scheme are you attempting now?
  For you insult the gods who gave you life,   210
  Betray the husband to whom your faith is given,
  Betray your hapless children whom you throw
  Under a rigorous yoke. Think that one day
  Will snatch their mother from them, and give up
  Their hopes to the stranger's son, to that proud foe   215
  Of you, and of your blood, the Amazon's son,
  Hippolytus.
PHAEDRA.   Ah Gods!
ŒNONE.   Does this reproach—?
PHAEDRA. Wretch! What name has issued from your mouth?   220
ŒNONE. You are right to be angry: I like to see you tremble
  At that ill-omened name. Then live! Both love and duty
  Reanimate you. Live. Do not let the son
  Of the Scythian,[4] crushing your children with his rule,   225
  Command the noblest blood of Greece and heaven.
  But don't delay: each moment threatens life.
  Repair your weakened strength, while yet life's torch
  Can be rekindled.
PHAEDRA.   I have too much prolonged   230
  Its guilty span.
ŒNONE.   What! are you torn apart

4. Scythia, home of the Amazons, was for the Greeks associated with barbarians.

By some remorse? What crime could have produced
Such agony? Your hands were never stained
With innocent blood.   235

PHAEDRA.   Thanks to the gods, my hands
Are guiltless still. But would to heaven my heart
Were innocent as they!

ŒNONE.   What frightful scheme
Have you conceived to terrify your heart?   240

PHAEDRA. I have said enough. Spare me the rest. I die
Because I cannot such confession make.

ŒNONE. Die then; and keep inhuman silence still.
But seek another hand to close your eyes.   245
Although there but remains a feeble flame
In you, my soul will journey to the dead
Before you, since there are a thousand ways
By which we can go thither—mine the shortest.
Cruel! When have I betrayed your confidence?
Think, that my arms received you at your birth,   250
For you I've left my country and my children.
Is this the price of my fidelity?

PHAEDRA. What fruit can come from so much violence?
You would be horror-struck if I should tell you.

ŒNONE. What will you say to me more horrible   255
Than seeing you expire before my eyes?

PHAEDRA. But when you know my crime and the dread fate
That crushes me, I shall die just the same,
And die more guilty.

ŒNONE.   Madam, by all the tears   260
That I have shed for you, by your weak knees
That I embrace now, free my mind from doubt.

PHAEDRA. You wish it: rise.

ŒNONE.   Speak: I am listening.

PHAEDRA. What shall I say? And where shall I begin?   265

ŒNONE. Cease to insult me by these needless fears.

PHAEDRA. O hate of Venus and her fatal wrath!
Love led my mother into desperate ways.

ŒNONE. Forget them, madam. Let an eternal silence
Hide their remembrance.

PHAEDRA.   My sister, Ariadne,[5]   270
Stricken with love, upon a desolate coast
Despairing died.

ŒNONE.   What are you doing, madam?
What mortal spite enkindles you today   275

---

5. Ariadne died on Naxos after Theseus' desertion of her.

Against your nearest . . . ?
PHAEDRA.   Since Venus so ordains,
  Last and most wretched of my tragic race,
  I too shall perish.
ŒNONE.   Are you in love?   280
PHAEDRA. All of love's frenzies I endure.
ŒNONE.   For whom?
PHAEDRA. You're going to hear the last extreme of horror.
  I love . . . I shudder at the fatal name . . .
  I love . . .   285
ŒNONE.   Whom do you love?
PHAEDRA.   You know the son
  Of the Amazon—the prince I've harshly used.
ŒNONE. Hippolytus! Great Gods!
PHAEDRA.   'Tis you have named him. 290
  Not I.
ŒNONE. O righteous heaven! The blood in my veins
  Is turned to ice. O crime! O hapless race!
  Disastrous voyage! O unlucky coast!
  Why did we travel to your perilous shores?   295
PHAEDRA. My evil comes from a more distant place.
  Scarce had I wedded Theseus and established
  My happiness it seemed, I saw in Athens
  My haughty foe. I saw him—blushed and blanched
  To see him—and my soul was all distraught.   300
  My eyes were blinded, and I could not speak.
  I felt my body freeze and burn; I knew
  The terrible fires of Venus, the tortures fated
  To one whom she pursues. I hoped to avert them
  By my assiduous prayers. I built for her   305
  A temple, and took pains to adorn its walls.
  Myself surrounded by the sacrifices,
  I sought for my lost reason in their entrails.
  Weak remedies of love incurable!
  In vain upon the altars I burnt incense;   310
  My lips implored the goddess, but I worshipped
  Only Hippolytus; and seeing him
  Each day even at the altar's foot
  I offered all to the god I dared not name.
  I shunned him everywhere. O heavy weight   315
  Of misery! My eyes beheld the son
  In the father's countenance. At length I dared
  To rebel against myself. I spurred my spirit
  To persecute him, striving thus to banish
  The enemy I worshipped by assuming   320

A stepmother's proverbial cruelty.
I clamored for his exile till my cries
Tore my dear enemy from his father's arms.
I breathed again, Œnone. In his absence
My calmer days flowed by in innocence,   325
Compliant to my husband, while my griefs
Lay hidden. I bore him children. But in vain
Were all precautions, for Fate intervened.
Brought by my husband to Troezen, once more
I saw the enemy I had sent away.   330
My keen wound bled again—it is no more
A passion hidden in my veins, but now
It's Venus fastened on her helpless prey.
I have a just abhorrence of my crime;
I hate my life, abominate my lust;   335
Longing by death to rescue my good name
And hide my black love from the light of day.
Your tears have conquered me. I have confessed
All my dark secret; and I won't regret it
If you respect now my approaching death,   340
And do not wound me with unjust reproofs,
Or with vain remedies keep alive within me
The last faint spark of life.

      SCENE 4. *Phaedra, Œnone, Panope*

PANOPE.   I would prefer
To hide these tidings from you, madam, but   345
I must reveal them. Death has robbed you now
Of your unconquerable husband, and
It is known to all but you.
ŒNONE.   What do you say?
PANOPE. That the mistaken Queen in vain demands   350
Theseus' return from heaven; and that from ships
Arrived in port, Hippolytus, his son,
Has just heard of his death.
PHAEDRA.   Heaven!
PANOPE.   For the choice 355
Of ruler, Athens is divided. Some
Vote for the Prince, your son, and others, madam,
Forgetting the laws of the State, dare give their voices
To the son of the stranger.[6] It is even said
An insolent faction has designed to place   360

---

6. Athenian law made the son of an Athenian and a non-Greek woman illegitimate; Hippolytus'
mother was Antiope the Amazon. It is not clear why Phaedra's children are not similarly classified.

Aricia on the throne. I thought you should
Be warned about this danger. Hippolytus
Is ready to depart, and it is feared,
If he becomes involved in this new storm,
Lest he draw to him all the fickle mob.   365
ŒNONE. No more, Panope. The Queen has heard you,
And won't neglect your warning.

SCENE 5. Phaedra and Œnone

ŒNONE. I had ceased,
Madam, to urge that you should live. Indeed,
I thought that I should follow you to the grave;   370
I had no further voice to change your mind.
But this new blow imposes other laws.
Your fortune shows a different face; the King
Is now no more, and his place must be filled.
His death has left you with a son to whom   375
You have a duty; slave if he loses you,
A king if you live. On whom in his misfortune
Do you wish that he should lean? His tears will have
No hand but yours to wipe them; and his cries,
Born even to the gods, would then incense   380
His ancestors against his mother. Live.
You have no longer reason to reproach
Yourself; your love becomes a usual love;
Theseus in dying cuts the sacred knots
Which made the crime and horror of your passion.   385
Hippolytus becomes less terrible to you,
And you can see him without guiltiness.
Perhaps, convinced of your aversion, he
Is going to lead the rebels. Undeceive him,
Appease his spirit. King of these happy shores,   390
Troezen is his portion; but he knows
That the laws give your son the lofty ramparts
Minerva[7] builded. Both of you, indeed,
Have a true enemy. Unite together   395
To combat Aricia.
PHAEDRA.   To your advice
I let myself be drawn. Well, let me live,
If I can be restored to life; and if
My love for a son can in this grievous moment
Reanimate the rest of my weak spirits.   400

---

7. The Greek goddess Athene, patroness of Athens.

Act II

SCENE 1. *Aricia and Ismene*

ARICIA. Hippolytus asks to see me in this place?
Hippolytus seeks me here to say good-by?
Ismene, is it true? You're not mistaken?

ISMENE. It is the first result of Theseus' death.
Madame, prepare yourself to see the hearts   5
Scattered by Theseus fly from every side
Towards you. Aricia at last is mistress
Of her fate, and soon will see the whole of Greece
Submit to her.

ARICIA.   It's not a false report?   10
Do I cease to be a slave, and have no foe?

ISMENE. No, madam, the gods are now no more against you,
And Theseus has rejoined your brothers' shades.

ARICIA. Is it known what caused his death?

ISMENE. They spread   15
An unbelievable tale of it. It is said
That stealing a new love this faithless husband
Was swallowed by the waves. It is even said—
A widespread rumor this—that he descended
To Hades with Peirithous,[8] and saw   20
Cocytus[9] and the gloomy banks, and living
Appeared to the infernal shades, but then
Could not emerge from those sad regions,
And cross the bourn from which there's no return.

ARICIA. Shall I believe a man before his hour   25
Can enter the dark dwelling of the dead?
What spell could draw him to those fearsome coasts?

ISMENE. Theseus is dead, madam, and you alone
Have doubts of it. Athens is mourning for it,
Troezen, informed of it, acknowledges   30
Hippolytus as King; and Phaedra, here
In this palace, trembling for her son, now seeks
The advice of anxious friends.

ARICIA.   Do you believe
Hippolytus, less cruel than his father,   35
Will make my chains less heavy, sympathize
With my misfortunes?

ISMENE.   Madam, I do believe it.

---

8. Theseus went with Peirithous, king of the Lapiths, with whom he had earlier abducted Helen,
to Hades to help his friend steal Persephone. Hercules freed Theseus, whom Pluto had imprisoned, but could not free Peirithous, who was later killed.   9. River in Hades, tributary to Acheron.

ARICIA. But do you really know that heartless man?
   By what fond hope do you think he'll pity me?   40
   In me alone respect a sex he scorns?
   You've seen how he avoids me, seeks those places
   Where I am not.
ISMENE.   I know all that is said
   About his coldness. But I've seen when near you   45
   This proud Hippolytus; and in seeing him,
   The rumor of his pride has doubly whetted
   My curiosity. His actual presence
   Seemed not to correspond. 'At your first glances
   I've seen him get confused. His eyes, which wished   50
   Vainly to shun you, could not leave your face.
   The name of lover would offend his heart,
   But yet he has a lover's tender eyes,
   If not his words.
ARICIA.   How my heart, dear Ismene,   55
   Drinks in a speech which may have little basis.
   Is it believable to you who know me
   That the sad plaything of a pitiless fate,
   Whose heart is fed on bitterness and tears,
   Should be acquainted with the trivial griefs   60
   Of love? The remnant of the blood of a king,
   Erechtheus, the noble son of Earth,
   Alone I have escaped war's ravages.
   I've lost six brothers in the flower of youth—
   Hope of a famous house!—all reaped by the sword.   65
   The moistened earth regretfully drank the blood
   Of the offspring of Erechtheus.[1] You know
   How since their death a cruel law was made,
   Forbidding Greeks to breathe a lover's sighs
   For me. It is feared the sister's reckless flames   70
   May kindle once again her brothers' ashes.
   But you know well with what disdainful eye
   I looked upon a conqueror's suspicions;
   And how, opposed to love, I often thanked
   The unjust Theseus whose convenient harshness   75
   Aided my scorn. But then my eyes had not
   Beheld his son. Not that by eyes alone
   Basely enchanted, I love his beauty and charm,
   Gifts with which nature wishes to honor him,
   And which he scorns, or seems unconscious of;   80
   I love in him his nobler wealth, his father's virtues,

---

1. Their ancestor, son of Earth and reared by Athene.

Without his faults. I love—I do confess it—
That generous pride that never yet has bowed
Beneath the amorous yoke. Phaedra took pride
In Theseus' practiced sighs. But as for me,   85
I am more proud, and shun the easy glory
Of gaining homage that a thousand others
Have had before me, and of penetrating
A heart completely open. But to bend
A heart inflexible, to make a soul   90
Insensible to love feel all its pain,
To enchain a captive by his bonds amazed,
In vain rebellion against the pleasing yoke,
That's what I wish; and that is what provokes me.
It's easier to disarm Hercules   95
Than Prince Hippolytus; and conquests soon
And often made will bring less glory to
The victor's eyes. But, dear Ismene, how
Unwise I am! for I shall be resisted
Only too much; and you perhaps will hear me   100
Lament the pride that I admire today.
If he would love! With what extreme delight
Would I make him . . .

ISMENE.   You'll hear him now, himself.
He comes to you.   105

SCENE 2. *Aricia, Ismene, Hippolytus*

HIPPOLYTUS. Madame, before I leave,
I thought that I should tell you of your fate.
My father lives no more. My apprehension
Presaged the reasons of his too long absence;
And death alone, stopping his famous deeds,   110
Could hide him for so long within this world.
The gods have yielded to the Fates at last
The friend and the successor of Alcides.[2]
I think your hatred, allowing him his virtues,
Will hear without regret what is his due.   115
One hope allays my deadly sorrow now.
From your strict tutelage I'll deliver you,
Revoke the laws whose rigor I've deplored.
Do what you will. Dispose of your own heart,
And in this Troezen, my heritage,   120
Which has forthwith accepted me as King,
I leave you as free, nay freer, than myself.

---

2. Theseus is "successor" to Alcides, or Hercules, as a destroyer of monsters.

ARICIA. Temper your generosity, my lord,
    For its excess embarrasses me. So
    To honor my disgrace will put me—more   125
    Than you think—under the harsh laws from which
    You would exempt me.
HIPPOLYTUS.   Athens, undecided
    In the choice of a successor, speaks of you,
    Names me and the Queen's son.   130
ARICIA.   Me, my lord?
HIPPOLYTUS. I know, without self-flattery, that a law
    Seems to reject me. Greece reproaches me
    With an alien mother. But if my brother were
    My only rival, over him I have   135
    Some veritable claims that I would save
    Out of the law's caprice. Another bridle,
    More lawful, checks my boldness. I yield to you,
    Or rather give you back what is your own,
    A scepter which your ancestors received   140
    From the most famous man that ever lived;
    Adoption placed it in Ægeus' hands;[3]
    Athens protected and enlarged by Theseus
    Joyfully recognized so good a king,
    And left in oblivion your luckless brothers.   145
    Now Athens calls you back within her walls;
    With a long quarrel she has groaned enough;
    Enough her fields have reeked with blood of thine.
    Troezen obeys me; and the plains of Crete
    Offer to Phaedra's son a rich domain.   150
    Attica is yours, and I am going
    On your behalf to reunite the suffrages
    We share between us.
ARICIA.   Astonished and confused
    At all I hear, I am afraid . . . afraid   155
    A dream abuses me. Am I awake?
    Can I believe in such a plan? What god,
    My lord, what god has put it in your breast?
    How justly is your glory spread abroad
    In every place! And how the truth surpasses   160
    Your fame! You would betray yourself for me?
    Would it not be enough for you to refrain
    From hating me? And to prevent your soul
    So long from this hostility . . .
HIPPOLYTUS.   I hate you,   165

---

3. Pandion's son by adoption, and Theseus' father.

Madam? However they depict my pride,
Do you think it bore a monster? What settled hate,
What savage manners could, in seeing you,
Not become milder? Could I have resisted
The charm that . . .   170
ARICIA.   What, my lord?
HIPPOLYTUS.   I've gone too far.
I see that reason yields to violence.
Since I've begun to speak, I must continue.
I must inform you, madam, of a secret   175
My heart no longer can contain. You see
Before you a lamentable prince, a type
Of headstrong pride. I, rebel against love,
For long have scorned its captives. I deplored
The shipwreck of weak mortals, and proposed   180
To contemplate the tempests from the shore.
But now enslaved under the common law,
I see myself transported. In a moment
My mad audacity has been subdued.
My proud soul is at last enslaved. For nearly   185
Six months, ashamed and desperate, and wearing
The marks of torture, against you, against myself,
Vainly I strove. Present I fled from you,
Absent I sought you. In the midst of forests
Your image followed me; the light of day,   190
The shadows of the night, brought to my eyes
The charms I shunned, and everything conspired
To make the rebel Hippolytus your captive.
Now for all fruit of my superfluous cares,
I seek but do not find myself. My bow, my spears, 195
My chariot call to me in vain. No more
Do I remember Neptune's lessons; the woods
Now echo to my groans. My idle steeds
Have now forgot my voice. Perhaps the tale
Of love so wild will make you, as you listen,   200
Blush for your work. What an uncouth recital
Of a heart that's offered you. What a strange captive
For bonds so beautiful! But to your eyes
The offering should be the richer for it;
Remember that I speak an alien tongue   205
And don't reject vows that are ill expressed,
Vows that without you I had never formed.

SCENE 3. *Aricia, Ismene, Hippolytus, Theramenes*

THERAMENES. My lord, the Queen is coming. I come before
To tell you that she seeks you.

HIPPOLYTUS.   Me?   210
THERAMENES.   I don't know why.
   But she has sent to ask for you. She wishes
   To speak with you before you go.
HIPPOLYTUS.   Phaedra!
   What shall I say to her? And what can she   215
   Expect . . .
ARICIA.   My lord, you can't refuse to hear her.
   Though you are sure of her hostility,
   You ought to have some pity for her tears.
HIPPOLYTUS. Yet you are going. And I depart, not knowing   220
   Whether I have offended by my words
   The charms that I adore. I do not know
   Whether this heart I leave now in your hands . . .
ARICIA. Go, Prince, pursue your generous designs;
   Put tributary Athens in my power   225
   And all those gifts that you have wished to make me,
   I accept. But yet that Empire, great and glorious,
   Is not to me the richest of your gifts.

SCENE 4. *Hippolytus and Theramenes*

HIPPOLYTUS. Friend, is all ready? But the Queen approaches.
   Go, see that all's prepared for our departure.   230
   Run, give the signal, and return at once
   To free me from a vexing interview.

SCENE 5. *Hippolytus, Phaedra, Œnone*

PHAEDRA. He's here: my blood retreats towards my heart,
   And I forget what I had meant to say.
ŒNONE. Think of a son whose sole hope lies in you.   235
PHAEDRA. It is said that your immediate departure
   Is sundering us, my lord. I come to wed
   My tears unto your griefs; and to explain
   My anxious fears to you. My son is now
   Without a father; and the day is near   240
   Which of my death will make him witness too.
   His youth is threatened by a thousand foes,
   And you alone can arm against them—but
   Secret remorse is fretting in my soul.
   I fear you're deaf to his cries, and that you'll wreak 245
   On him your wrath against an odious mother.
HIPPOLYTUS. Madam, I do not harbor such base feelings.
PHAEDRA. Although you hate me, I shall not complain,
   My lord: for you have seen me bent to harm you.
   You could not read the tables of my heart.   250
   I've taken care to invite your enmity,

And could not bear your presence where I dwelt.
In public, and in private, your known foe,
I've wished the seas to part us, and even forbidden
The mention of your name within my hearing.   255
But if one measures punishment by the offense,
If only hatred can attract your hate,
Never was woman who deserved more pity,
My lord, and less deserved your enmity.

HIPPOLYTUS. A mother jealous for her children's rights   260
Seldom forgives her stepson. I know it, madam.
Nagging suspicions are the commonest fruits
Of second marriage; and another wife
Would have disliked me just the same; and I
Might well have had to swallow greater wrongs.   265

PHAEDRA. Ah, my lord! Heaven—I dare avow it now—
Has made me an exception to that rule.
And what a different care perplexes me
And eats me up.

HIPPOLYTUS.   Madam, it is not time   270
To grieve. Perhaps your husband is alive.
Heaven to our tears may grant his swift return.
Neptune, his tutelary god, protects him,
To whom my father never prayed in vain.

PHAEDRA. None has beheld the marches[4] of the dead   275
A second time, my lord. Since he has seen
Those dismal shores, you hope in vain some god
Will send him back. The greedy Acheron
Never lets go its prey. What do I say?
He is not dead since he still lives in you.   280
Ever before my eyes I see my husband.
I see him, speak with him, and my heart still . . .
I'm wandering, my lord. My foolish feelings,
In spite of me, declare themselves.

HIPPOLYTUS.   I see   285
Love's wonderful effects. Dead though he is,
Theseus is always present to your eyes:
Your soul is ever burning with your love.

PHAEDRA. Yes, Prince, I pine and burn for Theseus.
I love him, not as when he visited   290
The underworld, a fickle lover, bent
To stain great Pluto's bed, but faithful, proud,
Attractive, young, and even a little shy,
Charming all hearts, an image of the gods,

4. Borderlands.

Or even as you are now. He had your bearing,   295
Your eyes, your speech; and such a modesty
Made flush his face when over the Cretan waves
He came and turned the hearts of Minos' daughters.[5]
What were you doing then? Why without you
Did he assemble there the flower of Greece?   300
And why were you too young to sail with him
Unto our shores? For then you would have slain
The Minotaur, despite the devious ways
Of his vast lair: my sister, to redeem you
From your confusion, with the fateful thread   305
Would have armed your hand[6]—but no, for I myself,
Inspired by love, would have forestalled her plan.
It would have been me, Prince; by timely aid,
I would have led you through the labyrinth.
How many cares that charming head of yours   310
Would then have cost me! I would not have trusted
To that weak thread alone, but walked before you,
Companion in the peril which you chose:
And going down into the labyrinth,
Phaedra would have returned with you, or else   315
Been lost with you.
HIPPOLYTUS.   O Gods! What do I hear?
Do you forget that Theseus is my father,
And you his wife?
PHAEDRA.   By what do you judge that I   320
Have done so, Prince? Would I forget my honor?
HIPPOLYTUS. Forgive me, madam. I admit, with blushing,
I misinterpreted an innocent speech.
I am ashamed to stay within your sight;
I'm going. . . .   325
PHAEDRA. Ah! cruel! You've understood too well.
I've said enough to save you from mistaking.
Know Phaedra, then, and all her madness. Yes,
I love; but do not think that I condone it,
Or think it innocent; nor that I ever   330
With base complaisance added to the poison
Of my mad passion. Hapless victim of
Celestial vengeance,[7] I abhor myself
More than you can. The gods are witnesses—
Those gods who kindled in my breast the flame   335

---

5. I.e., Phaedra and Ariadne.   6. The Minotaur inhabited the heart of a maze. Ariadne provided Theseus with a ball of thread by which he left a trail behind him and could retrace his steps
after killing the monster.   7. Phaedra feels herself a victim of Venus, the goddess of love; she
loves Hippolytus against her will.

Fatal to all my blood, whose cruel boast
Was to seduce a weak and mortal heart.
Recall what's past. I did not flee from you,
Hardhearted man, I drove you away. I wished
To seem to you both hateful and inhuman.   340
To resist you better I aroused your hatred.
But what have profited my useless pains?
You loathed me more: I did not love you less;
And your misfortunes lent you further charms.
I've languished, shriveled in the flames, in tears.   345
Your eyes will tell you so—if for a moment
Your eyes could look at me. What am I saying?
Think you that this confession I have made
Was voluntary? I trembled for a son
I did not dare betray and came to beg you   350
No more to hate him—futile schemes devised
By a heart too full of what it loves. Alas!
I could only speak to you about yourself.
Avenge yourself; punish an odious love,
Son worthy of a noble father, free   355
The universe of a monster who offends you.
Theseus' widow dares to love Hippolytus!
Believe me, Prince,
This dreadful monster would not seek to flee.
There is my heart: there you should aim your blow.   360
I feel it now, eager to expiate
Its sin, advance towards your arm. Strike.
Or if you think it unworthy of your blows,
Your hatred envying me a death so sweet,
Or if you think your hand with blood too vile   365
Would be imbrued, lend me your sword instead.
Give it me.   [*She takes sword.*]
ŒNONE. What are you doing, madam?
O righteous Gods! But someone's coming. Leave
These hateful testimonies. Come inside,
And flee a certain shame.

SCENE 6. *Hippolytus and Theramenes*

THERAMENES. Is it Phaedra who flees,   370
Or rather is led away? O why, my lord,
These marks of sorrow? I see you without sword,
Speechless and pale.
HIPPOLYTUS.   Theramenes, let's flee.
I am amazed, and cannot without horror   375

Behold myself. Phaedra . . . but no, great Gods!
In deep oblivion may this horrid secret
Remain entombed!
THERAMENES.   If you would now depart,
The sails are ready. But Athens has decided.   380
Her chiefs have taken the votes of all the tribes.
Your brother wins, and Phaedra gets her way.
HIPPOLYTUS. Phaedra?
THERAMENES.   A herald, bearing Athens' will,
Comes to remit the reins of government   385
Into her hands. Her son is King, my lord.
HIPPOLYTUS. O Gods, who know her heart, is it her virtue
That thus you recompense?
THERAMENES.   There is, however,
A muffled rumor that the King's alive.   390
It is said that in Epirus he's appeared.
But I, who sought him there, I know too well . . .
HIPPOLYTUS. No matter. Let us listen to everything,
And neglect nothing. Examine this report
And trace it to its source. If it should prove   395
Unfounded, let's depart. Whatever the cost,
Let's put the scepter into worthy hands.

Act III

SCENE 1. *Phaedra and Œnone*

PHAEDRA. O! that the honors which are brought to me
Were paid elsewhere! Why do you urge me so?
Can you wish me to be seen? What do you come with
To flatter my desolation? Hide me rather.
Not only have I spoken; but my frenzy   5
Is noised abroad. I've said those things which ought
Never to be heard. O heavens! The way he listened!
By devious means he somehow failed to grasp
What I was saying—then he recoiled. His blush
Doubled my shame. Why did you turn aside   10
The death I sought? Did he turn pale with fear
When with his sword I sought my breast, or seek
To snatch it from me? Since my hands had touched it
But once, it was made horrible in his eyes,
And would profane his hands.   15
ŒNONE.   Thus in your woes
Lamenting to yourself, you feed a flame
That ought to be put out. Would it not be better,

Worthy the blood of Minos, in nobler cares
To seek your peace. To spite a heartless man   20
Who had recourse to flight, assume the conduct
Of affairs, and reign.

PHAEDRA.   I reign? To place the State
Under my law, when reason reigns no longer
Over myself; when I have abdicated   25
From the empire of my senses; when beneath
A yoke of shame I scarcely breathe; when I
Am dying.

ŒNONE.   Fly.

PHAEDRA.   I cannot leave him.   30

ŒNONE.   You dared
To banish him, and dare not shun him now?

PHAEDRA. Too late. He knows of my mad passion.
I've crossed the bounds of rigid modesty,
Declared my shame before my conqueror's eyes,   35
And hope has slipped perforce into my heart.
It was you who rallied my declining strength,
When my departing soul was on my lips,
And by your flattering counsels knew the way
To bring me back to life. You made me glimpse   40
How I could love him.

ŒNONE.   To save you from your ills,
Guilty or innocent, what would I not
Have done? But if an insult ever touched you,
Can you forget his haughty scorn? And how   45
With cruel eyes his obstinate rigor let you
Lie prostrate at his feet. How his fierce pride
Rendered him odious! If only Phaedra
Had seen him, at that moment, with my eyes!

PHAEDRA. Œnone, he may leave this native pride   50
Which wounds you. Nurtured in the pathless woods,
He has their roughness. Hardened by savage laws,
He hears love spoken of for the first time;
Perhaps it was surprise that caused his silence;
Perhaps my pleas had too much violence.   55

ŒNONE. Remember a barbarian gave him birth.

PHAEDRA. Although a Scythian and barbarian,
She yet has loved.

ŒNONE.   He has for all our sex
A deadly hatred.   60

PHAEDRA.   So I shall not see him
Prefer a rival. All your counsels now
Are out of season. Serve my passion, Œnone,

And not my reason. He opposes now
To love a heart impenetrable; let us   65
Discover some more vulnerable place.
The charms of ruling have appeared to touch him.
Athens attracts him; he has not been able
To hide it. His ships have turned their prows; their sails
Flap in the wind. Find this ambitious youth,   70
Œnone; make the royal crown to glitter
Before his eyes. Let him wear upon his brow
The sacred diadem. I only wish
The honor of his love, and yield to him
The power I cannot keep. He will instruct   75
My son in the art of ruling, who may perhaps
Regard him as a father. Both son and mother
I put under his power. Try every means
To bend him; he will listen to your speech
More readily than to mine. Urge, weep, and moan.   80
Paint Phaedra dying; do not blush to use
The tone of a suppliant. I will approve
Of all you do. You are my only hope.
I await your coming to decide my fate.

SCENE 2. *Phaedra*

PHAEDRA. O thou who seest the shame to which I've come,   85
Venus implacable, am I confounded
Enough for thee? Thou canst not further urge
Thy cruelty; thy victory is complete.
O cruel! If thou wishest another triumph
Attack an enemy who is more rebellious.   90
Hippolytus flees thee; and, thy wrath defying,
Has never to thy altars bowed the knee.
Thy name appears to shock his haughty ears.
Goddess, avenge thyself. Thy cause is mine.
O let him love! Œnone is returned.   95
I am detested then. He would not hear you?

SCENE 3. *Phaedra and Œnone*

ŒNONE. Madam, you must repress the very thought
Of your vain passion, and recall again
Your former virtue. The King that we thought dead
Will soon appear before your eyes. Theseus   100
Is come. The people rush to see him. I went,
At your command, to seek Hippolytus,
When I heard a thousand shouts. . . .
PHAEDRA.   My husband lives,

Œnone. It is enough. I have confessed   105
A love which foully wrongs him. Theseus lives.
I wish to know no more.
ŒNONE.   What?
PHAEDRA.   I foretold it,
But you would not believe it. Your tears prevailed   110
Over my shame. I would have died today
Worthy of tears. I followed your advice—
I die dishonored.
ŒNONE.   Die?
PHAEDRA.   O righteous heaven!   115
What here I done today? My husband's coming,
And his son with him. I shall see the witness
Of my adulterous passion watch how boldly
I greet his father—my heart still full of sighs
To which he would not listen, and my eyes   120
Still moist with tears he scorned. Do you suppose
That he, so sensitive to Theseus' honor,
Will hide the fires that burn me—and betray
His father and his king? Could he contain
The horror I inspire? He would keep silence   125
In vain. I know my perfidies, Œnone;
I am not one of those who in their crimes
Enjoy a tranquil peace, and know the art
To keep their countenance without a blush.
I know my madness: I recall it all.   130
I think already that these walls, these arches,
Are going to speak; they but await my husband
Before they utter forth my crimes. Die, then.
My death will free me from a crowd of horrors.
Is it a great mischance to cease to live?   135
Death has no terrors for the unfortunate.
I only fear the name I leave behind me.
A dreadful heritage for my poor children!
The blood of Jupiter should puff up their courage,
With a just pride; but yet a mother's crime   140
Will be a heavy burden. One day, I fear,
A speech—too true!—will cast it in their teeth
They had a guilty mother; and I fear
That crushed by such a hateful load, they'll never
Dare raise their eyes.   145
ŒNONE.   It is true. I pity them.
Never was fear more justified than yours.
But why expose them to such insults? Why

Against yourself give evidence? All would be lost.
It will be said that guilty Phaedra fled   150
The terrible sight of husband she betrayed.
Hippolytus will rejoice that by your death
You corroborate his tale. What could I say
To your accuser? Face to face with him
I shall be easy to confound, and see him   155
Rejoicing in his triumph, while he tells
Your shame to all who listen. Rather let
Fire from heaven consume me! But tell me true
Is he still dear to you? And with what eyes
Do you behold this insolent prince?   160
PHAEDRA.   I see him
Even as a monster hideous to my eyes.
ŒNONE. Why yield him then a total victory?
You fear him, madam. Dare to accuse him first
Of the crime that he will charge you with today.   165
Who will contradict you? Everything
Speaks against him—his sword by lucky chance
Left in your hands, your present sore distress,
Your former sorrow, his father long ago
Warned by your outcries, and his actual exile   170
Obtained by you yourself.
PHAEDRA.   How should I dare
Oppress and slander innocence?
ŒNONE.   My zeal
Only requires your silence. Like you I shrink   175
From such an action. You would find me readier
To face a thousand deaths; but since I'd lose you
Without this painful rememdy, and your life
For me is of such value that all else
Must yield to it, I'll speak. And Theseus, angered   180
By what I tell him, will restrict his vengeance
To his son's exile. When he punishes,
A father is always father, satisfied
With a light penalty. But even if
His guiltless blood is spilt, your threatened honor   185
Is yet too valuable to be exposed.
Whatever it demands, you must submit,
Madam. And to save your threatened honor
All must be sacrificed, including virtue.
Someone is coming. I see Theseus.   190
PHAEDRA.   Ah!
I see Hippolytus. In his haughty eyes

I see my ruin written. Do what you will,
I resign myself to you. In my disorder,
I can do nothing for myself.   195

SCENE 4. *Phaedra, Œnone, Theseus, Hippolytus, Theramenes*

THESEUS. Now fortune,
Madam, no longer frowns, and in your arms . . .
PHAEDRA. Stay, Theseus. Do not profane the love you feel.
I am not worthy of your sweet caresses.
You are insulted. Fortune has not spared   200
Your wife during your absence. I am unworthy
To please you, or approach you; and hence forward
I ought to think only of where to hide.

SCENE 5. *Theseus, Hippolytus, Theramenes*

THESEUS. What is the reason for this strange reception?
HIPPOLYTUS. Phaedra alone the mystery can explain: 205
But if my ardent prayers can move your heart,
Permit me not to see her any more.
And let Hippolytus disappear forever
From places where she dwells.
THESEUS.   Leave me, my son?   210
HIPPOLYTUS. I sought her not: you brought her to these shores,
And when you left entrusted to the banks
Of Troezen, Aricia and the Queen,
I was instructed to look after them.
But what can now delay me? In my youth   215
I showed enough my prowess in the forests
Against unworthy foes; and could I not,
Escaping an ignoble idleness,
In blood more glorious stain my spears? Before
You reached my present age, already   220
More than one tyrant, more than one grim monster
Had felt your mighty strength; already you,
Chastiser of insolence, had secured the shores
Of the two seas; the private traveler feared   225
Outrage no more; and Hercules could rest
From his long labors, hearing of your deeds.
But I, an unknown son of famous sire,
Am even further from my mother's deeds![8]
Suffer my courage to be used at last;
And if some monster has escaped your arm,   230

---

8. Hippolytus' mother, an Amazon, also performed brave deeds.

Let me then lay the honorable skin
Before your feet; or by the lasting memory
Of a fine death perpetuate the days
So nobly ended, and prove to all the world
I was your son.   235
THESEUS.   What do I now behold?
What horror makes my frightened family
Flee from my sight? If I return so feared,
So little wanted, why, heaven, from my prison
Did you release me? I had one friend alone;   240
Imprudently he wished to steal the wife
Of the King of Epirus.[9] I aided, with regret,
His amorous designs; but angry fate
Blinded us both. The King surprised me there,
Defenseless, weaponless. I saw Peirithous,   245
Sad object of my tears, by this barbarian
Given to cruel monsters whom he fed
With blood of luckless mortals. He shut me up
In dismal caverns underground that neighbored
The empire of the shades. After six months   250
The gods again looked on me. I deceived
The eyes of those who guarded me. I cleansed
The world of a perfidious enemy;
To his own monsters he became a prey.
And when with joy I approach the dearest things   255
Now left me by the gods—what do I say?—
When to itself my soul returns and takes its fill
Of that dear sight, for welcome I receive
A shuddering fear and horror. All flee; all shrink
From my embraces. And I feel the terror   260
That I inspire. I'd like to be again
In the prisons of Epirus. Speak. Phaedra complains
That I am wronged. Who has betrayed me? Why
Have I not been avenged? Has Greece, to whom
So many times my arms proved useful, now   265
Granted asylum to a criminal?
You do not answer! Is my son, my own son,
Leagued with my enemies? Let us go in.
I cannot stay in doubt that overwhelms me.
Let me know both the offense and the offender.   270
Let Phaedra tell the cause of her distress.

9. A district in western Greece, on the Ionian Sea.

SCENE 6. *Hippolytus and Theramenes*

HIPPOLYTUS. Where did that speech, which petrified me, tend?
　　Does Phaedra, still a prey to her mad passion,
　　Wish to accuse, and so destroy, herself?
　　What will the King say? What destructive poison　　　　275
　　Is scattered over all his house by love.
　　And I, full of a love he will detest,
　　How different from the man that he remembers!
　　What black presentiments affright me now!
　　But innocence has nought to fear. Let's go:　　　　280
　　Seek by what happy art I can awaken
　　My father's tenderness—speak of a love
　　That he may wish to crush, though all his power
　　Will not be able to drive it from my heart.

Act IV

SCENE 1. *Theseus and Œnone*

THESEUS. What do I hear? A traitor, a rash traitor,
　　To plot this outrage to his father's honor?
　　How harshly, Destiny, dost thou pursue me!
　　I know not where I'm going, nor what I am!
　　O tenderness and bounty ill repaid!　　　　5
　　Audacious projects! evil thought! To reach
　　The goal of his black passion he sought the aid
　　Of violence. I recognize the sword—
　　The instrument of his rage—with which I armed him
　　For nobler purposes. All the ties of blood　　　　10
　　Could not restrain him! And Phaedra hesitated
　　To punish him! Her silence spared the villain!
ŒNONE. She rather spared a pitiable father.
　　Being ashamed of a violent lover's scheme
　　And of the wicked fire caught from her eyes,　　　　15
　　Phaedra desired to die; her murderous hand
　　Would have put out the pure light of her eyes.
　　I saw her raise her arm. I ran to stop her.
　　Alone I tried to save her for your love,
　　And, mourning for her troubles and your fears,　　　　20
　　I have unwillingly interpreted
　　The tears you saw.
THESEUS.　　　　　　　The villain! He was not able
　　To stop himself from turning pale. I saw him
　　Tremble with fear when he encountered me.　　　　25

I was astonished at his lack of joy;
His cold embraces froze my tenderness.
But was this guilty passion which devours him
Already manifest in Athens?

ŒNONE.   My lord,   30
Recall the Queen's complaints. A criminal love
Was cause of all her hatred.

THESEUS.   And did this passion
Kindle again at Troezen?

ŒNONE.   O my lord,   35
I have told you all that passed. Too long the Queen
Has in her mortal grief been left alone;
So let me leave, and hasten to her side.

SCENE 2. *Theseus and Hippolytus*

THESEUS. Ah! here he is. Great Gods! What eye, as mine,
Would not have been deceived? Why should the brow   40
Of a profane adulterer shine with virtue?
And should one not by certain signs perceive
The heart of villainous men?

HIPPOLYTUS.   May I inquire,
My lord, what dismal cloud is on your face?   45
Dare you confide in me?

THESEUS.   Villain! Do you then dare
To show yourself before me? Monster, whom
Too long the thunder's spared, vile brigand,
Of whom I purged the earth, as I believed,   50
After the transport of a horrible love
Had brought your lust even to your father's bed,
You show your hostile head! You would appear
In places full of your own infamy,
And do not seek, under an unknown sky   55
A country which my name has not yet reached.
Flee, traitor! Do not come to brave my hatred,
Or try a rage that I can scarcely hold.
I have enough opprobrium that I caused
The birth of such a criminal, without   60
Your shameful death should come to soil the glory
Of all my noble deeds. Flee! If you do not wish
A sudden death to add you to the villains
This hand has punished, take good care that never
The star that lights us see you in this place   65
Set a rash foot. Fly, I say; and hasten
To purge my territories forever from
Your horrible aspect. And thou, O Neptune!

If formerly my courage cleansed your shores
Of infamous assassins, remember now,   70
That for reward of all my happy efforts,
Thou promisedst to grant one prayer of mine.
In the long rigors of a cruel prison
I did not once implore thy immortal power;
Niggardly of the help that I expected,   75
I saved my prayers for greater needs. Today
I do implore thee. Avenge a wretched father!
This traitor I abandon to thy wrath.
In his own blood stifle his shameless lusts.
And by thy furies I shall recognize   80
Thy favors.

HIPPOLYTUS. Does Phaedra charge Hippolytus
With love incestuous? Such an excess of horror
Renders me speechless. So many sudden blows
Crush me at once, they take away my words   85
And choke my utterance.

THESEUS.   Traitor, you thought
Phaedra would bury in a cowardly silence
Your brutal conduct. You should not have left
The sword which in her hands has helped to damn you.   90
Or rather, piling up your perfidy,
You should have bought her silence with her life.

HIPPOLYTUS. With this black falsehood righteously incensed,
I would now speak the truth; but I suppress
A secret that would touch you too. Approve   95
The respect which seals my lips; and, without wishing
To augment your griefs, I urge you to examine
My life. Remember who I am. Small crimes
Always precede the great. Whoever crosses
The bounds of law may violate at last   100
The holiest rights. There are degrees of crime
Just as of virtue—never innocence
Changes to utter license at one stroke.
One day alone is not enough to turn
A good man to a treacherous murderer,   105
Still less to incest. Suckled at the breast
Of a chaste heroine, I have not belied
The fountain of her blood. Pitheus,[1] thought
To be the wisest of all men, did deign
To instruct me. I do not wish to give   110
Too favorable a picture of myself;

1. The most learned man of his age, Theseus' guardian. After marrying Phaedra, Theseus sent
Hippolytus to Pitheus, who adopted him as heir to the throne of Troezen.

But if some virtue's fallen to my share,
My lord, I think that I have clearly shown
My hatred of the crimes imputed to me.
By this Hippolytus is known in Greece.   115
I've pushed my virtue to the edge of harshness.
My moral inflexibility is known.
The day's not purer than my inmost heart,
And people wish Hippolytus could be smitten
By some profane love. . . .   120

THESEUS.   Yes, it is that same pride
Which now condemns you. I see the hateful cause
Of your frigidity. Phaedra alone
Charmed your lascivious eyes; your soul, indifferent
To every other object, disdained to burn   125
With innocent flames.

HIPPOLYTUS.   No, father, this my heart—
I cannot hide it longer—has not disdained
To burn with virtuous love. I do confess
My veritable offense. I love. I love   130
('Tis true) despite your prohibition, sir.
Aricia to her laws holds me enslaved.
The daughter of Pallas has overcome your son.
I worship her; rebellious to your orders
I can neither sigh nor burn, except for her.   135

THESEUS. You love her? Heavens! But no, the artifice
Is gross. You feign yourself a criminal
To justify yourself

HIPPOLYTUS.   For six months now,
My lord, I shunned her, but I loved. I came   140
Trembling to tell you. Can nothing disabuse you?
Or by what terrible oath can I convince you?
By earth, and heaven, and by the whole of nature . . .

THESEUS. Rogues always have recourse to perjury.
Cease, cease, and spare me further useless speech,   145
If your feigned virtue has no other aid.

HIPPOLYTUS. Although to you it may seem false and cunning,
Phaedra, within her heart, will be more just.

THESEUS. Ah! how your impudence excites my wrath!

HIPPOLYTUS. How long my exile? What the place prescribed?   150

THESEUS. Even if you should go beyond the pillars
Of Hercules,[2] I still would be too near you.

HIPPOLYTUS. Charged with this hideous crime, I should not have
One friend to plead for me when you desert me.

___

2. The two points of land on either side of the Strait of Gibraltar, at the western end of the
Mediterranean and thus representing one edge of the known world.

THESEUS. Go seek for friends who morbidly applaud   155
   Adultery and incest, ungrateful traitors,
   Dishonorable and lawless, fit protectors
   Of such a villain.
HIPPOLYTUS.   You speak to me once more
   Of incest and adultery. I hold   160
   My peace. Yet Phaedra's mother . . . Phaedra springs
   From a race, as you well know, my lord, more filled
   With horrors than mine is.
THESEUS.   What! will your rage
   Lose all restraint before me? For the last time,   165
   Out of my sight! Go, traitor. Do not wait
   For a wrathful father to have you driven out
   With infamy.

SCENE 3. *Theseus*

THESEUS.   O wretched man, you run
   To inevitable destruction. Neptune, feared
   Even by the gods themselves, has given his word,   170
   And he'll perform it. An avenging god
   Pursues you, and you'll not escape. I loved you,
   And feel that notwithstanding your offense
   My heart is yearning for you in advance.
   But it was you who forced me to condemn you.   175
   Was ever father more outraged than I?
   Just gods, you see the grief that overwhelms me.
   How could I father such a guilty child?

SCENE 4. *Theseus and Phaedra*

PHAEDRA. My lord, I come to you with fearful heart.
   I overheard your wrathful voice, and tremble   180
   Lest your dire threats should have a prompt result.
   If there is still time, spare your child, your blood.
   I dare to implore you. Save me from the horror
   Of hearing his blood cry. O do not cause me
   The everlasting grief of spilling it   185
   By a father's hand.
THESEUS.   No, madam, in my own blood
   My hand has not been steeped. But none the less
   He's not escaped me. An immortal hand
   Is charged with his destruction. Neptune himself   190
   Owes it to me, and you will be avenged.
PHAEDRA. Neptune owes it to you! Your wrathful prayers . . .
THESEUS. What! do you fear now lest they should be answered?
   Rather join yours unto my lawful prayers.

Recount to me his crimes in all their vileness;   195
Heat up my anger which is too restrained,
Too slow. For you are not acquainted yet
With all his crimes. His mad attempt against you
Has led to further wrongs. Your mouth, he says,
Is full of lies; and he maintains, his heart   200
And faith are given to Aricia—that he loves her.
PHAEDRA. What, my lord?
THESEUS.   That's what he said, but I
    Knew how to take this frivolous pretense.
    Let's hope from Neptune a swift stroke of justice.   205
    I'm going myself to pray before his altar,
    To accomplish his immortal vows with speed.

SCENE 5. *Phaedra*

PHAEDRA. He's gone. What news has beaten on my ears!
    What half-extinguished fire within my breast
    Revives! What thunderbolt! What dreadful news!   210
    I flew, with all my heart, to save his son,
    Breaking away from the restraining arms
    Of terrified Œnone; to my remorse
    I yielded. And who knows how far it would
    Have carried me? Perhaps to accuse myself;   215
    Perhaps, if my voice had failed not, the dread truth
    Might have escaped me. . . . Hippolytus feels love,
    But not for me. Aricia has his heart!
    Aricia has his faith! Gods! When the ingrate,
    Pitiless to my pleading, armed himself   220
    With eye so proud and brow so stern, I thought
    His heart to love would be forever closed,
    Invulnerable to all my sex; and yet
    Another has bent his will; and in his eyes
    Another has found favor. Perhaps he has   225
    A heart that's easily touched. I am alone
    The object of his scorn. And I undertook
    The task of his defense!

SCENE 6. *Phaedra and Œnone*

PHAEDRA.   Do you know   230
    Œnone, what I have just learnt?
ŒNONE.   No, madam.
    But trembling I have come to you, and pale,
    Aware of your intentions; and I feared
    A madness which might well be fatal to you.
PHAEDRA. Would you believe it, Œnone? I have a rival.   235

ŒNONE. What?

PHAEDRA. Hippolytus is in love. I cannot doubt it.
  That savage enemy no one could conquer
  Whom pleading and respect would both annoy,   240
  The tiger I encountered but with fear,
  Has recognized a conqueror at least.
  Aricia has found the way to his heart.

ŒNONE. Aricia?

PHAEDRA. O pain I never knew before!
  To what new torment am I now reserved!   245
  All I have suffered, all my frenzied fears,
  My passion's fury and its fierce remorse,
  The unbearable insult of his cruel repulse,
  Shadowed but feebly what I now endure.
  They love each other. By what potent spell   250
  Have I been hoodwinked? How have they met? Since when?
  And where? You must have known: why did you hide it?
  Could you not tell me of their furtive love?
  Were they not often seen to speak together,
  To seek each other? Did they go to hide   255
  Deep in the woods? But they, alas, could meet
  With perfect freedom. Heaven itself approved
  Their innocent desires. They could pursue
  Their amorous purposes without remorse,
  And every day, for them, broke clear and calm!   260
  While I, sad castaway of Nature, hid
  From day and light. Death is the only god
  I dared invoke; and I waited him,
  Feeding on gall and steeped in tears, but yet
  I did not dare (so closely I was watched)   265
  To weep my fill. I tasted that sour pleasure
  In fear and trembling; and with brow serene
  Disguising my distress, I was deprived
  Too often of my tears.

ŒNONE.   But their vain loves   270
  Will bear no fruit, for they will meet no more.

PHAEDRA. Forever and forever they will love.
  At the moment when I speak—ah! deadly thought!—
  They brave the fury of a maddened lover.
  Despite the exile which will sunder them,   275
  They vow eternal faith. I cannot bear
  A joy which is an outrage to me. Œnone,
  Take pity on my jealous rage. That girl
  Must be destroyed; the anger of my husband
  Against her hateful blood must be aroused   280

To no light penalty. The sister's crime
Exceeds the brothers'. In my jealous fury
I wish to urge him . . . But what am I doing?
Where has my reason fled? I jealous? I
To beg of Theseus? My husband is not dead,   285
And I am still aflame. For whom? Each word
Makes my hair stand on end. My crimes already
Have overflowed the measure. Both at once
I breathe the stench of incest and deceit.
My murderous hands, all apt for vengeance, burn   290
To plunge in innocent blood! Wretch! And I live!
And I endure the sight of sacred Phoebus
From whom I am derived. My ancestor
Is sire and master of the gods; and heaven,
Nay all the universe, is teeming now   295
With my forbears. Where then can I hide?
Flee to eternal night. What do I say?
For there my father holds the fatal urn,[3]
Put by the Fates in his stern hands, 'tis said.
Minos in Hades judges the pale ghosts.   300
Ah, how his shade will tremble when his eyes
Behold his daughter there, confessing sins—
Crimes yet unknown in hell! What wilt thou say,
Father, to see this hideous spectacle?
Methinks I now behold the dreadful urn   305
Fall from thy hand! Methinks I see thee search
For some new punishment, thyself become
The torturer of thine own blood. Forgive:
A cruel god has doomed thy family.
Behold his vengeance in thy daughter's lust.   310
But yet, alas, never has my sad heart
Once plucked the fruit of the atrocious crime
Whose shame pursues me. Dogged by miseries
To the last gasp, in torture, I render up
A life I long to lose.   315
ŒNONE.   Repel, madam,
An unreal terror! Behold with other eyes
A venial fault. You love. One's destiny
Cannot be overcome, and you were drawn
By a fatal spell. Is it a prodigy   320
Unknown before amongst us? And has love
Conquered no other hearts than yours alone?

---

3. After his death, Minos of Crete became, along with his brother Rhadamanthus, one of the
judges of souls in the underworld. The urn held the lots determining to what abode in the underworld the souls of the dead were to be sent.

Frailty is but too natural to us all.
You are a mortal—bow to mortals' lot.
The yoke that you bewail is nothing new: 325
The gods themselves—the dwellers on Olympus—
Who scare us from such crimes, have before now
Been scorched with lawless fires.

PHAEDRA.   What do I hear?
What counsels do you dare to give me now?   330
Would you thus poison me until the end?
Wretch! Thus you ruined me; and when I fled
You brought me back. It was your pleading
Made me forget my duty. When I avoided
Hippolytus, it was you who made me see him.   335
What have you done? Why has your wicked mouth
Blackened his honor? Perhaps he will be slain,
The father's impious prayer to Neptune answered.
No longer will I hearken to you. Go,
Thou execrable monster, go and leave me   340
To my unhappy fate. May the just gods
Reward thee with a punishment to fright
Those who by servile arts feed princes' vices,
Urging them down the path they wish to take,
And smoothing it before them—base flatterers,   345
The most pernicious gift the angry heavens
Can give to kings.   [*Exit* PHAEDRA.]

ŒNONE.   Ah! Gods! to do her service
I have done all, left all. And I receive
This for reward. I get but my deserts.   350

Act V

SCENE 1. *Hippolytus and Aricia*

ARICIA. How in this mortal danger can you still
Keep silence, and thus leave a loving father
In error? If you scorn my pleading tears,
And easily consent no more to see,
Go, separate yourself from sad Aricia: 5
But yet, before you leave, preserve your life;
Defend your honor from a vile reproach,
And force your father to revoke his prayers.
There is still time. Why, by what caprice,
Do you leave the field thus free to your accuser?   10
Enlighten Theseus.

HIPPOLYTUS. What have I not said?

Should I reveal the soiling of his bed?
Should I, by telling a too truthful tale,
Make flush my father's brow? For you alone   15
Have pierced the hateful mystery. My heart
Can be unbosomed only to the gods
And you. I could not hide from you—by this
Judge if I love you—all I would conceal
Even from myself. But yet remember, madam,   20
Under what seal I have revealed it to you.
Forget, if you are able, what I've said,
And may you never open your chaste lips
To tell of this affair. Let us rely
Upon the justice of the gods, for they   25
Are much concerned to justify me; and Phaedra
Sooner or later punished for her crime
Cannot avoid deserved ignominy.
That's all I ask of you. I permit all else
To my unbounded anger. Leave the serfdom   30
To which you are reduced, and follow me.
Dare to accompany my flight, Aricia.
Dare to come with me; snatch yourself away
From this unholy place, where virtue breathes
A poisoned air. To hide your disappearance,   35
Profit from the confusion that is caused
By my disgrace. I can assure the means
For your departure. All your guards are mine,
Powerful upholders of our cause. Argos
Holds out its arms to us, and Sparta calls us.   40
Let's bear our righteous cries to mutual friends;
And suffer not that Phaedra by our ruin
Should drive us from the throne, and to her son
Promise your spoil and mine. The chance is good;
We must embrace it. . . . What fear now restrains you?   45
You seem uncertain. Your interest alone
Inspires me to this boldness. When I am
Ablaze, what freezes you? Are you afraid
To tread with me the paths of exile?

ARICIA.   Alas!   50
How dear, my lord, would such an exile be!
Tied to your fate, with what delight would I
Live, by the rest of mortals quite forgotten!
But since I'm not united by such ties,
Can I, with honor, flee with you? I know   55
That without blemish I can free myself
From Theseus' hands—it would not be to leave

The bosom of my family—and flight
Is lawful if we flee from tyrants. But,
My lord, you love me, and my startled honor . . .   60
HIPPOLYTUS. No, no, I've too much care of your renown.
A nobler plan has brought me in your presence:
Flee from your enemies, and follow me,
Your husband. Free in our misfortunes, since
Heaven has ordained it so, our troth depends   65
Upon ourselves alone. Hymen need not
Be ringed with torches. At the gates of Troezen,
Among the tombs, the ancient sepulchers
Of the princes of my line, is a holy temple
Dreadful to perjurers. 'Tis there that mortals   70
Dare not make empty vows, lest they receive
Swift punishment; and, fearing there to meet
Inevitable death, the lie has not
A sterner bridle. There, if you will trust me,
We will confirm the solemn oath, and take   75
To witness it the god who's worshipped there,
Praying that he will act as father to us.
I'll call to witness the most sacred gods,
The chaste Diana, Juno the august,[4]
And all the gods who, witnessing my love,   80
Will guarantee my holy promises.
ARICIA. The King is coming. Fly, Prince; leave at once.
I will remain a moment, to conceal
My own departure. Go, but leave with me
Some faithful guide to lead my timid steps   85
To where you wait for me.

SCENE 2. *Aricia, Theseus, Ismene*

THESEUS [*Aside*].   O Gods! enlighten
My troubled heart, and deign to show the truth
That I am seeking here.
ARICIA [*To* ISMENE].   Remember all,   90
My dear Ismene, and prepare for flight.

SCENE 3. *Aricia and Theseus*

THESEUS. You change your color, and seem speechless, madam.
What was Hippolytus doing here?
ARICIA.   My lord,
To bid me an eternal farewell.   95
THESEUS.   Your eyes

---

4. Diana was goddess of the moon and of chastity; Juno, wife of Jupiter, was queen of the gods.

Have learnt to conquer that rebellious spirit,
And his first sighs were your accomplishment.
ARICIA. My lord, I cannot hide the truth from you.
  He's not inherited your unjust hate;   100
  He does not treat me as a criminal.
THESEUS. I see. He vows you an eternal love.
  Do not rely on his inconstant heart,
  For he would swear as much to others.
ARICIA.   He,   105
  My lord?
THESEUS. You ought to have made him less inconstant.
  How can you bear this horrible division
  Of his affections?
ARICIA.   And how do you endure   110
  That a horrible tale should smirch a blameless life?
  Have you so little knowledge of his heart?
  Do you discriminate so ill, my lord,
  'Twixt crime and innocence? Must a hateful cloud
  Conceal his virtue from your eyes alone,   115
  Which brightly shines for others? It is wrong
  To give him up to lying tongues. Cease now:
  Repent your murderous prayers. Fear lest the heavens
  Should bear you so much hatred as to grant
  What you implored. For often in their wrath   120
  They take our proferred victims; and their gifts
  Are but the punishments of our own crimes.
THESEUS. No. You wish in vain to hide his outrage.
  You're blinded by your love. I put my trust
  In sure and irreproachable witnesses: 125
  I've seen, I've seen a stream of genuine tears.
ARICIA. Take care, my lord. Your hands invincible
  Have freed mankind of monsters without number,
  But all are not destroyed, and you have left
  One still alive. . . . Your son, my lord, forbids me   130
  To tell you more. And knowing the respect
  He wishes to retain for you, I would
  Afflict him sorely if I dared to speak.
  I imitate his modesty, and flee
  Out of your presence, lest I should be forced   135
  To break my silence.

SCENE 4. *Theseus*

THESEUS.   What is in her mind?
  What does it hide, this speech of hers, begun
  So many times, and always interrupted?

Would they distract me with an empty feint?   140
Have they agreed together to torture me?
But I myself, in spite of my stern rigor,
What plaintive voice within my heart cried out?
I am afflicted by a secret pity,
And stand amazed. Let me a second time   145
Interrogate Œnone. I want to have
A clearer picture of the crime. Guards,
Send for Œnone. Let her come alone.

SCENE 5. *Theseus and Panope*

PANOPE. My lord, I know not what the Queen is planning,
But yet I fear her violent distress.   150
Mortal despair is painted on her face,
Marked with Death's pallor. Œnone, from her presence
Driven away with shame, has thrown herself
Into the deep sea: it is not known why
She took her desperate action; and the waves   155
Have hidden her forever.
THESEUS.   What do I hear?
PANOPE. The Queen has not been calmed by this dread deed.
Distress still grows within her doubtful soul.
Sometimes, to ease her secret griefs, she takes   160
Her children, bathing them with tears,
And then, renouncing her maternal love,
She suddenly repels them with her hand.
Then here and there she walks irresolute,
Her wandering eyes no longer knowing us.   165
Thrice she has written; then, with change of mind,
Thrice she has torn the letter she began.
Deign to see her, my lord, and try to help her.
THESEUS. O heavens! Œnone dead! and Phaedra now
Desires to die. Recall my son. Let him   170
Defend himself. Let him come and speak with me.
I'm ready to hear him. O Neptune, do not hasten
Thy deadly blessings. I would now prefer
That they should never be fulfilled. Perhaps
I have believed unfaithful witnesses   175
And raised too soon towards thee my cruel hands.
By what despair now will my prayers be followed!

SCENE 6. *Theseus and Theramenes*

THESEUS. Theramenes, is it you? What have you done
With Hippolytus? I entrusted him to you
From a tender age. But what has caused these tears   180

I see you shedding. What is my son doing?
THERAMENES. O tardy and superfluous cares, vain love!
  Hippolytus is no more.
THESEUS.   O Gods!
THERAMENES.   I have seen   185
  The most lovable of mortals die, and I must add,
  My lord, the least guilty.
THESEUS.   My son is dead?
  When I hold out my arms to him, the gods
  Have hastened his destruction. What dread blow   190
  Has snatched him from me? What sudden thunderclap?
THERAMENES. Scarce had we passed the gates of Troezen,
  He rode upon his chariot; his sad guards,
  Around him ranged, were silent as their lord.
  Brooding, he followed the Mycenæ road,   195
  And loosely held the reins. His splendid steeds,
  Which once with noble zeal obeyed his voice,
  Now with dejected eye and lowered head
  Seemed to adapt themselves to his sad thoughts.
  Then suddenly from out the waves there came   200
  A dreadful cry which broke the silent air
  And from the bosom of the earth a voice
  With dreadful groans replied. Our blood was frozen,
  Even to our hearts. The manes of the listening steeds
  Stood up. Then on the liquid plain arose   205
  A watery mountain which appeared to boil.
  The wave approached, then broke, and vomited
  Among the foamy seas a raging monster:
  His huge head armed with menacing horns, his body
  Covered with yellow scales, half-bull, half-dragon,   210
  With his croup curved in involuted folds.
  The seashore trembled with his bellowing;
  The sky with horror saw that savage monster;
  The earth was moved, the air infected with it;
  The sea which brought it started back amazed.   215
  Everyone fled; seeing all courage vain,
  They sought asylum in a neighboring temple.
  Hippolytus alone, a worthy son
  Of a heroic father, stopped his horses,
  Seized his javelins, approached the monster,   220
  And, with a dart, thrown with unerring aim,
  Wounded it in the flank. With rage and pain,
  The monster leapt, and at the horses' feet
  Fell roaring, rolled itself, and offered them
  Its flaming mouth, which covered them with fire,   225

And blood and smoke. Then terror seized them; deaf,
This time, nor voice nor bridle did they know.
Their master spent himself in useless efforts;
Their bits were reddened with a bloody foam.
'Tis said, that in this terrible confusion   230
A god was seen who spurred their dusty flanks.
Fear hurtled them across the rocks. The axle
Screeched and snapped. The bold Hippolytus
Saw all his chariot shiver into splinters;
And tangled in the reins, he fell. Excuse   235
My grief. That cruel sight will be for me
An everlasting source of tears. I've seen,
My lord, I've seen your most unlucky son
Dragged by the horses which his hands had fed.
He tried to check them; but, frightened by his voice,   240
They ran; and soon his body was a single wound.
The plain resounded with our grievous cries.
At last they slackened speed; they stopped not far
From those old tombs where his royal ancestors
Are the cold relics. There I ran, in tears,   245
And his guard followed me. A trail of blood
Showed us the way. The rocks were stained with it.
The loathsome brambles carried bloodstained scraps
Of hair torn from his head. I reached him, called
To him; he stretched his hand to me, and opened   250
His dying eyes, then closed them suddenly.
"The heavens," said he, "now snatch my guiltless life.
Look after Aricia when I am dead.
Dear friend, if my father one day learns the truth,
And weeps the tragic ending of a son   255
Falsely accused, in order to appease
My blood and plaintive ghost, tell him to treat
His captive kindly, to give her . . . ." At this word
The hero died and left within my arms
Only a corpse, disfigured, where the wrath   260
Of the gods had triumphed, one which his father's eyes
Would fail to recognize.
THESEUS.   My son! dear hope
Now taken from me! Inexorable gods,
Too well indeed you have fulfilled your word!   265
To what remorse my life is now reserved!
THERAMENES. Then gentle Aricia arrived; she came,
My lord, escaping from your wrath, to take him
Before the gods as husband. She approached.
She saw the red and reeking grass; she saw   270

(What an object for a lover's eyes!)
Hippolytus lying there a shapeless mass.
A while she wished to doubt of her disaster
And failed to recognize the man she loved.
She saw Hippolytus—and asked for him still.   275
At last too sure that he was lying there,
She with a mournful look reproached the gods;
Cold, moaning, almost lifeless, she fell down
At her lover's feet. Ismene was beside her;
Ismene, weeping, brought her back to life,   280
Or rather, back to grief. And I have come,
Hating the light, to tell you the last wish
Of a dead hero; and discharge, my lord,
The unhappy task his dying heart reposed
Upon me. But I see his mortal foe   285
Approaching.

SCENE 7. *Theseus, Theramenes, Phaedra, Panope, Guards*

THESEUS.   Well, you triumph, and my son
Is lifeless. Ah! how I have cause to fear!
A cruel suspicion, excusing him, alarms me.
But, madam, he is dead. Receive your victim,   290
Joy in his death, whether unjust or lawful.
I'll let my eyes forever be abused,
Believe him criminal, since you accuse him.
His death alone gives matter for my tears
Without my seeking harsh enlightenment,   295
Which could not bring him back, and might increase
The sum of my misfortunes. Let me, far from you,
Far from this coast flee from the bloody image
Of my rent son. Perplexed and persecuted
By deadly memories, I would banish me   300
From the whole world. Everything seems to rise
Against my injustice. Even my very fame
Augments my punishment. Less known of men,
I could the better hide. I hate the honors
The gods bestow upon me; and I'm going   305
To mourn their murderous favors, and no more
Tire them with useless prayers. Whate'er they granted,
Would never compensate me for the loss
Of what they've taken away.
PHAEDRA.   No, Theseus.   310
I must break an unjust silence; to your son
Restore his innocence. He was not guilty.
THESEUS. Unhappy father! It was by your word

That I condemned him. Cruel! do you think
That you can be excused . . . ?   315
PHAEDRA.   My time is precious.
　Hear me, Theseus. It was I myself
Who cast upon your chaste and modest son
Unholy and incestuous eyes. The heavens
Put in my breast that fatal spark—the rest   320
Was undertaken by the vile Œnone.
She trembled lest Hippolytus should disclose
A passion he abhorred. The traitress then,
Relying on my utter weakness, hastened
To accuse him to your face. She's punished for it.   325
Fleeing my wrath she sought amidst the waves
Too soft a punishment. The sword by now
Would have cut short my life, had I not left
Virtue suspected. Baring my remorse
Before you, I wished to take a slower road   330
To the house of Death. I have taken—I have made
Course through my burning veins a deadly poison
Medea⁵ brought to Athens. Already the venom
Has reached my dying heart, and thrown upon it
An unimagined cold. Already I see,   335
As through a mist, the sky above, the husband
My presence outrages; and Death, that robs
My eyes of clearness, to the day the soil
Restores its purity.
PANOPE.   She is dying, my lord.   340
THESEUS. Oh! that the memory of her black deed
Could perish with her! Of my error now
Only too well enlightened, let us go
To mix the blood of my unhappy son
With tears; to embrace the little that remains   345
Of that dear son, and expiate the madness
Of my detested prayer; to render him
The honors that he has too much deserved;
And, the better to appease his angry spirit,
Despite her family's plotting, from today   350
I'll hold Aricia as my own true child.

---

5. A sorceress who helped Jason get the Golden Fleece and later, deserted by him, killed her rival and her own children and burned her palace before fleeing to Athens. According to one legend, she tried to poison Theseus.

JONATHAN SWIFT

1667–1745

In virtually all his writing, Jonathan Swift displays his gift for making other people uncomfortable. He makes us uneasy by making us aware of our own moral inadequacies; and by his wit, his energy, his inventiveness, he actually compels us to enjoy the process of being brought to such awareness.

Born in Dublin to English parents, Swift was educated at Trinity College, Dublin. In 1689, the young man went to England, where he served as secretary to the statesman Sir William Temple. During his residence at Moor Park, Sir William's estate, Swift became friendly with Esther Johnson, daughter of the steward; he remained on close terms with her for the rest of his life. (His playful, intimate letters to her, under the name of Stella, were published in a collection called *Journal to Stella*.) In 1692, Swift received an M.A. from Oxford University; three years later, he took orders, becoming a clergyman in the Anglican Church but continuing in Sir William's employ, although with intermittent stays in Ireland. Early in the eighteenth century, he began his career of political journalism; he also published brilliant satiric works, including *A Tale of a Tub* (1704), of which he is supposed to have said, late in his life, "What a genius I had when I composed that book!" Although he had hoped for church advancement in England, as a reward for his writings in the Tory cause, in 1713 he was instead named dean of Saint Patrick's Cathedral, Dublin. He spent the rest of his life in Ireland, writing passionately on behalf of the oppressed Irish people. In his final years, he was declared mentally incompetent, suffering, presumably, from senility. As he had prophesied in his verses "On the Death of Dr. Swift," "He gave what little wealth he had / To build a house for fools and mad"; the mental hospital founded by his legacy still exists in Dublin.

Gulliver's Travels (1726) used the travel book, a form hovering between fact and fiction, as its model. Lemuel Gulliver, ship's surgeon, travels into four imagined nations. The first book takes him to Lilliput, where he duly observes the customs and traditions of a race of people six inches high. The narrative of their preoccupations and procedures mocks the pettiness of the English, although Gulliver, himself involved in the intrigues of his tiny hosts, fails to note the resemblance between Lilliput and his native land. His simple patriotism survives through the second book, where Gulliver encounters the giants of Brobdingnag, whose benevolent king, after hearing Gulliver's patriotic account of England, comments, "I cannot but conclude the bulk of your natives, to be the most pernicious race of little odious vermin that nature ever suffered to crawl upon the surface of the earth." The third book is more various, and Gulliver on the whole seems less gullible in his encounters with the ludicrous or dangerous results of abstract speculation divorced from practical concerns (philosophers, for instance, so deep in ratiocination that they have to be attended by "flappers," servants who "flap" them into awareness of immediate actuality), with the ghosts of great men from the past who stress the lies of historians and the moral and physical decline of their descendants, and with the terrifying Struldbrugs, who grow old but live forever in horrible senility.

Book Four, printed here, has always presented problems to critics. More directly than any other imaginative work of its period, it confronts problems inherent in the idealization of reason as sufficient guide to human conduct. It is easy enough to see that Swift has here imagined an absolute separation between the animal and the rational aspects of human nature. As Gulliver gradually and with horror realizes (the reader undergoing a comparable process), the disgusting Yahoos manifest degraded human form and embody characteristics of human beings deprived of all rational capacity. They act on the basis of pure—and ugly—passion: lust, envy, avarice, greed, rage. The Houyhnhnms, the governing class of horses, treat them as beasts, but consider them more ungovernable than other creatures; Gulliver, looking at them, sees a horrifying version of the human, become (by the absence of reason) subhuman.

As for the Houyhnhnms, those noble horses exemplify pure rationality. They lead monotonous, orderly lives, with no need for disagreement (the truth being self-evident to rational creatures) or excitement. Under their influence, Gulliver wants to stay forever in this land without literal or metaphorical salt. After the Houyhnhnms expel him, Gulliver can make no distinction among human beings: he condemns the benevolent Pedro Mendez as a Yahoo, resents his connection with his own wife and children, and spends as much time as possible in his stable. Life with the Houyhnhnms has driven him mad: he cannot adjust to English actuality.

The question is, why? By one interpretation, Gulliver judges rightly in perceiving his fellow human beings as essentially Yahoos. His Houyhnhnm master concludes, Gulliver says, that humans are "a sort of animals to whose share . . . some small pittance of reason had fallen, whereof we made no other use than by its assistance to aggravate our natural corruptions, and to acquire new ones which nature had not given us." Perhaps he is right. The Houyhnhnms exemplify an ideal to which human beings should aspire although they can never reach it; to call attention to the monotony of their lives or the failure of their curiosity only reveals the reader's participation in human depravity. Pedro Mendez is a good man, as men go, but the gulf between the best of men and a Houyhnhnm gapes so hugely that Gulliver sees correctly in detesting all humans. If he implicitly excepts himself, he thus acknowledges the difference his education by Houyhnhnms has made: at least he knows the gulf's existence.

Another view has it that the Houyhnhnms exemplify a way of being utterly irrelevant to humankind, as well as deeply boring. To hate the animal and glorify the rational denies the inextricable mixture of our nature. Gulliver's pride leads him to aspire to an essentially inhuman state; he wishes, sinfully, to exceed ordained natural limits. Moreover, he ignores the Christian virtue of charity, the command to love our neighbors. Captain Mendez demonstrates that virtue; Gulliver cannot perceive the moral distinction between the generous captain and the bloodthirsty natives who shoot the Englishman with an arrow shortly after he leaves the Houyhnhnms, producing a lasting scar. Gulliver's condemnation of pride in others emphasizes his blindness to his own flaws.

A compromise position might remind us that to declare the Houyhnhnms irrelevant perhaps leaves the reader in rather too comfortable a position, considering Swift's declared intention "to vex the world rather than divert it." *Gulliver's Travels*, this comment implies, involves serious attack. We can perhaps dismiss the Houyhnhnms as boring (they have virtually nothing to talk about) or heartless (they make no distinctions of parentage; they expel Gulliver despite his ardent desire to remain) because our natures include more than reason and we appropriately value principles of conduct beyond the rational. Gulliver becomes crazy when he returns to England, unable to accept his full human nature and to make necessary distinctions; given the limits of the human condition, men and women must find the way to operate within them. Gulliver fails and, failing, reminds us of necessities to which we must adapt. The Houyhnhnms provide no solution to human problems: their extirpation of passion, their narrow commitment to reason, prove "inhumane." (They are, after all, horses!) Humankind, as Swift suggested in a letter, is only capable of reason, not fully reasonable; perhaps the spontaneous generosity of the Portuguese captain exemplifies the greatest good to which human beings should aspire.

On the other hand, we claim to value reason; Gulliver has seen in pure form an ideal to which we pay lip service. His realization of the terrible discrepancy between ideal and actual has made it impossible for him to function in his own society; it has given him a harsh perspective by which he sees how morally intolerable social arrangements in fact are. The readiness of most people to compromise, given social necessity, shows how far they are from taking seriously the values they profess. Swift calls our attention to the divergences in our own lives between what we say we believe and how we actually behave. The reality of reason exceeds human capacities; *Gulliver's Travels* reminds us that we live by hypocrisies. The Houyhnhnms thus tell us something about ourselves despite their lack of humanity.

The problems in interpretation that *Gulliver's Travels* has always generated come partly from the fact that we receive all information about Gulliver's experience from the traveler himself, an untrustworthy source. In reading his narrative, we must assess his understanding: a slippery process, since we lack a point of reference. *Gulliver's Travels* abounds in allusions to such phenomena as corrupt lawyers and politicians, money-grubbing doctors, mass slaughter in wars over trivial pretexts—aspects of our experience as well as of Gulliver's, reminders that this narrative has something to do with us. The necessity of arriving at coherent judgment of Gulliver and his experiences implicates the reader in the moral problem of how to judge—and perhaps how to change—society.

Such implication of the reader in often uncomfortable processes of judgment typifies an important aspect of satire. *A Modest Proposal* (1729), Swift's attack on the economic oppression of the Irish by the English, keeps the reader constantly off balance, trying to understand exactly who is being criticized and why. Swift is writing out of his firsthand awareness of the suffering caused by English policies in Ireland. Absentee landlords who never saw the actual situation of their tenants, British politicians who made policy at a distance, presumably did not know that Ireland had become a land of the starving. The Irish people, however, in Swift's view, collaborated by their apathy with the oppressors. In *A Modest Proposal*, he attacks English and Irish alike.

Even more emphatically than Gulliver, the nameless speaker in *A Modest Proposal* proves an undependable guide, tempting us to identify with his tone of rationality and compassion, only to reveal that his plausible economic orientation leads to advocacy of cannibalism. He offers a series of morally sound and economically feasible suggestions for solutions to Ireland's problems, but draws back immediately, declaring them impossible, since no one will put them in practice. The satire indicts the English for inhumanity, the Irish for passivity, the economically oriented proposer of remedies for moral blindness; but it also reaches out to criticize the reader as representative of all who endure calmly the intolerable actuality in the world (but not, perhaps, where we have to see it ourselves) of man's inhumanity to man. Swift's self-chosen epitaph, on his tomb, may be translated, "Where fierce indignation no longer tears the heart." *A Modest Proposal* exemplifies the lacerating power of that indignation.

A good introduction to Swift's life and character is I. Ehrenpreis, *The Personality of Jonathan Swift* (1958). An interpretation of the writer in his intellectual context is K. Williams, *Jonathan Swift and the Age of Compromise* (1959). The annotated text of *Gulliver's Travels* with critical essays edited by R. A. Greenberg (1970) and the collection of critical essays, *Swift*, edited by E. Tuveson (1964), provide a useful range of responses.

Gulliver's Travels[1]

A *Letter from Captain Gulliver to His Cousin Sympson*[2]

I hope you will be ready to own publicly, whenever you shall be called to it, that by your great and frequent urgency you prevailed on me to publish a very loose and uncorrect account of my travels; with direction to hire some young gentlemen of either University to put them in order, and correct the style, as my Cousin Dampier[3] did by my advice, in his book called *A Voyage round the World*. But I do not remember I gave you power to consent that anything should be omitted, and much less that anything should be inserted: therefore, as to the latter, I do here renounce everything of that kind; particularly a paragraph about her Majesty the late Queen Anne, of most pious and glorious memory; although I did reverence and esteem her more than any of human species. But you, or your interpolator, ought to have considered that as it was not my inclination, so was it

---

1. Abridged. Swift's full title for this work was *Travels into Several Remote Nations of the World. In Four Parts. By Lemuel Gulliver, First a Surgeon, and then a Captain of several Ships.* The text is based on the Dublin edition of Swift's work (1735).   2. In this letter, first published in 1735, Swift complains, among other matters, of the alterations in his original text made by the publisher, Benjamin Motte, in the interest of what he considered political discretion.   3. William Dampier (1652–1715), the explorer, whose account of his circumnavigation of the globe Swift had read.

not decent to praise any animal of our composition before my master Houyhnhnm; and besides, the fact was altogether false; for to my knowledge, being in England during some part of her Majesty's reign, she did govern by a chief Minister; nay, even by two successively; the first whereof was the Lord of Godolphin, and the second the Lord of Oxford; so that you have made me *say the thing that was not*. Likewise, in the account of the Academy of Projectors, and several passages of my discourse to my master Houyhnhnm, you have either omitted some material circumstances, or minced or changed them in such a manner, that I do hardly know mine own work. When I formerly hinted to you something of this in a letter, you were pleased to answer that you were afraid of giving offense; that people in power were very watchful over the press; and apt not only to interpret, but to punish everything which looked like an *inuendo* (as I think you called it). But pray, how could that which I spoke so many years ago, and at above five thousand leagues distance, in another reign, be applied to any of the Yahoos, who now are said to govern the herd; especially, at a time when I little thought on or feared the unhappiness of living under them. Have not I the most reason to complain, when I see these very Yahoos carried by Houyhnhnms in a vehicle, as if these were brutes, and those the rational creatures? And, indeed, to avoid so monstrous and detestable a sight was one principal motive of my retirement hither.[4]

Thus much I thought proper to tell you in relation to yourself, and to the trust I reposed in you.

I do in the next place complain of my own great want of judgment, in being prevailed upon by the intreaties and false reasonings of you and some others, very much against mine own opinion, to suffer my travels to be published. Pray bring to your mind how often I desired you to consider, when you insisted on the motive of public good, that the Yahoos were a species of animals utterly incapable of amendment by precepts or examples; and so it hath proved; for instead of seeing a full stop put to all abuses and corruptions, at least in this little island, as I had reason to expect, behold, after above six months warning. I cannot learn that my book hath produced one single effect according to mine intentions; I desired you would let me know by a letter, when party and faction were extinguished; judges learned and upright; pleaders honest and modest, with some tincture of common sense; and Smithfield[5] blazing with pyramids of law books; the young nobility's education entirely changed; the physicians banished; the female Yahoos abounding in virtue, honor, truth, and good sense; courts and levees of great ministers thoroughly weeded and swept; wit, merit, and learning rewarded; all disgracers of the press in prose

4. To Nottinghamshire, central England.   5. A part of London containing many bookshops.

and verse, condemned to eat nothing but their own cotton, and quench
their thirst with their own ink. These, and a thousand other refor-
mations, I firmly counted upon by your encouragement; as indeed
they were plainly deducible from the precepts delivered in my book.
And, it must be owned that seven months were a sufficient time to
correct every vice and folly to which Yahoos are subject; if their
natures had been capable of the least disposition to virtue or wisdom;
yet so far have you been from answering mine expectation in any of
your letters, that on the contrary, you are loading our carrier every
week with libels, and keys, and reflections, and memoirs, and second parts; wherein I see myself accused of reflecting upon great sta-
tesfolk; of degrading human nature (for so they have still the confidence
to style it) and of abusing the female sex. I find likewise, that the
writers of those bundles are not agreed among themselves; for some
of them will not allow me to be author of mine own travels; and
others make me author of books to which I am wholly a stranger.

I find likewise that your printer hath been so careless as to confound the times, and mistake the dates of my several voyages and
returns; neither assigning the true year, or the true month, or day of
the month; and I hear the original manuscript is all destroyed, since
the publication of my book. Neither have I any copy left; however,
I have sent you some corrections, which you may insert, if ever there
should be a second edition; and yet I cannot stand to them, but shall
leave that matter to my judicious and candid readers, to adjust it as
they please.

I hear some of our sea Yahoos find fault with my sea language, as
not proper in many parts, nor now in use. I cannot help it. In my
first voyages, while I was young, I was instructed by the oldest mariners, and learned to speak as they did. But I have since found that
the sea Yahoos are apt, like the land ones, to become new fangled
in their words; which the latter change every year; insomuch, as I
remember upon each return to mine own country, their old dialect
was so altered, that I could hardly understand the new. And I observe,
when any Yahoo comes from London out of curiosity to visit me at
mine own house, we neither of us are able to deliver our conceptions
in a manner intelligible to the other.

If the censure of Yahoos could any way affect me, I should have
great reason to complain that some of them are so bold as to think
my book of travels a mere fiction out of mine own brain; and have
gone so far as to drop hints that the Houyhnhnms and Yahoos have
no more existence than the inhabitants of Utopia.

Indeed I must confess that as to the people of Lilliput, Brobding-
rag (for so the word should have been spelled, and not erroneously
Brobdingnag) and Laputa, I have never yet heard of any Yahoo so
presumptuous as to dispute their being, or the facts I have related

concerning them; because the truth immediately strikes every reader with conviction. And, is there less probability in my account of the Houyhnhnms or Yahoos, when it is manifest as to the latter, there are so many thousands even in this city, who only differ from their brother brutes in Houyhnhnmland, because they use a sort of a jabber, and do not go naked. I wrote for their amendment, and not their approbation. The united praise of the whole race would be of less consequence to me, than the neighing of those two degenerate Houyhnhnms I keep in my stable; because, from these, degenerate as they are, I still improve in some virtues, without any mixture of vice.

Do these miserable animals presume to think that I am so far degenerated as to defend my veracity; Yahoo as I am, it is well known through all Houyhnhnmland, that by the instructions and example of my illustrious master, I was able in the compass of two years (although I confess with the utmost difficulty) to remove that infernal habit of lying, shuffling, deceiving, and equivocating, so deeply rooted in the very souls of all my species; especially the Europeans.

I have other complaints to make upon this vexatious occasion; but I forbear troubling myself or you any further. I must freely confess that since my last return, some corruptions of my Yahoo nature have revived in me by conversing with a few of your species, and particularly those of mine own family, by an unavoidable necessity; else I should never have attempted so absurd a project as that of reforming the Yahoo race in this kingdom; but I have now done with all such visionary schemes for ever.

1727?   1735

The Publisher to the Reader

The author of these travels, Mr. Lemuel Gulliver, is my ancient and intimate friend; there is likewise some relation between us by the mother's side. About three years ago Mr. Gulliver, growing weary of the concourse of curious people coming to him at his house in Redriff,[6] made a small purchase of land, with a convenient house, near Newark, in Nottinghamshire, his native country; where he now lives retired, yet in good esteem among his neighbors.

Although Mr. Gulliver were born in Nottinghamshire, where his father dwelt, yet I have heard him say his family came from Oxfordshire; to confirm which, I have observed in the churchyard at Banbury, in that county, several tombs and monuments of the Gullivers.

Before he quitted Redriff, he left the custody of the following papers in my hands, with the liberty to dispose of them as I should think

6. Rotherhithe, a district in southern London then frequented by sailors.

fit. I have carefully perused them three times; the style is very plain and simple; and the only fault I find is that the author, after the manner of travelers, is a little too circumstantial. There is an air of truth apparent through the whole; and indeed the author was so distinguished for his veracity, that it became a sort of proverb among his neighbors at Redriff, when anyone affirmed a thing, to say, it was as true as if Mr. Gulliver had spoke it.

By the advice of several worthy persons, to whom, with the author's permission, I communicated these papers, I now venture to send them into the world; hoping they may be, at least for some time, a better entertainment to our young noblemen, than the common scribbles of politics and party.

This volume would have been at least twice as large, if I had not made bold to strike out innumerable passages relating to the winds and tides, as well as to the variations and bearings in the several voyages; together with the minute descriptions of the management of the ship in storms, in the style of sailors; likewise the account of the longitudes and latitudes, wherein I have reason to apprehend that Mr. Gulliver may be a little dissatisfied; but I was resolved to fit the work as much as possible to the general capacity of readers. However, if my own ignorance in sea affairs shall have led me to commit some mistakes, I alone am answerable for them; and if any traveler hath a curiosity to see the whole work at large, as it came from the hand of the author, I will be ready to gratify him.

As for any further particulars relating to the author, the reader will receive satisfaction from the first pages of the book.

RICHARD SYMPSON

Part IV. A Voyage to the Country of the Houyhnhnms[7]

CHAPTER I. *The Author sets out as Captain of a ship. His men conspire against him, confine him a long time to his cabin, set him on shore in an unknown land. He travels up into the country. The Yahoos, a strange sort of animal, described. The Author meets two Houyhnhnms.*

I continued at home with my wife and children about five months in a very happy condition, if I could have learned the lesson of knowing when I was well. I left my poor wife big with child, and accepted an advantageous offer made me to be Captain of the *Adventure*, a stout merchantman of 350 tons; for I understood navigation well, and being grown weary of a surgeon's employment at sea, which however I could exercise upon occasion, I took a skillful young man

---

7. Pronounced Hwin-ims, the word suggests a horse neighing.

of that calling, one Robert Purefoy, into my ship. We set sail from Portsmouth upon the 7th day of September, 1710; on the 14th we met with Captain Pocock of Bristol, at Tenariff, who was going to the Bay of Campeachy[8] to cut logwood. On the 16th he was parted from us by a storm; I heard since my return that his ship foundered and none escaped, but one cabin boy. He was an honest man and a good sailor, but a little too positive in his own opinions, which was the cause of his destruction, as it hath been of several others. For if he had followed my advice, he might at this time have been safe at home with his family as well as myself.

I had several men died in my ship of calentures,[9] so that I was forced to get recruits out of Barbadoes and the Leeward Islands,[1] where I touched by the direction of the merchants who employed me; which I had soon too much cause to repent, for I found afterwards that most of them had been buccaneers. I had fifty hands on board; and my orders were that I should trade with the Indians in the South Sea, and make what discoveries I could. These rogues whom I had picked up debauched my other men, and they all formed a conspiracy to seize the ship and secure me; which they did one morning, rushing into my cabin, and binding me hand and foot, threatening to throw me overboard, if I offered to stir. I told them I was their prisoner, and would submit. This they made me swear to do, and then unbound me, only fastening one of my legs with a chair near my bed, and placed a sentry at my door with his piece charged, who was commanded to shoot me dead if I attempted my liberty. They sent me down victuals and drink, and took the government of the ship to themselves. Their design was to turn pirates and plunder the Spaniards, which they could not do, till they got more men. But first they resolved to sell the goods in the ship, and then go to Madagascar for recruits, several among them having died since my confinement. They sailed many weeks, and traded with the Indians; but I knew not what course they took, being kept close prisoner in my cabin, and expecting nothing less than to be murdered, as they often threatened me.

Upon the 9th day of May, 1711, one James Welch came down to my cabin; and said he had orders from the Captain to set me ashore. I expostulated with him, but in vain; neither would he so much as tell me who their new Captain was. They forced me into the longboat, letting me put on my best suit of clothes, which were as good as new, and a small bundle of linen, but no arms except my hanger;[2] and they were so civil as not to search my pockets, into which I

8. Probably Campeche, in southeast Mexico, on the western side of the Yucatan peninsula. *Tenariff*: Largest of the Canary Islands, off northwest Africa in the Atlantic. 9. Tropical fever. 1. The northern group of the Lesser Antilles in the West Indies, extending southeast from Puerto Rico. Barbados is the easternmost of the West Indies. 2. A small sword.

conveyed what money I had, with some other little necessaries. They rowed about a league, and then set me down on a strand. I desired them to tell me what country it was; they all swore, they knew no more than myself, but said that the Captain (as they called him) was resolved, after they had sold the lading, to get rid of me in the first place where they discovered land. They pushed off immediately, advising me to make haste, for fear of being overtaken by the tide, and bade me farewell.

In this desolate condition I advanced forward, and soon got upon firm ground, where I sat down on a bank to rest myself, and consider what I had best to do. When I was a little refreshed, I went up into the country, resolving to deliver myself to the first savages I should meet, and purchase my life from them by some bracelets, glass rings, and other toys, which sailors usually provide themselves with in those voyages, and whereof I had some about me. The land was divided by long rows of trees, not regularly planted, but naturally growing; there was great plenty of grass, and several fields of oats. I walked very circumspectly for fear of being surprised, or suddenly shot with an arrow from behind, or on either side. I fell into a beaten road, where I saw many tracks of human feet, and some of cows, but most of horses. At last I beheld several animals in a field, and one or two of the same kind sitting in trees. Their shape was very singular, and deformed, which a little discomposed me, so that I lay down behind a thicket to observe them better. Some of them coming forward near the place where I lay, gave me an opportunity of distinctly marking their form. Their heads and breasts were covered with a thick hair, some frizzled and others lank; they had beards like goats, and a long ridge of hair down their backs, and the fore parts of their legs and feet; but the rest of their bodies were bare, so that I might see their skins, which were of a brown buff color. They had no tails, nor any hair at all on their buttocks, except about the anus; which, I presume Nature had placed there to defend them as they sat on the ground; for this posture they used, as well as lying down, and often stood on their hind feet. They climbed high trees, as nimbly as a squirrel, for they had strong extended claws before and behind, terminating in sharp points, and hooded. They would often spring, and bound, and leap with prodigious agility. The females were not so large as the males; they had long lank hair on their heads, and only a sort of down on the rest of their bodies, except about the anus, and pudenda. Their dugs hung between their forefeet, and often reached almost to the ground as they walked. The hair of both sexes was of several colors, brown, red, black, and yellow. Upon the whole, I never beheld in all my travels so disagreeable an animal, or one against which I naturally conceived so strong an antipathy. So that thinking I had seen enough, full of contempt and aversion, I got up and pursued the beaten road, hoping it might direct me to the cabin of some Indian: I had not gone far when I met one of these creatures full in my way, and coming up directly to me. The ugly monster, when he saw me, distorted several ways every feature of his visage, and stared as at an object he had never seen before; then approaching nearer, lifted up his forepaw, whether out of curiosity or mischief, I could not tell; but I drew my hanger, and gave him a good blow with the flat side of it; for I durst not strike him with the edge, fearing the inhabitants might be provoked against me, if they should come to know that I had killed or maimed any of their cattle. When the beast felt the smart, he drew back, and roared so loud, that a herd of at least forty came flocking about me from the next field, howling and making odious faces; but I ran to the body of a tree, and leaning my back against it, kept them off, by waving my hanger. Several of this cursed brood getting hold of the branches behind, leaped up into the tree, from whence they began to discharge their excrements on my head; however, I escaped pretty well, by sticking close to the stem of the tree, but was almost stifled with the filth, which fell about me on every side.

In the midst of this distress, I observed them all to run away on a sudden as fast as they could; at which I ventured to leave the tree, and pursue the road, wondering what it was that could put them into this fright. But looking on my left hand, I saw a horse walking softly in the field; which my persecutors having sooner discovered, was the cause of their flight. The horse started a little when he came near me, but soon recovering himself, looked full in my face with manifest tokens of wonder; he viewed my hands and feet, walking round me several times. I would have pursued my journey, but he placed himself directly in the way, yet looking with a very mild aspect, never offering the least violence. We stood gazing at each other for some time; at last I took the boldness, to reach my hand towards his neck, with a design to stroke it; using the common style and whistle of jockies when they are going to handle a strange horse. But, this animal seeming to receive my civilities with disdain, shook his head, and bent his brows, softly raising up his left forefoot to remove my hand. Then he neighed three or four times, but in so different a cadence, that I almost began to think he was speaking to himself in some language of his own.

While he and I were thus employed, another horse came up; who applying himself to the first in a very formal manner, they gently struck each others right hoof before, neighing several times by turns, and varying the sound, which seemed to be almost articulate. They went some paces off, as if it were to confer together, walking side by side, backward and forward, like persons deliberating upon some affair of weight; but often turning their eyes towards me, as it were to watch that I might not escape. I was amazed to see such actions and behavior in brute beasts; and concluded with myself that if the inhabitants of this country were endued with a proportionable degree of reason, they must needs be the wisest people upon earth. This thought gave me so much comfort, that I resolved to go forward until I could discover some house or village, or meet with any of the natives, leaving the two horses to discourse together as they pleased. But the first, who was a dapple grey, observing me to steal off, neighed after me in so expressive a tone that I fancied myself to understand what he meant; whereupon I turned back, and came near him, to expect his farther commands; but concealing my fear as much as I could; for I began to be in some pain, how this adventure might terminate; and the reader will easily believe I did not much like my present situation.

The two horses came up close to me, looking with great earnestness upon my face and hands. The grey steed rubbed my hat all round with his right fore hoof, and discomposed it so much that I was forced to adjust it better, by taking it off, and settling it again; whereat both he and his companion (who was a brown bay) appeared to be much surprised; the latter felt the lappet of my coat, and finding it to hang loose about me, they both looked with new signs of wonder. He stroked my right hand, seeming to admire the softness, and color; but he squeezed it so hard between his hoof and his pastern,[3] that I was forced to roar; after which they both touched me with all possible tenderness. They were under great perplexity about my shoes and stockings, which they felt very often, neighing to each other, and using various gestures, not unlike those of a philosopher, when he would attempt to solve some new and difficult phenomenon.

Upon the whole, the behavior of these animals was so orderly and rational, so acute and judicious, that I at last concluded, they must needs be magicians, who had thus metamorphosed themselves upon some design; and seeing a stranger in the way, were resolved to divert themselves with him; or perhaps were really amazed at the sight of a man so very different in habit, feature, and complexion from those who might probably live in so remote a climate. Upon the strength of this reasoning, I ventured to address them in the following manner: "Gentlemen, if you be conjurers, as I have good cause to believe, you can understand any language; therefore I make bold to let your worships know that I am a poor distressed Englishman, driven by his misfortunes upon your coast; and I entreat one of you, to let me ride upon his back, as if he were a real horse, to some house or village,

---

3. "The pastern of a horse . . . is the distance between the joint next the foot, and the coronet of the hoof." The definition is taken from the first edition of the *Encyclopaedia Britannica* (1768–1771), subsequently referred to as *E.B.*

where I can be relieved. In return of which favor, I will make you a present of this knife and bracelet" (taking them out of my pocket). The two creatures stood silent while I spoke, seeming to listen with great attention; and when I had ended, they neighed frequently towards each other, as if they were engaged in serious conversation. I plainly observed, that their language expressed the passions very well, and the words might with little pains be resolved into an alphabet more easily than the Chinese.

I could frequently distinguish the word *Yahoo*, which was repeated by each of them several times; and although it were impossible for me to conjecture what it meant, yet while the two horses were busy in conversation, I endeavored to practice this word upon my tongue; and as soon as they were silent, I boldly pronounced "Yahoo" in a loud voice, imitating, at the same time, as near as I could, the neighing of a horse; at which they were both visibly surprised, and the grey repeated the same word twice, as if he meant to teach me the right accent, wherein I spoke after him as well as I could, and found myself perceivably to improve every time, although very far from any degree of perfection. Then the bay tried me with a second word, much harder to be pronounced; but reducing it to the English orthography, may be spelt thus *Houyhnhnm*. I did not succeed in this so well as the former, but after two or three farther trials, I had better fortune; and they both appeared amazed at my capacity.

After some farther discourse, which I then conjectured might relate to me, the two friends took their leaves, with the same compliment of striking each other's hoof; and the grey made me signs that I should walk before him; wherein I thought it prudent to comply, till I could find a better director. When I offered to slacken my pace, he would cry, "Hhuun, Hhuun"; I guessed his meaning, and gave him to understand, as well as I could that I was weary, and not able to walk faster; upon which, he would stand a while to let me rest.

CHAPTER II. *The Author conducted by a Houyhnhnm to his house. The house described. The Author's reception. The food of the Houyhnhnms. The Author in distress for want of meat is at last relieved. His manner of feeding in that country.*

Having traveled about three miles, we came to a long kind of building, made of timber, stuck in the ground, and wattled across; the roof was low, and covered with straw. I now began to be a little comforted, and took out some toys, which travelers usually carry for presents to the savage Indians of America and other parts, in hopes the people of the house would be thereby encouraged to receive me kindly. The horse made me a sign to go in first; it was a large room with a smooth clay floor, and a rack and manger extending the whole length on one side. There were three nags, and two mares, not eating, but some of them sitting down upon their hams, which I very much wondered at; but wondered more to see the rest employed in domestic business; the last seemed but ordinary cattle; however this confirmed my first opinion, that a people who could so far civilize brute animals must needs excel in wisdom all the nations of the world. The grey came in just after, and thereby prevented any ill treatment, which the others might have given me. He neighed to them several times in a style of authority, and received answers.

Beyond this room there were three others, reaching the length of the house, to which you passed through three doors, opposite to each other, in the manner of a vista; we went through the second room towards the third; here the grey walked in first, beckoning me to attend; I waited in the second room, and got ready my presents, for the master and mistress of the house; they were two knives, three bracelets of false pearl, a small looking glass and a bead necklace. The horse neighed three or four times, and I waited to hear some answers in a human voice, but I heard no other returns than in the same dialect, only one or two a little shriller than his. I began to think that this house must belong to some person of great note among them, because there appeared so much ceremony before I could gain admittance. But, that a man of quality should be served all by horses, was beyond my comprehension. I feared my brain was disturbed by my sufferings and misfortunes; I roused myself, and looked about me in the room where I was left alone; this was furnished as the first, only after a more elegant manner. I rubbed my eyes often, but the same objects still occurred. I pinched my arms and sides, to awake myself, hoping I might be in a dream. I then absolutely concluded that all these appearances could be nothing else but necromancy and magic. But I had no time to pursue these reflections; for the grey horse came to the door, and made me a sign to follow him into the third room; where I saw a very comely mare, together with a colt and foal, sitting on their haunches, upon mats of straw, not unartfully made, and perfectly neat and clean.

The mare soon after my entrance, rose from her mat, and coming up close, after having nicely observed my hands and face, gave me a most contemptuous look; then turning to the horse, I heard the word Yahoo often repeated betwixt them; the meaning of which word I could not then comprehend, although it were the first I had learned to pronounce; but I was soon better informed, to my everlasting mortification: for the horse beckoning to me with his head, and repeating the word, "Hhuun, Hhuun," as he did upon the road, which I understood was to attend him, led me out into a kind of court, where was another building at some distance from the house. Here we entreed, and I saw three of those detestable creatures, which I first met after my landing, feeding upon roots, and the flesh of some animals, which I afterwards found to be that of asses and dogs, and now and then a cow dead by accident or disease. They were all tied by the neck with strong withes,[4] fastened to a beam; they held their food between the claws of their forefeet, and tore it with their teeth.

The master horse ordered a sorrel nag, one of his servants, to untie the largest of these animals, and take him into a yard. The beast and I were brought close together; and our countenances diligently compared, both by master and servant, who thereupon repeated several times the word "Yahoo." My horror and astonishment are not to be described, when I observed, in this abominable animal, a perfect human figure; the face of it indeed was flat and broad, the nose depressed, the lips large, and the mouth wide; but these differences are common to all savage nations, where the lineaments of the countenance are distorted by the natives suffering their infants to lie groveling on the earth, or by carrying them on their backs, nuzzling with their face against the mother's shoulders. The forefeet of the Yahoo differed from my hands in nothing else but the length of the nails, the coarseness and brownness of the palms, and the nairiness on the backs. There was the same resemblance between our feet, with the same differences, which I knew very well, although the horses did not, because of my shoes and stockings; the same in every part of our bodies, except as to hairiness and color, which I have already described.

The great difficulty that seemed to stick with the two horses was to see the rest of my body so very different from that of a Yahoo, for which I was obliged to my clothes, whereof they had no conception; the sorrel nag offered me a root, which he held (after their manner, as we shall describe in its proper place) between his hoof and pastern; I took it in my hand, and having smelled it, returned it to him again as civilly as I could. He brought out of the Yahoo's kennel a piece of ass's flesh, but it smelled so offensively that I turned from it with loathing; he then threw it to the Yahoo, by whom it was greedily devoured. He afterwards showed me a wisp of hay, and a fetlock[5] full of oats; but I shook my head, to signify that neither of these were food for me. And indeed, I now apprehended that I must absolutely starve, if I did not get to some of my own species; for as to those filthy Yahoos, although there were few greater lovers of mankind, at that time, than myself, yet I confess I never saw any sensitive being so detestable on all accounts; and the more I came near them, the more hateful they grew, while I stayed in that country. This the master horse observed by my behavior, and therefore sent the Yahoo back to his kennel. He then put his forehoof to his mouth, at which I was

---

4. Fibers braided into rope.   5. "A tuft of hair growing behind the pastern joint of many horses; for those of a low size have scarce any such tuft." E.B.

much surprised, although he did it with ease, and with a motion that appeared perfectly natural; and made other signs to know what I would eat; but I could not return him such an answer as he was able to apprehend; and if he had understood me, I did not see how it was possible to contrive any way for finding myself nourishment. While we were thus engaged, I observed a cow passing by; whereupon I pointed to her, and expressed a desire to let me go and milk her. This had its effect; for he led me back into the house, and ordered a mare-servant to open a room, where a good store of milk lay in earthen and wooden vessels, after a very orderly and cleanly manner. She gave me a large bowl full, of which I drank very heartily, and found myself well refreshed.

About noon I saw coming towards the house a kind of vehicle, drawn like a sledge by four Yahoos. There was in it an old steed, who seemed to be of quality; he alighted with his hind feet forward, having by accident got a hurt in his left forefoot. He came to dine with our horse, who received him with great civility. They dined in the best room, and had oats boiled in milk for the second course, which the old horse eat warm, but the rest cold. Their mangers were placed circular in the middle of the room, and divided into several partitions, round which they sat on their haunches upon bosses of straw. In the middle was a large rack with angles answering to every partition of the manger. So that each horse and mare eat their own hay, and their own mash of oats and milk, with much decency and regularity. The behavior of the young colt and foal appeared very modest; and that of the master and mistress extremely cheerful and complaisant to their guest. The grey ordered me to stand by him; and much discourse passed between him and his friend concerning me, as I found by the stranger's often looking on me, and the frequent repetition of the word Yahoo.

I happened to wear my gloves; which the master grey observing, seemed perplexed; discovering signs of wonder what I had done to my forefeet; he put his hoof three or four times to them, as if he would signify, that I should reduce them to their former shape, which I presently did, pulling off both my gloves, and putting them into my pocket. This occasioned farther talk, and I saw the company was pleased with my behavior, whereof I soon found the good effects. I was ordered to speak the few words I understood; and while they were at dinner, the master taught me the names for oats, milk, fire, water, and some others which I could readily pronounce after him, having from my youth a great facility in learning languages.

When dinner was done, the master horse took me aside, and by signs and words made me understand the concern he was in that I had nothing to eat. Oats in their tongue are called *hlunnh*. This word I pronounced two or three times; for although I had refused them at first, yet upon second thoughts, I considered that I could contrive to make a kind of bread, which might be sufficient with milk to keep me alive, till I could make my escape to some other country, and to creatures of my own species. The horse immediately ordered a white mare-servant of his family to bring me a good quantity of oats in a sort of wooden tray. These I heated before the fire as well as I could, and rubbed them till the husks came off, which I made a shift to winnow from the grain; I ground and beat them between two stones, then took water, and made them into a paste or cake, which I toasted at the fire, and eat warm with milk. It was at first a very insipid diet, although common enough in many parts of Europe, but grew tolerable by time; and having been often reduced to hard fare in my life, this was not the first experiment I had made how easily nature is satisfied. And I cannot but observe that I never had one hour's sickness, while I staid in this island. It is true, I sometimes made a shift to catch a rabbit, or bird, by springes made of Yahoos' hairs; and I often gathered wholesome herbs, which I boiled, or ate as salads with my bread; and now and then, for a rarity, I made a little butter, and drank the whey. I was at first at a great loss for salt; but custom soon reconciled the want of it; and I am confident that the frequent use of salt among us is an effect of luxury, and was first introduced only as a provocative to drink; except where it is necessary for preserving of flesh in long voyages, or in places remote from great markets. For we observe no animal to be fond of it but man;[6] and as to myself, when I left this country, it was a great while before I could endure the taste of it in anything that I eat.

This is enough to say upon the subject of my diet, wherewith other travelers fill their books, as if the readers were personally concerned whether we fare well or ill. However, it was necessary to mention this matter, lest the world should think it impossible that I could find sustenance for three years in such a country, and among such inhabitants.

When it grew towards evening, the master horse ordered a place for me to lodge in; it was but six yards from the house, and separated from the stable of the Yahoos. Here I got some straw, and covering myself with my own clothes, slept very sound. But I was in a short time better accommodated, as the reader shall know hereafter, when I come to treat more particularly about my way of living.

CHAPTER III. *The Author studious to learn the language, the Houyhnhnm his master assists in teaching him. The language described. Several Houyhnhnms of quality come out of curiosity to see the Author. He gives his master a short account of his voyage.*

6. Gulliver's error: many animals are very fond of salt.

My principal endeavor was to learn the language, which my master (for so I shall henceforth call him) and his children, and every servant of his house were desirous to teach me. For they looked upon it as a prodigy, that a brute animal should discover such marks of a rational creature. I pointed to everything, and enquired the name of it, which I wrote down in my journal book when I was alone, and corrected my bad accent, by desiring those of the family to pronounce it often. In this employment, a sorrel nag, one of the under servants, was very ready to assist me.

In speaking, they pronounce through the nose and throat, and their language approaches nearest to the High Dutch or German, of any I know in Europe; but is much more graceful and significant. The Emperor Charles V made almost the same observation, when he said, that if he were to speak to his horse, it should be in High Dutch.[7]

The curiosity and impatience of my master were so great, that he spent many hours of his leisure to instruct me. He was convinced (as he afterwards told me) that I must be a Yahoo, but my teachableness, civility, and cleanliness astonished him; which were qualities altogether so opposite to those animals. He was most perplexed about my clothes, reasoning sometimes with himself whether they were a part of my body; for I never pulled them off till the family were asleep, and got them on before they waked in the morning. My master was eager to learn from whence I came; how I acquired those appearances of reason, which I discovered in all my actions; and to know my story from my own mouth, which he hoped he should soon do by the great proficiency I made in learning and pronouncing their words and sentences. To help my memory, I formed all I learned into the English alphabet, and writ the words down with the translations. This last, after some time, I ventured to do in my master's presence. It cost me much trouble to explain to him what I was doing; for the inhabitants have not the least idea of books or literature.

In about ten weeks time I was able to understand most of his questions; and in three months could give him some tolerable answers. He was extremely curious to know from what part of the country I came, and how I was taught to imitate a rational creature; because the Yahoos (whom he saw I exactly resembled in my head, hands, and face, that were only visible) with some appearance of cunning, and the strongest disposition to mischief, were observed to be the most unteachable of all brutes. I answered that I came over the sea,

7. Charles was reputed to have said he would address his God in Spanish, his mistress in Italian, and his horse in German.

from a far place, with many others of my own kind, in a great hollow vessel made of the bodies of trees; that my companions forced me to land on this coast, and then left me to shift for myself. It was with some difficulty, and by the help of many signs, that I brought him to understand me. He replied that I must needs be mistaken, or that I *said the thing which was not*. (For they have no word in their language to express lying or falsehood.) He knew it was impossible that there could be a country beyond the sea, or that a parcel of brutes could move a wooden vessel whither they pleased upon water. He was sure no Houyhnhnm alive could make such a vessel, or would trust Yahoos to manage it.

The word Houyhnhnm, in their tongue, signifies a Horse; and in its etymology, the Perfection of Nature. I told my master that I was at a loss for expression, but would improve as fast as I could; and hoped in a short time I should be able to tell him wonders; he was pleased to direct his own mare, his colt, and foal, and the servants of the family to take all opportunities of instructing me; and every day for two or three hours, he was at the same pains himself; several horses and mares of quality in the neighborhood came often to our house, upon the report spread of a wonderful Yahoo, that could speak like a Houyhnhnm, and seemed in his words and actions to discover some glimmerings of reason. These delighted to converse with me; they put many questions, and received such answers as I was able to return. By all which advantages, I made so great a progress, that in five months from my arrival, I understood whatever was spoke, and could express myself tolerably well.

The Houyhnhnms who came to visit my master, out of a design of seeing and talking with me, could hardly believe me to be a right Yahoo, because my body had a different covering from others of my kind. They were astonished to observe me without the usual hair or skin, except on my head, face, and hands; but I discovered that secret to my master, upon an accident, which happened about a fortnight before.

I have already told the reader, that every night when the family were gone to bed, it was my custom to strip and cover myself with my clothes; it happened one morning early, that my master sent for me, by the sorrel nag, who was his valet; when he came, I was fast asleep, my clothes fallen off on one side, and my shirt above my waist. I awaked at the noise he made, and observed him to deliver his message in some disorder; after which he went to my master, and in a great fright gave him a very confused account of what he had seen; this I presently discovered; for going as soon as I was dressed, to pay my attendance upon his honor, he asked me the meaning of what his servant had reported; that I was not the same thing when I slept as I appeared to be at other times; that his valet assured him, some part of me was white, some yellow, at least not so white, and some brown.

I had hitherto concealed the secret of my dress, in order to distinguish myself as much as possible, from that cursed race of Yahoos; but now I found it in vain to do so any longer. Besides, I considered that my clothes and shoes would soon wear out, which already were in a declining condition, and must be supplied by some contrivance from the hides of Yahoos, or other brutes; whereby the whole secret would be known. I therefore told my master, that in the country from whence I came, those of my kind always covered their bodies with the hairs of certain animals prepared by art, as well for decency, as to avoid inclemencies of air both hot and cold; of which, as to my own person I would give him immediate conviction, if he pleased to command me; only desiring his excuse, if I did not expose those parts that nature taught us to conceal. He said, my discourse was all very strange, but especially the last part; for he could not understand why Nature should teach us to conceal what Nature had given. That neither himself nor family were ashamed of any parts of their bodies; but however I might do as I pleased. Whereupon, I first unbuttoned my coat, and pulled it off. I did the same with my waistcoat; I drew off my shoes, stockings, and breeches. I let my shirt down to my waist, and drew up the bottom, fastening it like a girdle about my middle to hide my nakedness.

My master observed the whole performance with great signs of curiosity and admiration. He took up all my clothes in his pastern, one piece after another, and examined them diligently; he then stroked my body very gently, and looked round me several times; after which he said, it was plain I must be a perfect Yahoo; but that I differed very much from the rest of my species, in the whiteness and smoothness of my skin, my want of hair in several parts of my body, the shape and shortness of my claws behind and before, and my affectation of walking continually on my two hinder feet. He desired to see no more; and gave me leave to put on my clothes again, for I was shuddering with cold.

I expressed my uneasiness at his giving me so often the appellation of Yahoo, an odious animal, for which I had so utter an hatred and contempt. I begged he would forbear applying that word to me, and take the same order in his family, and among his friends whom he suffered to see me. I requested likewise, that the secret of my having a false covering to my body might be known to none but himself, at least as long as my present clothing should last; for as to what the sorrel nag his valet had observed, his honor might command him to conceal it.

All this my master very graciously consented to; and thus the secret was kept till my clothes began to wear out, which I was forced to supply by several contrivances, that shall hereafter be mentioned. In the meantime, he desired I would go on with my utmost diligence to learn their language, because he was more astonished at my capacity for speech and reason, than at the figure of my body, whether it were covered or no; adding that he waited with some impatience to hear the wonders which I promised to tell him.

From thenceforward he doubled the pains he had been at to instruct me; he brought me into all company, and made them treat me with civility, because, as he told them privately, this would put me into good humor, and make me more diverting.

Every day when I waited on him, beside the trouble he was at in teaching, he would ask me several questions concerning myself, which I answered as well as I could; and by those means he had already received some general ideas, although very imperfect. It would be tedious to relate the several steps, by which I advanced to a more regular conversation, but the first account I gave of myself in any order and length was to this purpose:

That, I came from a very far country, as I already had attempted to tell him, with about fifty more of my own species; that we traveled upon the seas, in a great hollow vessel made of wood, and larger than his honor's house. I described the ship to him in the best terms I could; and explained by the help of my handkerchief displayed, how it was driven forward by the wind. That, upon a quarrel among us, I was set on shore on this coast, where I walked forward without knowing whither, till he delivered me from the persecution of those execrable Yahoos. He asked me who made the ship, and how it was possible that the Houyhnhnms of my country would leave it to the management of brutes? My answer was that I durst proceed no farther in my relation, unless he would give me his word and honor that he would not be offended; and then I would tell him the wonders I had so often promised. He agreed; and I went on by assuring him, that the ship was made by creatures like myself, who in all the countries I had traveled, as well as in my own, were the only governing, rational animals; and that upon my arrival hither, I was as much astonished to see the Houyhnhnms act like rational begins, as he or his friends could be in finding some marks of reason in a creature he was pleased to call a Yahoo; to which I owned my resemblance in every part, but could not account for their degenerate and brutal nature. I said farther, that if good fortune ever restored me to my native country, to relate my travels hither, as I resolved to do; everybody would believe that I *said the thing which was not*; that I invented the story out of my own head; and with all possible respect to himself, his family, and friends, and under his promise of not being offended, our countrymen would hardly think it probable, that a

Houyhnhnm should be the presiding creature of a nation, and a Yahoo the brute.

CHAPTER IV. *The Houyhnhnms' notion of truth and falsehood. The author's discourse disapproved by his master. The author gives a more particular account of himself, and the accidents of his voyages.*

My master heard me with great appearances of uneasiness in his countenance; because *doubting* or *not believing* are so little known in this country, that the inhabitants cannot tell how to behave themselves under such circumstances. And I remember in frequent discourses with my master concerning the nature of manhood, in other parts of the world, having occasion to talk of *lying* and *false representation*, it was with much difficulty that he comprehended what I meant; although he had otherwise a most acute judgment. For he argued thus: that the use of speech was to make us understand one another, and to receive information of facts; now if anyone *said the thing which was not*, these ends were defeated; because I cannot properly be said to understand him; and I am so far from receiving information, that he leaves me worse than in ignorance; for I am led to believe a thing *black* when it is *white*, and *short* when it is *long*. And these were all the notions he had concerning that faculty of *lying*, so perfectly well understood, and so universally practiced among human creatures.

To return from this digression; when I asserted that the Yahoos were the only governing animals in my country, which my master said was altogether past his conception, he desired to know, whether we had Houyhnhnms among us, and what was their employment; I told him we had great numbers; that in summer they grazed in the fields, and in winter were kept in houses, with hay and oats, where Yahoo servants were employed to rub their skins smooth, comb their manes, pick their feet, serve them with food, and make their beds. "I understand you well," said my master; "it is now very plain from all you have spoken, that whatever share of reason the Yahoos pretend to, the Houyhnhnms are your masters; I heartily wish our Yahoos would be so tractable." I begged his honor would please to excuse me from proceeding any farther, because I was very certain that the account he expected from me would be highly displeasing. But he insisted in commanding me to let him know the best and the worst; I told him he should be obeyed. I owned that the Houyhnhnms among us, whom we called Horses, were the most generous[8] and comely animal we had; that they excelled in strength and swiftness; and when they belonged to persons of quality, employed in traveling, racing, and drawing chariots, they were treated with much kind-

8. Noble.

ness and care, till they fell into diseases, or became foundered in the feet; but then they were sold, and used to all kind of drudgery till they died; after which their skins were stripped and sold for what they were worth, and their bodies left to be devoured by dogs and birds of prey. But the common race of horses had not so good fortune, being kept by farmers and carriers, and other mean people, who put them to greater labor, and feed them worse. I described as well as I could, our way of riding; the shape and use of a bridle, a saddle, a spur, and a whip; of harness and wheels. I added, that we fastened plates of a certain hard substance called iron at the bottom of their feet, to preserve their hoofs from being broken by the stony ways on which we often traveled.

My master, after some expressions of great indignation, wondered how we dared to venture upon a Houyhnhnm's back; for he was sure, that the weakest servant in his house would be able to shake off the strongest Yahoo; or by lying down, and rolling upon his back, squeeze the brute to death. I answered that our horses were trained up from three or four years old to the several uses we intended them for; that if any of them proved intolerably vicious, they were employed for carriages; that they were severely beaten while they were young for any mischievous tricks; that the males, designed for the common use of riding or draught, were generally castrated about two years after their birth, to take down their spirits, and make them more tame and gentle; that they were indeed sensible of rewards and punishments; but his honor would please to consider that they had not the least tincture of reason any more than the Yahoos in this country.

It put me to the pains of many circumlocutions to give my master a right idea of what I spoke; for their language doth not abound in variety of words, because their wants and passions are fewer than among us. But it is impossible to express his noble resentment at our savage treatment of the Houyhnhnm race; particularly after I had explained the manner and use of castrating horses among us, to hinder them from propagating their kind, and to render them more servile. He said, if it were possible there could be any country where Yahoos alone were endued with reason, they certainly must be the governing animal, because reason will in time always prevail against brutal strength. But, considering the frame of our bodies, and especially of mine, he thought no creature of equal bulk was so ill-contrived for employing that reason in the common offices of life; whereupon he desired to know whether those among whom I lived resembled me or the Yahoos of his country. I assured him that I was as well shaped as most of my age; but the younger and the females were much more soft and tender, and the skins of the latter generally as white as milk. He said I differed indeed from other Yahoos, being much more cleanly, and not altogether so deformed; but in point of real advantage, he thought I differed for the worse. That my nails were of no use either to my fore or hinder feet; as to my forefeet, he could not properly call them by that name, for he never observed me to walk upon them; that they were too soft to bear the ground; that I generally went with them uncovered, neither was the covering I sometimes wore on them of the same shape, or so strong as that on my feet behind. That I could not walk with any security; for if either of my hinder feet slipped, I must inevitably fall. He then began to find fault with other parts of my body; the flatness of my face, the prominence of my nose, my eyes placed directly in front, so that I could not look on either side without turning my head; that I was not able to feed myself without lifting one of my forefeet to my mouth; and therefore nature had placed those joints to answer that necessity. He knew not what could be the use of those several clefts and divisions in my feet behind; that these were too soft to bear the hardness and sharpness of stones without a covering made from the skin of some other brute; that my whole body wanted a fence against heat and cold, which I was forced to put on and off every day with tediousness and trouble. And lastly, that he observed every animal in his country naturally to abhor the Yahoos, whom the weaker avoided, and the stronger drove from them. So that supposing us to have the gift of reason, he could not see how it were possible to cure that natural antipathy which every creature discovered against us; nor consequently, how we could tame and render them serviceable. However, he would (as he said) debate the matter no farther, because he was more desirous to know my own story, the country where I was born, and the several actions and events of my life before I came hither.

I assured him how extremely desirous I was that he should be satisfied in every point; but I doubted much whether it would be possible for me to explain myself on several subjects whereof his honor could have no conception, because I saw nothing in his country to which I could resemble them. That however, I would do my best, and strive to express myself by similitudes, humbly desiring his assistance when I wanted proper words; which he was pleased to promise me.

I said, my birth was of honest parents, in an island called England, which was remote from this country, as many days journey as the strongest of his honor's servants could travel in the annual course of the sun. That I was bred a surgeon, whose trade it is to cure wounds and hurts in the body, got by accident or violence. That my country was governed by a female man, whom we called a queen.[9] That I left it to get riches, whereby I might maintain myself and family

9. Queen Anne (1665–1714), last Stuart ruler.

when I should return. That in my last voyage, I was Commander of the ship and had about fifty Yahoos under me, many of which died at sea, and I was forced to supply them by others picked out from several nations. That our ship was twice in danger of being sunk; the first time by a great storm, and the second, by striking against a rock. Here my master interposed, by asking me, how I could persuade strangers out of different countries to venture with me, after the losses I had sustained, and the hazards I had run. I said, they were fellows of desperate fortunes, forced to fly from the places of their birth, on account of their poverty or their crimes. Some were undone by law-suits; others spent all they had in drinking, whoring, and gaming; others fled for treason; many for murder, theft, poisoning, robbery, perjury, forgery, coining false money; for committing rapes or sodomy; for flying from their colors, or deserting to the enemy; and most of them had broken prison. None of these durst return to their native countries for fear of being hanged, or of starving in a jail; and there-fore were under a necessity of seeking livelihood in other places.

During this discourse, my master was pleased often to interrupt me. I had made use of many circumlocutions in describing to him the nature of the several crimes, for which most of our crew had been forced to fly their country. This labor took up several days con-versation before he was able to comprehend me. He was wholly at a loss to know what could be the use or necessity of practicing those vices. To clear up which I endeavored to give him some ideas of the desire of power and riches; of the terrible effects of lust, intemper-ance, malice, and envy. All this I was forced to define and describe by putting of cases, and making suppositions. After which, like one whose imagination was struck with something never seen or heard of before, he would lift up his eyes with amazement and indignation. Power, government, war, law, punishment, and a thousand other things had no terms, wherein that language could express them; which made the difficulty almost insuperable to give my master any con-ception of what I meant; but being of an excellent understanding, much improved by contemplation and converse, he at last arrived at a competent knowledge of what human nature in our parts of the world is capable to perform; and desired I would give him some particular account of that land, which we call Europe, especially, of my own country.

CHAPTER V. *The Author, at his master's commands, informs him of the state of England. The causes of war among the princes of Europe. The Author begins to explain the English Constitution.*

The reader may please to observe that the following extract of many conversations I had with my master contains a summary of the most material points, which were discoursed at several times for above two years; his honor often desiring fuller satisfaction as I farther improved in the Houyhnhnm tongue. I laid before him, as well as I could, the whole state of Europe; I discoursed of trade and manufactures, of arts and sciences; and the answers I gave to all the questions he made, as they arose upon several subjects, were a fund of conversation not to be exhausted. But I shall here only set down the substance of what passed between us concerning my own country, reducing it into order as well as I can, without any regard to time or other circumstances, while I strictly adhere to truth. My only concern is that I shall hardly be able to do justice to my master's arguments and expressions; which must needs suffer by my want of capacity, as well as by a translation into our barbarous English.

In obedience therefore to his honor's commands, I related to him the Revolution under the Prince of Orange; the long war with France entered into by the said Prince, and renewed by his successor the present queen; wherein the greatest powers of Christendom were engaged, and which still continued. I computed at his request, that about a million of Yahoos might have been killed in the whole progress of it; and perhaps a hundred or more cities taken, and five times as many ships burned or sunk.[1]

He asked me what were the usual causes or motives that made one country to go to war with another. I answered, they were innumerable; but I should only mention a few of the chief. Sometimes the ambition of princes, who never think they have land or people enough to govern; sometimes the corruption of ministers, who engage their master in a war in order to stifle or divert the clamor of the subjects against their evil administration. Difference in opinions hath cost many millions of lives; for instance, whether flesh be bread, or bread be flesh; whether the juice of a certain berry be blood or wine; whether whistling be a vice or a virtue; whether it be better to kiss a post, or throw it into the fire; what is the best color for a coat, whether black, white, red, or grey; and whether it should be long or short, narrow or wide, dirty or clean;[2] with many more. Neither are any wars so furious and bloody, or of so long continuance, as those occasioned by difference in opinion, especially if it be in things indifferent.

Sometimes the quarrel between two princes is to decide which of them shall dispossess a third of his dominions, where neither of them pretend to any right. Sometimes one prince quarreleth with another, for fear the other should quarrel with him. Sometimes a war is entered upon, because the enemy is too strong, and sometimes because he

---

1. Gulliver relates recent English history: the Glorious Revolution of 1688 and the War of Spanish Succession (1703–1713). He greatly exaggerates the casualties in the war.   2. Gulliver refers to the religious controversies of the Reformation and Counter Reformation: the doctrine of transubstantiation, the use of music in church services, the veneration of the crucifix, and the wearing of priestly vestments.

is too weak. Sometimes our neighbors want the things which we have, or have the things which we want; and we both fight, till they take ours or give us theirs. It is a very justifiable cause of war to invade a country after the people have been wasted by famine, destroyed by pestilence, or embroiled by factions amongst themselves. It is justifiable to enter into a war against our nearest ally, when one of his towns lies convenient for us, or a territory of land, that would render our dominions round and compact. If a prince send forces into a nation, where the people are poor and ignorant, he may lawfully put half of them to death, and make slaves of the rest, in order to civilize and reduce them from their barbarous way of living. It is a very kingly, honorable, and frequent practice, when one prince desires the assistance of another to secure him against an invasion, that the assistant, when he hath driven out the invader, should seize on the dominions himself, and kill, imprison, or banish the prince he came to relieve. Alliance by blood or marriage is a sufficient cause of war between princes; and the nearer the kindred is, the greater is their disposition to quarrel; poor nations are hungry, and rich nations are proud; and pride and hunger will ever be at variance. For these reasons, the trade of a soldier is held the most honorable of all others: because a soldier is a Yahoo hired to kill in cold blood as many of his own species, who have never offended him, as possibly he can.

There is likewise a kind of beggarly princes in Europe, not able to make war by themselves, who hire out their troops to richer nations for so much a day to each man; of which they keep three fourths to themselves, and it is the best part of their maintenance; such are those in many northern parts of Europe.

"What you have told me," said my master, "upon the subject of war, doth indeed discover most admirably the effects of that reason you pretend to; however, it is happy that the shame is greater than the danger; and that Nature hath left you utterly uncapable of doing much mischief; for your mouths lying flat with your faces, you can hardly bite each other to any purpose, unless by consent. Then, as to the claws upon your feet before and behind, they are so short and tender, that one of our Yahoos would drive a dozen of yours before him. And therefore in recounting the numbers of those who have been killed in battle, I cannot but think that you have *said the thing which is not*."

I could not forebear shaking my head and smiling a little at his ignorance. And, being no stranger to the art of war, I gave him a description of cannons, culverins, muskets, carabines, pistols, bullets, powder, swords, bayonets, battles, sieges, retreats, attacks, undermines, countermines, bombardments, sea fights; ships sunk with a thousand men; twenty thousand killed on each side; dying groans, limbs flying in the air; smoke, noise, confusion, trampling to death under horses' feet; flight, pursuit, victory; fields strewed with carcasses left for food to dogs, and wolves, and birds of prey; plundering, stripping, ravishing, burning, and destroying. And, to set forth the valor of my own dear countrymen, I assured him that I had seen them blow up a hundred enemies at once in a siege, and as many in a ship; and beheld the dead bodies drop down in pieces from the clouds, to the great diversion of all the spectators.

I was going on to more particulars, when my master commanded me silence. He said, whoever understood the nature of Yahoos might easily believe it possible for so vile an animal, to be capable of every action I had named, if their strength and cunning equaled their malice. But, as my discourse had increased his abhorrence of the whole species, so he found it gave him a disturbance in his mind, to which he was wholly a stranger before. He thought his ears being used to such abominable words, might by degrees admit them with less detestation. That, although he hated the Yahoos of this country, yet he no more blamed them for their odious qualities, than he did a *gnnayh* (a bird of prey) for its cruelty, or a sharp stone for cutting his hoof. But, when a creature pretending to reason could be capable of such enormities, he dreaded lest the corruption of that faculty might be worse than brutality itself. He seemed therefore confident, that instead of reason, we were only possessed of some quality fitted to increase our natural vices; as the reflection from a troubled stream returns the image of an ill-shapen body, not only larger, but more distorted.

He added that he had heard too much upon the subject of war, both in this and some former discourses. There was another point which a little perplexed him at present. I had said that some of our crew left their country on account of being ruined by law: that I had already explained the meaning of the word; but he was at a loss how it should come to pass, that the law which was intended for every man's preservation, should be any man's ruin. Therefore he desired to be farther satisfied what I meant by law, and the dispensers thereof, according to the present practice in my own country; because he thought nature and reason were sufficient guides for a reasonable animal, as we pretended to be, in showing us what we ought to do, and what to avoid.

I assured his honor that law was a science wherein I had not much conversed, further than by employing advocates, in vain, upon some injustices that had been done me. However, I would give him all the satisfaction I was able.

I said there was a society of men among us, bred up from their youth in the art of proving by words multiplied for the purpose, that white is black, and black is white, according as they are paid. To this society all the rest of the people are slaves.

"For example. If my neighbor hath a mind to my cow, he hires a lawyer to prove that he ought to have my cow from me. I must then hire another to defend my right; it being against all rules of law that any man should be allowed to speak for himself. Now in this case, I who am the true owner lie under two great disadvantages. First, my lawyer being practiced almost from his cradle in defending falsehood is quite out of his element when he would be an advocate for justice, which as an office unnatural, he always attempts with great awkwardness, if not with ill-will. The second disadvantage is that my lawyer must proceed with great caution, or else he will be reprimanded by the judges, and abhorred by his breathren, as one who would lessen the practice of the law. And therefore I have but two methods to preserve my cow. The first is to gain over my adversary's lawyer with a double fee; who will then betray his client, by insinuating that he hath justice on his side. The second way is for my lawyer to make my cause appear as unjust as he can; by allowing the cow to belong to my adversary; and this if it be skillfully done, will certainly bespeak the favor of the bench.

"Now, your honor is to know that these judges are persons appointed to decide all controversies of property, as well as for the trial of criminals; and picked out from the most dextrous lawyers who are grown old or lazy; and having been biased all their lives against truth and equity, lie under such a fatal necessity of favoring fraud, perjury, and oppression, that I have known some of them to have refused a large bribe from the side where justice lay, rather than injure the faculty,[3] by doing anything unbecoming their nature or their office.

"It is a maxim among these lawyers, that whatever hath been done before may legally be done again; and therefore they take special care to record all the decisions formerly made against common justice and the general reason of mankind. These, under the name of *precedents*, they produce as authorities to justify the most iniquitous opinions; and the judges never fail of directing accordingly.

"In pleading, they studiously avoid entering into the merits of the cause; but are loud, violent, and tedious in dwelling upon all circumstances which are not to the purpose. For instance, in the case already mentioned, they never desire to know what claim or title my adversary hath to my cow; but whether the said cow were red or black; her horns long or short; whether the field I graze her in be round or square; whether she were milked at home or abroad; what diseases she is subject to, and the like. After which they consult precedents, adjourn the cause, from time to time, and in ten, twenty, or thirty years come to an issue.

"It is likewise to be observed, that this society hath a peculiar cant and jargon of their own, that no other mortal can understand, and

3. Profession.

wherein all their laws are written, which they take special care to multiply; whereby they have wholly confounded the very essence of truth and falsehood, of right and wrong; so that it will take thirty years to decide whether the field, left me by my ancestors for six generations, belong to me, or to a stranger three hundred miles off.

"In the trial of persons accused for crimes against the state, the method is much more short and commendable: the judge first sends to sound the disposition of those in power; after which he can easily hang or save the criminal, strictly preserving all the forms of law."

Here my master interposing said it was a pity that creatures endowed with such prodigious abilities of mind as these lawyers, by the description I gave of them must certainly be, were not rather encouraged to be instructors of others in wisdom and knowledge. In answer to which, I assured his honor that in all points out of their own trade, they were usually the most ignorant and stupid generation among us, the most despicable in common conversation, avowed enemies to all knowledge and learning; and equally disposed to pervert the general reason of mankind, in every other subject of discourse as in that of their own profession.

CHAPTER VI. *A continuation of the state of England, under Queen Anne. The character of a first minister in the courts of Europe.*

My master was yet wholly at a loss to understand what motives could incite this race of lawyers to perplex, disquiet, and weary themselves by engaging in a confederacy of injustice, merely for the sake of injuring their fellow animals; neither could he comprehend what I meant in saying they did it for hire. Whereupon I was at much pains to describe to him the use of money, the materials it was made of, and the value of the metals; that when a Yahoo had got a great store of his precious substance, he was able to purchase whatever he had a mind to; the finest clothing, the noblest houses, great tracts of land, the most costly meats and drinks; and have his choice of the most beautiful females. Therefore since money alone was able to perform all these feats, our Yahoos thought they could never have enough of it to spend or to save, as they found themselves inclined from their natural bent either to profusion or avarice. That the rich man enjoyed the fruit of the poor man's labor, and the latter were a thousand to one in proportion to the former. That the bulk of our people was forced to live miserably, by laboring every day for small wages to make a few live plentifully. I enlarged myself much on these and many other particulars to the same purpose, but his honor was still to seek, for he went upon a supposition that all animals had a title to their share in the productions of the earth; and especially those who presided over the rest. Therefore he desired I would let him know what these costly meats were, and how any of us happened to want[4] them. Whereupon I enumerated as many sorts as came into my head, with the various methods of dressing them, which could not be done without sending vessels by sea to every part of the world, as well for liquors to drink, as for sauces, and innumerable other conveniencies. I assured him, that this whole globe of earth must be at least three times gone round, before one of our better female Yahoos could get her breakfast, or a cup to put it in. He said, "That must needs be a miserable country which cannot furnish food for its own inhabitants." But what he chiefly wondered at, was how such vast tracts of ground as I described, should be wholly without fresh water, and the people put to the necessity of sending over the sea for drink. I replied that England (the dear place of my nativity) was computed to produce three times the quantity of food, more than its inhabitants are able to consume, as well as liquors extracted from grain, or pressed out of the fruit of certain trees, which made excellent drink; and the same proportion in every other convenience of life. But, in order to feed the luxury and intemperance of the males, and the vanity of the females, we sent away the greatest part of our necessary things to other countries, from whence in return we brought the materials of diseases, folly, and vice, to spend among ourselves. Hence it follows of necessity, that vast numbers of our people are compelled to seek their livelihood by begging, robbing, stealing, cheating, pimping, foreswearing, flattering, suborning, forging, gaming, lying, fawning, hectoring, voting, scribbling, star gazing, poisoning, whoring, canting, libeling, freethinking, and the like occupations; every one of which terms, I was at much pains to make him understand.

That, wine was not imported among us from foreign countries, to supply the want of water or other drinks, but because it was a sort of liquid which made us merry, by putting us out of our senses; diverted all melancholy thoughts, begat wild extravagant imaginations in the brain, raised our hopes, and banished our fears; suspended every office of reason for a time, and deprived us of the use of our limbs, until we fell into a profound sleep; although it must be confessed, that we always awaked sick and dispirited; and that the use of this liquor filled us with diseases, which made our lives uncomfortable and short.

But beside all this, the bulk of our people supported themselves by furnishing the necessities or conveniencies of life to the rich, and to each other. For instance, when I am at home and dressed as I ought to be, I carry on my body the workmanship of an hundred tradesmen; the building and furniture of my house employ as many more; and five times the number to adorn my wife.

4. Lack.

I was going on to tell him of another sort of people, who get their livelihood by attending the sick; having upon some occasions informed his honor that many of my crew had died of diseases. But here it was with the utmost difficulty that I brought him to apprehend what I meant. He could easily conceive that a Houyhnhnm grew weak and heavy a few days before his death; or by some accident might hurt a limb. But that nature, who worketh all things to perfection, should suffer any pains to breed in our bodies, he thought impossible; and desired to know the reason of so unaccountable an evil. I told him, we fed on a thousand things which operated contrary to each other; that we eat when we were not hungry, and drank without the provocation of thirst; that we sat whole nights drinking strong liquors without eating a bit, which disposed us to sloth, inflamed our bodies, and precipitated or prevented digestion. That, prostitute female Yahoos acquired a certain malady, which bred rottenness in the bones of those who fell into their embraces; that this and many other diseases were propagated from father to son; so that great numbers come into the world with complicated maladies upon them; that it would be endless to give him a catalogue of all diseases incident to human bodies; for they could not be fewer than five or six hundred, spread over every limb, and joint; in short, every part, external and intestine, having diseases appropriated to each. To remedy which, there was a sort of people bred up among us, in the profession or pretense of curing the sick. And because I had some skill in the faculty, I would in gratitude to his honor let him know the whole mystery and method by which they proceed.

Their fundamental is that all diseases arise from repletion; from whence they conclude, that a great evacuation of the body is necessary, either through the natural passage, or upwards at the mouth. Their next business is, from herbs, minerals, gums, oils, shells, salts, juices, seaweed, excrements, barks of trees, serpents, toads, frogs, spiders, dead men's flesh and bones, birds, beasts and fishes, to form a composition for smell and taste the most abominable, nauseous, and detestable, that they can possibly contrive, which the stomach immediately rejects with loathing, and this they call a vomit. Or else from the same storehouse, with some other poisonous additions, they command us to take in at the orifice above or below (just as the physician then happens to be disposed) a medicine equally annoying and disgustful to the bowels; which relaxing the belly, drives down all before it; and this they call a purge, or a clyster. For nature (as the physicians allege) having intended the superior anterior orifice only for the intromission of solids and liquids, and the inferior posterior for ejection, these artists ingeniously considering that in all diseases nature is forced out of her seat; therefore to replace her in it, the body must be treated in a manner directly contrary, but interchanging the use of each orifice; forcing solids and liquids in at the anus, and making evacuations at the mouth.

But, besides real diseases, we are subject to many that are only imaginary, for which the physicians have invented imaginary cures; these have their several names, and so have the drugs that are proper for them; and with these our female Yahoos are always infested.

One great excellency in this tribe is their skill at prognostics, wherein they seldom fail; their predictions in real diseases, when they rise to any degree of malignity, generally portending death, which is always in their power, when recovery is not, and therefore, upon any unexpected signs of amendment, after they have pronounced their sentence rather than be accused as false prophets, they know how to approve[5] their sagacity to the world by a seasonable dose.

They are likewise of special use to husbands and wives, who are grown weary of their mates; to eldest sons, to great ministers of state, and often to princes.

I had formerly upon occasion discoursed with my master upon the nature of government in general, and particularly of our own excellent constitution, deservedly the wonder and envy of the whole world. But having here accidently mentioned a minister of state, he commanded me some time after to inform him what species of Yahoo I particularly meant by that appellation.

I told him that a first or chief minister of state, whom I intended to describe, was a creature wholly exempt from joy and grief, love and hatred, pity and anger; at least makes use of no other passions but a violent desire of wealth, power, and titles; that he applies his words to all uses, except to the indication of his mind; that he never tells a truth, but with an intent that you should take it for a lie; nor a lie, but with a design that you should take it for a truth; that those he speaks worst of behind their backs are in the surest way to preferment; and whenever he begins to praise you to others or to yourself, you are from that day forlorn. The worst mark you can receive is a promise, especially when it is confirmed with an oath; after which every wise man retires, and gives over all hopes.

There are three methods by which a man may rise to be chief minister: the first is by knowing how with prudence to dispose of a wife, a daughter, or a sister; the second, by betraying or undermining his predecessor; and the third is by a furious zeal in public assemblies against the corruptions of the court. But a wise prince would rather choose to employ those who practice the last of these methods; because such zealots prove always the most obsequious and subservient to the will and passions of their master. That, these ministers having all employments at their disposal, preserve themselves in power by brib-

5. Prove.

ing the majority of a senate or great council; and at last by an expedient called an Act of Indemnity (whereof I described the nature to him) they secure themselves from after reckonings, and retire from the public, laden with the spoils of the nation.

The palace of a chief minister is a seminary to breed up others in his own trade; the pages, lackies, and porter, by imitating their master, become ministers of state in their several districts, and learn to excel in the three principal ingredients, of insolence, lying, and bribery. Accordingly, they have a subaltern court paid to them by persons of the best rank; and sometimes by the force of dexterity and impudence, arrive through several gradations to be successors to their lord.

He is usually governed by a decayed wench, or favorite footman, who are the tunnels through which all graces are conveyed, and may properly be called, in the last resort, the governors of the kingdom.

One day, my master, having heard me mention the nobility of my country, was pleased to make me a compliment which I could not pretend to deserve: that, he was sure, I must have been born of some noble family, because I far exceeded in shape, color, and cleanliness, all the Yahoos of his nation, although I seemed to fail in strength, and agility, which must be imputed to my different way of living from those other brutes; and besides, I was not only endowed with the faculty of speech, but likewise with some rudiments of reason, to a degree, that with all his acquaintance I passed for a prodigy.

He made me observe, that among the Houyhnhnms, the white, the sorrel, and the iron grey were not so exactly shaped as the bay, the dapple grey, and the black; nor born with equal talents of mind, or a capacity to improve them; and therefore continued always in the condition of servants, without ever aspiring to match out of their own race, which in that country would be reckoned monstrous and unnatural.

I made his honor my most humble acknowledgements for the good opinion he was pleased to conceive of me; but assured him at the same time, that my birth was of the lower sort, having been born of plain, honest parents, who were just able to give me a tolerable education; that, nobility among us was altogether a different thing from the idea he had of it; that, our young noblemen are bred from their childhood in idleness and luxury; that, as soon as years will permit, they consume their vigor, and contract odious diseases among lewd females; and when their fortunes are almost ruined, they marry some woman of mean birth, disagreeable person, and unsound constitution, merely for the sake of money, whom they hate and despise. That, the productions of such marriages are generally scrofulous, rickety or deformed children; by which means the family seldom continues above three generations, unless the wife take care to provide a healthy father among her neighbors, or domestics, in order to improve and continue the breed. That a weak diseased body, a meager countenance, and sallow complexion are the true marks of noble blood; and a healthy robust appearance is so disgraceful in a man of quality, that the world concludes his real father to have been a groom or a coachman. The imperfections of his mind run parallel with those of his body; being a composition of spleen, dullness, ignorance, caprice, sensuality, and pride.

Without the consent of this illustrious body, no law can be enacted, repealed, or altered, and these nobles have likewise the decision of all our possessions without appeal.

CHAPTER VII. *The Author's great love of his native country. His master's observations upon the constitution and administration of England, as described by the Author, with parallel cases and comparisons. His master's observations upon human nature.*

The reader may be disposed to wonder how I could prevail on myself to give so free a representation of my own species, among a race of mortals who were already too apt to conceive the vilest opinion of humankind, from that entire congruity betwixt me and their Yahoos. But I must freely confess that the many virtues of those excellent quadrupeds placed in opposite view to human corruptions had so far opened my eyes, and enlarged my understanding, that I began to view the actions and passions of man in a very different light; and to think the honor of my own kind not worth managing; which, besides, it was impossible for me to do before a person of so acute a judgment as my master, who daily convinced me of a thousand faults in myself, whereof I had not the least perception before, and which with us would never be numbered even among human infirmities. I had likewise learned from his example an utter detestation of all falsehood or disguise; and truth appeared so amiable to me, that I determined upon sacrificing everything to it.

Let me deal so candidly with the reader as to confess that there was yet a much stronger motive for the freedom I took in my representation of things. I had not been a year in this country, before I contracted such a love and veneration for the inhabitants, that I entered on a firm resolution never to return to humankind, but to pass the rest of my life among these admirable Houyhnhnms in the contemplation and practice of every virtue; where I could have no example or incitement to vice. But it was decreed by fortune, my perpetual enemy, that so great a felicity should not fall to my share. However, it is now some comfort to reflect that in what I said of my countrymen, I extenuated their faults as much as I durst before so strict an examiner; and upon every article, gave as favorable a turn as the matter would bear. For, indeed, who is there alive that will not be swayed by his bias and partiality to the place of his birth?

I have related the substance of several conversations I had with my master, during the greatest part of the time I had the honor to be in his service; but have indeed for brevity sake omitted much more than is here set down.

When I had answered all his questions, and his curiosity seemed to be fully satisfied; he sent for me one morning early, and commanding me to sit down at some distance (an honor which he had never before conferred upon me), he said he had been very seriously considering my whole story, as far as it related both to myself and my country; that, he looked upon us as a sort of animals to whose share, by what accident he could not conjecture, some small pittance of reason had fallen, whereof we made no other use than by its assistance to aggravate our natural corruptions, and to acquire new ones which nature had not given us. That we disarmed ourselves of the few abilities she had bestowed; had been very successful in multiplying our original wants, and seemed to spend our whole lives in vain endeavors to supply them by our own inventions. That, as to myself, it was manifest I had neither the strength or agility of a common Yahoo; that I walked infirmly on my hinder feet; had found out a contrivance to make my claws of no use or defense, and to remove the hair from my chin, which was intended as a shelter from the sun and the weather. Lastly, that I could neither run with speed, nor climb trees like my brethren (as he called them) the Yahoos in this country.

That our institutions of government and law were plainly owing to our gross defects in reason, and by consequence, in virtue; because reason alone is sufficient to govern a rational creature; which was therefore a character we had no pretense to challenge, even from the account I had given of my own people; although he manifestly perceived, that in order to favor them, I had concealed many particulars, and often *said the thing which was not*.

He was the more confirmed in this opinion, because he observed that I agreed in every feature of my body with other Yahoos, except where it was to my real disadvantage in point of strength, speed, and activity, the shortness of my claws, and some other particulars where nature had no part; so, from the representation I had given him of our lives, our manners, and our actions, he found as near a resemblance in the disposition of our minds. He said the Yahoos were known to hate one another more than they did any different species of animals; and the reason usually assigned was the odiousness of their own shapes, which all could see in the rest, but not in themselves. He had therefore begun to think it not unwise in us to cover our bodies, and by that invention, conceal many of our deformities from each other, which would else be hardly supportable. But he now found he had been mistaken; and that the dissentions of those brutes in his country were owing to the same cause with ours, as I had described them. For, if (said he) you throw among five Yahoos as much food as would be sufficient for fifty, they will, instead of eating peaceably, fall together by the ears, each single one impatient to have all to itself; and therefore a servant was usually employed to stand by while they were feeding abroad, and those kept at home were tied at a distance from each other. That, if a cow died of age or accident, before a Houyhnhnm could secure it for his own Yahoos, those in the neighborhood would come in herds to seize it, and then would ensue such a battle as I had described, with terrible wounds made by their claws on both sides, although they seldom were able to kill one another, for want of such convenient instruments of death as we had invented. At other times the like battles have been fought between the Yahoos of several neighborhoods without any visible cause; those of one district watching all opportunities to surprise the next before they are prepared. But if they find their project hath miscarried, they return home, and for want of enemies, engage in what I call a civil war among themselves.

That, in some fields of his country, there are certain shining stones of several colors, whereof the Yahoos are violently fond; and when part of these stones are fixed in the earth, as it sometimes happeneth, they will dig with their claws for whole days to get them out, and carry them away, and hide them by heaps in their kennels; but still looking round with great caution, for fear their comrades should find out their treasure. My master said he could never discover the reason of this unnatural appetite, or how these stones could be of any use to a Yahoo; but now he believed it might proceed from the same principle of avarice, which I had ascribed to mankind. That he had once, by way of experiment, privately removed a heap of these stones from the place where one of his Yahoos had buried it, whereupon, the sordid animal missing his treasure, by his loud lamenting brought the whole herd to the place, there miserably howled, then fell to biting and tearing the rest; began to pine away, would neither eat nor sleep, nor work, till he ordered a servant privately to convey the stones into the same hole, and hide them as before; which when his Yahoo had found, he presently recovered his spirits and good humor; but took care to remove them to a better hiding place; and hath ever since been a very serviceable brute.

My master farther assured me, which I also observed myself; that in the fields where these shining stones abound, the fiercest and most frequent battles are fought, occasioned by perpetual inroads of the neighboring Yahoos.

He said it was common when two Yahoos discovered such a stone in a field, and were contending which of them should be the proprietor, a third would take the advantage, and carry it away from them both; which my master would needs contend to have some resemblance with our suits at law; wherein I thought it for our credit not to undeceive him; since the decision he mentioned was much more equitable than many decrees among us; because the plaintiff and defendant there lost nothing beside the stone they contended for; whereas our courts of equity would never have dismissed the cause while either of them had anything left.

My master continuing his discourse said there was nothing that rendered the Yahoos more odious, than their undistinguished appetite to devour everything that came in their way, whether herbs, roots, berries, corrupted flesh of animals, or all mingled together; and it was peculiar in their temper, that they were fonder of what they could get by rapine or stealth at a greater distance, than much better food provided for them at home. If their prey held out, they would eat till they were ready to burst, after which nature had pointed out to them a certain root that gave them a general evacuation.

There was also another kind of root very juicy, but something rare and difficult to be found, which the Yahoos fought for with much eagerness, and would suck it with great delight; it produced the same effects that wine hath upon us. It would make them sometimes hug, and sometimes tear one another; they would howl and grin, and chatter, and reel, and tumble, and then fall asleep in the mud.

I did indeed observe that the Yahoos were the only animals in this country subject to any diseases; which however, were much fewer than horses have among us, and contracted not by any ill treatment they meet with, but by the nastiness and greediness of that sordid brute. Neither has their language any more than a general appellation for those maladies; which is borrowed from the name of the beast, and called *Hnea Yahoo*, or the Yahoo's Evil; and the cure prescribed is a mixture of their own dung and urine, forcibly put down the Yahoo's throat. This I have since often known to have been taken with success, and do here freely recommend it to my countrymen, for the public good, as an admirable specific against all diseases produced by repletion.

As to learning, government, arts, manufactures, and the like, my master confessed he could find little or no resemblance between the Yahoos of that country and those in ours. For he only meant to observe what parity there was in our natures. He had heard indeed some curious Houyhnhnms observe that in most herds there was a sort of ruling Yahoo (as among us there is generally some leading or principal stag in a park) who was always more deformed in body, and mischievous in disposition, than any of the rest. That this leader had usually a favorite as like himself as he could get, whose employment was to lick his master's feet and posteriors, and drive the female Yahoos to his kennel; for which he was now and then rewarded with a piece of ass's flesh. This favorite is hated by the whole herd; and therefore to protect himself, keeps always near the person of his leader. He usually continues in office till a worse can be found; but the very moment he is discarded, his successor, at the head of all the Yahoos in that district, young and old, male and female, come in a body, and discharge their excrements upon him from head to foot. But how far this might be applicable to our courts and favorites, and ministers of state, my master said I could best determine.

I durst make no return to this malicious insinuation, which debased human understanding below the sagacity of a common hound, who hath judgment enough to distinguish and follow the cry of the ablest dog in the pack, without being ever mistaken.

My master told me there were some qualities remarkable in the Yahoos, which he had not observed me to mention, or at least very slightly, in the accounts I had given him of humankind. He said, those animals, like other brutes, had their females in common; but in this differed, that the she-Yahoo would admit the male while she was pregnant; and that the hes would quarrel and fight with the females as fiercely as with each other. Both which practices were such degrees of infamous brutality, that no other sensitive creature ever arrived at.

Another thing he wondered at in the Yahoos was their strange disposition to nastiness and dirt; whereas there appears to be a natural love of cleanliness in all other animals. As to the two former accusations, I was glad to let them pass without any reply, because I had not a word to offer upon them in defense of my species, which otherwise I certainly had done from my own inclinations. But I could have easily vindicated humankind from the imputation of singularity upon the last article, if there had been any swine in that country (as unluckily for me there were not) which although it may be a sweeter quadruped than a Yahoo, cannot I humbly conceive in justice pretend to more cleanliness; and so his honor himself must have owned, if he had seen their filthy way of feeding, and their custom of wallowing and sleeping in the mud.

My master likewise mentioned another quality, which his servants had discovered in several Yahoos, and to him was wholly unaccountable. He said, a fancy would sometimes take a Yahoo, to retire into a corner, to lie down and howl, and groan, and spurn away all that came near him, although he were young and fat, and wanted neither food nor water; nor did the servants imagine what could possibly ail him. And the only remedy they found was to set him to hard work, after which he would infallibly come to himself. To this I was silent out of partiality to my own kind; yet here I could plainly discover the true seeds of spleen,[6] which only seizeth on the lazy, the

6. Hypochondria.

luxurious, and the rich; who, if they were forced to undergo the same regimen, I would undertake for the cure.

His Honor had farther observed, that a female Yahoo would often stand behind a bank or a bush, to gaze on the young males passing by, and then appear, and hide, using many antic gestures and grimaces; at which time it was observed, that she had a most offensive smell; and when any of the males advanced, would slowly retire, looking back, and with a counterfeit show of fear, run off into some convenient place where she knew the male would follow her.

At other times, if a female stranger came among them, three or four of her own sex would get about her, and stare and chatter, and grin, and smell her all over; and then turn off with gestures that seemed to express contempt and disdain.

Perhaps my master might refine a little in these speculations, which he had drawn from what he observed himself, or had been told by others; however, I could not reflect without some amazement, and much sorrow, that the rudiments of lewdness, coquetry, censure, and scandal, should have place by instinct in womankind.

I expected every moment that my master would accuse the Yahoos of those unnatural appetites in both sexes, so common among us. But nature it seems hath not been so expert a school-mistress; and these politer pleasures are entirely the productions of art and reason, on our side of the globe.

CHAPTER VIII. *The Author relateth several particulars of the Yahoos. The great virtues of the Houyhnhnms. The education and exercises of their youth. Their general assembly.*

As I ought to have understood human nature much better than I supposed it possible for my master to do, so it was easy to apply the character he gave of the Yahoos to myself and my countrymen; and I believed I could yet make farther discoveries from my own observation. I therefore often begged his honor to let me go among the herds of Yahoos in the neighborhood; to which he always very graciously consented, being perfectly convinced that the hatred I bore those brutes would never suffer me to be corrupted by them; and his honor ordered one of his servants, a strong sorrel nag, very honest and good-natured, to be my guard; without whose protection I durst not undertake such adventures. For I have already told the reader how much I was pestered by those odious animals upon my first arrival. I afterwards failed very narrowly three or four times of falling into their clutches, when I happened to stray at any distance without my hanger. And I have reason to believe, they had some imagination that I was of their own species, which I often assisted myself, by stripping up my sleeves, and shewing my naked arms and breast in their sight, when my protector was with me; at which times they would approach as near as they durst, and imitate my actions after the manner of monkeys, but ever with great signs of hatred; as a tame jackdaw with cap and stockings is always persecuted by the wild ones, when he happens to be got among them.

They are prodigiously nimble from their infancy; however, I once caught a young male of three years old, and endeavored by all marks of tenderness to make it quiet; but the little imp fell a squalling, scratching, and biting with such violence, that I was forced to let it go; and it was high time, for a whole troop of old ones came about us at the noise; but finding the cub was safe (for away it ran) and my sorrel nag being by, they durst not venture near us. I observed the young animal's flesh to smell very rank, and the stink was somewhat between a weasel and a fox, but much more disagreeable. I forgot another circumstance (and perhaps I might have the reader's pardon, if it were wholly omitted) that while I held the odious vermin in my hands, it voided its filthy excrements of a yellow liquid substance, all over my clothes; but by good fortune there was a small brook hard by, where I washed myself as clean as I could; although I durst not come into my master's presence until I were sufficiently aired.

By what I could discover, the Yahoos appear to be the most unteachable of all animals, their capacities never reaching higher than to draw or carry burdens. Yet I am of opinion, this defect ariseth chiefly from a perverse, restive disposition. For they are cunning, malicious, treacherous and revengeful. They are strong and hardy, but of a cowardly spirit, and by consequence insolent, abject, and cruel. It is observed that the red-haired of both sexes are more libidinous and mischievous than the rest, whom yet they much exceed in strength and activity.

The Houyhnhnms keep the Yahoos for present use in huts not far from the house; but the rest are sent abroad to certain fields, where they dig up roots, eat several kinds of herbs, and search about for carrion, or sometimes catch weasels and *luhimuhs* (a sort of wild rat) which they greedily devour. Nature hath taught them to dig deep holes with their nails on the side of a rising ground, wherein they lie by themselves; only the kennels of the females are larger, sufficient to hold two or three cubs.

They swim from their infancy like frogs, and are able to continue long under water, where they often take fish, which the females carry home to their young. And upon this occasion, I hope the reader will pardon my relating an odd adventure.

Being one day abroad with my protector the sorrel nag, and the weather exceeding hot, I entreated him to let me bathe in a river that was near. He consented, and I immediately stripped myself stark naked, and went down softly into the stream. It happened that a

young female Yahoo standing behind a bank, saw the whole proceeding; and inflamed by desire, as the nag and I conjectured, came
running with all speed, and leaped into the water within five yards
of the place where I bathed. I was never in my life so terribly frighted;
the nag was grazing at some distance, not suspecting any harm; she
embraced me after a most fulsome manner; I roared as loud as I
could, and the nag came galloping towards me, whereupon she quitted her grasp, with the utmost reluctancy, and leaped upon the opposite
bank, where she stood gazing and howling all the time I was putting
on my clothes.

This was matter of diversion to my master and his family, as well
as of mortification to myself. For not I could no longer deny that I
was a real Yahoo, in every limb and feature, since the females had a
natural propensity to me as one of their own species; neither was the
hair of this brute of a red color (which might have been some excuse
for an appetite a little irregular) but black as a sole, and her countenance did not make an appearance altogether so hideous as the rest
of the kind; for I think, she could not be above eleven years old.

Having already lived three years in this country, the reader I suppose will expect that I should, like other travelers, give him some
account of the manners and customs of its inhabitants, which it was
indeed my principal study to learn.

As these noble Houyhnhnms are endowed by Nature with a general disposition to all virtues, and have no conceptions or ideas of
what is evil in a rational creature; so their grand maxim is to cultivate
reason, and to be wholly governed by it. Neither is reason among
them a point problematical as with us, where men can argue with
plausibility on both sides of a question; but strikes you with immediate conviction; as it must needs do where it is not mingled, obscured,
or discolored by passion and interest. I remember it was with extreme
difficulty that I could bring my master to understand the meaning of
the word "opinion," or how a point could be disputable; because
reason taught us to affirm or deny only where we are certain; and
beyond our knowledge we cannot do either. So that controversies,
wranglings, disputes, and positiveness in false or dubious propositions are evils unknown among the Houyhnhnms. In the like manner when I used to explain to him our several systems of natural
philosophy, he would laugh that a creature pretending to reason should
value itself upon the knowledge of other people's conjectures, and in
things, where that knowledge, if it were certain, could be of no use.
Wherein he agreed entirely with the sentiments of Socrates, as Plato
delivers them, which I mention as the highest honor I can do that
prince of philosophers. I have often since reflected what destruction
such a doctrine would make in the libraries of Europe; and how
many paths to fame would be then shut up in the learned world.

Friendship and benevolence are the two principal virtues among the Houyhnhnms; and these not confined to particular objects, but universal to the whole race. For a stranger from the remotest part is equally treated with the nearest neighbor, and wherever he goes, looks upon himself as at home. They preserve decency and civility in the highest degrees, but are altogether ignorant of ceremony. They have no fondness[7] for their colts or foals; but the care they take in educating them proceedeth entirely from the dictates of reason. And I observed my master to show the same affection to his neighbor's issue that he had for his own. They will have it that nature teaches them to love the whole species, and it is reason only that maketh a distinction of persons, where there is a superior degree of virtue.

When the matron Houyhnhnms have produced one of each sex, they no longer accompany with their consorts, except they lose one of their issue by some casualty, which very seldom happens; but in such a case they meet again; or when the like accident befalls a person whose wife is past bearing, some other couple bestows on him one of their own colts, and then go together a second time, until the mother be pregnant. This caution is necessary to prevent the country from being overburdened with numbers. But the race of inferior Houyhnhnms bred up to be servants is not so strictly limited upon this article; these are allowed to produce three of each sex, to be domestics in the noble families.

In their marriages they are exactly careful to choose such colors as will not make any disagreeable mixture in the breed. Strength is chiefly valued in the male, and comeliness in the female; not upon the account of love, but to preserve the race from degenerating; for, where a female happens to excel in strength, a consort is chosen with regard to comeliness. Courtship, love, presents, jointures, settlements, have no place in their thoughts, or terms whereby to express them in their language. The young couple meet and are joined, merely because it is the determination of their parents and friends; it is what they see done every day; and they look upon it as one of the necessary actions in a reasonable being. But the violation of marriage, or any other unchastity, was never heard of; and the married pair pass their lives with the same friendship and mutual benevolence that they bear to all others of the same species who come in their way, without jealousy, fondness, quarreling, or discontent.

In educating the youth of both sexes, their method is admirable, and highly deserveth our imitation. These are not suffered to taste a grain of oats, except upon certain days, till eighteen years old; nor milk, but very rarely; and in summer they graze two hours in the morning, and as many in the evening, which their parents likewise

7. Excessive doting.

observe; but the servants are not allowed above half that time; and a great part of the grass is brought home, which they eat at the most convenient hours, when they can be best spared from work.

Temperance, industry, exercise, and cleanliness are the lessons equally enjoined to the young ones of both sexes; and my master thought it monstrous in us to give the females a different kind of education from the males, except in some articles of domestic management; whereby, as he truly observed, one half of our natives were good for nothing but bringing children into the world; and to trust the care of their children to such useless animals, he said was yet a greater instance of brutality.

But the Houyhnhnms train up their youth to strength, speed, and hardiness, by exercising them in running races up and down steep hills, or over hard stony grounds; and when they are all in a sweat, they are ordered to leap over head and ears into a pond or a river. Four times a year the youth of certain districts meet to show their proficiency in running, and leaping, and other feats of strength or agility; where the victor is rewarded with a song made in his or her praise. On this festival the servants drive a herd of Yahoos into the field, laden with hay, and oats, and milk for a repast to the Houyhnhnms; after which these brutes are immediately driven back again, for fear of being noisome to the assembly.

Every fourth year, at the vernal equinox, there is a representative council of the whole nation, which meets in a plain about twenty miles from our house, and continueth about five or six days. Here they inquire into the state and condition of the several districts; whether they abound or be deficient in hay or oats, or cows or Yahoos? And wherever there is any want (which is but seldom) it is immediately supplied by unanimous consent and contribution. Here likewise the regulation of children is settled: as for instance, if a Houyhnhnm hath two males, he changeth one of them with another who hath two females, and when a child hath been lost by any casualty, where the mother is past breeding, it is determined what family in the district shall breed another to supply the loss.

CHAPTER IX. *A grand debate at the general assembly of the Houyhnhnms, and how it was determined. The learning of the Houyhnhnms. Their buildings. Their manner of burials. The defectiveness of their language.*

One of these grand assemblies was held in my time, about three months before my departure, whither my master went as the representative of our district. In this council was resumed their old debate, and indeed, the only debate that ever happened in their country; whereof my master after his return gave me a very particular account.

The question to be debated was whether the Yahoos should be exterminated from the face of the earth. One of the members for the affirmative offered several arguments of great strength and weight, alleging that, as the Yahoos were the most filthy, noisome, and deformed animal which nature ever produced, so they were the most restive and indocile, mischievous, and malicious; they would privately suck the teats of the Houyhnhnms' cows; kill and devour their cats, trample down their oats and grass, if they were not continually watched; and commit a thousand other extravagancies. He took notice of a general tradition, that Yahoos had not been always in their country, but that many ages ago, two of these brutes appeared together upon a mountain; whether produced by the heat of the sun upon corrupted mud and slime, or from the ooze and froth of the sea, was never known. That these Yahoos engendered, and their brood in a short time grew so numerous as to overrun and infest the whole nation. That the Houyhnhnms to get rid of this evil, made a general hunting, and at last enclosed the whole herd; and destroying the older, every Houyhnhnm kept two young ones in a kennel, and brought them to such a degree of tameness as an animal so savage by nature can be capable of acquiring, using them for draft and carriage. That there seemed to be much truth in this tradition, and that those creatures could not be *ylnhniamshy* (or aborigines of the land) because of the violent hatred the Houyhnhnms as well as all other animals bore them; which although their evil disposition sufficiently deserved, could never have arrived at so high a degree, if they had been aborigines, or else they would have long since been rooted out. That the inhabitants taking a fancy to use the service of the Yahoos, had very imprudently neglected to cultivate the breed of asses, which were a comely animal, easily kept, more tame and orderly, without any offensive smell, strong enough for labor, although they yield to the other in agility of body; and if their braying be no agreeable sound, it is far preferable to the horrible howlings of the Yahoos.

Several others declared their sentiments to the same purpose, when my master proposed an expedient to the assembly, whereof he had indeed borrowed the hint from me. He approved of the tradition, mentioned by the honorable member, who spoke before; and affirmed, that the two Yahoos said to be first seen among them, had been driven thither over the sea; that coming to land, and being forsaken by their companions, they retired to the mountains, and degenerating by degrees, became in process of time much more savage than those of their own species in the country from whence these two originals came. The reason of his assertion was that he had now in his possession a certain wonderful Yahoo (meaning myself) which most of them had heard of, and many of them had seen. He then related to them how he first found me; that my body was all covered with an artificial composure of the skins and hairs of other animals; that I spoke in a language of my own, and had thoroughly learned theirs; that I had related to him the accidents which brought me thither; that when he saw me without my covering, I was an exact Yahoo in every part, only of a whiter color, less hairy and with shorter claws. He added how I had endeavored to persuade him that in my own and other countries the Yahoos acted as the governing, rational animal, and held the Houyhnhnms in servitude; that he observed in me all the qualities of a Yahoo, only a little more civilized by some tincture of reason, which however was in a degree as far inferior to the Houyhnhnm race as the Yahoos of their country were to me; that among other things, I mentioned a custom we had of castrating Houyhnhnms when they were young, in order to render them tame; that the operation was easy and safe; that it was no shame to learn wisdom from brutes, as industry is taught by the ant, and building by the swallow (for so I translate the world *lyhannh*, although it be a much larger fowl). That this invention might be practiced upon the younger Yahoos here, which, besides rendering them tractable and fitter for use, would in an age put an end to the whole species without destroying life. That in the meantime the Houyhnhnms should be exhorted to cultivate the breed of asses, which, as they are in all respects more valuable brutes, so they have this advantage, to be fit for service at five years old, which the others are not till twelve.

This was all my master thought fit to tell me at that time, of what passed in the grand council. But he was pleased to conceal one particular, which related personally to myself, whereof I soon felt the unhappy effect, as the reader will know in its proper place, and from whence I date all the succeeding misfortunes of my life.

The Houyhnhnms have no letters, and consequently, their knowledge is all traditional. But there happening few events of any moment among a people so well united, naturally disposed to every virtue, wholly governed by reason, and cut off from all commerce with other nations, the historical part is easily preserved without burdening their memories. I have already observed that they are subject to no diseases, and therefore can have no need of physicians. However, they have excellent medicines composed of herbs, to cure accidental bruises and cuts in the pastern or frog of the foot by sharp stones, as well as other maims and hurts in the several parts of the body.

They calculate the year by the revolution of the sun and the moon, but use no subdivisions into weeks. They are well enough acquainted with the motions of those two luminaries, and understand the nature of eclipses; and this is the utmost progress of their astronomy.

In poetry they must be allowed to excel all other mortals; wherein the justness of their similes, and the minuteness, as well as exactness of their descriptions, are indeed inimitable. Their verses abound very much in both of these, and usually contain either some exalted notions of friendship and benevolence, or the praises of those who were victors in races and other bodily exercises. Their buildings, although very rude and simple, are not inconvenient, but well contrived to defend them from all injuries of cold and heat. They have a kind of tree, which at forty years old loosens in the root, and falls with the first storm; it grows very straight, and being pointed like stakes with a sharp stone (for the Houyhnhnms know not the use of iron), they stick them erect in the ground about ten inches asunder, and then weave in oat straw, or sometimes wattles, betwixt them. The roof is made after the same manner, and so are the doors.

The Houyhnhnms use the hollow part between the pastern and the hoof of their forefeet as we do our hands, and this with greater dexterity than I could at first imagine. I have seen a white mare of our family thread a needle (which I lent her on purpose) with that joint. They milk their cows, reap their oats, and do all the work which requires hands in the same manner. They have a kind of hard flints, which by grinding against other stones they form into instruments that serve instead of wedges, axes, and hammers. With tools made of these flints, they likewise cut their hay, and reap their oats, which there groweth naturally in several fields; the Yahoos draw home the sheaves in carriages, and the servants tread them in certain covered huts, to get out the grain, which is kept in stores. They make a rude kind of earthen and wooden vessels, and bake the former in the sun.

If they can avoid casualties, they die only of old age, and are buried in the obscurest places that can be found, their friends and relations expressing neither joy nor grief at their departure; nor does the dying person discover the least regret that he is leaving the world, any more than if he were upon returning home from a visit to one of his neighbors; I remember my master having once made an appointment with a friend and his family to come to his house upon some affair of importance; on the day fixed, the mistress and her two children came very late; she made two excuses, first for her husband, who, as she said, happened that very morning to *lhnuwnh*. The word is strongly expressive in their language, but not easily rendered into English; it signifies, *to retire to his first Mother.* Her excuse for not coming sooner was that her husband dying late in the morning, she was a good while consulting her servants about a convenient place where his body should be laid; and I observed she behaved herself at our house, as cheerfully as the rest; she died about three months after.

They live generally to seventy or seventy-five years, very seldom to fourscore; some weeks before their death they feel a gradual decay, but without pain. During this time they are much visited by their friends, because they cannot go abroad with their usual ease and satisfaction. However, about ten days before their death, which they seldom fail in computing, they return the visits that have been made by those who are nearest in the neighborhood, being carried in a convenient sledge drawn by Yahoos; which vehicle they use, not only upon this occasion, but when they grow old, upon long journeys, or when they are lamed by any accident. And therefore when the dying Houyhnhnms return those visits, they take a solemn leave of their friends, as if they were going to some remote part of the country, where they designed to pass the rest of their lives.

I know not whether it may be worth observing, that the Houyhnhnms have no word in their language to express anything that is evil, except what they borrow from the deformities or ill qualities of the Yahoos. Thus they denote the folly of a servant, an omission of a child, a stone that cuts their feet, a continuance of foul or unseasonable weather, and the like, by adding to each the epithet of Yahoo. For instance, *hhnm Yahoo, whnaholm Yahoo, ynlhmnd-wihlma Yahoo*, and an ill-contrived house, *ynholmhnmrohlnw Yahoo*.

I could with great pleasure enlarge farther upon the manners and virtues of this excellent people; but intending in a short time to publish a volume by itself expressly upon that subject, I refer the reader thither. And in the meantime, proceed to relate my own sad catastrophe.

CHAPTER X. *The Author's economy, and happy life among the Houyhnhnms. His great improvement in virtue, by conversing with them. Their conversations. The Author hath notice given him by his master that he must depart from the country. He falls into a swoon for grief, but submits. He contrives and finishes a canoe, by the help of a fellow servant, and puts to sea at a venture.*

I had settled my little economy to my own heart's content. My master had ordered a room to be made for me after their manner, about six yards from the house; the sides and floors of which I plastered with clay, and covered with rush mats of my own contriving; I had beaten hemp, which there grows wild, and made of it a sort of ticking; this I filled with the feathers of several birds I had taken with springes made of Yahoos' hairs, and were excellent food. I had worked two chairs with my knife, the sorrel nag helping me in the grosser and more laborious part. When my clothes were worn to rags, I made myself others with the skins of rabbits, and of a certain beautiful animal about the same size, called *nnuhnoh*, the skin of which is covered with a fine down. Of these I likewise made very tolerable stockings. I soled my shoes with wood which I cut from a tree, and fitted to the upper leather, and when this was worn out, I supplied it with the skins of Yahoos, dried in the sun. I often got honey out of hollow trees, which I mingled with water, or eat it with my bread. No man could more verify the truth of these two maxims, that *Nature is very easily satisfied*; and, that *Necessity is the mother of invention*. I enjoyed perfect health of body, and tranquility of mind; I did not feel the treachery or inconstancy of a friend, nor the inquiries of a secret or open enemy. I had no occasion of bribing, flattering, or pimping to procure the favor of any great man, or of his minion. I wanted no fence against fraud or oppression; here was neither physician to destroy my body, nor lawyer to ruin my fortune; no informer to watch my words and actions, or forge accusations against me for hire; here were no gibers, censurers, backbiters, pickpockets, highwaymen, housebreakers, attorneys, bawds, buffoons, gamesters, politicians, wits, splenetics, tedious talkers, controvertists, ravishers, murderers, robbers, virtuosos; no leaders or followers of party and faction; no encourages to vice, by seducement or examples; no dungeons, axes, gibbets, whipping posts, or pillories; no cheating shopkeepers or mechanics; no pride, vanity or affectation; no fops, bullies, drunkards, strolling whores, or poxes; no ranting, lewd, expensive wives; no stupid, proud pedants; no importunate, overbearing, quarrelsome, noisy, roaring, empty, conceited, swearing companions; no scoundrels raised from the dust upon the merit of their vices; or nobility thrown into it on account of their virtues; no lords, fiddlers, judges, or dancing masters.

I had the favor of being admitted to several Houyhnhnms, who came to visit or dine with my master; where his honor graciously suffered me to wait in the room, and listen to their discourse. Both he and his company would often descend to ask me questions, and receive my answers. I had also sometimes the honor of attending my master in his visits to others. I never presumed to speak, except in answer to a question; and then I did it with inward regret, because it was a loss of so much time for improving myself; but I was infinitely delighted with the station of an humble auditor in such conversations, where nothing passed but what was useful, expressed in the fewest and most significant words; where (as I have already said) the greatest decency was observed, without the least degree of ceremony; where no person spoke without being pleased himself, and pleasing his companions; where there was no interruption, tediousness, heat, or difference of sentiments. They have a notion, that when people are met together, a short silence doth much improve conversation; this I found to be true; for during those little intermissions of talk, new ideas would arise in their minds, which very much enlivened the discourse. Their subjects are generally on friendship and benevolence; on order and economy; sometimes upon the visible operations of nature, or ancient traditions; upon the bounds and limits of virtue; upon the unerring rules of reason; or upon some determinations, to be taken at the next great assembly; and often upon the various excellencies of poetry. I may add, without vanity, that my presence often gave them sufficient matter for discourse, because it afforded my master an occasion of letting his friends into the history of me and my country, upon which they were all pleased to discant in a manner not very advantageous to human kind; and for that reason I shall not repeat what they said; only I may be allowed to observe that his honor, to my great admiration, appeared to understand the nature of Yahoos much better than myself. He went through all our vices and follies, and discovered many which I had never mentioned to him; by only supposing what qualities a Yahoo of their country, with a small proportion of reason, might be capable of exerting; and concluded, with too much probability, how vile as well as miserable such a creature must be.

I freely confess, that all the little knowledge I have of any value was acquired by the lectures I received from my master, and from hearing the discourses of him and his friends; to which I should be prouder to listen, than to dictate to the greatest and wisest assembly in Europe. I admired the strength, comeliness, and speed of the inhabitants; and such a constellation of virtues in such amiable persons produced in me the highest veneration. At first, indeed, I did not feel that natural awe which the Yahoos and all other animals bear towards them; but it grew upon me by degrees, much sooner than I imagined, and was mingled with a respectful love and gratitude, that they would condescend to distinguish me from the rest of my species.

When I thought of my family, my friends, my countrymen, or human race in general, I considered them as they really were, Yahoos in shape and disposition, perhaps a little more civilized, and qualified with the gift of speech; but making no other use of reason than to improve and mutiply those vices, whereof their brethren in this country had only the share that nature allotted them. When I happened to behold the reflection of my own form in a lake or fountain, I turned away my face in horror and detestation of myself, and could better endure the sight of a common Yahoo than of my own person. By conversing with the Houyhnhnms, and looking upon them with delight, I fell to imitate their gait and gesture, which is now grown into a habit; and my friends often tell me in a blunt way, that I trot like a horse; which, however, I take for a great compliment; neither shall I disown, that in speaking I am apt to fall into the voice and manner of the Houyhnhnms, and hear myself ridiculed on that account without the least mortification.

In the midst of this happiness, when I looked upon myself to be fully settled for life, my master sent for me one morning a little earlier than his usual hour. I observed by his countenance that he was in some perplexity, and at a loss how to begin what he had to speak. After a short silence, he told me, he did not know how I would take what he was going to say; that, in the last general assembly, when the affair of the Yahoos was entered upon, the representatives had taken offense at his keeping a Yahoo (meaning myself) in his family more like a Houyhnhnm than a brute animal. That he was known frequently to converse with me, as if he could receive some advantage of pleasure in my company; that such a practice was not agreeable to reason or nature, or a thing ever heard of before among them. The assembly did therefore exhort him, either to employ me like the rest of my species, or command me to swim back to the place from whence I came. That the first of these expedients was utterly rejected by all the Houyhnhnms who had ever seen me at his house or their own; for, they alleged, that because I had some rudiments of reason, added to the natural pravity of those animals, it was to be feared, I might be able to seduce them into the woody and mountainous parts of the country, and bring them in troops by night to destroy the Houyhnhnms' cattle, as being naturally of the revenous kind, and averse from labor.

My master added that he was daily pressed by the Houyhnhnms of the neighborhood to have the assembly's exhortation executed, which he could not put off much longer. He doubted it would be impossible for me to swim to another country; and therefore wished I would contrive some sort of vehicle resembling those I had described to him, that might carry me on the sea; in which work I should have the assistance of his own servants, as well as those of his neighbors. He concluded that for his own part he could have been content to keep me in his service as long as I lived; because he found I had cured myself of some bad habits and dispositions, by endeavoring, as far as my inferior nature was capable, to imitate the Houyhnhnms.

I should here observe to the reader, that a decree of the general assembly in this country is expressed by the word *hnhloayn*, which signifies an exhortation, as near as I can render it; for they have no conception how a rational creature can be compelled, but only advised, or exhorted; because no person can disobey reason without giving up his claim to be a rational creature.

I was struck with the utmost grief and despair at my master's discourse; and being unable to support the agonies I was under, I fell into a swoon at his feet; when I came to myself, he told me that he concluded I had been dead (for these people are subject to no such imbecilities of nature). I answered, in a faint voice, that death would have been too great an happiness; that although I could not blame the assembly's exhortation, or the urgency of his friends; yet in my weak and corrupt judgment, I thought it might consist with reason to have been less rigorous. That I could not swim a league, and probably the nearest land to theirs might be distant above an hundred; that many materials, necessary for making a small vessel to carry me off, were wholly wanting in this country, which, however, I would attempt in obedience and gratitude to his honor, although I concluded the thing to be impossible, and therefore looked on myself as already devoted[8] to destruction. That the certain prospect of an unnatural death was the least of my evils; for, supposing I should escape with life by some strange adventure, how could I think with temper[9] of passing my days among Yahoos, and relapsing into my old corruptions, for want of examples to lead and keep me within the paths of virtue. That I knew too well upon what solid reasons all the determinations of the wise Houyhnhnms were founded, not to be shaken by arguments of mine, a miserable Yahoo; and therefore after presenting him with my humble thanks for the offer of his servants' assistance in making a vessel, and desiring a reasonable time for so difficult a work, I told him I would endeavor to preserve a wretched being; and, if ever I returned to England, was without hopes of being useful to my own species by celebrating the praises of the renowned Houyhnhnms, and proposing their virtues to the imitation of mankind.

My master in a few words made me a very gracious reply, allowed me the space of two months to finish my boat, and ordered the sorrel nag, my fellow servant (for so at this distance I may presume to call him), to follow my instructions, because I told my master that his help would be sufficient, and I knew he had a tenderness for me.

In his company my first business was to go to that part of the coast where my rebellious crew had ordered me to be set on shore. I got upon a height, and looking on every side into the sea, fancied I saw a small island towards the northeast; I took out my pocket glass, and could then clearly distinguish it about five leagues off, as I computed; but it appeared to the sorrel nag to be only a blue cloud; for, as he had no conception of any country besides his own, so he could not be as expert in distinguishing remote objects at sea, as we who so much converse in that element.

After I had discovered this island, I considered no farther; but resolved, it should, if possible, be the first place of my banishment, leaving the consequence to fortune.

I returned home, and consulting with the sorrel nag, we went into a copse at some distance, where I with my knife, and he with a sharp flint fastened very artificially,[1] after their manner, to a wooden handle, cut down several oak wattles about the thickness of a walking staff, and some larger pieces. But I shall not trouble the reader with

8. Doomed.   9. Equanimity.   1. Adroitly.

a particular description of my own mechanics; let it suffice to say, that in six weeks time, with the help of the sorrel nag, who performed the parts that required most labor, I finished a sort of Indian canoe; but much larger, covering it with the skins of Yahoos, well stitched together, with hempen threads of my own making. My sail was likewise composed of the skins of the same animal; but I made use of the youngest I could get, the older being too tough and thick; and I likewise provided myself with four paddles. I laid in a stock of boiled flesh, of rabbits and fowls; and took with me two vessels, one filled with milk, and the other with water.

I tried my canoe in a large pond near my master's house, and then corrected in it what was amiss, stopping all the chinks with Yahoo's tallow, till I found it staunch, and able to bear me and my freight. And when it was as complete as I could possibly make it, I had it drawn on a carriage very gently by Yahoos, to the seaside, under the conduct of the sorrel nag and another servant.

When all was ready, and the day came for my departure, I took leave of my master and lady, and the whole family, my eyes flowing with tears and my heart quite sunk with grief. But his honor, out of curiosity, and perhaps (if I may speak it without vanity) partly out of kindness, was determined to see me in my canoe; and got several of his neighboring friends to accompany him. I was forced to wait above an hour for the tide, and then observing the wind very fortunately bearing towards the island to which I intended to steer my course, I took a second leave of my master; but as I was going to prostrate myself to kiss his hoof, he did me the honor to raise it gently to my mouth. I am not ignorant how much I have been censured for mentioning this last particular. Detractors are pleased to think it improbable that so illustrious a person should descend to give so great a mark of distinction to a creature so inferior as I. Neither have I forgot how apt some travelers are to boast of extraordinary favors they have received. But, if these censurers were better acquainted with the noble and courteous disposition of the Houyhnhnms, they would soon change their opinion. I paid my respects to the rest of the Houyhnhnms in his honor's company; then getting into my canoe, I pushed off from shore.

CHAPTER XI. *The Author's dangerous voyage. He arrives at New Holland, hoping to settle there. Is wounded with an arrow by one of the natives. Is seized and carried by force into a Portuguese ship. The great civilities of the Captain. The Author arrives at England.*

I began this desperate voyage on February 15, 1714/5,[2] at 9 o'clock in the morning. The wind was very favorable; however, I made use

---

2. I.e., 1714. The year began on March 25th.

at first only of my paddles; but considering I should soon be weary, and that the wind might probably chop about, I ventured to set up my little sail; and thus, with the help of the tide, I went at the rate of a league and a half an hour, as near as I could guess. My master and his friends continued on the shore, till I was almost out of sight; and I often heard the sorrel nag (who always loved me) crying out, "*Hnuy illa nyha maiah Yahoo*" ("Take care of thyself, gentle Yahoo").

My design was, if possible, to discover some small island uninhabited, yet sufficient by my labor to furnish me with necessaries of life, which I would have thought a greater happiness than to be first minister in the politest court of Europe, so horrible was the idea I conceived of returning to live in the society and under the government of Yahoos. For in such a solitude as I desired, I could at least enjoy my own thoughts, and reflect with delight on the virtues of those inimitable Houyhnhnms, without any opportunity of degenerating into the vices and corruptions of my own species.

The reader may remember what I related when my crew conspired against me, and confined me to my cabin, how I continued there several weeks, without knowing what course we took; and when I was put ashore in the longboat, how the sailors told me with oaths, whether true or false, that they knew not in what part of the world we were. However, I did then believe us to be about 10 degrees southward of the Cape of Good Hope, or about 45 degrees southern latitude, as I gathered from some general words I overheard among them, being I supposed to the southeast in their intended voyage to Madagascar. And although this were but little better than conjecture, yet I resolved to steer my course eastward, hoping to reach the southwest coast of New Holland, and perhaps some such island as I desired, lying westward of it. The wind was full west, and by six in the evening I computed I had gone eastward at least eighteen leagues; when I spied a very small island about half a league off, which I soon reached. It was nothing but a rock with one creek,[3] naturally arched by the force of tempests. Here I put in my canoe, and climbing a part of the rock, I could plainly discover land to the east, extending from south to north. I lay all night in my canoe; and repeating my voyage early in the morning, I arrived in seven hours to the southeast point of New Holland.[4] This confirmed me in the opinion I have long entertained, that the maps and charts place this country at least three degrees more to the east than it really is; which thought I communicated many years ago to my worthy friend Mr. Herman Moll,[5] and gave him my reasons for it, although he hath rather chosen to follow other authors.

I saw no inhabitants in the place where I landed; and being

---

3. A bay.   4. Present-day Republic of South Africa.   5. A famous contemporary mapmaker.

unarmed, I was afraid of venturing far into the country. I found some shellfish on the shore, and eat them raw, not daring to kindle a fire, for fear of being discovered by the natives. I continued three days feeding on oysters and limpets, to save my own provisions; and I fortunately found a brook of excellent water, which gave me great relief.

On the fourth day, venturing out early a little too far, I saw twenty or thirty natives upon a height, not above five hundred yards from me. They were stark naked, men, women, and children round a fire, as I could discover by the smoke. One of them spied me, and gave notice to the rest; five of them advanced towards me, leaving the women and children at the fire. I made what haste I could to the shore, and getting into my canoe, shoved off; the savages observing me retreat, ran after me; and before I could get far enough into the sea, discharged an arrow, which wounded me deeply on the inside of my left knee. (I shall carry the mark to my grave.) I apprehended the arrow might be poisoned; and paddling out of the reach of their darts (being a calm day) I made a shift to suck the wound, and dress it as well as I could.

I was at a loss what to do, for I durst not return to the same landing place, but stood to the north, and was forced to paddle; for the wind, although very gentle, was against me, blowing northwest. As I was looking about for a secure landing place, I saw a sail to the north northeast, which appearing every minute more visible, I was in some doubt whether I should wait for them or no; but at last my detestation of the Yahoo race prevailed; and turning my canoe, I sailed and paddled together to the south, and got into the same creek from whence I set out in the morning, choosing rather to trust myself among these barbarians than live with European Yahoos. I drew up my canoe as close as I could to the shore, and hid myself behind a stone by the little brook, which, as I have already said, was excellent water.

The ship came within half a league of this creek, and sent out her longboat with vessels to take in fresh water (for the place it seems was very well known), but I did not observe it until the boat was almost on shore; and it was too late to seek another hiding place. The seamen at their landing observed my canoe, and rummaging it all over, easily conjectured that the owner could not be far off. Four of them well armed searched every cranny and lurking hole, till at last they found me flat on my face behind the stone. They gazed a while in admiration at my strange uncouth dress; my coat made of skins, my wooden-soled shoes, and my furred stockings; from whence, however, they concluded I was not a native of the place, who all go naked. One of the seamen in Portuguese bid me rise, and asked who I was. I understood that language very well, and getting upon my

feet, said I was a poor Yahoo, banished from the Houyhnhnms, and
desired they would please to let me depart. They admired to hear me
answer them in their own tongue, and saw by my complexion I must
be an European; but were at a loss to know what I meant by Yahoos
and Houyhnhnms, and at the same time fell a laughing at my strange
tone in speaking, which resembled the neighing of a horse. I trembled all the while betwixt fear and hatred; I again desired leave to
depart, and was gently moving to my canoe; but they laid hold on
me, desiring to know what country I was of? whence I came? with
many other questions. I told them I was born in England, from
whence I came about five years ago, and then their country and ours
was at peace. I therefore hoped they would not treat me as an enemy,
since I meant them no harm, but was a poor Yahoo, seeking some
desolate place where to pass the remainder of his unfortunate life.

When they began to talk, I thought I never heard or saw any thing
so unnatural; for it appeared to me as monstrous as if a dog or a cow
should speak in England, or a Yahoo in Houyhnhnmland. The honest Portuguese were equally amazed at my strange dress, and the odd
manner of delivering my words, which however they understood very
well. They spoke to me with great humanity, and said they were sure
their Captain would carry me *gratis* to Lisbon, from whence I might
return to my own country; that two of the seamen would go back to
the ship, to inform the Captain of what they had seen, and receive
his orders; in the meantime, unless I would give my solemn oath not
to fly, they would secure me by force. I thought it best to comply
with their proposal. They were very curious to know my story, but I
gave them very little satisfaction; and they all conjectured, that my
misfortunes had impaired my reason. In two hours the boat, which
went laden with vessels of water, returned with the Captain's commands to fetch me on board. I fell on my knees to preserve my
liberty; but all was in vain, and the men having tied me with cords,
heaved me into the boat, from whence I was taken into the ship, and
from thence into the Captain's cabin.

His name was Pedro de Mendez; he was a very courteous and
generous person; he entreated me to give some account of myself,
and desired to know what I would eat or drink; said I should be used
as well as himself, and spoke so many obliging things, that I wondered to find such civilities from a Yahoo. However, I remained
silent and sullen; I was ready to faint at the very smell of him and his
men. At last I desired something to eat out of my own canoe; but he
ordered me a chicken and some excellent wine, and then directed
that I should be put to bed in a very clean cabin. I would not undress
myself, but lay on the bedclothes; and in half an hour stole out,
when I thought the crew was at dinner; and getting to the side of the
ship, was going to leap into the sea, and swim for my life, rather

than continue among Yahoos. But one of the seamen prevented me, and having informed the Captain, I was chained to my cabin.

After dinner Don Pedro came to me, and desired to know my reason for so desperate an attempt; assured me he only meant to do me all the service he was able; and spoke so very movingly, that at last I descended to treat him like an animal which had some little portion of reason. I gave him a very short relation of my voyage; of the conspiracy against me by my own men; of the country where they set me on shore, and of my five years residence there. All which he looked upon as if it were a dream or a vision; whereat I took great offense; for I had quite forgot the faculty of lying, so peculiar to Yahoos in all countries where they preside, and consequently the disposition of suspecting truth in others of their own species. I asked him whether it were the custom of his country to *say the thing that was not?* I assured him I had almost forgot what he meant by falsehood; and if I had lived a thousand years in Houyhnhnmland, I should never have heard a lie from the meanest servant. That I was altogether indifferent whether he believed me or no; but however, in return for his favors, I would give so much allowance to the corruption of his nature, as to answer any objection he would please to make; and he might easily discover the truth.

The Captain, a wise man, after many endeavors to catch me tripping in some part of my story, at last began to have a better opinion of my veracity. But he added that since I professed so inviolable an attachment to truth, I must give him my word of honor to bear him company in this voyage without attempting anything against my life; or else he would continue me a prisoner till we arrived at Lisbon. I gave him the promise he required; but at the same time protested that I would suffer the greatest hardships rather than return to live among Yahoos.

Our voyage passed without any considerable accident. In gratitude to the Captain I sometimes sat with him at his earnest request, and strove to conceal my antipathy against humankind, although it often broke out; which he suffered to pass without observation. But the greatest part of the day, I confined myself to my cabin, to avoid seeing any of the crew. The Captain had often entreated me to strip myself of my savage dress, and offered to lend me the best suit of clothes he had. This I would not be prevailed on to accept, abhorring to cover myself with anything that had been on the back of a Yahoo. I only desired he would lend me two clean shirts, which having been washed since he wore them, I believed would not so much defile me. These I changed every second day, and washed them myself.

We arrived at Lisbon, Nov. 5, 1715. At our landing, the Captain forced me to cover myself with his cloak, to prevent the rabble from crowding about me. I was conveyed to his own house; and at my earnest request, he led me up to the highest room backwards.[6] I conjured him to conceal from all persons what I had told him of the Houyhnhnms; because the least hint of such a story would not only draw numbers of people to see me, but probably put me in danger of being imprisoned, or burned by the Inquisition. The Captain persuaded me to accept a suit of clothes newly made; but I would not suffer the tailor to take my measure; however, Don Pedro being almost of my size, they fitted me well enough. He accoutred me with other necessaries, all new, which I aired for twenty-four hours before I would use them.

The Captain had no wife, nor above three servants, none of which were suffered to attend at meals; and his whole deportment was so obliging, added to very good human understanding, that I really began to tolerate his company. He gained so far upon me, that I ventured to look out of the back window. By degrees I was brought into another room, from whence I peeped into the street, but drew my head back in a fright. In a week's time he seduced me down to the door. I found my terror gradually lessened, but my hatred and contempt seemed to increase. I was at last bold enough to walk the street in his company, but kept my nose well stopped with rue, or sometimes with tobacco.

In ten days, Don Pedro, to whom I had given some account of my domestic affairs, put it upon me as a point of honor and conscience that I ought to return to my native country, and live at home with my wife and children. He told me there was an English ship in the port just ready to sail, and he would furnish me with all things necessary. It would be tedious to repeat his arguments, and my contradictions. He said it was altogether impossible to find such a solitary island as I had desired to live in; but I might command in my own house, and pass my time in a manner as recluse as I pleased.

I complied at last, finding I could not do better. I left Lisbon the 24th day of November, in an English merchantman, but who was the Master I never inquired. Don Pedro accompanied me to the ship, and lent me twenty pounds. He took kind leave of me, and embraced me at parting; which I bore as well as I could. During this last voyage I had no commerce with the Master, or any of his men; but pretending I was sick kept close in my cabin. On the fifth of December, 1715, we cast anchor in the Downs about nine in the morning, and at three in the afternoon I got safe to my house at Redriff.

My wife and family received me with great surprise and joy, because they concluded me certainly dead; but I must freely confess, the sight

6. At the rear.

of them filled me only with hatred, disgust, and contempt; and the more, by reflecting on the near alliance I had to them. For, although since my unfortunate exile from the Houyhnhnm country, I had compelled myself to tolerate the sight of Yahoos, and to converse with Don Pedro de Mendez; yet my memory and imaginations were perpetually filled with the virtues and ideas of those exalted Houyhnhnms. And when I began to consider that by copulating with one of the Yahoo species, I had become a parent of more, it struck me with the utmost shame, confusion, and horror.

As soon as I entered the house, my wife took me in her arms, and kissed me; at which, having not been used to the touch of that odious animal for so many years, I fell in a swoon for almost an hour. At the time I am writing, it is five years since my last return to England; during the first year I could not endure my wife or children in my presence, the very smell of them was intolerable; much less could I suffer them to eat in the same room. To this hour they dare not presume to touch my bread, or drink out of the same cup; neither was I ever able to let one of them take me by the hand. The first money I laid out was to buy two young stone-horses,[7] which I keep in a good stable, and next to them the groom is my greatest favorite; for I feel my spirits revived by the smell he contracts in the stable. My horses understand me tolerably well; I converse with them at least four hours every day. They are strangers to bridle or saddle; they live in great amity with me, and friendship to each other.

CHAPTER XII. *The Author's veracity. His design in publishing this work. His censure of those travelers who swerve from the truth. The Author clears himself from any sinister ends in writing. An objection answered. The method of planting colonies. His native country commended. The right of the crown to those countries described by the Author is justified. The difficulty of conquering them. The Author takes his last leave of the reader; proposeth his manner of living for the future; gives good advice, and concludeth.*

Thus, gentle reader, I have given thee a faithful history of my travels for sixteen years, and above seven months; wherein I have not been so studious of ornament as of truth. I could perhaps like others have astonished thee with strange improbable tales; but I rather chose to relate plain matter of fact in the simplest manner and style; because my principal design was to inform, and not to amuse thee.

It is easy for us who travel into remote countries, which are seldom visited by Englishmen or other Europeans, to form descriptions of wonderful animals both at sea and land. Whereas a traveler's chief aim should be to make men wiser and better, and to improve their

7. Stallions.

minds by the bad as well as good example of what they deliver concerning foreign places.

I could heartily wish a law were enacted, that every traveler, before he were permitted to publish his voyages, should be obliged to make oath before the Lord High Chancellor that all he intended to print was absolutely true to the best of his knowledge; for then the world would no longer be deceived as it usually is, while some writers, to make their works pass the better upon the public, impose the grossest falsities on the unwary reader. I have perused several books of travels with great delight in my younger days; but, having since gone over most parts of the globe, and been able to contradict many fabulous accounts from my own observation, it hath given me a great disgust against this part of reading, and some indignation to see the credulity of mankind so impudently abused. Therefore, since my acquaintance were pleased to think my poor endeavors might not be unacceptable to my country; I imposed on myself as a maxim, never to be swerved from, that I would *strictly adhere to truth*; neither indeed can I be ever under the least temptation to vary from it, while I retain in my mind the lectures and example of my noble master, and the other illustrious Houyhnhnms, of whom I had so long the honor to be an humble hearer.

———*Nec si miserum Fortuna Sinonem
Finxit, vanum etiam, mendacemque improba finget.*[8]

I know very well how little reputation is to be got by writings which require neither genius nor learning, nor indeed any other talent, except a good memory, or an exact *Journal.* I know likewise, that writers of travels, like dictionary-makers, are sunk into oblivion by the weight and bulk of those who come last, and therefore lie uppermost. And it is highly probable that such travelers who shall hereafter visit the countries described in this work of mine, may be detecting my errors (if there be any) and adding many new discoveries of their own, jostle me out of vogue, and stand in my place, making the world forget that ever I was an author. This indeed would be too great a mortification if I wrote for fame; but, as my sole intention was the PUBLIC GOOD, I cannot be altogether disappointed. For, who can read the virtues I have mentioned in the glorious Houyhnhnms, without being ashamed of his own vices, when he considers himself as the reasoning, governing animal of his country? I shall say nothing of those remote nations where Yahoos preside; amongst which the least corrupted are the Brobdingnagians, whose wise maxims in

---

8. Virgil, *Aeneid* ll. 79–80: ". . . now, if Fortune had moulded Sinon for misery, will she also in spite mould him as false and lying."

morality and government it would be our happiness to observe. But I forbear descanting further, and rather leave the judicious reader to his own remarks and applications.

I am not a little pleased that this work of mine can possibly meet with no censurers; for what objections can be made against a writer who relates only plain facts that happened in such distant countries, where we have not the least interest with respect either to trade or negotiations? I have carefully avoided every fault with which common writers of travels are often too justly charged. Besides, I meddle not the least with any party, but write without passion, prejudice, or ill-will against any man or number of men whatsoever. I write for the noblest end, to inform and instruct mankind, over whom I may, without breach of modesty, pretend to some superiority, from the advantages I received by conversing so long among the most accomplished Houyhnhnms. I write without any view towards profit or praise. I never suffer a word to pass that may look like reflection, or possibly give the least offense even to those who are most ready to take it. So that, I hope, I may with justice pronounce myself an Author perfectly blameless; against whom the tribes of answerers, considerers, observers, reflectors, detecters, remarkers will never be able to find matter for exercising their talents.

I confess it was whispered to me that I was bound in duty as a subject of England, to have given in a memorial to a secretary of state, at my first coming over; because, whatever lands are discovered by a subject, belong to the Crown. But I doubt whether our conquests in the countries I treat of would be as easy as those of Ferdinando Cortez[9] over the naked Americans. The Lilliputians, I think, are hardly worth the charge of a fleet and army to reduce them; and I question whether it might be prudent or safe to attempt the Brobdingnagians; or, whether an English army would be much at their ease with the Flying Island over their heads. The Houyhnhnms, indeed, appear not to be so well prepared for war, a science to which they are perfect strangers, and especially against missive weapons. However, supposing myself to be a minister of state, I could never give my advice for invading them. Their prudence, unanimity, unacquaintedness with fear, and their love of their country would amply supply all defects in the military art. Imagine twenty thousand of them breaking into the midst of an European army, confounding the ranks, overturning the carriages, battering the warriors' faces into mummy, by terrible yerks[1] from their hinder hoofs: for they would well deserve the character given to Augustus, *Recalcitrat undique tutus.*[2] But instead of proposals for conquering that magnanimous

9. Hernando Cortez (1485–1547), who destroyed the Aztec Empire. 1. Kicks. *Mummy:* Pulp. 2. Horace, *Satires* II.i.20: ". . . he kicks backward, at every point on his guard."

nation, I rather wish they were in a capacity or disposition to send a sufficient number of their inhabitants for civilizing Europe; by teaching us the first principles of Honor, Justice, Truth, Temperance, Public Spirit, Fortitude, Chastity, Friendship, Benevolence, and Fidelity. The names of all which Virtues are still retained among us in most languages, and are to be met with in modern as well as ancient authors, which I am able to assert from my own small reading.

But I had another reason which made me less forward to enlarge his majesty's dominions by my discoveries: to say the truth, I had conceived a few scruples with relation to the distributive justice of princes upon those occasions. For instance, a crew of pirates are driven by a storm they know not whither; at length a boy discovers land from the topmast; they go on shore to rob and plunder; they see an harmless people, are entertained with kindness, they give the country a new name, they take formal possession of it for the king, they set up a rotten plank or a stone for a memorial, they murder two or three dozen of the natives, bring away a couple more by force for a sample, return home, and get their pardon. Here commences a new dominion acquired with a title by Divine Right. Ships are sent with the first opportunity; the natives driven out or destroyed, their princes tortured to discover their gold; a free license given to all acts of inhumanity and lust; the earth reeking with the blood of its inhabitants: and this execrable crew of butchers employed in so pious an expedition is a *modern colony* sent to convert and civilize an idolatrous and barbarous people.

But this description, I confess, doth by no means affect the British nation, who may be an example to the whole world for their wisdom, care, and justice in planting colonies; their liberal endowments for the advancement of religion and learning; their choice of devout and able pastors to propagate Christianity; their caution in stocking their provinces with people of sober lives and conversations from this the Mother Kingdom; their strict regard to the distribution of justice, in supplying the civil administration through all their colonies with officers of the greatest abilities, utter strangers to corruption: and to crown all, by sending the most vigilant and virtuous governors, who have no other views than the happiness of the people over whom they preside, and the honor of the king their master.

But, as those countries which I have described do not appear to have any desire of being conquered, and enslaved, murdered, or driven out by colonies, nor abound either in gold, silver, sugar, or tobacco, I did humbly conceive they were by no means proper objects of our zeal, our valor, or our interest. However, if those whom it may concern, think fit to be of another opinion, I am ready to depose, when I shall be lawfully called, that no European did ever visit these countries before me. I mean, if the inhabitants ought to be believed.

But, as to the formality of taking possession in my sovereign's name, it never came once into my thoughts; and if it had, yet as my affairs then stood, I should perhaps in point of prudence and self-preservation have put it off to a better opportunity.

Having thus answered the only objection that can be raised against me as a traveler, I here take a final leave of my courteous readers, and return to enjoy my own speculations in my little garden at Redriff; to apply those excellent lessons of virtue which I learned among the Houyhnhnms; to instruct the Yahoos of my own family as far as I shall find them docible animals; to behold my figure often in a glass, and thus if possible habituate myself by time to tolerate the sight of a human creature; to lament the brutality of Houyhnhnms in my own country, but always treat their persons with respect, for the sake of my noble master, his family, his friends, and the whole Houyhnhnm race, whom these of ours have the honor to resemble in all their lineaments, however their intellectuals came to degenerate.

I began last week to permit my wife to sit at dinner with me, at the farthest end of a long table; and to answer (but with the utmost brevity) the few questions I ask her. Yet the smell of a Yahoo continuing very offensive, I always keep my nose well stopped with rue, lavender, or tobacco leaves. And although it be hard for a man late in life to remove old habits, I am not altogether out of hopes in some time to suffer a neighbor Yahoo in my company, without the apprehensions I am yet under of his teeth or his claws.

My reconcilement to the Yahoo kind in general might not be so difficult, if they would be content with those vices and follies only which nature hath entitled them to. I am not in the least provoked at the sight of a lawyer, a pickpocket, a colonel, a fool, a lord, a gamester, a politician, a whoremonger, a physician, an evidence, a suborner, an attorney, a traitor, or the like: this is all according to the due course of things. But when I behold a lump of deformity, and diseases both in body and mind, smitten with pride, it immediately breaks all the measures of my patience; neither shall I be ever able to comprehend how such an animal and such a vice could tally together. The wise and virtuous Houyhnhnms, who abound in all excellencies that can adorn a rational creature, have no name for this vice in their language, which hath no terms to express anything that is evil, except those whereby they describe the detestable qualities of their Yahoos, among which they were not able to distinguish this of pride, for want of thoroughly understanding human nature, as it showeth itself in other countries, where that animal presides. But I, who had more experience, could plainly observe some rudiments of it among the wild Yahoos.

But the Houyhnhnms, who live under the government of reason, are no more proud of the good qualities they possess, than I should be for not wanting a leg or an arm, which no man in his wits would boast of, although he must be miserable without them. I dwell the longer upon this subject from the desire I have to make the society of an English Yahoo by any means not insupportable; and therefore I here entreat those who have any tincture of this absurd vice, that they will not presume to appear in my sight.   1726, 1735

A Modest Proposal for

Preventing the Children of poor People in Ireland, *from being a Burden to their Parents or Country; and for making them beneficial to the Publick.*[1]

WRITTEN IN THE YEAR 1729

It is a melancholly Object to those, who walk through this great Town,[2] or travel in the Country; when they see the *Streets*, the *Roads*, and *Cabbin-doors* crowded with *Beggars* of the Female Sex, followed by three, four, or six Children, *all in Rags*, and importuning every Passenger for an Alms. These *Mothers*, instead of being able to work for their honest Livelyhood, are forced to employ all their Time in stroling to beg Sustenance for their *helpless Infants*; who, as they grow up, either turn *Thieves* for want of Work; or leave their *dear Native Country, to fight for the Pretender* in Spain, or sell themselves to the *Barbadoes*.[3]

I THINK it is agreed by all Parties, that this prodigious Number of Children in the Arms, or on the Backs, or at the *Heels* of their *Mothers*, and frequently of their *Fathers*, is *in the present deplorable State of the Kingdom*, a very great additional Grievance; and therefore, whoever could find out a fair, cheap, and easy Method of making these Children sound and useful Members of the Commonwealth, would deserve so well of the Publick, as to have his Statue set up for a Preserver of the Nation.

BUT my Intention is very far from being confined to provide only for the Children of *professed Beggars*: It is of a much greater Extent, and shall take in the whole Number of Infants at a certain Age, who are born of Parents, in effect as little able to support them, as those who demand our Charity in the Streets.

---

1. The complete text edited by Herbert Davis.   2. Dublin.   3. A British possession at this time, with a prosperous sugar industry; workers were needed in the sugar plantations. *The Pretender:* James Edward (1688–1766), son of the Catholic King James II of England, called the "Old Pretender" (in distinction to his son Charles, nine years old at the time of this work, the "Young Pretender"). Many thought him a legitimate claimant to the throne.

As to my own Part, having turned my Thoughts for many Years, upon this important Subject, and maturely weighed the several *Schemes of other Projectors*,[4] I have always found them grosly mistaken in their Computation. It is true a Child, *just dropt from its Dam*, may be supported by her Milk, for a Solar Year with little other Nourishment; at most not above the Value of two Shillings; which the Mother may certainly get, or the Value in *Scraps*, by her lawful Occupation of *Begging*: And, it is exactly at one Year old, that I propose to provide for them in such a Manner, as, instead of being a Charge upon their *Parents*, or the *Parish*, or *wanting Food and Raiment* for the rest of their Lives; they shall, on the contrary, contribute to the Feeding, and partly to the Cloathing, of many Thousands.

THERE is likewise another great Advantage in my *Scheme*, that it will prevent those *voluntary Abortions*, and that horrid Practice of *Women murdering their Bastard Children*; alas! too frequent among us; sacrificing the *poor innocent Babes*, I doubt, more to avoid the Expence than the Shame; which would move Tears and Pity in the most Savage and inhuman Breast.

THE Number of Souls in *Ireland* being usually reckoned one Million and a half; of these I calculate there may be about Two hundred Thousand Couple whose Wives are Breeders; from which Number I subtract thirty thousand Couples, who are able to maintain their own Children; although I apprehend there cannot be so many, under *the present Distresses of the Kingdom*; but this being granted, there will remain an Hundred and Seventy Thousand Breeders. I again subtract Fifty Thousand, for those Women who miscarry, or whose Children die by Accident, or Disease, within the Year. There only remain an Hundred and Twenty Thousand Children of poor Parents, annually born: The Question therefore is, How this Number shall be reared, and provided for? Which, as I have already said, under the present Situation of Affairs, is utterly impossible, by all the Methods hitherto proposed: For we can *neither employ them in Handicraft* or *Agriculture*; we neither build Houses (I mean in the Country), nor cultivate Land: They can very seldom pick up a Livelyhood *by Stealing* until they arrive at six Years old; except where they are of towardly Parts;[5] although, I confess, they learn the Rudiments much earlier; during which Time, they can, however, be properly looked upon only as *Probationers*; as I have been informed by a principal Gentleman in the County of *Cavan*, who protested to me, that he never knew above one or two Instances under the Age of six, even in a Part of the Kingdom *so renowned for the quickest Proficiency in that Art*.

4. Planners.   5. Particularly talented, unusually gifted.

I AM assured by our Merchants, that a Boy or a Girl before twelve Years old, is no saleable Commodity; and even when they come to this Age, they will not yield above Three Pounds, or Three Pounds and half a Crown at most, on the Exchange; which cannot turn to Account either to the Parents or the Kingdom; the Charge of Nutriment and Rags, having been at least four Times that Value.

I SHALL now therefore humbly propose my own Thoughts; which I hope will not be liable to the least Objection.

I HAVE been assured by a very knowing *American* of my Acquaintance in *London*; that a young healthy Child, well nursed, is, at a Year old, a most delicious, nourishing, and wholesome Food; whether *Stewed, Roasted, Baked,* or *Boiled*; and, I make no doubt, that it will equally serve in a *Fricasie,* or *Ragoust.*

I DO therefore humbly offer it to *publick Consideration,* that of the Hundred and Twenty Thousand Children, already computed, Twenty thousand may be reserved for Breed; whereof only one Fourth Part to be Males; which is more than we allow to *Sheep, black Cattle,* or *Swine*; and my Reason is, that these Children are seldom the Fruits of Marriage, *a Circumstance not much regarded by our Savages*; therefore, *one Male* will be sufficient to serve *four Females.* That the remaining Hundred thousand, may, at a Year old, be offered in Sale to the *Persons of Quality* and *Fortune,* through the Kingdom; always advising the Mother to let them suck plentifully in the last Month, so as to render them plump, and fat for a good Table. A Child will make two Dishes at an Entertainment for Friends; and when the Family dines alone, the fore or hind Quarter will make a reasonable Dish; and seasoned with a little Pepper or Salt, will be very good Boiled on the fourth Day, especially in *Winter.*

I HAVE reckoned upon a Medium,[6] that a Child just born will weigh Twelve Pounds; and in a solar Year, if tolerably nursed, encreaseth to twenty eight Pounds.

I GRANT this Food will be somewhat dear,[7] and therefore very *proper for Landlords*; who, as they have already devoured most of the Parents, seem to have the best Title to the Children.

INFANTS Flesh will be in Season throughout the Year; but more plentiful in *March,* and a little before and after: For we are told by a grave Author,[8] an eminent *French* Physician, that *Fish being a prolifick Dyet,* there are more Children born in *Roman Catholick Countries* about Nine Months after *Lent,* than at any other Season: Therefore reckoning a Year after *Lent,* the Markets will be more glutted than usual; because the Number of *Popish Infants,* is, at

---

6. Average.   7. Expensive.   8. Rabelais [Swift's note]. François Rabelais (1494?–1553) was a French satirist and humorist.

least, three to one in this Kingdom; and therefore it will have one other Collateral Advantage, by lessening the Number of *Papists* among us.

I HAVE already computed the Charge of nursing a Beggar's Child (in which List I reckon all *Cottagers*, *Labourers*, and Four fifths of the *Farmers*) to be about two Shillings *per Annum*,[9] Rags included; and I believe, no Gentleman would repine to give Ten Shillings for the *Carcase of a good fat Child*; which, as I have said, will make four Dishes of excellent nutritive Meat, when he hath only some particular Friend, or his own Family, to dine with him. Thus the Squire will learn to be a good Landlord, and grow popular among his Tenants; the Mother will have Eight Shillings net Profit, and be fit for Work until she produceth another Child.

THOSE who are more thrifty (*as I must confess the Times require*) may flay the Carcase; the Skin of which, artificially dressed, will make admirable *Gloves for Ladies*, and *Summer Boots for fine Gentlemen*.

As to our City of *Dublin*; Shambles[1] may be appointed for this Purpose, in the most convenient Parts of it; and Butchers we may be assured will not be wanting; although I rather recommend buying the Children alive, and dressing them hot from the Knife, as we do *roasting Pigs*.

A VERY worthy Person, *a true Lover of his Country*, and whose Virtues I highly esteem, was lately pleased, in discoursing on this Matter, to offer a Refinement upon my Scheme. He said, that many Gentlemen of this Kingdom, having of late destroyed their Deer; he conceived, that the Want of Venison might be well supplied by the Bodies of young Lads and Maidens, not exceeding fourteen Years of Age, nor under twelve; so great a Number of both Sexes in every County being now ready to starve, for Want of Work and Service: And these to be disposed of by their Parents, if alive, or otherwise by their nearest Relations. But with due Deference to so excellent a Friend, and so deserving a Patriot, I cannot be altogether in his Sentiments. For as to the Males, my *American* Acquaintance assured me from frequent Experience, that their Flesh was generally tough and lean, like that of our School-boys, by continual Exercise, and their Taste disagreeable; and to fatten them would not answer the Charge. Then, as to the Females, it would, I think, with humble Submission, *be a Loss to the Publick*, because they soon would become Breeders themselves: And besides it is not improbable, that some scrupulous People might be apt to censure such a Practice (although indeed very unjustly) as a little bordering upon Cruelty; which, I

9. A year.   1. Slaughterhouses.

confess, hath always been with me the strongest Objection against any Project, how well soever intended.

But in order to justify my Friend; he confessed, that this Expedient was put into his Head by the famous *Salmanaazor*,[2] a Native of the Island *Formosa*, who came from thence to *London*, above twenty Years ago, and in Conversation told my Friend, that in his Country, when any young Person happened to be put to Death, the Executioner sold the Carcase to *Persons of Quality*, as a prime Dainty; and that, in his Time, the Body of a plump Girl of fifteen, who was crucified for an Attempt to poison the Emperor, was sold to his Imperial *Majesty's prime Minister of State*, and other great *Mandarins* of the Court, *in Joints from the Gibbet*,[3] at Four Hundred Crowns. Neither indeed can I deny, that if the same Use were made of several plump young girls in this Town, who, without one single Groat to their Fortunes, cannot stir Abroad without a Chair,[4] and appear at the *Play-house*, and *Assemblies* in foreign Fineries, which they never will pay for; the Kingdom would not be the worse.

Some Persons of a desponding Spirit are in great Concern about that vast Number of poor People, who are Aged, Diseased, or Maimed; and I have been desired to employ my Thoughts what Course may be taken, to ease the Nation of so grievous an Incumbrance. But I am not in the least Pain upon that Matter; because it is very well known, that they are every Day *dying*, and *rotting*, by *Cold* and *Famine*, and *Filth*, and *Vermin*, as fast as can be reasonably expected. And as to the younger Labourers, they are now in almost as hopeful a Condition: They cannot get Work, and consequently pine away for Want of Nourishment, to a Degree, that if at any Time they are accidentally hired to common Labour, they have not Strength to perform it; and thus the Country, and themselves, are in a fair Way of being soon delivered from the Evils to come.

I have too long digressed; and therefore shall return to my Subject. I think the Advantages by the Proposal which I have made, are obvious, and many, as well as of the highest Importance.

For, *First*, as I have already observed, it would greatly lessen the *Number of Papists*, with whom we are yearly overrun; being the principal Breeders of the Nation, as well as our most dangerous Enemies; and who stay at home on Purpose, with a Design to *deliver the Kingdom to the Pretender*; hoping to take their Advantage by the

---

2. George Psalmanazar (1679?–1763), a literary impostor born in the south of France who claimed to be a native of Formosa and a recent Christian convert. He published a catechism in an invented language which he called "Formosan" as well as a "Description" of Formosa with an introductory autobiography.   3. The post from which the bodies of criminals were hung in chains after execution. *Joints*: portions of a carcass carved up by a butcher.   4. Sedan chair, an enclosed seat carried on poles by men.

Absence *of so many good Protestants*, who have chosen rather to leave their Country, than stay at home, and pay Tithes against their Conscience, to an idolatrous *Episcopal Curate*.

SECONDLY, The poorer Tenants will have something valuable of their own, which, by Law, may be made liable to Distress,[5] and help to pay their Landlord's Rent; their Corn and Cattle being already seized, and *Money a Thing unknown*.

THIRDLY, Whereas the Maintenance of an Hundred Thousand Children, from two Years old, and upwards, cannot be computed at less than ten Shillings a Piece *per Annum*, the Nation's Stock will be thereby encreased Fifty Thousand Pounds *per Annum*; besides the Profit of a new Dish, introduced to the Tables of all *Gentlemen of Fortune* in the Kingdom, who have any Refinement in Taste; and the Money will circulate among ourselves, the Goods being entirely of our own Growth and Manufacture.

FOURTHLY, The constant Breeders, besides the Gain of Eight Shillings *Sterling per Annum*, by the Sale of their Children, will be rid of the Charge of maintaining them after the first Year.

FIFTHLY, This Food would likewise bring great *Custom to Taverns*, where the Vintners will certainly be so prudent, as to procure the best Receipts[6] for dressing it to Perfection; and consequently, have their Houses frequented by all the *fine Gentlemen*, who justly value themselves upon their Knowledge in good Eating; and a skilful Cook, who understands how to oblige his Guests, will contrive to make it as expensive as they please.

SIXTHLY, This would be a great Inducement to Marriage, which all wise Nations have either encouraged by Rewards, or enforced by Laws and Penalties. It would encrease the Care and Tenderness of Mothers towards their Children, when they were sure of a Settlement for Life, to the poor Babes, provided in some Sort by the Publick, to their annual Profit instead of Expence. We should soon see an honest Emulation among the married Women, *which of them could bring the fattest Child to the Market*. Men would become as *fond* of their Wives, during the Time of their Pregnancy, as they are now of their *Mares* in Foal, their *Cows* in Calf, or *Sows* when they ae ready to farrow; nor offer to beat or kick them, (as it is too *frequent* a Practice) for fear of a Miscarriage.

MANY other Advantages might be enumerated. For instance, the Addition of some Thousand Carcasses in our Exportation of barrelled Beef: The Propagation of *Swines Flesh*, and Improvement in the Art of making good *Bacon*; so much wanted among us by the

---

5. The legal seizing of goods to satisfy a debt, particularly for unpaid rent.   6. Recipes.

great Destruction of *Pigs*, too frequent at our Tables, and are no way comparable in Taste, or Magnificence, to a well-grown fat yearling Child; which, roasted whole, will make a considerable Figure at a *Lord Mayor's Feast*, or any other publick Entertainment. But this, and many others, I omit; being studious of Brevity.

SUPPOSING that one Thousand Families in this City, would be constant Customers for Infants Flesh; besides others who might have it at *merry Meetings*, particularly *Weddings* and *Christenings*; I compute that *Dublin* would take off, annually, about Twenty Thousand Carcasses; and the rest of the Kingdom (where probably they will be sold somewhat cheaper) the remaining Eighty Thousand.

I CAN think of no one Objection, that will possibly be raised against this Proposal; unless it should be urged, that the Number of People will be thereby much lessened in the Kingdom. This I freely own; and it was indeed one principal Design in offering it to the World. I desire the Reader will observe, that I calculate my Remedy *for this one individual Kingdom of* IRELAND, *and for no other that ever was, is, or I think ever can be upon Earth.* Therefore, let no man talk to me of other Expedients: *Of taxing our Absentees at five Shillings a Pound: Of using neither Cloaths, nor Houshold Furniture except what is of our own Growth and Manufacture: Of utterly rejecting the Materials and Instruments that promote foreign Luxury: Of curing the Expensiveness of Pride, Vanity, Idleness, and Gaming in our Women: Of introducing a Vein of Parsimony, Prudence and Temperance: Of learning to love our Country, wherein we differ even from* LAPLANDERS, *and the Inhabitants of* TOPINAMBOO:[7] *Of quitting our Animosities, and Factions; nor act any longer like the* Jews, *who were murdering one another at the very Moment their City was taken: Of being a little cautious not to sell our Country and Consciences for nothing: Of teaching Landlords to have, at least, one Degree of Mercy towards their Tenants. Lastly, Of putting a Spirit of Honesty, Industry, and Skill into our Shop-keepers; who, if a Resolution could now be taken to buy only our native Goods, would immediately unite to cheat and exact upon us in the Price, the Measure, and the Goodness; nor could ever yet be brought to make one fair Proposal of just Dealing, though often and earnestly invited to it.*[8]

THEREFORE I repeat, let no Man talk to me of these and the like Expedients; till he hath, at least, a Glimpse of Hope, that there will ever be some hearty and sincere Attempt to put *them in Practice.*

BUT, as to my self; having been wearied out for many Years with offering vain, idle, visionary Thoughts; and at length utterly despair-

---

7. In Brazil.   8. The italicized proposals are Swift's serious suggestions for remedying the situation of Ireland.

ing of Success, I fortunately fell upon this Proposal; which, as it is wholly new, so it hath something *solid* and *real*, of no Expence, and little Trouble, full in our own Power; and whereby we can incur no Danger in *disobliging* ENGLAND: For, this Kind of Commodity will not bear Exportation; the Flesh being of too tender a Consistence, to admit a long Continuance in Salt; *although, perhaps, I could name a Country,*[9] *which would be glad to eat up our whole Nation without it.*

AFTER all, I am not so violently bent upon my own Opinion, as to reject any Offer proposed by wise Men, which shall be found equally innocent, cheap, easy, and effectual. But before something of that Kind shall be advanced, in Contradiction to my Scheme, and offering a better; I desire the Author, or Authors, will be pleased maturely to consider two Points. *First*, As Things now stand, how they will be able to find Food and Raiment, for a Hundred Thousand useless Mouths and Backs? And *secondly*, There being a round Million of Creatures in human Figure, throughout this Kingdom; whose whole Subsistence, put into a common Stock, would leave them in Debt two Millions of Pounds *Sterling*; adding those, who are Beggars by Profession, to the Bulk of Farmers, Cottagers, and Labourers, with their Wives and Children, who are Beggars in Effect; I desire those Politicians, who dislike my Overture, and may perhaps be so bold to attempt an Answer, that they will first ask the Parents of these Mortals, Whether they would not, at this Day, think it a great Happiness to have been sold for Food at a Year old, in the Manner I prescribe; and thereby have avoided such a perpetual Scene of Misfortunes, as they have since gone through; by the *Oppression of Landlords*; the Impossibility of paying Rent, without Money or Trade; the Want of common Sustenance, with neither House nor Cloaths, to cover them from the Inclemencies of Weather; and the most inevitable Prospect of intailing the like, or greater Miseries upon their Breed for ever.

I PROFESS, in the Sincerity of my Heart, that I have not the least personal Interest, in endeavouring to promote this necessary Work; having no other Motive than the *publick Good of my Country, by advancing our Trade, providing for Infants, relieving the Poor, and giving some Pleasure to the Rich.* I have no Children, by which I can propose to get a single Penny; the youngest being nine Years old, and my Wife past Child-bearing.

9. England.

ALEXANDER POPE
1688–1744

"If Pope be not a poet, where is poetry to be found?" Dr. Johnson inquired. Transmuting the commonplace, claiming as subject matter everything from the minutiae of social existence to speculation about the nature of universal order, Alexander Pope made unlikely raw material into brilliant poetry.

Born to Roman Catholic parents in the year of the Glorious Revolution that deposed Catholic James II in favor of Protestant William and Mary, Pope lived when repressive legislation against Catholics restricted his financial, educational, professional, and residential possibilities. He could not attend a university or hold public employment; he had to live ten miles outside London. Sickly and undersized (he probably suffered a tubercular infection in infancy), he was educated largely at home. He also educated himself by literary friendships beginning in his youth; throughout his life, he enjoyed close associations with other men and with a few women, in particular his neighbor and intimate friend Martha Blount, to whom he left his estate. Increasingly, he won wealth and reputation by his writing, notably his translations of Homer. Following Candide's course of cultivating his garden, he perfected his grounds and grotto at Twickenham, living in retirement from the city. He died of asthma and dropsy.

Pope consciously wrote in most of the poetic genres of his period. Beginning, as Virgil had done, with pastorals, he later produced *An Essay on Criticism*, versified advice about proper literary and critical procedure, and went on to publish a great philosophic poem, the *Essay on Man*, and to edit Shakespeare's plays. The bulk of his verse, however, was satiric. In *The Dunciad* (1743), he provided a satiric epic for his age, a history of the progress of dullness.

Writing to a woman friend, Pope described *The Rape of the Lock* (1717) as "at once the most a satire, and the most inoffensive, of anything of mine. . . . 'Tis a sort of writing very like tickling." He thus suggests the tonal complexity of a work which conveys serious social criticism through a fanciful and playful fable narrated in verse of surpassing grace and elegance. The joke of the poem, as well as its serious point, derives from the cataclysmic disturbance a young woman makes over her loss of a lock of hair. Pope adapts epic conventions to his narrative of trivia, including even a supernatural species—the sylphs—parodying the functions of the Greek gods. These reminders of the epic, a genre by definition concerned with important matters, emphasize the poet's consciousness of the relative triviality of eighteenth-century high-society preoccupations. The world Belinda inhabits confuses small things with great; "Puffs, powders, patches, Bibles, billet-doux" occupy her dressing table in indiscriminate assembly. Members of this society take their own pleasure more seriously than anything else: "wretches hang that jurymen may dine." Men and women coexist in fascinated tension, tension that, given even slight provocation, explodes in hostilities. Sexual issues govern the conflict; women guard their "honor," the reputation of chastity, more intently than they preserve their physical purity; men seek to violate both. The ideals of good sense and good humor, expressed in the poem by Clarissa, govern no one in action; instead, both sexes value beauty (which, as Clarissa points out, fades) and accept it as an excuse for emotional self-indulgence (the theme of Umbriel's excursion to the Cave of Spleen). In its accounts of moral and psychological confusion, of hysterical fits and battles, the poem employs the familiar satiric techniques of exaggeration and distortion intended to reveal the truth and to inspire reform.

But *The Rape of the Lock* celebrates as well as criticizes. The delicacy and grace of the verse, the ethereal beauty of the sylphs, recapitulate Belinda's genuine grace and beauty: "If to her share some female errors fall, / Look on her face, and you'll forget 'em all." Like the society Mme. de La Fayette evokes, Belinda's world operates mainly on the basis of style. In its separation of style from moral substance, the society demands criticism; but the beauty it values—elegant conversation, boat trips on the Thames, magnificent women—like the beauty the poet creates, has meaning in itself. When the disputed lock of hair ascends to the constellations, when the poet calls attention to his own preservation of Belinda's beauty and fame, *The Rape of the Lock* reminds us that praise and blame sometimes appropriately attach to the same objects. Its mixture of playfulness and seriousness, of beauty and harshness, mark the poem's unique achievement.

In *An Essay on Man* (1733–4), a very different work, Pope set out to consider, in successive epistles, man in relation to the universe, to himself, to society, and to happiness: an enterprise of ambition almost comparable to Milton's in *Paradise Lost*. Indeed, in the first section of the poem Pope alludes specifically to his predecessor, describing the world as a "Garden, tempting with forbidden fruit" and declaring his own intention to "vindicate [Milton had said *justify*] the ways of God to man." Unlike Milton, Pope pursues this goal not through a dramatic fable but by an extended versified meditation on the philosophic issues involved. That meditation, however, generates its own drama.

Pope draws on a number of intellectual traditions to define the human situation in both cosmic and social terms. The breadth of his reference—to Catholic and Protestant theology, to Platonic and Stoic philosophy, to his period's notions of plenitude and natural order—itself reinforces the underlying assumption of universal, unchanging human nature. The poet evokes a timeless vision of humanity in the universe, poised at the middle of the Great Chain of Being that extends from God to the most minute forms of life, with the fullest possible range of being above and below humankind. Complaints that the poem's philosophy is "shallow" ignore the complexity of its synthesis and the seriousness of its ideas. The resounding assertion that concludes the first epistle, for instance ("One truth is clear, WHATEVER IS, IS RIGHT"), implies no unawareness of human misery or evil. Abundant examples of both have been presented in the text. The point is, rather, that the nature of God's plan—by definition not fully comprehensible to human reason—must allow evil for the sake of larger good. And human beings, in order to possess free will, must have available to them the choice of evil. Such assumptions belong to the intellectual position called "philosophical optimism"—by no means equivalent to what we usually think of as optimism, the faith that everything will turn out well in the long run. The belief expounded in *An Essay on Man*, on the contrary, allows the possibility that matters may turn out badly for individual men and women but assumes that personal misfortune takes its place in a larger, essentially benign, pattern.

The first epistle of the poem, here printed, progresses through ten logically connected sections. It begins by insisting on the necessary limitation of human judgment: we see only parts, not the whole. Nonetheless, this fact does not imply the imperfection of humankind; it means, rather, that we are adapted to our position in the general order of things. Our ignorance of future events and our hope for eternal life give us the possibility of happiness. The poem then indicts human beings for pride and impiety (we claim more power of judgment and more knowledge than we can have), for the absurdity of assuming themselves the center of the created universe, and for the unreasonableness of complaints against the providential order (we demand, the poet suggests, both the perfection of angels and the physical sensitivities of animals, although increase in our capacities would bring misery). Turning to the nature of the universal order, the argument insists on the gradations of faculties from the lower animals to humankind, then suggests that this order extends farther than we can know: any interference with it would destroy the whole. Even the speculative possibility of such interference suggests the insanity of human pride. Our only proper course is absolute submission to Providence.

This logical sequence structures the *Essay on Man*; but we should not read the poem only as a versified handbook of eighteenth-century philosophy. Here, as in *The Rape of the Lock*, Pope displays his poetic brilliance, converting philosophic argument into a rich emotional and intellectual texture. He draws us into the poem by addressing us directly, reminding us of our own tendencies to presumption, our own inevitable desire to understand the universe as revolving around us. "In Pride, in reas'ning Pride, our error lies": we all share bewilderment at our situation, we all need to interpret it, we all face, every day, our necessary limitations. The poet rapidly shifts tone, sometimes berating us, sometimes reminding us (and himself) of his own participation in the universal dilemma, sometimes assuming a godlike perspective and suggesting his superior knowledge. By his changing voice, his changing forms of address, he makes dramatic the futile, yet noble, effort to understand what only the deity can fully comprehend.

At its best, *An Essay on Man* transforms philosophy into emotional experience. It generates drama out of shifting, intersecting perspectives: the lamb licking the hand of its butcher, the Indian looking forward to a heaven his dog will share, the scientist trying to interpret the physical universe. It also makes the abstract vividly specific and concrete, as when reflection on the necessary limitation of human faculties produces the penetrating image of someone dying "of a rose in aromatic pain." Pope's imagination summons up a vast range of concrete reference, and it does not avoid the disturbing: we are invited to think of the human condition in the universe as comparable to that of the ox, which tills the fields, goes to slaughter, or finds itself worshipped as a god, according to accidents of situation. The fly's "microscopic eye" excels our powers; we resemble weeds more than oaks. Yet the poet, ranging from the conversational ease of his opening lines to the ringing certainties of his conclusion, incorporates perceptions of human inadequacy into assertions of a grand scheme which he makes not only rational but exciting.

Pope has been the subject of a great deal of writing. Biographies include G. Sherburn, *The Early Career of Alexander Pope* (1934), and M. Mack, *Alexander Pope* (1985). A range of responses is represented in *Pope: Recent Essays by Several Hands*, ed., M. Mack and J. A. Winn (1980). Perceptive critical books include R. A. Brower, *Alexander Pope: The Poetry of Allusion* (1959), and T. R. Edwards, *This Dark Estate: A Reading of Pope* (1963).

The Rape of the Lock[1]

AN HEROI-COMICAL POEM
Nolueram, Belinda, tuos violare capillos;
sed juvat hoc precibus me tribuisse tuis.
——MARTIAL

TO MRS. ARABELLA FERMOR

MADAM,
It will be in vain to deny that I have some regard for this piece, since I dedicate it to you. Yet you may bear me witness, it was intended only to divert a few young ladies, who have good sense and good humor enough to laugh not only at their sex's little unguarded follies, but at their own. But as it was communicated with the air of a secret, it soon found its way into the world. An imperfect copy having been offered to a bookseller, you had the good nature for my sake to consent to the publication of one more correct; this I was forced to, before I had executed half my design, for the machinery was entirely wanting to complete it.

The machinery, Madam, is a term invented by the critics, to signify that part which the deities, angels, or demons are made to act in a poem; for the ancient poets are in one respect like many modern ladies: let an action be never so trivial in itself, they always make it appear of the utmost importance. These machines I determined to raise on a very new and odd foundation, the Rosicrucian[2] doctrine of spirits.

I know how disagreeable it is to make use of hard words before a lady; but 'tis so much the concern of a poet to have his works under-

1. Text and notes by Samuel Holt Monk. The epigraph may be translated, "I was unwilling, Belinda, to ravish your locks; but I rejoice to have conceded this to your prayers" (Martial, *Epigrams* XII.lxxxiv.1–2). Pope substituted his heroine for Martial's Polytimus. The epigraph is intended to suggest that the poem was published at Miss Fermor's request.   2. A system of arcane philosophy introduced into England from Germany in the seventeenth century.

stood, and particularly by your sex, that you must give me leave to
explain two or three difficult terms.

The Rosicrucians are a people I must bring you acquainted with.
The best account I know of them is in a French book called *Le
Comte de Gabalis*,[3] which both in its title and size is so like a novel,
that many of the fair sex have read it for one by mistake. According
to these gentlemen, the four elements are inhabited by spirits, which
they call Sylphs, Gnomes, Nymphs, and Salamanders. The Gnomes
or Demons of earth delight in mischief; but the Sylphs, whose habitation is in the air, are the best-conditioned creatures imaginable.
For they say, any mortals may enjoy the most intimate familiarities
with these gentle spirits, upon a condition very easy to all true adepts,
an inviolate preservation of chastity.

As to the following cantos, all the passages of them are as fabulous
as the vision at the beginning, or the transformation at the end; (except
the loss of your hair, which I always mention with reverence). The
human persons are as fictitious as the airy ones; and the character of
Belinda, as it is now managed, resembles you in nothing but in
beauty.

If this poem had as many graces as there are in your person, or in
your mind, yet I could never hope it should pass through the world
half so uncensured as you have done. But let its fortune be what it
will, mine is happy enough, to have given me this occasion of assuring you that I am, with the truest esteem,

MADAM,

Your most obedient, humble servant,

A. POPE

CANTO I

> What dire offense from amorous causes springs,
> What mighty contests rise from trivial things,
> I sing—This verse to Caryll, Muse! is due:
> This, even Belinda may vouchsafe to view:
> Slight is the subject, but not so the praise,   5
> If she inspire, and he approve my lays.
>   Say what strange motive, Goddess! could compel
> A well-bred lord to assault a gentle belle?
> Oh, say what stranger cause, yet unexplored,
> Could make a gentle belle reject a lord?   10
> In tasks so bold can little men engage,
> And in soft bosoms dwells such mighty rage?
>   Sol through white curtains shot a timorous ray,
> And oped those eyes that must eclipse the day.

---

3. By the Abbé de Montfaucon de Villars, published in 1670.

Now lapdogs give themselves the rousing shake,   15
And sleepless lovers just at twelve awake:
Thrice rung the bell,[4] the slipper knocked the ground,
And the pressed watch returned a silver sound.
Belinda still her downy pillow pressed,
Her guardian Sylph prolonged the balmy rest: 20
'Twas he had summoned to her silent bed
The morning dream that hovered o'er her head.
A youth more glittering than a birthnight beau[5]
(That even in slumber caused her cheek to glow)
Seemed to her ear his winning lips to lay,   25
And thus in whispers said, or seemed to say:
    "Fairest of mortals, thou distinguished care
Of thousand bright inhabitants of air!
If e'er one vision touched thy infant thought,
Of all the nurse and all the priest have taught,   30
Of airy elves by moonlight shadows seen,
The silver token, and the circled green,[6]
Or virgins visited by angel powers,
With golden crowns and wreaths of heavenly flowers,
Hear and believe! thy own importance know,   35
Nor bound thy narrow views to things below.
Some secret truths, from learned pride concealed,
To maids alone and children are revealed:
What though no credit doubting wits may give?
The fair and innocent shall still believe.   40
Know, then, unnumbered spirits round thee fly,
The light militia of the lower sky:
These, though unseen, are ever on the wing,
Hang o'er the box,[7] and hover round the Ring.
Think what an equipage thou hast in air,   45
And view with scorn two pages and a chair.[8]
As now your own, our beings were of old,
And once enclosed in woman's beauteous mold
Thence, by a soft transition, we repair
From earthly vehicles to these of air.   50
Think not, when woman's transient breath is fled,
That all her vanities at once are dead:
Succeeding vanities she still regards,
And though she plays no more o'erlooks the cards.

4. Belinda thus summons her maid. A *pressed watch* chimes the hour and the quarter-hour when the stem is pressed down.   5. Courtiers wore especially fine clothes on the sovereign's birthday.   6. According to popular belief, fairies skim off the cream from jugs of milk left standing overnight and leave a coin in payment. *The circled green:* Rings of bright green grass, which are common in England even in winter, were held to be due to the round dances of fairies.   7. *Box* in the theater and the fashionable circular drive (*Ring*) in Hyde Park.   8. Sedan chair.

Her joy in gilded chariots, when alive,   55
And love of ombre,[9] after death survive.
For when the Fair in all their pride expire,
To their first elements[1] their souls retire:
The sprites of fiery termagants in flame
Mount up, and take a Salamander's name.[2]   60
Soft yielding minds to water glide away,
And sip, with Nymphs, their elemental tea.[3]
The graver prude sinks downward to a Gnome,
In search of mischief still on earth to roam.
The light coquettes in Sylphs aloft repair,   65
And sport and flutter in the fields of air.
    "Know further yet; whoever fair and chaste
Rejects mankind, is by some Sylph embraced:
For spirits, freed from mortal laws, with ease
Assume what sexes and what shapes they please.   70
What guards the purity of melting maids,
In courtly balls, and midnight masquerades,
Safe from the treacherous friend, the daring spark,
The glance by day, the whisper in the dark,
When kind occasion prompts their warm desires,   75
When music softens, and when dancing fires?
'Tis but their Sylph, the wise Celestials know,
Though Honor is the word with men below.
    "Some nymphs there are, too conscious of their face,
For life predestined to the Gnomes' embrace.   80
These swell their prospects and exalt their pride,
When offers are disdained, and love denied:'
Then gay ideas[4] crowd the vacant brain,
While peers, and dukes, and all their sweeping train,
And garters, stars, and coronets appear,   85
And in soft sounds, 'your Grace' salutes their ear.
'Tis these that early taint the female soul,
Instruct the eyes of young coquettes to roll,
Teach infant cheeks a bidden blush to know,
And little hearts to flutter at a beau.   90
    "Oft, when the world imagine women stray,
The Sylphs through mystic mazes guide their way,
Through all the giddy circle they pursue,

---

9. The popular card game. See III.27 ff. and note.   1. The four elements out of which all
things were believed to have been made were fire, water, earth, and air. One or another of these
elements was supposed to be predominant in both the physical and psychological make-up of each
human being. In this context they are spoken of as "humors."   2. Pope borrowed his supernatural beings from Rosicrucian mythology. Each element was inhabited by a spirit, as the following
lines explain. The salamander is a lizardlike animal, in antiquity believed to live in fire.
3. Pronounce *tay*.   4. Images.

And old impertinence expel by new.
What tender maid but must a victim fall 95
To one man's treat, but for another's ball?
When Florio speaks what virgin could withstand,
If gentle Damon did not squeeze her hand?
With varying vanities, from every part,
They shift the moving toyshop[5] of their heart; 100
Where wigs with wigs, with sword-knots sword-knots strive,
Beaux banish beaux, and coaches coaches drive.
This erring mortals levity may call;
Oh, blind to truth! the Sylphs contrive it all.
     "Of these am I, who thy protection claim, 105
A watchful sprite, and Ariel is my name.
Late, as I ranged the crystal wilds of air,
In the clear mirror of thy ruling star
I saw, alas! some dread event impend,
Ere to the main this morning sun descend, 110
But Heaven reveals not what, or how, or where:
Warned by the Sylph, O pious maid, beware!
This to disclose is all thy guardian can:
Beware of all, but most beware of Man!"
     He said; when Shock,[6] who thought she slept too long, 115
Leaped up, and waked his mistress with his tongue.
'Twas then, Belinda, if report say true,
Thy eyes first opened on a billet-doux;
Wounds, charms, and ardors were no sooner read,
But all the vision vanished from they head. 120
     And now, unveiled, the toilet stands displayed,
Each silver vase in mystic order laid.
First, robed in white, the nymph intent adores,
With head uncovered, the cosmetic powers.
A heavenly image in the glass appears; 125
To that she bends, to that her eyes she rears.
The inferior priestess, at her altar's side,
Trembling begins the sacred rites of Pride.
Unnumbered treasures ope at once, and here
The various offerings of the world appear; 130
From each she nicely culls with curious toil,
And decks the goddess with the glittering spoil.
This casket India's glowing gems unlocks,
And all Arabia breathes from yonder box.
The tortoise here and elephant unite, 135
Transformed to combs, the speckled and the white.

---

5. A shop stocked with baubles and trifles.   6. Belinda's lapdog.

Here files of pins extend their shining rows,
Puffs, powders, patches, Bibles, billet-doux.
Now awful Beauty puts on all its arms;
The fair each moment rises in her charms,   140
Repairs her smiles, awakens every grace,
And calls forth all the wonders of her face;
Sees by degrees a purer blush arise,
And keener lightnings quicken in her eyes.
The busy Sylphs surround their darling care,   145
These set the head, and those divide the hair,
Some fold the sleeve, whilst others plait the gown;
And Betty's[7] praised for labors not her own.

CANTO II

Not with more glories, in the ethereal plain,
The sun first rises o'er the purpled main,
Than, issuing forth, the rival of his beams
Launched on the bosom of the silver Thames.
Fair nymphs and well-dressed youths around her shone,   5
But every eye was fixed on her alone.
On her white breast a sparkling cross she wore,
Which Jews might kiss, and infidels adore.
Her lively looks a sprightly mind disclose,
Quick as her eyes, and as unfixed as those: 10
Favors to none, to all she smiles extends;
Oft she rejects, but never once offends.
Bright as the sun, her eyes the gazers strike,
And, like the sun, they shine on all alike.
Yet graceful ease, and sweetness void of pride,   15
Might hide her faults, if belles had faults to hide:
If to her share some female errors fall,
Look on her face, and you'll forget 'em all.
This nymph, to the destruction of mankind,
Nourished two locks which graceful hung behind   20
In equal curls, and well conspired to deck
With shining ringlets the smooth ivory neck.
Love in these labyrinths his slaves detains,
And mighty hearts are held in slender chains.
With hairy springes we the birds betray,   25
Slight lines of hair surprise the finny prey,
Fair tresses man's imperial race ensnare,
And beauty draws us with a single hair.
The adventurous Baron the bright locks admired,

7. Belinda's maid, the "inferior priestess" mentioned in line 127.

He saw, he wished, and to the prize aspired.   30
Resolved to win, he meditates the way,
By force to ravish, or by fraud betray;
For when success a lover's toil attends,
Few ask if fraud or force attained his ends.
    For this, ere Phoebus rose, he had implored   35
Propitious Heaven, and every power adored,
But chiefly Love—to Love an altar built,
Of twelve vast French romances, neatly gilt.
There lay three garters, half a pair of gloves,
And all the trophies of his former loves.   40
With tender billet-doux he lights the pyre,
And breathes three amorous sighs to raise the fire.
Then prostrate falls, and begs with ardent eyes
Soon to obtain, and long possess the prize:
The powers gave ear, and granted half his prayer,   45
The rest the winds dispersed in empty air.
    But now secure the painted vessel glides,
The sunbeams trembling on the floating tides,
While melting music steals upon the sky,
And softened sounds along the waters die.   50
Smooth flow the waves, the zephyrs gently play,
Belinda smiled, and all the world was gay.
All but the Sylph—with careful thoughts oppressed,
The impending woe sat heavy on his breast.
He summons straight his denizens of air;   55
The lucid squadrons round the sails repair:
Soft o'er the shrouds aërial whispers breathe
That seemed but zephyrs to the train beneath.
Some to the sun their insect-wings unfold,
Waft on the breeze, or sink in clouds of gold.   60
Transparent forms too fine for mortal sight,
Their fluid bodies half dissolved in light,
Loose to the wind their airy garments flew,
Thin glittering textures of the filmy dew,
Dipped in the richest tincture of the skies,   65
Where light disports in ever-mingling dyes,
While every beam new transient colors flings,
Colors that change whene'er they wave their wings.
Amid the circle, on the gilded mast,
Superior by the head was Ariel placed;   70
His purple[8] pinions opening to the sun,
He raised his azure wand, and thus begun:

---

8. In eighteenth-century poetic diction, the word might mean "bloodred," "purple," or simply (as is likely here) "brightly colored." The word derives from Virgil, *Eclogue* IX. 40, *purpureous.*

"Ye Sylphs and Sylphids, to your chief give ear!
Fays, Fairies, Genii, Elves, and Daemons, hear!
Ye know the spheres and various tasks assigned   75
By laws eternal to the aërial kind.
Some in the fields of purest ether play,
And bask and whiten in the blaze of day.
Some guide the course of wandering orbs on high,
Or roll the planets through the boundless sky.   80
Some less refined, beneath the moon's pale light
Pursue the stars that shoot athwart the night,
Or suck the mists in grosser air below,
Or dip their pinions in the painted bow,
Or brew fierce tempests on the wintry main,   85
Or o'er the glebe distill the kindly rain.
Others on earth o'er human race preside,
Watch all their ways, and all their actions guide:
Of these the chief the care of nations own,
And guard with arms divine the British Throne.   90
    "Our humbler province is to tend the Fair,
Not a less pleasing, though less glorious care:
To save the powder from too rude a gale,
Nor let the imprisoned essences exhale;
To draw fresh colors from the vernal flowers   95
To steal from rainbows e'er they drop in showers
A brighter wash;⁹ to curl their waving hairs,
Assist their blushes, and inspire their airs;
Nay oft, in dreams invention we bestow,
To change a flounce, or add a furbelow.   100
    "This day black omens threat the brightest fair,
That e'er deserved a watchful spirit's care;
Some dire disaster, or by force or slight,
But what, or where, the Fates have wrapped in night:
Whether the nymph shall break Diana's¹ law,   105
Or some frail china jar receive a flaw,
Or stain her honor or her new brocade,
Forget her prayers, or miss a masquerade,
Or lose her heart, or necklace, at a ball;
Or whether Heaven has doomed that Shock must fall.   110
Haste, then, ye spirits! to your charge repair:
The fluttering fan be Zephyretta's care;
The drops² to thee, Brillante, we consign;
And, Momentilla, let the watch be thine;
Do thou, Crispissa,³ tend her favorite Lock;   115

9. Cosmetic lotion.   1. Diana was the goddess of chastity.   2. Diamond earrings.   3. From
Latin *crispere*, to curl.

Ariel himself shall be the guard of Shock.
　"To fifty chosen Sylphs, of special note,
We trust the important charge, the petticoat;
Oft have we known that sevenfold fence to fail,
Though stiff with hoops, and armed with ribs of whale.　　120
Form a strong line about the silver bound,
And guard the wide circumference around.
　"Whatever spirit, careless of his charge,
His post neglects, or leaves the fair at large,
Shall feel sharp vengeance soon o'ertake his sins,　　125
Be stopped in vials, or transfixed with pins,
Or plunged in lakes of bitter washes lie,
Or wedged whole ages in a bodkin's eye;[4]
Gums and pomatums shall his flight restrain,
While clogged he beats his silken wings in vain,　　130
Or alum styptics with contracting power
Shrink his thin essence like a riveled[5] flower:
Or, as Ixion fixed,[6] the wretch shall feel
The giddy motion of the whirling mill,
In fumes of burning chocolate shall glow,　　135
And tremble at the sea that froths below!"
　He spoke; the spirits from the sails descend;
Some, orb in orb, around the nymph extend;
Some thread the mazy ringlets of her hair;
Some hang upon the pendants of her ear:　　140
With beating hearts the dire event they wait,
Anxious, and trembling for the birth of Fate.

CANTO III

　Close by those meads, forever crowned with flowers,
Where Thames with pride surveys his rising towers,
There stands a structure of majestic frame,
Which from the neighboring Hampton[7] takes its name.
Here Britain's statesmen oft the fall foredoom　　5
Of foreign tyrants and of nymphs at home;
Here thou, great Anna! whom three realms obey,
Dost sometimes counsel take—and sometimes tea.
　Hither the heroes and the nymphs resort,
To taste awhile the pleasures of a court;　　10
In various talk the instructive hours they passed,

---

4. A blunt needle with a large eye, used for drawing ribbon through eyelets in the edging of women's garments.　　5. To "rivel" is to "contract into wrinkles and corrugations" (Johnson's *Dictionary*).　　6. In the Greek myth Ixion was punished in the underworld by being bound on an ever-turning wheel.　　7. Hampton Court, the royal palace, about fifteen miles up the Thames from London.

Who gave the ball, or paid the visit last;
One speaks the glory of the British Queen,
And one describes a charming Indian screen;
A third interprets motions, looks, and eyes;   15
At every word a reputation dies.
Snuff, or the fan, supply each pause of chat,
With singing, laughing, ogling, and all that.
    Meanwhile, declining from the noon of day,
The sun obliquely shoots his burning ray;   20
The hungry judges soon the sentence sign,
And wretches hang that jurymen may dine;
The merchant from the Exchange returns in peace,
And the long labors of the toilet cease.
Belinda now, whom thirst of fame invites,   25
Burns to encounter two adventurous knights,
At ombre[8] singly to decide their doom
And swells her breast with conquests yet to come.
Straight the three bands prepare in arms to join,
Each band the number of the sacred nine.   30
Soon as she spreads her hand, the aërial guard
Descend, and sit on each important card:
First Ariel perched upon a Matadore,
Then each according to the rank they bore;
For Sylphs, yet mindful of their ancient race,   35
Are, as when women, wondrous fond of place.
    Behold, four Kings in majesty revered,
With hoary whiskers and a forky beard;
And four fair Queens whose hands sustain a flower,
The expressive emblem of their softer power;   40
Four Knaves in garbs succinct,[9] a trusty band,
Caps on their heads, and halberts in their hand;
And parti-colored troops, a shining train,
Draw forth to combat on the velvet plain.
    The skillful nymph reviews her force with care;   45
"Let Spades be trumps!" she said, and trumps they were.
    Now move to war her sable Matadores,
In show like leaders of the swarthy Moors.
Spadillio first, unconquerable lord!
Led off two captive trumps, and swept the board.   50

---

8. The game that Belinda plays against the Baron and another young man which is too complicated for complete explication here. Pope has carefully arranged the cards so that Belinda wins.
The Baron's hand is strong enough to be a threat, but the third player's is of little account. The
hand is played exactly according to the rules of ombre, and Pope's description of the cards is
equally accurate. Each player holds nine cards (1. 30). The "Matadores" (1. 33), when spades are
trumps, are "Spadillio" (1. 49), the ace of spades; "Manillio" (1. 51), the two of spades; "Basto"
(1. 53), the ace of clubs; Belinda holds all three of these.   9. Girded up.

As many more Manillio forced to yield,
And marched a victor from the verdant field.
Him Basto followed, but his fate more hard
Gained but one trump and one plebeian card.
With his broad saber next, a chief in years,   55
The hoary Majesty of Spades appears,
Puts forth one manly leg, to sight revealed,
The rest his many-colored robe concealed.
The rebel Knave, who dares his prince engage,
Proves the just victim of his royal rage.   60
Even mighty Pam,[1] that kings and queens o'erthrew
And mowed down armies in the fights of loo,
Sad chance of war! now destitute of aid,
Falls undistinguished by the victor Spade.
    Thus far both armies to Belinda yield;   65
Now to the Baron fate inclines the field.
His warlike amazon her host invades,
The imperial consort of the crown of Spades.
The Club's black tyrant first her victim died,
Spite of his haughty mien and barbarous pride.   70
What boots the regal circle on his head,
His giant limbs, in state unwieldy spread?
That long behind he trails his pompous robe,
And of all monarchs only grasps the globe?
    The Baron now his Diamonds pours apace;   75
The embroidered King who shows but half his face,
And his refulgent Queen, with powers combined
Of broken troops an easy conquest find.
Clubs, Diamonds, Hearts, in wild disorder seen,
With throngs promiscuous strew the level green.   80
Thus when dispersed a routed army runs,
Of Asia's troops, and Afric's sable sons,
With like confusion different nations fly,
Of various habit, and of various dye,
The pierced battalions disunited fall   85
In heaps on heaps; one fate o'erwhelms them all.
    The Knave of Diamonds tries his wily arts,
And wins (oh, shameful chance!) the Queen of Hearts.
At this, the blood the virgin's cheek forsook,
A livid paleness spreads o'er all her look;   90
She sees, and trembles at the approaching ill,
Just in the jaws of ruin, and Codille,[2]
And now (as oft in some distempered state)

1. The knave of clubs, the highest trump in the game of loo.   2. The term applied to losing a
hand at cards.

On one nice trick depends the general fate.
An Ace of Hearts steps forth: the King unseen   95
Lurked in her hand, and mourned his captive Queen.
He springs to vengeance with an eager pace,
And falls like thunder on the prostrate Ace.
The nymph exulting fills with shouts the sky,
The walls, the woods, and long canals reply.   100
   O thoughtless mortals! ever blind to fate,
Too soon dejected, and too soon elate:
Sudden these honors shall be snatched away,
And cursed forever this victorious day.
   For lo! the board with cups and spoons is crowned,   105
The berries crackle, and the mill turns round;[3]
On shining altars of Japan[4] they raise
The silver lamp; the fiery spirits blaze:
From silver spouts the grateful liquors glide,
While China's earth receives the smoking tide.   110
At once they gratify their scent and taste,
And frequent cups prolong the rich repast.
Straight hover round the fair her airy band;
Some, as she sipped, the fuming liquor fanned,
Some o'er her lap their careful plumes displayed,   115
Trembling, and conscious of the rich brocade.
Coffee (which makes the politician wise,
And see through all things with his half-shut eyes)
Sent up in vapors to the Baron's brain
New stratagems, the radiant Lock to gain.   120
Ah, cease, rash youth! desist ere 'tis too late,
Fear the just Gods, and think of Scylla's fate![5]
Changed to a bird, and sent to flit in air,
She dearly pays for Nisus' injured hair!
   But when to mischief mortals bend their will,   125
How soon they find fit instruments of ill!
Just then, Clarissa drew with tempting grace
A two-edged weapon from her shining case:
So ladies in romance assist their knight,
Present the spear, and arm him for the fight.   130
He takes the gift with reverence, and extends
The little engine on his fingers' ends;
This just behind Belinda's neck he spread,
As o'er the fragrant steams she bends her head.

3. I.e., coffee is roasted and ground.   **4.** I.e., small, lacquered tables. The word "altars" suggests the ritualistic character of coffee-drinking in Belinda's world.   **5.** Scylla, daughter of Nisus, was turned into a sea bird because, for the sake of her love for Minos of Crete, who was besieging her father's city of Megara, she cut from her father's head the purple lock on which his safety depended. She is not the Scylla of "Scylla and Charybdis."

Swift to the Lock a thousand sprites repair,   135
A thousand wings, by turns, blow back the hair,
And thrice they twitched the diamond in her ear,
Thrice she looked back, and thrice the foe drew near.
Just in that instant, anxious Ariel sought
The close recesses of the virgin's thought;   140
As on the nosegay in her breast reclined,
He watched the ideas rising in her mind,
Sudden he viewed, in spite of all her art,
An earthly lover lurking at her heart.
Amazed, confused, he found his power expired,   145
Resigned to fate, and with a sigh retired.
    The Peer now spreads the glittering forfex[6] wide,
To enclose the Lock; now joins it, to divide.
Even then, before the fatal engine closed,
A wretched Sylph too fondly interposed;   150
Fate urged the shears, and cut the Sylph in twain
(But airy substance soon unites again):
The meeting points the sacred hair dissever
From the fair head, forever, and forever!
    Then flashed the living lightning from her eyes,   155
And screams of horror rend the affrighted skies.
Not louder shrieks to pitying heaven are cast,
When husbands, or when lapdogs breathe their last;
Or when rich china vessels fallen from high,
In glittering dust and painted fragments lie!   160
"Let wreaths of triumph now my temples twine,"
The victor cried, "the glorious prize is mine!
While fish in streams, or birds delight in air,
Or in a coach and six the British Fair,
As long as _Atalantis_[7] shall be read,   165
Or the small pillow grace a lady's bed,
While visits shall be paid on solemn days,
When numerous wax-lights in bright order blaze,
While nymphs take treats, or assignations give,
So long my honor, name, and praise shall live!   170
What Time would spare, from Steel receives its date,
And monuments, like men, submit to fate!
Steel could the labor of the Gods destroy,
And strike to dust the imperial towers of Troy;
Steel could the works of mortal pride confound,   175
And hew triumphal arches to the ground.

---

6. Scissors.   7. Mrs. Manley's _New Atalantis_ (1709) was notorious for its thinly concealed allusions to contemporary scandals.

What wonder then, fair nymph! thy hairs should feel,
The conquering force of unresisted Steel?"

CANTO IV

But anxious cares the pensive nymph oppressed,
And secret passions labored in her breast.
Not youthful kings in battle seized alive,
Not scornful virgins who their charms survive,
Not ardent lovers robbed of all their bliss,   5
Not ancient ladies when refused a kiss,
Not tyrants fierce that unrepenting die,
Not Cynthia when her manteau's[8] pinned awry,
E'er felt such rage, resentment, and despair,
As thou, sad virgin! for thy ravished hair.   10
    For, that sad moment, when the Sylphs withdrew
And Ariel weeping from Belinda flew,
Umbriel,[9] a dusky, melancholy sprite
As ever sullied the fair face of light,
Down to the central earth, his proper scene,   15
Repaired to search the gloomy Cave of Spleen.[1]
    Swift on his sooty pinions flits the Gnome,
And in a vapor reached the dismal dome.
No cheerful breeze this sullen region knows,
The dreaded east is all the wind that blows.   20
Here in a grotto, sheltered close from air,
And screened in shades from day's detested glare,
She sighs forever on her pensive bed,
Pain at her side, and Megrim[2] at her head.
    Two handmaids wait the throne: alike in place,   25
But differing far in figure and in face.
Here stood Ill-Nature like an ancient maid,
Her wrinkled form in black and white arrayed;
With store of prayers for mornings, nights, and noons,
Her hand is filled; her bosom with lampoons.   30
    There Affectation, with a sickly mien,
Shows in her cheek the roses of eighteen,
Practiced to lisp, and hang the head aside,
Faints into airs, and languishes with pride,
On the rich quilt sinks with becoming woe,   35
Wrapped in a gown, for sickness and for show.
The fair ones feel such maladies as these,
When each new nightdress gives a new disease.

---

8. Negligee, or loose robe.   9. The name suggests shade and darkness.   1. Ill humor.
2. Headache.

A constant vapor[3] o'er the palace flies,
Strange phantoms rising as the mists arise;   40
Dreadful as hermit's dreams in haunted shades,
Or bright as visions of expiring maids.
Now glaring fiends, and snakes on rolling spires,[4]
Pale specters, gaping tombs, and purple fires;
Now lakes of liquid gold, Elysian scenes,   45
And crystal domes, and angels in machines.[5]
    Unnumbered throngs on every side are seen
Of bodies changed to various forms by Spleen.
Here living teapots stand, one arm held out,
One bent; the handle this, and that the spout: 50
A pipkin[6] there, like Homer's tripod, walks;
Here sighs a jar, and there a goose pie talks;
Men prove with child, as powerful fancy works,
And maids, turned bottles, call aloud for corks.
    Safe passed the Gnome through this fantastic band,   55
A branch of healing spleenwort[7] in his hand.
Then thus addressed the Power: "Hail, wayward Queen!
Who rule the sex to fifty from fifteen:
Parent of vapors and of female wit,
Who give the hysteric or poetic fit,   60
On various tempers act by various ways,
Make some take physic, others scribble plays;
Who cause the proud their visits to delay,
And send the godly in a pet to pray.
A nymph there is that all your power disdains,   65
And thousands more in equal mirth maintains.
But oh! if e'er thy Gnome could spoil a grace,
Or raise a pimple on a beauteous face,
Like citron-waters[8] matrons' cheeks inflame,
Or change complexions at a losing game;   70
If e'er with airy horns[9] I planted heads,
Or rumpled petticoats, or tumbled beds,
Or caused suspicion when no soul was rude,
Or discomposed the headdress of a prude,
Or e'er to costive lapdog gave disease,   75

3. Emblematic of "the vapors," i.e., hypochondria, melancholy, peevishness, often affected by
fashionable women.   4. Coils.   5. Mechanical devices used in the theaters for spectacular
effects. The fantasies of neurotic women here merge with the sensational stage effects popular
with contemporary audiences.   6. An earthen pot. In *Iliad* XVIII.373–377, Vulcan furnishes
the gods with self-propelling "tripods" (three-legged stools).   7. An herb, efficacious against the
spleen. Pope alludes to the golden bough that Aeneas and the Cumaean sybil carry with them for
protection into the underworld in *Aeneid* VI.   8. Brandy flavored with orange or lemon peel.
9. The symbol of the cuckold, the man whose wife has been unfaithful to him; here "airy,"
because they exist only in the jealous suspicions of the husband, the victim of the mischievous
Umbriel.

Which not the tears of brightest eyes could ease,
Hear me, and touch Belinda with chagrin:[1]
That single act gives half the world the spleen."
    The Goddess with a discontented air
Seems to reject him though she grants his prayer.   80
A wondrous bag with both her hands she binds,
Like that where once Ulysses held the winds;[2]
There she collects the force of female lungs,
Sighs, sobs, and passions, and the war of tongues.
A vial next she fills with fainting fears,   85
Soft sorrows, melting griefs, and flowing tears.
The Gnome rejoicing bears her gifts away,
Spreads his black wings, and slowly mounts to day.
    Sunk in Thalestris'[3] arms the nymph he found,
Her eyes dejected and her hair unbound.   90
Full o'er their heads the swelling bag he rent,
And all the Furies issued at the vent.
Belinda burns with more than mortal ire,
And fierce Thalestris fans the rising fire.
"O wretched maid!" she spread her hands, and cried   95
(While Hampton's echoes, "Wretched maid!" replied),
"Was it for this you took such constant care
The bodkin, comb, and essence to prepare?
For this your locks in paper durance bound,
For this with torturing irons wreathed around?   100
For this with fillets strained your tender head,
And bravely bore the double loads of lead?[4]
Gods! shall the ravisher display your hair,
While the fops envy, and the ladies stare!
Honor forbid! at whose unrivaled shrine   105
Ease, pleasure, virtue, all, our sex resign.
Methinks already I your tears survey,
Already hear the horrid things they say,
Already see you a degraded toast,
And all your honor in a whisper lost!   110
How shall I, then, your helpless fame defend?
'Twill then be infamy to seem your friend!
And shall this prize, the inestimable prize,
Exposed through crystal to the gazing eyes,
And heightened by the diamond's circling rays,   115

---

1. Ill humor.   2. Aeolus (later conceived of as god of the winds) gave Ulysses a bag containing all the winds adverse to his voyage home. When his ship was in sight of Ithaca, his companions opened the bag and the storms that ensued drove Ulysses far away (*Odyssey* X. 19 ff.).   3. The name is borrowed from a queen of the Amazons, hence a fierce and warlike woman. Thalestris, according to legend, traveled 30 days in order to have a child by Alexander the Great. Plutarch denies the story.   4. The frame on which the elaborate coiffures of the day were arranged.

On that rapacious hand forever blaze?
Sooner shall grass in Hyde Park Circus grow,
And wits take lodgings in the sound of Bow;[5]
Sooner let earth, air, sea, to chaos fall,
Men, monkeys, lapdogs, parrots, perish all!"   120
    She said; then raging to Sir Plume repairs,
And bids her beau demand the precious hairs
(Sir Plume of amber snuffbox justly vain,
And the nice conduct of a clouded cane).
With earnest eyes, and round unthinking face,   125
He first the snuffbox opened, then the case,
And thus broke out—"My Lord, why, what the devil!
Z——ds! damn the lock! 'fore Gad, you must be civil!
Plague on't! 'tis past a jest—nay prithee, pox!
Give her the hair"—he spoke, and rapped his box.   130
    "It grieves me much," replied the Peer again,
"Who speaks so well should ever speak in vain.
But by this Lock, this sacred Lock I swear
(Which never more shall join its parted hair;
Which never more its honors shall renew,   135
Clipped from the lovely head where late it grew),
That while my nostrils draw the vital air,
This hand, which won it, shall forever wear."
He spoke, and speaking, in proud triumph spread
The long-contended honors[6] of her head.   140
    But Umbriel, hateful Gnome, forbears not so;
He breaks the vial whence the sorrows flow.
Then see! the nymph in beauteous grief appears,
Her eyes half languishing, half drowned in tears;
On her heaved bosom hung her drooping head,   145
Which with a sigh she raised, and thus she said:
    "Forever cursed be this detested day,
Which snatched my best, my favorite curl away!
Happy! ah, ten times happy had I been,
If Hampton Court these eyes had never seen!   150
Yet am not I the first mistaken maid,
By love of courts to numerous ills betrayed.
Oh, had I rather unadmired remained
In some lone isle, or distant northern land;
Where the gilt chariot never marks the way,   155
Where none learn ombre, none e'er taste bohea![7]
There kept my charms concealed from mortal eye,

5. A person born within sound of the bells of St. Mary-le-Bow in Cheapside is said to be a
cockney. No fashionable wit would have so vulgar an address.   6. Ornaments, hence locks; a
Latinism.   7. A costly sort of tea.

Like roses that in deserts bloom and die.
What moved my mind with youthful lords to roam?
Oh, had I stayed, and said my prayers at home!   160
'Twas this the morning omens seemed to tell,
Thrice from my trembling hand the patch box[8] fell;
The tottering china shook without a wind,
Nay, Poll sat mute, and Shock was most unkind!
A Sylph too warned me of the threats of fate,   165
In mystic visions, now believed too late!
See the poor remnants of these slighted hairs!
My hands shall rend what e'en thy rapine spares.
These in two sable ringlets taught to break,
Once gave new beauties to the snowy neck;   170
The sister lock now sits uncouth, alone,
And in its fellow's fate foresees its own;
Uncurled it hangs, the fatal shears demands,
And tempts once more thy sacrilegious hands.
Oh, hadst thou, cruel! been content to seize   175
Hairs less in sight, or any hairs but these!"

CANTO V

She said: the pitying audience melt in tears.
But Fate and Jove had stopped the Baron's ears.
In vain Thalestris with reproach assails,
For who can move when fair Belinda fails?
Not half so fixed the Trojan[9] could remain,   5
While Anna begged and Dido raged in vain.
Then grave Clarissa graceful waved her fan;
Silence ensued, and thus the nymph began:
    "Say why are beauties praised and honored most,
The wise man's passion, and the vain man's toast?   10
Why decked with all that land and sea afford,
Why angels called, and angel-like adored?
Why round our coaches crowd the white-gloved beaux,
Why bows the side box from its inmost rows?
How vain are all these glories, all our pains,   15
Unless good sense preserve what beauty gains;
That men may say when we the front box grace,
'Behold the first in virtue as in face!'
Oh! if to dance all night, and dress all day,
Charmed the smallpox, or chased old age away,   20

---

8. A box to hold the ornamental patches of court plaster worn on the face by both sexes. Cf.
Spectator 81.   9. Aeneas, who forsook Dido at the bidding of the gods, despite her reproaches
and the supplications of her sister Anna. Virgil compares him to a steadfast oak that withstands a
storm (*Aeneid* IV.437–443).

Who would not scorn what housewife's cares produce,
Or who would learn one earthly thing of use?
To patch, nay ogle, might become a saint,
Nor could it sure be such a sin to paint.
But since, alas! frail beauty must decay,   25
Curled or uncurled, since locks will turn to gray;
Since painted, or not painted, all shall fade,
And she who scorns a man must die a maid;
What then remains but well our power to use,
And keep good humor still whate'er we lose?   30
And trust me, dear, good humor can prevail
When airs, and flights, and screams, and scolding fail.
Beauties in vain their pretty eyes may roll;
Charms strike the sight, but merit wins the soul."[1]
          So spoke the dame, but no applause ensued;   35
Belinda frowned, Thalestris called her prude.
"To arms, to arms!" the fierce virago cries,
And swift as lightning to the combat flies.
All side in parties, and begin the attack;
Fans clap, silks rustle, and tough whalebones crack;   40
Heroes' and heroines' shouts confusedly rise,
And bass and treble voices strike the skies.
No common weapons in their hands are found,
Like Gods they fight, nor dread a mortal wound.
          So when bold Homer makes the Gods engage,   45
And heavenly breasts with human passions rage;
'Gainst Pallas, Mars; Latona, Hermes arms;
And all Olympus rings with loud alarms:
Jove's thunder roars, heaven trembles all around,
Blue Neptune storms, the bellowing deeps resound: 50
Earth shakes her nodding towers, the ground gives way,
And the pale ghosts start at the flash of day!
          Triumphant Umbriel on a sconce's height
Clapped his glad wings, and sat to view the fight:
Propped on the bodkin spears, the sprites survey   55
The growing combat, or assist the fray.
          While through the press enraged Thalestris flies,
And scatters death around from both her eyes,
A beau and witling perished in the throng,
One died in metaphor, and one in song.   60
"O cruel nymph! a living death I bear,"
Cried Dapperwit, and sunk beside his chair.
A mournful glance Sir Fopling upwards cast,

1. The speech is a close parody of Pope's own translation of the speech of Sarpedon to Glaucus,
first published in 1709 and slightly revised in his version of the *Iliad* (XII.371–396).

"Those eyes are made so killing"—was his last.
Thus on Maeander's flowery margin lies   65
The expiring swan, and as he sings he dies.
    When bold Sir Plume had drawn Clarissa down,
Chloe stepped in, and killed him with a frown;
She smiled to see the doughty hero slain,
But, at her smile, the beau revived again.   70
Now Jove suspends his golden scales in air,
Weighs the men's wits against the lady's hair;
The doubtful beam long nods from side to side;
At length the wits mount up, the hairs subside.
    See, fierce Belinda on the Baron flies,   75
With more than usual lightning in her eyes;
Nor feared the chief the unequal fight to try,
Who sought no more than on his foe to die.
    But this bold lord with manly strength endued,
She with one finger and a thumb subdued: 80
Just where the breath of life his nostrils drew,
A charge of snuff the wily virgin threw;
The Gnomes direct, to every atom just,
The pungent grains of titillating dust.
Sudden, with starting tears each eye o'erflows,   85
And the high dome re-echoes to his nose.
    "Now meet thy fate," incensed Belinda cried,
And drew a deadly bodkin[2] from her side.
(The same, his ancient personage to deck,
Her great-great-grandsire wore about his neck,   90
In three seal rings; which after, melted down,
Formed a vast buckle for his widow's gown:
Her infant grandame's whistle next it grew,
The bells she jingled, and the whistle blew;
Then in a bodkin graced her mother's hairs,   95
Which long she wore, and now Belinda wears.)
    "Boast not my fall," he cried, "insulting foe!
Thou by some other shalt be laid as low.
Nor think to die dejects my lofty mind:
All that I dread is leaving you behind!   100
Rather than so, ah, let me still survive,
And burn in Cupid's flames—but burn alive."
    "Restore the Lock!" she cries; and all around
"Restore the Lock!" the vaulted roofs rebound.
Not fierce Othello in so loud a strain   105
Roared for the handkerchief that caused his pain.[3]
But see how oft ambitious aims are crossed,

---

2. An ornamental pin shaped like a dagger, to be worn in the hair.   3. *Othello* III.iv.

And chiefs contend till all the prize is lost!
The lock, obtained with guilt, and kept with pain,
In every place is sought, but sought in vain: 110
With such a prize no mortal must be blessed,
So Heaven decrees! with Heaven who can contest?
    Some thought it mounted to the lunar sphere,
Since all things lost on earth are treasured there.
There heroes' wits are kept in ponderous vases,   115
And beaux' in snuffboxes and tweezer cases.
There broken vows and deathbed alms are found,
And lovers' hearts with ends of riband bound,
The courtier's promises, and sick man's prayers,
The smiles of harlots, and the tears of heirs,   120
Cages for gnats, and chains to yoke a flea,
Dried butterflies, and tomes of casuistry.
    But trust the Muse—she saw it upward rise,
Though marked by none but quick, poetic eyes
(So Rome's great founder[4] to the heavens withdrew,   125
To Proculus alone confessed in view);
A sudden star, it shot through liquid air,
And drew behind a radiant trail of hair.
Not Berenice's[5] locks first rose so bright,
The heavens bespangling with disheveled light.   130
The Sylphs behold it kindling as it flies,
And pleased pursue its progress through the skies.
    This the beau monde shall from the Mall[6] survey,
And hail with music its propitious ray.
This the blest lover shall for Venus take,   135
And send up vows from Rosamonda's Lake.[7]
This Partridge soon shall view in cloudless skys,
When next he looks through Galileo's eyes;[8]
And hence the egregious wizard shall foredoom
The fate of Louis, and the fall of Rome.   140
    Then cease, bright nymph! to mourn thy ravished hair,
Which adds new glory to the shining sphere!
Not all the tresses that fair head can boast,
Shall draw such envy as the Lock you lost.
For, after all the murders of your eye,   145
When, after millions slain, yourself shall die:

---

4. Romulus, the "founder" and first king of Rome, was snatched to heaven in a storm cloud while reviewing his army in the Campus Martius (Livy I. xvi).   **5.** Berenice, the wife of Ptolemy III, dedicated a lock of her hair to the gods to ensure her husband's safe return from war. It was turned into a constellation.   **6.** A walk laid out by Charles II in St. James's Park, a resort for strollers of all sorts.   **7.** In St. James's Park; associated with unhappy lovers.   **8.** A telescope. John Partridge was an astrologer whose annually published predictions had been amusingly satirized by Swift and other wits in 1708.

When those fair suns shall set, as set they must,
And all those tresses shall be laid in dust,
This Lock the Muse shall consecrate to fame,
And 'midst the stars inscribe Belinda's name.   150
1714   1712

An Essay on Man

TO HENRY ST. JOHN, LORD BOLINGBROKE

EPISTLE I

ARGUMENT OF THE NATURE AND STATE OF MAN, WITH RESPECT TO
THE UNIVERSE. Of man in the abstract—I. That we can judge only
with regard to our own system, being ignorant of the relations of
systems and things, ver. 17, &c.—II. That man is not to be deemed
imperfect, but a being suited to his place and rank in the creation,
agreeable to the general order of things, and conformable to ends
and relations to him unknown, ver. 35, &c.—III. That it is partly
upon his ignorance of future events, and partly upon the hope of a
future state, that all his happiness in the present depends, ver. 77,
&c.—IV. The pride of aiming at more knowledge, and pretending
to more perfection, the cause of man's error and misery. The impiety
of putting himself in the place of God, and judging of the fitness or
unfitness, perfection or imperfection, justice or injustice of his dis-
pensations, ver. 113, &c.—V. The absurdity of conceiting himself
the final cause of the creation, or expecting that perfection in the
moral world which is not in the natural, ver. 131, &c.—VI. The
unreasonableness of his complaints against Providence, while on the
one hand he demands the perfections of the angels, and on the other
the bodily qualifications of the brutes; though, to possess any of the
sensitive faculties in a higher degree, would render him miserable,
ver. 173, &c.—VII. That throughout the whole visible world, an
universal order and gradation in the sensual and mental faculties is
observed, which causes a subordination of creature to creature, and
of all creatures to man. The gradations of sense, instinct, thought,
reflection, reason: that reason alone countervails all the other faculties, ver. 207.—VIII. How much further this order and subordination of living creatures may extend, above and below us; were any
part of which broken, not that part only, but the whole connected
creation must be destroyed, ver. 233—IX. The extravagance, madness, and pride of such a desire, ver. 259.—X. The consequence of
all, the absolute submission due to Providence, both as to our present and future state, ver. 281, &c., to the end.

Awake, my St. John![9] leave all meaner things
To low ambition, and the pride of Kings.
Let us (since Life can little more supply
Than just to look about us and to die)
Expatiate free o'er all this scene of Man;   5
A mighty maze! but not without a plan;
A Wild, where weeds and flow'rs promiscuous shoot;
Or Garden, tempting with forbidden fruit.
Together let us beat this ample field,
Try what the open, what the covert yield;   10
The latent tracts, the giddy heights, explore
Of all who blindly creep, or sightless soar;
Eye Nature's walks, shoot Folly as it flies,
And catch the Manners living as they rise;
Laugh where we must, be candid where we can;   15
But vindicate the ways of God to man.[1]
   I. Say first, of God above, or Man below,
What can we reason, but from what we know?
Of Man, what see we but his station here,
From which to reason, or to which refer?   20
Through worlds unnumbered though the God be known,
'Tis ours to trace him only in our own.
He, who through vast immensity can pierce,
See worlds on worlds compose one universe,
Observe how system into system runs,   25
What other planets circle other suns,
What varied Being peoples ev'ry star,
May tell why Heav'n has made us as we are.
But of this frame the bearings, and the ties,
The strong connections, nice dependencies,   30
Gradations just, has thy pervading soul
Looked through? or can a part contain the whole?
   Is the great chain,[2] that draws all to agree,
And drawn supports, upheld by God, or thee?
   II. Presumptuous Man! the reason wouldst thou find,   35
Why formed so weak, so little, and so blind?
First, if thou canst, the harder reason guess,
Why formed no weaker, blinder, and no less?
Ask of thy mother earth, why oaks are made
Taller or stronger than the weeds they shade?   40

9. Pope's friend, who had thus far neglected to keep his part of their friendly bargain: Pope was
to write his philosophical speculations in verse, Bolingbroke was to write his in prose.   1. Compare
Milton's *Paradise Lost*, Book I, 1. 26. Pope's theme is essentially the same as Milton's, and even
the opening image of the garden reminds us of the earlier poet's "Paradise."   2. The popular
eighteenth-century notion of the Great Chain of Being, in which elements of the universe took
their places in a hierarchy ranging from the lowest matter to God.

Or ask of yonder argent fields above,
Why Jove's satellites are less than JOVE?
   Of Systems possible, if it's confest.
That Wisdom infinite must form the best,
Where all must full[3] or not coherent be,   45
And all that rises, rise in due degree;
Then, in the scale of reas'ning life, 'tis plain,
There must be, somewhere, such a rank as Man:
And all the question (wrangle e'er so long)
Is only this, if God has placed him wrong?   50
   Respecting Man, whatever wrong we call,
May, must be right, as relative to all.
In human works, though laboured on with pain,
A thousand movements scarce one purpose gain;
In God's, one single can its end produce;   55
Yet serves to second too some other use.
So Man, who here seems principal alone,
Perhaps acts second to some sphere unknown,
Touches some wheel, or verges to some goal;
'Tis but a part we see, and not a whole.   60
   When the proud steed shall know why Man restrains
His fiery course, or drives him o'er the plains;
When the dull Ox, why now he breaks the clod,
Is now a victim, and now Egypt's God:
Then shall Man's pride and dullness comprehend   65
His actions', passions', being's use and end;
Why doing, suff'ring, checked, impelled; and why
This hour a slave, the next a deity.
   Then say not Man's imperfect, Heav'n in fault;
Say rather, Man's as perfect as he ought: 70
His knowledge measured to his state and place;
His time a moment, and a point his space.
If to be perfect in a certain sphere,
What matter, soon or late, or here or there?
The blest to-day is as completely so,   75
As who began a thousand years ago.
   III. Heav'n from all creatures hides the book of Fate,
All but the page prescribed, their present state:
From brutes what men, from men what spirits know:
Or who could suffer Being here below?   80
The lamb thy riot dooms to bleed to-day,
Had he thy Reason, would he skip and play?
Pleased to the last, he crops the flow'ry food,

---

3. According to the principle of plenitude, there can be no gaps in the Chain.

And licks the hand just raised to shed his blood.
Oh blindness to the future! kindly giv'n, 85
That each may fill the circle marked by Heav'n:
Who sees with equal eye, as God of all,
A hero perish, or a sparrow fall,
Atoms or systems into ruin hurled,
And now a bubble burst, and now a world. 90
   Hope humbly then; with trembling pinions soar;
Wait the great teacher Death; and God adore.
What future bliss, he gives not thee to know,
But gives that Hope to be thy blessing now.
Hope springs eternal in the human breast: 95
Man never Is, but always To be blest:
The soul, uneasy and confined from home,
Rests and expatiates in a life to come.
   Lo, the poor Indian! whose untutored mind
Sees God in clouds, or hears him in the wind; 100
His soul, proud Science never taught to stray
Far as the solar walk, or milky way;
Yet simple Nature to his hope has giv'n,
Behind the cloud-topt hill, an humbler heav'n;
Some safer world in depth of woods embraced, 105
Some happier island in the wat'ry waste,
Where slaves once more their native land behold,
No fiends torment, no Christians thirst for gold.
To Be, contents his natural desire,
He asks no Angel's wing, no Seraph's fire; 110
But thinks, admitted to that equal sky,
His faithful dog shall bear him company.
   IV. Go, wiser thou! and, in thy scale of sense,
Weigh thy Opinion against Providence;
Call imperfection what thou fanciest such, 115
Say, here he gives too little, there too much:
Destroy all Creatures for thy sport or gust,
Yet cry, If Man's unhappy, God's unjust;
If Man alone engross not Heav'n's high care,
Alone made perfect here, immortal there: 120
Snatch from his hand the balance and the rod,
Re-judge his justice, be the GOD of GOD.
In Pride, in reas'ning Pride, our error lies;
All quit their sphere, and rush into the skies.
Pride still is aiming at the blest abodes, 125
Men would be Angels, Angels would be Gods.
Aspiring to be Gods, if Angels fell,
Aspiring to be Angels, Men rebel:

And who but wishes to invert the laws
Of ORDER, sins against th' Eternal Cause.   130
    V. Ask for what end the heav'nly bodies shine,
Earth for whose use? Pride answers, " 'Tis for mine:
For me kind Nature wakes her genial Pow'r,
Suckles each herb, and spreads out ev'ry flow'r;
Annual for me, the grape, the rose, renew,   135
The juice nectareous, and the balmy dew;
For me, the mine a thousand treasures brings;
For me, health gushes from a thousand springs;
Seas roll to waft me, suns to light me rise;
My footstool earth, my canopy the skies."   140
    But errs not Nature from this gracious end,
From burning suns when livid deaths descend,
When earthquakes swallow, or when tempests sweep
Towns to one grave, whole nations to the deep?
"No," 'tis replied, "the first Almighty Cause   145
Acts not by partial, but by gen'ral laws;
Th' exceptions few; some change since all began:
And what created perfect?"—Why then Man?
If the great end be human happiness,
Then Nature deviates; and can man do less?   150
As much that end a constant course requires
Of show'rs and sunshine, as of man's desires;
As much eternal springs and cloudless skies,
As Men forever temp'rate, calm, and wise.
If plagues or earthquakes break not Heav'n's design,   155
Why then a Borgia, or a Catiline?[4]
Who knows but He whose hand the lightning forms,
Who heaves old Ocean, and who wings the storms;
Pours fierce Ambition in a Caesar's mind,
Or turns young Ammon[5] loose to scourge mankind?   160
From pride, from pride, our very reas'ning springs;
Account for moral, as for nat'ral things:
Why charge we Heav'n in those, in these acquit?
In both, to reason right is to submit.
    Better for Us, perhaps, it might appear,   165
Where there all harmony, all virtue here;
That never air or ocean felt the wind;
That never passion discomposed the mind.
But ALL subsists by elemental strife;
And Passions are the elements of Life.   170

---

4. Roman who conspired against the state in 63 B.C. *Borgia:* Cesare Borgia (1476–1507), Italian prince notorious for his crimes.   5. Alexander the Great, who when he visited the oracle of Zeus Ammon in Egypt was hailed by the priest there as son of the god.

The gen'ral ORDER, since the whole began,
Is kept in Nature, and is kept in Man.
    VI. What would this Man? Now upward will he soar,
And little less than Angel, would be more;
Now looking downwards, just as grieved appears   175
To want the strength of bulls, the fur of bears.
Made for his use all creatures if he call,
Say what their use, had he the pow'rs of all?
Nature to these, without profusion, kind,
The proper organs, proper pow'rs assigned;   180
Each seeming want compensated of course,
Here with degrees of swiftness, there of force;
All in exact proportion to the state;
Nothing to add, and nothing to abate.
Each beast, each insect, happy in its own: 185
Is Heav'n unkind to Man, and Man alone?
Shall he alone, whom rational we call,
Be pleased with nothing, if not blessed with all?
    The bliss of Man (could Pride that blessing find)
Is not to act or think beyond mankind;   190
No pow'rs of body or of soul to share,
But what his nature and his state can bear.
Why has not Man a microscopic eye?
For this plain reason, Man is not a Fly.
Say what the use, were finer optics[6] giv'n,   195
T' inspect a mite, not comprehend the heav'n?
Or touch, if tremblingly alive all o'er,
To smart and agonize at ev'ry pore?
Or quick effluvia[7] darting through the brain,
Die of a rose in aromatic pain?   200
If nature thundered in his op'ning ears,
And stunned him with the music of the spheres,[8]
How would he wish that Heav'n had left him still
The whisp'ring Zephyr, and the purling rill?
Who finds not Providence all good and wise,   205
Alike in what it gives, and what denies?
    VII. Far as Creation's ample range extends,
The scale of sensual, mental pow'rs ascends:
Mark how it mounts, to Man's imperial race,
From the green myriads in the peopled grass: 210
What modes of sight betwixt each wide extreme,
The mole's dim curtain, and the lynx's beam:[9]

---

6. Eyes.   7. Stream of minute particles.   8. The old notion that the movement of the planets created a "higher" music.   9. Legend made this animal one of the keenest-sighted. *Dim curtain:* The mole's poor vision.

Of smell, the headlong lioness between,
And hound sagacious[1] on the tainted green:
Of hearing, from the life that fills the Flood,   215
To that which warbles through the vernal wood:
The spider's touch, how exquisitely fine!
Feels at each thread, and lives along the line:
In the nice bee, what sense so subtly true
From pois'nous herbs extracts the healing dew?   220
How Instinct varies in the grov'lling swine,
Compared, half-reas'ning elephant, with thine!
'Twixt that, and Reason, what a nice barrier,
For ever sep'rate, yet for ever near!
Remembrance and Reflection how allied;   225
What thin partitions Sense from Thought divide:
And Middle natures,[2] how they long to join,
Yet never pass th' insuperable line!
Without this just gradation, could they be
Subjected, these to those, or all to thee?   230
The pow'rs of all subdued by thee alone,
Is not thy Reason all these pow'rs in one?
      VIII. See, through this air, this ocean, and this earth,
All matter quick, and bursting into birth.
Above, how high, progressive life may go!   235
Around, how wide! how deep extend below!
Vast chain of Being! which from God began,
Natures ethereal, human, angel, man,
Beast, bird, fish, insect, what no eye can see,
No glass can reach; from Infinite to thee,   240
From thee to Nothing.—On superior pow'rs
Were we to press, inferior might on ours:
Or in the full creation leave a void,
Where, one step broken, the great scale's destroyed:
From Nature's chain whatever link you strike,   245
Tenth or ten thousandth, breaks the chain alike.
      And, if each system in gradation roll
Alike essential to th' amazing Whole,
The least confusion but in one, not all
That system only, but the Whole must fall.   250
Let Earth unbalanced from her orbit fly,
Planets and Suns run lawless through the sky;
Let ruling angels from their spheres be hurled,
Being on Being wrecked, and world on world;
Heav'n's whole foundations to their center nod,   255

1. Here meaning "exceptionally quick of scent."   2. Animals that seem to share the characteristics of several different classes; for example, the duck-billed platypus.

And Nature trembles to the throne of God.
All this dread ORDER break—for whom? for thee?
Vile worm!—oh Madness! Pride! Impiety!
    IX. What if the foot, ordained the dust to tread,
Or hand, to toil, aspired to be the head?   260
What if the head, the eye, or ear repined
To serve mere engines to the ruling Mind?
Just as absurd for any part to claim
To be another, in this gen'ral frame:
Just as absurd, to mourn the tasks or pains,   265
The great directing MIND of ALL ordains.
   All are but parts of one stupendous whole,
Whose body Nature is, and God the soul;
That, changed through all, and yet in all the same;
Great in the earth, as in th' ethereal frame;   270
Warms in the sun, refreshes in the breeze,
Glows in the stars, and blossoms in the trees,
Lives through all life, extends through all extent,
Spreads undivided, operates unspent;
Breathes in our soul, informs our mortal part,   275
As full, as perfect, in a hair as heart;
As full, as perfect, in vile Man that mourns,
As the rapt Seraph that adores and burns:
To him no high, no low, no great, no small;
He fills, he bounds, connects, and equals all.   280
    X. Cease then, nor ORDER imperfection name:
Our proper bliss depends on what we blame.
Know thy own point: this kind, this due degree
Of blindness, weakness, Heav'n bestows on thee.
Submit.—In this, or any other sphere,   285
Secure to be as blest as thou canst bear:
Safe in the hand of one disposing Pow'r,
Or in the natal, or the mortal hour.
All Nature is but Art, unknown to thee;
All Chance, Direction, which thou canst not see;   290
All Discord, Harmony not understood;
All partial Evil, universal Good:
And, spite of Pride, in erring Reason's spite,
One truth is clear, WHATEVER IS, IS RIGHT.[3]

---

3. Epistle II deals with "the Nature and State of Man with respect to himself, as an Individual"; Episte III examines "the Nature and State of Man with respect to Society"; and the last Epistle concerns "the Nature and State of Man with respect to Happiness."

FRANÇOIS-MARIE AROUET DE VOLTAIRE
1694–1778

Voltaire's *Candide* (1759) brings to near perfection the art of black comedy. It subjects its characters to an accumulation of horrors so bizarre that they provoke a bewildered response of laughter as self-protection—even while they demand that the reader pay attention to the serious implications of such extravagance.

Voltaire had prepared himself to write such a work by varied experience—including that of political imprisonment. He was born François-Marie Arouet, son of a minor treasury official in Paris. After attending a Jesuit school, he took up the study of law, which, however, he soon abandoned. In his early twenties (1717–18), he spent eleven months in the Bastille for writing satiric verses about the aristocracy. His incarceration did not dissuade him from a literary career; by 1718 he was using the name *Voltaire* and beginning to acquire literary and social reputation—as well as some wealth: his speculations in the Compagnie des Indes made him rich by 1726. Money, however, did not protect him from spending more time in the Bastille during that year; after his release, he passed three years in exile, mainly in England. From 1734 to 1749, he studied widely, living with Mme. du Châtelet on her estate at Cirey. For the next three years he stayed with Frederick the Great of Prussia at his Potsdam court; after that arrangement collapsed, Voltaire bought property in Switzerland and in adjacent France, settling first at his own chateau, Les Delices, outside Geneva; then at nearby Ferney, in France. His international reputation as writer and social critic steadily increased; in the year of his death, he returned triumphantly to Paris.

Like his English contemporary, Samuel Johnson, Voltaire wrote in many important genres: tragedy, epic, history, philosophy, fiction. His *Philosophical Dictionary* (1764), with its witty and penetrating definitions, typifies his range and acumen and his participation in his period's effort to take control of experience by intellect. While still a young man, Voltaire wrote a *History of Charles XII* of Sweden, a work unusual for its time in its novelistic technique and its assumption that "history" includes the personal lives of powerful individuals and has nothing to do with divine intervention. Before *Candide* (1759), he had published another philosophic tale, *Zadig* (1748), following the pattern of Oriental narrative. Like Candide, Zadig goes through an educational process of experience; it teaches him inconclusive lessons about life's unforeseeable contingencies.

Candide mocks both the artificial order of fiction (through its ludicrously multiplied recognition scenes and its symmetrical division of the protagonist's travels into three equal parts) and what Voltaire suggests is the equally artificial order posited by philosophic optimists. The view of the universe suggested by Pope's *Essay on Man*, for instance, insists on the rationality of a pattern ungraspable by human reason. It does so, however, *Candide* implicitly argues, only by attending to the abstract and undemonstrable and ignoring the omnipresent pain of immediate experience. Gottfried Leibniz, the German philosopher, provides Voltaire's most specific target in *Can-*

dide, with the complexities of his version of optimism reduced for satiric purposes to the facile formula, "Everything is for the best in this best of all possible worlds." The formulation is of course unfair to Leibniz, whose philosophic optimism, like Pope's, implies belief in an unknowable universal order—roughly equivalent to Christian Providence—but no lack of awareness about the actual misery and depravity human beings experience.

The exuberance and extravagance of Voltaire's imagination force us to laugh at what we may feel embarrassed to laugh at: the plight of the woman whose buttock has been cut off to make rump steak for her hungry companions, the weeping of two girls whose monkey-lovers have been killed, the situation of six exiled, poverty-stricken kings. Like Swift, Voltaire keeps his readers off balance. Raped, cut to pieces, hanged, stabbed in the belly, the central characters of *Candide* keep coming back to life at opportune moments, as though no disaster could have permanent or ultimately destructive effects. Such reassuring fantasy suggests that we don't need to worry, it's all a joke, an outpouring of fertile fancy designed to ridicule an outmoded philosophic system with no particular relevance to us. On the other hand, historical reality keeps intruding. Those six hungry kings are real, actual figures, actually dispossessed. Candide sees Admiral Byng executed: an admiral who really lived, and really died by firing squad for not engaging an enemy with sufficient ferocity. The Lisbon earthquake actually occurred; thirty to forty thousand people literally lost their lives in it. The extravagances of reality equal those of the storyteller; Voltaire demands that the reader imaginatively confront and somehow come to terms with horrors that surround us still.

The real problem, *Candide* suggests, is not natural or human disaster so much as human complacency. When Candide sees Admiral Byng shot, he comments on the injustice of the execution. "That's perfectly true, came the answer; but in this country it is useful from time to time to kill one admiral in order to encourage the others." Early in the nineteenth century, William Wordsworth wrote, "much it grieved my heart to think / What man has made of man." His tone and perspective differ dramatically from Voltaire's, but his point is the same: human beings use their faculties to increase corruption. Failure to take seriously any human death is a form of moral corruption; failure to acknowledge the intolerability of war, in all its concrete detail of rape and butchery, epitomizes such corruption at its worst.

In a late chapter of *Candide*, the central character, less naïve than he once was, inquires about whether men have always massacred one another. Have they, he asks, "always been liars, traitors, ingrates, thieves, weaklings, sneaks, cowards, backbiters, gluttons, drunkards, misers, climbers, killers, calumniators, sensualists, fanatics, hypocrites, and fools?" His interlocutor, Martin, responds that, just as hawks have always devoured pigeons, human beings have always manifested the same vices. This ironic variation on the period's conviction of the universality and continuity of human nature epitomizes Voltaire's sense of outrage, which in some respects parallels Swift's in the fourth book of *Gulliver's Travels*. Swift demonstrates the implications of "reason" considered as an ideal and shows its irrelevance to actual human behavior; Voltaire shows how the claim of a rational universal order can provide a way to avoid the hard problems of living in a world where human beings have become liars, traitors, and so on. His Swiftian catalogue of vice and folly expresses the moral insufficiency and perversity of humankind.

Martin's cynical assumption that people are naturally corrupt, as hawks naturally eat smaller birds, constitutes another form of avoidance. The assumed inevitability of vice, like belief that all is for the best, justifies passivity. Nothing *can* be done, nothing *should* be done, or nothing *matters* (the view of Lord Pocucurante, another figure Candide encounters). So the characters of this fiction, including Candide himself, mainly pursue self-gratification. Even this course they do not follow judiciously: when Candide and Cacambo find themselves in the earthly paradise of Eldorado, "the two happy men resolved to be so no longer," driven by fantasies of improving their condition. Yet, unlike Gulliver, they acquire wisdom at last, learning to withstand "three great evils, boredom, vice, and poverty," by working hard at what comes to hand and avoiding futile theorizing about the nature of the universe.

Although Voltaire's picture of the human condition reveals the same indignation that marks Swift's, he allows at least conditional hope for moderate satisfaction in this life. Candide's beloved Cunegonde loses all her beauty, but she becomes an accomplished pastry cook; Candide possesses a garden he can cultivate. Greed, malice, and lust do not comprise the total possibility for humankind. If Voltaire's tone sometimes expresses outrage, at other times it verges on the playful. When, for example, he mocks the improbabilities of romance by his characters' miraculous resuscitations, or parodies the restrictions of classical form by sending Candide and his friends on an epic journey, one can feel his amused awareness of our human need to make order and our human desire to comfort ourselves by fictions. But as he insists that much of the order we claim to perceive itself comprises a comforting fiction, as he uses satire's fierce energies to challenge our complacencies, he reveals once more the underside of the Enlightenment ideal of reason. That we human beings have reason, Voltaire tells us, is no ground on which to flatter ourselves; rightly used, it exposes our insufficiencies.

Biographies and critical studies of Voltaire include R. Aldington, *Voltaire* (1934); G. Brandes, *The Life of Voltaire* (undated); I. O. Wade, *Voltaire and "Candide"* (1959); and T. Besterman, *Voltaire* (1969).

Candide, or Optimism[1]

translated from the German of Doctor Ralph with the additions which were found in the Doctor's pocket when he died at Minden in the Year of Our Lord 1759

CHAPTER I
How Candide Was Brought up in a Fine Castle and How He Was Driven Therefrom

There lived in Westphalia,[2] in the castle of the Baron of Thunder-Ten-Tronckh, a young man on whom nature had bestowed the per-

1. Translated with notes by Robert M. Adams.   2. A province of western Germany, near Holland and the lower Rhineland. Flat, boggy, and drab, it is noted chiefly for its excellent ham. In a letter to his niece, written during his German expedition of 1750, Voltaire described the "vast, sad, sterile, detestable countryside of Westphalia."

fection of gentle manners. His features admirably expressed his soul
he combined an honest mind with great simplicity of heart; and I
think it was for this reason that they called him Candide. The old
servants of the house suspected that he was the son of the Baron's
sister by a respectable, honest gentleman of the neighborhood, whom
she had refused to marry because he could prove only seventy-one
quarterings, [3] the rest of his family tree having been lost in the passage of time.

The Baron was one of the most mighty lords of Westphalia, for
his castle had a door and windows. His great hall was even hung
with a tapestry. The dogs of his courtyard made up a hunting pack
on occasion, with the stableboys as huntsmen; the village priest was
his grand almoner. They all called him "My Lord," and laughed at
his stories.

The Baroness, who weighed in the neighborhood of three hundred
and fifty pounds, was greatly respected for that reason, and did the
honors of the house with a dignity which rendered her even more
imposing. Her daughter Cunégonde, [4] aged seventeen, was a ruddy-
cheeked girl, fresh, plump, and desirable. The Baron's son seemed
in every way worthy of his father. The tutor Pangloss was the oracle
of the household, and little Candide listened to his lectures with all
the good faith of his age and character.

Pangloss gave instruction in metaphysico-theologico-cosmo-
loonig-ology. [5] He proved admirably that there cannot possibly be an
effect without a cause and that in this best of all possible worlds the
Baron's castle was the best of all castles and his wife the best of all
possible Baronesses.

—It is clear, said he, that things cannot be otherwise than they
are, for since everything is made to serve an end, everything necessarily serves the best end. Observe: noses were made to support spectacles, hence we have spectacles. Legs, as anyone can plainly see,
were made to be breeched, and so we have breeches. Stones were
made to be shaped and to build castles with; thus My Lord has a fine
castle, for the greatest Baron in the province should have the finest
house; and since pigs were made to be eaten, we eat pork all year
round. [6] Consequently, those who say everything is well are uttering
mere stupidities; they should say everything is for the best.

---

3. Genealogical divisions of one's family-tree. Seventy-one of them is a grotesque number to
have, representing something over 2,000 years of uninterrupted nobility.   4. Cunégonde gets
her odd name from Kunigunda, wife to Emperor Henry II, who walked barefoot and blindfolded
on red-hot irons to prove her chastity; Pangloss gets his name from Greek words meaning all-
tongue.   5. The "looney" I have buried in this burlesque word corresponds to a buried *nigaud*—
"booby" in the French. Christian Wolff, disciple of Leibniz, invented and popularized the word
"cosmology." The catch phrases in the following sentence, echoed by popularizers of Leibniz,
make reference to the determinism of his system, its linking of cause with effect, and its
optimism.   6. The argument from design supposes that everything in this world exists for a
specific reason; Voltaire objects not to the argument as a whole, but to the abuse of it.

Candide listened attentively and believed implicitly; for he found Miss Cunégonde exceedingly pretty, though he never had the courage to tell her so. He decided that after the happiness of being born Baron of Thunder-Ten-Tronckh, the second order of happiness was to be Miss Cunégonde; the third was seeing her every day, and the fourth was listening to Master Pangloss, the greatest philosopher in the province and consequently in the entire world.

One day, while Cunégonde was walking near the castle in the little woods that they called a park, she saw Dr. Pangloss in the underbrush; he was giving a lesson in experimental physics to her mother's maid, a very attractive and obedient brunette. As Miss Cunégonde had a natural bent for the sciences, she watched breathlessly the repeated experiments which were going on; she saw clearly the doctor's sufficient reason, observed both cause and effect, and returned to the house in a distracted and pensive frame of mind, yearning for knowledge and dreaming that she might be the sufficient reason of young Candide—who might also be hers.

As she was returning to the castle, she met Candide, and blushed; Candide blushed too. She greeted him in a faltering tone of voice; and Candide talked to her without knowing what he was saying. Next day, as everyone was rising from the dinner table, Cunégonde and Candide found themselves behind a screen; Cunégonde dropped her handkerchief, Candide picked it up; she held his hand quite innocently, he kissed her hand quite innocently with remarkable vivacity and emotion; their lips met, their eyes lit up, their knees trembled, their hands wandered. The Baron of Thunder-Ten-Tronckh passed by the screen and, taking note of this cause and this effect, drove Candide out of the castle by kicking him vigorously on the backside. Cunégonde fainted; as soon as she recovered, the Baroness slapped her face; and everything was confusion in the most beautiful and agreeable of all possible castles.

CHAPTER 2
What Happened to Candide Among the Bulgars[7]

Candide, ejected from the earthly paradise, wandered for a long time without knowing where he was going, weeping, raising his eyes to heaven, and gazing back frequently on the most beautiful of castles which contained the most beautiful of Baron's daughters. He slept without eating, in a furrow of a plowed field, while the snow drifted over him; next morning, numb with cold, he dragged himself into the neighboring village, which was called Waldberghoff-trarbk-

---

7. Voltaire chose this name to represent the Prussian troops of Frederick the Great because he wanted to make an insinuation of pederasty against both the soldiers and their master. *Cf.* French *bougre*, English "bugger."

dikdorff; he was penniless, famished, and exhausted. At the door of a tavern he paused forlornly. Two men dressed in blue[8] took note of him:

—Look, chum, said one of them, there's a likely young fellow of just about the right size.

They approached Candide and invited him very politely to dine with them.

—Gentlemen, Candide replied with charming modesty, I'm honored by your invitation, but I really don't have enough money to pay my share.

—My dear sir, said one of the blues, people of your appearance and your merit don't have to pay; aren't you five feet five inches tall?

—Yes, gentlemen, that is indeed my stature, said he, making a bow.

—Then, sir, you must be seated at once; not only will we pay your bill this time, we will never allow a man like you to be short of money; for men were made only to render one another mutual aid.

—You are quite right, said Candide; it is just as Dr. Pangloss always told me, and I see clearly that everything is for the best.

They beg him to accept a couple of crowns, he takes them, and offers an I.O.U.; they won't hear of it, and all sit down at table together.

—Don't you love dearly . . . . ?

—I do indeed, says he, I dearly love Miss Cunégonde.

—No, no, says one of the gentlemen, we are asking if you don't love dearly the King of the Bulgars.

—Not in the least, says he, I never laid eyes on him.

—What's that you say? He's the most charming of kings, and we must drink his health.

—Oh, gladly, gentlemen; and he drinks.

—That will do, they tell him; you are now the bulwark, the support, the defender, the hero of the Bulgars; your fortune is made and your future assured.

Promptly they slip irons on his legs and lead him to the regiment. There they cause him to right face, left face, present arms, order arms, aim, fire, doubletime, and they give him thirty strokes of the rod. Next day he does the drill a little less awkwardly and gets only twenty strokes; the third day, they give him only ten, and he is regarded by his comrades as a prodigy.

Candide, quite thunderstruck, did not yet understand very clearly how he was a hero. One fine spring morning he took it into his head to go for a walk, stepping straight out as if it were a privilege of the

8. The recruiting officers of Frederick the Great, much feared in eighteenth-century Europe, wore blue uniforms. Frederick had a passion for sorting out his soldiers by size; several of his regiments would accept only six-footers.

human race, as of animals in general, to use his legs as he chose.[9]
He had scarcely covered two leagues when four other heroes, each
six feet tall, overtook him, bound him, and threw him into a dungeon. At the court-martial they asked which he preferred, to be flogged
thirty-six times by the entire regiment or to receive summarily a dozen
bullets in the brain. In vain did he argue that the human will is free
and insist that he preferred neither alternative; he had to choose; by
virtue of the divine gift called "liberty" he decided to run the gauntlet
thirty-six times, and actually endured two floggings. The regiment
was composed of two thousand men. That made four thousand strokes,
which laid open every muscle and nerve from his nape to his butt.
As they were preparing for the third beating, Candide, who could
endure no more, begged as a special favor that they would have the
goodness to smash his head. His plea was granted; they bandaged his
eyes and made him kneel down. The King of the Bulgars, passing
by at this moment, was told of the culprit's crime; and as this king
had a rare genius, he understood, from everything they told him of
Candide, that this was a young metaphysician, extremely ignorant
of the ways of the world, so he granted his royal pardon, with a
generosity which will be praised in every newspaper in every age. A
worthy surgeon cured Candide in three weeks with the ointments
described by Dioscorides.[1] He already had a bit of skin back and was
able to walk when the King of the Bulgars went to war with the King
of the Abares.[2]

CHAPTER 3
How Candide Escaped from the Bulgars, and What Became of Him

Nothing could have been so fine, so brisk, so brilliant, so well-
drilled as the two armies. The trumpets, the fifes, the oboes, the
drums, and the cannon produced such a harmony as was never heard
in hell. First the cannons battered down about six thousand men on
each side; then volleys of musket fire removed from the best of worlds
about nine or ten thousand rascals who were cluttering up its surface. The bayonet was a sufficient reason for the demise of several
thousand others. Total casualties might well amount to thirty thou-

9. This episode was suggested by the experience of a Frenchman named Courtilz, who had
deserted from the Prussian army and been bastionadoed for it. Voltaire intervened with Frederick
to gain his release. But it also reflects the story that Wolff, Leibniz's disciple, got into trouble with
Frederick's father when someone reported that his doctrine denying free will had encouraged
several soldiers to desert. "The argument of the grenadier," who was said to have pleaded pre-
established harmony to justify his desertion, so infuriated the king that he had Wolff expelled from
the country.   1. Dioscorides' treatise on *materia medica*, dating from the first century A.D., was
not the most up to date.   2. A tribe of semicivilized Scythians, who might be supposed at war
with the Bulgars; allegorically, the Abares are the French, who opposed the Prussians in the Seven
Years' War (1756–1763). According to the title page of 1761, "Doctor Ralph," the dummy author
of *Candide*, himself perished at the battle of Minden (Westphalia) in 1759.

sand men or so. Candide, who was trembling like a philosopher, hid himself as best he could while this heroic butchery was going on.

Finally, while the two kings in their respective camps celebrated the victory by having *Te Deums* sung, Candide undertook to do his reasoning of cause and effect somewhere else. Passing by mounds of the dead and dying, he came to a nearby village which had been burnt to the ground. It was an Abare village, which the Bulgars had burned, in strict accordance with the laws of war. Here old men, stunned from beatings, watched the last agonies of their butchered wives, who still clutched their infants to their bleeding breasts; there, disemboweled girls, who had first satisfied the natural needs of various heroes, breathed their last; others, half-scorched in the flames, begged for their death stroke. Scattered brains and severed limbs littered the ground.

Candide fled as fast as he could to another village; this one belonged to the Bulgars, and the heroes of the Abare cause had given it the same treatment. Climbing over ruins and stumbling over corpses, Candide finally made his way out of the war area, carrying a little food in his knapsack and never ceasing to dream of Miss Cunégonde. His supplies gave out when he reached Holland; but having heard that everyone in that country was rich and a Christian, he felt confident of being treated as well as he had been in the castle of the Baron before he was kicked out for the love of Miss Cunégonde.

He asked alms of several grave personages, who all told him that if he continued to beg, he would be shut up in a house of correction and set to hard labor.

Finally he approached a man who had just been talking to a large crowd for an hour on end; the topic was charity. Looking doubtfully at him, the orator demanded:

—What are you doing here? Are you here to serve the good cause?

—There is no effect without a cause, said Candide modestly; all events are linked by the chain of necessity and arranged for the best. I had to be driven away from Miss Cunégonde, I had to run the gauntlet, I have to beg my bread until I can earn it; none of this could have happened otherwise.

—Look here, friend, said the orator, do you think the Pope is Antichrist?[3]

—I haven't considered the matter, said Candide; but whether he is or not, I'm in need of bread.

—You don't deserve any, said the other; away with you, you rascal, you rogue, never come near me as long as you live.

Meanwhile, the orator's wife had put her head out of the window, and, seeing a man who was not sure the Pope was Antichrist, emp-

3. Voltaire is satirizing extreme Protestant sects that have sometimes seemed to make hatred of Rome the sum and substance of their creed.

tied over his head a pot full of———Scandalous! The excesses into which women are led by religious zeal!

A man who had never been baptized, a good Anabaptist[4] named Jacques, saw this cruel and heartless treatment being inflicted on one of his fellow creatures, a featherless biped possessing a soul;[5] he took Candide home with him, washed him off, gave him bread and beer, presented him with two florins, and even undertook to give him a job in his Persian-rug factory—for these items are widely manufactured in Holland. Candide, in an ecstasy of gratitude, cried out:

—Master Pangloss was right indeed when he told me everything is for the best in this world; for I am touched by your kindness far more than by the harshness of that black-coated gentleman and his wife.

Next day, while taking a stroll about town, he met a beggar who was covered with pustules, his eyes were sunken, the end of his nose rotted off, his mouth twisted, his teeth black, he had a croaking voice and a hacking cough, and spat a tooth every time he tried to speak.

CHAPTER 4
How Candide Met His Old Philosophy Tutor, Doctor Pangloss, and What Came of It

Candide, more touched by compassion even than by horror, gave this ghastly beggar the two florins that he himself had received from his honest Anabaptist friend Jacques. The phantom stared at him, burst into tears, and fell on his neck. Candide drew back in terror.

—Alas, said one wretch to the other, don't you recognize your dear Pangloss any more?

—What are you saying? You, my dear master! you, in this horrible condition? What misfortune has befallen you? Why are you no longer in the most beautiful of castles? What has happened to Miss Cunégonde, that pearl among young ladies, that masterpiece of Nature?

—I am perishing, said Pangloss.

Candide promptly led him into the Anabaptist's stable, where he gave him a crust of bread, and when he had recovered:—Well, said he, Cunégonde?

—Dead, said the other.

Candide fainted. His friend brought him around with a bit of sour

4. Holland, as the home of religious liberty, had offered asylum to the Anabaptists, whose radical views on property and religious discipline had made them unpopular during the sixteenth century. Granted tolerance, they settled down into respectable burghers. Since this behavior confirmed some of Voltaire's major theses, he had a high opinion of contemporary Anabaptists.   5. Plato's famous minimal definition of a man, which he corrected by the addition of a soul to distinguish man from a plucked chicken.

vinegar which happened to be in the stable. Candide opened his eyes.

—Cunégonde, dead! Ah, best of worlds, what's become of you now? But how did she die? It wasn't of grief at seeing me kicked out of her noble father's elegant castle?

—Not at all, said Pangloss; she was disemboweled by the Bulgar soldiers, after having been raped to the absolute limit of human endurance; they smashed the Baron's head when he tried to defend her, cut the Baroness to bits, and treated my poor pupil exactly like his sister. As for the castle, not one stone was left on another, not a shed, not a sheep, not a duck, not a tree; but we had the satisfaction of revenge, for the Abares did exactly the same thing to a nearby barony belonging to a Bulgar nobleman.

At this tale Candide fainted again; but having returned to his senses and said everything appropriate to the occasion, he asked about the cause and effect, the sufficient reason, which had reduced Pangloss to his present pitiful state.

—Alas, said he, it was love; love, the consolation of the human race, the preservative of the universe, the soul of all sensitive beings, love, gentle love.

—Unhappy man, said Candide, I too have had some experience of this love, the sovereign of hearts, the soul of our souls; and it never got me anything but a single kiss and twenty kicks in the rear. How could this lovely cause produce in you such a disgusting effect?

Pangloss replied as follows:—My dear Candide! you knew Paquette, that pretty maidservant to our august Baroness. In her arms I tasted the delights of paradise, which directly caused these torments of hell, from which I am now suffering. She was infected with the disease, and has perhaps died of it. Paquette received this present from an erudite Franciscan, who took the pains to trace it back to its source; for he had it from an elderly countess, who picked it up from a captain of cavalry, who acquired it from a marquise, who caught it from a page, who had received it from a Jesuit, who during his novitiate got it directly from one of the companions of Christopher Columbus. As for me, I shall not give it to anyone, for I am a dying man.

—Oh, Pangloss, cried Candide, that's a very strange genealogy. Isn't the devil at the root of the whole thing?

—Not at all, replied that great man; it's an indispensable part of the best of worlds, a necessary ingredient; if Columbus had not caught, on an American island, this sickness which attacks the source of generation and sometimes prevents generation entirely—which thus strikes at and defeats the greatest end of Nature herself—we should have neither chocolate nor cochineal. It must also be noted that until the present time this malady, like religious controversy, has been wholly confined to the continent of Europe. Turks, Indians, Persians, Chinese, Siamese, and Japanese know nothing of it as yet; but there is a sufficient reason for which they in turn will make its acquaintance in a couple of centuries. Meanwhile, it has made splendid progress among us, especially among those big armies of honest, well-trained mercenaries who decide the destinies of nations. You can be sure that when thirty thousand men fight a pitched battle against the same number of the enemy, there will be about twenty thousand with the pox on either side.

—Remarkable indeed, said Candide, but we must see about curing you.

—And how can I do that, said Pangloss, seeing I don't have a cent to my name? There's not a doctor in the whole world who will let your blood or give you an enema without demanding a fee. If you can't pay yourself, you must find someone to pay for you.

These last words decided Candide; he hastened to implore the help of his charitable Anabaptist, Jacques, and painted such a moving picture of his friend's wretched state that the good man did not hesitate to take in Pangloss and have him cured at his own expense. In the course of the cure, Pangloss lost only an eye and an ear. Since he wrote a fine hand and knew arithmetic, the Anabaptist made him his bookkeeper. At the end of two months, being obliged to go to Lisbon on business, he took his two philosophers on the boat with him. Pangloss still maintained that everything was for the best, but Jacques didn't agree with him.

—It must be, said he, that men have corrupted Nature, for they are not born wolves, yet that is what they become. God gave them neither twenty-four-pound cannon nor bayonets, yet they have manufactured both in order to destroy themselves. Bankruptcies have the same effect, and so does the justice which seizes the goods of bankrupts in order to prevent the creditors from getting them.[6]

—It was all indispensable, replied the one-eyed doctor, since private misfortunes make for public welfare, and therefore the more private misfortunes there are, the better everything is.

While he was reasoning, the air grew dark, the winds blew from all directions, and the vessel was attacked by a horrible tempest within sight of Lisbon harbor.

CHAPTER 5
Tempest, Shipwreck, Earthquake, and What Happened to Doctor Pangloss, Candide, and the Anabaptist, Jacques

Half of the passengers, weakened by the frightful anguish of sea-sickness and the distress of tossing about on stormy waters, were inca-

6. Voltaire had suffered losses from various bankruptcy proceedings.

pable of noticing their danger. The other half shrieked aloud and fell to their prayers, the sails were ripped to shreds, the masts snapped, the vessel opened at the seams. Everyone worked who could stir, nobody listened for orders or issued them. The Anabaptist was lending a hand in the after part of the ship when a frantic sailor struck him and knocked him to the deck; but just at that moment, the sailor lurched so violently that he fell head first over the side, where he hung, clutching a fragment of the broken mast. The good Jacques ran to his aid, and helped him to climb back on board, but in the process was himself thrown into the sea under the very eyes of the sailor, who allowed him to drown without even glancing at him. Candide rushed to the rail, and saw his benefactor rise for a moment to the surface, then sink forever. He wanted to dive to his rescue; but the philosopher Pangloss prevented him by proving that the bay of Lisbon had been formed expressly for this Anabaptist to drown in. While he was proving the point *a priori*, the vessel opened up and everyone perished except for Pangloss, Candide, and the brutal sailor who had caused the virtuous Anabaptist to drown; this rascal swam easily to shore, while Pangloss and Candide drifted there on a plank.

When they had recovered a bit of energy, they set out for Lisbon; they still had a little money with which they hoped to stave off hunger after escaping the storm.

Scarcely had they set foot in the town, still bewailing the loss of their benefactor, when they felt the earth quake underfoot; the sea was lashed to a froth, burst into the port, and smashed all the vessels lying at anchor there. Whirlwinds of fire and ash swirled through the streets and public squares; houses crumbled, roofs came crashing down on foundations, foundations split; thirty thousand inhabitants of every age and either sex were crushed in the ruins.[7] The sailor whistled through his teeth, and said with an oath,—There'll be something to pick up here.

—What can be the sufficient reason of this phenomenon? asked Pangloss.

—The Last Judgment is here, cried Candide.

But the sailor ran directly into the middle of the ruins, heedless of danger in his eagerness for gain; he found some money, laid violent hands on it, got drunk, and, having slept off his wine, bought the favors of the first streetwalker he could find amid the ruins of smashed houses, amid corpses and suffering victims on every hand. Pangloss however tugged at his sleeve.

—My friend, said he, this is not good form at all; your behavior falls short of that required by the universal reason; it's untimely, to say the least.

7. The great Lisbon earthquake and fire occurred on November 1, 1755; between thirty and forty thousand deaths resulted.

—Bloody hell, said the other, I'm a sailor, born in Batavia; I've been four times to Japan and stamped four times on the crucifix;[8] get out of here with your universal reason.

Some falling stonework had struck Candide; he lay prostrate in the street, covered with rubble, and calling to Pangloss:—For pity's sake bring me a little wine and oil; I'm dying.

—This earthquake is nothing novel, Pangloss replied; the city of Lima, in South America, underwent much the same sort of tremor, last year; same causes, same effects; there is surely a vein of sulphur under the earth's surface reaching from Lima to Lisbon.

—Nothing is more probable, said Candide; but, for God's sake, a little oil and wine.

—What do you mean, probable? replied the philosopher; I regard the case as proved.

Candide fainted and Pangloss brought him some water from a nearby fountain.

Next day, as they wandered amid the ruins, they found a little food which restored some of their strength. Then they fell to work like the others, bringing relief to those of the inhabitants who had escaped death. Some of the citizens whom they rescued gave them a dinner as good as was possible under the circumstances; it is true that the meal was a melancholy one, and the guests watered their bread with tears; but Pangloss consoled them by proving that things could not possibly be otherwise.

—For, said he, all this is for the best, since if there is a volcano at Lisbon, it cannot be somewhere else, since it is unthinkable that things should not be where they are, since everything is well.

A little man in black, an officer of the Inquisition,[9] who was sitting beside him, politely took up the question, and said:—It would seem that the gentleman does not believe in original sin, since if everything is for the best, man has not fallen and is not liable to eternal punishment.

—I most humbly beg pardon of your excellency, Pangloss answered, even more politely, but the fall of man and the curse of original sin entered necessarily into the best of all possible worlds.

—Then you do not believe in free will? said the officer.

—Your excellency must excuse me, said Pangloss; free will agrees very well with absolute necessity, for it was necessary that we should be free, since a will which is determined . . .

Pangloss was in the middle of his sentence, when the officer nod-

8. The Japanese, originally receptive to foreign visitors, grew fearful that priests and proselytizers were merely advance agents of empire, and expelled both the Portuguese and Spanish early in the seventeenth century. Only the Dutch were allowed to retain a small foothold, under humiliating conditions, of which the notion of stamping on the crucifix is symbolic. It was never what Voltaire suggests here, an actual requirement for entering the country.	9. Specifically, a *familier* or *poursuivant*, an undercover agent with powers of arrest.

ded significantly to the attendant who was pouring him a glass of port, or Oporto, wine.

CHAPTER 6
How They Made a Fine Auto-da-Fé to Prevent Earthquakes, and How Candide Was Whipped

After the earthquake had wiped out three quarters of Lisbon, the learned men of the land could find no more effective way of averting total destruction than to give the people a fine auto-da-fé;[1] the University of Coimbra had established that the spectacle of several persons being roasted over a slow fire with full ceremonial rites is an infallible specific against earthquakes.

In consequence, the authorities had rounded up a Biscayan convicted of marrying a woman who had stood godmother to his child, and two Portuguese who while eating a chicken had set aside a bit of bacon used for seasoning.[2] After dinner, men came with ropes to tie up Doctor Pangloss and his disciple Candide, one for talking and the other for listening with an air of approval; both were taken separately to a set of remarkably cool apartments, where the glare of the sun is never bothersome; eight days later they were both dressed in *sanbenitos* and crowned with paper mitres;[3] Candide's mitre and *sanbenito* were decorated with inverted flames and with devils who had neither tails nor claws; but Pangloss's devils had both tails and claws, and his flames stood upright. Wearing these costumes, they marched in a procession, and listened to a very touching sermon, followed by a beautiful concert of plainsong. Candide was flogged in cadence to the music; the Biscayan and the two men who had avoided bacon were burned, and Pangloss was hanged, though hanging is not customary. On the same day there was another earthquake, causing frightful damage.[4]

Candide, stunned, stupefied, despairing, bleeding, trembling, said to himself:—If this is the best of all possible worlds, what are the others like? The flogging is not so bad, I was flogged by the Bulgars. But oh my dear Pangloss, greatest of philosophers, was it necessary for me to watch you being hanged, for no reason that I can see? Oh my dear Anabaptist, best of men, was it necessary that you should be drowned in the port? Oh Miss Cunégonde, pearl of young ladies, was it necessary that you should have your belly slit open?

He was being led away, barely able to stand, lectured, lashed,

1. Literally, "act of faith," a public ceremony of repentance and humiliation. Such an auto-da-fé was actually held in Lisbon, June 20, 1756.   2. The Biscayan's fault lay in marrying someone within the forbidden bounds of relationship, an act of spiritual incest. The men who declined pork or bacon were understood to be crypto-Jews.   3. The cone-shaped paper cap (intended to resemble a bishop's mitre) and flowing yellow cape were customary garb for those pleading before the Inquisition.   4. In fact, the second quake occurred December 21, 1755.

absolved, and blessed, when an old woman approached and said,—
My son, be of good cheer and follow me.

CHAPTER 7

*How an Old Woman Took Care of Candide, and How He
Regained What He Loved*

Candide was of very bad cheer, but he followed the old woman to
a shanty; she gave him a jar of ointment to rub himself, left him food
and drink; she showed him a tidy little bed; next to it was a suit of
clothing.

—Eat, drink, sleep, she said; and may Our Lady of Atocha, Our
Lord St. Anthony of Padua, and Our Lord St. James of Compostela
watch over you. I will be back tomorrow.

Candide, still completely astonished by everything he had seen
and suffered, and even more by the old woman's kindness, offered
to kiss her hand.

—It's not *my* hand you should be kissing, said she. I'll be back
tomorrow; rub yourself with the ointment, eat and sleep.

In spite of his many sufferings, Candide ate and slept. Next day
the old woman returned bringing breakfast; she looked at his back
and rubbed it herself with another ointment; she came back with
lunch; and then she returned in the evening, bringing supper. Next
day she repeated the same routine.

—Who are you? Candide asked continually. Who told you to be
so kind to me? How can I ever repay you?

The good woman answered not a word; she returned in the evening, and without food.

—Come with me, says she, and don't speak a word.

Taking him by the hand, she walks out into the countryside with
him for about a quarter of a mile; they reach an isolated house, quite
surrounded by gardens and ditches. The old woman knocks at a little
gate, it opens. She takes Candide up a secret stairway to a gilded
room furnished with a fine brocaded sofa; there she leaves him, closes
the door, disappears. Candide stood as if entranced; his life, which
had seemed like a nightmare so far, was now starting to look like a
delightful dream.

Soon the old woman returned; on her feeble shoulder leaned a
trembling woman, of a splendid figure, glittering in diamonds, and
veiled.

—Remove the veil, said the old woman to Candide.

The young man stepped timidly forward, and lifted the veil. What
an event! What a surprise! Could it be Miss Cunégonde? Yes, it
really was! She herself! His knees give way, speech fails him, he falls
at her feet, Cunégonde collapses on the sofa. The old woman plies

them with brandy, they return to their senses, they exchange words. At first they could utter only broken phrases, questions and answers at cross purposes, sighs, tears, exclamations. The old woman warned them not to make too much noise, and left them alone.

—Then it's really you, said Candide, you're alive, I've found you again in Portugal. Then you never were raped? You never had your belly ripped open, as the philosopher Pangloss assured me?

—Oh yes, said the lovely Cunégonde, but one doesn't always die of these two accidents.

—But your father and mother were murdered then?

—All too true, said Cunégonde, in tears.

—And your brother?

—Killed too.

—And why are you in Portugal? and how did you know I was here? and by what device did you have me brought to this house?

—I shall tell you everything, the lady replied; but first you must tell me what has happened to you since that first innocent kiss we exchanged and the kicking you got because of it.

Candide obeyed her with profound respect; and though he was overcome, though his voice was weak and hesitant, though he still had twinges of pain from his beating, he described as simply as possible everything that had happened to him since the time of their separation. Cunégonde lifted her eyes to heaven; she wept at the death of the good Anabaptist and at that of Pangloss; after which she told the following story to Candide, who listened to every word while he gazed on her with hungry eyes.

CHAPTER 8
Cunégonde's Story

—I was in my bed and fast asleep when heaven chose to send the Bulgars into our castle of Thunder-Ten-Tronckh. They butchered my father and brother, and hacked my mother to bits. An enormous Bulgar, six feet tall, seeing that I had swooned from horror at the scene, set about raping me; at that I recovered my senses, I screamed and scratched, bit and fought, I tried to tear the eyes out of the big Bulgar—not realizing that everything which had happened in my father's castle was a mere matter of routine. The brute then stabbed me with a knife on my left thigh, where I still bear the scar.

—What a pity! I should very much like to see it, said the simple Candide.

—You shall, said Cunégonde; but shall I go on?

—Please do, said Candide.

So she took up the thread of her tale:—A Bulgar captain appeared, he saw me covered with blood and the soldier too intent to get up.

Shocked by the monster's failure to come to attention, the captain killed him on my body. He then had my wound dressed, and took me off to his quarters, as a prisoner of war. I laundered his few shirts and did his cooking; he found me attractive, I confess it, and I won't deny that he was a handsome fellow, with a smooth, white skin; apart from that, however, little wit, little philosophical training; it was evident that he had not been brought up by Doctor Pangloss. After three months, he had lost all his money and grown sick of me; so he sold me to a Jew named Don Issachar, who traded in Holland and Portugal, and who was mad after women. This Jew developed a mighty passion for my person, but he got nowhere with it; I held him off better than I had done with the Bulgar soldier; for though a person of honor may be raped once, her virtue is only strengthened by the experience. In order to keep me hidden, the Jew brought me to his country house, which you see here. Till then I had thought there was nothing on earth so beautiful as the castle of Thunder-Ten-Tronckh; I was now undeceived.

—One day the Grand Inquisitor took notice of me at mass; he ogled me a good deal, and made known that he must talk to me on a matter of secret business. I was taken to his palace; I told him of my rank; he pointed out that it was beneath my dignity to belong to an Israelite. A suggestion was then conveyed to Don Issachar that he should turn me over to My Lord the Inquisitor. Don Issachar, who is court banker and a man of standing, refused out of hand. The inquisitor threatened him with an auto-da-fé. Finally my Jew, fearing for his life, struck a bargain by which the house and I would belong to both of them as joint tenants; the Jew would get Mondays, Wednesdays, and the Sabbath, the inquisitor would get the other days of the week. That has been the arrangement for six months now. There have been quarrels; sometimes it has not been clear whether the night from Saturday to Sunday belonged to the old or the new dispensation. For my part, I have so far been able to hold both of them off; and that, I think, is why they are both still in love with me.

—Finally, in order to avert further divine punishment by earthquake, and to terrify Don Issachar, My Lord the Inquisitor chose to celebrate an auto-da-fé. He did me the honor of inviting me to attend. I had an excellent seat; the ladies were served with refreshments between the mass and the execution. To tell you the truth, I was horrified to see them burn alive those two Jews and that decent Biscayan who had married his child's godmother; but what was my surprise, my terror, my grief, when I saw, huddled in a *san-benito* and wearing a mitre, someone who looked like Pangloss! I rubbed my eyes, I watched his every move, I saw him hanged; and I fell back in a swoon. Scarcely had I come to my senses again, when I saw you stripped for the lash; that was the peak of my horror, consternation, grief, and despair. I may tell you, by the way, that your skin is even whiter and more delicate than that of my Bulgar captain. Seeing you, then, redoubled the torments which were already over-whelming me. I shrieked aloud, I wanted to call out, 'Let him go, you brutes!' but my voice died within me, and my cries would have been useless. When you had been thoroughly thrashed: 'How can it be,' I asked myself, 'that agreeable Candide and wise Pangloss have come to Lisbon, one to receive a hundred whiplashes, the other to be hanged by order of My Lord the Inquisitor, whose mistress I am? Pangloss must have deceived me cruelly when he told me that all is for the best in this world.'

—Frantic, exhausted, half out of my senses, and ready to die of weakness, I felt as if my mind were choked with the massacre of my father, my mother, my brother, with the arrogance of that ugly Bul-gar soldier, with the knife slash he inflicted on me, my slavery, my cookery, my Bulgar captain, my nasty Don Issachar, my abominable inquisitor, with the hanging of Doctor Pangloss, with that great plainsong *miserere* which they sang while they flogged you—and above all, my mind was full of the kiss which I gave you behind the screen, on the day I saw you for the last time. I praised God, who had brought you back to me after so many trials. I asked my old woman to look out for you, and to bring you here as soon as she could. She did just as I asked; I have had the indescribable joy of seeing you again, hearing you and talking with you once more. But you must be frightfully hungry; I am, myself; let us begin with a dinner.

So then and there they sat down to table; and after dinner, they adjourned to that fine brocaded sofa, which has already been men-tioned; and there they were when the eminent Don Issachar, one of the masters of the house, appeared. It was the day of the Sabbath; he was arriving to assert his rights and express his tender passion.

CHAPTER 9

What Happened to Cunégonde, Candide, the Grand Inquisitor, and a Jew

This Issachar was the most choleric Hebrew seen in Israel since the Babylonian captivity.

—What's this, says he, you bitch of a Christian, you're not satis-fied with the Grand Inquisitor? Do I have to share you with this rascal, too?

So saying, he drew a long dagger, with which he always went armed, and, supposing his opponent defenceless, flung himself on Candide. But our good Westphalian had received from the old woman, along with his suit of clothes, a fine sword. Out it came, and though his manners were of the gentlest, in short order he laid the Israelite stiff and cold on the floor, at the feet of the lovely Cunégonde.

—Holy Virgin! she cried. What will become of me now? A man killed in my house! If the police find out, we're done for.

—If Pangloss had not been hanged, said Candide, he would give us good advice in this hour of need, for he was a great philosopher. Lacking him, let's ask the old woman.

She was a sensible body, and was just starting to give her opinion of the situation, when another little door opened. It was just one o'clock in the morning, Sunday morning. This day belonged to the inquisitor. In he came, and found the whipped Candide with a sword in his hand, a corpse at his feet, Cunégonde in terror, and an old woman giving them both good advice.

Here now is what passed through Candide's mind in this instant of time; this is how he reasoned:—If this holy man calls for help, he will certainly have me burned, and perhaps Cunégonde as well; he has already had me whipped without mercy; he is my rival; I have already killed once; why hesitate?

It was a quick, clear chain of reasoning; without giving the inquisitor time to recover from his surprise, he ran him through, and laid him beside the Jew.

—Here you've done it again, said Cunégonde; there's no hope for us now. We'll be excommunicated, our last hour has come. How is it that you, who were born so gentle, could kill in two minutes a Jew and a prelate?

—My dear girl, replied Candide, when a man is in love, jealous, and just whipped by the Inquisition, he is no longer himself.

The old woman now spoke up and said:—There are three Andalusian steeds in the stable, with their saddles and bridles; our brave Candide must get them ready: my lady has some gold coin and diamonds; let's take to horse at once, though I can only ride on one buttock; we will go to Cadiz. The weather is as fine as can be, and it is pleasant to travel in the cool of the evening.

Promptly, Candide saddled the three horses. Cunégonde, the old woman, and he covered thirty miles without a stop. While they were fleeing, the Holy Brotherhood[5] came to investigate the house; they buried the inquisitor in a fine church, and threw Issachar on the dunghill.

Candide, Cunégonde, and the old woman were already in the little town of Avacena, in the middle of the Sierra Morena; and there, as they sat in a country inn, they had this conversation.

5. A semireligious order with police powers, very active in eighteenth-century Spain.

CHAPTER 10
In Deep Distress, Candide, Cunégonde, and the Old Woman
Reach Cadiz; They Put to Sea

—Who then could have robbed me of my gold and diamonds? said Cunégonde, in tears. How shall we live? what shall we do? where shall I find other inquisitors and Jews to give me some more?

—Ah, said the old woman, I strongly suspect that reverend Franciscan friar who shared the inn with us yesterday at Badajoz. God save me from judging him unfairly! But he came into our room twice, and he left long before us.

—Alas, said Candide, the good Pangloss often proved to me that the fruits of the earth are a common heritage of all, to which each man has equal right. On these principles, the Franciscan should at least have left us enough to finish our journey. You have nothing at all, my dear Cunégonde?

—Not a maravedi, said she.

—What to do? said Candide.

—We'll sell one of the horses, said the old woman; I'll ride on the croup behind my mistress, though only on one buttock, and so we will get to Cadiz.

There was in the same inn a Benedictine prior; he bought the horse cheap. Candide, Cunégonde, and the old woman passed through Lucena, Chillas, and Lebrixa, and finally reached Cadiz. There a fleet was being fitted out and an army assembled, to reason with the Jesuit fathers in Paraguay, who were accused of fomenting among their flock a revolt against the kings of Spain and Portugal near the town of St. Sacrement.[6] Candide, having served in the Bulgar army, performed the Bulgar manual of arms before the general of the little army with such grace, swiftness, dexterity, fire, and agility, that they gave him a company of infantry to command. So here he is, a captain; and off he sails with Miss Cunégonde, the old woman, two valets, and the two Andalusian steeds which had belonged to My Lord the Grand Inquisitor of Portugal.

Throughout the crossing, they spent a great deal of time reasoning about the philosophy of poor Pangloss.

—We are destined, in the end, for another universe, said Candide; no doubt that is the one where everything is well. For in this one, it must be admitted, there is some reason to grieve over our physical and moral state.

—I love you with all my heart, said Cunégonde; but my soul is

---

6. Actually, Colonia del Sacramento. Voltaire took great interest in the Jesuit role in Paraguay, which he has much oversimplified and largely misrepresented here in the interests of his satire. In 1750 they did, however, offer armed resistance to an agreement made between Spain and Portugal. They were subdued and expelled in 1769.

still harrowed by thoughts of what I have seen and suffered.

—All will be well, replied Candide; the sea of this new world is already better than those of Europe, calmer and with steadier winds. Surely it is the New World which is the best of all possible worlds.

—God grant it, said Cunégonde; but I have been so horribly unhappy in the world so far, that my heart is almost dead to hope.

—You pity yourselves, the old woman told them; but you have had no such misfortunes as mine.

Cunégonde nearly broke out laughing; she found the old woman comic in pretending to be more unhappy than she.

—Ah, you poor old thing, said she, unless you've been raped by two Bulgars, been stabbed twice in the belly, seen two of your castles destroyed, witnessed the murder of two of your mothers and two of your fathers, and watched two of your lovers being whipped in an auto-da-fé, I do not see how you can have had it worse than me. Besides, I was born a baroness, with seventy-two quarterings, and I have worked in a scullery.

—My lady, replied the old woman, you do not know my birth and rank; and if I showed you my rear end, you would not talk as you do, you might even speak with less assurance.

These words inspired great curiosity in Candide and Cunégonde, which the old woman satisfied with this story.

CHAPTER 11
The Old Woman's Story

—My eyes were not always bloodshot and red-rimmed, my nose did not always touch my chin, and I was not born a servant. I am in fact the daughter of Pope Urban the Tenth and the Princess of Palestrina.[7] Till the age of fourteen, I lived in a palace so splendid that all the castles of all your German barons would not have served it as a stable; a single one of my dresses was worth more than all the assembled magnificence of Westphalia. I grew in beauty, in charm, in talent, surrounded by pleasures, dignities, and glowing visions of the future. Already I was inspiring the young men to love; my breast was formed—and what a breast! white, firm, with the shape of the Venus de Medici; and what eyes! what lashes, what black brows! What fire flashed from my glances and outshone the glitter of the stars, as the local poets used to tell me! The women who helped me dress and undress fell into ecstasies, whether they looked at me from in front or behind; and all the men wanted to be in their place.

—I was engaged to the ruling prince of Massa-Carrara; and what

7. Voltaire left behind a comment on this passage, a note first published in 1829: "Note the extreme discretion of the author; hitherto there has never been a pope named Urban X; he avoided attributing a bastard to a known pope. What circumspection! what an exquisite conscience!"

a prince he was! as handsome as I, softness and charm compounded, brilliantly witty, and madly in love with me. I loved him in return as one loves for the first time, with a devotion approaching idolatry. The wedding preparations had been made, with a splendor and magnificence never heard of before; nothing but celebrations, masks, and comic operas, uninterruptedly; and all Italy composed in my honor sonnets of which not one was even passable. I had almost attained the very peak of bliss, when an old marquise who had been the mistress of my prince invited him to her house for a cup of chocolate. He died in less than two hours, amid horrifying convulsions. But that was only a trifle. My mother, in complete despair (though less afflicted than I), wished to escape for a while the oppressive atmosphere of grief. She owned a handsome property near Gaeta.[8] We embarked on a papal galley gilded like the altar of St. Peter's in Rome. Suddenly a pirate ship from Salé swept down and boarded us. Our soldiers defended themselves as papal troops usually do; falling on their knees and throwing down their arms, they begged of the corsair absolution *in articulo mortis.*[9]

—They were promptly stripped as naked as monkeys, and so was my mother, and so were our maids of honor, and so was I too. It's a very remarkable thing, the energy these gentlemen put into stripping people. But what surprised me even more was that they stuck their fingers in a place where we women usually admit only a syringe. This ceremony seemed a bit odd to me, as foreign usages always do when one hasn't traveled. They only wanted to see if we didn't have some diamonds hidden there; and I soon learned that it's a custom of long standing among the genteel folk who swarm the seas. I learned that my lords the very religious knights of Malta never overlook this ceremony when they capture Turks, whether male or female; it's one of those international laws which have never been questioned.

—I won't try to explain how painful it is for a young princess to be carried off into slavery in Morocco with her mother. You can imagine everything we had to suffer on the pirate ship. My mother was still very beautiful; our maids of honor, our mere chambermaids, were more charming than anything one could find in all Africa. As for myself, I was ravishing, I was loveliness and grace supreme, and I was a virgin. I did not remain so for long; the flower which had been kept for the handsome prince of Massa-Carrara was plucked by the corsair captain; he was an abominable negro, who thought he was doing me a great favor. My Lady the Princess of Palestrina and I must have been strong indeed to bear what we did during our journey to Morocco. But on with my story; these are such common matters that they are not worth describing.

8. About halfway between Rome and Naples.   9. Literally, when at the point of death. Absolution from a corsair in the act of murdering one is of very dubious validity.

—Morocco was knee deep in blood when we arrived. Of the fifty sons of the emperor Muley-Ismael,[1] each had his faction, which produced in effect fifty civil wars, of blacks against blacks, of blacks against browns, halfbreeds against halfbreeds; thoughout the length and breadth of the empire, nothing but one continual carnage.

—Scarcely had we stepped ashore, when some negroes of a faction hostile to my captor arrived to take charge of his plunder. After the diamonds and gold, we women were the most prized possessions. I was now witness of a struggle such as you never see in the temperate climate of Europe. Northern people don't have hot blood; they don't feel the absolute fury for women which is common in Africa. Europeans seem to have milk in their veins; it is vitriol or liquid fire which pulses through these people around Mount Atlas. The fight for possession of us raged with the fury of the lions, tigers, and poisonous vipers of that land. A Moor snatched my mother by the right arm, the first mate held her by the left; a Moorish soldier grabbed one leg, one of our pirates the other. In a moment's time almost all our girls were being dragged four different ways. My captain held me behind him while with his scimitar he killed everyone who braved his fury. At last I saw all our Italian women, including my mother, torn to pieces, cut to bits, murdered by the monsters who were fighting over them. My captive companions, their captors, soldiers, sailors, blacks, browns, whites, mulattoes, and at last my captain, all were killed, and I remained half dead on a mountain of corpses. Similar scenes were occurring, as is well known, for more than three hundred leagues around, without anyone skimping on the five prayers a day decreed by Mohammed.

—With great pain, I untangled myself from this vast heap of bleeding bodies, and dragged myself under a great orange tree by a neighboring brook, where I collapsed, from terror, exhuastion, horror, despair, and hunger. Shortly, my weary mind surrendered to a sleep which was more of a swoon than a rest. I was in this state of weakness and languor, between life and death, when I felt myself touched by something which moved over my body. Opening my eyes, I saw a white man, rather attractive, who was groaning and saying under his breath: '*O che sciagura d'essere senza coglioni!*'[2]

CHAPTER 12
The Old Woman's Story Continued

—Amazed and delighted to hear my native tongue, and no less surprised by what this man was saying, I told him that there were

---

1. Having reigned for more than fifty years, a potent and ruthless sultan of Morocco, he died in 1727 and left his kingdom in much the condition described.　2. "Oh what a misfortune to have no testicles!"

worse evils than those he was complaining of. In a few words, I
described to him the horrors I had undergone, and then fainted again.
He carried me to a nearby house, put me to bed, gave me something
to eat, served me, flattered me, comforted me, told me he had never
seen anyone so lovely, and added that he had never before regretted
so much the loss of what nobody could give him back.

'I was born at Naples, he told me, where they caponize two or
three thousand children every year; some die of it, others acquire a
voice more beautiful than any woman's, still others go on to become
governors of kingdoms.[3] The operation was a great success with me,
and I became court musician to the Princess of Palestrina . . .'

'Of my mother,' I exclaimed.

'Of your mother,' cried he, bursting into tears; 'then you must be
the princess whom I raised till she was six, and who already gave
promise of becoming as beautiful as you are now!'

'I am that very princess; my mother lies dead, not a hundred yards
from here, buried under a pile of corpses.'

—I told him my adventures, he told me his: that he had been sent
by a Christian power to the King of Morocco, to conclude a treaty
granting him gunpowder, cannon, and ships with which to liquidate
the traders of the other Christian powers.

'My mission is concluded,' said this honest eunuch; 'I shall take
ship at Ceuta and bring you back to Italy. *Ma che sciagura d'essere
senza coglioni!*'

—I thanked him with tears of gratitude, and instead of returning
me to Italy, he took me to Algiers and sold me to the dey of that
country. Hardly had the sale taken place, when that plague which
has made the rounds of Africa, Asia, and Europe broke out in full
fury at Algiers. You have seen earthquakes; but tell me, young lady,
have you ever had the plague?

—Never, replied the baroness.

—If you had had it, said the old woman, you would agree that it
is far worse than an earthquake. It is very frequent in Africa, and I
had it. Imagine, if you will, the situation of a pope's daughter, fifteen
years old, who in three months' time had experienced poverty, slavery, had been raped almost every day, had seen her mother quartered, had suffered from famine and war, and who now was dying of
pestilence in Algiers. As a matter of fact, I did not die; but the eunuch
and the dey and nearly the entire seraglio of Algiers perished.

—When the first horrors of this ghastly plague had passed, the
slaves of the dey were sold. A merchant bought me and took me to
Tunis; there he sold me to another merchant, who resold me at
Tripoli; from Tripoli I was sold to Alexandria, from Alexandria resold

---

3. The castrato Farinelli (1705–1782), originally a singer, came to exercise considerable political
influence on the Kings of Spain, Philip V and Ferdinand VI.

to Smyrna, from Smyrna to Constantinople. I ended by belonging
to an aga of janizaries, who was shortly ordered to defend Azov against
the besieging Russians.[4]

—The aga, who was a gallant soldier, took his whole seraglio with
him, and established us in a little fort amid the Maeotian marshes,[5]
guarded by two black eunuchs and twenty soldiers. Our side killed a
prodigious number of Russians, but they paid us back nicely. Azov
was put to fire and sword without respect for age or sex; only our little
fort continued to resist, and the enemy determined to starve us out.
The twenty janizaries had sworn never to surrender. Reduced to the
last extremities of hunger, they were forced to eat our two eunuchs,
lest they violate their oaths. After several more days, they decided to
eat the women too.

—We had an imam,[6] very pious and sympathetic, who delivered
an excellent sermon, persuading them not to kill us altogether.

'Just cut off a single rumpsteak from each of these ladies,' he said,
'and you'll have a fine meal. Then if you should need another, you
can come back in a few days and have as much again; heaven will
bless your charitable action, and you will be saved.'

—His eloquence was splendid, and he persuaded them. We
underwent this horrible operation. The imam treated us all with the
ointment that they use on newly circumcised children. We were at
the point of death.

—Scarcely had the janizaries finished the meal for which we furnished the materials, when the Russians appeared in flat-bottomed
boats; not a janizary escaped. The Russians paid no attention to the
state we were in; but there are French physicians everywhere, and
one of them, who knew his trade, took care of us. He cured us, and
I shall remember all my life that when my wounds were healed, he
made me a proposition. For the rest, he counselled us simply to have
patience, assuring us that the same thing had happened in several
other sieges, and that it was according to the laws of war.

—As soon as my companions could walk, we were herded off to
Moscow. In the division of booty, I fell to a boyar who made me
work in his garden, and gave me twenty whiplashes a day; but when
he was broken on the wheel after about two years, with thirty other
boyars, over some little court intrigue,[7] I seized the occasion; I ran
away; I crossed all Russia; I was for a long time a chambermaid in
Riga, then at Rostock, Vismara, Leipzig, Cassel, Utrecht, Leyden,
The Hague, Rotterdam; I grew old in misery and shame, having only

---

4. Azov, near the mouth of the Don, was besieged by the Russians under Peter the Great in
1695–1696. *Janizaries:* An élite corps of the Ottoman armies.   5. The Roman name of the so-
called Sea of Azov, a shallow swampy lake near the town.   6. In effect, a chaplain.   7. Voltaire
had in mind an ineffectual conspiracy against Peter the Great known as the "revolt of the streltsy"
or musketeers, which took place in 1698. Though easily put down, it provoked from the emperor
a massive and atrocious program of reprisals.

half a backside and remembering always that I was the daughter of a Pope; a hundred times I wanted to kill myself, but always I loved life more. This ridiculous weakness is perhaps one of our worst instincts; is anything more stupid than choosing to carry a burden that really one wants to cast on the ground? to hold existence in horror, and yet to cling to it? to fondle the serpent which devours us till it has eaten out our heart?

—In the countries through which I have been forced to wander, in the taverns where I have had to work, I have seen a vast number of people who hated their existence; but I never saw more than a dozen who deliberately put an end to their own misery: three negroes, four Englishmen, four Genevans, and a German professor named Robeck.[8] My last post was as servant to the Jew Don Issachar; he attached me to your service, my lovely one; and I attached myself to your destiny, till I have become more concerned with your fate than with my own. I would not even have mentioned my own misfortunes, if you had not irked me a bit, and if it weren't the custom, on shipboard, to pass the time with stories. In a word, my lady, I have had some experience of the world, I know it; why not try this diversion? Ask every passenger on this ship to tell you his story, and if you find a single one who has not often cursed the day of his birth, who has not often told himself that he is the most miserable of men, then you may throw me overboard head first.

CHAPTER 13
How Candide Was Forced to Leave the Lovely Cunégonde and the Old Woman

Having heard out the old woman's story, the lovely Cunégonde paid her the respects which were appropriate to a person of her rank and merit. She took up the wager as well, and got all the passengers, one after another, to tell her their adventures. She and Candide had to agree that the old woman had been right.

—It's certainly too bad, said Candide, that the wise Pangloss was hanged, contrary to the custom of autos-da-fé; he would have admirable things to say of the physical evil and moral evil which cover land and sea, and I might feel within me the impulse to dare to raise several polite objections.

As the passengers recited their stories, the boat made steady progress, and presently landed at Buenos Aires. Cunégonde, Captain Candide, and the old woman went to call on the governor, Don Fernando d'Ibaraa y Figueroa y Mascarenes y Lampourdos y Souza. This nobleman had the pride appropriate to a man with so many

8. Johann Robeck (1672–1739) published a treatise advocating suicide and showed his conviction by drowning himself at the age of 67.

names. He addressed everyone with the most aristocratic disdain, pointing his nose so loftily, raising his voice so mercilessly, lording it so splendidly, and assuming so arrogant a pose, that everyone who met him wanted to kick him. He loved women to the point of fury; and Cunégonde seemed to him the most beautiful creature he had ever seen. The first thing he did was to ask directly if she were the captain's wife. His manner of asking this question disturbed Candide; he did not dare say she was his wife, because in fact she was not; he did not dare say she was his sister, because she wasn't that either; and though this polite lie was once common enough among the ancients,[9] and sometimes serves moderns very well, he was too pure of heart to tell a lie.

—Miss Cunégonde, said he, is betrothed to me, and we humbly beg your excellency to perform the ceremony for us.

Don Fernando d'Ibaraa y Figueroa y Mascarenes y Lampourdos y Souza twirled his moustache, smiled sardonically, and ordered Captain Candide to go drill his company. Candide obeyed. Left alone with My Lady Cunégonde, the governor declared his passion, and protested that he would marry her tomorrow, in church or in any other manner, as it pleased her charming self. Cunégonde asked for a quarter-hour to collect herself, consult the old woman, and make up her mind.

The old woman said to Cunégonde:—My lady, you have seventy-two quarterings and not one penny; if you wish, you may be the wife of the greatest lord in South America, who has a really handsome moustache; are you going to insist on your absolute fidelity? You have already been raped by the Bulgars; a Jew and an inquisitor have enjoyed your favors; miseries entitle one to privileges. I assure you that in your position I would make no scruple of marrying My Lord the Governor, and making the fortune of Captain Candide.

While the old woman was talking with all the prudence of age and experience, there came into the harbor a small ship bearing an alcalde and some alguazils.[1] This is what had happened.

As the old woman had very shrewdly guessed, it was a long-sleeved Franciscan who stole Cunégonde's gold and jewels in the town of Badajoz, when she and Candide were in flight. The monk tried to sell some of the gems to a jeweler, who recognized them as belonging to the Grand Inquisitor. Before he was hanged, the Franciscan confessed that he had stolen them, indicating who his victims were and where they were going. The flight of Cunégonde and Candide was already known. They were traced to Cadiz, and a vessel was hastily dispatched in pursuit of them. This vessel was now in the port of Buenos Aires. The rumor spread that an alcalde was aboard, in

9. Voltaire has in mind Abraham's adventures with Sarah (Genesis 12) and Isaac's with Rebecca (Genesis 26). 1. Police officers.

pursuit of the murderers of My Lord the Grand Inquisitor. The shrewd old woman saw at once what was to be done.

—You cannot escape, she told Cunégonde, and you have nothing to fear. You are not the one who killed my lord, and, besides, the governor, who is in love with you, won't let you be mistreated. Sit tight.

And then she ran straight to Candide:—Get out of town, she said, or you'll be burned within the hour.

There was not a moment to lose; but how to leave Cunégonde, and where to go?

CHAPTER 14
How Candide and Cacambo Were Received by the Jesuits of Paraguay

Candide had brought from Cadiz a valet of the type one often finds in the provinces of Spain and in the colonies. He was one quarter Spanish, son of a halfbreed in the Tucuman;[2] he had been choirboy, sacristan, sailor, monk, merchant, soldier, and lackey. His name was Cacambo, and he was very fond of his master because his master was a very good man. In hot haste he saddled the two Andalusian steeds.

—Hurry, master, do as the old woman says; let's get going and leave this town without a backward look.

Candide wept:—O my beloved Cunégonde! must I leave you now, just when the governor is about to marry us! Cunégonde, brought from so far, what will ever become of you?

—She'll become what she can, said Cacambo; women can always find something to do with themselves; God sees to it; let's get going.

—Where are you taking me? where are we going? what will we do without Cunégonde? said Candide.

—By Saint James of Compostela, said Cacambo, you were going to make war against the Jesuits, now we'll go make war for them. I know the roads pretty well, I'll bring you to their country, they will be delighted to have a captain who knows the Bulgar drill; you'll make a prodigious fortune. If you don't get your rights in one world, you will find them in another. And isn't it pleasant to see new things and do new things?

—Then you've already been in Paraguay? said Candide.

—Indeed I have, replied Cacambo; I was cook in the College of the Assumption, and I know the government of Los Padres[3] as I know the streets of Cadiz. It's an admirable thing, this government. The kingdom is more than three hundred leagues across; it is divided into thirty provinces. Los Padres own everything in it, and the people

2. A province of Argentina, to the northwest of Buenos Aires.   3. The Jesuit father.

nothing; it's a masterpiece of reason and justice. I myself know nothing so wonderful as Los Padres, who in this hemisphere make war on the kings of Spain and Portugal, but in Europe hear their confessions; who kill Spaniards here, and in Madrid send them to heaven; that really tickles me; let's get moving, you're going to be the happiest of men. Won't Los Padres be delighted when they learn they have a captain who knows the Bulgar drill!

As soon as they reached the first barricade, Cacambo told the frontier guard that a captain wished to speak with My Lord the Commander. A Paraguayan officer ran to inform headquarters by laying the news at the feet of the commander. Candide and Cacambo were first disarmed and deprived of their Andalusian horses. They were then placed between two files of soldiers; the commander was at the end, his three-cornered hat on his head, his cassock drawn up, a sword at his side, and a pike in his hand. He nods, and twenty-four soldiers surround the newcomers. A sergeant then informs them that they must wait, that the commander cannot talk to them, since the reverend father provincial has forbidden all Spaniards from speaking, except in his presence, and from remaining more than three hours in the country.

—And where is the reverend father provincial? says Cacambo.

—He is reviewing his troops after having said mass, the sergeant replies, and you'll only be able to kiss his spurs in three hours.

—But, says Cacambo, my master the captain, who, like me, is dying from hunger, is not Spanish at all, he is German; can't we have some breakfast while waiting for his reverence?

The sergeant promptly went off to report this speech to the commander.

—God be praised, said this worthy; since he is German, I can talk to him; bring him into my bower.

Candide was immediately led into a leafy nook surrounded by a handsome colonnade of green and gold marble and trellises amid which sported parrots, birds of paradise,[4] hummingbirds, guinea fowl, and all the rarest species of birds. An excellent breakfast was prepared in golden vessels; and while the Paraguayans ate corn out of wooden bowls in the open fields under the glare of the sun, the reverend father commander entered into his bower.

He was a very handsome young man, with an open face, rather blonde in coloring, with ruddy complexion, arched eyebrows, liquid eyes, pink ears, bright red lips, and an air of pride, but a pride somehow different from that of a Spaniard or a Jesuit. Their confiscated

4. In this passage and several later ones, Voltaire uses in conjunction two words, both of which mean hummingbird. The French system of classifying hummingbirds, based on the work of the celebrated Buffon, distinguishes *oiseaux-mouches* with straight bills from *colibris* with curved bills. This distinction is wholly fallacious. Hummingbirds have all manner of shaped bills, and the division of species must be made on other grounds entirely. At the expense of ornithological accuracy, I have therefore introduced birds of paradise to get the requisite sense of glitter and sheen.

weapons were restored to Candide and Cacambo, as well as their Andalusian horses; Cacambo fed them oats alongside the bower, always keeping an eye on them for fear of an ambush.

First Candide kissed the hem of the commander's cassock, then they sat down at the table.

—So you are German? said the Jesuit, speaking in that language.

—Yes, your reverence, said Candide.

As they spoke these words, both men looked at one another with great surprise, and another emotion which they could not control.

—From what part of Germany do you come? said the Jesuit.

—From the nasty province of Westphalia, said Candide; I was born in the castle of Thunder-Ten-Tronckh.

—Merciful heavens! cries the commander. Is it possible?

—What a miracle! exclaims Candide.

—Can it be you? asks the commander.

—It's impossible, says Candide.

They both fall back in their chairs, they embrace, they shed streams of tears.

—What, can it be you, reverend father! you, the brother of the lovely Cunégonde! you, who were killed by the Bulgars! you, the son of My Lord the Baron! you, a Jesuit in Paraguay! It's a mad world, indeed it is. Oh, Pangloss! Pangloss! how happy you would be, if you hadn't been hanged.

The commander dismissed his negro slaves and the Paraguayans who served his drink in crystal goblets. He thanked God and Saint Ignatius a thousand times, he clasped Candide in his arms, their faces were bathed in tears.

—You would be even more astonished, even more delighted, even more beside yourself, said Candide, if I told you that My Lady Cunégonde, your sister, who you thought was disemboweled, is enjoying good health.

—Where?

—Not far from here, in the house of the governor of Buenos Aires; and to think that I came to make war on you!

Each word they spoke in this long conversation added another miracle. Their souls danced on their tongues, hung eagerly at their ears, glittered in their eyes. As they were Germans, they sat a long time at table, waiting for the reverend father provincial; and the commander spoke in these terms to his dear Candide.

CHAPTER 15
How Candide Killed the Brother of His Dear Cunégonde

—All my life long I shall remember the horrible day when I saw my father and mother murdered and my sister raped. When the Bulgars left, that adorable sister of mine was nowhere to be found;

so they loaded a cart with my mother, my father, myself, two serving
girls, and three little murdered boys, to carry us all off for burial in
a Jesuit chapel some two leagues from our ancestral castle. A Jesuit
sprinkled us with holy water; it was horribly salty, and a few drops
got into my eyes; the father noticed that my lid made a little tremor;
putting his hand on my heart, he felt it beat; I was rescued, and at
the end of three weeks was as good as new. You know, my dear
Candide, that I was a very pretty boy; I became even more so; the
reverend father Croust,[5] superior of the abbey, conceived a most
tender friendship for me; he accepted me as a novice, and shortly
after, I was sent to Rome. The Father General had need of a resup-
ply of young German Jesuits. The rulers of Paraguay accept as few
Spanish Jesuits as they can; they prefer foreigners, whom they think
they can control better. I was judged fit, by the Father General, to
labor in this vineyard. So we set off, a Pole, a Tyrolean, and myself.
Upon our arrival, I was honored with the posts of subdeacon and
lieutenant; today I am a colonel and a priest. We are giving a vigorous reception to the King of Spain's men; I assure you they will be
excommunicated as well as trounced on the battlefield. Providence
has sent you to help us. But is it really true that my dear sister,
Cunégonde, is in the neighborhood, with the governor of Buenos
Aires?

Candide reassured him with a solemn oath that nothing could be
more true. Their tears began to flow again.

The baron could not weary of embracing Candide; he called him
his brother, his savior.

—Ah, my dear Candide, said he, maybe together we will be able
to enter the town as conquerors, and be united with my sister Cunégonde.

—That is all I desire, said Candide; I was expecting to marry her,
and I still hope to.

—You insolent dog, replied the baron, you would have the effron-
tery to marry my sister, who has seventy-two quarterings! It's a piece
of presumption for you even to mention such a crazy project in my
presence.

Candide, terrified by this speech, answered:—Most reverend father,
all the quarterings in the world don't affect this case; I have rescued
your sister out of the arms of a Jew and an inquisitor; she has many
obligations to me, she wants to marry me. Master Pangloss always
taught me that men are equal; and I shall certainly marry her.

—We'll see about that, you scoundrel, said the Jesuit baron of
Thunder-Ten-Tronckh; and so saying, he gave him a blow across
the face with the flat of his sword. Candide immediately drew his

---

5. A Jesuit rector at Colmar with whom Voltaire had quarreled in 1754.

own sword and thrust it up to the hilt in the baron's belly; but as he drew it forth all dripping, he began to weep.

—Alas, dear God! said he, I have killed my old master, my friend, my brother-in-law; I am the best man in the world, and here are three men I've killed already, and two of the three were priests.

Cacambo, who was standing guard at the entry of the bower, came running.

—We can do nothing but sell our lives dearly, said his master; someone will certainly come; we must die fighting.

Cacambo, who had been in similar scrapes before, did not lose his head; he took the Jesuit's cassock, which the commander had been wearing, and put it on Candide; he stuck the dead man's square hat on Candide's head, and forced him onto horseback. Everything was done in the wink of an eye.

—Let's ride, master; everyone will take you for a Jesuit on his way to deliver orders; and we will have passed the frontier before anyone can come after us.

Even as he was pronouncing these words, he charged off, crying in Spanish: —Way, make way for the reverend father colonel!

CHAPTER 16

What Happened to the Two Travelers with Two Girls,
Two Monkeys, and the Savages Named Biglugs

Candide and his valet were over the frontier before anyone in the camp knew of the death of the German Jesuit. Foresighted Cacambo had taken care to fill his satchel with bread, chocolate, ham, fruit, and several bottles of wine. They pushed their Andalusian horses forward into unknown country, where there were no roads. Finally a broad prairie divided by several streams opened before them. Our two travelers turned their horses loose to graze; Cacambo suggested that they eat too, and promptly set the example. But Candide said:
—How can you expect me to eat ham when I have killed the son of My Lord the Baron, and am now condemned never to see the lovely Cunégonde for the rest of my life? Why should I drag out my miserable days, since I must exist far from her in in the depths of despair and remorse? And what will the *Journal de Trévoux*[6] say of all this?

Though he talked this way, he did not neglect the food. Night fell. The two wanderers heard a few weak cries which seemed to be voiced by women. They could not tell whether the cries expressed grief or joy; but they leaped at once to their feet, with that uneasy suspicion which one always feels in an unknown country. The outcry arose from two girls, completely naked, who were running swiftly

6. A journal published by the Jesuit order, founded in 1701 and consistently hostile to Voltaire.

along the edge of the meadow, pursued by two monkeys who snapped
at their buttocks. Candide was moved to pity; he had learned marks-
manship with the Bulgars, and could have knocked a nut off a bush
without touching the leaves. He raised his Spanish rifle, fired twice,
and killed the two monkeys.

—God by praised, my dear Cacambo! I've saved these two poor
creatures from great danger. Though I committed a sin in killing an
inquisitor and a Jesuit, I've redeemed myself by saving the lives of
two girls. Perhaps they are two ladies of rank, and this good deed
may gain us special advantages in the country.

He had more to say, but his mouth shut suddenly when he saw
the girls embracing the monkeys tenderly, weeping over their bodies, and filling the air with lamentations.

—I wasn't looking for quite so much generosity of spirit, said he
to Cacambo; the latter replied: —You've really fixed things this time,
master; you've killed the two lovers of these young ladies.

—Their lovers! Impossible! You must be joking, Cacambo; how
can I believe you?

—My dear master, Cacambo replied, you're always astonished by
everything. Why do you think it so strange that in some countries
monkeys succeed in obtaining the good graces of women? They are
one quarter human, just as I am one quarter Spanish.

—Alas, Candide replied, I do remember now hearing Master Pangloss say that such things used to happen, and that from these mix-
tures there arose pans, fauns, and satyrs, and that these creatures had
appeared to various grand figures of antiquity; but I took all that for
fables.

—You should be convinced now, said Cacambo; it's true, and you
see how people make mistakes who haven't received a measure of
education. But what I fear is that these girls may get us into real
trouble.

These sensible reflections led Candide to leave the field and to
hide in a wood. There he dined with Cacambo; and there both of
them, having duly cursed the inquisitor of Portugal, the governor of
Buenos Aires, and the baron, went to sleep on a bed of moss. When
they woke up, they found themselves unable to move; the reason was
that during the night the Biglugs,[7] natives of the country, to whom
the girls had complained of them, had tied them down with cords of
bark. They were surrounded by fifty naked Biglugs, armed with arrows,
clubs, and stone axes. Some were boiling a caldron of water, others
were preparing spits, and all cried out: —It's a Jesuit, a Jesuit! We'll

7. Voltaire's name is "Oreillons" from Spanish "Orejones," a name mentioned in Garcilaso de
Vega's *Historia General del Perú* (1609), on which Voltaire drew from many of the details in his
picture of South America.

be revenged and have a good meal; let's eat some Jesuit, eat some Jesuit!

—I told you, my dear master, said Cacambo sadly, I said those two girls would play us a dirty trick.

Candide, noting the caldron and spits, cried out: —We are surely going to be roasted or boiled. Ah, what would Master Pangloss say if he could see these men in a state of nature? All is for the best, I agree; but I must say it seems hard to have lost Miss Cunégonde and to be stuck on a spit by the Biglugs.

Cacambo did not lose his head.

—Don't give up hope, said he to the disconsolate Candide; I understand a little of the jargon these people speak, and I'm going to talk to them.

—Don't forget to remind them, said Candide, of the frightful inhumanity of eating their fellow men, and that Christian ethics forbid it.

—Gentlemen, said Cacambo, you have a mind to eat a Jesuit today? An excellent idea; nothing is more proper than to treat one's enemies so. Indeed, the law of nature teaches us to kill our neighbor, and that's how men behave the whole world over. Though we Europeans don't exercise our right to eat our neighbors, the reason is simply that we find it easy to get a good meal elsewhere; but you don't have our resources, and we certainly agree that it's better to eat your enemies than to let the crows and vultures have the fruit of your victory. But, gentlemen, you wouldn't want to eat your friends. You think you will be spitting a Jesuit, and it's your defender, the enemy of your enemies, whom you will be roasting. For my part, I was born in your country; the gentleman whom you see is my master, and far from being a Jesuit, he has just killed a Jesuit, the robe he is wearing was stripped from him; that's why you have taken a dislike to him. To prove that I am telling the truth, take his robe and bring it to the nearest frontier of the kingdom of Los Padres; find out for yourselves if my master didn't kill a Jesuit officer. It won't take long; if you find that I have lied, you can still eat us. But if I've told the truth, you know too well the principles of public justice, customs, and laws, not to spare our lives.

The Biglugs found this discourse perfectly reasonable; they appointed chiefs to go posthaste and find out the truth; the two messengers performed their task like men of sense, and quickly returned bringing good news. The Biglugs united their two prisoners, treated them with great politeness, offered them girls, gave them refreshments, and led them back to the border of their state, crying joyously: —He isn't a Jesuit, he isn't a Jesuit!

Candide could not weary of exclaiming over his preservation.

—What a people! he said. What men! what customs! If I had not had the good luck to run a sword through the body of Miss Cunégonde's brother, I would have been eaten on the spot! But, after all, it seems that uncorrupted nature is good, since these folk, instead of eating me, showed me a thousand kindnesses as soon as they knew I was not a Jesuit.

CHAPTER 17
Arrival of Candide and His Servant at the Country of Eldorado, and What They Saw There

When they were out of the land of the Biglugs, Cacambo said to Candide: —You see that this hemisphere is no better than the other; take my advice, and let's get back to Europe as soon as possible.

—How to get back, asked Candide, and where to go? If I go to my own land, the Bulgars and Abares are murdering everyone in sight; if I go to Portugal, they'll burn me alive; if we stay here, we risk being skewered any day. But how can I ever leave that part of the world where Miss Cunégonde lives?

—Let's go toward Cayenne, said Cacambo, we shall find some Frenchmen there, for they go all over the world; they can help us; perhaps God will take pity on us.

To get to Cayenne was not easy; they knew more or less which way to go, but mountains, rivers, cliffs, robbers, and savages obstructed the way everywhere. Their horses died of weariness; their food was eaten; they subsisted for one whole month on wild fruits, and at last they found themselves by a little river fringed with coconut trees, which gave them both life and hope.

Cacambo, who was as full of good advice as the old woman, said to Candide: —We can go no further, we've walked ourselves out; I see an abandoned canoe on the bank, let's fill it with coconuts, get into the boat, and float with the current; a river always leads to some inhabited spot or other. If we don't find anything pleasant, at least we may find something new.

—Let's go, said Candide, and let Providence be our guide.

They floated some leagues between banks sometimes flowery, sometimes sandy, now steep, now level. The river widened steadily; finally it disappeared into a chasm of frightful rocks that rose high into the heavens. The two travelers had the audacity to float with the current into this chasm. The river, narrowly confined, drove them onward with horrible speed and a fearful roar. After twenty-four hours, they saw daylight once more; but their canoe was smashed on the snags. They had to drag themselves from rock to rock for an entire league; at last they emerged to an immense horizon, ringed with remote mountains. The countryside was tended for pleasure as well as profit; everywhere the useful was joined to the agreeable. The roads were covered, or rather decorated, with elegantly shaped carriages made of a glittering material, carrying men and women of singular beauty, and drawn by great red sheep which were faster than the finest horses of Andalusia, Tetuan, and Mequinez.

—Here now, said Candide, is a country that's better than Westphalia.

Along with Cacambo, he climbed out of the river at the first village he could see. Some children of the town, dressed in rags of gold brocade, were playing quoits at the village gate; our two men from the other world paused to watch them; their quoits were rather large, yellow, red, and green, and they glittered with a singular luster. On a whim, the travelers picked up several; they were of gold, emeralds, and rubies, and the least of them would have been the greatest ornament of the Great Mogul's throne.

—Surely, said Cacambo, these quoit players are the children of the king of the country.

The village schoolmaster appeared at that moment, to call them back to school.

—And there, said Candide, is the tutor of the royal household.

The little rascals quickly gave up their game, leaving on the ground their quoits and playthings. Candide picked them up, ran to the schoolmaster, and presented them to him humbly, giving him to understand by sign language that their royal highnesses had forgotten their gold and jewels. With a smile, the schoolmaster tossed them to the ground, glanced quickly but with great surprise at Candide's face, and went his way.

The travelers did not fail to pick up the gold, rubies, and emeralds.

—Where in the world are we? cried Candide. The children of this land must be well trained, since they are taught contempt for gold and jewels.

Cacambo was as much surprised as Candide. At last they came to the finest house of the village; it was built like a European palace. A crowd of people surrounded the door, and even more were in the entry; delightful music was heard, and a delicious aroma of cooking filled the air. Cacambo went up to the door, listened, and reported that they were talking Peruvian; that was his native language, for every reader must know that Cacambo was born in Tucuman, in a village where they talk that language exclusively.

—I'll act as interpreter, he told Candide; it's an hotel, let's go in.

Promptly two boys and two girls of the staff, dressed in cloth of gold, and wearing ribbons in their hair, invited them to sit at the host's table. The meal consisted of four soups, each one garnished with a brace of parakeets, a boiled condor which weighed two hundred pounds, two roast monkeys of an excellent flavor, three hundred birds of paradise in one dish and six hundred hummingbirds in another, exquisite stews, delicious pastries, the whole thing served up in plates of what looked like rock crystal. The boys and girls of the staff poured them various beverages made from sugar cane.

The diners were for the most part merchants and travelers, all extremely polite, who questioned Cacambo with the most discreet circumspection, and answered his questions very directly.

When the meal was over, Cacambo as well as Candide supposed he could settle his bill handsomely by tossing onto the table two of those big pieces of gold which they had picked up; but the host and hostess burst out laughing, and for a long time nearly split their sides. Finally they subsided.

—Gentlemen, said the host, we see clearly that you're foreigners; we don't meet many of you here. Please excuse our laughing when you offered us in payment a couple of pebbles from the roadside. No doubt you don't have any of our local currency, but you don't need it to eat here. All the hotels established for the promotion of commerce are maintained by the state. You have had meager entertainment here, for we are only a poor town; but everywhere else you will be given the sort of welcome you deserve.

Cacambo translated for Candide all the host's explanations, and Candide listened to them with the same admiration and astonishment that his friend Cacambo showed in reporting them.

—What is this country, then, said they to one another, unknown to the rest of the world, and where nature itself is so different from our own? This probably is the country where everything is for the best; for it's absolutely necessary that such a country should exist somewhere. And whatever Master Pangloss said of the matter, I have often had occasion to notice that things went badly in Westphalia.

CHAPTER 18
What They Saw in the Land of Eldorado

Cacambo revealed his curiosity to the host, and the host told him: —I am an ignorant man and content to remain so; but we have here an old man, retired from the court, who is the most knowing person in the kingdom, and the most talkative.

Thereupon he brought Cacambo to the old man's house. Candide now played second fiddle, and acted as servant to his own valet. They entered an austere little house, for the door was merely of silver and the paneling of the rooms was only gold, though so tastefully wrought that the finest paneling would not surpass it. If the truth must be told, the lobby was only decorated with rubies and emeralds;

but the patterns in which they were arranged atoned for the extreme simplicity.

The old man received the two strangers on a sofa stuffed with bird-of-paradise feathers, and offered them several drinks in diamond carafes; then he satisfied their curiosity in these terms.

—I am a hundred and seventy-two years old, and I heard from my late father, who was liveryman to the king, about the astonishing revolutions in Peru which he had seen. Our land here was formerly part of the kingdom of the Incas, who rashly left it in order to conquer another part of the world, and who were ultimately destroyed by the Spaniards. The wisest princes of their house were those who had never left their native valley; they decreed, with the consent of the nation, that henceforth no inhabitant of our little kingdom should ever leave it; and this rule is what has preserved our innocence and our happiness. The Spaniards heard vague rumors about this land, they called it El Dorado;[8] and an English knight named Raleigh even came somewhere close to it about a hundred years ago; but as we are surrounded by unscalable mountains and precipices, we have managed so far to remain hidden from the rapacity of the European nations, who have an inconceivable rage for the pebbles and mud of our land, and who, in order to get some, would butcher us all to the last man.

The conversation was a long one; it turned on the form of the government, the national customs, on women, public shows, the arts. At last Candide, whose taste always ran to metaphysics, told Cacambo to ask if the country had any religion.

The old man grew a bit red.

—How's that? he said. Can you have any doubt of it? Do you suppose we are altogether thankless scoundrels?

Cacambo asked meekly what was the religion of Eldorado. The old man flushed again.

—Can there be two religions? he asked. I suppose our religion is the same as everyone's, we worship God from morning to evening.

—Then you worship a single deity? said Cacambo, who acted throughout as interpreter of the questions of Candide.

—It's obvious, said the old man, that there aren't two or three or four of them. I must say the people of your world ask very remarkable questions.

Candide could not weary of putting questions to this good old man; he wanted to know how the people of Eldorado prayed to God.

—We don't pray to him at all, said the good and respectable sage;

8. The myth of this land of gold somewhere in Central or South America had been widespread since the sixteenth century. *The Discovery of Guiana*, published in 1595, described Sir Walter Raleigh's infatuation with the myth of Eldorado and served to spread the story still further.

we have nothing to ask him for, since everything we need has already been granted; we thank God continually.

Candide was interested in seeing the priests; he had Cacambo ask where they were. The old gentleman smiled.

—My friends, said he, we are all priests; the king and all the heads of household sing formal psalms of thanksgiving every morning, and five or six thousand voices accompany them.

—What! you have no monks to teach, argue, govern, intrigue, and burn at the stake everyone who disagrees with them?

—We should have to be mad, said the old man; here we are all of the same mind, and we don't understand what you're up to with your monks.

Candide was overjoyed at all these speeches, and said to himself:
—This is very different from Westphalia and the castle of My Lord the Baron; if our friend Pangloss had seen Eldorado, he wouldn't have called the castle of Thunder-Ten-Tronckh the finest thing on earth; to know the world one must travel.

After this long conversation, the old gentleman ordered a carriage with six sheep made ready, and gave the two travelers twelve of his servants for their journey to the court.

—Excuse me, said he, if old age deprives me of the honor of accompanying you. The king will receive you after a style which will not altogether displease you, and you will doubtless make allowance for the customs of the country if there are any you do not like.

Candide and Cacambo climbed into the coach; the six sheep flew like the wind, and in less than four hours they reached the king's palace at the edge of the capital. The entryway was two hundred and twenty feet high and a hundred wide; it is impossible to describe all the materials of which it was made. But you can imagine how much finer it was than those pebbles and sand which we call gold and jewels.

Twenty beautiful girls of the guard detail welcomed Candide and Cacambo as they stepped from the carriage, took them to the baths, and dressed them in robes woven of humming-bird feathers; then the high officials of the crown, both male and female, led them to the royal chamber between two long lines, each of a thousand musicians, as is customary. As they approached the throne room, Cacambo asked an officer what was the proper method of greeting his majesty: if one fell to one's knees or on one's belly; if one put one's hands on one's head or on one's rear; if one licked up the dust of the earth— in a word, what was the proper form?[9]

—The ceremony, said the officer, is to embrace the king and kiss him on both cheeks.

9. Candide's questions are probably derived from those of Gulliver on a similar occasion; see *Gulliver's Travels*, III ix.

Candide and Cacambo fell on the neck of his majesty, who received them with all the dignity imaginable, and asked them politely to dine.

In the interim, they were taken about to see the city, the public buildings rising to the clouds, the public markets and arcades, the fountains of pure water and of rose water, those of sugar cane liquors which flowed perpetually in the great plazas paved with a sort of stone which gave off odors of gillyflower and rose petals. Candide asked to see the supreme court and the hall of parliament; they told him there was no such thing, that lawsuits were unknown. He asked if there were prisons, and was told there were not. What surprised him more, and gave him most pleasure, was the palace of sciences, in which he saw a gallery two thousand paces long, entirely filled with mathematical and physical instruments.

Having passed the whole afternoon seeing only a thousandth part of the city, they returned to the king's palace. Candide sat down to dinner with his majesty, his own valet Cacambo, and several ladies. Never was better food served, and never did a host preside more jovially than his majesty. Cacambo explained the king's witty sayings to Candide, and even when translated they still seemed witty. Of all the things which astonished Candide, this was not, in his eyes, the least astonishing.

They passed a month in this refuge. Candide never tired of saying to Cacambo: —It's true, my friend, I'll say it again, the castle where I was born does not compare with the land where we now are; but Miss Cunégonde is not here, and you doubtless have a mistress somewhere in Europe. If we stay here, we shall be just like everybody else, whereas if we go back to our own world, taking with us just a dozen sheep loaded with Eldorado pebbles, we shall be richer than all the kings put together, we shall have no more inquisitors to fear, and we shall easily be able to retake Miss Cunégonde.

This harangue pleased Cacambo; wandering is such pleasure, it gives a man such prestige at home to be able to talk of what he has seen abroad, that the two happy men resolved to be so no longer, but to take their leave of his majesty.

—You are making a foolish mistake, the king told them; I know very well that my kingdom is nothing much; but when you are pretty comfortable somewhere, you had better stay there. Of course I have no right to keep strangers against their will, that sort of tyranny is not in keeping with our laws or our customs; all men are free; depart when you will, but the way out is very difficult. You cannot possibly go up the river by which you miraculously came; it runs too swiftly through its underground caves. The mountains which surround my land are ten thousand feet high, and steep as walls; each one is more than ten leagues across; the only way down is over precipices. But since you really must go, I shall order my engineers to make a machine which can carry you conveniently. When we take you over the mountains, nobody will be able to go with you, for my subjects have sworn never to leave their refuge, and they are too sensible to break their vows. Other than that, ask of me what you please.

—We only request of your majesty, Cacambo said, a few sheep loaded with provisions, some pebbles, and some of the mud of your country.

The king laughed.

—I simply can't understand, said he, the passion you Europeans have for our yellow mud; but take all you want, and much good may it do you.

He promptly gave orders to his technicians to make a machine for lifting these two extraordinary men out of his kingdom. Three thousand good physicists worked at the problem; the machine was ready in two weeks' time, and cost no more than twenty million pounds sterling, in the money of the country. Cacambo and Candide were placed in the machine; there were two great sheep, saddled and bridled to serve them as steeds when they had cleared the mountains, twenty pack sheep with provisions, thirty which carried presents consisting of the rarities of the country, and fifty loaded with gold, jewels, and diamonds. The king bade tender farewell to the two vagabonds.

It made a fine spectacle, their departure, and the ingenious way in which they were hoisted with their sheep up to the top of the mountains. The technicians bade them good-bye after bringing them to safety, and Candide had now no other desire and no other object than to go and present his sheep to Miss Cunégonde.

—We have, said he, enough to pay off the governor of Buenos Aires—if, indeed, a price can be placed on Miss Cunégonde. Let us go to Cayenne, take ship there, and then see what kingdom we can find to buy up.

CHAPTER 19
What Happened to Them at Surinam, and How Candide Got to Know Martin

The first day was pleasant enough for our travelers. They were encouraged by the idea of possessing more treasures than Asia, Europe, and Africa could bring together. Candide, in transports, carved the name of Cunégonde on the trees. On the second day two of their sheep bogged down in a swamp and were lost with their loads; two other sheep died of fatigue a few days later; seven or eight others starved to death in a desert; still others fell, a little after, from precipices. Finally, after a hundred days' march, they had only two sheep left. Candide told Cacambo:—My friend, you see how the riches of

this world are fleeting; the only solid things are virtue and the joy of
seeing Miss Cunégonde again.

—I agree, said Cacambo, but we still have two sheep, laden with
more treasure than the king of Spain will ever have; and I see in the
distance a town which I suspect is Surinam; it belongs to the Dutch.
We are at the end of our trials and on the threshold of our happiness.

As they drew near the town, they discovered a negro stretched on
the ground with only half his clothes left, that is, a pair of blue
drawers; the poor fellow was also missing his left leg and his right
hand.

—Good Lord, said Candide in Dutch, what are you doing in that
horrible condition, my friend?

—I am waiting for my master, Mr. Vanderdendur,[1] the famous
merchant, answered the negro.

—Is Mr. Vanderdendur, Candide asked, the man who treated you
this way?

—Yes, sir, said the negro, that's how things are around here. Twice
a year we get a pair of linen drawers to wear. If we catch a finger in
the sugar mill where we work, they cut off our hand; if we try to run
away, they cut off our leg: I have undergone both these experiences.
This is the price of the sugar you eat in Europe. And yet, when my
mother sold me for ten Patagonian crowns on the coast of Guinea,
she said to me: 'My dear child, bless our witch doctors, reverence
them always, they will make your life happy; you have the honor of
being a slave to our white masters, and in this way you are making
the fortune of your father and mother.' Alas! I don't know if I made
their fortunes, but they certainly did not make mine. The dogs,
monkeys, and parrots are a thousand times less unhappy than we
are. The Dutch witch doctors who converted me tell me every Sunday that we are all sons of Adam, black and white alike. I am no
genealogist; but if these preachers are right, we must all be remote
cousins; and you must admit no one could treat his own flesh and
blood in a more horrible fashion.

—Oh Pangloss! cried Candide, you had no notion of these abominations! I'm through, I must give up your optimism after all.

—What's optimism? said Cacambo.

—Alas, said Candide, it is a mania for saying things are well when
one is in hell.

And he shed bitter tears as he looked at his negro, and he was still
weeping as he entered Surinam.

The first thing they asked was if there was not some vessel in port

---

1. A name perhaps intended to suggest VanDuren, a Dutch bookseller with whom Voltaire had
quarreled. In particular, the incident of gradually raising one's price recalls VanDuren, to whom
Voltaire had successively offered 1,000, 1,500 2,000, and 3,000 florins for the return of the
manuscript of Frederick the Great's *Anti-Machiavel*.

which could be sent to Buenos Aires. The man they asked was a
Spanish merchant who undertook to make an honest bargain with
them. They arranged to meet in a café; Candide and the faithful
Cacambo, with their two sheep, went there to meet with him.

Candide, who always said exactly what was in his heart, told the
Spaniard of his adventures, and confessed that he wanted to recapture Miss Cunégonde.

—I shall take good care *not* to send you to Buenos Aires, said the
merchant; I should be hanged, and so would you. The lovely Cunégonde is his lordship's favorite mistress.

This was a thunderstroke for Candide; he wept for a long time;
finally he drew Cacambo aside.

—Here, my friend, said he, is what you must do. Each one of us
has in his pockets five or six millions' worth of diamonds; you are
cleverer than I; go get Miss Cunégonde in Buenos Aires. If the governor makes a fuss, give him a million; if that doesn't convince him,
give him two millions; you never killed an inquisitor, nobody will
suspect you. I'll fit out another boat and go wait for you in Venice.
That is a free country, where one need have no fear either of Bulgars
or Abares or Jews or inquisitors.

Cacambo approved of this wise decision. He was in despair at
leaving a good master who had become a bosom friend; but the pleasure of serving him overcame the grief of leaving him. They embraced,
and shed a few tears; Candide urged him not to forget the good old
woman. Cacambo departed that very same day; he was a very good
fellow, that Cacambo.

Candide remained for some time in Surinam, waiting for another
merchant to take him to Italy, along with the two sheep which were
left him. He hired servants and bought everything necessary for the
long voyage; finally Mr. Vanderdendur, master of a big ship, came
calling.

—How much will you charge, Candide asked this man, to take
me to Venice—myself, my servants, my luggage, and those two sheep
over there?

The merchant set a price of ten thousand piastres; Candide did
not blink an eye.

—Oh, ho, said the prudent Venderdendur to himself, this stranger
pays out ten thousand piastres at once, he must be pretty well fixed.

Then, returning a moment later, he made known that he could
not set sail under twenty thousand.

—All right, you shall have them, said Candide.

—Whew, said the merchant softly to himself, this man gives twenty
thousand piastres as easily as ten.

He came back again to say he could not go to Venice for less than
thirty thousand piastres.

—All right, thirty then, said Candide.

—Ah ha, said the Dutch merchant, again speaking to himself; so thirty thousand piastres mean nothing to this man; no doubt the two sheep are loaded with immense treasures; let's say no more; we'll pick up the thirty thousand piastres first, and then we'll see.

Candide sold two little diamonds, the least of which was worth more than all the money demanded by the merchant. He paid him in advance. The two sheep were taken aboard. Candide followed in a little boat, to board the vessel at its anchorage. The merchant bides his time, sets sail, and makes his escape with a favoring wind. Candide, aghast and stupified, soon loses him from view.

—Alas, he cries, now there is a trick worthy of the old world!

He returns to shore sunk in misery; for he had lost riches enough to make the fortunes of twenty monarchs.

Now he rushes to the house of the Dutch magistrate, and, being a bit disturbed, he knocks loudly at the door; goes in, tells the story of what happened, and shouts a bit louder than is customary. The judge begins by fining him ten thousand piastres for making such a racket; then he listens patiently to the story, promises to look into the matter as soon as the merchant comes back, and charges another ten thousand piastres as the costs of the hearing.

This legal proceeding completed the despair of Candide. In fact he had experienced miseries a thousand times more painful, but the coldness of the judge, and that of the merchant who had robbed him, roused his bile and plunged him into a black melancholy. The malice of men rose up before his spirit in all its ugliness, and his mind dwelt only on gloomy thoughts. Finally, when a French vessel was ready to leave for Bordeaux, since he had no more diamond-laden sheep to transport, he took a cabin at a fair price, and made it known in the town that he would pay passage and keep, plus two thousand piastres, to any honest man who wanted to make the journey with him, on condition that this man must be the most disgusted with his own condition and the most unhappy man in the province.

This drew such a crowd of applicants as a fleet could not have held. Candide wanted to choose among the leading candidates, so he picked out about twenty who seemed companionable enough, and of whom each pretended to be more miserable than all the others. He brought them together at his inn and gave them a dinner, on condition that each would swear to tell truthfully his entire history. He would select as his companion the most truly miserable and rightly discontented man, and among the others he would distribute various gifts.

The meeting lasted till four in the morning. Candide, as he listened to all the stories, remembered what the old woman had told him on the trip to Buenos Aires, and of the wager she had made, that there was nobody on the boat who had not undergone great misfortunes. At every story that was told him, he thought of Pangloss.

—That Pangloss, he said, would be hard put to prove his system. I wish he was here. Certainly if everything goes well, it is in Eldorado and not in the rest of the world.

At last he decided in favor of a poor scholar who had worked ten years for the booksellers of Amsterdam. He decided that there was no trade in the world with which one should be more disgusted.

This scholar, who was in fact a good man, had been robbed by his wife, beaten by his son, and deserted by his daughter, who had got herself abducted by a Portuguese. He had just been fired from the little job on which he existed; and the preachers of Surinam were persecuting him because they took him for a Socinian.[2] The others, it is true, were at least as unhappy as he, but Candide hoped the scholar would prove more amusing on the voyage. All his rivals declared that Candide was doing them a great injustice, but he pacified them with a hundred piastres apiece.

CHAPTER 20
What Happened to Candide and Martin at Sea

The old scholar, whose name was Martin, now set sail with Candide for Bordeaux. Both men had seen and suffered much; and even if the vessel had been sailing from Surinam to Japan via the Cape of Good Hope, they would have been able to keep themselves amused with instances of moral evil and physical evil during the entire trip.

However, Candide had one great advantage over Martin, that he still hoped to see Miss Cunégonde again, and Martin had nothing to hope for; besides, he had gold and diamonds, and though he had lost a hundred big red sheep loaded with the greatest treasures of the earth, though he had always at his heart a memory of the Dutch merchant's villainy, yet, when he thought of the wealth that remained in his hands, and when he talked of Cunégonde, especially just after a good dinner, he still inclined to the system of Pangloss.

—But what about you, Monsieur Martin, he asked the scholar, what do you think of all that? What is your idea of moral evil and physical evil?

—Sir, answered Martin, those priests accused me of being a Socinian, but the truth is that I am a Manichee.[3]

2. A follower of Faustus and Laelius Socinus, sixteenth-century Polish theologians, who proposed a form of "rational" Christianity which exalted the rational conscience and minimized such mysteries as the trinity. The Socinians, by a special irony, were vigorous optimists.   3. Mani, a Persian sage and philosopher of the third century A.D.., taught (probably under the influence of traditions stemming from Zoroaster and the worshippers of the sun god Mithra) that the earth is a field of dispute between two almost equal powers, one of light and one of darkness, both of which must be propitiated.

—You're joking, said Candide; there aren't any more Manichees in the world.

—There's me, said Martin; I don't know what to do about it, but I can't think otherwise.

—You must be possessed of the devil, said Candide.

—He's mixed up with so many things of this world, said Martin, that he may be in me as well as elsewhere; but I assure you, as I survey this globe, or globule, I think that God has abandoned it to some evil spirit—all of it except Eldorado. I have scarcely seen one town which did not wish to destroy its neighboring town, no family which did not wish to exterminate some other family. Everywhere the weak loathe the powerful, before whom they cringe, and the powerful treat them like brute cattle, to be sold for their meat and fleece. A million regimented assassins roam Europe from one end to the other, plying the trades of murder and robbery in an organized way for a living, because there is no more honest form of work for them; and in the cities which seem to enjoy peace and where the arts are flourishing, men are devoured by more envy, cares, and anxieties than a whole town experiences when it's under siege. Private griefs are worse even than public trials. In a word, I have seen so much and suffered so much, that I am a Manichee.

—Still there is some good, said Candide.

—That may be, said Martin, but I don't know it.

In the middle of this discussion, the rumble of cannon was heard. From minute to minute the noise grew louder. Everyone reached for his spyglass. At a distance of some three miles they saw two vessels fighting; the wind brought both of them so close to the French vessel that they had a pleasantly comfortable seat to watch the fight. Presently one of the vessels caught the other with a broadside so low and so square as to send it to the bottom. Candide and Martin saw clearly a hundred men on the deck of the sinking ship; they all raised their hands to heaven, uttering fearful shrieks; and in a moment everything was swallowed up.

—Well, said Martin, that is how men treat one another.

—It is true, said Candide, there's something devilish in this business.

As they chatted, he noticed something of a striking red color floating near the sunken vessel. They sent out a boat to investigate; it was one of his sheep. Candide was more joyful to recover this one sheep than he had been afflicted to lose a hundred of them, all loaded with big Eldorado diamonds.

The French captain soon learned that the captain of the victorious vessel was Spanish and that of the sunken vessel was a Dutch pirate. It was the same man who had robbed Candide. The enormous riches which this rascal had stolen were sunk beside him in the sea, and nothing was saved but a single sheep.

—You see, said Candide to Martin, crime is punished sometimes; this scoundrel of a Dutch merchant has met the fate he deserved.

—Yes, said Martin; but did the passengers aboard his ship have to perish too? God punished the scoundrel, and the devil drowned the others.

Meanwhile the French and Spanish vessels continued on their journey, and Candide continued his talks with Martin. They disputed for fifteen days in a row, and at the end of that time were just as much in agreement as at the beginning. But at least they were talking, they exchanged their ideas, they consoled one another. Candide caressed his sheep.

—Since I have found you again, said he, I may well rediscover Miss Cunégonde.

CHAPTER 21

Candide and Martin Approach the Coast of France: They Reason Together

At last the coast of France came in view.

—Have you ever been in France, Monsieur Martin? asked Candide.

—Yes, said Martin, I have visited several provinces. There are some where half the inhabitants are crazy, others where they are too sly, still others where they are quite gentle and stupid, some where they venture on wit; in all of them the principal occupation is love-making, the second is slander, and the third stupid talk.

—But, Monsieur Martin, were you ever in Paris?

—Yes, I've been in Paris; it contains specimens of all these types; it is a chaos, a mob, in which everyone is seeking pleasure and where hardly anyone finds it, at least from what I have seen. I did not live there for long; as I arrived, I was robbed of everything I possessed by thieves at the fair of St. Germain; I myself was taken for a thief, and spent eight days in jail, after which I took a proofreader's job to earn enough money to return on foot to Holland. I knew the writing gang, the intriguing gang, the gang with fits and convulsions.[4] They say there are some very civilized people in that town; I'd like to think so.

—I myself have no desire to visit France, said Candide; you no doubt realize that when one has spent a month in Eldorado, there is nothing else on earth one wants to see, except Miss Cunégonde. I am going to wait for her at Venice; we will cross France simply to get to Italy; wouldn't you like to come with me?

4. The Jansenists, a sect of strict Catholics, became notorious for spirtual ecstasies. Their public displays reached a height during the 1720s, and Voltaire described them in *Le Siècle de Louis XIV* (chap. 37), as well as in the article on "Convulsions" in the *Philosophical Dictionary*.

—Gladly, said Martin; they say Venice is good only for the Venetian nobles, but that on the other hand they treat foreigners very well when they have plenty of money. I don't have any; you do, so I'll follow you anywhere.

—By the way, said Candide, do you believe the earth was originally all ocean, as they assure us in that big book belonging to the ship's captain?[5]

—I don't believe that stuff, said Martin, nor any of the dreams which people have been peddling for some time now.

—But why, then, was this world formed at all? asked Candide.

—To drive us mad, answered Martin.

—Aren't you astonished, Candide went on, at the love which those two girls showed for the monkeys in the land of the Biglugs that I told you about?

—Not at all, said Martin, I see nothing strange in these sentiments; I have seen so many extraordinary things that nothing seems extraordinary any more.

—Do you believe, asked Candide, that men have always massacred one another as they do today? That they have always been liars, traitors, ingrates, thieves, weaklings, sneaks, cowards, backbiters, gluttons, drunkards, misers, climbers, killers, calumniators, sensualists, fanatics, hypocrites, and fools?

—Do you believe, said Martin, that hawks have always eaten pigeons when they could got them?

—Of course, said Condide.

—Well, said Martin, if hawks have always had the same character, why do you suppose that men have changed?

—Oh, said Candide, there's a great deal of difference, because freedom of the will . . .

As they were disputing in this manner, they reached Bordeaux.

CHAPTER 22
What Happened in France to Candide and Martin

Candide paused in Bordeaux only long enough to sell a couple of Dorado pebbles and to fit himself out with a fine two-seater carriage, for he could no longer do without his philosopher Martin; only he was very unhappy to part with his sheep, which he left to the academy of science in Bordeaux. They proposed, as the theme of that year's prize contest, the discovery of why the wool of the sheep was red; and the prize was awarded to a northern scholar[6] who demonstrated by A plus B minus C divided by Z that the sheep ought to be red and die of sheep rot.

5. The Bible: Genesis 1.   6. Maupertuis Le Lapon, philosopher and mathematician, whom Voltaire had accused of trying to adduce mathematical proofs of the existence of God.

But all the travelers with whom Candide talked in the roadside inns told him: —We are going to Paris.

This general consensus finally inspired in him too a desire to see the capital; it was not much out of his road to Venice.

He entered through the Faubourg Saint-Marceau,[7] and thought he was in the meanest village of Westphalia.

Scarcely was Candide in his hotel, when he came down with a mild illness caused by exhaustion. As he was wearing an enormous diamond ring, and people had noticed among his luggage a tremendously heavy safe, he soon found at his bedside two doctors whom he had not called, several intimate friends who never left him alone, and two pious ladies who helped to warm his broth. Martin said: — I remember that I too was ill on my first trip to Paris; I was very poor; and as I had neither friends, pious ladies, nor doctors, I got well.

However, as a result of medicines and bleedings, Candide's illness became serious. A resident of the neighborhood came to ask him politely to fill out a ticket, to be delivered to the porter of the other world.[8] Candide wanted nothing to do with it. The pious ladies assured him it was a new fashion; Candide replied that he wasn't a man of fashion. Martin wanted to throw the resident out the window. The cleric swore that without the ticket they wouldn't bury Candide. Martin swore that he would bury the cleric if he continued to be a nuisance. The quarrel grew heated; Martin took him by the shoulders and threw him bodily out the door; all of which caused a great scandal, from which developed a legal case.

Candide got better; and during his convalescence he had very good company in to dine. They played cards for money; and Candide was quite surprised that none of the aces were ever dealt to him, and Martin was not surprised at all.

Among those who did the honors of the town for Candide there was a little abbé from Perigord, one of those busy fellows, always bright, always useful, assured, obsequious, and obliging, who waylay passing strangers, tell them the scandal of the town, and offer them pleasures at any price they want to pay. This fellow first took Candide and Martin to the theatre. A new tragedy was being played. Candide found himself seated next to a group of wits. That did not keep him from shedding a few tears in the course of some perfectly played scenes. One of the commentators beside him remarked during the intermission: —You are quite mistaken to weep, this actress

---

7. A district on the left bank, notably grubby in the eighteenth century. "As I entered [Paris] through the Faubourg Saint-Marceau, I saw nothing but dirty stinking little streets, ugly black houses, a general air of squalor and poverty, beggars, carters, menders of clothes, sellers of herb-drinks and old hats." J.-J. Rousseau, *Confessions*, Book IV.   8. In the middle of the eighteenth century, it became customary to require persons who were grievously ill to sign *billets de confession*, without which they could not be given absolution, admitted to the last sacraments, or buried in consecrated ground.

is very bad indeed; the actor who plays with her is even worse; and the play is even worse than the actors in it. The author knows not a word of Arabic, though the action takes place in Arabia; and besides, he is a man who doesn't believe in innate ideas. Tomorrow I will show you twenty pamphlets written against him.

—Tell me, sir, said Candide to the abbé, how many plays are there for performance in France?

—Five or six thousand, replied the other.

—That's a lot, said Candide; how many of them are any good?

—Fifteen or sixteen, was the answer.

—That's a lot, said Martin.

Candide was very pleased with an actress who took the part of Queen Elizabeth in a rather dull tragedy[9] that still gets played from time to time.

—I like this actress very much, he said to Martin, she bears a slight resemblance to Miss Cunégonde; I should like to meet her.

The abbé from Perigord offered to introduce him. Candide, raised in Germany, asked what was the protocol, how one behaved in France with queens of England.

—You must distinguish, said the abbé; in the provinces, you take them to an inn; at Paris they are respected while still attractive, and thrown on the dunghill when they are dead.[1]

—Queens on the dunghill! said Candide.

—Yes indeed, said Martin, the abbé is right; I was in Paris when Miss Monime herself[2] passed, as they say, from this life to the other; she was refused what these folk call 'the honors of burial,' that is, the right to rot with all the beggars of the district in a dirty cemetery; she was buried all alone by her troupe at the corner of the Rue de Bourgogne; this must have been very disagreeable to her, for she had a noble character.

—That was extremely rude, said Candide.

—What do you expect? said Martin; that is how these folk are. Imagine all the contradictions, all the incompatibilities you can, and you will see them in the government, the courts, the churches, and the plays of this crazy nation.

—Is it true that they are always laughing in Paris? asked Candide.

—Yes, said the abbé, but with a kind of rage too; when people complain of things, they do so amid explosions of laughter; they even laugh as they perform the most detestable actions.

—Who was that fat swine, said Candide, who spoke so nastily

---

9. *Le Comte d'Essex* by Thomas Corneille.   1. Voltaire engaged in a long and vigorous campaign against the rule that actors and actresses could not be buried in consecrated ground. The superstition probably arose from a feeling that by assuming false identities they drained their own souls.   2. Adrienne Lecouvreur (1690–1730), so called because she made her debut as Monime in Racine's *Mithridate*. Voltaire had assisted at her secret midnight funeral and wrote an indignant poem about it.

about the play over which I was weeping, and the actors who gave me so much pleasure?

—He is a living illness, answered the abbé, who makes a business of slandering all the plays and books; he hates the successful ones, as eunuchs hate successful lovers; he's one of those literary snakes who live on filth and venom; he's a folliculator . . .

—What's this word *folliculator?* asked Candide.

—It's a folio filler, said the abbé, a Fréron.[3]

It was after this fashion that Candide, Martin, and the abbé from Perigord chatted on the stairway as they watched the crowd leaving the theatre.

—Although I'm in a great hurry to see Miss Cunégonde again, said Candide, I would very much like to dine with Miss Clairon,[4] for she seemed to me admirable.

The abbé was not the man to approach Miss Clairon, who saw only good company.

—She has an engagement tonight, he said; but I shall have the honor of introducing you to a lady of quality, and there you will get to know Paris as if you had lived here for years.

Candide, who was curious by nature, allowed himself to be brought to the lady's house, in the depths of the Faubourg St.-Honoré; they were playing faro;[5] twelve melancholy punters held in their hands a little sheaf of cards, blank summaries of their bad luck. Silence reigned supreme, the punters were pallid, the banker uneasy; and the lady of the house, seated beside the pitiless banker, watched with the eyes of a lynx for the various illegal redoublings and bets at long odds which the players tried to signal by folding the corners of their cards; she had them unfolded with a determination which was severe but polite, and concealed her anger lest she lose her customers. The lady caused herself to be known as the Marquise of Parolignac.[6] Her daughter, fifteen years old, sat among the punters and tipped off her mother with a wink to the sharp practices of these unhappy players when they tried to recoup their losses. The abbé from Perigord, Candide, and Martin came in; nobody arose or greeted them or looked at them; all were lost in the study of their cards.

—My Lady the Baroness of Thunder-Ten-Tronckh was more civil, thought Candide.

However, the abbé whispered in the ear of the marquise, who, half rising, honored Candide with a gracious smile and Martin with

<hr/>

3. A successful and popular journalist, who had attacked several of Voltaire's plays, including *Tancrède.*   4. Actually Claire Leris (1723–1803). She had played the lead role in *Tancrède* and was for many years a leading figure on the Paris stage.   5. A game of cards, about which it is necessary to know only that a number of punters play against a banker or dealer. The pack is dealt out two cards at a time, and each player may bet on any card as much as he pleases. The sharp practices of the punters consist essentially of tricks for increasing their winnings without corresponding risks.   6. A *paroli* is an illegal redoubling of one's bet; her name therefore implies a title grounded in cardsharping.

a truly noble nod; she gave a seat and dealt a hand of cards to Candide, who lost fifty thousand francs in two turns; after which they had a very merry supper. Everyone was amazed that Candide was not upset over his losses; the lackeys, talking together in their usual lackey language, said: —He must be some English milord.

The supper was like most Parisian suppers: first silence, then an indistinguishable rush of words; then jokes, mostly insipid, false news, bad logic, a little politics, a great deal of malice. They even talked of new books.

—Have you seen the new novel by Dr. Gauchat, the theologian?[7] asked the abbé from Perigord.

—Oh yes, answered one of the guests; but I couldn't finish it. We have a horde of impudent scribblers nowadays, but all of them put together don't match the impudence of this Gauchat, this doctor of theology. I have been so struck by the enormous number of detestable books which are swamping us that I have taken up punting at faro.

—And the *Collected Essays* of Archdeacon T——[8] asked the abbé, what do you think of them?

—Ah, said Madame de Parolignac, what a frightful bore he is! He takes such pains to tell you what everyone knows; he discourses so learnedly on matters which aren't worth a casual remark! He plunders, and not even wittily, the wit of other people! He spoils what he plunders, he's disgusting! But he'll never disgust me again; a couple of pages of the archdeacon have been enough for me.

There was at table a man of learning and taste, who supported the marquise on this point. They talked next of tragedies; the lady asked why there were tragedies which played well enough but which were wholly unreadable. The man of taste explained very clearly how a play could have a certain interest and yet little merit otherwise; he showed succinctly that it was not enough to conduct a couple of intrigues, such as one can find in any novel, and which never fail to excite the spectator's interest; but that one must be new without being grotesque, frequently touch the sublime but never depart from the natural; that one must know the human heart and give it words; that one must be a great poet without allowing any character in the play to sound like a poet; and that one must know the language perfectly, speak it purely, and maintain a continual harmony without ever sacrificing sense to mere sound.

—Whoever, he added, does not observe all these rules may write one or two tragedies which succeed in the theatre, but he will never

---

7. He had written against Voltaire, and Voltaire suspected him (wrongly) of having committed a novel, *L'Oracle des nouveaux philosophes*.   8. His name was Trublet, and he had said, among other disagreeable things, that Voltaire's epic poem, the *Henriade*, made him yawn and that Voltaire's genius was "the perfection of mediocrity."

be ranked among the good writers; there are very few good tragedies; some are idylls in well-written, well-rhymed dialogue, others are political arguments which put the audience to sleep, or revolting pompousities; still others are the fantasies of enthusiasts, barbarous in style, incoherent in logic, full of long speeches to the gods because the author does not know how to address men, full of false maxims and emphatic commonplaces.

Candide listened attentively to this speech and conceived a high opinion of the speaker; and as the marquise had placed him by her side, he turned to ask her who was this man who spoke so well.

—He is a scholar, said the lady, who never plays cards and whom the abbé sometimes brings to my house for supper; he knows all about tragedies and books, and has himself written a tragedy that was hissed from the stage and a book, the only copy of which ever seen outside his publisher's office was dedicated to me.

—What a great man, said Candide, he's Pangloss all over.

Then, turning to him, he said: —Sir, you doubtless think everything is for the best in the physical as well as the moral universe, and that nothing could be otherwise than as it is?

—Not at all, sir, replied the scholar, I believe nothing of the sort. I find that everything goes wrong in our world; that nobody knows his place in society or his duty, what he's doing or what he ought to be doing, and that outside of mealtimes, which are cheerful and congenial enough, all the rest of the day is spent in useless quarrels, as of Jansenists against Molinists,[9] parliament-men against churchmen, literary men against literary men, courtiers against courtiers, financiers against the plebs, wives against husbands, relatives against relatives—it's one unending warfare.

Candide answered: —I have seen worse; but a wise man, who has since had the misfortune to be hanged, taught me that everything was marvelously well arranged. Troubles are just the shadows in a beautiful picture.

—Your hanged philosopher was joking, said Martin; the shadows are horrible ugly blots.

—It is human beings who make the blots, said Candide, and they can't do otherwise.

—Then it isn't their fault, said Martin.

Most of the faro players, who understood this sort of talk not at all, kept on drinking; Martin disputed with the scholar, and Candide told part of his story to the lady of the house.

After supper, the marquise brought Candide into her room and sat him down on a divan.

9. The Jansenists (from Corneille Jansen, 1585–1638) were a relatively strict party of religious reform; the Molinists (from Luis Molina) were the party of the Jesuits. Their central issue of controversy was the relative importance of divine grace and human will to the salvation of man.

—Well, she said to him, are you still madly in love with Miss Cunégonde of Thunder-Ten-Tronckh?

—Yes, ma'am, replied Candide. The marquise turned upon him a tender smile.

—You answer like a young man of Westphalia, said she; a Frenchman would have told me: 'It is true that I have been in love with Miss Cunégonde; but since seeing you, madame, I fear that I love her no longer.'

—Alas, ma'am, said Candide, I will answer any way you want.

—Your passion for her, said the marquise, began when you picked up her handkerchief; I prefer that you should pick up my garter.

—Gladly, said Candide, and picked it up.

—But I also want you to put it back on, said the lady; and Candide put it on again.

—Look you now, said the lady, you are a foreigner; my Paris lovers I sometimes cause to languish for two weeks or so, but to you I surrender the very first night, because we must render the honors of the country to a young man from Westphalia.

The beauty, who had seen two enormous diamonds on the two hands of her young friend, praised them so sincerely that from the fingers of Candide they passed over to the fingers of the marquise.

As he returned home with his Perigord abbé, Candide felt some remorse at having been unfaithful to Miss Cunégonde; the abbé sympathized with his grief; he had only a small share in the fifty thousand francs which Candide lost at cards, and in the proceeds of the two diamonds which had been half-given, half-extorted. His scheme was to profit, as much as he could, from the advantage of knowing Candide. He spoke at length of Cunégonde, and Candide told him that he would beg forgiveness for his beloved for his infidelity when he met her at Venice.

The Perigordian overflowed with politeness and unction, taking a tender interest in everything Candide said, everything he did, and everything he wanted to do.

—Well, sir, said he, so you have an assignation at Venice?

—Yes indeed, sir, I do, said Candide; it is absolutely imperative that I go there to find Miss Cunégonde.

And then, carried away by the pleasure of talking about his love, he recounted, as he often did, a part of his adventures with that illustrious lady of Westphalia.

—I suppose, said the abbé, that Miss Cunégonde has a fine wit and writes charming letters.

—I never received a single letter from her, said Candide; for, as you can imagine, after being driven out of the castle for love of her, I couldn't write; shortly I learned that she was dead; then I rediscovered her; then I lost her again, and I have now sent, to a place more than twenty-five hundred leagues from here, a special agent whose return I am expecting.

The abbé listened carefully, and looked a bit dreamy. He soon took his leave of the two strangers, after embracing them tenderly. Next day Candide, when he woke up, received a letter, to the following effect:

—Dear sir, my very dear lover, I have been lying sick in this town for a week, I have just learned that you are here. I would fly to your arms if I could move. I heard that you had passed through Bordeaux; that was where I left the faithful Cacambo and the old woman, who are soon to follow me here. The governor of Buenos Aires took everything, but left me your heart. Come; your presence will either return me to life or cause me to die of joy.

This charming letter, coming so unexpectedly, filled Candide with inexpressible delight, while the illness of his dear Cunégonde covered him with grief. Torn between these two feelings, he took gold and diamonds, and had himself brought, with Martin, to the hotel where Miss Cunégonde was lodging. Trembling with emotion, he enters the room; his heart thumps, his voice breaks. He tries to open the curtains of the bed, he asks to have some lights.

—Absolutely forbidden, says the serving girl; light will be the death of her.

And abruptly she pulls shut the curtain.

—My dear Cunégonde, says Candide in tears, how are you feeling? If you can't see me, won't you at least speak to me?

—She can't talk, says the servant.

But then she draws forth from the bed a plump hand, over which Candide weeps a long time, and which he fills with diamonds, meanwhile leaving a bag of gold on the chair.

Amid his transports, there arrives a bailiff followed by the abbé from Perigord and a strong-arm squad.

—These here are the suspicious foreigners? says the officer; and he has them seized and orders his bullies to drag them off to jail.

—They don't treat visitors like this in Eldorado, says Candide.

—I am more a Manichee than ever, says Martin.

—But, please sir, where are you taking us? says Candide.

—To the lowest hole in the dungeons, says the bailiff.

Martin, having regained his self-possession, decided that the lady who pretended to be Cunégonde was a cheat, the abbé from Perigord was another cheat who had imposed on Candide's innocence, and the bailiff still another cheat, of whom it would be easy to get rid.

Rather than submit to the forms of justice, Candide, enlightened by Martin's advice and eager for his own part to see the real Cunégonde again, offered the bailiff three little diamonds worth about three thousand pistoles apiece.

—Ah, my dear sir! cried the man with the ivory staff, even if you have committed every crime imaginable, you are the most honest man in the world. Three diamonds! each one worth three thousand pistoles! My dear sir! I would gladly die for you, rather than take you to jail. All foreigners get arrested here; but let me manage it; I have a brother at Dieppe in Normandy; I'll take you to him; and if you have a bit of a diamond to give him, he'll take care of you, just like me.

—And why do they arrest all foreigners? asked Candide.

The abbé from Perigord spoke up and said: —It's because a beggar from Atrebatum[1] listened to some stupidities; that made him commit a parricide, not like the one of May, 1610, but like the one of December, 1594, much on the order of several other crimes committed in other years and other months by other beggars who had listened to stupidities.

The bailiff then explained what it was all about.[2]

—Foh! what beasts! cried Candide. What! monstrous behavior of this sort from a people who sing and dance? As soon as I can, let me get out of this country, where the monkeys provoke the tigers. In my own country I've lived with bears; only in Eldorado are there proper men. In the name of God, sir bailiff, get me to Venice where I can wait for Miss Cunégonde.

—I can only get you to Lower Normandy, said the guardsman.

He had the irons removed at once, said there had been a mistake, dismissed his gang, and took Candide and Martin to Dieppe, where he left them with his brother. There was a little Dutch ship at anchor. The Norman, changed by three more diamonds into the most helpful of men, put Candide and his people aboard the vessel, which was bound for Portsmouth in England. It wasn't on the way to Venice, but Candide felt like a man just let out of hell; and he hoped to get back on the road to Venice at the first possible occasion.

CHAPTER 23
*Candide and Martin Pass the Shores of England;
What They See There*

—Ah, Pangloss! Pangloss! Ah, Martin! Martin! Ah, my darling Cunégonde! What is this world of ours? sighed Candide on the Dutch vessel.

1. The Latin name for the district of Artois, from which came Robert-François Damiens, who tried to stab Louis XV in 1757. The assassination failed, like that of Châtel, who tried to kill Henri IV in 1594, but unlike that of Ravaillac, who succeeded in killing him in 1610.   2. The point, in fact, is not too clear since arresting foreigners is an indirect way at best to guard against home-grown fanatics, and the position of the abbé from Perigord in the whole transaction remains confused. Has he called in the officer just to get rid of Candide? If so, why is he sardonic about the very suspicions he is trying to foster? Candide's reaction is to the notion that Frenchmen should be capable of political assassination at all; it seems excessive.

—Something crazy, something abominable, Martin replied.

—You have been in England; are people as crazy there as in France?

—It's a different sort of crazy, said Martin. You know that these two nations have been at war over a few acres of snow near Canada, and that they are spending on this fine struggle more than Canada itself is worth.[3] As for telling you if there are more people in one country or the other who need a strait jacket, that is a judgment too fine for my understanding; I know only that the people we are going to visit are eaten up with melancholy.

As they chatted thus, the vessel touched at Portsmouth. A multitude of people covered the shore, watching closely a rather bulky man who was kneeling, his eyes blindfolded, on the deck of a man-of-war. Four soldiers, stationed directly in front of this man, fired three bullets apiece into his brain, as peaceably as you would want; and the whole assemblage went home, in great satisfaction.[4]

—What's all this about? asked Candide. What devil is everywhere at work?

He asked who was that big man who had just been killed with so much ceremony.

—It was an admiral, they told him.

—And why kill this admiral?

—The reason, they told him, is that he didn't kill enough people; he gave battle to a French admiral, and it was found that he didn't get close enough to him.

—But, said Candide, the French admiral was just as far from the English admiral as the English admiral was from the French admiral.

—That's perfectly true, came the answer; but in this country it is useful from time to time to kill one admiral in order to encourage the others.

Candide was so stunned and shocked at what he saw and heard, that he would not even set foot ashore; he arranged with the Dutch merchant (without even caring if he was robbed, as at Surinam) to be taken forthwith to Venice.

The merchant was ready in two days; they coasted along France, they passed within sight of Lisbon, and Candide quivered. They entered the straits, crossed the Mediterranean, and finally landed at Venice.

—God be praised, said Candide, embracing Martin; here I shall

---

3. The wars of the French and English over Canada dragged intermittently through the eighteenth century till the peace of Paris sealed England's conquest (1763). Voltaire thought the French should concentrate on developing Louisiana where the Jesuit influence was less marked.
4. Candide has witnessed the execution of Admiral John Byng, defeated off Minorca by the French fleet under Galisonnière and executed by firing squad on March 14, 1757. Voltaire had intervened to avert the execution.

recover the lovely Cunégonde. I trust Cacambo as I would myself. All is well, all goes well, all goes as well as possible.

CHAPTER 24
About Paquette and Brother Giroflée

As soon as he was in Venice, he had a search made for Cacambo in all the inns, all the cafés, all the stews—and found no trace of him. Every day he sent to investigate the vessels and coastal traders; no news of Cacambo.

—How's this? said he to Martin. I have had time to go from Surinam to Bordeaux, from Bordeaux to Paris, from Paris to Dieppe, from Dieppe to Portsmouth, to skirt Portugal and Spain, cross the Mediterranean, and spend several months at Venice—and the lovely Cunégonde has not come yet! In her place, I have met only that impersonator and that abbé from Perigord. Cunégonde is dead, without a doubt; and nothing remains for me too but death. Oh, it would have been better to stay in the earthly paradise of Eldorado than to return to this accursed Europe. How right you are, my dear Martin; all is but illusion and disaster.

He fell into a black melancholy, and refused to attend the fashionable operas or take part in the other diversions of the carnival season; not a single lady tempted him in the slightest. Martin told him: — You're a real simpleton if you think a half-breed valet with five or six millions in his pockets will go to the end of the world to get your mistress and bring her to Venice for you. If he finds her, he'll take her for himself; if he doesn't, he'll take another. I advice you to forget about your servant Cacambo and your mistress Cunégonde.

Martin was not very comforting. Candide's melancholy increased, and Martin never wearied of showing him that there is little virtue and little happiness on this earth, except perhaps in Eldorado, where nobody can go.

While they were discussing this important matter and still waiting for Cunégonde, Candide noticed in St. Mark's Square a young Theatine[5] monk who had given his arm to a girl. The Theatine seemed fresh, plump, and flourishing; his eyes were bright, his manner cocky, his glance brilliant, his step proud. The girl was very pretty, and singing aloud; she glanced lovingly at her Theatine, and from time to time pinched his plump cheeks.

—At least you must admit, said Candide to Martin, that these people are happy. Until now I have not found in the whole inhabited earth, except Eldorado, anything but miserable people. But this girl

---

5. A Catholic order founded in 1524 by Cardinal Cajetan and G. P. Caraffa, later Pope Paul IV.

and this monk, I'd be willing to bet, are very happy creatures.

—I'll bet they aren't, said Martin.

—We have only to ask them to dinner, said Candide, and we'll find out if I'm wrong.

Promptly he approached them, made his compliments, and invited them to his inn for a meal of macaroni, Lombardy partridges, and caviar, washed down with wine from Montepulciano, Cyprus, and Samos, and some Lacrima Christi. The girl blushed but the Theatine accepted gladly, and the girl followed him, watching Candide with an expression of surprise and confusion, darkened by several tears. Scarcely had she entered the room when she said to Candide:

—What, can it be that Master Candide no longer knows Paquette?

At these words Candide, who had not yet looked carefully at her because he was preoccupied with Cunégonde, said to her: —Ah, my poor child! so you are the one who put Doctor Pangloss in the fine fix where I last saw him.

—Alas, sir, I was the one, said Paquette; I see you know all about it. I heard of the horrible misfortunes which befell the whole household of My Lady the Baroness and the lovely Cunégonde. I swear to you that my own fate has been just as unhappy. I was perfectly innocent when you knew me. A Franciscan, who was my confessor, easily seduced me. The consequences were frightful; shortly after My Lord the Baron had driven you out with great kicks on the backside, I too was forced to leave the castle. If a famous doctor had not taken pity on me, I would have died. Out of gratitude, I became for some time the mistress of this doctor. His wife, who was jealous to the point of frenzy, beat me mercilessly every day; she was a gorgon. The doctor was the ugliest of men, and I the most miserable creature on earth, being continually beaten for a man I did not love. You will understand, sir, how dangerous it is for a nagging woman to be married to a doctor. This man, enraged by his wife's ways, one day gave her as a cold cure a medicine so potent that in two hours' time she died amid horrible convulsions. Her relatives brought suit against the bereaved husband; he fled the country, and I was put in prison. My innocence would never have saved me if I had not been rather pretty. The judge set me free on condition that he should become the doctor's successor. I was shortly replaced in this post by another girl, dismissed without any payment, and obliged to continue this abominable trade which you men find so pleasant and which for us is nothing but a bottomless pit of misery. I went to ply the trade in Venice. Ah, my dear sir, if you could imagine what it is like to have to caress indiscriminately an old merchant, a lawyer, a monk, a gondolier, an abbé; to be subjected to every sort of insult and outrage; to be reduced, time and again, to borrowing a skirt in order to go have it lifted by some disgusting man; to be robbed by this fellow of what one has gained from that; to be shaken down by the police, and to have before one only the prospect of a hideous old age, a hospital, and a dunghill, you will conclude that I am one of the most miserable creatures in the world.

Thus Paquette poured forth her heart to the good Candide in a hotel room, while Martin sat listening nearby. At last he said to Candide: —You see, I've already won half my bet.

Brother Giroflée[6] had remained in the dining room, and was having a drink before dinner.

—But how's this? said Candide to Paquette. You looked so happy, so joyous, when I met you; you were singing, you caressed the Theatine with such a natural air of delight; you seemed to me just as happy as you now say you are miserable.

—Ah, sir, replied Paquette, that's another one of the miseries of this business; yesterday I was robbed and beaten by an officer, and today I have to seem in good humor in order to please a monk.

Candide wanted no more; he conceded that Martin was right. They sat down to table with Paquette and the Theatine; the meal was amusing enough, and when it was over, the company spoke out among themselves with some frankness.

—Father, said Candide to the monk, you seem to me a man whom all the world might envy; the flower of health glows in your cheek, your features radiate pleasure; you have a pretty girl for your diversion, and you seem very happy with your life as a Theatine.

—Upon my word, sir, said Brother Giroflée, I wish that all the Theatines were at the bottom of the sea. A hundred times I have been tempted to set fire to my convent, and go turn Turk. My parents forced me, when I was fifteen years old, to put on this detestable robe, so they could leave more money to a cursed older brother of mine, may God confound him! Jealousy, faction, and fury spring up, by natural law, within the walls of convents. It is true, I have preached a few bad sermons which earned me a little money, half of which the prior stole from me; the remainder serves to keep me in girls. But when I have to go back to the monastery at night, I'm ready to smash my head against the walls of my cell; and all my fellow monks are in the same fix.

Martin turned to Candide and said with his customary coolness:
—Well, haven't I won the whole bet?

Candide gave two thousand piastres to Paquette and a thousand to Brother Giroflée.

—I assure you, said he, that with that they will be happy.

—I don't believe so, said Martin; your piastres may make them even more unhappy than they were before.

6. His name means "gillyflower," and Paquette means "daisy."

—That may be, said Candide; but one thing comforts me, I note that people often turn up whom one never expected to see again; it may well be that, having rediscovered my red sheep and Paquette, I will also rediscover Cunégonde.

—I hope, said Martin, that she will some day make you happy; but I very much doubt it.

—You're a hard man, said Candide.

—I've lived, said Martin.

—But look at these gondoliers, said Candide; aren't they always singing?

—You don't see them at home, said Martin, with their wives and squalling children. The doge has his troubles, the gondoliers theirs. It's true that on the whole one is better off as a gondolier than as a doge; but the difference is so slight, I don't suppose it's worth the trouble of discussing.

—There's a lot of talk here, said Candide, of this Senator Poco-curante,[7] who has a fine palace on the Brenta and is hospitable to foreigners. They say he is a man who has never known a moment's grief.

—I'd like to see such a rare specimen, said Martin.

Candide promptly sent to Lord Pococurante, asking permission to call on him tomorrow.

CHAPTER 25
Visit to Lord Pococurante, Venetian Nobleman

Candide and Martin took a gondola on the Brenta, and soon reached the palace of the noble Pococurante. The gardens were large and filled with beautiful marble statues; the palace was handsomely designed. The master of the house, sixty years old and very rich, received his two inquisitive visitors perfectly politely, but with very little warmth; Candide was disconcerted and Martin not at all displeased.

First two pretty and neatly dressed girls served chocolate, which they whipped to a froth. Candide could not forbear praising their beauty, their grace, their skill.

—They are pretty good creatures, said Pococurante; I sometimes have them into my bed, for I'm tired of the ladies of the town, with their stupid tricks, quarrels, jealousies, fits of ill humor and petty pride, and all the sonnets one has to make or order for them; but, after all, these two girls are starting to bore me too.

After lunch, Candide strolled through a long gallery, and was amazed at the beauty of the pictures. He asked who was the painter of the two finest.

7. His name means "small care."

—They are by Raphael, said the senator; I bought them for a lot of money, out of vanity, some years ago; people say they're the finest in Italy, but they don't please me at all; the colors have all turned brown, the figures aren't well modeled and don't stand out enough, the draperies bear no resemblance to real cloth. In a word, whatever people may say, I don't find in them a real imitation of nature. I like a picture only when I can see in it a touch of nature itself, and there are none of this sort. I have many paintings, but I no longer look at them.

As they waited for dinner, Pococurante ordered a concerto performed. Candide found the music delightful.

—That noise? said Pococurante. It may amuse you for half an hour, but if it goes on any longer, it tires everybody though no one dares to admit it. Music today is only the art of performing difficult pieces, and what is merely difficult cannot please for long. Perhaps I should prefer the opera, if they had not found ways to make it revolting and monstrous. Anyone who likes bad tragedies set to music is welcome to them; in these performances the scenes serve only to introduce, inappropriately, two or three ridiculous songs designed to show off the actress's sound box. Anyone who wants to, or who can, is welcome to swoon with pleasure at the sight of a castrate wriggling through the role of Caesar or Cato, and strutting awkwardly about the stage. For my part, I have long since given up these paltry trifles which are called the glory of modern Italy, and for which monarchs pay such ruinous prices.

Candide argued a bit, but timidly; Martin was entirely of a mind with the senator.

They sat down to dinner, and after an excellent meal adjourned to the library. Candide, seeing a copy of Homer in a splendid binding, complimented the noble lord on his good taste.

—That is an author, said he, who was the special delight of great Pangloss, the best philosopher in all Germany.

—He's no special delight of mine, said Pococurante coldly. I was once made to believe that I took pleasure in reading him; but that constant recital of fights which are all alike, those gods who are always interfering but never decisively, that Helen who is the cause of the war and then scarcely takes any part in the story, that Troy which is always under siege and never taken—all that bores me to tears. I have sometimes asked scholars if reading it bored them as much as it bores me; everyone who answered frankly told me the book dropped from his hands like lead, but that they had to have it in their libraries as a monument of antiquity, like those old rusty coins which can't be used in real trade.

Your Excellence doesn't hold the same opinion of Virgil? said Candide.

—I concede, said Pococurante, that the second, fourth, and sixth books of his *Aeneid* are fine; but as for his pious Aeneas, and strong Cloanthes, and faithful Achates, and little Ascanius, and that imbecile King Latinus, and middle-class Amata, and insipid Lavinia, I don't suppose there was ever anything so cold and unpleasant. I prefer Tasso and those sleepwalkers' stories of Ariosto.

—Dare I ask, sir, said Candide, if you don't get great enjoyment from reading Horace?

—There are some maxims there, said Pococurante, from which a man of the world can profit, and which, because they are formed into vigorous couplets, are more easily remembered; but I care very little for his trip to Brindisi, his description of a bad dinner, or his account of a quibblers' squabble between some fellow Pupilus, whose words he says *were full of pus*, and another whose words *were full of vinegar*.[8] I feel nothing but extreme disgust at his verses against old women and witches; and I can't see what's so great in his telling his friend Maecenas that if he is raised by him to the ranks of lyric poets, he will strike the stars with his lofty forehead. Fools admire everything in a well-known author. I read only for my own pleasure; I like only what is in my style.

Candide, who had been trained never to judge for himself, was much astonished by what he heard; and Martin found Pococurante's way of thinking quite rational.

—Oh, here is a copy of Cicero, said Candide. Now this great man I suppose you're never tired of reading.

—I never read him at all, replied the Venetian. What do I care whether he pleaded for Rabirius or Cluentius? As a judge, I have my hands full of lawsuits. I might like his philosophical works better, but when I saw that he had doubts about everything, I concluded that I knew as much as he did, and that I needed no help to be ignorant.

—Ah, here are eighty volumes of collected papers from a scientific academy, cried Martin; maybe there is something good in them.

—There would be indeed, said Pococurante, if one of these silly authors had merely discovered a new way of making pins; but in all those volumes there is nothing but empty systems, not a single useful discovery.

—What a lot of stage plays I see over there, said Candide, some in Italian, some in Spanish and French.

—Yes, said the senator, three thousand of them, and not three dozen good ones. As for those collections of sermons, which all

---

8. *Satires* I. vii; Pococurante, with gentlemanly negligence, has corrupted Rupilius to Pupilus. Horace's poems against witches are *Epodes* V, VIII, XII; the one about striking the stars with his lofty forehead is *Odes* I.i.

together are not worth a page of Seneca, and all these heavy volumes of theology, you may be sure I never open them, nor does anybody else.

Martin noticed some shelves full of English books.

—I suppose, said he, that a republican must delight in most of these books written in the land of liberty.

—Yes, replied Pococurante, it's a fine thing to write as you think; it is mankind's privilege. In all our Italy, people write only what they do not think; men who inhabit the land of the Caesars and Antonines dare not have an idea without the permission of a Dominican. I would rejoice in the freedom that breathes through English genius, if partisan passions did not corrupt all that is good in that precious freedom.

Candide, noting a Milton, asked if he did not consider this author a great man.

—Who? said Pococurante. That barbarian who made a long commentary on the first chapter of Genesis in ten books of crabbed verse? That clumsy imitator of the Greeks, who disfigures creation itself, and while Moses represents the eternal being as creating the world with a word, has the messiah take a big compass out of a heavenly cupboard in order to design his work? You expect me to admire the man who spoiled Tasso's hell and devil? who disguises Lucifer now as a toad, now as a pigmy? who makes him rehash the same arguments a hundred times over? who makes him argue theology? and who, taking seriously Ariosto's comic story of the invention of firearms, has the devils shooting off cannon in heaven? Neither I nor anyone else in Italy has been able to enjoy these gloomy extravagances. The marriage of Sin and Death, and the monster that Sin gives birth to, will nauseate any man whose taste is at all refined; and his long description of a hospital is good only for a gravedigger. This obscure, extravagant, and disgusting poem was despised at its birth; I treat it today as it was treated in its own country by its contemporaries. Anyhow, I say what I think, and care very little whether other people agree with me.

Candide was a little cast down by this speech; he respected Homer, and had a little affection for Milton.

—Alas, he said under his breath to Martin, I'm afraid this man will have a supreme contempt for our German poets.

—No harm in that, said Martin.

—Oh what a superior man, said Candide, still speaking softly, what a great genius this Pococurante must be! Nothing can please him.

Having thus looked over all the books, they went down into the garden. Candide praised its many beauties.

—I know nothing in such bad taste, said the master of the house; we have nothing but trifles here; tomorrow I am going to have one set out on a nobler design.

When the two visitors had taken leave of his excellency: —Well now, said Candide to Martin, you must agree that this was the happiest of all men, for he is superior to everything he possesses.

—Don't you see, said Martin, that he is disgusted with everything he possesses? Plato said, a long time ago, that the best stomachs are not those which refuse all food.

—But, said Candide, isn't there pleasure in criticizing everything, in seeing faults where other people think they see beauties?

—That is to say, Martin replied, that there's pleasure in having no pleasure?

—Oh well, said Candide, then I am the only happy man . . . or will be, when I see Miss Cunégonde again.

—It's always a good thing to have hope, said Martin.

But the days and the weeks slipped past; Cacambo did not come back, and Candide was so buried in his grief, that he did not even notice that Paquette and Brother Giroflée had neglected to come and thank him.

CHAPTER 26

About a Supper that Candide and Martin Had with Six Strangers, and Who They Were

One evening when Candide, accompanied by Martin, was about to sit down for dinner with the strangers staying in his hotel, a man with a soot-colored face came up behind him, took him by the arm, and said: —Be ready to leave with us, don't miss out.

He turned and saw Cacambo. Only the sight of Cunégonde could have astonished and pleased him more. He nearly went mad with joy. He embraced his dear friend.

—Cunégonde is here, no doubt? Where is she? Bring me to her, let me die of joy in her presence.

—Cunégonde is not here at all, said Cacambo, she is at Constantinople.

—Good Heavens, at Constantinople! but if she were in China, I must fly there, let's go.

—We will leave after supper, said Cacambo; I can tell you no more; I am a slave, my owner is looking for me, I must go wait on him at table; mum's the word; eat your supper and be prepared.

Candide, torn between joy and grief, delighted to have seen his faithful agent again, astonished to find him a slave, full of the idea of recovering his mistress, his heart in a turmoil, his mind in a whirl, sat down to eat with Martin, who was watching all these events coolly,

establishment four most serene highnesses, who had also lost their kingdoms through the luck of war, and who came to spend the rest of the carnival season at Venice. But Candide never bothered even to look at these newcomers because he was only concerned to go find his dear Cunégonde at Constantinople.

CHAPTER 27
Candide's Trip to Constantinople

Faithful Cacambo had already arranged with the Turkish captain who was returning Sultan Achmet to Constantinople to make room for Candide and Martin on board. Both men boarded ship after prostrating themselves before his miserable highness. On the way, Candide said to Martin: —Six dethroned kings that we had dinner with! and yet among those six there was one on whom I had to bestow charity! Perhaps there are other princes even more unfortunate. I myself have only lost a hundred sheep, and now I am flying to the arms of Cunégonde. My dear Martin, once again Pangloss is proved right, all is for the best.

—I hope so, said Martin.

—But, said Candide, that was a most unlikely experience we had at Venice. Nobody ever saw, or heard tell of, six dethroned kings eating together at an inn.

—It is no more extraordinary, said Martin, than most of the things that have happened to us. Kings are frequently dethroned; and as for the honor we had from dining with them, that's a trifle which doesn't deserve our notice.[7]

Scarcely was Candide on board than he fell on the neck of his former servant, his friend Cacambo.

—Well! said he, what is Cunégonde doing? Is she still a marvel of beauty? Does she still love me? How is her health? No doubt you have bought her a palace at Constantinople.

—My dear master, answered Cacambo, Cunégonde is washing dishes on the shores of the Propontis, in the house of a prince who has very few dishes to wash; she is a slave in the house of a onetime king named Ragotski,[8] to whom the Great Turk allows three crowns a day in his exile; but, what is worse than all this, she has lost all her beauty and become horribly ugly.

—Ah, beautiful or ugly, said Candide, I am an honest man, and my duty is to love her forever. But how can she be reduced to this wretched state with the five or six millions that you had?

—All right, said Cacambo, didn't I have to give two millions to

---

7. Another late change adds the following question: —What does it matter whom you dine with as long as you fare well at table?
I have omitted it, again on literary grounds.   8. Francis Leopold Rakoczy (1676–1735) who was briefly king of Transylvania in the early eighteenth century. After 1720 he was interned in Turkey.

Señor don Fernando d'Ibaraa y Figueroa y Mascarenes y Lampourdos y Souza, governor of Buenos Aires, for his permission to carry off Miss Cunégonde? And didn't a pirate cleverly strip us of the rest? And didn't this pirate carry us off to Cape Matapan, to Melos, Nicaria, Samos, Petra, to the Dardanelles, Marmora, Scutari? Cunégonde and the old woman are working for the prince I told you about, and I am the slave of the dethroned sultan.

—What a lot of fearful calamities linked one to the other, said Candide. But after all, I still have a few diamonds, I shall easily deliver Cunégonde. What a pity that she's become so ugly!

Then, turning toward Martin, he asked: —Who in your opinion is more to be pitied, the Emperor Achmet, the Emperor Ivan, King Charles Edward, or myself?

—I have no idea, said Martin; I would have to enter your hearts in order to tell.

—Ah, said Candide, if Pangloss were here, he would know and he would tell us.

—I can't imagine, said Martin, what scales your Pangloss would use to weigh out the miseries of men and value their griefs. All I will venture is that the earth holds millions of men who deserve our pity a hundred times more than King Charles Edward, Emperor Ivan, or Sultan Achmet.

—You may well be right, said Candide.

In a few days they arrived at the Black Sea canal. Candide began by repurchasing Cacambo at an exorbitant price; then, without losing an instant, he flung himself and his companions into a galley to go search out Cunégonde on the shores of Propontis, however ugly she might be.

There were in the chain gang two convicts who bent clumsily to the oar, and on whose bare shoulders the Levantine[9] captain delivered from time to time a few lashes with a bullwhip. Candide naturally noticed them more than the other galley slaves, and out of pity came closer to them. Certain features of their disfigured faces seemed to him to bear a slight resemblance to Pangloss and to that wretched Jesuit, that baron, that brother of Miss Cunégonde. The notion stirred and saddened him. He looked at them more closely.

—To tell you the truth, he said to Cacambo, if I hadn't seen Master Pangloss hanged, and if I hadn't been so miserable as to murder the baron, I should think they were rowing in this very galley.

At the names of 'baron' and 'Pangloss' the two convicts gave a great cry, sat still on their bench, and dropped their oars. The Levantine captain came running, and the bullwhip lashes redoubled.

—Stop, stop, captain, cried Candide. I'll give you as much money as you want.

9. From the eastern Mediterranean.

—What, can it be Candide? cried one of the convicts.

—What, can it be Candide? cried the other.

—Is this a dream? said Candide. Am I awake or asleep? Am I in this galley? Is that My Lord the Baron, whom I killed? Is that Master Pangloss, whom I saw hanged?

—It is indeed, they replied.

—What, is that the great philosopher? said Martin.

—Now, sir, Mr. Levantine Captain, said Candide, how much money do you want for the ransom of My Lord Thunder-Ten-Tronckh, one of the first barons of the empire, and Master Pangloss, the deepest metaphysician in all Germany?

—Dog of a Christian, replied the Levantine captain, since these two dogs of Christian convicts are barons and metaphysicians, which is no doubt a great honor in their country, you will give me fifty thousand sequins for them.

—You shall have them, sir, take me back to Constantinople and you shall be paid on the spot. Or no, take me to Miss Cunégonde.

The Levantine captain, at Candide's first word, had turned his bow toward the town, and he had them rowed there as swiftly as a bird cleaves the air.

A hundred times Candide embraced the baron and Pangloss.

—And how does it happen I didn't kill you, my dear baron? and my dear Pangloss, how can you be alive after being hanged? and why are you both rowing in the galleys of Turkey?

—Is it really true that my dear sister is in this country? asked the baron.

—Yes, answered Cacambo.

—And do I really see again my dear Candide? cried Pangloss.

Candide introduced Martin and Cacambo. They all embraced; they all talked at once. The galley flew, already they were back in port. A Jew was called, and Candide sold him for fifty thousand sequins a diamond worth a hundred thousand, while he protested by Abraham that he could not possibly give more for it. Candide immediately ransomed the baron and Pangloss. The latter threw himself at the feet of his liberator, and bathed them with tears; the former thanked him with a nod, and promised to repay this bit of money at the first opportunity.

—But is it really possible that my sister is in Turkey? said he.

—Nothing is more possible, replied Cacambo, since she is a dishwasher in the house of a prince of Transylvania.

At once two more Jews were called; Candide sold some more diamonds; and they all departed in another galley to the rescue of Cunégonde.

CHAPTER 28

What Happened to Candide, Cunégonde, Pangloss, Martin, &c.

—Let me beg your pardon once more, said Candide to the baron, pardon me, reverend father, for having run you through the body with my sword.

—Don't mention it, replied the baron. I was a little too hasty myself, I confess it; but since you want to know the misfortune which brought me to the galleys, I'll tell you. After being cured of my wound by the brother who was apothecary to the college, I was attacked and abducted by a Spanish raiding party; they jailed me in Buenos Aires at the time when my sister had just left. I asked to be sent to Rome, to the father general. Instead, I was named to serve as almoner in Constantinople, under the French ambassador. I had not been a week on this job when I chanced one evening on a very handsome young ichoglan.[1] The evening was hot; the young man wanted to take a swim; I seized the occasion, and went with him. I did not know that it is a capital offense for a Christian to be found naked with a young Moslem. A cadi sentenced me to receive a hundred blows with a cane on the soles of my feet, and then to be sent to the galleys. I don't suppose there was ever such a horrible miscarriage of justice. But I would like to know why my sister is in the kitchen of a Transylvanian king exiled among Turks.

—But how about you, my dear Pangloss, said Candide; how is it possible that we have met again?

—It is true, said Pangloss, that you saw me hanged; in the normal course of things, I should have been burned, but you recall that a cloudburst occurred just as they were about to roast me. So much rain fell that they despaired of lighting the fire; thus I was hanged, for lack of anything better to do with me. A surgeon bought my body, carried me off to his house, and dissected me. First he made a cross-shaped incision in me, from the navel to the clavicle. No one could have been worse hanged than I was. In fact, the executioner of the high ceremonials of the Holy Inquisition, who was a subdeacon, burned people marvelously well, but he was not in the way of hanging them. The rope was wet, and tightened badly; it caught on a knot; in short, I was still breathing. The cross-shaped incision made me scream so loudly that the surgeon fell over backwards; he thought he was dissecting the devil, fled in an agony of fear, and fell downstairs in his flight. His wife ran in, at the noise, from a nearby room; she found me stretched out on the table with my cross-shaped incision, was even more frightened than her husband, fled, and fell over him. When they had recovered a little, I heard her say to him: 'My dear, what were you thinking of, trying to dissect a heretic? Don't

---

1. A page to the sultan.

you know those people are always possessed of the devil? I'm going to get the priest and have him exorcised.' At these words, I shuddered, and collected my last remaining energies to cry: 'Have mercy on me!' At last the Portuguese barber[2] took courage; he sewed me up again; his wife even nursed me; in two weeks I was up and about. The barber found me a job and made me lackey to a Knight of Malta who was going to Venice; and when this master could no longer pay me, I took service under a Venetian merchant, whom I followed to Constantinople.

—One day it occurred to me to enter a mosque; no one was there but an old imam and a very attractive young worshipper who was saying her prayers. Her bosom was completely bare; and between her two breasts she had a lovely bouquet of tulips, roses, anemones, buttercups, hyacinths, and primroses. She dropped her bouquet, I picked it up, and returned it to her with the most respectful attentions. I was so long getting it back in place that the imam grew angry, and, seeing that I was a Christian, he called the guard. They took me before the cadi, who sentenced me to receive a hundred blows with a cane on the soles of my feet, and then to be sent to the galleys. I was chained to the same galley and precisely the same bench as My Lord the Baron. There were in this galley four young fellows from Marseilles, five Neapolitan priests, and two Corfu monks, who assured us that these things happen every day. My Lord the Baron asserted that he had suffered a greater injustice than I; I, on the other hand, proposed that it was much more permissible to replace a bouquet in a bosom than to be found naked with an ichoglan. We were arguing the point continually, and getting twenty lashes a day with the bullwhip, when the chain of events within this universe brought you to our galley, and you ransomed us.

—Well, my dear Pangloss, Candide said to him, now that you have been hanged, dissected, beaten to a pulp, and sentenced to the galleys, do you still think everything is for the best in this world?

—I am still of my first opinion, replied Pangloss; for after all I am a philosopher, and it would not be right for me to recant since Leibniz could not possibly be wrong, and besides pre-established harmony is the finest notion in the world, like the plenum and subtle matter.[3]

---

2. The two callings of barber and surgeon, since they both involved sharp instruments, were interchangeable in the early days of medicine.   3. Rigorous determinism requires that there be no empty spaces in the universe, so wherever it seems empty, one posits the existence of the "plenum." "Subtle matter" describes the soul, the mind, and all spiritual agencies—which can, therefore, be supposed subject to the influence and control of the great world machine, which is, of course, visibly material. Both are concepts needed to round out the system of optimistic determinism.

CHAPTER 29

How Candide Found Cunégonde and the Old Woman Again

While Candide, the baron, Pangloss, Martin, and Cacambo were telling one another their stories, while they were disputing over the contingent or non-contingent events of this universe, while they were arguing over effects and causes, over moral evil and physical evil, over liberty and necessity, and over the consolations available to one in a Turkish galley, they arrived at the shores of Propontis and the house of the prince of Transylvania. The first sight to meet their eyes was Cunégonde and the old woman, who were hanging out towels on lines to dry.

The baron paled at what he saw. The tender lover Candide, seeing his lovely Cunégonde with her skin weathered, her eyes bloodshot, her breasts fallen, her cheeks seamed, her arms red and scaly, recoiled three steps in horror, and then advanced only out of politeness. She embraced Candide and her brother; everyone embraced the old woman; Candide ransomed them both.

There was a little farm in the neighborhood; the old woman suggested that Candide occupy it until some better fate should befall the group. Cunégonde did not know she was ugly, no one had told her; she reminded Candide of his promises in so firm a tone that the good Candide did not dare to refuse her. So he went to tell the baron that he was going to marry his sister.

—Never will I endure, said the baron, such baseness on her part, such insolence on yours; this shame at least I will not put up with; why, my sister's children would not be able to enter the Chapters in Germany.[4] No, my sister will never marry anyone but a baron of the empire.

Cunégonde threw herself at his feet, and bathed them with her tears; he was inflexible.

—You absolute idiot, Candide told him, I rescued you from the galleys, I paid your ransom, I paid your sister's; she was washing dishes, she is ugly, I am good enough to make her my wife, and you still presume to oppose it! If I followed my impulses, I would kill you all over again.

—You may kill me again, said the baron, but you will not marry my sister while I am alive.

CHAPTER 30

Conclusion

At heart, Candide had no real wish to marry Cunégonde; but the baron's extreme impertinence decided him in favor of the marriage,

---

4. Knightly assemblies.

and Cunégonde was so eager for it that he could not back out. He consulted Pangloss, Martin, and the faithful Cacambo. Pangloss drew up a fine treatise, in which he proved that the baron had no right over his sister and that she could, according to all the laws of the empire, marry Candide morganatically.[5] Martin said they should throw the baron into the sea. Cacambo thought they should send him back to the Levantine captain to finish his time in the galleys, and then send him to the father general in Rome by the first vessel. This seemed the best idea; the old woman approved, and nothing was said to his sister; the plan was executed, at modest expense, and they had the double pleasure of snaring a Jesuit and punishing the pride of a German baron.

It is quite natural to suppose that after so many misfortunes, Candide, married to his mistress, and living with the philosopher Pangloss, the philosopher Martin, the prudent Cacambo, and the old woman—having, besides, brought back so many diamonds from the land of the ancient Incas—must have led the most agreeable life in the world. But he was so cheated by the Jews[6] that nothing was left but his little farm; his wife, growing every day more ugly, became sour-tempered and insupportable; the old woman was ailing and even more ill-humored than Cunégonde. Cacambo, who worked in the garden and went into Constantinople to sell vegetables, was worn out with toil, and cursed his fate. Pangloss was in despair at being unable to shine in some German university. As for Martin, he was firmly persuaded that things are just as bad wherever you are; he endured in patience. Candide, Martin, and Pangloss sometimes argued over metaphysics and morals. Before the windows of the farmhouse they often watched the passage of boats bearing effendis, pashas, and cadis into exile on Lemnos, Mytilene, and Erzeroum; they saw other cadis, other pashas, other effendis coming, to take the place of the exiles and to be exiled in their turn. They saw various heads, neatly impaled, to be set up at the Sublime Porte.[7] These sights gave fresh impetus to their discussions; and when they were not arguing, the boredom was so fierce that one day the old woman ventured to say:

—I should like to know which is worse, being raped a hundred times by negro pirates, having a buttock cut off, running the gauntlet in the Bulgar army, being flogged and hanged in an auto-da-fé, being dissected and rowing in the galleys—experiencing, in a word, all the miseries through which we have passed—or else just sitting here and doing nothing?

—It's a hard question, said Candide.

5. A morganatic marriage confers no rights on the partner of lower rank or on the offspring.
6. Voltaire's anti-Semitism, derived from various unhappy experiences with Jewish financiers, is not the most attractive aspect of his personality.   7. The gate of the sultan's palace is often used by extension to describe his government as a whole. But it was in fact a real gate where the heads of traitors and public enemies were gruesomely exposed.

These words gave rise to new reflections, and Martin in particular concluded that man was bound to live either in convulsions of misery or in the lethargy of boredom. Candide did not agree, but expressed no positive opinion. Pangloss asserted that he had always suffered horribly; but having once declared that everything was marvelously well, he continued to repeat the opinion and didn't believe a word of it.

One thing served to confirm Martin in his detestable opinions, to make Candide hesitate more than ever, and to embarrass Pangloss. It was the arrival one day at their farm of Paquette and Brother Giroflée, who were in the last stages of misery. They had quickly run through their three thousand piastres, had split up, made up, quarreled, been jailed, escaped, and finally Brother Giroflée had turned Turk. Paquette continued to ply her trade everywhere, and no longer made any money at it.

—I told you, said Martin to Candide, that your gifts would soon be squandered and would only render them more unhappy. You have spent millions of piastres, you and Cacambo, and you are no more happy than Brother Giroflée and Paquette.

—Ah ha, said Pangloss to Paquette, so destiny has brought you back in our midst, my poor girl! Do you realize you cost me the end of my nose, one eye, and an ear? And look at you now! eh! what a world it is, after all!

This new adventure caused them to philosophize more than ever.

There was in the neighborhood a very famous dervish, who was said to be the best philosopher in Turkey; they went to ask his advice. Pangloss was spokesman, and he said: —Master, we have come to ask you to tell us why such a strange animal as man was created.

—What are you getting into? answered the dervish. Is it any of your business?

—But, reverend father, said Candide, there's a horrible lot of evil on the face of the earth.

—What does it matter, said the dervish, whether there's good or evil? When his highness sends a ship to Egypt, does he worry whether the mice on board are comfortable or not?

—What shall we do then? asked Pangloss.

—Hold your tongue, said the dervish.

—I had hoped, said Pangloss, to reason a while with you concerning effects and causes, the best of possible worlds, the origin of evil, the nature of the soul, and pre-established harmony.

At these words, the dervish slammed the door in their faces.

During this interview, word was spreading that at Constantinople they had just strangled two viziers of the divan,[8] as well as the mufti, and impaled serveral of their friends. This catastrophe made a great

8. Intimate advisers of the sultan.

and general sensation for several hours. Pangloss, Candide, and Martin, as they returned to their little farm, passed a good old man who was enjoying the cool of the day at his doorstep under a grove of orange trees. Pangloss, who was as inquisitive as he was explanatory, asked the name of the mufti who had been strangled.

—I know nothing of it, said the good man, and I have never cared to know the name of a single mufti or vizier. I am completely ignorant of the episode you are discussing. I presume that in general those who meddle in public business sometimes perish miserably, and that they deserve their fate; but I never listen to the news from Constantinople; I am satisfied with sending the fruits of my garden to be sold there.

Having spoken these words, he asked the strangers into his house; his two daughters and two sons offered them various sherbets which they had made themselves, Turkish cream flavored with candied citron, orange, lemon, lime, pineapple, pistachio, and mocha coffee uncontaminated by the inferior coffee of Batavia and the East Indies. After which the two daughters of this good Moslem perfumed the beards of Candide, Pangloss, and Martin.

—You must possess, Candide said to the Turk, an enormous and splendid property?

I have only twenty acres, replied the Turk; I cultivate them with my children, and the work keeps us from three great evils, boredom, vice, and poverty.

Candide, as he walked back to his farm, meditated deeply over the words of the Turk. He said to Pangloss and Martin: —This good old man seems to have found himself a fate preferable to that of the six kings with whom we had the honor of dining.

—Great place, said Pangloss, is very perilous in the judgment of all the philosophers; for, after all, Eglon, king of the Moabites, was murdered by Ehud; Absalom was hung up by the hair and pierced with three darts; King Nadab, son of Jeroboam, was killed by Baasha; King Elah by Zimri; Ahaziah by Jehu; Athaliah by Jehoiada; and Kings Jehoiakim, Jeconiah, and Zedekiah were enslaved. You know how death came to Croesus, Astyages, Darius, Dionysius of Syracuse, Pyrrhus, Perseus, Hannibal, Jugurtha, Ariovistus, Caesar, Pompey, Nero, Otho, Vitellius, Domitian, Richard II of England, Edward II, Henry VI, Richard III, Mary Stuart, Charles I, the three Henrys of France, and the Emperor Henry IV? You know . . .

—I know also, said Candide, that we must cultivate our garden.

—You are perfectly right, said Pangloss; for when man was put into the garden of Eden, he was put there *ut operaretur eum*, so that he should work it; this proves that man was not born to take his ease.

—Let's work without speculating, said Martin; it's the only way of rendering life bearable.

The whole little group entered into this laudable scheme; each

one began to exercise his talents. The little plot yielded fine crops.
Cunégonde was, to tell the truth, remarkably ugly; but she became
an excellent pastry cook. Paquette took up embroidery; the old woman
did the laundry. Everyone, down even to Brother Giroflée, did
something useful; he became a very adequate carpenter, and even
an honest man; and Pangloss sometimes used to say to Candide: —
All events are linked together in the best of possible worlds; for, after
all, if you had not been driven from a fine castle by being kicked in
the backside for love of Miss Cunégonde, if you hadn't been sent
before the Inquisition, if you hadn't traveled across America on foot,
if you hadn't given a good sword thrust to the baron, if you hadn't
lost all your sheep from the good land of Eldorado, you wouldn't be
sitting here eating candied citron and pistachios.

—That is very well put, said Candide, but we must cultivate our
garden.

SAMUEL JOHNSON
1709–1784

In *The History of Rasselas, Prince of Abissinia* (1759), his longest philosophic tale, Samuel Johnson offers a dignified but moving account of the
futility of human endeavor. The narrative, written hastily and allegedly published in order to defray his mother's funeral expenses, distills the melancholy reflections of a fifty-year-old man whose observations and experience
alike convince him that human happiness depends mainly on the preservation of illusion.

Son of a Lichfield bookseller, Johnson received his early education at
Lichfield Grammar School. In 1728 he entered Pembroke College, Oxford,
but poverty forced him to leave without a degree three years later. An attempt
at teaching, and later a brief sequence as schoolmaster, proved unsuccessful;
in 1737 he went to London and began to earn a living by writing for the
Gentleman's Magazine. He had married, in 1735, a widow much older than
he; her death, in 1752, left him desolate.

Before long Johnson became distinguished as conversationalist and as writer,
known particularly for *The Rambler* (a periodical published from 1750 to
1752; Johnson himself wrote all but four and a half of its 208 numbers) and
the *Dictionary of the English Language* (1755), an almost incredible
achievement for one man. In 1762, he was granted a royal pension of three
hundred pounds a year; in 1775, his old university conferred upon him the
degree of Doctor in Civil Laws. Meanwhile, he had formed a close attachment to the Scotsman James Boswell, thirty-one years younger than he, of
whom he saw much in London and with whom he traveled through the
highlands and islands of Scotland. (Subsequently Boswell wrote a life of
Johnson.) His second intimate relationship was with Henry Thrale, a Lon-

don brewer, and his wife Hester, a woman of strong literary interests. With them Johnson made his only trip abroad, to Paris. A group of other distinguished men joined him in founding The Literary Club (1764), which met regularly for conversation. By the time of Johnson's death in 1784, he was unquestionably the most famous literary figure in England.

Johnson wrote poetic imitations of the classics; original verse in Latin and in English; a travel book; fiction; a tragic drama; literary criticism; philosophic, satiric, and meditative essays; biography; and a dictionary. He edited Shakespeare's plays, with a preface brilliantly defining the playwright's place for the mid-eighteenth-century consciousness; his final work, *Lives of the Poets* (1779–81), biographical and critical introductions to fifty-two English poets, exemplified at its best his gift for forceful judgment and discrimination. Sometimes he was wrong, by our standards: he disapproved, for example, of Milton's *Lycidas*. More often, he provided definitive statements about poetic careers and accomplishments.

Rasselas, published almost simultaneously with Voltaire's *Candide*, was immediately compared to the French work; Johnson himself found the resemblance striking. Both books employ the fictional device of a naïve protagonist whose travels educate him in the evils of the world. In tone and in implication, though, the two fictions differ greatly. Voltaire's satiric intensity and violence much exceed Johnson's; on the other hand, Candide, after far worse disasters than Rasselas faces, arrives at a more specific course of hopeful action than his English counterpart can discover.

Although Johnson was born eleven years after Voltaire, his point of view derives from an earlier era. The context in which Rasselas learns the futility of human endeavor is that of Christian humanism. When the princess, having seen the catacombs, concludes, "To me, . . . the choice of life is become less important; I hope hereafter to think only on the choice of eternity," she reveals the book's underlying assumptions. Human beings, because of their humanity, struggle to attain goals which, won, prove less than satisfactory. They live in illusion, governing themselves by hopes and fears disproportionate to actuality. The reality that should focus their attention, the afterlife of reward and punishment, seldom concerns them; they dwell resolutely in the irrelevant. They lack not only adequate reason, but sufficiently active faith.

Unlike Voltaire's Pangloss, Johnson's characters do not rely on universalizing interpretations. They do not worry about whether theirs is the best or the worst of possible worlds; their blinkered vision directs itself to personal and immediate concerns. Rasselas and his sister, trying to make their own "choice of life," seeking models of fulfillment and happiness, repeatedly find the inadequacy of human effort. Even more importantly, they discover what a chapter title calls "The Dangerous Prevalence [meaning dominance] of Imagination": the degree to which reason proves subject to desire, as individuals, seeing only what they want to see, beguile themselves into temporary satisfaction. The story ends with a "Conclusion, In Which Nothing Is Concluded"; the travelers, still not free of hopeful fantasy, return to Abyssinia. They have not encountered great natural disasters, striking instances of human malice or lust, or large-scale carnage; but neither have they found much ground for expecting earthly happiness. The satirist's tone, Voltaire's tone, by its very vehemence suggests belief that human beings, once aware of their own corruption, might at least minimally improve. Johnson's elevated, dignified, ponderous utterance, on the other hand, rings with the authority of conviction. The world he describes seems in no way subject to change.

This is not to say, however, that *Rasselas* makes its readers feel hopeless. The vigor and authority of the narrative voice carry comfort, conveying a sense of the possibility of knowledge and understanding. Rasselas and Nekayah, voices rather than developed characters, achieve no dazzling insight as a result of their efforts to understand the choices open to them. Never differentiated in personality, they serve mainly as mouthpieces for positions Johnson wishes to represent. Nonetheless, as instruments of communication they suggest a way of finding at least conditional value in this world. The fable that contains them implies the importance, the educational potential, of *experience*, exemplified by the travel and the purposeful investigations the characters undertake, and of *talk*. Rasselas and his sister learn not only by looking but by discussing. They talk with their mentor, Imlac, the voice of wisdom within the narrative—wisdom that has been derived from its possessor's previous experience, a fact reinforcing the stress on the moral significance of what the travelers see and do. But Rasselas and Nekayah also talk with one another, figuring out the meaning of what they have seen by a process of mutual assessment, of sharing and of questioning. If all faith in the possibility of ultimate earthly satisfaction proves illusory, what the travelers take for granted—their companionship—yet continues to sustain them. The human community contains the saving possibility of communal reassurance; the verbal sharing of experience intensifies its value. And the effort to say precisely what one knows is a self-sufficiently valuable enterprise, an enterprise corroborating the importance of Johnson's writing of the tale: for that, too, is an effort at *saying*.

So *Rasselas*, although somber in its assessments, does not imply despair. Reminding its readers as well as its characters of the vital "choice of eternity," it reiterates Johnson's typical insistence on human life as a condition offering much to endure, little to enjoy. But it also suggests the nature and the importance of the little enjoyment and insight possible to human beings; and it implicitly invites readers to take their own lives seriously, to understand and value the moral possibilities of all experience, and to share the restrained, ambiguous excitement of seeing things as they are.

J. Boswell, *The Life of Samuel Johnson* (1791), remains a brilliant account of its subject. The definitive modern biography is W. J. Bate, *Samuel Johnson* (1977). Bate's earlier, shorter book, *The Achievement of Samuel Johnson* (1955), provides an excellent introduction. *Johnson, The Critical Heritage*, ed., J. T. Boulton (1977), assembles critical statements from the eighteenth century onward.

The History of Rasselas, Prince of Abissinia[1]

Chapter I

DESCRIPTION OF A PALACE IN A VALLEY

Ye who listen with credulity to the whispers of fancy, and persue with eagerness the phantoms of hope; who expect that age will perform the promises of youth, and that the deficiencies of the present day will be supplied by the morrow; attend to the history of Rasselas prince of Abissinia.

Rasselas was the fourth son of the mighty emperour, in whose dominions the Father of Waters[2] begins his course; whose bounty pours down the streams of plenty, and scatters over half the world the harvests of Egypt.

According to the custom which has descended from age to age among the monarchs of the torrid zone, Rasselas was confined in a private palace, with the other sons and daughters of Abissinian royalty, till the order of succession should call him to the throne.

The place, which the wisdom or policy of antiquity had destined for the residence of the Abissinian princes, was a spacious valley in the kingdom of Amhara, surrounded on every side by mountains, of which the summits overhang the middle part. The only passage, by which it could be entered, was a cavern that passed under a rock, of which it has long been disputed whether it was the work of nature or of human industry. The outlet of the cavern was concealed by a thick wood, and the mouth which opened into the valley was closed with gates of iron, forged by the artificers of ancient days, so massy that no man could without the help of engines open or shut them.

From the mountains on every side, rivulets descended that filled all the valley with verdure and fertility, and formed a lake in the middle inhabited by fish of every species, and frequented by every fowl whom nature has taught to dip the wing in water. This lake discharged its superfluities by a stream which entered a dark cleft of the mountain on the northern side, and fell with dreadful noise from precipice to precipice till it was heard no more.

The sides of the mountains were covered with trees, the banks of the brooks were diversified with flowers; every blast shook spices from the rocks, and every month dropped fruits upon the ground. All animals that bite the grass, or brouse the shrub, whether wild or tame, wandered in this extensive circuit, secured from beasts of prey by the mountains which confined them. On one part were flocks and herds feeding in the pastures, on another all the beasts of chase frisking in the lawns; the sprightly kid was bounding on the rocks,

---

1. The text is that of the sixth edition (London, 1783). 2. The Nile.

the subtle[3] monkey frolicking in the trees, and the solemn elephant reposing in the shade. All the diversities of the world were brought together, the blessings of nature were collected, and its evils extracted and excluded.

The valley, wide and fruitful, supplied its inhabitants with the necessaries of life, and all delights and superfluities were added at the annual visit which the emperour paid his children, when the iron gate was opened to the sound of musick; and during eight days every one that resided in the valley was required to propose whatever might contribute to make seclusion pleasant, to fill up the vacancies of attention, and lessen the tediousness of time. Every desire was immediately granted. All the artificers of pleasure were called to gladden the festivity; the musicians exerted the power of harmony, and the dancers shewed their activity before the princes, in hope that they should pass their lives in this blissful captivity, to which these only were admitted whose performance was thought able to add novelty to luxury. Such was the appearance of security and delight which this retirement afforded, that they, to whom it was new, always desired that it might be perpetual; and as those, on whom the iron gate had once closed, were never suffered[4] to return, the effect of longer experience could not be known. Thus every year produced new schemes of delight, and new competitors for imprisonment.

The palace stood on an eminence raised about thirty paces above the surface of the lake. It was divided into many squares or courts, built with greater or less magnificence, according to the rank of those for whom they were designed. The roofs were turned into arches of massy stone joined by a cement that grew harder by time, and the building stood from century to century deriding the solstitial rains and equinoctial hurricanes, without need of reparation.

This house, which was so large as to be fully known to none but some ancient officers who successively inherited the secrets of the place, was built as if suspicion herself had dictated the plan. To every room there was an open and secret passage, every square had a communication with the rest, either from the upper stories by private galleries, or by subterranean passages from the lower apartments. Many of the columns had unsuspected cavities, in which a long race of monarchs had reposited their treasures. They then closed up the opening with marble, which was never to be removed but in the utmost exigencies of the kingdom; and recorded their accumulations in a book which was itself concealed in a tower not entered but by the emperour, attended by the prince who stood next in succession.

3. Cunning.　　4. Permitted.

Chapter 2

THE DISCONTENT OF RASSELAS IN THE HAPPY VALLEY

Here the sons and daughters of Abissinia lived only to know the soft vicissitudes[5] of pleasure and repose, attended by all that were skilful to delight, and gratified with whatever the senses can enjoy. They wandered in gardens of fragrance, and slept in the fortresses of security. Every art was practised to make them pleased with their own condition. The sages who instructed them, told them of nothing but the miseries of publick life, and described all beyond the mountains as regions of calamity, where discord was always raging, and where man preyed upon man.

To heighten their opinion of their own felicity, they were daily entertained with songs, the subject of which was the *happy valley*. Their appetites were excited by frequent enumerations of different enjoyments, and revelry and merriment was the business of every hour from the dawn of morning to the close of even.

These methods were generally successful; few of the princes had ever wished to enlarge their bounds, but passed their lives in full conviction that they had all within their reach that art or nature could bestow, and pitied those whom fate had excluded from this seat of tranquillity, as the sport of chance and the slaves of misery.

Thus they rose in the morning and lay down at night, pleased with each other and with themselves, all but Rasselas, who in the twenty-sixth year of his age, began to withdraw himself from their pastimes and assemblies, and to delight in solitary walks and silent meditation. He often sat before tables covered with luxury, and forgot to taste the dainties that were placed before him: he rose abruptly in the midst of the song, and hastily retired beyond the sound of musick. His attendants observed the change and endeavoured to renew his love of pleasure: he neglected their officiousness,[6] repulsed their invitations, and spent day after day on the banks of rivulets sheltered with trees, where he sometimes listened to the birds in the branches, sometimes observed the fish playing in the stream, and anon cast his eyes upon the pastures and mountains filled with animals, of which some were biting the herbage, and some sleeping among the bushes.

This singularity of his humour made him much observed. One of the Sages, in whose conversation he had formerly delighted, followed him secretly, in hope of discovering the cause of his disquiet. Rasselas, who knew not that any one was near him, having for some time fixed his eyes upon the goats that were brousing among the rocks, began to compare their condition with his own.

"What," said he, "makes the difference between man and all the

5. Alternations. 6. Helpfulness.

rest of the animal creation? Every beast that strays beside me has the same corporal necessities with myself; he is hungry and crops the grass, he is thirsty and drinks the stream, his thirst and hunger are appeased, he is satisfied and sleeps; he rises again and is hungry, he is again fed and is at rest. I am hungry and thirsty like him, but when thirst and hunger cease I am not at rest; I am, like him, pained with want, but am not, like him, satisfied with fulness. The intermediate hours are tedious and gloomy; I long again to be hungry that I may again quicken my attention. The birds peck the berries or the corn, and fly away to the groves where they sit in seeming happiness on the branches, and waste their lives in tuning one unvaried series of sounds. I likewise can call the lutanist and the singer, but the sounds that pleased me yesterday weary me to-day, and will grow yet more wearisome tomorrow. I can discover within me no power of perception which is not glutted with its proper pleasure, yet I do not feel myself delighted. Man surely has some latent sense for which this place affords no gratification, or he has some desires distinct from sense which must be satisfied before he can be happy."

After this he lifted up his head, and seeing the moon rising, walked towards the palace. As he passed through the fields, and saw the animals around him, "Ye, said he, are happy, and need not envy me that walk thus among you, burdened with myself; nor do I, ye gentle beings, envy your felicity; for it is not the felicity of man. I have many distresses from which ye are free; I fear pain when I do not feel it; I sometimes shrink at evils recollected, and sometimes start at evils anticipated: surely the equity of providence has balanced peculiar sufferings with peculiar enjoyments."

With observations like these the prince amused himself as he returned, uttering them with a plaintive voice, yet with a look that discovered[7] him to feel some complacence in his own perspicacity, and to receive some solace of the miseries of life, from consciousness of the delicacy with which he felt, and the eloquence with which he bewailed them. He mingled cheerfully in the diversions of the evening, and all rejoiced to find that his heart was lightened.

[Rasselas remains dissatisfied in the Happy Valley and attempts to escape by means of wings; the wings, however, drop their inventor in the lake.]

Chapter 7

THE PRINCE FINDS A MAN OF LEARNING

The prince was not much afflicted by this disaster, having suffered himself to hope for a happier event, only because he had no other

7. Revealed.

means of escape in view. He still persisted in his design to leave the happy valley by the first opportunity.

His imagination was now at a stand; he had no prospect of entering into the world; and, notwithstanding all his endeavours to support himself, discontent by degrees preyed upon him, and he began again to lose his thoughts in sadness, when the rainy season, which in these countries is periodical, made it inconvenient to wander in the woods.

The rain continued longer and with more violence than had been ever known: the clouds broke on the surrounding mountains, and the torrents streamed into the plain on every side, till the cavern was too narrow to discharge the water. The lake overflowed its banks, and all the level of the valley was covered with the inundation. The eminence, on which the palace was built, and some other spots of rising ground, were all that the eye could now discover. The herds and flocks left the pastures, and both the wild beasts and the tame retreated to the mountains.

This inundation confined all the princes to domestick amusements, and the attention of Rasselas was particularly seized by a poem, which Imlac rehearsed upon the various conditions of humanity. He commanded the poet to attend him in his apartment, and recite his verses a second time; then entering into familiar talk, he thought himself happy in having found a man who knew the world so well, and could so skilfully paint the scenes of life. He asked a thousand questions about things, to which, though common to all other mortals, his confinement from childhood had kept him a stranger. The poet pitied his ignorance, and loved his curiosity, and entertained him from day to day with novelty and instruction, so that the prince regretted the necessity of sleep, and longed till the morning should renew his pleasure.

As they were sitting together, the prince commanded Imlac to relate his history, and to tell by what accident he was forced, or by what motive induced, to close his life in the happy valley. As he was going to begin his narrative, Rasselas was called to a concert, and obliged to restrain his curiosity till the evening.

Chapter 8

THE HISTORY OF IMLAC

The close of the day is, in the regions of the torrid zone, the only season of diversion and entertainment, and it was therefore midnight before the musick ceased, and the princesses retired. Rasselas then called for his companion, and required him to begin the story of his life.

"Sir, said Imlac, my history will not be long: the life that is devoted to knowledge passes silently away, and is very little diversified by events. To talk in publick, to think in solitude, to read and to hear, to inquire, and answer inquiries, is the business of a scholar. He wanders about the world without pomp or terrour, and is neither known nor valued but by men like himself.

"I was born in the kingdom of Goiama, at no great distance from the fountain[8] of the Nile. My father was a wealthy merchant, who traded between the inland countries of Africk and the ports of the Red Sea. He was honest, frugal, and diligent, but of mean[9] sentiments, and narrow comprehension: he desired only to be rich, and to conceal his riches, lest he should be spoiled[1] by the governours of the province."

"Surely, said the prince, my father must be negligent of his charge, if any man in his dominions dares take that which belongs to another. Does he not know that kings are accountable for injustice permitted as well as done? If I were emperour, not the meanest[2] of my subjects should be oppressed with impunity. My blood boils when I am told that a merchant durst not enjoy his honest gains for fear of losing them by the rapacity of power. Name the governour who robbed the people, that I may declare his crimes to the emperour."

"Sir, said Imlac, your ardour is the natural effect of virtue animated by youth: the time will come when you will acquit your father, and perhaps hear with less impatience of the governour. Oppression is, in the Abissinian dominions, neither frequent nor tolerated; but no form of government has been yet discovered, by which cruelty can be wholly prevented. Subordination supposes power on one part, and subjection on the other; and if power be in the hands of men, it will sometimes be abused. The vigilance of the supreme magistrate may do much, but much will still remain undone. He can never know all the crimes that are committed, and can seldom punish all that he knows.

"This, said the prince, I do not understand, but I had rather hear thee than dispute. Continue thy narration."

"My father, proceeded Imlac, originally intended that I should have no other education, than such as might qualify me for commerce; and discovering in me great strength of memory, and quickness of apprehension, often declared his hope that I should be some time the richest man in Abissinia."

"Why, said the prince, did thy father desire the increase of his wealth, when it was already greater than he durst discover or enjoy? I am unwilling to doubt thy veracity, yet inconsistencies cannot both be true."

"Inconsistencies, answered Imlac, cannot both be right, but,

---

8. Source.   9. Ignoble, small-minded.   1. Plundered.   2. Lowliest.

imputed to man, they may both be true. Yet diversity is not inconsistency. My father might expect a time of greater security. However,
some desire is necessary to keep life in motion, and he, whose real
wants are supplied, must admit those of fancy."

"This, said the prince, I can in some measure conceive. I repent
that I interrupted thee."

"With this hope, proceeded Imlac, he sent me to school; but when
I had once found the delight of knowledge, and felt the pleasure of
intelligence and the pride of invention, I began silently to despise
riches, and determined to disappoint the purpose of my father, whose
grossness of conception raised my pity. I was twenty years old before
his tenderness would expose me to the fatigue of travel, in which
time I had been instructed, by successive masters, in all the literature
of my native country. As every hour taught me something new, I
lived in a continual course of gratifications; but, as I advanced towards
manhood, I lost much of the reverence with which I had been used
to look on my instructors; because, when the lesson was ended, I did
not find them wiser or better than common men.

"At length my father resolved to initiate me in commerce, and
opening one of his subterranean treasuries, counted out ten thousand pieces of gold. This, young man, said he, is the stock with
which you must negociate.[3] I began with less than the fifth part, and
you see how diligence and parsimony have increased it. This is your
own to waste or to improve. If you squander it by negligence or
caprice, you must wait for my death before you will be rich: if, in
four years, you double your stock, we will thenceforward let subordination cease, and live together as friends and partners; for he shall
always be equal with me, who is equally skilled in the art of growing
rich.

"We laid our money upon camels, concealed in bales of cheap
goods, and travelled to the shore of the Red Sea. When I cast my
eye on the expanse of waters, my heart bounded like that of a prisoner escaped. I felt an unextinguishable curiosity kindle in my mind,
and resolved to snatch this opportunity of seeing the manners of
other nations, and of learning sciences[4] unknown in Abissinia.

"I remembered that my father had obliged me to the improvement
of my stock, not by a promise which I ought not to violate, but by a
penalty which I was at liberty to incur; and therefore determined to
gratify my predominant desire, and by drinking at the fountains of
knowledge, to quench the thirst of curiosity.

"As I was supposed to trade without connexion with my father, it
was easy for me to become acquainted with the master of a ship, and
procure a passage to some other country. I had no motives of choice

3. Do business.   4. Forms of knowledge.

to regulate my voyage; it was sufficient for me that, wherever I wandered, I should see a country which I had not seen before. I therefore entered a ship bound for Surat,[5] having left a letter for my father declaring my intention."

Chapter 9

THE HISTORY OF IMLAC CONTINUED

"When I first entered upon the world of waters, and lost sight of land, I looked round about me with pleasing terrour, and thinking my soul enlarged by the boundless prospect, imagined that I could gaze round for ever without satiety; but, in a short time, I grew weary of looking on barren uniformity, where I could only see again what I had already seen. I then descended into the ship, and doubted for a while whether all my future pleasures would not end like this, in disgust and disappointment. Yet, surely, said I, the ocean and the land are very different; the only variety of water is rest and motion, but the earth has mountains and vallies, deserts and cities: it is inhabited by men of different customs and contrary opinions; and I may hope to find variety in life, though I should miss it in nature.

"With this thought I quieted my mind and amused myself during the voyage, sometimes by learning from the sailors the art of navigation, which I have never practised, and sometimes by forming schemes for my conduct in different situations, in not one of which I have been ever placed.

"I was almost weary of my naval amusements when we landed safely at Surat. I secured my money, and purchasing some commodities for show, joined myself to a caravan that was passing into the inland country. My companions, for some reason or other, conjecturing that I was rich, and, by my inquiries and admiration,[6] finding that I was ignorant, considered me as a novice whom they had a right to cheat, and who was to learn at the usual expence the art of fraud. They exposed me to the theft of servants, and the exaction of officers, and saw me plundered upon false pretences, without any advantage to themselves, but that of rejoicing in the superiority of their own knowledge."

"Stop a moment, said the prince. Is there such depravity in man, as that he should injure another without benefit to himself? I can easily conceive that all are pleased with superiority; but your ignorance was merely accidental, which being neither your crime nor your folly, could afford them no reason to applaud themselves; and the knowledge which they had, and which you wanted,[7] they might as effectually have shewn by warning, as betraying you."

5. An Indian port.   6. Astonishment.   7. Lacked.

"Pride, said Imlac, is seldom delicate, it will please itself with very mean advantages; and envy feels not its own happiness, but when it may be compared with the misery of others. They were my enemies, because they grieved to think me rich; and my oppressors, because they delighted to find me weak."

"Proceed, said the prince: I doubt not of the facts which you relate, but imagine that you impute them to mistaken motives."

"In this company, said Imlac, I arrived at Agra, the capital of Indostan, the city in which the great Mogul commonly resides. I applied myself to the language of the country, and in a few months was able to converse with the learned men; some of whom I found morose and reserved, and others easy and communicative; some were unwilling to teach another what they had with difficulty learned themselves; and some shewed that the end of their studies was to gain the dignity of instructing.

"To the tutor of the young princes I recommended myself so much, that I was presented to the emperour as a man of uncommon knowledge. The emperour asked me many questions concerning my country and my travels; and though I cannot now recollect any thing that he uttered above the power of a common man, he dismissed me astonished at his wisdom, and enamoured of his goodness.

"My credit was now so high, that the merchants, with whom I had travelled, applied to me for recommendations to the ladies of the Court. I was surprised at their confidence of solicitation, and gently reproached them with their practices on the road. They heard me with cold indifference, and shewed no tokens of shame or sorrow.

"They then urged their request with the offer of a bribe; but what I would not do for kindness, I would not do for money; and refused them, not because they had injured me, but because I would not enable them to injure others; for I knew they would have made use of my credit to cheat those who should buy their wares.

"Having resided at Agra till there was no more to be learned, I travelled into Persia, where I saw many remains of ancient magnificence, and observed many new accommodations[8] of life. The Persians are a nation eminently social, and their assemblies afforded me daily opportunities of remarking[9] characters and manners, and of tracing human nature through all its variations.

"From Persia I passed into Arabia, where I saw a nation at once pastoral and warlike; who live without any settled habitation; whose only wealth is their flocks and herds; and who have yet carried on, through all ages, an hereditary war with all mankind, though they neither covet nor envy their possessions."

8. Comforts, conveniences.   9. Noting.

Chapter 10

IMLAC'S HISTORY CONTINUED. A DISSERTATION UPON POETRY.

"Wherever I went, I found that poetry was considered as the highest learning, and regarded with a veneration somewhat approaching to that which man would pay to the Angelick Nature. And yet it fills me with wonder, that, in almost all countries, the most ancient poets are considered as the best: whether it be that every other kind of knowledge is an acquisition gradually attained, and poetry is a gift conferred at once; or that the first poetry of every nation surprised them as a novelty, and retained the credit by consent which it received by accident at first: or whether, as the province of poetry is to describe Nature and Passion, which are always the same, the first writers took possession of the most striking objects for description, and the most probable occurrences for fiction, and left nothing to those that followed them, but transcription of the same events, and new combinations of the same images. Whatever be the reason, it is commonly observed that the early writers are in possession of nature, and their followers of art: that the first excel in strength and invention, and the latter in elegance and refinement.

"I was desirous to add my name to this illustrious fraternity. I read all the poets of Persia and Arabia, and was able to repeat by memory the volumes that are suspended in the mosque of Mecca.[1] But I soon found that no man was ever great by imitation. My desire of excellence impelled me to transfer my attention to nature and to life. Nature was to be my subject, and men to be my auditors: I could never describe what I had not seen: I could not hope to move those with delight or terrour, whose interests and opinions I did not understand.

"Being now resolved to be a poet, I saw every thing with a new purpose; my sphere of attention was suddenly magnified: no kind of knowledge was to be overlooked. I ranged mountains and deserts for images and resemblances, and pictured upon my mind every tree of the forest and flower of the valley. I observed with equal care the crags of the rock and the pinnacles of the palace. Sometimes I wandered along the mazes of the rivulet, and sometimes watched the changes of the summer clouds. To a poet nothing can be useless. Whatever is beautiful, and whatever is dreadful, must be familiar to his imagination: he must be conversant with all that is awfully[2] vast or elegantly little. The plants of the garden, the animals of the wood, the minerals of the earth, and meteors of the sky, must all concur to store his mind with inexhaustible variety: for every idea is useful for

1. Because they have won prizes.   2. Impressively.

the enforcement or decoration of moral or religious truth; and he, who knows most, will have most power of diversifying his scenes, and of gratifying his reader with remote allusions and unexpected instruction.

"All the appearances of nature I was therefore careful to study, and every country which I have surveyed has contributed something to my poetical powers."

"In so wide a survey, said the prince, you must surely have left much unobserved. I have lived, till now, within the circuit of these mountains, and yet cannot walk abroad without the sight of something which I had never beheld before, or never heeded."

"The business of a poet, said Imlac, is to examine, not the individual, but the species; to remark general properties and large appearances; he does not number the streaks of the tulip, or describe the different shades in the verdure of the forest. He is to exhibit in his portraits of nature such prominent and striking features, as recall the original to every mind; and must neglect the minuter discriminations, which one may have remarked, and another have neglected, for those characteristicks which are alike obvious to vigilance and carelessness.

"But the knowledge of nature is only half the task of a poet; he must be acquainted likewise with all the modes of life. His character requires that he estimate the happiness and misery of every condition; observe the power of all the passions in all their combinations, and trace the changes of the human mind as they are modified by various institutions and accidental influences of climate or custom, from the sprightliness of infancy to the despondence of decrepitude. He must divest himself of the prejudices of his age or country; he must consider right and wrong in their abstracted and invariable state; he must disregard present laws and opinions, and rise to general and transcendental truths, which will always be the same: he must therefore content himself with the slow progress of his name; contemn the applause of his own time, and commit his claims to the justice of posterity. He must write as the interpreter of nature, and the legislator of mankind, and consider himself as presiding over the thoughts and manners of future generations; as a being superior to time and place.

"His labour is not yet at an end: he must know many languages and many sciences; and, that his style may be worthy of his thoughts, must, by incessant practice, familiarize to himself every delicacy of speech, and grace of harmony."

Chapter 11

IMLAC'S NARRATIVE CONTINUED, A HINT ON PILGRIMAGE

Imlac now felt the enthusiastic fit,[3] and was proceeding to aggrandize his own profession, when the prince cried out, "Enough! Thou hast convinced me, that no human being can ever be a poet. Proceed with thy narration."

"To be a poet, said Imlac, is indeed very difficult." "So difficult, returned the prince, that I will at present hear no more of his labours. Tell me whither you went when you had seen Persia."

"From Persia, said the poet, I travelled through Syria, and for three years resided in Palestine, where I conversed with great numbers of the northern and western nations of Europe; the nations which are now in possession of all power and all knowledge; whose armies are irresistible, and whose fleets command the remotest parts of the globe. When I compared these men with the natives of our own kingdom, and those that surround us, they appeared almost another order of beings. In their countries it is difficult to wish for any thing that may not be obtained: a thousand arts, of which we never heard, are continually labouring for their convenience and pleasure; and whatever their own climate has denied them is supplied by their commerce."

"By what means, said the prince, are the Europeans thus powerful, or why, since they can so easily visit Asia and Africa for trade or conquest, cannot the Asiaticks and Africans invade their coasts, plant colonies in their ports, and give laws to their natural princes? The same wind that carries them back would bring us thither."

"They are more powerful, Sir, than we, answered Imlac, because they are wiser; knowledge will always predominate over ignorance, as man governs the other animals. But why their knowledge is more than ours, I know not what reason can be given, but the unsearchable will of the Supreme Being."

"When, said the prince with a sigh, shall I be able to visit Palestine, and mingle with this mighty confluence of nations? Till that happy moment shall arrive, let me fill up the time with such representations as thou canst give me. I am not ignorant of the motive that assembles such numbers in that place, and cannot but consider it as the centre of wisdom and piety, to which the best and wisest men of every land must be continually resorting."

"There are some nations, said Imlac, that send few visitants to Palestine; for many numerous and learned sects in Europe concur to censure pilgrimage as superstitious, or deride it as ridiculous."

"You know, said the prince, how little my life has made me

---

3. I.e., a fit of extravagant emotion.

acquainted with diversity of opinions; it will be too long to hear the arguments on both sides; you, that have considered them, tell me the result."

"Pilgrimage, said Imlac, like many other acts of piety, may be reasonable or superstitious according to the principles upon which it is performed. Long journeys in search of truth are not commanded. Truth, such as is necessary to the regulation of life, is always found where it is honestly sought. Change of place is no natural cause of the increase of piety, for it inevitably produces dissipation of mind.[4] Yet, since men go every day to view the fields where great actions have been performed, and return with stronger impressions of the event, curiosity of the same kind may naturally dispose us to view that country whence our religion had its beginning; and I believe no man surveys those awful[5] scenes without some confirmation of holy resolutions. That the Supreme Being may be more easily propitiated in one place than in another, is the dream of idle superstition; but that some places may operate upon our own minds in an uncommon manner, is an opinion which hourly experience will justify. He who supposes that his vices may be more successfully combated in Palestine, will, perhaps, find himself mistaken, yet he may go thither without folly: he who thinks they will be more freely pardoned, dishonours at once his reason and religion."

"These, said the prince, are European distinctions. I will consider them another time. What have you found to be the effect of knowledge? Are those nations happier than we?"

"There is so much infelicity, said the poet, in the world, that scarce any man has leisure from his own distresses to estimate the comparative happiness of others. Knowledge is certainly one of the means of pleasure, as is confessed by the natural desire which every mind feels of increasing its ideas. Ignorance is mere privation, by which nothing can be produced: it is a vacuity in which the soul sits motionless and torpid for want of attraction; and, without knowing why, we always rejoice when we learn, and grieve when we forget. I am therefore inclined to conclude, that if nothing counteracts the natural consequence of learning, we grow more happy as our minds take a wider range.

"In enumerating the particular comforts of life we shall find many advantages on the side of the Europeans. They cure wounds and diseases with which we languish and perish. We suffer inclemencies of weather which they can obviate. They have engines[6] for the dispatch of many laborious works, which we must perform by manual industry. There is such communication between distant places, that one friend can hardly be said to be absent from another. Their policy

4. Scattering of attention.   5. Awe-inspiring.   6. Machines.

removes all publick inconveniencies: they have roads cut through their mountains, and bridges laid upon their rivers. And, if we descend to the privacies of life, their habitations are more commodious, and their possessions are more secure."

"They are surely happy, said the prince, who have all these conveniencies, of which I envy none so much as the facility with which separated friends interchange their thoughts."

"The Europeans, answered Imlac, are less unhappy than we, but they are not happy. Human life is every where a state in which much is to be endured, and little to be enjoyed."

[With the help of Imlac, Rasselas, joined by his sister Nekayah, tunnels to freedom. In Cairo, with the world before them, they begin to "review it at leisure."]

Chapter 18

THE PRINCE FINDS A WISE AND HAPPY MAN

As he [Rasselas] was one day walking in the street, he saw a spacious building which all were, by the open doors, invited to enter: he followed the stream of people, and found it a hall or school of declamation, in which professors read lectures to their auditory. He fixed his eye upon a sage raised above the rest, who discoursed with great energy on the government of the passions. His look was venerable, his action graceful, his pronunciation clear, and his diction elegant. He shewed, with great strength of sentiment, and variety of illustration, that human nature is degraded and debased, when the lower faculties predominate over the higher; that when fancy, the parent of passion, usurps the dominion of the mind, nothing ensues but the natural effect of unlawful government, perturbation and confusion; that she betrays the fortresses of the intellect to rebels, and excites her children to sedition against reason their lawful sovereign. He compared reason to the sun, of which the light is constant, uniform, and lasting: and fancy to a meteor, of bright but transitory lustre, irregular in its motion, and delusive in its direction.

He then communicated the various precepts given from time to time for the conquest of passion, and displayed the happiness of those who had obtained the important victory, after which man is no longer the slave of fear, nor the fool of hope; is no more emaciated by envy, inflamed by anger, emasculated by tenderness, or depressed by grief; but walks on calmly through the tumults or privacies of life, as the sun persues alike his course through the calm or the stormy sky.

He enumerated many examples of heroes immoveable by pain or pleasure, who looked with indifference on those modes or accidents to which the vulgar[7] give the names of good and evil. He exhorted his hearers to lay aside their prejudices, and arm themselves against the shafts of malice or misfortune, by invulnerable patience; concluding, that this state only was happiness, and that this happiness was in every one's power.

Rasselas listened to him with the veneration due to the instructions of a superiour being, and, waiting for him at the door, humbly implored the liberty of visiting so great a master of true wisdom. The lecturer hesitated a moment, when Rasselas put a purse of gold into his hand, which he received with a mixture of joy and wonder.

"I have found, said the prince, at his return to Imlac, a man who can teach all that is necessary to be known, who, from the unshaken throne of rational fortitude, looks down on the scenes of life changing beneath him. He speaks, and attention watches his lips. He reasons, and conviction closes his periods.[8] This man shall be my future guide: I will learn his doctrines, and imitate his life."

"Be not too hasty, said Imlac, to trust, or to admire, the teachers of morality: they discourse like angels, but they live like men."

Rasselas, who could not conceive how any man could reason so forcibly without feeling the cogency of his own arguments, paid his visit in a few days, and was denied admission. He had now learned the power of money, and made his way by a piece of gold to the inner apartment, where he found the philosopher in a room half darkened, with his eyes misty, and his face pale. "Sir, said he, you are come at a time when all human friendship is useless; what I suffer cannot be remedied, what I have lost cannot be supplied. My daughter, my only daughter, from whose tenderness I expected all the comforts of my age, died last night of a fever. My views, my purposes, my hopes are at an end: I am now a lonely being disunited from society."

"Sir, said the prince, mortality is an event by which a wise man can never be surprised; we know that death is always near, and it should therefore always be expected." "Young man, answered the philosopher, you speak like one that has never felt the pangs of separation." "Have you then forgot the precepts, said Rasselas, which you so powerfully enforced? Has wisdom no strength to arm the heart against calamity? Consider, that external things are naturally variable, but truth and reason are always the same." "What comfort, said the mourner, can truth and reason afford me? of what effect are they now, but to tell me, that my daughter will not be restored?"

7. Common people. 8. Sentences.

The prince, whose humanity would not suffer him to insult misery with reproof, went away convinced of the emptiness of rhetorical sound, and the inefficacy of polished periods and studied sentences.

[After various unsuccessful efforts to find examples of happiness, Rasselas and his sister decided to divide the enterprise between them. He will investigate the splendor of courts; she will look into the satisfactions of humbler life.]

Chapter 24

THE PRINCE EXAMINES THE HAPPINESS OF HIGH STATIONS

Rasselas applauded the design, and appeared next day with a splendid retinue at the court of the Bassa.[9] He was soon distinguished for his magnificence, and admitted as a prince whose curiosity had brought him from distant countries, to an intimacy with the great officers, and frequent conversation with the Bassa himself.

He was at first inclined to believe, that the man must be pleased with his own condition, whom all approached with reverence, and heard with obedience, and who had the power to extend his edicts to a whole kingdom. "There can be no pleasure, said he, equal to that of feeling at once the joy of thousands all made happy by wise administration. Yet, since, by the law of subordination, this sublime delight can be in one nation but the lot of one, it is surely reasonable to think, that there is some satisfaction more popular and accessible, and that millions can hardly be subjected to the will of a single man, only to fill his particular breast with incommunicable content."

These thoughts were often in his mind, and he found no solution of the difficulty. But as presents and civilities gained him more familiarity, he found that almost every man who stood high in employment hated all the rest, and was hated by them, and that their lives were a continual succession of plots and detections, stratagems and escapes, faction and treachery. Many of those, who surrounded the Bassa, were sent only to watch and report his conduct; every tongue was muttering censure, and every eye was searching for a fault.

At last the letters of revocation arrived, the Bassa was carried in chains to Constantinople, and his name was mentioned no more.

"What are we now to think of the prerogatives of power, said Rasselas to his sister; is it without any efficacy to good? or, is the subordinate degree only dangerous, and the supreme safe and glorious? Is the Sultan the only happy man in his dominions? or, is the Sultan

9. A high official in Egypt.

himself subject to the torments of suspicion, and the dread of enemies?"

In a short time the second Bassa was deposed. The Sultan, that
had advanced him, was murdered by the Janisaries,[1] and his successor had other views and different favourites.

Chapter 25

THE PRINCESS PURSUES HER INQUIRY WITH MORE DILIGENCE THAN SUCCESS

The princess, in the mean time, insinuated herself into many families; for there are few doors, through which liberality, joined with
good humour, cannot find its way. The daughters of many houses
were airy[2] and cheerful, but Nekayah had been too long accustomed
to the conversation of Imlac and her brother to be much pleased
with childish levity and prattle which had no meaning. She found
their thoughts narrow, their wishes low, and their merriment often
artificial. Their pleasures, poor as they were, could not be preserved
pure, but were embittered by petty competitions and worthless emulation. They were always jealous of the beauty of each other; of a
quality to which solicitude can add nothing, and from which detrac-
tion can take nothing away. Many were in love with triflets like
themselves, and many fancied that they were in love when in truth
they were only idle. Their affection was [seldom] fixed on sense or
virtue, and therefore seldom ended but in vexation. Their grief,
however, like their joy, was transient; every thing floated in their
mind unconnected with the past or future, so that one desire easily
gave way to another, as a second stone cast into the water effaces and
confounds the circles of the first.

With these girls she played as with inoffensive animals, and found
them proud of her countenance,[3] and weary of her company.

But her purpose was to examine more deeply, and her affability
easily persuaded the hearts that were swelling with sorrow to discharge their secrets in her ear: and those whom hope flattered, or
prosperity delighted, often courted her to partake their pleasures.

The princess and her brother commonly met in the evening in a
private summer-house on the bank of the Nile, and related to each
other the occurrences of the day. As they were sitting together, the
princess cast her eyes upon the river that flowed before her. "Answer,
said she, great father of waters, thou that rollest thy floods through
eighty nations, to the invocations of the daughter of thy native king.
Tell me if thou waterest, through all thy course, a single habitation

1. Turkish guards.   2. Lively.   3. Favor.

from which thou dost not hear the murmurs of complaint?"

"You are then, said Rasselas, not more successful in private houses than I have been in courts." "I have, since the last partition of our provinces, said the princess, enabled myself to enter familiarly into many families, where there was the fairest shew of prosperity and peace, and know not one house that is not haunted by some fury that destroys their quiet.

"I did not seek ease among the poor, because I concluded that there it could not be found. But I saw many poor, whom I had supposed to live in affluence. Poverty has, in large cities, very different appearances: it is often concealed in splendour, and often in extravagance. It is the care of a very great part of mankind to conceal their indigence from the rest: they support themselves by temporary expedients, and every day is lost in contriving for the morrow.

"This, however, was an evil, which, though frequent, I saw with less pain, because I could relieve it. Yet some have refused my bounties; more offended with my quickness to detect their wants, than pleased with my readiness to succour them: and others, whose exigencies compelled them to admit my kindness, have never been able to forgive their benefactress. Many, however, have been sincerely grateful, without the ostentation of gratitude, or the hope of other favours."

Chapter 26

THE PRINCESS CONTINUES HER REMARKS ON PRIVATE LIFE

Nekayah perceiving her brother's attention fixed, proceeded in her narrative.

"In families, where there is or is not poverty, there is commonly discord: if a kingdom be, as Imlac tells us, a great family, a family likewise is a little kingdom, torn with factions, and exposed to revolutions. An unpracticed observer expects the love of parents and children to be constant and equal; but this kindness seldom continues beyond the years of infancy: in a short time the children become rivals to their parents. Benefits are allayed by reproaches, and gratitude debased by envy.

"Parents and children seldom act in concert: each child endeavours to appropriate the esteem or fondness of the parents, and the parents, with yet less temptation, betray each other to their children; thus some place their confidence in the father, and some in the mother, and by degrees, the house is filled with artifices and feuds.

"The opinions of children and parents, of the young and the old, are naturally opposite, by the contrary effects of hope and despondence, of expectation and experience, without crime or folly on either side. The colours of life in youth and age appear different, as the face of nature in spring and winter. And how can children credit the assertions of parents, which their own eyes show them to be false?

"Few parents act in such a manner as much to enforce their maxims by the credit of their lives. The old man trusts wholly to slow contrivance and gradual progression: the youth expects to force his way by genius, vigour, and precipitance. The old man pays regard to riches, and the youth reverences virtue. The old man deifies prudence: the youth commits himself to magnanimity and chance. The young man, who intends no ill, believes that none is intended, and therefore acts with openness and candour:[4] but his father, having suffered the injuries of fraud, is impelled to suspect, and too often allured to practise it. Age looks with anger on the temerity of youth, and youth with contempt on the scrupulosity of age. Thus parents and children, for the greatest part, live on to love less and less: and, if those whom nature has thus closely united are the torments of each other, where shall we look for tenderness and consolation?"

"Surely, said the prince, you must have been unfortunate in your choice of acquaintance: I am unwilling to believe, that the most tender of all relations is thus impeded in its effects by natural necessity."

"Domestick discord, answered she, is not inevitably and fatally necessary; but yet it is not easily avoided. We seldom see that a whole family is virtuous: the good and evil cannot well agree; and the evil can yet less agree with one another: even the virtuous fall sometimes to variance, when their virtues are of different kinds, and tending to extremes. In general, those parents have most reverence who most deserve it: for he that lives well cannot be despised.

"Many other evils infest private life. Some are the slaves of servants whom they have trusted with their affairs. Some are kept in continual anxiety to the caprice of rich relations, whom they cannot please, and dare not offend. Some husbands are imperious, and some wives perverse: and, as it is always more easy to do evil than good, though the wisdom or virtue of one can very rarely make many happy, the folly or vice of one may often make many miserable."

"If such be the general effect of marriage, said the prince, I shall, for the future, think it dangerous to connect my interest with that of another, lest I should be unhappy by my partner's fault."

"I have met, said the princess, with many who live single for that reason; but I never found that their prudence ought to raise envy. They dream away their time without friendship, without fondness, and are driven to rid themselves of the day, for which they have no use, by childish amusements, or vicious delights. They act as beings

4. Generosity.

under the constant sense of some known inferiority, that fills their minds with rancour, and their tongues with censure. They are peevish at home, and malevolent abroad; and, as the outlaws of human nature, make it their business and their pleasure to disturb that society which debars them from its privileges. To live without feeling or exciting sympathy, to be fortunate without adding to the felicity of others, or afflicted with out tasting the balm of pity, is a state more gloomy than solitude: it is not retreat, but exclusion from mankind. Marriage has many pains, but celibacy has no pleasures."

"What then is to be done? said Rasselas; the more we inquire, the less we can resolve. Surely he is most likely to please himself that has no other inclination to regard."

Chapter 27

DISQUISITION UPON GREATNESS

The conversation had a short pause. The prince, having considered his sister's observations, told her, that she had surveyed life with prejudice, and supposed misery where she did not find it. "Your narrative, says he, throws yet a darker gloom upon the prospects of futurity: the predictions of Imlac were but faint sketches of the evils painted by Nekayah. I have been lately convinced that quiet is not the daughter of grandeur, or of power: that her presence is not to be bought by wealth, nor enforced by conquest. It is evident, that as any man acts in a wider compass, he must be more exposed to opposition from enmity or miscarriage from chance; whoever has many to please or to govern, must use the ministry of many agents, some of whom will be wicked, and some ignorant; by some he will be misled, and by others betrayed. If he gratifies one he will offend another: those that are not favoured will think themselves injured; and, since favours can be conferred but upon few, the greater number will be always discontented."

"The discontent, said the princess, which is thus unreasonable, I hope that I shall always have spirit to despise, and you, power to repress."

"Discontent, answered Rasselas, will not always be without reason under the most just and vigilant administration of publick affairs. None, however attentive, can always discover that merit which indigence or faction may happen to obscure; and none, however powerful, can always reward it. Yet, he that sees inferiour desert[5] advanced above him, will naturally impute that preference to partiality or caprice; and, indeed, it can scarcely be hoped that any man,

5. Merit, worth.

however magnanimous by nature, or exalted by condition, will be able to persist for ever in the fixed and inexorable justice of distribution: he will sometimes indulge his own affections, and sometimes those of his favourites; he will permit some to please him who can never serve him; he will discover in those whom he loves, qualities which in reality they do not possess; and to those, from whom he receives pleasure, he will in his turn endeavour to give it. Thus will recommendations sometimes prevail which were purchased by money, or by the more destructive bribery of flattery and servility.

"He that has much to do will do something wrong, and of that wrong must suffer the consequences; and, if it were possible that he should always act rightly, yet when such numbers are to judge of his conduct, the bad will censure and obstruct him by malevolence, and the good sometimes by mistake.

"The highest stations cannot therefore hope to be the abodes of happiness, which I would willingly believe to have fled from thrones and palaces to seats[6] of humble privacy and placid obscurity. For what can hinder the satisfaction, or intercept the expectations, of him whose abilities are adequate to his employments, who sees with his own eyes the whole circuit of his influence, who chooses by his own knowledge all whom he trusts, and whom none are tempted to deceive by hope or fear? Surely he has nothing to do but to love and to be loved, to be virtuous and to be happy."

"Whether perfect happiness would be procured by perfect goodness, said Nekayah, this world will never afford an opportunity of deciding. But this, at least, may be maintained, that we do not always find visible happiness in proportion to visible virtue. All natural, and almost all political evils, are incident alike to the bad and good: they are confounded in the misery of a famine, and not much distinguished in the fury of a faction; they sink together in a tempest, and are driven together from their country by invaders. All that virtue can afford is quietness of conscience, a steady prospect of a happier state; this may enable us to endure calamity with patience; but remember that patience must suppose pain."

Chapter 28

RASSELAS AND NEKAYAH CONTINUE THEIR CONVERSATION

"Dear princess, said Rasselas, you fall into the common errours of exaggeratory declamation, by producing, in a familiar disquisition, examples of national calamities, and scenes of extensive misery, which are found in books rather than in the world, and which, as they are

6. Residences.

horrid, are ordained to be rare. Let us not imagine evils which we do not feel, nor injure life by misrepresentations. I cannot bear that querulous eloquence which threatens every city with a siege like that of Jerusalem,[7] that makes famine attend on every flight of locusts, and suspends pestilence on the wing of every blast that issues from the south.

"On necessary and inevitable evils, which overwhelm kingdoms at once, all disputation is vain: when they happen they must be endured. But it is evident, that these bursts of universal distress are more dreaded than felt; thousands and ten thousands flourish in youth, and wither in age, without the knowledge of any other than domestick evils, and share the same pleasures and vexations, whether their kings are mild or cruel, whether the armies of their country persue their enemies, or retreat before them. While courts are disturbed with intestine[8] competitions, and ambassadors are negociating in foreign countries, the smith still plies his anvil, and the husbandman drives his plow forward; the necessaries of life are required and obtained; and the successive business of the seasons continues to make its wonted revolutions.

"Let us cease to consider what, perhaps, may never happen, and what, when it shall happen, will laugh at human speculation. We will not endeavour to modify the motions of the elements, or to fix the destiny of kingdoms. It is our business to consider what beings like us may perform; each labouring for his own happiness, by promoting within his circle, however narrow, the happiness of others.

"Marriage is evidently the dictate of nature; men and women are made to be companions of each other, and therefore I cannot be persuaded but that marriage is one of the means of happiness."

"I know not, said the princess, whether marriage be more than one of the innumerable modes of human misery. When I see and reckon the various forms of connubial infelicity, the unexpected causes of lasting discord, the diversities of temper, the oppositions of opinion, the rude collisions of contrary desire where both are urged by violent impulses, the obstinate contests of disagreeable virtues, where both are supported by consciousness of good intention, I am sometimes disposed to think with the severer casuists of most nations, that marriage is rather permitted than approved, and that none, but by the instigation of a passion too much indulged, entangle themselves with indissoluble compacts."

"You seem to forget, replied Rasselas, that you have, even now, represented celibacy as less happy than marriage. Both conditions may be bad, but they cannot both be worst. Thus it happens when

7. The siege of A.D. 70, after which Titus captured and destroyed the city.   8. Internal.

wrong opinions are entertained, that they mutually destroy each other, and leave the mind open to truth."

"I did not expect, answered the princess, to hear that imputed to falsehood which is the consequence only of frailty. To the mind, as to the eye, it is difficult to compare with exactness objects vast in their extent, and various in their parts. Where we see or conceive the whole at once, we readily note the discriminations, and decide the preference: but of two systems, of which neither can be surveyed by any human being in its full compass of magnitude and multiplicity of complication, where is the wonder, that judging of the whole by parts, I am alternately affected by one and the other as either presses on my memory or fancy? We differ from ourselves just as we differ from each other, when we see only part of the question, as in the multifarious relations of politicks and morality; but when we perceive the whole at once, as in numerical computations, all agree in one judgment, and none ever varies his opinion."

"Let us not add, said the prince, to the other evils of life, the bitterness of controversy, nor endeavour to vie with each other in subtilties of argument. We are employed in a search, of which both are equally to enjoy the success, or suffer by the miscarriage. It is therefore fit that we assist each other. You surely conclude too hastily from the infelicity of marriage against its institution: will not the misery of life prove equally that life cannot be the gift of heaven? The world must be peopled by marriage, or peopled without it."

"How the world is to be peopled, returned Nekayah, is not my care, and needs not be yours. I see no danger that the present generation should omit to leave successors behind them: we are not now inquiring for the world, but for ourselves."

Chapter 29

THE DEBATE OF MARRIAGE CONTINUED

"The good of the whole, says Rasselas, is the same with the good of all its parts. If marriage be best for mankind it must be evidently best for individuals, or a permanent and necessary duty must be the cause of evil, and some must be inevitably sacrificed to the convenience of others. In the estimate which you have made of the two states, it appears that the incommodities of a single life are, in a great measure, necessary and certain, but those of the conjugal state accidental and avoidable.

"I cannot forbear to flatter myself, that prudence and benevolence will make marriage happy. The general folly of mankind is the cause of general complaint. What can be expected but disappointment and repentance from a choice made in the immaturity of youth, in the ardour of desire, without judgment, without foresight, without inquiry after conformity of opinions, similarity of manners, rectitude of judgment, or purity of sentiment.

"Such is the common process of marriage. A youth or maiden meeting by chance, or brought together by artifice, exchange glances, reciprocate civilities, go home, and dream of one another. Having little to divert attention, or diversify thought, they find themselves uneasy when they are apart, and therefore conclude that they shall be happy together. They marry, and discover what nothing but voluntary blindness before had concealed; they wear out life in altercations, and charge nature with cruelty.

"From those early marriages proceeds likewise the rivalry of parents and children: the son is eager to enjoy the world before the father is willing to forsake it, and there is hardly room at once for two generations. The daughter begins to bloom before the mother can be content to fade, and neither can forbear to wish for the absence of the other.

"Surely all these evils may be avoided by that deliberation and delay which prudence prescribes to irrevocable choice. In the variety and jollity of youthful pleasures life may be well enough supported without the help of a partner. Longer time will increase experience, and wider views will allow better opportunities of inquiry and selection: one advantage, at least, will be certain; the parents will be visibly older than their children."

"What reason cannot collect, said Nekayah, and what experiment has not yet taught, can be known only from the report of others. I have been told that late marriages are not eminently happy. This is a question too important to be neglected, and I have often proposed it to those, whose accuracy of remark, and comprehensiveness of knowledge, made their suffrages[9] worthy of regard. They have generally determined, that it is dangerous for a man and woman to suspend their fate upon each other, at a time when opinions are fixed, and habits are established; when friendships have been contracted on both sides, when life has been planned into method, and the mind has long enjoyed the contemplation of its own prospects.

"It is scarcely possible that two travelling through the world under the conduct of chance, should have been both directed to the same path, and it will not often happen that either will quit the track which custom has made pleasing. When the desultory levity of youth has settled into regularity, it is soon succeeded by pride ashamed to yield, or obstinacy delighting to contend. And even though mutual esteem produces mutual desire to please, time itself, as it modifies

9. Opinions.

unchangeably the external mien, determines likewise the direction of the passions, and gives an inflexible rigidity to the manners. Long customs are not easily broken: he that attempts to change the course of his own life, very often labours in vain; and how shall we do that for others, which we are seldom able to do for ourselves?"

"But surely, interposed the prince, you suppose the chief motive of choice forgotten or neglected. Whenever I shall seek a wife, it shall be my first question, whether she be willing to be led by reason?"

"Thus it is, said Nekayah, that philosophers are deceived. There are a thousand familiar disputes which reason never can decide; questions that elude investigation, and make logick ridiculous; cases where something must be done, and where little can be said. Consider the state of mankind, and inquire how few can be supposed to act upon any occasions, whether small or great, with all the reasons of action present to their minds. Wretched would be the pair above all names of wretchedness, who should be doomed to adjust by reason, every morning, all the minute detail of a domestick day.

"Those who marry at an advanced age, will probably escape the encroachments of their children; but, in diminution of this advantage, they will be likely to leave them, ignorant and helpless, to a guardian's mercy: or, if that should not happen, they must at least go out of the world before they see those whom they love best either wise or great.

"From their children, if they have less to fear, they have less also to hope, and they lose, without equivalent, the joys of early love, and the convenience of uniting with manners pliant, and minds susceptible of new impressions, which might wear away their dissimilitudes by long cohabitation, as soft bodies by continual attrition, conform their surfaces to each other.

"I believe it will be found that those who marry late are best pleased with their children, and those who marry early with their partners."

"The union of these two affections, said Rasselas, would produce all that could be wished. Perhaps there is a time when marriage might unite them, a time neither too early for the father, nor too late for the husband."

"Every hour, answered the princess, confirms my prejudice in favour of the position so often uttered by the mouth of Imlac, 'That nature sets her gifts on the right hand and on the left.' Those conditions, which flatter hope and attract desire, are so constituted, that, as we approach one, we recede from another. There are goods so opposed that we cannot seize both but, by too much prudence, may pass between them at too great a distance to reach either. This is often the fate of long consideration; he does nothing who endeavours to do more than is allowed to humanity. Flatter not yourself with contrarieties of pleasure. Of the blessings set before you make your choice, and be content. No man can taste the fruits of autumn while he is delighting his scent with the flowers of the spring: no man can, at the same time, fill his cup from the source and from the mouth of the Nile."

[They decide to visit the pyramids, as monuments of the past. Nekayah's attendant, Pekuah, is frightened and remains behind.]

Chapter 31

THEY ENTER THE PYRAMID

Pekuah descended to the tents, and the rest entered the pyramid: they passed through the galleries, surveyed the vaults of marble, and examined the chest in which the body of the founder is supposed to have been reposited. They then sat down in one of the most spacious chambers to rest a while before they attempted to return.

"We have now, said Imlac, gratified our minds with an exact view of the greatest work of man, except the wall of China.

"Of the wall it is very easy to assign the motive. It secured a wealthy and timorous nation from the incursions of Barbarians, whose unskilfulness in arts made it easier for them to supply their wants by rapine than by industry, and who from time to time poured in upon the habitations of peaceful commerce, as vultures descend upon domestick fowl. Their celerity and fierceness made the wall necessary, and their ignorance made it efficacious.

"But for the pyramids no reason has ever been given adequate to the cost and labour of the work. The narrowness of the chambers proves that it could afford no retreat from enemies, and treasures might have been reposited at far less expence with equal security. It seems to have been erected only in compliance with that hunger of imagination which preys incessantly upon life, and must be always appeased by some employment. Those who have already all that they can enjoy, must enlarge their desires. He that has built for use, till use is supplied, must begin to build for vanity, and extend his plan to the utmost power of human performance, that he may not be soon reduced to form another wish.

"I consider this mighty structure as a monument of the insufficiency of human enjoyments. A king, whose power is unlimited, and whose treasures surmount all real and imaginary wants, is compelled to solace, by the erection of a pyramid, the satiety of dominion and tastelessness of pleasures, and to amuse the tediousness of declining life, by seeing thousands labouring without end, and one stone, for no purpose, laid upon another. Whoever thou art, that, not content with a moderate condition, imaginest happiness in royal magnificence, and dreamest that command or riches can feed the appetite of novelty with perpetual gratifications, survey the pyramids, and confess thy folly!"

[Pekuah is kidnapped by an Arab, but eventually returns to her friends.]

Chapter 34

THE HISTORY OF A MAN OF LEARNING

They returned to Cairo, and were so well pleased at finding themselves together, that none of them went much abroad. The prince began to love learning, and one day declared to Imlac, that he intended to devote himself to science,[1] and pass the rest of his days in literary solitude.

"Before you make your final choice, answered Imlac, you ought to examine its hazards, and converse with some of those who are grown old in the company of themselves. I have just left the observatory of one of the most learned astronomers in the world, who has spent forty years in unwearied attention to the motions and appearances of the celestial bodies, and has drawn out his soul in endless calculations. He admits a few friends once a month to hear his deductions and enjoy his discoveries. I was introduced as a man of knowledge worthy of his notice. Men of various ideas, and fluent conversation, are commonly welcome to those whose thoughts have been long fixed upon a single point, and who find the images of other things stealing away. I delighted him with my remarks; he smiled at the narrative of my travels, and was glad to forget the constellations, and descend for a moment into the lower world.

"On the next day of vacation I renewed my visit, and was so fortunate as to please him again. He relaxed from that time the severity of his rule, and permitted me to enter at my own choice. I found him always busy, and always glad to be relieved. As each knew much which the other was desirous of learning, we exchanged our notions with great delight. I perceived that I had every day more of his confidence, and always found new cause of admiration in the profundity of his mind. His comprehension is vast, his memory capacious and retentive, his discourse is methodical, and his expression clear.

"His integrity and benevolence are equal to his learning. His deepest researches and most favourite studies are willingly interrupted for any opportunity of doing good by his counsel or his riches. To his

1. Knowledge.

closest retreat, at his most busy moments, all are admitted that want his assistance: "For though I exclude idleness and pleasure, I will never, says he, bar my doors against charity. To man is permitted the contemplation of the skies, but the practice of virtue is commanded."

"Surely, said the princess, this man is happy."

"I visited him, said Imlac, with more and more frequency, and was every time more enamoured of his conversation: he was sublime without haughtiness, courteous without formality, and communicative without ostentation. I was at first, great princess, of your opinion, thought him the happiest of mankind, and often congratulated him on the blessing that he enjoyed. He seemed to hear nothing with indifference but the praises of his condition, to which he always returned a general answer, and diverted the conversation to some other topick."

"Amidst this willingness to be pleased, and labour to please, I had quickly reason to imagine that some painful sentiment pressed upon his mind. He often looked up earnestly towards the sun, and let his voice fall in the midst of his discourse. He would sometimes when we were alone, gaze upon me in silence with the air of a man who longed to speak what he was yet resolved to suppress. He would often send for me with vehement injunctions of haste, though, when I came to him, he had nothing extraordinary to say. And sometimes, when I was leaving him, would call me back, pause a few moments, and then dismiss me.

Chapter 40

THE ASTRONOMER DISCOVERS THE CAUSE OF HIS UNEASINESS

"At last the time came when the secret burst his reserve. We were sitting together last night in the turret of his house, watching the emersion[2] of a satellite of Jupiter. A sudden tempest clouded the sky, and disappointed our observation. We sat a while silent in the dark, and then he addressed himself to me in these words; "Imlac, I have long considered thy friendship as the greatest blessing of my life. Integrity without knowledge is weak and useless, and knowledge without integrity is dangerous and dreadful. I have found in thee all the qualities requisite for trust, benevolence, experience, and fortitude. I have long discharged an office which I must soon quit at the call of nature, and shall rejoice in the hour of imbecility and pain to devolve it upon thee."

"I thought myself honoured by this testimony, and protested, that

2. Reappearance (after having been obscured, for example, by clouds.)

whatever could conduce to his happiness would add likewise to mine."

"Hear Imlac, what thou wilt not without difficulty credit. I have possessed for five years the regulation of weather, and the distribution of the seasons: the sun has listened to my dictates, and passed from tropick to tropick by my direction; the clouds, at my call, have poured their waters, and the Nile has overflowed at my command; I have restrained the rage of the dogstar, and mitigated the fervours of the crab.[3] The winds alone, of all the elemental powers, have hitherto refused my authority, and multitudes have perished by equinoctial tempests, which I found myself unable to prohibit or restrain. I have administered this great office with exact justice, and made to the different nations of the earth an impartial dividend of rain and sunshine. What must have been the misery of half the globe, if I had limited the clouds to particular regions, or confined the sun to either side of the equator?"

Chapter 41

THE OPINION OF THE ASTRONOMER IS EXPLAINED AND JUSTIFIED

"I suppose he discovered in me, through the obscurity of the room, some tokens of amazement and doubt, for, after a short pause, he proceeded thus:"

"Not to be easily credited will neither surprise nor offend me; for I am, probably, the first of human beings to whom this trust has been imparted. Nor do I know whether to deem this distinction a reward or punishment; since I have possessed it I have been far less happy than before, and nothing but the consciousness of good intention could have enabled me to support the weariness of unremitted vigilance."

"How long, Sir, said I, has this great office been in your hands?"

"About ten years ago, said he, my daily observations of the changes of the sky led me to consider, whether, if I had the power of the seasons, I could confer greater plenty upon the inhabitants of the earth. This contemplation fastened on my mind, and I sat days and nights in imaginary dominion, pouring upon this country and that the showers of fertility, and seconding every fall of rain with a due proportion of sunshine. I had yet only the will to do good, and did not imagine that I should ever have the power."

"One day, as I was looking on the fields withering with heat, I felt in my mind a sudden wish that I could send rain on the southern mountains, and raise the Nile to an inundation. In the hurry of my imagination I commanded rain to fall, and by comparing the time

3. The constellation Cancer, associated with the summer solstice; *the dogstar*: Sirius, which rises in late summer and was supposed to cause insanity.

of my command, with that of the inundation, I found that the clouds
had listened to my lips."

"Might not some other cause, said I, produce this concurrence?
the Nile does not always rise on the same day."

"Do not believe, said he with impatience, that such objections
could escape me: I reasoned long against my own conviction, and
laboured against truth with the utmost obstinacy. I sometimes suspected myself of madness, and should not have dared to impart this
secret but to a man like you, capable of distinguishing the wonderful
from the impossible, and the incredible from the false."

"Why, Sir, said I, do you call that incredible, which you know,
or think you know, to be true?"

"Because, said he, I cannot prove it by any external evidence; and
I know too well the laws of demonstration to think that my conviction ought to influence another, who cannot, like me, be conscious
of its force. I, therefore, shall not attempt to gain credit by disputation. It is sufficient that I feel this power, that I have long possessed,
and every day exerted it. But the life of man is short, the infirmities
of age increase upon me, and the time will soon come, when the
regulator of the year must mingle with the dust. The care of appointing a successor has long disturbed me; the night and the day have
been spent in comparisons of all the characters which have come to
my knowledge, and I have yet found none so worthy as thyself.

Chapter 42

THE ASTRONOMER LEAVES IMLAC HIS DIRECTIONS

"Hear, therefore, what I shall impart with attention, such as the
welfare of a world requires. If the task of a king be considered as
difficult, who has the care only of a few millions, to whom he cannot
do much good or harm, what must be the anxiety of him, on whom
depends the action of the elements, and the great gifts of light and
heat!—Hear me therefore with attention.

"I have diligently considered the position of the earth and sun,
and formed innumerable schemes in which I changed their situation. I have sometimes turned aside the axis of the earth, and sometimes varied the ecliptick of the sun: but I have found it impossible
to make a disposition by which the world may be advantaged; what
one region gains, another loses by an imaginable alteration, even
without considering the distant parts of the solar system with which
we are unacquainted. Do not therefore, in thy administration of the
year, indulge thy pride by innovation; do not please thyself with
thinking that thou canst make thyself renowned to all future ages, by
disordering the seasons. The memory of mischief is no desirable fame.

Much less will it become thee to let kindness or interest[4] prevail. Never rob other countries of rain to pour it on thine own. For us the Nile is sufficient."

"I promised, that when I possessed the power, I would use it with inflexible integrity; and he dismissed me, pressing my hand." "My heart, said he, will be now at rest, and my benevolence will no more destroy my quiet; I have found a man of wisdom and virtue, to whom I can cheerfully bequeath the inheritance of the sun."

The prince heard this narration with very serious regard; but the princess smiled, and Pekuah convulsed herself with laughter. "Ladies, said Imlac, to mock the heaviest of human afflictions is neither charitable nor wise. Few can attain this man's knowledge, and few practise his virtues; but all may suffer his calamity. Of the uncertainties of our present state, the most dreadful and alarming is the uncertain continuance of reason."

The princess was recollected, and the favourite was abashed. Rasselas, more deeply affected, inquired of Imlac, whether he thought such maladies of the mind frequent, and how they were contracted?

Chapter 43

THE DANGEROUS PREVALENCE OF IMAGINATION

"Disorders of intellect, answered Imlac, happen much more often than superficial observers will easily believe. Perhaps, if we speak with rigorous exactness, no human mind is in its right state. There is no man whose imagination does not sometimes predominate over his reason, who can regulate his attention wholly by his will, and whose ideas will come and go at his command. No man will be found in whose mind airy notions do not sometimes tyrannize, and force him to hope or fear beyond the limits of sober probability. All power of fancy over reason is a degree of insanity; but while this power is such as we can control and repress, it is not visible to others, nor considered as any depravation of the mental faculties: it is not pronounced madness but when it comes ungovernable, and apparently[5] influences speech or action.

"To indulge the power of fiction, and send imagination out upon the wing, is often the sport of those who delight too much in silent speculation. When we are alone we are not always busy; the labour of excogitation is too violent to last long; the ardour of inquiry will sometimes give way to idleness or satiety. He who has nothing external that can divert him, must find pleasure in his own thoughts, and must conceive himself what he is not; for who is pleased with what

---

4. Self-interest.   5. Obviously; *comes*: becomes.

he is not; for who is pleased with what he is? He then expatiates in boundless futurity, and culls from all imaginable conditions that which for the present moment he should most desire, amuses his desires with impossible enjoyments, and confers upon his pride unattainable dominion. The mind dances from scene to scene, unites all pleasures in all combinations, and riots in delights, which nature and fortune, with all their bounty, cannot bestow.

"In time, some particular train of ideas fixes the attention, all other intellectual gratifications are rejected, the mind, in weariness or leisure, recurs constantly to the favourite conception, and feasts on the luscious falsehood, whenever she is offended with the bitterness of truth. By degrees the reign of fancy is confirmed; she grows first imperious, and in time despotick. The fictions begin to operate as realities, false opinions fasten upon the mind, and life passes in dreams of rapture or of anguish.

"This, Sir, is one of the dangers of solitude, which the hermit has confessed not always to promote goodness, and the astronomer's misery has proved to be not always propitious to wisdom."

"I will no more, said the favourite, imagine myself the queen of Abissinia. I have often spent the hours, which the princess gave to my own disposal, in adjusting ceremonies and regulating the court; I have repressed the pride of the powerful, and granted the petitions of the poor; I have built new palaces in more happy situations, planted groves upon the tops of mountains, and have exulted in the beneficence of royalty, till, when the princess entered, I had almost forgotten to bow down before her."

"And I, said the princess, will not allow myself any more to play the shepherdess in my waking dreams. I have often soothed my thoughts with the quiet and innocence of pastoral employments, till I have in my chamber heard the winds whistle, and the sheep bleat: sometimes freed the lamb entangled in the thicket, and sometimes with my crook encountered the wolf. I have a dress like that of the village maids, which I put on to help my imagination, and a pipe on which I play softly, and suppose myself followed by my flocks."

"I will confess, said the prince, an indulgence of fantastick delight more dangerous than yours. I have frequently endeavoured to image the possibility of a perfect government, by which all wrong should be restrained, all vice reformed, and all the subjects preserved in tranquillity and innocence. This thought produced innumerable schemes of reformation, and dictated many useful regulations and salutary edicts. This has been the sport, and sometimes the labour, of my solitude; and I start, when I think with how little anguish I once supposed the death of my father and my brothers."

"Such, says Imlac, are the effects of visionary schemes: when we first form them we know them to be absurd, but familiarize them by degrees, and in time lose sight of their folly."

Chapter 44

THEY DISCOURSE WITH AN OLD MAN

The evening was now far past, and they rose to return home. As they walked along the bank of the Nile, delighted with the beams of the moon quivering on the water, they saw at a small distance an old man, whom the prince had often heard in the assembly of the sages. "Yonder, said he, is one whose years have calmed his passions, but not clouded his reason: let us close the disquisitions of the night, by inquiring what are his sentiments of his own state, that we may know whether youth alone is to struggle with vexation, and whether any better hope remains for the latter part of life."

Here the sage approached and saluted them. They invited him to join their walk, and prattled a while, as acquaintances that had unexpectedly met one another. The old man was cheerful and talkative, and the way seemed short in his company. He was pleased to find himself not disregarded, accompanied them to their house, and, at the prince's request, entered with them. They placed him in the seat of honour, and set wine and conserves before him.

"Sir, said the princess, an evening walk must give to a man of learning, like you, pleasures which ignorance and youth can hardly conceive. You know the qualities and the causes of all that you behold, the laws by which the river flows, the periods in which the planets perform their revolutions. Every thing must supply you with contemplation, and renew the consciousness of your own dignity."

"Lady, answered he, let the gay and the vigorous expect pleasure in their excursions, it is enough that age can obtain ease. To me the world has lost its novelty: I look round, and see what I remember to have seen in happier days. I rest against a tree, and consider, that in the same shade I once disputed upon the annual overflow of the Nile with a friend who is now silent in the grave. I cast my eyes upwards, fix them on the changing moon, and think with pain on the vicissitudes of life. I have ceased to take much delight in physical truth; for what have I to do with those things which I am soon to leave?"

"You may at least recreate yourself, said Imlac, with the recollection of an honourable and useful life, and enjoy the praise which all agree to give you."

"Praise, said the sage, with a sigh, is to an old man an empty sound. I have neither mother to be delighted with the reputation of her son, nor wife to partake the honours of her husband. I have

outlived my friends and my rivals. Nothing is now of much importance; for I cannot extend my interest beyond myself. Youth is delighted
with applause, because it is considered as the earnest of some future
good, and because the prospect of life is far extended: but to me, who
am now declining to decrepitude, there is little to be feared from the
malevolence of men, and yet less to be hoped from their affection or
esteem. Something they may yet take away, but they can give me
nothing. Riches would now be useless, and high employment would
be pain. My retrospect of life recalls to my view many opportunities
of good neglected, much time squandered upon trifles, and more
lost in idleness and vacancy.[6] I leave many great designs unat-
tempted, and many great attempts unfinished. My mind is burdened
with no heavy crime, and therefore I compose myself to tranquillity;
endeavour to abstract my thoughts from hopes and cares, which,
though reason knows them to be vain, still try to keep their old possession of the heart; expect, with serene humility, that hour which
nature cannot long delay; and hope to possess, in a better state, that
happiness which here I could not find, and that virtue which here I
have not attained."

He rose and went away, leaving his audience not much elated
with the hope of long life. The prince consoled himself with remarking, that it was not reasonable to be disappointed by this account; for
age had never been considered as the season of felicity, and if it was
possible to be easy in decline and weakness, it was likely that the days
of vigour and alacrity might be happy: that the noon of life might be
bright, if the evening could be calm.

The princess suspected that age was querulous and malignant, and
delighted to repress the expectations of those who had newly entered
the world. She had seen the possessors of estates look with envy on
their heirs, and known many who enjoyed pleasure no longer than
they can confine it to themselves.

Pekuah conjectured, that the man was older than he appeared,
and was willing to impute his complaints to delirious dejection; or
else supposed that he had been unfortunate, and was therefore discontented: "For nothing, said she, is more common, than to call our
own condition the condition of life."

Imlac, who had no desire to see them depressed, smiled at the
comforts which they could so readily procure to themselves, and
remembered, that at the same age, he was equally confident of
unmingled prosperity, and equally fertile of consolatory expedients.
He forbore to force upon them unwelcome knowledge, which time
itself would too soon impress. The princess and her lady retired; the
madness of the astronomer hung upon their minds, and they desired

6. Inactivity.

Imlac to enter upon his office, and delay next morning the rising of the sun.

Chapter 45

THE PRINCESS AND PEKUAH VISIT THE ASTRONOMER

The princess and Pekuah having talked in private of Imlac's astronomer, thought his character at once so amiable and so strange, that they could not be satisfied without a nearer knowledge; and Imlac was requested to find the means of bringing them together.

This was somewhat difficult; the philosopher had never received any visits from women, though he lived in a city that had in it many Europeans who followed the manners of their own countries, and many from other parts of the world, that lived there with European liberty. The ladies would not be refused, and several schemes were proposed for the accomplishment of their design. It was proposed to introduce them as strangers in distress, to whom the sage was always accessible; but, after some deliberation, it appeared, that by this artifice, no acquaintance could be formed, for their conversation would be short, and they could not decently importune him often. "This, said Rasselas, is true; but I have yet a stronger objection against the misrepresentation of your state. I have always considered it as treason against the great republic of human nature, to make any man's virtues the means of deceiving him, whether on great or little occasions. All imposture weakens confidence, and chills benevolence. When the sage finds that you are not what you seemed, he will feel the resentment natural to a man who, conscious of great abilities, discovers that he has been tricked by understandings meaner than his own, and, perhaps, the distrust, which he can never afterwards wholly lay aside, may stop the voice of counsel, and close the hand of charity; and where will you find the power of restoring his benefactions to mankind, or his peace to himself?"

To this no reply was attempted, and Imlac began to hope that their curiosity would subside; but, next day, Pekuah told him, she had now found an honest pretence for a visit to the astronomer, for she would solicit permission to continue under him the studies in which she had been initiated by the Arab, and the princess might go with her either as a fellow-student, or because a woman could not decently come alone. "I am afraid, said Imlac, that he will be soon weary of your company: men advanced far in knowledge do not love to repeat the elements of their art, and I am not certain that even of the elements, as he will deliver them connected with inferences, and mingled with reflections, you are a very capable auditress." "That, said Pekuah, must be my care: I ask of you only to take me thither. My

knowledge is, perhaps, more than you imagine it, and, by concur-
ring always with his opinions, I shall make him think it greater than
it is."

The astronomer, in pursuance of this resolution, was told, that a
foreign lady, travelling in search of knowledge, had heard of his reputation, and was desirous to become his scholar. The uncommon-
ness of the proposal raised at once his surprise and curiosity, and
when, after a short deliberation, he consented to admit her; he could
not stay without impatience till the next day.

The ladies dressed themselves magnificently, and were attended
by Imlac to the astronomer, who was pleased to see himself approached
with respect by persons of so splendid an appearance. In the exchange
of the first civilities he was timorous and bashful; but when the talk
became regular, he recollected his powers, and justified the character[7]
which Imlac had given. Inquiring of Pekuah, what could have turned
her inclination towards astronomy? he received from her a history of
her adventure at the pyramid, and of the time passed in the Arab's
island. She told her tale with ease and elegance, and her conversation took possession of his heart. The discourse was then turned to
astronomy: Pekuah displayed what she knew: he looked upon her as
a prodigy of genius, and entreated her not to desist from a study
which she had so happily begun.

They came again and again, and were every time more welcome
than before. The sage endeavoured to amuse them, that they might
prolong their visits, for he found his thoughts grow brighter in their
company; the clouds of solicitude vanished by degrees, as he forced
himself to entertain them, and he grieved when he was left at their
departure to his old employment of regulating the seasons.

The princess and her favourite had now watched his lips for several months, and could not catch a single word from which they
could judge whether he continued, or not, in the opinion of his
preternatural commission. They often contrived to bring him to an
open declaration; but he easily eluded all their attacks, and on which
side soever they pressed him, escaped from them to some other topick.

As their familiarity increased, they invited him often to the house
of Imlac, where they distinguished him by extraordinary respect. He
began gradually to delight in sublunary pleasures. He came early,
and departed late; laboured to recommend himself by assiduity and
compliance; excited their curiosity after new arts, that they might
still want his assistance; and when they made any excursion of pleasure or inquiry, entreated to attend them.

By long experience of his integrity and wisdom, the prince and his
sister were convinced that he might be trusted without danger; and

7. Characterization.

lest he should draw any false hopes from the civilities which he received, discovered to him their condition, with the motives of their journey; and required his opinion on the choice of life.

"Of the various conditions which the world spreads before you, which you shall prefer, said the sage, I am not able to instruct you. I can only tell that I have chosen wrong. I have passed my time in study without experience; in the attainment of sciences which can, for the most part, be but remotely useful to mankind. I have purchased knowledge at the expence of all the common comforts of life: I have missed the endearing elegance of female friendship, and the happy commerce of domestick tenderness. If I have obtained any prerogatives above other students, they have been accompanied with fear, disquiet, and scrupulosity; but even of these prerogatives, whatever they were, I have, since my thoughts have been diversified by more intercourse with the world, begun to question the reality. When I have been for a few days lost in pleasing dissipation,[8] I am always tempted to think that my inquiries have ended in errour, and that I have suffered much, and suffered it in vain."

Imlac was delighted to find that the sage's understanding was breaking through its mists, and resolved to detain him from the planets till he should forget his task of ruling them, and reason should recover its original influence.

From this time the astronomer was received into familiar friendship, and partook of all their projects and pleasures: his respect kept him attentive, and the activity of Rasselas did not leave much time unengaged. Something was always to be done; the day was spent in making observations which furnished talk for the evening, and the evening was closed with a scheme for the morrow.

The sage confessed to Imlac, that since he had mingled in the gay tumults of life, and divided his hours by a succession of amusements, he found the conviction of his authority over the skies fade gradually from his mind, and began to trust less to an opinion which he never could prove to others, and which he now found subject to variation, from causes in which reason had no part. "If I am accidentally left alone for a few hours, said he, my inveterate persuasion rushes upon my soul, and my thoughts are chained down by some irresistible violence; but they are soon disentangled by the prince's conversation, and instantaneously released at the entrance of Pekuah. I am like a man habitually afraid of spectres, who is set at ease by a lamp, and wonders at the dread which harassed him in the dark; yet, if his lamp be extinguished, feels again the terrours which he knows that when it is light he shall feel no more. But I am sometimes afraid lest I indulge my quiet by criminal negligence, and voluntarily

8. Frivolity.

forget the great charge with which I am intrusted. If I favour myself in a known errour, or am determined by my own ease in a doubtful question of this importance, how dreadful is my crime!"

"No disease of the imagination, answered Imlac, is so difficult of cure, as that which is complicated with the dread of guilt: fancy and conscience then act interchangeably upon us, and so often shift their places, that the illusions of one are not distinguished from the dictates of the other. If fancy presents images not moral or religious, the mind drives them away when they give it pain, but when melancholick notions take the form of duty, they lay hold on the faculties without opposition, because we are afraid to exclude or banish them. For this reason the superstitious are often melancholy, and the melancholy almost always superstitious.

"But do not let the suggestions of timidity overpower your better reason: the danger of neglect can be but as the probability of the obligation, which when you consider it with freedom, you find very little, and that little growing every day less. Open your heart to the influence of the light, which, from time to time, breaks in upon you: when scruples importune you, which you in your lucid moments know to be vain, do not stand to parley, but fly to business or to Pekuah, and keep this thought always prevalent, that you are only one atom of the mass of humanity, and have neither such virtue nor vice, as that you should be singled out for supernatural favours or afflictions."

Chapter 46

THE PRINCE ENTERS, AND BRINGS A NEW TOPICK

"All this, said the astronomer, I have often thought, but my reason has been so long subjugated by an uncontrolable and overwhelming idea, that it durst not confide in its own decisions. I now see how fatally I betrayed my quiet, by suffering chimeras to prey upon me in secret; but melancholy shrinks from communication, and I never found a man before, to whom I could impart my troubles, though I had been certain of relief. I rejoice to find my own sentiments confirmed by yours, who are not easily deceived, and can have no motive or purpose to deceive. I hope that time and variety will dissipate the gloom that has so long surrounded me, and the latter part of my days will be spent in peace."

"Your learning and virtue, said Imlac, may justly give you hopes."

Rasselas then entered with the princess and Pekuah, and inquired, whether they had contrived any new diversion for the next day? "Such, said Nekayah, is the state of life, that none are happy but by the anticipation of change: the change itself is nothing; when we have made it, the next wish is to change again. The world is not yet exhausted; let me see something to-morrow which I never saw before."

[They visit the catacombs, "ancient repositories in which the bodies of the earliest generations were lodged."]

Chapter 47

IMLAC DISCOURSES ON THE NATURE OF THE SOUL

"What reason, said the prince, can be given why the Egyptians should thus expensively preserve those carcases which some nations consume with fire, others lay to mingle with the earth, and all agree to remove from their sight, as soon as decent rites can be performed?"

"The original[9] of ancient customs, said Imlac, is commonly unknown; for the practice often continues when the cause has ceased; and concerning superstitious ceremonies it is vain to conjecture; for what reason did not dictate, reason cannot explain. I have long believed that the practice of embalming arose only from tenderness to the remains of relations or friends, and to this opinion I am more inclined, because it seems impossible that this care should have been general: had all the dead been embalmed, their repositories must in time have been more spacious than the dwellings of the living. I suppose only the rich or honourable were secured from corruption, and the rest left to the course of nature.

"But it is commonly supposed that the Egyptians believed the soul to live as long as the body continued undissolved, and therefore tried this method of eluding death."

"Could the wise Egyptians, said Nekayah, think so grossly of the soul? If the soul could once survive its separation, what could it afterwards receive or suffer from the body?"

"The Egyptians would doubtless think erroneously, said the astronomer, in the darkness of heathenism, and the first dawn of philosophy. The nature of the soul is still disputed amidst all our opportunities of clearer knowledge: some yet say, that it may be material, who, nevertheless, believe it to be immortal."

"Some answered Imlac, have indeed said that the soul is material, but I can scarcely believe that any man has thought it, who knew how to think; for all the conclusions of reason enforce the immateriality of mind, and all the notices of sense and investigations of science concur to prove the unconsciousness of matter.

"It was never supposed that cogitation is inherent in matter, or that every particle is a thinking being. Yet, if any part of matter be

9. Origin.

devoid of thought, what part can we suppose to think? Matter can differ from matter only in form, density, bulk, motion, and direction of motion. To which of these, however varied or combined, can consciousness be annexed? To be round or square, to be solid or fluid, to be great or little, to be moved slowly or swiftly one way or another, are modes of material existence, all equally alien from the nature of cogitation. If matter be once without thought, it can only be made to think by some new modification, but all the modifications which it can admit are equally unconnected with cogitative powers."

"But the materialists, said the astronomer, urge that matter may have qualities with which we are unacquainted."

"He who will determine, returned Imlac, against that which he knows, because there may be something which he knows not; he that can set hypothetical possibility against acknowledged certainty, is not to be admitted among reasonable beings. All that we know of matter is, that matter is inert, senseless, and lifeless; and if this conviction cannot be opposed but by referring us to something that we know not, we have all the evidence that human intellect can admit. If that which is known may be over-ruled by that which is unknown, no being, not omniscient, can arrive at certainty."

"Yet let us not, said the astronomer, too arrogantly limit the Creator's power."

"It is no limitation of omnipotence, replied the poet, to suppose that one thing is not consistent with another, that the same proposition cannot be at once true and false, that the same number cannot be even and odd, that cogitation cannot be conferred on that which is created incapable of cogitation."

"I know not, said Nekayah, any great use of this question. Does that immateriality, which, in my opinion, you have sufficiently proved, necessarily include eternal duration?"

"Of immateriality, said Imlac, our ideas are negative, and therefore obscure. Immateriality seems to imply a natural power of perpetual duration as a consequence of exemption from all causes of decay: whatever perishes is destroyed by the solution of its contexture, and separation of its parts; nor can we conceive how that which has no parts, and therefore admits no solution, can be naturally corrupted or impaired."

"I know not, said Rasselas, how to conceive any thing without extension; what is extended must have parts, and you allow, that whatever has parts may be destroyed."

"Consider your own conceptions, replied Imlac, and the difficulty will be less. You will find substance without extension. An ideal form is no less real than material bulk: yet an ideal form has no extension. It is no less certain, when you think on a pyramid, that your mind possesses the idea of a pyramid, than that the pyramid itself is standing. What space does the idea of a pyramid occupy more than the idea of a grain of corn? or how can either idea suffer laceration? As is the effect such is the cause; as thought, such is the power that thinks; a power impassive and indiscernible."[1]

"But the Being, said Nekayah, whom I fear to name, the Being which made the soul, can destroy it."

"He, surely, can destroy it, answered Imlac, since, however unperishable, it receives from a superiour nature its power of duration. That it will not perish by any inherent cause of decay, or principle of corruption, may be shewn by philosophy; but philosophy can tell no more. That it will not be annihilated by him that made it, we must humbly learn from higher authority."

The whole assembly stood awhile silent and collected. "Let us return, said Rasselas, from this scene of mortality. How gloomy would be these mansions of the dead to him who did not know that he should never die; that what now acts shall continue its agency, and what now thinks shall think on for ever. Those that lie here stretched before us, the wise and the powerful of ancient times, warn us to remember the shortness of our present state: they were, perhaps, snatched away while they were busy like us in the choice of life."

"To me, said the princess, the choice of life is become less important; I hope hereafter to think only on the choice of eternity."

They then hastened out of the caverns, and, under the protection of their guard, returned to Cairo.

Chapter 48

THE CONCLUSION, IN WHICH NOTHING IS CONCLUDED

It was now the time of the inundation of the Nile: a few days after their visit to the catacombs, the river began to rise.

They were confined to their house. The whole region being under water gave them no invitation to any excursions, and, being well supplied with materials for talk, they diverted themselves with comparisons of the different forms of life which they had observed, and with various schemes of happiness, which each of them had formed.

Pekuah was never so much charmed with any place as the convent of St. Anthony, where the Arab restored her to the princess, and wished only to fill it with pious maidens, and to be made prioress of the order: she was weary of expectation and disgust, and would gladly be fixed in some unvariable state.

The princess thought, that of all sublunary things, knowledge was the best: She desired first to learn all sciences, and then purposed to

---

1. Incapable of being divided.

found a college of learned women, in which she would preside, that, by conversing with the old, and educating the young, she might divide her time between the acquisition and communication of wisdom, and raise up for the next age models of prudence, and patterns of piety.

The prince desired a little kingdom, in which he might administer justice in his own person, and see all the parts of government with his own eyes, but he could never fix the limits of his dominion, and was always adding to the number of his subjects.

Imlac and the astronomer were contented to be driven along the stream of life, without directing their course to any particular port.

Of these wishes that they had formed they well knew that none could be obtained. They deliberated awhile what was to be done, and resolved, when the inundation should cease, to return to Abissinia.

Masterpieces of the Nineteenth Century: Varieties of Romanticism

"Bliss was it in that dawn to be alive, / But to be young was very heaven." William Wordsworth alludes here to his experience, at the age of seventeen, of the French Revolution. The possibility of referring to a national cataclysm in such terms suggests the remarkable shift in sensibility, in dominant assumptions, in intellectual preoccupations, that occurred late in the eighteenth century. We call the evidence of that shift "Romanticism"—a designation so grandly inclusive as to defy definition. If our terms for the late seventeenth and early eighteenth centuries ("Enlightenment," "Age of Reason") emphasize one aspect of the prevailing intellectual culture to the exclusion of others equally important, the label of "Romanticism" refers to so many cultural manifestations that one can hardly pin it down. In general, it implies new emphasis on imagination, on feeling, on the value of the primitive and untrammeled, and particularly a narrowing of outlook from the universal to the particular, from humankind or "man" (the subject of Pope's *Essay*) to nation or ethnic group, and from the stability of community to the "fulfillment" of the individual. Such shifts have important political and philosophic as well as literary implications.

In the writings of individuals, one finds lines of continuity between the late and early parts of the eighteenth century; but when it comes to generalizations, all the important truths appear to have reversed themselves. In the middle of the century, reason was the guide to certainty; at the century's end, *feeling* tested authenticity. Earlier, tradition still anchored experience; now, the ideal of joyous liberation implied rejection of traditional authority. Wisdom had long associated itself with maturity, even with old age; by the 1790s, William Blake hinted at the child's superior insight, and Wordsworth openly claimed for the infant holy wisdom inevitably lost in the process of aging. Johnson had valued experience as a vital means of knowledge; at the beginning of the nineteenth century, innocence—in its nature evanescent—provided a more generally treasured resource.

Cause and effect, in such massive shifts of perspective, can never be ascertained. The French Revolution derived from new ideas about the sacredness of the individual; it also helped to generate such ideas. Without trying to distinguish causes from effects—indeed, with a strong suspicion that the period's striking phenomena constitute simultaneous causes and effects—

one can specify a number of ways that the world appeared to change, as the eighteenth century approached the nineteenth, as well as ways that these changes both solidified themselves and evoked challenges later in the nineteenth century.

NEW AND OLD

The embattled farmer of Concord fired the shot heard round the world in 1775; fourteen years later, the Bastille fell. Both the American and the French Revolution developed out of strong convictions about the innate rights of individual human beings—in other words, Protestantism in political form. Those who developed revolutionary theory glimpsed new human possibility. The hope of salvation lay in the overturn of established institutions. Swift, in *Gulliver's Travels*, had made a clear distinction between institutions as ideal constructions of human reason and their corruption in practice. Lawyers might be a money-grubbing, hypocritical lot, but the idea of law, of a social structure designed to assure the provision of justice, has its own inherent power. The theory of revolution implied radical assault on virtually all social institutions. Fundamental hierarchies of government, notions of sovereignty and of aristocracy, inherited systems of distinction—all fell. Old conventions, once emblems of social and of literary stability, now exemplified the dead hand of the past. Only a few years before, the old, the inherited, and the traditional embodied truth, its power attested by its survival. But the revolutionaries felt themselves to be originators; the newness of what they proposed gave it the almost religious authority suggested by Wordsworth's allusions to "bliss" and "heaven."

The blessed state evoked by the new political thinkers embodied a sense of infinite possibility. Pope had written, in the *Essay on Man*, "The bliss of Man (could Pride that blessing find) / Is not to act or think beyond mankind." By the century's end, people were doing their best to "think beyond mankind"—or, at any rate, beyond what mankind had considered normal limitations. Evidence of this abounds, in revolutionary sermons preached from pulpits even in England, in writings by such flamboyant defenders of human rights as Thomas Paine, in the development, even, of a political theory about women's social position. Mary Wollstonecraft was not the first to note the oppression of women; a century before her, Mary Astell had suggested the need for broader female education, and outcries on the subject emerged sporadically even earlier in the seventeenth century. But Wollstonecraft's *Vindication of the Rights of Women* (1792) offered the first detailed argument that the ideal of fulfilled human possibility for men and for women demanded political acknowledgement of women's equal humanity.

The very existence of such a work (which achieved a second edition in the year of its first publication) testifies to the atmosphere of political expectancy in which men and women could rethink "self-evident" principles. Replacing the ideal of hierarchy (what Dr. Johnson reverenced as "subordination"), for example, was the revolutionary notion of human brotherhood. Liberty, equality, and fraternity, the French proclaimed; the new American nation celebrated essentially the same ideals. In practice, though, "fraternity" turned out to involve the citizens specifically of France, or of the new United States. The emphasis on individual uniqueness extended itself to national uniqueness. In America particularly, ideas of national character and of national destiny developed almost talismanic force. Although peace generally prevailed among nations in the early nineteenth century, the developing distinctions dividing one country imaginatively from another foretold future danger.

New ideas with massive practical consequences included more than the political. In 1776, Adam Smith published *The Wealth of Nations,* a theory of laissez-faire economics presaging the enormous importance of money in subsequent history. Matters of exchange and acquisition, Smith argued, could be left to regulate themselves—a doctrine behind which still lurked unobtrusively the confidence, expressed in market terms, that Pope had expressed in religious ones: "All Chance, Direction that thou canst not see, / All Discord, Harmony, not understood." As manufacturing and trade developed increasing financial vitality, however, their importance as financial resources in fact heightened discord, through growing nationalism. Early in the century, at the end of "Windsor Forest" (1713), Pope had recognized in Britain's trade a form of power. A century later, the acceleration of this power would have astonished Pope. No longer did agriculture provide England's central economic resource. New forms of manufacture provided new substance for trade, generated new fortunes, produced a new social class—a "middle class" with the influence of wealth and without the inherited system of responsibilities, restrictions, decorums that had helped to control aristocratic possessors of wealth in preceding generations. Aristocrats had used their money, on the whole, to enlarge and beautify their estates. The new money-holders developed new ideas about what money might do. Re-invested, it could support innovation in manufacture and trade. It could educate the children of the uneducated; it could buy them (as it had been doing for a century) husbands and wives from the aristocracy; it could help to obviate ancient class distinctions. England's increasing economic ascendancy in the nineteenth century derived not only from new money but from the development of men willing and able to employ money ingeniously as power.

The enlarged possibilities of manufacture testified to practical applications of scientific research, another area of activity in which the new overwhelmingly replaced the old. In England and America especially, inventions multiplied: the steam engine, the spinning jenny, the cotton gin. Increasingly often, and in increasing numbers, men and women left their native rural environments to congregate in cities, where opportunities for relatively unskilled workers abounded—and where more and more people lived in congestion, poverty, and misery.

More vividly, perhaps, than ever before in history, the world was changing: was becoming, in fact, the world we ourselves assume, in which "mankind" as an ideal wanes, nations define themselves in psychic as well as military opposition to one another, money constitutes immediate power, science serves manufacture, hence commerce. From the beginning of these crucial changes, certain thinkers and writers realized the destructive possibilities inherent in every form of "progress." Blake, for example, glimpsed London's economic brutality and human wastefulness; his "revolutionary" impulses expressed themselves partly in resistance to the consequences of the new. That is to say, the new gave way to the newer, as it had not previously done on such a scale. No longer did the impulse to conserve past values express itself with the authority and power that Swift and Johnson had brought to the theme. As M. H. Abrams has written, "the Romantic period was eminently an age obsessed with the fact of violent change." Such change might provide ground for fear; it also supplied the substance for hope.

Individualism

Immanuel Kant (1724–1804), a German philosopher whose work influenced virtually all philosophers after him, questioned the power of reason to provide the most significant forms of knowledge—knowledge of the ultimately real. Feeling, on the other hand, might offer a guide. The individual will must engage itself in ethical struggle to locate and experience the good. Such followers of Kant as Johann Fichte (1762–1814) more clearly suggested an identification between will and what we call "ego." The idea of the self took on ever greater importance, for philosophers and for poets, for political thinkers, autobiographers, novelists.

To locate authority in the self rather than in society implies yet another radical break with the assumptions of the previous period. The idea of the self's importance is so familiar to us that it may be difficult to imagine the startling implications of the new focus. "I know the feelings of my heart, and I know men," Jean-Jacques Rousseau writes, at the beginning of his *Confessions*. "I am not made like any of those I have seen; I venture to believe that I am not made like any of those who are in existence." Dr. Johnson would have felt certain that a man who could write such words must be mad, like the astronomer in *Rasselas* who believes himself to control the weather. Yet faith in the absolute uniqueness of every consciousness became increasingly prevalent. Rousseau's significance for his period derives partly from the fact that his stress on the feelings of his heart and on his own specialness aroused recognition in his audience. No longer did the universality of human nature supply comfort to individuals; now they might seek reassurance instead in their uniqueness: the ultimate in protestantism— everyone his or her own church.

The new stress on and interest in the individual implied revaluation of inner as opposed to outer experience. Previously, life in the public arena had been assumed to test human capacities and to provide meaningful forms of experience. After Rousseau, however, psychic experience could provide the proper measure of an individual's emotional capacity. To place value *there* opened the possibility of taking women as seriously as men, children as seriously as adults, "savages" as seriously as civilized beings. Indeed, women, children, and savages were often thought to exceed cultivated adult males in their capacity both to feel and to express their feelings spontaneously—although the social subordination of such groups continued unchanged.

Even before Rousseau, the novel of sensibility in England and on the Continent revealed interest in highly developed emotional responsiveness. Johann Wolfgang von Goethe's *The Sorrows of Young Werther* (1774) made its author famous and inspired a cult of introverted, melancholy young people. In England, Henry Mackenzie's *The Man of Feeling* (1771) associated intense emotion with benevolent action. By the late century, the Gothic novel had become an important form—a novelistic mode often practiced by women which typically placed a young woman at the center of the action. The heroines of such novels confront a kind of experience (usually involving at least apparent supernatural elements) for which their social training, that important resource of earlier heroines, provided no help; instead, quick intuitions and subtle feelings insure their triumph over apparently insurmountable obstacles with no loss of feminine delicacy.

Given the view of feeling's centrality that replaced the earlier stress on passion's fruitful tension with reason, new kinds of feeling drew literary attention. From its beginnings (*The Princess of Clèves* is an early example), the novel had tended to emphasize (usually in decorous terms) love between the sexes. Now romantic love became a central subject of poetry and drama as well. More surprising kinds of emotion also attracted literary attention. William Blake imagined a chimney sweep's emotional relation to the idea of heaven; Samuel Taylor Coleridge and Percy Shelley made poetry of dejection; Alfred, Lord Tennyson, at the midpoint of the nineteenth century, wove his anxieties about the revelations of recent scientific inquiry into the texture of an elegiac poem. As these examples indicate, painful as well as pleasurable emotion interested readers and writers. The poet, Wordsworth said, is a man speaking to men; poetry originates in recollected emotion and recapitulates lost feeling. Lyric, not epic, typifies poetry for Wordsworth, who understands his genre as a form of emotional communication.

Wordsworth's definition ignores the fact that women too (including his own sister, Dorothy) also wrote poetry. Emily Brontë, Christina Rosetti, Elizabeth Barrett Browning, Emily Dickinson—all evoked intense passion in verse. In the Romantic novel, too, women excelled in the rendering of powerful feeling. The Brontë sisters, like George Eliot after them in England, like the equally passionate George Sand in France, wrote under male pseudonyms but established distinctively female visions of the struggle not only for love but for freedom and power within a context of social restriction. Mary Shelley (daughter of Mary Wollstonecraft and wife of the poet Percy Shelley) in her eloquent fable of creativity, *Frankenstein* (1818), epitomizes the peculiar intensity of much women's writing in this period.

As the nineteenth century wore on, hope for a new terrestrial Eden faded. The efflorescence of commerce and the innovations of science turned out to have negative as well as positive consequences. As the novels of Charles Dickens and of William Thackeray insist, the new middle class frequently became the repository of moral mediocrity. The autocracy of money had effects more brutal than those of inherited privilege. Science, once the emblem of progress, began to generate theological confusion. Charles Darwin's *Origin of Species* (1859) stated clearly humanity's mean rather than transcendent origins: animal and plant species had evolved over the centuries, adapting themselves to their environment by a process of natural selection. Fossils found in rocks provided supporting evidence for this theory, troubling to many Christians because it contradicted the Biblical account of creation. Five years after Darwin's revolutionary work, Karl Marx published *Das Kapital*, with its dialectical theory of history and its vision of capitalism's eventual decay and of the working class inevitably triumphant. In the United States, by the 1860s civil war raged, its central issue the morality of slavery—that by-product of agricultural capitalism. Neither the making of money nor the effort to fathom natural law seemed merely reassuring.

In the face of history's threats—the menace of Marx's prophecy and of Darwin's biology, the chaos of civil war—to insist on the importance of private experience offered tentative security, a standing place, a temporary source of authority. The voices of blacks as well as, in increasing numbers, of women could now be heard: placing high value on the personal implied respecting all persons. The American Civil War made blacks for the first time truly visible to the society that both contained and denied them. Slave narratives—sometimes wholly or partly fictionized, sometimes entirely authentic renditions of often horrifying experience—provided useful propaganda for the abolitionist cause, the ideology opposed to the institution of slavery, but they also opened a new emotional universe. In their typical emphasis, for instance, on the salvationary force of reading and writing (for most slaves officially forbidden knowledge), these narratives illuminated a new area of the taken-for-granted, thus extending the enterprise of Romantic poetry.

The capacity for revelatory illumination belonged, according to the dominant nineteenth-century view, to imagination, a mysterious and virtually sacred power of individual consciousness. When Dr. Johnson, in *Rasselas*, suggested that all predominance of imagination over reason constituted a degree of insanity, he intended, to put it crudely, an antithesis of true and false. Imagination, the faculty of generating images, had no necessary anchor in the communal, historical experience that tested truth. For Wordsworth and Coleridge and those who came after them, imagination was a visionary and unifying force (a new incarnation of the seventeenth century's inner light or candle of the Lord) through which the gifted person discovered and communicated new truth. (Johnson, of course, would have denied the possibility of "new" truth.) As Coleridge wrote,

> from the soul itself must issue forth
> A light, a glory, a fair luminous cloud
> Enveloping the Earth.

Imagination derived from the soul, the aspect of human being that links the human with the eternal. Through it, men and women can transcend earthly limitations, can express high aspiration, can escape, and help one another escape, the dreariness of mortality without necessarily positing a life beyond the present one.

A corollary of the high value attached to creative imagination was a new concern with originality. The notion of "the genius," the man or woman so gifted as to operate by principles unknown to ordinary mortals, developed only in the late eighteenth century. Previously, a person *had* rather than *was* a genius: the term designated a particular tendency or gift (a genius for cooking, say) rather than a human being with vast creative power. Now the genius was revered for his or her extraordinary difference from others, idealized as a being set apart; and the literary or artistic products of genius, it could be assumed, would correspondingly differ from everything previously produced. Newness itself became as never before a measure of value. The language, the themes, the forms of the preceding century would no longer suffice. In the early eighteenth century, literary figures wishing to congratulate themselves and their contemporaries would compare their artistic situation to that of Rome under the benevolent patronage of Augustus Caesar. A hundred years later, the note of self-congratulation would express itself in the claim of an unprecedented situation, unprecedented kinds of accomplishment. John Keats in a letter characterized Wordsworth as representing "the egotistical sublime." Such sublimity—authority and grandeur emanating from a unique self still in touch with something beyond itself—was the nineteenth century's special achievement.

NATURE

Nature and nature's laws, the rationally ordered universe, provided the foundation for much early eighteenth-century thought. In the nineteenth century, nature's importance possibly increased—but *nature* now meant something new. *Wuthering Heights* (1847) creates a setting of windswept moors for its romantic lovers—both environment and metaphor of their love. Wordsworth could value a host of daffodils, or fog-enveloped hills, or an icy lake. The physical reality of the natural world, in its varied abundance, became matter of absorbing interest for poets and novelists. Nature provided an alternative to the human, a possibility for imaginative as well as literal escape. Its imagery—flowers, clouds, ocean—became the common poetic stock. Workers still hastened from the country to the city, because the city housed possibilities of wealth; yet educated men and women increasingly declared their nostalgia for rural or sylvan landscapes embodying peace and beauty.

Nature, in the nineteenth-century mind, however, did not consist only in physical details. It also implied a totality, an enveloping whole greater than the sum of its parts, a vast unifying spirit. Wordsworth evokes

> a sense sublime
> Of something far more deeply interfused,
> Whose dwelling is the light of setting suns,
> And the round ocean and the living air,
> And the blue sky, and in the mind of man:
> A motion and a spirit, that impels
> All thinking things, all objects of all thought,
> And rolls through all things.

Coleridge and Shelley hint similar visions, vague yet comforting. The unifying whole, as Wordsworth's language suggests, depends less on rational system than on emotional association. Human beings link themselves with the infinite by what Wordsworth elsewhere terms "wise passiveness," the capacity to submit to feeling and be led by it to transcendence. Natural detail, too, acquires value by evoking and symbolizing emotion. Nature belongs to the realm of the nonrational, the superrational.

The idea of the natural can also imply the uncivilized, or precivilized. Philosophers have differed dramatically in their hypotheses about what humankind was like in its "natural" state. Thomas Hobbes, in the seventeenth century, argued that the natural human condition was one of conflict; society developed to curb the violent impulses human beings would manifest without its restraint. The prevailing nineteenth-century view, on the other hand, made civilization the agent of corruption. Rousseau expounded the crippling effect of institutions; the child raised with the greatest possible freedom, he maintained, would develop in more admirable ways than one subjected to system. By the second half of the eighteenth century, a French novelist could contrast the decadent life of Europe unfavorably with existence on an unspoiled island (Bernardin de Saint-Pierre, *Paul and Virginia*, 1788); Thomas Chatterton, before committing suicide in 1770 at the age of eighteen, wrote poems rich in nostalgia for a more primitive stage of social development which he tried to pass off as medieval works; the forged Ossian poems (1760–1763) of James Macpherson, purportedly ancient texts, attracted a large and enthusiastic audience. New interest manifested itself in ballads, poetic survivals of the primitive; Romantic poets imitated the form. The interest in a simpler past, a simpler life, continued throughout the nineteenth century: in Victorian England, Tennyson recast Arthurian legend in modern verse; the pre-Raphaelites evoked the medieval in visual and verbal arts.

The revolutionary fervor of the late eighteenth century had generated a vision of infinite human possibility, political and personal. The escapist implications of the increasing emphasis on nature, the primitive, the uncomplicated past, suggest, however, a sense of alienation. Blake, Wordsworth, Shelley, all write poems of social protest. "Society" would not help the individual work out his or her salvation; on the contrary, it embodied forces opposed to individual development. Melancholy marked the Romantic hero (Lord Byron in his poetic self-manifestations, Heathcliff in fiction, for example); melancholy tinged nineteenth-century poetry and fiction. The satiric spirit—that spirit of social reform—was in abeyance. Hope lay in the individual's separation from, not participation in, society. In the woods and mountains, one might feel free.

The Waste Land (1922), T. S. Eliot's twentieth-century epic, contains the line, "In the mountains, there you feel free," a line given complex ironic overtones by its context. Its occurrence, however, may remind us how powerfully ideas that came into currency in the late eighteenth and early nineteenth centuries survive into our own time. The world of the Romantic Period specifically prefigures our own, despite all the differences dividing the two cultures. We have developed more fully important Romantic tendencies: stress on the sacredness of the individual, suspicion of social institutions, belief in expressed feeling as the sign of authenticity ("Let it all hang out"), nostalgia for simpler ways of being, faith in genius, valuing of originality and imagination, an ambivalent relation to science. Although Wordsworth and Dickinson and Melville employ vocabularies and use references partly strange to us, they speak directly to twentieth-century preoccupations. By attending closely to them, we may learn more about ourselves: not only in the common humanity that we share with all our predecessors, but in our special historical situation as both direct inheritors of nineteenth-century assumptions and rebels against them.

FURTHER READING

Useful introductions to the Romantic period include L. Furst, *Romanticism in Perspective: A Comparative Study of Aspects of the Romantic Movements in England, France, and Germany* (1979); R. F. Gleckner and G. E. Enscoe, editors, *Romanticism: Points of View* (1962), a collection of essays by various contributors; R. W. Harris, *Romanticism and the Social Order, 1780–1830* (1969); and M. Butler, *Romantics, Rebels, and Reactionaries: English Literature and Its Background, 1760–1830* (1982).

JEAN-JACQUES ROUSSEAU
1712–1778

It would be difficult to overstate the historical importance of Jean-Jacques Rousseau's *Confessions* (composed between 1765 and 1770, published 1781–8), which inaugurated a new form of autobiography and suggested new ways of thinking about the self and its relation to other selves. Even for readers two centuries after its first publication, the book's sheer audacity compels attention, demanding that we rethink easy assumptions about important and trivial, right and wrong.

The facts of Rousseau's life are not altogether clear, partly because the *Confessions*, despite its claim of absolute truthfulness, sometimes appears more concerned to create a self-justifying story than to confine itself strictly to actuality. The son of a Geneva watchmaker, Jean-Jacques left home in his teens and lived for some time with Mme. de Warens, his protector and eventually his mistress, the "mamma" of the *Confessions*. He worked at many occupations, from secretary to government official (under the king of Sardinia). In Paris, where he settled in 1745, he lived with Thérèse le Vaseur; he claims she bore him five children, all consigned to an orphanage, but the claim has never been substantiated (or, for that matter, disproved). At various times his controversial writing forced Rousseau to leave France, usually for Switzerland; in 1766 he went to England as the guest of the philosopher David Hume. He was allowed to return to Paris in 1770 only on condition that he write nothing against the government or the church.

Rousseau's social ideas, stated in his didactic novels, *Julie, or the New Heloise* (1761) and *Emile* (1762), as well as in his autobiographical writings and political treatises (e.g., *The Social Contract*, 1762), stirred much contemporary discussion. He believed in the destructiveness of institutions, the gradual corruption of humankind throughout history, the importance of nature and of feeling in individual development and consequently in society. Also knowledgeable about music (he worked for a time as music teacher), he published several works on the subject, including a musical dictionary, as well as a comic opera, *The Village Soothsayer* (1752).

The *Confessions* presents its subject as a man (and boy) striving always to express natural impulses and recurrently frustrated by society's demands and assumptions. The central figure described here rather resembles Candide in his naïveté and good feeling. Experience chastens him less than it does Candide, however, although he reports many psychic hard knocks. For Voltaire's didactic purposes, his character's experience was more important than his personality; for Rousseau, his own nature has much more significance than anything that happens to him.

To read even a few pages of the work reveals how completely Rousseau exemplifies his period's dominant values. He describes himself as a being of powerful passions but confused ideas, he makes feeling the guide of conduct, he glorifies imagination and romantic love, he believes the common people morally superior to the upper classes. The emphasis on imagination and passion for him seems not a matter of ideology but of experience: life presents itself to him in this way. The fact emphasizes the degree to which the movement we call Romanticism involved genuine re-vision. Everything suddenly looked different in the late eighteenth century, everything demanded categories changed from those previously accepted without question. The new way of looking at the world that characterizes the Romantic Movement, inasmuch as it implies valuing the inner life of emotion and fancy for its own sake (not for the sake of any insight it might provide), always involves the danger of narcissism, a kind of concentration on the self that shuts out awareness of the reality and integrity of others. Rousseau, in the *Confessions*, vividly expresses the narcissistic side of Romanticism.

Implicit in Rousseau's ways of understanding himself and his life are new moral assumptions as well. Honesty of a particular kind becomes the highest value: however disreputable his behavior, Rousseau can feel comfortable about it because he reports it accurately. What Johnson or Pope would see as self-indulgence, care exclusively for one's own pleasure, seems acceptable to Rousseau because of the minute, exacting attention devoted to it. The autobiographer examines each nuance of his own happiness, as if to know it fully constituted moral achievement. To take the self this seriously as subject—not in relation to a progress of education or of salvation, merely in its moment-to-moment being—implies belief in self-knowledge (knowledge of feeling, thought, action) as a high moral achievement. This is not the slowly achieved, arduous discipline recommended by Socrates, but a much more indulgent form of self-contemplation. To connect it, as Rousseau does, with morality conveys the view that self-absorption without self-judgment provides valuable and sufficient insight.

The intensity of his self-concentration makes his subject compelling for others as well. However distasteful one finds Rousseau's obsessive focus, it is difficult to stop reading. The writer hints, makes us believe, that he will reveal all secrets about himself; and learning such secrets, despite Rousseau's insistence on his own uniqueness, tells us of human weakness, inconsistency, power, scope—tells us, therefore, something of ourselves.

F. C. Green, *Jean-Jacques Rousseau: A Critical Study of His Life and Writings* (1955), provides biography and criticism. I. Babbitt, *Rousseau and Romanticism* (1919), examines the relation of Rousseau's assumptions to those of the Romantic Movement. A thorough modern evaluation of Rousseau's achievement is L. G. Crocker, *Jean-Jacques Rousseau: A New Interpretative Analysis of His Works* (1973).

Confessions

Part I

BOOK I

[The Years 1712–1719.] I am commencing an undertaking, hitherto without precedent, and which will never find an imitator. I desire to set before my fellows the likeness of a man in all the truth of nature, and that man myself.

Myself alone! I know the feelings of my heart, and I know men. I am not made like any of those I have seen; I venture to believe that I am not made like any of those who are in existence. If I am not better, at least I am different. Whether Nature has acted rightly or wrongly in destroying the mould in which she cast me, can only be decided after I have been read.

Let the trumpet of the Day of Judgment sound when it will, I will present myself before the Sovereign Judge with this book in my hand. I will say boldly: "This is what I have done, what I have thought, what I was. I have told the good and the bad with equal frankness. I have neither omitted anything bad, nor interpolated anything good. If I have occasionally made use of some immaterial embellishments, this has only been in order to fill a gap caused by lack of memory. I may have assumed the truth of that which I knew might have been true, never of that which I knew to be false. I have shown myself as I was: mean and contemptible, good, high-minded and sublime, according as I was one or the other. I have unveiled my inmost self even as Thou hast seen it, O Eternal Being. Gather round me the countless host of my fellow-men; let them hear my confessions, lament for my unworthiness, and blush for my imperfections. Then let each of them in turn reveal, with the same frankness, the secrets of his heart at the foot of the Throne, and say, if he dare, *'I was better than that man!'* " . . .

I felt before I thought: this is the common lot of humanity. I experienced it more than others. I do not know what I did until I was five or six years old. I do not know how I learned to read; I only remember my earliest reading, and the effect it had upon me; from that time I date my uninterrupted self-consciousness. My mother had left some romances behind her, which my father and I began to read after supper. At first it was only a question of practising me in reading by the aid of amusing books; but soon the interest became so lively, that we used to read in turns without stopping, and spent whole nights in this occupation. We were unable to leave off until the volume was finished. Sometimes, my father, hearing the swallows begin to twitter in the early morning, would say, quite ashamed, "Let us go to bed; I am more of a child than yourself."

In a short time I acquired, by this dangerous method, not only extreme facility in reading and understanding what I read, but a knowledge of the passions that was unique in a child of my age. I had no idea of things in themselves, although all the feelings of actual life were already known to me. I had conceived nothing, but felt everything. These confused emotions which I felt one after the other, certainly did not warp the reasoning powers which I did not as yet possess; but they shaped them in me of a peculiar stamp, and gave me odd and romantic notions of human life, of which experience and reflection have never been able wholly to cure me. . . .

How could I become wicked, when I had nothing but examples of gentleness before my eyes, and none around me but the best people in the world? My father, my aunt, my nurse, my relations, our friends, our neighbours, all who surrounded me, did not, it is true, obey me, but they loved me; and I loved them in return. My wishes were so little excited and so little opposed, that it did not occur to me to have any. I can swear that, until I served under a master, I never knew what a fancy was. Except during the time I spent in reading or writing in my father's company, or when my nurse took me for a walk, I was always with my aunt, sitting or standing by her side, watching her at her embroidery or listening to her singing; and I was content. Her cheerfulness, her gentleness and her pleasant face have stamped so deep and lively an impression on my mind that I can still see her manner, look, and attitude; I remember her affectionate language: I could describe what clothes she wore and how her head was dressed, not forgetting the two little curls of black hair on her temples, which she wore in accordance with the fashion of the time.

I am convinced that it is to her I owe the taste, or rather passion, for music, which only became fully developed in me a long time afterwards. She knew a prodigious number of tunes and songs which she used to sing in a very thin, gentle voice. This excellent woman's cheerfulness of soul banished dreaminess and melancholy from herself and all around her. The attraction which her singing possessed for me was so great, that not only have several of her songs always remained in my memory, but even now, when I have lost her, and as I grew older, many of them, totally forgotten since the days of my childhood, return to my mind with inexpressible charm. Would anyone believe that I, an old dotard, eaten up by cares and troubles, sometimes find myself weeping like a child, when I mumble one of those little airs in a voice already broken and trembling?

. . . I have spent my life in idle longing, without saying a word, in the presence of those whom I loved most. Too bashful to declare my taste, I at least satisfied it in situations which had reference to it and kept up the idea of it. To lie at the feet of an imperious mistress, to obey her commands, to ask her forgiveness—this was for me a sweet enjoyment; and, the more my lively imagination heated my blood, the more I presented the appearance of a bashful lover. It may be easily imagined that this manner of making love does not lead to very speedy results, and is not very dangerous to the virtue of those who are its object. For this reason I have rarely possessed, but have none the less enjoyed myself in my own way—that is to say, in imagination. Thus it has happened that my senses, in harmony with my timid disposition and my romantic spirit, have kept my sentiments pure and my morals blameless, owing to the very tastes which, combined with a little more impudence, might have plunged me into the most brutal sensuality. . . .

I am a man of very strong passions, and, while I am stirred by them, nothing can equal my impetuosity; I forget all discretion, all feelings of respect, fear and decency; I am cynical, impudent, violent and fearless; no feeling of shame keeps me back, no danger frightens me; with the exception of the single object which occupies my thoughts, the universe is nothing to me. But all this lasts only for a moment, and the following moment plunges me into complete annihilation. In my calmer moments I am indolence and timidity itself; everything frightens and discourages me; a fly, buzzing past, alarms me; a word which I have to say, a gesture which I have to make, terrifies my idleness; fear and shame overpower me to such an extent that I would gladly hide myself from the sight of my fellow-creatures. If I have to act, I do not know what to do; if I have to speak, I do not know what to say; if anyone looks at me, I am put out of countenance. When I am strongly moved I sometimes know how to find the right words, but in ordinary conversation I can find absolutely nothing, and my condition is unbearable for the simple reason that I am obliged to speak.

Add to this, that none of my prevailing tastes centre in things that can be bought. I want nothing but unadulterated pleasures, and money poisons all. For instance, I am fond of the pleasures of the table; but, as I cannot endure either the constraint of good society or the drunkenness of the tavern, I can only enjoy them with a friend; alone, I cannot do so, for my imagination then occupies itself with other things, and eating affords me no pleasure. If my heated blood longs for women, my excited heart longs still more for affection. Women who could be bought for money would lose for me all their charms; I even doubt whether it would be in me to make use of them. I find it the same with all pleasures within my reach; unless they cost me nothing, I find them insipid. I only love those enjoyments which belong to no one but the first man who knows how to enjoy them.

. . . I worship freedom; I abhor restraint, trouble, dependence. As long as the money in my purse lasts, it assures my independence; it relieves me of the trouble of finding expedients to replenish it, a necessity which always inspired me with dread; but the fear of seeing it exhausted makes me hoard it carefully. The money which a man possesses is the instrument of freedom; that which we eagerly pursue is the instrument of slavery. Therefore I hold fast to that which I have, and desire nothing.

My disinterestedness is, therefore, nothing but idleness; the pleasure of possession is not worth the trouble of acquisition. In like manner, my extravagance is nothing but idleness; when the opportunity of spending agreeably presents itself, it cannot be too profitably employed. Money tempts me less than things, because between money and the possession of the desired object there is always an intermediary, whereas between the thing itself and the enjoyment of it there is none. If I see the thing, it tempts me; if I only see the means of gaining possession of it, it does not. For this reason I have committed thefts, and even now I sometimes pilfer trifles which tempt me, and which I prefer to take rather than to ask for; but neither when a child nor a grown-up man do I ever remember to have robbed anyone of a farthing, except on one occasion, fifteen years ago, when I stole seven *livres* ten *sous*. . . .

BOOK II

[The Years 1728–1731.] . . . I have drawn the great moral lesson, perhaps the only one of any practical value, to avoid those situations of life which bring our duties into conflict with our interests, and which show us our own advantage in the misfortunes of others; for it is certain that, in such situations, however sincere our love of virtue, we must, sooner or later, inevitably grow weak without perceiving it, and become unjust and wicked in act, without having ceased to be just and good in our hearts.

This principle, deeply imprinted on the bottom of my heart, which, although somewhat late, in practice guided my whole conduct, is one of those which have caused me to appear a very strange and foolish creature in the eyes of the world, and, above all, amongst my acquaintances. I have been reproached with wanting to pose as an original, and different from others. In reality, I have never troubled about acting like other people or differently from them. I sincerely desired to do what was right. I withdrew, as far as it lay in my power, from situations which opposed my interests to those of others, and might, consequently, inspire me with a secret, though involuntary, desire of injuring them.

. . . I loved too sincerely, too completely, I venture to say, to be able to be happy easily. Never have passions been at once more lively and purer than mine; never has love been tenderer, truer, more disinterested. I would have sacrificed my happiness a thousand times for that of the person whom I loved; her reputation was dearer to me than my life, and I would never have wished to endanger her repose for a single moment for all the pleasures of enjoyment. This feeling has made me employ such carefulness, such secrecy, and such precaution in my undertakings, that none of them have ever been successful. My want of success with women has always been caused by my excessive love for them. . . .

BOOK III

[The Years 1931–1732.] . . . I only felt the full strength of my attachment when I no longer saw her.[1] When I saw her, I was only content; but, during her absence, my restlessness became painful. The need of living with her caused me outbreaks of tenderness which often ended in tears. I shall never forget how, on the day of a great festival, while she was at vespers, I went for a walk outside the town, my heart full of her image and a burning desire to spend my life with her. I had sense enough to see that at present this was impossible, and that the happiness which I enjoyed so deeply could only be short. This gave to my reflections a tinge of melancholy, about which, however, there was nothing gloomy, and which was tempered by flattering hopes. The sound of the bells, which always singularly affects me, the song of the birds, the beauty of the daylight, the enchanting landscape, the scattered country dwellings in which my fancy placed our common home—all these produced upon me an impression so vivid, tender, melancholy and touching, that I saw myself transported, as it were, in ecstasy, into that happy time and place, wherein my heart, possessing all the happiness it could desire, tasted it with inexpressible rapture, without even a thought of sensual pleasure. I never remember to have plunged into the future with greater force and illusion than on that occasion; and what has struck me most in the recollection of this dream after it had been realised, is that I have found things again exactly as I had imagined them. If ever the dream of a man awake resembled a prophetic vision, it was assuredly that dream of mine. I was only deceived in the imaginary duration; for the days, the years, and our whole life were spent in serene and undisturbed tranquillity, whereas in reality it lasted only for a moment. Alas! my most lasting happiness belongs to a dream, the fulfilment of which was almost immediately followed by the awakening. . . .

Two things, almost incompatible, are united in me in a manner which I am unable to understand: a very ardent temperament, lively and tumultuous passions, and, at the same time, slowly developed and confused ideas, which never present themselves until it is too late. One might say that my heart and my mind do not belong to the same person. Feeling takes possession of my soul more rapidly than a flash of lightning; but, instead of illuminating, inflames and dazzles me. I feel everything and see nothing. I am carried away by my passions, but stupid; in order to think, I must be cool. The astonishing thing is that, notwithstanding, I exhibit tolerably sound judg-

---

1. Rousseau refers here to Mme. de Warens, whom he also calls "mamma."

ment, penetration, even finesse, if I am not hurried; with sufficient leisure I can compose excellent impromptus; but I have never said or done anything worthy of notice on the spur of the moment. I could carry on a very clever conversation through the post, as the Spaniards are said to carry on a game of chess. When I read of that Duke of Savoy, who turned round on his journey, in order to cry, "At your throat, Parisian huckster," I said, "There you have myself!"

This sluggishness of thought, combined with such liveliness of feeling, not only enters into my conversation, but I feel it even when alone and at work. My ideas arrange themselves in my head with almost incredible difficulty; they circulate in it with uncertain sound, and ferment till they excite and heat me, and make my heart beat fast; and, in the midst of this excitement, I see nothing clearly and am unable to write a single word—I am obliged to wait. Imperceptibly this great agitation subsides, the confusion clears up, everything takes its proper place, but slowly, and only after a period of long and confused agitation. . . .

BOOK IV

[The Years 1731–1732.] . . . I returned, not to Nyon, but to Lausanne. I wanted to sate myself with the sight of this beautiful lake, which is there seen in its greatest extent. Few of the secret motives which have determined me to act have been more rational. Things seen at a distance are rarely powerful enough to make me act. The uncertainty of the future has always made me look upon plans, which need considerable time to carry them out, as decoys for fools. I indulge in hopes like others, provided it costs me nothing to support them; but if they require continued attention, I have done with it. The least trifling pleasure which is within my reach tempts me more than the joys of Paradise. However, I make an exception of the pleasure which is followed by pain; this has no temptation for me, because I love only pure enjoyments, and these a man never has when he knows that he is preparing for himself repentance and regret. . . .

Why is it that, having found so many good people in my youth, I find so few in my later years? Is their race extinct? No; but the class in which I am obliged to look for them now, is no longer the same as that in which I found them. Among the people, where great passions only speak at intervals, the sentiments of nature make themselves more frequently heard; in the higher ranks they are absolutely stifled, and, under the mask of sentiment, it is only interest or vanity that speaks.

. . . Whenever I approach the Canton of Vaud, I am conscious of an impression in which the remembrance of Madame de Warens, who was born there, of my father who lived there, of Mademoiselle de Vulson who enjoyed the first fruits of my youthful love, of several pleasure trips which I made there when a child and, I believe, some other exciting cause, more mysterious and more powerful than all this, is combined. When the burning desire of this happy and peaceful life, which flees from me and for which I was born, inflames my imagination, it is always the Canton of Vaud, near the lake, in the midst of enchanting scenery, to which it draws me. I feel that I must have an orchard on the shore of this lake and no other, that I must have a loyal friend, a loving wife, a cow, and a little boat. I shall never enjoy perfect happiness on earth until I have all that. I laugh at the simplicity with which I have several times visited this country merely in search of this imaginary happiness. I was always surprised to find its inhabitants, especially the women, of quite a different character from that which I expected. How contradictory it appeared to me! The country and its inhabitants have never seemed to me made for each other.

During this journey to Vévay, walking along the beautiful shore, I abandoned myself to the sweetest melancholy. My heart eagerly flung itself into a thousand innocent raptures; I was filled with emotion, I sighed and wept like a child. How often have I stopped to weep to my heart's content, and, sitting on a large stone, amused myself with looking at my tears falling into the water! . . .

How greatly did the entrance into Paris belie the idea I had formed of it! The external decorations of Turin, the beauty of its streets, the symmetry and regularity of the houses, had made me look for something quite different in Paris. I had imagined to myself a city of most imposing aspect, as beautiful as it was large, where nothing was to be seen but splendid streets and palaces of gold and marble. Entering by the suburb of St. Marceau, I saw nothing but dirty and stinking little streets, ugly black houses, a general air of slovenliness and poverty, beggars, carters, menders of old clothes, criers of decoctions and old hats. All this, from the outset, struck me so forcibly, that all the real magnificence I have since seen in Paris has been unable to destroy this first impression, and I have always retained a secret dislike against residence in this capital. I may say that the whole time, during which I afterwards lived there, was employed solely in trying to find means to enable me to live away from it.

Such is the fruit of a too lively imagination, which exaggerates beyond human exaggeration, and is always ready to see more than it has been told to expect. I had heard Paris so much praised, that I had represented it to myself as the ancient Babylon, where, if I had ever visited it, I should, perhaps, have found as much to take off from the picture which I had drawn of it. The same thing happened to me at the Opera, whither I hastened to go the day after my arrival. The same thing happened to me later at Versailles; and again, when I saw the sea for the first time; and the same thing will always happen to me, when I see anything which has been too loudly announced; for it is impossible for men, and difficult for Nature herself, to surpass the exuberance of my imagination.

. . . The sight of the country, a succession of pleasant views, the open air, a good appetite, the sound health which walking gives me, the free life of the inns, the absence of all that makes me conscious of my dependent position, of all that reminds me of my condition—all this sets my soul free, gives me greater boldness of thought, throws me, so to speak, into the immensity of things, so that I can combine, select, and appropriate them at pleasure, without fear or restraint. I dispose of Nature in its entirety as its lord and master; my heart, roaming from object to object, mingles and identifies itself with those which soothe it, wraps itself up in charming fancies, and is intoxicated with delicious sensations. If, in order to render them permanent, I amuse myself by describing them by myself, what vigorous outlines, what fresh colouring, what power of expression I give them!

. . . At night I lay in the open air, and, stretched on the ground or on a bench, slept as calmly as upon a bed of roses. I remember, especially, that I spent a delightful night outside the city, on a road which ran by the side of the Rhône or Saône, I do not remember which. Raised gardens, with terraces, bordered the other side of the road. It had been very hot during the day; the evening was delightful; the dew moistened the parched grass; the night was calm, without a breath of wind; the air was fresh, without being cold; the sun, having gone down, had left in the sky red vapours, the reflection of which cast a rose-red tint upon the water; the trees on the terraces were full of nightingales answering one another. I walked on in a kind of ecstasy, abandoning my heart and senses to the enjoyment of all, only regretting, with a sigh, that I was obliged to enjoy it alone. Absorbed in my delightful reverie, I continued my walk late into the night, without noticing that I was tired. At last, I noticed it. I threw myself with a feeling of delight upon the shelf of a sort of niche or false door let into a terrace wall; the canopy of my bed was formed by the tops of trees; a nightingale was perched just over my head, and lulled me to sleep with his song; my slumbers were sweet, my awaking was still sweeter. . . .

In relating my journeys, as in making them, I do not know how to stop. My heart beat with joy when I drew near to my dear mamma, but I walked no faster. I like to walk at my ease, and to stop when I like. A wandering life is what I want. To walk through a beautiful country in fine weather, without being obliged to hurry, and with a pleasant prospect at the end, is of all kinds of life the one most suited to my taste. My idea of a beautiful country is already known. No flat country, however beautiful, has ever seemed so to my eyes. I must have mountain torrents, rocks, firs, dark forests, mountains, steep roads to climb or descend, precipices at my side to frighten me. . . .

BOOK V

[The Years 1732–1736.] . . . It is sometimes said that the sword wears out the scabbard. That is my history. My passions have made me live, and my passions have killed me. What passions? will be asked. Trifles, the most childish things in the world, which, however, excited me as much as if the possession of Helen or the throne of the universe had been at stake. In the first place—women. When I possessed one, my senses were calm; my heart, never. The needs of love devoured me in the midst of enjoyment; I had a tender mother, a dear friend; but I needed a mistress. I imagined one in her place; I represented her to myself in a thousand forms, in order to deceive myself. If I had thought that I held mamma in my arms when I embraced her, these embraces would have been no less lively, but all my desires would have been extinguished; I should have sobbed from affection, but I should never have felt any enjoyment. Enjoyment! Does this ever fall to the lot of man? If I had ever, a single time in my life, tasted all the delights of love in their fulness, I do not believe that my frail existence could have endured it; I should have died on the spot.

Thus I was burning with love, without an object; and it is this state, perhaps, that is most exhausting. I was restless, tormented by the hopeless condition of poor mamma's affairs, and her imprudent conduct, which were bound to ruin her completely at no distant date. My cruel imagination, which always anticipates misfortunes, exhibited this particular one to me continually, in all its extent and in all its results. I already saw myself compelled by want to separate from her to whom I had devoted my life, and without whom I could not enjoy it. Thus my soul was ever in a state of agitation; I was devoured alternately by desires and fears. . . .

BOOK VI

[The Year 1736.] . . . At this period commences the brief happiness of my life; here approach the peaceful, but rapid moments which have given me the right to say, *I have lived.* Precious and regretted moments! begin again for me your delightful course; and, if it be possible, pass more slowly in succession through my memory, than you did in your fugitive reality. What can I do, to prolong, as I should like, this touching and simple narrative, to repeat the same things over and over again, without wearying my readers by such repetition, any more than I was wearied of them myself, when I recommenced the life again and again? If all this consisted of facts, actions, and words, I could describe, and in a manner, give an idea of them; but how is it possible to describe what was neither said nor done, nor even thought, but enjoyed and felt, without being able to assign any other reason for my happiness than this simple feeling? I got up at sunrise, and was happy; I walked, and was happy; I saw mamma, and was happy; I left her, and was happy; I roamed the forests and hills, I wandered in the valleys, I read, I did nothing, I worked in the garden, I picked the fruit, I helped in the work of the house, and happiness followed me everywhere—happiness, which could not be referred to any definite object, but dwelt entirely within myself, and which never left me for a single instant. . . .

I should much like to know, whether the same childish ideas ever enter the hearts of other men as sometimes enter mine. In the midst of my studies, in the course of a life as blameless as a man could have led, the fear of hell still frequently troubled me. I asked myself: "In what state am I? If I were to die this moment, should I be damned?" According to my Jansenists,[2] there was no doubt about the matter; but, according to my conscience, I thought differently. Always fearful, and a prey to cruel uncertainty, I had recourse to the most laughable expedients to escape from it, for which I would unhesitatingly have anyone locked up as a madman if I saw him doing as I did. One day, while musing upon this melancholy subject, I mechanically amused myself by throwing stones against the trunks of trees with my usual good aim, that is to say, without hardly hitting one. While engaged in this useful exercise, it occurred to me to draw a prognostic from it to calm my anxiety. I said to myself: "I will throw this stone at the tree opposite; if I hit it, I am saved; if I miss it, I am damned." While speaking, I threw my stone with a trembling hand and a terrible palpitation of the heart, but with so successful an aim that it hit the tree right in the middle, which, to tell the truth, was no very difficult feat, for I had been careful to choose a tree with a thick trunk close at hand. From that time I have never had any doubt about my salvation! When I recall this characteristic incident, I do not know whether to laugh or cry at myself. You great men, who are most certainly laughing, may congratulate yourselves; but do not mock my wretchedness, for I swear to you that I feel it deeply. . . .

---

2. A sect of strict Catholics, named for Corneille Jansen (1585–1638).

JOHANN WILHELM VON GOETHE

1749–1832

Recasting the ancient legend of Faust, Johann Wilhelm von Goethe created a powerful symbol of the Romantic imagination in all its aspiration and anxiety. Faust himself, central character of the epic drama, emerges as a Romantic hero, ever testing the limits of possibility. Yet to achieve his ends he must make a contract with the devil: as if to say that giving full scope to imagination necessarily partakes of sin.

Goethe's *Faust* (Part I, 1808; Part II, 1833) constituted the crowning masterpiece of a life rich in achievement. Goethe exemplifies the nineteenth-century meaning of "genius." Accomplished as poet, dramatist, novelist, and autobiographer, he also practiced law, served as a diplomat, and pursued scientific research. He had a happy childhood in Frankfurt, after which he studied law at Leipzig and then at Strasbourg, where in 1770–71 he met Gottfried Herder, leader of a new literary movement called the Sturm und Drang (Storm and Stress) movement. Participants in this movement emphasized the importance of revolt against established standards; they interested Goethe in such newly discovered forms as the folk song and in the literary vitality of Shakespeare, as opposed to more formally constricted writers.

During the brief period when he practiced law, after an unhappy love affair, Goethe wrote *The Sorrows of Young Werther* (1774), a novel of immense influence in establishing the image of the introspective, self-pitying, melancholy Romantic hero. In 1775 he accepted an invitation to the court of Charles Augustus, duke of Saxe-Weimar. He remained in Weimar for the rest of his life, for ten years serving the duke as chief minister. A trip to Italy from 1786 to 1788 aroused his interest in classic sources. He wrote dramas based on classic texts, most notably *Iphigenia* (1787); novels (for example, *Elective Affinities*, 1809) that pointed the way to the psychological novel; lyric poetry; and an important autobiography, *Poetry and Truth* (1811–33). He also did significant work in botany and physiology. Increasingly famous, he became in his own lifetime a legendary figure; all Europe flocked to Weimar to visit him.

The legend of Dr. Faustus (the real Johannes Faustus, a scholar, lived from 1480 to 1540), in most versions a seeker after forbidden knowledge, had attracted other writers before Goethe. The most important previous literary embodiment of the tale was Christopher Marlowe's *Doctor Faustus* (c. 1588), a drama ending in its protagonist's damnation as a result of his search for illegitimate power through learning. Goethe's Faust meets no such fate. Pursuing not knowledge but experience, he embodies the ideal of limitless aspiration in all its glamour and danger. His contract with Mephistopheles provides that he will die at the moment he declares himself satisfied, content to rest in the present; he stakes his life and his salvation on his capacity ever to yearn for something beyond.

In Part I of Goethe's play, the protagonist's vision of the impossible locates itself specifically in the figure of Gretchen, the simple, innocent girl whom he possesses physically but with whom he can never attain total union. In a speech epitomizing Romantic attitudes toward nature and toward emotion (especially the emotion of romantic love), Faust responds to his beloved's question, "Do you believe in God?"

> Does not the Heaven vault itself above us?
> Is not the earth established fast below?
> And with their friendly glances do not
> Eternal stars rise over us?
> Do not my eyes look into yours,
> And all things thrust
> Into your head, into your heart,
> And weave in everlasting mystery
> Invisibly, visibly, around you?
> Fill your heart with *this*, great as it is,
> And when this feeling grants you perfect bliss,
> Then call it what you will—
> Happiness! Heart! Love! God!
> I have no name for it!
> Feeling is all.

The notion of "bliss," for Pope associated with respect for limitation, for Wordsworth connected with revolutionary vision, here designates an unnameable feeling, derived from experience of nature and of romantic love, possibly identical with God, but valued partly for its very vagueness.

Modern readers may feel that Faust bullies Gretchen, allowing her no reality except as instrument for his desires. In a poignant moment early in the play, interrupting Faust's rhapsody about her "simplicity" and "innocence," Gretchen suggests, "Only think of *me* one little minute." Faust seems incapable of any such awareness, too busy inventing his loved one to see her as she is. He dramatically represents the "egotistical sublime," with a kind of imaginative grandeur inseparable from his utter absorption in the wonder of his own being, his own experience.

Yet the action of Part I turns on Faust's development of just that consciousness of another's reality which seemed impossible for him, and Gretchen is the agent of his development. In the great final scene—Gretchen in prison, intermittently mad, condemned to death for murdering her illegitimate child by Faust—the woman again appeals to the man to think about her, to *know* her: "Do you know, my love, *whom* you are setting free?" Her anguish, his responsibility for it, force themselves on Faust. He wishes he had never been born: his lust for experience has eventuated in this terrible culpability, this agonizing loss. At the final moment of separation, with Gretchen's spiritual redemption proclaimed from above, Faust implicitly acknowledges the full reality of the woman he has lost and thus, even though he departs with Mephistopheles, distinguishes himself from his Satanic mentor. Mephistopheles in his nature cannot grasp a reality utterly apart from his own; he can only recognize what belongs to him. Faust, at least fleetingly, realizes the otherness of the woman and the value of what he has lost.

Mephistopheles, at the outset witty and powerful in his own imagination, gradually reveals his limitations. In the Prologue in Heaven, the devil seems energetic, perceptive, enterprising, fearless: as the Lord says, a "joker," apparently more playful than malign. His bargain with the Lord turns on his belief in the essentially "beastly" nature of humankind: like Gulliver's Houyhnhnm master, he emphasizes the human misuse of reason. Although the scene is modeled on the interchange between God and Satan in the Book of Job, it differs significantly in that the Lord gives an explicit reason for allowing the Tempter to function. "Men make mistakes as long as they strive," He says, but He adds that Mephistopheles' value is in prodding humanity into action. The introductory scene thus suggests that Mephistopheles will function as an agent of salvation rather than damnation. The devil's subsequent exchanges with Faust, in Mephistopheles' mind predicated on his own superior knowledge and comprehension, gradually make one realize that the man in significant respects knows more than does the devil. Mephistopheles, for example, can understand Faust's desire for Gretchen only in sexual terms. His witty cynicism seems more and more inadequate to the actual situation. By the end of Part I, Faust's suffering has enlarged him; but from the beginning, his capacity for sympathy marked his potential superiority to the devil.

The pattern of Faust's moral development in Part I prepares the reader for a nontragic denouement to the drama as a whole. In Part II, which he worked on for some thirty years, completing it only the year before his death, Goethe moves from the individual to the social. Faust marries Helen of Troy, who gives birth to Euphorion, symbol of new humanity. He turns soldier to save a kingdom; he reclaims land from the sea; finally he rests contented in a vision of happy community generated by the industry of mankind. Mephistopheles thinks this his moment of victory: now Faust has declared himself satisfied. But since his satisfaction depends still on aspiration, on a dream of the future, the angels rescue him at last and take him to heaven.

One cannot read *Faust* with twentieth-century expectations of what a play should be like. This is above all *poetic* drama, to be read with pleasure in the richness of its language, the fertility and daring of its imagination. Although its cast of characters natural and supernatural and its sequence of supernaturally generated events are far from "realistic," it addresses problems still very much with us. How can individual ambition and desire be reconciled with responsibility to others? Does a powerful imagination—an artist's, say, or a scientist's—justify its possessor in ignoring social obligations? Goethe investigates such perplexing issues in symbolic terms, drawing his readers into personal involvement by playing on their emotions even as he questions the proper functions and limitations of commitment to desire—that form of emotional energy that leads to the greatest human achievements, but involves the constant danger of debilitating narcissism.

E. Ludwig, *Goethe, The History of a Man, 1749–1832* (1928) is a solid biography. Also useful are *Goethe: A Collection of Critical Essays*, edited by V. Lange (1960), and the essays contained in the critical edition of *Faust*, edited by W. Arndt and C. Hamlin (1976). See also H. Hatfield, *Goethe: A Critical Introduction* (1963), and, specifically for *Faust*, L. Dieckmann, *Goethe's Faust: A Critical Reading* (1972).

Faust[1]

PROLOGUE IN HEAVEN[2]

The LORD. *The* HEAVENLY HOSTS. MEPHISTOPHELES[3] *following.*
[*The* THREE ARCHANGELS *step forward.*]

RAPHAEL. The chanting sun, as ever, rivals
  The chanting of his brother spheres
  And marches round his destined circuit—
  A march that thunders in our ears.
  His aspect cheers the Hosts of Heaven   5
  Though what his essence none can say;
  These inconceivable creations
  Keep the high state of their first day.

GABRIEL. And swift, with inconceivable swiftness,
  The earth's full splendour rolls around,   10
  Celestial radiance alternating
  With a dread night too deep to sound;
  The sea against the rocks' deep bases
  Comes foaming up in far-flung force,
  And rock and sea go whirling onward   15
  In the swift spheres' eternal course.

MICHAEL. And storms in rivalry are raging
  From sea to land, from land to sea,
  In frenzy forge the world a girdle
  From which no inmost part is free.   20
  The blight of lightning flaming yonder
  Marks where the thunder-bolt will play;
  And yet Thine envoys, Lord, revere
  The gentle movement of Thy day.

CHOIR OF ANGELS. Thine aspect cheers the Hosts of Heaven   25
  Though what Thine essence none can say,
    And all Thy loftiest creations
    Keep the high state of their first day.
  [*Enter* MEPHISTOPHELES.]

MEPHISTOPHELES. Since you, O Lord, once more approach and ask
  If business down with us be light or heavy—   30
  And in the past you've usually welcomed me—
  That's why you see me also at your levee.
  Excuse me, I can't manage lofty words—
  Not though your whole court jeer and find me low;
  My pathos certainly would make you laugh   35
  Had you not left off laughing long ago.

---

1. Translated by Louis MacNeice.   2. The scene is patterned on Job 1:6–12 and 2:1–6.
3. The origin of the name is still debatable. It may come from Hebrew, Persian, or Greek, with such meanings, as "destroyer-liar," "no friend of Faust," "no friend of light."

Your suns and worlds mean nothing much to me;
How men torment themselves, that's all I see.
The little god of the world, one can't reshape, reshade him;
He is as strange to-day as that first day you made him.   40
His life would be not so bad, not quite,
Had you not granted him a gleam of Heaven's light;
He calls it Reason, uses it not the least
Except to be more beastly than any beast.
He seems to me—if your Honour does not mind—   45
Like a grasshopper—the long-legged kind—
That's always in flight and leaps as it flies along
And then in the grass strikes up its same old song.
I could only wish he confined himself to the grass!
He thrusts his nose into every filth, alas.   50
LORD. Mephistopheles, have you no other news?
    Do you always come here to accuse?
    Is nothing ever right in your eyes on earth?
MEPHISTOPHELES. No, Lord! I find things there as downright bad as
    ever.
    I am sorry for men's days of dread and dearth;   55
    Poor things, *my* wish to plague 'em isn't fervent.
LORD. Do you know Faust?
MEPHISTOPHELES.   The Doctor?[4]
LORD.   Aye, my servant.
MEPHISTOPHELES. Indeed! He serves you[5] oddly enough, I think.   60
    The fool has no earthly habits in meat and drink.
    The ferment in him drives him wide and far,
    That he is mad he too has almost guessed;
    He demands of heaven each fairest star
    And of earth each highest joy and best,   65
    And all that is new and all that is far
    Can bring no calm to the deep-sea swell of his breast.
LORD. Now he may serve me only gropingly,
    Soon I shall lead him into the light.
    The gardener knows when the sapling first turns green   70
    That flowers and fruit will make the future bright.
MEPHISTOPHELES. What do you wager? You will lose him yet,
    Provided *you* give *me* permission
    To steer him gently the course I set.
LORD. So long as he walks the earth alive,   75
    So long you may try what enters your head;
    Men make mistakes as long as they strive.
MEPHISTOPHELES. I thank you for that; as regards the dead,

---

4. I.e., doctor of philosophy.   5. In the German text, Mephistopheles shifts from *du* to *ihr*, indicating his lack of respect for God.

The dead have never taken my fancy.
I favour cheeks that are full and rosy-red;   80
No corpse is welcome to my house;
I work as the cat does with the mouse.

LORD. Very well; you have my permission.
Divert this soul from its primal source
And carry it, if you can seize it,   85
Down with you upon your course—
And stand ashamed when you must needs admit:
A good man with his groping intuitions
Still knows the path that is true and fit.

MEPHISTOPHELES. All right—but it won't last for long.   90
I'm not afraid my bet will turn out wrong.
And, if my aim prove true and strong,
Allow me to triumph wholeheartedly.
Dust shall he eat—and greedily—
Like my cousin the Snake renowned in tale and song.   95

LORD. That too you are free to give a trial;
I have never hated the likes of you.
Of all the spirits of denial
The joker is the last that I eschew.
Man finds relaxation too attractive—   100
Too fond too soon of unconditional rest;
Which is why I am pleased to give him a companion
Who lures and thrusts and must, as devil, be active.
But ye, true sons of Heaven, it is your duty
To take your joy in the living wealth of beauty.   105
The changing Essence which ever works and lives
Wall you around with love, serene, secure!
And that which floats in flickering appearance
Fix ye it firm in thoughts that must endure.

CHOIR OF ANGELS. Thine aspect cheers the Hosts of Heaven   110
Though what Thine essence none can say,
And all Thy loftiest creations
Keep the high state of their first day.
    [*Heaven closes.*]

MEPHISTOPHELES. [*Alone*] I like to see the Old One now and then
And try to keep relations on the level.   115
It's really decent of so great a person
To talk so humanely even to the Devil.

The First Part of the Tragedy

NIGHT

In a high-vaulted narrow Gothic room FAUST, *restless, in a chair at his desk.*

FAUST. Here stand I, ach, Philosophy
Behind me and Law and Medicine too
And, to my cost, Theology— ·
All these I have sweated through and through
And now you see me a poor fool   5
As wise as when I entered school!
They call me Master, they call me Doctor,
Ten years now I have dragged my college
Along by the nose through zig and zag
Through up and down and round and round   10
And this is all that I have found—
The impossibility of knowledge!
It is this that burns away my heart;
Of course I am cleverer than the quacks,
Than master and doctor, than clerk and priest,   15
I suffer no scruple or doubt in the least,
I have no qualms about devil or burning,
Which is just why all joy is torn from me,
I cannot presume to make use of my learning,
I cannot presume I could open my mind   20
To proselytize and improve mankind.

Besides, I have neither goods nor gold,
Neither reputation nor rank in the world;
No dog would choose to continue so!
Which is why I have given myself to Magic   25
To see if the Spirit may grant me to know
Through its force and its voice full many a secret,
May spare the sour sweat that I used to pour out
In talking of what I know nothing about,
May grant me to learn what it is that girds   30
The world together in its inmost being,
That the seeing its whole germination, the seeing
Its workings, may end my traffic in words.

O couldst thou, light of the full moon,
Look now thy last upon my pain,   35
Thou for whom I have sat belated
So many midnights here and waited
Till, over books and papers, thou

Didst shine, sad friend, upon my brow!
O could I but walk to and fro   40
On mountain heights in thy dear glow
Or float with spirits round mountain eyries
Or weave through fields thy glances glean
And freed from all miasmal theories
Bathe in thy dew and wash me clean!   45

Oh! Am I still stuck in this jail?
This God-damned dreary hole in the wall
Where even the lovely light of heaven
Breaks wanly through the painted panes!
Cooped up among these heaps of books   50
Gnawed by worms, coated with dust,
Round which to the top of the Gothic vault
A smoke-stained paper forms a crust.
Retorts and canisters lie pell-mell
And pyramids of instruments,   55
The junk of centuries, dense and mat—
Your world, man! World? They call it that!

And yet you ask why your poor heart
Cramped in your breast should feel such fear,
Why an unspecified misery   60
Should throw your life so out of gear?
Instead of the living natural world
For which God made all men his sons
You hold a reeking mouldering court
Among assorted skeletons.   65

Away! There is a world outside!
And this one book of mystic art
Which Nostradamus[6] wrote himself,
Is this not adequate guard and guide?
By this you can tell the course of the stars,   70
By this, once Nature gives the word,
The soul begins to stir and dawn,
A spirit by a spirit heard.
In vain your barren studies here
Construe the signs of sanctity.   75
You Spirits, you are hovering near;
If you can hear me, answer me!
　　[*He opens the book and perceives the sign of the Macrocosm.*][7]

---

6. Latin name of the French astrologer and physician Michel de Notredame, born in 1503. His
collection of rhymed prophecies, *The Centuries*, appeared in 1555.　　7. Literally, "the great
world"; the universe as a whole.

Ha! What a river of wonder at this vision
Bursts upon all my senses in one flood!
And I feel young, the holy joy of life   80
Glows new, flows fresh, through nerve and blood!
Was it a god designed this hieroglyph to calm
The storm which but now raged inside me,
To pour upon my heart such balm,
And by some secret urge to guide me   85
Where all the powers of Nature stand unveiled around me?
Am I a God? It grows so light!
And through the clear-cut symbol on this page
My soul comes face to face with all creating Nature.
At last I understand the dictum of the sage: 90
'The spiritual world is always open,
Your mind is closed, your heart is dead;
Rise, young man, and plunge undaunted
Your earthly breast in the morning red.'
    [*He contemplates the sign.*]

Into one Whole how all things blend,   95
Function and live within each other!
Passing gold buckets to each other
How heavenly powers ascend, descend!
The odour of grace upon their wings,
They thrust from heaven through earthly things   100
And as all sing so *the* All sings!

What a fine show! Aye, but only a show!
Infinite Nature, where can I tap thy veins?
Where are thy breasts, those well-springs of all life
On which hang heaven and earth,   105
Towards which my dry breast strains?
They well up, they give drink, but I feel drought and dearth.
    [*He turns the pages and perceives the sign of the* EARTH SPIRIT.]

How differently this new sign works upon me!
Thy sign, thou Spirit of the Earth,[8] 'tis thine
And thou art nearer to me.   110
At once I feel my powers unfurled,
At once I glow as from new wine
And feel inspired to venture into the world,
To cope with the fortunes of earth benign or malign,
To enter the ring with the storm, to grapple and clinch,   115
To enter the jaws of the shipwreck and never flinch.
Over me comes a mist,

8. The Macrocosm represented the ordered, harmonious universe in its totality; this figure seems
to be a symbol for the energy of terrestrial nature—neither good nor bad, merely powerful.

The moon muffles her light,
The lamp goes dark.
The air goes damp. Red beams flash   120
Around my head. There blows
A kind of a shudder down from the vault
And seizes on me.
It is thou must be hovering round me, come at my prayers!
Spirit, unveil thyself!   125
My heart, oh my heart, how it tears!
And how each and all of my senses
Seem burrowing upwards towards new light, new breath!
I feel my heart as surrendered, I have no more defences.
Come then! Come! Even if it prove my death!   130
   [*He seizes the book and solemnly pronounces the sign of the*
   EARTH SPIRIT. *There is a flash of red flame and the* SPIRIT *appears*
   in it.]

SPIRIT. Who calls upon me?

FAUST. Appalling vision!

SPIRIT. You have long been sucking at my sphere,
   Now by main force you have drawn me here
   And now—   135

FAUST. No! Not to be endured!

SPIRIT. With prayers and with pantings you have procured
   The sight of my face and the sound of my voice—
   Now I am here. What a pitiable shivering
   Seizes the Superman. Where is the call of your soul?   140
   Where the breast which created a world in itself
   And carried and fostered it, swelling up, joyfully quivering,
   Raising itself to a level with Us, the Spirits?
   Where are you, Faust, whose voice rang out to me,
   Who with every nerve so thrust yourself upon me?   145
   Are you the thing that at a whiff of my breath
   Trembles throughout its living frame,
   A poor worm crawling off, askance, askew?

FAUST. Shall I yield to Thee, Thou shape of flame?
   I am Faust, I can hold my own with Thee.   150

SPIRIT. In the floods of life, in the storm of work,
   In ebb and flow,
   In warp and weft,
   Cradle and grave,
   An eternal sea,   155
   A changing patchwork,
   A glowing life,
   At the whirring loom of Time I weave
   The living clothes of the Deity.

FAUST. Thou who dost rove the wide world round,   160
   Busy Spirit, how near I feel to Thee!
SPIRIT. You are like that Spirit which you can grasp,
   Not me!
     [*The* SPIRIT *vanishes.*]
FAUST. Not thee!
   Whom then?   165
   I who am Godhead's image,
   Am I not even like Thee!
     [*A knocking on the door.*]
   Death! I know who that is. My assistant!
   So ends my happiest, fairest hour.
   The crawling pedant must interrupt   170
   My visions at their fullest flower!
     [WAGNER *enters in dressing-gown and nightcap, a lamp in his
     hand.*]
WAGNER. Excuse me but I heard your voice declaiming—
   A passage doubtless from those old Greek plays.
   That is an art from which I would gladly profit,
   It has its advantages nowadays.   175
   And I've often heard folks say it's true
   A preacher can learn something from an actor.
FAUST. Yes, when the preacher is an actor too;
   Which is a not uncommon factor.
WAGNER. Ah, when your study binds up your whole existence   180
   And you scarcely can see the world on a holiday
   Or through a spyglass—and always from a distance—
   How can your rhetoric make it walk your way?
FAUST. Unless you feel it, you cannot gallop it down,
   Unless it thrust up from your soul   185
   Forcing the hearts of all your audience
   With a primal joy beyond control.
   Sit there for ever with scissors and paste!
   Gather men's leavings for a rehash
   And blow up a little paltry flicker   190
   Out of your own little heap of ash!
   It will win you claps from apes and toddlers—
   Supposing your palate welcome such—
   But heart can never awaken a spark in heart
   Unless your own heart keep in touch.   195
WAGNER. However, it is the delivery wins all ears
   And I know that I am still far, too far, in arrears.
FAUST. Win your effects by honest means,
   Eschew the cap and bells of the fool!
   True insight and true sense will make   200

Their point without the rhetoric school
And, given a thought that must be heard,
Is there such need to chase a word?
Yes, your so glittering purple patches
In which you make cat's cradles of humanity　　　205
Are like the foggy wind which whispers in the autumn
Through barren leaves—a fruitless vanity.

WAGNER. Ah God, we know that art
　Is long and short our life!
　Often enough my analytical labours　　　210
　Pester both brain and heart.
　How hard it is to attain the means
　By which one climbs to the fountain head;
　Before a poor devil can reach the halfway house,
　Like as not he is dead.　　　215

FAUST. Your manuscript, is that your holy well
　A draught of which for ever quenches thirst?
　You have achieved no true refreshment
　Unless you can tap your own soul first.

WAGNER. Excuse me—it is considerable gratification　　　220
　To transport oneself into the spirit of times past,
　To observe what a wise man thought before our days
　And how we now have brought his ideas to consummation.

FAUST. Oh yes, consummated in heaven!
　There is a book, my friend, and its seals are seven—[9]　　　225
　The times that have been put on the shelf.
　Your so-called spirit of such times
　Is at bottom merely the spirit of the gentry
　In whom each time reflects itself,
　And at that it often makes one weep　　　230
　And at the first glance run away,
　A lumber-room and a rubbish heap,
　At best an heroic puppet play
　With excellent pragmatical Buts and Yets
　Such as are suitable to marionettes.　　　235

WAGNER. And yet the world! The heart and spirit of men!
　We all would wish to understand the same.

FAUST. Yes, what is known as understanding—
　But who dare call the child by his real name?
　The few who have known anything about it,　　　240
　Whose hearts unwisely overbrimmed and spake,
　Who showed the mob their feelings and their visions,
　Have ended on the cross or at the stake.

---

9. See Revelation 5:1.

My friend, I beg you, the night is now far gone;
We must break off for this occasion.   245
WAGNER. I'd have been happy sitting on and on
   To continue such a learned conversation.
   To-morrow however, as it is Easter Day,
   I shall put you some further questions if I may.
   Having given myself to knowledge heart and soul   250
   I have a good share of it, now I would like the whole.
      [*Exit* WAGNER.]
FAUST. [*Alone*] To think this head should still bring hope to birth
   Sticking like glue to hackneyed rags and tags,
   Delving with greedy hand for treasure
   And glad when it finds an earthworm in the earth!   255

That such a human voice should here intrude
Where spiritual fulness only now enclosed me!
And yet, my God, you poorest of all the sons
Of earth, this time you have earned my gratitude.
For you have snatched me away from that despair   260
Which was ripe and ready to destroy my mind;
Beside that gigantic vision I could not find
My normal self; only a dwarf was there.

I, image of the Godhead, who deemed myself but now
On the brink of the mirror of eternal truth and seeing   265
My rapturous fill of the blaze of clearest Heaven,
Having stripped off my earthly being;
I, more than an angel, I whose boundless urge
To flow through Nature's veins and in the act of creation
To revel it like the gods—what a divination,   270
What an act of daring—and what an expiation!
One thundering word has swept me over the verge.

To boast myself thine equal I do not dare.
Granted I owned the power to draw thee down,
I lacked the power to hold thee there.   275
In that blest moment I felt myself,
Felt myself so small, so great;
Cruelly thou didst thrust me back
Into man's uncertain fate.
Who will teach me? What must I shun?   280
Or must I go where that impulse drives?
Alas, our very actions like our sufferings
Put a brake upon our lives.
Upon the highest concepts of the mind
There grows an alien and more alien mould;   285

When we have reached what in this world is good
That which is better is labelled a fraud, a blind.
What gave us life, feelings of highest worth,
Go dead amidst the madding crowds of earth.

Where once Imagination on daring wing   290
Reached out to the Eternal, full of hope,
Now, that the eddies of time have shipwrecked chance on chance,
She is contented with a narrow scope.
Care makes her nest forthwith in the heart's deep places,
And there contrives her secret sorrows,   295
Rocks herself restlessly, destroying rest and joy;
And always she is putting on new faces,
Will appear as your home, as those that you love within it,
As fire or water, poison or steel;
You tremble at every blow that you do not feel   300
And what you never lose you must weep for every minute.

I am not like the gods—that I too deeply feel—
No, I am like the worm that burrows through the dust
Which, as it keeps itself alive in the dust,
Is annulled and buried by some casual heel.   305

Is it not dust that on a thousand shelves
Narrows this high wall round me so?
The junk that with its thousandfold tawdriness
In this moth world keeps me so low?
Shall I find here what I require?   310
Read maybe in a thousand books how men
Have in the general run tortured themselves,
With but a lucky one now and then?
Why do you grin at me, you hollow skull?
To point out that your brain was once, like mine, confused 315
And looked for the easy day but in the difficult dusk,
Lusting for truth was led astray and abused?
You instruments, I know you are mocking me
With cog and crank and cylinder.
I stood at the door, you were to be the key;   320
A key with intricate wards—but the bolt declines to stir.
Mysterious in the light of day
Nature lets none unveil her; if she refuse
To make some revelation to your spirit
You cannot force her with levers and with screws.   325
You ancient gear I have never used, it is only
Because my father used you that I retain you.[1]
You ancient scroll, you have been turning black

---

1. Later we find that Faust's father was a doctor of medicine.

Since first the dim lamp smoked upon this desk to stain you.
Far better to have squandered the little I have   330
Than loaded with that little to stay sweating here.
Whatever legacy your fathers left you,
To own it you must earn it dear.
The thing that you fail to use is a load of lead;
The moment can only use what the moment itself has bred.   335

But why do my eyes fasten upon that spot?
Is that little bottle a magnet to my sight?
Why do I feel of a sudden this lovely illumination
As when the moon flows round us in a dark wood at night?

Bottle, unique little bottle, I salute you   340
As now I devoutly lift you down. In you
I honour human invention and human skill.
You, the quintessence of all sweet narcotics,
The extract of all rare and deadly powers,
I am your master—show me your good will!   345
I look on you, my sorrow is mitigated,
I hold you and my struggles are abated,
The flood-tide of my spirit ebbs away, away.
The mirroring waters glitter at my feet,
I am escorted forth on the high seas,   350
Allured towards new shores by a new day.
A fiery chariot floats on nimble wings
Down to me and I feel myself upbuoyed
To blaze a new trail through the upper air
Into new spheres of energy unalloyed.   355
Oh this high life, this heavenly rapture! Do *you*
Merit this, you, a moment ago a worm?
Merit it? Aye—only turn your back on the sun
Which enchants the earth, turn your back and be firm!
And brace yourself to tear asunder the gates   360
Which everyone longs to shuffle past if he can;
Now is the time to act and acting prove
That God's height need not lower the merit of Man;
Nor tremble at that dark pit in which our fancy
Condemns itself to torments of its own framing,   365
But struggle on and upwards to that passage
At the narrow mouth of which all hell is flaming.
Be calm and take this step, though you should fall
Beyond it into nothing—nothing at all.

And you, you loving-cup of shining crystal—   370
I have not given a thought to you for years—
Down you come now out of your ancient chest!

You glittered at my ancestors' junketings
Enlivening the serious guest
When with you in his hand he proceeded to toast his
    neighbour—   375
But to-day no neighbour will take you from my hand.
Here is a juice that makes one drunk in a wink;
It fills you full, you cup, with its brown flood.
It was I who made this, I who had it drawn;
So let my whole soul now make my last drink   380
A high and gala greeting, a toast to the dawn![2]
> [*He raises the cup to his mouth. There is an outburst of bells and choirs.*]

CHORUS OF ANGELS. Christ is arisen![3]
                       Joy to mortality
                       Whom its own fatally
                       Earth-bound mortality   385
                       Bound in a prison.

FAUST. What a deep booming, what a ringing tone
Pulls back the cup from my lips—and with such power!
So soon are you announcing, you deep bells,
Easter Day's first festive hour?   390
You choirs, do you raise so soon the solacing hymn
That once round the night of the grave rang out from the sera-
    phim
As man's new covenant and dower?

CHORUS OF WOMEN. With balm and with spices
                       'Twas we laid him out,   395
                       We who tended him,
                       Faithful, devout;
                       We wound him in linen,
                       Made all clean where he lay,
                       Alas—to discover   400
                       Christ gone away.[4]

CHORUS OF ANGELS. Christ is arisen!
                       The loving one! Blest
                       After enduring the
                       Grievous, the curing, the   405
                       Chastening test.

FAUST. You heavenly music, strong as you are kind,
Why do you search me out in the dust?
Better ring forth where men have open hearts!
I hear your message, my faith it is that lags behind;   410

---

2. See line 248.   3. First line of an old medieval Easter hymn, freely adapted by Goethe.
4. Goethe makes free use of the New Testament here. None of the Evangelists says that Christ was laid in the tomb by women. According to Mark and Luke, they came on the third day *intending* to anoint the body, but He was gone from the tomb.

And miracle is the favourite child of faith.
Those spheres whence peals the gospel of forgiving,
Those are beyond what I can dare,
And yet, so used am I from childhood to this sound,
It even now summons me back to living.   415
Once I could feel the kiss of heavenly love
Rain down through the calm and solemn Sabbath air,
Could find a prophecy in the full-toned bell,
A spasm of happiness in a prayer.
An ineffably sweet longing bound me   420
To quest at random through field and wood
Where among countless burning tears
I felt a world rise up around me.
This hymn announced the lively games of youth, the lovely
Freedom of Spring's own festival;   425
Now with its childlike feelings memory holds me back
From the last and gravest step of all.
But you, sweet songs of heaven, keep sounding forth!
My tears well up, I belong once more to earth.

CHORUS OF DISCIPLES. Now has the Buried One,   430
                  Lowliness ended,
                  Living in lordliness,
                  Lordly ascended;
                  He in the zest of birth
                  Near to creating light;   435
                  We on the breast of earth
                  Still in frustrating night!
                  He left us, his own ones,
                  Pining upon this spot,
                  Ah, and lamenting   440
                  Master, thy lot.

CHORUS OF ANGELS. Christ is arisen
                  From the womb of decay!
                  Burst from your prison,
                  Rejoice in the day!   445
                  Praising him actively,
                  Practising charity,
                  Giving alms brotherly,
                  Preaching him wanderingly,
                  Promising sanctity,   450
                  You have your Master near,
                  You have him here!

EASTER HOLIDAY

Holidaymakers of all kinds come out through the city gate.[5]

FIRST STUDENT. Lord, these strapping wenches they go a lick!
    Hurry up, brother, we must give 'em an escort.
    My programme for to-day is a strong ale,
    A pipe of shag and a girl who's got up chic.
FIRST GIRL. Look! Will you look at the handsome boys!   5
    Really and truly it's degrading;
    They could walk out with the best of us
    And they have to run round scullery-maiding!
SECOND STUDENT. Hold on, hold on! There are two coming up behind
    With a very pretty taste in dress;   10
    One of those girls is a neighbour of mine,
    She appeals to me, I must confess.
    You see how quietly they go
    And yet in the end they'll be taking *us* in tow.
BEGGAR. [*Singing*] Good gentlemen and lovely ladies,   15
        Rosy of cheek and neat of dress,
        Be kind enough to look upon me
        And see and comfort my distress.
        Leave me not here a hopeless busker!
        Only the giver can be gay.   20
        A day when all the town rejoices,
        Make it for me a harvest day.
FIRST BURGHER. I know nothing better on Sundays or on holidays
    Than to have a chat about war and warlike pother
    When far away, in Turkey say,   25
    The peoples are socking one another.
    One stands at the window, drinks one's half of mild,
    And sees the painted ships glide down the waterways;
    Then in the evening one goes happily home
    And blesses peace and peaceful days.   30
SECOND BURGHER. Yes indeed, neighbour! That is all right with me.
    They can break heads if they like it so
    And churn up everything topsyturvy.
    But at home let us keep the status quo.
OLD WOMAN. Eh, but how smart they look! Pretty young things!   35
    Whoever saw you should adore you!
    But not so haughty! It's all right—
    Tell me your wish and I can get it for you.

---

5. It has been shown that Goethe had Frankfurt in mind for this scene, and the "gate" referred to is the Sachsenhausen Tor, or Affenthor. The translator omits a few lines here which include other local references—to a hunting lodge, or *Forsthaus*, two miles southwest of the gate; to an inn called the Gerbermühle on the Main River; and to a village, probably Oberrad.

FIRST GIRL. Come, Agatha! Such witches I avoid
　　In public places—it's much wiser really;　　　　　　　　　40
　　It's true, she helped me on St. Andrew's night[6]
　　To see my future sweetheart clearly.
SECOND GIRL Yes, mine she showed me in a crystal,
　　A soldier type with dashing chaps behind him;
　　I look around, I seek him everywhere　　　　　　　　　45
　　And yet—and yet I never find him.
SOLDIERS. [*Singing*] Castles with towering
　　　　　　　　　　　Walls to maintain them,
　　　　　　　　　　　Girls who have suitors
　　　　　　　　　　　But to disdain them,　　　　　　　50
　　　　　　　　　　　Would I could gain them!
　　　　　　　　　　　Bold is the venture,
　　　　　　　　　　　Lordly the pay.

　　　　　　　　　　　Hark to the trumpets!
　　　　　　　　　　　They may be crying　　　　　　　55
　　　　　　　　　　　Summons to gladness,
　　　　　　　　　　　Summons to dying.
　　　　　　　　　　　Life is a storming!
　　　　　　　　　　　Life is a splendour!
　　　　　　　　　　　Maidens and castles　　　　　　　60
　　　　　　　　　　　Have to surrender.
　　　　　　　　　　　Bold is the venture,
　　　　　　　　　　　Lordly the pay;
　　　　　　　　　　　Later the soldiers
　　　　　　　　　　　Go marching away.　　　　　　　65
　　[FAUST *and* WAGNER *are now walking off on the road to the
　　village.*]
FAUST. River and brook are freed from ice
　　By the lovely enlivening glance of spring
　　And hope grows green throughout the dale;
　　Ancient winter, weakening,
　　Has fallen back on the rugged mountains　　　　　　　70
　　And launches thence his Parthian shafts
　　Which are merely impotent showers of hail
　　Streaking over the greening mead;
　　But the sun who tolerates nothing white
　　Amidst all this shaping and stirring of seed,　　　　　　75
　　Wants to enliven the world with colour
　　And, flowers being lacking, in their lieu
　　Takes colourful crowds to mend the view.

---

6. Actually, St. Andrew's eve, November 29. This was the traditional time for young girls to
consult fortunetellers about their future lovers or husbands.

Turn round and look back from this rise
Towards the town. From the gloomy gate   80
Look, can you see them surging forth—
A harlequin-coloured crowd in fête!
Sunning themselves with one accord
In homage to the risen Lord
For they themselves to-day have risen: 85
Out of the dismal room in the slum,
Out of each shop and factory prison,
Out of the stuffiness of the garret,
Out of the squash of the narrow streets,
Out of the churches' reverend night—   90
One and all have been raised to light.
Look, only look, how quickly the gardens
And fields are sprinkled with the throng,
How the river all its length and breadth
Bears so many pleasure-boats along,   95
And almost sinking from its load
How this last dinghy moves away.
Even on the furthest mountain tracks
Gay rags continue to look gay.
Already I hear the hum of the village,   100
Here is the plain man's real heaven—
Great and small in a riot of fun;
Here I'm a man—and dare be one.
WAGNER. Doctor, to take a walk with you
Is a profit and a privilege for me   105
But I wouldn't lose my way alone round here,
Sworn foe that I am of all vulgarity.
This fiddling, screaming, skittle-playing,
Are sounds I loathe beyond all measure;
They run amuck as if the devil were in them   110
And call it music, call it pleasure.
   [*They have now reached the village.*]
OLD PEASANT. Doctor, it is most good of you
Not to look down on us to-day
And, pillar of learning that you are,
To mill around with folk at play.   115
So take this most particular jug
Which we have filled for you at the tap,
This is a pledge and I pray aloud
That it quench your thirst and more mayhap:
As many drops as this can give,   120
So many days extra may you live.
FAUST. Thank you for such a reviving beer

And now—good health to all men here.
  [*The people collect round him.*]
OLD PEASANT. Of a truth, Doctor, you have done rightly
  To appear on this day when all are glad,   125
  Seeing how in times past you proved
  Our own good friend when days were bad.
  Many a man stands here alive
  Whom your father found in the grip
  Of a raging fever and tore him thence[7]   130
  When he put paid to the pestilence.
  You too—you were a youngster then—
  Where any was ill you went your round,
  Right many a corpse left home feet first
  But you came out of it safe and sound,   135
  From many a gruelling trial—Aye,
  The helper got help from the Helper on high.
CROWD. Health to the trusty man. We pray
  He may live to help us many a day.
FAUST. Kneel to the One on high, our friend   140
  Who teaches us helpers, who help can send.
  [FAUST *and* WAGNER *leave the* CROWD *and move on.*]
WAGNER. You great man, how your heart must leap
  To be so honoured by the masses!
  How happy is he who has such talents
  And from them such a crop can reap!   145
  The father points you out to his boy,
  They all ask questions, run and jostle,
  The fiddles and the dancers pause
  And, as you pass, they stand in rows
  And caps go hurtling in the sky;   150
  They almost kneel to you as though
  The eucharist were passing by.
FAUST. Only a few steps more up to that stone!
  Here, after our walk, we will take a rest.
  Here I have often sat, thoughtful, alone,   155
  Torturing myself with prayer and fast.
  Rich in hope and firm in faith,
  With tears and sighs to seven times seven
  I thought I could end that epidemic
  And force the hand of the Lord of Heaven.   160
  But now the crowd's applause sounds to me like derision.
  O could you only read in my inmost heart

---

7. See l. 327 in the preceding scene. The old German Faust legend made Faust's father a peasant;
but Nostradamus and Paracelsus (1493–1541), two physician-astrologers closely linked to the Faust
myth, were famous for their plague-curing remedies.

How little father and son
Merited their great reputation!
My father was a worthy man who worked in the dark,   165
Who in good faith but on his own wise
Brooded on Nature and her holy circles
With laborious whimsicalities;
Who used to collect the connoisseurs
Into the kitchen and locked inside   170
Its black walls pour together divers
Ingredients of countless recipes;
Such was our medicine, the patients died
And no one counted the survivors.
And thus we with our hellish powders   175
Raged more perniciously than the plague
Throughout this district—valley and town.
Myself I have given the poison to thousands;
They drooped away, *I* must live on to sample
The brazen murderers' renown.   180

WAGNER. How can you let that weigh so heavily?
Does not a good man do enough
If he works at the art that he has received
Conscientiously and scrupulously?
As a young man you honour your father,   185
What he can teach, you take with a will;
As a man you widen the range of knowledge
And your son's range may be wider still.

FAUST. Happy the man who swamped in this sea of Error
Still hopes to struggle up through the watery wall;   190
What we don't know is exactly what we need
And what we know fulfils no need at all.
But let us not with such sad thoughts
Make this good hour an hour undone!
Look how the cottages on the green   195
Shine in the glow of the evening sun!
He backs away, gives way, the day is overspent,
He hurries off to foster life elsewhere.
Would I could press on his trail, on his trail for ever—
Alas that I have no wings to raise me into the air!   200
Then I should see in an everlasting sunset
The quiet world before my feet unfold,
All of its peaks on fire, all of its vales becalmed,
And the silver brook dispersed in streams of gold.
Not the wild peaks with all their chasms   205
Could interrupt my godlike flight;
Already the bays of the sea that the sun has warmed

Unfurl upon my marvelling sight.
But in the end the sungod seems to sink away,
Yet the new impulse sets me again in motion,   210
I hasten on to drink his eternal light,
With night behind me and before me day,
Above me heaven and below me ocean.
A beautiful dream—yet the sun leaves me behind.
Alas, it is not so easy for earthly wing   215
To fly on level terms with the wings of the mind.
Yet born with each of us is the instinct
That struggles upwards and away
When over our heads, lost in the blue,
The lark pours out her vibrant lay;   220
When over rugged pine-clad ranges
The eagle hangs on outspread wings
And over lake and over plain
We see the homeward-struggling crane.

WAGNER. I myself have often had moments of fancifulness   225
But I never experienced yet an urge like this.
Woods and fields need only a quick look
And *I* shall never envy the bird its pinions.
How differently the joys of the mind's dominions
Draw us from page to page, from book to book.   230
That's what makes winter nights lovely and snug—
The blissful life that warms you through your body—
And, ah, should you unroll a worthwhile manuscript,
You bring all heaven down into your study.

FAUST. You are only conscious of one impulse. Never   235
Seek an acquaintance with the other.
Two souls, alas, cohabit in my breast,
A contract one of them desires to sever.
The one like a rough lover clings
To the world with the tentacles of its senses;   240
The other lifts itself to Elysian Fields
Out of the mist on powerful wings.
Oh, if there be spirits in the air,
Princes that weave their way between heaven and earth,
Come down to me from the golden atmosphere   245
And carry me off to a new and colourful life.
Aye, if I only had a magic mantle
On which I could fly abroad, a-voyaging,
I would not barter it for the costliest raiment,
Not even for the mantle of a king.   250

WAGNER. Do not invoke the notorious host
Deployed in streams upon the wind,

Preparing danger in a thousand forms
From every quarter for mankind.
Thrusting upon you from the North   255
Come fanged spirits with arrow tongues;
From the lands of morning they come parching
To feed themselves upon your lungs;
The South despatches from the desert
Incendiary hordes against your brain   260
And the West a swarm which first refreshes,
Then drowns both you and field and plain.
They are glad to listen, adepts at doing harm,
Glad to obey and so throw dust in our eyes;
They make believe that they are sent from heaven   265
And lisp like angels, telling lies.
But let us move! The world has already gone grey,
The air is beginning to cool and the mist to fall.
It's in the evening one really values home—
But why do you look so astonished, standing there, staring that
    way?   270
What's there to see in the dusk that's worth the trouble?
FAUST. The black dog, do you mark him ranging through corn and
    stubble?
WAGNER. I noticed him long ago; he struck me as nothing much.
FAUST. Have a good look at the brute. What do you take him for?
WAGNER. For a poodle who, as is the way of such,   275
    Is trailing his master, worrying out the scent.
FAUST. But don't you perceive how in wide spirals around us
    He is getting nearer and nearer of set intent?
    And, unless I'm wrong, a running fire
    Eddies behind him in his wake.   280
WAGNER. I can see nothing but a black poodle;
    It must be your eyes have caused this mistake
FAUST. He is casting, it seems to me, fine nooses of magic
    About our feet as a snare.
WAGNER. I see him leaping round us uncertainly, timidly,   285
    Finding instead of his master two strangers there.
FAUST. The circle narrows; now he is near.
WAGNER. Just a dog, you see; no phantoms here.
    He growls and hesitates, grovels on the green
    And wags his tail. Pure dog routine.   290
FAUST. Heel, sir, heel! Come, fellow, come!
WAGNER. He is a real poodle noodle.
    Stand still and he'll sit up and beg;
    Speak to him and he's all over you;
    Lose something and he'll fetch it quick,   295

He'll jump in the water after your stick.
FAUST. I think you're right, I cannot find a trace
    Of a spirit here; it is all a matter of training.
WAGNER. If a dog is well brought up, a wise man even
    Can come to be fond of him in such a case.   300
    Yes, he fully deserves your name upon his collar,
    He whom the students have found so apt a scholar.

FAUST'S STUDY

He enters with the poodle.

FAUST. I have forsaken field and meadow
        Which night has laid in a deep bed,
        Night that wakes our better soul
        With a holy and foreboding dread.
        Now wild desires are wrapped in sleep   5
        And all the deeds that burn and break,
        The love of Man is waking now,
        The love of God begins to wake.

Poodle! Quiet! Don't run hither and thither!
Leave my threshold! Why are you snuffling there?   10
Lie down behind the stove and rest.
Here's a cushion; it's my best.
Out of doors on the mountain paths
You kept us amused by running riot;
But as my protégé at home   15
You'll only be welcome if you're quiet.

        Ah, when in our narrow cell
        The lamp once more imparts good cheer,
        Then in our bosom—in the heart
        That knows itself—then things grow clear.   20
        Reason once more begins to speak
        And the blooms of hope once more to spread;
        One hankers for the brooks of life,
        Ah, and for life's fountain head.

Don't growl, you poodle! That animal sound   25
Is not in tune with the holy music
By which my soul is girdled round.
We are used to human beings who jeer
At what they do not understand,
Who grouse at the good and the beautiful   30
Which often causes them much ado;
But must a dog snarl at it too?

But, ah, already, for all my good intentions
I feel contentment ebbing away in my breast.
Why must the stream so soon run dry   35
And we be left once more athirst?
I have experienced this so often;
Yet this defect has its compensation,
We learn to prize the supernatural
And hanker after revelation,   40
Which burns most bright and wins assent
Most in the New Testament.
I feel impelled to open the master text[8]
And this once, with true dedication,
Take the sacred original   45
And make in my mother tongue my own translation.
   [*He opens a Bible.*]

It is written: In the beginning was the Word.[9]
Here I am stuck at once. Who will help me on?
I am unable to grant the Word such merit,
I must translate it differently   50
If I am truly illumined by the spirit.
It is written: In the beginning was the Mind.
But why should my pen scour
So quickly ahead? Consider that first line well.
Is it the Mind that effects and creates all things?   55
It *should* read: In the beginning was the Power.
Yet, even as I am changing what I have writ,
Something warns me not to abide by it.
The spirit prompts me, I see in a flash what I need,
And write: In the beginning was the Deed!   60

Dog! If we two are to share this room,
Leave off your baying,
Leave off your barking!
I can't have such a fellow staying
Around me causing all this bother.   65
One of us or the other
Will have to leave the cell.
Well?
I don't really like to eject you so
But the door is open, you may go.   70

But what? What do I see?
Can this really happen naturally?
Is it a fact or is it a fraud?

8. I.e., the Greek.   9. John 1:1.

My dog is growing so long and broad!
He raises himself mightily,   75
That is not a dog's anatomy!
What a phantom have I brought to my house!
He already looks like a river horse
With fiery eyes and frightful jaws—
Aha! But I can give you pause!   80
For such a hybrid out of hell
Solomon's Key is a good spell.[1]
   [SPIRITS *are heard in the passage.*]

SPIRITS. Captured within there is one of us!
  Wait without, follow him none of us!
  Like a fox in a snare   85
  An old hell-cat's trembling there.
  But on the alert!
  Fly against and athwart,
  To starboard and port,
  And he's out with a spurt!   90
  If help you can take him,
  Do not forsake him!
  For often, to earn it, he
  Helped our fraternity.

FAUST. First, to confront the beast,   95
  Be the Spell of the Four[2] released:
    Salamander shall glow,
    Undine shall coil,
    Sylph shall vanish
    And gnome shall toil.   100
  One without sense
  Of the elements,
  Of their force
  And proper course,
  The spirits would never   105
  Own him for master.
    Vanish in flames,
    Salamander!
    Commingle in babble of streams,
    Undine!   110
    Shine meteor-like and majestic,
    Sylph!
    Bring help domestic,
    Lubber-fiend! Lubber-fiend!

1. The *Clavicula Salomonis*, a standard work used by magicians for conjuring; in many medieval legends, Solomon was noted as a great magician.   2. Salamanders were spirits of fire; undines, of water; sylphs, of air; and gnomes, of earth.

Step out of him and make an end!   115
None of the Four
Is the creature's core.
He lies quite quiet and grins at me,
I have not yet worked him injury.
To exercise you   120
I'll have to chastise you.
    Are you, rapscallion,
    A displaced devil?
    This sign can level
    Each dark battalion;   125
    Look at this sign!
He swells up already with bristling spine.
    You outcast! Heed it—
    This name! Can you read it?
    The unbegotten one,   130
    Unpronounceable,
    Poured throughout Paradise,
    Heinously wounded one?
Behind the stove, bound by my spells,
Look, like an elephant it swells,   135
Filling up all the space and more,
It threatens to melt away in mist.
Down from the ceiling! Down before—!
Down at your master's feet! Desist!
You see, I have not proved a liar;   140
I can burn you up with holy fire!
Do not await
The triply glowing light![3]
Do not await
My strongest brand of necromancy!   145
    [*The mist subsides and* MEPHISTOPHELES *comes forward from
    behind the stove, dressed like a travelling scholar.*]

MEPHISTOPHELES. What is the noise about? What might the gentle-
    man fancy?
FAUST. So that is what the poodle had inside him!
    A travelling scholar? That casus makes me laugh.
MEPHISTOPHELES. My compliments to the learned gentleman.
    You have put me a sweat—not half!   150
FAUST. What is your name?
MEPHISTOPHELES. The question strikes me as petty
    For one who holds the Word[4] in such low repute,
    Who, far withdrawn from all mere surface,

3. Perhaps the Trinity, or a triangle with divergent rays.   4. See l. 47 in this scene.

Aims only at the Essential Root. 155
FAUST. With you, you gentry, what is essential
  The name more often than not supplies,
  As is indeed only too patent
  When they call you Fly-God,[5] Corrupter, Father of Lies.
  All right, who are you then? 160
MEPHISTOPHELES. A part of that Power
  Which always wills evil, always procures good.
FAUST. What do you mean by this conundrum?
MEPHISTOPHELES. I am the Spirit which always denies.
  And quite rightly; whatever has a beginning 165
  Deserves to have an undoing;
  It would be better if nothing began at all.
  Thus everything that you call
  Sin, destruction, Evil in short,
  Is my own element, my resort. 170
FAUST. You call yourself a part, yet you stand before me whole?
MEPHISTOPHELES. This is the unassuming truth.
  Whereas mankind, that little world of fools,
  Commonly takes itself for a whole—
  I am a part of the Part which in the beginning was all, 175
  A part of the darkness[6] which gave birth to light,
  To that haughty light which is struggling now to usurp
  The ancient rank and realm of its mother Night,
  And yet has no success, try as it will,
  Being bound and clamped by bodies still. 180
  It streams from bodies, bodies it beautifies,
  A body clogs it when it would run,
  And so, I hope, it won't be long
  Till, bodies and all, it is undone.
FAUST. Ah, now I know your honourable profession! 185
  You cannot destroy on a large scale,
  So you are trying it on a small.
MEPHISTOPHELES. And, candidly, not getting far at all.
  That which stands over against the Nothing,
  The Something, I mean this awkward world, 190
  For all my endeavours up to date
  I have failed to get it under foot
  With waves, with storms, with earthquakes, fire—
  Sea and land after all stay put.
  And this damned stuff, the brood of beasts and men, 195
  There is no coming to grips with them;

---

5. An almost literal translation of the name of the Philistine deity Beelzebub. 6. Mephistopheles here speaks as the Prince of Darkness, the role in Christianity acquired by the devil from the Persian Manichaean deity Ahriman.

I've already buried heaps of them!
And always new blood, fresh blood, circulates again.
So it goes on, it's enough to drive one crazy.
A thousand embryos extricate themselves   200
From air, from water and from earth
In wet and dry and hot and cold.
Had I not made a corner in fire
I should find myself without a berth.
FAUST. So you when faced with the ever stirring,   205
    The creative force, the beneficent,
    Counter with your cold devil's fist
    Spitefully clenched but impotent.
    You curious son of Chaos, why
    Not turn your hand to something else?   210
MEPHISTOPHELES. We will give it our serious attention—
    But more on that subject by and by.
    Might I for this time take my leave?
FAUST. Why you ask I cannot see.
    I have already made your acquaintance;   215
    When you feel like it, call on me.
    Here is the window, here is the door—
    And a chimney too—if it comes to that.
MEPHISTOPHELES. I must confess; there's a slight impediment
    That stops me making my exit pat,   220
    The pentagram[7] upon your threshold—
FAUST. So the witch's foot[8] is giving you trouble?
    Then tell me, since you're worried by that spell,
    How did you ever enter, child of Hell?
    How was a spirit like you betrayed?   225
MEPHISTOPHELES. You study that sign! It's not well made;
    One of its corners, do you see,
    The outside one's not quite intact.
FAUST. A happy accident in fact!
    Which means you're in my custody?   230
    I did not intend to set a gin.
MEPHISTOPHELES. The dog—he noticed nothing, jumping in;
    The case has now turned round about
    And I, the devil, can't get out.
FAUST. Then why not leave there by the window?   235
MEPHISTOPHELES. It is a law for devils and phantoms all:
    By the way that we slip in by the same we must take our leave.
    One's free in the first, in the second one's a thrall.
FAUST. So Hell itself has its regulations?

---

7. A magic five-pointed star designed to keep away evil spirits, principally the female incubus or witch.   8. The pentagram.

That's excellent; a contract in that case   240
Could be made with you, you gentry—and definite?
MEPHISTOPHELES. What we promise, you will enjoy with no reser-
    vations,
Nothing will be nipped off from it.
But all this needs a little explaining
And will keep till our next heart-to-heart;   245
But now I beg and doubly beg you:
Let me, just for now, depart.
FAUST. But wait yet a minute and consent
To tell me first some news of moment.
MEPHISTOPHELES. Let me go now! I'll soon be back   250
To be questioned to your heart's content.
FAUST. It was not I laid a trap for you,
You thrust your own head in the noose.
A devil in the hand's worth two in hell!
The second time he'll be longer loose.   255
MEPHISTOPHELES. If you so wish it, I'm prepared
To keep you company and stay;
Provided that by my arts the time
Be to your betterment whiled away.
FAUST. I am in favour, carry on—   260
But let your art be a pleasing one.
MEPHISTOPHELES. My friend, your senses will have more
Gratification in this hour
Than in a year's monotony.
What the delicate spirits sing to you   265
And the beauties that they bring to you
Are no empty, idle wizardry.
You'll have your sense of smell delighted,
Your palate in due course excited,
Your feelings rapt enchantingly.   270
Preparation? There's no need,
We are all here. Strike up! Proceed!
    [*The* SPIRITS *sing.*]
SPIRITS.   Vanish, you darkling
        Arches above him,
        That a more witching   275
        Blue and enriching
        Sky may look in!
        If only the darkling
        Clouds were unravelled!
        Small stars are sparkling,   280
        Suns are more gently
        Shining within!

Spiritual beauty
Of the children of Heaven
Swaying and bowing   285
Floats in the air,
Leanings and longings
Follow them there;
And ribbons of raiment
The breezes have caught   290
Cover the country,
Cover the arbour
Where, drowning in thought,
Lovers exchange their
Pledges for life.   295
Arbour on arbour!
Creepers run rife!
Grapes in great wreathing
Clusters are poured into
Vats that are seething,   300
Wines that are foaming
Pour out in rivulets
Rippling and roaming
Through crystalline stones,
Leaving the sight of   305
The highlands behind them,
Widening to lakes
Amid the delight of
Green-growing foothills.
And the winged creatures   310
Sipping their ecstasy,
Sunwards they fly,
Fly to discover
The glittering islands
Which bob on the wave-tops   315
Deceiving the eye.
There we can hear
Huzzaing in chorus,
A landscape of dancers
Extending before us,   320
All in the open,
Free as the air.
Some of them climbing
Over the peaks,
Some of them swimming   325
Over the lakes,
Or floating in space—
All towards existence,

All towards the distance
Of stars that will love them   330
The blessing of grace.
MEPHISTOPHELES. He is asleep. That's fine, you airy, dainty young-
    sters
You have sung him a real cradle song.
For this performance I am in your debt.
You are not yet the man to hold the devil for long.   335
Play round him with your sweet dream trickeries
And sink him in a sea of untruth!
But to break the spell upon this threshold
What I need now is a rat's tooth.
And I needn't bother to wave a wand,   340
I can hear one rustling already, he'll soon respond.
The lord of rats, the lord of mice,
Of flies, frogs, bugs and lice,
Commands you to come out of that
And gnaw away this threshold, rat,   345
While he takes oil and gives it a few—
So there you come hopping? Quick on your cue!
Now get on the job! The obstructing point
Is on the edge and right in front.
One bite more and the work's done.   350
Now, Faust, till we meet again, dream on!
FAUST. [*Waking*] Am I defrauded then once more?
Does the throng of spirits vanish away like fog
To prove that the devil appeared to me in a dream
But what escaped was only a dog?   355

FAUST'S STUDY

The same room. Later.

FAUST. Who's knocking? Come in! *Now* who wants to annoy me?
MEPHISTOPHELES. [*Outside door*] It's I.
FAUST.   Come in!
MEPHISTOPHELES. [*Outside door*]
                          You must say 'Come in' three times.
FAUST. Come in then!   5
MEPHISTOPHELES. [*Entering*] Thank you; you overjoy me.
We two, I hope, we shall be good friends;
To chase those megrims of yours away
I am here like a fine young squire[9] to-day,
In a suit of scarlet trimmed with gold   10

---

9. In the popular plays based on the Faust legend, the devil often appeared as a monk when the play catered to a Protestant audience, and as a cavalier when the audience was predominantly Catholic.

And a little cape of stiff brocade,
With a cock's feather in my hat
And at my side a long sharp blade,
And the most succinct advice I can give
Is that you dress up just like me,   15
So that uninhibited and free
You may find out what it means to live.
FAUST. The pain of earth's constricted life, I fancy,
    Will pierce me still, whatever my attire;
    I am too old for mere amusement,   20
    Too young to be without desire.
    How can the world dispel my doubt?
    You must do without, you must do without!
    That is the everlasting song
    Which rings in every ear, which rings,   25
    And which to us our whole life long
    Every hour hoarsely sings.
    I wake in the morning only to feel appalled,
    My eyes with bitter tears could run
    To see the day which in its course   30
    Will not fulfil a wish for me, not one;
    The day which whittles away with obstinate carping
    All pleasures—even those of anticipation,
    Which makes a thousand grimaces to obstruct
    My heart when it is stirring in creation.   35
    And again, when night comes down, in anguish
    I must stretch out upon my bed
    And again no rest is granted me,
    For wild dreams fill my mind with dread.
    The God who dwells within my bosom   40
    Can make my inmost soul react;
    The God who sways my every power
    Is powerless with external fact.
    And so existence weighs upon my breast
    And I long for death and life—life I detest.   45
MEPHISTOPHELES. Yet death is never a wholly welcome guest.
FAUST. O happy is he whom death in the dazzle of victory
    Crowns with the bloody laurel in the battling swirl!
    Or he whom after the mad and breakneck dance
    He comes upon in the arms of a girl!   50
    O to have sunk away, delighted, deleted,
    Before the Spirit of the Earth, before his might!
MEPHISTOPHELES. Yet I know someone who failed to drink
    A brown juice on a certain night.
FAUST. Your hobby is espionage—is it not?   55

MEPHISTOPHELES. Oh I'm not omniscient—but I know a lot.
FAUST. Whereas that tumult in my soul
    Was stilled by sweet familiar chimes
    Which cozened the child that yet was in me
    With echoes of more happy times,   60
    I now curse all things that encompass
    The soul with lures and jugglery
    And bind it in this dungeon of grief
    With trickery and flattery.
    Cursed in advance be the high opinion   65
    That serves our spirit for a cloak!
    Cursed be the dazzle of appearance
    Which bows our senses to its yoke!
    Cursed be the lying dreams of glory,
    The illusion that our name survives!   70
    Cursed be the flattering things we own,
    Servants and ploughs, children and wives!
    Cursed be Mammon[1] when with his treasures
    He makes us play the adventurous man
    Or when for our luxurious pleasures   75
    He duly spreads the soft divan!
    A curse on the balsam of the grape!
    A curse on the love that rides for a fall!
    A curse on hope! A curse on faith!
    And a curse on patience most of all!   80
      [*The invisible* SPIRITS *sing again.*]
SPIRITS.   Woe! Woe!
               You have destroyed it,
               The beautiful world;
               By your violent hand
               'Tis downward hurled!   85
               A half-god has dashed it asunder!
               From under
               We bear off the rubble to nowhere
               And ponder
               Sadly the beauty departed.   90
               Magnipotent
               One among men,
               Magnificent
               Build it again,
               Build it again in your breast!   95
               Let a new course of life
               Begin

---

1. The Aramaic word for "riches," used in the New Testament; medieval writers interpreted the word as a proper noun, the name of the devil, as representing covetousness or avarice.

             With vision abounding

             To welcome it in!   100

MEPHISTOPHELES. These are the juniors

             Of my faction.

             Hear how precociously they counsel

             Pleasure and action.

             Out and away   105

             From your lonely day

             Which dries your senses and your juices

             Their melody seduces.

             Stop playing with your grief which battens

             Like a vulture on your life, your mind!   110

             The worst of company would make you feel

             That you are a man among mankind.

             Not that it's really my proposition

             To shove you among the common men:

             Though I'm not one of the Upper Ten,   115

             If you would like a coalition

             With me for your career through life,

             I am quite ready to fit in,

             I'm yours before you can say knife.

             I am your comrade;   120

             If you so crave,

             I am your servant, I am your slave.

FAUST. And what have I to undertake in return?

MEPHISTOPHELES. Oh it's early days to discuss what that is.

FAUST. No, no, the devil is an egoist   125

   And ready to do nothing gratis

   Which is to benefit a stranger.

   Tell me your terms and don't prevaricate!

   A servant like you in the house is a danger.

MEPHISTOPHELES. I will bind myself to your service in this world, 130

   To be at your beck and never rest nor slack;

   When we meet again on the other side,

   In the same coin you shall pay me back.

FAUST. The other side gives me little trouble;

   First batter this present world to rubble,   135

   Then the other may rise—if that's the plan.

   This earth is where my springs of joy have started,

   And this sun shines on me when broken-hearted;

   If I can first from them be parted,

   Then let happen what will and can!   140

   I wish to hear no more about it—

   Whether there too men hate and love

Or whether in those spheres too, in the future,
There is a Below or an Above.

MEPHISTOPHELES. With such an outlook you can risk it.   145
  Sign on the line! In these next days you will get
  Ravishing samples of my arts;
  I am giving you what never man saw yet.

FAUST. Poor devil, can *you* give anything ever?
  Was a human spirit in its high endeavour   150
  Even once understood by one of your breed?
  Have you got food which fails to feed?
  Or red gold which, never at rest,
  Like mercury runs away through the hand?
  A game at which one never wins?   155
  A girl who, even when on my breast,
  Pledges herself to my neighbour with her eyes?
  The divine and lovely delight of honour
  Which falls like a falling star and dies?
  Show me the fruits which, before they are plucked, decay   160
  And the trees which day after day renew their green!

MEPHISTOPHELES. Such a commission doesn't alarm me,
  I have such treasures to purvey.
  But, my good friend, the time draws on when we
  Should be glad to feast at our ease on something good.   165

FAUST. If ever I stretch myself on a bed of ease,
  Then I am finished! Is that understood?
  If ever your flatteries can coax me
  To be pleased with myself, if ever you cast
  A spell of pleasure that can hoax me—   170
  Then let *that* day be my last!
  That's my wager!

MEPHISTOPHELES. Done!

FAUST.   Let's shake!
  If ever I say to the passing moment   175
  'Linger a while! Thou art so fair!'
  Then you may cast me into fetters,
  I will gladly perish then and there!
  Then you may set the death-bell tolling,
  Then from my service you are free,   180
  The clock may stop, its hand may fall,
  And that be the end of time for me!

MEPHISTOPHELES. Think what you're saying, we shall not forget it.

FAUST. And you are fully within your rights;
  I have made no mad or outrageous claim.   185
  If I stay as I am, I am a slave—
  Whether yours or another's, it's all the same.

MEPHISTOPHELES. I shall this very day at the College Banquet[2]
    Enter your service with no more ado,
    But just one point—As a life-and-death insurance   190
    I must trouble you for a line or two.
FAUST. So you, you pedant, you too like things in writing?
    Have you never known a man? Or a man's word? Never?
    Is it not enough that my word of mouth
    Puts all my days in bond for ever?   195
    Does not the world rage on in all its streams
    And shall a promise hamper *me?*
    Yet this illusion reigns within our hearts
    And from it who would be gladly free?
    Happy the man who can inwardly keep his word;   200
    Whatever the cost, he will not be loath to pay!
    But a parchment, duly inscribed and sealed,
    Is a bogey from which all wince away.
    The word dies on the tip of the pen
    And wax and leather lord it then.   205
    What do you, evil spirit, require?
    Bronze, marble, parchment, paper?
    Quill or chisel or pencil of slate?
    You may choose whichever you desire.
MEPHISTOPHELES. How can you so exaggerate   210
    With such a hectic rhetoric?
    Any little snippet is quite good—
    And you sign it with one little drop of blood.[3]
FAUST. If that is enough and is some use,
    One may as well pander to your fad.   215
MEPHISTOPHELES. Blood is a very special juice.
FAUST. Only do not fear that I shall break this contract.
    What I promise is nothing more
    Than what all my powers are striving for.
    I have puffed myself up too much, it is only   220
    Your sort that really fits my case.
    The great Earth Spirit has despised me
    And Nature shuts the door in my face.
    The thread of thoughts is snapped asunder,
    I have long loathed knowledge in all its fashions.   225
    In the depths of sensuality
    Let us now quench our glowing passions!
    And at once make ready every wonder

---

2. Actually the *Doctorschmaus*, or dinner given by a successful candidate for a Ph.D. degree.
3. This method of confirming an agreement with the devil is older than the Faust legend—in which it always appears—and is partly a parody of the role of blood in the Christian Sacrament.

Of unpenetrated sorcery!
Let us cast ourselves into the torrent of time,   230
Into the whirl of eventfulness,
Where disappointment and success,
Pleasure and pain may chop and change
As chop and change they will and can;
It is restless action makes the man.   235
MEPHISTOPHELES. No limit is fixed for you, no bound;
    If you'd like to nibble at everything
    Or to seize upon something flying round—
    Well, may you have a run for your money!
    But seize your chance and don't be funny!   240
FAUST. I've told you, it is no question of happiness.
    The most painful joy, enamoured hate, enlivening
    Disgust—I devote myself to all excess.
    My breast, now cured of its appetite for knowledge,
    From now is open to all and every smart,   245
    And what is allotted to the whole of mankind
    That will I sample in my inmost heart,
    Grasping the highest and lowest with my spirit,
    Piling men's weal and woe upon my neck,
    To extend myself to embrace all human selves   250
    And to founder in the end, like them, a wreck.
MEPHISTOPHELES. O believe *me,* who have been chewing
    These iron rations many a thousand year,
    No human being can digest
    This stuff, from the cradle to the bier.   255
    This univers—believe a devil—
    Was made for no one but a god!
    He exists in eternal light
    But *us* he has brought into the darkness
    While *your* sole portion is day and night.   260
FAUST. I will all the same!
MEPHISTOPHELES.   That's very nice.
    There's only one thing I find wrong;
    Time is short, art is long.
    You could do with a little artistic advice.   265
    Confederate with one of the poets
    And let him flog his imagination
    To heap all virtues on your head,
    A head with such a reputation:
    Lion's bravery,   270
    Stag's velocity,
    Fire of Italy,
    Northern tenacity.

Let *him* find out the secret art
Of combining craft with a noble heart   275
And of being in love like a young man,
Hotly, but working to a plan.
Such a person—*I'd* like to meet him;
'Mr. Microcosm'[4] is how I'd greet him.

FAUST. What am I then if fate must bar   280
My efforts to reach that crown of humanity
After which all my senses strive?

MEPHISTOPHELES. You are in the end . . . what you are.
You can put on full-bottomed wigs with a million locks,
You can put on stilts instead of your socks,   285
You remain for ever what you are.

FAUST. I feel my endeavours have not been worth a pin
When I raked together the treasures of the human mind,
If at the end I but sit down to find
No new force welling up within.   290
I have not a hair's breadth more of height,
I am no nearer the Infinite.

MEPHISTOPHELES. My very good sir, you look at things
Just in the way that people do;
We must be cleverer than that   295
Or the joys of life will escape from you.
Hell! You have surely hands and feet,
Also a head and you-know-what;
The pleasures I gather on the wing,
Are they less mine? Of course they're not!   300
Suppose I can afford six stallions,
I can add that horse-power to my score
And dash along and be a proper man
As if my legs were twenty-four.
So good-bye to thinking! On your toes!   305
The world's before us. Quick! Here goes!
I tell you, a chap who's intellectual
Is like a beast on a blasted heath
Driven in circles by a demon
While a fine green meadow lies round beneath.   310

FAUST. How do we start?

MEPHISTOPHELES.   We just say go—and skip.
But please get ready for this pleasure trip.
     [*Exit* FAUST.]
Only look down on knowledge and reason,
The highest gifts that men can prize,   315

4. I.e., man viewed as the epitome of the universe.

Only allow the spirit of lies
To confirm you in magic and illusion,
And then I have you body and soul.
Fate has given this man a spirit
Which is always pressing onwards, beyond control,   320
And whose mad striving overleaps
All joys of the earth between pole and pole.
Him shall I drag through the wilds of life
And through the flats of meaninglessness,
I shall make him flounder and gape and stick   325
And to tease his insatiableness
Hang meat and drink in the air before his watering lips;
In vain he will pray to slake his inner thirst,
And even had he not sold himself to the devil
He would be equally accursed.[5]   330
   [*Re-enter* FAUST.]
FAUST. And now, where are we going?
MEPHISTOPHELES. Wherever you please.
  The small world, then the great for us.
  With what pleasure and what profit
  You will roister through the syllabus!   335
FAUST. But I, with this long beard of mine,
  I lack the easy social touch,
  I know the experiment is doomed;
  Out in the world I never could fit in much.
  I feel so small in company   340
  I'll be embarrassed constantly.
MEPHISTOPHELES. My friend, it will solve itself, any such misgiving;
  Just trust yourself and you'll learn the art of living.
FAUST. Well, then, how do we leave home?
  Where are your grooms? Your coach and horses?   345
MEPHISTOPHELES. We merely spread this mantle wide,
  It will bear us off on airy courses.
  But do not on this noble voyage
  Cumber yourself with heavy baggage.
  A little inflammable gas[6] which I'll prepare   350
  Will lift us quickly into the air.
  If we travel light we shall cleave the sky like a knife.
  Congratulations on your new course of life![7]

---

5. Between Faust's exit and entrance, the translator omits a scene in which Mephistopheles cynically interviews one of Faust's students.   6. Indicative of Goethe's scientific interests. The first hydrogen balloon was sent aloft in Paris in 1783, and several letters by Goethe refer to this new experiment.   7. The translator omits the next scene, in Auerbach's Cellar, where Faust and Mephistopheles join a group of genial drinking companions and Mephistopheles performs the trick—traditional in early Faust stories—of making wine flow from the table.

THE WITCH'S KITCHEN[8]

Every sort of witch prop. A large cauldron hangs over the fire.
MONKEYS *sit around it, seen through the fumes.*

MEPHISTOPHELES. Look, what a pretty species of monkey!
   She is the kitchen-maid, he is the flunkey.
   It seems your mistress isn't at home?
MONKEYS. Out at a rout!
          Out and about!   5
          By the chimney spout!
MEPHISTOPHELES. How long does she keep it up at night?
MONKEYS. As long as we warm our paws at this fire.
MEPHISTOPHELES. How do you like these delicate animals?
FAUST. I never saw such an outré sight.   10
   I find it nauseating, this crazy witchcraft![9]
   Do you promise me that I shall improve
   In this cesspit of insanity?
   Do I need advice from an old hag?
   And can this filthy brew remove   15
   Thirty years from my age? O vanity,
   If you know nothing better than this!
   My hope has already vanished away.
   Surely Nature, surely a noble spirit
   Has brought some better balm to the light of day?   20
MEPHISTOPHELES. My friend, you once more talk to the point.
   There is also a natural means of rejuvenation;
   But that is written in another book
   And is a chapter that needs some explanation.
FAUST. I want to know it.   25
MEPHISTOPHELES.   Right. There is a means requires
   No money, no physician, and no witch:
   Away with you this moment back to the land,
   And there begin to dig and ditch,
   Confine yourself, confine your mind,   30
   In a narrow round, ever repeating,
   Let your diet be of the simplest kind,
   Live with the beasts like a beast and do not think it cheating
   To use your own manure to insure your crops are weighty!
   Believe me, that is the best means   35
   To keep you young till you are eighty.
FAUST. I am not used to it, I cannot change
   My nature and take the spade in hand.

8. Certain transpositions have been made in this scene. [Translator's note.]   9. In composing
this scene, Goethe may have had in mind certain paintings by the Flemish artists David Teniers
the Younger (1610–1690) and Pieter Breughel the Younger (1564?–1638).

The narrow life is not my style at all.
MEPHISTOPHELES. Then it's a job for the witch to arrange.   40
FAUST. The hag—but why do we need just her?
    Can you yourself not brew the drink?
MEPHISTOPHELES. A pretty pastime! I'd prefer
    To build a thousand bridges[1] in that time.
    It is not only art and science   45
    That this work needs but patience too.
    A quiet spirit is busy at it for years
    And time but fortifies the subtle brew.
    And the most wonderful ingredients
    Go into it—you couldn't fake it!   50
    The devil taught it her, I admit;
    The devil, however, cannot make it.
    Tell me, you monkeys, you damned puppets,
    What are you doing with that great globe?
HE-MONKEY. This is the world: 55
            It rises and falls
            And rolls every minute;
            It rings like glass—
            But how soon it breaks!
            And there's nothing in it.   60
            It glitters here
            And here still more:
            I am alive!
            O my son, my dear,
            Keep away, keep away!   65
            You are bound to die!
            The shards are sharp,
            It was made of clay.
    [FAUST *has meanwhile been gazing in a mirror.*]

FAUST. What do I see in this magic mirror?
    What a heavenly image to appear!   70
    Oh Love, lend me the swiftest of your wings
    And waft me away into her sphere!
    But, alas, when I do not keep this distance,
    If to go nearer I but dare
    I can see her only as if there were mist in the air—   75
    The fairest image of a woman!
    But can Woman be so fair?
    In that shape in the mirror must I see the quintessence
    Of all the heavens—reclining there?

1. The folk legend existed that the devil built bridges at the request of men. As a reward, he caught either the first or the thirteenth soul to cross each new bridge.

Can such a thing be found on earth?   80
MEPHISTOPHELES. Naturally, when a God works six days like a black
    And at the end of it slaps himself on the back,
    Something should come of it of some worth.
    For this occasion look your fill.
    I can smell you out a sweetheart as good as this,   85
    And happy the man who has the luck
    To bear her home to wedded bliss.
    [*The* WITCH *enters down the chimney—violently.*]
WITCH. What goes on here?
      Who are you two?
      What d'you want here?   90
      Who has sneaked through?
      May the fever of fire
      Harrow your marrow!
MEPHISTOPHELES. Don't you know me, you bag of bones? You mons-
    ter, you!
    Don't you know your lord and master?   95
    What prevents me striking you
    And your monkey spirits, smashing you up like plaster?
    Has my red doublet no more claim to fame?
    Can you not recognize the cock's feather?
    Have I concealed my countenance?   100
    Must I myself announce my name?
WITCH. My lord, excuse this rude reception.
    It is only I miss your cloven foot.
    And where is your usual brace of ravens?[2]
MEPHISTOPHELES. I'll forgive you this once, as an exception;   105
    Admittedly some time has pass't
    Since we two saw each other last.
    Culture too, which is licking the whole world level,
    Has latterly even reached the devil.
    The Nordic spook no longer commands a sale;   110
    Where can you see horns, claws or tail?
    And as regards the foot, which is my *sine qua non,*
    It would prejudice me in the social sphere;
    Accordingly, as many young men have done,
    I have worn false calves this many a year.   115
WITCH. Really and truly I'm knocked flat
    To see Lord Satan here again!
MEPHISTOPHELES. Woman, you must not call me that!
WITCH. Why! What harm is there in the name?

---

2. Perhaps Goethe was thinking of the Norse god Odin, who owned two such birds: Hugin (Thought) and Munin (Memory).

MEPHISTOPHELES. Satan has long been a myth without sense or
    sinew;   120
    Not that it helps humanity all the same,
    They are quit of the Evil One but the evil ones continue.
    You may call me the Noble Baron, that should do;
    I am a cavalier among other cavaliers,
    You needn't doubt my blood is blue—   125
        [*He makes an indecent gesture.*]
WITCH. Ha! Ha! Always true to type!
    You still have the humour of a guttersnipe!
MEPHISTOPHELES. Observe my technique, my friend—not a single
    hitch;
    This is the way to get round a witch.
WITCH. Now tell me, gentlemen, what do you want?   130
MEPHISTOPHELES. A good glass of your well-known juice.
    And please let us have your oldest vintage;
    When it's been kept it's twice the use.
WITCH. Delighted! Why, there's some here on the shelf—
    I now and then take a nip myself—   135
    And, besides, this bottle no longer stinks;
    You're welcome while I've a drop to give.
    [Aside] But, if this man is unprepared when he drinks,
    You very well know he has not an hour to live.
MEPHISTOPHELES. He's a good friend and it should set him up;   140
    I'd gladly grant him the best of your kitchen,
    So draw your circle and do your witching
    And give the man a decent cup.
        [*The* WITCH *begins her conjuration.*]
FAUST. But, tell me, how will this mend my status?
    These lunatic gestures, this absurd apparatus,   145
    This most distasteful conjuring trick—
    I've known it all, it makes me sick.
MEPHISTOPHELES. Pooh, that's just fooling, get it in focus,
    And don't be such a prig for goodness' sake!
    As a doctor she must do her hocus-pocus   150
    So that when you have drunk your medicine it will take.
WITCH. The lofty power
        That is wisdom's dower,
        Concealed from great and clever,
        Don't use your brain
        And that's your gain—   155
        No trouble whatsoever.
FAUST. What nonsense is she saying to us?
    My head is splitting; I've the sensation

Of listening to a hundred thousand   160
   Idiots giving a mass recitation.
MEPHISTOPHELES. Enough, enough, you excellent Sibyl!
   Give us your drink and fill the cup
   Full to the brim and don't delay!
   This draught will do my friend no injury;   165
   He is a man of more than one degree
   And has drunk plenty in his day.
      [*The* WITCH *gives* FAUST *the cup.*]
   Now lower it quickly. Bottoms up!
   And your heart will begin to glow and perk.
   Now out of the circle! You mustn't rest.   170
WITCH. I hope the little drink will work.
MEPHISTOPHELES. [*To* WITCH] And you, if there's anything you want,
   all right;
   Just mention it to me on Walpurgis Night.[3]
   [*To* FAUST] Come now, follow me instantly!
   You've got to perspire, it's necessary,   175
   That the drug may pervade you inside and out.
   I can teach you later to value lordly leisure
   And you soon will learn with intensest pleasure
   How Cupid stirs within and bounds about.
FAUST. Just one more look, one quick look, in the mirror!   180
   That woman was too fair to be true.
MEPHISTOPHELES. No, no! The paragon of womanhood
   Will soon be revealed in the flesh to you.
   [*Aside*] With a drink like this in you, take care—
   You'll soon see Helens[4] everywhere.   185

IN THE STREET

FAUST *accosts* GRETCHEN *as she passes.*

FAUST. My pretty young lady, might I venture
   To offer you my arm and my escort too?
GRETCHEN. I'm not a young lady nor am I pretty
   And I can get home without help from you.
      [*She releases herself and goes off.*]
FAUST. By Heaven, she's beautiful, this child!   5
   I have never seen her parallel.
   So decorous, so virtuous,
   And just a little pert as well.

---

3. The eve of May Day (May 1), when witches are supposed to assemble on the Brocken, a peak
in the Hartz Mountains.   4. Faust marries Helen of Troy in the second part of *Faust*.

The light of her cheek, her lip so red,
I shall remember till I'm dead!   10
The way that she cast down her eye
Is stamped on my heart as with a die;
And the way that she got rid of me
Was a most ravishing thing to see!
    [*Enter* MEPHISTOPHELES.]
Listen to me! Get me that girl!   15
MEPHISTOPHELES. Which one?
FAUST.   The one that just went past.
MEPHISTOPHELES. She? She was coming from her priest,
    Absolved from her sins one and all;
    I'd crept up near the confessional.   20
    An innocent thing. Innocent? Yes!
    At church with nothing to confess!
    Over that girl I have no power.
FAUST. Yet she's fourteen if she's an hour.
MEPHISTOPHELES. Why, you're talking like Randy Dick[5]   25
    Who covets every lovely flower
    And all the favours, all the laurels,
    He fancies are for him to pick;
    But it doesn't always work out like that.
FAUST. My dear Professor[6] of Ancient Morals,   30
    Spare me your trite morality!
    I tell you straight—and hear me right—
    Unless this object of delight
    Lies in my arms this very night,
    At midnight we part company.   35
MEPHISTOPHELES. Haven't you heard: more haste less speed?
    A fortnight is the least I need
    Even to work up an occasion.
FAUST. If I had only seven hours clear,
    I should not need the devil here   40
    To bring *this* quest to consummation.
MEPHISTOPHELES. It's almost French, your line of talk;
    I only ask you not to worry.
    Why make your conquest in a hurry?
    The pleasure is less by a long chalk   45
    Than when you first by hook and by crook
    Have squeezed your doll and moulded her,
    Using all manner of poppycock

5. In the original German, "Hans Liederlich"—i.e., a profligate, since *liederlich* means "care-less" or "dissolute."   6. In the original German, Herr Magister Lobeasan ("Master Worship-ful")—stuffed shirt, or academic prig.

That foreign novels keep in stock.
FAUST. I am keen enough without all that.   50
MEPHISTOPHELES. Now, joking apart and without aspersion,
   You cannot expect, I tell you flat,
   This beautiful child in quick reversion.
   Immune to all direct attack—
   We must lay our plots behind her back.   55
FAUST. Get me something of my angel's!
   Carry me to her place of rest!
   Get me a garter of my love's!
   Get me a kerchief from her breast!
MEPHISTOPHELES. That you may see the diligent fashion   60
   In which I shall abet your passion,
   We won't let a moment waste away,
   I will take you to her room to-day.
FAUST. And shall I see her? Have her?
MEPHISTOPHELES.   No!   65
   She will be visiting a neighbour.
   But you in the meanwhile, quite alone,
   Can stay in her aura in her room
   And feast your fill on joys to come.
FAUST. Can we go now?   70
MEPHISTOPHELES.   It is still too soon.
FAUST. Then a present for her! Get me one!
      [*Exit* FAUST.]
MEPHISTOPHELES. Presents already? Fine. A certain hit!
   I know plenty of pretty places
   And of long-buried jewel-cases;   75
   I must take stock of them a bit.

GRETCHEN'S ROOM

GRETCHEN. [*Alone, doing her hair*] I'd give a lot to be able to say
   Who the gentleman was to-day.
   He cut a fine figure certainly
   And is sprung from nobility;
   His face showed that—Besides, you see,   5
   He'd otherwise not have behaved so forwardly.
      [*She goes out; then* MEPHISTOPHELES *and* FAUST *enter.*]
MEPHISTOPHELES. Come in—very quietly—Only come in!
FAUST. [*After a silence*] I ask you: please leave me alone!
MEPHISTOPHELES. Not all girls keep their room so clean.
FAUST. [*Looking around*] Welcome, sweet gleaming of the
   gloaming   10

That through this sanctuary falls aslope!
Seize on my heart, sweet fever of love
That lives and languishes on the dews of hope!
What a feeling of quiet breathes around me,
Of order, of contentedness!   15
What fulness in this poverty,
And in this cell what blessedness!

Here I could while away hour after hour.
It was here, O Nature, that your fleeting dreams
Brought this born angel to full flower.   20
Here lay the child and the warm life
Filled and grew in her gentle breast,
And here the pure and holy threads
Wove a shape of the heavenliest.

And you! What brought you here to-day?   25
Why do I feel this deep dismay?
What do you want here? Why is your heart so sore?
Unhappy Faust! You are Faust no more.

Is this an enchanted atmosphere?
To have her at once was all my aim,   30
Yet I feel my will dissolve in a lovesick dream.
Are we the sport of every current of air?
And were she this moment to walk in,
You would pay for this outrage, how you would pay!
The big man, now, alas, so small,   35
Would lie at her feet melted away.

MEPHISTOPHELES. Quick! I can see her coming below.

FAUST. Out, yes out! I'll never come back!

MEPHISTOPHELES. Here is a casket, it's middling heavy,
I picked it up in a place I know.   40
Only put it at once here in the cupboard,
I swear she won't believe her eyes;
I put some nice little trinkets in it
In order to win a different prize.
Still child is child and a game's a game.   45

FAUST. I don't know; shall I?

MEPHISTOPHELES.   You ask? For shame!
Do you perhaps intend to keep the spoil?
Then I advise Your Lustfulness
To save these hours that are so precious   50
And save me any further toil.
I hope you aren't avaricious.
After scratching my head so much and twisting my hands—
    [*He puts the casket in the cupboard.*]

Now quick! We depart!
In order to sway the dear young thing   55
To meet the dearest wish of your heart;
And *you* assume
A look that belongs to the lecture room,
As if Physics and Metaphysics too
Stood grey as life in front of you!   60
Come on!

    [*They go out; then* GRETCHEN *reappears.*]

GRETCHEN. It is so sultry, so fusty here,
    And it's not even so warm outside.
    I feel as if I don't know what—
    I wish my mother would appear.   65
    I'm trembling all over from top to toe—
    I'm a silly girl to get frightened so.

    [*She sings as she undresses.*]

    There was a king in Thule[7]
    Was faithful to the grave,
    To whom his dying lady   70
    A golden winecup gave.

    He drained it at every banquet—
    A treasure none could buy;
    Whenever he filled and drank it
    The tears o'erflowed his eye.   75

    And when his days were numbered
    He numbered land and pelf;
    He left his heir his kingdom,
    The cup he kept himself.

    He sat at the royal table   80
    With his knights of high degree
    In the lofty hall of his fathers
    In the castle on the sea.

    There stood the old man drinking
    The last of the living glow,   85
    Then threw the sacred winecup
    Into the waves below.

    He saw it fall and falter
    And founder in the main;
    His eyelids fell, thereafter   90

---

7. The fabled *ultima Thule* of Latin literature—those distant lands just beyond the reach of every explorer. In Roman times, the phrase probably denoted the Shetland Islands. Goethe wrote this ballad in 1774; it was published and set to music in 1782. The poem also served as the inspiration for the slow movement of Mendelssohn's *Italian Symphony*.

He never drank again.

[*She opens the cupboard to put away her clothes and sees the casket.*]

How did this lovely casket get in here?
I locked the cupboard, I'm quite sure.
But what can be in it? It's very queer.
Perhaps someone left it here in pawn   95
And my mother gave him a loan on it.
Here's a little key tied on with tape—
I've a good mind to open it.
What is all this? My God! But see!
I have never come across such things.   100
Jewels—that would suit a countess
At a really grand festivity.
To whom can these splendid things belong?

[*She tries on the jewels and looks in the looking glass.*]

If only the ear-rings belonged to me!
They make one look quite differently.   105
What is the use of looks and youth?
That's all very well and fine in truth
But people leave it all alone,
They praise you and pity you in one;
Gold is their sole   110
Concern and goal.
Alas for us who have none!

A WALK

Elsewhere and later. MEPHISTOPHELES *joins* FAUST.

MEPHISTOPHELES. By every despised love! By the elements of hell!
  I wish I knew something worse to provide a curse as well!
FAUST. What's the trouble? What's biting you?
  I never saw such a face in my life.
MEPHISTOPHELES. I would sell myself to the devil this minute   5
  If only I weren't a devil too.
FAUST. What is it? Are you mad? Or sick?
  It suits you to rage like a lunatic!
MEPHISTOPHELES. Imagine! The jewels that Gretchen got,
  A priest has gone and scooped the lot!   10
  Her mother got wind of it and she
  At once had the horrors secretly.
  That woman has a nose beyond compare,
  She's always snuffling in the Book of Prayer,
  And can tell by how each object smells   15
  If it is sacred or something else;

So the scent of the jewels tells her clear
There's nothing very blessed here.
'My child,' she cries, 'unrighteous wealth
Invests the soul, infects the health.   20
We'll dedicate it to the Virgin
And *she'll* make heavenly manna burgeon!'
Gretchen's face, you could see it fall;
She thought: 'It's a gift-horse after all,
And he *can't* be lacking in sanctity   25
Who brought it here so handsomely!'
The mother had a priest along
And had hardly started up her song
Before he thought things looked all right
And said: 'Very proper and above board!   30
Self-control is its own reward.
The Church has an excellent appetite,
She has swallowed whole countries and the question
Has never arisen of indigestion.
Only the Church, my dears, can take   35
Ill-gotten goods without stomach-ache!'
FAUST. That is a custom the world through,
    A Jew and a king observe it too.
MEPHISTOPHELES. So brooch, ring, chain he swipes at speed
    As if they were merely chicken-feed,   40
    Thanks them no more and no less for the casket
    Than for a pound of nuts in a basket,
    Promises Heaven will provide
    And leaves them extremely edified.
FAUST. And Gretchen?   45
MEPHISTOPHELES.   Sits and worries there,
    Doesn't know what to do and doesn't care,
    Thinks day and night on gold and gem,
    Still more on the man who presented them.
FAUST. My sweetheart's grief distresses me.   50
    Get her more jewels instantly!
    The first lot barely deserved the name.
MEPHISTOPHELES. So the gentleman thinks it all a nursery game!
FAUST. Do what I tell you and get it right;
    Don't let her neighbour out of your sight.   55
    And don't be a sloppy devil; contrive
    A new set of jewels. Look alive!
      [*Exit* FAUST.]
MEPHISTOPHELES. Yes, my dear sir, with all my heart.
    This is the way that a fool in love

Puffs away to amuse his lady   60
Sun and moon and the stars above.

MARTHA'S HOUSE

MARTHA. [*Alone*] My dear husband, God forgive him,
  His behaviour has *not* been without a flaw!
  Careers away out into the world
  And leaves me alone to sleep on straw.
  And yet I never trod on his toes,   5
  I loved him with all my heart, God knows.   [*Sobs.*]
    Perhaps he is even dead—O fate!
  If I'd only a death certificate!
    [GRETCHEN *enters.*]
GRETCHEN. Frau Martha!
MARTHA.   Gretelchen! What's up?   10
GRETCHEN. My legs are sinking under me,
  I've just discovered in my cupboard
  Another casket—of ebony,
  And things inside it, such a store,
  Far richer than the lot before.   15
MARTHA. You mustn't mention it to your mother;
  She'd take it straight to the priest—like the other.
GRETCHEN. But only look! Just look at this!
MARTHA. O you lucky little Miss!
GRETCHEN. I daren't appear in the street, I'm afraid,   20
  Or in church either, thus arrayed.
MARTHA. Just you visit me often here
  And put on the jewels secretly!
  Walk up and down for an hour in front of my glass
  And that will be fun for you and me;   25
  And then an occasion may offer, a holiday,
  Where one can let them be seen in a gradual way;
  A necklace to start with, then a pearl ear-ring; your mother
  Most likely won't see; if she does one can think up something or
    other.
GRETCHEN. But who brought these two cases, who could it be?   30
  It doesn't seem quite right to me.
    [*Knocking.*]
  My God! My mother? Is that her?
MARTHA. It is a stranger. Come in, sir!
    [*Enter* MEPHISTOPHELES.]
MEPHISTOPHELES. I have made so free as to walk straight in;
  The ladies will pardon me? May I begin   35

By inquiring for a Frau Martha Schwerdtlein?[8]

MARTHA. That's me. What might the gentleman want?

MEPHISTOPHELES. [*Aside to* MARTHA] Now I know who you are, that's
 enough for me;
 You have very distinguished company.
 Forgive my bursting in so soon;   40
 I will call again in the afternoon.

MARTHA. Imagine, child, in the name of Piety!
 The gentleman takes you for society.

GRETCHEN. I'm a poor young thing, not at all refined;
 My God, the gentleman is too kind.   45
 These jewels and ornaments aren't my own.

MEPHISTOPHELES. Oh, it's not the jewellery alone;
 She has a presence, a look so keen—
 How delighted I am that I may remain.

MARTHA. What is your news? I cannot wait—   50

MEPHISTOPHELES. I wish I'd a better tale to relate.
 I trust this will not earn me a beating:
 Your husband is dead and sends his greeting.

MARTHA. Dead? The good soul? Oh why! Oh why!
 My husband is dead! Oh I shall die!   55

GRETCHEN. Oh don't, dear woman, despair so.

MEPHISTOPHELES. Listen to my tale of woe!

GRETCHEN. Now, while I live, may I never love;
 Such a loss would bring me to my grave.

MEPHISTOPHELES. Joy must have grief, grief must have joy. 60

MARTHA. How was his end? Oh tell it me.

MEPHISTOPHELES. He lies buried in Padua
 At the church of Holy Anthony,[9]
 In properly consecrated ground
 Where he sleeps for ever cool and sound.   65

MARTHA. Have you nothing else for me? Is that all?

MEPHISTOPHELES. Yes, a request; it's heavy and fat.
 You must have three hundred masses said for his soul.
 My pockets are empty apart from that.

MARTHA. What! Not a trinket? Not a token?   70
 What every prentice keeps at the bottom of his bag
 And saves it up as a souvenir
 And would sooner starve and sooner beg—

MEPHISTOPHELES. Madam, you make me quite heart-broken.
 But, really and truly, he didn't squander his money. 75
 And, besides, he repented his mistakes,

---

8. Literally "little sword." Her husband is a soldier. 9. Mephistopheles' lie acquires added
irony from the fact that this is one of Padua's most famous churches, its basilica holding the bones
of St. Anthony.

Yes, and lamented still more his unlucky breaks.
GRETCHEN. Alas that men should be so unlucky!
   Be assured I shall often pray that he may find rest above.
MEPHISTOPHELES. *You* deserve to be taken straight to the altar;   80
   You are a child a man could love.
GRETCHEN. No, no, it's not yet time for that.
MEPHISTOPHELES. Then, if not a husband, a lover will do.
   It's one of the greatest gifts of Heaven
   To hold in one's arms a thing like you.   85
GRETCHEN. That is not the custom of our race.
MEPHISTOPHELES. Custom or not, it's what takes place.
MARTHA. But tell me!
MEPHISTOPHELES.   His deathbed, where I stood,
   Was something better than a dungheap—   90
   Half-rotten straw; however, he died like a Christian
   And found he had still a great many debts to make good.
   How thoroughly, he cried, I must hate myself
   To leave my job and my wife like that on the shelf!
   When I remember it, I die!   95
   If only she would forgive me here below!
MARTHA. Good man! I have forgiven him long ago.
MEPHISTOPHELES. All the same, God knows, she was more at fault
      than I.
MARTHA. That's a lie! To think he lied at the point of death!
MEPHISTOPHELES. He certainly fibbed a bit with his last breath,   100
   If I'm half a judge of the situation.
   I had no need, said he, to gape for recreation;
   First getting children, then getting bread to feed 'em—
   And bread in the widest sense, you know—
   And I couldn't even eat my share in peace.   105
MARTHA. So all my love, my loyalty, went for naught,
   My toiling and moiling without cease!
MEPHISTOPHELES. Not at all; he gave it profoundest thought.
   When I left Malta—that was how he began—
   I prayed for my wife and children like one demented   110
   And Heaven heard me and consented
   To let us capture a Turkish merchantman,
   With a treasure for the Sultan himself on board.
   Well, bravery got its due reward
   And I myself, as was only fit,   115
   I got a decent cut of it.
MARTHA. Eh! Eh! How? Where? Has he perhaps buried it?
MEPHISTOPHELES. Who knows where the four winds now have car-
      ried it?
   As he lounged round Naples, quite unknown,

A pretty lady made him her friend,   120
  She was so fond of him, so devoted,
  He wore her colours at his blessed end.
MARTHA. The crook! The robber of his children!
  Could no misery, no poverty,
  Check the scandalous life he led!   125
MEPHISTOPHELES. You see! That is just why he's dead.
  However, if I were placed like you,
  I would mourn him modestly for a year
  While looking round for someone new.
MARTHA. Ah God! My first one was so dear,   130
  His like in this world will be hard to discover.
  There could hardly be a more sweet little fool than mine.
  It was only he was too fond of playing the rover,
  And of foreign women and foreign wine,
  And of the God-damned gaming-table.   135
MEPHISTOPHELES. Now, now, he might have still got by
  If he on his part had been able
  To follow your suit and wink an eye.
  With that proviso, I swear, I too
  Would give an engagement ring to you.   140
MARTHA. The gentleman is pleased to be witty.
MEPHISTOPHELES. [*Aside*] I had better go while the going's good;
  She'd hold the devil to his word, she would!
  And how is it with *your* heart, my pretty?
GRETCHEN. What does the gentleman mean?   145
MEPHISTOPHELES. [*Aside*] Good, innocent child!
  Farewell, ladies!
GRETCHEN.   Farewell!
MARTHA.   O quickly! Tell me;
  I'd like to have the evidence filed   150
  Where, how and when my treasure died and was buried.
  I have always liked things orderly and decent
  And to read of his death in the weeklies would be pleasant.
MEPHISTOPHELES. Yes, Madam, when two witnesses are agreed,
  The truth, as we all know, is guaranteed;   155
  And I have a friend, an excellent sort,
  I'll get him to swear you this in court.
  I'll bring him here.
MARTHA.   O yes! Please do!
MEPHISTOPHELES. And the young lady will be here too?   160
  He's an honest lad. He's been around,
  His politeness to ladies is profound.
GRETCHEN. I'll be all blushes in his presence.
MEPHISTOPHELES. No king on earth should so affect you.

MARTHA. Behind the house there—in my garden—   165
　　This evening—both of you—we'll expect you.

IN THE STREET

FAUST. How is it? Going ahead? Will it soon come right?
MEPHISTOPHELES. Excellent! Do I find you all on fire?
　　Gretchen is yours before many days expire.
　　You will see her at Martha's, her neighbour's house to-night
　　And that's a woman with a special vocation,   5
　　As it were, for the bawd-cum-gipsy occupation.
FAUST. Good!
MEPHISTOPHELES. But there is something *we* must do.
FAUST. One good turn deserves another. True.
MEPHISTOPHELES. It only means the legal attesting   10
　　That her husband's played-out limbs are resting
　　At Padua in consecrated ground.
FAUST. Very smart! I suppose we begin by going to Padua!
MEPHISTOPHELES. There's no need for that. What a simple lad you
　　　are!
　　Only bear witness and don't ask questions.   15
FAUST. The scheme's at an end if you have no better suggestions.
MEPHISTOPHELES. Oh there you go! What sanctity!
　　Is this the first time in your life
　　You have committed perjury?
　　God and the world and all that moves therein,   20
　　Man and the way his emotions and thoughts take place,
　　Have you not given downright definitions
　　Of these with an iron breast and a brazen face?
　　And if you will only look below the surface,
　　You must confess you knew as much of these   25
　　As you know to-day of Herr Schwerdtlein's late decease.
FAUST. You are and remain a sophist and a liar.
MEPHISTOPHELES. Quite so—if that is as deep as you'll inquire.
　　Won't you to-morrow on your honour
　　Befool poor Gretchen and swear before her   30
　　That all your soul is set upon her?
FAUST. And from my heart.
MEPHISTOPHELES.　　　　　　　That's nice of you!
　　And your talk of eternal faith and love,
　　Of one single passion enthroned above   35
　　All others—will that be heartfelt too?
FAUST. Stop! It will! If I have feeling, if I
　　Feel this emotion, this commotion,
　　And can find no name to call it by;

If then I sweep the world with all my senses casting   40
Around for words and all the highest titles
And call this flame which burns my vitals
Endless, everlasting, everlasting,
Is that a devilish game of lies?
MEPHISTOPHELES. I'm right all the same.   45
FAUST.   Listen! Mark this well,
I beg you, and spare me talking till I'm hoarse:
The man who *will* be right, provided he has a tongue,
Why, he'll be right of course.
But come, I'm tired of listening to your voice;   50
You're right, the more so since I have no choice.

MARTHA'S GARDEN

They are walking in pairs: MARTHA *with* MEPHISTOPHELES, GRETCHEN
on FAUST'S *arm.*

GRETCHEN. The gentleman's only indulging me, I feel,
And condescending, to put me to shame.
You travellers are all the same,
You put up with things out of sheer good will.
I know too well that my poor conversation   5
Can't entertain a person of your station.
FAUST. One glance from you, one word, entertains me more
Than all this world's wisdom and lore.
     [*He kisses her hand.*]
GRETCHEN. Don't go to such inconvenience! How could you kiss my
     hand?
It is so ugly, it is so rough.   10
I have had to work at Heaven knows what!
My mother's exacting, true enough.
     [*They pass on.*]
MARTHA. And you, sir, do you always move round like this?
MEPHISTOPHELES. Oh, business[1] and duty keep us up to the minute!
With what regret one often leaves a place   15
And yet one cannot ever linger in it.
MARTHA. That may go in one's salad days—
To rush all over the world at random;
But the evil time comes on apace
And to drag oneself to the grave a lonely bachelor   20
Is never much good in any case.
MEPHISTOPHELES. The prospect alarms me at a distant glance.
MARTHA. Then, worthy sir, be wise while you have the chance.

---

1. Mephistopheles speaks as a traveling salesman.

[*They pass on.*]

GRETCHEN. Yes, out of sight, out of mind!
  You are polite to your finger-ends   25
  But you have lots of clever friends
  Who must leave me so far behind.
FAUST. Believe me, dearest, what the world calls clever
  More often is vanity and narrowness.
GRETCHEN.   What?   30
FAUST. Alas that simplicity, that innocence,
  Cannot assess itself and its sacred value ever!
  That humility, lowliness, the highest gifts
  That living Nature has shared out to men—
GRETCHEN. Only think of *me* one little minute,   35
  I shall have time enough to think of you again.
FAUST. You are much alone, I suppose?
GRETCHEN. Yes, our household's only small
  But it needs running after all.
  We have no maid; I must cook and sweep and knit   40
  And sew and be always on the run,
  And my mother looks into every detail—
  Each single one.
  Not that she has such need to keep expenses down;
  We could spread ourselves more than some others do;   45
  My father left us a decent property,
  A little house with a garden outside town.
  However, my days at the present are pretty quiet;
  My brother's in the army,
  My little sister is dead.   50
  The child indeed had worn me to a thread;
  Still, all that trouble, I'd have it again, I'd try it,
  I loved her so.
FAUST.   An angel, if she was like you!
GRETCHEN. I brought her up, she was very fond of me.   55
  She was born after my father died,
  We gave my mother up for lost,
  Her life was at such a low, low tide,
  And she only got better slowly, bit by bit;
  The poor little creature, she could not even   60
  Think for a minute of suckling it;
  And so I brought her up quite alone
  On milk and water; so she became my own.
  On my own arm, on my own knee,
  She smiled and kicked, grew fair to see.   65
FAUST. You felt, I am sure, the purest happiness.
GRETCHEN. Yes; and—be sure—many an hour of distress.

The little one's cradle stood at night
Beside my bed; she could hardly stir
But I was awake,   70
Now having to give her milk, now into my bed with her,
Now, if she went on crying, try to stop her
By getting up and dangling her up and down the room,
And then first thing in the morning stand at the copper;
Then off to the market and attend to the range,   75
And so on day after day, never a change.
Living like that, one can't always feel one's best;
But food tastes better for it, so does rest.
     [*They pass on.*]
MARTHA. No, the poor women don't come out of it well,
     A *vieux garçon* is a hard nut to crack.   80
MEPHISTOPHELES. It only rests with you and your like
     To put me on a better tack.
MARTHA. Tell me, sir: have you never met someone you fancy?
     Has your heart been nowhere involved among the girls?
MEPHISTOPHELES. The proverb says: A man's own fireside   85
     And a good wife are gold and pearls.
MARTHA. I mean, have you never felt any inclination?
MEPHISTOPHELES. I've generally been received with all consideration.
MARTHA. What I wanted to say: has your heart never been serious?
MEPHISTOPHELES. To make a joke to a woman is always pre-
     carious.   90
MARTHA. Oh you don't understand me!
MEPHISTOPHELES.   Now *that* I really mind!
     But I do understand—that you are very kind.
     [*They pass on.*]
FAUST. You knew me again, you little angel,
     As soon as you saw me enter the garden?   95
GRETCHEN. Didn't you see me cast down my eyes?
FAUST. And the liberty that I took you pardon?
     The impudence that reared its head
     When you lately left the cathedral door.
GRETCHEN. I was upset; it had never happened before;   100
     No one could ever say anything bad of me—
     Oh can he, I thought, have seen in my behaviour
     Any cheekiness, any impropriety?
     The idea, it seemed, had come to you pat:
     'I can treat this woman just like that.'   105
     I must admit I did not know what it was
     In my heart that began to make me change my view,
     But indeed I was angry with myself because
     I could not be angrier with you.
FAUST. Sweet love!   110

GRETCHEN.   Wait a moment!
   [*She plucks a flower and starts picking off the petals.*]
FAUST.   What is that? A bouquet?
GRETCHEN. No, only a game.
FAUST.   A what?
GRETCHEN.   You will laugh at me. Go away!   115
   [GRETCHEN *murmurs.*]
FAUST. What are you murmuring?
GRETCHEN.   Loves me—Loves me not—
FAUST. You flower from Heaven's garden plot!
GRETCHEN. Loves me—Not—Loves me—Not—   120
   Loves me!
FAUST.   Yes, child. What this flower has told you
   Regard it as God's oracle. He loves you!
   Do you know the meaning of that? He loves you!
   [*He takes her hands.*]
GRETCHEN. Oh I feel so strange.
FAUST. Don't shudder. Let this look,   125
   Let this clasp of the hand tell you
   What mouth can never express:
   To give oneself up utterly and feel
   A rapture which must be everlasting.
   Everlasting! Its end would be despair.   130
   No; no end! No end!
   [*She breaks away from him and runs off. After a moment's thought he follows her.*]
MARTHA. [*Approaching*] The night's coming on.
MEPHISTOPHELES. Yes—and we must go.
MARTHA. I would ask you to remain here longer
   But this is a terrible place, you know.   135
   It's as if no one were able to shape at
   Any vocation or recreation
   But must have his neighbour's comings and goings to gape at
   And, whatever one does, the talk is unleashed, unfurled.
   And our little couple?   140
MEPHISTOPHELES.   Carefree birds of summer!
   Flown to the summerhouse.
MARTHA.   He seems to like her.
MEPHISTOPHELES. And vice versa. That is the way of the world.

A SUMMERHOUSE

GRETCHEN *runs in and hides behind the door.*

GRETCHEN. He comes!
FAUST. [*Entering*]   You rogue! Teasing me so!

I've caught you!
    [*He kisses her.*]
GRETCHEN.   Dearest! I love you so!
    [MEPHISTOPHELES *knocks.*]   5
FAUST. Who's there?
MEPHISTOPHELES.   A friend.
FAUST.   A brute!
MEPHISTOPHELES.   It is time to part, you know.
MARTHA. [*Joining them*] Yes, it is late, sir.
FAUST.   May I not see you
    home?   10
GRETCHEN. My mother would—Farewell!
FAUST.   I must go then?
    Farewell:
MARTHA.   Adieu!
GRETCHEN.   Let us soon meet again!   15
    [FAUST *and* MEPHISTOPHELES *leave.*]
    Dear God! A man of such a kind,
    What things must go on in his mind!
    I can only blush when he talks to me;
    Whatever he says, I must agree.
    Poor silly child, I cannot see   20
    What it is he finds in me.

FOREST AND CAVERN

FAUST. [*Alone*] Exalted Spirit, you gave me, gave me all
    I prayed for. Aye, and it is not in vain
    That you have turned your face in fire upon me.
    You gave me glorious Nature for my kingdom
    With power to feel her and enjoy her. Nor   5
    Is it a mere cold wondering glance you grant me
    But you allow me to gaze into her depths
    Even as into the bosom of a friend.
    Aye, you parade the ranks of living things
    Before me and you teach me to know my brothers   10
    In the quiet copse, in the water, in the air.
    And when the storm growls and snarls in the forest
    And the giant pine falls headlong, bearing away
    And crushing its neighbours, bough and bole and all,
    With whose dull fall the hollow hill resounds,   15
    Then do you carry me off to a sheltered cave
    And show me myself, and wonders of my own breast
    Unveil themselves in their deep mystery.
    And now that the clear moon rises on my eyes

To soften things, now floating up before me   20
From walls of rocks and from the dripping covert
Come silver forms of the past which soothe and temper
The dour delight I find in contemplation.

That nothing perfect falls to men, oh now
I feel that true. In addition to the rapture   25
Which brings me near and nearer to the gods
You gave me that companion whom already
I cannot do without, though cold and brazen
He lowers me in my own eyes and with
One whispered word can turn your gifts to nothing.   30
He is always busily fanning in my breast
A fire of longing for that lovely image.
So do I stagger from desire to enjoyment
And in enjoyment languish for desire.
      [MEPHISTOPHELES *enters.*]
MEPHISTOPHELES. Haven't you yet had enough of this kind of life? 35
    How can it still appeal to you?
    It is all very well to try it once,
    Then one should switch to something new.
FAUST. I wish you had something else to do
    On my better days than come plaguing me.   40
MEPHISTOPHELES. Now, now! I'd gladly leave you alone;
    You needn't suggest it seriously.
    So rude and farouche and mad a friend
    Would certainly be little loss.
    One has one's hands full without end!   45
    One can never read in the gentleman's face
    What he likes or what should be left alone.
FAUST. That is exactly the right tone!
    He must be thanked for causing me ennui.
MEPHISTOPHELES. Poor son of earth, what sort of life   50
    Would you have led were it not for me?
    The flim-flams of imagination,
    I have cured you of those for many a day
    But for me, this terrestrial ball
    Would already have seen you flounce away.   55
    Why behave as an owl behaves
    Moping in rocky clefts and caves?
    Why do you nourish yourself like a toad that sips
    From moss that oozes, stone that drips?
    A pretty pastime to contrive!   60
    The doctor[2] in you is still alive.

2. I.e., the doctor of philosophy.

FAUST. Do you comprehend what a new and vital power
   This wandering in the wilderness has given me?
   Aye, with even an inkling of such joy,
   You would be devil enough to grudge it me.   65
MEPHISTOPHELES. A supernatural gratification!
   To lie on the mountain tops in the dark and dew
   Rapturously embracing earth and heaven,
   Swelling yourself to a godhead, ferreting through
   The marrow of the earth with divination,   70
   To feel in your breast the whole six days of creation,
   To enjoy I know not what in arrogant might
   And then, with the Old Adam discarded quite,
   To overflow into all things in ecstasy;
   After all which your lofty intuition   75
     [*He makes a gesture.*]
   Will end—hm—unmentionably.
FAUST. Shame on you!
MEPHISTOPHELES.   Am I to blame?
   You have the right to be moral and cry shame!
   One must not mention to the modest ear   80
   What the modest heart is ever agog to hear.
   And, in a word, you are welcome to the pleasure
   Of lying to yourself in measure;
   But this deception will not last.
   Already overdriven again,   85
   If this goes on you must collapse,
   Mad or tormented or aghast.
   Enough of this! Back there your love is sitting
   And all her world seems sad and small;
   You are never absent from her mind,   90
   Her love for you is more than all.
   At first your passion came overflowing
   Like a brook that the melted snows have bolstered high;
   You have poured your passion into her heart
   And now your brook once more is dry.   95
   I think, instead of lording it here above
   In the woods, the great man might think fit
   In view of that poor ninny's love
   To make her some return for it.
   She finds the time wretchedly long;   100
   She stands at the window, watches the clouds
   As over the old town walls they roll away.
   'If I had the wings of a dove'—so runs her song
   Half the night and all the day.
   Now she is cheerful, mostly low,   105

Now has spent all her tears,
Now calm again, it appears,
But always loves you so.
FAUST. You snake! You snake!
MEPHISTOPHELES. [*Aside*] Ha! It begins to take!   110
FAUST. You outcast! Take yourself away
    And do not name that lovely woman.
    Do not bring back the desire for her sweet body
    Upon my senses that are half astray.
MEPHISTOPHELES. Where's this to end? She thinks you have
    run off,   115
    And so you have—about half and half.
FAUST. I am still near her, though far removed,
    Her image must be always in my head;
    I already envy the body of the Lord
    When her lips rest upon the holy bread.   120
MEPHISTOPHELES. Very well, my friend. I have often envied you
    Those two young roes that are twins, I mean her two—
FAUST. Pimp! Get away!
MEPHISTOPHELES.   Fine! So you scold? I must laugh.
    The God who created girl and boy   125
    Knew very well the high vocation
    Which facilitates their joy.
    But come, this is a fine excuse for gloom!
    You should take the road to your sweetheart's room,
    Rather than that to death, you know.   130
FAUST. What is the joy of heaven in her arms?
    Even when I catch fire upon her breast
    Do I not always sense her woe?
    Am I not the runaway? The man without a home?
    The monster restless and purposeless   135
    Who roared like a waterfall from rock to rock in foam
    Greedily raging towards the precipice?
    And she on the bank in childlike innocence
    In a little hut on the little alpine plot
    And all her little household world   140
    Concentrated in that spot.
    And I, the loathed of God,
    I was not satisfied
    To seize and crush to powder
    The rocks on the river side!   145
    Her too, her peace, I must undermine as well!
    This was the sacrifice I owed to Hell!
    Help, Devil, to shorten my time of torment!
    What must be, must be; hasten it!

Let her fate hurtle down with mine,   150
    Let us go together to the pit!
MEPHISTOPHELES. How it glows again, how it boils again!
    Go in and comfort her, my foolish friend!
    When such a blockhead sees no outlet
    He thinks at once it is the end.   155
    Long live the man who does not flinch!
    But you've a devil in you, somewhere there.
    I know of nothing on earth more unattractive
    Than your devil who feels despair.

GRETCHEN'S ROOM

GRETCHEN *is alone, singing at the spinning-wheel.*

GRETCHEN. My peace is gone,
        My heart is sore,
        I shall find it never
        And never more.

        He has left my room   5
        An empty tomb,
        He has gone and all
        My world is gall.

        My poor head
        Is all astray,
        My poor mind   10
        Fallen away.

        My peace is gone,
        My heart is sore,
        I shall find it never
        And never more.   15

        'Tis he that I look through
        The window to see,
        He that I open
        The door for—he!   20

        His gait, his figure,
        So grand, so high!
        The smile of his mouth,
        The power of his eye,

        And the magic stream   25
        Of his words—what bliss!
        The clasp of his hand
        And, ah, his kiss!

My peace is gone,
My heart is sore,   30
I shall find it never
And never more.

My heart's desire
Is so strong, so vast;
Ah, could I seize him   35
And hold him fast

And kiss him for ever
Night and day—
And on his kisses
Pass away!   40

MARTHA'S GARDEN

GRETCHEN. Promise me, Heinrich![3]
FAUST.   If I can!
GRETCHEN. Tell me: how do you stand in regard to religion?
    You are indeed a good, good man
    But I think you give it scant attention.   5
FAUST. Leave that, my child! You feel what I feel for you;
    For those I love I would give my life and none
    Will I deprive of his sentiments and his church.
GRETCHEN. That is not right; one must believe thereon.
FAUST. Must one?   10
GRETCHEN.   If only I had some influence!
    Nor do you honour the holy sacraments.
FAUST. I honour them.
GRETCHEN.   Yes, but not with any zest.
    When were you last at mass, when were you last confessed?   15
    Do you believe in God?
FAUST.   My darling, who dare say:
    I believe in God?
    Ask professor or priest,
    Their answers will make an odd   20
    Mockery of you.
GRETCHEN.   You don't believe, you mean?
FAUST. Do not misunderstand me, my love, my queen!
    Who can name him?
    Admit on the spot: 25
    I believe in him?
    And who can dare

---

3. I.e., Faust. In the legend, Faust's first name was generally Johann (John). Goethe changed it
to Heinrich (Henry).

To perceive and declare:
I believe in him not?
The All-Embracing One, 30
All-Upholding One,
Does he not embrace, uphold,
You, me, Himself?
Does not the Heaven vault itself above us?
Is not the earth established fast below? 35
And with their friendly glances do not
Eternal stars rise over us?
Do not my eyes look into yours,
And all things thrust
Into your head, into your heart, 40
And weave in everlasting mystery
Invisibly, visibly, around you?
Fill your heart with *this,* great as it is,
And when this feeling grants you perfect bliss,
Then call it what you will— 45
Happiness! Heart! Love! God!
I have no name for it!
Feeling is all;
Name is mere sound and reek
Clouding Heaven's light. 50
GRETCHEN. That sounds quite good and right;
And much as the priest might speak,
Only not word for word.
FAUST. It is what all hearts have heard
In all the places heavenly day can reach, 55
Each in his own speech;
Why not I in mine?
GRETCHEN. I could almost accept it, you make it sound so fine,
Still there is something in it that shouldn't be;
For you have no Christianity. 60
FAUST. Dear child!
GRETCHEN.   It has long been a grief to me
To see you in such company.
FAUST. You mean?
GRETCHEN.   The man who goes about with you, 65
I hate him in my soul, right through and through.
And nothing has given my heart
In my whole life so keen a smart
As that man's face, so dire, so grim.
FAUST. Dear poppet, don't be afraid of him! 70
GRETCHEN. My blood is troubled by his presence.
All other people, I wish them well;

But much as I may long to see you,
He gives me a horror I cannot tell,
And I think he's a man too none can trust.   75
God forgive me if I'm unjust.
FAUST. Such queer fish too must have room to swim.
GRETCHEN. I wouldn't live with the like of him!
    Whenever that man comes to the door,
    He looks in so sarcastically,   80
    Half angrily,
    One can see he feels no sympathy;
    It is written on his face so clear
    There is not a soul he can hold dear.
    I feel so cosy in your arms,   85
    So warm and free from all restraint,
    And his presence ties me up inside.
FAUST. You angel, with your wild alarms!
GRETCHEN. It makes me feel so ill, so faint,
    That, if he merely happens to join us,   90
    I even think I have no more love for you.
    Besides, when he's there, I could never pray,
    And that is eating my heart away;
    You, Heinrich, you must feel it too.
FAUST. You suffer from an antipathy.   95
GRETCHEN. Now I must go.
FAUST.   Oh, can I never rest
    One little hour hanging upon your breast,
    Pressing both breast on breast and soul on soul?
GRETCHEN. Ah, if I only slept alone!   100
    I'd gladly leave the door unlatched for you to-night;
    My mother, however, sleeps so light
    And if she found us there, I own
    I should fall dead upon the spot.
FAUST. You angel, there is no fear of that.   105
    Here's a little flask. Three drops are all
    It needs—in her drink—to cover nature
    In a deep sleep, a gentle pall.
GRETCHEN. What would I not do for your sake!
    I hope it will do her no injury.   110
FAUST. My love, do you think that of me?
GRETCHEN. Dearest, I've only to look at you
    And I do not know what drives me to meet your will
    I have already done so much for you
    That little more is left me to fulfil.   115
        [*She goes out—and* MEPHISTOPHELES *enters.*]
MEPHISTOPHELLES. The monkey! Is she gone?

FAUST.   Have you been spying again?

MEPHISTOPHELES. I have taken pretty good note of it,
  The doctor has been catechised—
  And much, I hope, to his benefit;   120
  The girls are really keen to be advised
  If a man belongs to the old simple-and-pious school.
  'If he stand that,' they think, 'he'll stand *our* rule.'

FAUST. You, you monster, cannot see
  How this true and loving soul   125
  For whom faith is her whole
  Being and the only road
  To beatitude, must feel a holy horror
  Having to count her beloved lost for good.

MEPHISTOPHELES. You supersensual, sensual buck,   130
  Led by the nose by the girl you court!

FAUST. O you abortion of fire and muck!

MEPHISTOPHELES. And she also has skill in physiognomy;
  In my presence she feels she doesn't know what,
  She reads some hidden sense behind my little mask,   135
  She feels that I am assuredly a genius—
  Maybe the devil if she dared to ask.
  Now: to-night—

FAUST.   What is to-night to you?

MEPHISTOPHELES. I have my pleasure in it too.   140

AT THE WELL

GRETCHEN *and* LIESCHEN *with pitchers.*

LIESCHEN. Haven't you heard about Barbara? Not what's passed?

GRETCHEN. Not a word. I go out very little.

LIESCHEN. It's true, Sibylla[4] told me to-day:
  She has made a fool of herself at last.
  So much for her fine airs!   5

GRETCHEN.   Why?

LIESCHEN.   It stinks!
  Now she feeds two when she eats and drinks.

GRETCHEN. Ah!

LIESCHEN. Yes; she has got her deserts in the end.   10
  What a time she's been hanging on her friend!
  Going the rounds
  To the dances and the amusement grounds,
  She had to be always the first in the line,
  He was always standing her cakes and wine;   15

---

4. A friend of Gretchen's; not to be confused with the "Sibyl" named in l. 162 of the scene in the witch's kitchen.

She thought her looks so mighty fine,
She was so brazen she didn't waver
To take the presents that he gave her.
Such cuddlings and such carryings on—
But now the pretty flower is gone.   20
GRETCHEN. Poor thing!
LIESCHEN.   Is that the way you feel?
    When we were at the spinning-wheel
    And mother kept us upstairs at night,
    She was below with her heart's delight;   25
    On the bench or in the shady alley
    They never had long enough to dally.
    But now she must grovel in the dirt,
    Do penance in church in a hair shirt.
GRETCHEN. But surely he will marry her.   30
LIESCHEN. He'd be a fool! A smart young chap
    Has plenty of other casks to tap.
    Besides he's gone.
GRETCHEN.   That's not right.
LIESCHEN. If she hooks him she won't get off light!   35
    The boys will tear her wreath in half
    And we shall strew her door with chaff.⁵
        [LIESCHEN *goes off.*]
GRETCHEN. [*Going home*] What scorn I used to pour upon her
    When a poor maiden lost her honour!
    My tongue could never find a name   40
    Bad enough for another's shame!
    I thought it black and I blackened it,
    It was never black enough to fit,
    And I blessed myself and acted proud—
    And now I too am under a cloud.   45
    Yet, God! What drove me to this pass,
    It was all so good, so dear, alas!

RAMPARTS

*In a niche in the wall is an image of the Mater Dolorosa.⁶ In front
of it* GRETCHEN *is putting fresh flowers in the pots.*

GRETCHEN. Mary, bow down,
            Beneath thy woeful crown,
            Thy gracious face on me undone!

---

5. In contrast to the bridal bouquet. In Germany this treatment was reserved for girls who had
"fallen."   6. Literally, "sorrowful mother"; i.e., the Virgin Mary.

The sword in thy heart,
Smart upon smart,   5
Thou lookest up to thy dear son;

Sending up sighs
To the Father which rise
For his grief and for thine own.

Who can gauge   10
What torments rage
Through the whole of me and how—
How my poor heart is troubled in me,
How fears and longings undermine me?
Only thou knowest, only thou   15

Wherever I may go,
What woe, what woe, what woe
Is growing beneath my heart!
Alas, I am hardly alone,
I moan, I moan, I moan   20
And my heart falls apart.

The flower-pots in my window
I watered with tears, ah me,
When in the early morning
I picked these flowers for thee.   25

Not sooner in my bedroom
The sun's first rays were shed
Than I in deepest sorrow
Sat waking on my bed.

Save me from shame and death in one!   30
Ah, bow down
Thou of the woeful crown,
Thy gracious face on me undone.

NIGHT SCENE AT GRETCHEN'S DOOR

VALENTINE. When I was at some drinking bout
  Where big talk tends to blossom out,
  And my companions raised their voice
  To praise the maidens of their choice
  And drowned their praises in their drink,   5
  Then I would sit and never blink,
  Propped on my elbow listening
  To all their brags and blustering.
  Then smiling I would stroke my beard

And raise the bumper in my hand   10
And say: 'Each fellow to his taste!
But is there one in all the land
To hold a candle to my own
Dear sister, Gretchen? No, there's none!'
Hear! Hear! Kling! Kling! It went around;   15
Some cried: 'His judgment is quite sound,
She is the pearl of womanhood!'
That shut those boasters up for good.
And now! It would make one tear one's hair
And run up walls in one's despair!   20
Each filthy fellow in the place
Can sneer and jeer at my disgrace!
And I, like a man who's deep in debt,
Every chance word must make me sweat.
I could smash their heads for them if I tried—   25
I could not tell them that they lied.

    [FAUST *and* MEPHISTOPHELES *enter.*]

VALENTINE. Who comes there, slinking? Who comes there?
If I mistake not, they're a pair.
If it's he, I'll scrag him on the spot;
He'll be dead before he knows what's what!   30

FAUST. How from the window of the sacristy there
The undying lamp sends up its little flicker
Which glimmers sideways weak and weaker
And round it presses the dark air.
My heart too feels its night, its noose.   35

MEPHISTOPHELES. And I feel like a tom-cat on the loose,
Brushing along the fire escape
And round the walls, a stealthy shape;
Moreover I feel quite virtuous,
Just a bit burglarious, a bit lecherous.   40
You see, I'm already haunted to the marrow
By the glorious Walpurgis Night.
It returns to us the day after to-morrow,
Then one knows why one's awake all right.

FAUST. I'd like some ornament, some ring,   45
For my dear mistress. I feel sad
To visit her without anything.

MEPHISTOPHELES. It's really nothing to regret—
That you needn't pay for what you get.
Now that the stars are gems on heaven's brocade,   50
You shall hear a real masterpiece.
I will sing her a moral serenade
That her folly may increase.

[*He sings to the guitar.*]

MEPHISTOPHELES. Catherine, my dear,
     What? Waiting here   55
     At your lover's door
     When the stars of the night are fading?
     Oh don't begin!
     When he lifts the pin,
     A maid goes in—   60
     But she won't come out a maiden.

     So think aright!
     Grant him delight
     And it's good night,
     You poor, poor things— Don't linger! 65
     A girl who's wise
     Will hide her prize
     From robber's eyes—
     Unless she's a ring on her finger.[7]

 [VALENTINE *comes forward.*]

VALENTINE. Damn you! Who're you seducing here?   70
 You damned pied piper! You magician!
 First to the devil with your guitar!
 Then to the devil with the musician!

MEPHISTOPHELES. The guitar is finished. Look, it's broken in two.

VALENTINE. Now then, to break your heads for you!   75

MEPHISTOPHELES. Doctor! Courage! All you can muster!
 Stick by me and do as I say!
 Quick now, draw your feather duster!
 I'll parry his blows, so thrust away!

VALENTINE. Then parry that!   80

MEPHISTOPHELES.   Why not, why not?

VALENTINE. And that!

MEPHISTOPHELES.   Of course.

VALENTINE.   Is he the devil or what?
 What's this? My hand's already lamed.   85

MEPHISTOPHELES. Strike, you!

VALENTINE.   Oh!

 [VALENTINE *falls.*]

MEPHISTOPHELES.   Now the lout is tamed!
 But we must go! Vanish in the wink of an eye!
 They're already raising a murderous hue and cry. 90

MARTHA. [*At the window*] Come out! Come out!

GRETCHEN. [*At the window*]   Bring a light!

7. Lines 54–69 are adapted by Goethe from Shakespeare's *Hamlet* IV, 5.

MARTHA. [*As before*] There's a row and a scuffle, they're having a
    fight.
MAN. Here's one on the ground; he's dead.
MARTHA. [*Coming out*] The murderers, have they gone?   95
GRETCHEN. [*Coming out*] Who's here?
MAN.   Your mother's son.
GRETCHEN. O God! What pain! O God!
VALENTINE. I am dying—that's soon said
    And sooner done, no doubt.
    Why do you women stand howling and wailing?   100
    Come round and hear me out.
        [*They all gather round him.*]
    Look, my Gretchen, you're young still,
    You have not yet sufficient skill,
    You bungle things a bit.
    Here is a tip—you need no more—   105
    Since you are once for all a whore,
    Then make a job of it!
GRETCHEN. My brother? O God! Is it I you blame!
VALENTINE. Leave our Lord God out of the game!
    What is done I'm afraid is done,   110
    As one starts one must carry on.
    You began with one man on the sly,
    There will be more of them by and by,
    And when a dozen have done with you
    The whole town will have you too.   115

    When Shame is born, she first appears
    In this world in secrecy,
    And the veil of night is drawn so tight
    Over her head and ears;
    Yes, people would kill her and forget her.   120
    But she grows still more and more
    And brazenly roams from door to door
    And yet her appearance grows no better.
    The more her face creates dismay,
    The more she seeks the light of day.   125

    Indeed I see the time draw on
    When all good people in this town
    Will turn aside from you, you tart,
    As from a corpse in the plague cart.
    Then your heart will sink within you,   130
    When they look you in the eye!
    It's good-bye to your golden chains!

And church-going and mass—good-bye!
No nice lace collars any more
To make you proud on the dancing floor!   135
No, in some dark and filthy nook
You'll hide with beggars and crippled folk
And, if God pardon you, he may;
You are cursed on earth till your dying day.

MARTHA. Commend your soul to the mercy of God!   140
Will you add slander to your load?

VALENTINE. If I could get at your withered body,
You bawd, you sinner born and hardened!
Then I should hope that all my sins
And in full measure might be pardoned.   145

GRETCHEN. My brother! O hell's misery!

VALENTINE. I tell you: let your weeping be.
When you and your honour came to part,
It was you that stabbed me to the heart.
I go to God through the sleep of death,   150
A soldier—brave to his last breath.
   [*He dies.*]

CATHEDRAL

Organ and anthem. GRETCHEN *in the congregation. An* EVIL SPIRIT
whispers to her over her shoulder.

EVIL SPIRIT. How different it all was
                 Gretchen, when you came here
                 All innocent to the altar,
                 Out of the worn-out little book
                 Lisping your prayers,   5
                 Half a child's game,
                 Half God in the heart!
                 Gretchen!
                 How is your head?
                 And your heart—   10
                 What are its crimes?
                 Do you pray for your mother's soul, who thanks to you
                 And your sleeping draught overslept into a long, long
                     pain?
                 And whose blood stains your threshold?
                 Yes, and already under your heart   15
                 Does it now grow and quicken
                 And torture itself and you
                 With its foreboding presence?

GRETCHEN. Alas! Alas!
    If I could get rid of the thoughts   20
    Which course through my head hither and thither
    Despite me!
CHOIR. Dies irae, dies illa
    Solvet saeclum in favilla.[8]
[*The organ plays.*]
EVIL SPIRIT. Agony seizes you!   25
    The trumpet sounds!
    The graves tremble
    And your heart
    From its ashen rest
    To fiery torment   30
    Comes up recreated
    Trembling too!
GRETCHEN. Oh to escape from here!
    I feel as if the organ
    Were stifling me,   35
    And the music dissolving
    My heart in its depths.
CHOIR. Judex ergo cum sedebit,
    Quidquid latet adparebit,
    Nil inultum remanebit.[9]   40
GRETCHEN. I cannot breathe!
    The pillars of the walls
    Are round my throat!
    The vaulted roof
    Chokes me!—Air!   45
EVIL SPIRIT. Hide yourself! Nor sin nor shame
    Remains hidden.
    Air? Light?
    Woe to you!
CHOIR. Quid sum miser tunc dicturus?   50
    Quem patronum rogaturus?
    Cum vix justus sit securus.[1]
EVIL SPIRIT. The blessed turn
    Their faces from you.
    The pure shudder   55
    To reach out their hands to you.
    Woe!
CHOIR. Quid sum miser tunc dicturus?

---

8. Day of wrath, that day that dissolves the world into ashes. (The choir is singing the famous thirteenth-century hymn by Thomas Celano.) 9. When the judge shall be seated, what is hidden shall appear, nothing shall remain unavenged. 1. What shall I say in my wretchedness? To whom shall I appeal when scarcely the righteous man is safe?

GRETCHEN. Neighbour! Help! Your smelling bottle!
   [*She faints.*]

WALPURGIS NIGHT

FAUST *and* MEPHISTOPHELES *making their way through the Hartz Mountains.*

MEPHISTOPHELES. A broomstick—don't you long for such a convey-
   ance?
  I'd find the coarsest he-goat some assistance.
  Taking this road, our goal is still in the distance.
FAUST. No, so long as my legs are not in abeyance,
  I can make do with this knotted stick.   5
  What is the use of going too quick?
  To creep along each labyrinthine valley,
  Then climb this scarp, downwards from which
  The bubbling spring makes its eternal sally,
  This is the spice that makes such journeys rich.   10
  Already the spring is weaving through the birches,
  Even the pine already feels the spring;
  Should not our bodies too give it some purchase?
MEPHISTOPHELES. Candidly—*I* don't feel a thing.
  In my body all is winter,   15
  I would prefer a route through frost and snow.
  How sadly the imperfect disc
  Of the red moon rises with belated glow
  And the light it gives is bad, at every step
  One runs into some rock or tree!   20
  Permit me to ask a will o' the wisp.[2]
  I see one there, he's burning heartily.
  Ahoy, my friend! Might I call on you to help us?
  Why do you blaze away there to no purpose?
  Be so good as to light us along our road.   25
WILL O' THE WISP. I only hope my sense of your mightiness
  Will control my natural flightiness;
  A zigzag course is our accustomed mode.
MEPHISTOPHELES. Ha! Ha! So it's men you want to imitate.
  In the name of the Devil you go straight   30
  Or I'll blow out your flickering, dickering light!
WILL O' THE WISP. You're the head of the house, I can see that all
  right,

---

2. The Jack o' lantern, or ignis fatuus. In German folklore, this was thought of as leading travelers to their destruction.

You are welcome to use me at your convenience.
But remember, the mountain is magic-mad to-day
And if a will o' the wisp is to show you the way,   35
You too must show a little lenience.
FAUST, MEPHISTOPHELES, WILL O' THE WISP. [*Singing successively*]
              Into realms of dreams and witchcraft
              We, it seems, have found an ingress.
              Lead us well and show your woodcraft,
              That we may make rapid progress   40
              Through these wide and desert spaces.

              Trees on trees—how each one races,
              Pushing past—how each one hastens!
              And the crags that make obeisance!
              And the rocks with long-nosed faces—   45
              Hear them snorting, hear them blowing!

              Through the stones and lawns are flowing
              Brook and brooklet, downward hustling.
              Is that song—or is it rustling?
              Sweet, sad notes of love—a relic—   50
              Voices from those days angelic?
              Thus we hope, we love—how vainly!
              Echo like an ancient rumour
              Calls again, yes, calls back plainly.

              Now—Tu-whit!—we near the purlieu   55
              Of—Tu-whoo!—owl, jay and curlew;
              Are they all in waking humour?
              In the bushes are those lizards—
              Straggling legs and bloated gizzards?
              And the roots like snakes around us   60
              Coil from crag and sandy cranny,
              Stretch their mad and strange antennae
              Grasping at us to confound us;
              Stretch from gnarled and living timber
              Towards the passer-by their limber   65
              Polyp-suckers!
                            And in legions
              Through these mossy, heathy regions
              Mice, all colours, come cavorting!
              And above, a serried cohort,   70
              Fly the glow-worms as our escort—
              More confusing than escorting.

Tell me what our real case is!
Are we stuck or are we going?
Rocks and trees, they all seem flying   75
Round and round and making faces,
And the will o' the wisps are blowing
Up so big and multiplying.

MEPHISTOPHELES. Hold my coat-tails, hold on tight!
Standing on this central height   80
Marvelling see how far and wide
Mammon[3] lights the peaks inside.

FAUST. How strangely through the mountain hollows
A sad light gleams as of morning-red
And like a hound upon the scent   85
Probes the gorges' deepest bed!
Here fumes arise, there vapours float,
Here veils of mist catch sudden fire
Which creeps along, a flimsy threat,
Then fountains up, a towering spire.   90
Here a whole stretch it winds its way
With a hundred veins throughout the glen,
And here in the narrow neck of the pass
Is suddenly one strand again.
There, near by, are dancing sparks   95
Sprinkled around like golden sand.
But look! The conflagration climbs
The crags' full height, hand over hand.

MEPHISTOPHELES. Does not Sir Mammon light his palace
In splendid style for this occasion?   100
You are lucky to have seen it;
Already I sense the noisy guests' invasion.

FAUST. How the Wind Hag rages through the air!
What blows she rains upon the nape of my neck!

MEPHISTOPHELES. You must clamp yourself to the ancient ribs of the
    rock   105
Or she'll hurl you into this gorge, to find your grave down there.
A mist is thickening the night.
Hark to the crashing of the trees!
The owls are flying off in fright.
And the ever-green palaces—   110
Hark to their pillars sundering!
Branches moaning and breaking!
Tree-trunks mightily thundering!
Roots creaking and yawning!

3. Mammon is portrayed as leading a group of fallen angels in digging out gold and gems from
the ground of Hell, presumably for Satan's palace in Milton's *Paradise Lost*, Book I, ll. 678ff.

Tree upon tree in appalling 115
Confusion crashing and falling,
And through the wreckage on the scarps
The winds are hissing and howling.
Do you hear those voices in the air?
Far-off voices? Voices near? 120
Aye, the whole length of the mountain side
The witch-song streams in a crazy tide.

WITCHES. [*In chorus*]. The witches enter the Brocken scene,
 The stubble is yellow, the corn is green.
 There assembles the mighty horde, 125
 Urian[4] sits aloft as lord.
 So we go—over stock and stone—
 Farting witch on stinking goat.

A VOICE. But ancient Baubo[5] comes alone,
 She rides on a mother sow—take note. 130

CHORUS. So honour to whom honour is due!
 Let Mother Baubo head the queue!
 A strapping sow and Mother on top
 And we'll come after, neck and crop.

 The way is broad, the way is long, 135
 How is this for a crazy throng?
 The pitchfork pricks, the broomstick pokes,
 The mother bursts and the child chokes.

VOICE FROM ABOVE. Come along, come along, from Felsensee!

VOICES FROM BELOW. We'd like to mount with you straight away.
 We wash ourselves clean behind and before 140
 But we are barren for evermore.

CHORUS. The wind is silent, the star's in flight,
 The sad moon hides herself from sight.
 The soughing of the magic choir 145
 Scatters a thousand sparks of fire.

VOICE FROM BELOW. Wait! Wait!

VOICE FROM ABOVE. Who calls there from the cleft in the rock?

VOICE FROM BELOW. Don't leave me behind! Don't leave me behind!
 Three hundred years I've been struggling up 150
 And I can never reach the top;
 I want to be with my own kind.

CHORUS. Ride on a broom or ride on a stick,
 Ride on a fork or a goat—but quick!
 Who cannot to-night achieve the climb 155
 Is lost and damned till the end of time.

---

4. A name for the devil. 5. In Greek mythology, the nurse of Demeter, noted for her obscenity and bestiality.

HALF-WITCH. So long, so long, I've been on the trot;
      How far ahead the rest have got!
      At home I have neither peace nor cheer
      And yet I do not find it here.   160
CHORUS. Their ointment makes the witches hale,
      A rag will make a decent sail
      And any trough a ship for flight;
      You'll never fly, if not to-night.
      Once at the peak, you circle round   165
      And then you sweep along the ground
      And cover the heath far and wide—
      Witchhood in swarms on every side.
   [*The* WITCHES *land.*]
MEPHISTOPHELES. What a push and a crush and a rush and a clatter!
   How they sizzle and whisk, how they babble and batter!   170
   Kindle and sparkle and blaze and stink!
   A true witch-element, I think.
   Only stick to me or we shall be swept apart!
   Where are you?
FAUST.   Here!   175
MEPHISTOPHELES.   What! Carried so far already!
  I must show myself the master on this ground.
  Room! Here comes Voland![6] Room, sweet rabble! Steady!
  Here, Doctor, catch hold of me. Let's make one bound
  Out of this milling crowd and so get clear.   180
  Even for the likes of me it's *too* mad here.
  There's something yonder casting a peculiar glare,
  Something attracts me towards those bushes.
  Come with me! We will slip in there.
FAUST. You spirit of contradiction! Go on though! I'll follow.   185
   You have shown yourself a clever fellow. Quite!
   We visit the Brocken on Walpurgis Night
   To shut ourselves away in this lonely hollow!
MEPHISTOPHELES. Only look—what motley flames!
   It's a little club for fun and games   190
   One's not alone with a few, you know.
FAUST. I'd rather be above there though.
   Already there's fire and whorls of smoke.
   The Prince of Evil is drawing the folk;
   Many a riddle must there be solved.   195
MEPHISTOPHELES. And many a new one too evolved.
   Let the great world, if it likes, run riot;
   We will set up here in quiet.

---

6. One of Mephistopheles' names for himself. *V*oland, or *V*aland, is an old German word for "evil fiend."

It is a custom of old date
To make one's own small worlds within the great.   200
I see young witches here, bare to the buff,
And old ones dressed—wisely enough.
If only for my sake, do come on;
It's little trouble and great fun.
I hear some music being let loose too.   205
What a damned clack! It's what one must get used to.
Come along! Come along! You have no choice.
I'll lead the way and sponsor you
And you'll be obliged to me anew.
What do you say? This milieu isn't small   210
Just look! You can see no end to it at all.
A hundred fires are blazing in a row;
They dance and gossip and cook and drink and court—
Tell me where there is better sport!

FAUST. Do you intend, to introduce us here,   215
To play the devil or the sorcerer?

MEPHISTOPHELES. I am quite accustomed to go incognito
But one wears one's orders on gala days, you know.
I have no garter[7] for identification
But my cloven foot has here some reputation.   220
See that snail? Creeping up slow and steady?
Her sensitive feelers have already
Sensed out something odd in me.
Here I could *not* hide my identity.
But come! Let us go the round of the fires   225
And I'll play go-between to your desires.

COSTER-WITCH.[8] Gentlemen, don't pass me by!
Don't miss your opportunity!
Inspect my wares with careful eye;
I have a great variety.   230
And yet there is nothing on my stall
Whose like on earth you could not find,
That in its time has done no small
Harm to the world and to mankind.
No dagger which has not drunk of blood,   235
No goblet which has not poured its hot and searing
Poison into some healthy frame,
No gewgaw which has not ruined some endearing
Woman, no sword which has not been used to hack
A bond in two and stab a partner in the back.   240

MEPHISTOPHELES. Auntie! You are behind the times.

7. I.e., he has no decoration of nobility, such as the Order of the Garter.   8. The original
Trödelhexe, literally means "a witch (dealing in) old rags and clothes."

Past and done with! Past and done!
You must go in for novelties!
You'll lose our custom if you've none.
FAUST. I mustn't go crazy unawares!   245
  This is a fair to end all fairs.
MEPHISTOPHELES. The whole crowd's forcing its way above;
  You find you're shoved though you may think you shove.
FAUST. Who then is that?
MEPHISTOPHELES.   Look well at Madam;   250
  That's Lilith.[9]
FAUST.   Who?
MEPHISTOPHELES.   First wife of Adam.
  Be on your guard against her lovely hair,
  That shining ornament which has no match;   255
  Any young man whom those fair toils can catch,
  She will not quickly loose him from her snare.
FAUST. Look, an old and a young one, there they sit.
  They have already frisked a bit.
MEPHISTOPHELES. No rest to-night for 'em, not a chance.   260
  They're starting again. Come on! Let's join the dance.
    [FAUST *dances with a* YOUNG WITCH.]
FAUST. A lovely dream once came to me
    In which I saw an apple tree,
    On which two lovely apples shine,
    They beckon me, I start to climb.   265
YOUNG WITCH. Those little fruit you long for so
    Just as in Eden long ago.
    Joy runs through me, through and through;
    My garden bears its apples too.
    [FAUST *breaks away from the dance.*]
MEPHISTOPHELES. Why did you let that lovely maiden go   270
  Who danced with you and so sweetly sang?
FAUST. Ugh, in the middle of it there sprang
  Out of her mouth a little red mouse.
MEPHISTOPHELES. Why complain? That's nothing out of the way;
  You should be thankful it wasn't grey.   275
  In an hour of love! What a senseless grouse!
FAUST. And then I saw—
MEPHISTOPHELES.   What?
FAUST.   Mephisto, look over there!
  Do you see a girl in the distance, pale and fair?   280
  Who drags herself, only slowly, from the place?

---

9. According to an old rabbinical legend, Adam's first wife (the "female" mentioned in Genesis
1:27) was Lilith. After Eve was created, Lilith became a ghost who seduced men and inflicted evil
upon children.

And seems to walk with fetters on her feet?
I must tell you that I think I see
Something of dear Gretchen in her face.

MEPHISTOPHELES. That can do no good! Let it alone! Beware!   285
It is a lifeless phantom, an image of air.
It is a bad thing to behold;
Its cold look makes the blood of man run cold,
One turns to stone almost upon the spot;
You have heard of Medusa,[1] have you not?   290

FAUST. Indeed, they are the eyes of one who is dead,
Unclosed by loving hands, left open, void.
That is the breast which Gretchen offered me,
And that is the sweet body I enjoyed.

MEPHISTOPHELES. That is mere magic, you gullible fool! She can   295
Appear in the shape of his love to every man.

FAUST. What ravishment! What pain! Oh stay!
That look! I cannot turn away!
How strange that that adorable neck
In one red thread should be arrayed   300
As thin as the back of a knife-blade.

MEPHISTOPHELES. You are quite correct! I see it too.
She can also carry her head under her arm,
Perseus has cut it off for her.
Always this love of things untrue![2]   305
    [A CHOIR is heard, pianissimo.]

CHOIR. Drifting cloud and gauzy mist
    Brighten and dissever.
    Breeze on the leaf and wind in the reeds
    And all is gone for ever.

DREARY DAY—OPEN COUNTRY

FAUST. In misery! In despair! Long on the earth a wretched wanderer, now a prisoner! A criminal cooped in a dungeon for horrible torments, that dear and luckless creature! To end so! So!
Perfidious, worthless spirit—and this you have kept from me!
Stand, just stand there! Roll your devilish eyes spitefully round in
your head! Stand and brave me with your unbearable presence! A
prisoner! In irremediable misery! Abandoned to evil spirits, to
judging, unfeeling man! And I in the meantime—you lull me
with stale diversions, you hide her worsening plight from me, you
abandon her to perdition!

---

1. The Gorgon, with hair made of serpents, whose glance turned men to stone. She was finally
killed by Perseus, and her head was given to Athene.   2. The Walpurgis Night's Dream, which
is always cut from performances of *Faust*, is omitted. It occurs between l. 305 and l. 306 of our
text.

MEPHISTOPHELES. She is not the first.

FAUST. Dog! Loathsome monster! Change him, Thou eternal Spirit! Change this serpent back to his shape of a dog, in which he often delighted to trot before me at night—to roll about at the feet of the harmless wanderer and, as he tripped, to sink his teeth in his shoulders. Change him back to his fancy-shape that he may crouch in the sand on his belly before me, that I may trample over his vileness!

Not the first, you say! O the pity of it! What human soul can grasp that more than one creature has sunk to the depth of this misery, that the first did not pay off the guilt of all the rest, writhing and racked in death before the eyes of the Ever-Pardoning! It pierces me to my marrow and core, the torment of this one girl—and you grin calmly at the fate of thousands!

MEPHISTOPHELES. Now we're already back at our wits' end—the point where your human intelligence snaps. Why do you enter our company, if you can't carry it through? So you want to fly—and have no head for heights? Did we force ourselves on you—or you on us?

FAUST. Do not bare at me so those greedy fangs of yours! You sicken me! O great and glorious Spirit, Thou who didst deign to appear to me, Thou who knowest my heart and my soul, why fetter me to this odious partner who grazes on mischief and laps up destruction?

MEPHISTOPHELES. Have you finished?

FAUST. Save her! Or woe to you! The most withering curse upon you for thousands of years!

MEPHISTOPHELES. I cannot undo the avenger's bonds, his bolts I cannot open. Save her! Who was it plunged her into ruin? I or you?

[FAUST *looks wildly around.*]

MEPHISTOPHELES. Are you snatching at the thunder? Luckily, that is forbidden you wretched mortals. To smash to pieces his innocent critic, that is the way the tyrant relieves himself when in difficulties.

FAUST. Bring me to her! She shall be free!

MEPHISTOPHELES. And what of the risk you will run? Let me tell you; the town is still tainted with blood-guilt from your hand. Over the site of the murder there float avenging spirits who await the returning murderer.

FAUST. That too from *you?* Murder and death of a world on your monstrous head! Take me to her, I tell you; set her free!

MEPHISTOPHELES. I will take you, and what I *can* do—listen! Am I omnipotent in heaven and earth? I will cast a cloud on the gaoler's senses; do you get hold of the keys and carry her out with your

own human hands. I meanwhile wait, my magic horses are ready,
I carry you off. That much I can manage.

FAUST. Away! Away!

NIGHT

FAUST *and* MEPHISTOPHELES *fly past on black horses.*

FAUST. What do they weave round the Gallows Rock?[3]
MEPHISTOPHELES. Can't tell what they're cooking and hatching.
FAUST. Floating up, floating down, bending, descending.
MEPHISTOPHELES. A witch corporation.
FAUST. Black mass, black water.   5
MEPHISTOPHELES. Come on! Come on!

DUNGEON

FAUST *with a bunch of keys and a lamp, in front of an iron door.*

FAUST. A long unwonted trembling seizes me,
    The woe of all mankind seizes me fast.
    It is here she lives, behind these dripping walls,
    Her crime was but a dream too good to last!
    And *you,* Faust, waver at the door?   5
    You fear to see your love once more?
    Go in at once—or her hope of life is past.
        [*He tries the key.* GRETCHEN *starts singing inside.*]
GRETCHEN. My mother, the whore,
            Who took my life!
            My father, the rogue,   10
            Who ate my flesh!
            My little sister
            My bones did lay
            In a cool, cool glen;
            And there I turned to a pretty little wren;   15
            Fly away! Fly away!
        [FAUST *opens the lock.*]
FAUST. She does not suspect that her lover is listening—
    To the chains clanking, the straw rustling.
        [*He enters.*]
GRETCHEN. Oh! They come! O death! It's hard! Hard!
FAUST. Quiet! I come to set you free.   20
        [*She throws herself at his feet.*]
GRETCHEN. If you are human, feel my misery.

---

3. The masonry supporting a gallows.

FAUST. Do not cry out—you will wake the guard.

    [*He takes hold of the chains to unlock them.*]

GRETCHEN. [*On her knees*] Who has given you this power,

    Hangman, so to grieve me?

    To fetch me at this midnight hour!   25

    Have pity! O reprieve me!

    Will tomorrow not serve when the bells are rung?

      [*She gets up.*]

    I am still so young, I am still so young!

    Is my death so near?

    I was pretty too, that was what brought me here.   30

    My lover was by, he's far to-day;

    My wreath lies torn, my flowers have been thrown away.

    Don't seize on me so violently!

    What have I done to you? Let me be!

    Let me not vainly beg and implore;   35

    You know I have never seen you before.

FAUST. Can I survive this misery?

GRETCHEN. I am now completely in your power.

    Only let me first suckle my child.

    This night I cherished it, hour by hour;   40

    To torture me they took it away

    And now I murdered it, so they say.

    And I shall never be happy again.

    People make ballads about me—the heartless crew!

    An old story ends like this—   45

    Must mine too?

      [FAUST *throws himself on the ground.*]

FAUST. Look! At your feet a lover lies

    To loose you from your miseries.

      [GRETCHEN *throws herself beside him.*]

GRETCHEN. O, let us call on the saints on bended knee!

    Beneath these steps—but see—   50

    Beneath this sill

    The cauldron of Hell!

    And within,

    The Evil One in his fury

    Raising a din!   55

FAUST. Gretchen! Gretchen!

GRETCHEN. That was my lover's voice!

    [*She springs up: the chains fall off.*]

    I heard him calling. Where can he be?

    No one shall stop me. I am free!

    Quick! My arms round his neck!   60

    And lie upon his bosom! Quick!

He called 'Gretchen!' He stood at the door.
Through the whole of Hell's racket and roar,
Through the threats and jeers and from far beyond
I heard that voice so sweet, so fond.   65

FAUST. It is I!

GRETCHEN.   It's you? Oh say so once again!
    [*She clasps him.*]
It is! It is! Where now is all my pain?
And where the anguish of my captivity?
It's you; you have come to rescue me!   70
I am saved!
The street is back with me straight away
Where I saw you that first day,
And the happy garden too
Where Martha and I awaited you.   75

FAUST. Come! Come!

GRETCHEN.   Oh stay with me, oh do!
Where *you* stay, I would like to, too.

FAUST. Hurry!
If you don't,   80
The penalty will be sore.

GRETCHEN. What! Can you kiss no more?
So short an absence, dear, as this
And you've forgotten how to kiss!
Why do I feel so afraid, clasping your neck?   85
In the old days your words, your looks,
Were a heavenly flood I could not check
And you kissed me as if you would smother me—
Kiss me now!
Or I'll kill you!   90
    [*She kisses him.*]
Oh your lips are cold as stone!
And dumb!
What has become
Of your love?
Who has robbed me of my own?   95
    [*She turns away from him.*]

FAUST. Come! Follow me, my love! Be bold!
I will cherish you after a thousandfold.
Only follow me now! That is all I ask of you.

GRETCHEN. And is it you then? Really? Is it true?

FAUST. It is! But come!   100

GRETCHEN.   You are undoing each chain,
You take me to your arms again.
How comes it you are not afraid of me?

Do you know, my love, *whom* you are setting free?

FAUST. Come! The deep night is passing by and beyond.   105

GRETCHEN. My mother, I have murdererd her;

I drowned my child in the pond.

Was it not a gift to you and me?

To you too—You! Are you what you seem?

Give me your hand! It is not a dream!   110

Your dear hand—but, oh, it's wet!

Wipe it off! I think

There is blood on it.

Oh God! What have you done?

Put up your sword,   115

I beg you to.

FAUST. Let what is gone be gone!

You are killing me.

GRETCHEN. No! *You* must live on!

I will tell you about the graves—   120

You must get them put right

At morning light;

Give the best place to my mother,

The one next door to my brother,

Me a shade to the side—   125

A gap, but not too wide.

And the little one on my right breast.

No one else shall share my rest.

When it was you, when I could clasp you,

That was a sweet, a lovely day!   130

But I no longer can attain it,

I feel I must use force to grasp you,

As if you were thrusting me away.

And yet it's you and you look so kind, so just.

FAUST. If you feel it's I, then come with me? You must!   135

GRETCHEN. Outside there?

FAUST. Into the air!

GRETCHEN.   If the grave is there

And death on the watch, then come!

Hence to the final rest of the tomb   140

And not a step beyond—

You are going now? O Heinrich, if *I* could too!

FAUST. You can! The door is open. Only respond!

GRETCHEN. I dare not go out; for me there is no more hope.

They are lying in wait for me; what use is flight?   145

To have to beg, it is so pitiable

And that with a conscience black as night!

So pitiable to tramp through foreign lands—

And in the end I must fall into their hands!

FAUST. I shall stay by you. 150

GRETCHEN. Be quick! Be quick!
Save your poor child!
Go! Straight up the path—
Along by the brook—
Over the bridge— 155
Into the wood—
Left where the plank is—
In the pond!
Catch hold of it quickly!
It's trying to rise, 160
It's kicking still!
Save it! Save it!

FAUST. Collect yourself!
One step—just one—and you are free.

GRETCHEN. If only we were past the hill! 165
There sits my mother on a stone—
My brain goes cold and dead—
There sits my mother on a stone—
And wags and wags her head.
No sign, no nod, her head is such a weight 170
She'll wake no more, she slept so late.
She slept that we might sport and play.
What a time that was of holiday!

FAUST. If prayer and argument are no resource,
I will risk saving you by force. 175

GRETCHEN. No! I will have no violence! Let me go!
Don't seize me in that murderous grip!
I have done everything else for you, you know.

FAUST. My love! My love! The day is dawning!

GRETCHEN. Day! Yes, it's growing day! The last day breaks on me!
My wedding day it was to be! 180
Tell no one you had been before with Gretchen.
Alas for my garland!
There's no more chance!
We shall meet again— 185
But not at the dance.
The people are thronging—but silently;
Street and square
Cannot hold them there.
The bell tolls—it tolls for *me*. 190
How they seize me, bind me, like a slave!
Already I'm swept away to the block.
Already there jabs at every neck,

The sharp blade which jabs at mine.
The world lies mute as the grave.   195
FAUST. I wish I had never been born!
    [MEPHISTOPHELES *appears outside.*]
MEPHISTOPHELES. Away! Or you are lost.
    Futile wavering! Waiting and prating!
    My horses are shivering,
    The dawn's at the door.   200
GRETCHEN. What rises up from the floor?
    It's he! Send him away! It's he!
    What does he want in the holy place?
    It is I he wants!
FAUST.   You shall live!   205
GRETCHEN. Judgment of God! I have given myself to Thee!
MEPHISTOPHELES. [*To* FAUST] Come! Or I'll leave you both in the
    lurch.
GRETCHEN. O Father, save me! I am Thine!
    You angels! Hosts of the Heavenly Church,
    Guard me, stand round in serried line!   210
    Heinrich! I shudder to look at you.
MEPHISTOPHELES. She is condemned!
VOICE FROM ABOVE.   Redeemed!
MEPHISTOPHELES. Follow me!
    [*He vanishes with* FAUST.]
VOICE [*From within, dying away*] Heinrich! Heinrich!   215

WILLIAM BLAKE

1757–1827

Few works so ostentatiously "simple" as William Blake's *Songs of Innocence
and Experience* (1794) can ever have aroused such critical perplexity.
Employing uncomplicated vocabulary and, often, variants of traditional ballad structure; describing the experience usually of naïve subjects; supplying
no obvious intellectual substance, these short lyrics have long fascinated and
baffled their readers.

With no formal education, Blake, son of a London hosier, was at the age
of fourteen apprenticed to the engraver James Basire. He developed both as
painter and as engraver, partly influenced by the painter Henry Fuseli and
the sculptor John Flaxman, both his friends, but remaining always highly
individual in style and technique. An acknowledged mystic, he saw visions
from the age of four: trees filled with angels, God looking at him through
the window. His highly personal view of a world penetrated by the divine
helped to form both his visual and verbal art. In 1800, Blake moved from

London to Felpham, where the poet William Hayley was his patron. He returned to London in 1803 and remained there for the rest of his life, married but childless, engaged in writing, printing, and engraving.

Blake felt a close relation between the visual and the verbal; he illustrated the works of many poets, notably Milton and Dante. His first book, *Poetical Sketches* (1783), was conventionally published, but he produced all his subsequent books himself, combining pictorial engravings with lettering, striking off only a few copies of each work by hand. Gradually, in increasingly long poems, he developed an elaborate private mythology, with important figures appearing in one work after another. His major mythic poems include *The Marriage of Heaven and Hell* (1793), *America* (1793), *The Book of Los* (1795), *Milton* (1804), *Jerusalem* (1804), and *The Four Zoas*, which he never completed.

As his short poem, "Mock On, Mock On, Voltaire, Rousseau," testifies, Blake felt bitterly opposed to what he thought the destructive and repressive rationalism of the eighteenth century. Voltaire and Rousseau might have been surprised to find themselves thus associated; they belong together, in Blake's view, because both implicitly oppose not only orthodox Christianity but the more private variety of revealed religion so vital to Blake himself. Although, like his contemporaries, Blake idealizes imagination and emotion and believes in the sacredness of the individual, he entirely avoids the "egotistical sublime," neither speaking directly of himself in his poetry, as Wordsworth did, nor, like Goethe, creating self-absorbed characters. In his short lyrics he adopts many different voices; the difficulties of interpretation stem partly from this fact. He insistently deals with metaphysical questions about the human position in the universe and with social questions about the nature of human responsibility.

In *Songs of Innocence*, the speaker is often a child: asking questions of a lamb, meditating on his own blackness, describing the experience of a chimney sweep. Ostensibly these children in their innocence feel no anger or bitterness at the realities of the world where they find themselves. The little black boy assures himself of a future when the little English boy will resemble him and love him; the child addressing the lamb evokes a realm of pure delight; the chimney sweep comforts himself with conventional morality and with a companion's dream. When an adult observer watches children, as in "Holy Thursday," he too sees a benign arrangement, in which children are "flowers of London town," supervised by "aged men, wise guardians of the poor." In the "Introduction" to the volume, the adult speaker receives empowering advice from a child, who instructs him to write. Everything is for the best in this best of all possible worlds.

But not quite. Disturbing undertones reverberate through even the most "innocent" of these songs. Innocence is, after all, by definition a state automatically lost through experience and never possible to regain. If the children evoked by the text still possess their innocence, the adult reader does not. "The Little Black Boy" suggests the kind of ambiguity evoked by the conjunction between innocent speaker and experienced reader. The poem opens with a situation that the speaker does not entirely understand—but one likely to be painfully familiar to the reader. "White as an angel is the English child: / But I am black as if bereav'd of light": the child's similes indicate how completely he has incorporated the value judgments of his society, in which white suggests everything good, black means deficiency and deprivation. In this context, the mother's teaching, a comforting myth, becomes comprehensible as a way of dealing with her child's bewilderment and anxiety about his difference. At the end of the poem, the boy extends his mother's story into a prophetic vision in which black means protective power ("I'll shade him from the heat till he can bear / To lean in joy upon our father's knee"), and difference disappears into likeness, hostility into love. The vision evokes an ideal situation located in an imagined afterlife: it has only an antithetical connection to present actuality. Its emphatic divergence from real social conditions creates the subterranean disturbance characteristic of Blake's lyrics, the disturbance that calls attention to the serious social criticism implicit even in lyrics which may appear sweet to the point of blandness.

For all Blake's dislike of the earlier eighteenth century, he shares with his forebears one important assumption: his poetry, too, instructs as well as pleases. The innocent chimney sweep evokes parental death and betrayal, horrifying working conditions (soot and nakedness, darkness and shaved heads), and compensatory dreams. He never complains, but when he ends with the tag, "So if all do their duty, they need not fear harm," it generates moral shock. The discrepancy between the child's purity and his brutal exploitation indicts the society that allows such things. Innocence may be its own protection, these poems suggest, but that fact does not obviate social guilt.

If the *Songs of Innocence*, for all their atmosphere of brightness, cheer, and peace, convey outrage at the ways that social institutions harm those they should protect, the *Songs of Experience* more directly evoke a world worn, constricted, burdened with misery created by human beings. Now a new version of "The Chimney Sweeper" openly states what the earlier poem suggested:

> "And because I am happy, & dance & sing,
> They think they have done me no injury,
> And are gone to praise God & his Priest & King,
> Who make up a heaven of our misery."

The child understands the protective self-blinding of adults.

"London" in its sixteen lines sums up many of the collection's implications. Like most of the *Songs of Experience*, "London" presents an adult speaker, a wanderer through the city, who finds wherever he goes, in every face, "Marks of weakness, marks of woe." The city is the repository of suffering: men and infants and chimney sweepers cry; soldiers sigh; harlots curse. All are victims of corrupt institutions: blackening church, bloody palace. Marriage and death interpenetrate; the curses of illness and corruption pass through the generations. The speaker reports only what he sees and hears, without commentary. He evokes a society in dreadful decay, and he conveys his despairing rage at a situation he cannot remedy.

Blake's lyrics, in their mixture of the visionary and the observational, strike notes far different from those of satire. Like the visionary observations of Swift and Voltaire, though, they insist on the connection between literature and life. Literature has transformative capacity, but it works with the raw material of actual experience. And its visions have the power to insist on the necessity of change.

Blake has provided material for an enormous outpouring of critical material. Particularly useful for the student are the collection of critical essays, *Blake*, edited by N. Frye (1966); M. Schorer, *William Blake: The Politics of Vision* (1946); H. Adams, *William Blake: A Reading of the Shorter Poems* (1963); E. D. Hirsch, *Innocence and Experience* (1969); and D. G. Gilham, *William Blake* (1973).

From Songs of Innocence and of Experience
SHEWING THE TWO CONTRARY STATES OF THE HUMAN SOUL

From Songs of Innocence[1]
1789

The Author & Printer   W Blake
Introduction

> Piping down the valleys wild
> Piping songs of pleasant glee
> On a cloud I saw a child,
> And he laughing said to me,
>
> "Pipe a song about a Lamb";   5
> So I piped with merry chear;
> "Piper pipe that song again"—
> So I piped, he wept to hear.
>
> "Drop thy pipe thy happy pipe
> Sing thy songs of happy chear";   10
> So I sung the same again
> While he wept with joy to hear.
>
> "Piper sit thee down and write
> In a book that all may read"—
> So he vanish'd from my sight.   15
> And I pluck'd a hollow reed,
>
> And I made a rural pen,
> And I stain'd the water clear,

1. The text for all of Blake's works is edited by David V. Erdman and Harold Bloom. *Songs of Innocence* (1789) was later combined with *Songs of Experience* (1794); and the poems were etched and accompanied by Blake's illustrations, the process accomplished by copper engravings stamped on paper, then colored by hand.

And I wrote my happy songs
Every child may joy to hear.   20

The Lamb

Little Lamb, who made thee?
Dost thou know who made thee?
Gave thee life & bid thee feed,
By the stream & o'er the mead;
Gave thee clothing of delight,   5
Softest clothing wooly bright;
Gave thee such a tender voice,
Making all the vales rejoice!
Little Lamb who made thee?
Dost thou know who made thee?   10

Little Lamb I'll tell thee,
Little Lamb I'll tell thee!
He is calléd by thy name,
For he calls himself a Lamb:
He is meek & he is mild,   15
He became a little child:
I a child & thou a lamb,
We are calléd by his name.[2]
Little Lamb God bless thee.
Little Lamb God bless thee.

The Little Black Boy

My mother bore me in the southern wild,
And I am black, but O! my soul is white;
White as an angel is the English child:
But I am black as if bereav'd of light.

My mother taught me underneath a tree,   5
And sitting down before the heat of day,
She took me on her lap and kisséd me,
And pointing to the east, began to say:

"Look on the rising sun: there God does live,
And gives his light, and gives his heat away;   10
And flowers and trees and beasts and men receive
Comfort in morning, joy in the noon day.

"And we are put on earth a little space,
That we may learn to bear the beams of love,

2. Christians use the name of Christ to designate themselves.

And these black bodies and this sun-burnt face   15
Is but a cloud, and like a shady grove.

"For when our souls have learn'd the heat to bear,
The cloud will vanish; we shall hear his voice,
Saying: 'Come out from the grove, my love & care,
And round my golden tent like lambs rejoice.' "   20

Thus did my mother say, and kisséd me;
And thus I say to little English boy:
When I from black and he from white cloud free,
And round the tent of God like lambs we joy,

I'll shade him from the heat till he can bear   25
To lean in joy upon our father's knee;
And then I'll stand and stroke his silver hair,
And be like him, and he will then love me.

Holy Thursday

'Twas on a Holy Thursday,[3] their innocent faces clean,
The children walking two & two, in red & blue & green,[4]
Grey headed beadles[5] walk'd before with wands as white as snow,
Till into the high dome of Paul's they like Thames' waters flow.

O what a multitude they seemed, these flowers of London town! 5
Seated in companies they sit with radiance all their own.
The hum of multitudes was there, but multitudes of lambs,
Thousands of little boys & girls raising their innocent hands.

Now like a mighty wind they raise to heaven the voice of song,
Or like harmonious thunderings the seats of heaven among.   10
Beneath them sit the aged men, wise guardians[6] of the poor;
Then cherish pity, lest you drive an angel from your door.[7]
ca. 1784

The Chimney Sweeper

When my mother died I was very young,
And my father sold me[8] while yet my tongue

---

3. Ascension Day, forty days after Easter, when children from charity schools were marched to St. Paul's Cathedral.   4. Each school had its own distinctive uniform.   5. Ushers and minor functionaries, whose job was to maintain order.   6. The governors of the Charity Schools. 7. *Hebrews 13*: "Be not forgetful to entertain strangers; for thereby some have entertained angels unawares."   8. It was common practice in Blake's day for fathers to sell, or indenture, their children for this task. The average age of the child has been estimated at six and seven; they were generally employed for seven years, until they were too large for the task of ascending the chimneys.

Could scarcely cry " 'weep! 'weep! 'weep! 'weep!"[9]
So your chimneys I sweep & in soot I sleep.

There's little Tom Dacre, who cried when his head   5
That curl'd like a lambs back, was shav'd, so I said,
"Hush, Tom! never mind it, for when your head's bare,
You know that the soot cannot spoil your white hair."

And so he was quiet, & that very night,
As Tom was a-sleeping he had such a sight!   10
That thousands of sweepers, Dick, Joe, Ned, & Jack,
Were all of them lock'd up in coffins of black;

And by came an Angel who had a bright key,
And he open'd the coffins & set them all free;
Then down a green plain, leaping, laughing they run,   15
And wash in a river and shine in the Sun;

Then naked[1] & white, all their bags left behind,
They rise upon clouds, and sport in the wind.
And the Angel told Tom, if he'd be a good boy,
He'd have God for his father & never want joy.   20

And so Tom awoke; and we rose in the dark
And got with our bags & our brushes to work.
Tho' the morning was cold, Tom was happy & warm;
So if all do their duty, they need not fear harm.

From Songs of Experience

1794

The Author & Printer   W Blake

Introduction

Hear the voice of the Bard!
Who Present, Past, & Future sees;
Whose ears have heard
The Holy Word
That walk'd among the ancient trees;[2]   5

---

9. The child's lisping effort to say "sweep," as he walks the streets looking for work.   1. They climbed up the chimneys naked.   2. Genesis 3:8: "And [Adam and Eve] heard the voice of the Lord God walking in the garden in the cool of the day." Blake's ambiguous use of pronouns makes for interpretative difficulties. It would seem that "The Holy Word" (Jehovah, the Old Testament deity) calls "the lapsed soul," and weeps—not the Bard.

Calling the lapsèd Soul
And weeping in the evening dew;
That might controll
The starry pole,
And fallen, fallen light renew!   10

"O Earth, O Earth, return!
Arise from out the dewy grass;
Night is worn,
And the morn
Rises from the slumberous mass.   15

"Turn away no more;
Why wilt thou turn away?
The starry floor
The watry shore
Is giv'n thee till the break of day."   20

Earth's Answer

Earth rais'd up her head,
From the darkness dread & drear.
Her light fled:
Stony dread!
And her locks cover'd with grey despair.   5

"Prison'd on watry shore
Starry Jealousy does keep my den,
Cold and hoar
Weeping o'er
I hear the Father of the ancient men.[3]   10

"Selfish father of men,
Cruel, jealous, selfish fear!
Can delight
Chain'd in night
The virgins of youth and morning bear?   15

"Does spring hide its joy
When buds and blossoms grow?
Does the sower
Sow by night,
Or the plowman in darkness plow?   20

3. In Blake's later prophetic works one of the four Zoas, representing the four chief faculties of
man, is Urizen. In general he stood for the orthodox conception of the Divine Creator, sometimes
Jehovah in the Old Testament, often the God conceived by Newton and Locke; in all instances a
tyrant associated with excessive rationalism, sexual repression, the opponent of the imagination
and creativity. This may be "the Holy Word" in "Introduction."

"Break this heavy chain
That does freeze my bones around;
Selfish! vain!
Eternal bane!
That free Love with bondage bound."   25

The Tyger

Tyger! Tyger! burning bright
In the forests of the night,
What immortal hand or eye
Could frame thy fearful symmetry?

In what distant deeps or skies   5
Burnt the fire of thine eyes?
On what wings dare he aspire?
What the hand, dare seize the fire?

And what shoulder, & what art,
Could twist the sinews of thy heart?   10
And when thy heart began to beat,
What dread hand? & what dread feet?

What the hammer? what the chain?
In what furnace was thy brain?
What the anvil? what dread grasp   15
Dare its deadly terrors clasp?

When the stars threw down their spears,
And water'd heaven with their tears,
Did he smile his work to see?
Did he who made the Lamb make thee?   20

Tyger! Tyger! burning bright
In the forests of the night,
What immortal hand or eye
Dare frame thy fearful symmetry?

The Sick Rose

O Rose, thou art sick.
The invisible worm
That flies in the night
In the howling storm

Has found out thy bed   5
Of crimson joy,

And his dark secret love
Does thy life destroy.

London

I wander thro' each charter'd[4] street,
Near where the charter'd Thames does flow,
And mark in every face I meet
Marks of weakness, marks of woe.

In every cry of every Man,   5
In every Infant's cry of fear,
In every voice, in every ban,
The mind-forg'd manacles I hear.

How the Chimney-sweeper's cry
Every blackning Church appalls;[5]   10
And the hapless Soldier's sigh
Runs in blood down Palace walls.

But most thro' midnight streets I hear
How the youthful Harlot's curse
Blasts the new-born Infant's tear,[6]   15
And blights with plagues the Marriage hearse.

The Chimney Sweeper

A little black thing among the snow
Crying " 'weep, 'weep," in notes of woe!
"Where are thy father & mother? say?"
"They are both gone up to the church to pray.

"Because I was happy upon the heath,   5
And smil'd among the winter's snow;
They clothéd me in the clothes of death,
And taught me to sing the notes of woe.

"And because I am happy, & dance & sing,
They think they have done me no injury,   10
And are gone to praise God & his Priest & King,
Who make up a heaven of our misery."

---

4. Given liberty or freedom, but also taken over as private property.   5. Literally, makes
white   6. The harlot infects the parents with venereal disease, and thus the infant is inflicted
with prenatal blindness.

Mock on, Mock on, Voltaire, Rousseau

Mock on, Mock on, Voltaire, Rousseau;
Mock on, Mock on, 'tis all in vain.
You throw the sand against the wind,
And the wind blows it back again.

And every sand becomes a Gem   5
Reflected in the beams divine;
Blown back, they blind the mocking Eye,
But still in Israel's paths they shine.

The Atoms of Democritus[7]
And Newton's Particles of light[8]   10
Are sands upon the Red sea shore,
Where Israel's tents do shine so bright.

And Did Those Feet

And did those feet[9] in ancient time
Walk upon England's mountains green?
And was the holy Lamb of God
On England's pleasant pastures seen?

And did the Countenance Divine   5
Shine forth upon our clouded hills?
And was Jerusalem builded here,
Among these dark Satanic Mills?[1]

Bring me my Bow of burning gold:
Bring me my Arrows of desire: 10
Bring me my Spear: O clouds unfold!
Bring me my Chariot of fire!

I will not cease from Mental Fight,
Nor shall my Sword sleep in my hand,
Till we have built Jerusalem   15
In England's green & pleasant Land.
ca. 1804–1810   ca. 1804–1810

---

7. Greek philosopher (460?–362? B.C.) who advanced a theory that all things are merely patterns of atoms.   8. Newton's corpuscular theory of light. For Blake, both men were condemned as materialists.   9. A reference to an ancient legend that Jesus came to England with Joseph of Arimathea.   1. Possibly industrial England, but "mills" also meant for Blake eighteenth-century arid, mechanistic philosophy.

WILLIAM WORDSWORTH

1770–1850

William Wordsworth both proclaimed and embodied the *newness* of the Romantic Movement. In his preface to the second edition of *Lyrical Ballads* (1800), a collection of poems by him and his friend Samuel Taylor Coleridge, he announced the advent of a poetic revolution. Like other revolutionaries, Wordsworth and Coleridge created their identities by rebelling against and travestying their predecessors. Now no longer would poets write in "dead" forms; now they had discovered a "new" direction, "new" subject matter; now poetry could at last serve as an important form of human communication. Reading Wordsworth's poems with the excitement of that revolution long past, we can still feel the power of his desire to communicate. The human heart is his subject; he writes, in particular, of growth and of memory and of the perplexities inherent in the human condition.

Born at Cockermouth, Cumberland, to the family of an attorney, Wordsworth attended St. John's College, Cambridge, from 1787 to 1791. The next year, early in the French Revolution, he spent in France, where he met Annette Vallon and had a daughter by her. In 1795, Wordsworth met Coleridge; two years later, Wordsworth and his sister, Dorothy, moved to Alfoxden, near Coleridge's home in Nether Stowey, in the county of Somerset. There the two men conceived the idea of collaboration; in 1798, the first edition of *Lyrical Ballads* appeared, anonymously. The next year, Wordsworth and his sister settled in the Lake District of northwest England. In 1802, the poet married Mary Hutchinson, who bore him five children. He received the sinecure of stamp distributor in 1813 and in 1843 succeeded William Southey as poet laureate, having long since abandoned the political radicalism of his youth.

Wordsworth wrote little prose, except for the famous preface of 1800 and another preface in 1815; his accomplishment was almost entirely poetic. His early work employed conventional eighteenth-century techniques, but *Lyrical Ballads* marked a new direction: an effort to employ simple language and to reveal the high significance of simple themes, the transcendent importance of the everyday. Between 1798 and 1805, he composed his nineteenth-century version of an epic, *The Prelude*, an account of the development of a poet's mind—his own. His subsequent work included odes, sonnets, and many poems written to mark specific occasions.

It would be difficult to overestimate the extent of Wordsworth's historical and poetic importance. In *The Prelude*, not published until 1850, he not only made powerful poetry out of his own experience; he also specified a way of valuing experience.

> There are in our existence spots of time,
> That with distinct pre-eminence retain
> A renovating virtue, whence, depressed
> By false opinion and contentious thought,
> Or aught of heavier or more deadly weight,

> In trivial occupations, and the round
> Of ordinary intercourse, our minds
> Are nourished and invisibly repaired;
> A virtue, by which pleasure is enhanced,
> That penetrates, enables us to mount
> When high, more high, and lifts us up when fallen.

To take seriously the moment, this passage suggests, enables us to resist the dulling force of everyday life ("trivial occupations") and provides the means of personal salvation.

Wordsworth often uses religious language (a religious reference is hinted in the idea of being lifted up when fallen) to insist on the importance of his doctrine. He inaugurated an attempt that would last far into the century, an attempt to establish and sustain a secular religion to substitute for Christian faith. The attempt was, even for Wordsworth, only intermittently successful. *The Prelude* records experiences of persuasive visionary intensity, as when the poet speaks of seeing a shepherd in the distance:

> Or him have I descried in distant sky,
> A solitary object and sublime,
> Above all height! like an aerial cross
> Stationed alone upon a spiry rock
> Of the Chartreuse, for worship.

But such "spots of time" exist in isolation; it is difficult to maintain a saving faith on their basis.

The two long poems printed here treat the problem of discovering and sustaining faith. "Lines Composed a Few Miles Above Tintern Abbey," first published in *Lyrical Ballads*, and "Ode on Intimations of Immortality," published in 1807 but written between 1802 and 1806, share a preoccupation with loss and with the saving power of memory. Both speak of personal experience, although the ode, a more formal poem, also generalizes to a hypothetical "we." Both insist that nature—the external world experienced through the senses and the containing pattern assumed beyond that world—offers the possibility of wisdom to combat the pain inherent in human growth.

But it would be a mistake to assume that the poems exist to promulgate a doctrine of natural salvation, although some readers have considered their "pantheism" (the belief that God pervades every part of His created universe) their most important aspect. Both poems evoke an intellectual and emotional process, not a conclusion; they sketch dramas of human development.

In "Tintern Abbey," the speaker conveys his relief at returning to a sylvan scene that has been important to him in memory. His recollections of this natural beauty, he says, have helped sustain him in the confusion and weariness of city life; he thinks they may also have encouraged him toward goodness and serenity. But this second suggestion, that memories of nature have a moral effect, is only hypothetical, qualified in the text by such words and phrases as "I trust" and "perhaps." Indeed, the poem's next section opens with explicit statement that this may "Be but a vain belief." True or false, though, the belief comforts the speaker, who then recalls his more direct relation with nature in the past, when "The sounding cataract / Haunted me like a passion." He hopes, but cannot quite be sure, that his present aware-ness of "the still, sad music of humanity" and of the great "presence" that infuses nature compensates for what he has sacrificed in losing the imme-diacy of youthful experience.

The last section of "Tintern Abbey" emphasizes still more that the speaker is struggling with depression over his sense of loss; he observes that the pres-ence of his "dearest Friend," his sister, would protect his "genial spirits" from decay even without his faith in what he has learned. That sister now becomes the focus for his thoughts about nature; he imagines her growth as like his own, but perfected, and her power of memory as able to contain not only the beauties of the landscape but his presence as part of that landscape. The poem thus resolves itself with emphasis on a human relationship, between the man and his sister, as well as on the importance of nature. Its emotional power derives partly from its evocation of the *need* to believe in nature as a form of salvation and of the process of development through which that need manifests itself.

At about the same time that he wrote the "Ode on Intimations of Immor-tality," Wordsworth composed his sonnet, "The World Is Too Much With Us":

> . . . we lay waste our powers
> Little we see in Nature that is ours;
> . . . we are out of tune.

Despite the rhapsodic tone that dominates the ode, it too reveals itself as a hard-won act of faith, an effort to combat the view of the present world conveyed in the sonnet.

The ode opens with insistence on loss: "The things which I have seen I now can see no more." The speaker feels grief; he tries to deny it, because it seems at odds with the harmony and joy of the natural world. Yet the effort fails: even natural beauty speaks to him of what he no longer possesses. Stanzas five through eight emphasize the association of infancy with natural communion and the inevitable deprivation attending growth. In stanza nine, the speaker attempts to value what still remains to him: it's all he has, he's grateful for it. In the concluding stanzas, however, he arrives at a new rev-elation: now nature acquires value not as a form of unmixed ecstasy, but in connection with the experience of human suffering:

> Though nothing can bring back the hour
> Of splendour in the grass, of glory in the flower;
> We will grieve not, rather find
> Strength in what remains behind; . . .
> In the soothing thoughts that spring
> Out of human suffering . . .

It is "the human heart by which we live" that finally enables the poet to experience the wonder of a flower, now become the source of "Thoughts that do often lie too deep for tears."

The view that the processes of maturing involve giving up a kind of wisdom accessible only to children belongs particularly to the Romantic period, but most people at least occasionally feel that in growing up they have left behind something they would rather keep. Wordsworth's poetic expression of the effort to come to terms with such feelings may remind his readers of barely noticed aspects of their own experience.

G. M. Harper, *Wordsworth* (1916–1929), remains the standard biography. Other important works (critical in emphasis) include R. D. Havens, *The Mind of a Poet* (1950), G. Hartman, *Wordsworth's Poetry* (1964), and D. Perkins, *Wordsworth and the Poetry of Sincerity* (1964).

Lines

COMPOSED A FEW MILES ABOVE TINTERN ABBEY, ON REVISITING THE BANKS OF THE WYE DURING A TOUR. JULY 13, 1798.

Five years have past; five summers, with the length
Of five long winters! and again I hear
These waters, rolling from their mountain-springs
With a soft inland murmur.—Once again
Do I behold these steep and lofty cliffs,   5
That on a wild secluded scene impress
Thoughts of more deep seclusion; and connect
The landscape with the quiet of the sky.
The day is come when I again repose
Here, under this dark sycamore, and view   10
These plots of cottage-ground, these orchard-tufts,
Which at this season, with their unripe fruits,
Are clad in one green hue, and lose themselves
'Mid groves and copses. Once again I see
These hedge-rows, hardly hedge-rows, little lines   15
Of sportive wood run wild: these pastoral farms,
Green to the very door; and wreaths of smoke
Sent up, in silence, from among the trees!
With some uncertain notice, as might seem
Of vagrant dwellers in the houseless woods,   20
Or of some Hermit's cave, where by his fire
The Hermit sits alone.

                  These beauteous forms,
Through a long absence, have not been to me
As is a landscape to a blind man's eye:
But oft, in lonely rooms, and 'mid the din   25
Of towns and cities, I have owed to them,
In hours of weariness, sensations sweet,

Felt in the blood, and felt along the heart;
And passing even into my purer mind,
With tranquil restoration:—feelings too   30
Of unremembered pleasure: such, perhaps,
As have no slight or trivial influence
On that best portion of a good man's life,
His little, nameless, unremembered, acts
Of kindness and of love. Nor less, I trust,   35
To them I may have owed another gift,
Of aspect more sublime; that blessed mood,
In which the burthen of the mystery,
In which the heavy and the weary weight
Of all this unintelligible world,   40
Is lightened:—that serene and blessed mood,
In which the affections gently lead us on,—
Until, the breath of this corporeal frame
And even the motion of our human blood
Almost suspended, we are laid asleep   45
In body, and become a living soul:
While with an eye made quiet by the power
Of harmony, and the deep power of joy,
We see into the life of things.

                        If this
Be but a vain belief, yet, oh! how oft—   50
In darkness and amid the many shapes
Of joyless daylight; when the fretful stir
Unprofitable, and the fever of the world,
Have hung upon the beatings of my heart—
How oft, in spirit, have I turned to thee,   55
O sylvan Wye! thou wanderer thro' the woods,
How often has my spirit turned to thee!

    And now, with gleams of half-extinguished thought
With many recognitions dim and faint,
And somewhat of a sad perplexity,   60
The picture of the mind revives again:
While here I stand, not only with the sense
Of present pleasure, but with pleasing thoughts
That in this moment there is life and food
For future years. And so I dare to hope,   65
Though changed, no doubt, from what I was when first
I came among these hills; when like a roe
I bounded o'er the mountains, by the sides
Of the deep rivers, and the lonely streams,

Wherever nature led: more like a man   70
Flying from something that he dreads than one
Who sought the thing he loved. For nature then
(The coarser pleasures of my boyish days,
And their glad animal movements all gone by)
To me was all in all.—I cannot paint   75
What then I was. The sounding cataract
Haunted me like a passion: the tall rock,
The mountain, and the deep and gloomy wood,
Their colours and their forms, were then to me
An appetite; a feeling and a love,   80
That had no need for a remoter charm,
By thought supplied, nor any interest
Unborrowed from the eye.—That time is past,
And all its aching joys are now no more,
And all its dizzy raptures. Not for this   85
Faint I, nor mourn nor murmur; other gifts
Have followed; for such loss, I would believe,
Abundant recompense. For I have learned
To look on nature, not as in the hour
Of thoughtless youth; but hearing oftentimes   90
The still, sad music of humanity,
Nor harsh nor grating, though of ample power
To chasten and subdue. And I have felt
A presence that disturbs me with the joy
Of elevated thoughts; a sense sublime   95
Of something far more deeply interfused,
Whose dwelling is the light of setting suns,
And the round ocean and the living air,
And the blue sky, and in the mind of man:
A motion and a spirit, that impels   100
All thinking things, all objects of all thought,
And rolls through all things. Therefore am I still
A lover of the meadows and the woods,
And mountains; and of all that we behold
From this green earth; of all the mighty world   105
Of eye, and ear,—both what they half create,
And what perceive; well pleased to recognise
In nature and the language of the sense
The anchor of my purest thoughts, the nurse,
The guide, the guardian of my heart, and soul   110
Of all my moral being.

                        Nor perchance,
If I were not thus taught, should I the more

Suffer my genial spirits to decay:
For thou art with me here upon the banks
Of this fair river; thou my dearest Friend,   115
My dear, dear Friend; and in thy voice I catch
The language of my former heart, and read
My former pleasures in the shooting lights
Of thy wild eyes. Oh! yet a little while
May I behold in thee what I was once,   120
My dear, dear Sister! and this prayer I make,
Knowing that Nature never did betray
The heart that loved her; 'tis her privilege,
Through all the years of this our life, to lead
From joy to joy: for she can so inform   125
The mind that is within us, so impress
With quietness and beauty, and so feed
With lofty thoughts, that neither evil tongues,
Rash judgments, nor the sneers of selfish men,
Nor greetings where no kindness is, nor all   130
The dreary intercourse of daily life,
Shall e'er prevail against us, or disturb
Our cheerful faith, that all which we behold
Is full of blessings. Therefore let the moon
Shine on thee in thy solitary walk;   135
And let the misty mountain-winds be free
To blow against thee: and, in after years,
When these wild ecstasies shall be matured
Into a sober pleasure; when thy mind
Shall be a mansion for all lovely forms,   140
Thy memory be as a dwelling-place
For all sweet sounds and harmonies; oh! then,
If solitude, or fear, or pain, or grief
Should be thy portion, with what healing thoughts
Of tender joy wilt thou remember me,   145
And these my exhortations! Nor, perchance—
If I should be where I no more can hear
Thy voice, nor catch from thy wild eyes these gleams
Of past existence—wilt thou then forget
That on the banks of this delightful stream   150
We stood together; and that I, so long
A worshipper of Nature, hither came
Unwearied in that service: rather say
With warmer love—oh! with far deeper zeal
Of holier love. Nor wilt thou then forget   155
That after many wanderings, many years
Of absence, these steep woods and lofty cliffs,

And this green pastoral landscape, were to me
More dear, both for themselves and for thy sake!

Ode

INTIMATIONS OF IMMORTALITY FROM RECOLLECTIONS OF EARLY CHILDHOOD

> The Child is father of the Man;
> And I could wish my days to be
> Bound each to each by natural piety.

I

There was a time when meadow, grove, and stream,
   The earth, and every common sight,
      To me did seem
   Apparelled in celestial light,
The glory and the freshness of a dream.   5
It is not now as it hath been of yore;—
     Turn wheresoe'er I may,
       By night or day,
The things which I have seen I now can see no more.

II

   The Rainbow comes and goes   10
   And lovely is the Rose;
   The Moon doth with delight
Look round her when the heavens are bare,
    Waters on a starry night
    Are beautiful and fair;   15
   The sunshine is a glorious birth;
   But yet I know, where'er I go,
That there hath past away a glory from the earth.

III

Now, while the birds thus sing a joyous song,
   And while the young lambs bound   20
    As to the tabor's sound,
To me alone there came a thought of grief:
A timely utterance gave that thought relief,
    And I again am strong:
The cataracts blow their trumpets from the steep;   25
No more shall grief of mine the season wrong;
I hear the Echoes through the mountains throng,

The Winds come to me from the fields of sleep,
   And all the earth is gay;
     Land and sea   30
   Give themselves up to jollity,
    And with the heart of May
   Doth every Beast keep holiday;—
     Thou Child of Joy,
Shout round me, let me hear thy shouts, thou happy
    Shepherd-boy!   35

IV

Ye blessèd Creatures, I have heard the call
   Ye to each other make; I see
The heavens laugh with you in your jubilee;
   My heart is at your festival,   40
   My head hath its coronal,
The fulness of your bliss, I feel—I feel it all.
   Oh evil day! if I were sullen
   While Earth herself is adorning,
    This sweet May-morning,   45
    And the Children are culling
     On every side,
    In a thousand valleys far and wide,
    Fresh flowers; while the sun shines warm,
And the Babe leaps upon his Mother's arm:—   50
    I hear, I hear, with joy I hear!
    —But there's a Tree, of many, one,
A single Field which I have looked upon,
Both of them speak of something that is gone:
    The Pansy at my feet   55
    Doth the same tale repeat:
   Whither is fled the visionary gleam?
   Where is it now, the glory and the dream?

V

Our birth is but a sleep and a forgetting:
The Soul that rises with us, our life's Star,   60
   Hath had elsewhere its setting,
    And cometh from afar:
   Not in entire forgetfulness,
   And not in utter nakedness,
But trailing clouds of glory do we come   65
   From God, who is our home:
Heaven lies about us in our infancy!
Shades of the prison-house begin to close

Upon the growing Boy,
But He beholds the light, and whence it flows,   70
  He sees it in his joy;
The Youth, who daily farther from the east
  Must travel, still is Nature's Priest,
    And by the vision splendid
    Is on his way attended;   75
At length the Man perceives it die away,
And fade into the light of common day.

VI

Earth fills her lap with pleasures of her own;
Yearnings she hath in her own natural kind,
And, even with something of a Mother's mind,   80
    And no unworthy aim,
  The homely Nurse doth all she can
To make her Foster-child, her Inmate, Man,
  Forget the glories he hath known,
And that imperial palace whence he came.   85

VII

Behold the Child among his new-born blisses,
A six years' Darling of a pigmy size!
See, where 'mid work of his own hand he lies,
Fretted by sallies of his mother's kisses,
With light upon him from his father's eyes!   90
See, at his feet, some little plan or chart,
Some fragment from his dream of human life,
Shaped by himself with newly-learned art;
  A wedding or a festival,
  A mourning or a funeral;   95
    And this hath now his heart,
  And unto this he frames his song
    Then will he fit his tongue
To dialogues of business, love, or strife;
    But it will not be long   100
    Ere this will be thrown aside,
    And with new joy and pride
The little Actor cons another part;
Filling from time to time his 'humorous stage'
With all the Persons, down to palsied Age,   105
That Life brings with her in her equipage;
    As if his whole vocation
    Were endless imitation.

VIII

Thou, whose exterior semblance doth belie
    Thy Soul's immensity;   110
Thou best Philosopher, who yet dost keep
Thy heritage, thou Eye among the blind,
That, deaf and silent, read'st the eternal deep,
Haunted for ever by the eternal mind,—
    Mighty Prophet! Seer blest!   115
    On whom those truths do rest,
Which we are toiling all our lives to find,
In darkness lost, the darkness of the grave;
Thou, over whom thy Immortality
Broods like the Day, a Master o'er a Slave,   120
A presence which is not to be put by;
    [To whom the grave
Is but a lonely bed without the sense or sight
    Of day or the warm light
A place of thought where we in waiting lie;][1]   125
Thou little Child, yet glorious in the might
Of heaven-born freedom on thy being's height,
Why with such earnest pains dost thou provoke
The years to bring the inevitable yoke,
Thus blindly with thy blessedness at strife?   130
Full soon thy Soul shall have her earthly freight,
And custom lie upon thee with a weight,
Heavy as frost, and deep almost as life!

IX

    O joy! that in our embers
    Is something that doth live,   135
    That nature yet remembers
    What was so fugitive!
The thought of our past years in me doth breed
Perpetual benediction: not indeed
For that which is most worthy to be blest;   140
Delight and liberty, the simple creed
Of Childhood, whether busy or at rest,
With new-fledged hope still fluttering in his breast—
    Not for these I raise
    The song of thanks and praise;   145

1. These lines were included in the "Ode" in the 1807 and 1815 editions of Wordsworth's poems but were omitted in the 1820 and subsequent editions, as a result of Coleridge's severe censure of them.

But for those obstinate questionings
Of sense and outward things,
Fallings from us, vanishings;
Blank misgivings of a Creature
Moving about in worlds not realized,   150
High instincts before which our mortal Nature
Did tremble like a guilty Thing surprised:
    But for those first affections,
    Those shadowy recollections,
    Which, be they what they may,   155
Are yet the fountain-light of all our day,
Are yet a master-light of all our seeing;
Uphold us, cherish, and have power to make
Our noisy years seem moments in the being
Of the eternal Silence: truths that wake,   160
    To perish never:
Which neither listlessness, nor mad endeavour,
    Nor Man nor Boy,
Nor all that is at enmity with joy,
Can utterly abolish or destroy!   165
  Hence in a season of calm weather
    Though inland far we be,
Our Souls have sight of that immortal sea
    Which brought us hither,
    Can in a moment travel thither,   170
And see the Children sport upon the shore,
And hear the mighty waters rolling evermore.

X

Then sing, ye Birds, sing, sing a joyous song!
    And let the young Lambs bound
    As to the tabor's sound!   175
We in thought will join your throng,
  Ye that pipe and ye that play,
  Ye that through your hearts to-day
    Feel the gladness of the May!
What though the radiance which was once so bright   180
Be now for ever taken from my sight,
  Though nothing can bring back the hour
Of splendour in the grass, of glory in the flower;
    We will grieve not, rather find
    Strength in what remains behind;   185
    In the primal sympathy
    Which having been must ever be;
    In the soothing thoughts that spring

            Out of human suffering;
                In the faith that looks through death,   190
        In years that bring the philosophic mind.

                                XI

        And O, ye Fountains, Meadows, Hills, and Groves,
        Forebode not any severing of our loves!
        Yet in my heart of hearts I feel your might;
        I only have relinquished one delight   195
        To live beneath your more habitual sway.
        I love the Brooks which down their channels fret,
        Even more than when I tripped lightly as they;
        The innocent brightness of a new-born Day
                Is lovely yet;   200
        The Clouds that gather round the setting sun
        Do take a sober colouring from an eye
        That hath kept watch o'er man's mortality;
        Another race hath been, and other palms are won.
        Thanks to the human heart by which we live,   205
        Thanks to its tenderness, its joys, and fears,
        To me the meanest flower that blows can give
        Thoughts that do often lie too deep for tears.

Composed upon Westminster Bridge,
September 3, 1802

        Earth has not anything to show more fair:
        Dull would he be of soul who could pass by
        A sight so touching in its majesty;
        This City now doth, like a garment, wear
        The beauty of the morning; silent, bare,   5
        Ships, towers, domes, theatres, and temples lie
        Open unto the fields, and to the sky;
        All bright and glittering in the smokeless air.
        Never did sun more beautifully steep
        In his first splendour, valley, rock, or hill;   10
        Ne'er saw I, never felt, a calm so deep!
        The river glideth at his own sweet will:
        Dear God! the very houses seem asleep;
        And all that mighty heart is lying still!

The World Is Too Much With Us

        The world is too much with us; late and soon,
        Getting and spending, we lay waste our powers

Little we see in Nature that is ours;
We have given our hearts away, a sordid boon![2]
This Sea that bares her bosom to the moon,   5
The winds that will be howling at all hours,
And are up-gathered now like sleeping flowers,
For this, for everything, we are out of tune;
It moves us not.—Great God! I'd rather be
A Pagan suckled in a creed outworn;   10
So might I, standing on this pleasant lea,
Have glimpses that would make me less forlorn;
Have sight of Proteus[3] rising from the sea;
Or hear old Triton blow his wreathèd horn.

SAMUEL TAYLOR COLERIDGE
1772–1834

For Samuel Taylor Coleridge, the mystery of the imagination provided the most compelling and perplexing of subjects. In prose and in verse, by reasoned discussion and by poetic symbol making, he explored the subject, affirming imagination's virtually divine status as a creative power and suggesting his own emotional dependence on it.

Son of an English clergyman, Coleridge attended Jesus College, Cambridge, from 1791 to 1793. In 1795, he married Sara Fricker; the same year he met Wordsworth and began the fruitful collaboration leading to *Lyrical Ballads*. In 1810, his period of greatest poetic creativity already over, he separated from his wife; subsequently, he became increasingly addicted to opium. Known for his brilliant conversation, he spent much time talking and lecturing as well as writing.

The most intellectual of the English Romantics, Coleridge, after an early trip to Germany, was strongly influenced by the German Idealist philosophers, notably Emmanuel Kant and Johann Fichte. His best-known critical work, *Biographia Literaria* (1817), in which he develops most fully and explicitly his theory of imagination, contains many borrowings from German sources. His output of poetry was relatively small. In some of his most important poems (such as "The Rime of the Ancient Mariner"), he tries to incorporate the supernatural into essentially psychological narrative. He was also much interested in the native English ballad tradition, which on occasion influenced his choice of stanzaic form and meter.

Like other Romantic poets, Coleridge was fascinated by the Aeolian harp (it figures in the first stanza of "Dejection"), an instrument that makes music without human intervention, by the action of wind upon its strings. "Kubla Khan," a poem recording what the writer remembered of a dream stimulated

---

2. Gift; *sordid* refers to the act of giving the heart away.   3. An old man of the sea who, in the *Odyssey*, can assume a variety of shapes. *Triton:* A sea deity, usually represented as blowing on a conch shell.

by opium, comprises a kind of poetic equivalent for the Aeolian harp: a work for which its author disclaims conscious responsibility. It simply came to his mind, he says, to be broken off when he was interrupted by a person from Porlock. The poem therefore makes no claim to rational coherence, but it has always invited exegesis. Evoking a lush and splendid setting, it yet contains ominous suggestions: the ruler who presides over the magnificence of landscape ("deep romantic chasm," river, caves, incense-bearing trees) and building hears "Ancestral voices prophesying war." The theme of mingled beauty and danger intensifies as the poem focuses on the figure of a singer, a "damsel with a dulcimer," whose power the poem's speaker wishes to "revive" within himself. Then he could re-create the vision of Kubla's domain, and people would respond to him with "holy dread," recognizing his association with the magic, the sacred, the dangerous, the unpredictable and uncontrollable power of imagination. Thus the singer becomes an image for the poet, and we are reminded that the uncannily evocative scene of the poem's opening section itself issues from the poetic imagination, which creates for its possessor and for his readers a new version of reality, closer to the heart's desire than our workaday world, but not without danger—including the danger of becoming lost in it.

In "Dejection: An Ode," Coleridge concerns himself with the same theme in more extended personal terms. Paradoxically, this poem mourning his loss of creative imagination demonstrates the active presence of that quality whose absence it deplores, as it creates out of the dullness of depression a rich emotional and psychological texture. Like Wordsworth's "Ode on Intimations of Immortality," "Dejection" confronts the speaker's sense of diminishing power. He has lost the "joy" that he considers associated with the spontaneity of youth. More emphatically than Wordsworth, Coleridge attributes even the beauty of nature to the human imagination:

> O Lady! we receive but what we give,
> And in our life alone does Nature live: . . .
> Ah! from the soul itself must issue forth
> A light, a glory, a fair luminous cloud
> Enveloping the Earth.

One cannot hope for inspiration from nature, cannot expect to receive from without that reassurance and pleasure whose sources are within. As the poem develops, it demonstrates the operation of imagination on the external world by hearing meaning—meaning related to human action and suffering—in the sound of wind and storm. The imaginative activity provides its own solace; although the speaker never ceases to assert his dejection, he, like Wordsworth, is enabled finally to displace his vision of joy, harmony, and peace onto the figure of a woman who will embody all that he now feels impossible for himself.

In its emphasis on the "shaping spirit of Imagination," that presiding power of Romantic poetry, "Dejection" makes a strong statement of Coleridge's central concern. By its capacity to evoke emotional complexity—longing for what is lost, resentment at its passing, struggle to repossess what is mourned—and to demonstrate the patterns in which the mind deals with its own problems, it exemplifies the subtlety and the force of his poetic achievement.

E. K. Chambers, *Samuel Taylor Coleridge* (1938), is a solid biography. W. J. Bate, *Coleridge* (1968), combines biographical insight with critical commentary. J. L. Lowes, *The Road to Xanadu* (1927), provides a fascinating study of the sources of *Kubla Khan*. For criticism, see also J. Cornwell, *Coleridge* (1973), and J. Beer, *Coleridge's Poetic Intelligence* (1975).

Kubla Khan

OR, A VISION IN A DREAM, A FRAGMENT

The following fragment is here published at the request of a poet of great and deserved celebrity [Lord Byron], and, as far as the Author's own opinions are concerned, rather as a psychological curiosity, than on the ground of any supposed poetic merits.

In the summer of the year 1797, the Author, then in ill health, had retired to a lonely farm-house between Porlock and Linton, on the Exmoore confines of Somerset and Devonshire.[1] In consequence of a slight indisposition, an anodyne had been prescribed, from the effects of which he fell asleep in his chair at the moment that he was reading the following sentence, or words of the same substance, in "Purchas's Pilgraimage"[2]: "Here the Khan Kubla commanded a palace to be built, and a stately garden thereunto. And thus ten miles of fertile ground were inclosed with a wall." The Author continued for about three hours in a profound sleep, at least of the external senses, during which time he has the most vivid confidence, that he could not have composed less than from two to three hundred lines; if that indeed can be called composition in which all the images rose up before him as things, with a parallel production of the correspondent expressions, without any sensation or consciousness of effort.[3] On awaking he appeared to himself to have a distinct recollection of the whole, and taking his pen, ink, and paper, instantly and eagerly wrote down the lines that are here preserved. At this moment he was unfortunately called out by a person on business from Porlock, and detained by him above an hour, and on his return to his room, found, to his no small surprise and mortification, that though he still retained some vague and dim recollection of the

---

1. A high moorland shared by the two southwestern counties in England.   2. Samuel Purchas (1575?–1626) published *Purchas his Pilgrimage, or Relations of the World and the Religions observed in all Ages* in 1613. The passage in Purchas is slightly different: "In Xamdu did Cublai Can build a stately Palace, encompassing sixteene miles of plaine ground with a wall, wherein are fertile meddowes, pleasant Springs, delightfull Streames, and all sorts of beasts of chase and game, and in the middest thereof a sumptuous house of pleasure, which may be removed from place to place" (Book IV, Chap. 13).   3. Coleridge's statement that he dreamed the poem and wrote down what he could later remember *verbatim* has been queried, most recently by medical opinion. The belief that opium produces special dreams, or even any dreams at all, seems to lack confirmation.

general purport of the vision yet, with the exception of some eight or
ten scattered lines and images, all the rest had passed away like the
images on the surface of a stream into which a stone has been cast,
but, alas! without the after restoration of the latter!

> Then all the charm
> Is broken—all that phantom-world so fair
> Vanishes, and a thousand circlets spread,
> And each mis-shape['s] the other. Stay awhile,
> Poor youth! who scarcely dar'st lift up thine eyes—
> The stream will soon renew its smoothness, soon
> The visions will return! And lo, he stays,
> And soon the fragments dim of lovely forms
> Come trembling back, unite, and now once more
> The pool becomes a mirror.[4]

Yet from the still surviving recollections in his mind, the Author
has frequently purposed to finish for himself what had been originally, as it were, given to him.
Σαμερον αδιον ασω:[5] but the to-morrow is yet to come.

> In Xanadu did Kubla Khan[6]
> A stately pleasure-dome decree:
> Where Alph,[7] the sacred river, ran
> Through caverns measureless to man
>   Down to a sunless sea.   5
> So twice five miles of fertile ground
> With walls and towers were girdled round:
> And there were gardens bright with sinuous rills,
> Where blossomed many an incense-bearing tree;
> And here were forests ancient as the hills,   10
> Enfolding sunny spots of greenery.
>
> But oh! that deep romantic chasm which slanted
> Down the green hill athwart a cedarn cover!
> A savage place! as holy and enchanted
> As e'er beneath a waning moon was haunted   15
> By woman wailing for her demon-lover!
> And from this chasm, with ceaseless turmoil seething,
> As if this earth in fast thick pants were breathing,
> A mighty fountain momently was forced:

---

4. From Coleridge's poem *The Picture; or, the Lover's Resolution*, lines 91–100.   5. From
Theocritus, *Idylls*, I, 132: "to sing a sweeter song tomorrow."   6. Mongol emperor (1215?–
1294), visited by Marco Polo.   7. J. L. Lowes, in *The Road to Xanadu* (1927), thinks that
Coleridge may have had in mind the river Alpheus—linked with the Nile—mentioned by Virgil.

Amid whose swift half-intermitted burst   20
Huge fragments vaulted like rebounding hail,
Or chaffy grain beneath the thresher's flail:
And 'mid these dancing rocks at once and ever
It flung up momently the sacred river.
Five miles meandering with a mazy motion   25
Through wood and dale the sacred river ran,
Then reached the caverns measureless to man,
And sank in tumult to a lifeless ocean:
And 'mid this tumult Kubla heard from far
Ancestral voices prophesying war!   30
    The shadow of the dome of pleasure
    Floated midway on the waves;
    Where was heard the mingled measure
    From the fountain and the caves.
It was a miracle of rare device,   35
A sunny pleasure-dome with caves of ice!

    A damsel with a dulcimer
    In a vision once I saw:
    It was an Abyssinian maid,
    And on her dulcimer she played,   40
    Singing of Mount Abora.[8]
    Could I revive within me
    Her symphony and song,
    To such a deep delight 'twould win me,
That with music loud and long,   45
I would build that dome in air,
That sunny dome! those caves of ice!
And all who heard should see them there,
And all should cry, Beware! Beware!
His flashing eyes, his floating hair!   50
Weave a circle round him thrice,
And close your eyes with holy dread,
For he on honey-dew hath fed,
And drunk the milk of Paradise.

Dejection: An Ode

> *Late, late yestreen I saw the new Moon,*
> *With the old Moon in her arms;*
> *And I fear, I fear, my Master dear!*

8. Lowes argues that this may have been "Mt. Amara," mentioned by Milton in *Paradise Lost* (IV, 28), or Amhara in Samuel Johnson's *Rasselas*.

We shall have a deadly storm.
                    Ballad of Sir Patrick Spence   5

I

Well! If the Bard was weather-wise, who made
    The grand old ballad of Sir Patrick Spence,
    This night, so tranquil now, will not go hence
Unroused by winds, that ply a busier trade
Than those which mould yon cloud in lazy flakes,   10
Or the dull sobbing draft, that moans and rakes
Upon the strings of this Aeolian lute,[9]
        Which better far were mute.
    For lo! the New-moon winter-bright!
    And overspread with phantom light,   15
    (With swimming phantom light o'erspread
    But rimmed and circled by a silver thread)
I see the old Moon in her lap, foretelling
    The coming-on of rain and squally blast.
And oh! that even now the gust were swelling,   20
    And the slant night-shower driving loud and fast!
Those sounds which oft have raised me, whilst they awed,
        And sent my soul abroad,
Might now perhaps their wonted impulse give,
Might startle this dull pain, and make it move and live!   25

II

A grief without a pang, void, dark, and drear,
    A stifled, drowsy, unimpassioned grief,
    Which finds no natural outlet, no relief,
        In word, or sigh, or tear—
O Lady! in this wan and heartless mood,   30
To other thoughts by yonder throstle[1] woo'd,
    All this long eve, so balmy and serene,
Have I been gazing on the western sky,
    And its peculiar tint of yellow green:
And still I gaze—and with how blank an eye!   35
And those thin clouds above, in flakes and bars,
That give away their motion to the stars;
Those stars, that glide behind them or between,
Now sparkling, now bedimmed, but always seen:
Yon crescent Moon, as fixed as if it grew   40
In its own cloudless, starless lake of blue;

9. A frame fitted with strings or wires which produce musical tones when the wind hits them. Named after Aeolus, god of the winds.   1. The song-thrush.

I see them all so excellently[2] fair,
I see, not feel, how beautiful they are!

III

    My genial spirits[2] fail;
    And what can these avail   45
To lift the smothering weight from off my breast?
      It were a vain endeavour,
      Though I should gaze for ever
On that green light that lingers in the west:
I may not hope from outward forms to win   50
The passion and the life, whose fountains are within.

IV

O Lady! we receive but what we give,
And in our life alone does Nature live:
Ours is her wedding garment, ours her shroud!
    And would we aught behold of higher worth,   55
Than that inanimate cold world allowed
To the poor loveless ever-anxious crowd,
    Ah! from the soul itself must issue forth
A light, a glory, a fair luminous cloud
      Enveloping the Earth—   60
And from the soul itself must there be sent
    A sweet and potent voice, of its own birth,
Of all sweet sounds the life and element!

V

O pure of heart! thou need'st not ask of me
What this strong music in the soul may be!   65
What, and wherein doth exist,
This light, this glory, this fair luminous mist,
This beautiful and beauty-making power.
    Joy, virtuous Lady! Joy that ne'er was given,
Save to the pure, and in their purest hour,   70
Life, and Life's effluence, cloud at once and shower,
Joy, Lady! is the spirit and the power,
Which wedding Nature to us gives in dower
    A new Earth and new Heaven,
Undreamt of by the sensual and the proud—   75
Joy is the sweet voice, Joy the luminous cloud—
      We in ourselves rejoice!

2. Coleridge's generative spirits; in short, his creativity. The first version was written soon after Wordsworth had composed the first four stanzas of the *Ode on Intimations of Immortality*, and the themes are similar.

And thence flows all that charms or ear or sight,
   All melodies the echoes of that voice,
All colours a suffusion from that light.   80

VI

There was a time when, though my path was rough,
   This joy within me dallied with distress,
And all misfortunes were but as the stuff
   Whence Fancy[3] made me dreams of happiness:
For hope grew round me, like the twining vine,   85
And fruits, and foliage, not my own, seemed mine.
But now afflictions bow me down to earth:
Nor care I that they rob me of my mirth;
   But oh! each visitation[4]
Suspends what nature gave me at my birth,   90
   My shaping spirit of Imagination.
For not to think of what I needs must feel,
   But to be still and patient, all I can;
And haply by abstruse research to steal
   From my own nature all the natural man—   95
   This was my sole resource, my only plan:
Till that which suits a part infects the whole,
And now is almost grown the habit of my soul.

VI

Hence, viper thoughts, that coil around my mind,
   Reality's dark dream!   100
I turn from you, and listen to the wind,
   Which long has raved unnoticed. What a scream
Of agony by torture lengthened out
That lute sent forth! Thou Wind that rav'st without,
   Bare crag, or mountain-tairn,[5] or blasted tree,   105
Or pine-grove whither woodman never clomb,
Or lonely house, long held the witches' home,
   Methinks were fitter instruments for thee,
Mad Lutanist![6] who in this month of showers,
Of dark-brown gardens, and of peeping flowers,   110
Mak'st Devils' yule[7] with worse than wintry song,
The blossoms, buds, and timorous leaves among.
   Thou Actor, perfect in all tragic sounds!

---

3. Coleridge made much of the distinction between "fancy" and the "imagination" (line 86). Fancy makes pleasant combinations of images (cf. lines 78–79); the Imagination is a higher faculty of the mind that combines images in such a way that they create a higher reality, a poetic "truth" more valid than that which is perceived by the ordinary senses.   4. Of the misfortunes and afflictions in line 82.   5. Tarn or small mountain lake.   6. The storm wind in line 104. 7. Originally, yule was a heathen feast.

Thou mighty Poet, e'en to frenzy bold!
    What tell'st thou now about?   115
       'Tis of the rushing of an host in rout,
  With groans, of trampled men, with smarting wounds—
At once they groan with pain, and shudder with the cold!
But hush! there is a pause of deepest silence!
    And all that noise, as of a rushing crowd,   120
With groans, and tremulous shudderings—all is over—
It tells another tale,[8] with sounds less deep and loud!
    A tale of less affright,
    And tempered with delight,
As Otway's self[9] had framed the tender lay,—   125
    'Tis of a little child
    Upon a lonesome wild,
Not far from home, but she hath lost her way:
And now moans low in bitter grief and fear,
And now screams loud, and hopes to make her mother hear. 130

VIII

'Tis midnight, but small thoughts have I of sleep.
Full seldom may my friend such vigils keep!
Visit her, gentle Sleep! with wings of healing,
    And may this storm be but a mountain birth,
May all the stars hang bright above her dwelling,   135
    Silent as though they watched the sleeping Earth!
      With light heart may she rise,
      Gay fancy, cheerful eyes,
    Joy lift her spirit, joy attune her voice;
To her may all things live, from pole to pole   140
Their life the eddying of her living soul!
    O simple spirit, guided from above,
Dear Lady! friend devoutest of my choice,
Thus mayest thou ever, evermore rejoice.

PERCY BYSSHE SHELLEY
1792–1822

A longing for alternatives to things as they are dominates much of Shelley's poetry. Whether he writes of his own dejection, of the energizing force of the west wind, or of the political situation of England, he writes often from conviction that matters could and should be better.

8. The story of Wordsworth's *Lucy Gray.*   9. Originally "William" (Wordsworth). Thomas Otway (1652–1685) was a tragic dramatist.

Son of a country squire in Sussex, Shelley led a privileged early life, attending Eton and Oxford. He was, however, expelled from Oxford after a single year, for writing a work called *The Necessity of Atheism:* already he had begun to defy convention. He dramatized his defiance yet more forcefully in 1814, when, after three years of marriage with Harriet Westbrook, and two children, he eloped with Mary Wollstonecraft Godwin, daughter of two advanced social thinkers. Harriet committed suicide; the lovers married and had several children. Shelley was on friendly terms with other important Romantic writers; in Italy, where he moved in 1818, he associated closely with Byron. He was drowned while sailing off the Italian coast.

Productive as a poet, Shelley mastered tones ranging from the satiric to the prophetic. His most important works include *Prometheus Unbound* (1820), a philosophic-visionary-revolutionary expansion of a classical theme; *Epipsychidon* (1821), a defense of free love; and the elegy *Adonais* (1821), for the death of Keats. He also wrote a verse play having to do with the incest of a father and daughter, *The Cenci* (1819).

At the end of his essay, "A Defence of Poetry," posthumously published in 1840, Shelley insists on poetry's necessary connection with the future. Poets, he says, are "the mirrors of the gigantic shadows which futurity casts upon the present . . . : the influence which is moved not but moves. Poets are the unacknowledged legislators of the World." His own lyrics corroborate such grandiose claims by insistently establishing images of the possible. The sonnet, "England in 1819," for example, after twelve lines of nouns and noun clauses about the political and social horrors of the current English situation, concludes that all these phenomena "Are graves from which a glorious phantom may / Burst, to illumine our tempestuous day." The possibility—never the certainty—of good coming from evil always exists.

Like Coleridge, Shelley writes about his own dejection, interspersing penetrating images of natural beauty with detailed presentation of his painful psychic state. In the poem called "Stanzas Written in Dejection," the speaker dreams of death as a kind of mild fulfillment, a reabsorption into nature. The ending of the poem, however, has less dismal implications. Finally the speaker compares himself with the dying day as a presence in memory. Men do not love him, but would regret his passing; the day, which he has enjoyed, will linger "like joy in Memory." The comparison, which at first appears to sustain the mood of self-pity, also transcends that self-perpetuating emotion: it reminds the speaker of the capacity for enjoyment that he retains even in his bleakest mood. While he fancies his own easeful death, he still takes pleasure in the scene around him; that pleasure remains a lasting element in memory.

The "Ode to the West Wind" makes a particularly emphatic statement of the good-from-evil theme. Images of violence and sinister power ("Thou, from whose unseen presence the leaves dead / Are driven, like ghosts from an enchanter fleeing") dominate the early part of the poem. The third section creates an atmosphere of luxurious beauty, but ends with the depths of the sea growing suddenly "grey with fear" at the wind's advent. In the final section, however, the speaker places himself in relation with the natural force he has described, begging to be lifted, to "share / The impulse of thy strength." Finally, in imagination, the poet becomes the "lyre" (in effect, the Aeolian harp) of the wind, now revealed as a force of inspiration and change which enables him to function as "The trumpet of a prophecy!" The "Defence of Poetry" describes poets as "the trumpets which sing to battle"; in "To the West Wind," Shelley suggests that they acquire such inspirational capacity by imaginative union with nature, and particularly, as in the west wind blowing away the remnants of the past year, with the forces of regeneration and reform.

E. Blunden, *Shelley: A Life Story* (1946), provides a useful biography. For criticism, see C. Baker, *Shelley's Major Poetry: The Fabric of a Vision* (1948), E. Wasserman, *Shelley* (1971), and R. L. Holmes, *Shelley: The Pursuit* (1974).

Stanzas Written in Dejection— December 1818, Near Naples

The Sun is warm, the sky is clear,
The waves are dancing fast and bright,
Blue isles and snowy mountains wear
The purple noon's transparent might,
The breath of the moist earth is light   5
Around its unexpanded buds;
Like many a voice of one delight
The winds, the birds, the Ocean-floods;
The City's voice itself is soft, like Solitude's.

I see the Deep's untrampled floor   10
With green and purple seaweeds strown;
I see the waves upon the shore
Like light dissolved in star-showers, thrown;
I sit upon the sands alone;
The lightning of the noontide Ocean   15
Is flashing round me, and a tone
Arises from its measured motion,
How sweet! did any heart now share in my emotion.

Alas, I have nor hope nor health
Nor peace within nor calm around,   20
Nor that content surpassing wealth
The sage in meditation found,
And walked with inward glory crowned;
Nor fame nor power nor love nor leisure—
Others I see whom these surround,   25
Smiling they live and call life pleasure:
To me that cup has been dealt in another measure.

Yet now despair itself is mild,
Even as the winds and waters are;

I could lie down like a tired child   30
And weep away the life of care
Which I have borne and yet must bear
Till Death like Sleep might steal on me,
And I might feel in the warm air
My cheek grow cold, and hear the Sea   35
Breathe o'er my dying brain its last monotony.

Some might lament that I were cold,
As I, when this sweet day is gone,
Which my lost heart, too soon grown old,
Insults with this untimely moan—   40
They might lament,—for I am one
Whom men love not, and yet regret;
Unlike this day, which, when the Sun
Shall on its stainless glory set,
Will linger though enjoyed, like joy in Memory yet.   45

England in 1819

An old, mad, blind, despised, and dying King;[1]
Princes, the dregs of their dull race, who flow
Through public scorn,—mud from a muddy spring;
Rulers who neither see nor feel nor know,
But leechlike to their fainting country cling   5
Till they drop, blind in blood, without a blow.
A people starved and stabbed in th'untilled field;
An army, whom liberticide and prey
Makes as a two-edged sword to all who wield;
Golden[2] and sanguine laws which tempt and slay;   10
Religion Christless, Godless—a book sealed;
A senate, Time's worst statute,[3] unrepealed—
Are graves from which a glorious Phantom may
Burst, to illumine our tempestuous day.

Ode to the West Wind

I

O wild West Wind, thou breath of Autumn's being,
Thou, from whose unseen presence the leaves dead
Are driven, like ghosts from an enchanter fleeing,

1. George III (1738–1820). *Princes:* His sons, including the Prince-Regent, whose dissolute behavior gave rise to public scandals.   2. I.e., bought; the laws favor the rich and powerful. *Sanguine:* Bloody, causing bloodshed.   3. The law by which Roman Catholics and dissenters from the state religion (Anglicanism) were curtailed in their civil liberties.

Yellow, and black, and pale, and hectic red,
Pestilence-stricken multitudes: O Thou,   5
Who chariotest to their dark wintry bed

The winged seeds, where they lie cold and low,
Each like a corpse within its grave, until
Thine azure sister of the Spring shall blow

Her clarion o'er the dreaming earth, and fill   10
(Driving sweet buds like flocks to feed in air)
With living hues and odors plain and hill:

Wild Spirit, which are moving everywhere;
Destroyer and Preserver; hear, O hear!

II

Thou on whose stream, 'mid the steep sky's commotion,   15
Loose clouds like Earth's decaying leaves are shed,
Shook from the tangled boughs of Heaven and Ocean,

Angels of rain and lightning; there are spread
On the blue surface of thine aery surge,
Like the bright hair uplifted from the head   20

Of some fierce Mænad,[4] even from the dim verge
Of the horizon to the zenith's height,
The locks of the approaching storm. Thou Dirge

Of the dying year, to which this closing night
Will be the dome of a vast sepulchre,   25
Vaulted with all thy congregated might

Of vapors, from whose solid atmosphere
Black rain and fire and hail will burst: O hear!

III

Thou who didst waken from his summer dreams
The blue Mediterranean, where he lay,   30
Lulled by the coil of his crystalline streams,

Beside a pumice isle in Baiæ's bay,[5]
And saw in sleep old palaces and towers
Quivering within the wave's intenser day,

All overgrown with azure moss and flowers   35
So sweet, the sense faints picturing them! Thou
For whose path the Atlantic's level powers

4. Ecstatic female worshiper of Bacchus, god of wine.   **5.** West of Naples; the Roman emperors
built villas there.

Cleave themselves into chasms, while far below
The sea-blooms and the oozy woods which wear
The sapless foliage of the ocean, know   40

Thy voice, and suddenly grow grey with fear,
And tremble and despoil themselves: O hear!

IV

If I were a dead leaf thou mightest bear;
If I were a swift cloud to fly with thee;
A wave to pant beneath thy power, and share   45

The impulse of thy strength, only less free
Than thou, O Uncontrollable! If even
I were as in my boyhood, and could be

The comrade of thy wanderings over Heaven,
As then, when to outstrip thy skiey speed   50
Scarce seemed a vision; I would ne'er have striven

As thus with thee in prayer in my sore need.
Oh! lift me as a wave, a leaf, a cloud!
I fall upon the thorns of life! I bleed!

A heavy weight of hours has chained and bowed   55
One too like thee: tameless, and swift, and proud.

V

Make my thy lyre,[6] even as the forest is:
What if my leaves are falling like its own!
The tumult of thy mighty harmonies

Will take from both a deep, autumnal tone,   60
Sweet though in sadness. Be thou, Spirit fierce,
My spirit! Be thou me, impetuous one!

Drive my dead thoughts over the universe
Like withered leaves to quicken a new birth!
And, by the incantation of this verse,   65

Scatter, as from an unextinguished hearth
Ashes and sparks, my words among mankind!
Be through my lips to unawakened Earth

The trumpet of a prophecy! O Wind,
If Winter comes, can Spring be far behind?   70

---

6. Ancient harp. The allusion is also to the Aeolian harp, an instrument played upon by the wind, and a frequent image for the poet played upon by inspiration.

A Defence of Poetry[7]

. . . Poetry is the record of the best and happiest moments of the happiest and best minds. We are aware of evanescent visitations of thought and feeling sometimes associated with place or person, sometimes regarding our own mind alone, and always arising unforeseen and departing unbidden, but elevating and delightful beyond all expression: so that even in the desire and the regret they leave, there cannot but be pleasure, participating as it does in the nature of its object. It is as it were the interpenetration of a diviner nature through our own; but its footsteps are like those of a wind over a sea, which the coming calm erases, and whose traces remain only as on the wrinkled sand which paves it. These and corresponding conditions of being are experienced principally by those of the most delicate sensibility and the most enlarged imagination; and the state of mind produced by them is at war with every base desire. The enthusiasm of virtue, love, patriotism, and friendship is essentially linked with these emotions, and whilst they last, self appears as what it is, an atom to a Universe. Poets are not only subject to these experiences as spirits of the most refined organization, but they can color all that they combine with the evanescent hues of this ethereal world; a word, a trait in the representation of a scene or a passion, will touch the enchanted chord, and reanimate, in those who have ever experienced these emotions, the sleeping, the cold, the buried image of the past. Poetry thus makes immortal all that is best and most beautiful in the world; it arrests the vanishing apparitions which haunt the interlunations[8] of life, and veiling them or[9] in language or in form sends them forth among mankind, bearing sweet news of kindred joy to those with whom their sisters abide—abide, because there is no portal of expression from the caverns of the spirit which they inhabit into the universe of things. Poetry redeems from decay the visitations of the divinity in man.* * *

The first part of these remarks has related to Poetry in its elements and principles; and it has been shown, as well as the narrow limits assigned them would permit, that what is called poetry, in a restricted sense, has a common source with all other forms of order and of beauty according to which the materials of human life are susceptible of being arranged, and which is poetry in an universal sense.

The second part[1] will have for its object an application of these principles to the present state of the cultivation of Poetry, and a defence of the attempt to idealize the modern forms of manners and opinion, and compel them into a subordination to the imaginative and creative faculty. For the literature of England, an energetic

7. Our selection is the conclusion of the essay.   8. Dark periods between the old and new moon.   9. Either.   1. The second part was never written.

development of which has ever preceded or accompanied a great and free development of the national will, has arisen as it were from a new birth. In spite of the low-thoughted envy which would undervalue contemporary merit, our own will be a memorable age in intellectual achievements, and we live among such philosophers and poets as surpass beyond comparison any who have appeared since the last national struggle for civil and religious liberty.[2] The most unfailing herald, companion, and follower of the awakening of a great people to work a beneficial change in opinion or institution, is Poetry. At such periods there is an accumulation of the power of communicating and receiving intense and impassioned conceptions respecting man and nature. The persons in whom this power resides, may often, as far as regards many portions of their nature, have little apparent correspondence with that spirit of good of which they are the ministers. But even whilst they deny and abjure, they are yet compelled to serve, the Power which is seated upon the throne of their own soul. It is impossible to read the compositions of the most celebrated writers of the present day without being startled with the electric life which burns within their words. They measure the circumference and sound the depths of human nature with a comprehensive and all-penetrating spirit, and they are themselves perhaps the most sincerely astonished at its manifestations, for it is less their spirit than the spirit of the age. Poets are the hierophants[3] of an unapprehended inspiration, the mirrors of the gigantic shadows which futurity casts upon the present, the words which express what they understand not; the trumpets which sing to battle, and feel not what they inspire: the influence which is moved not, but moves. Poets are the unacknowledged legislators of the World.

JOHN KEATS
1795–1821

A poet "half in love with easeful Death," to quote a line from his "Ode to a Nightingale," John Keats expressed with compelling intensity the Romantic longing for the unattainable, a concept which he defined in ways very different from Goethe's. In a series of brilliant lyrics, he explored subtle links between the passion for absolute beauty, which provides an imagined alternative to the everyday world's sordidness and disappointment, and the desire to melt into extinction, another form of that alternative.

At the age of sixteen, Keats was apprenticed to a druggist and surgeon; in 1816, he was licensed as an apothecary. Son of a hostler (a groom for horses)

2. The English Civil War; the great poet of that age was Milton.   3. Interpreters, as priests who interpret sacred mysteries.

at a London inn, he had earlier attended school at Enfield, where he manifested an interest in literature encouraged by his friend Charles Cowden
Clarke, the headmaster's son. Through Leigh Hunt, whose literary circle he
joined in 1816, Keats came to know Shelley, William Hazlitt, and Charles
Lamb, important members of the Romantic movement. He had a brief love
affair with Fanny Brawne, to whom he became engaged in 1819; the next
year he went to Italy, seeking a cure for his tuberculosis, only to die in
Rome.

Although his first book, *Poems* (1817), met with some critical success, the
long mythological poem *Endymion* which he published a year later became
an object of attack by Tory literary reviews (*Blackwood's* and the *Quarterly*).
Shelley, in his elegy for Keats (*Adonais*, 1821), encouraged the myth that
the harsh reviews caused the poet's death. In fact, Keats lived long enough
to publish another important volume, *Lamia, Isabella, The Eve of St. Agnes,
and Other Poems* (1820), which won critical applause and contained most
of the poems for which he is remembered today.

Some of Keats's greatest works return to a form popular in the eighteenth
century: the ode addressed to an abstraction (e.g., melancholy) or another
nonhuman object (nightingale, urn, autumn). Although the basic literary
device seems highly artificial, Keats uses it powerfully to express his characteristic sense of beauty so intensely experienced that it almost corresponds
to pain.

> My heart aches, and a drowsy numbness pains
> My sense, as though of hemlock I had drunk . . . .
> 'Tis not through envy of thy happy lot,
> But being too happy in thy happiness. . . .

The "Ode on Melancholy," in its sharp contrast to Coleridge's and Shelley's
poems on dejection, as well as to seventeenth- and eighteenth-century evocations of melancholy, illustrates particularly well Keats's special exemplifi-
cation of the Romantic sensibility. In the first stanza, the speaker explicitly
rejects traditional concomitants of melancholy—yew, the death-moth, the
owl—because such associations suggest a kind of passivity or inertia that
might "drown the wakeful anguish of the soul," interfering with the immediate and intense experience of melancholy which he actively seeks. Instead,
he advocates trying to live as completely as possible in the immediacy of
emotion. Melancholy, he continues, dwells with beauty and joy and pleasure, all in their nature evanescent. To feel to the full the wonder of beauty
or happiness implies awareness that it will soon vanish. Only those capable
of active participation in their own positive emotions can hope to know
melancholy; paradoxically, the result of energetic commitment to the life of
feeling is the utter submission to melancholy's power: one can hope to "be
among her cloudy trophies hung."

Prose summary of such an argument risks sounding ridiculous or incomprehensible, for Keats's emotional logic inheres in the imagery and the music
of his poems, which exert their own compelling force. Without any previous
belief in the desirability of melancholy as an emotion, the reader, absorbed
into a rich sequence of images, feels swept into an experience comparable

to that which the poem endorses. The ode generates its own sense of beauty and of melancholy and of the close relation between the two. Its brilliantly evocative specificity of physical reference always suggests more than is directly said, more than paraphrase can encompass:

> Aye, in the very temple of Delight
> Veiled Melancholy has her sov'reign shrine,
>   Though seen of none save him whose strenuous tongue
>   Can burst Joy's grape against his palate fine.

Everyone can recall the sensuous pleasure of a grape releasing its juice into the mouth, but it would be difficult to elucidate the full implications of the "strenuous tongue" or of "Joy's grape." Keat's great poetic gift manifests itself most unmistakably in his extraordinary power of suggestion—not only in the odes, but in the ballad-imitation, "La Belle Dame Sans Merci," with its haunting, half-told story, and in the understated sonnets, asserting the speaker's feeling, but always hinting more emotion than they directly affirm.

A first-rate critical biography is A. Ward, *John Keats: The Making of a Poet* (1963). Also useful are W. J. Bate, *John Keats* (1963), and C. Ricks, *Keats and Embarrassment* (1974).

On First Looking into Chapman's Homer[1]

Much have I traveled in the realms of gold,
    And many goodly states and kingdoms seen;
    Round many western islands have I been
Which bards in fealty to Apollo[2] hold.
Oft of one wide expanse had I been told   5
    That deep-browed Homer ruled as his demesne;[3]
    Yet did I never breathe its pure serene
Till I heard Chapman speak out loud and bold:
Then felt I like some watcher of the skies
    When a new planet swims into his ken;   10
Or like stout Cortez[4] when with eagle eyes
    He stared at the Pacific—and all his men
Looked at each other with a wild surmise—
    Silent, upon a peak in Darien.

Bright Star

Bright star, would I were steadfast as thou art—
    Not in lone splendor hung aloft the night

---

1. Keats's friend and former teacher Charles Cowden Clarke had introduced Keats to George Chapman's translations of the *Iliad* (1611) and the *Odyssey* (1616) the night before this poem was written.   2. God of poetic inspiration.   3. Realm, kingdom.   4. In fact, Balboa, not Cortez, was the European explorer who first saw the Pacific from Darien, Panama.

And watching, with eternal lids apart,
  Like nature's patient, sleepless Eremite,[5]
The moving waters at their priestlike task   5
  Of pure ablution round earth's human shores,
Or gazing on the new soft fallen mask
  Of snow upon the mountains and the moors—
No—yet still steadfast, still unchangeable,
  Pillowed upon my fair love's ripening breast,   10
To feel forever its soft fall and swell,
  Awake forever in a sweet unrest,
Still, still to hear her tender-taken breath,
And so live ever—or else swoon to death.

La Belle Dame Sans Merci[6]

O what can ail thee, knight at arms,
  Alone and palely loitering?
The sedge has withered from the lake
  And no birds sing!

O what can ail thee, knight at arms,   5
  So haggard, and so woebegone?
The squirrel's granary is full
  And the harvest's done.

I see a lily on thy brow
  With anguish moist and fever dew,   10
And on thy cheeks a fading rose
  Fast withereth too.

I met a lady in the meads,[7]
  Full beautiful, a faery's child,
Her hair was long, her foot was light   15
  And her eyes were wild.

I made a garland for her head,
  And bracelets too, and fragrant zone;[8]
She looked at me as she did love
  And made sweet moan.   20

I set her on my pacing steed
  And nothing else saw all day long,
For sidelong would she bend and sing
  A faery's song.

5. Hermit.   6. The title is from a medieval poem by Alain Chartier: "The Beautiful Lady without Pity."   7. Meadows.   8. Girdle.

She found me roots of relish sweet,   25
   And honey wild, and manna[9] dew,
And sure in language strange she said
   "I love thee true."

She took me to her elfin grot
   And there she wept and sighed full sore,[1]   30
And there I shut her wild wild eyes
   With kisses four.

And there she lulléd me asleep,
   And there I dreamed, ah woe betide!
The latest[2] dream I ever dreamt   35
   On the cold hill side.

I saw pale kings, and princes too,
   Pale warriors, death-pale were they all;
They cried, "La belle dame sans merci
   Thee hath in thrall!"[3]   40

I saw their starved lips in the gloam[4]
   With horrid warning gapéd wide,
And I awoke, and found me here
   On the cold hill's side.

And this is why I sojourn here,   45
   Alone and palely loitering;
Though the sedge withered from the lake
   And no birds sing.

Ode on a Grecian Urn

I

Thou still unravished bride of quietness,
   Thou foster-child of silence and slow time,
Sylvan historian, who canst thus express
   A flowery tale more sweetly than our rhyme:
What leaf-fringed legend haunts about thy shape   5
   Of deities or of mortals, or of both,

     In Tempe or the dales of Arcady?[5]
   What men or gods are these? What maidens loth?

9. The supernatural substance with which God fed the Hebrews in the Wilderness. Cf. *Exodus* 16, *Numbers* 11:7–8, and Joshua 5:12.   1. With great grief. *Grot:* Cavern.   2. Last. 3. Bondage.   4. Twilight.   5. *Tempe:* A valley in Thessaly between Mount Olympus and Mount Ossa. A mountainous region in the Peloponnese, traditionally regarded as the place of ideal rustic, bucolic contentment.

What mad pursuit? What struggle to escape?
    What pipes and timbrels? What wild ecstasy?   10

II

Heard melodies are sweet, but those unheard
    Are sweeter; therefore, ye soft pipes, play on;
Not to the sensual ear, but, more endeared,
    Pipe to the spirit ditties of no tone:
Fair youth, beneath the trees, thou canst not leave   15
    Thy song, nor ever can those trees be bare;
      Bold lover, never, never canst thou kiss,
Though winning near the goal—yet, do not grieve;
      She cannot fade, though thou hast not thy bliss,
    For ever wilt thou love, and she be fair!   20

III

Ah, happy, happy boughs! that cannot shed
    Your leaves, nor ever bid the Spring adieu;
And, happy melodist, unwearièd,
    For ever piping songs for ever new;
More happy love! more happy, happy love!   25
    For ever warm and still to be enjoyed,
      For ever panting, and for every young;
All breathing human passion far above,
    That leaves a heart high-sorrowful and cloyed,
      A burning forehead, and a parching tongue.   30

IV

Who are these coming to the sacrifice?
    To what green altar, O mysterious priest,
Lead'st thou that heifer lowing at the skies,
    And all her silken flanks with garlands drest?
What little town by river or sea shore,   35
    Or mountain-built with peaceful citadel,
      Is emptied of this folk, this pious morn?
And, little town, thy streets for evermore
    Will silent be; and not a soul to tell
      Why thou art desolate, can e'er return.   40

V

O Attic shape! Fair attitude! with brede[6]
    Of marble men and maidens overwrought,
With forest branches and the trodden weed;

---

6. Pattern. *Attic:* Classical (literally, Athenian).

Thou, silent form, dost tease us out of thought
As doth eternity: Cold Pastoral!   45
    When old age shall this generation waste,
        Thou shalt remain, in midst of other woe
Than ours, a friend to man, to whom thou say'st,
    "Beauty is truth, truth beauty,"—that is all
        Ye know on earth, and all ye need to know.   50

Ode to a Nightingale

I

My heart aches, and a drowsy numbness pains
    My sense, as though of hemlock I had drunk,
Or emptied some dull opiate to the drains
    One minute past, and Lethe-wards[7] had sunk:
'Tis not through envy of thy happy lot,   5
    But being too happy in thy happiness,
        That thou, light-winged Dryad[8] of the trees,
            In some melodious plot
    Of beechen green, and shadows numberless,
        Singest of summer in full-throated ease.   10

II

O for a draught of vintage! that hath been
    Cooled a long age in the deep-delved earth,
Tasting of Flora[9] and the country green,
    Dance, and Provencal[1] song, and sunburnt mirth!
O for a beaker full of the warm South!   15
    Full of the true, the blushful Hippocrene,[2]
        With beaded bubbles winking at the brim,
            And purple-stained mouth;
    That I might drink, and leave the world unseen,
        And with thee fade away into the forest dim: 20

III

Fade far away, dissolve, and quite forget
    What thou among the leaves hast never known,
The weariness, the fever, and the fret
    Here, where men sit and hear each other groan;
Where palsy shakes a few, sad, last grey hairs,   25

---

7. I.e., toward Lethe, the river of forgetfulness in Greek mythology.   8. Wood nymph.
9. Flowers. Flora was the goddess of flowers and spring.   1. Provence was the district in France
associated with the troubadours.   2. The fountain on Mount Helicon, in Greece, sacred to the
Muse of poetry.

Where youth grows pale, and spectre-thin, and dies;
  Where but to think is to be full of sorrow
      And leaden-eyed despairs;
  Where beauty cannot keep her lustrous eyes,
    Or new love pine at them beyond tomorrow.   30

IV

Away! away! for I will fly to thee,
  Not charioted by Bacchus and his pards,[3]
But on the viewless wings of Poesy,
  Though the dull brain perplexes and retards:
Already with thee! tender is the night,   35
  And haply the Queen-Moon is on her throne,
    Clustered around by all her starry Fays;[4]
      But here there is no light,
  Save what from heaven is with the breezes blown
    Through verdurous glooms and winding mossy ways.   40

V

I cannot see what flowers are at my feet,
  Nor what soft incense hangs upon the boughs,
But, in embalmèd darkness, guess each sweet
  Wherewith the seasonable month endows
The grass, the thicket, and the fruit-tree wild;   45
  White hawthorn, and the pastoral eglantine;
    Fast-fading violets covered up in leaves;
      And mid-May's eldest child,
  The coming musk-rose, full of dewy wine,
    The murmurous haunt of flies on summer eves.   50

VI

Darkling[5] I listen; and for many a time
  I have been half in love with easeful Death,
Called him soft names in many a mused rhyme,
  To take into the air my quiet breath;
Now more than ever seems it rich to die,   55
  To cease upon the midnight with no pain,
    While thou art pouring forth thy soul abroad
      In such an ecstasy!
  Still wouldst thou sing, and I have ears in vain—
    To thy high requiem become a sod.[6]   60

---

3. Leopards. *Bacchus* (Dionysus) was traditionally supposed to be accompanied by leopards, lions, goats, and so on. 4. Fairies. *Haply:* Perhaps. 5. In the dark. 6. I.e., like dirt, unable to hear.

VII

Thou wast not born for death, immortal Bird!
  No hungry generations tread thee down;
The voice I hear this passing night was heard
  In ancient days by emperor and clown:
Perhaps the self-same song that found a path   65
    Through the sad heart of Ruth, when, sick for home,
      She stood in tears amid the alien corn;[7]
        The same that ofttimes hath
  Charmed magic casements, opening on the foam
    Of perilous seas, in faery lands forlorn.   70

VIII

Forlorn! the very word is like a bell
  To toll me back from thee to my sole self!
Adieu! the fancy cannot cheat so well
  As she is famed to do, deceiving elf.
Adieu! adieu! thy plaintive anthem fades   75
    Past the near meadows, over the still stream,
      Up the hill-side; and now 'tis buried deep
        In the next valley-glades:
  Was it a vision, or a waking dream?
    Fled is that music:—do I wake or sleep?   80

Ode on Melancholy

1

No, no, go not to Lethe,[8] neither twist
  Wolfsbane, tight-rooted, for its poisonous wine;
Nor suffer thy pale forehead to be kissed
  By nightshade, ruby grape of Proserpine;[9]
Make not your rosary of yew-berries,   5
    Nor let the beetle, nor the death-moth be
      Your mournful Psyche,[1] nor the downy owl
A partner in your sorrow's mysteries;
    For shade to shade will come too drowsily,
      And drown the wakeful anguish of the soul.   10

7. See Ruth 1:16. After her Israelite husband died, she returned to his native land with her mother-in-law.   8. The river of forgetfulness in Hades.   9. Wife of Pluto, queen of the Underworld. Wolfsbane, nightshade, and yew-berries are all poisonous.   1. The soul, portrayed by the Greeks as a butterfly. The death's-head moth has markings that resemble a skull; the beetle, from whose shape comes the scarab found in Egyptian tombs, was an emblem of death.

2

But when the melancholy fit shall fall
　　Sudden from heaven like a weeping cloud,
That fosters the droop-headed flowers all,
　　And hides the green hill in an April shroud;
Then glut thy sorrow on a morning rose,   15
　　Or on the rainbow of the salt sand-wave,
　　　Or on the wealth of globèd peonies;
Or if thy mistress some rich anger shows,
　　Imprison her soft hand, and let her rave,
　　　And feed deep, deep upon her peerless eyes.   20

3

She[2] dwells with Beauty—Beauty that must die;
　　And Joy, whose hand is ever at his lips
Bidding adieu; and aching Pleasure nigh,
　　Turning to Poison while the bee-mouth sips:
Aye, in the very temple of Delight   25
　　Veiled Melancholy has her sov'reign shrine,
　　　Though seen of none save him whose strenuous tongue
　　Can burst Joy's grape against his palate fine;
His soul shall taste the sadness of her might,
　　And be among her cloudy trophies hung.[3]   30

To Autumn

I

Season of mists and mellow fruitfulness,
　　Close bosom-friend of the maturing sun;
Conspiring with him how to load and bless
　　With fruit the vines that round the thatch-eves run;
To bend with apples the mossed cottage-trees,   5
　　And fill all fruit with ripeness to the core;
　　　To swell the gourd, and plump the hazel shells
With a sweet kernel; to set budding more,
　　And still more, later flowers for the bees,
　　Until they think warm days will never cease,   10
　　　For Summer has o'er-brimmed their clammy cells.

2. Melancholy.   3. The Greeks placed war trophies in their temples to commemorate victories.

II

Who hath not seen thee oft amid thy store?
   Sometimes whoever seeks abroad may find
Thee sitting careless on a granary floor,
   Thy hair soft-lifted by the winnowing wind;   15
Or on a half-reaped furrow sound asleep,
   Drowsed with the fume of poppies, while thy hook
      Spares the next swath and all its twinèd flowers:
And sometimes like a gleaner thou dost keep
   Steady thy laden head across a brook;   20
   Or by a cyder-press, with patient look,
      Thou watchest the last oozings hours by hours.

III

Where are the songs of Spring? Ay, where are they?
   Think not of them, thou hast thy music too,—
While barrèd clouds bloom the soft-dying day,   25
   And touch the stubble-plains with rosy hue;
Then in a wailful choir the small gnats mourn
   Among the river sallows,[4] borne aloft
      Or sinking as the light wind lives or dies;
And full-grown lambs loud bleat from hilly bourn;   30
   Hedge-crickets sing; and now with treble soft
   The red-breast whistles from a garden-croft;
      And gathering swallows twitter in the skies.

ALFRED, LORD TENNYSON
1809–1892

Tennyson's poetry expresses a conflict characteristic of his historical period but also of much human experience in all periods: between the tendency to despair and the desire to hope. Hope locates itself, for Tennyson, in the human capacity to struggle toward future goals, as well as, on occasion, in religious faith. Mortality causes despair: the death of others, the inevitable sense of increasing weakness as one ages, the scientific discovery that whole species have disappeared in the world's history. Tennyson's ability to remind us of both contradictory emotions, and of the degree to which they inevitably coexist and alternate, makes his poetry compelling.

   The poet's pervasive melancholy came partly from experience. Son of an Anglican clergyman, he spent four unhappy years in school before his father

4. Willows.

consented to allow him to be tutored at home. He attended Trinity College, Cambridge, where, with his friend Arthur Hallam, he belonged to an undergraduate society called "The Apostles," whose members discussed contemporary social, religious, scientific, and literary issues. The friendship with Hallam retained its intensity after his undergraduate years; by 1830, Hallam had become engaged to Tennyson's sister. Three years later, however, at the age of twenty-two, Hallam died suddenly in Vienna. The loss acutely affected Tennyson, who during the next seventeen years gradually composed the long elegiac poem *In Memoriam* to record the profound emotional and intellectual effects on him of his friend's death.

In 1836, Tennyson became engaged to Emily Sellwood, but, largely because of financial difficulties, he did not marry her until 1850, the year in which, after the publication of *In Memoriam*, he was made poet laureate. Five years earlier, he received a pension. He lived quietly for the rest of his life, increasingly famous; in 1884, he was created the first Baron Tennyson.

Tennyson's earliest independent collections of poems (1830 and 1833)— he had published a collaborative volume with his brother in 1827—were the target of fierce critical attack, another cause for melancholy. He published nothing more until 1842, when a collection called simply *Poems* met great critical success. Subsequently revered as a kind of national spokesman, Tennyson won popularity particularly with *The Princess* (1847, revised 1855), *Maud* (1855), and *The Idylls of the King* (1859, 1885), a retelling of the legends of King Arthur.

In "Ulysses" (1842), Tennyson, imagining the situation of the Greek hero after his return to domestic peace, evokes the excitement and moral grandeur of the human capacity for aspiration.

> that which we are, we are;
> One equal temper of heroic hearts,
> Made weak by time and fate, but strong in will
> To strive, to seek, to find, and not to yield.

In another meditation on classic themes, however, "Tithonus" (pub. 1860, first written in 1833), he puts the other side of the case. "The woods decay, the woods decay and fall," the poem begins; its imagined speaker, a man who has been granted immortality at his own request, wishes to return the gift. "Why should a man desire in any way / To vary from the kindly race of men . . . ?" Ulysses insists on the specialness of his sort of man; Tithonus knows the burden of specialness. In conjunction, the two poems call attention to the fact that neither the Enlightenment nor the early Romantic view of experience seems entirely adequate to this poet. Tithonus's desire to share the common fate of humankind throbs with melancholy; he feels that fate as doom, although he equally experiences his exemption from it as doom. Ulysses' condescension to his prudent son ("Most blameless is he. . . . / He works his work, I mine") underlines the sense of desperation in his insistent striving. No alternative form of action or commitment satisfies the imagination.

In *In Memoriam* (1850), his most ambitious work, Tennyson suggests reasons for his inability to imagine fulfillment. The problem is not merely temperament, but the impact on his consciousness of intellectual and social actuality as well as the loss and the possibility of loss made palpable to him by Hallam's death.

> Are God and Nature then at strife,
>   That Nature lends such evil dreams?
>   So careful of the type she seems,
> So careless of the single life.

That stanza comes from number 55 of the 125 linked poems that make up the whole. The next in the series begins,

> "So careful of the type?" but no, . . .
>   She [Nature] cries, "A thousand types are gone;
> I care for nothing, all shall go."

Reality offers not the slightest assurance of survival; contemporary scientists, studying fossils, had revealed the extinction of entire species. "Man, [Nature's] last work, who seemed so fair, / Such splendid purpose in his eyes"—with a Ulysses' capacity for fine imaginings—even man, humankind in general, may face extinction—a possibility that in the 1980s looks ever more compelling. The poem concludes with the faintest possible religious hope:

> O life as futile, then, as frail!
>   O for thy voice to soothe and bless!
>   What hope of answer, or redress?
> Behind the veil, behind the veil.

By the end of the entire sequence, the poet has arrived at a more affirmative vision; he claims to have discovered God through his own pain and through the processes of feeling, which he asserts as more revelatory than those of logic. Indeed, *In Memoriam* persuasively evokes the slow reconciliation of mourning, giving its readers vicarious experience of the despair, the false starts, the inconsistencies of grief. The poem's power, however, derives not only from its record of personal emotional experience but from its demonstration, its embodiment, of how the intellectual and the emotional intertwine. The private loss of a friend assimilates itself to a more general loss of faith and certainty characteristic of the Victorian period. The determination to strive, to seek, to find, and not to yield generated scientific discovery, industrial and mercantile development. As early as 1850, though, such achievements threatened established orders: traditional social and theological arrangements. Tennyson re-creates for us what such threats felt like to those actually experiencing them. He writes an elegy not only for Arthur Hallam but for the larger losses of his moment in history.

For useful biography, see H. Nicholson, *Tennyson* (1923, 1925). Important criticism includes J. Buckley, *Tennyson: The Growth of a Poet* (1961), and C. Ricks, *Tennyson* (1972).

Ulysses

It little profits that an idle king,
By this still hearth, among these barren crags,
Matched with an agèd wife, I mete and dole
Unequal laws unto a savage race,
That hoard, and sleep, and feed, and know not me.   5
I cannot rest from travel. I will drink
Life to the lees. All time I have enjoyed
Greatly, have suffered greatly, both with those
That loved me, and alone; on shore, and when
Through scudding drifts the rainy Hyades[1]   10
Vext the dim sea. I am become a name;
For always roaming with a hungry heart
Much have I seen and known,—cities of men
And manners, climates, councils, governments,
Myself not least, but honored of them all,—   15
And drunk delight of battle with my peers,
Far on the ringing plains of windy Troy.
I am a part of all that I have met;
Yet all experience is an arch where-through
Gleams that untravelled world whose margin fades   20
Forever and forever when I move.
How dull it is to pause, to make an end,
To rust unburnished, not to shine in use!
As though to breathe were life! Life piled on life
Were all too little, and of one to me   25
Little remains; but every hour is saved
From that eternal silence, something more,
A bringer of new things; and vile it were
For some three suns to store and hoard myself,
And this gray spirit yearning in desire   30
To follow knowledge like a sinking star,
Beyond the utmost bound of human thought.
    This is my son, mine own Telemachus,
To whom I leave the scepter and the isle[2]—
Well-loved of me, discerning to fulfill   35
This labor, by slow prudence to make mild
A rugged people, and through soft degrees
Subdue them to the useful and the good.
Most blameless is he, centered in the sphere
Of common duties, decent not to fail   40
In offices of tenderness, and pay

1. A cluster of seven stars in the constellation of Taurus. The ancients supposed that when they rose with the sun, rainy weather would follow.   2. Ithaca.

Meet adoration to my household gods,
When I am gone. He works his work, I mine.
   There lies the port; the vessel puffs her sail;
There gloom the dark broad seas. My mariners, 45
Souls that have toiled, and wrought, and thought with me—
That ever with a frolic welcome took
The thunder and the sunshine, and opposed
Free hearts, free foreheads—you and I are old;
Old age hath yet his honor and his toil; 50
Death closes all. But something ere the end,
Some work of noble note, may yet be done,
Not unbecoming men that strove with gods.
The lights begin to twinkle from the rocks;
The long day wanes; the slow moon climbs; the deep 55
Moans round with many voices. Come, my friends,
'Tis not too late to seek a newer world.
Push off, and sitting well in order smite
The sounding furrows; for my purpose holds
To sail beyond the sunset, and the baths 60
Of all the western stars, until I die.
It may be that the gulfs will wash us down;
It may be we shall touch the Happy Isles,[3]
And see the great Achilles, whom we knew.
Though much is taken, much abides; and though 65
We are not now that strength which in old days
Moved earth and heaven, that which we are, we are;
One equal temper of heroic hearts,
Made weak by time and fate, but strong in will
To strive, to seek, to find, and not to yield. 70

Tithonus[4]

   The woods decay, the woods decay and fall,
The vapors weep their burthen to the ground,
Man comes and tills the field and lies beneath,
And after many a summer dies the swan.
Me only cruel immortality 5
Consumes; I wither slowly in thine arms,
Here at the quiet limit of the world,
A white-haired shadow roaming like a dream
The ever-silent spaces of the East,

---

3. In Greek myth, the abode of the warriors after death. *Achilles:* Comrade-in-arms of Ulysses at Troy.   4. A prince of Troy loved by Aurora, goddess of dawn, in whose palace he is depicted as living. She obtained for him from Zeus the gift of immortality, but not of eternal youth.

Far-folded mists, and gleaming halls of morn.   10
    Alas! for this gray shadow, once a man—
So glorious in his beauty and thy choice,
Who madest him thy chosen, that he seemed
To his great heart none other than a God!
I asked thee, "Give me immortality."   15
Then didst thou grant mine asking with a smile,
Like wealthy men who care not how they give.
But thy strong Hours[5] indignant worked their wills,
And beat me down and marred and wasted me,
And tho' they could not end me, left me maimed   20
To dwell in presence of immortal youth,
Immortal age beside immortal youth,
And all I was in ashes. Can thy love,
Thy beauty, make amends, though even now,
Close over us, the silver star,[6] thy guide,   25
Shines in those tremulous eyes that fill with tears
To hear me? Let me go; take back thy gift.
Why should a man desire in any way
To vary from the kindly race of men,
Or pass beyond the goal of ordinance   30
Where all should pause, as is most meet[7] for all?
    A soft air fans the cloud apart; there comes
A glimpse of that dark world where I was born.
Once more the old mysterious glimmer steals
From thy pure brows, and from thy shoulders pure,   35
And bosom beating with a heart renewed.
Thy cheek begins to redden through the gloom,
Thy sweet eyes brighten slowly close to mine,
Ere yet they blind the stars, and the wild team[8]
Which love thee, yearning for thy yoke, arise,   40
And shake the darkness from their loosened manes,
And beat the twilight into flakes of fire.
    Lo! ever thus thou growest beautiful
In silence, then before thine answer given
Departest, and thy tears are on my cheek.   45
    Why wilt thou ever scare me with thy tears,
And make me tremble lest a saying learnt,
In days far-off, on that dark earth, be true?
"The Gods themselves cannot recall their gifts."
    Ay me! ay me! with what another heart   50

5. Or *Horae*, goddesses of the seasons and of growth and decay.   6. The morning star that precedes the dawn.   7. Suitable.   8. Of supernatural horses; they draw Aurora's chariot into the sky at dawn.

In days far-off, and with what other eyes
I used to watch—if I be he that watched—
The lucid outline forming round thee; saw
The dim curls kindle into sunny rings;
Changed with thy mystic change, and felt my blood   55
Glow with the glow that slowly crimsoned all
Thy presence and thy portals, while I lay,
Mouth, forehead, eyelids, growing dewy-warm
With kisses balmier than half-opening buds
Of April, and could hear the lips that kissed   60
Whispering I knew not what of wild and sweet,
Like that strange song I heard Apollo[9] sing,
While Ilion like a mist rose into towers.
    Yet hold me not forever in thine East;
How can my nature longer mix with thine?   65
Coldly thy rosy shadows bathe me, cold
Are all thy lights, and cold my wrinkled feet
Upon thy glimmering thresholds, when the steam
Floats up from those dim fields about the homes
Of happy men that have the power to die,   70
And grassy barrows[1] of the happier dead.
Release me, and restore me to the ground.
Thou seest all things, thou wilt see my grave;
Thou wilt renew thy beauty morn by morn,
I earth in earth forget these empty courts,   75
And thee returning on thy silver wheels.
But follow; let the torrent dance thee down
To find him in the valley; let the wild
Lean-headed eagles yelp alone, and leave   20
The monstrous ledges there to slope, and spill
Their thousand wreaths of dangling water-smoke,
That like a broken purpose waste in air.
So waste not thou, but come; for all the vales
Await thee; azure pillars[2] of the hearth   25
Arise to thee; the children call, and I
Thy shepherd pipe, and sweet is every sound,
Sweeter thy voice, but every sound is sweet;
Myriads of rivulets hurrying through the lawn,
The moan of doves in immemorial elms,   30
And murmuring of innumerable bees.

---

9. God of music and patron of Troy. According to legend, the walls of Troy (Ilion) were raised by the sound of his song.   1. Burial mounds.   2. Of smoke.

In Memoriam A. H. H.

Obit. MDCCCXXXIII

[Prologue]

Strong Son of God, immortal Love,[3]
  Whom we, that have not seen thy face,
  By faith, and faith alone, embrace,
Believing where we cannot prove;

Thine are these orbs of light and shade;[4]
  Thou madest Life in man and brute;
  Thou madest Death; and lo, thy foot
Is on the skull which thou hast made.[5]

Thou wilt not leave us in the dust:
  Thou madest man, he knows not why,   10
  He thinks he was not made to die;
And thou hast made him: thou art just.

Thou seemest human and divine,
  The highest, holiest manhood, thou.
  Our wills are ours, we know not how;   15
Our wills are ours, to make them thine.

Our little systems[6] have their day;
  They have their day and cease to be;
  They are but broken[7] lights of thee,
And thou, O Lord, art more than they.   20

We have but faith: we cannot know,
  For knowledge is of things we see;
  And yet we trust it comes from thee,
A beam in darkness: let it grow.

Let knowledge grow from more to more,   25
  But more of reverence in us dwell;
  That mind and soul, according well,
May make one music as before,

But vaster. We are fools and slight;
  We mock thee when we do not fear: 30

---

3. Cf 1 John 4:8, 15. "He that loveth not knoweth not God; for God is love." "Whosoever shall confess that Jesus is the Son of God, God dwelleth in him, and he in God."   4. I.e., the earth and the planets, part of each of which is sunlit, the rest in shadow.   5. I.e., Christ crushes Death underfoot, a common motif in painting and sculpture.   6. Transient theological and philosophical systems, contrasted with the enduring systems of the stars.   7. Refracted, as by a prism.

But help thy foolish ones to bear;
Help thy vain worlds to bear thy light.

Forgive what seemed my sin in me,
    What seemed my worth since I began;
    For merit lives from man to man,   35
And not from man, O Lord, to thee.

Forgive my grief for one removed,
    Thy creature, whom I found so fair.
    I trust he lives in thee, and there
I find him worthier to be loved.   40

Forgive these wild and wandering cries,
    Confusions of a wasted[8] youth;
    Forgive them where they fail in truth,
And in thy wisdom make me wise.

1

I held it truth, with him[9] who sings
    To one clear harp in divers tones,
    That men may rise on stepping-stones
Of their dead selves to higher things.

But who shall so forecast the years   5
    And find in loss a gain to match?
    Or reach a hand through time to catch
The far-off interest of tears?

Let Love clasp Grief lest both be drowned,
    Let darkness keep her raven gloss.   10
    Ah, sweeter to be drunk with loss,
To dance with Death, to beat the ground,

Than that the victor Hours[1] should scorn
    The long result of love, and boast,
    "Behold the man that loved and lost,   15
But all he was is overworn."[2]

2

Old yew,[3] which graspest at the stones
    That name the underlying dead,
    Thy fibers net the dreamless head,
Thy roots are wrapt about the bones.

8. Laid waste (by Hallam's loss).   9. Goethe, who in the second part of *Faust* and elsewhere voices his conception of spiritual progress through the outgrowing of one's former selves. *Divers:* Various.   1. Or Horae, goddesses of growth and decay.   2. Worn out, exhausted. 3. Evergreen capable of attaining to great age; hence often planted in graveyards as symbol of immortality.

The seasons bring the flower again,   5
  And bring the firstling[4] to the flock;
  And in the dusk of thee the clock
Beats out the little lives of men.

O, not for thee the glow, the bloom,
  Who changest not in any gale,   10
  Nor branding summer suns avail
To touch thy thousand years of gloom;

And gazing on thee, sullen tree,
  Sick for thy stubborn hardihood,
  I seem to fail from out my blood   15
And grow incorporate into thee.

3

O Sorrow, cruel fellowship,
  O Priestess in the vaults of Death,
  O sweet and bitter in a breath,
What whispers from thy lying lip?

"The stars," she whispers, "blindly run;   5
  A web is woven across the sky;
  From out waste places comes a cry,
And murmurs from the dying sun;

"And all the phantom, Nature, stands—
  With all the music in her tone,   10
  A hollow echo of my own,—
A hollow form with empty hands."

And shall I take a thing so blind,
  Embrace her as my natural good;
  Or crush her, like a vice of blood,   15
Upon the threshold of the mind?

*   *   *

5

I sometimes hold it half a sin
  To put in words the grief I feel;
  For words, like Nature, half reveal
And half conceal the Soul within.

But, for the unquiet heart and brain,   5
  A use in measured language lies;

4. Firstborn.

The sad mechanic exercise,
Like dull narcotics, numbing pain.

In words, like weeds,[5] I'll wrap me o'er,
    Like coarsest clothes against the cold;   10
    But that large grief which these enfold
Is given in outline and no more.

         ❋   ❋   ❋

7

Dark house,[6] by which once more I stand
    Here in the long unlovely street,
    Doors, where my heart was used to beat
So quickly, waiting for a hand,

A hand that can be clasped no more—   5
    Behold me, for I cannot sleep,
    And like a guilty thing I creep
At earliest morning to the door.

He is not here; but far away
    The noise of life begins again,   10
    And ghastly through the drizzling rain
On the bald street breaks the blank day.

         ❋   ❋   ❋

10

I hear the noise about thy keel;[7]
    I hear the bell struck in the night;
    I see the cabin-window bright;
I see the sailor at the wheel.

Thou bring'st the sailor to his wife,   5
    And traveled men from foreign lands;
    And letters unto trembling hands;
And, thy dark freight, a vanished life.

So bring him; we have idle dreams;
    This look of quiet flatters thus   10
    Our home-bred fancies. O, to us,
The fools of habit, sweeter seems

To rest beneath the clover sod,
    That takes the sunshine and the rains,

---

5. Garments (with allusion to mourning garments).   6. The Hallam family residence.   7. Of the ship bringing Hallam's body back from Vienna.

Or where the kneeling hamlet drains   15
The chalice of the grapes of God;[8]

Than if with thee the roaring wells
    Should gulf him fathom-deep in brine,
    And hands so often clasped in mine,
Should toss with tangle[9] and with shells.   20

11

Calm is the morn without a sound,
    Calm as to suit a calmer grief,
    And only through the faded leaf
The chestnut pattering to the ground;[1]

Calm and deep peace on this high wold,
    And on these dews that drench the furze,
    And all the silvery gossamers
That twinkle into green and gold;

Calm and still light on yon great plain
    That sweeps with all its autumn bowers,   10
    And crowded farms and lessening towers,
To mingle with the bounding main;

Calm and deep peace in this wide air,
    These leaves that redden to the fall,
    And in my heart, if calm at all,   15
If any calm, a calm despair;

Calm on the seas, and silver sleep,
    And waves that sway themselves in rest,
    And dead calm in that noble breast
Which heaves but with the heaving deep.   20

*   *   *

15

Tonight the winds begin to rise
    And roar from yonder dropping day;
    The last red leaf is whirled away,
The rooks[2] are blown about the skies;

The forest cracked, the waters curled,   5
    The cattle huddled on the lea;[3]

---

8. Lines 13–16 give alternate modes of burial: in the churchyard or under the chancel where worshippers kneel for the Sacrament.   9. Seaweed.   1. The time is September, when Hallam's body is still en route; the poet is at his home in Somersby among the high wolds (open uplands) of Lincolnshire.   2. European crow-like birds.   3. Pasture.

And wildly dashed on tower and tree
The sunbeam strikes along the world:

And but for fancies, which aver
   That all thy motions gently pass   10
   Athwart a plane of molten glass,
I scarce could brook the strain and stir

That makes the barren branches loud;[4]
   And but for fear it is not so,
   The wild unrest that lives in woe   15
Would dote and pore on yonder cloud

That rises upward always higher,
   And onward drags a laboring breast,
   And topples round the dreary west,
A looming bastion fringed with fire.   20

16

What words are these have fall'n from me?
   Can calm despair and wild unrest
   Be tenants of a single breast,
Or Sorrow such a changeling be?

Or doth she only seem to take   5
   The touch of change in calm or storm,
   But knows no more of transient form
In her deep self, than some dead lake

That holds the shadow of a lark
   Hung in the shadow of a heaven?   10
   Or has the shock, so harshly given,
Confused me like the unhappy bark[5]

That strikes by night a craggy shelf,
   And staggers blindly ere she sink?
   And stunned me from my power to think   15
And all my knowledge of myself;

And made me that delirious man
   Whose fancy fuses old and new,
   And flashes into false and true,
And mingles all without a plan?   20

*   *   *

4. In the midst of a gathering storm, the poet's imagination soothes him with the fancy that Hallam's ship moves gently toward England on a glass-calm sea. Only a fear that this fancy may delude him (and Hallam's crossing be really in danger) prevents the stormy unrest within him from romantically luxuriating in the stormy sunset all around him.   **5.** Ship.

19

The Danube to the Severn[6] gave
   The darkened heart that beat no more;
   They laid him by the pleasant shore,
And in the hearing of the wave.[7]

There twice a day the Severn fills;[8]
   The salt sea-water passes by,
   And hushes half the babbling Wye,
And makes a silence in the hills.

The Wye is hushed nor moved along,
   And hushed my deepest grief of all,   10
   When filled with tears that cannot fall,
I brim with sorrow drowning song.

The tide flows down, the wave again
   Is vocal in its wooded walls;
   My deeper anguish also falls,   15
And I can speak a little then.

      *   *   *

21

I sing to him that rests below,
   And, since the grasses round me wave,
   I take the grasses of the grave,
And make them pipes[9] whereon to blow.

The traveler hears me now and then,   5
   And sometimes harshly will he speak:
   "This fellow would make weakness weak,
And melt the waxen hearts of men."

Another answers: "Let him be,
   He loves to make parade of pain,   10
   That with his piping he may gain
The praise that comes to constancy."

A third is wroth:[1] "Is this an hour
   For private sorrow's barren song,
   When more and more the people throng   15
The chairs and thrones of civil power?

6. Vienna, where Hallam died, is on the Danube; the church at Clevedon, Somersetshire, where
he was buried, is on the Severn.   7. Tennyson was not present at the funeral and did not learn
till years later that Hallam had been buried in the church, not in the graveyard by the river.
8. The tides reach far up the bristol channel into the Severn and the Wye, its tributary.
9. Alluding to the pipes of mourning shepherds in pastoral elegy, the genre to which *In Memoriam* in part belongs.   1. Very angry.

"A time to sicken and to swoon,
    When Science reaches forth her arms
    To feel from world to world, and charms
Her secret from the latest moon?"[2]   20

Behold, ye speak an idle thing;
    Ye never knew the sacred dust.
    I do but sing because I must,
And pipe but as the linnets sing;

And one is glad; her note is gay,   25
    For now her little ones have ranged;
    And one is sad; her note is changed,
Because her brood is stolen away.

22

The path by which we twain did go,
    Which led by tracts that pleased us well,
    Through four sweet years arose and fell,
From flower to flower, from snow to snow;

And we with singing cheered the way,   5
    And, crowned with all the season lent,
    From April on to April went,
And glad at heart from May to May.

But where the path we walked began
    To slant the fifth autumnal slope,   10
    As we descended following Hope,
There sat the Shadow feared of man;

Who broke our fair companionship,
    And spread his mantle dark and cold,
    And wrapt thee formless in the fold,   15
And dulled the murmur on thy lip,

And bore thee where I could not see
    Nor follow, tho' I walk in haste,
    And think that somewhere in the waste[3]
The Shadow sits and waits for me.   20

23

Now, sometimes in my sorrow shut,
    Or breaking into song by fits,
    Alone, alone, to where he sits,
The Shadow cloaked from head to foot,

---

2. From 1846 to 1848, astronomers discovered the planet Neptune, the moon of Neptune, the satellites of Uranus, and the eighth moon of Saturn.   3. Wasteland.

Who keeps the keys of all the creeds,   5
   I wander, often falling lame,
   And looking back to whence I came,
Or on to where the pathway leads;

And crying, How changed from where it ran
   Through lands where not a leaf was dumb,   10
   But all the lavish hills would hum
The murmur of a happy Pan;[4]

When each by turns was guide to each,
   And Fancy light from Fancy caught,
   And Thought leapt out to wed with Thought   15
Ere Thought could wed itself with Speech;

And all we met was fair and good,
   And all was good that Time could bring,
   And all the secret of the Spring
Moved in the chambers of the blood;   20

And many an old philosophy
   On Argive heights divinely sang,
   And round us all the thicket rang
To many a flute of Arcady.[5]

        ❊   ❊   ❊

27

I envy not in any moods
   The captive void of noble rage,
   The linnet born within the cage,
That never knew the summer woods;

I envy not the beast that takes   5
   His license in the field of time,
   Unfettered by the sense of crime,
To whom a conscience never wakes;

Nor, what may count itself as blest,
   The heart that never plighted troth[6]   10
   But stagnates in the weeds of sloth;
Nor any want-begotten rest.[7]

---

4. God of flocks and shepherds, and hence of pastoral poetry like these verses.   5. I.e., they were like shepherds on the hills of Greece when what is now "old philosophy" was brand new; or on the plains of Arcady (home of pastoral poetry) when pastoral poetry was young.   6. Became engaged to be married.   7. I.e., any rest that comes from a lack or deficiency—specifically, from a failure to be fully human and therefore vulnerable.

I hold it true, whate'er befall;
    I feel it, when I sorrow most;
    'Tis better to have loved and lost   15
Than never to have loved at all.

28

The time draws near the birth of Christ.
    The moon is hid, the night is still;
    The Christmas bells from hill to hill
Answer each other in the mist.

Four voices of four hamlets round,   5
    From far and near, on mead and moor,
    Swell out and fail, as if a door
Were shut between me and the sound;

Each voice four changes on the wind,
    That now dilate, and now decrease,   10
    Peace and goodwill, goodwill and peace,
Peace and goodwill, to all mankind.

This year I slept and woke with pain,
    I almost wished no more to wake,
    And that my hold on life would break   15
Before I heard those bells again;

But they my troubled spirit rule,
    For they controlled me when a boy;
    They bring me sorrow touched with joy,
The merry, merry bells of Yule.   20

*   *   *

50

Be near me when my light is low,
    When the blood creeps, and the nerves prick
    And tingle; and the heart is sick,
And all the wheels of being slow.

Be near me when the sensuous frame   5
    Is racked with pangs that conquer trust;
    And Time, a maniac scattering dust,
And Life, a Fury slinging flame.[8]

---

8. The Furies of Greek myth carry torches. *Dust:* The dust from which life comes and to which it returns.

Be near me when my faith is dry,
 And men the flies of latter spring,   10
 That lay their eggs, and sting and sting
And weave their petty cells and die.

Be near me when I fade away,
 To point the term of human strife,
 And on the low dark verge of life   15
The twilight of eternal day.

* * *

54

O, yet we trust that somehow good
 Will be the final goal of ill,
 To pangs of nature, sins of will,
Defects of doubt, and taints of blood;

That nothing walks with aimless feet;   5
 That not one life shall be destroyed,
 Or cast as rubbish to the void,
When God hath made the pile complete;

That not a worm is cloven in vain;
 That not a moth with vain desire   10
 Is shriveled in a fruitless fire,
Or but subserves another's gain.

Behold, we know not anything;
 I can but trust that good shall fall
 At last—far off—at last, to all,   15
And every winter change to spring.

So runs my dream; but what am I?
 An infant crying in the night;
 An infant crying for the light,
And with no language but a cry.   20

55

The wish, that of the living whole
 No life may fail beyond the grave,
 Derives it not from what we have
The likest God within the soul?

Are God and Nature then at strife,   5
 That Nature lends such evil dreams?

So careful of the type she seems,
So careless of the single life,[9]

That I, considering everywhere
      Her secret meaning in her deeds
      And finding that of fifty seeds   10
She often brings but one to bear,

I falter where I firmly trod,
      And falling with my weight of cares
      Upon the great world's altar-stairs   15
That slope through darkness up to God,

I stretch lame hands of faith, and grope,
      And gather dust and chaff, and call
      To what I feel is Lord of all,
And faintly trust the larger hope.   20

                    56

"So careful of the type?" but no.
      From scarpèd cliff and quarried stone
      She cries, "A thousand types are gone;[1]
I care for nothing, all shall go.

"Thou makest thine appeal to me: 5
      I bring to life, I bring to death;
      The spirit does but mean the breath:
I know no more." And he, shall he,

Man, her last work, who seemed so fair,
      Such splendid purpose in his eyes,   10
      Who rolled the psalm to wintry skies,
Who built him fanes[2] of fruitless prayer,

Who trusted God was love indeed
      And love Creation's final law—
      Though Nature, red in tooth and claw   15
With ravin,[3] shrieked against his creed—

Who loved, who suffered countless ills,
      Who battled for the True, the Just,
      Be blown about the desert dust,
Or sealed within the iron hills?   20

9. The significance of Nature's prodigality and destructiveness was widely debated during Tennyson's lifetime. *Type*: Species.   1. That whole species had disappeared, not merely individuals, had become evident from Charles Lyell's researches, published in his *Principles of Geology* (3 vols., 1830–33) and *Elements of Geology* (1838). *Scarpèd*: Shorn away vertically to expose the rock strata of different ages.

No more? A monster then, a dream,
　　A discord. Dragons of the prime,[4]
　　That tare each other in their slime,
Were mellow music matched with him.

O life as futile, then, as frail!　　　　　　　　　25
　　O for thy voice[5] to soothe and bless!
　　What hope of answer, or redress?
Behind the veil, behind the veil.[6]

＊　　　＊　　　＊

78

Again at Christmas did we weave
　　The holly round the Christmas hearth;
　　The silent snow possessed the earth,
And calmly fell our Christmas-eve:

The yule-clog[7] sparkled keen with frost,　　　5
　　No wing of wind the region swept,
　　But over all things brooding slept
The quiet sense of something lost.

As in the winters left behind,
　　Again our ancient games had place,　　　　10
　　The mimic picture's breathing grace,
And dance and song and hoodman-blind.[8]

Who showed a token of distress?
　　No single tear, no mark of pain:
　　O sorrow, then can sorrow wane?
O grief, can grief be changed to less?

O last regret, regret can die!
　　No—mixt with all this mystic frame,
　　Her deep relations are the same,
But with long use her tears are dry.　　　　20

＊　　　＊　　　＊

95

By night we lingered on the lawn,
　　For underfoot the herb was dry;
　　And genial warmth; and o'er the sky
The silvery haze of summer drawn;

2. Temples.　　3. Prey.　　4. Prehistoric creatures.　　5. Hallam's.　　6. Death.　　7. Yule
log.　　8. Blind man's bluff. *Mimic picture*: The game may be charades.

And calm that let the tapers burn   5
    Unwavering; not a cricket chirred;
    The brook alone far-off was heard,
And on the board[9] the fluttering urn.

And bats went round in fragrant skies,
    And wheeled or lit the filmy shapes   10
    That haunt the dusk, with ermine capes
And woolly breasts and beaded eyes;

While now we sang old songs that pealed
    From knoll to knoll, where, couched at ease,
    The white kine[1] glimmered, and the trees   15
Laid their dark arms about the field.

But when those others, one by one,
    Withdrew themselves from me and night,
    And in the house light after light
Went out, and I was all alone,   20

A hunger seized my heart; I read
    Of that glad year which once had been,
    In those fall'n leaves which kept their green,
The noble letters of the dead.

And strangely on the silence broke   25
    The silent-speaking words, and strange
    Was love's dumb cry defying change
To test his worth; and strangely spoke

The faith, the vigor, bold to dwell
    On doubts that drive the coward back,   30
    And keen thro' wordy snares to track
Suggestion to her inmost cell.

So word by word, and line by line,
    The dead man touched me from the past,
    And all at once it seemed at last   35
The living soul was flashed on mine,

And mine in this was wound, and whirled
    About empyreal[2] heights of thought,
    And came on that which is, and caught
The deep pulsations of the world,   40

Æonian[3] music measuring out
    The steps of Time—the shocks of Chance—

9. Table. *Fluttering urn*: Boiling tea-urn.   1. Cattle.   2. Sublime.   3. Age-old.

The blows of Death. At length my trance
Was canceled, stricken through with doubt.

Vague words! but ah, how hard to frame   45
    In matter-molded forms of speech,
    Or even for intellect to reach
Through memory that which I became;

Till now the doubtful dusk revealed
    The knolls once more where, couched at ease,   50
    The white kine glimmered, and the trees
Laid their dark arms about the field;

And sucked from out the distant gloom
    A breeze began to tremble o'er
    The large leaves of the sycamore,   55
And fluctuate all the still perfume,

And gathering freshlier overhead
    Rock'd the full-foliaged elms, and swung
    The heavy-folded rose, and flung
The lilies to and fro, and said,   60

"The dawn, the dawn," and died away;
    And East and West, without a breath,
    Mixt their dim lights, like life and death,
To broaden into boundless day.

*   *   *

106

Ring out, wild bells, to the wild sky,
    The flying cloud, the frosty light:
    The year is dying in the night;
Ring out, wild bells, and let him die.

Ring out the old, ring in the new,   5
    Ring, happy bells, across the snow:
    The year is going, let him go;
Ring out the false, ring in the true.

Ring out the grief that saps the mind,
    For those that here we see no more;   10
    Ring out the feud of rich and poor,
Ring in redress to all mankind.

Ring out a slowly dying cause,
    And ancient forms of party strife;

Ring in the nobler modes of life,   15
With sweeter manners, purer laws.

Ring out the want, the care, the sin,
   The faithless coldness of the times;
   Ring out, ring out my mournful rhymes,
But ring the fuller minstrel in.   20

Ring out false pride in place and blood,
   The civic slander and the spite;
   Ring in the love of truth and right,
Ring in the common love of good.

Ring out old shapes of foul disease;   25
   Ring out the narrowing lust of gold;
   Ring out the thousand wars of old,
Ring in the thousand years of peace.[4]

Ring in the valiant man and free,
   The larger heart, the kindlier hand;
   Ring out the darkness of the land,
Ring in the Christ that is to be.   30

*　　　*　　　*

118

Contemplate all this work of Time,
   The giant laboring in his youth;
   Nor dream of human love and truth,
As dying Nature's earth and lime;[5]

But trust that those we call the dead   5
   Are breathers of an ampler day
   For ever nobler ends. They say,
The solid earth whereon we tread

In tracts of fluent heat began,
   And grew to seeming-random forms,   10
   The seeming prey of cyclic storms,
Till at the last arose the man;

Who throve and branched from clime to clime,
   The herald of a higher race,

---

4. The poet has in mind Revelation 20, where it is said that Satan will be bound in chains for a thousand years, during which time the martyrs will be "priests of God and of Christ, and shall reign with him."   5. The products of the decay of flesh and bone.

And of himself in higher place, 15
If so he type[6] this work of time

Within himself, from more to more;
    Or, crown'd with attributes of woe
    Like glories, move his course, and show
That life is not as idle ore, 20

But iron dug from central gloom,
    And heated hot with burning fears,
    And dipt in baths of hissing tears,
And battered with the shocks of doom

To shape and use. Arise and fly 25
    The reeling Faun, the sensual feast;
    Move upward, working out the beast,
And let the ape and tiger die.

*   *   *

124

That which we dare invoke to bless;
    Our dearest faith; our ghastliest doubt;
    He, They, One, All;[7] within, without;
The Power in darkness whom we guess,—

I found Him not in world or sun, 5
    Or eagle's wing, or insect's eye,
    Nor through the questions men may try,
The petty cobwebs we have spun.

If e'er when faith had fallen asleep,
    I heard a voice, "believe no more," 10
    And heard an ever-breaking shore
That tumbled in the Godless deep,

A warmth within the breast would melt
    The freezing reason's colder part,
    And like a man in wrath the heart 15
Stood up and answered, "I have felt."

No, like a child in doubt and fear:
    But that blind clamor made me wise;
    Then was I as a child that cries,
But, crying, knows his father near; 20

6. Copy, emulate.   7. Christ, as part of the Trinity, seen as three elements and as indivisible.

And what I am beheld again
   What is, and no man understands;
   And out of darkness came the hands
That reach through nature, molding men.

[*Epilogue*][8]

Today the grave is bright for me,
   For them[9] the light of life increased,
   Who stay to share the morning feast,   75
Who rest tonight beside the sea.

Let all my genial spirits advance
   To meet and greet a whiter[1] sun;
   My drooping memory will not shun
The foaming grape of eastern France.   80

It circles round, and fancy plays,
   And hearts are warmed and faces bloom,
   As drinking health to bride and groom
We wish them store of happy days.

Nor count me all to blame if I   85
   Conjecture of a stiller guest,
   Perchance, perchance, among the rest,
And, though in silence, wishing joy.

But they must go, the time draws on,
   And those white-favored[2] horses wait;   90
   They rise, but linger; it is late;
Farewell, we kiss, and they are gone.

A shade falls on us like the dark
   From little cloudlets on the grass,
   But sweeps away as out we pass   95
To range the woods, to roam the park,

Discussing how their courtship grew,
   And talk of others that are wed,
   And how she looked, and what he said,
And back we come at fall of dew.   100

Again the feast, the speech, the glee,
   The shade of passing thought, the wealth

8. The Epilogue celebrates the wedding of the poet's sister Cecilia to his friend Edmund Lushington (10 October 1842) and brings the poem of mourning full circle to its conclusion in a marriage and in the prospect of a new birth.   9. The new husband and wife.   1. More joyous and hopeful because of the marriage. *Foaming grape*: Champagne.   2. Wearing white ribbons for the wedding.

Of words and wit, the double health,
The crowning cup, the three-times-three,[3]

And last the dance;—till I retire.   105
     Dumb is that tower[4] which spake so loud,
     And high in heaven the streaming cloud,
And on the downs a rising fire:

And rise, O moon, from yonder down,
     Till over down and over dale   110
     All night the shining vapor sail
And pass the silent-lighted town,

The white-faced halls, the glancing rills,
     And catch at every mountain head,
     And o'er the friths[5] that branch and spread   115
Their sleeping silver through the hills;

And touch with shade the bridal doors,
     With tender gloom the roof, the wall;
     And breaking let the splendor fall
To spangle all the happy shores   120

By which they rest, and ocean sounds,
     And, star and system rolling past,
     A soul shall draw from out the vast
And strike his being into bounds,

And, moved through life of lower phase,   125
     Result in man, be born and think,
     And act and love, a closer link
Betwixt us and the crowning race

Of those that, eye to eye, shall look
     On knowledge; under whose command   130
     Is Earth and Earth's, and in their hand
Is Nature like an open book;

No longer half-akin to brute,
     For all we thought and loved and did,
     And hoped, and suffer'd, is but seed   135
Of what in them is flower and fruit;

Whereof the man that with me trod
     This planet was a noble type
     Appearing ere the times were ripe,
That friend of mine who lives in God,   140

---

3. Rousing cheers.   4. Church tower where wedding bells recently rang.   5. Arms of the sea.

That God, which ever lives and loves,
  One God, one law, one element,
  And one far-off divine event,
To which the whole creation moves.

ROBERT BROWNING
1812–1889

The pleasure of reading Robert Browning's dramatic monologues—the poems for which he is best known—involves delight in encountering a vividly realized personality but also, often, the kind of enjoyment one gets from detective fiction. An imaginary speaker utters words designed to generate a specific effect; from these words, typically, one can deduce a story never actually told. The poet allows us the fun of figuring out what has really happened as well as more familiar poetic pleasures.

Browning was the son of a bank clerk who later became a prosperous banker. After attending the University of London, he traveled on the Continent. Back in England, he became friendly with other important Victorian literary figures: Charles Dickens, Thomas Carlyle, and Leigh Hunt, for example. His romance with the semi-invalid Elizabeth Barrett, also a poet, eventuated in marriage in 1846; the two lived mainly in Italy for the remaining fifteen years of her life. Although Browning returned to England after his wife's death, he made frequent visits to the Continent and died in Venice.

Browning wrote verse plays and introspective Shelleyan lyrics, but his most popular poems have always been the dramatic monologues, originally included in such volumes as *Bells and Pomegranates* (1841–46), *Men and Women* (1855), and *Dramatis Personae* (1864). His most ambitious work was *The Ring and the Book* (1868–69), a linked series of blank verse dramatic monologues based on a Renaissance murder trial. In this long poem, in the course of which several people report the same events from very different points of view, Browning most clearly concentrates on the problem implicit in all his monologues, that of perspective. The nature of a story depends on who tells it: Browning's verse insistently reminds us of this fact.

"The Bishop Orders His Tomb at Saint Praxed's Church" (1845) invites complicated responses to the personality it evokes. The imagined sixteenth-century bishop reveals his lack of real allegiance to the Church he nominally serves. He has violated his vows of celibacy, having had at least one mistress and several children. He feels powerful competitive impulses, as well as rage and envy, toward his predecessor as bishop. Even on his deathbed, he remains utterly absorbed in the things of this world: the lump of lapis lazuli he has buried, the splendor of the marble he imagines for his tomb. The mass itself exists in his memory and imagination only as a sensuous experience:

> And then how I shall lie through centuries,
> And hear the blessed mutter of the mass,

> And see God made and eaten all day long,
> And feel the steady candle-flame, and taste
> Good strong thick stupefying incense-smoke!

If one wished to summarize this bishop in abstract terms, one might allude to "the corruption of the Church." Indeed, he exemplifies such corruption in many different ways, by what he fails to say as well as by what he says. "And thence ye may perceive the world's dream": occasionally such tag lines erupt in his speech, but his lack of real religious feeling is all too apparent. He imagines himself lying in his tomb in his church through eternity; he does not think of an afterlife in heaven—or, for that matter, in hell, perhaps his more likely destination. Browning, however, implicitly insists on the difference between people and abstractions. To sum up this bishop in terms of ecclesiastical corruption would leave out the fact of his enormous vitality, the vitality that informs the entire poem. The dramatic monologue makes the bishop's feeling come alive, makes the reader sympathetically understand his reluctance to leave behind beauty he has valued all his life.

Browning uses the superficially remote situation he has evoked to reiterate the great Romantic theme—we have encountered it most vividly in Wordsworth and in Keats—of the poignance and the inevitability of loss. Instead of considering the problem of loss in autobiographical terms, he enters imaginatively into the experience of an invented character.

> She, men would have to be your mother once,
> Old Gandolf envied me, so fair she was!
> What's done is done, and she is dead beside,
> Dead long ago, and I am Bishop since,
> And as she died so must we die ourselves.

The dying man's emotions recapitulate a feeling we have all had: the sadness of memory, even memory of happy experiences (in this case, love of a woman and triumph over an enemy), when it tells us of what is irretrievably gone. The bishop holds on still to what he knows he must lose. His speech, as Browning captures it, expresses in its rhythms and its idiom the enduring vigor of his personality, even on the edge of death.

> Ah, ye hope
> To revel down my villas while I gasp
> Bricked o'er with beggar's mouldy travertine
> Which Gandolf from his tomb-top chuckles at!

This is not a man who has given up: he insists on the preoccupations of his life as he faces his death. The poem, demanding no judgment of the bishop, suggests, rather, the inadequacy of judgment as a reaction to the multiplicity of any single human being.

Browning's greatest gift as a poet is his capacity to convey an energetic sense of pleasure in the reality of experience. "Grow old alone with me, / The best is yet to be," urges a character in one of his poems. But he also recognizes the cost of such intense living as that the bishop enjoys, since all human existence involves loss. The tonal complexity of "The Bishop Orders His Tomb" suggests the kind of richness typical of the Victorian period, with its faith and hope in the possibilities of human accomplishment mingled with doubt about what it all means after all.

A useful biography of Browning is B. Miller, *Robert Browning: A Portrait* (1952). W. C. De Vane, *A Browning Handbook* (1935), provides indispensable guidance. Valuable criticism includes N. Crowell, *The Convex Glass* (1968), and I. Jack, *Browning's Major Poetry* (1973).

The Bishop Orders His Tomb at Saint Praxed's Church[1]

ROME, 15—

Vanity, saith the preacher, vanity![2]
Draw round my bed: is Anselm keeping back?
Nephews—sons mine . . . ah God, I know not! Well—
She, men would have to be your mother once,
Old Gandolf[3] envied me, so fair she was!   5
What's done is done, and she is dead beside,
Dead long ago, and I am Bishop since,
And as she died so must we die ourselves,
And thence ye may perceive the world's a dream.
Life, how and what is it? As here I lie   10
In this state-chamber, dying by degrees,
Hours and long hours in the dead night, I ask
'Do I live, am I dead?' Peace, peace seems all.
Saint Praxed's ever was the church for peace;
And so, about this tomb of mine. I fought   15
With tooth and nail to save my niche, ye know:
—Old Gandolf cozened me, despite my care;
Shrewd was that snatch from out the corner South
He graced his carrion with, God curse the same!
Yet still my niche is not so cramped but thence   20
One sees the pulpit o' the epistle-side,[4]
And somewhat of the choir, those silent seats,
And up into the aery dome where live
The angels, and a sunbeam's sure to lurk:
And I shall fill my slab of basalt there,   25
And 'neath my tabernacle[5] take my rest,
With those nine columns round me, two and two,
The odd one at my feet where Anselm stands:

---

1. The Bishop, his tomb, and the character Gandolf are all fictional. Saint Praxed's church, seen by Browning in 1844, is named after a second-century Roman virgin.   2. See Ecclesiastes 1:2.
3. The Bishop's predecessor.   4. I.e., the right side as the congregation faces the altar.
5. Here, the canopy over his tomb.

Peach-blossom marble all, the rare, the ripe
As fresh-poured red wine of a mighty pulse.   30
—Old Gandolf with his paltry onion-stone,[6]
Put me where I may look at him! True peach,
Rosy and flawless: how I earned the prize!
Draw close: that conflagration of my church
—What then? So much was saved if aught were missed!   35
My sons, ye would not be my death? Go dig
The white-grape vineyard where the oil-press stood,
Drop water gently till the surface sink,
And if ye find . . . Ah God, I know not, I! . . .
Bedded in store of rotten fig-leaves soft,   40
And corded up in a tight olive-frail,[7]
Some lump, ah God, of lapis lazuli,
Big as a Jew's head cut off at the nape,
Blue as a vein o'er the Madonna's breast . . .
Sons, all have I bequeathed you, villas, all   45
That brave Frascati[8] villa with its bath,
So, let the blue lump poise between my knees,
Like God the Father's globe on both his hands
Ye worship in the Jesu Church[9] so gay,
For Gandolf shall not choose but see and burst!   50
Swift as a weaver's shuttle[1] fleet our years:
Man goeth to the grave, and where is he?
Did I say basalt for my slab, sons? Black—
'Twas ever antique-black[2] I meant! How else
Shall ye contrast my frieze to come beneath?   55
The bas-relief in bronze ye promised me,
Those Pans and Nymphs ye wot of, and perchance
Some tripod, thyrsus,[3] with a vase or so,
The Saviour at his sermon on the mount,
Saint Praxed in a glory, and one Pan   60
Ready to twitch the Nymph's last garment off,
And Moses with the tables[4] . . . but I know
Ye mark me not! What do they whisper thee,
Child of my bowels, Anselm? Ah, ye hope
To revel down my villas while I gasp   65
Bricked o'er with beggar's mouldy travertine[5]
Which Gandolf from his tomb-top chuckles at!
Nay, boys, ye love me—all of jasper, then!

6. A lesser grade of green marble.   7. Basket made of rushes, for figs, raisins, olives, and so
on. *Lapis lazuli*: A bright-blue semiprecious stone.   8. A wealthy Roman suburb.   9. *Jesu
Church*: The principal Jesuit church in Rome.   1. See Job 7:6.   2. A grade of good marble.
3. A staff tipped with a pine cone, associated with the Greek god Bacchus. *Wot*: Know. *Pans*:
Images of Greek nature deities.   4. The stone tablets on which the Decalogue was inscribed.
5. A cheap, flaky Italian building stone. *Jasper*: Reddish quartz.

'Tis jasper ye stand pledged to, lest I grieve.
My bath must needs be left behind, alas!   70
One block, pure green as a pistachio-nut,
There's plenty jasper somewhere in the world—
And have I not Saint Praxed's ear to pray
Horses for ye, and brown Greek manuscripts,
And mistresses with great smooth marbly limbs?   75
—That's if ye carve my epitaph aright,
Choice Latin, picked phrase, Tully's every word,
No gaudy ware like Gandolf's secondline—
Tully,[6] my masters? Ulpian serves his need!
And then how I shall lie through centuries,   80
And hear the blessed mutter of the mass,
And see God made and eaten[7] all day long,
And feel the steady candle-flame, and taste
Good strong thick stupefying incense-smoke!
For as I lie here, hours of the dead night,   85
Dying in state and by such slow degrees,
I fold my arms as if they clasped a crook,[8]
And stretch my feet forth straight as stone can point,
And let the bedclothes, for a mortcloth,[9] drop
Into great laps and folds of sculptor's-work: 90
And as yon tapers dwindle, and strange thoughts
Grow, with a certain humming in my ears,
About the life before I lived this life.
And this life too, popes, cardinals and priests,
Saint Praxed at his[1] sermon on the mount,   95
Your tall pale mother with her talking eyes,
And new-found agate urns as fresh as day,
And marble's language, Latin pure, discreet,
—Aha, *Elucescebat*[2] quoth our friend?
No Tully, said I, Ulpian at the best!   100
Evil and brief hath been my pilgrimage.
All lapis, all, sons! Else I give the Pope
My villas! Will ye ever eat my heart?
Ever your eyes were as a lizard's quick,
They glitter like your mother's for my soul,   105
Or ye would heighten my impoverished frieze,
Piece out its starved design, and fill my vase

---

6. Marcus Tullius Cicero (106–43 B.C.), Roman writer and master of Latin prose style. *Ulpian*:
Ulpianus Domitius (170–228 A.D.), lawyer, secretary to Emperor Alexander Severus, writer of
nonclassical Latin.   7. A reference to the sacrament of Communion.   8. The bishop's
crosier.   9. Funeral pall or winding sheet.   1. Browning's implication is evidently that the
Bishop is unaware that St. Prassede was a woman.   2. "He was illustrious," or "famous"; in
classical Latin the word would be *elucebat*. *Elucescebat* is an example of the less elegant Latin
associated with Ulpian's era.

With grapes, and add a vizor and a Term,[3]
And to the tripod ye would tie a lynx
That in his struggle throws the thyrsus down,   110
To comfort me on my entablature
Whereon I am to lie till I must ask
'Do I live, am I dead?' There, leave me, there!
For ye have stabbed me with ingratitude
To death—ye wish it—God, ye wish it! Stone—   115
Gritstone,[4] a-crumble! Clammy squares which sweat
As if the corpse they keep were oozing through—
And no more lapis to delight the world!
Well go! I bless ye. Fewer tapers there,
But in a row: and, going, turn your backs   120
—Ay, like departing altar-ministrants,
And leave me in my church, the church for peace,
That I may watch at leisure if he leers—
Old Gandolf, at me, from his onion-stone,
As still he envied me, so fair she was!   125

FREDERICK DOUGLASS
1818–1895

The *Narrative of the Life of Frederick Douglass, An American Slave* (1845) powerfully details the struggle for identity of a black man who, in the mid-nineteenth century, came to realize his own exclusion from the American myth of liberty and justice for all. His autobiographical record epitomizes the experience of many pre–Civil War slaves, but in its narrative skill it also suggests how the writer's effort to achieve selfhood and freedom partakes of a more nearly universal pattern, incident to men and women of whatever color.

Virtually everything that is known of Douglass's early life comes from the *Narrative* itself, which ends half a century before his death. The book became an immediate best-seller, but also a subject of controversy when accusations of fraud (promptly refuted) were made against it by a man who claimed to have known Douglass as a slave and to know him incapable of writing such a book. Because the autobiography's publication endangered its author, who might have been returned to slavery, Douglass subsequently went to Great Britain for two years of highly successful lecture appearances. At the end of 1846, two Englishwomen purchased his freedom from his old master, Hugh Auld, and Douglass returned to the United States in March 1847. He then began a journalistic career, writing and publishing a series of newspapers and making himself a leader of his race who continued to locate and to proclaim the injustices to which blacks were subject. Late in his life, he held

---

3. A pillar bearing a statue or a bust.   4. Sandstone—a cheap substitute for marble.

a number of diplomatic posts, including minister resident and consul general to the Republic of Haiti and chargé d'affaires for Santo Domingo. He died in Washington, D.C., and was buried in Rochester, N.Y.

Douglass gradually enlarged and elaborated his *Narrative*, which exists in three subsequent versions: *My Bondage and My Freedom* (1855) and two different editions of *Life and Times of Frederick Douglass* (1881, 1892). The earliest, shortest form has the greatest narrative integrity and clarity. For literary as well as historical reasons (its status as an important document in the Abolitionist crusade), it merits reprinting. It belongs to a genre familiar in its time: thousands of slave narratives were published in America, and in many cases translated into European languages, between the end of the eighteenth century and the beginning of the American Civil War. They won a large, enthusiastic readership; by making the horrors of slavery emotionally immediate, they intensified abolitionist sentiment. From the first publication of Douglass's work, it was acknowledged as unusually forceful by virtue of its rhetorical control and its narrative skill.

Douglass casts his autobiography as an account of self-discovery. The contrast between the openings of the *Narrative* and of Rousseau's *Confessions* is instructive. Rousseau begins by proclaiming that he differs importantly from everyone else in his unique and early established personality and character. Douglass, on the other hand, starts by reporting what he does *not* know of himself. He must guess his own age, he doesn't know his birthday, he has only rumor to tell him his father's identity. Although he knows his mother, he spends virtually no time with her; she comes to him and leaves him in the dark. Most children develop their sense of who they are by precisely the clues missing in Douglass's experience: age, parentage, such ritual occasions as birthdays. Douglass has only a generic identity: slave. Like other slave children, he wears nothing but a shirt—not the trousers that would symbolize his maleness, not shoes to protect his feet, nothing to differentiate him from others of his kind. Like the other children, he eats corn meal mush from a trough on the floor, thus, as he notes, treated like a pig and reduced to animality. Everything in Douglass's experience denies his individuality and declares his lack of particularized identity.

The narrative constructed by a man who has finally, arduously, discovered his selfhood recapitulates the process of that discovery: a process with language at its heart. The book ends with its author claiming his name: "I subscribe myself, FREDERICK DOUGLASS." The name itself is a triumph, not his father's or his mother's but the freshly bestowed name of his freedom. The author has won with difficulty the power to subscribe himself, to sign his name, for it involves the capacity to read and write, as well as the claim to a name. Each step of the winning—learning to read, learning to write, acquiring a name—involves painful self-testing, but the *word* proves for Douglass literally a means to salvation.

Douglass believes his arrival in Baltimore, to serve the Aulds, a sign of Providential intervention: in Baltimore he learns to read. Mrs. Auld, wife of his master, begins to teach the boy the alphabet; her husband warns her to desist. Reading, he says, "would forever unfit him to be a slave." Douglass comments, "It was a new and special revelation, explaining dark and mysterious things, with which my youthful understanding had struggled, but struggled in vain." The word *revelation* has almost religious force: the child's vision of reading as the key to freedom saves his soul. From this point on in his story—and he is only about eight years old at the time—*words* lead Douglass to succeeding revelations. He defies all efforts to shut him up "in mental darkness." From little white street urchins, he acquires the sustaining "bread of knowledge." At the age of twelve or thereabouts, he reads a book called *The Columbian Orator* which contains forceful antislavery arguments, and is thus enabled for the first time to utter his thoughts. Without the authority of the written word, the contact through it with other minds, he could not know how to articulate what he thinks, could hardly know what it is he thinks. He puzzles over the word *abolitionist*, hearing but not understanding it. When he figures out its meaning, he has passed another milestone. A slave's thoughts must be free, this account suggests, before he can hope for meaningful freedom of body; and freedom of thought comes only through knowledge of the word.

We know *that* the writer successfully achieves freedom, but he makes gripping drama out of the gradual reporting of *how*. First he must painfully learn to write, another step toward taking possession of language. For his first, agonizingly abortive attempt at escape, he writes passes for himself and his friends, briefly preempting the glory of being his own master. Subjected subsequently to more brutalized conditions, he sustains himself by making an imaginary speech, in what he remembers as elaborate literary language, to the fleet of ships he sees on Chesapeake Bay, images of freedom. He defies his brutal overseer, claims his manhood, teaches fellow slaves to read; finally, as though by magic, he escapes. (He withholds details of the escape to protect others; the effect of this suppression on the narrative is to suggest that the escape occurs almost as the inevitable, natural culmination of the process of self-discovery.) A friendly white man gives him a new name. And finally Douglass discovers his own voice as well as his own words: the *Narrative* concludes with his assuming the role of orator on behalf of his people.

Despite its emphasis on the power of language, the autobiography reminds us also that language can't say everything. Rousseau exhaustively explores his own feelings; Douglass recurrently comments on the inexpressibility of his deepest feelings. At the end of chapter 1, Frederick, a small child, watches his aunt whipped till she is covered with blood. "It was a most terrible spectacle. I wish I could commit to paper the feelings with which I beheld it." His feelings exceed the possibility of verbal representation. Other episodes of comparable brutality elicit the same response: the narrator feels more than he can say. The reader is recurrently reminded that the horrible reality to which Douglass's words refer is in fact a reality beyond words.

Douglass's development of identity, his ultimate subscription of his new name as the sign of his self, leads to no claim of uniqueness. On the contrary, the identity he claims is partly *communal*. "Sincerely and earnestly hoping that this little book may do something toward throwing light on the American slave system, and hastening the glad day of deliverance to the millions of my brethren in bonds—faithfully relying upon the power of truth, love, and justice, for success in my humble efforts—and solemnly pledging my self anew to the sacred cause,—I subscribe myself, FREDERICK

DOUGLASS." The "little book" exists not to establish Douglass's difference but to declare his unity. Now he possesses his own name, his own differentiating clothes, his own wife, his own self-defined occupation; but as much as when he was a half-naked child gobbling mush with the others, he feels part of a group. His love for fellow slaves, a recurrent theme of his story, provides the foundation for his identity—not, like Rousseau, emotionally isolated, but part of a sustaining community.

His language, both in the final paragraph just quoted and elsewhere, suggests that he partakes also of an even wider community. He evokes "truth" and "justice," proclaimed ideals of the American nation. He quotes John Greenleaf Whittier, "the slaves' poet," to express feelings he finds it hard to state for himself. Everywhere his prose rings with Biblical rhythms and allusions. Frederick Douglass is not only a slave, not only an ex-slave; he is a literary man, an American, a Christian, claiming, relying on, and valuing these larger forms of communion as well as his union with his race—and implicitly demanding that others who call themselves Americans or Christians acknowledge his participation with them and accept the responsibility such acknowledgment implies.

An illuminating biography of Douglass, which elaborates on the information of the *Narrative*, is N. Huggins, *Slave and Citizen: The Life of Frederick Douglass* (1980). D. J. Preston, *Young Frederick Douglass: The Maryland Years* (1980), concentrates on the earlier period. For critical treatments, see R. B. Stepto, "Narration, Authentication, and Authorial Control in Frederick Douglass' *Narrative* of 1845," *Afro-American Literature: The Reconstruction of Instruction*, ed., R. Stepto and D. Fisher (1978), and A. E. Stone, "Identity and Art in Frederick Douglass's *Narrative*," *College Language Association Journal* 17 (1973), 192–213.

Narrative of the Life of Frederick Douglass, An American Slave[1]

Chapter I

I was born in Tuckahoe, near Hillsborough, and about twelve miles from Easton, in Talbot county, Maryland. I have no accurate knowledge of my age, never having seen any authentic record containing it. By far the larger part of the slaves know as little of their ages as horses know of theirs, and it is the wish of most masters within my knowledge to keep their slaves thus ignorant. I do not remember to have ever met a slave who could tell of his birthday. They seldom come nearer to it than planting-time, harvest-time, cherry-time, spring-time, or fall-time. A want of information concerning my own was a source of unhappiness to me even during childhood. The white children could tell their ages. I could not tell

1. The text, printed in its entirety, is that of the first American edition, published by the Massachusetts Anti-Slavery Society in Boston in 1845.

why I ought to be deprived of the same privilege. I was not allowed to make any inquiries of my master concerning it. He deemed all such inquiries on the part of a slave improper and impertinent, and evidence of a restless spirit. The nearest estimate I can give makes me now between twenty-seven and twenty-eight years of age. I come to this, from hearing my master say, some time during 1835, I was about seventeen years old.

My mother was named Harriet Bailey. She was the daughter of Isaac and Betsey Bailey, both colored, and quite dark. My mother was of a darker complexion than either my grandmother or grandfather.

My father was a white man. He was admitted to be such by all I ever heard speak of my parentage. The opinion was also whispered that my master was my father; but of the correctness of this opinion, I know nothing; the means of knowing was withheld from me. My mother and I were separated when I was but an infant—before I knew her as my mother. It is a common custom, in the part of Maryland from which I ran away, to part children from their mothers at a very early age. Frequently, before the child has reached its twelfth month, its mother is taken from it, and hired out on some farm a considerable distance off, and the child is placed under the care of an old woman, too old for field labor. For what this separation is done, I do not know, unless it be to hinder the development of the child's affection toward its mother, and to blunt and destroy the natural affection of the mother for the child. This is the inevitable result.

I never saw my mother, to know her as such, more than four or five times in my life; and each of those times was very short in duration, and at night. She was hired by a Mr. Stewart, who lived about twelve miles from my home. She made her journeys to see me in the night, travelling the whole distance on foot, after the performance of her day's work. She was a field hand, and a whipping is the penalty of not being in the field at sunrise, unless a slave has special permission from his or her master to the contrary—a permission which they seldom get, and one that gives to him that gives it the proud name of being a kind master. I do not recollect of ever seeing my mother by the light of day. She was with me in the night. She would lie down with me, and get me to sleep, but long before I waked she was gone. Very little communication ever took place between us. Death soon ended what little we could have while she lived, and with it her hardships and suffering. She died when I was about seven years old, on one of my master's farms, near Lee's Mill. I was not allowed to be present during her illness, at her death, or burial. She was gone long before I knew any thing about it. Never having enjoyed, to any considerable extent, her soothing presence, her tender and watchful care, I received the tidings of her death with much the same emotions I should have probably felt at the death of a stranger.

Called thus suddenly away, she left me without the slightest intimation of who my father was. The whisper that my master was my father, may or may not be true; and, true or false, it is of but little consequence to my purpose whilst the fact remains, in all its glaring odiousness, that slaveholders have ordained, and by law established, that the children of slave women shall in all cases follow the condition of their mothers; and this is done too obviously to administer to their own lusts, and make a gratification of their wicked desires profitable as well as pleasurable; for by this cunning arrangement, the slaveholder, in cases not a few, sustains to his slaves the double relation of master and father.

I know of such cases; and it is worthy of remark that such slaves invariably suffer greater hardships, and have more to contend with, than others. They are, in the first place, a constant offence to their mistress. She is ever disposed to find fault with them; they can seldom do any thing to please her; she is never better pleased than when she sees them under the lash, especially when she suspects her husband of showing to his mulatto children favors which he withholds from his black slaves. The master is frequently compelled to sell this class of his slaves, out of deference to the feelings of his white wife; and, cruel as the deed may strike any one to be, for a man to sell his own children to human flesh-mongers, it is often the dictate of humanity for him to do so; for, unless he does this, he must not only whip them himself, but must stand by and see one white son tie up his brother, of but few shades darker complexion than himself, and ply the gory lash to his naked back; and if he lisp one word of disapproval, it is set down to his parental partiality, and only makes a bad matter worse, both for himself and the slave whom he would protect and defend.

Every year brings with it multitudes of this class of slaves. It was doubtless in consequence of a knowledge of this fact, that one great statesman of the south predicted the downfall of slavery by the inevitable laws of population. Whether this prophecy is ever fulfilled or not, it is nevertheless plain that a very different-looking class of people are springing up at the south, and are now held in slavery, from those originally brought to this country from Africa; and if their increase will do no other good, it will do away the force of the argument, that God cursed Ham,[2] and therefore American slavery is right. If the lineal descendants of Ham are alone to be scripturally enslaved, it is certain that slavery at the south must soon become unscriptural; for

2. Noah cursed his second son, Ham, for mocking him; it was thought that a black skin resulted from the curse and that all black people descended from Ham.

thousands are ushered into the world, annually, who, like myself, owe their existence to white fathers, and those fathers most frequently their own masters.

I have had two masters. My first master's name was Anthony. I do not remember his first name. He was generally called Captain Anthony—a title which, I presume, he acquired by sailing a craft on the Chesapeake Bay. He was not considered a rich slaveholder. He owned two or three farms, and about thirty slaves. His farms and slaves were under the care of an overseer. The overseer's name was Plummer. Mr. Plummer was a miserable drunkard, a profane swearer, and a savage monster. He always went armed with a cowskin and a heavy cudgel. I have known him to cut and slash the women's heads so horribly, that even master would be enraged at his cruelty, and would threaten to whip him if he did not mind himself. Master, however, was not a humane slaveholder. It required extraordinary barbarity on the part of an overseer to affect him. He was a cruel man, hardened by a long life of slaveholding. He would at times seem to take great pleasure in whipping a slave. I have often been awakened at the dawn of day by the most heart-rending shrieks of an own aunt of mine, whom he used to tie up to a joist, and whip upon her naked back till she was literally covered with blood. No words, no tears, no prayers, from his gory victim, seemed to move his iron heart from its bloody purpose. The louder she screamed, the harder he whipped; and where the blood ran fastest, there he whipped longest. He would whip her to make her scream, and whip her to make her hush; and not until overcome by fatigue, would he cease to swing the blood-clotted cowskin. I remember the first time I ever witnessed this horrible exhibition. I was quite a child, but I well remember it. I never shall forget it whilst I remember any thing. It was the first of a long series of such outrages, of which I was doomed to be a witness and a participant. It struck me with awful force. It was the blood-stained gate, the entrance to the hell of slavery, through which I was about to pass. It was a most terrible spectacle. I wish I could commit to paper the feelings with which I beheld it.

This occurrence took place very soon after I went to live with my old master, and under the following circumstances. Aunt Hester went out one night,—where or for what I do not know,—and happened to be absent when my master desired her presence. He had ordered her not to go out evenings, and warned her that she must never let him catch her in company with a young man, who was paying attention to her belonging to Colonel Lloyd. The young man's name was Ned Roberts, generally called Lloyd's Ned. Why master was so careful of her, may be safely left to conjecture. She was a woman of noble form, and of graceful proportions, having very few equals, and fewer superiors, in personal appearance, among the colored or white women of our neighborhood.

Aunt Hester had not only disobeyed his orders in going out, but had been found in company with Lloyd's Ned; which circumstance, I found, from what he said while whipping her, was the chief offence. Had he been a man of pure morals himself, he might have been thought interested in protecting the innocence of my aunt; but those who knew him will not suspect him of any such virtue. Before he commenced whipping Aunt Hester, he took her into the kitchen, and stripped her from neck to waist, leaving her neck, shoulders, and back, entirely naked. He then told her to cross her hands, calling her at the same time a d——d b——h. After crossing her hands, he tied them with a strong rope, and led her to a stool under a large hook in the joist, put in for the purpose. He made her get upon the stool, and tied her hands to the hook. She now stood fair for his infernal purpose. Her arms were stretched up at their full length, so that she stood upon the ends of her toes. He then said to her, "Now, you d——d b——h, I'll learn you how to disobey my orders!" and after rolling up his sleeves, he commenced to lay on the heavy cowskin, and soon the warm, red blood (amid heart-rending shrieks from her, and horrid oaths from him) came dripping to the floor. I was so terrified and horror-stricken at the sight, that I hid myself in a closet, and dared not venture out till long after the bloody transaction was over. I expected it would be my turn next. It was all new to me. I had never seen any thing like it before. I had always lived with my grandmother on the outskirts of the plantation, where she was put to raise the children of the younger women. I had therefore been, until now, out of the way of the bloody scenes that often occurred on the plantation.

Chapter II

My master's family consisted of two sons, Andrew and Richard; one daughter, Lucretia, and her husband, Captain Thomas Auld. They lived in one house, upon the home plantation of Colonel Edward Lloyd. My master was Colonel Lloyd's clerk and superintendent. He was what might be called the overseer of the overseers. I spent two years of childhood on this plantation in my old master's family. It was here that I witnessed the bloody transaction recorded in the first chapter; and as I received my first impressions of slavery on this plantation, I will give some description of it, and of slavery as it there existed. The plantation is about twelve miles north of Easton, in Talbot county, and is situated on the border of Miles River. The principal products raised upon it were tobacco, corn, and wheat.

These were raised in great abundance; so that, with the products of this and the other farms belonging to him, he was able to keep in almost constant employment a large sloop, in carrying them to market at Baltimore. This sloop was named *Sally Lloyd*, in honor of one of the colonel's daughters. My master's son-in-law, Captain Auld, was master of the vessel; she was otherwise manned by the colonel's own slaves. Their names were Peter, Isaac, Rich, and Jake. These were esteemed very highly by the other slaves, and looked upon as the privileged ones of the plantation; for it was no small affair, in the eyes of the slaves, to be allowed to see Baltimore.

Colonel Lloyd kept from three to four hundred slaves on his home plantation, and owned a large number more on the neighboring farms belonging to him. The names of the farms nearest to the home plantation were Wye Town and New Design. "Wye Town" was under the overseership of a man named Noah Willis. New Design was under the overseership of a Mr. Townsend. The overseers of these, and all the rest of the farms, numbering over twenty, received advice and direction from the managers of the home plantation. This was the great business place. It was the seat of government for the whole twenty farms. All disputes among the overseers were settled here. If a slave was convicted of any high misdemeanor, became unmanageable, or evinced a determination to run away, he was brought immediately here, severely whipped, put on board the sloop, carried to Baltimore, and sold to Austin Woolfolk, or some other slave-trader, as a warning to the slaves remaining.

Here, too, the slaves of all the other farms received their monthly allowance of food, and their yearly clothing. The men and women slaves received, as their monthly allowance of food, eight pounds of pork, or its equivalent in fish, and one bushel of corn meal. Their yearly clothing consisted of two coarse linen shirts, one pair of linen trousers, like the shirts, one jacket, one pair of trousers for winter, made of coarse negro cloth, one pair of stockings, and one pair of shoes; the whole of which could not have cost more than seven dollars. The allowance of the slave children was given to their mothers, or the old women having the care of them. The children unable to work in the field had neither shoes, stockings, jackets, nor trousers, given to them; their clothing consisted of two coarse linen shirts per year. When these failed them, they went naked until the next allowance-day. Children from seven to ten years old, of both sexes, almost naked, might be seen at all seasons of the year.

There were no beds given the slaves, unless one coarse blanket be considered such, and none but the men and women had these. This, however, is not considered a very great privation. They find less difficulty from the want of beds, than from the want of time to sleep; for when their day's work in the field is done, the most of them having their washing, mending, and cooking to do, and having few or none of the ordinary facilities for doing either of these, very many of their sleeping hours are consumed in preparing for the field the coming day; and when this is done, old and young, male and female, married and single, drop down side by side, on one common bed,— the cold, damp floor,—each covering himself or herself with their miserable blankets; and here they sleep till they are summoned to the field by the driver's horn. At the sound of this, all must rise, and be off to the field. There must be no halting; every one must be at his or her post; and woe betides them who hear not this morning summons to the field; for if they are not awakened by the sense of hearing, they are by the sense of feeling: no age nor sex finds any favor. Mr. Severe, the overseer, used to stand by the door of the quarter, armed with a large hickory stick and heavy cowskin, ready to whip any one who was so unfortunate as not to hear, or, from any other cause, was prevented from being ready to start for the field at the sound of the horn.

Mr. Severe was rightly named: he was a cruel man. I have seen him whip a woman, causing the blood to run half an hour at the time; and this, too, in the midst of her crying children, pleading for their mother's release. He seemed to take pleasure in manifesting his fiendish barbarity. Added to his cruelty, he was a profane swearer. It was enough to chill the blood and stiffen the hair of an ordinary man to hear him talk. Scarce a sentence escaped him but that was commenced or concluded by some horrid oath. The field was the place to witness his cruelty and profanity. His presence made it both the field of blood and of blasphemy. From the rising till the going down of the sun, he was cursing, raving, cutting, and slashing among the slaves of the field, in the most frightful manner. His career was short. He died very soon after I went to Colonel Lloyd's; and he died as he lived, uttering, with his dying groans, bitter curses and horrid oaths. His death was regarded by the slaves as the result of a merciful providence.

Mr. Severe's place was filled by a Mr. Hopkins. He was a very different man. He was less cruel, less profane, and made less noise, than Mr. Severe. His course was characterized by no extraordinary demonstrations of cruelty. He whipped, but seemed to take no pleasure in it. He was called by the slaves a good overseer.

The home plantation of Colonel Lloyd wore the appearance of a country village. All the mechanical operations for all the farms were performed here. The shoemaking and mending, the blacksmithing, cartwrighting, coopering, weaving, and grain-grinding, were all performed by the slaves on the home plantation. The whole place wore a business-like aspect very unlike the neighboring farms. The number of houses, too, conspired to give it advantage over the neighboring farms. It was called by the slaves the *Great House Farm*. Few privileges were esteemed higher, by the slaves of the out-farms, than that of being selected to do errands at the Great House Farm. It was associated in their minds with greatness. A representative could not be prouder of his election to a seat in the American Congress, than a slave on one of the out-farms would be of his election to do errands at the Great House Farm. They regarded it as evidence of great confidence reposed in them by their overseers; and it was on this account, as well as a constant desire to be out of the field from under the driver's lash, that they esteemed it a high privilege, one worth careful living for. He was called the smartest and most trusty fellow, who had this honor conferred upon him the most frequently. The competitors for this office sought as diligently to please their overseers, as the office-seekers in the political parties seek to please and deceive the people. The same traits of character might be seen in Colonel Lloyd's slaves, as are seen in the slaves of the political parties.

The slaves selected to go to the Great House Farm, for the monthly allowance for themselves and their fellow-slaves, were peculiarly enthusiastic. While on their way, they would make the dense old woods, for miles around, reverberate with their wild songs, revealing at once the highest joy and the deepest sadness. They would compose and sing as they went along, consulting neither time nor tune. The thought that came up, came out—if not in the word, in the sound;—and as frequently in the one as in the other. They would sometimes sing the most pathetic sentiment in the most rapturous tone, and the most rapturous sentiment in the most pathetic tone. Into all of their songs they would manage to weave something of the Great House Farm. Especially would they do this, when leaving home. They would then sing most exultingly the following words:—

> "I am going away to the Great House Farm!
> O, yea! O, yea! O!"

This they would sing, as a chorus, to words which to many would seem unmeaning jargon, but which, nevertheless, were full of meaning to themselves. I have sometimes thought that the mere hearing of those songs would do more to impress some minds with the horrible character of slavery, than the reading of whole volumes of philosophy on the subject could do.

I did not, when a slave, understand the deep meaning of those rude and apparently incoherent songs. I was myself within the circle; so that I neither saw nor heard as those without might see and hear. They told a tale of woe which was then altogether beyond my feeble comprehension; they were tones loud, long, and deep; they breathed the prayer and complaint of souls boiling over with the bitterest anguish. Every tone was a testimony against slavery, and a prayer to God for deliverance from chains. The hearing of those wild notes always depressed my spirit, and filled me with ineffable sadness. I have frequently found myself in tears while hearing them. The mere recurrence to those songs, even now, afflicts me; and while I am writing these lines, an expression of feeling has already found its way down my cheek. To those songs I trace my first glimmering conception of the dehumanizing character of slavery. I can never get rid of that conception. Those songs still follow me, to deepen my hatred of slavery, and quicken my sympathies for my brethren in bonds. If any one wishes to be impressed with the soul-killing effects of slavery, let him go to Colonel Lloyd's plantation, and, on allowance-day, place himself in the deep pine woods, and there let him, in silence, analyze the sounds that shall pass through the chambers of his soul,—and if he is not thus impressed, it will only be because "there is no flesh in his obdurate heart."

I have often been utterly astonished, since I came to the north, to find persons who could speak of the singing, among slaves, as evidence of their contentment and happiness. It is impossible to conceive of a greater mistake. Slaves sing most when they are most unhappy. The songs of the slave represent the sorrows of his heart; and he is relieved by them, only as an aching heart is relieved by its tears. At least, such is my experience. I have often sung to drown my sorrow, but seldom to express my happiness. Crying for joy, and singing for joy, were alike uncommon to me while in the jaws of slavery. The singing of a man cast away upon a desolate island might be as appropriately considered as evidence of contentment and happiness, as the singing of a slave; the songs of the one and of the other are prompted by the same emotion.

Chapter III

Colonel Lloyd kept a large and finely cultivated garden, which afforded almost constant employment for four men, besides the chief gardener, (Mr. M'Durmond). This garden was probably the greatest attraction of the place. During the summer months, people came from far and near—from Baltimore, Easton, and Annapolis—to see it. It abounded in fruits of almost every description, from the hardy apple of the north to the delicate orange of the south. This garden was not the least source of trouble on the plantation. Its excellent fruit was quite a temptation to the hungry swarms of boys, as well as the older slaves, belonging to the colonel, few of whom had the virtue or the vice to resist it. Scarcely a day passed, during the summer, but that some slave had to take the lash for stealing fruit. The colonel had to resort to all kinds of stratagems to keep his slaves out of the garden. The last and most successful one was that of tarring his fence all around; after which, if a slave was caught with tar upon his person, it was deemed sufficient proof that he had either been into the garden, or had tried to get in. In either case, he was severely whipped by the chief gardener. This plan worked well; the slaves became as fearful of tar as of the lash. They seemed to realize the impossibility of touching *tar* without being defiled.[3]

The colonel also kept a splendid riding equipage. His stable and carriage-house presented the appearance of some of our large city livery establishments. His horses were of the finest form and noblest blood. His carriage-house contained three splendid coaches, three or four gigs, besides dearborns and barouches of the most fashionable style.

This establishment was under the care of two slaves—old Barney and young Barney—father and son. To attend to this establishment was their sole work. But it was by no means an easy employment; for in nothing was Colonel Lloyd more particular than in the management of his horses. The slightest inattention to these was unpardonable, and was visited upon those, under whose care they were placed, with the severest punishment; no excuse could shield them, if the colonel only suspected any want of attention to his horses—a supposition which he frequently indulged, and one which, of course, made the office of old and young Barney a very trying one. They never knew when they were safe from punishment. They were frequently whipped when least deserving, and escaped whipping when most deserving it. Every thing depended upon the looks of the horses, and the state of Colonel Lloyd's own mind when his horses were brought to him for use. If a horse did not move fast enough, or hold his head high enough, it was owing to some fault of his keepers. It was painful to stand near the stable-door, and hear the various complaints against the keepers when a horse was taken out for use. "This horse has not had proper attention. He has not been sufficiently rubbed and curried, or he has not been properly fed; his food was too wet or too dry; he got it too soon or too late; he was too hot or too cold; he had too much hay, and not enough of grain; or he had too much grain, and not enough of hay; instead of old Barney's attending to the horse, he had very improperly left it to his son." To all these complaints, no matter how unjust, the slave must answer never a word. Colonel Lloyd could not brook any contradiction from a slave. When he spoke, a slave must stand, listen, and tremble; and such was literally the case. I have seen Colonel Lloyd make old Barney, a man between fifty and sixty years of age, uncover his bald head, kneel down upon the cold, damp ground, and receive upon

---

3. Cf. the proverb, "He who touches pitch shall be defiled."

his naked and toil-worn shoulders more than thirty lashes at the time. Colonel Lloyd had three sons—Edward, Murray, and Daniel,—and three sons-in-law, Mr. Winder, Mr. Nicholson, and Mr. Lowndes. All of these lived at the Great House Farm, and enjoyed the luxury of whipping the servants when they pleased, from old Barney down to William Wilkes, the coach-driver. I have seen Winder make one of the house-servants stand off from him a suitable distance to be touched with the end of his whip, and at every stroke raise great ridges upon his back.

To describe the wealth of Colonel Lloyd would be almost equal to describing the riches of Job.[4] He kept from ten to fifteen house-servants. He was said to own a thousand slaves, and I think this estimate quite within the truth. Colonel Lloyd owned so many that he did not know them when he saw them; nor did all the slaves of the out-farms know him. It is reported of him, that, while riding along the road one day, he met a colored man, and addressed him in the usual manner of speaking to colored people on the public highways of the south: "Well, boy, whom do you belong to?" "To Colonel Lloyd," replied the slave. "Well, does the colonel treat you well?" "No, sir," was the ready reply. "What, does he work you too hard?" "Yes, sir." "Well, don't he give you enough to eat?" "Yes, sir, he gives me enough, such as it is."

The colonel, after ascertaining where the slave belonged, rode on; the man also went on about his business, not dreaming that he had been conversing with his master. He thought, said, and heard nothing more of the matter, until two or three weeks afterwards. The poor man was then informed by his overseer that, for having found fault with his master, he was now to be sold to a Georgia trader. He was immediately chained and hand-cuffed; and thus, without a moment's warning, he was snatched away, and forever sundered, from his family and friends, by a hand more unrelenting than death. This is the penalty of telling the truth, of telling the simple truth, in answer to a series of plain questions.

It is partly in consequence of such facts, that slaves, when inquired of as to their condition and the character of their masters, almost universally say they are contented, and that their masters are kind. The slaveholders have been known to send in spies among their slaves, to ascertain their views and feelings in regard to their condition. The frequency of this has had the effect to establish among the slaves the maxim, that a still tongue makes a wise head. They suppress the truth rather than take the consequences of telling it, and in so doing prove themselves a part of the human family. If they have any thing

4. Job 1:3: "His substance also was seven thousand sheep, and three thousand camels, and five hundred yoke of oxen, and five hundred she asses, and a very great household; so that this man was the greatest of all the men of the east."

to say of their masters, it is generally in their masters' favor, especially when speaking to an untried man. I have been frequently asked, when a slave, if I had a kind master, and do not remember ever to have given a negative answer; nor did I, in pursuing this course, consider myself as uttering what was absolutely false; for I always measured the kindness of my master by the standard of kindness set up among slaveholders around us. Moreover, slaves are like other people, and imbibe prejudices quite common to others. They think their own better than that of others. Many, under the influence of this prejudice, think their own masters are better than the masters of other slaves; and this, too, in some cases, when the very reverse is true. Indeed, it is not uncommon for slaves even to fall out and quarrel among themselves about the relative goodness of their masters, each contending for the superior goodness of his own over that of the others. At the very same time, they mutually execrate their masters when viewed separately. It was so on our plantation. When Colonel Lloyd's slaves met the slaves of Jacob Jepson, they seldom parted without a quarrel about their masters; Colonel Lloyd's slaves contending that he was the richest, and Mr. Jepson's slaves that he was the smartest, and most of a man. Colonel Lloyd's slaves would boast his ability to buy and sell Jacob Jepson. Mr. Jepson's slaves would boast his ability to whip Colonel Lloyd. These quarrels would almost always end in a fight between the parties, and those that whipped were supposed to have gained the point at issue. They seemed to think that the greatness of their masters was transferable to themselves. It was considered as being bad enough to be a slave; but to be a poor man's slave was deemed a disgrace indeed!

Chapter IV

Mr. Hopkins remained but a short time in the office of overseer. Why his career was so short, I do not know, but suppose he lacked the necessary severity to suit Colonel Lloyd. Mr. Hopkins was succeeded by Mr. Austin Gore, a man possessing, in an eminent degree, all those traits of character indispensable to what is called a first-rate overseer. Mr. Gore had served Colonel Lloyd, in the capacity of overseer, upon one of the out-farms, and had shown himself worthy of the high station of overseer upon the home or Great House Farm.

Mr. Gore was proud, ambitious, and persevering. He was artful, cruel, and obdurate. He was just the man for such a place, and it was just the place for such a man. It afforded scope for the full exercise of all his powers, and he seemed to be perfectly at home in it. He was one of those who could torture the slightest look, word, or gesture, on the part of the slave, into impudence, and would treat it accordingly. There must be no answering back to him; no explanation was allowed a slave, showing himself to have been wrongfully accused. Mr. Gore acted fully up to the maxim laid down by slave-holders,—"It is better that a dozen slaves suffer under the lash, than that the overseer should be convicted, in the presence of the slaves, of having been at fault." No matter how innocent a slave might be—it availed him nothing, when accused by Mr. Gore of any misde-meanor. To be accused was to be convicted, and to be convicted was to be punished; the one always following the other with immutable certainty. To escape punishment was to escape accusation; and few slaves had the fortune to do either, under the overseership of Mr. Gore. He was just proud enough to demand the most debasing hom-age of the slave, and quite servile enough to crouch, himself, at the feet of the master. He was ambitious enough to be contented with nothing short of the highest rank of overseers, and persevering enough to reach the height of his ambition. He was cruel enough to inflict the severest punishment, artful enough to descend to the lowest trickery, and obdurate enough to be insensible to the voice of a reproving conscience. He was, of all the overseers, the most dreaded by the slaves. His presence was painful; his eye flashed confusion; and seldom was his sharp, shrill voice heard, without producing hor-ror and trembling in their ranks.

Mr. Gore was a grave man, and, though a young man, he indulged in no jokes, said no funny words, seldom smiled. His words were in perfect keeping with his looks, and his looks were in perfect keeping with his words. Overseers will sometimes indulge in a witty word, even with the slaves; not so with Mr. Gore. He spoke but to com-mand, and commanded but to be obeyed; he dealt sparingly with his words, and bountifully with his whip, never using the former where the latter would answer as well. When he whipped, he seemed to do so from a sense of duty, and feared no consequences. He did nothing reluctantly, no matter how disagreeable; always at his post, never inconsistent. He never promised but to fulfil. He was, in a word, a man of the most inflexible firmness and stone-like coolness.

His savage barbarity was equalled only by the consummate cool-ness with which he committed the grossest and most savage deeds upon the slaves under his charge. Mr. Gore once undertook to whip one of Colonel Lloyd's slaves, by the name of Demby. He had given Demby but few stripes, when, to get rid of the scourging, he ran and plunged himself into a creek, and stood there at the depth of his shoulders, refusing to come out. Mr. Gore told him that he would give him three calls, and that, if he did not come out at the third call, he would shoot him. The first call was given. Demby made no response, but stood his ground. The second and third calls were given with the same result. Mr. Gore then, without consultation or deliberation with any one, not even giving Demby an additional call, raised his musket to his face, taking deadly aim at his standing victim, and in an instant poor Demby was no more. His mangled body sank out of sight, and blood and brains marked the water where he had stood.

A thrill of horror flashed through every soul upon the plantation, excepting Mr. Gore. He alone seemed cool and collected. He was asked by Colonel Lloyd and my old master, why he resorted to this extraordinary expedient. His reply was, (as well as I can remember,) that Demby had become unmanageable. He was setting a dangerous example to the other slaves,—one which, if suffered to pass without some such demonstration on his part, would finally lead to the total subversion of all rule and order upon the plantation. He argued that if one slave refused to be corrected, and escaped with his life, the other slaves would soon copy the example; the result of which would be, the freedom of the slaves, and the enslavement of the whites. Mr. Gore's defence was satisfactory. He was continued in his station as overseer upon the home plantation. His fame as an overseer went abroad. His horrid crime was not even submitted to judicial investigation. It was committed in the presence of slaves, and they of course could neither institute a suit, nor testify against him; and thus the guilty perpetrator of one of the bloodiest and most foul murders goes unwhipped of justice, and uncensured by the community in which he lives. Mr. Gore lived in St. Michael's, Talbot county, Maryland, when I left there; and if he is still alive, he very probably lives there now; and if so, he is now, as he was then, as highly esteemed and as much respected as though his guilty soul had not been stained with his brother's blood.

I speak advisedly when I say this,—that killing a slave, or any colored person, in Talbot county, Maryland, is not treated as a crime, either by the courts or the community. Mr. Thomas Lanman, of St. Michael's, killed two slaves, one of whom he killed with a hatchet, by knocking his brains out. He used to boast of the commission of the awful and bloody deed. I have heard him do so laughingly, saying, among other things, that he was the only benefactor of his country in the company, and that when others would do as much as he had done, we should be relieved of "the d——d niggers."

The wife of Mr. Giles Hick [sic], living but a short distance from where I used to live, murdered my wife's cousin, a young girl between fifteen and sixteen years of age, mangling her person in the most horrible manner, breaking her nose and breastbone with a stick, so that the poor girl expired in a few hours afterward. She was immediately buried, but had not been in her untimely grave but a few hours before she was taken up and examined by the coroner, who decided that she had come to her death by severe beating. The offence for which this girl was thus murdered was this:—She had been set that night to mind Mrs. Hick's baby, and during the night she fell asleep, and the baby cried. She, having lost her rest for several nights previous, did not hear the crying. They were both in the room with Mrs. Hicks. Mrs. Hicks, finding the girl slow to move, jumped from her bed, seized an oak stick of wood by the fireplace, and with it broke the girl's nose and breastbone, and thus ended her life. I will not say this most horrid murder produced no sensation in the community. It did produce sensation, but not enough to bring the murderess to punishment. There was a warrant issued for her arrest, but it was never served. Thus she escaped not only punishment, but even the pain of being arraigned before a court for her horrid crime.

Whilst I am detailing bloody deeds which took place during my stay on Colonel Lloyd's plantation, I will briefly narrate another, which occurred about the same time as the murder of Demby by Mr. Gore.

Colonel Lloyd's slaves were in the habit of spending a part of their nights and Sundays in fishing for oysters, and in this way made up the deficiency of their scanty allowance. An old man belonging to Colonel Lloyd, while thus engaged, happened to get beyond the limits of Colonel Lloyd's, and on the premises of Mr. Beal Bondly. At this trespass, Mr. Bondly took offence, and with his musket came down to the shore, and blew its deadly contents into the poor old man.

Mr. Bondly came over to see Colonel Lloyd the next day, whether to pay him for his property, or to justify himself in what he had done, I know not. At any rate, this whole fiendish transaction was soon hushed up. There was very little said about it at all, and nothing done. It was a common saying, even among little white boys, that it was worth a half-cent to kill a "nigger," and a half-cent to bury one.

Chapter V

As to my own treatment while I lived on Colonel Lloyd's plantation, it was very similar to that of the other slave children. I was not old enough to work in the field, and there being little else than field work to do, I had a great deal of leisure time. The most I had to do was to drive up the cows at evening, keep the fowls out of the garden, keep the front yard clean, and run off errands for my old master's daughter, Mrs. Lucretia Auld. The most of my leisure time I spent in helping Master Daniel Lloyd in finding his birds, after he had shot them. My connection with Master Daniel was of some advantage to me. He became quite attached to me, and was a sort of protector of me. He would not allow the older boys to impose upon me, and would divide his cakes with me.

I was seldom whipped by my old master, and suffered little from any thing else than hunger and cold. I suffered much from hunger, but much more from cold. In hottest summer and coldest winter, I was kept almost naked—no shoes, no stockings, no jacket, no trousers, nothing on but a coarse tow linen shirt, reaching only to my knees. I had no bed. I must have perished with cold, but that, the coldest nights, I used to steal a bag which was used for carrying corn to the mill. I would crawl into this bag, and there sleep on the cold, damp, clay floor, with my head in and feet out. My feet had been so cracked with the frost, that the pen with which I am writing might be laid in the gashes.

We were not regularly allowanced. Our food was coarse corn meal boiled. This was called *mush*. It was put into a large wooden tray or trough, and set down upon the ground. The children were then called, like so many pigs, and like so many pigs they would come and devour the mush; some with oystershells, others with pieces of shingle, some with naked hands, and none with spoons. He that ate fastest got most; he that was strongest secured the best place; and few left the trough satisfied.

I was probably between seven and eight years old when I left Colonel Lloyd's plantation. I left it with joy. I shall never forget the ecstasy with which I received the intelligence that my old master (Anthony) had determined to let me go to Baltimore, to live with Mr. Hugh Auld, brother to my old master's son-in-law, Captain Thomas Auld. I received this information about three days before my departure. They were three of the happiest days I ever enjoyed. I spent the most part of all these three days in the creek, washing off the plantation scurf, and preparing myself for my departure.

The pride of appearance which this would indicate was not my own. I spent the time in washing, not so much because I wished to, but because Mrs. Lucretia had told me I must get all the dead skin off my feet and knees before I could go to Baltimore; for the people in Baltimore were very cleanly, and would laugh at me if I looked dirty. Besides, she was going to give me a pair of trousers, which I should not put on unless I got all the dirt off me. The thought of owning a pair of trousers was great indeed! It was almost a sufficient motive, not only to make me take off what would be called by pig-drovers the mange, but the skin itself. I went at it in good earnest, working for the first time with the hope of reward.

The ties that ordinarily bind children to their homes were all suspended in my case. I found no severe trial in my departure. My home was charmless; it was not home to me; on parting from it, I could not feel that I was leaving any thing which I could have enjoyed by staying. My mother was dead, my grandmother lived far off, so that I seldom saw her. I had two sisters and one brother, that lived in the same house with me; but the early separation of us from our mother had well nigh blotted the fact of our relationship from our memories. I looked for home elsewhere, and was confident of finding none which I should relish less than the one which I was leaving. If, however, I found in my new home hardship, hunger, whipping, and nakedness, I had the consolation that I should not have escaped any one of them by staying. Having already had more than a taste of them in the house of my old master, and having endured them there, I very naturally inferred my ability to endure them elsewhere, and especially at Baltimore; for I had something of the feeling about Baltimore that is expressed in the proverb, that "being hanged in England is preferable to dying a natural death in Ireland." I had the strongest desire to see Baltimore. Cousin Tom, though not fluent in speech, had inspired me with that desire by his eloquent description of the place. I could never point out any thing at the Great House, no matter how beautiful or powerful, but that he had seen something at Baltimore far exceeding, both in beauty and strength, the object which I pointed out to him. Even the Great House itself, with all its pictures, was far inferior to many buildings in Baltimore. So strong was my desire, that I thought a gratification of it would fully compensate for whatever loss of comforts I should sustain by the exchange. I left without a regret, and with the highest hopes of future happiness.

We sailed out of Miles River for Baltimore on a Saturday morning. I remember only the day of the week, for at that time I had no knowledge of the days of the month, nor the months of the year. On setting sail, I walked aft, and gave to Colonel Lloyd's plantation what I hoped would be the last look. I then placed myself in the bows of the sloop, and there spent the remainder of the day in looking ahead, interesting myself in what was in the distance rather than in things near by or behind.

In the afternoon of that day, we reached Annapolis, the capital of the State. We stopped but a few moments, so that I had no time to go on shore. It was the first large town that I had ever seen, and though it would look small compared with some of our New England factory villages, I thought it a wonderful place for its size—more imposing even than the Great House Farm!

We arrived at Baltimore early on Sunday morning, landing at Smith's Wharf, not far from Bowley's Wharf. We had on board the sloop a large flock of sheep; and after aiding in driving them to the slaughterhouse of Mr. Curtis on Louden Slater's Hill, I was conducted by Rich, one of the hands belonging on board of the sloop, to my new home in Alliciana Street, near Mr. Gardner's ship-yard, on Fells Point.

Mr. and Mrs. Auld were both at home, and met me at the door with their little son Thomas, to take care of whom I had been given. And here I saw what I had never seen before; it was a white face beaming with the most kindly emotions; it was the face of my new mistress, Sophia Auld. I wish I could describe the rapture that flashed through my soul as I beheld it. It was a new and strange sight to me, brightening up my pathway with the light of happiness. Little Thomas was told, there was his Freddy,—and I was told to take care of little Thomas; and thus I entered upon the duties of my new home with the most cheering prospect ahead.

I look upon my departure from Colonel Lloyd's plantation as one of the most interesting events of my life. It is possible, and even quite probable, that but for the mere circumstance of being removed from that plantation to Baltimore, I should have to-day, instead of being here seated by my own table, in the enjoyment of freedom and the happiness of home, writing this Narrative, been confined in the galling chains of slavery. Going to live at Baltimore laid the foundation, and opened the gateway, to all my subsequent prosperity. I have ever regarded it as the first plain manifestation of that kind providence which has ever since attended me, and marked my life with so many favors. I regarded the selection of myself as being somewhat remarkable. There were a number of slave children that might have been sent from the plantation to Baltimore. There were those younger, those older, and those of the same age. I was chosen from among them all, and was the first, last, and only choice.

I may be deemed superstitious, and even egotistical, in regarding this event as a special interposition of divine Providence in my favor. But I should be false to the earliest sentiments of my soul, if I suppressed the opinion. I prefer to be true to myself, even at the hazard of incurring the ridicule of others, rather than to be false, and incur my own abhorrence. From my earliest recollection, I date the entertainment of a deep conviction that slavery would not always be able to hold me within its foul embrace; and in the darkest hours of my career in slavery, this living word of faith and spirit of hope departed not from me, but remained like ministering angels to cheer me through the gloom. This good spirit was from God, and to him I offer thanksgiving and praise.

Chapter VI

My new mistress proved to be all she appeared when I first met her at the door,—a woman of the kindest heart and finest feelings. She had never had a slave under her control previously to myself, and prior to her marriage she had been dependent upon her own industry for a living. She was by trade a weaver; and by constant application to her business, she had been in a good degree preserved from the blighting and dehumanizing effects of slavery. I was utterly astonished at her goodness. I scarcely knew how to behave towards her. She was entirely unlike any other white woman I had ever seen. I could not approach her as I was accustomed to approach other white ladies. My early instruction was all out of place. The crouching servility, usually so acceptable a quality in a slave, did not answer when manifested toward her. Her favor was not gained by it; she seemed to be disturbed by it. She did not deem it impudent or unmannerly for a slave to look her in the face. The meanest slave was put fully at ease in her presence, and none left without feeling better for having seen her. Her face was made of heavenly smiles, and her voice of tranquil music.

But, alas! this kind heart had but a short time to remain such. The fatal poison of irresponsible power was already in her hands, and soon commenced its infernal work. That cheerful eye, under the influence of slavery, soon became red with rage; that voice, made all of sweet accord, changed to one of harsh and horrid discord; and that angelic face gave place to that of a demon.

Very soon after I went to live with Mr. and Mrs. Auld, she very kindly commenced to teach me the A, B, C. After I had learned this, she assisted me in learning to spell words of three or four letters. Just at this point of my progress, Mr. Auld found out what was going on, and at once forbade Mrs. Auld to instruct me further, telling her, among other things, that it was unlawful, as well as unsafe, to teach a slave to read. To use his own words, further, he said, "If you give a nigger an inch, he will take an ell. A nigger should know nothing but to obey his master—to do as he is told to do. Learning would *spoil* the best nigger in the world. Now," said he, "if you teach that nigger (speaking of myself) how to read, there would be no keeping him. It would forever unfit him to be a slave. He would at once become unmanageable, and of no value to his master. As to himself, it could do him no good, but a great deal of harm. It would make him discontented and unhappy." These words sank deep into my heart, stirred up sentiments within that lay slumbering, and called into existence an entirely new train of thought. It was a new and special revelation, explaining dark and mysterious things, with which my youthful understanding had struggled, but struggled in vain. I now understood what had been to me a most perplexing difficulty—to wit, the white man's power to enslave the black man. It was a grand achievement, and I prized it highly. From that moment, I understood the pathway from slavery to freedom. It was just what I wanted, and I got it at a time when I the least expected it. Whilst I was saddened by the thought of losing the aid of my kind mistress, I was gladdened by the invaluable instruction which, by the merest accident, I had gained from my master. Though conscious of the difficulty of learning without a teacher, I set out with high hope, and a fixed purpose, at whatever cost of trouble, to learn how to read.

The very decided manner with which he spoke, and strove to impress his wife with the evil consequences of giving me instruction, served to convince me that he was deeply sensible of the truths he was uttering. It gave me the best assurance that I might rely with the utmost confidence on the results which, he said, would flow from teaching me to read. What he most dreaded, that I most desired. What he most loved, that I most hated. That which to him was a great evil, to be carefully shunned, was to me a great good, to be diligently sought; and the argument which he so warmly urged, against my learning to read, only served to inspire me with a desire and determination to learn. In learning to read, I owe almost as much to the bitter opposition of my master, as to the kindly aid of my mistress. I acknowledge the benefit of both.

I had resided but a short time in Baltimore before I observed a marked difference, in the treatment of slaves, from that which I had witnessed in the country. A city slave is almost a freeman, compared with a slave on the plantation. He is much better fed and clothed, and enjoys privileges altogether unknown to the slave on the plantation. There is a vestige of decency, a sense of shame, that does much to curb and check those outbreaks of atrocious cruelty so commonly enacted upon the plantation. He is a desperate slaveholder, who will shock the humanity of his nonslaveholding neighbors with the cries of his lacerated slave. Few are willing to incur the odium attaching to the reputation of being a cruel master; and above all things, they would not be known as not giving a slave enough to eat. Every city slaveholder is anxious to have it known of him, that he feeds his slaves well; and it is due to them to say, that most of them do give their slaves enough to eat. There are, however, some painful exceptions to this rule. Directly opposite to us, on Philpot Street, lived Mr. Thomas Hamilton. He owned two slaves. Their names were Henrietta and Mary. Henrietta was about twenty-two years of age, Mary was about fourteen; and of all the mangled and emaciated creatures I ever looked upon, these two were the most so. His heart must be harder than stone, that could look upon these unmoved. The head, neck, and shoulders of Mary were literally cut to pieces. I have frequently felt her head, and found it nearly covered with festering sores, caused by the lash of her cruel mistress. I do not know that her master ever whipped her, but I have been an eye-witness to the cruelty of Mrs. Hamilton. I used to be in Mr. Hamilton's house nearly every day. Mrs. Hamilton used to sit in a large chair in the middle of the room, with a heavy cowskin always by her side, and scarce an hour passed during the day but was marked by the blood of one of these slaves. The girls seldom passed her without her saying, "Move faster, you *black gip!*"[5] at the same time giving

5. Cheat, swindler.

them a blow with the cowskin over the head or shoulders, often drawing the blood. She would then say, "Take that, you *black gip!*"—continuing, "If you don't move faster, I'll move you!" Added to the cruel lashings to which these slaves were subjected, they were kept nearly half-starved. They seldom knew what it was to eat a full meal. I have seen Mary contending with the pigs for the offal thrown into the street. So much was Mary kicked and cut to pieces, that she was oftener called "*pecked*" than by her name.

Chapter VII

I lived in Master Hugh's family about seven years. During this time, I succeeded in learning to read and write. In accomplishing this, I was compelled to resort to various stratagems. I had no regular teacher. My mistress, who had kindly commenced to instruct me, had, in compliance with the advice and direction of her husband, not only ceased to instruct, but had set her face against my being instructed by any one else. It is due, however, to my mistress to say of her, that she did not adopt this course of treatment immediately. She at first lacked the depravity indispensable to shutting me up in mental darkness. It was at least necessary for her to have some training in the exercise of irresponsible power, to make her equal to the task of treating me as though I were a brute.

My mistress was, as I have said, a kind and tender-hearted woman; and in the simplicity of her soul she commenced, when I first went to live with her, to treat me as she supposed one human being ought to treat another. In entering upon the duties of a slaveholder, she did not seem to perceive that I sustained to her the relation of a mere chattel, and that for her to treat me as a human being was not only wrong, but dangerously so. Slavery proved as injurious to her as it did to me. When I went there, she was a pious, warm, and tender-hearted woman. There was no sorrow or suffering for which she had not a tear. She had bread for the hungry, clothes for the naked, and comfort for every mourner that came within her reach. Slavery soon proved its ability to divest her of these heavenly qualities. Under its influence, the tender heart became stone, and the lamblike disposition gave way to one of tiger-like fierceness. The first step in her downward course was in her ceasing to instruct me. She now commenced to practise her husband's precepts. She finally became even more violent in her opposition than her husband himself. She was not satisfied with simply doing as well as he had commanded; she seemed anxious to do better. Nothing seemed to make her more angry than to see me with a newspaper. She seemed to think that here lay the danger. I have had her rush at me with a face made all up of fury, and snatch from me a newspaper, in a manner that fully revealed her apprehension. She was an apt woman; and a little experience soon demonstrated, to her satisfaction, that education and slavery were incompatible with each other.

From this time I was most narrowly watched. If I was in a separate room any considerable length of time, I was sure to be suspected of having a book, and was at once called to give an account of myself. All this, however, was too late. The first step had been taken. Mistress, in teaching me the alphabet, had given me the *inch*, and no precaution could prevent me from taking the *ell*.

The plan which I adopted, and the one by which I was most successful, was that of making friends of all the little white boys whom I met in the street. As many of these as I could, I converted into teachers. With their kindly aid, obtained at different times and in different places, I finally succeeded in learning to read. When I was sent of errands, I always took my book with me, and by going one part of my errand quickly, I found time to get a lesson before my return. I used also to carry bread with me, enough of which was always in the house, and to which I was always welcome; for I was much better off in this regard than many of the poor white children in our neighborhood. This bread I used to bestow upon the hungry little urchins, who, in return, would give me that more valuable bread of knowledge. I am strongly tempted to give the names of two or three of those little boys, as a testimonial of the gratitude and affection I bear them; but prudence forbids;—not that it would injure me, but it might embarrass them; for it is almost an unpardonable offence to teach slaves to read in this Christian country. It is enough to say of the dear little fellows, that they lived on Philpot Street, very near Durgin and Bailey's ship-yard. I used to talk this matter of slavery over with them. I would sometimes say to them, I wished I could be as free as they would be when they got to be men. "You will be free as soon as you are twenty-one, *but I am a slave for life!* Have not I as good a right to be free as you have?" These words used to trouble them; they would express for me the liveliest sympathy, and console me with the hope that something would occur by which I might be free.

I was now about twelve years old, and the thought of being *a slave for life* began to bear heavily upon my heart. Just about this time, I got hold of a book entitled "The Columbian Orator."[6] Every opportunity I got, I used to read this book. Among much of other interesting matter, I found in it a dialogue between a master and his slave. The slave was represented as having run away from his master three times. The dialogue represented the conversation which took place between them, when the slave was retaken the third time. In this

6. Caleb Bingham, *The Columbian Orator: Containing a Variety of Original and Selected Pieces: Together with Rules, Calculated to Improve Youth and Others in the Ornamental and Useful Art of Eloquence* (1807).

dialogue, the whole argument in behalf of slavery was brought forward by the master, all of which was disposed of by the slave. The slave was made to say some very smart as well as impressive things in reply to his master—things which had the desired though unexpected effect; for the conversation resulted in the voluntary emancipation of the slave on the part of the master.

In the same book, I met with one of Sheridan's[7] mighty speeches on and in behalf of Catholic emancipation. These were choice documents to me. I read them over and over again with unabated interest. They gave tongue to interesting thoughts of my own soul, which had frequently flashed through my mind, and died away for want of utterance. The moral which I gained from the dialogue was the power of truth over the conscience of even a slaveholder. What I got from Sheridan was a bold denunciation of slavery, and a powerful vindication of human rights. The reading of these documents enabled me to utter my thoughts, and to meet the arguments brought forward to sustain slavery; but while they relieved me of one difficulty, they brought on another even more painful than the one of which I was relieved. The more I read, the more I was led to abhor and detest my enslavers. I could regard them in no other light than a band of successful robbers, who had left their homes, and gone to Africa, and stolen us from our homes, and in a strange land reduced us to slavery. I loathed them as being the meanest as well as the most wicked of men. As I read and contemplated the subject, behold! that very discontentment which Master Hugh had predicted would follow my learning to read had already come, to torment and sting my soul to unutterable anguish. As I writhed under it, I would at times feel that learning to read had been a curse rather than a blessing. It had given me a view of my wretched condition, without the remedy. It opened my eyes to the horrible pit, but to no ladder upon which to get out. In moments of agony, I envied my fellow-slaves for their stupidity. I have often wished myself a beast. I preferred the condition of the meanest reptile to my own. Any thing, no matter what, to get rid of thinking! It was this everlasting thinking of my condition that tormented me. There was no getting rid of it. It was pressed upon me by every object within sight or hearing, animate or inanimate. The silver trump of freedom had roused my soul to eternal wakefulness. Freedom now appeared, to disappear no more forever. It was heard in every sound, and seen in every thing. It was ever present to torment me with a sense of my wretched condition. I saw nothing without seeing it, I heard nothing without hearing it, and felt nothing without feeling it. It looked from every star, it smiled in every calm, breathed in every wind, and moved in every storm.

---

7. Thomas Sheridan (1719–1788), lecturer and writer on elocution.

I often found myself regretting my own existence, and wishing myself dead; and but for the hope of being free, I have no doubt but that I should have killed myself, or done something for which I should have been killed. While in this state of mind, I was eager to hear any one speak of slavery. I was a ready listener. Every little while, I could hear something about the abolitionists. It was some time before I found what the word meant. It was always used in such connections as to make it an interesting word to me. If a slave ran away and succeeded in getting clear, or if a slave killed his master, set fire to a barn, or did any thing very wrong in the mind of a slaveholder, it was spoken of as the fruit of *abolition*. Hearing the word in this connection very often, I set about learning what it meant. The dictionary afforded me little or no help. I found it was "the act of abolishing;" but then I did not know what was to be abolished. Here I was perplexed. I did not dare to ask any one about its meaning, for I was satisfied that it was something they wanted me to know very little about. After a patient waiting, I got one of our city papers, containing an account of the number of petitions from the north, praying for the abolition of slavery in the District of Columbia, and of the slave trade between the States. From this time I understood the words *abolition* and *abolitionist*, and always drew near when that word was spoken, expecting to hear something of importance to myself and fellow-slaves. The light broke in upon me by degrees. I went one day down on the wharf of Mr. Waters; and seeing two Irishmen unloading a scow of stone, I went, unasked, and helped them. When we had finished, one of them came to me and asked me if I were a slave. I told him I was. He asked, "Are ye a slave for life?" I told him that I was. The good Irishman seemed to be deeply affected by the statement. He said to the other that it was a pity so fine a little fellow as myself should be a slave for life. He said it was a shame to hold me. They both advised me to run away to the north; that I should find friends there, and that I should be free. I pretended not to be interested in what they said, and treated them as if I did not understand them; for I feared they might be treacherous. White men have been known to encourage slaves to escape, and then, to get the reward, catch them and return them to their masters. I was afraid that these seemingly good men might use me so; but I nevertheless remembered their advice, and from that time I resolved to run away. I looked forward to a time at which it would be safe for me to escape. I was too young to think of doing so immediately; besides, I wished to learn how to write, as I might have occasion to write my own pass. I consoled myself with the hope that I should one day find a good chance. Meanwhile, I would learn to write.

The idea as to how I might learn to write was suggested to me by being in Durgin and Bailey's ship-yard, and frequently seeing the ship carpenters, after hewing, and getting a piece of timber ready for use, write on the timber the name of that part of the ship for which it was intended. When a piece of timber was intended for the larboard side, it would be marked thus—"L." When a piece was for the starboard side, it would be marked thus—"S." A piece for the larboard forward, would be marked thus—"L.F." When a piece was for starboard side forward, it would be marked thus—"S.F." For larboard aft, it would be marked thus—"L.A." For starboard aft, it would be marked thus—"S.A." I soon learned the names of these letters, and for what they were intended when placed upon a piece of timber in the ship-yard. I immediately commenced copying them, and in a short time was able to make the four letters named. After that, when I met with any boy who I knew could write, I would tell him I could write as well as he. The next word would be, "I don't believe you. Let me see you try it." I would then make the letters which I had been so fortunate as to learn, and ask him to beat that. In this way I got a good many lessons in writing, which it is quite possible I should never have gotten in any other way. During this time, my copy-book was the board fence, brick wall, and pavement; my pen and ink was a lump of chalk. With these, I learned mainly how to write. I then commenced and continued copying the Italics in Webster's Spelling Book, until I could make them all without looking on the book. By this time, my little Master Thomas had gone to school, and learned how to write, and had written over a number of copybooks. These had been brought home, and shown to some of our near neighbors, and then laid aside. My mistress used to go to class meeting at the Wilk Street meetinghouse every Monday afternoon, and leave me to take care of the house. When left thus, I used to spend the time in writing in the spaces left in Master Thomas's copy-book, copying what he had written. I continued to do this until I could write a hand very similar to that of Master Thomas. Thus, after a long, tedious effort for years, I finally succeeded in learning how to write.

Chapter VIII

In a very short time after I went to live at Baltimore, my old master's youngest son Richard died; and in about three years and six months after his death, my old master, Captain Anthony, died, leaving only his son, Andrew, and daughter, Lucretia, to share his estate. He died while on a visit to see his daughter at Hillsborough. Cut off thus unexpectedly, he left no will as to the disposal of his property. It was therefore necessary to have a valuation of the property, that it might be equally divided between Mrs. Lucretia and Master Andrew. I was immediately sent for, to be valued with the other property.

Here again my feelings rose up in detestation of slavery. I had now a new conception of my degraded condition. Prior to this, I had become, if not insensible to my lot, at least partly so. I left Baltimore with a young heart overborne with sadness, and a soul full of apprehension. I took passage with Captain Rowe, in the schooner *Wild Cat*, and, after a sail of about twenty-four hours, I found myself near the place of my birth. I had now been absent from it almost, if not quite, five years. I, however, remembered the place very well. I was only about five years old when I left it, to go and live with my old master on Colonel Lloyd's plantation; so that I was now between ten and eleven years old.

We were all ranked together at the valuation. Men and women, old and young, married and single, were ranked with horses, sheep, and swine. There were horses and men, cattle and women, pigs and children, all holding the same rank in the scale of being, and were all subjected to the same narrow examination. Silvery-headed age and sprightly youth, maids and matrons, had to undergo the same indelicate inspection. At this moment, I saw more clearly than ever the brutalizing effects of slavery upon both slave and slaveholder.

After the valuation, then came the division. I have no language to express the high excitement and deep anxiety which were felt among us poor slaves during this time. Our fate for life was now to be decided. We had no more voice in that decision than the brutes among whom we were ranked. A single word from the white men was enough—against all our wishes, prayers, and entreaties—to sunder forever the dearest friends, dearest kindred, and strongest ties known to human beings. In addition to the pain of separation, there was the horrid dread of falling into the hands of Master Andrew. He was known to us all as being a most cruel wretch,—a common drunkard, who had, by his reckless mismanagement and profligate dissipation, already wasted a large portion of his father's property. We all felt that we might as well be sold at once to the Georgia traders, as to pass into his hands; for we knew that that would be our inevitable condition,—a condition held by us all in the utmost horror and dread.

I suffered more anxiety than most of my fellow-slaves. I had known what it was to be kindly treated; they had known nothing of the kind. They had seen little or nothing of the world. They were in very deed men and women of sorrow, and acquainted with grief.[8] Their backs had been made familiar with the bloody lash, so that they had become callous; mine was yet tender; for while at Baltimore I got few whippings, and few slaves could boast of a kinder master and mistress than myself; and the thought of passing out of their hands into those of

8. In Isaiah 53:3, the Lord's servant is described as "a man of sorrows, and acquainted with grief."

Master Andrew—a man who, but a few days before, to give me a sample of his bloody disposition, took my little brother by the throat, threw him on the ground, and with the heel of his boot stamped upon his head till the blood gushed from his nose and ears—was well calculated to make me anxious as to my fate. After he had committed this savage outrage upon my brother, he turned to me, and said that was the way he meant to serve me one of these days,—meaning, I suppose, when I came into his possession.

Thanks to a kind Providence, I fell to the portion of Mrs. Lucretia, and was sent immediately back to Baltimore, to live again in the family of Master Hugh. Their joy at my return equalled their sorrow at my departure. It was a glad day to me. I had escaped a worse than lion's jaws. I was absent from Baltimore, for the purpose of valuation and division, just about one month, and it seemed to have been six.

Very soon after my return to Baltimore, my mistress, Lucretia, died, leaving her husband and one child, Amanda; and in a very short time after her death, Master Andrew died. Now all the property of my old master, slaves included, was in the hands of strangers,—strangers who had had nothing to do with accumulating it. Not a slave was left free. All remained slaves, from the youngest to the oldest. If any one thing in my experience, more than another, served to deepen my conviction of the infernal character of slavery, and to fill me with unutterable loathing of slaveholders, it was their base ingratitude to my poor old grandmother. She had served my old master faithfully from youth to old age. She had been the source of all his wealth; she had peopled his plantation with slaves; she had become a great grandmother in his service. She had rocked him in infancy, attended him in childhood, served him through life, and at his death wiped from his icy brow the cold death-sweat, and closed his eyes forever. She was nevertheless left a slave—a slave for life—a slave in the hands of strangers; and in their hands she saw her children, her grandchildren, and her great-grandchildren, divided, like so many sheep, without being gratified with the small privilege of a single word, as to their or her own destiny. And, to cap the climax of their base ingratitude and fiendish barbarity, my grandmother, who was now very old, having outlived my old master and all his children, having seen the beginning and end of all of them, and her present owners finding she was of but little value, her frame already racked with the pains of old age, and complete helplessness fast stealing over her once active limbs, they took her to the woods, built her a little hut, put up a little mud-chimney, and then made her welcome to the privilege of supporting herself there in perfect loneliness; thus virtually turning her out to die! If my poor old grandmother now lives, she lives to suffer in utter loneliness; she lives to

remember and mourn over the loss of children, the loss of grandchildren, and the loss of great-grandchildren. They are, in the language of the slave's poet, Whittier,—

> "Gone, gone, sold and gone
>   To the rice swamp dank and lone,
>   Where the slave-whip ceaseless swings,
>   Where the noisome insect stings,
>   Where the fever-demon strews
>   Poison with the falling dews,
>   Where the sickly sunbeams glare
>   Through the hot and misty air:—
>   Gone, gone, sold and gone
>   To the rice swamp dank and lone,
>   From Virginia hills and waters—
>   Woe is me, my stolen daughters!"[9]

The hearth is desolate. The children, the unconscious children, who
once sang and danced in her presence, are gone. She gropes her
way, in the darkness of age, for a drink of water. Instead of the voices
of her children, she hears by day the moans of the dove, and by
night the screams of the hideous owl. All is gloom. The grave is at
the door. And now, when weighed down by the pains and aches of
old age, when the head inclines to the feet, when the beginning and
ending of human existence meet, and helpless infancy and painful
old age combine together—at this time, this most needful time, the
time for the exercise of that tenderness and affection which children
only can exercise towards a declining parent—my poor old grandmother, the devoted mother of twelve children, is left all alone, in
yonder little hut, before a few dim embers. She stands—she sits—
she staggers—she falls—she groans—she dies—and there are none
of her children or grandchildren present, to wipe from her wrinkled
brow the cold sweat of death, or to place beneath the sod her fallen
remains. Will not a righteous God visit[1] for these things?

    In about two years after the death of Mrs. Lucretia, Master Thomas
married his second wife. Her name was Rowena Hamilton. She was
the eldest daughter of Mr. William Hamilton. Master now lived in
St. Michael's. Not long after his marriage, a misunderstanding took
place between himself and Master Hugh; and as a means of punishing his brother, he took me from him to live with himself at St.
Michael's. Here I underwent another most painful separation. It,
however, was not so severe as the one I dreaded at the division of

---

9. John Greenleaf Whittier, American poet (1807–1892) wrote a large group of antislavery poems.
This one is called "The rewell of a Virginia Slave Mother to her Daughters Sold into Southern
Bondage."   1. I.e., visit vengeance. Cf. Exodus 32:34: "Nevertheless, in the day when I visit,
I will visit their sin upon them."

property; for, during this interval, a great change had taken place in Master Hugh and his once kind and affectionate wife. The influence of brandy upon him, and of slavery upon her, had effected a disastrous change in the characters of both; so that, as far as they were concerned, I thought I had little to lose by the change. But it was not to them that I was attached. It was to those little Baltimore boys that I felt the strongest attachment. I had received many good lessons from them, and was still receiving them, and the thought of leaving them was painful indeed. I was leaving, too, without the hope of ever being allowed to return. Master Thomas had said he would never let me return again. The barrier betwixt himself and brother he considered impassable.

I then had to regret that I did not at least make the attempt to carry out my resolution to run away; for the chances of success are tenfold greater from the city than from the country.

I sailed from Baltimore for St. Michael's in the sloop *Amanda*, Captain Edward Dodson. On my passage, I paid particular attention to the direction which the steamboats took to go to Philadelphia. I found, instead of going down, on reaching North Point they went up the bay, in a north-easterly direction. I deemed this knowledge of the utmost importance. My determination to run away was again revived. I resolved to wait only so long as the offering of a favorable opportunity. When that came, I was determined to be off.

Chapter IX

I have now reached a period of my life when I can give dates. I left Baltimore, and went to live with Master Thomas Auld, at St. Michael's, in March, 1832. It was now more than seven years since I lived with him in the family of my old master, on Colonel Lloyd's plantation. We of course were now almost entire strangers to each other. He was to me a new master, and I to him a new slave. I was ignorant of his temper and disposition; he was equally so of mine. A very short time, however, brought us into full acquaintance with each other. I was made acquainted with his wife not less than with himself. They were well matched, being equally mean and cruel. I was now, for the first time during a space of more than seven years, made to feel the painful gnawings of hunger—a something which I had not experienced before since I left Colonel Lloyd's plantation. It went hard enough with me then, when I could look back to no period at which I had enjoyed a sufficiency. It was tenfold harder after living in Master Hugh's family, where I had always had enough to eat, and of that which was good. I have said Master Thomas was a mean man. He was so. Not to give a slave enough to eat, is regarded as the most aggravated development of meanness even among slaveholders. The rule is, no matter how coarse the food, only let there be enough of it. This is the theory; and in the part of Maryland from which I came, it is the general practice,—though there are many exceptions. Master Thomas gave us enough of neither coarse nor fine food. There were four slaves of us in the kitchen—my sister Eliza, my aunt Priscilla, Henny, and myself; and we were allowed less than a half of a bushel of corn-meal per week, and very little else, either in the shape of meat or vegetables. It was not enough for us to subsist upon. We were therefore reduced to the wretched necessity of living at the expense of our neighbors. This we did by begging and stealing, whichever came handy in the time of need, the one being considered as legitimate as the other. A great many times have we poor creatures been nearly perishing with hunger, when food in abundance lay mouldering in the safe and smoke-house, and our pious mistress was aware of the fact; and yet that mistress and her husband would kneel every morning, and pray that God would bless them in basket and store!

Bad as all slaveholders are, we seldom meet one destitute of every element of character commanding respect. My master was one of this rare sort. I do not know of one single noble act ever performed by him. The leading trait in his character was meanness; and if there were any other element in his nature, it was made subject to this. He was mean; and, like most other mean men, he lacked the ability to conceal his meanness. Captain Auld was not born a slaveholder. He had been a poor man, master only of a Bay craft. He came into possession of all his slaves by marriage; and of all men, adopted slaveholders are the worst. He was cruel, but cowardly. He commanded without firmness. In the enforcement of his rules, he was at times rigid, and at times lax. At times, he spoke to his slaves with the firmness of Napoleon and the fury of a demon; at other times, he might well be mistaken for an inquirer who had lost his way. He did nothing of himself. He might have passed for a lion, but for his ears.[2] In all things noble which he attempted, his own meanness shone most conspicuous. His airs, words, and actions, were the airs, words, and actions of born slaveholders, and, being assumed, were awkward enough. He was not even a good imitator. He possessed all the disposition to deceive, but wanted the power. Having no resources within himself, he was compelled to be the copyist of many, and being such, he was forever the victim of inconsistency; and of consequence he was an object of contempt, and was held as such even by his slaves. The luxury of having slaves of his own to wait upon him was something new and unprepared for. He was a slaveholder without the ability to hold slaves. He found himself incapable of

---

2. A variation on Aesop's fable of the ass in the lion's skin, in which the fox says, "I should have been frightened too, if I had not heard you bray."

managing his slaves either by force, fear, or fraud. We seldom called him "master;" we generally called him "Captain Auld," and were hardly disposed to title him at all. I doubt not that our conduct had much to do with making him appear awkward, and of consequence fretful. Our want of reverence for him must have perplexed him greatly. He wished to have us call him master, but lacked the firmness necessary to command us to do so. His wife used to insist upon our calling him so, but to no purpose. In August, 1832, my master attended a Methodist camp-meeting held in the Bay-side, Talbot county, and there experienced religion. I indulged a faint hope that his conversion would lead him to emancipate his slaves, and that, if he did not do this, it would, at any rate, make him more kind and humane. I was disappointed in both these respects. It neither made him to be humane to his slaves, nor to emancipate them. If it had any effect on his character, it made him more cruel and hateful in all his ways; for I believe him to have been a much worse man after his conversion than before. Prior to his conversion, he relied upon his own depravity to shield and sustain him in his savage barbarity; but after his conversion, he found religious sanction and support for his slaveholding cruelty. He made the greatest pretensions to piety. His house was the house of prayer. He prayed morning, noon, and night. He very soon distinguished himself among his brethren, and was soon made a class-leader and exhorter. His activity in revivals was great, and he proved himself an instrument in the hands of the church in converting many souls. His house was the preachers' home. They used to take great pleasure in coming there to put up; for while he starved us, he stuffed them. We have had three or four preachers there at a time. The names of those who used to come most frequently while I lived there, were Mr. Storks, Mr. Ewery, Mr. Humphry, and Mr. Hickey. I have also seen Mr. George Cookman at our house. We slaves loved Mr. Cookman. We believed him to be a good man. We thought him instrumental in getting Mr. Samuel Harrison, a very rich slaveholder, to emancipate his slaves; and by some means got the impression that he was laboring to effect the emancipation of all the slaves. When he was at our house, we were sure to be called in to prayers. When the others were there, we sometimes called in and sometimes not. Mr. Cookman took more notice of us than either of the other ministers. He could not come among us without betraying his sympathy for us, and, stupid as we were, we had the sagacity to see it.

While I lived with my master in St. Michael's, there was a white young man, a Mr. Wilson, who proposed to keep a Sabbath school for the instruction of such slaves as might be disposed to learn to read the New Testament. We met but three times, when Mr. West and Mr. Fairbanks, both class-leaders, with many others, came upon us with sticks and other missiles, drove us off, and forbade us to meet again. Thus ended our little Sabbath school in the pious town of St. Michael's.

I have said my master found religious sanction for his cruelty. As an example, I will state one of many facts going to prove the charge. I have seen him tie up a lame young woman, and whip her with a heavy cowskin upon her naked shoulders, causing the warm red blood to drip; and, in justification of the bloody deed, he would quote this passage of Scripture—"He that knoweth his master's will, and doeth it not, shall be beaten with many stripes."

Master would keep this lacerated young woman tied up in this horrid situation four or five hours at a time. I have known him to tie her up early in the morning, and whip her before breakfast; leave her, go to his store, return to dinner, and whip her again, cutting her in the places already made raw with his cruel lash. The secret of master's cruelty toward "Henny" is found in the fact of her being almost helpless. When quite a child, she fell into the fire, and burned herself horribly. Her hands were so burnt that she never got the use of them. She could do very little but bear heavy burdens. She was to master a bill of expense; and as he was a mean man, she was a constant offence to him. He seemed desirous of getting the poor girl out of existence. He gave her away once to his sister; but, being a poor gift, she was not disposed to keep her. Finally, my benevolent master, to use his own words, "set her adrift to take care of herself." Here was a recently-converted man, holding on upon the mother, and at the same time turning out her helpless child, to starve and die! Master Thomas was one of the many pious slaveholders who hold slaves for the very charitable purpose of taking care of them.

My master and myself had quite a number of differences. He found me unsuitable to his purpose. My city life, he said, had had a very pernicious effect upon me. It had almost ruined me for every good purpose, and fitted me for every thing which was bad. One of my greatest faults was that of letting his horse run away, and go down to his father-in-law's farm, which was about five miles from St. Michael's. I would then have to go after it. My reason for this kind of carelessness, or carefulness, was, that I could always get something to eat when I went there. Master William Hamilton, my master's father-in-law, always gave his slaves enough to eat. I never left there hungry, no matter how great the need of my speedy return. Master Thomas at length said he would stand it no longer. I had lived with him nine months, during which time he had given me a number of severe whippings, all to no good purpose. He resolved to put me out, as he said, to be broken; and, for this purpose, he let me for one year to a man named Edward Covey. Mr. Covey was a poor man, a farm-renter. He rented the place upon which he lived, as also the hands

with which he tilled it. Mr. Covey had acquired a very high reputation for breaking young slaves, and this reputation was of immense
value to him. It enabled him to get his farm tilled with much less
expense to himself than he could have had it done without such a
reputation. Some slaveholders thought it not much loss to allow Mr.
Covey to have their slaves one year, for the sake of the training to
which they were subjected, without any other compensation. He
could hire young help with great ease, in consequence of this reputation. Added to the natural good qualities of Mr. Covey, he was a
professor of religion—a pious soul—a member and a class-leader in
the Methodist church. All of this added weight to his reputation as a
"nigger-breaker." I was aware of all the facts, having been made
acquainted with them by a young man who had lived there. I nevertheless made the change gladly; for I was sure of getting enough to
eat, which is not the smallest consideration to a hungry man.

Chapter X

I left Master Thomas's house, and went to live with Mr. Covey,
on the 1st of January, 1833. I was now, for the first time in my life,
a field hand. In my new employment, I found myself even more
awkward than a country boy appeared to be in a large city. I had
been at my new home but one week before Mr. Covey gave me a
very severe whipping, cutting my back, causing the blood to run,
and raising ridges on my flesh as large as my little finger. The details
of this affair are as follows: Mr. Covey sent me, very early in the
morning of one of our coldest days in the month of January, to the
woods, to get a load of wood. He gave me a team of unbroken oxen.
He told me which was the in-hand ox, and which the off-hand ox.
He then tied the end of a large rope around the horns of the in-hand
ox, and gave me the other end of it, and told me, if the oxen started
to run, that I must hold on upon the rope. I had never driven oxen
before, and of course I was very awkward. I, however, succeeded in
getting to the edge of the woods with little difficulty; but I had got a
very few rods into the woods, when the oxen took fright, and started
full tilt, carrying the cart against trees, and over stumps, in the most
frightful manner. I expected every moment that my brains would be
dashed out against the trees. After running thus for a considerable
distance, they finally upset the cart, dashing it with great force against
a tree, and threw themselves into a dense thicket. How I escaped
death, I do not know. There I was, entirely alone, in a thick wood,
in a place new to me. My cart was upset and shattered, my oxen
were entangled among the young trees, and there was none to help
me. After a long spell of effort, I succeeded in getting my cart righted,
my oxen disentangled, and again yoked to the cart. I now proceeded

with my team to the place where I had, the day before, been chopping wood, and loaded my cart pretty heavily, thinking in this way to tame my oxen. I then proceeded on my way home. I had now consumed one half of the day. I got out of the woods safely, and now felt out of danger. I stopped my oxen to open the woods gate; and just as I did so, before I could get hold of my ox-rope, the oxen again started, rushed through the gate, catching it between the wheel and the body of the cart, tearing it to pieces, and coming within a few inches of crushing me against the gate-post. Thus twice, in one short day, I escaped death by the merest chance. On my return, I told Mr. Covey what had happened, and how it happened. He ordered me to return to the woods again immediately. I did so, and he followed on after me. Just as I got into the woods, he came up and told me to stop my cart, and that he would teach me how to trifle away my time, and break gates. He then went to a large gum-tree, and with his axe cut three large switches, and, after trimming them up neatly with his pocket-knife, he ordered me to take off my clothes. I made him no answer, but stood with my clothes on. He repeated his order. I still made him no answer, nor did I move to strip myself. Upon this he rushed at me with the fierceness of a tiger, tore off my clothes, and lashed me till he had worn out his switches, cutting me so savagely as to leave the marks visible for a long time after. This whipping was the first of a number just like it, and for similar offences.

I lived with Mr. Covey one year. During the first six months, of that year, scarce a week passed without his whipping me. I was seldom free from a sore back. My awkwardness was almost always his excuse for whipping me. We were worked fully up to the point of endurance. Long before day we were up, our horses fed, and by the first approach of day we were off to the field with our hoes and ploughing teams. Mr. Covey gave us enough to eat, but scarce time to eat it. We were often less than five minutes taking our meals. We were often in the field from the first approach of day till its last lingering ray had left us; and at saving-fodder time, midnight often caught us in the field binding blades.[3]

Covey would be out with us. The way he used to stand it was this. He would spend the most of his afternoons in bed. He would then come out fresh in the evening, ready to urge us on with his words, example, and frequently with the whip. Mr. Covey was one of the few slaveholders who could and did work with his hands. He was a hard-working man. He knew by himself just what a man or a boy could do. There was no deceiving him. His work went on in his absence almost as well as in his presence; and he had the faculty of making us feel that he was ever present with us. This he did by

---

3. Gathering cut grain into bundles or sheaves.

surprising us. He seldom approached the spot where we were at work openly, if he could do it secretly. He always aimed at taking us by surprise. Such was his cunning, that we used to call him, among ourselves, "the snake." When we were at work in the cornfield, he would sometimes crawl on his hands and knees to avoid detection, and all at once he would rise nearly in our midst, and scream out, "Ha, ha! Come, come! Dash on, dash on!" This being his mode of attack, it was never safe to stop a single minute. His comings were like a thief in the night. He appeared to us as being ever at hand. He was under every tree, behind every stump, in every bush, and at every window, on the plantation. He would sometimes mount his horse, as if bound to St. Michael's, a distance of seven miles, and in half an hour afterwards you would see him coiled up in the corner of the wood-fence, watching every motion of the slaves. He would, for this purpose, leave his horse tied up in the woods. Again, he would sometimes walk up to us, and give us orders as though he was upon the point of starting on a long journey, turn his back upon us, and make as though he was going to the house to get ready; and, before he would get half way thither, he would turn short and crawl into a fence-corner, or behind some tree, and there watch us till the going down of the sun.

Mr. Covey's *forte* consisted in his power to deceive. His life was devoted to planning and perpetrating the grossest deceptions. Every thing he possessed in the shape of learning or religion, he made conform to his disposition to deceive. He seemed to think himself equal to deceiving the Almighty. He would make a short prayer in the morning, and a long prayer at night; and, strange as it may seem, few men would at times appear more devotional than he. The exercises of his family devotions were always commenced with singing; and, as he was a very poor singer himself, the duty of raising the hymn generally came upon me. He would read his hymn, and nod at me to commence. I would at times do so; at others, I would not. My non-compliance would almost always produce much confusion. To show himself independent of me, he would start and stagger through with his hymn in the most discordant manner. In this state of mind, he prayed with more than ordinary spirit. Poor man! such was his disposition, and success at deceiving, I do verily believe that he sometimes deceived himself into the solemn belief, that he was a sincere worshipper of the most high God; and this, too, at a time when he may be said to have been guilty of compelling his woman slave to commit the sin of adultery. The facts in the case are these: Mr. Covey was a poor man; he was just commencing in life; he was only able to buy one slave; and, shocking as is the fact, he bought her, as he said, for a *breeder*. This woman was named Caroline. Mr. Covey bought her from Mr. Thomas Lowe, about six miles from St.

Michael's. She was a large, able-bodied woman, about twenty years old. She had already given birth to one child, which proved her to be just what he wanted. After buying her, he hired a married man of Mr. Samuel Harrison, to live with him one year; and him he used to fasten up with her every night! The result was, that, at the end of the year, the miserable woman gave birth to twins. At this result Mr. Covey seemed to be highly pleased, both with the man and the wretched woman. Such was his joy, and that of his wife, that nothing they could do for Caroline during her confinement was too good, or too hard, to be done. The children were regarded as being quite an addition to his wealth.

If at any one time of my life more than another, I was made to drink the bitterest dregs of slavery, that time was during the first six months of my stay with Mr. Covey. We were worked in all weathers. It was never too hot or too cold; it could never rain, blow, hail, or snow, too hard for us to work in the field. Work, work, work, was scarcely more the order of the day than of the night. The longest days were too short for him, and the shortest nights too long for him. I was somewhat unmanageable when I first went there, but a few months of this discipline tamed me. Mr. Covey succeeded in breaking me. I was broken in body, soul, and spirit. My natural elasticity was crushed, my intellect languished, the disposition to read departed, the cheerful spark that lingered about my eye died; the dark night of slavery closed in upon me; and behold a man transformed into a brute!

Sunday was my only leisure time. I spent this in a sort of beast-like stupor, between sleep and wake, under some large tree. At times I would rise up, a flash of energetic freedom would dart through my soul, accompanied with a faint beam of hope, that flickered for a moment, and then vanished. I sank down again, mourning over my wretched condition. I was sometimes prompted to take my life, and that of Covey, but was prevented by a combination of hope and fear. My sufferings on this plantation seem now like a dream rather than a stern reality.

Our house stood within a few rods of the Chesapeake Bay, whose broad bosom was ever white with sails from every quarter of the habitable globe. Those beautiful vessels, robed in purest white, so delightful to the eye of freemen, were to me so many shrouded ghosts, to terrify and torment me with thoughts of my wretched condition. I have often, in the deep stillness of a summer's Sabbath, stood all alone upon the lofty banks of that noble bay, and traced, with saddened heart and tearful eye, the countless number of sails moving off to the mighty ocean. The sight of these always affected me powerfully. My thoughts would compel utterance; and there, with no audience but the Almighty, I would pour out my soul's complaint, in my rude way, with an apostrophe[4] to the moving multitude of ships:—

"You are loosed from your moorings, and are free; I am fast in my chains, and am a slave! You move merrily before the gentle gale, and I sadly before the bloody whip! You are freedom's swift-winged angels, that fly round the world; I am confined in bands of iron! O that I were free! O, that I were on one of your gallant decks, and under your protecting wing! Alas! betwixt me and you, the turbid waters roll. Go on, go on. O that I could also go! Could I but swim! If I could fly! O, why was I born a man, of whom to make a brute! The glad ship is gone; she hides in the dim distance. I am left in the hottest hell of unending slavery. O God, save me! God, deliver me! Let me be free! Is there any God? Why am I a slave? I will run away. I will not stand it. Get caught, or get clear, I'll try it. I had as well die with ague as the fever. I have only one life to lose. I had as well be killed running as die standing. Only think of it; one hundred miles straight north, and I am free! Try it? Yes! God helping me, I will. It cannot be that I shall live and die a slave. I will take to the water. This very bay shall bear me into freedom. The steam boats steered in a north-east course from North Point. I will do the same; and when I get to the head of the bay, I will turn my canoe adrift, and walk straight through Delaware into Pennsylvania. When I get there, I shall not be required to have a pass; I can travel without being disturbed. Let but the first opportunity offer, and, come what will, I am off. Meanwhile, I will try to bear up under the yoke. I am not the only slave in the world. Why should I fret? I can bear as much as any of them. Besides, I am but a boy, and all boys are bound to some one. It may be that my misery in slavery will only increase my happiness when I get free. There is a better day coming."

Thus I used to think, and thus I used to speak to myself; goaded almost to madness at one moment, and at the next reconciling myself to my wretched lot.

I have already intimated that my condition was much worse, during the first six months of my stay at Mr. Covey's, than in the last six. The circumstances leading to the change in Mr. Covey's course toward me form an epoch in my humble history. You have seen how a man was made a slave; you shall see how a slave was made a man. On one of the hottest days of the month of August, 1833, Bill Smith, William Hughes, a slave named Eli, and myself, were engaged in fanning wheat.[5] Hughes was clearing the fanned wheat from before the fan, Eli was turning, Smith was feeding, and I was carrying wheat to the fan. The work was simple, requiring strength rather than intel-

---

4. An exclamatory form of address.   5. Separating the grain from the chaff.

lect; yet, to one entirely unused to such work, it came very hard. About three o'clock of that day, I broke down; my strength failed me; I was seized with a violent aching of the head, attended with extreme dizziness; I trembled in every limb. Finding what was coming, I nerved myself up, feeling it would never do to stop work. I stood as long as I could stagger to the hopper with grain. When I could stand no longer, I fell, and felt as if held down by an immense weight. The fan of course stopped; every one had his own work to do; and no one could do the work of the other, and have his own go on at the same time.

Mr. Covey was at the house, about one hundred yards from the treading-yard where we were fanning. On hearing the fan stop, he left immediately, and came to the spot where we were. He hastily inquired what the matter was. Bill answered that I was sick, and there was no one to bring wheat to the fan. I had by this time crawled away under the side of the post and rail-fence by which the yard was enclosed, hoping to find relief by getting out of the sun. He then asked where I was. He was told by one of the hands. He came to the spot, and, after looking at me awhile, asked me what was the matter. I told him as well as I could, for I scarce had strength to speak. He then gave me a savage kick in the side, and told me to get up. I tried to do so, but fell back in the attempt. He gave me another kick, and again told me to rise. I again tried, and succeeded in gaining my feet; but, stooping to get the tub with which I was feeding the fan, I again staggered and fell. While down in this situation, Mr. Covey took up the hickory slat with which Hughes had been striking off the half-bushel measure, and with it gave me a heavy blow upon the head, making a large wound, and the blood ran freely; and with this again told me to get up. I made no effort to comply, having now made up my mind to let him do his worst. In a short time after receiving this blow, my head grew better. Mr. Covey had now left me to my fate. At this moment I resolved, for the first time, to go to my master, enter a complaint, and ask his protection. In order to [do] this, I must that afternoon walk seven miles; and this, under the circumstances, was truly a severe undertaking. I was exceedingly feeble; made so as much by the kicks and blows which I received, as by the severe fit of sickness to which I had been subjected. I, however, watched my chance, while Covey was looking in an opposite direction, and started for St. Michael's. I succeeded in getting a considerable distance on my way to the woods, when Covey discovered me, and called after me to come back, threatening what he would do if I did not come. I disregarded both his calls and his threats, and made my way to the woods as fast as my feeble state would allow; and thinking I might be overhauled by him if I kept the road, I walked through the woods, keeping far enough from the road to avoid detection, and near enough to prevent losing my way. I had not gone far before my little strength again failed me. I could go no farther. I fell down, and lay for a considerable time. The blood was yet oozing from the wound on my head. For a time I thought I should bleed to death; and think now that I should have done so, but that the blood so matted my hair as to stop the wound. After lying there about three quarters of an hour, I nerved myself up again, and started on my way, through bogs and briers, barefooted and bareheaded, tearing my feet sometimes at nearly every step; and after a journey of about seven miles, occupying some five hours to perform it, I arrived at master's store. I then presented an appearance enough to affect any but a heart of iron. From the crown of my head to my feet, I was covered with blood. My hair was all clotted with dust and blood; my shirt was stiff with blood. My legs and feet were torn in sundry places with briers and thorns, and were also covered with blood. I suppose I looked like a man who had escaped a den of wild beasts, and barely escaped them. In this state I appeared before my master, humbly entreating him to interpose his authority for my protection. I told him all the circumstances as well as I could, and it seemed, as I spoke, at times to affect him. He would then walk the floor, and seek to justify Covey by saying he expected I deserved it. He asked me what I wanted. I told him, to let me get a new home; that as sure as I lived with Mr. Covey again, I should live with but to die with him; that Covey would surely kill me; he was in a fair way for it. Master Thomas ridiculed the idea that there was any danger of Mr. Covey's killing me, and said that he knew Mr. Covey; that he was a good man, and that he could not think of taking me from him; that, should he do so, he would lose the whole year's wages; that I belonged to Mr. Covey for one year, and that I must go back to him, come what might; and that I must not trouble him with any more stories, or that he would himself *get hold of me*. After threatening me thus, he gave me a very large dose of salts, telling me that I might remain in St. Michael's that night (it being quite late), but that I must be off back to Mr. Covey's early in the morning; and that if I did not, he would *get hold of me*, which meant that he would whip me. I remained all night, and, according to his orders, I started off to Covey's in the morning, (Saturday morning), wearied in body and broken in spirit. I got no supper that night, or breakfast that morning. I reached Covey's about nine o'clock; and just as I was getting over the fence that divided Mrs. Kemp's fields from ours, out ran Covey with his cowskin, to give me another whipping. Before he could reach me, I succeeded in getting to the cornfield; and as the corn was very high, it afforded me the means of hiding. He seemed very angry, and searched for me a long time. My behavior was altogether unaccountable. He finally gave up the chase, thinking, I suppose, that I must come home for something to eat; he would give himself no further trouble in looking for me. I spent that day mostly in the woods, having the alternative before me,—to go home and be whipped to death, or stay in the woods and be starved to death. That night, I fell in with Sandy Jenkins, a slave with whom I was somewhat acquainted. Sandy had a free wife who lived about four miles from Mr. Covey's; and it being Saturday, he was on his way to see her. I told him my circumstances, and he very kindly invited me to go home with him. I went home with him, and talked this whole matter over, and got his advice as to what course it was best for me to pursue. I found Sandy an old adviser. He told me, with great solemnity, I must go back to Covey; but that before I went, I must go with him into another part of the woods, where there was a certain *root*, which, if I would take some of it with me, carrying it *always on my right side*, would render it impossible for Mr. Covey, or any other white man, to whip me. He said he had carried it for years; and since he had done so, he had never received a blow, and never expected to while he carried it. I at first rejected the idea, that the simple carrying of a root in my pocket would have any such effect as he had said, and was not disposed to take it; but Sandy impressed the necessity with much earnestness, telling me it could do no harm, if it did no good. To please him, I at length took the root, and, according to his direction, carried it upon my right side. This was Sunday morning. I immediately started for home; and upon entering the yard gate, out came Mr. Covey on his way to meeting. He spoke to me very kindly, bade me drive the pigs from a lot near by, and passed on towards the church. Now, this singular conduct of Mr. Covey really made me begin to think that there was something in the *root* which Sandy had given me; and had it been on any other day than Sunday, I could have attributed the conduct to no other cause than the influence of that root; and as it was, I was half inclined to think the *root* to be something more than I at first had taken it to be. All went well till Monday morning. On this morning, the virtue of the *root* was fully tested. Long before daylight, I was called to go and rub, curry, and feed, the horses. I obeyed, and was glad to obey. But whilst thus engaged, whilst in the act of throwing down some blades from the loft, Mr. Covey entered the stable with a long rope; and just as I was half out of the loft, he caught hold of my legs, and was about tying me. As soon as I found what he was up to, I gave a sudden spring, and as I did so, he holding to my legs, I was brought sprawling on the stable floor. Mr. Covey seemed now to think he had me, and could do what he pleased; but at this moment—from whence came the spirit I don't know—I resolved to fight; and, suiting my action to the resolution, I seized Covey hard by the throat; and as I did so, I rose. He held on to me, and I to him. My resistance was so entirely unexpected, that Covey seemed taken all aback. He trembled like a leaf. This gave me assurance, and I held him uneasy, causing the blood to run where I touched him with the ends of my fingers. Mr. Covey soon called out to Hughes for help. Hughes came, and, while Covey held me, attempted to tie my right hand. While he was in the act of doing so, I watched my chance, and gave him a heavy kick close under the ribs. This kick fairly sickened Hughes, so that he left me in the hands of Mr. Covey. This kick had the effect of not only weakening Hughes, but Covey also. When he saw Hughes bending over with pain, his courage quailed. He asked me if I meant to persist in my resistance. I told him I did, come what might; that he had used me like a brute for six months, and that I was determined to be used so no longer. With that, he strove to drag me to a stick that was lying just out of the stable door. He meant to knock me down. But just as he was leaning over to get the stick, I seized him with both hands by his collar, and brought him by a sudden snatch to the ground. By this time, Bill came. Covey called upon him for assistance. Bill wanted to know what he could do. Covey said, "Take hold of him, take hold of him!" Bill said his master hired him out to work, and not to help to whip me; so he left Covey and myself to fight our own battle out. We were at it for nearly two hours. Covey at length let me go, puffing and blowing at a great rate, saying that if I had not resisted, he would not have whipped me half so much. The truth was, that he had not whipped me at all. I considered him as getting entirely the worst end of the bargain; for he had drawn no blood from me, but I had from him. The whole six months afterwards, that I spent with Mr. Covey, he never laid the weight of his finger upon me in anger. He would occasionally say, he didn't want to get hold of me again. "No," thought I, "you need not; for you will come off worse than you did before."

This battle with Mr. Covey was the turning-point in my career as a slave. It rekindled the few expiring embers of freedom, and revived within me a sense of my own manhood. It recalled the departed self-confidence, and inspired me again with a determination to be free. The gratification afforded by the triumph was a full compensation for whatever else might follow, even death itself. He only can understand the deep satisfaction which I experienced, who has himself repelled by force the bloody arm of slavery. I felt as I never felt before. It was a glorious resurrection, from the tomb of slavery, to the heaven of freedom. My long-crushed spirit rose, cowardice departed, bold defiance took its place; and I now resolved that, however long I might remain a slave in form, the day had passed forever when I could be a slave in fact. I did not hesitate to let it be known of me, that the white man who expected to succeed in whipping, must also succeed in killing me.

From this time I was never again what might be called fairly whipped, though I remained a slave four years afterwards. I had several fights, but was never whipped.

It was for a long time a matter of surprise to me why Mr. Covey did not immediately have me taken by the constable to the whipping-post, and there regularly whipped for the crime of raising my hand against a white man in defence of myself. And the only explanation I can now think of does not entirely satisfy me; but such as it is, I will give it. Mr. Covey enjoyed the most unbounded reputation for being a first-rate overseer and negro-breaker. It was of considerable importance to him. That reputation was at stake; and had he sent me—a boy about sixteen years old—to the public whipping-post, his reputation would have been lost; so, to save his reputation, he suffered me to go unpunished.

My term of actual service to Mr. Edward Covey ended on Christmas day, 1833. The days between Christmas and New Year's day are allowed as holidays; and, accordingly, we were not required to perform any labor, more than to feed and take care of the stock. This time we regarded as our own, by the grace of our masters; and we therefore used or abused it nearly as we pleased. Those of us who had families at a distance, were generally allowed to spend the whole six days in their society. This time, however, was spent in various ways. The staid, sober, thinking and industrious ones of our number would employ themselves in making corn-brooms, mats, horse-collars, and baskets; and another class of us would spend the time in hunting opossums, hares, and coons. But by far the larger part engaged in such sports and merriments as playing ball, wrestling, running foot-races, fiddling, dancing, and drinking whisky; and this latter mode of spending the time was by far the most agreeable to the feelings of our masters. A slave who would work during the holidays was considered by our masters as scarcely deserving them. He was regarded as one who rejected the favor of his master. It was deemed a disgrace not to get drunk at Christmas; and he was regarded as lazy indeed, who had not provided himself with the necessary means, during the year, to get whisky enough to last him through Christmas.

From what I know of the effect of these holidays upon the slave, I believe them to be among the most effective means in the hands of the slaveholder in keeping down the spirit of insurrection. Were the slaveholders at once to abandon this practice, I have not the slightest doubt it would lead to an immediate insurrection among the slaves. These holidays serve as conductors, or safety-valves, to carry off the rebellious spirit of enslaved humanity. But for these, the slave would be forced up to the wildest desperation; and woe betide the slaveholder, the day he ventures to remove or hinder the operation of those conductors! I warn him that, in such an event, a spirit will go forth in their midst, more to be dreaded than the most appalling earthquake.

The holidays are part and parcel of the gross fraud, wrong, and inhumanity of slavery. They are professedly a custom established by the benevolence of the slaveholders; but I undertake to say, it is the result of selfishness, and one of the grossest frauds committed upon the down-trodden slave. They do not give the slaves this time because they would not like to have their work during its continuance, but because they know it would be unsafe to deprive them of it. This will be seen by the fact, that the slaveholders like to have their slaves spend those days just in such a manner as to make them as glad of their ending as of their beginning. Their object seems to be, to disgust their slaves with freedom, by plunging them into the lowest depths of dissipation. For instance, the slaveholders not only like to see the slave drink of his own accord, but will adopt various plans to make him drunk. One plan is, to make bets on their slaves, as to who can drink the most whisky without getting drunk; and in this way they succeed in getting whole multitudes to drink to excess. Thus, when the slave asks for virtuous freedom, the cunning slaveholder, knowing his ignorance, cheats him with a dose of vicious dissipation, artfully labelled with the name of liberty. The most of us used to drink it down, and the result was just what might be supposed: many of us were led to think that there was little to choose between liberty and slavery. We felt, and very properly too, that we had almost as well be slaves to man as to rum. So, when the holidays ended, we staggered up from the filth of our wallowing, took a long breath, and marched to the field,—feeling, upon the whole, rather glad to go, from what our master had deceived us into a belief was freedom, back to the arms of slavery.

I have said that this mode of treatment is a part of the whole system of fraud and inhumanity of slavery. It is so. The mode here adopted to disgust the slave with freedom, by allowing him to see only the abuse of it, is carried out in other things. For instance, a slave loves molasses; he steals some. His master, in many cases, goes off to town, and buys a large quantity; he returns, takes his whip, and commands the slave to eat the molasses, until the poor fellow is made sick at the very mention of it. The same mode is sometimes adopted to make the slaves refrain from asking for more food than their regular allowance. A slave runs through his allowance, and applies for more. His master is enraged at him; but, not willing to send him off without food, gives him more than is necessary, and compels him to eat it within a given time. Then, if he complains that he cannot eat it, he is said to be satisfied neither full nor fasting, and is whipped for being hard to please! I have an abundance of such illustrations of the same principle, drawn from my own observation, but think the cases I have cited sufficient. The practice is a very common one.

On the first of January, 1834, I left Mr. Covey, and went to live with Mr. William Freeland, who lived about three miles from St. Michael's. I soon found Mr. Freeland a very different man from Mr. Covey. Though not rich, he was what would be called an educated southern gentleman. Mr. Covey, as I have shown, was a well-trained negro-breaker and slave-driver. The former (slaveholder though he was) seemed to possess some regard for honor, some reverence for justice, and some respect for humanity. The latter seemed totally insensible to all such sentiments. Mr. Freeland had many of the faults peculiar to slaveholders, such as being very passionate and fretful; but I must do him the justice to say, that he was exceedingly free from those degrading vices to which Mr. Covey was constantly addicted. The one was open and frank, and we always knew where to find him. The other was a most artful deceiver, and could be understood only by such as were skilful enough to detect his cunningly-devised frauds. Another advantage I gained in my new master was, he made no pretensions to, or profession of, religion; and this, in my opinion, was truly a great advantage. I assert most unhesitatingly, that the religion of the south is a mere covering for the most horrid crimes,—a justifier of the most appalling barbarity,—a sanctifier of the most hateful frauds,—and a dark shelter under which the darkest, foulest, grossest, and most infernal deeds of slaveholders find the strongest protection. Were I to be again reduced to the chains of slavery, next to that enslavement, I should regard being the slave of a religious master the greatest calamity that could befall me. For of all slaveholders with whom I have ever met, religious slaveholders are the worst. I have ever found them the meanest and basest, the most cruel and cowardly, of all others. It was my unhappy lot not only to belong to a religious slaveholder, but to live in a community of such religionists. Very near Mr. Freeland lived the Rev. Daniel Weeden, and in the same neighborhood lived the Rev. Rigby Hopkins. These were members and ministers in the Reformed Methodist Church. Mr. Weeden owned, among others, a woman slave, whose name I have forgotten. This woman's back, for weeks, was kept literally raw, made so by the lash of this merciless, *religious* wretch. He used to hire hands. His maxim was, Behave well or behave ill, it is the duty of a master occasionally to whip a slave, to remind him of his master's authority. Such was his theory, and such his practice.

Mr. Hopkins was even worse than Mr. Weeden. His chief boast was his ability to manage slaves. The peculiar feature of his government was that of whipping slaves in advance of deserving it. He always managed to have one or more of his slaves to whip every Monday morning. He did this to alarm their fears, and strike terror into those who escaped. His plan was to whip for the smallest offences, to prevent the commission of large ones. Mr. Hopkins could always find some excuse for whipping a slave. It would astonish one, unaccustomed to a slaveholding life, to see with what wonderful ease a slaveholder can find things, of which to make occasion to whip a slave. A mere look, word, or motion,—a mistake, accident, or want of power,—are all matters for which a slave may be whipped at any time. Does a slave look dissatisfied? It is said, he has the devil in him, and it must be whipped out. Does he speak loudly when spoken to by his master? Then he is getting high-minded, and should be taken down a button-hole lower. Does he forget to pull off his hat at the approach of a white person? Then he is wanting in reverence, and should be whipped for it. Does he ever venture to vindicate his conduct, when censured for it? Then he is guilty of impudence,— one of the greatest crimes of which a slave can be guilty. Does he ever venture to suggest a different mode of doing things from that pointed out by his master? He is indeed presumptuous, and getting above himself; and nothing less than a flogging will do for him. Does he, while ploughing, break a plough,—or, while hoeing, break a hoe? It is owing to his carelessness, and for it a slave must always be whipped. Mr. Hopkins could always find something of this sort to justify the use of the lash, and he seldom failed to embrace such opportunities. There was not a man in the whole county, with whom the slaves who had the getting their own home, would not prefer to live, rather than with this Rev. Mr. Hopkins. And yet there was not a man any where round, who made higher professions of religion, or was more active in revivals,—more attentive to the class, love-feast, prayer and preaching meetings, or more devotional in his family,—that prayed earlier, later, louder, and longer,—than this same reverend slave-driver, Rigby Hopkins.

But to return to Mr. Freeland, and to my experience while in his employment. He, like Mr. Covey, gave us enough to eat; but, unlike Mr. Covey, he also gave us sufficient time to take our meals. He worked us hard, but always between sunrise and sunset. He required a good deal of work to be done, but gave us good tools with which to work. His farm was large, but he employed hands enough to work it, and with ease, compared with many of his neighbors. My treatment, while in his employment, was heavenly, compared with what I experienced at the hands of Mr. Edward Covey.

Mr. Freeland was himself the owner of but two slaves. Their names were Henry Harris and John Harris. The rest of his hands he hired.

These consisted of myself, Sandy Jenkins,[6] and Handy Caldwell. Henry and John were quite intelligent, and in a very little while after I went there, I succeeded in creating in them a strong desire to learn how to read. This desire soon sprang up in the others also. They very soon mustered up some old spelling-books, and nothing would do but that I must keep a Sabbath school. I agreed to do so, and accordingly devoted my Sundays to teaching these my loved fellow-slaves how to read. Neither of them knew his letters when I went there. Some of the slaves of the neighboring farms found what was going on, and also availed themselves of this little opportunity to learn to read. It was understood, among all who came, that there must be as little display about it as possible. It was necessary to keep our religious masters at St. Michael's unacquainted with the fact, that, instead of spending the Sabbath in wrestling, boxing, and drinking whiskey, we were trying to learn how to read the will of God; for they had much rather see us engaged in those degrading sports, than to see us behaving like intellectual, moral, and accountable beings. My blood boils as I think of the bloody manner in which Messrs. Wright Fairbanks and Garrison West, both class-leaders, in connection with many others, rushed in upon us with sticks and stones, and broke up our virtuous little Sabbath school, at St. Michael's—all calling themselves Christians! humble followers of the Lord Jesus Christ! But I am again digressing.

I held my Sabbath school at the house of a free colored man, whose name I deem it imprudent to mention; for should it be known, it might embarrass him greatly, though the crime of holding the school was committed ten years ago. I had at one time over forty scholars, and those of the right sort, ardently desiring to learn. They were of all ages, though mostly men and women. I look back to those Sundays with an amount of pleasure not to be expressed. They were great days to my soul. The work of instructing my dear fellow-slaves was the sweetest engagement with which I was ever blessed. We loved each other, and to leave them at the close of the Sabbath was a severe cross indeed. When I think that these precious souls are to-day shut up in the prison-house of slavery, my feelings overcome me, and I am almost ready to ask, "Does a righteous God govern the universe? and for what does he hold the thunders in his right hand, if not to smite the oppressor, and deliver the spoiled out of the hand of the spoiler?" These dear souls came not to Sabbath school because it was popular to do so, nor did I teach them because it was reputable

6. This is the same man who gave me the roots to prevent my being whipped by Mr. Covey. He was "a clever soul." We used frequently to talk about the fight with Covey, and as often as we did so, he would claim my success as the result of the roots which he gave me. This superstition is very common among the more ignorant slaves. A slave seldom dies but that his death is attributed to trickery. [Douglass's note.]

to be thus engaged. Every moment they spent in that school, they were liable to be taken up, and given thirty-nine lashes. They came because they wished to learn. Their minds had been starved by their cruel masters. They had been shut up in mental darkness. I taught them, because it was the delight of my soul to be doing something that looked like bettering the condition of my race. I kept up my school nearly the whole year I lived with Mr. Freeland; and, beside my Sabbath school, I devoted three evenings in the week, during the winter, to teaching the slaves at home. And I have the happiness to know, that several of those who came to Sabbath school learned how to read; and that one, at least, is now free through my agency.

The year passed off smoothly. It seemed only about half as long as the year which preceded it. I went through it without receiving a single blow. I will give Mr. Freeland the credit of being the best master I ever had, *till I became my own master.* For the ease with which I passed the year, I was, however, somewhat indebted to the society of my fellow-slaves. They were noble souls; they not only possessed loving hearts, but brave ones. We were linked and inter-linked with each other. I loved them with a love stronger than any thing I have experienced since. It is sometimes said that we slaves do not love and confide in each other. In answer to this assertion, I can say, I never loved any or confided in any people more than my fellow-slaves, and especially those with whom I lived at Mr. Freeland's. I believe we would have died for each other. We never undertook to do any thing, of any importance, without a mutual consultation. We never moved separately. We were one; and as much so by our tempers and dispositions, as by the mutual hardships to which we were necessarily subjected by our condition as slaves.

At the close of the year 1834, Mr. Freeland again hired me of my master, for the year 1835. But, by this time, I began to want to live *upon free land* as well as *with Freeland;* and I was no longer content, therefore, to live with him or any other slaveholder. I began, with the commencement of the year, to prepare myself for a final strug-gle, which should decide my fate one way or the other. My tendency was upward. I was fast approaching manhood, and year after year had passed, and I was still a slave. These thoughts roused me—I must do something. I therefore resolved that 1835 should not pass without witnessing an attempt, on my part, to secure my liberty. But I was not willing to cherish this determination alone. My fellow-slaves were dear to me. I was anxious to have them participate with me in this, my life-giving determination. I therefore, though with great prudence, commenced early to ascertain their views and feel-ings in regard to their condition, and to imbue their minds with thoughts of freedom. I bent myself to devising ways and means for

our escape, and meanwhile strove, on all fitting occasions, to impress
them with the gross fraud and inhumanity of slavery. I went first to
Henry, next to John, then to the others. I found, in them all, warm
hearts and noble spirits. They were ready to hear, and ready to act
when a feasible plan should be proposed. This was what I wanted. I
talked to them of our want of manhood, if we submitted to our
enslavement without at least one noble effort to be free. We met
often, and consulted frequently, and told our hopes and fears,
recounted the difficulties, real and imagined, which we should be
called on to meet. At times we were almost disposed to give up, and
try to content ourselves with our wretched lot; at others, we were
firm and unbending in our determination to go. Whenever we suggested any plan, there was shrinking—the odds were fearful. Our
path was beset with the greatest obstacles; and if we succeeded in
gaining the end of it, our right to be free was yet questionable—we
were yet liable to be returned to bondage. We could see no spot, this
side of the ocean, where we could be free. We knew nothing about
Canada. Our knowledge of the north did not extend farther than
New York; and to go there, and be forever harassed with the frightful
liability of being returned to slavery—with the certainty of being treated
tenfold worse than before—the thought was truly a horrible one, and
one which it was not easy to overcome. The case sometimes stood
thus: At every gate through which we were to pass, we saw a watchman—at every ferry a guard—on every bridge a sentinel—and in
every wood a patrol. We were hemmed in upon every side. Here
were the difficulties, real or imagined—the good to be sought, and
the evil to be shunned. On the one hand, there stood slavery, a stern
reality, glaring frightfully upon us,—its robes already crimsoned with
the blood of millions, and even now feasting itself greedily upon our
own flesh. On the other hand, away back in the dim distance, under
the flickering light of the north star, behind some craggy hill or snow-
covered mountain, stood a doubtful freedom—half frozen—beckoning us to come and share its hospitality. This in itself was sometimes
enough to stagger us; but when we permitted ourselves to survey the
road, we were frequently appalled. Upon either side we saw grim
death, assuming the most horrid shapes. Now it was starvation, causing us to eat our own flesh;—now we were contending with the waves,
and were drowned;—now we were overtaken, and torn to pieces by
the fangs of the terrible bloodhound. We were stung by scorpions,
chased by wild beasts, bitten by snakes, and finally, after having nearly
reached the desired spot,—after swimming rivers, encountering wild
beasts, sleeping in the woods, suffering hunger and nakedness,—we
were overtaken by our pursuers, and, in our resistance, we were shot
dead upon the spot! I say, this picture sometimes appalled us, and
made us

> "rather bear those ills we had,
> Than fly to others, that we knew not of."[7]

In coming to a fixed determination to run away, we did more than Patrick Henry,[8] when he resolved upon liberty or death. With us it was a doubtful liberty at most, and almost certain death if we failed. For my part, I should prefer death to hopeless bondage.

Sandy, one of our number, gave up the notion, but still encouraged us. Our company then consisted of Henry Harris, John Harris, Henry Bailey, Charles Roberts, and myself. Henry Bailey was my uncle, and belonged to my master. Charles married my aunt: he belonged to my master's father-in-law, Mr. William Hamilton.

The plan we finally concluded upon was, to get a large canoe belonging to Mr. Hamilton, and upon the Saturday night previous to Easter holidays, paddle directly up the Chesapeake Bay. On our arrival at the head of the bay, a distance of seventy or eighty miles from where we lived, it was our purpose to turn our canoe adrift, and follow the guidance of the north star till we got beyond the limits of Maryland. Our reason for taking the water route was, that we were less liable to be suspected as runaways; we hoped to be regarded as fishermen; whereas, if we should take the land route, we should be subjected to interruptions of almost every kind. Any one having a white face, and being so disposed, could stop us, and subject us to examination.

The week before our intended start, I wrote several protections, one for each of us. As well as I can remember, they were in the following words, to wit:—

> "This is to certify that I, the undersigned, have given the bearer, my servant, full liberty to go to Baltimore, and spend the Easter holidays. Written with mine own hand, &c., 1835.
>
> "WILLIAM HAMILTON,
> "Near St. Michael's, in Talbot county, Maryland."

We were not going to Baltimore; but, in going up the bay, we went toward Baltimore, and these protections were only intended to protect us while on the bay.

As the time drew near for our departure, our anxiety became more and more intense. It was truly a matter of life and death with us. The strength of our determination was about to be fully tested. At this time, I was very active in explaining every difficulty, removing every doubt, dispelling every fear, and inspiring all with the firmness indispensable to success in our undertaking; assuring them that half

---

7. *Hamlet*, III.i.81–82: "rather bear those ills we have." 8. American statesman and orator (1736–1799) whose most famous utterance was "Give me liberty or give me death."

was gained the instant we made the move; we had talked long enough; we were now ready to move; if not now, we never should be; and if we did not intend to move now, we had as well fold our arms, sit down, and acknowledge ourselves fit only to be slaves. This, none of us were prepared to acknowledge. Every man stood firm; and at our last meeting, we pledged ourselves afresh, in the most solemn manner, that, at the time appointed, we would certainly start in pursuit of freedom. This was in the middle of the week, at the end of which we were to be off. We went, as usual, to our several fields of labor, but with bosoms highly agitated with thoughts of our truly hazardous undertaking. We tried to conceal our feelings as much as possible; and I think we succeeded very well.

After a painful waiting, the Saturday morning, whose night was to witness our departure, came. I hailed it with joy, bring what of sadness it might. Friday night was a sleepless one for me. I was, by common consent, at the head of the whole affair. The responsibility of success or failure lay heavily upon me. The glory of the one, and the confusion of the other, were alike mine. The first two hours of that morning were such as I never experienced before, and hope never to again. Early in the morning, we went, as usual, to the field. We were spreading manure; and all at once, while thus engaged, I was overwhelmed with an indescribable feeling, in the fulness of which I turned to Sandy, who was near by, and said, "We are betrayed!" "Well," said he, "that thought has this moment struck me." We said no more. I was never more certain of any thing.

The horn was blown as usual, and we went up from the field to the house for breakfast. I went for the form, more than for want of any thing to eat that morning. Just as I got to the house, in looking out at the lane gate, I saw four white men, with two colored men. The white men were on horseback, and the colored ones were walking behind, as if tied. I watched them a few moments till they got up to our lane gate. Here they halted, and tied the colored men to the gate-post. I was not yet certain as to what the matter was. In a few moments, in rode Mr. Hamilton, with a speed betokening great excitement. He came to the door, and inquired if Master William was in. He was told he was at the barn. Mr. Hamilton, without dismounting, rode up to the barn with extraordinary speed. In a few moments, he and Mr. Freeland returned to the house. By this time, the three constables rode up, and in great haste dismounted, tied their horses, and met Master William and Mr. Hamilton returning from the barn; and after talking awhile, they all walked up to the kitchen door. There was no one in the kitchen but myself and John. Henry and Sandy were up at the barn. Mr. Freeland put his head in at the door, and called me by name, saying, there were some gentlemen at the door who wished to see me. I stepped to the door, and inquired what they wanted. They at once seized me, and, without giving me any satisfaction, tied me—lashing my hands closely together. I insisted upon knowing what the matter was. They at length said, that they had learned I had been in a "scrape," and that I was to be examined before my master; and if their information proved false, I should not be hurt.

In a few moments, they succeeded in tying John. They then turned to Henry, who had by this time returned, and commanded him to cross his hands. "I won't!" said Henry, in a firm tone, indicating his readiness to meet the consequences of his refusal. "Won't you?" said Tom Graham, the constable. "No, I won't!" said Henry, in a still stronger tone. With this, two of the constables pulled out their shining pistols, and swore, by their Creator, that they would make him cross his hands or kill him. Each cocked his pistol, and, with fingers on the trigger, walked up to Henry, saying, at the same time, if he did not cross his hands, they would blow his damned heart out. "Shoot me, shoot me!" said Henry; "you can't kill me but once. Shoot, shoot,—and be damned! *I won't be tied!*" This he said in a tone of loud defiance; and at the same time, with a motion as quick as lightning, he with one single stroke dashed the pistols from the hand of each constable. As he did this, all hands fell upon him, and, after beating him some time, they finally overpowered him, and got him tied.

During the scuffle, I managed, I know not how, to get my pass out, and, without being discovered, put it into the fire. We were all now tied; and just as we were to leave for Easton jail, Betsy Freeland, mother of William Freeland, came to the door with her hands full of biscuits, and divided them between Henry and John. She then delivered herself of a speech, to the following effect:—addressing herself to me, she said, "*You devil! You yellow devil!* it was you that put it into the heads of Henry and John to run away. But for you, you long-legged mulatto devil! Henry nor John would never have thought of such a thing." I made no reply, and was immediately hurried off towards St. Michael's. Just a moment previous to the scuffle with Henry, Mr. Hamilton suggested the propriety of making a search for the protections which he had understood Frederick had written for himself and the rest. But, just at the moment he was about carrying his proposal into effect, his aid was needed in helping to tie Henry; and the excitement attending the scuffle caused them either to forget, or to deem it unsafe, under the circumstances, to search. So we were not yet convicted of the intention to run away.

When we got about half way to St. Michael's, while the constables having us in charge were looking ahead, Henry inquired of me what he should do with his pass. I told him to eat it with his biscuit, and own nothing; and we passed the word around, "*Own nothing*"; and

"*Own nothing!*" said we all. Our confidence in each other was unshaken. We were resolved to succeed or fail together, after the calamity had befallen us as much as before. We were now prepared for any thing. We were to be dragged that morning fifteen miles behind horses, and then to be placed in the Easton jail. When we reached St. Michael's, we underwent a sort of examination. We all denied that we ever intended to run away. We did this more to bring out the evidence against us, than from any hope of getting clear of being sold; for, as I have said, we were ready for that. The fact was, we cared but little where we went, so we went together. Our greatest concern was about separation. We dreaded that more than any thing this side of death. We found the evidence against us to be the testimony of one person; our master would not tell who it was; but we came to a unanimous decision among ourselves as to who their informant was. We were sent off to the jail at Easton. When we got there, we were delivered up to the sheriff, Mr. Joseph Graham, and by him placed in jail. Henry, John, and myself, were placed in one room together—Charles, and Henry Bailey, in another. Their object in separating us was to hinder concert.

We had been in jail scarcely twenty minutes, when a swarm of slave traders, and agents for slave traders, flocked into jail to look at us, and to ascertain if we were for sale. Such a set of beings I never saw before! I felt myself surrounded by so many fiends from perdition. A band of pirates never looked more like their father, the devil. They laughed and grinned over us, saying, "Ah, my boys! we have got you, haven't we?" And after taunting us in various ways, they one by one went into an examination of us, with intent to ascertain our value. They would impudently ask us if we would not like to have them for our masters. We would make them no answer, and leave them to find out as best they could. Then they would curse and swear at us, telling us that they could take the devil out of us in a very little while, if we were only in their hands.

While in jail, we found ourselves in much more comfortable quarters than we expected when we went there. We did not get much to eat, nor that which was very good; but we had a good clean room, from the windows of which we could see what was going on in the street, which was very much better than though we had been placed in one of the dark, damp cells. Upon the whole, we got along very well, so far as the jail and its keeper were concerned. Immediately after the holidays were over, contrary to all our expectations, Mr. Hamilton and Mr. Freeland came up to Easton, and took Charles, the two Henrys, and John, out of jail, and carried them home, leaving me alone. I regarded this separation as a final one. It caused me more pain than any thing else in the whole transaction. I was ready for any thing rather than separation. I supposed that they had consulted together, and had decided that, as I was the whole cause of the intention of the others to run away, it was hard to make the innocent suffer with the guilty; and that they had, therefore, concluded to take the others home, and sell me, as a warning to the others that remained. It is due to the noble Henry to say, he seemed almost as reluctant at leaving the prison as at leaving home to come to the prison. But we knew we should, in all probability, be separated, if we were sold; and since he was in their hands, he concluded to go peaceably home.

I was now left to my fate. I was all alone, and within the walls of a stone prison. But a few days before, and I was full of hope. I expected to have been safe in a land of freedom; but now I was covered with gloom, sunk down to the utmost despair. I thought the possibility of freedom was gone. I was kept in this way about one week, at the end of which, Captain Auld, my master, to my surprise and utter astonishment, came up, and took me out, with the intention of sending me, with a gentleman of his acquaintance, into Alabama. But, from some cause or other, he did not send me to Alabama, but concluded to send me back to Baltimore, to live again with his brother Hugh, and to learn a trade.

Thus, after an absence of three years and one month, I was once more permitted to return to my old home at Baltimore. My master sent me away, because there existed against me a very great prejudice in the community, and he feared I might be killed.

In a few weeks after I went to Baltimore, Master Hugh hired me to Mr. William Gardner, an extensive ship-builder, on Fell's Point. I was put there to learn how to calk. It, however, proved a very unfavorable place for the accomplishment of this object. Mr. Gardner was engaged that spring in building two large man-of-war brigs, professedly for the Mexican government. The vessels were to be launched in the July of that year, and in failure thereof, Mr. Gardner was to lose a considerable sum; so that when I entered, all was hurry. There was no time to learn any thing. Every man had to do that which he knew how to do. In entering the shipyard, my orders from Mr. Gardner were, to do whatever the carpenters commanded me to do. This was placing me at the beck and call of about seventy-five men. I was to regard all these as masters. Their word was to be my law. My situation was a most trying one. At times I needed a dozen pair of hands. I was called a dozen ways in the space of a single minute. Three or four voices would strike my ear at the same moment. It was—"Fred., come help me to cant this timber here."—"Fred., come carry this timber yonder."—"Fred., bring that roller here."—"Fred., go get a fresh can of water."—"Fred., come help saw off the end of this timber."—"Fred., go quick, and get the crow-bar."—"Fred., hold on the end of this fall."—"Fred., go to the blacksmith's shop, and get a new punch."—"Hurra,[9] Fred.! run and bring me a cold chisel."—"I say, Fred., bear a hand, and get up a fire as quick as lightning under that steam-box."—"Halloo, nigger! come, turn this grindstone."—"Come, come! move, move! and *bowse*[1] this timber forward."—"I say, darky, blast your eyes, why don't you heat up some pitch?"—"Halloo! halloo! halloo!" (Three voices at the same time.) "Come here!—Go there!—Hold on where you are! Damn you, if you move, I'll knock your brains out!"

This was my school for eight months, and I might have remained there longer, but for a most horrid fight I had with four of the white apprentices, in which my left eye was nearly knocked out, and I was horribly mangled in other respects. The facts in the case were these: Until a very little while after I went there, white and black ship-carpenters worked side by side, and no one seemed to see any impropriety in it. All hands seemed to be very well satisfied. Many of the black carpenters were freemen. Things seemed to be going on very well. All at once, the white carpenters knocked off, and said they would not work with free colored workmen. Their reason for this, as alleged, was, that if free colored carpenters were encouraged, they would soon take the trade into their own hands, and poor white men would be thrown out of employment. They therefore felt called upon at once to put a stop to it. And, taking advantage of Mr. Gardner's necessities, they broke off, swearing they would work no longer, unless he would discharge his black carpenters. Now, though this did not extend to me in form, it did reach me in fact. My fellow-apprentices very soon began to feel it degrading to them to work with me. They began to put on airs, and talk about the "niggers" taking the country, saying we all ought to be killed; and, being encouraged by the journeymen, they commenced making my condition as hard as they could, by hectoring me around, and sometimes striking me. I, of course, kept the vow I made after the fight with Mr. Covey, and struck back again, regardless of consequences; and while I kept them from combining, I succeeded very well; for I could whip the whole of them, taking them separately. They, however, at length combined, and came upon me, armed with sticks, stones, and heavy handspikes. One came in front with a half brick. There was one at each side of me, and one behind me. While I was attending to those in front, and on either side, the one behind ran up with the handspike, and struck me a heavy blow upon the head. It stunned me. I fell, and with this they all ran upon me, and fell to beating me with their fists. I let them lay on for a while, gathering strength. In an instant, I gave a sudden surge, and rose to my hands and knees. Just as I did that, one of their number gave me, with his heavy boot, a

9. I.e., hurry.   1. Lift or haul (usually with the help of block and tackle).

powerful kick in the left eye. My eyeball seemed to have burst. When they saw my eye closed, and badly swollen, they left me. With this I seized the handspike, and for a time pursued them. But here the carpenters interfered, and I thought I might as well give it up. It was impossible to stand my hand against so many. All this took place in sight of not less than fifty white ship-carpenters, and not one interposed a friendly word; but some cried, "Kill the damned nigger! Kill him! kill him! He struck a white person." I found my only chance for life was in flight. I succeeded in getting away without an additional blow, and barely so; for to strike a white man is death by Lynch law,—and that was the law in Mr. Gardner's ship-yard; nor is there much of any other out of Mr. Gardner's ship-yard.

I went directly home, and told the story of my wrongs to Master Hugh; and I am happy to say of him, irreligious as he was, his conduct was heavenly, compared with that of his brother Thomas under similar circumstances. He listened attentively to my narration of the circumstances leading to the savage outrage, and gave many proofs of his strong indignation of it. The heart of my once overkind mistress was again melted into pity. My puffed-out eye and blood-covered face moved her to tears. She took a chair by me, washed the blood from my face, and, with a mother's tenderness, bound up my head, covering the wounded eye with a lean piece of fresh beef. It was almost compensation for my suffering to witness, once more, a manifestation of kindness from this, my once affectionate old mistress. Master Hugh was very much enraged. He gave expression to his feelings by pouring out curses upon the heads of those who did the deed. As soon as I got a little the better of my bruises, he took me with him to Esquire Watson's, on Bond Street, to see what could be done about the matter. Mr. Watson inquired who saw the assault committed. Master Hugh told him it was done in Mr. Gardner's ship-yard, at midday, where there were a large company of men at work. "As to that," he said, "the deed was done, and there was no question as to who did it." His answer was, he could do nothing in the case, unless some white man would come forward and testify. He could issue no warrant on my word. If I had been killed in the presence of a thousand colored people, their testimony combined would have been insufficient to have arrested one of the murderers. Master Hugh, for once, was compelled to say this state of things was too bad. Of course, it was impossible to get any white man to volunteer his testimony in my behalf, and against the white young men. Even those who may have sympathized with me were not prepared to do this. It required a degree of courage unknown to them to do so; for just at that time, the slightest manifestation of humanity toward a colored person was denounced as abolitionism, and that name subjected its bearer to frightful liabilities. The watchwords of the bloody-

minded in that region, and in those days, were, "Damn the abolitionists!" and "Damn the niggers!" There was nothing done, and
probably nothing would have been done if I had been killed. Such
was, and such remains, the state of things in the Christian city of
Baltimore.

Master Hugh, finding he could get no redress, refused to let me
go back again to Mr. Gardner. He kept me himself, and his wife
dressed my wound till I was again restored to health. He then took
me into the ship-yard of which he was foreman, in the employment
of Mr. Walter Price. There I was immediately set to calking, and
very soon learned the art of using my mallet and irons. In the course
of one year from the time I left Mr. Gardner's, I was able to command the highest wages given to the most experienced calkers. I was
now of some importance to my master. I was bringing him from six
to seven dollars per week. I sometimes brought him nine dollars per
week: my wages were a dollar and a half a day. After learning how
to calk, I sought my own employment, made my own contracts, and
collected the money which I earned. My pathway became much
more smooth than before; my condition was now much more comfortable. When I could get no calking to do, I did nothing. During
these leisure times, those old notions about freedom would steal over
me again. When in Mr. Gardner's employment, I was kept in such
a perpetual whirl of excitement, I could think of nothing, scarcely,
but my life; and in thinking of my life, I almost forgot my liberty. I
have observed this in my experience of slavery,—that whenever my
condition was improved, instead of its increasing my contentment,
it only increased my desire to be free, and set me to thinking of plans
to gain my freedom. I have found that, to make a contented slave, it
is necessary to make a thoughtless one. It is necessary to darken his
moral and mental vision, and, as far as possible, to annihilate the
power of reason. He must be made to feel that slavery is right; and
he can be brought to that only when he ceases to be a man.

I was now getting, as I have said, one dollar and fifty cents per
day. I contracted for it; I earned it; it was paid to me; it was rightfully
my own; yet, upon each returning Saturday night, I was compelled
to deliver every cent of that money to Master Hugh. And why? Not
because he earned it,—not because he had any hand in earning it,—
not because I owed it to him,—nor because he possessed the slightest
shadow of a right to it; but solely because he had the power to compel
me to give it up. The right of the grim-visaged pirate upon the high
seas is exactly the same.

Chapter XI

I now come to that part of my life during which I planned, and
finally succeeded in making, my escape from slavery. But before

narrating any of the peculiar circumstances, I deem it proper to make known my intention not to state all the facts connected with the transaction. My reasons for pursuing this course may be understood from the following: First, were I to give a minute statement of all the facts, it is not only possible, but quite probable, that others would thereby be involved in the most embarrassing difficulties. Secondly, such a statement would most undoubtedly induce greater vigilance on the part of slaveholders than has existed heretofore among them; which would, of course, be the means of guarding a door whereby some dear brother bondman might escape his galling chains. I deeply regret the necessity that impels me to suppress any thing of importance connected with my experience in slavery. It would afford me great pleasure indeed, as well as materially add to the interest of my narrative, were I at liberty to gratify a curiosity, which I know exists in the minds of many, by an accurate statement of all the facts pertaining to my most fortunate escape. But I must deprive myself of this pleasure, and the curious of the gratification which such a statement would afford. I would allow myself to suffer under the greatest imputations which evil-minded men might suggest, rather than exculpate myself, and thereby run the hazard of closing the slightest avenue by which a brother slave might clear himself of the chains and fetters of slavery.

I have never approved of the very public manner in which some of our western friends have conducted what they call the *underground railroad*,[2] but which, I think, by their open declarations, has been made most emphatically the *upperground railroad*. I honor those good men and women for their noble daring, and applaud them for willingly subjecting themselves to bloody persecution, by openly avowing their participation in the escape of slaves. I, however, can see very little good resulting from such a course, either to themselves or the slaves escaping; while, upon the other hand, I see and feel assured that those open declarations are a positive evil to the slaves remaining, who are seeking to escape. They do nothing towards enlightening the slave, whilst they do much towards enlightening the master. They stimulate him to greater watchfulness, and enhance his power to capture his slave. We owe something to the slaves south of the line[3] as well as to those north of it; and in aiding the latter on their way to freedom, we should be careful to do nothing which would be likely to hinder the former from escaping from slavery. I would keep the merciless slaveholder profoundly ignorant of the means of flight adopted by the slave. I would leave him to imagine himself surrounded by myriads of invisible tormentors, ever ready to snatch from his infernal grasp his trembling prey. Let him be left to feel his

2. A system set up by opponents of slavery to help fugitive slaves from the South escape to free states and to Canada.   3. I.e., the Mason-Dixon line, the boundary between Pennsylvania and Maryland and between slave and free states.

way in the dark; let darkness commensurate with his crime hover over him; and let him feel that at every step he takes, in pursuit of the flying bondman, he is running the frightful risk of having his hot brains dashed out by an invisible agency. Let us render the tyrant no aid; let us not hold the light by which he can trace the footprints of our flying brother. But enough of this. I will now proceed to the statement of those facts, connected with my escape, for which I am alone responsible, and for which no one can be made to suffer but myself.

In the early part of the year 1838, I became quite restless. I could see no reason why I should, at the end of each week, pour the reward of my toil into the purse of my master. When I carried to him my weekly wages, he would, after counting the money, look me in the face with a robber-like fierceness, and ask, "Is this all?" He was satisfied with nothing less than the last cent. He would, however, when I made him six dollars, sometimes give me six cents, to encourage me. It had the opposite effect. I regarded it as a sort of admission of my right to the whole. The fact that he gave me any part of my wages was proof, to my mind, that he believed me entitled to the whole of them. I always felt worse for having received any thing; for I feared that the giving me a few cents would ease his conscience, and make him feel himself to be a pretty honorable sort of robber. My discontent grew upon me. I was ever on the look-out for means of escape; and, finding no direct means, I determined to try to hire my time, with a view of getting money with which to make my escape. In the spring of 1838, when Master Thomas came to Baltimore to purchase his spring goods, I got an opportunity, and applied to him to allow me to hire my time. He unhesitatingly refused my request, and told me this was another stratagem by which to escape. He told me I could go nowhere but that he could get me; and that, in the event of my running away, he should spare no pains in his efforts to catch me. He exhorted me to content myself, and be obedient. He told me, if I would be happy, I must lay out no plans for the future. He said, if I behaved myself properly, he would take care of me. Indeed, he advised me to complete thoughtlessness of the future, and taught me to depend solely upon him for happiness. He seemed to see fully the pressing necessity of setting aside my intellectual nature, in order to contentment in slavery. But in spite of him, and even in spite of myself, I continued to think, and to think about the injustice of my enslavement, and the means of escape.

About two months after this, I applied to Master Hugh for the privilege of hiring my time. He was not acquainted with the fact that I had applied to Master Thomas, and had been refused. He too, at first, seemed disposed to refuse; but, after some reflection, he granted me the privilege, and proposed the following terms: I was to be allowed all my time, make all contracts with those for whom I worked, and find my own employment; and, in return for this liberty, I was to pay him three dollars at the end of each week; find myself in calking tools, and in board and clothing. My board was two dollars and a half per week. This, with the wear and tear of clothing and calking tools, made my regular expenses about six dollars per week. This amount I was compelled to make up, or relinquish the privilege of hiring my time. Rain or shine, work or no work, at the end of each week the money must be forthcoming, or I must give up my privilege. This arrangement, it will be perceived, was decidedly in my master's favor. It relieved him of all need of looking after me. His money was sure. He received all the benefits of slaveholding without its evils; while I endured all the evils of a slave, and suffered all the care and anxiety of a freeman. I found it a hard bargain. But, hard as it was, I thought it better than the old mode of getting along. It was a step towards freedom to be allowed to bear the responsibilities of a freeman, and I was determined to hold on upon it. I bent myself to the work of making money. I was ready to work at night as well as day, and by the most untiring perseverance and industry, I made enough to meet my expenses, and lay up a little money every week. I went on thus from May till August. Master Hugh then refused to allow me to hire my time longer. The ground for his refusal was a failure on my part, one Saturday night, to pay him for my week's time. This failure was occasioned by my attending a camp meeting about ten miles from Baltimore. During the week, I had entered into an engagement with a number of young friends to start from Baltimore to the camp ground early Saturday evening; and being detained by my employer, I was unable to get down to Master Hugh's without disappointing the company. I knew that Master Hugh was in no special need of the money that night. I therefore decided to go to camp meeting, and upon my return pay him the three dollars. I staid at the camp meeting one day longer than I intended when I left. But as soon as I returned, I called upon him to pay him what he considered his due. I found him very angry; he could scarce restrain his wrath. He said he had a great mind to give me a severe whipping. He wished to know how I dared go out of the city without asking his permission. I told him I hired my time, and while I paid him the price which he asked for it, I did not know that I was bound to ask him when and where I should go. This reply troubled him; and, after reflecting a few moments, he turned to me, and said I should hire my time no longer; that the next thing he should know of, I would be running away. Upon the same plea, he told me to bring my tools and clothing home forthwith. I did so; but instead of seeking work, as I had been accustomed to do previously to hiring my time, I spent the whole week without the performance of a single stroke of work. I did this in retaliation. Saturday night, he called upon me as usual for my week's wages. I told him I had no wages; I had done no work that week. Here we were upon the point of coming to blows. He raved, and swore his determination to get hold of me. I did not allow myself a single word; but was resolved, if he laid the weight of his hand upon me, it should be blow for blow. He did not strike me, but told me that he would find me in constant employment in future. I thought the matter over during the next day, Sunday, and finally resolved upon the third day of September, as the day upon which I would make a second attempt to secure my freedom. I now had three weeks during which to prepare for my journey. Early on Monday morning, before Master Hugh had time to make any engagement for me, I went out and got employment of Mr. Butler, at his ship-yard near the draw-bridge, upon what is called the City Block, thus making it unnecessary for him to seek employment for me. At the end of the week, I brought him between eight and nine dollars. He seemed very well pleased, and asked me why I did not do the same the week before. He little knew what my plans were. My object in working steadily was to remove any suspicion he might entertain of my intent to run away; and in this I succeeded admirably. I suppose he thought I was never better satisfied with my condition than at the very time during which I was planning my escape. The second week passed, and again I carried him my full wages; and so well pleased was he, that he gave me twenty-five cents, (quite a large sum for a slaveholder to give a slave,) and bade me to make a good use of it. I told him I would.

Things went on without very smoothly indeed, but within there was trouble. It is impossible for me to describe my feelings as the time of my contemplated start drew near. I had a number of warm-hearted friends in Baltimore,—friends that I loved almost as I did my life,—and the thought of being separated from them forever was painful beyond expression. It is my opinion that thousands would escape from slavery, who now remain, but for the strong cords of affection that bind them to their friends. The thought of leaving my friends was decidedly the most painful thought with which I had to contend. The love of them was my tender point, and shook my decision more than all things else. Besides the pain of separation, the dread and apprehension of a failure exceeded what I had experienced at my first attempt. The appalling defeat I then sustained returned to torment me. I felt assured that, if I failed in this attempt, my case would be a hopeless one—it would seal my fate as a slave forever. I could not hope to get off with any thing less than the severest punishment, and being placed beyond the means of escape. It required no very vivid imagination to depict the most frightful scenes through which I should have to pass, in case I failed. The wretchedness of slavery, and the blessedness of freedom, were perpetually before me. It was life and death with me. But I remained firm, and, according to my resolution, on the third day of September, 1838, I left my chains, and succeeded in reaching New York without the slightest interruption of any kind. How I did so,—what means I adopted,— what direction I travelled, and by what mode of conveyance,—I must leave unexplained, for the reasons before mentioned.

I have been frequently asked how I felt when I found myself in a free State. I have never been able to answer the question with any satisfaction to myself. It was a moment of the highest excitement I ever experienced. I suppose I felt as one may imagine the unarmed mariner to feel when he is rescued by a friendly man-of-war from the pursuit of a pirate. In writing to a dear friend, immediately after my arrival at New York, I said I felt like one who had escaped a den of hungry lions. This state of mind, however, very soon subsided; and I was again seized with a feeling of great insecurity and loneliness. I was yet liable to be taken back, and subjected to all the tortures of slavery. This in itself was enough to damp the ardor of my enthusiasm. But the loneliness overcame me. There I was in the midst of thousands, and yet a perfect stranger; without home and without friends, in the midst of thousands of my own brethren— children of a common Father, and yet I dared not to unfold to any one of them my sad condition. I was afraid to speak to any one for fear of speaking to the wrong one, and thereby falling into the hands of money-loving kidnappers, whose business it was to lie in wait for the panting fugitive, as the ferocious beasts of the forest lie in wait for their prey. The motto which I adopted when I started from slavery was this—"Trust no man!" I saw in every white man an enemy, and in almost every colored man cause for distrust. It was a most painful situation; and, to understand it, one must needs experience it, or imagine himself in similar circumstances. Let him be a fugitive slave in a strange land—a land given up to be the hunting-ground for slaveholders—whose inhabitants are legalized kidnappers—where he is every moment subjected to the terrible liability of being seized upon by his fellow-men, as the hideous crocodile seizes upon his prey!—I say, let him place himself in my situation—without home or friends—without money or credit—wanting shelter, and no one to give it—wanting bread, and no money to buy it,—and at the same time let him feel that he is pursued by merciless men-hunters, and in total darkness as to what to do, where to go, or where to stay,— perfectly helpless both as to the means of defence and means of escape,—in the midst of plenty, yet suffering the terrible gnawings of hunger,—in the midst of houses, yet having no home,—among fellow-men, yet feeling as if in the midst of wild beasts, whose greediness to swallow up the trembling and half-famished fugitive is only equalled by that with which the monsters of the deep swallow up the helpless fish upon which they subsist,—I say, let him be placed in this most trying situation,—the situation in which I was placed,—then, and not till then, will he fully appreciate the hardships of, and know how to sympathize with, the toil-worn and whip-scarred fugitive slave.

Thank Heaven, I remained but a short time in this distressed situation. I was relieved from it by the humane hand of Mr. DAVID RUGGLES,[4] whose vigilance, kindness, and perseverance, I shall never forget. I am glad of an opportunity to express, as far as words can, the love and gratitude I bear him. Mr. Ruggles is now afflicted with blindness, and is himself in need of the same kind offices which he was once so forward in the performance of toward others. I had been in New York but a few days, when Mr. Ruggles sought me out, and very kindly took me to his boarding-house at the corner of Church and Lespenard Streets. Mr. Ruggles was then very deeply engaged in the memorable *Darg* case, as well as attending to a number of other fugitive slaves, devising ways and means for their successful escape; and, though watched and hemmed in on almost every side, he seemed to be more than a match for his enemies. Very soon after I went to Mr. Ruggles, he wished to know of me where I wanted to go; as he deemed it unsafe for me to remain in New York. I told him I was a calker, and should like to go where I could get work. I thought of going to Canada; but he decided against it, and in favor of my going to New Bedford, thinking I should be able to get work there at my trade. At this time, Anna,[5] my intended wife, came on; for I wrote to her immediately after my arrival at New York, (notwithstanding my homeless, houseless, and helpless condition,) informing her of my successful flight, and wishing her to come on forthwith. In a few days after her arrival, Mr. Ruggles called in the Rev. J. W. C. Pennington, who, in the presence of Mr. Ruggles, Mrs. Michaels, and two or three others, performed the marriage ceremony, and gave us a certificate, of which the following is an exact copy:—

"THIS may certify, that I joined together in holy matrimony Frederick Johnson[6] and Anna Murray, as man and wife, in the presence of Mr. David Ruggles and Mrs. Michaels.
"JAMES W. C. PENNINGTON.
"*New York, Sept.* 15, 1838."

Upon receiving this certificate, and a five-dollar bill from Mr. Ruggles, I shouldered one part of our baggage, and Anna took up the other, and we set out forthwith to take passage on board of the steam-

4. David Ruggles (1810–1849), a black abolitionist at this time living in New York, helped many slaves to escape.   5. She was free. [Douglass's note.]   6. I had changed my name from Frederick *Bailey* to that of *Johnson.* [Douglass's note.]

boat John W. Richmond for Newport, on our way to New Bedford. Mr. Ruggles gave me a letter to a Mr. Shaw in Newport, and told me, in case my money did not serve me to New Bedford, to stop in Newport and obtain further assistance; but upon our arrival at Newport, we were so anxious to get to a place of safety, that, notwithstanding we lacked the necessary money to pay our fare, we decided to take seats in the stage, and promise to pay when we got to New Bedford. We were encouraged to do this by two excellent gentlemen, residents of New Bedford, whose names I afterward ascertained to be Joseph Ricketson and William C. Taber. They seemed at once to understand our circumstances, and gave us such assurance of their friendliness as put us fully at ease in their presence. It was good indeed to meet with such friends, at such a time. Upon reaching New Bedford, we were directed to the house of Mr. Nathan Johnson, by whom we were kindly received, and hospitably provided for. Both Mr. and Mrs. Johnson took a deep and lively interest in our welfare. They proved themselves quite worthy of the name of abolitionists. When the stage-driver found us unable to pay our fare, he held on upon our baggage as security for the debt. I had but to mention the fact to Mr. Johnson, and he forthwith advanced the money.

We now began to feel a degree of safety, and to prepare ourselves for the duties and responsibilities of a life of freedom. On the morning after our arrival at New Bedford, while at the breakfast-table, the question arose as to what name I should be called by. The name given me by my mother was, "Frederick Augustus Washington Bailey." I, however, had dispensed with the two middle names long before I left Maryland so that I was generally known by the name of "Frederick Bailey." I started from Baltimore bearing the name of "Stanley." When I got to New York, I again changed my name to "Frederick Johnson," and thought that would be the last change. But when I got to New Bedford, I found it necessary again to change my name. The reason of this necessity was, that there were so many Johnsons in New Bedford, it was already quite difficult to distinguish between them. I gave Mr. Johnson the privilege of choosing me a name, but told him he must not take from me the name of "Frederick." I must hold on to that, to preserve a sense of my identity. Mr. Johnson had just been reading the "Lady of the Lake,"[7] and at once suggested that my name be "Douglass." From that time until now I have been called "Frederick Douglass"; and as I am more widely known by that name than by either of the others, I shall continue to use it as my own.

I was quite disappointed at the general appearance of things in New Bedford. The impression which I had received respecting the

---

7. A narrative poem by Sir Walter Scott (1810) about the fortunes of the Douglas clan in Scotland.

character and condition of the people of the north, I found to be singularly erroneous. I had very strangely supposed, while in slavery, that few of the comforts, and scarcely any of the luxuries, of life were enjoyed at the north, compared with what were enjoyed by the slave-holders of the south. I probably came to this conclusion from the fact that northern people owned no slaves. I supposed that they were about upon a level with the non-slaveholding population of the south. I knew *they* were exceedingly poor, and I had been accustomed to regard their poverty as the necessary consequence of their being non-slaveholders. I had somehow imbibed the opinion that, in the absence of slaves, there could be no wealth, and very little refinement. And upon coming to the north, I expected to meet with a rough, hard-handed, and uncultivated population, living in the most Spartan-like simplicity, knowing nothing of the ease, luxury, pomp, and grandeur of southern slaveholders. Such being my conjectures, any one acquainted with the appearance of New Bedford may very read-ily infer how palpably I must have seen my mistake.

In the afternoon of the day when I reached New Bedford, I visited the wharves, to take a view of the shipping. Here I found myself surrounded with the strongest proofs of wealth. Lying at the wharves, and riding in the stream, I saw many ships of the finest model, in the best order, and of the largest size. Upon the right and left, I was walled in by granite warehouses of the widest dimensions, stowed to their utmost capacity with the necessaries and comforts of life. Added to this, almost every body seemed to be at work, but noiselessly so, compared with what I had been accustomed to in Baltimore. There were no loud songs heard from those engaged in loading and unload-ing ships. I heard no deep oaths or horrid curses on the laborer. I saw no whipping of men; but all seemed to go smoothly on. Every man appeared to understand his work, and went at it with a sober, yet cheerful earnestness, which betokened the deep interest which he felt in what he was doing, as well as a sense of his own dignity as a man. To me this looked exceedingly strange. From the wharves I strolled around and over the town, gazing with wonder and admira-tion at the splendid churches, beautiful dwellings, and finely-culti-vated gardens; evincing an amount of wealth, comfort, taste, and refinement, such as I had never seen in any part of slaveholding Maryland.

Every thing looked clean, new, and beautiful. I saw few or no dilapidated houses, with poverty-stricken inmates; no half-naked children and barefooted women, such as I had been accustomed to see in Hillsborough, Easton, St. Michael's, and Baltimore. The peo-ple looked more able, stronger, healthier, and happier, than those of Maryland. I was for once made glad by a view of extreme wealth, without being saddened by seeing extreme poverty. But the most astonishing as well as the most interesting thing to me was the condition of the colored people, a great many of whom, like myself, had escaped thither as a refuge from the hunters of men. I found many, who had not been seven years out of their chains, living in finer houses, and evidently enjoying more of the comforts of life, than the average of slave-holders in Maryland. I will venture to assert that my **friend Mr. Nathan Johnson (of whom I can say with a grateful heart,** "I was hungry, and he gave me meat; I was thirsty, and he gave me drink; I was a stranger, and he took me in")[8] lived in a neater house; dined at a better table; took, paid for, and read, more newspapers; better understood the moral, religious, and political character of the nation,—than nine tenths of the slaveholders in Talbot county Maryland. Yet Mr. Johnson was a working man. His hands were hardened by toil, and not his alone, but those also of Mrs. Johnson. I found the colored people much more spirited than I had supposed they would be. I found among them a determination to protect each other from the blood-thirsty kidnapper, at all hazards. Soon after my arrival, I was told of a circumstance which illustrated their spirit. A colored man and a fugitive slave were on unfriendly terms. The former was heard to threaten the latter with informing his master of his whereabouts. Straightway a meeting was called among the colored people, under the stereotyped notice, "Business of importance!" The betrayer was invited to attend. The people came at the appointed hour, and organized the meeting by appointing a very religious old gentleman as president, who, I believe, made a prayer, after which he addressed the meeting as follows: *"Friends, we have got him here, and I would recommend that you young men just take him outside the door, and kill him!"* With this, a number of them bolted at him; but they were intercepted by some more timid than themselves, and the betrayer escaped their vengeance, and has not been seen in New Bedford since. I believe there have been no more such threats, and should there be hereafter, I doubt not that death would be the consequence.

I found employment, the third day after my arrival, in stowing a sloop with a load of oil. It was new, dirty, and hard work for me; but I went at it with a glad heart and a willing hand. I was now my own master. It was a happy moment, the rapture of which can be understood only by those who have been slaves. It was the first work, the reward of which was to be entirely my own. There was no Master Hugh standing ready, the moment I earned the money, to rob me of it. I worked that day with a pleasure I had never before experienced. I was at work for myself and newly-married wife. It was to me the starting-point of a new existence. When I got through with that job,

8. Cf. Matthew 25:35: "for I was ahungered, and ye gave me meat: I was thirsty, and ye gave me drink: I was a stranger, and ye took me in."

I went in pursuit of a job of calking; but such was the strength of prejudice against color, among the white calkers, that they refused to work with me, and of course I could get no employment.[9] Finding my trade of no immediate benefit, I threw off my calking habiliments, and prepared myself to do any kind of work I could get to do. Mr. Johnson kindly let me have his wood-horse and saw, and I very soon found myself a plenty of work. There was no work too hard—none too dirty. I was ready to saw wood, shovel coal, carry the hod, sweep the chimney, or roll oil casks,—all of which I did for nearly three years in New Bedford, before I became known to the anti-slavery world.

In about four months after I went to New Bedford there came a young man to me, and inquired if I did not wish to take the "Liberator."[1] I told him I did; but, just having made my escape from slavery, I remarked that I was unable to pay for it then. I, however, finally became a subscriber to it. The paper came, and I read it from week to week with such feelings as it would be quite idle for me to attempt to describe. The paper became my meat and my drink. My soul was set all on fire. Its sympathy for my brethren in bonds—its scathing denunciations of slaveholders—its faithful exposures of slavery—and its powerful attacks upon the upholders of the institution—sent a thrill of joy through my soul, such as I had never felt before!

I had not long been a reader of the "Liberator," before I got a pretty correct idea of the principles, measures and spirit of the anti-slavery reform. I took right hold of the cause. I could do but little; but what I could, I did with a joyful heart, and never felt happier than when in an anti-slavery meeting. I seldom had much to say at the meetings, because what I wanted to say was said so much better by others. But, while attending an anti-slavery convention at Nantucket, on the 11th of August, 1841, I felt strongly moved to speak, and was at the same time much urged to do so by Mr. William C. Coffin, a gentleman who had heard me speak in the colored people's meeting at New Bedford. It was a severe cross, and I took it up reluctantly. The truth was, I felt myself a slave, and the idea of speaking to white people weighed me down. I spoke but a few moments, when I felt a degree of freedom, and said what I desired with considerable ease. From that time until now, I have been engaged in pleading the cause of my brethren—with what success, and with what devotion, I leave those acquainted with my labors to decide.

---

9. I am told that colored persons can now get employment at calking in New Bedford—a result of antislavery effort. [Douglass's note.]   1. William Lloyd Garrison's antislavery newspaper, which began publication in 1831.

Appendix

I find, since reading over the foregoing Narrative that I have, in several instances, spoken in such a tone and manner, respecting religion, as may possibly lead those unacquainted with my religious views to suppose me an opponent of all religion. To remove the liability of such misapprehension, I deem it proper to append the following brief explanation. What I have said respecting and against religion, I mean strictly to apply to the *slaveholding religion* of this land, and with no possible reference to Christianity proper; for, between the Christianity of this land, and the Christianity of Christ, I recognize the widest possible difference—so wide, that to receive the one as good, pure, and holy, is of necessity to reject the other as bad, corrupt, and wicked. To be the friend of the one, is of necessity to be the enemy of the other. I love the pure, peaceable, and impartial Christianity of Christ: I therefore hate the corrupt, slaveholding, women-whipping, cradle-plundering, partial and hypocritical Christianity of this land. Indeed, I can see no reason, but the most deceitful one, for calling the religion of this land Christianity. I look upon it as the climax of all misnomers, the boldest of all frauds, and the grossest of all libels. Never was there a clearer case of "stealing the livery of the court of heaven to serve the devil in." I am filled with unutterable loathing when I contemplate the religious pomp and show, together with the horrible inconsistencies, which every where surround me. We have men-stealers for ministers, women-whippers for missionaries, and cradle-plunderers for church members. The man who wields the blood-clotted cowskin during the week fills the pulpit on Sunday, and claims to be a minister of the meek and lowly Jesus. The man who robs me of my earnings at the end of each week meets me as a class-leader on Sunday morning, to show me the way of life, and the path of salvation. He who sells my sister, for purposes of prostitution, stands forth as the pious advocate of purity. He who proclaims it a religious duty to read the Bible denies me the right of learning to read the name of the God who made me. He who is the religious advocate of marriage robs whole millions of its sacred influence, and leaves them to the ravages of wholesale pollution. The warm defender of the sacredness of the family relation is the same that scatters whole families,—sundering husbands and wives, parents and children, sisters and brothers,—leaving the hut vacant, and the hearth desolate. We see the thief preaching against theft, and the adulterer against adultery. We have men sold to build churches, women sold to support the gospel, and babes sold to purchase Bibles for the *poor heathen! all for the glory of God and the good of souls!* The slave auctioneer's bell and the church-going bell chime in with each other, and the bitter cries of the heart-broken slave are drowned in the religious shouts of his pious master. Revivals of religion and revivals in the slave-trade go hand in hand together. The slave prison and the church stand near each other. The clanking of fetters and the rattling of chains in the prison, and the pious psalm and solemn prayer in the church, may be heard at the same time. The dealers in the bodies and souls of men erect their stand in the presence of the pulpit, and they mutually help each other. The dealer gives his blood-stained gold to support the pulpit, and the pulpit, in return, covers **his infernal business with the garb of Christianity. Here we have religion and robbery the allies of each other—devils dressed in angels'** robes, and hell presenting the semblance of paradise.

> "Just God! and these are they,
>   Who minister at thine altar, God of right!
> Men who their hands, with prayer and blessing, lay
>   On Israel's ark of light.
>
> "What! preach, and kidnap men?
>   Give thanks, and rob thy own afflicted poor?
> Talk of thy glorious liberty, and then
>   Bolt hard the captive's door?
>
> "What! servants of thy own
>   Merciful Son, who came to seek and save
> The homeless and the outcast, fettering down
>   The tasked and plundered slave!
>
> "Pilate and Herod friends!
>   Chief priests and rulers, as of old, combine!
> Just God and holy! is that church which lends
>   Strength to the spoiler thine?"

The Christianity of America is a Christianity, of whose votaries it may be as truly said, as it was of the ancient scribes and Pharisees, "They bind heavy burdens, and grievous to be borne, and lay them on men's shoulders, but they themselves will not move them with one of their fingers. All their works they do for to be seen of men.——They love the uppermost rooms at feasts, and the chief seats in the synagogues, ... and to be called of men, Rabbi, Rabbi.——But woe unto you, scribes and Pharisees, hypocrites! for ye neither go in yourselves, neither suffer ye them that are entering to go in. Ye devour widows' houses, and for a pretence make long prayers; therefore ye shall receive the greater damnation. Ye compass sea and land to make one proselyte, and when he is made, ye make him twofold more the child of hell than yourselves.——Woe unto you, scribes and Pharisees, hypocrites! for ye pay tithe of mint, and anise, and cumin, and have omitted the weightier matters of the law, judgment, mercy, and faith; these ought ye to have done, and not to leave the other undone. Ye blind guides! which strain at a gnat, and swallow a camel. Woe unto you, scribes and Pharisees, hypocrites! for ye make clean the outside of the cup and of the platter; but within, they are full of extortion and excess.——Woe unto you, scribes and Pharisees, hypocrites! for ye are like unto whited sepulchres, which indeed appear beautiful outward, but are within full of dead men's bones, and of all uncleanness. Even so ye also outwardly appear righteous unto men, but within ye are full of hypocrisy and iniquity."[2]

Dark and terrible as is this picture, I hold it to be strictly true of the overwhelming mass of professed Christians in America. They strain at a gnat, and swallow a camel. Could any thing be more true of our churches? They would be shocked at the proposition of fellowshipping a *sheep*-stealer; and at the same time they hug to their communion a *man*-stealer, and brand me with being an infidel, if I find fault with them for it. They attend with Pharisaical strictness to the outward forms of religion, and at the same time neglect the weightier matters of the law, judgment, mercy, and faith. They are always ready to sacrifice, but seldom to show mercy. They are they who are represented as professing to love God whom they have not seen, whilst they hate their brother whom they have seen. They love the heathen on the other side of the globe. They can pray for him, pay money to have the Bible put into his hand, and missionaries to instruct him; while they despise and totally neglect the heathen at their own doors.

Such is, very briefly, my view of the religion of this land; and to avoid any misunderstanding, growing out of the use of general terms, I mean, by the religion of this land, that which is revealed in the words, deeds, and actions, of those bodies, north and south, calling themselves Christian churches, and yet in union with slaveholders. It is against religion, as presented by these bodies, that I have felt it my duty to testify.

I conclude these remarks by copying the following portrait of the religion of the south, (which is, by communion and fellowship, the religion of the north) which I soberly affirm is "true to the life," and without caricature or the slightest exaggeration. It is said to have been drawn, several years before the present anti-slavery agitation began, by a northern Methodist preacher, who, while residing at the south, had an opportunity to see slaveholding morals, manners, and piety, with his own eyes. "Shall I not visit for these things? saith the Lord. Shall not my soul be avenged on such a nation as this?"

2. Matthew 23:25–28.

"A PARODY.

"Come, saints and sinners, hear me tell
How pious priests whip Jack and Nell,
And women buy and children sell,
And preach all sinners down to hell,
　　And sing of heavenly union.

"They'll bleat and baa, dona like goats,
Gorge down black sheep, and strain at motes,
Array their backs in fine black coats,
Then seize their negroes by their throats,
　　And choke, for heavenly union.

"They'll church you if you sip a dram,
And damn you if you steal a lamb;
Yet rob old Tony, Doll, and Sam,
Of human rights, and bread and ham;
　　Kidnapper's heavenly union.

"They'll loudly talk of Christ's reward,
And bind his image with a cord,
And scold, and swing the lash abhorred,
And sell their brother in the Lord
　　To handcuffed heavenly union.

"They'll read and sing a sacred song,
And make a prayer both loud and long,
And teach the right and do the wrong,
Hailing the brother, sister throng,
　　With words of heavenly union.

"We wonder how such saints can sing,
Or praise the Lord upon the wing,
Who roar, and scold, and whip, and sting,
And to their slaves and mammon cling,
　　In guilty conscience union.

"They'll raise tobacco, corn, and rye,
And drive, and thieve, and cheat, and lie,
And lay up treasures in the sky,
By making switch and cowskin fly,
　　In hope of heavenly union.

"They'll crack old Tony on the skull,
And preach and roar like Bashan bull,
Or braying ass, of mischief full,
Then seize old Jacob by the wool,
　　And pull for heavenly union.

"A roaring, ranting, sleek man-thief,
Who lived on mutton, veal, and beef,

Yet never would afford relief
To needy, sable sons of grief,
  Was big with heavenly union.

" 'Love not the world,' the preacher said,
And winked his eye, and shook his head;
He seized on Tom, and Dick, and Ned,
Cut short their meat, and clothes, and bread,
  Yet still loved heavenly union.

"Another preacher whining spoke
Of One whose heart for sinners broke:
He tied old Nanny to an oak,
And drew the blood at every stroke,
  And prayed for heavenly union.

"Two others oped their iron jaws,
And waved their children-stealing paws;
There sat their children in gewgaws;
By stinting negroes' backs and maws,
  They kept up heavenly union.

"All good from Jack another takes,
And entertains their flirts and rakes,
Who dress as sleek as glossy snakes,
And cram their mouths with sweetened cakes;
  And this goes down for union."

Sincerely and earnestly hoping that this little book may do something toward throwing light on the American slave system, and hastening the glad day of deliverance to the millions of my brethren in bonds—faithfully relying upon the power of truth, love, and justice, for success in my humble efforts—and solemnly pledging my self anew to the sacred cause,—I subscribe myself,

FREDERICK DOUGLASS.

Lynn, Mass., April 28, 1845.

WALT WHITMAN
1819–1892

As insistently as Rousseau, but with a far richer sense of the nature and the importance of his social context, Walt Whitman in his poetry makes himself the center of the universe. He brings to his emphatic self-presentation a detailed, partly ironic, partly celebratory sense of what it means to be an American; his poetry suggests something of what life in the United States must have felt like in the middle of the nineteenth century.

Born in Long Island, Whitman in his childhood moved with his family to Brooklyn. He was christened Walter, but shortened his first name to distinguish himself from his father. As a young man, he functioned as schoolteacher, builder, bookstore owner, journalist, and poet, before moving to Washington to work as a government clerk. There he also served as a volunteer nurse, helping to care for the Civil War wounded. In 1873 he settled in Camden, New Jersey, where he remained for the rest of his life.

Whitman began writing in his youth, producing a good deal of bad poetry and a novel, a fictionalized temperance tract. He first published *Leaves of Grass* in 1855, after having become an admirer of Emerson and a Jeffersonian Democrat; he continued enlarging and revising the book for the rest of his life. In 1865, he published *Drum Taps*, poems derived from his Civil War experiences; in 1871, *Democratic Vistas*, a collection of political and philosophical essays.

Whitman's shifting diction (familiar, even slangy, to formal and rhetorical) makes possible a large range of tones in *Song of Myself*. In a single section (21), for example, these two sequences occur in close conjunction:

> I chant the chant of dilation or pride,
> We have had ducking and deprecating about enough,
> I show that size is only development.
>
> Smile O voluptuous cool-breath'd earth!
> Earth of the slumbering and liquid trees!
> Earth of departed sunset—earth of the mountains misty-
>   topt!
> Earth of the vitreous pour of the full moon just tinged
>   with blue!

The first three-line passage, after its formal opening, falls into a pattern like that of colloquial speech. "About enough" belongs to an informal vocabulary; the final line, turning on the word "only," makes the kind of joke one might make in conversation. ("Size doesn't matter, really, it only comes from growing.") The speaker's claim that he does not endorse conventional judgments, by which bigger is better, and his slightly mocking tone declare his independence and his willingness not to take himself with undue seriousness. Only a few lines later, when he turns to the "voluptuous cool-breath'd earth," he sounds like a different person, entirely serious, almost grandiose, about his personal perceptions. Now his rhapsodic tone unites him with the Romantic poets, though his vocabulary still insists on his individuality. The conjunction of "voluptuous" with "cool-breath'd," the use of "vitreous" (glass-like) to modify "pour" used as a noun, the idea of "liquid trees": such choices demand the reader's close attention to figure out exactly what the poem is saying, and they emphasize a fresh way of seeing, a precise attention to the look of things. But they also sound like poetry, in a sense familiar to readers of earlier nineteenth-century works—unlike the lines quoted just before, which resemble colloquial prose.

The range of tones here exemplified helps to communicate an important theme of Whitman's poem: the tension and exchange between desire for individuality and for community. *Narrative of the Life of Frederick Douglass* directly and without apparent conflict expresses a sense of community as part of a sense of personal identity. *Song of Myself,* on the other hand, alternates between assertions of specialness and of identification with others.

I am of old and young, of the foolish as much as the wise, . . .
One of the Nation of many nations, the smallest the same and the largest the same,
A Southerner soon as a Northerner, a planter nonchalant and hospitable down by the Oconee I live, . . .
At home on Kanadian snow-shoes or up in the bush, or with fishermen off Newfoundland,
At home in the fleet of ice-boats, sailing with the rest and tacking.

Declaring his union not, like Wordsworth, with the natural universe, but with the society of his compatriots, Whitman identifies himself with the enormous variety he perceives and celebrates in his country. But his poem opens, "I celebrate myself, and sing myself, / And what I assume you shall assume," insisting on his uniqueness and dominance. Toward the end, these two lines occur: "I too am not a bit tamed, I too am untranslatable, / I sound my barbaric yawp over the roofs of the world." One hears the note of defiant specialness: another characteristic aspect of *Song of Myself.* The poem's power derives partly from its capacity richly to embody both feelings, the feeling of uniqueness and the sense of shared humanity, feelings that most people experience, sometimes in confusing conjunction. Like his Romantic predecessors, Whitman values emotion, every kind of emotion, for its own sake. He suggests the irrelevance of the notion of contradiction to any understanding of inner life. In the realm of emotion, everything coexists. *Song of Myself* attempts to include that "everything."

The poetic daring of *Song of Myself* expresses itself not only in choice of subject matter but in poetic technique. Whitman's unrhymed lines, avoiding the blank verse that had been the norm, establish a new sort of rhythm— one that proved of crucial importance to twentieth-century American poets, who adapted it to their own purposes. Not metrical in any familiar sense, the verse establishes its own hypnotic rhythms, evoking an individual speaking voice, an individual idiom. It even risks the prosaic in its insistence that poetry implies, above all, personal perception and personal voice: "everything" can be included in technique as well as in material.

"Out of the Cradle Endlessly Rocking," another of Whitman's best-known pre–Civil War poems, develops a child's imaginative relation with nature in a way that Wordsworth might have approved. A man hears a bird song which evokes for him a past experience—just as, at the beginning of *Remembrance of Things Past,* Proust's narrator finds his childhood returning to his memory at the taste of a madeleine. Reduced to tears by the song and the memory, the speaker, "chanter of pains and joys, uniter of here and hereafter," records and explores his youthful revelation of lyric power, achieved by identification with the bird mourning the loss of its mate.

Now in a moment I know what I am for, I awake,
And already a thousand singers, a thousand songs,
    clearer, louder, and more sorrowful than yours,
A thousand warbling echoes have started to life
    within me, never to die.

The poem concludes with the adult speaker meditating on the nature of his creative force in terms recalling Keats's in "To A Nightingale." Whitman, too, muses about the attraction of death, feels the demonic and the beautiful united in the song that inspires him. His own songs merge in his imagination with the "strong and delicious word" spoken by the sea, another aspect of nature, and one traditionally associated with death (as well as with birth). In poetry marked, like *Song of Myself*, by his powerfully individual rhythm and meter, Whitman reminds us once more of a great Romantic theme: the mystery of creativity.

    G. W. Allen, *The Solitary Singer: A Critical Biography of Walt Whitman* (1959), provides both biography and criticism. *Walt Whitman: The Critical Heritage*, edited by M. Hindus (1971), contains nineteenth- and twentieth-century essays; J. E. Miller, Jr., *A Critical Guide to Leaves of Grass* (1957), is helpful. Also valuable is R. Chase, *Walt Whitman Reconsidered* (1955).

Song of Myself[1]

1

I celebrate myself, and sing myself,
And what I assume you shall assume,
For every atom belonging to me as good belongs to you.

I loafe and invite my soul,
I lean and loafe at my ease observing a spear of summer grass.   5

My tongue, every atom of my blood, form'd from this soil, this air,
Born here of parents born here from parents the same, and their
    parents the same,
I, now thirty-seven years old in perfect health begin,
Hoping to cease not till death.

Creeds and schools in abeyance,   10
Retiring back a while sufficed at what they are, but never forgotten,
I harbor for good or bad, I permit to speak at every hazard,
Nature without check with original energy.

            *   *   *

---

1. Selected sections. First published in 1855. Our text is from the 1891–1892 edition of *Leaves of Grass*, the so-called Deathbed Edition.

4

Trippers and askers surround me,
People I meet, the effect upon me of my early life or the ward and
    city I live in, or the nation,   15
The latest dates, discoveries, inventions, societies, authors old and
    new,
My dinner, dress, associates, looks, compliments, dues,
The real or fancied indifference of some man or woman I love,
The sickness of one of my folks or of myself, or ill-doing or loss or
    lack of money, or depressions or exaltations,
Battles, the horrors of fratricidal war, the fever of doubtful news, the
    fitful events;   20
These come to me days and nights and go from me again,
But they are not the Me myself.

Apart from the pulling and hauling stands what I am,
Stands amused, complacent, compassionating, idle, unitary,
Looks down, is erect, or bends an arm on an impalpable certain rest,
Looking with side-curved head curious what will come next,   26
Both in and out of the game and watching and wondering at it.

Backward I see in my own days where I sweated through fog with
    linguists and contenders,
I have no mockings or arguments, I witness and wait.

                    *   *   *

7

Has any one supposed it lucky to be born?   30
I hasten to inform him or her it is just as lucky to die, and I know it.

I pass death with the dying and birth with the new-wash'd babe, and
    am not contain'd between my hat and boots,
And peruse manifold objects, no two alike and every one good,
The earth good and the stars good, and their adjuncts all good.

I am not an earth nor an adjunct of an earth,   35
I am the mate and companion of people, all just as immortal and
    fathomless as myself,
(They do not know how immortal, but I know.)

Every kind for itself and its own, for me mine male and female,
For me those that have been boys and that love women,
For me the man that is proud and feels how it stings to be slighted,
For me the sweet-heart and the old maid, for me mothers and the
    mothers of mothers,   41
For me lips that have smiled, eyes that have shed tears,

For me children and the begetters of children.
Undrape! you are not guilty to me, nor stale nor discarded,
I see through the broadcloth and gingham whether or no,   45
And am around, tenacious, acquisitive, tireless, and cannot be shaken
    away.

✳   ✳   ✳

16

I am of old and young, of the foolish as much as the wise,
Regardless of others, ever regardful of others,
Maternal as well as paternal, a child as well as a man,
Stuff'd with the stuff that is coarse and stuff'd with the stuff that is
    fine,   50
One of the Nation of many nations, the smallest the same and the
    largest the same,
A Southerner soon as a Northerner, a planter nonchalant and hospi-
    table down by the Oconee[2] I live,
A Yankee bound my own was ready for trade, my joints the limberest
    joints on earth and the sternest joints on earth,
A Kentuckian walking the vale of the Elkhorn in my deer-skin leg-
    gings, a Louisianian or Georgian,
A boatman over lakes or bays or along coasts, a Hoosier, Badger,
    Buckeye;   55
At home on Kanadian snow-shoes or up in the bush, or with fisher-
    men off Newfoundland,
At home in the fleet of ice-boats, sailing with the rest and tacking,
At home on the hills of Vermont or in the woods of Maine, or the
    Texan ranch,
Comrade of Californians, comrade of free North-Westerners, (lov-
    ing their big proportions,)
Comrade of raftsmen and coalmen, comrade of all who shake hands
    and welcome to drink and meat,   60
A learner with the simplest, a teacher of the thoughtfullest,
A novice beginning yet experient of myriads of seasons,
Of every hue and caste am I, of every rank and religion,
A farmer, mechanic, artist, gentleman, sailor, quaker,
Prisoner, fancy-man, rowdy, lawyer, physician, priest.   65

I resist any thing better than my own diversity,
Breathe the air but leave plenty after me,
And am not stuck up, and am in my place.

2. River in Georgia.

(The moth and the fish-eggs are in their place,
The bright suns I see and the dark suns I cannot see are in their
place,   70
The palpable is in its place and the impalpable is in its place.)

✻   ✻   ✻

21

I am the poet of the Body and I am the poet of the Soul,
The pleasures of heaven are with me and the pains of hell are with
me,
The first I graft and increase upon myself, the latter I translate into
a new tongue.

I am the poet of the woman the same as the man,   76
And I say it is as great to be a woman as to be a man,
And I say there is nothing greater than the mother of men.

I chant the chant of dilation or pride,
We have had ducking and deprecating about enough,
I show that size is only development.   80

Have you outstript the rest? are you the President?
It is a trifle, they will more than arrive there every one, and still pass
on.

I am he that walks with the tender and growing night,
I call to the earth and sea half-held by the night.

Press close bare-bosom'd night—press close magnetic nourishing
night!   85
Night of south winds—night of the large few stars!
Still nodding night—mad naked summer night.

Smile O voluptuous cool-breath'd earth!
Earth of the slumbering and liquid trees!
Earth of departed sunset—earth of the mountains misty-topt!   90
Earth of the vitreous pour of the full moon just tinged with blue!
Earth of shine and dark mottling the tide of the river!
Earth of the limpid gray of clouds brighter and clearer for my sake!
Far-swooping elbow'd earth—rich apple-blossom'd earth!
Smile, for your lover comes.   95

Prodigal, you have given me love—therefore I to you give love!
O unspeakable passionate love.

✻   ✻   ✻

24

Walt Whitman, a kosmos, of Manhattan the son,
Turbulent, fleshy, sensual, eating, drinking and breeding,
No sentimentalist, no stander above men and women or apart from
    them,   100
No more modest than immodest.
Unscrew the locks from the doors!
Unscrew the doors themselves from their jambs!

Whoever degrades another degrades me,
And whatever is done or said returns at last to me.   105

Through me the afflatus surging and surging, through me the cur-
    rent and index.

I speak the pass-word primeval, I give the sign of democracy,
By God! I will accept nothing which all cannot have their counter-
    part of on the same terms.

                *   *   *

32

I think I could turn and live with animals, they are so placid and
    self-contain'd,
I stand and look at them long and long.   110

They do not sweat and whine about their condition,
They do not lie awake in the dark and weep for their sins,
They do not make me sick discussing their duty to God,
Not one is dissatisfied, not one is demented with the mania of own-
    ing things,
Not one kneels to another, nor to his kind that lived thousands of
    years ago,   115
Not one is respectable or unhappy over the whole earth.
So they show their relations to me and I accept them,
They bring me tokens of myself, they evince them plainly in their
    possession.

I wonder where they get those tokens,
Did I pass that way huge times ago and negligently drop them?   120

Myself moving forward then and now and forever,
Gathering and showing more always and with velocity,
Infinite and omnigenous,[3] and the like of these among them,
Not too exclusive toward the reachers of my remembrancers,

---

3. Belonging to all races.

Picking out here one that I love, and now go with him on brotherly
    terms. 125

A gigantic beauty of a stallion, fresh and responsive to my caresses,
Head high in the forehead, wide between the ears,
Limbs glossy and supple, tail dusting the ground,
Eyes full of sparkling wickedness, ears finely cut, flexibly moving.
His nostrils dilate as my heels embrace him, 130
His well-built limbs tremble with pleasure as we race around and
    return.
I but use you a minute, then I resign you, stallion,
Why do I need your paces when I myself out-gallop them?
Even as I stand or sit passing faster than you.

❈   ❈   ❈

46

I know I have the best of time and space, and was never measured
    and never will be measured. 135

I tramp a perpetual journey, (come listen all!)
My signs are a rain-proof coat, good shoes, and a staff cut from the
    woods,
No friend of mine takes his ease in my chair,
I have no chair, no church, no philosophy,
I lead no man to a dinner-table, library, exchange, 140
But each man and each woman of you I lead upon a knoll,
My left hand hooking you round the waist,
My right hand pointing to landscapes of continents and the public
    road.

Not I, not any one else can travel that road for you,
You must travel it for yourself. 145

It is not far, it is within reach,
Perhaps you have been on it since you were born and did not know,
Perhaps it is everywhere on water and on land.

Shoulder your duds dear son, and I will mine, and let us hasten
    forth,
Wonderful cities and free nations we shall fetch as we go. 150

❈   ❈   ❈

51

The past and present wilt—I have fill'd them, emptied them,
And proceed to fill my next fold of the future.

Listener up there! what have you to confide to me?
Look in my face while I snuff the sidle of evening,
(Talk honestly, no one else hears you, and I stay only a minute
      longer.)   155

Do I contradict myself?
Very well then I contradict myself,
(I am large, I contain multitudes.)
I concentrate toward them that are nigh, I wait on the door-slab.

Who has done his day's work? who will soonest be through with his
      supper?   160
Who wishes to walk with me?

Will you speak before I am gone? will you prove already too late?

52

The spotted hawk swoops by and accuses me, he complains of my
      gab and my loitering.

I too am not a bit tamed, I too am untranslatable,
I sound my barbaric yawp over the roofs of the world.   165

The last scud of day holds back for me,
It flings my likeness after the rest and true as any on the shadow'd
      wilds,
It coaxes me to the vapor and the dusk.

I depart as air, I shake my white locks at the runaway sun,
I effuse my flesh in eddies, and drift it in lacy jags.   170

I bequeath myself to the dirt to grow from the grass I love,
If you want me again look for me under your boot-soles.

You will hardly know who I am or what I mean,
But I shall be good health to you nevertheless,
And filter and fibre your blood.   175

Failing to fetch me at first keep encouraged,
Missing me one place search another,
I stop somewhere waiting for you.

Out of the Cradle Endlessly Rocking

Out of the cradle endlessly rocking,
Out of the mocking-bird's throat, the musical shuttle,

Out of the Ninth-month[4] midnight,
Over the sterile sands and the fields beyond, where the child leaving
    his bed wander'd alone, bareheaded, barefoot,
Down from the shower'd halo,   5
Up from the mystic play of shadows twining and twisting as if they
    were alive,
Out from the patches of briers and blackberries,
From the memories of the bird that chanted to me,
From your memories sad brother, from the fitful risings and fallings
    I heard,
From under that yellow half-moon late-risen and swollen as if with
    tears,   10
From those beginning notes of yearning and love there in the mist,
From the thousand responses of my heart never to cease,
From the myriad thence-arous'd words,
From the word stronger and more delicious than any,
From such as now they start the scene revisiting,   15
As a flock, twittering, rising, or overhead passing,
Borne hither, ere all eludes me, hurriedly,
A man, yet by these tears a little boy again,
Throwing myself on the sand, confronting the waves,
I, chanter of pains and joys, uniter of here and hereafter,   20
Taking all hints to use them, but swiftly leaping beyond them,
A reminiscence sing.

Once Paumanok,[5]
When the lilac-scent was in the air and Fifth-month grass was
    growing,   25
Up this seashore in some briers,
Two feather'd guests from Alabama, two together,
And their nest, and four light-green eggs spotted with brown,
And every day the he-bird to and fro at hand,
And every day the she-bird crouch'd on her nest, silent, with bright
    eyes,
And every day I, a curious boy, never too close, never disturbing
    them,   30
Cautiously peering, absorbing, translating.

Shine! shine! shine!
Pour down your warmth, great sun!
While we bask, we two together.

---

4. September, in Quaker usage.   5. The Indian name for Long Island, where Whitman grew
up. *Fifth-month*: May.

Two together!   35
Winds blow south, or winds blow north,
Day come white, or night come black,
Home, or rivers and mountains from home,
Singing all time, minding no time,
While we two keep together.   40

Till of a sudden,
Maybe kill'd, unknown to her mate,
One forenoon the she-bird crouch'd not on the nest,
Nor return'd that afternoon, nor the next,
Nor ever appear'd again.   45

And thenceforward all summer in the sound of the sea,
And at night under the full of the moon in calmer weather,
Over the hoarse surging of the sea,
Or flitting from brier to brier by day,
I saw, I heard at intervals the remaining one, the he-bird,   50
The solitary guest from Alabama.

Blow! blow! blow!
Blow up sea-winds along Paumanok's shore;
I wait and I wait till you blow my mate to me.

Yes, when the stars glisten'd,   55
All night long on the prong of a moss-scallop'd stake,
Down almost amid the slapping waves,
Sat the lone singer wonderful causing tears.

He call'd on his mate,
He pour'd forth the meanings which I of all men know.   60

Yes my brother I know,
The rest might not, but I have treasur'd every note,
For more than once dimly down to the beach gliding,
Silent, avoiding the moonbeams, blending myself with the shadows,
Recalling now the obscure shapes, the echoes, the sounds and sights
     after their sorts,   65
The white arms out in the breakers tirelessly tossing,
I, with bare feet, a child, the wind wafting my hair,
Listen'd long and long.

Listen'd to keep, to sing, now translating the notes,
Following you my brother.   70

Soothe! soothe! soothe!
Close on its wave soothes the wave behind,
And again another behind embracing and lapping, every one close,
But my love soothes not me, not me.

Low hangs the moon, it rose late,   75
It is lagging—O I think it is heavy with love, with love.

O madly the sea pushes upon the land,
With love, with love.
O night! do I not see my love fluttering out among the breakers?
What is that little black thing I see there in the white?   80

Loud! loud! loud!
Loud I call to you, my love!
High and clear I shoot my voice over the waves,
Surely you must know who is here, is here,
You must know who I am, my love.   85

Low-hanging moon!
What is that dusky spot in your brown yellow?
O it is the shape, the shape of my mate!
O moon do not keep her from me any longer.

Land! land! O land!   90
Whichever way I turn, O I think you could give me my mate back
       again if you only would,
For I am almost sure I see her dimly whichever way I look.

O rising stars!
Perhaps the one I want so much will rise, will rise with some of you.

O throat! O trembling throat!   95
Sound clearer through the atmosphere!
Pierce the woods, the earth,
Somewhere listening to catch you must be the one I want.

Shake out carols!
Solitary here, the night's carols!   100
Carols of lonesome love! death's carols!
Carols under that lagging, yellow, waning moon!
O under that moon where she droops almost down into the sea!
O reckless despairing carols.

But soft! sink low!   105
Soft! let me just murmur,
And do you wait a moment you husky-nois'd sea,
For somewhere I believe I heard my mate responding to me,
So faint, I must be still, be still to listen,
But not altogether still, for then she might not come immediately to
       me.   110

Hither my love!
Here I am! here!

With this just-sustain'd note I announce myself to you,
This gentle call is for you my love, for you.

Do not be decoy'd elsewhere,   115
That is the whistle of the wind, it is not my voice,
That is the fluttering, the fluttering of the spray,
Those are the shadows of leaves.

O darkness! O in vain!
O I am very sick and sorrowful.   120

O brown halo in the sky near the moon, drooping upon the sea!
O troubled reflection in the sea!
O throat! O throbbing heart!
And I singing uselessly, uselessly all the night.

O past! O happy life! O songs of joy!   125
In the air, in the woods, over fields,
Loved! loved! loved! loved! loved!
But my mate no more, no more with me!
We two together no more.

The aria sinking,   130
All else continuing, the stars shining,
The winds blowing, the notes of the bird continuous echoing,
With angry moans the fierce old mother incessantly moaning,
On the sands of Paumanok's shore gray and rustling,
The yellow half-moon enlarged, sagging down, drooping, the face
    of the sea almost touching,   135
The boy ecstatic, with his bare feet the waves, with his hair the
    atmosphere dallying,
The love in the heart long pent, now loose, now at last tumultously
    bursting,
The aria's meaning, the ears, the soul, swiftly depositing,
The strange tears down the cheeks coursing,
The colloquy there, the trio, each uttering,   140
The undertone, the savage old mother incessantly crying,
To the boy's soul's questions sullenly timing, some drown'd secret
    hissing,
To the outsetting bard.

Demon or bird! (said the boy's soul,)
Is it indeed toward your mate you sing? or is it really to me?   145
For I, that was a child, my tongue's use sleeping, now I have heard
    you,

Now in a moment I know what I am for, I awake,
And already a thousand singers, a thousand songs, clearer, louder

and more sorrowful than yours,
A thousand warbling echoes have started to life within me, never to
    die.

O you singer solitary, singing by yourself, projecting me,   150
O solitary me listening, never more shall I cease perpetuating you,
Never more shall I escape, never more the reverberations,
Never more the cries of unsatisfied love be absent from me,
Never again leave me to be the peaceful child I was before what there
    in the night,
By the sea under the yellow and sagging moon,   155
The messenger there arous'd, the fire, the sweet hell within,
The unknown want, the destiny of me.

O give me the clue! (it lurks in the night here somewhere,)
O if I am to have so much, let me have more!
A word then, (for I will conquer it,)   160
The word final, superior to all,
Subtle, sent up—what is it?—I listen;
Are you whispering it, and have been all the time, you sea-waves?
Is that it from your liquid rims and wet sands?

Whereto answering, the sea,   165
Delaying not, hurrying not,
Whisper'd me through the night, and very plainly before daybreak,
Lisp'd to me the low and delicious word death,
And again death, death, death, death,
Hissing melodious, neither like the bird nor like my arous'd child's
    heart,   170
But edging near as privately for me rustling at my feet,
Creeping thence steadily up to my ears and laving me softly all over.
Death, death, death, death, death.

Which I do not forget,
But fuse the song of my dusky demon and brother,   175
That he sang to me in the moonlight on Paumanok's gray beach,
With the thousand responsive songs at random,
My own songs awaked from that hour,
And with them the key, the word up from the waves,
The word of the sweetest song and all songs,   180
That strong and delicious word which, creeping to my feet,
(Or like some old crone rocking the cradle, swathed in sweet gar-
    ments, bending aside,)
The sea whisper'd me.

HERMAN MELVILLE

1819–1891

Herman Melville's *Billy Budd, Sailor* has always absorbed and puzzled its readers. Its story appears to deal with the eternal struggle of good and evil as manifested in mortal affairs, but critics disagree about who or what the author considered "good." It has something to say about the nature of justice and of the individual's relation to society—but what? Commentators have asserted that the book affirms Melville's final serene acceptance of life as it is but also that it documents his ironic defiance. We don't know whether Melville had completed the work before he died, or what he intended its title to be. The challenging experience of becoming implicated in the novel's dilemmas, of confronting its perplexing characters, of trying to follow its moral logic, may lead to no firm conclusions, but it can hardly fail to generate imaginative excitement.

Melville's father died when the boy was thirteen, leaving the family in near poverty. This fact helps to account for young Melville's varied money-making enterprises. He taught school, kept a store, and clerked in a bank; at the age of twenty, he for the first time shipped as a sailor. Subsequent ventures at sea included several whaling expeditions. On one of these, he jumped ship in the South Pacific, living for a month on an island in the Marquesas; on another whaling trip, he participated in a mutiny. In 1847, Melville married Elizabeth Shaw. The couple settled in Pittsfield, Massachusetts, where Melville spent his time writing. He attempted in vain to get an appointment to a foreign consulate as a means of support; his lecture tours, also intended to make money, were unsuccessful. Finally, with his wife and four children, he moved to New York City, where in 1867 he obtained a position at the Custom House which he held for the next eighteen years.

Melville's first novels, including *Typee* (1846) and *Omoo* (1847), seafaring adventure stories based on his own experience, won popular success. His masterpiece, *Moby-Dick* (1851), however, puzzled readers by its allegorical obscurity, its apparent shapelessness, and its highly elaborate language. Melville thought it his best work and felt disappointed and somewhat embittered by its critical failure. Although he continued writing and publishing short stories, novels, and poems, none of his later work achieved popularity.

Billy Budd, Sailor existed only in a heavily revised and at some points barely comprehensible manuscript at the time of the novelist's death. It was printed for the first time, in an imperfect version (*Billy Budd, Foretopman*), in a 1924 English edition of Melville's works. In 1948, Frederick Barron Freeman re-edited the novel as *Billy Budd*; his text was supplemented in 1956 by emendations from the manuscript by Elizabeth Treeman. In 1962, *Billy Budd, Sailor*, source of the present text, was produced by Harrison Hayford and Morton M. Sealts, Jr., who returned to the original manuscript, distinguished Mrs. Melville's handwriting in it from her husband's, and generated a version substantially different from its predecessors. Although the nature of Melville's intention must remain finally impossible to ascertain, this careful effort to recapture what the novelist actually wrote at least has clear authority for every editorial choice.

The issues raised by the French Revolution, so vivid a part of literary consciousness at the beginning of the nineteenth century, once more provide a novelistic theme at the century's end—but with a new perspective. The events reported in *Billy Budd, Sailor* are said to occur in 1797. The narrator speaks of "those invading waters of novel opinion social, political, and otherwise, which carried away as in a torrent no few minds in those days." His metaphor suggests disapproval of the "novel opinion" that so greatly excited the early Romantics. Captain Vere, an important character whose name associates him with truth ("verity"), utterly resists the "invading waters." The only direct evidence, within the novel, of the actual effects of revolution is the reported mutinies, of which the narrator also appears to disapprove. Such evidence suggests a negative view of the French Revolution in its moral and political effects.

On the other hand, the narrator provides evidence of abundant cause for mutiny, particularly in the brutal practice of impressment, by which men were removed forcibly from nonnaval ships (or from their hometown streets, or their farms) and pressed into navy service, with no legal or practical recourse. When Billy Budd says good-bye to his ship, *Rights of Man*, he intends no irony, but others hear irony, as well they may: the concept of human rights is violated in every instance of impressment. Captain Vere's absolute devotion to legality and rule, his lack of openness to new possibility, arguably amount to extreme rigidity, even, possibly, to insanity. The narrator's wariness about "invading waters" may, like Billy's good-bye, be heard as irony.

The conflicting claims of this series of statements, all supportable, need not be resolved; the important point is that by the end of the nineteenth century, everything that seemed true and exciting at the beginning has been called into question—not refuted, only made dubious. One can readily multiply examples from *Billy Budd, Sailor*. Billy, powerfully associated with images of innocence, resembles a child; a baby, even; a friendly dog; a big horse; Adam before the fall. A hundred years earlier, Blake had suggested the perceptive power of the innocent, the child who points out that the emperor wears no clothes (or that chimney sweepers must rely on dreams and a black child on his mother's wishful stories to compensate for social injustice). Billy's innocence, on the other hand, has ambiguous implications. What does it mean to be an unfallen man in a fallen world? Billy can neither acquire from experience nor learn from others the knowledge that might make him capable of self-protective suspicion. His utter helplessness indicts his society but also raises troubling questions about the desirability of innocence.

Of course, one might argue that we in the twentieth century, "cynical" in the same sense as the old Dansker in the novel, are suspicious of such figures as Billy and Captain Vere in ways that our forebears would not be. Perhaps so; yet virtually all the questions suggested in the last two paragraphs appear more or less directly in the novelistic text. The narrator reflects about troubling aspects of Billy's innocence; the surgeon raises the possibility that Captain Vere is "unhinged." At many points, the narrative's symbolic language calls insistent attention to itself. It too, however, typically leaves one poised between interpretive alternatives. Here, for instance, is the description of Billy's hanging. "At the same moment it chanced that the vapory fleece hanging low in the East was shot through with a soft glory as of the fleece of the Lamb of God seen in mystical vision, and simultaneously therewith, watched by the wedged mass of upturned faces, Billy ascended; and, ascending, took the full rose of dawn." Are we to take seriously the implicit identification of Billy with Christ? Billy has willingly taken guilt upon himself, has forgiven his condemner, dies in his innocence, and "ascends." On the other hand, he ascends not to heaven but to the yardarm, not in resurrection but in death. Is this a form of transcendence? Or irony again, at the expense of those who comfort themselves for social injustice by religious sentimentality?

Possiblities for interpretation depend, the novel tells us, on who formulates the story and who receives it. The book's subtitle, "An Inside Story," proves as ambiguous as everything else about it. This account, it suggests, will tell what really happened, as opposed to the newspaper report quoted late in the narrative which makes Billy into a suspicious foreigner who nefariously stabs the noble English Claggart. The storyteller recurs intermittently to his insistence that he deals with facts; hence he draws back from the climactic scene between Billy and Captain Vere. Because no one else was present, the narrator can only speculate; in this instance, we will never know what really happened. The dialogue between the purser and the surgeon about the physical peculiarities of the hanging exemplifies the universal difficulty of interpretation. The storyteller is only one more interpreter, with his own biases. Educating us in mistrust by the nature of his story, he leaves us no certainties. The last word on Billy is presented in the sailor's ballad at the end, in which Billy's execution becomes a matter of pathos, not of moral speculation. Perhaps this story does not after all involve the conflict of good and evil; maybe it only provides a record of social contingency. This final possibility explains events as adequately, and as inadequately, as any other hypothesis.

In its questioning of the Romantic verities, revolution and innocence, as in its possibly ironic use of nature ("a soft glory as of the fleece of the Lamb of God"), Melville's novel reminds us how much can happen in a century. It may also remind us how insistently the nineteenth century foretells the twentieth. We are accustomed to feeling that we never get enough dependable information to make accurate judgments in matters of morality, particularly international morality; we often distrust, if we think about it, the reliability of the "news" we are lavishly offered. *Billy Budd, Sailor* evokes a world that feels in many troubling respects like our own.

N. Arvin's *Herman Melville* is an excellent biographical study. Important critical works include L. Thompson, *Melville's Quarrel with God* (1952), W. Berthoff, *The Example of Melville* (1962), and J. Seelye, *Melville: The Ironic Diagram.* Beginning readers will be helped by J. Miller, Jr., *A Reader's Guide to Herman Melville* (1962).

Billy Budd, Sailor[1]

(An inside narrative)

1

In the time before steamships, or then more frequently than now, a stroller along the docks of any considerable seaport would occasionally have his attention arrested by a group of bronzed mariners, man-of-war's men or merchant sailors in holiday attire, ashore on liberty. In certain instances they would flank, or like a bodyguard quite surround, some superior figure of their own class, moving along with them like Aldebaran[2] among the lesser lights of his constellation. That signal object was the 'Handsome Sailor' of the less prosaic time alike of the military and merchant navies. With no perceptible trace of the vainglorious about him, rather with the offhand unaffectedness of natural regality, he seemed to accept the spontaneous homage of his shipmates.

A somewhat remarkable instance recurs to me. In Liverpool, now half a century ago, I saw under the shadow of the great dingy streetwall of Prince's Dock (an obstruction long since removed) a common sailor so intensely black that he must needs have been a native African of the unadulterate blood of Ham[3]—a symmetric figure much above the average height. The two ends of a gay silk handkerchief thrown loose about the neck danced upon the displayed ebony of his chest, in his ears were big hoops of gold, and a Highland bonnet with a tartan band set off his shapely head. It was a hot noon in July; and his face, lustrous with perspiration, beamed with barbaric good humor. In jovial sallies right and left, his white teeth flashing into view, he rollicked along, the center of a company of his shipmates. These were made up of such an assortment of tribes and complexions as would have well fitted them to be marched up by Anacharsis Cloots[4] before the bar of the first French Assembly as Representatives of the Human Race. At each spontaneous tribute rendered by the wayfarers to this black pagod[5] of a fellow—the tribute of a pause and stare, and less frequently an exclamation—the motley retinue showed that they took that sort of pride in the evoker of it which the Assyrian priests doubtless showed for their grand sculptured Bull when the faithful prostrated themselves.

1. Edited by Harrison Hayford and Merton M. Sealts, Jr.   2. A star of the first magnitude in the constellation of Taurus, the Bull, frequently used in navigation.   3. Ham, Noah's second son, was cursed by his father for mocking him. It was thought that a black skin was the result of the curse and that all black people descended from Ham.   4. Jean Baptiste du Val-de-Grace, Baron de Cloots, or Clootz (1755–1794), assembled a crowd of assorted nationalities and introduced them at the French National Assembly during the Revolution; he was popularly called "Anacharsis."   5. Meaning not only a pagoda but "an image of a deity, an idol" (O. E. D.).

To return. If in some cases a bit of a nautical Murat[6] in setting forth his person ashore, the Handsome Sailor of the period in question evinced nothing of the dandified Billy-be-Dam, an amusing character all but extinct now, but occasionally to be encountered, and in a form yet more amusing than the original, at the tiller of the boats on the tempestuous Erie Canal or, more likely, vaporing in the groggeries[7] along the towpath. Invariably a proficient in his perilous calling, he was also more or less of a mighty boxer or wrestler. It was strength and beauty. Tales of his prowess were recited. Ashore he was the champion; afloat the spokesman; on every suitable occasion always foremost. Close-reefing topsails in a gale, there he was, astride the weather yardarm-end, foot in the Flemish horse[8] as stirrup, both hands tugging at the earing as at a bridle, in very much the attitude of young Alexander curbing the fiery Bucephalus.[9] A superb figure, tossed up as by the horns of Taurus against the thunderous sky, cheerily hallooing to the strenuous file along the spar.

The moral nature was seldom out of keeping with the physical make. Indeed, except as toned by the former, the comeliness and power, always attractive in masculine conjunction, hardly could have drawn the sort of honest homage the Handsome Sailor in some examples received from his less gifted associates.

Such a cynosure, at least in aspect, and something such too in nature, though with important variations made apparent as the story proceeds, was welkin-eyed Billy Budd or Baby Budd, as more familiarly, under circumstances hereafter to be given, he at last came to be called—aged twenty-one, a foretopman[1] of the British fleet toward the close of the last decade of the eighteenth century. It was not very long prior to the time of the narration that follows that he had entered the King's service, having been impressed on the Narrow Seas from a homeward-bound English merchantman into a seventy-four[2] outward bound, H.M.S. *Bellipotent*; which ship, as was not unusual in those hurried days, having been obliged to put to sea short of her proper complement of men. Plump upon Billy at first sight in the gangway the boarding officer, Lieutenant Ratcliffe, pounced, even before the merchantman's crew was formally mustered on the quarterdeck for his deliberate inspection. And him only he elected. For whether it was because the other men when ranged before him showed to ill advantage after Billy, or whether he had some scruples in view of the merchantman's being rather short-handed, however it might

---

6. Joachim Murat (1767–1815), Marshall of France and king of Naples, Napoleon's brother-in-law, famous as a dandy.   7. Taverns. *Vaporing*: Boasting or blustering.   8. A hazardous activity: men go out on a yardarm (a spar supporting a sail) by means of foot ropes, one of which is called the "Flemish horse."   9. Alexander the Great's warhorse.   1. Junior to a maintopman like Jack Chase, to whom the book is dedicated.   2. A third-rate ship of the line, equivalent to a light cruiser today. The designation refers to the number of guns the ship carried. The "Narrow Seas" are the English Channel and the waters between England and Ireland.

be, the officer contented himself with his first spontaneous choice. To the surprise of the ship's company, though much to the lieutenant's satisfaction, Billy made no demur. But, indeed, any demur would have been as idle as the protest of a goldfish popped into a cage.

Noting this uncomplaining acquiescence, all but cheerful, one might say, the shipmaster turned a surprised glance of silent reproach at the sailor. The shipmaster was one of those worthy mortals found in every vocation, even the humbler ones—the sort of person whom everybody agrees in calling 'a respectable man.' And—nor so strange to report as it may appear to be—though a ploughman of the troubled waters, lifelong contending with the intractable elements, there was nothing this honest soul at heart loved better than simple peace and quiet. For the rest, he was fifty or thereabouts, a little inclined to corpulence, a prepossessing face, unwhiskered, and of an agreeable color—a rather full face, humanely intelligent in expression. On a fair day with a fair wind and all going well, a certain musical chime in his voice seemed to be the veritable unobstructed outcome of the innermost man. He had much prudence, much conscientiousness, and there were occasions when these virtues were the cause of overmuch disquietude in him. On a passage, so long as his craft was in any proximity to land, no sleep for Captain Graveling. He took to heart those serious responsibilities not so heavily borne by some shipmasters.

Now while Billy Budd was down in the forecastle getting his kit together, the *Bellipotent's* lieutenant, burly and bluff, nowise disconcerted by Captain Graveling's omitting to proffer the customary hospitalities on an occasion so unwelcome to him, an omission simply caused by preoccupation of thought, unceremoniously invited himself into the cabin, and also to a flask from the spirit locker, a receptacle which his experienced eye instantly discovered. In fact he was one of those sea dogs in whom all the hardship and peril of naval life in the great prolonged wars of his time never impaired the natural instinct for sensuous enjoyment. His duty he always faithfully did; but duty is sometimes a dry obligation, and he was for irrigating its aridity, whensoever possible, with a fertilizing decoction of strong waters. For the cabin's proprietor there was nothing left but to play the part of the enforced host with whatever grace and alacrity were practicable. As necessary adjuncts to the flask, he silently placed tumbler and water jug before the irrepressible guest. But excusing himself from partaking just then, he dismally watched the unembarrassed officer deliberately diluting his grog[3] a little, then tossing it off in three swallows, pushing the empty tumbler away, yet not so far as

---

3. A mixture of rum and water.

to be beyond easy reach, at the same time settling himself in his seat
and smacking his lips with high satisfaction, looking straight at the
host.

These proceedings over, the master broke the silence; and there
lurked a rueful reproach in the tone of his voice: 'Lieutenant, you
are going to take my best man from me, the jewel of 'em.'

'Yes, I know,' rejoined the other, immediately drawing back the
tumbler preliminary to a replenishing. 'Yes, I know. Sorry.'

'Beg pardon, but you don't understand, Lieutenant. See here, now.
Before I shipped that young fellow, my forecastle was a rat-pit of
quarrels. It was black times, I tell you, aboard the *Rights* here. I was
worried to that degree my pipe had no comfort for me. But Billy
came; and it was like a Catholic priest striking peace in an Irish
shindy. Not that he preached to them or said or did anything in
particular; but a virtue went out of him, sugaring the sour ones.
They took to him like hornets to treacle; all but the buffer[4] of the
gang, the big shaggy chap with the fire-red whiskers. He indeed, out
of envy, perhaps, of the newcomer, and thinking such a 'sweet and
pleasant fellow,' as he mockingly designated him to the others, could
hardly have the spirit of a gamecock, must needs bestir himself in
trying to get up an ugly row with him. Billy forebore with him and
reasoned with him in a pleasant way—he is something like myself,
Lieutenant, to whom aught like a quarrel is hateful—but nothing
served. So, in the second dogwatch[5] one day, the Red Whiskers in
presence of the others, under pretense of showing Billy just whence
a sirloin steak was cut—for the fellow had once been a butcher—
insultingly gave him a dig under the ribs. Quick as lightning Billy
let fly his arm. I dare say he never meant to do quite so much as he
did, but anyhow he gave the burly fool a terrible drubbing. It took
about half a minute, I should think. And lord bless you, the lubber
was astonished at the celerity. And will you believe it, Lieutenant,
the Red Whiskers now really loves Billy—loves him, or is the biggest
hypocrite that ever I heard of. But they all love him. Some of 'em
do his washing, darn his old trousers for him; the carpenter is at odd
times making a pretty little chest of drawers for him. Anybody will
do anything for Billy Budd; and it's the happy family here. But now,
Lieutenant, if that young fellow goes—I know how it will be aboard
the *Rights*. Not again very soon shall I, coming up from dinner, lean
over the capstan smoking a quiet pipe—no, not very soon again, I
think. Ay, Lieutenant, you are going to take away the jewel of 'em;
you are going to take away my peacemaker!' And with that the good
soul had really some ado in checking a rising sob.

'Well,' said the lieutenant, who had listened with amused interest

---

4. Big fellow.   5. Six to eight P.M.

to all this and now was waxing merry with his tipple: 'well, blessed are the peacemakers, especially the fighting peacemakers. And such are the seventy-four beauties some of which you see poking their noses out of the portholes of yonder warship lying to for me,' pointing through the cabin window at the *Bellipotent*. 'But courage! Don't look so downhearted, man. Why, I pledge you in advance the royal approbation. Rest assured that His Majesty will be delighted to know that in a time when his hardtack is not sought for by sailors with such avidity as should be, a time also when some shipmasters privily resent the borrowing from them a tar[6] or two for the service; His Majesty, I say, will be delighted to learn that *one* shipmaster at least cheerfully surrenders to the King the flower of his flock, a sailor who with equal loyalty makes no dissent.—But where's my beauty? Ah,' looking through the cabin's open door, 'here he comes; and, by Jove, lugging along his chest—Apollo with his portmanteau!—My man,' stepping out to him, 'you can't take that big box aboard a warship. The boxes there are mostly shot boxes. Put your duds in a bag, lad. Boot and saddle for the cavalryman, bag and hammock for the man-of-war's man.'

The transfer from chest to bag was made. And, after seeing his man into the cutter and then following him down, the lieutenant pushed off from the *Rights-of-Man*. That was the merchant ship's name, though by her master and crew abbreviated in sailor fashion into the *Rights*. The hardheaded Dundee owner was a staunch admirer of Thomas Paine,[7] whose book in rejoinder to Burke's arraignment of the French Revolution had then been published for some time and had gone everywhere. In christening his vessel after the title of Paine's volume the man of Dundee was something like his contemporary ship-owner, Stephen Girard[8] of Philadelphia, whose sympathies, alike with his native land and its liberal philosophers, he evinced by naming his ships after Voltaire, Diderot, and so forth.

But now, when the boat swept under the merchantman's stern, and officer and oarsmen were noting—some bitterly and others with a grin—the name emblazoned there; just then it was that the new recruit jumped up from the bow where the coxswain had directed him to sit, and waving hat to his silent shipmates sorrowfully looking over at him from the taffrail, bade the lads a genial good-bye. Then, making a salutation as to the ship herself, 'And good-bye to you too, old *Rights-of-Man*.'

'Down, sir!' roared the lieutenant, instantly assuming all the rigor of his rank, though with difficulty repressing a smile.

---

6. Sailor.   7. Paine (1737–1809), American Revolutionary patriot, born in England, published *The Rights of Man* in 1791 as a response to Edmund Burke's *Reflections on the Revolution in France* (1790). *Dundee* is a seaport in Scotland.   8. (1750–1831), merchant, banker, and philanthropist, a native of France who emigrated at the age of 27.

To be sure, Billy's action was a terrible breach of naval decorum. But in that decorum he had never been instructed; in consideration of which the lieutenant would hardly have been so energetic in reproof but for the concluding farewell to the ship. This he rather took as meant to convey a covert sally on the new recruit's part, a sly slur at impressment in general, and that of himself in especial. And yet, more likely, if satire it was in effect, it was hardly so by intention, for Billy, though happily endowed with the gaiety of high health, youth, and a free heart, was yet by no means of a satirical turn. The will to it and the sinister dexterity were alike wanting. To deal in double meanings and insinuations of any sort was quite foreign to his nature.

As to his enforced enlistment, that he seemed to take pretty much as he was wont to take any vicissitude of weather. Like the animals, though no philosopher, he was, without knowing it, practically a fatalist. And it may be that he rather liked this adventurous turn in his affairs, which promised an opening into novel scenes and martial excitements.

Aboard the *Bellipotent* our merchant sailor was forthwith rated as an able seaman and assigned to the starboard watch of the foretop. He was soon at home in the service, not at all disliked for his unpretentious good looks and a sort of genial happy-go-lucky air. No merrier man in his mess: in marked contrast to certain other individuals included like himself among the impressed portion of the ship's company; for these when not actively employed were sometimes, and more particularly in the last dogwatch when the drawing near of twilight induced revery, apt to fall into a saddish mood which in some partook of sullenness. But they were not so young as our foretopman, and no few of them must have known a hearth of some sort, others may have had wives and children left, too probably, in uncertain circumstances, and hardly any but must have had acknowledged kith and kin, while for Billy, as will shortly be seen, his entire family was practically invested in himself.

2

Though our new-made foretopman was well received in the top and on the gun decks, hardly here was he that cynosure he had previously been among those minor ship's companies of the merchant marine, with which companies only had he hitherto consorted. He was young; and despite his all but fully developed frame, in aspect looked even younger than he really was, owing to a lingering adolescent expression in the as yet smooth face all but feminine in purity of natural complexion but where, thanks to his seagoing,

the lily was quite suppressed and the rose had some ado visibly to
flush through the tan.

To one essentially such a novice in the complexities of factitious
life, the abrupt transition from his former and simpler sphere to the
ampler and more knowing world of a great warship; this might well
have abashed him had there been any conceit or vanity in his composition. Among her miscellaneous multitude, the *Bellipotent* mustered several individuals who however inferior in grade were of no
common natural stamp, sailors more signally susceptive of that air
which continuous martial discipline and repeated presence in battle
can in some degree impart even to the average man. As the Handsome Sailor, Billy Budd's position aboard the seventy-four was something analogous to that of a rustic beauty transplanted from the
provinces and brought into competition with the highborn dames of
the court. But this change of circumstances he scarce noted. As little
did he observe that something about him provoked an ambiguous
smile in one or two harder faces among the bluejackets. Nor less
unaware was he of the peculiar favorable effect his person and
demeanour had upon the more intelligent gentlemen of the quarter-
deck. Nor could this well have been otherwise. Cast in a mold peculiar to the finest physical examples of those Englishmen in whom
the Saxon strain would seem not at all to partake of any Norman or
other admixture, he showed in face that humane look of reposeful
good nature which the Greek sculptor in some instances gave to his
heroic strong man, Hercules. But this again was subtly modified by
another and pervasive quality. The ear, small and shapely, the arch
of the foot, the curve in mouth and nostril, even the indurated hand
dyed to the orange-tawny of the toucan's bill, a hand telling alike of
the halyards and tar bucket; but, above all, something in the mobile
expression, and every chance attitude and movement, something
suggestive of a mother eminently favored by Love and the Graces; all
this strangely indicated a lineage in direct contradiction to his lot.
The mysteriousness here became less mysterious through a matter of
fact elicited when Billy at the captain was being formally mustered
into the service. Asked by the officer, a small, brisk little gentleman
as it chanced, among other questions, his place of birth, he replied,
'Please, sir, I don't know.'

'Don't know where you were born? Who was your father?'

'God knows, sir.'

Struck by the straightforward simplicity of these replies, the officer
next asked, 'Do you know anything about your beginning?'

'No, sir. But I have heard that I was found in a pretty silk-lined
basket hanging one morning from the knocker of a good man's door
in Bristol.'

'*Found*, say you? Well,' throwing back his head and looking up and down the new recruit; 'well, it turns out to have been a pretty good find. Hope they'll find some more like you, my man; the fleet sadly needs them.'

Yes, Billy Budd was a foundling, a presumable by-blow, and, evidently, no ignoble one. Noble descent was as evident in him as in a blood horse.

For the rest, with little or no sharpness of faculty or any trace of the wisdom of the serpent, nor yet quite a dove, he possessed that kind and degree of intelligence going along with the unconventional rectitude of a sound human creature, one to whom not yet has been proffered the questionable apple of knowledge. He was illiterate; he could not read, but he could sing, and like the illiterate nightingale was sometimes the composer of his own song.

Of self-consciousness he seemed to have little or none, or about as much as we may reasonably impute to a dog of Saint Bernard's breed.

Habitually living with the elements and knowing little more of the land than as a beach, or, rather, that portion of the terraqueous globe providentially set apart for dance-houses, doxies, and tapsters, in short what sailors call a 'fiddler's green,'[9] his simple nature remained unsophisticated by those moral obliquities which are not in every case incompatible with that manufacturable thing known as respectability. But are sailors, frequenters of fiddler's greens, without vices? No; but less often than with landsmen do their vices, so called, partake of crookedness of heart, seeming less to proceed from viciousness than exuberance of vitality after long constraint: frank manifestations in accordance with natural law. By his original constitution aided by the co-operating influences of his lot, Billy in many respects was little more than a sort of upright barbarian, much such perhaps as Adam presumably might have been ere the urbane Serpent wriggled himself into his company.

And here be it submitted that apparently going to corroborate the doctrine of man's Fall, a doctrine now popularly ignored, it is observable that where certain virtues pristine and unadulterate peculiarly characterize anybody in the external uniform of civilization, they will upon scrutiny seem not to be derived from custom or convention, but rather to be out of keeping with these, as if indeed exceptionally transmitted from a period prior to Cain's city[1] and citified man. The character marked by such qualities has to an unvitiated taste an untampered-with flavor like that of berries, while the man thoroughly civilized, even in a fair specimen of the breed, has to the same moral palate a questionable smack as of a compounded

---

9. A sailor's utopia.   1. I.e., in the time of the Garden of Eden. Cain "builded a city" in Genesis 4:16–17.

wine. To any stray inheritor of these primitive qualities found, like
Caspar Hauser,[2] wandering dazed in any Christian capital of our
time, the good-natured poet's famous invocation, near two thousand
years ago, of the good rustic out of his latitude in the Rome of the
Caesars, still appropriately holds:

> Honest and poor, faithful in word and thought,
> What hath thee, Fabian, the city brought?[3]

Though our Handsome Sailor had as much of masculine beauty as
one can expect anywhere to see; nevertheless, like the beautiful woman
in one of Hawthorne's minor tales,[4] there was just one thing amiss
in him. No visible blemish indeed, as with the lady; no, but an
occasional liability to a vocal defect. Though in the hour of elemental uproar or peril he was everything that a sailor should be, yet
under sudden provocation of strong heart-feeling his voice, otherwise singularly musical, as if expressive of the harmony within, was
apt to develop an organic hesitancy, in fact more or less of a stutter
or even worse. In this particular Billy was a striking instance that the
arch interferer, the envious marplot of Eden, still has more or less to
do with every human consignment to this planet of Earth. In every
case, one way or another he is sure to slip in his little card, as much
as to remind us—I too have a hand here.

The avowal of such an imperfection in the Handsome Sailor should
be evidence not alone that he is not presented as a conventional
hero, but also that the story in which he is the main figure is no
romance.

3

At the time of Billy Budd's arbitrary enlistment into the *Bellipotent* that ship was on her way to join the Mediterranean fleet. No
long time elapsed before the junction was effected. As one of that
fleet the seventy-four participated in its movements, though at times
on account of her superior sailing qualities, in the absence of frigates, dispatched on separate duty as a scout and at times on less
temporary service. But with all this the story has little concernment,
restricted as it is to the inner life of one particular ship and the career
of an individual sailor.

It was the summer of 1797. In the April of that year had occurred
the commotion at Spithead followed in May by a second and yet
more serious outbreak in the fleet at the Nore. The latter is known,

---

2. A German foundling (1812?–1833) who claimed to have been brought up in a primitive
wilderness.   3. Martial, *Epigrams*, I.iv.1–2, from Cowley's translation in the Bohn edition.
4. "The Birthmark," in which the "blemish" is on the lady's cheek.

and without exaggeration in the epithet, as 'the Great Mutiny.' It
was indeed a demonstration more menacing to England than the
contemporary manifestoes and conquering and proselyting armies of
the French Directory.[5] To the British Empire the Nore Mutiny was
what a strike in the fire brigade would be to London threatened by
general arson. In a crisis when the kingdom might well have anticipated the famous signal that some years later published along the
naval line of battle what it was that upon occasion England expected
of Englishmen;[6] *that* was the time when at the mastheads of the
three-deckers and seventy-fours moored in her own roadstead—a fleet
the right arm of a Power then all but the sole free conservative one
of the Old World—the bluejackets, to be numbered by thousands,
ran up with huzzas the British colors with the union and cross[7] wiped
out; by that cancellation transmuting the flag of founded law and
freedom defined, into the enemy's red meteor of unbridled and
unbounded revolt. Reasonable discontent growing out of practical
grievances in the fleet had been ignited into irrational combustion as
by live cinders blown across the Channel from France in flames.

   The event converted into irony for a time those spirited strains of
Dibdin[8]—as a song-writer no mean auxiliary to the English government at that European conjuncture—strains celebrating, among other
things, the patriotic devotion of the British tar: 'And as for my life,
'tis the King's!'

   Such an episode in the Island's grand naval story her naval historians naturally abridge, one of them (William James[9]) candidly
acknowledging that fain would he pass it over did not 'impartiality
forbid fastidiousness.' And yet his mention is less a narration than a
reference, having to do hardly at all with details. Nor are these readily to be found in the libraries. Like some other events in every age
befalling states everywhere, including America, the Great Mutiny
was of such character that national pride along with views of policy
would fain shade it off into the historical background. Such events
cannot be ignored, but there is a considerate way of historically treating them. If a well-constituted individual refrains from blazoning
aught amiss or calamitous in his family, a nation in the like circumstance may without reproach be equally discreet.

   Though after parleyings between government and the ringleaders,
and concessions by the former as to some glaring abuses, the first
uprising—that at Spithead—with difficulty was put down, or matters

---

5. The five directors who governed France from 1795 to 1799, during the Revolution.
6. "England expects every man to do his duty!": Lord Nelson, before the battle at Trafalgar,
October 21, 1805.   7. The British Union Jack, or national flag, carries the crosses of St. Andrew,
St. George, and St. Patrick, patron saints of Scotland, England, and Ireland.   8. Charles Dibdin (1745–1814), English dramatist, chiefly remembered for his sea chanteys. The ballad quoted
is "Poor Jack."   9. *The Naval History of Great Britain* (1860). Melville mistakenly wrote "G.
P. R. James."

for the time pacified; yet at the Nore the unforeseen renewal of insurrection on a yet larger scale, and emphasized in the conferences that
ensured by demands deemed by the authorities not only inadmissible
but aggressively insolent, indicated—if the Red Flag did not sufficiently do so—what was the spirit animating the men. Final suppression, however, there was; but only made possible perhaps by the
unswerving loyalty of the marine corps and a voluntary resumption
of loyalty among influential sections of the crews.

To some extent the Nore Mutiny may be regarded as analogous to
the distempering irruption of contagious fever in a frame constitu-
tionally sound, and which anon throws it off.

At all events, of these thousands of mutineers were some of the
tars who not so very long afterwards—whether wholly prompted thereto
by patriotism, or pugnacious instinct, or by both—helped to win a
coronet for Nelson at the Nile, and the naval crown of crowns for
him at Trafalgar.[1] To the mutineers, those battles and especially
Trafalgar were a plenary absolution and a grand one. For all that
goes to make up scenic naval display and heroic magnificance in
arms, those battles, especially Trafalgar, stand unmatched in human
annals.

4

In this matter of writing, resolve as one may to keep to the main
road, some bypaths have an enticement not readily to be withstood.
I am going to err into such a bypath. If the reader will keep me
company I shall be glad. At the least, we can promise ourselves that
pleasure which is wickedly said to be in sinning, for a literary sin the
divergence will be.

Very likely it is no new remark that the inventions of our time
have at last brought about a change in sea warfare in degree corresponding to the revolution in all warfare effected by the original
introduction from China into Europe of gunpowder. The first European firearm, a clumsy contrivance, was, as is well known, scouted[2]
by no few of the knights as a base implement, good enough peradventure for weavers too craven to stand up crossing steel with steel in
frank fight. But as ashore knightly valor, though shorn of its bla-
zonry, did not cease with the knights, neither on the sea—though
nowadays in encounters there a certain kind of displayed gallantry be
fallen out of date as hardly applicable under changed circumstances—did the nobler qualities of such naval magnates as Don
John of Austria, Doria, Van Tromp, Jean Bart, the long line of Brit-

1. Nelson was made a baronet for his victory over the French at Aboukir in 1798; his 1805 victory
at Trafalgar is considered one of the greatest in naval history.   2. Scoffed at.

ish admirals, and the American Decaturs of 1812 become obsolete with their wooden walls.[3]

Nevertheless, to anybody who can hold the Present at its worth without being inappreciative of the Past, it may be forgiven, if to such an one the solitary old hulk at Portsmouth, Nelson's *Victory*, seems to float there, not alone as the decaying monument of a fame incorruptible, but also as a poetic reproach, softened by its picturesqueness, to the *Monitors*[4] and yet mightier hulls of the European ironclads. And this not altogether because such craft are unsightly, unavoidably lacking the symmetry and grand lines of the old battleships, but equally for other reasons.

There are some, perhaps, who while not altogether inaccessible to that poetic reproach just alluded to, may yet on behalf of the new order be disposed to parry it; and this to the extent of iconoclasm, if need be. For example, prompted by the sight of the star inserted in the *Victory*'s quarter-deck designating the spot where the Great Sailor fell, these martial utilitarians may suggest considerations implying that Nelson's ornate publication of his person in battle was not only unnecessary, but not military, nay, savored of foolhardiness and vanity. They may add, too, that at Trafalgar it was in effect nothing less than a challenge to death; and death came; and that but for his bravado the victorious admiral might possibly have survived the battle, and so, instead of having his sagacious dying injunctions overruled by his immediate successor in command, he himself when the contest was decided might have brought his shattered fleet to anchor, a proceeding which might have averted the deplorable loss of life by shipwreck in the elemental tempest that followed the martial one.

Well, should we set aside the more than disputable point whether for various reasons it was possible to anchor the fleet, then plausibly enough the Benthamites[5] of war may urge the above. But the *mighthave-been* is but boggy ground to build on. And, certainly, in foresight as to the larger issue of an encounter, and anxious preparations for it—buoying the deadly way and mapping it out, as at Copenhagen[6]—few commanders have been so painstakingly circumspect as this same reckless declarer of his person in fight.

Personal prudence, even when dictated by quite other than selfish considerations, surely is no special virtue in a military man; while

---

3. Don Juan of Austria (1547–1578) commanded a fleet against the Turks at Lepanto in 1571, the last major sea battle where oared ships predominated; *Andrea Doria* (1468–1560) liberated Genoa from the Turks; *Maarten Van Tromp* (1596–1653), Dutch admiral, fought successfully against the English under Charles II; *Jean Bart* (1651?–1702), a French captain, battled the Dutch; *Stephen Decatur* (1779–1820) won victories over the Barbary Coast pirates at Tripoli and over the British in the War of 1812. *Wooden walls* refers to the wooden ships made obsolete by ironclads.   **4.** The *Monitor* was an ironclad launched in 1862 to fight the Confederate *Merrimac* in a battle effectively ending the era of wooden ships.   **5.** Utilitarian thinkers and followers of Jeremy Bentham (1748–1832), who believed in the greatest good for the greatest number.   **6.** Where Nelson's careful planning defeated the Danish on 2 April 1801.

an excessive love of glory, impassioning a less burning impulse, the honest sense of duty, is the first. If the name *Wellington* is not so much of a trumpet to the blood as the simpler name *Nelson*, the reason for this may perhaps be inferred from the above. Alfred in his funeral ode on the victory of Waterloo ventures not to call him the greatest soldier of all time, though in the same ode he invokes Nelson as 'the greatest sailor since our world began.'[7]

At Trafalgar Nelson on the brink of opening the fight sat down and wrote his last brief will and testament. If under the presentiment of the most magnificent of all victories to be crowned by his own glorious death, a sort of priestly motive led him to dress his person in the jewelled vouchers of his own shining deeds; If thus to have adorned himself for the altar and the sacrifice were indeed vainglory, then affectation and fustian is each more heroic line in the great epics and dramas, since in such lines the poet but embodies in verse those exaltations of sentiment that a nature like Nelson, the opportunity being given, vitalizes into acts.

5

Yes, the outbreak at the Nore was put down. But not every grievance was redressed. If the contractors, for example, were no longer permitted to ply some practices peculiar to their tribe everywhere, such as providing shoddy cloth, rations not sound, or false in the measure; not the less impressment, for one thing, went on. By custom sanctioned for centuries, and judicially maintained by a Lord Chancellor as late as Mansfield,[8] that mode of manning the fleet, a mode now fallen into a sort of abeyance but never formally renounced, it was not practicable to give up in those years. Its abrogation would have crippled the indispensable fleet, one wholly under canvas, no steam power, its innumerable sails and thousands of cannon, everything in short, worked by muscle alone; a fleet the more insatiate in demand for men, because then multiplying its ships of all grades against contingencies present and to come of the convulsed Continent.

Discontent foreran the Two Mutinies, and more or less it lurkingly survived them. Hence it was not unreasonable to apprehend some return of trouble sporadic or general. One instance of such apprehensions: In the same year with this story, Nelson, then Rear Admiral Sir Horatio, being with the fleet off the Spanish coast, was directed by the admiral in command to shift his pennant from the *Captain* to the *Theseus*; and for this reason: that the latter ship hav-

7. The quotation comes from line 7 of Tennyson's ("Alfred") "Ode on the Death of the Duke of Wellington" (1852).   8. William Murray, Baron Mansfield (1705–1793), Lord Chief Justice of Great Britain from 1756.

ing newly arrived on the station from home, where it had taken part
in the Great Mutiny, danger was apprehended from the temper of
the men; and it was thought that an officer like Nelson was the one,
not indeed to terrorize the crew into base subjection, but to win
them, by force of his mere presence and heroic personality, back to
an allegiance if not as enthusiastic as his own yet as true.

So it was that for a time, on more than one quarter-deck, anxiety
did exist. At sea, precautionary vigilance was strained against relapse.
At short notice an engagement might come on. When it did, the
lieutenants assigned to batteries felt it incumbent on them, in some
instances, to stand with drawn swords behind the men working the
guns.

6

But on board the seventy-four in which Billy now swung his hammock, very little in the manner of the men and nothing obvious in
the demeanor of the officers would have suggested to an ordinary
observer that the Great Mutiny was a recent event. In their general
bearing and conduct the commissioned officers of a warship naturally take their tone from the commander, that is if he have that
ascendancy of character that ought to be his.

Captain the Honorable Edward Fairfax Vere, to give his full title,
was a bachelor of forty or thereabouts, a sailor of distinction even in
a time prolific of renowned seamen. Though allied to the higher
nobility, his advancement had not been altogether owing to influences connected with that circumstance. He had seen much service,
been in various engagements, always acquitting himself as an officer
mindful of the welfare of his men, but never tolerating an infraction
of discipline; thoroughly versed in the science of his profession, and
intrepid to the verge of temerity, though never injudiciously so. For
his gallantry in the West Indian waters as flag lietutenat under Rodney in that admiral's crowning victory over De Grasse,[9] he was made
a post captain.

Ashore, in the garb of a civilian, scarce anyone would have taken
him for a sailor, more especially that he never garnished unprofes-
sional talk with nautical terms, and grave in his bearing, evinced
little appreciation of mere humor. It was not out of keeping with
these traits that on a passage when nothing demanded his paramount
action, he was the most undemonstrative of men. Any landsman
observing this gentleman not conspicuous by his stature and wearing
no pronounced insignia, emerging from his cabin to the open deck,
and noting the silent deference of the officers retiring to leeward,
might have taken him for the King's guest, a civilian aboard the

9. The British admiral George Brydges, Baron Rodney (1719–1792), defeated the French Admiral De Grasse off Dominica, in the Leeward Islands, in 1782.

King's ship, some highly honorable discreet envoy on his way to an important post. But in fact this unobtrusiveness of demeanor may have proceeded from a certain unaffected modesty of manhood sometimes accompanying a resolute nature, a modesty evinced at all times not calling for pronounced action, which shown in any rank of life suggests a virtue aristocratic in kind. As with some others engaged in various departments of the world's more heroic activities, Captain Vere though practical enough upon occasion would at times betray a certain dreaminess of mood. Standing alone on the weather side of the quarter-deck, one hand holding by the rigging, he would absently gaze off at the blank sea. At the presentation to him then of some minor matter interrupting the current of his thoughts, he would show more or less irascibility; but instantly he would control it.

In the navy he was popularly known by the appellation 'Starry Vere.' How such a designation happened to fall upon one who whatever his sterling qualities was without any brilliant ones, was in this wise: A favorite kinsman, Lord Denton, a freehearted fellow, had been the first to meet and congratulate him upon his return to England from his West Indian cruise; and but the day previous turning over a copy of Andrew Marvell's[1] poems had lighted, not for the first time, however, upon the lines entitled 'Appleton House,' the name of one of the seats of their common ancestor, a hero in the German wars of the seventeenth century, in which poem occur the lines:

> This 'tis to have been from the first
> In a domestic heaven nursed,
> Under the discipline severe
> Of Fairfax and the starry Vere.

And so, upon embracing his cousin fresh from Rodney's great victory wherein he had played so gallant a part, brimming over with just family pride in the sailor of their house, he exuberantly exclaimed, 'Give ye joy, Ed; give ye joy, my starry Vere!' This got currency, and the novel prefix serving in familiar parlance readily to distinguish the *Bellipotent*'s captain from another Vere his senior, a distant relative, an officer of like rank in the navy, it remained permanently attached to the surname.

7

In view of the part that the commander of the *Bellipotent* plays in scenes shortly to follow, it may be well to fill out that sketch of him outlined in the previous chapter.

Aside from his qualities as a sea officer Captain Vere was an

---

1. English lyric poet (1621–1678).

exceptional character. Unlike no few of England's renowned sailors, long and arduous service with signal devotion to it had not resulted in absorbing and *salting* the entire man. He had a marked leaning toward everything intellectual. He loved books, never going to sea without a newly replenished library, compact but of the best. The isolated leisure, in some cases so wearisome, falling at intervals to commanders even during a war cruise, never was tedious to Captain Vere. With nothing of that literary taste which less heeds the thing conveyed than the vehicle, his bias was toward those books to which every serious mind of superior order occupying any active post of authority in the world naturally inclines: books treating of actual men and events no matter of what era—history, biography, and unconventional writers like Montaigne,[2] who, free from cant and convention, honestly and in the spirit of common sense philosophize upon realities. In this line of reading he found confirmation of his own more reserved thoughts—confirmation which he had vainly sought in social converse, so that as touching most fundamental topics, there had got to be established in him some positive convictions which he forefelt would abide in him essentially unmodified so long as his intelligent part remained unimpaired. In view of the troubled period in which his lot was cast, this was well for him. His settled convictions were as a dike against those invading waters of novel opinion social, political, and otherwise, which carried away as in a torrent no few minds in those days, minds by nature not inferior to his own. While other members of that aristocracy to which by birth he belonged were incensed at the innovators mainly because their theories were inimical to the privileged classes, Captain Vere disinterestedly opposed them not alone because they seemed to him insusceptible of embodiment in lasting institutions, but at war with the peace of the world and the true welfare of mankind.

With minds less stored than his and less earnest, some officers of his rank, with whom at times he would necessarily consort, found him lacking in the companionable quality, a dry and bookish gentleman, as they deemed. Upon any chance withdrawal from their company one would be apt to say to another something like this: 'Vere is a noble fellow, Starry Vere. 'Spite the gazettes,[3] Sir Horatio' (meaning him who became Lord Nelson) 'is at bottom scarce a better seaman or fighter. But between you and me now, don't you think there is a queer streak of the pedantic running through him? Yes, like the King's yarn in a coil of navy rope?'[4]

Some apparent ground there was for this sort of confidential criticism; since not only did the captain's discourse never fall into the

---

2. Michel Eyquem de Montaigne (1533–1592), French essayist.   3. Official gazettes that printed accounts of naval careers and honors.   4. A thread was worked into hempen cable to mark it as belonging to the Royal Navy.

jocosely familiar, but in illustrating of any point touching the stirring personages and events of the time he would be as apt to cite some historic character or incident of antiquity as he would be to cite from the moderns. He seemed unmindful of the circumstance that to his bluff company such remote allusions, however pertinent they might really be, were altogether alien to men whose reading was mainly confined to the journals. But considerateness in such matters is not easy to natures constituted like Captain Vere's. Their honesty prescribes to them directness, sometimes far-reaching like that of a migratory fowl that in its flight never heeds when it crosses a frontier.

8

THE lieutenants and other commissioned gentlemen forming Captain Vere's staff is not necessary here to particularize, nor needs it to make any mention of any of the warrant officers. But among the petty officers[5] was one who, having much to do with the story, may as well be forthwith introduced. His portrait I essay, but shall never hit it. This was John Claggart, the master-at-arms. But that sea title may to landsmen seem somewhat equivocal. Originally, doubtless, that petty officer's function was the instruction of the men in the use of arms, sword or cutlass. But very long ago, owing to the advance in gunnery making hand-to-hand encounters less frequent and giving to niter and sulphur the pre-eminence over steel, that function ceased; the master-at-arms of a great warship becoming a sort of chief of police charged among other matters with the duty of preserving order on the populous lower gun decks.

Claggart was a man about five-and-thirty, somewhat spare and tall, yet of no ill figure upon the whole. His hand was too small and shapely to have been accustomed to hard toil. The face was a notable one, the features all except the chin cleanly cut as those on a Greek medallion; yet the chin, beardless as Tecumseh's,[6] had something of strange protuberant broadness in its make that recalled the prints of the Reverend Dr Titus Oates,[7] the historic deponent with the clerical drawl in the time of Charles II and the fraud of the alleged Popish Plot. It served Claggart in his office that his eye could cast a tutoring glance. His brow was of the sort phrenologically associated with more than average intellect; silken jet curls partly clustering over it, making a foil to the pallor below, a pallor tinged with a faint shade of amber akin to the hue of time-tinted marbles of old. This complexion, singularly contrasting with the red or deeply bronzed visages of

5. Enlisted men corresponding in rank to noncommissioned officers in the army; *warrant officers* ranked above them and just below commissioned officers.   6. Shawnee chief (1768?–1813) who attempted to unite the Indian tribes against the United States.   7. In 1678 Oates (1649–1705) invented a plot accusing Jesuits of planning to assassinate Charles II, burn London, and slaughter English Protestants.

the sailors, and in part the result of his official seclusion from the sunlight, though it was not exactly displeasing, nevertheless seemed to hint of something defective or abnormal in the constitution and blood. But his general aspect and manner were so suggestive of an education and career incongruous with his naval function that when not actively engaged in it he looked like a man of high quality, social and moral, who for reasons of his own was keeping incog.[8] Nothing was known of his former life. It might be that he was an Englishman; and yet there lurked a bit of accent in his speech suggesting that possibly he was not such by birth, but through naturalization in early childhood. Among certain grizzled sea gossips of the gun decks and forecastle went a rumor perdue that the master-at-arms was a *chevalier* who had volunteered into the King's navy by way of compounding for some mysterious swindle whereof he had been arraigned at the King's Bench.[9] The fact that nobody could substantiate this report was, of course, nothing against its secret currency. Such a rumor once started on the gun decks in reference to almost anyone below the rank of a commissioned officer would, during the period assigned to this narrative, have seemed not altogether wanting in credibility to the tarry old wiseacres of a man-of-war crew. And indeed a man of Claggart's accomplishments, without prior nautical experience entering the navy at mature life, as he did, and necessarily allotted at the start to the lowest grade in it; a man too who never made allusion to his previous life ashore; these were circumstances which in the dearth of exact knowledge as to his true antecedents opened to the invidious a vague field for unfavorable surmise.

But the sailors' dogwatch gossip concerning him derived a vague plausibility from the fact that now for some period the British navy could so little afford to be squeamish in the matter of keeping up the muster rolls, that not only were press gangs notoriously abroad both afloat and ashore, but there was little or no secret about another matter, namely, that the London police were at liberty to capture any able-bodied suspect, any questionable fellow at large, and summarily ship him to the dockyard or fleet. Furthermore, even among voluntary enlistments there were instances where the motive thereto partook neither of patriotic impulse nor yet of a random desire to experience a bit of sea life and martial adventure. Insolvent debtors of minor grade, together with the promiscuous lame ducks of morality, found in the navy a convenient and secure refuge, secure because, once enlisted aboard a King's ship, they were as much in sanctuary as the transgressor of the Middle Ages harboring himself under the shadow of the altar. Such sanctioned irregularities, which for obvious reasons the government would hardly think to parade at the time and

8. Incognito, unrecognized.　9. Formerly the supreme court of common law in Great Britain; a *chevalier* here designates a man of high rank.

which consequently, and as affecting the least influential class of
mankind, have all but dropped into oblivion, lend color[1] to something for the truth whereof I do not vouch, and hence have some
scruple in stating; something I remember having seen in print though
the book I cannot recall; but the same thing was personally communicated to me now more than forty years ago by an old pensioner
in a cocked hat with whom I had a most interesting talk on the
terrace at Greenwich,[2] a Baltimore Negro, a Trafalgar man. It was
to this effect: In the case of a warship short of hands whose speedy
sailing was imperative, the deficient quota, in lack of any other way
of making it good, would be eked out by drafts culled direct from the
jails. For reasons previously suggested it would not perhaps be easy
at the present day directly to prove or disprove the allegation. But
allowed as a verity, how significant would it be of England's straits
at the time confronted by those wars which like a flight of harpies
rose shrieking from the din and dust of the fallen Bastille.[3] That era
appears measurably clear to us who look back at it, and but read of
it. But to the grandfathers of us graybeards, the more thoughtful of
them, the genius of it presented an aspect like that of Camoëns' Spirit
of the Cape,[4] an eclipsing menace mysterious and prodigious. Not
America was exempt from apprehension. At the height of Napoleon's unexampled conquests, there were Americans who had fought
at Bunker Hill who looked forward to the possibility that the Atlantic
might prove no barrier against the ultimate schemes of this French
portentous upstart from the revolutionary chaos who seemed in act
of fulfilling judgment prefigured in the Apocalypse.

But the less credence was to be given to the gun-deck talk touching
Claggart, seeing that no man holding his office in a man-of-war can
ever hope to be popular with the crew. Besides, in derogatory comments upon anyone against whom they have a grudge, or for any
reason or no reason mislike, sailors are much like landsmen: they
are apt to exaggerate or romance it.

About as much was really known to the *Bellipotent's* tars of the
master-at-arms' career before entering the service as an astronomer
knows about a comet's travels prior to its first observable appearance
in the sky. The verdict of the sea quidnuncs[5] has been cited only by
way of showing what sort of moral impression the man made upon
rude uncultivated natures whose conceptions of human wickedness
were necessarily of the narrowest, limited to ideas of vulgar rascality—a thief among the swinging hammocks during a night watch, or
the man-brokers and land-sharks of the seaports.

1. Appearance of truth.   2. Greenwich hospital near London, a home for retired personnel; a
"Trafalgar man" is a veteran of the Battle of Trafalgar.   3. The fall of the Bastille (July 14,
1789) signaled the beginning of the French Revolution.   4. The Portuguese poet Luiz Vaz de
Camoëns (1524–1580) describes in his epic poem, the *Lusiads*, a monster named Adamastor who
attempts to destroy Vasco da Gama and his crew.   5. Latin, "what now"; a busybody.

It was no gossip, however, but fact that though, as before hinted, Claggart upon his entrance into the navy was, as a novice, assigned to the least honorable section of a man-of-war's crew, embracing the drudgery, he did not long remain there. The superior capacity he immediately evinced, his constitutional sobriety, an ingratiating deference to superiors, together with a peculiar ferreting genius manifested on a singular occasion; all this, capped by a certain austere patriotism, abruptly advanced him to the position of master-at-arms.

Of this maritime chief of police the ship's corporals, so called, were the immediate subordinates, and compliant ones; and this, as is to be noted in some business departments ashore, almost to a degree inconsistent with entire moral volition. His place put various converging wires of underground influence under the chief's control, capable when astutely worked through his understrappers of operating to the mysterious discomfort, if nothing worse, of any of the sea commonalty.

9

Life in the foretop well agreed with Billy Budd. There, when not actually engaged on the yards yet higher aloft, the topmen, who as such had been picked out for youth and activity, constituted an aerial club lounging at ease against the smaller stun'sails rolled up into cushions, spinning yarns like the lazy gods, and frequently amused with what was going on in the busy world of the decks below. No wonder then that a young fellow of Billy's disposition was well content in such society. Giving no cause of offense to anybody, he was always alert at a call. So in the merchant service it had been with him. But now such a punctiliousness in duty was shown that his topmates would sometimes good-naturedly laugh at him for it. This heightened alacrity had its cause, namely, the impression made upon him by the first formal gangway-punishment he had ever witnessed, which befell the day following his impressment. It had been incurred by a little fellow, young, a novice afterguardsman absent from his assigned post when the ship was being put about; a dereliction resulting in a rather serious hitch to that maneuver, one demanding instantaneous promptitude in letting go and making fast. When Billy saw the culprit's naked back under the scourge, gridironed with red welts and worse, when he marked the dire expression in the liberated man's face as with his woolen shirt flung over him by the executioner he rushed forward from the spot to bury himself in the crowd, Billy was horrified. He resolved that never through remissness would he make himself liable to such a visitation or do or omit aught that might merit even verbal reproof. What then was his surprise and concern when ultimately he found himself getting into petty trouble occasionally about such matters as the stowage of his bag or something amiss in his hammock, matters under the police oversight of the ship's corporals of the lower decks, and which brought down on him a vague threat from one of them.

So heedful in all things as he was, how could this be? He could not understand it, and it more than vexed him. When he spoke to his young topmates about it they were either lightly incredulous or found something comical in his unconcealed anxiety. 'Is it your bag, Billy?' said one. 'Well, sew yourself up in it, bully boy, and then you'll be sure to know if anybody meddles with it.'

Now there was a veteran aboard who because his years began to disqualify him for more active work had been recently assigned duty as mainmastman in his watch, looking to the gear belayed at the rail roundabout that great spar near the deck. At off-times the foretopman had picked up some acquaintance with him, and now in his trouble it occurred to him that he might be the sort of person to go to for wise counsel. He was an old Dansker[6] long anglicized in the service, of few words, many wrinkles, and some honorable scars. His wizened face, time-tinted and weather-stained to the complexion of an antique parchment, was here and there peppered blue by the chance explosion of a gun cartridge in action.

He was an *Agamemnon* man, some two years prior to the time of this story having served under Nelson when still captain in that ship immortal in naval memory, which dismantled and in part broken up to her bare ribs is seen a grand skeleton in Haden's etching.[7] As one of a boarding party from the *Agamemnon* he had received a cut slantwise along one temple and cheek leaving a long pale scar like a streak of dawn's light falling athwart the dark visage. It was on account of that scar and the affair in which it was known that he had received it, as well as from his blue-peppered complexion, that the Dansker went among the *Bellipotent*'s crew by the name of 'Board-Her-in-the-Smoke.'

Now the first time that his small weasel eyes happened to light on Billy Budd, a certain grim internal merriment set all his ancient wrinkles into antic play. Was it that his eccentric unsentimental old sapience, primitive in its kind, saw or thought it saw something which in contrast with the warship's environment looked oddly incongruous in the Handsome Sailor? But after slyly studying him at intervals, the old Merlin's[8] equivocal merriment was modified; for now when the twain would meet, it would start in his face a quizzing[9] sort of look, but it would be but momentary and sometimes replaced by an expression of speculative query as to what might eventually befall a nature like that, dropped into a world not without some

6. Dane.   7. *Breaking up of the Agamemnon*, the masterpiece of Sir Francis Seymour Haden (1818–1910).   8. King Arthur's court magician.   9. Mocking.

mantraps and against whose subtleties simple courage lacking experience and address,[1] and without any touch of defensive ugliness, is of little avail; and where such innocence as man is capable of does yet in a moral emergency not always sharpen the faculties or enlighten the will.

However it was, the Dansker in his ascetic way rather took to Billy. Nor was this only because of a certain philosophic interest in such a character. There was another cause. While the old man's eccentricities, sometimes bordering on the ursine, repelled the juniors, Billy, undeterred thereby, revering him as a salt hero, would make advances, never passing the old *Agamemnon* man without a salutation marked by that respect which is seldom lost on the aged, however crabbed at times or whatever their station in life.

There was a vein of dry humor, or what not, in the mastman; and, whether in freak of patriarchal irony touching Billy's youth and athletic frame, or for some other and more recondite reason, from the first in addressing him he always substituted *Baby* for Billy, the Dansker in fact being the originator of the name by which the foretopman eventually became known aboard ship.

Well then, in his mysterious little difficulty going in quest of the wrinkled one, Billy found him off duty in a dogwatch ruminating by himself, seated on a shot box of the upper gun deck, now and then surveying with a somewhat cynical regard certain of the more swaggering promenaders there. Billy recounted his trouble, again wondering how it all happened. The salt seer attentively listened, accompanying the foretopman's recital with queer twitchings of his wrinkles and problematical little sparkles of his small ferret eyes. Making an end of his story, the foretopman asked, 'And now, Dansker, do tell me what you think of it.'

The old man, shoving up the front of his tarpaulin and deliberately rubbing the long slant scar at the point where it entered the thin hair, laconically said, 'Baby Budd, *Jemmy Legs*[2] (meaning the master-at-arms) 'is down on you.'

'*Jemmy Legs!*' ejaculated Billy, his welkin eyes expanding.

'What for? Why, he calls me "the sweet and pleasant young fellow," they tell me.'

'Does he so?' grinned the grizzled one; then said, 'Ay, Baby lad, a sweet voice has Jemmy Legs.'

'No, not always. But to me he has. I seldom pass him but there comes a pleasant word.'

'And that's because he's down upon you, Baby Budd.'

Such reiteration, along with the manner of it, incomprehensible to a novice, disturbed Billy almost as much as the mystery for which

---

1. Skill and tact in handling situations.   2. A disparaging nickname for the master-at-arms, still used in the American navy.

he had sought explanation. Something less unpleasingly oracular he tried to extract; but the old sea Chiron,[3] thinking perhaps that for the nonce he had sufficiently instructed his young Achilles, pursed his lips, gathered all his wrinkles together, and would commit himself to nothing further.

Years, and those experiences which befall certain shrewder men subordinated lifelong to the will of superiors, all this had developed in the Dansker the pithy guarded cynicism that was his leading characteristic.

10

THE next day an incident served to confirm Billy Budd in his incredulity as to the Dansker's strange summing up of the case submitted. The ship at noon, going large before the wind, was rolling on her course, and he below at dinner and engaged in some sportful talk with the members of his mess, chanced in a sudden lurch to spill the entire contents of his soup pan upon the new-scrubbed deck. Claggart, the master-at-arms, official rattan[4] in hand, happened to be passing along the battery in a bay of which the mess was lodged, and the greasy liquid streamed just across his path. Stepping over it, he was proceeding on his way without comment, since the matter was nothing to take notice of under the circumstances, when he happened to observe who it was that had done the spilling. His countenance changed. Pausing, he was about to ejaculate something hasty at the sailor, but checked himself, and pointing down to the streaming soup, playfully tapped him from behind with his rattan, saying in a low musical voice peculiar to him at times, 'Handsomely done, my lad! And handsome is as handsome did it, too!' And with that passed on. Not noted by Billy as not coming within his view was the involuntary smile, or rather grimace, that accompanied Claggart's equivocal words. Aridly it drew down the thin corners of his shapely mouth. But everybody taking his remark as meant for humorous, and at which therefore as coming from a superior they were bound to laugh 'with counterfeited glee,'[5] acted accordingly; and Billy, tickled, it may be, by the allusion to his being the Handsome Sailor, merrily joined in; then addressing his messmates exclaimed, 'There now, who says that Jemmy Legs is down on me!'

'And who said he was, Beauty?' demanded one Donald with some surprise. Whereat the foretopman looked a little foolish, recalling that it was only one person, Board-Her-in-the-Smoke, who had sug-

---

3. Chiron the Centaur, half man and half horse, skilled in healing and the wisest of his species, taught Achilles, Hercules, and Aesculapius.   4. Swagger stick, light whip.   5. Oliver Goldsmith, "The Deserted Village," 1:201, alluding to the response of students to a severe schoolmaster.

gested what to him was the smoky idea that his master-at-arms was in any peculiar way hostile to him. Meantime that functionary, resuming his path, must have momentarily worn some expression less guarded than that of the bitter smile, usurping the face from the heart—some distorting expression perhaps, for a drummer-boy heedlessly frolicking along from the opposite direction and chancing to come into light collision with his person was strangely disconcerted by his aspect. Nor was the impression lessened when the official, impetuously giving him a sharp cut with the rattan, vehemently exclaimed, 'Look where you go!'

11

What was the matter with the master-at-arms? And, be the matter what it might, how could it have direct relation to Billy Budd, with whom prior to the affair of the spilled soup he had never come into any special contact official or otherwise? What indeed could the trouble have to do with one so little inclined to give offense as the merchant-ship's 'peacemaker,' even him who in Claggart's own phrase was 'the sweet and pleasant young fellow'? Yes, why should Jemmy Legs, to borrow the Dansker's expression, be 'down' on the Handsome Sailor? But, at heart and not for nothing, as the late chance encounter may indicate to the discerning, down on him, secretly down on him, he assuredly was.

Now to invent something touching the more private career of Claggart, something involving Billy Budd, of which something the latter should be wholly ignorant, some romantic incident implying that Claggart's knowledge of the young bluejacket began at some period anterior to catching sight of him on board the seventy-four— all this, not so difficult to do, might avail in a way more or less interesting to account for whatever of enigma may appear to lurk in the case. But in fact there was nothing of the sort. And yet the cause necessarily to be assumed as the sole one assignable is in its very realism as much charged with that prime element of Radcliffian romance, the mysterious, as any that the ingenuity of the author of *The Mysteries of Udolpho*[6] could devise. For what can more partake of the mysterious than an antipathy spontaneous and profound such as is evoked in certain exceptional mortals by the mere aspect of some other mortal, however harmless he may be, if not called forth by this very harmlessness itself?

Now there can exist no irritating juxtaposition of dissimilar personalities comparable to that which is possible aboard a great warship fully manned and at sea. There, every day among all ranks, almost

6. An immensely popular Gothic novel by Ann Radcliffe (1764–1823).

every man comes into more or less of contact with almost every other man. Wholly there to avoid even the sight of an aggravating object one must needs give it Jonah's toss[7] or jump overboard himself. Imagine how all this might eventually operate on some peculiar human creature the direct reverse of a saint!

But for the adequate comprehending of Claggart by a normal nature these hints are insufficient. To pass from a normal nature to him one must cross 'the deadly space between.' And this is best done by indirection.

Long ago an honest scholar, my senior, said to me in reference to one who like himself is now no more, a man so unimpeachably respectable that against him nothing was ever openly said though among the few something was whispered, 'Yes, X——is a nut not to be cracked by the tap of a lady's fan. You are aware that I am the adherent of no organized religion, much less of any philosophy built into a system. Well, for all that, I think that to try and get into X——, enter his labyrinth and get out again, without a clue derived from some source other than what is known as "knowledge of the world"— that were hardly possible, at least for me.'

'Why,' said I, 'X——, however singular a study to some, is yet human, and knowledge of the world assuredly implies the knowledge of human nature, and in most of its varieties.'

'Yes, but a superficial knowledge of it, serving ordinary purposes. But for anything deeper, I am not certain whether to know the world and to know human nature be not two distinct branches of knowledge, which while they may co-exist in the same heart, yet either may exist with little or nothing of the other. Nay, in an average man of the world, his constant rubbing with it blunts that finer spiritual insight indispensable to the understanding of the essential in certain exceptional characters, whether evil ones or good. In a matter of some importance I have seen a girl wind an old lawyer about her little finger. Nor was it the dotage of senile love. Nothing of the sort. But he knew law better than he knew the girl's heart. Coke and Blackstone[8] hardly shed so much light into obscure spiritual places as the Hebrew prophets. And who were they? Mostly recluses.'

At the time, my inexperience was such that I did not quite see the drift of all this. It may be that I see it now. And, indeed, if that lexicon which is based on Holy Writ were any longer popular, one might with less difficulty define and denominate certain phenomenal men. As it is, one must turn to some authority not liable to the charge of being tinctured with the biblical element.

In a list of definitions included in the authentic translation of Plato,

---

7. Jonah 1:15: "So they took up Jonah, and cast him forth into the sea." A nautical expression when an unlucky object or person is put overboard.   8. Sir Edward Coke (1552–1634) and Sir William Blackstone (1723–1780), noted British jurists and writers on the law.

a list attributed to him, occurs this: 'Natural Depravity: a depravity
according to nature,' a definition which, though savoring of Calvin-
ism,[9] by no means involves Calvin's dogma as to total mankind.
Evidently its intent makes it applicable but to individuals. Not many
are the examples of this depravity which the gallows and jail supply.
At any rate, for notable instances, since these have no vulgar alloy
of the brute in them, but invariably are dominated by intellectuality,
one must go elsewhere. Civilization, especially if of the austerer sort,
is auspicious to it. It folds itself in the mantle of respectability. It has
certain negative virtues serving as silent auxiliaries. It never allows
wine to get within its guard. It is not going too far to say that it is
without vices or small sins. There is a phenomenal pride in it that
excludes them. It is never mercenary or avaricious. In short, the
depravity here meant partakes nothing of the sordid or sensual. It is
serious, but free from acerbity. Though no flatterer of mankind it
never speaks ill of it.

But the thing which in eminent instances signalizes so exceptional
a nature is this: Though the man's even temper and discreet bearing
would seem to intimate a mind peculiarly subject to the law of reason, not the less in heart he would seem to riot in complete exemption from that law, having apparently little to do with reason further
than to employ it as an ambidexter implement for effecting the irrational. That is to say: Toward the accomplishment of an aim which
in wantonness of atrocity would seem to partake of the insane, he
will direct a cool judgment sagacious and sound. These men are
madmen, and of the most dangerous sort, for their lunacy is not
continuous, but occasional, evoked by some special object; it is protectively secretive, which is as much as to say it is self-contained, so
that when, moreover, most active it is to the average mind not dis-
tinguishable from sanity, and for the reason above suggested: that
whatever its aims may be—and the aim is never declared—the method
and the outward proceeding are always perfectly rational.

Now something such an one was Claggart, in whom was the mania
of an evil nature, not engendered by vicious training or corrupting
books or licentious living, but born with him and innate, in short 'a
depravity according to nature.'

Dark sayings are these, some will say. But why? Is it because they
somewhat savor of Holy Writ in its phrase 'mystery of iniquity'?[1] If
they do, such savor was far enough from being intended, for little
will it commend these pages to many a reader of today.

The point of the present story turning on the hidden nature of the
master-at-arms has necessitated this chapter. With an added hint or

9. The religious system founded by John Calvin (1509–1564), which emphasizes
predestination.   1. 2 Thessalonians 2:7.

two in connection with the incident at the mess, the resumed narrative must be left to vindicate, as it may, its own credibility.

12

That Claggart's figure was not amiss, and his face, save the chin, well molded, has already been said. Of these favorable points he seemed not insensible, for he was not only neat but careful in his dress. But the form of Billy Budd was heroic; and if his face was without the intellectual look of the pallid Claggart's, not the less was it lit, like his, from within, though from a different source. The bonfire in his heart made luminous the rose-tan in his cheek.

In view of the marked contrast between the persons of the twain, it is more than probable that when the master-at-arms in the scene last given applied to the sailor the proverb 'Handsome is as handsome does,' he there let escape an ironic inkling, not caught by the young sailors who heard it, as to what it was that had first moved him against Billy, namely, his significant personal beauty.

Now envy and antipathy, passions irreconcilable in reason, nevertheless in fact may spring conjoined like Chang and Eng[2] in one birth. Is Envy than such a monster? Well, though many an arraigned mortal has in hopes of mitigated penalty pleaded guilty to horrible actions, did ever anybody seriously confess to envy? Something there is in it universally felt to be more shameful than even felonious crime. And not only does everybody disown it, but the better sort are inclined to incredulity when it is in earnest imputed to an intelligent man. But since its lodgment is in the heart not the brain, no degree of intellect supplies a guarantee against it. But Claggart's was no vulgar form of the passion. Nor, as directed toward Billy Budd, did it partake of that streak of apprehensive jealousy that marred Saul's visage perturbedly brooding on the comely young David.[3] Claggart's envy struck deeper. If askance he eyed the good looks, cheery health, and frank enjoyment of young life in Billy Budd, it was because these went along with a nature that, as Claggart magnetically felt, had in its simplicity never willed malice or experienced the reactionary bit of that serpent. To him, the spirit lodged within Billy, and looking out from his welkin eyes as from windows, that ineffability it was which made the dimple in his dyed cheek, suppled his joints, and dancing in his yellow curls made him pre-eminently the Handsome Sailor. One person expected, the master-at-arms was perhaps the only man in the ship intellectually capable of adequately appreciating the moral phenomenon presented in Billy Budd. And the insight

2. Famous Siamese twins (1811–1874) who toured the United States.   3. David's comeliness and Saul's jealousy are described in 1 Samuel 16:18, 18:8 ff.

but intensified his passion, which assuming various secret forms within him, at times assumed that of cynic disdain, disdain of innocence—to be nothing more than innocent! Yet in an aesthetic way he saw the charm of it, the courageous free-and-easy temper of it, and fain would have shared it, but he despaired of it.

With no power to annul the elemental evil in him, though readily enough he could hide it; apprehending the good, but powerless to be it; a nature like Claggart's, surcharged with energy as such natures almost invariably are, what recourse is left to it but to recoil upon itself and, like the scorpion for which the Creator alone is responsible, act out to the end the part allotted it.

13

Passion, and passion in its profoundest, is not a thing demanding a palatial stage whereon to play its part. Down among the groundlings,[4] among the beggars and rakers of the garbage, profound passion is enacted. And the circumstances that provoke it, however trivial or mean, are no measure of its power. In the present instance the stage is a scrubbed gun deck, and one of the external provocations a man-of-war's man's spilled soup.

Now when the master-at-arms noticed whence came that greasy fluid streaming before his feet, he must have taken it—to some extent wilfully, perhaps—not for the mere accident it assuredly was, but for the sly escape of a spontaneous feeling on Billy's part more or less answering to the antipathy on his own. In effect a foolish demonstration, he must have thought, and very harmless, like the futile kick of a heifer, which yet were the heifer a shod stallion would not be so harmless. Even so was it that into the gall of Claggart's envy he infused the vitriol of his contempt. But the incident confirmed to him certain telltale reports purveyed to his ear by 'Squeak,' one of his more cunning corporals, a grizzled little man, so nicknamed by the sailors on account of his squeaky voice and sharp visage ferreting about the dark corners of the lower decks after interlopers, satirically suggesting to them the idea of a rat in a cellar.

From his chief's employing him as an implicit tool in laying little traps for the worriment of the foretopman—for it was from the master-at-arms that the petty persecutions heretofore adverted to had proceeded—the corporal, having naturally enough concluded that his master could have no love for the sailor, made it his business, faithful understrapper that he was, to foment the ill blood by perverting to his chief certain innocent frolics of the good-natured foretopman, besides inventing for his mouth sundry contumelious epithets

---

4. The part of the audience which stood on the ground in an Elizabethan theater; the poorest spectators.

he claimed to have overheard him let fall. The master-at-arms never suspected the veracity of these reports, more especially as to the epithets, for he well knew how secretly unpopular may become a master-at-arms, at least a master-at-arms of those days, zealous in his function, and how the bluejackets shoot at him in private their raillery and wit; the nickname by which he goes among them (Jemmy Legs) implying under the form of merriment their cherished disrespect and dislike. But in view of the greediness of hate for pabulum[5] it hardly needed a purveyor to feed Claggart's passion.

An uncommon prudence is habitual with the subtler depravity, for it has everything to hide. And in case of an injury but suspected, its secretiveness voluntarily cuts it off from enlightenment or disillusion; and, not unreluctantly, action is taken upon surmise as upon certainty. And the retaliation is apt to be in monstrous disproportion to the supposed offense; for when in anybody was revenge in its exactions aught else but an inordinate usurer? But how with Claggart's conscience? For though consciences are unlike as foreheads, every intelligence, not excluding the scriptural devils who 'believe and tremble,'[6] has one. But Claggart's conscience being but the lawyer to his will, made ogres of trifles, probably arguing that the motive imputed to Billy in spilling the soup just when he did, together with the epithets alleged, these, if nothing more, made a strong case against him; nay, justified animosity into a sort of retributive righteousness. The Pharisee is the Guy Fawkes[7] prowling in the hid chambers underlying some natures like Claggart's. And they can really form no conception of an unreciprocated malice. Probably the master-at-arms' clandestine persecution of Billy was started to try the temper of the man; but it had not developed any quality in him that enmity could make official use of or even pervert into plausible self-justification; so that the occurrence at the mess, petty if it were, was a welcome one to that peculiar conscience assigned to be the private mentor of Claggart; and, for the rest, not improbably it put him upon new experiments.

14

Not many days after the last incident narrated, something befell Billy Budd that more graveled him than aught that had previously occurred.

It was a warm night for the latitude; and the foretopman, whose watch at the time was properly below, was dozing on the uppermost

5. Sustenance.   6. James 2:19: "The devils also believe, and tremble."   7. Instigator of the Gunpowder Plot, the plan to blow up the Houses of Parliament and King James I on November 5, 1605. *Pharisee*: Follower of a Jewish sect known for its strict observance of the Torah; hence anyone extremely rigid and dogmatic.

deck whither he had ascended from his hot hammock, one of hundreds suspended so closely wedged together over a lower gun deck that there was little or no swing to them. He lay as in the shadow of a hillside, stretched under the lee of the booms, a piled ridge of spare spars amidships between foremast and mainmast among which the ship's largest boat, the launch, was stowed. Alongside of three other slumberers from below, he lay near that end of the booms which approaches the foremast; his station aloft on duty as a foretopman being just over the deckstation of the forecastlemen, entitling him according to usage to make himself more or less at home in that neighborhood.

Presently he was stirred into semiconsciousness by somebody, who must have previously sounded the sleep of the others touching his shoulder, and then, as the foretopman raised his head, breathing into his ear in a quick whisper, 'Slip into the lee forechains, Billy; there is something in the wind. Don't speak. Quick, I will meet you there,' and disappearing.

Now Billy, like sundry other essentially good-natured ones, had some of the weaknesses inseparable from essential good nature; and among these was a reluctance, almost an incapacity of plumply[8] saying *no* to an abrupt proposition not obviously absurd on the face of it, nor obviously unfriendly, nor iniquitous. And being of warm blood, he had not the phlegm[9] tacitly to negative any proposition by unresponsive inaction. Like his sense of fear, his apprehension as to aught outside of the honest and natural was seldom very quick. Besides, upon the present occasion, the drowse from his sleep still hung upon him.

However it was, he mechanically rose and, sleepily wondering what could be in the wind, betook himself to the designated place, a narrow platform, one of six, outside of the high bulwarks and screened by the great deadeyes and multiple columned lanyards of the shrouds and backstays; and, in a great warship of that time, of dimensions commensurate to the hull's magnitude; a tarry balcony in short, overhanging the sea, and so secluded that one mariner of the *Bellipotent*, a Nonconformist old tar of a serious turn, made it even in daytime his private oratory.[1]

In this retired nook the stranger soon joined Billy Budd. There was no moon as yet; a haze obscured the starlight. He could not distinctly see the stranger's face. Yet from something in the outline and carriage, Billy took him, and correctly for one of the afterguard.

'Hist! Billy,' said the man, in the same quick cautionary whisper as before. 'You were impressed, weren't you? Well, so was I'; and he paused, as to mark the effect. But Billy, not knowing exactly what to

---

8. Bluntly.   9. Sluggishness, apathy.   1. A small chapel, especially for private prayer. A noncomformist is a Protestant dissenter from the Church of England.

make of this, said nothing. Then the other: 'We are not the only impressed ones, Billy. There's a gang of us.—Couldn't you—help—at a pinch?'

'What do you mean?' demanded Billy, here thoroughly shaking off his drowse.

'Hist, hist!' the hurried whisper now growing husky. 'See here,' and the man held up two small objects faintly twinkling in the night-light; 'see, they are yours, Billy, if you'll only—'

But Billy broke in, and in his resentful eagerness to deliver himself his vocal infirmity somewhat intruded. 'D—d—damme, I don't know what you are d—d—driving at, or what you mean, but you had betterg—g—go where you belong!' For the moment the fellow, as confounded, did not stir; and Billy, springing to his feet, said, 'If you d—don't start, I'll t—t—toss you back over the r—rail!' There was no mistaking this, and the mysterious emissary decamped, disappearing in the direction of the mainmast in the shadow of the booms.

'Hallo, what's the matter?' here came growling from a forecastle-man awakened from his deck-doze by Billy's raised voice. And as the foretopman reappeared and was recognized by him: 'Ah, Beauty, is it you? Well, something must have been the matter, for you st—st—stuttered.'

'Oh,' rejoined Billy, now mastering the impediment, 'I found an afterguardsman in our part of the ship here, and I bid him be off where he belongs.'

'And is that all you did about it, Foretopman?' gruffly demanded another, an irascible old fellow of brick-colored visage and hair who was known to his associate forecastlemen as 'Red Pepper.' 'Such sneaks I should like to marry to the gunner's daughter!'—by that expression meaning that he would like to subject them to disciplinary castigation over a gun.

However, Billy's rendering of the matter satisfactorily accounted to these inquirers for the brief commotion, since of all the sections of a ship's company the forecastlemen, veterans for the most part and bigoted in their sea prejudices, are the most jealous in resenting territorial encroachments, especially on the part of any of the afterguard, of whom they have but a sorry opinion—chiefly landsmen, never going aloft except to reef or furl the mainsail, and in no wise competent to handle a marlinspike or turn in a deadeye, say.

15

This incident sorely puzzled Billy Budd. It was an entirely new experience, the first time in his life that he had ever been personally approached in underhand intriguing fashion. Prior to this encounter he had known nothing of the afterguardsman, the two men being stationed wide apart, one forward and aloft during his watch, the other on deck and aft.

What could it mean? And could they really be guineas,[2] those two glittering objects the interloper had held up to his (Billy's) eyes? Where could the fellow get guineas? Why, even spare buttons are not so plentiful at sea. The more he turned the matter over, the more he was nonplussed, and made uneasy and discomfited. In his disgustful recoil from an overture which, though he but ill comprehended, he instinctively knew must involve evil of some sort, Billy Budd was like a young horse fresh from the pasture suddenly inhaling a vile whiff from some chemical factory, and by repeated snortings trying to get it out of his nostrils and lungs. This frame of mind barred all desire of holding further parley with the fellow, even were it but for the purpose of gaining some enlightenment as to his design in approaching him. And yet he was not without natural curiosity to see how such a visitor in the dark would look in broad day.

He espied him the following afternoon in his first dogwatch below, one of the smokers on that forward part of the upper gun deck allotted to the pipe. He recognized him by his general cut and build more than by his round freckled face and glassy eyes of pale blue, veiled with lashes all but white. And yet Billy was a bit uncertain whether indeed it were he—yonder chap about his own age chatting and laughing in freehearted way, leaning against a gun; a genial young fellow enough to look at, and something of a rattlebrain, to all appearance. Rather chubby too for a sailor, even an afterguardsman. In short, the last man in the world, one would think, to be overburdened with thoughts, especially those perilous thoughts that must needs belong to a conspirator in any serious project, or even to the underling of such a conspirator.

Although Billy was not aware of it, the fellow, with a sidelong watchful glance, had perceived Billy first, and then noting that Billy was looking at him, thereupon nodded a familiar sort of friendly recognition as to an old acquaintance, without interrupting the talk he was engaged in with the group of smokers. A day or two afterwards, chancing in the evening promenade on a gun deck to pass Bully, he offered a flying word of good-fellowship, as it were, which by its unexpectedness, and equivocalness under the circumstances, so embarrassed Billy that he knew not how to respond to it, and let it go unnoticed.

Billy was now left more at a loss than before. The ineffectual speculations into which he was led were so disturbingly alien to him that he did his best to smother them. It never entered his mind that here was a matter which, from its extreme questionableness, it was his

2. English gold coins, not minted after 1813, worth 21 shillings.

duty as a loyal bluejacket to report in the proper quarter. And, probably, had such a step been suggested to him, he would have been deterred from taking it by the thought, one of novice magnanimity, that it would savor overmuch of the dirty work of a telltale. He kept the thing to himself. Yet upon one occasion he could not forebear a little disburdening himself to the old Dansker, tempted thereto perhaps by the influence of a balmy night when the ship lay becalmed; the twain, silent for the most part, sitting together on deck, their heads propped against the bulwarks. But it was only a partial and anonymous account that Billy gave, the unfounded scruples above referred to preventing full disclosure to anybody. Upon hearing Billy's version, the sage Dansker seemed to divine more than he was told; and after a little meditation, during which his wrinkles were pursed as into a point, quite effacing for the time that quizzing expression his face sometimes wore: 'Didn't I say so, Baby Budd?'

'Say what?' demanded Billy.

'Why, *Jemmy Legs* is *down* on you.'

'And what,' rejoined Billy in amazement, 'has *Jemmy Legs* to do with that cracked afterguardsman?'

'Ho, it was an afterguardsman, then. A cat's-paw, a cat's-paw!'[3] And with that exclamation, whether it had reference to a light puff of air just then coming over the calm sea, or a subtler relation to the aftersguardsman, there is no telling, the old Merlin gave a twisting wrench with his black teeth at his plug of tobacco, vouchsafing no reply to Billy's impetuous question, though now repeated, for it was his wont to relapse into grim silence when interrogated in skeptical sort as to any of his sententious oracles, not always very clear ones, rather partaking of that obscurity which invests most Delphic[4] deliverances from any quarter.

Long experience had very likely brought this old man to that bitter prudence which never interferes in aught and never gives advice.

16

Yes, despite the Dansker's pithy insistence as to the master-at-arms being at the bottom of these strange experiences of Billy on board the *Bellipotent*, the young sailor was ready to ascribe them to almost anybody but the man who, to use Billy's own expression, 'always had a pleasant word for him.' This is to be wondered at. Yet not so much to be wondered at. In certain matters, some sailors even in mature life remain unsophisticated enough. But a young seafarer of the disposition of our athletic foretopman is much of a child-man.

3. A cat's paw can be either a light wind perceived by its impressions on the sea, or a seaman employed to entice volunteers.   4. Literally, issuing from the oracle of Apollo at Delphi, which made ambiguous prophecies; hence, obscure in meaning, ambiguous.

And yet a child's utter innocence is but its blank ignorance, and the innocence more or less wanes as intelligence waxes. But in Billy Budd intelligence, such as it was, had advanced while yet his simple-mindedness remained for the most part unaffected. Experience is a teacher indeed; yet did Billy's years make his experience small. Besides, he had none of that intuitive knowledge of the bad which in natures not good or incompletely so foreruns experience, and therefore may pertain, as in some instances it too clearly does pertain, even to youth.

And what could Billy know of man except of man as a mere sailor? And the old-fashioned sailor, the veritable man before the mast, the sailor from boyhood up, he, though indeed of the same species as a landsman, is in some respects singularly distinct from him. The sailor is frankness, the landsman is finesse. Life is not a game with the sailor, demanding the long head—no intricate games of chess where few moves are made in straightforwardness and ends are attained by indirection, an oblique, tedious, barren game hardly worth that poor candle burnt out in playing it.

Yes, as a class, sailors are in character a juvenile race. Even their deviations are marked by juvenility, this more especially holding true with the sailors of Billy's time. Then too, certain things which apply to all sailors do more pointedly operate here and there upon the junior one. Every sailor, too, is accustomed to obey orders without debating them; his life afloat is externally ruled for him; he is not brought into that promiscuous[5] commerce with mankind where unobstructed free agency on equal terms equal superficially, at least—soon teaches one that unless upon occasion he exercise a distrust keen in proportion to the fairness of the appearance, some foul turn may be served him. A ruled undemonstrative distrustfulness is so habitual, not with businessmen so much as with men who know their kind in less shallow relations than business, namely, certain men of the world, that they come at last to employ it all but unconsciously; and some of them would very likely feel real surprise at being charged with it as one of their general characteristics.

17

But after the little matter at the mess Billy Budd no more found himself in strange trouble at times about his hammock or his clothes bag or what not. As to that smile that occasionally sunned him, and the pleasant passing word, these were, if not more frequent, yet if anything more pronounced than before.

But for all that, there were certain other demonstrations now. When Claggart's unobserved glance happened to light on belted Billy roll-

5. Indiscriminate.

ing along the upper gun deck in the leisure of the second dogwatch, exchanging passing broadsides of fun with other young promenaders in the crowd, that glance would follow the cheerful sea Hyperion[6] with a settled meditative and melancholy expression, his eyes strangely suffused with incipient feverish tears. Then would Claggart look like the man of sorrows.[7] Yes, and sometimes the melancholy expression would have in it a touch of soft yearning, as if Claggart could even have loved Billy but for fate and ban. But this was an evanescence, and quickly repented of, as it were, by an immitigable look, pinching and shriveling the visage into the momentary semblance of a wrinkled walnut. But sometimes catching sight in advance of the foretopman coming in his direction, he would, upon their nearing, step aside a little to let him pass, dwelling upon Billy for the moment with the glittering dental satire of a Guise.[8] But upon any abrupt unforeseen encounter a red light would flash forth from his eye like a spark from an anvil in a dusk smithy. That quick, fierce light was a strange one, darted from orbs which in repose were of a color nearest approaching a deeper violet, the softest of shades.

Though some of these caprices of the pit[9] could not but be observed by their object, yet were they beyond the construing of such a nature. And the thews of Billy were hardly compatible with that sort of sensitive spiritual organization which in some cases instinctively conveys to ignorant innocence an admonition of the proximity of the malign. He thought the master-at-arms acted in a manner rather queer at times. That was all. But the occasional frank air and pleasant word went for what they purported to be, the young sailor never having heard as yet of the 'too fair-spoken man.'

Had the foretopman been conscious of having done or said anything to provoke the ill will of the official, it would have been different with him, and his sight might have been purged if not sharpened. As it was, innocence was his blinder.

So was it with him in yet another matter. Two minor officers, the armorer and captain of the hold, with whom he had never exchanged a word, his position in the ship not bringing him into contact with them, these men now for the first began to cast upon Billy, when they chanced to encounter him, that peculiar glance which evidences that the man from whom it comes has been some way tampered with, and to the prejudice of him upon whom the glance lights. Never did it occur to Billy as a thing to be noted or a thing suspicious, though he well knew the fact, that the armorer and captain of the hold, with the ship's yeoman, apothecary, and others of that

6. In Greek mythology, the Titan god who came to be identified with Apollo, god of youth and beauty.   7. Isaiah 53:3, the Lord's servant is described as "despised and rejected of men; a man of sorrows, and acquainted with grief."   8. Henri de Guise (1550–1588), a famed conspirator who could smile throughout his villainy.   9. I.e., of hell.

grade, were by neval usage messmates of the master-at-arms, men with ears convenient to his confidential tongue.

But the general popularity that came from our Handsome Sailor's manly forwardness upon occasion and irresistible good nature, indicating no mental superiority tending to excite an invidious feeling, this good will on the part of most of his shipmates made him the less to concern himself about such mute aspects toward him as those whereto allusion has just been made, aspects he could not so fathom as to infer their whole import.

As to the afterguardsman, though Billy for reasons already given necessarily saw little of him, yet when the two did happen to meet, invariably came the fellow's offhand cheerful recognition, sometimes accompanied by a passing pleasant word or two. Whatever that equivocal young person's original design may really have been, or the design of which he might have been the deputy, certain it was from his manner upon these occasions that he had wholly dropped it.

It was as if his precocity of crookedness (and every vulgar villain is precocious) had for once deceived him, and the man he had sought to entrap as a simpleton had through his very simplicity ignominiously baffled him.

But shrewd ones may opine that it was hardly possible for Billy to refrain from going up to the afterguardsman and bluntly demanding to know his purpose in the initial interview so abruptly closed in the forechains. Shrewd ones may also think it but natural in Billy to set about sounding some of the other impressed men of the ship in order to discover what basis, if any, there was for the emissary's obscure suggestions as to plotting disaffection aboard. Yes, shrewd ones may so think. But something more, or rather something else than mere shrewdness is perhaps needful for the due understanding of such a character as Billy Budd's.

As to Claggart, the monomania in the man—if that indeed it were—as involuntarily disclosed by starts in the manifestations detailed, yet in general covered over by his self-contained and rational demeanor; this, like a subterranean fire, was eating its way deeper and deeper in him. Something decisive must come of it.

18

After the mysterious interview in the forechains, the one so abruptly ended there by Billy, nothing especially germane to the story occurred until the events now about to be narrated.

Elsewhere it has been said that in the lack of frigates (of course better sailers than line-of-battle ships) in the English squadron up the Straits at that period, the *Bellipotent* 74 was occasionally employed not only as an available substitute for a scout, but at times on detached service of more important kind. This was not alone because of her sailing qualities, not common in a ship of her rate[1], but quite as much, probably, that the character of her commander, it was thought, specially adapted him for any duty where under unforeseen difficulties a prompt initiative might have to be taken in some matter demanding knowledge and ability in addition to those qualities implied in good seamanship. It was on an expedition of the latter sort, a somewhat distant one, and when the *Bellipotent* was almost at her furthest remove from the fleet, that in the latter part of an afternoon watch she unexpectedly came in sight of a ship of the enemy. It proved to be a frigate. The latter, perceiving through the glass that the weight of men and metal would be heavily against her, invoking her light heels crowded sail to get away. After a chase urged almost against hope and lasting until about the middle of the first dogwatch, she signally succeeded in effecting her escape.

Not long after the pursuit had been given up, and ere the excitement incident thereto had altogether waned away, the master-at-arms, ascending from his cavernous sphere, made his appearance cap in hand by the mainmast respectfully waiting the notice of Captain Vere, then solitary walking the weather side of the quarter-deck, doubtless somewhat chafed at the failure of the pursuit. The spot where Claggart stood was the place allotted to men of less grades seeking some more particular interview either with the officer of the deck or the captain himself. But from the latter it was not often that a sailor or petty officer of those days would seek a hearing; only some exceptional cause would, according to established custom, have warranted that.

Presently, just as the commander, absorbed in his reflections, was on the point of turning aft in his promenade, he became sensible of Claggart's presence, and saw the doffed cap held in deferential expectancy. Here be it said that Captain Vere's personal knowledge of his petty officer had only begun at the time of the ship's last sailing from home, Claggart then for the first, in transfer from a ship detained for repairs, supplying on board the *Bellipotent* the place of a previous master-at-arms disabled and ashore.

No sooner did the commander observe who it was that now deferentially stood awaiting his notice than a peculiar expression came over him. It was not unlike that which uncontrollably will flit across the countenance of one at unawares encountering a person who, though known to him indeed, has hardly been long enough known for thorough knowledge, but something in whose aspect nevertheless now for the first provokes a vaguely repellent distaste. But coming to

---

1. Classification.

a stand and resuming much of his wonted official manner, save that a sort of impatience lurked in the intonation of the opening word, he said 'Well? What is it, Master-at-arms?'

With the air of a subordinate grieved at the necessity of being a messenger of ill tidings, and while conscientiously determined to be frank yet equally resolved upon shunning overstatement, Claggart at this invitation, or rather summons to disburden, spoke up. What he said, conveyed in the language of no uneducated man, was to the effect following, if not altogether in these words, namely, that during the chase and preparations for the possible encounter he had seen enough to convince him that at least one sailor aboard was a dangerous character in a ship mustering some who not only had taken a guilty part in the late serious troubles, but others also who, like the man in question, had entered His Majesty's service under another form than enlistment.

At this point Captain Vere with some impatience interrupted him: 'Be direct, man; say *impressed men.*'

Claggart made a gesture of subservience, and proceeded. Quite lately he (Claggart) had begun to suspect that on the gun decks some sort of movement prompted by the sailor in question was covertly going on, but he had not thought himself warranted in reporting the suspicion so long as it remained indistinct. But from what he had that afternoon observed in the man referred to, the suspicion of something clandestine going on had advanced to a point less removed from certainty. He deeply felt, he added, the serious responsibility assumed in making a report involving such possible consequences to the individual mainly concerned, besides tending to augment those natural anxieties which every naval commander must feel in view of extraordinary outbreaks so recent as those which, he sorrowfully said it, it needed not to name.

Now at the first broaching of the matter Captain Vere, taken by surprise, could not wholly dissemble his disquietude. But as Claggart went on, the former's aspect changed into restiveness under something in the testifier's manner in giving his testimony. However, he refrained from interrupting him. And Claggart, continuing, concluded with this: 'God forbid, your honor, that the *Bellipotent's* should be the experience of the—'

'Never mind that!' here peremptorily broke in the superior, his face altering with anger, instinctively divining the ship that the other was about to name, one in which the Nore Mutiny had assumed a singularly tragical character that for a time jeopardized the life of its commander. Under the circumstances he was indignant at the purposed allusion. When the commissioned officers themselves were on all occasions very heedful how they referred to the recent events in the fleet, for a petty officer unnecessarily to allude to them in the presence of his captain, this struck him as a most immodest presumption. Besides, to his quick sense of self-respect it even looked under the circumstances something like an attempt to alarm him. Nor at first was he without some surprise that one who so far as he had hitherto come under his notice had shown considerable tact in his function should in this particular evince such lack of it.

But these thoughts and kindred dubious ones flitting across his mind were suddenly replaced by an intuitional surmise which, though as yet obscure in form, served practically to affect his reception of the ill tidings. Certain it is that, long versed in everything pertaining to the complicated gun-deck life, which like every other form of life has its secret mines and dubious side, the side popularly disclaimed, Captain Vere did not permit himself to be unduly disturbed by the general tenor of his subordinate's report.

Furthermore, if in view of recent events prompt action should be taken at the first palpable sign of recurring insubordination, for all that, not judicious would it be, he thought, to keep the idea of lingering disaffection alive by undue forwardness in crediting an informer, even if his own subordinate and charged among other things with police surveillance of the crew. This feeling would not perhaps have so prevailed with him were it not that upon a prior occasion the patriotic zeal officially evinced by Claggart had somewhat irritated him as appearing rather supersensible and strained. Furthermore something even in the official's self-possessed and somewhat ostentatious manner in making his specifications strangely reminded him of a bandsman, a perjurous witness in a capital case before a court-martial ashore of which when a lieutenant he (Captain Vere) had been a member.

Now the peremptory check given to Claggart in the matter of the arrested allusion was quickly followed up by this: 'You say that there is at least one dangerous man aboard. Name him.'

'William Budd, a foretopman, your honor.'

'William Budd!' repeated Captain Vere with unfeigned astonishment. 'And mean you the man that Lieutenant Ratcliffe took from the merchantman not very long ago, the young fellow who seems to be so popular with the men—Billy the Handsome Sailor, as they call him?'

'The same your honor; but for all his youth and good looks, a deep one. Not for nothing does he insinuate himself into the good will of his shipmates, since at the least they will at a pinch say—all hands will—a good word for him, and at all hazards. Did Lieutenant Ratcliffe happen to tell your honor of that adroit fling of Budd's, jumping up in the cutter's bow under the merchantman's stern when he was being taken off? It is even masked by that sort of good-humored air that at heart he resents his impressment. You have but noted his fair cheek. A mantrap may be under the ruddy-tipped daisies.'

Now the Handsome Sailor as a signal figure among the crew had naturally enough attracted the captain's attention from the first. Though in general not very demonstrative to his officers, he had congratulated Lieutenant Ratcliffe upon his good fortune in lighting on such a fine specimen of the *genus homo*, who in the nude might have posed for a statue of a young Adam before the Fall. As to Billy's adieu to the ship *Rights-of-Man*, which the boarding lieutenant had indeed reported to him, but, in a deferential way, more as a good story than aught else, Captain Vere, though mistakenly understanding it as a satiric sally, had but thought so much the better of the impressed man for it; as a military sailor, admiring the spirit that could take an arbitrary enlistment so merrily and sensibly. The foretopman's conduct, too, so far as it had fallen under the captain's notice, had confirmed the first happy augury, while the new recruit's qualities as a 'sailor-man' seemed to be such that he had thought of recommending him to the executive officer for promotion to a place that would more frequently bring him under his own observation, namely, the captaincy of the mizzentop, replacing there in the starboard watch a man not so young whom partly for that reason he deemed less fitted for the post. Be it parenthesized here that since the mizzentopmen have not to handle such breadths of heavy canvas as the lower sails on the mainmast and foremast, a young man if of the right stuff not only seems best adapted to duty there, but in fact is generally selected for the captaincy of that top, and the company under him are light hands and often but striplings. In sum, Captain Vere had from the beginning deemed Billy Budd to be what in the naval parlance of the time was called a 'King's bargain': that is to say, for His Britannic Majesty's navy a capital investment at small outlay or none at all.

After a brief pause, during which the reminiscences above mentioned passed vividly through his mind and he weighed the import of Claggart's last suggestion conveyed in the phrase 'mantrap under the daisies,' and the more he weighed it the less reliance he felt in the informer's good faith, suddenly he turned upon him and in a low voice demanded: 'Do you come to me, Master-at-arms, with so foggy a tale? As to Budd, cite me an act or spoken word of his confirmatory of what you in general charge against him. Stay,' drawing nearer to him; 'heed what you speak. Just now, and in a case like this, there is a yardarm-end for the false witness.'

'Ah, your honor!' sighed Claggart, mildly shaking his shapely head as in sad deprecation of such unmerited severity of tone. Then, bridling—erecting himself as in virtuous self-assertion—he circumstantially alleged certain words and acts which collectively, if credited, led to presumptions morally inculpating Budd. And for some of these averments, he added, substantiating proof was not far.

With gray eyes impatient and distrustful essaying to fathom to the bottom Claggart's calm violet ones, Captain Vere again heard him out; then for the moment stood ruminating. The mood he evinced, Claggart—himself for the time liberated from the other's scrutiny—steadily regarded with a look difficult to render: a look curious of the operation of his tactics, a look such as might have been that of the spokesman of the envious children of Jacob deceptively imposing upon the troubled patriarch the blood-dyed coat of young Joseph.[2]

Though something exceptional in the moral quality of Captain Vere made him, in earnest encounter with a fellow man, a veritable touchstone of that man's essential nature, yet now as to Claggart and what was really going on in him his feeling partook less of intuitional conviction than of strong suspicion clogged by strange dubieties. The perplexity he evinced proceeded less from aught touching the man informed against—as Claggart doubtless opined—than from considerations how best to act in regard to the informer. At first, indeed, he was naturally for summoning that substantiation of his allegations which Claggart said was at hand. But such a proceeding would result in the matter at once getting abroad, which in the present stage of it, he thought, might undesirably affect the ship's company. If Claggart was a false witness—that closed the affair. And therefore, before trying the accusation, he would first practically test the accuser; and he thought this could be done in a quiet, undemonstrative way.

The measure he determined upon involved a shifting of the scene, a transfer to a place less exposed to observation than the broad quarterdeck. For although the few gunroom officers there at the time had, in due observance of naval etiquette, withdrawn to leeward the moment Captain Vere had begun his promenade on the deck's weather side; and though during the colloquy with Claggart they of course ventured not to diminish the distance; and though throughout the interview Captain Vere's voice was far from him, and Claggart's silvery and low; and the wind in the cordage and the wash of the sea helped the more to put them beyond earshot; nevertheless, the interview's continuance already had attracted observation from some topmen aloft and other sailors in the waist or further forward.

Having determined upon his measures, Captain Vere forthwith took action. Abruptly turning to Claggart, he asked, 'Master-at-arms, is it now Budd's watch aloft?'

'No, your honor.'

---

2. Genesis 37:31–32: "And they took Joseph's coat, and killed a kid of the goats, and dipped the coat in the blood; and they sent the coat of many colours, and they brought it to their father; and said, This have we found: know now whether it be thy son's coat or no."

Whereupon, 'Mr Wilkes!' summoning the nearest midshipman. 'Tell Albert to come to me.' Albert was the captain's hammock-boy, a sort of sea valet in whose discretion and fidelity his master had much confidence. The lad appeared.

'You know Budd, the foretopman?'

'I do, sir.'

'Go find him. It is his watch off. Manage to tell him out of earshot that he is wanted aft. Contrive it that he speaks to nobody. Keep him in talk yourself. And not till you get well aft here, not till then let him know that the place where he is wanted is my cabin. You understand. Go.—Master-at-arms, show yourself on the decks below, and when you think it time for Albert to be coming with his man, stand by quietly to follow the sailor in.'

19

Now when the foretopman found himself in the cabin, closeted there, as it were, with the captain and Claggart, he was surprised enough. But it was a surprise unaccompanied by apprehension or distrust. To an immature nature essentially honest and humane, forewarning intimations of subtler danger from one's kind come tardily if at all. The only thing that took shape in the young sailor's mind was this: Yes, the captain, I have always thought, looks kindly upon me. Wonder if he's going to make me his coxswain. I should like that. And may be now he is going to ask the master-at-arms about me.

'Shut the door there, sentry,' said the commander; 'stand without, and let nobody come in.—Now, Master-at-arms, tell this man to his face what you told of him to me,' and stood prepared to scrutinize the mutually confronting visages.

With the measured step and calm collected air of an asylum physician approaching in the public hall some patient beginning to show indications of a coming paroxysm, Claggart deliberately advanced within short range of Billy and, mesmerically looking him in the eye, briefly recapitulated the accusation.

Not at first did Billy take it in. When he did, the rose-tan of his cheek looked struck as by white leprosy. He stood like one impaled and gagged. Meanwhile the accuser's eyes, removing not as yet from the blue dilated ones, underwent a phenomenal change, their wonted rich violet color blurring into a muddy purple. Those lights of human intelligence, losing human expression, were gelidly protruding like the alien eyes of certain uncatalogued creatures of the deep. The first mesmeristic glance was one of serpent fascination; the last was the paralyzing lurch of the torpedo fish.

'Speak, man!' said Captain Vere to the transfixed one, struck by his aspect even more than by Claggart's. 'Speak! Defend yourself!' Which appeal caused but a strange dumb gesturing and gurgling in Billy; amazement at such an accusation so suddenly sprung on inexperienced nonage; this, and, it may be, horror of the accuser's eyes, serving to bring out his lurking defect and in this instance for the time intensifying it into a convulsed tongue-tie; while the intent head and entire form straining forward in an agony of ineffectual eagerness to obey the injunction to speak and defend himself, gave an expression to the face like that of a condemned vestal priestess in the moment of being buried alive, and in the first struggle against suffocation.[3]

Though at the time Captain Vere was quite ignorant of Billy's liability to vocal impediment, he now immediately divined it, since vividly Billy's aspect recalled to him that of a bright young schoolmate of his whom he had once seen struck by much the same startling impotence in the act of eagerly rising in the class to be foremost in response to a testing question put to it by the master. Going close up to the young sailor, and laying a soothing hand on his shoulder, he said, 'There is no hurry, my boy. Take your time, take your time.' Contrary to the effect intended, these words so fatherly in tone, doubtless touching Billy's heart to the quick, prompted yet more violent efforts at utterance—efforts soon ending for the time in confirming the paralysis, and bringing to his face an expression which was as a crucifixion to behold. The next instant, quick as the flame from a discharged cannon at night, his right arm shot out, and Claggart dropped to the deck. Whether intentionally or but owing to the young athlete's superior height, the blow had taken effect full upon the forehead, so shapely and intellectual-looking a feature in the master-at-arms; so that the body fell over lengthwise, like a heavy plank tilted from erectness. A gasp or two, and he lay motionless.

'Fated boy,' breathed Captain Vere in tone so low as to be almost a whisper, 'what have you done! But here, help me.'

The twain raised the felled one from the loins up into a sitting position. The spare form flexibly acquiesced, but inertly. It was like handling a dead snake. They lowered it back. Regaining erectness, Captain Vere with one hand covering his face stood to all appearance as impassive as the object at his feet. Was he absorbed in taking in all the bearings of the event and what was best not only now at once to be done, but also in the sequel? Slowly he uncovered his face; and the effect was as if the moon emerging from eclipse should reappear with quite another aspect than that which had gone into hiding. The father in him, manifested towards Billy thus far in the

---

3. Vestal virgins in Rome were buried alive if they violated their vows.

scene, was replaced by the military disciplinarian. In his offical tone
he bade the foretopman retire to a stateroom aft (pointing it out), and
there remain till thence summoned. This order Billy in silence
mechanically obeyed. Then going to the cabin door where it opened
on the quarter-deck, Captain Vere said to the sentry without, 'Tell
somebody to send Albert here.' When the lad appeared, his master
so contrived it that he should not catch sight of the prone one. 'Albert,'
he said to him, 'tell the surgeon I wish to see him. You need not
come back till called.'

When the surgeon entered—a self-poised character of that grave
sense and experience that hardly anything could take him aback—
Captain Vere advanced to meet him, thus unconsciously intercepting his view of Claggart, and interrupting the other's wonted ceremonious salutation, said, 'Nay. Tell me how it is with yonder man,'
directing his attention to the prostrate one.

The surgeon looked, and for all his self-command somewhat started
at the abrupt revelation. On Claggart's always pallid complexion,
thick black blood was now oozing from nostril and ear. To the gaz-
er's professional eye it was unmistakably no living man that he saw.

'Is it so, then?' said Captain Vere, intently watching him. 'I thought
it. But verify it.' Whereupon the customary tests confirmed the surgeon's first glance, who now, looking up in unfeigned concern, cast
a look of intense inquisitiveness upon his superior. But Captain Vere,
with one hand to his brow, was standing motionless. Suddenly,
catching the surgeon's arm convulsively, he exclaimed, pointing down
to the body, 'It is the divine judgment on Ananias![4] Look!'

Disturbed by the excited manner he had never before observed in
the *Bellipotent*'s captain, and as yet wholly ignorant of the affair, the
prudent surgeon nevertheless held his peace, only again looking an
earnest interrogatory as to what it was that had resulted in such a
tragedy.

But Captain Vere was now again motionless, standing absorbed in
thought. Again starting, he vehemently exclaimed, 'Struck dead by
an angel of God! Yet the angel must hang!'

At these passionate interjections, mere incoherences to the listener as yet unapprised of the antecedents, the surgeon was profoundly discomposed. But now, as recollecting himself, Captain Vere
in less passionate tone briefly related the circumstances leading up
to the event. But come; we must dispatch,' he added. 'Help me to
remove him' (meaning the body) 'to yonder compartment,' designating one opposite that where the foretopman remained immured. Anew
disturbed by a request that, as implying a desire for secrecy, seemed

4. Acts 5:3–5: "Peter said, Ananias . . . thou has not lied unto men, but unto God. And Ananias
hearing these words fell down, and gave up the ghost."

unaccountably strange to him, there was nothing for the subordinate to do but comply.

'Go now,' said Captain Vere with something of his wonted manner. 'Go now. I presently shall call a drumhead court.[5] Tell the lieutenants what has happened, and tell Mr Mordant' (meaning the captain of marines), 'and charge them to keep the matter to themselves.'

20

Full of disquietude and misgiving, the surgeon left the cabin. Was Captain Vere suddenly affected in his mind, or was it but a transient excitement, brought about by so strange and extraordinary a tragedy? As to the drumhead court, it struck the surgeon as impolitic, if nothing more. The thing to do, he thought, was to place Billy Budd in confinement, and in a way dictated by usage, and postpone further action in so extraordinary a case to such time as they should rejoin the squadron, and then refer it to the admiral. He recalled the unwonted agitation of Captain Vere and his excited exclamations, so at variance with his normal manner. Was he unhinged?

But assuming that he is, it is not so susceptible of proof. What then can the surgeon do? No more trying situation is conceivable than that of an officer subordinate under a captain whom he suspects to be not mad, indeed, but yet not quite unaffected in his intellects. To argue his order to him would be insolence. To resist him would be mutiny.

In obedience to Captain Vere, he communicated what had happened to the lieutenants and captain of marines, saying nothing as to the captain's state. They fully shared his own surprise and concern. Like him too, they seemed to think that such a matter should be referred to the admiral.

21

Who in the rainbow can draw the line where the violet tint ends and the orange tint begins? Distinctly we see the difference of the colors, but where exactly does the one first blendingly enter into the other? So with sanity and insanity. In pronounced cases there is no question about them. But in some supposed cases, in various degrees supposedly less pronounced, to draw the exact line of demarcation few will undertake, though for a fee becoming considerate some

---

5. A court-martial, originally held around an upturned drum, to try offences committed during military operations.

professional experts will. There is nothing nameable but that some men will, or undertake to, do it for pay.

Whether Captain Vere, as the surgeon professionally and privately surmised, was really the sudden victim of any degree of aberration, every one must determine for himself by such light as this narrative may afford.

That the unhappy event which has been narrated could not have happened at a worse juncture was but too true. For it was close on the heel of the suppressed insurrections, an aftertime very critical to naval authority, demanding from every English sea commander two qualities not readily interfusable—prudence and rigor. Moreover, there was something crucial in the case.

In the jugglery of circumstances preceding and attending the event on board the *Bellipotent*, and in the light of that martial code whereby it was formally to be judged, innocence and guilt personified in Claggart and Budd in effect changed places. In a legal view the apparent victim of the tragedy was he who had sought to victimize a man blameless; and the indisputable deed of the latter, navally regarded, constituted the most heinous of military crimes. Yet more. The essential right and wrong involved in the matter, the clearer that might be, so much the worse for the responsibility of a loyal sea commander, inasmuch as he was not authorized to determine the matter on that primitive basis.

Small wonder then that the *Bellipotent*'s captain, though in general a man of rapid decision, felt that circumspectness not less than promptitude was necessary. Until he could decide upon his course, and in each detail; and not only so, but until the concluding measure was upon the point of being enacted, he deemed it advisable, in view of all the circumstances, to guard as much as possible against publicity. Here he may or may not have erred. Certain it is, however, that subsequently in the confidential talk of more than one or two gun rooms and cabins he was not a little criticized by some officers, a fact imputed by his friends and vehemently by his cousin Jack Denton to professional jealousy of Starry Vere. Some imaginative ground for invidious comment there was. The maintenance of secrecy in the matter, the confining all knowledge of it for a time to the place where the homicide occurred, the quarter-deck cabin; in these particulars lurked some resemblance to the policy adopted in those tragedies of the palace which have occurred more than once in the capital founded by Peter the Barbarian.[6]

The case indeed was such that fain would the *Bellipotent*'s captain have deferred taking any action whatever respecting it further than to keep the foretopman a close prisoner till the ship rejoined the

6. St. Petersburg (now Leningrad), founded by Peter the Great in 1703.

squadron and then submitting the matter to the judgment of his admiral.

But a true military officer is in one particular like a true monk. Not with more of self-abnegation will the latter keep his vows of monastic obedience than the former his vows of allegiance to martial duty.

Feeling that unless quick action was taken on it, the deed of the foretopman, so soon as it should be known on the gun decks, would tend to awaken any slumbering embers of the Nore among the crew, a sense of the urgency of the case overruled in Captain Vere every other consideration. But though a conscientious disciplinarian, he was no lover of authority for mere authority's sake. Very far was he from embracing opportunities for monopolizing to himself the perils of moral responsibility, none at least that could properly be referred to an official superior or shared with him by his official equals or even subordinates. So thinking, he was glad it would not be at variance with usage to turn the matter over to a summary court of his own officers, reserving to himself, as the one on whom the ultimate accountability would rest, the right of maintaining a supervision of it, or formally or informally interposing at need. Accordingly a drumhead court was summarily convened, he electing the individuals composing it: the first lieutenant, the captain of marines, and the sailing master.

In associating an officer of marines with the sea lieutenant and the sailing master in a case having to do with a sailor, the commander perhaps deviated from general custom. He was prompted thereto by the circumstance that he took that soldier to be a judicious person, thoughtful, and not altogether incapable of grappling with a difficult case unprecedented in his prior experience. Yet even as to him he was not without some latent misgiving, for withal he was an extremely good-natured man, an enjoyer of his dinner, a sound sleeper, and inclined to obesity—a man who though he would always maintain his manhood in battle might not prove altogether reliable in a moral dilemma involving aught of the tragic. As to the first lieutenant and the sailing master, Captain Vere could not but be aware that though honest natures, of approved gallantry upon occasion, their intelligence was mostly confined to the matter of active seamanship and the fighting demands of their profession.

The court was held in the same cabin where the unfortunate affair had taken place. This cabin, the commander's, embraced the entire area under the poop deck. Aft, and on either side, was a small stateroom, the one now temporarily a jail and the other a dead-house, and a yet smaller compartment, leaving a space between expanding forward into a goodly oblong of length coinciding with the ship's beam. A skylight of moderate dimension was overhead, and at each end of the oblong space were two sashed porthole windows easily convertible back into embrasures for short carronades.[7]

All being quickly in readiness, Billy Budd was arraigned, Captain Vere necessarily appearing as the sole witness in the case, and as such temporarily sinking his rank, though singularly maintaining it in a matter apparently trivial, namely, that he testified from the ship's weather side, with that object having caused the court to sit on the lee side. Concisely he narrated all that had led up to the catastrophe, omitting nothing in Claggart's accusation and deposing as to the manner in which the prisoner had received it. At this testimony the three officers glanced with no little surprise at Billy Budd, the last man they would have suspected either of the mutinous design alleged by Claggart or the undeniable deed he himself had done. The first lieutenant, taking judicial primacy and turning toward the prisoner, said, 'Captain Vere has spoken. Is it or is it not as Captain Vere says?'

In response came syllables not so much impeded in the utterance as might have been anticipated. They were these: 'Captain Vere tells the truth. It is just as Captain Vere says, but it is not as the master-at-arms said. I have eaten the King's bread and I am true to the King.'

'I believe you, my man,' said the witness, his voice indicating a suppressed emotion not otherwise betrayed.

'God will bless you for that, your honor!' not without stammering said Billy, and all but broke down. But immediately he was recalled to self-control by another question, to which with the same emotional difficulty of utterance he said, 'No, there was no malice between us. I never bore malice against the master-at-arms. I am sorry that he is dead. I did not mean to kill him. Could I have used my tongue I would not have struck him. But he foully lied to my face and in presence of my captain, and I had to say something, and I could only say it with a blow, God help me!'

In the impulsive aboveboard manner of the frank one the court saw confirmed all that was implied in words that just previously had perplexed them, coming as they did from the testifier to the tragedy and promptly following Billy's impassioned disclaimer of mutinous intent—Captain Vere's words, 'I believe you, my man.'

Next it was asked of him whether he knew of or suspected aught savoring of incipient trouble (meaning mutiny, though the explicit term was avoided) going on in any section of the ship's company.

The reply lingered. This was naturally imputed by the court to the same vocal embarrassment which had retarded or obstructed previous answers. But in main it was otherwise here, the question immediately recalling to Billy's mind the interview with the after-

7. Large pieces of artillery.

guardsman in the forechains. But an innate repugnance to playing a part at all approaching that of an informer against one's own shipmates—the same erring sense of uninstructed honor which had stood in the way of his reporting the matter at the time, though as a loyal man-of-war's man it was incumbent on him, and failure so to do, if charged against him and proven, would have subjected him to the heaviest of penalties; this, with the blind feeling now his that nothing really was being hatched, prevailed with him. When the answer came it was a negative.

'One question more,' said the officer of marines, now first speaking and with a troubled earnestness. 'You tell us that what the master-at-arms said against you was a lie. Now why should he have so lied, so maliciously lied, since you declare there was no malice between you?'

At that question, unintentionally touching on a spiritual sphere wholly obscure to Billy's thoughts, he was nonplussed, evincing a confusion indeed that some observers, such as can readily be imagined, would have construed into involuntary evidence of hidden guilt. Nevertheless, he strove some way to answer, but all at once relinquished the vain endeavor, at the same time turning an appealing glance towards Captain Vere as deeming him his best helper and friend. Captain Vere, who had been seated for a time, rose to his feet, addressing the interrogator. 'The question you put to him comes naturally enough. But how can he rightly answer it?—or anybody else, unless indeed it be he who lies within there,' designating the compartment where lay the corpse. 'But the prone one there will not rise to our summons. In effect, though, as it seems to me, the point you make is hardly material. Quite aside from any conceivable motive actuating the master-at-arms, and irrespective of the provocation to the blow, a martial court must needs in the provocation to the blow, a martial court must needs in the present case confine its attention to the blow's consequence, which consequence justly is to be deemed not otherwise than as the striker's deed.'

This utterance, the full significance of which it was not at all likely that Billy took in, nevertheless caused him to turn a wistful interrogative look toward the speaker, a look in its dumb expressiveness not unlike that which a dog of generous breed might turn upon his master, seeking in his face some elucidation of a previous gesture ambiguous to the canine intelligence. Nor was the same utterance without marked effect upon the three officers, more especially the soldier. Couched in it seemed to them a meaning unanticipated, involving a prejudgment on the speaker's part. It served to augment a mental disturbance previously evident enough.

The soldier once more spoke, in a tone of suggestive dubiety addressing at once his associates and Captain Vere: 'Nobody is present—none of the ship's company, I mean—who might shed lateral light, if any is to be had, upon what remains mysterious in this matter.'

'That is thoughtfully put,' said Captain Vere; 'I see your drift. Ay, there is a mystery; but, to use a scriptural phrase, it is a "mystery of iniquity," a matter for psychologic theologians to discuss. But what has a military court to do with it? Not to add that for us any possible investigation of it is cut off by the lasting tongue-tie of—him—in yonder,' again designating the mortuary stateroom. 'The prisoner's deed—with that alone we have to do.'

To this, and particularly the closing reiteration, the marine soldier, knowing not how aptly to reply, sadly abstained from saying aught. The first lieutenant, who at the outset had not unnaturally assumed primacy in the court, now overrulingly instructed by a glance from Captain Vere, a glance more effective than words, resumed that primacy. Turning to the prisoner, 'Budd,' he said, and scarce in equable tones, 'Budd, if you have aught further to say for yourself, say it now.'

Upon this the young sailor turned another quick glance toward Captain Vere; then, as taking a hint from that aspect, a hint confirming his own instinct that silence was now best, replied to the lieutenant, 'I have said all, sir.'

The marine—the same who had been the sentinel without the cabin door at the time that the foretopman, followed by the master-at-arms, entered it—he, standing by the sailor throughout these judicial proceedings was now directed to take him back to the after compartment originally assigned to the prisoner and his custodian. As the twain disappeared from view, the three officers, as partially liberated from some inward constraint associated with Billy's mere presence, simultaneously stirred in their seats. They exchanged looks of troubled indecision, yet feeling that decide they must and without long delay. For Captain Vere, he for the time stood—unconsciously with his back toward them, apparently in one of his absent fits—gazing out from a sashed porthole to windward upon the monotonous blank of the twilight sea. But the court's silence continuing, broken only at moments by brief consultations, in low earnest tones, this served to arouse him and energize him. Turning, he to-and-fro paced the cabin athwart; in the returning ascent to windward climbing the slant deck in the ship's lee roll, without knowing it symbolizing thus in his action a mind resolute to surmount difficulties even if against primitive instincts strong as the wind and the sea. Presently he came to a stand before the three. After scanning their faces he stood less as mustering his thoughts for expression than as one inly deliberating how best to put them to well-meaning men not intellectually mature, men with whom it was necessary to demonstrate certain principles that were axioms to himself. Similar impatience as to talking is perhaps one reason that deters some minds from addressing any popular assemblies.

When speak he did, something, both in the substance of what he said and his manner of saying it, showed the influence of unshared studies modifying and tempering the practical training of an active career. This, along with his phraseology, now and then was suggestive of the grounds whereon rested that imputation of a certain pedantry socially alleged against him by certain naval men of wholly practical cast, captains who nevertheless would frankly concede that His Majesty's navy mustered no more efficient officer of their grade than Starry Vere.

What he said was to this effect: 'Hitherto I have been but the witness, little more; and I should hardly think now to take another tone, that of your coadjutor for the time, did I not perceive in you— at the crisis too—a troubled hesitancy, proceeding, I doubt not, from the clash of military duty with moral scruple—scruple vitalized by compassion. For the compassion, how can I otherwise than share it? But, mindful of paramount obligations, I strive against scruples that may tend to enervate decision. Not, gentlemen, that I hide from myself that the case is an exceptional one. Speculatively regarded, it well might be referred to a jury of casuists. But for us here, acting not as casuists or moralists, it is a case practical, and under martial law practically to be dealt with.

'But your scruples: do they move as in a dusk? Challenge them. Make them advance and declare themselves. Come now; do they import something like this: If, mindless of palliating circumstances, we are bound to regard the death of the master-at-arms as the prisoner's deed, then does that deed constitute a capital crime whereof the penalty is a mortal one. But in natural justice is nothing but the prisoner's overt act to be considered? How can we adjudge to summary and shameful death a fellow creature innocent before God, and whom we feel to be so?—Does that state it aright? You sign sad assent. Well, I too feel that, the full force of that. It is Nature. But do these buttons that we wear attest that our allegiance is to Nature? No, to the King. Though the ocean, which is inviolate Nature primeval, though this be the element where we move and have our being as sailors, yet as the King's officers lies our duty in a sphere correspondingly natural? So little is that true, that in receiving our commissions we in the most important regards ceased to be natural free agents. When war is declared are we the commissioned fighters previously consulted? We fight at command. If our judgments approve the war, that is but coincidence. So in other particulars. So now. For suppose condemnation to follow these present proceedings. Would it be so much we ourselves that would condemn as it would be martial law operating through us? For that law and the rigor of it, we are not responsibile. Our vowed responsibility is in this: That however pitilessly that law may operate in any instances, we nevertheless adhere to it and administer it.

'But the exceptional in the matter moves the hearts within you. Even so too is mine moved. But let not warm hearts betray heads that should be cool. Ashore in a criminal case, will an upright judge allow himself off the bench to be waylaid by some tender kinswoman of the accused seeking to touch him with her tearful plea? Well, the heart here, sometimes the feminine in man, is as that piteous woman, and hard though it be, she must here be ruled out.'

He paused, earnestly studying them for a moment; then resumed.

'But something in your aspect seems to urge that it is not solely the heart that moves in you, but also the conscience, the private conscience. But tell me whether or not occupying the position we do, private conscience should not yield to that imperial one formulated in the code under which alone we officially proceed?'

Here the three men moved in their seats, less convinced than agitated by the course of an argument troubling but the more the spontaneous conflict within.

Perceiving which, the speaker paused for a moment; then abruptly changing his tone, went on.

'To steady us a bit, let us recur to the facts.—In wartime at sea a man-of-war's man strikes his superior in grade, and the blow kills. Apart from its effect the blow itself is, according to the Articles of War, a capital crime. Furthermore—'

'Ay, sir,' emotionally broke in the officer of marines, 'in one sense it was. But surely Budd proposed neither mutiny nor homicide.'

'Surely not, my good man. And before a court less arbitrary and more merciful than a martial one, that plea would largely extenuate. At the Last Assizes it shall acquit. But how here? We proceed under the law of the Mutiny Act.[8] In feature no child can resemble his father more than that Act resembles in spirit the thing from which it derives—War. In His Majesty's service—in this ship, indeed—there are Englishmen forced to fight for the King against their will. Against their conscience, for aught we know. Though as their fellow creatures some of us may appreciate their position, yet as navy officers what reck we of it? Still less recks the enemy. Our impressed men he would fain cut down in the same swath with our volunteers. As regards the enemy's naval conscripts, some of whom may even share our own abhorrence of the regicidal French Directory, it is the same on our side. War looks but to the frontage, the appearance. And the

---

8. The Mutiny Act, first passed in 1689, and its successors applied only to the army; the navy followed the King's Regulations and Admiralty Instructions of 1772. *Assizes:* the highest courts of appeal in Great Britain; Melville refers here to the Last Judgment.

Mutiny Act, War's child, takes after the father. Budd's intent or non-intent is nothing to the purpose.

'But while, put to it by those anxieties in you which I cannot but respect, I only repeat myself—while thus strangely we prolong proceedings that should be summary—the enemy may be sighted and an engagement result. We must do; and one of two things must we do—condemn or let go.'

'Can we not convict and yet mitigate the penalty?' asked the sailing master, here speaking, and falteringly, for the first.

'Gentlemen, were that clearly lawful for us under the circumstances, consider the consequences of such clemency. The people' (meaning the ship's company) 'have native sense; most of them are familiar with our naval usage and tradition; and how would they take it? Even could you explain to them—which our official position forbids—they, long molded by arbitrary discipline, have not that kind of intelligent responsiveness that might qualify them to comprehend and discriminate. No, to the people the foretopman's deed, however it be worded in the announcement, will be plain homicide committed in a flagrant act of mutiny. What penalty for that should follow, they know. But it does not follow. Why? they will ruminate. You know what sailors are. Will they not revert to the recent outbreak at the Nore? Ay. They know the well-founded alarm—the panic it struck throughout England. Your clement sentence they would account pusillanimous. They would think that we flinch, that we are afraid of them—afraid of practicing a lawful rigor singularly demanded at this juncture, lest it should provoke new troubles. What shame to us such a conjecture on their part, and how deadly to discipline. You see then, whither, prompted by duty and the law, I steadfastly drive. But I beseech you, my friends, do not take me amiss. I feel as you do for this unfortunate boy. But did he know our hearts, I take him to be of that generous nature that he would feel even for us on whom in this military necessity so heavy a compulsion is laid.'

With that, crossing the deck he resumed his place by the sashed porthole, tacitly leaving the three to come to a decision. On the cabin's opposite side the troubled court sat silent. Loyal lieges, plain and practical, though at bottom they dissented from some points Captain Vere had put to them, they were without the faculty, hardly had the inclination, to gainsay one whom they felt to be an earnest man, one too not less their superior in mind than in naval rank. But it is not improbable that even such of his words as were not without influence over them, less came home to them than his closing appeal to their instinct as sea officers: in the forethought he threw out as to the practical consequences to discipline, considering the unconfirmed tone of the fleet at the time, should a man-of-war's man's violent killing at sea of a superior in grade be allowed to pass for aught else than a capital crime demanding prompt infliction of the penalty.

Not unlikely they were brought to something more or less akin to that harassed frame of mind which in the year 1842 actuated the commander of the U.S. brig-of-war *Somers* to resolve, under the so-called Articles of War, Articles modeled upon the English Mutiny Act, to resolve upon the execution at sea of a midshipman and two sailors as mutineers designing the seizure of the brig.[9] Which resolution was carried out though in a time of peace and within not many days' sail of home. An act vindicated by a naval court of inquiry subsequently convened ashore. History, and here cited without comment. True, the circumstances on board the *Somers* were different from those on board the *Bellipotent*. But the urgency felt, well-warranted or otherwise, was much the same.

Says a writer whom few know,[1] 'Forty years after a battle it is easy for a noncombatant to reason about how it ought to have been fought. It is another thing personally and under fire to have to direct the fighting while involved in the obscuring smoke of it. Much so with respect to other emergencies involving considerations both practical and moral, and when it is imperative promptly to act. The greater the fog the more it imperils the steamer, and speed is put on though at the hazard of running somebody down. Little ween the snug card players in the cabin of the responsibilities of the sleepless man on the bridge.'

In brief, Billy Budd was formally convicted and sentenced to be hung at the yardarm in the early morning watch, it being now night. Otherwise, as is customary in such cases, the sentence would forthwith have been carried out. In wartime on the field or in the fleet, a mortal punishment decreed by a drumhead court—on the field sometimes decreed by but a nod from the general—follows without delay on the heel of conviction, without appeal.

22

It was Captain Vere himself who of his own motion communicated the finding of the court to the prisoner, for that purpose going to the compartment where he was in custody and bidding the marine there to withdraw for the time.

Beyond the communication of the sentence, what took place at this interview was never known. But in view of the character of the twain briefly closeted in that stateroom, each radically sharing in the rarer qualities of our nature—so rare indeed as to be all but incredi-

9. Melville's cousin, Guert Gansecoort, was first lieutenant of the *Somers* at the time of a mutiny. The incident may have been in the back of Melville's mind when he wrote *Billy Budd*. 1. Melville himself.

ble to average minds however much cultivated—some conjectures may be ventured.

It would have been in consonance with the spirit of Captain Vere should he on this occasion have concealed nothing from the condemned one—should he indeed have frankly disclosed to him the part he himself had played in bringing about the decision, at the same time revealing his actuating motives. On Billy's side it is not improbable that such a confession would have been received in much the same spirit that prompted it. Not without a sort of joy, indeed, he might have appreciated the brave[2] opinion of him implied in his captain's making such a confidant of him. Nor, as to the sentence itself, could he have been insensible that it was imparted to him as to one not afraid to die. Even more may have been. Captain Vere in end may have developed the passion sometimes latent under an exterior stoical or indifferent. He was old enough to have been Billy's father. The austere devotee of military duty, letting himself melt back into what remains primeval in our formalized humanity, may in end have caught Billy to his heart, even as Abraham may have caught young Isaac on the brink of resolutely offering him up in obedience to the exacting behest.[3] But there is no telling the sacrament, seldom if in any case revealed to the gadding world, wherever under circumstances at all akin to those here attempted to be set forth two of great Nature's nobler order embrace. There is privacy at the time, inviolable to the survivor; and holy oblivion, the sequel to each diviner magnanimity, providentially covers all at last.

The first to encounter Captain Vere in act of leaving the compartment was the senior lieutenant. The face he beheld, for the moment one expressive of the agony of the strong, was to that officer, though a man of fifty, a startling revelation. That the condemned one suffered less than he who mainly had effected the condemnation was apparently indicated by the former's exclamation in the scene soon perforce to be touched upon.

23

Of a series of incidents with a brief term rapidly following each other, the adequate narration may take up a term less brief, especially if explanation or comment here and there seem requisite to the better understanding of such incidents. Between the entrance into the cabin of him who never left it alive, and him who when he did leave it left

2. Fine, superior.   3. Genesis 22:1–18: "God did tempt Abraham, and said . . . Take now thy son, thine only son Isaac, whom thou lovest . . . and offer him . . . for a burnt offering. . . . And Abraham bound Isaac his son, and laid him on the altar upon the wood. And Abraham stretched forth his hand, and took the knife to slay his son. And the angel of the Lord said, Lay not thine hand upon the lad, neither do thou any thing unto him: for now I know that thou fearest God. And, saith the Lord, I will bless thee . . . because thou hast obeyed my voice."

it as one condemned to die; between this and the closeted interview just given, less than an hour and a half had elapsed. It was an interval long enough, however, to awaken speculations among no few of the ship's company as to what it was that could be detaining in the cabin the master-at-arms and the sailor; for a rumor that both of them had been seen to enter it and neither of them had been seen to emerge, this rumor had got abroad upon the gun decks and in the tops, the people of a great warship being in one respect like villagers, taking microscopic note of every outward movement or non-movement going on. When therefore, in weather not at all tempestuous, all hands were called in the second dogwatch, a summons under such circumstances not usual in those hours, the crew were not wholly unprepared for some announcement extraordinary, one having connection too with the continued absence of the two men from their wonted haunts.

There was a moderate sea at the time; and the moon, newly risen and near to being at its full, silvered the white spar deck wherever not blotted by the clear-cut shadows horizontally thrown of fixtures and moving men. On either side the quarter-deck the marine guard under arms was drawn up; and Captain Vere, standing in his place surrounded by all the wardroom officers, addressed his men. In so doing, his manner showed neither more nor less than that properly pertaining to his supreme position aboard his own ship. In clear terms and concise he told them what had taken place in the cabin: that the master-at-arms was dead, that he who had killed him had been already tried by a summary court and condemned to death, and that the execution would take place in the early morning watch. The word *mutiny* was not named in what he said. He refrained too from making the occasion an opportunity for any preachment as to the maintenance of disipline, thinking perhaps that under existing circumstances in the navy the consequence of violating discipline should be made to speak for itself.

Their captain's announcement was listened to by the throng of standing sailors in a dumbness like that of a seated congregation of believers in hell listening to the clergyman's announcement of his Calvinistic text.

At the close, however, a confused murmur went up. It began to wax. All but instantly, then, at a sign, it was pierced and suppressed by shrill whistles of the boatswain and his mates. The word was given to about ship.

To be prepared for burial Claggart's body was delivered to certain petty officers of his mess. And here, not to clog the sequel with lateral matters, it may be added that at a suitable hour, the master-at-arms was committed to the sea with every funeral honor properly belonging to his naval grade.

In this proceeding as in every public one growing out of the tragedy strict adherence to usage was observed. Nor in any point could it have been at all deviated from, either with respect to Claggart or Billy Budd, without begetting undersirable speculations in the ship's company, sailors, and more particularly men-of-war's men, being of all men the greatest sticklers for usage. For similar cause, all communication between Captain Vere and the condemned one ended with the closeted interview already given, the latter being now surrendered to the ordinary routine preliminary to the end. His transfer under guard from the captain's quarters was effected without unusual precautions—at least no visible ones. If possible, not to let the men so much as surmise that their officers anticipate aught amiss from them is the tacit rule in a military ship. And the more that some sort of trouble should really be apprehended, the more do the officers keep that apprehension to themselves, though not the less unostenatious vigilance may be augmented. In the present instance, the sentry placed over the prisoner had strict orders to let no one have communication with him but the chaplain. And certain unobtrusive measures were taken absolutely to insure this point.

24

In a seventy-four of the old order the deck known as the upper gun deck was the one covered over by the spar deck, which last, though not without its armament, was for the most part exposed to the weather. In general it was at all hours free from hammocks; those of the crew swinging on the lower gun deck and berth deck, the latter being not only a dormitory but also the place for the stowing of the sailors' bags, and on both sides lined with the large chests or movable pantries of the many messes of the men.

On the starboard side of the *Bellipotent*'s upper gun deck, behold Billy Budd under sentry lying prone in irons in one of the bays formed by the regular spacing of the guns comprising the batteries on either side. All these pieces were of the heavier caliber of that period. Mounted on lumbering wooden carriages, they were hampered with cumbersome harness of breeching and strong side-tackles for running them out. Guns and carriages, together with the long rammers and shorter linstocks lodged in loops overhead—all these, as customary, were painted black; and the heavy hempen breechings, tarred to the same tint, were the like livery of the undertakers. In contrast with the funereal hue of these surroundings, the prone sailor's exterior apparel, white jumper and white duck trousers, each more or less soiled, dimly glimmered in the obscure light of the bay like a patch of discolored snow in early April lingering at some upland cave's black mouth. In effect he is already in his shroud, or the garments that shall serve him in lieu of one. Over him but scarce illuminating him, two battle lanterns swing from two massive beams of the deck above. Fed with the oil supplied by the war contractors (whose gains, honest or otherwise, are in every land an anticipated portion of the harvest of death), with flickering splashes of dirty yellow light they pollute the pale moonshine all but ineffectually struggling in obstructed flecks through the open ports from which the tampioned[4] cannon protrude. Other lanterns at intervals serve but to bring out somewhat the obscurer bays which, like small confessionals or side-chapels in a cathedral, branch from the long dim-vistaed broad aisle between the two batteries of that covered tier.

Such was the deck where now lay the Handsome Sailor. Through the rose-tan of his complexion no pallor could have shown. It would have taken days of sequestration from the winds and the sun to have brought about the effacement of that. But the skeleton in the cheek-bone at the point of its angle was just beginning delicately to be defined under the warm-tinted skin. In fervid hearts self-contained, some brief experiences devour our human tissue as secret fire in a ship's hold consumes cotton in the bale.

But now lying between the two guns, as nipped in the vice of fate, Billy's agony, mainly proceeding from a generous young heart's virgin experience of the diabolical incarnate and effective in some men—the tension of that agony was over now. It survived not the something healing in the closeted interview with Captain Vere. Without movement, he lay as in a trance, that adolescent expression previously noted as his taking on something akin to the look of a slumbering child in the cradle when the warm hearthglow of the still chamber at night plays on the dimples that at whiles mysteriously form in the cheek, silently coming and going there. For now and then in the gyved[5] one's trance a serene happy light born of some wandering reminiscence or dream would diffuse itself over his face, and then wane away only anew to return.

The chaplain, coming to see him and finding him thus, and perceiving no sign that he was conscious of his presence, attentively regarded him for a space, then slipping aside, withdrew for the time, peradventure feeling that even he, the minister of Christ though receiving his stipend from Mars,[6] had no consolation to proffer which could result in a peace transcending that which he beheld. But in the small hours he came again. And the prisoner, now awake to his surroundings, noticed his approach, and civilly, all but cheerfully, welcomed him. But it was to little purpose that in the interview following, the good man sought to bring Billy Budd to some godly understanding that he must die, and at dawn. True, Billy himself

---

4. Plugged with a tampion, which fits into the muzzle of a gun not in use.   5. Shackled, chained.   6. I.e., paid by the navy. Mars was the god of war.

freely referred to his death as a thing close at hand; but it was something in the way that children will refer to death in general, who yet among their other sports will play a funeral with hearse and mourners.

Not that like children Billy was incapable of conceiving what death really is. No, but he was wholly without irrational fear of it, a fear more prevalent in highly civilized communities than those so-called barbarous ones which in all respects stand nearer to unadulterate Nature. And, as elsewhere said, a barbarian Billy radically was—as much so, for all the costume, as his countrymen the British captives, living trophies, made to march in the Roman triumph of Germanicus.[7] Quite as much so as those later barbarians, young men probably, and picked specimens among the earlier British converts to Christianity, at least nominally such, taken to Rome (as today converts from lesser isles of the sea may be taken to London), of whom the Pope at that time, admiring the strangeness of their personal beauty so unlike the Italian stamp, their clear ruddy complexion and curled flaxen locks, exclaimed, 'Angles' (meaning *English*, the modern derivative), 'Angles, do you call them? And is it because they look so like angels?'[8] Had it been later in time, one would think that the Pope had in mind Fra Angelico's seraphs, some of whom, plucking apples in gardens of the Hesperides, have the faint rosebud complexion of the more beautiful English girls.

If in vain the good chaplain sought to impress the young barbarian with ideas of death akin to those conveyed in the skull, dial and crossbones on old tombstones, equally futile to all appearance were his efforts to bring home to him the thought of salvation and a Savior. Billy listened, but less out of awe or reverence, perhaps, than from a certain natural politeness, doubtless at bottom regarding all that in much the same way that most mariners of his class take any discourse abstract or out of the common tone of the workaday world. And this sailor way of taking clerical discourse is not wholly unlike the way in which the primer of Christianity, full of transcendent miracles, was received long ago on tropic isles by any superior *savage*, so called—a Tahitian, say, of Captain Cook's time or shortly after that time.[9] Out of natural courtesy he received, but did not appropriate. It was like a gift placed in the palm of an outreached hand upon which the fingers do not close.

But the *Bellipotent*'s chaplain was a discreet man possessing the good sense of a good heart. So he insisted not in his vocation here. At the instance of Captain Vere, a lieutenant had apprised him of

---

7. Germanicus Caesar (15 B.C.–A.D. 19), granted a triumph in Rome in A.D. 17.   8. Bede's *Ecclesiastical History of the English People* tells this anecdote about Pope Gregory the Great (540?–604). *Fra Angelico*: The Florentine painter Giovanni da Fiesole (1387–1455). *Hesperides*: Daughters of Atlas who guarded a tree bearing golden apples on an enchanted island in the western sea. 9. James Cook (1728–1779) was in Tahiti in 1769 and from 1772 to 1775.

pretty much everything as to Billy; and since he felt that innocence was even a better thing than religion wherewith to go to Judgment, he reluctantly withdrew; but in his emotion not without first performing an act strange enough in an Englishman, and under the circumstances yet more so in any regular priest. Stooping over, he kissed on the fair cheek his fellow man, a felon in martial law, one whom though on the confines of death he felt he could never convert to a dogma; nor for all that did he fear for his future.

Marvel not that having been made acquainted with the young sailor's essential innocence the worthy man lifted not a finger to avert the doom of such a martyr to martial discipline. So to do would not only have been as idle as invoking the desert, but would also have been an audacious transgression of the bounds of his function, one as exactly prescribed to him by military law as that of the boatswain or any other naval officer. Bluntly put, a chaplain is the minister of the Prince of Peace serving in the host of the God of War—Mars. As such, he is as incongruous as a musket would be on the altar at Christmas. Why, then, is he there? Because he indirectly subserves the purpose attested by the cannon; because too he lends the sanction of the religion of the meek to that which practically is the abrogation of everything but brute Force.

25

The night so luminous on the spar deck, but otherwise on the cavernous ones below, levels so like the tiered galleries in a coal mine—the luminous night passed away. But like the prophet in the chariot disappearing in heaven and dropping his mantle to Elisha,[1] the withdrawing night transferred its pale robe to the breaking day. A meek, shy light appeared in the East, where stretched a diaphanous fleece of white furrowed vapor. That light slowly waxed. Suddenly *eight bells* was struck aft, responded to by one louder metallic stroke from forward. It was four o'clock in the morning. Instantly the silver whistles were heard summoning all hands to witness punishment. Up through the great hatchways rimmed with racks of heavy shot the watch below came pouring, overspreading with the watch already on deck the space between the mainmast and foremast including that occupied by the capacious launch and the black booms tiered on either side of it, boat and booms making a summit of observation for the powder-boys and younger tars. A different group comprising one watch of topmen leaned over the rail of that sea balcony, no small one in a seventy-four, looking down on the crowd below. Man or

---

1. 2 Kings 2:11–13: "There appeared a chariot of fire, and horses of fire, and parted them both asunder; and Elijah went up by a whirlwind into heaven. And Elisha . . . took up . . . the mantle of Elijah that fell from him."

boy, none spake but in whisper, and few spake at all. Captain Vere—as before, the central figure among the assembled commissioned officers—stood nigh the break of the poop deck facing forward. Just below him on the quarter-deck the marines in full equipment were drawn up much as at the scene of the promulgated sentence.

At sea in the old time, the execution by halter of a military sailor was generally from the foreyard. In the present instance, for special reasons[2] the mainyard was assigned. Under an arm of that yard the prisoner was presently brought up, the chaplain attending him. It was noted at the time, and remarked upon afterwards that in this final scene the good man evinced little or nothing of the perfunctory. Brief speech indeed he had with the condemned one, but the genuine Gospel was less on his tongue than in his aspect and manner towards him. The final preparations personal to the latter being speedily brought to an end by two boatswain's mates, the consummation impended. Billy stood facing aft. At the penultimate moment, his words, his only ones, words wholly unobstructed in the utterance, were these: 'God bless Captain Vere!' Syllables so unanticipated coming from one with the ignominious hemp about his neck—a conventional felon's benediction[3] directed aft towards the quarters of honor; syllables too delivered in the clear melody of a singing bird on the point of launching from the twig—had a phenomenal effect, not unenhanced by the rare personal beauty of the young sailor, spiritualized now through late experiences so poignantly profound.

Without volition, as it were, as if indeed the ship's populace were but the vehicles of some vocal current electric, with one voice from alow and aloft came a resonant sympathetic echo: 'God bless Captain Vere!' And yet at that instant Billy alone must hve been in their hearts, even as in their eyes.

At the pronounced words and the spontaneous echo that voluminously rebounded them, Captain Vere, either through stoic self-control or a sort of momentary paralysis induced by emotional shock, stood erectly rigid as a musket in the ship-armorer's rack.

The hull, deliberately recovering from the periodic roll to leeward, was just regaining an even keel when the last signal, a preconcerted dumb one, was given. At the same moment it chanced that the vapory fleece hanging low in the East was shot through with a soft glory as of the fleece of the Lamb of God seen in mystical vision, and simultaneously therewith, watched by the wedged mass of upturned faces, Billy ascended; and, ascending, took the full rose of the dawn.

2. The "special reasons" remain obscure. Hayford and Sealts suggest that the captain's motives were precautionary; the phrase, an insertion, previously read, "for strategic reasons."   3. It is a traditional ritual for the condemned man to forgive the official compelled by duty to order his death.

In the pinioned figure arrived at the yard-end, to the wonder of all no motion was apparent, none save that created by the slow roll of the hull in moderate weather, so majestic in a great ship ponderously cannoned.

26

When some days afterwards, in reference to the singularity just mentioned, the purser, a rather ruddy, rotund person more accurate as an accountant that profound as a philosopher, said at mess to the surgeon, "What testimony to the force lodged in will power,' the latter, saturnine, spare, and tall, one in whom a discreet causticity went along with a manner less genial than polite, replied. 'Your pardon, Mr Purser. In a hanging scientifically conducted—and under special orders I myself directed how Budd's was to be effected—any movement following the completed suspension and originating in the body suspended, such movement indicates mechanical spasm in the muscular system. Hence the absence of that is no more attributable to will power, as you call it, than to horsepower—begging your pardon.'

'But this muscular spasm you speak of, is not that in a degree more or less invariable in these cases?'

'Assuredly so, Mr Purser.'

'How then, my good sir, do you account for its absence in this instance?'

'Mr Purser, it is clear that your sense of the singularity in this matter equals not mine. You account for it by what you call will power—a term not yet included in the lexicon of science. For me, I do not, with my present knowledge, pretend to account for it at all. Even should we assume the hypothesis that at the first touch of the halyards the action of Budd's heart, intensified by extraordinary emotion at its climax, abruptly stopped—much like a watch when in carelessly winding it up you strain at the finish, thus snapping the chain—even under that hypothesis how account for the phenomenon that followed?'

'You admit, then, that the absence of spasmodic movement was phenomenal.'

'It was phenomenal, Mr Purser, in the sense that it was an appearance the cause of which is not immediately to be assigned.'

'But tell me, my dear sir,' pertinaciously continued the other, 'was the man's death effected by the halter, or was it a species of euthanasia?'[4]

'*Euthanasia*, Mr Purser, is something like your *will power*: I doubt

4. A quiet and easy death.

its authenticity as a scientific term—begging your pardon again. It is at once imaginative and metaphysical—in short, Greek.—But,' abruptly changing his tone, 'there is a case in the sick bay that I do not care to leave to my assistants. Beg your pardon, but excuse me.' And rising from the mess he formally withdrew.

27

The silence at the moment of execution and for a moment or two continuing thereafter, a silence but emphasized by the regular wash of the sea against the hull or the flutter of a sail caused by the helmsman's eyes being tempted astray, this emphasized silence was gradually disturbed by a sound not easily to be verbally rendered. Whoever has heard the freshet-wave of a torrent suddenly swelled by pouring showers in tropical mountains, showers not shared by the plain; whoever has heard the first muffled murmur of its sloping advance through precipitous woods may form some conception of the sound now heard. The seeming remoteness of its source was because of its murmurous indistinctness, since it came from close by, even from the men passed on the ship's open deck. Being inarticulate, it was dubious in significance further than it seemed to indicate some capricious revulsion of thought or feeling such as mobs ashore are liable to, in the present instance possibly implying a sullen revocation on the men's part of their involuntary echoing of Billy's benediction. But ere the murmur had time to wax into clamor it was met by a strategic command, the more telling that it came with abrupt unexpectedness: 'Pipe down the starboard watch, Boatswain, and see that they go.'

Shrill as the shriek of the sea hawk, the silver whistles of the boatswain and his mates pierced that ominous low sound, dissipating it; and yielding to the mechanism of discipline the throng was thinned by one-half. For the remainder, most of them were set to temporary employments connected with trimming the yards and so forth, business readily to be got up to serve occasion by any officer of the deck.

Now each proceeding that follows a mortal sentence pronounced at sea by a drumhead court is characterized by promptitude not perceptibly merging into hurry, though bordering that. The hammock, the one which had been Billy's bed when alive, having already been ballasted with shot and otherwise prepared to serve for his canvas coffin, the last offices of the sea undertakers, the sailmaker's mates, were now speedily completed. When everything was in readiness a second call for all hands, made necessary by the strategic movement before mentioned, was sounded, now to witness burial.

The details of this closing formality it needs not to give. But when the tilted plank let slide its freight into the sea, a second strange

human murmur was heard, blended now with another inarticulate
sound proceeding from certain larger seafowl who, their attention
having been attracted by the peculiar commotion in the water resulting from the heavy sloped dive of the shotted hammock into the sea,
flew screaming to the spot. So near the hull did they come, that the
stridor or bony creak of their gaunt double-jointed pinions was audible. As the ship under light airs passed on, leaving the burial spot
astern, they still kept circling it low down with the moving shadow
of their outstretched wings and the croaked requiem of their cries.

Upon sailors as superstitious as those of the age preceding ours,
men-of-war's men too who had just beheld the prodigy of repose in
the form suspended in air, and now foundering in the deeps; to such
mariners the action of the seafowl, though dictated by mere animal
greed for prey, was big with no prosaic significance. And uncertain
movement began among them, in which some encroachment was
made. It was tolerated but for a moment. For suddenly the drum
beat to quarters,[5] which familiar sound happening at least twice every
day, had upon the present occasion a signal peremptoriness in it.
True martial discipline long continued superinduces in average man
a sort of impulse whose operation at the official word of command
much resembles in its promptitude the effect of an instinct.

The drumbeat dissolved the multitude, distributing most of them
along the batteries of the two covered gun decks. There, as wonted,
the guns' crew stood by their respective cannon erect and silent. In
due course the first officer, sword under arm and standing in his
place on the quarter-deck, formally received the successive reports of
the sworded lieutenants commanding the sections of batteries below;
the last of which reports being made, the summed report he delivered with the customary salute to the commander. All this occupied
time, which in the present case was the object in beating to quarters
at an hour prior to the customary one. That such variance from
usage was authorized by an officer like Captain Vere, a martinet as
some deemed him, was evidence of the necessity for unusual action
implied in what he deemed to be temporarily the mood of his men:
'With mankind,' he would say, 'forms, measured forms, are everything; and this is the import couched in the story of Orpheus with
his lyre spellbinding the wild denizens of the wood.'[6] And this he
once applied to the disruption of forms going on across the Channel
and the consequences thereof.

At this unwonted muster at quarters, all proceeded as at the regular hour. The band on the quarter-deck played a sacred air, after
which the chaplain went through the customary morning service.

---

5. The signal for men to return to their assigned stations.   6. When Orpheus, in Greek mythology,
played his lyre and sang, wild animals were charmed, trees and stones followed him, fish left the
water in which they swam, and birds flew about his head.

That done, the drum beat the retreat; and toned by music and religious rites subserving the discipline and purposes of war, the men in their wonted orderly manner dispersed to the places allotted them when not at the guns.

And now it was full day. The fleece of low-hanging vapor had vanished, licked up by the sun that late had so glorified it. And the circumambient air in the clearness of its serenity was like smooth white marble in the polished block not yet removed from the marble-dealer's yard.

28

The symmetry of form attainable in pure fiction cannot so readily be achieved in a narration essentially having less to do with fable than with fact. Truth uncompromisingly told will always have its ragged edges; hence the conclusion of such a narration is apt to be less finished than an architectural finial.

How it fared with the Handsome Sailor during the year of the Great Mutiny has been faithfully given. But though properly the story ends with his life, something in way of sequel will not be amiss. Three brief chapters will suffice.

In the general rechristening under the Directory of the craft originally forming the navy of the French monarchy, the *St. Louis* line-of-battle ship was named the *Athée* (the *Atheist*). Such a name, like some other substituted ones in the Revolutionary fleet, while proclaiming the infidel audacity of the ruling power, was yet, though not so intended to be, the aptest name, if one consider it, ever given to a warship; far more so indeed than the *Devastation*, the *Erebus* (the *Hell*), and similar names bestowed upon fighting ships.

On the return passage to the English fleet from the detached cruise during which occurred the events already recorded, the *Bellipotent* fell in with the *Athée*. An engagement ensued, during which Captain Vere, in the act of putting his ship alongside the enemy with a view of throwing his boarders across her bulwarks, was hit by a musket ball from a porthole of the enemy's main cabin. More than disabled, he dropped to the deck and was carried below to the same cockpit where some of his men already lay. The senior lieutenant took command. Under him the enemy was finally captured, and though much crippled was by rare good fortune successfully taken into Gibraltar, an English port not very distant from the scene of the fight. There, Captain Vere with the rest of the wounded was put ashore. He lingered for some days, but the end came. Unhappily he was cut off too early for the Nile and Trafalgar. The spirit that 'spite its philosophic austerity may yet have indulged in the most secret of all passions, ambition, never attained to the fulness of fame.

Not long before death, while lying under the influence of that
magical drug which, soothing the physical frame, mysteriously operates on the subtler element in man, he was heard to murmur words
inexplicable to his attendant: 'Billy Budd, Billy Budd.' That these
were not the accents of remorse would seem clear from what the
attendant said to the *Bellipotent*'s senior officer of marines, who, as
the most reluctant to condemn of the members of the drumhead
court, too well knew, though here he kept the knowledge to himself,
who Billy Budd was.

29

Some few weeks after the execution, among other matters under the
head of 'News from the Mediterranean,' there appeared in a naval
chronicle of the time, an authorized weekly publication, an account
of the affair. It was doubtless for the most part written in good faith,
though the medium, partly rumor, through which the facts must
have reached the writer served to deflect and in part falsify them.
The account was as follows:

'On the tenth of the last month a deplorable occurrence took place
on board H.M.S. *Bellipotent*. John Claggart, the ship's master-at-
arms, discovering that some sort of plot was incipient among an inferior section of the ship's company, and that the ringleader was one
William Budd; he, Claggart, in the act of arraigning the man before
the captain, was vindictively stabbed to the heart by the suddenly
drawn sheath knife of Budd.

'The deed and the implement employed sufficiently suggest that
though mustered into the service under an English name the assassin
was no Englishman, but one of those aliens adopting English cog-
nomens whom the present extraordinary necessities of the service
have caused to be admitted into it in considerable number.

'The enormity of the crime and the extreme depravity of the criminal appear the greater in view of the character of the victim, a
middle-aged man respectable and discreet, belonging to that minor
official grade, the petty officers, upon whom, as none know better
than the commissioned gentlemen, the efficiency of His Majesty's
navy so largely depends. His function was a responsible one, at once
onerous and thankless; and his fidelity in it the greater because of his
strong patriotic impulse. In this instance as in so many other instances
in these days, the character of this unfortunate man signally refutes,
if refutation were needed, that peevish saying attributed to the late
Dr Johnson, that patriotism is the last refuge of a scoundrel.[7]

'The criminal paid the penalty of his crime. The promptitude of

---

7. The saying is quoted in James Boswell's *Life of Samuel Johnson, Ll. D.* (1791).

the punishment has proved salutary. Nothing amiss is now apprehended aboard H.M.S. *Bellipotent*.'

The above, appearing in a publication now long ago superannu-
ated and forgotten, is all that hitherto has stood in human record to
attest what manner of men respectively were John Claggart and Billy
Budd.

30

Everything is for a term venerated in navies. Any tangible object
associated with some striking incident of the service is converted into
a monument. The spar from which the foretopman was suspended
was for some few years kept trace of by the bluejackets. Their knowl-
edges followed it from ship to dockyard and again from dockyard to
ship, still pursuing it even when at last reduced to a mere dockyard
boom. To them a chip of it was as a piece of the Cross. Ignorant
though they were of the secret facts of the tragedy, and not thinking
but that the penalty was somehow unavoidably inflicted from the
naval point of view, for all that, they instinctively felt that Billy was
a sort of man as incapable of mutiny as of wilful murder. They recalled
the fresh young image of the Handsome Sailor, that face never
deformed by a sneer or subtler vile freak of the heart within. This
impression of him was doubtless deepened by the fact that he was
gone, and in a measure mysteriously gone. On the gun decks of the
Bellipotent the general estimate of his nature and its unconscious
simplicity eventually found rude utterance from another foretopman, one of his own watch, gifted, as some sailors are, with an
artless *poetic* temperament. The tarry hand made some lines which,
after circulating among the shipboard crews for a while, finally got
rudely printed at Portsmouth as a ballad. The title given to it was the
sailor's.

BILLY IN THE DARBIES[8]

> Good of the chaplain to enter Lone Bay
> And down on his marrowbones here and pray
> For the likes just o' me, Billy Budd.—But, look:
> Through the port comes the moonshine astray!
> It tips the guards's cutlass and silvers this nook;
> But 'twill die in the dawning of Billy's last day.
> A jewel-block[9] they'll make of me tomorrow,
> Pendant pearl from the yardarm-end
> Like the eardrop I gave to Bristol Molly—
> O, 'tis me, not the sentence they'll suspend.

---

8. Handcuffs or fetters.   9. Jewel-blocks carry the light sails called studding-sails to the very
ends of the yards where they are hoisted.

Ay, ay, all is up; and I must up too,
Early in the morning, aloft from alow.
On an empty stomach now never it would do.
They'll give me a nibble—bit o' biscuit ere I go.
Sure, a messmate will reach me the last parting cup;
But, turning heads away from the hoist and the belay,
Heaven knows who will have the running of me up!
No pipe to those halyards.—But aren't it all sham?
A blur's in my eyes; it is dreaming that I am.
A hatcher to my hawser? All adrift to go?
The drum roll to grog, and Billy never know?
But Donald he has promised to stand by the plank;
So I'll shake a friendly hand ere I sink.
But—no! It is dead then I'll be, come to think.
I remember Taff the Welshman when he sank.
And his cheek it was like the budding pink.
But me they'll lash in hammock, drop me deep.
Fathoms down, fathoms down, how I'll dream fast asleep.
I feel it stealing now. Sentry, are you there?
Just ease these darbies at the wrist,
And roll me over fair!
I am sleepy, and the oozy weeds about me twist.

EMILY DICKINSON
1830–1886

Emily Dickinson forces her readers to acknowledge the startling aspects of ordinary life. "Ordinary life" includes the mysterious actuality of death, but it also includes birds and woods and oceans, arguments between people, the weight of depression. In small facts and large, Dickinson perceives enormous meaning.

The poet's life, like her verse, was somewhat mysterious. Born to a prosperous and prominent Amherst, Massachusetts, family (her father, a lawyer, was also treasurer of Amherst College), Dickinson attended Amherst Academy and later, for a year, the Mount Holyoke Female Seminary. Thereafter, however, she remained almost entirely in her father's house, leading the life of a recluse. She had close family attachments and a few close friendships, pursued mainly through correspondence. The most important of these relationships, from a literary point of view, was with the Boston writer and critic Thomas Wentworth Higginson, who eventually published her poems. She had begun writing verse in the late 1850s; in 1862, after seeing an essay of Higginson's in the *Atlantic Monthly*, Dickinson wrote him to ask his opinion of her poems, about 300 of them in existence by this time. The correspondence thus begun continued to the end of Dickinson's life; Higginson also visited her in Amherst.

At Dickinson's death, 1775 poems survived; only seven had been published, anonymously. With the help of another friend, Mabel Todd Loomis, Higginson selected poems for a volume, published in 1890, which proved extremely popular. Further selections continued to appear, but not until 1955 did Dickinson's entire body of work reach print.

By 1843, the English woman poet, Elizabeth Barrett Browning, had written in verse an exhortation to social reform *(The Cry of the Children)*; in 1857, she published a long poem, *Aurora Leigh*, commenting on the oppressed situation of women. Christina Rossetti, born the same year as Emily Dickinson and like her unmarried, in poems like *Goblin Market* (1862) found indirect ways to meditate on female predicaments. Dickinson, on the other hand, seems only peripherally aware of social facts. She alludes to church services, locomotives, female costume; very occasionally (e.g., "My Life had stood—a Loaded Gun") she refers to the way a woman's life is defined in relation to a man's. More centrally, she finds brilliant and provocative formulations of the emotional import of universal phenomena. We may feel already that death amounts to an incomprehensible and undigestible fact, but we are unlikely to have imagined conversation within a tomb or a personified version of death as carriage driver. By using such images, Dickinson disarmingly suggests a kind of playful innocence. Only gradually does one realize that the naïve, childlike perception, devoid of obviously ominous suggestion, conceals a complex, disturbing sense of human self-deception and reluctance to face the truth of experience.

"Truth" is an important word in Dickinson's poetry. "Tell all the Truth but tell it slant," she advises, pointing out that "The Truth must dazzle gradually / Or every man be blind—." She tells of a man who preaches about " 'Truth' until it proclaimed him a Liar—": truth remains an absolute, both challenging and judging humankind. In one of her most haunting poems, she claims the identity of Beauty and Truth (an identity tellingly asserted earlier in Keats's "Ode on a Grecian Urn") through the fiction of two dead people discussing their profound commitments.

> I died for Beauty—but was scarce
> Adjusted in the Tomb
> When One who died for Truth, was lain
> In an adjoining Room—

Her neighbor asks her why she "failed"; when she explains, he says that beauty and truth "are One."

> And so, as Kinsmen, met a Night—
> We talked between the Rooms—
> Until the Moss had reached our lips—
> And covered up—our names—

Until the last two lines, about the moss, the poem appears to evoke a rather cozy vision of death: neighbors amiably conversing from one room to another, as though at a slumber party ("met a Night"), two "Kinsmen" dedicated to noble abstractions and comforted by the companionship of their dedication. Only the word "failed" (meaning "died") disturbs the comfortable atmosphere, by suggesting a view of death as defeat.

The Keats poem that ends by asserting the identity of truth and beauty implies the permanence of both, as embodied in the work of art, the Grecian urn that stimulates the poet's reflections. Dickinson's poem concludes with troubling suggestions of impermanence. Talk of beauty and truth may reassure the talkers, but death necessarily implies forgetfulness: the dead forget and are forgotten, their very identities ("names") lost, their capacity for communication eliminated. Death *is* defeat; the high Romanticism of Keats's ode, on which this poem implicitly comments, blurs that fact. Despite Dickinson's fanciful images and allegories, her poems insist on their own kind of uncompromising realism. They speak of the universal human effort to imagine experience in reassuring terms, but they do not suggest that reality offers much in the way of reassurance: only brief experiences of natural beauty; and even those challenge human constructions. "'Twas warm—at first—like Us—" a poem about the sea begins; but it ends with the sea encountering "the Solid Town— / No One He seemed to know—."

Dickinson's eccentric punctuation, with dashes as the chief mark of emphasis and interruption, emphasizes the movements of consciousness in her lyrics. In their early publication, the poems were typically given conventional punctuation; only in 1955 did the body of work appear as Dickinson wrote it. The highly personal mode of punctuation emphasizes the fact that this verse contains also a personal and demanding vision.

Emily Dickinson: An Interpretive Biography (1955), by T. H. Johnson, Dickinson's editor, is indispensable. Useful critical sources include *The Recognition of Emily Dickinson*, edited by C. Blake (1964), a collection of criticism since 1890, and Albert Gelpi, *Emily Dickinson: The Mind of the Poet* (1966). For a provocative feminist interpretation, see S. Gilbert and S. Gubar, *The Madwoman in the Attic* (1979).

216

Safe in their Alabaster Chambers—
Untouched by Morning
And untouched by Noon—
Sleep the meek members of the Resurrection—
Rafter of satin,
And Roof of stone.   5

Light laughs the breeze
In her Castle above them—
Babbles the Bee in a stolid Ear,
Pipe the Sweet Birds in ignorant cadence—   10
Ah, what sagacity perished here!

258

There's a certain Slant of light
Winter Afternoons—

That oppresses, like the Heft
Of Cathedral Tunes—

Heavenly Hurt, it gives us—   5
We can find no scar,
But internal difference,
Where the Meanings, are—

None may teach it—Any—
'Tis the Seal Despair—   10
An imperial affliction
Sent us of the Air—

When it comes, the Landscape listens—
Shadows—hold their breath—
When it goes, 'tis like the Distance   15
On the look of Death—

303

The Soul selects her own Society—
Then—shuts the Door—
To her divine Majority—
Present no more—

Unmoved—she notes the Chariots—pausing   5
At her low Gate—
Unmoved—an Emperor be kneeling
Upon her Mat—

I've known her—from an ample nation—
Choose One—   10
Then—close the Valves of her attention—
Like Stone—

328

A Bird came down the Walk—
He did not know I saw—
He bit an Angleworm in halves
And ate the fellow, raw,

And then he drank a Dew   5
From a convenient Grass—
And then hopped sidewise to the Wall
To let a Beetle pass—

He glanced with rapid eyes
That hurried all around—   10
They looked like frightened Beads, I thought—
He stirred his Velvet Head

Like one in danger, Cautious,
I offered him a Crumb
And he unrolled his feathers   15
And rowed him softer home—

Than Oars divide the Ocean,
Too silver for a seam—
Or Butterflies, off Banks of Noon
Leap, plashless as they swim.   20

341

After great pain, a formal feeling comes—
The Nerves sit ceremonious, like Tombs—
The stiff Heart questions was it He, that bore,
And Yesterday, or Centuries before?

The Feet, mechanical, go round—   5
Of Ground, or Air, or Ought[1]—
A Wooden way
Regardless grown,
A Quartz contentment, like a stone—

This is the Hour of Lead—   10
Remembered, if outlived,
As Freezing persons, recollect the Snow—
First—Chill—then Stupor—then the letting go—

435

Much Madness is divinest Sense—
To a discerning Eye—
Much Sense—the starkest Madness—
'Tis the Majority
In this, as All, prevail—   5
Assent—any you are sane—
Demur—you're straightway dangerous—
And handled with a Chain—

449

I died for Beauty—but was scarce
Adjusted in the Tomb
When One who died for Truth, was lain
In an adjoining Room—
He questioned softly "Why I failed"?   5
"For Beauty", I replied—

---

1. Zero

"And I—for Truth—Themself are One—
We Bretheren, are", He said—

And so, as Kinsmen, met a Night—
We talked between the Rooms—   10
Until the Moss had reached our lips—
And covered up—our names—

465

I heard a Fly buzz—when I died—
The Stillness in the Room
Was like the Stillness in the Air—
Between the Heaves of Storm—

The Eyes around—had wrung them dry—   5
And Breaths were gathering firm
For that last Onset—when the King
Be witnessed—in the Room—

I willed my Keepsakes—Signed away
What portion of me be   10
Assignable—and then it was
There interposed a Fly—

With Blue—uncertain stumbling Buzz—
Between the light—and me—
And then the Windows failed—and then   15
I could not see to see—

519

'Twas warm—at first—like Us—
Until there crept upon
A Chill—like frost upon a Glass—
Till all the scene—be gone.

And made as[2] He would eat me up—   5
As wholly as a Dew
Upon a Dandelion's Sleeve—
And then—I started—too—

And He—He followed—close behind—
I felt His Silver Heel   10
Upon my Ankle—Then my Shoes
Would overflow with Pearl—

2. As if.

Until We met the Solid Town—
No One He seemed to know—
And bowing—with a Mighty look—   15
At me—The Sea withdrew—

585

I like to see it lap the Miles—
And lick the Valleys up—
And stop to feed itself at Tanks—
And then—prodigious step

Around a Pile of Mountains—   5
And supercilious peer
In Shanties—by the sides of Roads—
And than a Quarry pare

To fit its Ribs
And crawl between   10

Complaining all the while
In horrid—hooting stanza—
Then chase itself down Hill—

And neigh like Boanerges[3]—
Then—punctual as a Star   15
Stop—docile and omnipotent
At its own stable door—

632

The Brain—is wider than the Sky—
For—put them side by side—
The one the other will contain
With ease—and You—beside—

The Brain is deeper than the sea—   5
For—hold them—Blue to Blue—
The one the other will absorb—
As Sponges—Buckets—do—

The Brain is just the weight of God—
For—Heft them—Pound for Pound—   10
And they will differ—if they do—
As Syllable from Sound—

---

3. "Sons of thunder," name given by Jesus to the brothers and disciples James and John, presumably because they were thunderous preachers.

657

I dwell in Possibility—
A fairer House than Prose—
More numberous of Windows—
Superior—for Doors—

Of Chambers as the Cedars—   5
Impregnable of Eye—
And for an Everlasting Roof
The Gambrels[4] of the Sky—

Of Vistors—the fairest—
For Occupation—This—   10
The spreading wide my narrow Hands
To gather Paradise—

712

Because I could not stop for Death—
He kindly stopped for me—
The Carriage held but just Ourselves—
And Immortality.

We slowly drove—He knew no haste   5
And I had put away
My labor and my lesire too,
For His Civility—

We passed School, where Children strove
At Recess—in the Ring—   10
We passed the Fields of Gazing Grain—
We passed the Setting Sun—

Or rather—He passed Us—
The Dews drew quivering and chill—
For only Gossamer, my Gown—   15
My Tippet—only Tulle[5]—

We paused before a House that seemed
A Swelling of the Ground—
The Roof was scarcely visible—
The Cornice—in the Ground—   20

Since then—'tis Centuries—and yet
Feels shorter than the Day

4. Slopes, as in the large, arched roofs often seen on barns.   5. Fine, silken netting. *Tippet:* A
scarf, usually of heavy material.

I first surmised the Horses' Heads
Were toward Eternity—

754

My Life had stood—a Loaded Gun
In Corners—till a Day
The Owner passed—identified—
And carried Me away—

And now We roam in Sovereign Woods—   5
And now We hunt the Doe—
And every time I speak for Him—
The Mountains straight reply—

And do I smile, such cordial light
Upon the Valley glow—   10
It is as a Vesuvian face[6]
Had let its pleasure through—

And when at Night—Our good Day done—
I guard My Master's Head—
'Tis better than the Eider-Duck's   15
Deep Pillow—to have shared—

To foe of His—I'm deadly foe—
None stir the second time—
On whom I lay a Yellow Eye—
Or an emphatic Thumb—   20

Though I than He—may longer live
He longer must—than I—
For I have but the power to kill,
Without—the power to die—

1084

At Half past Three, a single Bird
Unto a silent Sky
Propounded but a single term
Of cautious melody.

At Half past Four, Experiment   5
Had subjugated test
And lo, Her silver Principle
Supplanted all the rest.

At Half past Seven, Element
Nor Implement, be seen—   10

---

6. A face glowing with light like that from an erupting volcano.

And Place was where the Presence was
Circumference between.

1129

Tell all the Truth but tell it slant—
Success in Circuit lies
Too bright for our infirm Delight
The Truth's superb surprise
As Lightning to the Children eased   5
With explanation kind
The Truth must dazzle gradually
Or every man be blind—

1207

He preached upon "Breadth" till it argued him narrow—
The Broad are too broad to define
And of "Truth" until it proclaimed him a Liar—
The Truth never flaunted a Sign—

Simplicity fled from his counterfeit presence   5
As Gold the Pyrites[7] would shun—
What confusion would cover the innocent Jesus
To meet so enabled[8] a Man!

1564

Pass to thy Rendezvous of Light,
Pangless except for us—
Who slowly ford the Mystery
Which thou hast leaped across!

1593

There came a Wind like a Bugle—
It quivered through the Grass
And a Green Chill upon the Heat
So ominous did pass
We barred the Windows and the Doors   5
As from an Emerald Ghost—
The Doom's electric Moccasin[9]
That very instant passed—
On a strange Mob of panting Trees
And Fences fled away   10
And Rivers where the Houses ran

---

7. Iron bisulphide, sometimes called "fool's gold."   8. Competent.   9. I.e., water moccasin, a poisonous snake.

Those looked that lived—that Day—
The Bell within the steeple wild
The flying tidings told—
How much can come   15
And much can go,
And yet abide the World!

Masterpieces of
the Nineteenth Century:
Realism, Naturalism,
and the New Poetry

As was indicated in the preceding introduction, the nineteenth century is (apart from our own) the century of greatest change in the history of Western civilization. The upheavals following the French Revolution broke up the old order of Europe. The Holy Roman Empire and the Papal States were dissolved. Nationalism, nourished by the political and social aspirations of the middle classes, grew by leaps and bounds. "Liberty" became the main political slogan of the century. In different countries and different decades it meant different things: here liberation from the rule of the foreigner, there the emancipation of the serf; here the removal of economic restrictions on trade and manufacturing, there the introduction of a constitution, free speech, parliamentary institutions. Almost all over Europe, the middle classes established their effective rule, though monarchs often remained in more or less nominal power. Two large European countries, Germany and Italy, achieved their centuries-old dreams of political unification. The predominance of France, still marked at the beginning of the century, was broken, and England—or rather Great Britain—ruled the sea throughout the century. The smaller European nations, especially in the Balkans, began to emancipate themselves from foreign rule.

These major political changes were caused by, and in their turn caused, great social and economic changes. The Industrial Revolution which had begun in England in the eighteenth century spread over the Continent and transformed living conditions radically. The enormous increase in the speed and availability of transportation due to the development of railroads and steamships, the greatly increased urbanization following from the establishment of industries, changed the whole pattern of human life in most countries, and made possible, within a century, an unprecedented increase in the population (as much as threefold in most European countries), which was also fostered by the advances of medicine and hygiene. The increase of widespread wealth and prosperity is, in spite of the wretched living conditions and other hardships of the early factory workers, an undeniable fact. The barriers between the social classes diminished appreciably almost everywhere: both the social and the political power of the aristocracy declined. The industrial laborer began to be felt as a political force.

These social and economic changes were closely bound up with shifts in the prevailing outlooks and philosophies. Technological innovation is impossible without the discoveries of science. The scientific outlook, hitherto dominant only in a comparatively limited area, spread widely and permeated almost all fields of human thought and endeavor. It raised enormous hopes for the future betterment of man's condition on earth, especially when Darwin's evolutionary theories fortified the earlier, vaguer faith in unlimited progress. "Liberty," "science," "progress," "evolution" are the concepts which define the mental atmosphere of the nineteenth century.

But tendencies hostile to these were by no means absent. Feudal or Catholic conservatism succeeded, especially in Austria-Hungary, in Russia, and in much of the south of Europe, in preserving old regimes, and the philosophies of a conservative and religious society were reformulated in modern terms. At the same time, in England the very assumptions of the new industrial middle-class society were powerfully attacked by writers such as Carlyle and Ruskin who recommended a return to medieval forms of social co-operation and handicraft. The industrial civilization of the nineteenth century was also opposed by the fierce individualism of many artists and thinkers who were unhappy in the ugly commercial "Philistine" society of the age. The writings of Nietzsche, toward the end of the century, and the whole movement of "art for art's sake," which asserted the independence of the artist from society, are the most obvious symptoms of this revolt. The free enterprise system and the liberalism of the ruling middle classes also early clashed with the rising proletariat, which was won over to diverse forms of socialism, preaching a new collectivism with the stress on equality. Socialism could have Christian or romantic motivations, or it could become "scientific" and revolutionary, as Marx's brand of socialism (a certain stage of which he called "communism") claimed to be.

While up through the eighteenth century religion was, at least in name, a major force in European civilization, in the nineteenth century there was a marked decrease in its influence on both the intellectual leaders and the masses. Local intense revivals of religious consciousness, such as the Oxford Movement in England, did occur, and the traditional religious institutions were preserved everywhere, but the impact of science on religion was such that many tenets of the old faiths crumbled. The discoveries of astronomy, geology, evolutionary biology, archaeology, and biblical criticism forced, almost everywhere, a restatement of the old creeds. Religion, especially in the Protestant countries, was frequently confined to an inner feeling of religiosity or to a system of morality which preserved the ancient Christian virtues. During the early nineteenth century, in Germany, Hegel and his predecessors and followers tried to interpret the world in spiritual terms outside the bounds of traditional religion. There were many attempts even late in the century to restate this view, but the methods and discoveries of science seemed to invalidate it, and various formulas which took science as their base in building new lay religions of hope in humanity gained popularity. French Positivism, English utilitarianism, the evolutionism of Herbert Spencer, are some of the best-known examples. Meanwhile, for the first

time in history, at least in Europe, profoundly pessimistic and atheistic philosophies arose, of which Schopenhauer's was the most subtle, while a purely
physical materialism was the most widespread. Thus the whole gamut of
views of the universe was represented during the century in new and impressive formulations.

The plastic arts did not show a similar vitality. For a long time, in most
countries, painting and architecture floundered in a sterile eclecticism, in a
bewildering variety of historical masquerades in which the neo-Gothic style
was replaced by the neo-Renaissance and that by the neo-Baroque and other
decorative revivals of past forms. Only in France, painting, with the impres-
sionists, found a new style which was genuinely original. In music the highly
romantic art of Richard Wagner attracted most attention, but the individual
national schools either continued in their tradition, like Italian opera (Verdi)
or founded an idiom of their own, often based on a revival of folklore, as in
Russia (Tchaikovsky), Poland (Chopin), Bohemia (Dvořák), and Norway
(Grieg).

But literature was the most representative and the most widely influential
art of the nineteenth century. It found new forms and methods and expressed
the social and intellectual situation of the time most fully and memorably.

REALISM AND NATURALISM

After the great wave of the international romantic movement had spent its
force in the fourth decade of the nineteenth century, European literature
moved in the direction of what is usually called *realism*. Realism was not a
coherent general movement which established itself unchallenged for a long
period of time, as classicism had succeeded in doing during the eighteenth
century. Exceptions and reservations there were, but still in retrospect the
nineteenth century appears as the period of the great realistic writers: Flaubert in France, Dostoevsky and Tolstoy in Russia, Dickens in England, Henry
James in America, Ibsen in Norway.

What is meant by realism? The term, in literary use (there is a much
older philosophical use), apparently dates back to the Germans at the turn
of the century—to Schiller and the Schlegels. It cropped up in France as
early as 1826 but became a commonly accepted literary and artistic slogan
only in the 1850s. (A review called *Réalisme* began publication in 1856, and
a critic, Champfleury, published a volume of critical articles with the title
Le Réalisme in the following year.) Since then the word has been bandied
about, discussed, analyzed, and abused as all slogans are. It is frequently
confused with naturalism, an ancient philosophical term for materialism,
epicureanism, or any secularism. As a specifically literary term, it crystal-
lized only in France. In French, as in English, naturalist means, of course,
simply student of nature, and the analogy between the writer and the naturalist, specifically the botanist and zoologist, was ready at hand. Emile Zola,
in the Preface to a new edition of his early novel, *Thérèse Raquin* (1866),
proclaimed the naturalist creed most boldly. His book, he claims, is "an
analytical labor on two living bodies like that of a surgeon on corpses." He
proudly counts himself among the group of "naturalist writers."

The program of the groups of writers and critics who used these terms can
be easily summarized. The realists wanted a truthful representation in liter-

ature of reality—that is, of contemporary life and manners. They thought of their method as inductive, observational, and hence "objective." The personality of the author was to be suppressed, or was at least to recede into the background, since reality was to be seen "as it is." The naturalistic program, as formulated by Zola, was substantially the same except that Zola put greater stress on the analogies to science, considering the procedure of the novelist as identical with that of the experimenting scientist. He also more definitely and exclusively embraced the philosophy of scientific materialism, with its deterministic implications, its stress on heredity and environment, while the older realists were not always so clear in drawing the philosophical consequences. These French theories were anticipated, paralleled, or imitated all over the world of Western literature. In Germany, the movement called Young Germany, with which Heine was associated, had propounded a substantially antiromantic realistic program as early as the thirties, but versions of the French theories definitely triumphed there only in the 1880s. In Russia, as early as the forties, the most prominent critic of the time, Vissarion Belinsky, praised the "natural" school of Russian fiction, which described contemporary Russia with fidelity. Italy also, from the late seventies on, produced an analogous movement, which called itself *verismo*. The English-speaking countries were the last to adopt the critical programs and slogans of the Continent: George Moore and George Gissing brought the French theories to England in the late eighties, and in the United States William Dean Howells began his campaign for realism in 1886, when he became editor of *Harper's Magazine*. Realistic and naturalistic theories of literature have since been widely accepted in spite of many twentieth-century criticisms and the whole general trend of twentieth-century literature. Especially in the United States, the contemporary novel is usually considered naturalistic and judged by standards of nature and truth. The officially promoted doctrine in Russia is called "Socialist Realism."

The slogans "realism" and "naturalism" were thus new in the nineteenth century. They served as effective formulas directed against the romantic creed. Truth, contemporaneity, and objectivity were the obvious counterparts of romantic imagination, of romantic historicism and its glorification of the past, and of romantic subjectivity, the exaltation of the ego and the individual. But, of course, the emphasis on truth and objectivity was not really new: these qualities had been demanded by many older, classical theories of imitation, and in the eighteenth century there were great writers such as Diderot who wanted a literal "imitation of life" even on the stage.

The practice of realism, it could be argued, is very old indeed. There are realistic scenes in the *Iliad* and the *Odyssey*, and there is plenty of realism in ancient comedy and satire, in medieval stories (fabliaux) like some of Chaucer's and Boccaccio's, in many Elizabethan plays, in the Spanish rogue novels, in the English eighteenth-century novel beginning with Defoe, and so on almost ad infinitum. But while it would be easy to find in early literature anticipations of almost every single element of modern realism, still the systematic description of contemporary society, with a serious purpose, often even with a tragic tone as well, and with sympathy for heroes drawn from the middle and lower classes, was a real innovation of the nineteenth century.

It is usually rash to explain a literary movement in social and political terms. But the new realistic art surely has something to do with the triumph of the middle classes in France after the July revolution in 1830, and in England after the passage of the Reform Bill in 1832, and with the increasing influence of the middle classes in almost every country. Russia is somewhat of an exception as no large middle class could develop there during the nineteenth century. An absolute feudal regime continued in power and the special character of most of Russian literature must be due to this distinction, but even in Russia there emerged an "intelligentsia" (the term comes from Russia) which was open to Western ideas and was highly critical of the czarist regime and its official "ideology."

But while much nineteenth-century literature reflects the triumph of the middle classes, it would be an error to think of the great realistic writers as spokesmen or mouthpieces of the society they described. Balzac was politically a Catholic monarchist who applauded the Bourbon restoration after the fall of Napoleon, but he had an extraordinary imaginative insight into the processes leading to the victory of the middle classes. Flaubert despised the middle-class society of the Third Empire with an intense hatred and the pride of a self-conscious artist. Dickens became increasingly critical of the middle classes and the assumptions of industrial civilization. Dostoevsky, though he took part in a conspiracy against the Russian government early in his life and spent ten years in exile in Siberia, became the propounder of an extremely conservative nationalistic and religious creed which was definitely directed against the revolutionary forces in Russia. Tolstoy, himself a count and a landowner, was violent in his criticism of the czarist regime, especially later in his life, but he cannot be described as friendly to the middle classes, to the aims of the democratic movements in Western Europe, or to the science of the time. Ibsen's political attitude is that of a proud individualist who condemns the "compact majority" and its tyranny. Possibly all art is critical of its society, but in the nineteenth century this criticism became much more explicit, as social and political issues became much more urgent or, at least, were regarded as more urgent by the writing groups. To a far greater degree than in earlier centuries, writers felt their isolation from society, viewed the structure and problems of the prevailing order as debatable and reformable, and in spite of all demands for objectivity became, in many cases, social propagandists and reformers in their own right.

The program of realism, while defensible enough as a reaction against romanticism, raises critical questions which were not answered theoretically by its defenders. What is meant by "truth" of representation? Photographic copying? This seems the implication of many famous pronouncements. "A novel is a mirror walking along the road," said Stendhal as early as 1830. But such statements can hardly be taken literally. All art must select and represent; it cannot be and has never been a simple transcript of reality. What such analogies are intended to convey is rather a claim for an all-inclusiveness of subject matter, a protest against the exclusion of themes which before were considered "low," "sordid," or "trivial" (like the puddles along the road the mirror walks). Chekhov formulated this protest with the usual parallel between the scientist and the writer: "To a chemist nothing on earth is unclean. A writer must be as objective as a chemist; he must abandon the subjective line: he must know that dungheaps play a very respectable part in a landscape, and that evil passions are as inherent in life as good ones." Thus the "truth" of realistic art includes the sordid, the low, the disgusting, and the evil; and, the implication is, the subject is treated objectively, without interference and falsification by the artist's personality and his own desires.

But in practice, while the realistic artist succeeded in expanding the themes of art, he could not fulfill the demand for total objectivity. Works of art are written by human beings and inevitably express their personalities and their points of view. As Conrad admitted, "even the most artful of writers will give himself (and his morality) away in about every third sentence." Objectivity, in the sense which Zola had in mind when he proposed a scientific method in the writing of novels and conceived of the novelist as a sociologist collecting human documents, is impossible in practice. When it has been attempted, it has led only to bad art, to dullness and the display of inert materials, to the confusion between the art of the novel and reporting, "documentation." The demand for "objectivity" can be understood only as a demand for a specific method of narration, in which the author does not interfere explicitly, in his own name, and as a rejection of personal themes of introspection and reverie.

The realistic program, while it has made innumerable new subjects available to art, also implies a narrowing of its themes and methods—a condemnation of the fantastic, the historical, the remote, the idealized, the "unsullied," the idyllic. Realism professes to present us with a "slice of life." But one should recognize that it is an artistic method and convention like any other. Romantic art could, without offending its readers, use coincidences, improbabilities, and even impossibilities, which were not, theoretically at least, tolerated in realistic art. Ibsen, for instance, avoided many older conventions of the stage: asides, soliloquies, eavesdropping, sudden unmotivated appearances of new characters, and so on; but his dramas have their own marked conventions, which seem today almost as "unnatural" as those of the romantics. Realistic theories of literature cannot be upheld in their literal sense; objective and impersonal truth is unobtainable, at least in art, since all art is a "making," a creating of a world of symbols which differs radically from the world which we call reality. The value of realism lies in its negation of the conventions of romanticism, its expansion of the themes of art, and its new demonstration (never forgotten by artists) that literature has to deal also with its time and society and has, at its best, an insight into reality (not only social reality) which is not necessarily identical with that of science. Many of the great writers make us "realize" the world of their time, evoke an imaginative picture of it which seems truer and will last longer than that of historians and sociologists. But this achievement is due to their imagination and their art, or craft, two requisites which realistic theory tended to forget or minimize.

When we observe the actual practice of the great realistic writers of the nineteenth century, we notice a sharp contradiction between theory and practice, and an independent evolution of the art of the novel which is obscured for us if we pay too much attention to the theories and slogans of the time, even those that the authors themselves propounded. Flaubert, the high priest of a cult of "art for art's sake," the most consistent advocate of absolute objectivity, was actually, at least in a good half of his work, a writer of romantic fantasies of blood and gold, flesh and jewels. There is some truth in his saying that Madame Bovary is himself, for in the drab story of a provincial adulteress he castigated his own romanticism and romantic dreams.

So too with Dostoevsky. Although some of his settings resemble those of the "crime novel," he is actually a writer of high tragedy, of a drama of ideas in which ordinary reality is transformed into a symbol of the spiritual world. His technique is closely associated with Balzac's (it is significant that his first publication was a translation of Balzac's *Eugénie Grandet*) and thus with many devices of the sensational melodramatic novel of French romanticism. Tolstoy's art is more concretely real than that of any of the other great masters mentioned, yet he is, at the same time, the most personal and even literally autobiographical author in the history of the novel—a writer, besides, who knows nothing of detachment toward social and religious problems, but frankly preaches his own very peculiar religion. And if we turn to Ibsen, we find essentially the same situation. Ibsen began as a writer of historical and fantastic dramas and slowly returned to a style which is fundamentally symbolist. All his later plays are organized by symbols, from the duck of *The Wild Duck* (1884) to the white horses in *Rosmersholm* (1886), the burned manuscript in *Hedda Gabler* (1890), and the tower in *The Master Builder* (1892). Even Zola, the propounder of the most scientific theory, was in practice a novelist who used the most extreme devices of melodrama and symbolism. In *Germinal* (1885), his novel of mining, the mine is the central symbol, alive as an animal, heaving, breathing. It would be an odd reader who could find literal truth in the final catastrophe of the cave-in or even in such "naturalistic" scenes as a dance where the beer oozes from the nostrils of the drinkers.

One could assert, in short, that all the great realists were at bottom romanticists, but it is probably wiser to conclude that they were simply artists who created worlds of imagination and knew (at least instinctively) that in art one can say something about reality only through symbols. The attempts at documentary art, at mere reporting and transcribing, are today forgotten.

THE NEW POETRY

The later nineteenth century cannot, however, be considered simply an age of realism and naturalism. The great exception is poetry. Some poets continued to practice a substantially romantic art, Tennyson, for instance, and Victor Hugo. There were even movements which upheld a definitely romantic, escapist, antirealist program, such as that of the Pre-Raphaelites in England and the Parnassians in France. In France moreover one poet, Charles Baudelaire (1821–1867), was a completely new voice. He deeply influenced the later course of poetry, not in France only, and he remains even today the one French poet read widely outside France. He stimulated the later Symbolist movement which continued to dominate the early twentieth century.

Baudelaire deeply influenced two very different poets: Mallarmé and Rimbaud. Stéphane Mallarmé (1842–1898), an austere figure, a "hermetic" poet who cultivated obscurity, allusiveness, suggestion, was one of the first poets discontent with ordinary language. He attempted to create a separate poetic language, a language as "magic, words as things." He wanted the personality of the artist to disappear completely behind the work and went so far as to say: "All earthly existence exists to be contained in a book." In his poems he tried to express the mystery of the universe, which he felt to be insoluble and finally empty, Nothingness itself.

Arthur Rimbaud (1854–1891), quite differently, proposed in a famous letter written at the age of sixteen that "the poet should make himself a seer by a long, immense, deliberate disorder of all the senses," all forms of love (homosexual in particular), suffering, and madness. Alcohol and drugs were to encourage hallucination, which led to supernatural illuminations. The disorder of the mind seemed to him sacred. His verse and his prose-poems are a series of vivid images, linked by association, of childhood, nature, city, culminating in a utopia of innocence that he himself never achieved. He led a wandering Bohemian life; at the age of nineteen, he quit writing poetry. He finally came to Ethiopia making his living as a trader in ivory, contracted a disease, and died on a return trip to France in Marseilles in 1891. Rimbaud became a cult figure, his life a myth. He is the quintessential "cursed poet" (poète maudit), the rebellious tramp who renounced poetry and in his misanthropy turned to the most sordid trade in Africa, despising European civilization and bourgeois morality.

As a doctrine, Symbolism was proclaimed only in 1886 by a group headed by a Greek settled in France, Jean Moréas (actually Joannes Papadiaman-topoulos, 1856–1910). The group disintegrated quickly, but the name survived and also spread abroad. Symbolism as a term is vague and ambiguous. If it means symbols in religion and art, it permeates all history. In the French movement it means little more than a recommendation of musicality, suggestion, vagueness, and mystery. Often one can recognize Symbolist poetry by its reversal of the relation between thing and image. In most older poetry the thing is the theme and the image illustrates it, while in Symbolism the image assumes materiality and thing remains either hidden or is merely hinted at. The concrete situation is played down with the result that Symbolism lost its local flavor and became a genuinely international movement. Except for the language, poets in very different national traditions sound astonishingly alike. The later stages of Symbolism are best exemplified in the poetry of W. B. Yeats and T. S. Eliot; in prose its influence is marked in Marcel Proust, James Joyce, and Virginia Woolf, all represented in this anthology.

FURTHER READING

E. Auerbach, *Mimesis: The Representation of Reality in Western Literature* (1953), is a wide-ranging book (from Homer to Proust), with chapters on nineteenth-century realism. G. J. Becker, ed., *Documents of Literary Realism*, is a useful anthology. H. Levin, *The Gates of Horn. A Study of Five French Realists* (1963), contains much on realism in general, including Stendhal, Balzac, Flaubert, Zola, and Proust. Also helpful is R. Wellek, "The Concept of Realism in Literary Scholarship" in *Concepts of Criticism* (1963).

GUSTAVE FLAUBERT

1821–1880

Gustave Flaubert is rightly considered the exemplary realist novelist and *Madame Bovary* his masterpiece. He displays the objectivity, the detachment from his characters demanded by the theory and is a great virtuoso of the art of composition and of style while giving a clear picture of the society of his time. It is likewise a picture in which we can see much of ourselves.

Flaubert was born at Rouen, Normandy, on December 12, 1821, to the chief surgeon of the Hôtel Dieu. He was extremely precocious: by the age of sixteen he was writing stories in the romantic taste, which were published only after his death. In 1840 he went to Paris to study law (he had received his baccalaureate from the local *lycée*), but he failed in his examinations, and in 1843 suffered a sudden nervous breakdown which kept him at home. In 1846 he moved to Croisset, just outside of Rouen on the Seine, where he made his home for the rest of his life, devoting himself to writing. The same year, in Paris, Flaubert met Louise Colet, a minor poet and lady about town, who became his mistress. In 1849–1851 he visited the Levant, traveling extensively in Greece, Syria, and Egypt. After his return he settled down to the writing of *Madame Bovary*, which took him five full years and which was a great popular success. The remainder of his life was uneventful. He made occasional trips to Paris, and one trip, in 1860, to Tunisia to see the ruins of Carthage in preparation for the writing of his novel *Salammbô*. Three more novels followed: *The Sentimental Education* (1869), *The Temptation of St. Anthony* (1874), and the unfinished *Bouvard and Pecuchet* (1881), as well as *Three Tales* (1877), consisting of "A Simple Heart," "The Legend of St. Julian the Hospitaler," and "Herodias." Flaubert died at Croisset on May 8, 1880.

Flaubert's novel, *Madame Bovary* (1856), is deservedly considered the showpiece of French realism. It would be impossible to find a novel, certainly before Flaubert, in which humble persons in a humble setting are treated with such seriousness, restraint, verisimilitude, and imaginative clarity. At first sight, *Madame Bovary* is a solidly documented and clearly visualized account of life in a village of the French province of Normandy sometime in the forties of the last century. We meet a whole spectrum of social types found in such a time and place: the doctor (actually a "health officer" with a lower degree), a pharmacist, a storekeeper, a notary and his clerk, a tax collector, a woman innkeeper and her stableboy, the priest and his sacristan, a neighboring landowner, and a farmer. We are told the story of a young peasant woman brought up in a convent, who marries a dull man and commits adultery first with a ruthless philanderer and then with a spineless younger man. Overwhelmed by debts concealed from her unsuspecting husband, faced by sudden demands for repayment, disillusioned in love, rebuffed by everybody who might help her, she commits suicide by poisoning herself with arsenic. Nothing seems simpler and more ordinary, and the manner of telling seems completely objective, detached, impersonal. A case is presented which is observed with almost scientific curiosity. The descriptions are obviously accurate, sometimes based on expert knowledge; the clubfoot operation and the effects of arsenic poisoning agree with medical evidence. The setting—the topography of the two villages, the interior of the houses, the inn, the pharmacy, the city of Rouen, the cathedral there, the river landscape, and the particular things and sounds—imprints itself vividly on our memory. Every detail serves its purpose of characterization—from the absurd cap of the schoolboy Charles to the mirror and the crucifix in the deathbed scene; from the sound of Binet's lathe turning out napkin rings to the tap of the stableboy's wooden leg. "The technique of *Madame Bovary* has become the model of all novels" (Albert Thibaudet).

But surely the book could not have kept its grip on modern readers if it were only a superbly accurate description of provincial life in France (as the added subtitle, *Mœurs de province*, suggests). The book transcends its time and place if one thinks of Emma Bovary as the type of the unfulfilled dreamer, as the failed and foiled romanticist, as a female Don Quixote, corrupted by sentimental reading, caught in a trap of circumstance, pitiful and to be pitied in her horrible self-inflicted death.

This central theme has, however, remained ambiguous. What attracted and shocked readers was the uncertainty about the author's attitude toward Emma, particularly at the time of publication when readers were accustomed to being told clearly by addresses and comments what they were to think of the actions and morals of the characters of a novel. *Madame Bovary*, at publication, caused a scandal. The review *(Revue de Paris)* in which it was published serially and the author were hauled into court for immorality and blasphemy and the prosecutor described the book as an incitement to adultery and atheism. In his rebuttal, the defense counsel argued that the novel is rather a highly moral work in which adultery is punished even excessively. Flaubert was acquitted but neither the prosecutor nor the defending attorney interpreted the book correctly. It is neither a salacious novel nor a didactic tract. Some parts of the book are frankly satirical (and thus far from purely objective): The gross village priest who cannot even understand the distress of Emma is flanked by the fussy, shallow, pseudoscientific, enlightened, "progressive" pharmacist Homais. Though they argue and quarrel they are finally reduced to a common level when they eat and snore at the wake next to Emma's corpse. The rightly famous scene of the country fair satirizes and parodies the pompous rhetoric of the officials extolling the glories of agriculture, counterpointing it to the equally platitudinous love talk of Rodolphe and the lowing of the cattle in an amalgam which reduces men and women to a common level of animality. Even Emma is not spared: Her sentimental religiosity, her taste for luxury, her financial improvidence are diagnosed as disguised eroticism. She would not have minded if Rodolphe had drawn a pistol against her husband. In her desperate search for escape she asks Léon to steal for her. In the last attempt to get money she is ready to sell herself. She is indifferent to her child, deceitful even in small matters. Her longing for sensual satisfaction becomes, in the scenes with Léon in the hotel at Rouen, frantic and corrupt. The author weighed the scales against her: She married an excessively stupid and insensitive man; she met two callous lovers; she is tricked by a merciless usurer; she is utterly alone at last. When

Charles meeting Rodolphe after her death and after he had discovered her infidelities tells him, ineptly, awkwardly: "It was the fault of destiny," the author expressly approves of this saying. The novel conveys a sense of inexorable determinism, of the vanity of dreaming, of the impossibility of escape from one's nature and station. It conveys a sense of despair, of man's and woman's alienation in an incomprehensible universe but also a hatred for all the stupidity, mediocrity and baseness of people there and everywhere. (Flaubert called them "bourgeois," but included the proletarian masses in his contempt.) Emma is pitied because she has, at least, a spark of discontent, the yearning to escape the cage of her existence. But baseness triumphs and the book ends with a sudden change to the present tense: "Homais has just received the Cross of the Legion of Honor."

This sense of the inexorable, the fatal, the inescapable is secured also by the precision and firmness of Flaubert's style and the carefully planned architectonics of his composition. If we mean by style the systematic exploitation of the syntactical and lexical possibilities of a language we must class Flaubert with the great stylists: the exact descriptive epithet, the one right word (le mot juste) even when he uses the most trivial cliché or the most recondite scientific term coheres with the skillful modulations and rhythms of the sentences, the organization of the paragraphs and the divisions of the sections which are grouped around a series of pictorial scenes: the schoolroom, the rustic wedding, the ball, the visit to the priest, the country fair, the ride in the woods, the clubfoot operation, the opera, the cathedral, the cab ride, the deathbed, to mention only the most memorable.

Madame Bovary is constantly cited as an example for the handling of narrative perspective. The story begins in the schoolroom ostensibly told by a schoolfellow (the word "we" is used in the first pages); it shifts then to the narration of an omniscient author and, off and on, narrows to the point of view of Emma. Much is seen only through her eyes, but one cannot say that the author identifies with her or enters her mind sympathetically. He keeps his distance and on occasion conveys his own opinion. He is not averse even to moral judgments: He speaks of Emma's hard-hearted and tightfisted peasant nature (p. 874), he refers to her corruption (p. 1027), and Rodolphe is several times condemned for his brutality and cynicism (pp. 919, 964, 971). In the description of extreme unction (p. 1062) the author pronounces solemnly his forgiveness (which he suggests would be also God's) for her coveting all worldly goods, her greediness "for the warm breeze and scents of love," and even her sensuality and lust. But mostly Flaubert depicts the scenes by simple description or reproduction of speech or imagined silent reflections. Things and people become at times symbolic even in an obtrusive way: the wedding bouquet, the plate of boiled beef, and the apparition of the blind beggar who turns up conveniently at the hour of Emma's death. Much is said about her which she could not have observed herself. The famous saying "Madame Bovary c'est moi" ("I am Madame Bovary") cannot be traced back to an earlier date than 1909 when it is reported on distant hearsay in René Descharmes, Flaubert avant 1857 (p. 103). There are dozens of passages in the letters during the composition of Madame Bovary which express Flaubert's distaste for the "vulgarity of his subject," "the fetid smell of the milieu," and his opinion of Emma Bovary as "a woman of false poetry and false sentiments." Usually he defends his choice of theme as a "prodigious *tour de force*," as "an act of crude will power," as "a deliberate made-up thing" though we suspect him sometimes of exaggerating his efforts in order to impress his correspondent in Paris, a facile and prolific novelist and poet, Louise Colet.

Still, the saying "Madame Bovary c'est moi" has been widely quoted and accepted because it contains a kernel of truth. In Emma, Flaubert combats his own vices of daydreaming, romanticism, exoticism, of which he thought he could cure himself by writing this antiromantic book. But the identification with Emma distracts us from noticing Flaubert's deep-seated sympathies with the slow-witted, abused, but honest and loving Charles who rightly opens and closes the book and for the other good people: Emma's father, the farmer Rouault, kind and distressed by all he could not foresee; Justin, the pharmacist's apprentice adoring Emma from afar, praying on her grave; the clubfoot stableboy tortured and exploited for a dream of medical reputation; poor neglected Berthe sent to the cotton mill; the old peasant woman at the fair who for fifty-four years of service got a medal worth twenty-five francs; and even the blind beggar with his horrible skin disease. Moreover, there is the admirable Dr. Lavrière who appears fleetingly like an apparition from a saner, loftier world of good sense and professional devotion. Thus it seems unjust of Martin Turnell to say that the novel is "an onslaught on the whole basis of human feeling and on all spiritual and moral values."

In Flaubert's mind, the novel was also an assertion of the redeeming power of art. His long struggle with its composition, which took him more than five years of grinding drudgery: five days in which he had written a single page, five or six pages in a week, twenty-five pages in six weeks, thirteen pages in seven weeks, a whole night spent in hunting for the right adjective; the ruthless pruning to which he subjected his enormous manuscript, eliminating many fine touches, similes, metaphors, and descriptions of elusive mental states (as a study of the manuscripts has shown) were to him a victory of art over reality, a passionate search for Beauty, which he knew to be an illusion. But one wonders whether the conflict of Flaubert's scientific detachment and cruel observation with the intense adoration of beauty, the thirst for calculated purity and structure, for "style" as perfection, can be resolved. He tried to achieve this synthesis in *Madame Bovary*. Watching this struggle between heterogeneous elements, and even opposites, should explain some of the fascination of the book.

[*Editor's Note.* An explanation of the plot and the stage business is needed to understand properly the performance in *Madame Bovary* of the opera *Lucia di Lammermoor*, which occurs on pages 986–89 of this text. The French libretto by Alp. Royer and Gust. Vaez (published in Brussels in 1839) must be consulted, as it differs greatly from the original Italian libretto by Salvatore Cammarano and resembles only distantly the novel by Walter Scott. The story is one of family hatred: Edgar, the owner of the castle of Ravenswood in the Scottish Highlands, has been expelled by Lord Henry Ashton who had killed his father. He is in hiding as an outlaw. He loves and is loved clandestinely by Lucy, Lord Henry's sister. The opera opens with a hunting scene on the grounds of Ravenswood castle where Henry, his forester called Gilbert (Normanno in the Italian), and other followers comb the grounds for traces of a mysterious stranger whom they suspect to be the outcast Edgar. They are joined by Lord Arthur who is a suitor for Lucy's hand and is favored by her brother as he can save him from financial ruin. Arthur declares his love for Lucy (no such scene is in the Italian). Lucy in the next scene prepares to meet Edgar in a secluded spot; she gives a purse to Gilbert whom she believes to be her friend though Gilbert is actually scheming with Lord Henry against her. (The scene is not in the Italian original.) Then Lucy is left alone and sings a cavatina beginning: "Que n'avons-nous des ailes" ("If only we had wings"). Edgar appears then, played by Lagardy, a fictional tenor. He tells of his hatred for Lucy's brother because of the death of his father. He had sworn vengeance but is ready to forget it in his love for her. Edgar has to leave on a mission to France but in parting the lovers pledge their troth and exchange rings. The stretto contains the words, "Une fleur pour ma tombe" ("A flower for my tomb"), "donne une larme à l'exilé," ("give a tear for the exiled one"), phrases alluded to in Flaubert's account.

Charles is so obtuse that he thinks that Edgar is torturing Lucy, and Emma has to tell him that he is her lover. Charles protests that he heard him vowing vengeance on her family. He had heard him saying: "J'ai juré vengeance et guerre" ("I have sworn vengeance and war"). Charles has also heard Lord Arthur say, "J'aime Lucie et m'en crois aimé" ("I love Lucie and I believe she loves me") and has seen Lord Arthur going off with her father arm in arm. But Charles obviously takes her brother Henry for her father.

The second act begins with Gilbert telling his master Henry that he slipped Lucy's ring from the sleeping Edgar, had made a copy and will produce it in order to convince Lucy of Edgar's faithlessness. Charles mistakes the false ring which is shown Lucy for a love gift sent by Edgar. The business with the rings replaced an analogous deception with forged letters in the Italian libretto. Lucy appears dressed for the wedding with Lord Arthur, unhappily resisting and imploring, reminding Emma of her own wedding day and the contrast with her false joy soon turned to bitterness. Brandishing a sword Edgar suddenly returns voicing his indignation. There follows a sextet (Lucy, Henry, Edgar, Raimondo the minister, Arthur, Gilbert) which suggests to Emma her desire to flee and to be carried off as Edgar wants to carry off Lucy. But the marriage contract has been signed and Edgar curses her. The third act does not interest Emma any more as Léon has appeared in the interval. She does not care for the scene between Lord Henry and his retainer (called here "servant") Gilbert who introduces a disguised stranger, Edgar of course. The duet between Henry Lord Ashton and Edgar reaffirms their mutual hatred. The mad scene follows. Lucy flees the marriage chamber; she has stabbed her husband and gone mad. She dreams of Edgar and dies. The great aria which was considered the climax of coloratura singing was lost on Emma absorbed in Léon.

One must assume that Flaubert had the French libretto in front of him or remembered its wordings and stage business accurately. (He had seen the opera first in Rouen in 1840 and again in Constantinople in November 1850.) A modern reader who knows the Italian libretto from recordings may be puzzled by the discrepancies, and ascribe to Flaubert's imagination or confused memory what is actually an accurate description of the French version.]

Victor Brombert, *The Novels of Flaubert* (1966), is the best general book in English. Paul de Man, ed., *Gustave Flaubert: Madame Bovary. Backgrounds and Sources: Essays in Criticism* (1965), will help the reader, as will Alison Fairlie, *Flaubert: Madame Bovary* (1962), a good discussion of problems, structures, people, and values addressed to students. Raymond D. Giraud, *Flaubert: A Collection of Critical Essays*, contains selections of essays from modern criticism. Anthony Thorlby, *Gustave Flaubert and the Art of Realism* (1957), is a short book with an excellent chapter on *Madame Bovary*.

Madame Bovary[1]

Part One

I

We were in class when the headmaster came in, followed by a new boy, not wearing the school uniform, and a school servant carrying a large desk. Those who had been asleep woke up, and every one rose as if just surprised at his work.

The headmaster made a sign to us to sit down. Then, turning to the teacher, he said to him in a low voice:

"Monsieur Roger, here is a pupil whom I recommend to your care; he'll be in the second. If his work and conduct are satisfactory, he will go into one of the upper classes, as becomes his age."

The new boy, standing in the corner behind the door so that he could hardly be seen, was a country lad of about fifteen, and taller than any of us. His hair was cut square on his forehead like a village choir boy; he looked reliable, but very ill at ease. Although he was not broad-shouldered, his short jacket of green cloth with black buttons must have been tight about the armholes, and showed at the opening of the cuffs red wrists accustomed to being bare. His legs, in blue stockings, looked out from beneath yellowish trousers, drawn tight by suspenders. He wore stout, ill-cleaned, hob-nailed boots.

We began reciting the lesson. He listened with all his ears, as attentive as if at a sermon, not daring even to cross his legs or lean on his elbow; and when at two o'clock the bell rang, the master was obliged to tell him to fall into line with the rest of us.

When we came back to work, we were in the habit of throwing our caps on the ground so as to have our hands more free; we used from the door to toss them under the desk, so that they hit against

---

1. A substantially new translation by Paul De Man.

the wall and made a lot of dust: it was the fad of the moment.

But, whether he had not noticed the trick, or did not dare to attempt it, the new boy was still holding his cap on his knees even after prayers were over. It was one of those head-gears of composite order, in which we can find traces of the bear- and the coonskin, the shako, the bowler, and the cotton nightcap; one of those poor things, in fine, whose dumb ugliness has depths of expression, like an imbecile's face. Ovoid and stiffened with whalebone, it began with three circular strips; then came in succession lozenges of velvet and rabbit fur separated by a red band; after that a sort of bag that ended in a cardboard polygon covered with complicated braiding, from which hung, at the end of a long thin cord, small twisted gold threads in the manner of a tassel. The cap was new; its peak shone.

"Rise," said the master.

He stood up; his cap fell. The whole class began to laugh. He stooped to pick it up. A neighbour knocked it down again with his elbow; he picked it up once more.

"Get rid of your helmet," said the master, who liked to joke.

There was a burst of laughter from the boys, which so thoroughly put the poor lad out of countenance that he did not know whether to keep his cap in his hand, leave it on the ground, or put it on his head. He sat down again and placed it on his knee.

"Rise," repeated the master, "and tell me your name."

The new boy articulated in a stammering voice an unintelligible name.

"Again!"

The same sputtering of syllables was heard, drowned by the tittering of the class.

"Louder!" cried the master; "louder!"

The new boy then took a supreme resolution, opened an inordinately large mouth, and shouted at the top of his voice as if calling some one, the word "Charbovari."

A hubbub broke out, rose in crescendo with bursts of shrill voices (they yelled, barked, stamped, repeated "Charbovari! Charbovari!"), then died away into single notes, growing quieter only with great difficulty, and now and again suddenly recommencing along the line of a seat from where rose here and there, like a damp cracker going off, a stifled laugh.

However, amid a rain of penalties, order was gradually re-established in the class; and the master having succeeded in catching the name of "Charles Bovary," having had it dictated to him, spelt out, and re-read, at once ordered the poor devil to go and sit down on the punishment form at the foot of the master's desk. He got up, but before going hesitated.

"What are you looking for?" asked the master.

"My c-c-c-cap," said the new boy shyly, casting troubled looks round him.

"Five hundred verses for all the class!" shouted in a furious voice, stopped, like the *Quos ego*,[2] a fresh outburst. "Silence!" continued the master indignantly, wiping his brow with his handkerchief, which he had just taken from his cap. "As to you, Bovary, you will conjugate '*ridiculus sum*' twenty times." Then, in a gentler tone, "Come, you'll find your cap again; it hasn't been stolen."

Quiet was restored. Heads bent over desks, and the new boy remained for two hours in an exemplary attitude, although from time to time some paper pellet flipped from the tip of a pen came bang in his face. But he wiped his face with one hand and continued motionless, his eyes lowered.

In the evening, at study hall, he pulled out his sleeveguards from his desk, arranged his small belongings, and carefully ruled his paper. We saw him working conscientiously, looking up every word in the dictionary, and taking the greatest pains. Thanks, no doubt, to the willingness he showed, he had not to go down to the class below. But though he knew his rules passably, he lacked all elegance in composition. It was the curé of his village who had taught him his first Latin; his parents, from motives of economy, having sent him to school as late as possible.

His father, Monsieur Charles Denis Bartolomé Bovary, retired assistant-surgeon-major, compromised about 1812 in certain conscription scandals, and forced at this time to leave the service, had taken advantage of his fine figure to get hold of a dowry of sixty thousand francs in the person of a hosier's daughter who had fallen in love with his good looks. He was a fine man, a great talker, making his spurs ring as he walked, wearing whiskers that ran into his moustache, his fingers always garnished with rings; he dressed in loud colours, had the dash of a military man with the easy go of a commercial traveller. Once married, he lived for three or four years on his wife's fortune, dining well, rising late, smoking long porcelain pipes, not coming in at night till after the theatre, and haunting cafés. The father-in-law died, leaving little; he was indignant at this, tried his hand at the textile business, lost some money in it, then retired to the country, where he thought he would make the land pay off. But, as he knew no more about farming than calico, as he rode his horses instead of sending them to plough, drank his cider in bottle instead of selling it in cask, ate the finest poultry in his farm-yard, and greased his hunting-boots with the fat of his pigs, he was

---

2. Neptune becalming the winds in the *Aeneid* (I.135).

not long in finding out that he would do better to give up all speculation.

For two hundred francs[3] a year he managed to rent on the border of the provinces of Caux and Picardy, a kind of place half farm, half private house; and here, soured, eaten up with regrets, cursing his luck, jealous of every one, he shut himself up at the age of forty-five, sick of men, he said, and determined to live in peace.

His wife had adored him once on a time; she had loved him with a thousand servilities that had only estranged him the more. Lively once, expansive and affectionate, in growing older she had become (after the fashion of wine that, exposed to air, turns to vinegar) illtempered, grumbling, irritable. She had suffered so much without complaint at first, when she had seen him going after all the village harlots, and when a score of bad houses sent him back to her at night, weary, stinking drunk. Then her pride revolted. After that she was silent, burying her anger in a dumb stoicism that she maintained till her death. She was constantly going about looking after business matters. She called on the lawyers, the judges, remembered when notes fell due, got them renewed, and at home ironed, sewed, washed, looked after the workmen, paid the accounts, while he, troubling himself about nothing, eternally besotted in a sleepy sulkiness from which he only roused himself to say nasty things to her, sat smoking by the fire and spitting into the cinders.

When she had a child, it had to be sent out to nurse. When he came home, the lad was spoilt as if he were a prince. His mother stuffed him with jam; his father let him run about barefoot, and, playing the philosopher, even said he might as well go about quite naked like the young of animals. As opposed to the maternal ideas, he had a certain virile idea of childhood on which he sought to mould his son, wishing him to be brought up hardily, like a Spartan, to give him a strong constitution. He sent him to bed without any fire, taught him to drink off large draughts of rum and to jeer at religious processions. But, peaceable by nature, the boy responded poorly to his attempts. His mother always kept him near her; she cut out cardboard pictures for him, told him tales, entertained him with monologues full of melancholy gaiety, chatting and fondling in endless baby-talk. In her life's isolation she transferred on the child's head all her scattered, broken little vanities. She dreamed of high station; she already saw him, tall, handsome, clever, settled as an engineer or in the law. She taught him to read, and even on an old

3. It is very difficult to transpose monetary values from 1840 into present-day figures, since relationships between the actual value of the franc, the cost of living, and the relative cost of specific items (such as rent, rent estate, etc.) have undergone fundamental changes. One would not be too far off the mark by reading present-day dollars for Flaubert's francs; that would show Madame Bovary destroyed, at the end of the book, by an 8,000-dollar debt.

piano she had taught him two or three sentimental ballads. But to all this Monsieur Bovary, caring little for arts and letters, said "It was not worth while. Would they ever have the means to send him to a public school, to buy him a practice, or start him in business? Besides, with brashness a man can always make his way in the world." Madame Bovary bit her lips, and the child knocked about the village.

He followed the farm laborers, drove away with clods of earth the ravens that were flying about. He ate blackberries along the hedges, minded the geese with a long switch, went hay-making during harvest, ran about in the woods, played hopscotch under the church porch on rainy days, and at great fêtes begged the beadle to let him toll the bells, that he might hang all his weight on the long rope and feel himself borne upward by it in its swing.

So he grew like an oak; he was strong of hand, ruddy of complexion.

When he was twelve years old his mother had her own way; he began his lessons. The curé took him in hand; but the lessons were so short and irregular that they could not be of much use. They were given at spare moments in the sacristy, standing up, hurriedly, between a baptism and a burial; or else the curé, if he had not to go out, sent for his pupil after the *Angelus*. They went up to his room and settled down; the flies and moths fluttered round the candle. It was close, the child fell asleep, and the good man, beginning to doze with his hands on his stomach, was soon snoring with his mouth wide open. On other occasions, when Monsieur le Curé, on his way back after administering the holy oil to some sick person in the neighborhood, caught sight of Charles playing about the fields, he called him, lectured him for a quarter of an hour, and took advantage of the occasion to make him conjugate his verb at the foot of a tree. The rain interrupted them or an acquaintance passed. All the same he was always pleased with him, and even said the "young man" had a very good memory.

Charles could not go on like this. Madame Bovary took strong steps. Ashamed, or rather tired out, Monsieur Bovary gave in without a struggle, and they waited one year longer, so that the child could take his first communion.

Six months more passed, and the year after Charles was finally sent to school at Rouen. His father took him there towards the end of October, at the time of the St. Romain fair.

It would now be impossible for any of us to remember any thing about him. He was a youth of even temperament, who played in playtime, worked in school-hours, was attentive in class, slept well in the dormitory, and ate well in the refectory. He had for guardian a hardware merchant in the Rue Ganterie, who took him out once a month on Sundays after his shop was shut, sent him for a walk on the quay to look at the boats, and then brought him back to college at seven o'clock before supper. Every Thursday evening he wrote a long letter to his mother with red ink and three wax seals; then he went over his history note-books, or read an old volume of "Anarchasis"[4] that was lying about the study. When he went for walks he talked to the servant, who, like himself, came from the country.

By dint of hard work he kept always about the middle of the class; once even he got an honor mark in natural history. But at the end of his third year his parents withdrew him from the school to make him study medicine, convinced that he could make it to the bachelor's degree by himself.

His mother chose a room for him on the fourth floor of a dyer's she knew, overlooking the Eau-de-Robec.[5] She made arrangements for his board, got him furniture, table and two chairs, sent home for an old cherry-tree bedstead, and bought besides a small cast-iron stove with the supply of wood that was to warm her poor child. Then at the end of a week she departed, after a thousand injunctions to be good now that he was going to be left to himself.

The course list that he read on the notice-board stunned him: lectures on anatomy, lectures on pathology, lectures on physiology, lectures on pharmacy, lectures on botany and clinical medicine, and therapeutics, without counting hygiene and materia medica—all names of whose etymologies he was ignorant, and that were to him as so many doors to sanctuaries filled with magnificent darkness.

He understood nothing of it all; it was all very well to listen—he did not follow. Still he worked; he had bound note-books, he attended all the courses, never missed a single lecture. He did his little daily task like a mill-horse, who goes round and round with his eyes bandaged, not knowing what work it is grinding out.

To spare him expense his mother sent him every week by the carrier a piece of veal baked in the oven, with which he lunched when he came back from the hospital, while he sat kicking his feet against the wall. After this he had to run off to lectures, to the operation-room, to the hospital, and return to his home at the other end of the town. In the evening, after the poor dinner of his landlord, he went back to his room and set to work again in his wet clothes, that smoked as he sat in front of the hot stove.

On the fine summer evenings, at the time when the close streets are empty, when the servants are playing shuttle-cock at the doors, he opened his window and leaned out. The river, that makes of this

---

4. *Voyage du jeune Anarchasis en Grèce* (1788) was a popular account of ancient Greece, by Jean-Jacques Barthélemy (1716–1795).   5. Small river, now covered up, that flows through the poorest neighborhood of Rouen, used as a sewer by the factories that border it, thus suggesting Flaubert's description as *"une ignoble petite Venise"* (a wretched little Venice).

quarter of Rouen a wretched little Venice, flowed beneath him, between the bridges and the railings, yellow, violet, or blue. Working men, kneeling on the banks, washed their bare arms in the water. On poles projecting from the attics, skeins of cotton were drying in the air. Opposite, beyond the roofs, spread the pure sky with the red sun setting. How pleasant it must be at home! How fresh under the beech-tree! And he expanded his nostrils to breathe in the sweet odours of the country which did not reach him.

He grew thin, his figure became taller, his face took a saddened look that made it almost interesting.

Passively, through indifference, he abandoned all the resolutions he had made. Once he missed a lecture; the next day all the lectures; and, enjoying his idleness, little by little he gave up work altogether.

He got into the habit of going to the cafés, and had a passion for dominoes. To shut himself up every evening in the dirty public room, to push about on marble tables the small sheep-bones with black dots, seemed to him a fine proof of his freedom, which raised him in his own esteem. It was beginning to see life, the sweetness of stolen pleasures; and when he entered, he put his hand on the door-handle with a joy almost sensual. Then many things compressed within him expanded; he learned by heart student songs and sang them at gatherings, became enthusiastic about Béranger,[6] learnt how to make punch, and, finally how to make love.

Thanks to these preparatory labors, he failed completely in his examination for his degree of *officier de santé*.[7] He was expected home the same night to celebrate his success.

He started on foot, stopped at the beginning of the village, sent for his mother, and told her all. She excused him, threw the blame of his failure on the injustice of the examiners, encouraged him a little, and took upon herself to set matters straight. It was only five years later that Monsieur Bovary knew the truth; it was old then, and he accepted it. Moreover, he could not believe that a man born of him could be a fool.

So Charles set to work again and crammed for his examination, ceaselessly learning all the old questions by heart. He passed pretty well. What a happy day for his mother! They gave a grand dinner.

Where should he go to practise? To Tostes, where there was only one old doctor. For a long time Madame Bovary had been on the look-out for his death, and the old fellow had barely been packed off

6. Pierre-Jean de Béranger (1780–1857) was an extremely popular writer of songs often exalting the glories of the empire of Napoleon I.   7. Instituted during the Revolution, this was a kind of second-class medical degree, well below the doctorate. The student was allowed to attend a medical school without having passed the equivalence of the *baccalauréat*. He could only practice in the department in which the diploma had been conferred (Bovary is thus tied down to the vicinity of Rouen) and was not allowed to perform major operations except in the presence of a full-fledged doctor. The diploma was suppressed in 1892.

when Charles was installed, opposite his place, as his successor.

But it was not everything to have brought up a son, to have had him taught medicine, and discovered Tostes, where he could practise it; he must have a wife. She found him one—the widow of a bailiff at Dieppe, who was forty-five and had an income of twelve hundred francs.

Though she was ugly, as dry as a bone, her face with as many pimples as the spring has buds, Madame Dubuc had no lack of suitors. To attain her ends Madame Bovary had to oust them all, and she even succeeded in very cleverly baffling the intrigues of a pork-butcher backed up by the priests.

Charles had seen in marriage the advent of an easier life, thinking he would be more free to do as he liked with himself and his money. But his wife was master; he had to say this and not say that in company, to fast every Friday, dress as she liked, harass at her bidding those patients who did not pay. She opened his letters, watched his comings and goings, and listened at the partition-wall when women came to consult him in his surgery.

She had to have her chocolate every morning, attentions without end. She constantly complained of her nerves, her chest, her liver. The noise of footsteps made her ill; when people went away, solitude became odious to her; if they came back, it was doubtless to see her die. When Charles returned in the evening, she stretched forth two long thin arms from beneath the sheets, put them round his neck, and having made him sit down on the edge of the bed, began to talk to him of her troubles: he was neglecting her, he loved another. She had been warned she would be unhappy; and she ended by asking him for a dose of medicine and a little more love.

II

One night towards eleven o'clock they were awakened by the noise of a horse pulling up outside their door. The maid opened the garret-window and parleyed for some time with a man in the street below. He came for the doctor, had a letter for him. Nastasie came downstairs shivering and undid the locks and bolts one after the other. The man left his horse, and, following the servant, suddenly came in behind her. He pulled out from his wool cap with grey topknots a letter wrapped up in a rag and presented it gingerly to Charles, who rested on his elbow on the pillow to read it. Nastasie, standing near the bed, held the light. Madame in modesty had turned to the wall and showed only her back.

This letter, sealed with a small seal in blue wax, begged Monsieur Bovary to come immediately to the farm of the Bertaux to set a broken leg. Now from Tostes to the Bertaux was a good fifteen miles across country by way of Longueville and Saint-Victor. It was a dark night; Madame Bovary junior was afraid of accidents for her husband. So it was decided the stable-boy should go on first; Charles would start three hours later when the moon rose. A boy was to be sent to meet him, in order to show him the way to the farm and open the gates for him.

Towards four o'clock in the morning, Charles, well wrapped up in his cloak, set out for the Bertaux. Still sleepy from the warmth of his bed, he let himself be lulled by the quiet trot of his horse. When it stopped of its own accord in front of those holes surrounded with thorns that are dug on the margin of furrows, Charles awoke with a start, suddenly remembered the broken leg, and tried to call to mind all the fractures he knew. The rain had stopped, day was breaking, and on the branches of the leafless trees birds roosted motionless, their little feathers bristling in the cold morning wind. The flat country stretched as far as eye could see, and the tufts of trees around the farms seemed, at long intervals, like dark violet stains on the vast grey surface, fading on the horizon into the gloom of the sky. Charles from time to time opened his eyes but his mind grew weary, and sleep coming upon him, he soon fell into a doze wherein his recent sensations blending with memories, he became conscious of a double self, at once student and married man, lying in his bed as but now, and crossing the operation theatre as of old. The warm smell of poultices mingled in his brain with the fresh odour of dew; he heard the iron rings rattling along the curtain-rods of the bed and saw his wife sleeping . . . As he passed Vassonville he came upon a boy sitting on the grass at the edge of a ditch.

"Are you the doctor?" asked the child.

And on Charles's answer he took his wooden shoes in his hands and ran on in front of him.

The *officier de santé*, riding along, gathered from his guide's talk that Monsieur Rouault must be one of the well-to-do farmers. He had broken his leg the evening before on his way home from a Twelfth-night feast at a neighbor's. His wife had been dead for two years. There was only his daughter, who helped him to keep house, with him.

The ruts were becoming deeper; they were approaching the Bertaux. The little farmboy, slipping through a hole in the hedge, disappeared; then he came back to the end of a courtyard to open the gate. The horse slipped on the wet grass; Charles had to stoop to pass under the branches. The watchdogs in their kennels barked, dragging at their chains. As he entered the Bertaux the horse took fright and stumbled.

It was a substantial-looking farm. In the stables, over the top of the open doors, one could see great cart-horses quietly feeding from new racks. Right along the outbuildings extended a large dunghill, smoking at the top, while amidst fowls and turkeys five or six peacocks, the luxury of Cauchois farmyards, were foraging around. The sheepfold was long, the barn high, with walls smooth as a hand. Under the cart-shed were two large carts and four ploughs, with their whips, shafts and harnesses complete, whose fleeces of blue wool were getting soiled by the fine dust that fell from the granaries. The courtyard sloped upwards, planted with trees set out symmetrically, and the chattering noise of a flock of geese was heard near the pond.

A young woman in a blue merino dress with three flounces came to the threshold of the door to receive Monsieur Bovary; she led him to the kitchen, where a large fire was blazing. The servants' breakfast was boiling beside it in small pots of all sizes. Some damp clothes were drying inside the chimney-corner. The shovel, tongs, and the nozzle of the bellows, all of colossal size, shone like polished steel, while along the walls hung many pots and pans in which the clear flame of the hearth, mingling with the first rays of the sun coming in through the window, was mirrored fitfully.

Charles went up to the first floor to see the patient. He found him in his bed, sweating under his bed-clothes, having thrown his cotton nightcap right away from him. He was a fat little man of fifty, with white skin and blue eyes, the fore part of his head bald, and he wore ear-rings. By his side on a chair stood a large decanter of brandy, from which he poured himself out a little from time to time to keep up his spirits; but as soon as he caught sight of the doctor his elation subsided, and instead of swearing, as he had been doing for the last twelve hours, he began to groan feebly.

The fracture was a simple one, without any kind of complication. Charles could not have hoped for an easier case. Then calling to mind the devices of his masters at the bedside of patients, he comforted the sufferer with all sorts of kindly remarks, those caresses of the surgeon that are like the oil they put on scalpels. In order to make some splints a bundle of laths was brought up from the cart-house. Charles selected one, cut it into two pieces and planed it with a fragment of windowpane, while the servant tore up sheets to make bandages, and Mademoiselle Emma tried to sew some pads. As she was a long time before she found her workcase, her father grew impatient; she did not answer, but as she sewed she pricked her fingers, which she then put to her mouth to suck them.

Charles was surprised at the whiteness of her nails. They were shiny, delicate at the tips, more polished than the ivory of Dieppe, and almond-shaped. Yet her hand was not beautiful, perhaps not white enough, and a little hard at the knuckles; besides, it was too long, with no soft inflections in the outlines. Her real beauty was in her eyes. Although brown, they seemed black because of the lashes, and her look came at you frankly, with a candid boldness.

The bandaging over, the doctor was invited by Monsieur Rouault himself to have a bit before he left.

Charles went down into the room on the ground-floor. Knives and forks and silver goblets were laid for two on a little table at the foot of a huge bed that had a canopy of printed cotton with figures representing Turks. There was an odor of iris-root and damp sheets that escaped from a large oak chest opposite the window. On the floor in corners were sacks of flour stuck upright in rows. These were the overflow from the neighboring granary, to which three stone steps led. By way of decoration for the apartment, hanging to a nail in the middle of the wall, whose green paint scaled off from the effects of the saltpeter, was a crayon head of Minerva in a gold frame, underneath which was written in Gothic letters "To my dear Papa."

First they spoke of the patient, then of the weather, of the great cold, of the wolves that infested the fields at night. Mademoiselle Rouault did not at all like the country, especially now that she had to look after the farm almost alone. As the room was chilly, she shivered as she ate. This showed something of her full lips, that she had a habit of biting when silent.

Her neck stood out from a white turned-down collar. Her hair, whose two black folds seemed each of a single piece, so smooth were they, was parted in the middle by a delicate line that curved slightly with the curve of the head; and, just showing the tip of the ear, it was joined behind in a thick chignon, with a wavy movement at the temples that the country doctor saw now for the first time in his life. The upper part of her cheek was rose-coloured. Like a man, she wore a tortoise-shell eyeglass thrust between two buttons of her blouse.

When Charles, after bidding farewell to old Rouault, returned to the room before leaving, he found her standing, her forehead against the window, looking into the garden, where the beanpoles had been knocked down by the wind. She turned around. "Are you looking for something?" she asked.

"My riding crop, if you please," he answered.

He began rummaging on the bed, behind the doors, under the chairs. It had fallen to the ground, between the sacks and the wall. Mademoiselle Emma saw it, and bent over the flour sacks. Charles out of politeness made a dash also, and as he stretched out his arm, at the same moment felt his breast brush against the back of the young girl bending beneath him. She drew herself up, scarlet, and looked at him over her shoulder as she handed him his riding crop.

Instead of returning to the Bertaux in three days as he had promised, he went back the very next day, then regularly twice a week, without counting the visits he paid now and then as if by accident.

Everything, moreover, went well; the patient progressed favorably;

and when, at the end of forty-six days, old Rouault was seen trying
to walk alone in his "den," Monsieur Bovary began to be looked
upon as a man of great capacity. Old Rouault said that he could not
have been cured better by the first doctor of Yvetot, or even of Rouen.

As to Charles, he did not stay to ask himself why it was a pleasure
to him to go to the Bertaux. Had he done so, he would, no doubt
have attributed his zeal to the importance of the case, or perhaps to
the money he hoped to make by it. Was it for this, however, that his
visits to the farm formed a delightful exception to the barren occupations of his life? On these days he rose early, set off at a gallop,
urging on his horse, then got down to wipe his boots in the grass and
put on black gloves before entering. He liked seeing himself enter
the courtyard, and noticing the gate turn against his shoulder, the
cock crow on the wall, the farmboys run to meet him. He liked the
granary and the stables; he liked old Rouault, who pressed his hand
and called him his saviour; he liked the small wooden shoes of
Mademoiselle Emma on the scoured flags of the kitchen—her high
heels made her a little taller; and when she walked in front of him,
the wooden soles springing up quickly struck with a sharp sound
against the leather of her boots.

She always reconducted him to the first step of the porch. When
his horse had not yet been brought round she stayed there. They had
said "Good-bye"; there was no more talking. The open air wrapped
her round, playing with the soft down on the back of her neck, or
blew to and fro on her hips her apron-strings, that fluttered like
streamers. Once, during a thaw, the bark of the trees in the yard was
oozing, the snow melted on the roofs of the buildings; she stood on
the threshold, went to fetch her sunshade and opened it. The parasol, made of an iridescent silk that let the sunlight sift through, colored the white skin of her face with shifting reflections. Beneath it,
she smiled at the gentle warmth; drops of water fell one by one on
the taut silk.

During the first period of Charles's visits to the Bertaux, the younger
Madame Bovary never failed to inquire after the invalid, and she
had even chosen in the book that she kept on a system of double
entry a clean blank page for Monsieur Rouault. But when she heard
he had a daughter, she began to make inquiries, and she learnt that
Mademoiselle Rouault, brought up at the Ursuline Convent, had
received what is called "a good education"; and so knew dancing,
geography, drawing, how to embroider and play the piano. That was
the last straw.

"So that's why he looks so beaming when he goes to see her," she
thought. "That's why he puts on his new waist coat regardless of the
rain. Ah! that woman! that woman!"

And she detested her instinctively. At first she solaced herself by allusions that Charles did not understand, then by casual observations that he let pass for fear of a storm, finally by open apostrophes to which he knew no reply.—Why did he go back to the Bertaux now that Monsieur Rouault was cured and that the bill was still unpaid? Ah! it was because a certain person was there, some one who knew how to talk, to embroider, to be witty. So that was what he liked; he wanted city girls! And she went on:

"Imagine old Rouault's daughter being taken for a city girl! The grandfather was a shepherd and a cousin of theirs barely escaped being sentenced for nearly killing someone in a brawl. Hardly a reason to put on airs, or showing herself in church dressed in silk, like a countess. If it hadn't been for the colza crop last year, the old fellow would have been hard put paying his arrears."

For very weariness Charles left off going to the Bertaux. Héloïse made him swear, his hand on the prayer-book, that he would go there no more, after much sobbing and many kisses, in a great outburst of love. He obeyed then, but the strength of his desire protested against the servility of his conduct; and he thought, with a kind of naïve hypocrisy, that this interdict to see her gave him a sort of right to love her. And then the widow was thin; she had long teeth; wore in all weathers a little black shawl, the edge of which hung down between her shoulder-blades; her bony figure was sheathed in her clothes as if they were a scabbard; they were too short, and displayed her ankles with the laces of her large boots crossed over grey stockings.

Charles's mother came to see them from time to time, but after a few days the daughter-in-law seemed to put her own edge on her, and then, like two knives, they scarified him with their reflections and observations. It was wrong of him to eat so much. Why did he always offer a free drink to everyone who came along? How stubborn of him not to put on flannel underwear!

In the spring it came about that a notary at Ingouville, who managed the widow Dubuc's property, one fine day vanished, taking with him all the money in his office. Héloïse, it is true, still owned, besides a share in a boat valued at six thousand francs, her house in the Rue St. François; and yet, with all this fortune that had been so trumpeted abroad, nothing, excepting perhaps a little furniture and a few clothes, had appeared in the household. The matter had to be gone into. The house at Dieppe was found to be eaten up with mortgages to its foundations; what she had placed with the notary God only knew, and her share in the boat did not exceed three thousand francs. She had lied, the good lady! In his exasperation, Monsieur Bovary the elder, smashing a chair on the stone floor, accused his wife of having caused the misfortune of their son by harnessing him to such a harridan, whose harness wasn't worth her hide. They came to Tostes.

Explanations followed. There were scenes. Héloïse in tears, throwing her arms about her husband, conjured him to defend her from his parents. Charles tried to speak up for her. They grew angry and left the house.

But "the blow had struck home." A week after, as she was hanging up some washing in her yard, she was seized with a spitting of blood, and the next day, while Charles had his back turned and was closing the window curtains, she said, "O God!" gave a sigh and fainted. She was dead! What a surprise!

When all was over at the cemetery Charles went home. He found no one downstairs; he went up to the first floor to their room, saw her dress still hanging at the foot of the alcove; then leaning against the writing-table, he stayed until the evening, buried in a sorrowful reverie. She had loved him after all!

III

One morning old Rouault brought Charles the money for setting his leg—seventy-five francs in forty-sou pieces, and a turkey. He had heard of his loss, and consoled him as well as he could.

"I know what it is," said he, clapping him on the shoulder; "I've been through it. When I lost my poor wife, I went into the field to be alone. I fell at the foot of a tree; I cried; I called on God; I talked nonsense to Him. I wanted to be like the moles that I saw on the branches, their insides swarming with maggots, in short, dead, and an end of it. And when I thought that there were others at that very moment, with their wives in their arms, I struck great blows on the earth with my stick. I almost went out of my mind, to the point of not eating; the very idea of going to a café disgusted me—you wouldn't believe it. Well, very slowly, one day following another, a spring on a winter, and an autumn after a summer, this wore away, piece by piece, crumb by crumb; it passed away, it is gone, I should say it has sunk; for something always remains inside, as we would say—a weight here, at one's heart. But since it is the lot of all of us, one must not give way altogether, and, because others have died, want to die too. You must pull yourself together, Monsieur Bovary. It will pass away. Come and see us; my daughter thinks of you time and again, you know, and she says you are forgetting her. Spring will soon be here. We'll have you shoot a rabbit in the field to help you get over your sorrows."

Charles followed his advice. He went back to the Bertaux. He found all as he had left it, that is to say, as it was five months ago. The pear trees were already in blossom, and Farmer Rouault, on his legs again, came and went, making the farm more lively.

Thinking it his duty to heap the greatest attention upon the doctor because of his sad situation, he begged him not to take his hat off, spoke to him in whispers as if he had been ill, and even pretended to be angry because nothing lighter had been prepared for him than for the others, such as a little custard or stewed pears. He told stories. Charles found himself laughing, but the remembrance of his wife suddenly coming back to him depressed him. Coffee was brought in; he thought no more about her.

He thought less of her as he grew accustomed to living alone. The new delight of independence soon made his loneliness bearable. He could now change his meal-times, go in or out without explanation, and when he was very tired stretch himself at full length on his bed. So he nursed and coddled himself and accepted the consolations that were offered him. On the other hand, the death of his wife had not served him ill in his business, since for a month people had been saying, "The poor young man! what a loss!" His name had been talked about, his practice had increased; and, moreover, he could go to the Bertaux just as he liked. He had an aimless hope, and a vague happiness; he thought himself better looking as he brushed his whiskers before the looking-glass.

One day he got there about three o'clock. Everybody was in the fields. He went to the kitchen, but did not at once catch sight of Emma; the outside shutters were closed. Through the chinks of the wood the sun sent across the flooring long fine rays that were broken at the corners of the furniture and trembled along the ceiling. Some flies on the table were crawling up the glasses that had been used, and buzzing as they drowned themselves in the dregs of the cider. The daylight that came in by the chimney made velvet of the soot at the back of the fireplace, and touched with blue the cold cinders. Between the window and the hearth Emma was sewing; she wore no scarf; he could see small drops of perspiration on her bare shoulders.

After the fashion of country folks she asked him to have something to drink. He said no; she insisted, and at last laughingly offered to have a glass of liqueur with him. So she went to fetch a bottle of curacao from the cupboard, reached down two small glasses, filled one to the brim, poured scarcely anything into the other, and, after having clinked glasses, carried hers to her mouth. As it was almost empty she bent back to drink, her head thrown back, her lips pouting, her neck straining. She laughed at getting none, while with the tip of her tongue passing between her small teeth she licked drop by drop the bottom of her glass.

She sat down again and took up her work, a white cotton stocking she was darning. She worked with her head bent down; she did not speak, nor did Charles. The air coming in under the door blew a little dust over the stone floor; he watched it drift along, and heard nothing but the throbbing in his head and the faint clucking of a hen that had laid an egg in the yard. Emma from time to time cooled her cheeks with the palms of her hands, and cooled these again on the knobs of the huge fire-dogs.

She complained of suffering since the beginning of the spring from giddiness; she asked if sea-baths would do her any good; she began talking of her convent, Charles of his school; words came to them. They went up into her bed-room. She showed him her old music-books, the little prizes she had won, and the oak-leaf crowns, left at the bottom of a cupboard. She spoke to him, too, of her mother, of the country, and even showed him the bed in the garden where, on the first Friday of every month, she gathered flowers to put on her mother's tomb. But their gardener understood nothing about it; servants were so careless. She would have dearly liked, if only for the winter, to live in town, although the length of the fine days made the country perhaps even more wearisome in the summer. And, according to what she was saying, her voice was clear, sharp, or, suddenly all languor, lingering out in modulations that ended almost in murmurs as she spoke to herself, now joyous, opening big naïve eyes, then with her eyelids half closed, her look full of boredom, her thoughts wandering.

Going home at night, Charles went over her words one by one, trying to recall them, to fill out their sense, that he might piece out the life she had lived before he knew her. But he never saw her in his thoughts other than he had seen her the first time, or as he had just left her. Then he asked himself what would become of her—if she would be married, and to whom? Alas! old Rouault was rich, and she!—so beautiful! But Emma's face always rose before his eyes, and a monotone, like the humming of a top, sounded in his ears, "If you should marry after all! if you should marry!" At night he could not sleep; his throat was parched; he was thirsty. He got up to drink from the water-bottle and opened the window. The night was covered with stars, a warm wind blowing in the distance; the dogs were barking. He turned his head towards the Bertaux.

Thinking that, after all, he had nothing to lose, Charles promised himself to ask her in marriage at the earliest opportunity, but each time the fear of not finding the right words sealed his lips.

Old Rouault would not have been sorry to be rid of his daughter, who was of no use to him in the house. In his heart he excused her, thinking her too clever for farming, a calling under the ban of Heaven, since one never saw a millionaire in it. Far from having made a fortune; the old man was losing every year; for if he was good at bargaining and enjoyed the dodges of the trade, he was the poorest of growers or farm managers. He did not willingly take his hands out of his pockets, and did not spare expense for his own comforts, liking to eat and to sleep well, and never to suffer from the cold. He liked old cider, underdone legs of mutton, brandied coffee well beaten up. He took his meals in the kitchen, alone, opposite the fire on a little table brought to him already laid as on the stage.

When, therefore, he perceived that Charles's cheeks grew flushed if near his daughter, which meant that he would propose one of these days, he mulled over the entire matter beforehand. He certainly thought him somewhat weak, not quite the son-in-law he would have liked, but he was said to be well-behaved, prudent with his money as well as learned, and no doubt would not make too many difficulties about the dowry. Now, as old Rouault would soon be forced to sell twenty-two acres of his land as he owed a good deal to the mason, to the harnessmaker, and as the shaft of the cider-press wanted renewing, "If he asks for her," he said to himself, "I'll give her to him."

In the early fall Charles went to spend three days at the Bertaux. The last had passed like the others in procrastinating from hour to hour. Old Rouault was seeing him off; they were walking along a dirt road full of ruts; they were about to part. This was the time. Charles gave himself as far to the corner of the hedge, and at last, when past it . . .

"Monsieur Rouault," he murmured, "I should like to say something to you."

They stopped. Charles was silent.

"Well, tell me your story. Don't I know all about it?" said old Rouault, laughing softly.

"Monsieur Rouault—Monsieur Rouault," stammered Charles.

"I ask nothing better," the farmer went on. "Although, no doubt, the little one agrees with me, still we must ask her opinion. So yet get off—I'll go back home. If it is 'yes,' you needn't return because of all the people around, and besides it would upset her too much. But so that you may not be biting your fingernails with impatience, I'll open wide the outer shutter of the window against the wall; you can see it from the back by leaning over the hedge."

And he went off.

Charles fastened his horse to a tree; he ran into the road and waited. Half-an-hour passed, then he counted nineteen minutes by his watch. Suddenly a noise was heard against the wall; the shutter had been thrown back; the hook was still quivering.

The next day by nine o'clock he was at the farm. Emma blushed as he entered, and she gave a little forced laugh to hide her embarrassment. Old Rouault embraced his future son-in-law. The discussion of money matters was put off; moreover, there was plenty of time before them, as the marriage could not decently take place till Charles was out of mourning, that is to say, about the spring of the next year.

The winter passed waiting for this. Mademoiselle Rouault was busy with her trousseau. Part of it was ordered at Rouen, and she made herself slips and nightcaps after fashionplates that she borrowed. When Charles visited the farmer, the preparations for the wedding were talked over; they wondered in what room they should have dinner; they dreamed of the number of fishes that would be wanted, and what should be the entrées.

Emma would, on the contrary, have preferred to have a midnight wedding with torches, but old Rouault could not understand such an idea. So there was a wedding at which forty-three persons were present, at which they remained sixteen hours at table, began again the next day, and even carried a little into the following days.

IV

The guests arrived early in carriages, in one-horse chaises, two-wheeled cars, old open gigs, vans with leather curtains, and the young people from the nearer villages in carts, in which they stood up in rows, holding on to the sides so as not to fall, going at a trot and well shaken up. Some came from a distance of thirty miles, from Goderville, from Normanville, and from Cany. All the relatives of both families had been invited, old quarrels had been patched up and near-forgotten acquaintances written to for the occasion.

From time to time one heard the crack of a whip behind the hedge; then the gates opened, a chaise entered. Galloping up to the foot of the steps, it stopped short and emptied its load. They got down from all sides, rubbing knees and stretching arms. The ladies, wearing bonnets, had on dresses in the town fashion, gold watch chains, pelerines with the ends tucked into belts, or little coloured scarfs fastened down behind with a pin, and that left the back of the neck bare. The boys, dressed like their papas, seemed uncomfortable in their new clothes (many that day were wearing their first pair of boots), and by their sides, speaking never a word, wearing the white dress of their first communion lengthened for the occasion, were some big girls of fourteen or sixteen, cousins or elder sisters no doubt, scarlet, bewildered, their hair greasy with rose-pomade, and very much afraid of dirtying their gloves. As there were not enough stable-boys to unharness all the carriages, the gentlemen turned up their sleeves and set about it themselves. According to their different social positions they wore tail-coats, overcoats, shooting-jackets, cutaway-coats: fine tail-coats, redolent of family respectability, that only came out of the wardrobe on state occasions; overcoats with long tails flapping in the wind and round capes and pockets like sacks; shooting-jackets of coarse cloth, generally worn with a cap with a brass-bound peak; very short cutaway-coats with two small buttons in the back, close together like a pair of eyes, and the tails of which seemed cut out of one piece by a carpenter's hatchet. Some, too (but these, you may be sure, would sit at the bottom of the table), wore their best smocks— that is to say, with collars turned down to the shoulders, the back gathered into small plaits and the waist fastened very low down with a stitched belt.

And the shirts stood out from the chests like armour breastplates! Everyone had just had his hair cut; ears stood out from the heads; they had been close-shaven; a few, even, who had had to get up before daybreak, and not been able to see to shave, had diagonal gashes under their noses or cuts the size of a three-franc piece along the jaws, which the fresh air had enflamed during the trip, so that the great white beaming faces were mottled here and there with red spots.

The mairie was a mile and a half from the farm, and they went there on foot, returning in the same way after the ceremony in the church. The procession, first united like one long coloured scarf that undulated across the fields, along the narrow path winding amid the green wheat, soon lengthened out, and broke up into different groups that loitered to talk. The fiddler walked in front with his violin, gay with ribbons at its pegs. Then came the married pair, the relatives, the friends, all following pell-mell; the children stayed behind amusing themselves plucking the bell-flowers from oat-ears, or playing amongst themselves unseen. Emma's dress, too long, trailed a little on the ground; from time to time she stopped to pull it up, and then delicately, with her gloved hands, she picked off the coarse grass and the thistles, while Charles, empty handed, waited till she had finished. Old Rouault, with a new silk hat and the cuffs of his black coat covering his hands up to the nails, gave his arm to Madame Bovary senior. As to Monsieur Bovary senior, who, heartily despising all these people, had come simply in a frockcoat of military cut with one row of buttons—he was exchanging barroom banter with a blond young farmgirl. She bowed, blushed, and did not know what to say. The other wedding guests talked business or played tricks behind each other's backs, egging each other on in advance for the fun that was to come. Those who listened could always catch the squeaking of the fiddler, who went on playing across the fields. When he saw that the rest were far behind he stopped to take breath, slowly rosined his bow, so that the strings should squeak all the louder, then set off again, by turns lowering and raising the neck of his violin, the better to mark time for himself. The noise of the instrument drove away the little birds from afar.

The table was laid under the cart-shed. On it were four roasts of beef, six chicken fricassées, stewed veal, three legs of mutton, and in the middle a fine roast sucking-pig, flanked by four pork sausages with sorrel. At the corners were decanters of brandy. Sweet bottled-cider frothed round the corks, and all the glasses had been filled to the brim with wine beforehand. Large dishes of yellow cream, that trembled with the least shake of the table, had designed on their smooth surface the initials of the newly wedded pair in nonpareil arabesques. A confectioner of Yvetot had been entrusted with the pies and candies. As he had only just started out in the neighborhood, he had taken a lot of trouble, and at dessert he himself brought in a wedding cake that provoked loud cries of wonderment. At its base there was a square of blue cardboard, representing a temple with porticoes, colonnades, and stucco statuettes all round, and in the niches constellations of gilt paper stars; then on the second level was a dungeon of Savoy cake, surrounded by many fortifications in candied angelica, almonds, raisins, and quarters of oranges; and finally, on the upper platform a green field with rocks set in lakes of jam, nutshell boats, and a small Cupid balancing himself in a chocolate swing whose two uprights ended in real roses for balls at the top.

Until night they ate. When any of them were too tired of sitting, they went out for a stroll in the yard, or for a game of darts in the granary, and then returned to table. Some towards the end went to sleep and snored. But with the coffee every one woke up. Then they began songs, showed off tricks, raised heavy weights, competed to see who could pass his head under his arm while keeping a thumb on the table, tried lifting carts on their shoulders, made bawdy jokes, kissed the women. At night when they left, the horses, stuffed up to the nostrils with oats, could hardly be got into the shafts; they kicked, reared, the harness broke, their masters laughed or swore; and all night in the light of the moon along country roads there were runaway carts at full gallop plunging into the ditches, jumping over yard after yard of stones, clambering up the hills, with women leaning out from the tilt to catch hold of the reins.

Those who stayed at the Bertaux spent the night drinking in the kitchen. The children had fallen asleep under the seats.

The bride had begged her father to be spared the usual marriage pleasantries. However, a fishmonger, one of their cousins (who had brought a pair of soles for his wedding present), began to squirt water from his mouth through the keyhole, when old Rouault came up just in time to stop him, and explain to him that the distinguished position of his son-in-law would not allow of such liberties. The cousin was not easily convinced. In his heart he accused old Rouault of being proud, and he joined four or five other guests in a corner, who, through mere chance, had been served the poorer cuts of meat several times over and also considered themselves ill-treated. They were whispering about their host, hoping with covered hints that he would ruin himself.

Madame Bovary, senior, had not opened her mouth all day. She had been consulted neither as to the dress of her daughter-in-law nor as to the arrangement of the feast; she went to bed early. Her husband, instead of following her, sent to Saint-Victor for some cigars, and smoked till daybreak, drinking kirsch-punch, a mixture unknown to the company that added even more to the consideration in which he was held.

Charles, who was anything but quick-witted, did not shine at the wedding. He answered feebly to the puns, *doubles entendres*, compliments, and the customary pleasantries that were dutifully aimed at him as soon as the soup appeared.

The next day, on the other hand, he seemed another man. It was he who might rather have been taken for the virgin of the evening before, whilst the bride gave no sign that revealed anything. The shrewdest did not know what to make of it, and they looked at her when she passed near them with an unbounded concentration of mind. But Charles concealed nothing. He called her "my wife," addressed her by the familiar "tu," asked for her of everyone, looked for her everywhere, and often he dragged her into the yards, where he could be seen from far between the trees, putting his arm round her waist, and walking half-bending over her, ruffling the collar of her blouse with his head.

Two days after the wedding the married pair left. Charles, on account of his patients, could not be away longer. Old Rouault had them driven back in his cart, and himself accompanied them as far as Vassonville. Here he embraced his daughter for the last time, got down, and went his way. When he had gone about a hundred paces he stopped, and as he saw the cart disappearing, its wheels turning in the dust, he gave a deep sigh. Then he remembered his wedding, the old times, the first pregnancy of his wife; he, too, had been very happy the day when he had taken her from her father to his home, and had carried her off riding pillion, trotting through the snow, for it was near Christmas-time, and the country was all white. She held him by one arm, her basket hanging from the other; the wind blew the long lace of her Cauchois headdress so that it sometimes flapped across his mouth, and when he turned his head he saw near him, on his shoulder, her little rosy face, smiling silently under the gold bands of her cap. To warm her hands she put them from time to time in his breast. How long ago it all was! Their son would have been thirty by now. Then he looked back and saw nothing on the road. He felt dreary as an empty house; and tender memories mingling with sad thoughts in his brain, addled by the fumes of the feast, he felt inclined for a moment to take a turn towards the church. As he was afraid, however, that this sight would make him even sadder, he went right away home.

Monsieur and Madame Charles arrived at Tostes about six o'clock. The neighbors came to the windows to see their doctor's new wife.

The old servant presented herself, curtsied to her, apologised for not having dinner ready, and suggested that madame, in the meantime, should look over her house.

V

The brick front was just in a line with the street, or rather the road. Behind the door hung a cloak with a small collar, a bridle, and a black leather cap, and on the floor, in a corner, were a pair of leggings, still covered with dry mud. On the right was the one room that was both dining and sitting room. A canary-yellow paper, relieved at the top by a garland of pale flowers, was puckered everywhere over the badly-stretched canvas; white calico curtains with a red border hung crossways the length of the window; and on the narrow mantelpiece a clock with a head of Hippocrates shone resplendent between two plate candlesticks under oval shades. On the other side of the passage was Charles's consulting-room, a little room about six paces wide, with a table, three chairs, and an office-chair. Volumes of the "Dictionary of Medical Science," uncut, but the binding rather the worse for the successive sales through which they had gone, occupied almost alone the six shelves of a pinewood bookcase. The smell of sauces penetrated through the walls when he saw patients, just as in the kitchen one could hear the people coughing in the consulting-room and recounting their whole histories. Then, opening on the yard, where the stable was, came a large dilapidated room with a stove, now used as a wood-house, cellar, and pantry, full of old rubbish, of empty casks, discarded garden tools, and a mass of dusty things whose use it was impossible to guess.

The garden, longer than wide, ran between two mud walls covered with espaliered apricot trees, to a thorn hedge that separated it from the field. In the middle was a slate sundial on a brick pedestal; four flower-beds with eglantines surrounded symmetrically the more useful vegetable garden. Right at the bottom, under the spruce bushes, a plaster priest was reading his breviary.

Emma went upstairs. The first room was not furnished, but in the second, the conjugal bedroom, was a mahogany bedstead in an alcove with red drapery. A shell-box adorned the chest of drawers, and on the secretary near the window a bouquet of orange blossoms tied with white satin ribbons stood in a bottle. It was a bride's bouquet: the other one's. She looked at it. Charles noticed; he took the bouquet, carried it to the attic, while Emma seated in an armchair (they were putting her things down around her) thought of her bridal flowers packed up in a bandbox, and wondered, dreaming, what would be done with them if she were to die.

During the first days she kept busy thinking about changes in the house. She took the shades off the candlesticks, had new wall-paper put up, the staircase repainted, and seats made in the garden round the sundial; she even inquired how she could get a basin with a jet fountain and fishes. Finally her husband, knowing that she liked to drive out, picked up a second-hand dogcart, which, with new lamps and a splashboard in striped leather, looked almost like a tilbury.

He was happy then, and without a care in the world. A meal together, a walk in the evening on the highroad, a gesture of her hands over her hair, the sight of her straw hat hanging from the window-fastener, and many other things of which he had never suspected how pleasant they could be, now made up the endless round of his happiness. In bed, in the morning, by her side, on the pillow, he watched the sunlight sinking into the down on her fair cheek, half hidden by the ribbons of her nightcap. Seen thus closely, her eyes looked to him enlarged, especially when, on waking up, she opened and shut her eyelids rapidly many times. Black in the shade, dark blue in broad daylight, they had, as it were, depths of successive colors that, more opaque in the center, grew more transparent towards the surface of the eye. His own eyes lost themselves in these depths and he could see himself mirrored in miniature, down to his shoulders, with his scarf round his head and the top of his shirt open. He rose. She came to the window to see him off, and stayed leaning on the sill between two pots of geranium, clad in her dressing-gown hanging loosely about her. Charles, in the street, buckled his spurs, his foot on the mounting stone, while she talked to him from above, picking with her mouth some scrap of flower or leaf that she blew out at him and which, eddying, floating, described semicircles in the air like a bird, caught before it reached the ground in the ill-groomed mane of the old white mare standing motionless at the door. Charles from horseback threw her a kiss; she answered with a nod; she shut the window, and he set off. And then, along the endless dusty ribbon of the highroad, along the deep lanes that the trees bent over as in arbours, along paths where the wheat reached to the knees, with the sun on his back and the morning air in his nostrils, his heart full of the joys of the past night, his mind at rest, his flesh at ease, he went on, re-chewing his happiness, like those who after dinner taste again the truffles which they are digesting.

Until now what good had he had of his life? His time at school, when he remained shut up within the high walls, alone, in the midst of companions richer than he or cleverer at their work, who laughed at his accent, who jeered at his clothes, and whose mothers came to the school with cakes in their muffs? Later on, when he studied medicine, and never had his purse full enough to take out dancing

some little work-girl who would have become his mistress? Afterwards, he had lived fourteen months with the widow, whose feet in
bed were cold as icicles. But now he had for life this beautiful woman
whom he adored. For him the universe did not extend beyond the
silky circumference of her petticoat. He reproached himself for not
loving her enough; he wanted to see her again, turned back quickly,
ran up the stairs with a beating heart. Emma, in her room, was
dressing; he came up on tiptoe, kissed her back; she cried out in
surprise.

He could not keep from constantly touching her comb, her rings,
her scarf; sometimes he gave her great sounding kisses with all his
mouth on her cheeks, or else little kisses in a row all along her bare
arm from the tip of her fingers up to her shoulder, and she put him
away half-smiling, half-annoyed, as one does with a clinging child.

Before marriage she thought herself in love; but since the happiness that should have followed failed to come, she must, she thought,
have been mistaken. And Emma tried to find out what one meant
exactly in life by the words *bliss*, *passion*, *ecstasy*, that had seemed
to her so beautiful in books.

VI

She had read "Paul and Virginia,"[8] and she had dreamed of the
little bamboo-house, the negro Domingo, the dog Fidèle, but above
all of the sweet friendship of some dear little brother, who seeks red
fruit for you on trees taller than steeples, or who runs barefoot over
the sand, bringing you a bird's nest.

When she was thirteen, her father himself took her to town to
place her in the convent. They stopped in an inn in the St. Gervais
quarter, where, at their supper, they used painted plates that set forth
the story of Mademoiselle de la Vallière.[9] The explanatory legends,
chipped here and there by the scratching of knives, all glorified religion, the tendernesses of the heart, and the pomps of court.

Far from being bored at first at the convent, she took pleasure in
the society of the good sisters, who, to amuse her, took her to the
chapel, which one entered from the refectory by a long corridor. She
played very little during recreation hours, knew her catechism well,
and it was she was always answered the Vicar's difficult questions.
Living thus, without ever leaving the warm atmosphere of the class-
rooms, and amid these pale-faced women wearing rosaries with brass
crosses, she was softly lulled by the mystic languor exhaled in the

8. *Paul et Virginie* (1784) is a story of the sentimental and tragic love of two young people on the
tropical island of Ile de France (today, Mauritius). It was the most popular work of Bernardin de
Saint-Pierre (1737–1814).   9. One of Louis XIV's mistresses, whose mythologized character is
familiar to all readers of Alexandre Dumas's *Le Vicomte de Bragelonne* (a sequel to *The Three
Musketeers*).

perfumes of the altar, the freshness of the holy water, and the lights of the tapers. Instead of following mass, she looked at the pious vignettes with their azure borders in her book, and she loved the sick lamb, the sacred heart pierced with sharp arrows, or the poor Jesus sinking beneath the cross he carried. She tried, by way of mortification, to eat nothing a whole day. She puzzled her head to find some vow to fulfil.

When she sent to confession, she invented little sins in order that she might stay there longer, kneeling in the shadow, her hands joined, her face against the grating beneath the whispering of the priest. The comparisons of betrothed, husband, celestial lover, and eternal marriage, that recur in sermons, stirred within her soul depths of unexpected sweetness.

In the evening, before prayers, there was some religious reading in the study. On week-nights it was some abstract of sacred history or the Lectures of the Abbé Frayssinous, and on Sundays passages from the "Génie du Christianisme,"[1] as a recreation. How she listened at first to the sonorous lamentations of romantic melancholy re-echoing through the world and eternity! If her childhood had been spent in the shops of a busy city section, she might perhaps have opened her heart to those lyrical invasions of Nature, which usually come to us only through translation in books. But she knew the country too well; she knew the lowing of cattle, the milking, the ploughs. Accustomed to the quieter aspects of life, she turned instead to its tumultuous parts. She loved the sea only for the sake of its storms, and the green only when it was scattered among ruins. She had to gain some personal profit from things and she rejected as useless whatever did not contribute to the immediate satisfaction of her heart's desires—being of a temperament more sentimental than artistic, looking for emotions, not landscapes.

At the convent there was an old maid who came for a week each month to mend the linen. Patronised by the clergy, because she belonged to an ancient family of noblemen ruined by the Revolution, she dined in the refectory at the table of the good sisters, and after the meal chatted with them for a while before going back to her work. The girls often slipped out from the study to go and see her. She knew by heart the love-songs of the last century, and sang them in a low voice as she stitched away. She told stories, gave them news, ran their errands in the town, and on the sly lent the big girls some of the novels that she always carried in the pockets of her apron, and

1. An enormously influential book (1802) by François-René de Chateaubriand (1768–1848) celebrating the truths and beauties of Roman Catholicism, just before Napoleon's concordat with Rome. Denis de Frayssinous (1765–1841) was a popular preacher who wrote a *Défense du Christianisme* (1825). Under Louis XVIII he became a bishop and minister of ecclesiastical affairs.

of which the lady herself swallowed long chapters in the intervals of her work. They were all about love, lovers, sweethearts, persecuted ladies fainting in lonely pavilions, postilions killed at every relay, horses ridden to death on every page, sombre forests, heart-aches, vows, sobs, tears and kisses, little boatrides by moonlight, nightingales in shady groves, gentlemen brave as lions, gentle as lambs, virtuous as no one ever was, always well dressed, and weeping like fountains. For six months, then, a fifteen-year-old Emma dirtied her hands with the greasy dust of old lending libraries. With Walter Scott, later on, she fell in love with historical events, dreamed of guardrooms, old oak chests and minstrels. She would have liked to live in some old manor-house, like those long-waisted chatelaines who, in the shade of pointed arches, spent their days leaning on the stone, chin in hand, watching a white-plumed knight galloping on his black horse from the distant fields. At this time she had a cult for Mary Stuart and enthusiastic veneration for illustrious or unhappy women. Joan of Arc, Héloïse, Agnès Sorel, the beautiful Ferronière, and Clémence Isaure[2] stood out to her like comets in the dark immensity of history, where also were seen, lost in shadow, and all unconnected, St. Louis with his oak, the dying Bayard, some cruelties of Louis XI, a little of St. Bartholomew's, the plume of the Béarnais, and always the remembrance of the painted plates glorifying Louis XIV.[3]

In the music-class, the ballads she sang were all about little angels with golden wings, madonnas, lagunes, gondoliers; harmless-sounding compositions that, in spite of the inanity of the style and the vagueness of the melody, enabled one to catch a glimpse of the tantalizing phantasmagoria of sentimental realities. Some of her companions brought keepsakes given them as new year's gifts to the convent. These had to be hidden; it was quite an undertaking; they were read in the dormitory. Delicately handling the beautiful satin bindings, Emma looked with dazzled eyes at the names of the unknown authors, who had signed their verses for the most part as counts or viscounts.

She trembled as she blew back the thin transparent paper over the

2. *Héloïse* was famous for her love affair with the philosopher Abelard (1101–1164); *Agnès Sorel* (1422–1450) was a mistress of Charles VII, rumored to have been poisoned by the future Louis XI; *"la belle Ferronière"* (died in 1540) was one of François I's mistresses, wife of the lawyer Le Ferron who is said to have contracted syphilis for the mere satisfaction of passing it on to the king; *Clémence Isaure* is a half-fictional lady from Toulouse (fourteenth century), popularized in a novel by Florian as an incarnation of the mystical poetry of the troubadours.   3. St. Louis was King of France, Louis IX (1215–1270). He led the seventh and eighth crusades. He was canonized in 1297. According to tradition he dispensed justice under an oak tree at Vincennes (near Paris). *Bayard* (Pierre du Terrail, seigneur de, 1473–1524) was one of the most famous French captains, distinguishing himself by feats of bravery during the wars of Francis I. He was killed in 1524. Dying, he chided the connétable de Bourbon for his treason in a famous speech. *Louis XI* was born in 1421 and was king from 1461 to 1483. He ruthlessly suppressed the rebellious noblemen. *St. Bartholomew* was the massacre of the Protestants ordered by Catherine de Medici in the night of August 23, 1572.

engraving and saw it folded in two and fall gently against the page.
Here behind the balustrade of a balcony was a young man in a short
cloak, holding in his arms a young girl in a white dress who was
wearing an alms-bag at her belt; or there were nameless portraits of
English ladies with fair curls, who looked at you from under their
round straw hats with their large clear eyes. Some could be seen
lounging in their carriages, gliding through parks, a greyhound
bounding along ahead of the equipage, driven at a trot by two small
postilions in white breeches. Others, dreaming on sofas with an open
letter, gazed at the moon through a slightly open window half draped
by a black curtain. The innocent ones, a tear on their cheeks, were
kissing doves through the bars of a Gothic cage, or, smiling, their
heads on one side, were plucking the leaves of a marguerite with
their taper fingers, that curved at the tips like peaked shoes. And you,
too, were there, Sultans with long pipes reclining beneath arbours
in the arms of Bayadères; Giaours, curved swords, fezzes; and you
especially, pale landscapes of dithyrambic lands, that often show us
at once palm-trees and firs, tigers on the right, a lion to the left,
Tartar minarets on the horizon, Roman ruins in the foreground with
some kneeling camels besides; the whole framed by a very neat virgin
forest, and with a great perpendicular sunbeam trembling in the water,
where, sharply edged on a steel-grey background, white swans are
swimming here and there.

And the shade of the oil lamp fastened to the wall above Emma's
head lighted up all these pictures of the world, that passed before her
one by one in the silence of the dormitory, and to the distant noise
of some belated carriage still rolling down the Boulevards.

When her mother died she cried much the first few days. She had
a funeral picture made with the hair of the deceased, and, in a letter
sent to the Bertaux full of sad reflections on life, she asked to be
buried later on in the same grave. The old man thought she must be
ill, and came to see her. Emma was secretly pleased that she had
reached at a first attempt the rare ideal of delicate lives, never attained
by mediocre hearts. She let herself meander along with Lamartine,
listened to harps on lakes, to all the songs of dying swans, to the
falling of the leaves, the pure virgins ascending to heaven, and the
voice of the Eternal discoursing down the valleys. She soon grew
tired but wouldn't admit it, continued from habit first, then out of
vanity, and at last was surprised to feel herself consoled, and with no
more sadness at heart than wrinkles on her brow.

The good nuns, who had been so sure of her vocation, perceived
with great astonishment that Mademoiselle Rouault seemed to be
slipping from them. They had indeed been so lavish to her of prayers, retreats, novenas, and sermons, they had so often preached the
respect due to saints and martyrs, and given so much good advice as

to the modesty of the body and the salvation of her soul, that she did as tightly reigned horses: she pulled up short and the bit slipped from her teeth. This nature, positive in the midst of its enthusiasms, that had loved the church for the sake of the flowers, and music for the words of the songs, and literature for the passions it excites, rebelled against the mysteries of faith as it had rebelled against discipline, as something alien to her constitution. When her father took her from school, no one was sorry to see her go. The Lady Superior even thought that she had of late been less than reverent toward the community.

Emma, at home once more, first took pleasure in ruling over servants, then grew disgusted with the country and missed her convent. When Charles came to the Bertaux for the first time, she thought herself quite disillusioned, with nothing more to learn, and nothing more to feel.

But the uneasiness of her new position, or perhaps the disturbance caused by the presence of this man, had sufficed to make her believe that she at last felt that wondrous passion which, till then, like a great bird with rose-coloured wings, hung in the splendor of poetic skies—and now she could not think that the calm in which she lived was the happiness of her dreams.

VII

She thought, sometimes, that, after all, this was the happiest time of her life: the honeymoon, as people called it. To taste the full sweetness of it, it would no doubt have been necessary to fly to those lands with sonorous names where the days after marriage are full of the most suave laziness! In post-chaises behind blue silken curtains, one rides slowly up steep roads, listening to the song of the postilion re-echoed by the mountains, along with the bells of goats and the muffled sound of a waterfall. At sunset on the shores of gulfs one breathes in the perfume of lemon-trees; then in the evening on the villa-terraces above, one looks hand in hand at the stars, making plans for the future. It seemed to her that certain places on earth must bring happiness, as a plant peculiar to the soil, and that cannot thrive elsewhere. Why could not she lean over balconies in Swiss châlets, or enshrine her melancholy in a Scotch cottage, with a husband dressed in a black velvet coat with long tails, and thin shoes, a pointed hat and frills?

Perhaps she would have liked to confide all these things to some one. But how tell an undefinable uneasiness, changing as the clouds, unstable as the winds? Words failed her and, by the same token, the opportunity, the courage.

If Charles had but wished it, if he had guessed, if his look had but once met her thought, it seemed to her that a sudden bounty would have come from her heart, as the fruit falls from a tree when shaken by a hand. But as the intimacy of their life became deeper, the greater became the gulf that kept them apart.

Charles's conversation was commonplace as a street pavement, and every one's ideas trooped through it in their everyday garb, without exciting emotion, laughter, or thought. He had never had the curiosity, he said, while he lived at Rouen, to go to the theatre to see the actors from Paris. He could neither swim, nor fence, nor shoot, and one day he could not explain some term of horsemanship to her that she had come across in a novel.

A man, on the contrary, should he not know everything, excel in manifold activities, initiate you into the energies of passion, the refinements of life, all mysteries? But this one taught nothing, knew nothing, wished nothing. He thought her happy; and she resented this easy calm, this serene heaviness, the very happiness she gave him.

Sometimes she would draw; and it was great amusement to Charles to stand there bolt upright and watch her bend over her paper, with eyes half-closed the better to see her work, or rolling, between her fingers, little bread-pellets. As to the piano, the more quickly her fingers glided over it the more he wondered. She struck the notes with aplomb, and ran from top to bottom of the keyboard without a break. Thus shaken up, the old instrument, whose strings buzzed, could be heard at the other end of the village when the window was open, and often the bailiff's clerk, passing along the highroad bareheaded and in slippers, stopped to listen, his sheet of paper in his hand.

Emma, on the other hand, knew how to look after her house. She sent the patients' accounts in well-phrased letters that had no suggestion of a bill. When they had a neighbor to dinner on Sundays, she managed to have some tasty dish, knew how to pile the plums in pyramids on vine-leaves, how to serve jam turned out on a plate, and even spoke of buying finger bowls for dessert. From all this much consideration was extended to Bovary.

Charles finished by rising in his own esteem for possessing such a wife. He showed with pride in the sitting-room two small pencil sketches by her that he had had framed in very large frames, and hung up against the wall-paper by long green cords. People returning from mass saw him standing on his doorstep, wearing beautiful carpet slippers.

He came home late—at ten o'clock, at midnight sometimes. Then he asked for something to eat, and as the servant had gone to bed, Emma waited on him. He took off his coat to dine more at his ease. He told her, one after the other, the people he had met, the villages where he had been, the prescriptions he had written, and, well pleased with himself, he finished the remainder of the boiled beef, peeled the crust of his cheese, munched an apple, finished the wine, and then went to bed, lay on his back and snored.

As he had been for a long time accustomed to wear nightcaps, his handkerchief would not keep down over his ears, so that his hair in the morning was all dishevelled and whitened with the feathers of the pillow, whose strings came untied during the night. He always wore thick boots that had two long creases over the instep running obliquely towards the ankle, while the upper part continued in a straight line as if stretched on a wooden foot. He said that this was quite good enough for someone who lived in the country.

His mother approved of his thrift, for she came to see him as before, after there had been some violent row at her place; and yet the elder Madame Bovary seemed prejudiced against her daughter-in-law. She thought she was living above her means; the wood, sugar, and candles vanished as in a large establishment, and the amount of stovewood used in the kitchen would have been enough for twenty-five courses. She straightened the linen chests, and taught her to keep an eye on the butcher when he brought the meat. Emma had to accept these lessons lavished upon her, and the words "daughter" and "mother" were exchanged all day long, accompanied by little quiverings of the lips, each one uttering sweet words in a voice trembling with anger.

In Madame Dubuc's time the old woman felt that she was still the favourite; but now the love of Charles for Emma seemed to her a desertion from her tenderness, an encroachment upon what was hers, and she watched her son's happiness in sad silence, as a ruined man looks through the windows at people dining in his old house. She recalled to him as remembrances her troubles and her sacrifices, and, comparing these with Emma's casual ways, came to the conclusion that it was not reasonable to adore her so exclusively.

Charles knew not what to answer: he respected his mother, and he loved his wife infinitely; he considered the judgment of the one infallible, and yet he thought the conduct of the other irreproachable. When Madame Bovary had gone, he tried timidly and in the same terms to hazard one or two of the more anodyne observations he had heard from his mamma. Emma proved to him with a word that he was mistaken, and sent him off to his patients.

And yet, in accord with theories she believed right, she wanted to experience love with him. By moonlight in the garden she recited all the passionate rhymes she knew by heart, and, sighing, sang to him many melancholy adagios; but she found herself as calm after this as before, and Charles seemed neither more amorous, nor more moved.

When she had thus for a while struck the flint on her heart without getting a spark, incapable, moreover, of understanding what she did not experience or of believing anything that did not take on a conventional form, she persuaded herself without difficulty that Charles's passion was no longer very ardent. His outbursts became regular; he embraced her at certain fixed times. It was one habit among other habits, like a familiar dessert after the monotony of dinner.

A gamekeeper, whom the doctor had cured of a lung infection, had given madame a little Italian greyhound; she took her out walking, for she went out sometimes in order to be alone for a moment, and not to see before her eyes the eternal garden and the dusty road.

She went as far as the beeches of Banneville, near the deserted pavilion which forms an angle on the field side of the wall. Amidst the grass of the ditches grow long reeds with sharp-edged leaves that cut you.

She began by looking round her to see if nothing had changed since she had last been there. She found again in the same places the foxgloves and wallflowers, the beds of nettles growing round the big stones, and the patches of lichen along the three windows, whose shutters, always closed, were rotting away on their rusty iron bars. Her thoughts, aimless at first, wandered at random, like her greyhound, who ran round and round in the fields, yelping after the yellow butterflies, chasing the field-mice, or nibbling the poppies on the edge of a wheatfield. Then gradually her ideas took definite shape, and, sitting on the grass that she dug up with little pricks of her sunshade, Emma repeated to herself:—Why, for Heaven's sake, did I marry?

She asked herself if by some other chance combination it would not have been possible to meet another man; and she tried to imagine what would have been these unrealised events, this different life, this unknown husband. All, surely, could not be like this one. He might have been handsome, witty, distinguished, attractive, like, no doubt, the men her old companions of the convent had married. What were they doing now? In town, among the crowded streets, the buzzing theatres and the lights of the ball-room, they were living lives where the heart expands and the senses blossom out. As for her, her life was cold as a garret facing north, and ennui, the silent spider, was weaving its web in the darkness, in every corner of her heart. She recalled graduation day, when she mounted the platform to receive her little wreaths. With her hair in long plaits, in her white frock and open prunella shoes she had a pretty way, and when she went back to her seat, the gentlemen bent over to congratulate her; the courtyard was full of carriages; farewells were called to her through their windows; the music-master with his violin-case bowed in passing by. How far off all this! How far away!

She called Djali,[4] took her between her knees, and smoothed the long, delicate head, saying, "Come, kiss your mistress, you who are free of cares."

Then noting the melancholy face of the graceful animal, who yawned slowly, she softened, and comparing her to herself, spoke to her aloud as to somebody in pain whom one is consoling.

Occasionally there came gusts of wind, breezes from the sea rolling in one sweep over the whole plateau of the Caux country, which brought to these fields a salt freshness. The rushes, close to the ground, whistled; the branches of the beech trees trembled in a swift rustling, while their crowns, ceaselessly swaying, kept up a deep murmur. Emma drew her shawl round her shoulders and rose.

In the avenue a green light dimmed by the leaves lit up the short moss that crackled softly beneath her feet. The sun was setting; the sky showed red between the branches, and the trunks of the trees, uniform, and planted in a straight line, seemed a brown colonnade standing out against a background of gold. A fear took hold of her; she called Djali, and hurriedly returned to Tostes by the highroad, threw herself into an armchair, and for the rest of the evening did not speak.

But towards the end of September something extraordinary befell her: she was invited by the Marquis d'Andervilliers to Vaubyessard.

Secretary of State under the Restoration, the Marquis, anxious to re-enter political life, had long since been preparing for his candidature to the Chamber of Deputies. In the winter he distributed a great deal of firewood, and in the Conseil Général always enthusiastically demanded new roads for his arrondissement. During the height of the summer heat he had suffered from an abcess in the mouth, which Charles had cured as if by miracle by giving a timely little touch with the lancet. The steward sent to Tostes to pay for the operation reported in the evening that he had seen some superb cherries in the doctor's little garden. Now cherry-trees did not thrive at Vaubyessard; the Marquis asked Bovary for some offshoots. He made it his business to thank him personally and, on that occasion, saw Emma. He thought she had a pretty figure, and that she did not greet him like a peasant; so that he did not think he was going beyond the bounds of condescension, nor, on the other hand, making a mistake, in inviting the young couple.

One Wednesday at three o'clock, Monsieur and Madame Bovary, seated in their dog-cart, set out for Vaubyessard, with a great trunk strapped on behind and a hat-box in front on the apron. Besides these Charles held a carton between his knees.

4. Djali is the name of the little she-goat in Hugo's *Notre Dame de Paris.*

They arrived at nightfall, just as the lamps in the park were being lit to show the way for the carriages.

VIII

The château, a modern building in Italian style, with two projecting wings and three flights of steps, lay at the foot of an immense lawn, on which some cows were grazing among clumps of large trees set out at regular intervals, while large beds of arbutus, rhododendron, syringas, and snowballs bulged out their irregular clusters of green along the curve of the gravel path. A river flowed under a bridge; through the mist one could distinguish buildings with thatched roofs scattered over the field bordered by two gently sloping well-timbered hillocks, and in the background amid the trees rose in two parallel lines the coach-houses and stables, all that was left of the ruined old château.

Charles's dog-cart pulled up before the middle flight of steps; servants appeared; the Marquis came forward, and offering his arm to the doctor's wife, conducted her to the vestibule.

It was paved with marble slabs and seemed very lofty; the sound of footsteps and that of voices re-echoed through it as in a church. Opposite rose a straight staircase, and on the left a gallery overlooking the garden led to the billiard room, from where the click of the ivory balls could be heard immediately upon entering. As she crossed it to go to the drawing-room, Emma saw standing round the table men with grave faces, their chins resting on high cravats. They all wore orders, and smiled silently as they made their strokes. On the dark wainscoting of the walls large gold frames bore at the bottom names written in black letters. She read: "Jean-Antoine d'Andervilliers d'Yverbonville, Count de la Vaubyessard and Baron de la Fresnaye, killed at the battle of Coutras[5] on the 20th of October 1587." And on another: "Jean-Antoine-Henry-Guy d'Andervilliers de la Vaubyessard, Admiral of France and Chevalier of the Order of St. Michael, wounded at the battle of the Hougue-Saint-Vaast on the 29th of May 1692; died at Vaubyessard on the 23rd of January 1693." One could hardly make out the next ones, for the light of the lamps lowered over the green cloth threw a dim shadow round the room. Burnishing the horizontal pictures, it broke up in delicate lines among the cracks in the varnish, and from all these great black squares framed in gold stood out here and there some lighter portion of the painting—a pale brow, two eyes that looked at you, wigs resting on the powdered shoulder of red coats, or the buckle of a garter above a well-rounded calf.

5. Battle of Coutras (in the Gironde) was won by Henri de Navarre against the Duke de Joyeuse (1587).

The Marquis opened the drawing-room door; one of the ladies (the Marquise herself) came to meet Emma. She made her sit down by her on an ottoman, and began talking to her as amicably as if she had known her a long time. She was a woman of about forty, with fine shoulders, a hook nose, a drawling voice, and on this evening she wore over her brown hair a simple guipure fichu that fell in a point at the back. A blond young woman sat by her side in a high-backed chair, and gentlemen with flowers in their buttonholes were talking to ladies round the fire.

At seven dinner was served. The men, who were in the majority, sat down at the first table in the vestibule; the ladies at the second in the dining-room with the Marquis and Marquise.

Emma, on entering, felt herself wrapped round as by a warm breeze, a blending of the perfume of flowers and of the fine linen, of the fumes of the roasts and the odour of the truffles. The candles in the candelabra threw their lights on the silver dish covers; the cut crystal, covered with a fine mist of steam, reflected pale rays of light; bouquets were placed in a row the whole length of the table; and in the large-bordered plates each napkin, arranged after the fashion of a bishop's mitre, held between its two gaping folds a small oval-shaped roll. The red claws of lobsters hung over the dishes; rich fruit in woven baskets was piled up on moss; the quails were dressed in their own plumage, smoke was rising; and in silk stockings, knee-breeches, white cravat, and frilled shirt, the steward, grave as a judge, passed between the shoulders of the guests, offering ready-carved dishes and, with a flick of the spoon, landed on one's plate the piece one had chosen. On the large porcelain stove inlaid with copper baguettes the statue of a woman, draped to the chin, gazed motionless on the crowded room.

Madame Bovary noticed that many ladies had not put their gloves in their glasses.[6]

At the upper end of the table, alone amongst all these women, bent over his full plate, and his napkin tied round his neck like a child, an old man sat eating, letting drops of gravy drip from his mouth. His eyes were bloodshot, and he wore his hair in a little queue tied with a black ribbon. He was the Marquis's father-in-law, the old Duke de Laverdière, once on a time favourite of the Count d'Artois, in the days of the Marquis de Conflans' hunting-parties at le Vaudreuil, and had been, it was said, the lover of Queen Marie Antoinette, between Monsieur de Coigny and Monsieur de Lauzun. He had lived a life of loud dissipation, full of duels, bets, elope-

---

6. The ladies in the provinces, unlike their Paris counterparts, did not drink wine at public dinner parties, and signified their intention by putting their gloves in their wine-glasses. The fact that they fail to do so suggests to Emma the high degree of sophistication of the company.

ments; he had squandered his fortune and frightened all his family. A servant behind his chair shouted in his ear, in reply to his mutterings, the names of the dishes that he pointed to, and constantly Emma's eyes turned involuntarily to this old man with hanging lips, as to something extraordinary. He had lived at court and slept in the bed of queens!

Iced champagne was poured out. Emma shivered all over as she felt its cold in her mouth. She had never seen pomegranates nor tasted pineapples. Even the powdered sugar seemed to her whiter and finer than elsewhere.

The ladies afterwards retired to their rooms to prepare for the ball.

Emma made her toilette with the fastidious care of an actress on her début. She did her hair according to the directions of the hairdresser, and put on the barege dress spread out upon the bed. Charles's trousers were tight across the belly.

"My trouser-straps will be rather awkward for dancing," he said.

"Dancing?" repeated Emma.

"Yes!"

"Why, you must be mad! They would make fun of you; stay in your place, as it becomes a doctor."

Charles was silent. He walked up and down waiting for Emma to finish dressing.

He saw her from behind in the mirror between two lights. Her black eyes seemed blacker than ever. Her hair, gently undulating towards the ears, shone with a blue lustre; a rose in her chignon trembled on its mobile stalk, with artificial dewdrops on the tip of the leaves. She wore a gown of pale saffron trimmed with three bouquets of pompon roses mixed with green.

Charles came and kissed her on her shoulder.

"Don't touch me!" she cried; "I'll be all rumpled."

One could hear the flourish of the violin and the notes of a horn. She went downstairs restraining herself from running.

Dancing had begun. Guests were arriving and crowding the room. She sat down on a bench near the door.

The quadrille over, the floor was occupied by groups of talking men and by servants in livery bearing large trays. Along the line of seated women painted fans were fluttering, bouquets half-hid smiling faces, and gold-stoppered scent-bottles were turned in half-clenched hands, with white gloves outlining the nail and tightening on the flesh at the wrists. Lace trimmings, diamond brooches, medallion bracelets trembled on blouses, gleamed on breasts, clinked on bare arms. The hair, well smoothed over the temples and knotted at the nape, bore crowns, or bunches, or sprays of myosotis, jasmine, pomegranate blossoms, wheat-sprays and corn-flowers. Calmly seated in their places, mothers with forbidding countenances were wearing red turbans.

Emma's heart beat rather faster when, her partner holding her by the tips of the fingers, she took her place in a line with the dancers, and waited for the first note to start. But her emotion soon vanished, and, swaying to the rhythm of the orchestra, she glided forward with slight movements of the neck. A smile rose to her lips at certain delicate phrases of the violin, that sometimes played alone while the other instruments were silent; one could hear the clear clink of the louis d'or that were being thrown down upon the card-tables in the next room; then all struck in again, the trumpet uttered its sonorous note, feet marked time, skirts swelled and rustled, hands touched and parted; the same eyes that had been lowered returned to gaze at you again.

A few men (some fifteen or so), of twenty-five to forty, scattered here and there among the dancers or talking at the doorways, distinguished themselves from the crowd by a certain family-air, whatever their differences in age, dress, or countenance.

Their clothes, better made, seemed of finer cloth, and their hair, brought forward in curls towards the temples, glossy with more delicate pomades. They had the complexion of wealth,—that clear complexion that is heightened by the pallor of porcelain, the shimmer of satin, the veneer of old furniture, and that a well-ordered diet of exquisite food maintains at its best. Their necks moved easily in their low cravats, their long whiskers fell over their turned-down collars, they wiped their lips upon handkerchiefs with embroidered initials that gave forth a subtle perfume. Those who were beginning to grow old had an air of youth, while there was something mature in the faces of the young. Their indifferent eyes had the appeased expression of daily-satiated passions, and through all their gentleness of manner pierced that peculiar brutality that stems from a steady command over half-tame things, for the exercise of one's strength and the amusement of one's vanity—the handling of thoroughbred horses and the society of loose women.

A few steps from Emma a gentleman in a blue coat was talking of Italy with a pale young woman wearing a parure of pearls. They were praising the width of the columns of St. Peter's, Tivoli, Vesuvius, Castellamare, and the Cascine,[7] the roses of Genoa, the Coliseum by moonlight. With her other ear Emma was listening to a conversation full of words she did not understand. A circle gathered round a very young man who the week before had beaten "Miss Arabella," and "Romulus," and won two thousand louis jumping a ditch in

7. A park near Florence. *Castellamare:* A port south of Naples.

England. One complained that his racehorses were growing fat; another
of the printers' errors that had disfigured the name of his horse.

The atmosphere of the ball was heavy; the lamps were growing
dim. Guests were flocking to the billiard-room. A servant got upon
a chair and broke the window-panes. At the crash of the glass Madame Bovary turned her head and saw in the garden the faces of peasants pressed against the window looking in at them. Then the memory
of the Bertaux came back to her. She saw the farm again, the muddy
pond, her father in his apron under the apple-trees, and she saw
herself again as formerly, skimming with her finger the cream off the
milk-pans in the dairy. But in the splendor of the present hour her
past life, so distinct until then, faded away completely, and she almost
doubted having lived it. She was there; beyond the ball was only
shadow overspreading all the rest. She was eating a maraschino ice
that she held with her left hand in a silver-gilt cup, her eyes half-
closed, and the spoon between her teeth.

A lady near her dropped her fan. A gentleman was passing.

"Would you be good enough," said the lady, "to pick up my fan
that has fallen behind the sofa?"

The gentleman bowed, and as he moved to stretch out his arm,
Emma saw the hand of the young woman throw something white,
folded in a triangle, into his hat. The gentleman picking up the fan,
respectfully offered it to the lady; she thanked him with a nod and
breathed in the smell of her bouquet.

After supper, consisting of plenty of Spanish and Rhine wines,
bisque and almond-cream soups, Trafalgar puddings and all sorts of
cold meats with jellies that trembled in the dishes, the carriages began
to leave one after the other. Raising the corners of the muslin curtain, one could see the light of their lanterns glimmering through
the darkness. The seats began to empty, some card-players were still
left; the musicians were cooling the tips of their fingers on their
tongues. Charles was half asleep, his back propped against a door.

At three o'clock the cotillion began. Emma did not know how to
waltz. Every one was waltzing. Mademoiselle d'Andervilliers herself
and the Marquis; only the guests staying at the castle were still there,
about a dozen persons.

One of the waltzers, however, who was addressed as Viscount,
and whose low cut waistcoat seemed moulded to his chest, came a
second time to ask Madame Bovary to dance, assuring her that he
would guide her, and that she would get through it very well.

They began slowly, then increased in speed. They turned; all around
them was turning, the lamps, the furniture, the wainscoting, the
floor, like a disc on a pivot. On passing near the doors the train of
Emma's dress caught against his trousers. Their legs intertwined; he
looked down at her; she raised her eyes to his. A torpor seized her

and she stopped. They started again, at an even faster pace; the Viscount, sweeping her along, disappeared with her to the end of the gallery, where, panting, she almost fell, and for a moment rested her head upon his breast. And then, still turning, but more slowly, he guided her back to her seat. She leaned back against the wall and covered her eyes with her hands.

When she opened them again, in the middle of the drawing-room three waltzers were kneeling before a lady sitting on a stool. She chose the Viscount, and the violin struck up once more.

Every one looked at them. They kept passing by, she with rigid body, her chin bent down, and he always in the same pose, his figure curved, his elbow rounded, his chin thrown forward. That woman knew how to waltz! They kept it up a long time, and tired out all the others.

Then they talked a few moments longer, and after the good-nights, or rather good-mornings, the guests of the château retired to bed.

Charles dragged himself up by the banister. His knees were giving way under him. For five consecutive hours, he had stood bolt upright at the card-tables, watching them play whist, without understanding anything about it, and it was with a deep sigh of relief that he pulled off his boots.

Emma threw a shawl over her shoulders, opened the window, and leant out.

The night was dark; some drops of rain were falling. She breathed in the damp wind that refreshed her eyelids. The music of the ball was still echoing in her ears, and she tried to keep herself awake in order to prolong the illusion of this luxurious life that she would soon have to give up.

Day began to break. She looked long at the windows of the château, trying to guess which were the rooms of all those she had noticed the evening before. She would have wanted to know their lives, to penetrate into them, to blend with them.

But she was shivering with cold. She undressed, and cowered down between the sheets against Charles, who was asleep.

There were a great many people to luncheon. The meal lasted ten minutes; to the doctor's astonishment, no liqueurs were served. Next, Mademoiselle d'Andervilliers collected some rolls in a small basket to take them to the swans on the ornamental waters, and they went for a walk in the hothouses, where strange plants, bristling with hairs, rose in pyramids under hanging vases from where fell, as from over-filled nests of serpents, long green cords interlacing. The orangery, at the other end, led by a covered way to the tenant houses of the château. The Marquis, to amuse the young woman, took her to see the stables. Above the basket-shaped racks porcelain slabs bore the names of the horses in black letters. Each animal in its stall whisked

its tail when any one came near and clicked his tongue. The boards
of the harness-room shone like the flooring of a drawing-room. The
carriage harness was piled up in the middle against two twisted columns, and the bits, the whips, the spurs, the curbs, were lined up
in a row all along the wall.

Charles, meanwhile, went to ask a groom to harness his horse.
The dog-cart was brought to the foot of the steps, and all the parcels
being crammed in, the Bovarys paid their respects to the Marquis
and the Marquise and set out again for Tostes.

Emma watched the turning wheels in silence. Charles, on the
extreme edge of the seat, held the reins with his arms spread far
apart, and the little horse ambled along in the shafts that were too
big for him. The loose reins hanging over his crupper were wet with
foam, and the box fastened behind bumped regularly against the
cart.

They were on the heights of Thibourville when suddenly some
horsemen with cigars between their lips passed, laughing. Emma
thought she recognised the Viscount, turned back, and caught on
the horizon only the movement of the heads rising or falling with
the unequal cadence of the trot or gallop.

A mile farther on they had to stop to mend with some string the
traces that had broken.

But Charles, giving a last look to the harness, saw something on
the ground between his horse's legs, and he picked up a cigar-case
with a green silk border and a crest in the centre like the door of a
carriage.

"There are even two cigars in it," said he; "they'll do for this evening after dinner."

"Since when do you smoke?" she asked.

"Sometimes, when I get a chance."

He put his find in his pocket and whipped up the nag.

When they reached home the dinner was not ready. Madame lost
her temper. Nastasie answered rudely.

"Leave the room!" said Emma. "You are being insolent. I'll dismiss you."

For dinner there was onion soup and a piece of veal with sorrel.
Charles, seated opposite Emma, rubbed his hands gleefully.

"How good it is to be at home again!"

Nastasie could be heard crying. He was rather fond of the poor
girl. She had formerly, during the wearisome time of his widowhood, kept him company many an evening. She had been his first
patient, his oldest acquaintance in the place.

"Have you dismissed her for good?" he asked at last.

"Yes. Who is to prevent me?" she replied.

Then they warmed themselves in the kitchen while their room

was being made ready. Charles began to smoke. He smoked with lips protruded, spitting every moment, drawing back at every puff.

"You'll make yourself ill," she said scornfully.

He put down his cigar and ran to swallow a glass of cold water at the pump. Seizing the cigar case, Emma threw it quickly to the back of the cupboard.

The next day was a long one. She walked about her little garden, up and down the same walks, stopping before the beds, before the fruit tree, before the plaster priest, looking with amazement at all these things of the past that she knew so well. How far off the ball seemed already! What was it that thus set so far asunder the morning of the day before yesterday and the evening of to-day? Her journey to Vaubyessard had made a gap in her life, like the huge crevasses that a thunderstorm will sometimes carve in the mountains, in the course of a single night. Still she was resigned. She devoutly put away in her drawers her beautiful dress, down to the satin shoes whose soles were yellowed with the slippery wax of the dancing floor. Her heart resembled them: in its contact with wealth, something had rubbed off on it that could not be removed.

The memory of this ball, then, became an occupation for Emma. Whenever Wednesday came round she said to herself as she awoke, "Ah! I was there a week—a fortnight—three weeks ago." And little by little the faces grew confused in her remembrance. She forgot the tune of the quadrilles; she no longer saw the liveries and the guest-houses so distinctly; some of the details faded but the wistful feeling remained with her.

IX

Often when Charles was out she took from the cupboard, between the folds of the linen where she had left it, the green silk cigar-case.

She looked at it, opened it, and even smelt the odour of the lining, a mixture of verbena and tobacco. Whose was it? . . . The Viscount's? Perhaps it was a present from his mistress. It had been embroidered on some rosewood frame, a pretty piece of furniture, hidden from all eyes, that had occupied many hours, and over which had fallen the soft curls of the pensive worker. A breath of love had passed over the stitches on the canvas; each prick of the needle had fixed there a hope or a memory, and all those interwoven threads of silk were but the continued extension of the same silent passion. And then one morning the Viscount had taken it away with him. Of what had they spoken when it lay upon the wide-mantelled chimneys between flower-vases and Pompadour clocks? She was at Tostes; he was at Paris now, far away! What was this Paris like? What a bound-less name! She repeated it in a low voice, for the mere pleasure of it;

it rang in her ears like a great cathedral bell; it shone before her eyes, even on the labels of her jars of pomade.

At night, when the carts passed under her windows, carrying fish to Paris to the tune of "la Marjolaine," she awoke, and listened to the noise of the iron-bound wheels, which, as they gained the country road, was soon deadened by the earth. "They will be there tomorrow!" she said to herself.

And she followed them in thought up and down the hills, crossing villages, gliding along the highroads by the light of the stars. At the end of some indefinite distance there was always a confused spot, into which her dream died.

She bought a plan of Paris, and with the tip of her finger on the map she walked about the capital. She went up the boulevards, stopping at every turn, between the lines of the streets, in front of the white squares that represented the houses. At last she would close the lids of her weary eyes, and see in the darkness the gas jets flaring in the wind and the steps of carriages lowered noisily in front of the theatre-entrances.

She subscribed to "La Corbeille," a ladies' magazine, and the "Sylphe des Salons." She devoured, without skipping a word, all the accounts of first nights, races, and soirées, took an interest in the début of a singer, in the opening of a new shop. She knew the latest fashions, the addresses of the best tailors, the days of the Bois and the Opera. In Eugène Sue she studied descriptions of furniture; she read Balzac and George Sand,[8] seeking in them imaginary satisfaction for her own desires. She even brought her book to the table, and turned over the pages while Charles ate and talked to her. The memory of the Viscount always cropped up in everything she read. She made comparisons between him and the fictional characters in her books. But the circle of which he was the centre gradually widened round him, and the aureole that he bore, fading from his form and extending beyond his image, lit up her other dreams.

Paris, more vague than the ocean, glimmered before Emma's eyes with a silvery glow. The many lives that stirred amid this tumult were, however, divided into parts, classed as distinct pictures. Emma perceived only two or three that hid from her all the rest, and in themselves represented all humanity. The world of ambassadors moved over polished floors in drawing-rooms lined with mirrors, round oval tables covered with velvet and gold-fringed cloths. There were dresses with trains, deep mysteries, anguish hidden beneath smiles. Then came the society of the duchesses; all were pale; all got up at four o'clock; the women, poor angels, wore English point on their petti-

---

8. Pseudonym of Aurore Dupin, prolific woman novelist (1803–1876). *Eugène Sue* (1804–1857), a popular novelist, extremely successful at that period, both as a writer and as a fashionable dandy.

coats; and the men, their talents hidden under a frivolous appearance, rode horses to death at pleasure parties, spent the summer season at Baden, and ended up, on reaching their forties, by marrying heiresses. In the private rooms of restaurants, where one dines after midnight by the light of wax candles, the colorful crowd of writers and actresses held sway. They were prodigal as kings, full of ambitious ideals and fantastic frenzies. They lived far above all others, among the storms that rage between heaven and earth, partaking of the sublime. As for the rest of the world, it was lost, with no particular place, and as if non-existent. Anyway, the nearer things were the more her thoughts turned away from them. All her immediate surroundings, the wearisome countryside, the petty-bourgeois stupidity, the mediocrity of existence seemed to her the exception, an exception in which she had been caught by a stroke of fate, while beyond stretched as far as eye could see an immense land of joys and passions. In her wistfulness, she confused the sensuous pleasures of luxury with the delights of the heart, elegance of manners with delicacy of sentiment. Did not love, like Indian plants, need a special soil, a special temperature? Sighs by moonlight, long embraces, tears flowing over yielded hands, all the passions of the flesh and the languors of tenderness seemed to her inseparable from the balconies of great castles where life flows idly by, from boudoirs with silken curtains and thick carpets, well-filled flower-stands, a bed on a raised daïs, and from the flashing of precious stones and the golden braids of liveries.

The boy from the post-office who came to groom the mare every morning passed through the passage with his heavy wooden shoes; there were holes in his apron; his feet were bare in his slippers. And this was the groom in knee-breeches with whom she had to be content! His work done, he did not come back again all day, for Charles on his return put up his horse himself, unsaddled it and put on the halter, while the maid brought a bundle of straw and threw it as best she could into the manger.

To replace Nastasie (who finally left Tostes shedding torrents of tears) Emma hired a young girl of fourteen, an orphan with a sweet face. She forbade her wearing cotton caps, taught her to address her in the third person, to bring a glass of water on a plate, to knock before coming into a room, to iron, starch, and to dress her; she wanted to make a lady's-maid of her. The new servant obeyed without a murmur, so as not to be dismissed; and as madame usually left the key in the sideboard, Félicité every evening took a small supply of sugar that she ate alone in her bed after she had said her prayers.

Sometimes in the afternoon she went across the road to chat with the coachmen. Madame stayed upstairs.

She wore an open dressing-gown, that showed under the shawl-shaped collar a pleated blouse with three gold buttons. Her belt was a corded girdle with great tassels, and her small wine-red slippers had a large knot of ribbon that fell over her instep. She had bought herself a blotter, writing-case, pen-holder, and envelopes although she had no one to write to; she dusted her shelf, looked at herself in the mirror, picked up a book, and then, dreaming between the lines, let it drop on her knees. She longed to travel or to go back to her convent. She wanted to die, but she also wanted to live in Paris.

Charles trotted over the country-roads in snow and rain. He ate omelettes on farmhouse tables, poked his arm into damp beds, received the tepid spurt of blood-letting in his face, listened to death-rattles, examined basins, turned over a good deal of dirty linen; but every evening he found a blazing fire, his dinner ready, easy-chairs, and a well-dressed woman, charming and so freshly scented that it was impossible to say where the perfume came from; it might have been her skin that communicated its fragrance to her blouse.

She delighted him by numerous attentions; now it was some new way of arranging paper sconces for the candles, a flounce that she altered on her gown, or an extraordinary name for some very simple dish that the servant had spoilt, but that Charles swallowed with pleasure to the last mouthful. At Rouen she saw some ladies who wore a bundle of charms hanging from their watch-chains; she bought some. She wanted for her mantelpiece two large blue glass vases, and some time after an ivory nécessaire with a silver-gilt thimble. The less Charles understood these refinements the more they seduced him. They added something to the pleasure of the senses and to the comfort of his fireside. It was like a golden dust sanding all along the narrow path of his life.

He was well, looked well; his reputation was firmly established. The country-folk loved him because he was not proud. He petted the children, never went to the public-house, and, moreover, his good behavior inspired confidence. He was specially successful with heavy colds and chest ailments. Being much afraid of killing his patients, Charles, in fact, only prescribed sedatives, from time to time an emetic, a footbath, or leeches. It was not that he was afraid of surgery; he bled people copiously like horses, and for the pulling of teeth the strength of his grasp was second to no one.

Finally, to keep up with the times, he subscribed to "La Ruche Médicale," a new journal whose prospectus had been sent him. He read it a little after dinner, but in about five minutes, the warmth of the room added to the effect of his dinner sent him to sleep; and he sat there, his chin on his two hands and his hair spreading like a mane to the foot of the lamp. Emma looked at him and shrugged her shoulders. Why at least, was not her husband one of those silently determined men who work at their books all night, and at last, when at sixty the age of rheumatism was upon them, wear a string of medals on their ill-fitting black coat? She would have wished this name of Bovary, which was hers, to be illustrious, to see it displayed at the booksellers', repeated in the newspapers, known to all France. But Charles had no ambition. An Yvetot doctor whom he had lately met in consultation had somewhat humiliated him at the very bedside of the patient, before the assembled relatives. When, in the evening, Charles told this incident Emma inveighed loudly against his colleague. Charles was much touched. He kissed her forehead with a tear in his eyes. But she was angered with shame; she felt a wild desire to strike him; she went to open the window in the passage and breathed in the fresh air to calm herself.

"What a man! what a man!" she said in a low voice, biting her lips.

She was becoming more irritated with him. As he grew older his manner grew coarser; at dessert he cut the corks of the empty bottles; after eating he cleaned his teeth with his tongue; in eating his soup he made a gurgling noise with every spoonful; and, as he was getting fatter, the puffed-out cheeks seemed to push the eyes, always small, up to the temples.

Sometimes Emma tucked the red borders of his undervest into his waistcoat, rearranged his cravat, and threw away the faded gloves he was going to put on; and this was not, as he fancied, for his sake; it was for herself, by an expansion of selfishness, of nervous irritation. At other times, she told him what she had been reading, some passage in a novel, a new play, or an anecdote from high society found in a newspaper story; for, after all, Charles was someone to talk to, an ever-open ear, an ever-ready approbation. She even confided many a thing to her greyhound! She would have done so to the logs in the fireplace or to the pendulum of the clock.

All the while, however, she was waiting in her heart for something to happen. Like shipwrecked sailors, she turned despairing eyes upon the solitude of her life, seeking afar some white sail in the mists of the horizon. She did not know what this act of fortune would be, what wind would bring it, towards what shore it would drive her, if it would be a rowboat or an ocean liner with three decks, carrying anguish or laden to the gunwales with bliss. But each morning, as she awoke, she hoped it would come that day; she listened to every sound, sprang up with a start, wondered that it did not come; then at sunset, always more saddened, she longed for the next day.

Spring came round. With the first warm weather, when the pear-trees began to blossom, she had fainting-spells.

From the beginning of July she counted off on her fingers how many weeks there were to October, thinking that perhaps the Marquis d'Andervilliers would give another ball at Vaubyessard. But all

September passed without letters or visits.

After the shock of this disappointment her heart once more remained empty, and then the same series of identical days recommenced.

So now they would keep following one another, always the same, immovable, and bringing nothing new. Other lives, however flat, had at least the chance of some event. One adventure sometimes brought with it infinite consequences and the scene changed. But nothing happened to her; God had willed it so! The future was a dark corridor, with its door at the end shut tight.

She gave up music. What was the good of playing? Who would hear her? Since she could never, in a velvet gown with short sleeves, striking with her light fingers the ivory keys of an Erard concert piano, feel the murmur of ecstasy envelop her like a breeze, it was not worth while boring herself with practising. Her drawing cardboard and her embroidery she left in the cupboard. What was the use? What was the use? Sewing irritated her.

"I have read everything," she said to herself.

And she sat there, letting the tongs grow red-hot or looking at the rain falling.

How sad she was on Sundays when vespers sounded! She listened with dull attention to each stroke of the cracked bell. A cat slowly walking over some roof put up his back in the pale rays of the sun. The wind on the highroad blew up clouds of dust. A dog sometimes howled in the distance; and the bell, keeping time, continued at regular intervals its monotonous ringing that died away over the fields.

Then the people came out from church. The women had waxed their wooden shoes, the farmers wore new smocks, and with the little bareheaded children skipping along in front of them, all were going home. And till nightfall, five or six men, always the same, stayed playing at corks in front of the large door of the inn.

The winter was severe. Every morning, the windows were covered with rime, and the light that shone through them, dim as through ground-glass, sometimes did not change the whole day long. At four o'clock the lamp had to be lighted.

On fine days she went down into the garden. The dew had left a silver lace on the cabbages with long transparent threads spreading from one to the other. No birds were to be heard; everything seemed asleep, the fruit tree covered with straw, and the vine, like a great sick serpent under the coping of the wall, along which, on drawing near, one saw the many-footed woodlice crawling. Under the spruce by the hedgerow, the curé in the three-cornered hat reading his breviary had lost his right foot, and the very plaster, scaling off with the frost, had left white scabs on his face.

Then she went up again, shut her door, put on coals, and fainting with the heat of the hearth, felt her boredom weigh more heavily than ever. She would have liked to go down and talk to the maid, but a sense of shame restrained her.

Every day at the same time the schoolmaster in a black skull-cap opened the shutters of his house, and the village policeman, wearing his sword over his blouse, passed by. Night and morning the post-horses, three by three, crossed the street to water at the pond. From time to time the bell of a café would tinkle, and when it was windy one could hear the little brass basins that served as signs for the hair-dresser's shop creaking on their two rods. The shop was decorated with an old engraving of a fashion-plate stuck against a window-pane and with the wax bust of a woman with yellow hair. He, too, the hairdresser, lamented his wasted calling, his hopeless future, and dreaming of some shop in a big town—at Rouen, for example, over-looking the harbour, near the theatre—he walked up and down all day from the mairie to the church, sombre and waiting for custom-ers. When Madame Bovary looked up, she always saw him there, like a sentinel on duty, with his skull-cap over his ears and his woolen jacket.

Sometimes in the afternoon outside the window of her room, the head of a man appeared, a swarthy head with black whiskers, smiling slowly, with a broad, gentle smile that showed his white teeth. A waltz began, and on the barrel-organ, in a little drawing-room, dancers the size of a finger, women in pink turbans, Tyrolians in jackets, monkeys in frock-coats, gentlemen in knee breeches, turned and turned between the armchairs, the sofas and the tables, reflected in small pieces of mirror that strips of paper held together at the cor-ners. The man turned the handle, looking to the right, to the left and up at the windows. Now and again, while he shot out a long squirt of brown saliva against the milestone, he lifted his instrument with his knee, to relieve his shoulder from the pressure of the hard straps; and now, doleful and drawling, or merry and hurried, the music issued forth from the box, droning through a curtain of pink taffeta underneath an ornate brass grill. They were airs played in other places at the theatres, sung in drawing-rooms, danced to at night under lighted lustres, echoes of the world that reached even to Emma. Endless sarabands ran through her head, and, like an Ori-ental dancing-girl on the flowers of a carpet, her thoughts leapt with the notes, swung from dream to dream, from sadness to sadness. When the man had caught some pennies in his cap he drew down an old cover of blue cloth, hitched his organ on to his back, and went off with a heavy tread. She watched him going.

But it was above all the meal-times that were unbearable to her, in this small room on the ground-floor, with its smoking stove, its creaking door, the walls that sweated, the damp pavement; all the bitterness of life seemed served up on her plate, and with the smoke of the boiled beef there rose from her secret soul waves of nauseous disgust. Charles was a slow eater; she played with a few nuts, or, leaning on her elbow, amused herself drawing lines along the oil-cloth table-cover with the point of her knife.

She now let everybody in her household go its own way, and the elder Madame Bovary, when she came to spend part of Lent at Tostes, was much surprised at the change. She who was formerly so careful, so dainty, now spent whole days without dressing, wore grey cotton stockings, and used tallow candles to light the house. She kept saying they must be economical since they were not rich, adding that she was very contented, very happy, that Tostes pleased her very much, and other such statements that left her mother-in-law speechless. Besides, Emma no longer seemed inclined to follow her advice; on one occasion, when Madame Bovary had thought fit to maintain that masters ought to keep an eye on the religion of their servants, she had answered with a look so angry and a smile so cold that the old lady preferred to let the matter drop.

Emma was growing difficult, capricious. She ordered dishes for herself, then she did not touch them; one day drank only pure milk, and the next cups of tea by the dozen. Often she persisted in not going out, then, stifling, threw open the windows and put on light dresses. After she had well scolded her maid she gave her presents or sent her out to see neighbors. She sometimes threw beggars all the silver in her purse, although she was by no means tender-hearted or easily accessible to the feelings of others; like most country-bred people, she always retained in her soul something of the horny hardness of the paternal hands.

Towards the end of February old Rouault, in memory of his cure, personally brought a superb turkey to his son-in-law, and stayed three days at Tostes. Charles being with his patients, Emma kept him company. He smoked in the room, spat on the andirons, talked farming, calves, cows, poultry, and municipal council, so that when he left she closed the door on him with a feeling of satisfaction that surprised even herself. Moreover she no longer concealed her contempt for anything or anybody, and at times expressed singular opinions, finding fault with whatever others approved, and approving things perverse and immoral, all of which left her husband wide-eyed.

Would this misery last for ever? Would she never escape from it? Yet she was the equal of all the women who were living happily. She had seen duchesses at Vaubyessard with clumsier waists and commoner ways, and she hated the divine injustice of God. She leant her head against the walls to weep; she longed for lives of adventure, for masked balls, for shameless pleasures that were bound, she thought, to initiate her to ecstacies she had not yet experienced.

She grew pale and suffered from palpitations of the heart. Charles prescribed valerian drops and camphor baths. Everything that was tried only seemed to irritate her the more.

On certain days she chattered with feverish profusion, and this overexcitement was suddenly followed by a state of torpor, in which she remained without speaking, without moving. What then revived her was to pour a bottle of eau-de-cologne over her arms.

As she was constantly complaining about Tostes, Charles fancied that her illness was no doubt due to some local cause, and, struck by this idea, he began to think seriously of setting up practice elsewhere.

From that moment she drank vinegar to lose weight, contracted a sharp little cough, and lost all appetite.

It cost Charles much to give up Tostes after living there four years, just when he was beginning to get somewhere. Yet if it must be! He took her to Rouen to see his old master. It was a nervous condition; she needed a change of air.

After some looking around, Charles discovered that the doctor of a considerable market-town in the arrondissement of Neufchâtel, a former Polish refugee, had vanished a week earlier. Then he wrote to the local pharmacist to ask the size of the population, the distance from the nearest doctor, how much his predecessor had earned in a year, and so forth; and the answer being satisfactory, he made up his mind to move towards the spring, if Emma's health did not improve.

One day when, in view of her departure, she was tidying a drawer, something pricked her finger. It was a wire of her wedding-bouquet. The orange blossoms were yellow with dust and the silver-bordered satin ribbons frayed at the edges. She threw it into the fire. It flared up more quickly than dry straw. Then it was like a red bush in the cinders, slowly shrinking away. She watched it burn. The little pasteboard berries burst, the wire twisted, the gold lace melted; and the shrivelled paper petals, fluttering like black butterflies at the back of the stove, at last flew up the chimney.

When they left Tostes in the month of March, Madame Bovary was pregnant.

Part Two

I

Yonville-l'Abbaye (named after an old Capuchin abbey of which not even the ruins remain) is a market-town some twenty miles from Rouen, between the Abbeville and Beauvais roads. It lies at the foot of a valley watered by the Rieule, a little river that runs into the Andelle after turning three water-mills near its mouth; it contains a few trout and, on Sundays, the village boys entertain themselves by fishing.

Leaving the main road at la Boissière, one reaches the height of les Leux from where the valley comes into view. The river that runs through it has divided the area into two very distinct regions: on the left are pastures, while the right consists of tilled land. The meadow stretches under a bulge of low hills to join at the back with the pasture land of the Bray country, while on the eastern side, the plain, gently rising, broadens out, showing as far as the eye can reach its blond wheatfields. The water, flowing through the grass, divides with a white line the color of the meadows from that of the ploughed fields, and the country is like a great unfolded mantle with a green velvet cape bordered with a fringe of silver.

On the horizon rise the oaks of the forest of Argueil, with the steeps of the Saint Jean hills scarred from top to bottom with red irregular lines; they are rain-tracks, and these brick-tones standing out in narrow streaks against the grey colour of the mountain are due to the high iron content of the springs that flow beyond in the neighboring country.

These are the confines of Normandy, Picardy, and the Ile-de-France, a mongrel land whose language, like its landscape, is without accent or character. The worst Neufchâtel cheeses in the arrondissement are made here; and, on the other hand, farming is costly because so much manure is needed to enrich this brittle soil, full of sand and stones.

Up to 1835 no practicable road for getting to Yonville existed, but about this time a cross-road was cut, joining the Abbeville to the Amiens highway; it is occasionally used by the Rouen teamsters on their way to Flanders. Yonville-l'Abbaye has remained stationary in spite of its "new outlet." Instead of improving the soil they persist in keeping up the pasture lands, however depreciated they may be in value, and the lazy village, growing away from the plain, has naturally spread riverwards. It is seen from afar sprawling along the banks like a cowherd taking a nap by the side of the river.

At the foot of the hill beyond the bridge begins a roadway, planted with young aspens that leads in a straight line to the first houses in the place. These, fenced in by hedges, are in the middle of courtyards full of straggling buildings, wine-presses, cart-sheds, and distilleries scattered under thick trees, with ladders, poles, or scythes hooked over the branches. The thatched roofs, like fur caps drawn over eyes, reach down over about a third of the low windows, whose coarse convex glasses have bull's eyes in the middle, like the bottom of a bottle. A meagre pear-tree may be found leaning against some plaster wall crossed by black beans, and one enters the ground-floors through a door with a small swing-gate that keeps out the chicks when they pilfer, on the threshold, crumbs of bread steeped in cider. Gradually the courtyards grow narrower, the houses closer together, and the fences disappear; a bundle of ferns swings under a window from the end of a broomstick; there is a blacksmith's forge and then a wheelwright's, with two or three new carts outside that partly block the way. Then across an open space appears a white house at the end of a round lawn ornamented by a Cupid, his finger on his lips. Two cast-iron jars flank the high porch, copper signs gleam on the door. It is the notary's house, the finest in the place.

The church is on the other side of the street, twenty paces farther down, at the entrance of the square. The little graveyard that surrounds it, closed in by a breast-high wall, is so full of graves that the old stones, level with the ground, form a continuous pavement, on which the grass has, by itself, marked out regular green squares. The church was rebuilt during the last years of the reign of Charles X.[9] The wooden roof is beginning to rot from the top, and here and there black hollows appear in the blue paint. Over the door, where the organ should be, is a gallery for the men, with a spiral staircase that reverberates under the weight of their wooden shoes.

The daylight coming through the plain glass windows falls obliquely upon the pews perpendicular to the walls, here and there adorned with a straw mat inscribed, in large letters, with the name of some parishioner. Further on, where the nave grows narrow, the confessional faces a small Madonna, clothed in satin, wearing a tulle veil sprinkled with silver stars and with cheeks stained red like an idol of the Sandwich Islands;[1] finally, a painted copy entitled "The Holy Family, a gift from the Minister of the Interior," flanked by four candlesticks, crowns the main altar and rounds off the view. The choir stalls, of pine wood, have been left unpainted.

The market, that is to say, a tiled roof supported by some twenty posts, occupies by itself about half the public square of Yonville. The town hall, constructed "after the designs of a Paris architect," is a sort of Greek temple that forms the corner next to the pharmacy. On the ground-floor are three Ionic columns and on the first floor a gallery with arched windows, while the crowning frieze is occupied by a Gallic cock, resting one foot upon the Charter[2] and holding in the other the scales of Justice.

But what catches the eye most of all is Mr. Homais' pharmacy, right across from the Lion d'Or. In the evening especially its lamp is lit up and the red and green jars that embellish his shop-front cast their colored reflection far across the street; beyond them, as in a Bengal light, the silhouette of the pharmacist can be seen leaning

9. Charles X (1757–1836), son of Louis XV, was the last Bourbon king; he was expelled by the July Revolution (1830).   1. The old name for Hawaii. They were named after John Montagu, fourth Earl of Sandwich (1718–1792) who served as first Lord of Admiralty when the islands were discovered.   2. The *Charte constitutiouelle de la France*, basis of the French constitution after the Revolution, bestowed in 1814 by Louis XVIII and revised in 1830, after the downfall of Charles X.

over his desk. His house is plastered from top to bottom with inscriptions written in longhand, in round, in lower case: "Vichy, Seltzer and Barrège waters, depurative gum drops, Raspail patent medicine, Arabian racahout, Darcet lozenges, Regnault ointment, trusses, baths, laxative chocolate, etc." And the signboard, which stretches all the breadth of the shop, bears in gold letters "Homais, Pharmacist." Then at the back of the shop, behind the great scales fixed to the counter, the word "Laboratory" appears on a scroll above a glass door on which, about half-way up, the word Homais is once more repeated in gold letters on a black ground.

Beyond this there is nothing to see at Yonville. The street (the only one), a gunshot long and flanked by a few shops on either side, stops short at the turn of the high road. Turning right and following the foot of the Saint-Jean hills one soon reaches the graveyard.

At the time of the cholera epidemic, a piece of wall was pulled down and three acres of land purchased in order to make more room, but the new area is almost deserted; the tombs, as heretofore, continue to crowd together towards the gate. The keeper, who is at once gravedigger and church sexton (thus making a double profit out of the parish corpses), has taken advantage of the unused plot of ground to plant potatoes. From year to year, however, his small field grows smaller, and when there is an epidemic, he does not know whether to rejoice at the deaths or regret the added graves.

"You feed on the dead, Lestiboudois!" the curé told him one day.

This grim remark made him reflect; it checked him for some time; but to this day he carries on the cultivation of his little tubers, and even maintains stoutly that they grow naturally.

Since the events about to be narrated, nothing in fact has changed at Yonville. The tin tricolour flag still swings at the top of the church-steeple; the two streamers at the novelty store still flutter in the wind; the spongy white lumps, the pharmacist's foetuses, rot more and more in their cloudy alcohol, and above the big door of the inn the old golden lion, faded by rain, still shows passers-by its poodle mane.

On the evening when the Bovarys were to arrive in Yonville, the widow Lefrançois, the landlady of this inn, was so busy that she sweated great drops as she moved her saucepans around. To-morrow was market-day. The meat had to be cut beforehand, the chickens drawn, the soup and coffee made. Moreover, she had the boarders' meal to see to, and that of the doctor, his wife, and their maid; the billiard-room was echoing with bursts of laughter; three millers in the small parlour were calling for brandy; the wood was blazing, the charcoal crackling, and on the long kitchen-table, amid the quarters of raw mutton, rose piles of plates that rattled with the shaking of the block on which spinach was being chopped. From the poultry-yard was heard the screaming of the chickens whom the servant was chasing in order to wring their necks.

A slightly pockmarked man in green leather slippers, and wearing a velvet cap with a gold tassel, was warming his back at the chimney. His face expressed nothing but self-satisfaction, and he appeared as calmly established in life as the gold-finch suspended over his head in its wicker cage: he was the pharmacist.

"Artémise!" shouted the innkeeper, "chop some wood, fill the water bottles, bring some brandy, hurry up! If only I knew what dessert to offer the guests you are expecting! Good heavens! Those furniture-movers are beginning their racket in the billiard-room again; and their van has been left before the front door! The 'Hirondelle' might crash into it when it draws up. Call Polyte and tell him to put it away . . . Imagine, Monsieur Homais, that since morning they have had about fifteen games, and drunk eight pots of cider! . . . Why they'll tear my billiard-cloth to pieces!" she went on, looking at them from a distance, her strainer in her hand.

"That wouldn't be much of a loss," replied Monsieur Homais. "You would buy another."

"Another billiard-table!" exclaimed the widow.

"Since that one is coming to pieces, Madame Lefrançois. I tell you again you are doing yourself harm, much harm! And besides, players now want narrow pockets and heavy cues. They don't play the way they used to, everything is changed! One must keep pace with the times! Just look at Tellier!"

The hostess grew red with anger. The pharmacist added:

"You may say what you like; his table is better than yours; and if one were to think, for example, of getting up a patriotic tournament for Polish independence or for the victims of the Lyon floods . . ."[3]

"It isn't beggars like him that'll frighten us," interrupted the landlady, shrugging her fat shoulders. "Come, come, Monsieur Homais; as long as the Lion d'Or exists people will come to it. We are no fly-by-nights, we have feathered our nest! While one of these days you'll find the Café Français closed with a fine poster on the shutters. Change my billiard-table!" she went on, speaking to herself, "the table that comes in so handy for folding the washing, and on which, in the hunting season, I have slept six visitors! . . . But what can be keeping the slowpoke of a Hivert?"

"Are you waiting for him to serve your gentlemen's dinner?"

"Wait for him! And what about Monsieur Binet? As the clock

---

3. The allusion dates the action of the novel as taking place in 1840; during the winter of 1840, the Rhône overflowed with catastrophic results. At the same time, Louis Philippe was under steady attack for his failure to offer sufficient assistance to the victims of the repression that followed the insurrection of Warsaw (1831).

strikes six you'll see him come in, for he hasn't his equal under the sun for punctuality. He must always have his seat in the small parlour. He'd rather die than eat anywhere else. And he is finicky! and particular about his cider! Not like monsieur Léon; he sometimes comes at seven, or even half-past, and he doesn't so much as look at what he eats. Such a nice young man! Never speaks a cross word!"

"Well, you see, there's a great difference between an educated man and a former army man who is now a tax-collector."

Six o'clock struck. Binet came in.

He was dressed in a blue frock-coat falling in a straight line round his thin body, and his leather cap, with its lappets knotted over the top of his head with string, showed under the turned-up peak a bald forehead, flattened by the constant wearing of a helmet. He wore a black cloth vest, a hair collar, grey trousers, and, all the year round, well-blacked boots, that had two parallel swellings where the big toes protruded. Not a hair stood out from the regular line of fair whiskers, which, encircling his jaws, framed like a garden border his long, wan face, with smallish eyes and a hooked nose. Clever at all games of cards, a good hunter, and writing a fine hand, he had at home a lathe, and amused himself by turning napkin-rings, with which he crammed his house, jealous as an artist and selfish as a bourgeois.

He went to the small parlour, but the three millers had to be got out first, and during the whole time necessary for resetting the table, Binet remained silent in his place near the stove. Then he shut the door and took off his cap as usual.

"Politeness will not wear out his tongue," said the pharmacist, as soon as he was alone with the hostess.

"He never talks more," she replied. "Last week I had two travelling salesmen here selling cloth, really a cheerful pair, who spent the night telling jokes. They made me weep with laughter but he, he stood there mute as a fish, never opened his mouth."

"Yes," said the pharmacist, "no imagination, no wit, nothing that makes a man shine in society."

"Yet they say he is a man of means," objected the landlady.

"Of means?" replied the pharmacist. "He? In his own line, perhaps," he added in a calmer tone. And he went on:

"Now, that a businessman with numerous connections, a lawyer, a doctor, a pharmacist, should be thus absent-minded, that they should become whimsical or even peevish, I can understand; such cases are cited in history. But at least it is because they are thinking of something. How often hasn't it happened to me, for instance, to look on my desk for my pen when I had to write out a label, merely to discover, at last, that I had put it behind my ear?"

Madame Lefrançois just then went to the door to see if the "Hirondelle" was not coming. She started. A man dressed in black suddenly came into the kitchen. By the last gleam of the twilight one could see that he was red-faced and powerfully built.

"What can I do for you, Monsieur le curé?" asked the hostess, as she reached down a copper candlestick from the row of candles. "Will you have something to drink? A thimbleful of *Cassis*? A glass of wine?"

The priest declined very politely. He had come for his umbrella, that he had forgotten the other day at the Ernemont convent, and after asking Madame Lefrançois to have it sent to him at the rectory in the evening, he left for the church; the Angelus was ringing.

When the pharmacist no longer heard the noise of his boots along the square, he confessed that he had found the priest's behaviour just now very unbecoming. This refusal to take any refreshment seemed to him the most odious hypocrisy; all priests tippled on the sly, and were trying to bring back the days of the tithe.

The landlady took up the defence of her curé.

"Besides, he could double up four men like you over his knee. Last year he helped our people to bring in the hay, he carried as many as six bales at once, he is so strong."

"Bravo!" said the pharmacist. "Now just send your daughters to confess to such vigorous fellows! I, if I were the Government, I'd have the priests bled once a month. Yes, Madame Lefrançois, every month—a good phlebotomy, in the interests of the police and morals."

"Be quiet, Monsieur Homais. You are a godless man! You have no religion."

The chemist replied:

"I have a religion, my religion, and I even have more than all these others with their mummeries and their juggling. I adore God, on the contrary. I believe in the Supreme Being, in a Creator, whatever he may be. I care little who has placed us here below to fulfill our duties as citizens and parents; but I don't need to go to church to kiss silver plates, and fatten, out of my pocket, a lot of good-for-nothings who live better than we do. For one can know him as well in a wood, in a field, or even contemplating the ethereal heavens like the ancients. My God is the God of Socrates, of Franklin, of Voltaire, and of Béranger! I support the *Profession de Foi du Vicaire savoyard*[4] and the immortal principles of '89! And I can't admit of an old boy of a God who takes walks in his garden with a cane in his hand, who lodges his friends in the belly of whales, dies uttering a cry, and rises again at the end of three days; things absurd in themselves, and completely opposed, moreover, to all physical laws, which

4. Rousseau's declaration (1762) of faith in God, a religion of his heart, coupled with a criticism of revealed religion. It is included in Book IV of his pedagogic treatise *Émile* but was frequently reprinted as an independent pamphlet.

proves to us, by the way, that priests have always wallowed in squalid ignorance, and tried to drag whole nations down after them."

He stopped, looked around as if expecting to find an audience, for in his enthusiasm the pharmacist had for a moment fancied himself in the midst of the town council. But the landlady no longer heard him; she was listening to a distant rolling. One could distinguish the noise of a carriage mingled with the clattering of loose horseshoes that beat against the ground, and at last the "Hirondelle" stopped at the door.

It was a yellow box on two large wheels, that, reaching to the tilt, prevented travellers from seeing the road and dirtied their shoulders. The small panes of narrow windows rattled in their frames when the coach was closed, and retained here and there patches of mud amid the old layers of dust, that not even storms of rain had altogether washed away. It was drawn by three horses, the first a leader, and when it came down-hill its lower side jolted against the ground.

Some of the inhabitants of Yonville came out into the square; they all spoke at once, asking for news, for explanations of the delay, for their orders. Hivert did not know whom to answer first. He ran the errands in town for the entire village. He went to the shops and brought back rolls of leather for the shoemaker, old iron for the farrier, a barrel of herrings for his mistress, hats from the hat-shop and wigs from the hairdresser, and all along the road on his return journey he distributed his parcels, throwing them over fences as he stood upright on his seat and shouted at the top of his voice, while his horses went their own way.

An accident had delayed him. Madame Bovary's greyhound had escaped across the field. They had whistled for him a quarter of an hour; Hivert had even gone back a mile and a half expecting every moment to catch sight of her; but they had been forced to resume the journey. Emma had wept, grown angry; she had accused Charles of this misfortune. Monsieur Lheureux, a draper, who happened to be in the coach with her, had tried to console her by a number of examples of lost dogs recognising their masters at the end of long years. He had been told of one, he said, who had come back to Paris from Constantinople. Another had gone one hundred and fifty miles in a straight line, and swum four rivers; and his own father had owned a poodle, which, after twelve years of absence, had all of a sudden jumped on his back in the street as he was going to dine in town.

II

Emma got out first, then Félicité, Monsieur Lheureux, and a nurse, and they had to wake up Charles in his corner, where he had slept soundly since night set in.

Homais introduced himself; he offered his homages to madame and his respects to monsieur; said he was charmed to have been able to render them some slight service, and added cordially that he had taken the liberty to join them at dinner, his wife being away.

When Madame Bovary entered the kitchen she went up to the fireplace. With two fingertips she caught her dress at the knee, and having thus pulled it up to her ankle, held out her black-booted foot to the fire above the revolving leg of mutton. The flame lit up the whole of her, casting its harsh light over the pattern of her gown, the fine pores of her fair skin, and even her eyelids, when she blinked from time to time. A great red glow passed over her with the wind, blowing through the half-open door.

On the other side of the fireplace, a fair-haired young man watched her in silence.

As he was frequently bored at Yonville, where he was a clerk at Maître Guilleumin, the notary, Monsieur Léon Dupuis (the second of the Lion d'Or's daily customers) often delayed his dinner-hour in the hope that some traveller might come to the inn, with whom he could chat in the evening. On the days when his work was done early, he had, for want of something else to do, to come punctually, and endure from soup to cheese a *tête-à-tête* with Binet. It was therefore with delight that he accepted the hostess's suggestion that he should dine in company with the newcomers, and they passed into the large parlour where Madame Lefrançois, hoping to make an impression, had had the table laid for four.

Homais asked to be allowed to keep on his skull-cap, for fear of catching cold; then, turning to his neighbor:

"Madame is no doubt a little fatigued; one gets so frightfully shaken up in our Hirondelle."

"That is true," replied Emma; "but moving about always amuses me. I like a change."

"It is so tedious," sighed the clerk, "to be always riveted to the same places."

"If you were like me," said Charles, "constantly obliged to be in the saddle" . . .

"But," Léon went on, addressing himself to Madame Bovary, "nothing, it seems to me, is more pleasant—when one can," he added.

"Moreover," said the pharmacist, "the practice of medicine is not very hard work in our part of the world, for the state of our roads allows us the use of gigs, and generally, as the farmers are well off, they pay pretty well. We have, medically speaking, besides the ordinary cases of enteritis, bronchitis, bilious affections, &c., now and then a few intermittent fevers at harvest-time; but on the whole, little of a serious nature, nothing special to note, unless it be a great deal of scrofula, due, no doubt, to the deplorable hygienic conditions of our peasant dwellings. Ah! you will find many prejudices to combat, Monsieur Bovary, much obstinacy of routine, with which all the efforts of your science will daily come into collision; for people still have recourse to novenas, to relics, to the priest, rather than come straight to the doctor or the pharmacist. The climate, however, is truly not too bad, and we even have a few nonagenarians in our parish. The thermometer (I have made some observations) falls in winter to 4 degrees, and in the hottest season rises to 25 or 30 degrees Centigrade at the outside, which gives us 24 degrees Réaumur as the maximum, or otherwise stated 74 degrees Fahrenheit (English scale), not more. And, as a matter of fact, we are sheltered from the north winds by the forest of Argueil on the one side, from the west winds by the Saint Jean hills on the other; and this heat, moreover, which, on account of the watery vapours given off by the river and the considerable number of cattle in the fields, which, as you know, exhale much ammonia, that is to say, nitrogen, hydrogen, and oxygen (no, nitrogen and hydrogen alone), and which sucking up the humus from the soil, mixing together all those different emanations, unites them into a single bundle, so to speak, and combining with the electricity diffused through the atmosphere, when there is any, might in the long-run, as in tropical countries, engender poisonous fumes,— this heat, I say, finds itself perfectly tempered on the side from where it comes, or rather from where it ought to come, that is the south side, by the south-eastern winds, which, having cooled themselves in crossing the Seine, reach us sometimes all at once like blasts from Russia!"

"Do you at least have some walks in the neighborhood?" continued Madame Bovary, speaking to the young man.

"Oh, very few," he answered. "There is a place they call La Pâture, on the top of the hill, on the edge of the forest. Sometimes, on Sundays, I go and stay there with a book, watching the sunset."

"I think there is nothing so beautiful as sunsets," she resumed; "but especially by the seashore."

"Oh, I love the sea!" said Monsieur Léon.

"And doesn't it seem to you," continued Madame Bovary, "that the mind travels more freely on this limitless expanse, of which the contemplation elevates the soul, gives ideas of the infinite, the ideal?"

"It is the same with mountainous landscapes," continued Léon. "A cousin of mine who travelled in Switzerland last year told me that one could not picture to oneself the poetry of the lakes, the charm of the waterfalls, the gigantic effect of the glaciers. One sees pines of incredible size across torrents, cottages suspended over precipices, and, a thousand feet below one, whole valleys when the clouds open. Such spectacles must stir to enthusiasm, incline to prayer, to ecstasy; and I no longer wonder why a celebrated musician, in order to stimulate his imagination, was in the habit of playing the piano before some imposing view."

"Do you play?" she asked.

"No, but I am very fond of music," he replied.

"Ah! don't you listen to him, Madame Bovary," interrupted Homais, bending over his plate. "That's sheer modesty. Why, my friend, the other day in your room you were singing 'L'Ange Gardien'[5] to perfection. I heard you from the laboratory. You articulated with the skill of an actor."

Léon rented a small room at the pharmacist's, on the second floor overlooking the Square. He blushed at the compliment of his landlord, who had already turned to the doctor, and was enumerating to him, one after the other, all the principal inhabitants of Yonville. He was telling anecdotes, giving information; no one knew just how wealthy the notary was and there were, of course, the Tuvaches who put up a considerable front.

Emma continued, "And what music do you prefer?"

"Oh, German music; that which makes you dream."

"Have you been to the opera?"

"Not yet; but I shall go next year, when I'll be living in Paris to get a law degree."

"As I had the honour of putting it to your husband," said the pharmacist, "with regard to this poor Yanoda who has run away, you will find yourself, thanks to his extravagance, in the possession of one of the most comfortable houses of Yonville. Its greatest convenience for a doctor is a door giving on the Walk, where one can go in and out unseen. Moreover, it contains everything that is useful in a household—a laundry, kitchen with pantry, sitting-room, fruit bins, etc. He was a gay dog, who didn't care what he spent. At the end of the garden, by the side of the water, he had an arbour built just for the purpose of drinking beer in summer; and if madame is fond of gardening she will be able . . ."

"My wife doesn't care to," said Charles; "although she has been advised to take exercise, she prefers always sitting in her room reading."

"Just like me," replied Léon. "And indeed, what is better than to sit by one's fireside in the evening with a book, while the wind beats against the window and the lamp is burning? . . ."

"What, indeed?" she said, fixing her large black eyes wide open upon him.

"One thinks of nothing," he continued; "the hours slip by. Without having to move, we walk through the countries of our imagination, and your thought, blending with the fiction, toys with the details,

5. A sentimental romance written by Mme. Pauline Duchambre, author of several such songs that appeared in the keepsakes.

follows the outline of the adventures. It mingles with the characters, and it seems you are living their lives, that your own heart beats in their breast."

"That is true! that is true!" she said.

"Has it ever happened to you," Léon went on, "to discover some vague idea of one's own in a book, some dim image that comes back to you from afar, and as the fullest expression of your own slightest sentiment?"

"I have experienced it," she replied.

"That is why," he said, "I especially love the poets. I think verse more tender than prose, and that it makes one weep more easily."

"Still in the long-run it is tiring," continued Emma, "and now, on the contrary, I have come to love stories that rush breathlessly along, that frighten one. I detest commonplace heroes and moderate feelings, as one finds them in nature."

"You are right," observed the clerk, "since these works fail to touch the heart, they miss, it seems to me, the true end of art. It is so sweet, amid all the disenchantments of life, to be able to dwell in thought upon noble characters, pure affections, and pictures of happiness. For myself, living here far from the world, this is my one distraction. But there is so little to do in Yonville!"

"Like Tostes, no doubt," replied Emma; "and so I always subscribed to a lending library."

"If madame will do me the honor of making use of it," said the pharmacist, who had just caught the last words, "I have at her disposal a library composed of the best authors, Voltaire, Rousseau, Delille,[6] Walter Scott, the 'Echo des Feuilletons'; and in addition I receive various periodicals, among them the 'Fanal de Rouen' daily, being privileged to act as its correspondent for the districts of Buchy, Forges, Neufchâtel, Yonville, and vicinity."

They had been at the table for two hours and a half, for Artémise, the maid, listessly dragged her slippered feet over the tile-floor, brought in the plates one by one, forgot everything, understood nothing and constantly left the door of the billiard-room half open, so that the handle kept beating against the wall with its hooks.

Unconsciously, Léon, while talking, had placed his foot on one of the bars of the chair on which Madame Bovery was sitting. She wore a small blue silk necktie, which held upright, stiff as a ruff, a pleated batiste collar, and with the movements of her head the lower part of her face gently sunk into the linen or rose from it. Thus side by side, while Charles and the pharmacist chatted, they entered into one of those vague conversations where the hazard of all that is said brings you back to the fixed centre of a common sympathy. The

---

6. Jacques Delille (1738–1813) wrote idyllic descriptive poems; *Les Jardins* (1782) is best known.

Paris theatres, titles of novels, new quadrilles, and the world they did not know; Tostes, where she had lived, and Yonville, where they were; they examined all, talked of everything till the end of dinner.

When coffee was served Félicité left to prepare the room in the new house, and the guests soon rose from the table. Madame Lefrançois was asleep near the cinders, while the stable-boy, lantern in hand, was waiting to show Monsieur and Madame Bovary the way home. Bits of straw stuck in his red hair, and his left leg had a limp. When he had taken in his other hand the curé's umbrella, they started.

The town was asleep; the pillars of the market threw great shadows; the earth was all grey as on a summer's night.

But as the doctor's house was only some fifty paces from the inn, they had to say good-night almost immediately, and the company dispersed.

As soon as she entered the hallway, Emma felt the cold of the plaster fall about her shoulders like damp linen. The walls were new and the wooden stairs creaked. In their bedroom, on the first floor, a whitish light passed through the curtainless windows. She could catch glimpses of tree-tops, and beyond, the fields, half-drowned in the fog that lay like smoke over the course of the river. In the middle of the room, pell-mell, were scattered drawers, bottles, curtain-rods, gilt poles, with mattresses on the chains and basins on the floor—the two men who had brought the furniture had left everything about carelessly.

This was the fourth time that she had slept in a strange place. The first was the day she went to the convent; the second, of her arrival at Tostes; the third, at Vaubyessard; and this was the fourth; and it so happened that each one had marked in her life a new beginning. She did not believe that things could remain the same in different places, and since the portion of her life that lay behind her had been bad, no doubt that which remained to be lived would be better.

III

The next day, as she was getting up, she saw the clerk on the Place. She had on a dressing-gown. He looked up and bowed. She nodded quickly and reclosed the window.

Léon waited all day for six o'clock in the evening to come, but on going to the inn, he found only Monsieur Binet already seated at the table.

The dinner of the evening before had been a considerable event for him; he had never till then talked for two hours consecutively to a "lady." How then had he been able to express, and in such language, so many things that he could not have said so well before?

He was usually shy, and maintained that reserve which partakes at once of modesty and dissimulation. At Yonville, his manners were generally admired. He listened to the opinions of the older people, and seemed to have moderate political views, a rare thing for a young man. Then he had some accomplishments; he painted in water-colours, could read music, and readily talked literature after dinner when he did not play cards. Monsieur Homais respected him for his education; Madame Homais liked him for his good-nature, for he often took the little Homais into the garden—little brats who were always dirty, very much spoilt, and somewhat slow-moving, like their mother. They were looked after by the maid and by Justin, the pharmacist's apprentice, a second cousin of Monsieur Homais, who had been taken into the house out of charity and was also being put to work as a servant.

The druggist proved the best of neighbors. He advised Madame Bovary as to the tradespeople, sent expressly for his own cider merchant, tasted the wine himself, and saw that the casks were properly placed in the cellar; he explained how to stock up cheaply on butter, and made an arrangement with Lestiboudois, the sacristan, who, besides his ecclesiastical and funereal functions, looked after the main gardens at Yonville by the hour or the year, according to the wishes of the customers.

The need of looking after others was not the only thing that urged the pharmacist to such obsequious cordiality; there was a plan underneath it all.

He had infringed the law of the 19th Ventôse, year xi,[7] article 1, which forbade all persons not having a diploma to practise medicine; so that, after certain anonymous denunciations, Homais had been summoned to Rouen to see the royal prosecutor in his private office; the magistrate receiving him standing up, ermine on shoulder and cap on head. It was in the morning, before the court opened. In the corridors one heard the heavy boots of the gendarmes walking past, and like a far-off noise great locks that were shut. The druggist's ears tingled as if he were about to have a stroke; he saw the depths of dungeons, his family in tears, his shop sold, all the jars dispersed; and he was obliged to enter a café and take a glass of rum and soda water to recover his spirits.

Little by little the memory of this reprimand grew fainter, and he continued, as heretofore, to give anodyne consultations in his back-parlour. But the mayor resented it, his colleagues were jealous, he had everything and everyone to fear; gaining over Monsieur Bovary by his attentions was to earn his gratitude, and prevent his speaking

---

7. Ventôse ("windy") was the sixth month of the calendar established by the French Republic (from February 19 to March 20). The government of the Republic made the new year begin on September 22, 1792; thus the Year xi is 1801, and the 19th Ventôse March 10.

out later on, should he notice anything. So every morning Homais brought him the paper, and often in the afternoon left his shop for a few moments to have a chat with the Doctor.

Charles was depressed: he had no patients. He remained seated for hours without speaking, went into his consulting-room to sleep, or watched his wife sewing. Then for diversion he tried to work as a handyman around the house; he even tried to decorate the attic with some paint that had been left behind by the painters. But money matters worried him. He had spent so much for repairs at Tostes, for madame's toilette, and for the moving, that the whole dowry, over three thousand écus, had slipped away in two years. Then how many things had been spoilt or lost during their move from Tostes to Yonville, without counting the plaster curé, who, thrown out of the carriage by a particularly severe jolt, had broken in a thousand pieces on the pavement of Quincampoix!

A more positive worry came to distract him, namely, the pregnancy of his wife. As the time of birth approached he cherished her more. It was another bond of the flesh between them, and, as it were, a continued sentiment of a more complex union. When he caught sight of her indolent walk or watched her figure filling out over her uncorseted hips, when he had the opportunity to look at her undisturbed taking tired poses in her armchair, then his happiness knew no bounds; he got up, embraced her, passed his hands over her face, called her little mamma, wanted to make her dance, and, half-laughing, half-crying, uttered all kinds of caressing pleasantries that came into his head. The idea of having begotten a child delighted him. Now he wanted nothing more. He knew all there was to know of human life and sat down to enjoy it serenely, his elbows planted on the table as for a good meal.

Emma at first felt a great astonishment; then was anxious to be delivered that she might know what it felt like to be a mother. But not being able to spend as much as she would have liked on a suspended cradle with rose silk curtains, and embroidered caps, in a fit of bitterness she gave up looking for the layette altogether and had it all made by a village seamstress, without choosing or discussing anything.

Thus she did not amuse herself with those preparations that stimulate the tenderness of mothers, and so her affection was perhaps impaired from the start.

As Charles, however, spoke of the baby at every meal, she soon began to think of him more steadily.

She hoped for a son; he would be strong and dark; she would call him George; and this idea of having a male child was like an expected revenge for all her impotence in the past. A man, at least, is free; he can explore all passions and all countries, overcome obstacles, taste of the most distant pleasures. But a woman is always hampered. Being inert as well as pliable, she has against her the weakness of the flesh and the inequity of the law. Like the veil held to her hat by a ribbon, her will flutters in every breeze; she is always drawn by some desire, restrained by some rule of conduct.

She gave birth on a Sunday at about six o'clock, as the sun was rising.

"It is a girl!" said Charles.

She turned her head away and fainted.

Madame Homais, as well as Madame Lefrançois of the Lion d'Or, almost immediately came running in to embrace her. The pharmacist, as a man of discretion, only offered a few provisional felicitations through the half-opened door. He asked to see the child, and thought it well made.

During her recovery, she spent much time seeking a name for her daughter. First she went over all names that have Italian endings, such as Clara, Louisa, Amanda, Atala; she liked Galsuinde pretty well, and Yseult or Léocadie still better. Charles wanted the child to be called after her mother; Emma opposed this. They ran over the calendar from end to end, and then consulted outsiders.

"Monsieur Léon," said the chemist, "with whom I was talking about it the other day, wonders why you do not choose Madeleine. It is very much in fashion just now."

But Monsieur Bovary's mother protested loudly against this name of a sinner. As to Monsieur Homais, he had a preference for all names that recalled some great man, an illustrious fact, or a generous idea, and it was in accordance with this system that he had baptized his four children. Thus Napoleon represented glory and Franklin liberty; Irma was perhaps a concession to romanticism, but Athalie[8] was a homage to the greatest masterpiece of the French stage. For his philosophical convictions did not interfere with his artistic tastes; in him the thinker did not stifle the man of sentiment; he could make distinctions, make allowances for imagination and fanaticism. In this tragedy, for example, he found fault with the ideas, but admired the style; he detested the conception, but applauded all the details, and loathed the characters while he grew enthusiastic over their dialogue. When he read the fine passages he was transported, but when he thought that the Catholics would use it to their advantage, he was disconsolate; and in this confusion of sentiments in which he was involved he would have liked both to crown Racine with both his hands and take him to task for a good quarter of an hour.

At last Emma remembered that at the château of Vaubyessard she

8. A tragedy by Jean Racine (1639–1699) written in 1691 for the pupils of Saint-Cyr. Racine had abandoned the regular stage after a spiritual crisis and wrote two sacred tragedies *Esther* and *Athalie* for the young girls of Saint-Cyr.

had heard the Marquise call a young lady Berthe; from that moment this name was chosen; and as old Rouault could not come, Monsieur Homais was requested to be godfather. His gifts were all products from his establishment, to wit: six boxes of jujubes, a whole jar of racahout, three cakes of marsh-mallow paste, and six sticks of sugar-candy that he had come across in a cupboard. On the evening of the ceremony there was a grand dinner; the curé was present; there was much excitement. Towards liqueur time, Monsieur Homais began singing "Le Dieu des bonnes gens."[9] Monsieur Léon sang a barcarolle, and the elder Madame Bovary, who was god-mother, a romance of the time of the Empire; finally, M. Bovary, senior, insisted on having the child brought down, and began baptizing it with a glass of champagne that he poured over its head. This mockery of the first of the sacraments aroused the indignation of the Abbé Bournisien; Father Bovary replied by a quotation from "La Guerre des Dieux"; the curé wanted to leave; the ladies implored, Homais interfered; they succeeded in making the priest sit down again, and he quietly went on with the half-finished coffee in his saucer.

Monsieur Bovary père stayed at Yonville a month, dazzling the natives by a superb soldier's cap with silver tassels that he wore in the morning when he smoked his pipe in the square. Being also in the habit of drinking a good deal of brandy, he often sent the servant to the Lion d'Or to buy him a bottle, which was put down to his son's account, and to perfume his handkerchiefs he used up his daughter-in-law's whole supply of eau-de-cologne.

The latter did not at all dislike his company. He had knocked about the world, he talked about Berlin, Vienna, and Strasbourg, of his soldier times, of his mistresses, of the brilliant dinner-parties he had attended; then he was amiable, and sometimes even, either on the stairs or in the garden, would catch her by the waist, exclaiming:

"Charles, you better watch out!"

Then the elder Madame Bovary became alarmed for her son's happiness, and fearing that her husband might in the long run have an immoral influence upon the ideas of the young woman, she speeded up their departure. Perhaps she had more serious reasons for uneasiness. Monsieur Bovary was the man to stop at nothing.

One day Emma was suddenly seized with the desire to see her little girl, who had been put to nurse with the carpenter's wife, and, without looking at the calendar to see whether the six weeks of the Virgin[1] were yet passed, she set out for the Rollets' house, situated

---

9. A deistic song by Béranger (see p. 834, note 6). *"La Guerre des Dieux"* ("The War of the Gods," below) is a satirical poem by Évarite-Désiré Deforge (later Viscount de Parny, 1753–1814) published in 1799. It ridicules the Christian religion.   1. Originally the six weeks that separate Christmas from Purification (Feb. 2nd); in those days, the normal period of confinement for a woman after childbirth.

at the extreme end of the village, between the highroad and the fields.

It was mid-day, the shutters of the houses were closed, and the slate roofs that glittered beneath the fierce light of the blue sky seemed to strike sparks from the crest of their gables. A heavy wind was blowing; Emma felt weak as she walked; the stones of the pavement hurt her; she was doubtful whether she would not go home again, or enter somewhere to rest.

At the moment Monsieur Léon came out from a neighboring door with a bundle of papers under his arm. He came to greet her, and stood in the shade in front of Lheureux's shop under the projecting grey awning.

Madame Bovary said she was going to see her baby, but that she was getting tired.

"If . . ." said Léon, not daring to go on.

"Have you any business to attend to?" she asked.

And on the clerk's negative answer, she begged him to accompany her. That same evening this was known in Yonville, and Madame Tuvache, the mayor's wife, declared in the presence of her maid that Madame Bovary was jeopardizing her good name.

To get to the nurse's it was necessary to turn to the left on leaving the street, as if heading for the cemetery, and to follow between little houses and yards a small path bordered with privet hedges. They were in bloom, and so were the speedwells, eglantines, thistles, and the sweetbriar that sprang up from the thickets. Through openings in the hedges one could see into the huts, some pig on a dung-heap, or tethered cows rubbing their horns against the trunk of trees. The two, side by side, walked slowly, she leaning upon him, and he restraining his pace, which he regulated by hers; in front of them flies were buzzing in the warm air.

They recognised the house by an old walnut-tree which shaded it. Low and covered with brown tiles, there hung outside it, beneath the attic-window, a string of onions. Faggots upright against a thorn fence surrounded a bed of lettuces, a few square feet of lavender, and sweet peas strung on sticks. Dirty water was running here and there on the grass, and all round were several indefinite rags, knitted stockings, a red flannel undershirt, and a large sheet of coarse linen spread over the hedge. At the noise of the gate the wet nurse appeared with a baby she was suckling on one arm. With her other hand she was pulling along a poor puny little boy, his face covered with a scrofulous rash, the son of a Rouen hosier, whom his parents, too taken up with their business, left in the country.

"Go in," she said; "your baby is there asleep."

The room on the ground-floor, the only one in the dwelling, had at its farther end, against the wall, a large bed without curtains, while a kneading-trough took up the side by the window, one pane of which was mended with a piece of blue paper. In the corner behind the door, shining hob-nailed shoes stood in a row under the slab of the washstand, near a bottle of oil with a feather stuck in its mouth; a Mathieu Laensberg[2] lay on the dusty mantelpiece amid gunflints, candle-ends, and bits of tinder. Finally, the last extravagance in the room was a picture representing Fame blowing her trumpets, cut out, no doubt, from some perfumer's prospectus and nailed to the wall with six wooden shoe-pegs.

Emma's child was asleep in a wicker-cradle. She took it up in the wrapping that enveloped it and began singing softly as she rocked it to and fro.

Léon walked up and down the room; it seemed strange to him to see this beautiful woman in her silk dress in the midst of all this poverty. Madame Bovary blushed; he turned away, thinking perhaps there had been an impertinent look in his eyes. Then she put back the little girl, who had just thrown up over her collar. The nurse at once came to dry her, protesting that it wouldn't show.

"You should see some of the other tricks she plays on me," she said. "I always seem to be sponging her off. If you would have the goodness to order Camus, the grocer, to let me have a little soap; it would really be more convenient for you, as I needn't trouble you then."

"All right, all right!" said Emma. "Good-bye, Madame Rollet."

And she went out, wiping her shoes at the door.

The woman accompanied her to the end of the garden, complaining all the time of the trouble she had getting up nights.

"I'm so worn out sometimes that I drop asleep on my chair. You could at least give me a pound of ground coffee; that'd last me a month, and I'd take it in the morning with some milk."

After having submitted to her thanks, Madame Bovary left. She had gone a little way down the path when, at the sound of wooden shoes, she turned round. It was the nurse.

"What is it?"

Then the peasant woman, taking her aside behind an elm tree, began talking to her of her husband, who with his trade and six francs a year that the captain . . .

"Hurry up with your story," said Emma.

"Well," the nurse went on, heaving sighs between each word, "I'm afraid he'll be put out seeing me have coffee alone, you know men . . ."

"But I just told you you'll get some," Emma repeated; "I will give you some. Leave me alone!"

2. A farmer's almanac, begun in 1635 by Mathieu Laensberg, frequently found in farms and country houses.

"Oh, my dear lady! you see, his wounds give him terrible cramps in the chest. He even says that cider weakens him."

"Do make haste, Mère Rollet!"

"Well," the latter continued, making a curtsey, "if it weren't asking too much," and she curtsied once more, "if you would"—and her eyes begged—"a jar of brandy," she said at last, "and I'd rub your little one's feet with it; they're as tender as your tongue."

Once they were rid of the nurse, Emma again took Monsieur Léon's arm. She walked fast for some time, then more slowly, and looking straight in front of her, her eyes rested on the shoulder of the young man, whose frock-coat had a black-velvet collar. His brown hair fell over it, straight and carefully combed. She noticed his nails, which were longer than one wore them in Yonville. It was one of the clerk's chief concerns to trim them, and for this purpose he kept a special knife in his writing-desk.

They returned to Yonville by the water-side. In the warm season the bank, wider than at other times, showed to their foot the garden walls from where a few steps led to the river. It flowed noiselessly, swift, and cold to the eye; long, thin grasses huddled together in it as the current drove them, and spread themselves upon the limpid water like streaming hair. Sometimes at the top of the reeds or on the leaf of a water-lily an insect with fine legs crawled or rested. The sun pierced with a ray the small blue bubbles of the waves that broke successively on the bank; branchless old willows mirrored their grey barks in the water; beyond, all around, the meadows seemed empty. It was the dinner-hour at the farms, and the young woman and her companion heard nothing as they walked but the fall of their steps on the earth of the path, the words they spoke, and the sound of Emma's dress rustling round her.

The walls of the gardens, crested with pieces of broken bottle, were heated like the glass roof of a hothouse. Wallflowers had sprung up between the bricks, and with the tip of her own parasol Madame Bovary, as she passed, made some of their faded flowers crumble into yellow dust, or else a spray of overhanging honeysuckle and clematis would catch in the fringe of the parasol and scrape for a moment over the silk.

They were talking of a troupe of Spanish dancers who were expected shortly at the Rouen theatre.

"Are you going?" she asked.

"If I can," he answered.

Had they nothing else to say to one another? Yet their eyes were full of more serious speech, and while they forced themselves to find trivial phrases, they felt the same languor stealing over them both; it was like the deep, continuous murmur of the soul dominating that of their voices. Surprised with wonder at this strange sweetness, they did not think of speaking of the sensation or of seeking its cause. Future joys are like tropical shores; like a fragrant breeze, they extend their innate softness to the immense inland world of past experience, and we are lulled by this intoxication into forgetting the unseen horizons beyond.

In one place the ground had been trodden down by the cattle; they had to step on large green stones put here and there in the mud. She often stopped a moment to look where to place her foot, and tottering on the stone that shook, her arms outspread, her form bent forward with a look of indecision, she would laugh, afraid of falling into the puddles of water.

When they arrived in front of her garden, Madame Bovary opened the little gate, ran up the steps and disappeared.

Léon returned to his office. His employer was away; he just glanced at the briefs, then cut himself a pen, and finally took up his hat and went out.

He went to La Pâture at the top of the Argueil hills at the beginning of the forest; he stretched out under the pines and watched the sky through his fingers.

"How bored I am!" he said to himself, "how bored I am!"

He thought he was to be pitied for living in this village, with Homais for a friend and Monsieur Guillaumin for master. The latter, entirely absorbed by his business, wearing gold-rimmed spectacles and red whiskers over a white cravat, understood nothing of mental refinements, although he affected a stiff English manner, which in the beginning had impressed the clerk.

As for Madame Homais, she was the best wife in Normandy, gentle as a sheep, loving her children, her father, her mother, her cousins, weeping for others' woes, letting everything go in her household, and detesting corsets; but so slow of movement, such a bore to listen to, so common in appearance, and of such restricted conversation, that although she was thirty and he only twenty, although they slept in rooms next each other and he spoke to her daily, he never thought that she might be a woman to anyone, or that she possessed anything else of her sex than the gown.

And what else was there? Binet, a few shopkeepers, two or three innkeepers, the curé, and, finally, Monsieur Tuvache, the mayor, with his two sons, rich, haughty, obtuse people, who farmed their own lands and had feasts among themselves, devout Christians at that, but altogether unbearable as companions.

But from the general background of all these human faces the figure of Emma stood out isolated and yet farthest off; for between her and him he seemed to sense a vague abyss.

In the beginning he had called on her several times along with the pharmacist. Charles had not appeared particularly anxious to see

him again, and Léon did not know what to do between his fear of
being indiscreet and the desire for an intimacy that seemed almost
impossible.

IV

When the first cold days set in Emma left her bedroom for the
parlour, a long, low-ceilinged room, with on the mantelpiece a large
bunch of coral spread out against the looking-glass. Seated in her
armchair near the window, she could see the villagers pass along the
pavement.

Twice a day Léon went from his office to the Lion d'Or, Emma
could watch him coming from afar; she leant forward listening, and
the young man glided past the curtain, always dressed in the same
way, and without turning his head. But in the twilight, when, her
chin resting on her left hand, she let her begun embroidery fall on
her knees, she often shuddered at the apparition of this shadow suddenly gliding past. She would get up and order the table to be laid.

Monsieur Homais called at dinner-time. Skull-cap in hand, he
came in on tiptoe, in order to disturb no one, always repeating the
same phrase, "Good evening, everybody." Then, when he had taken
his seat at table between them, he asked the doctor about his patients,
and the latter consulted him as to the probability of their payment.
Next they talked of "what was in the paper." By this hour of the day,
Homais knew it almost by heart, and he repeated from beginning to
end, including the comments of the journalist, all the stories of individual catastrophes that had occurred in France or abroad. But the
subject becoming exhausted, he was not slow in throwing out some
remarks on the dishes before him. Sometimes even, half-rising, he
delicately pointed out to madame the tenderest morsel, or turning to
the maid, gave her some advice on the manipulation of stews and
the hygiene of seasoning. He talked aroma, osmazome, juices, and
gelatine in a bewildering manner. Moreover, Homais, with his head
fuller of recipes than his shop of jars, excelled in making all kinds of
preserves, vinegars, and sweet liqueurs; he knew also all the latest
inventions in economic stoves, together with the art of preserving
cheeses and of curing sick wines.

At eight o'clock Justin came to fetch him to shut up the shop.
Then Monsieur Homais gave him a sly look, especially if Félicité
was there, for he had noticed that his apprentice was fond of the
doctor's house.

"The young man," he said, "is beginning to have ideas, and the
devil take me if I don't believe he's in love with your maid!"

But a more serious fault with which he reproached Justin was his constantly listening to conversation. On Sunday, for example, one could not get him out of the parlor, even when Madame Homais called him to fetch the children, who had fallen asleep in the arm-chairs, dragging down with their backs the overwide slip-covers.

Not many people came to the pharmacist's evening parties, his scandal-mongering and political opinions having successfully alien-ated various persons. The clerk never failed to be there. As soon as he heard the bell he ran to meet Madame Bovary, took her shawl, and put away under the shop-counter the heavy overshoes she wore when it snowed.

First they played some hands at trente-et-un; next Monsieur Homais played écarté with Emma; Léon standing behind her, gave advice. Standing up with his hands on the back of her chair, he saw the teeth of her comb that bit into her chignon. With every movement that she made to throw her cards the right side of her dress was drawn up. From her turned-up hair a dark colour fell over her back, and growing gradually paler, lost itself little by little in the shade. Her dress dropped on both sides of her chair, blowing out into many folds before it spread on the floor. When Léon occasionally felt the sole of his boot resting on it, he drew back as if he had trodden on some-thing alive.

When the game of cards was over, the pharmacist and the Doctor played dominoes, and Emma, changing her place, leant her elbow on the table, turning over the pages of "L'Illustration." She had brought her ladies' journal with her. Léon sat down near her; they looked at the engravings together, and waited for one another at the bottom of the pages. She often begged him to read her the verses; Léon declaimed them in a languid voice, to which he carefully gave a dying fall in the love passages. But the noise of the dominoes annoyed him. Monsieur Homais was strong at the game; he could beat Charles and give him a double-six. Then the three hundred finished, they both stretched in front of the fire, and were soon asleep. The fire was dying out in the cinders; the teapot was empty, Léon was still reading. Emma listened to him, mechanically turning round the lampshade, its gauze decorated with painted clowns in carriages, and tightrope dancers with balancing-poles. Léon stopped, pointing with a gesture to his sleeping audience; then they talked in low tones, and their conversation seemed the sweeter to them because it was unheard.

Thus a kind of bond was established between them, a constant exchange of books and of romances. Little inclined to jealousy, Monsieur Bovary thought nothing of it.

On his birthday he received a beautiful phrenological head, all marked with figures to the thorax and painted blue. This was a gift of the clerk's. He showed him many other attentions, to the point of running errands for him at Rouen: and a novel having made the mania for cactuses fashionable, Léon bought some for Madame Bovary, bringing them back on his knees in the "Hirondelle," pricking his fingers on their hard spikes.

She had a railed shelf suspended against her window to hold the pots. The clerk, too, had his small hanging garden; they saw each other tending their flowers at their windows.

One of the village windows was even more often occupied; for on Sundays from morning to night, and every morning when the weather was bright, one could see at an attic-window the profile of Monsieur Binet bending over his lathe; its monotonous humming could be heard at the Lion d'Or.

One evening on coming home Léon found in his room a rug in velvet and wool with leaves on a pale ground. He called Madame Homais, Monsieur Homais, Justin, the children, the cook; he spoke of it to his employer; every one wanted to see this rug. Why did the doctor's wife give the clerk presents? It looked odd; and they decided that he must be her lover.

He gave plenty of reason for this belief, so ceaselessly did he talk of her charms and of her wit; so much so, that Binet once roughly interrupted him:

"What do I care since I'm not one of her friends?"

He tortured himself to find out how he could make his declaration to her, and always halting between the fear of displeasing her and the shame of being such a coward, he wept with discouragement and desire. Then he took energetic resolutions, wrote letters that he tore up, put it off to times that he again deferred. Often he set out with the determination to dare all; but this resolution soon deserted him in Emma's presence; and when Charles, dropping in, invited him to jump into his carriage to go with him to see some patient in the neighborhood, he at once accepted, bowed to madame, and left. Wasn't the husband also a part of her after all?

As for Emma, she did not ask herself whether she loved him. Love, she thought, must come suddenly, with great outbursts and lightnings,—a hurricane of the skies, which sweeps down on life, upsets everything, uproots the will like a leaf and carries away the heart as in an abyss. She did not know that on the terrace of houses the rain makes lakes when the pipes are choked, and she would thus have remained safe in her ignorance when she suddenly discovered a rent in the wall.

v

It was a Sunday in February, an afternoon when the snow was falling.

Monsieur and Madame Bovary, Homais, and Monsieur Léon had

all gone to see a yarn-mill that was being built in the valley a mile and a half from Yonville. The druggist had taken Napoleon and Athalie to give them some exercise, and Justin accompanied them, carrying the umbrellas over his shoulder.

Nothing, however, could be less worth seeing than this sight. A great piece of waste ground, on which, amid a mass of sand and stones, were scattered a few rusty cogwheels, surrounded by a long rectangular building pierced with numerous little windows. The building was unfinished; the sky could be seen through the beams of the roofing. Attached to the ridgepole of the gable a bunch of straw mixed with corn-ears fluttered its tricoloured ribbons in the wind.

Homais was talking. He explained to the company the future importance of this establishment, computed the strength of the floorings, the thickness of the walls, and regretted extremely not having a yard-stick such as Monsieur Binet possessed for his own special use.

Emma, who had taken his arm, bent lightly against his shoulder, and she looked at the sun's disc shining afar through the mist with pale splendour. She turned; there was Charles. His cap was drawn down over his eyebrows, and his two thick lips were trembling, which added a look of stupidity to his face; his very back, his calm back, was irritating to behold, and she saw all his platitude spelled out right there, on his very coat.

While she was considering him thus, savoring her irritation with a sort of depraved pleasure, Léon made a step forward. The cold that made him pale seemed to add a more gentle languor to his face; between his cravat and his neck the somewhat loose collar of his shirt showed the skin; some of his ear was showing beneath a lock of hair, and his large blue eyes, raised to the clouds, seemed to Emma more limpid and more beautiful than those mountain-lakes which mirror the heavens.

"Look out there!" suddenly cried the pharmacist.

And he ran to his son, who had just jumped into a pile of lime in order to whiten his boots. Overcome by his father's reproaches, Napoleon began to howl, while Justin dried his shoes with a wisp of straw. But a knife was needed; Charles offered his.

"Ah!" she said to herself, "he carries a knife in his pocket like a peasant."

It was beginning to snow and they turned back to Yonville.

In the evening Madame Bovary did not go to her neighbor's, and when Charles had left and she felt herself alone, the comparison again forced itself upon her, almost with the clarity of direct sensation, and with that lengthening of perspective which memory gives to things. Looking from her bed at the bright fire that was burning, she still saw, as she had down there, Léon standing up with one hand bending his cane, and with the other holding Athalie, who was quietly sucking a piece of ice. She thought him charming; she could not tear herself away from him; she recalled his other attitudes on other days, the words he had spoken, the sound of his voice, his whole person; and she repeated, pouting out her lips as if for a kiss?

"Yes, charming! charming! Is he not in love?" . . . she asked herself; "but with whom? . . . With me!"

All the evidence asserted itself at once; her heart leapt. The flame of the fire threw a joyous light upon the ceiling; she turned on her back, stretched out her arms.

Then began the eternal lamentation: "Oh, if Heaven had but willed it! And why not? What prevented it?"

When Charles came home at midnight, she seemed to have just awakened, and as he made a noise undressing, she complained of a headache, then asked casually what had happened that evening.

"Monsieur Léon," he said, "went to his room early."

She could not help smiling, and she fell asleep, her soul filled with a new delight.

The next day, at dusk, she received a visit from Monsieur Lheureux, the owner of the local general store.

He was a smart man, this shopkeeper.

Born in Gascony but bred a Norman, he grafted upon his southern volubility the cunning of the Cauchois. His fat, flabby, beardless face seemed dyed by a decoction of liquorice, and his white hair made even more vivid the keen brilliance of his small black eyes. No one knew what he had been formerly; some said he was a peddler, others that he was a banker at Routot. One thing was certain: he could make complex figurings in his head that would have frightened Binet himself. Polite to obsequiousness, he always held himself with his back bent in the attitude of one who bows or who invites.

After leaving at the door his black-bordered hat, he put down a green cardboard box on the table, and began by complaining to madame, with many civilities, that he should have remained till that day without the benefit of her confidence. A poor shop like his was not made to attract a lady of fashion; he stressed the words; yet she had only to command, and he would undertake to provide her with anything she might wish, whether it be lingerie or knitwear, hats or dresses, for he went to town regularly four times a month. He was connected with the best houses. His name could be mentioned at the "Trois Frères," at the "Barbe d'Or," or at the "Grand Sauvage"; all these gentlemen knew him inside out. Today, then, he had come to show madame, in passing, various articles he happened to have by an unusual stroke of luck. And he pulled out half-a-dozen embroidered collars from the box.

Madame Bovary examined them.

"I don't need anything," she said.

Then Monsieur Lheureux delicately exhibited three Algerian scarves, several packages of English needles, a pair of straw slippers, and, finally, four eggcups in cocoa-nut wood, carved in open work by convicts. Then, with both hands on the table, his neck stretched out, leaning forward with open mouth, he watched Emma's gaze wander undecided over the merchandise. From time to time, as if to remove some dust, he flicked his nail against the silk of the scarves spread out at full length, and they rustled with a little noise, making the gold spangles of the material sparkle like stars in the greenish twilight.

"How much are they?"

"A mere trifle," he replied, "a mere trifle. But there's no hurry; whenever it's convenient. We are no Jews."

She reflected for a few moments, and ended by again declining Monsieur Lheureux's offer. Showing no concern, he replied:

"Very well! Better luck next time. I have always got on with ladies . . . even if I didn't with my own!"

Emma smiled.

"I wanted to tell you," he went on good-naturedly, after his joke, "that it isn't the money I should trouble about. Why, I could give you some, if need be."

She made a gesture of surprise.

"Ah!" he said quickly and in a low voice, "I shouldn't have to go far to find you some, rely on that."

And he began asking after Père Tellier, the owner of the Café Français, who was being treated by Monsieur Bovary at the time.

"What's the matter with Père Tellier? He makes the whole house shake with his coughing, and I'm afraid he'll soon need a pine coat rather than a flannel jacket. He certainly lived it up when he was young! These people, madame, they never know when to stop! He burned himself up with brandy. Still it's sad, all the same, to see an acquaintance go."

And while he fastened up his box he discoursed about the doctor's patients.

"It's the weather, no doubt," he said, looking frowningly at the floor, "that causes these illnesses. I myself don't feel just right. One of these days I shall even have to consult the doctor for a pain I have in my back. Well, good-bye, Madame Bovary. At your service; your very humble servant."

And he gently closed the door behind him.

Emma had her dinner served in her bedroom on a tray by the fireside; she took a long time eating; everything seemed wonderful.

"How good I was!" she said to herself, thinking of the scarves.

She heard steps on the stairs. It was Léon. She got up and took from the chest of drawers the first pile of dusters to be hemmed.

When he came in she seemed very busy.

The conversation languished; Madame Bovary let it drop every few minutes, while he himself seemed quite embarrassed. Seated on a low chair near the fire, he kept turning the ivory thimble case with his fingers. She stitched on, or from time to time turned down the hem of the cloth with her nail. She did not speak; he was silent, captivated by her silence, as he would have been by her speech.

"Poor fellow!" she thought.

"How have I displeased her?" he asked himself.

At last, however, Léon said that one of these days, he had to go to Rouen on business.

"Your music subscription has expired; shall I renew it?"

"No," she replied.

"Why?"

"Because . . ."

And pursing her lips she slowly drew a long stitch of grey thread.

This work irritated Léon. It seemed to roughen the ends of her fingers. A gallant phrase came into his head, but he did not risk it.

"Then you are giving up?" he went on.

"What?" she asked hurriedly. "Music? Ah! yes! Have I not my house to look after, my husband to attend to, a thousand things, in fact, many duties that must be considered first?"

She looked at the clock. Charles was late. Then she affected anxiety. Two or three times she even repeated, "He is so good!"

The clerk was fond of Monsieur Bovary. But this tenderness on his behalf came as an unpleasant surprise; still, he sang his praise: everyone did, he said, especially the pharmacist.

"Ah! he is a good man," continued Emma.

"Certainly," replied the clerk.

And he began talking of Madame Homais, whose very untidy appearance generally made them laugh.

"What does it matter?" interrupted Emma. "A good housewife does not trouble about her appearance."

Then she relapsed into silence.

It was the same on the following days; her talks, her manners, everything changed. She took interest in the housework, went to church regularly, and looked after her maid with more severity.

She took Berthe away from the nurse. When visitors called, Félicité brought her in, and Madame Bovary undressed her to show off her limbs. She claimed to love children; they were her consolation, her joy, her passion, and she accompanied her caresses with lyrical outbursts that would have reminded any one but the Yonvillians of Sachette in "Notre Dame de Paris."[3]

---

3. A historical novel (1831) by Victor Hugo (1802–1885). *Sachette* ("sackcloth"); Paguette la Chantefleurie is the mother of Agnes, the girl abducted by gypsies who takes the name Esmeralda. She worshipped a shoe of her stolen child.

When Charles came home he found his slippers put to warm near the fire. His waistcoat now never wanted lining, nor his shirt buttons, and it was quite a pleasure to see in the cupboard the nightcaps arranged in piles of the same height. She no longer grumbled as before when asked to take a walk in the garden; what he proposed was always done, although she never anticipated the wishes to which she submitted without a murmur; and when Léon saw him sit by his fireside after dinner, his two hands on his stomach, his two feet on the fender, his cheeks flushed with wine, his eyes moist with happiness, the child crawling along the carpet, and this woman with the slender waist who came behind his armchair to kiss his forehead:

"What madness!" he said to himself. "How could I ever hope to reach her?"

She seemed so virtuous and inaccessible to him that he lost all hope, even the faintest. But, by thus renouncing her, he made her ascend to extraordinary heights. She transcended, in his eyes, those sensuous attributes which were forever out of his reach; and in his heart she rose forever, soaring away from him like a winged apotheosis. It was one of those pure feelings that do not interfere with life, that are cultivated for their rarity, and whose loss would afflict more than their fulfilment rejoices.

Emma grew thinner, her cheeks paler, her face longer. With her black hair, her large eyes, her straight nose, her birdlike walk, and always silent now, did she not seem to be passing through life scarcely touching it, bearing on her brow the slight mark of a sublime destiny? She was so sad and so calm, at once so gentle and so reserved, that near her one came under the spell of an icy charm, as we shudder in churches at the perfume of the flowers mingling with the cold of the marble. Even others could not fail to be impressed. The pharmacist said:

"She is a real lady! She would not be out of place in a sous-préfecture!"

The housewives admired her thrift, the patients her politeness, the poor her charity.

But she was eaten up with desires, with rage, with hate. The rigid folds of her dress covered a tormented heart of which her chaste lips never spoke. She was in love with Léon, and sought solitude that she might more easily delight in his image. His physical presence troubled the voluptuousness of this meditation. Emma thrilled at the sound of his step; then in his presence the emotion subsided, and afterwards there remained in her only an immense astonishment that ended in sorrow.

Léon did not know that when he left her in despair she rose after he had gone to see him in the street. She concerned herself about his comings and goings; she watched his face; she invented quite a story to find an excuse for going to his room. She envied the pharmacist's wife for sleeping under the same roof, and her thoughts constantly centered upon this house, like the Lion d'Or pigeons who alighted there to dip their pink feet and white wings in the rainpipes. But the more Emma grew conscious of her love, the more she repressed it, hoping thus to hide and to stifle her true feeling. She would have liked Léon to know, and she imagined circumstances, catastrophes that would make this possible. What restrained her was, no doubt, idleness and fear, as well as a sense of shame. She thought she had repulsed him too much, that the time was past, that all was lost. Then, pride, the joy of being able to say to herself, "I am virtuous," and to look at herself in the mirror striking resigned poses, consoled her a little for the sacrifice she thought she was making.

Then the desires of the flesh, the longing for money, and the melancholy of passion all blended into one suffering, and instead of putting it out of her mind, she made her thoughts cling to it, urging herself to pain and seeking everywhere the opportunity to revive it. A poorly served dish, a half-open door would aggravate her; she bewailed the clothes she did not have, the happiness she had missed, her overexalted dreams, her too cramped home.

What exasperated her was that Charles did not seem to be aware of her torment. His conviction that he was making her happy looked to her a stupid insult, and his self-assurance on this point sheer ingratitude. For whom, then, was she being virtuous? Was it not for him, the obstacle to all happiness, the cause of all misery, and, as it were, the sharp clasp of that complex strap that buckled her in all sides?

Thus he became the butt of all the hatred resulting from her frustrations; but all efforts to conquer them augmented her suffering—for this useless humiliation still added to her despair and widened the gap between them. His very gentleness would drive her at times to rebellion. Domestic mediocrity urged her on to wild extravagance, matrimonial tenderness to adulterous desires. She would have liked Charles to beat her, that she might have a better right to hate him, to revenge herself upon him. She was surprised sometimes at the shocking thoughts that came into her head, and she had to go on smiling, to hear repeated to her at all hours that she was happy, to pretend to be happy and let it be believed.

Yet, at moments, she loathed this hypocrisy. She was tempted to flee somewhere with Léon and try a new life; but at once a dark, shapeless chasm would open within her soul.

"Besides, he no longer loves me," she thought. "What is to become of me? What help can I hope for, what consolation, what relief?"

Such thoughts would leave her shattered, exhausted, frozen, sobbing silently, with flowing tears.

"Why don't you tell monsieur?" the maid asked her when she came in during these crises.

"It is nerves," said Emma. "Don't mention it to him, he would worry."

"Ah! yes," Félicité went on, "you are just like La Guérine, the daughter of Père Guérin, the fisherman at le Pollet,[4] that I used to know at Dieppe before I came to see you. She was so sad, so sad, that to see her standing on the threshold of her house, she looked like a winding-sheet spread out before the door. Her illness, it appears, was a kind of fog that she had in the head, and the doctors could do nothing about it, neither could the priest. When she had a bad spell, she went off by herself to the sea-shore, so that the customs officer, going his rounds, often found her flat on her face, crying on the pebbles. Then, after her marriage, it stopped, they say."

"But with me," replied Emma, "it was after marriage that it began."

VI

One evening when she was sitting by the open window, watching Lestiboudois, the sexton, trim the boxwood, she suddenly heard the Angelus ringing.

It was the beginning of April, when the primroses are in bloom, and a warm wind blows over the newly-turned flower beds, and the gardens, like women, seem to be getting ready for the summer dances. Through the bars of the arbour and away beyond, the river could be seen in the fields, meandering through the grass in sinuous curves. The evening vapors rose between the leafless poplars, touching their outlines with a violet tint, paler and more transparent than a subtle gauze caught amidst their branches. Cattle moved around in the distance; neither their steps nor their lowing could be heard; and the bell, still ringing through the air, kept up its peaceful lamentation.

This repeated tinkling stirred in the young woman distant memories of her youth and school-days. She remembered the great candlesticks that rose above the vases full of flowers on the altar, and the tabernacle with its small columns. She would have liked to be once more lost in the long line of white veils, marked off here and there by the stiff black hoods of the good sisters bending over their praying-chairs. At mass on Sundays, when she looked up, she saw the gentle face of the Virgin amid the blue smoke of the rising incense. The image awoke a tender emotion in her; she felt limp and helpless, like the down of a bird whirled by the tempest, and it was unconsciously that she went towards the church, ready for any kind of devotion, provided she could humble her soul and lose all sense of selfhood.

4. Suburb of Dieppe, where the fishermen live.

On the Square she met Lestiboudois on his way back, for, in order not to lose out on a full day's wages, he preferred to interrupt his gardening-work and go ring the Angelus when it suited him best. Besides, the earlier ringing warned the boys that catechism time had come.

Already a few who had arrived were playing marbles on the stones of the cemetery. Others, astride the wall, swung their legs, trampling with their wooden shoes the large nettles that grew between the little enclosure and the newest graves. This was the only green spot. All the rest was but stones, always covered with a fine dust, in spite of Lestiboudois' broom.

The children played around in their socks, as if they were on their own ground. The shouts of their voices could be heard through the humming of the bell. The noise subsided with the swinging of the great rope that, hanging from the top of the belfry, dragged its end on the ground. Swallows flitted to and fro uttering little cries, cutting the air with the edge of their wings, and swiftly returned to their yellow nests under the eave-tiles of the coping. At the end of the church a lamp was burning, the wick of a night-light hung up in a glass. Seen from a distance, it looked like a white stain trembling in the oil. A long ray of the sun fell across the nave and seemed to darken the lower sides and the corners.

"Where is the priest?" Madame Bovary asked one of the boys, who was entertaining himself by shaking the turnstile in its too loose socket.

"He is coming," he answered.

Indeed, the door of the rectory creaked and the Abbé Bournisien appeared; the children fled in a heap into the church.

"The little brats!" muttered the priest, "always the same!" Then, picking up a ragged catechism on which he had stepped:

"They have respect for nothing!"

But, as soon as he caught sight of Madame Bovary:

"Excuse me," he said; "I did not recognise you."

He thrust the catechism into his pocket, and stopped, balancing the heavy key of the sacristy between his two fingers.

The full light of the setting sun upon his face made the cloth of his cassock, shiny at the elbows and frayed at the hem, seem paler. Grease and tobacco stains ran along his broad chest, following the line of his buttons, growing sparser in the vicinity of his neckcloth, in which rested the massive folds of his red chin; it was dotted with yellow spots that disappeared beneath the coarse hair of his greyish beard. He had just eaten his dinner, and was breathing noisily.

"And how are you?" he added.

"Not well," replied Emma; "I am suffering."

"So do I," answered the priest. "The first heat of the year is hard to bear, isn't it? But, after all, we are born to suffer, as St. Paul says.

But, what does Monsieur Bovary think of it?"

"He!" she said with a gesture of contempt.

"What!" he replied, genuinely surprised, "doesn't he prescribe something for you?"

"Ah!" said Emma, "it is no earthly remedy I need."

But the curé time and again was looking into the church, where the kneeling boys were shouldering one another, and tumbling over like packs of cards.

"I should like to know . . ." she went on.

"You look out, Riboudet," the priest cried angrily, "I'll box your ears, you scoundrel!" Then turning to Emma. "He's Boudet the carpenter's son; his parents are well off, and let him do just as he pleases. Yet he could learn quickly if he would, for he is very sharp. And so sometimes for a joke I call him Riboudet (like the road one takes to go to Maromme), and I even say 'Mon Riboudet.' Ha! ha! 'Mont Riboudet.' The other day I repeated this little joke to the bishop, and he laughed. Can you imagine? He deigned to laugh. And how is Monsieur Bovary?"

She seemed not to hear him. And he went on . . .

"Always very busy, no doubt; for he and I are certainly the busiest people in the parish. But he is doctor of the body," he added with a thick laugh, "and I of the soul."

She fixed her pleading eyes upon the priest. "Yes," she said, "you solace all sorrows."

"Ah! don't tell me of it, Madame Bovary. This morning I had to go to Bas-Diauville for a cow was all swollen; they thought it was under a spell. All their cows, I don't know how it is . . . But pardon me! Longuemarre and Boudet! Bless me! Will you stop it?"

And he bounded into the church.

The boys were just then clustering round the large desk, climbing over the cantor's footstool, opening the missal; and others on tiptoe were just about to venture into the confessional. But the priest suddenly distributed a shower of blows among them. Seizing them by the collars of their coats, he lifted them from the ground, and deposited them on their knees on the stones of the choir, firmly, as if he meant to plant them there.

"Yes," said he, when he returned to Emma, unfolding his large cotton handkerchief, one corner of which he put between his teeth, "farmers are much to be pitied."

"Others, too," she replied.

"Certainly. Workingmen in the cities, for instance."

"I wasn't thinking of them . . ."

"Oh, but excuse me! I've known housewives there, virtuous women. I assure you, real saints, who didn't even have bread to eat."

"But those," replied Emma, and the corners of her mouth twitched as she spoke, "those, Monsieur le Curé, who have bread and have no . . ."

"Fire in the winter," said the priest.

"Oh, what does it matter?"

"What! What does it matter? It seems to me that when one has firing and food . . . for, after all . . ."

"My God! my God!" she sighed.

"Do you feel unwell?" he asked, approaching her anxiously. "It is indigestion, no doubt? You must get home, Madame Bovary; drink a little tea, that will strengthen you, or else a glass of fresh water with a little moist sugar."

"Why?"

And she looked like one awaking from a dream.

"Well, you see, you were putting your hand to your forehead. I thought you felt faint."

Then, bethinking himself: "But you were asking me something? What was it? I don't remember."

"I? Oh, nothing . . . nothing," Emma repeated.

And the glance she cast round her slowly fell upon the old man in the cassock. They looked at each other face to face without speaking.

"Well then, Madame Bovary," he said at last, "excuse me, but duty comes first as the saying goes; I must look after my brats. The first communion will soon be upon us, and I fear we shall be behind, as ever. So after Ascension Day I regularly keep them an extra hour every Wednesday. Poor children! One cannot lead them too soon into the path of the Lord . . . He Himself advised us to do so, through the mouth of His Divine Son. Good health to you, madame; my respects to your husband."

And he went into the church making a genuflexion as soon as he reached the door.

Emma saw him disappear between the double row of benches, walking with heavy tread, his head a little bent over his shoulder, and with his two half-open hands stretched sidewards.

Then she turned on her heel all of one piece, like a statue on a pivot, and went homewards. But the loud voice of the priest, the clear voices of the boys still reached her ears, and pursued her:

"Are you a Christian?"

"Yes, I am a Christian."

"What is a Christian?"

"He who, being baptized . . . baptized . . . baptized . . ."

She climbed the steps of the staircase holding on to the banisters, and when she was in her room threw herself into an arm-chair.

The whitish light of the window-panes was softly wavering. The pieces of furniture seemed more frozen in their places, about to lose themselves in the shadow as in an ocean of darkness. The fire was out, the clock went on ticking, and Emma vaguely wondered at this calm of all things while within herself there was such tumult. But little Berthe was there, between the window and the work-table, tottering on her knitted shoes, and trying to reach the end of her mother's apron-strings.

"Leave me alone," Emma said, pushing her back with her hand.

The little girl soon came up closer against her knees, and leaning on them with her arms, she looked up with her large blue eyes, while a small thread of clear saliva drooled from her lips on to the silk of her apron.

"Leave me alone," repeated the young woman quite angrily.

Her expression frightened the child, who began to scream.

"Will you leave me alone?" she said, forcing her away with her elbow.

Berthe fell at the foot of the chest of drawers against the brass handle; she cut her cheek, blood appeared. Madame Bovary rushed to lift her up, broke the bell-rope, called for the maid with all her might, and she was just going to curse herself when Charles appeared. It was dinner time; he was coming home.

"Look, dear!" said Emma calmly, "the child fell down while she was playing, and she hurt herself."

Charles reassured her; it was only a slight cut, and he went for some adhesive plaster.

Madame Bovary did not go downstairs to the dining-room; she wished to remain alone to look after the child. Then watching her sleep, the little anxiety she still felt gradually wore off, and she seemed very stupid to herself, and very kind to have been so worried just now at so little. Berthe, in fact, no longer cried. Her breathing now imperceptibly raised the cotton covering. Big tears lay in the corner of the half-closed eyelids, through whose lashes one could see two pale sunken pupils; the adhesive plaster on her cheek pulled the skin aside.

"It is very strange," thought Emma, "how ugly this child is!"

When at eleven o'clock Charles came back from the pharmacist's shop, where he had gone after dinner to return the remainder of the plaster, he found his wife standing by the cradle.

"I assure you it's nothing," he said, kissing her on the forehead. "Don't worry, my poor darling; you will make yourself ill."

He had stayed a long time at the pharmacist's. Although he had not seemed much concerned, Homais, nevertheless, had exerted himself to buoy him up, to "raise his spirits." Then they had talked of the various dangers that threaten childhood, of the carelessness of servants. Madame Homais knew what he meant: she still carried on her chest the scars of a load of charcoal that a cook dropped on her when she was a child. Hence that her kind parents took all sorts of precautions. The knives were not sharpened, nor the floors waxed; there were iron gratings in front of the windows and strong bars across the fireplace. In spite of their spirit, the little Homais could not stir without some one watching them; at the slightest cold their father stuffed them with cough-syrups; and until they turned four they all were mercilessly forced to use padded headwear. This, it is true, was a fancy of Madame Homais'; her husband was secretly afflicted by it. Fearing the possible consequences of such compression to the intellectual organs, he even went so far as to say to her:

"Do you want to make them into Caribs or Botocudos?"

Charles, however, had several times tried to interrupt the conversation.

"I would like a word with you," he whispered, addressing the clerk who preceded him on the stairs.

"Can he suspect anything?" Léon asked himself. His heart beat faster, and all sorts of conjectures occured to him.

At last, Charles, having closed the door behind him, begged him to inquire at Rouen after the price of a fine daguerreotype. It was a sentimental surprise he intended for his wife, a delicate attention: his own portrait in black tail coat. But he wanted first to know how much it would cost. It wouldn't cause Monsieur Léon too much trouble to find out, since he went to town almost every week.

Why? Monsieur Homais suspected some love affair, an intrigue. But he was mistaken. Léon was carrying on no flirtations. He was sadder than ever, as Madame Lefrançois saw from the amount of food he left on his plate. To find out more about it she questioned the tax-collector. Binet answered roughly that he wasn't being paid to spy on him.

All the same, his companion's behavior seemed very strange to him, for Léon often threw himself back in his chair, and stretching out his arms, complained vaguely about life.

"It's because you have no distractions," said the collector.

"What distractions?"

"If I were you I'd have a lathe."

"But I don't know how to turn," answered the clerk.

"Ah! that's true," said the other, rubbing his chin with an air of mingled contempt and satisfaction.

Léon was weary of loving without success; moreover, he was beginning to feel that depression caused by the repetition of the same life, with no interest to inspire and no hope to sustain it. He was so bored with Yonville and the Yonvillers, that the sight of certain persons, of certain houses, irritated him beyond endurance; and the pharmacist, good companion though he was, was becoming absolutely unbearable to him. Yet the prospect of a new condition of life frightened as much as it seduced him.

This apprehension soon changed into impatience, and then Paris beckoned from afar with the music of its masked balls, the laughter of the grisettes. Since he was to go to law-school there anyway, why not set out at once? Who prevented him? And, inwardly, he began making preparations; he arranged his occupations beforehand. In his mind, he decorated an apartment. He would lead an artist's life there! He would take guitar lessons! He would have a dressing-gown, a Basque béret, blue velvet slippers! He already admired two crossed foils over his chimney-piece, with a skull on the guitar above them.

The main difficulty was to obtain his mother's consent, though nothing could seem more reasonable. Even his employer advised him to go to some other law office where he could learn more rapidly. Taking a middle course, then, Léon looked for some position as second clerk in Rouen; found none, and at last wrote his mother a long letter full of details, in which he set forth the reasons for going to live in Paris at once. She consented.

He did not hurry. Every day for a month Hivert carried boxes, valises, parcels for him from Yonville to Rouen and from Rouen to Yonville; and when Léon had rounded out his wardrobe, had his three armchairs restuffed, bought a supply of neckties, in a word, had made more preparations than for a trip round the world, he put it off from week to week, until he received a second letter from his mother urging him to leave, since he wanted to pass his examination before the vacation.

When the moment for the farewells had come, Madame Homais wept, Justin sobbed; Homais, as a strong man, concealed his emotion; he wished to carry his friend's overcoat himself as far as the gate of the notary, who was taking Léon to Rouen in his carriage. The latter had just time to bid farewell to Monsieur Bovary.

When he reached the head of the stairs he stopped, he was so out of breath. When he entered, Madame Bovary rose hurriedly.

"It is I again!" said Léon.

"I was sure of it!"

She bit her lips, and a rush of blood flowing under her skin made her red from the roots of her hair to the top of her collar. She remained standing, leaning with her shoulder against the wainscot.

"The doctor is not here?" he went on.

"He is out."

She repeated:

"He is out."

Then there was silence. They looked one at the other, and their thoughts, united in the same agony, clung together like two hearts in a passionate embrace.

"I would like to kiss little Berthe good-bye," said Léon.

Emma went down a few steps and called Félicité.

He threw one long look around him that took in the walls, the shelves, the fireplace, as if to appropriate everything, to carry it with him.

She returned, and the servant brought Berthe, who was swinging an upside down windmill at the end of a string. Léon kissed her several times on the neck.

"Good-bye poor child! good-bye, dear little one! good-bye!" And he gave her back to her mother.

"Take her away," she said.

They remained alone—Madame Bovary, her back turned, her face pressed against a window-pane; Léon held his cap in his hand, tapping it softly against his thigh.

"It is going to rain," said Emma.

"I have a coat," he answered.

"Ah!"

She turned round, her chin lowered, her forehead bent forward. The light covered it to the curve of the eyebrows, like a single piece of marble, without revealing what Emma was seeing on the horizon or what she was thinking within herself.

"Well, good-bye," he sighed.

She raised her head with a quick movement.

"Yes, good-bye . . . go!"

They faced each other; he held out his hand; she hesitated.

"In the English manner, then," she said, offering him her hand and forcing a laugh.

Léon felt it between his fingers, and the very substance of all his being seemed to pass into that moist palm.

He opened his hand; their eyes met again, and he disappeared. When he reached the market-place, he stopped and hid behind a pillar to look for the last time at this white house with the four green blinds. He thought he saw a shadow behind the window in the room; but the curtain, sliding along the rod as though no one were touching it, slowly opened its long oblique folds, that spread out all at once, and thus hung straight and motionless as a plaster wall. Léon ran away.

From afar he saw his employer's buggy in the road, and by it a man in a coarse apron holding the horse. Homais and Monsieur Guillaumin were talking. They were waiting for him.

"Embrace me," said the pharmacist with tears in his eyes. "Here is your coat, my good friend. Mind the cold; take care of yourself; don't overdo it!"

"Come, Léon, jump in," said the notary.

Homais bent over the splash-board, and in a voice broken by sobs uttered these three sad words:

"A pleasant journey!"

"Good-night," said Monsieur Guillaumin. "Go ahead!"

They departed and Homais went home.

Madame Bovary had opened her window that looked out over the garden and watched the clouds. They were gathering round the sunset in the direction of Rouen, and rolling back swiftly in black swirls, behind which the great rays of the sun looked out like the golden arrows of a suspended trophy, while the rest of the empty heavens was white as porcelain. But a gust of wind bowed the poplars, and suddenly the rain fell; it rattled against the green leaves. Then the sun reappeared, the hens clucked, sparrows shook their wings in the damp thickets, and the pools of water on the gravel as they flowed away carried off the pink flowers of an acacia. "Ah! How far off he must be already!" she thought.

Monsieur Homais, as usual, came at half-past six during dinner.

"Well," said he, "so we've sent off our young friend!"

"So it seems," replied the doctor.

Then, turning on his chair: "Any news at home?"

"Nothing much. Only my wife was a little out of sorts this afternoon. You know women—a nothing upsets them, especially my wife. And we shouldn't object to that, since their nervous system is much more fragile than ours."

"Poor Léon!" said Charles. "How will he live at Paris? Will he get used to it?"

Madame Bovary sighed.

"Of course!" said the pharmacist, smacking his lips. "The late night suppers! the masked balls, the champagne—he won't be losing his time, I assure you."

"I don't think he'll go wrong," objected Bovary.

"Nor do I," said Monsieur Homais quickly; "although he'll have to do like the rest for fear of passing for a Jesuit. And you don't know what a life those jokers lead in the Latin quarter, actresses and the rest! Besides, students are thought a great deal of in Paris. Provided they have a few accomplishments, they are received in the best society; there are even ladies of the Faubourg Saint-Germain[5] who fall in love with them, which later gives them opportunities for making very good matches."

"But," said the doctor, "I fear for him that . . . down there . . ."

"You are right," interrupted the pharmacist, "that is the other side of the coin. And you are constantly obliged to keep your hand in your pocket there. Let us say, for instance, you are in a public garden. A fellow appears, well dressed, even wearing a decoration, and

---

5. The aristocratic quarter of Paris.

whom one would take for a diplomat. He addresses you, you chat with him; he forces himself upon you; offers you a pinch of snuff, or picks up your hat. Then you become more intimate; he takes you to a café, invites you to his countryhouse, introduces you, between two drinks, to all sorts of people; and three fourths of the time it's only to get hold of your money or involve you in some shady deal."

"That is true," said Charles; "but I was thinking specially of illnesses—of typhoid fever, for example, that attacks students from the provinces."

Emma shuddered.

"Because of the change of diet," continued the pharmacist, "and of the resulting upset for the whole system. And then the water at Paris, don't you know! The dishes at restaurants, all the spiced food, end by heating the blood, and are not worth, whatever people may say of them, a good hearty stew. As for me, I have always preferred home cooking; it is healthier. So when I was studying pharmacy at Rouen, I boarded in a boarding-house; and dined with the professors."

And thus he went on, expounding his general opinions and his personal preferences, until Justin came to fetch him for a mulled egg for a customer.

"Not a moment's peace!" he cried; "always at it! I can't go out for a minute! Like a plough-horse, I have always to be sweating blood and water! What drudgery!" Then, when he was at the door, "By the way, do you know the news?"

"What news?"

"It is very likely," Homais went on, raising his eyebrows and assuming one of his gravest expressions, "that the agricultural fair of the Seine-Inférieure will be held this year at Yonville-l'Abbaye.

"The rumor, at all events, is going the round. This morning the paper alluded to it. It would be of the utmost importance for our district. But we'll talk it over later. I can see, thank you; Justin has the lantern."

VII

The next day was a dreary one for Emma. Everything seemed shrouded in an atmosphere of bleakness that hung darkly over the outward aspect of things, and sorrow blew into her soul with gentle moans, as the winter wind makes in ruined castles. Her reverie was that of things gone forever, the exhaustion that seizes you after everything is done; the pain, in short, caused by the interruption of a familiar motion, the sudden halting of a long drawn out vibration.

As on the return from Vaubyessard, when the quadrilles were running in her head, she was full of a gloomy melancholy, of a numb despair. Léon reappeared, taller, handsomer, more charming, more vague. Though separated from her, he had not left her; he was there, and the walls of the house seemed to hold his shadow. She could not detach her eyes from the carpet where he had walked, from those empty chairs where he had sat. The river still flowed on and slowly drove its ripples along the slippery banks. They had often walked there listening to the murmur of the waves over the moss-covered pebbles. How bright the sun had been! What happy afternoons they had known, alone, in the shade at the end of the garden! He read aloud, bare-headed, sitting on a footstool of dry sticks; the fresh wind of the meadow set trembling the leaves of the book and the nasturtiums of the arbour. Ah! he was gone, the only charm of her life, the only possible hope of joy. Why had she not seized this happiness when it came to her? Why did she not keep him from leaving, beg him on her knees, when he was about to flee from her? And she cursed herself for not having loved Léon. She thirsted for his lips. She wanted to run after him, to throw herself into his arms and say to him, "It is I; I am yours." But Emma recoiled beforehand at the difficulties of the enterprise, and her desires, increased by regret, became only the more acute.

Henceforth the memory of Léon was the center of her boredom; it burnt there more brightly than the fires left by travellers on the snow of a Russian steppe. She threw herself at his image, pressed herself against it; she stirred carefully the dying embers, sought all around her anything that could make it flare; and the most distant reminiscences, like the most immediate occasions, what she experienced as well as what she imagined, her wasted voluptuous desires that were unsatisfied, her projects of happiness that crackled in the wind like dead boughs, her sterile virtue, her lost hopes, the yoke of domesticity,—she gathered it all up, took everything, and made it all serve as fuel for her melancholy.

The flames, however, subsided, either because the supply had exhausted itself, or because it had been piled up too much. Love, little by little, was quelled by absence; regret stifled beneath habit; and the bright fire that had empurpled her pale sky was overspread and faded by degrees. In her slumbering conscience, she took her disgust for her husband for aspirations towards her lover, the burning of hate for the warmth of tenderness; but as the tempest still raged, and as passion burnt itself down to the very cinders, and no help came, no sun rose, there was night on all sides, and she was lost in the terrible cold that pierced her through.

Then the evil days of Tostes began again. She thought herself now far more unhappy; for she had the experience of grief, with the certainty that it would not end.

A woman who had consented to such sacrifices could well allow herself certain whims. She bought a gothic prie-Dieu, and in a month spent fourteen francs on lemons for polishing her nails; she wrote to Rouen for a blue cashmere gown; she chose one of Lheureux's finest scarves, and wore it knotted round her waist over her dressing-gown; thus dressed, she lay stretched out on the couch with closed blinds.

She often changed her hairdo; she did her hair à la Chinoise, in flowing curls, in plaited coils; she parted it on one side and rolled it under, like a man's.

She wanted to learn Italian; she bought dictionaries, a grammar, and a supply of white paper. She tried serious reading, history, and philosophy. Sometimes in the night Charles woke up with a start, thinking he was being called to a patient:

"I'm coming," he stammered.

It was the noise of a match Emma had struck to relight the lamp. But her reading fared like her pieces of embroidery, all of which, only just begun, filled her cupboard; she took it up, left it, passed on to other books.

She had attacks in which she could easily have been driven to commit any folly. She maintained one day, to contradict her husband, that she could drink off a large glass of brandy, and, as Charles was stupid enough to dare her to, she swallowed the brandy to the last drop.

In spite of her vaporish airs (as the housewives of Yonville called them), Emma, all the same, never seemed gay, and usually she had at the corners of her mouth that immobile contraction that puckers the faces of old maids, and those of men whose ambition has failed. She was pale all over, white as a sheet; the skin of her nose was drawn at the nostrils, her eyes had a vague look. After discovering three grey hairs on her temples, she talked much of her old age.

She often had spells. One day she even spat blood, and, as Charles fussed round her showing his anxiety . . .

"Bah!" she answered, "what does it matter?"

Charles fled to his study and wept there, both his elbows on the table, sitting in his office chair under the phrenological head.

Then he wrote to his mother to beg her to come, and they had many long consultations together on the subject of Emma.

What should they decide? What was to be done since she rejected all medical treatment?

"Do you know what your wife wants?" replied Madame Bovary senior. "She wants to be forced to occupy herself with some manual work. If she were obliged, like so many others, to earn her living, she wouldn't have these vapors, that come to her from a lot of ideas she stuffs into her head, and from the idleness in which she lives."

"Yet she is always busy," said Charles.

"Ah! always busy at what? Reading novels, bad books, works against religion, and in which they mock at priests in speeches taken from Voltaire. But all that leads you far astray, my poor child. A person who has no religion is bound to go astray."

So it was decided to keep Emma from reading novels. The enterprise did not seem easy. The old lady took it upon herself: She was, when she passed through Rouen, to go herself to the lending library and represent that Emma had discontinued her subscription. Would they not have a right to call in the police if the bookseller persisted all the same in his poisonous trade?

The farewells of mother and daughter-in-law were cold. During the three weeks that they had been together they had not exchanged half-a-dozen words except for the usual questions and greetings when they met at table and in the evening before going to bed.

Madame Bovary left on a Wednesday, the market-day at Yonville.

Since morning, the Square had been crowded by end on end of carts, which, with their shafts in the air, spread all along the line of houses from the church to the inn. On the other side there were canvas booths for the sale of cotton goods, blankets, and woolen stockings, together with harness for horses, and packages of blue ribbon, whose ends fluttered in the wind. The coarse hardware was spread out on the ground between pyramids of eggs and hampers of cheeses showing pieces of sticky straw. Near the wheat threshers clucking hens passed their necks through the bars of flat cages. The crowds piled up in one place and refused to budge; they threatened at times to smash the window of the pharmacy. On Wednesdays his shop was never empty, and the people pushed in less to buy drugs than for consultations, so great was Homais' reputation in the neighboring villages. His unshakable assurance deeply impressed the country people. They considered him a greater doctor than all the doctors.

Emma was standing in the open window (she often did so: in the provinces, the window takes the place of the theatre and the promenade) and she amused herself with watching the rustic crowd, when she saw a gentleman in a green velvet coat. Although he was wearing heavy boots, he had on yellow gloves; he was coming towards the doctor's house, followed by a worried looking peasant with lowered head and quite a thoughtful air.

"Can I see the doctor?" he asked Justin, who was talking on the doorsteps with Félicité.

And, mistaking him for a servant of the house, he added,

"Tell him that M. Rodolphe Boulanger de la Huchette is here."

It was not out of affectation that the new arrival added "de la Huchette" to his name, but to make himself the better known. La Huchette, in fact, was an estate near Yonville, where he had just bought the château and two farms that he cultivated himself, without, however, taking too many pains. He lived as a bachelor, and was supposed to have an income of "at least fifteen thousand francs a year."

Charles came into the room. Monsieur Boulanger introduced his man, who wanted to be bled because he felt "as if ants were crawling all over him."

"It will clear me out," was his answer to all reasonable objections.

So Bovary brought a bandage and a basin, and asked Justin to hold it. Then addressing the peasant, who was already turning pale:

"Don't be scared, my friend."

"No, no, sir," said the other; "go ahead!"

And with an air of bravado he held out his heavy arm. At the prick of the lancet the blood spurted out, splashing against the looking-glass.

"Hold the basin nearer," exclaimed Charles.

"Look!" said the peasant, "one would swear it was a little fountain flowing. How red my blood is! That's a good sign, isn't it?"

"Sometimes," answered the *officier de santé*, "one feels nothing at first, and then they start fainting, especially when they're strong like this one."

At these words the peasant dropped the lancet-case he was holding back of his chair. A shudder of his shoulders made the chairback creak. His hat fell off.

"I thought as much," said Bovary, pressing his finger on the vein.

The basin was beginning to tremble in Justin's hands; his knees shook, he turned pale.

"My wife! get my wife!" called Charles.

With one bound she rushed down the staircase.

"Vinegar," he cried. "Lord, two at a time!"

And he was so upset he could hardly put on the compress.

"It is nothing," said Monsieur Boulanger quietly, taking Justin in his arms. He seated him on the table with his back resting against the wall.

Madame Bovary opened the collar of his shirt. The strings of his shirt had got into a knot, and she was for some minutes moving her light fingers about the young fellow's neck. Then she poured some vinegar on her cambric handkerchief; she moistened his temples with little dabs, and then blew delicately upon them.

The ploughman revived, but Justin remained unconscious. His eyeballs disappeared in their whites like blue flowers in milk.

"We must hide this from him," said Charles.

Madame Bovary took the basin to put it under the table. With the movement she made in bending down, her dress (it was a summer dress with four flounces, yellow, long in the waist and wide in the skirt) spread out around on the tiles; and as Emma, stooping, staggered a little in stretching out her arms, the pull of her dress made it hug more closely the line of her bosom. Then she went to fetch a bottle of water, and she was melting some pieces of sugar when the pharmacist arrived. The maid had gone for him at the height of the confusion; seeing his pupil with his eyes open he gave a sigh of relief; then going round him he looked at him from head to foot.

"You fool!" he said, "you're a real fool! A capital idiot! And all that for a little blood-letting! and coming from a fellow who isn't afraid of anything! a real squirrel, climbing to incredible heights in order to steal nuts! You can be proud of yourself! showing a fine talent for the pharmaceutical profession; for, later on, you may be called before the courts of justice in serious circumstances, to enlighten the consciences of the magistrates, and you would have to keep your head then, to reason, show yourself a man, or else pass for an imbecile."

Justin did not answer. The pharmacist went on:

"Who asked you to come? You are always pestering the doctor and madame. Anyway, on Wednesday, I need you in the shop. There are over twenty people there now waiting to be served. I left them just out of concern for you. Get going! hurry! Wait for me there and keep an eye on the jars."

When Justin, who was rearranging his clothes, had gone, they talked for a little while about fainting-fits. Madame Bovary had never fainted.

"That is most unusual for a lady," said Monsieur Boulanger; "but some people are very susceptible. Thus in a duel, I have seen a witness faint away at the mere sound of the loading of pistols."

"As for me," said the pharmacist, "the sight of other people's blood doesn't affect me in the least, but the mere thought of my own flowing would make me faint if I reflected upon it too much."

Monsieur Boulanger, however, dismissed his servant and told him to be quiet, now that his whim was satisfied.

"It gave me the opportunity of making your acquaintance," he added, and he looked at Emma as he said this.

Then he put three francs on the corner of the table, bowed casually, and went out.

He soon had crossed to the other bank of the river (this was his way back to La Huchette), and Emma saw him in the meadow, walking under the poplars, slackening his pace now and then as one who reflects.

"She is nice, very nice, that doctor's wife," he said to himself. "Fine teeth, black eyes, a dainty foot, a figure like a Parisienne's. Where the devil does she come from? Where did that boor ever pick her up?"

Monsieur Rodolphe Boulanger was thirty-four; he combined brutality of temperament with a shrewd judgment, having had much experience with women and being something of a connoisseur. This one had seemed pretty to him; so he kept dreaming about her and her husband.

"I think he is very stupid. She must be tired of him, no doubt. He has dirty nails, and hasn't shaven for three days. While he is trotting after his patients, she sits there mending socks. How bored she gets! How she'd want to be in the city and go dancing every night! Poor little woman! She is gaping after love like a carp on the kitchen table after water. Three gallant words and she'd adore me, I'm sure of it. She'd be tender, charming. Yes; but how get rid of her afterwards?"

The prospect of love's involvements brought to mind, by contrast, his present mistress. She was an actress in Rouen whom he kept, and when he had pondered over this image, even in memory he found himself satiated.

"Madame Bovary," he thought, "is much prettier, much fresher too. Virginie is decidedly beginning to grow fat. Her enthusiasms bore me to tears. And that habit of hers of eating prawns all the time . . .!"

The fields were empty; around him Rodolphe only heard the noise of the grass as it rubbed against his boots, and the chirping of the cricket hidden away among the oats. He again saw Emma in her room, dressed as he had seen her, and he undressed her.

"Oh, I will have her," he cried, smashing, with a blow of his cane, a clod of earth before him.

At once, he began to consider the strategy. He wondered:

"Where shall we meet? And how? We shall always be having the brat on our hands, and the maid, the neighbors, the husband, all sorts of worries. Bah!" he concluded, "it would be too time-consuming!"

Then he started again:

"But she really has eyes that bore into your heart. And that pale complexion! And I, who love pale women!"

When he reached the top of the Argueil hills he had made up his mind.

"All that remains is to create the proper opportunity. Well, I will call in now and then, I'll send game and poultry; I'll have myself bled, if need be. We shall become friends; I'll invite them to my place. Of course!" he added, "the agricultural fair is coming on; she'll be there, I'll see her. We'll begin boldly, for that's the surest way."

VIII

At last it came, the much-awaited agricultural fair. Ever since the morning of the great day, the villagers, on their doorsteps, were discussing the preparations. The facade of the townhall had been hung with garlands of ivy; a tent had been erected in a meadow for the banquet; and in the middle of the Place, in front of the church, a kind of a small cannon was to announce the arrival of the prefect and the names of the fortunate farmers who had won prizes. The National Guard of Buchy (there was none at Yonville) had come to join the corps of firemen, of whom Binet was captain. On that day he wore a collar even higher than usual; and, tightly buttoned in his tunic, his figure was so stiff and motionless that all life seemed to be confined to his legs, which moved in time with the music, with a single motion. As there was some rivalry between the tax-collector and the colonel, both, to show off their talents, drilled their men separately. The red epaulettes and the black breastplates kept parading up and down, one after the other; there was no end to it, and it constantly began again. Never had there been such a display of pomp. Several citizens had washed down their houses the evening before; tricolor flags hung from half-open windows; all the cafés were full; and in the lovely weather the starched caps, the golden crosses, and the colored neckerchiefs seemed whiter than snow, shone in the sun, and relieved with their motley colors the somber monotony of the frock-coats and blue smocks. The neighboring farmers' wives, when they got off their horses, removed the long pin with which they had gathered their dresses tight around them for fear of getting them spattered; while their husbands protected their hats by covering them with handkerchiefs, of which they held one corner in their teeth.

The crowd came into the main street from both ends of the village. People poured in from the lanes, the alleys, the houses; and from time to time one heard the banging of doors closing behind ladies of the town in cotton gloves, who were going out to see the fête. Most admired of all were two long lamp-stands covered with lanterns, that flanked a platform on which the authorities were to sit. Aside from this, a kind of pole had been placed against the four columns of the townhall, each bearing a small standard of greenish cloth, embellished with inscriptions in gold letters. On one was written, "To Commerce"; on the other, "To Agriculture"; on the third, "To Industry"; and on the fourth, "To the Fine Arts".

But the jubilation that brightened all faces seemed to darken that of Madame Lefrançois, the innkeeper. Standing on her kitchen-steps she muttered to herself:

"How stupid! How stupid they are with their canvas booth! Do they think the prefect will be glad to dine down there under a tent like a gipsy? They call all this fussing for the good of the town! As if it helped the town to send to Neufchâtel for the keeper of a cookshop! And for whom? For cowheads! for tramps!"

The pharmacist passed by. He was wearing a frock-coat, nankeen trousers, beaver shoes, and, to everyone's surprise, a hat—a low crowned hat.

"Your servant," he said. "Excuse me, I am in a hurry."

And as the fat widow asked where he was going . . .

"It seems odd to you, doesn't it, I who am always more cooped up in my laboratory than the man's rat in his cheese."

"What cheese?" asked the landlady.

"Oh, nothing, never mind!" Homais continued. "I merely wished to convey to you, Madame Lefrançois, that I usually live at home like a recluse. To-day, however, considering the circumstances, it is necessary . . ."

"Oh, are you going down there?" she said contemptuously.

"Yes, I am going," replied the pharmacist, astonished. "Am I not a member of the Advisory committee?"

Mère Lefrançois looked at him for a few moments, and ended by saying with a smile:

"That's another matter! But is agriculture any of your business? Do you understand anything about it?"

"Certainly I understand it, since I am a pharmacist,—that is to say, a chemist. And the object of chemistry, Madame Lefrançois, being the knowledge of the reciprocal and molecular action of all natural bodies, it follows that agriculture is comprised within its domain. And, in fact, the composition of the manure, the fermentation of liquids, the analyses of gases, and the effects of miasmas, what, I ask you, is all this, if it isn't chemistry, pure and simple?"

The landlady did not answer. Homais went on:

"Do you think that to be an agriculturist it is necessary to have tilled the earth or fattened fowls oneself? It is much more important to know the composition of the substances in question—the geological strata, the atmospheric actions, the quality of the soil, the minerals, the waters, the density of the different bodies, their capillarity, and what not. And one must be master of all the principles of hygiene in order to direct, criticise the construction of buildings, the feeding of animals, the diet of the servants. And, moreover, Madame Lefrançois, one must know botany, be able to distinguish between plants, you understand, which are the wholesome and those that are deleterious, which are unproductive and which nutritive, if it is well to pull them up here and re-sow them there, to propagate some, destroy others; in brief, one must keep pace with science by reading publications and papers, be always on the alert to detect improvements."

The landlady never took her eyes off the "Café Français" and the pharmacist went on:

"Would to God our agriculturists were chemists, or that at least they would pay more attention to the counsels of science. Thus lately I myself wrote a substantial paper, a memoir of over seventy-two pages, entitled, 'Cider, its Manufacture and its Effects, together with some New Reflections on this Subject,' that I sent to the Agricultural Society in Rouen, and which even procured me the honor of being received among its members—Section, Agriculture; Class, Pomology. Well, if my work had been given to the public . . ."

But the pharmacist stopped, so distracted did Madame Lefrançois seem.

"Just look at them!" she said. "It's past comprehension! Such a hash-house!" And with a shrug of the shoulders that stretched out the stitches of her sweater, she pointed with both hands at the rival establishment, from where singing erupted. "Well, it won't last long," she added, "It'll be over before a week."

Homais drew back in surprise. She came down three steps and whispered in his ear:

"What! you didn't know it? They'll foreclose this week. It's Lheureux who does the selling; he killed them off with his notes."

"What a dreadful catastrophe!" exclaimed the pharmacist, who always found expressions that filled all imaginable circumstances.

Then the landlady began telling him this story, that she had heard from Theodore, Monsieur Guillaumin's servant, and although she detected Tellier, she blamed Lheureux. He was "a wheedler, a fawner."

"There!" she said. "Look at him! There he goes down the square; he is greeting Madame Bovary, who's wearing a green hat. And she is on Monsieur Boulanger's arm."

"Madame Bovary!" exclaimed Homais. "I must go at once and pay her my respects. Perhaps she'll be pleased to have a seat in the enclosure under the peristyle." And, without heeding Madame Lefrançois, who was calling him back for more gossip, the pharmacist walked off rapidly with a smile on his face and his walk jauntier than ever, bowing copiously to right and left, and taking up much room with the large tails of his frock-coat that fluttered behind him in the wind.

Rodolphe having caught sight of him from afar, quickened his pace, but Madame Bovary couldn't keep up; so he walked more slowly, and, smiling at her, said roughly:

"It's only to get away from that fat fellow, you know, the pharmacist."

She nudged him with her elbow.

"How shall I understand that?" he asked himself.

And, walking on, he looked at her out of the corner of his eyes.

Her profile was so calm that it revealed nothing.

It stood out in the light from the oval of her hat that was tied with pale ribbons like waving rushes. Her eyes with their long curved lashes looked straight before her, and though wide open, they seemed slightly slanted at the cheek-bones, because of the blood pulsing gently under the delicate skin. A rosy light shone through the partition between her nostrils. Her head was bent upon her shoulder, and the tips of her teeth shone through her lips like pearls.

"Is she making fun of me?" thought Rodolphe.

Emma's gesture, however, had only been meant for a warning; for Monsieur Lheureux was accompanying them, and spoke now and again as if to enter into the conversation.

"What a beautiful day! Everybody is outside! The wind is from the east!"

Neither Madame Bovary nor Rodolphe answered him, but their slightest movement made him draw near saying, "I beg your pardon!" and raising his hat.

When they reached the blacksmith's house, instead of following the road up to the fence, Rodolphe suddenly turned down a path, drawing Madame Bovary with him. He called out:

"Good evening, Monsieur Lheureux! We'll see you soon!"

"How you got rid of him!" she said, laughing.

"Why," he went on, "allow oneself to be intruded upon by others? And as to-day I have the happiness of being with you . . ."

Emma blushed. He did not finish his sentence. Then he talked of the fine weather and of the pleasure of walking on the grass. A few daisies had sprung up again.

"Here are some pretty Easter daisies," he said, "and enough to provide oracles for all the lovers in the vicinity."

He added,

"Shall I pick some? What do you think?"

"Are you in love?" she asked, coughing a little.

"H'm, h'm! who knows?" answered Rodolphe.

The meadow was beginning to fill up, and the housewives were hustling about with their great umbrellas, their baskets and their babies. One often had to make way for a long file of country girls, servant-maids with blue stockings, flat shoes, and silver rings, who smelt of milk when one passed close to them. They walked along holding one another by the hand, and thus they spread over the whole field from the row of open trees to the banquet tent. But this was the judging time, and the farmers one after the other entered a kind of enclosure formed by ropes supported on sticks.

The beasts were there, their noses turned toward the rope, and making a confused line with their unequal rumps. Drowsy pigs were burrowing in the earth with their snouts, calves were lowing and bleating; the cows, one leg folded under them, stretched their bellies on the grass, slowly chewing their cud, and blinking their heavy eyelids at the gnats that buzzed around them. Ploughmen with bare arms were holding by the halter prancing stallions that neighed with dilated nostrils looking in the direction of the mares. These stood quietly, stretching out their heads and flowing manes, while their foals rested in their shadow, or sucked them from time to time. And above the long undulation of these crowded bodies one saw some white mane rising in the wind like a wave, or some sharp horns sticking out, and the heads of men running about. Apart, outside the enclosure, a hundred paces off, was a large black bull, muzzled, with an iron ring in its nostrils, and who moved no more than if he had been in bronze. A child in rags was holding him by a rope.

Between the two lines the committee-men were walking with heavy steps, examining each animal, then consulting one another in a low voice. One who seemed of more importance now and then took notes in a book as he walked along. This was the president of the jury, Monsieur Derozerays de la Panville. As soon as he recognised Rodolphe he came forward quickly, and smiling amiably, said:

"What! Monsieur Boulanger, you are deserting us?"

Rodolphe protested that he would come. But when the president had disappeared:

"To tell the truth," he said, "I shall not go. Your company is better than his."

And while poking fun at the show, Rodolphe, to move about more easily, showed the gendarme his blue card, and even stopped now and then in front of some fine beast, which Madame Bovary did not at all admire. He noticed this, and began jeering at the Yonville ladies and their dresses; then he apologised for his own casual attire. It had the inconsistency of things at once commonplace and refined which enchants or exasperates the ordinary man because he suspects that it reveals an unconventional existence, a dubious morality, the affectations of the artist, and, above all, a certain contempt for established conventions. The wind, blowing up his batiste shirt with pleated cuffs revealed a waistcoat of grey linen, and his broad-striped trousers disclosed at the ankle nankeen boots, with patent leather gaiters. These were so polished that they reflected the grass. He trampled on horse's dung, one hand in the pocket of his jacket and his straw hat tilted on one side.

"Anyway," he added, "when one lives in the country. . . ."

"Nothing is worthwhile," said Emma.

"That is true," replied Rodolphe. "To think that not one of these people is capable of understanding even the cut of a coat!"

Then they talked about provincial mediocrity, of the lives it stifles, the lost illusions.

"No wonder," said Rodolphe, "that I am more and more sinking in gloom."

"You!" she said in astonishment; "I thought you very light-hearted."

"Oh, yes, it seems that way because I know how to wear a mask

of mockery in society, and yet, how many a time at the sight of a
cemetery by moonlight have I not asked myself whether it were not
better to join those sleeping there!"

"Oh! and your friends?" she said. "How can you forget them."

"My friends! What friends? Have I any? Who cares about me?"
And he followed up the last words with a kind of hissing whistle.

They were obliged to separate because of a great pile of chairs that
a man was carrying behind them. He was so overladen that one
could only see the tips of his wooden shoes and the ends of his two
outstretched arms. It was Lestiboudois, the gravedigger, who was
carrying the church chairs about amongst the people. Alive to all
that concerned his interests, he had hit upon this means of turning
the agricultural show to his advantage, and his idea was succeeding,
for he no longer knew which way to turn. In fact, the villagers, who
were tired and hot, quarrelled for these seats, whose straw smelt of
incense, and they leant against the thick backs, stained with the wax
of candles, with a certain veneration.

Madame Bovary again took Rodolphe's arm; he went on as if
speaking to himself:

"Yes, I have missed so many things. Always alone! Ah! if I had
some aim in life, if I had met some love, if I had found some one!
Oh, how I would have spent all the energy of which I am capable,
surmounted everything, overcome everything!"

"Yet it seems to me," said Emma, "that you are not to be pitied."

"Ah! you think so?" said Rodolphe.

"For, after all," she went on, "you are free . . ."

She hesitated,

"Rich . . ."

"Don't mock me," he replied.

And she protested that she was not mocking him, when the sound
of a cannon was heard; immediately all began crowding one another
towards the village.

It was a false alarm. The prefect seemed not to be coming, and
the members of the jury felt much embarrassed, not knowing if they
ought to begin the meeting or wait longer.

At last, at the end of the Place a large hired landau appeared,
drawn by two thin horses, generously whipped by a coachman in a
white hat. Binet had only just time to shout, "Present arms!" and
the colonel to imitate him. There was a rush towards the guns; every
one pushed forward. A few even forgot their collars.

But the prefectoral coach seemed to sense the trouble, for the two
yoked nags, dawdling in their harness, came at a slow trot in front of
the townhall at the very moment when the National Guard and firemen deployed, beating time with their boots.

"Present arms!" shouted Binet.

"Halt!" shouted the colonel. "By the left flank, march!"

And after presenting arms, during which the clang of the band, letting loose, rang out like a brass kettle rolling downstairs, all the guns were lowered.

Then was seen stepping down from the carriage a gentleman in a short coat with silver braiding, with bald brow, and wearing a tuft of hair at the back of his head, of a sallow complexion and the most benign of aspects. His eyes, very large and covered by heavy lids, were half-closed to look at the crowd, while at the same time he raised his sharp nose, and forced a smile upon his sunken mouth. He recognised the mayor by his scarf, and explained to him that the prefect was not able to come. He himself was a councillor at the prefecture; then he added a few apologies. Monsieur Tuvache reciprocated with polite compliments, humbly acknowledged by the other; and they remained thus, face to face, their foreheads almost touching, surrounded by members of the jury, the municipal council, the notable personages, the National Guard and the crowd. The councillor pressing his little cocked hat to his breast repeated his greetings, while Tuvache, bent like a bow, also smiled, stammered, tried to say something, protested his devotion to the monarchy and the honor that was being done to Yonville.

Hippolyte, the groom from the inn, took the head of the horses from the coachman, and, limping along with his clubfoot, led them to the door of the Lion d'Or where a number of peasants collected to look at the carriage. The drum beat, the howitzer thundered, and the gentlemen one by one mounted the platform, where they sat down in red utrecht velvet arm-chairs that had been lent by Madame Tuvache.

All these people looked alike. Their fair flabby faces, somewhat tanned by the sun, were the color of sweet cider, and their puffy whiskers emerged from stiff collars, kept up by white cravats with broad bows. All the waistcoats were of velvet, double-breasted; all the watches had, at the end of a long ribbon, an oval seal; all rested their two hands on their thighs, carefully stretching the stride of their trousers, whose unspunged glossy cloth shone more brilliantly than the leather of their heavy boots.

The ladies of the company stood at the back under the porch between the pillars, while the common herd was opposite, standing up or sitting on chairs. Lestiboudois had brought there all the chairs that he had moved from the field, and he even kept running back every minute to fetch others from the church. He caused such confusion with this piece of business that one had great difficulty in getting to the small steps of the platform.

"I think," said Monsieur Lheureux to the pharmacist who was heading for his seat, "that they ought to have put up two Venetian masts with something rather severe and rich for ornaments; it would have been a very pretty sight."

"Certainly," replied Homais; "but what can you expect? The mayor took everything on his own shoulders. He hasn't much taste. Poor Tuvache! he is completely devoid of what is called the genius of art."

Meanwhile, Rodolphe and Madame Bovary had ascended to the first floor of the townhall, to the "council-room," and, as it was empty, he suggested that they could enjoy the sight there more comfortably. He fetched three chairs from the round table under the bust of the monarch, and having carried them to one of the windows, they sat down together.

There was commotion on the platform, long whisperings, much parleying. At last the councillor got up. It was known by now that his name was Lieuvain, and in the crowd the name was now passing from lip to lip. After he had reshuffled a few pages, and bent over them to see better, he began:

"Gentlemen! May I be permitted first of all (before addressing you on the object of our meeting to-day, and this sentiment will, I am sure, be shared by you all), may I be permitted, I say, to pay a tribute to the higher administration, to the government, to the monarch, gentlemen, our sovereign, to that beloved king to whom no branch of public or private prosperity is a matter of indifference, and who directs with a hand at once so firm and wise the chariot of the state amid the incessant perils of a stormy sea, knowing, moreover, how to make peace respected as well as war, industry, commerce, agriculture, and the fine arts."

"I ought," said Rodolphe, "to get back a little further."

"Why?" said Emma.

But at this moment the voice of the councillor rose to an extraordinary pitch. He declaimed—

"This is no longer the time, gentlemen, when civil discord made blood flow in our market squares, when the landowner, the businessman, the working-man himself, lying down to peaceful sleep, trembled lest he should be awakened suddenly by the noise of alarming tocsins, when the most subversive doctrines audaciously sapped foundations . . ."

"Well, some one down there might see me," Rodolphe resumed, "then I should have to invent excuses for a fortnight; and with my bad reputation . . ."

"Oh, you are slandering yourself," said Emma.

"No! It is dreadful, I assure you."

"But, gentlemen," continued the councillor, "if, banishing from my memory the remembrance of these sad pictures, I carry my eyes back to the present situation of our dear country, what do I see there?

Everywhere commerce and the arts are flourishing; everywhere new means of communication, like so many new arteries in the body politic, establish within it new relations. Our great industrial centers have recovered all their activity; religion, more consolidated, smiles in all hearts; our ports are full, confidence is born again, and France breathes once more! . . ."

"Besides," added Rodolphe, "perhaps from the world's point of view they are right."

"How so?" she asked.

"What!" said he. "Don't you know that there are souls constantly tormented? They need by turns to dream and to act, the purest passions and the most turbulent joys, and thus they fling themselves into all sorts of fantasies, of follies."

Then she looked at him as one looks at a traveler who has voyaged over strange lands, and went on:

"We have not even this distraction, we poor women!"

"A sad distraction, for happiness isn't found in it."

"But is it ever found?" she asked.

"Yes; one day it comes," he answered.

"And this is what you have understood," said the councillor. "You, farmers, agricultural laborers! you pacific pioneers of a work that belongs wholly to civilisation! you, men of progress and morality, you have understood, I say, that political storms are even more redoubtable than atmospheric disturbances!"

"A day comes," repeated Rodolphe, "one is near despair. Then the horizon expands; it is as if a voice cried, 'It is here!' You feel the need of confiding the whole of your life, of giving everything, sacrificing everything to this person. There is no need for explanations; one understands each other, having met before in dreams!" (And he looked at her.) "At last, here it is, this treasure so sought after, here before you. It glitters, it flashes; yet one still doubts, one does not believe it; one remains dazzled, as if one went out from darkness into light."

And as he ended Rodolphe suited the action to the word. He passed his hand over his face, like a man about to faint. Then he let it fall on Emma's. She drew hers back. But the councillor was still reading.

"And who would be surprised at it, gentlemen? He only who was so blind, so imprisoned (I do not fear to say it), so imprisoned by the prejudices of another age as still to misunderstand the spirit of our rural populations. Where, indeed, is more patriotism to be found than in the country, greater devotion to the public welfare, in a word, more intelligence? And, gentlemen, I do not mean that superficial intelligence, vain ornament of idle minds, but rather that profound and balanced intelligence that applies itself above all else to useful objects, thus contributing to the good of all, to the common amelioration and to the support of the state, born of respect for law and the practice of duty . . ."

"Ah! again!" said Rodolphe. "Always 'duty.' I am sick of the word. They are a lot of old jackasses in woolen vests and old bigots with foot-warmers and rosaries who constantly drone into our ears 'Duty, duty!' Ah! by Jove! as if one's real duty were not to feel what is great, cherish the beautiful, and not accept all the conventions of society with the hypocrisy it forces upon us."

"Yet . . . yet . . ." objected Madame Bovary.

"No, no! Why cry out against the passions? Are they not the one beautiful thing on earth, the source of heroism, of enthusiasm, of poetry, music, the arts, in a word, of everything?"

"But one must," said Emma, "to some extent bow to the opinion of the world and accept its morality."

"Ah, but there are two moralities," he replied, "the petty one, the morality of small men that constantly keeps changing, but yells itself hoarse; crude and loud like the crowd of imbeciles that you see down there. But the other, the eternal, that is about us and above, like the landscape that surrounds us, and the blue heavens that give us light."

Monsieur Lieuvain had just wiped his mouth with a pocket handkerchief. He continued:

"It would be presumptuous of me, gentlemen, to point out to you the uses of agriculture. Who supplies our wants, who provides our means of subsistence, if not the farmer? It is the farmer, gentlemen, who sows with laborious hand the fertile furrows of the country, brings forth the wheat, which, being ground, is made into a powder by means of ingenious machinery, issues from there under the name of flour, and is then transported to our cities, soon delivered to the baker, who makes it into food for poor and rich alike. Again, is it not the farmer who fattens his flocks in the pastures in order to provide us with warm clothing? For how should we clothe or nourish ourselves without his labor? And, gentlemen, is it even necessary to go so far for examples? Who has not frequently reflected on all the momentous things that we get out of that modest animal, the ornament of poultry-yards, that provides us at once with a soft pillow for our bed, with succulent flesh for our tables, and eggs? But I should never end if I were to enumerate one after the other all the different products which the earth, well cultivated, like a generous mother, lavishes upon her children. Here it is the vine; elsewhere apple trees for cider; there colza; further, cheeses, and flax; gentlemen, let us not forget flax, which has made such great strides forward these last years and to which I call your special attention!"

He had no need to call it, for all the mouths of the multitude were wide open, as if to drink in his words. Tuvache by his side listened to him with staring eyes. Monsieur Derozerays from time to time softly closed his eyelids, and farther on the pharmacist, with his son Napoleon between his knees, put his hand behind his ear in order not to lose a syllable. The chins of the other members of the jury nodded slowly up and down in their waistcoats in sign of approval. The firemen at the foot of the platform rested on their bayonets; and Binet, motionless, stood with out-turned elbows, the point of his sabre in the air. Perhaps he could hear, but he certainly couldn't see a thing, for the visor of his helmet fell down on his nose. His lieutenant, the youngest son of Monsieur Tuvache, had an even bigger one; it was so large that he could hardly keep it on, in spite of the cotton scarf that peeped out from underneath. He wore a smile of childlike innocence, and his thin pale face, dripping with sweat, expressed satisfaction, some exhaustion and sleepiness.

The square was crowded up to the houses. People were leaning on their elbows at all the windows, others were standing on their doorsteps, and Justin, in front of the pharmacy, seemed fascinated by the spectacle. In spite of the silence Monsieur Lieuvain's voice was lost in the air. It reached you in fragments of phrases, interrupted here and there by the creaking of chairs in the crowd; then, the long bellowing of an ox would suddenly burst forth from behind, or else the bleating of the lambs, who answered one another from street to street. Even the cowherds and shepherds had driven their beasts this far, and one could hear their lowing from time to time, while with their tongues they tore down some scrap of foliage that hung over their muzzles.

Rodolphe had drawn nearer to Emma, and was whispering hurriedly in her ear:

"Doesn't this conspiracy of society revolt you? Is there a single sentiment it does not condemn? The noblest instincts, the purest feelings are persecuted, slandered; and if at length two poor souls do meet, all is organized in such a way as to keep them from becoming one. Yet they will try, they will call to each other. Not in vain, for sooner or later, be it in six or ten years, they will come together in love; for fate has decreed it, and they are born for each other."

His arms were folded across his knees, and thus lifting his face at her from close by, he looked fixedly at her. She noticed in his eyes small golden lines radiating from the black pupils; she even smelt the perfume of the pomade that made his hair glossy. Then something gave way in her; she recalled the Viscount who had waltzed with her at Vaubyessard, and whose beard exhaled a similar scent of vanilla and lemon, and mechanically she half-closed her eyes the better to breathe it in. But in making this movement, as she leant back in her chair, she saw in the distance, right on the line of the horizon, the old diligence the "Hirondelle," that was slowly descending the hill of Leux, dragging after it a long trail of dust. It was in this yellow carriage that Léon had so ofter come back to her, and by this route down there that he had gone for ever. She fancied she saw him opposite at his window; then all grew confused; clouds gathered; it seemed to her that she was again turning in the waltz under the light of the lustres on the arm of the Viscount, and that Léon was not far away, that he was coming . . . and yet all the time she was conscious of Rodolphe's head by her side. The sweetness of this sensation revived her past desires, and like grains of sand under a gust of wind, they swirled around in the subtle breath of the perfume that diffused over her soul. She breathed deeply several times to drink in the freshness of the ivy round the columns. She took off her gloves and wiped her hands; then she fanned her face with her handkerchief while she kept hearing, through the throbbing of her temples, the murmur of the crowd and the voice of the councillor intoning his phrases.

He was saying:

"Persevere! listen neither to the suggestions of routine, nor to the over-hasty councils of a rash empiricism. Apply yourselves, above all, to the amelioration of the soil, to good manures, to the development of the breeds, whether equine, ovine, or porcine. May these shows be to you pacific arenas, where the victor in leaving will hold forth a hand to the vanquished, and will fraternise with him in the hope of even greater success. And you, aged servants! humble helpers, whose hard labor no Government up to this day has taken into consideration, receive the reward of your silent virtues, and be assured that the state henceforward has its eye upon you; that it encourages you, protects you; that it will accede to your just demands, and alleviate as much as possible the heavy burden of your painful sacrifices."

Monsieur Lieuvain sat down; Monsieur Derozerays got up, beginning another speech. His was not perhaps so florid as that of the councillor, but it stood out by a more direct style, that is to say, by more specific knowledge and more elevated considerations. Thus the praise of the Government took up less space; religion and agriculture more. He showed the relation between both, and how they had always contributed to civilisation. Rodolphe was talking dreams, forebodings, magnetism with Madame Bovary. Going back to the cradle of society, the orator painted those fierce times when men lived on acorns in the heart of woods. Then they had left off the skins of beasts, had put on cloth, tilled the soil, planted the vine. Was this a good, or wasn't there more harm than good in this discovery? That was the problem to which Monsieur Derozerays addressed himself. From magnetism little by little Rodolphe had come to affinities, and while the president was citing Cincinnatus and his plough, Diocletian planting his cabbages,[6] and the Emperors of China inaugurating the year by the sowing of seed, the young man was explaining to the young woman that these irresistible attractions find their cause in some previous state of existence.

"Take us, for instance," he said, "how did we happen to meet? What chance willed it? It was because across infinite distances, like two streams uniting, our particular inclinations pushed us toward one another."

And he seized her hand; she did not withdraw it.

"First prize for general farming!" announced the president.

"—Just now, for example, when I went to your home . . ."

"To Mr. Bizat of Quincampoix."

"—Did I know I would accompany you?"

"Seventy francs!"

"—A hundred times I tried to leave; yet I followed you and stayed . . ."

"For manures!"

"—As I would stay to-night, to-morrow, all other days, all my life!"

"To Monsieur Caron of Argueil, a gold medal!"

"—For I have never enjoyed anyone's company so much."

"To Monsieur Bain of Givry-Saint-Martin."

"—And I will never forget you."

"For a merino ram . . ."

"—Whereas you will forget me; I'll pass through your life as a mere shadow . . ."

"To Monsieur Belot of Notre-Dame."

"—But no, tell me there can be a place for me in your thoughts, in your life, can't there?"

"Hog! first prize equally divided between Messrs. Lehérissé and Cullembourg, sixty francs!"

Rodolphe was holding her hand on his; it was warm and quivering like a captive dove that wants to fly away; perhaps she was trying to take it away or perhaps she was answering his pressure, at any rate, she moved her fingers; he exclaimed,

"Oh, thank you! You do not repulse me! You are kind! You

6. *Cincinnatus* was a Roman Consul (460 B.C.), who was supposedly called to his office while found plowing. *Diocletian* (A.D. 245–313) was Roman emperor from 284 to 305. He resigned in 305 and retired to Salone (now Split) in Dalmatia, to cultivate his garden.

understand that I am yours! Let me see you, let me look at you!"

A gust of wind that blew in at the window ruffled the cloth on the table, and in the square below all the large bonnets rose up like the fluttering wings of white butterflies.

"Use of oil-cakes!" continued the president.

He was hurrying now: "Flemish manure, flax-growing, drainage, long term leases . . . domestic service."

Rodolphe was no longer speaking. They looked at each other. As their desire increased, their dry lips trembled and languidly, effortlessly, their fingers intertwined.

"Catherine Nicaise Elizabeth Leroux, of Sassetot-la-Guerrière, for fifty-four years of service at the same farm, a silver medal—value, twenty-five francs!"

"Where is Catherine Leroux?" repeated the councillor.

She did not appear, and one could hear whispering voices:

"Go ahead!"

"No."

"To the left!"

"Don't be afraid!"

"Oh, how stupid she is!"

"Well, is she there?" cried Tuvache.

"Yes; here she is."

"Then what's she waiting for?"

There came forward on the platform a frightened-looking little old lady who seemed to shrink within her poor clothes. On her feet she wore heavy wooden shoes, and from her hips hung a large blue apron. Her pale face framed in a borderless cap was more wrinkled than a withered russet apple, and from the sleeves of her red jacket looked out two large hands with gnarled joints. The dust from the barns, washing soda, and grease from the wool had so encrusted, roughened, hardened them that they seemed dirty, although they had been rinsed in clear water; and by dint of long service they remained half open, as if to bear humble witness of so much suffering endured. Something of monastic rigidity dignified her. No trace of sadness or tenderness weakened her pale face. Having lived so long among animals, she had taken on their silent and tranquil ways. It was the first time that she found herself in the midst of so large a company; and inwardly scared by the flags, the drums, the gentlemen in frock-coats, and the decorations of the councillor, she stood motionless, not knowing whether she should advance or run away, nor why the crowd was cheering and the jury smiling at her. Thus, a half century of servitude confronted these beaming bourgeois.

"Step forward, venerable Catherine Nicaise Elizabeth Leroux!" said the councillor, who had taken the list of prize-winners from the president; and, looking at the piece of paper and the old woman by turns, he repeated in a fatherly tone:

"Step forward, step forward!"

"Are you deaf?" said Tuvache, who was jumping around in his arm-chair; and he began shouting in her ear, "Fifty-four years of service. A silver medal! Twenty-five francs! For you!"

Then, when she had her medal, she looked at it, and a smile of beatitude spread over her face; and as she walked away they could hear her muttering:

"I'll give it to our curé at home, to say some masses for me!"

"What fanaticism!" exclaimed the pharmacist, leaning across to the notary.

The meeting was over, the crowd dispersed, and now that the speeches had been read, everything fell back into place again, and everything into the old grooves; the masters bullied the servants, the servants beat the animals, indolent victors returning to their stables with a green wreath between their horns.

The National Guards, however, had climbed up to the second floor of the townhall; brioches were stuck on their bayonets, and the drummer of the battalion carried a basket with bottles. Madame Bovary took Rodolphe's arm; he saw her home; they separated at her door; then he walked about alone in the meadow while waiting for the banquet to start.

The feast was long, noisy, ill served; the guests were so crowded that they could hardly move their elbows; and the narrow planks that served as benches almost broke under their weight. They ate huge amounts. Each one stuffed himself with all he could lay hands on. Sweat stood on every brow, and a whitish steam, like the vapour of a stream on an autumn morning, floated above the table between the hanging lamps. Rodolphe, leaning against the canvas of the tent, was thinking so intently of Emma that he heard nothing. Behind him on the grass the servants were piling up the dirty plates, his neighbors were talking; he did not answer them; they filled his glass, and there was silence in his thoughts in spite of the noise around him. He was dreaming of what she had said, of the line of her lips; her face, as in a magic mirror, shone on the plates of the shakos, the folds of her gown fell along the walls, and endless days of love unrolled before him in the future.

He saw her again in the evening during the fireworks, but she was with her husband, Madame Homais, and the pharmacist, who was worrying about the danger of stray rockets. Time and again he left the company to give some advice to Binet.

The fireworks sent to Monsieur Tuvache had, through an excess of caution, been locked in his cellar; so the damp powder would not

light, and the main piece, that was to represent a dragon biting his
tail, failed completely. From time to time, a meagre Roman-candle
went off; then the gaping crowd sent up a roar that mingled with the
giggling of the women who were being tickled in the darkness. Emma
silently nestled against Charles's shoulder; then, raising her chin, she
watched the luminous rays of the rockets against the dark sky. Rodolphe
gazed at her in the light of the burning lanterns.

One by one, they went out. Stars appeared. A few drops of rain
began to fall. She tied her scarf over her bare head.

At this moment the councillor's carriage came out from the inn.
His coachman, who was drunk, suddenly fell asleep, and one could
see the mass of his body from afar above the hood, framed by the
two lanterns, swaying from right to left with the motion of the springs.

"Truly," said the pharmacist, "severe measures should be taken
against drunkenness! I should like to see written up weekly at the
door of the townhall on a board *ad hoc* the names of all those who
during the week got intoxicated on alcohol. Besides, with regard to
statistics, one would thus have, as it were, public records that one
could refer to if needed . . . But excuse me!"

And he once more ran off to the captain. The latter was returning
to see his lathe.

"You might do well," said Homais to him, "to send one of your
men, or to go yourself . . ."

"Oh, leave me alone!" answered the tax-collector. "I'm telling
you everything is taken care of."

"There is nothing for you to worry about," said the pharmacist,
when he returned to his friends. "Monsieur Binet has assured me
that all precautions have been taken. No sparks have fallen; the pumps
are full. Let's go to bed."

"I can certainly use some sleep," said Madame Homais with a
huge yawn. "But never mind; we've had a beautiful day for our fête."

Rodolphe repeated in a low voice, and with a tender look, "Oh,
yes! very beautiful!"

And after a final good night, they parted ways.

Two days later, in the "Fanal de Rouen," there was a long article
on the show. Homais had composed it on the spur of the moment,
the very morning after the banquet.

"Why these festoons, these flowers, these garlands? Whereto was
the crowd hurrying, like the waves of a furious sea under the torrents
of a tropical sun pouring its heat upon our meadows?"

Then he spoke of the condition of the peasants. Certainly the
Government was doing much, but not enough. "Be bold!" he told
them; "a thousand reforms are needed; let us carry them out!" Then,
reporting on the entry of the councillor, he did not forget, "the mar-

tial spirit of our militia," nor "our dazzling village maidens," nor the "bald-headed elders like patriarchs, some of whom, left over from our immortal phalanxes, still felt their hearts beat at the manly sound of the drums." He cited himself among the first of the members of the jury, and he even called attention in a note to the fact that Monsieur Homais, pharmacist, had sent a memoir on cider to the agricultural society. When he came to the distribution of the prizes, he painted the joy of the prize-winners in dithyrambic strophes. "The father embraced the son, the brother the brother, the husband his wife. More than one showed his humble medal with pride; and no doubt when he got home to his good housewife, he hung it up weeping on the modest walls of his cottage.

"About six o'clock a banquet prepared in the meadow of Monsieur Leigeard brought together the main participants in the festivities. The utmost merriment reigned throughout. Several toasts were proposed: Monsieur Lieuvain, To the king! Monsieur Tuvache, To the prefect! Monsieur Derozerays, To Agriculture! Monsieur Homais, To the twin sisters, Industry and Fine Arts! Monsieur Leplichey, To Improvements! At night some brilliant fireworks suddenly lit up the sky. It was a real kaleidoscope, an operatic scene; and for a moment our little locality might have thought itself transported into the midst of a dream from the 'Thousand and One Nights.'

"Let us state that no untoward event disturbed this family meeting."

And he added: "Only the absence of the clergy was noted. No doubt the priests do not understand progress in the same way. Just as you please, *messieurs de Loyola!*"[7]

IX

Six weeks passed. Rodolphe did not come again. At last one evening he appeared.

The day after the fair he told himself:

"Let's not go back too soon; that would be a mistake."

And at the end of a week he had gone off hunting. After the hunting he first feared that too much time had passed, and then he reasoned thus:

"If she loved me from the first day, impatience must make her love me even more. Let's persist!"

And he knew that his calculation had been right when, on entering the room, he saw Emma turn pale.

She was alone. Night was falling. The small muslin curtain along

7. Ignatius Loyola (1491–1556), a Spaniard, founded the Order of the Jesuits in 1534. The Jesuits were expelled from France in 1762.

the windows deepened the twilight, and the gilding of the barometer, on which the rays of the sun fell, shone in the looking-glass between the meshes of the coral.

Rodolphe remained standing, and Emma hardly answered his first conventional phrases.

"I have been busy," he said, "I have been ill."

"Nothing serious?" she cried.

"Well," said Rodolphe, sitting down at her side on a footstool, "no . . . It was because I did not want to come back."

"Why?"

"Can't you guess?"

He looked at her again, but so hard that she lowered her head, blushing. He pursued:

"Emma . . ."

"Monsieur!" she exclaimed, drawing back a little.

"Ah! you see," he replied in a melancholy voice, "that I was right not to come back; for this name, this name that fills my whole soul, and that escaped me, you forbid me its use! Madame Bovary! . . . why, the whole world calls you thus! Moreover, it is not your name; it is the name of another!"

He repeated,

"Of another!"

And he hid his face in his hands.

"Yes, I think of you constantly! . . . The thought of you drives me to despair. Ah! forgive me! . . . I'll go . . . Adieu . . . I'll go far away, so far that you will never hear of me again; yet . . . today . . . I don't know what force made me come here. For one does not struggle against Heaven; it is impossible to resist the smile of angels; one is carried away by the beautiful, the lovely, the adorable."

It was the first time that Emma had heard such words addressed to her, and her pride unfolded languidly in the warmth of this language, like someone stretching in a hot bath.

"But if I didn't come," he continued, "if I couldn't see you, at least I have gazed long on all that surrounds you. At night, every night, I arose; I came here; I watched your house, the roof glimmering in the moon, the trees in the garden swaying before your window, and the little lamp, a gleam shining through the window-panes in the darkness. Ah! you never knew that there, so near you, so far from you, was a poor wretch . . ."

She turned towards him with a sob.

"Oh, you are kind!" she said.

"No, I love you, that is all! You do not doubt that! Tell me; one word, one single word!"

And Rodolphe imperceptibly glided from the footstool to the ground; but a sound of wooden shoes was heard in the kitchen, and he noticed that the door of the room was not closed.

"You would do an act of charity," he went on, rising, "if you accepted to gratify a whim!" It was to visit her home, he wished to see it, and since Madame Bovary could see no objection to this, they both rose just when Charles came in.

"Good morning, doctor," Rodolphe said to him.

Flattered by this unexpected title, Charles launched into elaborate displays of politeness. Of this the other took advantage to pull himself together.

"Madame was speaking to me," he then said, "about her health."

Charles interrupted; she was indeed giving him thousands of worries; her palpitations were beginning again. Then Rodolphe asked if riding would not be helpful.

"Certainly! excellent, just the thing! What a good idea! You ought to try it."

And as she objected that she had no horse, Monsieur Rodolphe offered one. She refused his offer; he did not insist. Then to explain his visit he said that his ploughman, the man of the blood-letting, still suffered from dizziness.

"I'll drop by," said Bovary.

"No, no! I'll send him to you; we'll come; that will be more convenient for you."

"Ah! very good! I thank you."

And as soon as they were alone, "Why don't you accept Monsieur Boulanger's offer? It was so gracious of him."

She seemed to pout, invented a thousand excuses, and finally declared that perhaps it would look odd.

"That's the least of my worries!" said Charles, turning on his heel. "Health first! You are making a mistake."

"Could I go riding without proper clothes?"

"You must order a riding outfit," he answered.

The riding-habit decided her.

When it was ready, Charles wrote to Monsieur Boulanger that his wife was able to accept his invitation and thanked him in advance for his kindness.

The next day at noon Rodolphe appeared at Charles's door with two saddle-horses. One had pink rosettes at his ears and a deerskin side-saddle.

Rodolphe had put on high soft boots, assuming that she had never seen the likes of them. In fact, Emma was charmed with his appearance as he stood on the landing in his great velvet coat and white corduroy breeches. She was ready; she was waiting for him.

Justin escaped from the store to watch her depart, and the pharmacist himself also came out. He was giving Monsieur Boulanger some good advice.

"An accident happens so easily. Be careful! Your horses may be skittish!"

She heard a noise above her; it was Félicité drumming on the window-panes to amuse little Berthe. The child blew her a kiss; her mother answered with a wave of her whip.

"Have a pleasant ride!" cried Monsieur Homais. "Be careful! above all, be careful!"

And he flourished his newspaper as he saw them disappear.

As soon as he felt the ground, Emma's horse set off at a gallop. Rodolphe galloped by her side. Now and then they exchanged a word. With slightly bent head, her hand well up, and her right arm stretched out, she gave herself up to the cadence of the movement that rocked her in her saddle.

At the bottom of the hill Rodolphe gave his horse its head; they set off together at a bound, then at the top suddenly the horses stopped, and her large blue veil fell about her.

It was early in October. There was fog over the land. Hazy clouds hovered on the horizon between the outlines of the hills; others, rent asunder, floated up and disappeared. Sometimes through a rift in the clouds, beneath a ray of sunshine, gleamed from afar the roofs of Yonville, with the gardens at the water's edge, the yards, the walls and the church steeple. Emma half closed her eyes to pick out her house, and never had this poor village where she lived appeared so small. From the height on which they were the whole valley seemed an immense pale lake sending off its vapour into the air. Clumps of trees here and there stood out like black rocks, and the tall lines of the poplars that rose above the mist were like a beach stirred by the wind.

By the side, on the grass between the pines, a brown light shimmered in the warm atmosphere. The earth, ruddy like the powder of tobacco, deadened the noise of their steps, and as they walked, the horses kicked up fallen pine cones before them.

Rodolphe and Emma thus skirted the woods. She turned away from time to time to avoid his look, and then she saw only the line of pine trunks, whose monotonous succession made her a little giddy. The horses were panting; the leather of the saddles creaked.

Just as they were entering the forest the sun came out.

"God is with us!" said Rodolphe.

"Do you think so?" she said.

"Forward! forward!" he continued.

He clucked with his tongue. The horses set off at a trot.

Long ferns by the roadside caught in Emma's stirrup. Rodolphe leant forward and removed them as they rode along. At other times, to turn aside the branches, he passed close to her, and Emma felt his knee brushing against her leg. The sky was blue now. The leaves no longer stirred. There were spaces full of heather in flower, and patches of purple alternated with the confused tangle of the trees, grey, fawn, or golden colored, according to the nature of their leaves. Often in the thicket one could hear the fluttering of wings, or else the hoarse, soft cry of the ravens flying off amidst the oaks.

They dismounted. Rodolphe fastened up the horses. She walked on in front of the moss between the paths.

But her long dress got in her way, although she held it up by the skirt; and Rodolphe, walking behind her, saw between the black cloth and the black shoe the delicacy of her white stocking, that seemed to him as if it were a part of her nakedness.

She stopped.

"I am tired," she said.

"Come, try some more," he went on. "Courage!"

Some hundred paces further on she stopped again, and through her veil, that fell sideways from her man's hat over her hips, her face appeared in a bluish transparency as if she were floating under azure waves.

"But where are we going?"

He did not answer. She was breathing irregularly. Rodolphe looked round him biting his moustache.

They came to a larger space which had been cleared of undergrowth. They sat down on the trunk of a fallen tree, and Rodolphe began speaking to her of his love.

He did not frighten her at first with compliments. He was calm, serious, melancholy.

Emma listened to him with bowed head, and stirred the bits of wood on the ground with the tip of her foot.

But at the words, "Are not our destinies now forever united?"

"Oh, no!" she replied. "You know they aren't. It is impossible!"

She rose to go. He seized her by the wrist. She stopped. Then, having gazed at him for a few moments with an amorous and moist look, she said hurriedly:

"Well, let's not speak of it again! Where are the horses? Let's go back."

He made a gesture of anger and annoyance. She repeated:

"Where are the horses? Where are the horses?"

Then smiling a strange smile, looking straight at her, his teeth set, he advanced with outstretched arms. She recoiled trembling. She stammered:

"Oh, you frighten me! You hurt me! Take me back!"

"If it must be," he went on, his face changing; and he again became respectful, caressing, timid. She gave him her arm. They went back. He said:

"What was the matter with you? Why? I do not understand. You were mistaken, no doubt. In my soul you are as a Madonna on a pedestal, in a place lofty, secure, immaculate. But I cannot live without you! I need your eyes, your voice, your thought! Be my friend, my sister, my angel!"

And he stretched out his arm and caught her by the waist. Gently she tried to disengage herself. He supported her thus as they walked along.

They heard the two horses browsing on the leaves.

"Not quite yet!" said Rodolphe. "Stay a minute longer! Please stay!"

He drew her farther on to a small pool where duckweeds made a greenness on the water. Faded waterlilies lay motionless between the reeds. At the noise of their steps in the grass, frogs jumped away to hide themselves.

"I shouldn't, I shouldn't!" she said. "I am out of my mind listening to you!"

"Why? . . . Emma! Emma!"

"Oh, Rodolphe! . . ." she said slowly and she pressed against his shoulder.

The cloth of her dress clung to the velvet of his coat. She threw back her white neck which swelled in a sigh, and, faltering, weeping, and hiding her face in her hands, with one long shudder, she abandoned herself to him.

The shades of night were falling; the horizontal sun passing between the branches dazzled the eyes. Here and there around her, in the leaves or on the ground, trembled luminous patches, as if humming-birds flying about had scattered their feathers. Silence was everywhere; something sweet seemed to come forth from the trees. She felt her heartbeat return, and the blood coursing through her flesh like a river of milk. Then far away, beyond the wood, on the other hills, she heard a vague prolonged cry, a voice which lingered, and in silence she heard it mingling like music with the last pulsations of her throbbing nerves. Rodolphe, a cigar between his lips, was mending with his penknife one of the two broken bridles.

They returned to Yonville by the same road. On the mud they saw again the traces of their horses side by side, the same thickets, the same stones in the grass; nothing around them seemed changed; and yet for her something had happened more stupendous than if the mountains had moved in their places. Rodolphe now and again bent forward and took her hand to kiss it.

She was charming on horseback—upright, with her slender waist, her knee bent on the mane of her horse, her face somewhat flushed by the fresh air in the red of the evening.

On entering Yonville she made her horse prance in the road.

People looked at her from the windows.

At dinner her husband thought she looked well, but she pretended not to hear him when he inquired about her ride, and she remained sitting there with her elbow at the side of her plate between the two lighted candles.

"Emma!" he said.

"What?"

"Well, I spent the afternoon at Monsieur Alexandre's. He has an old filly, still very fine, just a little broken in the knees, and that could be bought, I am sure, for a hundred crowns." He added, "And thinking it might please you, I have reserved her . . . I bought her . . . Have I done right? Do tell me!"

She nodded her head in assent; then a quarter of an hour later:

"Are you going out to-night?" she asked.

"Yes. Why?"

"Oh, nothing, nothing, dear!"

And as soon as she had got rid of Charles she went and shut herself up in her room.

At first she felt stunned; she saw the trees, the paths, the ditches, Rodolphe, and she again felt the pressure of his arms, while the leaves rustled and the reeds whistled.

But when she saw herself in the mirror she wondered at her face. Never had her eyes been so large, so black, nor so deep. Something subtle about her being transfigured her.

She repeated: "I have a lover! a lover!" delighting at the idea as if a second puberty had come to her. So at last she was to know those joys of love, that fever of happiness of which she had despaired! She was entering upon a marvelous world where all would be passion, ecstasy, delirium. She felt herself surrounded by an endless rapture. A blue space surrounded her and ordinary existence appeared only intermittently between these heights, dark and far away beneath her.

Then she recalled the heroines of the books that she had read, and the lyric legion of these adulterous women began to sing in her memory with the voice of sisters that charmed her. She became herself, as it were, an actual part of these lyrical imaginings; at long last, as she saw herself among those lovers she had so envied, she fulfilled the love-dream of her youth. Besides, Emma felt a satisfaction of revenge. How she had suffered! But she had won out at last, and the love so long pent up erupted in joyous outbursts. She tasted it without remorse, without anxiety, without concern.

The next day brought a new-discovered sweetness. They exchanged vows. She told him of her sorrows. Rodolphe interrupted her with kisses; and she, looking at him through half-closed eyes, asked him to call her again by her name and to say that he loved her. They were in the forest, as yesterday, this time in the hut of some *sabot* makers. The walls were of straw, and the roof so low they had to stoop. They were seated side by side on a bed of dry leaves.

From that day on they wrote to one another regularly every evening. Emma placed her letter at the end of the garden, by the river, in a crack of the wall. Rodolphe came to fetch it, and put another in its place that she always accused of being too short.

One morning, when Charles had gone out before daybreak, she felt the urge to see Rodolphe at once. She would go quickly to La Huchette, stay there an hour, and be back again at Yonville while every one was still asleep. The idea made her breathless with desire, and she soon found herself in the middle of the field, walking with rapid steps, without looking behind her.

Day was just breaking. Emma recognised her lover's house from a distance. Its two dove-tailed weathercocks stood out black against the pale dawn.

Beyond the farmyard there was a separate building that she assumed must be the château. She entered it as if the doors at her approach had opened wide of their own accord. A large straight staircase led up to the corridor. Emma raised the latch of a door, and suddenly at the end of the room she saw a man sleeping. It was Rodolphe. She uttered a cry.

"You here? You here?" he repeated. "How did you manage to come? Ah! Your dress is wet."

"I love you!" she answered, winding her arm around his neck.

This first bold attempt having been successful, now every time Charles went out early Emma dressed quickly and slipped on tiptoe down the steps that led to the waterside.

But when the cow plank was taken up, she had to follow the walls alongside the river; the bank was slippery; to keep from falling, she had to catch hold of the tufts of faded wall-flowers. Then she went across ploughed fields, stumbling, her thin shoes sinking in the heavy mud. Her scarf, knotted round her head, fluttered to the wind in the meadows. She was afraid of the oxen; she began to run; she arrived out of breath, with rosy cheeks, and breathing out from her whole person a fresh perfume of sap, of verdure, of the open air. At this hour Rodolphe was still asleep. It was like a spring morning bursting into his room.

The golden curtains along the windows let a heavy, whitish light filter into the room. Emma would find her way gropingly, with blinking eyes, the drops of dew hanging from her hair, making a topaz halo around her face. Rodolphe, laughing, would draw her to him and press her to his breast.

Then she inspected the room, opened the drawers of the tables, combed her hair with his comb, and looked at herself in his shaving mirror. Often she put between her teeth the big pipe that lay on the bedtable, amongst lemons and pieces of sugar near the water bottle.

It took them a good quarter of an hour to say good-bye. Then Emma cried: she would have wished never to leave Rodolphe. Something stronger than herself drew her to him; until, one day, when she arrived unexpectedly, he frowned as one put out.

"What is wrong?" she said. "Are you ill? tell me!"

He ended up declaring earnestly that her visits were too dangerous and that she was compromising herself.

X

Gradually Rodolphe's fears took possession of her. At first, love had intoxicated her, and she had thought of nothing beyond. But now that he was indispensable to her life, she feared losing the smallest part of his love or upsetting him in the least. When she came back from his house, she looked all about her, anxiously watching every form that passed in the horizon, and every village window from which she could be seen. She listened for steps, cries, the noise of the ploughs, and she stopped short, white, and trembling more than the aspen leaves swaying overhead.

One morning as she was thus returning, she suddenly thought she saw the long barrel of a carbine that seemed to be aimed at her. It stuck out sideways from the end of a small barrel half-buried in the grass on the edge of a ditch. Emma, half-fainting with terror, nevertheless walked on, and a man stepped out of the barrel like a Jack-in-the-box jumping out of his cage. He had gaiters buckled up to the knees, his cap pulled down over his eyes; his lips shivered in the cold and his nose was red. It was Captain Binet lying in ambush for wild ducks.

"You ought to have called out long ago!" he exclaimed. "When one sees a gun, one should always give warning."

The tax-collector was thus trying to hide his own fright, for a prefectorial order prohibited duck-hunting except in boats. Monsieur Binet, despite his respect for the laws, was breaking the law and he expected to see the garde champêtre turn up any moment. But this anxiety whetted his pleasure, and, all alone in his barrel, he congratulated himself on his luck and his cleverness.

The sight of Emma seemed to relieve him of a great weight, and he at once opened the conversation.

"Pretty cold, isn't it; it's nippy!"

Emma didn't answer. He pursued:

"You're certainly off to an early start today."

"Yes," she stammered; "I am just coming from the nurse who is keeping my child."

"Ah, yes indeed, yes indeed. As for myself, I am here, just as you see me, since break of day; but the weather is so muggy, that unless one had the bird at the mouth of the gun . . ."

"Good day, Monsieur Binet," she interrupted, turning her back on him.

"Your servant, madame," he replied drily.

And he went back into his barrel.

Emma regretted having left the tax-collector so abruptly. No doubt he would jump to the worst conclusions. The story about the nurse was the weakest possible excuse, for every one at Yonville knew that the Bovary baby had been at home with her parents for a year. Besides, no one was living in this direction; this path led only to La Huchette. Binet, then, could not fail to guess where she came from, and he would not remain silent; he would talk, that was certain. She remained until evening racking her brain with every lie she could think up, but the image of that idiot with his game bag would not leave her.

Seeing her so gloomy, Charles proposed after dinner to take her to the pharmacist by way of distraction, and the first person she caught sight of in the shop was him again, the tax-collector! He was standing in front of the counter, lit up by the gleams of the red jar, saying:

"Could I have half an ounce of vitriol, please?"

"Justin," cried the pharmacist, "bring us the sulphuric acid."

Then to Emma, who was going up to Madame Homais' room, "Don't go up, it's not worth the trouble, she is just coming down. Why not warm yourself by the fire . . . Excuse me . . . Good-day, doctor" (for the pharmacist much enjoyed pronouncing the word "doctor," as if addressing another by it reflected on himself some of the grandeur of the title). "Justin, take care not to upset the mortars! You'd better fetch some chairs from the little room; you know very well that the arm-chairs are not to be taken out of the drawing-room."

And he was just about to put his arm-chair back in its place when Binet asked him for half an ounce of sugar acid.

"Sugar acid!" said the pharmacist contemptuously, "never heard of it! There is no such thing. Perhaps it is Oxalic acid you want. It is Oxalic, isn't it?"

Binet explained that he wanted a corrosive to make himself some copper-water with which to remove rust from his hunting things. Emma shuddered. The pharmacist was saying:

"Indeed, the dampness we're having is certainly not propitious."

"Nevertheless," replied the tax-collector, with a sly look, "some people seem to like it." She was stifling.

"And give me . . ."

"Will he never go?" she thought.

"Half an ounce of resin and turpentine, four ounces of beeswax, and three half ounces of animal charcoal, if you please, to clean the leather of my togs."

The druggist was beginning to cut the wax when Madame Homais appeared with Irma in her arms, Napoleon by her side, and Athalie following. She sat down on the velvet seat by the window, and the boy squatted down on a footstool, while his eldest sister hovered round the jujube box near her papa. The latter was filling funnels and corking phials, sticking on labels, making up parcels. Around him all were silent; only from time to time could one hear the weights jingling in the scales, and a few words of advice from the pharmacist to his apprentice.

"And how is your little girl?" Madame Homais asked suddenly.

"Silence!" exclaimed her husband, who was writing down some figures on a scratch pad.

"Why didn't you bring her?" she went on in a low voice.

"Hush! hush!" said Emma, pointing a finger at the pharmacist.

But Binet, quite absorbed in checking over his bill, had probably heard nothing. At last he went out. Then Emma, relieved, uttered a deep sigh.

"How heavily you are breathing!" said Madame Homais.

"It is so hot in here," she replied.

So the next day they agreed to arrange their rendezvous. Emma wanted to bribe her servant with a present, but it would be better to find some safe house at Yonville. Rodolphe promised to look for one.

All through the winter, three or four times a week, in the dead of night he came to the garden. Emma had on purpose taken away the key of the gate, letting Charles think it was lost.

To call her, Rodolphe threw a handful of sand at the shutters. She jumped up with a start; but sometimes he had to wait, for Charles had the habit of talking endlessly by the fireside.

She was wild with impatience; if her eyes could have done it, they would have hurled him out of the window. At last she would begin to undress, then take up a book, and go on reading very quietly as if the book amused her. But Charles, who was in bed, would call her to bed.

"Come, now, Emma," he said, "it is time."

"Yes, I am coming," she answered.

Then, as the candles shone in his eyes, he turned to the wall and fell asleep. She escaped, holding her breath, smiling, half undressed.

Rodolphe had a large cloak; he wrapped it around her, and putting his arm round her waist, he drew her without a word to the end of the garden.

It was in the arbour, on the same bench of half rotten sticks where formerly Léon had stared at her so amorously on the summer evenings. She never thought of him now.

The stars shone through the leafless jasmine branches. Behind them they heard the river flowing, and now and again on the bank the rustling of the dry reeds. Masses of deeper darkness stood out here and there in the night and sometimes, shaken with one single motion, they would rise up and sway like immense black waves pressing forward to engulf them. The cold of the nights made them clasp each other more tightly; the sighs of their lips seemed to them deeper; their eyes, that they could hardly see, larger; and in the midst of the silence words softly spoken would fall on their souls with a crystalline sound, that echoed in endless reverberations.

When the night was rainy, they took refuge in the consulting-room between the cart-shed and the stable. She would light one of the kitchen candles that she had hidden behind the books. Rodolphe settled down there as if at home. The sight of the library, of the desk, of the entire room, in fine, would arouse his mirth; and he could not refrain from making jokes at Charles's expense despite Emma's embarrassment. She would have liked to see him more serious, and even on occasions more dramatic; as, for example, when she thought she heard a noise of approaching steps in the alley.

"Some one is coming!" she said.

He blew out the light.

"Have you your pistols?"

"Why?"

"Why, to defend yourself," replied Emma.

"From your husband? Oh, the poor fellow!" And Rodolphe finished his sentence with a gesture that said, "I could crush him with a flip of my finger."

She was awed at his bravery, although she felt in it a sort of indecency and a naïve coarseness that scandalised her.

Rodolphe reflected a good deal on the pistol incident. If she had spoken in earnest, he thought it most ridiculous, even odious; for he had no reason whatever to hate the good Charles, not exactly being devoured by jealousy; and in this same connection, Emma had made him a solemn promise that he did not think in the best of taste.

Besides, she was becoming dreadfully sentimental. She had insisted on exchanging miniatures; handfuls of hair had been cut off, and now she was asking for a ring—a real wedding-ring, in token of eternal union. She often spoke to him of the evening chimes, of the "voices of nature." Then she talked to him of their respective mothers. Rodolphe's had died twenty years ago. Emma none the less consoled him with conventional phrases, like those one would use with a bereaved child; sometimes she even said to him, gazing at the moon:

"I am sure that, from up there, both approve our love."

But she was so pretty! He had possessed so few women of similar ingenuousness. This love without debauchery was a new experience for him, and, drawing him out of his lazy habits, caressed at once his pride and his sensuality. Although his bourgeois common sense disapproved of it, Emma's exaltations, deep down in his heart, enchanted him, since they were directed his way. Then, sure of her love, he no longer made an effort, and insensibly his manner changed.

No longer did he, as before, find words so tender that they made her cry, nor passionate caresses that drove her into ecstasy; their great love, in which she had lived immersed, seemed to run out beneath her, like the water of a river absorbed by its own bed; and she could see the bottom. She would not believe it; she redoubled in tenderness, and Rodolphe concealed his indifference less and less.

She did not know if she regretted having yielded to him, or whether she did not wish, on the contrary, to love him even more. The humiliation of having given in turned into resentment, tempered by their voluptuous pleasures. It was not tenderness; it was like a continual seduction. He held her fully in his power; she almost feared him.

On the surface, however, things seemed calm enough, Rodolphe having carried out his adultery just as he had wanted; and at the end of six months, when the spring-time came, they were to one another like a married couple, tranquilly keeping up a domestic flame.

It was the time of year when old Rouault sent his turkey in rememberance of the setting of his leg. The present always arrived with a letter. Emma cut the string that tied it to the basket, and read the following lines:

> My Dear Children,—I hope this will find you in good health, and that it will be as good as the others, for it seems to me a little more tender, if I may venture to say so, and heavier. But next time, for a change, I'll give you a turkeycock, unless you would prefer a capon; and send me back the hamper, if you please, with the two old ones. I have had an accident with sheds; the coverings flew off one windy night among the trees. The harvest has not been over-good either. Finally, I don't know when I shall come to see you. It is so difficult now to leave the house since I am alone, my poor Emma.

Here there was a break in the lines as if the old fellow had dropped his pen to dream a little while.

> As for myself, I am very well, except for a cold I caught the other day at Yvetot, where I had gone to hire a shepherd, having got rid of mine because no cooking was good enough for his taste. We are to be pitied with rascals like him! Moreover, he was dishonest.
> I heard from a peddler who had a tooth pulled out when he passed through your part of the country this winter, that Bovary was as usual working hard. That doesn't surprise me; and he showed me his tooth; we had some coffee together. I asked him if he had seen you, and he said no, but that he had seen two horses in the stables, from which I conclude that business is looking up. So much the better, my dear children, and may God send you every imaginable happiness!

It grieves me not yet to have seen my dear little grand-daughter, Berthe Bovary. I have planted an Orleans plum-tree for her in the garden under your room, and I won't have it touched until we can make jam from it, that I will keep in the cupboard for her when she comes.

Good-bye, my dear children. I kiss you, my girl, you too, my son-in-law, and the little one on both cheeks. I am, with best compliments, your loving father.

THEODORE ROUAULT

She held the coarse paper in her fingers for some minutes. A continuous stream of spelling mistakes ran through the letter, and Emma followed the kindly thought that cackled right through it like a hen half hidden in a hedge of thorns. The writing had been dried with ashes from the hearth, for a little grey powder slipped from the letter on her dress, and she almost thought she saw her father bending over the hearth to take up the tongs. How long since she had been with him, sitting on the footstool in the chimney-corner, where she used to burn the end of a stick in the crackling flame of the sea-sedges! She remembered the summer evenings all full of sunshine. The colts whinnied when one passed by, and galloped, galloped . . . Under her window there was a beehive and at times, the bees wheeling round in the light, struck against her window like rebounding balls of gold. What happiness she had known at that time, what freedom, what hope! What a wealth of illusions! It was all gone now. She had lost them one by one, at every stage in the growth of her soul, in the succession of her conditions; maidenhood, marriage and love—shedding them along her path like a traveller who leaves something of his wealth at every inn along his road.

But who was it, then, who made her so unhappy? What extraordinary catastrophe had destroyed her life? And she raised her head, as if seeking around her for the cause of all that suffering.

An April sunray was dancing on the china in the shelves; the fire burned; beneath her slippers she felt the softness of the carpet; the day was bright, the air warm, and she heard her child shouting with laughter.

In fact, the little girl was just then rolling on the lawn in the new-mown grass. She was lying flat on her stomach at the top of a rick. The maid was holding her by her skirt. Lestiboudois was raking by her side, and every time he came near she bent forward, beating the air with both her arms.

"Bring her to me," said her mother, rushing over to kiss her. "How I love you, my poor child! How I love you!"

Then noticing that the tips of her ears were rather dirty, she rang at once for warm water, and washed her, changed her underwear, her stockings, her shoes, asked a thousand questions about her health, as if on the return from a long journey, and finally, kissing her again and crying a little, she gave her back to the maid, who was dumbfounded at this sudden outburst.

That evening Rodolphe found her more reserved than usual.

"It will blow over," he thought, "a passing whim . . ."

And he missed three successive rendezvous. When he did appear, her attitude was cold, almost contemptuous.

"Ah! you're wasting time, sweetheart!"

And he pretended not to notice her melancholy sighs, nor the handkerchief she pulled out.

Then Emma knew what it was to repent!

She even wondered why she hated Charles; wouldn't it have been better trying to love him? But he offered little hold for these reawakened sentiments, so she remained rather embarrassed with her sacrificial intentions until the pharmacist provided her with a timely opportunity.

XI

He had recently read a paper praising a new method for curing club-foot, and since he was a partisan of progress, he conceived the patriotic idea that Yonville should show its pioneering spirit by having some club-foot operations performed there.

"Look here," he told Emma, "what do we risk?" and he ticked off on his fingers the advantages of the attempt, "success practically assured, relief and better appearance for the patient, quick fame for the surgeon. Why, for example, should not your husband relieve poor Hippolyte of the Lion d'Or? He is bound to tell all passing travellers about his cure, and then" (Homais lowered his voice and looked round him) "who is to prevent me from sending a short piece on the subject to the paper? And! My God! an article gets around . . . people talk about it . . . it snowballs! And who knows? who knows?"

After all, Bovary might very well succeed. Emma had no reason to suppose he lacked skill, it would be a satisfaction for her to have urged him to a step by which his reputation and fortune would be increased! She only longed to lean on something more solid than love.

Pressed by her and the pharmacist, Charles allowed himself to be persuaded. He went to Rouen for Dr. Duval's volume, and every evening, with his head between his hands, he embarked on his reading assignment.

While he struggled with the equinus, varus, and valgus—that is to say, *katastrephopody*, *endostrephopody*, and *exostrephopody*, or in other words, the various deviations of the foot, to the inside, outside, or downwards, as well as with *hypostrephopody* and *anastrephopody*

or torsion below and contraction above,—Monsieur Homais was trying
out all possible arguments on the stable boy in order to persuade him
to submit to the operation.

"At the very most you'll feel a slight pain, a small prick, like a
little blood letting, less than the extraction of certain corns."

Hippolyte thought it over, rolling his stupid eyes.

"Anyway," continued the pharmacist, "it is none of my business.
I am telling you this for your own sake! out of pure humanity! I
would like to see you freed from that hideous caudication as well as
that swaying in your lumbar region which, whatever you say, must
considerably interfere with the proper performance of your work."

Then Homais represented to him how much more dashing and
nimble he would feel afterwards, and even hinted that he would be
more likely to please the women; and the stable boy broke into a
stupid grin. Then he attacked him through his vanity:

"Come on, act like a man! Think what would have happened if
you had been called into the army, and had to fight under our national
banner! . . . Ah! Hippolyte!"

And Homais left him, declaring that he could not understand such
blindness, such obstinacy, in refusing the benefits of science.

The poor wretch finally gave in, for it was like a conspiracy. Binet,
who never interfered with other people's business, Madame Lefrançois, Artémise, the neighbors, even the mayor, Monsieur Tuvache—
every one tried to convince him by lecture and reproof; but what
finally won him over was that it would cost him nothing. Bovary
even undertook to provide the machine for the operation. This generosity was an idea of Emma's, and Charles consented to it, thinking
in his heart of hearts that his wife was an angel.

So with the advice of the pharmacist, and after three fresh starts,
he had a kind of box made by the carpenter, with the assistance of
the locksmith; it weighed about eight pounds, for iron, wood, sheet-
iron, leather, screws, and nuts had not been spared.

Yet, to know which of Hippolyte's tendons had to be cut, it was
necessary first of all to find out what kind of club-foot he had.

His foot almost formed a straight line with the leg, which, however, did not prevent it from being turned in, so that it was an equinus
combined with something of a varus, or else a slight varus with a
strong tendency to equinus. But on the equine foot, wide indeed as
a horse's hoof, with its horny skin, and large toes, whose black nails
resembled the nails of a horse shoe, the cripple ran about like a deer
from morn till night. He was constantly to be seen on the Square,
jumping round the carts, thrusting his limping foot forwards. He
seemed even stronger on that leg than the other. By dint of hard
service it had acquired, as it were, moral qualities of patience and
energy; and when he was given some heavy work to do, he would

support himself on it in preference to the sound one.

Now, as it was an equinus, it was necessary to cut the Achilles tendon first; if need be, the anterior tibial muscle could be seen to afterwards to take care of the varus. For the doctor did not dare to risk both operations at once; he was already sufficiently worried for fear of injuring some important region that he did not know.

Neither Ambroise Paré, applying a ligature to an artery, for the first time since Celsus did it fifteen centuries before; nor Dupuytren, cutting open abscesses through a thick layer of brain; nor Gensoul on first removing the superior maxilla, had hearts that trembled, hands that shook, minds that strained as Monsieur Bovary's when he approached Hippolyte, his tenotomy knife between his fingers. Just as in a hospital, near by on a table lay a heap of lint, with waxed thread, many bandages—a pyramid of bandages—every bandage to be found at the pharmacy. It was Monsieur Homais who since morning had been organising all these preparations, as much to dazzle the multitude as to keep up his illusions. Charles pierced the skin; a dry crackling was heard. The tendon was cut, the operation over. Hippolyte could not believe his eyes: he bent over Bovary's hands to cover them with kisses.

"Come, be calm," said the pharmacist; "later on you will show your gratitude to your benefactor."

And he went down to report the result to five or six bystanders who were waiting in the yard, and who fancied that Hippolyte would reappear walking straight up. Then Charles, having strapped his patient into the machine, went home, where Emma was anxiously waiting for him on the doorstep. She threw herself on his neck; they sat down at the table; he ate much, and at dessert he even wanted to take a cup of coffee, a luxury he only permitted himself on Sundays when there was company.

The evening was charming, full of shared conversation and common dreams. They talked about their future success, of the improvements to be made in their house; with his rising reputation, he saw his comforts increasing, his wife always loving him; and she was happy to refresh herself with a new sentiment, healthier and purer, and to feel at last some tenderness for this poor man who adored her. The thought of Rodolphe for one moment passed through her mind, but her eyes turned again to Charles; she even noticed with surprise that he had rather handsome teeth.

They were in bed when Monsieur Homais, sidestepping the cook, suddenly entered the room, holding in his hand a newly written sheet of paper. It was the article he intended for the "Fanal de Rouen." He brought it them to read.

"You read it," said Bovary.

He read:

" 'Braving the prejudices that still spread over the face of Europe like a net, the light nevertheless begins to penetrate into our country places. Thus on Tuesday our little town of Yonville found itself the scene of a surgical operation which was at the same time an act of loftiest philanthropy. Monsieur Bovary, one of our most distinguished practitioners . . .' "

"Oh, that is too much! too much!" said Charles, choking with emotion.

—"But certainly not! far from it! . . . 'operated on a club-foot.' I have not used the scientific term, because you know in newspapers . . . not everyone would understand . . . the masses, after all, must . . ."

"Certainly," said Bovary; "please go on!"

"I proceed," said the pharmacist. " 'Monsieur Bovary, one of our most distinguished practitioners, performed an operation on a club-footed man, one Hippolyte Tautain, stable-man for the last twenty-five years at the hotel of the Lion d'Or, kept by Widow Lefrançois, at the Place d'Armes. The novelty of the experiment and the general interest in the patient had attracted such a number of people that a crowd gathered on the threshold of the establishment. The operation, moreover, was performed as if by magic, and barely a few drops of blood appeared on the skin, as though to say that the rebellious tendon had at last given way under the efforts of the medical arts. The patient, strangely enough (we affirm it *de visu*), complained of no pain. His condition up to the present time leaves nothing to be desired. Everything tends to show that his convalescence will be brief; and who knows if, at our next village festivity we shall not see our good Hippolyte appear in the midst of a bacchic dance, surrounded by a group of gay companions, and thus bear witness to all assembled, by his spirit and his capers, of his total recovery? Honor, then, to those generous men of science! Honor to those tireless spirits who consecrate their vigils to the improvement and relief of their kind! Honor to them! Hasn't the time come to cry out that the blind shall see, the deaf hear, the lame walk? What fanaticism formerly promised to a few elect, science now accomplishes for all men. We shall keep our readers informed as to the subsequent progression of this remarkable cure.' "

All this did not prevent Mère Lefrançois from coming five days later, scared out of her wits and shouting:

"Help! he is dying! I am going out of my mind!"

Charles rushed to the Lion d'Or, and the pharmacist, who caught sight of him passing along the Square without a hat, left his shop. He arrived himself breathless, flushed, anxious, and asked from every one who was going up the stairs:

"What can be the matter with our interesting patient?"

The interesting patient was writhing, in dreadful convulsions, so violent that the contraption in which his foot was locked almost beat down the wall.

With many precautions, in order not to disturb the position of the limb, the box was removed, and an awful spectacle came into view. The outlines of the foot disappeared in such a swelling that the entire skin seemed about to burst; moreover, the leg was covered with bruises caused by the famous machine. Hippolyte had abundantly complained, but nobody had paid any attention to him; now they admitted he might have some grounds for protest and he was freed for a few hours. But hardly had the oedema somewhat gone down, that the two specialists thought fit to put back the limb in the machine, strapping it even tighter to speed up matters. At last, three days after, when Hippolyte could not stand it any longer, they once more removed the machine, and were much surprised at the result they saw. A livid tumescence spread over the entire leg, and a black liquid oozed from several blisters. Things had taken a turn for the worse. Hippolyte was getting bored, and Mère Lefrançois had him installed in the little room near the kitchen, so that he might at least have some distraction.

But the tax-collector, who dined there every day, complained bitterly of such companionship. Then Hippolyte was removed to the billiard-room.

He lay there moaning under his heavy blankets, pale and unshaven, with sunken eyes; from time to time he rubbed his sweating head over the fly-covered pillow. Madame Bovary came to see him. She brought him linen for his poultices; she comforted, and encouraged him. Besides, he did not want for company, especially on market days, when farmers around him were hitting the billiard balls around and fencing with the cues while they drank, sang and brawled.

"How are things?" they would say, clapping him on the shoulder. "Ah! not so well from what we hear. But that's your fault. You should do this! do that!"

And then they told him stories of people who had all been cured by other means. Then by way of consolation they added:

"You pamper yourself too much! You should get up; you coddle yourself like a king. Just the same, old boy, you do smell pretty awful!"

Gangrene was indeed spreading higher and higher. It made Bovary ill to think of it. He came every hour, every moment. Hippolyte looked at him with terrified eyes and sobbed:

"When will I be cured?—Oh, please save me! . . . How unhappy I am! . . . How unhappy I am!"

And the doctor left him, prescribing a strict diet.

"Don't listen to him," said Mère Lefrançois. "Haven't they tortured you enough already? You'll grow still weaker. Here! swallow this."

And she gave him some strong broth, a slice of mutton, a piece of bacon, and sometimes small glasses of brandy, that he had not the strength to put to his lips.

The abbé Bournisien, hearing that he was growing worse, asked to see him. He began by pitying his sufferings, declaring at the same time that he ought to rejoice since it was the will of the Lord, and hasten to reconcile himself with Heaven.

"For," said the ecclesiastic in a paternal tone, "you rather neglected your duties; you were rarely seen at divine worship. How many years is it since you approached the holy table? I understand that your work, that the whirl of the world may have distracted you from your salvation. But now the time has come. Yet don't despair. I have known great sinners, who, about to appear before God (you are not yet at this point I know), had implored His mercy, and who certainly died in a truly repenting frame of mind. Let us hope that, like them, you will set us a good example! Thus, as a precaution, what is to prevent you from saying morning and evening a Hail Mary and an Our Father? Yes, do that, for my sake, to oblige me. That won't cost you anything. Will you promise me?"

The poor devil promised. The curé came back day after day. He chatted with the landlady, and even told anecdotes interspersed with jokes and puns that Hippolyte did not understand. Then, as soon as he could, he would return to religious considerations, putting on an appropriate expression.

His zeal seemed to bring results, for the club-foot soon manifested a desire to go on a pilgrimage to Bon-Secours if he were cured; to which Monsieur Bournisien replied that he saw no objection; two precautions were better than one; moreover, it certainly could do no harm.

The pharmacist was incensed by what he called the priest's machinations; they were prejudicial, he said, to Hippolyte's convalescence, and he kept repeating to Madame Lefrançois, "Leave him alone! leave him alone! You're ruining his morale with your mysticism."

But the good woman would no longer listen to him; she blamed him for being the cause of it all. In sheer rebellion, she hung near the patient's bedside a well-filled basin of holy water and a sprig of boxwood.

Religion, however, seemed no more able than surgery to bring relief and the irresistible putrefaction kept spreading from the foot to the groin. It was all very well to vary the potions and change the poultices; the muscles each day rotted more and more; Charles replied by an affirmative nod of the head when Mère Lefrançois asked him if she could not, as a last resort, send for Monsieur Canivet, a famous surgeon from Neufchâtel.

Charles' fifty-year old colleague, a doctor of medicine with a well established practice and a solid self-confidence, did not refrain from laughing disdainfully when he had uncovered the leg, gangrened to the knee. Then having flatly declared that it must be amputated, he went off to the pharmacist's to rail at the asses who could have reduced a poor man to such a state. Shaking Monsieur Homais by his coat-button, he shouted for everyone to hear:

"That is what you get from listening to the fads from Paris! What will they come up with next, these gentlemen from the capital! It is like strabismus, chloroform, lithotrity, monstrosities the Government ought to prohibit. But they want to be clever and cram you full of remedies without troubling about the consequences. We are not so clever out here, not we! We are no specialists, no cure-alls, no fancy talkers! We are practitioners; we cure people, and we wouldn't dream of operating on someone who is in perfect health. Straighten club-feet! As if one could straighten club-feet indeed! It is as if one wished to make a hunchback straight!"

Homais suffered as he listened to this discourse, and he concealed his discomfort beneath a courtier's smile; for he needed to humour Monsieur Canivet, whose prescriptions sometimes came as far as Yonville. So he did not take up the defence of Bovary; he did not even make a single remark, and, renouncing his principles, he sacrificed his dignity to the more serious interests of his business.

This thigh amputation by Doctor Canivet was a great event in the village. On that day all the inhabitants got up earlier, and the Grande Rue, crowded as it was, had something lugubrious about it, as though one were preparing for an execution. At the grocers they discussed Hippolyte's illness; the shops did no business, and Madame Tuvache, the mayor's wife, did not stir from her window, such was her impatience to see the surgeon arrive.

He came in his gig, which he drove himself. The springs of the right side had all given way beneath his corpulence and the carriage tilted a little as it rolled along, revealing on the cushion near him a large case covered in red sheep-leather, whose three brass clasps shone grandly.

Like a whirlwind, the doctor entered the porch of the Lion d'Or and, shouting loudly, he ordered to unharness. Then he went into the stable to see that his horse was eating his oats all right; for on arriving at a patient's he first of all looked after his mare and his gig. The habit made people say, "Ah, that Monsieur Canivet, what a character!" but he was the more esteemed for his composure. The universe as a whole might have been blown apart, and he would not have changed the least of his habits.

Homais introduced himself.

"I count on you," said the doctor. "Are you ready? Come along!"

But the pharmacist blushingly confessed that he was too sensitive to witness such an operation.

"When one is a simple spectator," he said, "the imagination, you know, is easily impressed. And then, my nerves are so . . ."

"Bah!" interrupted Canivet; "on the contrary, you seem like the apoplectic type to me. But I am not surprised, for you gentlemen pharmacists are always poking about your kitchens, which must end by spoiling your constitutions. Now just look at me. I get up every day at four o'clock; I shave with cold water (and am never cold). I don't wear flannel underwear, and I never catch cold; my carcass is good enough! I take things in my stride, philosophically, as they come my way. That is why I am not squeamish like you, and it doesn't matter to me whether I carve up a Christian or the first fowl that comes my way. Habit, you'll say . . . mere habit! . . ."

Then, without any consideration for Hippolyte, who was sweating with agony between his sheets, these gentlemen began a conversation, in which the druggist compared the coolness of a surgeon to that of a general; and his comparison was pleasing to Canivet, who held forth on the demands of his art. He looked upon it as a sacred office, although the ordinary practitioners dishonored it. At last, coming back to the patient, he examined the bandages brought by Homais, the same that had appeared for the club-foot, and asked for some one to hold the limb for him. Lestiboudois was sent for, and Monsieur Canivet having turned up his sleeves, passed into the billiard-room, while the druggist stayed with Artémise and the landlady, both whiter than their aprons, and with ears strained towards the door.

Meanwhile, Bovary didn't dare to stir from his house.

He kept downstairs in the sitting-room by the side of the fireless chimney, his chin on his breast, his hands clasped, his eyes staring. "What a misfortune," he thought, "what a disappointment!" Yet, he had taken all possible precautions. Luck must have been against him. All the same, if Hippolyte died later on, he would be considered the murderer. And how would he defend himself against the questions his patients were bound to ask him during his calls? Maybe, after all, he had made some slip. He thought and thought, but nothing came. The most famous surgeons also made mistakes. But no one would ever believe that; on the contrary, people would laugh, jeer! The news would spread as far as Neufchâtel, as Rouen, everywhere! Who could say if his colleagues would not write against him? Polemics would ensue; he would have to answer in the papers. Hippolyte might even prosecute him. He saw himself dishonored, ruined, lost; and his imagination, assailed by numberless hypotheses, tossed amongst them like an empty cask dragged out to sea and pitched about by the waves.

Emma, opposite, watched him; she did not share his humiliation; she felt another—that of having imagined that such a man could have any worth, as if twenty times already she had not sufficiently perceived his mediocrity.

Charles was pacing the room. His boots creaked on the floor.

"Sit down," she said; "you irritate me!"

He sat down again.

How was it that she—she, who was so intelligent—could have allowed herself to be deceived again? Moreover, what madness had driven her to ruin her life by continual sacrifices! She recalled all her instincts of luxury, all the privations of her soul, the sordidness of marriage, of the household, her dreams sinking into the mire like wounded swallows; all that she had longed for, all that she had denied herself, all that she might have had! And for what? for what?

In the midst of the silence that hung over the village a heart-rending cry pierced the air. Bovary turned white as a sheet. She knit her brows with a nervous gesture, then returned to her thought. And it was for him, for this creature, for this man, who understood nothing, who felt nothing! For he sat there as if nothing had happened, not even suspecting that the ridicule of his name would henceforth sully hers as well as his. She had made efforts to love him, and she had repented with tears for having yielded to another!

"But it was perhaps a valgus after all!" exclaimed Bovary suddenly, interrupting his meditations.

At the unexpected shock of this phrase falling on her thought like a leaden bullet on a silver plate, Emma shuddered and raised her head in an effort to find out what he meant to say; and they gazed at one another in silence, almost amazed to see each other, so far sundered were they by their respective states of consciousness. Charles gazed at her with the dull look of a drunken man, while he listened motionless to the last cries of the sufferer, following each other in long-drawn modulations, broken by sharp spasms like the far-off howling of some beast being slaughtered. Emma bit her wan lips, and rolling between her fingers a piece of wood she had peeled from the coral-tree, fixed on Charles the burning glance of her eyes like two arrows of fire about to dart forth. Everything in him irritated her now; his face, his dress, all the things he did not say, his whole person, in short, his existence. She repented of her past virtue as of a crime, and what still remained of it crumbled away beneath the furious blows of her pride. She revelled in all the evil ironies of triumphant adultery. The memory of her lover came back to her with irresistible, dizzying attractions; she threw her whole soul towards this image, carried by renewed passion; and Charles seemed to her as removed from her life, as eternally absent, as incongruous and annihilated, as if he were dying under her very eyes.

There was a sound of steps on the pavement. Charles looked up, and through the lowered blinds he saw Dr. Canivet standing in broad sunshine at the corner of the market, wiping his brow with his handkerchief. Homais, behind him, was carrying a large red bag in his hand, and both were going towards the pharmacy.

Then with a feeling of sudden tenderness and discouragement Charles turned to his wife and said:

"Oh, kiss me, my dear!"

"Don't touch me!" she cried, flushed with anger.

"What is it? what is it?" he repeated, in utter bewilderment. "Don't be upset! calm down! You know that I love you . . . come! . . ."

"Stop it!" she cried with a terrible look.

And rushing from the room, Emma closed the door so violently that the barometer fell from the wall and smashed on the floor.

Charles sank back into his arm-chair thoroughly shaken, wondering what could have come over her, imagining it might be some nervous disease, weeping, and vaguely feeling something fatal and incomprehensible was whirling around him.

When Rodolphe came to the garden that evening, he found his mistress waiting for him at the foot of the steps on the lowest stair. They threw their arms round one another, and all their rancor melted like snow beneath the warmth of that kiss.

XII

Their love resumed its course. Often in the middle of the day, Emma would suddenly write to him, then beckon Justin through the window; he quickly untied his apron and flew to La Huchette. Rodolphe would come; she had to tell him again how bored she was, that her husband was odious, her life dreadful.

"What do you expect me to do about it?" he asked one day impatiently.

"Ah, if only you wanted . . ."

She was sitting on the floor between his knees, her hair loosened, staring in a void.

"Wanted what?" said Rodolphe.

She sighed.

"We would go and live elsewhere . . . anywhere . . ."

"Are you out of your mind!" he said laughing. "How could we?"

She mentioned it again; he pretended not to understand, and changed the subject. What he did not understand was all this worry about so simple an affair as love. But she had a motive, a reason that gave added grounds to her attachment.

Her tenderness, in fact, grew daily as her repulsion toward her husband increased. The more she yielded to the one, the more she loathed the other. Never did Charles seem so unattractive, slow-witted, clumsy and vulgar as when she met him after her rendezvous with Rodolphe. Then while playing the part of the virtuous wife, she would burn with passion at the thought of his head, the black curl falling over the sun-tanned brow; of his figure, both elegant and strong, of the man so experienced in his thought, so impetuous in his desires! It was for him that she filed her nails with a sculptor's care, that there was never enough cold-cream for her skin, nor patchouli for her handkerchiefs. She loaded herself with bracelets, rings, and necklaces. When she expected him, she filled her two large blue glass vases with roses, and prepared herself and her room like a courtesan receiving a prince. The servant was kept busy steadily laundering her linen, and all day Félicité did not stir from the kitchen, where little Justin, who often kept her company, watched her at work.

With his elbows on the long board on which she was ironing, he greedily watched all these women's garments spread out about him, the dimity petticoats, the fichus, the collars, and the drawers with running strings, wide at the hips and narrowing below.

"What is that for?" asked the young boy, passing his hand over the crinoline or the hooks and eyes.

"Why, haven't you ever seen anything?" Félicité answered laughing. "As if your mistress, Madame Homais, didn't wear the same."

"Oh, well, Madame Homais . . ."

And he added thoughtfully,

"Is she a lady like Madame?"

But Félicité grew impatient of seeing him hanging round her. She was six years older than he, and Theodore, Monsieur Guillaumin's servant, was beginning to pay court to her.

"Leave me alone," she said, moving her pot of starch. "You'd better be off and pound almonds; you are always snooping around women. Before you bother with such things, naughty boy, wait till you've got a beard to your chin."

"Oh, don't be cross! I'll go and clean her boots."

And he hurriedly took down Emma's boots from the shelf all coated with mud—the mud of the rendezvous—that crumbled into powder beneath his fingers, and that he watched as it gently rose in a ray of sunlight.

"How scared you are of spoiling them!" said the maid, who wasn't so particular when she cleaned them herself, because if the boots looked slightly worn Madame would give them to her.

Emma kept a number in her cupboard that she squandered one

after the other, without Charles allowing himself the slightest observation.

He also spent three hundred francs for a wooden leg that she thought had to be given to Hippolyte. The top was covered with cork, and it had spring joints, a complicated mechanism, covered over by black trousers ending in a patent-leather boot. But Hippolyte didn't dare use such a handsome leg every day, and he begged Madame Bovary to get him another more convenient one. The doctor, of course, had to pay for this purchase as well.

So little by little the stable-boy returned to work. One saw him running about the village as before, and when Charles heard from afar the tap of the wooden leg on the pavement, he quickly went in another direction.

It was Monsieur Lheureux, the shopkeeper, who had ordered the wooden leg. This provided him with an excuse for visiting Emma. He chatted with her about the new goods from Paris, about a thousand feminine trifles, made himself very obliging and never asked for his money. Emma yielded to this lazy mode of satisfying all her caprices. When she wanted to give Rodolphe a handsome riding-crop from an umbrella store in Rouen, Monsieur Lheureux placed it on her table the very next week.

But the next day he called on her with a bill for two hundred and seventy francs, not counting the centimes. Emma was much embarrassed; all the drawers of the writing-table were empty; they owed over a fortnight's wages to Lestiboudois, six months to the maid, and there were several other bills. Bovary was impatiently waiting to hear from Monsieur Derozeray who was in the habit of settling every year about Midsummer.

She succeeded at first in putting off Lheureux. At last he lost patience; he was being sued; he was short of capital and unless he could collect on some of his accounts, he would be forced to take back all the goods she had received.

"Oh, very well, take them!" said Emma.

"I was only joking," he replied; "the only thing I regret is the riding crop. Well, I'll have to ask Monsieur to return it to me."

"No, no!" she said.

"Ah! I've got you!" thought Lheureux.

And, certain of his discovery, he went out muttering to himself and with his usual low whistle . . .

"Good! we shall see! we shall see!"

She was wondering how to handle the situation when the maid entered and put on the mantelpiece a small roll of blue paper "with the compliments of Monsieur Derozeray." Emma grasped it, tore it open. It contained fifteen napoleons: the account paid in full. Hearing Charles on the stairs, she threw the money to the back of her drawer, and took out the key.

Three days later, Lheureux returned.

"I have a suggestion to make," he said. "If, instead of the sum, agreed on, you would take. . . ."

"Here it is," she said handing him fourteen napoleons.

The shopkeeper was taken aback. Then, to conceal his disappointment, he was profuse in apologies and offers of service, all of which Emma declined; she remained a few moments fingering in the pocket of her apron the two five-franc pieces of change he had returned to her. She told herself she would economise in order to pay back later . . . "Bah!" she thought, "he'll forget all about it."

Besides the riding-crop with its silver-gilt top, Rodolphe had received a signet with the motto *Amor nel cor*, furthermore, a scarf for a muffler, and, finally, a cigar-case exactly like the Viscount's, that Charles had formerly picked up in the road, and that Emma had kept. These presents, however, humiliated him; he refused several; she insisted, and he ended by obeying, thinking her tyrannical and over-exacting.

Then she had strange ideas.

"When midnight strikes," she said, "you must think of me."

And if he confessed that he had not thought of her, there were floods of reproaches that always ended with the eternal question:

"Do you love me?"

"Why, of course I love you," he answered.

"A great deal?"

"Certainly!"

"You haven't loved any others?"

"Did you think you'd got a virgin?" he exclaimed laughing.

Emma cried, and he tried to console her, adorning his protestations with puns.

"Oh," she went on, "I love you! I love you so that I could not live without you, do you see? There are times when I long to see you again, when I am torn by all the anger of love. I ask myself, where is he? Perhaps he is talking to other women. They smile upon him; he approaches. Oh no; no one else pleases you. There are some more beautiful, but I love you best. I know how to love best. I am your servant, your concubine! You are my king, my idol! You are good, you are beautiful, you are clever, you are strong!"

He had so often heard these things said that they did not strike him as original. Emma was like all his mistresses; and the charm of novelty, gradually falling away like a garment, laid bare the eternal monotony of passion, that has always the same shape and the same language. He was unable to see, this man so full of experience, the

variety of feelings hidden within the same expressions. Since libertine or venal lips had murmured similar phrases, he only faintly
believed in the candor of Emma's; he thought one should beware of
exaggerated declarations which only serve to cloak a tepid love; as
though the abundance of one's soul did not sometimes overflow with
empty metaphors, since no one ever has been able to give the exact
measure of his needs, his concepts, or his sorrows. The human tongue
is like a cracked cauldron on which we beat out tunes to set a bear
dancing when we would make the stars weep with our melodies.

But with the superiority of critical insight of the person who holds
back his emotions in any engagement, Rodolphe perceived that there
were other pleasures to be exploited in this love. He discarded all
modesty as inconvenient. He treated her without consideration. And
he made her into something at once malleable and corrupt. It was
an idiotic sort of attachment, full of admiration on his side and
voluptuousness on hers, a beatitude which left her numb; and her
soul sunk deep into this intoxication and drowned in it, all shrivelled
up, like the duke of Clarence in his butt of malmsey.[8]

Solely as a result of her amorous practices, Madame Bovary began
to change in appearance. Her glances were bolder, her speech freer;
she even went as far as to go out walking with Rodolphe, a cigarette
in her mouth, "just to scandalize the town"; finally, those who had
doubted doubted no longer when they saw her descend one day from
the "Hirondelle" wearing a tight-fitting waistcoat cut like a man's.
And Madame Bovary senior who, after a frightful scene with her
husband, had come to seek refuge with her son, was not the least
scandalized lady in town. Many other things displeased her too: first
of all, Charles had not followed her advice in banning novels from
the house; then, the "tone" of the house upset her; she allowed herself to make observations, and there were arguments, especially, on
one occasion, concerning Felicité.

The previous evening, while crossing the corridor, Madame Bovary senior had come upon her in the company of a man of about
forty wearing a brown collar, who on hearing footsteps, had quickly
fled from the kitchen. Emma had burst out laughing; but the good
woman was furious, declaring that anyone who took morality seriously ought to keep an eye on their servant's behavior.

"What kind of society do you come from?" asked the daughter-in-
law, with so impertinent a look that Madame Bovary asked her if she
were not perhaps defending her own case.

"Get out!" said the young woman, rising in fury.

8. The duke of Clarence was the younger brother of King Edward IV of England and the elder
brother of Richard Duke of Gloucester. He was condemned to death for treason and, according
to rumor, drowned in a butt of malmsey (a sweet aromatic wine) in February 1478. See Shakespeare, *Richard III*, 1:4, 155.

"Emma! . . . Mother! . . ." cried Charles, trying to reconcile them.

But both had fled in their exasperation. Emma was stamping her feet as she repeated:

"Oh! what manners! What a peasant!"

He ran to his mother; she was beside herself. She stammered:

"How insolent she is! and how flighty! worse perhaps!"

And she was ready to leave at once if the other did not apologise. So Charles went back again to his wife and implored her to give way; he threw himself at her feet; finally, she said:

"Very well! I'll go to her."

And she actually held out her hand to her mother-in-law with the dignity of a marquise as she said:

"Excuse me, madame."

Then, having returned to her room, she threw herself flat on her bed and cried there like a child, her face buried in the pillow.

She and Rodolphe had agreed that in the event of anything extraordinary occurring, she should fasten a small piece of white paper to the blind, so that if by chance he happened to be in Yonville, he could hurry to the lane behind the house. Emma made the signal; she had been waiting three-quarters of an hour when she suddenly caught sight of Rodolphe at the corner of the square. She felt tempted to open the window and call him, but he had already disappeared. She fell back in despair.

Soon, however, it seemed to her that someone was walking on the pavement. It was he, no doubt. She went downstairs, crossed the yard. He was there outside. She threw herself into his arms.

"Watch out!" he said.

"Ah! if only you knew!" she replied.

And she began telling him everything, hurriedly, disjointedly, exaggerating the facts, inventing many, and with so many digressions that he understood nothing at all.

"Come now, my poor angel, be brave, console yourself, be patient!"

"But I have been patient; I have suffered for four years. A love like ours ought to show itself in the face of heaven. They torture me! I can bear it no longer! Save me!"

She clung to Rodolphe. Her eyes, full of tears, flashed like flames beneath a wave; her panting made her breast rise and fall; never had she seemed more lovely, so much so that he lost his head and said:

"What do you want me to do?"

"Take me away," she cried, "carry me off! . . . I beg you!"

She pressed her lips against his mouth, as if to capture the unhoped for consent the moment it was breathed forth in a kiss.

"But . . ." Rodolphe began.

"What?"

"Your little girl!"

She reflected a few moments, then replied:

"We'll take her with us, there is no other way!"

"What a woman!" he said to himself, watching her as she went. For she had run into the garden. Some one was calling her.

On the following days the elder Madame Bovary was much surprised at the change in her daughter-in-law. Emma, in fact, was showing herself more docile, and even carried her deference to the point of asking for a recipe for pickles.

Was it the better to deceive them both? Or did she wish by a sort of voluptuous stoicism to feel the more profoundly the bitterness of the things she was about to leave? But she paid no heed to them; on the contrary, she lived as lost in the anticipated delight of her coming happiness. It was an eternal subject for conversation with Rodolphe. She leant on his shoulder murmuring:

"Think, we will soon be in the mail-coach! Can you imagine? Is it possible? It seems to me that the moment the carriage will start, it will be as if we were rising in a balloon, as if we were setting out for the clouds. Do you know that I count the hours? . . . Don't you?"

Never had Madame Bovary been so beautiful as at this period; she had that indefinable beauty that results from joy, from enthusiasm, from success, and that expresses the harmony between temperament and circumstances. Her cravings, her sorrows, her sensuous pleasures and her ever-young illusions had slowly brought her to full maturity, and she blossomed forth in the fullness of her being, like a flower feeding on manure, on rain, wind and sunshine. Her half-closed eyelids seemed perfectly shaped for the long languid glances that escaped from them; her breathing dilated the fine nostrils and raised the fleshy corners of her mouth, shaded in the light by a slight black down. Some artist skilled in corruption seemed to have devised the shape of her hair as it fell on her neck, coiled in a heavy mass, casually reassembled after being loosened daily in adultery. Her voice now took more mellow inflections, her figure also; something subtle and penetrating escaped even from the folds of her gown and from the line of her foot. Charles thought her exquisite and altogether irresistible, as when they were first married.

When he came home in the middle of the night, he did not dare to wake her. The porcelain night-light threw a round trembling gleam upon the ceiling, and the drawn curtains of the little cot formed as it were a white hut standing out in the shade by the bedside. Charles looked at them. He seemed to hear the light breathing of his child. She would grow big now; every season would bring rapid progress. He already saw her coming from school as the day drew in, laughing, with ink-stains on her jacket, and carrying her basket on her arm. Then she would have to be sent to a boarding-school; that would cost much; how was it to be done? He kept thinking about it. He thought of renting a small farm in the neighborhood, that he would supervise every morning on his way to his patients. He would not spend what he brought in; he would put it in the savings-bank. Then he would invest in some stocks, he didn't know which; besides, his practice would increase; he counted on it, for he wanted Berthe to be well-educated, to be accomplished, to learn to play the piano. Ah! how pretty she would be later on when she was fifteen, when, resembling her mother, she would, like her, wear large straw hats in the summer-time; from a distance they would be taken for two sisters. He pictured her to himself working in the evening by their side beneath the light of the lamp; she would embroider him slippers; she would look after the house; she would fill all the home with her charm and her gaiety. At last, they would think of her marriage; they would find her some good young fellow with a steady business; he would make her happy; this would last for ever.

Emma was not asleep; she pretended to be; and while he dozed off by her side she awakened to other dreams.

To the gallop of four horses she was carried away for a week towards a new land, from where they would never return. They went on and on, their arms entwined, without speaking a word. Often from the top of a mountain there suddenly appeared some splendid city with domes, and bridges, and ships, forests of lemon trees, and cathedrals of white marble, their pointed steeples crowned with storks' nests. The horses slowed down to a walk because of the wide pavement, and on the ground there were bouquets of flowers, offered by women dressed in red. They heard the chiming of bells, the neighing of mules, together with the murmur of guitars and the noise of fountains, whose rising spray refreshed heaps of fruit arranged like a pyramid at the foot of pale statues that smiled beneath playing waters. And then, one night they came to a fishing village, where brown nets were drying in the wind along the cliffs and in front of the huts. It was there that they would stay; they would live in a low, flat-roofed house, shaded by a palm-tree in the heart of a gulf, by the sea. They would row in gondolas, swing in hammocks, and their existence would be easy and free as their wide silk gowns, warm and star-spangled as the nights they would contemplate. However, in the immensity of this future that she conjured up, nothing specific stood out; the days, all magnificent, resembled each other like waves; and the vision swayed in the horizon, infinite, harmonised, azure, and bathed in sunshine. But the child began to cough in her cot or Bovary snored more loudly, and Emma did not fall asleep till morning, when the dawn whitened the windows, and when little Justin was already in the square taking down the shutters of the pharmacy.

She had sent for Monsieur Lheureux, and had said to him:

"I want a cloak—a large lined cloak with a deep collar."

"You are going on a journey?" he asked.

"No; but . . . never mind. I count on you to get it in a hurry."

He bowed.

"Besides, I shall want," she went on, "a trunk . . . not too heavy . . . a handy size."

"Yes, yes, I understand. About three feet by a foot and a half, as they are being made just now."

"And a travelling bag."

"No question about it," thought Lheureux, "she is up to something."

"And," said Madame Bovary, taking her watch from her belt, "take this; you can pay yourself out of it."

But the shopkeeper protested that it was not necessary; as if he didn't know and trust her. She was being childish!

She insisted, however, on his taking at least the chain, and Lheureux had already put it in his pocket and was going, when she called him back.

"You will leave everything at your place. As to the cloak"—she seemed to be reflecting—"do not bring it either; you can give me the maker's address, and tell him to have it ready for me."

It was the next month that they were to run away. She was to leave Yonville as if she was going on some business to Rouen. Rodolphe would have booked the seats, obtained the passports, and even have written to Paris in order to have the whole mail-coach reserved for them as far as Marseilles, where they would buy a carriage, and go on from there straight by the Genoa road. She would have sent her luggage to Lheureux, from where it would be taken directly to the "Hirondelle," so that no one would have any suspicion. And in all this there never was any allusion to the child. Rodolphe avoided the subject; it may be that he had forgotten about it.

He wished to have two more weeks before him to arrange some affairs; then at the end of a week he wanted two more; then he said he as ill; next he went on a journey. The month of August passed, and, after all these delays, they decided that it was to be irrevocably fixed for the 4th September—a Monday.

At last the Saturday before arrived.

Rodolphe came in the evening earlier than usual.

"Is everything ready?" she asked him.

"Yes."

Then they walked round a garden-bed, and sat down near the terrace on the kerb-stone of the wall.

"You are sad," said Emma.

"No; why?"

And yet he looked at her strangely, though with tenderness.

"Is it because you are going away?" she went on; "because you are leaving behind what is dear to you, your own life? I can understand that·. . . But I have nothing in the world! You are everything I have, and I'll be everything to you. I'll be your family, your country; I'll look after you, I'll love you."

"How sweet you are!" he said, taking her in his arms.

"Am I really?" she said with a voluptuous laugh. "Do you love me? Swear it then!"

"Do I love you? Do I? But I adore you, my love!"

The moon, full and purple-colored, was rising right out of the earth at the end of the meadow. It rose quickly between the branches of the poplar trees, partly hidden as by a tattered black curtain. Then it appeared dazzling white, lighting up the empty sky; slowing down, it let fall upon the river a great stain that broke up into an infinity of stars; and the silver sheen seemed to writhe through the very depths like a headless serpent covered with luminous scales; it also resembled some monster candelabra from which sparkling diamonds fell like molten drops. The soft night was about them; masses of shadow filled the branches. Emma, her eyes half closed, breathed in with deep sighs the fresh wind that was blowing. They did not speak, caught as they were in their dream. The tenderness of the old days came back to their hearts, full and silent as the flowing river, with the soft perfume of the syringas, and threw across their memories shadows more immense and more sombre than those of the still willows that lengthened out over the grass. Often some night-animal, hedgehog or weasel, setting out on the hunt, disturbed the lovers, or sometimes they heard a ripe peach fall by itself from the tree.

"Ah! what a lovely night!" said Rodolphe.

"We shall have others," replied Emma.

Then, as if speaking to herself:

"Yes, it will be good to travel. And yet, why should my heart be so heavy? Is it dread of the unknown? The weight of old habits? . . . Or else? No, it is the excess of happiness. How weak I am! You must forgive me!"

"There is still time!" he cried. "Think! You may regret it later!"

"Never!" she cried impetuously.

And, drawing closer to him:

"What ill could come to me? There is no desert, no precipice, no ocean I would not traverse with you. The longer we live together the more it will be like an embrace, every day closer, more complete. There will be nothing to trouble us, no cares, no obstacle. We shall be alone, all to ourselves forever . . . Say something, answer me!"

At regular intervals he answered, "Yes . . . Yes . . ." She had passed her hands through his hair, and she repeated on a childlike voice through her tears:

"Rodolphe! Rodolphe! . . . Sweet little Rodolphe!"

Midnight struck.

"Midnight!" she said. "Come, it is to-morrow. One more day!"

He rose to go; and as if the movement he made had been the signal for their flight, Emma suddenly seemed gay:

"You have the passports?"

"Yes."

"You are forgetting nothing?"

"No."

"Are you sure?"

"Absolutely."

"You'll be waiting for me at the Hotel de Provence, won't you? . . . at noon?"

He nodded.

"Till to-morrow then!" said Emma in a last caress; and she watched him go.

He did not turn round. She ran after him, and, leaning over the water's edge between the bushes:

"Till to-morrow!" she cried.

He was already on the other side of the river and walking fast across the meadow.

After a few moments Rodolphe stopped; and when he saw her with her white gown gradually fade away in the shade like a ghost, his heart beat so wildly that he had to support himself against a tree.

"What a fool I am!" he said, swearing a dreadful oath. "All the same, she was the prettiest mistress ever."

And immediately Emma's beauty, with all the pleasures of their love, came back to him. For a moment he weakened, but then he rebelled against her.

"For, after all," he exclaimed, gesticulating, "I can't exile myself, and with a child on my hands to boot!"

He was saying these things to strengthen his determination.

"And besides, the worries, the cost! No, no, a thousand times no! It would have been too stupid."

XIII

No sooner was Rodolphe at home than he sat down quickly at his desk under the stag's head that hung as a trophy on the wall. But when he had the pen between his fingers, he could think of nothing, so that, resting on his elbows, he began to reflect. Emma seemed to him to have receded into a far-off past, as if the resolution he had taken had suddenly placed an immeasurable distance between them.

In order to recapture something of her presence, he fetched from the cupboard at the bedside an old Rheims cookie-box, in which he usually kept his love letters. An odour of dry dust and withered roses emanated from it. First he saw a handkerchief stained with pale drops. It was a handkerchief of hers. Once when they were walking her nose had bled; he had forgotten it. Near it, almost too large for the box, was Emma's miniature: her dress seemed pretentious to him, and her languishing look in the worst possible taste. Then, from looking at this image and recalling the memory of the original, Emma's features little by little grew confused in his remembrance, as if the living and the painted face, rubbing one against the other, had erased each other. Finally, he read some of her letters; they were full of explanations relating to their journey, short, technical, and urgent, like business notes. He wanted to see the long ones again, those of old times. In order to find them at the bottom of the box, Rodolphe disturbed all the others, and mechanically began rummaging among this mass of papers and things, finding pell-mell bouquets, garters, a black mask, pins, and hair . . . lots of hair! Some dark, some fair, some, catching in the hinges of the box, even broke when he opened it.

Following his memories, he examined the writing and the style of the letters, as varied as their spelling. They were tender or jovial, facetious, melancholy; there were some that asked for love, others that asked for money. A word recalled faces to him, certain gestures, the sound of a voice; sometimes, however, he remembered nothing at all.

All these women, crowding into his consciousness, rather shrank in size, levelled down by the uniformity of his feeling. Seizing the letters at random, he amused himself for a while by letting them cascade from his right into his left hand. At last, bored and weary, Rodolphe took back the box to the cupboard, saying to himself:

"What a lot of nonsense!"

Which summed up his opinion; for pleasures, like schoolboys in a school courtyard, had so trampled upon his heart that no green thing was left; whatever entered there, more heedless than children, did not even, like them, leave a name carved upon the wall.

"Come," he said, "let's go."

He wrote:

> Courage, Emma! you must be brave! I don't want to be the one to ruin your life . . .

"After all, that's true," thought Rodolphe. "I am acting in her interest; I am honest."

> Have you carefully weighed your resolution? Do you know to what an abyss I was dragging you, poor angel? No, you don't, I assure you.

> You were coming confident and fearless, believing in a future happiness . . . Ah! the wretched creatures we are! We nearly lost our minds!

Rodolphe paused to think of some good excuse.

"If I told her that I lost all my money? No! Besides, that would stop nothing. It would all start again later on. As if one could make women like that listen to reason!"

He thought for a moment, then added:

> I shall not forget you, believe me; and I shall forever have a profound devotion for you; but some day, sooner or later, this ardour (such is the fate of human things) would doubtlessly have diminished. Weariness would have been unavoidable, and who knows if I would not even have had the atrocious pain of witnessing your remorse, of sharing it myself, since I would have been its cause? The mere idea of the grief that would come to you tortures me, Emma. Forget me! Why did I ever know you? Why were you so beautiful? Is it my fault? God, no! only fate is to blame!

"That's a word that always helps," he said to himself.

> Ah, if you had been one of those shallow women of which there are so many, I might, out of selfishness, have tried an experiment, in that case without danger for you. But your exquisite sensitivity, at once your charm and your torment, has prevented you from understanding, adorable woman that you are, the falseness of our future position. I myself had not fully realized this till now; I was living in the bliss of this ideal happiness as under the shade of a poisonous tree, without forseeing the consequences.

"She may suspect that it is out of stinginess that I am giving her up . . . But never mind, let's get this over with!"

> This is a cruel world, Emma. Wherever we might have gone, it would have persecuted us. You would have had to put up with indiscreet questions, calumny, contempt, insult perhaps. Imagine you being insulted! It is unbearable! . . . I who would place you on a throne! I who bear with me your memory as a talisman! For I am going to punish myself by exile for all the ill I have done you. I am going away. I don't know where, I am too close to madness to think. Farewell! Continue to be good! Remember the unfortunate man who caused your undoing. Teach my name to your child; let her repeat it in her prayers.

The wicks of the candles flickered. Rodolphe got up to close the window, and when he saw down again:

"I think that covers it. Ah, let me add this for fear she might pursue me here."

> I shall be far away when you read these sad lines, for I have wished to flee as quickly as possible to shun the temptation of seeing you again.

No weakness! I shall return, and perhaps later on we shall be able to talk coldly of our past love. Adieu!

And there was a last "adieu" divided into two words: "A Dieu!" which he thought in very excellent taste.

"Now how am I to sign?" he asked himself. " 'Yours devotedly?' No! 'Your friend?' Yes, that's it."

YOUR FRIEND.

He re-read his letter and thought it quite good.

"Poor little woman!" he thought tenderly. "She'll think me harder than a rock. There ought to have been some tears on this; but I can't cry; it isn't my fault." Then, having emptied some water into a glass, Rodolphe dipped his finger into it, and let a big drop fall on the paper, making a pale stain on the ink. Then looking for a seal, he came upon the one "*Amor nel cor.*"

"Hardly the right thing under the circumstances . . . But who cares?"

Whereupon he smoked three pipes and went to bed.

Upon arising the next morning—around two o'clock in the afternoon, for he had slept late—Rodolphe had a basket of apricots picked. He put his letter at the bottom under some vine leaves, and at once ordered Girard, his ploughman, to take it with care to Madame Bovary. They used to correspond this way before and he would send her fruit or game according to season.

"If she asks about me," he said, "tell her that I have gone on a journey. You must give the basket to her herself, into her own hands. Get going now, and be careful!"

Girard put on his new smock, knotted his handkerchief round the apricots, and, walking heavily in his hobnailed boots, quietly made his way to Yonville.

When he got to the house, Madame Bovary was arranging a bundle of linen on the kitchen-table with Félicité.

"Here," said the ploughboy, "is something for you from my master."

She was seized with apprehension, and as she sought in her pocket for some small change, she looked at the peasant with haggard eyes, while he himself stared at her with amazement, not understanding how such a small present could stir up such violent emotions. Finally he left. Félicité stayed. She could bear it no longer; she ran into the sitting room as if to take the apricots there, overturned the basket, tore away the leaves, found the letter, opened it, and, as if pursued by some fearful fire, Emma flew in terror to her room.

Charles was there; she saw him; he spoke to her; she heard nothing, and she ran quickly up the stairs, breathless, distraught, crazed, and ever holding this horrible piece of paper, that crackled between her fingers like a plate of sheet-iron. On the second floor she stopped before the closed attic-door.

Then she tried to calm herself; she recalled the letter; she must finish it but she didn't care. Where and how was she to read it? She would be seen!

"Here," she thought, "I'll be safe here."

Emma pushed open the door and went in.

The slates projected a heavy heat that gripped her temples, stifled her; she dragged herself to the closed window, drew back the bolt, and the dazzling sunlight burst in.

Opposite, beyond the roofs, the open country stretched as far as the eye could reach. Down below, underneath her, the village square was empty; the stones of the pavement glittered, the weathercocks on the houses stood motionless. At the corner of the street, from a lower story, rose a kind of humming with strident modulations. It was Binet turning.

She leant against the window-frame, and re-read the letter with angry sneers. But the more she concentrated on it, the more confused she grew. She could see him, hear him, feel his embrace; the throbbing of her heart, beating irregularly in her breast like the blows of a battering ram, grew faster and faster. She looked about her wishing that the earth might crumble. Why not end it all? What restrained her? She was free. She advanced, looked at the paving-stones, saying to herself, "Jump! jump!"

The ray of light reflected straight from below drew the weight of her body towards the abyss. The ground of the village square seemed to tilt over and climb up the walls, the floor to pitch forward like in a tossing boat. She was right at the edge, almost hanging, surrounded by vast space. The blue of the sky invaded her, the air was whirling in her hollow head; she had but to yield, to let herself be taken; and the humming of the lathe never ceased, like an angry voice calling her.

"My wife! my wife!" cried Charles.

She stopped.

"Where have you gone? Come here!"

The thought that she had just escaped from death almost made her faint with terror. She closed her eyes; then she started at the touch of a hand on her sleeve; it was Félicité.

"Monsieur is waiting for you, madame; the soup is on the table."

And she had to go down! and sit at the table!

She tried to eat. The food choked her. Then she unfolded her napkin as if to examine the darns, and really tried to concentrate on this work, counting the stitches in the linen. Suddenly she remembered the letter. How had she lost it? Where could it be found? But she felt such weariness of spirit that she could not even invent a pretext for leaving the table. Then she became a coward; she was afraid of Charles; he knew all, that was certain! Just then, he said, in an odd tone:

"We are not likely to see Monsieur Rodolphe soon again, it seems."

"Who told you?" she said, shuddering.

"Who told me!" he replied, rather astonished at her abrupt tone. "Why, Girard, whom I met just now at the door of the Café Français. He has gone on a journey, or is about to go."

She could not suppress a sob.

"What is so surprising about that? He goes away like that from time to time for a change, and I certainly can't blame him. A bachelor, and rich as he is! And from what I hear, he isn't exactly starved for pleasures, our friend! he enjoys life. Monsieur Langlois told me . . ."

He stopped for propriety's sake because the maid had just come in.

She collected the apricots that were strewn over the sideboard and put them back in the basket. Charles, unaware that his wife had turned scarlet, had them brought to him, took one, and bit into it.

"Perfect!" he said. "Have a taste!"

And he handed her the basket, which she gently put away from her.

"Smell them! Such perfume!" he insisted, moving it back and forth under her nose.

"I am choking," she exclaimed, leaping up.

By sheer willpower, she succeeded in forcing back the spasm.

"It is nothing," she said, "it is nothing! Just nerves. Sit down and eat."

For she dreaded most of all that he would question her, try to help and not leave her to herself.

Charles, to obey her, sat down again, and he spat the stones of the apricots into his hands, afterwards putting them on his plate.

Suddenly a blue tilbury passed across the square at a rapid trot. Emma uttered a cry and fell back rigid on the floor.

After many hesitations, Rodolphe had finally decided to set out for Rouen. Now, as from La Huchette to Buchy there is no other way than by Yonville, he had to go through the village, and Emma had recognised him by the rays of the lanterns, which like lightning flashed through the twilight.

The general commotion which broke out in the house brought the pharmacist over in a hurry. The table, with all the plates, had been knocked over; sauce, meat, knives, the salt, and cruet-stand were strewn over the room; Charles was calling for help; Berthe, scared, was crying; and Félicité, whose hands trembled, was unlacing her mistress, whose whole body shivered convulsively.

"I'll run to my laboratory for some aromatic vinegar," said the pharmacist.

Then as she opened her eyes on smelling the bottle:

"I thought so," he said, "this thing would resuscitate a corpse!"

"Speak to us," said Charles, "try to recover! It is Charles, who loves you . . . Do you know me? Look, here is your little girl; kiss her, darling!"

The child stretched out her arms to cling to her mother's neck. But turning away her head, Emma said in a broken voice:

"No, no . . . I want no one!"

She fainted again. They carried her to her bed.

She lay there stretched at full length, her lips apart, her eyelids closed, her hands open, motionless, and white as a waxen image. Two streams of tears flowed from her eyes and fell slowly upon the pillow.

Charles stood at the back of the alcove, and the pharmacist, near him, maintained the meditative silence that is fitting on the serious occasions of life.

"Don't worry," he said, touching his elbow; "I think the paroxysm is past."

"Yes, she is resting a little now," answered Charles, watching her sleep. "Poor girl! poor girl! She has dropped off now!"

Then Homais asked how the accident had occurred. Charles answered that she had been taken ill suddenly while she was eating some apricots.

"Extraordinary!" continued the pharmacist. "It is quite possible that the apricots caused the syncope. Some natures are so sensitive to certain smells; it would even be a very fine question to study both from a pathological and physiological point of view. The priests know all about it; that's why they use aromatics in all their ceremonies. It is to stupefy the senses and to bring on ecstasies,—a thing, moreover, very easy in persons of the weaker sex, who are more sensitive than we are. Some are reported fainting at the smell of burnt horn, or fresh bread . . ."

"Be careful not to wake her!" warned Bovary.

But the pharmacist was not to be stopped. "Not only," he resumed, "are human beings subject to such anomalies, but animals also. You are of course not ignorant of the singularly aphrodisiac effect produced by the *Nepeta cataria*, vulgarly called catnip, on the feline race; and, on the other hand, to quote an example whose authenticity I can vouch for, Bridaux (one of my old schoolmates, at present established in the Rue Malpalu) owns a dog that falls into convulsions as soon as you hold out a snuff-box to him. He often performs the experiment before his friends at his summerhouse in Bois-Guil-laume. Could you believe that a simple sternutative could cause such damage to a quadrupedal organism? Wouldn't you agree that it is extremely curious?"

"Yes," said Charles, who was not listening.

"It just goes to show," pursued the pharmacist, smiling with benign self-satisfaction, "the numberless irregularities of the nervous system. With regard to madame, I must say that she has always seemed extremely susceptible to me. And so I should by no means recommend to you, my dear friend, any of those so-called remedies that, under the pretence of attacking the symptoms, attack the constitution. No, no gratuitous medications! Diet, that is all; sedatives, emollients, dulcifiers. And then, don't you think we ought to stimulate the imagination?"

"In what way? How?" said Bovary.

"Ah, that is the problem. 'That is the question' (he said it in English) as I lately read in a newspaper."

But Emma, awaking, cried out:

"The letter! Where is the letter?"

They thought she was delirious; and she was by midnight. Brain-fever had set in.

For forty-three days Charles did not leave her. He gave up all his patients; he no longer went to bed; he was constantly feeling her pulse, applying mustard plasters and cold-water compresses. He sent Justin as far as Neufchâtel for ice; the ice melted on the way; he sent him back again. He called Monsieur Canivet into consultation; he sent for Dr. Larivière, his old master, from Rouen; he was in despair. What alarmed him most was Emma's prostration, for she did not speak, did not listen, did not even seem to suffer—as if both her body and her soul were resting after all their tribulations.

About the middle of October she could sit up in bed supported by pillows. Charles wept when he saw her eat her first piece of bread and jam. Her strength returned; she got up for a few hours of an afternoon, and one day, when she felt better, he tried to take her, leaning on his arm, for a walk round the garden. The sand of the paths was disappearing beneath the dead leaves; she walked slowly, dragging her slippers, and leaning against Charles's shoulder. She smiled all the time.

They went thus to the end of the garden near the terrace. She drew herself up slowly, shading her eyes with her hand. She looked far off, as far as she could, but on the horizon were only great bonfires of grass smoking on the hills.

"You will tire yourself, darling!" said Bovary.

And, pushing her gently to make her enter the arbour: "Sit down on this seat; you'll be comfortable."

"Oh! no; not there!" she said in a faltering voice.

She was seized with giddiness, and that evening, she suffered a relapse, less specific in character, it is true, and with more complex symptoms. At times it was her heart that troubled her, then her head or her limbs; she had vomitings, in which Charles thought he detected the first signs of cancer.

And, on top of all this, the poor fellow had money troubles!

XIV

To begin with, he did not know how to reimburse Monsieur Homais for all the drugs he had supplied and although, as a doctor, he could have forgone paying for them, he blushed at the thought of such an obligation. Then the expenses of the household, now that the maid was in charge, became staggering. Bills flooded the house; the tradesmen grumbled; Monsieur Lheureux especially harassed him. At the height of Emma's illness, he had taken advantage of the situation to increase his bill; he hurriedly brought the cloak, the travelling-bag, two trunks instead of one, and a number of other things. Charles protested in vain; the shopkeeper rudely replied that the merchandise had been ordered and that he had no intention of taking it back. Besides, it would interfere with madame's convalescence; the doctor had better think it over; in short, he was resolved to sue him rather than give up his rights and take it off his hands. Charles subsequently ordered them sent back to the shop. Félicité forgot and, having other things on his mind, Charles thought no more about it. Monsieur Lheureux did not desist and, alternating threats with whines, he finally forced Bovary into signing him a six months' promissory note. But hardly had he signed the note than a bold idea occurred to him: he meant to borrow a thousand francs from Lheureux. So, with an embarrassed air, he asked if he could get them, adding that it would be for a year, at any interest. Lheureux ran off to his shop, brought back the money, and dictated another note by which Bovary undertook to pay for his order on the 1st of September next the sum of one thousand and seventy francs, which, with the hundred and eighty already agreed to, made just twelve hundred and fifty. He was thus lending at six per cent in addition to one-fourth for commission; and since the merchandise brought him a good third profit at least, he stood to make one hundred and thirty francs in twelve months. He hoped that the business would not stop there; that the notes would not be paid on time and would have to be renewed, and that his puny little investment, thriving in the doctor's care like a patient in a rest home, would return to him one day considerably plumper, fat enough to burst the bag.

All of Lheureux's enterprises were thriving. He got the franchise for supplying the Neufchâtel hospital with cider; Monsieur Guillau-min promised him some shares in the turf-bogs of Gaumesnil, and he dreamt of establishing a new coach service between Argueil and Rouen, which no doubt would not be long in putting the ramshackle van of the Lion d'Or out of business. Travelling faster, at a cheaper rate, and carrying more luggage, it would concentrate into his hands all of Yonville's business.

Charles often wondered how he would ever be able to pay back so much money next year. He tried to think of solutions, such as apply-ing to his father or selling something. But his father would be deaf, and he—he had nothing to sell. He foresaw such difficulties that he quickly dismissed so disagreeable a subject of meditation from his mind. He reproached himself with forgetting Emma, as if, all his thoughts belonging to this woman, it was robbing her of something not to be constantly thinking of her.

It was a severe winter. Madame Bovary's convalescence was slow. On good days they wheeled her arm-chair to the window that over-looked the square, for she now disliked the garden, and the blinds on that side were always down. She wanted her horse to be sold; what she formerly liked now displeased her. The limit of her con-cerns seemed to be her own health. She stayed in bed taking light meals, rang for the maid to inquire about her tea or merely to chat. The snow on the market-roof threw a white, still light into the room; then the rain began to fall; and every day Emma would wait with a kind of anxiety for the inevitable return of some trifling event that was of little or no concern to her. The most important was the arrival of the "Hirondelle" in the evening. Then the inn-keeper would shout and other voices answered, while Hippolyte's lantern, as he took down the luggage from the roof, was like a star in the darkness. At noontime, Charles came home; then he left again; next she took some broth, and towards five o'clock, as night fell, the children com-ing back from school, dragging their wooden shoes along the pave-ment, beat with their rulers against the clapper of the shutters.

Around this time of day, Monsieur Bournisien came to see her. He inquired after her health, gave her news, exhorted her to religion in a playful, gossipy tone that was not without charm. The mere sight of his cassock comforted her.

Once, at the height of her illness, she thought she was about to die and asked for communion; and while they were making the prep-arations in her room for the sacrament, while they were clearing the night table of its medicine bottles and turning it into an altar, and while Félicité was strewing dahlia flowers on the floor, Emma felt some power passing over her that freed her from her pains, from all perception, from all feeling. Her body, relieved, no longer thought; another life was beginning; it seemed to her that her being, mounting toward God, would be annihilated in that love like a burning incense that melts into vapour. The bed-clothes were sprinkled with holy water, the priest drew the white host from the holy pyx and she fainted with celestial joy as she advanced her lips to accept the body of the Saviour presented to her. The curtains of the alcove floated gently round her like clouds, and the rays of the two tapers burning on the night table seemed to shine like dazzling halos. Then she let her head fall back, fancying she heard in space the music of seraphic harps, and perceived in an azure sky, on a golden throne in the midst of saints holding green palms, God the Father, resplendent with majesty, who ordered to earth angels with wings of fire to carry her away in their arms.

This splendid vision dwelt in her memory as the most beautiful thing that it was possible to dream, so that now she strove to recall her sensation; it was still with her, albeit in a less overpowering manner, but with the same profound sweetness. Her soul, tortured by pride, at length found rest in Christian humility, and, tasting the joy of weakness, she saw within herself the destruction of her will opening wide the gates for heavenly grace to conquer her. She realised the existence of a bliss that could replace happiness, another love beyond all loves, without pause and without end, that would grow forever! Amid the illusions of her hope, she saw a state of purity floating above the earth, mingling with heaven. She wanted to become a saint. She bought rosaries and wore holy medals; she wished to have in her room, by the side of her bed, a reliquary set in emeralds that she might kiss it every evening.

The priest was delighted with her new state of mind, although he couldn't help worrying that Emma's excessive fervor might lead to heresy, to extravagance. But not being much versed in these matters once they went beyond a certain point he wrote to Monsieur Boulard, the bishop's bookseller, to send him "something first rate for a lady with a very distinguished mind." With as much concern as if he were shipping kitchen ware to savages, the bookseller made a random package of whatever happened to be current in the religious booktrade at the time. It contained little question and answer manuals, pamphlets written in the brusque tone of Joseph de Maistre,[9] pseudo-novels in rose-coloured bindings and a sugary style, manufactured by sentimental seminarists or penitent blue-stockings. There were titles such as "Consider carefully: the Man of the World at the Feet of the Virgin Mary, by Monsieur de * * * , decorated with many Orders"; "The Errors of Voltaire, for the Use of the Young," &c.

9. The main theorist (1753–1821) of Catholic conservatism. His books, *Du Pape* (1819) and *Soirées de Saint-Petersbourg* (1821), defended the power of the pope and the sovereign king and argued that the reign of evil on earth has to be curbed by authority.

Madame Bovary's mind was not yet sufficiently clear to apply herself seriously to anything; moreover, she began this reading in too great a hurry. She grew provoked at the doctrines of religion; the arrogance of the polemic writings displeased her by their ferocious attacks on people she did not know; and the secular stories, sprinkled with religious seasoning, seemed to her written in such ignorance of the world, that they rather led her away from the truths she wanted to see confirmed. Nevertheless, she persevered; and when the volume slipped from her hands, she fancied herself seized with the finest Catholic melancholy ever conceived by an ethereal soul.

As for the memory of Rodolphe, she had locked it away in the deepest recesses of her heart, and it remained there solemn and motionless as a pharaoh's mummy in a catacomb. A fragrance escaped from this embalmed love, that, penetrating through everything, perfumed with tenderness the immaculate atmosphere in which she longed to live. When she knelt on her Gothic prie-Dieu, she addressed to the Lord the same suave words that she had murmured formerly to her lover in the outpourings of adultery. She was searching for faith; but no delights descended from the heavens, and she arose with aching limbs and the vague feeling that she was being cheated.

Yet she thought this search all the more admirable, and in the pride of her devoutness Emma compared herself to those grand ladies of long ago whose glory she had dreamed of over a portrait of La Vallière, and who, trailing with so much majesty the lace-trimmed trains of their long gowns, retired into solitude to shed at the feet of Christ the tears of hearts that life had wounded.

Then she indulged in excessive charity. She sewed clothes for the poor, she sent wood to women in childbirth; and on coming home one day, Charles found three tramps eating soup in the kitchen. Her little girl, whom her husband had sent back to the nurse during her illness, returned home. She wanted to teach her to read; even Berthe's crying no longer irritated her. She was resigned, universally tolerant. Her speech was full of elevated expressions. She would say:

"Is your stomach-ache any better, my angel?"

The elder Madame Bovary couldn't find fault with anything except perhaps this mania of knitting jackets for orphans instead of mending her own dishtowels; but, harassed with domestic quarrels, the good woman took pleasure in this quiet house, and she even stayed there till after Easter, to escape the sarcasms of old Bovary, who never failed to order a big pork sausage on Good Friday.

Besides the companionship of her mother-in-law, who strengthened her resolutions somewhat by the rigor of her judgment and her stern appearance, Emma almost every day had other visitors: Madame Langlois, Madame Caron, Madame Dubreuil, Madame Tuvache, and regularly from two to five o'clock the sterling Madame

Homais who, for her part, had never believed any of the gossip about her neighbor. The Homais children also came to see her, accompanied by Justin. He went up with them to her bedroom, and remained standing near the door without daring to move or to utter a word. Often enough Madame Bovary, taking no heed of him, would start dressing. She began by taking out her comb and tossing her head, in a brusque gesture, and when for the first time the poor boy saw this mass of hair fall in ringlets to her knees, it was as if he entered suddenly into a new and strange world, whose splendour terrified him.

Emma probably did not notice his silent attentions or his timidity. She had no inkling that love, which presumably had left her life forever, was pulsating right there, under that coarse shirt, in that adolescent heart open to the emanations of her beauty. Besides, she now wrapped all things in the same mood of indifference, she combined gentleness of speech with such haughty looks, affected such contradictory ways, that one could no longer distinguish selfishness from charity, or corruption from virtue. One evening, for example, she first got angry with the maid, who had asked to go out, and stammered as she tried to find some pretext; then suddenly:

"So you love him, don't you?" she said.

And without waiting for an answer from Félicité, who was blushing, she added sadly:

"All right! run along, and have a good time!"

In early spring she had the garden all changed around, over Bovary's objections; yet he was pleased to see her at last express some will of her own. She did so more and more as her strength returned. First, she found occasion to expel Mère Rollet, the nurse, who during her convalescence had taken to visiting the kitchen in the company of her two nurslings and her young boarder, whose appetite surpassed that of a cannibal. She cut down on the visits of the Homais family, gradually freed herself from the other visitors, and even went to church less assiduously, to the great approval of the pharmacist, who remarked to her:

"I suspect you were beginning to fall for the priest's sales talk!"

As before, Monsieur Bournisien would drop in every day after catechism class. He preferred to take the air in the "grove," as he called the arbour. This was the time when Charles came home. They were hot; some sweet cider was brought out, and they drank together to madame's complete recovery.

Binet was often there, that is to say, a little lower down against the terrace wall, fishing for crayfish. Bovary invited him to have a drink, and he proved to be a real expert on the uncorking of the stone bottles.

Looking around with utter self-satisfaction, first at his companions, then at the furthest confines of the landscape, he would say:

"You must first hold the bottle perpendicularly on the table, and after the strings are cut, press the cork upwards inch by inch, gently, very gently—the way they handle soda water in restaurants."

But during his demonstration the cider often spurted right into their faces, and the priest, laughing his thick laugh, would never fail to make his little joke:

"Its excellence certainly strikes the eye!"

He was undoubtedly a kindly fellow and one day he was not even scandalised at the pharmacist, who advised Charles to give madame some distraction by taking her to the theatre at Rouen to hear the illustrious tenor, Lagardy. Homais, surprised at this silence, wanted to know his opinion, and the priest declared that he considered music less dangerous for morals than literature.

But the pharmacist took up the defence of letters. The theatre, he contended, served to decry prejudices and, while pretending to amuse, it taught virtue.

"*Castigat ridendo mores*,[1] Monsieur Bournisien! Look at most of Voltaire's tragedies: they contain a wealth of philosophical considerations that make them into a real school of morals and diplomacy for the people."

"I," said Binet, "once saw a play called the 'Gamin de Paris,'[2] in which there is a really fine part of an old general. He settles the account of a rich young fellow who has seduced a working girl, and at the end . . ."

"Of course," pursued Homais, "there is bad literature as there is bad pharmacy, but to condemn in a lump the most important of the fine arts seems to me a stupidity, a Gothic aberration worthy of the abominable times that imprisoned Galileo."[3]

"I know very well," objected the curé, "that there are good works, good authors. Still, the very fact of crowding people of different sexes into the same room, made to look enticing by displays of worldly pomp, these pagan disguises, the makeup, the lights, the effeminate voices, all this must, in the long-run, engender a certain mental libertinage, give rise to immodest thoughts and impure temptations. Such, at any rate, is the opinion of all the church fathers. Moreover," he added, suddenly assuming a mystic tone of voice while he rolled a pinch of snuff between his fingers, "if the Church has condemned the theatre, she must be right; we must bow to her decrees."

"Why," asked the druggist, "should she excommunicate actors

---

1. "It [comedy] reproves the manners, through laughter"—a slogan for comedy invented by the poet Jean de Santeuil (1630–1697), and given to the harlequin Dominique to put on the curtain of his theater.   2. A comedy by Bayard and Vanderbusch performed in 1836 in Paris. 3. Galileo Galilei (1564–1642), the astronomer, was confined to his house in Arcetri (near Florence) after his book propounding the view that the earth circled around the sun was condemned by the Inquisition (in 1633).

when formerly they used to take part openly in religious ceremonies? They would play right in the middle of the choir and perform a kind of farce called "mystery plays" that frequently offended against the laws of decency."

The curé merely groaned and the pharmacist persisted:

"It's like in the Bible; you know . . . there are things in it . . . certain details . . . I'd call them downright daring . . . bordering on obscenity!"

And as Monsieur Bournisien signaled his annoyance:

"Ah! you'll admit that it is not a book to place in the hands of a young girl, and I wouldn't at all like it if Athalie . . ."

"But it is the Protestants, and not we," protested the other impatiently, "who recommend the Bible."

"All the same," said Homais. "I am surprised that in our days, in this century of enlightenment, any one should still persist in proscribing an intellectual relaxation that is inoffensive, morally uplifting, and sometimes even good for the health—isn't that right, doctor?"

"Quite," the doctor replied in a non-committal tone, either because, sharing the same ideas, he wished to offend no one, or else because he simply had no ideas on the subject.

The conversation seemed at an end when the pharmacist thought fit to try a parting shot.

"I've known priests who put on civilian clothes to go watch burlesque shows."

"Come, come!" said the cure.

"Ah yes, I've known some!"

And, separating the words, he repeated:

"I—have—known—some!"

"Well, they did wrong," said Bournisien, prepared to listen to anything with resignation.

"And they didn't stop at that, either!" persisted the pharmacist.

"That's enough! . . ." exclaimed the priest, looking so fierce that the other thought safe to retreat.

"I only mean to say," he replied in a much less aggressive tone, "that tolerance is the surest way to draw people to religion."

"That is true! that is true!" conceded the priest, sitting down again.

But he stayed only a few minutes. Hardly had he left that Monsieur Homais said to the doctor:

"That's what I call a good fight! See how I found his weak spot? I didn't give him much of a chance . . . Now take my advice. Take madame to the theatre, if only to get for once the better of one of these rooks! If someone could keep the store in my absence, I'd go with you. But hurry! Lagardy is only going to give one performance; he's going to play in England for a tremendous fee. From what I hear, he's quite a character. He's simply loaded with money! He travels with three mistresses and a cook. All these great artists burn the candle at both ends; they need to lead a dissolute life to stir the imagination of the public. But they die at the poorhouse, because they don't have the sense to save their money when it comes in. Well, enjoy your dinner! See you to-morrow."

This theatre idea quickly grew in Bovary's mind; he at once communicated it to his wife, who at first refused, alleging the fatigue, the worry, the expense; but, for once, Charles did not give in, so sure was he that this occasion would do her good. He saw nothing to prevent it: his mother had sent three hundred francs he no longer counted on, the current bills were far from staggering and Lheureux's notes were not due for such a long time that he could dismiss them from his mind. Besides, imagining that she was refusing out of consideration for him, he insisted all the more, until she finally consented. The next day at eight o'clock they set out in the "Hirondelle."

The pharmacist, who had nothing whatever to keep him at Yonville but fancied himself to be indispensable, sighed with envy as he saw them go.

"Well, a pleasant journey!" he said to them; "happy mortals that you are!"

Then addressing himself to Emma, who was wearing a blue silk gown with four flounces:

"You are prettier than ever. You'll make quite an impression in Rouen."

The diligence stopped at the Croix-Rouge on the Place Beavoisine. It was a typical provincial inn, with large stables and small bedrooms and chickens in the courtyard, picking at the oats under the muddy gigs of travelling salesmen;—a fine old place, with worm-eaten balconies that creak in the wind on winter nights, always crowded, noisy and full of food, its black tables stained with coffee and brandy, the thick windows yellowed by flies, the napkins spotted with cheap red wine. Like farmboys dressed in Sunday-clothes, the place still reeks of the country; it has a café on the street and a vegetable-garden on the back. Charles at once set out on his errands. He confused stage-boxes and gallery, orchestra seats and regular boxes, asked for explanations which he did not understand, was sent from the box-office to the manager, came back to the inn, returned to the theatre and ended up by crossing the full length of the town, from theatre to outer boulevard, several times.

Madame bought herself a hat, gloves, and a bouquet. Monsieur worried greatly about missing the beginning, and, without having had time to swallow a plate of soup, they arrived at the gates of the theatre well before opening time.

XV

The crowd was lined up against the wall, evenly distributed on both sides of the entrance rails. At the corner of the neighbouring streets huge bills, printed in Gothic letters, announced "Lucie de Lammermoor-Lagardy-Opera &c."[4] The weather was fine, the people hot; sweat trickled among fancy coiffures and pocket handkerchiefs were mopping red foreheads; now and then a warm wind that blew from the river gently stirred the edges of the canvas awnings hanging from the doors of the cafés. A little lower down, however, one was refreshed by a current of icy air that smelt of tallow, leather, and oil, breathed forth from the Rue des Charrettes with its huge, dark warehouses resounding with the noise of rolling barrels.

For fear of seeming ridiculous, Emma first wanted to take a little stroll in the harbor, and Bovary carefully kept clutching the tickets in his trouser pockets, pressed against his stomach.

Her heart began to beat as soon as she reached the entrance hall. She involuntarily smiled with vanity on seeing the crowd rushing to the right by the other corridor while she went up the staircase to the reserved seats. She was as pleased as a child to push the large tapestried door open with her finger; she breathed deeply the dusty smell of the lobbies, and when she was seated in her box she drew herself up with the self-assurance of a duchess.

The theatre was beginning to fill; opera-glasses were taken from their cases, and the subscribers greeted and bowed as they spotted each other at a distance. They sought relief from the pressures of commerce in the arts, but, unable to take their minds off business matters, they still talked about cotton, spirits of wine, or indigo. The placid and meek heads of the old men, with their pale whitish hair and complexion, resembled silver medals tarnished by lead fumes. The young beaux were strutting about in the orchestra, exhibiting their pink or apple-green cravats under their gaping waistcoats; sitting above them, Madame Bovary admired how they leant the tight-drawn palm of their yellow gloves on the golden knobs of their canes.

Now the lights of the orchestra were lit; the chandelier, let down from the ceiling, threw the sudden gaiety of its sparkling crystals over the theatre; then the musicians began to file in; and first there was the protracted hubbub of roaring cellos, squeaking violins, blaring trumpets, and piping flutes. But three knocks were heard on the stage, a rolling of drums began, the brass instruments played some chords, and the curtain rose, discovering a country-scene.

It was the cross-roads of a wood, with a fountain on the left, shaded

---

4. *Lucia di Lammermoor* is an opera by Gaetano Donizetti (1797–1848) first performed in Naples in 1835 (in Paris in 1837). It is based on Walter Scott's novel, *The Bride of Lammermoor* (1819). See the extended note p. 826.

by an oak tree. Peasants and lords with tartans over their shoulders were singing a hunting-song in chorus; a captain suddenly appeared, who evoked the spirit of evil by lifting both his arms to heaven. Another followed; they departed, and the hunters started afresh.

She felt herself carried back to the reading of her youth, into the midst of Walter Scott. She seemed to hear through the mist the sound of the Scotch bagpipes re-echoing over the moors. Her remembrance of the novel helping her to understand the libretto, she followed the story phrase by phrase, while the burst of music dispersed the fleeting thoughts that came back to her. She gave herself up to the flow of the melodies, and felt all her being vibrate as if the violin bows were being drawn over her nerves. Her eyes could hardly take in all the costumes, the scenery, the actors, the painted trees that shook whenever someone walked, and the velvet caps, cloaks, swords—all those imaginary things that vibrated in the music as in the atmosphere of another world. But a young woman stepped forward, throwing a purse to a squire in green. She was left alone on the stage, and the flute was heard like the murmur of a fountain or the warbling of birds. Lucie bravely attacked her cavatina in G major. She begged for love, longed for wings. Emma, too, would have liked to flee away from life, locked in a passionate embrace. Suddenly Edgar Lagardy appeared.

He had that splendid pallor that gives something of the majesty of marble to the ardent races of the South. His vigourous form was tightly clad in a brown-coloured doublet; a small chiselled dagger swung against his left thigh, and he rolled languid eyes while flashing his white teeth. They said that a Polish princess having heard him sing one night on the beach at Biarritz, where he used to be a boatsman, had fallen in love with him. She had lost her entire fortune for his sake. He had deserted her for other women, and this sentimental fame did not fail to enhance his artistic reputation. A skilled ham actor, he never forgot to have a phrase on his seductiveness and his sensitive soul inserted in the accounts about him. He had a fine voice, colossal aplomb, more temperament than intelligence, more pathos than lyric feeling; all this made for an admirable charlatan type, in which there was something of the hairdresser as well as of the bullfighter.

From the first scene he brought down the house. He pressed Lucie in his arms, he left her, he came back, he seemed desperate; he had outbursts of rage, then elegiac gurglings of infinite sweetness, and tones like sobs and kisses escaped from his bare throat. Emma bent forward to see him, scratching the velvet of the box with her nails. Her heart filled with these melodious lamentations that were accompanied by the lugubrious moanings of the double-basses, like the cries of the drowning in the tumult of a tempest. She recognised all the intoxication and the anguish that had brought her close to death. The voice of the prima donna seemed to echo her own conscience, and the whole fictional story seemed to capture something of her own life. But no one on earth had loved her with such love. He had not wept like Edgar that last moonlit night when they had said "Till tomorrow! Till tomorrow! . . ." The theatre rang with cheers; they repeated the entire stretto; the lovers spoke of the flowers on their tomb, of vows, exile, fate, hopes; and when they uttered the final farewell, Emma gave a sharp cry that mingled with the vibrations of the last chords.

"But why," asked Bovary, "is that lord torturing her like that?"

"No, no!" she answered; "he is her lover!"

"Yet he vows vengeance on her family, while the other one who came on before said, 'I love Lucie and she loves me!' Besides, he went off with her father arm in arm. For he certainly is her father, isn't he—the ugly little man with a cock's feather in his hat?"

Despite Emma's explanations, as soon as the recitative duet began in which Gilbert lays bare his abominable machinations to his master Ashton, Charles, seeing the false engagement ring that is to deceive Lucie, thought it was a love-gift sent by Edgar. He confessed, moreover, that he did not understand the story because of the music, which interfered very much with the words.

"What does it matter?" said Emma. "Do be quiet!"

"Yes, but you know," he went on, leaning against her shoulder, "I like to understand things."

"Be quiet! be quiet!" she cried impatiently.

Lucie came on, half supported by her women, a wreath of orange blossoms in her hair, and paler than the white satin of her gown. Emma dreamed of her marriage day; she saw herself at home again among the fields in the little path as they walked to the church. Why didn't she, like this woman, resist and implore? Instead, she had walked joyously and unwittingly towards the abyss . . . Ah! if in the freshness of her beauty, before the degradation of marriage and the disillusions of adultery, she could have anchored her life upon some great, strong heart! Virtue, affection, sensuous pleasure and duty would have combined to give her eternal bliss. But such happiness, she realized, was a lie, a mockery to taunt desire. She knew now how small the passions were that art magnified. So, striving for detachment, Emma resolved to see in this reproduction of her sorrows a mere formal fiction for the entertainment of the eye, and she smiled inwardly in scornful pity when from behind the velvet curtains at the back of the stage a man appeared in a black cloak.

His large Spanish hat fell at a gesture he made, and immediately the instruments and the singers began the sextet. Edgar, flashing with fury, dominated all the others with his clearer voice; Ashton hurled homicidal provocations at him in deep notes; Lucie uttered her shrill lament; Arthur sang modulated asides in a middle register and the deep basso of the minister pealed forth like an organ, while the female voices re-echoed his words in a delightful chorus. They were lined up in one single gesticulating row, breathing forth anger, vengeance, jealousy, terror, mercy and surprise all at once from their open mouths. The outraged lover brandished his naked sword; his lace ruff rose and fell jerkily with the movements of his chest, and he walked from right to left with long strides, clanking against the boards the silver-gilt spurs of his soft, flaring boots. She thought that he must have inexhaustible supplies of love in him to lavish it upon the crowd with such effusion. All her attempts at critical detachment were swept away by the poetic power of the acting, and, drawn to the man by the illusion of the part, she tried to imagine his life— extraordinary, magnificent, notorious, the life that could have been hers if fate had willed it. If only they had met! He would have loved her, they would have travelled together through all the kingdoms of Europe from capital to capital, sharing in his success and in his hardships, picking up the flowers thrown to him, mending his clothes. Every night, hidden behind the golden lattice of her box, she would have drunk in eagerly the expansions of this soul that would have sung for her alone; from the stage, even as he acted, he would have looked at her. A mad idea took possession of her: he was looking at her right now! She longed to run to his arms, to take refuge in his strength, as in the incarnation of love itself, and to say to him, to cry out, "Take me away! carry me with you! let us leave! All my passion and all my dreams are yours!"

The curtain fell.

The smell of gas mingled with the people's breath and the waving fans made the air even more suffocating. Emma wanted to go out; the crowd filled the corridors, and she fell back in her arm-chair with palpitations that choked her. Charles, fearing that she would faint, ran to the refreshment-room to get a glass of orgeat.

He had great difficulty in getting back to his seat, for as he was holding the glass in his hands, his elbows bumped into someone at every step; he even spilt three-fourths on the shoulders of a Rouen lady in short sleeves, who feeling the cold liquid running down her back, started to scream like a peacock, as if she were being murdered. Her mill-owner husband lashed out at his clumsiness, and while she used her handkerchief to wipe off the stains from her handsome cherry-coloured taffeta gown, he angrily muttered about indemnity, costs, reimbursement. Charles was quite out of breath when he finally reached his wife:

"I thought I'd never make it. What a crowd! . . . What a crowd!"

And he added:

"Just guess whom I met up there! Monsieur Léon!"

"Léon?"

"Himself! He's coming along to pay his respects."

And as he finished these words the ex-clerk of Yonville entered the box.

He held out his hand with the casual ease of a gentleman; and Madame Bovary extended hers, yielding no doubt to the pressure of a stronger will. She had not felt it since that spring evening when the rain fell upon the green leaves, and they had said good-bye while standing near the window. But soon recalling herself to the necessities of the situation, she managed to shake off the torpor of her memories, and began stammering a few hurried words.

"Ah! good evening . . . What, you here?"

"Silence!" cried a voice from the orchestra, for the third act was beginning.

"So you are at Rouen?"

"Yes."

"And since when?"

"Be quiet! Throw them out!"

People were looking at them; they fell silent.

But from that moment she listened no more; and the chorus of the guests, the scene between Ashton and his servant, the grand duet in D major, all became more distant, as if the instruments had grown less sonorous and the characters more remote. She remembered the card games at the pharmacist, the walk to the nurse, the poetry readings in the arbour, the tête-à-têtes by the fireside—all the sadness of their love, so calm and so protracted, so discreet, so tender, and that she had nevertheless forgotten. And why had he come back? What combination of circumstances had brought him back into her life? He was standing behind her, leaning with his shoulder against the wall of the box; now and again she felt herself shudder as she felt the warmth of his breath on her hair.

"Do you find this amusing?" he said, bending over her so closely that the end of his moustache brushed her cheek.

She replied flippantly:

"Heavens, no! not particularly."

Then he suggested that they leave the theatre and have an ice somewhere.

"Oh, not yet; let us stay," said Bovary. "Her hair's undone; this is going to be tragic."

But the madness scene did not interest Emma, and she thought the singer was overacting.

"She screams too loud," she said, turning to Charles who was listening.

"Yes . . . perhaps . . . a little," he replied, torn between his genuine enjoyment and his respect for his wife's opinion.

Then Léon sighed:

"Don't you find it hot . . ."

"Unbearably so! Yes!"

"Don't you feel well?" Bovary inquired.

"Yes, I am stifling; let's go."

Monsieur Léon draped her long lace shawl carefully about her shoulders, and the three of them left and sat down near the harbor, on the terrace of a café. First they spoke of her illness, although Emma interrupted Charles from time to time, for fear, she said, of boring Monsieur Léon; and the latter told them that he had come to spend two years in a big Rouen law firm, in order to gain some experience of how business is conducted in Normandy—so different from Paris. Then he inquired after Berthe, the Homais, Mère Lefrançois, and as they had, in the husband's presence, nothing more to say to one another, the conversation soon came to an end.

People coming out of the theatre walked along the pavement, humming or shouting at the top of their voices, "*O bel ange, ma Lucie!*" Then Léon, playing the dilettante, began to talk music. He had seen Tamburini, Rubini, Persiani, Grisi,[5] and, compared with them, Lagardy, despite his grand outbursts, was nowhere.

"Yet," interrupted Charles, who was slowly sipping his rum-sherbet, "they say that he is quite admirable in the last act. I regret leaving before the end, just when I was beginning to enjoy myself."

"Why," said the clerk, "he will soon give another performance."

But Charles replied that they had to leave the next day. "Unless," he added, turning to his wife, "you'd like to stay by yourself, my darling?"

And changing his tactics at the unexpected opportunity that presented itself to his hopes, the young man sang the praises of Lagardy in the last aria. It was really superb, sublime. Then Charles insisted:

"You'll come back on Sunday. Come, make up your mind. If you feel that this is doing you the least bit of good, you shouldn't hesitate to stay."

The adjoining tables, however, were emptying; a waiter came and stood discreetly near them. Charles, who understood, took out his purse; the clerk held back his arm, and made a point of leaving two extra pieces of silver that he made chink on the marble.

"I am really sorry," said Bovary, "for all the money you are . . ."

The other silenced him with a gesture of affable disdain and, taking his hat, said:

"So, we are agreed, to-morrow at six o'clock?"

---

5. Antonio Tamburini (1800–1876), Gian-Battista Rubini (1795–1854), Fanny Facchinardi Persiani (who was the first Lucia), and Ciulia Grisi (1811–1869) were all famous bel-canto singers who appeared in Paris in the operas of Rossini and Donizetti.

Charles explained once more that he could not absent himself longer, but that nothing prevented Emma . . .

"But," she stammered, with a strange smile, "I don't know if I ought . . ."

"Well, you must think it over. Sleep over it and we'll see in the morning."

Then, to Léon, who was walking along with them:

"Now that you are in our part of the world, I hope you'll come and have dinner with us from time to time."

The clerk declared he would not fail to do so, being obliged, moreover, to go to Yonville on some business for his office. And they parted before the passage Saint-Herbland just as the cathedral struck half-past eleven.

Part Three

I

Monsieur Léon, while studying law, had been a fairly assiduous customer at the Chaumière, a dance-hall where he was particularly successful with the grisettes who thought him distinguished looking. He was the best-mannered of the students; he wore his hair neither too long nor too short, didn't spend all his quarter's money on the first day of the month, and kept on good terms with his professors. As for excesses, he had always abstained from them, as much from cowardice as from refinement.

Often when he stayed in his room to read, or else when sitting in the evening under the linden-trees of the Luxembourg,[6] he let his law-code fall to the ground, and the memory of Emma came back to him. But gradually this feeling grew weaker, and other desires took the upperhand, although the original passion still acted through them. For Léon did not lose all hope; there was for him, as it were, a vague promise floating in the future, like a golden fruit suspended from some fantastic tree.

Then, seeing her again after three years of absence, his passion reawakened. He must, he thought, finally make up his mind to possess her. Moreover, his timidity had worn off in the gay company of his student days, and he returned to the provinces in utter contempt of whoever had not set foot on the asphalt of the boulevards. In the presence of a genuine Parisienne, in the house of some famous physician surrounded by honors and luxury, the poor clerk would no

6. The gardens of the Palace of Luxembourg (built between 1615 and 1620 for Marie de Medici). The gardens are open to the public and much frequented by students, as they are near the Sorbonne.

doubt have trembled like a child; but here, on the quays of Rouen, with the wife of a small country-doctor, he felt at his ease, sure to shine. Self-confidence depends on environment: one does not speak in the same tone in the drawing room than in the kitchen; and the wealthy woman seems to have about her, to guard her virtue, all her bank-notes, like an armour, in the lining of her corset.

On leaving the Bovarys the night before, Léon had followed them through the streets at a distance; when he saw them enter the Croix-Rouge, he returned home and spent the night planning his strategy.

So the next afternoon about five o'clock he walked into the kitchen of the inn, pale and apprehensive, driven by a coward's resolution that stops at nothing.

"Monsieur isn't in," a servant told him.

This seemed to him a good omen. He went upstairs.

She didn't seem surprised at his arrival; on the contrary, she apologized for having failed to tell him where they were staying.

"Oh, I guessed it!" said Léon.

He pretended he had found her by chance, guided by instinct. When he saw her smile, he tried to repair his blunder by telling her he had spent the morning looking for her in all the hotels in the town.

"So you have made up your mind to stay?" he added.

"Yes," she said, "and I shouldn't have. One should avoid getting used to inaccessible pleasures when one is burdened by so many responsibilities . . ."

"Oh, I can imagine . . ."

"No, you can't, you are not a woman."

But men too had their trials, and the conversation started off by some philosophical considerations. Emma expatiated on the frailty of earthly affections, and the eternal isolation that stifles the human heart.

To show off, or in a naive imitation of this melancholy which stirred his own, the young man declared that he had been dreadfully despondent. He was bored by the law, attracted by other vocations and his mother had never ceased to harass him in all her letters. As they talked, they stated the reasons for their respective unhappiness with more precision and they felt a shared exaltation in this growing confidence. But they sometimes stopped short of revealing their thought in full, and then sought to invent a phrase that might nevertheless express it. She did not confess her passion for another; he did not say that he had forgotten her.

Perhaps he no longer remembered the suppers with girls after masked balls; and no doubt she did not recollect the rendezvous of old when she ran across the fields in the morning to her lover's house. The noises of the town hardly reached them, and the room seemed small, as if to bring them even closer together in their solitude. Emma, in a dimity dressing gown, leant her chignon against the back of the old arm-chair; the yellow wall-paper formed, as it were, a golden background behind her, and her bare head was reflected in the mirror with the white parting in the middle, the tip of her ears peeping out from the folds of her hair.

"How bad of me!" she said, "you must forgive me for boring you with my eternal complaints."

"No, never, never!"

"If only you knew," she went on, raising to the ceiling her beautiful eyes, in which a tear was trembling, "if only you knew all I dreamed!"

"So did I! Oh, I too have suffered! Often I went out; I went away. I left, dragging myself along the quays, seeking distraction amid the din of the crowd without being able to banish the heaviness that weighed upon me. In an engraver's shop on the boulevard I found an Italian print of one of the Muses. She is draped in a tunic, and she is looking at the moon, with forget-me-nots in her flowing hair. Something continually drove me there. I would stay for hour after hour."

Then, in a trembling voice:

"She looked a little like you."

Madame Bovary turned away her head that he might not see the irrepressible smile she felt rising to her lips.

"Often," he want on, "I wrote you letters that I tore up."

She did not answer. He continued;

"I sometimes fancied that some chance would bring you. I thought I recognised you at street-corners, and I ran after carriages when I saw a shawl or a veil like yours flutter in the window . . ."

She seemed resolved to let him speak without interruption. With arms crossed and her head lowered, she stared at the rosettes on her slippers, and from time to time moved her toes under the satin.

At last she sighed.

"But what I find worst of all is to drag out, as I do, a useless existence. If our pains could be of use to some one, we should find consolation in the thought of the sacrifice."

He started off in praise of virtue, duty, and silent immolation, having himself an incredible longing for self-sacrifice that he could not satisfy.

"What I would like," she said "is to work in a hospital as a nursing Sister."

"Unfortunately," he replied, "no such holy vocations are open to men, and I can think of no profession . . . except perhaps a doctor's . . ."

With a slight shrug of the shoulders, Emma interrupted him to speak of her illness, which had almost killed her. How she regretted her cure! if she had died, she would not now be suffering. Léon was quick to express his own longing for "the quiet of the tomb"; one night, he had even made his will, asking to be buried in that beautiful coverlet with velvet stripes he had received from her. For this was how they would have wished to be, each setting up an ideal to which they were now trying to adapt their past life. Besides, speech is like a rolling machine that always stretches the sentiment it expresses.

But this made-up story of the coverlet made her ask:

"Why?"

"Why?" He hesitated.

"Because I loved you so!"

And congratulating himself at having surmounted the obstacle, Léon watched her face out of the corner of his eye.

It was like the sky when a gust of wind sweeps the clouds away. The mass of darkening sad thoughts lifted from her blue eyes; her whole face shone.

He waited. At last she replied:

"I always suspected it."

Then they went over all the trifling events of that far-off existence, of which the joys and sorrows had just been conjured up by that one word. He remembered the clematis arbour, the dresses she had worn, the furniture of her room, the entire house.

"And our poor cactuses, where are they?"

"The cold killed them this winter."

"How often did I think of them! I see them again as they looked when on summer mornings the sun shone on your blinds, and I saw your two bare arms among the flowers.

"Poor friend!" she said, holding out her hand.

Léon swiftly pressed his lips to it. Then, when he had taken a deep breath:

"In those days, you were like an incomprehensible power to me which held me captive. Once, for instance, I came to see you, but you probably don't remember."

"I do," she said; "go on."

"You were downstairs in the hall, ready to go out, standing on the last stair; you were wearing a hat with small blue flowers; and without being invited, in spite of myself, I went with you. But I grew more and more conscious of my folly every moment, and I kept walking by your side, not daring to follow you completely but unable to leave. When you went into a shop, I waited in the street, and I watched you through the window taking off your gloves and counting the change on the counter. Then you rang at Madame Tuvache's; you were let in, and I stood like an idiot in front of the great heavy door that had closed after you."

Madame Bovary, as she listened to him, wondered that she was so old. All these things reappearing before her seemed to expand her existence; it was like some sentimental immensity to which she returned; and from time to time she said in a low voice, her eyes half closed:

"Yes, it is true . . . it is true . . ."

They heard eight o'clock strike on the different towers that surround the Place Beauvoisine, a neighborhood of schools, churches, and large empty private dwellings. They no longer spoke, but as they looked upon each other, they felt their heads whirl, as if waves of sound had escaped from their fixed glances. They were hand in hand now, and the past, the future, reminiscences and dreams, all were confounded in the sweetness of this ecstasy. Night was darkening over the walls, leaving visible only, half hidden in the shade, the coarse colours of four bills representing scenes from *La Tour de Nesle*,[7] with Spanish and French captains underneath. Through the sash-window they could see a patch of sky between the pointed roofs.

She rose to light two wax-candles on the chest of drawers, then she sat down again.

"Well . . . ?" said Léon.

"Well . . . ?" she replied.

He was wondering how to resume the interrupted conversation, when she said to him:

"How is it that no one until now has ever expressed such sentiments to me?"

The clerk retorted that idealistic natures rarely found understanding. But he had loved her from the very first moment; the thought of their possible happiness filled him with despair. If only they had met earlier, by some stroke of chance, they would have been forever bound together.

"I have sometimes thought of it," she went on.

"What a dream!" murmured Léon.

And fingering gently the blue border of her long white belt, he added,

"Who prevents us from starting all over again?"

"No, my friend," she replied; "I am too old . . . You are too young . . . forget me! Others will love you . . . you will love them."

"Not as I love you!"

"What a child you are! Come, let us be sensible, I want it."

She told him again that their love was impossible, that they must remain, as before, like brother and sister to each other.

Was she speaking seriously? No doubt Emma did not herself know, absorbed as she was by the charm of the seduction and the necessity

7. A melodrama by Alexandre Dumas the elder (1803–1870) and Gaillardet (1832) in which Marie de Bourgogne, famous for her crimes, is the main heroine.

of defending herself; looking tenderly at the young man, she gently repulsed the timid caresses that his trembling hands attempted.

"Ah! forgive me!" he cried, drawing back.

Emma was seized with a vague fear at this shyness, more dangerous to her than the boldness of Rodolphe when he advanced to her open-armed. No man had ever seemed to her so beautiful. His demeanor suggested an exquisite candor. He lowered his long curling eyelashes. The soft skin of his cheek was flushed, she thought, with desire for her, and Emma felt an invincible longing to press her lips to it. Then, leaning towards the clock as if to see the time:

"How late it is!" she exclaimed. "How we have been chattering!"

He understood the hint and took up his hat.

"You made me forget about the opera! And poor Bovary who left me here especially for that! Monsieur Lormeaux, of the Rue Grand-Pont, was to take me and his wife."

And there would be no other opportunity, as she was to leave the next day.

"Really?" said Léon.

"Yes."

"But I must see you again," he went on. "I had something to tell you . . ."

"What?"

"Something . . . important, serious. I cannot possibly let you go like this. If only you knew . . . Listen to me . . . Haven't you understood? Can't you guess?"

"You made yourself very clear," said Emma.

"Ah! you can jest! But you shouldn't. Have mercy, and allow me to see you again . . . only once . . . one single time."

"Well . . ."

She stopped; then, as if changing her mind:

"But not here!"

"Wherever you say."

"Will you . . ."

She seemed to think; then suddenly:

"To-morrow at eleven o'clock in the cathedral."

"I shall be there," he cried, seizing her hands, which she withdrew.

And as they were both standing up, he behind and Emma with lowered head, he stooped over her and pressed long kisses on her neck.

"You are crazy, you are crazy!" she cried between bursts of laughter, as the kisses multiplied.

Then bending his head over her shoulder, he seemed to beg the consent of her eyes, but when they met his, they seemed icy and distant.

Léon took three paces backwards. He stopped on the threshold; then he whispered in a trembling voice:

"Till to-morrow."

She answered with a nod, and vanished like a bird into the next room.

In the evening Emma wrote the clerk an interminable letter, in which she cancelled the rendezvous; all was over between them; they must not, for the sake of their happiness, meet again. But when the letter was finished, as she did not know Leon's address, she was puzzled.

"I'll give it to him myself," she said; "he'll come."

The next morning, humming a tune while he stood on his balcony by the open window, Léon polished his shoes with special care. He put on white trousers, silken socks, a green coat, emptied all the scent he had into his handkerchief, then having had his hair curled, he uncurled it again, in order to give it a more natural elegance.

"It is still too early," he thought, looking at the barber's cuckoo-clock, that pointed to the hour of nine.

He read an old fashion journal, went out, smoked a cigar, walked up three streets, thought the time had come and walked slowly towards the porch of Notre Dame.

It was a beautiful summer morning. Silver sparkled in the window of the jeweler's store and the light, falling obliquely on the cathedral, threw shimmering reflections on the edges of the grey stones; a flock of birds fluttered in the grey sky round the trefoiled turrets; the square, resounding with cries, was fragrant with the flowers that bordered the pavement, roses, jasmines, carnations, narcissus, and tuberoses, unevenly spaced out between moist grasses, catnip, and chickweed for the birds; the fountains gurgled in the center, and under large umbrellas, amidst heaps of piled up melons, bare-headed flower vendors wrapped bunches of violets in pieces of paper.

The young man took one. It was the first time that he had bought flowers for a woman, and his breast, as he smelt them, swelled with pride, as if this homage that he meant for another had been reflected upon himself.

But he was afraid of being seen and resolutely entered the church.

The verger was just then standing on the threshold in the middle of the left doorway, under the figure of Salomé dancing, known in Rouen as the "dancing Marianne." He wore a feather cap, a rapier dangled against his leg and he looked more majestic than a cardinal, as shining as a pyx.

He came towards Léon, and, with the bland benign smile of a priest when questioned a child, asked:

"I gather that Monsieur is a visitor in this town? Would Monsieur care to be shown the church?"

"No!" said Léon.

And he first went round the lower aisles. Then he went out to look at the Place. Emma was not coming yet, so he returned as far as the choir.

The nave was reflected in the full fonts together with the base of the arches and some fragments of the stained glass windows. But the reflections of the painted glass, broken by the marble rim, were continued farther on upon the pavement, like a many-coloured carpet. The broad daylight from outside entered the church in three enormous rays through the three opened portals. From time to time a sacristan crossed the far end of the church, making the sidewise genuflection of a hurried worshipper in the direction of the altar. The crystal lustres hung motionless. In the choir a silver lamp was burning, and from the side chapels and dark places in the church sounds like sighs arose, together with the clang of a closing grating that echoed under the lofty vaults.

Léon walked solemnly alongside the walls. Life had never seemed so good to him. She would soon appear, charming and agitated, looking back to see if anyone was watching her—with her flounced dress, her gold eyeglass, her delicate shoes, with all sorts of elegant trifles that he had never been allowed to taste, and with the ineffable seduction of yielding virtue. The church was set around her like a huge boudoir; the arches bent down to shelter in their darkness the avowal of her love; the windows shone resplendent to light up her face, and the censers would burn that she might appear like an angel amid sweet-smelling clouds.

Meanwhile, she did not come. He sat down on a chair, and his eyes fell upon a blue stained window representing boatmen carrying baskets. He looked at it long, attentively, and he counted the scales of the fishes and the button-holes of the doublets, while his thoughts wandered off in search of Emma.

The verger, left to himself, resented the presence of someone who dared to admire the cathedral without his assistance. He considered this a shocking way to behave, robbing him of his due, close to committing sacrilege.

There was a rustle of silk on the pavement, the edge of a hat, a hooded cape—it was she! Leon rose and ran to meet her.

Emma was pale. She walked hurriedly.

"Read this!" she said, holding out a piece of paper to him. "Oh, no!"

And she abruptly withdrew her hand to enter the chapel of the Virgin, where, kneeling on a chair, she began to pray.

The young man was irritated by this display of piety; then he nevertheless felt a certain charm in seeing her thus lost in devotions in the middle of a rendezvous, like an Andalusian marquise; then he grew bored, for she seemed to go on for ever.

Emma prayed, or rather tried to pray, hoping that some sudden resolution might descend to her from heaven; and to draw down divine aid she filled her eyes with the splendors of the tabernacle. She breathed in the perfumes of the full-blown flowers in the large vases, and listened to the stillness of the church—a stillness that only heightened the tumult in her own heart.

She rose, and they were about to leave, when the verger quickly approached:

"Madame is perhaps a stranger here? Madame would like to visit the church?"

"Oh, no!" the clerk cried.

"Why not?" she said.

For, with her expiring virtue, she clung to the Virgin, the sculptures, the tombs—to anything.

Then, in order to do things right, the verger took them to the entrance near the square, where, pointing out with his cane a large circle of black stones, without inscription or carving:

"This," he said majestically, "is the circumference of the beautiful bell of Ambroise. It weighed forty thousand pounds. There was not its equal in all Europe. The workman who cast it died of joy . . ."

"Let's go," said Léon.

The old man started off again; then, having got back to the chapel of the Virgin, he waved his arm in a theatrical gesture of demonstration, and, prouder than a country squire showing his orchard, he announced:

"This simple stone covers Pierre de Brézé, lord of Varenne and of Brissac, grand marshal of Poitou, and governor of Normandy, who died at the battle of Montlhéry on the 16th of July, 1465."

Léon was furiously biting his lips of impatience.

"And on the right, this gentleman in full armour, on the prancing horse, is his grandson, Louis de Brézé, lord of Breval and of Montchauvet, Count de Maulevrier, Baron de Mauny, chamberlain to the king, Knight of the Order, and also governor of Normandy; he died on the 23rd of July, 1531—a Sunday, as the inscription specifies; and below, this figure, about to descend into the tomb, portrays the same person. How could one conceive of a better way to depict the void of human destiny?"

Madame Bovary lifted her eyeglass. Motionless, Léon watched her without even trying to protest, to make a gesture, so discouraged was he by this double display of idle talk and indifference.

Nothing could stop the guide:

"Near him, this kneeling woman who weeps is his spouse, Diane de Poitiers, comtesse de Brézé, duchesse de Valentinois, born in 1499, died in 1566, and to the left, the one with the child is the

Holy Virgin. Now if you turn to this side, you will see the tombs of the Ambroise. They were both cardinals and archbishops of Rouen. That one was minister under Louis XII. He did a great deal for the cathedral. In his will he left thirty thousand gold crowns for the poor."

And without ceasing to talk, he pushed them into a chapel crowded with wooden railings; he pushed some aside and discovered a kind of wooden block that looked vaguely like a poorly carved statue.

"It seems hard to believe," he sighed sadly, "but this used to adorn the tomb of Richard Coeur de Lion,[8] King of England and Duke of Normandy. It was the Calvinists, Monsieur, who reduced it to this condition. They were mean enough to bury it in the earth, under the episcopal throne of Monseigneur the bishop. You can see from here the door by which Monseigneur passes to his house. Let's move on to the gargoyle windows."

But Léon hastily extracted some silver coins from his pocket and seized Emma's arm. The verger stood dumbfounded, not able to understand this untimely munificence when there were still so many things for the stranger to see. He called after him:

"Monsieur! The steeple! the steeple!"[9]

"No, thank you!" said Léon.

"You are missing the best! It is four hundred and forty feet high, nine less than the great pyramid of Egypt. It is all cast iron, it . . ."

Léon was fleeing, for it seemed to him that his love, that for nearly two hours had been frozen in the church like the stones, would now vanish like a vapor through that sort of truncated funnel, rectangular cage or open chimney that rises so grotesquely from the cathedral like the extravagant brainchild of some fantastic roofer.

"But where are we going?" she said.

He pushed on without answering, and Madame Bovary was already dipping her finger in the holy water when behind them they heard a panting breath interrupted by the regular sound of a tapping cane, Léon turned around.

"Monsieur!"

"What is it?"

And he recognised the verger, holding under his arms and bracing against his stomach some twenty large volumes, all of them works on the cathedral.

"Idiot!" muttered Léon, rushing out of the church.

A boy was playing on the sidewalk:

"Go and get me a cab!"

8. Richard the Lion Hearted (born 1175), was king of England from 1189–1199. He died at the siege of the Castle of Châlus.   9. Added to the Cathedral of Rouen, built in the Gothic style in stages from the thirteenth century to the early sixteenth, was a high cast iron spire (485 feet), which is generally considered a tasteless disfigurement. Construction was begun in 1824 but not finished until 1876.

The child bounded off like a ball by the rue des Quatre-Vents; then they were alone a few minutes, face to face, and a little embarrassed.

"Oh Léon! Truly . . . I don't know . . . if I should . . ."

She simpered. Then, in a serious tone:

"It's very improper, you know, it isn't done."

"Everybody does it in Paris!" replied the clerk.

This, like a decisive argument, entirely convinced her. She had made up her mind.

But no cab arrived. Léon shuddered at the thought that she might return into the church. At last the cab appeared.

"At least, you should go out by the northern gate," cried the verger, who was left alone on the threshold, "and look at the Resurrection, the Last Judgment, Paradise, King David, and the damned burning in the flames of Hell!"

"Where to, sir?" asked the coachman.

"Anywhere!" said Léon, pushing Emma into the cab.

And the lumbering machine set out.

It went down the Rue Grand-Pont, crossed the Place des Arts, the Quai Napoleon, the Pont Neuf, and stopped short before the statue of Pierre Corneille.

"Go on," cried a voice that came from within.

The cab went on again, and as soon as it reached the Carrefour Lafayette, set off down-hill, and entered the railroad station at a gallop.

"No, straight on!" cried the same voice.

The cab came out by the gate, and soon having reached the Mall, trotted quietly beneath the elm-trees. The coachman wiped his brow, put his leather hat between his knees, and drove his carriage beyond the side alley by the meadow to the margin of the waters.

It went along by the river, along the towing-path paved with sharp pebbles, and for a long while in the direction of Oyssel, beyond the islands.

But suddenly it turned sideways across Quatremares, Sotteville, La Grande-Chaussée, the Rue d'Elbeuf, and made its third halt in front of the Jardin des Plantes.

"Get on, will you?" cried the voice more furiously.

And at once resuming its course, it passed by Saint Sever, by the Quai des Curandiers, the Quai aux Meules, once more over the bridge, by the Place du Champ de Mars, and behind the hospital gardens, where old men in black coats were walking in the sun along the ivy-covered terraces. It went up the Boulevard Bouvreuil, along the Boulevard Cauchoise, then the whole of Mont-Riboudet to the Deville hills.

It came back; and then, without any fixed plan or direction, wandered about at random. The cab was seen at Saint-Pol, at Lescure, at Mont Gargan, at La Rougue-Marc and Place du Gaillardbois; in the Rue Maladrerie, Rue Dinanderie, before Saint-Romain, Saint-Vivien, Saint-Maclou, Saint-Nicaise—in front of the Customs, at the Basse-Vieille-Tour, the "Trois Pipes," and the Cimetière monumental. From time to time the coachman on his seat cast despairing glances at the passing cafés. He could not understand what furious locomotive urge prevented these people from ever coming to a stop. Time and again he would try, but exclamations of anger would at once burst forth behind him. Then he would whip his two sweating nags, but he no longer bothered dodging bumps in the road; the cab would hook on to things on all sides but he couldn't have cared less, demoralised as he was, almost weeping with thirst, fatigue, and despair.

Near the harbor, among the trucks and the barrels, and along the street corners and the sidewalks, bourgeois stared in wonder at this thing unheard of in the provinces: a cab with all blinds drawn that reappeared incessantly, more tightly sealed than a tomb and tossed around like ship on the waves.

One time, around noon, in the open country, just as the sun beat most fiercely against the old plated lanterns, a bare hand appeared under the yellow canvass curtain, and threw out some scraps of paper that scattered in the wind, alighting further off like white butterflies on a field of red clover all in bloom.

Then, at about six o'clock the carriage stopped in a back street of the Beauvoisine Quarter, and a woman got out, walking with her veil down and without looking back.

II

On reaching the inn, Madame Bovary was surprised not to see the stage coach. Hivert had waited for her fifty-three minutes, but finally left without her.

Nothing forced her to go, but she had promised to return that same evening. Moreover, Charles expected her, and in her heart she felt already that cowardly docility that is for some women at once the chastisement and atonement of adultery.

She packed her bag quickly, paid her bill, took a cab in the yard, hurrying on the driver, urging him on, every moment inquiring about time and distance traversed. He succeeded in catching up with the Hirondelle as it neared the first houses of Quincampoix.

Hardly was she seated in her corner that she closed her eyes, and opened them at the foot of the hill, when from afar she recognised Félicité, who was on the look-out in front of the blacksmith's. Hivert pulled up his horses, and the maid, reaching up to the window, said in a tone of mystery:

"Madame, you must go at once to Monsieur Homais. It's for something urgent."

The village was silent as usual. At the corner of the streets little pink mounds lay smoking in the air, for this was the time for jam-making, and every one at Yonville prepared his supply on the same day. But in front of the pharmacist's shop one might admire a far larger heap; it surpassed the others with the superiority that a laboratory must have over domestic ovens, a general need over individual fancy.

She went in. The big arm-chair had fallen over and even the "Fanal de Rouen" lay on the ground, outspread between two pestles. She pushed open the door of the hall, and in the middle of the kitchen, amid brown jars full of picked currants, powdered and lump sugar, scales on the table and pans on the fire, she saw assembled all the Homais, big and little, with aprons reaching to their chins, and holding forks in their hands. Justin was standing with bowed head, and the pharmacist was screaming:

"Who told you to go fetch it in the *Capharnaum?*"

"What is it? What is the matter?"

"What is it?" replied the pharmacist. "We are making jelly; it is cooking; but it threatens to boil over because there is too much juice, and I ask for another pan. Then this one here, out of laziness, goes to my laboratory, and dares to take the key to the Capharnaum from the nail!"

This name had been given to a small room under the eaves, crammed with the tools and the goods of his trade. He often spent long hours there alone, labelling, decanting, and packaging. He looked upon it not as a simple store-room, but as a veritable sanctuary from where the creations of his own hands were to set forth: pills, lotions, and potions that would spread far and wide his rising fame. No one in the world was allowed to set foot there, and he revered it to the point of sweeping it himself. If the pharmacy, open to all comers, was the stage where he displayed his pride, the Capharnaum was the refuge where in selfish concentration, Homais indulged in his most relished pursuits. Therefore, Justin's thoughtlessness seemed to him a monstrous piece of irreverence, and, his face redder than the currants, he continued:

"Yes, the key to the Capharnaum! The key that locks up the acids and caustic alkalis! To go and get a spare pan! a pan with a lid! and that I shall perhaps never use! Everything is of importance in the delicate operations of our art! One must maintain the proper distinctions, and not employ for nearly domestic purposes, what is destined for a pharmaceutical science! It is as if one were to carve a fowl with a scalpel; as if a magistrate . . ."

"Quiet down," Madame Homais was saying.

And Athalie, pulling at his coat, cried:

"Papa! papa!"

"No, leave me alone!" the pharmacist cried, "leave me alone! I tell you, I might as well be running a grocery store. Just keep at it, don't mind me and break everything to pieces! Smash the test-tubes, let the leeches loose, burn the marshmallows, put pickles in the medical jars, tear up the bandages!"

"I thought you wanted to . . ."

"In a moment . . . Do you know what risks you took? Didn't you see something in the corner, on the left, on the third shelf? Speak! Answer me! Say something!"

"I . . . don't . . . know . . ." stammered the boy.

"Ah! you don't know! Well, *I* do! You saw a bottle of blue glass sealed with yellow wax, that contains a white powder carefully marked *Dangerous!* And do you know what is in it? Arsenic! And you go and touch it! You take a pan that stands right next to it!"

"Right next to it!" cried Madame Homais, clasping her hands. "Arsenic! You might have poisoned us all."

And the children began to scream as if they already felt dreadful stomach pains.

"Or poison a patient!" continued the pharmacist. "Do you want to see me dragged into court like a common criminal? or taken to the scaffold? As if you didn't know how careful one has to be in handling chemicals, even I who spent my life doing nothing else. Often I am horrified when I think of my responsibility; the Government persecutes us, and the absurd legislation that rules us is a veritable Damocles' sword suspended over our heads."

Emma gave up trying to find out what they wanted her for, and the pharmacist continued without pausing for breath:

"That is how you thank us for the many kindnesses we have shown you! That is how you reward me for the truly paternal care that I lavish on you! Where would you be if I hadn't taken you in hand? What would you be doing? Who provides you with food, education, clothes, and all the means to rise to a respectable level in society? But if you want to get there, you'll have to learn to pull hard at the oars—get callouses on your hands, as the saying goes. *Fabricando fit faber, age quod agis.*"[1]

He was so exasperated he quoted Latin. He would have used Chinese or Greenlandic had he known them, for he was rocked by one of these crises in which the soul reveals all it contains, just as the storm lays bare the ocean from the seaweed on the shore down to the sand on its deepest bottom.

And he went on:

---

1. The artisan becomes proficient through practice; practice what you are supposed to do.

"I am beginning to regret that I ever took you in charge! I would have done a lot better if I'd let you wallow in poverty and filth, where you were born. The best you can hope for is to be a cowhand. You are not fit to be a scientist! You hardly know how to stick on a label! And there you are, dwelling with me snug as a parson, living in clover, taking your ease!"

Emma turned in despair to Madame Homais:

"I was told to come . . ."

"Heavens!" the lady exclaimed in a mournful tone "How am I to tell you? . . . Such a misfortune!"

She could not finish. The pharmacist was thundering:

"Empty it! Clean it! Take it back! And hurry!"

And seizing Justin by the collar of his apron, he shook him so vigorously that a book fell out of his pocket. The boy stooped, but Homais was the quicker, and, having picked up the volume, he stared at it with bulging eyes and open mouth.

"Conjugal . . . love!" he said, slowly separating the two words. "Ah! very good! very good! very pretty! And with illustrations! . . . Truly, this is too much!"

Madame Homais drew near.

"No, don't touch it!"

The children wanted to look at the pictures.

"Leave the room," he said imperiously.

They went out.

First he walked up and down, with the open gook in his hand, rolling his eyes, choking, fuming, apoplectic. Then he came straight to his apprentice, and, planting himself in front of him with folded arms:

"So you are blessed with all the vices under the sun, you little wretch? Watch out! you are following a dangerous path! . . . Did it never occur to you that this infamous book might fall into the hands of my children, kindle a spark in their minds, tarnish the purity of Athalie, corrupt Napoleon! He is close to being a man. Are you quite sure, at least, that they have not read it? Can you certify to me . . ."

"But, Monsieur," said Emma, "you wished to tell me . . ."

"Oh yes, Madame . . . your father-in-law is dead."

Indeed, the elder Bovary had suddenly died from a stroke the evening before, as he got up from the table; overanxious to spare Emma's sensitive nerves, Charles had asked Monsieur Homais to break the horrible news to her as carefully as possible.

Homais had meditated at length over his speech; he had rounded, polished it, given it the proper cadence; it was a masterpiece of prudence and transitions, of subtle turns and delicacy; but anger had got the better of rhetoric.

Emma, abandoning all hope to learn any further details, left the pharmacy; for Monsieur Homais had resumed his vituperations. He was growing calmer, however, and was now grumbling in a paternal tone whilst he fanned himself with his skull-cap.

"It is not that I entirely disapprove of the book. The author was a doctor! It contains scientific information that a man might well want to know; I'd go as far as saying that he ought to know. But later . . . later! You should at least wait till you are yourself full-grown, and your character formed."

When Emma knocked at the door, Charles, who was waiting for her, came forward with open arms and said in a tearful voice:

"Ah! my dear wife. . . ."

And he leant over gently to kiss her. But at the contact of his lips the memory of the other returned; she passed her hand over her face and shuddered.

Yet, she answered:

"Yes, I know . . . I know . . . ."

He showed her the letter in which his mother told the event without any sentimental hypocrisy. Her only regret was that her husband had not received the consolation of religion; he had died at Doudeville, in the street, at the door of a café after a patriotic dinner with some ex-officers.

Emma gave him back the letter; then at dinner, for appearance's sake, she affected a lack of appetite. But as he urged her to try, she resolutely began eating, while Charles opposite her sat motionless and dejected.

Now and then he raised his head and gave her a long, distressed look. Once he sighed:

"I'd have liked to see him again!"

She was silent. At last, realizing that she must say something:

"How old was your father?" she asked.

"Fifty-eight."

"Ah!"

And that was all.

A quarter of an hour later, he added: "My poor mother! what will become of her now?"

She made a gesture of ignorance.

Seeing her so taciturn, Charles imagined her much affected, and forced himself to say nothing, not to reawaken this sorrow which moved him. And, shaking off his own:

"Did you enjoy yourself yesterday?" he asked.

"Yes."

When the cloth was removed, Bovary did not rise, nor did Emma; and as she looked at him, the monotony of the spectacle drove little by little all pity from her heart. He seemed to her paltry, weak, a nonentity—a sorry creature in every way. How to get rid of him? What an interminable evening! She felt a stupor invading her, as if from opium fumes.

They heard the sharp noise of a wooden leg on the boards of the entrance hall. It was Hippolyte bringing back Emma's luggage.

To put them down, he had to bring around his wooden stump painfully in a quarter circle.

"He doesn't even seem to remember" she thought, looking at the poor devil, whose coarse red hair was wet with perspiration.

Bovary was searching for a coin at the bottom of his purse; he did not seem to realize how humiliating the man's presence was for him, standing there as the living embodiment of his hopeless ineptitude.

"Oh, you have a pretty bouquet," he said, noticing Léon's violets on the mantlepiece.

"Yes," she replied indifferently, "it's a bouquet I bought just now . . . from a beggar-woman."

Charles picked up the flowers and, bathing his tear-stained eyes in their freshness, he delicately sniffed their perfume. She took them quickly from his hand and put them in a glass of water.

The next day the elder Madame Bovary arrived. She and her son spent much time weeping. Pretending to be busy in the house, Emma managed to stay by herself.

The following day, they had to discuss together the arrangements for the period of mourning. They went and sat down with their workboxes by the waterside under the arbor.

Charles was thinking of his father, and was surprised to feel so much affection for this man, whom up till now he thought he cared little about. The older Madmae Bovary was thinking of her husband. The worst days of the past seemed enviable to her. All was forgotten beneath the instinctive regret of such a long habit, and from time to time, while sewing, a big tear rolled down her nose and hung suspended there a moment.

Emma was thinking that it was scarcely forty-eight hours since they had been together, far from the world, lost in ecstasy, and not having eyes enough to gaze upon each other. She tried to recall the slightest details of that past day. But the presence of her husband and mother-in-law bothered her. She would have liked to stop hearing and seeing, in order to keep intact the stillness of her love; but, try as she would, the memory would vanish under the impact of outer sensations.

She was removing the lining of a dress, and the strips were scattered around her. Mother Bovary, without looking up, kept her scissors busy, and Charles, in his felt slippers and his old brown coat that he used as a dressing gown, sat in silence with both hands in his pockets; near them Berthe, in a little white apron, was raking the sandwalks with her spade.

Suddenly they saw Monsieur Lheureux, the storekeeper, come in through the gate.

He came to offer his services "on this sad occasion." Emma replied that none were needed, but the shopkeeper wouldn't take no for an answer.

"I beg your pardon," he said, "but I should like to have a word in private."

Then, in a low voice, he added:

"It is about this little matter . . . you know . . . ." Charles turned crimson.

"Oh yes . . . . of course."

And, in his confusion, he turned to his wife:

"Darling, could you perhaps . . . ?"

She seemed to understand him, for she rose; and Charles said to his mother:

"Nothing important. Some household trifle, I suppose."

Fearing her reproaches, he didn't want her to know about the note.

As soon as they were alone, Monsieur Lheureux began by congratulating Emma outspokenly on the inheritance, then talked of this and that, the fruit trees, the harvest, his own health which had endless ups and downs. He had to work like devil and, regardless of what people thought, didn't make enough to buy butter for his bread.

Emma let him talk. She had been so dreadfully bored, these last two days!

"And so you're quite well again?" he went on. "Believe me, your husband was in quite a state. He's a good fellow, though we did have a little misunderstanding."

She asked what the misunderstanding was about, for Charles had told her nothing of the dispute about the goods supplied to her.

"As if you didn't know!" exclaimed Lheureux. "It was about your little caprice . . . the trunks."

He had drawn his hat over his eyes, and, with his hands behind his back, smiling and whistling, he looked straight at her in an unbearable manner. Did he suspect anything? She was lost in all kinds of apprehensions. Finally he said:

"We made it up, and I've come to propose still another arrangement."

He offered to renew the note Bovary had signed. The doctor, of course, would do as he pleased; he was not to trouble himself, especially just now, when he would have a lot to attend to.

"It seems to me he'd do well to turn it all over to some one else,—

to you, for example. With a power of attorney it could be easily managed, and then the two of us could have our little business transactions together . . ."

She did not understand. He did not insist, and brought the conversation back to his trade; it was impossible that Madame didn't need anything. He would send her a black barège, twelve yards, just enough to make a dress.

"The one you've on is good enough for the house, but you want another for calls. I saw that the very moment that I came in. I've got a quick eye for these things!"

He did not send the material, he brought it. Then he came again to take her measurements; he came again on other pretexts, always trying to make himself agreeable, useful, like a vassal serving his master, as Homais might have put it, and never failing to drop a hint about the power of attorney. He never mentioned the note. She didn't think of it; although Charles doubtlessly had mentioned something at the beginning of her convalescence, so many emotions had passed through her head that she no longer remembered it. Besides, she made it a point never to bring up any money questions. Charles' mother seemed surprised at this, and attributed the change in her ways to the religious sentiments she had contracted during her illness.

But as soon as she left, Emma greatly astounded Bovary by her practical good sense. They would have to make inquiries, look into the mortgages, decide whether it would be more advantageous to sell by auction or by other means.

She quoted legal jargon at random, and grand words such as "order," "the future," "foresight." She constantly exaggerated the difficulties of settling his father's affairs; at last, one day she showed him the rough draft of a power of attorney to manage and administer his business, arrange all notes, sign and endorse all bills, pay all sums, etc. She had profited by Lheureux's lessons.

Charles naively asked her where this paper came from.

"From Master Guillaumin."

And with the utmost coolness she added:

"I don't trust him overmuch. Notaries have such a bad reputation. Perhaps we ought to consult . . . But the only person we know . . . There is no one."

"Unless perhaps Léon . . ." replied Charles, who was thinking.

But it was difficult to explain matters by letter. Then she offered to make the journey. He refused. She insisted. It was quite a contest of mutual consideration. At last she exclaimed, in a childish tone of mock-rebellion:

"No, enough, I will!"

"How good you are!" he said, kissing her on the forehead.

The next morning she set out in the "Hirondelle" for Rouen to consult Monsieur Léon, and she stayed there three days.

III

They were three full, exquisite, magnificent days—a true honeymoon. They stayed at the Hôtel-de-Boulogne, on the harbor; and they lived there behind drawn blinds and closed doors, with flowers on the floor, and iced fruit syrups that were brought them early in the morning.

Towards evening they took a covered boat and went to dine on one of the islands.

At this time of the day, one could hear the caulking irons sound against the hulls in the dockyard. Tar smoke rose up between the trees and large oily patches floated on the water, undulating unevenly in the purple sunlight like surfaces of Florentine bronze.

They drifted down among moored ships whose long slanting cables grazed lightly the top of their boat.

The sounds of the city gradually fainted in the distance, the rattling of carriages, the tumult of voices, the yelping of dogs on the decks of barges. She loosened her hat and they landed on their island.

They sat down in the low-ceilinged room of a tavern with black fishing-nets hanging across the door. They ate fried smelts, cream and cherries. They lay down upon the grass, kissed behind the poplar trees; like two Robinson Crusoes, they would gladly have lived forever in this spot; in their bliss, it seemed to them the most magnificent place on earth. It was not the first time that they had seen trees, a blue sky, meadows; or heard the water flow and the wind blow in the branches. But they had never really felt any of this; it was as if nature had not existed before, or had only begun to be beautiful since the gratification of their desires.

At nightfall they returned. The boat glided along the shores of the islands. They stayed below, hidden in darkness, without saying a word. The square-tipped oars sounded against the iron oar-locks; in the stillness, they seemed to mark time like the beat of a metronome, while the rope that trailed behind never ceased its gentle splash against the water.

One night the moon rose, and they did not fail to make fine phrases about how melancholical and poetic it appeared to them. She even began to sing:

> One night, do you remember,
> We were sailing . . .

Her thin musical voice died away over the water; Léon could hear the wind-borne trills pass by him like a fluttering of wings.

She faced him, leaning against the wall of the cabin while the moon shone through the open blinds. Her black dress, falling around her like a fan, made her seem more slender, taller. Her head was raised, her hands clasped, her eyes turned towards heaven. At times the shadow of the willows hid her completely; then she reappeared suddenly, like a vision in the moonlight.

Léon, on the floor by her side, found under his hand a ribbon of scarlet silk.

The boatman looked at it, and said at last:

"Perhaps it belongs to the party I took out the other day. They were a jolly bunch of ladies and gentlemen, with cakes, champagne, trumpets—everything in style! There was one especially, a tall hand-some man with small moustaches, who was the life of the party. They kept asking him 'Come on, Adolphe—or Dodolphe, or some-thing like that—tell us a story . . .'"

She shuddered.

"Don't you feel well?" Léon inquired, coming closer.

"Oh, it's nothing! Just a chill from the cold night air."

"He's another one who seems to have trouble finding women," the old sailor added softly, intending to pay Léon a compliment.

Then, spitting on his hands, he took the oars again.

Yet the time to part had come. The farewells were sad. He was to send his letters to Mère Rollet, and she gave him such precise instructions about a double envelope that he was much impressed with her shrewdness in love matters.

"So you can guarantee me that everything is in order?" she said with her last kiss.

"Yes, certainly."

"But why," he thought afterwards as he came back through the streets alone, "is she so very anxious to get this power of attorney?"

IV

Léon soon put on superior airs with his friends, avoided their company, and completely neglected his work.

He waited for her letters, read and re-read them. He wrote to her. He called her to mind with all the strength of his desires and of his memories. Instead of lessening with absence, his longing to see her kept growing to the point where, one Saturday morning he escaped from his office.

When, from the summit of the hill, he saw in the valley below the church-spire with its metal flag swinging in the wind, he felt that delight mingled with triumphant vanity and selfish benevolence that millionaires must experience when they come back to their native village.

He went prowling around round her house. A light was burning in the kitchen. He watched for her shadow behind the curtains, but nothing appeared.

Mère Lefrançois, on seeing him, uttered many exclamations. She thought he had grown taller and thinner, while Artémise, on the contrary, thought him stouter and darker.

He ate in the little dining-room, as in the past, but alone, without the tax collector; for Binet, tired of waiting for the "Hirondelle," had definitely moved his meal an hour earlier. Now he dined punctually at five, which didn't keep him from complaining that the rickety old carriage was late.

Léon finally made up his mind, and knocked at the doctor's door. Madame was in her room, and did not come down for a quarter of an hour. The doctor seemed delighted to see him, but he never left the house that evening, nor the next day.

He saw her alone in the evening, very late, behind the garden in the lane;—in the lane, as with the other one! It was a stormy night, and they talked under an umbrella by lightning flashes.

They couldn't bear the thought of parting.

"I'd rather die!" said Emma.

She seized his arm convulsively, and wept.

"Good bye! When shall I see you again?"

They came back again to embrace once more, and it was then that she promised him to find soon, no matter how, some assured way of meeting in freedom at least once a week. Emma was certain to find a way. She was generally in a hopeful frame of mind: the inheritance money was bound to come in soon.

On the strength of it she bought a pair of yellow curtains with large stripes for her room; Monsieur Lheureux had recommended them as a particularly good buy. She dreamt of getting a carpet, and Lheureux, declaring that it wasn't that much of an investment after all, politely undertook to supply her with one. She could no longer do without his services. Twenty times a day she sent for him, and he at once interrupted whatever he was doing, without a murmur. Neither could people understand why Mère Rollet ate at her house every day, and even paid her private visits.

It was about this time, in the early part of the Winter, that a sudden urge to make music seemed to come over her.

One evening when Charles was listening to her, she began the same piece four times over, each time with much vexation, while he, totally oblivious to her mistakes, exclaimed:

"Bravo! . . . Very good! . . . Don't stop. Keep going!"

"Oh, no. It's awful! My fingers are much too rusty!"

The next day he begged her to play for him again.

"Very well, if you wish."

And Charles had to confess that she had slipped a little. She played wrong notes and blundered; then, stopping short:

"Ah! it's no use. I ought to take some lessons, but . . ."

Biting her lip, she added:

"Twenty francs a lesson, that's too expensive!"

"Maybe it is . . . a little," said Charles with a stupid giggle. "But it seems to me that one might be able to do it for less; for there are artists of little reputation, who are often better than the celebrities."

"Find them!" said Emma.

The next day on coming home, he gave her a sly look, and finally could no longer repress what he had to say:

"How stubborn you can be at times! I went to Barfuchéres to-day. Well, Madame Liégard assured me that her three daughters, who go to school at Miséricorde, take lessons at fifty sous apiece, and that from an excellent teacher!"

She shrugged her shoulders and did not open her piano again.

But whenever she passed in front ot it (provided Bovary was present), she sighed:

"Ah! my poor piano!"

And whenever someone came to call, she did not fail to inform them that she had given up music, and could not begin again now for important reasons. People would commiserate. What a pity! She had so much talent! They even spoke to Bovary about it. They put him to shame, especially the pharmacist.

"You are wrong. One should never let any natural faculties lie fallow. Besides, just think, my good friend, that by inducing madame to study, you are economising on the subsequent musical education of your child. For my own part, I think that mothers ought themselves to instruct their children. It's an idea of Rousseau's, still rather new perhaps, but bound to win out sooner or later, like vaccination and breast-feeding."

So Charles returned once more to this question of the piano. Emma replied bitterly that it would be better to sell it. Poor piano! it had given his vanity so many satisfactions that to see it go was for Bovary, in an undefinable manner, like Emma's partial suicide.

"I you really want it . . ." he said, "a lesson from time to time wouldn't ruin us after all."

"But lessons," she replied, "are only of use if one persists."

And this is how she managed to obtain her husband's permission to go to town once a week to see her lover. At the end of a month she was even considered to have made considerable progress.

V

She went on Thursdays. She got up and dressed silently, in order not to awaken Charles, who would have reproached her for getting ready too early. Then she walked up and down, stood at the windows, and looked out over the Square. The early dawn was broadening between the pillars of the market, and the pharmacy, still boarded up, showed in the pale light of the dawn the large letters of the signboard.

When the clock pointed to a quarter past seven, she went to the Lion d'Or, where a yawning Artémise unlocked the door for her. She would poke the fire in Madame's honor, and Emma remained alone in the kitchen. Now and again she went out. Hivert was leisurely harnessing his horses while listening to the Mère Lefrançois who, sticking her head and night cap through a window, was instructing him on his errands and giving him explanations that would have bewildered any one else. Emma tapped her boots on the cobblestones of the yard.

At last, when he had eaten his soup, put on his cloak, lighted his pipe, and grasped his whip, he calmly took his place on the seat.

The "Hirondelle" started at a slow trot, and for about a mile stopped time and again to pick up waiting passengers along the roadside, before their house-gates. Those who had booked seats the night before kept it waiting; some even were still in bed in their houses. Hivert called, shouted, swore; then he got down from his seat and knocked loudly at the doors. The wind blew through the cracked windows.

Gradually, the four benches filled up. The carriage rolled off; rows of apple-trees followed one upon another, and the road between its two long ditches, full of yellow water, rose, constantly narrowing towards the horizon.

Emma knew every inch of the road: after a certain meadow there was a sign post, then a barn or roadmender's hut. Sometimes, in hope of being surprised, she would close her eyes, but she never lost a clear sense of the distance still to be covered.

At last the brick houses began to follow one another more closely, the earth resounded beneath the wheels, the "Hirondelle" glided between the gardens, revealing through an occasional opening, statues, a summer pavillion, trimmed yew trees, a swing. Then all at once, the city came into sight.

Sloping down like an amphitheatre, and drowned in the fog, it overflowed unevenly beyond its bridges. Then the open country mounted again in a monotonous sweep until it touched in the distance the elusive line of the pale sky. Seen thus from above, the whole landscape seemed frozen, like a picture; the anchored ships were massed in one corner, the river curved round the foot of the green hills, and the oblong islands looked like giant fishes lying motionless on the water. The factory chimneys belched forth immense plumes of brown smoke, their tips carried off in the wind. One heard the rumbling of the foundries, mingled with the clear chimes of the churches, dimly outlined in the fog. The leafless trees on the bou-

levards seemed violet thickets in the midst of the houses, and the
roofs, shining from the rain, threw back unequal reflections, according to the heights of the various districts. From time to time a gust
of wind would drive the clouds towards the slopes of Saint Catherine, like aerial waves breaking silently against a cliff.

Something seemed to emanate from this mass of human lives that
left her dizzy; her heart swelled as though the hundred and twenty
thousand souls palpitating there had all at once wafted to her the
passions with which her imagination had endowed them. Her love
grew in the presence of this vastness, and filled with the tumult of
the vague murmuring which rose from below. She poured it out,
onto the squares, the avenues, the streets; and the old Norman city
spread out before her like some incredible capital, a Babylon into
which she was about to enter. She lifted the window with both hands
to lean out, drinking in the breeze; the three horses galloped, the
stones grated in the mud, the diligence rocked, and Hivert, from
afar, hailed the carts on the road, while the well-to-do residents of
Bois Guillaume sedately descended the hill to town in their little
family carriages.

The coach made a stop at the city gates; Emma undid her overshoes, put on other gloves, rearranged her shawl, and some twenty
paces farther she descended from the "Hirondelle."

The town was beginning to awake. Shop-boys in caps were polishing the front windows of the stores, and women, with baskets balanced on their hips, would stand on the street corners calling out
from time to time some sonorous cry. She walked with downcast
eyes, close to the walls, and smiling with pleasure beneath her lowered black veil.

For fear of being seen, she did not usually take the most direct
road. She would plunge into dark alleys, and emerge, all in a sweat,
near the little fountain at the beginning of the Rue Nationale. This
was the quarter of the theaters, cabarets, and prostitutes. Often, a
cart loaded with shaking scenery passed close by her. Waiters in aprons
were sprinkling sand on the flagstones between green shrubs. There
was a smell of absinthe, cigars, and oysters.

She turned a corner; she recognised him by his curling hair that
escaped from beneath his hat.

Léon kept on walking ahead of her along the sidewalk. She followed him into the hotel. He went up, opened the door, entered—
What an embrace!

Then, after the kisses, the words rushed forth. They told each
other the sorrows of the week, the forebodings, the anxiety for the
letters; but now everything was forgotten; they gazed at each other
with voluptuous laughs, and tender names.

The bed was a large one, made of mahogany and shaped like a
boat. The red silk curtains which hung from the ceiling, were gath-

ered together too low, close to the lyre-shaped headboards;—and nothing in the world was so lovely as her brown hair and white skin set off against that deep crimson color, when with a gesture of modesty, she closed her arms and hid her face in her hands.

The warm room, with its subdued carpet, its frivolous ornaments and its soft light, seemed made for the intimacies of passion. The curtain-rods, ending in arrows, the brass pegs and the great balls of the andirons would suddenly light up if a ray of sunlight entered. On the chimney, between the candelabra there were two of those pink shells in which one hears the murmur of the sea when one holds them against one's ear.

How they loved that room, so full of gaiety, despite its somewhat faded splendour! They always found the furniture arranged the same way, and sometimes hairpins, that she had forgotten the Thursday before, under the pedestal of the clock. They lunched by the fireside on a little round table, inlaid with rosewood. Emma carved, put bits on his plate while playing all sorts of coquettish tricks; she would laugh a ringing libertine laugh when the froth from the champagne overflowed the fragile glass onto the rings of her fingers. They were so completely lost in the possession of each other that they thought themselves in their own house, that they would go on living there until separated by death, like an eternally young married couple. They said "our room," "our carpet," she even said "my slippers," referring to the gift Léon had bought to satisfy a whim of hers. They were rose-colored satin, bordered with swansdown. When she sat on his lap, her leg, which was then too short, hung in the air, and the dainty shoe having no back, was held on only by the toes of her bare foot.

He savoured for the first time the inexpressible delights of feminine refinement. He had never encountered this grace of language, this direction in dress, these poses of a weary dove. He admired the exaltation of her soul and the lace on her petticoat. Besides, was she not a "woman of the world," and a married woman! in short a real mistress!

According to her changing moods, in turn meditative and gay, talkative and silent, passionate and langorous, she awakened in him a thousand desires, called up instincts or memories. She was the mistress of all the novels, the heroine of all the dramas, the vague "she" of all the volumes of verse. On her shoulders, he rediscovered the amber color of the "Odalisque au Bain"; her waist was long like the feudal chatelaines; she resembled Musset's "Femme Pâle de Barcelone."[2] Above all, she was his Angel.

It often seemed to him that his soul, fleeing toward her, broke like

2. Alfred de Musset (1810–1857) frequently incarnates, for Flaubert, the type of stilted romantic sensibility he despises. *Odalisque au Bain*: Famous painting, a nude, by Jean Auguste Dominique Ingres (1780–1867).

a wave against the contours of her head, and was drawn irresistibly down into the whiteness of her breast.

He knelt on the ground before her; and resting his elbows on her lap, he would gaze at her smilingly, his face uplifted.

She bent over him, and murmured, as if choking with intoxication:

"Oh! don't move! don't speak! Look at me! There is something so tender that comes from your eyes. It does me so much good!"

She called him child.

"Do you love me, child?"

And she never heard his reply, his lips always rose so fast to find her mouth.

There was a little bronze cupid on the clock, who simpered as he held up his arms under a golden garland. They had laughed at it many a time, but when they had to part everything seemed serious.

Motionless, they looked at each other and kept repeating:

"Till Thursday! . . . Till Thursday! . . ."

Suddenly she would take his head between her hands and kiss him quickly on the forehead while crying "Adieu" and rush down the stairs.

She went next to a hairdresser in the Rue de la Comédie to have her hair arranged. Night would be falling; they lit the gas in the shop.

She heard the bell in the theatre calling the actors to the performance; and she saw white-faced men and women in faded dresses pass by on the other side of the street and enter in at the stage door.

It was hot in the little low-ceilinged room with its stove humming amidst the wigs and pommades. The smell of the tongs together with the oily hands that were manipulating her hair, would soon stupefy her and she would begin to doze a bit in her dressing gown. Often, as he did her hair, the man offered her tickets for a masked ball.

Then she left! She remounted the streets; reached the Croix-Rouge, retrieved her overshoes which she had hidden under the bench that morning, and settled into her place among the impatient passengers. The other passengers got out at the foot of the hill in order to spare the horses. She remained alone in the carriage.

At every turn, they could see more and more of the city below, forming a luminous mist above the mass of houses. Emma knelt on the cushions, and let her eyes wander over the dazzling light. She sobbed, called to Léon, sent him tender words and kisses which were lost in the wind.

There was a wretched creature on the hillside, who would wander about with his stick right in the midst of the carriages. A mass of rags covered his shoulders, and an old staved-in beaver hat, shaped like a basin, hid his face; but when he took it off he revealed two gaping bloody orbits in the place of eyelids. The flesh hung in red strips; and from them flowed a liquid which congealed into green scales reaching down to his nose with its black nostrils, which kept sniffing convulsively. To speak to you he threw back his head with an idiotic laugh;—then his blueish eyeballs, rolling round and round, would rub against the open wound near the temples.

He sang a little song as he followed the carriages:

> Often the warmth of a summer day
> Makes a young girl dream her heart away.

And all the rest was about birds and sunshine and green leaves.

Sometimes he would appear behind Emma, his head bare. She would draw back with a cry. Hivert liked to tease him. He would advise him to get a booth at the Saint Romain fair, or else ask him, laughing, how his girl friend was.

Often the coach was already in motion when his hat would be thrust violently in at the window, while he clung with his other arm to the footboard, between the spattering of the wheels. His voice, at first weak and quavering, would grow sharp. It lingered into the night like an inarticulate lament of some vague despair; and, heard through the jingling of the horses' bells, the murmuring of the trees, and the rumble of the empty coach, it had something so distant and sad that it filled Emma with dread. It went to the very depths of her soul, like whirlwind in an abyss, and carried her away to a boundless realm of melancholy. But Hivert, noticing a weight behind, would lash out savagely at the blind man with his whip. The thong lashed his wounds and he fell back into the mud with a shriek.

The passengers in the "Hirondelle" would all finally drop off to sleep, some with their mouths open, others their chins pressed against their chests, leaning on their neighbor's shoulder, or with their arm passed through the strap, all the time swaying regularly with the jolting of the carriage; and the sight of the lantern, that was swinging back and forth outside and reflecting on the rumps of the shaft horses, penetrated into the coach through the chocolate-colored curtains, throwing blood-red shadows over all those motionless beings within. Emma, drunk with grief, shivered under her coat and felt her feet grow colder and colder, with death in her soul.

Charles at home would be waiting for her; the "Hirondelle" was always late on Thursdays. Madame arrived at last! She scarcely kissed the child. The dinner was not ready, no matter! She excused the cook. The girl now seemed allowed to do just as she liked.

Often her husband, noting her pallor, asked if she were unwell.

"No," said Emma.

"But," he replied, "you seem so strange this evening."

"Oh, it's nothing! nothing!"

There were even days when she had no sooner come in than she went up to her room; and Justin, who would happen to be there, moved about noiselessly, more adroit at helping her than the best of maids. He put the matches ready, the candlestick, a book, arranged her nightgown, turned back the bedclothes.

"All right," she'd say, "that's fine, get going!"

For he stood there, his hands hanging down and his eyes wide open, as if enmeshed in the innumerable threads of a sudden reverie.

The following day was frightful, and those that came after still more unbearable, because of her impatience to once again seize her happiness,—this fierce lust, enflamed by recent memories, which on the seventh day would erupt freely within Léon's embraces. His own passion was manifested by continual expressions of wonder and gratitude. Emma tasted this love discreetly, and with all her being, nourished it by every tender device she knew, and trembled a little that some day it might be lost.

She often said to him, with a sweet melancholy in her voice:

"Ah! you too, you will leave me! You will marry! You will be like all the others."

He asked:

"What others?"

"Why, like all men," she replied.

Then added, repulsing him with a languid movement:

"You are all of you wretches!"

One day, as they were talking philosophically of earthly disillusions she happened to mention (in order to provoke his jealousy, or perhaps through some irresistible urge to confide in him) that in the past, before she knew him, she had loved someone else. "Not like you," she went on quickly, swearing on the head of her child "that nothing had happened."

The young man believed her, but none the less questioned her to find out what kind of a man *He* was.

"He was a ship's captain, my dear."

Was this not preventing any inquiry, and, at the same time, assuming a higher ground because of the aura of fascination which is supposed to surround a man who must have been of warlike nature and accustomed to receive homage?

The clerk then felt the lowliness of his position; he longed for epaulettes, crosses, titles. These things would please her; he suspected as much from her extravagant habits.

However, Emma never mentioned a number of her most extravagant ideas, such as her desire to have a blue tilbury to drive into Rouen, drawn by an English horse and driven by a groom in turned down boots. It was Justin who had inspired her with this whim, by begging her to take him into service as footman; and if the privation of it did not lessen the pleasure of her arrival at each of their weekly rendez-vous, it certainly augmented the bitterness of the return.

Often, when they were talking together of Paris, she would end by murmuring,

"Ah, how happy we could be living there."

"Are we not happy?" the young man would gently ask, passing his hands over her hair.

"Yes, that is true," she said. "I am mad: kiss me!"

To her husband she was more charming than ever. She made him pistachio-creams and played him waltzes after dinner. He thought himself the most fortunate of men, and Emma was without uneasiness, when, suddenly one evening:

"It is Mademoiselle Lempereur, isn't it, who gives you lessons?"

"Yes."

"Well, I saw her just now," Charles went on, "at Madame Lié-gard's. I spoke to her about you; and she doesn't know you."

This was like a thunderbolt. However, she replied quite naturally:

"She must have forgotten my name."

"But perhaps," said the doctor, "there are several Demoiselles Lempereur at Rouen who are music teachers."

"Possibly!"

Then she added quickly:

"Nevertheless, I have her receipts, here! Look."

And she went to the writing-table, ransacked all the drawers, mixed up the papers, and at last lost her head so completely that Charles earnestly begged her not to take so much trouble about those wretched receipts.

"Oh! I will find them," she said.

And, in fact, on the following Friday, as Charles was putting on one of his boots in the dark closet where his clothes were kept, he felt a piece of paper between the leather and his sock. He took it out and read:

"Received, for three months' lessons and several pieces of music, the sum of sixty-three francs.—FELICIE LEMPEREUR, professor of music."

"How the devil did it get into my boots?"

"It must," she replied, "have fallen from the old box of bills that is on the edge of the shelf."

From that moment on, her existence was one long tissue of lies, in which she wrapped her love as under a veil in order to hide it. It became a need, an obsession, a delight, to such a point that, if she claimed to have walked on the right side of the street the previous day, one could be sure she had walked on the left.

One morning, when she had gone, as usual, rather lightly clothed, it suddenly began to snow, and as Charles was watching the weather from the window, he caught sight of Monsieur Bournisien in the chaise of Monsieur Tuvache, who was driving him to Rouen. Then he went down to give the priest a thick shawl that he was to hand over to Emma as soon as he reached the Croix-Rouge. When he got to the inn, Monsieur Bournisien asked for the wife of the Yonville doctor. The landlady replied that she very rarely came to her establishment. So that evening, when he recognised Madame Bovary in the "Hirondelle," the curé told her his dilemma, without, however, appearing to attach much importance to it, for he began praising a preacher who was doing wonders at the Cathedral, and whom all the ladies were rushing to hear.

Still, even if he had not asked for any explanations, others, later on, might prove less discreet. So she thought it would be a good idea to get out of the coach at the Croix-Rouge each time she came so that the good folk of her village seeing her on the stairs would not become suspicious.

One day, however, Monsieur Lheureux met her coming out of the Hôtel de Boulogne on Léon's arm; and she was frightened, thinking he would gossip. He was not such a fool.

But three days after he came to her room, shut the door, and said: "I must have some money."

She declared she could not give him any. Lheureux began to moan, reminding her of all the favors he had done her.

In fact, of the two bills signed by Charles, Emma up to the present had paid only one. As to the second, the shopkeeper, at her request, had consented to replace it by another, which again had been renewed for a long date. Then he drew from his pocket a list of goods not paid for; to wit, the curtains, the carpet, the material for the arm-chairs, several dresses, and diverse articles of dress, totaling in all a sum of about two thousand francs.

She hung her head; he continued:

"But if you haven't any ready money, you do have some property."

And he called to her attention a miserable little shack situated at Barneville, near Aumale, that brought in almost nothing. It had formerly been part of a small farm sold by Monsieur Bovary senior; for Lheureux knew everything, even down to the number of acres and the names of the neighbors.

"If I were in your place," he said, "I'd get it off my hands, and have some money left over."

She pointed out the difficulty of finding a buyer; he said he thought he could find one; but she asked him how she should manage to sell it.

"Haven't you your power of attorney?" he replied.

The phrase came to her like a breath of fresh air. "Leave me the bill," said Emma.

"Oh, it isn't worth while," answered Lheureux.

He came back the following week boasting that after having gone to a great deal of trouble, he had finally tracked down a certain man named Langlois, who had had his eye on the property for a long time but had never mentioned a price.

"Never mind the price!" she cried.

On the contrary, he said, they must take their time and sound the fellow out. The affair was certainly worth the trouble of a trip, and, as she could not undertake it, he offered to go to the place and bargain with Langlois. On his return he announced that the purchaser proposed four thousand francs.

Emma's heart rose at this news.

"Frankly," he added, "that's a good price."

She drew half the sum at once, and when she was about to pay her account the shopkeeper said:

"It grieves me, it really does, to see you give up such a considerable sum of money as that all at once." She stared at the bank notes and began to dream of the countless rendez-vous with Léon that those two thousand francs represented.

"What! What do you mean!" she stammered.

"Oh!" he went on, laughing good-naturedly, "one puts anything one likes on receipts. Don't you think I know what household affairs are?"

And he looked at her fixedly, while in his hand he held two long papers which he kept sliding between his nails. At last, opening his billfold, he spread out on the table four bills to order, each for a thousand francs.

"Sign these," he said, "and keep it all!"

She cried out, scandalised.

"But if I give you the balance," replied Monsieur Lheureux impudently, "isn't that doing you a service?"

And taking a pen he wrote at the bottom of the account, "Received from Madame Bovary four thousand francs."

"What is there to worry about, since in six months you'll draw the arrears for your cottage, and I don't make the last bill due till after you've been paid?"

Emma was becoming somewhat confused in her calculations and her ears rang as though gold pieces were bursting out of their bags and tinkling onto the floor all around her. At last Lheureux explained that he had a very good friend named Vinçart, a banker in Rouen, who would discount these four bills. Then he himself would hand over to madame the remainder after the actual debt was paid.

But instead of two thousand francs he brought her only eighteen hundred, for his friend Vinçart (which was "only fair") had deducted two hundred francs for commission and discount.

Then he carelessly asked for a receipt.

"You understand . . . in business . . . sometimes . . . And with the date, please don't forget the date."

A whole horizon of new possibilities now opened up before Emma. She was wise enough to set aside three thousand francs, with which the first three bills were paid when they fell due; but the fourth happened to arrive at the house on a Thursday, and a stunned Charles patiently awaited his wife's return for an explanation.

If she had not told him about this note, it was only to spare him such domestic worries; she sat on his lap, caressed him, cooed at him, gave a long enumeration of all the indispensable things that had been got on credit.

"Really, you must confess, considering the number of things, it isn't too expensive."

Charles, at his wit's end, soon had recourse to the eternal Lheureux, who promised to arrange everything if Charles would sign two more notes, one of which was for seven hundred francs and would be payable in three months. To take care of this he wrote his mother a pathetic letter. Instead of sending a reply she came herself; and when Emma wanted to know whether he had got anything out of her:

"Yes," he replied; "but she wants to see the account."

The next morning at daybreak Emma ran to Lheureux to beg him to make out another account for not more than a thousand francs: for to show the one for four thousand it would be necessary to say that she had paid two-thirds, and confess, consequently, the sale of the property, for the transaction had been well handled by the shopkeeper and only came to light later on.

Despite the low price of each article, Madame Bovary senior of course thought the expenditure extravagant.

"Couldn't you do without a carpet? Why did you re-cover the arm-chairs? In my time there was a single arm-chair in a house, for elderly persons,—at any rate it was so at my mother's, who was a respectable woman, I assure you.—Everybody can't be rich! No fortune can hold out against waste! I should be ashamed to pamper myself as you do! And yet I am old, I need looking after . . . and look at this! Look at this! alterations! frills and finery! What is that! silk for lining at two francs; . . . when you get jaconet for ten sous, or even for eight which does just as well!"

Emma lying on a lounge, replied as calmly as she could "Ah! Madame, enough! enough! . . ."

The other went on lecturing her, predicting they would end in the workhouse. But it was Bovary's fault. Luckily he had promised to destroy that power of attorney.

"What?"

"Ah! he swore he would," went on the good woman.

Emma opened the window, called Charles, and the poor fellow was obliged to confess the promise torn from him by his mother.

Emma disappeared, then came back quickly, and majestically handed her a large sheet of paper.

"Thank you," said the old woman. And she threw the power of attorney into the fire.

Emma began to laugh, a strident, piercing, continuous laugh; she had an attack of hysterics.

"Oh! my God!" cried Charles. "Ah! You are in the wrong too! You come here and make scenes with her! . . . "

His mother, shrugging her shoulders, declared it was "all put on."

But Charles, rebelling for the first time, took his wife's part, so that Madame Bovary senior said she would leave. She went the very next day, and on the threshold, as he was trying to detain her, she replied:

"No, no! You love her better than me, and you are right. It is natural. Take care of yourself! . . . for I'm not likely to be back again soon to 'make scenes' as you say."

Charles nevertheless was very crestfallen before Emma, who did not hide the resentment she still felt at his want of confidence, and it needed many prayers before she would consent to another power of attorney. He even accompanied her to Monsieur Guillaumin to have a second one, just like the other, drawn up.

"I know how it is," said the notary, "a man of science can't be worried with the practical details of life."

And Charles felt relieved by this comfortable reflection, which gave his weakness the flattering appearance of higher preoccupation.

How exalted she was the following Thursday at the hotel in their room with Léon! She laughed, cried, sang, sent for sherbets, wanted to smoke cigarettes, seemed to him wild and extravagant, but adorable, superb.

He did not know what combination of forces within her was driving her to throw herself so recklessly after the pleasures of life. She became irritable, greedy, voluptuous. She walked boldly through the streets with him, her head high, unconcerned, she said, about being compromised. At times, however, Emma shuddered at the sudden thought of meeting Rodolphe, for it seemed to her that, although they were separated forever, she was not completely free from the power he held over her.

One night she did not return to Yonville at all. Charles lost his head with anxiety, and little Berthe refusing to go to bed without her mamma, sobbed as though her heart would break. Justin had gone out searching the road at random. Monsieur Homais even had left his pharmacy.

At last, at eleven o'clock, able to bear it no longer, Charles harnessed his chaise, jumped in, whipped up his horse, and reached the Croix-Rouge about two o'clock in the morning. No one there! He thought that the clerk had perhaps seen her; but where did he live? Happily, Charles remembered his employer's address, and rushed off there.

Day was breaking, and he could make out some letters over the door; he knocked. Some one, without opening the door, shouted out the required information and added a generous number of insults concerning people who disturb others in the middle of the night.

The house inhabited by the clerk had neither bell, knocker, nor porter. Charles beat on the shutters with his fists. A policeman happened to pass by; he felt nervous and left.

"What a fool I am" he said. "M. Lormeaux must have asked her to stay to dinner."

The Lormeaux no longer lived in Rouen.

"She probably stayed to look after Madame Dubreuil. Oh, but Madame Dubreuil has been dead these ten months . . . Then where can she be?"

An idea occurred to him. At a café he asked for a Directory, and hurriedly looked for the name of Mademoiselle Lempereur, who turned out to live at No. 74 Rue de la Renelle-des-Maroquiniers.

As he was turning into the street, Emma herself appeared at the other end of it; he threw himself upon her rather than embraced her, crying:

"What kept you yesterday?"

"I was not well."

"What! . . . Where! . . . How! . . ."

She passed her hand over her forehead and answered,

"At Mme. Lempereur's."

"I was sure of it! I was just on my way there."

"Oh!" said Emma. "It's not worth while now. She just stepped out a minute ago; don't get so excited. I will never feel free, you understand, if the slightest delay is going to make you lose your head like this."

This was a sort of permission that she gave herself, so as to get perfect freedom in her escapades. And she took full and free advantage of it. Whenever she was seized with the desire to see Léon, she would set out upon any pretext whatever, and if he were not expecting her that day, she would go to fetch him at his office.

It was a great delight at first, but soon he no longer concealed the truth, which was, that his master complained very much about these interruptions.

"Oh, who cares!" she said, "come along."

And he slipped out.

She wanted him to dress all in black, and grow a pointed beard, to look like the portraits of Louis XIII.[3] She asked to see his rooms and found them lacking in taste. This embarrassed him but she paid no attention; she then advised him to buy curtains like hers, and when he objected to the expense:

"Ah! ah! you hold onto your pennies!" she said laughing.

Each time Léon had to tell her everything that he had done since their last meeting. She asked him for some verses—some verses "for herself," a "love poem" in honor of her. But he never succeeded in getting a rhyme for the second verse; and at last ended by copying a sonnet from a Keepsake.

He did this less from vanity, than simply out of a desire to please her. He never questioned her ideas; he accepted all her tastes; he was becoming her mistress rather than she his. She had tender words and kisses that thrilled his soul. Where could she have learnt this corruption so deep and well masked as to be almost unseizable?

VI

On his trips to see her, Léon often dined at the pharmacist's, and he felt obliged out of politeness to invite him in turn.

"With pleasure!" Monsieur Homais had replied; "besides, I must recharge my mind a bit, for I am getting rusty here. We'll go to the theatre, to the restaurant. We'll do the town."

"Oh, my dear!" tenderly murmured Madame Homais, alarmed at the vague perils he was preparing to brave.

"Well, what? Do you think I'm not sufficiently ruining my health living here amid the continual emanations of the pharmacy? But there! That's just like woman! They are jealous of science, and then are opposed to our taking the most legitimate distractions. No matter! Count upon me. One of these days I shall turn up at Rouen, and we'll paint the town together."

The pharmacist would formerly have taken good care not to use such an expression, but he was cultivating a flippant Parisian manner which he thought very stylish; and, like his neighbor, Madame Bovary, he questioned the clerk avidly about life in the capital; he even used slang in order to impress . . . the "bourgeois," saying

3. Born 1601, ruled 1610–1643; the father of Louis XIV.

"flip," "cool," "sweet," "neat-o," and "I must break it up," for "I must leave."

So one Thursday Emma was surprised to meet Monsieur Homais in the kitchen of the Lion d'Or, wearing a traveller's costume, that is to say, wrapped in an old cloak which no one knew he had, while he carried a valise in one hand and the foot-warmer of his establishment in the other. He had confided his intentions to no one, for fear of causing the public anxiety by his absence.

The prospect of seeing again the scenes of his youth no doubt excited him for he never stopped talking during the whole trip; the coach had barely stopped when he leaped out in search of Léon; and in vain the clerk struggled to free himself. M. Homais dragged him off to the flashy Café de la Normandie, where he entered majestically, without taking off his hat, for he thought it highly provincial to uncover in any public place.

Emma waited for Léon three quarters of an hour. At last she ran to his office, and, lost in all sorts of conjectures, accusing him of indifference, and reproaching herself for her weakness, she spent the afternoon, her face pressed against the window-panes.

At two o'clock they were still at table opposite each other. The large room was emptying; the stove-pipe, in the shape of a palm-tree, spread its gilt leaves over the white ceiling; and near them, just outside the window, in the full sun, a little fountain gurgled into a white basin, where, among the watercress and asparagus, sluggish lobsters stretched out their claws towards a heap of quail lying on their sides.

Homais relished it all. He was more intoxicated by the luxury than by the fine food and drink, but nevertheless, the Pommard wine began to go to his head, and by the time the "omelette au rhum" appeared, he began expounding scandalous theories on women. What attracted him above all else, was "chic." He adored an elegant outfit and hairdo in a well-furnished apartment, and when it came to their physical proportions, he didn't mind them on the plump side.

Léon watched the clock in despair. The pharmacist went on drinking, eating, and talking.

"You must be completely deprived here in Rouen," he said suddenly. "But then the object of your affections doesn't live far away."

And, when the other blushed:

"Come now, be frank. Can you deny that at Yonville . . ."

The young man began to stammer.

"At Madame Bovary's, can you deny that you were courting . . ."

"Whom do you mean?"

"The maid!"

He was not joking; but vanity getting the better of his judgment,

Léon protested indignantly in spite of himself. Besides, he only liked dark women.

"I approve of your taste," said the pharmacist; "they have more temperament."

And whispering into his friend's ear, he pointed out the symptoms by which one could detect temperament in a woman. He even launched into an ethnographic digression: the German was romantic, the French woman licentious, the Italian passionate.

"And negresses?" asked the clerk.

"They are for artistic tastes!" said Homais. "Waiter! Two demitasses!"

"Shall we go?" asked Léon, at last reaching the end of his patience.

"Yes" said Homais in English.

But before leaving he wanted to see the proprietor of the establishment and made him a few compliments. Then the young man, to be alone, alleged he had some business engagement.

"Ah! I will escort you," said Homais.

And all the while he was walking through the streets with him he talked of his wife, his children, of their future, and of his business; told him in what a dilapidated condition he had found it, and to what a state of perfection he had now raised it.

When they arrived in front of the Hôtel de Boulogne, Léon left him abruptly, ran up the stairs, and found his mistress almost hysterical.

On hearing the name of the pharmacist, she flew into a passion. Nevertheless, he kept overwhelming her with good reasons; it wasn't his fault; didn't she know Homais? Could she believe that he would prefer his company? But she turned away; he held her back, and falling on his knees, he encircled her waist with his arm, in a pose at once langorous, passionate, and imploring.

She stood there looking at him, her large flashing eyes were serious, almost terrible. Then her tears clouded them over, her pink eyelids lowered, and she gave him her hands. Léon was just pressing them to his lips when a servant appeared to say that someone wanted to see the gentleman.

"You will come back?" she said.

"Yes."

"But when?"

"Immediately."

"It's a trick," said the pharmacist, when he saw Léon. "I wanted to interrupt this visit, that seemed to me to annoy you. Let's go and have a glass of *garus*[4] at Bridoux'."

Léon swore that he must get back to his office. Then the phar-

---

4. A liqueur named after its inventor.

macist began making jokes about legal papers and procedure.

"Forget about Cujas and Barthole[5] a bit, what the Devil! Who's going to stop you? Be a man! Let's go to Bridoux'. You'll see his dog. It's very interesting."

And as the clerk still insisted:

"I'll go with you. I'll read a paper while I wait for you, or thumb through a code."

Léon, bewildered by Emma's anger, Monsieur Homais' chatter, and perhaps, by the heaviness of the luncheon, was undecided, and, as though he were under the spell of the pharmacist who kept repeating:

"Let's go to Bridoux'. It's just by here, in the Rue Malpalu."

Then, out of cowardice, out of stupidity, out of that undefinable necessity that leads us towards those actions we are most set against, he allowed himself to be led off to Bridoux'; they found him in his small courtyard overseeing three workmen who panted as they turned the huge wheel of a seltzer water machine. Homais gave them some advice; he embraced Bridoux; they drank some *garus*. Twenty times Léon tried to escape, but the other seized him by the arm saying:

"Wait a minute! I'm coming! We'll go to the 'Fanal de Rouen' to see the fellows there. I'll introduce you to Thomassin."

He finally got rid of him, however, and flew to the hotel. Emma was gone.

She had just left in exasperation. She detested him now. His failure to come as he had promised she took as an insult, and she looked for other reasons for separating from him: he was incapable of heroism, weak, banal, more spiritless than a woman, avaricious, and timorous as well.

Later when she was calmer, she realized that she had doubtless been unjust to him. But the picking apart of those we love always alienates us from them. One must not touch one's idols, a little of the gilt always comes off on one's fingers.

They gradually began to talk more frequently of matters outside their love, and in the letters that Emma wrote him she spoke of flowers, poetry, the moon and the stars, naïve resources of a waning passion, striving to keep itself alive by all external aids. She was constantly promising herself a profound happiness on her next trip; then she confessed to herself that she had felt nothing extraordinary. This disappointment quickly gave way to a new hope, and Emma returned to him more avid and inflamed than before. She undressed brutally, ripping off the thin laces of her corset so violently that they would whistle round her hips like a gliding snake. She went on tiptoe, barefooted, to see once more that the door was locked, then with one

---

5. Jacques Cugar (1522–1590) was a famous jurist who interpreted Roman Law in contemporary terms. *Barthole*, or Bartole: An early Italian jurist (1313–1357) in Bologna.

movement, she would let her clothes fall at once to the ground;—
then, pale and serious, without a word, she would throw herself
against his breast with a long shudder.

Yet there was upon that brow covered with cold drops, on those
stammering lips, in those wild eyes, in the grip of those arms, something strange, vague, and sinister that seemed to Léon to be subtly
gliding between them to force them apart.

He did not dare to question her; but finding how experienced she
was, he told himself that she must have passed through all the extremes
of both pleasure and pain. What had once charmed now frightened
him a little. Furthermore, he revolted against the daily increased
absorption of his personality into hers. He resented her, because of
this constant victory. He even strove not to love her; then, when he
heard the creaking of her boots, he felt his courage desert him, like
drunkards at the sight of strong liquor.

It is true, she showered him with every sort of attention, from
exotic foods, to little coquettish refinements in her dress and languishing glances. She used to bring roses from Yonville hidden in
her bosom which she would toss up into his face; she was worried
about his health, advised him how he should behave; and in order
to bind him closer to her, hoping perhaps that heaven would take
her part, she hung a medal of the Virgin round his neck. She inquired
like a virtuous mother about his companions. She said to him:

"Don't see them; don't go out; only think of us; love me!"

She would have liked to be able to watch over his life, and the
idea occurred to her of having him followed in the streets. Near the
hotel there was always a kind of vagabond who accosted travellers,
and who would surely not refuse . . . But her pride revolted at this.

"Ah! So what! What does it matter if he betrays me! What do I
care?"

One day, when they had parted early and she was returning alone
along the boulevard, she saw the walls of her convent; she sat down
on a bench in the shade of the elms. How calm her life had been in
those days! How she envied her first undefinable sentiments of love
which she had tried to construct from the books she read.

The first months of her marriage, her rides in the forest, the viscount who had waltzed with her, and Lagardy singing, all repassed
before her eyes . . . And Léon suddenly appeared to her as far off
as the others.

"I do love him!" she said to herself.

No matter! She was not happy, she never had been. Why was her
life so unsatisfactory, why did everything she leaned on instantly rot
and give way? . . . But suppose there existed somewhere some one
strong and beautiful, a man of valor, passionate yet refined, the heart
of a poet in the form of an angel, a bronze stringed lyre, playing

elegaic epithalamia to the heavens, why might she not someday happen on him? What a vain thought! Besides, nothing was worth the trouble of seeking it; everything was a lie. Every smile concealed a yawn of boredom, every joy a curse, every pleasure its own disgust, and the sweetest kisses left upon your lips only the unattainable desire for a greater delight.

A coarse metallic rattle sounded around her, and the convent bell struck four. And it seemed to her that she had been sitting on that bench since the beginning of time. But an infinity of time can be compressed into a minute like a crowd of people into a small space.

Emma lived all absorbed in her passions and worried no more about money matters than an archduchess.

There came a day, however, when a seedy-looking man with a red face and a bald head came to her house, saying he had been sent by Monsieur Vinçart of Rouen. He took out the pins that held together the side-pockets of his long green overcoat, stuck them into his sleeve, and politely handed her a paper.

It was a bill for seven hundred francs, signed by her, and which Lheureux, in spite of all his promises had endorsed to Vinçart.

She sent her servant for him. He could not come.

Then the stranger who had remained standing, casting around him to the right and left curious glances which were hidden behind his blond eyebrows, asked with an innocent air:

"What answer am I to take Vinçart?"

"Well!" said Emma, "tell him . . . that I haven't got it . . . I'll pay him next week . . . He must wait . . . yes, next week."

And the fellow went without another word.

But the next day at twelve o'clock she received a summons, and the sight of the stamped paper, on which appeared several times in large letters, "Maître Hereng, bailiff at Buchy," so frightened her that she rushed in all haste to Lheureux. She found him in his shop, tying up a parcel.

"At your service," he said. "What can I do for you?"

But Lheureux continued what he was doing, aided by a young girl of about thirteen, somewhat hunchbacked, who was both his clerk and his servant.

Then, his sabots clattering on the wooden planks of the shop, he mounted in front of Madame Bovary to the second floor and showed her into a narrow closet, where, in a large pine wood desk, lay some ledgers, protected by an iron bar laid horizontally across them and padlocked down. Against the wall, under some remnants of calico, one caught sight of a safe, but of such dimensions that it must contain something besides promissory notes and cash. Monsieur Lheureux, in fact, went in for pawnbroking, and it was there that he had put Madame Bovary's gold chain, together with the earrings of poor old Tellier, who had been forced, at last, to sell his café, and had bought a small grocery store in Quincampoix, where he was dying of catarrh amongst his candles, that were less yellow than his face.

Lheureux sat down in a large cane arm-chair, saying:

"What's new?"

"Look here!"

"Well, what do you want me to do about it?"

Then she lost her temper, reminding him that he had promised not to endorse her notes away. He admitted it.

"But I was pressed myself; they were holding a knife against my throat too."

"And what will happen now?" she went on.

"Oh, it's very simple; a judgment and then a seizure . . . that's about it!"

Emma kept down a desire to strike him, and asked gently if there was no way of quieting Monsieur Vinçart.

"Oh, sure! appease Vinçart, indeed! You don't know him; he's fiercer than an Arab!"

Nevertheless, Monsieur Lheureux had to help her.

"All right then, listen, it seems to me that I've been pretty good to you so far."

And opening one of his ledgers:

"Look!" he said.

Then moving his finger up the page:

"Let's see . . . let's see . . . ! August 3d, two hundred francs . . . June 17th, a hundred and fifty . . . March 23d, forty-six . . . In April . . ."

He stopped, as if afraid of making some mistake.

"I won't even mention the bills signed by Monsieur Bovary, one for seven hundred francs, and another for three hundred. As to the little payments on your account and the interest, I'd never get to the end of the list, I can't figure that high. I'll have nothing more to do with it."

She wept; she even called him "her good Monsieur Lheureux." But he always fell back upon "that rascal Vinçart." Besides, he hadn't a penny, no one was paying him these days, they were eating his coat off his back, a poor shopkeeper like himself couldn't advance money.

Emma was silent, and Monsieur Lheureux, who was biting the feathers of a quill, no doubt became uneasy at her silence, for he went on:

"Perhaps, if something were paid on this, one of these days . . . I might . . ."

"Well," she said, "as soon as the balance on the Barneville property . . ."

"What? . . ."

And on hearing that Langlois had not yet paid he seemed much surprised. Then in a honied voice:

"Then we'll agree, what do you say to . . . ?"

"Oh! Whatever you say!"

On this he closed his eyes, to reflect, wrote down a few figures, and saying that this was really going to hurt him, it was a risky affair, that he was "bleeding" himself for her, he wrote out four bills for two hundred and fifty francs each, to fall due month by month.

"Provided that Vinçart will listen to me! However, it's settled. I don't back down on my word. I'm as square as a brick."

Next he carelessly showed her several new goods; not one of which, however, was in his opinion worthy of madame.

"When I think that there's a dress that costs seven cents a yard and guaranteed color-fast! And they actually swallow it all down! Of course you understand one doesn't tell them what it really is!" He hoped by this confession of chicanery towards others to convince her of his honesty with her.

Then he called her back to show her three yards of guipure that he had lately picked up "at a sale."

"Isn't it lovely?" said Lheureux. "It is very much used now for the backs of arm-chairs. It's quite the rage."

And, quicker than a juggler, he wrapped up the guipure in some blue paper and put it in Emma's hands.

"But at least let me know . . ."

"Yes, some other time," he replied, turning on his heel.

That same evening she urged Bovary to write to his mother, to ask her to send at once the whole of the balance due from the father's estate. The mother-in-law replied that she had nothing more: that the liquidation was complete, and, aside from Barneville, there remained for them an income of six hundred francs, that she would pay them punctually.

Madame Bovary then sent bills to two or three patients, and was soon making great use of this method which turned out to be very successful. She was always careful to add a postscript: "Do not mention this to my husband; you know how proud he is . . . forgive my having to . . . your humble servant. . . ." There were a few complaints; she intercepted them.

To get money she began selling her old gloves, her old hats, all sorts of old odds and ends, and she bargained rapaciously, her peasant blood standing her in good stead. Then on her trips to town she searched the second hand stores for knick-knacks which she was sure, if no one else, Monsieur Lheureux would certainly take off her hands. She bought ostrich feathers, Chinese porcelain, and trunks; she borrowed from Félicité, from Madame Lefrançois, from the landlady at the Croix-Rouge, from everybody, no matter where. With the money she at last received from Barneville she paid two bills; the other fifteen hundred francs fell due. She renewed the notes, and then renewed them again!

Sometimes, it is true, she tried to add up her accounts, but the results were always so staggering, she couldn't believe they were possible. Then she would begin over again, soon get confused, leave everything where it was and forget about it.

The house was a dreary place now! Tradesmen were seen leaving it with angry faces. Handkerchiefs hung drying on the stoves, and little Berthe, to the great scandal of Madame Homais, wore stockings with holes in them. If Charles timidly ventured a remark, she would snap back at him savagely that it certainly wasn't her fault!

What was the meaning of all these fits of temper? He explained everything by her old nervous illness, and reproaching himself with having taken her infirmities for faults, accused himself of egotism, and longed to go and take her in his arms.

"Ah, no!" he said to himself; "I would only annoy her."

And he stayed where he was.

After dinner he would walk about alone in the garden; he took little Berthe on his lap and unfolding his medical journal, tried to teach her to read. But the child, who had never had any schooling at all, would soon open wide her large eyes in bewilderment and begin to cry. Then he would comfort her; he fetched water in her watering can to make rivers on the sand path, or broke off branches from the privet hedges to plant trees in the flower beds. This did not spoil the garden much, which was now overgrown with long weeks. They owed Lestiboudois for so many day's wages. Then the child would grow cold and ask for her mother.

"Go call your nurse," said Charles. "You know, my darling, that mama does not like to be disturbed!"

Autumn was setting in, and the leaves were already falling—as they had two years ago when she was ill!—Where would it all end! . . . And he would continue to pace up and down, his hands behind his back.

Madame was in her room. No one was allowed to enter. There she stayed from morning to night, listless and hardly dressed, from time to time lighting a tablet of Turkish incense she had bought at the shop of an Algerian in Rouen. In order to get rid of this sleeping man stretched out beside her at night, she finally managed by continual badgering to relegate him to a room on the third floor; then she would read until morning, lurid novels where there would be scenes of orgies, violence, and bloodshed. Often she would be seized by a sudden terror and cry out. Charles would come running.

"Oh! Leave me alone!" she would say.

Or at other times, when she was burnt more fiercely by that inner flame which her adultery kept feeding, panting and overcome with desire, she would throw open the window breathing in the chill air and letting the wind blow back her hair which hung too heavy on her neck, and, looking up at the stars, she would long for the love of a prince. She thought of him, of Léon. She would then have given anything for a single one of those meetings which would appease her.

These were her gala days. She was determined that they should be magnificent! When he could not pay all the expenses himself, she made up the deficit liberally, which happened pretty well every time. He tried to convince her that they would be just as well off somewhere else, in a more modest hotel, but she always found some objection.

One day she drew six small silver-gilt spoons from her bag (they were old Rouault's wedding present), begging him to pawn them at once for her; Léon obeyed, although the errand annoyed him. He was afraid of compromising himself.

Then, on reflection, he began to think that his mistress was beginning to behave rather strangely, and perhaps they were not wrong in wishing to separate him from her.

In fact, some one had sent his mother a long anonymous letter to warn her that he was "ruining himself with a married woman"; and immediately the good woman had visions of the eternal bug-a-boo of every family, that is to say, that vague and terrible creature, the siren, the fantastic monster which makes its home in the treacherous depths of love. She wrote to Maître Dubocage, his employer, who behaved perfectly in the affair. He kept him for three quarters of an hour trying to open his eyes, to warn him of the abyss into which he was falling. Such an intrigue would damage him later on in his career. He implored him to break with her, and, if he would not make this sacrifice in his own interest, to do it at least for his, Dubocage's sake.

Léon finally swore he would not see Emma again; and he reproached himself with not having kept his word, considering all the trouble and reproaches she was likely to bring down on him, not counting the jokes made by his fellow clerks as they sat around the stove in the morning. Besides, he was soon to be head clerk; it was time to settle down. So he gave up his flute, his exalted sentiments, his poetic imagination; for every bourgeois in the flush of his youth, were it but for a day, a moment, had believed himself capable of immense passions, of lofty enterprises. The most mediocre libertine has dreamed of sultanas; every notary bears within him the débris of a poet.

He was bored now when Emma suddenly began to sob on his

breast; and his heart, like the people who can only stand a certain amount of music; became drowsy through indifference to the vibrations of a love whose subtleties he could no longer distinguish.

They knew one another too well to experience any of those sudden surprises which multiply the enjoyment of a possession a hundred-fold. She was as sick of him as he was weary of her. Emma found again in adultery all the platitudes of marriage.

But how to get rid of him? Then, though she felt humiliated by the sordidity of such a happiness, she clung to it out of habit, or out of degeneration; she pursued it more desperately than ever, destroying every pleasure by always wishing for it to be too great. She blamed Léon for her disappointed hopes, as if he had betrayed her; and she even longed for some catastrophe that would bring about their separation, since she had not the courage to do it herself.

She none the less went on writing him love letters, in keeping with the notion that a woman must write to her lover.

But while writing to him, it was another man she saw, a phantom fashioned out of her most ardent memories, of her favorite books, her strongest desires, and at last he became so real, so tangible, that her heart beat wildly in awe and admiration, though unable to see him distinctly, for, like a god, he was hidden beneath the abundance of his attributes. He dwelt in that azure land where silken ladders swung from balconies in the moonlight, beneath a flower-scented breeze. She felt him near her; he was coming and would ravish her entire being in a kiss. Then she would fall back to earth again shattered; for these vague ecstasies of imaginary love, would exhaust her more than the wildest orgies.

She now felt a constant pain throughout her body. Often she even received summonses, stamped paper that she barely looked at. She would have liked not to be alive, or to be always asleep.

On the day of Mid-Lent she did not return to Yonville; that evening she went to a masked ball. She wore velvet breeches, red stockings, a peruke, and a three-cornered hat cocked over one ear. She danced all night to the wild sounds of the trombones; people gathered around her, and in the morning she found herself on the steps of the theatre together with five or six other masked dancers, dressed as stevadores or sailors, friends of Léon's who were talking about going out to find some supper.

The neighboring cafés were full. They found a dreadful-looking restaurant at the harbor, where the proprietor showed them to a little room on the fifth floor.

The men were whispering in a corner, no doubt consulting about expenses. There were a clerk, two medical students, and a shop assistant: what company for her! As to the women, Emma soon perceived from the tone of their voices that most of them probably came from the lowest class. This frightened her, she drew back her chair and lowered her eyes.

The others began to eat; she ate nothing. Her head was on fire, her eyes smarted, and her skin was ice-cold. In her head she seemed to feel the floor of the ball-room rebounding again beneath the rhythmical pulsation of thousands of dancing feet. The smell of punch and cigar smoke made her dizzy. She fainted: they carried her to the window.

Day was breaking, and a large purple stain was spreading across the pale sky in the direction of the St. Catherine hills. The ashen river was shivering in the wind; there was no one on the bridges; the street lamps were going out.

She came to herself, however, and began to think of Berthe asleep at home in the maid's room. But just then a cart loaded with long strips of iron passed by, and made a deafening metallic vibration against the walls of the house.

She abruptly slipped out of the room; removed her costume; told Léon she had to return; and found herself alone at last in the Hôtel de Boulogne. Everything, herself included, was now unbearable to her. She would have liked to take wing like a bird, and fly off far away to become young again in the realms of immaculate purity.

She left the hotel, crossed the Boulevard, the Place Cauchoise, and the Faubourg, as far as an open street that overlooked the park. She walked rapidly, the fresh air calmed her; and, little by little, the faces of the crowd, the masks, the quadrilles, the lights, the supper, those women, all, disappeared like rising mists. Then, reaching the "Croix-Rouge," she threw herself on the bed in her little room on the second floor, where there were pictures of the "Tour de Nesle." At four o'clock Hivert awoke her.

When she got home, Félicité showed her a grey paper stuck behind the clock. She read:

"In virtue of the seizure in execution of a judgment."

What judgment . . . ? As a matter of fact, the evening before another paper had been brought that she had not yet seen, and she was stunned by these words:

"By power of the king, the law, and the courts, Mme. Bovary is hereby ordered . . ."

Then, skipping several lines, she read:

"Within twenty-four hours, at the latest . . ." But what? "To pay the sum of eight thousand francs." There was even written at the bottom of the page, "She will be constrained thereto by every form of law, and notably by a writ of distraint on her furniture and effects."

What should she do? . . . In twenty-four hours; tomorrow! Lheureux, she thought, probably wanted to frighten her again, for, all at once, she saw through his manoeuvres, the reason for his favors.

The only thing that reassured her was the extraordinary amount of the figure.

Nevertheless, as a result of buying and not paying, of borrowing, signing notes, and renewing these notes which gres ever larger each time they fell due, she had ended by preparing a capital for Monsieur Lheureux which he was impatiently waiting to collect to use in his own financial speculations.

She went over to his place, assuming an air of indifference.

"Do you know what has happened to me? It's a joke, I'm sure!"

"No."

"What do you mean?"

He slowly turned around, and, folding his arms, said to her:

"Did you think, my dear lady, that I was going to go on to the end of time providing you with merchandise and cash, just for the love of God? I certainly have to get back what I laid out, let's be fair."

She objected to the amount of the debt.

"Ah! Too bad! The court has recognised it! There's a judgment. You've been notified. Besides, it isn't my fault. It's Vinçart's."

"But couldn't you . . . ?"

"No! Not a single thing!"

"But . . . Still . . . let's talk it over."

And she began beating about the bush; she had known nothing about it . . . it was a surprise . . .

"Whose fault is that?" said Lheureux, bowing ironically. "While I'm slaving like a nigger, you go gallivanting about."

"Ah! Don't preach to me!"

"It never does any harm," he replied.

She turned coward; she implored him; she even pressed her pretty white and slender hand against the shopkeeper's knee.

"There, that'll do! Any one'd think you wanted to seduce me!"

"You are a wretch!" she cried.

"Oh, oh! What a fuss you are making!"

"I will show you up. I'll tell my husband . . ."

"All right! I too, I'll show your husband something!"

And Lheureux drew from his strong box the receipt for eighteen hundred francs that she had given him when Vinçart had discounted the bills.

"Do you think," he added, "that he won't catch on to your little theft, the poor dear man?"

She collapsed, more overcome than if felled by the blow of a club. He was walking up and down from the window to the bureau, repeating all the while:

"I'll show him all right . . . I'll show him all right . . ." Then he approached her, and said in a soft voice:

"It's no fun, I know; but after all it hasn't killed anyone, and, since that is the only way that is left for you paying back my money . . ."

"But where am I to get any?" said Emma, wringing her hands.

"Bah! when one has friends like you!"

And he looked at her with such a knowing and terrible stare, that she shuddered to the very core of her heart.

"I promise you," she said, "I'll sign . . ."

"I've enough of your signatures!"

"I will sell something else . . ."

"Oh come!" he said, shrugging his shoulders. "You've nothing left to sell."

And he called through the peep-hole that looked down into the shop:

"Annette, don't forget the three coupons of No. 14."

The servant appeared; Emma caught the hint and asked how much money would be needed to put a stop to the proceedings.

"It is too late."

"But if I were to bring you several thousand francs, a quarter of the sum, a third, almost all?"

"No; it's no use!"

And he pushed her gently towards the staircase.

"I implore you, Monsieur Lheureux, just a few days more!"

She was sobbing.

"Ah that's good! let's have some tears!"

"You'll drive me to do something desperate!"

"Don't make me laugh!" said he, shutting the door.

VII

She was stoical the next day when Maître Hareng, the bailiff, with two assistants arrived at her house to draw up inventory for the seizure.

They began with Bovary's consulting-room, and did not write down the phrenological head, which was considered an "instrument of his profession"; but in the kitchen they counted the plates, the saucepans, the chairs, the candlesticks, and in the bedroom all the knick-knacks on the wall-shelf. They examined her dresses, the linen, the dressing-room; and her whole existence, to its most intimate details, was stretched out like a cadaver in an autopsy before the eyes of these three men.

Maître Hareng, buttoned up in his thin black coat, wearing a white choker and very tight foot-straps, repeated from time to time:

"Allow me madame? Allow me?"

Often he uttered exclamations:

"Charming! very pretty."

Then he began writing again, dipping his pen into the horn ink-stand he carried in his left hand.

When they had done with the rooms they went up to the attic.

She kept a desk there in which Rodolphe's letters were locked. It had to be opened.

"Ah! a correspondence!" said Maître Hareng, with a discreet smile. "But allow me! for I must make sure the box contains nothing else." And he tipped up the papers lightly, as if to let the napoleons fall out. This made her furious to see this coarse hand, with red moist fingers like slugs, touching these pages against which her heart had beaten.

They went at last! Félicité came back. Emma had sent her out to watch for Bovary in order to keep him away, and they hastily installed the man set to guard the seizure, in the attic, where he swore he would not stir.

During the evening Charles seemed to her careworn. Emma watched him with a look of anguish, fancying she saw an accusation in every line of his face. Then, when her eyes wandered over the chimney-piece ornamented with Chinese screens, over the large curtains, the arm-chairs, all those things that had softened the bitterness of her life, remorse seized her, or rather an immense regret, that, far from destroying her passion, rather irritated it. Charles placidly poked the fire, both his feet on the andirons.

Once the man, no doubt bored in his hiding-place, made a slight noise.

"Is any one walking upstairs?" said Charles.

"No," she replied; "it is a window that has been left open, and is banging in the wind."

The next day which was Sunday, she went to Rouen to call on all the brokers whose names she knew. They were either in the country, or away on a trip. She was not discouraged; and those whom she did manage to see she asked for money, insisting that she absolutely had to have it, that she would pay it back. Some laughed in her face; all refused.

At two o'clock she ran to Léon's apartment, and knocked at the door. No one answered. At length he appeared.

"What brings you here?"

"Am I disturbing you?"

"No . . . but . . ." And he admitted that his landlord didn't like his having "women" there.

"I must speak to you," she went on.

Then he took down the key, but she stopped him.

"No, no! Over there, in our home!"

And they went to their room at the Hôtel de Boulogne.

On arriving she drank off a large glass of water. She was very pale. She said to him:

"Léon, I have a favor to ask you."

And, shaking him by both hands which she held tightly in hers, she added:

"Listen, I must have eight thousand francs."

"But you are mad!"

"Not yet."

And thereupon, telling him the story of the seizure, she explained her distress to him; for Charles knew nothing of it; her mother-in-law detested her; old Rouault could do nothing; but he, Léon, he would set about finding this indispensable sum . . .

"But what do you want me . . . ?"

"What a coward you are!" she cried.

Then he said stupidly, "You're making things out to be worse than they are. Your fellow there could probably be quieted with three thousand francs."

All the more reason to try and do something; it was inconceivable that they couldn't find three thousand francs. Besides, Léon could sign the notes instead of her.

"Go! try! you must! run! . . . Oh! Try! try! I will love you so!"

He went out, and came back at the end of an hour, saying, with a solemn face:

"I have been to three people . . . with no success!"

Then they sat there facing each other on either side of the fireplace, motionless, without speaking. Emma shrugged her shoulders as she tapped her foot impatiently. He heard her murmur:

"If I were in your place I'd certainly find some!"

"Where?"

"At your office."

And she looked at him.

A diabolical determination showed in her burning eyes which were half closed in a lascivious and encouraging manner;—so that the young man felt himself growing weak beneath the mute will of this woman who was urging him to commit a crime. Then he was afraid, and to avoid any explanation he smote his forehead crying:

"Morel is coming back tonight! He will not refuse me, I hope" (this was one of his friends, the son of a very rich merchant); "and I will bring it you to-morrow," he added.

Emma did not seem to welcome this new hope with all the joy he had expected. Did she suspect the lie? He went on, blushing:

"However, if you don't see me by three o'clock, do not wait for me, my darling. I must leave now, forgive me. Good-bye!"

He pressed her hand, but it felt quite lifeless. Emma had no strength left for any sentiment whatever.

Four o'clock struck; and she rose to return to Yonville, mechanically obeying the force of old habits.

The weather was beautiful; it was one of those March days, clear and sharp, when the sun shines in a perfectly white sky. The people of Rouen, dressed in their Sunday-clothes, seemed happy as they strolled by. She reached the Place du Parvis. People were coming out of the cathedral after vespers; the crowd flowed out through the three portals like a river through the three arches of a bridge, and in the middle, more immobile than a rock, stood the verger.

Then she remembered the day when, eager and full of hope, she had entered beneath this large nave, that had opened out before her, less profound than her love; and she walked on weeping beneath her veil, dazed, staggering, almost fainting.

"Look out!" cried a voice issuing from behind a carriage gate which was swinging open.

She stopped to let pass a black horse, prancing between the shafts of a tilbury, driven by a gentleman dressed in sables. Who was it? She knew him . . . The carriage sprang forward and disappeared.

Why, it was he, the Viscount! She turned away; the street was empty. She was so crushed, so sad, that she had to lean against a wall to keep herself from falling.

Then she thought she had been mistaken.

How could she tell? Everything, within herself and without, was abandoning her. She felt that she was lost, that she was wandering about at random within undefinable abysses, and she was almost happy, on reaching the Croix-Rouge, to see the good Homais, who was watching a large box full of pharmaceutical stores being hoisted on to the "Hirondelle"; holding in his hand a silk handkerchief containing six "cheminots" for his wife.

Madame Homais was very fond of these small, heavy rolls shaped like turbans which are eaten during Lent with salt butter: a last relic of Gothic fare, going back, perhaps, to the Crusades, and with which the hardy Normans would stuff themselves in times gone-by, thinking that they saw, illuminated in the golden light of the torches, between the tankards of Hippocras[6] and the gigantic slabs of meat, the heads of Saracens to be devoured. The druggist's wife crunched them up as they had done, heroically, in spite of her wretched teeth; so whenever Homais made a trip to town, he never failed to bring her home some which he bought at the great baker's in the Rue Massacre.

"Charmed to see you," he said, offering Emma a hand to help her into the "Hirondelle."

Then he tied his "cheminots" to the baggage net and remained

---

6. An aromatic, highly spiced wine of medieval Europe; after Hippocrates, the Greek physician.

with his head bare and his arms folded in an attitude pensive and Napoleonic.

But when the blind man appeared as usual at the foot of the hill he exclaimed indignantly:

"I can't understand why the authorities continue to tolerate such criminal occupations! These unfortunate people should be locked up, forced to do some work. I give you my word, Progress marches at a snail's pace! We are paddling about in a state of total barbarism!"

The blind man held out his hat which flapped about in the window as though it were a pocket in the upholstery which had come loose.

"This," said the pharmacist, "is a scrofulous disease."

And though he knew the poor devil, he pretended to see him for the first time, muttering such words as "cornea," "opaque cornea," "sclerotic," "facies," then asked him in a paternal tone:

"My friend, have you suffered long from this dreadful affliction? Instead of getting drunk in the café you would do better to follow a diet."

He advised him to drink good wine, good beer and to eat good roasts of meat. The blind man went on with his song. He actually seemed almost insane. At last Monsieur Homais opened his purse.

"Now there's a sou; give me back two liards: don't forget what I told you, you'll find it does you good."

Hivert openly cast some doubt on its efficacy. But the druggist said that he would cure the man himself with an antiphlogistic salve of his own composition, and he gave his address: "Monsieur Homais, near the market, everyone knows me."

"All right!" said Hivert, "in payment, you can 'put on your act' for us."

The blind man squatted down on his haunches with his head thrown back, and rolling his greenish eyes and sticking out his tongue, he rubbed his stomach with both hands while uttering a sort of low howl like a famished dog. Emma, overcome with disgust, threw him a five franc piece over her shoulder. It was all her fortune. It seemed like a grand thing to her to throw it away like this.

The coach had already started again when Monsieur Homais suddenly leaned out of the window and shouted:

"No farinacious foods or dairy products, wear woolen clothing next to the skin, and expose the diseased areas to the smoke of juniper berries."

The sight of the familiar things that passed before her eyes gradually diverted Emma from her present suffering. An intolerable fatigue overwhelmed her, and she reached home stupefied, discouraged, almost asleep.

"Let come what may!" she told herself.

Besides, anything could happen. Couldn't some extraordinary event occur at any moment? Lheureux might even die.

At nine o'clock in the morning she was awakened by the sound of voices in the square. A crowd around the market was reading a large bill fixed to one of the posts, and she saw Justin climb on a milepost and tear down the bill. The local policeman had just seized him by the collar. Monsieur Homais came out of his shop, and Mère Lefrançois, in the midst of the crowd, was talking the loudest of all.

"Madame! madame!" cried Félicité, running in, "it's an outrage!"

And the poor girl, all in tears, handed her a yellow paper that she had just torn off the door. Emma read with a glance that her furniture was for sale.

Then they looked at one another in silence. Servant and master had no secrets from each other. At last Félicité whispered:

"If I were you, madame, I'd go see Monsieur Guillaumin."

"You think so?"

The question meant:

"You who know all about the house from the butler, has the master sometimes spoken of me?"

"Yes, you'd do well to go there."

She dressed, put on her black gown, and her cape with jet beads, and that she might not be seen (there was still a crowd on the Square), she took the path by the river, outside the village.

She was out of breath when she reached the notary's gate. The sky was sombre, and a little snow was falling.

At the sound of the bell, Theodore in a red waistcoat appeared on the steps; he came to open the door with a casual air, as if she were an old acquaintance, and showed her into the dining-room.

A large porcelain stove crackled beneath a cactus that filled up the niche in the wall, and in black wood frames against the oak-stained paper hung Steuben's "Esmeralda" and Schopin's "Putiphar."[7] The ready-laid table, the two silver chafing-dishes, the crystal door-knobs, the parquet and the furniture, all shone with a scrupulous, English cleanliness; the windows were ornamented at each corner with stained glass.

"Now this," thought Emma, "is the kind of dining-room I ought to have."

The notary came in. With his left hand, he pressed his palm-embroidered dressing gown against his body, while with his other hand he quickly took off and replaced his brown velvet skullcap, which he wore jauntily cocked to the right. After circling around his

7. Karl Steuben (1788–1856) was a German history painter. Esmeralda is the gypsy girl in Hugo's *Notre Dame de Paris* (a picture, "Esmeralda et Quasimodo"—the Dwarf—was exhibited in 1839). *Schopin* was (with a different spelling) the brother of the composer Chopin. Putiphar is the official of the court of Egypt who was Joseph's master—the wife of Putiphar tried to seduce him. The picture represents the seduction scene.

bald cranium, the end of three strains of blond hair stuck out from underneath the cap.

After he had offered her a seat he sat down to breakfast, apologising profusely for his rudeness.

"I have come," she said, "to beg you, sir . . ."

"What, madame! I am listening."

And she began telling him about her situation.

Monsieur Guillaumin knew all about it. He was working in secret partnership with the shopkeeper, who always provided him with the capital for the mortgage loans he was asked to arrange.

So he knew (and better than she herself) the long story of these notes, small at first, bearing the names of several endorsers, made out for long terms and constantly renewed up to the day when, gathering together all the protested notes, the shopkeeper had asked his friend Vinçart to take in his own name all the necessary legal steps to collect the money, not wishing to appear as a shark in the eyes of his fellow-citizens.

She mingled her story with recriminations against Lheureux, to which the notary from time to time gave meaningless replies. Eating his cutlet and drinking his tea, he buried his chin in his sky-blue cravat, into which were thrust two diamond pins, held together by a small gold chain; and he smiled a singular smile, in a sugary, ambiguous fashion. Noticing that her feet were damp:

"Do get closer to the stove," he said, "put your feet up against the porcelain."

She was afraid of dirtying it but the notary replied gallantly:

"Pretty things never spoil anything."

Then she tried to appeal to his better feelings and, growing moved herself, she began telling him about the tightness of her household, her worries, her wants. He could understand that—such an elegant woman!—and, without interrupting his lunch, he turned completely round towards her, so that his knee brushed against her boot; the sole was beginning to curl in the heat of the stove.

But when she asked for three thousand francs, his lips drew tight and he said how sorry he was not to have had the management of her capital before, for there were hundreds of ways very convenient, even for a lady, of turning her money to account. In the turf-pits of Gaumesnil or in Le Havre real estate, they could have ventured, with hardly any risk, on some excellent speculations; and he let her consume herself with rage at the thought of the fabulous sums that she would certainly have made.

"How was it," he went on, "that you didn't come to me?"

"I don't know," she said.

"Why not! Did I frighten you so much? It is I, on the contrary, who ought to complain. We hardly know one another; yet I am very devoted to you. You do not doubt that any longer, I hope?"

He held out his hand, took hers, kissed it greedily, then held it on his knee; and he played delicately with her fingers, while muttering thousands of compliments.

His bland voice rustled like a running brook; a light shone in his eyes through the glimmering of his spectacles, and his hand was advancing up Emma's sleeve to press her arm. She felt against her cheek his panting breath. This man was intolerable.

She sprang to her feet and told him:

"Sir, I am waiting."

"For what?" said the notary, who suddenly became very pale.

"This money."

"But . . ."

Then, yielding to an irresistible wave of desire:

"Well then, . . . yes!"

He dragged himself towards her on his knees, regardless of his dressing gown.

"I beg you, stay! I love you!"

He seized her by the waist. Madame Bovary's face flushed purple. She recoiled with a terrible look, exclaiming:

"You shamelessly take advantage of my distress, sir! I am to be pitied—not to be sold."

And she went out.

The notary remained dumbfounded, his eyes fixed on his fine embroidered slippers. They were a love gift, and their sight finally consoled him. Besides, he reflected that such an adventure might have carried him too far.

"The wretch! the scoundrel! . . . what an infamy!" she said to herself, as she fled with nervous steps under the aspens that lined the road. The disappointment of her failure increased the indignation of her outraged modesty; it seemed to her that Providence pursued her implacably, and, strengthening herself in her pride, she had never felt so much esteem for herself nor so much contempt for others. A spirit of warfare transformed her. She would have liked to strike all men, to spit in their faces, to crush them; she kept walking straight on, as quickly as she could, pale, shaking and furious, searching the empty horizon with tear-dimmed eyes, almost rejoicing in the hatred that was choking her.

When she saw her house a numbness came over her. She could not go on; yet she had to. Besides, what escape was there for her?

Félicité was waiting for her at the door.

"Well?"

"No!" said Emma.

And for a quarter of an hour the two of them went over the various persons in Yonville who might perhaps be inclined to help her. But each time that Félicité named some one Emma replied:

"Out of the question! they won't!"

"And the master'll soon be in."

"I know that well enough . . . Now leave me alone."

She had tried everything; there was nothing more to be done now; and when Charles came in she would have to tell him:

"Step aside! This rug on which you are walking is no longer ours. In your own house you don't own a chair, a pin, a straw, and it is I, poor man, who have ruined you."

Then there would be a great sob; next he would weep abundantly, and at last, the surprise past, he would forgive her.

"Yes," she murmured, grinding her teeth, "*he* will forgive me, the man I could never forgive for having known me, even if he had a million to spare! . . . Never! never!"

The thought of Bovary's magnanimity exasperated her. He was bound to find out the catastrophe, whether she confessed or not, now, soon, or to-morrow; so there was no escape from the horrible scene and she would have to bear the weight of his generosity. She wanted to return to Lheureux, but what good would it do? To write to her father—it was too late; and perhaps she began to repent now that she had not yielded to the notary, when she heard the trot of a horse in the alley. It was he; he was opening the gate; he was whiter than the plaster wall. Rushing to the stairs, she fled to the Square; and the wife of the mayor, who was talking to Lestiboudois in front of the church, saw her enter the house of the tax-collector.

She hurried off to tell Madame Caron, and the two ladies went up to the attic; hidden behind a sheet strung up on two poles, they stationed themselves comfortably in full command of Binet's room.

He was alone in his garret, busily copying in wood one of those indescribable bits of ivory, composed of crescents, of spheres hollowed out one within the other, the whole as straight as an obelisk, and of no use whatever; and he was beginning on the last piece—he was nearing his goal! In the twilight of the workshop the white dust was flying from his tools like a shower of sparks under the hoofs of a galloping horse; the two wheels were turning, droning; Binet smiled, his chin lowered, his nostrils distended. He seemed lost in the state of complete bliss that only the most menial tasks can offer: distracting the mind by easily overcome obstacles, they satisfy it completely, leading to a fulfilled achievement that leaves no room for dreams beyond.

"Ah! there she is!" exclaimed Madame Tuvache.

But the noise of the lathe made it impossible to hear what she was saying.

At last the two ladies thought they made out the word "francs," and Madame Tuvache whispered in a low voice:

"She's asking for extra time to pay her taxes."

"Apparently!" replied the other.

They saw her walking up and down, examining the napkin-rings, the candlesticks, the banister rails against the walls, while Binet stroked his beard with satisfaction.

"Do you think she wants to order something from him?" said Madame Tuvache.

"Why, he never sells anything," objected her neighbor.

The tax-collector seemed to be listening with wide-open eyes, as if he did not understand. She went on in a tender, suppliant manner. She came nearer to him, her breast heaving; they no longer spoke.

"Is she making advances to him?" said Madame Tuvache.

Binet was scarlet to his very ears. She took hold of his hands.

"Oh, it's too much!"

And no doubt she was suggesting something abominable to him; for the tax-collector—yet he was brave, had fought at Bautzen and at Lützen, had been through the French campaign,[8] and had even been proposed for the Croix de Guerre—suddenly, as at the sight of a serpent, recoiled as far as he could from her, exclaiming:

"Madame! How dare you? . . ."

"Women like that ought to be whipped," said Madame Tuvache.

"But where did she go?" Madame Caron asked. For while they talked, she had vanished out of sight, till they discovered her running up the Grande Rue and turning right as if making for the graveyard, leaving them lost in wonder.

"Mère Rollet," she cried on reaching the nurse's home, "I am choking; unlace me!" She fell sobbing on the bed. Nurse Rollet covered her with a petticoat and remained standing by her side. Then, as she did not answer, the woman withdrew, took her wheel and began spinning flax.

"Please, stop that!" she murmured, fancying she heard Binet's lathe.

"What's bothering her?" said the nurse to herself. "Why has she come here?"

She had come, impelled by a kind of horror that drove her from her home.

Lying on her back, motionless, and with staring eyes, she saw things but vaguely, although she tried with idiotic persistence to focus her attention on them. She looked at the scaling walls, two logs smoking end to end in the fireplace, and a long spider crawling over her head in a cracked beam. At last she began to collect her thoughts.

8. The battles in France before the Allies captured Paris and forced the abdication of Napoleon and his banishment to Elba in 1814. *Bautzen* (in Saxony, now in Poland, called Budyszin): The scene of a battle in 1813 where Napoleon defeated the Prussians and Russians. *Lützen*, in Saxony: The scene of another battle of Napoleon.

She remembered—one day, with Léon . . . Oh! how long ago that was—the sun was shining on the river, and the air full of the scent from the clematis . . . Then, carried by her memories as by a rushing torrent, she soon remembered what had happened the day before.

"What time is it?" she asked.

Mère Rollet went out, raised the fingers of her right hand to that side of the sky that was brightest, and came back slowly, saying:

"Nearly three."

"Ah! thank you, thank you!"

For he would come, he was bound to. He would have found the money. But he would, perhaps, go down to her house, not guessing where she was, and she told the nurse to run and fetch him.

"Be quick!"

"I'm going, my dear lady, I'm going!"

She wondered now why she had not thought of him from the first. Yesterday he had given his word; he would not break it. And she already saw herself at Lheureux's spreading out her three bank-notes on his desk. Then she would have to invent some story to explain matters to Bovary. What would she tell him?

The nurse, however, was a long time returning. But, as there was no clock in the cot, Emma feared she was perhaps exaggerating the length of time. She began walking round the garden, step by step; she went into the path by the hedge, and returned quickly, hoping that the woman would have come back by another road. At last, weary of waiting, assailed by fears that she thrust from her, no longer conscious whether she had been here a century or a moment, she sat down in a corner, closed her eyes, and stopped her ears. The gate grated; she sprang up. Before she could speak, Mère Rollet told her:

"There is no one at your house!"

"What?"

"He isn't there. And Monsieur is crying. He is calling for you. Everybody is looking for you."

Emma did not answer. She gasped with wild, rolling eyes, while the peasant woman, frightened at her face drew back instinctively, thinking her mad. Suddenly she struck her brow and uttered a cry; for the thought of Rodolphe, like a flash of lightning in a dark night, had struck into her soul. He was so good, so tender, so generous! And besides, should he hesitate to come to her assistance, she would know well enough how one single glance would reawaken their lost love. So she set out towards La Huchette, unaware that she was hastening to offer what had so angered her a while ago, not in the least conscious of her prostitution.

VIII

She asked herself as she walked along. "What am I going to say? How shall I begin?" And as she went on she recognised the thickets, the trees, the sea-rushes on the hill, the château beyond. All the sensations of her first love came back to her, and her poor oppressed heart expanded in the warmth of this tenderness. A warm wind blew in her face; melting snow fell drop by drop from the leave-buds onto the grass.

She entered, as in the past, through the small park-gate, reached the main courtyard, planted with a double row of lindens, their long whispering branches swaying in the wind. The dogs in their kennels barked, but their resounding voices brought no one out.

She went up the large straight staircase with wooden banisters that led to the hallway paved with dusty flagstones, into which a row of doors opened, as in a monastery or an inn. He was at the top, right at the end, on the left. When she placed her fingers on the lock her strength suddenly deserted her. She was afraid, almost wished he would not be there, though this was her only hope, her last chance of salvation. She collected her thoughts for one moment, and, strengthening herself by the feeling of present necessity, went in.

He was sitting in front of the fire, both his feet propped against the mantelpiece, smoking a pipe.

"Oh, it's you!" he said, getting up hurriedly.

"Yes, it is I . . . I have come, Rodolphe, to ask your advice."

And, despite all her efforts, it was impossible for her to open her lips.

"You have not changed; you're as charming as ever!"

"Oh," she replied bitterly, "they are poor charms since you disdained them."

Then he began a long justification of his conduct, excusing himself in vague terms, since he was unable to invent better.

She yielded to his words, still more to his voice and the sight of him, so that she pretended to believe, or perhaps believed, in the pretext he gave for their break; it was a secret on which depended the honor, the very life of a third person.

"Never mind," she said, looking at him sadly. "I have suffered much."

He replied philosophically:

"Life is that way!"

"Has life," Emma went on, "been kind to you at least since our separation?"

"Oh, neither good . . . nor bad."

"Perhaps it would have been better never to have parted."

"Yes, perhaps."

"You think so?" she said, drawing nearer.

Then, with a sigh:

"Oh, Rodolphe! if only you knew! . . . I loved you so!"

It was then that she took his hand, and they remained some time, their fingers intertwined, like that first day at the Agricultural Fair. With a gesture of pride he struggled against this emotion. But sinking upon his breast she told him:

"How did you think I could live without you? One cannot lose the habit of happiness. I was desperate, I thought I was going to die! I'll tell you about it . . . But you, you fled from me!"

With the natural cowardice that characterizes the stronger sex, he had carefully avoided her for the last three years; now Emma persisted, with coaxing little motions of the head, playful and feline:

"I know you love others, you may as well admit it. Oh! I don't blame them, I understand! You seduced them just as you seduced me. You're a man, a real man! you have all it takes to make yourself loved. But we'll start all over, won't we? We'll love each other as before! Look, I am laughing, I am happy! . . . Say something!"

She was irresistible, with a tear trembling in her eye, like a raindrop in a blue flower-cup, after the storm.

He had drawn her upon his knees, and with the back of his hand was caressing her smooth hair; a last ray of the sun was mirrored there, like a golden arrow. She lowered her head; at last he kissed her on the eylids quite gently with the tips of his lips.

"Why, you have been crying! Why?"

She burst into tears. Rodolphe thought this was an outburst of her love. As she did not speak, he took this silence to be a last remnant of resistance, so he exclaimed:

"Oh, forgive me! You are the only one who really pleases me. I was a fool, a wicked fool! I love you, I'll always love you! What is the matter? Tell me . . ."

He knelt before her.

"Well, Rodolphe . . . I am ruined! You must lend me three thousand francs."

"But . . ." he said, as he slowly rose to his feet, "but . . ." His face assumed a grave expression.

"You know," she went on quickly, "that my husband had entrusted his money to a notary to invest, and he absconded. So we borrowed; the patients don't pay us. Moreover, the estate isn't settled yet; we shall have the money later on. But to-day, for want of three thousand francs, we are to be sold out, right now, this very minute. Counting on your friendship, I have come to you for help."

"Ah!" thought Rodolphe, turning very pale, "so that's what she came for."

At last he said, very calmly:

"My dear lady, I haven't got them."

He did not lie. If he had had it, he would probably have given the money, although it is generally unpleasant to do such fine things: a demand for money being, of all the winds that blow upon love, the coldest and most destructive.

She stared at him in silence for minutes.

"You haven't got them!"

She repeated several times:

"You haven't got them! . . . I ought to have spared myself this last shame. You never loved me. You are no better than the others."

She was losing her head, giving herself away.

Rodolphe interrupted her, declaring he was himself "hard up."

"Oh! I feel sorry for you!" said Emma, "exceedingly sorry!"

And fixing her eyes upon an embossed rifle that shone against its panoply:

"But when one is so poor one doesn't have silver on the butt of one's gun. One doesn't buy a clock inlaid with tortoiseshell," she went on, pointing to the Boulle clock, "nor silver-gilt whistles for one's whips," and she touched them, "nor charms for one's watch. Oh, he has all he needs! even a liqueur-stand in his bedroom; for you pamper yourself, you live well. You have a château, farms, woods; you go hunting; you travel to Paris. Why, if it were but that," she cried, taking up two cuff-links from the mantlepiece, "even for the least of these trifles, one could get money . . . Oh, I don't want anything from you; you can keep them!"

And she flung the links away with such force that their gold chain broke as it struck against the wall.

"But I! I would have given you everything. I would have sold all, worked for you with my hands, I would have begged on the high-roads for a smile, for a look, to hear you say 'Thank you!' And you sit there quietly in your arm-chair, as if you had not made me suffer enough already! But for you, and you know it, I might have lived happily. What made you do it? Was it a bet? Yet you loved me . . . you said so. And but a moment ago . . . Ah! it would have been better to have driven me away. My hands are hot with your kisses, and there is the spot on the carpet where at my knees you swore an eternity of love! You made me believe you; for two years you held me in the most magnificent, the sweetest dream! . . . Our plans for the journey, do you remember? Oh, your letter! your letter! it tore my heart! And then when I come back to him—to him, rich, happy, free—to implore the help the first stranger would give, a suppliant, and bringing back to him all my tenderness, he repulses me because it could cost him three thousand francs!"

"I haven't got them," replied Rodolphe, with that perfect calm with which resigned rage covers itself as with a shield.

She went out. The walls trembled, the ceiling was crushing her, and she passed back through the long alley, stumbling against the heaps of dead leaves scattered by the wind. At last she reached the low hedge in front of the gate; she broke her nails against the lock in her haste to open it. Then a hundred paces beyond, breathless, almost falling, she stopped. And now turning round, she once more saw the impassive château, with the park, the gardens, the three courts, and all the windows of the façade.

She remained lost in stupor, and only conscious of herself through the beating of her arteries, that seemed to burst forth like a deafening music filling all the fields. The earth beneath her feet was more yielding than the sea, and the furrows seemed to her immense brown waves breaking into foam. All the memories and ideas that crowded her head seemed to explode at once like a thousand pieces of fire-works. She saw her father, Lheureux's closet, their room at home, another landscape. Madness was coming upon her; she grew afraid, and managed to recover herself, in a confused way, it is true, for she did not remember the cause of her dreadful confusion, namely the money. She suffered only in her love, and felt her soul escaping from her in this memory, as wounded men, dying, feel their life ebb from their bleeding wounds.

Night was falling, crows were flying about.

Suddenly it seemed to her that fiery spheres were exploding in the air like bullets when they strike, and were whirling, whirling, to melt at last upon the snow between the branches of the trees. In the midst of each of them appeared the face of Rodolphe. They multiplied and drew near, they penetrated her. It all disappeared; she recognised the lights of the houses that shone through the fog.

Now her plight, like an abyss, loomed before her. She was panting as if her heart would burst. Then in an ecstasy of heroism, that made her almost joyous, she ran down the hill, crossed the cow-plank, the footpath, the alley, the market, and reached the pharmacy. She was about to enter, but at the sound of the bell some one might come, and slipping in by the gate, holding her breath, feeling her way along the walls, she went as far as the door of the kitchen, where a candle was burning on the stove. Justin in his shirt-sleeves was carrying out a dish.

"Ah! they're eating; let's wait."

He returned; she tapped at the window. He came out.

"The key! the one for upstairs where he keeps the . . ."

"What?"

And he looked at her, astonished at the pallor of her face, that stood out white against the black background of the night. She seemed to him extraordinarily beautiful and majestic as a phantom. Without understanding what she wanted, he had the presentiment of something terrible.

But she went on quickly in a low voice that was sweet and melting:
"I want it; give it to me."

As the partition wall was thin, they could hear the clatter of the forks on the plates in the dining-room.

She pretended that she wanted to kill the rats that kept her from sleeping.

"I must go ask Monsieur."

"No, stay!"

Then with a casual air:

"Oh, it's not worth bothering him about, I'll tell him myself later. Come, hold the light for me."

She entered the corridor into which the laboratory door opened. Against the wall was a key labelled *Capharnaum*.

"Justin!" called the pharmacist, growing impatient.

"Let's go up."

And he followed her. The key turned in the lock, and she went straight to the third shelf, so well did her memory guide her, seized the blue jar, tore out the cork, plunged in her hand, and withdrawing it full of white powder, she ate it greedily.

"Stop!" he cried, throwing himself upon her.

"Quiet! They might hear us . . ."

He was in despair, ready to call out.

"Say nothing, or all the blame will fall on your master."

Then she went home, suddenly calmed, with something of the serenity of one that has done his duty.

When Charles, thunderstruck at the news of the execution, rushed home, Emma had just gone out. He cried aloud, wept, fainted, but she did not return. Where could she be? He sent Félicité to Homais, to Monsieur Tuvache, to Lheureux, to the Lion d'Or, everywhere, and in between the waves of his anxiety he saw his reputation destroyed, their fortune lost, Berthe's future ruined. By what?—Not a word! He waited till six in the evening. At last, unable to bear it any longer, and fancying she had gone to Rouen, he set out along the highroad, walked a mile, met no one, again waited, and returned home.

She had come back.

"What happened? . . . Why did you? . . . Tell me . . ."

She sat down at her writing-table and wrote a letter, which she sealed slowly, adding the date and the hour.

Then she said in a solemn tone:

"You are to read it to-morrow; till then, I beg you, don't ask me a single question. No, not one!"

"But . . .

"Oh, leave me!"

She lay down full length on her bed.

A bitter taste in her mouth awakened her. She saw Charles, and again closed her eyes.

She was studying herself curiously, to detect the first signs of suffering. But no! nothing as yet. She heard the ticking of the clock, the cracking of the fire, and Charles breathing as he stood upright by her bed.

"Ah! it is but a little thing, death!" she thought. "I shall fall asleep and all will be over."

She drank a mouthful of water and turned her face to the wall. The frightful taste of ink persisted.

"I am thirsty; oh! so thirsty," she sighed.

"What is the matter?" said Charles, who was handing her a glass.

"It's nothing . . . Open the window, I'm choking."

She was seized with a sickness so sudden that she had hardly time to draw out her handkerchief from under the pillow.

"Take it away," she said quickly; "throw it away."

He spoke to her; she did not answer. She lay motionless, afraid that the slightest movement might make her vomit. But she felt an icy cold creeping from her feet to her heart.

"Ah! It's beginning," she murmured.

"What did you say?"

She gently rocked her head to and fro in anguish, opening her jaws as if something very heavy were weighing upon her tongue. At eight o'clock the vomiting began again.

Charles noticed that at the bottom of the basin there was a trace of white sediment sticking to the sides of the porcelain.

"This is extraordinary, very strange!" he repeated.

"No!" she loudly replied, "you are mistaken."

Then gently, almost caressingly, he passed his hand over her stomach. She uttered a sharp cry. He recoiled in terror.

Then she began to moan, faintly at first. Her shoulders were shaken by a strong shudder, and she was growing paler than the sheets in which she buried her clenched fists. Her unequal pulse was now almost imperceptible.

Drops of sweat oozed from her face, that had turned blue and rigid as under the effect of a metallic vapor. Her teeth chattered, her dilated eyes looked vaguely about her, and to all questions she replied only with a shake of the head; she even smiled once or twice. Gradually, her moaning grew louder; she couldn't repress a muffled scream; she pretended she felt better and that she'd soon get up. But she was seized with convulsions and cried out:

"God! It's horrible!"

He threw himself on his knees by her bed.

"Tell me! what have you eaten? Answer, for heaven's sake!"

And he looked at her with a tenderness in his eyes such as she had never seen.

"Well, there . . . there . . ." she said in a faltering voice.

He flew to the writing-table, tore open the seal, and read aloud: "Let no one be blamed . . ." He stopped, passed his hands over his eyes, and read it over again.

"What! . . . Help! Help!"

He could only keep repeating the word: "Poisoned! poisoned!" Félicité ran to Homais, who proclaimed it in the market-place; Madame Lefrançois heard it at the Lion d'Or; some got up to go and tell their neighbors, and all night the village was on the alert.

Distracted, stammering, reeling, Charles wandered about the room. He knocked against the furniture, tore his hair, and the pharmacist had never believed that there could be so terrible a sight.

He went home to write to Monsieur Canivet and to Doctor Larivière. His mind kept wandering, he had to start over fifteen times. Hippolyte went to Neufchâtel, and Justin so spurred Bovary's horse that he left it foundered and three parts dead by the hill at Bois-Guillaume.

Charles tried to look up his medical dictionary, but could not read it; the lines were jumping before his eyes.

"Be calm," said the pharmacist; "we must administer a powerful antidote. What is the poison?"

Charles showed him the letter. It was arsenic.

"Very well," said Homais, "we must make an analysis."

For he knew that in cases of poisoning an analysis must be made; and the other, who did not understand, answered:

"Oh, do it! Do anything! Save her . . ."

Then going back to her, he sank upon the carpet, and lay there with his head leaning against the edge of her bed, sobbing.

"Don't cry," she said to him. "Soon I won't trouble you any longer."

"Why did you do it? Who made you?"

She replied:

"There was no other way!"

"Weren't you happy? Is it my fault? But I did the best I could!"

"Yes, that's true . . . you're good, not like the others."

And she slowly passed her hand over his hair. The sweetness of this sensation deepened his sadness; he felt his whole being dissolving in despair at the thought that he must lose her, just when she was confessing more love for him than she ever did. He didn't know what to do, felt paralyzed by fear; the need for an immediate decision took away his last bit of self-control.

Emma thought that, at last, she was through with lying, cheating and with the numberless desires that had tortured her. She hated no one now; a twilight dimness was settling upon her thoughts, and, of all earthly noises, Emma heard none but the intermittent lamentations of this poor heart, sweet and remote like the echo of a symphony dying away.

"Bring me the child," she said, raising herself on her elbow.

"You're not feeling worse, are you?" asked Charles.

"No, no!"

The child, serious, and still half-asleep, was carried in on the maid's arm in her long white nightgown, from which her bare feet peeped out. She looked wonderingly at the disordered room, and half-closed her eyes, dazzled by the burning candles on the table. They reminded her, no doubt of the morning of New Year's day and Mid-Lent, when thus awakened early by candlelight she came to her mother's bed to fetch her presents.

"But where is it, mamma?" she asked.

And as everybody was silent, "But I can't see my little stocking."

Félicité held her over the bed while she still kept looking towards the mantelpiece.

"Did nurse take it away?" she asked.

At the mention of this name, that carried her back to the memory of her adulteries and her calamities, Madame Bovary turned away her head, as at the loathing of another bitter poison that rose to her mouth. But Berthe remained perched on the bed.

"Oh, how big your eyes are, mamma! How pale you are! how you sweat!"

Her mother looked at her.

"I'm frightened!" cried the child, recoiling.

Emma took her hand to kiss it; the child struggled.

"Enough! Take her away!" cried Charles, who was sobbing at the foot of the bed.

Then the symptoms ceased for a moment; she seemed less agitated; and at every insignificant word she spoke, every time she drew breath a little easier, his hopes revived. At last, when Canivet came in, he threw himself into his arms.

"Ah; it's you. Thank you! How good of you to come. But she's better. See! look at her."

His colleague was by no means of this opinion, and "never beating about the bush"—as he put it—he prescribed an emetic in order to empty the stomach completely.

She soon began vomiting blood. Her lips became drawn. Her limbs were convulsed, her whole body covered with brown spots, and her pulse slipped beneath the fingers like a stretched thread, like a harpstring about to break.

After this she began to scream horribly. She cursed the poison, railed at it, and implored it to be quick, and thrust away with her stiffened arms everything that Charles, in more agony than herself, tried to make her drink. He stood up, his handkerchief to his lips, moaning, weeping, and choked by sobs that shook his whole body. Félicité was running up and down the room. Homais, motionless, uttered great sighs; and Monsieur Canivet, always retaining his self-command, nevertheless began to feel uneasy.

"The devil! yet she has been purged, and since the cause has been removed . . ."

"The effect must cease," said Homais, "that's obvious."

"Oh, save her!" cried Bovary.

And, without listening to the pharmacist, who was still venturing the hypothesis. "It is perhaps a salutary paroxysm," Canivet was about to administer theriaca, when they heard the cracking of a whip; all the windows rattled, and a postchaise drawn by three horses abreast, up to their ears in mud, drove at a gallop round the corner of market. It was Doctor Larivière.

The apparition of a god would not have caused more commotion. Bovary raised his hands; Canivet stopped short; and Homais pulled off his cap long before the doctor had come in.

He belonged to that great school of surgeons created by Bichat,[9] to that generation, now extinct, of philosophical practitioners, who, cherishing their art with a fanatical love, exercised it with enthusiasm and wisdom. Every one in his hospital trembled when he was angry: and his students so revered him that they tried, as soon as they were themselves in practice, to imitate him as much as possible. They could be found in all the neighboring towns wearing exactly the same merino overcoat and black frock. The doctor's buttoned cuffs slightly covered his fleshy hands—very beautiful hands, never covered by gloves, as though to be more ready to plunge into suffering. Disdainful of honors, of titles, and of academies, hospitable, generous, fatherly to the poor, and practising virtue without believing in it, he would almost have passed for a saint if the keenness of his intellect had not caused him to be feared as a demon. His glance, more penetrating than his scalpels, looked straight into your soul, and would detect any lie, regardless how well hidden. He went through life with the benign dignity that goes with the assurance of talent and wealth, with forty years of a hard-working, blameless life.

He frowned as soon as he had passed the door when he saw the cadaverous face of Emma stretched out on her back with her mouth open. Then, while apparently listening to Canivet, he rubbed his fingers up and down beneath his nostrils, repeating:

"I see, yes, yes . . ."

9. Marie-Françoise-Xavier Bichat (1771–1802) was the author of an *Anatomie générale*.

But he slowly shrugged his shoulders. Bovary watched him; they looked at one another; and this man, accustomed as he was to the sight of pain, could not keep back a tear that fell on his shirt front.

He tried to take Canivet into the next room. Charles followed him.

"She is sinking, isn't she? If we put on poultices? Anything! Oh, think of something, you who have saved so many!"

Charles put both arms around him, and looked at him in anxious supplication, half-fainting against his breast.

"Come, my poor boy, courage! There is nothing more to be done."

And Doctor Larivière turned away.

"You are leaving?"

"I'll be back."

He went out as if to give an order to the coachman, followed by Canivet, who was equally glad to escape from the spectacle of Emma dying.

The pharmacist caught up with them on the Square. He could not by temperament keep away from celebrities, so he begged Monsieur Larivière to do him the signal honor of staying for lunch.

He sent quickly to the Lion d'Or for some pigeons; to the butcher's for all the cutlets that could be found; to Tuvache for cream; and to Lestiboudois for eggs; and Homais himself aided in the preparations, while Madame Homais was saying as she tightened her apron-strings:

"I hope you'll forgive us, sir, for in this village, if one is caught unawares . . ."

"Stemmed glasses!" whispered Homais.

"If only we were in the city, I'd be able to find stuffed pig's feet . . ."

"Be quiet . . . Please doctor, *à table!*"

He thought fit, after the first few mouthfuls, to supply some details about the catastrophe.

"We had a feeling of siccity in the pharynx, then intolerable pains at the epigastrium, super-purgation, coma."

"But how did she poison herself?"

"I don't know, doctor, and I don't even know where she can have procured the arsenious acid."

Justin, who was just bringing in a pile of plates, began to tremble.

"What's the matter?" said the pharmacist.

At this question the young man dropped the whole lot on the floor with a dreadful crash.

"Imbecile!" cried Homais, "clumsy lout! blockhead! confounded ass!"

But suddenly controlling himself:

"I wished, doctor, to make an analysis, and *primo* I delicately introduced a tube . . ."

"You would have done better," said the physician, "to introduce your fingers into her throat."

His colleague was silent, having just before privately received a severe lecture about his emetic, so that this good Canivet, so arrogant and so verbose at the time of the club-foot, was to-day very modest. He smiled an incessantly approving smile.

Homais dilated in Amphitryonic pride,[1] and the affecting thought of Bovary vaguely contributed to his pleasure by a kind of selfish comparison with his own lot. Moreover, the presence of the surgeon exalted him. He displayed his erudition, spoke effusively about cantharides, upas, the manchineel, adder bites.

"I have even read that various persons have found themselves under toxicological symptoms, and, as it were, paralyzed by blood sausage that had been too strongly smoked. At least, this was stated in a very fine paper prepared by one of our pharmaceutical authorities, one of our masters, the illustrious Cadet de Gassicourt!"[2]

Madame Homais reappeared, carrying one of those shaky machines that are heated with spirits of wine; for Homais liked to make his coffee at the table, having, moreover, torrefied it, pulverised it, and mixed it himself.

"*Saccharum*, doctor?" he said, offering sugar.

Then he had all his children brought down, anxious to have the physician's opinion on their constitutions.

At last Monsieur Larivière was about to leave, when Madame Homais asked for a consultation about her husband. He was making his blood too thick by falling asleep every evening after dinner.

"Oh, it isn't his blood I'd call too thick," said the physician.

And, smiling a little at his unnoticed joke, the doctor opened the door. But the shop was full of people; he had the greatest difficult in getting rid of Monsieur Tuvache, who feared his wife would get pneumonia because she was in the habit of spitting on the ashes; then of Monseiur Binet, who sometimes experienced sudden attacks of great hunger; and of Madame Caron, who suffered from prickling sensations; of Lheureux, who had dizzy spells; of Lestiboudois, who had rheumatism; and of Madame Lefrançois, who had heartburn. At last the three horses started; and it was the general opinion that he had not shown himself at all obliging.

Public attention was distracted by the appearance of Monsieur

---

1. A host's pride. *Amphitryon* is a comedy by Molière (1668). The verse: "Le véritable Amphitryon / Est l'Amphitryon où l'on dîne" has become a proverb. It means a man who brings companions to his table, a rich and powerful man whom we flatter.   2. Cadet de Gassicourt (1769–1821) was the pharmacist of Emperor Napoleon I who had considerable trouble under the Restoration because of his liberal ideas.

Bournisien, who was going across the square carrying the holy oil.

Homais, as was due to his principles, compared priests to ravens attracted by the smell of death. The sight of an ecclesiastic was personally disagreeable to him, for the cassock made him think of the shroud, and his dislike of the one matched his fear of the other.

Nevertheless, not shrinking from what he called his "Mission," he returned to Bovary's house with Canivet, who had been strongly urged by Dr. Larivière to make this call; and he would, but for his wife's objections, have taken his two sons with him, in order to accustom them to great occasions; that this might be a lesson, an example, a solemn picture, that should remain in their heads later on.

The room when they went in was full of mournful solemnity. On the work-table, covered over with a white cloth, there were five or six small balls of cotton in a silver dish, near a large crucifix between two lighted candles.

Emma, her chin sunken upon her breast, had her eyes inordinately wide open, and her poor hands wandered over the sheets with that hideous and gentle movement of the dying, that seems as if they already wanted to cover themselves with the shroud. Pale as a statue and with eyes red as fire, Charles, beyond weeping, stood opposite her at the foot of the bed, while the priest, bending one knee, was muttering in a low voice.

She turned her face slowly, and seemed filled with joy on suddenly seeing the violet stole. She was doubtlessly reminded, in this moment of sudden serenity, of the lost bliss of her first mystical flights, mingling with the visions of eternal beatitude that were beginning.

The priest rose to take the crucifix; then she stretched forward her neck like one suffering from thirst, and gluing her lips to the body of the Man-God, she pressed upon it with all her expiring strength the fullest kiss of love that she had ever given. Then he recited the *Misereatur* and the *Indulgentiam*, dipped his right thumb in the oil, and began to give extreme unction. First, upon the eyes, that had so coveted all wordly goods; then upon the nostrils, that had been so greedy of the warm breeze and the scents of love; then upon the mouth, that had spoken lies, moaned in pride, and cried out in lust; then upon the hands that had taken delight in the texture of sensuality; and finally upon the soles of the feet, so swift when she had hastened to satisfy her desires, and that would now walk no more.

The curé wiped his fingers, threw the bit of oil-stained cotton into the fire, and came and sat down by the dying woman, to tell her that she must now blend her sufferings with those of Jesus Christ and abandon herself to the divine mercy.

Finishing his exhortations, he tried to place in her hand a blessed candle, symbol of the celestial glory with which she was soon to be surrounded. Emma, too weak, could not close her fingers, and if it hadn't been for Monsieur Bournisien, the taper would have fallen to the ground.

Yet she was no longer quite so pale, and her face had an expression of serenity as if the sacrament had cured her.

The priest did not fail to point this out; he even explained to Bovary that the Lord sometimes prolonged the life of persons when he thought it useful for their salvation; and Charles remembered the day when, so near death, she had received communion. Perhaps there was no need to despair, he thought.

In fact, she looked around her slowly, as one awakening from a dream; then in a distinct voice she asked for her mirror, and remained bent over it for some time, until big tears fell from her eyes. Then she turned away her head with a sigh and fell back upon the pillows.

Her chest soon began heaving rapidly; the whole of her tongue protruded from her mouth; her eyes, as they rolled, grew paler, like the two globes of a lamp that is going out, so that one might have thought her already dead but for the fearful labouring of her ribs, shaken by violent breathing, as if the soul were struggling to free itself. Félicité knelt down before the crucifix, and the pharmacist himself slightly bent his knees, while Monsieur Canivet looked out vaguely at the Square. Bournisien had resumed his praying, his face bowed against the edge of the bed, his long black cassock trailing behind him in the room. Charles was on the other side, on his knees, his arms outstretched towards Emma. He had taken her hands and pressed them, shuddering at every heartbeat, as at the tremors of a falling ruin. As the death-rattle became stronger the priest prayed faster; his prayers mingled with Bovary's stifled sobs, and sometimes all seemed lost in the muffled murmur of the Latin syllables that sounded like a tolling bell.

Suddenly from the pavement outside came the loud noise of wooden shoes and the clattering of stick; and a voice rose—a raucous voice— that sang

> Often the heat of a summer's day
> Makes a young girl dream her heart away.

Emma raised herself like a galvanised corpse, her hair streaming, her eyes fixed, staring.

> To gather up all the new-cut stalks
> Of wheat left by the scythe's cold swing,
> Nanette bends over as she walks
> Toward the furrows from where they spring.

"The blind man!" she cried.

And Emma began to laugh, an atrocious, frantic, desperate laugh, thinking she saw the hideous face of the poor wretch loom out of the eternal darkness like a menace.

The wind blew very hard that day
It blew her petticoat away.

A final spasm threw her back upon the mattress. They all drew near. She had ceased to exist.

IX

Someone's death always causes a kind of stupefaction; so difficult it is to grasp this advent of nothingness and to resign ourselves to the fact that it has actually taken place. But still, when he saw that she did not move, Charles flung himself upon her, crying:

"Farewell! farewell!"

Homais and Canivet dragged him from the room.

"Control yourself!"

"Yes," he said, struggling, "I'll be quiet. I won't do anything. But let me stay. I want to see her. She is my wife!"

And he wept.

"Cry," said the pharmacist; "let nature take its course; that will relieve you."

Weaker than a child, Charles let himself be led downstairs into the sitting-room, and Monsieur Homais soon went home. On the Square he was accosted by the blind man, who, having dragged himself as far as Yonville in the hope of getting the antiphlogistic salve, was asking every passer-by where the pharmacist lived.

"Good heavens, man, as if I didn't have other fish to fry! I can't help it, but you'll have to come back later."

And he hurried into the shop.

He had to write two letters, to prepare a soothing position for Bovary, to invent some lie that would conceal the poisoning, and work it up into an article for the "Fanal," without counting the people who were waiting to get the news from him; and when the Yonvillers had all heard his story of the arsenic that she had mistaken for sugar in making a vanilla cream, Homais once more returned to Bovary's.

He found him alone (Monsieur Canivet had left), sitting in an arm-chair near the window, staring with a vacant look at the stone floor.

"Well," Homais said, "you ought yourself to fix the hour for the ceremony."

"Why? What ceremony?"

Then, in a stammering, frightened voice:

"Oh, no! not that. No! I want to keep her here."

Homais, to save face, took up a pitcher from the whatnot to water the geraniums.

"Ah! thank you," said Charles; "how kind of you!"

But he did not finish, choked by the flow of memories that Homais' action had released in him.

Then to distract him, Homais thought fit to talk a little about horticulture: plants wanted moisture. Charles bowed his head in approval.

"Besides, we'll soon be having fine weather again."

"Ah!" said Bovary.

The pharmacist, at his wit's end, gently drew aside the small window-curtain.

"Look! there's Monsieur Tuvache passing by."

Charles repeated mechanically:

"Monsieur Tuvache passing by!"

Homais did not dare to bring up the funeral arrangements again; it was the priest who finally convinced him of the necessity to bury Emma.

He shut himself up in his consulting-room, took a pen, and after sobbing for some time, wrote:

"I wish her to be buried in her wedding dress, with white shoes, and a wreath. Her hair is to be spread out over her shoulders. Three coffins, one oak, one mahogany, one of lead. Let no one try to overrule me; I shall have the strength to resist him. She is to be covered with a large piece of green velvet. This is my wish; see that it is done."

The two men were much taken aback by Bovary's romantic ideas. The pharmacist was first to remonstrate with him:

"This velvet seems excessive to me. Besides, think of the expense . . ."

"What's that to you?" cried Charles. "Leave me alone! You didn't love her. Go away!"

The priest took him by the arm for a walk in the garden. He discoursed on the vanity of earthly things. God was very great, very good: one must submit to his decrees without a murmur, even learn to be grateful for one's suffering.

Charles burst into blasphemy:

"I hate your God!"

"The spirit of rebellion is still upon you," sighed the priest.

Bovary was far away. He was striding along by the wall, near the espalier, and he ground his teeth; he raised to heaven looks of malediction, but not so much as a leaf stirred.

A fine rain was falling: Charles, whose chest was bare, at last began to shiver; he went in and sat down in the kitchen.

At six o'clock a noise like a clatter of old iron was heard on the square; it was the "Hirondelle" coming in, and he remained with his forehead pressed against the window-pane, watching all the passengers get out, one after the other. Félicité put down a mattress for him in the drawing-room. He threw himself upon it and fell asleep.

Although a philosopher, Monsieur Homais respected the dead. So bearing poor Charles no grudge, he returned in the evening to sit up with the body, bringing with him three books and a writing-pad for taking notes.

Monsieur Bournisien was there, and two large candles were burning at the head of the bed, which had been taken out of the alcove.

The pharmacist, unable to keep silent, soon began to express some regrets about this "unfortunate young woman," and the priest replied that there was nothing to do now but pray for her.

"Still," Homais insisted, "it is one of two things; either she died in a state of grace (as the Church calls it), and then she doesn't need our prayers; or else she died unrepentant (that is, I believe, the correct technical term), and then . . ."

Bournisien interrupted him, replying testily that it was none the less necessary to pray.

"But," the pharmacist objected, "since God knows all our needs, what can be the good of prayer?"

"What!" the priest exclaimed, "of prayer? Why, aren't you a Christian?"

"I beg your pardon," said Homais; "I admire Christianity. It freed the slaves, brought morality into the world . . ."

"That isn't the point. Look at the texts . . ."

"Oh! oh! As to texts, look at history; everybody knows that the Jesuits have falsified all the texts!"

Charles came in, and advancing towards the bed, slowly drew the curtains.

Emma's head was turned towards her right shoulder, the corner of her mouth, which was open, seemed like a black hole at the lower part of her face; her two thumbs were bent into the palms of her hands; a kind of white dust besprinkled her lashes, and her eyes were beginning to disappear in a viscous pallor, as if covered by a spider-web. The sheet sunk in from her breast to her knees, and then rose at the tips of her toes, and it seemed to Charles that infinite masses, an enormous load, were weighing upon her.

The church clock struck two. They could hear the loud murmur of the river flowing in the darkness at the terrace. Monsieur Bournisien noisily blew his nose from time to time, and Homais' pen was scratching over the paper.

"Come, my good friend," he said, "don't stay here; the sight is too much for you."

When Charles had left, the pharmacist and the priest resumed their argument.

"Read Voltaire," said the one, "read D'Holbach, read the *Encyclopédie!*"[3]

"Read the 'Letters of some Portuguese Jews,' " said the other; "read 'The Meaning of Christianity,'[4] by the former magistrate Nicolas."

They grew warm, they grew red, they both talked at once without listening to each other. Bournisien was scandalised at such audacity; Homais marvelled at such stupidity; and they were about to come to blows when Charles suddenly reappeared. He couldn't resist coming upstairs as though he were spellbound.

He stood at the foot of the bed to see her better, and he lost himself in a contemplation so deep that it was no longer painful.

He recalled stories of catalepsy, the marvels of magnetism, and he said to himself that by willing it with all his force he might perhaps succeed in reviving her. Once he even bent towards her, and cried in a low voice, "Emma! Emma!" His strong breathing made the flames of the candles tremble against the wall.

At daybreak the elder Madame Bovary arrived. As he embraced her, Charles burst into another flood of tears. She tried, as the pharmacist had done, to remonstrate with him on the expenses for the funeral. He became so angry that she was silent, and he even commissioned her to go to town at once and buy what was necessary.

Charles remained alone the whole afternoon; they had taken Berthe to Madame Homais'; Félicité was in the room upstairs with Madame Lefrançois.

In the evening he had some visitors. He rose and shook hands with them, unable to speak. Then they sat down together, and formed a large semicircle in front of the fire. With lowered head, they crossed and uncrossed their legs, and uttered from time to time a deep sigh. They were bored to tears, yet none would be the first to go.

Homais, when he returned at nine o'clock (for the last two days Homais seemed to have made the public Square his residence), was laden with a supply of camphor, benzoin, and aromatic herbs. He also carried a large jar full of chlorine water, to keep off the miasma. Just then the servant, Madame Lefrançois and the elder Madame Bovary were busy getting Emma dressed, and they were drawing down

---

3. Paul-Henri Dietrich, baron d'Holbach (1723–1789), friend and disciple of Diderot, was one of the most outspoken opponents of religion in the French Enlightenment. The *Encyclopedie*, a dictionary of the sciences, arts and letters, edited by Diderot and d'Alembert (1751–1772), is the intellectual monument of the French Enlightenment, a fountainhead of later secular and agnostic thought.   4. One of the many books defending Roman Catholicism by Jean-Jacques-Auguste Nicolas (1807–1888). *Letters of Some Portuguese Jews* (1769) refers to a book by the Abbé Antoine Guéné directed against Voltaire.

the long stiff veil that covered her to her satin shoes.

Félicité was sobbing:

"Oh, my poor mistress! my poor mistress!"

"Look at her," said the innkeeper, sighing; "how pretty she still is! Now, couldn't you swear she was going to get up in a minute?"

Then they bent over her to put on her wreath. They had to raise the head a little, and a rush of black liquid poured from her mouth, as if she wre vomiting.

"Heavens! Watch out for her dress!" cried Madame Lefrançois. "Now, just come and help us," she said to the pharmacist, "or are you afraid?"

"Afraid?" he replied, "I? As if I hadn't seen a lot worse when I was a student at the Hôtel-Dieu. We used to make punch in the dissecting room! Nothingness does not frighten a philosopher; I have often said that I intend to leave my body to the hospitals, to serve the cause of science."

On arriving, the curé inquired after Monsieur Bovary and, at Homais' reply, he said:

"Of course, the blow is still too recent."

Then Homais congratulated him on not being exposed, like other people, to the loss of a beloved companion; this lead to a discussion on the celibracy of priests.

"You must admit," said the pharmacist, "that it is against nature for a man to do without women. There have been crimes . . ."

"For Heaven's sake!" exclaimed the priest, "how do you expect an individual who is married to keep the secrets of the confessional, for example?"

Homais attacked confession. Bournisien defended it; he discoursed on the acts of restitution that it brought about. He cited various anecdotes about thieves who had suddenly become honest. Military men on approaching the tribunal of penitence had finally seen the light. At Fribourg there was a minister . . .

His companion had fallen asleep. Then he felt somewhat stifled by the over-heavy atmosphere of the room; he opened the window; this awoke the pharmacist.

"Come, take a pinch of snuff," he told him. "Take it, it'll do you good."

A continual barking was heard in the distance.

"Do you hear that dog howling?" said the pharmacist.

"They smell the dead," replied the priest. "It's like bees; they leave their hives when there is a death in the neighborhood."

Homais failed to object to these prejudices, for he had again dropped asleep. Monsieur Bournisien, stronger than he, went on moving his lips and muttering for some time, then insensibly his chin sank down, he dropped his big black book, and began to snore.

They sat opposite one another, with bulging stomachs, puffed-up faces, and frowning looks, after so much disagreement uniting at last in the same human weakness, and they moved no more than the corpse by their side, that also seemed to be sleeping.

Charles coming in did not wake them. It was the last time; he came to bid her farewell.

The aromatic herbs were still smoking, and spirals of bluish vapour blended at the window with the entering fog. There were few stars, and the night was warm.

The wax of the candles fell in great drops upon the sheets of the bed. Charles watched them burn, straining his eyes in the glare of their yellow flame.

The watered satin of her gown shimmered white as moonlight. Emma was lost beneath it; and it seemed to him that, spreading beyond her own self, she blended confusedly with everything around her—the silence, the night, the passing wind, the damp odors rising from the ground.

Then suddenly he saw her in the garden at Tostes, on a bench against the thorn hedge, or else at Rouen in the streets, on the threshold of their house, in the yard at Bertaux. He again heard the laughter of the happy boys dancing under the appletrees: the room was filled with the perfume of her hair; and her dress rustled in his arms with a crackling noise. It was the same dress she was wearing now!

For a long while he thus recalled all his lost joys, her attitudes, her movements, the sound of her voice. Wave upon wave of despair came over him, like the tides of an overflowing sea.

He was seized by a terrible curiosity. Slowly, with the tips of his fingers, his heart pounding, he lifted her veil. But he uttered a cry of horror that awoke the other two.

They dragged him down into the sitting-room. Then Félicité came up to say that he wanted some of her hair.

"Cut some off," replied the pharmacist.

And as she did not dare to, he himself stepped forward, scissors in hand. He trembled so that he nicked the skin of the temple in several places. At last, stiffening himself against emotion, Homais gave two or three great cuts at random that left white patches amongst that beautiful black hair.

The pharmacist and the curé resumed their original occupations, not without time and again falling asleep—something of which they accused each other whenever they awoke. Monsieur Bournisien sprinkled the room with holy water and Homais threw a little chlorine on the floor.

Félicité had been so considerate as to put on the chest of drawers, for each of them, a bottle of brandy, some cheese, and a large brioche, and about four o'clock in the morning, unable to restrain himself any longer, the pharmacist sighed:

"I must say that I wouldn't mind taking some sustenance."

The priest did not need any persuading; he left to say mass and, upon his return, they ate and drank, chuckling a little without knowing why, stimulated by that vague gaiety that comes upon us after times of sadness. At the last glass the priest said to the pharmacist, as he clapped him on the shoulder:

"We'll end up good friends, you and I."

In the passage downstairs they met the undertaker's men, who were coming in. Then for two hours Charles had to suffer the torture of hearing the hammer resound against the wood. Next day they lowered her into her oak coffin, that was fitted into the other two; but as the bier was too large, they had to fill up the gaps with the wool of a mattress. At last, when the three lids had been planed down, nailed, soldered, it was placed outside in front of the door; the house was thrown open, and the people of Yonville began to flock round.

Old Rouault arrived, and fainted on the square at the sight of the black cloth.

X

He had only received Homais' letter thirty-six hours after the event; and, to cushion the blow, he had worded it in such a manner that it was impossible to make out just what had happened.

First, the old man had been shaken as if struck by apoplexy. Next, he understood that she was not dead, but she might be . . . At last, he had put on his smock, taken his hat, fastened his spurs to his boots, and set out at full speed; and the whole of the way old Rouault, panting, had been devoured by anxiety. He felt so dizzy that he was forced to dismount. He fancied he heard voices around him and thought he was losing his mind.

Day broke. He saw three black hens asleep in a tree. He shuddered, horrified at this omen. Then he promised the Holy Virgin three chasubles for the church, and vowed that he would go barefooted from the cemetery at Bertaux to the chapel of Vassonville.

He entered Maromme calling out ahead at the people of the inn, burst open the door with a thrust of his shoulder, made for a sack of oats and emptied a bottle of sweet cider into the manger; then he remounted his nag, whose feet struck sparks as it galloped along.

He told himself that they would certainly save her; the doctors were bound to discover a remedy. He remembered all the miraculous cures he had been told about.

Then she appeared to him dead: She was there, before his eyes, lying on her back in the middle of the road. He reined in his horse, and the hallucination disappeared.

At Quincampoix, to give himself heart, he drank three cups of coffee one after the other.

He imagined that they had written the wrong name on the letter. He looked for the letter in his pocket, felt it there, but did not dare to open it.

At last he began to think it was all a bad joke, a spiteful farce, somebody's idea of a fine prank; besides, if she were dead, he would have known. It couldn't be! the countryside looked as usual: the sky was blue, the trees swayed; a flock of sheep passed by. He reached the village; they saw him coming, hunched over his horse, whipping it savagely till its saddle-girths dripped with blood.

When he recovered consciousness, he fell, weeping, into Bovary's arms:

"My daughter! Emma! my child! tell me . . ."

The other replied between sobs:

"I don't know! I don't know! It's a curse!"

The pharmacist pulled them apart.

"Spare him the horrible details. I'll tell monsieur all about it. People are coming, show some dignity, for heaven's sake! Let's behave like philosophers."

Poor Charles tried as hard as he could, and repeated several times: "Yes, be brave . . ."

"Damn it, I'll be brave," cried the old man, "I'll stay with her till the end!"

The bell was tolling. All was ready; they had to start.

Seated together in a stall of the choir, they saw the three chanting choristers continually pass and repass in front of them. The serpent-player was blowing with all his might. Monsieur Bournisien, in full regalia, was singing in a shrill voice. He bowed before the tabernacle, raising his hands, stretched out his arms. Lestiboudois went about the church with his verger's staff. The bier stood near the lectern, between four rows of candles. Charles felt an urge to get up and put them out.

Yet he tried to stir into himself the proper devotional feelings, to throw himself into the hope of a future life in which he would see her again. He tried to convince himself that she had gone on a long journey, far away, for a long time. But when he thought of her lying there, and that it was all over and that they would put her in the earth, he was seized with a fierce, gloomy, desperate rage. It seemed at times that he felt nothing, and he welcomed this lull in his pain, while blaming himself bitterly for being such a scoundrel.

The sharp noise of an iron-tipped stick was heard on the stones, striking them at irregular intervals. It came from the end of the church, and stopped short at the lower aisles. A man in a coarse brown jacket knelt down painfully. It was Hippolyte, the stable-boy at the "Lion d'Or." He had put on his new leg.

One of the choir boys came round the nave taking collection, and the coppers chinked one after the other on the silver plate.

"Oh hurry up!" cried Bovary, angrily throwing him a five-franc piece. "I can't stand it any longer."

The singer thanked him with a deep bow.

They sang, they knelt, they stood up; it was endless! He remembered how once, in the early days of their marriage, they had been to mass together, and they had sat down on the other side, on the right, by the wall. The bell began again. There was a great shuffling of chairs; the pall bearers slipped their three poles under the coffin, and every one left the church.

Then Justin appeared in the doorway of the pharmacy, but retreated suddenly, pale and staggering.

People stood at the windows to see the procession pass by. Charles walked fast, as straight as he could. He tried to look brave and nodded to those who joined the crowd, coming from the side streets or from the open doors. The six men, three on either side, walked slowly, painting a little. The priests, the choristers, and the two choir-boys recited the *De profundis*, and their voices echoed over the fields, rising and falling with the shape of the hills. Sometimes they disappeared in the windings of the path; but the great silver cross always remained visible among the trees.

The women followed, wearing black coats with turned-down hoods; each of them carried a large lighted candle, and Charles felt himself grow faint at this continual repetition of prayers and torch-lights, oppressed by the sweetish smell of wax and of cassocks. A fresh breeze was blowing; the rye and colza were turning green and along the roadside, dewdrops hung from the hawthorn hedges. All sorts of joyous sounds filled the air; the jolting of a cart rolling way off in the ruts, the crowing of a cock, repeated again and again, or the gamboling of a foal under the apple-trees. The pure sky was dappled with rosy clouds; a bluish haze hung over the iris-covered cottages. Charles recognized each courtyard as he passed. He remembered mornings like this, when, after visiting a patient, he left one of those houses to return home, to his wife.

The black cloth decorated with silver tears flapped from time to time in the wind, baring the coffin underneath. The tired bearers walked more slowly, and the bier advanced jerkily, like a boat that pitches with every wave.

They reached the cemetery.

The men went right down to a place in the grass where a grave had been dug. They grouped themselves all round; and while the

priest spoke, the red soil thrown up at the sides kept noiselessly slipping down at the corners.

Then, when the four ropes were laid out, the coffin was pushed
onto them. He watched it go down; it seemed to go down forever.

At last a thud was heard; the ropes creaked and were drawn up.
Then Bournisien took the spade handed to him by Lestiboudois;
while his right hand kept sprinkling holy water, he vigorously threw
in a spadeful of earth with the left; and the wood of the coffin, struck
by the pebbles, gave forth that dread sound that seems to us the
reverberation of eternity.

The priest passed the holy water sprinkler to his neighbor, Monsieur Homais. The pharmacist swung it gravely, then handed it to
Charles, who sank to his knees and threw in handfuls of earth, crying,
"Adieu!" He sent her kisses; he dragged himself towards the grave, as
if to engulf himself with her.

They led him away, and he soon grew calmer, feeling perhaps,
like the others, a vague satisfaction that it was all over.

Old Rouault on his way back began quietly smoking a pipe, to
Homais' silent disapproval. He also noticed that Monsieur Binet had
not come, that Tuvache had disappeared after mass, and that Theodore, the notary's servant, wore a blue coat—"as if he couldn't respect
customs, and wear a black coat, for Heaven's sake!" And to share his
observations with others he went from group to group. They were
deploring Emma's death, especially Lheureux, who had not failed
to come to the funeral.

"Poor little lady! What a blow for her husband!"

"Can you imagine," the pharmacist replied, "that he would have
done away with himself if I hadn't intervened?"

"Such a fine person! To think that I saw her only last Saturday in
my store."

"I haven't had leisure," said Homais, "to prepare a few words that
I would cast over her tomb."

On getting home, Charles undressed, and old Rouault put on his
blue smock. It was new, and as he had repeatedly wiped his eyes on
the sleeves during his journey, the dye had stained his face, and
traces of tears lined the layer of dust that covered it.

Mother Bovary joined them. All three were silent. At last the old
man sighed:

"Do you remember, my friend, I came to Tostes once when you
had just lost your first deceased? I consoled you that time. I could
think of something to say then, but now . . ."

Then, with a loud groan that shook his whole chest,

"Ah! this is the end for me! I saw my wife go . . . then my son
. . . and now today my daughter!"

He wanted to go back to Bertaux, saying that he couldn't sleep in this house. He even refused to see his grand-daughter.

"No, no! It would grieve me too much. You'll kiss her many times for me. Good-bye . . . You're a good man! And I'll never forget this," he said, slapping his thigh. "Never fear, you shall always have your turkey."

But when he reached the top of the hill he turned back, as he had turned once before on the road of Saint-Victor when he had parted from her. The windows of the village were all ablaze in the slanting rays of the sun that was setting behind the meadow. He put his hand over his eyes, and saw at the horizon a walled enclosure, with black clusters of trees among the white stones; then he went on his way at a gentle trot, for his nag was limping.

Despite their fatigue, Charles and his mother stayed up talking very long that evening. They spoke of the days of the past and of the future. She would come to live at Yonville; she would keep house for him; they would never part again. She was subtly affectionate, rejoicing in her heart at regaining some of the tenderness that had wandered from her for so many years. Midnight struck. The village was silent as usual, and Charles lay awake, never ceasing to think of her.

Rodolphe, who, to distract himself, had been roaming in the woods all day, was quietly asleep in his château; and Léon, away in the city, also slept.

There was another who at that hour was not asleep.

On the grave between the pine-trees a child was on his knees weeping, and his heart, rent by sobs, was panting in the dark under the weight of an immense sorrow, tender as the moon and unfathomable as the night.

The gate suddenly grated. It was Lestiboudois coming to fetch the spade he had forgotten. He recognised Justin climbing over the wall, and knew at last who had been stealing his potatoes.

XI

The next day Charles had the child brought back. She asked for her mamma. They told her she was away; that she would bring her back some toys. Berthe mentioned her again several times, then finally forgot her. The child's gaiety broke Bovary's heart, and he had to put up besides with the intolerable consolations of the pharmacist.

Before long, money troubles started again. Monsieur Lheureux was putting his friend Vinçart back on the warpath, and before long Charles was signing notes for exorbitant amounts. For he would never consent to let the smallest of the things that had belonged to *her* be sold. His mother was exasperated with him; he grew even more angry than she did. He was a changed man. She left the house.

Then every one began to collect what they could. Mademoiselle Lempereur presented a bill for six months' teaching, although Emma had never taken a lesson (despite the receipted bill she had shown Bovary); it was an arrangement between the two women. The lending library demanded three years' subscriptions; Mère Rollet claimed postage for some twenty letters, and when Charles asked for an explanation, she was tactful enough to reply:

"Oh, I know nothing about it. It was her business."

With every debt he paid Charles thought he had reached the end. But others followed ceaselessly.

He tried to collect accounts due him from patients. He was shown the letters his wife had written. Then he had to apologise.

Félicité now wore Madame Bovary's dresses; not all, for he had kept some, and he locked himself up in Emma's room to look at them. Félicité was about her former mistress's height and often, on seeing her from behind, Charles thought she had come back and cried out:

"Oh, stay, don't go away!"

But at Pentecost she ran away from Yonville, carried off by Theodore, stealing all that was left of the wardrobe.

It was about this time that the widow Dupuis had the honor to inform him of the "marriage of Monsieur Léon Dupuis her son, notary at Yvetot, to Mademoiselle Léocadié Lebœuf Bondeville." Charles, among the other congratulations he sent him, wrote this sentence:

"How happy this would have made my poor wife!"

One day when, wandering aimlessly about the house, he had gone up to the attic, he felt a crumpled piece of paper under his slipper. He opened it and read: "Courage, Emma, courage. I would not bring misery into your life." It was Rodolphe's letter, fallen to the ground between the boxes, where it had remained till now, when the wind from the open dormer had blown it toward the door. And Charles stood, motionless and staring, in the very same place where, long ago, Emma, in despair, and paler even than he had thought of dying. At last he discovered a small R at the bottom of the second page. What did this mean? He remembered Rodolphe's attentions, his sudden disappearance, his embarrassed air on two or three subsequent occasions. But the respectful tone of the letter deceived him.

"Perhaps they loved one another platonically," he told himself.

Besides, Charles was not of those who go to the root of things; he shrank from the proofs, and his vague jealousy was lost in the immensity of his sorrow.

Every one, he thought, must have adored her; all men inevitably must have coveted her. This made her seem even more beautiful, and it awoke in him a fierce and persistent desire, which inflamed his despair and grew boundless, since it could never be assuaged.

To please her, as if she were still living, he adopted her taste, her ideas; he bought patent leather boots and took to wearing white cravats. He waxed his moustache and, just like her, signed promissory notes. She corrupted him from beyond the grave.

He was obliged to sell his silver piece by piece; next he sold the drawing-room furniture. All the rooms were stripped; but the bedroom, her own room, remained as before. After his dinner Charles went up there. He pushed the round table in front of the fire, and drew up her arm-chair. He sat down facing it. A candle burnt in one of the gilt candlesticks. Berthe, at his side, colored pictures.

He suffered, poor man, at seeing her so badly dressed, with laceless boots, and the arm-holes of her pinafore torn down to the hips; for the cleaning woman took no care of her. But she was so sweet, so pretty, and her little head bent forward so gracefully, letting her fair hair fall over her rosy cheeks, that an infinite joy came upon him, a happiness mingled with bitterness, like those ill-made wines that taste of resin. He mended her toys, made her puppets from cardboard, or sewed up half-torn dolls. Then, if his eyes fell upon the sewing kit, a ribbon lying about, or even a pin left in a crack of the table, he began to dream, and looked so sad that she became as sad as he.

No one now came to see them, for Justin had run away to Rouen, where he worked in a grocery, and the pharmacist's children saw less and less of the child. In view of the difference in their social positions, Monsieur Homais had chosen to discontinue the former intimacy.

The blind man, whom his salve had not cured, had gone back to the hill of Bois-Guillaume, where he told the travellers of his failure, to such an extent, that Homais when he went to town hid himself behind the curtains of the "Hirondelle" to avoid meeting him. He detested him, and wishing, in the interests of his own reputation, to get rid of him at all costs, he directed against him a secret campaign, that betrayed the depth of his intellect and the baseness of his vanity. Thus, for six consecutive months, one could read in the "Fanal de Rouen" editorials such as these:

"Anyone who has ever wended his way towards the fertile plains of Picardy has, no doubt, remarked, by the Bois-Guillaume hill, an unfortunate wretch suffering from a horrible facial wound. He bothers the passers-by, pursues them and levies a regular tax on all travellers. Are we still living in the monstrous times of the Middle Ages, when vagabonds were permitted to display in our public places leprosy and scrofulas they had brought back from the Crusades?"

Or:

"In spite of the laws against vagrancy, the approaches to our great towns continue to be infected by bands of beggars. Some are seen going about alone, and these are, by no means, the least dangerous. Why don't our City Authorities intervene?"

Then Homais invented incidents:

"Yesterday, by the Bois-Guillaume hill, a skittish horse . . ." And then followed the story of an accident caused by the presence of the blind man.

He managed so well that the fellow was locked up. But he was released. He began again, and so did Homais. It was a struggle. Homais won out, for his foe was condemned to lifelong confinement in an asylum.

This success emboldened him, and henceforth there was no longer a dog run over, a barn burnt down, a woman beaten in the parish, of which he did not immediately inform the public, guided always by the love of progress and the hatred of priests. He instituted comparisons between the public and parochial schools to the detriment of the latter; called to mind the massacre of St. Bartholomew à propos of a grant of one hundred francs to the church; denounced abuses and kept people on their toes. That was his phrase. Homais was digging and delving; he was becoming dangerous.

However, he was stifling in the narrow limits of journalism, and soon a book, a major work, became a necessity. Then he composed "General Statistics of the Canton of Yonville, followed by Climatological Remarks." The statistics drove him to philosophy. He busied himself with great questions: the social problem, the moral plight of the poorer classes, a pisciculture, rubber, railways, &c. He even began to blush at being a bourgeois. He affected bohemian manners, he smoked. He bought two chic Pompadour statuettes to adorn his drawing-room.

He by no means gave up his store. On the contrary, he kept well abreast of new discoveries. He followed the great trend towards chocolates; he was the first to introduce *Cho-ca* and *Revalenta* into the Seine-Inférieure. He was enthusiastic about the hydro-electric Pulvermacher health-belts; he wore one himself, and when at night he took off his flannel undershirt, Madame Homais was dazzled by the golden spiral that almost hid him from view. Her ardor would redouble for that man, swaddled more than a Scythian and as resplendent as one of the Magi.

He had fine ideas about Emma's tomb. First he proposed a broken column surmounted by a drapery, next a pyramid, then a Temple of Vesta, a sort of rotunda . . . or else a large pile of ruins. And in all his plans Homais always stuck to the weeping willow, which he looked upon as the indispensable symbol of sorrow.

Charles and he made a journey to Rouen together to look at some tombs, accompanied by an artist, one Vaufrylard, a friend of Bridoux's, who never ceased to make puns. At last, after having examined some hundred drawings, having ordered an estimate and made another journey to Rouen, Charles decided in favor of a mausoleum, whose two principal sides were to be decorated with "a spirit bearing an extinguished torch."

As to the inscription, Homais could think of nothing finer than *Sta viator*, and he got no further; he racked his brain in vain; all that he could come up with was *Sta viator*. At last he hit upon *Amabilem conjugem calcas*,[5] which was adopted.

A strange thing was happening to Bovary: while continually thinking of Emma, he was nevertheless forgetting her. He grew desperate as he felt this image fading from his memory in spite of all efforts to retain it. Yet every night he dreamt of her; it was always the same dream. He approached her, but when he was about to embrace her she fell into decay in his arms.

For a week he was even going to church in the evening. Monsieur Bournisien even paid him two or three visits, then gave him up. Moreover, the old man was growing bigoted and fanatic, according to Homais. He thundered against the spirit of the age, and never failed, every other week, in his sermon, to recount the death agony of Voltaire, who died devouring his excrements, as every one knows.

In spite of Bovary's thrifty life, he was far from being able to pay off his old debts. Lheureux refused to renew any more notes. Execution became imminent. Then he appealed to his mother, who consented to let him take a mortgage on her property, but with a great many recriminations against Emma; and in return for her sacrifice she asked for a shawl that had escaped from Félicité's raids. Charles refused to give it to her; they quarrelled.

She made the first peace overtures by offering to let the little girl, who could help her in the house, live with her. Charles consented to this, but when the time for parting came, all his courage failed him. Then there was a final, complete break between them.

As his affections vanished, he clung more closely to the love of his child. She worried him, however, for she coughed sometimes, and had red patches on her cheeks.

Across the square, facing his house, the prospering family of the pharmacist was more flourishing and thriving than ever. Napoleon helped him in the laboratory, Athalie embroidered him a skullcap, Irma cut out rounds of paper to cover the preserves, and Franklin recited the tables of Pythagoras by rote, without the slightest hesitation. He was the happiest of fathers, the most fortunate of men.

Not quite, however! A secret ambition devoured him. Homais

---

5. "You are treading upon the beloved spouse." *Sta viator*: "Stop, traveler."

hankered after the cross of the Legion of Honour. He had plenty of claims to it.

"First, having at the time of the cholera distinguished myself by a boundless devotion; second, by having published, at my expense, various works of public usefulness, such as" (and he recalled his pamphlet entitled *On Cider, its Manufacture and Effects*, besides observations on the wooly aphis that he had sent to the Academy; his volume of statistics, and down to his pharmaceutical thesis); "without counting that I am a member of several learned societies" (he was member of a single one).

"And if this won't do," he said, turning on his heels, "there always is the assistance I give at fires!"

Homais' next step was trying to win over the Government to his cause. He secretly did the prefect several favors during the elections. He sold, in a word, prostituted himself. He even addressed a petition to the sovereign in which he implored him to "do him justice;" he called him "our good king," and compared him to Henri IV.

And every morning the pharmacist rushed for the paper to see if his nomination appeared. It was never there. At last, unable to bear it any longer, he had a grass plot in his garden designed to represent the Star of the Cross of Honour, with two little strips of grass running from the top to imitate the ribbon. He walked round it with folded arms, meditating on the folly of the Government and the ingratitude of men.

Out of respect, or because he took an almost sensuous pleasure in dragging out his investigations, Charles had not yet opened the secret drawer of Emma's rosewood desk. One day, however, he sat down before it, turned the key, and pressed the spring. All Léon's letters were there. There could be no doubt this time. He devoured them to the very last, ransacked every corner, all the furniture, all the drawers, behind the walls, sobbing and shouting in mad distress. He discovered a box and kicked it open. Rodolphe's portrait flew out at him, from among the pile of love-letters.

People wondered at his despondency. He never went out, saw no one, refused even to visit his patients. Then they said "he shut himself up to drink."

At times, however, someone would climb on the garden hedge, moved by curiosity. They would stare in amazement at this long-bearded, shabbily clothed, wild figure of a man, who wept aloud as he walked up and down.

On summer evenings, he would take his little girl with him to visit the cemetery. They came back at nightfall, when the only light left in the village was that in Binet's window.

He was unable, however, to savor his grief to the full, for he had no one to share it with. He paid visits to Madame Lefrançois to be able to speak of her. But the innkeeper only listened with half an ear, having troubles of her own. For Monsieur Lheureux had finally set up his own business, *les Favorites du Commerce*, and Hivert, every one's favorite messenger, threatened to go to work for the competition unless he received higher wages.

One day when he had gone to the market at Argueil to sell his horse—his last resource—he met Rodolphe.

They both turned pale when they caught sight of one another. Rodolphe, who had only sent his card for the funeral, first stammered some apologies, then grew bolder, and even invited Charles (it was in the month of August and very hot) to share a bottle of beer with him at the terrace of a café.

Leaning his elbows on the table, he chewed his cigar as he talked, and Charles was lost in reverie at the sight of the face she had loved. He seemed to find back something of her there. It was quite a shock to him. He would have liked to have been this man.

The other went on talking of agriculture, cattle, and fertilizers, filling with banalities all the gaps where an allusion might slip in. Charles was not listening to him; Rodolphe noticed it, and he could follow the sequence of memories that crossed his face. This face gradually reddened; Charles's nostrils fluttered, his lips quivered. For a moment, Charles stared at him in somber fury and Rodolphe, startled and terrified, stopped talking. But soon the same look of mournful weariness returned to his face.

"I can't blame you for it," he said.

Rodolphe remained silent. And Charles, his head in his hands, went on in a broken voice, with the resigned accent of infinite grief:

"No, I can't blame you any longer."

He even made a phrase, the only one he'd ever made:

"Fate willed it this way."

Rodolphe, who had been the agent of this fate, thought him very meek for a man in his situation, comic even and slightly despicable.

The next day Charles sat down on the garden seat under the arbor. Rays of light were straying through the trellis, the vine leaves threw their shadows on the sand, jasmines perfumed the blue air, Spanish flies buzzed round the lilies in bloom, and Charles was panting like an adolescent under the vague desires of love that filled his aching heart.

At seven o'clock little Berthe who had not seen him all afternoon, came to fetch him for dinner.

His head was leaning against the wall, with closed eyes and open mouth, and in his hand was a long tress of black hair.

"Papa, come!"

And thinking he wanted to play, she gave him a gentle push. He fell to the ground. He was dead.

Thirty-six hours later, at the pharmacist's request, Monsieur Carnivet arrived. He performed an autopsy, but found nothing.

When everything had been sold, there remained twelve francs and seventy-five centimes, just enough to send Mademoiselle Bovary off to her grandmother. The woman died the same year; and since Rouault was paralyzed, it was an aunt who took charge of her. She is poor, and sends her to a cotton-mill to earn a living.

Since Bovary's death three doctors have succeeded one another in Yonville without any success, so effectively did Homais hasten to eradicate them. He has more customers than there are sinners in hell; the authorities treat him kindly and he has the public on his side.

He has just been given the cross of the Legion of Honor.

FYODOR DOSTOEVSKY

1821–1881

Fyodor Dostoevsky has become a central figure in the formation of the modern sensibility. He formulated in fictional terms, in dramatic and even sensational scenes, some of the main predicaments of our time: the choices between God and atheism, good and evil, freedom and tyranny; the recognition of the limits and even of the fall of man against the belief in progress, revolution, and utopia. Most important, he captured unforgettably the enormous contradictions of which our common human nature is capable and by which it is torn.

Fyodor Mikhailovich Dostoevsky was born in Moscow on October 30, 1821. His father was a staff doctor at the Hospital for the Poor. Later he acquired an estate and serfs. In 1839 he was killed by one of his peasants in a quarrel. Dostoevsky was sent to the Military Engineering Academy in St. Petersburg, from which he graduated in 1843. He became a civil servant, a draftsman in the St. Petersburg Engineering Corps, but resigned soon because he feared that he would be transferred to the provinces when his writing was discovered. His first novel, *Poor People* (1846), proved a great success with the critics; his second, *The Double* (1846), which followed immediately, was a failure.

Subsequently, Dostoevsky became involved in the Petrashevsky circle, a secret society of antigovernment and socialist tendencies. He was arrested on April 23, 1849, and condemned to be shot. On December 22 he was led to public execution, but he was reprieved at the last moment and sent to penal servitude in Siberia (near Omsk), where he worked for four years in a stockade, wearing fetters, completely cut off from communications with Russia. On his release in February 1854, he was assigned as a common soldier to Semipalatinsk, a small town near the Mongolian frontier. There he received several promotions (eventually becoming an ensign); his rank of nobility, forfeited by his sentence, was restored; and he married the widow of a customs official. In July 1859, Dotoevsky was permitted to return to Russia, and finally, in December 1859, to St. Petersburg—after ten years of his life had been spent in Siberia.

In the last year of his exile, Dostoevsky had resumed writing, and in 1861, shortly after his return, he founded a review, *Time (Vremya)*. This was suppressed in 1863, though Dostoevsky had changed his political opinions and was now strongly nationalistic and conservative in outlook. He made his first trip to France and England in 1862, and traveled in Europe again in 1863 and 1865, in order to follow a young woman friend, Apollinaria Suslova, and to indulge in gambling. After his wife's death in 1864, and another unsuccessful journalistic venture, *The Epoch (Epokha)*, 1864–1865, Dostoevsky was for a time almost crushed by gambling debts, emotional entanglements, and frequent epileptic seizures. He barely managed to return from Germany in 1865. In the winter of 1866 he wrote *Crime and Punishment*, and before he had finished it, dictated a shorter novel, *The Gambler*, to meet a deadline. He married his secretary, Anna Grigoryevna Snitkina, early in 1867 and left Russia with her to avoid his creditors. For years they wandered over Germany, Italy, and Switzerland, frequently in abject poverty. Their first child died. In 1871, when the initial chapters of *The Possessed* proved a popular success, Dostoevsky returned to St. Petersburg. He became the editor of a weekly, *The Citizen (Grazhdanin)*, for a short time and then published a periodical written by himself, *The Diary of a Writer* (1876–1881), which won great acclaim. His last novel, *The Brothers Karamazov* (1880), was an immense success, and honors and some prosperity came to him at last. At a Pushkin anniversary celebrated in Moscow in 1880 he gave the main speech. But soon after his return to St. Petersburg he died, on January 28, 1881, not yet sixty years old.

Dostoevsky, like every great writer, can be approached in different ways and read on different levels. We can try to understand him as a religious philosopher, a political commentator, a psychologist, and a novelist, and if we know much about his fascinating and varied life, we can interpret his works as biographical.

The biographical interpretation is the one that has been pushed furthest. The lurid crimes of Dostoevsky's characters (such as the rape of a young girl) have been ascribed to him, and all his novels have been studied as if they constituted a great personal confession. Dostoevsky certainly did use many of his experiences in his books (as every writer does): he several times described the feelings of a man facing a firing squad as he himself faced it on December 22, 1849, only to be reprieved at the last moment. His writings also reflect his years in Siberia: four years working in a loghouse, in chains, as he describes it in an oddly impersonal book, *Memoirs from the House of the Dead* (1862), and six more years as a common soldier on the borders of Mongolia, in a small, remote provincial town. Similarly, he used the experience of his disease (epilepsy), ascribing great spiritual significance to the ecstatic rapture preceding the actual seizure. He assigned his disease to both his most angelic "good" man, the "Idiot," Prince Myshkin, and his most diabolical, inhuman figure, the cold-blooded unsexed murderer of the old Karamazov, the flunky Smerdyakov. Dostoevsky also used something of his experiences in Germany, where in the 1860s he succumbed to a passion for gambling which he overcame only much later, during his second marriage. The short novel *The Gambler* (1866) gives an especially vivid account of this life and its moods.

There are other autobiographical elements in Dostoevsky's works, but it seems a gross misunderstanding of his methods and the procedures of art in general to conclude from his writings (as Thomas Mann has done) that he was a "saint and criminal" in one. Dostoevsky, after all, was an extremely hard worker who wrote and rewrote some twenty volumes. He was a novelist who employed the methods of the French sensational novel, he was constantly on the lookout for the most striking occurrences—the most shocking crimes and the most horrible disasters and scandals—because only in such fictional situations could he exalt his characters to their highest pitch, bringing out the clash of ideas and temperaments, revealing the deepest layers of their souls. But these fictions cannot be taken as literal transcripts of reality and actual experience.

Whole books have been written to explain Dostoevsky's religious philosophy and conception of man. The Russian philosopher Berdayev concludes his excellent study by saying, "So great is the value of Dostoevsky that to have produced him is by itself sufficient justification for the existence of the Russian people in the world." But there is no need for such extravagance. Dostoevsky's philosophy of religion is rather a personal version of extreme mystical Christianity, and assumes flesh and blood only in the context of the novels. Reduced to the bare bones of abstract propositions, it amounts to saying that man is fallen but is free to choose between evil and Christ. And choosing Christ means taking upon oneself the burden of humanity in love and pity, since "everybody is guilty for all and before all." Hence in Dostoevsky there is tremendous stress on personal freedom of choice, and his affirmation of the worth of every individual is combined, paradoxically, with an equal insistence on the substantial identity of all men, their equality before God, the bond of love which unites them.

Dostoevsky also develops a philosophy of history, with practical political implications, based upon this point of view. According to him, the West is in complete decay; only Russia has preserved Christianity in its original form. The West is either Catholic—and Catholicism is condemned by Dostoevsky as an attempt to force salvation by magic and authority—or bourgeois, and hence materialistic and fallen away from Christ; or socialist, and socialism is to Dostoevsky identical with atheism, as it dreams of a utopia in which man would not be free to choose even at the expense of suffering. Dostoevsky—who himself had belonged to a revolutionary group and come into contact with Russian revolutionaries abroad—had an extraordinary insight into the mentality of the Russian underground. In *The Possessed* (1871–1872) he gave a lurid satiric picture of these would-be saviors of Russia and mankind. But while he was afraid of the revolution, Dostoevsky himself hoped and prophesied that Russia would save Europe from the dangers of communism, as Russia alone was the uncorrupted Christian land. Put in terms of political propositions (as Dostoevsky himself preached them in his journal, *The Diary of a Writer*, 1876–1881), what he propounds is a conservative Russian nationalism with messianic hopes for Russian Christianity. It is hard to imagine a political creed more remote from present-day realities.

When translated into abstractions, Dostoevsky's psychology is as unimpressive as his political theory. It is merely a derivative of theories propounded by German writers about the unconscious, the role of dreams, the ambivalence of human feelings. What makes it electric in the novels is his ability to dramatize it in scenes of sudden revulsions, in characters who in today's terminology would be called split personalities, in people twisted by isolation, lust, humiliation, and resentment. The dreams of Raskolnikov may be interpreted according to Freudian psychology, but to the reader without any knowledge of science they are comprehensible in their place in the novel and function as warnings and anticipations.

Dostoevsky is first of all an artist—a novelist who succeeded in using his ideas (many old and venerable, many new and fantastic) and psychological insights for the writing of stories of absorbing interest. As an artist, Dostoevsky treated the novel like a drama, constructing it in large, vivid scenes which end with a scandal or a crime or some act of violence, filling it with unforgettable "stagelike" figures torn by great passions and swayed by great ideas. Then he set this world in an environment of St. Petersburg slums, or of towns, monasteries, and country houses, all so vividly realized that we forget how the setting, the figures, and the ideas melt together into one cosmos of the imagination only remotely and obliquely related to any reality of nineteenth-century Russia. We take part in a great drama of pride and humility, good and evil, in a huge allegory of man's search for God and himself. We understand and share in this world because it is not merely Russia in the nineteenth century, where people could hardly have talked and behaved as Dostoevsky's people do, but a myth of humanity, universalized as all art is.

Notes from Underground (1864) precedes the four great novels, *Crime and Punishment* (1866), *The Idiot* (1868), *The Possessed*, and *The Brothers Karamazov* (1880). The *Notes* can be viewed as a prologue, an introduction to the cycle of the four great novels, an anticipation of the mature Dostoevsky's method and thought. Though it cannot compare in dramatic power and scope with these, the story has its own peculiar and original artistry. It is made up of two parts, at first glance seemingly independent: the monologue of the Underground man and the confession which he makes about himself, called "À Propos of the Wet Snow." The monologue, though it includes no action, is dramatic—a long address to an imaginary hostile reader, whom the Underground man ridicules, defies, jeers at, but also flatters. The confession is an autobiographical reminiscence of the Underground man. It describes events which occurred long before the delivery of the monologue, but it functions as a confirmation in concrete terms of the self-portrait drawn in the monologue and as an explanation of the isolation of the hero.

The narrative of the confession is a comic variation on the old theme of the rescue of a fallen woman from vice, a seesaw series of humiliations permitting Dostoevsky to display all the cruelty of his probing psychology. The hero, out of spite and craving for human company, forces himself into the company of former schoolfellows and is shamefully humiliated by them. He reasserts his ego (as he cannot revenge himself on them) in the company of a humble prostitute by impressing her with florid and moving speeches, which he knows to be insincere, about her horrible future. Ironically, he converts her, but when she comes to him and surprises him in a degrading scene with his servant, he humiliates her again. When, even then, she understands and forgives and thus shows her moral superiority, he crowns his spite by deliberately misunderstanding her and forcing money on her. She is the moral victor and the Underground man returns to his hideout to jeer at humanity. It is hard not to feel that we are shown a tortured and twisted soul almost too despicable to elicit our compassion.

Still it would be a complete misunderstanding of Dostoevsky's story to take the philosophy expounded jeeringly in the long monologue of the first part merely as the irrational railings of a sick soul. The Underground man, though abject and spiteful, represents not only a specific Russian type of the time—the intellectual divorced from the soil and his nation—but also modern humanity, even Everyman, and, strangely enough, even the author, who through the mouth of this despicable character, as through a mask, expresses his boldest and most intimate convictions. In spite of all the exaggerated pathos, wild paradox, and jeering irony used by the speaker, his self-criticism and his criticism of society and history must be taken seriously and interpreted patiently if we are to extract the meaning accepted by Dostoevsky.

The Underground man is the hyperconscious man who examines himself as if in a mirror, and sees himself with pitiless candor. His very self-consciousness cripples his will and poisons his feelings. He cannot escape from his ego; he knows that he has acted badly toward the girl but at the same time he cannot help acting as he does. He knows that he is alone, that there is no bridge from him to humanity, that the world is hostile to him, and that he is being humiliated by everybody he meets. But though he resents the humiliation, he cannot help courting it, provoking it, and liking it in his perverse manner. He understands (and knows from his own experience) that man is not good but enjoys evil and destruction.

His self-criticism widens, then, into a criticism of the assumptions of modern civilization, of nineteenth-century optimism about human nature and progress, of utilitarianism, and of all kinds of utopias. It is possible to identify definite allusions to a contemporary novel by a radical socialist and revolutionary, Chernyshevsky, entitled *What Shall We Do?* (1863), but we do not need to know the exact target of Dostoevsky's satire to recognize what he attacks: the view that man is good, that he always seeks his enlightened self-interest, that science propounds immutable truths, and that a paradise on earth will be just around the corner once society is reformed along scientific lines. In a series of vivid symbols these assumptions are represented, parodied, exposed. Science says that "twice two makes four" but the Underground man laughs that "twice two makes five is sometimes a very charming thing too." Science means to him (and to Dostoevsky) the victory of the doctrine of fatality, of iron necessity, of determinism, and thus finally of death. Man would become an "organ-stop," a "piano key," if deterministic science were valid.

Equally disastrous are the implications of the social philosophy of liberalism and of socialism (which Dostoevsky considers its necessary consequence). Man, in this view, need only follow his enlightened self-interest, need only be rational, and he will become noble and good and the earth will be a place of prosperity and peace. But the Underground man knows that this conception of man is entirely false. What if mankind does not follow, and never will follow, its own enlightened self-interest, is consciously and purposely irrational, even bloodthirsty and evil? History seems to the Underground man to speak a clear language: ". . . civilization has made mankind if not more bloodthirsty, at least more vilely, more loathsomely bloodthirsty." Man wills the irrational and evil because he does not want to become an organ-stop, a piano key, because he wants to be left with the freedom to choose between good and evil. This freedom of choice, even at the expense of chaos and destruction, is what makes him man.

Actually, man loves something other than his well-being and happiness, loves even suffering and pain, because he is a man and not an animal inhabiting some great organized rational "ant heap." The ant heap, the hen house, the block of tenements, and finally the Crystal Palace (then the newest wonder of architecture, a great hall of iron and glass erected for the Universal Exhibition in London) are the images used by the Underground man to represent his hated utopia. The heroine of *What Shall We Do?* had dreamed of a building, made of cast iron and glass and placed in the middle of a beautiful garden where there would be eternal spring and summer, eternal joy. Dostoevsky had recognized there the utopian dream of Fourier, the French socialist whom he had admired in his youth and whose ideals he had come to hate with a fierce revulsion. But we must realize that the Underground man, and Dostoevsky, despises this "ant heap," this perfectly organized society of robots, in the name of something higher, in the name of freedom. Dostoevsky does not believe that man can achieve freedom and happiness at the same time; he thinks that man can buy happiness only at the expense of freedom, and all utopian schemes seem to him devices to lure man into the yoke of slavery. This freedom is, of course, not political freedom but freedom of choice, indeterminism, even caprice and willfulness, in the paradoxical formulation of the Underground man.

There are hints at a positive solution only in the one section (Section X), which was mutilated by the censor. A letter by Dostoevsky to his brother about the "swine of a censor who let through the passages where I jeered at everything and blasphemed ostensibly" refers to the fact that he "suppressed everything where I drew the conclusion that faith in Christ is needed." In Section XI of the present text (and Dostoevsky never restored the suppressed passages) the Underground man says merely, "I am lying because I know myself that it is not underground that is better, but something different, quite different, for which I am thirsting, but which I cannot find!" This "something . . . quite different" all the other writings of Dostoevsky show to be the voluntary following of Christ even at the expense of suffering and pain.

In a paradoxical form, through the mouth of one of his vilest characters, Dostoevsky reveals in the story his view of man and history—of the evil in man's nature and of the blood and tragedy in history—and his criticism of the optimistic, utilitarian, utopian, progressive view of man which was spreading to Russia from the West during the nineteenth century and which found its most devoted adherents in the Russian revolutionaries. Preoccupied with criticism, Dostoevsky does not here suggest any positive remedy.

But if we understand the *Notes* we can understand how Raskolnikov, the murderer out of intellect in *Crime and Punishment*, can find salvation at last, and how Dmitri, the guilty-guiltless parricide of *The Brothers Karamazov*, can sing his hymn to joy in the Siberian mines. We can even understand the legend of the Great Inquisitor told by Ivan Karamazov, in which we meet the same criticism of a utopia (this time that of Catholicism) and the same exaltation of human freedom even at the price of suffering.

Monroe C. Beardsley, "Dostoevsky's Metaphor of the 'Underground,' " *Journal of the History of Ideas* (June 1942) III: 265–90, is a subtle interpretation of the central metaphor of the *Notes*. Joseph Frank, "Nihilism and *Notes from Underground*," *Sewanee Review* (1961) LXIX, interprets the *Notes* in the context of the history of the times. Robert L. Jackson, *The Underground Man in Russian Literature* (1958), traces the impact of the *Notes* on Russian literature. Konstantin Mochulsky, *Dostoevsky: Life and Work*, trans., Michael Minihan (1967), is the best general work translated from Russian, the work of an emigré in Paris. René Wellek, ed., *Dostoevsky: A Collection of Critical Essays* (1962), contains an essay by the editor on the history of Dostoevsky criticism.

Notes from Underground[1]

Part I

(UNDERGROUND)

I

I am a sick man. . . . I am a spiteful man. I am an unattractive man. I believe my liver is diseased. However, I know nothing at all about my disease, and do not know for certain what ails me. I don't consult a doctor for it, and never have, though I have a respect for medicine and doctors. Besides, I am extremely superstitious, sufficiently so to respect medicine anyway (I am well-educated enough not to be superstitious, but I am superstitious). No, I refuse to consult a doctor from spite. That you probably will not understand. Well, I understand it, though. Of course I can't explain who it is precisely that I am mortifying in this case by my spite: I am perfectly well aware that I cannot "pay out" the doctors by not consulting them; I know better than any one that by all this I am only injuring

---

1. Translated by Constance Garnett. The punctuation ". . ." does not indicate omissions from this text. "The author of the diary and the diary itself are, of course, imaginary. Nevertheless it is clear that such persons as the writer of these notes not only may, but positively must, exist in our society, when we consider the circumstances in the midst of which our society is formed. I have tried to expose to the view of the public more distinctly than is commonly done, one of the characters of the recent past. He is one of the representatives of a generation still living. In this fragment, entitled 'Underground,' this person introduces himself and his views, and, as it were, tries to explain the causes owing to which he has made his appearance and was bound to make his appearance in our midst. In the second fragment there are added the actual notes of this person concerning certain events in his life." [Author's note.]

myself and no one else. But still, if I don't consult a doctor it is from spite. My liver is bad, well—let it get worse!

I have been going on like that for a long time—twenty years. Now I am forty. I used to be in the government service, but am no longer. I was a spiteful official. I was rude and took pleasure in being so. I did not take bribes, you see, so I was bound to find a recompense in that, at least. (A poor jest, but I will not scratch it out. I wrote it thinking it would sound very witty; but now that I have seen myself that I only wanted to show off in a despicable way, I will not scratch it out on purpose!)

When petitioners used to come for information to the table at which I sat, I used to grind my teeth at them, and felt intense enjoyment when I succeeded in making anybody unhappy. I almost always did succeed. For the most part they were all timid people—of course, they were petitioners. But of the uppish ones there was one officer in particular I could not endure. He simply would not be humble, and clanked his sword in a disgusting way. I carried on a feud with him for eighteen months over that sword. At last I got the better of him. He left off clanking it. That happened in my youth, though.

But do you know, gentlemen, what was the chief point about my spite? Why, the whole point, the real sting of it lay in the fact that continually, even in the moment of the acutest spleen, I was inwardly conscious with shame that I was not only not a spiteful but not even an embittered man, that I was simply scaring sparrows at random and amusing myself by it. I might foam at the mouth, but bring me a doll to play with, give me a cup of tea with sugar in it, and maybe I should be appeased. I might even be genuinely touched, though probably I should grind my teeth at myself afterwards and lie awake at night with shame for months after. That was my way.

I was lying when I said just now that I was a spiteful official. I was lying from spite. I was simply amusing myself with the petitioners and with the officer, and in reality I never could become spiteful. I was conscious every moment in myself of many, very many elements absolutely opposite to that. I felt them positively swarming in me, these opposite to that. I felt them positively swarming in me all my life and craving some outlet from me, but I would not let them, would not let them, purposely would not let them come out. They tormented me till I was ashamed: they drove me to convulsions and—sickened me, at last, how they sickened me! Now, are not you fancying that . . . However, I assure you I do not care if you are. . . .

It was not only that I could not become spiteful, I did not know how to become anything: neither spiteful nor kind, neither a rascal nor an honest man, neither a hero nor an insect. Now, I am living out my life in my corner, taunting myself with the spiteful and useless consolation that an intelligent man cannot become anything

seriously, and it is only the fool who becomes anything. Yes, a man
in the nineteenth century must and morally ought to be pre-eminently a characterless creature; a man of character, an active man is
pre-eminently a limited creature. That is my conviction of forty years.
I am forty years old now, and you know forty years is a whole lifetime; you know it is extreme old age. To live longer than forty years
is bad manners, is vulgar, immoral. Who lives beyond forty? Answer
that, sincerely and honestly. I will tell you who do: fools and worthless fellows. I tell all old men that to their face, all these venerable
old men, all these silver-haired and reverend seniors! I tell the whole
world that to its face! I have a right to say so, for I shall go on living
to sixty myself. To seventy! To eighty! . . . Stay, let me take
breath. . . .

You imagine no doubt, gentlemen, that I want to amuse you. You
are mistaken in that, too. I am by no means such a mirthful person
as you imagine, or as you may imagine; however, irritated by all this
babble (and I feel that you are irritated) you think fit to ask me who
am I—then my answer is, I am a collegiate assessor. I was in the
service that I might have something to eat (and solely for that reason), and when last year a distant relation left me six thousand roubles in his will I immediately retired from the service and settled
down in my corner. I used to live in this corner before, but now I
have settled down in it. My room is a wretched, horrid one in the
outskirts of the town. My servant is an old country-woman, ill-natured
from stupidity, and moreover, there is always a nasty smell about
her. I am told that the Petersburg climate is bad for me, and that
with my small means it is very expensive to live in Petersburg. I know
all that better than all these sage and experienced counsellors and
monitors. . . . But I am remaining in Petersburg; . . . I am not
going away from Petersburg! I am not going away because . . . ech!
Why, it is absolutely no matter whether I am going away or not
going away.

But what can a decent man speak of with most pleasure?

Answer: Of himself.

Well, so I will talk about myself.

II

I want now to tell you, gentlemen, whether you care to hear it or
not, why I could not even become an insect. I tell you solemnly,
that I have many times tried to become an insect. But I was not equal
even to that. I swear, gentlemen, that to be too conscious is an illness—a real thoroughgoing illness. For man's everyday needs, it would
have been quite enough to have the ordinary human consciousness,
that is, half or a quarter of the amount which falls to the lot of a

cultivated man of our unhappy nineteenth century, especially one who has the fatal ill-luck to inhabit Petersburg, the most theoretical and intentional town on the whole terrestrial globe. (There are intentional and unintentional towns.) It would have been quite enough, for instance, to have the consciousness by which all so-called direct persons and men of action live. I bet you think I am writing all this from affection, to be witty at the expense of men of action; and what is more, that from ill-bred affection, I am clanking a sword like my officer. But, gentlemen, whoever can pride himself on his diseases and even swagger over them?

Though, after all, every one does do that; people do pride them-selves on their diseases, and I do, may be, more than any one else. We will not dispute it; my contention was absurd. But yet I am firmly persuaded that a great deal of consciousness, every sort of consciousness, in fact, is a disease. I stick to that. Let us leave that, too, for a minute. Tell me this: why does it happen that at the very, yes, at the very moments when I am most capable of feeling every refinement of all that is "good and beautiful," as they used to say at one time, it would, as though of design, happen to me not only to feel but to do such ugly things, such that . . . Well, in short, actions that all, perhaps, commit; but which, as though purposely, occurred to me at the very time when I was most conscious that they ought not to be committed. The more conscious I was of goodness and of all that was "good and beautiful," the more deeply I sank into my mire and the more ready I was to sink in it altogether. But the chief point was that all this was, as it were, not accidental in me, but as though it were bound to be so. It was as though it were my most normal condition, and not in the least disease or depravity, so that at last all desire in me to struggle against this depravity passed. It ended by my almost believing (perhaps actually believing) that this was perhaps my normal condition. But at first, in the beginning, what agonies I endured in that struggle! I did not believe it was the same with other people, and all my life I hid this fact about myself as a secret. I was ashamed (even now, perhaps, I am ashamed): I got to the point of feeling a sort of secret abnormal, despicable enjoy-ment in returning home to my corner on some disgusting Petersburg night, acutely conscious that that day I had committed a loathsome action again, that what was done could never be undone, and secretly, inwardly gnawing, gnawing at myself for it, tearing and consuming myself till at last the bitterness turned into a sort of shameful accursed sweetness, and at last—into positive real enjoyment! Yes into enjoy-ment, into enjoyment! I insist upon that. I have spoken of this because I keep wanting to know for a fact whether other people feel such enjoyment? I will explain; the enjoyment was just from the too intense consciousness of one's own degradation; it was from feeling oneself that one had reached the last barrier, that it was horrible, but that it could not be otherwise; that there was no escape for you; that you never could become a different man; that even if time and faith were still left you to change into something different you would most likely not wish to change; or if you did wish to, even then you would do nothing; because perhaps in reality there was nothing for you to change into.

And the worst of it was, and the root of it all, that it was all in accord with the normal fundamental laws of over-acute consciousness, and with the inertia that was the direct result of those laws, and that consequently one was not only unable to change but could do absolutely nothing. Thus it would follow, as the result of acute consciousness, that one is not to blame in being a scoundrel; as though that were any consolation to the scoundrel once he has come to realize that he actually is a scoundrel. But enough. . . . Ech, I have talked a lot of nonsense, but what have I explained? How is enjoyment in this to be explained? But I will explain it. I will get to the bottom of it! That is why I have taken up my pen. . . .

I, for instance, have a great deal of *amour propre*. I am as suspicious and prone to take offence as a hunchback or a dwarf. But upon my word I sometimes have had moments when if I had happened to be slapped in the face I should, perhaps, have been positively glad of it. I say, in earnest, that I should probably have been able to discover even in that a peculiar sort of enjoyment—the enjoyment, of course, of despair; but in despair there are the most intense enjoyments, especially when one is very acutely conscious of the hopelessness of one's position. And when one is slapped in the face—why then the consciousness of being rubbed into a pulp would positively overwhelm one. The worst of it is, look at it which way one will, it still turns out that I was always the most to blame in everything. And what is most humiliating of all, to blame for no fault of my own but, so to say, through the laws of nature. In the first place, to blame because I am cleverer than any of the people surrounding me. (I have always considered myself cleverer than any of the people surrounding me, and sometimes, would you believe it, have been positively ashamed of it. At any rate, I have all my life, as it were, turned my eyes away and never could look people straight in the face.) To blame, finally, because even if I had had magnanimity, I should only have had more suffering from the sense of its uselessness. I should certainly have never been able to do anything from being magnanimous—neither to forgive, for my assailant would perhaps have slapped me from the laws of nature, and one cannot forgive the laws of nature; nor to forget, for even if it were owing to the laws of nature, it is insulting all the same. Finally even if I had wanted to be anything but magnanimous, had desired on the contrary to revenge myself on my assailant, I could not have revenged myself on any one for anything because I should certainly never have made up my mind to do anything, even if I had been able to. Why should I not have made up my mind? About that in particular I want to say a few words.

III

With people who know how to revenge themselves and to stand up for themselves in general, how is it done? Why, when they are possessed, let us suppose, by the feeling of revenge, then for the time there is nothing else but that feeling left in their whole being. Such a gentleman simply dashes straight for his object like an infuriated bull with its horns down, and nothing but a wall will stop him. (By the way: facing the wall, such gentlemen—that is, the "direct" persons and men of action—are genuinely nonplussed. For them a wall is not an evasion, as for us people who think and consequently do nothing; it is not an excuse for turning aside, an excuse for which we are always very glad, though we scarcely believe in it ourselves, as a rule. No, they are nonplussed in all sincerity. The wall has for them something tranquillizing, morally soothing, final—maybe even something mysterious . . . but of the wall later.)

Well, such a direct person I regard as the real normal man, as his tender mother nature wished to see him when she graciously brought him into being on the earth. I envy such a man till I am green in the face. He is stupid. I am not disputing that, but perhaps the normal man should be stupid, how do you know? Perhaps it is very beautiful, in fact. And I am the more persuaded of that suspicion, if one can call it so, by the fact that if you take, for instance, the antithesis of the normal man, that is, the man of acute consciousness, who has come, of course, not out of the lap of nature but out a retort (this is almost mysticism, gentlemen, but I suspect this, too), this retort-made man is sometimes so nonplussed in the presence of his antithesis that with all his exaggerated consciousness he genuinely thinks of himself as a mouse and not a man. It may be an acutely conscious mouse, yet it is a mouse, while the other is a man, and therefore, et cætera, et cætera. And the worst of it is, he himself, his very own self, looks on himself as a mouse; no one asks him to do so; and that is an important point. Now let us look at this mouse in action. Let us suppose, for instance, that it feels insulted, too (and it almost always does feel insulted), and wants to revenge itself, too. There may even be a greater accumulation of spite in it than in *l'homme de la nature et de la vérité.*[2] The base and nasty desire to

2. "The man of nature and truth"; Rousseau's description of himself in the *Confessions* (1781–1788), which created an enormous stir because they professed to tell the whole truth about the author and were sometimes self-accusing.

vent that spite on its assailant rankles perhaps even more nastily in it than in *l'homme de la nature et de la vérité*. For through his innate stupidity the latter looks upon his revenge as justice pure and simple; while in consequence of his acute consciousness the mouse does not believe in the justice of it. To come at last to the deed itself, to the very act of revenge. Apart from the one fundamental nastiness the luckless mouse succeeds in creating around it so many other nastinesses in the form of doubts and questions, adds to the one question so many unsettled questions that there inevitably works up around it a sort of fatal brew, a stinking mess, made up of its doubts, emotions, and of the contempt spat upon it by the direct men of action who stand solemnly about it as judges and arbitrators, laughing at it till their healthy sides ache. Of course the only thing left for it is to dismiss all that with a wave of its paw, and, with a smile of assumed contempt in which it does not even itself believe, creep ignominiously into its mouse-hole. There in its nasty, stinking, underground home our insulted, crushed, and ridiculed mouse promptly becomes absorbed in cold, malignant and, above all, everlasting spite. For forty years together it will remember its injury down to the smallest, most ignominious details, and every time will add, of itself, details still more ignominious, spitefully teasing and tormenting itself with its own imagination. It will itself be ashamed of its imaginings, but yet it will recall it all, it will go over and over every detail, it will invent unheard of things against itself, pretending that those things might happen, and will forgive nothing. Maybe it will begin to revenge itself, too, but, as it were, piecemeal, in trivial ways, from behind the stove, incognito, without believing either in its own right to vengeance, or in the success of its revenge knowing that from all its efforts at revenge it will suffer a hundred times more than he on whom it revenges itself, while he, I daresay, will not even scratch himself. On its deathbed it will recall it all over again, with interest accumulated over all the years and. . . .

But it is just in that cold, abominable half despair, half belief, in that conscious burying oneself alive for grief in the underworld for forty years, in that acutely recognized and yet partly doubtful hopelessness of one's position, in that hell of unsatisfied desires turned inward, in that fever of oscillations, or resolutions determined for ever and repented of again a minute later—that the savour of that strange enjoyment of which I have spoken lies. It is so subtle, so difficult of analysis, that persons who are a little limited, or even simply persons of strong nerves, will not understand a single atom of it. "Possibly," you will add on your own account with a grin, "people will not understand it either who have never received a slap in the face," and in that way you will politely hint to me that I, too, perhaps, have had the experience of a slap in the face in my life, and so I speak as one who knows. I bet that you are thinking that. But set your minds at rest, gentlemen, I have not received a slap in the face, though it is absolutely a matter of indifference to me what you may think about it. Possibly, I even regret, myself, that I have given so few slaps in the face during my life. But enough . . . not another word on that subject of such extreme interest to you.

I will continue calmly concerning persons with strong nerves who do not understand a certain refinement of enjoyment. Though in certain circumstances these gentlemen bellow their loudest like bulls, though this, let us suppose, does them the greatest credit, yet, as I have said already, confronted with the impossible they subside at once. The impossible means the stone wall! What stone wall? Why, of course, the laws of nature, the deductions of natural science, mathematics. As soon as they prove to you, for instance, that you are descended from a monkey, then it is no use scowling, accept it for a fact. When they prove to you that in reality one drop of your own fat must be dearer to you than a hundred thousand of your fellow-creatures, and that this conclusion is the final solution of all so-called virtues and duties and all such prejudices and fancies, then you have just to accept it, there is no help for it, for twice two is a law of mathematics. Just try refuting it.

"Upon my word," they will shout at you, "it is no use protesting: it is a case of twice two makes four! Nature does not ask your permission, she has nothing to do with your wishes, and whether you like her laws or dislike them, you are bound to accept her as she is, and consequently all her conclusions. A wall, you see, is a wall . . ." and so on, and so on.

Merciful Heavens! but what do I care for the laws of nature and arithmetic, when, for some reason I dislike those laws and the fact that twice two makes four? Of course I cannot break through the wall by battering my head against it if I really have not the strength to knock it down, but I am not going to be reconciled to it simply because it is a stone wall and I have not the strength.

As though such a stone wall really were a consolation, and really did contain some word of conciliation, simply because it is as true as twice two makes four. Oh, absurdity of absurdities! How much better it is to understand it all, to recognize it all, all the impossibilities and the stone wall; not to be reconciled to one of those impossibilities and stone walls if it disgusts you to be reconciled to it; by the way of the most inevitable, logical combinations to reach the most revolting conclusions on the everlasting theme, that even for the stone wall you are yourself somehow to blame, though again it is as clear as day you are not to blame in the least, and therefore grinding your teeth in silent impotence to sink into luxurious inertia, brooding on the fact that there is no one even for you to feel vindictive against, that you have not, and perhaps never will have, an object for your spite, that it is a sleight of hand, a bit of juggling, a card-sharper's trick, that it is simply a mess, no knowing what and no knowing who, but in spite of all these uncertainties and jugglings, still there is an ache in you, and the more you do not know, the worse the ache.

IV

"Ha, ha, ha! You will be finding enjoyment in toothache next," you cry, with a laugh.

"Well? Even in toothache there is enjoyment," I answer. I had toothache for a whole month and I know there is. In that case, of course, people are not spiteful in silence, but moan; but they are not candid moans, they are malignant moans, and the malignancy is the whole point. The enjoyment of the sufferer finds expression in those moans; if he did not feel enjoyment in them he would not moan. It is a good example, gentlemen, and I will develop it. Those moans express in the first place all the aimlessness of your pain, which is so humiliating to your consciousness; the whole legal system of nature on which you spit disdainfully, of course, but from which you suffer all the same while she does not. They express the consciousness that you have no enemy to punish, but that you have pain; the consciousness that in spite of all possible Wagenheims[3] you are in complete slavery to your teeth; that if some one wishes it, your teeth will leave off aching, and if he does not, they will go on aching another three months; and that finally if you are still contumacious and still protest, all that is left you for your own gratification is to thrash yourself or beat your wall with your fist as hard as you can, and absolutely nothing more. Well, these mortal insults, these jeers on the part of some one unknown, end at last in an enjoyment which sometimes reaches the highest degree of voluptuousness. I ask you, gentlemen, listen sometimes to the moans of an educated man of the nineteenth century suffering from toothache, on the second or third day of the attack, when he is beginning to moan, not as he moaned on the first day, that is, not simply because he has toothache, not just as any coarse peasant, but as a man affected by progress and European civilization, a man who is "divorced from the soil and the national elements," as they express it now-a-days. His moans become nasty, disgustingly malignant, and go on for whole days and nights. And of course he knows himself that he is doing himself no sort of good with his moans; he knows better than any one that he is only lacerating and harassing himself and others for nothing; he knows that even the audience before whom he is making his efforts, and his whole family, listen to him with loathing, do not put the least faith in him,

---

3. Wagenheim was apparently a German who advertised painless dentistry; he may have used hypnosis or autosuggestion.

and inwardly understand that he might moan differently, more simply, without trills and flourishes, and that he is only amusing himself
like that from ill-humour, from malignancy. Well, in all these recognitions and disgraces it is that there lies a voluptuous pleasure. As
though he would say: "I am worrying you, I am lacerating your hearts,
I am keeping every one in the house awake. Well, stay awake then,
you, too, feel every minute that I have toothache. I am not a hero
to you now, as I tried to seem before, but simply a nasty person, an
impostor. Well, so be it, then! I am very glad that you see through
me. It is nasty for you to hear my despicable moans: well, let it be
nasty; here I will let you have a nastier flourish in a minute. . . . "
You do not understand even now, gentlemen? No, it seems our
development and our consciousness must go further to understand
all the intricacies of this pleasure. You laugh? Delighted. My jests,
gentlemen, are of course in bad taste, jerky, involved, lacking self-
confidence. But of course that is because I do not respect myself.
Can a man of perception respect himself at all?

V

Come, can a man who attempts to find enjoyment in the very
feeling of his own degradation possibly have a spark of respect for
himself? I am not saying this now from any mawkish kind of remorse.
And, indeed, I could never endure saying, "Forgive me, Papa, I
won't do it again," not because I am incapable of saying that—on
the contrary, perhaps just because I have been too capable of it, and
in what a way, too! As though of design I used to get into trouble in
cases when I was not to blame in any way. That was the nastiest part
of it. At the same time I was genuinely touched and penitent, I used
to shed tears and, of course, deceived myself, though I was not acting
in the least and there was a sick feeling in my heart at the time.
 . . . . For that one could not blame even the laws of nature, though
the laws of nature have continually all my life offended me more
than anything. It is loathsome to remember it all, but it was loathsome even them. Of course, a minute or so later I would realize
wrathfully that it was all a lie, a revolting lie, an affected lie, that is,
all this penitence, this emotion, these vows of reform. You will ask
why did I worry myself with such antics: answer, because it was very
dull to sit with one's hands folded, and so one began cutting capers.
That is really it. Observe yourselves more carefully, gentlemen, then
you will understand that it is so. I invented adventures for myself and
made up a life, so as at least to live in some way. How many times
it has happened to me—well, for instance, to take offence simply on
purpose, for nothing; and one knows oneself, of course, that one is
offended at nothing, that one is putting it on, but yet one brings

oneself, at last to the point of being really offended. All my life I have had an impulse to play such pranks, so that in the end I could not control it in myself. Another time, twice, in fact, I tried hard to be in love. I suffered, too, gentlemen, I assure you. In the depth of my heart there was no faith in my suffering, only a faint stir of mockery, but yet I did suffer, and in the real, orthodox way; I was jealous, beside myself . . . and it was all from *ennui*, gentlemen, all from *ennui*; inertia overcame me. You know the direct, legitimate fruit of consciousness is inertia, that is, conscious sitting-with-the-hands-folded. I have referred to this already. I repeat, I repeat with emphasis: all "direct" persons and men of action are active just because they are stupid and limited. How explain that? I will tell you: in consequence of their limitation they take immediate and secondary causes for primary ones, and in that way persuade themselves more quickly and easily than other people do that they have found an infallible foundation for their activity, and their minds are at ease and you know that is the chief thing. To begin to act, you know, you must first have your mind completely at ease and no trace of doubt left in it. Why, how am I, for example to set my mind at rest? Where are the primary causes on which I am to build? Where are my foundations? Where am I to get them from? I exercise myself in reflection, and consequently with me every primary cause at once draws after itself another still more primary, and so on to infinity. That is just the essence of every sort of consciousness and reflection. It must be a case of the laws of nature again. What is the result of it in the end? Why, just the same. Remember I spoke just now of vengeance. (I am sure you did not take it in.) I said that a man revenges himself because he sees justice in it. Therefore he has found a primary cause, that is, justice. And so he is at rest on all sides, and consequently he carries out his revenge calmly and successfully, being persuaded that he is doing a just and honest thing. But I see no justice in it, I find no sort of virtue in it either, and consequently if I attempt to revenge myself, it is only out of spite. Spite, of course, might overcome everything, all my doubts, and so might serve quite successfully in place of a primary cause, precisely because it is not a cause. But what is to be done if I have not even spite (I began with that just now, you know). In consequence again of those accursed laws of consciousness, anger in me is subject to chemical disintegration. You look into it, the object flies off into air, your reasons evaporate, the criminal is not to be found, the wrong becomes not a wrong but a phantom, something like the toothache, for which no one is to blame, and consequently there is only the same outlet left again— that is, to beat the wall as hard as you can. So you give it up with a wave of the hand because you have not found a fundamental cause. And try letting yourself be carried away by your feelings, blindly, without reflection, without a primary cause, repelling consciousness at least for a time; hate or love, if only not to sit with your hands folded. The day after to-morrow, at the latest, you will begin despising yourself for having knowingly deceived yourself. Result: a soap-bubble and inertia. Oh, gentlemen, do you know, perhaps I consider myself an intelligent man, only because all my life I have been able neither to begin nor to finish anything. Granted I am a babbler, a harmless vexatious babbler, like all of us. But what is to be done if the direct and sole vocation of every intelligent man is babble, that is, the intentional pouring of water through a sieve?

VI

Oh, if I had done nothing simply from laziness! Heavens, how I should have respected myself, then. I should have respected myself because I should at least have been capable of being lazy; there would at least have been one quality, as it were, positive in me, in which I could have believed myself. Question: What is he? Answer: A sluggard; how very pleasant it would have been to hear that of oneself! It would mean that I was positively defined, it would mean that there was something to say about me. "Sluggard"—why, it is a calling and vocation, it is a career. Do not jest, it is so. I should then be a member of the best club by right, and should find my occupation in continually respecting myself. I knew a gentlemen who prided himself all his life on being a connoisseur of Lafitte. He considered this as his positive virtue, and never doubted himself. He died, not simply with a tranquil, but with a triumphant, conscience, and he was quite right, too. Then I should have chosen a career for myself, I should have been a sluggard and a glutton, not a simple one, but, for instance, one with sympathies for everything good and beautiful. How do you like that? I have long had visions of it. That "good and beautiful" weighs heavily on my mind at forty. But that is at forty; then—oh, then it would have been different! I should have found for myself a form of activity in keeping with it, to be precise, drinking to the health of everything "good and beautiful." I should have snatched at every opportunity to drop a tear into my glass and then to drain it to all that is "good and beautiful." I should then have turned everything into the good and the beautiful; in the nastiest, unquestionable trash, I should have sought out the good and the beautiful. I should have exuded tears like a wet sponge. An artist, for instance, paints a picture worthy of Gay.[4] At once I drink to the health of the artist who painted the picture worthy of Gay, because I love all that is "good and beautiful." An author has written *What*

---

4. Nikolay Nikolaevich Gay (1831–1894), Russian painter of historical pictures who then had a great reputation. His father was a French emigrant.

you will:[5] at once I drink to the health of "what you will" because I love all that is "good and beautiful."

I should claim respect for doing so. I should persecute any one who would not show me respect. I should live at ease, I should die with dignity, why, it is charming, perfectly charming! And what a good round belly I should have grown, what a triple chin I should have established, what a ruby nose I should have coloured for myself, so that every one would have said, looking at me: "Here is an asset! Here is something real and solid!" And, say what you like, it is very agreeable to hear such remarks about oneself in this negative age.

VII

But these are all golden dreams. Oh, tell me, who was it first announced, who was it first proclaimed, that man only does nasty things because he does not know his own interests; and that if he were enlightened, if his eyes were opened to his real normal interests, man would at once cease to do nasty things, would at once become good and noble because, being enlightened and understanding his real advantage, he would see his own advantage in the good and nothing else, and we all know that not one man can, consciously, act against his own interests, consequently, so to say, through necessity, he would begin doing good? Oh, the babe! Oh, the pure, innocent child! Why, in the first place, when in all these thousands of years has there been a time when man has acted only from his own interest? What is to be done with the millions of facts that bear witness that men, *consciously*, that is fully understanding their real interests, have left them in the background and have rushed headlong on another path, to meet peril and danger, compelled to this course by nobody and by nothing, but, as it were, simply disliking the beaten track, and have obstinately, wilfully, struck out another difficult, absurd way, seeking it almost in the darkness. So, I suppose, this obstinacy and perversity were pleasanter to them than any advantage. . . . Advantage! What is advantage? And will you take it upon yourself to define with perfect accuracy in what the advantage of man consists? And what if it so happens that a man's advantage, *sometimes*, not only may, but even must, consist in his desiring in certain cases what is harmful to himself and not advantageous. And if so, if there can be such a case, the whole principle falls into dust. What do you think—are there such cases? You laugh; laugh away, gentlemen, but only answer me: have man's advantages been reckoned up with perfect certainty? Are there not some which not only have not been included but cannot possibly be included under any

5. Subtitle of Shakespeare's comedy *Twelfth Night*, generally used on the Continent instead of the main title, which is difficult to translate.

classification? You see, you gentlemen have, to the best of my knowledge, taken your whole register of human advantages from the averages of statistical figures and politico-economical formulas. Your advantages are prosperity, wealth, freedom, peace—and so on, and so on. So that the man who should, for instance, go openly and knowingly in opposition to all that list would, to your thinking, and indeed mine, too, of course, be obscurantist or an absolute madman: would not he? But, you know, this is what is surprising: why does it so happen that all these statisticians, sages and lovers of humanity, when they reckon up human advantages invariably leave out one? They don't even take it into their reckoning in the form in which it should be taken, and the whole reckoning depends upon that. It would be no great matter, they would simply have to take it, this advantage, and add it to the list. But the trouble is, that this strange advantage does not fall under any classification and is not in place in any list. I have a friend for instance . . . Ech! gentlemen, but of course he is your friend, too; and indeed there is no one, no one, to whom he is not a friend! When he prepares for any undertaking this gentleman immediately explains to you, elegantly and clearly, exactly how he must act in accordance with the laws of reason and truth. What is more, he will talk to you with excitement and passion of the true normal interests of man; with irony he will upbraid the short-sighted fools who do not understand their own interests, nor the true significance of virtue; and, within a quarter of an hour, without any sudden outside provocation, but simply through something inside him which is stronger than all his interests, he will go off on quite a different tack—that is, act in direct opposition to what he has just been saying about himself, in opposition to the laws of reason, in opposition to his own advantage, in fact in opposition to everything . . . I warn you that my friend is a compound personality, and there-fore it is difficult to blame him as an individual. The fact is, gentle-men, it seems there must really exist something that is dearer to almost every man than his greatest advantages, or (not to be illogical) there is a most advantageous advantage (the very one omitted of which we spoke just now) which is more important and more advantageous than all other advantages, for the sake of which a man if necessary is ready to act in opposition to all laws; that is, in opposition to reason, honour, peace, prosperity—in fact, in opposition to all those excel-lent and useful things if only he can attain that fundamental, most advantageous advantage which is dearer to him than all. "Yes, but it's advantage all the same," you will retort. But excuse me, I'll make the point clear, and it is not a case of playing upon words. What matters is, that this advantage is remarkable from the very fact that it breaks down all our classifications, and continually shatters every system constructed by lovers of mankind for the benefit of mankind.

In fact, it upsets everything. But before I mention this advantage to you, I want to compromise myself personally, and therefore I boldly declare that all these fine systems, all these theories for explaining to mankind their real normal interests, in order that inevitably striving to pursue these interests they may at once become good and noble— are, in my opinion, so far, mere logical exercises! Yes, logical exercises. Why, to maintain this theory of the regeneration of mankind of means of the pursuit of his own advantage is to my mind almost the same thing as . . . as to affirm, for instance, following Buckle,[6] that through civilization mankind becomes softer, and consequently less bloodthirsty and less fitted for warfare. Logically it does seem to follow from his arguments. But man has such a predilection for systems and abstract deductions that he is ready to distort the truth intentionally, he is ready to deny the evidence of his senses only to justify his logic. I take this example because it is the most glaring instance of it. Only look about you: blood is being split in streams, and in the merriest way, as though it were champagne. Take the whole of the nineteenth century in which Buckle lived. Take Napoleon—the Great and also the present one. Take North America— the eternal union. Take the farce of Schleswig-Holstein.[7] . . . And what is it that civilization softens in us? The only gain of civilization for mankind is the greater capacity for variety of sensations—and absolutely nothing more. And through the development of this many-sidedness man may come to finding enjoyment in bloodshed. In fact, this has already happened to him. Have you noticed that it is the most civilized gentlemen who have been the subtlest slaughterers, to whom the Attilas and Stenka Razins[8] could not hold a candle, and if they are not so conspicuous as the Attilas and Stenka Razins it is simply because they are so often met with, are so ordinary and have become so familiar to us. In any case civilization has made mankind if not more bloodthirsty, at least more vilely, more loathsomely bloodthirsty. In old days he saw justice in bloodshed and with his conscience at peace exterminated those he thought proper. Now we do think bloodshed abominable and yet we engage in this abomination, and with more energy than ever. Which is worse? Decide that for yourselves. They say that Cleopatra (excuse an instance from Roman history) was fond of sticking gold pins into her slave-girls' breasts and derived gratification from their screams and writhings.

6. Henry Thomas Buckle (1821–1862), the author of the *History of Civilization in England* (two volumes, 1857, 1861), which held that all progress is due to the march of mind. There is no moral progress except indirectly, as a result of intellectual enlightenment.   7. Austria and Prussia invaded Denmark and annexed its southernmost part, Schleswig-Holstein, in 1864.   8. A Don Cossack leader who in 1670 conquered many cities along the Volga. He was finally defeated, captured, and executed in 1671. *Attila* (406?–453 A.D.) was king of the Huns (433?–453). In 451 his armies penetrated as far as Orléans, in what today is France. He was defeated in the battle of Châlons on the Catalaunian plains and retired to Hungary. In 452 he led an expedition against Rome.

You will say that that was in the comparatively barbarous times; that these are barbarous times too, because also, comparatively speaking, pins are stuck in even now; that though man has now learned to see more clearly than in barbarous ages, he is still far from having learnt to act as reason and science would dictate. But yet you are fully convinced that he will be sure to learn when he gets rid of certain old bad habits, and when common sense and science have completely re-educated human nature and turned it in a normal direction. You are confident that then man will cease from *intentional* error and will, so to say, be compelled not to want to set his will against his normal interests. That is not all; then, you say, science itself will teach man (though to my mind it's a superfluous luxury) that he never has really had any caprice or will of his own, and that he himself is something of the nature of a piano-key or the stop of an organ, and that there are, besides, things called the laws of nature; so that everything he does is not done by his willing it, but is done of itself, by the laws of nature. Consequently we have only to discover these laws of nature, and man will no longer have to answer for his actions and life will become exceedingly easy for him. All human actions, will then, of course, be tabulated according to these laws, mathematically like tables of logarithms up to 108,000, and entered in an index; or, better still, there would be published certain edifying works of the nature of encyclopædic lexicons, in which everything will be so clearly calculated and explained that there will be no more incidents or adventures in the world.

Then—this is all what you say—new economic relations will be established all ready-made and worked out with mathematical exactitude, so that every possible question will vanish in the twinkling of any eye, simply because every possible answer to it will be provided. Then the "Crystal Palace"[9] will be built. Then . . . In fact those will be halcyon days. Of course there is no guaranteeing (this is my comment) that it will not be, for instance, frightfully dull then (for what will one have to do when everything will be calculated and tabulated), but of course boredom may lead you to anything . It is boredom sets one sticking golden pins into people, but all that would not matter. What is bad (this is my comment again) is that I dare say people will be thankful for the gold pins then. Man is stupid, you know, phenomenally stupid; or rather he is not at all stupid, but he is so ungrateful that you could not find another like him in all creation. I, for instance, would not be in the least surprised if all of a sudden, *à propos* of nothing, in the midst of general prosperity a gentleman with an ignoble, or rather with a reactionary and ironical,

9. A structure of glass and iron built in London in 1851–1854, and at that time admired as the newest wonder of architecture. The nave was five hundred yards long. The building burned down in 1936.

countenance were to arise and, putting his arms akimbo, say to us all: "I say, gentlemen, hadn't we better kick over the whole show and scatter rationalism to the winds, simply to send these logarithms to the devil, and to enable us to live once more at our own sweet foolish will!" That again would not matter, but what is annoying is that he would be sure to find followers—such is the nature of man. And all that for the most foolish reason, which, one would think, was hardly worth mentioning: that is, that man everywhere and at all times, whoever he may be, has preferred to act as he chose and not in the least as his reason and advantage dictated. And one may choose what is contrary to one's own interests, and sometimes one *positively ought* (that is my idea). One's own free unfettered choice, one's own caprice, however wild it may be, one's own fancy worked up at times to frenzy—is that very "most advantageous advantage" which we have over-looked, which comes under no classification and against which all systems and theories are continually being shattered to atoms. And how do these wiseacres know that man wants a normal, a virtuous choice? What has made them conceive that man must want a ration-ally advantageous choice? What man wants is simply *independent* choice, whatever that independence may cost and wherever it may lead. And choice, of course, the devil only knows what choice.

VIII

"Ha! ha! ha! But you know there is no such thing as choice in reality, say what you like," you will interpose with a chuckle. "Sci-ence has succeeded in so far analysing man that we know already that choice and what is called freedom of will is nothing else than——"

Stay, gentlemen, I meant to begin with that myself. I confess, I was rather frightened. I was just going to say that the devil only knows what choice depends on, and that perhaps that was a very good thing, but I remembered the teaching of science . . . and pulled myself up. And here you have begun upon it. Indeed, if there really is some day discovered a formula for all our desires and caprices—that is, an explanation of what they depend upon, by what laws they arise, how they develop, what they are aiming at in one case and in another and so on, that is a real mathematical formula—then, most likely man will at once cease to feel desire, indeed, he will be certain to. For who would want to choose by rule? Besides, he will at once be transformed from a human being into an organ-stop or something of the sort; for what is a man without desires, without free will and without choice, if not a stop in an organ? What do you think? Let us reckon the chances—can such a thing happen or not?

"H'm!" you decide. "Our choice is usually mistaken from a false view of our advantage. We sometimes choose absolute nonsense because in our foolishness we see in that nonsense the easiest means for attaining a supposed advantage. But when all that is explained and worked out on paper (which is perfectly possible, for it is contemptible and senseless to suppose that some laws of nature man will never understand), then certainly so-called desires will no longer exist. For if a desire should come into conflict with reason we shall then reason and not desire, because it will be impossible retaining our reason to be senseless in our desires, and in that way knowingly act against reason and desire to injure ourselves. And as all choice and reasoning can be really calculated—because there will some day be discovered the laws of our so-called freewill—so, joking apart, there may one day be something like a table constructed of them, so that we really shall choose in accordance with it. If, for instance, some day they calculate and prove to me that I make a long nose at some one because I could not help making a long nose at him and that I had to do it in that particular way, what freedom is left me, especially if I am a learned man and have taken my degree somewhere? Then I should be able to calculate my whole life for thirty years beforehand. In short, if this could be arranged there would be nothing left for us to do; anyway, we should have to understand that. And, in fact, we ought unwearyingly to repeat to ourselves that at such and such a time and in such and such circumstances nature does not ask our leave; that we have got to take her as she is and not fashion her to suit our fancy, and if we really aspire to formulas and tables of rules, and well, even . . . to the chemical retort, there's no help for it, we must accept the retort too, or else it will be accepted without our consent. . . .

Yes, but here I come to a stop! Gentlemen, you must excuse me for being over-philosophical; it's the result of forty years underground! Allow me to indulge my fancy. You see, gentlemen, reason is an excellent thing, there's no disputing that, but reason is nothing but reason and satisfies only the rational side of man's nature, while will is a manifestation of the whole life, that is, of the whole human life including reason and all the impulses. And although our life, in this manifestation of it, is often worthless, yet it is life and not simply extracting square roots. Here I, for instance, quite naturally want to live, in order to satisfy all my capacities for life, and not simply my capacity for reasoning, that is, not simply one twentieth of my capacity for life. What does reason know? Reason only knows what it has succeeded in learning (some things, perhaps, it will never learn; this is a poor comfort, but why not say so frankly?) and human nature acts as a whole, with everything that is in it, consciously or unconsciously, and, even if it goes wrong, it lives. I suspect, gentlemen, that you are looking at me with compassion; you tell me again that an enlightened and developed man, such, in short, as the future man will be, cannot consciously desire anything disadvantageous to himself, that that can be proved mathematically. I thoroughly agree, it can—by mathematics. But I repeat for the hundredth time, there is one case, one only, when man may consciously, purposely, desire what is injurious to himself, what is stupid, very stupid—simply in order to have the right to desire for himself even what is very stupid and not to be found by an obligation to desire only what is sensible. Of course, this very stupid thing, this caprice of ours, may be in reality, gentlemen, more advantageous for us than anything else on earth, especially in certain cases. And in particular it may be more advantageous than any advantage even when it does us obvious harm, and contradicts the soundest conclusions of our reason concerning our advantage—for in any circumstances it preserves for us what is most precious and most important—that is, our personality, our individuality. Some, you see, maintain that this really is the most precious thing for mankind; choice can, of course, if it chooses, be in agreement with reason; and especially if this be not abused but kept within bounds. It is profitable and sometimes even praiseworthy. But very often, and even most often, choice is utterly and stubbornly opposed to reason . . . and . . . and . . . do you know that that, too, is profitable, sometimes even praiseworthy? Gentlemen, let us suppose that man is not stupid. (Indeed one cannot refuse to suppose that, if only from the one consideration, that, if man is stupid, then who is wise?) But if he is not stupid, he is monstrously ungrateful! Phenomenally ungrateful. In fact, I believe that the best definition of man is the ungrateful biped. But that is not all, that is not his worst defect; his worst defect is his perpetual moral obliquity, perpetual—from the days of the Flood to the Schleswig-Holstein period. Moral obliquity and consequently lack of good sense; for it has long been accepted that lack of good sense is due to no other cause than moral obliquity. Put it to the test and cast your eyes upon the history of mankind. What will you see? Is it a grand spectacle? Grand, if you like. Take the Colossus of Rhodes,[1] for instance, that's worth something. With good reason Mr. Anaevsky testifies of it that some say that it is the work of man's hands, while others maintain that it has been created by nature herself. Is it many-coloured? May be it is many-coloured, too: if one takes the dress uniforms, military and civilian, of all peoples in all ages—that alone is worth something, and if you take the undress uniforms you will never get to the end of it; no historian would be equal to the job. Is it monotonous? May be it's monotonous too: it's fighting and fighting; they are fight-

1. A statue of Helios (Apollo) at Rhodes (an island in the Aegean Sea), about a hundred feet high, which was considered one of the Seven Wonders of the World. It was erected about 290 B.C.

ing now, they fought first and they fought last—you will admit, that it is almost too monotonous. In short, one may say anything about the history of the world—anything that might enter the most disordered imagination. The only thing one can't say is that it's rational. The very word sticks in one's throat. And, indeed, this is the odd thing that is continually happening: there are continually turning up in life moral and rational persons, sages and lovers of humanity who make it their object to live all their lives as morally and rationally as possible, to be, so to speak, a light to their neighbours simply in order to show them that it is possible to live morally and rationally in this world. And yet we all know that those very people sooner or later have been false to themselves, playing some queer trick, often a most unseemly one. Now I ask you: what can be expected of man since he is a being endowed with such strange qualities? Shower upon him every earthly blessing, drown him in a sea of happiness, so that nothing but bubbles of bliss can be seen on the surface; give him economic prosperity, such that he should have nothing else to do but sleep, eat cakes and busy himself with the continuation of his species, and even then out of sheer ingratitude, sheer spite, man would play you some nasty trick. He would even risk his cakes and would deliberately desire the most fatal rubbish, the most uneconomical absurdity, simply to introduce into all his fantastic dreams, his vulgar folly that he will desire to retain, simply in order to prove to himself—as though that were so necessary—that men still are men and not the keys of a piano, which the laws of nature threaten to control so completely that soon one will be able to desire nothing but by the calendar. And that is not all: even if man really were nothing but a piano-key, even if this were proved to him by natural science and mathematics, even then he would not become reasonable, but would purposely do something perverse out of simple ingratitude, simply to gain his point. And if he does not find means he will contrive destruction and chaos, will contrive sufferings of all sorts, only to gain his point! He will launch a curse upon the world, and as only man can curse (it is his privilege, the primary distinction between him and other animals), may be by his curse alone he will attain his object—that is, convince himself that he is a man and not a piano-key! If you say that all this, too, can be calculated and tabulated—chaos and darkness and curses, so that the mere possibility of calculating it all beforehand would stop it all, and reason would reassert itself, then man would purposely go mad in order to be rid of reason and gain his point! I believe in it, I answer for it, for the whole work of man really seems to consist in nothing but proving to himself every minute that he is a man and not a piano-key! It may be at the cost of his skin, it may be by cannibalism! And this being so, can one help being tempted to rejoice that it has not yet come off, and that desire still depends on something we don't know?

You will scream at me (that is, if you condescend to do so) that no one is touching my free will, that all they are concerned with is that my will should of itself, of its own free will, coincide with my own normal interests, with the laws of nature and arithmetic.

Good Heavens, gentlemen, what sort of free will is left when we come to tabulation and arithmetic, when it will all be a case of twice two makes four? Twice two makes four without my will. As if free will meant that!

IX

Gentlemen, I am joking, and I know myself that my jokes are not brilliant, but you know one can't take everything as a joke. I am, perhaps, jesting against the grain. Gentlemen, I am tormented by questions; answer them for me. You, for instance, want to cure men of their old habits and reform their will in accordance with science and good sense. But how do you know, not only that it is possible, but also that it is *desirable*, to reform man in that way? And what leads you to the conclusion that man's inclinations *need* reforming? In short, how do you know that such a reformation will be a benefit to man? And to go to the root of the matter, why are you so positively convinced that not to act against his real normal interests guaranteed by the conclusions of reason and arithmetic is certainly always advantageous for man and must always be a law for mankind? So far, you know, this is only your supposition. It may be the law of logic, but not the law of humanity. You think, gentlemen, perhaps that I am mad? Allow me to defend myself. I agree that man is pre-eminently a creative animal, predestined to strive consciously for an object and to engage in engineering—that is, incessantly and eternally to make new roads, *wherever they may lead*. But the reason why he wants sometimes to go off at a tangent may just be that he is *predestined* to make the road, and perhaps, too, that however stupid the "direct" practical man may be, the thought sometimes will occur to him that the road almost always does lead *somewhere*, and that the destination it leads to is less important than the process of making it, and that the chief thing is to save the well-conducted child from despising engineering, and so giving way to the fatal idleness, which, as we all know, is the mother of all the vices. Man likes to make roads and to create, that is a fact beyond dispute. But why has he such a passionate love for destruction and chaos also? Tell me that! But on that point I want to say a couple of words myself. May it not be that he loves chaos and destruction (there can be no disputing that he does sometimes love it) because he is instinctively afraid of attaining his object and completing the edifice he is constructing?

Who knows, perhaps he only loves that edifice from a distance, and is by no means in love with it at close quarters; perhaps he only loves building it and does not want to live in it, but will leave it, when completed, for the use of *les animaux domestiques*—such as the ants, the sheep, and so on. Now the ants have quite a different taste. They have a marvellous edifice of that pattern which endures for ever—the ant-heap.

With the ant-heap the respectable race of ants began and with the ant-heap they will probably end, which does the greatest credit to their perseverance and good sense. But man is a frivolous and incongruous creature, and perhaps, like a chess player, loves the process of the game, not the end of it. And who knows (there is no saying with certainty), perhaps the only goal on earth to which mankind is striving lies in this incessant process of attaining, in other words, in life itself, and not in the thing to be attained, which must always be expressed as a formula, as positive as twice two makes four, and such positiveness is not life, gentlemen, but is the beginning of death. Anyway, man has always been afraid of this mathematical certainty, and I am afraid of it now. Granted that man does nothing but seek that mathematical certainty, he traverses oceans, sacrifices his life in the quest, but to succeed, really to find it, he dreads, I assure you. He feels that when he has found it there will be nothing for him to look for. When workmen have finished their work they do at least receive their pay, they go to the tavern, then they are taken to the police-station—and there is occupation for a week. But where can man go? Anyway, one can observe a certain awkwardness about him when he has attained such objects. He loves the process of attaining, but does not quite like to have attained, and that, of course, is very absurd. In fact, man is a comical creature; there seems to be a kind of jest in it all. But yet mathematical certainty is, after all, something insufferable. Twice two makes four seems to me simply a piece of insolence. Twice two makes four is a pert coxcomb who stands with arms akimbo barring your path and spitting. I admit that twice two makes four is an excellent thing, but if we are to give everything its due, twice two makes five is sometimes a very charming thing too.

And why are you so firmly, so triumphantly, convinced that only the normal and the positive—in other words, only what is conducive to welfare—is for the advantage of man? Is not reason in error as regards advantage? Does not man, perhaps, love something besides well-being? Perhaps he is just as fond of suffering? Perhaps suffering is just as great a benefit to him as well-being? Man is sometimes extraordinarily, passionately, in love with suffering, and that is a fact. There is no need to appeal to universal history to prove that; only ask yourself, if you are a man and have lived at all. As far as my personal opinion is concerned, to care only for well-being seems to

me positively ill-bred. Whether it's good or bad, it is sometimes very
pleasant, too, to smash things. I hold no brief for suffering nor for
well-being either. I am standing for . . . my caprice, and for its being
guaranteed to me when necessary. Suffering would be out of place
in vaudevilles, for instance; I know that. In the "Crystal Palace" it is
unthinkable; suffering means doubt, negation, and what would be
the good of a crystal palace if there could be any doubt about it? And
yet I think man will never renounce real suffering, that is, destruction and chaos. Why, suffering is the sole origin of consciousness.
Though I did lay it down at the beginning that consciousness is the
greatest misfortune for man, yet I know man prizes it and would not
give it up for any satisfaction. Consciousness, for instance, is infinitely superior to twice two makes four. Once you have mathematical certainty there is nothing left to do or to understand. There will
be nothing left but to bottle up your five senses and plunge into
contemplation. While if you stick to consciousness, even though the
same result is attained, you can at least flog yourself at times, and
that will, at any rate, liven you up. Reactionary as it is, corporal
punishment is better than nothing.

$$X^2$$

You believe in a crystal palace that can never be destroyed—a
palace at which one will not be able to put out one's tongue or make
a long nose on the sly. And perhaps that is just why I am afraid of
this edifice, that it is of crystal and can never be destroyed and that
one cannot put one's tongue out at it even on the sly.

You see, if it were not a palace, but a hen-house, I might creep
into it to avoid getting wet, and yet I would not call the hen-house a
palace out of gratitude to it for keeping me dry. You laugh and say
that in such circumstances a hen-house is as good as a mansion.
Yes, I answer, if one had to live simply to keep out of the rain.

But what is to be done, if I have taken it into my head that that is
not the only object in life, and that if one must live one had better
live in a mansion. That is my choice, my desire. You will only
eradicate it when you have changed my preference. Well, do change
it, allure me with something else, give me another ideal. But meanwhile I will not take a hen-house for a mansion. The crystal palace
may be an idle dream, it may be that it is inconsistent with the laws
of nature and that I have invented it only through my own stupidity,
through the old-fashioned irrational habits of my generation. But
what does it matter to me that it is inconsistent? That makes no
difference since it exists in my desires, or rather exists as long as my

2. Section X was badly mutilated by the censor, as Dostoevsky makes clear in the letter to his
brother Mikhail, dated March 26, 1864, which is quoted in our introduction.

desires exist. Perhaps you are laughing again? Laugh away; I will put up with any mockery rather than pretend that I am satisfied when I am hungry. I know, anyway, that I will not be put off with a compromise, with a recurring zero, simply because it is consistent with the laws of nature and actually exists. I will not accept as the crown of my desires a block of slum tenements on a lease of a thousand years, and perhaps with a sign-board of Wagenheim the dentist hanging out. Destroy my desires, eradicate my ideals, show me something better, and I will follow you. You will say, perhaps, that it is not worth your trouble; but in that case I can give you the same answer. We are discussing things seriously; but if you won't deign to give me your attention, I will drop your acquaintance. I can retreat into my underground hole.

But while I am alive and have desires I would rather my hand were withered off than bring one brick to such a building! Don't remind me that I have just rejected the crystal place for the sole reason that no cannot put one's tongue to it. I did not say because I am so fond of putting my tongue out. Perhaps the thing I resented was, that of all your edifices there has not been one at which one could not put out one's tongue. On the contrary, I would let my tongue be cut off out of gratitude if things could be so arranged, that I should lose all desire to put it out. It is not my fault that things cannot be so arranged, and that one must be satisfied with model flats. Then why am I made with such desires? Can I have been constructed simply in order to come to the conclusion that all my construction is a cheat? Can this be my whole purpose? I do not believe it.

But do you know what: I am convinced that we underground folk ought to be kept on a curb. Though we may sit forty years underground without speaking, when we do come out into the light of day and break out we talk and talk and talk. . . .

XI

The long and the short of it is, gentlemen, that it is better to do nothing! Better conscious inertia! And so hurrah for underground! Though I have said that I envy the normal man to the last drop of my bile, yet I should not care to be in his place such as he is now (though I shall not cease envying him). No, no; anyway the underground life is more advantageous. There, at any rate, one can. . . . Oh, but even now I am lying! I am lying because I know myself that it is not underground that is better, but something different, quite different, for which I am thirsting, but which I cannot find! Damn underground!

I will tell you another thing that would be better, and that is, if I myself believed in anything of what I have just written. I swear to you, gentlemen, there is not one thing, not one word of what I have written that I really believe. That is, I believe it, perhaps, but at the same time I feel and suspect that I am lying like a cobbler.

"Then why have you written all this?" you will say to me. "I ought to put you underground for forty years without anything to do and then come to you in your cellar, to find out what stage you have reached. How can a man be left with nothing to do for forty years?"

"Isn't that shameful, isn't that humiliating?" you will say, perhaps, wagging your heads contemptuously. "You thirst for life and try to settle the problems of life by a logical tangle. And how persistent, how insolent are your sallies, and at the same time what a scare you are in! You talk nonsense and are pleased with it, you say impudent things and are in continual alarm and apologizing for them. You declare that you are afraid of nothing and at the same time try to ingratiate yourself in our good opinion. You declare that you are gnashing your teeth and at the same time you try to be witty so as to amuse us. You know that your witticisms are not witty, but you are evidently well satisfied with their literary value. You may, perhaps, have really suffered, but you have no respect for your own suffering. You may have sincerity, but you have no modesty; out of the pettiest vanity you expose your sincerity to publicity and ignominy. You doubtlessly mean to say something, but hide your last word through fear, because you have not the resolution to utter it, and only have a cowardly impudence. You boast of consciousness, but you are not sure of your ground, for though your mind works, yet your heart is darkened and corrupt, and you cannot have a full, genuine consciousness without a pure heart. And how intrusive you are, how you insist and grimace! Lies, lies, lies!"

Of course I have myself made up all the things you say. That, too, is from underground. I have been for forty years listening to you through a crack under the floor. I have invented them myself, there was nothing else I could invent. It is no wonder that I have learned it by heart and it has taken a literary form. . . .

But can you really be so credulous as to think that I will print all this and give it to you to read too? And another problem: why do I call you "gentlemen," why do I address you as though you really were my readers? Such confessions as I intend to make are never printed nor given to other people to read. Anyway, I am not strongminded enough for that, and I don't see why I should be. But you see a fancy has occurred to me and I want to realize it at all costs. Let me explain.

Every man has reminiscences which he would not tell to every one, but only to his friends. He has other matters in his mind which he would not reveal even to his friends, but only to himself, and that in secret. But there are other things which a man is afraid to tell even to himself, and every decent man has a number of such things stored away in his mind. The more decent he is, the greater the number of such things in his mind. Anyway, I have only lately determined to remember some of my early adventures. Till now I have always avoided them, even with a certain uneasiness. Now, when I am not only recalling them, but have actually decided to write an account of them, I want to try the experiment whether one can, even with oneself, be perfectly open and not take fright at the whole truth. I will observe, in parenthesis, that Heine[3] says that a true autobiography is almost an impossibility, and that man is bound to lie about himself. He considers that Rousseau certainly told lies about himself in his *Confessions*, and even intentionally lied, out of vanity. I am convinced that Heine is right; I quite understand how sometimes one may, out of sheer vanity, attribute regular crimes to oneself, and indeed I can very well conceive that kind of vanity. But Heine judged of people who made their confessions to the public. I write only for myself, and I wish to declare once and for all that if I write as though I were addressing readers, that is simply because it is easier for me to write in that form. It is a form, an empty form—I shall never have readers. I have made this plain already. . . .

I don't wish to be hampered by any restrictions in the compilation of my notes. I shall not attempt any system or method. I will jot things down as I remember them.

But here, perhaps, some one will catch at the word and ask me: if you really don't reckon on readers, why do you make such compacts with yourself—and on paper too—that is, that you won't attempt any system or method, that you jot things down as you remember them, and so on, and so on? Why are you explaining? Why do you apologize?

Well, there it is, I answer.

There is a whole psychology in all this, though. Perhaps it is simply that I am a coward. And perhaps that I purposely imagine an audience before me in order that I may be more dignified while I write. There are perhaps thousands of reasons. Again, what is my object precisely in writing? If it is not for the benefit of the public why should I not simply recall these incidents in my own mind without putting them on paper?

Quite so; but yet it is more imposing on paper. There is something more impressive in it; I shall be better able to criticize myself and improve my style. Besides, I shall perhaps obtain actual relief from writing. To-day, for instance, I am particularly oppressed by one memory of a distant past. It came back vividly to my mind a few days ago, and has remained haunting me like an annoying tune that one cannot get rid of. And yet I must get rid of it somehow. I have

---

3. Dostoevsky alludes to *Confessions* (1854), fragmentary memoirs written by the German poet Heinrich Heine (1797–1856), in which on the very first page Heine speaks of Rousseau as lying and inventing disgraceful incidents about himself for his *Confessions*.

hundreds of such reminiscences; but at times some one stands out from the hundred and oppresses me. For some reason I believe that if I write it down I should get rid of it. Why not try?

Besides, I am bored, and I never have anything to do. Writing will be a sort of work. They say work makes man kind-hearted and honest. Well, here is a chance for me, anyway.

Snow is falling to-day, yellow and dingy. It fell yesterday, too, and a few days ago. I fancy it is the wet snow that has reminded me of that incident which I cannot shake off now. And so let it be a story *à propos* of the falling snow.

Part II

À PROPOS OF THE WET SNOW

When from dark error's subjugation
My words of passionate exhortation
   Had wrenched thy fainting spirit free;
And writhing prone in thine affliction
Thou didst recall with malediction
   The vice that had encompassed thee:
And when thy slumbering conscience, fretting
   By recollection's torturing flame,
Thou didst reveal the hideous setting
   Of thy life's current ere I came:
When suddenly I saw thee sicken,
   And weeping, hide thine anguished face,
Revolted, maddened, horror-stricken,
   At memories of foul disgrace, etc., etc., etc. . . . .

               NEKRASOV[4] *(translated by Juliet Soskice)*

I

At that time I was only twenty-four. My life was even then gloomy, ill-regulated, and as solitary as that of a savage. I made friends with no one and positively avoided talking, and buried myself more and more in my hole. At work in the office I never looked at any one, and I was perfectly well aware that my companions looked upon me, not only as a queer fellow, but even looked upon me—I always fancied this—with a sort of loathing. I sometimes wondered why it was that nobody except me fancied that he was looked upon with aversion? One of the clerks had a most repulsive, pock-marked face,

---

4. Nikolay A. Nekrasov (1821–1878) was a famous Russian poet and editor of radical sympathies. The poem quoted dates from 1845, and is without title. The poem ends with the lines, "Into my house come bold and free, Its rightful mistress there to be."

which looked positively villainous. I believe I should not have dared to look at any one with such an unsightly countenance. Another had such a very dirty old uniform that there was an unpleasant odor in his proximity. Yet not one of these gentlemen showed the slightest self-consciousness—either about their clothes or their countenance or their character in any way. Neither of them ever imagined that they were looked at with repulsion; if they had imagined it they would not have minded—so long as their superiors did not look at them in that way. It is clear to me now that, owing to my unbounded vanity and to the high standard I set for myself, I often looked at myself with furious discontent, which verged on loathing, and so I inwardly attributed the same feeling to every one. I hated my face, for instance: I thought it disgusting, and even suspected that there was something base in my expression, and so every day when I turned up at the office I tried to behave as independently as possible, and to assume a lofty expression, so that I might not be suspected of being abject. "My face may be ugly," I thought, "but let it be lofty, expressive, and, above all, *extremely* intelligent." But I was positively and painfully certain that it was impossible for my countenance ever to express those qualities. And what was worst of all, I thought it actually stupid-looking, and I would have been quite satisfied if I could have looked intelligent. In fact, I would even have put up with looking base if, at the same time, my face could have been thought strikingly intelligent.

Of course, I hated my fellow clerks one and all, and I despised them all, yet at the same time I was, as it were, afraid of them. In fact, it happened at times that I thought more highly of them than of myself. It somehow happened quite suddenly that I alternated between despising them and thinking them superior to myself. A cultivated and decent man cannot be vain without setting a feafully high standard for himself, and without despising and almost hating himself at certain moments. But whether I despised them or thought them superior I dropped my eyes almost every time I met any one. I even made experiments whether I could face so and so's looking at me, and I was always the first to drop my eyes. This worried me to distraction. I had a sickly dread, too, of being ridiculous, and so had a slavish passion for the conventional in everything external. I loved to fall into the common rut, and had a whole-hearted terror of any kind of eccentricity in myself. But how could I live up to it? I was morbidly sensitive, as a man of our age should be. They were all stupid, and as like one another as so many sheep. Perhaps I was the only one in the office who fancied that I was a coward and a slave, and I fancied it just because I was more highly developed. But it was not only that I fancied it, it really was so. I was a coward and a slave. I say this without the slightest embarrassment. Every decent man of our age must be a coward and a slave. That is his normal condition.

Of that I am firmly persuaded. He is made and constructed to that very end. And not only at the present time owing to some casual circumstances, but always, at all times, a decent man is bound to be a coward and a slave. It is the law of nature for all decent people all over the earth. If any one of them happens to be valiant about something, he need not be comforted nor carried away by that; he would show the white feather just the same before something else. That is how it invariably and inevitably ends. Only donkeys and mules are valiant, and they only till they are pushed up to the wall. It is not worth while to pay attention to them for they really are of no consequence.

Another circumstance, too, worried me in those days: that there was no one like me and I was unlike any one else. "I am unique and they are all alike," I thought—and pondered.

From that it is evident that I was still a youngster.

The very opposite sometimes happened. It was loathsome sometimes to go to the office; things reached such a point that I often came home ill. But all at once, à propos of nothing, there would come a phase of scepticism and indifference (everything happened in phases to me), and I would laugh myself at any intolerance and fastidiousness, I would reproach myself with being *romantic*. At one time I was unwilling to speak to any one, while at other times I would not only talk, but go to the length of contemplating making friends with them. All my fastidiousness would suddenly, for no rhyme or reason, vanish. Who knows, perhaps I never had really had it, and it had simply been affected, and got out of books. I have not decided that question even now. Once I quite made friends with them, visited their homes, played preference, drank vodka, talked of promotions. . . . But here let me make a digression.

We Russians, speaking generally, have never had those foolish transcendental "romantics"—German, and still more French—on whom nothing produces any effect; if there were an earthquake, if all France perished at the barricades, they would still be the same, they would not even have the decency to affect a change, but would still go on singing their transcendental songs to the hour of their death, because they are fools. We, in Russia, have no fools; that is well known. That is what distinguishes us from foreign lands. Consequently these transcendental natures are not found amongst us in their pure form. The idea that they are is due to our "realistic" journalists and critics of that day, always on the look out for Kostanzhoglos and Uncle Pyotr Ivanichs[5] and foolishly accepting them as our ideal; they have slandered our romantics, taking them for the same

---

5. A character in Ivan Goncharov's novel *A Common Story* (1847); a high bureaucrat, a factory owner who teaches lessons of sobriety and good sense to the romantic hero, Alexander Aduyev. *Konstanzhoglo*: The ideal efficient landowner in the second part of Gogol's novel *Dead Souls* (1852).

transcendental sort as in Germany or France. On the contrary, the characteristics of our "romantics" are absolutely and directly opposed to the transcendental European type, and no European standard can be applied to them. (Allow me to make use of this word "romantic"—an old-fashioned and much respected word which has done good service and is familiar to all.) The characteristics of our romantic are to understand everything, *to see everything and to see it often incomparably more clearly than our most realistic minds see it*; to refuse to accept anyone or anything, but at the same time not to despise anything; to give way, to yield, from policy; never to lose sight of a useful practical object (such as rent-free quarters at the government expense, pensions, decorations), to keep their eye on that object through all the enthusiasm and volumes of lyrical poems, and at the same time to preserve "the good and the beautiful" inviolate within them to the hour of their death, and to preserve themselves also, incidentally, like some precious jewel wrapped in cotton wool if only for the benefit of "the good and the beautiful." Our "romantic" is a man of great breadth and the greatest rogue of all our rogues, I assure you. . . . I can assure you from experience, indeed. Of course, that is, if he is intelligent. But what am I saying! The romantic is always intelligent, and I only meant to observe that although we have had foolish romantics they don't count, and they were only so because in the flower of their youth they degenerated into Germans, and to preserve their precious jewel more comfortably, settled somewhere out there—by preference in Weimar or the Black Forest.

I, for instance, genuinely despised my official work and did not openly abuse it simply because I was in it myself and got a salary for it. Anyway, take note, I did not openly abuse it. Our romantic would rather go out of his mind—a thing, however, which very rarely happens—than take to open abuse, unless he had some other career in view; and he is never kicked out. At most, they would take him to the lunatic asylum as "the King of Spain"[6] if he should go mad. But it is only the thin, fair people who go out of their minds in Russia. Innumerable "romantics" attain later in life to considerable rank in the service. Their many-sidedness is remarkable! And what a faculty they have for the most contradictory sensations! I was comforted by this thought even in those days, and I am of the same opinion now. That is why there are so many "broad natures" among us who never lose their ideal even in the depths of degradation; and though they never stir a finger for their ideal, though they are arrant thieves and knaves, yet they tearfully cherish their first ideal and are extraordinarily honest at heart. Yes, it is only among us that the most incor-

6. An allusion to Gogol's story "Memoirs of a Madman" (1835). The narrator imagines himself "the King of Spain" and is finally carried off to a lunatic asylum.

rigible rogue can be absolutely and loftily honest at heart without in the least ceasing to be a rogue. I repeat, our romantics, frequently, become such accomplished rascals (I use the term "rascals" affectionately), suddenly display such a sense of reality and practical knowledge that their bewildered superiors and the public generally can only ejaculate in amazement.

Their many-sidedness is really amazing, and goodness knows what it may develop into later on, and what the future has in store for us. It is not a poor material! I do not say this from any foolish or boastful patriotism. But I feel sure that you are again imagining that I am joking. Or perhaps it's just the contrary and you are convinced that I really think so. Anyway, gentlemen, I shall welcome both views as an honour and a special favour. And do forgive my digression.

I did not, of course, maintain friendly relations with my comrades and soon was at loggerheads with them, and in my youth and inexperience I even gave up bowing to them, as though I had cut off all relations. That, however, only happened to me once. As a rule, I was always alone.

In the first place I spent most of my time at home, reading. I tried to stifle all that was continually seething within me by means of external impressions. And the only external means I had was reading. Reading, of course, was a great help—exciting me, giving me pleasure and pain. But at times it bored me fearfully. One longed for movement in spite of everything, and I plunged all at once into dark, underground, loathsome vice of the pettiest kind. My wretched passions were acute, smarting, from my continual, sickly irritability. I had hysterical impulses, with tears and convulsions. I had no resource except reading, that is, there was nothing in my surroundings which I could respect and which attracted me. I was overwhelmed with depression, too; I had a hysterical craving for incongruity and for contrast, and so I took to vice. I have not said all this to justify myself. . . . But, no! I am lying. I did want to justify myself. I make that little observation for my own benefit, gentlemen. I don't want to lie. I vowed to myself I would not.

And so, furtively, timidly, in solitude, at night, I indulged in filthy vice, with a feeling of shame which never deserted me, even at the most loathsome moments, and which at such moments nearly made me curse. Already even then I had my underground world in my soul. I was fearfully afraid of being seen, of being met, of being recognized. I visited various obscure haunts.

One night as I was passing a tavern I saw through a lighted window some gentlemen fighting with billiard cues, and saw one of them thrown out of a window. At other times I should have felt very much disgusted, but I was in such a mood at the time, that I actually envied the gentleman thrown out of a window—and I envied him so much that I even went into the tavern and into the billiard-room. "Perhaps," I thought, "I'll have a fight, too, and they'll throw me out of the window."

I was not drunk—but what is one to do—depression will drive a man to such a pitch of hysteria? But nothing happened. It seemed that I was not even equal to being thrown out of the window and I went away without having my fight.

An officer put me in my place from the first moment.

I was standing by the billiard-table and in my ignorance blocking up the way, and he wanted to pass; he took me by the shoulders and without a word—without a warning or explanation—moved me from where I was standing to another spot and passed by as though he had not noticed me. I could have forgiven blows, but I could not forgive his having moved me without noticing me.

Devil knows what I would have given for a real regular quarrel— a more decent, a more *literary* one, so to speak. I had been treated like a fly. This officer was over six foot, while I was a spindly little fellow. But the quarrel was in my hands. I had only to protest and I certainly would have been thrown out of the window. But I changed my mind and preferred to beat a resentful retreat.

I went out of the tavern straight home, confused and troubled, and the next night I went out again with the same lewd intentions, still more furtively, abjectly and miserably than before, as it were, with tears in my eyes—but still I did go out again. Don't imagine, though, it was cowardice made me slink away from the officer: I never have been a coward at heart, though I have always been a coward in action. Don't be in a hurry to laugh—I assure you I can explain it all.

Oh, if only that officer had been one of the sort who would consent to fight a duel! But no, he was one of those genetlemen (alas, long extinct!) who preferred fighting with cues or, like Gogol's Lieutenant Pirogov,[7] appealing to the police. They did not fight duels and would have thought a duel with a civilian like me an utterly unseemly procedure in any case—and they looked upon the duel altogether as something impossible, something free-thinking and French. But they were quite ready to bully, especially when they were over six foot.

I did not slink away through cowardice, but through an unbounded vanity. I was afraid not of his six foot, not of getting a sound thrashing and being thrown out of the window; I should have had physical courage enough, I assure you; but I had not the moral courage. What I was afraid of was that every one present, from the insolent

---

7. A character in Gogol's story "The Nevsky Prospekt" (1835). He pays violent court to the wife of a German tradesman and is thrown out by him and his friends. He does not actually call the police.

marker down to the lowest little stinking, pimply clerk in a greasy collar, would jeer at me and fail to understand when I began to protest and to address them in literary language. For of the point of honour—not of honour, but of the point of honour *(point d'honneur)*—one cannot speak among us except in literary language. You can't allude to the "point of honour" in ordinary language. I was fully convinced (the sense of reality, in spite of all my romanticism!) that they would all simply split their sides with laughter, and that the officer would not simply beat me, that is, without insulting me, but would certainly prod me in the back with his knee, kick me round the billiard-table, and only then perhaps have pity and drop me out of the window.

Of course, this trivial incident could not with me end in that. I often met that officer afterwards in the street and noticed him very carefully. I am not quite sure whether he recognized me, I imagine not; I judge from certain signs. But I—I stared at him with spite and hatred and so it went on . . . for several years! My resentment grew even deeper with years. At first I began making stealthy inquiries about this officer. It was difficult for me to do so, for I knew no one. But one day I heard some one shout his surname in the street as I was following him at a distance, as though I were tied to him—and so I learnt his surname. Another time I followed him to his flat, and for ten kopecks learned from the porter where he lived, on which storey, whether he lived alone or with others, and so on—in fact, everything one could learn from a porter. One morning, though I had never tried my hand with the pen, it suddenly occurred to me to write a satire on this officer in the form of a novel which would unmask his villainy. I wrote the novel with relish. I did unmask his villainy, I even exaggerated it; at first I so altered his surname that it it could easily be recognized, but on second thoughts I changed it, and sent the story to the *Otechestvennye Zapiski.*[8] But at that time such attacks were not the fashion and my story was not printed. That was a great vexation to me.

Sometimes I was positively choked with resentment. At last I determined to challenge my enemy to a duel. I composed a splendid, charming letter to him, imploring him to apologize to me, and hinting rather plainly at a duel in case of refusal. The letter was so composed that if the officer had had the least understanding of the good and the beautiful he would certainly have flung himself on my neck and have offered me his friendship. And how fine that would have been! How we should have got on together! "He could have shielded me with his higher rank, while I could have improved his mind with my culture, and, well . . . my ideas, and all sorts of

8. *Notes of the Fatherland*, the most famous radical Russian journal, founded in 1839.

things might have happened." Only fancy, this was two years after his insult to me, and my challenge would have been a ridiculous anachronism, in spite of all the ingenuity of my letter in disguising and explaining away the anchronism. But, thank God (to this day I thank the Almighty with tears in my eyes) I did not send the letter to him. Cold shivers run down my back when I think of what might have happened if I had sent it.

And all at once I revenged myself in the simplest way, by a stroke of genius! A brilliant thought suddenly dawned upon me. Sometimes on holidays I used to stroll along the sunny side of the Nevsky[9] about four o'clock in the afternoon. Though it was hardly a stroll so much as a series of innumerable miseries, humiliations, and resentments; but no doubt that was just what I wanted. I used to wriggle along in a most unseemingly fashion, like an eel, continually moving aside to make way for generals, for officers of the guards and the hussars, or for ladies. At such minutes there used to be a convulsive twinge at my heart, and I used to feel hot all down my back at the mere thought of the wretchedness of my attire, of the wretchedness and abjectness of my little scurrying figure. This was a regular martyrdom, a continual, intolerable humiliation at the thought, which passed into an incessant and direct sensation, that I was a mere fly in the eyes of all this world, a nasty, disgusting fly—more intelligent, more highly developed, more refined in feeling than any of them, of course—but a fly that was continually making way for every one, insulted and injured by every one. Why I inflicted this torture upon myself, why I went to the Nevsky, I don't know. I felt simply drawn there at every possible opportunity.

Already then I began to experience a rush of the enjoyment of which I spoke in the first chapter. After my affair with the officer I felt even more drawn there than before: it was on the Nevsky that I met him most frequently, there I could admire him. He, too, went there chiefly on holidays. He, too, turned out of his path for generals and persons of high rank, and he, too, wriggled between them like an eel; but people, like me, or even better dressed like me, he simply walked over; he made straight for them as though there wqs nothing but empty space before him, and never, under any circumstances, turned aside. I gloated over my resentment watching him and . . . always resentfully made way for him. It exasperated me that even in the street I could not be an an even footing with him.

"Why must you invariably be the first to move aside?" I kept asking myself in hysterical rage waking up sometimes at three o'clock in the morning. "Why is it you and not he? There's no regulation about it; there's no written law. Let the making way be equal as it usually

9. Nevsky Prospekt, the most elegant main street in St. Petersburg, about three miles long; now called "Prospekt of the 25th October."

is when refined people meet: he moves half-way and you move half-way; you pass with mutual respect."

But that never happened, and I always moved aside, while he did not even notice my making way for him. And lo and behold a bright idea dawned up on! "What," I thought, "if I meet him and don't move on one side? What if I don't move aside on purpose, even if I knock up against him? How would that be?" This audacious idea took such a hold on me that it gave me no peace. I was dreaming of it continually, horribly, and I purposely went more frequently to the Nevsky in order to picture more vividly how I should do it when I did do it. I was delighted. This intention seemed to me more and more practical and possible.

"Of course I shall not really push him," I thought, already more good-natured in my joy. "I will simply not turn aside, will run up against him, not very violently, but just shouldering each other— just as much as decency permits. I will push against him just as much as he pushes against me." At last I made up my mind completely. But my preparations took a great deal of time. To begin with, when I carried out my plan I should need to be looking rather more decent, and so I had to think of my get-up. "In case of emergency, if, for instance, there were any sort of public scandal (and the public there is of the most *recherché*: the Countess walks there; Prince D. walks there; all of the literary world is there), I must be well dressed; that inspires respect and of itself puts on an an equal footing in the eyes of society."

With this object I asked for some of my salary in advance, and bought at Churkin's a pair of black gloves and a decent hat. Black gloves seemed to me both more dignified and *bon ton* than the lemon-coloured ones which I had contemplated at first. "The colour is too gaudy, it looks as though one were trying to be conspicuous," and I did not take the lemon-coloured ones. I had got ready long before-hand a good shirt, with white bone studs; my overcoat was the only thing that held me back. The coat in itself was a very good one, it kept me warm; but it was wadded and it had a raccoon collar which was the height of vulgarity. I had to change the collar at any sacrifice, and to have a beaver one like an officer's. For this purpose I began visiting the Gostiny Dvor[1] and after several attempts I pitched upon a piece of cheap German beaver. Though these German beavers soon grow shabby and look wretched, yet at first they look exceedingly well, and I only needed it for one occasion. I asked the price; even so, it was too expensive. After thinking it over thoroughly I decided to sell my raccoon collar. The rest of the money—a considerable sum for me, I decided to borrow from Anton Antonich

---

1. Originally a guesthouse for foreign merchants; later used for displaying their wares.

Syetochkin, my immediate superior, an unassumng person, though grave and judicious. He never lent money to any one, but I had, on entering the service, been specially recommended to him by an important personage who had got me my berth. I was horribly worried. To borrow from Anton Antonich seemed to me monstrous and shameful. I did not sleep for two or three nights. Indeed, I did not sleep well at that time, I was in a fever; I had a vague sinking at my heart or else a sudden throbbing, throbbing, throbbing! Anton Antonich was surprised at first, then he frowned, then he reflected, and did after all lend me the money, receiving from me a written authorization to take from my salary a fortnight later the sum that he had lent me.

In this way everything was at last ready. The handsome beaver replaced the mean-looking raccoon, and I began by degrees to get to work. I would never have done to act off-hand, at random; the plan had to be carried out skilfully, by degrees. But I must confess that after many efforts I began to despair: we simply could not run into each other. I made every preparation, I was quite determined—it seemed as though we should run into one another directly—and before I knew what I was doing I had stepped aside for him again and he had passed without noticing me. I even prayed as I approached him that God would grant me determination. One time I had made up my mind thoroughly, but it ended in my stumbling and falling at his feet because at the very last instant when I was six inches from him my courage failed me. He very calmly stepped over me, while I flew on one side like a ball. That night I was ill again, feverish and delirious.

And suddenly it ended most happily. The night before I had made up my mind not to carry out my fatal plan and to abandon it all, and with that object I went to the Nevsky for the last time, just to see how I would abandon it all. Suddenly, three paces from my enemy, I unexpectedly made up my mind—I closed my eyes, and we ran full tilt, shoulder to shoulder, against one another! I did not budge an inch and passed him on a perfectly equal footing! He did not even look round and pretended not to notice it; but he was only pretending, I am convinced of that. I am convinced of that to this day! Of course, I got the worst of it—he was stronger, but that was not he point. The point was that I had attained my object, I had kept up my dignity, I had not yielded a step, and had put myself publicly on an equal social footing with him. I returned home feeling that I was fully avenged for everything. I was delighted. I was triumphant and sang Italian arias. Of course, I will not describe to you what happened to me three days later; if you have read my first chapter you can guess that for yourself. The officer was afterwards transferred; I have not seen him now for fourteen years. What is the dear fellow doing now? Whom is he walking over?

II

But the period of my dissipation would end and I always felt very sick afterwards. It was followed by remorse—I tried to drive it away: I felt too sick. By degrees, however, I grew used to that too. I grew used to everything, or rather I voluntarily resigned myself to enduring it. But I had a means of escape that reconciled everything—that was to find refuge in "the good and the beautiful," in dreams, of course. I was a terrible dreamer, I would dream for three months on end, tucked away in my corner, and you may believe me that at those moments I had no resemblance to the gentleman who, in the perturbation of his chicken heart, put a collar of German beaver on his great coat. I suddenly became a hero. I would not have admitted my six-foot lieutenant even if he had called on me. I could not even picture him before me then. What were my dreams and how I could satisfy myself with them—it is hard to say now, but at the time I was satisfied with them. Though, indeed, even now, I am to some extent satisfied with them. Dreams were particularly sweet and vivid after a spell of dissipation; they came with remorse and with tears, with curses and transports. There were moments of such positive intoxication, of such happiness, that there was not the faintest trace of irony within me, on my honour. I had faith, hope, love. I believed blindly at such times that by some miracle, by some external circumstance, all this would suddenly open out, expand; that suddenly a vista of suitable activity—beneficent, good, and, above all, *ready made* (what sort of activity I had no idea, but the great thing was that it should be all ready for me)—would rise up before me—and I should come out into the light of day, almost riding a white horse and crowned with laurel. Anything but the foremost place I could not conceive for myself, and for that very reason I quite contentedly occupied the lowest in reality. Either to be a hero or to grovel in the mud—there was nothing between. That was my ruin, for when I was in the mud I comforted myself with the thought that at other times I was a hero, and the hero was a cloak for the mud: for an ordinary man it was shameful to defile himself, but a hero was too lofty to be utterly defiled, and so he might defile himself. It is worth noting that these attacks of the "good and the beautiful" visited me even during the period of dissipation and just at the times when I was touching bottom. They came in separate spurts, as though reminding me of themselves, but did not banish the dissipation by their appearance. On the contrary, they seemed to add a zest to it by contrast, and were only sufficiently present to serve as an appetizing sauce. That sauce was made up of contradictions and sufferings, of agonizing inward analysis, and all these pangs and pinpricks gave a certain piquancy, even a significance to my dissipation—in fact, completely answered the purpose of an appetizing sauce. There was a certain depth of meaning in it. And I could hardly have resigned myself to the simple, vulgar, direct debauchery of a clerk and have endured all the filthiness of it. What could have allured me about it then and have drawn me at night into the street? No, I had a lofty way of getting out of it all.

And what loving-kindness, oh Lord, what loving-kindness I felt at times in those dreams of mine! in those "flights into the good and the beautiful"; though it was fantastic love, though it was never applied to anything human in reality, yet there was so much of this love that one did not feel afterwards even the impulse to apply it in reality; that would have been superfluous. Everything, however, passed satisfactorily by a lazy and fascinating transition into the sphere of art, that is, into the beautiful forms of life, lying ready, largely stolen from the poets and novelists and adapted to all sorts of needs and uses. I, for instance, was triumphant over every one; every one, of course, was in dust and ashes, and was forced spontaneously to recognize my superiority, and I forgave them all. I was a poet and a grand gentleman, I fell in love; I came in for countless millions and immediately devoted them to humanity, and at the same time I confessed before all the people my shameful deeds, which, of course, were not merely shameful, but had in them much that was "good and beautiful" something in the Manfred[2] style. Every one would kiss me and weep (what idiots they would be if they did not), while I should go barefoot and hungry preaching new ideas and fighting a victorious Austerlitz[3] against the obscurantists. Then the band would play a march, an amnesty would be declared, the Pope would agree to retire from Rome to Brazil; then there would be a ball for the whole of Italy at the Villa Borghese on the shores of the Lake of Como,[4] the Lake of Como being for that purpose transferred to the neighbourhood of Rome; then would come a scene in the bushes, and so on, and so on—as though you did not know all about it? You will say that it is vulgar and contemptible to drag all this into public after all the tears and transports which I have myself confessed. But why is it contemptible? Can you imagine that I am ashamed of it all, and that it was stupider than anything in your life, gentlemen? And I can assure you that some of these fancies were by no means badly

---

2. The hero of Lord Byron's verse drama *Manfred* (1817), who was oppressed by a mysterious guilt.   3. A village near Brno, the capital of Moravia, now in Czechoslovakia, where Napoleon defeated the combined Austrian and Russian armies in 1805.   4. Villa Borghese is in Rome, Lake Como on the border between Italy and Switzerland.

composed. . . . It did not all happen on the shores of Lake Como. And yet you are right—it really is vulgar and contemptible. And most contemptible of all it is that now I am attempting to justify myself to you. And even more contemptible than that is my making this remark now. But that's enough, or there will be no end to it: each step will be more contemptible than the last. . . .

I could never stand more than three months of dreaming at a time without feeling an irresistible desire to plunge into society. To plunge into society meant to visit my superior at the office, Anton Antonich Syetochkin. He was the only permanent acquaintance I have had in my life, and wonder at the fact myself now. But I only went to see him when that phase came over me, and when my dreams had reached such a point of bliss that it became essential at once to embrace my fellows and all mankind; and for that purpose I needed, at least, one human being, actually existing. I had to call on Anton Antonich, however, on Tuesday—his at-home day; so I had always to time my passionate desire to embrace humanity so that it might fall on a Tuesday.

This Anton Antonich lived on the fourth storey in a house in Five Corners, in four low-pitched rooms, one smaller than the other, of a particularly frugal and sallow appearance. He had two daughters and their aunt, who used to pour out the tea. Of the daughters one was thirteen and another fourteen, they both had snub noses, and I was awfully shy of them because they were always whispering and giggling together. The master of the house usually sat in his study on a leather couch in front of the table with some grey-headed gentlemen, usually a colleague from our office or some other department. I never saw more than two or three visitors there, always the same. They talked about the excise duty; about business in the Senate,[5] about salaries, about promotions, about His Excellency, and the best means of pleasing him, and so on. I had the patience to sit like a fool beside these people for four hours at a stretch, listening to them without knowing what to say to them or venturing to say a word. I became stupefied, several times I felt myself perspiring, I was overcome by a sort of paralysis; but this was pleasant and good for me. On returning home I deferred for a time my desire to embrace all mankind.

I had however one other acquaintance of a sort, Simonov, who was an old schoolfellow. I had a number of schoolfellows, indeed, in Petersburg, but I did not associate with them and had even given up nodding to them in the street. I believe I had transferred into the department I was in simply to avoid their company and to cut off all connection with my hateful childhood. Curses on that school and

---

5. The Russian Senate was at that time not a parliamentary body, but a high court.

all those terrible years of penal servitude! In short, I parted from my schoolfellows as soon as I got out into the world. There were two or three left to whom I nodded in the street. One of them was Simonov, who had been in no way distinguished at school, was of a quiet and equable disposition; but I discovered in him a certain independence of character and even honesty. I don't even suppose that he was particularly stupid. I had at one time spent some rather soulful moments with him, but these had not lasted long and had somehow been suddenly clouded over. He was evidently uncomfortable at these reminiscences, and was, I fancy, always afraid that I might take up the same tone again. I suspected that he had an aversion for me, but still I went on going to see him, not being quite certain of it.

And so on one occasion, unable to endure my solitude and knowing that as it was Thursday Anton Antonich's door would be closed, I thought of Simonov. Climbing up to his fourth storey I was thinking that the man disliked me and that it was a mistake to go and see him. But as it always happened that such reflections impelled me, as though purposely, to put myself into a false position, I went in. It was almost a year since I had last seen Simonov.

III

I found two of my old schoolfellows with him. They seemed to be discussing an important matter. All of them took scarcely any notice of my entrance, which was strange, for I had not met them for years. Evidently they looked upon me as something on the level of a common fly. I had not been treated like that even at school, though they all hated me. I knew, of course, that they must despise me now for my lack of success in the service, and for my having let myself sink so low, going about badly dressed and so on—which seemed to them a sign of my incapacity and insignificance. But I had not expected such contempt. Simonov was positively surprised at my turning up. Even in old days he had always seemed surprised at my coming. All this disconcerted me: I sat down, feeling rather miserable, and began listening to what they were saying.

They were engaged in warm and earnest conversation about a farewell dinner which they wanted to arrange for the next day to a comrade of theirs called Zverkov, an officer in the army, who was going away to a distant province. This Zverkov had been all the time at school with me too. I had begun to hate him particularly in the upper grades. In the lower grades he had simply been a pretty, playful boy whom everybody liked. I had hated him, however, even in the lower grades, just because he was a pretty and playful boy. He was always bad at his lessons and got worse and worse as he went on;

however, he left with a good certificate, as he had powerful interest. During his last year at school he came in for an estate of two hundred serfs, and as almost all of us were poor he took up a swaggering tone among us. He was vulgar in the extreme, but at the same time he was a good-natured fellow, even in his swaggering. In spite of superficial, fantastic, and sham notions of honour and dignity, all but very few of us positively grovelled before Zverkov, and the more so the more he swaggered. And it was not from any interested motive that they grovelled, but simply because he had been favoured by the gifts of nature. Moreover, it was, as it were, an accepted idea among us that Zverkov was a specialist in regard to tact and ths social graces. This last particularly infuriated me. I hated the abrupt self-confident tone of his voice, his admiration of his own witticisms, which were often frightfully stupid, though he was bold in his language; I hated his handsome, but stupid face (for which I would, however, have gladly exchanged my intelligent one), and the free-and-easy military manners in fashion in the 'forties. I hated the way in which he used to talk of his future conquests of women (he did not venture to begin his attack upon women until he had the epaulettes of an officer, and was looking forward to them with impatience), and boasted of the duels he would constantly be fighting. I remember how I, invariably so taciturn, suddenly fastened upon Zverkov, when one day talking at a leisure moment with his schoolfellows of his future relations with the fair sex, and growing as sportive as a puppy in the sun, he all at once declared that he would not leave a single village girl on his estate unnoticed, that that was his *droit de seigneur*,[6] and that if the peasants dared to protest he would have them all flogged and double the tax on them, the bearded rascals. Our servile rabble applauded, but I attacked him, not from compassion for the girls and their fathers, but simply because they were applauding such an insect. I got the better of him on that occasion, but though Zverkov was stupid he was lively and impudent, and so laughed it off, and in such a way that my victory was not really complete: the laugh was on his side. He got the better of me on several occasions afterwards, but without malice, jestingly, casually. I remained angrily and contemptuously silent and would not answer him. When we left school he made advances to me; I did not rebuff them, for I was flattered, but we soon parted and quite naturally. Afterwards I heard of his barrack-room success as a lieutenant, and of the fast life he was leading. Then there came other rumours—of his successes in the service. By then he had taken to cutting me in the street, and I suspected that he was afraid of compromising himself by greeting a personage as

6. "The right of the master," i.e., to all the women serfs.

insignificant as me. I saw him once in the theatre, in the third tier of boxes. By then he was wearing shoulder-straps. He was twisting and twirling about, ingratiating himself with the daughters of an ancient General. In three years he had gone off considerably, though he was still rather handsome and adroit. One could see that by the time he was thirty he could be corpulent. So it was to this Zverkov that my school-fellows were going to give a dinner on his departure. They had kept up with him for those three years, though privately they did not consider themselves on an equal footing with him, I am convinced of that.

Of Simonov's two visitors, one was Ferfichkin, a Russianized German—a little fellow with the face of a monkey, a blockhead who was always deriding every one, a very bitter enemy of mine from our days in the lower grades—a vulgar, impudent, swaggering fellow, who affected a most sensitive feeling of personal honour, though, of course, he was a wretched little coward at heart. He was one of those worshippers of Zverkov who made up to the latter from interested motives, and often borrowed money from him. Simonov's other visitor, Trudolyubov, was a person in no way remarkable—a tall young fellow, in the army, with a cold face, fairly honest, though he worshipped success of every sort, and was only capable of thinking of promotion. He was some sort of distant relation of Zverkov's, and this, foolish as it seems, gave him a certain importance among us. He always thought me of no consequence whatever; his behaviour to me, though not quite courteous, was tolerable.

"Well, with seven roubles each," said Trudolyubov, "twenty-one roubles between the three of us, we ought to be able to get a good dinner. Zverkov, of course, won't pay."

"Of course not, since we are inviting him," Simonov decided.

"Can you imagine," Ferfichkin interrupted hotly and conceitedly, like some insolent flunkey boasting of his master the General's decorations, "can you imagine that Zverkov will let us pay alone? He will accept from delicacy, but he will order half a dozen bottles of champagne."

"Do we want half a dozen for the four of us?" observed Trudolyubov, taking notice only of the half-dozen.

"So the three of us, with Zverkov for the fourth, twenty-one roubles, at the Hôtel de Paris at five o'clock to-morrow," Simonov, who had been asked to make the arrangements, concluded finally.

"How twenty-one roubles?" I asked in some agitation, with a show of being offended; "if you count me it will not be twenty-one, but twenty-eight roubles."

It seemed to me that to invite myself so suddenly and unexpectedly would be positively graceful, and that they would all be conquered at once and would look at me with respect.

"Do you want to join, too?" Simonov observed, with no appearance of pleasure, seeming to avoid looking at me. He knew me through and through.

It infuriated me that he knew me so thoroughly.

"Why not? I am an old schoolfellow of his, too, I believe, and I must own I feel hurt that you have left me out," I said, boiling over again.

"And where were we to find you?" Ferfichkin put in roughly.

"You never were on good terms with Zverkov," Trudolyubov added, frowning.

But I had already clutched at the idea and would not give it up.

"It seems to me that no one has a right to form an opinion upon that," I retorted in a shaking voice, as though something tremendous had happened. "Perhaps that is just my reason for wishing it now, that I have not always been on good terms with him."

"Oh, there's no making you out . . . with these refinements," Trudolyubov jeered.

"We'll put your name down," Simonov decided, addressing me. "To-morrow at five o'clock at the Hôtel de Paris."

"What about the money?" Ferfichkin began in an undertone, indicating me to Simonov, but he broke off, for even Simonov was embarrassed.

"That will do," said Trudolyubov, getting up. "If he wants to come so much, let him."

"But it's a private thing, between us friends," Ferfichkin said crossly, as he, too, picked up his hat. "It's not an official gathering."

"We do not want at all, perhaps . . ."

They went away. Ferfichkin did not greet me in any way as he went out, Trudolyubov barely nodded. Simonov, with whom I was left *tête-à-tête*, was in a state of vexation and perplexity, and looked at me queerly. He did not sit down and did not ask me to.

"H'm . . . yes . . . to-morrow, then. Will you pay your subscription now? I just ask so as to know," he muttered in embarrassment.

I flushed crimson, and as I did so I remembered that I had owed Simonov fifteen roubles for ages—which I had, indeed, never forgotten, though I had not paid it.

"You will understand, Simonov, that I could have no idea when I came here. . . . I am very much vexed that I have forgotten. . . ."

"All right, all right, that doesn't matter. You can pay to-morrow after the dinner. I simply wanted to know. . . . Please don't . . ."

He broke off and began pacing the room still more vexed. As he walked he began to stamp with his heels.

"Am I keeping you?" I asked, after two minutes of silence.

"Oh!" he said, starting, "that is—to be truthful—yes. I have to go and see some one . . . not far from here," he added in an apologetic voice, somewhat abashed.

"My goodness, why didn't you say so?" I cried, seizing my cap, with an astonishingly free-and-easy air, which was the last thing I should have expected of myself.

"It's close by . . . not two passes away," Simonov repeated, accompanying me to the front door with a fussy air which did not suit him at all. "So five o'clock, punctually, to-morrow," he called down the stairs after me. He was very glad to get rid of me. I was in a fury.

"What possessed me, what possessed me to force myself upon them?" I wondered, grinding my teeth as I strode along the street, "for a scoundrel, a pig like that Zverkov! Of course, I had better not go; of course, I must just snap my fingers at them. I am not bound in any way. I'll send Simonov a note by to-morrow's post. . . ."

But what made me furious was that I knew for certain that I should go, that I should make a point of going; and the more tactless, the more unseemly my going would be, the more certainly I would go.

And there was a positive obstacle to my going: I had no money. All I had was nine roubles, I had to give seven of that to my servant, Apollon, for his monthly wages. That was all I paid him—he had to keep himself.

Not to pay him was impossible, considering his character. But I will talk about that fellow, about that plague of mine, another time. However, I knew I should go and should not pay him his wages.

That night I had the most hideous dreams. No wonder; all the evening I had been oppressed by memories of my miserable days at school, and I could not shake them off. I was sent to the school by distant relations, upon whom I was dependent and of whom I have heard nothing since—they sent me there a forlorn, silent boy, already crushed by their reproaches, already troubled by doubt, and looking with savage distrust at every one. My schoolfellows met me with spiteful and merciless jibes because I was not like any of them. But I could not endure their taunts; I could not give in to them with the ignoble readiness with which they gave in to one another. I hated them from the first, and shut myself away from every one in timid, wounded, and disproportionate pride. Their coarseness revolted me. They laughed cynically at my face, at my clumsy figure; and yet what stupid faces they had themselves. In our school the boys' faces seemed in a special way to degenerate and grow stupider. How many fine-looking boys came to us! In a few years they became repulsive. Even at sixteen I wondered at them morosely; even then I was struck by the pettiness of their thoughts, the stupidity of their pursuits, their games, their conversations. They had no understanding of such essential things, they took no interest in such striking, impressive subjects, that I could not help considering them inferior to myself. It was not wounded vanity that drove me to it, and for God's sake do not thrust open me your hackneyed remarks, repeated to nausea, that "I was only a dreamer," while they even then had an understanding of life. They understood nothing, they had no idea of real life, and I swear that that was what made me most indignant with them. On the contrary, the most obvious, striking reality they accepted with fantastic stupidity and even at that time were accustomed to respect success. Everything that was just, but oppressed and looked down upon, they laughed at heartlessly and shamefully. They took rank for intelligence; even at sixteen they were already talking about a snug berth. Of course, a great deal of it was due to their stupidity, to the bad examples with which they had always been surrounded in their childhood and boyhood. They were monstrously depraved. Of course a great deal of that, too, was superficial and an assumption of cynicism; of course there were glimpses of youth and freshness even in their depravity; but even that freshness was not attractive, and showed itself in a certain rakishness. I hated them horribly, though perhaps I was worse than any of them. They repaid me in the same way, and did not conceal their aversion for me. But by then I did not desire their affection: on the contrary I continually longed for their humiliation. To escape from their derision I purposely began to make all the progress I could with my studies and forced my way to the very top. This impressed them. Moreover, they all began by degrees to grasp that I had already read books none of them could read, and understood things (not forming part of our school curriculum) of which they had not even heard. They took a savage and sarcastic view of it, but were morally impressed, especially as the teachers began to notice me on those grounds. The mockery ceased, but the hostility remained, and cold and strained relations became permanent between us. In the end I could not put up with it: with years a craving for society, for friends, developed in me. I attempted to get on friendly terms with some of my schoolfellows; but somehow or other my intimacy with them was always strained and soon ended of itself. Once, indeed, I did have a friend. But I was already a tyrant at heart; I wanted to exercise unbounded sway over him; I tried to instil into him a contempt for his surroundings; I required of him a disdainful and complete break with those surroundings. I frightened him with my passionate affection; I reduced him to tears, to hysterics. He was a simple and devoted soul; but when he devoted himself to me entirely I began to hate him immediately and repulsed him— as though all I needed him for was to win a victory over him, to subjugate him and nothing else. But I could not subjugate all of them; my friend was not at all like them either, he was, in fact, a rare exception. The first thing I did on leaving school was to give up the special job for which I had been destined so as a to break all ties, to curse my past and shake the dust from off my feet. . . . And goodness knows why, after all that, I should go trudging off to Simonov's!

Early next morning I roused myself and jumped out of bed with excitement, as though it were all about to happen at once. But I believed that some radical change in my life was coming, and would inevitably come that day. Owing to its rarity, perhaps, any external event, however trivial, always made me feel as though some radical change in my life were at hand. I went to the office, however, as usual, but sneaked away home two hours earlier to get ready. The great thing, I thought, is not to be the first to arrive, or they will think I am overjoyed at coming. But there were thousands of such great points to consider, and they all agitated and overwhelmed me. I polished my boots a second time with my own hands; nothing in the world would have induced Apollon to clean them twice a day, as he considered that it was more than his duties required of him. I stole the brushes to clean them from the passage, being careful he should not detect it, for fear of his contempt. Then I minutely examined my clothes and thought that everything looked old, worn, and threadbare. I had let myself get too slovenly. My uniform, perhaps, was tidy, but I could not go out to dinner in my uniform. The worst of it was that on the knee of my trousers was a big yellow stain. I had a foreboding that that stain would deprive me of nine-tenths of my personal dignity. I knew, too, that it was very bad to think so. "But this is no time for thinking: now I am in for the real thing," I thought, and my heart sank. I knew, too, perfectly well even then, that I was monstrously exaggerating the facts. But how could I help it? I could not control myself and was already shaking with fever. With despair I pictured to myself how coldly and disdainfully that "scoundrel" Zverkov would meet me; with what dull-witted, invincible contempt the blockhead Trudolyubov would look at me; with what impudent rudeness the insect Ferfichkin would snigger at me in order to curry favour with Zverkov; how completely Simonov would take it all in, and how he would despise me for the abjectness of my vanity and lack of spirit—and, worst of all, how paltry, *unliterary*, commonplace it would all be. Of course, the best thing would be not to go at all. But that was most impossible of all: if I feel impelled to do anything, I seem to be pitchforked into it. I should have jeered at myself ever afterwards: "So you funked it, you funked it, you funked the *real thing!*" On the contrary, I passionately longed to show all that "rabble" that I was by no means such a spiritless creature as I seemed to myself. What is more, even in the acutest paroxysm of this cowardly fever, I dreamed of getting the upper hand, of dominating them,

carrying them away, making them like me—if only for my "elevation of thought and unmistakable wit." They would abandon Zverkov, he would sit on one side, silent and ashamed, while I should
crush him. Then, perhaps, we would be reconciled and drink to our
everlasting friendship; but what was most bitter and most humiliating
for me was that I knew even then, knew fully and for certain, that I
needed nothing of all this really, that I did not really want to crush,
to subdue, to attract them, and that I did not care a straw really for
the result, even if I did achieve it. Oh, how I prayed for the day to
pass quickly! In unutterable anguish I went to the window, opened
the movable pane and looked out into the troubled darkness of the
thickly falling wet snow. At last my wretched little clock hissed out
five. I seized my hat and trying not to look at Apollon, who had been
all day expecting his month's wages, but in his foolishness was
unwilling to be the first to speak about it, I slipt between him and
the door and jumping into a high-class sledge, on which I spent my
last half rouble, I drove up in grand style to the Hôtel de Paris.

IV

I had been certain the day before that I should be the first to arrive.
But it was not a question of being the first to arrive. Not only were
they not there, but I had difficulty in finding our room. The table
was not laid even. What did it mean? After a good many questions I
elicited from the waiters that the dinner had been ordered not for
five, but for six o'clock. This was confirmed at the buffet too. I felt
really ashamed to go on questioning them. It was only twenty-five
minutes past five. If they changed the dinner hour they ought at least
to have let me know—that is what the post is for, and not to have
put me in an absurd position in my own eyes and . . . and even
before the waiters. I sat down; the servant began laying the table; I
felt even more humiliated when he was present. Toward six o'clock
they brought in candles, though there were lamps burning in the
room. It had not occurred to the waiter, however, to bring them in
at once when I arrived. In the next room two gloomy, angry-looking
persons were eating their dinners in silence at two different tables.
There was a great deal of noise, even shouting, in a room further
away; one could hear the laughter of a crowd of people, and nasty
little shrieks in French: there were ladies at the dinner. It was sick-
ening, in fact. I rarely passed more unpleasant moments, so much
so that when they did arrive all together punctually at six I was overjoyed to see them, as though they were my deliverers, and even
forgot that it was incumbent upon me to show resentment.

Zverkov walked in at the head of them; evidently he was the leading spirit. He and all of them were laughing; but, seeing me, Zver-

kov drew himself up a little, walked up to me deliberately with a slight, rather jaunty bend from the waist. He shook hands with me in a friendly, but not over-friendly, fashion, with a sort of circumspect courtesy like that of a General, as though in giving me his hand he were warding off something. I had imagined, on the contrary, that on coming in he would at once break into his habitual thin, shrill laugh and fall to making his insipid jokes and witticisms. I had been preparing for them ever since the previous day, but I had not expected such condescension, such high-official courtesy. So, then, he felt himself ineffably superior to me in every respect! If he only meant to insult me by that high-official tone, if would not matter, I thought—I could pay him back for it one way or another. But what if, in reality, without the least desire to be offensive, that sheepshead had a notion in earnest that he was superior to me and could only look at me in a patronizing way? The very supposition made me gasp.

"I was surprised to hear of your desire to join us," he began, lisping and drawling, which was something new. "You and I seem to have seen nothing of one another. You fight shy of us. You shouldn't. We are not such terrible people as you think. Well, anyway, I am glad to renew our acquaintance."

And he turned carelessly to put down his hat on the window.

"Have you been waiting long?" Trudolyubov inquired.

"I arrived at five o'clock as you told me yesterday," I answered aloud, with an irritability that threatened an explosion.

"Didn't you let him know that we had changed the hour?" said Trudolyubov to Simonov.

"No, I didn't. I forgot," the latter replied, with no sign of regret, and without even apologizing to me he went off to order the *hors d'œuvres*.

"So you've been here a whole hour? Oh, poor fellow!" Zverkov cried ironically, for to his notions this was bound to be extremely funny. That rascal Ferfichkin followed with his nasty little snigger like a puppy yapping. My position struck him, too, as exquisitely ludicrous and embarrassing.

"It isn't funny at all!" I cried to Ferfichkin, more and more irritated. "It wasn't my fault, but other people's. They neglected to let me know. It was . . . it was . . . it was simply absurd."

"It's not only absurd, but something else as well," muttered Trudolyubov, naïvely taking my part. "You are not hard enough upon it. It was simply rudeness—unintentional, of course. And how could Simonov . . . h'm!"

"If a trick like that had been played on me," observed Ferfichkin, "I should . . ."

"But you should have ordered something for yourself," Zverkov interrupted, "or simply asked for dinner without waiting for us."

"You will allow that I might have done that without your permission," I rapped out. "If I waited, it was . . ."

"Let us sit down, gentlemen," cried Simonov, coming in. "Everything is ready; I can answer for the champagne; it is capitally frozen. . . . You see, I did not know your address, where was I to look for you?" he suddenly turned to me, but again he seemed to avoid looking at me. Evidently he had something against me. It must have been what happened yesterday.

All sat down; I did the same. It was a round table. Trudolyubov was on my left, Simonov on my right. Zverkov was sitting opposite, Ferfichkin next to him, between him and Trudolyubov.

"Tell me, are you . . . in a government office?" Zverkov went on attending to me. Seeing that I was embarrassed he seriously thought that he ought to be friendly to me, and, so to speak, cheer me up.

"Does he want me to throw a bottle at his head?" I thought, in a fury. In my novel surroundings I was unnaturally ready to be irritated.

"In the N—— office," I answered jerkily, with my eyes on my plate.

"And ha-ave you a go-ood berth? I say, what ma-a-de you leave your original job?"

"What ma-a-de me was that I wanted to leave my original job," I drawled more than he, hardly able to control myself. Ferfichkin went off into a guffaw. Simonov looked at me ironically. Trudolyubov left off eating and began looking at me with curiosity.

Zverkov winced, but he tried not to notice it.

"And the remuneration?"

"What remuneration?"

"I mean, your sa-a-lary?"

"Why are you cross-examining me?" However, I told him at once what my salary was. I turned horribly red.

"It is not very handsome," Zverkov observed majestically.

"Yes, you can't afford to dine at cafés on that," Ferfichkin added insolently.

"To my thinking it's very poor," Trudolyubov observed gravely.

"And how thin you have grown! How you have changed!" added Zverkov, with a shade of venom in his voice, scanning me and my attire with a sort of insolent compassion.

"Oh, spare his blushes," cried Ferfichkin, sniggering.

"My dear sir, allow me to tell you I am not blushing," I broke out at last; "do you hear? I am dining here, at this café, at my own expense, not at other people's—note that, Mr. Ferfichkin."

"Wha-at? Isn't every one here dining at his own expense? You would seem to be . . ." Ferfichkin flew out at me, turning as red as a lobster, and looking me in the face with fury.

"Tha-at," I answered, feeling I had gone too far, "and I imagine it would be better to talk of something more intelligent."

"You intend to show off your intelligence, I suppose?"

"Don't disturb yourself, that would be quite out of place here."

"Why are you clacking away like that, my good sir, eh? Have you gone out of yours wits in your office?"

"Enough, gentlemen, enough!" Zverkov cried, authoritatively.

"How stupid it is!" muttered Simonov.

"It really is stupid. We have met here, a company of friends, for a farewell dinner to a comrade and you carry on an altercation," said Trudolyubov, rudely addressing himself to me alone. "You invited yourself to join us, so don't disturb the general harmony."

"Enough, enough!" cried Zverkov. "Give over, gentlemen, it's out of place. Better let me tell you how I nearly got married the day before yesterday. . . ."

And then followed a burlesque narrative of how this gentleman had almost been married two days before. There was not a word about the marriage, however, but the story was adorned with generals, colonels, and gentlemen-in-waiting, while Zverkov almost took the lead among them. It was greeted with approving laughter; Ferfichkin positively squealed.

No one paid any attention to me, and I sat crushed and humiliated.

"Good Heavens, these are not the people for me!" I thought. "And what a fool I have made of myself before them! I let Ferfichkin go too far, though. The brutes imagine they are doing me an honour in letting me sit down with them. They don't understand that it's an honour to them and not to me! I've grown thinner! My clothes! Oh, damn my trousers! Zverkov noticed the yellow stain on the knee as soon as he came in. . . . But what's the use! I must get up at once, this very minute, take my hat and simply go without a word . . . with contempt! And to-morrow I can send a challenge. The scoundrels! As though I cared about the seven roubles. They may think. . . . Damn it! I don't care about the seven roubles. I'll go this minute!"

Of course I remained. I drank sherry and Lafitte by the glassful in my discomfiture. Being unaccustomed to it, I was quickly affected. My annoyance increased as the wine went to my head. I longed all at once to insult them all in a most flagrant manner and then go away. To seize the moment and show what I could do, so that they would say, "He's clever, though he is absurd," and . . . and . . . in fact, damn them all!

I scanned them all insolently with my drowsy eyes. But they seemed to have forgotten me altogether. They were noisy, vociferous, cheerful. Zverkov was talking all the time. I began listening. Zverkov wa̍ talking of some exuberant lady whom he had at last led on to declaring her love (of course, he was lying like a horse), and how he had been helped in this affair by an intimate friend of his, a Prince Kolya, an officer in the hussars, who had three thousand serfs.

"And yet this Kolya, who has three thousand serfs, has not put in an appearance here to-night to see you off," I cut in suddenly.

For a minute every one was silent. "You are drunk already." Trudolyubov deigned to notice me at last, glancing contemptuously in my direction. Zverkov, without a word, examined me as though I were an insect. I dropped my eyes. Simonov made haste to fill up the glasses with champagne.

Trudolyubov raised his glass, as did every one else but me.

"Your health and good luck on the journey!" he cried to Zverkov. "To old times, to our future, hurrah!"

They all tossed off their glasses, and crowded round Zverkov to kiss him. I did not move; my full glass stood untouched before me.

"Why, aren't you going to drink it?" roared Trudolyubov, losing patience and turning menacingly to me.

"I want to make a speech separately, on my own account . . . and then I'll drink it, Mr. Trudolyubov."

"Spiteful brute!" muttered Simonov. I drew myself up in my chair and feverishly seized my glass, prepared for something extraordinary, though I did not know myself precisely what I was going to say.

"Silence!" cried Ferfichkin. "Now for a display of wit!"

Zverkov waited very gravely, knowing what was coming.

"Mr. Lieutenant Zverkov," I began, "let me tell you that I hate phrases, phrasemongers, and men in corsets . . . that's the first point, and there is a second one to follow it."

There was a general stir.

"The second point is: I hate ribaldry and ribald talkers. Especially ribald talkers! The third point: I love justice, truth, and honesty." I went on almost mechanically, for I was beginning to shiver with horror myself and had no idea how I came to be talking like this. "I love thought, Monsieur Zverkov; I love true comradeship, on an equal footing and not . . . H'm . . . I love. . . . But, however, why not? I will drink your health, too, Mr. Zverkov. Seduce the Circassian girls, shoot the enemies of the fatherland and . . . and . . . to your health, Monsieur Zverkov!"

Zverkov got up from his seat, bowed to me and said:

"I am very much obliged to you." He was frightfully offended and turned pale.

"Damn the fellow!" roared Trudolyubov, bringing his fist down on the table.

"Well, he wants a punch in the face for that," squealed Ferfichkin.

"We ought to turn him out," muttered Simonov.

"Not a word, gentlemen, not a movement!" cried Zverkov solemnly, checking the general indignation. "I thank you all, but I can show him for myself how much value I attach to his words."

"Mr. Ferfichkin, you will give me satisfaction to-morrow for your words just now!" I said aloud, turning with dignity to Ferfichkin.

"A duel, you mean? Certainly," he answered. But probably I was so ridiculous as I challenged him and it was so out of keeping with my appearance that everyone, including Ferfichkin, was prostrate with laughter.

"Yes, let him alone, of course! He is quite drunk," Trudolyubov said with disgust.

"I shall never forgive myself for letting him join us," Simonov muttered again.

"Now is the time to throw a bottle at their heads," I thought to myself. I picked up the bottle . . . and filled my glass. . . . "No, I'd better sit on to the end," I went on thinking; "you would be pleased, my friends if I went away. Nothing will induce me to go. I'll go on sitting here and drinking to the end, on purpose, as a sign that I don't think you of the slightest consequence. I will go on sitting and drinking, because this a public-house and I paid my entrance money. I'll sit here and drink, for I look upon you as so many pawns, as inanimate pawns. I'll sit here and drink . . . and sing if I want to, yes, sing, for I have the right to . . . to sing . . . H'm!"

But I did not sing. I simply tried not to look at any of them. I assumed most unconcerned attitudes and waited with impatience for them to speak first. But alas, they did not address me! And oh, how I wished, how I wished at that moment to be reconciled to them! It struck eight, at last nine. They moved from the table to the sofa. Zverkov stretched himself on a lounge and put one foot on a round table. Wine was brought there. He did, as a fact, order three bottles on his own account. I, of course, was not invited to join them. They all sat round him on the sofa. They listened to him, almost with reverence. It was evident that they were fond of him. "What for? What for?" I wondered. From time to time they were moved to drunken enthusiasm and kissed each other. They talked of the Caucasus, of the nature of true passion, of snug berths in the service, of the income of an hussar called Podkharzhevsky, whom none of them knew personally, and rejoiced in the largeness of it, of the extraordinary grace and beauty of a Princess D., whom none of them had ever seen; then it came to Shakespeare's being immortal.

I smiled contemptuously and walked up and down the other side of the room, opposite the sofa, from the table to the stove and back again. I tried my very utmost to show them that I could do without them, and yet I purposely made a noise with my boots, thumping with my heels. But it was all in vain. They paid no attention. I had the patience to walk up and down in front of them from eight o'clock till eleven, in the same place, from the table to the stove and back again. "I walk up and down to please myself and no one can prevent me." The waiter who came into the room stopped, from time to time, to look at me. I was somewhat giddy from turning round so often; at moments it seemed to me that I was in delirium. During those three hours I was three times soaked with sweat and dry again. At times, with an intense, acute pang I was stabbed to the heart by the thought that ten years, twenty years, forty years would pass, and that even in forty years I would remember with loathing and humiliation those filthiest, most ludicrous, and most awful moments of my life. No one could have gone out of his way to degrade himself more shamelessly, and I fully realized it, fully, and yet I went on pacing up and down from the table to the stove. "Oh, if you only knew what thoughts and feelings I am capable of, how cultured I am!" I thought at moments, mentally addressing the sofa on which my enemies were sitting. But my enemies behaved as though I were not in the room. Once—only once—they turned towards me, just when Zverkov was talking about Shakespeare, and I suddenly gave a contemptuous laugh. I laughed in such an affected and disgusting way that they all at once broke off their conversation, and silently and gravely for two minutes watched me walking up and down from the table to the stove, *taking no notice of them.* But nothing came of it: they said nothing, and two minutes later they ceased to notice me again. It struck eleven.

"Friends," cried Zverkov getting up from the sofa, "let us all be off now, *there!*"

"Of course, of course," the others assented. I turned sharply to Zverkov. I was so harassed, so exhausted, that I would have cut my throat to put an end to it. I was in a fervor; my hair, soaked with perspiration, stuck to my forehead and temples.

"Zverkov, I beg your pardon," I said abruptly and resolutely. "Ferfichkin, yours too, and every one's, every one's: I have insulted you all!"

"Aha! A duel is not in your line, old man," Ferfichkin hissed venomously.

It sent a sharp pang to my heart.

"No, it's not the duel I am afraid of, Ferfichkin! I am ready to fight you to-morrow, after we are reconciled. I insist upon it, in fact, and you cannot refuse. I want to show you that I am not afraid of a duel. You shall fire first and I shall fire into the air."

"He is comforting himself," said Simonov.

"He's simply raving," said Trudolyubov.

"But let us pass. Why are you barring our way? What do you want?" Zverkov answered disdainfully.

They were all flushed, their eyes were bright: they had been drinking heavily.

"I ask for your friendship, Zverkov; I insulted you, but . . ."

"Insulted? *You* insulted *me*? Understand, sir, that you never, under any circumstances, could possibly insult *me*."

"And that's enough for you. Out of the way!" concluded Trudolyubov.

"Olympia is mine, friends, that's agreed!" cried Zverkov.

"We won't dispute your right, we won't dispute your right," the others answered, laughing.

I stood as though spat upon. The party went noisily out of the room. Trudolyubov struck up some stupid song. Simonov remained behind for a moment to tip the waiters. I suddenly went up to him.

"Simonov! give me six roubles!" I said, with desperate resolution.

He looked at me in extreme amazement, with vacant eyes. He, too, was drunk.

"You don't mean you are coming with us?"

"Yes."

"I've no money," he snapped out, and with a scornful laugh he went out of the room.

I clutched at his overcoat. It was a nightmare.

"Simonov, I saw you had money. Why do you refuse me? Am I a scoundrel? Beware of refusing me: if you knew, if you knew why I am asking! My whole future, my whole plans depend upon it!"

Simonov pulled out the money and almost flung it at me.

"Take it, if you have no sense of shame!" he pronounced pitilessly, and ran to overtake them.

I was left for a moment alone. Disorder, the remains of dinner, a broken wine-glass on the floor, spilt wine, cigarette ends, fumes of drink and delirium in my brain, an agonizing misery in my heart and finally the waiter, who had seen and heard all and was looking inquisitively into my face.

"I am going there!" I cried. "Either they shall all go down on their knees to beg for my friendship, or I will give Zverkov a slap in the face!"

V

"So this is it, this is it at last—contact with real life," I muttered as I ran headlong downstairs. "This is very different from the Pope's leaving Rome and going to Brazil, very different from the ball on Lake Como!"

"You are a scoundrel," a thought flashed through my mind, "if you laugh at this now."

"No matter!" I cried, answering myself. "Now everything is lost!"

There was no trace to be seen of them, but that made no differ-ence—I knew where they had gone.

At the steps was standing a solitary night sledge-driver in a rough peasant coat, powdered over with the still falling, wet, and as it were warm, snow. It was hot and steamy. The little shaggy piebald horse was also covered with snow and coughing, I remember that very well. I made a rush for the roughly made sledge; but as soon as I raised my foot to get into it, the recollection of how Simonov had just given me six roubles seemed to double me up and I tumbled into the sledge like a sack.

"No, I must do a great deal to make up for all that," I cried. "But I will make up for it or perish on the spot this very night. Start!"

We set off. There was a perfect whirl in my head.

"They won't go down on their knees to beg for my friendship. That is a mirage, cheap mirage, revolting, romantic and fantasti-cal—that's another ball on Lake Como. And so I am bound to slap Zverkov's face! It is my duty to. And so it is settled; I am flying to give him a slap in the face. Hurry up!"

The driver tugged at the reins.

"As soon as I go in I'll give it him. Ought I before giving him the slap to say a few words by way of preface? No. I'll simply go in and give it him. They will all be sitting in the drawing-room, and he with Olympia on the sofa. That damned Olympia! She laughed at my looks on one occasion and refused me. I'll pull Olympia's hair, pull Zverkov's ears! No, better one ear, and pull him by it round the room. Maybe they will all begin beating me and will kick me out. That's most likely, indeed. No matter! Anyway, I shall first slap him; the initiative will be mine; and by the laws of honour that is everything: he will be branded and cannot wipe off the slap by any blows, by nothing but a duel. He will be forced to fight. And let them beat me now. Let them, the ungrateful wretches! Trudolyubov will beat me hardest, he is so strong; Ferfichkin will be sure to catch hold sideways and tug at my hair. But no matter, no matter! That's what I am going for. The blockheads will be forced at last to see the tragedy of it all! When they drag me to the door I shall call out to them that in reality they are not worth my little finger. Get on, driver, get on!" I cried to the driver. He started and flicked his whip, I shouted so savagely.

"We shall fight at daybreak, that's a settled thing. I've done with the office. Ferfichkin made a joke about it just now. But where can I get pistols? Nonsense! I'll get my salary in advance and buy them. And powder, and bullets? That's the second's business. And how can it all be done by daybreak? And where am I to get a second? I have no friends. Nonsense!" I cried, lashing myself up more and more. "It's of no consequence! the first person I meet in the street is bound to be my second, just as he would be bound to pull a drowning man out of water. The most eccentric things may happen. Even if I were to ask the director himself to be my second to-morrow, and to keep the secret! Anton Antonich. . . ."

The fact is, that at that very minute the disgusting absurdity of my plan and the other side of the question was clearer and more vivid to my imagination than it could be to any one on earth. But. . . .

"Get on, driver, get on, you rascal, get on!"

"Ugh, sir!" said the son of toil.

Cold shivers suddenly ran down me.

Wouldn't it be better . . . to go straight home? My God, my God! Why did I invite myself to this dinner yesterday? But no, it's impossible. And my walking up and down for three hours from the table to the stove? No, they, they and no one else must pay for my walking up and down! They must wipe out this dishonour! Drive on!

And what if they give me into custody? They won't dare! They'll be afraid of the scandal. And what if Zverkov is so contemptuous that he refuses to fight a duel? He is sure to; but in that case I'll show them . . . I will turn up at the posting station when he is setting off to-morrow, I'll catch him by the leg, I'll pull off his coat when he gets into the carriage. I'll get my teeth into his hand, I'll bite him. "See what lengths you can drive a desperate man to!" He may hit me on the head and they may belabour me from behind. I will shout to the assembled multitude: "Look at this young puppy who is driving off to captivate the Circassian girls after letting me spit in his face!"

Of course, after that everything will be over! The office will have vanished off the face of the earth. I shall be arrested, I shall be tried, I shall be dismissed from the service, thrown in prison, sent to Siberia. Never mind! In fifteen years when they let me out of prison I will trudge off to him, a beggar, in rags. I shall find him in some provincial town. He will be married and happy. He will have a grown-up daughter. . . . I shall say to him: "Look, monster, at my hollow cheeks and my rags! I've lost everything—my career, my happiness, art, science, *the woman I loved*, and all through you. Here are pistols. I have come to discharge my pistol and . . . and I . . . forgive you. Then I shall fire into the air and he will hear nothing more of me. . . ."

I was actually on the point of tears, though I knew perfectly well at that moment that all this was out of Pushkin's *Silvio* and Lermontov's *Masquerade*.[7] And all at once I felt horribly ashamed, so ashamed that I stopped the horse, got out of the sledge, and stood still in the

---

7. A verse play by the poet Mikhail Yu. Lermontov (1814–1841). *Silvio:* Actually "The Shot" (1830), by the Russian Poet Alexander Pushkin (1799–1837), a story in which the hero, Silvio, finally gives up the idea of revenging himself for a slap on the face.

snow in the middle of the street. The driver gazed at me, sighing and astonished.

What was I to do? I could not go in there—it was evidently stupid, and I could not leave things as they were, because that would seem as though . . . Heavens, how could I leave things! And after such insults! "No!" I cried, throwing myself into the sledge again. "It is ordained! It is fate! Drive on, drive on!"

And in my impatience I punched the sledge-driver on the back of the neck.

"What are you up to? What are you hitting me for?" the peasant shouted, but he whipped up his nag so that it began kicking.

The wet snow was falling in big flakes; I unbuttoned myself, regardless of it. I forgot everything else, for I had finally decided on the slap, and felt with horror that it was going to happen *now*, *at once*, and that *no force could stop it*. The deserted street lamps gleamed sullenly in the snowy darkness like torches at a funeral. The snow drifted under my great-coat, under my coat, under my cravat, and melted there. I did not wrap myself up—all was lost, anyway.

At last we arrived. I jumped out, almost unconscious, ran up the steps and began knocking and kicking at the door. I felt fearfully weak, particularly in my legs and my knees. The door was opened quickly as though they knew I was coming. As a fact, Simonov had warned them that perhaps another gentleman would arrive, and this was a place in which one had to give notice and to observe certain precautions. It was one of those "millinery establishments" which were abolished by the police a good time ago. By day it really was a shop; but at night, if one had an introduction, one might visit it for other purposes.

I walked rapidly through the dark shop into the familiar drawing-room, where there was only one candle burning, and stood still in amazement: there was no one there. "Where are they?" I asked somebody. But by now, of course, they had separated. Before me was standing a person with a stupid smile, the "madam" herself, who had seen me before. A minute later a door opened and another person came in.

Taking no notice of anything I strode about the room, and, I believe, I talked to myself. I felt as though I had been saved from death and was conscious of this, joyfully, all over: I should have given that slap, I should certainly certainly have given it! But now they were not here and . . . everything had vanished and changed! I looked round. I could not realize my condition yet. I looked mechanically at the girl who had come in: and had a glimpse of a fresh, young, rather pale face, with straight, dark eyebrows, and with grave, as it were wondering, eyes that attracted me at once; I should have hated her if she had been smiling. I began looking at her more intently and, as it were, with effort. I had not fully collected my thoughts. There was something simple and good-natured in her face, but something strangely grave. I am sure that this stood in her way here, and no one of those fools had noticed her. She could not, however, have been called a beauty, though she was tall, strong-looking, and well built. She was very simply dressed. Something loathsome stirred within me. I went straight up to her.

I chanced to look into the glass. My harassed face struck me as revolting in the extreme, pale, angry, abject, with dishevelled hair. "No matter, I am glad of it," I thought; "I am glad that I shall seem repulsive to her; I like that."

VI

. . . Somewhere behind a screen a clock began wheezing, as though oppressed by something, as though some one were strangling it. After an unnaturally prolonged wheezing there followed a shrill, nasty, and as it were unexpectedly rapid, chime—as though some one were suddenly jumping forward. It struck two. I woke up, though I had indeed not been asleep but lying half conscious.

It was almost completely dark in the narrow, cramped, low-pitched room, cumbered up with an enormous wardrobe and piles of cardboard boxes and all sorts of frippery and litter. The candle end that had been burning on the table was going out and gave a faint flicker from time to time. In a few minutes there would be complete darkness.

I was not long in coming to myself; everything came back to my mind at once, without an effort, as though it had been in ambush to pounce upon me again. And, indeed, even while I was unconscious a point seemed continually to remain in my memory unforgotten, and round it my dreams moved drearily. But strange to say, everything that had happened to me in that day seemed to me now, on waking, to be in the far, far away past, as though I had long, long ago lived all that down.

My head was full of fumes. Something seemed to be hovering over me, rousing me, exciting me, and making me restless. Misery and spite seemed surging up in me again and seeking an outlet. Suddenly I saw beside me two wide eyes scrutinizing me curiously and persistently. The look in those eyes was coldly detached, sullen, as it were utterly remote; it weighed upon me.

A grim idea came into my brain and passed all over my body, as a horrible sensation, such as one feels when one goes into a damp and mouldy cellar. There was something unnatural in those two eyes, beginning to look at me only now. I recalled, too, that during those two hours I had not said a single word to this creature, and

had, in fact, considered it utterly superfluous; in fact, the silence had
for some reason gratified me. Now I suddenly realized vividly the
hideous idea—revolting as a spider—of vice, which, without love,
grossly and shamelessly begins with that in which true love finds its
consummation. For a long time we gazed at each other like that,
but she did not drop her eyes before mine and her expression did not
change, so that at last I felt uncomfortable.

"What is your name?" I asked abruptly, to put an end to it.

"Liza," she answered almost in a whisper, but somehow far from
graciously, and she turned her eyes away.

I was silent.

"What weather! The snow . . . it's disgusting!" I said, almost to
myself, putting my arm under my head despondently, and gazing at
the ceiling.

She made no answer. This was horrible.

"Have you always lived in Petersburg?" I asked a minute later,
almost angrily, turning my head slightly towards her.

"No."

"Where do you come from?"

"From Riga," she answered reluctantly.

"Are you a German?"

"No, Russian."

"Have you been here long?"

"Where?"

"In this house?"

"A fortnight."

She spoke more and more jerkily. The candle went out; I could
no longer distinguish her face.

"Have you a father and mother?"

"Yes . . . no . . . I have."

"Where are they?"

"There . . . in Riga."

"What are they?"

"Oh, nothing."

"Nothing? Why, what class are they?"

"Tradespeople."

"Have you always lived with them?"

"Yes."

"How old are you?"

"Twenty."

"Why did you leave them?"

"Oh, for no reason."

That answer meant "Let me alone; I feel sick, sad."

We were silent.

God knows why I did not go away. I felt myself more and more sick and dreary. The images of the previous day began of themselves, apart from my will, flitting through my memory in confusion. I suddenly recalled something I had seen that morning when, full of anxious thoughts, I was hurrying to the office.

"I saw them carrying a coffin out yesterday and they nearly dropped it," I suddenly said aloud, not that I desired to open the conversation, but as it were by accident.

"A coffin?"

"Yes, in the Haymarket; they were bringing it up out of a cellar."

"From a cellar?"

"Not from a cellar, but from a basement. Oh, you know . . . down below . . . from a house of ill-fame. It was filthy all round . . . Egg-shells, litter . . . stench. It was loathsome."

Silence.

"A nasty day to be buried," I began, simply to avoid being silent.

"Nasty, in what way?"

"The snow, the wet." (I yawned.)

"It makes no difference," she said suddenly, after a brief silence.

"No, it's horrid." (I yawned again.) "The gravediggers must have sworn at getting drenched by the snow. And there must have been water in the grave."

"Why water in the grave?" she asked, with a sort of curiosity, but speaking even more harshly and abruptly than before.

I suddenly began to feel provoked.

"Why, there must have been water at the bottom a foot deep. You can't dig a dry grave in Volkovo Cemetery."

"Why?"

"Why? Why, the place is waterlogged. It's a regular marsh. So they bury them in water. I've seen it myself . . . many times."

(I had never seen it once, indeed I had never been in Volkovo, and had only heard stories of it.)

"Do you mean to say, you don't mind how you die?"

"But why should I die?" she answered, as though defending herself.

"Why, some day you will die, and you will die just the same as that dead woman. She was . . . a girl like you. She died of consumption."

"A wench would have died in a hospital . . ." (She knows all about it already; she said "wench," not "girl.")

"She was in debt to her madam," I retorted, more and more provoked by the discussion; "and went on earning money for her up to the end, though she was in consumption. Some sledge-drivers standing by were talking about her to some soldiers and telling them so. No doubt they knew her. They were laughing. They were going to meet in a pot-house to drink to her memory."

A great deal of this was my invention. Silence followed, profound silence. She did not stir.

"And is it better to die in a hospital?"

"Isn't it just the same? Besides, why should I die?" she added irritably.

"If not now, a little later."

"Why, a little later?"

"Why, indeed? Now you are young, pretty, fresh, you fetch a high price. But after another year of this life you will be very different— you will go off."

"In a year?"

"Anyway, in a year you will be worth less," I continued malignantly. "You will go from here to something lower, another house; a year later—to a third, lower and lower, and in seven years you will come to a basement in the Haymarket. That will be if you were lucky. But it would be much worse if you got some disease, consumption, say . . . and caught a chill, or something or other. It's not easy to get over an illness in your way of life. If you catch anything you may not get rid of it. And so you would die."

"Oh, well, then I shall die," she answered, quite vindictively, and she made a quick movement.

"But one is sorry."

"Sorry for whom?"

"Sorry for life."

Silence.

"Have you been engaged to be married? Eh?"

"What's that to you?"

"Oh, I am not cross-examining you. It's nothing to me. Why are you so cross? Of course you may have had your own troubles. What is it to me? It's simply that I felt sorry."

"Sorry for whom?"

"Sorry for you."

"No need," she whispered hardly audibly, and again made a faint movement.

That incensed me at once. What! I was so gentle with her, and she. . . .

"Why, do you think that you are on the right path?"

"I don't think anything."

"That's what's wrong, that you don't think. Realize it while there is still time. There still is time. You are still young, good-looking; you might love, be married, be happy. . . ."

"Not all married women are happy," she snapped out in the rude abrupt tone she had used at first.

"Not all, of course, but anyway it is much better than the life here. Infinitely better. Besides, with love one can live even without happiness. Even in sorrow life is sweet; life is sweet, however one lives. But here what is there but . . . filth? Phew!"

I turned away with disgust; I was no longer reasoning coldly. I began to feel myself what I was saying and warmed to the subject. I was already longing to expound the cherished ideas I had brooded over in my corner. Something suddenly flared up in me. An object had appeared before me.

"Never mind my being here, I am not an example for you. I am, perhaps, worse than you are. I was drunk when I came here, though," I hastened, however, to say in self-defence. "Besides, a man is no example for a woman. It's a different thing. I may degrade and defile myself, but I am not any one's slave. I come and go, and that's an end of it. I shake it off, and I am a different man. But you are a slave from the start. Yes, a slave! You give up everything, your whole freedom. If you want to break your chains afterwards, you won't be able to: you will be more and more fast in the snares. It is an accursed bondage. I know it. I won't speak of anything else, maybe you won't understand, but tell me: no doubt you are in debt to your madam? There, you see," I added, though she made no answer, but only listened in silence, entirely absorbed, "that's a bondage for you! You will never buy your freedom. They will see to that. It's like selling your soul to the devil. . . . And besides . . . perhaps I, too, am just as unlucky—how do you know—and wallow in the mud on purpose, out of misery? You know, men take to drink from grief; well, maybe I am here from grief. Come, tell me, what is there good here? Here you and I . . . came together . . . just now and did not say one word to one another all the time, and it was only afterwards you began staring at me like a wild creature, and I at you. Is that loving? Is that how one human being should meet another? It's hideous, that's what it is!"

"Yes!" she assented sharply and hurriedly.

I was positively astounded by the promptitude of this "Yes." So the same thought may have been straying through her mind when she was staring at me just before. So she, too, was capable of certain thoughts? "Damn it all, this was interesting, this was a point of likeness!" I thought, almost rubbing my hands. And indeed it's easy to turn a young soul like that!

It was the exercise of my power that attracted me most.

She turned her head nearer to me, and it seemed to me in the darkness that she propped herself on her arm. Perhaps she was scrutinizing me. How I regretted that I could not see her eyes. I heard her deep breathing.

"Why have you come here?" I asked her, with a note of authority already in my voice.

"Oh, I don't know."

"But how nice it would be to be living in your father's house! It's warm and free; and you have a home of your own."

"But what if it's worse than this?"

"I must take the right tone," flashed through my mind. "I may not get far with sentimentality." But it was only a momentary thought. I swear she really did interest me. Besides, I was exhausted and moody. And cunning so easily goes hand-in-hand with feeling.

"Who denies it!" I hastened to answer. "Anything may happen. I am convinced that some one has wronged you, and that you are more sinned against than sinning. Of course, I know nothing of your story, but it's not likely a girl like you has come here of her own inclination. . . ."

"A girl like me?" she whispered, hardly audibly; but I heard it.

Damn it all, I was flattering her. That was horrid. But perhaps it was a good thing. . . . . . She was silent.

"See, Liza, I will tell you about myself. If I had had a home from childhood, I shouldn't be what I am now. I often think that. However bad it may be at home, anyway they are your father and mother, and not enemies, strangers. Once a year at least, they'll show their love of you. Anyway, you know you are at home. I grew up without a home; and perhaps that's why I've turned so . . . unfeeling."

I waited again. "Perhaps she doesn't understand," I thought, "and, indeed, it is absurd—it's moralizing."

"If I were a father and had a daughter, I believe I should love my daughter more than my sons, really," I began indirectly, as though talking of something else, to distract her attention. I must confess I blushed.

"Why so?" she asked.

Ah! so she was listening!

"I don't know, Liza. I knew a father who was a stern, austere man, but used to go down on his knees to his daughter, used to kiss her hands, her feet, he couldn't make enough of her, really. When she danced at parties he used to stand for five hours at a stretch, gazing at her. He was mad over her: I understand that! She would fall asleep tired at night, and he would wake to kiss her in her sleep and make the sign of the cross over her. He would go about in a dirty old coat, he was stingy to every one else, but would spend his last penny for her, giving her expensive presents, and it was his greatest delight when she was pleased with what he gave her. Fathers always love their daughters more than the mothers do. Some girls live happily at home! And I believe I should never let my daughters marry."

"What next?" she said, with a faint smile.

"I should be jealous, I really should. To think that she should kiss any one else! That she should love a stranger more than her father! It's painful to imagine it. Of course, that's all nonsense, of course every father would be reasonable at last. But I believe before I should let her marry, I should worry myself to death; I should find fault with all her suitors. But I should end by letting her marry whom she herself loved. The one whom the daughter loves always seems the worst to the father, you know. That is always so. So many family troubles come from that."

"Some are glad to sell their daughters, rather than marrying them honourably."

Ah, so that was it!

"Such a thing, Liza, happens in those accursed families in which there is neither love nor God," I retorted warmly, "and where there is no love, there is no sense either. There are such families, it's true, but I am not speaking of them. You must have seen wickedness in your own family, if you talk of that. Truly, you must have been unlucky. H'm! . . . that sort of thing mostly comes about through poverty."

"And is it any better with the gentry? Even among the poor, honest people live happily."

"H'm . . . yes. Perhaps. Another thing, Liza, man is fond of reckoning up his troubles, but does not count his joys. If he counted them up as he ought, he would see that every lot has enough happiness provided for it. And what if all goes well with the family, if the blessing of God is upon it, if the husband is a good one, loves you, cherishes you, never leaves you! There is happiness in such a family! Even sometimes there is happiness in the midst of sorrow; and indeed sorrow is everywhere. If you marry *you will find out for yourself.* But think of the first years of married life with one you love: what happiness, what happiness there sometimes is in it! And indeed it's the ordinary thing. In those early days even quarrels with one's husband end happily. Some women get up quarrels with their husbands just because they love them. Indeed, I knew a woman like that: she seemed to say that because she loved him, she would torment him and make him feel it. You know that you may torment a man on purpose through love. Women are particularly given to that, thinking to themselves 'I will love him so, I will make so much of him afterwards, that it's no sin to torment him a little now.' And all in the house rejoice in the sight of you, and you are happy and gay and peaceful and honourable. . . . Then there are some women who are jealous. If he went off anywhere—I knew one such woman, she couldn't restrain herself, but would jump up at night and run off on the sly to find out where he was, whether he was with some other woman. That's a pity. And the woman knows herself it's wrong, and her heart fails her and she suffers, but she loves—it's all through love. And how sweet it is to make it up after quarrels, to own herself in the wrong or to forgive him! And they are both so happy all at once—as though they had met anew, been married over again; as though their love had begun afresh. And no one, no one should know what passes between husband and wife if they love one another. And whatever quarrels there may be between them they ought not to call in their own mother to judge between them and tell tales of one another. They are their own judges. Love is a holy mystery and ought to be hidden from all other eyes, whatever happens. That makes it holier and better. They respect one another more, and much is built on respect. And if once there has been love, if they have been married for love, why should love pass away? Surely one can keep it! It is rare that one cannot keep it. And if the husband is kind and straightforward, why should not love last? The first phase of married love will pass, it is true, but then there will come a love that is better still. Then there will be the union of souls, they will have everything in common, there will be no secrets between them. And once they have children, the most difficult times will seem to them happy, so long as there is love and courage. Even toil will be a joy, you may deny yourself bread for your children and even that will be a joy. They will love you for it afterwards; so you are laying by for your future. As the children grow up you feel that you are an example, a support for them; that even after you die your children will always keep your thoughts and feelings, because they have received them from you, they will take on your semblance and likeness. So you see this is a great duty. How can it fail to draw the father and mother nearer? People say it's a trial to have children. Who says that? It is heavenly happiness! Are you fond of little children, Liza? I am awfully fond of them. You know—a little rosy baby boy at your bosom, and what husband's heart is not touched, seeing his wife nursing his child! A plump little rosy baby, sprawling and snuggling, chubby little hands and feet, clean tiny little nails, so tiny that it makes one laugh to look at them; eyes that look as if they understand everything. And while it sucks it clutches at your bosom with its little hand, plays. When its father comes up, the child tears itself away from the bosom, flings itself back, looks at its father, laughs, as though it were fearfully funny and falls to sucking again. Or it will bite its mother's breast when its little teeth are coming, while it looks sideways at her with its little eyes as though to say, 'Look, I am biting!' Is not all that happiness when they are the three together, husband, wife and child? One can forgive a great deal for the sake of such moments. Yes, Liza, one must first learn to live oneself before one blames others!"

"It's by pictures, pictures like that one must get at you," I thought to myself, though I did speak with real feeling, and all at once I flushed crimson. "What if she were suddenly to burst out laughing, what should I do then?" That idea drove me to fury. Towards the end of my speech I really was excited, and now my vanity was somehow wounded. The silence continued. I almost nudged her.

"Why are you——" she began and stopped. But I understood: there was a quiver of something different in her voice, not abrupt, harsh and unyielding as before, but something soft and shamefaced, so shamefaced that I suddenly felt ashamed and guilty.

"What?" I asked, with tender curiosity.

"Why, you . . ."

"What?"

"Why, you . . . speak somehow like a book," she said, and again there was a note of irony in her voice.

That remark sent a pang to my heart. It was not what I was expecting.

I did not understand that she was hiding her feelings under irony, that this is usually the last refuge of modest and chaste-souled people when the privacy of their soul is coarsely and intrusively invaded, and that their pride makes them refuse to surrender till the last moment and shrink from giving expression to their feelings before you. I ought to have guessed the truth from the timidity with which she had repeatedly approached her sarcasm, only bringing herself to utter it, at last with an effort. But I did not guess, and an evil feeling took possession of me.

"Wait a bit!" I thought.

VII

"Oh, hush, Liza! How can you talk about being like a book, when it makes even me, an outsider, feel sick? Though I don't look at it as an outsider, for, indeed, it touches me to the heart. . . . Is it possible, is it possible that you do not feel sick at being here yourself? Evidently habit does wonders! God knows what habit can do with any one. Can you seriously think that you will never grow old, that you will always be good-looking, and that they will keep you here for ever and ever? I say nothing of the loathsomeness of the life here. . . . Though let me tell you this about it—about your present life, I mean; here though you are young now, attractive, nice, with soul and feeling, yet you know as soon as I came to myself just now I felt as once sick at being here with you! One can only come here when one is drunk. But if you were anywhere else, living as good people live, I should perhaps be more than attracted by you, should fall in love with you, should be glad of a look from you, let alone a word; I should hang about your door, should go down on my knees to you, should look upon you as my betrothed and think it an honour to be allowed to. I should not dare to have an impure thought about you. But here, you see, I know that I have only to whistle and you have to come with me whether you like it or not. I don't consult your wishes, but you mine. The lowest labourer hires himself as a workman, but he doesn't make a slave of himself altogether; besides, he knows that he will be free again presently. But when are you free? Only think what you are giving up here? What is it you are making a slave of? It is your soul, together with your body; you are selling your soul which you have no right to dispose of! You give your love to be outraged by every drunkard! Love! But that's everything, you know, it's a priceless diamond, it's a maiden's treasure, love—why, a man would be ready to give his soul, to face death to gain that love. But how much is your love worth now? You are sold, all of you, body and soul, and there is no need to strive for love when you can have everything without love. And you know there is no greater insult to a girl than that, do you understand? To be sure, I have heard that they comfort you, poor fools, they let you have lovers of your own here. But you know that's simply a farce, that's simply a sham, it's just laughing at you, and you are taken in by it! Why, do you suppose he really loves you, that lover of yours? I don't believe it. How can he love you when he knows you may be called away from him any minute? He would be a low fellow if he did! Will he have a grain of respect for you? What have you in common with him? He laughs at you and robs you—that is all his love amounts to! You are lucky if he does not beat you. Very likely he does beat you, too. Ask him, if you have got one, whether he will marry you. He will laugh in your face, if he doesn't spit in it or give you a blow—though maybe he is not worth a bad halfpenny himself. And for what have you ruined your life, if you come to think of it? For the coffee they give you to drink and the plentiful meals? But with what object are they feeding you up? An honest girl couldn't swallow the food, for she would know what she was being fed for. You are in debt here, and, of course, you will always be in debt, and you will go on in debt to the end, till the visitors here begin to scorn you. And that will soon happen, don't rely upon your youth—all that flies by express train here, you know. You will be kicked out. And not simply kicked out; long before that she'll begin nagging at you, scolding you, abusing you, as though you had not sacrificed your health for her, had not thrown away your youth and your soul for her benefit, but as though you had ruined her, beggared her, robbed her. And don't expect any one to take your part: the others, your companions, will attack you, too, to win her favour, for all are in slavery here, and have lost all conscience and pity here long ago. They have become utterly vile, and nothing on earth is viler, more loathsome, and more insulting than their abuse. And you are laying down everything here, unconditionally, youth and health and beauty and hope, and at twenty-two you will look like a woman of five-and-thirty, and you will be lucky if you are not diseased, pray to God for that! No doubt you are thinking now that you have a gay time and no work to do! Yet there is no work harder or more dreadful in the world or ever has been. One would think that the heart alone would be worn out with tears. And you won't dare to say a word, not half a word when they drive you away from here; you will go away as though you were to blame. You will change to another house, then to a third, then somewhere else, till you come down at last to the Haymarket. There you will be beaten at every turn; that is good manners there, the visitors don't know how to be friendly without beating you. You don't believe that it is so hateful there? Go and look for yourself some time, you can see with your own eyes. Once, one New Year's Day, I saw a woman at a door. They had turned her out as a joke, to give her a taste of the frost because she had been crying too much, and they shut the door behind her. At nine o'clock in the morning she was already quite drunk, dishevelled, half-naked, covered with bruises, her face was powdered, but she had a black-eye, blood was trickling from her nose and her teeth; some cabman had just given her a drubbing. She was sitting on the stone steps, a salt fish of some sort was in her hand; she was crying, wailing something about her luck and beating with the fish on the steps, and cabmen and drunken soldiers were crowding in the doorway taunting her. You don't believe that you will ever be like that? I should be sorry to believe it, too, but how do you know; maybe ten years, eight years ago that very woman with the salt fish came here fresh as a cherub, innocent, pure, knowing no evil, blushing at every word. Perhaps she was like you, proud, ready to take offence, not like the others; perhaps she looked like a queen, and knew what happiness was in store for the man who should love her and whom she should love. Do you see how it ended? And what if at that very minute when she was beating on the filthy steps with that fish, drunken and dishevelled—what if at that very minute she recalled the pure early days in her father's house, when she used to go to school and the neighbour's son watched for her on the way, declaring that he would love her as long as he lived, that he would devote his life to her, and when they vowed to love one another for ever and be married as soon as they were grown up! No, Liza, it would be happy for you if you were to die soon of consumption in some corner, in some cellar like that woman just now. In the hospital, do you say? You will be lucky if they take you, but what if you are still of use to the madam here? Consumption is a queer disease, it is not like fever. The patient goes on hoping till the last minute and says he is all right. He deludes himself. And that just suits your madam. Don't doubt it, that's how it is; you have sold your soul, and what is more you owe money, so you daren't say a word. But when you are dying, all will abandon you, all will turn away from you, for then there will be nothing to get from you. What's more, they will reproach you for cumbering the place, for being so long over dying. However you beg you won't get a drink of water without abuse: 'Whenever are you going off, you nasty hussy, you won't let us sleep with your moaning, you make the gentlemen sick.' That's true, I have heard such things said myself. They will thrust you dying into the filthiest corner in the cellar—in the damp and darkness; what will your thoughts be, lying there alone? When you die, strange hands will lay you out, with grumbling and impatience; no one will bless you, no one will sigh for you, they only want to get rid of you as soon as may be; they will buy a coffin, take you to the grave as they did that poor woman to-day, and celebrate your memory at the tavern. In the gravest sleet, filth, wet snow—no need to put themselves out for you—'Let her down, Vanyukha; it's just like her luck—even here, she is head-foremost, the hussy. Shorten the cord, you rascal.' 'It's all right as it is.' 'All right, is it? Why, she's on her side! She was a fellow-creature, after all! But, never mind, throw the earth on her.' And they won't care to waste much time quarreling over you. They will scatter the wet blue clay as quick as they an and go off to the tavern . . . and there your memory on earth will end; other women have children to go to their graves, fathers, husbands. While for you neither tear, nor sigh, nor remembrance; no one in the whole world will ever come to you, your name will vanish from the face of the earth—as though you had never existed, never been born at all! Nothing but filth and mud, however you knock at your coffin lid at night, when the dead arise, however you cry: 'Let me out, kind people, to live in the light of day! My life was no life at all; my life has been thrown away like a dish-clout; it was drunk away in the tavern at the Haymarket; let me out, kind people, to live in the world again.' "

And I worked myself up to such a pitch that I began to have a lump in my throat myself, and . . . and all at once I stopped, sat up in dismay, and bending over apprehensively, began to listen with a beating heart. I had reason to be troubled.

I had felt for some time that I was turning her soul upside down and rending her heart, and—and the more I was convinced of it, the more eagerly I desired to gain my object as quickly and as effectually as possible. It was the exercise of my skill that carried me away; yet it was not merely sport. . . .

I knew I was speaking stiffly, artificially, even bookishly, in fact, I could not speak except "like a book." But that did not trouble me: I knew, I felt that I should be understood and that this very bookishness might be an assistance. But now, having attained my effect, I was suddenly panic-stricken. Never before had I witnessed such despair! She was lying on her face, thrusting her face into the pillow and clutching it in both hands. Her heart was being torn. Her youthful body was shuddering all over as though in convulsions. Suppressed sobs rent her bosom and suddenly burst out in weeping and wailing, then she pressed closer into the pillow: she did not want any one here, not a living soul, to know of her anguish and her tears. She bit the pillow, bit her hand till it bled (I saw that afterwards), or, thrusting her fingers into her dishevelled hair seemed rigid with the effort of restraint, holding her breath and clenching her teeth. I began saying something, begging her to calm herself, but felt that I did not dare; and all at once, in a sort of cold shiver, almost in terror, began fumbling in the dark, trying hurriedly to get dressed to go. It was dark: though I tried my best I could not finish dressing quickly. Suddenly I felt a box of matches and a candlestick with a whole candle in it. As soon as the room was lighted up, Liza sprang up, sat up in bed, and with a contorted face, with a half insane smile, looked at me almost senselessly. I sat down beside her and took her hands; she came to herself, made an impulsive movement towards me, would have caught hold of me, but did not dare, and slowly bowed her head before me.

"Liza, my dear, I was wrong . . . forgive me, my dear," I began, but she squeezed my hand in her fingers so tightly that I felt I was saying the wrong thing and stopped.

"This is my address, Liza, come to me."

"I will come," she answered resolutely, her head still bowed.

"But now I am going, good-bye . . . till we meet again."

I got up; she, too, stood up and suddenly flushed all over, gave a shudder, snatched up a shawl that was lying on a chair and muffled herself in it to her chin. As she did this she gave another sickly smile, blushed and looked at me strangely. I felt wretched; I was in haste to get away—to disappear.

"Wait a minute," she said suddenly, in the passage just at the doorway, stopping me with her hand on my overcoat. She put down the candle in hot haste and ran off; evidently she had thought of something or wanted to show me something. As she ran away she flushed, her eyes shone, and there was a smile on her lips—what was the meaning of it? Against my will I waited: she came back a minute later with an expression that seemed to ask forgiveness for something. In fact, it was not the same face, not the same look as the evening before: sullen, mistrustful, and obstinate. Her eyes now were imploring, soft, and at the same time trustful, caressing, timid. The expression with which children look at people they are very fond of, of whom they are asking a favour. Her eyes were a light hazel, they were lovely eyes, full of life, and capable of expressing love as well as sullen hatred.

Making no explanation, as though I, as a sort of higher being, must understand everything without explanations, she held out a piece of paper to me. Her whole face was positively beaming at that instant with naïve, almost childish, triumph. I unfolded it. It was a letter to her from a medical student or some one of that sort—a very high-flown and flowery, but extremely respectful, love-letter. I don't recall the words now, but I remember well that through the high-flown phrases there was apparent a genuine feeling, which cannot be feigned. When I had finished reading it I met her glowing, questioning, and childishly impatient eyes fixed upon me. She fastened her eyes upon my face and waited impatiently for what I should say. In a few words, hurriedly, but with a sort of joy and pride, she explained to me that she had been to a dance somewhere in a private house, a family of "very nice people *who knew nothing*, absolutely nothing, for she had only come here so lately and it had all happened . . . and she hadn't made up her mind to stay and was certainly going away as soon as she had paid her debt . . ."and at that party there had been the student who had danced with her all the evening. He had talked to her, and it turned out that he had known her in old days at Riga when he was a child, they had played together, but a very long time ago—and he knew her parents, but *about this* he knew nothing, nothing whatever, and had no suspicion! And the day after the dance (three days ago) he had sent her that letter through the friend with whom she had gone to the party . . . and . . . well, that was all.

She dropped her shining eyes with a sort of bashfulness as she finished.

The poor girl was keeping that student's letter as a precious treasure, and had run to fetch it, her only treasure, because she did not want me to go away without knowing that she, too, was honestly and genuinely loved; that she, too, was addressed respectfully. No doubt that letter was destined to lie in her box and lead to nothing. But none the less, I am certain that she would keep it all her life as a precious treasure, as her pride and justification, and now at such a minute she had thought of that letter and brought it with naïve pride to raise herself in my eyes that I might see, that I, too, might think well of her. I said nothing, pressed her hand and went out. I so longed to get away. . . . I walked all the way home, in spite of the fact that the melting snow was still falling in heavy flakes. I was exhausted, shattered, in bewilderment. But behind the bewilderment the truth was already gleaming. The loathsome truth.

VIII

It was some time, however, before I consented to recognize that truth. Waking up in the morning after some hours of heavy, leaden sleep, and immediately realizing all that had happened on the previous day, I was positively amazed at my last night's *sentimentality* with Liza, at all those "outcries of horror and pity." "To think of having such an attack of womanish hysteria, pah!" I concluded. And what did I thrust my address upon her for? What if she comes? Let her come, though; it doesn't matter. . . . But *obviously*, that was not now the chief and the most important matter: I had to make haste and at all costs save my reputation in the eyes of Zverkov and Simonov as quickly as possible; that was the chief business. And I was so taken up that morning that I actually forgot all about Liza.

First of all I had at once to repay what I had borrowed the day before from Simonov. I resolved on a desperate measure: to borrow fifteen roubles straight off from Anton Antonich. As luck would have it he was in the best of humours that morning, and gave it to me at once, on the first asking. I was so delighted at this that, as I signed the I O U with a swaggering air, I told him casually that the night before "I had been keeping it up with some friends at the Hôtel de Paris; we were giving a farewell party to a comrade, in fact, I might say a friend of my childhood, and you know—a desperate rake, fearfully spoilt—of course, he belongs to a good family, and has considerable means, a brilliant career; he is witty, charming, a regular Lovelace, you understand; we drank an extra 'half-dozen' and . . ."

And it went off all right; all this was uttered very easily, unconstrainedly and complacently.

On reaching home I promptly wrote to Simonov.

To this hour I am lost in admiration when I recall the truly gentlemanly, good-humoured, candid tone of my letter. With tact and good-breeding, and, above all, entirely without superfluous words, I blamed myself for all that had happened. I defended myself, "if I really may be allowed to defend myself," by alleging that being utterly unaccustomed to wine, I had been intoxicated with the first glass, which I said, I had drunk before they arrived, while I was waiting for them at the Hôtel de Paris between five and six o'clock. I begged Simonov's pardon especially; I asked him to convey my explanations to all the others, especially to Zverkov, whom "I seemed to remember as though in a dream" I had insulted. I added that I would have called upon all of them myself, but my head ached, and besides I had not the face to. I was particularly pleased with a certain lightness, almost carelessness (strictly within the bounds of politeness, however), which was apparent in my style, and better than any possible arguments, gave them at once to understand that I took rather an independent view of "all that unpleasantness last night;" that I was by no means so utterly crushed as you, my friends, probably imagine; but on the contrary, looked upon it as a gentleman serenely respecting himself should look upon it. "On a young hero's past no censure is cast!"

"There is actually an aristocratic playfulness about it!" I thought admiringly, as I read over the letter. And it's all because I am an intellectual and cultivated man! Another man in my place would not have known how to extricate himself, but here I have got out of it and am as jolly as ever again, and all because I am "a cultivated and educated man of our day." And, indeed, perhaps, everything was due to the wine yesterday. H'm! . . . no, it was not the wine. I did not drink anything at all between five and six when I was waiting for them. I had lied to Simonov; I had lied shamelessly; and indeed I wasn't ashamed now. . . . Hang it all though, the great thing was that I was rid of it.

I put six roubles in the letter, sealed it up, and asked Apollon to take it to Simonov. When he learned that there was money in the letter, Apollon became more respectful and agreed to take it. Towards evening I went out for a walk. My head was still aching and giddy after yesterday. But as evening came on and the twilight grew denser, my impressions and, following them, my thoughts, grew more and more different and confused. Something was not dead within me, in the depths of my heart and conscience it would not die, and it showed itself in acute depression. For the most part I jostled my way through the most crowded business streets, along Myeshchansky Street, along Sadovy Street and in Yusupov Garden. I always liked particularly sauntering along these streets in the dusk, just when there were crowds of working people of all sorts going home from their daily work, with faces looking cross with anxiety. What I liked was just that cheap bustle, that bare prose. On this occasion the jostling of the streets irritated me more than ever. I could not make out what was wrong with me, I could not find the clue, something seemed rising up continually in my soul, painfully, and refusing to be appeased. I returned home completely upset, it was just as though some crime were lying on my conscience.

The thought that Liza was coming worried me continually. It seemed queer to me that of all my recollections of yesterday this tormented me, as it were, especially, as it were, quite separately. Everything else I had quite succeeded in forgetting by the evening; I dismissed it all and was still perfectly satisfied with my letter to Simonov. But on this point I was not satisfied at all. It was as though I were worried only by Liza. "What if she comes," I thought incessantly, "well, it doesn't matter, let her come! H'm! it's horrid that she should see, for instance, how I live. Yesterday I seemed such a hero to her, while now, h'm! It's horrid, though, that I have let myself go so, the room looks like a beggar's. And I brought myself to go out to dinner in such a suit! And my American leather sofa with the stuffing sticking out. And my dressing-gown, which will not cover me, such tatters, and she will see all this and she will see Apollon. That beast is certain to insult her. He will fasten upon her in order to be rude to me. And I, of course, shall be panic-stricken as usual, I shall begin bowing and scraping before her and pulling my dressing-gown round me, I shall begin smiling, telling lies. Oh, the beastliness! And it isn't the beastliness of it that matters most! There is something more important, more loathsome, viler! Yes, viler! And to put on that dishonest lying mask again!" . . .

When I reached that thought I fired up all at once.

"Why dishonest? How dishonest? I was speaking sincerely last night. I remember there was real feeling in me, too. What I wanted was to excite an honourable feeling in her. . . . Her crying was a good thing, it will have a good effect."

Yet I could not feel at ease. All that evening, even when I had come back home, even after nine o'clock, when I calculated that Liza could not possibly come, she still haunted me, and what was worse, she came back to my mind always in the same position. One moment out of all that had happened last night stood vividly before my imagination; the moment when I struck a match and saw her pale, distorted face, with its look of torture. And what a pitiful, what an unnatural, what a distorted smile she had at that moment! But I did not know then, that fifteen years later I should still in my imagination see Liza, always with the pitiful, distorted, inappropriate smile which was on her face at that minute.

Next day I was ready again to look upon it all as nonsense, due to over-excited nerves, and, above all, as *exaggerated*, I was always conscious of that weak point of mine, and sometimes very much afraid of it. "I exaggerate everything, that is where I go wrong," I repeated to myself every hour. But, however, "Liza will very likely come all the same," was the refrain with which all my reflections ended. I was so uneasy that I sometimes flew into a fury: "She'll come, she is certain to come!" I cried, running about the room, "if not to-day, she will come to-morrow; she'll find me out! The damnable romanticism of these pure hearts! Oh, the vileness—oh, the silliness—oh, the stupidity of these 'wretched sentimental souls!' Why, how fail to understand? How could one fail to understand? . . ."

But at this point I stopped short, and in great confusion, indeed.

And how few, how few words, I thought, in passing, were needed; how little of the idyllic (and affectedly, bookishly, artificially idyllic too) had sufficed to turn a whole human life at once according to my will. That's virginity, to be sure! Freshness of soil!

At times a thought occurred to me, to go to her, "to tell her all," and beg her not to come to me. But this thought stirred such wrath in me that I believed I should have crushed that "damned" Liza if she had chanced to be near me at the time. I should have insulted her, have spat at her, have turned her out, have struck her!

One day passed, however, another and another; she did not come and I began to grow calmer. I felt particularly bold and cheerful after nine o'clock, I even sometimes began dreaming, and rather sweetly: I, for instance, became the salvation of Liza, simply through her coming to me and my talking to her. . . . I develop her, educate her. Finally, I notice that she loves me, loves me passionately. I pretend not to understand (I don't know, however, why I pretend, just for effect, perhaps). At last all confusion, transfigured, trembling and sobbing, she flings herself at my feet and says that I am her saviour, and that she loves me better than anything in the world. I am amazed, but. . . . "Liza," I say, "can you imagine that I have not noticed your love, I saw it all, I divined it, but I did not dare to approach you first, because I had an influence over you and was afraid that you would force yourself, from gratitude, to respond to my love, would try to rouse in your heart a feeling which was perhaps absent, and I did not wish that . . . because it would be tyranny . . . it would be indelicate (in short, I launch off at that point into European, inexplicably lofty subtleties à la George Sand[8]) but now, now you are mine, you are my creation, you are pure, you are good, you are my noble wife.

> 'Into my house come bold and free,
> Its rightful mistress there to be.' "[9]

Then we begin living together, go abroad and so on, and so on. In fact, in the end it seemed vulgar to me myself, and I began putting out my tongue at myself.

Besides, they won't let her out, "the hussy!" I thought. They don't let them go out very readily, especially in the evening (for some reason I fancied she would come in the evening, and at seven o'clock precisely). Though she did say she was not altogether a slave there yet, and had certain rights; so, h'm! Damn it all, she will come, she is sure to come!

It was a good thing, in fact, that Apollon distracted my attention at that time by his rudeness. He drove me beyond all patience! He was the bane of my life, the curse laid upon me by Providence. We had been squabbling continually for years, and I hated him. My

---

8. Pseudonym of the French woman novelist Mme. Aurore Dudevant (1804–1876), famous also as a promoter of feminism.   9. The last lines of the poem by Nekrasov used as the epigraph of Part II of this story.

God, how I hated him! I believe I had never hated any one in my life as I hated him, especially at some moments. He was an elderly, dignified man, who worked part of his time as a tailor. But for some unknown reason he despised me beyond all measure, and looked down upon me insufferably. Though, indeed, he looked down upon every one. Simply to glance at that flaxen, smoothly brushed head, at the tuft of hair he combed up on his forehead and oiled with sunflower oil, at that dignified mouth, compressed into the shape of the letter V, made one feel one was confronting a man who never doubted of himself. He was a pedant, to the most extreme point, the greatest pedant I had met on earth, and with that had a vanity only befitting Alexander of Macedon. He was in love with every button on his coat, every nail on his fingers—absolutely in love with them, and he looked it! In his behaviour to me he was a perfect tyrant, he spoke very little to me, and if he chanced to glance at me he gave me a firm, majestically self-confident and invariably ironical look that drove me sometimes to fury. He did his work with the air of doing me the greatest favour. Though he did scarcely anything for me, and did not, indeed, consider himself bound to do anything. There could be no doubt that he looked upon me as the greatest fool on earth, and that "he did not get rid of me" was simply that he could get wages from me every month. Many sins should be forgiven me for what I suffered from him. My hatred reached such a point that sometimes his very step almost threw me into convulsions. What I loathed particularly was his lisp. His tongue must have been a little too long or something of that sort, for he continually lisped, and seemed to be very proud of it, imagining that it greatly added to his dignity. He spoke in a slow, measured tone, with his hands behind his back and his eyes fixed on the ground. He maddened me particularly when he read aloud the psalms to himself behind his partition. Many a battle I waged over that reading! But he was awfully fond of reading aloud in the evenings, in a slow, even, sing-song voice, as though over the dead. It is interesting that that is how he has ended: he hires himself out to read the psalms over the dead, and at the same time he kills rats and makes blacking. But at that time I could not get rid of him, it was as though he were chemically combined with my existence. Besides, nothing would have induced him to consent to leave me. I could not live in furnished lodgings: my lodging was my private solitude, my shell, my cave, in which I concealed myself from all mankind, and Apollon seemed to me, for some reason, an integral part of that flat, and for seven years I could not turn him away.

To be two or three days behind with his wages for instance, was impossible. He would have made such a fuss, I should not have known where to hide my head. But I was so exasperated with every one during those days, that I made up my mind for some reason and with some object to *punish* Apollon and not to pay him for a fortnight the wages that were owing him. I had for a long time—for the last two years—been intending to do this, simply in order to teach him not to give himself airs with me, and to show him that if I liked I could withhold his wages. I purposed to say nothing to him about it, and was purposely silent indeed, in order to score off his pride and force him to be the first to speak of his wages. Then I would take the seven roubles out of a drawer, show him I have the money put aside on purpose, but that I won't, I won't, I simply won't pay him his wages, I won't just because that is "what I wish," because "I am master, and it is for me to decide," because he has been disrespectful, because he has been rude; but if he were to ask respectfully I might be softened and give it to him, otherwise he might wait another fortnight, another three weeks, a whole month. . . .

But angry as I was, yet he got the better of me. I could not hold out for four days. He began as he always did begin in such cases, for there had been such cases already, there had been attempts (and it may be observed I knew all this beforehand, I knew his nasty tactics by heart). He would begin by fixing upon me an exceedingly severe stare, keeping it up for several minutes at a time, particularly on meeting me or seeing me out of the house. If I held out and pretended not to notice these stares, he would, still in silence, proceed to further tortures. All at once, *à propos* of nothing, he would walk softly and smoothly into my room, when I was pacing up and down or reading, stand by the door, one hand behind his back and one foot behind the other, and fix upon me a stare more than severe, utterly contemptuous. If I suddenly asked him what he wanted, he would make me no answer, but continue staring at me persistently for some seconds, then, with a peculiar compression of his lips and a most significant air, deliberately turn round and deliberately go back to his room. Two hours later he would come out again and again present himself before me in the same way. It had happened that in my fury I did not even ask him what he wanted, but simply raised my head sharply and imperiously and began staring back at him. So we stared at one another for two minutes; at last he turned with deliberation and dignity and went back again for two hours.

If I were still not brought to reason by all this, but persisted in my revolt, he would suddenly begin sighing while he looked at me, long, deep sighs as though measuring by them the depths of my moral degradation, and, of course, it ended at last by his triumphing completely: I raged and shouted, but still was forced to do what he wanted.

This time the usual staring manœuvres had scarcely begun when I lost my temper and flew at him in a fury. I was irritated beyond endurance apart from him.

"Stay," I cried, in a frenzy, as he was slowly and silently turning, with one hand behind his back, to go to his room, "stay! Come back, come back, I tell you!" and I must have bawled so unnaturally, that he turned round and even looked at me with some wonder. However, he persisted in saying nothing, and that infuriated me.

"How dare you come and look at me like that without being sent for? Answer!"

After looking at me calmly for half a minute, he began turning round again.

"Stay!" I roared, running up to him, "don't stir! There. Answer, now: what did you come in to look at?"

"If you have any order to give me it's my duty to carry it out," he answered, after another silent pause, with a slow, measured lisp, raising his eyebrows and calmly twisting his head from one side to another, all this with exasperating composure.

"That's not what I am asking you about, you torturer!" I shouted, turning crimson with anger. "I'll tell you why you came here myself: you see, I don't give you your wages, you are so proud you don't want to bow down and ask for it, and so you come to punish me with your stupid stares, to worry me and you have no sus . . . pic . . . ion how stupid it is—stupid, stupid, stupid, stupid!" . . .

He would have turned round again without a word, but I seized him.

"Listen," I shouted to him. "Here's the money, do you see, here it is" (I took it out of the table drawer); "here's the seven roubles complete, but you are not going to have it, you . . . are . . . not . . . going . . . to . . . have it until you come respectfully with bowed head to beg my pardon. Do you hear?"

"That cannot be," he answered, with the most unnatural self-confidence.

"It shall be so," I said, "I give you my word of honour, it shall be!"

"And there's nothing for me to beg your pardon for," he went on, as though he had not noticed my exclamations at all. "Why, besides, you called me a 'torturer,' for which I can summon you at the police-station at any time for insulting behaviour."

"Go, summon me," I roared, "go at once, this very minute, this very second! You are a torturer all the same! a torturer!"

But he merely looked at me, then turned, and regardless of my loud calls to him, he walked to his room with an even step and without looking round.

"If it had not been for Liza nothing of this would have happened," I decided inwardly. Then, after waiting a minute, I went myself behind his screen with a dignified and solemn air, though my heart was beating slowly and violently.

"Apollon," I said quietly and emphatically, though I was breathless, "go at once without a minute's delay and fetch the police-officer."

He had meanwhile settled himself at his table, put on his spectacles and taken up some sewing. But, hearing my order, he burst into a guffaw.

"At once, go this minute! Go on, or else you can't imagine what will happen."

"You are certainly out of your mind," he observed, without even raising his head, lisping as deliberately as ever and threading his needle. "Whoever heard of a man sending for the police against himself? And as for being frightened—you are upsetting yourself about nothing, for nothing will come of it."

"Go!" I shrieked, clutching him by the shoulder. I felt I should strike him in a minute.

But I did not notice the door from the passage softly and slowly open at that instant and a figure come in, stop short, and begin staring at us in perplexity. I glanced, nearly swooned with shame, and rushed back to my room. There, clutching at my hair with both hands, I leaned my head against the wall and stood motionless in that position.

Two minutes later I heard Apollon's deliberate footsteps. "There is some woman asking for you," he said, looking at me with peculiar severity. Then he stood aside and let in Liza. He would not go away, but stared at us sarcastically.

"Go away, go away," I commanded in desperation. At that moment my clock began whirring and wheezing and struck seven.

IX

> 'Into my house come bold and free,
> Its rightful mistress there to be.'
> (From the same poem)

I stood before her crushed, crestfallen, revoltingly confused, and I believe I smiled as I did my utmost to wrap myself in the skirts of my ragged wadded dressing-gown—exactly as I had imagined the scene not long before in a fit of depression. After standing over us for a couple of minutes Apollon went away, but that did not make me more at ease. What made it worse was that she, too, was overwhelmed with confusion, more so, in fact, than I should have expected. At the sight of me, of course.

"Sit down," I said mechanically, moving a chair up to the table, and I sat down on the sofa. She obediently sat down at once and gazed at me open-eyed, evidently expecting something from me at once. This naïveté of expectation drove me to fury, but I restrained myself.

She ought to have tried not to notice, as though everything had been as usual, while instead of that, she . . . and I dimly felt that I should make her pay dearly for *all this*.

"You have found me in a strange position, Liza," I began, stammering and knowing that this was the wrong way to begin. "No, no, don't imagine anything," I cried, seeing that she had suddenly flushed. "I am not ashamed of my poverty. . . . On the contrary I look with pride on my poverty. I am poor but honourable. . . . One can be poor and honourable," I muttered. "However . . . would you like tea?" . . .

"No," she was beginning.

"Wait a minute."

I leapt up and ran to Apollon. I had to get out of the room somehow.

"Apollon," I whispered in feverish haste, flinging down before him the seven roubles which had remained all the time in my clenched fist, "here are your wages, you see I give them to you; but for that you must come to my rescue: bring me tea and a dozen rusks from the restaurant. If you won't go, you'll make me a miserable man! You don't know what this woman is. . . . This is—everything! You may be imagining something. . . . But you don't know what that woman is!" . . .

Apollon, who had already sat down to his work and put on his spectacles again, at first glanced askance at the money without speaking or putting down his needle; then, without paying the slightest attention to me or making any answer he went on busying himself with his needle, which he had not yet threaded. I waited before him for three minutes with my arms crossed *à la Napoléon*. My temples were moist with sweat. I was pale, I felt it. But, thank God, he must have been moved to pity, looking at me. Having threaded his needle he deliberately got up from his seat, deliberately moved back his chair, deliberately took off his spectacles, deliberately counted the money, and finally asking me over his shoulder: "Shall I get a whole portion?" deliberately walked out of the room. As I was going back to Liza, the thought occurred to me on the way: shouldn't I run away just as I was in my dressing-gown, no matter where, and then let happen what would.

I sat down again. She looked at me uneasily For some minutes we were silent.

"I will kill him," I shouted suddenly, striking the table with my fist so that the ink spurted out of the inkstand.

"What are you saying!" she cried, starting.

"I will kill him! kill him!" I shrieked, suddenly striking the table in absolute frenzy, and at the same time fully understanding how stupid it was to be in such a frenzy. "You don't know, Liza, what that torturer is to me. He is my torturer. . . . He has gone now to fetch some rusks; he . . ."

And suddenly I burst into tears. It was an hysterical attack. How ashamed I felt in the midst of my sobs; but still I could not restrain them.

She was frightened.

"What is the matter? What is wrong?" she cried, fussing about me.

"Water, give me water, over there!" I muttered in a faint voice, though I was inwardly conscious that I could have got on very well without water and without muttering in a faint voice. But I was, what is called, *putting it on*, to save appearances, though the attack was a genuine one.

She gave me water, looking at me in bewilderment. At that moment Apollon brought in the tea. It suddenly seemed to me that this commonplace, prosaic tea was horribly undignified and paltry after all that had happened, and I blushed crimson. Liza looked at Apollon with positive alarm. He went out without a glance at either of us.

"Liza, do you despise me?" I asked, looking at her fixedly, trembling with impatience to know what she was thinking.

She was confused, and did not know what to answer.

"Drink your tea," I said to her angrily. I was angry with myself, but, of course, it was she who would have to pay for it. A horrible spite against her suddenly surged up in my heart; I believe I could have killed her. To revenge myself on her I swore inwardly not to say a word to her all the time. "She is the cause of it all," I thought.

Our silence lasted for five minutes. The tea stood on the table; we did not touch it. I had got to the point of purposely refraining from beginning in order to embarrass her further; it was awkward for her to begin alone. Several times she glanced at me with mournful perplexity. I was obstinately silent. I was, of course, myself the chief sufferer, because I was fully conscious of the disgusting meanness of my spiteful stupidity, and yet at the same time I could not restrain myself.

"I want to . . . get away . . . from there altogether," she began, to break the silence in some way, but, poor girl, that was just what she ought not to have spoken about at such a stupid moment to a man so stupid as I was. My heart positively ached with pity for her tactless and unnecessary straightforwardness. But something hideous at once stifled all compassion in me; it even provoked me to greater venom. I did not care what happened. Another five minutes passed.

"Perhaps I am in your way," she began timidly, hardly audibly, and was getting up.

But as soon as I saw this first impulse of wounded dignity I positively trembled with spite, and at once burst out.

"Why have you come to me, tell me that, please?" I began, gasping for breath and regardless of logical connection in my words. I longed to have it all out at once, at one burst; I did not even trouble how to begin. "Why have you come? Answer, answer," I cried, hardly knowing what I was doing. "I'll tell you, my good girl, why you have come. You've come because I talked sentimental stuff to you then. So now you are soft as butter and longing for fine sentiments again. So you may as well know that I was laughing at you then. And I am laughing at you now. Why are you shuddering? Yes, I was laughing at you! I had been insulted just before, at dinner, by the fellows who came that evening before me. I came to you, meaning to thrash one of them, an officer; but I didn't succeed, I didn't find him; I had to avenge the insult on some one to get back my own again; you turned up, I vented my spleen on you and laughed at you. I had been humiliated, so I wanted to humiliate; I had been treated like a rag, so I wanted to show my power. . . . That's what it was, and you imagined I had come there on purpose to save you. Yes? You imagined that? You imagined that?"

I knew that she would perhaps be muddled and not take it all in exactly, but I knew, too, that she would grasp the gist of it, very well indeed. And so, indeed, she did. She turned white as a handkerchief, tried to say something, and her lips worked painfully; but she sank on a chair as though she had been felled by an axe. And all the time afterwards she listened to me with her lips parted and her eyes wide open, shuddering with awful terror. The cynicism, the cynicism of my words overwhelmed her. . . .

"Save you!" I went on, jumping up from my chair and running up and down the room before her. "Save you from what? But perhaps I am worse than you myself. Why didn't you throw it in my teeth when I was giving you that sermon: 'But what did you come here yourself for? was it to read us a sermon?' Power, power was what I wanted then, sport was what I wanted, I wanted to ring out your tears, your humiliation, your hysteria—that was what I wanted then! Of course, I couldn't keep it up then, because I am a wretched creature, I was frightened, and, the devil knows why, gave you my address in my folly. Afterwards, before I got home, I was cursing and swearing at you because of that address, I hated you already because of the lies I had told you. Because I only like playing with words, only dreaming, but, do you know, what I really want is that you should all go to hell. That is what I want. I want peace; yes, I'd sell the whole world for a farthing, straight off, so long as I was left in peace. Is the world to go to pot, or am I to go without my tea? I say that the world may go to pot for me so long as I always get my tea. Did you know that, or not? Well, anyway, I know that I am a blackguard, a scoundrel, an egoist, a sluggard. Here I have been shuddering for the last three days at the thought of your coming. And do you know what has worried me particularly for these three days? That I posed as such a hero to you, and now you would see me in a wretched torn dressing-gown, beggarly, loathsome. I told you just now that I was not ashamed of my poverty; so you may as well know that I am ashamed of it; I am more ashamed of it than of anything, more afraid of it than of being found out if I were a thief, because I am as vain as though I had been skinned and the very air blowing on my hurts. Surely by now you must realize that I shall never forgive you for having found me in this wretched dressing-gown, just as I was flying at Apollon like a spiteful cur. The saviour, the former hero, was flying like a mangy, unkempt sheep-dog at his lackey, and the lackey was jeering at him! And I shall never forgive you for the tears I could not help shedding before you just now, like some silly woman put to shame! And for what I am confessing to you now, I shall never forgive *you* either! Yes—you must answer for it all because you turned up like this, because I am a blackguard, because I am the nastiest, stupidest, absurdest, and most envious of all the worms on earth, who are not a bit better than I am, but, the devil knows why, are never put to confusion; while I shall always be insulted by every louse, that is my doom! And what is it to me that you don't understand a word of this! And what do I care, what do I care about you, and whether you go to ruin there or not? Do you understand? How I shall hate you now after saying this, for having been here and listening. Why, it's not once in a lifetime a man speaks out like this, and then it is in hysterics! . . . What more do you want? Why do you still stand confronting me, after all this? Why are you worrying me? Why don't you go?"

But at this point a strange thing happened. I was so accustomed to think and imagine everything from books, and to picture everything in the world to myself just as I had made it up in my dreams beforehand, that I could not all at once take in this strange circumstance. What happened was this: Liza, insulted and crushed by me, understood a great deal more than I imagined. She understood from all this what a woman understands first of all, if she feels genuine love, that is, that I was myself unhappy.

The frightened and wounded expression on her face was followed first by a look of sorrowful perplexity. When I began calling myself a scoundrel and a blackguard and my tears flowed (the tirade was accompanied throughout by tears) her whole face worked convulsively. She was on the point of getting up and stopping me; when I finished she took no notice of my shouting: "Why are you here, why don't you go away?" but realized only that it must have been very bitter to me to say all this. Besides, she was so crushed, poor girl; she considered herself infinitely beneath me; how could she feel anger or resentment? She suddenly leapt up from her chair with an irresistible impulse and held out her hands, yearning towards me, though still timid and not daring to stir. . . . At this point there was a revulsion in my heart, too. Then she suddenly rushed to me, threw her arms round me and burst into tears. I, too, could not restrain myself, and sobbed as I never had before.

"They won't let me . . . I can't be good!" I managed to articulate; then I went to the sofa, fell on it face downwards, and sobbed on it for a quarter of an hour in genuine hysterics. She came close to me, put her arms round me and stayed motionless in that position. But the trouble was that the hysterics could not go on for ever, and (I am writing the loathsome truth) lying face downwards on the sofa with my face thrust into my nasty leather pillow, I began by degrees to be aware of a far-away, involuntary but irresistible feeling that it would be awkward now for me to raise my head and look Liza straight in the face. Why was I ashamed? I don't know, but I was ashamed. The thought, too, came into my over-wrought brain that our parts now were completely changed, that she was now the heroine, while I was just such a crushed and humiliated creature as she had been before me that night—four days before. . . . And all this came into my mind during the minutes I was lying on my face on the sofa.

My God! surely I was not envious of her then.

I don't know, to this day I cannot decide, and at the time, of course, I was still less able to understand what I was feeling than now. I cannot get on without domineering and tyrannizing over some one, but . . . there is no explaining anything by reasoning and so it is useless to reason.

I conquered myself, however, and raised my head; I had to do so sooner or later . . . and I am convinced to this day that it was just because I was ashamed to look at her that another feeling was suddenly kindled and flamed up in my heart . . . a feeling of mastery and possession. My eyes gleamed with passion, and I gripped her hands tightly. How I hated her and how I was drawn to her at that minute! The one feeling intensified the other. It was almost like an act of vengeance. At first there was a look of amazement, even of terror on her face, but only for one instant. She warmly and rapturously embraced me.

X

A quarter of an hour later I was rushing up and down the room in frenzied impatience, from minute to minute I went up to the screen and peeped through the crack at Liza. She was sitting on the ground with her head leaning against the bed, and must have been crying. But she did not go away, and that irritated me. This time she understood it all. I had insulted her finally, but . . . there's no need to describe it. She realized that my outburst of passion had been simply revenge, a fresh humiliation, and that to my earlier, almost causeless hatred was added a *personal hatred*, born of envy. . . . Though I do not maintain positively that she understood all this distinctly; but she certainly did fully understand that I was a despicable man, and what was worse, incapable of loving her.

I know I shall be told that this is incredible—but it is incredible to be as spiteful and stupid as I was; it may be added that it was strange I should not love her, or at any rate, appreciate her love. Why is it strange? In the first place, by then I was incapable of love, for I repeat, with me loving meant tyrannizing and showing my moral superiority. I have never in my life been able to imagine any other sort of love, and have nowadays come to the point of sometimes thinking that love really consists in the right—freely given by the beloved object—to tyrannize over her.

Even in my underground dreams I did not imagine love except as a struggle. I began it always with hatred and ended it with moral subjugation, and afterwards I never knew what to do with the sub-jugated object. And what is there to wonder at in that, since I had succeeded in so corrupting myself, since I was so out of touch with "real life," as to have actually thought of reproaching her, and putting her to shame for having come to me to hear "fine sentiments"; and did not even guess that she had come not to hear fine sentiments, but to love me, because to a woman all reformation, all salvation from any sort of ruin, and all moral renewal is included in love and can only show itself in that form.

I did not hate her so much, however, when I was running about the room and peeping through the crack in the screen. I was only insufferably oppressed by her being here. I wanted her to disappear. I wanted "peace," to be left alone in my underground world. Real life oppressed me with its novelty so much that I could hardly breathe.

But several minutes passed and she still remained, without stirring, as though she were unconscious. I had the shamelessness to tap softly at the screen as though to remind her. . . . She started, sprang up, and flew to seek her kerchief, her hat, her coat, as though making her escape from me. . . . Two minutes later she came from behind the screen and looked with heavy eyes at me. I gave a spiteful grin, which was forced, however, to *keep up appearances*, and I turned away from her eyes.

"Good-bye," she said, going towards the door.

I ran up to her, seized her hand, opened it, thrust something in it and closed it again. Then I turned at once and dashed away in haste to the other corner of the room to avoid seeing her, anyway. . . .

I did not mean a moment since to tell a lie—to write that I did this accidentally, not knowing what I was doing through foolishness, through losing my head. But I don't want to lie, and so I will say straight out that I opened her hand and put the money in it . . . from spite. It came into my head to do this while I was running up and down the room and she was sitting behind the screen. But this I can say for certain: though I did that cruel thing purposely, it was not an impulse from the heart, but came from my evil brain. This cruelty was so affected, so purposely made up, so completely a product of the brain, of books, that I could not even keep it up a minute—first I dashed away to avoid seeing her, and then in shame and despair rushed after Liza. I opened the door in the passage and began listening.

"Liza! Liza!" I cried on the stairs, but in a low voice, not boldly.

There was no answer, but I fancied I heard her footsteps, lower down on the stairs.

"Liza!" I cried, more loudly.

No answer. But at that minute I heard the stiff outer glass door open heavily with a creak and slam violently, the sound echoed up the stairs.

She had gone. I went back to my room in hesitation. I felt horribly oppressed.

I stood still at the table, beside the chair on which she had sat and looked aimlessly before me. A minute passed, suddenly I started; straight before me on the table I saw. . . . In short, I saw a crumpled blue five-rouble note, the one I had thrust into her hand a minute before. It was the same note; it could be no other, there was no other in the flat. So she had managed to fling it from her hand on the table at the moment when I had dashed into the further corner.

Well! I might have expected that she would do that. Might I have expected it? No, I was such an egoist, I was so lacking in respect for my fellow-creatures that I could not even imagine she would do so. I could not endure it. A minute later I flew like a madman to dress, flinging on what I could at random and ran headlong after her. She could not have got two hundred paces away when I ran out into the street.

It was a still night and the snow was coming down in masses and falling almost perpendicularly, covering the pavement and the empty street as though with a pillow. There was no one in the street, no sound was to be heard. The street lamps gave a disconsolate and useless glimmer. I ran two hundred paces to the cross-roads and stopped short.

Where had she gone? And why was I running after her?

Why? To fall down before her, to sob with remorse, to kiss her feet, to entreat her forgiveness! I longed for that, my whole breast was being rent to pieces, and never, never shall I recall that minute with indifference. But—what for? I thought. Should I not begin to hate her, perhaps, even to-morrow, just because I had kissed her feet to-day? Should I give her happiness? Had I not recognized that day, for the hundredth time, what I was worth? Should I not torture her?

I stood in the snow, gazing into the troubled darkness and pondered this.

"And will it not be better?" I mused fantastically, afterwards at home, stifling the living pang of my heart with fantastic dreams. "Will it not be better that she should keep the resentment of the insult for ever? Resentment—why, it is purification; it is a most stinging and painful consciousness! To-morrow I should have defiled her soul and have exhausted her heart, while now the feeling of insult will never die in her heart, and however loathsome the filth awaiting her—the feeling of insult will elevate and purify her . . . by hatred . . . h'm! . . . perhaps, too, by forgiveness. . . . Will all that make things easier for her though? . . ."

And, indeed, I will ask on my own account here, an idle question: which is better—cheap happiness or exalted sufferings? Well, which is better?

So I dreamed as I sat at home that evening, almost dead with the pain in my soul. Never had I endured such suffering and remorse, yet could there have been the faintest doubt when I ran out from my lodging that I should turn back half-way? I never met Liza again and I have heard nothing of her. I will add, too, that I remained for a long time afterwards pleased with the phrase about the benefit from resentment and hatred in spite of the fact that I almost fell ill from misery.

Even now, so many years later, all this is somehow a very evil memory. I have many evil memories now, but . . . hadn't I better end my "Notes" here? I believe I made a mistake in beginning to write them, anyway I have felt ashamed all the time I've been writing this story; so it's hardly literature so much as a corrective punishment. Why, to tell long stories, showing how I have spoiled my life through morally rotting in my corner,, through lack of fitting environment, through divorce from real life, and rankling spite in my underground world, would certainly not be interesting; a novel needs a hero, and all the traits for an anti-hero are *expressly* gathered together here, and what matters most, it all produces an unpleasant impres-

sion, for we are all divorced from life, we are all cripples, every one
of us, more or less. We are so divorced from it that we feel at once a
sort of loathing for real life, and so cannot bear to be reminded of it.
Why, we have come almost to looking upon real life as an effort,
almost as hard labour, and we are all privately agreed that it is better
in books. And why do we fuss and fume sometimes? Why are we
perverse and ask for something else? We don't know what ourselves.
It would be the worse for us if our petulant prayers were answered.
Come, try, give any one of us, for instance, a little more independence, untie our hands, widen the spheres of our activity, relax the
control and we . . . yes, I assure you . . . we should be begging to
be under control again at once. I know that you will very likely be
angry with me for that, and will begin shouting and stamping. Speak
for yourself, you will say, and for your miseries in your underground
holes, and don't dare to say "all of us"—excuse me, gentlemen, I
am not justifying myself with that "all of us." As for what concerns
me in particular I have only in my life carried to an extreme what
you have not dared to carry half-way, and what's more, you have
taken your cowardice for good sense, and have found comfort in
deceiving yourselves. So that perhaps, after all, there is more life in
me than in you. Look into it more carefully! Why, we don't even
know what living means now, what it is, and what it is called? Leave
us alone without books and we shall be lost and in confusion at once.
We shall not know what to join on to, what to cling to, what to love
and what to hate, what to respect and what to despise. We are oppressed
at being men—men with a real individual flesh and blood, we are
ashamed of it, we think it a disgrace and try to contrive to be some
sort of impossible generalized man. We are stillborn, and for generations past have been begotten, not by living fathers, and that suits
us better and better. We are developing a taste for it. Soon we shall
contrive to be born somehow from an idea. But enough; I don't want
to write more from "Underground."

*(The notes of this paradoxalist do not end here, however. He could
not refrain from going on with them, but it seems to us that we may
stop here.)*

LEO TOLSTOY
1828–1910

Count Leo Tolstoy excited the interest of the West mainly as a public figure:
a count owning large estates who decided to give up his wealth and live like
a simple Russian peasant—to dress in a blouse, to eat peasant food, and

even to plow the fields and make shoes with his own hands. By the time of his death he had become the leader of a religious cult, the propounder of a new religion. It was, in substance, a highly simplified primitive Christianity which he put into a few moral commands (such as, "Do not resist evil") and from which he drew, with radical consistency, a complete condemnation of modern civilization: the state, courts and law, war, patriotism, marriage, modern art and literature, science and medicine. In debating this Christian anarchism people have tended to forget that Tolstoy established his command of the public ear as a novelist, or they have exaggerated the contrast between the early worldly novelist and the later prophet who repudiated all his early novelistic work: *War and Peace*, the enormous epic of the 1812 invasion of Russia, and *Anna Karenina*, the story of an adulterous love, superbly realized in accurately imagined detail.

Tolstoy was born at Yásnaya Polyána, his mother's estate near Tula (about 130 miles south of Moscow), on August 28, 1828. His father was a retired lieutenant colonel; one of his ancestors, the first count, had served Peter the Great as an ambassador. His mother's father was a Russian general in chief. Tolstoy lost both parents early in his life and was brought up by aunts. He went to the University of Kazan between 1844 and 1847, drifted along aimlessly for a few years more, and in 1851 became a cadet in the Caucasus. As an artillery officer he saw action in the wars with the mountain tribes and again, in 1854–1855, during the Crimean War against the French and English. Tolstoy had written fictional reminiscences of his childhood while he was in the Caucasus, and during the Crimean War he wrote war stories which established his literary reputation. For some years he lived on his estate, where he founded and himself taught an extremely "progressive" school for peasant children. He made two trips to western Europe, in 1857 and in 1860–61. In 1862 he married the daughter of a physician, Sonya Bers, who bore him thirteen children.

In the first years of his married life, between 1863 and 1869, he wrote his enormous novel *War and Peace*. The book made him famous in Russia but was not translated into English until long afterward. Superficially, *War and Peace* is a historical novel about the Napoleonic invasion of Russia in 1812, a huge swarming epic of a nation's resistance to the foreigner. Tolstoy himself interprets history in general as a struggle of anonymous collective forces which are moved by unknown irrational impulses, waves of communal feeling. Heroes, great men, are actually not heroes but merely insignificant puppets; the best general is the one who does nothing to prevent the unknown course of Providence. But *War and Peace* is not only an impressive and vivid panorama of historical events but also the profound story—centered in two main characters, Pierre Bezukhov and Prince Andrey Bolkonsky—of a search for the meaning of life. Andrey finds the meaning of life in love and forgiveness of his enemies. Pierre, at the end of a long groping struggle, an education by suffering, finds it in an acceptance of ordinary existence, its duties and pleasures, the family, the continuity of the race.

Tolstoy's next long novel, *Anna Karenina* (1875–1877), resumes this second thread of *War and Peace*. It is a novel of contemporary manners, a narrative of adultery and suicide. But this vivid story, told with incomparable concrete imagination, is counterpointed and framed by a second story, that of Levin, another seeker after the meaning of life, a figure who represents the author as Pierre did in the earlier book; the work ends with a promise of solution, with the ideal of a life in which we should "remember God." Thus *Anna Karenina* also anticipates the approaching crisis in Tolstoy's life. When it came, with the sudden revulsion he describes in *A Confession* (1879), he condemned his earlier books and spent the next years in writing pamphlets and tracts expounding his religion.

Only slowly did Tolstoy return to the writing of fiction, now regarded entirely as a means of presenting his creed. The earlier novels seemed to him unclear in their message, overdetailed in their method. Hence Tolstoy tried to simplify his art; he wrote plays with a thesis, stories which are like fables or parables, and one long, rather inferior novel, *The Resurrection* (1899), his most savage satire on Russian and modern institutions.

In 1901 Tolstoy was excommunicated. A disagreement with his wife about the nature of the good life and about financial matters sharpened into a conflict over his last will, which finally led to a complete break: he left home in the company of a doctor friend. He caught cold on the train journey south and died in the house of the stationmaster of Astápovo, on November 20, 1910.

If we look back on Tolstoy's work as a whole, we must recognize its continuity. From the very beginning he was a Rousseauist. As early as 1851, when he was in the Caucasus, his diary announced his intention of founding a new, simplified religion. Even as a young man on his estate he had lived quite simply, like a peasant, except for occasional sprees and debauches. He had been horrified by war from the very beginning, though he admired the heroism of the individual soldier and had remnants of patriotic feeling. All his books concern the same theme, the good life, and they all say that the good life lies outside of civilization, near to the soil, in simplicity and humility, in love of one's neighbor. Power, the lust for power, luxury, are always evil.

As a novelist Tolstoy is rooted in the tradition of the older realism. He read and knew the English writers of the eighteenth century, and also Thackeray and Trollope. He did not care for the recent French writers (he was strong in his disapproval of Flaubert) except for Maupassant, who struck him as truthful and useful in his struggle against hypocrisy. Tolstoy's long novels are loosely plotted, though they have large over-all designs. They work by little scenes vividly visualized, by an accumulation of exact detail. Each character is drawn by means of repeated emphasis on certain physical traits, like Pierre's shortsightedness and his hairy, clumsy hands, or Princess Marya's luminous eyes, the red patches on her face, and her shuffling gait. This concretely realized surface, however, everywhere recedes into depths: to the depiction of disease, delirium, and death and to glimpses into eternity. In *War and Peace* the blue sky is the recurrent symbol for the metaphysical relationships of man. Tolstoy is so robust, has his feet so firmly on the ground, presents what he sees with such clarity and objectivity, that one can be easily deluded into considering his dominating quality to be physical, sensual, antithetical to Dostoevsky's spirituality. The contrasts between the two greatest Russian novelists are indeed obvious. While Tolstoy's method can be called epic, Dostoevsky's is dramatic; while Tolstoy's view of man is

Rousseauistic, Dostoevsky stresses the fall of man; while Tolstoy rejects history and status, Dostoevsky appeals to the past and wants a hierarchical society, and so on. But these profound differences should not obscure one basic similarity: the deep spirituality of both, their rejection of the basic materialism and the conception of truth propounded by modern science and theorists of realism.

The Death of Iván Ilyich (1886) belongs to the period after Tolstoy's religious conversion when he slowly returned to fiction writing. It represents a happy medium between his early and late manner. Its story and moral are simple and obvious, as always with Tolstoy (in contrast to Dostoevsky). And it says what almost all of his works are intended to convey—that man is leading the wrong kind of life, that he should return to essentials, to "nature." In *The Death of Iván Ilyich* Tolstoy combines a savage satire on the futility and hypocrisy of conventional life with a powerful symbolic presentation of man's isolation in the struggle with death and of man's hope for a final resurrection. Iván Ilyich is a Russian judge, an official, but he is also the average man of the prosperous middle classes of his time and ours, and he is also Everyman confronted with disease and dying and death. He is an ordinary person, neither virtuous nor particularly vicious, a "go-getter" in his profession, a "family man," as marriages go, who has children but has drifted apart from his wife. Through his disease, which comes about by a trivial accident in the trivial business of fixing a curtain, Iván Ilyich is slowly awakened to self-consciousness and a realization of the falsity of his life and ambitions. The isolation which disease imposes upon him, the wall of hypocrisy erected around him by his family and his doctors, his suffering and pain, drive him slowly to the recognition of *It:* to a knowledge, not merely theoretical but proved on his pulses, of his own mortality. At first he would like simply to return to his former pleasant and normal life—even in the last days of his illness, knowing he must die, he screams in his agony, "I won't!"—but at the end, struggling in the black sack into which he is being pushed, he sees the light at the bottom. " 'Death is finished,' he said to himself. 'It is no more!' "

All the people around him are egotists and hypocrites: his wife, who can remember only how she suffered during his agony; his daughter, who thinks only of the delay in her marriage; his colleagues, who speculate only about the room his death will make for promotions in the court; the doctors, who think only of the name of the disease and not of the patient; all except his shy and frightened son, Vásya, and the servant Gerásim. Gerásim is a healthy peasant lad, assistant to the butler, but because he is near to nature, he is free from hypocrisy, helps his master to be comfortable, and even mentions death, while all the others conceal the truth from him. The doctors, especially, are shown as mere specialists, inhuman and selfish. The first doctor is like a judge, like Iván himself when he sat in court, summing up and cutting off further questions of the patient (or is it the prisoner?). The satire at points appears ineffectively harsh in its violence, but it will not seem exceptional to those who know the older Tolstoy's general attitude toward courts, medicine, marriage, and even modern literature. The cult of art is jeered at, in small touches, only incidentally; it belongs, according to Tolstoy, to the falsities of modern civilization, alongside marriage (which merely

hides bestial sensuality), and science (which merely hides rapacity and ignorance).

The story is deliberately deprived of any element of suspense, not only by
the announcement contained in the title but by the technique of the cut-
back. We first hear of Iván Ilyich's death and see the reaction of the widow
and friends, and only then listen to the story of his life. The detail, as always
in Tolstoy, is superbly concrete and realistic: he does not shy away from the
smell of disease, the physical necessity of using a chamber-pot, or the sound
of screaming. He can employ the creaking of a hassock as a recurrent motif
to point up the comedy of hypocrisy played by the widow and her visitor.
He can seriously and tragically use the humble image of a black sack or the
illusion of the movement of a train.

But all this naturalistic detail serves the one purpose of making us realize,
as Iván Ilyich realizes, that not only Caius is mortal but you and I also, and
that the life of most of us civilized people is a great lie because it disguises
and ignores its dark background, the metaphysical abyss, the reality of Death.
While the presentation of *The Death of Iván Ilyich* approaches, at moments,
the tone of a legend or fable ("Iván Ilyich's life had been most simple and
most ordinary and therefore most terrible"), Tolstoy in this story manages to
stay within the concrete situation of our society and to combine the aesthetic
method of realism with the universalizing power of symbolic art.

R. F. Christian, *Tolstoy: A Critical Introduction* (1969), is clear, instructive, informative. E. B. Greenwood, *Tolstoy: The Comprehensive Vision*
(1975), contains an excellent chapter, "Death: A *Confession* and *Ivan Ilyich*."
Ralph E. Matlaw, *Tolstoy: A Collection of Critical Essays* (1967), and Philip
Rahv, *Image and Idea* (1949), both present essays on "The Death of Ivan
Ilyich." Theodore Redpath, *Tolstoy* (1960), provides a brief introduction
with good criticism of ideas. Ernest J. Simmons, *Leo Tolstoy* (1946), is the
fullest biography in English.

The Death of Iván Ilyich[1]

I

During an interval in the Melvínski trial in the large building of
the Law Courts the members and public prosecutor met in Iván
Egórovich Shébek's private room, where the conversation turned on
the celebrated Krasóvski case. Fëdor Vasílievich warmly maintained
that it was not subject to their jurisdiction, Iván Egórovich maintained the contrary, while Peter Ivánovich, not having entered into
the discussion at the start, took no part in it but looked through the
Gazette which had just been handed in.

"Gentlemen," he said, "Iván Ilyich has died!"

"You don't say!"

1. Translated by Louise and Aylmer Maude.

"Here read it yourself," replied Peter Ivánovich, handing Fëdor Vasílievich the paper still damp from the press. Surrounded by a black border were the words: "Praskóvya Fëdorovna Golovíná, with profound sorrow, informs relatives and friends of the demise of her beloved husband Iván Illyich Golovín, Member of the Court of Justice, which occurred on February the 4th of this year 1882. The funeral will take place on Friday at one o'clock in the afternoon."

Iván Ilyich had been a colleague of the gentlemen present and was liked by them all. He had been ill for some weeks with an illness said to be incurable. His post had been kept open for him, but there had been conjectures that in case of his death, Alexéev might receive his appointment, and that either Vínnikov or Shtábel would succeed Alexéev. So on receiving the news of Iván Ilyich's death the first thought of each of the gentlemen in that private room was of the changes and promotions it might occasion among themselves or their acquaintances.

"I shall be sure to get Shtábel's place or Vínnikov's," thought Fëdor Vasílievich. "I was promised that long ago, and the promotion means an extra eight hundred rubles a year for me besides the allowance."

"Now I must apply for my brother-in-law's transfer from Kalúga," thought Peter Ivánovich. "My wife will be very glad, and then she won't be able to say that I never do anything for her relations."

"I thought he would never leave his bed again," said Peter Ivánovich aloud. "It's very sad."

"But what really was the matter with him?"

"The doctors couldn't say—at least they could, but each of them said something different. When last I saw him I thought he was getting better."

"And I haven't been to see him since the holidays. I always meant to go."

"Had he any property?"

"I think his wife had a little—but something quite trifling."

"We shall have to go to see her, but they live so terribly far away."

"Far away from you, you mean. Everything's far away from your place."

"You see, he never can forgive my living on the other side of the river," said Peter Ivánovich, smiling at Shébek. Then, still talking of the distances between different parts of the city, they returned to the Court.

Besides considerations as to the possible transfers and promotions likely to result from Iván Ilyich's death, the mere fact of the death of a near acquaintance aroused, as usual, in all who heard of it the complacent feeling that, "it is he who is dead and not I."

Each one thought or felt, "Well, he's dead but I'm alive!" But the more intimate of Iván Ilyich's acquaintances, his so-called friends, could not help thinking also that they would now have to fulfil the very tiresome demands of propriety by attending the funeral service and paying a visit of condolence to the widow.

Fëdor Vasílievich and Peter Ivánovich had been his nearest acquaintances. Peter Ivánovich had studied law with Iván Ilyich and had considered himself to be under obligations to him.

Having told his wife at dinner-time of Iván Ilyich's death, and of his conjecture that it might be possible to get her brother transferred to their circuit, Peter Ivánovich sacrificed his usual nap, put on his evening clothes, and drove to Iván Ilyich's house.

At the entrance stood a carriage and two cabs. Leaning against the wall in the hall downstairs near the cloak-stand was a coffin-lid covered with cloth of gold, ornamented with gold cord and tassels, that had been polished up with metal powder. Two ladies in black were taking off their fur cloaks. Peter Ivánovich recognized one of them as Iván Ilyich's sister, but the other was a stranger to him. His colleague Schwartz was just coming downstairs, but on seeing Peter Ivánovich enter he stopped and winked at him, as if to say: "Iván Ilyich has made a mess of things—not like you and me."

Schwartz's face with his Piccadilly whiskers, and his slim figure in evening dress, had as usual an air of elegant solemnity which contrasted with the playfulness of his character and had a special piquancy here, or so it seemed to Peter Ivánovich.

Peter Ivánovich allowed the ladies to precede him and slowly followed them upstairs. Schwartz did not come down but remained where he was, and Peter Ivánovich understood that he wanted to arrange where they should play bridge that evening. The ladies went upstairs to the widow's room, and Schwartz with seriously compressed lips but a playful look in his eyes, indicated by a twist of his eyebrows the room to the right where the body lay.

Peter Ivánovich, like everyone else on such occasions, entered feeling uncertain what he would have to do. All he knew was that at such times it is always safe to cross oneself. But he was not quite sure whether one should make obeisances while doing so. He therefore adopted a middle course. On entering the room he began crossing himself and made a slight movement resembling a bow. At the same time, as far as the motion of his head and arm allowed, he surveyed the room. Two young men—apparently nephews, one of whom was a high-school pupil—were leaving the room, crossing themselves as they did so. An old woman was standing motionless, and a lady with strangely arched eyebrows was saying something to her in a whisper. A vigorous, resolute Church Reader, in a frock-coat, was reading something in a loud voice with an expression that precluded any contradiction. The butler's assistant, Gerásim, stepping lightly in front of Peter Ivánovich, was strewing something on the floor. Noticing this, Peter Ivánovich was immediately aware of a faint odour of a decomposing body.

The last time he had called on Iván Ilyich, Peter Ivánovich had seen Gerásim in the study. Iván Ilyich had been particularly fond of him and he was performing the duty of a sick nurse.

Peter Ivánovich continued to make the sign of the cross slightly inclining his head in an intermediate direction between the coffin, the Reader, and the icons on the table in a corner of the room. Afterwards, when it seemed to him that this movement of his arm in crossing himself had gone on too long, he stopped and began to look at the corpse.

The dead man lay, as dead men always lie, in a specially heavy way, his rigid limbs sunk in the soft cushions of the coffin, with the head forever bowed on the pillow. His yellow waxen brow with bald patches over his sunken temples was thrust up in the way peculiar to the dead, the protruding nose seeming to press on the upper lip. He was much changed and had grown even thinner since Peter Ivánovich had last seen him, but, as is always the case with the dead, his face was handsomer and above all more dignified than when he ws alive. The expression on the face said that what was necessary had been accomplished, and accomplished rightly. Besides this there was in that expression a reproach and a warning to the living. This warning seemed to Peter Ivánovich out of place, or at least not applicable to him. He felt a certain discomfort and so he hurriedly crossed himself once more and turned and went out of the door—too hurriedly and too regardless of propriety, as he himself was aware.

Schwartz was waiting for him in the adjoining room with legs spread wide apart and both hands toying with his top-hat behind his back. The mere sight of that playful, well-groomed, and elegant figure refreshed Peter Ivánovich. He felt that Schwartz was above all these happenings and could not surrender to any depressing influences. His very look said that this incident of a church service for Iván Ilyich could not be a sufficient reason for infringing the order of the session—in other words, that it would certainly not prevent his unwrapping a new pack of cards and shuffling them that evening while a footman placed four fresh candles on the table: in fact, that there was no reason for supposing that this incident would hinder their spending the evening agreeably. Indeed he said this in a whisper as Peter Ivánovich passed him, proposing that they should meet for a game at Fëdor Vasílievich's. But apparently Peter Ivánovich was not destined to play bridge that evening. Praskóvya Fëdorovna (a short, fat woman who despite all efforts to the contrary had continued to broaden steadily from her shoulders downwards and who had the same extraordinary arched eyebrows as the lady who had been standing by the coffin), dressed all in black, her head covered with lace, came out of her own room with some other ladies, conducted them to the room where the dead body lay, and said: "The service will begin immediately. Please go in."

Schwartz, making an indefinite bow, stood still, evidently neither accepting nor declining this invitation. Praskóvya Fëdorovna recognizing Peter Ivánovich, sighed, went close up to him, took his hand, and said: "I know you were a true friend to Iván Ilyich . . ." and looked at him awaiting some suitable response. And Peter Ivánovich knew that, just as it had been the right thing to cross himself in that room, so what he had to do here was to press her hand, sigh, and say, "Believe me . . ." So he did all this and as he did it felt that the desired result had been achieved: that both he and she were touched.

"Come with me. I want to speak to you before it begins," said the widow. "Give me your arm."

Peter Ivánovich gave her his arm and they went to the inner rooms, passing Schwartz who winked at Peter Ivánovich compassionately.

"That does for our bridge! Don't object if we find another player. Perhaps you can cut in when you do escape," said his playful look.

Peter Ivánovich sighed still more deeply and despondently, and Praskóvya Fëdorovna pressed his arm gratefully. When they reached the drawing-room, upholstered in pink cretonne and lighted by a dim lamp, they sat down at the table—she on a sofa and Peter Ivánovich on a low hassock, the springs of which yielded spasmodically under his weight. Praskóvya Fëdorovna had been on the point of warning him to take another seat, but felt that such a warning was out of keeping with her present condition and so changed her mind. As he sat down on the hassock Peter Ivánovich recalled how Iván Ilyich had arranged this room and had consulted him regarding this pink cretonne with green leaves. The whole room was full of furniture and knick-knacks, and on her way to the sofa the lace of the widow's black shawl caught on the carved edge of the table. Peter Ivánovich rose to detach it, and the springs of the hassock, relieved of his weight, rose also and gave him a push. The widow began detaching her shawl herself, and Peter Ivánovich again sat down, suppressing the rebellious springs of the hassock under him. But the widow had not quite freed herself and Peter Ivánovich got up again, and again the hassock rebelled and even creaked. When this was all over she took out a clean cambric handkerchief and began to weep. The episode with the shawl and the struggle with the hassock had cooled Peter Ivánovich's emotions and he sat there with a sullen look on his face. This awkward situation was interrupted by Sokolóv, Iván Ilyich's butler, who came to report that the plot in the cemetery that Praskóvya Fëdorovna had chosen would cost two hundred rubles.

She stopped weeping and, looking at Peter Ivánovich with the air of a victim, remarked in French that it was very hard for her. Peter Ivánovich made a silent gesture signifying his full conviction that it must indeed be so.

"Please smoke," she said in a magnanimous yet crushed voice, and turned to discuss with Sokolóv the price of the plot for the grave.

Peter Ivánovich while lighting his cigarette heard her inquiring very circumstantially into the prices of different plots in the cemetery and finally decide which she would take. When that was done she gave instructions about engaging the choir. Sokolóv then left the room.

"I look after everything myself," she told Peter Ivánovich, shifting the albums that lay on the table; and noticing that the table was endangered by his cigarette-ash, she immediately passed him an ash-tray, saying as she did so: "I consider it an affectation to say that my grief prevents my attending to practical affairs. On the contrary, if anything can—I won't say console me, but—distract me, it is seeing to everything concerning him." She again took out her handkerchief as if preparing to cry, but suddenly, as if mastering her feeling, she shook herself and began to speak calmly. "But there is something I want to talk to you about."

Peter Ivánovich bowed, keeping control of the springs of the hassock, which immediately began quivering under him.

"He suffered terribly the last few days."

"Did he?" said Peter Ivánovich.

"Oh, terribly! He screamed unceasingly, not for minutes but for hours. For the last three days he screamed incessantly. It was unendurable. I cannot understand how I bore it; you could hear him three rooms off. Oh, what I have suffered!"

"Is it possible that he was conscious all that time?" asked Peter Ivánovich.

"Yes," she whispered. "To the last moment. He took leave of us a quarter of an hour before he died, and asked us to take Volódya away."

The thought of the sufferings of this man he had known so intimately, first as a merry little boy, then as a school-mate, and later as a grown-up colleague, suddenly struck Peter Ivánovich with horror, despite an unpleasant consciousness of his own and this woman's dissimulation. He again saw that brow, and that nose pressing down on the lip, and felt afraid for himself.

"Three days of frightful suffering and then death! Why, that might suddenly, at any time, happen to me," he thought, and for a moment felt terrified. But—he did not himself know how—the customary reflection at once occurred to him that this had happened to Iván Ilyich and not to him, and that it should not and could not happen to him, and that to think that it could would be yielding to depression which he ought not to do, as Schwartz's expression plainly showed. After which reflection Peter Ivánovich felt reassured, and began to ask with interest about the details of Iván Ilyich's death, as though death was an accident natural to Iván Ilyich but certainly not to himself.

After many details of the really dreadful physical sufferings Iván Ilyich had endured (which details he learnt only from the effect those sufferings had produced on Praskóvya Fëdorovna's nerves) the widow apparently found it necessary to get to business.

"Oh, Peter Ivánovich, how hard it is! How terribly, terribly hard!" and she again began to weep.

Peter Ivánovich sighed and waited for her to finish blowing her nose. When she had done so he said, "Believe me . . ." and she again began talking and brought out what was evidently her chief concern with him—namely, to question him as to how she could obtain a grant of money from the government on the occasion of her husband's death. She made it appear that she was asking Peter Ivánovich's advice about her pension, but he soon saw that she already knew about that to the minutest detail, more even than he did himself. She knew how much could be got out of the government in consequence of her husband's death, but wanted to find out whether she could possibly extract something more. Peter Ivánovich tried to think of some means of doing so, but after reflecting for a while and, out of propriety, condemning the government for its niggardliness, he said he thought that nothing more could be got. Then she sighed and evidently began to devise means of getting rid of her visitor. Noticing this, he put out his cigarette, rose, pressed her hand, and went out into the anteroom.

In the dining-room where the clock stood that Iván Ilyich had liked so much and had bought at an antique shop, Peter Ivánovich met a priest and a few acquaintances who had come to attend the service, and he recognized Iván Ilyich's daughter, a handsome young woman. She was in black and her slim figure appeared slimmer than ever. She had a gloomy, determined, almost angry expression, and bowed to Peter Ivánovich as though he were in some way to blame. Behind her, with the same offended look, stood a wealthy young man, an examining magistrate, whom Peter Ivánovich also knew and who was her fiancé, as he had heard. He bowed mournfully to them and was about to pass into the death-chamber, when from under the stairs appeared the figure of Iván Ilyich's schoolboy son, who was extremely like this father. He seemed a little Iván Ilyich, such as Peter Ivánovich remembered when they studied law together. His tear-stained eyes had in them the look that is seen in the eyes of boys of thirteen or fourteen who are not pure-minded.

When he saw Peter Ivánovich he scowled morosely and shame-facedly. Peter Ivánovich nodded to him and entered the death-chamber. The service began: candles, groans, incense, tears, and sobs. Peter Ivánovich stood looking gloomily down at his feet. He did not look once at the dead man, did not yield to any depressing influence, and was one of the first to leave the room. There was no one in the anteroom, but Gerásim darted out of the dead man's room, rummaged with his strong hands among the fur coats to find Peter Ivánovich's and helped him on with it.

"Well, friend Gerásim," said Peter Ivánovich, so as to say something. "It's a sad affair, isn't it?"

"It's God's will. We shall all come to it some day," said Gerásim, displaying his teeth—the even, white teeth of a healthy peasant—and, like a man in the thick of urgent work, he briskly opened the front door, called the coachman, helped Peter Ivánovich into the sledge, and sprang back to the porch as if in readiness for what he had to do next.

Peter Ivánovich found the fresh air particularly pleasant after the smell of incense, the dead body, and carbolic acid.

"Where to, sir?" asked the coachman.

"It's not too late even now. . . . I'll call round on Fëdor Vasílie-vich."

He accordingly drove there and found them just finishing the first rubber, so that it was quite convenient for him to cut in.

II

Iván Ilyich's life had been most simple and most ordinary and therefore most terrible.

He had been a member of the Court of Justice, and died at the age of forty-five. His father had been an official who after serving in various ministries and departments in Petersburg had made the sort of career which brings men to positions from which by reason of their long service they cannot be dismissed, though they are obviously unfit to hold any responsible position, and for whom therefore posts are specially created, which though fictitious, carry salaries of from six to ten thousand rubles that are not fictitious, and in receipt of which they live on to a great age.

Such was the Privy Councillor and superfluous member of various superfluous institutions, Ilya Efímovich Golovín.

He had three sons, of whom Iván Ilyich was the second. The eldest son was following in his father's footsteps only in another department, and was already approaching that stage in the service at which a similar sinecure would be reached. The third son was a failure. He had ruined his prospects in a number of positions and was now serving in the railway department. His father and brothers, and still more their wives, not merely disliked meeting him, but avoided remembering his existence unless compelled to do so. His sister had married Baron Greff, a Petersburg official of her father's type. Iván Ilyich was *le phénix de la famille*[2] as people said. He was neither as cold and formal as his elder brother nor as wild as the younger, but was a happy mean between them—an intelligent, polished, lively and agreeable man. He had studied with his younger brother at the School of Law, but the latter had failed to complete the course and was expelled when he was in the fifth class. Iván Ilyich finished the course well. Even when he was at the School of Law he was just what he remained for the rest of his life: a capable, cheerful, good-natured, and sociable man, though strict in the fulfilment of what he considered to be his duty: and he considered his duty to be what was so considered by those in authority. Neither as a boy nor as a man was he a toady, but from early youth was by nature attracted to people of high station as a fly is drawn to the light, assimilating their ways and views of life and establishing friendly relations with them. All the enthusiasms of childhood and youth passed without leaving much trace on him; he succumbed to sensuality, to vanity, and latterly among the highest classes to liberalism, but always within limits which his instinct unfailingly indicated to him as correct.

At school he had done things which had formerly seemed to him very horrid and made him feel disgusted with himself when he did them; but when later on he saw that such actions were done by people of good position and that they did not regard them as wrong, he was able not exactly to regard them as right, but to forget about them entirely or not be at all troubled at remembering them.

Having graduated from the School of Law and qualified for the tenth rank of the civil service, and having received money from his father for his equipment, Iván Ilyich ordered himself clothes at Scharmer's, the fashionable tailor, hung a medallion inscribed *respice finem*[3] on his watch-chain, took leave of his professor and the prince who was patron of the school, had a farewell dinner with his comrades at Donon's first-class restaurant, and with his new and fashionable portmanteau, linen, clothes, shaving and other toilet appliances, and a travelling rug, all purchased at the best shops, he set off for one of the provinces where, through his father's influence, he had been attached to the governor as an official for special service.

In the province Iván Ilyich soon arranged as easy and agreeable a position for himself as he had at the School of Law. He performed his official tasks, made his career, and at the same time amused

---

2. "The phoenix of the family." The word "phoenix" is used here to mean "rare bird, "prodigy."   3. "Regard the end" (a Latin motto).

himself pleasantly and decorously. Occasionally he paid official visits to country districts, where he behaved with dignity both to his superiors and inferiors, and performed the duties entrusted to him, which related chiefly to the sectarians,[4] with an exactness and incorruptible honesty of which he could not but feel proud.

In official matters, despite his youth and taste for frivolous gaiety, he was exceedingly reserved, punctilious, and even severe; but in society he was often amusing and witty, and always good-natured, correct in his manner, and *bon enfant*, as the governor and his wife—with whom he was like one of the family—used to say of him.

In the province he had an affair with a lady who made advances to the elegant young lawyer, and there was also a milliner; and there were carousals with aides-de-camp who visited the district, and after-supper visits to a certain outlying street of doubtful reputation; and there was too some obsequiousness to his chief and even to his chief's wife, but all this was done with such a tone of good breeding that no hard names could be applied to it. It all came under the heading of the French saying: *"Il faut que jeunesse se passe."*[5] It was all done with clean hands, in clean linen, with French phrases, and above all among people of the best society and consequently with the approval of people of rank.

So Iván Ilyich served for five years and then came a change in his official life. The new and reformed judicial institutions were introduced, and new men were needed. Iván Ilyich became such a new man. He was offered the post of Examining Magistrate, and he accepted it though the post was in another province and obliged him to give up the connexions he had formed and to make new ones. His friends met to give him a send-off; they had a group-photograph taken and presented him with a silver cigarette-case, and he set off to his new post.

As examining magistrate Iván Ilyich was just as *comme il faut* and decorous a man, inspiring general respect and capable of separating his official duties from his private life, as he had been when acting as an official on special service. His duties now as examining magistrate were far more interesting and attractive than before. In his former position it had been pleasant to wear an undress uniform made by Scharmer, and to pass through the crowd of petitioners and officials who were timorously awaiting an audience with the governor, and who envied him as with free and easy gait he went straight into his chief's private room to have a cup of tea and a cigarette with him. But not many people had then been directly dependent on him—only police officials and the sectarians when he went on spe-

4. The Old Believers, a large group of Russians (about twenty-five million in 1900), members of a sect which originated in a break with the Orthodox Church in the seventeenth century; they were subject to many legal restrictions.   5. Youth must have its fling. [Translator's note.]

cial missions—and he liked to treat them politely, almost as comrades, as if he were letting them feel that he who had the power to
crush them was treating them in this simple, friendly way. There
were then but few such people. But now, as an examining magistrate, Iván Ilyich felt that everyone without exception, even the most
important and self-satisfied, was in his power, and that he need only
write a few words on a sheet of paper with a certain heading, and
this or that important, self-satisfied person would be brought before
him in the role of an accused person or a witness, and if he did not
choose to allow him to sit down, would have to stand before him
and answer his questions. Iván Ilyich never abused his power; he
tried on the contrary to soften its expression, but the consciousness
of it and of the possibility of softening its effect, supplied the chief
interest and attraction of his office. In his work itself, especially in
his examinations, he very soon acquired a method of eliminating all
considerations irrelevant to the legal aspect of the case, and reducing
even the most complicated case to a form in which it would be presented on paper only in its externals, completely excluding his personal opinion of the matter, while above all observing every prescribed
formality. The work was new and Iván Ilyich was one of the first
men to apply the new Code of 1864.[6]

On taking up the post of examining magistrate in a new town, he
made new acquaintances and connexions, placed himself on a new
footing, and assumed a somewhat different tone. He took up an attitude of rather dignified aloofness towards the provincial authorities,
but picked out the best circle of legal gentlemen and wealthy gentry
living in the town and assumed a tone of slight dissatisfaction with
the government, of moderate liberalism, and of enlightened citizenship. At the same time, without at all altering the elegance of his
toilet, he ceased shaving his chin and allowed his beard to grow as it
pleased.

Iván Ilyich settled down very pleasantly in this new town. The
society there, which inclined towards opposition to the governor,
was friendly, his salary was larger, and he began to play *vint* [a form
of bridge], which he found added not a little to the pleasure of life,
for he had a capacity for cards, played good-humouredly, and calculated rapidly and astutely, so that he usually won.

After living there for two years he met his future wife, Praskóvya
Fëdorovna Míkhel, who was the most attractive, clever, and brilliant
girl of the set in which he moved, and among other amusements and
relaxations from his labours as examining magistrate, Iván Ilyich
established light and playful relations with her.

While he had been an official on special service he had been

6. The emancipation of the serfs in 1861 was followed by a thorough all-round reform of judicial
proceedings. [Translator's note.]

accustomed to dance, but now as an examining magistrate it was exceptional for him to do so. If he danced now, he did it as if to show that though he served under the reformed order of things, and had reached the fifth official rank, yet when it came to dancing he could do it better than most people. So at the end of an evening he sometimes danced with Praskóvya Fëdorovna, and it was chiefly during these dances that he captivated her. She fell in love with him. Iván Ilyich had at first no definite intention of marrying, but when the girl fell in love with him he said to himself: "Really, why shouldn't I marry?"

Praskóvya Fëdorovna came of a good family, was not bad looking, and had some little property. Iván Ilyich might have aspired to a more brilliant match, but even this was good. He had his salary, and she, he hoped, would have an equal income. She was well connected, and was a sweet, pretty, and thoroughly correct young woman. To say that Iván Ilyich married because he fell in love with Praskóvya Fëdorovna and found that she sympathized with his views of life would be as incorrect as to say that he married because his social circle approved of the match. He was swayed by both these considerations: the marriage gave him personal satisfaction, and at the same time it was considered the right thing by the most highly placed of his associates.

So Iván Ilyich got married.

The preparations for marriage and the beginning of married life, with its conjugal caresses, the new furniture, new crockery, and new linen, were very pleasant until his wife became pregnant—so that Iván Ilyich had begun to think that marriage would not impair the easy, agreeable, gay, and always decorous character of his life, approved of by society and regarded by himself as natural, but would even improve it. But from the first months of his wife's pregnancy, something new, unpleasant, depressing, and unseemly, and from which there was no way of escape, unexpectedly showed itself.

His wife, without any reason—*de gaieté de coeur* as Iván Ilyich expressed it to himself—began to disturb the pleasure and propriety of their life. She began to be jealous without any cause, expected him to devote his whole attention to her, found fault with everything, and made coarse and ill-mannered scenes.

At first Iván Ilyich hoped to escape from the unpleasantness of this state of affairs by the same easy and decorous relation to life that had served him heretofore: he tried to ignore his wife's disagreeable moods, continued to live in his usual easy and pleasant way, invited friends to his house for a game of cards, and also tried going out to his club or spending his evenings with friends. But one day his wife began upbraiding him so vigorously, using such coarse words, and continued to abuse him every time he did not fulfil her demands, so resolutely and with such evident determination not to give way till he submitted—that is, till he stayed at home and was bored just as she was—that he became alarmed. He now realized that matrimony—at any rate with Praskóvya Fëdorovna—was not always conducive to the pleasures and amenities of life, but on the contrary often infringed both comfort and propriety, and that he must therefore entrench himself against such infringement. And Iván Ilyich began to seek for means of doing so. His official duties were the one thing that imposed upon Praskóvya Fëdorovna, and by means of his official work and the duties attached to it he began struggling with his wife to secure his own independence.

With the birth of their child, the attempts to feed it and the various failures in doing so, and with the real and imaginary illnesses of mother and child, in which Iván Ilyich's sympathy was demanded but about which he understood nothing, the need of securing for himself an existence outside his family life became still more imperative.

As his wife grew more irritable and exacting and Iváan Ilyich transferred the centre of gravity of his life more and more to his official work, so did he grow to like his work better and became more ambitious than before.

Very soon, within a year of his wedding, Iván Ilyich had realized that marriage, though it may add some comforts to life, is in fact a very intricate and difficult affair towards which in order to perform one's duty, that is, to lead a decorous life approved of by society, one must adopt a definite attitude just as towards one's official duties.

And Iván Ilyich evolved such an attitude towards married life. He only required of it those conveniences—dinner at home, housewife, and bed—which it could give him, and above all that propriety of external forms required by public opinion. For the rest he looked for light-hearted pleasure and propriety, and was very thankful when he found them, but if he met with antagonism and querulousness he at once retired into his separate fenced-off world of official duties, where he found satisfaction.

Iván Ilyich was esteemed a good official, and after three years was made Assistant Public Prosecutor. His new duties, their importance, the possibility of indicting and imprisoning anyone he chose, the publicity his speeches received, and the success he had in all these things, made his work still more attractive.

More children came. His wife became more and more querulous and ill-tempered, but the attitude Iván Ilyich had adopted towards his home life rendered him almost impervious to her grumbling.

After seven years' service in that town he was transferred to another province as Public Prosecutor. They moved, but were short of money and his wife did not like the place they moved to. Though the salary was higher the cost of living was greater, besides which two of their children died and family life became still more unpleasant for him.

Praskóvya Fëdorovna blamed her husband for every inconvenience they encountered in their new home. Most of the conversations between husband and wife, especially as to the children's education, led to topics which recalled former disputes, and those disputes were apt to flare up again at any moment. There remained only those are rare periods of amorousness which still came to them at times but did not last long. These were islets at which they anchored for a while and then again set out upon that ocean of veiled hostility which showed itself in their aloofness from one another. This aloofness might have grieved Iván Ilyich had he considered that it ought not to exist, but he now regarded the position as normal, and even made it the goal at which he aimed in family life. His aim was to free himself more and more from those unpleasantnesses and to give them a semblance of harmlessness and propriety. He attained this by spending less and less time with his family, and when obliged to be at home he tried to safeguard his position by the presence of outsiders. The chief thing however was that he had his official duties. The whole interest of his life now centered in the official world and that interest absorbed him. The consciousness of his power, being able to ruin anybody he wished to ruin, the importance, even the external dignity of his entry into court, or meetings with his subordinates, his success with superiors and inferiors, and above all his masterly handling of cases, of which he was conscious—all this gave him pleasure and filled his life, together with chats with his colleagues, dinners, and bridge. So that on the whole Iván Ilyich's life continued to flow as he considered it should do—pleasantly and properly.

So things continued for another seven years. His eldest daughter was already sixteen, another child had died, and only one son was left, a schoolboy and a subject of dissensions. Iván Ilyich wanted to put him in the School of Law, but to spite him Praskóvya Fëdorovna entered him at the High School. The daughter had been educated at home and had turned out well: the boy did not learn badly either.

III

So Iván Ilyich lived for seventeen years after his marriage. He was already a Public Prosecutor of long standing, and had declined several proposed transfers while awaiting a more desirable post, when an unanticipated and unpleasant occurrence quite upset the peaceful course of his life. He was expecting to be offered the post of presiding judge in a University town, but Hoppe somehow came to the front and obtained the appointment instead. Iván Ilyich became irritable, reproached Hoppe, and quarrelled both with him and with his immediate superiors—who became colder to him and again passed him over when other appointments were made.

This was in 1880, the hardest year of Iván Ilyich's life. It was then that it became evident on the one hand that his salary was insufficient for them to live on, and on the other that he had been forgotten, and not only this, but that what was for him the greatest and most cruel injustice appeared to others a quite ordinary occurrence. Even his father did not consider it his duty to help him. Iván Ilyich felt himself abandoned by everyone, and that they regarded his position with a salary of 3,500 rubles as quite normal and even fortunate. He alone knew that with the consciousness of the injustices done him, with his wife's incessant nagging, and with the debts he had contracted by living beyond his means his position was far from normal.

In order to save money that summer he obtained leave of absence and went with his wife to live in the country at her brother's place.

In the country, without his work, he experienced *ennui* for the first time in his life, and not only *ennui* but intolerable depression, and he decided that it was impossible to go on living like that, and that it was necessary to take energetic measures.

Having passed a sleepless night pacing up and down the veranda, he decided to go to Petersburg and bestir himself, in order to punish those who had failed to appreciate him and to get transferred to another ministry.

Next day, despite many protests from his wife and her brother, he started for Petersburg with the sole object of obtaining a post with a salary of five thousand rubles a year. He was no longer bent on any particular department, or tendency, or kind of activity. All he now wanted was an appointment to another post with a salary of five thousand rubles, either in the administration, in the banks, with the railways, in one of the Empress Márya's Institutions,[7] or even in the customs—but it had to carry with it a salary of five thousand rubles and be in a ministry other than that in which they had failed to appreciate him.

And this quest of Iván Ilyich's was crowned with remarkable and unexpected success. At Kursk an acquaintance of his, F. I. Ilyín, got into the first-class carriage, sat down beside Iván Ilyich, and told him of a telegram just received by the governor of Kursk announcing that a change was about to take place in the ministry: Peter Ivánovich was to be superseded by Iván Semënovich.

The proposed change, apart from its significance for Russia, had a special significance for Iván Ilyich, because by bringing forward a

---

7. Reference to the charitable organization founded by the Empress Márya, wife of Paul I, late in the eighteenth century.

new man, Peter Petróvich, and consequently his friend Zachár Ivánovich, it was highly favourable for Iván Ilyich, since Zachár Ivánovich was a friend and colleague of his.

In Moscow his news was confirmed, and on reaching Petersburg
Iván Ilyich found Zachár Ivánovich and received a definite promise
of an appointment in his former department of Justice.

A week later he telegraphed to his wife: "Zachár in Miller's place.
I shall receive appointment on presentation of report."

Thanks to this change of personnel, Iván Ilyich had unexpectedly
obtained an appointment in his former ministry which placed him
two stages above his former colleagues besides giving him five thousand rubles salary and three thousand five hundred rubles for expenses
connected with his removal. All his ill humour towards his former
enemies and the whole department vanished, and Iván Ilyich was
completely happy.

He returned to the country more cheerful and contented than he
had been for a long time. Praskóvya Fëdorovna also cheered up and
a truce was arranged between them. Iván Ilyich told of how he had
been fêted by everybody in Petersburg, how all those who had been
his enemies were put to shame and now fawned on him, how envious
they were of his appointment, and how much everybody in Petersburg had liked him.

Praskóvya Fëdorovna listened to all this and appeared to believe
it. She did not contradict anything, but only made plans for their
life in the town to which they were going. Iván Ilyich saw with delight
that these plans were his plans, that he and his wife agreed, and that,
after a stumble, his life was regaining its due and natural character
of pleasant lightheartedness and decorum.

Iván Ilyich had come back for a short time only, for he had to take
up his new duties on the 10th of September. Moreover, he needed
time to settle into the new place, to move all his belongings from the
province, and to buy and order many additional things: in a word, to
make such arrangements as he had resolved on, which were almost
exactly what Praskóvya Fëdorovna too had decided on.

Now that everything had happened so fortunately, and that he and
his wife were at one in their aims and moreover saw so little of one
another they got on together better than they had done since the first
years of marriage. Iván Ilyich had thought of taking his family away
with him at once, but the insistence of his wife's brother and her
sister-in-law, who had suddenly become particularly amiable and
friendly to him and his family, induced him to depart alone.

So he departed, and the cheerful state of mind induced by his
success and by the harmony between his wife and himself, the one
intensifying the other, did not leave him. He found a delightful house,
just the thing both he and his wife had dreamt of. Spacious, lofty

reception rooms in the old style, a convenient and dignified study, rooms for his wife and daughter, a study for his son—it might have been specially built for them. Iván Ilyich himself superintended the arrangements, chose the wallpapers, supplemented the furniture (preferably with antiques which he considered particularly *comme il faut*), and supervised the upholstering. Everything progressed and progressed and approached the ideal he had set himself: even when things were only half completed they exceeded his expectations. He saw what a refined and elegant character, free from vulgarity, it would all have when it was ready. On falling asleep he pictured to himself how the reception-room would look. Looking at the yet unfinished drawing-room he could see the fireplace, the screen, the what-not, the little chairs dotted here and there, the dishes and plates on the walls, and the bronzes, as they would be when everything was in place. He was pleased by the thought of how his wife and daughter, who shared his taste in this matter, would be impressed by it. They were certainly not expecting as much. He had been particularly successful in finding, and buying cheaply, antiques which gave a particularly aristocratic character to the whole place. But in his letters he intentionally understated everything in order to be able to surprise them. All this so absorbed him that his new duties—though he liked his official work—interested him less than he had expected. Sometimes he even had moments of absent-mindedness during the Court Sessions, and would consider whether he should have straight or curved cornices for his curtains. He was so interested in it all that he often did things himself, rearranging the furniture, or rehanging the curtains. Once when mounting a step-ladder to show the upholsterer, who did not understand, how he wanted the hangings draped, he made a false step and slipped, but being a strong and agile man he clung on and only knocked his side against the knob of the window frame. The bruised place was painful but the pain soon passed, and he felt particularly bright and well just then. He wrote: "I feel fifteen years younger." He thought he would have everything ready by September, but it dragged on till mid-October. But the result was charming not only in his eyes but to everyone who saw it.

In reality it was just what is usually seen in the houses of people of moderate means who want to appear rich, and therefore succeed only in resembling others like themselves: there were damasks, dark wood, plants, rugs, and dull and polished bronzes—all the things people of a certain class have in order to resemble other people of that class. His house was so like the others that it would never have been noticed, but to him it all seemed to be quite exceptional. He was very happy when he met his family at the station and brought them to the newly furnished house all lit up, where a footman in a white tie opened the door into the hall decorated with plants, and when they went on into the drawing room and the study uttering exclamations of delight. He conducted them everywhere, drank in their praises eagerly, and beamed with pleasure. At tea that evening, when Praskóvya Fëdorovna among other things asked him about his fall, he laughed, and showed them how he had gone flying and had frightened the upholsterer.

"It's a good thing I'm a bit of an athlete. Another man might have been killed, but I merely knocked myself, just here; it hurts when it's touched, but it's passing off already—it's only a bruise."

So they began living in their new home—in which, as always happens, when they got thoroughly settled in they found they were just one room short—and with the increased income, which as always was just a little (some five hundred rubles) too little, but it was all very nice.

Things went particularly well at first, before everything was finally arranged and while something had still to be done: this thing bought, that thing ordered, another thing moved, and something else adjusted. Though there were some disputes between husband and wife, they were both so well satisfied and had so much to do that it all passed off without any serious quarrels. When nothing was left to arrange it became rather dull and something seemed to be lacking, but they were then making acquaintances, forming habits, and life was growing fuller.

Iván Ilyich spent his mornings at the law court and came home to dinner, and at first he was generally in a good humour, though he occasionally became irritable just on account of his house. (Every spot on the tablecloth or the upholstery, and every broken window-blind string, irritated him. He had devoted so much trouble to arranging it all that every disturbance of it distressed him.) But on the whole his life ran its course as he believed life should do: easily, pleasantly, and decorously.

He got up at nine, drank his coffee, read the paper, and then put on his undress uniform and went to the law courts. There the harness in which he worked had already been stretched to fit him and he donned it without a hitch: petitioners, inquiries at the chancery, the chancery itself, and the sittings public and administrative. In all this the thing was to exclude everything fresh and vital, which always disturbs the regular course of official business, and to admit only official relations with people, and then only on official grounds. A man would come, for instance, wanting some information. Iván Ilyich, as one in whose sphere the matter did not lie, would have nothing to do with him: but if the man had some business with him in his official capacity, something that could be expressed on officially stamped paper, he would do everything, positively everything he could within the limits of such relations, and in doing so would maintain

the semblance of friendly human relations, that is, would observe
the courtesies of life. As soon as the official relations ended, so did
everything else. Iván Ilyich possessed this capacity to separate his real
life from the official side of affairs and not mix the two, in the highest
degree, and by long practice and natural aptitude again and drop the
human relation. And he did it all easily, pleasantly, correctly, and
even artistically. In the intervals between the sessions he smoked,
drank tea, chatted a little about politics, a little about general topics,
a little about cards, but most of all about official appointments. Tired,
but with the feelings of a virtuoso—one of the first violins who has
played his part in an orchestra with precision—he would return home
to find that his wife and daughter had been out paying calls, or had
a visitor, and that his son had been to school, had done his homework with his tutor, and was duly learning what is taught at High
Schools. Everything was as it should be. After dinner, if they had no
visitors, Iván Ilyich sometimes read a book that was being much
discussed at the time, and in the evening settled down to work, that
is, read official papers, compared the depositions of witnesses, and
noted paragraphs of the Code applying to them. This was neither
dull nor amusing. It was dull when he might have been playing
bridge, but if no bridge was available it was at any rate better than
doing nothing or sitting with his wife. Iván Ilyich's chief pleasure
was giving little dinners to which he invited men and women of good
social position, and just as his drawing-room resembled all other
drawing-rooms so did his enjoyable little parties resemble all other
such parties.

Once they even gave a dance. Iván Ilyich enjoyed it and everything went off well, except that it led to a violent quarrel with his
wife about the cakes and sweets. Praskóvya Fëdorovna had made her
own plans, but Iván Ilyich insisted on getting everything from an
expensive confectioner and ordered too many cakes, and the quarrel
occurred because some of those cakes were left over and the confectioner's bill came to forty-five rubles. It was a great and disagreeable
quarrel. Praskóvya Fëdorovna called him "a fool and an imbecile,"
and he clutched at his head and made angry allusions to divorce.

But the dance itself had been enjoyable. The best people were
there, and Iván Ilyich had danced with Princess Trúfonova, a sister
of the distinguished founder of the Society "Bear my Burden."

The pleasures connected with his work were pleasures of ambition; his social pleasures were those of vanity; but Iván Ilyich's greatest pleasure was playing bridge. He acknowledged that whatever
disagreeable incident happened in his life, the pleasure that beamed
like a ray of light above everything else was to sit down to bridge with
good players, not noisy partners, and of course to four-handed bridge
(with five players it was annoying to have to stand out, though one

pretended not to mind), to play a clever and serious game (when the cards allowed it) and then to have supper and drink a glass of wine. After a game of bridge, especially if he had won a little (to win a large sum was unpleasant), Iván Ilyich went to bed in specially good humour.

So they lived. They formed a circle of acquaintances among the best people and were visited by people of importance and by young folk. In their views as to their acquaintances, husband, wife, and daughter were entirely agreed, and tacitly and unanimously kept at arm's length and shook off the various shabby friends and relations who, with much show of affection, gushed into the drawing-room with its Japanese plates on the walls. Soon these shabby friends ceased to obtrude themselves and only the best people remained in the Golovíns' set.

Young men made up to Lisa, and Petríshchev, an examining magistrate and Dmítri Ivánovich Petríshchev's son and sole heir, began to be so attentive to her that Iván Ilyich had already spoken to Praskóvya Fëdorovna about it, and considered whether they should not arrange a party for them, or get up some private theatricals.

So they lived, and all went well, without change, and life flowed pleasantly.

IV

They were all in good health. It could not be called ill health if Iván Ilyich sometimes said that he had a queer taste in his mouth and felt some discomfort in his left side.

But this discomfort increased and, though not exactly painful, grew into a sense of pressure in his side accompanied by ill humour. And his irritability became worse and worse and began to mar the agreeable, easy, and correct life that had established itself in the Golovín family. Quarrels between husband and wife became more and more frequent, and soon the ease and amenity disappeared and even the decorum was barely maintained. Scenes again became frequent, and very few of those islets remained on which husband and wife could meet without an explosion. Praskóvya Fëdorovna now had good reason to say that her husband's temper was trying. With characteristic exaggeration she said he had always had a dreadful temper, and that it had needed all her good nature to put up with it for twenty years. It was true that now the quarrels were started by him. His bursts of temper always came just before dinner, often just as he began to eat his soup. Sometimes he noticed that a plate or dish was chipped, or the food was not right, or his son put his elbow on the table, or his daughter's hair was not done as he liked it, and for all this he blamed Praskóvya Fëdorovna. At first she retorted and said disagreeable things to him, but once or twice he fell into such a rage at the beginning of dinner that she realized it was due to some physical derangement brought on by taking food, and so she restrained herself and did not answer, but only hurried to get the dinner over. She regarded this self-restraint as highly praiseworthy. Having come to the conclusion that her husband had a dreadful temper and made her life miserable, she began to feel sorry for herself, and the more she pitied herself the more she hated her husband. She began to wish he would die; yet she did not want him to die because then his salary would cease. And this irritated her against him still more. She considered herself dreadfully unhappy just because not even his death could save her, and though she concealed her exasperation, that hidden exasperation of hers increased his irritation also.

After one scene in which Iván Ilyich had been particularly unfair and after which he had said in explanation that he certainly was irritable but that it was due to his not being well, she said that if he was ill it should be attended to, and insisted on his going to see a celebrated doctor.

He went. Everything took place as he had expected and as it always does. There was the usual waiting and the important air assumed by the doctor, with which he was so familiar (resembling that which he himself assumed in court), and the sounding and listening, and the questions which called for answers that were foregone conclusions and were evidently unnecessary, and the look of importance which implied that "if only you put yourself in our hands we will arrange everything—we know indubitably how it has to be done, always in the same way for everybody alike." It was all just as it was in the law courts. The doctor put on just the same air towards him as he himself put on towards an accused person.

The doctor said that so-and-so indicated that there was so-and-so inside the patient, but if the investigation of so-and-so did not confirm this, then he must assume that and that. If he assumed that and that, then . . . and so on. To Iván Ilyich only one question was important: was his case serious or not? But the doctor ignored that inappropriate question. From his point of view it was not the one under consideration, the real question was to decide between a floating kidney, chronic catarrh, or appendicitis. It was not a question of Iván Ilyich's life or death, but one between a floating kidney and appendicitis. And that question the doctor solved brilliantly, as it seemed to Iván Ilyich, in favour of the appendix, with the reservation that should an examination of the urine give fresh indications the matter would be reconsidered. All this was just what Iván Ilyich had himself brilliantly accomplished a thousand times in dealing with men on trial. The doctor summed up just as brilliantly, looking over his spectacles triumphantly and even gaily at the accused. From the doctor's summing up Iván Ilyich concluded that things were bad, but that for the doctor, and perhaps for everybody else, it was a matter of indifference, though for him it was bad. And this conclusion struck him painfully, arousing in him a great feeling of pity for himself and of bitterness towards the doctor's indifference to a matter of such importance.

He said nothing of this, but rose, placed the doctor's fee on the table, and remarked with a sigh: "We sick people probably often put inappropriate questions. But tell me, in general, is this complaint dangerous or not? . . ."

The doctor looked at him sternly over his spectacles with one eye, as if to say: "Prisoner, if you will not keep to the questions put to you, I shall be obliged to have you removed from the court."

"I have already told you what I consider necessary and proper. The analysis may show something more." And the doctor bowed.

Iván Ilyich went out slowly, seated himself disconsolately in his sledge, and drove home. All the way home he was going over what the doctor had said, trying to translate those complicated, obscure, scientific phrases into plain language and find in them an answer to the question: "Is my condition bad? Is it very bad? Or is there as yet nothing much wrong?" And it seemed to him that the meaning of what the doctor had said was it was very bad. Everything in the streets seemed depressing. The cabmen, the houses, the passers-by, and the shops, were dismal. His ache, this dull gnawing ache that never ceased for a moment, seemed to have acquired remarks. Iván Ilyich now watched it with a new and oppressive feeling.

He reached home and began to tell his wife about it. She listened, but in the middle of his account his daughter came in with her hat on, ready to go out with her mother. She sat down reluctantly to listen to this tedious story, but could not stand it long, and her mother too did not hear him to the end.

"Well, I am very glad," she said. "Mind now to take your medicine regularly. Give me the prescription and I'll send Gerásim to the chemist's." And she went to get ready to go out.

While she was in the room Iván Ilyich had hardly taken time to breathe, but he sighed deeply when she left it.

"Well," he thought, "perhaps it isn't so bad after all."

He began taking his medicine and following the doctor's directions, which had been altered after the examination of the urine. But then it happened that there was a contradiction between the indications drawn from the examination of the urine and the symptoms that showed themselves. It turned out that what was happening differed from what the doctor had told him, and that he had either forgotten, or blundered, or hidden something from him. He could not, however, be blamed for that, and Iván Ilyich still obeyed his orders implicitly and at first derived some comfort from doing so.

From the time of his visit to the doctor, Iván Ilyich's chief occupation was the exact fulfilment of the doctor's instructions regarding
hygiene and the taking of medicine, and the observation of his pain
and his excretions. His chief interests came to be people's ailments
and people's health. When sickness, deaths, or recoveries were mentioned in his presence, especially when the illness resembled his own,
he listened with agitation which he tried to hide, asked questions,
and applied what he heard to his own case.

The pain did not grow less, but Iván Ilyich made efforts to force
himself to think that he was better. And he could do this so long as
nothing agitated him. But as soon as he had any unpleasantness with
his wife, any lack of success in his official work, or held bad cards at
bridge, he was at once acutely sensible of his disease. He had formerly borne such mischances, hoping soon to adjust what was wrong,
to master it and attain success, or make a grand slam. But how every
mischance upset him and plunged him into despair. He would say
to himself. "There now, just as I was beginning to get better and the
medicine had begun to take effect, comes this accursed misfortune,
or unpleasantness . . ." And he was furious with the mishap, or with
the people who were causing the unpleasantness and killing him, for
he felt that this fury was killing him but could not restrain it. One
would have thought that it should have been clear to him that this
exasperation with circumstances and people aggravated his illness,
and that he ought therefore to ignore unpleasant occurrences. But
he drew the very opposite conclusion: he said that he needed peace,
and he watched for everything that might disturb it and became irritable at the slightest infringement of it. His condition was rendered
worse by the fact that he read medical books and consulted doctors.
The progress of his disease was so gradual that he could deceive
himself when comparing one day with another—the difference was
so slight. But when he consulted the doctors it seemed to him that
he was getting worse, and even very rapidly. Yet despite this he was
continually consulting them.

That month he went to see another celebrity, who told him almost
the same as the first had done but put his questions rather differently,
and the interview with this celebrity only increased Iván Ilyich's
doubts and fears. A friend of a friend of his, a very good doctor,
diagnosed his illness again quite differently from the others, and though
he predicted recovery, his questions and suppositions bewildered Iván
Ilyich still more and increased his doubts. A homeopathist diagnosed
the disease in yet another way, and prescribed medicine which Iván
Ilyich took secretly for a week. But after a week, not feeling any
improvement and having lost confidence both in the former doctor's
treatment and in this one's, he became still more despondent. One

day a lady acquaintance mentioned a cure effected by a wonder-working icon. Iván Ilyich caught himself listening attentively and beginning to believe that it had occurred. This incident alarmed him. "Has my mind really weakened to such an extent?" he asked himself. "Nonsense! It's all rubbish. I mustn't give way to nervous fears but having chosen a doctor must keep strictly to his treatment. That is what I will do. Now it's all settled. I won't think about it, but will follow the treatment seriously till summer, and then we shall see. From now there must be no more of this wavering!" This was easy to say but impossible to carry out. The pain in his side oppressed him and seemed to grow worse and more incessant, while the taste in his mouth grew stranger and stranger. It seemed to him that his breath had a disgusting smell, and he was conscious of a loss of appetite and strength. There was no deceiving himself: something terrible, new, and more important than anything before in his life, was taking place within him of which he alone was aware. Those about him did not understand or would not understand it, but thought everything in the world was going on as usual. That tormented Iván Ilyich more than anything. He saw that his household, especially his wife and daughter who were in a perfect whirl of visiting, did not understand anything of it and were annoyed that he was so depressed and so exacting, as if he were to blame for it. Though they tried to disguise it he saw that he was an obstacle in their path, and that his wife had adopted a definite line in regard to his illness and kept to it regardless of anything he said or did. Her attitude was this: "You know," she would say to her friends, "Iván Ilyich can't do as other people do, and keep to the treatment prescribed for him. One day he'll take his drops and keep strictly to his diet and go to bed in good time, but the next day unless I watch him he'll suddenly forget his medicine, eat sturgeon—which is forbidden—and sit up playing cards till one o'clock in the morning."

"Oh, come, when was that?" Iván Ilyich would ask in vexation. "Only once at Peter Ivánovich's."

"And yesterday with Shébek."

"Well, even if I hadn't stayed up, this pain would have kept me awake."

"Be that as it may you'll never get well like that, but will always make us wretched."

Praskóvya Fédorovna's attitude to Iván Ilyich's illness, as she expressed it both to others and to him, was that it was his own fault and was another of the annoyances he caused her. Iván Ilyich felt that this opinion escaped her involuntarily—but that did not make it easier for him.

At the law courts too, Iván Ilyich noticed, or thought he noticed, a strange attitude towards himself. It sometimes seemed to him that people were watching him inquisitively as a man whose place might soon be vacant. Then again, his friends would suddenly begin to chaff him in a friendly way about his low spirits, as if the awful, horrible, and unheard-of thing that was going on within him, incessantly gnawing at him and irresistibly drawing him away, was a very agreeable subject for jests. Schwartz in particular irritated him by his jocularity, vivacity, and *savoir-faire*, which reminded him of what he himself had been ten years ago.

Friends came to make up a set and they sat down to cards. They dealt, bending the new cards to soften them, and he sorted the diamonds in his hand and found he had seven. His partner said "No trumps" and supported him with two diamonds. What more could be wished for? It ought to be jolly and lively. They would make a grand slam. But suddenly Iván Ilyich was ridiculous that in such circumstances he should be pleased to make a grand slam.

He looked at his partner Mikháil Mikháylovich, who rapped the table with his strong hand and instead of snatching up the tricks pushed the cards courteously and indulgently towards Iváan Ilyich that he might have the pleasure of gathering them up without the trouble of stretching out his hand for them. "Does he think I am too weak to stretch out my arm?" thought Iván Ilyich, and forgetting what he was doing he over-trumped his partner, missing the grand slam by three tricks. And what was most awful of all was that he saw how upset Mikháil Mikháylovich was about it but did not himself care. And it was dreadful to realize why he did not care.

They all saw that he was suffering, and said: "We can stop if you are tired. Take a rest." Lie down? No, he was not at all tired, and he finished the rubber. All were gloomy and silent. Iván Ilyich felt that he had diffused this gloom over them and could not dispel it. They had supper and went away, and Iván Ilyich was left alone with the consciousness that his life was poisoned and was poisoning the lives of others, and that this poison did not weaken but penetrated more and more deeply into his whole being.

With this consciousness, and with physical pain besides the terror, he must go to bed, often to lie awake the greater part of the night. Next morning he had to get up again, dress, go to the law courts, speak, and write; or if he did not go out, spend at home those twenty-four hours a day each of which was a torture. And he had to live thus all alone on the brink of an abyss, with no one who understood or pitied him.

V

So one month passed and then another. Just before the New Year his brother-in-law came to town and stayed at their house. Iván Ilyich was at the law courts and Praskóvya Fëdorovna had gone shopping. When Iván Ilyich came home and entered his study he found his brother-in-law there—a healthy, florid man—unpacking his portmanteau himself. He raised his head on hearing Iván Ilyich's footsteps and looked up at him for a moment without a word. That stare told Iván everything. His brother-in-law opened his mouth to utter an exclamation of surprise but checked himself, and that action confirmed it all.

"I have changed, eh?"

"Yes, there is a change."

And after that, try as he would to get his brother-in-law to return to the subject of his looks, the latter would say nothing about it. Praskóvya Fëdorovna came home and her brother went out to her. Iván Ilyich locked the door and began to examine himself in the glass, first full face, then in profile. He took up a portrait of himself taken with his wife, and compared it with what he saw in the glass. The change in him was immense. Then he bared his arms to the elbow, looked at them, drew the sleeves down again, sat down on an ottoman, and grew blacker than night.

"No, no, this won't do!" he said to hikmself, and jumped up, went to the table, took up some law papers and began to read them, but could not continue. He unlocked the door and went into the reception-room. The door leading to the drawing-room was shut. He approached it on tiptoe and listened.

"No, you are exaggerating!" Praskóvya Fëdorovna was saying.

"Exaggerating! Don't you see it? Why, he's a dead man! Look at his eyes—there's no light in them. But what is it that is wrong with him?"

"No one knows. Nikoláevich [that was another doctor] said something, but I don't know what. And Leshchetítsky [this was the celebrated specialist] said quite the contrary. . ."

Iván Ilyich walked away, went to his own room, lay down and began musing: "The kidney, a floating kidney." He recalled all the doctors had told him of how it detached itself and swayed about. And by an effort of imagination he tried to catch that kidney and arrest it and support it. So little was needed for this, it seemed to him. "No, I'll go to see Peter Ivánovich again." [That was the friend whose friend was a doctor.] He rang, ordered the carriage, and got ready to go.

"Where are you going, *Jean?*" asked his wife, with a specially sad and exceptionally kind look.

This exceptionally kind look irritated him. He looked morosely at her.

"I must go to see Peter Ivánovich."

He went to see Peter Ivánovich, and together they went to see his friend, the doctor. He was in, and Iván Ilyich had a long talk with him.

Reviewing the anatomical and physiological details of what in the doctor's opinion was going on inside him, he understood it all.

There was something, a small thing, in the vermiform appendix. It might all come right. Only stimulate the energy of one organ and check the activity of another, then absorption would take place and everything would come right. He got home rather late for dinner, ate his dinner, and conversed cheerfully, but could not for a long time bring himself to go back to work in his room. At last, however, he went to his study and did what was necessary, but the conscious-ness that he had put something aside—an important, intimate mat-ter which he would revert to when his work was done—never left him. When he had finished his work he remembered that this inti-mate matter was the thought of his vermiform appendix. But he did not give himself up to it, and went to the drawing-room for tea. There were callers there, including the examining magistrate who was a desirable match for his daughter, and they were conversing, playing the piano, and singing. Iván Ilyich, as Praskóvya Fëdorovna remarked, spent that evening more cheerfully than usual, but he never for a moment forgot that he had postponed the important mat-ter of the appendix. At eleven o'clock he said good-night and went to his bedroom. Since his illness he had slept alone in a small room next to his study. He undressed and took up a novel by Zola,[8] but instead of reading it he fell into thought, and in his imagination that desired improvement in the vermiform appendix occurred. There was the absorption and evacuation and the reestablishment of nor-mal activity. "Yes, that's it!" he said to himself. "One need only assist nature, that's all." He remembered his medicine, rose, took it, and lay down on his back watching for the beneficent action of the medicine and for it to lessen the pain. "I need only take it regularly and avoid all injurious influences. I am already feeling better, much better." He began touching his side: it was not painful to the touch. "There, I really don't feel it. It's much better already." He put out the light and turned on his side. . . . "The appendix is getting better, absorption is occurring." Suddenly he felt the old, familiar, dull, gnawing pain, stubborn and serious. There was the same familiar loathsome taste in his mouth. His heart sank and he felt dazed. "My God! My God!" he muttered. "Again, again! And it will never cease." And suddenly the matter presented itself in a quite different aspect. "Vermiform appendix! Kidney!" he said to himself. "It's not a ques-

<hr>

8. Émile Zola (1840–1902), French novelist, author of the *Rougon-Macquart* novels (*Nana, Germinal,* and so on). Tolstoy condemned Zola for his naturalistic theories and considered his novels crude and gross.

tion of appendix or kidney, but of life and . . . death. Yes, life was there and now it is going, going and I cannot stop it. Yes. Why deceive myself? Isn't it obvious to everyone but me that I'm dying, and that it's only a question of weeks, days . . . it may happen this moment. There was light and now there is darkness. I was here and now I'm going there! Where?" A chill came over him, his breathing ceased, and he felt only the throbbing of his heart.

"When I am not, what will there be? There will be nothing. Then where shall I be when I am no more? Can this be dying? No, I don't want to!" He jumped up and tried to light the candle, felt for it with trembling hands, dropped candle and candlestick on the floor, and fell back on his pillow.

"What's the use? It makes no difference," he said to himself, staring with wide-open eyes into the darkness. "Death. Yes, death. And none of them know or wish to know it, and they have no pity for me. Now they are playing." (He heard through the door the distant sound of a song and its accompaniment.) "It's all the same to them, but they will die too! Fools! I first, and they later, but it will be the same for them. And now they are merry . . . the beasts!"

Anger choked him and he was agonizingly, unbearably miserable. "It is impossible that all men have been doomed to suffer this awful horror!" He raised himself.

"Something must be wrong. I must calm myself—must think it all over from the beginning." And he again began thinking. "Yes, the beginning of my illness: I knocked my side, but I was still quite well that day and the next. It hurt a little, then rather more. I saw the doctors, then followed despondency and anguish, more doctors, and I drew nearer to the abyss. My strength grew less and I kept coming nearer and nearer, and now I have wasted away and there is no light in my eyes. I think of the appendix—but this is death! I think of mending the appendix, and all the while here is death! Can it really be death!" Again terror seized him and he gasped for breath. He leant down and began feeling for the matches, pressing with his elbow on the stand beside the bed. It was in his way and hurt him, he grew furious with it, pressed on it still harder, and upset it. Breathless and in despair he fell on his back, expecting death to come immediately.

Meanwhile the visitors were leaving. Praskóvya Fëdorovna was seeing them off. She heard something fall and came in.

"What has happened?"

"Nothing. I knocked it over accidentally."

She went out and returned with a candle. He lay there panting heavily, like a man who has run a thousand yards, and stared upwards at her with a fixed look.

"What is it, *Jean?*"

"No . . . o . . . thing. I upset it." ("Why speak of it? She won't understand," he thought.)

And in truth she did not understand. She picked up the stand, lit his candle, and hurried away to see another visitor off. When she came back he still lay on his back, looking upwards.

"What is it? Do you feel worse?"

"Yes."

She shook her head and sat down.

"Do you know, *Jean*, I think we must ask Leshchetísky to come and see you here."

This meant calling in the famous specialist, regardless of expense. He smiled malignantly and said "No." She remained a little longer and then went up to him and kissed his forehead.

While she was kissing him he hated her from the bottom of his soul and with difficulty refrained from pushing her away.

"Good-night. Please God you'll sleep."

"Yes."

VI

Iván Ilyich saw that he was dying, and he was in continual despair.

In the depth of his heart he knew he was dying, but not only was he not accustomed to the thought, he simply did not and could not grasp it.

The syllogism he had learned from Kiesewetter's *Logic*:[9] "Caius is a man, men are mortal, therefore Caius is mortal," had always seemed to him correct as applied to Caius, but certainly not as applied to himself. That Caius—man in the abstract—was mortal, was perfectly correct, but he was not Caius, not an abstract man, but a creature quite, quite separate from all others. He had been little Ványa, with a mamma and a papa, with Mítya and Volódya, with the toys, a coachman and a nurse, afterwards with Kátenka and with all the joys, griefs, and delights of childhood, boyhood, and youth. What did Caius know of the smell of that striped leather ball Ványa had been so fond of? Had Caius kissed his mother's hand like that, and did the silk of her dress rustle so for Caius? Had he rioted like that at school when the pastry was bad? Had Caius been in love like that? Could Caius preside at a session as he did? "Caius really was mortal, and it was right for him to die; but for me, little Ványa, Iván Ilyich, with all my thoughts and emotions, it's altogether a different matter. It cannot be that I ought to die. That would be too terrible."

9. Karl Kiesewetter (1766–1819) was a German popularizer of Kant's philosophy. His *Outline of Logic According to Kantian Principles* (1796) was widely used in Russian adaptations as a schoolbook.

Such was his feeling.

"If I had to die like Caius I should have known it was so. An inner voice would have told me so, but there was nothing of the sort in me and I and all my friends felt that our case was quite different from that of Caius. And now here it is!" he said to himself. "It can't be. It's impossible! But here it is. How is this? How is one to understand it?"

He could not understand it, and tried to drive this false, incorrect, morbid thought away and to replace it by other proper and healthy thoughts. But that thought, and not the thought only but the reality itself, seemed to come and confront him.

And to replace that thought he called up a succession of others, hoping to find in them some support. He tried to get back into the former current of thoughts that had once screened the thought of death from him. But strange to say, all that had formerly shut off, hidden, and destroyed, his consciousness of death, no longer had that effect. Iván Ilyich now spent most of his time in attempting to re-establish that old current. He would say to himself: "I will take up my duties again—after all I used to live by them." And banishing all doubts he would go to the law courts, enter into conversation with his colleagues, and sit carelessly as was his wont, scanning the crowd with a thoughtful look and leaning both his emaciated arms on the arms of his oak chair; bending over as usual to a colleague and drawing his papers nearer he would interchange whispers with him, and then suddenly raising his eyes and sitting erect would pronounce certain words and open the proceedings. But suddenly in the midst of those proceedings the pain in his side, regardless of the stage the proceedings had reached, would begin its own gnawing work. Iván Ilyich would turn his attention to it and try to drive the thought of it away, but without success. *It* would come and stand before him and look at him, and he would be petrified and the light would die out of his eyes, and he would again begin asking himself whether *It* alone was true. And his colleagues and subordinates would see with surprise and distress that he, the brilliant and subtle judge, was becoming confused and making mistakes. He would shake himself, try to pull himself together, manage somehow to bring the sitting to a close, and return home with the sorrowful consciousness that his judicial labours could not as formerly hide from him what he wanted them to hide, and could not deliver him from *It*. And what was worst of all was that *It* drew his attention to itself not in order to make him take some action but only that he should look at *It*, look it straight in the face: look at it without doing anything, suffer inexpressibly.

And to save himself from this condition Iván Ilyich looked for consolations—new screens—and new screens were found and for a while seemed to save him, but then they immediately fell to pieces or rather became transparent, as *It* penetrated them and nothing could veil *It*.

In these latter days he would go into the drawing-room he had arranged—that drawing-room where he had fallen and for the sake of which (how bitterly ridiculous it seemed) he had sacrificed his life—for he knew that his illness originated with that knock. He would enter and see that something had scratched the polished table. He would look for the cause of this and find that it was the bronze orna-mentation of an album, that had got bent. He would take up the expensive album which he had lovingly arranged, and feel vexed with his daughter and her friends for their untidiness—for the album was torn here and there and some of the photographs turned upside down. He would put it carefully in order and bend the ornamenta-tion back into position. Then it would occur to him to place all those things in another corner of the room, near the plants. He would call the footman, but his daughter or wife would contradict him, and he would dispute and grow angry. But that was all right, for then he did not think about *It*. *It* was invisible.

But then, when he was moving something himself, his wife would say: "Let the servants do it. You will hurt yourself again." And sud-denly *It* would flash through the screen and he would see it. It was just a flash, and he hoped it would disappear, but he would involun-tarily pay attention to his side. "It sits there as before, gnawing just the same!" And he could no longer forget *It*, but could distinctly see it looking at him from behind the flowers. "What is it all for?"

"It really is so! I lost my life over that curtain as I might have done when storming a fort. Is that possible? How terrible and how stupid. It can't be true! It can't, but it is."

He would go to his study, lie down, and again be alone with *It*: face to face with *It*. And nothing could be done with *It* except to look at it and shudder.

VII

How it happened it is impossible to say because it came about step by step, unnoticed, but in the third month of Iván Ilyich's illness, his wife, his daughter, his son, his acquaintances, the doctors, the servants, and above all he himself, were aware that the whole interest he had for other people was whether he would soon vacate his place, and at last release the living from the discomfort caused by his pres-ence and be himself released from his sufferings.

He slept less and less. He was given opium and hypodermic injec-tions of morphine, but this did not relieve him. The dull depression he experienced in a somnolent condition at first gave him a little relief, but only as something new, afterwards it became as distressing as the pain itself or even more so.

Special foods were prepared for him by the doctors' orders, but all those foods became increasingly distasteful and disgusting to him.

For his excretions also special arrangements had to be made, and this was a torment to him every time—a torment from the uncleanliness, the unseemliness, and the smell, and from knowing that another person had to take part in it.

But just through this most unpleasant matter, Iván Ilyich obtained comfort. Gerásim, the butler's young assistant, always came in to carry the things out. Gerásim was a clean, fresh peasant lad, grown stout on town food and always cheerful and bright. At first the sight of him, in his clean Russian peasant costume, engaged on that disgusting task embarrassed Iván Ilyich.

Once when he got up from the commode too weak to draw up his trousers, he dropped into a soft armchair and looked with horror at his bare, enfeebled thighs with the muscles so sharply marked on them.

Gerásim with a firm light tread, his heavy boots emitting a pleasant smell of tar and fresh winter air, came in wearing a clean Hessian apron, the sleeves of his print shirt tucked up over his strong bare young arms; and refraining from looking at his sick master out of consideration for his feelings, and restraining the joy of life that beamed from his face, he went up to the commode.

"Gerásim!" said Iván Ilyich in a weak voice.

Gerásim started, evidently afraid he might have committed some blunder, and with a rapid movement turned his fresh, kind, simple young face which just showed the first downy sign of a beard.

"Yes, sir?"

"That must be very unpleasant for you. You must forgive me. I am helpless."

"Oh, why, sir," and Gerásim's eyes beamed and he showed his glistening white teeth, "what's a little trouble? It's a case of illness with you, sir."

And his deft strong hands did their accustomed task, and he went out of the room stepping lightly. Five minutes later he as lightly returned.

Iván Ilyich was still sitting in the same position in the armchair.

"Gerásim," he said when the latter had replaced the freshly-washed utensil. "Please come here and help me." Gerásim went up to him. "Lift me up. It is hard for me to get up, and I have sent Dmítri away."

Gerásim went up to him, grasped his master with his strong arms deftly but gently, in the same way that he stepped—lifted him, supported him with one hand, and with the other drew up his trousers and would have set him down again, but Iván Ilyich asked to be led to the sofa. Gerásim, without an effort and without apparent pressure, led him, almost lifting him, to the sofa and placed him on it.

"Thank you. How easily and well you do it all!"

Gerásim smiled again and turned to leave the room. But Iván Ilyich felt his presence such a comfort that he did not want to let him go.

"One thing more, please move up that chair. No, the other one— under my feet. It is easier for me when my feet are raised."

Gerásim brought the chair, set it down gently in place, and raised Iván Ilyich's legs on to it. It seemed to Iván Ilyich that he felt better while Gerásim was holding up his legs.

"It's better when my legs are higher," he said. "Place that cushion under them."

Gerásim did so. He again lifted the legs and placed them, and again Iván Ilyich felt better while Gerásim held his legs. When he set them down Iván Ilyich fancied he felt worse.

"Gerásim," he said. "Are you busy now?"

"Not at all, sir," said Gerásim, who had learnt from the townsfolk how to speak to gentlefolk.

"What have you still to do?"

"What have I to do? I've done everything except chopping the logs for to-morrow."

"Then hold my legs up a bit higher, can you?"

"Of course I can. Why not?" And Gerásim raised his master's legs higher and Iván Ilyich thought that in that position he did not feel any pain at all.

"And how about the logs?"

"Don't trouble about that, sir. There's plenty of time."

Iván Ilyich told Gerásim to sit down and hold his legs, and began to talk to him. And strange to say it seemed to him that he felt better while Gerásim held his legs up.

After that Iván Ilyich would sometimes call Gerásim and get him to hold his legs on his shoulders, and he liked talking to him. Gerásim did it all easily, willingly, simply, and with a good nature that touched Iván Ilyich. Health, strength, and vitality in other people were offensive to him, but Gerásim's strength and vitality did not mortify but soothed him.

What tormented Iván Ilyich most was the deception, the lie, which for some reason they all accepted, that he was not dying but was simply ill, and that he only need keep quiet and undergo a treatment and then something very good would result. He however knew that do what they would nothing would come of it, only still more agonizing suffering and death. This deception tortured him—their not wishing to admit what they all knew and what he knew, but wanting to lie to him concerning his terrible condition, and wishing and forcing him to participate in that lie. Those lies—lies enacted over him on the eve of his death and destined to degrade this awful, solemn act to the level of their visitings, their curtains, their sturgeon for dinner—were a terrible agony for Iván Ilyich. And strangely enough, many times when they were going through their antics over him he had been within a hairbreadth of calling out to them: "Stop lying! You know and I know that I am dying. Then at least stop lying about it!" But he had never had the spirit to do it. The awful, terrible act of his dying was, he could see, reduced by those about him to the level of a casual, unpleasant, and almost indecorous incident (as if someone entered a drawing-room diffusing an unpleasant odour) and this was done by that very decorum which he had served all his life long. He saw that no one felt for him, because no one even wished to grasp his position. Only Gerásim recognized and pitied him. And so Iván Ilyich felt at ease only with him. He felt comforted when Gerásim supported his legs (sometimes all night long) and refused to go to bed, saying: "Don't you worry, Iván Ilyich. I'll get sleep enough later on," or when he suddenly became familiar and exclaimed: "If you weren't sick it would be another matter, but as it is, why should I grudge a little trouble?" Gerásim alone did not lie; everything showed that he alone understood the facts of the case and did not consider it necessary to disguise them, but simply felt sorry for his emaciated and enfeebled master. Once when Iván Ilyich was sending him away he even said straight out: "We shall all of us die, so why should I grudge a little trouble?"—expressing the fact that he did not think his work burdensome, because he was doing it for a dying man and hoped someone would do the same for him when his time came.

Apart from this lying, or because of it, what most tormented Iván Ilyich was that no one pitied him as he wished to be pitied. At certain moments after prolonged suffering he wished most of all (though he would have been ashamed to confess it) for someone to pity him as a sick child is pitied. He longed to be petted and comforted. He knew he was an important functionary, that he had a beard turning grey, and that therefore what he longed for was impossible, but still he longed for it. And in Gerásim's attitude towards him there was something akin to what he wished for, and so that attitude comforted him. Iván Ilyich wanted to weep, wanted to be petted and cried over, and then his colleague Shébek would come, and instead of weeping and being petted, Iván Ilyich would assume a serious, severe, and profound air, and by force of habit would express his opinion on a decision of the Court of Appeal and would stubbornly insist on that view. This falsity around him and within him did more than anything else to poison his last days.

VIII

It was morning. He knew it was morning because Gerásim had gone, and Peter the footman had come and put out the candles, drawn back one of the curtains, and begun quietly to tidy up. Whether it was morning or evening, Friday or Sunday, made no difference, it was all just the same: the gnawing, unmitigated, agonizing pain, never ceasing for an instant, the consciousness of life inexorably waning but not yet extinguished, the approach of that ever dreaded and hateful Death which was the only reality, and always the same falsity. What were days, weeks, hours, in such a case?

"Will you have some tea, sir?"

"He wants things to be regular, and wishes the gentlefolk to drink tea in the morning," thought Iván Ilyich, and only said "No."

"Wouldn't you like to move onto the sofa, sir?"

"He wants to tidy up the room, and I'm in the way. I am uncleanliness and disorder," he thought, and said only:

"No, leave me alone."

The man went on bustling about. Iván Ilyich stretched out his hand. Peter came up, ready to help.

"What is it, sir?"

"My watch."

Peter took the watch which was close at hand and gave it to his master.

"Half-past eight. Are they up?"

"No sir, except Vladímir Ivánich" (the son) "who has gone to school. Praskóvya Fëdorovna ordered me to wake her if you asked for her. Shall I do so?"

"No, there's no need to." "Perhaps I'd better have some tea," he thought, and added aloud: "Yes, bring me some tea."

Peter went to the door, but Iván Ilyich dreaded being left alone. "How can I keep him here? Oh yes, my medicine." "Peter, give me my medicine." "Why not? Perhaps it may still do me some good." He took a spoonful and swallowed it. "No, it won't help. It's all tomfoolery, all deception," he decided as soon as he became aware of the familiar, sickly, hopeless taste. "No, I can't believe in it any longer. But the pain, why this pain? If it would only cease just for a moment!" And he moaned. Peter turned towards him. "It's all right. Go and fetch me some tea."

Peter went out. Left alone Iván Ilyich groaned not so much with pain, terrible though, that was, as from mental anguish. Always and forever the same, always these endless days and nights. If only it would come quicker! If only *what* would come quicker? Death, darkness? . . . No, no! Anything rather than death!

When Peter returned with the tea on a tray, Iván Ilyich stared at him for a time in perplexity, not realizing who and what he was. Peter was disconcerted by that look and his embarrassment brought Iván Ilyich to himself.

"Oh, tea! All right, put it down. Only help me to wash and put on a clean shirt."

And Iván Ilyich began to wash. With pauses for rest, he washed his hands and then his face, cleaned his teeth, brushed his hair, and looked in the glass. He was terrified by what he saw, especially by the limp way in which his hair clung to his pallid forehead.

While his shirt was being changed he knew that he would be still more frightened at the sight of his body, so he avoided looking at it. Finally he was ready. He drew on a dressing-gown, wrapped himself in a plaid, and sat down in the armchair to take his tea. For a moment he felt refreshed, but as soon as he began to drink the tea he was again aware of the same taste, and the pain also returned. He finished it with an effort, and then lay down stretching out his legs, and dismissed Peter.

Always the same. Now a spark of hope flashes up, then a sea of despair rages, and always pain; always pain, always despair, and always the same. When alone he had a dreadful and distressing desire to call someone, but he knew beforehand that with others present it would be still worse. "Another dose of morphine—to lose consciousness. I will tell him, the doctor, that he must think of something else. It's impossible, impossible, to go on like this."

An hour and another pass like that. But now there is a ring at the door bell. Perhaps it's the doctor? It is. He comes in fresh, hearty, plump, and cheerful, with that look on his face that seems to say: "There now, you're in a panic about something, but we'll arrange it all for you directly!" The doctor knows this expression is out of place here, but he has put it on once for all and can't take it off—like a man who has put on a frock-coat in the morning to pay a round of calls.

The doctor rubs his hands vigorously and reassuringly.

"Brr! How cold it is! There's such a sharp frost; just let me warm myself!" he says, as if it were only a matter of waiting till he was warm, and then he would put everything right.

"Well now, how are you?"

Iván Ilyich feels that the doctor would like to say: "Well, how are our affairs?" but that even he feels that this would not do, and says instead: "What sort of a night have you had?"

Iván Ilyich looks at him as much as to say: "Are you really never ashamed of lying?" But the doctor does not wish to understand this question, and Iván Ilyich says: "Just as terrible as ever. The pain never leaves me and never subsides. If only something . . ."

"Yes, you sick people are always like that. . . . There, now I think I'm warm enough. Even Praskóvya Fëdorovna, who is so particular, could find no fault with my temperature. Well, now I can say good-morning," and the doctor presses his patient's hand.

Then, dropping his former playfulness, he begins with a most serious face to examine the patient, feeling his pulse and taking his temperature, and then begins the sounding and auscultation.

Iván Ilyich knows quite well and definitely that all this is nonsense and pure deception, but when the doctor, getting down on his knee, leans over him, putting his ear first higher then lower, and performs various gymnastic movements over him with a significant expression on his face, Iván Ilyich submits to it all as he used to submit to the speeches of the lawyers, though he knew very well that they were all lying and why they were lying.

The doctor, kneeling on the sofa, is still sounding him when Praskóvya Fëdorovna's silk dress rustles at the door and she is heard scolding Peter for not having let her know of the doctor's arrival.

She comes in, kisses her husband, and at once proceeds to prove that she has been up a long time already, and only owing to a misunderstanding failed to be there when the doctor arrived.

Iván Ilyich looks at her, scans her all over, sets against her the whiteness and plumpness and cleanness of her hands and neck, the gloss of her hair, and the sparkle of her vivacious eyes. He hates her with his whole soul. And the thrill of hatred he feels for her makes him suffer from her touch.

Her attitude towards him and his disease is still the same. Just as the doctor had adopted a certain relation to his patient which he could not abandon, so had she formed one towards him—that he was not doing something he ought to do and was himself to blame, and that she reproached him lovingly for this—and she could not now change that attitude.

"You see he doesn't listen to me and doesn't take his medicine at the proper time. And above all he lies in a position that is no doubt bad for him—with his legs up."

She described how he made Gerásim hold his legs up.

The doctor smiled with a contemptuous affability that said: "What's to be done? These sick people do have foolish fancies of that kind, but we must forgive them."

When the examination was over the doctor looked at his watch, and then Praskóvya Fëdorovna announced to Iván Ilyich that it was of course as he pleased, but she had sent to-day for a celebrated specialist who would examine him and have a consultation with

Michael Danílovich (their regular doctor).

"Please don't raise any objections. I am doing this for my own sake," she said ironically, letting it be felt that she was doing it all for his sake and only said this to leave him no right to refuse. He remained silent, knitting his brows. He felt that he was so surrounded and involved in a mesh of falsity that it was hard to unravel anything.

Everything she did for him was entirely for her own sake, and she told him she was doing for herself what she actually was doing for herself, as if that was so incredible that he must understand the opposite.

At half-past eleven the celebrated specialist arrived. Again the sounding began and the significant conversations in his presence and in other room, about the kidneys and the appendix, and the questions and answers, with such an air of importance that again, instead of the real question of life and death which now alone confronted him, the question arose of the kidney and the appendix which were not behaving as they ought to and would now be attacked by Michael Danílovich and the specialist and forced to amend their ways.

The celebrated specialist took leave of him with a serious though not hopeless look, and in reply to the timid question in Iván Ilyich, with eyes glistening with fear and hope, put to him as to whether there was a chance of recovery, said that he could not vouch for it but there was a possibility. The look of hope with which Iván Ilyich watched the doctor out was so pathetic that Praskóvya Fëdorovna, seeing it, even wept as she left the room to hand the doctor his fee.

The gleam of hope kindled by the doctor's encouragement did not last long. The same room, the same pictures, curtains, wallpaper, medicine bottles, were all there, and the same aching suffering body, and Iván Ilyich began to moan. They gave him a subcutaneous injection and he sank into oblivion.

It was twilight when he came to. They brought him his dinner and he swallowed some beef tea with difficulty, and then everything was the same again and night was coming on.

After dinner, at seven o'clock, Praskóvya Fëdorovna came into the room in evening dress, her full bosom pushed up by her corset, and with traces of powder on her face. She had reminded him in the morning that they were going to the theatre. Sarah Bernhardt was visiting the town and they had a box, which he had insisted on their taking. Now he had forgotten about it and her toilet offended him, but he concealed his vexation when he remembered that he had himself insisted on their securing a box and going because it would be an instructive and aesthetic pleasure for the children.

Praskóvya Fëdorovna came in, self-satisfied but yet with a rather guilty air. She sat down and asked how he was, but, as he saw, only for the sake of asking and not in order to learn about it, knowing that there was nothing to learn—and then went on to what she really wanted to say: that she would not on any account have gone but that the box had been taken and Helen and their daughter were going, as well as Petríshchev (the examining magistrate, their daughter's fiancé) and that it was out of the question to let them go alone; but that she would have much preferred to sit with him for a while; and he must be sure to follow the doctor's orders while she was away.

"Oh, and Fëdor Petróvich" (the fiancé) "would like to come in. May he? And Lisa?"

"All right."

Their daughter came in in full evening dress, her fresh young flesh exposed (making a show of that very flesh which in his own case caused so much suffering), strong, healthy, evidently in love, and impatient with illness, suffering, and death, because they interfered with her happiness.

Fëdor Petróvich came in too, in evening dress, his hair curled *a la Capoul*, a tight stiff collar round his long sinewy neck, an enormous white shirt-front and narrow black trousers tightly stretched over his strong thighs. He had one white glove tightly drawn on, and was holding his opera hat in his hand.

Following him the schoolboy crept in unnoticed, in a new uniform, poor little fellow, and wearing gloves. Terribly dark shadows showed under his eyes, the meaning of which Iván Ilyich knew well.

His son had always seemed pathetic to him, and now it was dreadful to see the boy's frightened look of pity. It seemed to Iván Ilyich that Vásya was the only one besides Gerásim who understood and pitied him.

They all sat down and again asked how he was. A silence followed. Lisa asked her mother about the opera-glasses, and there was an altercation between mother and daughter as to who had taken them and where they had been put. This occasioned some unpleasantness.

Fëdor Petróvich inquired of Iván Ilyich whether he had ever seen Sarah Bernhardt. Iván Ilyich did not at first catch the question, but then replied: "No, have you seen her before?"

"Yes, in *Adrienne Lecouvreur*."[1]

Praskóvya Fëdorovna mentioned some rôles in which Sarah Bernhardt was particularly good. Her daughter disagreed. Conversation sprang up as to the elegance and realism of her acting—the sort of conversation that is always repeated and is always the same.

In the midst of the conversation Fëdor Petróvich glanced at Iván

---

1. A play (1849) by the French dramatist Eugène Scribe (1791–1861), in which the heroine was a famous actress of the eighteenth century. Tolstoy considered Scribe, who wrote over four hundred plays, a shoddy, commercial playwright.

Ilyich and became silent. The others also looked at him and grew silent. Iván Ilyich was staring with glittering eyes straight before him, evidently indignant with them. This had to be rectified, but it was impossible to do so. The silence had to be broken, but for a time no one dared to break it and they all became afraid that the conventional deception would suddenly become obvious and the truth become plain to all. Lisa was the first to pluck up courage and break that silence, but by trying to hide what everybody was feeling, she betrayed it.

"Well, if we are going it's time to start," she said, looking at her watch, a present from her father, and with a faint and significant smile at Fëdor Petróvich relating to something known only to them. She got up with a rustle of her dress.

They all rose, said good-night, and went away.

When they had gone it seemed to Iván Ilyich that he felt better; the falsity had gone with them. But the pain remained—that same pain and that same fear that made everything monotonously alike, nothing harder and nothing easier. Everything was worse.

Again minute followed minute and hour followed hour. Everything remained the same and there was no cessation. And the inevitable end of it all became more and more terrible.

"Yes, send Gerásim here," he replied to a question Peter asked.

IX

His wife returned late at night. She came in on tiptoe, but he heard her, opened his eyes, and made haste to close them again. She wished to send Gerásim away and to sit with him herself, but he opened his eyes and said: "No, go away."

"Are you in great pain?"

"Always the same."

"Take some opium."

He agreed and took some. She went away.

Till about three in the morning he was in a state of stupefied misery. It seemed to him that he and his pain were being thrust into a narrow, deep black sack, but though they were pushed further and further in they could not be pushed to the bottom. And this, terrible enough in itself, was accompanied by suffering. He was frightened yet wanted to fall through the sack, he struggled but yet co-operated. And suddenly he broke through, fell, and regained consciousness. Gerásim was sitting at the foot of the bed dozing quietly and patiently, while he himself lay with his emaciated stockinged legs resting on Gerásim's shoulders; the same shaded candle was there and the same unceasing pain.

"Go away, Gerásim," he whispered.

"It's all right, sir. I'll stay a while."

"No. Go away."

He removed his legs from Gerásim's shoulders, turned sideways onto his arm, and felt sorry for himself. He only waited till Gerásim had gone into the next room and then restrained himself no longer but wept like a child. He wept on account of his helplessness, his terrible loneliness, the cruelty of man, the cruelty of God, and the absence of God.

"Why hast Thou done all this? Why hast Thou brought me here? Why, dost Thou torment me so terribly?"

He did not expect an answer and yet wept because there was no answer and could be none. The pain again grew more acute, but he did not stir and did not call. He said to himself: "Go on! Strike me! But what is it for? What have I done to Thee? What is it for?"

Then he grew quiet and not only ceased weeping but even held his breath and became all attention. It was as though he were listening not to an audible voice but to a voice of his soul, to the current of thoughts arising within him.

"What is it you want?" was the first clear conception capable of expression in words, that he heard.

"What do you want? What do you want?" he repeated to himself.

"What do I want? To live and not to suffer," he answered.

And again he listened with such concentrated attention that even his pain did not distract him.

"To live? How?" asked his inner voice.

"Why, to live as I used to—well and pleasantly."

"As you lived before, well and pleasantly?" the voice repeated.

And in imagination he began to recall the moments of his pleasant life. But strange to say none of those best moments of his pleasant life now seemed at all what they had then seemed—none of them except the first recollections of childhood. There, in childhood, there had been something really pleasant with which it would be possible to live if it could return. But the child who had experienced that happiness existed no longer, it was like a reminiscence of somebody else.

As soon as the period began which had produced the present Iván Ilyich, all that had then seemed joys now melted before his sight and turned into something trivial and often nasty.

And the further he departed from childhood and the nearer he came to the present the more worthless and doubtful were the joys. This began with the School of Law. A little that was really good was still found there—there was light-heartedness, friendship, and hope. But in the upper classes there had already been fewer of such good moments. Then during the first years of his official career, when he was in the service of the Governor, some pleasant moments again occurred: they were the memories of love for a woman. Then all became confused and there was still less of what was good; later on again there was still less that was good, and the further he went the less there was. His marriage, a mere accident, then the disenchantment that followed it, his wife's bad breath and the sensuality and hypocrisy: then that deadly official life and those preoccupations about money, a year of it, and two, and ten, and twenty, and always the same thing. And the longer it lasted the more deadly it became. "It is as if I had been going downhill while I imagined I was going up. And that is really what it was. I was going up in public opinion, but to the same extent life was ebbing away from me. And now it is all done and there is only death."

"Then what does it mean? Why? It can't be that life is so senseless and horrible. But if it really has been so horrible and senseless, why must I die and die in agony? There is something wrong!"

"Maybe I did not live as I ought to have done," it suddenly occurred to him. "But how could that be, when I did everything properly?" he replied, and immediately dismissed from his mind this, the sole solution of all the riddles of life and death, as something quite impossible.

"Then what do you want now? To live? Live how? Live as you lived in the law courts when the usher proclaimed 'The judge is coming!' The judge is coming, the judge!" he repeated to himself. "Here he is, the judge. But I am not guilty!" he exclaimed angrily. "What is it for?" And he ceased crying, but turning his face to the wall continued to ponder on the same question: Why, and for what purpose, is there all this horror? But however much he pondered he found no answer. And whenever the thought occurred to him, as it often did, that it all resulted from his not having lived as he ought to have done, he at once recalled the correctness of his whole life, and dismissed so strange an idea.

X

Another fortnight passed. Iván Ilyich now no longer left his sofa. He would not lie in bed but lay on the sofa, facing the wall nearly all the time. He suffered ever the same unceasing agonies and in his loneliness pondered always on the same insoluble question: "What is this? Can it be that it is Death?" And the inner voice answered: "Yes, it is Death."

"Why these sufferings?" And the voice answered, "For no reason—they just are so." Beyond and besides this there was nothing.

From the very beginning of his illness, ever since he had first been to see the doctor, Iván Ilyich's life had been divided between two contrary and alternating moods: now it was despair and the expectation of this uncomprehended and terrible death, and now hope and an intently interested observation of the functioning of his organs. Now before his eyes there was only a kidney or an intestine that temporarily evaded its duty, and now only that incomprehensible and dreadful death from which it was impossible to escape.

These two states of mind had alternated from the very beginning of his illness, but the further it progressed the more doubtful and fantastic became the conception of the kidney, and the more real the sense of impending death.

He had but to call to mind what he had been three months before and what he was now, to call to mind with what regularity he had been going downhill, for every possible of hope to be shattered.

Latterly during that loneliness in which he found himself as he lay facing the back of the sofa, a loneliness in the midst of a populous town and surrounded by numerous acquaintances and relations but that yet could not have been more complete anywhere—either at the bottom of the sea or under the earth—during that terrible loneliness Iván Ilyich had lived only in memories of the past. Pictures of his past rose before him one after another. They always began with what was nearest in time and then went back to what was most remote—to his childhood—and rested there. If he thought of the stewed prunes that had been offered him that day, his mind went back to the raw shrivelled French plums of his childhood, their peculiar flavour and the flow of saliva when he sucked their stones, and along with the memory of that taste came a whole series of memories of those days: his nurse, his brother, and their toys. "No, I mustn't think of that. . . . It is too painful," Iván Ilyich said to himself, and brought himself back to the present—to the button on the back of the sofa and the creases in its morocco. "Morocco is expensive, but it does not wear well: there had been a quarrel about it. It was a different kind of quarrel and a different kind of morocco that time when we tore father's portfolio and were punished, and mamma brought us some tarts. . . ." And again his thoughts dwelt on his childhood, and again it was painful and he tried to banish them and fix his mind on something else.

Then again together with that chain of memories another series passed through his mind—of how his illness had progressed and grown worse. There also the further back he looked the more life there had been. There had been more of what was good in life and more of life itself. The two merged together. "Just as the pain went on getting worse and worse, so my life grew worse and worse," he thought. "There is one bright spot there at the back, at the beginning of life, and afterwards all becomes blacker and blacker and proceeds more and more rapidly—in inverse ratio to the square of the distance from death," thought Iván Ilyich. And the example of a stone falling downwards with increasing velocity entered his mind. Life, a series of increasing sufferings, flies further and further towards its end— the most terrible suffering. "I am flying. . . ." He shuddered, shifted himself, and tried to resist, but was already aware that resistance was impossible, and again with eyes weary of gazing but unable to cease seeing what was before them, he stared at the back of the sofa and waited—awaiting that dreadful fall and shock and destruction.

"Resistance is impossible!" he said to himself. "If I could only understand what it is all for! But that too is impossible. An explanation would be possible if it could be said that I have not lived as I ought to. But it is impossible to say that," and he remembered all the legality, correctitude, and propriety of his life. "That at any rate can certainly not be admitted," he thought, and his lips smiled ironically as if someone could see that smile and be taken in by it. "There is no explanation! Agony, death. . . . What for?"

XI

Another two weeks went by in this way and during that fortnight an event occurred that Iván Ilyich and his wife had desired. Petríshchev formally proposed. It happened in the evening. The next day Praskóvya Fëdorovna came into her husband's room considering how best to inform him of it, but that very night there had been a fresh change for the worse in his condition. She found him still lying on the sofa but in a different position. He lay on his back, groaning and staring fixedly straight in front of him.

She began to remind him of his medicines, but he turned his eyes towards her with such a look that she did not finish what she was saying; so great an animosity, to her in particular, did that look express.

"For Christ's sake let me die in peace!" he said.

She would have gone away, but just then their daughter came in and went up to say good morning. He looked at her as he had done at his wife, and in reply to her inquiry about his health said dryly that he would soon free them all of himself. They were both silent and after sitting with him for a while went away.

"Is it our fault?" Lisa said to her mother. "It's as if we were to blame! I am sorry for papa, but why should we be tortured?"

The doctor came at his usual time. Iván Ilyich answered "Yes" and "No," never taking his angry eyes from him, and at last said: "You know you can do nothing for me, so leave me alone."

"We can ease your sufferings."

"You can't even do that. Let me be."

The doctor went into the drawing-room and told Praskóvya Fëdorovna that the case was very serious and that the only resource left was opium to allay her husband's sufferings, which must be terrible.

It was true, as the doctor said, that Iván Ilyich's physical sufferings were terrible, but worse than the physical sufferings were his mental sufferings which were his chief torture.

His mental sufferings were due to the fact that that night, as he looked at Gerásim's sleepy, good-natured face with its prominent cheek-bones, the question suddenly occurred to him: "What if my whole life has really been wrong?"

It occurred to him that what had appeared perfectly impossible before, namely that he had not spent his life as he should have done, might after all be true. It occurred to him that his scarcely perceptible attempts to struggle against what was considered good by the most highly placed people, those scarcely noticeable impulses which he had immediately suppressed, might have been the real thing, and all the rest false. And his professional duties and the whole arrangement of his life and of his family, and all his social and official interests, might all have been false. He tried to defend all those things to himself and suddenly felt the weakness of what he was defending. There was nothing to defend.

"But if that is so," he said to himself, "and I am leaving this life with the consciousness that I have lost all that was given me and it is impossible to rectify it—what then?"

He lay on his back and began to pass his life in review in quite a new way. In the morning when he saw first his footman, then his wife, then his daughter, and then the doctor, their every word and movement confirmed to him the awful truth that had been revealed to him during the night. In them he saw himself—all that for which he had lived—and saw clearly that it was not real at all, but a terrible and huge deception which had hidden both life and death. This consciousness intensified his physical suffering tenfold. He groaned and tossed about, and pulled at his clothing which choked and stifled him. And he hated them on that account.

He was given a large dose of opium and became unconscious, but at noon his sufferings began again. He drove everybody away and tossed from side to side.

His wife came to him and said:

"*Jean*, my dear, do this for me. It can't do any harm and often helps. Healthy people often do it."

He opened his eyes wide.

"What? Take communion? Why? It's unnecessary! However . . ."

She began to cry.

"Yes, do, my dear. I'll send for our priest. He is such a nice man."

"All right. Very well," he muttered.

When the priest came and heard his confession, Iván Ilyich was softened and seemed to feel a relief from his doubts and consequently from his sufferings, and for a moment there came a ray of hope. He again began to think of the vermiform appendix and the possibility of correcting it. He received the sacrament with tears in his eyes.

When they laid him down again afterwards he felt a moment's ease, and the hope that he might live awoke in him again. He began to think of the operation that had been suggested to him. "To live! I want to live!" he said to himself.

His wife came in to congratulate him after his communion, and when uttering the usual conventional words she added:

"You feel better, don't you?"

Without looking at her he said "Yes."

Her dress, her figure, the expression of her face, the tone of her voice, all revealed the same thing. "This is wrong, it is not as it should be. All you have lived for and still live for is falsehood and deception, hiding life and death from you." And as soon as he admitted that thought, his hatred and his agonizing physical suffering again sprang up, and with that suffering a consciousness of the unavoidable, approaching end. And to this was added a new sensation of grinding shooting pain and a feeling of suffocation.

The expression of his face when he uttered that "yes" was dreadful. Having uttered it, he looked her straight in the eyes, turned on his face with a rapidity extraordinary in his weak state and shouted:

"Go away! Go away and leave me alone!"

XII

From that moment the screaming began that continued for three days, and was so terrible that one could not hear it through two closed doors without horror. At the moment he answered his wife he realized that he was lost, that there was no return, that the end had come, the very end, and his doubts were still unsolved and remained doubts.

"Oh! Oh! Oh!" he cried in various intonations. He had begun by screaming "I won't!" and continued screaming on the letter "o."

For three whole days, during which time did not exist for him, he struggled in that black sack into which he was being thrust by an invisible, resistless force. He struggled as a man condemned to death struggles in the hands of the executioner, knowing that he cannot save himself. And every moment he felt that despite all his efforts he was drawing nearer and nearer to what terrified him. He felt that his agony was due to his being thrust into that black hole and still more to his not being able to get right into it. He was hindered from getting into it by his conviction that his life had been a good one. That very justification of his life held him fast and prevented his moving forward, and it caused him most torment of all.

Suddenly some force struck him in the chest and side, making it still harder to breathe, and he fell through the hole and there at the bottom was a light. What had happened to him was like the sensation one sometimes experiences in a railway carriage when one thinks one is going backwards while one is really going forwards and suddenly becomes aware of the real direction.

"Yes, it was all not the right thing," he said to himself, "but that's no matter. It can be done. But what *is* the right thing?" he asked himself, and suddenly grew quiet.

This occurred at the end of the third day, two hours before his death. Just then his schoolboy son had crept softly in and gone up to the bedside. The dying man was still screaming desperately and waving his arms. His hand fell on the boy's head, and the boy caught it, pressed it to his lips, and began to cry.

At that very moment Iván Ilyich fell through and caught sight of the light, and it was revealed to him that though his life had not been what it should have been, this could still be rectified. He asked himself, "What *is* the right thing?" and grew still, listening. Then he felt that someone was kissing his hand. He opened his eyes, looked at his son, and felt sorry for him. His wife came up to him and he glanced at her. She was gazing at him open-mouthed, with undried tears on her nose and cheek and a despairing look on her face. He felt sorry for her too.

"Yes, I am making them wretched," he thought. "They are sorry, but it will be better for them when I die." He wished to say this but had not the strength to utter it. "Besides, why speak? I must act," he thought. With a look at his wife he indicated his son and said: "Take him away . . . sorry for him . . . sorry for you too. . . ." He tried to add, "forgive me," but said "forego" and waved his hand, knowing that He whose understanding mattered would understand.

And suddenly it grew clear to him that what had been oppressing him and would not leave him was all dropping away at once from two sides, from ten sides, and from all sides. He was sorry for them, he must act so as not to hurt them: release them and free himself from these sufferings. "How good and how simple!" he thought. "And the pain?" he asked himself. "What has become of it? Where are you, pain?"

He turned his attention to it.

"Yes, here it is. Well, what of it? Let the pain be."

"And death . . . where is it?"

He sought his former accustomed fear of death and did not find it. "Where is it? What death?" There was no fear because there was no death.

In place of death there was light.

"So that's what it is!" he suddenly exclaimed aloud. "What joy!"

To him all this happened in a single instant, and the meaning of that instant did not change. For those present his agony continued for another two hours. Something rattled in his throat, his emaciated body twitched, then the gasping and rattle became less and less frequent.

"It is finished!" said someone near him.

He heard these words and repeated them in his soul.

"Death is finished," he said to himself. "It is no more!"

He drew in a breath, stopped in the midst of a sigh, stretched out, and died.

HENRIK IBSEN
1828–1906

Henrik Ibsen was the foremost playwright of his time, treating social themes and ideas (the subjection of women, hereditary disease, man's illusions and self-delusions) and often satirizing the nineteenth-century bourgeoisie—not only in Norway, his native land. His plays may be viewed historically as the culmination point of the *bourgeois* drama which has flourished fitfully, in France and Germany particularly, since the eighteenth century, when Diderot advocated and wrote plays about the middle classes, their "conditions" and problems. But they may also be seen as the fountainhead of much modern drama—of the plays of Shaw and Galsworthy, who discuss social problems, and of Maeterlinck and Chekhov, who learned from the later "symbolist" Ibsen.

Ibsen was born at Skien, in Norway, on March 20, 1828. His family had sunk into poverty and finally complete bankruptcy. In 1844, at the age of sixteen, he was sent to Grimstad, another small coastal town, as an apothecary's apprentice. There he lived in almost complete isolation and cut himself off from his family, except for his sister Hedvig. In 1850 he managed to get to Oslo (then Christiana) and to enroll at the university. But he never passed his examinations and in the following year left for Bergen, where he had acquired the position of playwright and assistant stage manager at the newly founded Norwegian Theater. Ibsen supplied the small theater with several historical and romantic plays. In 1857 he was appointed artistic director at the Mollergate Theater in Christiana, and a year later he married Susannah Thoresen. *Love's Comedy* (1862) was his first major success on the stage. Ibsen was then deeply affected by Scandinavianism, the movement for the solidarity of the Northern nations, and when in 1864 Norway refused to do anything to support Denmark in her war with Prussia and Austria over Schleswig-Holstein, he was so disgusted with his country that he left it for what he thought would be permanent exile. After that, Ibsen led a life of wandering. He lived in Rome, in Dresden, in Munich, and in smaller summer resorts, and during this time wrote all his later plays.

After a long period of incubation and experimentation with romantic and historical themes, Ibsen wrote a series of "problem" plays, beginning with *The Pillars of Society* (1877), which in their time created a furor by their fearless criticism of the nineteenth-century social scene: the subjection of women, hypocrisy, hereditary disease, seamy politics, and corrupt journalism. He wrote these plays using naturalistic modes of presentation: ordinary colloquial speech, a simple setting in a drawing room or study, a natural way of introducing or dismissing characters. Ibsen had learned from the "well-made" Parisian play (typified by those of Scribe) how to confine his action to one climactic situation and how gradually to uncover the past by retrogressive exposition. But he went far beyond it in technical skill and intellectual honesty.

The success of Ibsen's problem plays was international. But we must not forget that he was a Norwegian, the first writer of his small nation (its population at that time was less than two million) to win a reputation outside of Norway. Ibsen more than anyone else widened the scope of world literature beyond the confines of the great modern nations, which had entered its community roughly in this order: Italy, Spain, France, England, Germany, Russia. Since the time of Ibsen, the other small nations have begun to play their part in the concert of European literature. Paradoxically, however, Ibsen rejected his own land. He had dreamed of becoming a great national poet. Instead, the plays he wrote during his voluntary exile depicted Norwegian society as consisting largely of a stuffy, provincial middle class, redeemed by a few upright, even fiery, individuals of initiative and courage. Only in 1891, when he was sixty-three, did Ibsen return to Christiana for good. He was then famous and widely honored, but lived a very retired life. In 1900 he suffered a stroke which made him a complete invalid for the last years of his life. He died on May 23, 1906, at Christiana.

Ibsen could hardly have survived his time if he had been merely a painter of society, a dialectician of social issues, and a magnificent technician of the theater. True, many of his discussions are now dated. We smile at some of the doings in *A Doll's House* (1879) and *Ghosts* (1881). His stagecraft is not unusual, even on Broadway. But Ibsen stays with us because he has more to offer—because he was an artist who managed to create, at his best, works of poetry which, under their mask of sardonic humor, express his dream of humanity reborn by intelligence and self-sacrifice.

Hedda Gabler (1890) surprised and puzzled the large audience all over Europe that Ibsen had won in the 1880s. The play shows nothing of Ibsen's reforming zeal: no general theme emerges which could be used in spreading progressive ideas such as the emancipation of women dramatized in *A Doll's House* (1879), nor is the play an example of Ibsen's peculiar technique of retrospective revelation exhibited in *Rosmersholm* (1886). At first glance it seems mainly a study of a complex, exceptional, and even unique woman. Henry James, reviewing the first English performance, saw it as the picture of "a state of nerves as well as of soul, a state of temper, of health, of chagrin, of despair." Undoubtedly, Hedda is the central figure of the play, but she is no conventional heroine. She behaves atrociously to everyone with whom she comes in contact, and her moral sense is thoroughly defective: she is perverse, egotistical, sadistic, callous, even evil and demonic, truly a *femme fatale.* Still, this impression, while not mistaken, ignores another side of her personality and her situation. The play is, after all, a tragedy (though there are comic touches) and we are to feel pity and terror. Hedda is not simply evil and perverse. We must imagine her as distinguished, well-bred, proud, beautiful, and even grand in her defiance of her surroundings and in the final gesture of her suicide. Not for nothing have great actresses excelled in this role. We must pity her as a tortured, tormented creature caught in a web of circumstance, as a victim, in spite of her lashings-out to dominate and control the fate of those around her.

We are carefully prepared to understand her heritage. She is General Gabler's daughter. Ibsen tells us himself (in a letter to Count Moritz Prozor, 4 December 1890) that "I intended to indicate thereby that as a personality she is to be regarded rather as her father's daughter than as her husband's wife." She has inherited an aristocratic view of life. Her father's portrait hangs in her apartment. His pistols tell of the code of honor and the ready escape they offer in a self-inflicted death. Hedda lives in Ibsen's Norway, a stuffy, provincial, middle-class society, and is acutely, even morbidly afraid of scandal. She has, to her own regret, rejected the advances of Eilert, theatrically threatening him with her father's pistol. She envies Thea for the boldness with which she deserted her husband to follow Eilert. She admires Eilert for his escapades, which she romanticizes with the recurrent metaphor of his returning with "vine-leaves in his hair." But she cannot break out of the narrow confines of her society. She is not an emancipated woman.

When she is almost thirty, in reduced circumstances, she accepts a suitable husband, Jörgen Tesman. The marriage of convenience turns out to be a ghastly error for which she cannot forgive herself. Tesman is an amiable bore absorbed in his research into the "Domestic Industries of Brabant During the Middle Ages." His expectations of a professorship in his home town turn out to be uncertain. He has gone into debt, even to his guileless old aunt, in renting an expensive house and, supreme humiliation for her, Hedda is with child by him. The dream of luxury, of becoming a hostess, of keeping thoroughbred horses, is shattered the very first day after their return from the prolonged honeymoon which for Tesman was also a trip to rummage around in archives. Hedda is deeply stirred by the return of Eilert, her first suitor. She seems vaguely to think of a new relationship, at least, by spoiling his friendship with Thea. She plays with the attentions of Judge Brack. But everything quickly comes to nought: she is trapped in her marriage, unable and unwilling to become unfaithful to her husband; she is deeply disappointed by Eilert's ugly death, saying, "Everything I touch seems destined to turn into something mean and farcical." She fears the scandal which will follow when her role in Eilert's suicide is discovered and she is called before the police; she can avoid it only by coming under the power of Judge Brack, who is prepared to blackmail her with his knowledge of the circumstances. Her plot to destroy Thea and Eilert's brainchild is frustrated by Thea's having preserved notes and drafts which Thea eagerly starts to reconstruct with the help of Tesman. Still, while Hedda is in a terrible *impasse,* her suicide remains a shock, an abrupt, even absurd deed, eliciting the final line from the commonsensical Judge Brack: "Good God—people don't do things like that!" But we must assume that Hedda had pondered suicide long before:

the pistol she gave to Eilert implies an unspoken suicide pact. He bungled it; she does it the right way, dying in beauty, shot in the temple and not in the abdomen.

The play is not, however, simply a character study, though Hedda is an extraordinarily complex, contradictory, subtle woman whose portrait, at least on the stage, could not be easily paralleled before Ibsen. It is also an extremely effective, swiftly moving play of action, deftly plotted in its clashes and climaxes. At the end of act 1 Hedda seems to have won. The Tesmans, husband and aunt, are put in their place. Thea is lured into making confidences. The scene in act 2 in which Hedda appeals to Eilert's pride in his independence and induces him to join in Judge Brack's party is a superb display of Hedda's power and skill. Act 2 ends with Eilert going off and the two women left alone in their tense though suppressed antagonism. Act 3 ends with Hedda alone, burning the precious manuscript about the "forces that will shape our civilization and the direction in which that civilization may develop," an obvious contrast to Tesman's research into an irrelevant past. (Ibsen himself always believed in progress, in a utopia he called "the Third Empire.")

The action is compressed into about thirty-six hours and located in a house where only the moving of furniture (the piano into the back room) or the change of light or costumes indicates the passing of time. Tesman is something of a fool. He is totally unaware of Hedda's inner turmoil, he obtusely misunderstands allusions to her pregnancy, he comically encourages the advances of Judge Brack, he complacently settles down to the task of assembling the fragments of Eilert's manuscript, recognizing that "putting other people's papers into order is rather my specialty." Though he seems amiably domestic in his love for his aunts, proud of having won Hedda, ambitious to provide an elegant home for her, his behavior is by no means above reproach. He envies and fears Eilert, gloats over his bad reputation, surreptitiously brings home the lost manuscript, conceals its recovery from Thea; when Hedda tells of its being burned, he is at first shocked, reacting comically with the legal phrase about "appropriating lost property," but is then easily persuaded to accept it when Hedda tells him that she did it for his sake and completely won over when she reveals her pregnancy. After Eilert's death he feels, however, some guilt and tries to make up by helping in the reconstruction of the manuscript, now that his rival no longer threatens his career. Tesman is given strong speech mannerisms: the frequent use of "what?" which Hedda, commenting at the end on the progress of the work on the manuscript, imitates sarcastically, and the use of "fancy that." His last inappropriate words, "She's shot herself! Shot herself in the head! Fancy that!" lend a grotesque touch to the tragic end. Aunt Juliana belongs with him: she is a fussy, kindly person, proud of her nephew, awed by his new wife, eager to help with the expected baby, but also easily consoled after the death of her sister: "There's always some poor invalid who needs care and attention."

Judge Brack is a "man of the world," a sensualist who hardly conceals his desire to make Hedda his mistress, by blackmail if necessary, and is dismayed when she escapes his clutches: in his easy-going philosophy "people usually learn to accept the inevitable."

The other pair, Eilert Loevborg and Thea Elvsted, are sharply contrasted.

Thea had the courage to leave her husband; she is devoted to Eilert and seems to have cured him of his addiction to drink but fears that he cannot resist a new temptation. Eilert tells Hedda unkindly that Thea is "stupid," and there is some truth to that, inasmuch as she is so easily taken in by Hedda. Her quick settling down to work on the manuscript after Eilert's death suggests some obtuseness, though we must, presumably, excuse it as a theatrical foreshortening.

Eilert, we must assume, is some kind of genius. His book, we have to take on trust, is an important work. We are told that he had squandered an inheritance, had engaged in orgies, and had regaled Hedda with tales of his exploits before she chased him with her pistol. When he comes back to town, ostensibly reformed, dressed conventionally, he immediately starts courting Hedda again. Stung by her contempt for his abstinence, he rushes off to Brack's party, which degenerates into a disgraceful brawl in a house of ill fame. His relapse and the loss of the manuscript destroy his self-esteem and hope for any future. He accepts Hedda's pistol but dies an ignominious, ugly death. We see Eilert mainly reflected in Hedda's imagination as a figure of pagan freedom who, she thinks, has done something noble, beautiful, and courageous in "rising from the feast of life so early." She dies in beauty as she wanted Eilert to die.

This aesthetic suicide must seem to us a supremely futile gesture of revolt. Ibsen always admired the great rebels, the fighters for freedom, but *Hedda Gabler* will appear almost a parodic version of his persistent theme: the individual against society, defying it and escaping it in death.

J. W. McFarlane, ed., *Discussions of Henrik Ibsen* (1962), contains Henry James, "On the Occasion of 'Hedda Gabler.'" John Northan, *Ibsen: A Critical Study* (1973), has a chapter on *Hedda Gabler*, as do Bernard Shaw, *The Quintessence of Ibsenism* (1913), and Hermann J. Weigand, *The Modern Ibsen* (1925).

Hedda Gabler[1]

Characters

GEORGE TESMAN, *research graduate in cultural history*
HEDDA, *his wife*
MISS JULIANA TESMAN, *his aunt*

MRS. ELVSTED
JUDGE BRACK
EILERT LOEVBORG
BERTHA, *a maid*

The action takes place in TESMAN'S *villa in the fashionable quarter of town.*

Act I

SCENE—*A large drawing room, handsomely and tastefully furnished; decorated in dark colors. In the rear wall is a broad open*

---

1. Translated by Michael Meyer.

*doorway, with curtains drawn back to either side. It leads to a smaller
room, decorated in the same style as the drawing room. In the right-
hand wall of the drawing room, a folding door leads out to the hall.
The opposite wall, on the left, contains french windows, also with
curtains drawn back on either side. Through the glass we can see
part of a verandah, and trees in autumn colors. Downstage stands an
oval table, covered by a cloth and surrounded by chairs. Downstage
right, against the wall, is a broad stove tiled with dark porcelain; in
front of it stand a high-backed armchair, a cushioned footrest, and
two footstools. Upstage right, in an alcove, is a corner sofa, with a
small, round table. Downstage left, a little away from the wall, is
another sofa. Upstage of the french windows, a piano. On either side
of the open doorway in the rear wall stand what-nots holding ornaments of terra cotta and majolica. Against the rear wall of the smaller
room can be seen a sofa, a table, and a couple of chairs. Above this
sofa hangs the portrait of a handsome old man in general's uniform.
Above the table a lamp hangs from the ceiling, with a shade of opa-
lescent, milky glass. All round the drawing room bunches of flowers
stand in vases and glasses. More bunches lie on the tables. The floors
of both rooms are covered with thick carpets. Morning light. The
sun shines in through the french windows.*

MISS JULIANA TESMAN, *wearing a hat and carrying a parasol, enters
from the hall, followed by* BERTHA, *who is carrying a bunch of flowers wrapped in paper.* MISS TESMAN *is about sixty-five, of pleasant
and kindly appearance. She is neatly but simply dressed in grey outdoor clothes.* BERTHA, *the maid, is rather simple and rustic-looking.
She is getting on in years.*

MISS TESMAN. [*Stops just inside the door, listens, and says in a hushed
voice*] No, bless my soul! They're not up yet.

BERTHA. [*Also in hushed tones*] What did I tell you, miss? The boat
didn't get in till midnight. And when they did turn up—Jesus,
miss, you should have seen all the things Madam made me unpack
before she'd go to bed!

MISS TESMAN. Ah, well. Let them have a good lie in. But let's have
some nice fresh air waiting for them when they do come down.
[*Goes to the french windows and throws them wide open*]

BERTHA. [*Bewildered at the table, the bunch of flowers in her hand*]
I'm blessed if there's a square inch left to put anything. I'll have
to let it lie here, miss.
[*Puts it on the piano*]

MISS TESMAN. Well, Bertha dear, so now you have a new mistress.
Heaven knows it nearly broke my heart to have to part with you.

BERTHA. [*Snivels*] What about me, Miss Juju? How do you suppose
I felt? After all the happy years I've spent with you and Miss Rena?

MISS TESMAN. We must accept it bravely, Bertha. It was the only way. George needs you to take care of him. He could never manage without you. You've looked after him ever since he was a tiny boy.

BERTHA. Oh, but Miss Juju, I can't help thinking about Miss Rena, lying there all helpless, poor dear. And that new girl! She'll never learn the proper way to handle an invalid.

MISS TESMAN. Oh, I'll manage to train her. I'll do most of the work myself, you know. You needn't worry about my poor sister, Bertha dear.

BERTHA. But Miss Juju, there's another thing. I'm frightened Madam may not find me suitable.

MISS TESMAN. Oh, nonsense, Bertha. There may be one or two little things to begin with——

BERTHA. She's a real lady. Wants everything just so.

MISS TESMAN. But of course she does! General Gabler's daughter! Think of what she was accustomed to when the General was alive. You remember how we used to see her out riding with her father? In that long black skirt? With the feather in her hat?

BERTHA. Oh, yes, miss. As if I could forget! But, Lord! I never dreamed I'd live to see a match between her and Master Georgie.

MISS TESMAN. Neither did I. By the way, Bertha, from now on you must stop calling him Master Georgie. You must say: Dr. Tesman.

BERTHA. Yes, Madam said something about that too. Last night—the moment they'd set foot inside the door. Is it true, then, miss?

MISS TESMAN. Indeed it is. Just imagine, Bertha, some foreigners have made him a doctor. It happened while they were away. I had no idea till he told me when they got off the boat.

BERTHA. Well, I suppose there's no limit to what he won't become. He's that clever. I never thought he'd go in for hospital work, though.

MISS TESMAN. No, he's not that kind of doctor. [*Nods impressively*] In any case, you may soon have to address him by an even grander title.

BERTHA. You don't say! What might that be, miss?

MISS TESMAN. [*Smiles*] Ah! If you only knew! [*Moved*] Dear God, if only poor dear Joachim could rise out of his grave and see what his little son has grown into! [*Looks round*] But Bertha, why have you done this? Taken the chintz covers off all the furniture!

BERTHA. Madam said I was to. Can't stand chintz covers on chairs, she said.

MISS TESMAN. But surely they're not going to use this room as a parlor?

BERTHA. So I gathered, miss. From what Madam said. He didn't say anything. The Doctor.

[GEORGE TESMAN *comes into the rear room, from the right,*

humming, with an open, empty travelling bag in his hand. He is about thirty-three, of medium height and youthful appearance, rather plump, with an open, round, contented face, and fair hair and beard. He wears spectacles, and is dressed in comfortable, indoor clothes.]

MISS TESMAN. Good morning! Good morning, George!

TESMAN. [*In open doorway*] Auntie Juju! Dear Auntie Juju! [*Comes forward and shakes her hand*] You've come all the way out here! And so early! What?

MISS TESMAN. Well, I had to make sure you'd settled in comfortably.

TESMAN. But you can't have had a proper night's sleep.

MISS TESMAN. Oh, never mind that.

TESMAN. We were so sorry we couldn't give you a lift. But you saw how it was—Hedda had so much luggage—and she insisted on having it all with her.

MISS TESMAN. Yes, I've never seen so much luggage.

BERTHA. [*To* TESMAN] Shall I go and ask Madam if there's anything I can lend her a hand with?

TESMAN. Er—thank you, Bertha; no, you needn't bother. She says if she wants you for anything she'll ring.

BERTHA. [*Over to right*] Oh. Very good.

TESMAN. Oh, Bertha—take this bag, will you?

BERTHA. [*Takes it.*] I'll put it in the attic.

[*Goes out into the hall*]

TESMAN. Just fancy, Auntie Juju, I filled that whole bag with notes for my book. You know, it's really incredible what I've managed to find rooting through those archives. By Jove! Wonderful old things no one even knew existed——

MISS TESMAN. I'm sure you didn't waste a single moment of your honeymoon, George dear.

TESMAN. No, I think I can truthfully claim that. But, Auntie Juju, do take your hat off. Here. Let me untie it for you. What?

MISS TESMAN. [*As he does so*] Oh dear, oh dear! It's just as if you were still living at home with us.

TESMAN. [*Turns the hat in his hand and looks at it*] I say! What a splendid new hat!

MISS TESMAN. I bought it for Hedda's sake.

TESMAN. For Hedda's sake? What?

MISS TESMAN. So that Hedda needn't be ashamed of me, in case we ever go for a walk together.

TESMAN. [*Pats her cheek*] You still think of everything, don't you, Auntie Juju? [*Puts the hat down on a chair by the table*] Come on, let's sit down here on the sofa. And have a little chat while we wait for Hedda.

[*They sit. She puts her parasol in the corner of the sofa.*]

MISS TESMAN. [*Clasps both his hands and looks at him*] Oh, George, it's so wonderful to have you back, and be able to see you with my own eyes again! Poor dear Joachim's own son!

TESMAN. What about me! It's wonderful for me to see you again, Auntie Juju. You've been a mother to me. And a father, too.

MISS TESMAN. You'll always keep a soft spot in your heart for your old aunties, won't you. George dear?

TESMAN. I suppose Auntie Rena's no better? What?

MISS TESMAN. Alas, no. I'm afraid she'll never get better, poor dear. She's lying there just as she has for all these years. Please God I may be allowed to keep her for a little longer. If I lost her I don't know what I'd do. Especially now I haven't you to look after.

TESMAN. [*Pats her on the back*] There, there, there!

MISS TESMAN. [*With a sudden change of mood*] Oh but George, fancy you being a married man! And to think it's you who've won Hedda Gabler! The beautiful Hedda Gabler! Fancy! She was always so surrounded by admirers.

TESMAN. [*Hums a little and smiles contentedly*] Yes, I suppose there are quite a few people in this town who wouldn't mind being in my shoes. What?

MISS TESMAN. And what a honeymoon! Five months! Nearly six.

TESMAN. Well, I've done a lot of work, you know. All those archives to go through. And I've had to read lots of books.

MISS TESMAN. Yes, dear, of course. [*Lowers her voice confidentially*] But tell me, George—haven't you any—any extra little piece of news to give me?

TESMAN. You mean, arising out of the honeymoon?

MISS TESMAN. Yes.

TESMAN. No, I don't think there's anything I didn't tell you in my letters. My doctorate, of course—but I told you about that last night, didn't I?

MISS TESMAN. Yes, yes, I didn't mean that kind of thing. I was just wondering—are you—are you expecting——?

TESMAN. Expecting what?

MISS TESMAN. Oh, come on George, I'm your old aunt!

TESMAN. Well actually—yes, I am expecting something.

MISS TESMAN. I knew it!

TESMAN. You'll be happy to hear that before very long I expect to become a professor.

MISS TESMAN. Professor?

TESMAN. I think I may say that the matter has been decided. But, Auntie Juju, you know about this.

MISS TESMAN. [*Gives a little laugh*] Yes, of course. I'd forgotten. [*Changes her tone*] But we were talking about your honeymoon. It must have cost a dreadful amount of money, George?

TESMAN. Oh well, you know, that big research grant I got helped a good deal.

MISS TESMAN. But how on earth did you manage to make it do for two?

TESMAN. Well, to tell the truth it was a bit tricky. What?

MISS TESMAN. Especially when one's traveling with a lady. A little bird tells me that makes things very much more expensive.

TESMAN. Well, yes, of course it does make things a little more expensive. But Hedda has to do things in style, Auntie Juju. I mean, she has to. Anything less grand wouldn't have suited her.

MISS TESMAN. No, no, I suppose not. A honeymoon abroad seems to be the vogue nowadays. But tell me, have you had time to look round the house?

TESMAN. You bet. I've been up since the crack of dawn.

MISS TESMAN. Well, what do you think of it?

TESMAN. Splendid. Absolutely splendid. I'm only wondering what we're going to do with those two empty rooms between that little one and Hedda's bedroom.

MISS TESMAN. [*Laughs slyly*] Ah, George dear, I'm sure you'll manage to find some use for them—in time.

TESMAN. Yes, of course, Auntie Juju, how stupid of me. You're thinking of my books. What?

MISS TESMAN. Yes, yes, dear boy. I was thinking of your books.

TESMAN. You know, I'm so happy for Hedda's sake that we've managed to get this house. Before we became engaged she often used to say this was the only house in town she felt she could really bear to live in. It used to belong to Mrs. Falk—you know, the Prime Minister's widow.

MISS TESMAN. Fancy that! And what a stroke of luck it happened to come into the market. Just as you'd left on your honeymoon.

TESMAN. Yes, Auntie Juju, we've certainly had all the luck with us. What?

MISS TESMAN. But, George dear, the expense! It's going to make a dreadful hole in your pocket, all this.

TESMAN. [*A little downcast*] Yes, I—I suppose it will, won't it?

MISS TESMAN. Oh, George, really!

TESMAN. How much do you think it'll cost? Roughly, I mean? What?

MISS TESMAN. I can't possibly say till I see the bills.

TESMAN. Well, luckily Judge Brack's managed to get it on very favorable terms. He wrote and told Hedda so.

MISS TESMAN. Don't you worry, George dear. Anyway I've stood security for all the furniture and carpets.

TESMAN. Security? But dear, sweet Auntie Juju, how could you possibly stand security?

MISS TESMAN. I've arranged a mortgage on our annuity.

TESMAN. [*jumps up*] What? On your annuity? And—Auntie Rena's?

MISS TESMAN. Yes. Well, I couldn't think of any other way.

TESMAN. [*Stands in front of her*] Auntie Juju, have you gone completely out of your mind? That annuity's all you and Auntie Rena have.

MISS TESMAN. All right, there's no need to get so excited about it. It's a pure formality, you know. Judge Brack told me so. He was so kind as to arrange it all for me. A pure formality; those were his very words.

TESMAN. I dare say. All the same——

MISS TESMAN. Anyway, you'll have a salary of your own now. And, good heavens, even if we did have to fork out a little—tighten our belts for a week or two—why, we'd be happy to do so for your sake.

TESMAN. Oh, Auntie Juju! Will you never stop sacrificing yourself for me?

MISS TESMAN. [*Gets up and puts her hands on his shoulders*] What else have I to live for but to smooth your road a little, my dear boy? You've never had any mother or father to turn to. And now at last we've achieved our goal. I won't deny we've had our little difficulties now and then. But now, thank the good Lord, George dear, all your worries are past.

TESMAN. Yes, it's wonderful really how everything's gone just right for me.

MISS TESMAN. Yes! And the enemies who tried to bar your way have been struck down. They have been made to bite the dust. The man who was your most dangerous rival has had the mightiest fall. And now he's lying there in the pit he dug for himself, poor misguided creature.

TESMAN. Have you heard any news of Eilert? Since I went away?

MISS TESMAN. Only that he's said to have published a new book.

TESMAN. What! Eilert Loevborg? You mean—just recently? What?

MISS TESMAN. So they say. I don't imagine it can be of any value, do you? When your new book comes out, that'll be another story. What's it going to be about?

TESMAN. The domestic industries of Brabant[2] in the Middle Ages.

MISS TESMAN. Oh, George! The things you know about!

TESMAN. Mind you, it may be some time before I actually get down to writing it. I've made these very extensive notes, and I've got to file and index them first.

MISS TESMAN. Ah, yes! Making notes; filing and indexing; you've always been wonderful at that. Poor dear Joachim was just the same.

TESMAN. I'm looking forward so much to getting down to that. Espe-

---

2. In the Middle Ages, a duchy located in parts of what are now Belgium and the Netherlands.

cially now I've a home of my own to work in.

MISS TESMAN. And above all, now that you have the girl you set your heart on, George dear.

TESMAN. [*Embraces her*] Oh, yes, Auntie Juju, yes! Hedda's the loveliest thing of all! [*Looks towards the doorway*] I think I hear her coming. What?

> [HEDDA *enters the rear room from the left, and comes into the drawing room. She is a woman of twenty-nine. Distinguished, aristocratic face and figure. Her complexion is pale and opalescent. Her eyes are steel-grey, with an expression of cold, calm serenity. Her hair is of a handsome auburn color, but is not especially abundant. She is dressed in an elegant, somewhat loose-fitting morning gown.*]

MISS TESMAN. [*Goes to greet her*] Good morning, Hedda dear! Good morning!

HEDDA. [*Holds out her hand*] Good morning, dear Miss Tesman. What an early hour to call. So kind of you.

MISS TESMAN. [*Seems somewhat embarrassed*] And has the young bride slept well in her new home?

HEDDA. Oh—thank you, yes. Passably well.

TESMAN. [*Laughs*] Passably. I say, Hedda, that's good! When I jumped out of bed, you were sleeping like a top.

HEDDA. Yes. Fortunately. One has to accustom oneself to anything new, Miss Tesman. It takes time. [*Looks left*] Oh, that maid's left the french windows open. This room's flooded with sun.

MISS TESMAN. [*Goes towards the windows*] Oh—let me close them.

HEDDA. No, no, don't do that. Tesman dear, draw the curtains. This light's blinding me.

TESMAN. [*At the windows*] Yes, yes, dear. There, Hedda, now you've got shade and fresh air.

HEDDA. This room needs fresh air. All these flowers—But my dear Miss Tesman, won't you take a seat?

MISS TESMAN. No, really not, thank you. I just wanted to make sure you have everything you need. I must see about getting back home. My poor dear sister will be waiting for me.

TESMAN. Be sure to give her my love, won't you? Tell her I'll run over and see her later today.

MISS TESMAN. Oh yes, I'll tell her that. Oh, George——[*Fumbles in the pocket of her skirt*] I almost forgot. I've brought something for you.

TESMAN. What's that, Auntie Juju? What?

MISS TESMAN. [*Pulls out a flat package wrapped in newspaper and gives it to him*] Open and see, dear boy.

TESMAN. [*Opens the package*] Good heavens! Auntie Juju, you've kept them! Hedda, this is really very touching. What?

HEDDA. [*By the what-nots, on the right*] What is it, Tesman?

TESMAN. My old shoes! My slippers, Hedda!

HEDDA. Oh, them. I remember you kept talking about them on our honeymoon.

TESMAN. Yes, I missed them dreadfully. [*Goes over to her*] Here, Hedda, take a look.

HEDDA. [*Goes away towards the stove*] Thanks, I won't bother.

TESMAN. [*Follows her*] Fancy, Hedda, Auntie Rena's embroidered them for me. Despite her being so ill. Oh, you can't imagine what memories they have for me.

HEDDA. [*By the table*] Not for me.

MISS TESMAN. No, Hedda's right there, George.

TESMAN. Yes, but I thought since she's one of the family now——

HEDDA. [*Interrupts*] Tesman, we really can't go on keeping this maid.

MISS TESMAN. Not keep Bertha?

TESMAN. What makes you say that, dear? What?

HEDDA. [*Points*] Look at that! She's left her old hat lying on the chair.

TESMAN. [*Appalled, drops his slippers on the floor*] But, Hedda——!

HEDDA. Suppose someone came in and saw it?

TESMAN. But Hedda—that's Auntie Juju's hat.

HEDDA. Oh?

MISS TESMAN. [*Picks up the hat*] Indeed it's mine. And it doesn't happen to be old, Hedda dear.

HEDDA. I didn't look at it very closely, Miss Tesman.

MISS TESMAN. [*Tying on the hat*] As a matter of fact, it's the first time I've worn it. As the good Lord is my witness.

TESMAN. It's very pretty, too. Really smart.

MISS TESMAN. Oh, I'm afraid it's nothing much really. [*Looks round*] My parasol? Ah, here it is. [*Takes it*] This is mine, too. [*Murmurs*] Not Bertha's.

TESMAN. A new hat and a new parasol! I say, Hedda, fancy that!

HEDDA. Very pretty and charming.

TESMAN. Yes, isn't it? What? But Auntie Juju, take a good look at Hedda before you go. Isn't she pretty and charming?

MISS TESMAN. Dear boy, there's nothing new in that. Hedda's been a beauty ever since the day she was born.
[*Nods and goes right.*]

TESMAN. [*Follows her*] Yes, but have you noticed how strong and healthy she's looking? And how she's filled out since we went away?

MISS TESMAN. [*Stops and turns*] Filled out?

HEDDA. [*Walks across the room*] Oh, can't we forget it?

TESMAN. Yes, Auntie Juju—you can't see it so clearly with that dress on. But I've good reason to know——

HEDDA. [*By the french windows, impatiently*] You haven't good reason to know anything.

TESMAN. It must have been the mountain air up there in the Tyrol——

HEDDA. [*Curtly, interrupts him*] I'm exactly the same as when I went away.

TESMAN. You keep on saying so. But you're not. I'm right, aren't I, Auntie Juju?

MISS TESMAN. [*Has folded her hands and is gazing at her*] She's beautiful—beautiful. Hedda is beautiful. [*Goes over to* HEDDA, *takes her head between her hands, draws it down and kisses her hair*] God bless and keep you, Hedda Tesman. For George's sake.

HEDDA. [*Frees herself politely*] Oh—let me go, please.

MISS TESMAN. [*Quietly, emotionally*] I shall come see you both every day.

TESMAN. Yes, Auntie Juju, please do. What?

MISS TESMAN. Good-bye! Good-bye!

> [*She goes out into the hall.* TESMAN *follows her. The door remains open.* TESMAN *is heard sending his love to* AUNT RENA *and thanking* MISS TESMAN *for his slippers. Meanwhile* HEDDA *walks up and down the room raising her arms and clenching her fists as though in desperation. Then she throws aside the curtains from the french windows and stands there, looking out. A few moments later,* TESMAN *returns and closes the door behind him.*]

TESMAN. [*Picks up his slippers from the floor*] What are you looking at, Hedda?

HEDDA. [*Calm and controlled again*] Only the leaves. They're so golden. And withered.

TESMAN. [*Wraps up the slippers and lays them on the table*] Well, we're in September now.

HEDDA. [*Restless again*] Yes. We're already into September.

TESMAN. Auntie Juju was behaving rather oddly, I thought, didn't you? Almost as though she was in church or something. I wonder what came over her. Any idea?

HEDDA. I hardly know her. Does she often act like that?

HESMAN. Not to the extent she did today.

HEDDA. [*Goes away from the french windows*] Do you think she was hurt by what I said about the hat?

TESMAN. Oh, I don't think so. A little at first, perhaps——

HEDDA. But what a thing to do, throw her hat down in someone's drawing room. People don't do such things.

TESMAN. I'm sure Auntie Juju doesn't do it very often.

HEDDA. Oh well, I'll make it up with her.

TESMAN. Oh Hedda, would you?

HEDDA. When you see them this afternoon invite her to come out here this evening.

TESMAN. You bet I will! I say, there's another thing which would please her enormously.

HEDDA. Oh?

TESMAN. If you could bring yourself to call her Auntie Juju. For my sake, Hedda? What?

HEDDA. Oh no, really Tesman, you mustn't ask me to do that. I've told you so once before. I'll try to call her Aunt Juliana. That's as far as I'll go.

TESMAN. [*After a moment*] I say, Hedda, is anything wrong? What?

HEDDA. I'm just looking at my old piano. It doesn't really go with all this.

TESMAN. As soon as I start getting my salary we'll see about changing it.

HEDDA. No, no, don't let's change it. I don't want to part with it. We can move it into that little room and get another one to put in here.

TESMAN. [*A little downcast*] Yes, we—might do that.

HEDDA. [*Picks up the bunch of flowers from the piano*] These flowers weren't here when we arrived last night.

TESMAN. I expect Auntie Juju brought them.

HEDDA. Here's a card. [*Takes it out and reads*] "Will come back later today." Guess who it's from?

TESMAN. No idea. Who? What?

HEDDA. It says: "Mrs. Elvsted."

TESMAN. No, really? Mrs. Elvsted! She used to be Miss Rysing, didn't she?

HEDDA. Yes. she was the one with that irritating hair she was always showing off. I hear she used to be an old flame of yours.

TESMAN. [*Laughs*] That didn't last long. Anyway, that was before I got to know you, Hedda. By Jove, fancy her being in town!

HEDDA. Strange she should call. I only knew her at school.

TESMAN. Yes, I haven't seen her for—oh, heaven knows how long. I don't know how she manages to stick it out up there in the north. What?

HEDDA. [*Thinks for a moment, then says suddenly*] Tell me, Tesman, doesn't he live somewhere up in those parts? You know— Eilert Loevborg?

TESMAN. Yes, that's right. So he does.

[BERTHA *enters from the hall.*]

BERTHA. She's here again, madam. The lady who came and left the flowers. [*Points*] The ones you're holding.

HEDDA. Oh, is she? Well, show her in.

[BERTHA *opens the door for* MRS. ELVSTED *and goes out.* MRS. ELVSTED *is a delicately built woman with gentle, attractive fea-*

*tures. Her eyes are light blue, large, and somewhat prominent,
with a frightened, questioning expression. Her hair is extremely
fair, almost flaxen, and is exceptionally wavy and abundant.
She is two or three years younger than* HEDDA. *She is wearing a
dark visiting dress, in good taste but not quite in the latest fashion.*]

HEDDA. [*Goes cordially to greet her*] Dear Mrs. Elvsted, good morning. How delightful to see you again after all this time.

MRS. ELVSTED. [*Nervously, trying to control herself*] Yes, it's many
years since we met.

TESMAN. And since *we* met. What?

HEDDA. Thank you for your lovely flowers.

MRS. ELVSTED. Oh, please—I wanted to come yesterday afternoon.
But they told me you were away——

TESMAN. You've only just arrived in town, then? What?

MRS. ELVSTED. I got here yesterday, around midday. Oh, I became
almost desperate when I heard you weren't here.

HEDDA. Desperate? Why?

TESMAN. My dear Mrs. Rysing—Elvsted——

HEDDA. There's nothing wrong, I hope?

MRS. ELVSTED. Yes, there is. And I don't know anyone else here
whom I can turn to.

HEDDA. [*Puts the flowers down on the table*] Come and sit with me
on the sofa——

MRS. ELVSTED. Oh, I feel too restless to sit down.

HEDDA. You must. Come along, now.

[*She pulls* MRS. ELVSTED *down on to the sofa and sits beside
her.*]

TESMAN. Well? Tell us, Mrs.—er——

HEDDA. Has something happened at home?

MRS. ELVSTED. Yes—that is, yes and no. Oh, I do hope you won't
misunderstand me——

HEDDA. Then you'd better tell us the whole story, Mrs. Elvsted.

TESMAN. That's why you've come. What?

MRS. ELVSTED. Yes—yes, it is. Well, then—in case you don't already
know—Eilert Loevborg is in town.

HEDDA. Loevborg here?

TESMAN. Eilert back in town? By Jove, Hedda, did you hear that?

HEDDA. Yes, of course I heard.

MRS. ELVSTED. He's been here a week. A whole week! In this city.
Alone. With all those dreadful people——

HEDDA. But my dear Mrs. Elvsted, what concern is he of yours?

MRS. ELVSTED. [*Gives her a frightened look and says quickly*] He's
been tutoring the children.

HEDDA. Your children?

MRS. ELVSTED. My husband's. I have none.

HEDDA. Oh, you mean your stepchildren.

MRS. ELVSTED. Yes.

TESMAN. [*Gropingly*] But was he sufficiently—I don't know how to put it—sufficiently regular in his habits to be suited to such a post? What?

MRS. ELVSTED. For the past two to three years he has been living irreproachably.

TESMAN. You don't say! By Jove, Hedda, hear that?

HEDDA. I hear.

MRS. ELVSTED. Quite irreproachably, I assure you. In every respect. All the same—in this big city—with money in his pockets—I'm so dreadfully frightened something may happen to him.

TESMAN. But why didn't he stay up there with you and your husband?

MRS. ELVSTED. Once his book had come out, he became restless.

TESMAN. Oh, yes—Auntie Juju said he's brought out a new book.

MRS. ELVSTED. Yes, a big new book about the history of civilization. A kind of general survey. It came out a fortnight ago. Everyone's been buying it and reading it—it's created a tremendous stir——

TESMAN. Has it really? It must be something he's dug up, then.

MRS. ELVSTED. You mean from the old days?

TESMAN. Yes.

MRS. ELVSTED. No, he's written it all since he came to live with us.

TESMAN. Well, that's splendid news, Hedda. Fancy that!

MRS. ELVSTED. Oh, yes! If only he can go on like this!

HEDDA. Have you met him since you came here?

MRS. ELVSTED. No, not yet. I had such dreadful difficulty finding his address. But this morning I managed to track him down at last.

HEDDA. [*Looks searchingly at her*] I must say I find it a little strange that your husband—hm——

MRS. ELVSTED. [*Starts nervously*] My husband! What do you mean?

HEDDA. That he should send you all the way here on an errand of this kind. I'm surprised he didn't come himself to keep an eye on his friend.

MRS. ELVSTED. Oh, no, no—my husband hasn't the time. Besides, I—er—wanted to do some shopping here.

HEDDA. [*With a slight smile*] Ah. Well, that's different.

MRS. ELVSTED. [*Gets up quickly, restlessly*] Please, Mr. Tesman, I beg you—be kind to Eilert Loevborg if he comes here. I'm sure he will. I mean, you used to be such good friends in the old days. And you're both studying the same subject, as far as I can understand. You're in the same field, aren't you?

TESMAN. Well, we used to be, anyway.

MRS. ELVSTED. Yes—so I beg you earnestly, do please, please, keep an eye on him. Oh, Mr. Tesman, do promise me you will.

TESMAN. I shall be only too happy to do so, Mrs. Rysing.

HEDDA. Elvsted.

TESMAN. I'll do everything for Eilert that lies in my power. You can rely on that.

MRS. ELVSTED. Oh, how good and kind you are! [*Presses his hands*] Thank you, thank you, thank you. [*Frightened*] My husband's so fond of him, you see.

HEDDA. [*Gets up*] You'd better send him a note, Tesman. He may not come to you of his own accord.

TESMAN. Yes, that'd probably be the best plan, Hedda. What?

HEDDA. The sooner the better. Why not do it now?

MRS. ELVSTED. [*Pleasingly*] Oh yes, if only you would!

TESMAN. I'll do it this very moment. Do you have his address, Mrs.— er—Elvsted?

MRS. ELVSTED. Yes.

   [*Takes a small piece of paper from her pocket and gives it to him.*]

TESMAN. Good, good. Right, well I'll go inside and——[*Looks round*] Where are my slippers? Oh yes, here.

   [*Picks up the package and is about to go*]

HEDDA. Try to sound friendly. Make it a nice long letter.

TESMAN. Right, I will.

MRS. ELVSTED. Please don't say anything about my having seen you.

TESMAN. Good heavens no, of course not. What?

   [*Goes out through the rear room to the right*]

HEDDA. [*Goes over to* MRS. ELVSTED, *smiles, and says softly*] Well! Now we've killed two birds with one stone.

MRS. ELVSTED. What do you mean?

HEDDA. Didn't you realize I wanted to get him out of the room?

MRS. ELVSTED. So that he could write the letter?

HEDDA. And so that I could talk to you alone.

MRS. ELVSTED. [*Confused*] About this?

HEDDA. Yes, about this.

MRS. ELVSTED. [*In alarm*] But there's nothing more to tell, Mrs. Tesman. Really there isn't.

HEDDA. Oh, yes there is. There's a lot more. I can see that. Come along, let's sit down and have a little chat.

   [*She pushes* MRS. ELVSTED *down into the armchair by the stove and seats herself on one of the footstools.*]

MRS. ELVSTED. [*Looks anxiously at her watch*] Really, Mrs. Tesman, I think I ought to be going now.

HEDDA. There's no hurry. Well? How are things at home?

MRS. ELVSTED. I'd rather not speak about that.

HEDDA. But my dear, you can tell me. Good heavens, we were at school together.

MRS. ELVSTED. Yes, but you were a year senior to me. Oh, I used to be terribly frightened of you in those days.

HEDDA. Frightened of me?

MRS. ELVSTED. Yes, terribly frightened. Whenever you met me on the staircase you used to pull my hair.

HEDDA. No, did I?

MRS. ELVSTED. Yes. And once you said you'd burn it all off.

HEDDA. Oh, that was only in fun.

MRS. ELVSTED. Yes, but I was so silly in those days. And then afterwards—I mean, we've drifted so far apart. Our backgrounds were so different.

HEDDA. Well, now we must try to drift together again. Now listen. When we were at school we used to call each other by our Christian names——

MRS. ELVSTED. No, I'm sure you're mistaken.

HEDDA. I'm sure I'm not. I remember it quite clearly. Let's tell each other our secrets, as we used to in the old days. [*Moves closer on her footstool*] There, now. [*Kisses her on the cheek*] You must call me Hedda.

MRS. ELVSTED. [*Squeezes her hands and pats them*] Oh, you're so kind. I'm not used to people being so nice to me.

HEDDA. Now, now, now. And I shall call you Tora, the way I used to.

MRS. ELVSTED. My name is Thea.

HEDDA. Yes, of course. Of course. I meant Thea. [*Looks at her sympathetically*] So you're not used to kindness, Thea? In your own home?

MRS. ELVSTED. Oh, if only I had a home! But I haven't. I've never had one.

HEDDA. [*Looks at her for a moment*] I thought that was it.

MRS. ELVSTED. [*Stares blankly and helplessly*] Yes—yes—yes.

HEDDA. I can't remember exactly now, but didn't you first go to Mr. Elvsted as a housekeeper?

MRS. ELVSTED. Governess, actually. But his wife—at the time, I mean—she was an invalid, and had to spend most of her time in bed. So I had to look after the house too.

HEDDA. But in the end, you became mistress of the house.

MRS. ELVSTED. [*Sadly*] Yes, I did.

HEDDA. Let me see. Roughly how long ago was that?

MRS. ELVSTED. When I got married, you mean?

HEDDA. Yes.

MRS. ELVSTED. About five years.

HEDDA. Yes; it must be about that.

MRS. ELVSTED. Oh, those five years! Especially that last two or three. Oh, Mrs. Tesman, if you only knew——

HEDDA. [*Slaps her hand gently*] Mrs. Tesman? Oh, Thea!

MRS. ELVSTED. I'm sorry, I'll try to remember. Yes—if you had any idea——

HEDDA. [*Casually*] Eilert Loevborg's been up here too, for about three years, hasn't he?

MRS. ELVSTED. [*Looks at her uncertainly*] Eilert Loevborg? Yes, he has.

HEDDA. Did you know him before? When you were here?

MRS. ELVSTED. No, not really. That is—I knew him by name, of course.

HEDDA. But up there, he used to visit you?

MRS. ELVSTED. Yes, he used to come and see us every day. To give the children lessons. I found I couldn't do that as well as manage the house.

HEDDA. I'm sure you couldn't. And your husband——? I suppose being a magistrate he has to be away from home a good deal?

MRS. ELVSTED. Yes. You see, Mrs.——you see, Hedda, he has to cover the whole district.

HEDDA. [*Leans against the arm of* MRS. ELVSTED'S *chair*] Poor, pretty little Thea! Now you must tell me the whole story. From beginning to end.

MRS. ELVSTED. Well—what do you want to know?

HEDDA. What kind of a man is your husband, Thea? I mean, as a person. Is he kind to you?

MRS. ELVSTED. [*Evasively*] I'm sure he does his best to be.

HEDDA. I only wonder if he isn't too old for you. There's more than twenty years between you, isn't there?

MRS. ELVSTED. [*Irritably*] Yes, there's that too. Oh, there are so many things. We're different in every way. We've nothing in common. Nothing whatever.

HEDDA. But he loves you, surely? In his own way?

MRS. ELVSTED. Oh, I don't know. I think he just finds me useful. And then I don't cost much to keep. I'm cheap.

HEDDA. Now you're being stupid.

MRS. ELVSTED. [*Shakes her head*] It can't be any different. With him. He doesn't love anyone except himself. And perhaps the children—a little.

HEDDA. He must be fond of Eilert Loevborg, Thea.

MRS. ELVSTED. [*Looks at her*] Eilert Loevborg? What makes you think that?

HEDDA. Well, if he sends you all the way down here to look for him——[*Smiles almost imperceptibly*] Besides, you said so yourself to Tesman.

MRS. ELVSTED. [*With a nervous twitch*] Did I? Oh yes, I suppose I did. [*Impulsively, but keeping her voice low*] Well, I might as well tell you the whole story. It's bound to come out sooner or later.

HEDDA. But my dear Thea——?

MRS. ELVSTED. My husband had no idea I was coming here.

HEDDA. What? Your husband didn't know?

MRS. ELVSTED. No, of course not. As a matter of fact, he wasn't even there. He was away at the assizes. Oh, I couldn't stand it any longer, Hedda! I just couldn't. I'd be so dreadfully lonely up there now.

HEDDA. Go on.

MRS. ELVSTED. So I packed a few things. Secretly. And went.

HEDDA. Without telling anyone?

MRS. ELVSTED. Yes. I caught the train and came straight here.

HEDDA. But my dear Thea! How brave of you!

MRS. ELVSTED. [*Gets up and walks across the room*] Well, what else could I do?

HEDDA. But what do you suppose your husband will say when you get back?

MRS. ELVSTED. [*By the table, looks at her*] Back there? To him?

HEDDA. Yes. Surely——?

MRS. ELVSTED. I shall never go back to him.

HEDDA. [*Gets up and goes closer*] You mean you've left your home for good?

MRS. ELVSTED. Yes. I didn't see what else I could do.

HEDDA. But to do it so openly!

MRS. ELVSTED. Oh, it's no use trying to keep a thing like that secret.

HEDDA. But what do you suppose people will say?

MRS. ELVSTED. They can say what they like. [*Sits sadly, wearily on the sofa*] I had to do it.

HEDDA. [*After a short silence*] What do you intend to do now? How are you going to live?

MRS. ELVSTED. I don't know. I only know that I must live wherever Eilert Loevborg is. If I am to go on living.

HEDDA. [*Moves a chair from the table, sits on it near* MRS. ELVSTED *and strokes her hands*] Tell me, Thea, how did this—friendship between you and Eilert Loevborg begin?

MRS. ELVSTED. Oh, it came about gradually. I developed a kind of—power over him.

HEDDA. Oh?

MRS. ELVSTED. He gave up his old habits. Not because I asked him to. I'd never have dared to do that. I suppose he just noticed I didn't like that kind of thing. So he gave it up.

HEDDA. [*Hides a smile*] So you've made a new man of him. Clever little Thea!

MRS. ELVSTED. Yes—anyway, he says I have. And he's made a —sort of—real person of me. Taught me to think—and to understand all kinds of things.

HEDDA. Did he give you lessons too?

MRS. ELVSTED. Not exactly lessons. But he talked to me. About—oh, you've no idea—so many things! And then he let me work with him. Oh, it was wonderful. I was so happy to be allowed to help him.

HEDDA. Did he allow you to help him!

MRS. ELVSTED. Yes. Whenever he wrote anything we always—did it together.

HEDDA. Like good pals?

MRS. ELVSTED. [*Eagerly*] Pals! Yes—why, Hedda, that's exactly the word he used! Oh, I ought to feel so happy. But I can't. I don't know if it will last.

HEDDA. You don't seem very sure of him.

MRS. ELVSTED. [*Sadly*] Something stands between Eilert Loevberg and me. The shadow of another woman.

HEDDA. Who can that be?

MRS. ELVSTED. I don't know. Someone he used to be friendly with in—in the old days. Someone he's never been able to forget.

HEDDA. What has he told you about her?

MRS. ELVSTED. Oh, he only mentioned her once, casually.

HEDDA. Well! What did he say?

MRS. ELVSTED. He said when he left her she tried to shoot him with a pistol.

HEDDA. [*Cold, controlled*] What nonsense. People don't do such things. The kind of people we know.

MRS. ELVSTED. No, I think it must have been that red-haired singer he used to——

HEDDA. Ah yes, very probably.

MRS. ELVSTED. I remember they used to say she always carried a loaded pistol.

HEDDA. Well then, it must be her.

MRS. ELVSTED. But Hedda, I hear she's come back, and is living here. Oh, I'm so desperate——!

HEDDA. [*Glances toward the rear room*] Ssh! Tesman's coming. [*Gets up and whispers*] Thea, we mustn't breathe a word about this to anyone.

MRS. ELVSTED. [*Jumps up*] Oh, no, no! Please don't!

[GEORGE TESMAN *appears from the right in the rear room with a letter in his hand, and comes into the drawing room.*]

TESMAN. Well, here's my little epistle all signed and sealed.

HEDDA. Good. I think Mrs. Elvsted wants to go now. Wait a moment— I'll see you as far as the garden gate.

TESMAN. Er—Hedda, do you think Bertha could deal with this?

HEDDA. [*Takes the letter*] I'll give her instructions.

[BERTHA *enters from the hall.*]

BERTHA. Judge Brack is here and asks if he may pay his respects to Madam and the Doctor.

HEDDA. Yes, ask him to be so good as to come in. And—wait a moment—drop this letter in the post box.

BERTHA. [*Takes the letter*] Very good, madam.

[*She opens the door for* JUDGE BRACK, *and goes out.* JUDGE BRACK *is forty-five; rather short, but well-built, and elastic in his movements. He has a roundish face with an aristocratic profile. His hair, cut short, is still almost black, and is carefully barbered. Eyes lively and humorous. Thick eyebrows. His moustache is also thick, and is trimmed square at the ends. He is wearing outdoor clothes which are elegant but a little too youthful for him. He has a monocle in one eye; now and then he lets it drop.*]

BRACK. [*Hat in hand, bows*] May one presume to call so early?

HEDDA. One may presume.

TESMAN. [*Shakes his hand*] You're welcome here any time. Judge Brack—Mrs. Rysing.

[HEDDA *sighs.*]

BRACK. [*Bows*] Ah—charmed——

HEDDA. [*Looks at him and laughs*] What fun to be able to see you by daylight for once, Judge.

BRACK. Do I look—different?

HEDDA. Yes. A little younger, I think.

BRACK. Obliged.

TESMAN. Well, what do you think of Hedda? What? Doesn't she look well? Hasn't she filled out——?

HEDDA. Oh, do stop it. You ought to be thanking Judge Brack for all the inconvenience he's put himself to——

BRACK. Nonsense, it was a pleasure——

HEDDA. You're a loyal friend. But my other friend is pining to get away. Au revoir, Judge. I won't be a minute.

[*Mutual salutations.* MRS. ELVSTED *and* HEDDA *go out through the hall.*]

BRACK. Well, is your wife satisfied with everything?

TESMAN. Yes, we can't thank you enough. That is—we may have to shift one or two things around, she tells me. And we're short of one or two little items we'll have to purchase.

BRACK. Oh? Really?

TESMAN. But you musn't worry your head about that. Hedda says she'll get what's needed. I say, why don't we sit down? What?

BRACK. Thanks, just for a moment. [*Sits at the table*] There's something I'd like to talk to you about, my dear Tesman.

TESMAN. Oh? Ah yes, of course. [*Sits*] After the feast comes the reckoning. What?

BRACK. Oh, never mind about the financial side—there's no hurry about that. Though I could wish we'd arranged things a little less palatially.

TESMAN. Good heavens, that'd never have done. Think of Hedda, my dear chap. You know her. I couldn't possibly ask her to live like a suburban housewife.

BRACK. No, no—that's just the problem.

TESMAN. Anyway, it can't be long now before my nomination[3] comes through.

BRACK. Well, you know, these things often take time.

TESMAN. Have you heard any more news? What?

BRACK. Nothing definite. [*Changing the subject*] Oh, by the way, I have one piece of news for you.

TESMAN. What?

BRACK. Your old friend Eilert Loevborg is back in town.

TESMAN. I know that already.

BRACK. Oh? How did you hear that?

TESMAN. She told me. That lady who went out with Hedda.

BRACK. I see. What was her name? I didn't catch it.

TESMAN. Mrs. Elvsted.

BRACK. Oh, the magistrate's wife. Yes, Loevborg's been living up near them, hasn't he?

TESMAN. I'm delighted to hear he's become a decent human being again.

BRACK. Yes, so they say.

TESMAN. I gather he's published a new book, too. What?

BRACK. Indeed he has.

TESMAN. I hear it's created rather a stir.

BRACK. Quite an unusual stir.

TESMAN. I say, isn't that splendid news! He's such a gifted chap—and I was afraid he'd gone to the dogs for good.

BRACK. Most people thought he had.

TESMAN. But I can't think what he'll do now. How on earth will he manage to make ends meet? What?

[*As he speaks his last words,* HEDDA *enters from the hall.*]

HEDDA. [*To* BRACK, *laughs slightly scornfully*] Tesman is always worrying about making ends meet.

TESMAN. We were talking about poor Eilert Loevborg, Hedda dear.

HEDDA. [*Gives him a quick look*] Oh, were you? [*Sits in the armchair by the stove and asks casually*] Is he in trouble?

---

3. For the professorship. Professors at European universities were less numerous and more socially prominent than their contemporary American counterparts.

TESMAN. Well, he must have run through his inheritance long ago by now. And he can't write a new book every year. What? So I'm wondering what's going to become of him.

BRACK. I may be able to enlighten you there.

TESMAN. Oh?

BRACK. You mustn't forget he has relatives who wield a good deal of influence.

TESMAN. Relatives? Oh, they've quite washed their hands of him, I'm afraid.

BRACK. They used to regard him as the hope of the family.

TESMAN. Used to, yes. But he's put an end to that.

HEDDA. Who knows? [*With a little smile*] I hear the Elvsteds have made a new man of him.

BRACK. And then this book he's just published——

TESMAN. Well, let's hope they find something for him. I've just written him a note. Oh, by the way, Hedda, I asked him to come over and see us this evening.

BRACK. But my dear chap, you're coming to me this evening. My bachelor party.[4] You promised me last night when I met you at the boat.

HEDDA. Had you forgotten, Tesman?

TESMAN. Good heavens, yes, I'd quite forgotten.

BRACK. Anyway, you can be quite sure he won't turn up here.

TESMAN. Why do you think that? What?

BRACK. [*A little unwillingly, gets up and rests his hands on the back of his chair*] My dear Tesman—and you, too, Mrs. Tesman— there's something I feel you ought to know.

TESMAN. Concerning Eilert?

BRACK. Concerning him and you.

TESMAN. Well, my dear Judge, tell us, please!

BRACK. You must be prepared for your nomination not to come through quite as quickly as you hope and expect.

TESMAN. [*Jumps up uneasily*] Is anything wrong? What?

BRACK. There's a possibility that the appointment may be decided by competition——

TESMAN. Competition! By Jove, Hedda, fancy that!

HEDDA. [*Leans further back in her chair*] Ah! How interesting!

TESMAN. But who else——? I say, you don't mean——?

BRACK. Exactly. By competition with Eilert Loevborg.

TESMAN. [*Clasps his hands in alarm*] No, no, but this is inconceivable! It's absolutely impossible! What?

BRACK. Hm. We may find it'll happen, all the same.

TESMAN. No, but—Judge Brack, they couldn't be so inconsiderate

---

4. A party for men only, whether single or married.

toward me! [*Waves his arms*] I mean, by Jove, I—I'm a married man! It was on the strength of this that Hedda and I *got* married! We ran up some pretty hefty debts. And borrowed money from Auntie Juju! I mean, good heavens, they practically promised me the appointment. What?

BRACK. Well, well, I'm sure you'll get it. But you'll have to go through a competition.

HEDDA. [*Motionless in her armchair*] How exciting, Tesman. It'll be a kind of duel, by Jove.

TESMAN. My dear Hedda, how can you take it so lightly?

HEDDA. [*As before*] I'm not. I can't wait to see who's going to win.

BRACK. In any case, Mrs. Tesman, it's best you should know how things stand. I mean before you commit yourself to these little items I hear you're threatening to purchase.

HEDDA. I can't allow this to alter my plans.

BRACK. Indeed? Well, that's your business. Good-bye. [*To* TESMAN] I'll come and collect you on the way home from my afternoon walk.

TESMAN. Oh, yes, yes. I'm sorry, I'm all upside down just now.

HEDDA. [*Lying in her chair, holds out her hand*] Good-bye, Judge. See you this afternoon.

BRACK. Thank you. Good-bye, good-bye.

TESMAN. [*Sees him to the door*] Good-bye, my dear Judge. You will excuse me, won't you?

[JUDGE BRACK *goes out through the hall.*]

TESMAN. [*Pacing up and down*] Oh, Hedda! One oughtn't to go plunging off on wild adventures. What?

HEDDA. [*Looks at him and smiles*] Like you're doing?

TESMAN. Yes. I mean, there's no denying it, it was a pretty big adventure to go off and get married and set up house merely on expectation.

HEDDA. Perhaps you're right.

TESMAN. Well, anyway, we have our home, Hedda. By Jove, yes. The home we dreamed of. And set our hearts on. What?

HEDDA. [*Gets up slowly, wearily*] You agreed that we should enter society. And keep open house. That was the bargain.

TESMAN. Yes. Good heavens, I was looking forward to it all so much. To seeing you play hostess to a select circle! By Jove! What? Ah, well, for the time being we shall have to make do with each other's company, Hedda. Perhaps have Auntie Juju in now and then. Oh dear, this wasn't all what you had in mind——

HEDDA. I won't be able to have a liveried footman.[5] For a start.

TESMAN. Oh no, we couldn't possibly afford a footman.

---

5. A uniformed servant.

HEDDA. And that thoroughbred horse you promised me——

TESMAN. [*Fearfully*] Thoroughbred horse!

HEDDA. I mustn't even think of that now.

TESMAN. Heaven forbid!

HEDDA. [*Walks across the room*] Ah, well. I still have one thing left to amuse myself with.

TESMAN. [*Joyfully*] Thank goodness for that. What's that, Hedda? What?

HEDDA. [*In the open doorway, looks at him with concealed scorn*] My pistols, George darling.

TESMAN. [*Alarmed*] Pistols!

HEDDA. [*Her eyes cold*] General Gabler's pistols.

[*She goes into the rear room and disappears.*]

TESMAN. [*Runs to the doorway and calls after her*] For heaven's sake, Hedda dear, don't touch those things. They're dangerous. Hedda— please—for my sake! What?

Act II

SCENE—*The same as in Act I except that the piano has been removed and an elegant little writing table, with a bookcase, stands in its place. By the sofa on the left a smaller table has been placed. Most of the flowers have been removed.* MRS. ELVSTED's *bouquet stands on the larger table, downstage. It is afternoon.*

HEDDA, *dressed to receive callers, is alone in the room. She is standing by the open french windows, loading a revolver. The pair to it is lying in an open pistol case on the writing table.*

HEDDA. [*Looks down into the garden and calls*] Good afternoon, Judge.

BRACK. [*In the distance, below*] Afternoon, Mrs. Tesman.

HEDDA. [*Raises the pistol and takes aim*] I'm going to shoot you, Judge Brack.

BRACK. [*Shouts from below*] No no, no! Don't aim that thing at me!

HEDDA. This'll teach you to enter houses by the back door. [*Fires*]

BRACK. [*Below*] Have you gone completely out of your mind?

HEDDA. Oh dear! Did I hit you?

BRACK. [*Still outside*] Stop playing these silly tricks.

HEDDA. All right, Judge. Come along in.

[JUDGE BRACK, *dressed for a bachelor party, enters through the french windows. He has a light overcoat on his arm.*]

BRACK. For God's sake! Haven't you stopped fooling around with those things yet? What are you trying to hit?

HEDDA. Oh, I was just shooting at the sky.

BRACK. [*Takes the pistol gently from her hand*] By your leave, ma'am. [*Looks at it*] Ah, yes—I know this old friend well. [*Looks around*] Where's the case? Oh, yes. [*Puts the pistol in the case and closes it*] That's enough of that little game for today.

HEDDA. Well, what on earth *am* I to do?

BRACK. You haven't had any visitors?

HEDDA. [*Closes the french windows*] Not one. I suppose the best people are all still in the country.

BRACK. Your husband isn't home yet?

HEDDA. [*Locks the pistol case away in a drawer of the writing table*] No. The moment he'd finished eating he ran off to his aunties. He wasn't expecting you so early.

BRACK. Ah, why didn't I think of that? How stupid of me.

HEDDA. [*Turns her head and looks at him*] Why stupid?

BRACK. I'd have come a little sooner.

HEDDA. [*Walks across the room*] There'd have been no one to receive you. I've been in my room since lunch, dressing.

BRACK. You haven't a tiny crack in the door through which we might have negotiated?

HEDDA. You forgot to arrange one.

BRACK. Another stupidity.

HEDDA. Well, Well, we'll have to sit down here. And wait. Tesman won't be back for some time.

BRACK. Sad. Well, I'll be patient.

    [HEDDA *sits on the corner of the sofa.* BRACK *puts his coat over the back of the nearest chair and seats himself, keeping his hat in his hand. Short pause. They look at each other.*]

HEDDA. Well?

BRACK. [*In the same tone of voice*] Well?

HEDDA. I asked first.

BRACK. [*Leans forward slightly*] Yes, well, now we can enjoy a nice, cosy little chat—Mrs. Hedda.

HEDDA. [*Leans further back in her chair*] It seems such ages since we had a talk. I don't count last night or this morning.

BRACK. You mean: *à deux?*[6]

HEDDA. Mm—yes. That's roughly what I meant.

BRACK. I've been longing so much for you to come home.

HEDDA. So have I.

BRACK. You? Really, Mrs. Hedda? And I thought you were having such a wonderful honeymoon.

HEDDA. Oh, yes. Wonderful!

BRACK. But your husband wrote such ecstatic letters.

HEDDA. He! Oh, yes! He thinks life has nothing better to offer than rooting around in libraries and copying old pieces of parchment, or whatever it is he does.

BRACK. [*A little maliciously*] Well, that *is* his life. Most of it, anyway.

HEDDA. Yes, I know. Well, it's all right for him. But for me! Oh no,

---

6. Just the two of us.

my dear Judge. I've been bored to death.

BRACK. [*Sympathetically*] Do you mean that? Seriously?

HEDDA. Yes. Can you imagine? Six whole months without ever meeting a single person who was one of us, and to whom I could talk about the kind of things we talk about.

BRACK. Yes, I can understand. I'd miss that, too.

HEDDA. That wasn't the worst, though.

BRACK. What was?

HEDDA. Having to spend every minute of one's life with—with the same person.

BRACK. [*Nods*] Yes. What a thought! Morning; noon; and——

HEDDA. [*Coldly*] As I said: every minute of one's life.

BRACK. I stand corrected. But dear Tesman is such a clever fellow, I should have thought one ought to be able——

HEDDA. Tesman is only interested in one thing, my dear Judge. His special subject.

BRACK. True.

HEDDA. And people who are only interested in one thing don't make the most amusing company. Not for long, anyway.

BRACK. Not even when they happen to be the person one loves?

HEDDA. Oh, don't use that sickly, stupid word.

BRACK. [*Starts*] But, Mrs. Hedda——!

HEDDA. [*Half laughing, half annoyed*] You just try it, Judge. Listening to the history of civilization morning, noon and——

BRACK. [*Corrects her*] Every minute of one's life.

HEDDA. All right. Oh, and those domestic industries of Brabant in the Middle Ages! That really is beyond the limit.

BRACK. [*Looks at her searchingly*] But, tell me—if you feel like this why on earth did you—? Ha——

HEDDA. Why on earth did I marry George Tesman?

BRACK. If you like to put it that way.

HEDDA. Do you think it so very strange?

BRACK. Yes—and no, Mrs. Hedda.

HEDDA. I'd danced myself tired, Judge. I felt my time was up—— [*Gives a slight shudder*] No, I mustn't say that. Or even think it.

BRACK. You've no rational cause to think it.

HEDDA. Oh—cause, cause——[*Looks searchingly at him*] After all, George Tesman—well, I mean, he's a very respectable man.

BRACK. Very respectable, sound as a rock. No denying that.

HEDDA. And there's nothing exactly ridiculous about him. Is there?

BRACK. Ridiculous? No-no, I wouldn't say that.

HEDDA. Mm. He's very clever at collecting material and all that, isn't he? I mean, he may go quite far in time.

BRACK. [*Looks at her a little uncertainly*] I thought you believed, like everyone else, that he would become a very prominent man.

HEDDA. [*Looks tired*] Yes, I did. And when he came and begged me on his bended knees to be allowed to love and to cherish me, I didn't see why I shouldn't let him.

BRACK. No, well—if one looks at it like that——

HEDDA. It was more than my other admirers were prepared to do, Judge dear.

BRACK. [*Laughs*] Well, I can't answer for the others. As far as I myself am concerned, you know I've always had a considerable respect for the institution of marriage. As an institution.

HEDDA. [*Lightly*] Oh, I've never entertained any hopes of you.

BRACK. All I want is to have a circle of friends whom I can trust, whom I can help with advice or—or by any other means, and into whose houses I may come and go as a—trusted friend.

HEDDA. Of the husband?

BRACK. [*Bows*] Preferably, to be frank, of the wife. And of the husband too, of course. Yes, you know, this kind of—triangle is a delightful arrangement for all parties concerned.

HEDDA. Yes, I often longed for a third person while I was away. Oh, those hours we spent alone in railway compartments——

BRACK. Fortunately your honeymoon is now over.

HEDDA. [*Shakes her head*] There's a long way still to go. I've only reached a stop on the line.

BRACK. Why not jump out and stretch your legs a little, Mrs. Hedda?

HEDDA. I'm not the jumping sort.

BRACK. Aren't you?

HEDDA. No. There's always someone around who——

BRACK. [*Laughs*] Who looks at one's legs?

HEDDA. Yes. Exactly.

BRACK. Well, but surely——

HEDDA. [*With a gesture of rejection*] I don't like it. I'd rather stay where I am. Sitting in the compartment. *À deux.*

BRACK. But suppose a third person were to step into the compartment?

HEDDA. That would be different.

BRACK. A trusted friend—someone who understood——

HEDDA. And was lively and amusing——

BRACK. And interested in—more subjects than one——

HEDDA. [*Sighs audibly*] Yes, that'd be a relief.

BRACK. [*Hears the front door open and shut*] The triangle is completed.

HEDDA. [*Half under breath*] And the train goes on.

[GEORGE TESMAN, *in grey walking dress with a soft felt hat, enters from the hall. He has a number of paper-covered books under his arm and in his pockets.*]

TESMAN. [*Goes over to the table by the corner sofa*] Phew! It's too hot to be lugging all this around. [*Puts the books down*] I'm positively sweating, Hedda. Why, hullo, hullo! You here already, Judge? What? Bertha didn't tell me.

BRACK. [*Gets up*] I came in through the garden.

HEDDA. What are all those books you've got there?

TESMAN. [*Stands glancing through them*] Oh, some new publications dealing with my special subject. I had to buy them.

HEDDA. Your special subject?

BRACK. His special subject, Mrs. Tesman.

    [BRACK *and* HEDDA *exchange a smile.*]

HEDDA. Haven't you collected enough material on your special subject?

TESMAN. My dear Hedda, one can never have too much. One must keep abreast of what other people are writing.

HEDDA. Yes. Of course.

TESMAN. [*Rooting among the books*] Look—I bought a copy of Eilert Loevborg's new book, too. [*Holds it out to her*] Perhaps you'd like to have a look at it, Hedda? What?

HEDDA. No, thank you. Er—yes, perhaps I will, later.

TESMAN. I glanced through it on my way home.

BRACK. What's your opinion—as a specialist on the subject?

TESMAN. I'm amazed how sound and balanced it is. He never used to write like that. [*Gathers his books together*] Well, I must get down to these at once. I can hardly wait to cut the pages.[7] Oh, I've got to change, too. [*To* BRACK] We don't have to be off just yet, do we? What?

BRACK. Heavens, no. We've plenty of time yet.

TESMAN. Good, I needn't hurry, then. [*Goes with his books, but stops and turns in the doorway*] Oh, by the way, Hedda, Auntie Juju won't be coming to see you this evening.

HEDDA. Won't she? Oh—the hat, I suppose.

TESMAN. Good heavens, no. How could you think such a thing of Auntie Juju? Fancy——! No, Auntie Rena's very ill.

HEDDA. She always is.

TESMAN. Yes, but today she's been taken really bad.

HEDDA. Oh, then it's quite understandable that the other one should want to stay with her. Well, I shall have to swallow my disappointment.

TESMAN. You can't imagine how happy Auntie Juju was in spite of everything. At your looking so well after the honeymoon!

HEDDA. [*Half beneath her breath, as she rises*] Oh, these everlasting aunts!

TESMAN. What?

7. Books used to be sold with the pages folded but uncut as they came from the printing press; the owner had to cut the pages in order to read the book.

HEDDA. [*Goes over to the french windows*] Nothing.

TESMAN. Oh. All right.

[*Goes into the rear room and out of sight*]

BRACK. What was that about the hat?

HEDDA. Oh, something that happened with Miss Tesman this morning. She'd put her hat down on a chair. [*Looks at him and smiles*]
And I pretended to think it was the servant's.

BRACK. [*Shakes his head*] But my dear Mrs. Hedda, how could you
do such a thing? To that poor old lady?

HEDDA. [*Nervously, walking across the room*] Sometimes a mood
like that hits me. And I can't stop myself. [*Throws herself down
in the armchair by the stove*] Oh, I don't know how to explain it.

BRACK. [*Behind her chair*] You're not really happy. That's the answer.

HEDDA. [*Stares ahead of her*] Why on earth should I be happy? Can
you give me a reason?

BRACK. Yes. For one thing you've got the home you always wanted.

HEDDA. [*Looks at him*] You really believe that story?

BRACK. You mean it isn't true?

HEDDA. Oh, yes, it's partly true.

BRACK. Well?

HEDDA. It's true I got Tesman to see me home from parties last summer——

BRACK. It was a pity my home lay in another direction.

HEDDA. Yes. Your interests lay in another direction, too.

BRACK. [*Laughs*] That's naughty of you, Mrs. Hedda. But to return
to you and Tesman——

HEDDA. Well, we walked past this house one evening. And poor
Tesman was fidgeting in his boots trying to find something to talk
about. I felt sorry for the great scholar——

BRACK. [*Smiles incredulously*] Did you? Hm.

HEDDA. Yes, honestly I did. Well, to help him out of his misery, I
happened to say quite frivolously how much I'd love to live in this
house.

BRACK. Was that all?

HEDDA. That evening, yes.

BRACK. But—afterwards?

HEDDA. Yes. My little frivolity had its consequences, my dear Judge.

BRACK. Our little frivolities do. Much too often, unfortunately.

HEDDA. Thank you. Well, it was our mutual admiration for the late
Prime Minister's house that brought George Tesman and me
together on common ground. So we got engaged, and we got married, and we went on our honeymoon, and—Ah well, Judge, I've—
made my bed and I must lie in it, I was about to say.

BRACK. How utterly fantastic! And you didn't really care in the least
about the house?

HEDDA. God knows I didn't.

BRACK. Yes, but now that we've furnished it so beautifully for you?

HEDDA. Ugh—all the rooms smell of lavender and dried roses. But perhaps Auntie Juju brought that in.

BRACK. [*Laughs*] More likely the Prime Minister's widow, rest her soul.

HEDDA. Yes, it's got the odor of death about it. It reminds me of the flowers one has worn at a ball—the morning after. [*Clasps her hands behind her neck, leans back in the chair and looks up at him*] Oh, my dear Judge, you've no idea how hideously bored I'm going to be out here.

BRACK. Couldn't you find some kind of occupation, Mrs. Hedda? Like your husband?

HEDDA. Occupation? That'd interest me?

BRACK. Well—preferably.

HEDDA. God knows what. I've often thought——[*Breaks off*] No, that wouldn't work either.

BRACK. Who knows? Tell me about it.

HEDDA. I was thinking—if I could persuade Tesman to go into politics, for example.

BRACK. [*Laughs*] Tesman! No, honestly, I don't think he's quite cut out to be a politician.

HEDDA. Perhaps not. But if I could persuade him to have a go at it?

BRACK. What satisfaction would that give you? If he turned out to be no good? Why do you want to make him do that?

HEDDA. Because I'm bored. [*After a moment*] You feel there's absolutely no possibility of Tesman becoming Prime Minister, then?

BRACK. Well, you know, Mrs. Hedda, for one thing he'd have to be pretty well off before he could become that.

HEDDA. [*Gets up impatiently*] There you are! [*Walks across the room*] It's this wretched poverty that makes life so hateful. And ludicrous. Well, it is!

BRACK. I don't think that's the real cause.

HEDDA. What is, then?

BRACK. Nothing really exciting has ever happened to you.

HEDDA. Nothing serious, you mean?

BRACK. Call it that if you like. But now perhaps it may.

HEDDA. [*Tosses her head*] Oh, you're thinking of this competition for that wretched professorship? That's Tesman's affair. I'm not going to waste my time worrying about that.

BRACK. Very well, let's forget about that then. But suppose you were to find yourself faced with what people call—to use the conventional phrase—the most solemn of human responsibilities? [*Smiles*] A new responsibility, little Mrs. Hedda.

HEDDA. [*Angrily*] Be quiet! Nothing like that's going to happen.

BRACK. [*Warily*] We'll talk about it again in a year's time. If not earlier.

HEDDA. [*Curtly*] I've no leanings in that direction, Judge. I don't want any—responsibilities.

BRACK. But surely you must feel some inclination to make use of that—natural talent which every woman—

HEDDA. [*Over by the french windows*] Oh, be quiet, I say! I often think there's only one thing for which I have any natural talent.

BRACK. [*Goes closer*] And what is that, if I may be so bold as to ask?

HEDDA. [*Stands looking out*] For boring myself to death. Now you know. [*Turns, looks toward the rear room and laughs*] Talking of boring, here comes the Professor.

BRACK. [*Quietly, warningly*] Now, now, now, Mrs. Hedda!
   [GEORGE TESMAN, *in evening dress, with gloves and hat in his hand, enters through the rear room from the right.*]

TESMAN. Hedda, hasn't any message come from Eilert? What?

HEDDA. No.

TESMAN. Ah, then we'll have him here presently. You wait and see.

BRACK. You really think he'll come?

TESMAN. Yes, I'm almost sure he will. What you were saying about him this morning is just gossip.

BRACK. Oh?

TESMAN. Yes. Auntie Juju said she didn't believe he'd ever dare to stand in my way again. Fancy that!

BRACK. Then everything in the garden's lovely.

TESMAN. [*Puts his hat, with his gloves in it, on a chair, right*] Yes, but you really must let me wait for him as long as possible.

BRACK. We've plenty of time. No one'll be turning up at my place before seven or half past.

TESMAN. Ah, then we can keep Hedda company a little longer. And see if he turns up. What?

HEDDA. [*Picks up* BRACK's *coat and hat and carries them over to the corner sofa*] And if the worst comes to the worst, Mr. Loevborg can sit here and talk to me.

BRACK [*Offering to take his things from her*] No, please. What do you mean by "if the worst comes to the worst"?

HEDDA. If he doesn't want to go with you and Tesman.

TESMAN. [*Looks doubtfully at her*] I say, Hedda, do you think it'll be all right for him to stay here with you? What? Remember Auntie Juju isn't coming.

HEDDA. Yes, but Mrs. Elvsted is. The three of us can have a cup of tea together.

TESMAN. Ah, that'll be all right then.

BRACK. [*Smiles*] It's probably the safest solution as far as he's concerned.

HEDDA. Why?

BRACK. My dear Mrs. Tesman, you always say of my little bachelor parties that they should be attended only by men of the strongest principles.

HEDDA. But Mr. Loevborg is a man of principle now. You know what they say about a reformed sinner——

[BERTHA *enters from the hall.*]

BERTHA. Madam, there's a gentleman here who wants to see you——

HEDDA. Ask him to come in.

TESMAN. [*Quietly*] I'm sure it's him. By Jove. Fancy that!

[EILERT LOEVBORG *enters from the hall. He is slim and lean, of the same age as* TESMAN, *but looks older and somewhat haggard. His hair and beard are of a blackish-brown; his face is long and pale, but with a couple of reddish patches on his cheekbones. He is dressed in an elegant and fairly new black suit, and carries black gloves and a top hat in his hand. He stops just inside the door and bows abruptly. He seems somewhat embarrassed.*]

TESMAN. [*Goes over and shakes his hand*] My dear Eilert! How grand to see you again after all these years!

EILERT LOEVBORG. [*Speaks softly*] It was good of you to write, George. [*Goes nearer to* HEDDA] May I shake hands with you, too, Mrs. Tesman?

HEDDA. [*Accepts his hand*] Delighted to see you, Mr. Loevborg. [*With a gesture*] I don't know if you two gentlemen——

LOEVBORG. [*Bows slightly*] Judge Brack, I believe.

BRACK. [*Also with a slight bow*] Correct. We—met some years ago——

TESMAN. [*Puts his hands on* LOEVBORG'S *shoulders*] Now you're to treat this house just as though it were your own home, Eilert. Isn't that right, Hedda? I hear you've decided to settle here again? What?

LOEVBORG. Yes, I have.

TESMAN. Quite understandable. Oh, by the bye—I've just bought your new book. Though to tell the truth I haven't found time to read it yet.

LOEVBORG. You needn't bother.

TESMAN. Oh? Why?

LOEVBORG. There's nothing much in it.

TESMAN. By Jove, fancy hearing that from you!

BRACK. But everyone's praising it.

LOEVBORG. That was exactly what I wanted to happen. So I only wrote what I knew everyone would agree with.

BRACK. Very sensible.

TESMAN. Yes, but my dear Eilert——

LOEVBORG. I want to try to re-establish myself. To begin again—from the beginning.

TESMAN. [*A little embarrassed*] Yes, I—er—suppose you do. What?

LOEVBORG. [*Smiles, puts down his hat and takes a package wrapped in paper from his coat pocket*] But when this gets published— George Tesman—read it. This is my real book. The one in which I have spoken with my own voice.

TESMAN. Oh, really? What's it about?

LOEVBORG. It's the sequel.

TESMAN. Sequel? To what?

LOEVBORG. To the other book.

TESMAN. The one that's just come out?

LOEVBORG. Yes.

TESMAN. But my dear Eilert, that covers the subject right up to the present day.

LOEVBORG. It does. But this is about the future.

TESMAN. The future! But, I say, we don't know anything about that.

LOEVBORG. No. But there are one or two things that need to be said about it. [*Opens the package*] Here, have a look.

TESMAN. Surely that's not your handwriting?

LOEVBORG. I dictated it [*Turns the pages*] It's in two parts. The first deals with the forces that will shape our civilization. [*Turns further on towards the end*] And the second indicates the direction in which that civilization may develop.

TESMAN. Amazing! I'd never think of writing about anything like that.

HEDDA. [*By the french windows, drumming on the pane*] No. You wouldn't.

LOEVBORG. [*Puts the pages back into their cover and lays the package on the table*] I brought it because I thought I might possibly read you a few pages this evening.

TESMAN. I say, what a kind idea! Oh, but this evening——? [*Glances at* BRACK] I'm not quite sure whether——

LOEVBORG. Well, some other time, then. There's no hurry.

BRACK. The truth is, Mr. Loevborg, I'm giving a little dinner this evening. In Tesman's honor, you know.

LOEVBORG. [*Looks round for his hat*] Oh—then I mustn't——

BRACK. No, wait a minute. Won't you do me the honor of joining us?

LOEVBORG. [*Curtly, with decision*] No I can't. Thank you so much.

BRACK. Oh, nonsense. Do—please. There'll only be a few of us. And I can promise you we shall have some good sport, as Mrs. Hed— as Mrs. Tesman puts it.

LOEVBORG. I've no doubt. Nevertheless——

BRACK. You could bring your manuscript along and read it to Tesman at my place. I could lend you a room.

TESMAN. By Jove, Eilert, that's an idea. What?

HEDDA. [*Interposes*] But Tesman, Mr. Loevborg doesn't want to go. I'm sure Mr. Loevborg would much rather sit here and have supper with me.

LOEVBORG. [*Looks at her*] With you, Mrs. Tesman?

HEDDA. And Mrs. Elvsted.

LOEVBORG. Oh. [*Casually*] I ran into her this afternoon.

HEDDA. Did you? Well, she's coming here this evening. So you really must stay, Mr. Loevborg. Otherwise she'll have no one to see her home.

LOEVBORG. That's true. Well—thank you, Mrs. Tesman, I'll stay then.

HEDDA. I'll just tell the servant.

[*She goes to the door which leads into the hall, and rings.* BERTHA *enters.* HEDDA *talks softly to her and points towards the rear room.* BERTHA *nods and goes out.*]

TESMAN. [*To* LOEVBORG, *as* HEDDA *does this*] I say, Eilert. This new subject of yours—the—er—future—is that the one you're going to lecture about?

LOEVBORG. Yes.

TESMAN. They told me down at the bookshop that you're going to hold a series of lectures here during the autumn.

LOEVBORG. Yes, I am, I—hope you don't mind, Tesman.

TESMAN. Good heavens, no! But——?

LOEVBORG. I can quite understand it might queer your pitch a little.

TESMAN. [*Dejectedly*] Oh well, I can't expect you to put them off for my sake.

LOEVBORG. I'll wait till your appointment's been announced.

TESMAN. You'll wait! But—but—aren't you going to compete with me for the post? What?

LOEVBORG. No. I only want to defeat you in the eyes of the world.

TESMAN. Good heavens! Then Auntie Juju was right after all! Oh, I knew it, I knew it! Hear that, Hedda? Fancy! Eilert *doesn't* want to stand in our way.

HEDDA. [*Curtly*] Our? Leave me out of it, please.

[*She goes towards the rear room, where* BERTHA *is setting a tray with decanters and glasses on the table.* HEDDA *nods approval, and comes back into the drawing room.* BERTHA *goes out.*]

TESMAN. [*While this is happening*] Judge Brack, what do you think about all this? What?

BRACK. Oh, I think honor and victory can be very splendid things——

TESMAN. Of course they can. Still——

HEDDA. [*Looks at* TESMAN *with a cold smile*] You look as if you'd been hit by a thunderbolt.

TESMAN. Yes, I feel rather like it.

BRACK. There was a black cloud looming up, Mrs. Tesman. But it seems to have passed over.

HEDDA. [*Points toward the rear room*] Well, gentlemen, won't you go in and take a glass of cold punch?

BRACK. [*Glances at his watch*] A stirrup cup?[8] Yes, why not?

TESMAN. An admirable suggestion, Hedda. Admirable! Oh, I feel so relieved!

HEDDA. Won't you have one, too, Mr. Loevborg?

LOEVBORG. No, thank you. I'd rather not.

BRACK. Great heavens, man, cold punch isn't poison. Take my word for it.

LOEVBORG. Not for everyone, perhaps.

HEDDA. I'll keep Mr. Loevborg company while you drink.

TESMAN. Yes, Hedda dear, would you?

[*He and* BRACK *go into the rear room, sit down, drink punch, smoke cigarettes and talk cheerfully during the following scene.* EILERT LOEVBORG *remains standing by the stove.* HEDDA *goes to the writing table.*]

HEDDA [*Raising her voice slightly*] I've some photographs I'd like to show you, if you'd care to see them. Tesman and I visited the Tyrol on our way home.

[*She comes back with an album, places it on the table by the sofa and sits in the upstage corner of the sofa.* EILERT LOEVBORG *comes toward her, stops and looks at her. Then he takes a chair and sits down on her left, with his back toward the rear room.*]

HEDDA. [*Opens the album*] You see these mountains, Mr. Loevborg? That's the Ortler group. Tesman has written the name underneath. You see: "The Ortler Group near Meran."[9]

LOEVBORG. [*Has not taken his eyes from her; says softly, slowly*] Hedda—Gabler!

HEDDA. [*Gives him a quick glance*] Ssh!

LOEVBORG. [*Repeats softly*] Hedda Gabler!

HEDDA. [*Looks at the album*] Yes, that used to be my name. When we first knew each other.

LOEVBORG. And from now on—for the rest of my life—I must teach myself never to say: Hedda Gabler.

HEDDA. [*Still turning the pages*] Yes, you must. You'd better start

8. A drink before parting. (Originally, it was taken by riders on horseback just before setting forth.) 9. Or Merano, a city in the Austrian Tyrol, since 1918 in Italy. The scenic features mentioned here and later are tourist attractions. The Ortler Group and the Dolomites are ranges of the Alps; the Ampezzo Valley lies beyond the Dolomites to the east; and the Brenner Pass is a major route through the Alps to Austria.

getting into practice. The sooner the better.

LOEVBORG. [*Bitterly*] Hedda Gabler married? And to George Tesman?

HEDDA. Yes. Well—that's life.

LOEVBORG. Oh, Hedda, Hedda! How could you throw yourself away like that?

HEDDA. [*Looks sharply at him*] Stop it.

LOEVBORG. What do you mean?

[TESMAN *comes in and goes toward the sofa.*]

HEDDA. [*Hears him coming and says casually*] And this, Mr. Loevborg, is the view from the Ampezzo valley. Look at those mountains. [*Glances affectionately up at* TESMAN] What did you say those curious mountains were called, dear?

TESMAN. Let me have a look. Oh, those are the Dolomites.

HEDDA. Of course. Those are the Dolomites, Mr. Loevborg.

TESMAN. Hedda, I just wanted to ask you, can't we bring some punch in here? A glass for you, anyway. What?

HEDDA. Thank you, yes. And a biscuit[1] or two, perhaps.

TESMAN. You wouldn't like a cigarette?

HEDDA. No.

TESMAN. Right.

[*He goes into the rear room and over to the right.* BRACK *is sitting there, glancing occasionally at* HEDDA *and* LOEVBORG.]

LOEVBORG. [*Softly, as before*] Answer me, Hedda. How could you do it?

HEDDA. [*Apparently absorbed in the album*] If you go on calling me Hedda I won't talk to you any more.

LOEVBORG. Mayn't I even when we're alone?

HEDDA. No. You can think it. But you mustn't say it.

LOEVBORG. Oh, I see. Because you love George Tesman.

HEDDA. [*Glances at him and smiles*] Love? Don't be funny.

LOEVBORG. You don't love him?

HEDDA. I don't intend to be unfaithful to him. That's not what I want.

LOEVBORG. Hedda—just tell me one thing——

HEDDA. Ssh!

[TESMAN *enters from the rear room, carrying a tray.*]

TESMAN. Here we are! Here come the goodies!

[*Puts the tray down on the table*]

HEDDA. Why didn't you ask the servant to bring it in?

TESMAN. [*Fills the glasses*] I like waiting on you, Hedda.

HEDDA. But you've filled both glasses. Mr. Loevborg doesn't want to drink.

1. Tea biscuit, or cookie.

TESMAN. Yes, but Mrs. Elvsted'll be here soon.

HEDDA. Oh yes, that's true. Mrs. Elvsted——

TESMAN. Had you forgotten her? What?

HEDDA. We're so absorbed with these photographs. [*Shows him one*] You remember this little village?

TESMAN. Oh, that one down by the Brenner Pass. We spent a night there——

HEDDA. Yes, and met all those amusing people.

TESMAN. Oh yes, it was there, wasn't it? By Jove, if only we could have had you with us, Eilert! Ah, well.

    [*Goes back into the other room and sits down with* BRACK]

LOEVBORG. Tell me one thing, Hedda.

HEDDA. Yes?

LOEVBORG. Didn't you love me either? Not—just a little?

HEDDA. Well now, I wonder? No, I think we were just good pals— Really good pals who could tell each other anything. [*Smiles*] You certainly poured your heart out to me.

LOEVBORG. You begged me to.

HEDDA. Looking back on it, there was something beautiful and fascinating—and brave—about the way we told each other everything. That secret friendship no one else knew about.

LOEVBORG. Yes, Hedda, yes! Do you remember? How I used to come up to your father's house in the afternoon—and the General sat by the window and read his newspapers—with his back toward us——

HEDDA. And we sat on the sofa in the corner——

LOEVBORG. Always reading the same illustrated magazine——

HEDDA. We hadn't any photograph album.

LOEVBORG. Yes, Hedda. I regarded you as a kind of confessor. Told you things about myself which no one else knew about—then. Those days and nights of drinking and— Oh, Hedda, what power did you have to make me confess such things?

HEDDA. Power? You think I had some power over you?

LOEVBORG. Yes—I don't know how else to explain it. And all those— oblique questions you asked me——

HEDDA. You knew what they meant.

LOEVBORG. But that you could sit there and ask me such questions! So unashamedly——

HEDDA. I thought you said they were oblique.

LOEVBORG. Yes, but you asked them so unashamedly. That you could question me about—about that kind of thing!

HEDDA. You answered willingly enough.

LOEVBORG. Yes—that's what I can't understand—looking back on it. But tell me, Hedda—what you felt for me—wasn't that—love? When you asked me those questions and made me confess my sins to you, wasn't it because you wanted to wash me clean?

HEDDA. No, not exactly.

LOEVBORG. Why did you do it, then?

HEDDA. Do you find it so incredible that a young girl, given the chance to do so without anyone knowing, should want to be allowed a glimpse into a forbidden world of whose existence she is supposed to be ignorant?

LOEVBORG. So that was it?

HEDDA. One reason. One reason—I think.

LOEVBORG. You didn't love me, then. You just wanted—knowledge. But if that was so, why did you break it off?

HEDDA. That was your fault.

LOEVBORG. It was you who put an end to it.

HEDDA. Yes, when I realized that our friendship was threatening to develop into something—something else. Shame on you, Eilert Loevborg! How could you abuse the trust of your dearest friend?

LOEVBORG. [Clenches his fists] Oh, why didn't you do it? Why didn't you shoot me dead? As you threatened to?

HEDDA. I was afraid. Of the scandal.

LOEVBORG. Yes, Hedda. You're a coward at heart.

HEDDA. A dreadful coward. [Changes her tone] Luckily for you. Well, now you've found consolation with the Elvsteds.

LOEVBORG. I know what Thea's been telling you.

HEDDA. I dare say you told her about us.

LOEVBORG. Not a word. She's too silly to understand that kind of thing.

HEDDA. Silly?

LOEVBORG. She's silly about that kind of thing.

HEDDA. And I am a coward. [Leans closer to him, without looking him in the eyes, and says quietly] But let me tell you something. Something you don't know.

LOEVBORG. [Tensely] Yes?

HEDDA. My failure to shoot you wasn't my worst act of cowardice that evening.

LOEVBORG. [Looks at her for a moment, realizes her meaning and whispers passionately] Oh, Hedda! Hedda Gabler! Now I see what was behind those questions. Yes! It wasn't knowledge you wanted! It was life!

HEDDA. [Flashes a look at him and says quietly] Take care! Don't you delude yourself!

[It has begun to grow dark. BERTHA, from outside, opens the door leading into the hall.]

HEDDA. [Closes the album with a snap and cries, smiling] Ah, at last! Come in, Thea dear!

[MRS. ELVSTED enters from the hall, in evening dress. The door is closed behind her.]

HEDDA. [On the sofa, stretches out her arms toward her] Thea darling, I thought you were never coming!

[MRS. ELVSTED *makes a slight bow to the gentlemen in the rear room as she passes the open doorway, and they to her. Then she goes to the table and holds out her hand to* HEDDA. EILERT LOEVBORG *has risen from his chair. He and* MRS. ELVSTED *nod silently to each other.*]

MRS. ELVSTED. Perhaps I ought to go in and say a few words to your husband?

HEDDA. Oh, there's no need. They're happy by themselves. They'll be going soon.

MRS. ELVSTED. Going?

HEDDA. Yes, they're off on a spree this evening.

MRS. ELVSTED. [*Quickly, to* LOEVBORG] You're not going with them?

LOEVBORG. No.

HEDDA. Mr. Loevborg is staying here with us.

MRS. ELVSTED. [*Takes a chair and is about to sit down beside him*] Oh, how nice it is to be here!

HEDDA. No, Thea darling, not there. Come over here and sit beside me. I want to be in the middle.

MRS. ELVSTED. Yes, just as you wish.

[*She goes right the table and sits on the sofa, on* HEDDA'S *right.* LOEVBORG *sits down again in his chair.*]

LOEVBORG. [*After a short pause, to* HEDDA] Isn't she lovely to look at?

HEDDA. [*Strokes her hair gently*] Only to look at?

LOEVBORG. Yes. We're just good pals. We trust each other implicitly. We can talk to each other quite unashamedly.

HEDDA. No need to be oblique?

MRS. ELVSTED. [*Nestles close to* HEDDA *and says quietly*] Oh, Hedda I'm so happy. Imagine—he says I've inspired him!

HEDDA. [*Looks at her with a smile*] Dear Thea! Does he really?

LOEVBORG. She has the courage of her convictions, Mrs. Tesman.

MRS. ELVSTED. I? Courage?

LOEVBORG. Absolute courage. Where friendship is concerned.

HEDDA. Yes. Courage. Yes. If only one had that——

LOEVBORG. Yes?

HEDDA. One might be able to live. In spite of everything. [*Changes her tone suddenly*] Well, Thea darling, now you're going to drink a nice glass of cold punch.

MRS. ELVSTED. No, thank you. I never drink anything like that.

HEDDA. Oh. You, Mr. Loevborg?

LOEVBORG. Thank you, I don't either.

MRS. ELVSTED. No, he doesn't, either.

HEDDA. [*Looks into his eyes*] But if I want you to?

LOEVBORG. That doesn't make any difference.

HEDDA. [*Laughs*] Have I no power over you at all? Poor me!

LOEVBORG. Not where this is concerned.

HEDDA. Seriously, I think you should. For your own sake.

MRS. ELVSTED. Hedda!

LOEVBORG. Why?

HEDDA. Or perhaps I should say for other people's sake.

LOEVBORG. What do you mean?

HEDDA. People might think you didn't feel absolutely and unashamedly sure of yourself. In your heart of hearts.

MRS. ELVSTED. [*Quietly*] Oh, Hedda, no!

LOEVBORG. People can think what they like. For the present.

MRS. ELVSTED. [*Happily*] Yes, that's true.

HEDDA. I saw it so clearly in Judge Brack a few minutes ago.

LOEVBORG. Oh. What did you see?

HEDDA. He smiled so scornfully when he saw you were afraid to go in there and drink with them.

LOEVBORG. Afraid! I wanted to stay here and talk to you.

MRS. ELVSTED. That was only natural, Hedda.

HEDDA. But the Judge wasn't to know that. I saw him wink at Tesman when you showed you didn't dare to join their wretched little party.

LOEVBORG. Didn't dare! Are you saying I didn't dare?

HEDDA. I'm not saying so. But that was what Judge Brack thought.

LOEVBORG. Well, let him.

HEDDA. You're not going, then?

LOEVBORG. I'm staying here with you and Thea.

MRS. ELVSTED. Yes, Hedda, of course he is.

HEDDA. [*Smiles, and nods approvingly to* LOEVBORG] Firm as a rock! A man of principle! That's how a man should be! [*Turns to* MRS. ELVSTED *and strokes her cheek*] Didn't I tell you so this morning when you came here in such a panic——

LOEVBORG. [*Starts*] Panic?

MRS. ELVSTED. [*Frightened*] Hedda! But—Hedda!

HEDDA. Well, now you can see for yourself. There's no earthly need for you to get scared to death just because——[*Stops*] Well! Let's all three cheer up and enjoy ourselves.

LOEVBORG. Mrs. Tesman, would you mind explaining to me what this is all about?

MRS. ELVSTED. Oh, my God, my God, Hedda, what are you saying? What are you doing?

HEDDA. Keep calm. That horrid Judge has his eye on you.

LOEVBORG. Scared to death, were you? For my sake?

MRS. ELVSTED. [*Quietly, trembling*] Oh, Hedda! You've made me so unhappy!

LOEVBORG. [*Looks coldly at her for a moment. His face is distorted.*] So that was how much you trusted me.

MRS. ELVSTED. Eilert dear, please listen to me——

LOEVBORG. [*Takes one of the glasses of punch, raises it and says quietly, hoarsely*] Skoal, Thea!

   [*Empties the glass, puts it down and picks up one of the others.*]

MRS. ELVSTED. [*Quietly*] Hedda, Hedda! Why did you want this to happen?

HEDDA. I—want it? Are you mad?

LOEVBORG. Skoal to you too, Mrs. Tesman. Thanks for telling me the truth. Here's to the truth!

   [*Empties his glass and refills it*]

HEDDA. [Puts her hand on his arm] Steady. That's enough for now. Don't forget the party.

MRS. ELVSTED. No, no, no!

HEDDA. Ssh! They're looking at you.

LOEVBORG. [*Puts down his glass*] Thea, tell me the truth——

MRS. ELVSTED. Yes!

LOEVBORG. Did your husband know you were following me?

MRS. ELVSTED. Oh, Hedda!

LOEVBORG. Did you and he have an agreement that you should come here and keep an eye on me? Perhaps he gave you the idea? After all, he's a magistrate.[2] I suppose he needed me back in his office. Or did he miss my companionship at the card table?

MRS. ELVSTED. [*Quietly, sobbing*] Eilert, Eilert!

LOEVBORG. [*Seizes a glass and is about to fill it*] Let's drink to him, too.

HEDDA. No more now. Remember you're going to read your book to Tesman.

LOEVBORG. [*Calm again, puts down his glass*] That was silly of me, Thea. To take it like that, I mean. Don't be angry with me, my dear. You'll see—yes, and they'll see, too—that though I fell, I— I have raised myself up again. With your help, Thea.

MRS. ELVSTED. [*Happily*] Oh, thank God!

   [BRACK *has meanwhile glanced at his watch. He and* TESMAN *get up and come into the drawing room.*]

BRACK. [*Takes his hat and overcoat*] Well, Mrs. Tesman. It's time for us to go.

HEDDA. Yes, I suppose it must be.

LOEVBORG. [*Gets up*] Time for me too, Judge.

MRS. ELVSTED. [*Quietly, pleadingly*] Eilert, please don't!

HEDDA. [*Pinches her arm*] They can hear you.

MRS. ELVSTED. [*Gives a little cry*] Oh!

LOEVBORG. [*To* BRACK] You were kind enough to ask me to join you.

---

2. Also translated *sheriff*. A civil official with duties associated with the courts.

BRACK. Are you coming?

LOEVBORG. If I may.

BRACK. Delighted.

LOEVBORG. [*Puts the paper package in his pocket and says to* TES-MAN] I'd like to show you one or two things before I send it off to the printer.

TESMAN. I say, that'll be fun. Fancy——! Oh, but Hedda, how'll Mrs. Elvsted get home? What?

HEDDA. Oh, we'll manage somehow.

LOEVBORG. [*Glances over toward the ladies*] Mrs. Elvsted? I shall come back and collect her, naturally. [*Goes closer*] About ten o'clock, Mrs. Tesman? Will that suit you?

HEDDA. Yes. That'll suit me admirably.

TESMAN. Good, that's settled. But you mustn't expect me back so early, Hedda.

HEDDA. Stay as long as you c—as long as you like, dear.

MRS. ELVSTED. [*Trying to hide her anxiety*] Well then, Mr. Loevborg, I'll wait here till you come.

LOEVBORG. [*His hat in his hand*] Pray do, Mrs. Elvsted.

BRACK. Well, gentlemen, now the party begins. I trust that, in the words of a certain fair lady, we shall enjoy good sport.

HEDDA. What a pity the fair lady can't be there, invisible.

BRACK. Why invisible?

HEDDA. So as to be able to hear some of your uncensored witticisms, your honor.

BRACK. [*Laughs*] Oh, I shouldn't advise the fair lady to do that.

TESMAN. [*Laughs too*] I say, Hedda, that's good. By Jove! Fancy that!

BRACK. Well, good night, ladies, good night!

LOEVBORG. [*Bows farewell*] About ten o'clock, then.

[BRACK, LOEVBORG *and* TESMAN *go out through the hall. As they do so* BERTHA *enters from the rear room with a lighted lamp. She puts it on the drawing-room table, then goes out the way she came.*]

MRS. ELVSTED. [*Has got up and is walking uneasily to and fro*] Oh Hedda, Hedda! How is all this going to end?

HEDDA. At ten o'clock, then. He'll be here. I can see him. With a crown of vine-leaves in his hair. Burning and unashamed!

MRS. ELVSTED. Oh, I do hope so!

HEDDA. Can't you see? Then he'll be himself again! He'll be a free man for the rest of his days!

MRS. ELVSTED. Please God you're right.

HEDDA. That's how he'll come! [*Gets up and goes closer*] You can doubt him as much as you like. I believe in him! Now we'll see which of us——

MRS. ELVSTED. You're after something, Hedda.

HEDDA. Yes, I am. For once in my life I want to have the power to shape a man's destiny.

MRS. ELVSTED. Haven't you that power already?

HEDDA. No, I haven't. I've never had it.

MRS. ELVSTED. What about your husband?

HEDDA. Him! Oh, if you could only understand how poor I am. And you're allowed to be so rich, so rich! [*Clasps her passionately*] I think I'll burn your hair off after all!

MRS. ELVSTED. Let me go! Let me go! You frighten me, Hedda!

BERTHA. [*In the open doorway*] I've laid tea in the dining room, madam.

HEDDA. Good, we're coming.

MRS. ELVSTED. No, no, no! I'd rather go home alone! Now—at once!

HEDDA. Rubbish! First you're going to have some tea, you little idiot. And then—at ten o'clock—Eilert Loevborg will come. With a crown of vine-leaves in his hair![3]

[*She drags* MRS. ELVSTED *almost forcibly toward the open doorway.*]

Act III

SCENE—*The same. The curtains are drawn across the open doorway, and also across the french windows. The lamp, half turned down, with a shade over it, is burning on the table. In the stove, the door of which is open, a fire has been burning, but it is now almost out.*

MRS. ELVSTED, *wrapped in a large shawl and with her feet resting on a footstool, is sitting near the stove, huddled in the armchair.* HEDDA *is lying asleep on this sofa, fully dressed, with a blanket over her.*

MRS. ELVSTED. [*After a pause, suddenly sits up in her chair and listens tensely. Then she sinks wearily back again and sighs.*] Not back yet! Oh, God! Oh, God! Not back yet!

[BERTHA *tiptoes cautiously in front the hall. She has a letter in her hand.*]

MRS. ELVSTED. [*Turns and whispers*] What is it? Has someone come?

BERTHA. [*Quietly*] Yes, a servant's just called with this letter.

MRS. ELVSTED. [*Quickly, holding out her hand*] A letter! Give it to me!

BERTHA. But it's for the Doctor, madam.

MRS. ELVSTED. Oh. I see.

BERTHA. Miss Tesman's maid brought it. I'll leave it here on the table.

3. Like Bacchus, the god of wine, and his followers.

MRS. ELVSTED. Yes, do.

BERTHA. [*Puts down the letter*] I'd better put the lamp out. It's starting to smoke.

MRS. ELVSTED. Yes, put it out. It'll soon be daylight.

BERTHA. [*Puts out the lamp*] It's daylight already, madam.

MRS. ELVSTED. Yes. Broad day. And not home yet.

BERTHA. Oh dear, I was afraid this would happen.

MRS. ELVSTED. Were you?

BERTHA. Yes. When I heard that a certain gentleman had returned to town, and saw him go off with them. I've heard all about him.

MRS. ELVSTED. Don't talk so loud. You'll wake your mistress.

BERTHA. [*Looks at the sofa and sighs*] Yes. Let her go on sleeping, poor dear. Shall I put some more wood on the fire?

MRS. ELVSTED. Thank you, don't bother on my account.

BERTHA. Very good.

   [*Goes quietly out through the hall*]

HEDDA. [*Wakes as the door closes and looks up*] What's that?

MRS. ELVSTED. It was only the maid.

HEDDA. [*Looks round*] What am I doing here? Oh, now I remember. [*Sits up on the sofa, stretches herself and rubs her eyes*] What time is it, Thea?

MRS. ELVSTED. It's gone seven.

HEDDA. When did Tesman get back?

MRS. ELVSTED. He's not back yet.

HEDDA. Not home yet?

MRS. ELVSTED. [*Gets up*] No one's come.

HEDDA. And we sat up waiting for them till four o'clock.

MRS. ELVSTED. God! How I waited for him!

HEDDA. [*Yawns and says with her hand in front of her mouth*] Oh, dear. We might have saved ourselves the trouble.

MRS. ELVSTED. Did you manage to sleep?

HEDDA. Oh, yes. Quite well, I think. Didn't you get any?

MRS. ELVSTED. Not a wink. I couldn't, Hedda. I just couldn't.

HEDDA. [*Gets up and comes over to her*] Now, now, now. There's nothing to worry about. I know what's happened.

MRS. ELVSTED. What? Please tell me.

HEDDA. Well, obviously the party went on very late——

MRS. ELVSTED. Oh dear, I suppose it must have. But——

HEDDA. And Tesman didn't want to come home and wake us all up in the middle of the night. [*Laughs*] Probably wasn't too keen to show his face either, after a spree like that.

MRS. ELVSTED. But where could he have gone?

HEDDA. I should think he's probably slept at his aunts'. They keep his old room for him.

MRS. ELVSTED. No, he can't be with them. A letter came for him just now from Miss Tesman. It's over there.

HEDDA. Oh? [*Looks at the envelope*] Yes, it's Auntie Juju's hand-writing. Well, he must still be at Judge Brack's, then. And Eilert Loevborg is sitting there, reading to him. With a crown of vine-leaves in his hair.

MRS. ELVSTED. Hedda, you're only saying that. You don't believe it.

HEDDA. Thea, you really are a little fool.

MRS. ELVSTED. Perhaps I am.

HEDDA. You look tired to death.

MRS. ELVSTED. Yes. I am tired to death.

HEDDA. Go to my room and lie down for a little. Do as I say, now; don't argue.

MRS. ELVSTED. No, no. I couldn't possibly sleep.

HEDDA. Of course you can.

MRS. ELVSTED. But your husband'll be home soon. And I must know at once——

HEDDA. I'll tell you when he comes.

MRS. ELVSTED. Promise me, Hedda?

HEDDA. Yes, don't worry. Go and get some sleep.

MRS. ELVSTED. Thank you. All right, I'll try.

[*She goes out through the rear room.* HEDDA *goes to the french windows and draws the curtains. Broad daylight floods into the room. She goes to the writing table, takes a small hand mirror from it and arranges her hair. Then she goes to the door leading into the hall and presses the bell. After a few moments,* BERTHA *enters.*]

BERTHA. Did you want anything, madam?

HEDDA. Yes, put some more wood on the fire. I'm freezing.

BERTHA. Bless you, I'll soon have this room warmed up. [*She rakes the embers together and puts a fresh piece of wood on them. Suddenly she stops and listens.*] There's someone at the front door, madam.

HEDDA. Well, go and open it. I'll see to the fire.

BERTHA. It'll burn up in a moment.

[*She goes out through the hall.* HEDDA *kneels on the footstool and puts more wood in the stove. After a few seconds,* GEORGE TESMAN *enters from the hall. He looks tired, and rather worried. He tiptoes toward the open doorway and is about to slip through the curtains.*]

HEDDA. [*At the stove, without looking up*] Good morning.

TESMAN. [*Turns*] Hedda! [*Comes nearer*] Good heavens, are you up already? What?

HEDDA. Yes, I got up very early this morning.

TESMAN. I was sure you'd still be sleeping. Fancy that!

HEDDA. Don't talk so loud. Mrs. Elvsted's asleep in my room.

TESMAN. Mrs. Elvsted? Has she stayed the night here?

HEDDA. Yes. No one came to escort her home.

TESMAN. Oh. No, I suppose not.

HEDDA. [*Closes the door of the stove and gets up*] Well. Was it fun?

TESMAN. Have you been anxious about me? What?

HEDDA. Not in the least. I asked if you'd had fun.

TESMAN. Oh yes, rather! Well, I thought, for once in a while—The first part was the best; when Eilert read his book to me. We arrived over an hour too early—what about that, eh? By Jove! Brack had a lot of things to see to, so Eilert read to me.

HEDDA. [*Sits at the right-hand side of the table*] Well? Tell me about it.

TESMAN. [*Sits on a footstool by the stove*] Honestly, Hedda, you've no idea what a book that's going to be. It's really one of the most remarkable things that's ever been written. By Jove!

HEDDA. Oh, never mind about the book——

TESMAN. I'm going to make a confession to you, Hedda. When he'd finished reading a sort of beastly feeling came over me.

HEDDA. Beastly feeling?

TESMAN. I found myself envying Eilert for being able to write like that. Imagine that, Hedda!

HEDDA. Yes. I can imagine.

TESMAN. What a tragedy that with all those gifts he should be so incorrigible.

HEDDA. You mean he's less afraid of life than most men?

TESMAN. Good heavens, no. He just doesn't know the meaning of the word moderation.

HEDDA. What happened afterwards?

TESMAN. Well, looking back on it I suppose you might almost call it an orgy, Hedda.

HEDDA. Had he vine-leaves in his hair?

TESMAN. Vine-leaves? No, I didn't see any of them. He made a long, rambling oration in honor of the woman who'd inspired him to write this book. Yes, those were the words he used.

HEDDA. Did he name her?

TESMAN. No. But I suppose it must be Mrs. Elvsted. You wait and see!

HEDDA. Where did you leave him?

TESMAN. On the way home. We left in a bunch—the last of us, that is—and Brack came with us to get a little fresh air. Well, then, you see, we agreed we ought to see Eilert home. He'd had a drop too much.

HEDDA. You don't say?

TESMAN. But now comes the funny part, Hedda. Or I should really say the tragic part. Oh, I'm almost ashamed to tell you. For Eilert's sake, I mean——

HEDDA. Why, what happened?

TESMAN. Well, you see, as we were walking toward town I happened to drop behind for a minute. Only for a minute—er—you understand——

HEDDA. Yes, yes——?

TESMAN. Well then, when I ran on to catch them up, what do you think I found by the roadside. What?

HEDDA. How on earth should I know?

TESMAN. You mustn't tell anyone, Hedda. What? Promise me that—for Eilert's sake. [*Takes a package wrapped in paper from his coat pocket*] Just fancy! I found this.

HEDDA. Isn't this the one he brought here yesterday?

TESMAN. Yes! The whole of that precious, irreplaceable manuscript! And he went and lost it! Didn't even notice! What about that? By Jove! Tragic.

HEDDA. But why didn't you give it back to him?

TESMAN. I didn't dare to, in the state he was in.

HEDDA. Didn't you tell any of the others?

TESMAN. Good heavens, no. I didn't want to do that. For Eilert's sake, you understand.

HEDDA. Then on one else knows you have his manuscript?

TESMAN. No. And no one must be allowed to know.

HEDDA. Didn't it come up in the conversation later?

TESMAN. I didn't get a chance to talk to him any more. As soon as we got into the outskirts of town, he and one or two of the others gave us the slip. Disappeared, by Jove!

HEDDA. Oh? I suppose they took him home.

TESMAN. Yes, I imagine that was the idea. Brack left us, too.

HEDDA. And what have you been up to since then?

TESMAN. Well, I and one or two of the others—awfully jolly chaps, they were—went back to where one of them lived, and had a cup of morning coffee. Morning-after coffee—what? Ah, well. I'll just lie down for a bit and give Eilert time to sleep it off, poor chap, then I'll run over and give this back to him.

HEDDA. [*Holds out her hand for the package*] No, don't do that. Not just yet. Let me read it first.

TESMAN. Oh no, really, Hedda dear, honestly, I daren't do that.

HEDDA. Daren't?

TESMAN. No—imagine how desperate he'll be when he wakes up and finds his manuscript's missing. He hasn't any copy, you see. He told me so himself.

HEDDA. Can't a thing like that be rewritten?

TESMAN. Oh no, not possibly, I shouldn't think. I mean, the inspiration, you know——

HEDDA. Oh, yes. I'd forgotten that. [*Casually*] By the way, there's a letter for you.

TESMAN. Is there? Fancy that!

HEDDA. [*Holds it out to him*] It came early this morning.

TESMAN. I say, it's from Auntie Juju! What on earth can it be? [*Puts the package on the other footstool, opens the letter, reads it and jumps up*] Oh, Hedda! She says poor Auntie Rena's dying.

HEDDA. Well, we've been expecting that.

TESMAN. She says if I want to see her I must go quickly. I'll run over at once.

HEDDA. [*Hides a smile*] Run?

TESMAN. Hedda dear, I suppose you wouldn't like to come with me? What about that, eh?

HEDDA. [*Gets up and says wearily and with repulsion*] No, no, don't ask me to do anything like that. I can't bear illness or death. I loathe anything ugly.

TESMAN. Yes, yes. Of course. [*In a dither*] My hat? My overcoat? Oh yes, in the hall. I do hope I won't get there too late, Hedda? What?

HEDDA. You'll be all right if you run.

[BERTHA *enters from the hall.*]

BERTHA. Judge Brack's outside and wants to know if he can come in.

TESMAN. At this hour? No, I can't possibly receive him now.

HEDDA. I can. [*To* BERTHA] Ask his honor to come in.

[BERTHA *goes.*]

HEDDA. [*Whispers quickly*] The manuscript, Tesman.

[*She snatches it from the footstool.*]

TESMAN. Yes, give it to me.

HEDDA. No, I'll look after it for now.

[*She goes over to the writing table and puts it in the bookcase.* TESMAN *stands dithering, unable to get his gloves on.* JUDGE BRACK *enters from the hall.*]

HEDDA. [*Nods to him*] Well, you're an early bird.

BRACK. Yes, aren't I? [*To* TESMAN] Are you up and about, too?

TESMAN. Yes, I've got to go and see my aunts. Poor Auntie Rena's dying.

BRACK. Oh dear, is she? Then you mustn't le me detain you. At so tragic a——

TESMAN. Yes, I really must run. Good-bye! Good-bye!

[*Runs out through the hall*]

HEDDA. [*Goes nearer*] You seem to have had excellent sport last night—Judge.

BRACK. Indeed yes, Mrs. Hedda. I haven't even had time to take my clothes off.

HEDDA. *You* haven't either?

BRACK. As you see. What's Tesman told you about last night's escapades?

HEDDA. Oh, only some boring story about having gone and drunk coffee somewhere.

BRACK. Yes, I've heard about that coffee party. Eilert Loevborg wasn't with them, I gather?

HEDDA. No, they took him home first.

BRACK. Did Tesman go with him?

HEDDA. No, one or two of the others, he said.

BRACK. [*Smiles*] George Tesman is a credulous man, Mrs. Hedda.

HEDDA. God knows. But—has something happened?

BRACK. Well, yes, I'm afraid it has.

HEDDA. I see. Sit down and tell me.

[*She sits on the left of the table,* BRACK *at the long side of it, near her.*]

HEDDA. Well?

BRACK. I had a special reason for keeping track of my guests last night. Or perhaps I should say some of my guests.

HEDDA. Including Eilert Loevborg?

BRACK. I must confess—yes.

HEDDA. You're beginning to make me curious.

BRACK. Do you know where he and some of my other guests spent the latter half of last night, Mrs. Hedda?

HEDDA. Tell me. If it won't shock me.

BRACK. Oh, I don't think it'll shock you. They found themselves participating in an exceedingly animated *soirée.*[4]

HEDDA. Of a sporting character?

BRACK. Of a highly sporting character.

HEDDA. Tell me more.

BRACK. Loevborg had received an invitation in advance—as had the others. I knew all about that. But he had refused. As you know, he's become a new man.

HEDDA. Up at the Elvsteds', yes. But he went?

BRACK. Well, you see, Mrs. Hedda, last night at my house, unhappily, the spirit moved him.

HEDDA. Yes, I hear he became inspired.

BRACK. Somewhat violently inspired. And as a result, I suppose, his thoughts strayed. We men, alas, don't always stick to our principles as firmly as we should.

HEDDA. I'm sure you're an exception, Judge Brack. But go on about Loevborg.

BRACK. Well, to cut a long story short, he ended up in the establish-

4. Evening party.

ment of a certain Mademoiselle Danielle.

HEDDA. Mademoiselle Danielle?

BRACK. She was holding the *soirée*. For a selected circle of friends and admirers.

HEDDA. Has she got red hair?

BRACK. She has.

HEDDA. A singer of some kind?

BRACK. Yes—among other accomplishments. She's also a celebrated huntress—of men, Mrs. Hedda. I'm sure you've heard about her. Eilert Loevborg used to be one of her most ardent patrons. In his salad days.[5]

HEDDA. And how did all this end?

BRACK. Not entirely amicably, from all accounts. Mademoiselle Danielle began by receiving him with the utmost tenderness and ended by resorting to her fists.

HEDDA. Against Loevborg?

BRACK. Yes. He accused her, or her friends, of having robbed him. He claimed his pocketbook had been stolen. Among other things. In short, he seems to have made a bloodthirsty scene.

HEDDA. And what did this lead to?

BRACK. It led to a general free-for-all, in which both sexes participated. Fortunately, in the end the police arrived.

HEDDA. The police too?

BRACK. Yes. I'm afraid it may turn out to be rather an expensive joke for Master Eilert. Crazy fool!

HEDDA. Oh?

BRACK. Apparently he put up a very violent resistance. Hit one of the constables on the ear and tore his uniform. He had to accompany them to the police station.

HEDDA. Where did you learn all this?

BRACK. From the police.

HEDDA. [*To herself*] So that's what happened. He didn't have a crown of vine-leaves in his hair.

BRACK. Vine-leaves, Mrs. Hedda?

HEDDA. [*In her normal voice again*] But, tell me, Judge, why do you take such a close interest in Eilert Loevborg?

BRACK. For one thing it'll hardly be a matter of complete indifference to me if it's revealed in court that he came there straight from my house.

HEDDA. Will it come to court?

BRACK. Of course. Well, I don't regard that as particularly serious. Still, I thought it my duty, as a friend of the family, to give you and your husband a full account of his nocturnal adventures.

5. Indiscreet youth.

HEDDA. Why?

BRACK. Because I've a shrewd suspicion that he's hoping to use you as a kind of screen.

HEDDA. What makes you think that?

BRACK. Oh, for heaven's sake, Mrs. Hedda, we're not blind. You wait and see. This Mrs. Elvsted won't be going back to her husband just yet.

HEDDA. Well, if there were anything between those two there are plenty of other places where they could meet.

BRACK. Not in anyone's home. From now on every respectable house will once again be closed to Eilert Loevborg.

HEDDA. And mine should be too, you mean?

BRACK. Yes. I confess I should find it more than irksome if this gentleman were to be granted unrestricted access to this house. If he were superfluously to intrude into——

HEDDA. The triangle?

BRACK. Precisely. For me it would be like losing a home.

HEDDA. [Looks at him and smiles] I see. You want to be the cock of the walk.

BRACK. [Nods slowly and lowers his voice] Yes, that is my aim. And I shall fight for it with—every weapon at my disposal.

HEDDA. [As her smile fades] You're a dangerous man, aren't you? When you really want something.

BRACK. You think so?

HEDDA. Yes. I'm beginning to think so. I'm deeply thankful you haven't any kind of hold over me.

BRACK. [Laughs equivocally] Well, well, Mrs. Hedda—perhaps you're right. If I had, who knows what I might not think up?

HEDDA. Come, Judge Brack. That sounds almost like a threat.

BRACK. [Gets up] Heaven forbid! In the creation of a triangle—and its continuance—the question of compulsion should never arise.

HEDDA. Exactly what I was thinking.

BRACK. Well, I've said what I came to say. I must be getting back. Good-bye, Mrs. Hedda.

[Goes toward the french windows]

HEDDA. [Gets up] Are you going out through the garden?

BRACK. Yes, it's shorter.

HEDDA. Yes. And it's the back door, isn't it?

BRACK. I've nothing against back doors. They can be quite intriguing—sometimes.

HEDDA. When people fire pistols out of them, for example?

BRACK. [In the doorway, laughs] Oh, people don't shoot tame cocks.

HEDDA. [Laughs too] I suppose not. When they've only got one.

[They nod good-bye, laughing. He goes. She closes the french windows behind him, and stands for a moment, looking out *pensively. Then she walks across the room and glances through the curtains in the open doorway. Goes to the writing table, takes* LOEVBORG's *package from the bookcase and is about to leaf through the pages when* BERTHA *is heard remonstrating loudly in the hall.* HEDDA *turns and listens. She hastily puts the package back in the drawer, locks it and puts the key on the inkstand.* EILBERT LOEVBORG, *with his overcoat on and his hat in his hand, throws the door open. He looks somehat confused and excited.*]

LOEVBORG. [*Shouts as he enters*] I must come in, I tell you! Let me pass!

[*He closes the door, turns, sees* HEDDA, *controls himself immediately and bows.*]

HEDDA. [*At the writing table*] Well, Mr. Loevborg, this is rather a late hour to be collecting Thea.

LOEVBORG. And an early hour to call on you. Please forgive me.

HEDDA. How do you know she's still here?

LOEVBORG. They told me at her lodgings that she has been out all night.

HEDDA. [*Goes to the table*] Did you notice anything about their behavior when they told you?

LOEVBORG. [*Looks at her, puzzled*] Notice anything?

HEDDA. Did they sound as if they thought it—strange?

LOEVBORG. [*Suddenly understands*] Oh, I see what you mean. I'm dragging her down with me. No, as a matter of fact I didn't notice anything. I suppose Tesman isn't up yet?

HEDDA. No, I don't think so.

LOEVBORG. When did he get home?

HEDDA. Very late.

LOEVBORG. Did he tell you anything?

HEDDA. Yes. I gather you had a merry party at Judge Brack's last night.

LOEVBORG. He didn't tell you anything else?

HEDDA. I don't think so. I was so terribly sleepy——

[MRS. ELVSTED *comes through the curtains in the open doorway.*]

MRS. ELVSTED. [*Runs toward him*] Oh, Eilert! At last!

LOEVBORG. Yes—at last. And too late.

MRS. ELVSTED. What is too late?

LOEVBORG. Everything—now. I'm finished, Thea.

MRS. ELVSTED. Oh, no, no! Don't say that!

LOEVBORG. You'll say it yourself, when you've heard what I——

MRS. ELVSTED. I don't want to hear anything!

HEDDA. Perhaps you'd rather speak to her alone? I'd better go.

LOEVBORG. No, stay.

MRS. ELVSTED. But I don't want to hear anything, I tell you!

LOEVBORG. It's not about last night.

MRS. ELVSTED. Then what——?

LOEVBORG. I want to tell you that from now on we must stop seeing each other.

MRS. ELVSTED. Stop seeing each other!

HEDDA. [*Involuntarily*] I knew it!

LOEVBORG. I have no further use for you, Thea.

MRS. ELVSTED. You can stand there and say that! No further use for me! Surely I can go on helping you? We'll go on working together, won't we?

LOEVBORG. I don't intend to do any more work from now on.

MRS. ELVSTED. [*Desperately*] Then what use have I for my life?

LOEVBORG. You must try to live as if you had never known me.

MRS. ELVSTED. But I can't!

LOEVBORG. Try to, Thea. Go back home——

MRS. ELVSTED. Never! I want to be wherever you are! I won't let myself be driven away like this! I want to stay here—and be with you when the book comes out.

HEDDA. [*Whispers*] Ah, yes! The book!

LOEVBORG. [*Looks at her*] Our book; Thea's and mine. It belongs to both of us.

MRS. ELVSTED. Oh, yes! I feel that, too! And I've a right to be with you when it comes into the world. I want to see people respect and honor you again. And the joy! The joy! I want to share it with you!

LOEVBORG. Thea—our book will never come into the world.

HEDDA. Ah!

MRS. ELVSTED. Not——?

LOEVBORG. It cannot. Ever.

MRS. ELVSTED. Eilert—what have you done with the manuscript? Where is it?

LOEVBORG. Oh Thea, please don't ask me that!

MRS. ELVSTED. Yes, yes—I must know. I've a right to know. Now!

LOEVBORG. The manuscript. I've torn it up.

MRS. ELVSTED. [*Screams*] No, no!

HEDDA. [*Involuntarily*] But that's not——!

LOEVBORG. [*Looks at her*] Not true, you think?

HEDDA. [*Controls herself*] Why—yes, of course it is, if you say so. It just sounded so incredible——

LOEVBORG. It's true, nevertheless.

MRS. ELVSTED. Oh, my God, my God, Hedda—he's destroyed his own book!

LOEVBORG. I have destroyed my life. Why not my life's work, too?

MRS. ELVSTED. And you—did this last night?

LOEVBORG. Yes, Thea. I tore it into a thousand pieces. And scattered them out across the fjord.[6] It's good, clean, salt water. Let it carry them away; let them drift in the current and the wind. And in a little while, they will sink. Deeper and deeper. As I shall, Thea.

MRS. ELVSTED. Do you know, Eilert—this book—all my life I shall feel as though you'd killed a little child?

LOEVBORG. You're right. It is like killing a child.

MRS. ELVSTED. But how could you? It was my child, too!

HEDDA. [*Almost inaudibly*] Oh—the child——!

MRS. ELVSTED. [*Breathes heavily*] It's all over, then. Well—I'll go now, Hedda.

HEDDA. You're not leaving town?

MRS. ELVSTED. I don't know what I'm going to do. I can't see anything except—darkness.

[*She goes out through the hall.*]

HEDDA. [*Waits a moment*] Aren't you going to escort her home, Mr. Loevborg?

LOEVBORG. I? Through the streets? Do you want me to let people see her with me?

HEDDA. Of course I don't know what else may have happened last night. But is it so utterly beyond redress?

LOEVBORG. It isn't just last night. It'll go on happening. I know it. But the curse of it is, I don't want to live that kind of life. I don't want to start all that again. She's broken my courage. I can't spit in the eyes of the world any longer.

HEDDA. [*As though to herself*] That pretty little fool's been trying to shape a man's destiny. [*Looks at him*] But how could you be so heartless toward her?

LOEVBORG. Don't call me heartless!

HEDDA. To go and destroy the one thing that's made her life worth living? You don't call that heartless?

LOEVBORG. Do you want to know the truth, Hedda?

HEDDA. The truth?

LOEVBORG. Promise me first—give me your word—that you'll never let Thea know about this.

HEDDA. I give you my word.

LOEVBORG. Good. Well; what I told her just now was a lie.

HEDDA. About the manuscript?

LOEVBORG. Yes. I didn't tear it up. Or throw it in the fjord.

HEDDA. You didn't? But where is it, then?

LOEVBORG. I destroyed it, all the same. I destroyed it, Hedda!

HEDDA. I don't understand.

LOEVBORG. Thea said that what I had done was like killing a child.

---

6. Inlet of the sea (pronounced *fyord*).

HEDDA. Yes. That's what she said.

LOEVBORG. But to kill a child isn't the worst thing a father can do to it.

HEDDA. What could be worse than that?

LOEVBORG. Hedda—suppose a man came home one morning, after a night of debauchery, and said to the mother of his child: "Look here. I've been wandering round all night. I've been to—such-and-such a place and such-and-such a place. And I had our child with me. I took him to—these places. And I've lost him. Just—lost him. God knows where he is or whose hands he's fallen into."

HEDDA. I see. But when all's said and done, this was only a book—

LOEVBORG. Thea's heart and soul were in that book. It was her whole life.

HEDDA. Yes. I understand.

LOEVBORG. Well, then you must also understand that she and I cannot possibly ever see each other again.

HEDDA. Where will you go?

LOEVBORG. Nowhere. I just want to put an end to it all. As soon as possible.

HEDDA. [*Takes a step toward him*] Eilert Loevborg, listen to me. Do it—beautifully!

LOEVBORG. Beautifully? [*Smiles*] With a crown of vine-leaves in my hair? The way you used to dream of me—in the old days?

HEDDA. No. I don't believe in that crown any longer. But—do it beautifully, all the same. Just this once. Good-bye. You must go now. And don't come back.

LOEVBORG. Adieu, madam. Give my love to George Tesman.
     [*Turns to go*]

HEDDA. Wait. I want to give you a souvenir to take with you.
     [*She goes over to the writing table, opens the drawer and the pistol-case, and comes back to* LOEVBORG *with one of the pistols.*]

LOEVBORG. [*Looks at her*] This? Is this the souvenir?

HEDDA. [*Nods slowly*] You recognize it? You looked down its barrel once.

LOEVBORG. You should have used it then.

HEDDA. Here! Use it now!

LOEVBORG. [*Puts the pistol in his breast pocket*] Thank you.

HEDDA. Do it beautifully, Eilert Loevborg. Only promise me that!

LOEVBORG. Good-bye, Hedda Gabler.
     [*He goes out through the hall.* HEDDA *stands by the door for a moment, listening. Then she goes over to the writing table, takes out the package containing the manuscript, glances inside it, pulls some of the pages half out and looks at them. Then she takes it to the armchair by the stove and sits down with the*

package in her lap. After a moment, she opens the door of the stove; then she opens the packet.]

HEDDA. [*Throws one of the pages into the stove and whispers to herself*] I'm burning your child, Thea! You with your beautiful wavy hair! [*She throws a few more pages into the stove.*] The child Eilert Loevborg gave you. [*Throws the rest of the manuscript in*] I'm burning it! I'm burning your child!

Act IV

SCENE—*The same. It is evening. The drawing room is in darkness. The small room is illuminated by the hanging lamp over the table. the curtains are drawn across the french windows.* HEDDA, *dressed in black, is walking up and down in the darkened room. Then she goes into the small room and crosses to the left. A few chords are heard from the paino. She comes back into the drawing room.*

BERTHA *comes through the small room from the right with a lighted lamp, which she places on the table in front of the corner sofa in the drawing room. Her eyes are red with crying, and she has black ribbons on her cap. She goes quietly out, right.* HEDDA *goes over to the french windows, draws the curtains slightly to one side and looks out into the darkness.*

A few moments later, MISS TESMAN *enters from the hall. She is dressed in mourning, with a black hat and veil.* HEDDA *goes to meet her and holds out her hand.*

MISS TESMAN. Well, Hedda, here I am in the weeds of sorrow. My poor sister has ended her struggles at last.

HEDDA. I've already heard. Tesman sent me a card.

MISS TESMAN. Yes, he promised me he would. But I thought, no, I must go and break the news of death to Hedda myself—here, in the house of life.

HEDDA. It's very kind of you.

MISS TESMAN. Ah, Rena shouldn't have chosen a time like this to pass away. This is no moment for Hedda's house to be a place of mourning.

HEDDA. [*Changing the subject*] She died peacefully, Miss Tesman?

MISS TESMAN. Oh, it was quite beautiful! The end came so calmly. And she was so happy at being able to see George once again. And say good-bye to him. Hasn't he come home yet?

HEDDA. No. He wrote that I mustn't expect him too soon. But please sit down.

MISS TESMAN. No, thank you, Hedda dear—bless you. I'd like to.

But I've so little time. I must dress her and lay her out as well as I can. She shall go to her grave looking really beautiful.

HEDDA. Can't I help with anything?

MISS TESMAN. Why, you mustn't think of such a thing! Hedda Tesman mustn't let her hands be soiled by contact with death. Or her thoughts. Not at this time.

HEDDA. One can't always control one's thoughts.

MISS TESMAN. [*Continues*] Ah, well, that's life. Now we must start to sew poor Rena's shroud. There'll be sewing to be done in this house too before long, I shouldn't wonder. But not for a shroud, praise God.

[GEORGE TESMAN *enters from the hall.*]

HEDDA. You've come at last! Thank heavens!

TESMAN. Are you here, Auntie Juju? With Hedda? Fancy that!

MISS TESMAN. I was just on the point of leaving, dear boy. Well, have you done everything you promised me?

TESMAN. No, I'm afraid I forgot half of it. I'll have to run over again tomorrow. My head's in a complete whirl today. I can't collect my thoughts.

MISS TESMAN. But George dear, you mustn't take it like this.

TESMAN. Oh? Well—er—how should I?

MISS TESMAN. You must be happy in your grief. Happy for what's happened. As I am.

TESMAN. Oh, yes, yes. You're thinking of Aunt Rena.

HEDDA. It'll be lonely for you now, Miss Tesman.

MISS TESMAN. For the first few days, yes. But it won't last long, I hope. Poor dear Rena's little room isn't going to stay empty.

TESMAN. Oh? Whom are you going to move in there? What?

MISS TESMAN. Oh, there's always some poor invalid who needs care and attention.

HEDDA. Do you really want another cross like that to bear?

MISS TESMAN. Cross! God forgive you, child. It's been no cross for me.

HEDDA. But now—if a complete stranger comes to live with you——?

MISS TESMAN. Oh, one soon makes friends with invalids. And I need so much to have someone to live for. Like you, my dear. Well, I expect there'll soon be work in this house too for an old aunt, praise God!

HEDDA. Oh—please!

TESMAN. By Jove, yes! What a splendid time the three of us could have together if——

HEDDA. If?

TESMAN. [*Uneasily*] Oh, never mind. It'll all work out. Let's hope so—what?

MISS TESMAN. Yes, yes. Well, I'm sure you two would like to be alone. [*Smiles*] Perhaps Hedda may have something to tell you, George. Good-bye. I must go home to Rena. [*Turns to the door*] Dear God, how strange! Now Rena is with me and with poor dear Joachim.

TESMAN. Fancy that. Yes, Auntie Juju! What?

[MISS TESMAN *goes out through the hall.*]

HEDDA. [*Follows* TESMAN *coldly and searchingly with her eyes*] I really believe this death distresses you more than it does her.

TESMAN. Oh, it isn't just Auntie Rena. It's Eilert I'm so worried about.

HEDDA. [*Quickly*] Is there any news of him?

TESMAN. I ran over to see him this afternoon. I wanted to tell him his manuscript was in safe hands.

HEDDA. Oh? You didn't find him?

TESMAN. No. He wasn't at home. But later I met Mrs. Elvsted and she told me he'd been here early this morning.

HEDDA. Yes, just after you'd left.

TESMAN. It seems he said he'd torn the manuscript up. What?

HEDDA. Yes, he claimed to have done so.

TESMAN. You told him we had it, of course?

HEDDA. No. [*Quickly*] Did you tell Mrs. Elvsted?

TESMAN. No, I didn't like to. But you ought to have told him. Think if he should go home and do something desperate! Give me the manuscript, Hedda. I'll run over to him with it right away. Where did you put it?

HEDDA. [*Cold and motionless, leaning against the armchair*] I haven't got it any longer.

TESMAN. Haven't got it? What on earth do you mean?

HEDDA. I've burned it.

TESMAN. [*Starts, terrified*] Burned it! Burned Eilert's manuscript!

HEDDA. Don't shout. The servant will hear you.

TESMAN. Burned it! But in heaven's name——! Oh, no, no, no! This is impossible!

HEDDA. Well, it's true.

TESMAN. But Hedda, do you realize what you've done? That's appropriating lost property! It's against the law! By Jove! You ask Judge Brack and see if I'm not right.

HEDDA. You'd be well advised not to talk about it to Judge Brack or anyone else.

TESMAN. But how could you go and do such a dreadful thing? What on earth put the idea into your head? What came over you? Answer me! What?

HEDDA. [*Represses on almost imperceptible smile*] I did it for your sake, George.

TESMAN. For my sake?

HEDDA. When you came home this morning and described how he'd read his book to you——

TESMAN. Yes, yes?

HEDDA. You admitted you were jealous of him.

TESMAN. But, good heavens, I didn't mean it literally!

HEDDA. No matter. I couldn't bear the thought that anyone else should push you into the background.

TESMAN. [*Torn between doubt and joy*] Hedda—is this true? But—but—but I never realized you loved me like that! Fancy——

HEDDA. Well, I suppose you'd better know. I'm going to have—— [*Breaks off and says violently*] No, no—you'd better ask your Auntie Juju. She'll tell you.

TESMAN. Hedda! I think I understand what you mean. [*Clasps his hands*] Good heavens, can it really be true! What?

HEDDA. Don't shout. The servant will hear you.

TESMAN. [*Laughing with joy*] The servant! I say, that's good! The servant! Why, that's Bertha! I'll run out and tell her at once!

HEDDA. [*Clenches her hands in despair*] Oh, it's destroying me, all this—it's destroying me!

TESMAN. I say, Hedda, what's up? What?

HEDDA. [*Cold, controlled*] Oh, it's all so—absurd—George.

TESMAN. Absurd? That I'm so happy? But surely——? Ah, well—perhaps I won't say anything to Bertha.

HEDDA. No, do. She might as well know too.

TESMAN. No, no, I won't tell her yet. But Auntie Juju—I must let her know! And you—you called me George! For the first time! Fancy that! Oh, it'll make Auntie Juju so happy, all this! So very happy!

HEDDA. Will she be happy when she hears I've burned Eilert Loevborg's manuscript—for your sake?

TESMAN. No, I'd forgotten about that. Of course no one must be allowed to know about the manuscript. But that you're burning with love for me, Hedda, I must certainly let Auntie Juju know that. I say, I wonder if young wives often feel like that toward their husbands? What?

HEDDA. You might ask Auntie Juju about that too.

TESMAN. I will, as soon as I get the chance. [*Looks uneasy and thoughtful again*] But I say, you know, that manuscript. Dreadful business. Poor Eilert!

[MRS. ELVSTED, *dressed as on her first visit, with hat and overcoat, enters from the hall.*]

MRS. ELVSTED. [*Greets them hastily and tremulously*] Oh, Hedda dear, do please forgive me for coming here again.

HEDDA. Why, Thea, what's happened?

TESMAN. Is it anything to do with Eilert Loevborg? What?

MRS. ELVSTED. Yes—I'm so dreadfully afraid he may have met with an accident.

HEDDA. [*Grips her arm*] You think so?

TESMAN. But, good heavens, Mrs. Elsted, what makes you think that?

MRS. ELVSTED. I heard them talking about him at the boarding-house, as I went in. Oh, there are the most terrible rumors being spread about him in town today.

TESMAN. Fancy. Yes, I heard about them too. But I can testify that he went straight home to bed. Fancy that!

HEDDA. Well—what did they say in the boarding-house?

MRS. ELVSTED. Oh, I couldn't find out anything. Either they didn't know, or else—— They stopped talking when they saw me. And I didn't dare to ask.

TESMAN. [*Fidgets uneasily*] We must hope—we must hope you misheard them, Mrs. Elvsted.

MRS. ELVSTED. No, no, I'm sure it was he they were talking about. I heard them say something about a hospital——

TESMAN. Hospital!

HEDDA. Oh no, surely that's impossible!

MRS. ELVSTED. Oh, I became so afraid. So I went up to his rooms and asked to see him.

HEDDA. Do you think that was wise, Thea?

MRS. ELVSTED. Well, what else could I do? I couldn't bear the uncertainty any longer.

TESMAN. But you didn't manage to find him either? What?

MRS. ELVSTED. No. And they had no idea where he was. They said he hadn't been home since yesterday afternoon.

TESMAN. Since yesterday? Fancy that!

MRS. ELVSTED. I'm sure he must have met with an accident.

TESMAN. Hedda, I wonder if I ought to go into town and make one or two enquiries?

HEDDA. No, no, don't you get mixed up in this.

> [JUDGE BRACK *enters from the hall, hat in hand.* BERTHA, *who has opened the door for him, closes it. He looks serious and greets them silently.*]

TESMAN. Hullo, my dear Judge. Fancy seeing you!

BRACK. I had to come and talk to you.

TESMAN. I can see Auntie Juju's told you the news.

BRACK. Yes, I've heard about that too.

TESMAN. Tragic, isn't it?

BRACK. Well, my dear chap, that depends how you look at it.

TESMAN. [*Looks uncertainly at him*] Has something else happened?

BRACK. Yes.

HEDDA. Another tragedy?

BRACK. That also depends on how you look at it, Mrs. Tesman.

MRS. ELVSTED. Oh, it's something to do with Eilert Loevborg!

BRACK. [*Looks at her for a moment*] How did you guess? Perhaps you've heard already——?

MRS. ELVSTED. [*Confused*] No, no, not at all—I——

TESMAN. For heaven's sake, tell us!

BRACK. [*Shrugs his shoulers*] Well, I'm afraid they've taken him to the hospital. He's dying.

MRS. ELVSTED. [*Screams*] Oh God, God!

TESMAN. The hospital! Dying!

HEDDA. [*Involuntarily*] So quickly!

MRS. ELVSTED. [*Weeping*] Oh, Hedda! And we parted enemies!

HEDDA. [*Whispers*] Thea—Thea!

MRS. ELVSTED. [*Ignoring her*] I must see him! I must see him before he dies!

BRACK. It's no use, Mrs. Elvsted. No one's allowed to see him now.

MRS. ELVSTED. But what's happened to him? You must tell me!

TESMAN. He hasn't tried to do anything to himself? What?

HEDDA. Yes, he has. I'm sure of it.

TESMAN. Hedda, how can you——?

BRACK. [*Who has not taken his eyes from her*] I'm afraid you've guessed correctly, Mrs. Tesman.

MRS. ELVSTED. How dreadful!

TESMAN. Attempted suicide! Fancy that!

HEDDA. Shot himself!

BRACK. Right again, Mrs. Tesman.

MRS. ELVSTED. [*Tries to compose herself*] When did this happen, Judge Brack?

BRACK. This afternoon. Between three and four.

TESMAN. But, good heavens—where? What?

BRACK. [*A little hesitantly*] Where? Why, my dear chap, in his rooms of course.

MRS. ELVSTED. No, that's impossible. I was there soon after six.

BRACK. Well, it must have been somewhere else, then. I don't know exactly. I only know that they found him. He'd shot himself—through the breast.

MRS. ELVSTED. Oh, how horrible! That he should end like that!

HEDDA. [*To* BRACK] Through the breast, you said?

BRACK. That is what I said.

HEDDA. Not through the head?

BRACK. Through the breast, Mrs. Tesman.

HEDDA. The breast. Yes; yes. That's good, too.

BRACK. Why, Mrs. Tesman?

HEDDA. Oh—no, I didn't mean anything.

TESMAN. And the wound's dangerous you say? What?

BRACK. Mortal. He's probably already dead.

MRS. ELVSTED. Yes, yes—I feel it! It's all over. All over. Oh Hedda——!

TESMAN. But, tell me, how did you manage to learn all this?

BRACK. [*Curtly*] From the police. I spoke to one of them.

HEDDA. [*Loudly, clearly*] At last! Oh, thank God!

TESMAN. [*Appalled*] For God's sake, Hedda, what are you saying?

HEDDA. I am saying there's beauty in what he has done.

BRACK. Mm—Mrs. Tesman——

TESMAN. Beauty! Oh, but I say!

MRS. ELVSTED. Hedda, how can you talk of beauty in connection with a thing like this?

HEDDA. Eilert Loevborg has settled his account with life. He's had the courage to do what—what he had to do.

MRS. ELVSTED. No, that's not why it happened. He did it because he was mad.

TESMAN. He did it because he was desperate.

HEDDA. You're wrong! I know!

MRS. ELVSTED. He must have been mad. The same as when he tore up the manuscript.

BRACK. [*Starts*] Manuscript? Did he tear it up?

MRS. ELVSTED. Yes. Last night.

TESMAN. [*Whispers*] Oh, Hedda, we shall never be able to escape from this.

BRACK. Hm. Strange.

TESMAN. [*Wanders round the room*] To think of Eilert dying like that. And not leaving behind him the thing that would have made his name endure.

MRS. ELVSTED. If only it could be pieced together again!

TESMAN. Yes, fancy! If only it could! I'd give anything——

MRS. ELVSTED. Perhaps it can, Mr. Tesman.

TESMAN. What do you mean?

MRS. ELVSTED. [*Searches in the pocket of her dress*] Look! I kept the notes he dictated it from.

HEDDA. [*Takes a step nearer*] Ah!

TESMAN. You kept them, Mrs. Elvsted! What?

MRS. ELVSTED. Yes, here they are. I brought them with me when I left home. They've been in my pocket ever since.

TESMAN. Let me have a look.

MRS. ELVSTED. [*Hands him a wad of small sheets of paper*] They're in a terrible muddle. All mixed up.

TESMAN. I say, just fancy if we can sort them out! Perhaps if we work on them together——?

MRS. ELVSTED. Oh, yes! Let's try, anyway!

TESMAN. We'll manage it. We must! I shall dedicate my life to this.

HEDDA. *You,* George? Your life?

TESMAN. Yes—well, all the time I can spare. My book'll have to wait. Hedda, you do understand? What? I owe it to Eilert's memory.

HEDDA. Perhaps.

TESMAN. Well, my dear Mrs. Elvsted, you and I'll have to pool our brains. No use crying over spilt milk, what? We must try to approach this matter calmly.

MRS. ELVSTED. Yes, yes, Mr. Tesman. I'll do my best.

TESMAN. Well, come over here and let's start looking at these notes right away. Where shall we sit? Here? No, the other room. You'll excuse us, won't you, Judge? Come along with me, Mrs. Elvsted.

MRS. ELVSTED. Oh, God! If only we can manage to do it!

[TESMAN *and* MRS. ELVSTED *go into the rear room. He takes off his hat and overcoat. They sit at the table beneath the hanging lamp and absorb themselves in the notes.* HEDDA *walks across to the stove and sits in the armchair. After a moment,* BRACK *goes over to her.*]

HEDDA. [*Half aloud*] Oh, Judge! This act of Eilert Loevborg's—doesn't it give one a sense of release!

BRACK. Release, Mrs. Hedda? Well, it's a release for him, of course——

HEDDA. Oh, I don't mean him—I mean me! The release of knowing that someone can do something really brave! Something beautiful!

BRACK. [*Smiles*] Hm—my dear Mrs. Hedda——

HEDDA. Oh, I know what you're going to say. You're a bourgeois at heart too, just like—ah, well!

BRACK. [*Looks at her*] Eilert Loevborg has meant more to you than you're willing to admit to yourself. Or am I wrong?

HEDDA. I'm not answering questions like that from you. I only know that Eilert Loevborg has had the courage to live according to his own principles. And now, at last, he's done something big! Something beautiful! To have the courage and the will to rise from the feast of life so early!

BRACK. It distresses me deeply, Mrs. Hedda, but I'm afraid I must rob you of that charming illusion.

HEDDA. Illusion?

BRACK. You wouldn't have been allowed to keep it for long, anyway.

HEDDA. What do you mean?

BRACK. He didn't shoot himself on purpose.

HEDDA. Not on purpose?

BRACK. No. It didn't happen quite the way I told you.

HEDDA. Have you been hiding something? What is it?

BRACK. In order to spare poor Mrs. Elvsted's feelings, I permitted myself one or two small—equivocations.

HEDDA. What?

BRACK. To begin with, he is already dead.

HEDDA. He died at the hospital?

BRACK. Yes. Without regaining consciousness.

HEDDA. What else haven't you told us?

BRACK. The incident didn't take place at his lodgings.

HEDDA. Well, that's utterly unimportant.

BRACK. Not utterly. The fact is, you see, that Eilert Loevborg was found shot in Mademoiselle Danielle's boudoir.

HEDDA. [*Almost jumps up, but instead sinks back in her chair*] That's impossible. He can't have been there today.

BRACK. He was there this afternoon. He went to ask for something he claimed they'd taken from him. Talked some crazy nonsense about a child which had got lost——

HEDDA. Oh! So that was the reason!

BRACK. I thought at first he might have been referring to his manuscript. But I hear he destroyed that himself. So he must have meant his pocketbook—I suppose.

HEDDA. Yes, I suppose so. So they found him there?

BRACK. Yes; there. With a discharged pistol in his breast pocket. The shot had wounded him mortally.

HEDDA. Yes. In the breast.

BRACK. No. In the—hm—stomach. The—lower part——

HEDDA. [*Looks at him with an expression of repulsion*] That too! Oh, why does everything I touch become mean and ludicrous? It's like a curse!

BRACK. There's something else, Mrs. Hedda. It's rather disagreeable, too.

HEDDA. What?

BRACK. The pistol he had on him——

HEDDA. Yes? What about it?

BRACK. He must have stolen it.

HEDDA. [*Jumps up*] Stolen it! That isn't true! He didn't!

BRACK. It's the only explanation. He must have stolen it. Ssh!

[TESMAN *and* MRS. ELVSTED *have got up from the table in the rear room and come into the drawing room.*]

TESMAN. [*His hands full of papers*] Hedda, I can't see properly under that lamp. Think!

HEDDA. I am thinking.

TESMAN. Do you think we could possibly use your writing table for a little? What?

HEDDA. Yes, of course. [*Quickly*] No, wait! Let me tidy it up first.

TESMAN. Oh, don't you trouble about that. There's plenty of room.

HEDDA. No, no, let me tidy it up first, I say. I'll take this in and put them on the piano. Here.

[*She pulls an object, covered with sheets of music, out from under the bookcase, puts some more sheets on top and carries it all into the rear room and away to the left.* TESMAN *puts his papers on the writing table and moves the lamp over from the corner table. He and* MRS. ELVSTED *sit down and begin working again.* HEDDA *comes back.*]

HEDDA. [*Behind* MRS. ELVSTED's *chair, ruffles her hair gently*] Well, my pretty Thea! And how is work progressing on Eilert Loevborg's memorial?

MRS. ELVSTED. [*Looks up at her, dejectedly*] Oh, it's going to be terribly difficult to get these into any order.

TESMAN. We've got to do it. We must! After all, putting other people's papers into order is rather my specialty, what?

[HEDDA *goes over to the stove and sits on one of the footstools.* BRACK *stands over her, leaning against the armchair.*]

HEDDA. [*Whispers*] What was that you were saying about the pistol?

BRACK. [*Softly*] I said he must have stolen it.

HEDDA. Why do you think that?

BRACK. Because any other explanation is unthinkable, Mrs. Hedda, or ought to be.

HEDDA. I see.

BRACK. [*Looks at her for a moment*] Eilert Loevborg was here this morning. Wasn't he?

HEDDA. Yes.

BRACK. Were you alone with him?

HEDDA. For a few moments.

BRACK. You didn't leave the room while he was here?

HEDDA. No.

BRACK. Think again. Are you sure you didn't go out for a moment?

HEDDA. Oh—yes, I might have gone into the hall. Just for a few seconds.

BRACK. And where was your pistol-case during this time?

HEDDA. I'd locked it in that——

BRACK. Er—Mrs. Hedda?

HEDDA. It was lying over there on my writing table.

BRACK. Have you looked to see if both the pistols are still there?

HEDDA. No.

BRACK. You needn't bother. I saw the pistol Loevborg had when they found him. I recognized it at once. From yesterday. And other occasions.

HEDDA. Have you got it?

BRACK. No. The police have it.

HEDDA. What will the police do with this pistol?

BRACK. Try to trace the owner.

HEDDA. Do you think they'll succeed?

BRACK. [*Leans down and whispers*] No, Hedda Gabler. Not as long as I hold my tongue.

HEDDA. [*Looks nervously at him*] And if you don't?

BRACK. [*Shrugs his shoulders*] You could always say he'd stolen it.

HEDDA. I'd rather die!

BRACK. [*Smiles*] People say that. They never do it.

HEDDA. [*Not replying*] And suppose the pistol wasn't stolen? And they trace the owner? What then?

BRACK. There'll be a scandal, Hedda.

HEDDA. A scandal!

BRACK. Yes, a scandal. The thing you're so frightened of. You'll have to appear in court. Together with Mademoiselle Danielle. She'll have to explain how it all happened. Was it an accident, or was it—homicide? Was he about to take the pistol from his pocket to threaten her? And did it go off? Or did she snatch the pistol from his hand, shoot him and then put it back in his pocket? She might quite easily have done it. She's a resourceful lady, is Mademoiselle Danielle.

HEDDA. But I had nothing to do with this repulsive business.

BRACK. No. But you'll have to answer one question. Why did you give Eiiert Loevborg this pistol? And what conclusions will people draw when it is proved you did give it to him?

HEDDA. [*Bows her head*] That's true. I hadn't thought of that.

BRACK. Well, luckily there's no danger as long as I hold my tongue.

HEDDA. [*Looks up at him*] In other words, I'm in your power, Judge. From now on, you've got your hold over me.

BRACK. [*Whispers, more slowly*] Hedda, my dearest—believe me—I will not abuse my position.

HEDDA. Nevertheless, I'm in your power. Dependent on your will, and your demands. Not free. Still not free! [*Rises passionately*] No. I couldn't bear that. No.

BRACK. [*Looks half-derisively at her*] Most people resign themselves to the inevitable, sooner or later.

HEDDA. [*Returns his gaze*] Possibly they do.

  [*She goes across to the writing table.*]

HEDDA. [*Represses an involuntary smile and says in* TESMAN's *voice*] Well, George. Think you'll be able to manage? What?

TESMAN. Heaven knows, dear. This is going to take months and months.

HEDDA. [*In the same tone as before*] Fancy that, by Jove! [*Runs her hands gently through* MRS. ELVSTED's *hair*] Doesn't it feel strange, Thea? Here you are working away with Tesman just the way you used to work with Eilert Loevborg.

MRS. ELVSTED. Oh—if only I can inspire your husband too!

HEDDA. Oh, it'll come. In time.

TESMAN. Yes—do you know, Hedda, I really think I'm beginning to feel a bit—well—that way. But you go back and talk to Judge Brack.

HEDDA. Can't I be of use to you two in any way?

TESMAN. No, none at all. [*Turns his head*] You'll have to keep Hedda company from now on, Judge, and see she doesn't get bored. If you don't mind.

BRACK. [*Glances at* HEDDA] It'll be a pleasure.

HEDDA. Thank you. But I'm tired this evening. I think I'll lie down on the sofa in there for a little while.

TESMAN. Yes, dear—do. What?

[HEDDA *goes into the rear room and draws the curtain behind her. Short pause. Suddenly she begins to play a frenzied dance melody on the piano.*]

MRS. ELVSTED. [*Starts up from her chair*] Oh, what's that?

TESMAN. [*Runs to the doorway*] Hedda dear, please! Don't play dance music tonight! Think of Auntie Rena. And Eilert.

HEDDA. [*Puts her head out through the curtains*] And Auntie Juju. And all the rest of them. From now on I'll be quiet.

[*Closes the curtains behind her*]

TESMAN. [*At the writing table*] It distresses her to watch us doing this. I say, Mrs. Elvsted, I've an idea. Why don't you move in with Auntie Juju? I'll run over each evening, and we can sit and work there. What?

MRS. ELVSTED. Yes, that might be the best plan.

HEDDA. [*From the rear room*] I can hear what you're saying, Tesman. But how shall I spend the evenings out here?

TESMAN. [*Looking through his papers*] Oh, I'm sure Judge Brack'll be kind enough to come over and keep you company. You won't mind my not being here, Judge?

BRACK. [*In the armchair, calls gaily*] I'll be delighted, Mrs. Tesman. I'll be here every evening. We'll have great fun together, you and I.

HEDDA. [*Loud and clear*] Yes, that'll suit you, won't it, Judge? The only cock on the dunghill——!

[*A shot is heard from the rear room.* TESMAN, MRS. ELVSTED *and* JUDGE BRACK *start from their chairs.*]

TESMAN. Oh, she's playing with those pistols again.

[*He pulls the curtains aside and runs in.* MRS. ELVSTED *follows him.* HEDDA *is lying dead on the sofa. Confusion and shouting.* BERTHA *enters in alarm from the right.*]

TESMAN. [*Screams to* BRACK] She's shot herself! Shot herself in the head! By Jove! Fancy that!

BRACK. [*Half paralyzed in the armchair*] But, good God! People don't do such things!

ANTON CHEKHOV
1860–1904

In plays and stories Anton Chekhov depicts Russia around 1900 with great pity, gentleness, and kindness of heart. More important: with a deep humanity which has outlasted all the problems of his time he dramatizes universal and almost timeless feelings rather than ideas that date and pass. He differs sharply from the two giants of Russian literature. For one thing, his work is of smaller scope. With the exception of an immature, forgotten novel and a travel book, he never wrote anything but short stories and plays. He belongs, furthermore, to a very different moral and spiritual atmosphere. Chekhov had studied medicine, and practiced it for a time. He shared the scientific outlook of his age and had too skeptical a mind to believe in Christianity or in any metaphysical system. He confessed that an intelligent believer was a puzzle to him. His attitude toward his materials and characters is detached, "objective." He is thus much more in the stream of Western realism than either Tolstoy or Dostoevsky, and his affinities with Maupassant (to whom he is related also in technical matters) are obvious. But extended reading of Chekhov does convey an impression of his view of life. There is implied in his stories a philosophy of kindness and humanity, a sense of the unexplainable mystery of life, a sense, especially, of man's utter loneliness in this universe and among his fellow men. Chekhov's pessimism has nothing of the defiance of the universe or the horror at it which we meet in other writers with similar attitudes; it is somehow merely sad, pathetic, and yet also comforting and comfortable.

The Russia depicted in Chekhov's stories and plays is of a later period than that presented by Tolstoy and Dostoevsky. It seems to be nearing its end; there is a sense of decadence and frustration which heralds the approach of catastrophe. The aristocracy still keeps up a beautiful front, but is losing its fight without much resistance, resignedly. Officialdom is stupid and venal. The Church is backward and narrow-minded. The intelligentsia are hopelessly ineffectual, futile, lost in the provinces or absorbed in their egos. The peasants live subject to the lowest degradations of poverty and drink, apparently rather aggravated than improved since the much-heralded emancipation of the serfs in 1861. There seems no hope for society except in a gradual spread of enlightenment, good sense, and hygiene, for Chekhov is skeptical of the revolution and revolutionaries as well as of Tolstoy's followers.

Anton Pavlovich Chekhov was born on January 17, 1860, at Taganrog, a small town on the Sea of Azov. His father was a grocer and haberdasher; his grandfather, a serf who had bought his freedom. Chekhov's father went bankrupt in 1876, and the family moved to Moscow, leaving Anton to finish school in his home town. After his graduation in 1879, he followed his family to Moscow, where he studied medicine. In order to earn additional money for his family and himself, he started to write humorous sketches and stories for magazines. In 1884 he became a doctor and published his first collection of stories, *Tales of Melpomene*. In the same year he had his first hemorrhage. All the rest of his life he struggled against tuberculosis. His first play, *Ivanov*, was performed in 1887. Three years later, he undertook an arduous journey through Siberia to the island of Sakhalin (north of Japan) and back by boat through the Suez Canal. He saw there the Russian penal settlements and wrote a moving account of his trip in *Sakhalin Island* (1892). In 1898 his play *The Sea Gull* was a great success at the Moscow Art Theater. The next year he moved to Yalta, in the Crimea, and in 1901 married the actress Olga Knipper. He died on July 2, 1904, at Badenweiler in the Black Forest.

The plays of Chekhov seem to go furthest in the direction of naturalism, the depiction of a "slice of life" on stage. Compared to Ibsen's plays they seem plotless; they could be described as a succession of little scenes, composed like a mosaic or like the dots on an impressionist painting. The characters often do not engage in the usual dialogue; they speak often in little soliloquies, hardly justified by the situation and they often do not listen to the words of their ostensible partners. They seem alone even in a crowd. Human communication seems difficult and even impossible. There is no clear message, no zeal for social reform; life seems to flow quietly, even sluggishly, until interrupted by some desperate outbreak or even a pistol shot.

Chekhov's last play, *The Cherry Orchard* (composed in 1903, first performed at the Moscow Art Theater on January 17, 1904) differs, however, from this pattern in several respects. It has a strongly articulated central theme: the loss of the orchard, and it has a composition which roughly follows the traditional scheme of a well-made play. Arrival and departure from the very same room, the nursery, frame the two other acts: the outdoor idyll of act 2 and the dance in act 3. Act 3 is the turning point of the action: Lopahin appears and announces, somewhat shamefacedly, that he has bought the estate. The orchard was lost from the very beginning—there is no real struggle to prevent its sale—but still the news of Lopahin's purchase is a surprise as he had no intention of buying it but did so only when during the auction sale a rival seemed to have a chance of acquiring it. A leading action runs its course, and one may even argue, many—too many—subplots crisscross each other: the shy and awkward love affair of the student Trofimov and the gay daughter Anya; the love triangle among the three dependents, Yepihodov, the unlucky clerk, Dunyasha, the silly chambermaid, and Yasha, the conceited and insolent footman. Varya, the practical, spinsterish stepdaughter, has her troubles with Lopahin, and Simeonov-Pishchik is beset by the same financial problems as the owners of the orchard and is rescued by the discovery of some white clay on his estate. The German governess Charlotta drifts around alluding to her obscure origins and past. There are undeveloped references to events preceding the action on stage: the lover in Paris, the drowned boy Grisha, but there is no revelation of the past as in Ibsen, no mystery, no intrigue.

While the events on the stage follow each other naturally, though hardly always in a logical, causal order, a symbolic device is used conspicuously: In act 2 after a pause, "suddenly a distant sound is heard, coming from the sky as it were, the sound of a snapping string, mournfully dying away." It occurs again at the very end of the play followed by "the stroke of an ax felling a tree far away in the orchard." An attempt is made to explain this sound at its first occurrence as a bucket's fall in a faraway pit, or as the cries of a heron or an owl, but the effect is weird and even supernatural; it establishes an ominous mood. Even the orchard carries more than its obvious meaning: It is white, drowned in blossoms when the party arrives in the spring; it is bare and desolate in the autumn when the axes are heard cutting it down. "The old bark on the trees gleams faintly, and the cherry trees seem to be dreaming of things that happened a hundred, two hundred years ago and to be tormented by painful visions," declaims Trofimov, defining his feeling for the orchard as a symbol of repression and serfdom. For Lubov Ranevskaya it is an image of her lost innocence and of the happier past, while Lopahin sees it only as an investment. It seems to draw together the meaning of the play.

But what is this meaning? Can we even decide whether it is a tragedy or a comedy? It has been commonly seen as the tragedy of the downfall of the Russian aristocracy (or more correctly, the landed gentry) victimized by the newly rich, upstart peasantry. One could see the play as depicting the defeat of a group of feckless people at the hand of a ruthless "developer" who destroys nature and natural beauty for profit. Or one can see it as prophesying, through the mouth of the student Trofimov, the approaching end of feudal Russia and the coming happier future. Soviet interpretations and performances lean that way.

Surely none of these interpretations can withstand inspection in the light of the actual play. They all run counter to Chekhov's professed intentions. He called the play a comedy. In a letter of September 15, 1903, he declared expressly that the play "has not turned out as drama but as comedy, in places even a farce" and a few days later (September 21, 1903) he wrote that "the whole play is gay and frivolous." Chekhov did not like the staging of the play at the Moscow Art Theater and complained of its tearful tone and its slow pace. He objected that "they obstinately call my play a drama in playbill and newspaper advertisements" while he had called it a comedy (April 10, 1904).

No doubt, there are many comical and even farcical characters and scenes in the play. Charlotta with her dog eating nuts, her card tricks, her ventriloquism, her disappearing acts, is a clownish figure. Gayev, the landowner, though "suave and elegant," is a windbag obsessed by his passion for billiards, constantly popping candy into his mouth, telling the waiters in a restaurant about the "decadents" in Paris. Yepihodov, the clerk, carries a revolver and, threatening suicide, asks foolishly whether you have read Buckle (the English historian) and complains of his ill-luck: a spider on his chest, a cockroach in his drink. Simeonov-Pishchik empties a whole bottle of pills, eats a gallon and a half of cucumbers, quotes Nietzsche supposedly recommending the forging of banknotes and, fat as he is, puffs and prances at the dance ordering the "cavaliers à genoux." Even the serious characters are put into ludicrous predicaments: Trofimov falls down the stairs; Lopahin, coming to announce the purchase of the estate, is almost hit with a stick by Varya (and was hit in the original version). Lopahin, teasing his intended Varya, "moos like a cow." The ball with the Jewish orchestra, the hunting for the galoshes, and the champagne drinking by Yasha in the last act have all a touch of absurdity. The grand speeches, Gayev's addresses to the bookcase and to nature or Trofimov's about "mankind going forward" and "All Russia is our orchard," are undercut by the contrast between the sentiment and the character: Gayev is callous and shallow, the "eternal student;" Trofimov never did a stitch of work. He is properly ridiculed and insulted by Lubov for his scant beard and his silly professions of being "above love." One can sympathize with Chekhov's irritation at the pervading gloom imposed by the Moscow production.

Still, I believe, we cannot, in spite of the author, completely dismiss the genuine pathos of the central situation and of the central figure, Lubov Ranevskaya. Whatever one may say about her recklessness in financial matters and her guilt in relation to her lover in France, we must feel her deep attachment to the house and the orchard, to the past and her lost innocence, clearly and unhumorously expressed in the first act on her arrival, again and again at the impending sale of the estate, and finally at the parting from her house: "Oh, my orchard—my dear, sweet, beautiful orchard! . . . My life, my youth, my happiness—Good-bye!" That Gayev, before the final parting, seems to have overcome the sense of loss and even looks forward to his job in the bank and that Lubov acknowledges that her "nerves are better" and that "she sleeps well" testifies to the indestructible spirit of brother and sister, but cannot minimize the sense of loss, the pathos of parting, the nostalgia for happier times. Nor is the conception of Lopahin simple. Chekhov emphasized, in a letter to Konstantin Stanislavsky who was to play the part, that "Lopahin is a decent person in the full sense of the word, and his bearing must be that of a completely dignified and intelligent man." He is not, he says, a profiteering peasant (*kulachok*, October 30, 1903). He admires Lubov and thinks of her with gratitude. He senses the beauty of the poppies in his fields. Even the scene of the abortive encounter with Varya at the end has its quiet pathos in spite of all its awkwardness and the comic touches such as the reference to the broken thermometer. Firs, the old valet, aged eighty-six, may be grotesque in his deafness and his nostalgia for the good old days of serdom, but the very last scene when we see him abandoned in the locked-up house surely concludes the play on a note of desolation and even despair.

Chekhov, we must conclude, achieved a highly original and even paradoxical blend of comedy and tragedy or rather of farce and pathos. The play gives a social picture firmly set in a specific historical time: the dissolution of the landed gentry, the rise of the peasant, the encroachment of the city; but it does not propound an obvious social thesis. Chekhov, in his tolerance and tenderness, in his distrust of ideologies and heroics, extends his sympathy to all his characters (with the exception of the crudely ambitious valet Yasha). The glow of his humanity, untrammeled by time and place, keeps *The Cherry Orchard* alive in quite different social and political conditions, as it has the universalizing power of great art.

Francis Fergusson, "*Ghosts* and *The Cherry Orchard*" in *The Idea of the Theatre* (1949), presents a sensitive comparison of the two plays. Beverly Hahn, *Chekhov: A Study of Major Stories and Plays* (1977), and Harvey Pitcher, *The Chekhov Play: A New Interpretation* (1973) have good chapters on *Cherry Orchard*. Ernest J. Simmons, *Chekhov: A Biography* (1962), is the fullest biography in English. L. J. Styan, *Chekhov in Performance: A Commentary on the Major Plays* (1971), contains a detailed analysis of *Cherry Orchard*. René and N. D. Wellek, eds., *Chekhov: New Perspectives* (1984), is a selection from modern criticism with a sketch, by the editor, of Chekhov criticism in England and America.

The Cherry Orchard[1]

Characters

LUBOV ANDREYEVNA RANEVSKAYA, *a landowner*
ANYA, *her seventeen-year-old daughter*
VARYA, *her adopted daughter, twenty-two years old*
LEONID ANDREYEVICH GAYEV, Mme. *Ranevskaya's brother*
YERMOLAY ALEXEYEVICH LOPAHIN, *a merchant*
PYOTR SERGEYEVICH TROFIMOV, a student
SIMEONOV-PISHCHIK, *a landowner*
CHARLOTTA IVANOVNA, *a governess*
SEMYON YEPIHODOV, *a clerk*
DUNYASHA, *a maid*
FIRS (pronounced *fierce*), *a manservant, aged eighty-seven*
YASHA, *a young valet*
A TRAMP
STATIONMASTER
POST OFFICE CLERK
GUESTS
SERVANTS

The action takes place on Mme. Ranevskaya's estate.

Act I

A room that is still called the nursery. One of the doors leads into ANYA's *room. Dawn, the sun will soon rise. It is May, the cherry trees are in blossom, but it is cold in the orchard; there is a morning frost. The windows are shut. Enter* DUNYASHA *with a candle, and* LOPAHIN *with a book in his hand.*

LOPAHIN. The train is in, thank God. What time is it?
DUNYASHA. Nearly two. [*Puts out the candle.*] It's light already.
LOPAHIN. How late is the train, anyway? Two hours at least. [*Yawns and stretches.*] I'm a fine one! What a fool I've made of myself! I came here on purpose to meet them at the station, and then I went and overslept. I fell asleep in my chair. How annoying! You might have waked me . . .

1. Translated by Avraham Yarmolinksy.

DUNYASHA. I thought you'd left. [*Listens.*] I think they're coming!

LOPAHIN. [*Listens.*] No, they've got to get the luggage, and one thing and another . . . [*Pause.*] Lubov Andreyevna spent five years abroad, I don't know what she'd like now. . . . She's a fine person—light-hearted, simple. I remember when I was a boy of fifteen, my poor father—he had a shop here in the village then—punched me in the face with his fist and made my nose bleed. We'd come into the yard, I don't know what for, and he'd had a drop too much. Lubov Andreyevna, I remember her as if it were yesterday—she was still young and so slim—led me to the wash-basin, in this very room . . . in the nursery. "Don't cry, little peasant," she said, "it'll heal in time for your wedding . . ." [*Pause.*] Little peasant . . . my father was a peasant, it's true, and here I am in a white waistcoat and yellow shoes. A pig in a pastry shop, you might say. It's true I'm rich. I've got a lot of money. . . . But when you look at it closely, I'm a peasant through and through. [*Pages the book.*] Here I've been reading this book and I didn't understand a word of it. . . . I was reading it and feel asleep . . . [*Pause.*]

DUNYASHA. And the dogs were awake all night, they feel that their masters are coming.

LOPAHIN. Dunyasha, why are you so—

DUNYASHA. My hands are trembling. I'm going to faint.

LOPAHIN. You're too soft, Dunyasha. You dress like a lady, and look at the way you do your hair. That's not right. One should remember one's place.

[*Enter* YEPIHODOV *with a bouquet; he wears a jacket and highly polished boots that squeak badly. He drops the bouquet as he comes in.*]

YEPIHODOV. [*Picking up the bouquet.*] Here, the gardener sent these, said you're to put them in the dining room. [*Hands the bouquet to* DUNYASHA.]

LOPAHIN. And bring me some kvass.

DUNYASHA. Yes, sir. [*Exits.*]

YEPIHODOV. There's a frost this morning—three degrees below—and yet the cherries are all in blossom. I cannot approve of our climate. [*Sighs.*] I cannot. Our climate does not activate properly. And, Yermolay Alexeyevich, allow me to make a further remark. The other day I bought myself a pair of boots, and I make bold to assure you, they squeak so that it is really intolerable. What should I grease them with?

LOPAHIN. Oh, get out! I'm fed up with you.

YEPIHODOV. Every day I meet with misfortune. And I don't complain, I've got used to it, I even smile.

[DUNYASHA *enters, hands* LOPAHIN *the kvass.*]

YEPIHODOV. I am leaving. [*Stumbles against a chair, which falls over.*]

There! [*Triumphantly, as it were.*] There again, you see what sort of circumstance, pardon the expression. . . . It is absolutely phenomenal! [*Exits.*]

DUNYASHA. You know, Yermolay Alexeyevich, I must tell you, Yepihodov has proposed to me.

LOPAHIN. Ah!

DUNYASHA. I simply don't know . . . he's a quiet man, but sometimes when he starts talking, you can't make out what he means. He speaks nicely—and it's touching—but you can't undersand it. I sort of like him though, and he is crazy about me. He's an unlucky man . . . every day something happens to him. They tease him about it here . . . they call him, Two-and-Twenty Troubles.

LOPAHIN. [*Listening.*] There! I think they're coming.

DUNYASHA. They *are* coming! What's the matter with me? I feel cold all over.

LOPAHIN. They really are coming. Let's go and meet them. Will she recognize me? We haven't seen each other for five years.

DUNYASHA. [*In a flutter.*] I'm going to faint this minute. . . . Oh, I'm going to faint!

[*Two carriages are heard driving up to the house.* LOPAHIN *and* DUNYASHA *go out quickly. The stage is left empty. There is a noise in the adjoining rooms.* FIRS, *who had driven to the station to meet* LUBOV ANDREYEVNA RANEVSKAYA, *crosses the stage hurriedly, leaning on a stick. He is wearing an old-fashioned livery and a tall hat. He mutters to himself indistinctly. The hubbub offstage increases. A* VOICE: "Come, let's go this way."
Enter LUBOV ANDREYEVNA, ANYA, *and* CHARLOTTA IVANOVNA *with a pet dog on a leash, all in traveling dresses;* VARYA, *wearing a coat and kerchief;* GAYEV, SIMEONOV-PISHCHIK, LOPAHIN, DUNYASHA *with a bag and an umbrella, servants with luggage. All walk across the room.*]

ANYA: Let's go this way. Do you remember what room this is, Mamma?

MME. RANEVSKAYA. [*Joyfully, through her tears.*] The nursery!

VARYA. How cold it is! My hands are numb. [*To* MME. RANEVSKAYA.] Your rooms are just the same as they were, Mamma, the white one and the violet.

MME. RANEVSKAYA. The nursery! My darling, lovely room! I slept here when I was a child . . . [*Cries.*] And here I am, like a child again! [*Kisses her brother and* VARYA, *and then her brother again.*] Varya's just the same as ever, like a nun. And I recognized Dunyasha. [*Kisses* DUNYASHA.]

GAYEV. The train was two hours late. What do you think of that? What a way to manage things!

CHARLOTTA. [*To* PISHCHIK.] My dog eats nuts, too.

PISHCHIK. [*In amazement.*] You don't say!

[*All go out, except* ANYA *and* DUNYASHA.]

DUNYASHA. We've been waiting for you for hours. [*Takes* ANYA's *hat and coat.*]

ANYA. I didn't sleep on the train for four nights and now I'm frozen . . .

DUNYASHA. It was Lent when you left; there was snow and frost, and now . . . My darling! [*Laughs and kisses her.*] I have been waiting for you, my sweet, my darling! But I must tell you something . . . I can't put it off another minute . . .

ANYA. [*Listlessly.*] What now?

DUNYASHA. The clerk, Yephihodov, proposed to me, just after Easter.

ANYA. There you are, at it again . . . [*Straightening her hair.*] I've lost all my hairpins . . . [*She is staggering with exhaustion.*]

DUNYASHA. Really, I don't know what to think. He loves me—he loves me so!

ANYA. [*Looking toward the door of her room, tenderly.*] My own room, my windows, just as though I'd never been away. I'm home! Tomorrow morning I'll get up and run into the orchard. Oh, if I could only get some sleep. I didn't close my eyes during the whole journey—I was so anxious.

DUNYASHA. Pyotr Sergeyevich came the day before yesterday.

ANYA. [*Joyfully.*] Petya!

DUNYASHA. He's asleep in the bathhouse. He has settled there. He said he was afraid of being in the way. [*Looks at her watch.*] I should wake him, but Miss Varya told me not to. "Don't you wake him," she said.

[*Enter* VARYA *with a bunch of keys at her belt.*]

VARYA. Dunyasha, coffee, and be quick. . . . Mamma's asking for coffee.

DUNYASHA. In a minute. [*Exits.*]

VARYA. Well, thank God, you've come. You're home again. [*Fondling* ANYA.] My darling is here again. My pretty one is back.

ANYA. Oh, what I've been through!

VARYA. I can imagine.

ANYA. When we left, it was Holy Week, it was cold then, and all the way Charlotta chattered and did her tricks. Why did you have to saddle me with Charlotta?

VARYA. You couldn't have travelled all alone, darling—at seventeen!

ANYA. We got to Paris, it was cold there, snowing. My French is dreadful. Mamma lived on the fifth floor; I went up there, and found all kinds of Frenchmen, ladies, an old priest with a book. The place was full of tobacco smoke, and so bleak. Suddenly I felt sorry for Mamma, so sorry, I took her head in my arms and hugged her and couldn't let go of her. Afterward Mamma kept fondling me and crying . . .

VARYA. [*Through tears.*] Don't speak of it . . . don't.

ANYA. She had already sold her villa at Mentone, she had nothing left, nothing. I hadn't a kopeck left either, we had only just enough to get home. And Mamma wouldn't understand! When we had dinner at the stations, she always ordered the most expensive dishes, and tipped the waiters a whole ruble. Charlotta, too. And Yasha kept ordering, too—it was simply awful. You know Yasha's Mamma's footman now, we brought him here with us.

VARYA. Yes, I've seen the blackguard.

ANYA. Well, tell me—have you paid the interest?

VARYA. How could we?

ANYA. Good heavens, good heavens!

VARYA. In August the estate will be put up for sale.

ANYA. My God!

LOPAHIN. [*Peeps in at the door and bleats*]. Meh-h-h. [*Disappears.*]

VARYA. [*Through tears*]. What I couldn't do to him! [*Shakes her fist threateningly.*]

ANYA. [*Embracing* VARYA, *gently.*] Varya, has he proposed to you? [VARYA *shakes her head.*] But he loves you. Why don't you come to an undersatanding? What are you waiting for?

VARYA. Oh, I don't think anything will ever come of it. He's too busy, he has no time for me . . . pays no attention to me. I've washed my hands of him—I can't bear the sight of him. They all talk about our getting married, they all congratulate me—and all the time there's really nothing to it—it's all like a dream. [*In another tone.*] You have a new brooch—like a bee.

ANYA. [*Sadly.*] Mamma bought it. [*She goes into her own room and speaks gaily like a child.*] And you know, in Paris I went up in a balloon.

VARYA. My darling's home, my pretty one is back! [DUNYASHA *returns with the coffeepot and prepares coffee.* VARYA *stands at the door of* ANYA's *room.*] All day long, darling, as I go about the house, I keep dreaming. If only we could marry you off to a rich man, I should feel at ease. Then I would go into a convent, and afterward to Kiev, to Moscow . . . I would spend my life going from one holy place to another . . . I'd go on and on. . . . What a blessing that would be!

ANYA. The birds are singing in the orchard. What time is it?

VARYA. It must be after two. Time you were asleep, darling. [*Goes into* ANYA's *room.*] What a blessing that would be!

[YASHA *enters with a plaid and a traveling bag, crosses the stage.*]

YASHA. [*Finically.*] May I pass this way, please?

DUNYASHA. A person could hardly recognize you, Yasha. Your stay abroad has certainly done wonders for you.

YASHA. Hm-m . . . and who are you?

DUNYASHA. When you went away I was that high—[*Indicating with her hand.*] I'm Dunyasha—Fyodor Kozoyedev's daughter. Don't you remember?

YASHA. Hm! What a peach! [*He looks round and embraces her. She cries out and drops a saucer.* YASHA *leaves quickly.*]

VARYA. [*In the doorway, in a tone of annoyance.*] What's going on here?

DUNYASHA. [*Through tears.*] I've broken a saucer.

VARYA. Well, that's good luck.

ANYA. [*Coming out of her room.*] We ought to warn Mamma that Petya's here.

VARYA. I left orders not to wake him.

ANYA. [*Musingly.*] Six years ago father died. A month later brother Grisha was drowned in the river. . . . Such a pretty little boy he was—only seven. It was more than Mamma could bear, so she went away, went away without looking back . . . [*Shudders.*] How well I understand her, if she only knew! [*Pause.*] And Petya Trofimov was Grisha's tutor, he may remind her of it all . . .

[*Enter* FIRS, *wearing a jacket and a white waistcoat. He goes up to the coffeepot.*]

FIRS. [*Anxiously.*] The mistress will have her coffee here. [*Puts on white gloves.*] Is the coffee ready? [*Sternly, to* DUNYASHA.] Here, you! And where's the cream?

DUNYASHA. Oh, my God! [*Exits quickly.*]

FIRS. [*Fussing over the coffeepot.*] Hah! the addlehead! [*Mutters to himself.*] Home from Paris. And the old master used to go to Paris too . . . by carriage. [*Laughs.*]

VARYA. What is it, Firs?

FIRS. What is your pleasure, Miss? [*Joyfully.*] My mistress has come home, and I've seen her at last! Now I can die. [*Weeps with joy.*]

[*Enter* MME. RANEVSKAYA, GAYEV, *and* SIMEONOV-PISHCHIK. *The latter is wearing a tight-waisted, pleated coat of fine cloth, and full trousers.* GAYEV, *as he comes in, goes through the motions of a billiard player with his arms and body.*]

MME. RANEVSKAYA. Let's see, how does it go? Yellow ball in the corner! Bank shot in the side pocket!

GAYEV. I'll tip it in the corner! There was a time, Sister, when you and I used to sleep in this very room and now I'm fifty-one, strange as it may seem.

LOPAHIN. Yes, time flies.

GAYEV. Who?

LOPAHIN. I say, time flies.

GAYEV. It smells of patchouli here.

ANYA. I'm going to bed. Good night, Mamma. [*Kisses her mother.*]

MME. RANEVSKAYA: My darling child! [*Kisses her hands.*] Are you happy to be home? I can't come to my senses.

ANYA. Good night, Uncle.

GAYEV. [*Kissing her face and hands.*] God bless you, how like your
mother you are! [*To his sister.*] At her age, Luba, you were just
like her.

> [ANYA *shakes hands with* LOPAHIN *and* PISHCHIK, *then goes out,
> shutting the door behind her.*]

MME. RANEVSKAYA. She's very tired.

PISHCHIK. Well, it was a long journey.

VARYA. [*To* LOPAHIN *and* PISHCHIK.] How about it, gentlemen? It's
past two o'clock—isn't it time for you to go?

MME. RANEVSKAYA. [*Laughs.*] You're just the same as ever, Varya.
[*Draws her close and kisses her.*] I'll have my coffee and then we'll
all go. [FIRS *puts a small cushion under her feet.*] Thank you, my
dear. I've got used to coffee. I drink it day and night. Thanks, my
dear old man. [*Kisses him.*]

VARYA. I'd better see if all the luggage has been brought in. [*Exits.*]

MME. RANEVSKAYA. Can it really be I sitting here? [*Laughs.*] I feel
like dancing, waving my arms about. [*Covers her face with her
hands.*] But maybe I am dreaming! God knows I love my country,
I love it tenderly; I couldn't look out of the window in the train, I
kept crying so. [*Through tears.*] But I must have my coffee. Thank
you, Firs, thank you, dear old man. I'm so happy that you're still
alive.

FIRS. Day before yesterday.

GAYEV. He's hard of hearing.

LOPAHIN. I must go soon, I'm leaving for Kharkov about five o'clock.
How annoying! I'd like to have a good look at you, talk to you.
. . . You're just as splendid as ever.

PISHCHIK. [*Breathing heavily.*] She's even better-looking. . . . Dressed
in the latest Paris fashion. . . . Perish my carriage and all its four
wheels. . . .

LOPAHIN. Your brother, Leonid Andreyevich, says I'm a vulgarian
and an exploiter. But it's all the same to me—let him talk. I only
want you to trust me as you used to. I want you to look at me with
your touching, wonderful eyes, as you used to. Dear God! My
father was a serf of your father's and grandfather's, but you, you
yourself, did so much for me once . . . so much . . . that I've
forgotten all about that; I love you as though you were my sister—
even more.

MME. RANEVSKAYA. I can't sit still, I simply can't. [*Jumps up and
walks about in violent agitation.*] This joy is too much for me.
. . . . Laugh at me, I'm silly! My own darling bookcase! My darling table! [*Kisses it.*]

GAYEV. While you were away, nurse died.

MME. RANEVSKAYA. [*Sits down and takes her coffee.*] Yes, God rest her soul; they wrote me about it.

GAYEV. And Anastasy is dead. Petrushka Kossoy has left me and has gone into town to work for the police inspector. [*Takes a box of sweets out of his pocket and begins to suck one.*]

PISHCHIK. My daughter Dashenka sends her regards.

LOPAHIN. I'd like to tell you something very pleasant—cheering. [*Glancing at his watch.*] I am leaving directly. There isn't much time to talk. But I will put it in a few words. As you know, your cherry orchard is to be sold to pay your debts. The sale is to be on the twenty-second of August; but don't you worry, my dear, you may sleep in peace; there is a way out. Here is my plan. Give me your attention! Your estate is only fifteen miles from the town; the railway runs close by it; and if the cherry orchard and the land along the riverbank were cut up into lots and these leased for summer cottages, you would have an income of at least 25,000 rubles a year out of it.

GAYEV. Excuse me. . . . What nonsense.

MME. RANEVSKAYA. I don't quite understand you, Yermolay Alexeyevich.

LOPAHIN. You will get an annual rent of at least ten rubles per acre, and if you advertise at once, I'll give you any guarantee you like that you won't have a square foot of ground left by autumn, all the lots will be snapped up. In short, congratulations, you're saved. The location is splendid—by that deep river. . . . Only, of course, the ground must be cleared . . . all the old buildings, for instance, must be torn down, and this house, too, which is useless, and, of course, the old cherry orchard must be cut down.

MME. RANEVSKAYA. Cut down? My dear, forgive me, but you don't know what you're talking about. If there's one thing that's interesting—indeed, remarkable—in the whole province, it's precisely our cherry orchard.

LOPAHIN. The only remarkable thing about this orchard is that it's a very large one. There's a crop of cherries every other year, and you can't do anything with them; no one buys them.

GAYEV. This orchard is even mentioned in the encyclopedia.

LOPAHIN. [*Glancing at his watch.*] If we can't think of a way out, if we don't come to a decision, on the twenty-second of August the cherry orchard and the whole estate will be sold at auction. Make up your minds! There's no other way out—I swear. None, none.

FIRS. In the old days, forty or fifty years ago, the cherries were dried, soaked, pickled, and made into jam, and we used to—

GAYEV. Keep still, Firs.

FIRS. And the dried cherries would be shipped by the cartload. It meant a lot of money! And in those days the dried cherries were soft and juicy, sweet, fragrant. . . . They knew the way to do it, then.

MME. RANEVSKAYA. And why don't they do it that way now?

FIRS. They've forgotten. Nobody remembers it.

PISHCHIK. [*To* MME. RANEVSKAYA.] What's doing in Paris? Eh? Did you eat frogs there?

MME. RANEVSKAYA. I ate crocodiles.

PISHCHIK. Just imagine!

LOPAHIN. There used to be only landowners and peasants in the country, but now these summer people have appeared on the scene. . . . All the towns, even the small ones, are surrounded by these summer cottages; and in another twenty years, no doubt, the summer population will have grown enormously. Now the summer resident only drinks tea on his porch, but maybe he'll take to working his acre, too, and then your cherry orchard will be a rich, happy, luxuriant place.

GAYEV. [*Indignantly.*] Poppycock!

[*Enter* VARYA *and* YASHA.]

VARYA. There are two telegrams for you, Mamma dear. [*Picks a key from the bunch at her belt and noisily opens an old-fashioned bookcase.*] Here they are.

MME. RANEVSKAYA. They're from Paris. [*Tears them up without reading them.*] I'm through with Paris.

GAYEV. Do you know, Luba, how old this bookcase is? Last week I pulled out the bottom drawer and there I found the date burnt in it. It was made exactly a hundred years ago. Think of that! We could celebrate its centenary. True, it's an inanimate object, but nevertheless, a bookcase . . .

PISHCHIK. [*Amazed.*] A hundred years! Just imagine!

GAYEV. Yes. [*Tapping it.*] That's something. . . . Dear, honored bookcase, hail to you who for more than a century have served the glorious ideals of goodness and justice! Your silent summons to fruitful toil has never weakened in all those hundred years [*through tears*], sustaining, through successive generations of our family, courage and faith in a better future, and fostering in us ideals of goodness and social consciousness. . . . [*Pauses.*]

LOPAHIN. Yes . . .

MME. RANEVSKAYA. You haven't changed a bit, Leonid.

GAYEV. [*Somewhat embarrassed.*] I'll play it off the red in the corner! Tip it in the side pocket!

LOPAHIN. [*Looking at his watch.*] Well, it's time for me to go . . .

YASHA. [*Handing pillbox to* MME. RANEVSKAYA.] Perhaps you'll take your pills now.

PISHCHIK. One shouldn't take medicines, dearest lady, they do neither harm nor good. . . . Give them here, my valued friend. [*Takes the pillbox, pours the pills into his palm, blows on them, puts them in his mouth, and washes them down with some kvass.*] There!

MME. RANEVSKAYA. [*Frightened.*] You must be mad!

PISHCHIK. I've taken all the pills.

LOPAHIN. What a glutton!

[*All laugh.*]

FIRS. The gentleman visited us in Easter week, ate half a bucket of pickles, he did . . . [*Mumbles.*]

MME. RANEVSKAYA. What's he saying?

VARYA. He's been mumbling like that for the last three years—we're used to it.

YASHA. His declining years!

[CHARLOTTA IVANOVNA, *very thin, tightly laced, dressed in white, a lorgnette at her waist, crosses the stage.*]

LOPAHIN. Forgive me, Charlotta Ivanovna, I've not had time to greet you. [*Tries to kiss her hand.*]

CHARLOTTA. [*Pulling away her hand.*] If I let you kiss my hand, you'll be wanting to kiss my elbow next, and then my shoulder.

LOPAHIN. I've no luck today. [*All laugh.*] Charlotta Ivanovna, show us a trick.

MME. RANEVSKAYA. Yes, Charlotta, do a trick for us.

CHARLOTTA. I don't see the need. I want to sleep. *Exits.*]

LOPAHIN. In three weeks we'll meet again. [*Kisses* MME. RANEVSKAYA'*s hand.*] Good-bye till then. Time's up. [*To* GAYEV.] Bye-bye. [*Kisses* PISHCHIK.] Bye-bye. [*Shakes hands with* VARYA, *then with* FIRS *and* YASHA.] I hate to leave. [*To* MME. RANEVSKAYA.] If you make up your mind about the cottages, let me know; I'll get you a loan of 50,000 rubles. Think it over seriously.

VARYA. [*Crossly.*] Will you never go!

LOPAHIN. I'm going, I'm going. [*Exits.*]

GAYEV. The vulgarian. But, excuse me . . . Varya's going to marry him, he's Varya's fiancé.

VARYA. You talk too much, Uncle.

MME. RANEVSKAYA. Well, Varya, it would make me happy. He's a good man.

PISHCHIK. Yes, one must admit, he's a most estimable man. And my Dashenka . . . she too says that . . . she says . . . lots of things. [*Snores; but wakes up at once.*] All the same, my valued friend, could you oblige me . . . with a loan of 240 rubles? I must pay the interest on the mortgage tomorrow.

VARYA. [*Alarmed.*] We can't, we can't!

MME. RANEVSKAYA. I really haven't any money.

PISHCHIK. It'll turn up. [*Laughs.*] I never lose hope, I thought everything was lost, that I was done for, when lo and behold, the railway ran through my land . . . and I was paid for it. . . . And something else will turn up again, if not today, then tomorrow . . . Dashenka will win two hundred thousand . . . she's got a lottery ticket.

MME. RANEVSKAYA. I've had my coffee, now let's go to bed.

FIRS. [*Brushes off* GAYEV; *admonishingly.*] You've got the wrong trousers on again. What am I to do with you?

VARYA. [*Softly.*] Anya's asleep. [*Gently opens the window.*] The sun's up now, it's not a bit cold. Look, Mamma dear, what wonderful trees. And heavens, what air! The starlings are singing!

GAYEV. [*Opens the other window.*] The orchard is all white. You've not forgotten it? Luba? That's the long alley that runs straight, straight as an arrow; how it shines on moonlight nights, do you remember? You've not forgotten?

MME. RANEVSKAYA. [*Looking out of the window into the orchard.*] Oh, my childhood, my innocent childhood. I used to sleep in this nursery—I used to look out into the orchard, happiness waked with me every morning, the orchard was just the same then . . . nothing has changed. [*Laughs with joy.*] All, all white! Oh, my orchard! After the dark, rainy autumn and the cold winter, you are young again, and full of happiness, the heavenly angels have not left you. . . . If I could free my chest and my shoulders from this rock that weighs on me, if I could only forget the past!

GAYEV. Yes, and the orchard will be sold to pay our debts, strange as it may seem.

MME. RANEVSKAYA. Look! There is our poor mother walking in the orchard . . . all in white . . . [*Laughs with joy.*] It is she!

GAYEV. Where?

VARYA. What are you saying, Mamma dear!

MME. RANEVSKAYA. There's no one there, I just imagined it. To the right, where the path turns toward the arbor, there's a little white tree, leaning over, that looks like a woman . . .

[TROFIMOV *enters, wearing a shabby student's uniform and spectacles.*]

MME. RANEVSKAYA. What an amazing orchard! White masses of blossom, the blue sky . . .

TROFIMOV. Lubov Andreyevna! [*She looks round at him.*] I just want to pay my respects to you, then I'll leave at once. [*Kisses her hand ardently.*] I was told to wait until morning, but I hadn't the patience . . . [MME. RANEVSKAYA *looks at him, perplexed.*]

VARYA. [*Through tears.*] This is Petya Trofimov.

TROFIMOV. Petya Trofimov, formerly your Grisha's tutor. . . . Can I have changed so much? [MME. RANEVSKAYA *embraces him and weeps quietly.*]

GAYEV. [*Embarrassed.*] Don't, don't, Luba.

VARYA. [*Crying.*] I told you, Petya, to wait until tomorrow.

MME. RANEVSKAYA. My Grisha . . . my little boy . . . Grisha . . . my son.

VARYA. What can one do, Mamma dear, it's God's will.

TROFIMOV. [*Softly, through tears.*] There . . . there.

MME. RANEVSKAYA. [*Weeping quietly.*] My little boy was lost . . . drowned. Why? Why, my friend? [*More quietly.*] Anya's asleep in there, and here I am talking so loudly . . . making all this noise. . . . But tell me, Petya, why do you look so badly? Why have you aged so?

TROFIMOV. A mangy master, a peasant woman in the train called me.

MME. RANEVSKAYA. You were just a boy then, a dear little student, and now your hair's thin—and you're wearing glasses! Is it possible you're still a student? [*Goes toward the door.*]

TROFIMOV. I suppose I'm a perpetual student.

MME. RANEVSKAYA. [*Kisses her brother, then* VARYA.] Now, go to bed. . . . You have aged, too, Leonid.

PISHCHIK. [*Follows her.*] So now we turn in. Oh, my gout! I'm staying the night here . . . Lubov Andreyevna, my angel, tomorrow morning . . . I do need 240 rubles.

GAYEV. He keeps at it.

PISHCHIK. I'll pay it back, dear . . . it's a trifling sum.

MME. RANEVSKAYA. All right, Leonid will give it to you. Give it to him, Leonid.

GAYEV. Me give it to him! That's a good one!

MME. RANEVSKAYA. It can't be helped. Give it to him! He needs it. He'll pay it back.

> [MME. RANEVSKAYA, TROFIMOV, PISHCHIK, *and* FIRS *go out;* GAYEV, VARYA, *and* YASHA *remain.*]

GAYEV. Sister hasn't got out of the habit of throwing money around. [*To* YASHA.] Go away, my good fellow, you smell of the barnyard.

YASHA. [*With a grin.*] And you, Leonid Andreyevich, are just the same as ever.

GAYEV. Who? [*To* VARYA.] What did he say?

VARYA. [*To* YASHA.] Your mother's come from the village; she's been sitting in the servants' room since yesterday, waiting to see you.

YASHA. Botheration!

VARYA. You should be ashamed of yourself!

YASHA. She's all I needed! She could have come tomorrow. [*Exits.*]

VARYA. Mamma is just the same as ever; she hasn't changed a bit. If she had her own way, she'd keep nothing for herself.

GAYEV. Yes . . . [*Pauses.*] If a great many remedies are offered for some disease, it means it is incurable; I keep thinking and racking my brains; I have many remedies, ever so many, and that really means more. It would be fine if we came in for a legacy; it would be fine if we married off our Anya to a very rich man; or we might go to Yaroslavl and try our luck with our aunt, the Countess. She's very rich, you know . . .

VARYA. [*Weeping.*] If only God would help us!

GAYEV. Stop bawling. Aunt's very rich, but she doesn't like us. In the first place, Sister married a lawyer who was no nobleman . . . [ANYA *appears in the doorway.*] She married beneath her, and it can't be said that her behavior has been very exemplary. She's good, kind, sweet, and I love her, but no matter what extenuating circumstances you may adduce, there's no denying that she has no morals. You sense it in her least gesture.

VARYA. [*In a whisper.*] Anya's in the doorway.

GAYEV. Who? [*Pauses.*] It's queer, something got into my right eye— my eyes are going back on me. . . . And on Thursday, when I was in the circuit court—

[*Enter* ANYA.]

VARYA. Why aren't you asleep, Anya?

ANYA. I can't get to sleep, I just can't.

GAYEV. My little pet! [*Kisses* ANYA's *face and hands.*] My child! [*Weeps.*] You are not my niece, you're my angel! You're everything to me. Believe me, believe—

ANYA. I believe you, Uncle. Everyone loves you and respects you . . . but, Uncle dear, you must keep still. . . . You must. What were you saying just now about my mother? Your own sister? What made you say that?

GAYEV. Yes, yes . . . [*Covers his face with her hand.*] Really, that was awful! Good God! Heaven help me! Just now I made a speech to the bookcase . . . so stupid! And only after I was through, I saw how stupid it was.

VARYA. It's true, Uncle dear, you ought to keep still. Just don't talk, that's all.

ANYA. If you could only keep still, it would make things easier for you, too.

GAYEV. I'll keep still. [*Kisses* ANYA's *and* VARYA's *hands.*] I will. But now about business. On Thursday I was in court; well, there were a number of us there, and we began talking of one thing and another, and this and that, and do you know, I believe it will be possible to raise a loan on a promissory note to pay the interest at the bank.

VARYA. If only God would help us!

GAYEV. On Tuesday I'll go and see about it again. [*To* VARYA.] Stop bawling. [*To* ANYA.] Your mamma will talk to Lopahin, and he, of course, will not refuse her . . . and as soon as you're rested, you'll go to Yaroslavl to the Countess, your great-aunt. So we'll be working in three directions at once, and the thing is in the bag.

We'll pay the interest—I'm sure of it. [*Puts a candy in his mouth.*] I swear on my honor, I swear by anything you like, the estate shan't be sold. [*Excitedly.*] I swear by my own happiness! Here's my hand on it, you can call me a swindler and a scoundrel if I let it come to an auction! I swear by my whole being.

ANYA. [*Relieved and quite happy again.*] How good you are, Uncle, and how clever! [*Embraces him.*] Now I'm at peace, quite at peace, I'm happy.

[*Enter* FIRS.]

FIRS. [*Reproachfully.*] Leonid Andreyevich, have you no fear of God? When are you going to bed?

GAYEV. Directly, directly. Go away, Firs, I'll . . . yes, I will undress myself. Now, children, 'nightie-'nightie. We'll consider details tomorrow, but now go to sleep. [*Kisses* ANYA *and* VARYA.] I am a man of the eighties; they have nothing good to say of that period nowadays. Nevertheless, in the course of my life, I have suffered not a little for my convictions. It's not for nothing that the peasant loves me; one should know the peasant; one should know from which—

ANYA. There you go again, Uncle.

VARYA. Uncle dear, be quiet.

FIRS. [*Angrily.*] Leonid Andreyevich!

GAYEV. I'm coming, I'm coming! Go to bed! Double bank shot in the side pocket! Here goes a clean shot . . .

[*Exits,* FIRS *hobbling after him.*]

ANYA. I am at peace now. I don't want to go to Yaroslavl—I don't like my great-aunt, but still, I am at peace, thanks to Uncle. [*Sits down.*]

VARYA. We must get some sleep. I'm going now. While you were away, something unpleasant happened. In the old servants' quarters, there are only the old people as you know; Yefim, Polya, Yevstigney, and Karp, too. They began letting all sorts of rascals in to spend the night. . . . I didn't say anything. Then I heard they'd been spreading a report that I gave them nothing but dried peas to eat—out of stinginess, you know . . . and it was all Yevstigney's doing. . . . All right, I thought, if that's how it is, I thought, just wait. I sent for Yevstigney . . . [*Yawns.*] He comes. . . . "How's this, Yevstigney?" I say, "You fool . . ." [*Looking at* ANYA.] Anichka! [*Pauses.*] She's asleep. [*Puts her arm around* ANYA.] Come to your little bed. . . . Come . . . [*Leads her.*] My darling has fallen asleep. . . . Come.

[*They go out. Far away beyond the orchard, a shepherd is piping.* TROFIMOV *crosses the stage and, seeing* VARYA *and* ANYA, *stands still.*]

VARYA. Sh! She's asleep . . . asleep. . . . Come, darling.

ANYA. [*Softly, half-asleep.*] I'm so tired. Those bells . . . Uncle . . . dear. . . . Mamma and Uncle . . .

VARYA. Come, my precious, come along. [*They go into* ANYA'S *room.*]

TROFIMOV. [*With emotion.*] My sunshine, my spring!

Act II

A meadow. An old, long-abandoned, lopsided little chapel; near it a well, large slabs, which had apparently once served as tomb-stones, and an old bench. In the background the road to the Gayev estate. To one side poplars loom darkly, where the cherry orchard begins. In the distance a row of telegraph poles, and far off, on the horizon, the faint outline of a large city which is seen only in fine, clear weather. The sun will soon be setting. CHARLOTTA, YASHA, *and* DUNYASHA *are seated on the bench.* YEPIHODOV *stands near and plays a guitar. All are pensive.* CHARLOTTA *wears an old peaked cap. She has taken a gun from her shoulder and is straightening the buckle on the strap.*

CHARLOTTA. [*Musingly.*] I haven't a real passport, I don't know how old I am, and I always feel that I am very young. When I was a little girl, my father and mother used to go from fair to fair and give performances, very good ones. And I used to do the *salto mortale,* and all sorts of other tricks. And when papa and mamma died, a German lady adopted me and began to educate me. Very good. I grew up and became a governess. But where I come from and who am I, I don't know. . . . Who were my parents? Perhaps they weren't even married. . . . I don't know . . . [*Takes a cucumber out of her pocket and eats it.*] I don't know a thing. [*Pause.*] One wants so much to talk, and there isn't anyone to talk to. . . . I haven't anybody.

YEPIHODOV. [*Plays the guitar and sings.*] "What care I for the jarring world? What's friend or foe to me? . . ." How agreeable it is to play the mandolin.

DUNYASHA. That's a guitar, not a mandolin. [*Looks in a hand mirror and powders her face.*]

YEPIHODOV. To a madman in love it's a mandolin. [*Sings.*] "Would that the heart were warmed by the fire of mutual love!" [YASHA *joins in.*]

CHARLOTTA. How abominably these people sing. Pfui! Like jackals!

DUNYASHA. [*To* YASHA.] How wonderful it must be though to have stayed abroad!

YASHA. Ah, yes, of course, I cannot but agree with you there.
     [*Yawns and lights a cigar.*]

YEPIHODOV. Naturally. Abroad, everything has long since achieved full perplexion.

YASHA. That goes without saying.

YEPIHODOV. I'm a cultivated man, I read all kinds of remarkable books. And yet I can never make out what direction I should take, what is it that I want, properly speaking. Should I live, or should I shoot myself, properly speaking? Nevertheless, I always carry a revolver about me. . . . Here it is . . . [*Shows revolver.*]

CHARLOTTA. I've finished. I'm going. [*Puts the gun over her shoulder.*] You are a very clever man, Yepihodov, and a very terrible one; women must be crazy about you. Br-r-r! [*Starts to go.*] These clever men are all so stupid; there's no one for me to talk to . . . always alone, alone, I haven't a soul . . . and who I am, and why I am, nobody knows. [*Exits unhurriedly.*]

YEPIHODOV. Properly speaking and letting other subjects alone, I must say regarding myself, among other things, that fate treats me mercifully, like a storm treats a small boat. If I am mistaken, let us say, why then do I wake up this morning, and there on my chest is a spider of enormous dimensions . . . like this . . . [*Indicates with both hands.*] Again, I take up a pitcher of kvass to have a drink, and in it there is something unseemly to the highest degree, something like a cockroach. [*Pause.*] Have you read Buckle?[2] [*Pause.*] I wish to have a word with you, Avdotya Fyodorovna, if I may trouble you.

DUNYASHA. Well, go ahead.

YEPIHODOV. I wish to speak with you alone. [*Sighs.*]

DUNYASHA. [*Embarassed.*] Very well. Only first bring me my little cape. You'll fine it near the wardrobe. It's rather damp here.

YEPIHODOV. Certainly, ma'am; I will fetch it, ma'am. Now I know what to do with my revolver. [*Takes the guitar and goes offplaying it.*]

YASHA. Two-and-Twenty Troubles! An awful fool, between you and me. [*Yawns.*]

DUNYASHA. I hope to God he doesn't shoot himself! [*Pause.*] I've become so nervous, I'm always fretting. I was still a little girl when I was taken into the big house, I am quite unused to the simple life now, and my hands are white, as white as a lady's. I've become so soft, so delicate, so refined, I'm afraid of everything. It's so terrifying; and if you deceive me, Yasha, I don't know what will happen to my nerves. [YASHA *kisses her.*]

YASHA. You're a peach! Of course, a girl should never forget herself; and what I dislike more than anything is when a girl don't behave properly.

---

2. Henry Thomas Buckle (1821–1862) wrote a *History of Civilization in England* (1857–1861) which was considered daringly materialistic and free thinking.

DUNYASHA. I've fallen passionately in love with you; you're educated—you have something to say about everything. [*Pause.*]

YASHA. [*Yawns.*] Yes, ma'am. Now the way I look at it, if a girl loves someone, it means she is immoral. [*Pause.*] It's agreeable smoking a cigar in the fresh air. [*Listens.*] Someone's coming this way. . . . It's our madam and the others. [DUNYASHA *embraces him impulsively.*] You go home, as though you'd been to the river to bathe; go to the little path, or else they'll run into you and suspect me of having arranged to meet you here. I can't stand that sort of thing.

DUNYASHA. [*Coughing softly.*] Your cigar's made my head ache. [*Exits.* YASHA *remains standing near the chapel. Enter* MME. RANEVSKAYA, GAYEV, *and* LOPAHIN.]

LOPAHIN. You must make up your mind once and for all—there's no time to lose. It's quite a simple question, you know. Do you agree to lease your land for summer cottages or not? Answer in one word, yes or no; only one word!

MME. RANEVSKAYA. Who's been smoking such abominable cigars here? [*Sits down.*]

GAYEV. Now that the railway line is so near, it's made things very convenient. [*Sits down.*] Here we've been able to have lunch in town. Yellow ball in the side pocket! I feel like going into the house and playing just one game.

MME. RANEVSKAYA. You can do that later.

LOPAHIN. Only one word! [*Imploringly.*] Do give me an answer!

GAYEV. [Yawning.] Who?

MME. RANEVSKAYA. [*Looks into her purse.*] Yesterday I had a lot of money and now my purse is almost empty. My poor Varya tries to economize by feeding us just milk soup; in the kitchen the old people get nothing but dried peas to eat, while I squander money thoughtlessly. [*Drops the purse, scattering gold pieces.*] You see, there they go . . . [*Shows vexation.*]

YASHA. Allow me—I'll pick them up. [*Picks up the money.*]

MME. RANEVSKAYA. Be so kind. Yasha. And why did I go to lunch in town? That nasty restaurant, with its music and the tablecloth smelling of soap. . . . Why drink so much, Leonid? Why eat so much? Why talk so much? Today again you talked a lot, and all so inappropriately about the seventies, about the decadents.[3] And to whom? Talking to waiters about decadents!

LOPAHIN. Yes.

GAYEV. [*Waving his hand.*] I'm incorrigible; that's obvious.[*Irritably, to* YASHA.] Why do you keep dancing about in front of me?

YASHA. [*Laughs.*] I can't hear your voice without laughing—

---

3. A group of French poets (Mallarmé is today the most famous) of the 1880's were labeled "decadents" by their enemies and sometimes adopted the name themselves, proud of their refinement and sensitivity.

GAYEV. Either he or I—

MME. RANEVSKAYA. Go away, Yasha; run along.

YASHA. [*Handing* MME. RANEVSKAYA *her purse.*] I'm going at once. [*Hardly able to suppress his laughter.*] This minute. [*Exits.*]

LOPAHIN. That rich man, Deriganov, wants to buy your estate. They say he's coming to the auction himself.

MME. RANEVSKAYA. Where did you hear that?

LOPAHIN. That's what they are saying in town.

GAYEV. Our aunt in Yaroslavl has promised to help, but when she will send the money, and how much, no one knows.

LOPAHIN. How much will she send? A hundred thousand? Two hundred?

MME. RANEVSKAYA. Oh, well, ten or fifteen thousand; and we'll have to be grateful for that.

LOPAHIN. Forgive me, but such frivolous people as you are, so queer and unbusinesslike—I never met in my life. One tells you in plain language that your estate is up for sale, and you don't seem to take it in.

MME. RANEVSKAYA. What are we to do? Tell us what to do.

LOPAHIN. I do tell you, every day; every day I say the same thing! You must lease the cherry orchard and the land for summer cottages, you must do it and as soon as possible—right away. The auction is close at hand. Please understand! Once you've decided to have the cottages, you can raise as much money as you like, and you're saved.

MME. RANEVSKAYA. Cottages—summer people—forgive me, but it's all so vulgar.

GAYEV. I agree with you absolutely.

LOPAHIN. I shall either burst into tears or scream or faint! I can't stand it! You've worn me out! [*To* GAYEV.] You're an old woman!

GAYEV. Who?

LOPAHIN. An old woman! [*Gets up to go.*]

MME. RANEVSKAYA. [*Alarmed.*] No, don't go! Please stay, I beg you, my dear. Perhaps we shall think of something.

LOPAHIN. What is there to think of?

MME. RANEVSKAYA. Don't go, I beg you. With you here it's more cheerful anyway. [*Pause.*] I keep expecting something to happen, it's as though the house were going to crash about our ears.

GAYEV. [*In deep thought.*] Bank shot in the corner. . . . Three cushions in the side pocket. . . .

MME. RANEVSKAYA. We have been great sinners . . .

LOPAHIN. What sins could you have committed?

GAYEV. [*Putting a candy in his mouth.*] They say I've eaten up my fortune in candy! [*Laughs.*]

MME. RANEVSKAYA. Oh, my sins! I've squandered money away reck-

lessly, like a lunatic, and I married a man who made nothing but
debts. My husband drank himself to death on champagne, he was
a terrific drinker. And then, to my sorrow, I fell in love with
another man, and I lived with him. And just then—that was my
first punishment—a blow on the head: my little boy was drowned
here in the river. And I went abroad, went away forever . . . never
to come back, never to see this river again . . . I closed my eyes
and ran, out of my mind. . . . But he followed me, pitiless, brutal. I bought a villa near Mentone, because he fell ill there; and
for three years, day and night, I knew no peace, no rest. The sick
man wore me out, he sucked my soul dry. Then last year, when
the villa was sold to pay my debts, I went to Paris, and there he
robbed me, abandoned me, took up with another woman, I tried
to poison myself—it was stupid, so shameful—and then suddenly
I felt drawn back to Russia, back, to my own country, to my little
girl. [*Wipes her tears away.*] Lord, Lord! Be merciful, forgive me
my sins—don't punish me anymore! [*Takes a telegram out of her
pocket.*] This came today from Paris—he begs me to forgive him,
implores me to go back . . . [*Tears up the telegram.*] Do I hear
music? [*Listens.*]

GAYEV. That's our famous Jewish band, you remember? Four violins, a flute, and a double bass.

MME. RANEVSKAYA. Does it still exist? We ought to send for them
some evening and have a party.

LOPAHIN. [*Listens.*] I don't hear anything. [*Hums softly.*] "The Germans for a fee will Frenchify a Russian." [*Laughs.*] I saw a play at
the theater yesterday—awfully funny.

MME. RANEVSKAYA. There was probably nothing funny about it. You
shouldn't go to see plays, you should look at yourselves more often.
How drab your lives are—how full of unnecessary talk.

LOPAHIN. That's true; come to think of it, we do live like fools. [*Pause.*]
My pop was a peasant, an idiot; he understood nothing, never
taught me anything, all he did was beat me when he was drunk,
and always with a stick. Fundamentally, I'm just the same kind of
blockhead and idiot. I was never taught anything—I have a terrible handwriting. I write so that I feel ashamed before people, like
a pig.

MME. RANEVSKAYA. You should get married, my friend.

LOPAHIN. Yes . . . that's true.

MME. RANEVSKAYA. To our Varya, she's a good girl.

LOPAHIN. Yes.

MME. RANEVSKAYA. She's a girl who comes of simple people, she
works all day long; and above all, she loves you. Besides, you've
liked her for a long time now.

LOPAHIN. Well, I've nothing against it. She's a good girl. [*Pause.*]

GAYEV. I've been offered a place in the bank—6,000 a year. Have you heard?

MME. RANEVSKAYA. You're not up to it. Stay where you are.

[FIRS *enters, carrying an overcoat.*]

FIRS. [*To* GAYEV.] Please put this on, sir, it's damp.

GAYEV. [*Putting it on.*] I'm fed up with you, brother.

FIRS. Never mind. This morning you drove off without saying a word. [*Looks him over.*]

MME. RANEVSKAYA. How you've aged, Firs.

FIRS. I beg your pardon?

LOPAHIN. The lady says you've aged.

FIRS. I've lived a long time; they were arranging my wedding and your papa wasn't born yet. [*Laughs.*] When freedom[4] came I was already head footman. I wouldn't consent to be set free then; I stayed on with the master . . . [*Pause.*] I remember they were all very happy, but why they were happy, they didn't know themselves.

LOPAHIN. It was fine in the old days! At least there was flogging!

FIRS. [*Not hearing.*] Of course. The peasants kept to the masters, the masters kept to the peasants; but now they've all gone their own ways, and there's no making out anything.

GAYEV. Be quiet, Firs. I must go to town tomorrow. They've promised to introduce me to a general who might let us have a loan.

LOPAHIN. Nothing will come of that. You won't even be able to pay the interest, you can be certain of that.

MME. RANEVSKAYA. He's raving, there isn't any general. [*Enter* TROFIMOV, ANYA, *and* VARYA.]

GAYEV. Here come our young people.

ANYA. There's Mamma, on the bench.

MME. RANEVSKAYA. [*Tenderly.*] Come here, come along, my darlings. [*Embraces* ANYA *and* VARYA.] If you only knew how I love you both! Sit beside me—there, like that. [*All sit down.*]

LOPAHIN. Our perpetual student is always with the young ladies.

TROFIMOV. That's not any of your business.

LOPAHIN. He'll soon be fifty, and he's still a student!

TROFIMOV. Stop your silly jokes.

LOPAHIN. What are you so cross about, you queer bird?

TROFIMOV. Oh, leave me alone.

LOPAHIN. [*Laughs.*] Allow me to ask you, what do you think of me?

TROFIMOV. What I think of you, Yermolay Alexeyevich, is this: you are a rich man who will soon be a millionaire. Well, just as a beast of prey, which devours everything that comes in its way, is

4. Tsar Alexander II (ruled 1855–1881) emancipated the serfs in 1861.

necessary for the process of metabolism to go on, so you, too, are necessary. [*All laugh.*]

VARYA. Better tell us something about the planets, Petya.

MME. RANEVSKAYA. No, let's go on with yesterday's conversation.

TROFIMOV. What was it about?

GAYEV. About man's pride.

TROFIMOV. Yesterday we talked a long time, but we came to no conclusion. There is something mystical about man's pride in your sense of the word. Perhaps you're right, from your own point of view. But if you reason simply, without going into subtleties, then what call is there for pride? Is there any sense in it, if man is so poor a thing physiologically, and if, in the great majority of cases, he is coarse, stupid, profoundly unhappy? We should stop admiring ourselves. We should work, and that's all.

GAYEV. You die, anyway.

TROFIMOV. Who knows? And what does it mean—to die? Perhaps man has a hundred senses, and at his death only the five we know perish, while the other ninety-five remain alive.

MME. RANEVSKAYA. How clever you are, Petya!

LOPAHIN. [*Ironically.*] Awfully clever!

TROFIMOV. Mankind goes forward, developing its powers. Everything that is now unattainable for it will one day come within man's reach and be clear to him; only we must work, helping with all our might those who seek the truth. Here among us in Russia only the very few work as yet. The great majority of the intelligentsia, as far as I can see, seek nothing, do nothing, are totally unfit for work of any kind. They call themselves the intelligentsia, yet they are uncivil to their servants, treat the peasants like animals, are poor students, never read anything serious, do absolutely nothing at all, only talk about science, and have little appreciation of the arts. They are all solemn, have grim faces, they all philosophize and talk of weighty matters. And meanwhile the vast majority of us, ninety-nine out of a hundred, live like savages. At the least provocation—a punch in the jaw, and curses. They eat disgustingly, sleep in filth and stuffiness, bedbugs everywhere, stench and damp and moral slovenliness. And obviously, the only purpose of all our fine talk is to hoodwink ourselves and others. Show me where the public nurseries are that we've heard so much about, and the libraries. We read about them in novels, but in reality they don't exist, there is nothing but dirt, vulgarity, and Asiatic backwardness. I don't like very solemn faces, I'm afraid of them, I'm afraid of serious conversations. We'd do better to keep quiet for a while.

LOPAHIN. Do you know, I get up at five o'clock in the morning, and

I work from morning till night; and I'm always handling money, my own and other people's, and I see what people around me are really like. You've only to start doing anything to see how few honest, decent people there are. Sometimes when I lie awake at night, I think: "Oh, Lord, thou hast given us immense forests, boundless fields, the widest horizons, and living in their midst, we ourselves ought really to be giants."

MME. RANEVSKAYA. Now you want giants! They're only good in fairy tales; otherwise they're frightening.

[YEPIHODOV *crosses the stage at the rear, playing the guitar.*]

MME. RANEVSKAYA. [*Pensively*] There goes Yepihodov.

GAYEV. Ladies and gentlemen, the sun has set.

TROFIMOV. Yes.

GAYEV. [*In a low voice, declaiming as it were.*] Oh, Nature, wondrous Nature, you shine with eternal radiance, beautiful and indifferent! You, whom we call our mother, unite within yourself life and death! You animate and destroy!

VARYA. [*Pleadingly.*] Uncle dear!

ANYA. Uncle, again!

TROFIMOV. You'd better bank the yellow ball in the side pocket.

GAYEV. I'm silent, I'm silent . . .

[*All sit plunged in thought. Stillness reigns. Only* FIRS's *muttering is audible. Suddenly a distant sound is heard, coming from the sky as it were, the sound of a snapping string, mournfully dying away.*]

MME. RANEVSKAYA. What was that?

LOPAHIN. I don't know. Somewhere far away, in the pits, a bucket's broken loose; but somewhere very far away.

GAYEV. Or it might be some sort of bird, perhaps a heron.

TROFIMOV. Or an owl . . .

MME. RANEVSKAYA. [*Shudders.*] It's weird, somehow. [*Pause.*]

FIRS. Before the calamity the same thing happened—the owl screeched, and the samovar hummed all the time.

GAYEV. Before what calamity?

FIRS. Before the Freedom. [*Pause.*]

MME. RANEVSKAYA. Come, my friends, let's be going. It's getting dark. [*To* ANYA.] You have tears in your eyes. What is it, my little one? [*Embraces her.*]

ANYA. I don't know, Mamma; it's nothing.

TROFIMOV. Somebody's coming.

[*A* TRAMP *appears, wearing a shabby white cap and an overcoat. He is slightly drunk.*]

TRAMP. Allow me to inquire, will this short cut take me to the station?

GAYEV. It will. Just follow that road.

TRAMP. My heartfelt thanks. [*Coughing.*] The weather is glorious. [*Recites.*] "My brother, my suffering brother. . . . Go down to the Volga![5] Whose groans . . . ?' [*To* VARYA.] Mademoiselle, won't you spare 30 kopecks for a hungry Russian?

VARYA. [*Frightened, cries out.*]

LOPAHIN. [*Angrily.*] Even panhandling has its proprieties.

MME. RANEVSKAYA. [*Scared.*] Here, take this. [*Fumbles in her purse.*] I haven't any silver . . . never mind, here's a gold piece.

TRAMP. My heartfelt thanks. [*Exits. Laughter.*]

VARYA. [*Frightened.*] I'm leaving. I'm leaving. . . . Oh, Mamma dearest, at home the servants have nothing to eat, and you gave him a gold piece!

MME. RANEVSKAYA. What are you going to do with me? I'm such a fool. When we get home, I'll give you everything I have. Yermo-lay Alexeyevich, you'll lend me some more . . .

LOPAHIN. Yes, ma'am.

MME. RANEVSKAYA. Come, ladies and gentlemen, it's time to be going. Oh! Varya, we've settled all about your marriage. Congratula-tions!

VARYA. [*Through tears.*] Really, Mamma, that's not a joking matter.

LOPAHIN. "Aurelia, get thee to a nunnery, go . . ."

GAYEV. And do you know, my hands are trembling: I haven't played billiards in a long time.

LOPAHIN. "Aurelia, nymph, in your orisons, remember me!"[6]

MME. RANEVSKAYA. Let's go, it's almost suppertime.

VARYA. He frightened me! My heart's pounding.

LOPAHIN. Let me remind you, ladies and gentlemen, on the twenty-second of August the cherry orchard will be up for sale. Think about that! Think!

    [*All except* TROFIMOV *and* ANYA *go out.*]

ANYA. [*Laughs.*] I'm grateful to that tramp, he frightened Varya and so we're alone.

TROFIMOV. Varya's afraid we'll fall in love with each other all of a sudden. She hasn't left us alone for days. Her narrow mind can't grasp that we're above love. To avoid the petty and illusory, every-thing that prevents us from being free and happy—that is the goal and meaning of our life. Forward! Do not fall behind, friends!

ANYA. [*Strikes her hands together.*] How well you speak! [*Pause.*] It's wonderful here today.

TROFIMOV. Yes, the weather's glorious.

ANYA. What have you done to me, Petya? Why don't I love the

---

5. Lines from poems by Semyon Nadson (1862–1878) and Nikolay Nekrasov (1821–1878).
6. Lopahin makes comic use of Hamlet's meeting with Ophelia (in the Russian distorted to "Okh-melia"). Hamlet, seeing her approaching, says: "Nymph, in thy orisons / Be all my sins remem-bered" (III: 1, 89–90), and later, suspecting her of spying for her father, sends her off with "Get thee to a nunnery" (1. 121).

cherry orchard as I used to? I loved it so tenderly. It seemed to me there was no spot on earth lovelier than our orchard.

TROFIMOV. All Russia is our orchard. Our land is vast and beautiful, there are many wonderful places in it. [*Pause.*] Think of it, Anya, your grandfather, your great-grandfather and all your ancestors were serf owners, owners of living souls, and aren't human beings looking at you from every tree in the orchard, from every leaf, from every trunk? Don't you hear voices? Oh, it's terrifying! Your orchard is a fearful place, and when you pass through it in the evening or at night, the old bark on the trees gleams faintly, and the cherry trees seem to be dreaming of things that happened a hundred, two hundred years ago and to be tormented by painful visions. What is there to say? We're at least two hundred years behind, we've really achieved nothing yet, we have no definite attitude to the past, we only philosophize, complain of the blues, or drink vodka. It's all so clear: in order to live in the present, we should first redeem our past, finish with it, and we can expiate it only by suffering, only by extraordinary, unceasing labor. Realize that, Anya.

ANYA. The house in which we live has long ceased to be our own, and I will leave it, I give you my word.

TROFIMOV. If you have the keys, fling them into the well and go away. Be free as the wind.

ANYA. [*In ecstasy.*] How well you put that!

TROFIMOV. Believe me, Anya, believe me! I'm not yet thirty, I'm young, I'm still a student—but I've already suffered so much. In winter I'm hungry, sick, harassed, poor as a beggar, and where hasn't Fate driven me? Where haven't I been? And yet always, every moment of the day and night, my soul is filled with inexplicable premonitions. . . . I have a premonition of happiness, Anya. . . . I see it already!

ANYA. [*Pensively.*] The moon is rising.

[YEPIHODOV *is heard playing the same mournful tune on the guitar. The moon rises. Somewhere near the poplars* VARYA *is looking for* ANYA *and calling, "Anya, where are you?"*]

TROFIMOV. Yes, the moon is rising. [*Pause.*] There it is, happiness, it's approaching, it's coming nearer and nearer, I can already hear its footsteps. And if we don't see it, if we don't know it, what does it matter? Others will!

VARYA'S VOICE. Anya! Where are you?

TROFIMOV. That Varya again! [*Angrily.*] It's revolting!

ANYA. Never mind, let's go down to the river. It's lovely there.

TROFIMOV. Come on. [*They go.*]

VARYA'S VOICE. Anya! Anya!

Act III

*A drawing room separated by an arch from a ballroom. Evening.
Chandelier burning. The Jewish band is heard playing in the anteroom. In the ballroom they are dancing the Grand Rond.* PISCHIK *is
heard calling,* "Promenade à une paire." PISCHIK *and* CHARLOTTA,
TROFIMOV *and* MME. RANEVSKAYA, ANYA *and the* POST OFFICE CLERK,
VARYA *and the* STATIONMASTER, *and others enter the drawing room
in couples.* DUNYASHA *is in the last couple.* VARYA *weeps quietly,
wiping her tears as she dances. All parade through drawing room.*
PISCHICK *calling,* "Grand rond, balancez!" *and* "Les cavaliers à genoux et remerciez vos dames!" FIRS, *wearing a dress coat, brings in
soda water on a tray.* PISCHIK *and* TROFIMOV *enter the drawing room.*

PISCHIK. I have high blood pressure; I've already had two strokes.
Dancing's hard work for me; but as they say, "If you run with the
pack, you can bark or not, but at least wag your tail." Still, I'm as
strong as a horse. My late lamented father, who would have his
joke, God rest his soul, used to say, talking about our origin, that
the ancient line of the Simeonov-Pischiks was descended from the
very horse that Caligula had made a senator. [*Sits down.*] But the
trouble is, I have no money. A hungry dog believes in nothing
but meat. [*Snores, and wakes up at once.*] It's the same with me—
I can think of nothing but money.
TROFIMOV. You know, there *is* something equine about your figure.
PISHCHIK. Well, a horse is a fine animal—one can sell a horse.
  [*Sound of billards being played in an adjoining room.* VARYA
  appears in the archway.]
TROFIMOV. [*Teasing her.*] Madam Lopahina! Madam Lopahina!
VARYA. [*Angrily.*] Mangy master!
TROFIMOV. Yes, I am a mangy master and I'm proud of it.
VARYA. [*Reflecting bitterly.*] Here we've hired musicians, and what
shall we pay them with? [*Exits.*]
TROFIMOV. [*To* PISHCHIK.] If the energy you have spent during your
lifetime looking for money to pay interest had gone into some-
thing else, in the end you could have turned the world upside
down.
PISHCHIK. Nietzsche, the philosopher, the greatest, most famous of
men, that colossal intellect, says in his works that it is permissible
to forge banknotes.
TROFIMOV. Have you read Nietzsche?
PISHCHIK. Well . . . Dashenka told me. . . . And now I've got to the
point where forging banknotes is the only way out for me. . . .
The day after tomorrow I have to pay 310 rubles—I already have
130 . . . [*Feels in his pockets. In alarm.*] The money's gone! I've

lost my money! [*Through tears.*] Where's my money? [*Joyfully.*]
Here it is! Inside the lining . . . I'm all in a sweat . . .
    [*Enter* MME. RANEVSKAYA *and* CHARLOTTA.]

MME.. RANEVSKAYA. [*Hums the "Lezginka."*] Why isn't Leonid back
yet? What is he doing in town? [*To* DUNYASHA.] Dunyasha, offer
the musicians tea.

TROFIMOV. The auction hasn't taken place, most likely.

MME. RANEVSKAYA. It's the wrong time to have the band, and the
wrong time to give a dance. Well, never mind. [*Sits down and
hums softly.*]

CHARLOTTA. [*Hands* PISHCHIK *a pack of cards.*] Here is a pack of cards.
Think of any card you like.

PISHCHIK. I've thought of one.

CHARLOTTA. Shuffle the pack now. That's right. Give it here, my
dear Mr. Pishchik. *Eins, zwei, drei!*[7] Now look for it—it's in your
side pocket.

PISHCHIK. [*Taking the card out of his pocket.*] The eight of spades!
Perfectly right! Just imagine!

CHARLOTTA. [*Holding the pack of cards in her hands. To* TROFIMOV.]
Quickly, name the top card.

TROFIMOV. Well, let's see—the queen of spades.

CHARLOTTA. Right! [*To* PISHCHIK.] Now name the top card.

PISHCHIK. The ace of hearts.

CHARLOTTA. Right! [*Claps her hands and the pack of cards disappears.*] Ah, what lovely weather it is today! [*A mysterious feminine voice, which seems to come from under the floor, answers
her:* "Oh, yes, it's magnificent weather, madam."] You are my
best ideal. [*Voice:* "And I find you pleasing too, madam."]

STATIONMASTER.[*Applauding.*] The lady ventriloquist, bravo!

PISHCHIK. [*Amazed.*] Just imagine! Enchanting Charlotta Ivanovna,
I'm simply in love with you.

CHARLOTTA. In love? [*Shrugs her shoulders.*] Are you capable of love?
Guter Mensch, aber schlechter Musikant![8]

TROFIMOV. [*Claps* PISHCHIK *on the shoulder.*] You old horse, you!

CHARLOTTA. Attention please! One more trick! [*Takes a plaid from a
chair.*] Here is a very good plaid; I want to sell it. [*Shaking it out.*]
Does anyone want to buy it?

PISHCHIK. [*In amazement.*] Just imagine!

CHARLOTTA. *Eins, zwei, drei!* [*Raises the plaid quickly, behind it
stands* ANYA. *She curtsies, runs to her mother, embraces her, and*

---

7. German for "one, two, three."   8. "A good man, but a bad musician," usually quoted in
the plural: "*Gute Leute, schlechte Musikanten.*" It comes from *Das Buch le Grand* (1826) of
German poet Heinrich Heine (1799–1856). Here it suggests that Pishchik may be a good man
but a bad lover.

runs back into the ballroom, amid general enthusiasm.]

MME. RANEVSKAYA. [*Applauds.*] Bravo! Bravo!

CHARLOTTA. Now again! *Eins, zwei, drei!* [*Lifts the plaid; behind it
stands* VARYA, *bowing.*]

PISHCHIK. [*In amazement.*] Just imagine!

CHARLOTTA. [*Throws the plaid at* PISHCHIK, *curtsies, and runs into
the ballroom.*]

PISHCHIK. [*Running after her.*] The rascal! What a woman, what a
woman! [*Exits.*]

MME. RANEVSKAYA. And Leonid still isn't here. What is he doing in
town so long? I don't understand. It must be all over by now.
Either the estate has been sold, or the auction hasn't taken place.
Why keep us in suspense so long?

VARYA. [*Trying to console her.*] Uncle's bought it, I feel sure of that.

TROFIMOV. [*Mockingly.*] Oh, yes!

VARYA. Great-aunt sent him an authorization to buy it in her name,
and to transfer the debt. She's doing it for Anya's sake. And I'm
sure that God will help us, and Uncle will buy it.

MME. RANEVSKAYA. Great-aunt sent fifteen thousand to buy the estate
in her name, she doesn't trust us, but that's not even enough to
pay the interest. [*Covers her face with her hands.*] Today my fate
will be decided, my fate—

TROFIMOV. [*Teasing* VARYA.] Madam Lopahina!

VARYA. [*Angrily.*] Perpetual student! Twice already you've been
expelled from the university.

MME. RANEVSKAYA. Why are you so cross, Varya? He's teasing you
about Lopahin. Well, what of it? If you want to marry Lopahin,
go ahead. He's a good man, and interesting; if you don't want to,
don't. Nobody's compelling you, my pet!

VARYA. Frankly, Mamma dear, I take this thing seriously; he's a good
man and I like him.

MME. RANEVSKAYA. All right then, marry him. I don't know what
you're waiting for.

VARYA. But, Mamma, I can't propose to him myself. For the last two
years, everyone's been talking to me about him—talking. But he
either keeps silent, or else cracks jokes. I understand; he's growing
rich, he's absorbed in business—he has no time for me. If I had
money, even a little, say, 100 rubles, I'd throw everything up and
go far away—I'd go into a nunnery.

TROFIMOV. What a blessing . . .

VARYA. A student ought to be intelligent. [*Softly, with tears in her
voice.*] How homely you've grown, Petya! How old you look! [*To*
MME. RANEVSKAYA, *with dry eyes.*] But I can't live without work,
Mamma dear; I must keep busy every minute.

[*Enter* YASHA.]

YASHA. [*Hardly restraining his laughter.*] Yepihodov has broken a
billiard cue! [*Exits.*]

VARYA. Why is Yepihodov here? Who allowed him to play billiards?
I don't understand these people! [*Exits.*]

MME. RANEVSKAYA. Don't tease her, Petya. She's unhappy enough
with that.

TROFIMOV. She bustles so—and meddles in other people's business.
All summer long she's given Anya and me no peace. She's afraid
of a love affair between us. What business is it of hers? Besides,
I've given no grounds for it, and I'm far from such vulgarity. We
are above love.

MME. RANEVSKAYA. And I suppose I'm beneath love? [*Anxiously.*]
What can be keeping Leonid? If I only knew whether the estate
has been sold or not. Such a calamity seems so incredible to me
that I don't know what to think—I feel lost. . . . I could scream.
. . . I could do something stupid. . . . Save me, Petya, tell me
something, talk to me!

TROFIMOV. Whether the estate is sold today or not, isn't it all one?
That's all done with long ago—there's no turning back, the path
is overgrown. Calm yourself, my dear. You mustn't deceive yourself. For once in your life you must face the truth.

MME. RANEVSKAYA. What truth? You can see the truth, you can tell
it from falsehood, but I seem to have lost my eyesight, I see nothing. You settle every great problem so boldly, but tell me, my dear
boy, isn't it because you're young, because you don't yet know
what one of your problems means in terms of suffering? You look
ahead fearlessly, but isn't it because you don't see and don't expect
anything dreadful, because life is still hidden from your young
eyes? You're bolder, more honest, more profound than we are,
but think hard, show just a bit of magnanimity, spare me. After
all, I was born here, my father and mother lived here, and my
grandfather; I love this house. Without the cherry orchard, my
life has no meaning for me, and if it really must be sold, then sell
me with the orchard. [*Embraces* TROFIMOV, *kisses him on the
forehead.*] My son was drowned here. [*Weeps.*] Pity me, you good,
kind fellow!

TROFIMOV. You know, I feel for you with all my heart.

MME. RANEVSKAYA. But that should have been said differently, so
differently! [*Takes out her handkerchief—a telegram falls on the
floor.*] My heart is so heavy today—you can't imagine! The noise
here upsets me—my inmost being trembles at every sound—I'm
shaking all over. But I can't go into my own room; I'm afraid to
be alone. Don't condemn me, Petya. . . . I love you as though
you were one of us, I would gladly let you marry Anya—I swear I

would—only, my dear boy, you must study—you must take your degree—you do nothing, you let yourself be tossed by Fate from place to place—it's so strange. It's true, isn't it? And you should do something about your beard, to make it grow somehow! [*Laughs.*] You're so funny!

TROFIMOV. [*Picks up the telegram.*] I've no wish to be a dandy.

MME. RANEVSKAYA. That's a telegram from Paris. I get one every day. One yesterday and one today. That savage is ill again—he's in trouble again. He begs forgiveness, implores me to go to him, and really I ought to go to Paris to be near him. Your face is stern, Petya; but what is there to do, my dear boy? What am I to do? He's ill, he's alone and unhappy, and who is to look after him, who is to keep him from doing the wrong thing, who is to give him his medicine on time? And why hide it or keep still about it—I love him! That's clear. I love him, love him! He's a millstone round my neck, he'll drag me to the bottom, but I love that stone, I can't live without it. [*Presses* TROFIMOV's *hand.*] Don't think badly of me. Petya, and don't say anything, don't say . . .

TROFIMOV. [*Through tears.*] Forgive me my frankness in heaven's name; but, you know, he robbed you!

MME. RANEVSKAYA. No, no, no, you mustn't say such things! [*Covers her ears.*]

TROFIMOV. But he's a scoundrel! You're the only one who doesn't know it. He's a petty scoundrel—a nonentity!

MME. RANEVSKAYA. [*Controlling her anger.*] You are twenty-six or twenty-seven years old, but you're still a schoolboy.

TROFIMOV. That may be.

MME. RANEVSKAYA. You should be a man at your age. You should understand people who love—and ought to be in love yourself. You ought to fall in love! [*Angrily.*] Yes, yes! And it's not purity in you, it's prudishness, you're simply a queer fish, a comical freak!

TROFIMOV. [*Horrified.*] What is she saying?

MME. RANEVSKAYA. "I am above love!" You're not above love, but simple, as our Firs says, you're an addlehead. At your age not to have a mistress!

TROFIMOV. [*Horrified.*] This is frightful! What is she saying! [*Goes rapidly into the ballroom, clutching his head.*] It's frightful—I can't stand it, I won't stay! [*Exits, but returns at once.*] All is over between us! [*Exits into anteroom.*]

MME. RANEVSKAYA. [*Shouts after him.*] Petya! Wait! You absurd fellow, I was joking. Petya!

[*Sound of somebody running quickly downstairs and suddenly falling down with a crash.* ANYA *and* VARYA *scream. Sound of laughter a moment later.*]

MME. RANEVSKAYA. What's happened?

    [ANYA *runs in.*]

ANYA.[*Laughing.*] Petya's fallen downstairs! [*Runs out.*]

MME. RANEVSKAYA. What a queer bird that Petya is!

    [STATIONMASTER, *standing in the middle of the ballroom, recites Alexey Tolstoy's "Magdalene,"[9] to which all listen, but after a few lines, the sound of a waltz is heard from the anteroom and the reading breaks off. All dance.* TROFIMOV, ANYA, VARYA *and* MME. RANEVSKAYA *enter from the anteroom.*]

MME. RANEVSKAYA. Petya, you pure soul, please forgive me. . . . Let's dance.

    [*Dances with* PETYA, ANYA *and* VARYA *dance.* FIRS *enters, puts his stick down by the side door.* YASHA *enters from the drawing room and watches the dancers.*]

YASHA. Well, Grandfather?

FIRS. I'm not feeling well. In the old days it was generals, barons, and admirals that were dancing at our balls, and now we have to send for the Post Office Clerk and the Stationmaster, and even they aren't too glad to come. I feel kind of shaky. The old master that's gone, their grandfather, dosed everyone with sealing wax, whatever ailed 'em. I've been taking sealing wax every day for twenty years or more. Perhaps that's what's kept me alive.

YASHA. I'm fed up with you, Grandpop. [*Yawns.*] It's time you croaked.

FIRS. Oh, you addlehead! [*Mumbles.*]

    [TROFIMOV *and* MME. RANEVSKAYA *dance from the ballroom into the drawing room.*]

MME. RANEVSKAYA. *Merci.* I'll sit down a while. [*Sits down.*] I'm tired.

    [*Enter* ANYA.]

ANYA. [*Excitedly.*] There was a man in the kitchen just now who said the cherry orchard was sold today.

MME. RANEVSKAYA. Sold to whom?

ANYA. He didn't say. He's gone. [*Dances off with* TROFIMOV.]

YASHA. It was some old man gabbing, a stranger.

FIRS. And Leonid Andreyevich isn't back yet, he hasn't come. And he's wearing his lightweight between-season overcoat; like enough, he'll catch cold. Ah, when they're young they're green.

MME. RANEVSKAYA. This is killing me. Go, Yasha, find out to whom it has been sold.

YASHA. But the old man left long ago. [*Laughs.*]

MME RANEVSKAYA. What are you laughing at? What are you pleased about?

---

9. Called "The Sinning Woman" in Russian, begins thus: "A bustling crowd with happy laughter, / with twanging lutes and clashing cymbals / with flowers and foliage all around / the colonnaded portico." Alexey Tolstoy (1817–1875) was a distant relative of Leo Tolstoy, popular in his time as a dramatist and poet.

YASHA. That Yepihodov is such a funny one. A funny fellow, Two-and-Twenty Troubles!

MME. RANEVSKAYA. Firs, if the estate is sold, where will you go?

FIRS. I'll go where you tell me.

MME. RANEVSKAYA. Why do you look like that? Are you ill? You ought to go to bed.

FIRS. Yes! [*With a snigger.*] Me go to bed, and who's to hand things round? Who's to see to things? I'm the only one in the whole house.

YASHA. [*To* MME. RANEVSKAYA.] Lubov Andreyevna, allow me to ask a favor of you, be so kind! If you go back to Paris, take me with you, I beg you. It's positively impossible for me to stay here. [*Looking around; sotto voce.*] What's the use of talking? You see for yourself, it's an uncivilized country, the people have no morals, and then the boredom! The food in the kitchen's revolting, and besides there's this Firs wanders about mumbling all sorts of inappropriate words. Take me with you, be so kind!

[*Enter* PISHCHIK.]

PISHCHIK. May I have the pleasure of a waltz with you, charming lady? [MME. RANEVSKAYA *accepts.*] All the same, enchanting lady, you must let me have 180 rubles. . . . You must let me have [*dancing*] just one hundred and eighty rubles. [*They pass into the ballroom.*]

YASHA. [*Hums softly.*] "Oh, wilt thou understand the tumult in my soul?"

[*In the ballroom a figure in a gray top hat and checked trousers is jumping about and waving its arms; shouts:* "Bravo, Charlotta Ivanovna!"]

DUNYASHA. [*Stopping to powder her face; to* FIRS.] The young miss has ordered me to dance. There are so many gentlemen and not enough ladies. But dancing makes me dizzy, my heart begins to beat fast, Firs Nikolayevich. The Post Office Clerk said something to me just now that quite took my breath away. [*Music stops.*]

FIRS. What did he say?

DUNYASHA. "You're like a flower," he said.

YASHA. [*Yawns.*] What ignorance. [*Exits.*]

DUNYASHA. "Like a flower!" I'm such a delicate girl. I simply adore pretty speeches.

FIRS. You'll come to a bad end.

[*Enter* YEPIHODOV.]

YEPIHODOV. [*To* DUNYASHA.] You have no wish to see me, Avdotya Fyodorovna . . . as though I was some sort of insect. [*Sighs.*] Ah, life!

DUNYASHA. What is it you want?

YEPIHODOV. Indubitably you may be right. [*Sighs.*] But of course, if one looks at it from the point of view, if I may be allowed to say so, and apologizing for my frankness, you have completely reduced me to a state of mind. I know my fate. Every day some calamity befalls me, and I grew used to it long ago, so that I look upon my fate with a smile. You gave me your word, and though I—

DUNYASHA. Let's talk about it later, please. But just now leave me alone, I am daydreaming. [*Plays with a fan.*]

YEPIHODOV. A misfortune befalls me every day; and if I may be allowed to say so, I merely smile, I even laugh.

[*Enter* VARYA.]

VARYA. [*To* YEPIHODOV.] Are you still here? What an impertinent fellow you are really! Run along, Dunyasha. [*To* YEPIHODOV.] Either you're playing billiards and breaking a cue, or you're wandering about the drawing room as though you were a guest.

YEPIHODOV. You cannot, permit me to remark, penalize me.

VARYA. I'm not penalizing you; I'm just telling you. You merely wander from place to place, and don't do your work. We keep you as a clerk, but heaven knows what for.

YEPIHODOV. [*Offended.*] Whether I work or whether I walk, whether I eat or whether I play billiards, is a matter to be discussed only by persons of understanding and of mature years.

VARYA. [*Enraged.*] You dare say that to me—you dare? You mean to say I've no understanding? Get out of here at once! This minute!

YEPIHODOV. [*Scared.*] I beg you to express yourself delicately.

VARYA. [*Beside herself.*] Clear out this minute! Out with you!

[YEPIHODOV *goes toward the door,* VARYA *following.*]

VARYA. Two-and-Twenty Troubles! Get out—don't let me set eyes on you again!

[*Exit* YEPIHODOV. *His voice is heard behind the door:* "I shall lodge a complaint against you!"]

VARYA. Oh, you're coming back? [*She seizes the stick left near door by* FIRS.] Well, come then . . . come . . . I'll show you. . . . Ah, you're coming? You're coming? . . . Come . . . [*Swings the stick just as* LOPAHIN *enters.*]

LOPAHIN. Thank you kindly.

VARYA. [*Angrily and mockingly.*] I'm sorry.

LOPAHIN. It's nothing. Thank you kindly for your charming reception.

VARYA. Don't mention it. [*Walks away, looks back and asks softly.*] I didn't hurt you, did I?

LOPAHIN. Oh, no, not at all. I shall have a large bump, though.

[*Voices from the ballroom:* "Lopahin is here! Lopahin!"] [*Enter* PISHCHIK.]

PISHCHIK. My eyes do see, my ears do hear! [*Kisses* LOPAHIN.] You smell of cognac, my dear friend. And we've been celebrating here, too.

[*Enter* MME. RANEVSKAYA.]

MME. RANEVSKAYA. Is that you, Yermolay Alexeyevich? What kept you so long? Where's Leonid?

LOPAHIN. Leonid Andreyevich arrived with me. He's coming.

MME. RANEVSKAYA. Well, what happened? Did the sale take place? Speak!

LOPAHIN. [*Embarrassed, fearful of revealing his joy.*] The sale was over at four o'clock. We missed the train—had to wait till half-past nine. [*Sighing heavily.*] Ugh. I'm a little dizzy.

[*Enter* GAYEV. *In his right hand he holds parcels, with his left he is wiping away his tears.*]

MME. RANEVSKAYA. Well, Leonid? What news? [*Impatiently, through tears.*] Be quick, for God's sake!

GAYEV. [*Not answering, simply waves his hand. Weeping, to* FIRS.] Here, take these; anchovies, Kerch herrings . . . I haven't eaten all day. What I've been through! [*The click of billiard balls comes through the open door of the billiard room and* YASHA's *voice is heard: "Seven and eighteen!"* GAYEV's *expression changes, he no longer weeps.*] I'm terribly tired. Firs, help me change. [*Exits, followed by* FIRS.]

PISHCHIK. How about the sale? Tell us what happened.

MME. RANEVSKAYA. Is the cherry orchard sold?

LOPAHIN. Sold.

MME. RANEVSKAYA: Who bought it?

LOPAHIN. I bought it.

[*Pause,* MME. RANEVSKAYA *is overcome. She would fall to the floor, were it not for the chair and table near which she stands.* VARYA *takes the keys from her belt, flings them on the floor in the middle of the drawing room and goes out.*]

LOPAHIN. I bought it. Wait a bit, ladies and gentlemen, please, my head is swimming, I can't talk. [*Laughs.*] We got to the auction and Deriganov was there already. Leonid Andreyevich had only 15,000 and straight off Deriganov bid 30,000 over and above the mortgage. I saw how the land lay, got into the fight, bid 40,000. He bid 45,000. I bid fifty-five. He kept adding five thousands, I ten. Well . . . it came to an end. I bid ninety above the mortgage and the estate was knocked down to me. Now the cherry orchard's mine! Mine! [*Laughs uproariously.*] Lord! God in Heaven! The cherry orchard's mine! Tell me that I'm drunk—out of my mind— that it's all a dream. [*Stamps his feet.*] Don't laugh at me! If my father and my grandfather could rise from their graves and see all that has happened—how their Yermolay, who used to be flogged, their half-literate Yermolay, who used to run about barefoot in winter, how that very Yermolay has bought the most magnificent estate in the world. I bought the estate where my father and grandfather were slaves, where they weren't even allowed to enter the kitchen. I am asleep—it's only a dream—I only imagine it. . . . It's the fruit of your imagination, wrapped in the darkness of the unknown! [*Picks up the keys, smiling genially.*] She threw down the keys, wants to show she's no longer mistress here. [*Jingles keys.*] Well, no matter. [*The band is warming up.*] Hey, musicians! Strike up! I want to hear you! Come, everybody, and see how Yermolay Lopahin will lay the ax to the cherry orchard and how the trees will fall to the ground. We will build summer cottages there, and our grandsons and great grandsons will see a new life here. Music! Strike up!

[*The band starts to play.* MME RANEVSKAYA *has sunk into a chair and is weeping bitterly.*]

LOPAHIN. [*Reproachfully.*] Why, why didn't you listen to me? My dear friend, my poor friend, you can't bring it back now. [*Tearfully.*] Oh, if only this were over quickly! Oh, if only our wretched, disordered life were changed!

PISHCHIK. [*Takes him by the arm; sotto voce.*] She's crying. Let's go into the ballroom. Let her be alone. Come. [*Takes his arm and leads him into the ballroom.*]

LOPAHIN. What's the matter? Musicians, play so I can hear you! Let me have things the way I want them.[*Ironically.*] Here comes the new master, the owner of the cherry orchard. [*Accidentally he trips over a little table, almost upsetting the candelabra.*] I can pay for everything. [*Exits with* PISHCHIK.]

[MME. RANEVSKAYA, *alone, sits huddled up, weeping bitterly. Music plays softly. Enter* ANYA *and* TROFIMOV *quickly.* ANYA *goes to her mother and falls on her knees before her.* TROFIMOV *stands in the doorway.*]

ANYA. Mamma, Mamma, you're crying! Dear, kind, good Mamma, my precious, I love you, I bless you! The cherry orchard is sold, it's gone, that's true, quite true. But don't cry, Mamma, life is still before you, you still have your kind, pure heart. Let us go, let us go away from here, darling. We will plant a new orchard, even more luxuriant than this one. You will see it, you will understand, and like the sun at evening, joy—deep, tranquil joy—will sink into your soul, and you will smile, Mamma. Come, darling, let us go.

Act IV

Scene as in Act I. No window curtains or pictures, only a little furniture, piled up in a corner, as if for sale. A sense of emptiness. Near the outer door and at the back, suitcases, bundles, etc., are piled up. A door open on the left and the voices of VARYA *and* ANYA *are heard.* LOPAHIN *stands waiting.* YASHA *holds a tray with glasses full of champagne.* YEPIHODOV *in the anteroom is tying up a box. Behind the scene a hum of voices: peasants have come to say good-bye. Voice of* GAYEV: "Thanks, brothers, thank you."

YASHA. The country folk have come to say good-bye. In my opinion, Yermolay Alexeyevich, they are kindly souls, but there's nothing in their heads.

    [*The hum dies away. Enter* MME. RANEVSKAYA *and* GAYEV. *She is not crying, but is pale, her face twitches and she cannot speak.*]

GAYEV. You gave them your purse, Luba. That won't do! That won't do!

MME. RANEVSKAYA. I couldn't help it! I couldn't! [*They go out.*]

LOPAHIN. [*Calls after them.*] Please, I beg you, have a glass at parting. I didn't think of bringing any champagne from town and at the station I could find only one bottle. Please, won't you? [*Pause.*] What's the matter, ladies and gentlemen, don't you want any? [*Moves away from the door.*] If I'd known, I wouldn't have bought it. Well, then I won't drink any, either. [YASHA *carefully sets the tray down on a chair.*] At least you have a glass, Yasha.

YASHA. Here's to the travelers! And good luck to those that stay! [*Drinks.*] This champagne isn't the real stuff, I can assure you.

LOPAHIN. Eight rubles a bottle. [*Pause.*] It's devilishly cold here.

YASHA. They didn't light the stoves today—it wasn't worth it, since we're leaving. [*Laughs.*]

LOPAHIN. Why are you laughing?

YASHA. It's just that I'm pleased.

LOPAHIN. It's October, yet it's as still and sunny as though it were summer. Good weather for building. [*Looks at his watch, and speaks off.*] Bear in mind, ladies and gentlemen, the train goes in forty-seven minutes, so you ought to start for the station in twenty minutes. Better hurry up!

    [*Enter* TROFIMOV, *wearing an overcoat.*]

TROFIMOV. I think it's time to start. The carriages are at the door. The devil only knows what's become of my rubbers; they've disappeared. [*Calling off.*] Anya! My rubbers are gone. I can't find them.

LOPAHIN. I've got to go to Kharkov. I'll take the same train you do. I'll spend the winter in Kharkov. I've been hanging round here with you, till I'm worn out with loafing. I can't live without work— I don't know what to do with my hands, they dangle as if they didn't belong to me.

TROFIMOV. Well, we'll soon be gone, then you can go on with your useful labors again.

LOPAHIN. Have a glass.

TROFIMOV. No, I won't.

LOPAHIN. So you're going to Moscow now?

TROFIMOV. Yes, I'll see them into town, and tomorrow I'll go on to Moscow.

LOPAHIN. Well, I'll wager the professors aren't giving any lectures, they're waiting for you to come.

TROFIMOV. That's none of your business.

LOPAHIN. Just how many years have you been at the university?

TROFIMOV. Can't you think of something new? Your joke's stale and flat. [*Looking for his rubbers.*] We'll probably never see each other again, so allow me to give you a piece of advice at parting: don't wave your hands about! Get out of the habit. And another thing: building bungalows, figuring that summer residents will eventually become small farmers, figuring like that is just another form of waving your hands about. . . . Never mind, I love you anyway; you have fine, delicate fingers, like an artist; you have a fine delicate soul.

LOPAHIN. [*Embracing him.*] Good-bye, my dear fellow. Thank you for everything. Let me give you some money for the journey, if you need it.

TROFIMOV. What for? I don't need it.

LOPAHIN. But you haven't any.

TROFIMOV. Yes, I have, thank you. I got some money for a translation—here it is in my pocket. [*Anxiously.*] But where are my rubbers?

VARYA. [*from the next room.*] Here! Take the nasty things. [*Flings a pair of rubbers onto the stage.*]

TROFIMOV. What are you so cross about, Varya? Hm . . . and these are not my rubbers.

LOPAHIN. I sowed three thousand acres of poppies in the spring, and now I've made 40,000 on them, clear profit; and when my poppies were in bloom, what a picture it was! So, as I say, I made 40,000; and I am offering you a loan because I can afford it. Why turn up your nose at it? I am a peasant—I speak bluntly.

TROFIMOV. Your father was a peasant, mine was a druggist—that proves absolutely nothing whatever. [LOPAHIN *takes out his wallet.*] Don't, put that away! If you were to offer me two hundred thousand, I wouldn't take it. I'm a free man. And everything that all of you, rich and poor alike, value so highly and hold so dear hasn't the slightest power over me. It's like so much fluff floating in the air. I can get on without you, I can pass you by, I'm strong and proud. Mankind is moving toward the highest truth, toward the highest happiness possible on earth, and I am in the front ranks.

LOPAHIN. Will you get there?

TROFIMOV. I will. [*Pause.*] I will get there, or I will show others the way to get there.

[*The sound of axes chopping down trees is heard in the distance.*]

LOPAHIN. Well, good-bye, my dear fellow. It's time to leave. We turn up our noses at one another, but life goes on just the same. When I'm working hard, without resting, my mind is easier, and it seems to me that I, too, know why I exist. But how many people are there in Russia, brother, who exist nobody knows why? Well, it doesn't matter. That's not what makes the wheels go round. They say Leonid Andreyevich has taken a position in the bank, 6,000 rubles a year. Only, of course, he won't stick to it, he's too lazy. . . .

ANYA. [*In the doorway.*] Mamma begs you not to start cutting down the cherry trees until she's gone.

TROFIMOV. Really, you should have more tact! [*Exits.*]

LOPAHIN. Right away—right away! Those men . . . [*Exits.*]

ANYA. Has Firs been taken to the hospital?

YASHA. I told them this morning. They must have taken him.

ANYA. [*To* YEPIHODOV, *who crosses the room.*] Yepihodov, please find out if Firs has been taken ot the hospital.

YASHA. [*Offended.*] I told Yegor this morning. Why ask a dozen times?

YEPIHODOV. The aged Firs, in my definitive opinion, is beyond mending. It's time he was gathered to his fathers. And I can only envy him. [*Puts a suitcase down on a hat box and crushes it.*] There now, of course, I knew it! [*Exits.*]

YASHA. [*Mockingly.*] Two-and-Twenty Troubles!

VARYA. [*Through the door.*] Has Firs been taken to the hospital?

ANYA. Yes.

VARYA. Then why wasn't the note for the doctor taken too?

ANYA. Oh! Then someone must take it to him. [*Exits.*]

VARYA. [*From adjoining room.*] Where's Yasha? Tell him his mother's come and wants to say good-bye.

YASHA. [*Waves his hand.*] She tries my patience.

[DUNYASHA *has been occupied with the luggage. Seeing* YASHA *alone, she goes up to him.*]

DUNYASHA. You might just give me one little look, Yasha. You're going away. . . . You're leaving me . . . [*Weeps and throws herself on his neck.*]

YASHA. What's there to cry about? [*Drinks champagne.*] In six days I shall be in Paris again. Tomorrow we get into an express train and off we go, that's the last you'll see of us. . . . I can scarcely believe it. *Vive la France!* It don't suit me here, I just can't live here. That's all there is to it. I'm fed up with the ignorance here, I've had enough of it. [*Drinks champagne.*] What's there to cry about?

Behave yourself properly, and you'll have no cause to cry.

DUNYASHA. [*Powders her face, looking in pocket mirror.*] Do send me a letter from Paris. You know I loved you, Yasha, how I loved you! I'm a delicate creature, Yasha.

YASHA. Somebody's coming! [*Busies himself with the luggage; hums softly.*]

[*Enter* MME. RANEVSKAYA, GAYEV, ANYA, *and* CHARLOTTA.]

GAYEV. We ought to be leaving. We haven't much time. [*Looks at* YASHA.] Who smells of herring?

MME. RANEVSKAYA. In about ten minutes we should be getting into the carriages. [*Looks around the room.*] Good-bye, dear old home, good-bye, grandfather. Winter will pass, spring will come, you will no longer be here, they will have torn you down. How much these walls have seen! [*Kisses* ANYA *warmly.*] My treasure, how radiant you look! Your eyes are sparkling like diamonds. Are you glad? Very?

ANYA. [*Gaily.*] Very glad. A new life is beginning, Mamma.

GAYEV. Well, really, everything is all right now. Before the cherry orchard was sold, we all fretted and suffered; but afterward, when the question was settled finally and irrevocably, we all calmed down, and even felt quite cheerful. I'm a bank employee now, a financier. The yellow ball in the side pocket! And anyhow, you are looking better, Luba, there's no doubt of that.

MME. RANEVSKAYA. Yes, my nerves are better, that's true. [*She is handed her hat and coat.*] I sleep well. Carry out my things, Yasha. It's time. [*To* ANYA.] We shall soon see each other again, my little girl. I'm going to Paris, I'll live there on the money your great-aunt sent us to buy the estate with—long live Auntie! But that money won't last long.

ANYA. You'll come back soon, soon, Mamma, won't you? Meanwhile I'll study. I'll pass my high school examination, and then I'll go to work and help you. We'll read all kinds of books together, Mamma, won't we? [*Kisses her mother's hands.*] We'll read in the autumn evenings, we'll read lots of books, and a new wonderful world will open up before us. [*Falls into a revery.*] Mamma, do come back.

MME. RANEVSKAYA. I will come back, my precious. [*Embraces her daughter. Enter* LOPAHIN *and* CHARLOTTA *who is humming softly.*]

GAYEV. Charlotta's happy: she's singing.

CHARLOTTA. [*Picks up a bundle and holds it like a baby in swaddling clothes.*] Bye, baby, bye. [*A baby is heard crying: "Wah! Wah!"*] Hush, hush, my pet, my little one. ["Wah! Wah!"] I'm so sorry for you! [*Throws the bundle down.*] You will find me a position, won't you? I can't go on like this.

LOPAHIN. We'll find one for you, Charlotta Ivanovna, don't worry.

GAYEV. Everyone's leaving us. Varya's going away. We've suddenly become of no use.

CHARLOTTA. There's no place for me to live in town, I must go away. [*Hums.*]

[*Enter* PISHCHIK.]

LOPAHIN. There's nature's masterpiece!

PISHCHIK. [*Gasping.*] Oh . . . let me get my breath . . . I'm in agony. . . . Esteemed friends . . . Give me a drink of water. . . .

GAYEV. Wants some money, I suppose. No, thank you . . . I'll keep out of harm's way. [*Exits.*]

PISHCHIK. It's a long while since I've been to see you, most charming lady. [*To* LOPAHIN.] So you are here . . . glad to see you, you intellectual giant . . . There . . . [*Gives* LOPAHIN *money.*] Here's 400 rubles, and I still owe you 840.

LOPAHIN. [*Shrugging his shoulders in bewilderment.*] I must be dreaming. . . . Where did you get it?

PISHCHIK. Wait a minute . . . it's hot. . . . A most extraordinary event! Some Englishmen came to my place and found some sort of white clay on my land . . . [*To* MME. RANEVSKAYA.] And 400 for you . . . most lovely . . . most wonderful . . . [*Hands her the money.*] The rest later. [*Drinks water.*] A young man in the train was telling me just now that a great philosopher recommends jumping off roofs. "Jump!" says he; "that's the long and the short of it!" [*In amazement.*] Just imagine! Some more water!

LOPAHIN. What Englishmen?

PISHCHIK. I leased them the tract with the clay on it for twenty-four years. . . . And now, forgive me, I can't stay. . . . I must be dashing on. . . . I'm going over to Znoikov . . . to Kardamanov . . . I owe them all money . . . [*Drinks water.*] Good-bye, everybody . . . I'll look in on Thursday . . .

MME. RANEVSKAYA. We're just moving into town; and tomorrow I go abroad.

PISHCHIK. [*Upset.*] What? Why into town? That's why the furniture is like that . . . and the suitcases. . . . Well, never mind! [*Through tears.*] Never mind . . . men of colossal intellect, these Englishmen. . . . Never mind . . . Be happy. God will come to your help. . . . Never mind . . . everything in this world comes to an end. [*Kisses* MME. RANEVSKAYA*'s hand.*] If the rumor reaches you that it's all up with me, remember this old . . . horse, and say: "Once there lived a certain . . . Simeonov-Pishchik . . . the kingdom of Heaven be his. . . ." Glorious weather! . . . Yes . . . [*Exits, in great confusion, but at once returns and says in the doorway.*] My daughter Dashenka sends her regards. [*Exits.*]

MME. RANEVSKAYA. Now we can go. I leave with two cares weighing on me. The first is poor old Firs. [*Glancing at her watch.*] We still have about five minutes.

ANYA. Mamma, Firs has already been taken to the hospital. Yasha sent him there this morning.

MME. RANEVSKAYA. My other worry is Varya. She's used to getting up early and working; and now, with no work to do, she is like a fish out of water. She has grown thin and pale, and keeps crying, poor soul. [*Pause.*] You know this very well, Yermolay Alexeyevich; I dreamed of seeing her married to you, and it looked as though that's how it would be. [*Whispers to* ANYA, *who nods to* CHARLOTTA *and both go out.*] She loves you. You find her attractive. I don't know, I don't know why it is you seem to avoid each other; I can't understand it.

LOPAHIN. To tell you the truth, I don't understand it myself. It's all a puzzle. If there's still time, I'm ready now, at once. Let's settle it straight off, and have done with it! Without you, I feel I'll never be able to propose.

MME. RANEVSKAYA. That's splendid. After all, it will only take a minute. I'll call her once. . . .

LOPAHIN. And luckily, here's champagne, too. [*Looks at the glasses.*] Empty! Somebody's drunk it all. [*Yasha coughs.*] That's what you might call guzzling . . .

MME. RANEVSKAYA. [*Animatedly.*] Excellent! We'll go and leave you alone. Yasha, *allez!* I'll call her. [*At the door.*] Varya, leave everything and come here. Come! [*Exits with* YASHA.]

LOPAHIN. [*Looking at his watch.*] Yes . . . [*Pause behind the door, smothered laughter and whispering; at last, enter* VARYA.]

VARYA. [*Looking over the luggage in leisurely fashion.*] Strange, I can't find it . . .

LOPAHIN. What are you looking for?

VARYA. Packed it myself, and I don't remember . . . [*Pause.*]

LOPAHIN. Where are you going now, Varya?

VARYA. I? To the Ragulins'. I've arranged to take charge there—as housekeeper, if you like.

LOPAHIN. At Yashnevo? About fifty miles from here. [*Pause.*] Well, life in this house is ended!

VARYA. [*Examining luggage.*] Where is it? Perhaps I put it in the chest. Yes, life in this house is ended. . . . There will be no more of it.

LOPAHIN. And I'm just off to Kharkov—by this next train. I've a lot to do there. I'm leaving Yepihodov here . . . I've taken him on.

VARYA. Oh!

LOPAHIN. Last year at this time, it was snowing, if you remember, but now it's sunny and there's no wind. It's cold, though. . . . It must be three below.

VARYA. I didn't look. [*Pause.*] And besides, our thermometer's broken. [*Pause. Voice from the yard:* "Yermolay Alexeyevich!"]

LOPAHIN. [*As if he had been waiting for the call.*] This minute! [*Exits quickly.*]

   [VARYA *sits on the floor and sobs quietly, her head on a bundle of clothes. Enter* MME. RANEVSKAYA *cautiously.*]

MME. RANEVSKAYA. Well? [*Pause.*] We must be going.

VARYA. [*Wiping her eyes.*] Yes, it's time, Mamma dear. I'll be able to get to the Ragulins' today, if only we don't miss the train.

MME. RANEVSKAYA. [*At the door.*] Anya, put your things on. [*Enter* ANYA, GAYEV, CHARLOTTA. GAYEV *wears a heavy overcoat with a hood. Enter servants and coachmen.* YEPIHODOV *bustles about the luggage.*]

MME. RANEVSKAYA. Now we can start on our journey.

ANYA. [*Joyfully.*] On our journey!

GAYEV. My friends, my dear, cherished friends, leaving this house forever, can I be silent? Can I, at leave-taking, refrain from giving utterance to those emotions that now fill my being?

ANYA. [*Imploringly.*] Uncle!

VARYA. Uncle, Uncle dear, don't.

GAYEV. [*Forlornly.*] I'll bank the yellow in the side pocket . . . I'll be silent . . .

   [*Enter* TROFIMOV, *then* LOPAHIN.]

TROFIMOV. Well, ladies and gentlemen, it's time to leave.

LOPAHIN. Yepihodov, my coat.

MME. RANEVSKAYA. I'll sit down just a minute. It seems as though I'd never before seen what the walls of this house were like, the ceilings, and now I look at them hungrily, with such tender affection.

GAYEV. I remember when I was six years old sitting on that window sill on Whitsunday, watching my father going to church.

MME. RANEVSKAYA. Has everything been taken?

LOPAHIN. I think so. [*Putting on his overcoat.*] Yepihodov, see that everything's in order.

YEPIHODOV. [*In a husky voice.*] You needn't worry, Yermolay Alexeyevich.

LOPAHIN. What's the matter with your voice?

YEPIHODOV. I just had a drink of water. I must have swallowed something.

YASHA. [*Contemptuously.*] What ignorance!

MME. RANEVSKAYA. When we're gone, not a soul will be left here.

LOPAHIN. Until the spring.

   [VARYA *pulls an umbrella out of a bundle, as though about to hit someone with it.* LOPAHIN *pretends to be frightened.*]

VARYA. Come, come, I had no such idea!

TROFIMOV. Ladies and gentlemen, let's get into the carriages—it's time. The train will be in directly.

VARYA. Petya, there they are, your rubbers, by that trunk. [*Tearfully.*] And what dirty old things, they are!

TROFIMOV. [*Puts on rubbers.*] Let's go, ladies and gentlemen.

GAYEV. [*Greatly upset, afraid of breaking down.*] The train . . . the station. . . . Three cushions in the side pocket, I'll bank this one in the corner . . .

MME. RANEVSKAYA. Let's go.

LOPAHIN. Are we all here? No one in there? [*Locks the side door on the left.*] There are some things stored here, better lock up. Let us go!

ANYA. Good-bye, old house! Good-bye, old life!

TROFIMOV. Hail to you, new life!

[*Exits with* ANYA. VARYA *looks round the room and goes out slowly.* YASHA *and* CHARLOTTA *with her dog go out.*]

LOPAHIN. And so, until the spring. Go along, friends . . . Bye-bye! [*Exits.*]

[MME. RANEVSKAYA *and* GAYEV *remain alone. As though they had been waiting for this, they throw themselves on each other's necks, and break into subdued, restrained sobs, afraid of being overheard.*]

GAYEV. [*In despair.*] My sister! My sister!

MME. RANEVSKAYA. Oh, my orchard—my dear, sweet, beautiful orchard! My life, my youth, my happiness—good-bye! Good-bye! [*Voice of* ANYA, *gay and summoning:* "Mamma!" *Voice of* TROFIMOV, *gay and excited:* "Halloo!"]

MME. RANEVSKAYA. One last look at the walls, at the windows. . . . Our poor mother loved to walk about this room . . .

GAYEV. My sister, my sister! [*Voice of* ANYA: "MAMMA!" VOICE OF TROFIMOV: "Halloo!"]

MME. RANEVSKAYA. We're coming.

[*They go out. The stage is empty. The sound of doors being locked, of carriages driving away. Then silence. In the stillness is heard the muffled sound of the ax striking a tree, a mournful, lonely sound.*

Footsteps are heard. FIRS *appears in the doorway on the right. He is dressed as usual in a jacket and white waistcoat and wears slippers. He is ill.*]

FIRS. [*Goes to the door, tries the handle.*] Locked! They've gone . . . [*Sits down on the sofa.*] They've forgotten me. . . . Never mind . . . I'll sit here a bit . . . I'll wager Leonid Andreyevich hasn't put his fur coat on, he's gone off in his light overcoat . . . [*Sighs anxiously.*] I didn't keep an eye on him. . . . Ah, when they're young, they're green . . . [*Mumbles something indistinguishable.*] Life has gone by as if I had never lived. [*Lies down.*] I'll lie down a while. . . There's no strength left in you, old fellow; nothing is left, nothing. Ah, you addlehead! [*Lies motionless. A distant sound is heard coming from the sky, as it were, the sound of a snapping string mournfully dying away. All is still again, and nothing is heard but the strokes of the ax against a tree far away in the orchard.*]

CHARLES BAUDELAIRE
1821–1867

The impact of Charles Baudelaire is due mainly to the novelty of his sensibility and to the shock effect of his themes, never before presented in traditional forms. The clash between the austere beauty of the verse and the often tortured, morbid, and even perverse content is suggested in the very title of his collection of poems, *Flowers of Evil* (1857). It appeared in the same year as Flaubert's *Madame Bovary* and was, like Flaubert's novel, prosecuted for obscenity and blasphemy. The publisher was forced to suppress six poems, two of which were explicit depictions of lesbianism. Baudelaire wrote a review of *Madame Bovary* in which he praised Emma for that "double character of calculus and dreaming which makes a perfect human being." This double character is Baudelaire's rather than Emma's.

Baudelaire was born in Paris on April 9, 1821. His father died when the boy was six, and in 1828 his widowed mother married Captain Jacques Aupick, later to become a general and an ambassador. Throughout his life Baudelaire remained greatly attached to his mother and detested his stepfather. His independent behavior having caused alarm, in 1841 he was dispatched on a voyage to the tropics. The following year saw the beginning of his lifelong liaison with Jeanne Duval, a mulatto woman, and of his frequent changes of residence in Paris. Disturbed by his extravagance, the family in 1844 placed him under a financial tutelage which was never to be lifted. The revolutionary disturbances of 1848 awakened his enthusiasm, though later he expressed reactionary political views. The same year he published the first of his many translations from Edgar Allan Poe. His long-heralded collection of poems *Flowers of Evil* (*Les Fleurs du mal*), at last appeared in 1857. In 1862 he noted that he had felt on his forehead "the breeze from imbecility's wing," probably the result of a venereal infection acquired many years before. Two years later he left Paris, and his creditors, for Brussels. There, in 1866, he was stricken with aphasia and hemiplegia, and he was brought back to Paris. After prolonged suffering he died in his mother's arms, on August 31, 1867. He was interred beside the body of General Aupick.

Baudelaire distrusted inspiration. He translated, paraphrased, and identified himself with Edgar Allan Poe, who had ridiculed the romantic cult of spontaneity and described the process of creation as an intellectual calculus. This is also Baudelaire's view, who composed the *Flowers of Evil* in a clearly thought-out order or even architecture and wrote every poem with meticulous care for the metrical pattern and the sound and associative values of every word. Many of his lines sound like Racine's. His classicist ambition opposes the loose sentimentalism of the French romantic poets. He wants and achieves sublimity, grandiose pathos, and ultimately "objectivity." There are, to be sure, many personal references in his poetry, and one can hardly deny that the picture of a personality emerges from the collection, but the book is meant rather to be a panorama of our civilization and an allegory of the pilgrimage of man from cradle to grave. Baudelaire is also antiromantic in his rejection of nature worship. Nature appears as the enemy of man: not only as the eventual victor in death over life, but as the implicit opponent in Baudelaire's very self-conscious glorification of the artificial, in his praise of makeup, jewels, glittering stones, and all the artifices of prostitution. Baudelaire is also one of the first poets in love with the city, with Paris, in spite of all the horror of its poverty and corruption.

Still, Baudelaire inherits much from the romantics; his cult of beauty, his defense of "art for art's sake," and his assertion of the mission of the grand artist go back to the cults of the early century, as does his boastful dandyism, not only in elegant dress, but in a superior disdain for the crowd. There is a strong residue of romanticism in his nostalgia for a lost paradise, for miraculous moments of ecstasy and happiness which he often locates in childhood or faraway tropical lands. There are a few poems of Platonic love, of yearning for an ideal that remains, however, empty and vague. His aesthetics, developed at length in his writings on art (collected posthumously as *L'Art romantique*, 1868), is ultimately romantic in its reliance on creative imagination and the role of dreams. He thinks of poetry as extracting flowers from evil, as the triumph of beauty over the ugly and even the repulsive. He widened the repertory of themes unheard or seldom heard in earlier poetry. His erotic poetry differs from anything that preceded it: no more frivolous, amusing, or leering than it is adoring of an unreachable beauty in the manner of Petrarch. At most, Donne and the sonnets of Shakespeare could be cited as antecedents. An entirely new sensibility finds its voice here: feelings of disgust and guilt attached to the sexual act; an attraction to venal women, in spite of contempt and loathing for them; the appeal of and the fear of woman as man's destroyer; preoccupation with death not as a faraway event, but concretely as smelly putrefaction; inner conflict between spirit and flesh that divides man in two. Baudelaire grew up as a Roman Catholic, and much is phrased in religious terms: the fall of man, the sense of sin. But Baudelaire engages in blasphemy, even in the cult of Satan. If we exclude what was possibly a late conversion, he was an atheist and even a nihilist, who did not yearn for God's grace and redemption, did not believe in immortality, and hardly mentions Jesus Christ. We could consider his expansion of themes as an aesthetics of the ugly well in tune with realism, although Baudelaire detested the term and its propounders and quickly transforms realistic detail into a dream landscape or even phantasmagoria.

Baudelaire is today called the forerunner or even father of symbolism, which as a term and movement was established in France in 1886, long after his death. Only his early sonnet, "Correspondences" (1852), picks up the old idea of universal analogy, the concept of nature as a "forest of symbols," and the idea of the unity of the senses, "synaesthesia." But the rest of Baudelaire's work shows hardly any trace of this doctrine, for which this sonnet became the key text. Rather, Baudelaire abandons all such pretensions and celebrates "modernity": "the ephemeral and fleeting beauty of modern life," life in the city, lived with detachment, irony, and even revulsion. The poet has become an outcast and at the very least an outsider, who, as a little poem in prose tells us, loses his halo in the mud of the street and does not even bother to pick it up (XLV. "Perte d'Aureole," in *Petits Poëmes en Prose*).

Thus Baudelaire stands at the crossroads: he rejects romanticism, its reliance on inspiration and its nature-worship, though he preserves some of its apparatus and otherworldly nostalgia. To call him the father of Symbolism is misleading. He must be mainly seen as the poet of a new sensibility: in his preoccupation with death and sex, his view of the futility of all human endeavor, his horror of ugliness and evil in the modern metropolis, and his personal feelings of depression, of what he himself called "spleen" or most often *ennui*, boredom, even disgust. Baudelaire sees his time as an age of decadence, man's fate inexorably subject to a hostile power above him, and man and woman condemned to an internecine war. Man, primarily as artist, can escape into a world of dreams, but disillusion waits for him in any case. The cult of beauty is desperate defiance; it is the artist's or simply the sensitive man's revolt against the ugliness of industrial and commercial civilization, against the complacency of its belief in progress. But he himself is infected with the gloom and despair around him. In "Voyage," the last poem in *Flowers of Evil*, Death, the Captain, takes over, and we are consoled only with the vague hope: "Through the unknown, we'll find the new." This Baudelaire certainly did. Without him modern poetry would be different.

Our selection of poems from Baudelaire's *Flowers of Evil* offers characteristic poems in the translation of eminent modern English and American poets who try to give a feeling for Baudelaire's form. Prose translations and translations in loose rhythmic prose make the poetry evaporate, though they may be more accurate and literal.

Joseph D. Bennett, *Baudelaire: A Criticism* (1944), gives a close reading of the *Flowers of Evil*. Henri Peyre, ed., *Baudelaire: A Collection of Critical Essays* (1962), presents a selection from modern criticism. Enid Starkie, *Baudelaire* (1953), is the best biography in English. Martin Turnell, *Baudelaire* (1954), is a critical examination of his works.

The Flowers of Evil

Correspondences[1]

Nature is a temple whose living colonnades
Breathe forth a mystic speech in fitful sighs;

---

1. Translated by Richard Wilbur.

Man wanders among symbols in those glades
Where all things watch him with familiar eyes.

Like dwindling echoes gathered far away
Into a deep and thronging unison
Huge as the night or as the light of day,
All scents and sounds and colors meet as one.

Perfumes there are as sweet as the oboe's sound,
Green as the prairies, fresh as a child's caress,
—And there are others, rich, corrupt, profound

And of an infinite pervasiveness,
Like myrrh, or musk, or amber, that excite
The ecstasies of sense, the soul's delight.

Correspondances

La Nature est un temple où de vivants piliers
Laissent parfois sortir de confuses paroles;
L'homme y passe à travers des forêts de symboles
Qui l'observent avec des regards familiers.

Comme de longs échos qui de loin se confondent
Dans une ténébreuse et profonde unité,
Vaste comme la nuit et comme la clarté,
Les parfums, les couleurs et les sons se répondent.

Il est des parfums frais comme des chairs d'enfants,
Doux comme les hautbois, verts comme les prairies,
—Et d'autres, corrompus, riches et triomphants,

Ayant l'expansion des choses infinies,
Comme l'ambre, le musc, le benjoin et l'encens,
Qui chantent les transports de l'esprit et des sens.

Her Hair[2]

O fleece that down her nape rolls, plume on plume!
O curls! O scent of nonchalance and ease!
What ecstasy! To populate this room
With memories it harbours in its gloom,
I'd shake it like a banner on the breeze.

---

2. Translated by Roy Campbell.

Hot Africa and languid Asia play
(An absent world, defunct, and far away)
Within that scented forest, dark and dim.
As other souls on waves of music swim,
Mine on its perfume sails, as on the spray.

I'll journey there, where man and sap-filled tree
Swoon in hot light for hours. Be you my sea,
Strong tresses! Be the breakers and the gales
That waft me. Your black river holds, for me,
A dream of masts and rowers, flames and sails.

A port, resounding there, my soul delivers
With long deep draughts of perfumes, scent, and clamour,
Where ships, that glide through gold and purple rivers,
Fling wide their vast arms to embrace the glamour
Of skies wherein the heat forever quivers.

I'll plunge my head in it, half drunk with pleasure—
In this black ocean that engulfs her form.
My soul, caressed with wavelets there may measure
Infinite rockings in embalmèd leisure,
Creative idleness that fears no storm!

Blue tresses, like a shadow-stretching tent,
You shed the blue of heavens round and far.
Along its downy fringes as I went
I reeled half-drunken to confuse the scent
Of oil of coconuts, with musk and tar.

My hand forever in your mane so dense,
Rubies and pearls and sapphires there will sow,
That you to my desire be never slow—
Oasis of my dreams, and gourd from whence
Deep draughted wines of memory will flow.

You'd Take the Entire Universe to Bed with You[3]

You'd take the entire universe to bed with you,
I think, just out of boredom, you lecherous, idle shrew!
You need, to keep your teeth sound, exercise your jaws,
Daily, for dinner, some new heart between your paws!
Your eyes, all lighted up like shops, like public fairs,

---

3. Translated by Edna St. Vincent Millay.

How insolent they are!—as if their power were theirs
Indeed!—this borrowed power, this Beauty, you direct
And use, whose law, however, you do not suspect.

Unwholesome instrument for health, O deaf machine
And blind, fecund in tortures!—how is it you have not seen,
You drinker of the world's blood, your mirrored loveliness
Blench and recoil? how is it you feel no shame? Confess:
Has never, then, this evil's very magnitude
Caused you to stagger?—you, who think yourself so shrewd
In evil?—seeing how Nature, patient and abstruse—
O Woman, Queen of Sins, Vile Animal,—has made use
Of you, to mould a genius?—employed you all this time?

O muddy grandeur!—ignominy ironic and sublime!

A Carrion[4]

Remember now, my Love, what piteous thing
   We saw on a summer's gracious day:
By the roadside a hideous carrion, quivering
   On a clean bed of pebbly clay,

Her legs flexed in the air like a courtesan,
   Burning and sweating venomously,
Calmly exposed its belly, ironic and wan,
   Clamorous with foul ecstasy.

The sun bore down upon this rottenness
   As if to roast it with gold fire,
And render back to nature her own largess
   A hundredfold of her desire.

Heaven observed the vaunting carcass there
   Blooming with the richness of a flower;
And that almighty stink which corpses wear
   Choked you with sleepy power!

The flies swarmed on the putrid vulva, then
   A black tumbling rout would seethe
Of maggots, thick like a torrent in a glen,
   Over those rags that lived and seemed to breathe.

4. Translated by Allen Tate.

They darted down and rose up like a wave
    Or buzzed impetuously as before;
One would have thought the corpse was held a slave
    To living by the life it bore!

This world had music, its own swift emotion
    Like water and the wind running,
Or corn that a winnower in rhythmic motion
    Fans with fiery cunning.

All forms receded, as in a dream were still,
    Where white visions vaguely start
From the sketch of a painter's long-neglected idyl
    Into a perfect art!

Behind the rocks a restless bitch looked on
    Regarding us with jealous eyes,
Waiting to tear from the livid skeleton
    Her loosed morsel quick with flies.

And even you will come to this foul shame,
    This ultimate infection,
Star of my eyes, my being's inner flame,
    My angel and my passion!

Yes: such shall you be, O queen of heavenly grace,
    Beyond the last sacrament,
When through your bones the flowers and sucking grass
    Weave their rank cerement.

Speak, then, my Beauty, to this dire putrescence,
    To the worm that shall kiss your proud estate,
That I have kept the divine form and the essence
    Of my festered loves inviolate!

The Balcony[5]

Mother of memories, queen of paramours,
Yourself are all my pleasures, all my duty;
You will recall caresses that were yours
And fireside evenings in their warmth and beauty.
Mother of memories, queen of paramours.

---

5. Translated by Roy Campbell.

On eves illumined by the light of coal,
The balcony beneath a rose-veiled sky,
Your breast how soft! Your heart how good and whole!
We spoke eternal things that cannot die—
On eves illumined by the light of coal!

How splendid sets the sun of a warm evening!
How deep is space! the heart how full of power!
When, queen of the adored, towards you leaning,
I breathed the perfume of your blood in flower.
How spendid sets the sun of a warm evening!

The evening like an alcove seemed to thicken,
And as my eyes astrologised your own,
Drinking your breath, I felt sweet poisons quicken,
And in my hands your feet slept still as stone.
The evening like an alcove seemed to thicken.

I know how to resuscitate dead minutes.
I see my past, its face hid in your knees.
How can I seek your languorous charm save in its
Own source, your heart and body formed to please.
I know how to resuscitate dead minutes.

These vows, these perfumes, and these countless kisses,
Reborn from gulfs that we could never sound,
Will they, like suns, once bathed in those abysses,
Rejuvenated from the deep, rebound—
These vows, these perfumes, and these countless kisses?

To One Who is Too Gay[6]

Your head, your gestures, and your air
Are lovely as a landscape; smiles
Rimple upon your face at whiles
Like winds in the clear sky up there.

The grumpy passers that you graze
Are dazzled by the radiant health,
And the illimitable wealth
Your arms and shoulders seem to blaze.

---

6. Translated by Roy Campbell.

The glaring colours that, in showers,
Clash in your clothes with such commotion,
In poets' minds suggest the notion
Of a mad ballet-dance of flowers.

These garish dresses illustrate
Your spirit, striped with every fad.
O madwoman, whom, quite as mad,
I love as madly as I hate.

Sometimes in gardens, seeking rest,
Where I have dragged my soul atonic,
I've felt the sun with gaze ironic
Tearing the heart within my breast.

The spring and verdure, dressed to stagger,
Humiliate me with such power
That I have punished, in a flower,
The insolence of Nature's swagger.

And so, one night, I'd like to sneak,
When darkness tolls the hour of pleasure,
A craven thief, towards the treasure
Which is your person, plump and sleek.

To punish your bombastic flesh,
To bruise your breast immune to pain,
To furrow down your flank a lane
Of gaping crimson, deep and fresh.

And, most vertiginous delight!
Into those lips, so freshly striking
And daily lovelier to my liking—
Infuse the venom of my spite.

Spleen[7]

I'm like the king of a rain-country, rich
but sterile, young but with an old wolf's itch,
one who escapes his tutor's monologues,
and kills the day in boredom with his dogs;

7. Translated by Robert Lowell.

nothing cheers him, darts, tennis, falconry,
his people dying by the balcony;
the bawdry of the pet hermaphrodite
no longer gets him through a single night;
his bed of fleur-de-lys becomes a tomb;
even the ladies of the court, for whom
all kings are beautiful, cannot put on
shameful enough dresses for this skeleton;
the scholar who makes his gold cannot invent
washes to cleanse the poisoned element;
even in baths of blood, Rome's legacy,
our tyrants' solace in senility,
he cannot warm up his shot corpse, whose food
is syrup-green Lethean[8] ooze, not blood.

Parisian Dream[9]

I

That marvellous landscape of my dream—
Which no eye knows, nor ever will—
At moments, wide awake, I seem
To grasp, and it excites me still.

Sleep, how miraculous you are—
A strange caprice had urged my hand
To banish, as irregular,
All vegetation from that land;

And, proud of what my art had done,
I viewed my painting, knew the great
Intoxicating monotone
Of marble, water, steel and slate.

Staircases and arcades there were
In a long labyrinth, which led
To a vast palace; fountains there
Were gushing gold, and gushing lead.

And many a heavy cataract
Hung like a curtain,—did not fall,
As water does, but hung, compact,
Crystal, on many a metal wall.

8. Lethe is the river of forgetfulness in the underworld.   9. Translated by Edna St. Vincent Millay.

Tall nymphs with Titan breasts and knees
Gazed at their images unblurred,
Where groves of colonnades, not trees,
Fringed a deep pool where nothing stirred.

Blue sheets of water, left and right,
Spread between quays of rose and green,
To the world's end and out of sight,
And still expanded, though unseen.

Enchanted rivers, those—with jade
And jasper were their banks bedecked;
Enormous mirrors, dazzled, made
Dizzy by all they did reflect.

And many a Ganges, taciturn
And heedless, in the vaulted air,
Poured out the treasure of its urn
Into a gulf of diamond there.

As architect, it tempted me
To tame the ocean at is source;
And this I did,—I made the sea
Under a jeweled culvert course.

And every colour, even black,
Became prismatic, polished, bright;
The liquid gave its glory back
Mounted in iridescent light.

There was no moon, there was no sun,—
For why should sun and moon conspire
To light such prodigies?—each one
Blazed with its own essential fire!

A silence like eternity
Prevailed, there was no sound to hear;
These marvels all were for the eye,
And there was nothing for the ear.

II

I woke; my mind was bright with flame;
I saw the cheap and sordid hole

I live in, and my cares all came
Burrowing back into my soul.

Brutally the twelve strokes of noon
Against my naked ear were hurled;
And a grey sky was drizzling down
Upon this sad, lethargic world.

Voyage to Cythera[1]

My heart, a seagull rocketed and spun
about the rigging, dipping joyfully;
our slow prow rocking under cloudless sky
was like an angel drunk with the live sun.

What's that out there? Those leagues of hovering sand?
"It's Cythera famous in the songs,
the gay old dogs' El Dorado, it belongs
to legend. Look closely, it's a poor land."

Island of secret orgies none profess,
the august shade of Aphrodite plays
like clouds of incense over your blue bays,
and weights the heart with love and weariness.

Island whose myrtle esplanades arouse
our nerves, here heart-sighs and the adoration
of every land and age and generation
ramble like coal-red roses on a house

to the eternal cooing of the dove.
"No, Cythera crumbles, cakes and dries,
a rocky desert troubled by shrill cries . . .
And yet I see one portent stretch above
us. Is it a temple where the pagan powers
hover in naked majesty to bless
the arbors, gold-fish ponds and terraces;
and the young priestess is in love with flowers?"

No, nosing through these shoals, and coming near
enough to scare the birds with our white sails,

---

1. Translated by Robert Lowell. Cythera is an island off the Peloponnese and the mythic birthplace of Aphrodite.

we saw a man spread-eagled on the nails
of a cross hanging like a cypress there.

Ferocious vultures choking down thick blood
gutted the hanging man, already foul;
each smacked its beak like the flat of a trowel
into the private places of their food.

His eyes were holes and his important paunch
oozed lazy, looping innards down his hips;
those scavengers, licking sweetmeats from their lips,
had hung his pouch and penis on a branch.

Under his foot-soles, shoals of quadrupeds
with lifted muzzles nosed him round and guzzled;
a huge ante-diluvian reptile muscled
through them like an executioner with his aides.

Native of Cythera, initiate,
how silently you hung and suffered insult
in retribution for your dirty cult
and orgasms only death could expiate.

Ridiculous hanged man, my sins confirm
your desecration; when I saw you seethe,
I felt my nausea mounting to my teeth,
the drying bile-stream of my wasted sperm.

Poor devil with sweet memories, your laws
are mine; before you, I too felt those jaws:
black panther, lancing crow, the Noah's Ark
that loved to chafe my flesh and leave their mark.

I'd lost my vision clinging to those shrouds,
I feared the matching blues of sky and sea;
all things were henceforth black with blood for me,
and plunged my heart in allegoric clouds . . .

Nothing stands upright in your land, oh Lust,
except my double, hanging at full length—
Oh God, give me the courage and the strength
to see my heart and body without disgust.

The Voyage[2]

TO MAXIME DU CAMP

For children crazed with postcards, prints, and stamps
All space can scarce suffice their appetite.
How vast the world seems by the light of lamps,
But in the eyes of memory how slight!

One morning we set sail, with brains on fire,
And hearts swelled up with rancorous emotion,
Balancing, to the rhythm of its lyre,
Our infinite upon the finite ocean.

Some wish to leave their venal native skies,
Some flee their birthplace, others change their ways,
Astrologers who've drowned in Beauty's eyes,
Tyrannic Circe[3] with the scent that slays.

Not to be changed to beasts, they have their fling
With space, and splendour, and the burning sky,
The suns that bronze them and the frosts that sting
Efface the mark of kisses by and by.

But the true travellers are those who go
Only to get away: hearts like balloons
Unballasted, with their own fate aglow,
Who know not why they fly with the monsoons:

Those whose desires are in the shape of clouds.
And dream, as raw recruits of shot and shell,
Of mighty raptures in strange, transient crowds
Of which no human soul the name can tell.

II

Horror! We imitate the top and bowl
In swerve and bias. Through our sleep it runs.
It's Curiosity that makes us roll
As the fierce Angel whips the whirling suns.

Singular game! where the goal changes places;
The winning-post is nowhere, yet all round;

---

2. Translated by Roy Campbell.   3. An enchantress who lured sailors onto her island and changed them into beasts (see, for example, the *Odyssey* X).

Where Man tires not of the mad hope he races
Thinking, some day, that respite will be found.

Our soul's like a three-master, where one hears
A voice that from the bridge would warn all hands.
Another from the foretop madly cheers
"Love, joy, and glory" . . . Hell! we're on the sands!

The watchmen think each isle that heaves in view
An Eldorado, shouting their belief.
Imagination riots in the crew
Who in the morning only find a reef.

The fool that dotes on far, chimeric lands—
Put him in irons, or feed him to the shark!
The drunken sailor's visionary lands
Can only leave the bitter truth more stark.

So some old vagabond, in mud who grovels,
Dreams, nose in air, of Edens sweet to roam.
Wherever smoky wicks illumine hovels
He sees another Capua[4] or Rome.

III

Amazing travellers, what noble stories
We read in the deep oceans of your gaze!
Show us your memory's casket, and the glories
Streaming from gems made out of stars and rays!

We, too, would roam without a sail or steam,
And to combat the boredom of our jail,
Would stretch, like canvas on our souls, a dream,
Framed in horizons, of the seas you sail.

What have you seen?

IV

    "We have seen stars and waves.
We have seen sands and shores and oceans too,
In spite of shocks and unexpected graves,
We have been bored, at times, the same as you.

---

4. City in southern Italy famous as the center of corruption and luxury.

The solar glories on the violet ocean
And those of spires that in the sunset rise,
Lit, in our hearts, a yearning, fierce emotion
To plunge into those ever-luring skies.

The richest cities and the scenes most proud
In nature, have no magic to enamour
Like those which hazard traces in the cloud
While wistful longing magnifies their glamour.

Enjoyment adds more fuel for desire,
Old tree, to which all pleasure is manure;
As the bark hardens, so the boughs shoot higher,
And nearer to the sun would grow mature.

Tree, will you always flourish, more vivacious
Than cypress?—None the less, these views are yours:
We took some photographs for your voracious
Album, who only care for distant shores.

We have seen idols elephantine-snouted,
And thrones with living gems bestarred and pearled,
And palaces whose riches would have routed
The dreams of all the bankers in the world.

We have seen wonder-striking robes and dresses,
Women whose nails and teeth the betel stains
And jugglers whom the rearing snake caresses."

V

What then? What then?

VI

   "O childish little brains,
Not to forget the greatest wonder there—
We've seen in every country, without searching,
From top to bottom of the fatal stair
Immortal sin ubiquitously lurching:

Woman, a vile slave, proud in her stupidity,
Self-worshipping, without the least disgust:
Man, greedy, lustful, ruthless in cupidity,
Slave to a slave, and sewer to her lust:

The torturer's delight, the martyr's sobs,
The feasts where blood perfumes the giddy rout:
Power sapping its own tyrants: servile mobs
In amorous obeisance to the knout:

Some similar religions to our own,
All climbing skywards: Sanctity who treasures,
As in his downy couch some dainty drone,
In horsehair, nails, and whips, his dearest pleasures.

Prating Humanity, with genius raving,
As mad today as ever from the first,
Cries in fierce agony, its Maker braving,
'O God, my Lord and likeness, be thou cursed!'

But those less dull, the lovers of Dementia,
Fleeing the herd which fate has safe impounded,
In opium seek for limitless adventure.
—That's all the record of the globe we rounded."

VII

It's bitter knowledge that one learns from travel.
The world so small and drab, from day to day,
The horror of our image will unravel,
A pool of dread in deserts of dismay.

Must we depart, or stay? Stay if you can.
Go if you must. One runs: another hides
To baffle Time, that fatal foe to man.
And there are runners, whom no rest betides,

Like the Apostles or the Wandering Jew,[5]
Whom neither ship nor waggon can enable
To cheat the retiary.[6] But not a few
Have killed him without stirring from their cradle.

But when he sets his foot upon our nape
We still can hope and cry "Leave all behind!"
As in old times to China we'll escape
With eyes turned seawards, hair that fans the wind,—

---

5. A Jew, according to a medieval legend, who mocked Christ on his way to the cross and was condemned to a life of wandering until Judgment Day.   6. Net (i.e., of Time).

We'll sail once more upon the sea of Shades
With heart like that of a young sailor beating.
I hear the rich, sad voices of the Trades
Who cry "This Way! all you who would be eating

The scented Lotus. Here it is they range
The piles of magic fruit. O hungry friend,
Come here and swoon away into the strange
Trance of an afternoon that has no end."

In the familiar tones we sense the spectre.
Our Pylades stretch arms across the seas,
"To salve your heart, now swim to your Electra"[7]
She cries, of whom we used to kiss the knees.

VIII

O Death, old Captain, it is time. Weigh anchor!
To sail beyond the doldrums of our days.
Though black as pitch the sea and sky, we hanker
For space; you know our hearts are full of rays.

Pour us your poison to revive our soul!
It cheers the burning quest that we pursue,
Careless if Hell or Heaven be our goal,
Beyond the known world to seek out the New!

7. The sister of Orestes. *Pylades:* Orestes' friend.

Masterpieces of the Twentieth Century: Varieties of Modernism

Twentieth-century authors (like those of the Renaissance, or "Rebirth," and of the Enlightenment) often make a point of being "modern" and "new." There are many aspects to twentieth-century "newness," and they usually center in the claim to have achieved a more accurate representation of reality, and a better understanding of human consciousness. It is worth remembering, of course, that artists and philosophers have for centuries sought effective ways to perceive and express the "truth" of the world and the human condition. If, in reading a modern text, you sense an aim or attitude comparable with those of an earlier work, you are probably right. In some instances, we have tried to point out such echoes. Yet there is a recurrent emphasis on *how* we know, on structures of perception themselves, that runs through the claims to newness of almost all these writers and thinkers and which must be taken—no matter what individual comparisons can be made to previous eras—as the typifying mark of twentieth-century vision. This vision implies, generally, a criticism of the preceding century as a period of comfortable certainty and positive assurance that was dangerously unreal. It suggests that nineteenth-century philosophers and scientists placed too much faith in the possibility of finding unambiguous answers to age-old problems and that, in consequence, a belief in the provable "rightness" of certain ideas created uncompromising attitudes which, transposed into politics, ultimately brought on the bloody conflict of World Wars I and II. Only time will tell what criticism will be made of our own age by the twenty-first century.

This twentieth-century view of the flaws of the nineteenth has been influential but is, of course, inaccurate insofar as it neglects the roots of modern consciousness in nineteenth-century science, sociology, and art. Modernity was already a subject of widespread anxiety and argument in the nineteenth century, as the industrial revolution transformed social, economic, and political life faster, it seemed, than changes could peacefully be absorbed. To some, it seemed a time of decadence and the loss of stable values; others saw it as an era in which a progressive Europe would lead the rest of the world to its own pinnacle of achievement (a point of view obviously not shared by the colonial countries). In science, philosophy, social theory, and the arts, the nineteenth century prepared both the evolution and the rebellion of the twentieth.

SCIENTIFIC RATIONALISM

By the end of the nineteenth century, unprecedented developments in science had encouraged people to believe that they would soon master all the secrets of the universe. The Enlightenment notion of the world as a machine—something whose parts could be named and seen to function—came back into favor. Discoveries in different fields seemed to make the universe more rational and hence predictable: in chemistry, there was Dalton's atomic theory and Mendeleyev's periodic table of elements; in physics, Maxwell's field theory unifying the study of. electricity, magnetism, and light. The development of Newtonian analysis made it possible to study the fixed stars, and spectral analysis showed the essential homogeneity of the universe. Technological applications suggested that these discoveries would serve humanity, not master it. Thermodynamics explained the processes of energy transformation, and locomotives and steamships promised rapid transportation throughout the world. Daguerreotype photography provided a documentary record. Finally, the history of living nature itself became an object of study when Charles Darwin examined the evolution of species according to material evidence, without reference to divine laws or purpose.

The enthusiasm for scientific discovery was not confined to scientists. Auguste Comte (1798–1857), a philosopher known as the founder of Positivism, held that scientific method constituted a total world view in which everything would ultimately be explained, including human society. Comte proposed a science of humanity which would analyze and define the laws governing human society (the first sociology). Soon it would be evident, however, that the results of "scientific method" depended on the objectivity of the scientist's point of view. Count Gobineau (1816–1882) proposed a "scientific" description of society in which there were three races with innate qualities and in which the white race (predictably, for this white Frenchman) was the superior category; his theory laid the groundwork for much "scientific" racism later on. In literature, the historian and critic Hippolyte Taine (1828–1893) proposed a science of culture in which each literary work could be categorized as the combined product of its "race, milieu, and time." The novelist Emile Zola offered as scientific justification for his series on the degeneracy of the Rougon-Macquart family, an *Introduction to the Study of Experimental Medicine* by Dr. Claude Bernard (1813–1878). The mixed attraction and repulsion of scientific method—its promise of objective truth, its risk of unrecognized bias, its description of individual subjects in terms of collective statistical evidence—would be recognized within as well as outside the scientific community in the twentieth century.

Social theorists shared with the philosopher Comte the vision of creating a perfect society by understanding social "laws." Utopian socialists like Charles Fourier (1772–1837), the Comte de Saint-Simon (1760–1825), and the Welsh industrialist Robert Owen (1771–1858) envisaged various methods for organizing society and planning its economy. John Stuart Mill (1806–1876) preached the dignity of man, the rights of women, and the possibility of happiness for all. By far the most important and influential theorist was Karl Marx (1819–1883), whose *Communist Manifesto* (1848) and *Capital* (1867) proposed a scientific theory of impersonal economic forces driving world history. Marx's vision of modern man as an alienated cog in the industrial economic machine, no longer in control of his own productivity, expressed for many the antihuman aspect of modern technological progress. Yet he too believed in the power of rational systems to find answers for social ills, as is evident in his division of modern industrial society into the two competing forces of capital and labor (the proletariat) and in his schema of dialectical materialism to explain the process of history.

All, however, was not an unbroken picture of hope and enthusiasm. One of the strongest voices against positivism and its belief in rational solutions was the German philosopher Friedrich Nietzsche (1844–1900). Nietszche focused on the individual, not society, and admired only the superhero who refused to be bound by the prevailing social paradigms of nationalism, Christianity, faith in science, loyalty to the state, or bourgeois civilized comfort. Nietzsche's distinction between the Dionysiac (instinctual) and the Apollonian (intellectual) forces in human beings, his insistence on the individual's complete freedom (and responsibility) in a world that lacks transcendental law ("God is dead"), and his attack on the unimaginative mediocrity of mass society in the modern industrial world, all made him a powerful influence in the early years of the twentieth century.

REACTIONS TO RATIONALISM

The debate about scientific rationalism was inevitably a debate about knowledge and human values, and as such would change its focus along with the evolution of the different disciplines. The shape and intensity of this debate, however, as well as its impact on the world at large, were dictated for many years by a historical event that turned the generations of the early twentieth century against everything inherited from the recent past: the Great War (World War I, 1914–1918). In spite of the confident rationalism of the political leaders of "Papa's Europe" (a term of resentment used by many to describe an authoritarian, patriarchial society that claimed to have all the answers), World War I had for the first time involved the whole continent of Europe and the United States in battle, and was the first "total war" in which modern weapons spared no one, including civilians. Clearly, something was wrong. A generation of European and American youth was lost in the trenches, and the survivors emerged resolved to reexamine the bases of certainty, the structures of knowledge, the systems of belief, and the repositories of authority in a society which had allowed such a war to occur. Their reaction would also be reflected in literature, not only in subject matter but—for many—in a new use of language, in new ways of representing our knowledge of the world.

Several thinkers stand out as particularly important in formulating alternatives to the narrow rationalism of positivist philosophy. The French philosopher Henri Bergson (1859–1941) had attacked scientific rationality as artificial and unreal because it froze everything in conceptual space; it ignored the whole dimension of life as it is actually experienced. For Bergson, reality was a fluid, living force (élan vital) that could only be apprehended by consciousness. Instead of quantitative and logical inquiry, he proposed intuiting the "immediate data of consciousness" as an alternate, nonscientific means of knowledge. Authors were not slow to perceive the implications of his prescription for representing reality. Proust, searching to discover his identity through layers of "lost time," or Joyce, imitating the stream of consciousness in the written flow of words, both reflect a Bergsonian change in the way reality is perceived and represented. Bergson himself received the Nobel Prize in Literature in 1927, both for the creative imagination shown in his own work and for his literary influence.

Sigmund Freud (1856–1939), the founder of psychoanalysis, is another influential figure. Freud's study of subconscious motives and instinctual drives revealed a level of activity that had been largely ignored, and that was certainly not considered a productive subject for continued "rational" inquiry. His essays and case studies argued that dreams and manias contain their own networks of meaning, and that human beings cannot properly be understood without taking into consideration the irrational as well as the rational level of their existence. All are caught up, he suggested, in the process of mediating the same sexual drives and civilizational repressions that caused neurosis in his own patients. While many of Freud's theories are questioned today (his assumption that every woman considers herself an incomplete man, for example), he focused attention on the way everyday, "rational" behavior is shaped by unconscious impulses and hidden motivations, and on the way human beings actually create (and modify) their images of self through engaging in dialogue with others. It is probably impossible for any author after Freud to write without taking into consideration the psychological undercurrents of human behavior—and this without implying that the author has ever read Freud. Some derive themes and images from the idea of subconscious motivations guiding interpersonal relations and social behavior (Lawrence, Lessing, Ellison); others employ a "stream of consciousness" technique very much like Freud's therapeutic tactic of free association (Joyce, Faulkner); others exploit the aesthetic possibilities of a surface pattern of apparent intentions concealing a contradictory pattern of repressed intentions (Porter); others exploit the pattern of otherwise-empty dialogue creating its own reality (Beckett); the surrealists, while quoting Freud, totally reverse his aim by pronouncing madness an insight into a larger reality instead of an illness to be cured. Freud, like Bergson, was honored as a creative artist when he received the Goethe Prize in 1930.

Literature, however, is a matter of words, and not disembodied themes and patterns of consciousness. Much twentieth-century literature exploits patterns of language to the limit of comprehensibility (and perhaps past, as some have said of Joyce's *Finnegans Wake* or Beckett's later novels). If some liberation of language derives from Freudian free association, from the complex inner patterns favored by nineteenth-century Symbolist poetry, or from attempts to reproduce the effects of impressionist or cubist painting, a number of later texts (Beckett, Borges, Robbe-Grillet) also reflect the "gamelike" theories of language stemming from the Swiss linguist Ferdinand de Saussure (1857–1913) and the Austrian philosopher Ludwig Wittgenstein (1889–1951). Here readers of literature are likely to feel that the theorists are only catching up with what poets have always known: that the "reality" of literature is created on the page, in the manipulation of words. The French poet Mallarmé had already responded to the painter and sculptor Degas, when the latter claimed that he too had a lot of ideas for poems: "Poems are not made with ideas, but with words." Gertrude Stein employed words to create a different way of looking at the world when she created the relationships of "A Carafe, That Is a Blind Glass":

> A kind of glass and a cousin, a spectacle and nothing strange a single hurt color and an arrangement in a system to pointing. All this and not ordinary, not unordered in not resembling. The difference is spreading. (*Tender Buttons*, 1914)

Modern linguistic theory contributed nonetheless by formulating theoretical objections to the positivist understanding of language. Where nineteenth-century positivism had assumed that language was a specific, accurate tool for direct reference to reality, and Bertrand Russell's "logical positivism" of 1913 proposed the construction of an ideal language whose "syntax" would be clear, precise, and allow us to comprehend the structures of reality, Saussure and Wittgenstein emphasized instead the artificial or culture-bound nature of language: that it does not give "real" names but only socially-agreed-upon titles (a *signifier* pointing to a *signified*). The sun remains the same gaseous ball no matter what it is called; what is of interest is the network of meanings and associations the word can achieve in different contexts (along with its homonym *son*). Here literature and linguistic systems are seen as *games*, combinations of moves which have a particular meaning in each arrangement (and, as any sports or chess fan knows, there are "good games" and "bad games" depending on the relative elegance and efficiency of the play). Words and word-fragments combine to stress patterns of surface relationships, instead of trying to peel away associations and name a single core of meaning. Joyce, in *Finnegans Wake*, chooses verbal associations over direct referent when he describes Anna Livia Plurabelle as "babbling, bubbling, chattering to herself, deloothering the fields on their elbows leaning with the sloothering side of her, giddgaddy, grannyma, gossipacious Anna Livia." Samuel Beckett's tongue-tied characters in *Endgame*, or the excessively voluble narrators of his novels, make immediate conversational sense but finally express very little, unless it be the absurd inexpressibility of the human condition. At its most extreme, the "game" theory leads to a view of all language as an endless networking of associations: a situation in which communication, as well as value judgment, is impossible. Yet it also gives a linguistic explanation for one of the traditional attributes of the literary masterwork: that it can bear rereading and rereading because of its connotative richness, because it manipulates words so as to pull together many dimensions of meaning.

These insights are not isolated from current developments in the sciences, or from the impact of historical events. In psychology, anthropology, and physics, there were not only new definitions of human nature and the material world, but also new ideas of how we pursue such knowledge. Gestalt psychology (*Gestalt* is German for *form*) after 1912 suggested that the meaning of individual phenomena was not to be found in further analysis of the separate pieces but in the organized wholes of which they were a part: it was the "shape of things" that mattered. Shapes and the relation of parts were also important in structural anthropology, with the anthropologist Claude

Lévi-Strauss (1908—) defining human society as a system of world views or "codes" that could be compared from culture to culture. From his early research on the primitive Nambikwara Indian tribe of Brazil to his later comparisons of primitive with modern cultures, Lévi-Strauss insisted that each society could only be understood from the inside, by an imaginative participation that recognized the codes or system of relationships (kinship rules, taboos, habits of social interaction, folkloric imagination) governing its daily life. Less scientific but more influential on modern writers was Jungian psychology (Carl Gustav Jung, 1875–1961), which proposed that humanity shared a "collective unconscious"—a buried level of universal experience tapped by myth, religion, and art. According to Jung, the common experience of our species was revealed in archetypes (master patterns) like the figures of the hero, seer, or Great Mother, the image of the quest, or the process of death and regeneration. A number of writers (for example, T. S. Eliot in *The Waste Land*) openly incorporated archetypal images in their work in order to allude to a universal level of human experience.

Gestalt psychology and structural anthropology had both emphasized the relationship of parts, and directed attention to modes of perception as part of scientific inquiry. Physics and mathematics were doing the same thing, with results that shocked the general public and intrigued writers and artists. Albert Einstein's theory of relativity (1905) abandoned the concepts of absolute motion and the absolute difference of space and time and, working from pure mathematical logic, proposed that reality should be understood as a four-dimensional continuum (called space-time) that literally could not be expressed either in words or in the old three-dimensional models of Newtonian physics. "Relativity" implied "relativism" in the popular mind, and Einstein's discovery was widely thought to pull the ground out from under any certainty—scientific or religious—about the physical world. Worse yet, Werner Heisenberg's "uncertainty principle" (1927) proclaimed that scientific measurement (in this case, the measurement of electrons) was always a matter of statistical approximation, a "probability function" and not an exact description. Ironically, what was scientifically an increasingly *accurate* perception of the nature of things often seemed just the opposite to the general public. It was not possible for them to find self-evident truths, or go "back to basics," when scientists had just shown that the "basic" world of three-dimensional reality did not even exist. Many writers, however (and Proust among the earliest), welcomed what they saw as scientific confirmation that reality could be represented in a shifting and fluid perspective.

Although all the attitudes mentioned thus far have been concerned with one or another aspect of the perception of reality, the issue itself belongs more squarely to the philosophy known as phenomenology (the analysis of phenomena or things *as they appear to us*) and its offshoot, existentialism. The phenomenology of Edmund Husserl (1859–1938) described all consciousness as consciousness *of* something *by* someone, and concluded that every object of study should be imagined in "brackets"—not as a thing in itself, but as part of a relationship between perceiver and perceived. The ethical implications of this view were taken up by the philosophers Martin Heidegger (1889–1976) and Jean-Paul Sartre (1905–1980), who questioned what existence could mean in a world without preexisting truths, values, or general laws. Heidegger's profoundly somber vision of the "absurd" condition of human beings, "thrown into the world" without any understanding of their fate, influenced many writers and especially the "Theater of the Absurd" that flourished after World War II, of which Samuel Beckett (1906—) and Eugène Ionesco (1912—) are the best-known writers. Sartre, who was much more of a social activist, derived from the same "absurd" freedom an ideal of human "authenticity" which consists in choosing our actions at each point, avoiding the "bad faith" of pretending that others are responsible for our choices, and choosing not just for oneself but "for all" inasmuch as each choice envisages the creation of a new world. This kind of existentialism, with its appealing image of the lonely tragic hero who acts to benefit society without any hope of reward (Sartre portrayed such a hero as Orestes in *The Flies*, based on Aeschylus' *Oresteia*), had tremendous influence on young writers immediately after World War II. Albert Camus, writing at the same time as Sartre, offers in "The Guest" a good example of the emphasis on freedom, responsibility, and social "engagement" that typifies much "existentialist" writing. Although existentialism was attacked by those who felt that "total freedom" necessarily meant an abdication of moral commitment, a glance at the works of Sartre and Camus (or at the Christian existentialists Gabriel Marcel, Jacques Maritain, Karl Jaspers, and Paul Tillich) will show that the existentialist rejection of exterior laws leads immediately to the question of responsible choice and to a sharpening of moral issues.

Existentialism's popular appeal in the forties and fifties was undoubtedly enhanced by the fact that it was a philosophic attempt to recover clear vision—and a basis for action—in a confused and meaningless world. The notion of philosophical "absurdity" corresponded to a very real confusion felt by the general public in the face of the radical historical changes taking place ever since World War I and the Russian Revolution of 1917. By the middle of the century, there had been two world wars, the second of which had reached all the way around the globe to Japan; almost all the old monarchies had been overthrown and colonial empires were being dismantled as the emerging nations of Africa and Asia struggled for independence and self-definition; the wielders of authority became the enormous bureaucracy of the modern state, multinational corporations, international governmental organizations, and ethnic alliances. Transportation and telecommunications progressed to an extent only envisaged in earlier ages' science fiction and effectively shrank the global community; and the rise of the modern industrial state set up new political, cultural, and economic tensions not only in the West but between the West and the "less developed" countries of the world.

The change in historical conditions had visible effects on literature and art. Cultural parochialism—the belief that there is only one correct view of the world (ours)—was much harder to maintain when people traveled widely and experienced different ways of life. Racial and ethnic stereotypes were challenged, and traditional ideas of identity and social class broken down. Romantic heroism and aristocratic "rank" seemed irrelevant to men who died anonymously in the trenches of World War I, or to the masses killed at a distance by bombing raids in both wars. The appropriate symbol for modern, impersonal warfare was the Tomb of the Unknown Soldier, and in literature it was the "common man," not the Romantic hero, whose plight was portrayed. The conventional roles of the sexes came under examination. Western women achieved civil rights unparalleled in previous centuries: the right to vote (1920 in the United States), the right to have bank accounts and to own and control their own property, the right to be educated equally with men, and the right to enter professions not previously open to them. When women held many jobs previously thought to be masculine ("Rosie the Riveter" was a famous poster in World War II), it was no longer possible to pretend that they were incapable of work outside the home. Technology became part of the modern literary consciousness, inspiring both enthusiasm and fear, and initiating all over again the question of human values in a society where so much could be done (and so many controlled) by the use of machines.

A CENTURY OF ISMS

The literary and artistic movements of the twentieth century are part of this evolution; they were shaped by it, and helped shape it for others. There are many such movements: in fact, the twentieth century has been called by some a "century of isms," or of "vanguardism," reflecting the fact that so many different groups have tried to find the appropriate artistic response to contemporary history. Expressionism, Dadaism, Surrealism, and Futurism—each worth exploring in itself—are all different ways of expressing the "reality" of the world: some appearing very unreal at first glance, but all trying to adopt a point of view that will reveal an inner (presumably more important) truth than could be shown by documentary detail alone. Expressionists refused the direct representation of reality, or even impressions of it (as in Impressionism), in favor of expressing an inner vision, emotion, or spiritual reality. *The Scream*, a painting by Edward Munch (1863–1944) evokes a whole realm of spiritual agony, and expressionist writers like Frank Wedekind (1864–1918) and Gottfried Benn (1886–1956) assert their alienation from an industrial society whose inhumanity repels them. In order to bring out an underlying psychological distress that "objective" descriptions fail to capture, expressionist writers subordinate conventional (rational) style and let emotion dictate the structure of their works, emphasizing rhythm, disrupted narrative line and broken syntax, and distorted imagery.

Futurism loudly proclaimed its enthusiasm for the dynamic new machine age. F. T. Marinetti (1876–1944) wrote in the first Futurist Manifesto (1908) that "a roaring motor car which seems to run on machine-gun fire is more beautiful than the Winged Victory of Samothrace" (a famous Greek statue). Italian Futurism is still clouded by Marinetti's glorification of terrorism and war, and his delighted description (from the pilot's point of view) of bombs bursting in the air. However, the Futurists' experiments in typography, in free association, in rapid shifts and breaks of syntax; their manipulation of sounds and word placement for special effects apart from semantic meaning; their harshness and stark vision; and above all their eagerness to depict the new age, were all widely imitated.

Dada-Surrealism is the best known of the movements, and the only one to have adherents today. Dada began in Zurich in 1916 as a movement of absolute revolt agains "Papa's Europe," and the word *dada* is a nonsense word which represents the disgust the Dadaists felt for the traditional middle-class values (patriotism, religion, morality, and rationalism) that they blamed for World War I. Dada set out to contradict authority and break all the rules (including those of art), hoping to liberate the creative imagination. Marcel Duchamp (1887–1968) reversed a series of expectations when he named a piece "Why Not Sneeze, Rrose Sélavy?" (1921): it was a small birdcage filled with what looked like sugar lumps and turned out (when you tried to lift the cage) to be carved marble cubes. Tristan Tzara (1896–1963) attacked the notion of the inspired genius by giving a recipe for the Dada poem: the "poet" was to cut words out of a newspaper, shake them in a paper bag, and pull them out one at a time. Dada creations were attacks on the mind and emotions: for Dadaists and Surrealists alike the important thing was to bring about a "revolution of the mind" in which ordinary habits of seeing yielded to a different, "surreal" or "superreal" vision.

Surrealists especially aimed to bring about a fuller awareness of human experience, including both conscious and unconscious states. The Surrealist Manifestoes of 1924 and 1930 proclaimed that Surrealism was a means of expressing "the actual functioning of thought," "the total recuperation of our psychic force by a means that is nothing else than the dizzying descent into ourselves. . . ." André Breton, the Surrealist leader, had been a medical intern in a psychiatric clinic during World War I and was interested in Freud's theories of the unconscious. The Surrealists experimented with various means to liberate the unconscious imagination and reach what they called the "marvelous" point of view: dream-writing, automatic writing (writing rapidly and continuously whatever comes to mind), and chiefly the creation of startling images. The Surrealist image forcibly yokes two seemingly unrelated elements to suggest buried connections, possible relationships not to be discovered by the logical mind. A poem by Paul Eluard, for example, will begin "Earth is blue like an orange, / Never a mistake; words don't lie . . ." and leave it to the reader to make the connections of shape, color, distance, and the fact that the whole vision is brought about in the realm of words (they don't lie). The dreamlike quality and startling imagery of Surrealism has made "surrealist" a convenient word for many unconventional or fantastic works that have no real connection with the movement.

The most generally used term for the change in tastes and artistic strategy at the beginning of the century is modernism, and in its broadest sense modernism will embrace all the separate movements just described. Taken more narrowly, it refers to a group of Anglo-American writers (many associated with the Imagists, 1908–1917) who favored clear, precise images and "common speech" and thought of the work as an art object produced by consummate craft rather than as a statement of emotion. James Joyce, Ezra Pound, T. S. Eliot, William Faulkner, and Virginia Woolf are examples of Anglo-American modernism, and of the larger modernism too. Modernism in general is an attempt to use language in a new way, to reconstruct the world of art much as the philosophers and scientists had redefined the world of their own disciplines. Modernist writers played with shifting and contradictory appearances to suggest the shifting and uncertain nature of reality (Pirandello): they broke up the logically developing plot typical of the nineteenth-century novel, and offered instead unexpected connections or sudden changes of perspective (Woolf); they used interior monologues and free association to express the rhythm of consciousness (Joyce, Woolf); they made much greater use of image clusters, thematic associations, and "musical" patterning to supply the basic structures of both fiction and poetry (Proust, Porter; Stevens, Eliot); they drew attention to style instead of trying to make it "transparent" (Eliot, Brecht); they blended fantasy with reality while representing real historical or psychological dilemmas (Kafka); they raised age-old questions of human identity in terms of contemporary philosophy and psychology (Proust, Camus). Yet there is another element which unites these figures: their experiments with perspective and language are carried on inside still-traditional concepts of individual psychological depth, and of the art work as a coherent aesthetic whole. The combination of discontinuous, experimental style with a continuing belief in the wholeness of the human personality and of the art work carries with it the stamp of what we call the Modernist tradition.

FURTHER READING

The Modern Tradition, edited by Richard Ellmann and Charles Feidelson, Jr. (1965), is a valuable collection of statements by writers, artists, philosophers and scientists, arranged by themes. Willson Coates and Hayden White's *The Ordeal of Liberal Humanism; An Intellectual History of Western Europe* (1970) is an excellent intellectual history of Western Europe after the French Revolution. Harry Levin, "What Was Modernism?" (1962, reprinted in *Refractions*, 1966), is an influential survey of modernist writers as humanists and inheritors of the Enlightenment. Renato Poggioli's *Theory of the Avant-Garde* (1968, translated by Gerald Fitzgerald), locates basic categories of attitudes toward society inside the different arts of the twentieth-century American avant-garde. *History of Modern Art, Painting, Sculpture, Architecture*, by H. H. Arnason (1977), illustrated with many photographs and plates (black-and-white and color), follows the evolution of the arts in the West from the nineteenth century to the 1960s. Examples of Impressionism, Expressionism, Cubism, Surrealism, and contemporary abstract, concrete, and "new realist" art introduce the reader to changes in artistic perception throughout the modern era. Matei Calinescu's *Faces of Modernity* (1977) is a subtly argued, informative collection of essays on the aesthetics of modernism, avant-garde, decadence, and kitsch. *Romanticism, Modernism, Postmodernism*, edited by Harry R. Garvin (1980), is a useful collection of essays that attempt to define changing views of the artistic imagination and its place in society.

WILLIAM BUTLER YEATS

1865–1939

The major figure in the Irish Literary Renaissance defies national boundaries, for William Butler Yeats is also known as the twentieth century's greatest poet in the English language. If that language has a Symbolist poet it is
certainly Yeats, whose use of allusive imagery and symbolic structure underlies many poems that seem first of all merely extraordinarily evocative and
sensuous descriptions. Yeats's symbolism is to be distinguished from that of
his continental predecessors, however, for the European Symbolists did not
share his fascination with occult wisdom, and his construction of a cyclical
model of history for which the rise and fall of civilizations are predetermined
inside a series of interweaving evolutionary spirals. Such mythic vision allowed
Yeats to come to terms with both personal and cultural pain, and helped to
explain—as symptoms of a civilization's declining spiral—the plight of contemporary Irish society and the chaos of European culture around World
War I. Yeats shares with writers like Rilke and T. S. Eliot the quest for
larger meaning in a time of trouble and the use of symbolic language to
articulate that quest.

Yeats was born in a Dublin suburb on June 13, 1865, the oldest of four
children born to John Butler and Susan Pollexfen Yeats. His father, a cosmopolitan man who had turned from law to painting, took over Yeats's
education when he found that, at age nine, the boy could not read. J. B.
Yeats was a highly argumentative religious skeptic who alternately terrorized
his son and awakened his interest in poetry and the visual arts, inspiring at
one and the same time both rebellion against scientific rationalism and belief
in the higher knowledge of art. His mother's strong ties to her home in
County Sligo (where Yeats spent many summers and school holidays) introduced him to the beauties of the Irish countryside and the Irish folklore and
supernatural legends that appear throughout his work. Living alternately in
Ireland and England for much of his youth, Yeats became part of literary
society in both countries and—though an Irish nationalist—was unable to
adopt a narrowly patriotic point of view. Even the Irish Rebellion of 1916
that he celebrated in "Easter 1916," and the revolutionary figures who were
beloved friends, took their place in a larger mythic historical framework. By
the end of his life, he had abandoned all practical politics and devoted himself to the reality of personal experience inside a mystic view of history.

For many, it is Yeats's mastery of images that defines his work. From his
early use of symbols as private keys, or dramatic metaphors for complex
personal emotions, to the immense cosmology of his last work, he continued
to create a highly visual poetry whose power derives from the dramatic interweaving of specific images. Symbols like the Tower, Byzantium, Helen of
Troy, the opposition of sun and moon, birds of prey, the blind man and the
fool recur frequently and draw their meaning not from inner connections
established inside the poem (as for the French Symbolists) but from an
underlying myth based upon occult tradition, Irish folklore, history, and
Yeats's own personal experience. Symbols as Yeats used them, however,
make sense in and among themselves: the "gyre" or spiral unfolding of his-

tory is simultaneously the falcon's spiral flight, and the sphinx-like beast slouching blank-eyed toward Bethlehem in "The Second Coming" is a comprehensible horror capable of many explicit interpretations but resistant to all, and therefore the more terrifying. Even readers unacquainted with Yeats's mythic system will respond to images precisely expressing a situation or state of mind (e.g., golden Byzantium for intellect, art, wisdom—all that "body" cannot supply), and to a visionary organization that proposes shape and context for twentieth-century anxieties.

The nine poems presented here cover the range of Yeats's career, which embraced several periods and styles. Yeats had attended art school and planned to be an artist before he turned fully to literature in 1886, and his early works show the influence of the Pre-Raphaelite school in art and literature. Pre-Raphaelitism called for a return to the sensuous representation and concrete particulars found in Italian painting before Raphael (1483–1520), and Pre-Raphaelite poetry evoked a poetic realm of luminous supernatural beauty described in allusive and erotically sensuous detail. Rossetti's "Blessed Damozel," yearning for her beloved "from the gold bar of heaven," has eyes "deeper than the depth / Of waters stilled at even; / She had three lilies in her hand, / And the stars in her hair were seven." The Pre-Raphaelite fascination with the medieval past (William Morris wrote a "Defense of Guenevere," King Arthur's adulterous wife) joined Yeats's own interest in Irish legend, and in 1889 a long poem describing a traveler in fairyland (The Wanderings of Oisin) established his reputation and won Morris's praise. The musical, evocative style of Yeats's Pre-Raphaelite period is well shown in "The Lake Isle of Innisfree" (1890), with its hidden "bee-loud glade" where "peace comes dropping slow" and evening, after the "purple glow" of noon, is "full of the linnet's wings." Another poem from the same period, "When You Are Old," pleads his love for the beautiful actress and Irish nationalist Maud Gonne, whom he met in 1889 and who repeatedly refused to marry him. From the love poems of his youth to his old age, when "The Circus Animals' Desertion" described her as prey to fanaticism and hate, Yeats returned again and again to examine his feelings for this woman, who personified love, beauty, and Irish nationalism along with hope, frustration, and despair.

Yeats's family moved to London in 1887, where he continued an earlier interest in mystical philosophy by taking up theosophy under its Russian interpreter Madame Blavatsky. Madame Blavatsky claimed mystic knowledge from Tibetan monks and preached a doctrine of the Universal Oversoul, individual spiritual evolution through cycles of incarnation, and the world as a conflict of opposites. Yeats was taken with her grandiose cosmology, although he inconveniently wished to test it by experiment and analysis and was ultimately expelled from the society in 1890. He found a more congenial literary model in the works of a fellow Irishman, William Blake, which he co-edited in 1893 with E. J. Ellis. Yeats's interest in large mystical systems later waned but never altogether disappeared.

Several collections of Irish folk and fairy tales and a book describing Irish traditions (The Celtic Twilight, 1893) demonstrated a corresponding interest in Irish national identity. In 1896 he had met Lady Gregory, an Irish nationalist who invited him to spend summers at her country house in Galway, Coole Park, and worked closely with him (and later J. M. Synge) in founding the Irish National Theatre (later the Abbey Theatre). Along with other participants in what was once called the Irish Literary Renaissance, he aimed to create "a national literature that made Ireland beautiful in the memory . . . freed from provincialism by an exacting criticism." To this end, he wrote *Cathleen ni Houlihan* (1902), a play in which the title character personifies Ireland and which became immensely popular with Irish nationalists. He also established Irish literary societies in Dublin and Ireland, promoted and reviewed Irish books, and lectured and wrote about the need for Irish community. In 1922 he was elected an Irish senator, serving until 1928.

Gradually Yeats became embittered by the split between narrow Irish nationalism and the free expression of Irish culture. He was outraged at the attacks on Synge's *Playboy of the Western World* for its supposed derogatory picture of Irish culture, and he commented scathingly in *Poems Written in Discouragement* (1913, reprinted in *Responsibilities*, 1914) on the inability of the Irish middle class to appreciate art or literature. When he celebrates the abortive Easter uprisings of 1916, it is with a more universal, aesthetic view; "A terrible beauty is born" in the self-sacrifice that leads even a "drunken, vainglorious lout" to be "transformed utterly" by political martyrdom. Except for summers at Coole Park, Yeats in his middle age was spending more time in England than in Ireland. He began his *Autobiographies* in 1914, and wrote symbolic plays intended for small audiences on the model of the Japanese Noh theater. There is a change in the tone of his works at this time, a new precision and epigrammatic quality that is partly due to his disappointment with the narrowness of Irish nationalism and partly to the new tastes in poetry promulgated by his friend Ezra Pound and by T. S. Eliot after the example of John Donne and the metaphysical poets.

Yeats's marriage in 1917 to Georgie Hyde-Lees provided him with much-needed stability and also an impetus to work out a larger symbolic scheme. He interpreted his wife's experiments with automatic writing (writing whatever comes to mind, without correction or rational intent) as glimpses into a hidden cosmic order, and gradually evolved a total system which he explained in *A Vision* (1925). The wheel of history takes 26,000 years to turn, and inside that wheel civilizations evolve in roughly 2,000-year *gyres*, spirals expanding outward until they collapse at the beginning of a new gyre which will reverse the direction of the old. Human personalities fall into different types within the system, and both gyres and types are related to the different phases of the moon. Yeats's later poems in *The Tower* (1928), *The Winding Stair* (1933), and the *Last Poems* (1939) are set in the context of this system. Even when it is not literally present, it suggests an organizing pattern that resolves contraries inside an immense historical perspective. "Leda and the Swan," on one level an erotic retelling of a mythic rape, also foreshadows the Trojan War—brute force mirroring brute force. In the two poems on Byzantium, Yeats admired an artistic civilization which "could answer all my questions," but which was also only a moment in history. Byzantine art, with its stylized perspectives and mosaics made by arranging tiny colored pieces of stone, was the exact opposite of the Western tendency to imitate nature, and it provided a kind of escape, or healing distance, for the poet. The idea of an inhuman, metallic, abstract beauty separated "out of nature" by art expresses a mystic and Symbolist quest for an invulnerable world distinct from the ravages of time. This world was to be found in an idealized

Byzantium, where the poet's body would be transmuted into "such a form as Grecian goldsmiths make / Of hammered gold and gold enamelling / To keep a drowsy Emperor awake; / Or set upon a golden bough to sing / To lords and ladies of Byzantium / Of what is past, or passing, or to come." At the end of "Among School Children," the sixty-year-old "public man" compensates for the passing of youth by dreaming of pure "Presences" that never fade. Yeats had often adopted the persona of the old man for whom the perspectives of age, idealized beauty, or of history were ways to keep human agony at a distance. In "Lapis Lazuli," the tragic figures of history transcend their roles by the calm "gaiety" with which they accept their fate; the ancient Chinamen carved in the poem's damaged blue stone climb toward a vantage point where they stare detachedly down on the world's tragedies: "Their eyes mid many wrinkles, their eyes, / Their ancient, glittering eyes, are gay."

But the world is still there; its tragedies still take place; and Yeats's poetry is always aware of the physical and emotional roots from which it sprang. Whatever the wished-for distance, his poems are full of passionate feelings, erotic desire and disappointment, delight in sensuous beauty, horror at civil war and anarchy, dismay at degradation and change. By the time of his death on January 28, 1939, Yeats had rejected his Byzantine identity as the golden songbird, and sought out "the brutality, the ill breeding, the barbarism of truth." "The Wild Old Wicked Man" replaced earlier druids or ancient Chinamen as spokesman, and in "The Circus Animals' Desertion" Yeats described his former themes as so many circus animals put on display. No matter how much these themes embodied "pure mind," they were based in "a mound of refuse or the sweepings of a street . . . the foul rag-and-bone shop of the heart"—the rose springing from the dunghill. Yeats's poetry, which draws its initial power from the mastery of images and verbal rhythm, continues to resonate in the reader's mind for this attempt to come to terms with reality, to grasp and make sense of human experience in the transfiguring language of art.

Edward Malins presents a brief introduction with biography, illustrations, and maps in *A Preface to Yeats* (1977). Richard Ellmann's *The Identity of Yeats*, 2nd ed. (1964), is an excellent discussion of Yeats's work as a whole. Norman A. Jeffares has revised his major study, *A New Commentary on the Collected Poems of W. B. Yeats* (1983).

When You Are Old[1]

When you are old and gray and full of sleep,
And nodding by the fire, take down this book,
And slowly read, and dream of the soft look
Your eyes had once, and of their shadows deep;

How many loved your moments of glad grace,   5
And loved your beauty with love false or true,

---

1. An adaptation of a love sonnet by the French Renaissance poet, Pierre de Ronsard, which begins similarly ("Quand vous serez bien vieille . . .") but ends by asking the beloved to "pluck the roses of life today."

But one man loved the pilgrim soul in you,
And loved the sorrows of your changing face;

And bending down beside the glowing bars,
Murmur, a little sadly, how Love fled   10
And paced upon the mountains overhead
And hid his face amid a crowd of stars.

Easter 1916[2]

I have met them at close of day
Coming with vivid faces
From counter or desk among grey
Eighteenth-century houses.
I have passed with a nod of the head   5
Or polite meaningless words,
Or have lingered awhile and said
Polite meaningless words,
And thought before I had done
Of a mocking tale or a gibe   10
To please a companion
Around the fire at the club,
Being certain that they and I
But lived where motley is worn:
All changed, changed utterly: 15
A terrible beauty is born.

That woman's days were spent
In ignorant good-will,
Her nights in argument
Until her voice grew shrill.   20
What voice more sweet than hers
When, young and beautiful,
She rode to harriers?[3]
This man had kept a school
And rode our wingèd horse;   25
This other his helper and friend
Was coming into his force;[4]
He might have won fame in the end,
So sensitive his nature seemed,
So daring and sweet his thought.   30
This other man I had dreamed

2. On Easter Sunday, 1916, Irish nationalists began an unsuccessful rebellion against British rule
which lasted throughout the week and ended in the surrender and execution of its leaders.
3. Constance Gore-Booth, later Countess Markiewicz, an ardent nationalist.   4. Patrick Pearse
and his friend Thomas MacDonagh, both schoolmasters and both executed by the British. As a
Gaelic poet, Pearse symbolically rode the winged horse of the Muses, Pegasus.

A drunken, vainglorious lout.
He had done most bitter wrong
To some who are near my heart,[5]
Yet I number him in the song;   35
He, too, has resigned his part
In the casual comedy;
He, too, has been changed in his turn,
Transformed utterly:
A terrible beauty is born.   40

Hearts with one purpose alone
Through summer and winter seem
Enchanted to a stone
To trouble the living stream.
The horse that comes from the road,   45
The rider, the birds that range
From cloud to tumbling cloud,
Minute by minute they change;
A shadow of cloud on the stream
Changes minute by minute;   50
A horse-hoof slides on the brim,
And a horse plashes within it;
The long-legged moor-hens dive,
And hens to moor-cocks call;
Minute by minute they live: 55
The stone's in the midst of all.

Too long a sacrifice
Can make a stone of the heart.
O when may it suffice?
That is Heaven's part, our part   60
To murmur name upon name,
As a mother names her child
When sleep at last has come
On limbs that had run wild.
What is it but nightfall?   65
No, no, not night but death;
Was it needless death after all?
For England may keep faith
For all that is done and said.
We know their dream; enough   70
To know they dreamed and are dead;
And what if excess of love
Bewildered them till they died?
I write it out in a verse—

5. Major John MacBride, who had married and separated from Maud Gonne, Yeats's great love.

MacDonagh and MacBride   75
And Connolly[6] and Pearse
Now and in time to be,
Wherever green is worn,
Are changed, changed utterly:
A terrible beauty is born.   80

September 25, 1916

The Second Coming[7]

Turning and turning in the widening gyre[8]
The falcon cannot hear the falconer;
Things fall apart; the centre cannot hold;
Mere anarchy is loosed upon the world,
The blood-dimmed tide is loosed, and everywhere   5
The ceremony of innocence is drowned;
The best lack all conviction, while the worst
Are full of passionate intensity.

Surely some revelation is at hand;
Surely the Second Coming is at hand.   10
The Second Coming! Hardly are those words out
When a vast image out of *Spiritus Mundi*[9]
Troubles my sight: somewhere in sands of the desert
A shape with lion body and the head of a man
A gaze blank and pitiless as the sun,   15
Is moving its slow thighs, while all about it
Reel shadows of the indignant desert birds.
The darkness drops again; but now I know
That twenty centuries of stony sleep
Were vexed to nightmare by a rocking cradle,   20
And what rough beast, its hour come round at last,
Slouches towards Bethlehem to be born?

Leda and the Swan[1]

A sudden blow: the great wings beating still
Above the staggering girl, her thighs caressed
By the dark webs, her nape caught in his bill,
He holds her helpless breast upon his breast.

6. James Connolly, labor leader and nationalist executed by the British.   7. The Second Coming of Christ, believed by Christians to herald the end of the world, is transformed here into the prediction of a new birth initiating a new era and terminating the 2000-year cycle of Christianity.   8. The gyre (pronounced by Yeats with a hard "g") is the cone-pattern of the falcon's flight and of historical cycles, in Yeats's vision.   9. "World-soul" or, as *Anima Mundi* in Yeats's *Per Amica Silentia Lunae*, a "great memory" containing archetypal images; recalls C. G. Jung's "collective unconscious."   1. Zeus, ruler of the Greek gods, took the form of a swan to rape the mortal Leda; she gave birth to Helen of Troy, whose beauty caused the Trojan War.

How can those terrified vague fingers push   5
The feathered glory from her loosening thighs?
And how can body, laid in that white rush,
But feel the strange heart beating where it lies?

A shudder in the loins engenders there
The broken wall, the burning roof and tower   10
And Agamemnon dead.[2]
                              Being so caught up,
So mastered by the brute blood of the air,
Did she put on his knowledge with his power
Before the indifferent beak could let her drop?

Sailing to Byzantium[3]

I

That is no country for old men. The young
In one another's arms, birds in the trees
—Those dying generations—at their song,
The salmon-falls, the mackerel-crowded seas,
Fish, flesh, or fowl, commend all summer long   5
Whatever is begotten, born, and dies.
Caught in the sensual music all neglect
Monuments of unageing intellect.

II

An aged man is but a paltry thing,
A tattered coat upon a stick, unless   10
Soul clap its hands and sing, and louder sing
For every tatter in its mortal dress,
Nor is there singing school but studying
Monuments of its own magnificence;
And therefore I have sailed the seas and come   15
To the holy city of Byzantium.

III

O sages standing in God's holy fire
As in the gold mosaic of a wall,
Come from the holy fire, perne in a gyre,[4]
And be the singing-masters of my soul.   20
Consume my heart away; sick with desire

2. The ruins of Troy and the death of Agamemnon, the Greek leader, whose sacrifice of his
daughter Iphigenia to win the gods' favor caused his wife, Clytemnestra (also a daughter of Leda),
to assassinate him on his return.   3. Byzantium, the ancient name for modern Istanbul, was
the capital of the eastern Roman Empire and represented for Yeats (who had seen Byzantine
mosaics in Italy) a highly stylized and perfectly integrated artistic world where "religious, aesthetic,
and practical life were one."   4. "Come spinning down in a spiral." (Pirn, a spool or bobbin;
for gyre, see note to "The Second Coming.")

And fastened to a dying animal
It knows not what it is; and gather me
Into the artifice of eternity.

IV

Once out of nature I shall never take   25
My bodily form from any natural thing,
But such a form as Grecian goldsmiths make
Of hammered gold and gold enamelling
To keep a drowsy Emperor awake;
Or set upon a golden bough to sing   30
To lords and ladies of Byzantium
Of what is past, or passing, or to come.

Among School Children

1

I walk through the long schoolroom questioning;
A kind old nun in a white hood replies;
The children learn to cipher and to sing,
To study reading-books and history,
To cut and sew, be neat in everything   5
In the best modern way—the children's eyes
In momentary wonder stare upon
A sixty-year-old smiling public man.[5]

2

I dream of a Ledaean body,[6] bent
Above a sinking fire, a tale that she   10
Told of a harsh reproof, or trivial event
That changed some childish day to tragedy—
Told, and it seemed that our two natures blent
Into a sphere from youthful sympathy,
Or else, to alter Plato's parable,   15
Into the yolk and white of the one shell.[7]

3

And thinking of that fit of grief or rage
I look upon one child or t'other there
And wonder if she stood so at that age—
For even daughters of the swan can share   20
Something of every paddler's heritage—

5. Yeats was elected senator of the Irish Free State in 1922.   6. Beautiful as Leda, or as her daughter Helen of Troy.   7. In Plato's *Symposium*, Socrates explains love by telling how the gods split human beings into two halves—like halves of an egg—so that each half seeks its opposite throughout life. Yeats compares the two parts to the yolk and white of an egg.

And had that color upon cheek or hair,
And thereupon my heart is driven wild:
She stands before me as a living child.

4

Her present image floats into the mind—   25
Did Quattrocento finger fashion it
Hollow of cheek as though it drank the wind
And took a mess of shadows for its meat?[8]
And I though never of Ledaean kind
Had pretty plumage once—enough of that,   30
Better to smile on all that smile, and show
There is a comfortable kind of old scarecrow.

5

What youthful mother, a shape upon her lap
Honey of generation had betrayed,
And that must sleep, shriek, struggle to escape   35
As recollection or the drug decide,[9]
Would think her son, did she but see that shape
With sixty or more winters on its head,
A compensation for the pang of his birth,
Or the uncertainty of his setting forth?   40

6

Plato thought nature but a spume that plays
Upon a ghostly paradigm of things;
Solider Aristotle played the taws
Upon the bottom of a king of kings;
World-famous golden-thighed Pythagoras   45
Fingered upon a fiddle-stick or strings
What a star sang and careless Muses heard:[1]
Old clothes upon old sticks to scare a bird.

7

Both nuns and mothers worship images,
But those the candles light are not as those   50

8. The Italian fifteenth century is known as the Quattrocento; painters like Botticelli (1444–1510)
were known for their delicate figures.   9. Yeats's note to this poem recalls the third-century
scholar Porphyry, who associates "honey" with "the pleasure arising from copulation" that engenders children; the poet further describes honey as a "drug" destroying the child's " 'recollection'
of pre-natal freedom."   1. Three Greek philosophers: *Plato* (427–437 B.C.) believed that nature
was only a series of illusionistic reflections or appearances cast by abstract "forms" which were the
only true realities; *Aristotle* (384–322 B.C.), more pragmatic, was Alexander the Great's tutor and
spanked him with the "taws" (leather straps); *Pythagoras* (582–407 B.C., a demigod to his disciples
and thought to have a golden thigh-bone) pondered the relationship of music, mathematics, and
the stars.

That animate a mother's reveries,
But keep a marble or a bronze repose.
And yet they too break hearts—O Presences
That passion, piety, or affection knows,
And that all heavenly glory symbolize—   55
O self-born mockers of man's enterprise;

8

Labor is blossoming or dancing where
The body is not bruised to pleasure soul,
Nor beauty born out of its own despair,
Nor blear-eyed wisdom out of midnight oil.   60
O chestnut tree, great-rooted blossomer,
Are you the leaf, the blossom, or the bole?
O body swayed to music, O brightening glance,
How can we know the dancer from the dance?

Byzantium[2]

The unpurged images of day recede;
The Emperor's drunken soldiery are abed;
Night resonance recedes, night-walkers' song
After great cathedral gong;
A starlit or a moonlit dome[3] disdains
All that man is,
All mere complexities,
The fury and the mire of human veins.

Before me floats an image, man or shade,
Shade more than man, more image than a shade;   10
For Hades' bobbin bound in mummy-cloth
May unwind the winding path;[4]
A mouth that has no moisture and no breath
Breathless mouths may summon;
I hail the superhuman;   15
I call it death-in-life and life-in-death.

Miracle, bird or golden handiwork,
More miracle than bird or handiwork,
Planted on the starlit golden bough,

---

2. The "holy city" of "Sailing to Byzantium," seen here as it resists and transforms the blood and mire of human life into its own transcendent world of art.   3. According to Yeats's system in A *Vision*, the first "starlit" phase in which the moon does not shine, and the fifteenth, opposing phase of the full moon, represent complete objectivity (potential being) and complete subjectivity (the achievement of complete beauty). In between these absolute phases lie the evolving "mere complexities" of human life.   4. Unwinding the spool of fate that leads from mortal death (Hades, the realm of the dead in Greek mythology) to the superhuman.

Can like the cocks of Hades crow,[5]　　　　　　　　　　20
Or, by the moon embittered, scorn aloud
In glory of changeless metal
Common bird or petal
And all complexities of mire or blood.

At midnight on the Emperor's pavement flit　　　　　　25
Flames that no faggot feeds, nor steel has lit,
Nor storm disturbs, flames begotten of flame,
Where blood-begotten spirits come
And all complexities of fury leave,
Dying into a dance,　　　　　　　　　　　　　　　30
An agony of trance,
An agony of flame that cannot singe a sleeve.

Astraddle on the dolphin's mire and blood,[6]
Spirit after spirit! The smithies break the flood,
The golden smithies of the Emperor!
Marbles of the dancing floor
Break bitter furies of complexity,
Those images that yet
Fresh images beget,
That dolphin-torn, that gong-tormented sea.

Lapis Lazuli[7]

For Harry Clifton

I have heard that hysterical women say
They are sick of the palette and fiddle-bow,
Of poets that are always gay,
For everybody knows or else should know
That if nothing drastic is done　　　　　　　　　　5
Aeroplane and Zeppelin will come out,
Pitch like King Billy bomb-balls in
Until the town lie beaten flat.[8]

5. To mark the transition from death to the dawn of new life.　　6. A dolphin rescued the famous singer Arion by carrying him on his back over the sea. Dolphins were associated with Apollo, Greek god of music and prophecy, and in ancient art they are often shown escorting the souls of the dead to the Isles of the Blessed. Here, the dolphin is also flesh and blood, a part of life. 7. A deep blue semiprecious stone. One of Yeats's letters describes a Chinese carving in lapis lazuli that depicts an ascetic and pupil about to climb a mountain. "Ascetic, pupil, hard stone, eternal theme of the sensual east . . . the east has its solutions always and therefore knows nothing of tragedy." [Letter to Dorothy Wellesley, July 6, 1935.]　　8. Zeppelins—long, cylindrical airships supported by internal gas chambers—were used for bombing by the Germans during World War I. King Billy: another linkage of past and present. According to an Irish ballad, William III, King of England, "threw his bomb-balls in" and set fire to the tents of the deposed James II at the Battle of the Boyne in 1690; also a reference to Kaiser Wilhelm II (King William II) of Germany, who sent the zeppelins to bomb London.

All perform their tragic play,
There struts Hamlet, there is Lear, 10
That's Ophelia, that Cordelia;[9]
Yet they, should the last scene be there,
The great stage curtain about to drop,
If worthy their prominent part in the play,
Do not break up their lines to weep. 15
They know that Hamlet and Lear are gay;
Gaiety transfiguring all that dread.
All men have aimed at, found and lost;
Black out;[1] Heaven blazing into the head:
Tragedy wrought to its uttermost. 20
Though Hamlet rambles and Lear rages,
And all the drop-scenes drop at once
Upon a hundred thousand stages,
It cannot grow by an inch or an ounce.

On their own feet they came, or on shipboard, 25
Camel-back, horse-back, ass-back, mule-back,
Old civilisations put to the sword.
Then they and their wisdom went to rack:
No handiwork of Callimachus,[2]
Who handled marble as if it were bronze, 30
Made draperies that seemed to rise
When sea-wind swept the corner, stands;
His long lamp-chimney shaped like the stem
Of a slender palm, stood but a day;
All things fall and are built again, 35
And those that build them again are gay.

Two Chinamen, behind them a third,
Are carved in lapis lazuli,
Over them flies a long-legged bird,
A symbol of longevity;[3] 40
The third, doubtless a serving-man,
Carries a musical instrument.

Every discoloration of the stone,
Every accidental crack or dent,
Seems a water-course or an avalanche, 45
Or lofty slope where it still snows
Though doubtless plum or cherry-branch

9. Tragic figures in Shakespeare. 1. The loss of rational consciousness making way for the
blaze of inner revelation or "mad" tragic vision. (Also suggestion of final curtain, and of air raid
curfew.) 2. Fifth-century B.C. Athenian sculptor famous for a gold lamp in the Erechtheum
(temple on the Acropolis) and for using drill lines in marble to give the effect of flowing drapery.
3. The crane.

Sweetens the little half-way house
Those Chinamen climb towards, and I
Delight to imagine them seated there;   50
There, on the mountain and the sky,
On all the tragic scene they stare.
One asks for mournful melodies;
Accomplished fingers begin to play.
Their eyes mid many wrinkles, their eyes,   55
Their ancient, glittering eyes, are gay.

The Circus Animals' Desertion

I

I sought a theme and sought for it in vain,
I sought it daily for six weeks or so.
Maybe at last, being but a broken man,
I must be satisfied with my heart, although
Winter and summer till old age began   5
My circus animals were all on show,
Those stilted boys, that burnished chariot,
Lion and woman[4] and the Lord knows what.

II

What can I but enumerate old themes?
First that sea-rider Oisin led by the nose   10
Through three enchanted islands, allegorical dreams,[5]
Vain gaiety, vain battle, vain repose,
Themes of the embittered heart, or so it seems,
That might adorn old songs or courtly shows;
But what cared I that set him on to ride,   15
I, starved for the bosom of his faery bride?

And then a counter-truth filled out its play,
The Countess Cathleen[6] was the name I gave it;
She, pity-crazed, had given her soul away,
But masterful Heaven had intervened to save it.   20
I thought my dear must her own soul destroy,
So did fanaticism and hate enslave it,
And this brought forth a dream and soon enough
This dream itself had all my thought and love.

4. Yeats enumerates images and themes from his earlier work: here, the sphinx of "The Double
Vision of Michael Robartes." 5. In The Wanderings of Oisin (1889), an early poem where
Yeats describes a legendary Irish hero who wandered in fairyland for 150 years. 6. Title of a
play (1892, dedicated to Maud Gonne) in which the countess is saved by Heaven after having sold
her soul to the devil in exchange for food for the poor. The figure of Cathleen comes up frequently
in Yeats's work, and is often taken as a personification of nationalist Ireland.

And when the Fool and Blind Man stole the bread   25
Cuchulain[7] fought the ungovernable sea;
Heart-mysteries there, and yet when all is said
It was the dream itself enchanted me:
Character isolated by a deed
To engross the present and dominate memory.   30
Players and painted stage took all my love,
And not those things that they were emblems of.

III

Those masterful images because complete
Grew in pure mind, but out of what began?
A mound of refuse or the sweepings of a street,   35
Old kettles, old bottles, and a broken can,
Old iron, old bones, old rags, that raving slut
Who keeps the till. Now that my ladder's gone,
I must lie down where all the ladders start,
In the foul rag-and-bone shop of the heart.   40

LUIGI PIRANDELLO
1867–1936

Although Pirandello's basic themes reappear throughout his novels, short stories, and plays, he is best known as an innovative dramatist who revolutionized stage techniques at the same time that he dramatized issues later known as "existential": the difficulty of achieving a sense of identity, the impossibility of communication, and the overlapping frontiers of appearance and reality. Instead of the late nineteenth-century's "well-made play," with its neatly constructed plot offering a conventional beginning, middle, and end, and characters who remained safely on the other side of the footlights, Pirandello offered plays that sometimes seemed merely improvised and that always raised questions about the roles assumed in everyday life. It is not easy to know the truth, he suggests, or to make oneself known behind the "naked mask" that each of us wears in society. Pirandello composes a fully self-reflexive theater that readily displays its own nature as illusion: plays exist within plays until one is not sure where the "real" play begins, and characters question their own reality and that of the audience. In their manipulation of contradictory appearances and often tragicomic effects, these plays foreshadow the absurdist theater of Samuel Beckett and Eugène Ionesco, the cosmic irony of Antonin Artaud's "Theater of Cruelty," and the emphasis on spectacle and illusion in works by Jean Genet.

Pirandello was born in Girgenti (now Agrigento), Sicily, on June 28, 1867. His father was a sulphur merchant who intended his son to go into business

7. In *On Baile's Strand*, a 1904 play. *Cuchulain* (KOO-hoo-lin) is a legendary Irish hero.

like himself, but Pirandello preferred language and literature. After studying in Palermo and the University of Rome, he traveled to the University of Bonn in 1888 where he received a doctorate in Romance Philology in 1891 with a thesis on the dialect of his home town. In 1894, Pirandello made an arranged marriage with the daughter of a rich sulphur merchant. They lived for ten years in Rome, where he wrote poetry and short stories, until the collapse of the sulphur mines destroyed the fortunes of both families. Not only was Pirandello suddenly forced to earn a living, but his wife became insane with a jealous paranoia that lasted until her death in 1918. Pirandello himself died on December 1, 1936.

Pirandello's early poetry was indebted to nineteenth-century Italian predecessors like Giosuè Carducci (1835–1907). He also translated Goethe's *Roman Elegies* in 1896. Soon, however, he turned to short stories or *novelle* under the influence of a narrative style called *verismo* (realism) exemplified in the work of the Sicilian writer Giovanni Verga (1840–1922). Pirandello wrote hundreds of stories of all lengths and, in his clarity, realism, and psychological acuteness, which did not rule out a liking for a certain grotesqueness, is recognized as an Italian master of the story much as was Guy de Maupassant (1850–1893) in France. Collections include the 1894 *Love Without Love* and an anthology in 1922 titled *A Year's Worth of Stories.*

In such stories, and in his early novels, Pirandello begins to develop his characteristic themes: the questioning of appearance and reality and problems of identity. In *The Outcast* (1901), an irate husband drives his innocent wife out of the house only to take her back when—without his knowing it— the supposed adultery has actually occurred. The hero of Pirandello's best-known novel, *The Late Mattia Pascal*, tries to create a fresh identity for himself and leave behind the old Mattia Pascal. When things become too difficult he returns to his "late" self and begins to write his life story: an early example of the tendency in Pirandello's works to comment on their own composition. The protagonists in these and other works are visibly commonplace, middle-class citizens, neither heroic nor villainous, but prototypes of the twentieth-century "antihero" who takes the center of the stage while remaining aggressively average.

The questions of identity that obsessed Pirandello (he speaks of them as reflecting the "pangs of my spirit") are explored on social, psychological, and metaphysical levels. He was acquainted with the experimental psychology of his day, and learned from works like Alfred Binet's *Personality Alterations* (1892) about the existence of a subconscious personality beneath our everyday awareness (a theme Pirandello shares with Proust and Freud). Successive layers of personality, conflicts among the various parts, and the simultaneous existence of multiple perspectives shape an identity that is never fixed but always fluid and changing. This identity escapes the grasp of onlookers and subject alike, and expresses a basic incongruity in human existence that challenges the most earnest attempts to create a unified self. The protagonist of a later novel, *One, None, and a Hundred Thousand* (1925–26) finds that what "he" is depends on the viewpoint of a great number of people. Such incongruity can be tragic or comic—or both at once—according to one's attitude, a topic which Pirandello explored in a 1908 essay, *On Humor*, and which is echoed in the double-edged humor of his plays. The "Pirandellian" themes of ambiguous identity, lack of communication, and deceptive appearance reappear in all the genres, however, reaching a particular intensity in his first dramatic success (*It Is So [If You Think So]*, 1917), and in the play printed here, *Six Characters in Search of an Author.*

First performed in Paris in 1923, *Six Characters in Search of an Author* (1921) represented a change from the mimetic realism and unified character portrayals of nineteenth-century drama and offered a new psychological realism emphasizing the ambiguity of language and motivation and the impossibility of communication between individuals. These ideas were also being explored by existentialist thinkers at the same time, and through Pirandello made their way into the repertory of the theater. Later playwrights like Eugène Ionesco, Samuel Beckett, Edward Albee, and Harold Pinter (and, to a lesser degree, Jean-Paul Sartre and T. S. Eliot) show the influence of Pirandellian attitudes and dialogue in their work.

Six Characters in Search of an Author and *Henry IV* established Pirandello's stature as a major dramatist. He directed his own company (the Teatro d'Arte di Roma) from 1924 to 1928 and received the Nobel Prize for Literature in 1934. His later plays, featuring fantastic and grotesque elements, did not achieve the wide popularity of their predecessors. In 1936, he published a collection of 43 plays as *Naked Masks*, a title conceived in 1918 after Luigi Chiarelli's "grotesque theater." Pirandello's characters are "naked" and vulnerable inside their social roles or masks: Henry IV, trapped for life inside a pretense of insanity, or the Father in *Six Characters*, forced to play out a demeaning role in which, he insists, only part of his true nature is revealed. The term "naked mask" also suggests Pirandello's superb manipulation of theatrical ambiguity—the confusion between the actor and the character he portrays—that ultimately prolongs the confusion of appearance and reality which is one of his chief themes. Pirandello is famous in twentieth-century theater for his use of the "play within a play," a technique of embedded dramatic episodes that maintain a life of their own while serving as foil to the overall or governing plot. Dividing lines are sometimes hard to draw when stage dialogue can be taken as referring to either context, a situation that allows for double meanings at the same time that it reiterates the impossibility of real communication.

Six Characters in Search of an Author combines all these elements in an extraordinarily self-reflexive style. From the beginning, where the audience apparently sees the rehearsal of another Pirandellian play (including comments in which the author pokes fun at his reputation for obscurity), to the invasion of the stage by characters out of an unwritten novel, demanding to be given dramatic existence, the play is continually in the process of being composed: composed as the interwoven double plot we see on stage, written down in shorthand by the prompter for the actors to reproduce, and potentially composed as the characters' inner drama finally achieves its rightful existence as a work of art. The conflicts between the different levels of the play finally prevent the completion of any but the first work, but it has created a convincing dramatic illusion in the meantime (it is difficult not to believe in Madame Pace when she walks on stage) that incorporates the psychological drama of the "six characters," as well as a discussion of the relationship of life and art.

The initial absurdity of the play appears when six admittedly fictional characters arrive with their claim to be "truer and more real" than the "real" characters they confront. (Of course, to the audience all the actors on stage are equally unreal.) Their greater "truth" is the truth of art with its profound but formally fixed glimpses into human nature. Each character represents, specifically and in depth, a particular identity created by the author. They are incapable of developing outside that role and are condemned, in their search for existence, painfully to re-enact their essential selves.

Conversely, the fictional characters have a more stable personality than "real" people who are still "nobody," incomplete, open to change and misinterpretation. Characters are "somebody" because their nature has been decided once and for all. Yet there is a further complication to this contrast between real and fictional characters: the characters have real anxieties in that they want to play their own roles, and are disturbed at the prospect of having actors represent them incorrectly. All human beings, suggests Pirandello, whether fictional or real, are subject to misunderstanding. We even misunderstand ourselves when we think we are the same person in all situations. "We have this illusion of being one person for all," says the Father, "but it isn't true." When he explains himself as a very human philosopher driven by the Demon of Experiment, his self-image is quite different from the picture held by his vengeful Step-Daughter or the passive Mother who blames him for her expulsion from the house. The Step-Daughter, in turn, appears to love an innocent little sister because she reminds her of an earlier self. It is an entanglement of motives and "deceit of mutual understanding" that goes beyond the tabloid level of a sordid family scandal and claims a broader scope. Pirandello, in fact, does not intend merely to describe a particular setting or situation: that is the concern of what he calls "historical writers." He belongs to the opposite category of "philosophical writers" whose characters and situations embody "a particular sense of life and acquire from it a universal value."

Pirandello does not hold his audience by uttering grand philosophical truths, however. There is constant suspense and a process of discovery in *Six Characters*, from the moment that the rehearsal with its complaining actors and Manager is interrupted and the initial hints of melodrama and family scandal catch our attention in the Step-Daughter's and Mother's complaints. It is a story that could be found in the most sensational papers: an adulterous wife thrust out of her home and supporting herself and her children after her lover's death by sewing; the daughter's turn to prostitution to support the family; the father's unknowing attempt to seduce his step-daughter (interpreted by the latter as the continuation of an old and perverse impulse); and the final drowning and suicide of the two youngest children. Pirandello plays with the sensational aspect of his story by focusing the play around the characters' repeated attempts to portray the seduction scene; actors and Manager perceive the saleable quality of such "human-interest" events and are eager to let the story unfold. The daughter's protective fondness for her doomed baby sister, and her puzzling reproach to the little boy ("Instead of killing myself, I'd have shot one of those two") hints at an inner plot which is revealed only as the action continues. The level of illusion and the level of "reality" persist to the very end, when the little boy's suicide is seen alternately as death and make-believe. If the Manager dismisses what has just occurred with the cry "I've lost a whole day over these people, a whole day!" the audience—which sees both Manager and characters as illusions—is more willing to entertain the possibility that this play is a "real" description of the human condition.

A good biography and general introduction is found in Susan Bassnett-McGuire, *Pirandello* (1984). Walter Starkie's *Luigi Pirandello, 1867–1936,* 3rd. ed., revised and enlarged (1965), is a general study against the background of twentieth-century Italian literature: novels, stories, plays, and themes. The study *Pirandello: A Collection of Critical Essays* (1967), edited by Glauco Cambon, lays emphasis to the plays.

Six Characters in Search of an Author[1]

A Comedy in the Making

Characters of the Comedy in the Making

THE FATHER	THE BOY
THE MOTHER	THE CHILD
THE STEP-DAUGHTER	*(The last two do not speak)*
THE SON	MADAME PACE

Actors of the Company

THE MANAGER	OTHER ACTORS AND ACTRESSES
LEADING LADY	PROPERTY MAN
LEADING MAN	PROMPTER
SECOND LADY	MACHINIST
LEAD	MANAGER'S SECRETARY
L'INGÉNUE	DOOR-KEEPER
JUVENILE LEAD	SCENE-SHIFTERS

Daytime. The Stage of a Theatre

N.B. The Comedy is without acts or scenes. The performance is interrupted once, without the curtain being lowered, when the manager and the chief characters withdraw to arrange the scenario. A second interruption of the action takes place when, by mistake, the stage hands let the curtain down.

ACT I

The spectators will find the curtain raised and the stage as it usually is during the day time. It will be half dark, and empty, so that

1. English version by Edward Storer.

from the beginning the public may have the impression of an impromptu performance.

Prompter's box and a small table and chair for the manager.

Two other small tables and several chairs scattered about as during rehearsals.

The ACTORS *and* ACTRESSES *of the company enter from the back of the stage: first one, then another, then two together; nine or ten in all. They are about to rehearse a Pirandello play: Mixing It Up.*[2] *Some of the company move off towards their dressing rooms. The* PROMPTER *who has the "book" under his arm, is waiting for the manager in order to begin the rehearsal.*

The ACTORS *and* ACTRESSES, *some standing, some sitting, chat and smoke. One perhaps reads a paper; another cons his part.*

Finally, the MANAGER *enters and goes to the table prepared for him. His* SECRETARY *brings him his mail, through which he glances. The* PROMPTER *takes his seat, turns on a light, and opens the "book."*

THE MANAGER [*throwing a letter down on the table*]. I can't see [*To* PROPERTY MAN.] Let's have a little light, please!

PROPERTY MAN. Yes sir, yes, at once. [*A light comes down on to the stage.*]

THE MANAGER [*clapping his hands*]. Come along! Come along! Second act of "Mixing It Up." [*Sits down.*]

[*The* ACTORS *and* ACTRESSES *go from the front of the stage to the wings, all except the three who are to begin the rehearsal.*]

THE PROMPTER [*reading the "book"*]. "Leo Gala's house. A curious room serving as dining-room and study."

THE MANAGER [*to* PROPERTY MAN]. Fix up the old red room.

PROPERTY MAN [*noting it down*]. Red set. All right!

THE PROMPTER [*continuing to read from the "book"*]. "Table already laid and writing desk with books and papers. Book-shelves. Exit rear to Leo's bedroom. Exit left to kitchen. Principal exit to right."

THE MANAGER [*energetically*]. Well, you understand: The principal exit over there; here, the kitchen. [*Turning to actor who is to play the part of* SOCRATES.][3] You make your entrances and exits here. [*To* PROPERTY MAN.] The baize doors at the rear, and curtains.

PROPERTY MAN [*noting it down*]. Right!

PROMPTER [*reading as before*]. "When the curtain rises, Leo Gala, dressed in cook's cap and apron, is busy beating an egg in a cup. Philip, also dressed as a cook, is beating another egg. Guido Venanzi is seated and listening."

---

2. *Il giuoco delle parti*, written in 1918. The hero, Leone Gala, pretends to ignore the infidelity of his wife, Silia, until the end, when he takes revenge by tricking her lover, Guido Venanzi, into taking his place in a fatal duel she had engineered to get rid of her husband.   3. Nickname given to Gala's servant, Philip, in *Mixing It Up*.

LEADING MAN [*To* MANAGER]. Excuse me, but must I absolutely wear a cook's cap?

THE MANAGER [*annoyed*]. I imagine so. It says so there anyway. [*Pointing to the "book."*]

LEADING MAN. But it's ridiculous!

THE MANAGER [*jumping up in a rage*]. Ridiculous? Ridiculous? Is it my fault if France won't send us any more good comedies,[4] and we are reduced to putting on Pirandello's works, where nobody understands anything, and where the author plays the fool with us all? [*The* ACTORS *grin. The* MANAGER *goes to* LEADING MAN *and shouts.*] Yes sir, you put on the cook's cap and beat eggs. Do you suppose that with all this egg-beating business you are on an ordinary stage? Get that out of your head. You represent the shell of the eggs you are beating! [*Laughter and comments among the* ACTORS.] Silence! and listen to my explanations, please! [*To* LEADING MAN.] "The empty form of reason without the fullness of instinct, which is blind."—You stand for reason, your wife is instinct. It's a mixing up of the parts, according to which you who act your own part become the puppet of yourself.[5] Do you understand?

LEADING MAN. I'm hanged if I do.

THE MANAGER. Neither do I. But let's get on with it. It's sure to be a glorious failure anyway. [*Confidentially.*] But I say, please face three-quarters. Otherwise, what with the abstruseness of the dialogue, and the public that won't be able to hear you, the whole thing will go to hell. Come on! come on!

PROMPTER. Pardon sir, may I get into my box? There's a bit of a draught.

THE MANAGER. Yes, yes, of course!

At this point, the DOOR-KEEPER *has entered from the stage door and advances towards the manager's table, taking off his braided cap. During this manoeuvre, the* SIX CHARACTERS *enter, and stop by the door at back of stage, so that when the* DOOR-KEEPER *is about to announce their coming to the* MANAGER, *they are already on the stage. A tenuous light surrounds them, almost as if irradiated by them—the faint breath of their fantastic reality.*

This light will disappear when they come forward towards the actors. They preserve, however, something of the dream lightness in which they seem almost suspended; but this does not detract from the essential reality of their forms and expressions.

---

4. The tightly constructed, realistic, and "well-made" plays of French theater were internationally popular, and a staple in Italian theaters at the beginning of the century.   5. Leo Gala is a rationalist and an aesthete—the opposite of his impulsive, passionate wife, Silia. By masking his feelings and constantly playing the role of gourmet cook, he chooses his own role and thus becomes his own "puppet."

He who is known as THE FATHER *is a man of about 50: hair, reddish in colour, thin at the temples; he is not bald, however; thick moustaches, falling over his still fresh mouth, which often opens in an empty and uncertain smile. He is fattish, pale; with an especially wide forehead. He has blue, oval-shaped eyes, very clear and piercing. Wears light trousers and a dark jacket. He is alternatively mellifluous and violent in his manner.*

THE MOTHER *seems crushed and terrified as if by an intolerable weight of shame and abasement. She is dressed in modest black and wears a thick widow's veil of crêpe. When she lifts this, she reveals a wax-like face. She always keeps her eyes downcast.*

THE STEP-DAUGHTER, *is dashing, almost impudent, beautiful. She wears mourning too, but with great elegance. She shows contempt for the timid half-frightened manner of the wretched* BOY *(14 years old, and also dressed in black); on the other hand, she displays a lively tenderness for her little sister,* THE CHILD *(about four), who is dressed in white, with a black silk sash at the waist.*

THE SON *(22) tall, severe in his attitude of contempt for* THE FATHER, *supercilious and indifferent to* THE MOTHER. *He looks as if he had come on the stage against his will.*

DOOR-KEEPER [*cap in hand*]. Excuse me, sir . . .

THE MANAGER [*rudely*]. Eh? What is it?

DOOR-KEEPER [*timidly*]. These people are asking for you, sir.

THE MANAGER [*furious*]. I am rehearsing, and you know perfectly well no one's allowed to come in during rehearsals! [*Turning to the* CHARACTERS.] Who are you, please? What do you want?

THE FATHER [*coming forward a little, followed by the others who seem embarrassed*]. As a matter of fact . . . we have come here in search of an author . . .

THE MANAGER [*half angry, half amazed*]. An author? What author?

THE FATHER. Any author, sir.

THE MANAGER. But there's no author here. We are not rehearsing a new piece.

THE STEP-DAUGHTER [*vivaciously*]. So much the better, so much the better! We can be your new piece.

AN ACTOR [*coming forward from the others*]. Oh, do you hear that?

THE FATHER [*to* STEP-DAUGHTER]. Yes, but if the author isn't here . . . [*To* MANAGER.] unless you would be willing . . .

THE MANAGER. You are trying to be funny.

THE FATHER. No, for Heaven's sake, what are you saying? We bring you a drama, sir.

THE STEP-DAUGHTER. We may be your fortune.

THE MANAGER. Will you oblige me by going away? We haven't time to waste with mad people.

THE FATHER [*mellifluously*]. Oh sir, you know well that life is full of
   infinite absurdities, which, strangely enough, do not even need to
   appear plausible, since they are true.

THE MANAGER. What the devil is he talking about?

THE FATHER. I say that to reverse the ordinary process may well be
   considered a madness: that is, to create credible situations, in order
   that they may appear true. But permit me to observe that if this be
   madness, it is the sole *raison d'être* of your profession, gentlemen.
   [*The* ACTORS *look hurt and perplexed.*]

THE MANAGER [*getting up and looking at him*]. So our profession
   seems to you one worthy of madmen then?

THE FATHER. Well, to make seem true that which isn't true . . .
   without any need . . . for a joke as it were . . . Isn't that your
   mission, gentlemen: to give life to fantastic characters on the stage?

THE MANAGER [*interpreting the rising anger of the* COMPANY]. But I
   would beg you to believe, my dear sir, that the profession of the
   comedian is a noble one. If today, as things go, the playwrights
   give us stupid comedies to play and puppets to represent instead of
   men, remember we are proud to have given life to immortal works
   here on these very boards! [*The* ACTORS, *satisfied, applaud their*
   MANAGER.]

THE FATHER [*interrupting furiously*]. Exactly, perfectly, to living beings
   more alive than those who breathe and wear clothes: beings less
   real perhaps, but truer! I agree with you entirely. [*The* ACTORS
   look at one another in amazement.]

THE MANAGER. But what do you mean? Before, you said . . .

THE FATHER. No, excuse me, I meant it for you, sir, who were crying
   out that you had no time to lose with madmen, while no one
   better than yourself knows that nature uses the instrument of human
   fantasy in order to pursue her high creative purpose.

THE MANAGER. Very well,—but where does all this take us?

THE FATHER. Nowhere! It is merely to show you that one is born to
   life in many forms, in many shapes, as tree, or as stone, as water,
   as butterfly, or as woman. So one may also be born a character in
   a play.

THE MANAGER [*with feigned comic dismay*]. So you and these other
   friends of yours have been born characters?

THE FATHER. Exactly, and alive as you see! [MANAGER *and* ACTORS
   burst out laughing.]

THE FATHER [*hurt*]. I am sorry you laugh, because we carry in us a
   drama, as you can guess from this woman here veiled in black.

THE MANAGER [*losing patience at last and almost indignant*]. Oh,
   chuck it! Get away please! Clear out of here! [*To* PROPERTY MAN.]
   For Heaven's sake, turn them out!

THE FATHER [*resisting*]. No, no, look here, we . . .

THE MANAGER [*roaring*]. We come here to work, you know.

LEADING ACTOR. One cannot let oneself be made such a fool of.

THE FATHER [*determined, coming forward*]. I marvel at your incredulity, gentlemen. Are you not accustomed to see the characters created by an author spring to life in yourselves and face each other? Just because there is no "book" [*Pointing to the* PROMPTER'S *box.*] which contains us, you refuse to believe . . .

THE STEP-DAUGHTER [*advances towards* MANAGER, *smiling and coquettish*]. Believe me, we are really six most interesting characters, sir; side-tracked however.

THE FATHER. Yes, that is the word! [*To* MANAGER *all at once.*] In the sense, that is, that the author who created us alive no longer wished, or was no longer able, materially to put us into a work of art.[6] And this was a real crime, sir; because he who has had the luck to be born a character can laugh even at death. He cannot die. The man, the writer, the instrument of the creation will die, but his creation does not die. And to live for ever, it does not need to have extraordinary gifts or to be able to work wonders. Who was Sancho Panza? Who was Don Abbondio?[7] Yet they live eternally because—live germs as they were—they had the fortune to find a fecundating matrix, a fantasy which could raise and nourish them: make them live for ever!

THE MANAGER. That is quite all right. But what do you want here, all of you?

THE FATHER. We want to live.

THE MANAGER [*ironically*]. For Eternity?

THE FATHER. No, sir, only for a moment . . . in you.

AN ACTOR. Just listen to him!

LEADING LADY. They want to live, in us . . . !

JUVENILE LEAD [*pointing to the* STEP-DAUGHTER]. I've no objection, as far as that one is concerned!

THE FATHER. Look here! look here! The comedy has to be made. [*To the* MANAGER.] But if you and your actors are willing, we can soon concert it among ourselves.

THE MANAGER [*annoyed*]. But what do you want to concert? We don't go in for concerts here. Here we play dramas and comedies!

THE FATHER. Exactly! That is just why we have come to you.

THE MANAGER. And where is the "book"?

THE FATHER. It is in us! [*The* ACTORS *laugh.*] The drama is in us, and we are the drama. We are impatient to play it. Our inner passion drives us on to this.

---

6. In the 1925 preface to *Six Characters*, Pirandello explains that these characters came to him first as characters for a novel, which he later abandoned. Haunted by their half-realized personalities, he decided to use the situation in a play.   7. Sancho Panza was Don Quixote's servant in Cervantes' novel *Don Quixote* (1605–15). Don Abbondio is the priest in Manzoni's novel *The Betrothed* (1828).

THE STEP-DAUGHTER [*disdainful, alluring, treacherous, full of impudence*]. My passion, sir! Ah, if you only knew! My passion for him! [*Points to the* FATHER *and makes a pretence of embracing him. Then she breaks out into a loud laugh.*]

THE FATHER [*angrily*]. Behave yourself! And please don't laugh in that fashion.

THE STEP-DAUGHTER. With your permission, gentlemen, I, who am a two months' orphan, will show you how I can dance and sing. [*Sings and then dances* Prenez garde à Tchou-Tchin-Tchou.]

> Les chinois sont un peuple malin,
> De Shangaî à Pekin,
> Ils ont mis des écriteaux partout:
> Prenez garde à Tchou-Tchin-Tchou.[8]

ACTORS AND ACTRESSES. Bravo! Well done! Tip-top!

THE MANAGER. Silence! This isn't a café concert, you know! [*Turning to the* FATHER *in consternation.*] Is she mad?

THE FATHER. Mad? No, she's worse than mad.

THE STEP-DAUGHTER [*to* MANAGER]. Worse? Worse? Listen! Stage this drama for us at once! Then you will see that at a certain moment I . . . when this little darling here . . . [*Takes the* CHILD *by the hand and leads her to the* MANAGER.] Isn't she a dear? [*Takes her up and kisses her.*] Darling! Darling! [*Puts her down again and adds feelingly.*] Well, when God suddenly takes this dear little child away from that poor mother there; and this imbecile here [*Seizing hold of the* BOY *roughly and pushing him forward.*] does the stupidest things, like the fool he is, you will see me run away. Yes, gentlemen, I shall be off. But the moment hasn't arrived yet. After what has taken place between him and me [*indicates the* FATHER *with a horrible wink.*] I can't remain any longer in this society, to have to witness the anguish of this mother here for that fool . . . [*Indicates the* SON.] Look at him! Look at him! See how indifferent, how frigid he is, because he is the legitimate son. He despises me, despises him [*Pointing to the* BOY.], despises this baby here; because . . . we are bastards. [*Goes to the* MOTHER *and embraces her.*] And he doesn't want to recognize her as his mother—she who is the common mother of us all. He looks down upon her as if she were only the mother of us three bastards. Wretch! [*She says all this very rapidly, excitedly.*

---

8. A popular musical comedy, *Chu-Chin-Chow*, ran in London from 1916 to 1921, and inspired the song *Chu-Chin-Chow* by Dave Stamper for the Ziegfeld Follies in 1917. Stamper's song was translated into the French, which Pirandello cites. Retranslated, the lines say "The Chinese are a crafty people, / From Shanghai to Peking, / They have put up their signs everywhere: / Watch out for Chu-Chin-Chow."

At the word "bastards" she raises her voice, and almost spits out
the final "Wretch!"]

THE MOTHER [to the MANAGER, in anguish]. In the name of these two
little children, I beg you . . . [She grows faint and is about to fall.]
Oh God!

THE FATHER [coming forward to support her as do some of the ACTORS].
Quick, a chair, a chair for this poor widow!

THE ACTORS. Is it true? Has she really fainted?

THE MANAGER. Quick, a chair! Here!

[One of the ACTORS brings a chair, the OTHERS proffer assistance.
The MOTHER tries to prevent the FATHER from lifting the veil
which covers her face.]

THE FATHER. Look at her! Look at her!

THE MOTHER. No, no; stop it please!

THE FATHER [raising her veil]. Let them see you!

THE MOTHER [rising and covering her face with her hands, in desper-
ation]. I beg you, sir, to prevent this man from carrying out his
plan which is loathsome to me.

THE MANAGER [dumbfounded]. I don't understand at all. What is the
situation? Is this lady your wife? [To the FATHER.]

THE FATHER. Yes, gentlemen: my wife!

THE MANAGER. But how can she be a widow if you are alive? [The
ACTORS find relief for their astonishment in a loud laugh.]

THE FATHER. Don't laugh! Don't laugh like that, for Heaven's sake.
Her drama lies just here in this: she has had a lover, a man who
ought to be here.

THE MOTHER [with a cry]. No! No!

THE STEP-DAUGHTER. Fortunately for her, he is dead. Two months
ago as I said. We are in mourning, as you see.

THE FATHER. He isn't here you see, not because he is dead. He isn't
here—look at her a moment and you will understand—because
her drama isn't a drama of the love of two men for whom she was
incapable of feeling anything except possibly a little gratitude—
gratitude not for me but for the other. She isn't a woman, she is a
mother, and her drama—powerful sir, I assure you—lies, as a
matter of fact, all in these four children she has had by two men.

THE MOTHER. I had them? Have you got the courage to say that I
wanted them? [To the COMPANY.] It was his doing. It was he who
gave me that other man, who forced me to go away with him.

THE STEP-DAUGHTER. It isn't true.

THE MOTHER [startled]. Not true, isn't it?

THE STEP-DAUGHTER. No, it isn't true, it just isn't true.

THE MOTHER. And what can you know about it?

THE STEP-DAUGHTER. It isn't true. Don't believe it. [To MANAGER.]
Do you know why she says so? For that fellow there. [Indicates

the SON.] She tortures herself, destroys herself on account of the neglect of that son there; and she wants him to believe that if she abandoned him when he was only two years old, it was because he [*Indicates the* FATHER.] made her do so.

THE MOTHER [*vigorously*]. He forced me to it, and I call God to witness it. [*To the* MANAGER.] Ask him [*Indicates* HUSBAND.] if it isn't true. Let him speak. You [*To* DAUGHTER.] are not in a position to know anything about it.

THE STEP-DAUGHTER. I know you lived in peace and happiness with my father while he lived. Can you deny it?

THE MOTHER. No, I don't deny it . . .

THE STEP-DAUGHTER. He was always full of affection and kindness for you. [*To the* BOY, *angrily*.] It's true, isn't it? Tell them! Why don't you speak, you little fool?

THE MOTHER. Leave the poor boy alone. Why do you want to make me appear ungrateful, daughter? I don't want to offend your father. I have answered him that I didn't abandon my house and my son through any fault of mine, nor from any wilful passion.

THE FATHER. It is true. It was my doing.

LEADING MAN [*to the* COMPANY]. What a spectacle!

LEADING LADY. We are the audience this time.

JUVENILE LEAD. For once, in a way.

THE MANAGER [*beginning to get really interested*]. Let's hear them out. Listen!

THE SON. Oh yes, you're going to hear a fine bit now. He will talk to you of the Demon of Experiment.

THE FATHER. You are a cynical imbecile, I've told you so already a hundred times. [*To the* MANAGER.] He tries to make fun of me on account of this expression which I have found to excuse myself with.

THE SON [*with disgust*]. Yes, phrases! phrases!

THE FATHER. Phrases! Isn't everyone consoled when faced with a trouble or fact he doesn't understand, by a word, some simple word, which tells us nothing and yet calms us?

THE STEP-DAUGHTER. Even in the case of remorse. In fact, especially then.

THE FATHER. Remorse? No, that isn't true. I've done more than use words to quieten the remorse in me.

THE STEP-DAUGHTER. Yes, there was a bit of money too. Yes, yes, a bit of money. There were the hundred lire he was about to offer me in payment, gentlemen . . . [*Sensation of horror among the* ACTORS.]

THE SON [*to the* STEP-DAUGHTER]. This is vile.

THE STEP-DAUGHTER. Vile? There they were in a pale blue envelope on a little mahogany table in the back of Madame Pace's shop.

You know Madame Pace—one of those ladies who attract poor girls of good family into their ateliers, under the pretext of their selling *robes et manteaux.*[9]

THE SON. And he thinks he has bought the right to tyrannize over us all with those hundred lire he was going to pay; but which, fortunately—note this, gentlemen—he had no chance of paying.

THE STEP-DAUGHTER. It was a near thing, though, you know! [*Laughs ironically.*]

THE MOTHER [*protesting*]. Shame, my daughter, shame!

THE STEP-DAUGHTER. Shame indeed! This is my revenge! I am dying to live that scene . . . The room . . . I see it . . . Here is the window with the mantles exposed, there the divan, the looking-glass, a screen, there in front of the window the little mahogany table with the blue envelope containing one hundred lire. I see it. I see it. I could take hold of it . . . But you, gentlemen, you ought to turn your backs now: I am almost nude, you know. But I don't blush: I leave that to him. [*Indicating* FATHER.]

THE MANAGER. I don't understand this at all.

THE FATHER. Naturally enough. I would ask you, sir, to exercise your authority a little here, and let me speak before you believe all she is trying to blame me with. Let me explain.

THE STEP-DAUGHTER. Ah yes, explain it in your own way.

THE FATHER. But don't you see that the whole trouble lies here. In words, words. Each one of us has within him a whole world of things, each man of us his own special world. And how can we ever come to an understanding if I put in the words I utter the sense and value of things as I see them; while you who listen to me must inevitably translate them according to the conception of things each one of you has within himself. We think we understand each other, but we never really do. Look here! This woman [*Indicating the* MOTHER.] takes all my pity for her as a specially ferocious form of cruelty.

THE MOTHER. But you drove me away.

THE FATHER. Do you hear her? I drove her away! She believes I really sent her away.

THE MOTHER. You know how to talk, and I don't; but, believe me, sir [*To* MANAGER], after he had married me . . . who knows why? . . . I was a poor insignificant woman . . .

THE FATHER. But, good Heavens! it was just for your humility that I married you. I loved this simplicity in you. [*He stops when he sees she makes signs to contradict him, opens his arms wide in sign of desperation, seeing how hopeless it is to make himself understood.*] You see she denies it. Her mental deafness, believe me, is

9. An atelier is a studio: the implication is that Madame Pace runs a call-girl operation under the guise of selling fashionable "dresses and coats."

phenomenal, the limit: [*Touches his forehead.*] deaf, deaf, mentally deaf! She has plenty of feeling. Oh yes, a good heart for the children; but the brain—deaf, to the point of desperation——!

THE STEP-DAUGHTER. Yes, but ask him how his intelligence has helped us.

THE FATHER. If we could see all the evil that may spring from good, what should we do? [*At this point the* LEADING LADY *who is biting her lips with rage at seeing the* LEADING MAN *flirting with the* STEP-DAUGHTER, *comes forward and says to the* MANAGER.]

LEADING LADY. Excuse me, but are we going to rehearse today?

MANAGER. Of course, of course; but let's hear them out.

JUVENILE LEAD. This is something quite new.

L'INGÉNUE. Most Interesting!

LEADING LADY. Yes, for the people who like that kind of thing. [*Casts a glance at* LEADING MAN.]

THE MANAGER [*to* FATHER]. You must please explain yourself quite clearly. [*Sits down.*]

THE FATHER. Very well then: listen! I had in my service a poor man, a clerk, a secretary of mine, full of devotion, who became friends with her. [*Indicating the* MOTHER.] They understood one another, were kindred souls in fact, without, however, the least suspicion of any evil existing. They were incapable even of thinking of it.

THE STEP-DAUGHTER. So he thought of it—for them!

THE FATHER. That's not true. I meant to do good to them—and to myself, I confess, at the same time. Things had come to the point that I could not say a word to either of them without their making a mute appeal, one to the other, with their eyes. I could see them silently asking each other how I was to be kept in countenance, how I was to be kept quiet. And this, believe me, was just about enough of itself to keep me in a constant rage, to exasperate me beyond measure.

THE MANAGER. And why didn't you send him away then—this secretary of yours?

THE FATHER. Precisely what I did, sir. And then I had to watch this poor woman drifting forlornly about the house like an animal without a master, like an animal one has taken in out of pity.

THE MOTHER. Ah yes . . . !

THE FATHER [*suddenly turning to the* MOTHER]. It's true about the son anyway, isn't it?

THE MOTHER. He took my son away from me first of all.

THE FATHER. But not from cruelty. I did it so that he should grow up healthy and strong by living in the country.

THE STEP-DAUGHTER [*pointing to him ironically*]. As one can see.

THE FATHER [*quickly*]. Is it my fault if he has grown up like this? I sent him to a wet nurse in the country, a peasant, as *she* did not seem to me strong enough, though she is of humble origin. That was, anyway, the reason I married her. Unpleasant all this may be, but how can it be helped? My mistake possibly, but there we are! All my life I have had these confounded aspirations towards a certain moral sanity. [*At this point the* STEP-DAUGHTER *bursts into a noisy laugh.*] Oh, stop it! Stop it! I can't stand it.

THE MANAGER. Yes, please stop it, for Heaven's sake.

THE STEP-DAUGHTER. But imagine moral sanity from him, if you please—the client of certain ateliers like that of Madame Pace!

THE FATHER. Fool! That is the proof that I am a man! This seeming contradiction, gentlemen, is the strongest proof that I stand here a live man before you. Why, it is just for this very incongruity in my nature that I have had to suffer what I have. I could not live by the side of that woman [*Indicating the* MOTHER.] any longer; but not so much for the boredom she inspired me with as for the pity I felt for her.

THE MOTHER. And so he turned me out—.

THE FATHER. —Well, provided for! Yes, I sent her to that man, gentlemen . . . to let her go free of me.

THE MOTHER. And to free himself.

THE FATHER. Yes, I admit it. It was also a liberation for me. But great evil has come of it. I meant well when I did it; and I did it more for her sake than mine. I swear it. [*Crosses his arms on his chest; then turns suddenly to the* MOTHER.] Did I ever lose sight of you until that other man carried you off to another town, like the angry fool he was? And on account of my pure interest in you . . . my pure interest, I repeat, that had no base motive in it . . . I watched with the tenderest concern the new family that grew up around her. She can bear witness to this. [*Points to the* STEP-DAUGHTER.]

THE STEP-DAUGHTER. Oh yes, that's true enough. When I was a kid-die, so so high, you know, with plaits over my shoulders and knickers longer than my skirts, I used to see him waiting outside the school for me to come out. He came to see how I was growing up.

THE FATHER. This is infamous, shameful!

THE STEP-DAUGHTER. No. Why?

THE FATHER. Infamous! infamous! [*Then excitedly to* MANAGER *explaining.*] After she [*Indicating* MOTHER.] went away, my house seemed suddenly empty. She was my incubus, but she filled my house. I was like a dazed fly alone in the empty rooms. This boy here [*Indicating the* SON.] was educated away from home, and when he came back, he seemed to me to be no more mine. With no mother to stand between him and me, he grew up entirely for himself, on his own, apart, with no tie of intellect or affection binding him to me. And then—strange but true—I was driven, by curiosity at first and then by some tender sentiment, towards her family, which had come into being through my will. The thought of her began gradually to fill up the emptiness I felt all around me. I wanted to know if she were happy in living out the simple duties of life. I wanted to think of her as fortunate and happy because far away from the complicated torments of my spirit. And so, to have proof of this, I used to watch that child coming out of school.

THE STEP-DAUGHTER. Yes, yes. True. He used to follow me in the street and smiled at me, waved his hand, like this. I would look at him with interest, wondering who he might be. I told my mother, who guessed at once. [*The* MOTHER *agrees with a nod.*] Then she didn't want to send me to school for some days; and when I finally went back, there he was again—looking so ridiculous—with a paper parcel in his hands. He came close to me, caressed me, and drew out a fine straw hat from the parcel, with a bouquet of flowers— all for me!

THE MANAGER. A bit discursive this, you know!

THE SON [*contemptuously*]. Literature! Literature!

THE FATHER. Literature indeed! This is life, this is passion!

THE MANAGER. It may be, but it won't act.

THE FATHER. I agree. This is only the part leading up. I don't suggest this should be staged. She [*Pointing to the* STEP-DAUGHTER.], as you see, is no longer the flapper with plaits down her back—

THE STEP-DAUGHTER. —and the knickers showing below the skirt!

THE FATHER. The drama is coming now, sir; something new, complex, most interesting.

THE STEP-DAUGHTER. As soon as my father died . . .

THE FATHER. —there was absolute misery for them. They came back here, unknown to me. Through her stupidity! [*Pointing to the* MOTHER.] It is true she can barely write her own name; but she could anyhow have got her daughter to write to me that they were in need . . .

THE MOTHER. And how was I to divine all this sentiment in him?

THE FATHER. That is exactly your mistake, never to have guessed any of my sentiments.

THE MOTHER. After so many years apart, and all that had happened . . .

THE FATHER. Was it my fault if that fellow carried you away? It happened quite suddenly; for after he had obtained some job or other, I could find no trace of them; and so, not unnaturally, my interest in them dwindled. But the drama culminated unforeseen and violent on their return, when I was impelled by my miserable flesh that still lives . . . Ah! what misery, what wretchedness is that of the man who is alone and disdains debasing *liaisons!* Not old enough to do without women, and not young enough to go and look for one without shame. Misery? It's worse than misery; it's a horror; for no woman can any longer give him love; and when a man feels this . . . One ought to do without, you say? Yes, yes, I know. Each of us when he appears before his fellows is clothed in a certain dignity. But every man knows what unconfessable things pass within the secrecy of his own heart. One gives way to the temptation, only to rise from it again, afterwards, with a great eagerness to re-establish one's dignity, as if it were a tombstone to place on the grave of one's shame, and a monument to hide and sign the memory of our weaknesses. Everybody's in the same case. Some folks haven't the courage to say certain things, that's all!

THE STEP-DAUGHTER. All appear to have the courage to do them though.

THE FATHER. Yes, but in secret. Therefore, you want more courage to say these things. Let a man but speak these things out, and folks at once label him a cynic. But it isn't true. He is like all the others, better indeed, because he isn't afraid to reveal with the light of the intelligence the red shame of human bestiality on which most men close their eyes so as not to see it.

Woman—for example, look at her case! She turns tantalizing inviting glances on you. You seize her. No sooner does she feel herself in your grasp than she closes her eyes. It is the sign of her mission, the sign by which she says to man: "Blind yourself, for I am blind."

THE STEP-DAUGHTER. Sometimes she can close them no more: when she no longer feels the need of hiding her shame to herself, but dry-eyed and dispassionately, sees only that of the man who has blinded himself without love. Oh, all these intellectual complications make me sick, disgust me—all this philosophy that uncovers the beast in man, and then seeks to save him, excuse him . . . I can't stand it, sir. When a man seeks to "simplify" life bestially, throwing aside every relic of humanity, every chaste aspiration, every pure feeling, all sense of ideality, duty, modesty, shame . . . then nothing is more revolting and nauseous than a certain kind of remorse—crocodiles' tears, that's what it is.

THE MANAGER. Let's come to the point. This is only discussion.

THE FATHER. Very good, sir! But a fact is like a sack which won't stand up when it is empty. In order that it may stand up, one has to put into it the reason and sentiment which have caused it to exist. I couldn't possibly know that after the death of that man, they had decided to return here, that they were in misery, and that she [*Pointing to the* MOTHER.] had gone to work as a modiste, and at a shop of the type of that of Madame Pace.

THE STEP-DAUGHTER. A real high-class modiste, you must know, gentlemen. In appearance, she works for the leaders of the best society; but she arranges matters so that these elegant ladies serve her purpose . . . without prejudice to other ladies who are . . . well . . . only so-so.

THE MOTHER. You will believe me, gentlemen, that it never entered my mind that the old hag offered me work because she had her eye on my daughter.

THE STEP-DAUGHTER. Poor mamma! Do you know, sir, what that woman did when I brought her back the work my mother had finished? She would point out to me that I had torn one of my frocks, and she would give it back to my mother to mend. It was I who paid for it, always I; while this poor creature here believed she was sacrificing herself for me and these two children here, sitting up at night sewing Madame Pace's robes.

THE MANAGER. And one day you met there . . .

THE STEP-DAUGHTER. Him, him. Yes sir, an old client. There's a scene for you to play! Superb!

THE FATHER. She, the Mother arrived just then . . .

THE STEP-DAUGHTER [*treacherously*]. Almost in time!

THE FATHER [*crying out*]. No, in time! in time! fortunately I recognized her . . . in time. And I took them back home with me to my house. You can imagine now her position and mine; she, as you see her; and I who cannot look her in the face.

THE STEP-DAUGHTER. Absurd! How can I possibly be expected—after that—to be a modest young miss, a fit person to go with his confounded aspirations for "a solid moral sanity"?

THE FATHER. For the drama lies all in this—in the conscience[1] that I have, that each one of us has. We believe this conscience to be a single thing, but it is many-sided. There is one for this person, and another for that. Diverse consciences. So we have this illusion of being one person for all, of having a personality that is unique in all our acts. But it isn't true. We perceive this when, tragically perhaps, in something we do, we are as it were, suspended, caught up in the air on a kind of hook. Then we perceive that all of us was not in that act, and that it would be an atrocious injustice to judge us by that action alone, as if all our existence were summed up in that one deed. Now do you understand the perfidy of this girl? She surprised me in a place, where she ought not to have known me, just as I could not exist for her; and she now seeks to attach to me a reality such as I could never suppose I should have to assume for her in a shameful and fleeting moment of my life. I feel this above all else. And the drama, you will see, acquires a tremendous value from this point. Then there is the position of

---

1. *Coscienza*: a word with a double meaning, better translated here as "consciousness" (awareness of identity) although it can also mean the English "conscience."

the others . . . his . . . [*Indicating the* SON.]

THE SON. [*shrugging his shoulders scornfully*]. Leave me alone! I don't come into this.

THE FATHER. What? You don't come into this?

THE SON. I've got nothing to do with it, and don't want to have; because you know well enough I wasn't made to be mixed up in all this with the rest of you.

THE STEP-DAUGHTER. We are only vulgar folk! He is the fine gentleman. You may have noticed, Mr. Manager, that I fix him now and again with a look of scorn while he lowers his eyes—for he knows the evil he has done me.

THE SON [*scarcely looking at her*]. I?

THE STEP-DAUGHTER. You! you! I owe my life on the streets to you. Did you or did you not deny us, with your behaviour, I won't say the intimacy of home, but even that mere hospitality which makes guests feel at their ease? We were intruders who had come to disturb the kingdom of your legitimacy. I should like to have you witness, Mr. Manager, certain scenes between him and me. He says I have tyrannized over everyone. But it was just his behaviour which made me insist on the reason for which I had come into the house,—this reason he calls "vile"—into his house, with my mother who is his mother too. And I came as mistress of the house.

THE SON. It's easy for them to put me always in the wrong. But imagine, gentlemen, the position of a son, whose fate it is to see arrive one day at his home a young woman of impudent bearing, a young woman who inquires for his father, with whom who knows what business she has. This young man has then to witness her return bolder than ever, accompanied by that child there. He is obliged to watch her treat his father in an equivocal and confidential manner. She asks money of him in a way that lets one suppose he must give it her, *must*, do you understand, because he has every obligation to do so.

THE FATHER. But I have, as a matter of fact, this obligation. I owe it to your mother.

THE SON. How should I know? When had I ever seen or heard of her? One day there arrive with her [*Indicating* STEP-DAUGHTER.] that lad and this baby here. I am told: "This is *your* mother too, you know." I divine from her manner [*Indicating* STEP-DAUGHTER *again.*] why it is they have come home. I shouldn't even care to confess to myself. No action can therefore be hoped for from me in this affair. Believe me, Mr. Manager, I am an "unrealized" character, dramatically speaking; and I find myself not at all at ease in their company. Leave me out of it, I beg you.

THE FATHER. What? It is just because you are so that . . .

THE SON. How do you know what I am like? When did you ever
bother your head about me?

THE FATHER. I admit it. I admit it. But isn't that a situation in itself?
This aloofness of yours which is so cruel to me and to your mother,
who returns home and sees you almost for the first time grown
up, who doesn't recognize you but knows you are her son . . .
[*Pointing out the* MOTHER *to the* MANAGER.] See, she's crying!

THE STEP-DAUGHTER [*angrily, stamping her foot*]. Like a fool!

THE FATHER [*indicating* STEP-DAUGHTER]. She can't stand him you
know. [*Then referring again to the* SON.] He says he doesn't come
into the affair, whereas he is really the hinge of the whole action.
Look at that lad who is always clinging to his mother, frightened
and humiliated. It is on account of this fellow here. Possibly his
situation is the most painful of all. He feels himself a stranger
more than the others. The poor little chap feels mortified, humiliated at being brought into a home out of charity as it were. [*In
confidence.*] He is the image of his father. Hardly talks at all.
Humble and quiet.

THE MANAGER. Oh, we'll cut him out. You've no notion what a
nuisance boys are on the stage . . .

THE FATHER. He disappears soon, you know. And the baby too. She
is the first to vanish from the scene. The drama consists finally in
this: when that mother re-enters my house, her family born outside of it, and shall we say superimposed on the original, ends
with the death of the little girl, the tragedy of the boy and the
flight of the elder daughter. It cannot go on, because it is foreign
to its surroundings. So after much torment, we three remain: I,
the mother, that son. Then, owing to the disappearance of that
extraneous family, we too find ourselves strange to one another.
We find we are living in an atmosphere of mortal desolation which
is the revenge, as he [*Indicating* SON.] scornfully said of the Demon
of Experiment, that unfortunately hides in me. Thus, sir, you see
when faith is lacking, it becomes impossible to create certain states
of happiness, for we lack the necessary humility. Vaingloriously,
we try to substitute ourselves for this faith, creating thus for the
rest of the world a reality which we believe after their fashion,
while, actually, it doesn't exist. For each one of us has his own
reality to be respected before God, even when it is harmful to
one's very self.

THE MANAGER. There is something in what you say. I assure you all
this interests me very much. I begin to think there's the stuff for a
drama in all this, and not a bad drama either.

THE STEP-DAUGHTER [*coming forward*]. When you've got a character
like me.

THE FATHER [*shutting her up, all excited to learn the decision of the* MANAGER]. You be quiet!

THE MANAGER [*reflecting, heedless of interruption*]. It's new . . . hem . . . yes . . .

THE FATHER. Absolutely new!

THE MANAGER. You've got a nerve though, I must say, to come here and fling it at me like this . . .

THE FATHER. You will understand, sir, born as we are for the stage . . .

THE MANAGER. Are you amateur actors then?

THE FATHER. No. I say born for the stage, because . . .

THE MANAGER. Oh, nonsense. You're an old hand, you know.

THE FATHER. No sir, no. We act that rôle for which we have been cast, that rôle which we are given in life. And in my own case, passion itself, as usually happens, becomes a trifle theatrical when it is exalted.

THE MANAGER. Well, well, that will do. But you see, without an author . . . I could give you the address of an author if you like . . .

THE FATHER. No, no. Look here! You must be the author.

THE MANAGER. I? What are you talking about?

THE FATHER. Yes, you, you! Why not?

THE MANAGER. Because I have never been an author: that's why.

THE FATHER. Then why not turn author now? Everybody does it. You don't want any special qualities. Your task is made much easier by the fact that we are all here alive before you . . .

THE MANAGER. It won't do.

THE FATHER. What? When you see us live our drama . . .

THE MANAGER. Yes, that's all right. But you want someone to write it.

THE FATHER. No, no. Someone to take it down, possibly, while we play it, scene by scene! It will be enough to sketch it out at first, and then try it over.

THE MANAGER. Well . . . I am almost tempted. It's a bit of an idea. One might have a shot at it.

THE FATHER. Of course. You'll see what scenes will come out of it. I can give you one, at once . . .

THE MANAGER. By Jove, it tempts me. I'd like to have a go at it. Let's try it out. Come with me to my office. [*Turning to the* ACTORS.] You are at liberty for a bit, but don't step out of the theatre for long. In a quarter of an hour, twenty minutes, all back here again! [*To the* FATHER.] We'll see what can be done. Who knows if we don't get something really extraordinary out of it?

THE FATHER. There's no doubt about it. They [*Indicating the* CHAR-ACTERS.] had better come with us too, hadn't they?

THE MANAGER. Yes, yes. Come on! come on! [*Moves away and then turning to the* ACTORS.] *Be punctual, please!* [MANAGER *and the*

SIX CHARACTERS *cross the stage and go off. The other* ACTORS *remain, looking at one another in astonishment.*]

LEADING MAN. Is he serious? What the devil does he want to do?

JUVENILE LEAD. This is rank madness.

THIRD ACTOR. Does he expect to knock up a drama in five minutes?

JUVENILE LEAD. Like the improvisers![2]

LEADING LADY. If he thinks I'm going to take part in a joke like this . . .

JUVENILE LEAD. I'm out of it anyway.

FOURTH ACTOR. I should like to know who they are. [*Alludes to* CHARACTERS].

THIRD ACTOR. What do you suppose? Madmen or rascals!

JUVENILE LEAD. And he takes them seriously!

L'INGÉNUE. Vanity! He fancies himself as an author now.

LEADING MAN. It's absolutely unheard of. If the stage has come to this . . . well I'm . . .

FIFTH ACTOR. It's rather a joke.

THIRD ACTOR. Well, we'll see what's going to happen next.

Thus talking, the ACTORS *leave the stage; some going out by the little door at the back; others retiring to their dressing-rooms.*

The curtain remains up.

The action of the play is suspended for twenty minutes.

ACT II

The stage call-bells ring to warn the company that the play is about to begin again.

The STEP-DAUGHTER *comes out of the* MANAGER'S *office along with the* CHILD *and the* BOY. *As she comes out of the office, she cries:*—

Nonsense! nonsense! Do it yourselves! I'm not going to mix myself up in this mess. [*Turning to the* CHILD *and coming quickly with her on to the stage.*] Come on, Rosetta, let's run!

[*The* BOY *follows them slowly, remaining a little behind and seeming perplexed.*]

THE STEP-DAUGHTER [*stops, bends over the* CHILD *and takes the latter's face between her hands*]. My little darling! You're frightened, aren't you? You don't know where we are, do you? [*Pretending to reply to a question of the* CHILD.] What is the stage? It's a place, baby, you know, where people play at being serious, a place where they act comedies. We've got to act a comedy now, dead serious, you know; and you're in it also, little one. [*Embraces her, pressing the little head to her breast, and rocking the* CHILD *for a moment.*]

---

2. Literally, like players in the *Commedia dell'arte*, an improvisational form popular beginning with the sixteenth century in which actors improvised their dialogue according to basic plots and audience reaction.

Oh darling, darling, what a horrid comedy you've got to play! What a wretched part they've found for you! A garden . . . a fountain . . . look . . . just suppose, kiddie, it's here. Where, you say? Why, right here in the middle. It's all make-believe here. It's better to imagine it though, because if they fix it up for you, it'll only be painted cardboard, painted cardboard for the rockery, the water, the plants. . . . Ah, but I think a baby like this one would sooner have a make-believe fountain than a real one, so she could play with it. What a joke it'll be for the others! But for you, alas! not quite such a joke: you who are real, baby dear, and really play by a real fountain that is big and green and beautiful, with ever so many bamboos around it that are reflected in the water, and a whole lot of little ducks swimming about . . . No, Rosetta, no, your mother doesn't bother about you on account of that wretch of a son there. I'm in the devil of a temper, and as for that lad . . . [*Seizes* BOY *by the arm to force him to take one of his hands out of his pockets.*] What have you got there? What are you hiding? [*Pulls his hand out of his pocket, looks into it and catches the glint of a revolver.*] Ah! where did you get this? [*The* BOY, *very pale in the face, looks at her, but does not answer*]. Idiot! If I'd been in your place, instead of killing myself, I'd have shot one of those two, or both of them: father and son.

> [*The* FATHER *enters from the office, all excited from his work. The* MANAGER *follows him.*]

THE FATHER. Come on, come on dear! Come here for a minute! We've arranged everything. It's all fixed up.

THE MANAGER [*also excited*]. If you please, young lady, there are one or two points to settle still. Will you come along?

THE STEP-DAUGHTER [*following him towards the office*]. Ouff! what's the good, if you've arranged everything.

> [*The* FATHER, MANAGER *and* STEP-DAUGHTER *go back into the office again (off) for a moment. At the same time, the* SON *followed by The* MOTHER, *comes out.*]

THE SON [*looking at the three entering office*]. Oh this is fine, fine! And to think I can't even get away!

> [*The* MOTHER *attempts to look at him, but lowers her eyes immediately when* HE *turns away from her.* SHE *then sits down. The* BOY *and the* CHILD *approach her.* SHE *casts a glance again at the* SON, *and speaks with humble tones, trying to draw him into conversation.*]

THE MOTHER. And isn't my punishment the worst of all? [*Then seeing from the* SON's *manner that he will not bother himself about her.*] My God! Why are you so cruel? Isn't it enough for one person to support all this torment? Must you then insist on others seeing it also?

THE SON [*half to himself, meaning the* MOTHER *to hear, however*].
And they want to put it on the stage! If there was at least a reason
for it! He thinks he has got at the meaning of it all. Just as if each
one of us in every circumstance of life couldn't find his own explanation of it! [*Pauses.*] He complains he was discovered in a place
where he ought not to have been seen, in a moment of his life
which ought to have remained hidden and kept out of the reach
of that convention which he has to maintain for other people. And
what about my case? Haven't I had to reveal what no son ought
ever to reveal: how father and mother live and are man and wife
for themselves quite apart from that idea of father and mother
which we give them? When this idea is revealed, our life is then
linked at one point only to that man and that woman; and as such
it should shame them, shouldn't it?

[*The* MOTHER *hides her face in her hands. From the dressing-
rooms and the little door at the back of the stage the* ACTORS
and STAGE MANAGER *return, followed by the* PROPERTY MAN,
and the PROMPTER. *At the same moment, The* MANAGER *comes
out of his office, accompanied by the* FATHER *and the* STEP-
DAUGHTER.]

THE MANAGER. Come on, come on, ladies and gentlemen! Heh! you
there, machinist!

MACHINIST. Yes sir?

THE MANAGER. Fix up the white parlor with the floral decorations.
Two wings and a drop with a door will do.[3] Hurry up!

[*The* MACHINIST *runs off at once to prepare the scene, and arranges
it while the* MANAGER *talks with the* STAGE MANAGER, *the* PROP-
ERTY MAN, *and the* PROMPTER *on matters of detail.*]

THE MANAGER [*to* PROPERTY MAN]. Just have a look, and see if there
isn't a sofa or divan in the wardrobe . . .

PROPERTY MAN. There's the green one.

THE STEP-DAUGHTER. No no! Green won't do. It was yellow, ornamented with flowers—very large! and most comfortable!

PROPERTY MAN. There isn't one like that.

THE MANAGER. It doesn't matter. Use the one we've got.

THE STEP-DAUGHTER. Doesn't matter? It's most important!

THE MANAGER. We're only trying it now. Please don't interfere. [*To*
PROPERTY MAN.] See if we've got a shop window—long and nar-
rowish.

THE STEP-DAUGHTER. And the little table! The little mahogany table
for the pale blue envelope!

PROPERTY MAN [*to* MANAGER]. There's that little gilt one.

THE MANAGER. That'll do fine.

THE FATHER. A mirror.

3. Stage sets: a backdrop with a door painted on it and two side walls.

THE STEP-DAUGHTER. And the screen! We must have a screen. Otherwise how can I manage?

PROPERTY MAN. That's all right, Miss. We've got any amount of them.

THE MANAGER [*to the* STEP-DAUGHTER]. We want some .clothes pegs too, don't we?

THE STEP-DAUGHTER. Yes, several, several!

THE MANAGER. See how many we've got and bring them all.

PROPERTY MAN. All right!

> [*The* PROPERTY MAN *hurries off to obey his orders. While he is putting the things in their places, the* MANAGER *talks to the* PROMPTER *and then with the* CHARACTERS *and the* ACTORS.]

THE MANAGER [*to* PROMPTER]. Take your seat. Look here: this is the outline of the scenes, act by act. [*Hands him some sheets of paper.*] And now I'm going to ask you to do something out of the ordinary.

PROMPTER. Take it down in shorthand?

THE MANAGER [*pleasantly surprised*]. Exactly! Can you do shorthand?

PROMPTER. Yes, a little.

THE MANAGER. Good! [*Turning to a* STAGE HAND.] Go and get some paper from my office, plenty, as much as you can find.

> [*The* STAGE HAND *goes off, and soon returns with a handful of paper which he gives to the* PROMPTER.]

THE MANAGER [*to* PROMPTER]. You follow the scenes as we play them, and try and get the points down, at any rate the most important ones. [*Then addressing the* ACTORS.] Clear the stage, ladies and gentlemen! Come over here [*Pointing to the left.*] and listen attentively.

LEADING LADY. But, excuse me, we . . .

THE MANAGER [*guessing her thought*]. Don't worry! You won't have to improvise.

LEADING MAN. What have we to do then?

THE MANAGER. Nothing. For the moment you just watch and listen. Everybody will get his part written out afterwards. At present we're going to try the thing as best we can. They're going to act now.

THE FATHER [*as if fallen from the clouds into the confusion of the stage*]. We? What do you mean, if you please, by a rehearsal?

THE MANAGER. A rehearsal for them. [*Points to the* ACTORS.]

THE FATHER. But since we are the characters . . .

THE MANAGER. All right: "characters" then, if you insist on calling yourselves such. But here, my dear sir, the characters don't act. Here the actors do the acting. The characters are there, in the "book" [*Pointing towards* PROMPTER's *box.*]—when there is a "book"!

THE FATHER. I won't contradict you; but excuse me, the actors aren't the characters. They want to be, they pretend to be, don't they? Now if these gentlemen here are fortunate enough to have us alive before them . . .

THE MANAGER. Oh this is grand! You want to come before the public yourselves then?

THE FATHER. As we are . . .

THE MANAGER. I can assure you it would be a magnificent spectacle!

LEADING MAN. What's the use of us here anyway then?

THE MANAGER. You're not going to pretend that you can act? It makes me laugh! [*The* ACTORS *laugh.*] There, you see, they are laughing at the notion. But, by the way, I must cast the parts. That won't be difficult. They cast themselves. [*To the* SECOND LADY LEAD.] You play the Mother. [*To the* FATHER.] We must find her a name.

THE FATHER. Amalia, sir.

THE MANAGER. But that is the real name of your wife. We don't want to call her by her real name.

THE FATHER. Why ever not, if it is her name? . . . Still, perhaps, if that lady must . . . [*Makes a slight motion of the hand to indicate the* SECOND LADY LEAD.] I see this woman here [*Means the* MOTHER.] as Amalia. But do as you like. [*Gets more and more confused.*] I don't know what to say to you. Already, I begin to hear my own words ring false, as if they had another sound . . .

THE MANAGER. Don't you worry about it. It'll be our job to find the right tones. And as for her name, if you want her Amalia, Amalia it shall be; and if you don't like it, we'll find another! For the moment though, we'll call the characters in this way: [*To* JUVENILE LEAD.] You are the Son. [*To the* LEADING LADY.] You naturally are the Step-Daughter . . .

THE STEP-DAUGHTER [*excitedly*]. What? what? I, that woman there? [*Bursts out laughing.*]

THE MANAGER [*angry*]. What is there to laugh at?

LEADING LADY [*indignant*]. Nobody has ever dared to laugh at me. I insist on being treated with respect; otherwise I go away.

THE STEP-DAUGHTER. No, no, excuse me . . . I am not laughing at you . . .

THE MANAGER [*to* STEP-DAUGHTER]. You ought to feel honored to be played by . . .

LEADING LADY [*at once, contemptuously*]. "That woman there" . . .

THE STEP-DAUGHTER. But I wasn't speaking of you, you know. I was speaking of myself—whom I can't see at all in you! That is all. I don't know . . . but . . . you . . . aren't in the least like me . . .

THE FATHER. True. Here's the point. Look here, sir, our temperaments, our souls . . .

THE MANAGER. Temperament, soul, be hanged! Do you suppose the spirit of the piece is in you? Nothing of the kind!

THE FATHER. What, haven't we our own temperaments, our own souls?

THE MANAGER. Not at all. Your soul or whatever you like to call it takes shape here. The actors give body and form to it, voice and gesture. And my actors—I may tell you—have given expression to much more lofty material than this little drama of yours, which may or may not hold up on the stage. But if it does, the merit of it, believe me, will be due to my actors.

THE FATHER. I don't dare contradict you, sir; but believe me, it is a terrible suffering for us who are as we are, with these bodies of ours, these features to see . . .

THE MANAGER [*cutting him short and out of patience*]. Good heavens! The make-up will remedy all that, man, the make-up . . .

THE FATHER. Maybe. But the voice, the gestures . . .

THE MANAGER. Now, look here! On the stage, you as yourself, cannot exist. The actor here acts you, and that's an end to it!

THE FATHER. I understand. And now I think I see why our author who conceived us as we are, all alive, didn't want to put us on the stage after all. I haven't the least desire to offend your actors. Far from it! But when I think that I am to be acted by . . . I don't know by whom . . .

LEADING MAN [*on his dignity*]. By me, if you've no objection!

THE FATHER [*humbly, mellifluously*]. Honored, I assure you, sir. [*Bows.*] Still, I must say that try as this gentleman may, with all his good will and wonderful art, to absorb me into himself . . .

LEADING MAN. Oh chuck it! "Wonderful art!" Withdraw that, please!

THE FATHER. The performance he will give, even doing his best with make-up to look like me . . .

LEADING MAN. It will certainly be a bit difficult! [*The* ACTORS *laugh.*]

THE FATHER. Exactly! It will be difficult to act me as I really am. The effect will be rather—apart from the make-up—according as to how he supposes I am, as he senses me—if he does sense me—and not as I inside of myself feel myself to be. It seems to me then that account should be taken of this by everyone whose duty it may become to criticize us . . .

THE MANAGER. Heavens! The man's starting to think about the critics now! Let them say what they like. It's up to us to put on the play if we can. [*Looking around.*] Come on! come on! Is the stage set? [*To the* ACTORS *and* CHARACTERS.] Stand back—stand back! Let me see, and don't let's lose any more time! [*To the* STEP-DAUGHTER.] Is it all right as it is now?

THE STEP-DAUGHTER. Well, to tell the truth, I don't recognize the scene.

THE MANAGER. My dear lady, you can't possibly suppose that we can construct that shop of Madame Pace piece by piece here? [*To the* Father.] You said a white room with flowered wall paper, didn't you?

THE FATHER. Yes.

THE MANAGER. Well then. We've got the furniture right more or less. Bring that little table a bit further forward. [*The* STAGE HANDS *obey the order. To* PROPERTY MAN.] You go and find an envelope, if possible, a pale blue one; and give it to that gentleman. [*Indicates* FATHER.]

PROPERTY MAN. An ordinary envelope?

MANAGER AND FATHER. Yes, yes, an ordinary envelope.

PROPERTY MAN. At once, sir. [*Exit.*]

THE MANAGER. Ready, everyone! First scene—the Young Lady. [*The* LEADING LADY *comes forward.*] No, no, you must wait. I meant her [*Indicating the* STEP-DAUGHTER.] You just watch—

THE STEP-DAUGHTER [*adding at once*]. How I shall play it, how I shall live it! . . .

LEADING LADY [*offended*]. I shall live it also, you may be sure, as soon as I begin!

THE MANAGER [*with his hands to his head*]. Ladies and gentlemen, if you please! No more useless discussions! Scene I: the young lady with Madame Pace: Oh! [*Looks around as if lost.*] And this Madame Pace, where is she?

THE FATHER. She isn't with us, sir.

THE MANAGER. Then what the devil's to be done?

THE FATHER. But she is alive too.

THE MANAGER. Yes, but where is she?

THE FATHER. One minute. Let me speak! [*Turning to the* ACTRESSES.] If these ladies would be so good as to give me their hats for a moment . . .

THE ACTRESSES [*half surprised, half laughing, in chorus*]. What?
Why?
Our hats?
What does he say?

THE MANAGER. What are you going to do with the ladies' hats? [*The* ACTORS *laugh.*]

THE FATHER. Oh nothing. I just want to put them on these pegs for a moment. And one of the ladies will be so kind as to take off her mantle . . .

THE ACTORS. Oh, what d'you think of that?
Only the mantle?
He must be mad.

SOME ACTRESSES. But why?
Mantles as well?

THE FATHER. To hang them up here for a moment. Please be so kind, will you?

THE ACTRESSES [*taking off their hats, one or two also their cloaks, and going to hang them on the racks*]. After all, why not?
There you are!

This is really funny.

We've got to put them on show.

THE FATHER. Exactly; just like that, on show.

THE MANAGER. May we know why?

THE FATHER. I'll tell you. Who knows if, by arranging the stage for her, she does not come here herself, attracted by the very articles of her trade? [*Inviting the* ACTORS *to look towards the exit at back of stage.*] Look! Look!

> [*The door at the back of stage opens and* MADAME PACE *enters and takes a few steps forward. She is a fat, oldish woman with puffy oxygenated hair.*[4] *She is rouged and powdered, dressed with a comical elegance in black silk. Round her waist is a long silver chain from which hangs a pair of scissors. The* STEP-DAUGHTER *runs over at once amid the stupor of the actors.*]

THE STEP-DAUGHTER [*turning towards her*]. There she is! There she is!

THE FATHER [*radiant*]. It's she! I said so, didn't I? There she is!

THE MANAGER [*conquering his surprise, and then becoming indignant*]. What sort of a trick is this?

LEADING MAN [*almost at the same time*]. What's going to happen next?

JUVENILE LEAD. Where does *she* come from?

L'INGÉNUE. They've been holding her in reserve, I guess.

LEADING LADY. A vulgar trick!

THE FATHER [*dominating the protests*]. Excuse me, all of you! Why are you so anxious to destroy in the name of a vulgar, common-place sense of truth, this reality which comes to birth attracted and formed by the magic of the stage itself, which has indeed more right to live here than you, since it is much truer than you—if you don't mind my saying so? Which is the actress among you who is to play Madame Pace! Well, here is Madame Pace herself. And you will allow, I fancy, that the actress who acts her will be less true than this woman here, who is herself in person. You see my daughter recognized her and went over to her at once. Now you're going to witness the scene!

> [*But the scene between the* STEP-DAUGHTER *and* MADAME PACE *has already begun despite the protest of the actors and the reply of the* FATHER. *It has begun quietly, naturally, in a manner impossible for the stage. So when the actors, called to attention by the* FATHER, *turn round and see* MADAME PACE, *who has placed one hand under the* STEP-DAUGHTER's *chin to raise her head, they observe her at first with great attention, but hearing*

---

4. Bleached.

her speak in an unintelligible manner their interest begins to wane.]

THE MANAGER. Well? well?

LEADING MAN. What does she say?

LEADING LADY. One can't hear a word.

JUVENILE LEAD. Louder! Louder please!

THE STEP-DAUGHTER [*leaving* MADAME PACE, *who smiles a Sphinx-like smile, and advancing towards the actors*]. Louder? Louder? What are you talking about? These aren't matters which can be shouted at the top of one's voice. If I have spoken them out loud, it was to shame him and have my revenge. [*Indicates* FATHER.] But for Madame it's quite a different matter.

THE MANAGER. Indeed? indeed? But here, you know, people have got to make themselves heard, my dear. Even we who are on the stage can't hear you. What will it be when the public's in the theatre? And anyway, you can very well speak up now among yourselves, since we shan't be present to listen to you as we are now. You've got to pretend to be alone in a room at the back of a shop where no one can hear you.

[*The* STEP-DAUGHTER *coquettishly and with a touch of malice makes a sign of disagreement two or three times with her finger.*]

THE MANAGER. What do you mean by no?

THE STEP-DAUGHTER [*sotto voce, mysteriously*]. There's someone who will hear us if she [*Indicating* MADAME PACE.] speaks out loud.

THE MANAGER [*in consternation*]. What? Have you got someone else to spring on us now? [*The* ACTORS *burst out laughing.*]

THE FATHER. No, no sir. She is alluding to me. I've got to be here— there behind that door, in waiting; and Madame Pace knows it. In fact, if you will allow me, I'll go there at once, so I can be quite ready. [*Moves away.*]

THE MANAGER [*stopping him*]. No! Wait! wait! We must observe the conventions of the theatre. Before you are ready . . .

THE STEP-DAUGHTER [*interrupting him*]. No, get on with it at once! I'm just dying, I tell you, to act this scene. If he's ready, I'm more than ready.

THE MANAGER [*shouting*]. But, my dear young lady, first of all, we must have the scene between you and this lady . . . [*Indicates* MADAME PACE.] Do you understand? . . .

THE STEP-DAUGHTER. Good Heavens! She's been telling me what you know already; that mamma's work is badly done again, that the material's ruined; and that if I want her to continue to help us in our misery I must be patient . . .

MADAME PACE [*coming forward with an air of great importance*]. Yes

indeed, sir, I no wanta take advantage of her, I no wanta be hard . . .
[*Note.* MADAME PACE *is supposed to talk in a jargon half Italian, half English.*]

THE MANAGER [*alarmed*]. What? What? She talks like that? [*The* ACTORS *burst out laughing again.*]

THE STEP-DAUGHTER [*also laughing*]. Yes yes, that's the way she talks, half English, half Italian! Most comical it is!

MADAME PACE. Itta seem not verra polite gentlemen laugha atta me eef I trya best speaka English.

THE MANAGER. *Diamine!*[5] Of course! Of course! Let her talk like that! Just what we want. Talk just like that, Madame, if you please! The effect will be certain. Exactly what was wanted to put a little comic relief into the crudity of the situation. Of course she talks like that! Magnificent!

THE STEP-DAUGHTER. Magnificent? Certainly! When certain suggestions are made to one in language of that kind, the effect is certain, since it seems almost a joke. One feels inclined to laugh when one hears her talk about an "old signore"[6] "who wanta talka nicely with you." Nice old signore, eh, Madame?

MADAME PACE. Not so old my dear, not so old! And even if you no lika him, he won't make any scandal!

THE MOTHER [*jumping up amid the amazement and consternation of the actors who had not been noticing her.* THEY *move to restrain her*]. You old devil! You murderess!

THE STEP-DAUGHTER [*running over to calm her* MOTHER]. Calm yourself, Mother, calm yourself! Please don't . . .

THE FATHER [*going to her also at the same time*]. Calm yourself! Don't get excited! Sit down now!

THE MOTHER. Well then, take that woman away out of my sight!

THE STEP-DAUGHTER [*to* MANAGER]. It is impossible for my mother to remain here.

THE FATHER [*to* MANAGER]. They can't be here together. And for this reason, you see: that woman there was not with us when we came . . . If they are on together, the whole thing is given away inevitably, as you see.

THE MANAGER. It doesn't matter. This is only a first rough sketch—just to get an idea of the various points of the scene, even confusedly . . . [*Turning to the* MOTHER *and leading her to her chair.*] Come along, my dear lady, sit down now, and let's get on with the scene . . .
[*Meanwhile, the* STEP-DAUGHTER, *coming forward again, turns to* MADAME PACE.]

THE STEP-DAUGHTER. Come on, Madame, come on!

5. "Devil take it!" 6. "Old gentleman."

MADAME PACE [*offended*]. No, no, *grazie*.[7] I not do anything witha your mother present.

THE STEP-DAUGHTER. Nonsense! Introduce this "old signore" who wants to talk nicely to me. [*Addressing the* COMPANY *imperiously*.] We've got to do this scene one way or another, haven't we? Come on! [*To* MADAME PACE.] You can go!

MADAME PACE. Ah yes! I go'way! I go'way! Certainly! [*Exits furious*.]

THE STEP-DAUGHTER [*to the* FATHER]. Now you make your entry. No, you needn't go over here. Come here. Let's suppose you've already come in. Like that, yes! I'm here with bowed head, modest like. Come on! Out with your voice! Say "Good morning, Miss" in that peculiar tone, that special tone . . .

THE MANAGER. Excuse me, but are you the Manager, or am I? [*To the* FATHER, *who looks undecided and perplexed*.] Get on with it, man! Go down there to the back of the stage. You needn't go off. Then come right forward here.

[*The* FATHER *does as he is told, looking troubled and perplexed at first. But as soon as he begins to move, the reality of the action affects him, and he begins to smile and to be more natural. The* ACTORS *watch intently*.]

THE MANAGER [*sotto voce, quickly to the* PROMPTER *in his box*]. Ready! ready? Get ready to write now.

THE FATHER [*coming forward and speaking in a different tone*]. Good afternoon, Miss!

THE STEP-DAUGHTER [*head bowed down slightly, with restrained disgust*]. Good afternoon!

THE FATHER [*looks under her hat which partly covers her face. Perceiving she is very young, he makes an exclamation, partly of surprise, partly of fear lest he compromise himself in a risky adventure*]. Ah . . . but . . . ah . . . I say . . . this is not the first time that you have come here, is it?

THE STEP-DAUGHTER [*modestly*]. No sir.

THE FATHER. You've been here before, eh? [*Then seeing her nod agreement*.] More than once? [*Waits for her to answer, looks under her hat, smiles, and then says*.] Well then, there's no need to be so shy, is there? May I take off your hat?

THE STEP-DAUGHTER [*anticipating him and with veiled disgust*]. No sir . . . I'll do it myself. [*Takes it off quickly*.]

[*The* MOTHER, *who watches the progress of the scene with The* SON *and the other two children who cling to her, is on thorns; and follows with varying expressions of sorrow, indignation, anxiety, and horror the words and actions of the other two. From time to time* SHE *hides her face in her hands and sobs*.]

7. "Thank you."

THE MOTHER. Oh, my God, my God!

THE FATHER [*playing his part with a touch of gallantry*]. Give it to me! I'll put it down. [*Takes hat from her hands.*] But a dear little head like yours ought to have a smarter hat. Come and help me choose one from the stock, won't you?

L'INGÉNUE [*interrupting*]. I say . . . those are our hats you know.

THE MANAGER [*furious*]. Silence! silence! Don't try and be funny, if you please . . . We're playing the scene now I'd have you notice. [*To the* STEP-DAUGHTER.] Begin again, please!

THE STEP-DAUGHTER [*continuing*]. No thank you, sir.

THE FATHER. Oh, come now. Don't talk like that. You must take it. I shall be upset if you don't. There are some lovely little hats here; and then—Madame will be pleased. She expects it, anyway, you know.

THE STEP-DAUGHTER. No, no! I couldn't wear it!

THE FATHER. Oh, you're thinking about what they'd say at home if they saw you come in with a new hat? My dear girl, there's always a way round these little matters, you know.

THE STEP-DAUGHTER [*all keyed up*]. No, it's not that. I couldn't wear it because I am . . . as you see . . . you might have noticed . . . [*Showing her black dress.*]

THE FATHER. . . . in mourning! Of course: I beg your pardon: I'm frightfully sorry . . .

THE STEP-DAUGHTER [*forcing herself to conquer her indignation and nausea*]. Stop! Stop! It's I who must thank you. There's no need for you to feel mortified or specially sorry. Don't think any more of what I've said. [*Tries to smile.*] I must forget that I am dressed so . . .

THE MANAGER [*interrupting and turning to the* PROMPTER]. Stop a minute! Stop! Don't write that down. Cut out that last bit. [*Then to the* FATHER *and* STEP-DAUGHTER.] Fine! it's going fine! [*To the* FATHER *only.*] And now you can go on as we arranged. [*To the* ACTORS.] Pretty good that scene, where he offers her the hat, eh?

THE STEP-DAUGHTER. The best's coming now. Why can't we go on?

THE MANAGER. Have a little patience! [*To the* ACTORS.] Of course, it must be treated rather lightly.

LEADING MAN. Still, with a bit of go in it!

LEADING LADY. Of course! It's easy enough! [*To* LEADING MAN.] Shall you and I try it now?

LEADING MAN. Why, yes! I'll prepare my entrance. [*Exit in order to make his entrance.*]

THE MANAGER [*to* LEADING LADY]. See here! The scene between you and Madame Pace is finished. I'll have it written out properly after. You remain here . . . oh, where are you going?

LEADING LADY. One minute. I want to put my hat on again. [*Goes to hat-rack and puts her hat on her head.*]

THE MANAGER. Good! You stay here with your head bowed down a bit.

THE STEP-DAUGHTER. But she isn't dressed in black.

LEADING LADY. But I shall be, and much more effectively than you.

THE MANAGER [*to* STEP-DAUGHTER]. Be quiet please, and watch! You'll be able to learn something. [*Clapping his hands.*] Come on! come on! Entrance, please!

> [*The door at rear of stage opens, and the* LEADING MAN *enters with the lively manner of an old gallant. The rendering of the scene by the* ACTORS *from the very first words is seen to be quite a different thing, though it has not in any way the air of a parody. Naturally, the* STEP-DAUGHTER *and the* FATHER, *not being able to recognize themselves in the* LEADING LADY *and the* LEAD-ING MAN, *who deliver their words in different tones and with a different psychology, express, sometimes with smiles, sometimes with gestures, the impression they receive.*]

LEADING MAN. Good afternoon, Miss . . .

THE FATHER [*at once unable to contain himself*]. No! no!

> [*The* STEP-DAUGHTER *noticing the way the* LEADING MAN *enters, bursts out laughing.*]

THE MANAGER [*furious*]. Silence! And you please just stop that laughing. If we go on like this, we shall never finish.

THE STEP-DAUGHTER. Forgive me, sir, but it's natural enough. This lady [*Indicating* LEADING LADY.] stands there still; but if she is supposed to be me, I can assure you that if I heard anyone say "Good afternoon" in that manner and in that tone, I should burst out laughing as I did.

THE FATHER. Yes, yes, the manner, the tone . . .

THE MANAGER. Nonsense! Rubbish! Stand aside and let me see the action.

LEADING MAN. If I've got to represent an old fellow who's coming into a house of an equivocal character . . .

THE MANAGER. Don't listen to them, for Heaven's sake! Do it again! It goes fine. [*Waiting for the* ACTORS *to begin again.*] Well?

LEADING MAN. Good afternoon, Miss.

LEADING LADY. Good afternoon.

LEADING MAN [*imitating the gesture of the* FATHER *when he looked under the hat, and then expressing quite clearly first satisfaction and then fear*]. Ah, but . . . I say . . . this is not the first time that you have come here, is it?

THE MANAGER. Good, but not quite so heavily. Like this. [*Acts himself.*] "This isn't the first time that you have come here" . . . [*To*

LEADING LADY.] And you say: "No, sir."

LEADING LADY. No, sir.

LEADING MAN. You've been here before, more than once.

THE MANAGER. No, no, stop! Let her nod "yes" first. "You've been here before, eh?" [*The* LEADING LADY *lifts up her head slightly and closes her eyes as though in disgust. Then* SHE *inclines her head twice.*]

THE STEP-DAUGHTER [*unable to contain herself*]. Oh my God! [*Puts a hand to her mouth to prevent herself from laughing.*]

THE MANAGER [*turning round*]. What's the matter?

THE STEP-DAUGHTER. Nothing, nothing!

THE MANAGER [*to* LEADING MAN]. Go on!

LEADING MAN. You've been here before, eh? Well then, there's no need to be so shy, is there? May I take off your hat?

    [*The* LEADING MAN *says this last speech in such a tone and with such gestures that the* STEP-DAUGHTER, *though she has her hand to her mouth, cannot keep from laughing.*]

LEADING LADY [*indignant*]. I'm not going to stop here to be made a fool of by that woman there.

LEADING MAN. Neither am I! I'm through with it!

THE MANAGER [*shouting to* STEP-DAUGHTER]. Silence! for once and all, I tell you!

THE STEP-DAUGHTER. Forgive me! forgive me!

THE MANAGER. You haven't any manners: that's what it is! You go too far.

THE FATHER [*endeavouring to intervene*]. Yes, it's true, but excuse her . . .

THE MANAGER. Excuse what? It's absolutely disgusting.

THE FATHER. Yes, sir, but believe me, it has such a strange effect when . . .

THE MANAGER. Strange? Why strange? Where is it strange?

THE FATHER. No, sir; I admire your actors—this gentleman here, this lady; but they are certainly not us!

THE MANAGER. I should hope not. Evidently they cannot be you, if they are actors.

THE FATHER. Just so: actors! Both of them act our parts exceedingly well. But, believe me, it produces quite a different effect on us. They want to be us, but they aren't, all the same.

THE MANAGER. What is it then anyway?

THE FATHER. Something that is . . . that is theirs—and no longer ours . . .

THE MANAGER. But naturally, inevitably. I've told you so already.

THE FATHER. Yes, I understand . . . I understand . . .

THE MANAGER. Well then, let's have no more of it! —*Turning to the*

ACTORS.] We'll have the rehearsals by ourselves, afterwards, in the ordinary way. I never could stand rehearsing with the author present. He's never satisfied! [*Turning to* FATHER *and* STEP-DAUGHTER.] Come on! Let's get on with it again; and try and see if you can't keep from laughing.

THE STEP-DAUGHTER. Oh, I shan't laugh any more. There's a nice little bit coming for me now: you'll see.

THE MANAGER. Well then: when she says "Don't think any more of what I've said. I must forget, etc.," you [*Adressing the* FATHER.] come in sharp with "I understand, I understand"; and then you ask her . . .

THE STEP-DAUGHTER [*interrupting*]. What?

THE MANAGER. Why she is in mourning.

THE STEP-DAUGHTER. Not at all! See here: when I told him that it was useless for me to be thinking about my wearing mourning, do you know how he answered me? "Ah well," he said, "then let's take off this little frock."

THE MANAGER. Great! Just what we want, to make a riot in the theatre!

THE STEP-DAUGHTER. But it's the truth!

THE MANAGER. What does that matter? Acting is our business here. Truth up to a certain point, but no further.

THE STEP-DAUGHTER. What do you want to do then?

THE MANAGER. You'll see, you'll see! Leave it to me.

THE STEP-DAUGHTER. No sir! What you want to do is to piece together a little romantic sentimental scene out of my disgust, out of all the reasons, each more cruel and viler than the other, why I am what I am. He is to ask me why I'm in mourning; and I'm to answer with tears in my eyes, that it is just two months since papa died. No sir, no! He's got to say to me; as he did say: "Well, let's take off this little dress at once." And I; with my two months' mourning in my heart, went there behind that screen, and with these fingers tingling with shame . . .

THE MANAGER [*running his hands through his hair*]. For Heaven's sake! What are you saying?

THE STEP-DAUGHTER [*crying out excitedly*]. The truth! The truth!

THE MANAGER. It may be. I don't deny it, and I can understand all your horror; but you must surely see that you can't have this kind of thing on the stage. It won't go.

THE STEP-DAUGHTER. Not possible, eh? Very well! I'm much obliged to you—but I'm off!

THE MANAGER. Now be reasonable! Don't lose your temper!

THE STEP-DAUGHTER. I won't stop here! I won't! I can see you've fixed it all up with him in your office. All this talk about what is possible for the stage . . . I understand! He wants to get at his complicated "cerebral drama," to have his famous remorses and torments acted; but I want to act my part, *my part!*

THE MANAGER [*annoyed, shaking his shoulders*]. Ah! Just *your* part! But, if you will pardon me, there are other parts than yours: His [*Indicating the* FATHER.] and hers! [*Indicating the* MOTHER.] On the stage you can't have a character becoming too prominent and overshadowing all the others. The thing is to pack them all into a neat little framework and then act what is actable. I am aware of the fact that everyone has his own interior life which he wants very much to put forward. But the difficulty lies in this fact: to set out just so much as is necessary for the stage, taking the other characters into consideration, and at the same time hint at the unrevealed interior life of each. I am willing to admit, my dear young lady, that from your point of view it would be a fine idea if each character could tell the public all his troubles in a nice monologue or a regular one-hour lecture. [*Good-humoredly.*] You must restrain yourself, my dear, and in your own interest, too; because this fury of yours, this exaggerated disgust you show, may make a bad impression, you know. After you have confessed to me that there were others before him at Madame Pace's and more than once . . .

THE STEP-DAUGHTER [*bowing her head, impressed*]. It's true. But remember those others mean him for me all the same.

THE MANAGER [*not understanding*]. What? The others? What do you mean?

THE STEP-DAUGHTER. For one who has gone wrong, sir, he who was responsible for the first fault is responsible for all that follow. He is responsible for my faults, was, even before I was born. Look at him, and see if it isn't true!

THE MANAGER. Well, well! And does the weight of so much responsibility seem nothing to you? Give him a chance to act it, to get it over!

THE STEP-DAUGHTER. How? How can he act all his "noble remorses," all his "moral torments," if you want to spare him the horror of being discovered one day—after he had asked her what he did ask her—in the arms of her, that already fallen woman, that child, sir, that child he used to watch come out of school? [SHE *is moved.*]

[*The* MOTHER *at this point is overcome with emotion, and breaks out into a fit of crying. ALL are touched. A long pause.*]

THE STEP-DAUGHTER [*as soon as the* MOTHER *becomes a little quieter, adds resolutely and gravely*]. At present, we are unknown to the public. Tomorrow, you will act us as you wish, treating us in your own manner. But do you really want to see drama, do you want to see it flash out as it really did?

THE MANAGER. Of course! That's just what I do want, so I can use as much of it as is possible.

THE STEP-DAUGHTER. Well then, ask that Mother there to leave us.

THE MOTHER [*changing her low plaint into a sharp cry*]. No! No! Don't permit it, sir, don't permit it!

THE MANAGER. But it's only to try it.

THE MOTHER. I can't bear it. I can't.

THE MANAGER. But since it has happened already . . . I don't understand!

THE MOTHER. It's taking place now. It happens all the time. My torment isn't a pretended one. I live and feel every minute of my torture. Those two children there—have you heard them speak? They can't speak any more. They cling to me to keep up my torment actual and vivid for me. But for themselves, they do not exist, they aren't any more. And she [*Indicating the* STEP-DAUGHTER.] has run away, she has left me, and is lost. If I now see her here before me, it is only to renew for me the tortures I have suffered for her too.

THE FATHER. The eternal moment! She [*Indicating the* STEP-DAUGHTER.] is here to catch me, fix me, and hold me eternally in the stocks for that one fleeting and shameful moment of my life. She can't give it up! And you sir, cannot either fairly spare me it.

THE MANAGER. I never said I didn't want to act it. It will form, as a matter of fact, the nucleus of the whole first act right up to her surprise. [*Indicates the* MOTHER.]

THE FATHER. Just so! This is my punishment: the passion in all of us that must culminate in her final cry.

THE STEP-DAUGHTER. I can hear it still in my ears. It's driven me mad, that cry!—You can put me on as you like; it doesn't matter. Fully dressed, if you like—provided I have at least the arm bare; because, standing like this [*She goes close to the* FATHER *and leans her head on his breast.*] with my head so, and my arms round his neck, I saw a vein pulsing in my arm here; and then, as if that live vein had awakened disgust in me, I closed my eyes like this, and let my head sink on his breast. [*Turning to the* MOTHER.] Cry out mother! Cry out! [*Buries head in* FATHER's *breast, and with her shoulders raised as if to prevent her hearing the cry, adds in tones of intense emotion.*] Cry out as you did then!

THE MOTHER [*coming forward to separate them*]. No! My daughter, my daughter! [*And after having pulled her away from him.*] You brute! you brute! She is my daughter! Don't you see she's my daughter?

THE MANAGER [*walking backwards towards footlights*]. Fine! fine!

Damned good! And then, of course—curtain!

THE FATHER [*going towards him excitedly*]. Yes, of course, because
that's the way it really happened.

THE MANAGER [*convinced and pleased*]. Oh, yes, no doubt about it.
Curtain here, curtain!

> [*At the reiterated cry of the* MANAGER, *the* MACHINIST *lets the
> curtain down, leaving the* MANAGER *and the* FATHER *in front of
> it before the footlights.*]

THE MANAGER. The darned idiot! I said "curtain" to show the act
should end there, and he goes and lets it down in earnest. [*To the*
FATHER, *while he pulls the curtain back to go on to the stage
again.*] Yes, yes, it's all right. Effect certain! That's the right ending. I'll guarantee the first act at any rate.

ACT III

*When the curtain goes up again, it is seen that the stage hands
have shifted the bit of scenery used in the last part, and have rigged
up instead at the back of the stage a drop, with some trees, and one
or two wings. A portion of a fountain basin is visible. The* MOTHER
is sitting on the right with the two children by her side. The SON *is
on the same side, but away from the others. He seems bored, angry,
and full of shame. The* FATHER *and the* STEP-DAUGHTER *are also
seated towards the right front. On the other side (left) are the* ACTORS,
*much in the positions they occupied before the curtain was lowered.
Only the* MANAGER *is standing up in the middle of the stage, with his
hand closed over his mouth in the act of meditating.*

THE MANAGER [*shaking his shoulders after a brief pause*]. Ah yes: the
second act! Leave it to me, leave it all to me as we arranged, and
you'll see! It'll go fine!

THE STEP-DAUGHTER. Our entry into his house [*Indicates* FATHER.]
in spite of him . . . [*Indicates the* SON.]

THE MANAGER [*out of patience*]. Leave it to me, I tell you!

THE STEP-DAUGHTER. Do let it be clear, at any rate, that it is in spite
of my wishes.

THE MOTHER [*from her corner, shaking her head*]. For all the good
that's come of it . . .

THE STEP-DAUGHTER [*turning towards her quickly*]. It doesn't matter.
The more harm done us, the more remorse for him.

THE MANAGER [*impatiently*]. I understand! Good Heavens! I understand! I'm taking it into account.

THE MOTHER [*supplicatingly*]. I beg you, sir, to let it appear quite
plain that for conscience' sake I did try in every way . . .

THE STEP-DAUGHTER [*interrupting indignantly and continuing for the*

MOTHER]. . . . to pacify me, to dissuade me from spiting him. [*To* MANAGER.] Do as she wants: satisfy her, because it is true! I enjoy it immensely. Anyhow, as you can see, the meeker she is, the more she tries to get at his heart, the more distant and aloof does he become.

THE MANAGER. Are we going to begin this second act or not?

THE STEP-DAUGHTER. I'm not going to talk any more now. But I must tell you this: you can't have the whole action take place in the garden, as you suggest. It isn't possible!

THE MANAGER. Why not?

THE STEP-DAUGHTER. Because he [*Indicates the* SON *again.*] is always shut up alone in his room. And then there's all the part of that poor dazed-looking boy there which takes place indoors.

THE MANAGER. Maybe! On the other hand, you will understand— we can't change scenes three or four times in one act.

THE LEADING MAN. They used to once.

THE MANAGER. Yes, when the public was up to the level of that child there.

THE LEADING LADY. It makes the illusion easier.

THE FATHER [*irritated*]. The illusion! For Heaven's sake, don't say illusion. Please don't use that word, which is particularly painful for us.

THE MANAGER [*astounded*]. And why, if you please?

THE FATHER. It's painful, cruel, really cruel; and you ought to under- stand that.

THE MANAGER. But why? What ought we to say then? The illusion, I tell you, sir, which we've got to create for the audience . . .

THE LEADING MAN. With our acting.

THE MANAGER. The illusion of a reality.

THE FATHER. I understand; but you, perhaps, do not understand us. Forgive me! You see . . . here for you and your actors, the thing is only—and rightly so . . . a kind of game . . .

THE LEADING LADY [*interrupting indignantly*]. A game! We're not children here, if you please! We are serious actors.

THE FATHER. I don't deny it. What I mean is the game, or play, of your art, which has to give, as the gentleman says, a perfect illu- sion of reality.

THE MANAGER. Precisely—!

THE FATHER. Now, if you consider the fact that we [*Indicates himself and the other five* CHARACTERS.], as we are, have no other reality outside of this illusion . . .

THE MANAGER [*astonished, looking at his* ACTORS, *who are also amazed*]. And what does that mean?

THE FATHER [*after watching them for a moment with a wan smile*]. As I say, sir, that which is a game of art for you is our sole reality.

[*Brief pause. He goes a step or two nearer the* MANAGER *and adds.*] But not only for us, you know, by the way. Just you think it over well. [*Looks him in the eyes.*] Can you tell me who you are?

THE MANAGER [*perplexed, half smiling*]. What? Who am I? I am myself.

THE FATHER. And if I were to tell you that that isn't true, because you and I . . . ?

THE MANAGER. I should say you were mad—! [*The* ACTORS *laugh.*]

THE FATHER. You're quite right to laugh: because we are all making believe here. [*To* MANAGER.] And you can therefore object that it's only for a joke that that gentleman there [*Indicates the* LEADING MAN.], who naturally is himself, has to be me, who am on the contrary myself—this thing you see here. You see I've caught you in a trap! [*The* ACTORS *laugh.*]

THE MANAGER [*annoyed*]. But we've had all this over once before. Do you want to begin again?

THE FATHER. No, no! That wasn't my meaning! In fact, I should like to request you to abandon this game of art [*Looking at the* LEADING LADY *as if anticipating her.*] which you are accustomed to play here with your actors, and to ask you seriously once again: who are you?

THE MANAGER [*astonished and irritated, turning to his* ACTORS]. If this fellow here hasn't got a nerve! A man who calls himself a character comes and asks me who I am!

THE FATHER [*with dignity, but not offended*]. A character, sir, may always ask a man who he is. Because a character has really a life of his own, marked with his especial characteristics; for which reason he is always "somebody." But a man—I'm not speaking of you now—may very well be "nobody."

THE MANAGER. Yes, but you are asking these questions of me, the boss, the manager! Do you understand?

THE FATHER. But only in order to know if you, as you really are now, see yourself as you once were with all the illusions that were yours then, with all the things both inside and outside of you as they seemed to you—as they were then indeed for you. Well, sir, if you think of all those illusions that mean nothing to you now, of all those things which don't even *seem* to you to exist any more, while once they *were* for you, don't you feel that—I won't say these boards—but the very earth under your feet is sinking away from you when you reflect that in the same way this *you* as you feel it today—all this present reality of yours—is fated to seem a mere illusion to you tomorrow?

THE MANAGER [*without having understood much, but astonished by the specious argument*]. Well, well! And where does all this take us anyway?

THE FATHER. Oh, nowhere! It's only to show you that if we [*Indicating the* CHARACTERS.] have no other reality beyond the illusion, you too must not count overmuch on your reality as you feel it today, since, like that of yesterday, it may prove an illusion for you tomorrow.

THE MANAGER [*determining to make fun of him*]. Ah, excellent! Then you'll be saying next that you, with this comedy of yours that you brought here to act, are truer and more real than I am.

THE FATHER [*with the greatest seriousness*]. But of course; without doubt!

THE MANAGER. Ah, really?

THE FATHER. Why, I thought you'd understand that from the beginning.

THE MANAGER. More real than I?

THE FATHER. If your reality can change from one day to another . . .

THE MANAGER. But everyone knows it can change. It is always changing, the same as anyone else's.

THE FATHER [*with a cry*]. No, sir, not ours! Look here! That is the very difference! Our reality doesn't change: it can't change! It can't be other than what it is, because it is already fixed for ever. It's terrible. Ours is an immutable reality which should make you shudder when you approach us if you are really conscious of the fact that your reality is a mere transitory and fleeting illusion, taking this form today and that tomorrow, according to the conditions, according to your will, your sentiments, which in turn are controlled by an intellect that shows them to you today in one manner and tomorrow . . . who knows how? . . . Illusions of reality represented in this fatuous comedy of life that never ends, nor can ever end! Because if tomorrow it were to end . . . then why, all would be finished.

THE MANAGER. Oh for God's sake, will you *at least* finish with this philosophizing and let us try and shape this comedy which you yourself have brought me here? You argue and philosophize a bit too much, my dear sir. You know you seem to me almost, almost . . . [*Stops and looks him over from head to foot.*] Ah, by the way, I think you introduced yourself to me as a—what shall . . . we say—a "character," created by an author who did not afterward care to make a drama of his own creations.

THE FATHER. It is the simple truth, sir.

THE MANAGER. Nonsense! Cut that out, please! None of us believes it, because it isn't a thing, as you must recognize yourself, which one can believe seriously. If you want to know, it seems to me you are trying to imitate the manner of a certain author whom I heartily detest—I warn you—although I have unfortunately bound myself to put on one of his works. As a matter of fact, I was just starting

to rehearse it, when you arrived. [*Turning to the* ACTORS.]
And this is what we've gained—out of the frying-pan into the fire!

THE FATHER. I don't know to what author you may be alluding, but
believe me I feel what I think; and I seem to be philosophizing
only for those who do not think what they feel, because they blind
themselves with their own sentiment. I know that for many people
this self-blinding seems much more "human"; but the contrary is
really true. For man never reasons so much and becomes so
introspective as when he suffers; since he is anxious to get at the
cause of his sufferings, to learn who has produced them, and
whether it is just or unjust that he should have to bear them. On
the other hand, when he is happy, he takes his happiness as it
comes and doesn't analyze it, just as if happiness were his right.
The animals suffer without reasoning about their sufferings. But
take the case of a man who suffers and begins to reason about it.
Oh no! it can't be allowed! Let him suffer like an animal, and
then—ah yet, he is "human"!

THE MANAGER. Look here! Look here! You're off again, philosophizing worse than ever.

THE FATHER. Because I suffer, sir! I'm not philosophizing: I'm crying
aloud the reason of my sufferings.

THE MANAGER [*makes brusque movement as he is taken with a new
idea*]. I should like to know if anyone has ever heard of a character
who gets right out of his part and perorates and speechifies as you
do. Have you ever heard of a case? I haven't.

THE FATHER. You have never met such a case, sir, because authors,
as a rule, hide the labour of their creations. When the characters
are really alive before their author, the latter does nothing but
follow them in their action, in their words, in the situations which
they suggest to him; and he has to will them the way they will
themselves—for there's trouble if he doesn't. When a character is
born, he acquires at once such an independence, even of his own
author, that he can be imagined by everybody even in many other
situations where the author never dreamed of placing him; and so
he acquires for himself a meaning which the author never thought
of giving him.

THE MANAGER. Yes, yes, I know this.

THE FATHER. What is there then to marvel at in us? Imagine such a
misfortune for characters as I have described to you: to be born of
an author's fantasy, and be denied life by him; and then answer
me if these characters left alive, and yet without life, weren't right
in doing what they did do and are doing now, after they have
attempted everything in their power to persuade him to give them
their stage life. We've all tried him in turn, I, she [*Indicating the*

STEP-DAUGHTER.] and she. [*Indicating the* MOTHER.]

THE STEP-DAUGHTER. It's true. I too have sought to tempt him, many, many times, when he has been sitting at his writing table, feeling a bit melancholy, at the twilight hour. He would sit in his armchair too lazy to switch on the light, and all the shadows that crept into his room were full of our presence coming to tempt him. [*As if she saw herself still there by the writing table, and was annoyed by the presence of the* ACTORS.] Oh, if you would only go away, go away and leave us alone—mother here with that son of hers— I with that Child—that Boy there always alone—and then I with him [*Just hints at the* FATHER.]—and then I alone, alone . . . in those shadows! [*Makes a sudden movement as if in the vision she has of herself illuminating those shadows she wanted to seize hold of herself.*] Ah! my life! my life! Oh, what scenes we proposed to him—and I tempted him more than any of the others!

THE FATHER. Maybe. But perhaps it was your fault that he refused to give us life: because you were too insistent, too troublesome.

THE STEP-DAUGHTER. Nonsense! Didn't he make me so himself? [*Goes close to the* MANAGER *to tell him as if in confidence.*] In my opinion he abandoned us in a fit of depression, of disgust for the ordinary theatre as the public knows it and likes it.

THE SON. Exactly what it was, sir; exactly that!

THE FATHER. Not at all! Don't believe it for a minute. Listen to me! You'll be doing quite right to modify, as you suggest, the excesses both of this girl here, who wants to do too much, and of this young man, who won't do anything at all.

THE SON. No, nothing!

THE MANAGER. You too get over the mark occasionally, my dear sir, if I may say so.

THE FATHER. I? When? Where?

THE MANAGER. Always! Continuously! Then there's this insistence of yours in trying to make us believe you are a character. And then too, you must really argue and philosophize less, you know, much less.

THE FATHER. Well, if you want to take away from me the possibility of representing the torment of my spirit which never gives me peace, you will be suppressing me: that's all. Every true man, sir, who is a little above the level of the beasts and plants does not live for the sake of living, without knowing how to live; but he lives so as to give a meaning and a value of his own to life. For me this is *everything*. I cannot give up this, just to represent a mere fact as she [*Indicating the* STEP-DAUGHTER.] wants. It's all very well for her, since her "vendetta" lies in the "fact." I'm not going to do it. It destroys my *raison d'être*.

THE MANAGER. Your *raison d'être!* Oh, we're going ahead fine! First she starts off, and then you jump in. At this rate, we'll never finish.

THE FATHER. Now, don't be offended! Have it your own way—provided, however, that within the limits of the parts you assign us each one's sacrifice isn't too great.

THE MANAGER. You've got to understand that you can't go on arguing at your own pleasure. Drama is action, sir, action and not confounded philosophy.

THE FATHER. All right. I'll do just as much arguing and philosophizing as everybody does when he is considering his own torments.

THE MANAGER. If the drama permits! But for Heaven's sake, man, let's get along and come to the scene.

THE STEP-DAUGHTER. It seems to me we've got too much action with our coming into his house. [*Indicating* FATHER.] You said, before, you couldn't change the scene every five minutes.

THE MANAGER. Of course not. What we've got to do is to combine and group up all the facts in one simultaneous, close-knit action. We can't have it as you want, with your little brother wandering like a ghost from room to room, hiding behind doors and meditating a project which—what did you say it did to him?

THE STEP-DAUGHTER. Consumes him, sir, wastes him away!

THE MANAGER. Well, it may be. And then at the same time, you want the little girl there to be playing in the garden . . . one in the house, and the other in the garden: isn't that it?

THE STEP-DAUGHTER. Yes, in the sun, in the sun! That is my only pleasure: to see her happy and careless in the garden after the misery and squalor of the horrible room where we all four slept together. And I had to sleep with her—I, do you understand?—with my vile contaminated body next to hers; with her folding me fast in her loving little arms. In the garden, whenever she spied me, she would run to take me by the hand. She didn't care for the big flowers, only the little ones; and she loved to show me them and pet me.

THE MANAGER. Well then, we'll have it in the garden. Everything shall happen in the garden; and we'll group the other scenes there. [*Calls a* STAGE HAND.] Here, a backcloth with trees and something to do as a fountain basin. [*Turning round to look at the back of the stage.*] Ah, you've fixed it up. Good! [*To* STEP-DAUGHTER.] This is just to give an idea, of course. The Boy, instead of hiding behind the doors, will wander about here in the garden, hiding behind the trees. But it's going to be rather difficult to find a child to do that scene with you where she shows you the flowers. [*Turning to the* BOY.] Come forward a little, will you please? Let's try it now! Come along! come along! [*Then seeing him come shyly forward, full of fear and looking lost.*] It's a nice business, this lad here. What's the matter with him? We'll have to give him a word or two to say. [*Goes close to him, puts a hand on his shoulders, and leads him behind one of the trees.*] Come on! come on! Let me see you a little! Hide here . . . yes, like that. Try and show your head just a little as if you were looking for someone . . . [*Goes back to observe the effect, when the* BOY *at once goes through the action.*] Excellent! fine! [*Turning to* STEP-DAUGHTER.] Suppose the little girl there were to surprise him as he looks round, and run over to him, so we could give him a word or two to say?

THE STEP-DAUGHTER. It's useless to hope he will speak, as long as that fellow there is here . . . [*Indicates the* SON.] You must send him away first.

THE SON [*jumping up*]. Delighted! Delighted! I don't ask for anything better. [*Begins to move away.*]

THE MANAGER [*at once stopping him*]. No! No! Where are you going? Wait a bit!

[*The* MOTHER *gets up alarmed and terrified at the thought that he is really about to go away. Instinctively she lifts her arms to prevent him, without, however, leaving her seat.*]

THE SON [*to* MANAGER *who stops him*]. I've got nothing to do with this affair. Let me go please! Let me go!

THE MANAGER. What do you mean by saying you've got nothing to do with this?

THE STEP-DAUGHTER [*calmly, with irony*]. Don't bother to stop him: he won't go away.

THE FATHER. He has to act the terrible scene in the garden with his mother.

THE SON [*suddenly resolute and with dignity*]. I shall act nothing at all. I've said so from the very beginning. [*To the* MANAGER.] Let me go!

THE STEP-DAUGHTER [*going over to the* MANAGER]. Allow me? [*Puts down the* MANAGER'S *arm which is restraining the* SON.] Well, go away then, if you want to! [*The* SON *looks at her with contempt and hatred. She laughs and says.*] You see, he can't, he can't go away! He is obliged to stay here, indissolubly bound to the chain. If I, who fly off when that happens which has to happen, because I can't bear him—if I am still here and support that face and expression of his, you can well imagine that he is unable to move. He has to remain here, has to stop with that nice father of his, and that mother whose only son he is. [*Turning to the* MOTHER.] Come on, mother, come along! [*Turning to* MANAGER *to indicate her.*] You see, she was getting up to keep him back. [*To the* MOTHER, *beckoning her with her hand.*] Come on! come on! [*Then to* MANAGER]. You can imagine how little she wants to show these actors of yours what she really feels; but so eager is she to get near him that . . . There, you see? She is willing to act her part. [*And in fact, the* MOTHER *approaches him; and as soon as the* STEP-DAUGHTER *has finished speaking, opens her arms to signify that she consents.*]

THE SON [*suddenly*]. No! no! If I can't go away, then I'll stop here; but I repeat: I act nothing!

THE FATHER [*to* MANAGER *excitedly*]. You can force him, sir.

THE SON. Nobody can force me.

THE FATHER. I can.

THE STEP-DAUGHTER. Wait a minute, wait . . . First of all, the baby has to go to the fountain . . . [*Runs to take the* CHILD *and leads her to the fountain.*]

THE MANAGER. Yes, yes of course; that's it. Both at the same time.
[*The second* LADY LEAD *and the* JUVENILE LEAD *at this point separate themselves from the group of* ACTORS. *One watches the* MOTHER *attentively; the other moves about studying the movements and manner of the* SON *whom he will have to act.*]

THE SON [*to* MANAGER]. What do you mean by both at the same time? It isn't right. There was no scene between me and her. [*Indicates the* MOTHER.] Ask her how it was!

THE MOTHER. Yes, it's true. I had come into his room . . .

THE SON. Into my room, do you understand? Nothing to do with the garden.

THE MANAGER. It doesn't matter. Haven't I told you we've got to group the action?

THE SON [*observing the* JUVENILE LEAD *studying him*]. What do you want?

THE JUVENILE LEAD. Nothing! I was just looking at you.

THE SON [*turning towards the second* LADY LEAD]. Ah! she's at it too: to re-act her part! [*Indicating the* MOTHER.]

THE MANAGER. Exactly! And it seems to me that you ought to be grateful to them for their interest.

THE SON. Yes, but haven't you yet perceived that it isn't possible to live in front of a mirror which not only freezes us with the image of ourselves, but throws our likeness back at us with a horrible grimace?

THE FATHER. That is true, absolutely true. You must see that.

THE MANAGER [*to second* LADY LEAD *and* JUVENILE LEAD]. He's right! Move away from them!

THE SON. Do as you like. I'm out of this!

THE MANAGER. Be quiet, you, will you? And let me hear your mother! [*To* MOTHER.] You were saying you had entered . . .

THE MOTHER. Yes, into his room, because I couldn't stand it any longer. I went to empty my heart to him of all the anguish that tortures me . . . But as soon as he saw me come in . . .

THE SON. Nothing happened! There was no scene. I went away, that's all! I don't care for scenes!

THE MOTHER. It's true, true. That's how it was.

THE MANAGER. Well now, we've got to do this bit between you and him. It's indispensable.

THE MOTHER. I'm ready . . . when you are ready. If you could only find a chance for me to tell him what I feel here in my heart.

THE FATHER [*going to* SON *in a great rage*]. You'll do this for your mother, for your mother, do you understand?

THE SON [*quite determined*]. I do nothing!

THE FATHER [*taking hold of him and shaking him*]. For God's sake, do as I tell you! Don't you hear your mother asking you for a favor? Haven't you even got the guts to be a son?

THE SON [*taking hold of the* FATHER]. No! No! And for God's sake stop it, or else . . . [*General agitation. The* MOTHER, *frightened, tries to separate them.*]

THE MOTHER [*pleading*]. Please! please!

THE FATHER [*not leaving hold of the* SON]. You've got to obey, do you hear?

THE SON [*almost crying from rage*]. What does it mean, this madness you've got? [*They separate.*] Have you no decency, that you insist on showing everyone our shame? I won't do it! I won't! And I stand for the will of our author in this. He didn't want to put us on the stage, after all!

THE MANAGER. Man alive! You came here . . .

THE SON [*indicating* FATHER]. *He* did! I didn't!

THE MANAGER. Aren't you here now?

THE SON. It was his wish, and he dragged us along with him. He's told you not only the things that did happen, but also things that have never happened at all.

THE MANAGER. Well, tell me then what did happen. You went out of your room without saying a word?

THE SON. Without a word, so as to avoid a scene!

THE MANAGER. And then what did you do?

THE SON. Nothing . . . walking in the garden . . . [*Hesitates for a moment with expression of gloom.*]

THE MANAGER [*coming closer to him, interested by his extraordinary reserve*]. Well, well . . . walking in the garden . . .

THE SON [*exasperated*]. Why on earth do you insist? It's horrible! [*The* MOTHER *trembles, sobs, and looks towards the fountain.*]

THE MANAGER [*slowly observing the glance and turning towards the* SON *with increasing apprehension*]. The baby?

THE SON. There in the fountain . . .

THE FATHER [*pointing with tender pity to the* MOTHER]. She was following him at the moment . . .

THE MANAGER [*to the* SON *anxiously*]. And then you . . .

THE SON. I ran over to her; I was jumping in to drag her out when I saw something that froze my blood . . . the boy standing stock still, with eyes like a madman's, watching his little drowned sister, in the fountain! [*The* STEP-DAUGHTER *bends over the fountain to hide the* CHILD. *She sobs.*] Then . . . [*A revolver shot rings out behind the trees where the* BOY *is hidden.*]

THE MOTHER [*with a cry of terror runs over in that direction together with several of the* ACTORS *amid general confusion*]. My son! My son! [*Then amid the cries and exclamations one hears her voice.*] Help! Help!

THE MANAGER [*pushing the* ACTORS *aside while* THEY *lift up the* BOY *and carry him off.*] Is he really wounded?

SOME ACTORS. He's dead! dead!

OTHER ACTORS. No, no, it's only make believe, it's only pretence!

THE FATHER [*with a terrible cry*]. Pretence? Reality, sir, reality!

THE MANAGER. Pretence? Reality? To hell with it all! Never in my life has such a thing happened to me. I've lost a whole day over these people, a whole day!

Curtain.

MARCEL PROUST
1871–1922

Proust's influence in twentieth-century letters is unequalled by any other writer. His massive novel sequence, *Remembrance of Things Past* (À *la recherche du temps perdu*), broke from nineteenth-century tradition to provide the example of a new kind of characterization and narrative line, a monumentally complex and precisely coordinated aesthetic structure, and a concept of the individual's cumulatively created profound identity—much of it buried in the experience of our senses—that has influenced writers everywhere modern Western literature is known. All of these innovations refer to an exploration of time in terms that parallel the influential work of Proust's contemporary, the philosopher Henri Bergson, with its emphasis on experience as duration, or *lived* time (rather than the artificial measurements of clock or calendar), and the importance of intuitive knowledge. Proust's plot refuses the immediate sense of direction given by traditional nineteenth-century novels: it acquires purpose gradually, through the relationship of different themes, and its collective intent appears only at the end when Marcel's suddenly catalyzed memory grasps the relationship of all parts. Characters are not sketched in fully from the beginning but are revealed piece by piece, evolving inside the different perspectives of individual chapters: even the protagonist is not fully outlined before the end. Proust's novel is a monumental construction coordinated down to its smallest parts not by the development of traditional novel form but by a new structural vision; it suggested the availability of intuitive or nonrational elements as organizational principles in an example that continues to be a reference point for twentieth-century writers.

Marcel Proust was born on July 10, 1871, the older of two sons in a wealthy middle-class Parisian family. His father was a well-known doctor and professor of medicine, a Catholic from a small town outside Paris. His mother, a sensitive, scrupulous, and highly educated woman to whom Marcel was devoted, came from an urban Jewish family. Proust fell ill with severe asthma when he was nine, and thereafter spent his childhood holidays at a seaside resort in Normandy that became the fictional model for Balbec. In spite of his illness, which limited what he could do, he graduated with honors from the Lycée Condorcet in Paris in 1889 and did a year's military service at Orléans (the fictional Doncières). As a student, Proust had met many young writers and composers, and he began to frequent the salons of the wealthy bourgeoisie and the aristocracy of the Faubourg Saint Germain (an elegant area of Paris), from which he drew much of the material for his portraits of society. He wrote for symbolist magazines like *Le Banquet* and *La Revue blanche*, published a collection of essays, poems, and stories in an elegant book, *Pleasures and Days* (1896), with drawings by Madeleine Lemaire and music by Reynaldo Hahn. In 1899 (with his mother's help since he knew no English), he began to translate the English moralist and art critic, John Ruskin.

Proust is known as the author of one work: the enormous, fifteen-volume exploration of time and consciousness called *Remembrance of Things Past*. As early as 1895, he had begun work on a shorter novel that traced the same themes and autobiographical awareness, but *Jean Santeuil* (published posthumously in 1952) never found a coherent structure for its numerous episodes and Proust abandoned it in 1899. Many episodes from the unfinished manuscript reflected Proust's interest in current events, and especially the Dreyfus Affair that was dividing France around issues of military honor, anti-Semitism, and national security. Themes, ideas, and some episodes from the earlier novel were absorbed into *Remembrance of Things Past*, and it is striking that the major difference (aside from the length) between the two works is simply the extremely sophisticated and subtle structure that Proust devised for the later one.

Proust's health started seriously to decline in 1902, and to make matters worse, he lost both parents by 1905. The following year, his asthma worsening, he moved into a cork-lined, fumigated room at 102 Boulevard Haussmann in Paris, where he stayed until forced to move in 1919. From 1907 to 1914, he spent summers in the seacoast town of Cabourg (another source of material for the fictional Balbec), but when in Paris emerged rarely from his apartment and then only late at night for dinners with friends. In 1909 he conceived the structure of his novel as a whole, and wrote its first and last chapters together. A first draft was finished by September 1912, but Proust had difficulty finding a publisher and finally published the first volume at his own expense in 1913. Though *Swann's Way (Du côté de chez Swann)* was a success, World War I delayed publication of subsequent volumes, and Proust began the painstaking revision and enlargement of the whole manuscript (from 1,500 to 4,000 pages, and three to seven parts) that was to occupy him until his death on November 18, 1922. *Within a Budding Grove* (À *l'ombre des jeunes filles en fleurs*—"In the Shadow of Young Girls in Flower") won the prestigious Goncourt Prize in 1919, and *The Guermantes' Way* (*Le Côté de Guermantes*) followed in 1920–21. The last volume published in Proust's lifetime was *Cities of the Plain II* (*Sodome et Gomorrhe II*—"Sodom and Gomorrah II," 1922), and the remaining volumes (*The Captive* [*La Prisonnière*, 1923], *The Fugitive* [*Albertine disparue*—"Albertine Disappeared," 1925], and *Time Regained* [*Le Temps retrouvé*, 1927]) were published posthumously from manuscripts on which he had been working. Written almost completely in the first person, and based on events in the author's life (although by no means purely autobiographical), the novel is famous both for its evocation of the closed world of Parisian society at the turn of the century and as a meditation on time and human emotions.

When *Swann's Way* appeared in 1913, it was immediately seen as a new kind of fiction. Unlike nineteenth-century novels such as Flaubert's *Madame Bovary*, *Remembrance of Things Past* has no clear and continuous plot line building to a dénouement, nor (until the last volume, published in 1927) could the reader detect a consistent development of the central character, Marcel. Only at the end does the narrator recognize the meaning and value of what has preceded, and when he retells his story it is not from an omniscient, explanatory point of view but rather as a re-living and gradual assessment of Marcel's lifelong experience. Most of the novel sets forth a roughly chronological sequence of events, yet its opening pages swing through recollections of many times and places before settling on the narrator's childhood in Combray. The second section, *Swann in Love (Un Amour de Swann)*, is a story told about another character and in the third person. Thus the novel proceeds by apparently discontinuous blocks of recollection, all bound together by the central consciousness of the narrator. This was always Proust's plan: he insisted that he had from the beginning a fixed structure and goal for the whole novel that reached down to the "solidity of the smallest parts," and his substantial revisions of the shorter first draft enriched an already existing structure without changing the sequence of scenes and events.

The overall theme of the novel is suggested by a literal translation of its title: "In Search of Lost Time." The narrator, a "Marcel" who suggests but is not identical with the author, is an old man weakened by a long illness who puzzles over the events of his past, trying to find in them a significant pattern. He begins with his childhood, ordered within the comfortable security of accepted manners and ideals in the family home at Combray. In succeeding volumes he goes out into the world, experiences love and disappointment, discovers the disparity between idealized images of places and their crude, sometimes banal reality, and is increasingly overcome by disillusionment with himself and society. Until the end of the novel, Marcel remains a *grand nerveux* ("nervous" or high-strung person), an extremely sensitive person impelled by the major experiences of his life—love, betrayal, art, separation, and death—to discard his earlier naive perspective and seek out a largely intuited meaning for life.

In the short ending chapter, things suddenly come into focus as Marcel reaches a new understanding of the role of time. Abruptly reliving a childhood experience when he sees a familiar book, and recognizing the ravages of time in the aged and enfeebled figures of his old friends, Marcel faces the approach of death with a new sense of existential continuity and realizes that his vocation as an artist lies in giving form to this buried existence. Apparently lost, the past is still alive within us, a part of our being, and memory can recapture it to give coherence and depth to present identity. "Marcel" has not yet begun to write by the end of the last volume, *Time Regained*, but paradoxically the book that he plans to write is already there: Proust's *Remembrance of Things Past*.

The larger subject of the novel, penetrating its description of society and Marcel's experience, is "that invisible substance called time." Although neither ever claimed any direct connection (and Proust recognized more readily the influence of his lycée philosophy professor, Darlu), Proust echoes the concerns of contemporary philosopher Henri Bergson when he looks to intuition and a sense of lived experience for a way to represent reality. Bergson's opposition of intellect and intuition, his preference for *duration* (everyday lived time) as opposed to abstract or clock time as a means of knowledge, and his distinction between the interactive "social ego" and the individually "profound" or intuitive ego all correspond to themes in Proust. Marcel's awareness of his life in time is created through memory—not rational or "forced," but spontaneous or "involuntary" memory—the chance recollection that wells up from his subconscious mind when he repeats a previous action such as dipping cookies in lime-blossom tea, stumbling on a paving stone, hearing a spoon clatter, or glimpsing a familiar book. Involuntary memory is more powerful because it draws upon a buried level of experience where the five senses are still linked. Life thus recalled comes to us in one piece, not separated into different categories for easier intellectual understanding. Sounds are connected with colors (the name *Brabant* with gold), and emotions with the settings in which they were experienced (sorrow with the smell of varnish on the stairway up to bed). Involuntary memory recreates a whole past world in all its concrete reality—and so does art. When Proust attributes such an absolute metaphysical value to art, making it a special means of knowledge and the focus of his book, he joins a special French tradition of "moralist" writers: those who, from Montaigne to Camus, strive for clear vision and a sense of universal human values.

Proust's style has a unique "architectural" design that coordinates large blocks of material: themes, situations, places, and events recur and are transformed across time. His long sentences and mammoth paragraphs reflect the slow and careful progression of thought among the changing objects of its perception. The ending paragraph of the "Overture" is composed of two long sentences that encompass an enormous range of meditative detail as the narrator not only recalls his childhood world—the old gray house, garden, public square and country roads, Swann's park, the river, the villagers, and indeed the whole town of Combray—but simultaneously compares the suddenly arisen house to a stage set, and the unfolding village itself to the twists and turns of a Japanese flower taking on color and form inside a bowl of water: here, in the narrator's cup of lime-blossom tea. Characters are remembered in different settings and perspectives, creating a "multiple self" who is free to change and still remain the same. Thus Charles Swann appears first as the visitor who often delays the child Marcel's bedtime kiss from his mother, next as an anxious and disappointed lover, and finally as a tragic, dying man rejected by his friends, the Guermantes, in their haste to get to a ball. Marcel's grandmother appears throughout the scenes in Combray, later during a visit to the seaside resort of Balbec, still later in her death agonies when Marcel is unable truly to grieve, and finally as a sudden recollection when Marcel has trouble tying his shoelace in Balbec. Nor is it characters alone who undergo cumulative transformations. The little musical phrase which Marcel first hears as part of a sonata by the composer Vinteuil, and which is associated with love in various settings, recurs towards the end of the novel as part of a septet and becomes a revelation of the subtle constructions of art. Places overlap in the memory: the imagined and the real Balbec or Venice confront one another, and the church steeples of Vieuxvicq and Martinville are juxtaposed. On a linguistic level, Proust juxtaposes entire social roles and habits of mind through the interaction of different types of speech. When Charlus and the Princesse de Guermantes meet in a bourgeois salon, their manner of speaking to each other creates a small "ingroup" dialogue of the aristocracy and sets them off from everyone else. The flexibility of Proust's style, representing thought and habits of speech rather than following a superimposed common code, makes him an example of verbal and visionary innovation that is paralleled by other writers of the same period such as Joyce and Woolf, and is enormously influential on later writers of the "new novel" tradition.

The selection given here, "Overture," is the first chapter of *Swann's Way* (*Du côté de chez Swann*, 1913), the first full volume of Proust's novel. "Swann's way" is one of the two directions in which Marcel's family used to take walks from their home in Combray, toward Tansonville, home of Charles Swann, and is associated with various scenes and anecdotes of love and private life. The longer walk toward the estate of the Guermantes (*The Guermantes' Way*), a fictional family of the highest aristocracy appearing frequently in the novel, evokes an aura of high society and French history, a more public sphere. Fictional people and places mingle throughout with the real; where a name is not annotated, it is Proust's invention. The narrator of "Overture" is Marcel as an old man, and the French verb tense used in his recollections (here and throughout all but the final volume) is appropriately the imperfect, a tense of uncompleted action ("I used to . . . . I would ask myself").

As the chapter title suggests, "Overture" introduces the work's themes and methods rather like the overture of an opera. All but one of the main characters appear or are mentioned, and the patterns of future encounters are set. Marcel, waiting anxiously for his beloved mother's response to a note sent down to her during dinner, suffers the same agony of separation as does Swann in his love for the promiscuous Odette, or the older Marcel himself for Albertine. The strange world of half-sleep, half-waking with which the novel begins prefigures later awakenings of memory. Long passages of intricate introspection, and sudden shifts of time and space, introduce us to the style and point of view of the rest of the book. The narrator shares the painful anxiety of little Marcel's desperate wait for his mother's bedtime kiss; for though his observations and judgments are tempered with mature wisdom, he is only at the beginning of his progress to full consciousness. The remembrance of things past is a key to further discovery but not an end in itself.

"Overture" ends with Proust's most famous image, summing up for many readers the world, the style, and the process of discovery of the Proustian vision. Nibbling at a madeleine (a small rich pastry) that he has dipped in lime-blossom tea, Marcel suddenly has an overwhelming feeling of happiness. He soon associates this tantalizing, puzzling phenomenon with the memory of earlier times when he sipped tea with his Aunt Leonie. He realizes that there is something valuable about such passive, spontaneous, and sensuous memory, quite different from the abstract operations of reason. Although the Marcel of "Combray" does not yet know it, he will pursue the elusive significance of this moment of happiness until, in *Time Regained*, he can as a complete artist bring it to the surface and link past and present time in a fuller and richer identity.

Roger Shattuck's *Proust* (1974) is a general study including advice on "how to read" Proust; it is still useful although it predates the revised translation used here. An excellent general study is Germaine Brée's *Marcel Proust and Deliverance from Time*, translated by R. J. Richards and A. D. Truitt (1969). A *Reader's Guide to Remembrance of Things Past* (1984), by Terence Kilmartin, is a handbook guide to Proust's characters, to persons referred to in the text, to places, and to themes, all keyed to the revised translation by the translator. René Girard, *Proust: A Collection of Critical Essays* (1962) is also recommended.

Remembrance of Things Past[1]

Overture[2]

For a long time I used to go to bed early. Sometimes, when I had put out my candle, my eyes would close so quickly that I had not even time to say to myself: "I'm falling asleep." And half an hour later the thought that it was time to go to sleep would awaken me; I would make as if to put away the book which I imagined was still in my hands, and to blow out the light; I had gone on thinking, while I was asleep, about what I had just been reading, but these thoughts had taken a rather peculiar turn; it seemed to me that I myself was the immediate subject of my book: a church, a quartet, the rivalry between François I and Charles V.[3] This impression would persist for some moments after I awoke; it did not offend my reason, but lay like scales upon my eyes and prevented them from registering the fact that the candle was no longer burning. Then it would begin to seem unintelligible, as the thoughts of a former existence must be to a reincarnate spirit; the subject of my book would separate itself from

---

1. Translated by C. K. Scott Moncrieff and Terence Kilmartin.   2. The opening section of Combray, the first volume of *Swann's Way*.   3. Francis I (1496–1567), King of France, and Charles V (1500–1558), Holy Roman Emperor and King of Spain, fought four wars over the Empire's expansion in Europe.

me, leaving me free to apply myself to it or not; and at the same time my sight would return and I would be astonished to find myself in a state of darkness, pleasant and restful enough for my eyes, but even more, perhaps, for my mind, to which it appeared incomprehensible, without a cause, something dark indeed.

I would ask myself what time it could be; I could hear the whistling of trains, which, now nearer and now farther off, punctuating the distance like the note of a bird in a forest, showed me in perspective the deserted countryside through which a traveller is hurrying towards the nearby station; and the path he is taking will be engraved in his memory by the excitement induced by strange surroundings, by unaccustomed activities, by the conversation he has had and the farewells exchanged beneath an unfamiliar lamp, still echoing in his ears amid the silence of the night, by the imminent joy of going home.

I would lay my cheeks gently against the comfortable cheeks of my pillow, as plump and blooming as the cheeks of babyhood. I would strike a match to look at my watch. Nearly midnight. The hour when an invalid, who has been obliged to set out on a journey and to sleep in a strange hotel, awakened by a sudden spasm, sees with glad relief a streak of daylight showing under his door. Thank God, it is morning! The servants will be about in a minute: he can ring, and someone will come to look after him. The thought of being assuaged gives him strength to endure his pain. He is certain he heard footsteps: they come nearer, and then die away. The ray of light beneath his door is extinguished. It is midnight; someone has just turned down the gas; the last servant has gone to bed, and he must lie all night in agony with no one to bring him relief.

I would fall asleep again, and thereafter would reawaken for short snatches only, just long enough to hear the regular creaking of the wainscot,[4] or to open my eyes to stare at the shifting kaleidoscope of the darkness, to savour, in a momentary glimmer of consciousness, the sleep which lay heavy upon the furniture, the room, the whole of which I formed but an insignificant part and whose insensibility I should very soon return to share. Or else while sleeping I had drifted back to an earlier stage in my life, now for ever outgrown, and had come under the thrall of one of my childish terrors, such as that old terror of my great-uncle's pulling my curls which was effectually dispelled on the day—the dawn of a new era to me—when they were finally cropped from my head. I had forgotten that event during my sleep, but I remembered it again immediately I had succeeded in waking myself up to escape my great-uncle's fingers, and as a mea-

4. The wooden paneling of the walls.

sure of precaution I would bury the whole of my head in the pillow before returning to the world of dreams.

Sometimes, too, as Eve was created from a rib of Adam, a woman would be born during my sleep from some strain in the position of my thighs. Conceived from the pleasure I was on the point of consummating, she it was, I imagined, who offered me that pleasure. My body, conscious that its own warmth was permeating hers, would strive to become one with her, and I would awake. The rest of humanity seemed very remote in comparison with this woman whose company I had left but a moment ago; my cheek was still warm from her kiss, my body ached beneath the weight of hers. If, as would sometimes happen, she had the features of some woman whom I had known in waking hours, I would abandon myself altogether to the sole quest of her, like people who set out on a journey to see with their eyes some city of their desire, and imagine that one can taste in reality what has charmed one's fancy. And then, gradually, the memory of her would dissolve and vanish, until I had forgotten the girl of my dream.

When a man is asleep, he has in a circle round him the chain of the hours, the sequence of the years, the order of the heavenly host. Instinctively, when he awakes, he looks to these, and in an instant reads off his own position on the earth's surface and the time that has elapsed during his slumbers; but this ordered procession is apt to grow confused, and to break its ranks. Suppose that, towards morning, after a night of insomnia, sleep descends upon him while he is reading, in quite a different position from that in which he normally goes to sleep, he has only to lift his arm to arrest the sun and turn it back in its course,[5] and, at the moment of waking, he will have no idea of the time, but will conclude that he has just gone to bed. Or suppose that he dozes off in some even more abnormal and divergent position, sitting in an armchair, for instance, after dinner: then the world will go hurtling out of orbit, the magic chair will carry him at full speed through time and space, and when he opens his eyes again he will imagine that he went to sleep months earlier in another place. But for me it was enough if, in my own bed, my sleep was so heavy as completely to relax my consciousness; for then I lost all sense of the place in which I had gone to sleep, and when I awoke in the middle of the night, not knowing where I was, I could not even be sure at first who I was; I had only the most rudimentary sense of existence, such as may lurk and flicker in the depths of an animal's consciousness; I was more destitute than the cave-dweller; but then the memory—not yet of the place in which I was, but of various

5. If his uplifted arm prevents him from seeing the sunlight, he will think it is still night.

other places where I had lived and might now very possibly be—
would come like a rope let down from heaven to draw me up out of
the abyss of not-being, from which I could never have escaped by
myself: in a flash I would traverse centuries of civilisation, and out
of a blurred glimpse of oil-lamps, then of shirts with turned-down
collars, would gradually piece together the original components of
my ego.

Perhaps the immobility of the things that surround us is forced
upon them by our conviction that they are themselves and not anything else, by the immobility of our conception of them. For it always
happened that when I awoke like this, and my mind struggled in an
unsuccessful attempt to discover where I was, everything revolved
around me through the darkness: things, places, years. My body, still
too heavy with sleep to move, would endeavour to construe from the
pattern of its tiredness the position of its various limbs, in order to
deduce therefrom the direction of the wall, the location of the furniture, to piece together and give a name to the house in which it
lay. Its memory, the composite memory of its ribs, its knees, its
shoulder-blades, offered it a whole series of rooms in which it had at
one time or another slept, while the unseen walls, shifting and adapting
themselves to the shape of each successive room that it remembered,
whirled round it in the dark. And even before my brain, lingering in
cogitation over when things had happened and what they had looked
like, had reassembled the circumstances sufficiently to identify the
room, it, my body, would recall from each room in succession the
style of the bed, the position of the doors, the angle at which the
daylight came in at the windows, whether there was a passage outside, what I had had in my mind when I went to sleep and found
there when I awoke. The stiffened side on which I lay would, for
instance, in trying to fix its position, imagine itself to be lying face
to the wall in a big bed with a canopy; and at once I would say to
myself, "Why, I must have fallen asleep before Mamma came to say
good night," for I was in the country at my grandfather's, who died
years ago; and my body, the side upon which I was lying, faithful
guardians of a past which my mind should never have forgotten,
brought back before my eyes the glimmering flame of the night-light
in its urn-shaped bowl of Bohemian glass that hung by chains from
the ceiling, and the chimney-piece of Siena marble[6] in my bedroom
at Combray, in my grandparents' house, in those far distant days
which at this moment I imagined to be in the present without being
able to picture them exactly, and which would become plainer in a
little while when I was properly awake.

---

6. From central Italy, mottled and reddish in color. *Bohemian glass:* Likely to have been ornately
engraved. (Bohemia, now the western part of Czechoslovakia, was a major center of the glass
industry.)

Then the memory of a new position would spring up, and the wall would slide away in another direction; I was in my room in Mme de Saint-Loup's[7] house in the country; good heavens, it must be ten o'clock, they will have finished dinner! I must have overslept myself in the little nap which I always take when I come in from my walk with Mme de Saint-Loup, before dressing for the evening. For many years have now elapsed since the Combray days when, coming in from the longest and latest walks, I would still be in time to see the reflection of the sunset glowing in the panes of my bedroom window. It is a very different kind of life that one leads at Tansonville, at Mme de Saint-Loup's, and a different kind of pleasure that I derive from taking walks only in the evenings, from visiting by moonlight the roads on which I used to play as a child in the sunshine; while the bedroom in which I shall presently fall asleep instead of dressing for dinner I can see from the distance as we return from our walk, with its lamp shining through the window, a solitary beacon in the night.

These shifting and confused gusts of memory never lasted for more than a few seconds; it often happened that, in my brief spell of uncertainty as to where I was, I did not distinguish the various suppositions of which it was composed any more than, when we watch a horse running, we isolate the successive positions of its body as they appear upon a bioscope.[8] But I had seen first one and then another of the rooms in which I had slept during my life, and in the end I would revisit them all in the long course of my waking dream: rooms in winter, where on going to bed I would at once bury my head in a nest woven out of the most diverse materials—the corner of my pillow, the top of my blankets, a piece of a shawl, the edge of my bed, and a copy of a children's paper—which I had contrived to cement together, bird-fashion, by dint of continuous pressure; rooms where, in freezing weather, I would enjoy the satisfaction of being shut in from the outer world (like the sea-swallow which builds at the end of a dark tunnel and is kept warm by the surrounding earth), and where, the fire keeping in all night, I would sleep wrapped up, as it were, in a great cloak of snug and smoky air, shot with the glow of the logs intermittently breaking out again in flame, a sort of alcove without walls, a cave of warmth dug out of the heart of the room itself, a zone of heat whose boundaries were constantly shifting and altering in temperature as gusts of air traversed them to strike freshly upon my face, from the corners of the room or from parts near the window or far from the fireplace which had therefore remained cold;—or rooms in summer, where I would delight to feel myself a part of the warm night, where the moonlight striking upon the half-opened

7. Charles Swann's daughter, Gilberte, who has married Robert de Saint-Loup, a nephew of the Guermantes.   8. An early moving-picture machine that showed photographs in rapid succession.

shutters would throw down to the foot of my bed its enchanted ladder, where I would fall asleep, as it might be in the open air, like a
titmouse which the breeze gently rocks at the tip of a sunbeam;—or
sometimes the Louis XVI room,[9] so cheerful that I never felt too
miserable in it, even on my first night, and in which the slender
columns that lightly supported its ceiling drew so gracefully apart to
reveal and frame the site of the bed;—sometimes, again, the little
room with the high ceiling, hollowed in the form of a pyramid out
of two separate storeys, and partly walled with mahogany, in which
from the first moment, mentally poisoned by the unfamiliar scent of
vetiver,[1] I was convinced of the hostility of the violet curtains and of
the insolent indifference of a clock that chattered on at the top of its
voice as though I were not there; in which a strange and pitiless
rectangular cheval-glass, standing across one corner of the room,
carved out for itself a site I had not looked to find tenanted in the
soft plenitude of my normal field of vision;[2] in which my mind,
striving for hours on end to break away from its moorings, to stretch
upwards so as to take on the exact shape of the room and to reach to
the topmost height of its gigantic funnel, had endured many a painful night as I lay stretched out in bed, my eyes staring upwards, my
ears straining, my nostrils flaring, my heart beating; until habit had
changed the colour of the curtains, silenced the clock, brought an
expression of pity to the cruel, slanting face of the glass, disguised or
even completely dispelled the scent of vetiver, and appreciably reduced
the apparent loftiness of the ceiling. Habit! that skilful but slow-
moving arranger who begins by letting our minds suffer for weeks on
end in temporary quarters, but whom our minds are none the less
only too happy to discover at last, for without it, reduced to their
own devices, they would be powerless to make any room seem habitable.

Certainly I was now well awake; my body had veered round for
the last time and the good angel of certainty had made all the surrounding objects stand still, had set me down under my bedclothes,
in my bedroom, and had fixed, approximately in their right places
in the uncertain light, my chest of drawers, my writing-table, my
fireplace, the window overlooking the street, and both the doors. But
for all that I now knew that I was not in any of the houses of which
the ignorance of the waking moment had, in a flash, if not presented
me with a distinct picture, at least persuaded me of the possible presence, my memory had been set in motion; as a rule I did not attempt
to go to sleep again at once, but used to spend the greater part of the

9. Furnished in late-18th-century style, named for the French monarch of the time, and marked
by great elegance. The room is that in which Marcel visits Robert de Saint-Loup in *Guermantes'
Way*.   1. The aromatic root of a tropical grass packaged as a moth-preventive.   2. The narrator's room at the fictional seaside resort of Balbec, a setting in *Within a Budding Grove*.

night recalling our life in the old days at Combray with my great-aunt, at Balbec, Paris, Doncières, Venice, and the rest; remembering again all the places and people I had known, what I had actually seen of them, and what others had told me.

At Combray, as every afternoon ended, long before the time when I should have to go to bed and lie there, unsleeping, far from my mother and grandmother, my bedroom became the fixed point on which my melancholy and anxious thoughts were centred. Someone had indeed had the happy idea of giving me, to distract me on evenings when I seemed abnormally wretched, a magic lantern,[3] which used to be set on top of my lamp while we waited for dinner-time to come; and, after the fashion of the master-builders and glass-painters of gothic days, it substituted for the opaqueness of my walls an impalpable iridescence, supernatural phenomena of many colours, in which legends were depicted as on a shifting and transitory window. But my sorrows were only increased thereby, because this mere change of lighting was enough to destroy the familiar impression I had of my room, thanks to which, save for the torture of going to bed, it had become quite endurable. Now I no longer recognised it, and felt uneasy in it, as in a room in some hotel or chalet, in a place where I had just arrived by train for the first time.

Riding at a jerky trot, Golo,[4] filled with an infamous design, issued from the little triangular forest which dyed dark-green the slope of a convenient hill, and advanced fitfully towards the castle of poor Geneviève de Brabant. This castle was cut off short by a curved line which was in fact the circumference of one of the transparent ovals in the slides which were pushed into position through a slot in the lantern. It was only the wing of a castle, and in front of it stretched a moor on which Geneviève stood lost in contemplation, wearing a blue girdle.[5] The castle and the moor were yellow, but I could tell their colour without waiting to see them, for before the slides made their appearance the old-gold sonorous name of Brabant had given me an unmistakable clue. Golo stopped for a moment and listened sadly to the accompanying patter read aloud by my great-aunt,[6] which he seemed perfectly to understand, for he modified his attitude with a docility not devoid of a degree of majesty, so as to conform to the indications given in the text; then he rode away at the same jerky trot. And nothing could arrest his slow progress. If the lantern were moved I could still distinguish Golo's horse advancing across the window-curtains, swelling out with their curves and diving into their folds. The body of Golo himself, being of the same supernatural

3. A kind of slide projector.   4. Villain of a fifth-century legend. He falsely accuses Geneviève de Brabant of adultery. (Brabant was a principality in what is now Belgium.)   5. Belt.
6. Marcel's great-aunt is reading the story to him as they wait for dinner.

substance as his steed's, overcame every material obstacle—every-thing that seemed to bar his way—by taking it as an ossature[7] and embodying it in himself: even the door-handle, for instance, over which, adapting itself at once, would float irresistibly his red cloak or his pale face, which never lost its nobility or its melancholy, never betrayed the least concern at this transvertebration.

And, indeed, I found plenty of charm in these bright projections, which seemed to emanate from a Merovingian[8] past and shed around me the reflections of such ancient history. But I cannot express the discomfort I felt at this intrusion of mystery and beauty into a room which I had succeeded in filling with my own personality until I thought no more of it than of myself. The anaesthetic effect of habit being destroyed, I would begin to think—and to feel—such melan-choly things. The door-handle of my room, which was different to me from all the other door-handles in the world, inasmuch as it seemed to open of its own accord and without my having to turn it, so unconscious had its manipulation become—lo and behold, it was now an astral body[9] for Golo. And as soon as the dinner-bell rang I would hurry down to the dining-room, where the big hanging lamp, ignorant of Golo and Bluebeard[1] but well acquainted with my family and the dish of stewed beef, shed the same light as on every other evening; and I would fall into the arms of my mother, whom the misfortunes of Geneviève de Brabant had made all the dearer to me, just as the crimes of Golo had driven me to a more than ordinarily scrupulous examination of my own conscience.

But after dinner, alas, I was soon obliged to leave Mamma, who stayed talking with the others, in the garden if it was fine, or in the little parlour where everyone took shelter when it was wet. Everyone except my grandmother, who held that "It's a pity to shut oneself indoors in the country," and used to have endless arguments with my father on the very wettest days, because he would send me up to my room with a book instead of letting me stay out of doors. "That is not the way to make him strong and active," she would say sadly, "especially this little man, who needs all the strength and will-power that he can get." My father would shrug his shoulders and study the barometer, for he took an interest in meteorology, while my mother, keeping very quiet so as not to disturb him, looked at him with tender respect, but not too hard, not wishing to penetrate the mysteries of his superior mind. But my grandmother, in all weathers, even when the rain was coming down in torrents and Françoise had rushed the precious wicker armchairs indoors so that they should not get soaked,

7. Skeleton.   8. The first dynasty of French kings, 500–751 A.D.   9. Spiritual counterpart of the physical body; according to the doctrine of Theosophy (a spiritualist movement originating in 1875), the astral body survives the death of the physical body.   1. The legendary wife-mur-derer, presumably depicted on another set of slides.

was to be seen pacing the deserted rain-lashed garden, pushing back her disordered grey locks so that her forehead might be freer to absorb the health-giving draughts of wind and rain. She would say, "At last one can breathe!" and would trot up and down the sodden paths—too straight and symmetrical for her liking, owing to the want of any feeling for nature in the new gardener, whom my father had been asking all morning if the weather were going to improve—her keen, jerky little step regulated by the various effects wrought upon her soul by the intoxication of the storm, the power of hygiene, the stupidity of my upbringing and the symmetry of gardens, rather than by any anxiety (for that was quite unknown to her) to save her plum-coloured skirt from the mudstains beneath which it would gradually disappear to a height that was the constant bane and despair of her maid.

When these walks of my grandmother's took place after dinner there was one thing which never failed to bring her back to the house: this was if (at one of those points when her circular itinerary brought her back, moth-like, in sight of the lamp in the little parlour where the liqueurs were set out on the card-table) my great-aunt called out to her: "Bathilde! Come in and stop your husband drinking brandy!" For, simply to tease her (she had brought so different a type of mind into my father's family that everyone made fun of her), my great-aunt used to make my grandfather, who was forbidden liqueurs, take just a few drops. My poor grandmother would come in and beg and implore her husband not to taste the brandy; and he would get angry and gulp it down all the same, and she would go out again sad and discouraged, but still smiling, for she was so humble of heart and so gentle that her tenderness for others and her disregard for herself and her own troubles blended in a smile which, unlike those seen on the majority of human faces, bore no trace of irony save for herself, while for all of us kisses seemed to spring from her eyes, which could not look upon those she loved without seeming to bestow upon them passionate caresses. This torture inflicted on her by my great-aunt, the sight of my grandmother's vain entreaties, of her feeble attempts, doomed in advance, to remove the liqueur-glass from my grandfather's hands—all these were things of the sort to which, in later years, one can grow so accustomed as to smile at them and to take the persecutor's side resolutely and cheerfully enough to persuade oneself that it is not really persecution; but in those days they filled me with such horror that I longed to strike my great-aunt. And yet, as soon as I heard her "Bathilde! Come in and stop your husband drinking brandy," in my cowardice I became at once a man, and did what all we grown men do when face to face with suffering and injustice: I preferred not to see them; I ran up to the top of the house to cry by myself in a little room beside the schoolroom and beneath the roof, which smelt of orris-root[2] and was scented also by a wild currant-bush which had climbed up between the stones of the outer wall and thrust a flowering branch in through the half-opened window. Intended for a more special and a baser use,[3] this room, from which, in the daytime, I could see as far as the keep[4] of Roussainville-le-Pin, was for a long time my place of refuge, doubtless because it was the only room whose door I was allowed to lock, whenever my occupation was such as required an inviolable solitude: reading or day-dreaming, secret tears or sensual gratification. Alas! I little knew that my own lack of will-power, my delicate health, and the consequent uncertainty as to my future, weighed far more heavily on my grandmother's mind than any little dietary indiscretion by her husband in the course of those endless perambulations, afternoon and evening, during which we used to see her handsome face passing to and fro, half raised towards the sky, its brown and wrinkled cheeks, which with age had acquired almost the purple hue of tilled fields in autumn, covered, if she were "going out," by a half-lifted veil, while upon them either the cold or some sad reflection invariably left the drying traces of an involuntary tear.

My sole consolation when I went upstairs for the night was that Mamma would come in and kiss me after I was in bed. But this good night lasted for so short a time, she went down again so soon, that the moment in which I heard her climb the stairs, and then caught the sound of her garden dress of blue muslin, from which hung little tassels of plaited straw, rustling along the double-doored corridor, was for me a moment of the utmost pain; for it heralded the moment which was bound to follow it, when she would have left me and gone downstairs again. So much so that I reached the point of hoping that this good night which I loved so much would come as late as possible, so as to prolong the time of respite during which Mamma would not yet have appeared. Sometimes when, after kissing me, she opened the door to go, I longed to call her back, to say to her "Kiss me just once more," but I knew that then she would at once look displeased, for the concession which she made to my wretchedness and agitation in coming up to give me this kiss of peace always annoyed my father, who thought such rituals absurd, and she would have liked to try to induce me to outgrow the need, the habit, of having her there at all, let alone get into the habit of asking her for an additional kiss when she was already crossing the threshold. And to see her look displeased destroyed all the calm and serenity she had brought me a moment before, when she had bent her loving face down over my bed, and held it out to me like a host[5] for an act of

2. A powder then used as a deodorizer for rooms.   3. As a toilet.   4. The best-fortified tower of a medieval castle.   5. Communion wafer.

peace-giving communion in which my lips might imbibe her real presence and with it the power to sleep. But those evenings on which Mamma stayed so short a time in my room were sweet indeed compared to those on which we had guests to dinner, and therefore she did not come at all. Our "guests" were usually limited to M. Swann, who, apart from a few passing strangers, was almost the only person who ever came to the house at Combray, sometimes to a neighbourly dinner (but less frequently since his unfortunate marriage, as my family did not care to receive his wife) and sometimes after dinner, uninvited. On those evenings when, as we sat in front of the house round the iron table beneath the big chestnut-tree, we heard, from the far end of the garden, not the shrill and assertive alarm bell which assailed and deafened with its ferruginous,[6] interminable, frozen sound any member of the household who set it off on entering "without ringing," but the double tinkle, timid, oval, golden, of the visitors' bell, everyone would at once exclaim "A visitor! Who in the world can it be?" but they knew quite well that it could only be M. Swann. My great-aunt, speaking in a loud voice to set an example, in a tone which she endeavoured to make sound natural, would tell the others not to whisper so; that nothing could be more offensive to a stranger coming in, who would be led to think that people were saying things about him which he was not meant to hear; and then my grandmother, always happy to find an excuse for an additional turn in the garden, would be sent out to reconnoitre, and would take the opportunity to remove surreptitiously, as she passed, the stakes of a rose-tree or two, so as to make the roses look a little more natural, as a mother might run her hand through her boy's hair after the barber has smoothed it down, to make it look naturally wavy.

We would all wait there in suspense for the report which my grandmother would bring back from the enemy lines, as though there might be a choice between a large number of possible assailants, and then, soon after, my grandfather would say: "I can hear Swann's voice." And indeed one could tell him only by his voice, for it was difficult to make out his face with its arched nose and green eyes, under a high forehead fringed with fair, almost red hair, done in the Bressant style,[7] because in the garden we used as little light as possible, so as not to attract mosquitoes; and I would slip away unobtrusively to order the liqueurs to be brought out, for my grandmother made a great point, thinking it "nicer," of their not being allowed to seem anything out of the ordinary, which we kept for visitors only. Although a far younger man, M. Swann was very much attached to my grandfather, who had been an intimate friend of Swann's father,

6. Iron-like.   7. Close-cropped, like a crew cut; named after a French actor.

an excellent but eccentric man the ardour of whose feelings and the current of whose thoughts would often be checked or diverted by the most trifling thing. Several times in the course of a year I would hear my grandfather tell at table the story, which never varied, of the behaviour of M. Swann the elder upon the death of his wife, by whose bedside he had watched day and night. My grandfather, who had not seen him for a long time, hastened to join him at the Swanns' family property on the outskirts of Combray, and managed to entice him for a moment, weeping profusely, out of the death-chamber, so that he should not be present when the body was laid in its coffin. They took a turn or two in the park, where there was a little sunshine. Suddenly M. Swann seized my grandfather by the arm and cried, "Ah, my dear old friend, how fortunate we are to be walking here together on such a charming day! Don't you see how pretty they are, all these trees, my hawthorns, and my new pond, on which you have never congratulated me? You look as solemn as the grave. Don't you feel this little breeze? Ah! whatever you may say, it's good to be alive all the same, my dear Amédée!" And then, abruptly, the memory of his dead wife returned to him, and probably thinking it too complicated to inquire into how, at such a time, he could have allowed himself to be carried away by an impulse of happiness, he confined himself to a gesture which he habitually employed whenever any perplexing question came into his mind: that is, he passed his hand across his forehead, rubbed his eyes, and wiped his glasses. And yet he never got over the loss of his wife, but used to say to my grandfather, during the two years by which he survived her, "It's a funny thing, now; I very often think of my poor wife, but I cannot think of her for long at a time." "Often, but a little at a time, like poor old Swann," became one of my grandfather's favourite sayings, which he would apply to all manner of things. I should have assumed that this father of Swann's had been a monster if my grandfather, whom I regarded as a better judge than myself, and whose word was my law and often led me in the long run to pardon offences which I should have been inclined to condemn, had not gone on to exclaim, "But, after all, he had a heart of gold."

For many years, during the course of which—especially before his marriage—M. Swann the younger came often to see them at Combray, my great-aunt and my grandparents never suspected that he had entirely ceased to live in the society which his family had frequented, and that, under the sort of incognito which the name of Swann gave him among us, they were harbouring—with the complete innocence of a family of respectable innkeepers who have in their midst some celebrated highwayman without knowing it—one of the most distinguished members of the Jockey Club, a particular friend of the Comte de Paris and of the Prince of Wales, and one of

the men most sought after in the aristocratic world of the Faubourg
Saint-Germain.[8]

Our utter ignorance of the brilliant social life which Swann led
was, of course, due in part to his own reserve and discretion, but
also to the fact that middle-class people in those days took what was
almost a Hindu view of society, which they held to consist of sharply
defined castes, so that everyone at his birth found himself called to
that station in life which his parents already occupied, and from
which nothing, save the accident of an exceptional career or of a
"good" marriage, could extract you and translate you to a superior
caste. M. Swann the elder had been a stockbroker; and so "young
Swann" found himself immured for life in a caste whose members'
fortunes, as in a category of tax-payers, varied between such and
such limits of income. One knew the people with whom his father
had associated, and so one knew his own associates, the people with
whom he was "in a position to mix." If he knew other people besides,
those were youthful acquaintances on whom the old friends of his
family, like my relatives, shut their eyes all the more good-naturedly
because Swann himself, after he was left an orphan, still came most
faithfully to see us; but we would have been ready to wager that the
people outside our acquaintance whom Swann knew were of the sort
to whom he would not have dared to raise his hat if he had met them
while he was walking with us. Had it been absolutely essential to
apply to Swann a social coefficient peculiar to himself, as distinct
from all the other sons of other stockbrokers in his father's position,
his coefficient would have been rather lower than theirs, because,
being very simple in his habits, and having always had a craze for
"antiques" and pictures, he now lived and amassed his collections in
an old house which my grandmother longed to visit but which was
situated on the Quai d'Orléans,[9] a neighbourhood in which my great-
aunt thought it most degrading to be quartered. "Are you really a
connoisseur, now?" she would say to him: "I ask for your own sake,
as you are likely to have fakes palmed off on you by the dealers," for
she did not, in fact, endow him with any critical faculty, and had no
great opinion of the intelligence of a man who, in conversation,
would avoid serious topics and showed a very dull preciseness, not
only when he gave us kitchen recipes, going into the most minute
details, but even when my grandmother's sisters were talking to him
about art. When challenged by them to give an opinion, or to express

8. A fashionable area of Paris on the left bank of the Seine; many of the French aristocracy lived
there. The *Jockey Club* was an exclusive men's club devoted not only to horseracing but to other
diversions (such as the Opera). The *Comte de Paris* (1838–1894) was heir apparent to the French
throne, in the unlikely event that the monarchy were reinstated; the *Prince of Wales* became in
1901 King Edward VII of England. The implication is that Swann's social connections were not
merely of the highest but of an idle and somewhat hedonistic sort.   9. A beautiful though less
fashionable section in the heart of Paris, along the Seine.

his admiration for some picture, he would remain almost offensively silent, and would then make amends by furnishing (if he could) some fact or other about the gallery in which the picture was hung, or the date at which it had been painted. But as a rule he would content himself with trying to amuse us by telling us about his latest adventure with someone whom we ourselves knew, such as the Combray chemist,[1] or our cook, or our coachman. These stories certainly used to make my great-aunt laugh, but she could never decide whether this was on account of the absurd rôle which Swann invariably gave himself therein, or of the wit that he showed in telling them: "I must say you really are a regular character, M. Swann!"

As she was the only member of our family who could be described as a trifle "common," she would always take care to remark to strangers, when Swann was mentioned, that he could easily, had he so wished, have lived in the Boulevard Haussmann or the Avenue de l'Opéra,[2] and that he was the son of old M. Swann who must have left four or five million francs, but that it was a fad of his. A fad which, moreover, she thought was bound to amuse other people so much that in Paris, when M. Swann called on New Year's Day bringing her a little packet of *marrons glacés*,[3] she never failed, if there were strangers in the room, to say to him: "Well, M. Swann, and do you still live next door to the bonded vaults,[4] so as to be sure of not missing your train when you go to Lyons?" and she would peep out of the corner of her eye, over her glasses, at the other visitors.

But if anyone had suggested to my great-aunt that this Swann, who, in his capacity as the son of old M. Swann, was "fully qualified" to be received by any of the "best people," by the most respected barristers and solicitors[5] of Paris (though he was perhaps a trifle inclined to let this hereditary privilege go by default), had another almost secret existence of a wholly different kind; that when he left our house in Paris, saying that he must go home to bed, he would no sooner have turned the corner than he would stop, retrace his steps, and be off to some salon on whose like no stockbroker or associate of stockbrokers had ever set eyes—that would have seemed to my aunt as extraordinary as, to a woman of wider reading, the thought of being herself on terms of intimacy with Aristaeus[6] and of learning that after having a chat with her he would plunge deep into the realms of Thetis, into an empire veiled from mortal eyes, in which Virgil depicts him as being received with open arms; or—to be con-

---

1. Pharmacist.   2. Two large modern avenues where the wealthy *bourgeoisie* (or middle class) liked to live. *Four or five million francs* would have been nearly a million dollars in the currency of the day.   3. Candied chestnuts, a traditional gift on New Year's Day, then a more common day for exchanging gifts than Christmas.   4. A wine warehouse in southeastern Paris, close to the *Gare de Lyon*, the terminal from which trains depart for the industrial city of Lyon and other destinations in southeastern France.   5. Trial lawyers and lawyers of other kinds.   6. Son of the Greek god Apollo. In Virgil's *Fourth Georgic*, Aristaeus seeks help from the sea nymph Thetis.

tent with an image more likely to have occurred to her, for she had seen it painted on the plates we used for biscuits at Combray—as the thought of having had to dinner Ali Baba,[7] who, as soon as he finds himself alone and unobserved, will make his way into the cave, resplendent with its unsuspected treasures.

One day when he had come to see us after dinner in Paris, apologising for being in evening clothes, Françoise told us after he had left that she had got it from his coachman that he had been dining "with a princess." "A nice sort of princess,"[8] retorted my aunt, shrugging her shoulders without raising her eyes from her knitting, serenely sarcastic.

Altogether, my great-aunt treated him with scant ceremony. Since she was of the opinion that he ought to feel flattered by our invitations, she thought it only right and proper that he should never come to see us in summer without a basket of peaches or raspberries from his garden, and that from each of his visits to Italy he should bring back some photographs of old masters for me.

It seemed quite natural, therefore, to send for him whenever a recipe for some special sauce or for a pineapple salad was needed for one of our big dinner-parties, to which he himself would not be invited, being regarded as insufficiently important to be served up to new friends who might be in our house for the first time. If the conversation turned upon the princes of the House of France,[9] "gentlemen you and I will never know, will we, and don't want to, do we?" my great-aunt would say tartly to Swann, who had, perhaps, a letter from Twickenham[1] in his pocket; she would make him push the piano into place and turn over the music on evenings when my grandmother's sister sang, manipulating this person who was elsewhere so sought after with the rough simplicity of a child who will play with a collectors' piece with no more circumspection than if it were a cheap gewgaw. Doubtless the Swann who was a familiar figure in all the clubs of those days differed hugely from the Swann created by my great-aunt when, of an evening, in our little garden at Combray, after the two shy peals had sounded from the gate, she would inject and vitalise with everything she knew about the Swann family the obscure and shadowy figure who emerged, with my grandmother in his wake, from the dark background and who was identified by his voice. But then, even in the most insignificant details of our daily life, none of us can be said to constitute a material whole, which is identical for everyone, and need only be turned up like a page in an account-book or the record of a will; our social

7. Hero of an *Arabian Nights* tale, a poor youth who discovers a robber's cave filled with treasure.   8. That is, a "princess" of some shady level of society.   9. The male members of the French royal family, such as the Comte de Paris. The spirit of the times was anti-Royalist, and in fact all claimants to the French throne and their heirs were banished from France by law in 1886.   1. Fashionable London suburb. The French royal family had a house there.

personality is a creation of the thoughts of other people. Even the simple act which we describe as "seeing someone we know" is to some extent an intellectual process. We pack the physical outline of the person we see with all the notions we have already formed about him, and in the total picture of him which we compose in our minds those notions have certainly the principal place. In the end they come to fill out so completely the curve of his cheeks, to follow so exactly the line of his nose, they blend so harmoniously in the sound of his voice as if it were no more than a transparent envelope, that each time we see the face or hear the voice it is these notions which we recognise and to which we listen. And so, no doubt, from the Swann they had constructed for themselves my family had left out, in their ignorance, a whole host of details of his life in the world of fashion, details which caused other people, when they met him, to see all the graces enthroned in his face and stopping at the line of his aquiline nose as at a natural frontier; but they had contrived also to put into this face divested of all glamour, vacant and roomy as an untenanted house, to plant in the depths of these undervalued eyes, a lingering residuum, vague but not unpleasing—half-memory and half-oblivion—of idle hours spent together after our weekly dinners, round the card-table or in the garden, during our companionable country life. Our friend's corporeal envelope had been so well lined with this residuum, as well as various earlier memories of his parents, that their own special Swann had become to my family a complete and living creature; so that even now I have the feeling of leaving someone I know for another quite different person when, going back in memory, I pass from the Swann whom I knew later and more intimately to this early Swann—this early Swann in whom I can distinguish the charming mistakes of my youth, and who in fact is less like his successor than he is like the other people I knew at that time, as though one's life were a picture gallery in which all the portraits of any one period had a marked family likeness, a similar tonality—this early Swann abounding in leisure, fragrant with the scent of the great chestnut-tree, of baskets of raspberries and of a sprig of tarragon.

And yet one day, when my grandmother had gone to ask some favour of a lady whom she had known at the Sacré Cœur[2] (and with whom, because of our notions of caste, she had not cared to keep up any degree of intimacy in spite of several common interests), the Marquise de Villeparisis,[3] of the famous house of Bouillon, this lady had said to her:

---

2. A convent school in Paris, attended by daughters of the aristocracy and the wealthy *bourgeoisie*. 3. Member of the Guermantes family. Proust enhances the apparent reality of the Guermantes by relating them to the historical house of Bouillon, a famous aristocratic family tracing its descent from the Middle Ages. The des Laumes, on the other hand, are fictional.

"I believe you know M. Swann very well; he's a great friend of my nephews, the des Laumes."

My grandmother had returned from the call full of praise for the house, which overlooked some gardens, and in which Mme de Villeparisis had advised her to rent a flat, and also for a repairing tailor and his daughter who kept a little shop in the courtyard, into which she had gone to ask them to put a stitch in her skirt, which she had torn on the staircase. My grandmother had found these people perfectly charming: the girl, she said, was a jewel, and the tailor the best and most distinguished man she had ever seen. For in her eyes distinction was a thing wholly independent of social position. She was in ecstasies over some answer the tailor had made to her, saying to Mamma:

"Sévigné[4] would not have put it better!" and, by way of contrast, of a nephew of Mme de Villeparisis whom she had met at the house:

"My dear, he is so common!"

Now, the effect of the remark about Swann had been, not to raise him in my great-aunt's estimation, but to lower Mme de Villeparisis. It appeared that the deference which, on my grandmother's authority, we owed to Mme de Villeparisis imposed on her the reciprocal obligation to do nothing that would render her less worthy of our regard, and that she had failed in this duty by becoming aware of Swann's existence and in allowing members of her family to associate with him. "What! She knows Swann? A person who, you always made out, was related to Marshal MacMahon!"[5] This view of Swann's social position which prevailed in my family seemed to be confirmed later on by his marriage with a woman of the worst type, almost a prostitute, whom, to do him justice, he never attempted to introduce to us—for he continued to come to our house alone, though more and more seldom—but from whom they felt they could establish, on the assumption that he had found her there, the circle, unknown to them, in which he ordinarily moved.

But on one occasion my grandfather read in a newspaper that M. Swann was one of the most regular attendants at the Sunday luncheons given by the Duc de X——, whose father and uncle had been among our most prominent statesmen in the reign of Louis-Philippe.[6] Now my grandfather was curious to learn all the smallest details which might help him to take a mental share in the private lives of men like Molé, the Duc Pasquier, or the Duc de Broglie.[7]

4. The Marquise de Sévigné (1626–1696), known for the lively style of her letters.   5. (1808–1893), Marshal of France, elected President of the French Republic in 1873.   6. King of France from 1830 to 1848, father of the Comte de Paris.   7. Comte Louis Mathieu Molé (1781–1855) held various cabinet positions before becoming premier of France in 1836; Duc Etienne Denis de Pasquier (1767–1862) also held important public positions up to 1837; and Duc Achille Charles Leonce Victor de Broglie (1785–1870) had a busy public career that ended in 1851. All were active during the reign of Louis Philippe.

He was delighted to find that Swann associated with people who had known them. My great-aunt, on the other hand, interpreted this piece of news in a sense discreditable to Swann; for anyone who chose his associates outside the caste in which he had been born and bred, outside his "proper station," automatically lowered himself in her eyes. It seemed to her that such a one abdicated all claim to enjoy the fruits of the splendid connections with people of good position which prudent parents cultivate and store up for their children's benefit, and she had actually ceased to "see" the son of a lawyer of our acquaintance because he had married a "Highness" and had thereby stepped down—in her eyes—from the respectable position of a lawyer's son to that of those adventurers, upstart footmen or stable-boys mostly, to whom, we are told, queens have sometimes shown their favours. She objected, therefore, to my grandfather's plan of questioning Swann, when next he came to dine with us, about these people whose friendship with him we had discovered. At the same time my grandmother's two sisters, elderly spinsters who shared her nobility of character but lacked her intelligence, declared that they could not conceive what pleasure their brother-in-law could find in talking about such trifles. They were ladies of lofty aspirations, who for that reason were incapable of taking the least interest in what might be termed gossip, even if it had some historical import, or, generally speaking, in anything that was not directly associated with some aesthetic or virtuous object. So complete was their negation of interest in anything which seemed directly or indirectly connected with worldly matters that their sense of hearing—having finally come to realise its temporary futility when the tone of the conversation at the dinner-table became frivolous or merely mundane without the two old ladies' being able to guide it back to topics dear to themselves—would put its receptive organs into abeyance to the point of actually becoming atrophied. So that if my grandfather wished to attract the attention of the two sisters, he had to resort to some such physical stimuli as alienists adopt in dealing with their distracted patients: to wit, repeated taps on a glass with the blade of a knife, accompanied by a sharp word and a compelling glance, violent methods which these psychiatrists are apt to bring with them into their everyday life among the sane, either from force of professional habit or because they think the whole world a trifle mad.

Their interest grew, however, when, the day before Swann was to dine with us, and when he had made them a special present of a case of Asti,[8] my great-aunt, who had in her hand a copy of the *Figaro* in which to the name of a picture then on view in a Corot[9] exhibition were added the words, "from the collection of M. Charles

8. An Italian white wine.   9. (1796–1875), French landscape painter, very popular at the time. *Figaro*: Leading Parisian newspaper.

Swann," asked: "Did you see that Swann is 'mentioned' in the *Figaro*?"

"But I've always told you," said my grandmother, "that he had a great deal of taste."

"You would, of course," retorted my great-aunt, "say anything just to seem different from *us*." For, knowing that my grandmother never agreed with her, and not being quite confident that it was her own opinion which the rest of us invariably endorsed, she wished to extort from us a wholesale condemnation of my grandmother's views, against which she hoped to force us into solidarity with her own. But we sat silent. My grandmother's sisters having expressed a desire to mention to Swann this reference to him in the *Figaro*, my great-aunt dissuaded them. Whenever she saw in others an advantage, however trivial, which she herself lacked, she would persuade herself that it was no advantage at all, but a drawback, and would pity so as not to have to envy them.

"I don't think that would please him at all; I know very well that I should hate to see my name printed like that, as large as life, in the paper, and I shouldn't feel at all flattered if anyone spoke to me about it."

She did not, however, put any very great pressure upon my grandmother's sisters, for they, in their horror of vulgarity, had brought to such a fine art the concealment of a personal allusion in a wealth of ingenious circumlocution, that it would often pass unnoticed even by the person to whom it was addressed. As for my mother, her only thought was of trying to induce my father to speak to Swann, not about his wife but about his daughter, whom he worshipped, and for whose sake it was understood that he had ultimately made his unfortunate marriage.

"You need only say a word; just ask him how she is. It must be so very hard for him."

My father, however, was annoyed: "No, no; you have the most absurd ideas. It would be utterly ridiculous."

But the only one of us in whom the prospect of Swann's arrival gave rise to an unhappy foreboding was myself. This was because on the evenings when there were visitors, or just M. Swann, in the house, Mamma did not come up to my room. I dined before the others, and afterwards came and sat at table until eight o'clock, when it was understood that I must go upstairs; that frail and precious kiss which Mamma used normally to bestow on me when I was in bed and just going to sleep had to be transported from the dining-room to my bedroom where I must keep it inviolate all the time that it took me to undress, without letting its sweet charm be broken, without letting its volatile essence diffuse itself and evaporate; and it was precisely on those very evenings when I needed to receive it with special care that I was obliged to take it, to snatch it brusquely and

in public, without even having the time or the equanimity to bring
to what I was doing the single-minded attention of lunatics who compel
themselves to exclude all other thoughts from their minds while they
are shutting a door, so that when the sickness of uncertainty sweeps
over them again they can triumphantly oppose it with the recollection of the precise moment when they shut the door.

We were all in the garden when the double tinkle of the visitors'
bell sounded shyly. Everyone knew that it must be Swann, and yet
they looked at one another inquiringly and sent my grandmother to
reconnoitre.

"See that you thank him intelligibly for the wine," my grandfather
warned his two sisters-in-law. "You know how good it is, and the
case is huge."

"Now, don't start whispering!" said my great-aunt. "How would
you like to come into a house and find everyone muttering to themselves?"

"Ah! There's M. Swann," cried my father. "Let's ask him if he
thinks it will be fine to-morrow."

My mother fancied that a word from her would wipe out all the
distress which my family had contrived to cause Swann since his
marriage. She found an opportunity to draw him aside for a moment.
But I followed her: I could not bring myself to let her out of my sight
while I felt that in a few minutes I should have to leave her in the
dining-room and go up to my bed without the consoling thought, as
on ordinary evenings, that she would come up later to kiss me.

"Now, M. Swann," she said, "do tell me about your daughter.
I'm sure she already has a taste for beautiful things, like her papa."

"Come along and sit down here with us all on the verandah," said
my grandfather, coming up to him. My mother had to abandon her
quest, but managed to extract from the restriction itself a further
delicate thought, like good poets whom the tyranny of rhyme forces
into the discovery of their finest lines.

"We can talk about her again when we are by ourselves," she said,
or rather whispered to Swann. "Only a mother is capable of understanding these things. I'm sure that hers would agree with me."

And so we all sat down round the iron table. I should have liked
not to think of the hours of anguish which I should have to spend
that evening alone in my room, without being able to go to sleep: I
tried to convince myself that they were of no importance since I
should have forgotten them next morning, and to fix my mind on
thoughts of the future which would carry me, as on a bridge, across
the terrifying abyss that yawned at my feet. But my mind, strained
by this foreboding, distended like the look which I shot at my mother,
would not allow any extraneous impression to enter. Thoughts did
indeed enter it, but only on the condition that they left behind them

every element of beauty, or even of humour, by which I might have been distracted or beguiled. As a surgical patient, thanks to a local anaesthetic, can look on fully conscious while an operation is being performed upon him and yet feel nothing, I could repeat to myself some favourite lines, or watch my grandfather's efforts to talk to Swann about the Duc d' Audiffret-Pasquier,[1] without being able to kindle any emotion from the one or amusement from the other. Hardly had my grandfather begun to question Swann about that orator when one of my grandmother's sisters, in whose ears the question echoed like a solemn but untimely silence which her natural politeness bade her interrupt, addressed the other with:

"Just fancy, Flora, I met a young Swedish governess today who told me some most interesting things about the co-operative movement in Scandinavia. We really must have her to dine here one evening."

"To be sure!" said her sister Flora, "but I haven't wasted my time either. I met such a clever old gentleman at M. Vinteuil's who knows Maubant[2] quite well, and Maubant has told him every little thing about how he gets up his parts. It's the most interesting thing I ever heard. He's a neighbour of M. Vinteuil's, and I never knew; and he is so nice besides."

"M. Vinteuil is not the only one who has nice neighbours," cried my aunt Céline in a voice that was loud because of shyness and forced because of premeditation, darting, as she spoke, what she called a "significant glance" at Swann. And my aunt Flora, who realised that this veiled utterance was Céline's way of thanking Swann for the Asti, looked at him also with a blend of congratulation and irony, either because she simply wished to underline her sister's little witticism, or because she envied Swann his having inspired it, or because she imagined that he was embarrassed, and could not help having a little fun at his expense.

"I think it would be worth while," Flora went on, "to have this old gentleman to dinner. When you get him going on Maubant or Mme Materna[3] he will talk for hours on end."

"That must be delightful," sighed my grandfather, in whose mind nature had unfortunately forgotten to include any capacity whatsoever for becoming passionately interested in the Swedish co-operative movement or in the methods employed by Maubant to get up his parts, just as it had forgotten to endow my grandmother's two sisters with a grain of that precious salt which one has oneself to "add to taste" in order to extract any savour from a narrative of the private life of Molé or of the Comte de Paris.

---

1. A fictitious nobleman. 2. Actor at the Comédie Française, the French national theater. M. Vinteuil: A fictitious composer and neighbor of the family. 3. Austrian soprano, who took part in the premiere of Wagner's *Ring* cycle at Bayreuth in 1876.

"By the way," said Swann to my grandfather, "what I was going to tell you has more to do than you might think with what you were asking me just now, for in some respects there has been very little change. I came across a passage in Saint-Simon[4] this morning which would have amused you. It's in the volume which covers his mission to Spain; not one of the best, little more in fact than a journal, but at least a wonderfully well written journal, which fairly distinguishes it from the tedious journals we feel bound to read morning and evening."

"I don't agree with you: there are some days when I find reading the papers very pleasant indeed," my aunt Flora broke in, to show Swann that she had read the note about his Corot in the *Figaro*.

"Yes," aunt Céline went one better, "when they write about things or people in whom we are interested."

"I don't deny it," answered Swann in some bewilderment. "The fault I find with our journalism is that it forces us to take an interest in some fresh triviality or other every day, whereas only three or four books in a lifetime give us anything that is of real importance. Suppose that, every morning, when we tore the wrapper off our paper with fevered hands, a transmutation were to take place, and we were to find inside it—oh! I don't know; shall we say Pascal's *Pensées?*"[5] He articulated the title with an ironic emphasis so as not to appear pedantic. "And then, in the gilt and tooled volumes which we open once in ten years," he went on, showing that contempt for worldly matters which some men of the world like to affect, "we should read that the Queen of the Hellenes had arrived at Cannes, or that the Princesse de Léon had given a fancy dress ball. In that way we should arrive at a happy medium." But at once regretting that he had allowed himself to speak of serious matters even in jest, he added ironically: "What a fine conversation we're having! I can't think why we climb to these lofty heights," and then, turning to my grandfather: "Well, Saint-Simon tells how Maulévrier had had the audacity to try to shake hands with his sons. You remember how he says of Maulévrier, 'Never did I find in that coarse bottle anything but ill-humour, boorishness, and folly.' "[6]

"Coarse or not, I know bottles in which there is something very different," said Flora briskly, feeling bound to thank Swann as well as her sister, since the present of Asti had been addressed to them both. Céline laughed.

---

4. The memoirs of the Duc de Saint-Simon (1675–1755) describe court life and intrigue during the reigns of Louis XIV and Louis XV. He was sent to Spain in 1721 to arrange the marriage of Louis XV and the daughter of the King of Spain.   5. The *Thoughts* of the French mathematician and religious philosopher Blaise Pascal (1623–1662) are comments on the human condition, and one of the triumphant works of French classicism.   6. Maulévrier was the French ambassador to Spain. Saint-Simon considered him of inferior birth, and refused to let his own children shake Maulévrier's hand. (*Memoirs*, vol. XXXIX.)

Swann was puzzled, but went on: "I cannot say whether it was ignorance or cozenage,' writes Saint-Simon. 'He tried to give his hand to my children. I noticed it in time to prevent him.' "

My grandfather was already in ecstasies over "ignorance or cozenage," but Mlle Céline—the name of Saint-Simon, a "man of letters," having arrested the complete paralysis of her auditory faculties—was indignant:

"What! You admire that? Well, that's a fine thing, I must say! But what's it supposed to mean? Isn't one man as good as the next? What difference can it make whether he's a duke or a groom so long as he's intelligent and kind? He had a fine way of bringing up his children, your Saint-Simon, if he didn't teach them to shake hands with all decent folk. Really and truly, it's abominable. And you dare to quote it!"

And my grandfather, utterly depressed, realising how futile it would be, against this opposition, to attempt to get Swann to tell him the stories which would have amused him, murmured to my mother: "Just tell me again that line of yours which always comforts me so much on these occasions. Oh, yes: 'What virtues, Lord, Thou makest us abhor!'[7] How good that is!"

I never took my eyes off my mother. I knew that when they were at table I should not be permitted to stay there for the whole of dinner-time, and that Mamma, for fear of annoying my father, would not allow me to kiss her several times in public, as I would have done in my room. And so I promised myself that in the dining-room, as they began to eat and drink and as I felt the hour approach, I would put beforehand into this kiss, which was bound to be so brief and furtive, everything that my own efforts could muster, would carefully choose in advance the exact spot on her cheek where I would imprint it, and would so prepare my thoughts as to be able, thanks to these mental preliminaries, to consecrate the whole of the minute Mamma would grant me to the sensation of her cheek against my lips, as a painter who can have his subject for short sittings only prepares his palette, and from what he remembers and from rough notes does in advance everything which he possibly can do in the sitter's absence. But to-night, before the dinner-bell had sounded, my grandfather said with unconscious cruelty: "The little man looks tired; he'd better go up to bed. Besides, we're dining late to-night."

And my father, who was less scrupulous than my grandmother or my mother in observing the letter of a treaty, went on: "Yes; run along; off to bed."

I would have kissed Mamma then and there, but at that moment the dinner-bell rang.

7. From *Pompey's Death* (line 1072), a tragedy by the French dramatist Pierre Corneille (1606–1684).

"No, no, leave your mother alone. You've said good night to one another, that's enough. These exhibitions are absurd. Go on upstairs."

And so I must set forth without viaticum;[8] must climb each step of the staircase "against my heart," as the saying is, climbing in opposition to my heart's desire, which was to return to my mother, since she had not, by kissing me, given my heart leave to accompany me forth. That hateful staircase, up which I always went so sadly, gave out a smell of varnish which had, as it were, absorbed and crystallised the special quality of sorrow that I felt each evening, and made it perhaps even crueller to my sensibility because, when it assumed this olfactory guise, my intellect was powerless to resist it. When we have gone to sleep with a raging toothache and are conscious of it only as of a little girl whom we attempt, time after time, to pull out of the water, or a line of Molière[9] which we repeat incessantly to ourselves, it is a great relief to wake up, so that our intelligence can disentangle the idea of toothache from any artificial semblance of heroism or rhythmic cadence. It was the converse of this relief which I felt when my anguish at having to go up to my room invaded my consciousness in a manner infinitely more rapid, instantaneous almost, a manner at once insidious and brutal, through the inhalation—far more poisonous than moral penetration—of the smell of varnish peculiar to that staircase.

Once in my room I had to stop every loophole, to close the shutters, to dig my own grave as I turned down the bedclothes, to wrap myself in the shroud of my nightshirt. But before burying myself in the iron bed which had been placed there because, on summer nights, I was too hot among the rep curtains of the four-poster,[1] I was stirred to revolt, and attempted the desperate stratagem of a condemned prisoner. I wrote to my mother begging her to come upstairs for an important reason which I could not put in writing. My fear was that Françoise, my aunt's cook who used to be put in charge of me when I was at Combray, might refuse to take my note. I had a suspicion that, in her eyes, to carry a message to my mother when there was a guest would appear as flatly inconceivable as for the door-keeper of a theatre to hand a letter to an actor upon the stage. On the subject of things which might or might not be done she possessed a code at once imperious, abundant, subtle, and uncompromising on points themselves imperceptible or irrelevant, which gave it a resemblance to those ancient laws which combine such cruel ordinances as the massacre of infants at the breast with prohibitions of exaggerated refinement against "seething the kid in his mother's milk," or "eating of the sinew which is upon the hollow of the thigh."[2] This code,

---

8. The communion wafer and wine given to the dying in Catholic rites.   9. (1622–1673), French dramatist.   1. Bed with corner pillars to support a canopy and curtains. *rep:* a heavy, ribbed fabric.   2. Refers to the strict dietary laws of Deuteronomy 14:21 and Genesis 32:32.

judging by the sudden obstinacy which she would put into her refusal to carry out certain of our instructions, seemed to have provided for social complexities and refinements of etiquette which nothing in Françoise's background or in her career as a servant in a village household could have put into her head; and we were obliged to assume that there was latent in her some past existence in the ancient history of France, noble and little understood, as in those manufacturing towns where old mansions still testify to their former courtly days, and chemical workers toil among delicately sculptured scenes from Le Miracle de Théophile or Les quatre fils Aymon.[3]

In this particular instance, the article of her code which made it highly improbable that—barring an outbreak of fire—Françoise would go down and disturb Mamma in the presence of M. Swann for so unimportant a person as myself was one embodying the respect she showed not only for the family (as for the dead, for the clergy, or for royalty), but also for the stranger within our gates; a respect which I should perhaps have found touching in a book, but which never failed to irritate me on her lips, because of the solemn and sentimental tones in which she would express it, and which irritated me more than usual this evening when the sacred character with which she invested the dinner-party might have the effect of making her decline to disturb its ceremonial. But to give myself a chance of success I had no hesitation in lying, telling her that it was not in the least myself who had wanted to write to Mamma, but Mamma who, on saying good night to me, had begged me not to forget to send her an answer about something she had asked me to look for, and that she would certainly be very angry if this note were not taken to her. I think that Françoise disbelieved me, for, like those primitive men whose senses were so much keener than our own, she could immediately detect, from signs imperceptible to the rest of us, the truth or falsehood of anything that we might wish to conceal from her. She studied the envelope for five minutes as though an examination of the paper itself and the look of my handwriting could enlighten her as to the nature of the contents, or tell her to which article of her code she ought to refer the matter. Then she went out with an air of resignation which seemed to imply: "It's hard lines on parents having a child like that."

A moment later she returned to say that they were still at the ice stage and that it was impossible for the butler to deliver the note at once, in front of everybody; but that when the finger-bowls were put round he would find a way of slipping it into Mamma's hand. At once my anxiety subsided; it was now no longer (as it had been a moment ago) until to-morrow that I had lost my mother, since my

3. Théophile was saved from damnation by the Virgin Mary after having signed a pact with the devil, and the four sons of Aymon were heroic knights who together rode the magic horse Bayard.

little note—though it would annoy her, no doubt, and doubly so because this stratagem would make me ridiculous in Swann's eyes—would at least admit me, invisible and enraptured, into the same room as herself, would whisper about me into her ear; since that forbidden and unfriendly dining-room, where but a moment ago the ice itself—with burned nuts in it—and the finger-bowls seemed to me to be concealing pleasures that were baleful and of a mortal sadness because Mamma was tasting of them while I was far away, had opened its doors to me and, like a ripe fruit which bursts through its skin, was going to pour out into my intoxicated heart the sweetness of Mamma's attention while she was reading what I had written. Now I was no longer separated from her; the barriers were down; an exquisite thread united us. Besides, that was not all: for surely Mamma would come.

As for the agony through which I had just passed, I imagined that Swann would have laughed heartily at it if he had read my letter and had guessed its purpose; whereas, on the contrary, as I was to learn in due course, a similar anguish[4] had been the bane of his life for many years, and no one perhaps could have understood my feelings at that moment so well as he; to him, the anguish that comes from knowing that the creature one adores is in some place of enjoyment where oneself is not and cannot follow—to him that anguish came through love, to which it is in a sense predestined, by which it will be seized upon and exploited; but when, as had befallen me, it possesses one's soul before love has yet entered into one's life, then it must drift, awaiting love's coming, vague and free, without precise attachment, at the disposal of one sentiment to-day, of another to-morrow, of filial piety or affection for a friend. And the joy with which I first bound myself apprentice, when Françoise returned to tell me that my letter would be delivered, Swann, too, had known well—that false joy which a friend or relative of the woman we love can give us, when, on his arrival at the house or theatre where she is to be found, for some ball or party or "first-night" at which he is to meet her, he sees us wandering outside, desperately awaiting some opportunity of communicating with her. He recognises us, greets us familiarly, and asks what we are doing there. And when we invent a story of having some urgent message to give to his relative or friend, he assures us that nothing could be simpler, takes us in at the door, and promises to send her down to us in five minutes. How we love him—as at that moment I loved Françoise—the good-natured intermediary who by a single word has made supportable, human, almost propitious the inconceivable, infernal scene of gaiety in the thick of which we had been imagining swarms of enemies, perverse and

4. That is, his unhappy love for Odette de Crécy, described in *Swann in Love*.

seductive, beguiling away from us, even making laugh at us, the
woman we love! If we are to judge of them by him—this relative
who has accosted us and who is himself an initiate in those cruel
mysteries—then the other guests cannot be so very demoniacal. Those
inaccessible and excruciating hours during which she was about to
taste of unknown pleasures—suddenly, through an unexpected breach,
we have broken into them; suddenly we can picture to ourselves, we
possess, we intervene upon, we have almost created, one of the
moments the succession of which would have composed those hours,
a moment as real as all the rest, if not actually more important to us
because our mistress is more intensely a part of it: namely, the moment
in which he goes to tell her that we are waiting below. And doubtless
the other moments of the party would not have been so very different
from this one, would be no more exquisite, no more calculated to
make us suffer, since this kind friend has assured us that "Of course,
she will be delighted to come down! It will be far more amusing for
her to talk to you than to be bored up there." Alas! Swann had
learned by experience that the good intentions of a third party are
powerless to influence a woman who is annoyed to find herself pursued even into a ballroom by a man she does not love. Too often,
the kind friend comes down again alone.

My mother did not appear, but without the slightest consideration
for my self-respect (which depended upon her keeping up the fiction
that she had asked me to let her know the result of my search for
something or other) told Françoise to tell me, in so many words:
"There is no answer"—words I have so often, since then, heard the
hall-porters in grand hotels and the flunkeys in gambling-clubs and
the like repeat to some poor girl who replies in bewilderment: "What!
he said nothing? It's not possible. You did give him my letter, didn't
you? Very well, I shall wait a little longer." And, just as she invariably protests that she does not need the extra gas which the porter
offers to light for her, and sits on there, hearing nothing further
except an occasional remark on the weather which the porter exchanges
with a bell-hop whom he will send off suddenly, when he notices
the time, to put some customer's wine on the ice, so, having declined
Françoise's offer to make me some tea or to stay beside me, I let her
go off again to the pantry, and lay down and shut my eyes, trying
not to hear the voices of my family who were drinking their coffee
in the garden.

But after a few seconds I realised that, by writing that note to
Mamma, by approaching—at the risk of making her angry—so near
to her that I felt I could reach out and grasp the moment in which I
should see her again, I had cut myself off from the possibility of
going to sleep until I actually had seen her, and my heart began to
beat more and more painfully as I increased my agitation by ordering

myself to keep calm and to acquiesce in my ill-fortune. Then, suddenly, my anxiety subsided, a feeling of intense happiness coursed
through me, as when a strong medicine begins to take effect and
one's pain vanishes: I had formed a resolution to abandon all attempts
to go to sleep without seeing Mamma, had made up my mind to kiss
her at all costs, even though this meant the certainty of being in
disgrace with her for long afterwards—when she herself came up to
bed. The calm which succeeded my anguish filled me with an
extraordinary exhilaration, no less than my sense of expectation, my
thirst for and my fear of danger. Noiselessly I opened the window
and sat down on the foot of my bed. I hardly dared to move in case
they should hear me from below. Outside, things too seemed frozen,
rapt in a mute intentness not to disturb the moonlight which, dupli-
cating each of them and throwing it back by the extension in front
of it of a shadow denser and more concrete than its substance, had
made the whole landscape at once thinner and larger, like a map
which, after being folded up, is spread out upon the ground. What
had to move—a leaf of the chestnut-tree, for instance—moved. But
its minute quivering, total, self-contained, finished down to its minutest gradation and its last delicate tremor, did not impinge upon the
rest of the scene, did not merge with it, remained circumscribed.
Exposed upon this surface of silence which absorbed nothing of them,
the most distant sounds, those which must have come from gardens
at the far end of the town, could be distinguished with such exact
"finish" that the impression they gave of coming from a distance
seemed due only to their "pianissimo" execution, like those movements on muted strings so well performed by the orchestra of the
Conservatoire[5] that, even though one does not miss a single note,
one thinks nonetheless that they are being played somewhere outside, a long way from the concert hall, so that all the old subscribers—my grandmother's sisters too, when Swann had given them
his seats—used to strain their ears as if they had caught the distant
approach of an army on the march, which had not yet rounded the
corner of the Rue de Trévise.[6]

I was well aware that I had placed myself in a position than which
none could be counted upon to involve me in graver consequences
at my parents' hands; consequences far graver, indeed, than a stranger
would have imagined, and such as (he would have thought) could
follow only some really shameful misdemeanour. But in the
upbringing which they had given me faults were not classified in the
same order as in that of other children, and I had been taught to
place at the head of the list (doubtless because there was no other

class of faults from which I needed to be more carefully protected) those in which I can now distinguish the common feature that one succumbs to them by yielding to a nervous impulse. But such a phrase had never been uttered in my hearing; no one had yet accounted for my temptations in a way which might have led me to believe that there was some excuse for my giving in to them, or that I was actually incapable of holding out against them. Yet I could easily recognise this class of transgressions by the anguish of mind which preceded as well as by the rigour of the punishment which followed them; and I knew that what I had just done was in the same category as certain other sins for which I had been severely punished, though infinitely more serious than they. When I went out to meet my mother on her way up to bed, and when she saw that I had stayed up in order to say good night to her again in the passage, I should not be allowed to stay in the house a day longer, I should be packed off to school[7] next morning; so much was certain. Very well: had I been obliged, the next moment, to hurl myself out of the window, I should still have preferred such a fate. For what I wanted now was Mamma, to say good night to her. I had gone too far along the road which led to the fulfilment of this desire to be able to retrace my steps.

I could hear my parents' footsteps as they accompanied Swann to the gate, and when the clanging of the bell assured me that he had really gone, I crept to the window. Mamma was asking my father if he had thought the lobster good, and whether M. Swann had had a second helping of the coffee-and-pistachio ice. "I thought it rather so-so," she was saying. "Next time we shall have to try another flavour."

"I can't tell you," said my great-aunt, "what a change I find in Swann. He is quite antiquated!" She had grown so accustomed to seeing Swann always in the same stage of adolescence that it was a shock to her to find him suddenly less young than the age she still attributed to him. And the others too were beginning to remark in Swann that abnormal, excessive, shameful and deserved senescence of bachelors, of all those for whom it seems that the great day which knows no morrow must be longer than for other men, since for them it is void of promise, and from its dawn the moments steadily accumulate without any subsequent partition[8] among offspring.

"I fancy he has a lot of trouble with that wretched wife of his, who lives with a certain Monsieur de Charlus,[9] as all Combray knows. It's the talk of the town."

My mother observed that, in spite of this, he had looked much less unhappy of late. "And he doesn't nearly so often do that trick of

---

7. Boarding school.   8. Sharing, as under a will.   9. Brother of the Duc de Guermantes.

his, so like his father, of wiping his eyes and drawing his hand across
his forehead. I think myself that in his heart of hearts he no longer
loves that woman."

"Why, of course he doesn't," answered my grandfather. "He wrote
me a letter about it, ages ago, to which I took care to pay no attention, but it left no doubt as to his feelings, or at any rate his love, for
his wife. Hullo! you two; you never thanked him for the Asti," he
went on, turning to his sisters-in-law.

"What! we never thanked him? I think, between you and me, that
I put it to him quite neatly," replied my aunt Flora.

"Yes, you managed it very well; I admired you for it," said my
aunt Céline.

"But you did it very prettily, too."

"Yes; I was rather proud of my remark about 'nice neighbours.' "

"What! Do you call that thanking him?" shouted my grandfather.
"I heard that all right, but devil take me if I guessed it was meant for
Swann. You may be quite sure he never noticed it."

"Come, come; Swann isn't a fool. I'm sure he understood. You
didn't expect me to tell him the number of bottles, or to guess what
he paid for them."

My father and mother were left alone and sat down for a moment;
then my father said: "Well, shall we go up to bed?"

"As you wish, dear, though I don't feel at all sleepy. I don't know
why; it can't be the coffee-ice—it wasn't strong enough to keep me
awake like this. But I see a light in the servants' hall: poor Françoise
has been sitting up for me, so I'll get her to unhook me while you
go and undress."

My mother opened the latticed door which led from the hall to
the staircase. Presently I heard her coming upstairs to close her window. I went quietly into the passage; my heart was beating so violently that I could hardly move, but at least it was throbbing no
longer with anxiety, but with terror and joy. I saw in the well of the
stair a light coming upwards, from Mamma's candle. Then I saw
Mamma herself and I threw myself upon her. For an instant she
looked at me in astonishment, not realising what could have happened. Then her face assumed an expression of anger. She said not
a single word to me; and indeed I used to go for days on end without
being spoken to, for far more venial offences than this. A single word
from Mamma would have been an admission that further intercourse with me was within the bounds of possibility, and that might
perhaps have appeared to me more terrible still, as indicating that,
with such a punishment as was in store for me, mere silence and
black looks would have been puerile. A word from her then would
have implied the false calm with which one addresses a servant to
whom one has just decided to give notice; the kiss one bestows on a

son who is being packed off to enlist, which would have been denied him if it had merely been a matter of being angry with him for a few days. But she heard my father coming from the dressing-room, where he had gone to take off his clothes, and, to avoid the "scene" which he would make if he saw me, she said to me in a voice half-stifled with anger: "Off you go at once. Do you want your father to see you waiting there like an idiot?"

But I implored her again: "Come and say good night to me," terrified as I saw the light from my father's candle already creeping up the wall, but also making use of his approach as a means of blackmail, in the hope that my mother, not wishing him to find me there, as find me he must if she continued to refuse me, would give in and say: "Go back to your room. I will come."

Too late: my father was upon us. Instinctively I murmured, though no one heard me, "I'm done for!"

I was not, however. My father used constantly to refuse to let me do things which were quite clearly allowed by the more liberal charters granted me by my mother and grandmother, because he paid no heed to "principles," and because for him there was no such thing as the "rule of law."[1] For some quite irrelevant reason, or for no reason at all, he would at the last moment prevent me from taking some particular walk, one so regular, so hallowed, that to deprive me of it was a clear breach of faith; or again, as he had done this evening, long before the appointed hour he would snap out: "Run along up to bed now; no excuses!" But at the same time, because he was devoid of principles (in my grandmother's sense), he could not, strictly speaking, be called intransigent. He looked at me for a moment with an air of surprise and annoyance, and then when Mamma had told him, not without some embarrassment, what had happened, said to her: "Go along with him, then. You said just now that you didn't feel very sleepy, so stay in his room for a little. I don't need anything."

"But, my dear," my mother answered timidly, "whether or not I feel sleepy is not the point; we mustn't let the child get into the habit . . ."

"There's no question of getting into a habit," said my father, with a shrug of the shoulders; "you can see quite well that the child is unhappy. After all, we aren't jailers. You'll end by making him ill, and a lot of good that will do. There are two beds in his room; tell Françoise to make up the big one for you, and stay with him for the rest of the night. Anyhow, I'm off to bed; I'm not so nervy as you. Good night."

1. Reference to the *ius gentium*, the "law of nations" or natural law supposed to govern international and public relations. Marcel sees the relationship between himself and his mother and grandmother as a social contract; his father is the unpredictable tyrant.

It was impossible for me to thank my father; he would have been exasperated by what he called mawkishness. I stood there, not daring to move; he was still in front of us, a tall figure in his white night-shirt, crowned with the pink and violet cashmere scarf which he used to wrap around his head since he had begun to suffer from neuralgia, standing like Abraham in the engraving after Benozzo Gozzoli[2] which M. Swann had given me, telling Sarah that she must tear herself away from Isaac. Many years have passed since that night. The wall of the staircase up which I had watched the light of his candle grad-ually climb was long ago demolished. And in myself, too, many things have perished which I imagined would last for ever, and new ones have arisen, giving birth to new sorrows and new joys which in those days I could not have foreseen, just as now the old are hard to understand. It is a long time, too, since my father has been able to say to Mamma: "Go along with the child." Never again will such moments be possible for me. But of late I have been increasingly able to catch, if I listen attentively, the sound of the sobs which I had the strength to control in my father's presence, and which broke out only when I found myself alone with Mamma. In reality their echo has never ceased; and it is only because life is now growing more and more quiet round about me that I hear them anew, like those convent bells which are so effectively drowned during the day by the noises of the street that one would suppose them to have stopped, until they ring out again through the silent evening air.

Mamma spent that night in my room: when I had just committed a sin so deadly that I expected to be banished from the household, my parents gave me a far greater concession than I could ever have won as the reward of a good deed. Even at the moment when it manifested itself in this crowning mercy, my father's behaviour towards me still retained that arbitrary and unwarranted quality which was so characteristic of him and which arose from the fact that his actions were generally dictated by chance expediencies rather than based on any formal plan. And perhaps even what I called his severity, when he sent me off to bed, deserved that title less than my mother's or my grandmother's attitude, for his nature, which in some respects differed more than theirs from my own, had probably prevented him from realising until then how wretched I was every evening, some-thing which my mother and grandmother knew well; but they loved me enough to be unwilling to spare me that suffering, which they hoped to teach me to overcome, so as to reduce my nervous sensi-bility and to strengthen my will. Whereas my father, whose affection for me was of another kind, would not, I suspect, have had the same courage, for as soon as he had grasped the fact that I was unhappy

2. (1420–1497). Florentine painter whose frescoes at Pisa contain scenes from the life of the Hebrew patriarch Abraham.

he had said to my mother: "Go and comfort him."

Mamma stayed that night in my room, and it seemed that she did not wish to mar by recrimination those hours which were so different from anything that I had had a right to expect, for when Françoise (who guessed that something extraordinary must have happened when she saw Mamma sitting by my side, holding my hand and letting me cry unchided) said to her: "But, Madame, what is young master crying for?" she replied: "Why, Françoise, he doesn't know himself: it's his nerves. Make up the big bed for me quickly and then go off to your own." And thus for the first time my unhappiness was regarded no longer as a punishable offence but as an involuntary ailment which had been officially recognised, a nervous condition for which I was in no way responsible: I had the consolation of no longer having to mingle apprehensive scruples with the bitterness of my tears; I could weep henceforth without sin. I felt no small degree of pride, either, in Françoise's presence at this return to humane conditions which, not an hour after Mamma had refused to come up to my room and had sent the snubbing message that I was to go to sleep, raised me to the dignity of a grown-up person, brought me of a sudden to a sort of puberty of sorrow, a manumission of tears. I ought to have been happy; I was not. It struck me that my mother had just made a first concession which must have been painful to her, that it was a first abdication on her part from the ideal she had formed for me, and that for the first time she who was so brave had to confess herself beaten. It struck me that if I had just won a victory it was over her, that I had succeeded, as sickness or sorrow or age might have succeeded, in relaxing her will, in undermining her judgment; a black date in the calendar. And if I had dared now, I should have said to Mamma: "No, I don't want you to, you mustn't sleep here." But I was conscious of the practical wisdom, of what would nowadays be called the realism, with which she tempered the ardent idealism of my grandmother's nature, and I knew that now the mischief was done she would prefer to let me enjoy the soothing pleasure of her company, and not to disturb my father again. Certainly my mother's beautiful face seemed to shine again with youth that evening, as she sat gently holding my hands and trying to check my tears; but this was just what I felt should not have been; her anger would have saddened me less than this new gentleness, unknown to my childhood experience; I felt that I had with an impious and secret finger traced a first wrinkle upon her soul and brought out a first white hair on her head. This thought redoubled my sobs, and then I saw that Mamma, who had never allowed herself to indulge in any undue emotion with me, was suddenly overcome by my tears and had to struggle to keep back her own. When she realised that I had noticed this, she said to me with a smile: "Why, my little buttercup, my little

canary-boy, he's going to make Mamma as silly as himself if this
goes on. Look, since you can't sleep, and Mamma can't either, we
mustn't go on in this stupid way; we must do something; I'll get one
of your books." But I had none there. "Would you like me to get
out the books now that your grandmother is going to give you for
your birthday? Just think it over first, and don't be disappointed if
there's nothing new for you then."

I was only too delighted, and Mamma went to fetch a parcel of
books of which I could not distinguish, through the paper in which
they were wrapped, any more than their short, wide format but which,
even at this first glimpse, brief and obscure as it was, bade fair to
eclipse already the paintbox of New Year's Day and the silkworms of
the year before. The books were *La Mare au Diable*, *François le
Champi*, *La Petite Fadette* and *Les Maîtres Sonneurs*.[3] My grandmother, as I learned afterwards, had at first chosen Musset's poems,
a volume of Rousseau, and *Indiana*; for while she considered light
reading as unwholesome as sweets and cakes, she did not reflect that
the strong breath of genius might have upon the mind even of a child
an influence at once more dangerous and less invigorating than that
of fresh air and sea breezes upon his body. But when my father had
almost called her an imbecile on learning the names of the books
she proposed to give me,[4] she had journeyed back by herself to Jouy-
le-Vicomte to the bookseller's, so that there should be no danger of
my not having my present in time (it was a boiling hot day, and she
had come home so unwell that the doctor had warned my mother
not to allow her to tire herself so), and had fallen back upon the four
pastoral novels of George Sand.

"My dear," she had said to Mamma, "I could not bring myself to
give the child anything that was not well written."

The truth was that she could never permit herself to buy anything
from which no intellectual profit was to be derived, above all the
profit which fine things afford us by teaching us to seek our pleasures
elsewhere than in the barren satisfaction of worldly wealth. Even
when she had to make someone a present of the kind called "useful,"
when she had to give an armchair or some table-silver or a walking-
stick, she would choose "antiques," as though their long desuetude
had effaced from them any semblance of utility and fitted them rather
to instruct us in the lives of the men of other days than to serve the
common requirements of our own. She would have liked me to have
in my room photographs of ancient buildings or of beautiful places.
But at the moment of buying them, and for all that the subject of

3. *The Devil's Pool*, *François the Founding Discovered in the Fields*, *Little Fadette*, and *The
Master Bellringers*, novels of idealized country life by the French woman writer George Sand
(1806–1876).　　4. The works of Alfred de Musset (1810–1857) and Jean-Jacques Rousseau (1712–
1778), often romantic and sometimes confessional, and some works by Sand (*Indiana* was a novel
of free love), would be thought unsuitable reading for a young child.

the picture had an aesthetic value, she would find that vulgarity and
utility had too prominent a part in them, through the mechanical
nature of their reproduction by photography. She attempted by a
subterfuge, if not to eliminate altogether this commercial banality,
at least to minimise it, to supplant it to a certain extent with what
was art still, to introduce, as it were, several "thicknesses" of art:
instead of photographs of Chartres Cathedral, of the Fountains of
Saint-Cloud, or of Vesuvius, she would inquire of Swann whether
some great painter had not depicted them, and preferred to give me
photographs of "Chartres Cathedral" after Corot, of the "Fountains
of Saint-Cloud" after Hubert Robert, and of "Vesuvius" after Turner,[5]
which were a stage higher in the scale of art. But although the photographer had been prevented from reproducing directly these masterpieces or beauties of nature, and had there been replaced by a
great artist, he resumed his odious position when it came to reproducing the artist's interpretation. Accordingly, having to reckon again
with vulgarity, my grandmother would endeavour to postpone the
moment of contact still further. She would ask Swann if the picture
had not been engraved, preferring, when possible, old engravings
with some interest of association apart from themselves, such, for
example, as show us a masterpiece in a state in which we can no
longer see it to-day (like Morghen's print of Leonardo's "Last Supper" before its defacement).[6] It must be admitted that the results of
this method of interpreting the art of making presents were not always
happy. The idea which I formed of Venice, from a drawing by Titian[7]
which is supposed to have the lagoon in the background, was certainly far less accurate than what I should have derived from ordinary
photographs. We could no longer keep count in the family (when
my great-aunt wanted to draw up an indictment of my grandmother)
of all the armchairs she had presented to married couples, young
and old, which on a first attempt to sit down upon them had at once
collapsed beneath the weight of their recipients. But my grandmother would have thought it sordid to concern herself too closely
with the solidity of any piece of furniture in which could still be
discerned a flourish, a smile, a brave conceit of the past. And even
what in such pieces answered a material need, since it did so in a
manner to which we are no longer accustomed, charmed her like
those old forms of speech in which we can still see traces of a metaphor whose fine point has been worn away by the rough usage of our
modern tongue. As it happened, the pastoral novels of George Sand

5. The Cathedral of Chartres, painted in 1830 by Corot; the fountains in the old park at Saint-
Cloud, outside Paris, painted by Hubert Robert (1733–1809), and Vesuvius, the famous volcano
near Naples, painted by J. M. W. Turner (1775–1851).   6. Leonardo da Vinci's *Last Supper*
was the subject of a famous engraving by Morghen, a late eighteenth-century engraver. The paints
in the original fresco had deteriorated rapidly, and a major restoration took place in the nineteenth
century.   7. Venetian painter (1477–1576).

which she was giving me for my birthday were regular lumber-rooms full of expressions that have fallen out of use and become quaint and picturesque, and are now only to be found in country dialects. And my grandmother had bought them in preference to other books, as she would more readily have taken a house with a gothic dovecot or some other such piece of antiquity as will exert a benign influence on the mind by giving it a hankering for impossible journeys through the realms of time.

Mamma sat down by my bed; she had chosen *François le Champi*, whose reddish cover and incomprehensible title[8] gave it, for me, a distinct personality and a mysterious attraction. I had not then read any real novels. I had heard it said that George Sand was a typical novelist. This predisposed me to imagine that *François le Champi* contained something inexpressibly delicious. The narrative devices designed to arouse curiosity or melt to pity, certain modes of expression which disturb or sadden the reader, and which, with a little experience, he may recognise as common to a great many novels, seemed to me—for whom a new book was not one of a number of similar objects but, as it were, a unique person, absolutely self-contained—simply an intoxicating distillation of the peculiar essence of *François le Champi*. Beneath the everyday incidents, the ordinary objects and common words, I sensed a strange and individual tone of voice. The plot began to unfold: to me it seemed all the more obscure because in those days, when I read, I used often to daydream about something quite different for page after page. And the gaps which this habit left in my knowledge of the story were widened by the fact that when it was Mamma who was reading to me aloud she left all the love-scenes out. And so all the odd changes which take place in the relations between the miller's wife and the boy, changes which only the gradual dawning of love can explain, seemed to me steeped in a mystery the key to which (I readily believed) lay in that strange and mellifluous name of *Champi*, which invested the boy who bore it, I had no idea why, with its own vivid, ruddy, charming colour. If my mother was not a faithful reader, she was none the less an admirable one, when reading a work in which she found the note of true feeling, in the respectful simplicity of her interpretation and the beauty and sweetness of her voice. Even in ordinary life, when it was not works of art but men and women whom she was moved to pity or admire, it was touching to observe with what deference she would banish from her voice, her gestures, from her whole conversation, now the note of gaiety which might have distressed some mother who had once lost a child, now the recollection of an event or anniversary which might have reminded some old gentleman of

8. *Champi* is an old French word the child Marcel would not have known.

the burden of his years, now the household topic which might have bored some young man of letters. And so, when she read aloud the prose of George Sand, prose which is everywhere redolent of that generosity and moral distinction which Mamma had learned from my grandmother to place above all other qualities in life, and which I was not to teach her until much later to refrain from placing above all other qualities in literature too, taking pains to banish from her voice any pettiness or affectation which might have choked that powerful stream of language, she supplied all the natural tenderness, all the lavish sweetness which they demanded to sentences which seemed to have been composed for her voice and which were all, so to speak, within the compass of her sensibility. She found, to tackle them in the required tone, the warmth of feeling which pre-existed and dictated them, but which is not to be found in the words themselves, and by this means she smoothed away, as she read, any harshness or discordance in the tenses of verbs, endowing the imperfect and the preterite[9] with all the sweetness to be found in generosity, all the melancholy to be found in love, guiding the sentence that was drawing to a close towards the one that was about to begin, now hastening, now slackening the pace of the syllables so as to bring them, despite their differences of quantity, into a uniform rhythm, and breathing into this quite ordinary prose a kind of emotional life and continuity.

My aching heart was soothed; I let myself be borne upon the current of this gentle night on which I had my mother by my side. I knew that such a night could not be repeated; that the strongest desire I had in the world, namely, to keep my mother in my room through the sad hours of darkness, ran too much counter to general requirements and to the wishes of others for such a concession as had been granted me this evening to be anything but a rare and artificial exception. To-morrow night my anguish would return and Mamma would not stay by my side. But when my anguish was assuaged, I could no longer understand it; besides, to-morrow was still a long way off; I told myself that I should still have time to take preventive action, although that time could bring me no access of power since these things were in no way dependent upon the exercise of my will, and seemed not quite inevitable only because they were still separated from me by this short interval.

And so it was that, for a long time afterwards, when I lay awake at night and revived old memories of Combray, I saw no more of it than this sort of luminous panel, sharply defined against a vague and shadowy background, like the panels which the glow of a Bengal

9. The imperfect is the tense of continued and incomplete action in the past, while the preterite describes a single completed action.

light[1] or a searchlight beam will cut out and illuminate in a building the other parts of which remain plunged in darkness: broad enough at its base, the little parlour, the dining-room, the opening of the dark path from which M. Swann, the unwitting author of my sufferings, would emerge, the hall through which I would journey to the first step of that staircase, so painful to climb, which constituted, all by itself, the slender cone of this irregular pyramid; and, at the summit, my bedroom, with the little passage through whose glazed[2] door Mamma would enter; in a word, seen always at the same evening hour, isolated from all its possible surroundings, detached and solitary against the dark background, the bare minimum of scenery necessary (like the decor one sees prescribed on the title-page of an old play, for its performance in the provinces) to the drama of my undressing; as though all Combray had consisted of but two floors joined by a slender staircase, and as though there had been no time there but seven o'clock at night. I must own[3] that I could have assured any questioner that Combray did include other scenes and did exist at other hours than these. But since the facts which I should then have recalled would have been prompted only by voluntary memory, the memory of the intellect, and since the pictures which that kind of memory shows us preserve nothing of the past itself, I should never have had any wish to ponder over this residue of Combray. To me it was in reality all dead.

Permanently dead? Very possibly.

There is a large element of chance in these matters, and a second chance occurrence, that of our own death, often prevents us from awaiting for any length of time the favours of the first.

I feel that there is much to be said for the Celtic belief that the souls of those whom we have lost are held captive in some inferior being, in an animal, in a plant, in some inanimate object, and thus effectively lost to us until the day (which to many never comes) when we happen to pass by the tree or to obtain possession of the object which forms their prison.[4] Then they start and tremble, they call us by our name, and as soon as we have recognised their voice the spell is broken. Delivered by us, they have overcome death and return to share our life.

And so it is with our own past. It is a labour in vain to attempt to recapture it: all the efforts of our intellect must prove futile. The past is hidden somewhere outside the realm, beyond the reach of intellect, in some material object (in the sensation which that material object will give us) of which we have no inkling. And it depends on chance whether or not we come upon this object before we ourselves must die.

---

1. Fireworks.   2. I.e., with glass panes.   3. Admit.   4. A belief attributed to Druids, the priests of the Celtic peoples.

Many years had elapsed during which nothing of Combray, save what was comprised in the theatre and the drama of my going to bed there, had any existence for me, when one day in winter, on my return home, my mother, seeing that I was cold, offered me some tea, a thing I did not ordinarily take. I declined at first, and then, for no particular reason, changed my mind. She sent for one of those squat, plump little cakes called "petites madeleines," which look as though they had been moulded in the fluted valve of a scallop shell. And soon, mechanically, dispirited after a dreary day with the prospect of a depressing morrow, I raised to my lips a spoonful of the tea in which I had soaked a morsel of the cake. No sooner had the warm liquid mixed with the crumbs touched my palate than a shudder ran through me and I stopped, intent upon the extraordinary thing that was happening to me. An exquisite pleasure had invaded my senses, something isolated, detached, with no suggestion of its origin. And at once the vicissitudes of life had become indifferent to me, its disasters innocuous, its brevity illusory—this new sensation having had on me the effect which love has of filling me with a precious essence; or rather this essence was not in me, it *was* me. I had ceased now to feel mediocre, contingent, mortal. Whence could it have come to me, this all-powerful joy? I sensed that it was connected with the taste of the tea and the cake, but that it infinitely transcended those savours, could not, indeed, be of the same nature. Whence did it come? What did it mean? How could I seize and apprehend it?

I drink a second mouthful, in which I find nothing more than in the first, then a third, which gives me rather less than the second. It is time to stop; the potion is losing its magic. It is plain that the truth I am seeking lies not in the cup but in myself. The drink has called it into being, but does not know it, and can only repeat indefinitely, with a progressive diminution of strength, the same message which I cannot interpret, though I hope at least to be able to call it forth again and to find it there presently, intact and at my disposal, for my final enlightenment. I put down the cup and examine my own mind. It alone can discover the truth. But how? What an abyss of uncertainty, whenever the mind feels overtaken by itself; when it, the seeker, is at the same time the dark region through which it must go seeking and where all its equipment will avail it nothing. Seek? More than that: create. It is face to face with something which does not yet exist, to which it alone can give reality and substance, which it alone can bring into the light of day.

And I begin again to ask myself what it could have been, this unremembered state which brought with it no logical proof, but the indisputable evidence, of its felicity, its reality, and in whose presence other states of consciousness melted and vanished. I decide to attempt to make it reappear. I retrace my thoughts to the moment at which I drank the first spoonful of tea. I rediscover the same state, illuminated by no fresh light. I ask my mind to make one further effort, to bring back once more the fleeting sensation. And so that nothing may interrupt it in its course I shut out every obstacle, every extraneous idea, I stop my ears and inhibit all attention against the sounds from the next room. And then, feeling that my mind is tiring itself without having any success to report, I compel it for a change to enjoy the distraction which I have just denied it, to think of other things, to rest and refresh itself before making a final effort. And then for the second time I clear an empty space in front of it; I place in position before my mind's eye the still recent taste of that first mouthful, and I feel something start within me, something that leaves its rest-ing-place and attempts to rise, something that has been embedded like an anchor at a great depth; I do not know yet what it is, but I can feel it mounting slowly; I can measure the resistance, I can hear the echo of great spaces traversed.

Undoubtedly what is thus palpitating in the depths of my being must be the image, the visual memory which, being linked to that taste, is trying to follow it into my conscious mind. But its struggles are too far off, too confused and chaotic; scarcely can I perceive the neutral glow into which the elusive whirling medley of stirred-up colours is fused, and I cannot distinguish its form, cannot invite it, as the one possible interpreter, to translate for me the evidence of its contemporary, its inseparable paramour, the taste, cannot ask it to inform me what special circumstance is in question, from what period in my past life.

Will it ultimately reach the clear surface of my consciousness, this memory, this old, dead moment which the magnetism of an identi-cal moment has travelled so far to importune, to disturb, to raise up out of the very depths of my being? I cannot tell. Now I feel nothing; it has stopped, has perhaps sunk back into its darkness, from which who can say whether it will ever rise again? Ten times over I must essay the task, must lean down over the abyss. And each time the cowardice that deters us from every difficult task, every important enterprise, has urged me to leave the thing alone, to drink my tea and to think merely of the worries of to-day and my hopes for to-morrow, which can be brooded over painlessly.

And suddenly the memory revealed itself. The taste was that of the little piece of madeleine which on Sunday mornings at Combray (because on those mornings I did not go out before mass), when I went to say good morning to her in her bedroom, my aunt Léonie used to give me, dipping it first in her own cup of tea or tisane. The sight of the little madeleine had recalled nothing to my mind before I tasted it; perhaps because I had so often seen such things in the meantime, without tasting them, on the trays in pastry-cooks' win-dows, that their image had dissociated itself from those Combray days to take its place among others more recent; perhaps because of those memories, so long abandoned and put out of mind, nothing now survived, everything was scattered; the shapes of things, including that of the little scallop-shell of pastry, so richly sensual under its severe, religious folds, were either obliterated or had been so long dormant as to have lost the power of expansion which would have allowed them to resume their place in my consciousness. But when from a long-distant past nothing subsists, after the people are dead, after the things are broken and scattered, taste and smell alone, more fragile but more enduring, more unsubstantial, more persistent, more faithful, remain poised a long time, like souls, remembering, waiting, hoping, amid the ruins of all the rest; and bear unflinchingly, in the tiny and almost impapable drop of their essence, the vast structure of recollection.

And as soon as I had recognised the taste of the piece of madeleine soaked in her decoction of lime-blossom which my aunt used to give me (although I did not yet know and must long postpone the discovery of why this memory made me so happy) immediately the old grey house upon the street, where her room was, rose up like a stage set to attach itself to the little pavilion opening on to the garden which had been built out behind it for my parents (the isolated segment which until that moment had been all that I could see); and with the house the town, from morning to night and in all weathers, the Square where I used to be sent before lunch, the streets along which I used to run errands, the country roads we took when it was fine. And as in the game wherein the Japanese amuse themselves by filling a porcelain bowl with water and steeping in it little pieces of paper which until then are without character or form, but, the moment they become wet, stretch and twist and take on colour and distinctive shape, become flowers or houses or people, solid and recognisable, so in that moment all the flowers in our garden and in M. Swann's park, and the water-lilies on the Vivonne[5] and the good folk of the village and their little dwellings and the parish church and the whole of Combray and its surroundings, taking shape and solidity, sprang into being, town and gardens alike, from my cup of tea.

THOMAS MANN
1875–1955

Thomas Mann's reputation as the great German novelist of the twentieth century represents only part of his stature; by the time of his death in 1955, he had become an international figure to whom people looked for statements

5. The local river.

on art, modern society, and the human condition. Continuing the great nineteenth-century tradition of psychological realism, Mann took as his subject the cultural and spiritual crises of Europe at the turn of the century. His career spanned a time of great change, including as it did the upheaval of two world wars and the visible disintegration of a whole society. Where other modern novelists, such as Joyce, Faulkner, or Woolf stressed innovative language and style, Mann emphasized instead the society of his time and—inside that society—the universal human conflicts between art and life, sensuality and intellect, individual and social will.

Many of Mann's themes derive from the nineteenth-century German aesthetic tradition in which he grew up. The philosophers Schopenhauer and Nietzsche and the composer Wagner had the most influence on his work: Arthur Schopenhauer (1788–1860) for his vision of artistic suffering and development; Friedrich Nietzsche (1844–1900) for his portrait of the diseased artist overcoming chaos and decay to produce, through discipline and will, art works that justify existence; and Richard Wagner (1813–1883) for embodying the complete artist who controlled all aspects of his work: music, lyrics, the very staging of his operas. Mann's well-known use of the verbal *leitmotif* (pronounced "light-moteef") is also borrowed from Wagner, who would use in his operas a recurrent musical theme (the leitmotif) associated with a particular person, thing, action, or state of being. In Mann's literary adaptation, evocative phrases, repeated almost without change, link memories throughout the text and establish a cumulative emotional resonance. In the story "Tonio Kröger," for example, Tonio's dual ancestry is repeatedly suggested by the contrasting phrases of the "dark, fiery mother, who played the piano and mandolin," and the father with his "thoughtful blue eyes" and "wild flower in the buttonhole." Inside the tradition of realistic narration, Mann created a highly organized literary structure with subtly interrelated themes and images that built up rich associations of ideas: in his own words, an "epic prose composition . . . understood by me as spiritual thematic pattern, as a musical complex of associations."

Mann was born in an historic seaport and commercial city, Lübeck, on June 6, 1875. His father was a grain merchant and head of the family firm; his mother came from a German-Brazilian family and was known for her beauty and musical talent. The contrast of Nordic and Latin that plays such a large part in Mann's work begins in his consciousness of his own heritage and is expanded to far-reaching symbolic levels. He disliked the scientific emphasis of his secondary education, and left school in 1894 after repeating two years. Rejoining his family in Munich, where they had moved in 1891 after his father's death, he worked as an unpaid apprentice in a fire insurance business but found more interest in university lectures in history, political economy, and art. He decided against a business career after his first published story, "Fallen" (1896), received praise from the noted poet Richard Dehmel, and from 1896 to 1898 lived and wrote in Italy before returning to Munich for a two-year stint as manuscript reader for the satiric weekly *Simplicissimus*. In 1905, he married Katia Pringsheim, with whom he had six children. The short stories collected in *Little Herr Friedemann* (1899) were a success, and enabled Mann to find a publisher for his first major work, *Buddenbrooks* (1901).

Buddenbrooks describes the decline of a prosperous German family through four generations, and is to some extent based on the history of the Mann family business. Nonetheless, the elements of autobiography are quickly absorbed into the more universal themes of the inner decay of the German burgher ("bourgeois," or middle-class) tradition and its growing isolation from other segments of society, a decline paralleled in the portrait of a developing artistic sensitivity and its relation to death. Children in the family of the self-confident, aggressive, and disciplined Consul Johann Buddenbrooks become increasingly introspective, hesitant, unhealthy, and artistic. The end of the family comes with young Hanno, a musical genius who is completely absorbed in his piano improvisations and the fatal temptation to the infinite that music implies. In this novel, as in many later works, Mann's fictional world is governed by a tension or dualism between sensuous experience and intellect or will. A diseased and alienated imaginative soul is set against a healthy, gregarious, somewhat obtuse normal citizen; the erratic and poor artist against the disciplined and prosperous burgher; the dark, brown-eyed Latin against the blond, blue-eyed Nordic; warm, unselfconscious feelings against icy intellect; freedom against authority; immorality and decadence against moral respectability; a longing for the eternal and infinite against active participation in everyday life.

There is no recommended resolution of these polarities, for if either overwhelms the other, tragedy must follow. In the seemingly autobiographical "Tonio Kröger," the protagonist is portrayed as sensitive to the claims of both, and his growing awareness of their combined importance is a sign of maturity. Ideally, the artist must live both extremes at once, in constant lucidity and pain. In *Death in Venice*, the author Gustave Aschenbach suffers and dies for having been unable to keep the balance; in the late novel *Doctor Faustus*, the composer Adrian Leverkühn sells his soul to the devil in order to draw on both extremes for his art. In "Mario and the Magician," the sadistic hypnotist Cipolla is an artist in his fashion, exercising a fatally corrupt art in which all his psychological insight, cutting intellect, and iron will produce only torment for himself and others. Mann's letters and essays show that he felt deeply involved in the relations of the artist's life to that of the art work, but his protagonists have their own identity and symbolize much more than Mann's own artistic career. As artist and craftsman, he always insisted on distinguishing the work of art from its raw material, the emotions and experiences of life. He cultivated objectivity, distance, and irony in his own works, and no character—including the narrator—is immune from the author's critical eye.

Mann's most famous novella, *Death in Venice*, was published in 1912, shortly after a trip to Venice and shortly before World War I. Its sense of impending doom involves the cultural disintegration of the "European soul" (soon to be expressed in the Great War) symbolized by the corruption and death of the writer Gustave Aschenbach during an epidemic. The story pictures a loss of psychological balance, a sickness of the artistic soul to match that of plague-ridden Venice masking its true condition before unsuspecting tourists. Erotic and artistic themes mingle as the respected Aschenbach, escaping a lifetime of laborious creation and self-discipline, allows himself to be swept away by the classical beauty of a young boy until he becomes a grotesque figure, dyeing his hair and rouging his cheeks in a vain attempt to appear young. The issue, however, is not Aschenbach's obsession with Tadzio but rather his alternate repression of and abandonment to emotion. On the one hand, the will which drove him to compose masterworks is now gutted from within as he sinks into a passive, fatalistic acceptance of his feelings and remains in the plague-stricken city. On the other, Aschenbach has clearly sacrificed an integral part of artistic vision in his former repression of emotions. He has developed an "official" note and been anthologized in textbooks, but he no longer takes joy in his work, lives with the tension of a clenched fist, and suffers from repressed yearnings for freedom and mystic beauty. "Who shall unriddle the puzzle of the artist's nature?" asks the narrator. *Death in Venice* is a crystallization of Mann's work at its best, displaying the penetrating detail of his social and psychological realism, the power of his tightly interwoven symbolic structure, and the cumulative impact of his artist-hero's quest for meaning.

Throughout his writings up to and during World War I, Mann established himself as an important spokesman for modern Germany. His early conservatism and defense of an authoritarian nationalist government (*Reflections of a Non-Political Man*, 1918) gave way to an ardent defense of democracy and liberal humanism as the Nazis came to power. Mann's most famous novel, *The Magic Mountain* (1924), is a *Bildungsroman* (novel of the protagonist's education and development) that uses the isolation of a mountain-top sanitorium to gain perspective on the philosophic issues of twentieth-century Europe. The hero, Hans Castorp, has to decide how to live as he listens to the competing dogmas of the humanist Settembrini and the fanatic antirationalist Naphta, and undergoes a double temptation of oblivion through eroticism (Clavdia Chauchat) and death (symbolized by the isolated sanitorium). The novel ends with Castorp choosing active participation in a world at war; whether or not he survives the trenches is left unresolved, but he has taken charge of his own destiny. *The Magic Mountain* was immensely popular, and its author received the Nobel Prize in 1929. He was so much an international figure when he went into voluntary exile in Switzerland as Hitler came to power in 1933 that the Nazis, stung by his criticism, revoked his citizenship. Moving to America in 1938, he wrote and lectured against Hitlerism and in 1944 became an American citizen.

Mann's later works cover a range of themes. *Joseph and His Brothers* (1933–45) is a tetralogy on the Biblical tale of Joseph who, abandoned for dead by his brothers, survives and comes to power in Egypt. *Dr. Faustus* (1947), which Mann called "the novel of my epoch, dressed up in the story of a highly precarious and sinful artistic life," portrayed the composer Adrian Leverkühn as a modern Faust who personifies the temptation and corruption of contemporary Germany. Leverkühn makes a pact with the devil to become aware of the extremes of his own personality, thus enriching his experience and his music. His pieces are rationally composed by using patterns derived from the twelve-tone row, and his "Lamentation of Doctor Faustus" is a direct challenge to the traditional tonality and freer form of the earlier German masterpiece, Beethoven's Ninth Symphony with its concluding "Ode to Joy." A somber and compelling work, *Doctor Faustus* symbolizes the negation of life Mann found inherent in Hitler's attempt to reshape German culture. Well after the war, when Mann had moved to Zurich, he published a final, comic picture of the artist-figure as a confidence man who uses his skill and ironic insight to manipulate society (*The Confessions of Felix Krull*, 1954). Mann's last work before his death on August 12, 1955, the *Confessions* recapitulate his familiar themes but in a light-hearted parody of traditional *Bildungsromans* that is a far cry from the moral seriousness of earlier tales.

"Mario and the Magician" is both a specific commentary on a period in history—the Fascist era in which the dictators Mussolini and Hitler came to power in Italy and Germany—and a larger and still valid examination of the relation between individual and society, freedom and authority, artistic power and its corruption. Published in 1929, the short story pictures Italy falling under the spell of a militant nationalism, indirectly referring to the dictatorship of Benito Mussolini and his dream of a second Roman Empire. In 1928, the Italian dictator had ended parliamentary government and reorganized the economy as a centralized, corporate state; he controlled the press, encouraged terrorism by nationalist groups, and began an ambitious building program which sought to enhance national pride by constructing modern Italian monuments to rival those of ancient Rome. Small wonder that the northern European tourists who traditionally visited Italy in search of sun and sea began to feel unwelcome, inexplicably attacked by swaggering locals eager to establish their own superiority. In the same years, Adolph Hitler was using his extraordinary skills as a speaker, and his insight into mass psychology, to sway crowds in a new, hate-filled German nationalism that also aimed at world domination. He was the "Leader" (literally: *Führer* in Germany and *Duce* for Mussolini in Italy) wedded to his people in a complex rhetoric of love, hate, and mastery whose erotic overtones have often been observed. Like Mussolini, Hitler loved grand spectacles and prophesied the rebirth of ancient glories: in his case, the powerful gods of Nordic mythology to replace "weak" Christianity, the assertion of an Aryan master race archetypally superior to all others (especially Jews), and the abandonment of rational inquiry and individual will in favor of his own mythic vision.

The story is subtitled "A Tragic Travel Experience" and is viewed throughout from the slightly alienated eyes of the narrator, a German tourist on holiday with his family in the small Italian resort of Torre di Venere. The tragedy is viewed first from the outside, in the hotel and on the beach, and then in more personal terms as the magician Cipolla brings various members of the audience under his control. Mann leads the reader through different levels and seriousness of attack: the anonymous Italian defending his will and the "honour of the human race," Sofronia's loyalty to family ties, and the "utter abandonment of the inmost soul" when simple, kindly Mario's hidden love is travestied before an entire audience. "In that evil span of time, crowded with a sense of the illusiveness of all joy, one sound became audible, and that not quite at once, but on the instant of the melancholy and ribald meeting between Mario's lips and the repulsive flesh which thrust itself forward for his caress. It was the sound of a laugh. . . ." Cipolla, receiving the kiss, is himself a grotesque, tormented figure; a cripple who cannot endure either physical beauty or human love, a demon nourished by alcohol who ultimately falls puppet-like into a "huddled heap of clothing," he is the fountainhead and personification of the whole unhealthy atmosphere in Torre di Venere.

Cipolla uses his mastery of stage technique and repartee to win his audience's admiration in spite of their initial dislike, and then—whip in hand—proceeds ruthlessly to demolish all resistance. It is a complicated performance, alternating between outright aggression and an emotional plea for sympathy and identification. The magician suffers for them all, he suggests, and both artist and audience are partners in the reciprocal enactment of a higher goal, a "mysterious common will" which only he can formulate. In its successive triumphs, Cipolla's performance also demonstrates the difficulty of maintaining free will before determined attack: first, the defensive posture is negative and therefore weak, and second, the very openness of free will—its refusal to be enclosed in a set doctrine—leaves it vulnerable to more aggressive beliefs. "A will that aims at its own freedom aims at the unknown," taunts Cipolla. One of the disturbing aspects of "Mario and the Magician" is that free will, in fact, does not triumph: it is the instinctive revulsion of an outraged Mario, revolver in hand, that puts an end to Cipolla and accomplishes what the narrator calls "a liberation." The conclusion is doubly ambiguous, expressing in 1929 both the unfinished tragedy of history and a somber view of the resources of human individualism.

Ignace Feuerlicht's *Thomas Mann* (1969) provides a general biographical introduction. In *Thomas Mann: A Collection of Critical Essays* (1964) Henry Hatfield presents essays on different works, including one by Mann on humor; there is a short biographical sketch at the end. Terence J. Reed's *Thomas Mann: The Uses of Tradition* (1974) is an excellent, well-written general study incorporating recent material. Richard Winston, *Thomas Mann: The Making of an Artist 1875–1911* (1981), the first volume of an unfinished study, is a detailed and authoritative presentation by the translator of Mann's diaries and letters.

Mario and the Magician[1]

The atmosphere of Torre di Venere[2] remains unpleasant in the memory. From the first moment the air of the place made us uneasy, we felt irritable, on edge; then at the end came the shocking business of Cipolla, that dreadful being who seemed to incorporate, in so fateful and so humanly impressive a way, all the peculiar evilness of the situation as a whole. Looking back, we had the feeling that the horrible end of the affair had been preordained and lay in the nature of things; that the children had to be present at it was an added impropriety, due to the false colours in which the weird creature presented himself. Luckily for them, they did not know where the comedy left off and the tragedy began; and we let them remain in

---

1. Subtitled "A Tragic Travel Experience."   2. "Tower of Venus" (Italian).

their happy belief that the whole thing had been a play up till the end.

Torre di Venere lies some fifteen kilometres from Portoclemente, one of the most popular summer resorts on the Tyrrhenian Sea.[3] Portoclemente is urban and elegant and full to overflowing for months on end. Its gay and busy main street of shops and hotels runs down to a wide sandy beach covered with tents and pennanted sand-castles and sunburnt humanity, where at all times a lively social bustle reigns, and much noise. But this same spacious and inviting fine-sanded beach, this same border of pine grove and near, presiding mountains, continues all the way along the coast. No wonder then that some competition of a quiet kind should have sprung up further on. Torre di Venere—the tower that gave the town its name is gone long since, one looks for it in vain—is an offshoot of the larger resort, and for some years remained an idyll for the few, a refuge for more unworldly spirits. But the usual history of such places repeated itself: peace has had to retire further along the coast, to Marina Petriera and dear knows where else. We all know how the world at once seeks peace and puts her to flight—rushing upon her in the fond idea that they two will wed, and where she is, there it can be at home. It will even set up its Vanity Fair in a spot and be capable of thinking that peace is still by its side. Thus Torre—though its atmosphere so far is more modest and contemplative than that of Portoclemente—has been quite taken up, by both Italians and foreigners. It is no longer the thing to go to Portoclemente—though still so much the thing that it is as noisy and crowded as ever. One goes next door, so to speak: to Torre. So much more refined, even, and cheaper to boot. And the attractiveness of these qualities persists, though the qualities themselves long ago ceased to be evident. Torre has got a Grand Hotel. Numerous pensions have sprung up, some modest, some pretentious. The people who own or rent the villas and pinetas[4] overlooking the sea no longer have it all their own way on the beach. In July and August it looks just like the beach at Portoclemente: it swarms with a screaming, squabbling, merrymaking crowd, and the sun, blazing down like mad, peels the skin off their necks. Garish little flat-bottomed boats rock on the glittering blue, manned by children, whose mothers hover afar and fill the air with anxious cries of Nino! and Sandro! and Bice! and Maria! Pedlars step across the legs of recumbent sun-bathers, selling flowers and corals, oysters, lemonade, and *cornetti al burro*,[5] and crying their wares in the breathy, full-throated southern voice.

Such was the scene that greeted our arrival in Torre: pleasant

---

3. Part of the Mediterranean Sea, between Italy and Sicily and Sardinia. *Portoclemente* means "merciful harbors."   4. Small pine groves. *Pension*: a boardinghouse.   5. Buttered rolls or croissants.

enough, but after all, we thought, we had come too soon. It was the middle of August, the Italian season was still at its height, scarcely the moment for strangers to learn to love the special charms of the place. What an afternoon crowd in the cafés on the front! For instance, in the Esquisito, where we sometimes sat and were served by Mario, that very Mario of whom I shall have presently to tell. It is well-nigh impossible to find a table; and the various orchestras contend together in the midst of one's conversation with bewildering effect. Of course, it is in the afternoon that people come over from Portoclemente. The excursion is a favourite one for the restless denizens of that pleasure resort, and a Fiat motor-bus plies to and fro, coating inch-thick with dust the oleander and laurel hedges along the highroad—a notable if repulsive sight.

Yes, decidedly one should go to Torre in September, when the great public has left. Or else in May, before the water is warm enough to tempt the Southerner to bathe. Even in the before and after seasons Torre is not empty, but life is less national and more subdued. English, French, and German prevail under the tent-awnings and in the pension dining-rooms; whereas in August—in the Grand Hotel, at least, where, in default of private addresses, we had engaged rooms—the stranger finds the field so occupied by Florentine and Roman society that he feels quite isolated and even temporarily *déclassé*.[6]

We had, rather to our annoyance, this experience on the evening we arrived, when we went in to dinner and were shown to our table by the waiter in charge. As a table, it had nothing against it, save that we had already fixed our eyes upon those on the veranda beyond, built out over the water, where little red-shaded lamps glowed—and there were still some tables empty, though it was as full as the dining-room within. The children went into raptures at the festive sight, and without more ado we announced our intention to take our meals by preference in the veranda. Our words, it appeared, were prompted by ignorance; for we were informed with somewhat embarrassed politeness, that the cosy nook outside was reserved for the clients of the hotel: *ai nostri clienti*.[7] Their clients? But we were their clients. We were not tourists or trippers, but boarders for a stay of some three or four weeks. However, we forbore to press for an explanation of the difference between the likes of us and that clientèle to whom it was vouchsafed to eat out there in the glow of the red lamps, and took our dinner by the prosaic common light of the dining-room chandelier—a thoroughly ordinary and monotonous hotel bill of fare, be it said. In Pensione Eleonora, a few steps landward, the table, as we were to discover, was much better.

And thither it was that we moved, three or four days later, before

---

6. Socially inferior; "lower class" (French).   7. "Our clients" (Italian).

we had had time to settle in properly at the Grand Hotel. Not on account of the veranda and the lamps. The children, straightway on the best of terms with waiters and pages, absorbed in the joys of life on the beach, promptly forgot those colourful seductions. But now there arose, between ourselves and the veranda clientèle—or perhaps more correctly with the compliant management—one of those little unpleasantnesses which can quite spoil the pleasure of a holiday. Among the guests were some high Roman aristocracy, a Principe[8] X and his family. These grand folk occupied rooms close to our own, and the Principessa, a great and a passionately maternal lady, was thrown into a panic by the vestiges of a whooping-cough which our little ones had lately got over, but which now and then still faintly troubled the unshatterable slumbers of our youngest-born. The nature of this illness is not clear, leaving some play for the imagination. So we took no offence at our elegant neighbour for clinging to the widely held view that whooping-cough is acoustically contagious and quite simply fearing lest her children yield to the bad example set by ours. In the fullness of her feminine self-confidence she protested to the management, which then, in the person of the proverbial frock-coated manager, hastened to represent to us, with many expressions of regret, that under the circumstances they were obliged to transfer us to the annexe. We did our best to assure him that the disease was in its very last stages, that it was actually over, and presented no danger of infection to anybody. All that we gained was permission to bring the case before the hotel physician—not one chosen by us—by whose verdict we must then abide. We agreed, convinced that thus we should at once pacify the Princess and escape the trouble of moving. The doctor appeared, and behaved like a faithful and honest servant of science. He examined the child and gave his opinion: the disease was quite over, no danger of contagion was present. We drew a long breath and considered the incident closed—until the manager announced that despite the doctor's verdict it would still be necessary for us to give up our rooms and retire to the *dépendance*.[9] Byzantinism like this outraged us. It is not likely that the Principessa was responsible for the wilful breach of faith. Very likely the fawning management had not even dared to tell her what the physician said. Anyhow, we made it clear to his understanding that we preferred to leave the hotel altogether and at once—and packed our trunks. We could do so with a light heart, having already set up casual friendly relations with Casa Eleonora. We had noticed its pleasant exterior and formed the acquaintance of its proprietor, Signora Angiolieri, and her husband: she slender and black-haired, Tuscan[1] in type,

8. "Prince" (Italian); *Principessa*, "Princess."   9. Annex (French). *Byzantinism:* officious behavior and worship of rank (a reference to the Eastern Roman or Byzantine Empire, A.D. 330–1453).
1. From Tuscany, a region in north central Italy.

probably at the beginning of the thirties, with the dead ivory complexion of the southern woman, he quiet and bald and carefully dressed. They owned a larger establishment in Florence and presided only in summer and early autumn over the branch in Torre di Venere. But earlier, before her marriage, our new landlady had been companion, fellow-traveller, wardrobe mistress, yes, friend, of Eleonora Duse[2] and manifestly regarded that period as the crown of her career. Even at our first visit she spoke of it with animation. Numerous photographs of the great actress, with affectionate inscriptions, were displayed about the drawing-room, and other souvenirs of their life together adorned the little tables and étagères. This cult of a so interesting past was calculated, of course, to heighten the advantages of the signora's present business. Nevertheless our pleasure and interest were quite genuine as we were conducted through the house by its owner and listened to her sonorous and staccato Tuscan voice relating anecdotes of that immortal mistress, depicting her suffering saintliness, her genius, her profound delicacy of feeling.

Thither, then, we moved our effects, to the dismay of the staff of the Grand Hotel, who, like all Italians, were very good to children. Our new quarters were retired and pleasant, we were within easy reach of the sea through the avenue of young plane trees that ran down to the esplanade. In the clean, cool dining-room Signora Angiolieri daily served the soup with her own hands, the service was attentive and good, the table capital. We even discovered some Viennese acquaintances, and enjoyed chatting with them after luncheon, in front of the house. They, in their turn, were the means of our finding others—in short, all seemed for the best, and we were heartily glad of the change we had made. Nothing was now wanting to a holiday of the most gratifying kind.

And yet no proper gratification ensued. Perhaps the stupid occasion of our change of quarters pursued us to the new ones we had found. Personally, I admit that I do not easily forget these collisions with ordinary humanity, the naïve misuse of power, the injustice, the sycophantic corruption. I dwelt upon the incident too much, it irritated me in retrospect—quite futilely, of course, since such phenomena are only all too natural and all too much the rule. And we had not broken off relations with the Grand Hotel. The children were as friendly as ever there, the porter mended their toys, and we sometimes took tea in the garden. We even saw the Principessa. She would come out, with her firm and delicate tread, her lips emphatically corallined, to look after her children, playing under the supervision of their English governess. She did not dream that we were anywhere near, for so soon as she appeared in the offing we sternly

2. Famous Italian actress (1859–1924).

forbade our little one even to clear his throat.

The heat—if I may bring it in evidence—was extreme. It was African. The power of the sun, directly one left the border of the indigo-blue wave, was so frightful, so relentless, that the mere thought of the few steps between the beach and luncheon was a burden, clad though one might be only in pyjamas.[3] Do you care for that sort of thing? Weeks on end? Yes, of course, it is proper to the south, it is classic weather, the sun of Homer,[4] the climate wherein human culture came to flower—and all the rest of it. But after a while it is too much for me, I reach a point where I begin to find it dull. The burning void of the sky, day after day, weighs one down; the high coloration, the enormous naïveté of the unrefracted light—they do, I dare say, induce light-heartedness, a carefree mood born of immunity from downpours and other meteorological caprices. But slowly, slowly, there makes itself felt a lack: the deeper, more complex needs of the northern soul remain unsatisfied. You are left barren—even it may be, in time, a little contemptuous. True without that stupid business of the whooping-cough I might not have been feeling these things. I was annoyed, very likely I wanted to feel them and so half-unconsciously seized upon an idea lying ready to hand to induce, or if not to induce, at least to justify and strengthen, my attitude. Up to this point, then, if you like, let us grant some ill will on our part. But the sea; and the mornings spent extended upon the fine sand in face of its eternal splendours—no, the sea could not conceivably induce such feelings. Yet it was none the less true that, despite all previous experience, we were not at home on the beach, we were not happy.

It was too soon, too soon. The beach, as I have said, was still in the hands of the middle-class native. It is a pleasing breed to look at, and among the young we saw much shapeliness and charm. Still, we were necessarily surrounded by a great deal of very average humanity—a middle-class mob, which, you will admit, is not more charming under this sun than under one's own native sky. The voices these women have! It was sometimes hard to believe that we were in the land which is the western cradle of the art of song. *"Fuggièro!"* I can still hear that cry, as for twenty mornings long I heard it close behind me, breathy, full-throated, hideously stressed, with a harsh open *e*, uttered in accents of mechanical despair. *"Fuggièro! Rispondi almeno!"* Answer when I call you! The *sp* in *rispondi* was pronounced like *shp*, as Germans pronounce it; and this, on top of what I felt already, vexed my sensitive soul. The cry was addressed to a repulsive youngster whose sunburn had made disgusting raw sores on his shoulders. He outdid anything I have ever seen for ill-

---

3. Loungewear.   4. Greek epic poet; German tourists came south to vacation in the homeland of the ancient Greco-Roman civilization they so much admired.

breeding, refractoriness, and temper and was a great coward to boot, putting the whole beach in an uproar, one day, because of his outrageous sensitiveness to the slightest pain. A sand-crab had pinched his toe in the water, and the minute injury made him set up a cry of heroic proportions—the shout of an antique hero in his agony—that pierced one to the marrow and called up visions of some frightful tragedy. Evidently he considered himself not only wounded, but poisoned as well; he crawled out on the sand and lay in apparently intolerable anguish, groaning *"Ohi!"* and *"Ohimè!"* and threshing about with arms and legs to ward off his mother's tragic appeals and the questions of the bystanders. An audience gathered round. A doctor was fetched—the same who had pronounced objective judgment on our whooping-cough—and here again acquitted himself like a man of science. Good-naturedly he reassured the boy, telling him that he was not hurt at all, he should simply go into the water again to relieve the smart. Instead of which, Fuggièro was borne off the beach, followed by a concourse of people. But he did not fail to appear next morning, nor did he leave off spoiling our children's sand-castles. Of course, always by accident. In short, a perfect terror.

And this twelve-year-old lad was prominent among the influences that, imperceptibly at first, combined to spoil our holiday and render it unwholesome. Somehow or other, there was a stiffness, a lack of innocent enjoyment. These people stood on their dignity—just why, and in what spirit, it was not easy at first to tell. They displayed much self-respectingness; towards each other and towards the foreigner their bearing was that of a person newly conscious of a sense of honour. And wherefore? Gradually we realized the political implications and understood that we were in the presence of a national ideal. The beach, in fact, was alive with patriotic children—a phenomenon as unnatural as it was depressing. Children are a human species and a society apart, a nation of their own, so to speak. On the basis of their common form of life, they find each other out with the greatest ease, no matter how different their small vocabularies. Ours soon played with natives and foreigners alike. Yet they were plainly both puzzled and disappointed at times. There were wounded sensibilities, displays of assertiveness—or rather hardly assertiveness, for it was too self-conscious and too didactic to deserve the name. There were quarrels over flags, disputes about authority and precedence. Grownups joined in, not so much to pacify as to render judgment and enunciate principles. Phrases were dropped about the greatness and dignity of Italy, solemn phrases that spoilt the fun. We saw our two little ones retreat, puzzled and hurt, and were put to it to explain the situation. These people, we told them, were just passing through a certain stage, something rather like an illness, perhaps; not very pleasant, but probably unavoidable.

We had only our own carelessness to thank that we came to blows
in the end with this "stage"—which, after all, we had seen and sized
up long before now. Yes, it came to another "cross-purposes," so
evidently the earlier ones had not been sheer accident. In a word,
we became an offence to the public morals. Our small daughter—
eight years old, but in physical development a good year younger
and thin as a chicken—had had had a good long bathe and gone
playing in the warm sun in her wet costume. We told her that she
might take off her bathing-suit, which was stiff with sand, rinse it in
the sea, and put it on again, after which she must take care to keep
it cleaner. Off goes the costume and she runs down naked to the sea,
rinses her little jersey, and comes back. Ought we to have foreseen
the outburst of anger and resentment which her conduct, and thus
our conduct, called forth? Without delivering a homily on the subject, I may say that in the last decade our attitude towards the nude
body and our feelings regarding it have undergone, all over the world,
a fundamental change. There are things we "never think about" any
more, and among them is the freedom we had permitted to this by
no means provocative little childish body. But in these parts it was
taken as a challenge. The patriotic children hooted. Fuggièro whistled on his fingers. The sudden buzz of conversation among the
grown people in our neighbourhood boded no good. A gentleman
in city togs, with a not very apropos bowler hat on the back of his
head, was assuring his outraged womenfolk that he proposed to take
punitive measures; he stepped up to us, and a philippic[5] descended
on our unworthy heads, in which all the emotionalism of the sense-
loving south spoke in the service of mortality and discipline. The
offence against decency of which we had been guilty was, he said,
the more to be condemned because it was also a gross ingratitude
and an insulting breach of his country's hospitality. We had crimi-
nally injured not only the letter and spirit of the public bathing regulations, but also the honour of Italy; he, the gentleman in the city
togs, knew how to defend that honour and proposed to see to it that
our offence against the national dignity should not go unpunished.

We did our best, bowing respectfully, to give ear to this eloquence. To contradict the man, overheated as he was, would probably
be to fall from one error into another. On the tips of our tongues we
had various answers: as, that the word "hospitality," in its strictest
sense, was not quite the right one, taking all the circumstances into
consideration. We were not literally the guests of Italy, but of Signora Angiolieri, who had assumed the rôle of dispenser of hospitality
some years ago on laying down that of familiar friend to Eleonora
Duse. We longed to say that surely this beautiful country had not

5. A scathing denunciation; named after the attacks on Philip II of Macedon by the Greek orator
Demosthenes (384–322 B.C.).

sunk so low as to be reduced to a state of hypersensitive prudishness. But we confined ourselves to assuring the gentleman that any lack of respect, any provocation on our parts, had been the furthest from our thoughts. And as a mitigating circumstance we pointed out the tender age and physical slightness of the little culprit. In vain. Our protests were waved away, he did not believe in them; our defence would not hold water. We must be made an example of. The authorities were notified, by telephone, I believe, and their representatives appeared on the beach. He said the case was *"molto grave."*[6] We had to go with him to the Municipio up in the Piazza, where a higher official confirmed the previous verdict of *"molto grave,"* launched into a stream of the usual didactic phrases—the selfsame tune and words as the man in the bowler hat—and levied a fine and ransom of fifty lire. We felt that the adventure must willy-nilly be worth to us this much of a contribution to the economy of the Italian government; paid, and left. Ought we not at this point to have left Torre as well?

If we only had! We should thus have escaped that fatal Cipolla. But circumstances combined to prevent us from making up our minds to a change. A certain poet says that it is indolence that makes us endure uncomfortable situations. The *aperçu*[7] may serve as an explanation for our inaction. Anyhow, one dislikes voiding the field immediately upon such an event. Especially if sympathy from other quarters encourages one to defy it. And in the Villa Eleonora they pronounced as with one voice upon the injustice of our punishment. Some Italian after-dinner acquaintances found that the episode put their country in a very bad light, and proposed taking the man in the bowler hat to task, as one fellow-citizen to another. But the next day he and his party had vanished from the beach. Not on our account, of course. Though it might be that the consciousness of his impending departure had added energy to his rebuke; in any case his going was a relief. And, furthermore, we stayed because our stay had by now become remarkable in our own eyes, which is worth something in itself, quite apart from the comfort or discomfort involved. Shall we strike sail, avoid a certain experience so soon as it seems not expressly calculated to increase our enjoyment or our self-esteem? Shall we go away whenever life looks like turning in the slightest uncanny, or not quite normal, or even rather painful and mortifying? No, surely not. Rather stay and look matters in the face, brave them out; perhaps precisely in so doing lies a lesson for us to learn. We stayed on and reaped as the awful rward of our constancy the unholy and staggering experience with Cipolla.

I have not mentioned that the after season had begun, almost on the very day we were disciplined by the city authorities. The worshipful gentleman in the bowler hat, our denouncer, was not the only person to leave the resort. There was a regular exodus, on every hand you saw luggage-carts on their way to the station. The beach denationalized itself. Life in Torre, in the cafés and the pinetas, became more homelike and more European. Very likely we might even have eaten at a table in the glass veranda, but we refrained, being content at Signora Angiolieri's—as content, that is, as our evil star would let us be. But at the same time with this turn for the better came a change in the weather: almost to an hour it showed itself in harmony with the holiday calendar of the general public. The sky was overcast; not that it grew any cooler, but the unclouded heat of the entire eighteen days since our arrival, and probably long before that, gave place to a stifling sirocco air, while from time to time a little ineffectual rain sprinkled the velvety surface of the beach. Add to which, that two-thirds of our intended stay at Torre had passed. The colourless, lazy sea, with sluggish jellyfish floating in its shallows, was at least a change. And it would have been silly to feel retrospective longings after a sun that had caused us so many sighs when it burned down in all its arrogant power.

At this juncture, then, it was that Cipolla announced himself. Cavaliere[8] Cipolla he was called on the posters that appeared one day stuck up everywhere, even in the dining-room of Pensione Eleonora. A travelling virtuoso, an entertainer, *"forzatore, illusionista, prestidigatore,"* as he called himself, who proposed to wait upon the highly respectable population of Torre di Venere with a display of extraordinary phenomena of a mysterious and staggering kind. A conjuror! The bare announcement was enough to turn our children's heads. They had never seen anything of the sort, and now our present holiday was to afford them this new excitement. From that moment on they besieged us with prayers to take tickets for the performance. We had doubts, from the first, on the score of the lateness of the hour, nine o'clock; but gave way, in the idea that we might see a little of what Cipolla had to offer, probably no great matter, and then go home. Besides, of course, the children could sleep late next day. We bought four tickets of Signora Angiolieri herself, she having taken a number of the stalls on commission to sell them to her guests. She could not vouch for the man's performance, and we had no great expectations. But we were conscious of a need for diversion, and the children's violent curiosity proved catching.

The Cavaliere's performance was to take place in a hall where during the season there had been a cinema with a weekly programme. We had never been there. You reached it by following the

---

8. "Knight" or "Sir" Cipolla (*Cipolla* is also Italian for "onion"); he is a "strong man, illusionist, conjuror."

main street under the wall of the *"palazzo,"*[9] a ruin with a "For sale" sign, that suggested a castle and had obviously been built in lordlier days. In the same street were the chemist,[1] the hairdresser, and all the better shops; it led, so to speak, from the feudal past the bourgeois into the proletarian, for it ended off between two rows of poor fishing-huts, where old women sat mending nets before the doors. And here, among the proletariat, was the hall, not much more, actually, than a wooden shed, though a large one, with a turreted entrance, plastered on either side with layers of gay placards. Some while after dinner, then, on the appointed evening, we wended our way thither in the dark, the children dressed in their best and blissful with the sense of so much irregularity. It was sultry, as it had been for days; there was heat lightning now and then, and a little rain; we proceeded under umbrellas. It took us a quarter of an hour.

Our tickets were collected at the entrance, our places we had to find ourselves. They were in the third row left, and as we sat down we saw that, late though the hour was for the performance, it was to be interpreted with even more laxity. Only very slowly did an audience—who seemed to be relied upon to come late—begin to fill the stalls. These comprised the whole auditorium; there were no boxes. This tardiness gave us some concern. The children's cheeks were already flushed as much with fatigue as with excitement. But even when we entered, the standing-room at the back and in the side aisles was already well occupied. There stood the manhood of Torre di Venere, all and sundry, fisherfolk, rough-and-ready youths with bare forearms crossed over their striped jerseys. We were well pleased with the presence of this native assemblage, which always adds colour and animation to occasions like the present; and the children were frankly delighted. For they had friends among these people—acquaintances picked up on afternoon strolls to the further ends of the beach. We would be turning homeward, at the hour when the sun dropped into the sea, spent with the huge effort it had made and gilding with reddish gold the oncoming surf; and we would come upon bare-legged fisherfolk standing in rows, bracing and hauling with long-drawn cries as they drew in the nets and harvested in dripping baskets their catch, often so scanty, of *frutto di mare*.[2] The children looked on, helped to pull, brought out their little stock of Italian words, made friends. So now they exchanged nods with the "standing-room" clientèle; there was Guiscardo, there Antonio, they knew them by name and waved and called across in half-whispers, getting answering nods and smiles that displayed rows of healthy white teeth. Look, there is even Mario, Mario from the Esquisito, who brings us the chocolate. He wants to see the conjuror, too, and he

9. Mansion.   1. Drugstore.   2. Seafood.

must have come early, for he is almost in front; but he does not see us, he is not paying attention; that is a way he has, even though he is a waiter. So we wave instead to the man who lets out the little boats on the beach; he is there too, standing at the back.

It had got to a quarter past nine, it got to almost half past. It was natural that we should be nervous. When would the children get to bed? It had been a mistake to bring them, for now it would be very hard to suggest breaking off their enjoyment before it had got well under way. The stalls had filled in time; all Torre, apparently, was there: the guests of the Grand Hotel, the guests of Villa Eleonora, familiar faces from the beach. We heard English and German and the sort of French that Rumanians speak with Italians. Madame Angiolieri herself sat two rows behind us, with her quiet, bald-headed spouse, who kept stroking his moustache with the two middle fingers of his right hand. Everybody had come late, but nobody too late. Cipolla made us wait for him.

He made us wait. That is probably the way to put it. He heightened the suspense by his delay in appearing. And we could see the point of this, too—only not when it was carried to extremes. Towards half past nine the audience began to clap—an amiable way of expressing justifiable impatience, evincing as it does an eagerness to applaud. For the little ones, this was a joy in itself—all children love to clap. From the popular sphere came loud cries of *"Pronti!"* *"Cominciamo!"*[3] And lo, it seemed now as easy to begin as before it had been hard. A gong sounded, greeted by the standing rows with a many-voiced "Ah-h!" and the curtains parted. They revealed a platform furnished more like a schoolroom than like the theatre of a conjuring performance—largely because of the blackboard in the left foreground. There was a common yellow hat-stand, a few ordinary straw-bottomed chairs, and further back a little round table holding a water carafe and glass, also a tray with a liqueur glass and a flask of pale yellow liquid. We had still a few seconds of time to let these things sink in. Then, with no darkening of the house, Cavaliere Cipolla made his entry.

He came forward with a rapid step that expressed his eagerness to appear before his public and gave rise to the illusion that he had already come a long way to put himself at their service—whereas, of course, he had only been standing in the wings. His costume supported the fiction. A man of an age hard to determine, but by no means young; with a sharp, ravaged face, piercing eyes, compressed lips, small black waxed moustache, and a so-called imperial[4] in the curve between mouth and chin. He was dressed for the street with a sort of complicated evening elegance, in a wide black pelerine[5] with

3. "Ready! Let's begin!"   4. A small pointed beard, named after Napoleon III, Emperor of France (1808–1873).   5. Cloak.

velvet collar and satin lining; which, in the hampered state of his
arms, he held together in front with his white-gloved hands. He had
a white scarf round his neck; a top hat with a curving brim sat far
back on his head. Perhaps more than anywhere else the eighteenth
century is still alive in Italy, and with it the charlatan and mounte-
bank type so characteristic of the period. Only there, at any rate,
does one still encounter really well-preserved specimens. Cipolla had
in his whole appearance much of the historic type; his very clothes
helped to conjure up the traditional figure with its blatantly, fantastically foppish air. His pretentious costume sat upon him, or rather
hung upon him, most curiously, being in one place drawn too tight,
in another a mass of awkward folds. There was something not quite
in order about his figure, both front and back—that was plain later
on. But I must emphasize the fact that there was not a trace of personal jocularity or clownishness in his pose, manner, or behaviour.
On the contrary, there was complete seriousness, an absence of any
humorous appeal; occasionally even a cross-grained pride, along with
that curious, self-satisfied air so characteristic of the deformed. None
of all this, however, prevented his appearance from being greeted
with laughter from more than one quarter of the hall.

All the eagerness had left his manner. The swift entry had been
merely an expression of energy, not of zeal. Standing at the footlights
he negligently drew off his gloves, to display long yellow hands, one
of them adorned with a seal ring with a lapis-lazuli in a high setting.
As he stood there, his small hard eyes, with flabby pouches beneath
them, roved appraisingly about the hall, not quickly, rather in a
considered examination, pausing here and there upon a face with
his lips clipped together, not speaking a word. Then with a display
of skill as surprising as it was casual, he rolled his gloves into a ball
and tossed them across a considerable distance into the glass on the
table. Next from an inner pocket he drew forth a packet of cigarettes;
you could see by the wrapper that they were the cheapest sort the
government sells. With his fingertips he pulled out a cigarette and
lighted it, without looking, from a quick-firing benzine lighter. He
drew the smoke deep into his lungs and let it out again, tapping his
foot, with both lips drawn in an arrogant grimace and the grey smoke
streaming out between broken and saw-edged teeth.

With a keenness equal to his own his audience eyed him. The
youths at the rear scowled as they peered at this cocksure creature to
search out his secret weaknesses. He betrayed none. In fetching out
and putting back the cigarettes his clothes got in his way. He had to
turn back his pelerine, and in so doing revealed a riding-whip with
a silver claw-handle that hung by a leather thong from his left forearm
and looked decidedly out of place. You could see that he had on not
evening clothes but a frock-coat, and under this, as he lifted it to get

at his pocket, could be seen a striped sash worn about the body. Somebody behind me whispered that this sash went with his title of Cavaliere. I give the information for what it may be worth—personally, I never heard that the title carried such insignia with it. Perhaps the sash was sheer pose, like the way he stood there, without a word, casually and arrogantly puffing smoke into his audience's face.

People laughed, as I said. The merriment had become almost general when somebody in the "standing seats," in a loud, dry voice, remarked: "*Buona sera.*"[6]

Cipolla cocked his head. "Who was that?" asked he, as though he had been dared. "Who was that just spoke? Well? First so bold and now so modest? *Paura*,[7] eh?" He spoke with a rather high, asthmatic voice, which yet had a metallic quality. He waited.

"That was me," a youth at the rear broke into the stillness, seeing himself thus challenged. He was not far from us, a handsome fellow in a woollen shirt, with his coat hanging over one shoulder. He wore his surly, wiry hair in a high, dishevelled mop, the style affected by the youth of the awakened Fatherland; it gave him an African appearance that rather spoiled his looks. "*Bè!* That was me. It was your business to say it first, but I was trying to be friendly."

More laughter. The chap had a tongue in his head. "*Ha sciolto la scilinguágnolo*,"[8] I heard near me. After all, the retort was deserved.

"Ah, bravo!" answered Cipolla. "I like you, *giovanotto*. Trust me, I've had my eye on you for some time. People like you are just in my line. I can use them. And you are the pick of the lot, that's plain to see. You do what you like. Or is it possible you have ever not done what you liked—or even, maybe, what you didn't like? What somebody else liked, in short? Hark ye, my friend, that might be a pleasant change for you, to divide up the willing and the doing and stop tackling both jobs at once. Division of labour, *sistema americano, sa!* For instance, suppose you were to show your tongue to this select and honourable audience here—your whole tongue, right down to the roots?"

"No, I won't," said the youth, hostilely. "Sticking out your tongue shows a bad bringing-up."

"Nothing of the sort," retorted Cipolla. "You would only be *doing* it. With all due respect to your bringing-up, I suggest that before I count ten, you will perform a right turn and stick out your tongue at the company here further than you knew yourself that you could stick it out."

He gazed at the youth, and his piercing eyes seemed to sink deeper into their sockets. "*Uno!*"[9] said he. He had let his riding-whip slide down his arm and made it whistle once through the air. The boy

6. "Good evening." 7. "Afraid?" 8. "His tongue is well attached" (he speaks glibly). *Giovanotto*: young man. *Sistema americano*: the American way. 9. One!

faced about and put out his tongue, so long, so extendedly, that you could see it was the very uttermost in tongue which he had to offer. Then turned back, stony-faced, to his former position.

"That was me," mocked Cipolla, with a jerk of his head towards the youth. "*Bè!* That was me." Leaving the audience to enjoy its sensations, he turned towards the little round table, lifted the bottle, poured out a small glass of what was obviously cognac, and tipped it up with a practised hand.

The children laughed with all their hearts. They had understood practically nothing of what had been said, but it pleased them hugely that something so funny should happen, straightaway, between that queer man up there and somebody out of the audience. They had no preconception of what an "evening" would be like and were quite ready to find this a priceless beginning. As for us, we exchanged a glance and I remember that involuntarily I made with my lips the sound that Cipolla's whip had made when it cut the air. For the rest, it was plain that people did not know what to make of a preposterous beginning like this to a sleight-of-hand performance. They could not see why the *giovanotto*, who after all in a way had been their spokes-man, should suddenly have turned on them to vent his incivility. They felt that he had behaved like a silly ass and withdrew their countenances from him in favour of the artist, who now came back from his refreshment table and addressed them as follows:

"Ladies and gentlemen," said he, in his wheezing, metallic voice, "you saw just now that I was rather sensitive on the score of the rebuke this hopeful young linguist saw fit to give me"—"*questo lin-guista di belle speranze*"[1] was what he said, and we all laughed at the pun. "I am a man who sets some store by himself, you may take it from me. And I see no point in being wished a good-evening unless it is done courteously and in all seriousness. For anything else there is no occasion. When a man wishes me a good-evening he wishes himself one, for the audience will have one only if I do. So this lady-killer of Torre di Venere" (another thrust) "did well to tes-tify that I have one tonight and that I can dispense with any wishes of his in the matter. I can boast of having good evenings almost without exception. One not so good does come my way now and again, but very seldom. My calling is hard and my health not of the best. I have a little physical defect which prevented me from doing my bit in the war for the greater glory of the Fatherland. It is perforce with my mental and spiritual parts that I conquer life—which after all only means conquering oneself. And I flatter myself that my achievements have aroused interest and respect among the educated public. The leading newspapers have lauded me, the *Corriere della*

---

1. "This would-be master of tongues."

Sera[2] did me the courtesy of calling me a phenomenon, and in Rome the brother of the *Duce* honoured me by his presence at one of my evenings. I should not have thought that in a relatively less important place" (laughter here, at the expense of poor little Torre) "I should have to give up the small personal habits which brilliant and elevated audiences had been ready to overlook. Nor did I think I had to stand being heckled by a person who seems to have been rather spoilt by the favours of the fair sex." All this of course at the expense of the youth whom Cipolla never tired of presenting in the guise of *donnaiuolo*[3] and rustic Don Juan. His persistent thin-skinnedness and animosity were in striking contrast to the self-confidence and the worldly success he boasted of. One might have assumed that the *giovanotto* was merely the chosen butt of Cipolla's customary professional sallies, had not the very pointed witticisms betrayed a genuine antagonism. No one looking at the physical parts of the two men need have been at a loss for the explanation, even if the deformed man had not constantly played on the other's supposed success with the fair sex. "Well," Cipolla went on, "before beginning our entertainment this evening, perhaps you will permit me to make myself comfortable."

And he went towards the hat-stand to take off his things.

"*Parla benissimo*,"[4] asserted somebody in our neighbourhood. So far, the man had done nothing; but what he had said was accepted as an achievement, by means of that he had made an impression. Among southern peoples speech is a constituent part of the pleasure of living, it enjoys far livelier social esteem than in the north. That national cement, the mother tongue, is paid symbolic honours down here, and there is something blithely symbolical in the pleasure people take in their respect for its forms and phonetics. They enjoy speaking, they enjoy listening; and they listen with discrimination. For the way a man speaks serves as a measure of his personal rank; carelessness and clumsiness are greeted with scorn, elegance and mastery are rewarded with social éclat. Wherefore the small man too, where it is a question of getting his effect, chooses his phrase nicely and turns it with care. On this count, then, at least, Cipolla had won his audience; though he by no means belonged to the class of men which the Italian, in a singular mixture of moral and æsthetic judgments, labels "*simpatico*."[5]

After removing his hat, scarf, and mantle he came to the front of the stage, settling his coat, pulling down his cuffs with their large cuff-buttons, adjusting his absurd sash. He had very ugly hair; the top of his head, that is, was almost bald, while a narrow, black-

2. Major evening newspaper in Rome; *Duce* [Leader] refers to Benito Mussolini, the head of the Italian government at the time.   3. "Lady-killer."   4. "He speaks well."   5. "Sympathetic": pleasant to be with.

varnished frizz of curls ran from front to back as though stuck on;
the side hair, likewise blackened, was brushed forward to the corners
of the eyes—it was, in short, the hairdressing of an old-fashioned
circus-director, fantastic, but entirely suited to his outmoded personal type and worn with so much assurance as to take the edge off
the public's sense of humour. The little physical defect of which he
had warned us was now all too visible, though the nature of it was
even now not very clear; the chest was too high, as is usual in such
cases, but the corresponding malformation of the back did not sit
between the shoulders, it took the form of a sort of hips or buttocks
hump, which did not indeed hinder his movements but gave him a
grotesque and dipping stride at every step he took. However, by mentioning his deformity beforehand he had broken the shock of it, and
a delicate propriety of feeling appeared to reign throughout the hall.

"At your service," said Cipolla. "With your kind permission, we
will begin the evening with some arithmetical tests."

Arithmetic? That did not sound much like sleight-of-hand. We
began to have our suspicions that the man was sailing under a false
flag, only we did not yet know which was the right one. I felt sorry
on the children's account; but for the moment they were content
simply to be there.

The numerical test which Cipolla now introduced was as simple
as it was baffling. He began by fastening a piece of paper to the upper
right-hand corner of the blackboard; then lifting it up, he wrote
something underneath. He talked all the while, relieving the dryness
of his offering by a constant flow of words, and showed himself a
practised speaker, never at a loss for conversational turns of phrase.
It was in keeping with the nature of his performance, and at the same
time vastly entertained the children, that he went on to eliminate
the gap between stage and audience, which had already been bridged
over by the curious skirmish with the fisher lad; he had representatives from the audience mount the stage, and himself descended the
wooden steps to seek personal contact with his public. And again,
with individuals, he fell into his former taunting tone. I do not know
how far that was a deliberate feature of his system; he preserved a
serious, even a peevish air, but his audience, at least the more popular section, seemed convinced that that was all part of the game.
So then, after he had written something and covered the writing by
the paper, he desired that two persons should come up on the platform and help to perform the calculations. They would not be difficult, even for people not clever at figures. As usual, nobody
volunteered, and Cipolla took care not to molest the more select
portion of his audience. He kept to the populace. Turning to two
sturdy young louts standing behind us, he beckoned them to the
front, encouraging and scolding by turns. They should not stand

there gaping, he said, unwilling to oblige the company. Actually he got them in motion; with clumsy tread they came down the middle aisle, climbed the steps, and stood in front of the blackboard, grinning sheepishly at their comrades' shouts and applause. Cipolla joked with them for a few minutes, praised their heroic firmness of limb and the size of their hands, so well calculated to do this service for the public. Then he handed one of them the chalk and told him to write down the numbers as they were called out. But now the creature declared that he could not write! *"Non so scrivere,"* said he in his gruff voice, and his companion added that neither did he.

God knows whether they told the truth or whether they wanted to make game of Cipolla. Anyhow, the latter was far from sharing the general merriment which their confession aroused. He was insulted and disgusted. He sat there on a straw-bottomed chair in the centre of the stage with his legs crossed, smoking a fresh cigarette out of his cheap packet; obviously it tasted the better for the cognac he had indulged in while the yokels were stumping up the steps. Again he inhaled the smoke and let it stream out between curling lips. Swinging his leg, with his gaze sternly averted from the two shamelessly chuckling creatures and from the audience as well, he stared into space as one who withdraws himself and his dignity from the contemplation of an utterly despicable phenomenon.

"Scandalous," said he, in a sort of icy snarl. "Go back to your places! In Italy everybody can write—in all her greatness there is no room for ignorance and unenlightenment. To accuse her of them, in the hearing of this international company, is a cheap joke, in which you yourselves cut a very poor figure and humiliate the government and the whole country as well. If it is true that Torre di Venere is indeed the last refuge of such ignorance, than I must blush to have visited the place—being, as I already was, aware of its inferiority to Rome in more than one respect—"

Here Cipolla was interrupted by the youth with the Nubian[6] coiffure and his jacket across his shoulder. His fighting spirit, as we now saw, had only abdicated temporarily, and he now flung himself into the breach in defence of his native heath. "That will do," said he loudly. "That's enough jokes about Torre. We all come from the place and we won't stand strangers making fun of it. These two chaps are our friends. Maybe they are no scholars, but even so they may be straighter than some folks in the room who are so free with their boasts about Rome, though they did not build it either."

That was capital. The young man had certainly cut his eye-teeth. And this sort of spectacle was good fun, even though it still further delayed the regular performance. It is always fascinating to listen to

6. African.

an altercation. Some people it simply amuses, they take a sort of kill-joy pleasure in not being principals. Others feel upset and uneasy, and my sympathies are with these latter, although on the present occasion I was under the impression that all this was part of the show—the analphabetic yokels no less than the *giovanotto* with the jacket. The children listened well pleased. They understood not at all, but the sound of the voices made them hold their breath. So this was a "magic evening"—at least it was the kind they have in Italy. They expressly found it "lovely." Cipolla had stood up and with two of his scooping strides was at the footlights.

"Well, well, see who's here!" said he with grim cordiality. "An old acquaintance! A young man with his heart at the end of his tongue" (he used the word *linguaccia*, which means a coated tongue, and gave rise to much hilarity). "That will do, my friends," he turned to the yokels. "I do not need you now, I have business with this deserving young man here, *con questo torregiano di Venere*, this tower of Venus, who no doubt expects the gratitude of the fair as a reward for his prowess—"

"*Ah, non scherziamo!*[7] We're talking earnest," cried out the youth. His eyes flashed, and he actually made as though to pull off his jacket and proceed to direct methods of settlement.

Cipolla did not take him too seriously. We had exchanged apprehensive glances; but he was dealing with a fellow-countryman and had his native soil beneath his feet. He kept quite cool and showed complete mastery of the situation. He looked at his audience, smiled, and made a sideways motion of the head towards the young cockerel as though calling the public to witness how the man's bumptiousness only served to betray the simplicity of his mind. And then, for the second time, something strange happened, which set Cipolla's calm superiority in an uncanny light, and in some mysterious and irritating way turned all the explosiveness latent in the air into matter for laughter.

Cipolla drew still nearer to the fellow, looking him in the eye with a peculiar gaze. He even came half-way down the steps that led into the auditorium on our left, so that he stood directly in front of the trouble-maker, on slightly higher ground. The riding-whip hung from his arm.

"My son, you do not feel much like joking," he said. "It is only too natural, for anyone can see that you are not feeling too well. Even your tongue, which leaves something to be desired on the score of cleanliness, indicates acute disorder of the gastric system. An evening entertainment is no place for people in your state; you yourself, I can tell, were of several minds whether you would not do better to

7. "We aren't joking!"

put on a flannel bandage and go to bed. It was not good judgment to drink so much of that very sour white wine this afternoon. Now you have such a colic you would like to double up with the pain. Go ahead, don't be embarrassed. There is a distinct relief that comes from bending over, in cases of intestinal cramp."

He spoke thus, word for word, with quiet impressiveness and a kind of stern sympathy, and his eyes, plunged the while deep in the young man's, seemed to grow very tired and at the same time burning above their enlarged tear-ducts—they were the strangest eyes, you could tell that not manly pride alone was preventing the young adversary from withdrawing his gaze. And presently, indeed, all trace of its former arrogance was gone from the bronzed young face. He looked open-mouthed at the Cavaliere and the open mouth was drawn in a rueful smile.

"Double over," repeated Cipolla. "What else can you do? With a colic like that you *must* bend. Surely you will not struggle against the performance of a perfectly natural action just because somebody suggests it to you?"

Slowly the youth lifted his forearms, folded and squeezed them across his body; it turned a little sideways, then bent, lower and lower, the feet shifted, the knees turned inward, until he had become a picture of writhing pain, until he all but grovelled upon the ground. Cipolla let him stand for some seconds thus, then made a short cut through the air with his whip and went with his scooping stride back to the little table, where he poured himself out a cognac.

"*Il boit beaucoup*,"[8] asserted a lady behind us. Was that the only thing that struck her? We could not tell how far the audience grasped the situation. The fellow was standing upright again, with a sheepish grin—he looked as though he scarcely knew how it had all happened. The scene had been followed with tense interest and applauded at the end; there were shouts of "*Bravo, Cipolla!*" and "*Bravo, giovanotto!*" Apparently the issue of the duel was not looked upon as a personal defeat for the young man. Rather the audience encouraged him as one does an actor who succeeds in an unsympathetic rôle. Certainly his way of screwing himself up with cramp had been highly picturesque, its appeal was directly calculated to impress the gallery—in short, a fine dramatic performance. But I am not sure how far the audience were moved by that natural tactfulness in which the south excels, or how far it penetrated into the nature of what was going on.

The Cavaliere, refreshed, had lighted another cigarette. The numerical tests might now proceed. A young man was easily found in the back row who was willing to write down on the blackboard the

8. "He drinks a lot" (French).

numbers as they were dictated to him. Him too we knew; the whole
entertainment had taken on an intimate character through our
acquaintance with so many of the actors. This was the man who
worked at the greengrocer's in the main street; he had served us several times, with neatness and dispatch. He wielded the chalk with
clerkly confidence, while Cipolla descended to our level and walked
with his deformed gait through the audience, collecting numbers as
they were given, in two, three, and four places, and calling them
out to the grocer's assistant, who wrote them down in a column. In
all this, everything on both sides was calculated to amuse, with its
jokes and its oratorical asides. The artist could not fail to hit on
foreigners, who were not ready with their figures, and with them he
was elaborately patient and chivalrous, to the great amusement of
the natives, whom he reduced to confusion in their turn, by making
them translate numbers that were given in English or French. Some
people gave dates concerned with great events in Italian history. Cipolla
took them up at once and made patriotic comments. Somebody
shouted "Number one!" The Cavaliere, incensed at this as at every
attempt to make game of him, retorted over his shoulder that he
could not take less than two-place figures. Whereupon another joker
cried out "Number two!" and was greeted with the applause and
laughter which every reference to natural functions is sure to win
among southerners.

When fifteen numbers stood in a long straggling row on the board,
Cipolla called for a general adding-match. Ready reckoners might
add in their heads, but pencil and paper were not forbidden. Cipolla,
while the work went on, sat on his chair near the blackboard, smoked
and grimaced, with the complacent, pompous air cripples so often
have. The five-place addition was soon done. Somebody announced
the answer, somebody else confirmed it, a third had arrived at a
slightly different result, but the fourth agreed with the first and second. Cipolla got up, tapped some ash from his coat, and lifted the
paper at the upper right-hand corner of the board to display the writing. The correct answer, a sum close on a million, stood there; he
had written it down beforehand.

Astonishment, and loud applause. The children were overwhelmed. How had he done that, they wanted to know. We told
them it was a trick, not easily explainable offhand. In short, the man
was a conjuror. This was what a sleight-of-hand evening was like, so
now they knew. First the fisherman had a cramp, and then the right
answer was written down beforehand—it was all simply glorious, and
we saw with dismay that despite the hot eyes and the hand of the
clock at almost half past ten, it would be very hard to get them away.
There would be tears. And yet it was plain that this magician did not
"magick"—at least not in the accepted sense, of manual dexterity—

and that the entertainment was not at all suitable for children. Again, I do not know, either, what the audience really thought. Obviously there was grave doubt whether its answers had been given of "free choice"; here and there an individual might have answered of his own motion, but on the whole Cipolla certainly selected his people and thus kept the whole procedure in his own hands and directed it towards the given result. Even so, one had to admire the quickness of his calculations, however much one felt disinclined to admire anything else about the performance. Then his patriotism, his irritable sense of dignity—the Cavaliere's own countrymen might feel in their element with all that and continue in a laughing mood; but the combination certainly gave us outsiders food for thought.

Cipolla himself saw to it—though without giving them a name— that the nature of his powers should be clear beyond a doubt to even the least-instructed person. He alluded to them, of course, in his talk—and he talked without stopping—but only in vague, boastful, self-advertising phrases. He went on awhile with experiments on the same lines as the first, merely making them more complicated by introducing operations in multiplying, subtracting, and dividing; then he simplified them to the last degree in order to bring out the method. He simply had numbers "guessed" which were previously written under the paper; and the guess was nearly always right. One guesser admitted that he had had in mind to give a certain number, when Cipolla's whip went whistling through the air, and a quite different one slipped out, which proved to be the "right" one. Cipolla's shoulders shook. He pretended admiration for the powers of the people he questioned. But in all his compliments there was something fleering and derogatory; the victims could scarcely have relished them much, although they smiled, and although they might easily have set down some part of the applause to their own credit. Moreover, I had not the impression that the artist was popular with his public. A certain ill will and reluctance were in the air, but courtesy kept such feelings in check, as did Cipolla's competency and his stern self-confidence. Even the riding-whip, I think, did much to keep rebellion from becoming overt.

From tricks with numbers he passed to tricks with cards. There were two packs, which he drew out of his pockets, and so much I still remember, that the basis of the tricks he played with them was as follows: from the first pack he drew three cards and thrust them without looking at them inside his coat. Another person then drew three out of the second pack, and these turned out to be the same as the first three—not invariably all the three, for it did happen that only two were the same. But in the majority of cases Cipolla triumphed, showing his three cards with a little bow in acknowledgment of the applause with which his audience conceded his possession of strange powers—strange whether for good or evil. A young man in the front row, to our right, an Italian, with proud, finely chiselled features, rose up and said that he intended to assert his own will in his choice and consciously to resist any influence, of whatever sort. Under these circumstances, what did Cipolla think would be the result? "You will," answered the Cavaliere, "make my task somewhat more difficult thereby. As for the result, your resistance will not alter it in the least. Freedom exists, and also the will exists; but freedom of the will does not exist, for a will that aims at its own freedom aims at the unknown. You are free to draw or not to draw. But if you draw, you will draw the right cards—the more certainly, the more wilfully obstinate your behaviour."

One must admit that he could not have chosen his words better, to trouble the waters and confuse the mind. The refractory youth hesitated before drawing. Then he pulled out a card and at once demanded to see if it was among the chosen three. "But why?" queried Cipolla. "Why do things by halves?" Then, as the other defiantly insisted, "E servito,"[9] said the juggler, with a gesture of exaggerated servility; and held out the three cards fanwise, without looking at them himself. The left-hand card was the one drawn.

Amid general applause, the apostle of freedom sat down. How far Cipolla employed small tricks and manual dexterity to help out his natural talents, the deuce only knew. But even without them the result would have been the same: the curiosity of the entire audience was unbounded and universal, everybody both enjoyed the amazing character of the entertainment and unanimously conceded the professional skill of the performer. "Lavora bene,"[1] we heard, here and there in our neighbourhood; it signified the triumph of objective judgment over antipathy and repressed resentment.

After his last, incomplete, yet so much the more telling success, Cipolla had at once fortified himself with another cognac. Truly he did "drink a lot," and the fact made a bad impression. But obviously he needed the liquor and the cigarettes for the replenishment of his energy, upon which, as he himself said, heavy demands were made in all directions. Certainly in the intervals he looked very ill, exhausted and hollow-eyed. Then the little glassful would redress the balance, and the flow of lively, self-confident chatter run on, while the smoke he inhaled gushed out grey from his lungs. I clearly recall that he passed from the card-tricks to parlour games—the kind based on certain powers which in human nature are higher or else lower than human reason: on intuition and "magnetic" transmission; in short, upon a low type of manifestation. What I do not remember is the precise order things came in. And I will not bore you with a descrip-

9. "At your service."   1. "He does a good job."

tion of these experiments; everybody knows them, everybody has at one time or another taken part in this finding of hidden articles, this blind carrying out of a series of acts, directed by a force that proceeds from organism to organism by unexplored paths. Everybody has had his little glimpse into the equivocal, impure, inexplicable nature of the occult, has been conscious of both curiosity and contempt, has shaken his head over the human tendency of those who deal in it to help themselves out with humbuggery, though, after all, the hum-buggery is no disproof whatever of the genuineness of the other ele-ments in the dubious amalgam. I can only say here that each single circumstance gains in weight and the whole greatly in impressiveness when it is a man like Cipolla who is the chief actor and guiding spirit in the sinister business. He sat smoking at the rear of the stage, his back to the audience while they conferred. The object passed from hand to hand which it was his task to find, with which he was to perform some action agreed upon beforehand. Then he would start to move zigzag through the hall, with his head thrown back and one hand out-stretched, the other clasped in that of a guide who was in on the secret but enjoined to keep himself perfectly passive, with his thoughts directed upon the agreed goal. Cipolla moved with the bearing typical in these experiments: now groping upon a false start, now with a quick forward thrust, now pausing as though to listen and by sudden inspiration correcting his course. The rôles seemed reversed, the stream of influence was moving in the contrary direc-tion, as the artist himself pointed out, in his ceaseless flow of dis-course. The suffering, receptive, performing part was now his, the will he had before imposed on others was shut out, he acted in obe-dience to a voiceless common will which was in the air. But he made it perfectly clear that it all came to the same thing. The capacity for self-surrender, he said, for becoming a tool, for the most uncondi-tional and utter self-abnegation, was but the reverse side of that other power to will and to command. Commanding and obeying formed together one single principle, one indissoluble unity; he who knew how to obey knew also how to command, and conversely; the one idea was comprehended in the other, as people and leader were com-prehended in one another. But that which was *done*, the highly exacting and exhausting performance, was in every case his, the leader's and mover's, in whom the will became obedience, the obedience will, whose person was the cradle and womb of both, and who thus suffered enormous hardship. Repeatedly he emphasized the fact that his lot was a hard one—presumably to account for his need of stim-ulant and his frequent recourse to the little glass.

Thus he groped his way forward, like a blind seer, led and sus-tained by the mysterious common will. He drew a pin set with a stone out of its hiding-place in an English-woman's shoe, carried it,

halting and pressing on by turns, to another lady—Signora Angiolieri—and handed it to her on bended knee, with the words it had
been agreed he was to utter. "I present you with this in token of my
respect," was the sentence. Their sense was obvious, but the words
themselves not easy to hit upon, for the reason that they had been
agreed on in French; the language complication seemed to us a little
malicious, implying as it did a conflict between the audience's natural interest in the success of the miracle, and their desire to witness
the humiliation of this presumptuous man. It was a strange sight:
Cipolla on his knees before the signora, wrestling, amid efforts at
speech, after knowledge of the preordained words. "I must say something," he said, "and I feel clearly what it is I must say. But I also
feel that if it passed my lips it would be wrong. Be careful not to help
me unintentionally!" he cried out, though very likely that was precisely what he was hoping for. "*Pensez très fort,*"[2] he cried all at
once, in bad French, and then burst out with the required words—
in Italian, indeed, but with the final substantive pronounced in the
sister tongue, in which he was probably far from fluent: he said *vén-
ération* instead of *venerazione*, with an impossible nasal. And this
partial success, after the complete success before it, the finding of
the pin, the presentation of it on his knees to the right person—was
almost more impressive than if he had got the sentence exactly right,
and evoked bursts of admiring applause.

Cipolla got up from his knees and wiped the perspiration from his
brow. You understand that this experiment with the pin was a single
case, which I describe because it sticks in my memory. But he changed
his method several times and improvised a number of variations suggested by his contact with his audience; a good deal of time thus
went by. He seemed to get particular inspiration from the person of
our landlady; she drew him on to the most extraordinary displays of
clairvoyance. "It does not escape me, madame," he said to her, "that
there is something unusual about you, some special and honourable
distinction. He who has eyes to see descries about your lovely brow
an aureola—if I mistake not, it once was stronger than now—a slowly
paling radiance . . . hush, not a word! Don't help me. Beside you
sits your husband—yes?" He turned towards the silent Signor
Angiolieri. "You are the husband of this lady, and your happiness is
complete. But in the midst of this happiness memories rise . . . the
past, signora, so it seems to me, plays an important part in your
present. You knew a king . . . has not a king crossed your path in
bygone days?"

"No," breathed the dispenser of our midday soup, her golden-
brown eyes gleaming in the noble pallor of her face.

2. "Think very hard" (French).

"No? No, not a king; I meant that generally, I did not mean literally a king. Not a king, not a prince, and a prince after all, a king
of a loftier realm; it was a great artist, at whose side you once—you
would contradict me, and yet I am not wholly wrong. Well, then! It
was a woman, a great, a world-renowned woman artist, whose
friendship you enjoyed in your tender years, whose sacred memory
overshadows and transfigures your whole existence. Her name? Need
I utter it, whose fame has long been bound up with the Fatherland's,
immortal as its own? Eleonora Duse," he finished, softly and with
much solemnity.

The little woman bowed her head, overcome. The applause was
like a patriotic demonstration. Nearly everyone there knew about
Signora Angiolieri's wonderful past; they were all able to confirm the
Cavaliere's intuition—not least the present guests of Casa Eleonora.
But we wondered how much of the truth he had learned as the result
of professional inquiries made on his arrival. Yet I see no reason at
all to cast doubt, on rational grounds, upon powers which, before
our very eyes, became fatal to their possessor.

At this point there was an intermission. Our lord and master withdrew. Now I confess that almost ever since the beginning of my tale
I have looked forward with dread to this moment in it. The thoughts
of men are mostly not hard to read; in this case they are very easy.
You are sure to ask why we did not choose this moment to go away—
and I must continue to owe you an answer. I do not know why. I
cannot defend myself. By this time it was certainly eleven, probably
later. The children were asleep. The last series of tests had been too
long, nature had had her way. They were sleeping in our laps, the
little one on mine, the boy on his mother's. That was, in a way, a
consolation; but at the same time it was also ground for compassion
and a clear leading to take them home to bed. And I give you my
word that we wanted to obey this touching admonition, we seriously
wanted to. We roused the poor things and told them it was now high
time to go. But they were no sooner conscious than they began to
resist and implore—you know how horrified children are at the thought
of leaving before the end of a thing. No cajoling has any effect, you
have to use force. It was so lovely, they wailed. How did we know
what was coming next? Surely we could not leave until after the
intermission; they liked a little nap now and again—only not go home,
only not go to bed, while the beautiful evening was still going on!

We yielded, but only for the moment, of course—so far as we
knew—only for a little while, just a few minutes longer. I cannot
excuse our staying, scarcely can I even understand it. Did we think,
having once said A, we had to say B—having once brought the children hither we had to let them stay? No, it is not good enough. Were
we ourselves so highly entertained? Yes, and no. Our feelings for

Cavaliere Cipolla were of a very mixed kind, but so were the feelings of the whole audience, if I mistake not, and nobody left. Were we under the sway of a fascination which emanated from this man who took so strange a way to earn his bread; a fascination which he gave out independently of the programme and even between the tricks and which paralysed our resolve? Again, sheer curiosity may account for something. One was curious to know how such an evening turned out; Cipolla in his remarks having all along hinted that he had tricks in his bag stranger than any he had yet produced.

But all that is not it—or at least it is not all of it. More correct it would be to answer the first question with another. Why had we not left Torre di Venere itself before now? To me the two questions are one and the same, and in order to get out of the impasse I might simply say that I had answered it already. For, as things had been in Torre in general: queer, uncomfortable, troublesome, tense, oppressive, so precisely they were here in this hall tonight. Yes, more than precisely. For it seemed to be the fountainhead of all the uncanniness and all the strained feelings which had oppressed the atmosphere of our holiday. This man whose return to the stage we were awaiting was the personification of all that; and, as we had not gone away in general, so to speak, it would have been inconsistent to do it in the particular case. You may call this an explanation, you may call it inertia, as you see fit. Any argument more to the purpose I simply do not know how to adduce.

Well, there was an interval of ten minutes, which grew into nearly twenty. The children remained awake. They were enchanted by our compliance, and filled the break to their own satisfaction by renewing relations with the popular sphere, with Antonio, Guiscardo, and the canoe man. They put their hands to their mouths and called messages across, appealing to us for the Italian words. "Hope you have a good catch tomorrow, a whole netful!" They called to Mario, Esquisito Mario: "*Mario, una ciocolata e biscotti!*" And this time he heeded and answered with a smile: "*Subito, signorini!*"[3] Later we had reason to recall this kindly, if rather absent and pensive smile.

Thus the interval passed, the gong sounded. The audience, which had scattered in conversation, took their places again, the children sat up straight in their chairs with their hands in their laps. The curtain had not been dropped. Cipolla came forward again, with his dipping stride, and began to introduce the second half of the programme with a lecture.

Let me state once for all that this self-confident cripple was the most powerful hypnotist I have ever seen in my life. It was pretty plain now that he threw dust in the public eye and advertised himself

---

3. "Mario, a hot chocolate and cookies!" "Right away, young sirs."

as a prestidigitator on account of police regulations which would have prevented him from making his living by the exercise of his powers. Perhaps this eye-wash is the usual thing in Italy; it may be permitted or even connived at by the authorities. Certainly the man had from the beginning made little concealment of the actual nature of his operations; and this second half of the programme was quite frankly and exclusively devoted to one sort of experiment. While he still practised some rhetorical circumlocutions, the tests themselves were one long series of attacks upon the will-power, the loss or compulsion of volition. Comic, exciting, amazing by turns, by midnight they were still in full swing; we ran the gamut of all the phenomena this natural-unnatural field has to show, from the unimpressive at one end of the scale to the monstrous at the other. The audience laughed and applauded as they followed the grotesque details; shook their heads, clapped their knees, fell very frankly under the spell of this stern, self-assured personality. At the same time I saw signs that they were not quite complacent, not quite unconscious of the peculiar ignominy which lay, for the individual and for the general, in Cipolla's triumphs.

Two main features were constant in all the experiments: the liquor glass and the claw-handled riding-whip. The first was always invoked to add fuel to his demoniac fires; without it, apparently, they might have burned out. On this score we might even have felt pity for the man; but the whistle of his scourge, the insulting symbol of his domination, before which we all cowered, drowned out every sensation save a dazed and outbraved submission to his power. Did he then lay claim to our sympathy to boot? I was struck by a remark he made—it suggested no less. At the climax of his experiments, by stroking and breathing upon a certain young man who had offered himself as a subject and already proved himself a particularly susceptible one, he had not only put him into the condition known as deep trance and extended his insensible body by neck and feet across the backs of two chairs, but had actually sat down on the rigid form as on a bench, without making it yield. The sight of this unholy figure in a frock-coat squatted on the stiff body was horrible and incredible; the audience, convinced that the victim of this scientific diversion must be suffering, expressed its sympathy: "Ah, *poveretto!*" Poor soul, poor soul! "*Poor soul!*" Cipolla mocked them, with some bitterness. "Ladies and gentlemen, you are barking up the wrong tree. *Sono io il poveretto.*[4] I am the person who is suffering, I am the one to be pitied." We pocketed the information. Very good. Maybe the experiment was at his expense, maybe it was he who had suffered the cramp when the *giovanotto* over there had made the faces. But appearances

4. "*I am the poor soul.*"

were all against it; and one does not feel like saying *poveretto* to a man who is suffering to bring about the humiliation of others.

I have got ahead of my story and lost sight of the sequence of events. To this day my mind is full of the Cavaliere's feats of endurance; only I do not recall them in their order—which does not matter. So much I do know: that the longer and more circumstantial tests, which got the most applause, impressed me less than some of the small ones which passed quickly over. I remember the young man whose body Cipolla converted into a board, only because of the accompanying remarks which I have quoted. An elderly lady in a cane-seated chair was lulled by Cipolla in the delusion that she was on a voyage to India and gave a voluble account of her adventures by land and sea. But I found this phenomenon less impressive than one which followed immediately after the intermission. A tall, well-built, soldierly man was unable to lift his arm, after the hunchback had told him that he could not and given a cut through the air with his whip. I can still see the face of that stately, mustachioed colonel smiling and clenching his teeth as he struggled to regain his lost freedom of action. A staggering performance! He seemed to be exerting his will, and in vain; the trouble, however, was probably simply that he could not will. There was involved here that recoil of the will upon itself which paralyses choice—as our tyrant had previously explained to the Roman gentleman.

Still less can I forget the touching scene, at once comic and horrible, with Signora Angiolieri. The Cavaliere, probably in his first bold survey of the room, had spied out her ethereal lack of resistance to his power. For actually he bewitched her, literally drew her out of her seat, out of her row, and away with him whither he willed. And in order to enhance his effect, he bade Signor Angiolieri call upon his wife by her name, to throw, as it were, all the weight of his existence and his rights in her into the scale, to rouse by the voice of her husband everything in his spouse's soul which could shield her virtue against the evil assaults of magic. And how vain it all was! Cipolla was standing at some distance from the couple, when he made a single cut with his whip through the air. It caused our landlady to shudder violently and turn her face towards him. "Sofronia!" cried Signor Angiolieri—we had not known that Signora Angiolieri's name was Sofronia. And he did well to call, everybody saw that there was no time to lose. His wife kept her face turned in the direction of the diabolical Cavaliere, who with his ten long yellow fingers was making passes at his victim, moving backwards as he did so, step by step. Then Signora Angiolieri, her pale face gleaming, rose up from her seat, turned right round, and began to glide after him. Fatal and forbidding sight! Her face as though moonstruck, stiff-armed, her lovely hands lifted a little at the wrists, the feet as it were together, she seemed to float slowly out of her row and after the tempter. "Call her, sir, keep on calling," prompted the redoubtable man. And Signor Angiolieri, in a weak voice, called: "Sofronia!" Ah, again and again he called; as his wife went further off he even curved one hand round his lips and beckoned with the other as he called. But the poor voice of love and duty echoed unheard, in vain, behind the lost one's back; the signora swayed along, moonstruck, deaf, enslaved; she glided into the middle aisle and down it towards the fingering hunchback, towards the door. We were driven to the conviction, that she would have followed her master, had he so willed it, to the ends of the earth.

"*Accidente!*"[5] cried out Signor Angiolieri, in genuine affright, springing up as the exit was reached. But at the same moment the Cavaliere put aside, as it were, the triumphal crown and broke off. "Enough, signora, I thank you," he said, and offered his arm to lead her back to her husband. "Signor," he greeted the latter, "here is your wife. Unharmed, with my compliments, I give her into your hands. Cherish with all the strength of your manhood a treasure which is so wholly yours, and let your zeal be quickened by knowing that there are powers stronger than reason or virtue, and not always so magnanimously ready to relinquish their prey!"

Poor Signor Angiolieri, so quiet, so bald! He did not look as though he would know how to defend his happiness, even against powers much less demoniac than these which were now adding mockery to frightfulness. Solemnly and pompously the Cavaliere retired to the stage, amid applause to which his eloquence gave double strength. It was this particular episode, I feel sure, that set the seal upon his ascendancy. For now he made them dance, yes, literally; and the dancing lent a dissolute, abandoned, topsy-turvy air to the scene, a drunken abdication of the critical spirit which had so long resisted the spell of this man. Yes, he had had to fight to get the upper hand—for instance against the animosity of the young Roman gentleman, whose rebellious spirit threatened to serve others as a rallying-point. But it was precisely upon the importance of example that the Cavaliere was so strong. He had the wit to make his attack at the weakest point and to choose as his first victim that feeble, ecstatic youth whom he had previously made into a board. The master had but to look at him, when this young man would fling himself back as though struck by lightning, place his hands rigidly at his sides, and fall into a state of military somnambulism, in which it was plain to any eye that he was open to the most absurd suggestion that might be made to him. He seemed quite content in his abject state, quite pleased to be relieved of the burden of voluntary choice. Again and

5. "Blast it!"

again he offered himself as a subject and gloried in the model facility
he had in losing consciousness. So now he mounted the platform,
and a single cut of the whip was enough to make him dance to the
Cavaliere's orders, in a kind of complacent ecstasy, eyes closed, head
nodding, lank limbs flying in all directions.

It looked unmistakably like enjoyment, and other recruits were
not long in coming forward: two other young men, one humbly and
one well dressed, were soon jigging alongside the first. But now the
gentleman from Rome bobbed up again, asking defiantly if the Cavaliere would engage to make him dance too, even against his will.

"Even against your will," answered Cipolla, in unforgettable accents.
That frightful "*anche se non vuole*"[6] still rings in my ears. The struggle began. After Cipolla had taken another little glass and lighted a
fresh cigarette he stationed the Roman at a point in the middle aisle
and himself took up a position some distance behind, making his
whip whistle through the air as he gave the order: "*Balla!*" His opponent did not stir. "*Balla!*" repeated the Cavaliere incisively, and
snapped his whip. You saw the young man move his neck round in
his collar; at the same time one hand lifted slightly at the wrist, one
ankle turned outward. But that was all, for the time at least; merely
a tendency to twitch, now sternly repressed, now seeming about to
get the upper hand. It escaped nobody that here a heroic obstinacy,
a fixed resolve to resist, must needs be conquered; we were beholding
a gallant effort to strike out and save the honour of the human race.
He twitched but danced not; and the struggle was so prolonged that
the Cavaliere had to divide his attention between it and the stage,
turning now and then to make his riding-whip whistle in the direction of the dancers, as it were to keep them in leash. At the same
time he advised the audience that no fatigue was involved in such
activities, however long they went on, since it was not the automa-
tons up there who danced, but himself. Then once more his eye
would bore itself into the back of the Roman's neck and lay siege to
the strength of purpose which defied him.

One saw it waver, that strength of purpose, beneath the repeated
summons and whip-crackings. Saw with an objective interest which
yet was not quite free from traces of sympathetic emotion—from
pity, even from a cruel kind of pleasure. If I understand what was
going on, it was the negative character of the young man's fighting
position which was his undoing. It is likely that not willing is not a
practicable state of mind; *not* to want to do something may be in the
long run a mental content impossible to subsist on. Between not
willing a certain thing and not willing at all—in other words, yielding to another person's will—there may lie too small a space for the

6. "Even if you don't want to." *Balla!*: "Dance!"

idea of freedom to squeeze into. Again, there were the Cavaliere's persuasive words, woven in among the whip-crackings and commands, as he mingled effects that were his own secret with others of a bewilderingly psychological kind. "*Balla!*" said he. "Who wants to torture himself like that? Is forcing yourself your idea of freedom? *Una ballatina!* Why, your arms and legs are aching for it. What a relief to give way to them—there, you are dancing already! That is no struggle any more, it is a pleasure!" And so it was. The jerking and twitching of the refractory youth's limbs had at last got the upper hand; he lifted his arms, then his knees, his joints quite suddenly relaxed, he flung his legs and danced, and amid bursts of applause the Cavaliere led him to join the row of puppets on the stage. Up there we could see his face as he "enjoyed" himself; it was clothed in a broad grin and the eyes were half-shut. In a way, it was consoling to see that he was having a better time than he had had in the hour of his pride.

His "fall" was, I may say, an epoch. The ice was completely broken, Cipolla's triumph had reached its height. The Circe's wand,[7] that whistling leather whip with the claw handle, held absolute sway. At one time—it must have been well after midnight—not only were there eight or ten persons dancing on the little stage, but in the hall below a varied animation reigned, and a long-toothed Anglo-Saxoness in a pince-nez left her seat of her own motion to perform a tarantella[8] in the centre aisle. Cipolla was lounging in a cane-seated chair at the left of the stage, gulping down the smoke of a cigarette and breathing it impudently out through his bad teeth. He tapped his foot and shrugged his shoulders, looking down upon the abandoned scene in the hall; now and then he snapped his whip backwards at a laggard upon the stage. The children were awake at the moment. With shame I speak of them. For it was not good to be here, least of all for them; that we had not taken them away can only be explained by saying that we had caught the general devil-may-careness of the hour. By that time it was all one. Anyhow, thank goodness, they lacked understanding for the disreputable side of the entertainment, and in their innocence were perpetually charmed by the unheard-of indulgence which permitted them to be present at such a thing as a magician's "evening." Whole quarter-hours at a time they drowsed on our laps, waking refreshed and rosy-cheeked, with sleep-drunken eyes, to laugh to bursting at the leaps and jumps the magician made those people up there make. They had not thought it would be so jolly; they joined with their clumsy little hands in every round of applause. And jumped for joy upon their chairs, as

7. In Homer's *Odyssey* (Book X) the goddess Circe changed men into animals with a stroke of her wand. 8. A lively Southern Italian dance. *Pince-nez:* Eyeglasses clipped to the bridge of the nose (without earpieces).

was their wont, when Cipolla beckoned to their friend Mario from the Esquisito, beckoned to him just like a picture in a book, holding his hand in front of his nose and bending and straightening the forefinger by turns.

Mario obeyed. I can see him now going up the stairs to Cipolla, who continued to beckon him, in that droll, picture-book sort of way. He hesitated for a moment at first; that, too, I recall quite clearly. During the whole evening he had lounged against a wooden pillar at the side entrance, with his arms folded, or else with his hands thrust into his jacket pockets. He was on our left, near the youth with the militant hair, and had followed the performance attentively, so far as we had seen, if with no particular animation and God knows how much comprehension. He could not much relish being summoned thus, at the end of the evening. But it was only too easy to see why he obeyed. After all, obedience was his calling in life; and then, how should a simple lad like him find it within his human capacity to refuse compliance to a man so throned and crowned as Cipolla at that hour? Willy-nilly he left his column and with a word of thanks to those making way for him he mounted the steps with a doubtful smile on his full lips.

Picture a thickset youth of twenty years, with clipt hair, a low forehead, and heavy-lidded eyes of an indefinite grey, shot with green and yellow. These things I knew from having spoken with him, as we often had. There was a saddle of freckles on the flat nose, the whole upper half of the face retreated behind the lower, and that again was dominated by thick lips that parted to show the salivated teeth. These thick lips and the veiled look of the eyes lent the whole face a primitive melancholy—it was that which had drawn us to him from the first. In it was not the faintest trace of brutality—indeed, his hands would have given the lie to such an idea, being unusually slender and delicate even for a southerner. They were hands by which one liked being served.

We knew him humanly without knowing him personally, if I may make that distinction. We saw him nearly every day, and felt a certain kindness for his dreamy ways, which might at times be actual inattentiveness, suddenly transformed into a redeeming zeal to serve. His mien was serious, only the children could bring a smile to his face. It was not sulky, but uningratiating, without intentional effort to please—or, rather, it seemed to give up being pleasant in the conviction that it could not succeed. We should have remembered Mario in any case, as one of those homely recollections of travel which often stick in the mind better than more important ones. But of his circumstances we knew no more than that his father was a petty clerk in the Municipio and his mother took in washing.

His white waiter's-coat became him better than the faded striped suit he wore, with a gay coloured scarf instead of a collar, the ends tucked into his jacket. He neared Cipolla, who however did not leave off that motion of his finger before his nose, so that Mario had to come still closer, right up to the chair-seat and the master's legs. Whereupon the latter spread out his elbows and seized the lad, turning him so that we had a view of his face. Then gazed him briskly up and down, with a careless, commanding eye.

"Well, *ragazzo mio*,[9] how comes it we make acquaintance so late in the day? But believe me, I made yours long ago. Yes, yes, I've had you in my eye this long while and known what good stuff you were made of. How could I go and forget you again? Well, I've had a good deal to think about. . . . Now tell me, what is your name? The first name, that's all I want."

"My name is Mario," the young man answered, in a low voice.

"Ah, Mario. Very good. Yes, yes, there is such a name, quite a common name, a classic name too, one of those which preserve the heroic traditions of the Fatherland. *Bravo! Salve!*" And he flung up his arm slantingly above his crooked shoulder, palm outward, in the Roman salute. He may have been slightly tipsy by now, and no wonder; but he spoke as before, clearly, fluently, and with emphasis. Though about this time there had crept into his voice a gross, autocratic note, and a kind of arrogance was in his sprawl.

"Well, now, Mario *mio*," he went on, "it's a good thing you came this evening, and that's a pretty scarf you've got on; it is becoming to your style of beauty. It must stand you in good stead with the girls, the pretty pretty girls of Torre—"

From the row of youths, close by the place where Mario had been standing, sounded a laugh. It came from the youth with the militant hair. He stood there, his jacket over his shoulder, and laughed outright, rudely and scornfully.

Mario gave a start. I think it was a shrug, but he may have started and then hastened to cover the movement by shrugging his shoulders, as much as to say that the neckerchief and the fair sex were matters of equal indifference to him.

The Cavaliere gave a downward glance.

"We needn't trouble about him," he said. "He is jealous, because your scarf is so popular with the girls, maybe partly because you and I are so friendly up here. Perhaps he'd like me to put him in mind of his colic—I could do it free of charge. Tell me, Mario. You've come here this evening for a bit of fun—and in the daytime you work in an iron-monger's shop?"

"In a café," corrected the youth.

"Oh, in a café. That's where Cipolla nearly came a cropper! What

9. "My boy."

you are is a cup-bearer, a Ganymede[1]—I like that, it is another classical allusion—*Salvietta!*" Again the Cavaliere saluted, to the huge
gratification of his audience.

Mario smiled too. "But before that," he interpolated, in the interest of accuracy, "I worked for a while in a shop in Portoclemente."
He seemed visited by a natural desire to assist the prophecy by dredg-
ing out its essential features.

"There, didn't I say so? In an ironmonger's shop?"

"They kept combs and brushes," Mario got round it.

"Didn't I say that you were not always a Ganymede? Not always
at the sign of the serviette? Even when Cipolla makes a mistake, it is
a kind that makes you believe in him. Now tell me: Do you believe
in me?"

An indefinite gesture.

"A half-way answer," commented the Cavaliere. "Probably it is
not easy to win your confidence. Even for me, I can see, it is not so
easy. I see in your features a reserve, a sadness, *un tratto di malinconia*[2]
. . . tell me" (he seized Mario's hand persuasively) "have you troubles?"

"*Nossignore*," answered Mario, promptly and decidedly.

"You *have* troubles," insisted the Cavaliere, bearing down the denial
by the weight of his authority. "Can't I see? Trying to pull the wool
over Cipolla's eyes, are you? Of course, about the girls—it is a girl,
isn't it? You have love troubles?"

Mario gave a vigorous head-shake. And again the *giovanotto*'s brutal
laugh rang out. The Cavaliere gave heed. His eyes were roving about
somewhere in the air: but he cocked an ear to the sound, then swung
his whip backwards, as he had once or twice before in his conversation with Mario, that none of his puppets might flag in their zeal.
The gesture had nearly cost him his new prey: Mario gave a sudden
start in the direction of the steps. But Cipolla had him in his clutch.

"Not so fast," said he. "That would be fine, wouldn't it? So you
want to skip, do you, Ganymede, right in the middle of the fun, or,
rather, when it is just beginning? Stay with me, I'll show you something nice. I'll convince you. You have no reason to worry, I promise you. This girl—you know her and others know her too—what's
her name? Wait! I read the name in your eyes, it is on the tip of my
tongue and yours too—"

"Silvestra!" shouted the *giovanotto* from below.

The Cavaliere's face did not change.

"Aren't there the forward people?" he asked, not looking down,
more as in undisturbed converse with Mario. "Aren't there the young
fighting-cocks that crow in season and out? Takes the word out of

1. A young boy, waiter or cup-bearer to the gods. *Salvietta*: "Napkin!"   2. "A melancholy air."
Nossignore: "No sir."

your mouth, the conceited fool, and seems to think he has some
special right to it. Let him be. But Silvestra, your Silvestra—ah,
what a girl that is! What a prize! Brings your heart into your mouth
to see her walk or laugh or breathe, she is so lovely. And her round
arms when she washes, and tosses her head back to get the hair out
of her eyes! An angel from paradise!"

Mario started at him, his head thrust forward. He seemed to have
forgotten the audience, forgotten where he was. The red rings round
his eyes had got larger, they looked as though they were painted on.
His thick lips parted.

"And she makes you suffer, this angel," went on Cipolla, "or,
rather, you make yourself suffer for her—there is a difference, my
lad, a most important difference, let me tell you. There are misun-
derstandings in love, maybe nowhere else in the world are there so
many. I know what you are thinking: what does this Cipolla, with
his little physical defect, know about love? Wrong, all wrong, he
knows a lot. He has a wide and powerful understanding of its workings, and it pays to listen to his advice. But let's leave Cipolla out,
cut him out altogether and think only of Silvestra, your peerless Silvestra! What! Is she to give any young gamecock the preference, so
that he can laugh while you cry? To prefer him to a chap like you,
so full of feeling and so sympathetic? Not very likely, is it? It is
impossible—we know better, Cipolla and she. If I were to put myself
in her place and choose between the two of you, a tarry lout like
that—a codfish, a sea-urchin—and a Mario, a knight of the serviette, who moves among gentlefolk and hands round refreshments
with an air—my word, but my heart would speak in no uncertain
tones—it knows to whom I gave it long ago. It is time that he should
see and understand, my chosen one! It is time that you see me and
recognize me, Mario, my beloved! Tell me, who am I?"

It was grisly, the way the betrayer made himself irresistible, wreathed
and coquetted with his crooked shoulder, languished with the puffy
eyes, and showed his splintered teeth in a sickly smile. And alas, at
his beguiling words, what was come of our Mario? It is hard for me
to tell, hard as it was for me to see; for here was nothing less than an
utter abandonment of the inmost soul, a public exposure of timid
and deluded passion and rapture. He put his hands across his mouth,
his shoulders rose and fell with his pantings. He could not, it was
plain, trust his eyes and ears for joy, and the one thing he forgot was
precisely that he could not trust them. "Silvestra!" he breathed, from
the very depths of his vanquished heart.

"Kiss me!" said the hunchback. "Trust me, I love thee. Kiss me
here." And with the tip of his index finger, hand, arm, and little
finger outspread, he pointed to his cheek, near the mouth. And Mario
bent and kissed him.

It had grown very still in the room. There was a monstrous moment, grotesque and thrilling, the moment of Mario's bliss. In that evil span of time, crowded with a sense of the illusiveness of all joy, one sound became audible, and that not quite at once, but on the instant of the melancholy and ribald meeting between Mario's lips and the repulsive flesh which thrust itself forward for his caress. It was the sound of a laugh, from the *giovanotto* on our left. It broke into the dramatic suspense of the moment, coarse, mocking, and yet—or I must have been grossly mistaken—with an undertone of compassion for the poor bewildered, victimized creature. It had a faint ring of that *"Poveretto"* which Cipolla had declared was wasted on the wrong person, when he claimed the pity for his own.

The laugh still rang in the air when the recipient of the caress gave his whip a little swish, low down, close to his chair-leg, and Mario started up and flung himself back. He stood in that posture staring, his hands one over the other on those desecrated lips. Then he beat his temples with his clenched fists, over and over; turned and staggered down the steps, while the audience applauded, and Cipolla sat there with his hands in his lap, his shoulders shaking. Once below, and even while in full retreat, Mario hurled himself round with legs flung wide apart; one arm flew up, and two flat shattering detonations crashed through applause and laughter.

There was instant silence. Even the dancers came to a full stop and stared about, struck dumb. Cipolla bounded from his seat. He stood with his arms spread out, slanting as though to ward everybody off, as though next moment he would cry out: "Stop! Keep back! Silence! What was that?" Then, in that instant, he sank back in his seat, his head rolling on his chest; in the next he had fallen sideways to the floor, where he lay motionless, a huddled heap of clothing, with limbs awry.

The commotion was indescribable. Ladies hid their faces, shuddering, on the breasts of their escorts. There were shouts for a doctor, for the police. People flung themselves on Mario in a mob, to disarm him, to take away the weapon that hung from his fingers—that small, dull-metal, scarcely pistol-shaped tool with hardly any barrel—in how strange and unexpected a direction had fate levelled it!

And now—now finally, at last—we took the children and led them towards the exit, past the pair of *carabinieri*[3] just entering. Was that the end, they wanted to know, that they might go in peace? Yes, we assured them, that was the end. An end of horror, a fatal end. And yet a liberation—for I could not, and I cannot, but find it so!

---

3. Policemen.

RAINER MARIA RILKE
1875–1926

In many ways, Rilke exists between traditions: inheritor of the Symbolist tradition in his allusive imagery and intuitions of universal order, modernist in the "thing-centered" concreteness of his individual descriptions, precursor of the existentialists in his constant struggle to comprehend the self's relation to the universe. The best-known and most influential German poet of the twentieth century, Rilke has been read and translated outside Europe in countries as far apart as the United States and Japan—visibly able to speak to a variety of cultures and audiences in spite of the fact that he is perhaps the least socially-oriented poet of his time.

Born in Prague on December 4, 1875, to German-speaking parents who separated when he was nine, Rainer Maria Rilke had an unhappy childhood that included being dressed as a girl when he was young (thus his mother compensated for the earlier loss of a baby daughter) and being sent to military academies, where he was lonely and miserable, from 1886 to 1891. Illness caused his departure from the second academy and, after a year in business school, he worked in his uncle's law firm and studied at the University of Prague. Rilke hoped to persuade his family that he should devote himself to a literary career rather than business or law, and energetically wrote poetry (*Sacrifice to the Lares*, 1895, *Crowned by Dream*, 1896), plays, stories, and reviews. Moving to Munich in 1897, he met and fell in love with a fascinating and cultured older woman, Lou Andreas-Salomé, who would be a constant influence on him throughout his life. He accompanied Andreas-Salomé and her husband to Russia in 1899, where he met Tolstoy and the painter Leonid Pasternak and—fascinated with Russian mysticism and the Russian landscape—wrote most of the poems later published as *The Book of Hours, The Book of Monastic Life* (1905), as well as a romantic verse tale that became extremely popular, *The Tale of Love and Death of Cornet Christoph Rilke* (1906). After a second trip to Russia, Rilke spent some time at an artists' colony called Worpswede where he met his future wife, the sculptress Clara Westhoff. They were married in March 1901 and settled in a cottage near the colony where Rilke wrote the second part of *The Book of Hours, The Book of Pilgrimage*. He and Clara separated in the following year, and Rilke moved to Paris where he embarked on a study of the sculptor Auguste Rodin (1903).

Unhappy in Paris, where he felt lonely and isolated, he fled to Italy in 1903 to write the last section of *The Book of Hours, The Book of Poverty and Death*. Nonetheless, he found there a new kind of literary and artistic inspiration. He read French writers and especially Baudelaire, whose minutely realistic but strangely beautiful description of a rotting carcass ("A Carcass") initiated, he felt, "the entire development toward objective expression, which we now recognize in Cézanne." In Rodin, too, he recognized a workmanlike dedication to the technical demands of his craft, an intense concentration on visible, tangible objects, and above all, a belief in art as an essentially religious activity. Although he wrote in distress to his friend Lou Andreas-

Salomé, complaining of nightmares and a sense of failure, it is at this time (and with her encouragement) that Rilke began his major work. The anguished, semi-autobiographical spiritual confessions of *The Notebooks of Malte Laurids Brigge* (1910) date to this period, as do a series of *New Poems* (1907–08) in which he abandoned his earlier, impressionistic and romantic style and developed a more intense symbolic vision focused on objects. The *New Poems* emphasized physical reality, the absolute otherness and "thing-like" nature of what was observed—be it fountain, panther, flower, human being, or the "Archaic Torso of Apollo" presented here. "Thing-poems" (*Dinggedichte*), in fact, is a term often used to describe Rilke's writing at this time, with its open emphasis on material description. In a letter to Lou Andreas-Salomé, he described the way that ancient art objects took on a peculiar luster once they were detached from history and seen as "things" in and for themselves: "No subject matter is attached to them, no irrelevant voice interrupts the silence of their concentrated reality . . . no history casts a shadow over their naked clarity—: they *are*. That is all . . . one day one of them reveals itself to you, and shines like a first star."

Such "things" are not dead or inanimate but supremely alive, filled with a strange vitality before the poet's glance: the charged sexuality of the marble torso, the metamorphosis of the Spanish dance in which the dancer's flame-like dress "becomes a furnace / from which, like startled rattlesnakes, the long / naked arms uncoil, aroused and clicking" ("Spanish Dancer"), or the caged panther's circling "like a ritual dance around a center / in which a mighty will stands paralyzed" ("The Panther"). If "things" are not dead, neither is death unambiguous: when Rilke retells the ancient myth of Orpheus and his lost wife, Eurydice, the dead woman is seen as achieving a new and fuller existence in the underworld. "Deep within herself. Being dead / filled her beyond fulfillment. . . . She was already loosened like long hair, / poured out like fallen rain, / shared like a limitless supply. / She was already root." Themes of the interpenetration of life and death, the visible and invisible world, and creativity itself are taken up in Rilke's next major work, the sequence of ten elegies called the *Duino Elegies* (1923) which he was to begin in 1912 while spending the winter in Duino Castle near Trieste.

The composition of the *Duino Elegies** came in two bursts of inspiration separated by ten years. Despite Rilke's increasing reputation and the popularity of his earlier work, he felt frustrated and unhappy. It was not that he lacked friends or activity: based in Paris, he corresponded actively and traveled widely, visiting Italy, Flanders, Germany, Austria, Egypt, and Algeria. But social pressures and everyday anxieties kept him overly occupied, and when a patroness, Princess Marie von Thurn und Taxis-Hohenlohe, proposed that he stay by himself in her castle at Duino during the winter of 1911–12, he was delighted. "The necessity to be alone, alone for a long time, builds stronger in me every day. . . . People (whether it be my fault or theirs) wear me out." The story has been told many times of how Rilke, walking on the rocks above the sea and puzzling over how to answer a both-ersome business letter that had just arrived, seemed to hear in the roar of the wind the first lines of his elegy: "Who, if I cried out, would hear me among

* An elegy is a mournful lyric poem, usually a lament for loss, and generally of medium length.

the angels' / hierarchies?" By February he had written the first and second elegies, and when he left Duino Castle in May he had conceived the whole cycle and written fragments of the third, sixth, ninth, and tenth.

Completion did not come easily in the following years, with the advent of World War I. After writing the third Duino elegy in Paris in 1913, Rilke left for Munich—never dreaming that his apartment and personal property would soon be confiscated as that of an enemy alien. In April 1915, everything was sold at public auction; that summer, Duino Castle was bombarded and reduced to ruins. Rilke wrote the somber fourth elegy in Munich on November 22 and 23, and the next day was called up for the draft. Three weeks later, he was a clerk in the War Archives Office in Vienna where he drew precise vertical and horizontal lines on paper until June 1916, when the intercession of friends released him from military service. Rilke composed little after this experience and feared that he would never be able to complete the Duino sequence. In 1922, however, a friend's purchase of the tiny Château de Muzot (pronounced Muzotte) in Switzerland gave him a peaceful place to retire and write. He not only completed the *Duino Elegies* in Muzot, but wrote in addition—as a memorial for the young daughter of a friend—a two-part sequence of fifty-five sonnets, the *Sonnets to Orpheus* (1923).

With the *Duino Elegies* and the *Sonnets to Orpheus*, Rilke's last great works were complete. The melancholy philosophic vision of the early elegies had described an Angel of absolute reality, whose self-contained perfection was terrifyingly separate from mortal concerns; in the later elegies and the *Sonnets*, the poet balanced the idea of Angelic perfection with a newly important human role for the artist, who serves as a bridge between two worlds. To the poet's initial sense of helplessness and alienation, the later poems respond that all creatures need the artist's transforming glance in order to reach full being. If the Angel is "that creature in whom the transformation of the visible into the invisible . . . already appears in its completion . . . who guarantees the recognition of a higher level of reality in the invisible," then also the artist has the mission of bringing about this transformation. "It is our task to imprint this temporary, perishable earth into ourselves so deeply, so painfully and passionately, that its essence can rise again, 'invisibly,' inside us. We are the bees of the invisible. We wildly collect the honey of the visible, to store it in the great golden hive of the invisible." *Elegies* and *Sonnets* support each other in this shared endeavor, and move toward a more positive statement of artistic "praise"—the celebration of simple Things—as the dominant Angel of the *Elegies* gives way to the human poet Orpheus, who in turn retires into the background of the later *Sonnets* before Eurydice, the woman whose passing into the realm of the dead brings her fuller being. With this major affirmation of the essential unity of life and death, Rilke closed his two complementary sequences ("the little rust-colored sail of the Sonnets and the Elegies' gigantic white canvas") and wrote little—chiefly poems in French—over the next few years. Increasingly ill with leukemia, he died on December 29, 1926, as the result of a sudden infection after pricking himself on roses he cut for a friend in his garden.

Despite their differences of length and style, the "Archaic Torso of Apollo" and the first and ninth Duino elegies are all concerned with the contrast of angelic perfection and flawed human existence. Art is the key in each case, although what the poet feels intuitively in the first poem remains to be analyzed and affirmed in the latter two. The "Archaic Torso of Apollo" is written in Petrarchan sonnet form, and takes as its point of departure a fifth-century B.C. Greek sculpture on display in the Louvre Museum in Paris. This headless marble torso is only a "thing": it should strike us as a lifeless, even defaced chunk of stone. Yet such is the perfection of its luminous sensuality—descended, the speaker suggests, from the brilliant gaze of its missing head and "ripening" eyes—that it seems impossibly alive, and an inner radiance bursts star-like from the marble. The *human* perfection of this marble torso, a perfection achieved through artistic vision, challenges and puts to shame the observer's own puny existence. Nor is there any place to escape from the lesson, once it is recognized: instead, "You must change your life."

The ten *Duino Elegies* also explore the same ambiguous relationship of life and art but in a more extended narrative style; they take up in addition one of Rilke's favorite themes, the complex tension between life and death in which human beings often appear puppets on a falsely real stage, ephemeral beings whose greatest achievements are finally reduced to nothing. The first and ninth elegies have a special corresponding relationship inside the overall sequence. To the question phrased desperately in the first: "Whom can we ever turn to / in our need?" the ninth responds that we must turn to ourselves, and to the artist's ability to comprehend and transmute the objects of this earth. In "The First Elegy," human alienation and distress are evident even to the beasts who, more attuned to nature, know that human beings are "not really at home" in the world. The poet himself fails to notice the simplest things as they call out for recognition—a star, a wave, or the sound of a violin—because he yearns for purer existence. Yet he too cannot attain the ideal: reaching out for perfect love, his arms embrace only emptiness. If there is an ideal essence of human qualities, he realizes, it is lifted above earthly ties: heroes survive in their reputation, and the purest love is a "soaring, objectless love" that does not depend on being answered, and recognizes that there is no permanence on earth—"no place where we can remain." Rilke's characteristic examples of an idealized human essence are women, unrequited love, and those dying young: "What speaks to me of humanity," he wrote, "is the phenomenon of those have died young and, even more absolutely, purely, inexhaustibly: *the woman in love*." To these he gives his entire sympathy and he evokes, at the end of "The First Elegy," the gentle surprise of the newly-dead for whom "it is strange to inhabit the earth no longer, to give up customs one barely had time to learn. . . ." Rilke celebrates the passage into eternity of these crucially "human" lives, and suggests that the celebration itself is important because it provides a nourishing myth for the living, who are otherwise overwhelmed by their sense of mortal loss. Such is the role of art: when the poet assumes the all-embracing perspective of angelic vision his lament (like the ancient dirge for Linus) transcends grief by filling the Void with unexpected and comforting harmony.

"The Ninth Elegy" begins by stressing the peculiar paradox of the human condition: why, being mortal, do we not live serenely and happily as part of nature—like the laurel leaf? Why is it "human" to long for some further destiny? The response, as in "The First Elegy," involves art; but whereas earlier it was the poet's special mission to give profundity to human lives, here he responds to a universal need. "Everything here / apparently needs us . . . Us, the most fleeting of all." The "unsayable" reality of the Angel is not the reality of earth, and the poet's human magic resides in finding some "pure word" that names things in their essence, says them "*more* intensely than the Things themselves / ever dreamed of existing." Such a poet presents earthly Things to the unearthly Angel in a way the latter, astonished, can never know. Ultimately, Rilke is celebrating the power of human creativity: like the rope maker in Rome, or the potter along the Nile, he observes reality and creates from it a new being. For the poet, however, it is a process of making the visible angelically "invisible," and a bridge between two worlds; he "delivers" Things by absorbing them into his imagination's inner dimension. "Earth, isn't this what you want: to arise within us, / *invisible?*" Rilke's poetic journey, in the *Elegies* as in the *Sonnets to Orpheus* which follow, was an inward journey that preserved what was most alive and valuable in human existence by subjecting it to the transfiguring perspective of art.

    J. F. Hendry's *The Sacred Threshold*, *A Life of Rainer Maria Rilke* (1983) is a brief and readable biography with numerous citations from Rilke's letters and work. Heinz F. Peters', *Rainer Maria Rilke: Masks and the Man* (1977; reprint 1960), is a biographical and thematic study of Rilke's work and influence. Romano Guardini examines the elegies in *Rilke's Duino Elegies* (1961).

Archaic Torso of Apollo[1]

We cannot know his legendary head[2]
with eyes like ripening fruit. And yet his torso
is still suffused with brilliance from inside,
like a lamp, in which his gaze, now turned to low,

gleams in all its power. Otherwise   5
the curved breast could not dazzle you so, nor could
a smile run through the placid hips and thighs
to that dark center where procreation flared.

Otherwise this stone would seem defaced
beneath the translucent cascade of the shoulders   10
and would not glisten like a wild beast's fur:

---

1. Translated by Stephen Mitchell. The first poem in the second volume of Rilke's *New Poems* (1908), which were dedicated "to my good friend, Auguste Rodin" (the French sculptor, 1840–1917, whose secretary Rilke was for a brief period and on whom he wrote two monographs in 1903 and 1907). The poem itself was inspired by an ancient Greek statue discovered at Miletus (a Greek colony on the coast of Asia Minor) that was called simply the *Torso of a Youth from Miletus*; since the god Apollo was an ideal of youthful male beauty, his name was often associated with such statues.   2. In a torso, the head and limbs are missing.

would not, from all the borders of itself,
burst like a star: for here there is no place
that does not see you. You must change your life.

Archaïscher Torso Apollos

Wir kannten nicht sein unerhörtes Haupt,
darin die Augenäpfel reiften. Aber
sein Torso glüht noch wie ein Kandelaber,
in dem sein Schauen, nur zurückgeschraubt,

sich hält und glänzt. Sonst könnte nicht der Bug   5
der Brust dich blenden, und im leisen Drehen
der Lenden könnte nicht ein Lächeln gehen
zu jener Mitte, die die Zeugung trug.

Sonst stünde dieser Stein entstellt und kurz
unter der Schultern durchsichtigem Sturz   10
und flimmerte nicht so wie Raubtierfelle;

und bräche nicht aus allen seinen Rändern
aus wie ein Stern: denn da ist keine Stelle,
die dich nicht sieht. Du mußt dein Leben ändern.

Duino Elegies[3]

The First Elegy

Who, if I cried out, would hear me among the angels'[4]
hierarchies? and even if one of them pressed me
suddenly against his heart: I would be consumed
in that overwhelming existence. For beauty is nothing
but the beginning of terror, which we still are just able to endure,   5
and we are so awed because it serenely disdains
to annihilate us. Every angel is terrifying.
    And so I hold myself back and swallow the call-note
of my dark sobbing. Ah, whom can we ever turn to
in our need? Not angels, not humans,   10
and already the knowing animals are aware
that we are not really at home in
our interpreted[5] world. Perhaps there remains for us

---

3. Translated by Stephen Mitchell.   4. "The 'angel' of the Elegies has nothing to do with the
angel of the Christian heaven. . . . The angel of the Elegies is that being which stands for the
idea of recognizing a higher order of reality in invisibility." [Rilke: Letter to his Polish translator
Witold Hulewicz, November 13, 1925.]   5. Unlike animals, who live in unconscious harmony
with earth, human beings conceptualize whatever they see.

some tree on a hillside, which every day we can take
into our vision; there remains for us yesterday's street   15
and the loyalty of a habit so much at ease
when it stayed with us that it moved in and never left.
 Oh and night: there is night, when a wind full of infinite space
gnaws at our faces. Whom would it not remain for—that longed-
  after,
mildly disillusioning presence, which the solitary heart   20
so painfully meets. Is it any less difficult for lovers?
But they keep on using each other to hide their own fate.
 Don't you know *yet*? Fling the emptiness out of your arms
into the spaces we breathe; perhaps the birds
will feel the expanded air with more passionate flying.   25

Yes—the springtimes needed you. Often a star
was waiting for you to notice it. A wave rolled toward you
out of the distant past, or as you walked
under an open window, a violin
yielded itself to your hearing. All this was mission.   30
But could you accomplish it? Weren't you always
distracted by expectation, as if every event
announced a beloved? (Where can you find a place
to keep her, with all the huge strange thoughts inside you
going and coming and often staying all night.)   35
But when you feel longing, sing of women in love;
for their famous passion is still not immortal. Sing
of women abandoned and desolate (you envy them, almost)
who could love so much more purely than those who were gratified.
Begin again and again the never-attainable praising;   40
remember: the hero lives on; even his downfall was
merely a pretext for achieving his final birth.
But Nature, spent and exhausted, takes lovers back
into herself, as if there were not enough strength
to create them a second time. Have you imagined   45
Gaspara Stampa[6] intensely enough so that any girl
deserted by her beloved might be inspired
by that fierce example of soaring, objectless love
and might say to herself, "Perhaps I can be like her"?
Shouldn't this most ancient of sufferings finally grow   50
more fruitful for us? Isn't it time that we lovingly
freed ourselves from the beloved and, quivering, endured:[7]

6. An Italian poet (1523–1554) who wrote a series of two hundred sonnets recording her unhappy love for Count Collalto, who abandoned her. 7. Rilke recalls a passage from the *Portuguese Letters* (a seventeenth-century French novel supposedly written by a Portuguese nun) in which the heroine, Marianna Alcoforado, writes that her love no longer depends on its being reciprocated by the man who has clearly abandoned her.

as the arrow endures the bowstring's tension, so that
gathered in the snap of release it can be more than
itself. For there is no place where we can remain.   55

Voices. Voices. Listen, my heart, as only
saints have listened: until the gigantic call lifted them
off the ground; yet they kept on, impossibly,
kneeling and didn't notice at all:
so complete was their listening. Not that you could endure   60
God's voice—far from it. But listen to the voice of the wind
and the ceaseless message that forms itself out of silence.
It is murmuring toward you now from those who died young.
Didn't their fate, whenever you stepped into a church
in Naples or Rome, quietly come to address you?   65
Or high up, some eulogy entrusted you with a mission,
as, last year, on the plaque in Santa Maria Formosa. [8]
What they want of me is that I gently remove the appearance
of injustice about their death—which at times
slightly hinders their souls from proceeding onward.   70
Of course, it is strange to inhabit the earth no longer,
to give up customs one barely had time to learn,
not to see roses and other promising Things
in terms of a human future; no longer to be
what one was in infinitely anxious hands; to leave   75
even one's own first name behind, forgetting it
as easily as a child abandons a broken toy.
Strange to no longer desire one's desires. Strange
to see meanings that clung together once, floating away
in every direction. And being dead is hard work   80
and full of retrieval before one can gradually feel
a trace of eternity.—Though the living are wrong to believe
in the too-sharp distinctions which they themselves have created.
Angels (they say) don't know whether it is the living
they are moving among, or the dead. The eternal torrent   85
whirls all ages along in it, through both realms
forever, and their voices are drowned out in its thunderous roar.

In the end, those who were carried off early no longer need us:
they are weaned from earth's sorrows and joys, as gently as children
outgrow the soft breasts of their mothers. But we, who do need   90
such great mysteries, we for whom grief is so often
the source of our spirit's growth—: could we exist without *them*?

8. A church in Venice (which Rilke visited in 1911) where a plaque commemorating the death
of a Hermann Wilhelm in 1593 reads, in part, "I have not perished but live for myself in cold
marble" (*non perii at gelido in marmore vivo mihi*).

Is the legend meaningless that tells how, in the lament for Linus,[9]
the daring first notes of song pierced through the barren numbness;
and then in the startled space which a youth as lovely as a god   95
had suddenly left forever, the Void felt for the first time
that harmony which now enraptures and comforts and helps us.

The Ninth Elegy

Why, if this interval of being can be spent serenely
in the form of a laurel,[1] slightly darker than all
other green, with tiny waves on the edges
of every leaf (like the smile of a breeze)—: why then
have to be human—and, escaping from fate,   5
keep longing for fate? . . .

         Oh *not* because happiness *exists*,
that too-hasty profit snatched from approaching loss.
Not out of curiosity, not as practice for the heart, which
would exist in the laurel too. . . .   10

But because *truly* being here is so much; because everything here
apparently needs us, this fleeting world, which in some strange way
keeps calling to us. Us, the most fleeting of all.
Once for each thing. Just once; no more. And we too,
just once. And never again. But to have been   15
this once, completely, even if only once:
to have been at one with the earth, seems beyond undoing.

And so we keep pressing on, trying to achieve it,
trying to hold it firmly in our simple hands,
in our overcrowded gaze, in our speechless heart.   20
Trying to become it.—Whom can we give it to? We would
hold on to it all, forever . . . Ah, but what can we take along
into that other realm? Not the art of looking,
which is learned so slowly, and nothing that happened here. Noth-
    ing.
The sufferings, then. And, above all, the heaviness,   25
and the long experience of love,—just what is wholly
unsayable. But later, among the stars,
what good is it—*they* are *better* as they are: unsayable.

9. The Linus-song (Homer, *Iliad* XVIII, 570) is a dirge for a youth who died young and whose death is associated with the passing of summer; those paralyzed by his loss were revived only by the perfect music of the song of mourning (attributed to Apollo or Orpheus).   1. The nymph Daphne, escaping from the pursuit of her would-be lover Apollo, was changed by that god into a laurel tree. [Ovid, *Metamorphoses*, I, 548ff.]

For when the traveler returns from the mountain-slopes into the
     valley,
he brings, not a handful of earth, unsayable to others, but instead 30
some word he has gained, some pure word, the yellow and blue
gentian. Perhaps we are *here* in order to say: house,
bridge, fountain, gate, pitcher, fruit-tree, window—
at most: column, tower. . . . But to *say* them, you must understand,
oh to say them *more* intensely than the Things themselves   35
ever dreamed of existing. Isn't the secret intent
of this taciturn earth, when it forces lovers together,
that inside their boundless emotion all things may shudder with joy?
Threshold: what it means for two lovers
to be wearing down, imperceptibly, the ancient threshold of their
     door—   40
they too, after the many who came before them
and before those to come. . . . . , lightly.

Here is the time for the *sayable*, *here* is its homeland.
Speak and bear witness. More than ever   45
the Things that we might experience are vanishing, for
what crowds them out and replaces them is an imageless act.
An act under a shell, which easily cracks open as soon as
the business inside outgrows it and seeks new limits.
Between the hammers our heart
endures, just as the tongue does   50
between the teeth and, despite that,
still is able to praise.

Praise this world to the angel, not the unsayable one,
you can't impress *him* with glorious emotion; in the universe
where he feels more powerfully, you are a novice. So show him   55
something simple which, formed over generations,
lives as our own, near our hand and within our gaze.
Tell him of Things. He will stand astonished; as *you* stood
by the rope-maker in Rome or the potter along the Nile.
Show him how happy a Thing can be, how innocent and ours,   60
how even lamenting grief purely decides to take form,
serves as a Thing, or dies into a Thing—, and blissfully
escapes far beyond the violin.—And these Things,
which live by perishing, know you are praising them; transient,
they look to us for deliverance: us, the most transient of all.   65
They want us to change them, utterly, in our invisible heart,
within—oh endlessly—within us! Whoever we may be at last.

Earth, isn't this what you want: to arise within us,
invisible? Isn't it your dream

to be wholly invisible someday?—O Earth: invisible!   70
What, if not transformation, is your urgent command?
Earth, my dearest, I will. Oh believe me, you no longer
need your springtimes to win me over—one of them,
ah, even one, is already too much for my blood.
Unspeakably I have belonged to you, from the first.   75
You were always right, and your holiest inspiration
is our intimate companion, Death.

Look, I am living. On what? Neither childhood nor future
grows any smaller. . . . Superabundant being
wells up in my heart.   80

WALLACE STEVENS
1879–1955

A Hartford businessman as well as major American poet, Wallace Stevens was not really a part of the contemporary literary scene with its movements and isms. He was acquainted with current New York writers and artists, he collected modern art (which is often reflected in his poems), and later in his career he wrote and lectured about poetry, but it is not through these connections that he joins the mainstream of modern European and American letters. Stevens combines two aspects of modern tradition: the free verse and sensuous, significant imagery of Symbolism, which he especially admired in the French poet Paul Verlaine, and the exploration of material reality and its philosophical implications that characterizes more "existential" writers like Albert Camus and Alain Robbe-Grillet. The dualism of concrete reality and human imagination that is Stevens's constant theme also preoccupied the Symbolists and, like them, Stevens finds the ultimate human value in the artist's freedom to imagine the world anew in a "supreme fiction." This fiction is not yet the ungraspable "fictionality" of writers like Beckett or Robbe-Grillet, for it does not dissolve in a series of competing perspectives. Instead, it seeks the essence of an ideal or "supreme" artistic transformation whose creation is enough to give meaning to an otherwise meaningless universe.

Stevens was born in Reading, Pennsylvania, on October 2, 1879, the second of five children. His father was a schoolteacher and then attorney with diverse interests, and his mother also taught school. He enrolled at Harvard in 1897 as a special student (not in a degree program) and while at college contributed poems, stories, and sketches to the Harvard *Advocate* (of which he became president) and the Harvard *Monthly*. He also came to know the philosopher and writer George Santayana, whose assertion of a common imaginative essence in religion and poetry appealed greatly to him.

Stevens left Harvard in 1900 to try journalism and then law school in New York; he received his degree and was admitted to the bar in 1904. After working as an attorney for several firms he finally entered the insurance business in 1908. In 1916 he joined a subsidiary of the Hartford Accident and Indemnity Company, becoming vice-president of the parent company in 1934 and remaining with them until his death in 1955. He dictated business correspondence and poems to the same secretary. In 1922 business affairs took him to Florida, and until 1940 he returned frequently to its warm and lush landscape, which contrasted in his poetry both physically and emotionally with the chillier climate of the north.

Stevens married Elsie V. Kachel in 1909, and in 1924 a daughter was born, Holly, who later edited her father's letters. He published individual poems in little magazines and was a friend of *Poetry* editor Harriet Monroe and of the poets William Carlos Williams and Marianne Moore. *Harmonium*, his first collection of poetry, appeared in 1923. In following years, Stevens's insurance career occupied most of his time and he published little poetry until 1936, when *Ideas of Order* appeared. Later volumes included *The Man with the Blue Guitar* (1937), *Parts of a World* (1942), and a collection of prose essays called *The Necessary Angel* (1951). Stevens kept the two parts of his career quite separate, but gradually became a well-known and influential poet, winning the Bollingen Prize for Poetry in 1949 and the National Book Award in 1951 (for *The Auroras of Autumn*) and 1955 (for *The Collected Poems of Wallace Stevens*). He died of cancer on August 2, 1955.

Wallace Stevens's poetry expresses the dualism between reality and imagination, between things as they really are and as we perceive and then shape them. For we can never know reality directly; our five senses see, touch, taste, smell, and hear what is outside us, constructing an image of the world in which we live, but this world also exists separate from us and beyond our image of it. This paradox underlies all Stevens's poetry, which swings between the two poles of the shaping, creative imagination and the material world of which we are only partly aware. The names of real Connecticut towns or the state of Tennessee, an inventory of the trash on a dump, descriptions of coffee and oranges at breakfast, and marred old pieces of furniture, inhabit his poems side by side with the most abstract speculations, transformations of everyday scenes, and visions of the edge of space. Poetic artifice—the playful and imaginative use of language—clothes the most mundane observations, as if to assert a counterpart between verbal style and the real subject about which it tries to speak. Stevens once said that "it is pleasant to hear the milkman, and yet . . . the imaginative world is the only real world after all," and this balancing of dualities continues throughout his work.

"Sunday Morning," one of Stevens's earlier poems, already reflects this dualism on several levels. The opening lines present a contrast between the comfortable self-indulgence of the Sunday morning breakfast table, warmly alive with sun and bright colors, and the traditional Christian dedication of the day to thoughts of human mortality redeemed by Christ's death. The contrast continues in a quasi dialogue between the poet, who protests any attempt to transcend this world or death, and the woman who speaks of paradise and some "imperishable bliss." Earth itself is sufficient paradise, says the poet, and "friendlier" than the untouchable sky or supernatural explanations of different religions; death is a necessary part of life's constant renewal, and sharpens our awareness of love and beauty while they exist. The wholly natural beauty of the New England landscape at the poem's end, with its acceptance of death and change, suggests a more real and human ideal than the unchanging perfection of eternal life.

The softer, more consolatory tone of "Sunday Morning" (which derives in part from Stevens's recollection of his mother's death in 1912), becomes bold and gaudier in "The Emperor of Ice-Cream," which also deals—but more ironically—with the contrast of life and death. The scene is a wake: a dead woman lies covered with the same sheet on which she once embroidered fantail pigeons. Stevens, however, begins his poem in the kitchen with the festivities in which the survivors are taking part. For the day is devoted not only to the dead but to the living, in whose imperial court the ice cream server is emperor, and the women dressed in their best clothes are hand-maidens. Words with erotic overtones (*concupiscent*, *wenches*) reinforce the scene's essential hedonism, in which the only reality that counts is the pleasure of the moment.

Yet there is another reality, that of the dead woman, who has now become a mere object much like her own furniture, and Stevens painstakingly registers its details. The dresser is made of pine wood and lacks three glass knobs; the dead woman's calloused feet protrude from the too-short embroidered sheet. Such close-up observation puts the woman in a new imaginative context, in a world of lifeless inanimate things whose stillness comments with grim finality on the first stanza's boisterous celebration. The empire of ice cream contains both life and death; people, flowers, and yesterday's newspapers all ultimately come down to the same level of bare physicality. Wisdom lies in accepting the common outcome of all earthly appearances— "Let be be finale of seem"—and in celebrating life while it remains.

Stevens's juxtaposition of reality and our imaginative perception of it is echoed throughout his writing by a dialectic of other oppositions, one idea being raised seemingly only to be challenged and tested by another. Thus southern warmth and creativity in "The Idea of Order at Key West" oppose "The Snow Man" 's "mind of winter" and "junipers shagged with ice"; the jar on a hill in Tennessee juxtaposes human intellect and aesthetic imagination against the unshaped wilderness of nature; "Peter Quince at the Clavier" celebrates the immortal presence—in the memory—of a long-dead woman's physical beauty. Such balancing or counterpoint rejects a single perspective and opens up avenues for continued meditation.

"Counterpoint" is basically a musical term, and Stevens's work is filled with the imagery of musical performance: the harpsichord of "Peter Quince at the Clavier," the singer in "The Idea of Order at Key West," and the nightingale and even grackles of "The Man on the Dump." Other poems speak of a blue guitar (the image taken from a painting by Picasso), an old horn, a lute, citherns, saxophones, not to mention the "tink and tank and tunk-a-tunk-tunk" of an unnamed instrument (perhaps a banjo). Musical images are used to describe events, such as the tambourinelike rhythm of Susanna's attendants arriving (with the additional musical end rhymes of *tambourines* and *Byzantines*), or emotions, like the erotic intensity of the elders' lustful glance ("The basses of their beings throb / In witching chords") and the comic counterpoint of their quivering nerves pulsing "pizzicati of

Hosanna." Even the title of Stevens's book is the name of a musical instrument, *Harmonium*, and he had wanted to name his collected poems *The
Whole of Harmonium.*

Music for Stevens was not however merely musical images in a poem, or
the notion of harmonizing the sounds of words or holding contrasted ideas
in counterpoint. It implied for him a supreme, intuited language, the "foreign song" of the gold-feathered bird on the edge of space in "Of Mere
Being," perhaps the same bird that sang to the emperor in Yeats's "Sailing
to Byzantium." The singer, bird or human, is the type of the poet, the "one
of fictive music" who creates the world anew through the incantatory power
of imagination.

The singer of "The Idea of Order at Key West" is such a poet, embodying
imagination at its most ambitious: "She was the single artificer of the world
/ In which she sang." Nature itself cannot create such a world, for it lacks
the igniting spark; while the sea may imitate human gestures and sounds, it
cannot truly speak, and makes only "meaningless plungings of water and
wind." Imagination is supreme; the singer has "the maker's rage to order
words" (*poet* comes from a Greek word meaning *maker*) and her song creates
for herself and for her listeners a world of imagination in which lights from
the fishing boats seem to map out the night against which they shine.

The luminous beauty of the singer's world is only one of many possible
poetic worlds, all of which take their place on the accumulated heap of
poetry where the latest artificer sits as "The Man on the Dump." The trash
heap of history is the place to find outworn poetic images, from dewy clichés
to the nightingale as traditional symbol for poetry (see Keats's "Ode to a
Nightingale," p. 611). In a poem filled with the debris of modern times,
from old tires to dead cats, Stevens suggests that poetry's philosophical quest
to name the "the" of existence cannot employ previous ages' images and
ideas, but must develop its own, even if they appear only the grating music
of grackles or beatings on an old tin can. Yet all are engaged in the same
enterprise, creating what he elsewhere called "supreme fictions" to give
meaning to our lives.

Stevens's poetry focuses on the ability of the individual imagination to
conceive its own world. Whether expressed in realistic images or in abstract
speculations, this theme could not please the politically minded critics of
the thirties, who accused him of being escapist and "a single artificer of his
own world of mannerism." Stevens responded that he had "confidence in
the spiritual role of the poet," and that this role was not to take sides on
political issues, but to uncover for his society the possible relations between
the subjective mind and the objective world in which it lives. Despite this
explanation, his early work was at first unappreciated; its gaudy exuberance
made it seem less serious than the poetry of political commitment and visionary
mysticism that Yeats was then writing, or Eliot's evocation in *The Waste
Land* of a universal and profound despair. Only after World War II did
Americans, and Europeans, realize that Stevens, too, was a master worthy
to stand beside his greatest contemporaries.

A good general introduction is Robert Pack, *Wallace Stevens: An Approach
to His Poetry* (1958). Robert Buttel's *Wallace Stevens: The Makings of Harmonium* (1967) discusses Stevens's early and middle work. Many views on

Stevens are presented in Marie Borroff, ed., *Wallace Stevens: A Collection
of Critical Essays* (1963). Michel Benamou, *Wallace Stevens and the Symbolist Imagination* (1972), is an interesting study of Stevens's themes and
style compared with those of French Symbolist poets.

Sunday Morning[1]

I

Complacencies of the peignoir, and late
Coffee and oranges in a sunny chair,
And the green freedom of a cockatoo
Upon a rug mingle to dissipate
The holy hush of ancient sacrifice.   5
She dreams a little, and she feels the dark
Encroachment of that old catastrophe,
As a calm darkens among water-lights.
The pungent oranges and bright, green wings
Seem things in some procession of the dead,   10
Winding across wide water, without sound.
The day is like wide water, without sound,
Stilled for the passing of her dreaming feet
Over the seas, to silent Palestine,
Dominion of the blood and sepulchre.[2]   15

II

Why should she give her bounty to the dead?
What is divinity if it can come
Only in silent shadows and in dreams?
Shall she not find in comforts of the sun,
In pungent fruit and bright, green wings, or else   20
In any balm or beauty of the earth,
Things to be cherished like the thought of heaven?[3]
Divinity must live within herself:
Passions of rain, or moods in falling snow;
Grievings in loneliness, or unsubdued   25
Elations when the forest blooms; gusty
Emotions on wet roads on autumn nights;
All pleasures and all pains, remembering
The bough of summer and the winter branch.
These are the measures destined for her soul.   30

1. Although the central figure of the poem is clearly a woman sitting over late breakfast on Sunday
morning instead of going to church, Stevens comments that "this is not essentially a woman's
meditation on religion and the meaning of life. It is anybody's meditation." [Stevens, *Letters*, p.
250].   2. Throughout the stanza there are hints of Christ's Crucifixion and the celebration of
the Mass.   3. "The poem is simply an expression of paganism." [Stevens, *Letters* p. 250.]

III

Jove[4] in the clouds had his inhuman birth.
No mother suckled him, no sweet land gave
Large-mannered motions to his mythy mind
He moved among us, as a muttering king,
Magnificent, would move among his hinds,[5]   35
Until our blood, commingling, virginal,
With heaven, brought such requital to desire
The very hinds discerned it, in a star.[6]
Shall our blood fail? Or shall it come to be
The blood of paradise? And shall the earth   40
Seem all of paradise that we shall know?
The sky will be much friendlier then than now,
A part of labor and a part of pain,
And next in glory to enduring love,
Not this dividing and indifferent blue.   45

IV

She says, "I am content when wakened birds,
Before they fly, test the reality
Of misty fields, by their sweet questionings;
But when the birds are gone, and their warm fields
Return no more, where, then, is paradise?"   50
There is not any haunt of prophecy,[7]
Nor any old chimera of the grave,
Neither the golden underground, nor isle
Melodious, where spirits gat them home,[8]
Nor visionary south, nor cloudy palm   55
Remote on heaven's hill, that has endured
As April's green endures; or will endure
Like her remembrance of awakened birds,
Or her desire for June and evening, tipped
By the consummation of the swallow's wings.   60

V

She says, "But in contentment I still feel
The need of some imperishable bliss."
Death is the mother of beauty; hence from her,
Alone, shall come fulfilment to our dreams
And our desires. Although she strews the leaves   65

---

4. Ruler of the gods in Roman myth.   5. Shepherds.   6. An allusion to the doctrine of the
Immaculate Conception and the star over Bethlehem.   7. Like, for example, the oracle at
Delphi.   8. The Elysian Fields, or Isles of the Blessed, where the heroes of Greek myth went
after death.

Of sure obliteration on our paths,
The path sick sorrow took, the many paths
Where triumph rang its brassy phrase, or love
Whispered a little out of tenderness,
She makes the willow shiver in the sun   70
For maidens who were wont to sit and gaze
Upon the grass, relinquished to their feet.
She causes boys to pile new plums and pears
On disregarded plate.[9] The maidens taste
And stray impassioned in the littering leaves.   75

VI

Is there no change of death in paradise?
Does ripe fruit never fall? Or do the boughs
Hang always heavy in that perfect sky,
Unchanging, yet so like our perishing earth,
With rivers like our own that seek for seas   80
They never find, the same receding shores
That never touch with inarticulate pang?
Why set the pear upon those river-banks
Or spice the shores with odors of the plum?
Alas, that they should wear our colors there,   85
The silken weavings of our afternoons,
And pick the strings of our insipid lutes!
Death is the mother of beauty, mystical,
Within whose burning bosom we devise
Our earthly mothers waiting, sleeplessly.   90

VII

Supple and turbulent, a ring of men
Shall chant in orgy on a summer morn
Their boisterous devotion to the sun,
Not as a god, but as a god might be,
Naked among them, like a savage source.   95
Their chant shall be a chant of paradise,
Out of their blood, returning to the sky;
And in their chant shall enter, voice by voice,
The windy lake wherein their lord delights,
The trees, like serafin,[1] and echoing hills,   100
That choir among themselves long afterward.
They shall know well the heavenly fellowship

---

9. "Plate is used in the sense of so-called family plate. Disregarded refers to the disuse into which
things fall that have been possessed for a long time. I mean, therefore, that death releases and
renews. What the old have come to disregard, the young inherit and make use of." [Stevens,
Letters, p. 183.]   1. Angels of the highest rank.

Of men that perish and of summer morn.
And whence they came and whither they shall go
The dew upon their feet shall manifest.[2]   105

VIII

She hears, upon that water without sound,
A voice that cries, "The tomb in Palestine
Is not the porch of spirits lingering.[3]
It is the grave of Jesus, where he lay."
We live in an old chaos of the sun,   110
Or old dependency of day and night,
Or island solitude, unsponsored, free,
Of that wide water, inescapable.
Deer walk upon our mountains, and the quail
Whistle about us their spontaneous cries;   115
Sweet berries ripen in the wilderness;
And, in the isolation of the sky,
At evening, casual flocks of pigeons make
Ambiguous undulations as they sink.
Downward to darkness, on extended wings.   120

Peter Quince at the Clavier[4]

I

Just as my fingers on these keys
Make music, so the selfsame sounds
On my spirit make a music, too.

Music is feeling, then, not sound;
And thus it is that what I feel,   5
Here in this room, desiring you,

Thinking of your blue-shadowed silk,
Is music. It is like the strain
Waked in the elders by Susanna.[5]

Of a green evening, clear and warm,   10
She bathed in her still garden, while
The red-eyed elders watching, felt

---

2. "Life is as fugitive as dew upon the feet of men dancing in dew. Men do not either come from
any direction or disappear in any direction. Life is as meaningless as dew." [Stevens, *Letters*, p.
250.]   3. That is, remaining on earth after the body is dead.   4. In Shakespeare's *Midsummer Night's Dream*, Peter Quince is the carpenter-playwright who directs his own play about the
tragic lovers Pyramus and Thisbe. Both the play and the production amuse the noble audience.
Clavier: General term in Shakespeare's day for a keyboard instrument, such as a harpsichord.
5. In the Apocrypha, a Babylonian woman falsely accused of adultery by lecherous elders who
spied on her bathing.

The basses of their beings throb
In witching chords, and their thin blood
Pulse pizzicati of Hosanna.[6]   15

                                        II

In the green water, clear and warm,
Susanna lay.
She searched
The touch of springs,
And found   20
Concealed imaginings.
She sighed,
For so much melody.

Upon the bank, she stood
In the cool   25
Of spent emotions.
She felt, among the leaves,
The dew
Of old devotions.

She walked upon the grass,   30
Still quavering.
The winds were like her maids,
On timid feet,
Fetching her woven scarves,
Yet wavering.   35

A breath upon her hand
Muted the night.
She turned—
A cymbal crashed,
And roaring horns.   40

                                        III

Soon, with a noise like tambourines,
Came her attendant Byzantines.[7]

They wondered why Susanna cried
Against the elders by her side;

And as they whispered, the refrain   45
Was like a willow swept by rain.

6. A cry of praise to God. *Pizzicati:* Notes sounded by plucking a string (as on a violin).
7. Inhabitants of ancient Byzantium, a Christian empire of the Near East. "Somebody once
called my attention to the fact that there were no Byzantines in Susanna's time. I hope that that
bit of previous pedantry will seem as unimportant to you as it does to me." [Stevens, *Letters,* p.
250.]

Anon,[8] their lamps' uplifted flame
Revealed Susanna and her shame.

And then, the simpering Byzantines
Fled, with a noise like tambourines.   50

IV

Beauty is momentary in the mind—
The fitful tracing of a portal;
But in the flesh it is immortal.
The body dies; the body's beauty lives.
So evenings die, in their green going,   55
A wave, interminably flowing.
So gardens die, their meek breath scenting
The cowl of winter, done repenting.
So maidens die,[9] to the auroral
Celebration of a maiden's choral.[1]   60
Susanna's music touched the bawdy strings
Of those white elders; but, escaping,
Left only Death's ironic scraping.[2]
Now, in its immortality, it plays
On the clear viol[3] of her memory,   65
And makes a constant sacrament of praise.

Anecdote of the Jar

I placed a jar in Tennessee.
And round it was, upon a hill.
It made the slovenly wilderness
Surround that hill.

The wilderness rose up to it,   5
And sprawled around, no longer wild.
The jar was round upon the ground
And tall and of a port[4] in air.

It took dominion everywhere.
The jar was gray and bare.   10
It did not give of bird or bush,
Like nothing else in Tennessee.

---

8. Soon.   9. As maidens; i.e., on becoming women.   1. Choral song.   2. Rasping fiddle
music.   3. A stringed instrument of the sixteenth and seventeenth centuries, played with a bow;
also a pun on *violation*.   4. Dignified bearing, manner.

The Emperor of Ice-Cream[5]

Call the roller of big cigars,
The muscular one, and bid him whip
In kitchen cups concupiscent[6] curds.
Let the wenches dawdle in such dress
As they are used to wear, and let the boys   5
Bring flowers in last month's newspapers.
Let be be finale of seem.[7]
The only emperor is the emperor of ice-cream.

Take from the dresser of deal,[8]
Lacking the three glass knobs, that sheet   10
On which she embroidered fantails[9] once
And spread it so as to cover her face.
If her horny feet protrude, they come
To show how cold she is, and dumb.
Let the lamp affix its beam.   15
The only emperor is the emperor of ice-cream.

The Idea of Order at Key West[1]

She sang beyond the genius of the sea.[2]
The water never formed to mind or voice,
Like a body wholly body, fluttering
Its empty sleeves; and yet its mimic motion
Made constant cry, caused constantly a cry,   5
That was not ours although we understood,
Inhuman, of the veritable ocean.

The sea was not a mask.[3] No more was she.
The song and water were not medleyed sound

---

5. "I think I should select from my poems as my favorite 'The Emperor of Ice-Cream.' This wears a deliberately commonplace costume, and yet seems to me to contain something of the essential gaudiness of poetry; that is the reason why I like it." (1933) [Stevens, *Letters*, p. 263.]   6. Lusty, sensual. "The words 'concupiscent curds' . . . express the concupiscence of life, but, by contrast with the things in relation to them in the poem they express or accentuate life's destitution." [Stevens, *Letters*, p. 500.]   7. ". . . the true sense of 'Let be be the finale of seem' is let being become the conclusion or denouement of appearing to be: in short, icecream is an absolute good. The poem is obviously not about icecream, but about being as distinguished from seeming to be." [Stevens, *Letters*, p. 341.]   8. Fir or pine wood.   9. Fantail pigeons.   1. Published in *Ideas of Order* (1936). "In 'The Idea of Order at Key West' life has ceased to be a matter of chance. It may be that every man introduces his own order into the life about him. . . . But still there is order. . . . These are tentative ideas for the purposes of poetry." [Stevens, *Letters*, p. 293.] Key West is the southernmost of the Florida keys, and Stevens spent midwinter vacations there for almost twenty years.   2. Beyond the power of the sea to respond.   3. The movement of the waves, imitating fluttering sleeves, also emits an inhuman cry. The sea mimics the human body, but without a mind; it is not even as close as the mask worn by actors in ancient Greek drama.

Even if what she sang was what she heard.   10
Since what she sang was uttered word by word.
It may be that in all her phrases stirred
The grinding water and the gasping wind;
But it was she and not the sea we heard.

For she was the maker of the song she sang.   15
The ever-hooded, tragic-gestured sea
Was merely a place by which she walked to sing.
Whose spirit is this? we said, because we knew
It was the spirit that we sought and knew
That we should ask this often as she sang.   20

If it was only the dark voice of the sea
That rose, or even colored by many waves;
If it was only the outer voice of sky
And cloud, of the sunken coral water-walled,
However clear, it would have been deep air,   25
The heaving speech of air, a summer sound
Repeated in a summer without end
And sound alone. But it was more than that,
More even than her voice, and ours, among
The meaningless plungings of water and the wind,   30
Theatrical distances, bronze shadows heaped
On high horizons, mountainous atmospheres
Of sky and sea.
                    It was her voice that made
The sky acutest at its vanishing.   35
She measured to the hour its solitude.
She was the single artificer of the world
In which she sang. And when she sang, the sea,
Whatever self it had, became the self
That was her song, for she was the maker. Then we,   40
As we beheld her striding there alone,
Knew that there never was a world for her
Except the one she sang and, singing, made.

Ramon Fernandez,[4] tell me, if you know,
Why, when the singing ended and we turned   45
Toward the town, tell why the glassy lights,
The lights in the fishing boats at anchor there,
As the night descended, tilting in the air,
Mastered the night and portioned out the sea,

---

4. (1894–1944), French critic who described the way impressionistic techniques in literature impose a subjective order on reality. Stevens had read some of Fernandez' criticism, but denied that he intended any specific reference here.

Fixing emblazoned[5] zones and fiery poles,   50
Arranging, deepening, enchanting night.

Oh! Blessed rage for order, pale Ramon,
The maker's rage to order words of the sea,
Words of the fragrant portals, dimly-starred,
And of ourselves and of our origins,   55
In ghostlier demarcations, keener sounds.

The Man on the Dump

Day creeps down. The moon is creeping up.
The sun is a corbeil[6] of flowers the moon Blanche
Places there, a bouquet. Ho-ho . . . The dump is full
Of images. Days pass like papers[7] from a press.
The bouquets come here in the papers. So the sun,   5
And so the moon, both come, and the janitor's poems
Of every day, the wrapper on the can of pears,
The cat in the paper-bag, the corset, the box
From Esthonia:[8] the tiger chest, for tea.

The freshness of night has been fresh a long time.   10
The freshness of morning, the blowing of day, one says
That it puffs as Cornelius Nepos[9] reads, it puffs
More than, less than or it puffs like this or that.
The green smacks in the eye, the dew in the green
Smacks like fresh water in a can, like the sea   15

On a cocoanut—how many men have copied dew
For buttons, how many women have covered themselves
With dew, dew dresses, stones and chains of dew, heads
Of the floweriest flowers dewed with the dewiest dew.
One grows to hate these things except on the dump.   20

Now, in the time of spring (azaleas, trilliams,
Myrtle, viburnums, daffodils, blue phlox),[1]
Between that disgust and this, between the things
That are on the dump (azaleas and so on)
And those that will be (azaleas and so on).   25
One feels the purifying change. One rejects
The trash.

---

5. Ornamented, usually with heraldic symbols. *Zones . . . poles:* As with the geographic zones and poles of the earth.   6. Basket. *Blanche:* A woman's name, etymologically signifying whiteness.   7. Newspapers.   8. A Baltic republic, since 1940 part of the U.S.S.R.   9. Roman historian (first century B.C.), now little read, the author of brief anecdotal and highly moralized *Lives of Famous Men.*   1. Spring flowers.

> That's the moment when the moon creeps up
To the bubbling of bassoons. That's the time
One looks at the elephant-colorings of tires: 30
Everything is shed; and the moon comes up as the moon
(All its images are in the dump) and you see
As a man (not like an image of a man),
You see the moon rise in the empty sky.

One sits and beats an old tin can, lard pail.   35
One beats and beats for that which one believes.
That's what one wants to get near. Could it after all
Be merely oneself, as superior as the ear
To a crow's voice? Did the nightingale[2] torture the ear,
Pack the heart and scratch the mind? And does the ear   40
Solace itself in peevish birds? Is it peace,
Is it a philosopher's honeymoon,[3] one finds
On the dump? Is it to sit among mattresses of the dead,
Bottles, pots, shoes and grass and murmur *aptest eve:*
Is it to hear the blatter of grackles[4] and say   45
Invisible priest; is it to eject, to pull
The day to pieces and cry *stanza my stone?*[5]
Where was it one first heard of the Truth? The the.[6]

JAMES JOYCE
1882–1941

An Irish writer who spent most of his life outside Ireland and became an international figure, James Joyce is the most important and influential exponent of literary modernism in prose. He created a narrative style that changed the way modern novelists could afford to write about the world, and writers as widely separated as the American William Faulkner, the Irishman Samuel Beckett, the Colombian Gabriel García Márquez, and the French "new novelists" Alain Robbe-Grillet and Nathalie Sarraute are indebted to his twentieth-century revision of the art of the novel. Joyce's playful manipulation of language, perspective, and blocks of time is not entirely new to literary history—Laurence Sterne's *Tristram Shandy* gave the example in 1760— but his progressive exploration of the resources of literary language inspired many contemporary authors eager to break away from the traditions of the

2. Traditional image for lyric poetry, for example in Keats's *Ode to a Nightingale* (p. 611).
3. A respite from philosophizing. 4. Noisy birds. 5. Suggests a romantic, mystical, "nightingale" poetry that turns its back on material reality. "Invisible priest" may recall Rilke's proposed artistic transformation of reality into an invisible higher reality (see Ninth Duino Elegy, p. 1527). 6. "The truth" is an intangible absolute (like "*the* good"); what it specifies cannot be defined. The *the* itself however represents an urge to seek absolute meaning: to say *the*, not merely *a*.

immediate past and to express, in newly relevant form, the intricacies of modern consciousness. Joyce himself exemplified this development when he moved from the early naturalistic style of *Dubliners*, where he described in linear chronology and realistic detail the repressive social setting of his native Dublin, to the symbolism, complicated construction, mythic parallels, and linguistic experimentation of *Ulysses* and *Finnegans Wake*. His best-known contribution to modern literature is the "stream of consciousness" technique, influential not only because it allows the reader apparent access to the very workings of a character's mind but because—in its rejection of orthodox sentence structure and logical transition—it reminds us that literary texts achieve their most realistic effects only by manipulating language: a theme especially favored by postmodernist writers who make such fictionality their chief concern.

Born in Dublin on February 2, 1882, to May Murray and John Stanislaus Joyce, he was given the impressive name of James Augustine Aloysius Joyce. The Joyce family was initially well-to-do, and the father held a well-paid and easy post in the civil service until 1891, when his job was eliminated with a small pension and he declined to take up more demanding work elsewhere. The Joyce family (there were ten children) moved steadily down the social and economic scale, and life became difficult under the improvident guidance of a man whom Joyce later portrayed as "a drinker, a good fellow, a storyteller, somebody's secretary, something in a distillery, a tax-gatherer, a bankrupt, and at present a praiser of his own past." Joyce attended the well-known Catholic preparatory school of Clongowes Wood College from six to nine years of age, leaving when his family could no longer afford the tuition; two years later, he was admitted as a scholarship student to Belvedere College in Dublin. Both were Jesuit schools, and provided a rigorous Catholic training against which Joyce violently rebelled but which he was never able to forget. In Belvedere College, shaken by a dramatic hell-fire sermon shortly after his first experience with sex, he even thought of becoming a priest; the life of the senses and his vocation as an artist won out, however, and the sermon and his reaction to it became part of *Portrait of the Artist as a Young Man*. After graduating from Belvedere in 1898, Joyce entered another Irish Catholic institution: University College, Dublin, where he consciously rebelled against Irish tradition and looked abroad for new values. Teaching himself Norwegian to read Henrik Ibsen in the original, he criticized the writers of the Irish Literary Renaissance as provincial and had no interest in joining their ranks. Like his hero, Stephen Dedalus, he decided in 1902 to escape the stifling conventions of his native land and leave for Europe.

This first trip did not last long. For six months, he supported himself in Paris by giving English lessons but when his mother turned seriously ill he was called home. After her death, he taught school awhile in Dublin and then returned to the Continent with Nora Barnacle, a country girl from western Ireland with whom he had two children and whom he married in 1931. The young couple moved to Trieste, where Joyce taught English in a Berlitz school and where he started writing both the short stories collected as *Dubliners* and the early version (partially published as *Stephen Hero* in 1944) of *Portrait of the Artist as a Young Man*. *Dubliners* sketches aspects of life in Dublin as Joyce knew it, which means that the parochiality, piety, and repressive conventions of Irish life are shown stifling individual development and especially the artist's soul. Whether it be the young boy who arrives too late at the fair in "Araby," the poor-aunt laundress of "Clay," or the frustrated writer Gabriel Conroy of "The Dead," characters in *Dubliners* dream of a better life against a dismal and impoverishing background whose cumulative effect is one of despair. The style of *Dubliners* is more realistic than Joyce's later fiction, but he is already employing a structure of symbolic meanings and revelatory moments called "epiphanies." The all-blanketing white snow at the end of "The Dead" suggests the chill uniformity of death and Gabriel Conroy's alienation from the rest of his world. It is Gabriel who observes the scene, and whose suddenly expanded vision of the whole universe being swallowed up in oblivion constitutes an epiphany, a moment when everything fuses and makes sense in a larger spiritual perspective.

Portrait of the Artist as a Young Man is based on Joyce's life until 1902, but it is not mere autobiography and the reader recognizes in the first pages a radical experiment in fictional language. From the toddler's early echoing of his parents' baby talk ("nicens little boy," "baby tuckoo") to the mature rhetoric of the end ("Old father, old artificer, stand me now and ever in good stead"), everything in *Portrait* is artistically shaped to make the most powerful cumulative impact. Even the naïveté of Stephen's first thoughts prepares themes and imagery later on: the attention paid to sense impressions, from the clammy bed to his mother's smell; the political symbolism of Dante's green and maroon hairbrushes; the bird imagery and threat of punishment on high in Dante's reproach; and the small boy's habit of thinking over things and rephrasing them in poetic language. Events that stand out in the young boy's mind, like the humiliation of receiving an unfair spanking in school, convey their full impression because they are not simply first-person or third-person descriptions but an imaginative combination of the two, where an outside observer who seems to have access to all Stephen's feelings follows the course of events. *Portrait*, like *Dubliners*, is still in the tradition of naturalist narrative and specifically of the *Künstlerroman* or artist-novel, which follows chronologically the career of its artist hero. Its sophisticated symbolism, use of epiphanies, and stress on dramatic dialogue, however, hint at the radical break with narrative tradition that Joyce was preparing in *Ulysses*.

Ulysses, published in 1922, is one of the most celebrated instances of literary censorship. Its serial publication in the New York *Little Review* from 1918 to 1920 was stopped as obscene by the U.S. Post Office, and the novel was banned and all available copies actually burned in England and America until a 1933 decision by Judge Woolsey in a U.S. District Court lifted the ban in America. The problem was not new: Joyce's realistic descriptions of sensory experience from bedroom to bathroom, his playfully allusive use of language, and his antinationalist and antireligious attitudes had already offended many readers from *Dubliners* (which an Irish printer refused to print) to *Portrait* (which was refused as a "work of doubtful character even though it may be a classic"). While Joyce's evocations have lost none of their pungency, it is hard to imagine a reader who would not be struck also by the "classical" density and enormous mythic scope of this complex, symbolic, and linguistically innovative novel. Openly referring to an ancient predecessor, the *Odyssey* of Homer ("Ulysses" is the Latin name for Homer's hero Odysseus), *Ulysses* structures numerous episodes on ancient parallels and transforms the twenty-year Homeric journey home into the day-long wanderings through Dublin of an unheroic advertising man, Leopold Bloom, and a rebellious young teacher and writer, Stephen Dedalus. Odysseus' faithful wife, Penelope, and his son, Telemachus, reappear in a distorted modern version as Bloom's promiscuous wife, Molly, and as the combined image of Bloom's dead son, Rudy, and the young Dedalus. Bloom and Dedalus cross paths but miss each other for most of the day, but finally meet in Bella Cohen's brothel where Stephen gets roaring drunk. After hallucinations and a scuffle, Stephen is taken home and cared for paternally by Bloom.

Bloom is in one sense a perfectly ordinary man, the "common man" of modern society. He comes to no great decisions (whereas Stephen decides to leave Ireland and dedicate himself to art), and his life will continue its uneventful and somewhat downtrodden way. Yet Bloom is the most fully developed character in the book, a man whose dimensions encompass the mythic overtones of the outcast (Ulysses or Wandering Jew), the psychological tension of a father and husband cut off from family relationships, and (in bathroom, bedroom, and meat market) the most mundane domestic details. The ancient Ulysses was a man of many roles, and so is the modern Bloom; the *Odyssey* has been described as one of the first voyages of Everyman, and *Ulysses* shows Everyman in the twentieth century. According to T. S. Eliot, Joyce's paralleling of ancient myth and modern life is more than literary homage; it is "a way of controlling, of ordering, of giving a shape and significance to the immense panorama of futility and anarchy which is contemporary history."

There is no classical parallel, however, for the language of *Ulysses*. Its quick shifts in points of view, changes of narrative voice, and blendings of the most exacting realism with hallucinatory scenes that combine memory and distorted current vision have been called the literary equivalent of cinematic *montage*. In addition, Joyce abandoned the regular syntax and logical sequences of traditional narrative for a more imitative style that tried to represent what was going on in a character's mind. A development of the "interior monologue" that recounted a character's thoughts and meditations, Joyce's "stream of consciousness" technique was far looser and freer in its fragmented, punning, freely associating and at times almost unrecognizable representation of consciousness. Sometimes it is a sleepy jangle where the relaxed mind lazily plays with sound associations: "Sinbad the Sailor and Tinbad the Tailor and Jinbad the Jailer and Whinbad the Whaler and Ninbad the Nailer and . . ." Sometimes it is more obscure, as in the introduction to a bar scene with its associative, fragmented vision and evocations of sound: "Bronze by gold heard the hoofirons, steelyringing Imperthnthn thnthnthn. Chips, picking chips off rocky thumbnail, chips. Horrid! And gold flushed more. A husky fifenote blew. Blew. Blue bloom in on the Gold pinnacled hair." In the famous ending to the novel, it combines emotions and response with very specific remembered images, as Molly recalls her first yielding to Bloom: "O that awful deepdown torrent O and the sea the sea crimson sometimes like fire and the glorious sunsets and the figtrees in the Alameda gardens yes and all the queer little streets and pink and blue and yellow houses and the rosegardens and the jessamine and geraniums and cactuses . . . yes and then he asked me would I yes to say yes my mountain flower and first I put my arms around him yes and drew him down to me so he could feel my breasts all perfume yes and his heart was going like mad and yes I said yes I will Yes." The extraordinary thing about Joyce's stream of consciousness technique, as the perspicacious Judge Woolsey commented in his court decision, was that it represented the many layers of experience making up each individual's current consciousness: "Not only what is in the focus of each man's observation of the actual things about him, but also in a penumbral zone residua of past impressions, some recent and some drawn up by association from the domain of the subconscious." Taken to the extreme, it is so completely individualized that a reader outside the personal code cannot break in; however, stream of consciousness technique at its best can draw upon echoes and clues already present in the text. The sample in *Ulysses* provided a glimpse of unparalleled richness into human awareness, and set a challenging example for narrative style after Joyce.

After the publication of *Ulysses*, Joyce spent the next seventeen years writing an even more complex work: *Finnegans Wake* (1939). Despite the title, which refers to a ballad in which the bricklayer Tim Finnegan is brought back to life at his wake when somebody spills whisky on him, the novel is the multivoiced, multidimensional dream of Humphrey Chimpden Earwicker: HCE, Here Comes Everybody, Haveth Childers Everywhere, Tristan, Humpty-Dumpty, and Allmen. HCE's dream includes his wife Anna Earwicker as Anna Livia Plurabelle, ALP, the voice of the river Liffey, or a suggestion of historical "holy wars," and together they constitute the originating pair of Adam and Eve. *Finnegans Wake* expands upon the encyclopedic series of literary and cultural references underlying *Ulysses*, and does so in language that has been even more radically broken apart and reassembled. Digressing exuberantly in all directions at once, with complex puns and hybrid words that mix languages, *Finnegans Wake* is—in spite of its cosmic symbolism—a game of language and reference by an artist "hoppy on akkant of his joyicity." It has not achieved the wide audience of *Portrait*, or *Ulysses*, but when Joyce died in Zurich in 1941 he considered it the culmination of his career as a writer.

Portrait of the Artist as a Young Man shows only the beginnings of the fanciful and allusive use of language to come. The novel falls into three general sections: Stephen Dedalus' infancy and boyhood until age sixteen, by which time he has found religious doubt and had his first sexual experience; his painful alternation between religious belief and doubt at Belvedere College (this section includes the famous hell-fire sermon but also Stephen's conscious acceptance of the world of nature and of himself as Stephanoforos, the ritually-crowned artist—*stephanos* being the Greek word for a victory wreath); and a last section in which Stephen examines his experience, develops a theory of art, and prepares for exile and the solitary life of an artist: "Amen. So be it. Welcome, O life! I go to encounter for the millionth time the reality of experience and to forge in the smithy of my soul the uncreated conscience of my race." In the first chapter, printed here, Stephen's earliest memories of home and school are presented through still-naive eyes and the short, choppy sentences of a child's groping attempts to make sense of the world. Forced to espouse the rhythms of the child's thought, the reader participates in the young boy's wonder at tastes, textures, and smells, or at the peculiar language and behavior of adults; in his half-formed curiosity about sex and religious belief; in his pain and frustrated rage at an unjust punishment, and his hesitation and triumph as he appeals to authority against the unjust Father Dolan. The drops of water falling into the brimming bowl at the end of Chapter I are an appropriate image for the way Stephen's early experiences merge into the undivided whole that underlies the *Portrait of the Artist as a Young Man*.

Harry Levin's *James Joyce: A Critical Introduction* (1941) is an excellent and readable general introduction. The standard and detailed biography, with illustrations, is Richard Ellmann's *James Joyce*, rev. ed. (1982). William M. Chace, ed., *Joyce: A Collection of Critical Essays* (1974), will give the reader insight into Joyce's prose. Don Gifford's *Joyce Annotated: Notes for Dubliners and Portrait of the Artist as a Young Man*, 2nd ed. (illustrated, 1982), is an invaluable, copiously detailed, analytic examination of Joyce's sources and allusions.

A Portrait of the Artist as a Young Man

One

Once upon a time and a very good time it was there was a moocow coming down along the road and this moocow that was coming down along the road met a nicens little boy named baby tuckoo. . . .

His father told him that story: his father looked at him through a glass: he had a hairy face.

He was baby tuckoo. The moocow came down the road where Betty Byrne lived: she sold lemon platt.[1]

> O, the wild rose blossoms
> On the little green place.

He sang that song. That was his song.

> O, the green wothe botheth.

When you wet the bed first it is warm then it gets cold. His mother put on the oilsheet. That had the queer smell.

His mother had a nicer smell than his father. She played on the piano the sailor's hornpipe for him to dance. He danced:

---

1. Barley-sugar candy.

> *Tralala lala*
> *Tralala tralaladdy*
> *Tralala lala*
> *Tralala lala.*

Uncle Charles and Dante clapped. They were older than his father and mother but uncle Charles was older than Dante.

Dante had two brushes in her press. The brush with the maroon velvet back was for Michael Davitt and the brush with the green velvet back was for Parnell.[2] Dante gave him a cachou every time he brought her a piece of tissue paper.

The Vances lived in number seven. They had a different father and mother. They were Eileen's father and mother. When they were grown up he was going to marry Eileen. He hid under the table. His mother said:

—O, Stephen will apologise.

Dante said:

—O, if not, the eagles will come and pull out his eyes.[3]

> *Pull out his eyes,*
> *Apologise,*
> *Apologise,*
> *Pull out his eyes.*
>
> *Apologise,*
> *Pull out his eyes,*
> *Pull out his eyes,*
> *Apologise.*

*   *   *

The wide playgrounds were swarming with boys. All were shouting and the prefects urged them on with strong cries. The evening air was pale and chilly and after every charge and thud of the footballers the greasy leather orb flew like a heavy bird through the grey light. He kept on the fringe of his line, out of sight of his prefect, out of the reach of the rude feet, feigning to run now and then. He felt his body small and weak amid the throng of players and his eyes were weak and watery. Rody Kickham was not like that: he would be

---

2. Irish patriots. *Davitt* (1846–1906) broke with *Parnell* (1846–1891) when the latter was accused of adultery by Captain O'Shea in 1889. Parnell was leader of the Irish Parliamentary Party in the British House of Commons, and the Irish nationalists were split over whether he should continue in that position. His power was broken when the Irish Roman Catholic hierarchy denounced him. *Cachou:* Cashew-nut candy.   3. Echo of a song for children by the hymnologist Isaac Watts, based on Proverbs 30:17, "The eye that mocketh at his father, and despiseth to obey his mother, the ravens of the valley shall pick it out, and the young eagles shall eat it."

captain of the third line[4] all the fellows said.

Rody Kickham was a decent fellow but Nasty Roche was a stink. Rody Kickham had greaves in his number[5] and a hamper in the refectory. Nasty Roche had big hands. He called the Friday pudding dog-in-the-blanket. And one day he had asked:

—What is your name?

Stephen had answered:

—Stephen Dedalus.

Then Nasty Roche had said:

—What kind of a name is that?

And when Stephen had not been able to answer Nasty Roche had asked:

—What is your father?

Stephen had answered:

—A gentleman.

Then Nasty Roche had asked:

—Is he a magistrate?

He crept about from point to point on the fringe of his line, making little runs now and then. But his hands were bluish with cold. He kept his hands in the sidepockets of his belted grey suit. That was a belt round his pocket. And belt was also to give a fellow a belt. One day a fellow had said to Cantwell:

—I'd give you such a belt in a second.

Cantwell had answered:

—Go and fight your match. Give Cecil Thunder a belt. I'd like to see you. He'd give you a toe in the rump for yourself.

That was not a nice expression. His mother had told him not to speak with the rough boys in the college. Nice mother! The first day in the hall of the castle[6] when she had said goodbye she had put up her veil double to her nose to kiss him: and her nose and eyes were red. But he had pretended not to see that she was going to cry. She was a nice mother but she was not so nice when she cried. And his father had given him two fiveshilling pieces for pocket money. And his father had told him if he wanted anything to write home to him and, whatever he did, never to peach on a fellow. Then at the door of the castle the rector had shaken hands with his father and mother, his soutane fluttering in the breeze, and the car had driven off with his father and mother on it. They had cried to him from the car, waving their hands:

—Goodbye, Stephen, goodbye!

—Goodbye, Stephen, goodbye!

---

4. Students at Clongowes were divided into three groups: the third line, those under thirteen (including Stephen); the lower line, from thirteen to fifteen, and the higher line, from fifteen to eighteen.   5. Shin guards in his locker.   6. The central buildings of the Jesuit boys' school at Clongowes Wood College were part of an old castle.

He was caught in the whirl of a scrimmage and, fearful of the flashing eyes and muddy boots, bent down to look through the legs. The fellows were struggling and groaning and their legs were rubbing and kicking and stamping. Then Jack Lawton's yellow boots dodged out the ball and all the other boots and legs ran after. He ran after them a little way and then stopped. It was useless to run on. Soon they would be going home for the holidays. After supper in the studyhall he would change the number pasted up inside his desk from seventyseven to seventysix.

It would be better to be in the studyhall than out there in the cold. The sky was pale and cold but there were lights in the castle. He wondered from which window Hamilton Rowan[7] had thrown his hat on the haha and had there been flowerbeds at that time under the windows. One day when he had been called to the castle the butler had shown him the marks of the soldiers' slugs in the wood of the door and had given him a piece of shortbread that the community[8] ate. It was nice and warm to see the lights in the castle. It was like something in a book. Perhaps Leicester Abbey was like that. And there were nice sentences in Doctor Cornwell's Spelling Book.[9] They were like poetry but they were only sentences to learn the spelling from.

> *Wolsey died in Leicester Abbey*
> *Where the abbots buried him.*
> *Canker is a disease of plants,*
> *Cancer one of animals.*

It would be nice to lie on the hearthrug before the fire, leaning his head upon his hands, and think on those sentences. He shivered as if he had cold slimy water next his skin. That was mean of Wells to shoulder him into the square ditch because he would not swop his little snuffbox for Wells's seasoned hacking chestnut,[1] the conqueror of forty. How cold and slimy the water had been! A fellow had once seen a big rat jump into the scum. Mother was sitting at the fire with Dante waiting for Brigid to bring in the tea. She had her feet on the fender[2] and her jewelly slippers were so hot and they had such a lovely warm smell! Dante knew a lot of things. She had taught him where the Mozambique Channel was and what was the longest river in America and what was the name of the highest

---

7. An Irish patriot who tricked his British pursuers by pretending to have escaped out a window at Clongowes Wood Castle: he threw his hat on the "haha" (a ditch with raised bank intended to keep cattle away from gardens) and hid. 8. The faculty. 9. An English-oriented grammar book stressing items of English history, such as the name of the abbey in which English Cardinal Wolsey (1475–1530) died, one hundred miles north of London. 1. Used in a game where two chestnuts, suspended on strings, are knocked against each other until one breaks. 2. Firescreen.

mountain in the moon. Father Arnall knew more than Dante because he was a priest but both his father and uncle Charles said that Dante was a clever woman and a wellread woman. And when Dante made that noise after dinner and then put up her hand to her mouth: that was heartburn.

A voice cried far out on the playground:

—All in!

Then other voices cried from the lower and third lines:

—All in! All in!

The players closed around, flushed and muddy, and he went among them, glad to go in. Rody Kickham held the ball by its greasy lace. A fellow asked him to give it one last: but he walked on without ever answering the fellow. Simon Moonan told him not to because the prefect was looking. The fellow turned to Simon Moonan and said:

—We all know why you speak. You are McGlade's suck.

Suck was a queer word. The fellow called Simon Moonan that name because Simon Moonan used to tie the prefect's false sleeves[3] behind his back and the prefect used to let on to be angry. But the sound was ugly. Once he had washed his hands in the lavatory of the Wicklow Hotel[4] and his father pulled the stopper up by the chain after and the dirt water went down through the hole in the basin. And when it had all gone down slowly the hole in the basin had made a sound like that: suck. Only louder.

To remember that and the white look of the lavatory made him feel cold and then hot. There were two cocks[5] that you turned and water came out: cold and hot. He felt cold and then a little hot: and he could see the names printed on the cocks. That was a very queer thing.

And the air in the corridor chilled him too. It was queer and wettish. But soon the gas would be lit and in burning it made a light noise like a little song. Always the same: and when the fellows stopped talking in the playroom you could hear it.

It was the hour for sums. Father Arnall wrote a hard sum on the board and then said:

—Now then, who will win? Go ahead, York! Go ahead, Lancaster![6]

Stephen tried his best but the sum was too hard and he felt confused. The little silk badge with the white rose on it that was pinned on the breast of his jacket began to flutter. He was no good at sums but he tried his best so that York might not lose. Father Arnall's face looked very black but he was not in a wax:[7] he was laughing. Then

---

3. Strips of cloth that hang down over the sleeves of the soutane or cassock. Simon "sucks up to" or flatters the prefect.   4. In Dublin.   5. Faucets.   6. To encourage competition, the teams are named after rival claimants to the throne in the English Wars of the Roses (1445–85): the house of Lancaster, symbolized by the red rose, and the house of York, symbolized by the white. 7. Rage.

Jack Lawton cracked his fingers and Father Arnall looked at his copybook and said:

—Right. Bravo Lancaster! The red rose wins. Come on now, York! Forge ahead!

Jack Lawton looked over from his side. The little silk badge with the red rose on it looked very rich because he had a blue sailor top on. Stephen felt his own face red too, thinking of all the bets about who would get first place in elements,[8] Jack Lawton or he. Some weeks Jack Lawton got the card for first and some weeks he got the card for first. His white silk badge fluttered and fluttered as he worked at the next sum and heard Father Arnall's voice. Then all his eagerness passed away and he felt his face quite cool. He thought his face must be white because it felt so cool. He could not get out the answer for the sum but it did not matter. White roses and red roses: those were beautiful colours to think of. And the cards for first place and second place and third place were beautiful colours too: pink and cream and lavender. Lavender and cream and pink roses were beautiful to think of. Perhaps a wild rose might be like those colours and he remembered the song about the wild rose blossoms on the little green place. But you could not have a green rose. But perhaps somewhere in the world you could.

The bell rang and then the classes began to file out of the rooms and along the corridors towards the refectory. He sat looking at the two prints of butter on his plate but could not eat the damp bread. The tablecloth was damp and limp. But he drank off the hot weak tea which the clumsy scullion, girt with a white apron, poured into his cup. He wondered whether the scullion's apron was damp too or whether all white things were cold and damp. Nasty Roche and Saurin drank cocoa that their people sent them in tins. They said they could not drink the tea; that it was hogwash. Their fathers were magistrates, the fellows said.

All the boys seemed to him very strange. They had all fathers and mothers and different clothes and voices. He longed to be at home and lay his head on his mother's lap. But he could not: and so he longed for the play and study and prayers to be over and to be in bed.

He drank another cup of hot tea and Fleming said:

—What's up? Have you a pain or what's up with you?

—I don't know, Stephen said.

—Sick in your breadbasket, Fleming said, because your face looks white. It will go away.

—O yes, Stephen said.

But he was not sick there. He thought that he was sick in his heart

---

8. The "third line" subjects of spelling, grammar, writing, arithmetic, geography, history, and Latin.

if you could be sick in that place. Fleming was very decent to ask him. He wanted to cry. He leaned his elbows on the table and shut and opened the flaps of his ears. Then he heard the noise of the refectory every time he opened the flaps of his ears. It made a roar like a train at night. And when he closed the flaps the roar was shut off like a train going into a tunnel. That night at Dalkey[9] the train had roared like that and then, when it went into the tunnel, the roar stopped. He closed his eyes and the train went on, roaring and then stopping; roaring again, stopping. It was nice to hear it roar and stop and then roar out the tunnel again and then stop.

Then the higher line fellows began to come down along the matting in the middle of the refectory, Paddy Rath and Jimmy Magee and the Spaniard who was allowed to smoke cigars and the little Portuguese who wore the woolly cap. And then the lower line tables and the tables of the third line. And every single fellow had a different way of walking.

He sat in a corner of the playroom pretending to watch a game of dominos and once or twice he was able to hear for an instant the little song of the gas.[1] The prefect was at the door with some boys and Simon Moonan was knotting his false sleeves. He was telling them something about Tullabeg.[2]

Then he went away from the door and Wells came over to Stephen and said:

—Tell us, Dedalus, do you kiss your mother before you go to bed?

Stephen answered:

—I do.

Wells turned to the other fellows and said:

—O, I say, here's a fellow says he kisses his mother every night before he goes to bed.

The other fellows stopped their game and turned round, laughing. Stephen blushed under their eyes and said:

—I do not.

Wells said:

—O, I say, here's a fellow says he doesn't kiss his mother before he goes to bed.

They all laughed again. Stephen tried to laugh with them. He felt his whole body hot and confused in a moment. What was the right answer to the question? He had given two and still Wells laughed. But Wells must know the right answer for he was in third of grammar.[3] He tried to think of Wells's mother but he did not dare to raise his eyes to Wells's face. He did not like Wells's face. It was Wells who had shouldered him into the square ditch the day before because

9. Coastal village eight miles southeast of Dublin, on the railroad line connecting Dublin with Stephen's home in Bray.   1. The bubbling noise of the gas lamp.   2. Fifty-five miles west of Dublin, site of St. Stanislaus's College.   3. Just above Stephen's class.

he would not swop his little snuffbox for Wells's seasoned hacking chestnut, the conqueror of forty. It was a mean thing to do; all the fellows said it was. And how cold and slimy the water had been! And a fellow had once seen a big rat jump plop into the scum.

The cold slime of the ditch covered his whole body; and, when the bell rang for study and the lines filed out of the playrooms, he felt the cold air of the corridor and staircase inside his clothes. He still tried to think what was the right answer. Was it right to kiss his mother or wrong to kiss his mother? What did that mean, to kiss? You put your face up like that to say goodnight and then his mother put her face down. That was to kiss. His mother put her lips on his cheek; her lips were soft and they wetted his cheek; and they made a tiny little noise: kiss. Why did people do that with their two faces?

Sitting in the studyhall he opened the lid of his desk and changed the number pasted up inside from seventyseven to seventysix. But the Christmas vacation was very far away: but one time it would come because the earth moved round always.

There was a picture of the earth on the first page of his geography: a big ball in the middle of clouds. Fleming had a box of crayons and one night during free study he had coloured the earth green and the clouds maroon. That was like the two brushes in Dante's press, the brush with the green velvet back for Parnell and the brush with the maroon velvet back for Michael Davitt. But he had not told Fleming to colour them those colours. Fleming had done it himself.

He opened the geography to study the lesson; but he could not learn the names of places in America. Still they were all different places that had those different names. They were all in different countries and the countries were in continents and the continents were in the world and the world was in the universe.

He turned to the flyleaf of the geography and read what he had written there: himself, his name and where he was.

> *Stephen Dedalus*
> *Class of Elements*
> *Clongowes Wood College*
> *Sallins*
> *County Kildare*
> *Ireland*
> *Europe*
> *The World*
> *The Universe*

That was in his writing: and Fleming one night for a cod[4] had written on the opposite page:

4. Joke.

> *Stephen Dedalus is my name,*
> *Ireland is my nation.*
> *Clongowes is my dwellingplace*
> *And heaven my expectation.*

He read the verses backwards but then they were not poetry. Then he read the flyleaf from the bottom to the top till he came to his own name. That was he: and he read down the page again. What was after the universe? Nothing. But was there anything round the universe to show where it stopped before the nothing place began? It could not be a wall but there could be a thin thin line there all round everything. It was very big to think about everything and everywhere. Only God could do that. He tried to think what a big thought that must be but he could think only of God. God was God's name just as his name was Stephen. *Dieu* was the French for God and that was God's name too; and when anyone prayed to God and said *Dieu* then God knew at once that it was a French person that was praying. But though there were different names for God in all the different languages in the world and God understood what all the people who prayed said in their different languages still God remained always the same God and God's real name was God.

It made him very tired to think that way. It made him feel his head very big. He turned over the flyleaf and looked wearily at the green round earth in the middle of the maroon clouds. He wondered which was right, to be for the green or for the maroon, because Dante had ripped the green velvet back off the brush that was for Parnell one day with her scissors and had told him that Parnell was a bad man. He wondered if they were arguing at home about that. That was called politics. There were two sides in it: Dante was on one side and his father and Mr Casey were on the other side but his mother and uncle Charles were on no side. Every day there was something in the paper about it.

It pained him that he did not know well what politics meant and that he did not know where the universe ended. He felt small and weak. When would he be like the fellows in poetry and rhetoric?[5] They had big voices and big boots and they studied trigonometry. That was very far away. First came the vacation and then the next term and then vacation again and then again another term and then again the vacation. It was like a train going in and out of tunnels and that was like the noise of the boys eating in the refectory when you opened and closed the flaps of the ears. Term, vacation; tunnel, out; noise, stop. How far away it was! It was better to go to bed to sleep. Only prayers in the chapel and then bed. He shivered and yawned.

5. The highest levels at Clongowes.

It would be lovely in bed after the sheets got a bit hot. First they were so cold to get into. He shivered to think how cold they were first. But then they got hot and then he could sleep. It was lovely to be tired. He yawned again. Night prayers and then bed: he shivered and wanted to yawn. It would be lovely in a few minutes. He felt a warm glow creeping up from the cold shivering sheets, warmer and warmer till he felt warm all over, ever so warm; ever so warm and yet he shivered a little and still wanted to yawn.

The bell rang for night prayers and he filed out of the studyhall after the others and down the staircase and along the corridors to the chapel. The corridors were darkly lit and the chapel was darkly lit. Soon all would be dark and sleeping. There was cold night air in the chapel and the marbles were the colour the sea was at night. The sea was cold day and night: but it was colder at night. It was cold and dark under the seawall beside his father's house. But the kettle would be on the hob[6] to make punch.

The prefect of the chapel prayed above his head and his memory knew the responses:

> *O Lord, open our lips*
> *And our mouth shall announce Thy praise.*
> *Incline unto our aid, O God!*
> *O Lord, make haste to help us!*[7]

There was a cold night smell in the chapel. But it was a holy smell. It was not like the smell of the old peasants who knelt at the back of the chapel at Sunday mass. That was a smell of air and rain and turf and corduroy. But they were very holy peasants. They breathed behind him on his neck and sighed as they prayed. They lived in Clane, a fellow said: there were little cottages there and he had seen a woman standing at the halfdoor of a cottage with a child in her arms, as the cars had come past from Sallins. It would be lovely to sleep for one night in that cottage before the fire of smoking turf, in the dark lit by the fire, in the warm dark, breathing the smell of the peasants, air and rain and turf and corduroy. But, O, the road there between the trees was dark! You would be lost in the dark. It made him afraid to think of how it was.

He heard the voice of the prefect of the chapel saying the last prayer. He prayed it too against the dark outside under the trees.

> *Visit, we beseech Thee, O Lord, this habitation and drive*
> *away from it all the snares of the enemy. May Thy holy angels*
> *dwell herein to preserve us in peace and may Thy blessing be*
> *always upon us through Christ, Our Lord. Amen.*[8]

6. Heating shelf in the fireplace.   7. The beginning of Matins, or morning prayers.   8. From the Compline, or last prayers for the day.

His fingers trembled as he undressed himself in the dormitory. He told his fingers to hurry up. He had to undress and then kneel and say his own prayers and be in bed before the gas was lowered so that he might not go to hell when he died. He rolled his stockings off and put on his nightshirt quickly and knelt trembling at his bedside and repeated his prayers quickly quickly, fearing that the gas would go down. He felt his shoulders shaking as he murmured:

> *God bless my father and my mother and spare them to me!*
> *God bless my little brothers and sisters and spare them to me!*
> *God bless Dante and uncle Charles and spare them to me!*

He blessed himself and climbed quickly into bed and, tucking the end of the nightshirt under his feet, curled himself together under the cold white sheets, shaking and trembling. But he would not go to hell when he died; and the shaking would stop. A voice bade the boys in the dormitory goodnight. He peered out for an instant over the coverlet and saw the yellow curtains round and before his bed that shut him off on all sides. The light was lowered quietly.

The prefect's shoes went away. Where? Down the staircase and along the corridors or to his room at the end? He saw the dark. Was it true about the black dog that walked there at night with eyes as big as carriagelamps? They said it was the ghost of a murderer. A long shiver of fear flowed over his body. He saw the dark entrance hall of the castle. Old servants in old dress were in the ironingroom[9] above the staircase. It was long ago. The old servants were quiet. There was a fire there but the hall was still dark. A figure came up the staircase from the hall. He wore the white cloak of a marshal; his face was pale and strange; he held his hand pressed to his side. He looked out of strange eyes at the old servants. They looked at him and saw their master's face and cloak and knew that he had received his deathwound. But only the dark was where they looked: only dark silent air. Their master had received his deathwound on the battlefield of Prague far away over the sea. He was standing on the field; his hand was pressed to his side; his face was pale and strange and he wore the white cloak of a marshal.[1]

O how cold and strange it was to think of that! All the dark was cold and strange. There were pale strange faces there, great eyes like carriagelamps. They were the ghosts of murderers, the figures of marshals who had received their deathwound on battlefields far away over the sea. What did they wish to say that their faces were so strange?

---

9. The room where armor was stored.   1. Maximilian Ulysses, Count von Browne (1705–1757) and a marshal in the Austrian army, was supposed to have appeared as a ghost in the castle on the day he died abroad: his family owned the castle at that time.

> *Visit, we beseech Thee, O Lord, this habitation and drive away from it all . . .*

Going home for the holidays! That would be lovely: the fellows had told him. Getting up on the cars in the early wintry morning outside the door of the castle. The cars were rolling on the gravel. Cheers for the rector!

Hurray! Hurray! Hurray!

The cars drove past the chapel and all caps were raised. They drove merrily along the country roads. The drivers pointed with their whips to Bodenstown. The fellows cheered. They passed the farmhouse of the Jolly Farmer. Cheer after cheer after cheer. Through Clane they drove, cheering and cheered. The peasant women stood at the halfdoors, the men stod here and there. The lovely smell there was in the wintry air: the smell of Clane: rain and wintry air and turf smouldering and corduroy.

The train was full of fellows: a long long chocolate train with cream facings. The guards went to and fro opening, closing, locking, unlocking the doors. They were men in dark blue and silver; they had silvery whistles and their keys made a quick music: click, click: click, click.

And the train raced on over the flat lands and past the Hill of Allen. The telegraphpoles were passing, passing. The train went on and on. It knew. There were coloured lanterns in the hall of his father's house and ropes of green branches. There were holly and ivy round the pierglass[2] and holly and ivy, green and red, twined round the chandeliers. There were red holly and green ivy round the old portraits on the walls. Holly and ivy for him and for Christmas.

Lovely . . .

All the people. Welcome home, Stephen! Noises of welcome. His mother kissed him. Was that right? His father was a marshal now: higher than a magistrate. Welcome home, Stephen!

Noises . . .

There was a noise of curtainrings running back along the rods, of water being splashed in the basins. There was a noise of rising and dressing and washing in the dormitory: a noise of clapping of hands as the prefect went up and down telling the fellows to look sharp. A pale sunlight showed the yellow curtains drawn back, the tossed beds. His bed was very hot and his face and body were very hot.

He got up and sat on the side of his bed. He was weak. He tried to pull on his stocking. It had a horrid rough feel. The sunlight was queer and cold.

Fleming said:

---

2. A tall mirror often placed between two windows.

—Are you not well?

He did not know; and Fleming said:

—Get back into bed. I'll tell McGlade you're not well.

—He's sick.

—Who is?

—Tell McGlade.

—Get back into bed.

—Is he sick?

A fellow held his arms while he loosened the stocking clinging to his foot and climbed back into the hot bed.

He crouched down between the sheets, glad of their tepid glow. He heard the fellows talk among themselves about him as they dressed for mass. It was a mean thing to do, to shoulder him into the square ditch, they were saying.

Then their voices ceased; they had gone. A voice at his bed said:

—Dedalus, don't spy on us, sure you won't?

Wells's face was there. He looked at it and saw that Wells was afraid.

—I didn't mean to. Sure you won't?

His father had told him, whatever he did, never to peach on a fellow. He shook his head and answered no and felt glad. Wells said:

—I didn't mean to, honour bright. It was only for cod. I'm sorry.

The face and the voice went away. Sorry because he was afraid. Afraid that it was some disease. Canker was a disease of plants and cancer one of animals: or another different. That was a long time ago then out on the playgrounds in the evening light, creeping from point to point on the fringe of his line, a heavy bird flying low through the grey light. Leicester Abbey lit up. Wolsey died there. The abbots buried them themselves.

It was not Wells's face, it was the prefect's. He was not foxing. No, no: he was sick really. He was not foxing. And he felt the prefect's hand on his forehead; and he felt his forehead warm and damp against the prefect's cold damp hand. That was the way a rat felt, slimy and damp and cold. Every rat had two eyes to look out of. Sleek slimy coats, little little feet tucked up to jump, black shiny eyes to look out of. They could understand how to jump. But the minds of rats could not understand trigonometry. When they were dead they lay on their sides. Their coats dried then. They were only dead things.

The prefect was there again and it was his voice that was saying that he was to get up, that Father Minister[3] had said he was to get up and dress and go to the infirmary. And while he was dressing himself as quickly as he could the prefect said:

---

3. The priest supervising all nonacademic activities.

—We must pack off to Brother Michael because we have the collywobbles! Terrible thing to have the collywobbles! How we wobble
when we have the collywobbles!

He was very decent to say that. That was all to make him laugh.
But he could not laugh because his cheeks and lips were all shivery;
and then the prefect had to laugh by himself.

The prefect cried:

—Quick march! Hayfoot! Strawfoot!⁴

They went together down the staircase and along the corridor and
past the bath. As he passed the door he remembered with a vague
fear the warm turfcoloured bogwater, the warm moist air, the noise
of plunges, the smell of the towels, like medicine.

Brother Michael was standing at the door of the infirmary and
from the door of the dark cabinet on his right came a smell like
medicine. That came from the bottles on the shelves. The prefect
spoke to Brother Michael and Brother Michael answered and called
the prefct sir. He had reddish hair mixed with grey and a queer look.
It was queer that he would always be a brother. It was queer too that
you could not call him sir because he was a brother and had a different kind of look. Was he not holy enough or why could he not
catch up on the others?

There were two beds in the room and in one bed there was a
fellow: and when they went in he called out:

—Hello! It's young Dedalus! What's up?

—The sky is up, Brother Michael said.

He was a fellow out of the third of grammar and, while Stephen
was undressing, he asked Brother Michael to bring him a round of
buttered toast.

—Ah, do! he said.

—Butter you up! said Brother Michael. You'll get your walking
papers in the morning when the doctor comes.

—Will I? the fellow said. I'm not well yet.

Brother Michael repeated:

You'll get your walking papers, I tell you.

He bent down to rake the fire. He had a long back like the long
back of a tramhorse. He shook the poker gravely and nodded his
head at the fellow out of third of grammar.

Then Brother Michael went away and after a while the fellow out
of third of grammar turned in towards the wall and fell asleep.

That was the infirmary. He was sick then. Had they written home
to tell his mother and father? But it would be quicker for one of the
priests to go himself to tell them. Or he would write a letter for the
priest to bring.

---

4. Marching orders: uneducated rural recruits traditionally were supposed to distinguish their feet
in learning to march by having hay tied to the left foot, and straw to the right.

Dear Mother

I am sick. I want to go home. Please come and take me home. I am in the infirmary.

Your fond son,
Stephen

How far away they were! There was cold sunlight outside the window. He wondered if he would die. You could die just the same on a sunny day. He might die before his mother came. Then he would have a dead mass in the chapel like the way the fellows had told him it was when Little had died. All the fellows would be at the mass, dressed in black, all with sad faces. Wells too would be there but no fellow would look at him. The rector would be there in a cope of black and gold[5] and there would be tall yellow candles on the altar and round the catafalque. And they would carry the coffin out of the chapel slowly and he would be buried in the little graveyard of the community off the main avenue of lime. And Wells would be sorry then for what he had done. And the bell would toll slowly.

He could hear the tolling. He said over to himself the song that Brigid had taught him.

> Dingdong! The castle bell!
> Farewell, my mother!
> Bury me in the old churchyard
> Beside my eldest brother.
> My coffin shall be black,
> Six angels at my back,
> Two to sing and two to pray
> And two to carry my soul away.

How beautiful and sad that was! How beautiful the words were where they said *Bury me in the old Churchyard!* A tremor passed over his body. How sad and how beautiful! He wanted to cry quietly but not for himself: for the words, so beautiful and sad, like music. The bell! The bell! Farewell! O farewell!

The cold sunlight was weaker and Brother Michael was standing at his bedside with a bowl of beeftea. He was glad for his mouth was hot and dry. He could hear them playing on the playgrounds. And the day was going on in the college just as if he were there.

Then Brother Michael was going away and the fellow out of third of grammar told him to be sure and come back and tell him all the news in the paper. He told Stephen that his name was Athy and that his father kept a lot of racehorses that were spiffing jumpers and that his father would give a good tip to Brother Michael any time he

---

5. The priest's mantle for the Funeral Mass.

wanted it because Brother Michael was very decent and always told him the news out of the paper they got every day up in the castle. There was every kind of news in the paper: accidents, shipwrecks, sports and politics.

—Now it is all about politics in the paper, he said. Do your people talk about that too?

—Yes, Stephen said.

—Mine too, he said.

Then he thought for a moment and said:

—You have a queer name, Dedalus, and I have a queer name too, Athy. My name is the name of a town. Your name is like Latin.

Then he asked:

—Are you good at riddles?

Stephen answered:

—Not very good.

Then he said:

—Can you answer me this one? Why is the county Kildare like the leg of a fellow's breeches?

Stephen thought what could be the answer and then said:

—I give it up.

—Because there is a thigh[6] in it, he said. Do you see the joke? Athy is the town in the county Kildare and a thigh is the other thigh.

—O, I see, Stephen said.

—That's an old riddle, he said.

After a moment he said:

—I say!

—What? asked Stephen.

—You know, he said, you can ask that riddle another way?

—Can you? said Stephen.

—The same riddle, he said. Do you know the other way to ask it?

—No, said Stephen.

—Can you not think of the other way? he said.

He looked at Stephen over the bedclothes as he spoke. Then he lay back on the pillow and said:

—There is another way but I won't tell you what it is.

Why did he not tell it? His father, who kept the racehorses, must be a magistrate too like Saurin's father and Nasty Roche's father. He thought of his own father, of how he sang songs while his mother played and of how he always gave him a shilling when he asked for sixpence and he felt sorry for him that he was not a magistrate like the other boys' fathers. Then why was he sent to that place with them? But his father had told him that he would be no stranger there because his granduncle had presented an address to the liberator[7]

---

6. Athy is pronounced "a thigh."   7. Daniel O'Connell (1775–1847), Irish politician who brought about the repeal in 1829 of laws restricting Catholic civil and political rights.

there fifty years before. You could know the people of that time by their old dress. It seemed to him a solemn time: and he wondered if that was the time when the fellows in Clongowes wore blue coats with brass buttons and yellow waistcoats and caps of rabbitskin and drank beer like grownup people and kept greyhounds of their own to course the hares with.

He looked at the window and saw that the daylight had grown weaker. There would be cloudy grey light over the playgrounds. There was no noise on the playgrounds. The class must be doing the themes or perhaps Father Arnall was reading a legend[8] out of the book.

It was queer that they had not given him any medicine. Perhaps Brother Michael would bring it back when he came. They said you got stinking stuff to drink when you were in the infirmary. But he felt better now than before. It would be nice getting better slowly. You could get a book then. There was a book in the library about Holland. There were lovely foreign names in it and pictures of strangelooking cities and ships. It made you feel so happy.

How pale the light was at the window! But that was nice. The fire rose and fell on the wall. It was like waves. Someone had put coal on and he heard voices. They were talking. It was the noise of the waves. Or the waves were talking among themselves as they rose and fell.

He saw the sea of waves, long dark waves rising and falling, dark under the moonless night. A tiny light twinkled at the pierhead where the ship was entering: and he saw a multitude of people gathered by the waters' edge to see the ship that was entering their harbour. A tall man stood on the deck, looking out towards the flat dark land: and by the light at the pierhead he saw his face, the sorrowful face of Brother Michael.

He saw him lift his hand towards the people and heard him say in a loud voice of sorrow over the waters:

—He is dead. We saw him lying upon the catafalque.

A wail of sorrow went up from the people.

—Parnell! Parnell! He is dead![9]

They fell upon their knees, moaning in sorrow.

And he saw Dante in a maroon velvet dress and with a green velvet mantle hanging from her shoulders walking proudly and silently past the people who knelt by the waters' edge.

*   *   *

A great fire, banked high and red, flamed in the grate and under the ivytwined branches of the chandelier the Christmas table was

8. A saint's life, from the collection of such lives called (in English) *The Golden Legend*.
9. Parnell was buried in Dublin with great pomp and a massive funeral procession on October 11, 1891.

spread. They had come home a little late and still dinner was not
ready: but it would be ready in a jiffy, his mother had said. They
were waiting for the door to open and for the servants to come in,
holding the big dishes covered with their heavy metal covers.

All were waiting: uncle Charles, who sat far away in the shadow
of the window, Dante and Mr Casey, who sat in the easychairs at
either side of the hearth, Stephen, seated on a chair between them,
his feet resting on the toasted boss.[1] Mr Dedalus looked at himself
in the pierglass above the mantelpiece, waxed out his moustache-
ends and then, parting his coattails, stood with his back to the glowing fire: and still, from time to time, he withdrew a hand from his
coattail to wax out one of his moustache-ends. Mr Casey leaned his
head to one side and, smiling, tapped the gland of his neck with his
fingers. And Stephen smiled too for he knew now that it was not true
that Mr Casey had a purse of silver in his throat. He smiled to think
how the silvery noise which Mr Casey used to make had deceived
him. And when he had tried to open Mr Casey's hand to see if the
purse of silver was hidden there he had seen that the fingers could
not be straightened out: and Mr Casey had told him that he had got
those three cramped fingers making a birthday present for Queen
Victoria.[2]

Mr Casey tapped the gland of his neck and smiled at Stephen with
sleepy eyes: and Mr Dedalus said to him:

—Yes. Well now, that's all right. O, we had a good walk, hadn't
we, John? Yes . . . I wonder if there's any likelihood of dinner this
evening. Yes . . . O, well now, we got a good breath of ozone round
the Head[3] today. Ay, bedad.

He turned to Dante and said:

—You didn't stir out at all, Mrs Riordan?

Dante frowned and said shortly:

—No.

Mr Dedalus dropped his coattails and went over to the sideboard.
He brought forth a great stone jar of whisky from the locker and filled
the decanter slowly, bending now and then to see how much he had
poured in. Then replacing the jar in the locker he poured a little of
the whisky into two glasses, added a little water and came back with
them to the fireplace.

—A thimbleful, John, he said, just to whet your appetite.

Mr Casey took the glass, drank, and placed it near him on the
mantelpiece. Then he said:

—Well, I can't help thinking of our friend Christopher manufacturing . . .

1. A hassock.   2. Mr. Casey, an ardent Irish nationalist, may have been in a British prison
picking oakum (a form of hard labor).   3. Bray Head, on the coast thirteen miles south of
Dublin.

He broke into a fit of laughter and coughing and added:

—. . . manufacturing that champagne for those fellows.

Mr Dedalus laughed loudly.

—Is it Christy? he said. There's more cunning in one of those warts on his bald head than in a pack of jack foxes.

He inclined his head, closed his eyes, and, licking his lips profusely, began to speak with the voice of the hotelkeeper.

—And he has such a soft mouth when he's speaking to you, don't you know. He's very moist and watery about the dewlaps, God bless him.

Mr Casey was still struggling through his fit of coughing and laughter. Stephen, seeing and hearing the hotelkeeper through his father's face and voice, laughed.

Mr Dedalus put up his eyeglass and, staring down at him, said quietly and kindly:

—What are you laughing at, you little puppy, you?

The servants entered and placed the dishes on the table. Mrs Dedalus followed and the places were arranged.

—Sit over, she said.

Mr Dedalus went to the end of the table and said:

—Now, Mrs Riordan, sit over. John, sit you down, my hearty.

He looked round to where uncle Charles sat and said:

—Now then, sir, there's a bird here waiting for you.

When all had taken their seats he laid his hand on the cover and then said quickly, withdrawing it:

—Now, Stephen.

Stephen stood up in his place to say the grace before meals:

Bless us, O Lord, and these Thy gifts which through Thy bounty we are about to receive through Christ Our Lord. Amen.

All blessed themselves and Mr Dedalus with a sigh of pleasure lifted from the dish the heavy cover pearled around the edge with glistening drops.

Stephen looked at the plump turkey which had lain, trussed and skewered, on the kitchen table. He knew that his father had paid a guinea for it in Dunn's of D'Olier Street and that the man had prodded it often at the breastbone to show how good it was: and he remembered the man's voice when he had said:

—Take that one, sir. That's the real Ally Daly.[4]

Why did Mr Barrett in Clongowes call his pandybat[5] a turkey? But Clongowes was far away: and the warm heavy smell of turkey and ham and celery rose from the plates and dishes and the great fire was banked high and red in the grate and the green ivy and red holly

---

4. "The very best" (Dublin slang).   5. A leather strap reinforced with whalebone used to spank schoolboys' hands, whereupon they turn "turkey" red.

made you feel so happy and when dinner was ended the big plum-pudding would be carried in, studded with peeled almonds and sprigs of holly, with bluish fire running around it and a little green flag flying from the top.

It was his first Christmas dinner and he thought of his little brothers and sisters who were waiting in the nursery, as he had often waited, till the pudding came. The deep low collar and the Eton jacket made him feel queer and oldish: and that morning when his mother had brought him down to the parlour, dressed for mass, his father had cried. That was because he was thinking of his own father. And uncle Charles had said so too.

Mr Dedalus covered the dish and began to eat hungrily. Then he said:

—Poor old Christy, he's nearly lopsided now with roguery.

—Simon, said Mrs Dedalus, you haven't given Mrs Riordan any sauce.

Mr Dedalus seized the sauceboat.

—Haven't I? he cried. Mrs Riordan, pity the poor blind.

Dante covered her plate with her hands and said:

—No, thanks.

Mr Dedalus turned to uncle Charles.

—How are you off, sir?

—Right as the mail, Simon.

—You, John?

—I'm all right. Go on yourself.

—Mary? Here, Stephen, here's something to make your hair curl.

He poured sauce freely over Stephen's plate and set the boat again on the table. Then he asked uncle Charles was it tender. Uncle Charles could not speak because his mouth was full but he nodded that it was.

—That was a good answer our friend made to the canon. What? said Mr Dedalus.

—I didn't think he had that much in him, said Mr Casey.

—*I'll pay you your dues, father, when you cease turning the house of God into a pollingbooth.*[6]

—A nice answer, said Dante, for any man calling himself a catholic to give to his priest.

—They have only themselves to blame, said Mr Dedalus suavely. If they took a fool's advice they would confine their attention to religion.

—It is religion, Dante said. They are doing their duty in warning the people.

—We go to the house of God, Mr Casey said, in all humility to

6. The Irish clergy preached against Parnell and Parnellite candidates, causing the defeat of one of them in an 1890 Kilkenny by-election.

pray to our Maker and not to hear election addresses.

—It is religion, Dante said again. They are right. They must direct their flocks.

—And preach politics from the altar, is it? asked Mr Dedalus.

—Certainly, said Dante. It is a question of public morality. A priest would not be a priest if he did not tell his flock what is right and what is wrong.

Mrs Dedalus laid down her knife and fork, saying:

—For pity's sake and for pity sake let us have no political discussion on this day of all days in the year.

—Quite right, ma'am, said uncle Charles. Now, Simon, that's quite enough now. Not another word now.

—Yes, yes, said Mr Dedalus quickly.

He uncovered the dish boldly and said:

—Now then, who's for more turkey?

Nobody answered. Dante said:

—Nice language for any catholic to use!

—Mrs Riordan, I appeal to you, said Mrs Dedalus, to let the matter drop now.

Dante turned on her and said:

—And am I to sit here and listen to the pastors of my church being flouted?

—Nobody is saying a word against them, said Mr Dedalus, so long as they don't meddle in politics.

—The bishops and priests of Ireland have spoken, said Dante, and they must be obeyed.

—Let them leave politics alone, said Mr Casey, or the people may leave their church alone.

—You hear? said Dante turning to Mrs Dedalus.

—Mr Casey! Simon! said Mrs Dedalus. Let it end now.

—Too bad! Too bad! said uncle Charles.

—What? cried Mr Dedalus. Were we to desert him at the bidding of the English people?[7]

—He was no longer worthy to lead, said Dante. He was a public sinner.

—We are all sinners and black sinners, said Mr Casey coldly.

—*Woe be to the man by whom the scandal cometh!* said Mrs Riordan. *It would be better for him that a millstone were tied about his neck and that he were cast into the depth of the sea rather than that he should scandalise one of these, my least little ones.*[8] That is the language of the Holy Ghost.

—And very bad language if you ask me, said Mr Dedalus coolly.

7. Prime Minister Gladstone, pressured by his own Liberal Party, tried to persuade Parnell to leave politics after the scandal and—when the latter refused—issued an ultimatum that the Irish could choose between Parnell and Gladstone's support of Home Rule.   8. Luke 17:1–2.

—Simon! Simon! said uncle Charles. The boy.

—Yes, yes, said Mr Dedalus. I meant about the . . . I was thinking about the bad language of that railway porter. Well now, that's
all right. Here, Stephen, show me your plate, old chap. Eat away
now. Here.

He heaped up the food on Stephen's plate and served uncle Charles
and Mr Casey to large pieces of turkey and splashes of sauce. Mrs
Deadalus was eating little and Dante sat with her hands in her lap.
She was red in the face. Mr Dedalus rooted with the carvers at the
end of the dish and said:

—There's a tasty bit here we call the pope's nose.[9] If any lady or
gentleman . . .

He held a piece of fowl up on the prong of the carving-fork. Nobody
spoke. He put it on his own plate, saying:

—Well, you can't say but you were asked. I think I had better eat
it myself because I'm not well in my health lately.

He winked at Stephen and, replacing the dishcover, began to eat
again.

There was a silence while he ate. Then he said:

—Well now, the day kept up fine after all. There were plenty of
strangers down too.

Nobody spoke. He said again:

—I think there were more strangers down than last Christmas.

He looked round at the others whose faces were bent towards their
plates and, receiving no reply, waited for a moment and said bitterly:

—Well, my Christmas dinner has been spoiled anyhow.

—There could be neither luck nor grace, Dante said, in a house
where there is no respect for the pastors of the church.

Mr Dedalus threw his knife and fork noisily on his plate.

—Respect! he said. Is it for Billy with the lip or for the tub of guts
up in Armagh?[1] Respect!

—Princes of the church, said Mr Casey with slow scorn.

—Lord Leitrim's coachman,[2] yes, said Mr Dedalus.

—They are the Lord's anointed, Dante said. They are an honour
to their country.

—Tub of guts, said Mr Dedalus coarsely. He has a handsome
face, mind you, in repose. You should see that fellow lapping up his
bacon and cabbage of a cold winter's day. O Johnny!

He twisted his features into a grimace of heavy bestiality and made
a lapping noise with his lips.

9. The roasted turkey's tail end, so called because it has no feathers and looks like a "Roman"
nose.   1. The archbishop of Dublin, William J. Walsh (1841–1921), and the archbishop of
Armagh, Michael Logue (1840–1924).   2. Lord Leitrim was the English absentee landlord of
an enormous estate in western Ireland. His Irish coachman tried to save him when he was murdered in 1877, presumably by Irish nationalists.

—Really, Simon, said Mrs Dedalus, you should not speak that way before Stephen. It's not right.

—O, he'll remember all this when he grows up, said Dante hotly— the language he heard against God and religion and priests in his own home.

—Let him remember too, cried Mr Casey to her from across the table, the language with which the priests and the priests' pawns broke Parnell's heart and hounded him into his grave. Let him remember that too when he grows up.

—Sons of bitches! cried Mr Dedalus. When he was down they turned on him to betray him and rend him like rats in a sewer. Lowlived dogs! And they look it! By Christ, they look it!

—They behaved rightly, cried Dante. They obeyed their bishops and their priests. Honour to them!

—Well, it is perfectly dreadful to say that not even for one day in the year, said Mrs Dedalus, can we be free from these dreadful disputes!

Uncle Charles raised his hands mildly and said:

—Come now, come now, come now! Can we not have our opinions whatever they are without this bad temper and this bad language? It is too bad surely.

Mrs Dedalus spoke to Dante in a low voice but Dante said loudly:

—I will not say nothing. I will defend my church and my religion when it is insulted and spit on by renegade catholics.

Mr Casey pushed his plate rudely into the middle of the table and, resting his elbows before him, said in a hoarse voice to his host:

—Tell me, did I tell you that story about a very famous spit?

—You did not, John, said Mr Dedalus.

—Why then, said Mr Casey, it is a most instructive story. It happened not long ago in the county Wicklow where we are now.

He broke off and, turning towards Dante, said with quiet indignation:

—And I may tell you, ma'am, that I, if you mean me, am no renegade catholic. I am a catholic as my father was and his father before him and his father before him again when we gave up our lives rather than sell our faith.

—The more shame to you now, Dante said, to speak as you do.

—The story, John, said Mr Dedalus smiling. Let us have the story anyhow.

—Catholic indeed! repeated Dante ironically. The blackest protestant in the land would not speak the language I have heard this evening.

Mr Dedalus began to sway his head to and fro, crooning like a country singer.

—I am no protestant, I tell you again, said Mr Casey flushing.

Mr Dedalus, still crooning and swaying his head, began to sing in a grunting nasal tone:

> O, come all you Roman catholics
> That never went to mass.[3]

He took up his knife and fork again in good humour and set to eating, saying to Mr Casey:

—Let us have the story, John. It will help us to digest.

Stephen looked with affection at Mr Casey's face which stared across the table over his joined hands. He liked to sit near him at the fire, looking up at his dark fierce face. But his dark eyes were never fierce and his slow voice was good to listen to. But why was he then against the priests? Because Dante must be right then. But he had heard his father say that she was a spoiled nun and that she had come out of the convent in the Alleghanies when her brother had got the money from the savages for the trinkets and the chainies.[4] Perhaps that made her severe against Parnell. And she did not like him to play with Eileen because Eileen was a protestant and when she was young she knew children that used to play with protestants and the protestants used to make fun of the litany of the Blessed Virgin. *Tower of Ivory*, they used to say, *House of Gold!*[5] How could a woman be a tower of ivory or a house of gold? Who was right then? And he remembered the evening in the infirmary in Clongowes, the dark waters, the light at the pierhead and the moan of sorrow from the people when they had heard.

Eileen had long white hands. One evening when playing tig[6] she had put her hands over his eyes: long and white and thin and cold and soft. That was ivory: a cold white thing. That was the meaning of *Tower of Ivory*.

—The story is very short and sweet, Mr Casey said. It was one day down in Arklow, a cold bitter day, not long before the chief died.[7] May God have mercy on him!

He closed his eyes wearily and paused. Mr Dedalus took a bone from his plate and tore some meat from it with his teeth, saying:

—Before he was killed, you mean.

Mr Casey opened his eyes, sighed and went on:

—It was down in Arklow one day. We were down there at a meeting and after the meeting was over we had to make our way to the railway station through the crowd. Such booing and baaing, man, you never heard. They called us all the names in the world. Well

3. Parody of the street ballad, "Come all you loyal Irishmen . . ."   4. Damaged china.
5. Phrases taken from a Roman Catholic litany celebrating the Virgin Mary as the gateway to heaven.   6. Tag.   7. Parnell.

there was one old lady, and a drunken old harridan she was surely, that paid all her attention to me. She kept dancing along beside me in the mud bawling and screaming into my face: *Priest-hunter! The Paris Funds! Mr Fox! Kitty O'Shea!*[8]

—And what did you do, John? asked Mr Dedalus.

—I let her bawl away, said Mr Casey. It was a cold day and to keep up my heart I had (saving your presence, ma'am) a quid of Tullamore in my mouth and sure I couldn't say a word in any case because my mouth was full of tobacco juice.

—Well, John?

—Well. I let her bawl away, to her heart's content, *Kitty O'Shea* and the rest of it till at last she called that lady a name that I won't sully this Christmas board nor your ears, ma'am, nor my own lips by repeating.

He paused. Mr Dedalus, lifting his head from the bone, asked:

—And what did you do, John?

—Do! said Mr Casey. She stuck her ugly old face up at me when she said it and I had my mouth full of tobacco juice. I bent down to her and *Phth!* says I to her like that.

He turned aside and made the act of spitting.

—*Phth!* says I to her like that, right into her eye.

He clapped a hand to his eye and gave a hoarse scream of pain.

—*O Jesus, Mary and Joseph!* says she. *I'm blinded! I'm blinded and drownded!*

He stopped in a fit of coughing and laughter, repeating:

—*I'm blinded entirely.*

Mr Dedalus laughed loudly and lay back in his chair while uncle Charles swayed his head to and fro.

Dante looked terribly angry and repeated while they laughed:

—Very nice! Ha! Very nice!

It was not nice about the spit in the woman's eye. But what was the name the woman had called Kitty O'Shea that Mr Casey would not repeat? He thought of Mr Casey walking through the crowds of people and making speeches from a wagonette. That was what he had been in prison for and he remembered that one night Sergeant O'Neill had come to the house and had stood in the hall, talking in a low voice with his father and chewing nervously at the chinstrap of his cap. And that night Mr Casey had not gone to Dublin by train but a car had come to the door and he had heard his father say something about the Cabinteely road.[9]

---

8. Parnell, a Protestant, struck back at the Irish Catholic hierarchy that was preaching against him. The Paris Funds were money (drawn chiefly from American supporters) placed in a Paris bank so that the English would not be able to confiscate them; Parnell had control of them, and after the split the funds were an object of suspicion and rumor. Parnell had used the name *Mr. Fox* when corresponding with Mrs. O'Shea; the diminutive *Kitty* is insulting.   9. An indirect route from Bray to Dublin.

He was for Ireland and Parnell and so was his father: and so was Dante too for one night at the band on the esplanade she had hit a gentleman on the head with her umbrella because he had taken off his hat when the band played *God save the Queen* at the end.

Mr Dedalus gave a snort of contempt.

—Ah, John, he said. It is true for them. We are an unfortunate priestridden race and always were and always will be till the end of the chapter.

Uncle Charles shook his head, saying:

—A bad business! A bad business!

Mr Dedalus repeated:

—A priestridden Godforsaken race!

He pointed to the portrait of his grandfather on the wall to his right.

—Do you see that old chap up there, John? he said. He was a good Irishman when there was no money in the job. He was condemned to death as a whiteboy.[1] But he had a saying about our clerical friends, that he would never let one of them put his two feet under his mahogany.[2]

Dante broke in angrily:

—If we are a priestridden race we ought to be proud of it! They are the apple of God's eye. *Touch them not,* says Christ, *for they are the apple of My eye.*[3]

—And can we not love our country then? asked Mr Casey. Are we not to follow the man that was born to lead us?

—A traitor to his country! replied Dante. A traitor, an adulterer! The priests were right to abandon him. The priests were always the true friends of Ireland.

—Were they, faith? said Mr Casey.

He threw his fist on the table and, frowning angrily, protruded one finger after another.

—Didn't the bishops of Ireland betray us in the time of the union when bishop Lanigan presented an address of loyalty to the Marquess Cornwallis? Didn't the bishops and priests sell the aspirations of their country in 1829 in return for catholic emancipation? Didn't they denounce the fenian movement from the pulpit and in the confessionbox? And didn't they dishonour the ashes of Terence Bellew MacManus?[4]

His face was glowing with anger and Stephen felt the glow rise to

---

1. Agitators for tax reform who wore white clothes to be able to recognize each other during night raids; the movement began in the late eighteenth century.   2. Dining room table.   3. After Zechariah 2:8–9.   4. In 1800, and after much political maneuvering which included promising Catholic bishops the emancipation of their faith from various civil and political restrictions, the British were able to persuade the Irish Parliament to dissolve and merge with the British Parliament in London (the Act of Union). The fenian movement is the Irish Republican Brotherhood, whose terrorist activities were condemned by the clergy. MacManus was an Irish patriot who died in exile and was brought back to Ireland for burial over clerical opposition.

his own cheek as the spoken words thrilled him. Mr Dedalus uttered a guffaw of coarse scorn.

—O, by God, he cried, I forgot little old Paul Cullen![5] Another apple of God's eye!

Dante bent across the table and cried to Mr Casey:

—Right! Right! They were always right! God and morality and religion come first.

Mrs Dedalus, seeing her excitement, said to her:

—Mrs Riordan, don't excite yourself answering them.

—God and religion before everything! Dante cried. God and religion before the world!

Mr Casey raised his clenched fist and brought it down on the table with a crash.

—Very well, then, he shouted hoarsely, if it comes to that, no God for Ireland!

—John! John! cried Mr Dedalus, seizing his guest by the coat-sleeve.

Dante stared across the table, her cheeks shaking. Mr Casey struggled up from his chair and bent across the table towards her, scraping the air from before his eyes with one hand as though he were tearing aside a cobweb.

—No God for Ireland! he cried. We have had too much God in Ireland. Away with God!

—Blasphemer! Devil! screamed Dante, starting to her feet and almost spitting in his face.

Uncle Charles and Mr Dedalus pulled Mr Casey back into his chair again, talking to him from both sides reasonably. He stared before him out of his dark flaming eyes, repeating:

—Away with God, I say!

Dante shoved her chair violently aside and left the table, upsetting her napkinring which rolled slowly along the carpet and came to rest against the foot of an easychair. Mrs Dedalus rose quickly and followed her towards the door. At the door Dante turned round violently and shouted down the room, her cheeks flushed and quivering with rage:

—Devil out of hell! We won! We crushed him to death! Fiend!

The door slammed behind her.

Mr Casey, freeing his arms from his holders, suddenly bowed his head on his hands with a sob of pain.

—Poor Parnell! he cried loudly. My dead king![6]

He sobbed loudly and bitterly.

Stephen, raising his terrorstricken face, saw that his father's eyes were full of tears.

5. Archbishop of Dublin, later cardinal and ruler of the Catholic Church in Ireland. He supported the British.   6. Parnell was called "the uncrowned king of Ireland."

*   *   *

The fellows talked together in little groups.

One fellow said:

—They were caught near the Hill of Lyons.[7]

—Who caught them?

—Mr Gleeson and the minister. They were on a car.

The same fellow added:

—A fellow in the higher line told me.

Fleming asked:

—But why did they run away, tell us?

—I know why, Cecil Thunder said. Because they had fecked[8] cash
out of the rector's room.

—Who fecked it?

—Kickham's brother. And they all went shares in it.

But that was stealing. How could they have done that?

—A fat lot you know about it, Thunder! Wells said. I know why
they scut.

—Tell us why.

—I was told not to, Wells said.

—O, go on, Wells, all said. You might tell us. We won't let it
out.

Stephen bent forward his head to hear. Wells looked round to see
if anyone was coming. Then he said secretly:

—You know the altar wine they keep in the press in the sacristy?

—Yes.

—Well, they drank that and it was found out who did it by the
smell. And that's why they ran away, if you want to know.

And the fellow who had spoken first said:

—Yes, that's what I heard too from the fellow in the higher line.

The fellows were all silent. Stephen stood among them, afraid to
speak, listening. A faint sickness of awe made him feel weak. How
could they have done that? He thought of the dark silent sacristy.
There were dark wooden presses there where the crimped surplices
lay quietly folded. It was not the chapel but still you had to speak
under your breath. It was a holy place. He remembered the summer
evening he had been there to be dressed as boatbearer,[9] the evening
of the procession to the little altar in the wood.[1] A strange and holy
place. The boy that held the censer had swung it gently to and fro
near the door with the silvery cap lifted by the middle chain to keep
the coals lighting. That was called charcoal: and it had burned qui-

---

7. A hill between Clongowes Wood College and Dublin.   8. Stolen ("fetched"). *Scut*: ran
away.   9. The person who carries the boat or incense container to be blessed during Mass.
Incense is then taken from the boat and burned in the censer.   1. Processions on holy days
went from the College to a little altar in the nearby park.

etly as the fellow had swung it gently and had given off a weak sour smell. And then when all were vested he had stood holding out the boat to the rector and the rector had put a spoonful of incense in it and it had hissed on the red coals.

The fellows were talking together in little groups here and there on the playground. The fellows seemed to him to have grown smaller: that was because a sprinter[2] had knocked him down the day before, a fellow out of second of grammar. He had been thrown by the fellow's machine lightly on the cinderpath and his spectacles had been broken in three pieces and some of the grit of the cinders had gone into his mouth.

That was why the fellows seemed to him smaller and farther away and the goalposts so thin and far and the soft grey sky so high up. But there was no play on the football grounds for cricket was coming: and some said that Barnes would be the prof[3] and some said it would be Flowers. And all over the playgrounds they were playing rounders and bowling twisters and lobs.[4] And from here and from there came the sounds of the cricketbats through the soft grey air. They said: pick, pack, pock, puck: like drops of water in a fountain slowly falling in the brimming bowl.

Athy, who had been silent, said quietly:

—You are all wrong.

All turned towards him eagerly.

—Why?

—Do you know?

—Who told you?

—Tell us, Athy.

Athy pointed across the playground to where Simon Moonan was walking by himself kicking a stone before him.

—Ask him, he said.

The fellows looked there and then said:

—Why him?

—Is he in it?

—Tell us, Athy. Go on. You might if you know.

Athy lowered his voice and said.

—Do you know why those fellows scut? I will tell you but you must not let on you know.

He paused for a moment and then said mysteriously:

—They were caught with Simon Moonan and Tusker Boyle in the square[5] one night.

The fellows looked at him and asked:

—Caught?

—What doing?

2. A high-speed bicyclist.   3. Captain of the team.   4. Rounders is a game like baseball; twisters (curve balls) and lobs are pitches in cricket.   5. The urinal.

Athy said:

—Smugging.[6]

All the fellows were silent: and Athy said:

—And that's why.

Stephen looked at the faces of the fellows but they were all looking across the playground. He wanted to ask somebody about it. What did that mean about the smugging in the square? Why did the five fellows out of the higher line run away for that? It was a joke, he thought. Simon Moonan had nice clothes and one night he had shown him a ball of creamy sweets that the fellows of the football fifteen[7] had rolled down to him along the carpet in the middle of the refectory when he was at the door. It was the night of the match against the Bective Rangers and the ball was made just like a red and green apple only it opened and it was full of the creamy sweets. And one day Boyle had said that an elephant had two tuskers instead of two tusks and that was why he was called Tusker Boyle but some fellows called him Lady Boyle because he was always at his nails, paring them.

Eileen had long thin cool white hands too because she was a girl. They were like ivory; only soft. That was the meaning of *Tower of Ivory* but protestants could not understand it and made fun of it. One day he had stood beside her looking into the hotel grounds. A waiter was running up a trail of bunting on the flagstaff and a fox terrier was scampering to and fro on the sunny lawn. She had put her hand into his pocket where his hand was and he had felt how cool and thin and soft her hand was. She had said that pockets were funny things to have: and then all of a sudden she had broken away and had run laughing down the sloping curve of the path. Her fair hair had streamed out behind her like gold in the sun. *Tower of Ivory. House of Gold.* By thinking of things you could understand them.

But why in the square? You went there when you wanted to do something. It was all thick slabs of slate and water trickled all day out of tiny pinholes and there was a queer smell of stale water there. And behind the door of one of the closets there was a drawing in red pencil of a bearded man in a Roman dress with a brick in each hand and underneath was the name of the drawing:

Balbus was building a wall.[8]

Some fellows had drawn it there for a cod. It had a funny face but it was very like a man with a beard. And on the wall of another closet there was written in backhand in beautiful writing:

Julius Cæsar wrote The Calico Belly.[9]

---

6. An obsolete word that implies, in this case, schoolboy homosexuality. 7. The Irish football team. 8. Graffito after a Latin text in which Cicero criticized Balbus (*Letters to Atticus* XII:2) and which the students probably had to study. 9. Mimicking the sound of a famous title: the "Calico Belly" is *De Bello Gallico*, or Caesar's *Gallic Wars*.

Perhaps that was why they were there because it was a place where some fellows wrote things for cod. But all the same it was queer what Athy said and the way he said it. It was not a cod because they had run away. He looked with the others in silence across the playground and began to feel afraid.

At last Fleming said:

—And we are all to be punished for what other fellows did?

—I won't come back, see if I do, Cecil Thunder said. Three days' silence in the refectory and sending us up for six and eight[1] every minute.

—Yes, said Wells. And old Barrett has a new way of twisting the note so that you can't open it and fold it again to see how many ferulæ you are to get. I won't come back too.

—Yes, said Cecil Thunder, and the prefect of studies was in second of grammar this morning.

—Let us get up a rebellion, Fleming said. Will we?

All the fellows were silent. The air was very silent and you could hear the cricketbats but more slowly than before: pick, pock.

Wells asked:

—What is going to be done to them?

—Simon Moonan and Tusker are going to be flogged, Athy said, and the fellows in the higher line got their choice of flogging or being expelled.

—And which are they taking? asked the fellow who had spoken first.

—All are taking expulsion except Corrigan, Athy answered. He's going to be flogged by Mr Gleeson.

—Is it Corrigan that big fellow? said Fleming. Why, he'd be able for two of Gleeson!

—I know why, Cecil Thunder said. He is right and the other fellows are wrong because a flogging wears off after a bit but a fellow that has been expelled from college is known all his life on account of it. Besides Gleeson won't flog him hard.

—It's best of his play not to, Fleming said.

—I wouldn't like to be Simon Moonan and Tusker, Cecil Thunder said. But I don't believe they will be flogged. Perhaps they will be sent up for twice nine.

—No, no, said Athy. They'll both get it on the vital spot.

Wells rubbed himself and said in a crying voice:

—Please, sir, let me off!

Athy grinned and turned up the sleeves of his jacket, saying:

> *It can't be helped;*
> *It must be done.*

1. The number of strokes (*ferulae*) that the boys received on the palm of the hands for misbehavior (first three on each hand, then four).

> So down with your breeches
> And out with your bum.

The fellows laughed; but he felt that they were a little afraid. In the silence of the soft grey air he heard the cricketbats from here and from there: pock. That was a sound to hear but if you were hit then you would feel a pain. The pandybat made a sound too but not like that. The fellows said it was made of whalebone and leather with lead inside: and he wondered what was the pain like. There were different kinds of pains for all the different kinds of sounds. A long thin cane would have a high whistling sound and he wondered what was that pain like. It made him shivery to think of it and cold: and what Athy said too. But what was there to laugh at in it? It made him shivery: but that was because you always felt like a shiver when you let down your trousers. It was the same in the bath when you undressed yourself. He wondered who had to let them down, the master or the boy himself. O how could they laugh about it that way?

He looked at Athy's rolledup sleeves and knuckly inky hands. He had rolled up his sleeves to show how Mr Gleeson would roll up his sleeves. But Mr Gleeson had round shiny cuffs and clean white wrists and fattish white hands and the nails of them were long and pointed. Perhaps he pared them too like Lady Boyle. But they were terribly long and pointed nails. So long and cruel they were though the white fattish hands were not cruel but gentle. And though he trembled with cold and fright to think of the cruel long nails and of the high whistling sound of the cane and of the chill you felt at the end of your shirt when you undressed yourself yet he felt a feeling of queer quiet pleasure inside him to think of the white fattish hands, clean and strong and gentle. And he thought of what Cecil Thunder had said; that Mr Gleeson would not flog Corrigan hard. And Fleming had said he would not because it was best of his play not to. But that was not why.

A voice from far out on the playground cried:

—All in!

And other voices cried:

—All in! All in!

During the writing lesson he sat with his arms folded, listening to the slow scraping of the pens. Mr Harford went to and fro making little signs in red pencil and sometimes sitting beside the boy to show him how to hold the pen. He had tried to spell out the headline for himself though he knew already what it was for it was the last of the book. *Zeal without prudence is like a ship adrift.* But the lines of the letters were like fine invisible threads and it was only by closing his right eye tight tight and staring out of the left eye that he could make out the full curves of the capital.

But Mr Harford was very decent and never got into a wax. All the other masters got into dreadful waxes. But why were they to suffer for what fellows in the higher line did? Wells had said that they had drunk some of the altar wine out of the press in the sacristy and that it had been found out who had done it by the smell. Perhaps they had stolen a monstrance[2] to run away with it and sell it somewhere. That must have been a terrible sin, to go in there quietly at night, to open the dark press and steal the flashing gold thing into which God was put on the altar in the middle of flowers and candles at benediction while the incense went up in clouds at both sides as the fellow swung the censer and Dominic Kelly sang the first part by himself in the choir. But God was not in it of course when they stole it. But still it was a strange and a great sin even to touch it. He thought of it with deep awe; a terrible and strange sin: it thrilled him to think of it in the silence when the pens scraped lightly. But to drink the altar wine out of the press and be found out by the smell was a sin too: but it was not terrible and strange. It only made you feel a little sickish on account of the smell of the wine. Because on the day when he had made his first holy communion in the chapel he had shut his eyes and opened his mouth and put out his tongue a little: and when the rector had stooped down to give him the holy communion he had smelt a faint winy smell off the rector's breath after the wine of the mass. The word was beautiful: wine. It made you think of dark purple because the grapes were dark purple that grew in Greece outside houses like white temples. But the faint smell off the rector's breath had made him feel a sick feeling on the morning of his first communion. The day of your first communion was the happiest day of your life. And once a lot of generals had asked Napoleon what was the happiest day of his life. They thought he would say the day he won some great battle or the day he was made an emperor. But he said:

—Gentlemen, the happiest day of my life was the day on which I made my first holy communion.

Father Arnall came in and the Latin lesson began and he remained still, leaning on the desk with his arms folded. Father Arnall gave out the themebooks and he said that they were scandalous and that they were all to be written out again with the corrections at once. But the worst of all was Fleming's theme because the pages were stuck together by a blot: and Father Arnall held it up by a corner and said it was an insult to any master to send him up such a theme. Then he asked Jack Lawton to decline the noun *mare* and Jack Lawton stopped at the ablative singular and could not go on with the plural.

—You should be ashamed of yourself, said Father Arnall sternly. You, the leader of the class!

2. Vessel where the Host is kept.

Then he asked the next boy and the next and the next. Nobody knew. Father Arnall became very quiet, more and more quiet as each boy tried to answer and could not. But his face was blacklooking and his eyes were staring though his voice was so quiet. Then he asked Fleming and Fleming said that that word had no plural. Father Arnall suddenly shut the book and shouted at him:

—Kneel out there in the middle of the class. You are one of the idlest boys I ever met. Copy out your themes again the rest of you.

Fleming moved heavily out of his place and knelt between the two last benches. The other boys bent over their themebooks and began to write. A silence filled the classroom and Stephen, glancing timidly at Father Arnall's dark face, saw that it was a little red from the wax he was in.

Was that a sin for Father Arnall to be in a wax or was he allowed to get into a wax when the boys were idle because that made them study better or was he only letting on to be in a wax? It was because he was allowed because a priest would know what a sin was and would not do it. But if he did it one time by mistake what would he do to go to confession? Perhaps he would go to confession to the minister. And if the minister did it he would go to the rector: and the rector to the provincial: and the provincial to the general of the jesuits. That was called the order: and he had heard his father say that they were all clever men. They could all have become highup people in the world if they had not become jesuits. And he wondered what Father Arnall and Paddy Barrett would have become and what Mr McGlade and Mr Gleeson would have become if they had not become jesuits. It was hard to think what because you would have to think of them in a different way with different coloured coats and trousers and with beards and moustaches and different kinds of hats.

The door opened quietly and closed. A quick whisper ran through the class: the prefect of studies. There was an instant of dead silence and then the loud crack of a pandybat on the last desk. Stephen's heart leapt up in fear.

—Any boys want flogging here, Father Arnall? cried the prefect of studies. Any lazy idle loafers that want flogging in this class?

He came to the middle of the class and saw Fleming on his knees.

—Hoho! he cried. Who is this boy? Why is he on his knees? What is your name, boy?

—Fleming, sir.

—Hoho, Fleming! An idler of course. I can see it in your eye. Why is he on his knees, Father Arnall?

—He wrote a bad Latin theme, Father Arnall said, and he missed all the questions in grammar.

—Of course he did! cried the prefect of studies. Of course he did! A born idler! I can see it in the corner of his eye.

He banged his pandybat down on the desk and cried:

—Up, Fleming! Up, my boy!

Fleming stood up slowly.

—Hold out! cried the prefect of studies.

Fleming held out his hand. The pandybat came down on it with a loud smacking sound: one, two, three, four, five, six.

—Other hand!

The pandybat came down again in six loud quick smacks.

—Kneel down! cried the prefect of studies.

Fleming knelt down squeezing his hands under his armpits, his face contorted with pain, but Stephen knew how hard his hands were because Fleming was always rubbing rosin into them. But perhaps he was in great pain for the noise of the pandies was terrible. Stephen's heart was beating and fluttering.

—At your work, all of you! shouted the prefect of studies. We want no lazy idle loafers here, lazy idle little schemers. At your work, I tell you. Father Doland will be in to see you every day. Father Dolan will be in tomorrow.

He poked one of the boys in the side with the pandybat, saying:

—You, boy! When will Father Dolan be in again?

—Tomorrow, sir, said Tom Furlong's voice.

—Tomorrow and tomorrow and tomorrow, said the prefect of studies. Make up your minds for that. Every day Father Dolan. Write away. You, boy, who are you?

Stephen's heart jumped suddenly.

—Dedalus, sir.

—Why are you not writing like the others?

—I . . . my . . .

He could not speak with fright.

—Why is he not writing, Father Arnall?

—He broke his glasses, said Father Arnall, and I exempted him from work.

—Broke? What is this I hear? What is this your name is? said the prefect of studies.

—Dedalus, sir.

—Out here, Dedalus. Lazy little schemer. I see schemer in your face. Where did you break your glasses?

Stephen stumbled into the middle of the class, blinded by fear and haste.

—Where did you break your glasses? repeated the prefect of studies.

—The cinderpath, sir.

—Hoho! The cinderpath! cried the prefect of studies. I know that trick.

Stephen lifted his eyes in wonder and saw for a moment Father

Dolan's whitegrey not young face, his baldy whitegrey head with fluff at the sides of it, the steel rims of his spectacles and his nocoloured eyes looking through the glasses. Why did he say he knew that trick?

—Lazy idle little loafer! cried the prefect of studies. Broke my glasses! An old schoolboy trick! Out with your hand this moment!

Stephen closed his eyes and held out in the air his trembling hand with the palm upwards. He felt the prefect of studies touch it for a moment at the fingers to straighten it and then the swish of the sleeve of the soutane as the pandybat was lifted to strike. A hot burning stinging tingling blow like the loud crack of a broken stick made his trembling hand crumple together like a leaf in the fire: and at the sound and the pain scalding tears were driven into his eyes. His whole body was shaking with fright, his arm was shaking and his crumpled burning livid hand shook like a loose leaf in the air. A cry sprang to his lips, a prayer to be let off. But though the tears scalded his eyes and his limbs quivered with pain and fright he held back the hot tears and the cry that scalded his throat.

—Other hand! shouted the prefect of studies.

Stephen drew back his maimed and quivering right arm and held out his left hand. The soutane sleeve swished again as the pandybat was lifted and a loud crashing sound and a fierce maddening tingling burning pain made his hand shrink together with the palms and fingers in a livid quivering mass. The scalding water burst forth from his eyes and, burning with shame and agony and fear, he drew back his shaking arm in terror and burst out into a whine of pain. His body shook with a palsy of fright and in shame and rage he felt the scalding cry come from his throat and the scalding tears falling out of his eyes and down his flaming cheeks.

—Kneel down! cried the prefect of studies.

Stephen knelt down quickly pressing his beaten hands to his sides. To think of them beaten and swollen with pain all in a moment made him feel so sorry for them as if they were not his own but someone else's that he felt sorry for. And as he knelt, calming the last sobs in his throat and feeling the burning tingling pain pressing in to his sides, he thought of the hands which he had held out in the air with the palms up and of the firm touch of the prefect of studies when he had steadied the shaking fingers and of the beaten swollen reddened mass of palm and fingers that shook helplessly in the air.

—Get at your work, all of you, cried the prefect of studies from the door. Father Dolan will be in every day to see if any boy, any lazy idle little loafer wants flogging. Every day. Every day.

The door closed behind him.

The hushed class continued to copy out the themes. Father Arnall rose from his seat and went among them, helping the boys with gentle words and telling them the mistakes they made. His voice was very gentle and soft. Then he returned to his seat and said to Fleming and Stephen:

—You may return to your places, you two.

Fleming and Stephen rose and, walking to their seats, sat down. Stephen, scarlet with shame, opened a book quickly with one weak hand and bent down upon it, his face close to the page.

It was unfair and cruel because the doctor had told him not to read without glasses and he had written home to his father that morning to send him a new pair. And Father Arnall had said that he need not study till the new glasses came. Then to be called a schemer before the class and to be pandied when he always got the card for first or second and was the leader of the Yorkists! How could the prefect of studies know that it was a trick? He felt the touch of the prefect's fingers as they had steadied his hand and at first he had thought he was going to shake hands with him because the fingers were soft and firm: but then in an instant he had heard the swish of the soutane sleeve and the crash. It was cruel and unfair to make him kneel in the middle of the class then: and Father Arnall had told them both that they might return to their places without making any difference between them. He listened to Father Arnall's low and gentle voice as he corrected the themes. Perhaps he was sorry now and wanted to be decent. But it was unfair and cruel. The prefect of studies was a priest but that was cruel and unfair. And his whitegrey face and the nocoloured eyes behind the steelrimmed spectacles were cruel looking because he had steadied the hand first with his firm soft fingers and that was to hit it better and louder.

—It's a stinking mean thing, that's what it is, said Fleming in the corridor as the classes were passing out in file to the refectory, to pandy a fellow for what is not his fault.

—You really broke your glasses by accident, didn't you? Nasty Roche asked.

Stephen felt his heart filled by Fleming's words and did not answer.

—Of course he did! said Fleming. I wouldn't stand it. I'd go up and tell the rector on him.

—Yes, said Cecil Thunder eagerly, and I saw him lift the pandybat over his shoulder and he's not allowed to do that.

—Did they hurt much? Nasty Roche asked.

—Very much, Stephen said.

—I wouldn't stand it, Fleming repeated, from Baldyhead or any other Baldyhead. It's a stinking mean low trick, that's what it is. I'd go straight up to the rector and tell him about it after dinner.

—Yes, do. Yes, do, said Cecil Thunder.

—Yes, do. Yes, go up and tell the rector on him, Dedalus, said Nasty Roche, because he said that he'd come in tomorrow again to pandy you.

—Yes, yes. Tell the rector, all said.

And there were some fellows out of second of grammar listening and one of them said:

—The senate and the Roman people declared that Dedalus had been wrongly punished.[3]

It was wrong; it was unfair and cruel: and, as he sat in the refectory, he suffered time after time in memory the same humiliation until he began to wonder whether it might not really be that there was something in his face which made him look like a schemer and he wished he had a little mirror to see. But there could not be; and it was unjust and cruel and unfair.

He could not eat the blackish fish fritters they got on Wednesdays in Lent and one of his potatoes had the mark of the spade in it. Yes, he would do what the fellows had told him. He would go up and tell the rector that he had been wrongly punished. A thing like that had been done before by somebody in history, by some great person whose head was in the books of history. And the rector would declare that he had been wrongly punished because the senate and the Roman people always declared that the men who did that had been wrongly punished. Those were the great men whose names were in Richmal Magnall's questions. History was all about those men and what they did and that was what Peter Parley's Tales about Greece and Rome were all about.[4] Peter Parley himself was on the first page in a picture. There was a road over a heath with grass at the side and little bushes: and Peter Parley had a broad hat like a protestant minister and a big stick and he was walking fast along the road to Greece and Rome.

It was easy what he had to do. All he had to do was when the dinner was over and he came out in his turn to go on walking but not out to the corridor but up the staircase on the right that led to the castle. He had nothing to do but that: to turn to the right and walk fast up the staircase and in half a minute he would be in the low dark narrow corridor that led through the castle to the rector's room. And every fellow had said that it was unfair, even the fellow out of second of grammar who had said that about the senate and the Roman people.

What would happen? He heard the fellows of the higher line stand up at the top of the refectory and heard their steps as they came down the matting: Paddy Rath and Jimmy Magee and the Spaniard and

3. Another echo of their Latin studies: decrees of the Roman Senate began "Senatus populusque Romanus," or "The Senate and the Roman People. . . ."   4. Richmal Magnall wrote a popular elementary history text called *Historical and Miscellaneous Questions for the Use of Young People* (1800). Peter Parley (a pseudonym) published educational books for children.

the Portuguese and the fifth was big Corrigan who was going to be flogged by Mr Gleeson. That was why the prefect of studies had called him a schemer and pandied him for nothing: and, straining his weak eyes, tired with the tears, he watched big Corrigan's broad shoulders and big hanging black head passing in the file. But he had done something and besides Mr Gleeson would not flog him hard: and he remembered how big Corrigan looked in the bath. He had skin the same colour as the turfcoloured bogwater in the shallow end of the bath and when he walked along the side his feet slapped loudly on the wet tiles and at every step his thighs shook a little because he was fat.

The refectory was half empty and the fellows were still passing out in file. He could go up the staircase because there was never a priest or a prefect outside the refectory door. But he could not go. The rector would side with the prefect of studies and think it was a schoolboy trick and then the prefect of studies would come in every day the same only it would be worse because he would be dreadfully waxy at any fellow going up to the rector about him. The fellows had told him to go but they would not go themselves. They had forgotten all about it. No, it was best to forget all about it and perhaps the prefect of studies had only said he would come in. No, it was best to hide out of the way because when you were small and young you could often escape that way.

The fellows at his table stood up. He stood up and passed out among them in the file. He had to decide. He was coming near the door. If he went on with the fellows he could never go up to the rector because he could not leave the playground for that. And if he went and was pandied all the same all the fellows would make fun and talk about young Dedalus going up to the rector to tell on the prefect of studies.

He was walking down along the matting and he saw the door before him. It was impossible: he could not. He thought of the baldy head of the prefect of studies with the cruel nocoloured eyes looking at him and he heard the voice of the prefect of studies asking him twice what his name was. Why could he not remember the name when he was told the first time? Was he not listening the first time or was it to make fun out of the name? The great men in the history had names like that and nobody made fun of them. It was his own name that he should have made fun of if he wanted to make fun. Dolan: it was like the name of a woman that washed clothes.

He had reached the door and, turning quickly up to the right, walked up the stairs and, before he could make up his mind to come back, he had entered the low dark narrow corridor that led to the castle. And as he crossed the threshold of the door of the corridor he saw, without turning his head to look, that all the fellows were looking after him as they went filing by.

He passed along the narrow dark corridor, passing little doors that were the doors of the rooms of the community. He peered in front of him and right and left throgh the gloom and thought that those must be portraits. It was dark and silent and his eyes were weak and tired with tears so that he could not see. But he thought they were the portraits of the saints and great men of the order who were looking down on him silently as he passed: saint Ignatius Loyola holding an open book and pointing to the words *Ad Majorem Dei Gloriam* in it, saint Francis Xavier pointing to his chest, Lorenzo Ricci with his berretta on his head like one of the prefects of the lines, the three patrons of holy youth, saint Stanislaus Kostka, saint Aloysius Gonzaga and blessed John Berchmans, all with young faces because they died when they were young, and Father Peter Kenny sitting in a chair wrapped in a big cloak.[5]

He came out on the landing above the entrance hall and looked about him. That was where Hamilton Rowan had passed and the marks of the soldiers' slugs were there. And it was there that the old servants had seen the ghost in the white cloak of a marshal.

An old servant was sweeping at the end of the landing. He asked him where was the rector's room and the old servant pointed to the door at the far end and looked after him as he went on to it and knocked.

There was no answer. He knocked again more loudly and his heart jumped when he heard a muffled voice say:

—Come in!

He turned the handle and opned the door and fumbled for the handle of the green baize door inside. He found it and pushed it open and went in.

He saw the rector sitting at a desk writing. There was a skull[6] on the desk and a strange solemn smell in the room like the old leather of chairs.

His heart was beating fast on account of the solemn place he was in and the silence of the room: and he looked at the skull and at the rector's kindlooking face.

—Well, my little man, said the rector, what is it?

Stephen swallowed down the thing in his throat and said:

—I broke my glasses, sir.

The rector opened his mouth and said:

—O!

---

5. St. Ignatius of Loyola founded the Jesuit order in 1534: the Latin inscription means "To the greater glory of God," which is the Jesuit motto. Saint Francis Xavier was a Jesuit missionary to India, and Lorenzo Ricci—general of the Jesuits in 1758—wears the berretta (square cap). The remaining three saints (Berchmans was also canonized) died young and are therefore patron saints for Jesuit boys' schools. Father Peter Kenny founded Clongowes Wood College.   6. A traditional reminder that one should always be prepared for death.

Then he smiled and said:

—Well, if we broke our glasses we must write home for a new pair.

—I wrote home, sir, said Stephen, and Father Arnall said I am not to study till they come.

—Quite right! said the rector.

Stephen swallowed down the thing again and tried to keep his legs and his voice from shaking.

—But, sir . . .

—Yes?

—Father Dolan came in today and pandied me because I was not writing my theme.

The rector looked at him in silence and he could feel the blood rising to his face and the tears about to rise to his eyes.

The rector said:

—Your name is Dedalus, isn't it?

—Yes, sir.

—And where did you break your glasses?

—On the cinderpath, sir. A fellow was coming out of the bicycle house and I fell and they got broken. I don't know the fellow's name.

The rector looked at him again in silence. Then he smiled and said:

—O, well, it was a mistake; I am sure Father Dolan did not know.

—But I told him I broke them, sir, and he pandied me.

—Did you tell him that you had written home for a new pair? the rector asked.

—No, sir.

—O well then, said the rector, Father Dolan did not understand. You can say that I excused you from your lessons for a few days.

Stephen said quickly for fear his trembling would prevent him:

—Yes, sir, but Father Dolan said he will come in tomorrow to pandy me again for it.

Very well, the rector said, it is a mistake and I shall speak to Father Dolan myself. Will that do now?

Stephen felt the tears wetting his eyes and murmured:

—O yes sir, thanks.

The rector held his hand across the side of the desk where the skull was and Stephen, placing his hand in it for a moment, felt a cool moist palm.

—Good day now, said the rector, withdrawing his hand and bowing.

—Good day, sir, said Stephen.

He bowed and walked quietly out of the room, closing the doors carefully and slowly.

But when he had passed the old servant on the landing and was again in the low narrow dark corridor he began to walk faster and faster. Faster and faster he hurried on through the gloom excitedly. He bumped his elbow against the door at the end and, hurrying down the staircase, walked quickly through the two corridors and out into the air.

He could hear the cries of the fellows on the playgrounds. He broke into a run and, running quicker and quicker, ran across the cinderpath and reached the third line playground, panting.

The fellows had seen him running. They closed round him in a ring, pushing one against another to hear.

—Tell us! Tell us!

—What did he say?

—Did you go in?

—What did he say?

—Tell us! Tell us!

He told them what he had said and what the rector had said and, when he had told them, all the fellows flung their caps spinning up into the air and cried:

—Hurroo!

They caught their caps and sent them up again spinning skyhigh and cried again:

—Hurroo! Hurroo!

They made a cradle of their locked hands and hoisted him up among them and carried him along till he struggled to get free. And when he had escaped from them they broke away in all directions, flinging their caps again into the air and whistling as they went spinning up and crying:

—Hurroo!

And they gave three groans for Baldyhead Dolan and three cheers for Conmee and they said he was the decentest rector that was ever in Clongowes.

The cheers died away in the soft grey air. He was alone. He was happy and free: but he would not be anyway proud with Father Dolan. He would be very quiet and obedient: and he wished that he could do something kind for him to show him that he was not proud.

The air was soft and grey and mild and evening was coming. There was the smell of evening in the air, the smell of the fields in the country where they digged up turnips to peel them and eat them when they went out for a walk to Major Barton's,[7] the smell there was in the little wood beyond the pavilion where the gallnuts were.

The fellows were practising long shies and bowing lobs and slow twisters. In the soft grey silence he could hear the bump of the balls: and from here and from there through the quiet air the sound of the

7. A local magistrate whose estate was a little over two miles from Clongowes.

cricket bats: pick, pack, pock, puck: like drops of water in a fountain falling softly in the brimming bowl.

VIRGINIA WOOLF
1882–1941

An experimental novelist who developed the model of a particular poetic style for prose fiction, Virginia Woolf is known for her precise evocations of states of mind—the sensuous as well as rational perceptions that make up human consciousness. It is through this recording of moments of awareness that she joins Proust and Joyce in the move away from the linear development and objective descriptions of the nineteenth-century novel, and develops a different way of structuring both her protagonists' personal awareness and the relationships of different parts of the text. Blocks of time are juxtaposed in the memory or in different points of view; incomplete perspectives play off one another to create a larger pattern; alternating modes of narration remind the reader that a poetic (or fictional) creation is involved. Adapting the "stream of consciousness" technique inside a narrative style that ranges from precise, mundane details to lyric elaboration, and keenly aware of the way perception is further shaped by cultural habits, Woolf shows the creative imagination to be as basic an element in human fulfillment as it is in the creation of artistic texts.

She was born Adeline Virginia Stephen on January 25, 1882, one of the four children of the eminent Victorian editor and historian Leslie Stephen and his wife, Julia. The family actively pursued intellectual and artistic interests, and Julia was admired and sketched by some of the most famous Pre-Raphaelite artists. Following the customs of the day, only the sons, Adrian and Thoby, were given formal and university education; Virginia and her sister, Vanessa (later the painter Vanessa Bell), were instructed at home by their parents, and depended for further education on their father's immense library. Virginia bitterly resented this unequal treatment and the systematic discouragement of women's intellectual development that it implied. Throughout her own work, themes of society's different attitudes toward men and women play a strong role, especially in the essays *A Room of One's Own* (1929)—which contains the famous anecdote of her having been warned off the grass and forbidden entrance to a university library because she was a woman—and *Three Guineas* (1938). *A Room of One's Own* examines the history of literature written by women and contains also an impassioned plea that women writers be given conditions equal to those available for men: specifically, the privacy of a room in which to write and economic independence. (At the time Woolf wrote, it was very unusual for women to have any money of their own or to be able to devote themselves to a career with the same freedom as men.) After her mother's death in 1895, Woolf was expected to take over the supervision of the family household, which she did until her father's death in 1904. Of fragile physical health after an attack of whooping cough when she was six, she suffered in addition a nervous break-down after the death of each parent.

Woolf moved to central London with her sister and brother Adrian after their father's death, and took a house in the Bloomsbury district (where the British Museum is located). They soon became the focus of what was later called the "Bloomsbury Group," a group of writers, artists, and intellectuals impatient with conservative Edwardian society and eager to explore new modes of thought. Members of the group included the novelist E. M. Forster, the historian Lytton Strachey, the economist John Maynard Keynes, and the art critics Clive Bell (who married Vanessa) and Roger Fry (who introduced the group to Postimpressionist painters like Manet and Cézanne). Woolf was not yet writing fiction, but contributed reviews to the *Times Literary Supplement*, taught literature and composition at Morley College (an institution with a volunteer faculty that provided educational opportunities for workers), and worked for the adult suffrage movement and a feminist group. In 1912 she married Leonard Woolf, who encouraged her to write and with whom she founded the Hogarth Press in 1917. The Press became one of the most respected of the small literary presses and published works by such major authors as Eliot, Mansfield, Strachey, Forster, Gorky, and Middleton Murry as well as Woolf's own novels and translations of Freud. Over the next two decades she produced her best-known fiction while coping with frequent bouts of physical and mental illness. Already depressed during World War II, and exhausted after the completion of her last novel, she sensed the approach of a serious attack of insanity and the confinement it would entail: in such situations, she was obliged to "rest" and forbidden to read or write. In March 1941, she drowned herself in a river close to her Sussex home.

As a writer, Woolf is best known for her poetic evocations of the way we think and feel. Like Proust and Joyce, she is superbly capable of evoking all the concrete, sensuous detail of everyday experience; like them, she explores the structures of consciousness. What she really deplored was the microscopic, documentary realism that contemporaries like Arnold Bennett and John Galsworthy drew from the nineteenth-century masters. To the "appalling narrative business of . . . getting from lunch to dinner," and the pretense of scientific objectivity, Woolf preferred a more subjective—and thereby more accurate—account of the real. Her focus was not so much the object under observation as the observer's own reaction: "Let us record the atoms as they fall upon the mind in the order in which they fall, let us trace the pattern, however disconnected and incoherent in appearance, which each sight or incident scores upon the consciousness."

Woolf's writing has been compared to Postimpressionist art in the way that it emphasizes the abstract arrangement of perspectives to suggest additional networks of meaning. After two relatively traditional novels, she began to develop a more flexible approach that openly manipulated fictional structure. The continuously developing plot gave way to an organization by juxtaposed points of view; the experience of "real" or chronological time was displaced (although not completely) by a mind ranging ambiguously among its memories; and an intricate pattern of symbolic themes connected otherwise unrelated characters in the same story. All these techniques made new demands on the reader's ability to synthesize and re-create a whole picture. In *Jacob's Room* (1922), a picture of the hero must be assembled from a series of partial points of view. In *The Waves* (1931), the multiple perspective of different characters soliloquizing on their relationship to the dead Percival is broken by ten interludes that together construct an additional, interacting perspective when they describe the passage of a single day from dawn to dusk. The same novel may expand or telescope the sense of time: *Mrs. Dalloway* (1925) focuses apparently on Clarissa Dalloway's preparations for a party that evening, but at the same time calls up—at different times, and according to different contexts—her whole life from childhood to her present age of fifty. Problems of identity are a constant concern in these shifting perspectives, and Woolf often portrayed the search of unfulfilled personalities for whatever will complete them. Her work is studded with moments of heightened awareness (comparable to Joyce's "epiphanies") in which a character suddenly *sees into* a person or situation. With Woolf, this moment is less a matter of mystical insight (as it is with Joyce) than a real creation of the mind using all its faculties.

No one can read Woolf without being struck by the importance she gives to the creative imagination. Her major characters display a sensitivity that reacts on wavelengths beyond rational logic, and her narrative style celebrates the aesthetic impulse to coordinate many dimensions inside one harmoniously significant whole. Human beings are not complete, Woolf suggests, without exercising their intuitive and imaginative faculties. Like other modernist writers, she is fascinated by the creative process and often makes reference to it in her work. Whether describing the struggles of a painter in *To the Lighthouse* (1927) or of a writer in "An Unwritten Novel," she simultaneously illustrates the exploratory and creative work of the human imagination. Not all this work is visible in the finished painting or novel: observing, sifting, coordinating, projecting different interpretations and relationships, the mind performs an enormous labor of coordinating consciousness that cannot be captured entirely in any fixed form.

In "An Unwritten Novel," Woolf humorously describes the embryonic stages of composition by taking the reader through the tentative beginnings of a novel that might have been. The story moves back and forth between two sides of imagination and reality, both contributing to the potential novel, as the narrator mentally tests out possible versions based on her observation of a particular person in the railway carriage. On the one hand, she records the actual words and gestures of her fellow passengers on the train: on the other, she projects their imagined life into a completely fictional creation as she perceives, empathizes, and shapes what she sees to fit her own preconceptions. The process of composition appears in all its experiments, false starts, and corrections for tone and consistency: the narrator must find the appropriate imagined crime for Minnie's repressed air, supply ferns instead of rhododendrons to fit a given scene, and add or subtract characters to round out the story. Nor does Woolf ignore the narrator's own character as a motivating force: although the narrator prides herself on starting from a solid base of concrete observation, her artist's joy in the pure exercise of creativity quickly leads to elaboration for its own sake (the broken eggshell that becomes a map, blocks of marble, and Spanish silver and gold: her delighted transformation of James Moggridge into a clinically functioning organism as her X-ray vision penetrates "the spine tough as whalebone, straight as oaktree; the ribs radiating branches; the flesh taut tarpaulin; the red hollows; the suck and regurgitation of the heart; while from above meat falls in brown cubes and beer gushes to be churned to blood again"). Like Baudelaire in "The Windows," she triumphantly asserts the value of creativity over mere factual evidence. When her first tale has comically been disproved and she is left "bare as a bone," it is not long before instinct takes over and she starts spinning stories anew. In this richly textured short story, which combines the dimensions of objective reality and self-deception with a passionate statement of the liberating power of art, Woolf pokes gentle fun at herself and at the whole tradition of the novel as a mirror of reality. The essayist's critical and self-analytic perspective gives way at the end, however, to a lyric reaffirmation of the artist's obsession with the fascinating, "adorable world" of colorful sights and mysterious figures, all waiting to be created.

Phyllis Rose's *Woman of Letters: A Life of Virginia Woolf* (1978) is a valuable biography incorporating much recent material and critical perspectives. A useful and readable introduction to the texts is provided by Avrom Fleishmann, *Virginia Woolf, A Critical Reading* (1975). Patricia Clements and Isobel Grundy are editors of *Virginia Woolf: New Critical Essays* (1983), a collection of modern essays examining Woolf in relation to contemporary writers, to modernism, and to her perspectives on writing. Virginia Woolf's autobiographical writings are collected in *Moments of Being*, edited by Jeanne Schulkind (1976).

An Unwritten Novel

Such an expression of unhappiness was enough by itself to make one's eyes slide above the paper's edge to the poor woman's face— insignificant without that look, almost a symbol of human destiny with it. Life's what you see in people's eyes; life's what they learn, and, having learnt it, never, though they seek to hide it, cease to be aware of—what? That life's like that, it seems. Five faces opposite— five mature faces—and the knowledge in each face. Strange, though, how people want to conceal it! Marks of reticence are on all those faces: lips shut, eyes shaded, each one of the five doing something to hide or stultify his knowledge. One smokes; another reads; a third checks entries in a pocket book; a fourth stares at the map of the line framed opposite; and the fifth—the terrible thing about the fifth is that she does nothing at all. She looks at life. Ah, but my poor, unfortunate woman, do play the game—do, for all our sakes, conceal it!

As if she heard me, she looked up, shifted slightly in her seat and sighed. She seemed to apologize and at the same time to say to me, "If only you knew!" Then she looked at life again. "But I do know,"

I answered silently, glancing at the *Times*[1] for manners' sake. "I know the whole business. 'Peace between Germany and the Allied Powers was yesterday officially ushered in at Paris—Signor Nitti, the Italian Prime Minister—a passenger train at Doncaster was in collision with a goods train . . .' We all know—the *Times* knows—but we pretend we don't." My eyes had once more crept over the paper's rim. She shuddered, twitched her arm queerly to the middle of her back and shook her head. Again I dipped into my great reservoir of life. "Take what you like," I continued, "births, deaths, marriages, Cort Circular, the habits of birds, Leonardo da Vinci, the Sandhills murder, high wages and the cost of living—oh, take what you like," I repeated, "it's all in the *Times*!" Again with infinite weariness she moved her head from side to side until, like a top exhausted with spinning, it settled on her neck.

The *Times* was no protection against such sorrow as hers. But other human beings forbade intercourse. The best thing to do against life was to fold the paper so that it made a perfect square, crisp, thick, impervious even to life. This done, I glanced up quickly, armed with a shield of my own. She pierced through my shield; she gazed into my eyes as if searching any sediment of courage at the depths of them and damping it to clay. Her twitch alone denied all hope, discounted all illusion.

So we rattled through Surrey and across the border into Sussex.[2] But with my eyes upon life I did not see that the other travellers had left, one by one, till, save for the man who read, we were alone together. Here was Three Bridges station. We drew slowly down the platform and stopped. Was he going to leave us? I prayed both ways— I prayed last that he might stay. At that instant he roused himself, crumpled his paper contemptuously, like a thing done with, burst open the door, and left us alone.

The unhappy woman, leaning a little forward, palely and colourlessly addressed me—talked of stations and holidays, of brothers at Eastbourne, and the time of year, which was, I forget now, early or late. But at last looking from the window and seeing, I knew, only life, she breathed, "Staying away—that's the drawback of it—" Ah, now we approached the catastrophe.[3] "My sister-in-law"—the bitterness of her tone was like lemon on cold steel, and speaking, not to me, but to herself, she muttered, "nonsense, she would say—that's what they all say," and while she spoke she fidgeted as though the skin on her back were as a plucked fowl's in a poulterer's shop-window.

1. Major London newspaper, reputed to cover everything from international and royal news [the Court Circular] to a variety of local topics.   2. The train is passing through the southeastern English countryside, headed away from London. Eastbourne a seaside resort.   3. In the literary sense: a dénouement or crucial revelation.

"Oh, that cow!" she broke off nervously, as though the great wooden cow in the meadow had shocked her and saved her from some indiscretion. Then she shuddered, and then she made the awkward angular movement that I had seen before, as if, after the spasm, some spot between the shoulders burnt or itched. Then again she looked the most unhappy woman in the world, and I once more reproached her, though not with the same conviction, for if there were a reason, and if I knew the reason, the stigma was removed from life.

"Sisters-in-law," I said—

Her lips pursed as if to spit venom at the word; pursed they remained. All she did was to take her glove and rub hard at a spot on the window-pane. She rubbed as if she would rub something out for ever—some stain, some indelible contamination. Indeed, the spot remained for all her rubbing, and back she sank with the shudder and the clutch of the arm I had come to expect. Something impelled me to take my glove and rub my window. There, too, was a little speck on the glass. For all my rubbing it remained. And then the spasm went through me; I crooked my arm and plucked at the middle of my back. My skin, too, felt like the damp chicken's skin in the poulterer's shop-window; one spot between the shoulders itched and irritated, felt clammy, felt raw. Could I reach it? Surreptitiously I tried. She saw me. A smile of infinite irony, infinite sorrow, flitted and faded from her face. But she had communicated, shared her secret, passed her poison; she would speak no more. Leaning back in my corner, shielding my eyes from her eyes, seeing only the slopes and hollows, greys and purples, of the winter's landscape, I read her message, deciphered her secret, reading it beneath her gaze.

Hilda's the sister-in-law. Hilda? Hilda? Hilda Marsh—Hilda the blooming, the full bosomed, the matronly. Hilda stands at the door as the cab draws up, holding a coin. "Poor Minnie, more of a grasshopper than ever—old cloak she had last year. Well, well, with two children these days one can't do more. No, Minnie, I've got it; here you are, cabby—none of your ways with me. Come in, Minnie. Oh, I could carry *you*, let alone your basket!" So they go into the dining-room. "Aunt Minnie, children."

Slowly the knives and forks sink from the upright. Down they get (Bob and Barbara), hold out hands stiffly; back again to their chairs, staring between the resumed mouthfuls. [But this we'll skip; ornaments, curtains, trefoil china plate, yellow oblongs of cheese, white squares of biscuit—skip, oh, but wait! Halfway through luncheon one of those shivers; Bob stares at her, spoon in mouth. "Get on with your pudding, Bob"; but Hilda disapproves. "Why *should* she twitch?" Skip, skip, till we reach the landing on the upper floor; stairs brass-bound; linoleum worn; oh, yes! little bedroom looking out over the roofs of Eastbourne—zigzagging roofs like the spines of caterpillars,

this way, that way, striped red and yellow, with blue-black slating.]
Now, Minnie, the door's shut; Hilda heavily descends to the basement; you unstrap the straps of your basket, lay on the bed a meagre
nightgown, stand side by side furred felt slippers. The looking-glass—
no, you avoid the looking-glass. Some methodical disposition of hat-
pins. Perhaps the shell box has something in it? You shake it; it's the
pearl stud there was last year—that's all. And then the sniff, the sigh,
the sitting by the window. Three o'clock on a December afternoon;
the rain drizzling! one light low in the skylight of a drapery empor-
ium; another high in a servant's bedroom—this one goes out. That
gives her nothing to look at. A moment's blankness—then, what are
you thinking? (Let me peep across at her opposite; she's asleep or
pretending it; so what would she think about sitting at the window at
three o'clock in the afternoon? Health, money, hills, her God?) Yes,
sitting on the very edge of the chair looking over the roofs of Eastbourne, Minnie Marsh prays to God. That's all very well; and she
may rub the pane too, as though to see God better; but what God
does she see? Who's the God of Minnie Marsh, the God of the back
streets of Eastbourne, the God of three o'clock in the afternoon? I,
too, see roofs, I see sky; but, oh, dear—this seeing of Gods! More
like President Kruger than Prince Albert[4]—that's the best I can do
for him; and I see him on a chair, in a black frock-coat, not so very
high up either; I can manage a cloud or two for him to sit on; and
then his hand trailing in the cloud holds a rod, a truncheon is it?—
black, thick, thorned—a brutal old bully—Minnie's God! Did he
send the itch and the patch and the twitch? Is that why she prays?
What she rubs on the window is the stain of sin. Oh, she committed
some crime!

I have my choice of crimes. The woods flit and fly—in summer
there are bluebells; in the opening there, when spring comes, primroses. A parting, was it, twenty years ago? Vows broken? Not Minnie's! . . . She was faithful. How she nursed her mother! All her
savings on the tombstone—wreaths under glass—daffodils in jars.
But I'm off the track. A crime. . . . They would say she kept her
sorrow, suppressed her secret—her sex, they'd say—the scientific
people. But what flummery to saddle *her* with sex! No—more like
this. Passing down the streets of Croydon twenty years ago, the violet
loops of ribbon in the draper's window spangled in the electric light
catch her eye. She lingers—past six. Still by running she can reach
home. She pushes through the glass wing door. It's sale-time. Shallow trays brim with ribbons. She pauses, pulls this, fingers that with

---

4. Paul Kruger (1825–1904), Transvaal statesman strongly opposed to British influence in South
Africa, president of the Boer Republic for twenty years. Contemporary pictures show him in
formal frock coat with a severe, bearded face. *Prince Albert* (1819–61), husband of the British
Queen Victoria, was a popular figure known for political moderation.

the raised roses on it—no need to choose, no need to buy, and each tray with its surprises. "We don't shut till seven," and then it *is* seven. She runs, she rushes, home she reaches, but too late. Neighbours— the doctor—baby brother—the kettle—scalded—hospital—dead—or only the shock of it, the blame? Ah, but the detail matters nothing! It's what she carries with her; the spot, the crime, the thing to expiate, always there between her shoulders. "Yes," she seems to nod to me, "it's the thing I did."

Whether you did, or what you did, I don't mind; it's not the thing I want. The draper's window looped with violet—that'll do; a little cheap perhaps, a little commonplace—since one has a choice of crimes, but then so many (let me peep across again—still sleeping, or pretending sleep! white, worn, the mouth closed—a touch of obstinacy, more than one would think—no hint of sex)—so many crimes aren't *your* crime; your crime was cheap, only the retribution solemn; for now the church door opens, the hard wooden pew receives her; on the brown tiles she kneels; every day, winter, summer, dusk, dawn (here she's at it) prays. All her sins fall, fall, for ever fall. The spot receives them. It's raised, it's red, it's burning. Next she twitches. Small boys point. "Bob at lunch today"—But elderly women are the worst.

Indeed now you can't sit praying any longer. Kruger's sunk beneath the clouds—washed over as with a painter's brush of liquid grey, to which he adds a tinge of black—even the tip of the truncheon gone now. That's what always happens! Just as you've seen him, felt him, someone interrupts. It's Hilda now.

How you hate her! She'll even lock the bathroom door overnight, too, though it's only cold water you want, and sometimes when the night's been bad it seems as if washing helped. And John at break-fast—the children—meals are worst, and sometimes there are friends— ferns don't altogether hide 'em—they guess, too; so out you go along the front,[5] where the waves are grey, and the papers blow, and the glass shelters green and draughty, and the chairs cost tuppence—too much—for there must be preachers along the sands. Ah, that's a nigger—that's a funny man—that's a man with parakeets—poor little creatures! Is there no one here who thinks of God?—just up there, over the pier, with his rod—but no—there's nothing but grey in the sky or if it's blue the white clouds hide him, and the music—it's military music—and what they are fishing for? Do they catch them? How the children stare! Well, then home a back way—"Home a back way!" The words have meaning; might have been spoken by the old man with whiskers—no, no, he didn't really speak; but every-thing has meaning—placards leaning against doorways—names above

5. Waterfront; chairs were available for rent.

shop-windows—red fruit in baskets—women's heads in the hairdresser's—all say "Minnie Marsh!" But here's a jerk. "Eggs are cheaper!"[6]
That's what always happens! I was heading her over the waterfall,
straight for madness, when, like a flock of dream sheep, she turns
t'other way and runs between my fingers. Eggs are cheaper. Tethered
to the shores of the world, none of the crimes, sorrows, rhapsodies,
or insanities for poor Minnie Marsh; never late for luncheon; never
caught in a storm without a mackintosh; never utterly unconscious
of the cheapness of eggs. So she reaches home—scrapes her boots.

    Have I read you right? But the human face—the human face at
the top of the fullest sheet of print holds more, withholds more.
Now, eyes open, she looks out; and in the human eye—how d'you
define it?—there's a break—a division—so that when you've grasped
the stem the butterfly's off—the moth that hangs in the evening over
the yellow flower—move, raise your hand, off, high, away. I won't
raise my hand. Hang still, then, quiver, life, soul, spirit, whatever
you are of Minnie Marsh—I, too, on my flower—the hawk over the
down—alone, or what were the worth of life? To rise; hang still in
the evening, in the midday; hang still over the down. The flicker of
a hand—off, up! then poised again. Alone, unseen; seeing all so still
down there, all so lovely. None seeing, none caring. The eyes of
others our prisons; their thoughts our cages. Air above, air below.
And the moon and immortality. . . . Oh, but I drop to the turf! Are
you down too, you in the corner, what's your name—woman—Minnie
Marsh; some such name as that? There she is, tight to her blossom;
opening her hand-bag, from which she takes a hollow shell—an egg—
who was saying that eggs were cheaper? You or I? Oh, it was you
who said it on the way home, you remember, when the old gentleman, suddenly opening his umbrella—or sneezing was it? Anyhow,
Kruger went, and you came "home a back way," and scraped your
boots. Yes. And now you lay across your knees a pocket-handker-
chief into which drop little angular fragments of eggshell—fragments
of a map—a puzzle. I wish I could piece them together! If you would
only sit still. She's moved her knees—the map's in bits again. Down
the slopes of the Andes the white blocks of marble go bounding and
hurtling, crushing to death a whole troop of Spanish muleteers, with
their convoy—Drake's booty, gold and silver.[7] But to return—

    To what, to where? She opened the door, and, putting her umbrella
in the stand—that goes without saying; so, too, the whiff of beef from
the basement; dot, dot, dot. But what I cannot thus eliminate, what

6. The narrator's silent imaginings are interrupted and brought down to earth when "Minnie
Marsh," preparing to eat her snack of hard-boiled egg, comments out loud that "Eggs are
cheaper!"   7. The yellow and white fragments of egg inspire another series of images. Sir Francis Drake (1540?—96) was an English explorer and sea captain who captured Spanish ships returning from South America laden with gold and silver stolen from the Indians; the Indians are
imagined as rolling blocks of marble down the Andes mountains to crush the invaders.

I must, head down, eyes shut, with the courage of a battalion and the blindness of a bull, charge and disperse are, indubitably, the figures behind the ferns, commercial travellers. There, I've hidden them all this time in the hope that somehow they'd disappear, or better still emerge, as indeed they must, if the story's to go on gathering richness and rotundity, destiny and tragedy, as stories should, rolling along with it two, if not three, commercial travellers and a whole grove of aspidistra. "The fronds of the aspidistra only partly concealed the commercial traveller—" Rhododendrons would conceal him utterly, and into the bargain give me my fling of red and white, for which I starve and strive; but rhododendrons in Eastbourne—in December—on the Marshes' table—no, no, I dare not;[8] it's all a matter of crusts and cruets, frills and ferns. Perhaps there'll be a moment later by the sea. Moreover, I feel, pleasantly pricking through the green fretwork and over the glacis of cut glass, a desire to peer and peep at the man opposite—one's as much as I can manage. James Moggridge is it, whom the Marshes call Jimmy? [Minnie, you must promise not to twitch till I've got this straight.] James Moggridge travels in[9]—shall we say buttons?—but the time's not come for bringing *them* in—the big and the little on the long cards, some peacock-eyed, others dull gold; cairngorms some, and others coral sprays—but I say the time's not come. He travels, and on Thursdays, his Eastbourne day, takes his meals with the Marshes. His red face, his little steady eyes—but no means altogether commonplace—his enormous appetite (that's safe; he won't look at Minnie till the bread's swamped the gravy dry), napkin tucked diamond-wise—but this is primitive, and, whatever it may do the reader, don't take me in. Let's dodge to the Moggridge household, set that in motion. Well, the family boots are mended on Sundays by James himself. He reads *Truth*.[1] But his passion? Roses—and his wife a retired hospital nurse—interesting—for God's sake let me have one woman with a name I like! But no; she's of the unborn children of the mind, illicit, none the less loved, like my rhododendrons. How many die in every novel that's written—the best, the dearest, while Moggridge lives. It's life's fault. Here's Minnie eating her egg at the moment opposite and at t'other end of the line—are we past Lewes?[2]—there must be Jimmy—what's her twitch for?

There must be Moggridge—life's fault. Life imposes her laws; life blocks the way; life's behind the fern; life's the tyrant; oh, but not the bully! No, for I assure you I come willingly; I come wooed by Heaven knows what compulsion across ferns and cruets, table splashed and

8. Aspidistra (a long-leaved, common house plant) is more appropriate for the imagined story's middle-class setting than rhododendron, which would not fit the season or context. 9. The commercial traveler (traveling salesman) given the name James Moggridge is imagined as selling buttons; there follows a brief description of his merchandise on its display cards (*cairngorm* is a yellow quartz). 1. A popular weekly magazine. 2. County town in East Sussex.

bottles smeared. I come irresistibly to lodge myself somewhere on the firm flesh, in the robust spine, wherever I can penetrate or find foothold on the person, in the soul, of Moggridge the man. The enormous stability of the fabric; the spine tough as whalebone, straight as oaktree; the ribs radiating branches; the flesh taut tarpaulin; the red hollows; the suck and regurgitation of the heart; while from above meat falls in brown cubes and beer gushes to be churned to blood again—and so we reach the eyes. Behind the aspidistra they see something: black, white, dismal; now the plate again; behind the aspidistra they see elderly woman; "Marsh's sister, Hilda's more my sort"; the tablecloth now. "Marsh would know what's wrong with Morrises . . ." talk that over; cheese has come; the plate again; turn it round—the enormous fingers; now the woman opposite. "Marsh's sister—not a bit like Marsh; wretched, elderly female. . . . You should feed your hens. . . . God's truth, what's set her twitching? Not what I said? Dear, dear, dear! these elderly women. Dear, dear!"

[Yes, Minnie; I know you've twitched, but one moment—James Moggridge.]

"Dear, dear, dear!" How beautiful the sound is! like the knock of a mallet on seasoned timber, like the throb of the heart of an ancient whaler when the seas press thick and the green is clouded. "Dear, dear!" what a passing bell for the souls of the fretful to soothe them and solace them, lap them in linen, saying, "So long. Good luck to you!" and then, "What's your pleasure?" for though Moggridge would pluck his rose for her, that's done, that's over. Now what's the next thing? "Madam, you'll miss your train," for they don't linger.

That's the man's way; that's the sound that reverberates; that's St. Paul's,[3] and the motor-omnibuses. But we're brushing the crumbs off. Oh, Moggridge, you won't stay? You must be off? Are you driving through Eastbourne this afternoon in one of those little carriages? Are you the man who's walled up in green cardboard boxes, and sometimes sits so solemn staring like a sphinx; and always there's a look of the sepulchral, something of the undertaker, the coffin, and the dusk about horse and driver? Do tell me—but the doors slammed. We shall never meet again. Moggridge, farewell!

Yes, yes, I'm coming. Right up to the top of the house. One moment I'll linger. How the mud goes round in the mind—what a swirl these monsters leave, the waters rocking, the weeds waving and green here, black there, striking to the sand, till by degrees the atoms reassemble, the deposit sifts itself, and again through the eyes one sees clear and still, and there comes to the lips some prayer for the departed, some obsequy for the souls of those one nods to, the people one never meets again.

---

3. St. Paul's Cathedral in London.

James Moggridge is dead now, gone for ever. Well, Minnie—"I can face it no longer." If she said that—(Let me look at her. She is brushing the eggshell into deep declivities). She said it certainly, leaning against the wall of the bedroom, and plucking at the little balls which edge the claret-coloured curtain. But when the self speaks to the self, who is speaking?—the entombed soul, the spirit driven in, in, in to the central catacomb; the self that took the veil[4] and left the world—a coward perhaps, yet somehow beautiful, as it flits with its lantern restlessly up and down the dark corridors. "I can bear it no longer," her spirit says. "That man at lunch—Hilda—the children." Oh, heavens, her sob! It's the spirit wailing its destiny, the spirit driven hither, thither, lodging on the diminishing carpets— meagre footholds—shrunken shreds of all the vanishing universe— love, life, faith, husband, children, I know not what splendours and pageantries glimpsed in girlhood. "Not for me—not for me."

But then—the muffins, the bald elderly dog? Bead mats I should fancy and the consolation of underlinen. If Minnie Marsh were run over and taken to hospital, nurses and doctors themselves would exclaim.[5] . . . There's the vista and the vision—there's the distance—the blue blot at the end of the avenue, while, after all, the tea is rich, the muffin hot, and the dog—"Benny, to your basket, sir, and see what mother's brought you!" So, taking the glove with the worn thumb, defying once more the encroaching demon of what's called going in holes, you renew the fortifications, threading the grey wool, running it in and out.

Running it in and out, across and over, spinning a web through which God himself—hush, don't think of God! How firm the stitches are! You must be proud of your darning. Let nothing disturb her. Let the light fall gently, and the clouds show an inner vest of the first green leaf. Let the sparrow perch on the twig and shake the raindrop hanging to the twig's elbow. . . . Why look up? Was it a sound, a thought? Oh, heavens! Back again to the thing you did, the plate glass with the violet loops? But Hilda will come. Ignominies, humiliations, oh! Close the breach.

Having mended her glove, Minnie Marsh lays it in the drawer. She shuts the drawer with decision. I catch sight of her face in the glass. Lips are pursed. Chin held high. Next she laces her shoes. Then she touches her throat. What's your brooch? Mistletoe or merrythought?[6] And what is happening? Unless I'm much mistaken, the pulse's quickened, the moment's coming, the threads are racing, Niagara's ahead. Here's the crisis! Heaven be with you! Down she goes. Courage, courage! Face it, be it! For God's sake don't wait on

---

4. Became a nun. 5. The hospital attendants are to exclaim at the neatness of Minnie Marsh's underwear. Immaculate and well-kept clothing—both inside and out—were the signs of a proper lady. 6. Wishbone.

the mat now! There's the door! I'm on your side. Speak! Comfort her, confound her soul![7]

"Oh, I beg your pardon! Yes, this is Eastbourne. I'll reach it down for you. Let me try the handle." [But Minnie, though we keep up pretences, I've read you right—I'm with you now.]

"That's all your luggage?"

"Much obliged, I'm sure."

(But why do you look about you? Hilda won't come to the station, nor John; and Moggridge is driving at the far side of Eastbourne.)

"I'll wait by my bag, ma'am, that's safest. He said he'd meet me. . . . Oh, there he is! That's my son."

So they walk off together.

Well, but I'm confounded. . . . Surely, Minnie, you know better! A strange young man. . . . Stop! I'll tell him—Minnie!—Miss Marsh!—I don't know though. There's something queer in her cloak as it blows. Oh, but it's untrue, it's indecent. . . . Look how he bends as they reach the gateway. She finds her ticket. What's the joke? Off they go, down the road, side by side. . . . Well, my world's done for! What do I stand on? What do I know? That's not Minnie. There never was Moggridge. Who am I? Life's bare as bone.

And yet the last look of them—he stepping from the kerb and she following him round the edge of the big building brims me with wonder—floods me anew. Mysterious figures! Mother and son. Who are you? Why do you walk down the street? Where tonight will you sleep, and then, tomorrow? Oh, how it whirls and surges—floats me afresh! I start after them. People drive this way and that. The white light splutters and pours. Plate-glass windows. Carnations; chrysanthemums. Ivy in dark gardens. Milk carts at the door. Wherever I go, mysterious figures, I see you, turning the corner, mothers and sons; you, you, you. I hasten, I follow. This, I fancy, must be the sea. Grey is the landscape; dim as ashes; the water murmurs and moves. If I fall on my knees, if I go through the ritual, the ancient antics, it's you, unknown figures, you I adore; if I open my arms, it's you I embrace, you I draw to me—adorable world!

FRANZ KAFKA

1883–1924

Although Kafka was born in Prague in 1883 and died in 1924, generations of twentieth-century readers have considered him their contemporary and a

7. The narrator imagines a major confrontation between the poor spinster "Minnie Marsh" and "Hilda."

representative of the age. His predicament, as W. H. Auden put it, is the "predicament of modern man," and the world of his imagination held many terrors which are all too familiar today. The vision and structure of Kafka's fictional world have long fascinated contemporary writers, who see in them a peculiarly timely combination of the most mundane, pedestrian realism and a nightmare imagination that lifts daily events to an allusively symbolic and infinitely interpretable level. Whether evoking the multilayered bureaucracy of the modern state, the sense of guilt experienced by those facing powerful and incomprehensible authority (patriarchal, political, or religious), or the frustrated vulnerability of characters who are unable to establish viable human relations, Kafka finds familiar images to convey the most prevalent themes of modern literature: the helpless yearning towards meaning in a universe that will not respond, and the oppressive alienation of individual lives in modern industrial society. It is the ordinariness of his world that helps convince the reader, even when that ordinariness is later distorted by illogical events and their grotesque implications. Such a combination of ordinariness and expanded meaning is found in writers—however different—who have read and absorbed Kafka's lesson: Beckett, Pinter, Robbe-Grillet, García Márquez.

Kafka was born into cultural alienation. Jewish (though not truly part of the Jewish community) in Catholic Czechoslovakia; son of a German-speaking shopkeeper when German was the language of the imposed Austro-Hungarian government; and drawn to literature when his father—a domineering, self-made man—pushed him toward success in business, he was constantly part of two incompatible contexts. Nor was he happier at home. Resenting his father's overbearing nature and feeling deprived of maternal love, he nonetheless lived with his parents for most of his life and complained in long letters about his coldness and inability to love (despite numerous liaisons). Kafka took a degree in law in order to qualify himself for a position in a large accident-insurance corporation, where he worked until illness forced his retirement in 1922. By the time of his death from tuberculosis two years later, he had published a number of short stories and two novellas (*The Metamorphosis*, 1915; *In the Penal Colony*, 1919), but left behind him the manuscripts of three near-complete novels which—considering himself a failure—he asked to have burned. Instead, Kafka's executor Max Brod published the novels (*The Trial*, 1925; *The Castle*, 1926; *Amerika*, 1927) and a biography celebrating the genius of his tormented, guilt-ridden friend.

In spite of the indubitable fact that Franz Kafka became a respected senior executive handling claims, litigations, public relations, and his institute's annual reports, and was one of the few top German executives retained when Czechoslovakia finally gained independence in 1918, his image in the modern imagination is derived from the portraits of inner anguish given in his fiction, diaries, and letters. This "Kafka" is a tormented and sensitive soul, guiltily resentful of his job in a giant bureaucracy, unable to free himself from his family or to cope with the demands of love, physically feeble, and constantly beset by feelings of inferiority and doom in an existence whose laws he can never quite understand. "Before the Law," a parable published in Kafka's lifetime and included in *The Trial*, recounts the archetypal setting of the "Kafka" character: a countryman waits and waits throughout his lifetime for permission to enter a crucial Gate, where the doorkeeper (the first of many) constantly refuses him entrance. He tries everything from good behavior to bribes without success. Finally, as the now-aged countryman dies in frustration, he is told that the gate existed only for him, and that it is now being closed. For the countryman (as for Vladimir and Estragon in Beckett's later *Waiting for Godot*, and indeed for much modern literature), there is no response. The Law that governs our existence is all-powerful but irrational; at least it is not to be understood by its human suppliants, a lesson which Kafka could have derived equally well from his readings in the Danish philosopher Søren Kierkegaard, in Nietzsche, or in the Jewish Talmud.

The combination of down-to-earth, matter-of-fact setting and unreal or nightmarish events is the hallmark of Kafka's style. His characters speak everyday language and react in a common-sense way when such a response (given the situation) is utterly grotesque. A young businessman is changed overnight into a giant beetle (*The Metamorphosis*) or charged with undefined crimes and finally executed (*The Trial*); a would-be land surveyor is unable to communicate with the castle that employs him and keeps sending incomprehensible messages (*The Castle*); a visitor to a penal colony observes a gigantic machine whose function is to execute condemned criminals by inscribing their sentence deeper and deeper into the flesh (*In the Penal Colony*). The term "surrealist" is often attached to this blend of everyday reality and dream configuration, with its implication of psychic undercurrents and cosmic significance stirring beneath the most ordinary-seeming existence. Kafka, however, had no connection with the Surrealists, whose vision of a miraculous level of existence hidden behind everyday life is the obverse of his heroes' vain attempts to maintain control over the impossible.

Kafka's stories are not allegories, although many readers have been tempted to find in them a particular underlying message. A political reading sees them as indictments of faceless bureaucracy controlling individual lives in the modern totalitarian state, and in fact Kafka's works cannot be published in Czechoslovakia. The sense of being found guilty by an entire society recalls the traditional theme of the Wandering Jew, and predicts for many the Holocaust of World War II (in fact, Kafka's three sisters died in concentration camps). His heroes' self-conscious quest to fit into some meaningful structure, their attempt ceaselessly to do the right thing when there is no rational way of knowing what that is, is the very picture of absurdity and alienation that existentialist philosophers and writers examined during and after World War II. The assumption that there is a Law, and the presence of protagonists who die in search for purity ("The Hunger Artist") or in a humble admission of guilt (*The Trial*) allow the stories to be taken as religious metaphors. Kafka's desperately lucid analysis of the way his parents' influence shaped an impressionable child into an unhappy adult ("Letter to My Father") articulates emotional tangles and parent-child rivalry wih an openness and detail that recalls decades of psychoanalytical criticism following Freud. The picture of a sick society where individual rights and sensitivity no longer count, and unreasoning torment is visited on the ignorant, has been read as an indictment of disintegrating modern culture. Yet no one allegorical interpretation is finally possible, for all these potential meanings overlap as they expand towards social, familial, political, philosophical, and religious dimensions and constitute the richly allusive texture of separate tales by a master storyteller.

The Metamorphosis, Kafka's longest complete work published in his life-time, is first of all a consummate story in which the question "What happens next?" never loses interest from the moment that Gregor Samsa wakes up to find himself transformed. "It was no dream," no nightmarish fantasy in which Gregor temporarily identified himself with other downtrodden ver-min of society. Instead, this grotesque transformation is permanent, a single unshakable fact that renders almost comic his family's calculations and attempts to adjust. "The terror of art," said Kafka in a conversation about The Met-amorphosis, is that "the dream reveals the reality," and this dream become reality sheds light on the intolerable nature of Gregor's daily existence. The other side of his job is its mechanical rigidity, personal rivalries, and threat-ening suspicion of any deviation from the norm. Gregor himself is part of this world, as he shows when he fawns on the manager and tries to manip-ulate him by criticizing the boss.

More disturbing is the transformation that takes place in Gregor's family, where the expected love and support turns into shamed acceptance and ani-mal resentment now that Gregor has let the family down. Mother and sister are ineffectual, and their sympathy slowly disappears in disgust. Gregor's father quickly reassumes his position of authority and beats the beetle back into his room: first with the businesslike newspaper and manager's cane, and later with a barrage of apples from the family table. Just before his death Gregor has become an "it" whose death is warmly wished by the whole family—and perhaps they are right, in one of Kafka's ironies. The beetle's death brings not remorse but a new lease on life to his family. Weak and passive when Gregor took care of them, they regain strength and vitality under the pressure of earning a living. Mother, father, and sister celebrate Gregor's death with a holiday trip out of town, into the sunshine and open air, where they make plans for the future.

Gregor Samsa may be a pathetic figure but he is not a tragic one. In his passiveness and unvoiced resentment, his willingness to exist at a surface level of adjustment to job and family, he has become an accomplice in his own fate. His descent into animal consciousness is not a true pilgrimage to inner awareness, even though it involves letting go the trappings of civiliza-tion. Rather, it is an obscuring of consciousness that is perfectly represented when he is swept out onto the dustheap at the end. From that point on, it is the family's story, continuing a career that has meant death for Gregor and joyous survival for his family, but in which both are reduced to existence on an animal level.

Anthony Thorlby, Kafka: A Study (1972) is a brief general introduction. Heinz Politzer, Franz Kafka: Parable and Paradox (rev. 1966), presents an interesting, readable study of symbolic relationships. Ernest Pawel's The Nightmare of Reason, A Life of Franz Kafka (1984), is an excellent contem-porary biography with penetrating descriptions of his family and friends. Max Brod, Franz Kafka: A Biography, translated by G. Humphrey Roberts and Richard Winston (1960), is an early, admiring biography by a close friend and Kafka's executor.

The Metamorphosis[1]

I

When Gregor Samsa woke up one morning from unsettling dreams, he found himself changed in his bed into a monstrous vermin. He was lying on his back as hard as armor plate, and when he lifted his head a little, he saw his vaulted brown belly, sectioned by arch-shaped ribs, to whose dome the cover, about to slide off completely, could barely cling. His many legs, pitifully thin compared with the size of the rest of him, were waving helplessly before his eyes.

"What's happened to me?" he thought. It was no dream. His room, a regular human room, only a little on the small side, lay quiet between the four familiar walls. Over the table, on which an unpacked line of fabric samples was all spread out—Samsa was a traveling salesman—hung the picture which he had recently cut out of a glossy magazine and lodged in a pretty gilt frame. It showed a lady done up in a fur hat and a fur boa, sittng upright and raising up against the viewer a heavy fur muff in which her whole forearm had disappeared.

Gregor's eyes then turned to the window, and the overcast weather—he could hear raindrops hitting against the metal window ledge—completely depressed him. "How about going back to sleep for a few minutes and forgetting all this nonsense," he thought, but that was completely impracticable, since he was used to sleeping on his right side and in his present state could not get into that position. No matter how hard he threw himself onto his right side, he always rocked onto his back again. He must have tried it a hundred times, closing his eyes so as not to have to see his squirming legs, and stopped only when he began to feel a slight, dull pain in his side, which he had never felt before.

"Oh God," he thought, "what a grueling job I've picked. Day in, day out—on the road. The upset of doing business is much worse than the actual business in the home office, and besides, I've got the torture of traveling, worrying about changing trains, eating miserable food at all hours, constantly seeing new faces, no relationships that last or get more intimate. To the devil with it all!" He felt a slight itching up on top of his belly; shoved himself slowly on his back closer to the bedpost, so as to be able to lift his head better; found the itchy spot, studded with small white dots which he had no idea what to make of; and wanted to touch the spot with one of his legs but immediately pulled it back, for the contact sent a cold shiver through him.

1. Translated by Stanley Corngold.

He slid back again into his original position. "This getting up so early," he thought, "makes anyone a complete idiot. Human beings have to have their sleep. Other traveling salesmen live like harem women. For instance, when I go back to the hotel before lunch to write up the business I've done, these gentlemen are just having breakfast. That's all I'd have to try with my boss; I'd be fired on the spot. Anyway, who knows if that wouldn't be a very good thing for me. If I didn't hold back for my parents' sake, I would have quit long ago, I would have marched up to the boss and spoken my piece from the bottom of my heart. He would have fallen off the desk! It is funny, too, the way he sits on the desk and talks down from the heights to the employees, especially when they have to come right up close on account of the boss's being hard of hearing. Well, I haven't given up hope completely; once I've gotten the money together to pay off my parents' debt to him—that will probably take another five or six years—I'm going to do it without fail. Then I'm going to make the big break. But for the time being I'd better get up, since my train leaves at five."

And he looked over at the alarm clock, which was ticking on the chest of drawers. "God Almighty!" he thought. It was six-thirty, the hands were quietly moving forward, it was actually past the half-hour, it was already nearly a quarter to. Could it be that the alarm hadn't gone off? You could see from the bed that it was set correctly for four o'clock; it certainly had gone off, too. Yes, but was it possible to sleep quietly through a ringing that made the furniture shake? Well, he certainly hadn't slept quietly, but probably all the more soundly for that. But what should he do now? The next train left at seven o'clock; to make it, he would have to hurry like a madman, and the line of samples wasn't packed yet, and he himself didn't feel especially fresh and ready to march around. And even if he did make the train, he could not avoid getting it from the boss, because the messenger boy had been waiting at the five-o'clock train and would have long ago reported his not showing up. He was a tool of the boss, without brains or backbone. What if he were to say he was sick? But that would be extremely embarrassing and suspicious because during his five years wth the firm Gregor had not been sick even once. The boss would be sure to come with the health-insurance doctor, blame his five years with the firm Gregor had not been sick even once. The health-insurance doctor, for whom the world consisted of people who were completely healthy but afraid to work. And, besides, in this case would he be so very wrong? In fact, Gregor felt fine, with the exception of his drowsiness, which was really unnecessary after sleeping so late, and he even had a ravenous appetite.

Just as he was thinking all this over at top speed, without being able to decide to get out of bed—the alarm clock had just struck a quarter to seven—he heard a cautious knocking at the door next to the head of his bed. "Gregor," someone called—it was his mother— "it's a quarter to seven. Didn't you want to catch the train?" What a soft voice! Gregor was shocked to hear his own voice answering, unmistakably his own voice, true, but in which, as if from below, an insistent distressed chirping intruded, which left the clarity of his words intact only for a moment really, before so badly garbling them as they carried that no one could be sure if he had heard right. Gregor had wanted to answer in detail and to explain everything, but, given the circumstances, confined himself to saying, "Yes, yes, thanks, Mother, I'm just getting up." The wooden door must have prevented the change in Gregor's voice from being noticed outside, because his mother was satisfied with this explanation and shuffled off. But their little exchange had made the rest of the family aware that, contrary to expectations, Gregor was still in the house, and already his father was knocking on one of the side doors, feebly but with this fist. "Gregor, Gregor," he called, "what's going on?" And after a little while he called again in a deeper, warning voice, "Gregor! Gregor!" At the other side door, however, his sister moaned gently, "Gregor? Is something the matter with you? Do you want anything?" Toward both sides Gregor answered: "I'm all ready," and made an effort, by meticulous pronunciation and by inserting long pauses between individual words, to eliminate everything from his voice that might betray him. His father went back to his breakfast, but his sister whispered, "Gregor, open up, I'm pleading with you." But Gregor had absolutely no intention of opening the door and complimented himself instead on the precaution he had adopted from his business trips, of locking all the doors during the night even at home.

First of all he wanted to get up quietly, without any excitement; get dressed; and the main thing, have breakfast, and only then think about what to do next, for he saw clearly that in bed he would never think things through to a rational conclusion. He remembered how even in the past he had often felt some kind of slight pain, possibly caused by lying in an uncomfortable position, which, when he got up, turned out to be purely imaginary, and he was eager to see how today's fantasy would gradually fade away. That the change in his voice was nothing more than the first sign of a bad cold, an occupational ailment of the traveling salesman, he had no doubt in the least.

It was very easy to throw off the cover; all he had to do was puff himself up a little, and it fell off by itself. But after this, things got difficult, especially since he was so unusually broad. He would have needed hands and arms to lift himself up, but instead of that he had only his numerous little legs, which were in every different kind of perpetual motion and which, besides, he could not control. If he wanted to bend one, the first thing that happened was that it stretched itself out; and if he finally succeeded in getting this leg to do what he wanted, all the others in the meantime, as if set free, began to work in the most intensely painful agitation. "Just don't stay in bed being useless," Gregor said to himself.

First he tried to get out of bed with the lower part of his body, but this lower part—which by the way he had not seen yet and which he could not form a clear picture of—proved too difficult to budge; it was taking so long; and when finally, almost out of his mind, he lunged forward with all his force, without caring, he had picked the wrong direction and slammed himself violently against the lower bedpost, and the searing pain he felt taught him that exactly the lower part of his body was, for the moment anyway, the most sensitive.

He therefore tried to get the upper part of his body out of bed first and warily turned his head toward the edge of the bed. This worked easily, and in spite of its width and weight, the mass of his body finally followed, slowly, the movement of his head. But when at last he stuck his head over the edge of the bed into the air, he got too scared to continue any further, since if he finally let himself fall in this position, it would be a miracle if he didn't injure his head. And just now he had better not for the life of him lose consciousness; he would rather stay in bed.

But when, once again, after the same exertion, he lay in his original position, sighing, and again watched his little legs struggling, if possible more fiercely, with each other and saw no way of bringing peace and order into this mindless motion, he again told himself that it was impossible for him to stay in bed and that the most rational thing was to make any sacrifice for even the smallest hope of freeing himself from the bed. But at the same time he did not forget to remind himself occasionally that thinking things over calmly—indeed, as calmly as possible—was much better than jumping to desperate decisions. At such moments he fixed his eyes as sharply as possible on the window, but unfortunately there was little confidence and cheer to be gotten from the view of the morning fog, which shrouded even the other side of the narrow street. "Seven o'clock already," he said to himself as the alarm clock struck again, "seven o'clock already and still such a fog." And for a little while he lay quietly, breathing shallowly, as if expecting, perhaps, from the complete silence the return of things to the way they really and naturally were.

But then he said to himself, "Before it strikes a quarter past seven, I must be completely out of bed without fail. Anyway, by that time someone from the firm will be here to find out where I am, since the office opens before seven." And now he started rocking the complete length of his body out of the bed with a smooth rhythm. If he let himself topple out of bed in this way, his head, which on falling he planned to lift up sharply, would presumably remain unharmed. His back seemed to be hard; nothing was likely to happen to it when it fell onto the carpet. His biggest misgiving came from his concern about the loud crash that was bound to occur and would probably create, if not terror, at least anxiety behind all the doors. But that would have to be risked.

When Gregor's body already projected halfway out of bed—the new method was more of a game than a struggle, he only had to keep on rocking and jerking himself along—he thought how simple everything would be if he could get some help. Two strong persons—he thought of his father and the maid—would have been completely sufficient; they would only have had to shove their arms under his arched back, in this way scoop him off the bed, bend down with their burden, and then just be careful and patient while he managed to swing himself down onto the floor, where his little legs would hopefully acquire some purpose. Well, leaving out the fact that the doors were locked, should he really call for help? In spite of all his miseries, he could not repress a smile at this thought.

He was already so far along that when he rocked more strongly he could hardly keep his balance, and very soon he would have to commit himself, because in five minutes it would be a quarter past seven—when the doorbell rang. "It's someone from the firm," he said to himself and almost froze, while his little legs only danced more quickly. For a moment everything remained quiet. "They're not going to answer," Gregor said to himself, captivated by some senseless hope. But then, of course, the maid went to the door as usual with her firm stride and opened up. Gregor only had to hear the visitor's first word of greeting to know who it was—the office manager himself. Why was only Gregor condemned to work for a firm where at the slightest omission they immediately suspected the worst? Were all employees louts without exception, wasn't there a single loyal, dedicated worker among them who, when he had not fully utilized a few hours of the morning for the firm, was driven half-mad by pangs of conscience and was actually unable to get out of bed? Really, wouldn't it have been enough to send one of the apprentices to find out—if this prying were absolutely necessary—did the manager himself have to come, and did the whole innocent family have to be shown in this way that the investigation of this suspicious affair could be entrusted only to the intellect of the manager? And more as a result of the excitement produced in Gregor by these thoughts than as a result of any real decision, he swung himself out of bed with all his might. There was a loud thump, but it was not a real crash. The fall was broken a little by the carpet, and Gregor's back was more elastic than he had thought, which explained the not very noticeable muffled sound. Only he had not held his head carefully enough and hit it; he turned it and rubbed it on the carpet in anger and pain.

"Something fell in there," said the manager in the room on the left. Gregor tried to imagine whether something like what had happened to him today could one day happen even to the manager; you really had to grant the possibility. But, as if in rude reply to this question, the manager took a few decisive steps in the next room and made his patent leather boots creak. From the room on the right his sister whispered, to inform Gregor, "Gregor, the manager is here." "I know," Gregor said to himself; but he did not dare raise his voice enough for his sister to hear.

"Gregor," his father now said from the room on the left, "the manager has come and wants to be informed why you didn't catch the early train. We don't know what we should say to him. Besides, he wants to speak to you personally. So please open the door. He will certainly be so kind as to excuse the disorder of the room." "Good morning, Mr. Samsa," the manager called in a friendly voice. "There's something the matter with him," his mother said to the manager while his father was still at the door, talking. "Believe me, sir, there's something the matter with him. Otherwise how would Gregor have missed a train? That boy has nothing on his mind but the business. It's almost begun to rile me that he never goes out nights. He's been back in the city for eight days now, but every night he's been home. He sits there with us at the table, quietly reading the paper or studying timetables. It's already a distraction for him when he's busy working with his fretsaw. For instance, in the span of two or three evenings he carved a little frame. You'll be amazed how pretty it is; it's hanging inside his room. You'll see it right away when Gregor opens the door. You know, I'm glad that you've come, sir. We would never have gotten Gregor to open the door by ourselves; he's so stubborn. And there's certainly something wrong with him, even though he said this morning there wasn't." "I'm coming right away," said Gregor slowly and deliberately, not moving in order not to miss a word of the conversation. "I haven't any other explanation myself," said the manager. "I hope it's nothing serious. On the other hand, I must say that we businessmen—fortunately or unfortunately, whichever you prefer—very often simply have to overcome a slight indisposition for business reasons." "So can the manager come in now?" asked his father, impatient, and knocked on the door again. "No," said Gregor. In the room on the left there was an embarrassing silence; in the room on the right his sister began to sob.

Why didn't his sister go in to the others? She had probably just got out of bed and not even started to get dressed. Then what was she crying about? Because he didn't get up and didn't let the manager in, because he was in danger of losing his job, and because then the boss would start hounding his parents about the old debts? For the time being, certainly, her worries were unnecessary. Gregor was still here and hadn't the slightest intention of letting the family down. True, at the moment he was lying on the carpet, and no one knowing his condition could seriously have expected him to let the manager in. But just because of this slight discourtesy, for which an appropriate excuse would easily be found later on, Gregor could not simply be dismissed. And to Gregor it seemed much more sensible to leave him alone now than to bother him with crying and persuasion. But it was just the uncertainty that was tormenting the others and excused their behavior.

"Mr. Samsa," the manager now called, raising his voice, "what's the matter? You barricade yourself in your room, answer only 'yes' and 'no,' cause your parents serious, unnecessary worry, and you neglect—I mention this only in passing—your duties to the firm in a really shocking manner. I am speaking here in the name of your parents and of your employer and ask you in all seriousness for an immediate, clear explanation. I'm amazed, amazed. I thought I knew you to be a quiet, reasonable person, and now you suddenly seem to want to start strutting about, flaunting strange whims. The head of the firm did suggest to me this morning a possible explanation for your tardiness—it concerned the cash payments recently entrusted to you—but really, I practically gave my word of honor that this explanation could not be right. But now, seeing your incomprehensible obstinacy, I am about to lose even the slightest desire to stick up for you in any way at all. And your job is not the most secure. Originally I intended to tell you all this in private, but since you make me waste my time here for nothing, I don't see why your parents shouldn't hear too. Your performance of late has been very unsatisfactory; I know it is not the best season for doing business, we all recognize that; but a season for not doing any business, there is no such thing, Mr. Samsa, such a thing cannot be tolerated."

"But sir," cried Gregor, beside himself, in his excitement forgetting everything else, "I'm just opening up, in a minute. A slight indisposition, a dizzy spell, prevented me from getting up. I'm still in bed. But I already feel fine again. I'm just getting out of bed. Just be patient for a minute! I'm not as well as I thought yet. But really I'm fine. How something like this could just take a person by surprise! Only last night I was fine, my parents can tell you, or wait, last night I already had a slight premonition. They must have been able to tell by looking at me. Why didn't I report it to the office! But you always think that you'll get over a sickness without staying home. Sir! Spare my parents! There's no basis for any of the accusations that you're making against me now; no one has ever said a word to me about them. Perhaps you haven't seen the last orders I sent in. Anyway, I'm still going on the road with the eight o'clock train; these few hours of rest have done me good. Don't let me keep you, sir. I'll be at the office myself right away, and be so kind as to tell them this, and give my respects to the head of the firm."

And while Gregor hastily blurted all this out, hardly knowing what he was saying, he had easily approached the chest of drawers, probably as a result of the practice he had already gotten in bed, and now he tried to raise himself up against it. He actually intended to open the door, actually present himself and speak to the manager; he was eager to find out what the others, who were now so anxious to see him, would say at the sight of him. If they were shocked, then Gregor had no further responsibility and could be calm. But if they took everything calmly, then he, too, had no reason to get excited and could, if he hurried, actually be at the station by eight o'clock. At first he slid off the polished chest of drawers a few times, but at last, giving himself a final push, he stood upright; he no longer paid any attention to the pains in his abdomen, no matter how much they were burning. Now he let himself fall against the back of a nearby chair, clinging to its slats with his little legs. But by doing this he had gotten control of himself and fell silent, since he could now listen to what the manager was saying.

"Did you understand a word?" the manager was asking his parents. "He isn't trying to make fools of us, is he?" "My God," cried his mother, already in tears, "maybe he's seriously ill, and here we are, torturing him. Grete! Grete!" she then cried. "Mother?" called his sister from the other side. They communicated by way of Gregor's room. "Go to the doctor's immediately. Gregor is sick. Hurry, get the doctor. Did you just hear Gregor talking?" "That was the voice of an animal," said the manager, in a tone conspicuously soft compared with the mother's yelling. "Anna!" "Anna!" the father called through the foyer into the kitchen, clapping his hands, "get a locksmith right away!" And already the two girls were running with rustling skirts through the foyer—how could his sister have gotten dressed so quickly?—and tearing open the door to the apartment. The door could not be heard slamming; they had probably left it open, as is the custom in homes where a great misfortune has occurred.

But Gregor had become much calmer. It was true that they no longer understood his words, though they had seemed clear enough to him, clearer than before, probably because his ear had grown accustomed to them. But still, the others now believed that there was something the matter with him and were ready to help him. The assurance and confidence with which the first measures had been taken did him good. He felt integrated into human society once again and hoped for marvelous, amazing feats from both the doctor and the locksmith, without really distinguishing sharply between them. In order to make his voice as clear as possible for the crucial discussions that were approaching, he cleared his throat a little—taking pains, of course, to do so in a very muffled manner, since this noise, too, might sound different from human coughing, a thing he no longer trusted himself to decide. In the next room, meanwhile, everything had become completely still. Perhaps his parents were sitting at the table with the manager, whispering; perhaps they were all leaning against the door and listening.

Gregor slowly lugged himself toward the door, pushing the chair in front of him, then let go of it, threw himself against the door, held himself upright against it—the pads on the bottom of his little legs exuded a little sticky substance—and for a moment rested there from the exertion. But then he got started turning the key in the lock with his mouth. Unfortunately it seemed that he had no real teeth—what was he supposed to grip the key with?—but in compensation his jaws, of course, were very strong; with their help he actually got the key moving and paid no attention to the fact that he was undoubtedly hurting himself in some way, for a brown liquid came out of his mouth, flowed over the key, and dripped onto the floor. "Listen," said the manager in the next room, "he's turning the key." This was great encouragement to Gregor; but everyone should have cheered him on, his father and mother too. "Go, Gregor," they should have called, "keep going, at that lock, harder, harder!" And in the delusion that they were all following his efforts with suspense, he clamped his jaws madly on the key with all the strength he could muster. Depending on the progress of the key, he danced around the lock; holding himself upright only by his mouth, he clung to the key, as the situation demanded, or pressed it down again with the whole weight of his body. The clearer click of the lock as it finally snapped back literally woke Gregor up. With a sigh of relief he said to himself, "So I didn't need the locksmith after all," and laid his head down on the handle in order to open wide one wing of the double doors.

Since he had to use this method of opening the door, it was really opened very wide while he himself was still invisible. He first had to edge slowly around the one wing of the door, and do so very carefully if he was not to fall flat on his back just before entering. He was still busy with this difficult maneuver and had no time to pay attention to anything else when he heard the manager burst out with a loud "Oh!"—it sounded like a rush of wind—and now he could see him, standing closest to the door, his hand pressed over his open mouth, slowly backing away, as if repulsed by an invisible, unrelenting force. His mother—in spite of the manager's presence she stood with her hair still unbraided from the night, sticking out in all directions—first looked at his father with her hands clasped, then took two steps toward Gregor, and sank down in the midst of her skirts spreading out around her, her face completely hidden on her breast. With a hostile expression his father clenched his fist, as if to drive Gregor back into his room, then looked uncertainly around the living room, shielded his eyes with his hands, and sobbed with heaves of his powerful chest.

Now Gregor did not enter the room after all but leaned against the inside of the firmly bolted wing of the door, so that only half his body was visible and his head above it, cocked to one side and peeping out at the others. In the meantime it had grown much lighter; across the street one could see clearly a section of the endless, grayish-black building opposite—it was a hospital—with its regular windows starkly piercing the façade; the rain was still coming down, but only in large, separately visible drops that were also pelting the ground literally one at a time. The breakfast dishes were laid out lavishly on the table, since for his father breakfast was the most important meal of the day, which he would prolong for hours while reading various newspapers. On the wall directly opposite hung a photograph of Gregor from his army days, in a lieutenant's uniform, his hand on his sword, a carefree smile on his lips, demanding respect for his bearing and his rank. The door to the foyer was open, and since the front door was open too, it was possible to see out onto the landing and the top of the stairs going down.

"Well," said Gregor—and he was thoroughly aware of being the only one who had kept calm—"I'll get dressed right away, pack up my samples, and go. Will you, will you please let me go? Now, sir, you see, I'm not stubborn and I'm willing to work; traveling is a hardship, but without it I couldn't live. Where are you going, sir? To the office? Yes? Will you give an honest report of everything? A man might find for a moment that he was unable to work, but that's exactly the right time to remember his past accomplishments and to consider that later on, when the obstacle has been removed, he's bound to work all the harder and more efficiently. I'm under so many obligations to the head of the firm, as you know very well. Besides, I also have my parents and my sister to worry about. I'm in a tight spot, but I'll also work my way out again. Don't make things harder for me than they already are. Stick up for me in the office, please. Traveling salesmen aren't well liked there, I know. People think they make a fortune leading the gay life. No one has any particular reason to rectify this prejudice. But you, sir, you have a better perspective on things than the rest of the office, an even better perspective, just between the two of us, than the head of the firm himself, who in his capacity as owner easily lets his judgment be swayed against an employee. And you also know very well that the traveling salesman, who is out of the office practically the whole year round, can so easily become the victim of gossip, coincidences, and unfounded accusations, against which he's completely unable to defend himself, since in most cases he knows nothing at all about them except when he returns exhausted from a trip, and back home gets to suffer on his own person the grim consequences, which can no longer be traced back to their causes. Sir, don't go away without a word to tell me you think I'm at least partly right!"

But at Gregor's first words the manager had already turned away and with curled lips looked back at Gregor only over his twitching shoulder. And during Gregor's speech he did not stand still for a minute but, without letting Gregor out of his sight, backed toward the door, yet very gradually, as if there were some secret prohibition against leaving the room. He was already in the foyer, and from the sudden movement with which he took his last step from the living room, one might have thought he had just burned the sole of his foot. In the foyer, however, he stretched his right hand far out toward the staircase, as if nothing less than an unearthly deliverance were awaiting him there.

Gregor realized that he must on no account let the manager go away in this mood if his position in the firm were not to be jeopardized in the extreme. His parents did not understand this too well; in the course of the years they had formed the conviction that Gregor was set for life in this firm; and furthermore, they were so preoccupied with their immediate troubles that they had lost all consideration for the future. But Gregor had this forethought. The manager must be detained, calmed down, convinced, and finally won over; Gregor's and the family's future depended on it! If only his sister had been there! She was perceptive; she had already begun to cry when Gregor was still lying calmly on his back. And certainly the manager, this ladies' man, would have listened to her; she would have shut the front door and in the foyer talked him out of his scare. But his sister was not there, Gregor had to handle the situation himself. And without stopping to realize that he had no idea what his new faculties of movement were, and without stopping to realize either that his speech had possibly—indeed, probably—not been understood again, he let go of the wing of the door; he shoved himself through the opening, intending to go to the manager, who was already on the landing, ridiculously holding onto the banisters with both hands; but groping for support, Gregor immediately fell down with a little cry onto his numerous little legs. This had hardly happened when for the first time that morning he had a feeling of physical well-being; his little legs were on firm ground; they obeyed him completely, as he noted to his joy; they even strained to carry him away wherever he wanted to go; and he already believed that final recovery from all his sufferings was imminent. But at that very moment, as he lay on the floor rocking with repressed motion, not far from his mother and just opposite her, she, who had seemed so completely self-absorbed, all at once jumped up, her arms stretched wide, her fingers spread, and cried, "Help, for God's sake, help!" held her head bent as if to see Gregor better, but inconsistently darted madly backward instead; had forgotten that the table laden with the break-fast dishes stood behind her; sat down on it hastily, as if her thoughts were elsewhere, when she reached it; and did not seem to notice at all that near her the big coffeepot had been knocked over and coffee was pouring in a steady stream onto the rug.

"Mother, Mother," said Gregor softly and looked up at her. For a minute the manager had completely slipped his mind; on the other hand at the sight of the spilling coffee he could not resist snapping his jaws several times in the air. At this his mother screamed once more, fled from the table, and fell into the arms of his father, who came rushing up to her. But Gregor had no time now for his parents; the manager was already on the stairs; with his chin on the banister, he was taking a last look back. Gregor was off to a running start, to be as sure as possible of catching up with him; the manager must have suspected something like this, for he leaped down several steps and disappeared; but still he shouted "Agh," and the sound carried through the whole staircase. Unfortunately the manager's flight now seemed to confuse his father completely, who had been relatively calm until now, for instead of running after the manager himself, or at least not hindering Gregor in his pursuit, he seized in his right hand the manager's cane, which had been left behind on a chair with his hat and overcoat, picked up in his left hand a heavy news-paper from the table, and stamping his feet, started brandishing the cane and the newspaper to drive Gregor back into his room. No plea of Gregor's helped, no plea was even understood; however humbly he might turn his head, his father merely stamped his feet more forcefully. Across the room his mother had thrown open a window in spite of the cool weather, and leaning out, she buried her face, far outside the window, in her hands. Between the alley and the staircase a strong draft was created, the window curtains blew in, the newspapers on the table rustled, single sheets fluttered across the floor. Pitilessly his father came on, hissing like a wild man. Now Gregor had not had any practice at all walking in reverse, it was really very slow going. If Gregor had only been allowed to turn around, he could have gotten into his room right away, but he was afraid to make his father impatient by this time-consuming gyration, and at any minute the cane in his father's hand threatened to come down on his back or his head with a deadly blow. Finally, however, Gregor had no choice, for he noticed with horror that in reverse he could not even keep going in one direction; and so, incessantly throwing uneasy side-glances at his father, he began to turn around as quickly as possible, in reality turning only very slowly. Perhaps his father realized his good intentions, for he did not interfere with him; instead, he even now and then directed the maneuver from afar with the tip of his cane. If only his father did not keep making this intolerable hissing sound! It made Gregor lose his head completely. He had almost finished the turn when—his mind continually on this hissing—he made a mistake and even started turning back around to his original position. But when he had at last successfully managed to get his head in front of the opened door, it turned out that his body was too broad to get through as it was. Of course in his father's present state of mind it did not even remotely occur to him to open the other wing of the door in order to give Gregor enough room to pass through. He had only the fixed idea that Gregor must return to his room as quickly as possible. He would never have allowed the complicated preliminaries Gregor needed to go through in order to stand up on one end and perhaps in this way fit through the door. Instead he drove Gregor on, as if there were no obstacle, with exceptional loudness; the voice behind Gregor did not sound like that of only a single father; now this was really no joke any more, and Gregor forced himself—come what may—into the doorway. One side of his body rose up, he lay lop-sided in the opening, one of his flanks was scraped raw, ugly blotches marred the white door, soon he got stuck and could not have budged any more by himself, his little legs on one side dangled tremblingly in midair, those on the other were painfully crushed against the floor—when from behind his father gave him a hard shove, which was truly his salvation, and bleeding profusely, he flew far into his room. The door was slammed shut with the cane, then at last everything was quiet.

II

It was already dusk when Gregor awoke from his deep, comalike sleep. Even if he had not been disturbed, he would certainly not have woken up much later, for he felt that he had rested and slept long enough, but it seemed to him that a hurried step and a cautious shutting of the door leading to the foyer had awakened him. The light of the electric street-lamps lay in pallid streaks on the ceiling and on the upper parts of the furniture, but underneath, where Gregor was, it was dark. Groping clumsily with his antennae, which he was only now beginning to appreciate, he slowly dragged himself toward the door to see what had been happening there. His left side felt like one single long, unpleasantly tautening scar, and he actually

had to limp on his two rows of legs. Besides, one little leg had been
seriously injured in the course of the morning's events—it was almost
a miracle that only one had been injured—and dragged along life-
lessly.

Only after he got to the door did he notice what had really attracted
him— the smell of something to eat. For there stood a bowl filled
with fresh milk, in which small slices of white bread were floating.
He could almost have laughed for joy, since he was even hungrier
than he had been in the morning, and he immediately dipped his
head into the milk, almost to over his eyes. But he soon drew it back
again in disappointment; not only because he had difficulty eating
on account of the soreness in his left side—and he could eat only if
his whole panting body cooperated—but because he didn't like the
milk at all, although it used to be his favorite drink, and that was
certainly why his sister had put it in the room; in fact, he turned
away from the bowl almost with repulsion and crawled back to the
middle of the room.

In the living room, as Gregor saw through the crack in the door,
the gas had been lit, but while at this hour of the day his father was
in the habit of reading the afternoon newspaper in a loud voice to
his mother and sometimes to his sister too, now there wasn't a sound.
Well, perhaps this custom of reading aloud, which his sister was
always telling him and writing him about, had recently been discontinued altogether. But in all the other rooms too it was just as still,
although the apartment certainly was not empty. "What a quiet life
the family has been leading," Gregor said to himself, and while he
stared rigidly in front of him into the darkness, he felt very proud
that he had been able to provide such a life in so nice an apartment
for his parents and his sister. But what now if all the peace, the
comfort, the contentment were to come to a horrible end? In order
not to get involved in such thoughts, Gregor decided to keep moving, and he crawled up and down the room.

During the long evening first one of the side doors and then the
other was opened a small crack and quickly shut again; someone had
probably had the urge to come in and then had had second thoughts.
Gregor now settled into position right by the living-room door, determined somehow to get the hesitating visitor to come in, or at least to
find out who it might be; but the door was not opened again, and
Gregor waited in vain. In the morning, when the doors had been
locked, everyone had wanted to come in; now that he had opened
one of the doors and the others had evidently been opened during
the day, no one came in, and now the keys were even inserted on
the outside.

It was late at night when the light finally went out in the living
room, and now it was easy for Gregor to tell that his parents and his

sister had stayed up so long, since, as he could distinctly hear, all three were now retiring on tiptoe. Certainly no one would come in to Gregor until the morning; and so he had ample time to consider undisturbed how best to rearrange his life. But the empty high-ceilinged room in which he was forced to lie flat on the floor made him nervous, without his being able to tell why—since it was, after all, the room in which he had lived for the past five years—and turning half unconsciously and not without a slight feeling of shame, he scuttled under the couch where, although his back was a little crushed and he could not raise his head any more, he immediately felt very comfortable and was only sorry that his body was too wide to go completely under the couch.

There he stayed the whole night, which he spent partly in a sleepy trance, from which hunger pangs kept waking him with a start, partly in worries and vague hopes, all of which, however, led to the conclusion that for the time being he would have to lie low and, by being patient and showing his family every possible consideration, help them bear the inconvenience which he simply had to cause them in his present condition.

Early in the morning—it was still almost night—Gregor had the opportunity of testing the strength of the resolutions he had just made, for his sister, almost fully dressed, opened the door from the foyer and looked in eagerly. She did not see him right away, but when she caught sight of him under the couch—God, he had to be somewhere, he couldn't just fly away—she became so frightened that she lost control of herself and slammed the door shut again. But, as if she felt sorry for her behavior, she immediately opened the door again and came in on tiptoe, as if she were visiting someone seriously ill or perhaps even a stranger. Gregor had pushed his head forward just to the edge of the couch and was watching her. Would she notice that he had left the milk standing, and not because he hadn't been hungry, and would she bring in a dish of something he'd like better? If she were not going to do it of her own free will, he would rather starve than call it to her attention, although, really, he felt an enormous urge to shoot out from under the couch, throw himself at his sister's feet, and beg her for something good to eat. But his sister noticed at once, to her astonishment, that the bowl was still full, only a little milk was spilled around it; she picked it up immediately—not with her bare hands, of course, but with a rag—and carried it out. Gregor was extremely curious to know what she would bring him instead, and he racked his brains on the subject. But he would never have been able to guess what his sister, in the goodness of her heart, actually did. To find out his likes and dislikes, she brought him a wide assortment of things, all spread out on an old newspaper: old, half-rotten vegetables; bones left over from the eve-

ning meal, caked with congealed white sauce; some raisins and
almonds; a piece of cheese, which two days before Gregor had declared
inedible; a plain slice of bread, a slice of bread and butter, and one
with butter and salt. In addition to all this she put down some water
in the bowl apparently permanently earmarked for Gregor's use. And
out of a sense of delicacy, since she knew that Gregor would not eat
in front of her, she left hurriedly and even turned the key, just so
that Gregor should know that he might make himself as comfortable
as he wanted. Gregor's legs began whirring now that he was going to
eat. Besides, his bruises must have completely healed, since he no
longer felt any handicap, and marveling at this he thought how, over
a month ago, he had cut his finger very slightly with a knife and how
this wound was still hurting him only the day before yesterday. "Have
I become less sensitive?" he thought, already sucking greedily at the
cheese, which had immediately and forcibly attracted him ahead of
all the other dishes. One right after the other, and with eyes streaming with tears of contentment, he devoured the cheese, the vegetables, and the sauce; the fresh foods, on the other hand, he did not
care for; he couldn't even stand their smell and even dragged the
things he wanted to eat a bit further away. He had finished with
everything long since and was just lying lazily at the same spot when
his sister slowly turned the key as a sign for him to withdraw. That
immediately startled him, although he was almost asleep, and he
scuttled under the couch again. But it took great self-control for him
to stay under the couch even for the short time his sister was in the
room, since his body had become a little bloated from the heavy
meal, and in his cramped position he could hardly breathe. In between
slight attacks of suffocation he watched with bulging eyes as his
unsuspecting sister took a broom and swept up, not only his leavings,
but even the foods which Gregor had left completely untouched—
as if they too were no longer usable—and dumping everything hastily into a pail, which she covered with a wooden lid, she carried
everything out. She had hardly turned her back when Gregor came
out from under the couch, stretching and puffing himself up.

This, then, was the way Gregor was fed each day, once in the
morning, when his parents and the maid were still asleep, and a
second time in the afternoon after everyone had had dinner, for then
his parents took a short nap again, and the maid could be sent out
by his sister on some errand. Certainly they did not want him to
starve either, but perhaps they would not have been able to stand
knowing any more about his meals than from hearsay, or perhaps
his sister wanted to spare them even what was possibly only a minor
torment, for really, they were suffering enough as it was.

Gregor could not find out what excuses had been made to get rid
of the doctor and the locksmith on that first morning, for since the

others could not understand what he said, it did not occur to any of them, not even to his sister, that he could understand what they said, and so he had to be satisfied, when his sister was in the room, with only occasionally hearing her sighs and appeals to the saints. It was only later, when she had begun to get used to everything—there could never, of course, be any question of a complete adjustment—that Gregor sometimes caught a remark which was meant to be friendly or could be interpreted as such. "Oh, he liked what he had today," she would say when Gregor had tucked away a good helping, and in the opposite case, which gradually occurred more and more frequently, she used to say, almost sadly, "He's left everything again."

But if Gregor could not get any news directly, he overheard a great deal from the neighboring rooms, and as soon as he heard voices, he would immediately run to the door concerned and press his whole body against it. Especially in the early days, there was no conversation that was not somehow about him, if only implicitly. For two whole days there were family consultations at every mealtime about how they should cope; this was also the topic of discussion between meals, for at least two members of the family were always at home, since no one probably wanted to stay home alone and it was impossible to leave the apartment completely empty. Besides, on the very first day the maid—it was not completely clear what and how much she knew of what had happened—had begged his mother on bended knees to dismiss her immediately; and when she said goodbye a quarter of an hour later, she thanked them in tears for the dismissal, as if for the greatest favor that had ever been done to her in this house, and made a solemn vow, without anyone asking her for it, not to give anything away to anyone.

Now his sister, working with her mother, had to do the cooking too; of course that did not cause her much trouble, since they hardly ate anything. Gregor was always hearing one of them pleading in vain with one of the others to eat and getting no answer except, "Thanks, I've had enough," or something similar. They did not seem to drink anything either. His sister often asked her father if he wanted any beer and gladly offered to go out for it herself; and when he did not answer, she said, in order to remove any hesitation on his part, that she could also send the janitor's wife to get it, but then his father finally answered with a definite "No," and that was the end of that.

In the course of the very first day his father explained the family's financial situation and prospects to both the mother and the sister. From time to time he got up from the table to get some kind of receipt or notebook out of the little strongbox he had rescued from the collapse of his business five years before. Gregor heard him open the complicated lock and secure it again after taking out what he had been looking for. These explanations by his father were to some extent the first pleasant news Gregor had heard since his imprisonment. He had always believed that his father had not been able to save a penny from the business, at least his father had never told him anything to the contrary, and Gregor, for his part, had never asked him any questions. In those days Gregor's sole concern had been to do every-thing in his power to make the family forget as quickly as possible the business disaster which had plunged everyone into a state of total despair. And so he had begun to work with special ardor and had risen almost overnight from stock clerk to traveling salesman, which of course had opened up very different money-making possibilities, and in no time his successes on the job were transformed, by means of commissions, into hard cash that could be plunked down on the table at home in front of his astonished and delighted family. Those had been wonderful times, and they had never returned, at least not with the same glory, although later on Gregor earned enough money to meet the expenses of the entire family and actually did so. They had just gotten used to it, the family as well as Gregor, the money was received with thanks and given with pleasure, but no special feeling of warmth went with it any more. Only his sister had remained close to Gregor, and it was his secret plan that she who, unlike him, loved music and could play the violin movingly, should be sent next year to the Conservatory, regardless of the great expense involved, which could surely be made up for in some other way. Often during Gregor's short stays in the city, the Conservatory would come up in his conversations with his sister, but always merely as a beautiful dream which was not supposed to come true, and his parents were not happy to hear even these innocent allusions; but Gregor had very concrete idea on the subject and he intended solemnly to announce his plan on Christmas Eve.

Thoughts like these, completely useless in his present state, went through his head as he stood glued to the door, listening. Sometimes out of general exhaustion he could not listen any more and let his head bump carelessly against the door, but immediately pulled it back again, for even the slight noise he made by doing this had been heard in the next room and made them all lapse into silence. "What's he carrying on about in there now?" said his father after a while, obviously turning toward the door, and only then would the inter-rupted conversation gradually be resumed.

Gregor now learned in a thorough way—for his father was in the habit of often repeating himself in his explanations, partly because he himself had not dealt with these matters for a long time, partly, too, because his mother did not understand everything the first time around—that in spite of all their misfortunes a bit of capital, a very little bit, certainly, was still intact from the old days, which in the meantime had increased a little through the untouched interest. But

besides that, the money Gregor had brought home every month—
he had kept only a few dollars for himself—had never been completely used up and had accumulated into a tidy principal. Behind
his door Gregor nodded emphatically, delighted at this unexpected
foresight and thrift. Of course he actually could have paid off more
of his father's debt to the boss with this extra money, and the day on
which he could have gotten rid of his job would have been much
closer, but now things were undoubtedly better the way his father
had arranged them.

Now this money was by no means enough to let the family live
off the interest; the principal was perhaps enough to support the family for one year, or at the most two, but that was all there was. So it
was just a sum that really should not be touched and that had to be
put away for a rainy day; but the money to live on would have to be
earned. Now his father was still healthy, certainly, but he was an old
man who had not worked for the past five years and who in any case
could not be expected to undertake too much; during these five years,
which were the first vacation of his hard-working yet unsuccessful
life, he had gained a lot of weight and as a result had become fairly
sluggish. And was his old mother now supposed to go out and earn
money, when she suffered from asthma, when a walk through the
apartment was already an ordeal for her, and when she spent every
other day lying on the sofa under the open window, gasping for breath?
And was his sister now supposed to work—who for all her seventeen
years was still a child and whom it would be such a pity to deprive
of the life she had led until now, which had consisted of wearing
pretty clothes, sleeping late, helping in the house, enjoying a few
modest amusements, and above all playing the violin? At first,
whenever the conversation turned to the necessity of earning money,
Gregor would let go of the door and throw himself down on the cool
leather sofa which stood beside it, for he felt hot with shame and
grief.

Often he lay there the whole long night through, not sleeping a
wink and only scrabbling on the leather for hours on end. Or, not
balking at the huge effort of pushing an armchair to the window, he
would crawl up to the window sill and, propped up in the chair, lean
against the window, evidently in some sort of remembrance of the
feeling of freedom he used to have from looking out the window.
For, in fact, from day to day he saw things even a short distance
away less and less distinctly; the hospital opposite, which he used to
curse because he saw so much of it, was now completely beyond his
range of vision, and if he had not been positive that he was living in
Charlotte Street—a quiet but still very much a city street—he might
have believed that he was looking out of his window into a desert
where the gray sky and the gray earth were indistinguishably fused.

It took his observant sister only twice to notice that his armchair was standing by the window for her to push the chair back to the same place by the window each time she had finished cleaning the room, and from then on she even left the inside casement of the window open.

If Gregor had only been able to speak to his sister and thank her for everything she had to do for him, he could have accepted her services more easily; as it was, they caused him pain. Of course his sister tried to ease the embarrassment of the whole situation as much as possible, and as time went on, she naturally managed it better and better, but in time Gregor, too, saw things much more clearly. Even the way she came in was terrible for him. Hardly had she entered the room than she would run straight to the window without taking time to close the door—though she was usually so careful to spare everyone the sight of Gregor's room—then tear open the casements with eager hands, almost as if she were suffocating, and remain for a little while at the window even in the coldest weather, breathing deeply. With this racing and crashing she frightened Gregor twice a day; the whole time he cowered under the couch, and yet he knew very well that she would certainly have spared him this if only she had found it possible to stand being in a room with him with the window closed.

One time—it must have been a month since Gregor's metamorphosis, and there was certainly no particular reason any more for his sister to be astonished at Gregor's appearance—she came a little earlier than usual and caught Gregor still looking out the window, immobile and so in an excellent position to be terrifying. It would not have surprised Gregor if she had not come in, because his position prevented her from immediately opening the window, but not only did she not come in, she even sprang back and locked the door; a stranger might easily have thought that Gregor had been lying in wait for her, wanting to bite her. Of course Gregor immediately hid under the couch, but he had to wait until noon before his sister came again, and she seemed much more uneasy than usual. He realized from this that the sight of him was still repulsive to her and was bound to remain repulsive to her in the future, and that she probably had to overcome a lot of resistance not to run away at the sight of even the small part of his body that jutted out from under the couch. So, to spare her even this sight, one day he carried the sheet on his back to the couch—the job took four hours—and arranged it in such a way that he was now completely covered up and his sister could not see him even when she stooped. If she had considered this sheet unnecessary, then of course she could have removed it, for it was clear enough that it could not be for his own pleasure that Gregor shut himself off altogether, but she left the sheet the way it was, and

Gregor thought that he had even caught a grateful look when one time he cautiously lifted the sheet a little with his head in order to see how his sister was taking the new arrangement.

During the first two weeks, his parents could not bring themselves to come in to him, and often he heard them say how much they appreciated his sister's work, whereas until now they had frequently been annoyed with her because she had struck them as being a little useless. But now both of them, his father and his mother, often waited outside Gregor's room while his sister straightened it up, and as soon as she came out she had to tell them in great detail how the room looked, what Gregor had eaten, how he had behaved this time, and whether he had perhaps shown a little improvement. His mother, incidentally, began relatively soon to want to visit Gregor, but his father and his sister at first held her back with reasonable arguments to which Gregor listened very attentively and of which he whole-heartedly approved. But later she had to be restrained by force, and then when she cried out, "Let me go to Gregor, he is my unfortunate boy! Don't you understand that I have to go to him?" Gregor thought that it might be a good idea after all if his mother did come in, not every day of course, but perhaps once a week; she could still do everything much better than his sister, who, for all her courage, was still only a child and in the final analysis had perhaps taken on such a difficult assignment only out of childish flightiness.

Gregor's desire to see his mother was soon fulfilled. During the day Gregor did not want to show himself at the window, if only out of consideration for his parents, but he couldn't crawl very far on his few square yards of floor space, either; he could hardly put up with just lying still even at night; eating soon stopped giving him the slightest pleasure, so, as a distraction, he adopted the habit of crawling cris-scross over the walls and the ceiling. He especially liked hanging from the ceiling; it was completely different from lying on the floor; one could breathe more freely; a faint swinging sensation went through the body; and in the almost happy absent-mindedness which Gregor felt up there, it could happen to his own surprise that he let go and plopped onto the floor. But now, of course, he had much better control of his body than before and did not hurt himself even from such a big drop. His sister immediately noticed the new entertain-ment Gregor had discovered for himself—after all, he left behind traces of his sticky substance wherever he crawled—and so she got it into her head to make it possible for Gregor to crawl on an altogether wider scale by taking out the furniture which stood in his way—mainly the chest of drawers and the desk. But she was not able to do this by herself; she did not dare ask her father for help; the maid would certainly not have helped her, for although this girl, who was about sixteen, was bravely sticking it out after the previous cook had left, she had asked for the favor of locking herself in the kitchen at all times and of only opening the door on special request. So there was nothing left for his sister to do except to get her mother one day when her father was out. And his mother did come, with exclamations of excited joy, but she grew silent at the door of Gregor's room. First his sister looked to see, of course, that everything in the room was in order; only then did she let her mother come in. Hurrying as fast as he could, Gregor had pulled the sheet down lower still and pleated it more tightly—it really looked just like a sheet accidently thrown over the couch. This time Gregor also refrained from spying from under the sheet; he renounced seeing his mother for the time being and was simply happy that she had come after all. "Come on, you can't see him," his sister said, evidently leading her mother in by the hand. Now Gregor could hear the two frail women moving the old chest of drawers—heavy for anyone—from its place and his sister insisting on doing the harder part of the job herself, ignoring the warnings of her mother, who was afraid that she would overexert herself. It went on for a long time. After struggling for a good quarter of an hour, his mother said that they had better leave the chest where it was, because, in the first place, it was too heavy, they would not finish before his father came, and with the chest in the middle of the room, Gregor would be completely barricaded; and, in the second place, it was not at all certain that they were doing Gregor a favor by removing his furniture. To her the opposite seemed to be the case; the sight of the bare wall was heart-breaking; and why shouldn't Gregor also have the same feeling, since he had been used to his furniture for so long and would feel abandoned in the empty room. "And doesn't it look," his mother concluded very softly—in fact she had been almost whispering the whole time, as if she wanted to avoid letting Gregor, whose exact whereabouts she did not know, hear even the sound of her voice, for she was convinced that he did not understand the words—"and doesn't it look as if by removing his furniture we were showing him that we have given up all hope of his getting better and are leaving him to his own devices without any consideration? I think the best thing would be to try to keep the room exactly the way it was before, so that when Gregor comes back to us again, he'll find everything unchanged and can forget all the more easily what's happened in the meantime."

When he heard his mother's words, Gregor realized that the monotony of family life, combined with the fact that not a soul had addressed a word directly to him, must have addled his brain in the course of the past two months, for he culd not explain to himself in any other way how in all seriousness he could have been anxious to have his room cleared out. Had he really wanted to have his warm room, comfortably fitted with furniture that had always been in the family, changed into a cave, in which, of course, he would be able to crawl around unhampered in all directions but at the cost of simultaneously, rapidly, and totally forgetting his human past? Even now he had been on the verge of forgetting, and only his mother's voice, which he had not heard for so long, had shaken him up. Nothing should be removed; everything had to stay; he could not do without the beneficial influence of the furniture on his state of mind; and if the furniture prevented him from carrying on this senseless crawling around, then that was no loss but rather a great advantage.

But his sister unfortunately had a different opinion; she had become accustomed, certainly not entirely without justification, to adopt with her parents the role of the particularly well-qualified expert whenever Gregor's affairs were being discussed; and so her mother's advice was now sufficient reason for her to insist, not only on the removal of the chest of drawers and the desk, which was all she had been planning at first, but also on the removal of all the furniture with the exception of the indispensable couch. Of course it was not only childish defiance and the self-confidence she had recently acquired so unexpectedly and at such a cost that led her to make this demand; she had in fact noticed that Gregor needed plenty of room to crawl around in; and on the other hand, as best she could tell, he never used the furniture at all. Perhaps, however, the romantic enthusiasm of girls her age, which seeks to indulge itself at every opportunity, played a part, by tempting her to make Gregor's situation even more terrifying in order that she might do even more for him. Into a room in which Gregor ruled the bare walls all alone, no human being beside Grete was ever likely to set foot.

And so she did not let herself be swerved from her decision by her mother, who, besides, from the sheer anxiety of being in Gregor's room, seemed unsure of herself, soon grew silent, and helped her daughter as best she could to get the chest of drawers out of the room. Well, in a pinch Gregor could do without the chest, but the desk had to stay. And hardly had the women left the room with the chest, squeezing against it and groaning, than Gregor stuck his head out from under the couch to see how he could feel his way into the situation as considerately as possible. But unfortunately it had to be his mother who came back first, while in the next room Grete was clasping the chest and rocking it back and forth by herself, without of course budging it from the spot. His mother, however, was not used to the sight of Gregor, he could have made her ill, and so Gregor, frightened, scuttled in reverse to the far end of the couch but could not stop the sheet from shifting a little at the front. That was enough to put his mother on the alert. She stopped, stood still for a moment, and then went back to Grete.

Although Gregor told himself over and over again that nothing special was happening, only a few pieces of furniture were being moved, he soon had to admit that this coming and going of the women, their little calls to each other, the scraping of the furniture along the floor had the effect on him of a great turmoil swelling on all sides, and as much as he tucked in his head and his legs and shrank until his belly touched the floor, he was forced to admit that he would not be able to stand it much longer. They were clearing out his room; depriving him of everything that he loved; they had already carried away the chest of drawers, in which he kept the fret-saw and other tools; were now budging the desk firmly embedded in the floor, the desk he had done his homework on when he was a student at business college, in high school, yes, even in public school— now he really had no more time to examine the good intentions of the two women, whose existence, besides, he had almost forgotten, for they were so exhausted that they were working in silence, and one could hear only the heavy shuffling of their feet.

And so he broke out—the women were just leaning against the desk in the next room to catch their breath for a minute—changed his course four times, he really didn't know what to salvage first, then he saw hanging conspicuously on the wall, which was otherwise bare already the picture of the lady all dressed in furs, hurriedly crawled up on it and pressed himself against the glass, which gave a good surface to stick to and soothed his hot belly. At least no one would take away this picture, while Gregor completely covered it up. He turned his head toward the living-room door to watch the women when they returned.

They had not given themselves much of a rest and were already coming back; Grete had put her arm around her mother and was practically carrying her. "So what should we take now?" said Grete and looked around. At that her eyes met Gregor's as he clung to the wall. Probably only because of her mother's presence she kept her self-control, bent her head down to her mother to keep her from looking around, and said, though in a quavering and thoughtless voice: "Come, we'd better go back into the living room for a min-ute." Grete's intent was clear to Gregor, she wanted to bring his mother into safety and then chase him down from the wall. Well, just let her try! He squatted on his picture and would not give it up. He would rather fly in Grete's face.

But Grete's words had now made her mother really anxious; she stepped to one side, caught sight of the gigantic brown blotch on the flowered wallpaper, and before it really dawned on her that what she saw was Gregor, cried in a hoarse, bawling voice: "Oh, God, Oh, God!"; and as if giving up completely, she fell with outstretched arms across the couch and did not stir. "You, Gregor!" cried his sister with raised fist and piercing eyes. These were the first words she had addressed directly to him since his metamorphosis. She ran into the next room to get some kind of spirits to revive her mother; Gregor wanted to help too—there was time to rescue the picture—but he was stuck to the glass and had to tear himself loose by force; then he too ran into the next room, as if he could give his sister some sort of advice, as in the old days; but then had to stand behind her doing nothing while she rummaged among various little bottles; moreover, when she turned around she was startled, a bottle fell on the floor and broke, a splinter of glass wounded Gregor in the face, some kind of corrosive medicine flowed around him; now without waiting any longer, Grete grabbed as many little bottles as she could carry and ran with them inside to her mother; she slammed the door behind her with her foot. Now Gregor was cut off from his mother, who was perhaps near death through his fault; he could not dare open the door if he did not want to chase away his sister, who had to stay with his mother; now there was nothing for him to do except wait; and tormented by self-reproaches and worry, he began to crawl, crawled over everything, walls, furniture and ceiling, and finally in desperation, as the whole room was beginning to spin, fell down onto the middle of the big table.

A short time passed; Gregor lay there prostrate; all around, things were quiet, perhaps that was a good sign. Then the doorbell rang. The maid, of course, was locked up in her kitchen and so Grete had to answer the door. His father had come home. "What's happened?" were his first words; Grete's appearance must have told him everything. Grete answered in a muffled voice, her face was obviously pressed atainst her father's chest; "Mother fainted, but she's better now. Gregor's broken out." "I knew it," his father said. "I kept telling you, but you women don't want to listen." It was clear to Gregor that his father had put the worst interpretation on Grete's all-too-brief announcement and assumed that Gregor was guilty of some outrage. Therefore Gregor now had to try to calm his father down, since he had neither the time nor the ability to enlighten him. And so he fled to the door of his room and pressed himself against it for his father to see, as soon as he came into the foyer, that Gregor had the best intentions of returning to his room immediately and that it was not necessary to drive him back; if only the door were opened for him, he would disappear at once.

But his father was in no mood to notice such subtleties; "Ah!" he cried as he entered, in a tone that sounded as if he were at once furious and glad. Gregor turned his head away from the door and lifted it toward his father. He had not really imagined his father looking like this, as he stood in front of him now; admittedly Gregor had been too absorbed recently in his newfangled crawling to bother as much as before about events in the rest of the house and should

really have been prepared to find some changes. And yet, and yet—
was this still his father? Was this the same man who in the old days
used to lie wearily buried in bed when Gregor left on a business trip;
who greeted him on his return in the evening, sitting in his bathrobe
in the armchair, who actually had difficulty getting to his feet but as
a sign of joy only lifted up his arms; and who, on the rare occasions
when the whole family went out for a walk, on a few Sundays in
June and on the major holidays, used to shuffle along with great
effort between Gregor and his mother, who were slow walkers themselves, always a little more slowly than they, wrapped in his old overcoat, always carefully planting down his crutch-handled cane, and,
when he wanted to say something, nearly always stood still and
assembled his escort around him? Now, however, he was holding
himself very erect, dressed in a tight-fitting blue uniform with gold
buttons, the kind worn by messengers at banking concerns; above
the high stiff collar of the jacket his heavy chin protruded; under his
bushy eyebrows his black eyes darted bright, piercing glances; his
usually rumpled white hair was combed flat, with a scrupulously
exact, gleaming part. He threw his cap—which was adorned with a
gold monogram, probably that of a bank—in an arc across the entire
room onto the couch, and with the tails of his long uniform jacket
slapped back, his hands in his pants pockets, went for Gregor with a
sullen look on his face. He probably did not know himself what he
had in mind; still he lifted his feet unusually high off the floor, and
Gregor staggered at the gigantic size of the soles of his boots. But he
did not linger over this, he had known right from the first day of his
new life that his father considered only the strictest treatment called
for in dealing with him. And so he ran ahead of his father, stopped
when his father stood still, and scooted ahead again when his father
made even the slightest movement. In this way they made more than
one tour of the room, without anything decisive happening; in fact
the whole movement did not even have the appearance of a chase
because of its slow tempo. So Gregor kept to the floor for the time
being, especially since he was afraid that his father might interpret a
flight onto the walls or the ceiling as a piece of particular nastiness.
Of course Gregor had to admit that he would not be able to keep up
even this running for long, for whenever his father took one step,
Gregor had to execute countless movements. He was already beginning to feel winded, just as in the old days he had not had very
reliable lungs. As he now staggered around, hardly keeping his eyes
open in order to gather all his strength for the running; in his obtuseness not thinking of any escape other than by running; and having
almost forgotten that the walls were at his disposal, though here of
course they were blocked up with elaborately carved furniture full of
notches and points—at that moment a lightly flung object hit the

floor right near him and rolled in front of him. It was an apple; a second one came flying right after it; Gregor stopped dead with fear; further running was useless, for his father was determined to bombard him. He had filled his pockets from the fruit bowl on the buffet and was now pitching one apple after another, for the time being without taking good aim. These little red apples rolled around on the floor as if electrified, clicking into each other. One apple, thrown weakly, grazed Gregor's back and slid off harmlessly. But the very next one that came flying after it literally forced its way into Gregor's back; Gregor tried to drag himself away, as if the startling, unbelievable pain might disappear with a change of place; but he felt nailed to the spot and stretched out his body in a complete confusion of all his senses. With his last glance he saw the door of his room burst open, as his mother rushed out ahead of his screaming sister, in her chemise, for his sister had partly undressed her while she was unconscious in order to let her breathe more freely; saw his mother run up to his father and on the way her unfastened petticoats slide to the floor one by one; and saw as, stumbling over the skirts, she forced herself onto his father, and embracing him, in complete union with him—but now Gregor's sight went dim—her hands clasping his father's neck, begged for Gregor's life.

III

Gregor's serious wound, from which he suffered for over a month—the apple remained imbedded in his flesh as a visible souvenir since no one dared to remove it—seemed to have reminded even his father that Gregor was a member of the family, in spite of his present pathetic and repulsive shape, who could not be treated as an enemy; that, on the contrary, it was the commandment of family duty to swallow their disgust and endure him, endure him and nothing more.

And now, although Gregor had lost some of his mobility probably for good because of his wound, and although for the time being he needed long, long minutes to get across his room, like an old war veteran—crawling above ground was out of the question—for this deterioration of his situation he was granted compensation which in his view was entirely satisfactory: every day around dusk the living-room door—which he was in the habit of watching closely for an hour or two beforehand—was opened, so that, lying in the darkness of his room, invisible from the living room, he could see the whole family sitting at the table under the lamp and could listen to their conversation, as it were with general permission; and so it was completely different from before.

Of course these were no longer the animated conversations of the old days, which Gregor used to remember with a certain nostalgia in small hotel rooms when he'd had to throw himself wearily into the damp bedding. Now things were mostly very quiet. Soon after supper his father would fall asleep in his armchair; his mother and sister would caution each other to be quiet; his mother, bent low under the light, sewed delicate lingerie for a clothing store; his sister, who had taken a job as a salesgirl, was learning shorthand and French in the evenings in order to attain a better position some time in the future. Sometimes his father woke up, and as if he had absolutely no idea that he had been asleep, said to his mother, "Look how long you're sewing again today!" and went right back to sleep, while mother and sister smiled wearily at each other.

With a kind of perverse obstinacy his father refused to take off his official uniform even in the house; and while his robe hung uselessly on the clothes hook, his father dozed, completely dressed, in his chair, as if he were always ready for duty and were waiting even here for the voice of his superior. As a result his uniform, which had not been new to start with, began to get dirty in spite of all the mother's and sister's care, and Gregor would often stare all evening long at this garment, covered with stains and gleaming with its constantly polished gold buttons, in which the old man slept most uncomfortably and yet peacefully.

As soon as the clock struck ten, his mother tried to awaken his father with soft encouraging words and then persuade him to go to bed, for this was no place to sleep properly, and his father badly needed his sleep, since he had to be at work at six o'clock. But with the obstinacy that had possessed him ever since he had become a messenger, he always insisted on staying at the table a little longer, although he invariably fell asleep and then could be persuaded only with the greatest effort to exchange his armchair for bed. However much mother and sister might pounce on him with little admonitions, he would slowly shake his head for a quarter of an hour at a time, keeping his eyes closed, and would not get up. Gregor's mother plucked him by the sleeves, whispered blandishments into his ear, his sister dropped her homework in order to help her mother, but all this was of no use. He only sank deeper into his armchair. Not until the women lifted him up under his arms did he open his eyes, look alternately at mother and sister, and usually say, "What a life. So this is the peace of my old age." And leaning on the two women, he would get up laboriously, as if he were the greatest weight on himself, and let the women lead him to the door, where, shrugging them off, he would proceed independently, while Gregor's mother threw down her sewing and his sister her pen as quickly as possible so as to run after his father and be of further assistance.

Who in this overworked and exhausted family had time to worry about Gregor any more than was absolutely necessary? The household was stinted more and more; now the maid was let go after all; a gigantic bony cleaning woman with white hair fluttering about her head came mornings and evenings to do the heaviest work; his mother took care of everything else, along with all her sewing. It even happened that various pieces of family jewelry, which in the old days his mother and sister had been overjoyed to wear at parties and celebrations, were sold, as Gregor found out one evening from the general discussion of the prices they had fetched. But the biggest complaint was always that they could not give up the apartment, which was much too big for their present needs, since no one could figure out how Gregor was supposed to be moved. But Gregor understood easily that it was not only consideration for him which prevented their moving, for he could easily have been transported in a suitable crate with a few air holes; what mainly prevented the family from moving was their complete hopelessness and the thought that they had been struck by a misfortune as none of their relatives and acquaintances had ever ben hit. What the world demands of poor people they did to the utmost of their ability; his father brought breakfast for the minor officials at the bank, his mother sacrificed herself to the underwear of strangers, his sister ran back and forth behind the counter at the request of the customers; but for anything more than this they did not have the strength. And the wound in Gregor's back began to hurt anew when mother and sister, after getting his father to bed, now came back, dropped their work, pulled their chairs close to each other and sat cheek to cheek; when his mother, pointing to Gregor's room, said, "Close that door, Grete"; and when Gregor was back in darkness, while in the other room the women mingled their tears or stared dry-eyed at the table.

Gregor spent the days and nights almost entirely without sleep. Sometimes he thought that the next time the door opened he would take charge of the family's affairs again, just as he had done in the old days; after this long while there again appeared in his thoughts the boss and the manager, the salesmen and the trainees, the handyman who was so dense, two or three friends from other firms, a chambermaid in a provincial hotel—a happy fleeting memory—a cashier in a millinery store, whom he had courted earnestly but too slowly—they all appeared, intermingled with strangers or people he had already forgotten; but instead of helping him and his family, they were all inaccessible, and he was glad when they faded away. At other times he was in no mood to worry about his family, he was completely filled with rage at his miserable treatment, and although he could not imagine anything that would pique his appetite, he still made plans for getting into the pantry to take what was coming to him, even if he wasn't hungry. No longer considering what she could do to give Gregor a special treat, his sister, before running to business

every morning and afternoon, hurriedly shoved any old food into
Gregor's room with her foot; and in the evening, regardless of whether
the food had only been toyed with or—the most usual case—had
been left completely untouched, she swept it out with a swish of the
broom. The cleaning up of Gregor's room, which she now always
did in the evenings, could not be done more hastily. Streaks of dirt
ran along the walls, fluffs of dust and filth lay here and there on the
floor. At first, whenever his sister came in, Gregor would place himself in those corners which were particularly offending, meaning by
his position in a sense to reproach her. But he could probably have
stayed there for weeks without his sister's showing any improvement;
she must have seen the dirt as clearly as he did, but she had just
decided to leave it. At the same time she made sure—with an irrita-
bleness that was completely new to her and which had in fact infected
the whole family—that the cleaning of Gregor's room remain her
province. One time his mother had submitted Gregor's room to a
major housecleaning, which she managed only after employing a
couple of pails of water—all this dampness, of course, irritated Gregor too and he lay prostrate, sour and immobile, on the couch—but
his mother's punishment was not long in coming. For hardly had
his sister noticed the difference in Gregor's room that evening than,
deeply insulted, she ran into the living room and, in spite of her
mother's imploringly uplifted hands, burst out in a fit of crying, which
his parents—his father had naturally been startled out of his armchair—at first watched in helpless amazement; until they too got
going; turning to the right, his father blamed his mother for not
letting his sister clean Gregor's room; but turning to the left, he
screamed at his sister that she would never again be allowed to clean
Gregor's room; while his mother tried to drag his father, who was
out of his mind with excitement, into the bedroom; his sister, shaken
with sobs, hammered the table with her small fists; and Gregor hissed
loudly with rage because it did not occur to any of them to close the
door and spare him such a scene and a row.

But even if his sister, exhausted from her work at the store, had
gotten fed up with taking care of Gregor as she used to, it was not
necessary at all for his mother to take her place and still Gregor did
not have to be neglected. For now the cleaning woman was there.
This old widow, who thanks to her strong bony frame had probably
survived the worst in a long life, was not really repelled by Gregor.
Without being in the least inquisitive, she had once accidentally
opened the door of Gregor's room, and at the sight of Gregor—who,
completely taken by surprise, began to race back and forth although
no one was chasing him—she had remained standing, with her hands
folded on her stomach, marveling. From that time on she never
failed to open the door a crack every morning and every evening and

peek in hurriedly at Gregor. In the beginning she also used to call
him over to her with words she probably considered friendly, like,
"Come over here for a minute, you old dung beetle!" or "Look at
that old dung beetle!" To forms of address like these Gregor would
not respond but remained immobile where he was, as if the door had
not been opened. If only they had given this cleaning woman orders
to clean up his room every day, instead of letting her disturb him
uselessly whenever the mood took her. Once, early in the morning—heavy rain, perhaps already a sign of approaching spring, was
beating on the window panes—Gregor was so exasperated when the
cleaning woman started in again with her phrases that he turned on
her, of course slowly and decrepitly, as if to attack. But the cleaning
woman, instead of getting frightened, simply lifted up high a chair
near the door, and as she stood there with her mouth wide open, her
intention was clearly to shut her mouth only when the chair in her
hand came crashing down on Gregor's back. "So, is that all there
is?" she asked when Gregor turned around again, and she quietly put
the chair back in the corner.

Gregor now hardly ate anything anymore. Only when he accidentally passed the food laid out for him would he take a bite into his
mouth just for fun, hold it in for hours, and then mostly spit it out
again. At first he thought that his grief at the state of his room kept
him off food, but it was the very changes in his room to which he
quickly became adjusted. His family had gotten into the habit of
putting in this room things for which they could not find any other
place, and now there were plenty of these, since one of the rooms in
the apartment had been rented to three boarders. These serious
gentlemen—all three had long beards, as Gregor was able to register
once through a crack in the door—were obsessed with neatness, not
only in their room, but since they had, after all, moved in here,
throughout the entire household and especially in the kitchen. They
could not stand useless, let alone dirty junk. Besides, they had brought
along most of their own household goods. For this reason many
things had become superfluous, and though they certainly weren't
salable, on the other hand they could not just be thrown out. All
these things migrated into Gregor's room. Likewise the ash can and
the garbage can from the kitchen. Whatever was not being used at
the moment was just flung into Gregor's room by the cleaning woman,
who was always in a big hurry; fortunately Gregor generally saw only
the object involved and the hand that held it. Maybe the cleaning
woman intended to reclaim the things as soon as she had a chance
or else to throw out everything together in one fell swoop, but in fact
they would have remained lying wherever they had been thrown in
the first place if Gregor had not squeezed through the junk and set
it in motion, at first from necessity, because otherwise there would

have been no room to crawl in, but later with growing pleasure, although after such excursions, tired to death and sad, he did not budge again for hours.

Since the roomers sometimes also had their supper at home in the common living room, the living-room door remained closed on certain evenings, but Gregor found it very easy to give up the open door, for on many evenings when it was opened he had not taken advantage of it, but instead, without the family's noticing, had lain in the darkest corner of his room. But once the cleaning woman had left the living-room door slightly open, and it also remained opened a little when the roomers came in in the evening and the lamp was lit. They sat down at the head of the table where in the old days his father, his mother, and Gregor had eaten, unfolded their napkins, and picked up their knives and forks. At once his mother appeared in the doorway with a platter of meat, and just behind her came his sister with a platter piled high with potatoes. A thick vapor steamed up from the food. The roomers bent over the platters set in front of them as if to examine them before eating, and in fact the one who sat in the middle, and who seemed to be regarded by the other two as an authority, cut into a piece of meat while it was still on the platter, evidently to find out whether it was tender enough or whether it should perhaps be sent back to the kitchen. He was satisfied, and mother and sister, who had been watching anxiously, sighed with relief and began to smile.

The family itself ate in the kitchen. Nevertheless, before going into the kitchen, his father came into this room and, bowing once, cap in hand, made a turn around the table. The roomers rose as one man and mumbled something into their beards. When they were alone again, they ate in almost complete silence. It seemed strange to Gregor that among all the different noises of eating he kept picking up the sound of their chewing teeth, as if this were a sign to Gregor that you needed teeth to eat with and that even with the best make of toothless jaws you couldn't do a thing. "I'm hungry enough," Gregor said to himself, full of grief, "but not for these things. Look how these roomers are gorging themselves, and I'm dying!"

On this same evening—Gregor could not remember having heard the violin during the whole time—the sound of violin playing came from the kitchen. The roomers had already finished their evening meal, the one in the middle had taken out a newspaper, given each of the two others a page, and now, leaning back, they read and smoked. When the violin began to play, they became attentive, got up, and went on tiptoe to the door leading to the foyer, where they stood in a huddle. They must have been heard in the kitchen, for his father called, "Perhaps the playing bothers you, gentlemen? It can be stopped right away." "On the contrary," said the middle roomer. "Wouldn't the young lady like to come in to us and play in here where it's much roomier and more comfortable?" "Oh, certainly," called Gregor's father, as if he were the violinist. The boarders went back into the room and waited. Soon Gregor's father came in with the music stand, his mother with the sheet music, and his sister with the violin. Calmly his sister got everything ready for playing; his parents—who had never rented out rooms before and therefore behaved toward the roomers with excessive politeness—did not even dare sit down on their own chairs; his father leaned against the door, his right hand inserted between two buttons of his uniform coat, which he kept closed; but his mother was offered a chair by one of the roomers, and since she left the chair where the roomer just happened to put it, she sat in a corner to one side.

His sister began to play. Father and mother, from either side, attentively followed the movements of her hands. Attracted by the playing, Gregor had dared to come out a little further and already had his head in the living room. It hardly surprised him that lately he was showing so little consideration for the others; once such consideration had been his greatest pride. And yet he would never have had better reason to keep hidden; for now, because of the dust which lay all over his room and blew around at the slightest movement, he too was completely covered with dust; he dragged around with him on his back and along his sides fluff and hairs and scraps of food; his indifference to everything was much too deep for him to have gotten on his back and scrubbed himself clean against the carpet, as once he had done several times a day. And in spite of his state, he was not ashamed to inch out a little farther on the immaculate living-room floor.

Admittedly no one paid any attention to him. The family was completely absorbed by the violin-playing; the roomers, on the other hand, who at first had stationed themselves, hands in pockets, much too close behind his sister's music stand, so that they could all have followed the score, which certainly must have upset his sister, soon withdrew to the window, talking to each other in an undertone, their heads lowered, where they remained, anxiously watched by his father. It now seemed only too obvious that they were disappointed in their expectation of hearing beautiful or entertaining violin-playing, had had enough of the whole performance, and continued to let their peace be disturbed only out of politeness. Especially the way they all blew the cigar smoke out of their nose and mouth toward the ceiling suggested great nervousness. And yet his sister was playing so beautifully. Her face was inclined to one side, sadly and probingly her eyes followed the lines of music. Gregor crawled forward a little farther, holding his head close to the floor, so that it might be possible to catch her eye. Was he an animal, that music could move him so?

He felt as if the way to the unknown nourishment he longed for were coming to light. He was determined to force himself on until he reached his sister, to pluck at her skirt, and to let her know in this way that she should bring her violin into his room, for no one here appreciated her playing the way he would appreciate it. He would never again let her out of his room—at least not for as long as he lived; for once, his nightmarish looks would be of use to him; he would be at all the doors of his room at the same time and hiss and spit at the aggressors; his sister, however, should not be forced to stay with him, but would do so of her own free will; she should sit next to him on the couch, bending her ear down to him, and then he would confide to her that he had had the firm intention of sending her to the Conservatory, and that, if the catastrophe had not intervened, he would have announced this to everyone last Christmas—certainly Christmas had come and gone?—without taking notice of any objections. After this declaration his sister would burst into tears of emotion, and Gregor would raise himself up to her shoulder and kiss her on the neck which, ever since she started going out to work, she kept bare, without a ribbon or collar.

"Mr. Samsa!" the middle roomer called to Gregor's father and without wasting another word pointed his index finger at Gregor, who was slowly moving forward. The violin stopped, the middle roomer smiled first at his friends, shaking his head, and then looked at Gregor again. Rather than driving Gregor out, his father seemed to consider it more urgent to start by soothing the roomers although they were not at all upset, and Gregor seemed to be entertaining them more than the violin-playing. He rushed over to them and tried with outstretched arms to drive them into their room and at the same time with his body to block their view of Gregor. Now they actually did get a little angry—it was not clear whether because of his father's behavior or because of their dawning realization of having had without knowing it such a next door neighbor as Gregor. They demanded explanations from his father; in their turn they raised their arms, plucked excitedly at their beards, and, dragging their feet, backed off toward their room. In the meantime his sister had overcome the abstracted mood into which she had fallen after her playing had been so suddenly interrupted; and all at once, after holding violin and bow for a while in her slackly hanging hands and continuing to follow the score as if she were still playing, she pulled herself together, laid the instrument on the lap of her mother—who was still sitting in her chair, fighting for breath, her lungs violently heaving—and ran into the next room, which the roomers, under pressure from her father, were nearing more quickly than before. One could see the covers and bolsters on the beds, obeying his sister's practiced hands, fly up and arrange themselves. Before the boarders had reached the room, she had finished turning down the beds and had slipped out. Her father seemed once again to be gripped by his perverse obstinacy to such a degree that he completely forgot any respect still due his tenants. He drove them on and kept on driving until, already at the bedroom door, the middle boarder stamped his foot thunderingly and thus brought him to a standstill. "I herewith declare," he said, raising his hand and casting his eyes around for Gregor's mother and sister too, "that in view of the disgusting conditions prevailing in this apartment and family"—here he spat curtly and decisively on the floor—"I give notice as of now. Of course I won't pay a cent for the days I have been living here; either; on the contrary, I shall consider taking some sort of action against you with claims that—believe me—will be easy to substantiate." He stopped and looked straight in front of him, as if he were expecting something. And in fact his two friends at once chimed in with the words, "We too give notice as of now." Thereupon he grabbed the door knob and slammed the door with a bang.

Gregor's father, his hands groping, staggered to his armchair and collapsed into it; it looked as if he were stretching himself out for his usual evening nap, but the heavy drooping of his head, as if it had lost all support, showed that he was certainly not asleep. All this time Gregor had lain quietly at the spot where the roomers had surprised him. His disappointment at the failure of his plan—but perhaps also the weakness caused by so much fasting—made it impossible for him to move. He was afraid with some certainty that in the very next moment a general debacle would burst over him, and he waited. He was not even startled by the violin as it slipped from under his mother's trembling fingers and fell off her lap with a reverberating clang.

"My dear parents," said his sister and by way of an introduction pounded her hand on the table, "things can't go on like this. Maybe you don't realize it, but I do. I won't pronounce the name of my brother in front of this monster, and so all I say is: we have to try to get rid of it. We've done everything humanly possible to take care of it and to put up with it; I don't think anyone can blame us in the least."

"She's absolutely right," said his father to himself. His mother, who still could not catch her breath, began to cough dully behind her hand, a wild look in her eyes.

His sister rushed over to his mother and held her forehead. His father seemed to have been led by Grete's words to more definite thoughts, had sat up, was playing with the cap of his uniform among the plates which were still lying on the table from the roomers' supper, and from time to time looked at Gregor's motionless form.

"We must try to get rid of it," his sister now said exclusively to her father, since her mother was coughing too hard to hear anything. "It will be the death of you two, I can see it coming. People who already have to work as hard as we do can't put up with this constant torture at home, too. I can't stand it anymore either." And she broke out crying so bitterly that her tears poured down onto her mother's face, which she wiped off with mechanical movements of her hand.

"Child," said her father kindly and with unusual understanding, "but what can we do?"

Gregor's sister only shrugged her shoulders as a sign of the bewildered mood that had now gripped her as she cried, in contrast with her earlier confidence.

"If he could understand us," said her father, half questioning; in the midst of her crying Gregor's sister waved her hand violently as a sign that that was out of the question.

"If he could understand us," his father repeated and by closing his eyes, absorbed his daughter's conviction of the impossibility of the idea, "then maybe we could come to an agreement with him. But the way things are————"

"It has to go," cried his sister. "That's the only answer, Father. You just have to try to get rid of the idea that it's Gregor. Believing it for so long, that is our real misfortune. But how can it be Gregor? If it were Gregor, he would have realized long ago that it isn't possible for human beings to live with such a creature, and he would have gone away of his own free will. Then we wouldn't have a brother, but we'd be able to go on living and honor his memory. But as things are, this animal persecutes us, drives the roomers away, obviously wants to occupy the whole apartment and for us to sleep in the gutter. Look, Father," she suddenly shrieked, "he's starting in again!" And in a fit of terror that was completely incomprehensible to Gregor, his sister abandoned even her mother, literally shoved herself off from her chair, as if she would rather sacrifice her mother than stay near Gregor, and rushed behind her father, who, upset only by her behavior, also stood up and half-lifted his arms in front of her as if to protect her.

But Gregor had absolutely no intention of frightening anyone, let alone his sister. He had only begun to turn around in order to trek back to his room; certainly his movements did look peculiar, since his ailing condition made him help the complicated turning maneuver along with his head, which he lifted up many times and knocked against the floor. He stopped and looked around. His good intention seemed to have been recognized; it had only been a momentary scare. Now they all watched him, silent and sad. His mother lay in her armchair, her legs stretched out and pressed together, her eyes almost closing from exhaustion; his father and his sister sat side by side, his sister had put her arm around her father's neck.

Now maybe they'll let me turn around, Gregor thought and began his labors again. He could not repress his panting from the exertion, and from time to time he had to rest. Otherwise no one harassed him, he was left completely on his own. When he had completed the turn, he immediately began to crawl back in a straight line. He was astonished at the great distance separating him from his room and could not understand at all how, given his weakness, he had covered the same distance a little while ago almost without realizing it. Constantly intent only on rapid crawling, he hardly noticed that not a word, not an exclamation from his family interrupted him. Only when he was already in the doorway did he turn his head—not completely, for he felt his neck stiffening; nevertheless he still saw that behind him nothing had changed except that his sister had gotten up. His last glance ranged over his mother, who was now fast asleep.

He was hardly inside his room when the door was hurriedly slammed shut, firmly bolted, and locked. Gregor was so frightened at the sudden noise behind him that his little legs gave way under him. It was his sister who had been in such a hurry. She had been standing up straight, ready and waiting, then she had leaped forward nimbly, Gregor had not even heard her coming, and she cried "Finally!" to her parents as she turned the key in the lock.

"And now?" Gregor asked himself, looking around in the darkness. He soon made the discovery that he could no longer move at all. It did not surprise him; rather, it seemed unnatural that until now he had actually been able to propel himself on these thin little legs. Otherwise he felt relatively comfortable. He had pains, of course, throughout his whole body, but it seemed to him that they were gradually getting fainter and fainter and would finally go away altogether. The rotten apple in his back and the inflamed area around it, which were completely covered with fluffy dust, already hardly bothered him. He thought back on his family with deep emotion and love. His conviction that he would have to disappear was, if possible, even firmer than his sister's. He remained in this state of empty and peaceful reflection until the tower clock struck three in the morning. He still saw that outside the window everything was beginning to grow light. Then, without his consent, his head sank down to the floor, and from his nostrils streamed his last weak breath.

When early in the morning the cleaning woman came—in sheer energy and impatience she would slam all the doors so hard although she had often been asked not to, that once she had arrived, quiet sleep was no longer possible anywhere in the apartment—she did not at first find anything out of the ordinary on paying Gregor her usual short visit. She thought that he was deliberately lying motionless, pretending that his feelings were hurt; she credited him with unlimited intelligence. Because she happened to be holding the long broom, she tried from the doorway to tickle Gregor with it. When this too produced no results, she became annoyed and jabbed Gregor a little, and only when she had shoved him without any resistance to another spot did she begin to take notice. When she quickly became aware of the true state of things, she opened her eyes wide, whistled softly, but did not dawdle; instead, she tore open the door of the bedroom and shouted at the top of her voice into the darkness: "Come and have a look, it's croaked; it's lying there, dead as a doornail!"

The couple Mr. and Mrs. Samsa sat up in their marriage bed and had a struggle overcoming their shock at the cleaning woman before they could finally grasp her message. But then Mr. and Mrs. Samsa hastily scrambled out of bed, each on his side, Mr. Samsa threw the blanket around his shoulders, Mrs. Samsa came out in nothing but her nightgown; dressed this way, they entered Gregor's room. In the meantime the door of the living room had also opened, where Grete had been sleeping since the roomers had moved in; she was fully dressed, as if she had not been asleep at all; and her pale face seemed to confirm this. "Dead?" said Mrs. Samsa and looked inquiringly at the cleaning woman, although she could scrutinize everything for herself and could recognize the truth even without scrutiny. "I'll say," said the cleaning woman, and to prove it she pushed Gregor's corpse with her broom a good distance sideways. Mrs. Samsa made a movement as if to hold the broom back but did not do it. "Well," said Mr. Samsa, "now we can thank God!" He crossed himself, and the three women followed his example. Grete, who never took her eyes off the corpse, said, "Just look how thin he was. Of course he didn't eat anything for such a long time. The food came out again just the way it went in." As a matter of fact, Gregor's body was completely flat and dry; this was obvious now for the first time, really, since the body was no longer raised up by his little legs and nothing else distracted the eye.

"Come in with us for a little while, Grete," said Mrs. Samsa with a melancholy smile, and Grete, not without looking back at the corpse, followed her parents into their bedroom. The cleaning woman shut the door and opened the window wide. Although it was early in the morning, there was already some mildness mixed in with the fresh air. After all, it was already the end of March.

The three boarders came out of their room and looked around in astonishment for their breakfast; they had been forgotten. "Where's breakfast?" the middle roomer grumpily asked the cleaning woman. But she put her finger to her lips and then hastily and silently beckoned the boarders to follow her into Gregor's room. They came willingly and then stood, their hands in the pockets of their somewhat shabby jackets, in the now already very bright room, surrounding Gregor's corpse.

At that point the bedroom door opened, and Mr. Samsa appeared in his uniform, his wife on one arm, his daughter on the other. They all looked as if they had been crying; from time to time Grete pressed her face against her father's sleeve.

"Leave my house immediately," said Mr. Samsa and pointed to the door, without letting go of the women. "What do you mean by that?" said the middle roomer, somewhat nonplussed, and smiled with a sugary smile. The two others held their hands behind their back and incessantly rubbed them together, as if in joyful anticipation of a big argument, which could only turn out in their favor. "I mean just what I say," answered Mr. Samsa and with his two companions marched in a straight line toward the roomer. At first the roomer stood still and looked at the floor, as if the thoughts inside his head were fitting themselves together in a new order. "So, we'll go, then," he said and looked up at Mr. Samsa as if, suddenly overcome by a fit of humility, he were asking for further permission even for this decision. Mr. Samsa merely nodded briefly several times, his eyes wide open. Thereupon the roomer actually went immediately into the foyer, taking long strides; his two friends had already been listening for a while, their hands completely still, and now they went hopping right after him, as if afraid that Mr. Samsa might get into the foyer ahead of them and interrupt the contact with their leader. In the foyer all three took their hats from the coatrack, pulled their canes from the umbrella stand, bowed silently, and left the apartment. In a suspicious mood which proved completely unfounded, Mr. Samsa led the two women out onto the landing; leaning over the banister, they watched the three roomers slowly but steadily going down the long flight of stairs, disappearing on each landing at a particular turn of the stairway and a few moments later emerging again; the farther down they got, the more the Samsa family's interest in them wore off, and when a butcher's boy with a carrier on his head came climbing up the stairs with a proud bearing, toward them and then up on past them, Mr. Samsa and the women quickly left the banister and all went back, as if relieved, into their apartment.

They decided to spend this day resting and going for a walk; they not only deserved a break in their work, they absolutely needed one. And so they sat down at the table and wrote three letters of excuse, Mr. Samsa to the management of the bank, Mrs. Samsa to her employer, and Grete to the store owner. While they were writing, the cleaning woman came in to say that she was going, since her morning's work was done. The three letter writers at first simply nodded without looking up, but as the cleaning woman still kept lingering, they looked up, annoyed. "Well?" asked Mr. Samsa. The cleaning woman stood smiling in the doorway, as if she had some great good news to announce to the family but would do so only if she were thoroughly questioned. The little ostrich feather which stood almost upright on her hat and which had irritated Mr. Samsa the whole time she had been with them swayed lightly in all directions. "What do you want?" asked Mrs. Samsa, who inspired the most respect in the cleaning woman. "Well," the cleaning woman answered, and for good-natured laughter could not immediately go on, "look, you don't have to worry about getting rid of the stuff next door. It's already been taken care of." Mrs. Samsa and Grete bent down over their letters, as if to continue writing; Mr. Samsa, who noticed that the cleaning woman was now about to start describing everything in detail, stopped her with a firmly outstretched hand. But since she was not going to be permitted to tell her story, she remembered that she was in a great hurry, cried, obviously insulted, "So long, everyone," whirled around wildly, and left the apartment with a terrible slamming of doors.

"We'll fire her tonight," said Mr. Samsa, but did not get an answer from either his wife or his daughter, for the cleaning woman seemed to have ruined their barely regained peace of mind. They got up, went to the window, and stayed there, holding each other tight. Mr. Samsa turned around in his chair toward them and watched them quietly for a while. Then he called, "Come on now, come over here. Stop brooding over the past. And have a little consideration for me, too." The women obeyed him at once, hurried over to him, fondled him, and quickly finished their letters.

Then all three of them left the apartment together, something they had not done in months, and took the trolley into the open country on the outskirts of the city. The car, in which they were the only passengers, was completely filled with warm sunshine. Leaning back comfortably in their seats, they discussed their prospects for the time to come, and it seemed on closer examination that these weren't bad at all, for all three positions—about which they had never really asked one another in any detail—were exceedingly advantageous and especially promising for the future. The greatest immediate improvement in their situation would come easily, of course, from a change in apartments; they would now take a smaller and cheaper apartment, but one better situated and in every way simpler to manage than the old one, which Gregor had picked for them. While they were talking in this vein, it occurred almost simultaneously to Mr. and Mrs. Samsa, as they watched their daughter getting livelier and livelier, that lately, in spite of all the troubles which had turned her cheeks pale, she had blossomed into a good-looking, shapely girl. Growing quieter and communicating almost unconsciously through glances, they thought that it would soon be time, too, to find her a good husband. And it was like a confirmation of their new dreams and good intentions when at the end of the ride their daughter got up first and stretched her young body.

D. H. LAWRENCE
1885–1930

Few novelists have expressed the opposition between nature and society, intuitive instincts and the industrial age, as insistently as D. H. Lawrence. Widely known for portrayals of erotic passion that shocked his contemporaries, Lawrence took as his mission the exploration of individual human psychology and a struggle against everything that hindered its fulfillment. A master of striking descriptions that seemed to reproduce the very sight and smell of physical reality, Lawrence also worked on another plane: that of symbolic allusions to an underlying, elementary or archetypal reality which actually explained the human interactions being portrayed. Whether he wrote about the stunted, dreary landscape of the coal mining district, the deadening influence of gentility and social inhibitions, or about human possessiveness and its destruction of personal relationships, Lawrence tried to suggest an alternate world in which men and women related freely with one another and in perfect harmony with nature. Such a world is almost a mystic vision: it will come about, he argues, only if we remain true to the darker, irrational life-forces within us, and reject any intellectualized attempt to master our basic instincts. As often happens, the fictional definition of this supreme vision is less generous than its aim: Lawrence usually associates repression and convention with women, and the mutely powerful expression of life forces with men or animals. Nonetheless, his fiction is remarkable for its artistry and power, and for evoking—inside realistically portrayed personal relationships—some of the deepest currents of human psychology.

David Herbert Lawrence was born on September 11, 1885, the fourth of five children born to the coal miner Arthur Lawrence and his wife, Lydia, a former schoolteacher. They lived in Eastwood, a mining town near Nottingham, England, where the father went down to dig in the pits each day and David's mother—who had come from a more prosperous family—struggled against poverty and her husband's alcoholism to give her children a better opportunity in life. After the death of his older brother, Ernest, in 1901, young David—already physically frail—became increasingly the focus of his mother's anxious care. Violent quarrels between father and mother marked the early years of the children, who were usually sympathetic to their mother although Lawrence came later to feel that he had underestimated his father's warmth and vitality. Echoes of this early struggle, of his mother's ultimately unhealthy and possessive love, and of the mining community itself occur repeatedly in Lawrence's work, notably the novel *Sons and Lovers* and the short story, "Odor of Chrysanthemums," included here.

Lawrence was a good student, and at twelve won a county council scholarship that let him attend Nottingham High School. After graduation he became a clerk in a factory making artificial limbs, and then a teacher in local schools. He had taken up painting by now and started writing poetry in 1902. Teaching at the British School in Eastwood, Lawrence became close friends with a neighbor, Jessie Chambers, who shared his love of literature. The two might well have married if it had not been for the jealous disapproval of his mother, a situation Lawrence reconstructed with a pitiless perspective on both women in his third novel, *Sons and Lovers*. Memories of the countryside and the women he came to know reappear in several novels: Louise Burrows, whom he met in 1903, furnished elements of the "modern woman" Ursula Brangwen in *The Rainbow* (1915), and the tragic love affair of a later friend, Helen Corke, became the basis of his second novel, *The Trespasser* (1912).

In 1904 Lawrence won first place in all England and Wales in the King's Scholarship Examination. Although he had to postpone entrance into Nottingham University College until he could earn money for fees, the scholarship enabled him to begin the College's two-year teaching certificate course in 1906 and in 1908 he began teaching at a school in south London. His mother died in December 1910, and illness forced Lawrence to retire from teaching the next year. In 1912, on a visit to his former French professor, Lawrence met the man's much younger wife—Frieda von Richthofen Weekley—and fell in love. The two left the same year for Germany and then Italy, although they were not able to marry until Frieda received her divorce in 1914. The marriage lasted, passionate and quarrelsome, until Lawrence's death on March 2, 1930.

During World War I Frieda's German birth and Lawrence's general disgust with patriotic sentiments made the couple a focus of local suspicion. After much harassment, they were ordered in 1917 to leave the cottage in Cornwall where they had lived for two years and to stay away from coastal areas altogether; yet their application for passports was denied and they could not leave England. Lawrence wrote his most celebrated novels in this period: after the moderate success of *Sons and Lovers* (1913), he turned to a longer study of love relationships in modern society that became *The Rainbow* (1915) and *Women in Love* (1920). The latter novel continued the earlier tale of Ursula Brangwen's quest for love inside the story of two couples, themselves modeled on aspects of the Lawrences and their friends, the short story writer Katherine Mansfield and the critic John Middleton Murry. *The Rainbow* and *Women in Love*, with their depictions of erotic consciousness inside a suggested mythic and symbolic framework, were stylistically far more innovative than *Sons and Lovers*. The explicit love scenes, criticism of modern industrial society, and scorn for patriotic values shocked many, and *The Rainbow* was declared obscene and all copies destroyed in November 1915.

Embittered by his experiences in England, Lawrence left for Italy with Frieda in 1919. In subsequent years they traveled widely, living for brief periods in Sicily, Ceylon, Australia, and finally New Mexico and Mexico, where Lawrence thought to find in Indian primitivism a key to the elemental "blood-knowledge" he sought as an antidote to overly intellectualized modern society. The travel book, *Sea and Sardinia*, dates to this period, as does a series of "leadership" novels (*Aaron's Rod*, 1922, *Kangaroo*, 1923, and *The Plumed Serpent*, 1926) in which the protagonist seeks direction from a charismatic leader or cause. Although Lawrence has often been accused of fascism in these novels (and he certainly had no use for democracy or the rule of the masses), his main concern was to assert individual rights against society's encroaching claims, and to rebalance the human personality by emphasizing intuition over intellect. After finishing *The Plumed Serpent* in February 1925, Lawrence fell seriously ill with the tuberculosis that would cause his death five years later. He and Frieda returned to Italy and settled in 1926 in the Villa Mirenda outside Florence, where he took up painting again and completed work on *Lady Chatterley's Lover*. Privately printed in Florence in 1928, the novel could not be published or circulated unexpurgated in England or America until 1959 because of its explicit sexual scenes (*Ulysses*, in contrast, was judged not obscene in 1933). Lawrence and Frieda left the Villa Mirenda in 1928 and traveled in France and Spain before returning to Florence. His paintings had been exhibited in London in 1929 and provoked the same scandal and legal suppression as *Lady Chatterley's Lover*. Lawrence was extremely ill with tuberculosis in these years, although he also wrote poems (*Pansies*, 1929), essays, and a blasphemous variation on the Biblical account of the Resurrection (*The Man Who Died*, 1929) in which the resurrected prophet renounces prophecy for human love. In February 1930 the sick man moved to a sanitorium in Vence, in southern France. He died in Vence on March 2, and his body was later cremated and the ashes buried in a tomb on the New Mexico ranch where he had finished *The Plumed Serpent*.

From the beginning, "Odor of Chrysanthemums" evokes the childhood scenery and psychological themes of Lawrence's first novels, especially *Sons and Lovers*. The contrast between the industrial ugliness of the mining community and the thwarted beauty of nature is emphasized and given moral significance by the juxtaposition of locomotive and startled colt, the picture of the woman standing "insignificantly trapped" between the tracks and the hedge, and the dreary landscape's "bony vines," "ragged cabbages," and faded pink chrysanthemums. The conflict between husband and wife is also familiar, although here it appears at an earlier stage: Mrs. Bates's two children are still young as she tries, pregnant, to keep the household going in spite of her unruly and alcoholic husband. She is portrayed as imperious, practical, responsible, and disillusioned, and most of the story focuses on what seems to be one more evening of waiting for Walter Bates to come home drunk after having spent most of his pay at a local bar. Our knowledge of the situation develops through scenes of family friction as mother and children wait by the fire, and through the cautious sympathy of her father and neighbors, so that Elizabeth Bates's impatience and hostility toward her irresponsible husband seem totally justified by the time of the shocking announcement of his death in a mine accident. From that point on, the portrait of the wife does not change but a new counterpoint is introduced in the person of the dead man: solid, unreachable, mysteriously alien and inviolate in his death.

In the last pages of the story, the physical presence of her husband's dead body forces Elizabeth Bates to recognize for the first time the absolute difference between their two natures: a complete separation of individual identities which was true all along but which it took the permanent separation of death to make visible. Her image of Walter Bates while alive was not the measure of the man, whose stock of vitality and warmth Lawrence hints at when he repeatedly associates with him the natural symbol of chrysanthemum flowers. Husband and wife had not known each other, "had denied each other in life," and the wrong is now forever irreparable. The horror with which Elizabeth Bates comes to this realization extends beyond the loss of her husband, and beyond the tears her mother-in-law expects. It is the horror of "utter, intact separateness" that can exist between human beings in the closest relationships.

George Becker's *D. H. Lawrence* (1980) provides a general introduction and biography, and Frank Kermode's *D. H. Lawrence* (1971) is an excellent general study. See E. T. (Jessie Chambers), *D. H. Lawrence*, 2nd ed. (1965), for an account of Lawrence's youth by a close friend who figures in *Sons and Lovers*. A good critical study of the fiction is Julian Moynahan, *The Deed of Life: The Novels and Tales of D. H. Lawrence* (1963).

Odor of Chrysanthemums

I

The small locomotive engine, Number 4, came clanking, stumbling down from Selston with seven full wagons. It appeared round the corner with loud threats of speed, but the colt that it startled from among the gorse, which still flickered indistinctly in the raw afternoon, out-distanced it at a canter. A woman, walking up the railway line to Underwood, drew back into the hedge, held her basket aside, and watched the footplate of the engine advancing. The trucks thumped heavily past, one by one, with slow inevitable movement, as she stood insignificantly trapped between the jolting black wagons and the hedge; then they curved away towards the coppice where the withered oak leaves dropped noiselessly, while the birds, pulling at the scarlet hips beside the track, made off into the dusk that had already crept into the spinney. In the open, the smoke from the engine sank and cleaved to the rough grass. The fields were dreary and forsaken, and in the marshy strip that led to the whimsey, a reedy pit pond, the fowls had already abandoned their run among the alders, to roost in the tarred fowl house. The pit bank[1] loomed up beyond the pond, flames like red sores licking its ashy sides, in the afternoon's stagnant light. Just beyond rose the tapering chimneys and the clumsy black headstocks[2] of Brinsley Colliery. The two wheels were spinning fast up against the sky, and the winding engine rapped out its little spasms. The miners were being turned up.

The engine whistled as it came into the wide bay of railway lines beside the colliery, where rows of trucks stood in harbor.

Miners, single, trailing, and in groups, passed like shadows diverging home. At the edge of the ribbed level of sidings squat a low

---

1. Bank formed by waste materials extracted from the mine.	2. Aboveground structures over mine shafts.

cottage, three steps down from the cinder track. A large bony vine clutched at the house, as if to claw down the tiled roof. Round the bricked yard grew a few wintry primroses. Beyond, the long garden sloped down to a bush-covered brook course. There were some twiggy apple trees, winter-crack trees, and ragged cabbages. Beside the path hung disheveled pink chrysanthemums, like pink cloths hung on bushes. A woman came stooping out of the felt-covered fowl house, halfway down the garden. She closed and padlocked the door, then drew herself erect, having brushed some bits from her white apron.

She was a tall woman of imperious mien, handsome, with definite black eyebrows. Her smooth black hair was parted exactly. For a few moments she stood steadily watching the miners as they passed along the railway: then she turned towards the brook course. Her face was calm and set, her mouth was closed with disillusionment. After a moment she called:

"John!" There was no answer. She waited, and then said distinctly:

"Where are you?"

"Here!" replied a child's sulky voice from among the bushes. The woman looked piercingly through the dusk.

"Are you at that brook?" she asked sternly.

For answer the child showed himself before the raspberry canes that rose like whips. He was a small, sturdy boy of five. He stood quite still, defiantly.

"Oh!" said the mother, conciliated. "I thought you were down at that wet brook—and you remember what I told you——"

The boy did not move or answer.

"Come, come on in," she said more gently, "it's getting dark. There's your grandfather's engine coming down the line!"

The lad advanced slowly, with resentful, taciturn movement. He was dressed in trousers and waistcoat of cloth that was too thick and hard for the size of the garments. They were evidently cut down from a man's clothes.

As they went slowly towards the house he tore at the ragged wisps of chrysanthemums and dropped the petals in handfuls among the path.

"Don't do that—it does look nasty," said his mother. He refrained, and she, suddenly pitiful, broke off a twig with three or four wan flowers and held them against her face. When mother and son reached the yard her hand hesitated, and instead of laying the flower aside, she pushed it in her apron-band. The mother and son stood at the foot of the three steps looking across the bay of lines at the passing home of the miners. The trundle of the small train was imminent. Suddenly the engine loomed past the house and came to a stop opposite the gate.

The engine-driver, a short man with round gray beard, leaned out of the cab high above the woman.

"Have you got a cup of tea?" he said in a cheery, hearty fashion.

It was her father. She went in, saying she would mash. Directly, she returned.

"I didn't come to see you on Sunday," began the little gray-bearded man.

"I didn't expect you," said his daughter.

The engine driver winced; then, reassuming his cheery, airy manner, he said:

"Oh, have you heard then? Well, and what do you think——?"

"I think it is soon enough," she replied.

At her brief censure the little man made an impatient gesture, and said coaxingly, yet with dangerous coldness:

"Well, what's a man to do? It's no sort of life for a man of my years, to sit at my own hearth like a stranger. And if I'm going to marry again it may as well be soon as late—what does it matter to anybody?"

The woman did not reply, but turned and went into the house. The man in the engine-cab stood assertive, till she returned with a cup of tea and a piece of bread and butter on a plate. She went up the steps and stood near the footplate of the hissing engine.

"You needn't 'a' brought me bread an' butter," said her father. "But a cup of tea"—he sipped appreciatively—"it's very nice." He sipped for a moment or two, then: "I hear as Walter's got another bout on," he said.

"When hasn't he?" said the woman bitterly.

"I heerd tell of him in the Lord Nelson braggin' as he was going to spend that b—— afore he went: half a sovereign that was."

"When?" asked the woman.

"A' Sat'day night—I know that's true."

"Very likely," she laughed bitterly. "He gives me twenty-three shillings."

"Aye, it's a nice thing, when a man can do nothing with his money but make a beast of himself!" said the gray-whiskered man. The woman turned her head away. Her father swallowed the last of his tea and handed her the cup.

"Aye," he sighed, wiping his mouth. "It's a settler,[3] it is——"

He put his hand on the lever. The little engine strained and groaned, and the train rumbled towards the crossing. The woman again looked across the metals. Darkness was settling over the spaces of the railway and trucks: the miners, in gray somber groups, were still passing home. The winding engine pulsed hurriedly, with brief pauses. Eliz-

---

3. Grave problem, something hard to bear.

abeth Bates looked at the dreary flow of men, then she went indoors. Her husband did not come.

The kitchen was small and full of firelight; red coals piled glowing up the chimney mouth. All the life of the room seemed in the white, warm hearth and the steel fender reflecting the red fire. The cloth was laid for tea; cups glinted in the shadows. At the back, where the lowest stairs protruded into the room, the boy sat struggling with a knife and a piece of white wood. He was almost hidden in the shadow. It was half-past four. They had but to await the father's coming to begin tea. As the mother watched her son's sullen little struggle with the wood, she saw herself in his silence and pertinacity; she saw the father in her child's indifference to all but himself. She seemed to be occupied by her husband. He had probably gone past his home, slunk past his own door, to drink before he came in, while his dinner spoiled and wasted in waiting. She glanced at the clock, then took the potatoes to strain them in the yard. The garden and fields beyond the brook were closed in uncertain darkness. When she rose with the saucepan, leaving the drain steaming into the night behind her, she saw the yellow lamps were lit along the high road that went up the hill away beyond the space of the railway lines and the field.

Then again she watched the men trooping home, fewer now and fewer.

Indoors the fire was sinking and the room was dark red. The woman put her saucepan on the hob, and set a batter pudding near the mouth of the oven. Then she stood unmoving. Directly, gratefully, came quick young steps to the door. Someone hung on the latch a moment, then a little girl entered and began pulling off her outdoor things, dragging a mass of curls, just ripening from gold to brown, over her eyes with her hat.

Her mother chid her for coming late from school, and said she would have to keep her at home the dark winter days.

"Why, mother, it's hardly a bit dark yet. The lamp's not lighted, and my father's not home."

"No, he isn't. But it's a quarter to five! Did you see anything of him?"

The child became serious. She looked at her mother with large, wistful blue eyes.

"No, mother, I've never seen him. Why? Has he come up an' gone past, to Old Brinsley? He hasn't, mother, 'cos I never saw him."

"He'd watch that," said the mother bitterly, "he'd take care as you didn't see him. But you may depend upon it, he's seated in the Prince o' Wales. He wouldn't be this late."

The girl looked at her mother piteously.

"Let's have our teas, mother, should we?" said she.

The mother called John to table. She opened the door once more and looked out across the darkness of the lines. All was deserted: she could not hear the winding engines.[4]

"Perhaps," she said to herself, "he's stopped to get some ripping done."

They sat down to tea. John, at the end of the table near the door, was almost lost in the darkness. Their faces were hidden from each other. The girl crouched against the fender slowly moving a thick piece of bread before the fire. The lad, his face a dusky mark on the shadow, sat watching her who was transfigured in the red glow.

"I do think it's beautiful to look in the fire," said the child.

"Do you?" said her mother. "Why?"

"It's so red, and full of little caves—and it feels so nice, and you can fair smell it."

"It'll want mending directly," replied her mother, "and then if your father comes he'll carry on and say there never is a fire when a man comes home sweating from the pit. A public house is always warm enough."

There was silence till the boy said complainingly: "Make haste, our Annie."

"Well, I am doing! I can't make the fire do it no faster, can I?"

"She keeps wafflin'[5] it about so's to make 'er slow," grumbled the boy.

"Don't have such an evil imagination, child," replied the mother.

Soon the room was busy in the darkness with the crisp sound of crunching. The mother ate very little. She drank her tea determinedly, and sat thinking. When she rose her anger was evident in the stern unbending of her head. She looked at the pudding in the fender, and broke out:

"It is a scandalous thing as a man can't even come home to his dinner! If it's crozzled[6] up to a cinder I don't see why I should care. Past his very door he goes to get to a public house, and here I sit with his dinner waiting for him——"

She went out. As she dropped piece after piece of coal on the red fire, the shadows fell on the walls, till the room was almost in total darkness.

"I canna see," grumbled the invisible John. In spite of herself, the mother laughed.

"You know the way to your mouth," she said. She set the dustpan outside the door. When she came again like a shadow on the hearth, the lad repeated, complaining sulkily:

"I canna see."

"Good gracious!" cried the mother irritably, "you're as bad as your father if it's a bit dusk!"

4. For raising and lowering men and materials.   5. Separating, breaking up embers.   6. Burnt up.

Nevertheless, she took a paper spill[7] from a sheaf on the mantelpiece and proceeded to light the lamp that hung from the ceiling in the middle of the room. As she reached up, her figure displayed itself just rounding with maternity.

"Oh, mother——!" exclaimed the girl.

"What?" said the woman, suspended in the act of putting the lamp glass over the flame. The copper reflector shone handsomely on her, as she stood with uplifted arm, turning to face her daughter.

"You've got a flower in your apron!" said the child, in a little rapture at this unusual event.

"Goodness me!" exclaimed the woman, relieved. "One would think the house was afire." She replaced the glass and waited a moment before turning up the wick. A pale shadow was seen floating vaguely on the floor.

"Let me smell!" said the child, still rapturously, coming forward and putting her face to her mother's waist.

"Go along, silly!" said the mother, turning up the lamp. The light revealed their suspense so that the woman felt it almost unbearable. Annie was still bending at her waist. Irritably, the mother took the flowers out from her apron band.

"Oh, mother—don't take them out!" Annie cried, catching her hand and trying to replace the sprig.

"Such nonsense!" said the mother, turning away. The child put the pale chrysanthemums to her lips, murmuring:

"Don't they smell beautiful!"

Her mother gave a short laugh.

"No," she said, "not to me. It was chrysanthemums when I married him, and chrysanthemums when you were born, and the first time they ever brought him home drunk, he'd got brown chrysanthemums in his buttonhole."

She looked at the children. Their eyes and their parted lips were wondering. The mother sat rocking in silence for some time. Then she looked at the clock

"Twenty minutes to six!" In a tone of fine bitter carelessness she continued: "Eh, he'll not come now till they bring him. There he'll stick! But he needn't come rolling in here in his pit dirt, for *I* won't wash him. He can lie on the floor——Eh, what a fool I've been, what a fool! And this is what I came here for, to this dirty hole, rats and all, for him to slink past his very door. Twice last week—he's begun now——"

She silenced herself, and rose to clear the table.

While for an hour or more the children played, subduedly intent, fertile of imagination, united in fear of the mother's wrath, and in

---

7. Long twist of paper.

dread of their father's home-coming, Mrs. Bates sat in her rocking chair making a "singlet" of thick cream-colored flannel, which gave a dull wounded sound as she tore off the gray edge. She worked at her sewing with energy, listening to the children, and her anger wearied itself, lay down to rest, opening its eyes from time to time and steadily watching, its ears raised to listen. Sometimes even her anger quailed and shrank, and the mother suspended her sewing, tracing the footsteps that thudded along the sleepers outside; she would lift her head sharply to bid the children "hush," but she recovered herself in time, and the footsteps went past the gate, and the children were not flung out of their play-world.

But at last Annie sighed, and gave in. She glanced at her wagon of slippers, and loathed the game. She turned plaintively to her mother.

"Mother!"—but she was inarticulate.

John crept out like a frog from under the sofa. His mother glanced up.

"Yes," she said, "just look at those shirt-sleeves!"

The boy held them out to survey them, saying nothing. Then somebody called in a hoarse voice away down the line, and suspense bristled in the room, till two people had gone by outside, talking.

"It is time for bed," said the mother.

"My father hasn't come," wailed Annie plaintively. But her mother was primed with courage.

"Never mind. They'll bring him when he does come—like a log." She meant there would be no scene. "And he may sleep on the floor till he wakes himself. I know he'll not go to work to-morrow after this!"

The children had their hands and faces wiped with a flannel. They were very quiet. When they had put on their nightdresses, they said their prayers, the boy mumbling. The mother looked down at them, at the brown silken bush of intertwining curls in the nape of the girl's neck, at the little black head of the lad, and her heart burst with anger at their father, who caused all three such distress. The children hid their faces in her skirts for comfort.

When Mrs. Bates came down, the room was strangely empty, with a tension of expectancy. She took up her sewing and stitched for some time without raising her head. Meantime her anger was tinged with fear.

II

The clock struck eight and she rose suddenly, dropping her sewing on her chair. She went to the stair-foot door, opened it, listening. Then she went out, locking the door behind her.

Something scuffled in the yard, and she started, though she knew it was only the rats with which the place was over-run. The night was very dark. In the great bay of railway lines, bulked with trucks, there was no trace of light, only away back she could see a few yellow lamps at the pit top, and the red smear of the burning pit bank on the night. She hurried along the edge of the track, then, crossing the converging lines, came to the stile by the white gates, whence she emerged on the road. Then the fear which had led her shrank. People were walking up to New Brinsley; she saw the lights in the houses; twenty yards farther on were the broad windows of the Prince of Wales, very warm and bright, and the loud voices of men could be heard distinctly. What a fool she had been to imagine that anything had happened to him! He was merely drinking over there at the Prince of Wales. She faltered. She had never yet been to fetch him, and she never would go. So she continued her walk towards the long straggling line of houses, standing back on the highway. She entered a passage between the dwellings.

"Mr. Rigley?—Yes! Did you want him? No, he's not in at this minute."

The raw-boned woman leaned foward from her dark scullery and peered at the other, upon whom fell a dim light through the blind of the kitchen window.

"Is it Mrs. Bates?" she asked in a tone tinged with respect.

"Yes. I wondered if your Master[8] was at home. Mine hasn't come yet."

" 'Asn't 'e! Oh, Jack's been 'ome an' 'ad 'is dinner an' gone out. 'E's just gone for 'alf an hour afore bedtime. Did you call at the Prince of Wales?"

"No——"

"No, you didn't like——! It's not very nice." The other woman was indulgent. There was an awkward pause. "Jack never said nothink about—about your Master," she said.

"No!—I expect he's stuck in there!"

Elizabeth Bates said this bitterly, and with recklessness. She knew that the woman across the yard was standing at her door listening, but she did not care. As she turned:

"Stop a minute! I'll just go an' ask Jack if 'e knows anythink," said Mrs. Rigley.

"Oh no—I wouldn't like to put——!"

"Yes, I will, if you'll just step inside an' see as th' childer' doesn't come downstairs and set theirselves afire."

Elizabeth Bates, murmuring a remonstrance, stepped inside. The other woman apologized for the state of the room.

The kitchen needed apology. There were little frocks and trousers

8. Husband

and childish undergarments on the squab[9] and on the floor, and a litter of playthings everywhere. On the black American cloth of the table were pieces of bread and cake, crusts, slops,[1] and a teapot with cold tea.

"Eh, ours is just as bad," said Elizabeth Bates, looking at the woman, not at the house. Mrs. Rigley put a shawl over her head and hurried out, saying:

"I shanna be a minute."

The other sat, noting with faint disapproval the general untidiness of the room. Then she fell to counting the shoes of various sizes scattered over the floor. There were twelve. She sighed and said to herself: "No wonder!"—glancing at the litter. There came the scratching of two pairs of feet on the yard, and the Rigleys entered. Elizabeth Bates rose. Rigley was a big man, with very large bones. His head looked particularly bony. Across his temple was a blue scar, caused by a wound got in the pit, a wound in which the coal dust remained blue like tattooing.

" 'Asna 'e come whoam yit?" asked the man, without any form of greeting, but with deference and sympathy. "I couldna say wheer he is—'e's non ower theer!"[2]—he jerked his head to signify the Prince of Wales.

" 'E's 'appen gone up to th'Yew," said Mrs. Rigley.

There was another pause. Rigley had evidently something to get off his mind:

"Ah left 'im finishin' a stint," he began. "Loose-all[3] 'ad bin gone about ten minutes when we com'n away, an' I shouted: 'Are ter comin', Walt?' an' 'e said: 'Go on, Ah shanna be but a'ef a minnit,' so we com'n ter th' bottom, me an' Bowers, thinkin' as 'e wor just behint, an' 'ud come up i' th' next bantle[4]——"

He stood perplexed, as if answering a charge of deserting his mate. Elizabeth Bates, now again certain of disaster, hastened to reassure him:

"I expect 'e's gone up to th' Yew Tree, as you say. It's not the first time. I've fretted myself into a fever before now. He'll come home when they carry him."

"Ay, isn't it too bad!" deplored the other woman.

"I'll just step up to Dick's an' see if 'e *is* theer," offered the man, afraid of appearing alarmed, afraid of taking liberties.

"Oh, I wouldn't think of bothering you that far," said Elizabeth Bates, with emphasis, but he knew she was glad of his offer.

As they stumbled up the entry, Elizabeth Bates heard Rigley's wife run across the yard and open her neighbor's door. At this, suddenly all the blood in her body seemed to switch away from her heart.

9. Couch.   1. Undrunk remains of tea, emptied out of the cups into a "slop bowl." *American cloth*: oilcloth.   2. "Hasn't he come home yet?" "He's not over there!"   3. End of day's shift.   4. Platform of elevator in mine shaft.

"Mind!" warned Rigley. "Ah've said many a time as Ah'd fill up them ruts in this entry, sumb'dy 'll be breakin' their legs yit."

She recovered herself and walked quickly along with the miner.

"I don't like leaving the children in bed, and nobody in the house," she said.

"No, you dunna!" he replied courteously. They were soon at the gate of the cottage.

"Well, I shanna be many minnits. Dunna you be frettin' now, 'e'll be all right," said the butty.[5]

"Thank you very much, Mr. Rigley," she replied.

"You're welcome!" he stammered, moving away. "I shanna be many minnits."

The house was quiet. Elizabeth Bates took off her hat and shawl, and rolled back the rug. When she had finished, she sat down. It was a few minutes past nine. She was startled by the rapid chuff of the winding engine at the pit, and the sharp whirr of the brakes on the rope as it descended. Again she felt the painful sweep of her blood, and she put her hand to her side, saying aloud: "Good gracious!—it's only the nine o'clock deputy going down," rebuking herself.

She sat still, listening. Half an hour of this, and she was wearied out.

"What am I working myself up like this for?" she said pitiably to herself, "I s'll only be doing myself some damage."

She took out her sewing again.

At a quarter to ten there were footsteps. One person! She watched for the door to open. It was an elderly woman, in a black bonnet and a black woolen shawl—his mother. She was about sixty years old, pale, with blue eyes, and her face all wrinkled and lamentable. She shut the door and turned to her daughter-in-law peevishly.

"Eh, Lizzie, whatever shall we do, whatever shall we do!" she cried.

Elizabeth drew back a little, sharply.

"What is it, mother?" she said.

The elder woman seated herself on the sofa.

"I don't know, child, I can't tell you!"—she shook her head slowly. Elizabeth sat watching her, anxious and vexed.

"I don't know," replied the grandmother, sighing very deeply. "There's no end to my troubles, there isn't. The things I've gone through, I'm sure it's enough——!" She wept without wiping her eyes, the tears running.

"But, mother," interrupted Elizabeth, "what do you mean? What is it?"

The grandmother slowly wiped her eyes. The fountains of her

5. Buddy, work companion.

tears were stopped by Elizabeth's directness. She wiped her eyes slowly.

"Poor child! Eh, you poor thing!" she moaned. "I don't know what we're going to do, I don't—and you as you are—it's a thing, it is indeed!"

Elizabeth waited.

"Is he dead?" she asked, and at the words her heart swung violently, though she felt a slight flush of shame at the ultimate extravagance of the question. Her words sufficiently frightened the old lady, almost brought her to herself.

"Don't say so, Elizabeth! We'll hope it's not as bad as that; no, may the Lord spare us that, Elizabeth. Jack Rigley came just as I was sittin' down to a glass afore going to bed, an' 'e said: ' 'Appen you'll go down th' line, Mrs. Bates. Walt's had an accident. 'Appen you'll go an' sit wi' 'er till we can get him home.' I hadn't time to ask him a word afore he was gone. An' I put my bonnet on an' come straight down, Lizzie. I thought to myself: 'Eh, that poor blessed child, if anybody should come an' tell her of a sudden, ther's no knowin' what'll 'appen to 'er.' You mustn't let it upset you, Lizzie—or you know what to expect. How long is it, six months—or is it five, Lizzie? Ay!"—the old woman shook her head—"time slips on, it slips on! Ay!"

Elizabeth's thoughts were busy elsewhere. If he was killed—would she be able to manage on the little pension and what she could earn?—she counted up rapidly. If he was hurt—they wouldn't take him to the hospital—how tiresome he would be to nurse!—but perhaps she'd be able to get him away from the drink and his hateful ways. She would—while he was ill. The tears offered to come to her eyes at the picture. But what sentimental luxury was this she was beginning? She turned to consider the children. At any rate she was absolutely necessary for them. They were her business.

"Ay!" repeated the old woman, "it seems but a week or two since he brought me his first wages. Ay—he was a good lad, Elizabeth, he was, in his way. I don't know why he got to be such a trouble, I don't. He was a happy lad at home, only full of spirits. But there's no mistake he's been a handful of trouble, he has! I hope the Lord'll spare him to mend his ways. I hope so, I hope so. You've had a sight o' trouble with him, Elizabeth, you have indeed. But he was a jolly enough lad wi' me, he was, I can assure you. I don't know how it is. . . ."

The old woman continued to muse aloud, a monotonous irritating sound, while Elizabeth thought concentratedly, startled once, when she heard the winding engine chuff quickly, and the brakes skirr with a shriek. Then she heard the engine more slowly, and the brakes made no sound. The old woman did not notice. Elizabeth waited in suspense. The mother-in-law talked, with lapses into silence.

"But he wasn't your son, Lizzie, an' it makes a difference. What-ever he was, I remember him when he was little, an' I learned to understand him and to make allowances. You've got to make allow-ances for them———"

It was half-past ten, and the old woman was saying: "But it's trou-ble from beginning to end; you're never too old for trouble, never too old for that———" when the gate banged back, and there were heavy feet on the steps.

"I'll go, Lizzie, let me go," cried the old woman, rising. But Eliz-abeth was at the door. It was a man in pit clothes.

"They're bringin' 'im, Missis," he said. Elizabeth's heart halted a moment. Then it surged on again, almost suffocating her.

"Is he—is it bad?" she asked.

The man turned away, looking at the darkness:

"The doctor says 'e'd been dead hours. 'E saw 'im i' th' lamp-cabin."

The old woman, who stood just behind Elizabeth, dropped into a chair, and folded her hands, crying: "Oh, my boy, my boy!"

"Hush!" said Elizabeth, with a sharp twitch of a frown. "Be still, mother, don't waken th' children: I wouldn't have them down for anything!"

The old woman moaned softly, rocking herself. The man was drawing away. Elizabeth took a step forward.

"How was it?" she asked.

"Well, I couldn't say for sure," the man replied, very ill at ease. " 'E wor finishin' a stint an' th' butties 'ad gone, an' a lot o'stuff come down atop 'n 'im."

"And crushed him?" cried the widow, with a shudder.

"No," said the man, "it fell at th' back of 'im. 'E wor under th' face[6] an' it niver touched 'im. It shut 'im in. It seems 'e wor smoth-ered."

Elizabeth shrank back. She heard the old woman behind her cry:

"What?—what did 'e say it was?"

The man replied, more loudly: " 'E wor smothered!"

Then the old woman wailed aloud, and this relieved Elizabeth.

"Oh, mother," she said, putting her hand on the old woman, "don't waken th' children, don't waken th' children."

She wept a little, unknowing, while the old mother rocked herself and moaned. Elizabeth remembered that they were bringing him home, and she must be ready. "They'll lay him in the parlor," she said to herself, standing a moment pale and perplexed.

Then she lighted a candle and went into the tiny room. The air was cold and damp, but she could not make a fire, there was no

6. Coal face.

fireplace. She set down the candle and looked round. The candle-light glittered on the luster-glasses, on the two vases that held some of the pink chrysanthemums, and on the dark mahogany. There was a cold, deathly smell of chrysanthemums in the room. Elizabeth stood looking at the flowers. She turned away, and calculated whether there would be room to lay him on the floor, between the couch and the chiffonier. She pushed the chairs aside. There would be room to lay him down and to step round him. Then she fetched the old red tablecloth, and another old cloth, spreading them down to save her bit of carpet. She shivered on leaving the parlor; so, from the dresser drawer she took a clean shirt and put it at the fire to air. All the time her mother-in-law was rocking herself in the chair and moaning.

"You'll have to move from there, mother," said Elizabeth. "They'll be bringing him in. Come in the rocker."

The old mother rose mechanically, and seated herself by the fire, continuing to lament. Elizabeth went into the pantry for another candle, and there, in the little penthouse under the naked tiles, she heard them coming. She stood still in the pantry doorway, listening. She heard them pass the end of the house, and come awkwardly down the three steps, a jumble of shuffling footsteps and muttering voices. The old woman was silent. The men were in the yard.

Then Elizabeth heard Matthews, the manager of the pit, say: "You go in first, Jim. Mind!"

The door came open, and the two women saw a collier backing into the room, holding one end of a stretcher, on which they could see the nailed pit boots of the dead man. The two carriers halted, the man at the head stooping to the lintel of the door.

"Wheer will you have him?" asked the manager, a short, white-bearded man.

Elizabeth roused herself and came from the pantry carrying the unlighted candle.

"In the parlor," she said.

"In there, Jim!" pointed the manager, and the carriers backed round into the tiny room. The coat with which they had covered the body fell off as they awkwardly turned through the two doorways, and the women saw their man, naked to the waist, lying stripped for work. The old woman began to moan in a low voice of horror.

"Lay th' stretcher at th' side," snapped the manager, "an' put 'im on th' cloths. Mind now, mind! Look you now——!"

One of the men had knocked off a vase of chrysanthemums. He stared awkwardly, then they set down the stretcher. Elizabeth did not look at her husband. As soon as she could get in the room, she went and picked up the broken vase and the flowers.

"Wait a minute!" she said.

The three men waited in silence while she mopped up the water with a duster.

"Eh, what a job, what a job, to be sure!" the manager was saying, rubbing his brow with trouble and perplexity. "Never knew such a thing in my life, never! He'd no business to ha' been left. I never knew such a thing in my life! Fell over him clean as a whistle, an' shut him in. Not four foot of space, there wasn't—yet it scarce bruised him."

He looked down at the dead man, lying prone, half naked, all grimed with coal dust.

" ' 'Sphyxiated', the doctor said. It *is* the most terrible job I've ever known. Seems as if it was done o' purpose. Clean over him, an' shut 'im in, like a mouse-trap"—he made a sharp, descending gesture with his hand.

The colliers standing by jerked aside their heads in hopeless comment.

The horror of the thing bristled upon them all.

Then they heard the girl's voice upstairs calling shrilly: "Mother, mother—who is it? Mother, who is it?"

Elizabeth hurried to the foot of the stairs and opened the door:

"Go to sleep!" she commanded sharply. "What are you shouting about? Go to sleep at once—there's nothing——"

Then she began to mount the stairs. They could hear her on the boards, and on the plaster floor of the little bedroom. They could hear her distinctly:

"What's the matter now?—what's the matter with you, silly thing?"—her voice was much agitated, with an unreal gentleness.

"I thought it was some men come," said the plaintive voice of the child. "Has he come?"

"Yes, they've brought him. There's nothing to make a fuss about. Go to sleep now, like a good child."

They could hear her voice in the bedroom, they waited whilst she covered the children under the bedclothes.

"Is he drunk?" asked the girl, timidly, faintly.

"No! No—he's not! He—he's asleep."

"Is he asleep downstairs?"

"Yes—and don't make a noise."

There was silence for a moment, then the men heard the frightened child again:

"What's that noise?"

"It's nothing, I tell you, what are you bothering for?"

The noise was the grandmother moaning. She was oblivious of everything, sitting on her chair rocking and moaning. The manager put his hand on her arm and bade her "Sh—sh! !"

The old woman opened her eyes and looked at him. She was shocked by this interruption, and seemed to wonder.

"What time is it?" the plaintive thin voice of the child, sinking back unhappily into sleep, asked this last question.

"Ten o'clock," answered the mother more softly. Then she must have bent down and kissed the children.

Matthews beckoned to the men to come away. They put on their caps and took up the stretcher. Stepping over the body, they tiptoed out of the house. None of them spoke till they were far from the wakeful children.

When Elizabeth came down she found her mother alone on the parlor floor, leaning over the dead man, the tears dropping on him.

"We must lay him out," the wife said. She put on the kettle, then returning knelt at the feet, and began to unfasten the knotted leather laces. The room was clammy and dim with only one candle, so that she had to bend her face almost to the floor. At last she got off the heavy boots and put them away.

"You must help me now," she whispered to the old woman. Together they stripped the man.

When they arose, saw him lying in the naïve dignity of death, the women stood arrested in fear and respect. For a few moments they remained still, looking down, the old mother whimpering. Elizabeth felt countermanded. She saw him, how utterly inviolable he lay in himself. She had nothing to do with him. She could not accept it. Stooping, she laid her hand on him, in claim. He was still warm, for the mine was hot where he had died. His mother had his face between her hands, and was murmuring incoherently. The old tears fell in succession as drops from wet leaves; the mother was not weeping, merely her tears flowed. Elizabeth embraced the body of her husband, with cheek and lips. She seemed to be listening, inquiring, trying to get some connection. But she could not. She was driven away. He was impregnable.

She rose, went into the kitchen, where she poured warm water into a bowl, brought soap and flannel and a soft towel. "I must wash him," she said.

Then the old mother rose stiffly, and watched Elizabeth as she carefully washed his face, carefully brushing his big blond moustache from his mouth with the flannel. She was afraid with a bottomless fear, so she ministered to him. The old woman, jealous, said:

"Let me wipe him!"—and she kneeled on the other side drying slowly as Elizabeth washed, her big black bonnet sometimes brushing the dark head of her daughter-in-law. They worked thus in silence for a long time. They never forgot it was death, and the touch of the man's dead body gave them strange emotions, different in each of the women; a great dread possessed them both, the mother felt the lie was given to her womb, she was denied; the wife felt the utter isolation of the human soul, the child within her was a weight apart from her.

At last it was finished. He was a man of handsome body, and his face showed no traces of drink. He was blond, full fleshed, with fine limbs. But he was dead.

"Bless him," whispered his mother, looking always at his face, and speaking out of sheer terror. "Dear lad—bless him!" She spoke in a faint, sibilant ecstasy of fear and mother love.

Elizabeth sank down again to the floor, and put her face against his neck, and trembled and shuddered. But she had to draw away again. He was dead, and her living flesh had no place against his. A great dread and weariness held her: she was so unavailing. Her life was gone like this.

"White as milk he is, clear as a twelve-month baby, bless him, the darling!" the old mother murmured to herself. "Not a mark on him, clear and clean and white, beautiful as ever a child was made," she murmured with pride. Elizabeth kept her face hidden.

"He went peaceful, Lizzie—peaceful as sleep. Isn't he beautiful, the lamb? Ay—he must ha' made his peace, Lizzie. 'Appen he made it all right, Lizzie, shut in there. He'd have time. He wouldn't look like this if he hadn't made his peace. The lamb, the dear lamb. Eh, but he had a hearty laugh. I loved to hear it. He had the heartiest laugh, Lizzie, as a lad——"

Elizabeth looked up. The man's mouth was fallen back, slightly open under the cover of the moustache. The eyes, half shut, did not show glazed in the obscurity. Life with its smoky burning gone from him, had left him apart and utterly alien to her. And she knew what a stranger he was to her. In her womb was ice of fear, because of this separate stranger with whom she had been living as one flesh. Was this what it all meant—utter, intact separateness, obscured by heat of living? In dread she turned her face away. The fact was too deadly. There had been nothing between them, and yet they had come together, exchanging their nakedness repeatedly. Each time he had taken her, they had been two isolated beings, far apart as now. He was no more responsible than she. The child was like ice in her womb. For as she looked at the dead man, her mind, cold and detached, said clearly: "Who am I? What have I been doing? I have been fighting a husband who did not exist. *He* existed all the time. What wrong have I done? What was that I have been living with? There lies the reality, this man." And her soul died in her for fear: she knew she had never seen him, he had never seen her, they had met in the dark and had fought in the dark, not knowing whom they met or whom they fought. And now she saw, and turned silent in seeing. For she had been wrong. She had said he was something he was not; she had felt familiar with him. Whereas he was apart all the while, living as she never lived, feeling as she never felt.

In fear and shame she looked at his naked body, that she had known falsely. And he was the father of her children. Her soul was torn from her body and stood apart. She looked at his naked body and was ashamed, as if she had denied it. After all, it was itself. It seemed awful to her. She looked at his face, and she turned her own face to the wall. For his look was other than hers, his way was not her way. She had denied him what he was—she saw it now. She had refused him as himself. And this had been her life, and his life. She was grateful to death, which restored the truth. And she knew she was not dead.

And all the while her heart was bursting with grief and pity for him. What had he suffered? What stretch of horror for this helpless man! She was rigid with agony. She had not been able to help him. He had been cruelly injured, this naked man, this other being, and she could make no reparation. There were the children—but the children belonged to life. This dead man had nothing to do with them. He and she were only channels through which life had flowed to issue in the children. She was a mother—but how awful she knew it now to have been a wife. And he, dead now, how awful he must have felt it to be a husband. She felt that in the next world he would be a stranger to her. If they met there, in the beyond, they would only be ashamed of what had been before. The children had come, for some mysterious reason, out of both of them. But the children did not unite them. Now he was dead, she knew how eternally he was apart from her, how eternally he had nothing more to do with her. She saw this episode of her life closed. They had denied each other in life. Now he had withdrawn. An anguish came over her. It was finished then: it had become hopeless between them long before he died. Yet he had been her husband. But how little!

"Have you got his shirt, 'Lizabeth?"

Elizabeth turned without answering, though she strove to weep and behave as her mother-in-law expected. But she could not, she was silenced. She went into the kitchen and returned with the garment.

"It is aired," she said, grasping the cotton shirt here and there to try. She was almost ashamed to handle him; what right had she or anyone to lay hands on him; but her touch was humble on his body. It was hard work to clothe him. He was so heavy and inert. A terrible dread gripped her all the while: that he could be so heavy and utterly inert, unresponsive, apart. The horror of the distance between them was almost too much for her—it was so infinite a gap she must look across.

At last it was finished. They covered him with a sheet and left him lying, with his face bound. And she fastened the door of the little parlor, lest the children should see what was lying there. Then, with peace sunk heavy on her heart, she went about making tidy the kitchen.

She knew she submitted to life, which was her immediate master.
But from death, her ultimate master, she winced with fear and shame.

T. S. ELIOT
1888–1965

In poetry and in literary criticism, Thomas Stearns Eliot has a unique position as a writer who not only expressed but helped to define modernist taste
and style. He rejected the narrative, moralizing, and frequently "noble" style
of late Victorian poetry, employing instead precisely focused and often startling images, and an elliptical, allusive, and ironic voice that had enormous
influence on modern American poetry. His early essays on literature and
literary history helped bring about not only a new appreciation of seventeenth-century "metaphysical" poetry but also a different understanding of
the text, no longer seen as the inspired overflow of spontaneous emotion but
as a carefully made aesthetic object. Yet much of Eliot's immediate impact
was not merely formal, but spiritual or philosophical. The search for meaning that pervades his work created a famous picture of the barrenness of
modern culture in *The Waste Land*, which juxtaposed images of past nobility and present decay, civilizations near and far, and Biblical, mythical, and
Buddhist allusions to evoke the dilemma of a composite, anxious, and infinitely vulnerable modern soul. Readers in different countries who know
nothing of Eliot's other works are often familiar with *The Waste Land* as a
literary-historical landmark representing a cultural crisis in European society
after the Great War. In many ways, Eliot's combination of spiritual insight
and technical innovation carries on the tradition of the Symbolist poet who
was both visionary artist and consummate craftsman.

Two countries, England and America, claim Eliot as part of their national
literature. Born September 26, 1888, to a prosperous and educated family
in St. Louis, Eliot went to Harvard University for his undergraduate and
graduate education and moved to England only in 1915, where he became
a British citizen in 1927. While at Harvard, Eliot was influenced by the
anti-Romantic humanist Irving Babbitt and the philosopher and aesthetician
George Santayana. He later wrote a doctoral dissertation on the philosophy
of F. H. Bradley, whose examination of private consciousness *(Appearance
and Reality)* appears in Eliot's own later essays and poems. Eliot also found
literary examples that would be important for him in future years: the poetry
of Dante and Donne, and the Elizabethan and Jacobean dramatists. In 1908
he read Arthur Symons's *The Symbolist Movement in Literature* and became
acquainted with the French Symbolist poets whose richly allusive images,
as well as a highly self-conscious, ironic, and craftsmanlike technique, he
would adopt for his own. Eliot began writing poetry while in college, and
published his first major poem—"The Love Song of J. Alfred Prufrock"—in
Chicago's *Poetry* magazine in 1915. When he moved to England, however,
he began a many-sided career as poet, reviewer, essayist, editor, and later

playwright. By the time he received the Nobel Prize for Literature in 1948, Eliot was recognized as one of the most influential twentieth-century writers in English.

Eliot's first poems, in 1915, already displayed the evocative yet startling images, abrupt shifts in focus, and combination of human sympathy and ironic wit that would attract and puzzle his readers. The "Preludes" linked the "notion of some infinitely gentle / Infinitely suffering thing" with a harsh fatalism in which "The worlds revolve like ancient women / Gathering fuel in vacant lots." Prufrock's dramatic monologue openly tried to startle readers by asking them to imagine the evening spread out "like a patient etherised upon a table" and by changing focus abruptly between imaginary land-scapes, metaphysical questions, drawing-room chatter, literary and Biblical allusions, and tones of high seriousness set against the most banal and even sing-song speech. "I grow old . . . I grow old . . . . / I shall wear the bottoms of my trousers rolled." The individual stanzas of "Prufrock" are individual scenes, each with its own coherence (e.g., the third stanza's yellow fog as a cat). Together, they compose a symbolic landscape sketched in the narrator's mind as a combination of factual observation and subjective feelings: the delicately stated eroticism of the arm "downed with light brown hair," and the frustrated aggression in "I should have been a pair of ragged claws / Scuttling across the floors of silent seas." In its discontinuity, precise yet evocative imagery, mixture of romantic and everyday reference, formal and conversational speech, and in the complex and ironic self-consciousness of its most unheroic hero, "The Love Song of J. Alfred Prufrock" already dis-plays many of the "modernist" traits typical of Eliot's entire work. Peculiarly his, as well, is the theme of spiritual void, and of a disoriented protagonist who—at least at this point—does not know how to cope with a crisis which is as much that of modern Western culture as it is his own personal tragedy.

Once established in London, Eliot married, taught briefly before taking a job in the foreign department of Lloyd's Bank (1917–25), and in 1925 joined the publishing firm of Faber and Faber. He wrote a number of essays and book reviews that were published in *The Sacred Wood* (1920) and *Homage to Dryden* (1924) and enjoyed a great deal of influence as assistant editor of the *Egoist* (1917–1919) and founding editor of the quarterly *Criterion* from 1922 until it folded in 1939. Eliot helped shape changing literary tastes as much by his essays and literary criticism as by his poetry. Influenced himself by T. E. Hulme's proposal that the time had come for a classical literature of "hard, dry wit" after Romantic vagueness and religiosity and by Imagism's goal of clear, precise physical images phrased in everyday language, he out-lined his own definitions of literature and literary history and contributed to a theoretical approach later known as the "New Criticism." In "Tradition and the Individual Talent" (1919), Eliot proclaimed that there existed a special level of great works—"masterpieces"—which formed among them-selves an "ideal order" of quality even though, as individual works, they expressed the characteristic sensibility of their age. The best poets were aware of fitting into the cumulative "mind of Europe" (Eliot describes a Western tradition like that presented in these volumes), and thus of being to some extent depersonalized in their works. Eliot's "impersonal theory of poetry" emphasizes the medium in which a writer works, rather than his inner state;

craft and control rather than the Romantic ideal of a spontaneous overflow of private emotion. In a famous passage which compares the creative mind to the untouched catalyst of a chemistry experiment, he insists that the writer makes the art object out of language and the experience of any number of people. "The poet's mind is in fact a receptacle for seizing and storing up numberless feelings, phrases, images, which remain there until all the particles which can unite to form a new compound are present together." Poetry can and should express the whole being—intellectual and emotional, conscious and unconscious. In a review of Herbert Grierson's edition of the seventeenth-century "metaphysical" poets (1921), Eliot praised the complex mixture of intellect and passion that characterized John Donne and the other metaphysicals (and that characterized Eliot himself), and criticized the tendency of English literature after the seventeenth century to separate the language of analysis from that of feeling. His criticism of this "dissociation of sensibility" implied a change in literary tastes: from Milton to Donne, from Tennyson to Gerard Manley Hopkins, from Romanticism to Classicism, from simplicity to complexity.

The great poetic example of this change came with *The Waste Land* in 1922. Eliot dedicated the poem to Ezra Pound, who had helped him revise the first draft, with a quotation from Dante praising the "better craftsman." Quotations from, or allusions to, a wide range of sources, including Shakespeare, Dante, Baudelaire, Wagner, Ovid, St. Augustine, Buddhist sermons, folk songs, and the anthropologists Jessie Weston and James Frazer, punctuate this lengthy poem, to which Eliot actually added explanatory notes when it was first published in book form. *The Waste Land* describes modern society in a time of cultural and spiritual crisis, and sets off the fragmentation of modern experience against references (some in foreign languages) to our common cultural heritage. The ancient prophet Tiresias is juxtaposed with the contemporary charlatan Madame Sosostris; celebrated lovers like Antony and Cleopatra with a house-agent's clerk who mechanically seduces a disinterested typist at the end of her day; the religious vision of St. Augustine and Buddhist sermons with a sterile world of rock and dry sand where "one can neither stand nor lie nor sit." The modern wasteland could be redeemed if it learned to answer (or rather, to ask) the right questions: a situation Eliot symbolized by oblique references to the legend of a knight passing an evening of trial in a Chapel Perilous, and healing a Fisher King by asking the right questions about the holy Grail and its lance. The series of references (many from literary masterworks) that Eliot integrated into his poem were so many "fragments I have shored against my ruins," pieces of a puzzle whose resolution would bring "shantih" or the peace which passes understanding, but which is still out of reach as the poem's final lines in a foreign language suggest.

The most influential technical innovation in *The Waste Land* was the deliberate use of fragmentation and discontinuity. Eliot pointedly refused to supply any transitional passages or narrative thread, and expected the reader to construct a pattern whose implications would make sense as a whole. This was a direct attack on linear habits of reading, which are here broken up with sudden introductions of a different scene or unexplained literary reference, shifts in perspective, interpolation of a foreign language, changes from elegant description to barroom gossip, from Elizabethan to modern scenes, from formal to colloquial language. Eliot's rupture of traditional expectations served several functions. It contributed to the general picture of cultural disintegration which the poem expressed, it allowed him to exploit the symbolist or allusive powers of language inasmuch as they now carried the burden of meaning, and finally—by drawing attention to its own technique—it exemplified modernist "self-reflexive" or self-conscious style. It is impossible to read a triple shift like "I remember / Those are pearls that were his eyes. / 'Are you alive, or not? Is there nothing in your head?' "—moving from the narrator's meditative recall to a quotation from Shakespeare and the woman's blunt attack—without noticing the abrupt changes in style and tone. Eliot's "heap of broken images" and "fragments shored against my ruins" also took the shape of fragments of thought and speech, and as such embodied a new tradition of literary language.

The spiritual search of "Prufrock," "Gerontion" (1919), and *The Waste Land* entered a new phase for Eliot in 1927, when he became a member of the Anglican Catholic Church. "Ash Wednesday" (1930) and a verse play on the death of Saint Thomas à Becket (*Murder in the Cathedral*, 1935) display the same distress over the human condition but now within a framework of hope for those who have accepted religious discipline. Eliot began writing plays to reach a larger audience, of which the best known are *The Family Reunion* (1939), which recast the Orestes story from Greek tragedy, and *The Cocktail Party* (1949), a drawing room comedy that also explored its characters' search for salvation. He is still best known for his poetry, however, and his last major work in that genre is the *Four Quartets* begun in 1934 and published entire in 1943.

As their title suggests, the *Four Quartets* are divided into sections much like the movement of a musical quartet. Each has five sections, inside which themes are introduced, developed, and resolved, and each has the title of a place. "Little Gidding" is a village in Huntingdonshire, England, which was the home of a seventeenth-century Anglican Catholic religious community of which only a chapel (rebuilt after the civil wars) remained. All the *Quartets* use varying forms of free verse, ranging from the most intense short lyrics to—for the first time—continuous narrative passages of the kind Eliot once disdained. Throughout, the poet ponders the relationship of historical change and eternal order.

Eliot's experiences in World War II as a watchman checking for fires during bombing raids enter into "Little Gidding," and he uses the chapel in that village as the point of departure for a meditation on the meaning of strife and change in a universe which the mind strives to structure, always imperfectly, by the timeless truths of religion. The *Quartet* opens in a section that is itself divided into three separate movements, first establishing the season of "midwinter spring" with the sun blazing on ice, then the chapel as the goal of any season's journey, and finally the chapel as a place so consecrated by prayer that the dead may communicate with the living. The lyrics opening the second section mourn the place's present decay by all four elements of earth, air, fire, and water, and pass on to an imaginary conversation between the poet, wandering after the last bomb and before the All Clear signal, and an anonymous "dead master." The mood is pessimistic, and the dead master (a "compound ghost" with elements of Eliot, Dante's Virgil, and W. B. Yeats) prophesies a bitter old age full of remorse and impotent rage at human folly. Their conversation suggests a comparison between the air-raid scene and Dante's Inferno, for it echoes the triple-line stanzaic form of the *Divine Comedy* and recalls the Italian poet's own encounter with his former master Brunetto Latini, in Hell (*Inferno*, 15: 23–124). The rest of the poem, however, moves forward to a kind of resolution out of time. The third section's beginning rhetoric of logical persuasion ("There are three conditions") introduces the concept of memory expanding our perspectives and enabling us to transcend the narrow commitments of history and civil war; the intense lyrics of the short fourth section propose that the flames of the annunciatory dove (or bomb) may be purgation as well as destruction; and in the final section, as the afternoon draws to a close, the poet ends his meditation on past and present, time and eternity, by asserting his faith in a condition of mind and spirit that combines both *now* and *always*, a transcendental vision that is a "condition of complete simplicity" and "crowned knot of fire."

The poem's conclusion is thus a religious one, moving from the agony of history to an eternal, purifying flame that may recall a similar mystic vision of all-penetrating light at the end of Dante's *Paradiso*. It may seem paradoxical that the poet who is known for expressing the dilemma of modern consciousness and for developing a new poetic style appropriate to twentieth-century experience, should resolve that experience in a metaphor of transcendence. From his earliest work, however, Eliot was preoccupied with the spiritual implications of the most mundane reality, and the yoking of concrete with transcendental vision defines at once the range and depth of his modernist style.

Bernard Bergonzi's *T. S. Eliot* (1972) is a brief, readable introduction to the life and works. *Twentieth-Century Interpretations of the Waste Land* (1968), edited by Martin Jay, provides five full-length essays and a series of excerpts from a range of critics. Another recommended collection of essays is *T. S. Eliot: A Collection of Criticism* (1974), Linda Wagner, ed.

The Love Song of J. Alfred Prufrock

S'io credesse che mia risposta fosse
A persona che mai tornasse al mondo,
Questa fiamma staria senza piu scosse.
Ma perciocche giammai di questo fondo
Non torno vivo alcun, s'i'odo il vero,
Senza tema d'infamia ti rispondo.[1]

Let us go then, you and I,
When the evening is spread out against the sky

1. From Dante's *Inferno* (27:61–66), where the false counselor Guido da Montefeltro, enveloped in flame, explains that he would never reveal his past if he thought the traveler could report it: "If I thought that my reply would be to one who would ever return to the world, this flame would stay without further movement. But since none has ever returned alive from this depth, if what I hear is true, I answer you without fear of infamy."

Like a patient etherised upon a table;
Let us go, through certain half-deserted streets,
The muttering retreats 5
Of restless nights in one-night cheap hotels
And sawdust restaurants with oyster-shells:
Streets that follow like a tedious argument
Of insidious intent
To lead you to an overwhelming question . . . 10
Oh, do not ask, "What is it?"
Let us go and make our visit.
   In the room the women come and go
Talking of Michelangelo.[2]

   The yellow fog that rubs its back upon the window-panes, 15
The yellow smoke that rubs its muzzle on the window-panes
Licked its tongue into the corners of the evening,
Lingered upon the pools that stand in drains,
Let fall upon its back the soot that falls from chimneys,
Slipped by the terrace, made a sudden leap, 20
And seeing that it was a soft October night,
Curled once about the house, and fell asleep.

   And indeed there will be time[3]
For the yellow smoke that slides along the street,
Rubbing its back upon the window-panes; 25
There will be time, there will be time
To prepare a face to meet the faces that you meet;
There will be time to murder and create,
And time for all the works and days of hands[4]
That lift and drop a question on your plate; 30
Time for you and time for me,
And time yet for a hundred indecisions,
And for a hundred visions and revisions,
Before the taking of a toast and tea.

   In the room the women come and go 35
Talking of Michelangelo.

   And indeed there will be time
To wonder, "Do I dare?" and, "Do I dare?"
Time to turn back and descend the stair,

2. Michelangelo Buonarroti (1475–1564), famous Italian Renaissance sculptor, painter, architect, and poet: here, merely a topic of fashionable conversation.   3. Echo of a love poem by
Andrew Marvell (1621–1678), "To His Coy Mistress": "Had we but world enough and
time . . ."   4. An implied contrast with the more productive agricultural labor of hands in the
Works and Days of the Greek poet Hesiod (eighth century B.C.).

With a bald spot in the middle of my hair—   40
[They will say: "How his hair is growing thin!"]
My morning coat, my collar mounting firmly to the chin,
My necktie rich and modest, but asserted by a simple pin—
[They will say: "But how his arms and legs are thin!"]
Do I dare   45
Disturb the universe?
In a minute there is time
For decisions and revisions which a minute will reverse.

       For I have known them all already, known them all:—
Have known the evenings, mornings, afternoons,   50
I have measured out my life with coffee spoons;
I know the voices dying with a dying fall
Beneath the music from a farther room.[5]
       So how should I presume?

       And I have known the eyes already, known them all—   55
The eyes that fix you in a formulated phrase,
And when I am formulated, sprawling on a pin,
When I am pinned and wriggling on the wall,
Then how should I begin
To spit out all the butt-ends of my days and ways?   60
       And how should I presume?

       And I have known the arms already, known them all—
Arms that are braceleted and white and bare
[But in the lamplight, downed with light brown hair!]
Is it perfume from a dress   65
That makes me so digress?
Arms that lie along a table, or wrap about a shawl.
       And should I then presume?
       And how should I begin?

                    .   .   .   .   .
Shall I say, I have gone at dusk through narrow streets   70
And watched the smoke that rises from the pipes
Of lonely men in shirt-sleeves, leaning out of windows? . . .

       I should have been a pair of ragged claws
Scuttling across the floors of silent seas.

                    .   .   .   .   .
And the afternoon, the evening, sleeps so peacefully!   75
Smoothed by long fingers,

5. Recalls Duke Orsino's description of a musical phrase in Shakespeare's "Twelfth Night" (I.i.4):
"It has a dying fall."

Asleep . . . tired . . . or it malingers,
Stretched on the floor, here beside you and me.
Should I, after tea and cakes and ices,
Have the strength to force the moment to its crisis?   80
But though I have wept and fasted, wept and prayed,
Though I have seen my head [grown slightly bald] brought in upon
    a platter,
I am no prophet[6]—and here's no great matter;
I have seen the moment of my greatness flicker,
And I have seen the eternal Footman hold my coat, and snicker,   85
And in short, I was afraid.

   And would it have been worth it, after all,
After the cups, the marmalade, the tea,
Among the porcelain, among some talk of you and me,
Would it have been worth while,   90
To have bitten off the matter with a smile,
To have squeezed the universe into a ball
To roll it toward some overwhelming question,[7]
To say: "I am Lazarus, come from the dead,[8]   95
Come back to tell you all, I shall tell you all"—
If one, settling a pillow by her head,
   Should say: "That is not what I meant at all.
   That is not it, at all."

   And would it have been worth it, after all,
Would it have been worth while,   100
After the sunsets and the dooryards and the sprinkled streets,
After the novels, after the teacups, after the skirts that trail along the
    floor—
And this, and so much more?—
Is it impossible to say just what I mean!
But as if a magic lantern[9] threw the nerves in patterns on a screen:

                                              105

Would it have been worth while
If one, settling a pillow or throwing off a shawl,
And turning toward the window, should say:
   "That is not it at all,   110
   That is not what I meant, at all."

No! I am not Prince Hamlet, nor was meant to be;
Am an attendant lord, one that will do

---

6. Salome obtained the head of the prophet John the Baptist on a platter as a reward for dancing
before the tetrarch Herod (Matthew 14:3–11).   7. Another echo of "To His Coy Mistress,"
when the lover suggests rolling "all our strength and all / our sweetness up into one ball" to send
against the "iron gates of life."   8. The story of Lazarus, raised from the dead, is told in John
11:1–44.   9. A slide projector.

To swell a progress,[1] start a scene or two,
Advise the prince; no doubt, an easy tool,
Deferential, glad to be of use,   115
Politic, cautious, and meticulous;
Full of high sentence, but a bit obtuse;
At times, indeed, almost ridiculous—
Almost, at times, the Fool.

    I grow old . . . I grow old . . .   120
I shall wear the bottoms of my trousers rolled.

    Shall I part my hair behind? Do I dare to eat a peach?
I shall wear white flannel trousers, and walk upon the beach.
I have heard the mermaids singing, each to each.

    I do not think that they will sing to me.   125

    I have seen them riding seaward on the waves
Combing the white hair of the waves blown back
When the wind blows the water white and black.

    We have lingered in the chambers of the sea
By sea-girls wreathed with seaweed red and brown   130
Till human voices wake us, and we drown.

The Waste Land[2]

"Nam Sibyllam quidem Cumis ego ipse oculis meis vidi in ampulla
pendere, et cum illi pueri dicerent: Σίβυλλα τί θέλειφ; respondebat
illa: ἀποθανειν θέλω."[3]

For Ezra Pound
il miglior fabbro.[4]

I. The Burial of the Dead[5]

April is the cruellest month, breeding
Lilacs out of the dead land, mixing

---

1. An official journey in Elizabethan times. 2. Eliot provided footnotes for *The Waste Land* when it was first published in book form; these notes are included below. A general note at the beginning referred readers to the religious symbolism described in Jessie L. Weston's study of the Grail legend, *From Ritual to Romance* (1920), and to fertility myths and vegetation ceremonies (especially those involving Adonis, Attis, and Osiris) as described in the *The Golden Bough* (1890–1918) by the anthropologist Sir James Frazer. 3. Lines from the *Satyricon* of the Latin writer Petronius (d. A.D. 66) describing the Sibyl, a prophetess shriveled with age and suspended in a bottle. "For indeed I myself have seen with my own eyes the Sibyl at Cumae, hanging in a bottle, and when those boys would say to her: 'Sibyl, what do you want?' she would reply: 'I want to die.' " 4. The dedication to Ezra Pound, who suggested cuts and changes in the first manuscript of *The Waste Land*, borrows words used by Guido Guinizelli to describe his predecessor, the Provençal poet Arnaut Daniel, in Dante's *Purgatorio* (XXVI:117): he is "the better craftsman." 5. From the burial service of the Anglican Church.

Memory and desire, stirring
Dull roots with spring rain.
Winter kept us warm, covering   5
Earth in forgetful snow, feeding
A little life with dried tubers.
Summer surprised us, coming over the Starnbergersee[6]
With a shower of rain; we stopped in the colonnade,
And went on in sunlight, into the Hofgarten,   10
And drank coffee, and talked for an hour.
Bin gar keine Russin, stamm' aus Litauen, echt deutsch.[7]
And when we were children, staying at the archduke's,
My cousin's, he took me out on a sled,
And I was frightened. He said, Marie,   15
Marie, hold on tight. And down we went.
In the mountains, there you feel free.
I read, much of the night, and go south in the winter.
    What are the roots that clutch, what branches grow
Out of this stony rubbish? Son of man,[8]   20
You cannot say, or guess, for you know only
A heap of broken images, where the sun beats,
And the dead tree gives no shelter, the cricket no relief,[9]
And the dry stone no sound of water. Only
There is shadow under this red rock,   25
(Come in under the shadow of this red rock),
And I will show you something different from either
Your shadow at morning striding behind you
Or your shadow at evening rising to meet you;
I will show you fear in a handful of dust.   30

> Frisch weht der Wind
> Der Heimat zu
> Mein Irisch Kind,
> Wo weilest du?[1]

"You gave me hyacinths first a year ago;   35
"They called me the hyacinth girl."
—Yet when we came back, late, from the Hyacinth garden,
Your arms full, and your hair wet, I could not
Speak, and my eyes failed, I was neither
Living nor dead, and I knew nothing,   40

6. Lines 8–16 recall *My Past*, the memoirs of Countess Marie Larisch. The Starnbergersee is a lake near Munich; the Hofgarten is a public park.   7. "I am certainly no Russian, I come from Lithuania and am pure German." German settlers in Lithuania considered themselves superior to the Slavic natives.   8. "Cf. Ezekiel II,i" [Eliot's note]. The passage reads "Son of man, stand upon thy feet, and I will speak unto thee."   9. "Cf. Ecclesiastes XII,v" [Eliot's note]. "Also when they shall be afraid of that which is high, and fears shall be in the way . . . the grasshopper shall be a burden, and desire shall fail . . ."   1. "V. *Tristan und Isolde*, I, verses 5–8" [Eliot's note]. A sailor in Wagner's opera sings "The wind blows fresh / Towards the homeland / My Irish child / Where are you waiting?"

Looking into the heart of light, the silence.
Oed' und leer das Meer.[2]

   Madame Sosostris, famous clairvoyante,[3]
Had a bad cold, nevertheless
Is known to be the wisest woman in Europe,   45
With a wicked pack of cards.[4] Here, said she,
Is your card, the drowned Phoenician Sailor,
(Those are pearls that were his eyes.[5] Look!)
Here is Belladonna, the Lady of the Rocks,
The lady of situations.   50
Here is the man with three staves, and here the Wheel,
And here is the one-eyed merchant, and this card,
Which is blank, is something he carries on his back,
Which I am forbidden to see. I do not find
The Hanged Man. Fear death by water.   55
I see crowds of people, walking round in a ring.
Thank you. If you see dear Mrs. Equitone,
Tell her I bring the horoscope myself:
One must be so careful these days.

   Unreal City,[6]   60
Under the brown fog of a winter dawn,
A crowd flowed over London Bridge, so many,
I had not thought death had undone so many.[7]

---

2. "Id. III, verse 24" [Eliot's note]. "Barren and empty is the sea" is the report the dying Tristan
hears as he waits for Isolde's ship in the third act of Wagner's opera.   3. A fortune-teller with
an assumed Egyptian name, possibly suggested by a similar figure in a novel by Aldous Huxley
(*Crome Yellow*, 1921).   4. "I am not familiar with the exact constitution of the Tarot pack of
cards, from which I have obviously departed to suit my own convenience. The Hanged Man, a
member of the traditional pack, fits my purpose in my mind: because he is associated in my mind
with the Hanged God of Frazer, and because I associate him with the hooded figure in the passage
of the disciples to Emmaus in Part V. The Phoenician Sailor and the Merchant appear later; also
the 'crowds of people,' and Death by Water is executed in Part IV. The Man with Three Staves
(an authentic member of the Tarot pack) I associate, quite arbitrarily, with the Fisher King himself" [Eliot's note]. Tarot cards are used for telling fortunes; the four suits (cup, lance, sword, and
dish) are life-symbols related to the Grail legend and, as Eliot suggests, various figures on the cards
are associated with different characters and situations in *The Waste Land*. For example: the "drowned
Phoenician Sailor" recurs in the merchant from Smyrna (III) and Phlebas the Phoenician (IV);
Belladonna (a poison, hallucinogen, medicine, and cosmetic; literally, "beautiful lady"; also an
echo of Leonardo's painting of the Virgin, *Madonna of the Rocks*) heralds the neurotic society
woman amidst her jewels and perfumes (II); the Wheel is the wheel of fortune; the Hanged Man
becomes the sacrificed fertility god whose death insures resurrection and new life for his people.
5. A line from Ariel's song in Shakespeare's *The Tempest* (I,ii,398), which describes the transformation of a drowned man.   6. "Cf. Baudelaire: 'Fourmillante cité, cité pleine de rêves, / Où
le spectre en plein jour raccroche le passant' " [Eliot's note]. "Swarming city, city full of dreams,
/ Where the specter in broad daylight accosts the passerby": a description of Paris from "The Seven
Old Men" in *Flowers of Evil* (1857).   7. "Cf. *Inferno* III, 55–57: 'si lunga tratta / di gente, ch'io
non avrei mai creduto / che morte tant n'avesse disfatta' " [Eliot's note]. "So long a train / of
people, that I would never have believed / death had undone so many": not only is Dante amazed
at the number of people who have died, but he is also describing a crowd of people who were
neither good nor bad—nonentities denied even the entrance to Hell.

Sighs, short and infrequent, were exhaled,[8]
And each man fixed his eyes before his feet.
Flowed up the hill and down King William Street,
To where Saint Mary Woolnoth kept the hours
With a dead sound on the final stroke of nine.[9]
There I saw one I knew, and stopped him, crying: "Stetson!
"You who were with me in the ships at Mylae![1]   70
"That corpse you planted last year in your garden,
"Has it begun to sprout? Will it bloom this year?
"Or has the sudden frost disturbed its bed?
"Oh keep the Dog far hence, that's friend to men,[2]
"Or with his nails he'll dig it up again!   75
"You! hypocrite lecteur!—mon semblable,—mon frère!"[3]

II. A Game of Chess[4]

The Chair she sat in, like a burnished throne,[5]
Glowed on the marble, where the glass
Held up by standards wrought with fruited vines
From which a golden Cupidon peeped out   80
(Another hid his eyes behind his wing)
Doubled the flames of sevenbranched candelabra
Reflecting light upon the table as
The glitter of her jewels rose to meet it,
From satin cases poured in rich profusion;   85
In vials of ivory and coloured glass
Unstoppered, lurked her strange synthetic perfumes,
Unguent, powdered, or liquid—troubled, confused

8. "Cf. *Inferno* IV, 25–27: 'Quivi, secondo che per ascoltare, / non avea pianto, ma' che di sospiri, / che l'aura eterna facevan tremare' " [Eliot's note]. "Here, so far as I could tell by listening, there was no weeping but so many sighs that they caused the everlasting air to tremble": the first circle of Hell, or Limbo, contained the souls of virtuous people who lived before Christ or had not been baptized.   9. "A phenomenon which I have often noticed" [Eliot's note]. The church is in the financial district of London, where King William Street is also located.   1. An "average" modern name (with business associations) linked to the ancient battle of Mylae (260 B.C.) where Rome was victorious over her commercial rival, Carthage.   2. "Cf. the Dirge in Webster's *White Devil*" [Eliot's note]. The dirge, or song of lamentation, sung by Cornelia in Webster's play (1625), asks to "keep the wolf far thence, that's foe to men," so that the wolf's nails may not dig up the bodies of her murdered relatives. Eliot's reversal of dog for wolf, and friend for foe, domesticates the grotesque scene; it may also foreshadow rebirth since (according to Weston's book), the rise of the Dog Star Sirius announced the flooding of the Nile and the consequent return of fertility to Egyptian soil.   3. "V. Baudelaire, Preface to *Fleurs du Mal*" [Eliot's note]. Baudelaire's preface, titled "To the Reader," ended "Hypocritical reader!—my likeness!—my brother!" The poet challenges the reader to recognize that both are caught up the worst sin of all—the moral wasteland of "ennui" (boredom) as lack of will, the refusal to care one way or the other.   4. Reference to a play (*A Game of Chess*, 1627) by Thomas Middleton (1580–1627): see note to line 137. Part II juxtaposes two scenes of modern sterility: an initial setting of wealthy boredom, neurosis, and lack of communication, and a pub scene where similar concerns of appearance, sexual attraction, and thwarted childbirth are brought out more visibly, and in more vulgar language.   5. "Cf. *Antony and Cleopatra*, II, ii, l. 190" [Eliot's note]. A paler version of Cleopatra's splendor as she met her future lover Antony: "The barge she sat in, like a burnish'd throne, / Burn'd on the water."

And drowned the sense in odours; stirred by the air
That freshened from the window, these ascended   90
In fattening the prolonged candle-flames,
Flung their smoke into the laquearia,[6]
Stirring the pattern on the coffered ceiling.
Huge sea-wood fed with copper
Burned green and orange, framed by the coloured stone,   95
In which sad light a carvèd dolphin swam.
Above the antique mantel was displayed
As though a window gave upon the sylvan scene[7]
The change of Philomel,[8] by the barbarous king
So rudely forced; yet there the nightingale[9]   100
Filled all the desert with inviolable voice
And still she cried, and still the world pursues,
"Jug Jug" to dirty ears.
And other withered stumps of time
Were told upon the walls; staring forms   105
Leaned out, leaning, hushing the room enclosed.
Footsteps shuffled on the stair.
Under the firelight, under the brush, her hair
Spread out in fiery points
Glowed into words, then would be savagely still.   110

       "My nerves are bad to-night. Yes, bad. Stay with me.
"Speak to me. Why do you never speak. Speak.
       "What are you thinking of? What thinking? What?
"I never know what you are thinking. Think."

       I think we are in rats' alley[1]   115
Where the dead men lost their bones.

       "What is that noise?"
                                    The wind under the door.[2]
"What is that noise now? What is the wind doing?"
                                    Nothing again nothing.   120
            "Do

6. "Laquearia. V. *Aeneid*, I, 726: dependent lychni laquearibus aureis incensi, et noctem flammis funalia vincunt" [Eliot's note]. "Glowing lamps hang from the gold-paneled ceiling, and the torches conquer night with their flames": the banquet setting of another classical love scene, where Dido is inspired with a fatal passion for Aeneas.   7. "Sylvan scene. V. Milton, *Paradise Lost*, IV, 140" [Eliot's note]. Eden as first seen by Satan.   8. "V. Ovid, *Metamorphoses*, VI, Philomela" [Eliot's note]. Philomela was raped by her brother-in-law, King Tereus, who cut out her tongue so that she could not tell her sister, Procne. Later Procne is changed into a swallow, and Philomela a nightingale, to save them from the king's rage after they have revenged themselves by killing his son.   9. "Cf. Part III, l. 204" [Eliot's note]. "Jug jug" represents the nightingale's song in Elizabethan poetry.   1. "Cf. Part III, l. 195" [Eliot's note].   2. "Cf. Webster: 'Is the wind in that door still?'" [Eliot's note]. From *The Devil's Law Case* (1623), III, 2, 162, with the implied meaning "is there still breath in him?"

"You know nothing? Do you see nothing? Do you remember
"Nothing?"

     I remember 125
Those are pearls that were his eyes.
"Are you alive, or not? Is there nothing in your head?"

                                                 But

     O O O O that Shakespeherian Rag—
It's so elegant
So intelligent 130
"What shall I do now? What shall I do?"
"I shall rush out as I am, and walk the street
"With my hair down, so. What shall we do to-morrow?
"What shall we ever do?"
                          The hot water at ten. 135
And if it rains, a closed car at four.
And we shall play a game of chess,
Pressing lidless eyes and waiting for a knock upon the door.[3]

     When Lil's husband got demobbed,[4] I said—
I didn't mince my words, I said to her myself, 140
HURRY UP PLEASE ITS TIME[5]
Now Albert's coming back, make yourself a bit smart.
He'll want to know what you done with that money he gave you
To get yourself some teeth. He did, I was there.
You have them all out, Lil, and get a nice set, 145
He said, I swear, I can't bear to look at you.
And no more can't I, I said, and think of poor Albert,
He's been in the army four years, he wants a good time,
And if you don't give it him, there's others will, I said.
Oh is there, she said. Something o' that, I said. 150
Then I'll know who to thank, she said, and give me a
     straight look.
HURRY UP PLEASE ITS TIME
If you don't like it you can get on with it, I said.
Others can pick and choose if you can't.
But if Albert makes off, it won't be for lack of telling. 155
You ought to be ashamed, I said, to look so antique.
(And her only thirty-one.)
I can't help it, she said, pulling a long face,
It's them pills I took, to bring it off, she said.

3. "Cf. the game of chess in Middleton's *Women Beware Women* [Eliot's note]. In this scene, a woman is seduced in a series of strategic steps that parallel the moves of a chess game occupying her mother-in-law at the same time.   4. Demobilized, discharged from the army.   5. The British bartender's warning that the pub is about to close.

(She's had five already, and nearly died of young George.)   160
The chemist[6] said it would be all right, but I've never been the same.
You are a proper fool, I said.
Well, if Albert won't leave you alone, there it is, I said,
What you get married for if you don't want children?
HURRY UP PLEASE ITS TIME   165
Well, that Sunday Albert was home, they had a hot gammon,[7]
And they asked me in to dinner, to get the beauty of it hot—
HURRY UP PLEASE ITS TIME
HURRY UP PLEASE ITS TIME
Goonight Bill. Goonight Lou. Goonight May. Goonight.   170
Ta ta. Goonight. Goonight.
Good night, ladies, good night, sweet ladies, good night, good night.[8]

III. The Fire Sermon[9]

The river's tent is broken: the last fingers of leaf
Clutch and sink into the wet bank. The wind   175
Crosses the brown land, unheard. The nymphs are departed.
Sweet Thames, run softly, till I end my song.[1]
The river bears no empty bottles, sandwich papers,
Silk handkerchiefs, cardboard boxes, cigarette ends
Or other testimony of summer nights. The nymphs are departed.
And their friends, the loitering heirs of city directors;   180
Departed, have left no addresses.
By the waters of Leman I sat down and wept . . .[2]
Sweet Thames, run softly till I end my song,
Sweet Thames, run softly, for I speak not loud or long.
But at my back in a cold blast I hear[3]   185
The rattle of the bones, and chuckle spread from ear to ear.
A rat crept softly through the vegetation
Dragging its slimy belly on the bank
While I was fishing in the dull canal
On a winter evening round behind the gashouse   190
Musing upon the king my brother's wreck

6. The druggist, who gave her pills to cause a miscarriage.   7. Ham.   8. The popular song for a party's end ("Good night, ladies") shifts into Ophelia's last words in *Hamlet* (IV,5,72) as she goes off to drown herself.   9. Reference to the Buddha's Fire Sermon (see note to line 308) in which he denounced the fiery lusts and passions of earthly experience. "All things are on fire . . . with the fire of passion . . . of hatred . . . of infatuation." Part III describes the degeneration of even these passions in the sterile decadence of the modern Waste Land.   1. "V. Spenser, *Prothalamion*" [Eliot's note]; the line is the refrain of a marriage song by the Elizabethan poet Edmund Spenser (1552?—1599), and evokes a river of unpolluted pastoral beauty.   2. Lake Leman is Lake Geneva (where Eliot wrote much of *The Waste Land*); a "leman" is a mistress or lover; in Psalm 137.1, the exiled Hebrews sit by the rivers of Babylon and weep for their lost homeland. 3. Distorted echo of Andrew Marvell, "To His Coy Mistress": "But at my back I always hear / Time's winged chariot hurrying near" (see also line 196).

And on the king my father's death before him.[4]
White bodies naked on the low damp ground
And bones cast in a little low dry garret,
Rattled by the rat's foot only, year to year.   195
But at my back from time to time I hear[5]
The sound of horns and motors, which shall bring[6]
Sweeney to Mrs. Porter in the spring.
O the moon shone bright on Mrs. Porter[7]
And on her daughter   200
They wash their feet in soda water
Et O ces voix d'enfants, chantant dans la coupole![8]

    Twit twit twit
Jug jug jug jug jug jug
So rudely forc'd.   205
Tereu[9]

    Unreal City
Under the brown fog of a winter noon
Mr. Eugenides, the Smyrna merchant
Unshaven, with a pocket full of currants   210
C.i.f. London: documents at sight,[1]
Asked me in demotic French
To luncheon at the Cannon Street Hotel
Followed by a weekend at the Metropole.[2]

At the violet hour, when the eyes and back   215
Turn upward from the desk, when the human engine waits
Like a taxi throbbing waiting,
I Tiresias,[3] though blind, throbbing between two lives,

---

4. "Cf. *The Tempest*, I,ii" [Eliot's note]; Ferdinand, the king's son, believes his father drowned and mourns his death.   5. Cf. Marvell, "To His Coy Mistress" [Eliot's note].   6. "Cf. Day, *Parliament of Bees*: 'When of the sudden, listening, you shall hear, / A noise of horns and hunting, which shall bring / Actaeon to Diana in the spring, / Where all shall see her naked skin . . .'" [Eliot's note]. The young hunter Actaeon was changed into a stag, hunted down, and killed when he came upon the goddess Diana bathing. Sweeney is in no such danger from his visit to Mrs. Porter.   7. "I do not know the origin of the ballad from which these lines are taken: it was reported to me from Sydney, Australia" [Eliot's note]. A song popular among Allied troops during World War I. One version continues lines 199–201 as follows: "And so they oughter / To keep them clean."   8. "V. Verlaine, *Parsifal*" [Eliot's note]: "And O these children's voices, singing in the dome!": the last lines of a sonnet by Paul Verlaine (1844–1896), which ambiguously celebrates the Grail hero's chaste restraint. In Wagner's opera, Parsifal's feet are washed to purify him before entering the presence of the Grail.   9. Tereus, who raped Philomela (see line 99); also the nightingale's song.   1. "The currants were quoted at a price 'carriage and insurance free to London'; and the Bill of Lading etc. were to be handed to the buyer upon payment of the sight draft" [Eliot's note].   2. Smyrna is an ancient Phoenician seaport, and early Smyrna merchants spread the Eastern fertility cults. In contrast, their descendant Mr. Eugenides ("Well-born") invites the poet to lunch in a large commercial hotel and a weekend at a seaside resort in Brighton.   3. "Tiresias, although a mere spectator and not indeed a 'character,' is yet the most important personage in the poem, uniting all the rest. Just as the one-eyed merchant, seller of currants, melts into the Phoenician Sailor, and the latter is not wholly distinct from Ferdinand

Old man with wrinkled female breasts, can see
At the violet hour, the evening hour that strives   220
Homeward, and brings the sailor home from sea,[4]
The typist home at teatime, clears her breakfast, lights
Her stove, and lays out food in tins.
Out of the window perilously spread
Her drying combinations touched by the sun's last rays,   225
On the divan are piled (at night her bed)
Stockings, slippers, camisoles, and stays.
I Tiresias, old man with wrinkled dugs
Perceived the scene, and foretold the rest—
I too awaited the expected guest.   230
He, the young man carbuncular, arrives,
A small house agent's clerk, with one bold stare,
One of the low on whom assurance sits
As a silk hat on a Bradford[5] millionaire.
The time is now propitious, as he guesses,   235
The meal is ended, she is bored and tired,
Endeavours to engage her in caresses
Which still are unreproved, if undesired.
Flushed and decided, he assaults at once;
Exploring hands encounter no defence;   240
His vanity requires no response,
And makes a welcome of indifference.
(And I Tiresias have foresuffered all
Enacted on this same divan or bed;
I who have sat by Thebes below the wall   245
And walked among the lowest of the dead.)[6]
Bestows one final patronising kiss,
And gropes his way, finding the stairs unlit . . .

    She turns and looks a moment in the glass,
Hardly aware of her departed lover;   250
Her brain allows one half-formed thought to pass:
"Well now that's done: and I'm glad it's over."
When lovely woman stoops to folly and[7]

Prince of Naples, so all the women are one woman, and the two sexes meet in Tiresias. What
Tiresias *sees*, in fact, is the substance of the poem. The whole passage from Ovid is one of great
anthropological interest . . ." [Eliot's note]. The passage then quoted from Ovid's *Metamorphoses*
(3:320–38) describes how Tiresias spent seven years of his life as a woman, and thus experienced
love from the point of view of both sexes. Blinded by Juno, he was recompensed by Jove with the
gift of prophecy.   **4.** "This may or may not appear as exact as Sappho's lines, but I had in mind
the 'longshore' or 'dory' fisherman, who returns at nightfall" [Eliot's note]. Sappho's poem describes
how the evening star brings home those whom dawn has sent abroad; there is also an echo of
Robert Louis Stevenson's (1850–1894) "Requiem," 1:221: "Home is the sailor, home from the
sea."   **5.** A manufacturing town in Yorkshire which prospered greatly during World War I.
6. Tiresias prophesied in the marketplace at Thebes for many years before dying and continuing
to prophesy in Hades.   **7.** "V. Goldsmith, the song in *The Vicar of Wakefield*" [Eliot's note].
"When lovely woman stoops to folly / And finds too late that men betray / What charm can soothe
her melancholy, / What art can wash her guilt away?"

Paces about her room again, alone,
She smoothes her hair with automatic hand,   255
And puts a record on the gramophone.
  "This music crept by me upon the waters"[8]
And along the Strand, up Queen Victoria Street.
O City city,[9] I can sometimes hear
Beside a public bar in Lower Thames Street,   260
The pleasant whining of a mandoline
And a clatter and a chatter from within
Where fishmen lounge at noon: where the walls
Of Magnus Martyr hold[1]
Inexplicable splendour of Ionian white and gold.   265

               The river sweats[2]
               Oil and tar
               The barges drift
               With the turning tide
               Red sails   270
               Wide
               To leeward, swing on the heavy spar.
               The barges wash
               Drifting logs
               Down Greenwich reach   275
               Past the Isle of Dogs.
                         Weialala leia
                         Wallala leialala

               Elizabeth and Leicester[3]
               Beating oars   280
               The stern was formed
               A gilded shell
               Red and gold

---

8. "V. *The Tempest*, as above" [Eliot's note, referring to line 191]; spoken by Ferdinand as he hears Ariel sing.   9. A double invocation: the city of London, the "City" as London's central financial district (see lines 60, 207); see later the great cities of Western civilization (lines 375–76).   1. "The interior of St. Magnus Martyr is to my mind one of the finest among Wren's interiors. See *The Proposed Demolition of Nineteen City Churches*: (P. S. King & Son, Ltd)" [Eliot's note]. The architect was Christopher Wren (1632–1723), and the church was located just below London Bridge on Lower Thames Street.   2. "The Song of the (three) Thames-daughters begins here. From line 292 to 306 inclusive they speak in turn. V. *Götterdämmerung*, III, i: the Rhine-daughters" [Eliot's note]. In Wagner's opera *The Twilight of the Gods* (1876), the three Rhine-maidens mourn the loss of their gold, which gave the river its sparkling beauty; lines 177–78 here echo the Rhine-maidens' refrain. The Isle of Dogs is a peninsula opposite Greenwich on the Thames.   3. "V. Froude, *Elizabeth*, vol. I, ch. iv, letter of De Quadra to Philip of Spain: 'In the afternoon we were in a barge, watching the games on the river. (The queen) was alone with Lord Robert and myself on the poop, when they began to talk nonsense, and went so far that Lord Robert at last said, as I was on the spot there was no reason why they should not be married if the queen pleased" [Eliot's note]. Sir Robert Dudley (1532–88) was the Earl of Leicester, a favorite of Queen Elizabeth who at one point hoped to marry her.

The brisk swell
Rippled both shores   285
Southwest wind
Carried down stream
The peal of bells
White towers
       Weialala leia   290
       Wallala leialala
"Trams and dusty trees.
Highbury bore me. Richmond and Kew
Undid me.[4] By Richmond I raised my knees
Supine on the floor of a narrow canoe."   295

"My feet are at Moorgate,[5] and my heart
Under my feet. After the event
He wept. He promised 'a new start.'
I made no comment. What should I resent?"

"On Margate Sands.   300
I can connect
Nothing with nothing.
The broken fingernails of dirty hands.
My people humble people who expect
Nothing."   305
       la la

To Carthage then I came[6]

Burning burning burning burning[7]
O Lord Thou pluckest me out[8]
O Lord Thou pluckest   310

burning

---

4. "Cf. *Purgatorio*, V, 133: 'Ricorditi di me, che son la Pia; / Siena mi fe', disfecemi Maremma' "
[Eliot's note]. La Pia, in Purgatory, recalls her seduction: "Remember me, who am La Pia. /
Siena made me, Maremma undid me." Eliot's parody substitutes Highbury (a London suburb)
and Richmond and Kew, popular excursion points on the Thames.   **5.** A London slum; Mar-
gate is a seaside resort on the Thames.   **6.** "V. St. Augustine's *Confessions:* 'to Carthage then I
came, where a cauldron of unholy loves sang all about mine ears' " [Eliot's note]. The youthful
Augustine is described. For Carthage, see line 92.   **7.** "The complete text of the Buddha's Fire
Sermon (which corresponds in importance to the Sermon on the Mount) from which these words
are taken, will be found translated in the late Henry Clarke Warren's *Buddhism in Translation*
(Harvard Oriental Studies). Mr. Warren was one of the great pioneers of Buddhist studies in the
Occident" [Eliot's note]. The Sermon on the Mount may be found in Matthew 5–7.   **8.** "From
St. Augustine's *Confessions* again. The collocation of these two representatives of eastern and
western asceticism, as the culmination of this part of the poem is not an accident" [Eliot's note].
See also Zechariah 3:2, where the high priest Joshua is described as a "brand plucked out of the
fire."

IV. *Death by Water*

Phlebas the Phoenician, a fortnight dead,
Forgot the cry of gulls, and the deep sea swell
And the profit and loss.
　　　　　　　　A current under sea　　　　　　315
Picked his bones in whispers. As he rose and fell
He passed the stages of his age and youth
Entering the whirlpool.
　　　　　　　　Gentile or Jew
O you who turn the wheel and look to windward,　　320
Consider Phlebas, who was once handsome and tall as you.

V. *What the Thunder Said*[9]

After the torchlight red on sweaty faces
After the frosty silence in the gardens
After the agony in stony places
The shouting and the crying　　　　　　　　325
Prison and palace and reverberation
Of thunder of spring over distant mountains
He who was living is now dead[1]
We who were living are now dying
With a little patience　　　　　　　　　　330

　Here is no water but only rock
Rock and no water and the sandy road
The road winding above among the mountains
Which are mountains of rock without water
If there were water we should stop and drink　　335
Amongst the rock one cannot stop or think
Sweat is dry and feet are in the sand
If there were only water amongst the rock
Dead mountain mouth of carious teeth that cannot spit
Here one can neither stand nor lie nor sit　　　340
There is not even silence in the mountains
But dry sterile thunder without rain
There is not even solitude in the mountains

9. "In the first part of Part V three themes are employed: the journey to Emmaus, the approach to the Chapel Perilous (see Miss Weston's book) and the present decay of eastern Europe" [Eliot's note]. On their journey to Emmaus (Luke 24:13–34), the disciples were joined by a stranger who later revealed himself to be the crucified and resurrected Christ. The Thunder of the title is a divine voice in the Hindu Upanishads (see line 401).　1. Allusions to stages in Christ's Passion: the betrayal, prayer in the garden of Gethsemane, imprisonment, trial, crucifixion, and burial. Despair reigns, for this is death before the Resurrection.

But red sullen faces sneer and snarl
From doors of mudcracked houses   345
            If there were water
    And no rock
    If there were rock
    And also water
    And water   350
    A spring
    A pool among the rock
    If there were the sound of water only
    Not the cicada[2]
    And dry grass singing   355
    But sound of water over a rock
    Where the hermit-thrush[3] sings in the pine trees
    Drip drop drip drop drop drop drop
    But there is no water

    Who is the third who walks always beside you?   360
When I count, there are only you and I together[4]
But when I look ahead up the white road
There is always another one walking beside you
Gliding wrapt in a brown mantle, hooded
I do not know whether a man or a woman   365
—But who is that on the other side of you?

    What is that sound high in the air[5]
Murmur of maternal lamentation
Who are those hooded hordes swarming
Over endless plains, stumbling in cracked earth   370
Ringed by the flat horizon only
What is the city over the mountains
Cracks and reforms and bursts in the violet air
Falling towers
Jerusalem Athens Alexandria   375
Vienna London
Unreal

---

2. Grasshopper or cricket: see line 23.   3. ". . . the hermit-thrush which I have heard in Que-
bec Province. . . . Its 'water-dripping song' is justly celebrated" [Eliot's note].   4. "The following lines were stimulated by the account of one of the Antarctic expeditions (I forget which, but I
think one of Shackleton's): it was related that the party of explorers, at the extremity of their
strength, had the constant delusion that there was *one more member* than could actually be counted"
[Eliot's note]; see also the journey to Emmaus, previously mentioned.   5. Eliot's note to lines
367–77 refers to Hermann Hesse's *Blick ins Chaos* ("Glimpse into Chaos"), and a passage that
reads, translated, "Already half of Europe, already at least half of Eastern Europe is on the way to
Chaos, drives drunk in holy madness on the edge of the abyss and sings at the same time, sings
drunk and hymn-like, as Dimitri Karamazov sang [in Dostoevsky's *The Brothers Karamazov*]. The
offended bourgeois laughs at the songs; the saint and the seer hear them with tears."

A woman drew her long black hair out tight
And fiddled whisper music on those strings
And bats with baby faces in the violet light   380
Whistled, and beat their wings
And crawled head downward down a blackened wall
And upside down in air were towers
Tolling reminiscent bells, that kept the hours
And voices singing out of empty cisterns and exhausted wells.   385
    In this decayed hole among the mountains
In the faint moonlight, the grass is singing
Over the tumbled graves, about the chapel
There is the empty chapel, only the wind's home.
It has no windows, and the door swings,   390
Dry bones can harm no one.
Only a cock stood on the rooftree
Co co rico co co rico[6]
In a flash of lightning. Then a damp gust
Bringing rain   395

Ganga[7] was sunken, and the limp leaves
Waited for rain, while the black clouds
Gathered far distant, over Himavant.
The jungle crouched, humped in silence.
Then spoke the thunder
Da   400
Datta: what have we given?[8]
My friend, blood shaking my heart
The awful daring of a moment's surrender
Which an age of prudence can never retract   405
By this, and this only, we have existed
Which is not to be found in our obituaries
Or in memories draped by the beneficent spider[9]
Or under seals broken by the lean solicitor
In our empty rooms   410
Da
Dayadhvam: I have heard the key[1]

---

6. European version of the cock's crow: cock-a-doodle-doo. The cock crowed in Matthew 26:34,74,
after Peter had denied Christ three times.   7. The River Ganges in India. Himavant is a mountain in the Himalayas.   8. " 'Datta, dayadhvam, damyata' (Give, sympathise, control). The
fable of the meaning of the Thunder is found in the *Brihadaranyaka*—Upanishad, 5,1" [Eliot's
note]. In the fable, the word DA, spoken by the supreme being Prajapati, is interpreted as *Datta*
(to give alms), *Dayadhvam* (to sympathize or have compassion), and *Damyata* (to have self-
control) by gods, human beings, and demons respectively. The conclusion is that when the thunder booms DA DA DA, Prajapati is commanding that all three virtues be practiced
simultaneously.   9. "Cf. Webster, *The White Devil*, V, vi: '. . . they'll remarry / Ere the worm
pierce your winding-sheet, ere the spider / Make a thin curtain for your epitaphs" [Eliot's note].
1. Eliot's note on the command to "sympathize" or reach outside the self cites two descriptions
of helpless isolation. The first comes from Dante's *Inferno* 33,46: "ed io sentii chiavar l'uscio di

Turn in the door once and turn once only
We think of the key, each in his prison
Thinking of the key, each confirms a prison   415
Only at nightfall, aethereal rumours
Revive for a moment a broken Coriolanus[2]
DA
Damyata: The boat responded
Gaily, to the hand expert with sail and oar   420
The sea was calm, your heart would have responded
Gaily, when invited, beating obedient
To controlling hands

                            I sat upon the shore
Fishing,[3] with the arid plain behind me   425
Shall I at least set my lands in order?
London Bridge is falling down falling down falling down
Poi s'ascose nel foco che gli affina[4]
Quando fiam uti chelidon[5]—O swallow swallow
Le Prince d'Aquitaine à la tour abolie[6]   430
These fragments I have shored against my ruins
Why then Ile fit you. Hieronymo's mad againe.[7]
Datta. Dayadhvam. Damyata.
            Shantih   shantih   shantih[8]

---

sotto / all'orribile torre," as Ugolino, imprisoned in a tower with his children to die of starvation, says "And I heard below the door of the horrible tower being locked up." The second is a modern description by the English philosopher F. H. Bradley (1846–1924) of the inevitably self-enclosed or private nature of consciousness: "My external sensations are no less private to myself than are my thoughts or my feelings. In either case my experience falls within my own circle, a circle closed on the outside; and, with all its elements alike, every sphere is opaque to the others which surround it . . . In brief, regarded as an existence which appears in a soul, the whole world for each is peculiar and private to that soul" (*Appearance and Reality*, p. 346).   **2.** A self-willed Roman patrician who was exiled and led an army against his homeland. In Shakespeare's play, both his grandeur and his downfall come from a desire to be ruled only by himself.   **3.** "V. Weston: *From Ritual to Romance*; chapter on the Fisher King" [Eliot's note].   **4.** Eliot's note quotes a passage in the *Purgatorio* in which Arnaut Daniel (see note to dedication) asks Dante to remember his pain; the line cited here, "then he hid himself in the fire which refines them" [*Purgatorio* 148], shows the Provençal poet departing in fire which—in Purgatory—exists as a purifying rather than a destructive element.   **5.** "V. *Pervigilium Veneris*. Cf. Philomela in Parts II and III [Eliot's note]: "When shall I be as a swallow?" A line from the *Vigil of Venus*, a late Latin poem, that asks for the gift of song: here associated with Philomela as a swallow, not the nightingale of lines 99–103, 203–06.   **6.** "V. Gerard de Nerval, Sonnet *El Desdichado*" [Eliot's note]. The Spanish title means "The Disinherited One," and the sonnet is a monologue describing the speaker as a melancholy, ill-starred dreamer: "the Prince of Aquitaine in his ruined tower." Another line recalls the scene at the end of "Prufrock": "I dreamed in the grotto where sirens swim."   **7.** "V. Kyd's *Spanish Tragedy*" [Eliot's note]. Thomas Kyd's revenge play (1594) is subtitled "Hieronymo's Mad Againe." The protagonist "fits" his son's murderers into appropriate roles in a court entertainment so that they may all be killed.   **8.** "Shantih. Repeated as here, a formal ending to an Upanishad. 'The Peace which passeth understanding' is our equivalent to this word'" [Eliot's note]. The Upanishads comment on the sacred Hindu scriptures, the Vedas (cf. note to line 400).

Four Quartets

Little Gidding[9]

I

Midwinter spring is its own season
Sempiternal though sodden towards sundown,
Suspended in time, between pole and tropic.
When the short day is brightest, with frost and fire,
The brief sun flames the ice, on pond and ditches,   5
In windless cold that is the heart's heat,
Reflecting in a watery mirror
A glare that is blindness in the early afternoon.
And glow more intense than blaze of branch, or brazier,
Stirs the dumb spirit: no wind, but pentecostal fire[1]   10
In the dark time of the year. Between melting and freezing
The soul's sap quivers. There is no earth smell
Or smell of living thing. This is the spring time
But not in time's covenant. Now the hedgerow
Is blanched for an hour with transitory blossom   15
Of snow, a bloom more sudden
Than that of summer, neither budding nor fading,
Not in the scheme of generation.
Where is the summer, the unimaginable
Zero summer?

            If you came this way,   20
Taking the route you would be likely to take
From the place you would be likely to come from,
If you came this way in may time, you would find the hedges
White again, in May, with voluptuary sweetness.
It would be the same at the end of the journey,   25
If you came at night like a broken king,[2]
If you came by day not knowing what you came for,
It would be the same, when you leave the rough road
And turn behind the pig-sty to the dull façade
And the tombstone. And what you thought you came for   30
Is only a shell, a husk of meaning
From which the purpose breaks only when it is fulfilled
If at all. Either you had no purpose

---

9. A village in Huntingdonshire that housed a religious community in the seventeenth century;
Eliot visited the (rebuilt) chapel on a midwinter day.   1. On the Pentecost day after Christ's
resurrection, the apostles saw "cloven tongues like as of fire" and were "filled with the Holy Ghost"
(Acts 2).   2. Charles I, King of England (1600–1649), had visited the religious community
several times and went there secretly after his final defeat in the Civil War.

Or the purpose is beyond the end you figured
And is altered in fulfilment. There are other places   35
Which also are the world's end, some at the sea jaws,
Or over a dark lake, in a desert or a city—
But this is the nearest, in place and time,
Now and in England.

                  If you came this way,   40
Taking any route, starting from anywhere,
At any time or at any season,
It would always be the same: you would have to put off
Sense and notion. You are not here to verify,
Instruct yourself, or inform curiosity   45
Or carry report. You are here to kneel
Where prayer has been valid. And prayer is more
Than an order of words, the conscious occupation
Of the praying mind, or the sound of the voice praying.
And what the dead had no speech for, when living,   50
They can tell you, being dead: the communication
Of the dead is tongued with fire beyond the language of the living.
Here, the intersection of the timeless moment
Is England and nowhere. Never and always.

II

Ash on an old man's sleeve   55
Is all the ash the burnt roses leave.
Dust in the air suspended
Marks the place where a story ended.
Dust inbreathed was a house—
The wall, the wainscot and the mouse.   60
The death of hope and despair,
    This is the death of air.[3]
    There are flood and drouth
Over the eyes and in the mouth,
Dead water and dead sand   65
Contending for the upper hand.
The parched eviscerate soil
Gapes at the vanity of toil,
Laughs without mirth.
      This is the death of earth.   70

---

3. "Fire lives in the death of air": a phrase from the pre-Socratic philosopher Heraclitus (535–475 B.C.) describing how one element (here, fire) lives at the expense of another (here, air).

Water and fire succeed
The town, the pasture and the weed.
Water and fire deride
The sacrifice that we denied.
Water and fire shall rot   75
The marred foundations we forgot,
Of sanctuary and choir.
        This is the death of water and fire.

    In the uncertain hour before the morning[4]
        Near the ending of interminable night   80
        At the recurrent end of the unending
After the dark dove with the flickering tongue
        Had passed below the horizon of his homing
        While the dead leaves still rattled on like tin
Over the asphalt where no other sound was   85
        Between three districts whence the smoke arose
        I met one walking, loitering and hurried
As if blown towards me like the metal leaves
        Before the urban dawn wind unresisting.
        And as I fixed upon the down-turned face   90
That pointed scrutiny with which we challenge
        The first-met stranger in the waning dusk
        I caught the sudden look of some dead master
Whom I had known, forgotten, half recalled
        Both one and many; in the brown baked features   95
        The eyes of a familiar compound ghost
Both intimate and unidentifiable.
        So I assumed a double part,[5] and cried
        And heard another's voice cry: 'What! are _you_ here?'
Although we were not. I was still the same,   100
        Knowing myself yet being someone other—
        And he a face still forming; yet the words sufficed
To compel the recognition they preceded.
        And so, complaint to the common wind,
        Too strange to each other for misunderstanding,   105
In concord at this intersection time
        Of meeting nowhere, no before and after,
        We trod the pavement in a dead patrol.
I said: 'The wonder that I feel is easy,   110
        Yet ease is cause of wonder. Therefore speak:

---

4. The narrative passage from here to the end of Part II is written in tercets, a form that recalls
Dante's use of _terza rima_ (triple rhyme) in the _Divine Comedy_; Eliot later commented that this
section was "the nearest equivalent to a canto of the _Inferno_ or _Purgatorio_" that he could create.
5. The role of questioner of souls (after Dante in the _Divine Comedy_) and the role of one inter-
rogating himself.

I may not comprehend, may not remember.'
And he: 'I am not eager to rehearse
   My thought and theory which you have forgotten.
   These things have served their purpose: let them be.
So with your own, and pray they be forgiven   115
   By others, as I pray you to forgive
   Both bad and good. Last season's fruit is eaten
And the fullfed beast shall kick the empty pail.
   For last year's words belong to last year's language
   And next year's words await another voice.   120
But, as the passage now presents no hindrance
   To the spirit unappeased and peregrine
   Between two worlds become much like each other,
So I find words I never thought to speak
   In streets I never thought I should revisit   125
   When I left my body on a distant shore.
Since our concern was speech, and speech impelled us
   To purify the dialect of the tribe[6]
   And urge the mind to aftersight and foresight,
Let me disclose the gifts reserved for age   130
   To set a crown upon your lifetime's effort.
   First, the cold friction of expiring sense
Without enchantment, offering no promise
   But bitter tastelessness of shadow fruit
   As body and soul begin to fall asunder.   135
Second, the conscious impotence of rage
   At human folly, and the laceration
   Of laughter at what ceases to amuse.
And last, the rending pain of re-enactment
   Of all that you have done, and been; the shame   140
   Of motives late revealed, and the awareness
Of things ill done and done to others' harm
   Which once you took for exercise of virtue.
   Then fools' approval stings, and honour stains.
From wrong to wrong the exasperated spirit   145
   Proceeds, unless restored by that refining fire
   Where you must move in measure, like a dancer.'[7]
The day was breaking. In the disfigured street
   He left me, with a kind of valediction,
   And faded on the blowing of the horn.[8]   150

---

6. In his epitaph-sonnet for Edgar Allan Poe, "The Tomb of Edgar Poe," the French poet Stéphane Mallarmé (1842–1898) defines the poet's role as purifying speech by using ordinary language ("the dialect of the tribe") in a more precise and yet complex way, creating a new structure
of interlocking or multiple meanings. (See line 227.)   7. In Dante's *Purgatorio* (26,148), fire is
seen as a purgative or refining element, and characters are enveloped in flames that move in
accord with their bodies.   8. The horn that marks the All Clear signal after an air raid; also the
disappearance of Hamlet's father's ghost (*Hamlet* I, 2,157): "It faded on the crowing of the cock."

III

There are three conditions which often look alike
Yet differ completely, flourish in the same hedgerow:
Attachment to self and to things and to persons; detachment
From self and from things and from persons; and, growing between
        them, indifference
Which resembles the others as death resembles life,   155
Being between two lives—unflowering, between
The live and the dead nettle. This is the use of memory:
For liberation—not less of love but expanding
Of love beyond desire, and so liberation
From the future as well as the past. Thus, love of a country   160
Begins as attachment to our own field of action
And comes to find that action of little importance
Though never indifferent. History may be servitude,
History may be freedom. See, now they vanish,
The faces and places, with the self which, as it could, loved them,
                                                                                                 165
To become renewed, transfigured, in another pattern.

   Sin is Behovely,[9] but
All shall be well, and
All manner of thing shall be well.
If I think, again, of this place,
And of people, not wholly commendable,   170
Of no immediate kin or kindness,
But some of peculiar genius,
All touched by a common genius,
United in the strife which divided them;
If I think of a king at nightfall,   175
Of three men, and more, on the scaffold[1]
And a few who died forgotten
In other places, here and abroad,
And of one who died blind and quiet,[2]
Why should we celebrate   180
These dead men more than the dying?
It is not to ring the bell backward
Nor is it an incantation
To summon the spectre of a Rose.
We cannot revive old factions   185

9. Inevitable. These three lines repeat the consoling words of Dame Juliana of Norwich, a fourteenth-century English mystic: "Sin is behovabil, but all shall be well and all manner of thing
shall be well."   1. Charles I and his chief advisers were executed on the scaffold after the
English Civil War.   2. The poet John Milton (1608–1874), who supported Parliament and the
Commonwealth in the Civil War.

We cannot restore old policies
Or follow an antique drum.
These men, and those who opposed them
And those whom they opposed
Accept the constitution of silence   190
And are folded in a single party.
Whatever we inherit from the fortunate
We have taken from the defeated
What they had to leave us—a symbol:
A symbol perfected in death.   195
And all shall be well and
All manner of thing shall be well
By the purification of the motive
In the ground of our beseeching.

                              IV

The dove descending breaks the air   200
With flame of incandescent terror
Of which the tongues declare
The one discharge from sin and error.
The only hope, or else despair
    Lies in the choice of pyre or pyre—   205
    To be redeemed from fire by fire.

    Who then devised the torment? Love.
Love is the unfamiliar Name
Behind the hands that wove
The intolerable shirt of flame[3]   210
Which human power cannot remove.
    We only live, only suspire
    Consumed by either fire or fire.

                              V

What we call the beginning is often the end
And to make an end is to make a beginning.   220
The end is where we start from. And every phrase
And sentence that is right (where every word is at home,
Taking its place to support the others,
The word neither diffident nor ostentatious,
An easy commerce of the old and the new,   225

3. The shirt, poisoned with the blood of Nessus the centaur, that Deianeira (unknowingly) gave
her husband Hercules in order to strengthen his love for her. Instead, the shirt burned Hercules'
flesh so that he chose death on a funeral pyre to escape the agony.

The common word exact without vulgarity,
The formal word precise but not pedantic,
The complete consort[4] dancing together)
Every phrase and every sentence is an end and a beginning,
Every poem an epitaph. And any action   230
Is a step to the block, to the fire, down the sea's throat
Or to an illegible stone: and that is where we start.
We die with the dying:
See, they depart, and we go with them.
We are born with the dead: 235
See, they return, and bring us with them.
The moment of the rose and the moment of the yew-tree
Are of equal duration. A people without history
Is not redeemed from time, for history is a pattern
Of timeless moments. So, while the light fails   240
On a winter's afternoon, in a secluded chapel
History is now and England.
With the drawing of this Love and the voice of this Calling[5]

　　We shall not cease from exploration
And the end of all our exploring   245
Will be to arrive where we started
And know the place for the first time.
Through the unknown, remembered gate
When the last of earth left to discover
Is that which was the beginning;   250
At the source of the longest river
The voice of the hidden waterfall
And the children in the apple-tree
Not known, because not looked for
But heard, half-heard, in the stillness   255
Between two waves of the sea.
Quick now, here, now, always—[6]
A condition of complete simplicity
(Costing not less than everything)
And all shall be well and   260
All manner of thing shall be well
When the tongues of flame are in-folded
Into the crowned knot of fire
And the fire and the rose are one.

---

4. Both "harmony" and "company."   5. Line from *The Cloud of Unknowing*, a fourteenth-
century mystical book.   6. This same line occurs towards the end of *Burnt Norton*, the first of
the *Four Quartets*, where it also follows voices of children hidden in foliage: there is a suggestion
of sudden insight gained in a moment of passive openness to illumination.

KATHERINE ANNE PORTER
1890–1980

The short stories of Katherine Anne Porter are widely known as models of subtly constructed, precisely phrased, and realistically presented explorations of human psychology. She is not an avant-garde or experimental writer, but continues the realist tradition with its emphasis on linear chronology, historical context, and the development of consistent characterization. Inside a fundamentally realistic style, however, she takes full advantage of strategies such as the interior monologue, symbolic associations, and networks of inner reference to establish a compact, densely interconnected structure that achieves both psychological and artistic impact. A regional writer in the sense that she comes from and often writes about the American South, she does not construct a mythical southern community (like Faulkner) but uses her southern background to suggest characters and situations that will then be examined in terms of *individual* psychology. Her protagonists exist at a specific moment in history and in a real, even documented society: whether Denver, New York, Mexico, or the South. They are often caught at crucial moments when issues of life and death, love, betrayal, and disappointment are involved; when their identity evolves, under pressure, in a particular direction, or when it seems suddenly to have been decided for all time. Throughout, Porter describes individual psychology with an ironic awareness of its complexity and a verbal spareness and precision that have come to represent her mastery of the modern short story.

She was born on May 15, 1890, in Indian Creek, Texas, the third of five children and the descendant of a family that remembered "solid wealth and property in Kentucky, Louisiana, and Virginia" but had fallen on poorer days in Texas after the Civil War. Her mother died in 1892, and the family went to live with her paternal grandmother in Kyle, Texas. She was educated in convent schools in Louisiana, but was a rebellious student and ran away from school at sixteen and married. At nineteen, she was divorced; at twenty-one she worked in Chicago on a newspaper and briefly as an extra in the movies; at twenty-four, she returned to Texas, supporting herself as a ballad singer; and at twenty-eight she moved to a job as reporter for the *The Rocky Mountain News* in Denver, where she nearly died during the influenza epidemic of 1918. Porter used material in her life as the basis for much of her fiction; stories and novellas like *Old Mortality* and "The Grave" reflect the experience of a young Southern girl named Miranda, and an older Miranda in the novella *Pale Horse, Pale Rider* encounters love, sickness, and death during the great epidemic. Her one novel, *Ship of Fools* (1961), derives from a cruise she took from Veracruz, Mexico, to Bremerhaven, Germany, in 1931.

Yet Porter's writing must not be taken as purely autobiographical: the heroine of "Flowering Judas," for example, shares aspects of the author's own background but is also based on the figure of a friend, an American schoolteacher living in Mexico at the same time. Porter's experience is a vantage point from which she can observe people reacting to a variety of situations, all of them integrated into a larger and more complex interpersonal perspective. She is much concerned with the relations between people, especially within the family, and probes the ambiguous and often self-deluding attitudes inherent in the closest emotional ties. "My whole attempt," she has said, "has been to discover and understand human motives, human feelings, to make a distillation of what human relations and experiences my mind has been able to absorb."

Porter lived briefly in New York after the war, and then moved to Mexico where she played a small part in revolutionary politics during the Obrègon revolution in 1920–21. She had continuing sympathy for revolutionary or liberal causes: anything that promised help for the "anguish that human beings inflict on each other—the never-ending wrong, forever incurable." (The Never-Ending Wrong is also the title of her 1977 book on the Sacco-Vanzetti case: a famous trial in which two Italian immigrants were condemned and executed on evidence that was later discredited, and probably on the basis of their reputation as radicals. In 1927 Porter had joined demonstrations in Boston against the executions.) Her sympathy for the revolution did not prevent her taking a realistic view of its various groups and individuals, as is shown in her description of the revolutionary Braggioni in "Flowering Judas." In 1921 Porter left Mexico for Forth Worth, and over the next ten years wrote stories, reviews, and articles on Mexican culture, as well as acting in amateur theater and traveling as often as she could. Many of the stories published during the twenties and collected in Flowering Judas draw on her Mexican experience. Some characters are based on actual persons—Uspensky in "Hacienda" suggests the film director Sergei Eisenstein, who made a massive documentary about Mexico—and some are unknown people, glimpsed for a moment whose lives are then imagined (as in her first published story, "María Concepción"). Reality is a crucial raw material for Porter's fiction, and she has described the way that scattered memories of different people and scenes observed over the years combine into a new tale with a structure all its own: "Now and again thousands of memories converge, harmonize, arrange themselves around a central idea in a coherent form, and I write a story."

Porter's stories describe the situation of individuals caught within the broad movements of history. Ordinary people act out their destinies inside a culture and society—whether of the American South or West, Mexico, Europe, or an ocean liner—that shapes much of what they can be. Often the protagonist is an inquiring, independent, and uncompromising woman, like Laura in "Flowering Judas" or Miranda in Pale Horse, Pale Rider, who rejects the oversimplifications and stupidities of wartime propaganda and seeks refuge from its pressures in a love affair about which she is nonetheless fearfully hesitant. Yet these apparently simple and straightforward stories of personal experience open out upon larger historical and metaphysical planes. A pessimistic sense of history informs much of Porter's fiction: World War I is not merely the setting for Pale Horse, Pale Rider, but an atmosphere and influence that motivates what its characters do, say, and think. Beyond history, there is spiritual anguish, the natural human condition in Porter's profoundly pessimistic religious vision. No happy resolution is possible, but only an increasing awareness of the conditions of existence. This view of human life as painful and incomplete is accompanied by a dedication to art, the "true testimony" that outlives its own society and civilization. "The arts," Porter has said, "represent the substance of faith and the only reality. They are what we find again when the ruins are cleared away." As with Mann, many of her protagonists are artists or have artistic sensibilities, and the clarity, balance, and fine discriminations of her own style become a way of ordering reality into art.

Porter was a perfectionist who published only a small part of her writings before her death in 1980. A collection of three novellas, *Old Mortality*, *Noon Wine*, and *Pale Horse, Pale Rider* appeared in 1939, and her second collection of stories, *The Leaning Tower* (chiefly about Miranda's childhood), in 1944. In 1962 she gained a wider audience with the publication of *Ship of Fools*, which—although initially deriving from her own trip in 1931—was also modeled on Sebastian Brant's fifteenth-century allegory of the same name, and constituted her own exploration of the quest for meaning in modern society. *Collected Stories* followed in 1965 and *Collected Essays* in 1970.

Recognized as a consummate stylist, Porter received a number of awards including the Pulitzer Prize and National Book Award for fiction in 1966. She writes in the tradition of the realistic novel, with a single narrator who tells the story from a consistent point of view, and events that follow upon each other in rational and usually chronological order. What makes her world distinctive is a precise thoughtful style that seeks the exact word to render each shade of intellectual and emotional perception (Flaubert's ideal of *le mot juste*), and—included in her realism and its intricate imagery—a darkly pessimistic view of human life. Both elements are present in "Flowering Judas," the title story from her first collection.

The "Flowering Judas" is a tree, whose flowers Laura eats in a dream at the end of the story, but it is clearly more than that. The name of Judas, the betrayer of Christ, immediately evokes themes of betrayal and faith, and the religious overtones are confirmed when the dream ends with the words from the Mass asserting the presence of Christ in the communion wafer and wine: "This is my body and blood." Laura cries "No!" because the communion is not complete. The Judas tree exists in a barren landscape where religious faith and human communion are equally lacking ("not water but a desert of crumbling stone"), a wasteland like that of T. S. Eliot who also wrote (in "Gerontion") of a depraved springtime with "dogwood and chestnut, flowering judas / To be eaten, to be divided, to be drunk / Among whispers." Laura is in many ways a prisoner in this wasteland: drawn by political idealism to help the revolution, she feels isolated inside an alien culture (she is "Gringita," something close to "Little Yankee"); she refuses love, whether that of Braggioni or the young captain; she is too realistic or too complicated not to register the grotesque appearance and behavior of the revolutionary heroes (Braggioni bursting out of his gaudy clothes, or the Roumanian and Polish agitators maneuvering for political advantage); she performs small errands to help the cause but they lead in one case to the death of the prisoner Eugenio—and no one cares. Throughout, her typical reaction is to help on a mechanical level but at the same time to close herself off from any real emotional involvement. "No. No. No" is the "holy talismanic word" that is to keep her safe from some unnameable disaster, but in the end it leads her to the brink of the final negation—death—when she dreams of the prisoner whose approaching death has been on her mind all day. Eugenio, for whose fate she feels subconsciously guilty, represents the possibility of authentic human relationships when he pities her imprisoned state and offers her flowers to eat; but the time is past. As Laura is about to take his hand he turns into a skeleton, the scarlet flowers "bleed," and he accuses her of murder—worse, of cannibalism, inasmuch as she made the gesture of communion without having the necessary faith to transform body and blood into divine nourishment. Porter's heroine awakens into a fearful consciousness of alienation and loss that goes beyond the particular historical moment to a vision of human existence denied all underlying principles of faith and love.

Joan Givner's lengthy study, *Katherine Anne Porter: A Life* (1982), is the only complete biography. Collections of her essays include Robert Penn Warren, ed., *Katherine Anne Porter: A Collection of Critical Essays* (1979), and *The Collected Essays and Occasional Writings* (1970), which contains discussions of her own reading tastes and concept of art. A recommended study is Jane Krause DeMouy's *Katherine Anne Porter's Women: The Eye of Her Fiction* (1983).

Flowering Judas

Braggioni sits heaped upon the edge of a straight-backed chair much too small for him, and sings to Laura in a furry, mournful voice. Laura has begun to find reasons for avoiding her own house until the latest possible moment, for Braggioni is there almost every night. No matter how late she is, he will be sitting there with a surly, waiting expression, pulling at his kinky yellow hair, thumbing the strings of his guitar, snarling a tune under his breath. Lupe the Indian maid meets Laura at the door, and says with a flicker of a glance towards the upper room, "He waits."

Laura wishes to lie down, she is tired of her hairpins and the feel of her long tight sleeves, but she says to him, "Have you a new song for me this evening?" If he says yes, she asks him to sing it. If he says no, she remembers his favorite one, and asks him to sing it again. Lupe brings her a cup of chocolate and a plate of rice, and Laura eats at the small table under the lamp, first inviting Braggioni, whose answer is always the same: "I have eaten, and besides, chocolate thickens the voice."

Laura says, "Sing, then," and Braggioni heaves himself into song. He scratches the guitar familiarly as though it were a pet animal, and sings passionately off key, taking the high notes in a prolonged painful squeal. Laura, who haunts the markets listening to the ballad singers, and stops every day to hear the blind boy playing his reed-

flute in Sixteenth of September Street,[1] listens to Braggioni with pitiless courtesy, because she dares not smile at his miserable performance. Nobody dares to smile at him. Braggioni is cruel to everyone,
with a kind of specialized insolence, but he is so vain of his talents,
and so sensitive to slights, it would require a cruelty and vanity greater
than his own to lay a finger on the vast cureless wound of his self-
esteem. It would require courage, too, for it is dangerous to offend
him, and nobody has this courage.

Braggioni loves himself with such tenderness and amplitude and
eternal charity that his followers—for he is a leader of men, a skilled
revolutionist, and his skin has been punctured in honorable warfare—warm themselves in the reflected glow, and say to each other:
"He has a real nobility, a love of humanity raised above mere personal affections." The excess of this self-love has flowed out, inconveniently for her, over Laura, who, with so many others, owes her
comfortable situation and her salary to him. When he is in a very
good humor, he tells her, "I am tempted to forgive you for being a
gringa. Gringita!"[2] and Laura, burning, imagines herself leaning
forward suddenly, and with a sound back-handed slap wiping the
suety smile from his face. If he notices her eyes at these moments he
gives no sign.

She knows what Braggioni would offer her, and she must resist
tenaciously without appearing to resist, and if she could avoid it she
would not admit even to herself the slow drift of his intention. During these long evenings which have spoiled a long month for her,
she sits in her deep chair with an open book on her knees, resting
her eyes on the consoling rigidity of the printed page when the sight
and sound of Braggioni singing threaten to identify themselves with
all her remembered afflictions and to add their weight to her uneasy
premonitions of the future. The gluttonous bulk of Braggioni has
become a symbol of her many disillusions, for a revolutionist should
be lean, animated by heroic faith, a vessel of abstract virtues. This is
nonsense, she knows it now and is ashamed of it. Revolution must
have leaders, and leadership is a career for energetic men. She is,
her comrades tell her, full of romantic error, for what she defines as
cynicism in them is merely "a developed sense of reality." She is
almost too willing to say, "I am wrong, I suppose I don't really
understand the principles," and afterward she makes a secret truce
with herself, determined not to surrender her will to such expedient
logic. But she cannot help feeling that she has been betrayed irre-
parably by the disunion between her way of living and her feeling of
what life should be, and at times she is almost contented to rest in

1. On September 16, 1810, revolt broke out against Spanish rule; the date has become a common
street name in Mexico.   2. Feminine diminutive of *gringo*, a contemptuous Latin-American
term for foreigner (especially North American).

this sense of grievance as a private store of consolation. Sometimes she wishes to run away, but she stays. Now she longs to fly out of this room, down the narrow stairs, and into the street where the houses lean together like conspirators under a single mottled lamp, and leave Braggioni singing to himself.

Instead she looks at Braggioni, frankly and clearly, like a good child who understands the rules of behavior. Her knees cling together under sound blue serge, and her round white collar is not purposely nun-like. She wears the uniform of an idea, and has renounced vanities. She was born Roman Catholic, and in spite of her fear of being seen by someone who might make a scandal of it, she slips now and again into some crumbling little church, kneels on the chilly stone, and says a Hail Mary[3] on the gold rosary she bought in Tehuantepec. It is no good and she ends by examining the altar with its tinsel flowers and ragged brocades, and feels tender about the battered doll-shape of some male saint whose white, lace-trimmed drawers hang limply around his ankles below the hieratic dignity of his velvet robe. She has encased herself in a set of principles derived from her early training, leaving no detail of gesture or of personal taste untouched, and for this reason she will not wear lace made on machines. This is her private heresy, for in her special group the machine is sacred, and will be the salvation of the workers. She loves fine lace, and there is a tiny edge of fluted cobweb on this collar, which is one of twenty precisely alike, folded in blue tissue paper in the upper drawer of her clothes chest.

Braggioni catches her glance solidly as if he had been waiting for it, leans forward, balancing his paunch between his spread knees, and sings with tremendous emphasis, weighing his words. He has, the song relates, no father and no mother, nor even a friend to console him; lonely as a wave of the sea he comes and goes, lonely as a wave. His mouth opens round and yearns sideways, his balloon cheeks grow oily with the labor of song. He bulges marvelously in his expensive garments. Over his lavender collar, crushed upon a purple necktie, held by a diamond hoop: over his ammunition belt of tooled leather worked in silver, buckled cruelly around his gasping middle: over the tops of his glossy yellow shoes Braggioni swells with ominous ripeness, his mauve silk hose stretched taut, his ankles bound with the stout leather thongs of his shoes.

When he stretches his eyelids at Laura she notes again that his eyes are the true tawny yellow cat's eyes. He is rich, not in money, he tells her, but in power, and this power brings with it the blameless ownership of things, and the right to indulge his love of small luxuries. "I have a taste for the elegant refinements," he said once, flour-

---

3. Roman Catholic prayer, the "Ave Maria." *Tehuantepec*: town in southern Mexico.

ishing a yellow silk handkerchief before her nose. "Smell that? It is Jockey Club,[4] imported from New York." Nonetheless he is wounded by life. He will say so presently. "It is true everything turns to dust in the hand, to gall on the tongue." He sighs and his leather belt creaks like a saddle girth. "I am disappointed in everything as it comes. Everything." He shakes his head. "You, poor thing, you will be disappointed too. You are born for it. We are more alike than you realize in some things. Wait and see. Some day you will remember what I have told you, you will know that Braggioni was your friend."

Laura feels a slow chill, a purely physical sense of danger, a warning in her blood that violence, mutilation, a shocking death, wait for her with lessening patience. She has translated this fear into something homely, immediate, and sometimes hesitates before crossing the street. "My personal fate is nothing, except as the testimony of a mental attitude," she reminds herself, quoting from some forgotten philosophic primer, and is sensible enough to add, "Anyhow, I shall not be killed by an automobile if I can help it."

"It may be true I am as corrupt, in another way, as Braggioni," she thinks in spite of herself, "as callous, as incomplete," and if this is so, any kind of death seems preferable. Still she sits quietly, she does not run. Where could she go? Uninvited she has promised herself to this place; she can no longer imagine herself as living in another country, and there is no pleasure in remembering her life before she came here.

Precisely what is the nature of this devotion, its true motives, and what are its obligations? Laura cannot say. She spends part of her days in Xochimilco,[5] near by, teaching Indian children to say in English, "The cat is on the mat." When she appears in the classroom they crowd about her with smiles on their wise, innocent, clay-colored faces, crying, "Good morning, my titcher!" in immaculate voices, and they make of her desk a fresh garden of flowers every day.

During her leisure she goes to union meetings and listens to busy important voices quarreling over tactics, methods, internal politics. She visits the prisoners of her own political faith in their cells, where they entertain themselves with counting cockroaches, repenting of their indiscretions, composing their memoirs, writing out manifestoes and plans for their comrades who are still walking about free, hands in pockets, sniffing fresh air. Laura brings them food and cigarettes and a little money, and she brings messages disguised in equivocal phrases from the men outside who dare not set foot in the prison for fear of disappearing into the cells kept empty for them. If the prisoners confuse night and day, and complain, "Dear little Laura, time doesn't pass in this infernal hole, and I won't know when it is

4. Expensive cologne.   5. Suburb of Mexico City (the Indian word means "flower plantation").

time to sleep unless I have a reminder," she brings them their favorite narcotics, and says in a tone that does not wound them with pity, "Tonight will really be night for you," and though her Spanish amuses them, they find her comforting, useful. If they lose patience and all faith, and curse the slowness of their friends in coming to their rescue with money and influence, they trust her not to repeat everything, and if she inquires, "Where do you think we can find money, or influence?" they are certain to answer, "Well, there is Braggioni, why doesn't he do something?"

She smuggles letters from headquarters to men hiding from firing squads in back streets in mildewed houses, where they sit in tumbled beds and talk bitterly as if all Mexico were at their heels, when Laura knows positively they might appear at the band concert in the Alameda[6] on Sunday morning, and no one would notice them. But Braggioni says, "Let them sweat a little. The next time they may be careful. It is very restful to have them out of the way for a while." She is not afraid to knock on any door in any street after midnight, and enter in the darkness, and say to one of these men who is really in danger: "They will be looking for you—seriously—tomorrow morning after six. Here is some money from Vicente. Go to Vera Cruz and wait."

She borrows money from the Roumanian agitator to give to his bitter enemy the Polish agitator. The favor of Braggioni is their disputed territory, and Braggioni holds the balance nicely, for he can use them both. The Polish agitator talks love to her over café tables, hoping to exploit what he believes is her secret sentimental preference for him, and he gives her misinformation which he begs her to repeat as the solemn truth to certain persons. The Roumanian is more adroit. He is generous with his money in all good causes, and lies to her with an air of ingenious candor, as if he were her good friend and confidant. She never repeats anything they may say. Braggioni never asks questions. He has other ways to discover all that he wishes to know about them.

Nobody touches her, but all praise her gray eyes, and the soft, round under lip which promises gayety, yet is always grave, nearly always firmly closed: and they cannot understand why she is in Mexico. She walks back and forth on her errands, with puzzled eyebrows, carrying her little folder of drawings and music and school papers. No dancer dances more beautifully than Laura walks, and she inspires some amusing, unexpected ardors, which cause little gossip, because nothing comes of them. A young captain who had been a soldier in Zapata's[7] army attempted, during a horseback ride near Cuernavaca, to express his desire for her with the noble simplicity befitting a rude folk-hero: but gently, because he was gentle.

---

6. Public mall. 7. Emiliano Zapata (1879–1919), Mexican revolutionary and agrarian reformer of Indian descent. *Cuernavaca* is in southern Mexico.

This gentleness was his defeat, for when he alighted, and removed her foot from the stirrup, and essayed to draw her down into his arms, her horse, ordinarily a tame one, shied fiercely, reared and plunged away. The young hero's horse careered blindly after his stable-mate, and the hero did not return to the hotel until rather late that evening. At breakfast he came to her table in full charro[8] dress, gray buckskin jacket and trousers with strings of silver buttons down the leg, and he was in a humorous, careless mood. "May I sit with you?" and "You are a wonderful rider. I was terrified that you might be thrown and dragged. I should never have forgiven myself. But I cannot admire you enough for your riding!"

"I learned to ride in Arizona," said Laura.

"If you will ride with me again this morning, I promise you a horse that will not shy with you," he said. But Laura remembered that she must return to Mexico City at noon.

Next morning the children made a celebration and spent their playtime writing on the blackboard, "We lov ar ticher," and with tinted chalks they drew wreaths of flowers around the words. The young hero wrote her a letter: "I am a very foolish, wasteful, impulsive man. I should have first said I love you, and then you would not have run away. But you shall see me again." Laura thought, "I must send him a book of colored crayons," but she was trying to forgive herself for having spurred her horse at the wrong moment.

A brown, shock-haired youth came and stood in her patio one night and sang like a lost soul for two hours, but Laura could think of nothing to do about it. The moonlight spread a wash of gauzy silver over the clear spaces of the garden, and the shadows were cobalt blue. The scarlet blossoms of the Judas tree[9] were dull purple, and the names of the colors repeated themselves automatically in her mind, while she watched not the boy, but his shadow, fallen like a dark garment across the fountain rim, trailing in the water. Lupe came silently and whispered expert counsel in her ear: "If you will throw him one little flower, he will sing another song or two and go away." Laura threw the flower, and he sang a last song and went away with the flower tucked in the band of his hat. Lupe said, "He is one of the organizers of the Typographers Union, and before that he sold corridos[1] in the Merced market, and before that, he came from Guanajuato, where I was born. I would not trust any man, but I trust least those from Guanajuato."

She did not tell Laura that he would be back again the next night, and the next, nor that he would follow her at a certain fixed distance around the Merced market, through the Zócolo, up Francisco I.

8. A flamboyant traditional costume, often worn at festivals.   9. The redbud tree; in legend, the tree from which Judas Iscariot hanged himself after betraying Christ.   1. Popular ballads that also passed along news.

Madero[2] Avenue, and so along the Paseo de la Reforma to Chapul-
tepec Park, and into the Philosopher's Footpath, still with that flower
withering in his hat, and an indivisible attention in his eyes.

Now Laura is accustomed to him, it means nothing except that
he is nineteen years old and is observing a convention with all propriety, as though it were founded on a law of nature, which in the
end it might well prove to be. He is beginning to write poems which
he prints on a wooden press, and he leaves them stuck like handbills
in her door. She is pleasantly disturbed by the abstract, unhurried
watchfulness of his black eyes which will in time turn easily towards
another object. She tells herself that throwing the flower was a mistake, for she is twenty-two years old and knows better; but she refuses
to regret it, and persuades herself that her negation of all external
events as they occur is a sign that she is gradually perfecting herself
in the stoicism she strives to cultivate against that disaster she fears,
though she cannot name it.

She is not at home in the world. Every day she teaches children
who remain strangers to her, though she loves their tender round
hands and their charming opportunist savagery. She knocks at unfamiliar doors not knowing whether a friend or a stranger shall answer,
and even if a known face emerges from the sour gloom of that unknown
interior, still it is the face of a stranger. No matter what this stranger
says to her, nor what her message to him, the very cells of her flesh
reject knowledge and kinship in one monotonous word. No. No.
No. She draws her strength from this one holy talismanic word which
does not suffer her to be led into evil. Denying everything, she may
walk anywhere in safety, she looks at everything without amazement.

No, repeats this firm unchanging voice of her blood; and she looks
at Braggioni without amazement. He is a great man, he wishes to
impress this simple girl who covers her great round breasts with thick
dark cloth, and who hides long, invaluably beautiful legs under a
heavy skirt. She is almost thin except for the incomprehensible fullness of her breasts, like a nursing mother's, and Braggioni, who considers himself a judge of women, speculates again on the puzzle of
her notorious virginity, and takes the liberty of speech which she
permits without a sign of modesty, indeed, without any sort of sign,
which is disconcerting.

"You think you are so cold, *gringita!* Wait and see. You will surprise yourself some day! May I be there to advise you!" He stretches
his eyelids at her, and his ill-humored cat's eyes waver in a separate
glance for the two points of light marking the opposite ends of a
smoothly drawn path between the swollen curve of her breasts. He

2. Mexican statesman and reformer; President 1911–13.

is not put off by that blue serge, nor by her resolutely fixed gaze. There is all the time in the world. His cheeks are bellying with the wind of song. "O girl with the dark eyes," he sings, and reconsiders. "But yours are not dark. I can change all that. O girl with the green eyes, you have stolen my heart away!" then his mind wanders to the song, and Laura feels the weight of his attention being shifted elsewhere. Singing thus, he seems harmless, he is quite harmless, there is nothing to do but sit patiently and say "No," when the moment comes. She draws a full breath, and her mind wanders also, but not far. She dares not wander too far.

Not for nothing has Braggioni taken pains to be a good revolutionist and a professional lover of humanity. He will never die of it. He has the malice, the cleverness, the wickedness, the sharpness of wit, the hardness of heart, stipulated for loving the world profitably. *He will never die of it.* He will live to see himself kicked out from his feeding trough by other hungry world-saviors. Traditionally he must sing in spite of his life which drives him to bloodshed, he tells Laura, for his father was a Tuscany[3] peasant who drifted to Yucatan and married a Maya woman: a woman of race, an aristocrat. They gave him the love and knowledge of music, thus: and under the rip of his thumbnail, the strings of the instrument complain like exposed nerves.

Once he was called Delgadito[4] by all the girls and married women who ran after him; he was so scrawny all his bones showed under his thin cotton clothing, and he could squeeze his emptiness to the very backbone with his two hands. He was a poet and the revolution was only a dream then; too many women loved him and sapped away his youth, and he could never find enough to eat anywhere, anywhere! Now he is a leader of men, crafty men who whisper in his ear, hungry men who wait for hours outside his office for a word with him, emaciated men with wild faces who waylay him at the street gate with a timid, "Comrade, let me tell you . . ." and they blow the foul breath from their empty stomachs in his face.

He is always sympathetic. He gives them handfuls of small coins from his own pocket, he promises them work, there will be demonstrations, they must join the unions and attend the meetings, above all they must be on the watch for spies. They are closer to him than his own brothers, without them he can do nothing—until tomorrow, comrade!

Until tomorrow. "They are stupid, they are lazy, they are treacherous, they would cut my throat for nothing," he says to Laura. He has good food and abundant drink, he hires an automobile and drives in the Paseo on Sunday morning, and enjoys plenty of sleep in a soft bed beside a wife who dares not disturb him; and he sits pampering

3. From central Italy. *Yucatan:* a state in southeastern Mexico, home of the ancient Maya civilization which flourished from approximately 1000 B.C.   4. Skinny.

his bones in easy billows of fat, singing to Laura, who knows and thinks these things about him. When he was fifteen, he tried to drown himself because he loved a girl, his first love, and she laughed at him. "A thousand women have paid for that," and his tight little mouth turns down at the corners. Now he perfumes his hair with Jockey Club, and confides to Laura: "One woman is really as good as another for me, in the dark. I prefer them all."

His wife organizes unions among the girls in the cigarette factories, and walks in picket lines, and even speaks at meetings in the evening. But she cannot be brought to acknowledge the benefits of true liberty. "I tell her I must have my freedom, net. She does not understand my point of view." Laura has heard this many times. Braggioni scratches the guitar and meditates. "She is an instinctively virtuous woman, pure gold, no doubt of that. If she were not, I should lock her up, and she knows it."

His wife, who works so hard for the good of the factory girls, employs part of her leisure lying on the floor weeping because there are so many women in the world, and only one husband for her, and she never knows where nor when to look for him. He told her: "Unless you can learn to cry when I am not here, I must go away for good." That day he went away and took a room at the Hotel Madrid.

It is this month of separation for the sake of higher principles that has been spoiled not only for Mrs. Braggioni, whose sense of reality is beyond criticism, but for Laura, who feels herself bogged in a nightmare. Tonight Laura envies Mrs. Braggioni, who is alone, and free to weep as much as she pleases about a concrete wrong. Laura has just come from a visit to the prison, and she is waiting for tomorrow with a bitter anxiety as if tomorrow may not come, but time may be caught immovably in this hour, with herself transfixed, Braggioni singing on forever, and Eugenio's body not yet discovered by the guard.

Braggioni says: "Are you going to sleep?" Almost before she can shake her head, he begins telling her about the May-day disturbances coming on in Morelia,[5] for the Catholics hold a festival in honor of the Blessed Virgin, and the Socialists celebrate their martyrs on that day. "There will be two independent processions, starting from either end of town, and they will march until they meet, and the rest depends . . ." He asks her to oil and load his pistols. Standing up, he unbuckles his ammunition belt, and spreads it laden across her knees. Laura sits with the shells slipping through the cleaning cloth dipped in oil, and he says again he cannot understand why she works so hard for the revolutionary idea unless she loves some man who is in it. "Are you not in love with someone?" "No," says Laura.

---

5. Capital of Michoacan state in western Mexico and home of a seventeenth-century Spanish cathedral.

"And no one is in love with you?" "No." "Then it is your own fault. No woman need go begging. Why, what is the matter with you? The legless beggar woman in the Alameda has a perfectly faithful lover. Did you know that?"

Laura peers down the pistol barrel and says nothing, but a long, slow faintness rises and subsides in her; Braggioni curves his swollen fingers around the throat of the guitar and softly smothers the music out of it, and when she hears him again he seems to have forgotten her, and is speaking in the hypnotic voice he uses when talking in small rooms to a listening, close-gathered crowd. Some day this world, now seemingly so composed and eternal, to the edges of every sea shall be merely a tangle of gaping trenches, of crashing walls and broken bodies. Everything must be torn from its accustomed place where it has rotted for centuries, hurled skyward and distributed, cast down again clean as rain, without separate identity. Nothing shall survive that the stiffened hands of poverty have created for the rich and no one shall be left alive except the elect spirits destined to pro-create a new world cleansed of cruelty and injustice, ruled by benev-olent anarchy: "Pistols are good, I love them, cannon are even better, but in the end I pin my faith to good dynamite," he concludes, and strokes the pistol lying in her hands. "Once I dreamed of destroying this city, in case it offered resistance to General Ortíz, but it fell into his hands like an over-ripe pear."

He is made restless by his own words, rises and stands waiting. Laura holds up the belt to him: "Put that on, and go kill somebody in Morelia, and you will be happier," she says softly. The presence of death in the room makes her bold. "Today, I found Eugenio going into a stupor. He refused to allow me to call the prison doctor. He had taken all the tablets I brought him yesterday. He said he took them because he was bored."

"He is a fool, and his death is his own business," says Braggioni, fastening his belt carefully.

"I told him if he had waited only a little while longer, you would have got him set free," says Laura. "He said he did not want to wait."

"He is a fool and we are well rid of him," says Braggioni, reaching for his hat.

He goes away. Laura knows his mood has changed, she will not see him any more for a while. He will send word when he needs her to go on errands into strange streets, to speak to the strange faces that will appear, like clay masks with the power of human speech, to mutter their thanks to Braggioni for his help. Now she is free, and she thinks, I must run while there is time. But she does not go.

Braggioni enters his own house where for a month his wife has spent many hours every night weeping and tangling her hair upon her pillow. She is weeping now, and she weeps more at the sight of him, the cause of all her sorrows. He looks about the room. Nothing is changed, the smells are good and familiar, he is well acquainted with the woman who comes toward him with no reproach except grief on her face. He says to her tenderly: "You are so good, please don't cry any more, you dear good creature." She says, "Are you tired, my angel? Sit here and I will wash your feet." She brings a bowl of water, and kneeling, unlaces his shoes, and when from her knees she raises her sad eyes under her blackened lids, he is sorry for everything, and bursts into tears. "Ah, yes, I am hungry, I am tired, let us eat something together," he says, between sobs. His wife leans her head on his arm and says, "Forgive me!" and this time he is refreshed by the solemn, endless rain of her tears.

Laura takes off her serge dress and puts on a white linen night-gown and goes to bed. She turns her head a little to one side, and lying still, reminds herself that it is time to sleep. Numbers tick in her brain like little clocks, soundless doors close of themselves around her. If you would sleep, you must not remember anything, the children will say tomorrow, good morning, my teacher, the poor prisoners who come every day bringing flowers to their jailor. 1-2-3-4-5—it is monstrous to confuse love with revolution, night with day, life with death—ah, Eugenio!

The tolling of the midnight bell is a signal, but what does it mean? Get up, Laura, and follow me: come out of your sleep, out of your bed, out of this strange house. What are you doing in this house? Without a word, without fear she rose and reached for Eugenio's hand, but he eluded her with a sharp, sly smile and drifted away. This is not all, you shall see—Murderer, he said, follow me, I will show you a new country, but it is far away and we must hurry. No, said Laura, not unless you take my hand, no; and she clung first to the stair rail, and then to the topmost branch of the Judas tree that bent down slowly and set her upon the earth, and then to the rocky ledge of a cliff, and then to the jagged wave of a sea that was not water but a desert of crumbling stone. Where are you taking me, she asked in wonder but without fear. To death, and it is a long way off, and we must hurry, said Eugenio. No, said Laura, not unless you take my hand. Then eat these flowers, poor prisoner, said Eugenio in a voice of pity, take and eat: and from the Judas tree he stripped the warm bleeding flowers, and held them to her lips. She saw that his hand was fleshless, a cluster of small white petrified branches, and his eye sockets were without light, but she ate the flowers greedily for they satisfied both hunger and thirst. Murderer! said Eugenio, and Cannibal! This is my body and my blood.[6] Laura cried No! and

---

6. Christ's words to his disciples at the Last Supper as he gave them bread and wine (Matthew 26; Mark 14; Luke 22:1); a transubstantiation and participation in divine essence that is supposed to take place during the Christian sacrament of communion.

at the sound of her own voice, she awoke trembling, and was afraid
to sleep again.

JEAN RENOIR
1894–1979

When a film critic called Jean Renoir "one of the four or five great *auteurs*
[authors] in all the history of the cinema," he was not referring to the director's "literary" quality so much as recognizing that Renoir put his own creative or "authorial" stamp on each of his films. A film by Jean Renoir has
something to say about the human condition; it shows human beings caught
in complicated social and psychological relationships that are often a microcosm of larger social problems; it presents complex personalities whose many
sides are revealed by comparison with other, similar-yet-different characters;
it describes the conflict of values in terms of historical change and of opposing social classes; and it conveys the complex patterns of social relationships
by emphasizing aesthetic patterns of similarity and difference, of parallelism
and exchange. Although much of Renoir's work develops a realistic (and
often satirical) portrayal of life in society, he aims also to express a second,
"inner realism"—the implied truth that emerges through the artistic
arrangement of documentary detail. Like so many twentieth-century literary
artists from Pirandello to Beckett, Renoir exploits his artistic medium in
order to represent reality over as full a range as possible. In tragedy and
comedy, with the silent film *The Little Match Girl* (based on a tragic fairy
tale by Hans Christian Andersen), the satirical comedy *Boudu Saved From
Drowning*, the bitter social criticism of *Rules of the Game*, and the color
spectacle of *The Golden Coach*, Renoir combines realistic and theatrical
dimensions to comment on human nature and "civilized" behavior.

   Grand Illusion comes in the middle of Renoir's career, after the early
silent films, but toward the end of his European work before his departure
(forced by World War II) for the United States in 1940. In the history of the
cinema, it is located as part of a period of French film called "poetic realism," a development of the mid-thirties that is located stylistically somewhere between a documentary, "naturalist" style and the lyric imagination
of surrealist or German expressionist film. A combination of social realism
and a strongly interpretive perspective, often verging on romantic pessimism
while it treats life as a form of theater, "poetic realism" creates characters
and situations that become metaphors for aspects of society or the human
condition. Poetic realism is still a form of realism, with chronological development and consistent psychological characterization, and as such is far
from the formal experiments of the French "new wave" and a film like Alain
Robbe-Grillet and Alain Resnais's *Last Year at Marienbad* (1961) with its
contradictory perspectives and ambiguous plot. However, its emphasis on
the director's visual *interpretation* of reality, its use of camera angles and
composition in depth to create a desired atmosphere, and its frequent reminders

of the ambiguous interplay of art and life, helped to prepare the way for later experimental cinema.

The film script printed here is the combined work of Charles Spaak (1903–1974) and Jean Renoir, with additional changes during filming that reflect the presence of actor-director Erich von Stroheim and even the observations of a friend chatting on the set. Spaak, one of the major screenwriters of poetic realism, sketched out an original script (tentatively titled *The Escapes of Captain Maréchal*) around the paired characters of Maréchal and Boeldieu. When Erich von Stroheim was added to the cast at the last minute, Renoir enlarged the part of Rauffenstein and created a second pairing: that between Rauffenstein and Boeldieu. Stroheim suggested the emphasis on Rauffenstein's broken body, including the visual symbol of the iron chinstrap supporting his jaw; Albert Pinkovitch, chatting with Renoir during the shooting, gave Renoir the idea of developing the character of Rosenthal as Maréchal's companion in escape, which in turn allowed the director to incorporate an additional ethnic or cultural layer into this microcosm of European society at war with itself. Thus the decisive aesthetic effects in this film come not merely from a printed script but from the way the script evolved in the imagination of an ensemble: writers, actors, and technical experts (photographer, set designer, sound engineer, technical adviser, editor), all coordinated by the director's "authorial" imagination. The result is an art object, the film *Grand Illusion*: not a play, where each performance is slightly different, but a single performance where intonation and gesture are fixed for all time, close-ups and panoramic views repeated in exactly the same order at each showing. A director is thus an author in the sense that he or she is responsible for the shape of the cinematic world as it unfolds on screen.

Some effects are more purely "literary" in the sense that they transpose effects attainable in writing: the juxtaposition of French and German bars; the symbolism of von Rauffenstein's geranium—the only flower in the fortress—or of the aristocratic white gloves; Boeldieu's solitary climb up the fortress tower; the repetition and cumulative effect of the song "Il était un petit navire" in different circumstances. Some effects exploit the technical capacities of film as a medium, manipulating the camera's ability to move quickly among planes, bringing out facial expressions and small gestures; to juxtapose simultaneous action in two places (Boeldieu's climb; the escape); to dissolve or overlap one image into another, and choose different angles of vision; to comment visually on dialogue (the teacher's wig and clown ruff); to intensify suspense by speeding the rhythm of short individual shots; to draw attention to emotions by sustained longer shots (the prisoners' response to Douaumont's recapture). In addition, as with plays, the actors' performances establish nuances and character relationships that may not be apparent in the script.

The script of *Grand Illusion* printed here includes camera directions reconstructed after a frame-by-frame analysis of the film. Inserted in the same format as a play's stage directions, they should be read along with the dialogue as guidelines to interpretation and creation of aesthetic effect. One difference from play technique will become immediately apparent: while a play progresses in acts produced on a central stage, the film alternates rapidly from scene to scene (indicated here within brackets), and sets up a different rhythm of expectations in its viewer. *Grand Illusion* possesses an unusually full dialogue script and can easily be read as a fascinating story of heroism and social change during World War I, but it takes on its full dimensions when viewed as a cinematic and not merely a verbal creation.

Jean Renoir, the son of Impressionist painter Pierre-Auguste Renoir (1841–1915), had made a range of silent and sound films before directing *Grand Illusion* in 1936–37. Adaptations of novels (Zola's *Nana*, 1926, and Flaubert's *Madame Bovary*, 1934), a detective thriller (*Night at the Crossroads*, 1931), comedies (*Boudu Saved From Drowning*, 1932, and *Chotard and Company*, 1933), socialist realist drama (*The Bitch*, 1932, *Toni*, 1934, *The Crime of Monsieur Lange*, 1935), and election propaganda (*Life Is Ours*, 1936) demonstrated Renoir's concern for social themes and his ability to find cinematic strategies for expressing ideas and values. In 1936, with Hitler and Mussolini in power and Europe fearful of another war, he undertook *Grand Illusion* as a statement that emphasized the common humanity of people in all nations and classes, and the foolishness of going to war for national pride. First shown in June 1937, the film was an international success in spite of being banned in Italy and Germany (Hitler's Minister of Propaganda, Joseph Goebbels, called it "the cinema enemy number one"). At the 1958 World's Fair in Brussels, an international film jury voted it one of the twelve best films ever made. Renoir's last French film of this period, *Rules of the Game* (1939), was a brilliantly photographed development of the themes of cultural collapse portrayed in *Grand Illusion*.

In 1940, while Renoir was teaching and directing in Rome, Italy joined Hitler in the war against France and the director was forced to flee. Emigrating to the United States, he made a number of films, of which the best known is *The Southerner* (1945). Gradually more interested in the possibilities of cinema as theater and spectacle, he abandoned his earlier realistic style and made *The River* in India (color, 1951), and *The Golden Coach* (color, 1952) in Italy. The story of an eighteenth-century *commedia dell'arte* (living theater) troupe in Peru, *The Golden Coach* allowed Renoir to unite themes of theater, real life, and film. In 1954 he returned to France and made a series of lighter films, sometimes experimenting with color and pictorial effects as in the 1954 *French Cancan* and 1959 *Déjeuner sur l'herbe*. Before his death in 1979, Renoir retired to Southern California, where he wrote novels, plays, and memoirs.

Grand Illusion and *Rules of the Game* together established Renoir's reputation as a pioneer of composition in depth, or "deep-focus realism." Instead of depending on *montage* (cutting in a variety of separate shots to cover a lot of material in a short time), Renoir arranged to move the camera through different levels of focus in the same frame (a "long take" or "sequence shot") so as to include action in the foreground, middle ground, and background for a unified "real" perspective. Instead of separate scenes arbitrarily linked, the camera appears to pick up different details of a single dramatic event. Boeldieu's death scene, for example, includes a medium close-up of the two officers talking; a close-up of Boeldieu's pained face; a longer continuous shot as von Rauffenstein rises, goes to the corner to pour himself a drink, hears the nurse announce Boeldieu's death, drinks, and returns to the bed;

another shot showing von Rauffenstein's hand closing Boeldieu's eyes; and a culminating sequence that shows von Rauffenstein pacing around the room, looking out the window, seeing his prized geranium, and finally cutting the only blossom off the plant. Moving among spatial planes according to the desired focus, Renoir filled the whole frame with dramatically significant activity. In this respect, he considered himself a "technician," a term he used in a letter written to projectionists for a 1957 screening of *Grand Illusion*. "I have composed each image to fill this surface and not leave anything empty. I accumulated details both on top and on the bottom of the frame," he said, asking that the projectionist use a screen of the same dimensions current in 1936 so that details would not be eliminated and a truncated effect obtained which would be "unaesthetic." Renoir is clearly more than a master technician, of course. He is also—as he described himself in another context—a storyteller. The pioneering "deep-focus" effects of *Grand Illusion* do not call attention to themselves, but disappear into the story they help to tell.

The story line is a magnificently suspenseful escape plot that gathers momentum from the abortive tunnel to Boeldieu's sacrifice and the final tense, argumentative walk toward freedom of the two survivors, Maréchal and Rosenthal. Punctuating the escape plot are episodes that—even when comic—heighten the feeling of tension. The escape is part of a cat-and-mouse game inside the larger game of war: a game that Renoir feels is unnecessary, artificial, and perhaps an illusion of meaningful activity while real human relationships go on by themselves. As the end suggests, the illusion is also that there will be no more wars. Renoir and others who had fought in World War I remembered it as the promised final battle against evil, the "war to end war" and to "make the world safe for democracy." By 1937, these ideals were beginning to look like battered illusions, and the time seemed to have come to remind Europeans that they were part of a common humanity. *Grand Illusion* takes national divisions at their most intense, in a wartime prison camp with differences of nation, language, class, religion, and race, and shows a common humanity through those differences as well as the struggle of a new order to emerge from the ruins of the old.

In the camp, the nationalist habits that lead countries to war appear artificial and irrelevant to more basic human relationships. Friendship, love, class identity, and human sympathy easily transcend national boundaries. Von Rauffenstein befriends Boeldieu as a fellow aristocrat just as Maréchal delightedly recognizes a fellow mechanic at the German bar; Maréchal and Elsa fall in love although her family has been killed in battle by French soldiers; the old German soldier pities Maréchal and gives him his harmonica. Only the old aristocratic class has been bred to "career officership": common people will fight for their freedom but have as little interest in the protocol of war as they do in the etiquette of white gloves. For all their eccentricity, however, von Rauffenstein and Boeldieu are sympathetic characters in their lucidity, idealism, and aesthetic imagination. Boeldieu's climb is more than an efficient diversion: it is a theatrical grand gesture to which von Rauffenstein's sole flower appropriately responds. Yet both are part of a bankrupt society which has been falling apart ever since the French Revo-

lution, and it is the new international classes of worker (Maréchal) and bourgeoisie (Rosenthal) who will escape and create the future. Creating the new
order will not be an easy task, as the quarrels and anti-Semitic outburst on
the road home show. The prison camps of Hallbach and Wintersborn had
established a situation in which microcosms of European society, with its
different nations, classes, and ingrained prejudices, found themselves working together to escape the imprisonment of war. The end of *Grand Illusion*
remains open not because the war had not ended by 1937, but because the
questions raised by the film still remained to be answered.

André Bazin's *Jean Renoir*, translated by W. W. Halsey II and William
H. Simon (1974), is an important book by a major theoretician of modern
cinema (completed by colleagues after the author's death); it contains a
description of the early script of *Grand Illusion* before changes introduced
in the filming. Renoir's autobiography, *My Life and My Films*, translated
by Norman Denny (1974), contains much information on the making of his
films. Two works dealing with the films are Alexander Sesonske, *Jean Renoir:
The French Years, 1924–1939* (1980), a study of the cinematic techniques
and historical context of Renoir's films in the years including *Grand Illusion*, and Raymond Durgnat, *Jean Renoir* (1975), a major historical and
critical study of Renoir the filmmaker, proceeding film by film (bibliography).

Grand Illusion[1]

*Titles: then the legend: THE EVENTS DESCRIBED IN THIS FILM
TOOK PLACE DURING THE WAR OF 1914–1918.*
> [*French Front: Officers' Bar*]
> *In the officers' mess of an air squadron on the French front,
> camera tracks into close-up of a gramophone with a horn, play-
> ing the music of the song 'Frou-Frou, Frou-Frou . . . ,'[2] also
> being hummed by a man's voice. Pan up to Lieutenant* MARE-
> CHAL *who is bending over the gramophone as though hypno-
> tized by the spinning record. He seems lost in distant memories,
> as he sings the chorus.*

MARECHAL *close-up.* Frou-Frou . . . Frou-Frou-Frou . . . Tra la la
la . . . la . . . la . . . Frou-Frou . . .
> MARECHAL *is a mechanic whom circumstance has made an offi-
> cer. He is wearing a uniform, his képi[3] pushed slightly towards
> the back of his head, his airman's jacket unbuttoned, his scarf
> loosely knotted round his neck. It is winter, one of the terrible
> winters of that war, and this officers' mess behind the French
> front is not very warm. Behind* MARECHAL *in a blurred back-*

---

1. Translated by Marianne Alexandre and Andrew Sinclair. Scene indications have been added
from the French text, in brackets, for clarity; the English translation employs a more general
background description.   2. A popular French song, played on a record player with a horn-
shaped speaker.   3. Visored soldier's cap.

*ground, a few officers are seen sitting at tables near the bar,
talking together. Suddenly,* MARECHAL *snaps out of his reverie
and lifts his head. Camera follows him towards the bar, where
he speaks to a soldier,* HALPHEN.

MARECHAL. Hey! I say, waiter, are you going to Epernay?[4]

HALPHEN. Yes, of course.

MARECHAL. When?

HALPHEN. In half-an-hour.

MARECHAL, *near him now.* In the lorry?[5] HALPHEN *nods.* Well then,
be a sport . . . try to wait for me.

HALPHEN. Joséphine?

MARECHAL, *as though it were obvious.* Well naturally . . . Joséphine.

HALPHEN *smiling.* You're not the only one.

MARECHAL *shrugging.* I don't care!

> *Pan towards the door, revealing the other officers talking and
> drinking together at different tables; the record plays the same
> song. Captain* RINGIS *bursts in. Camera pans back with him as
> he spots* MARECHAL *and goes over to speak with him.*

RINGIS. Hey, Maréchal . . . there's a fellow there from the General
Staff. . . . You've got to show him around.

MARECHAL *disappointed.* A bloke from the General Staff? . . . Hmmm,
well. . . . He's come at the wrong time.

RINGIS *ironically.* Joséphine? *Sceptically.* Where are you going to get
with all that?

> MARECHAL *follows him as far as the door.*

MARECHAL. All right. She'll wait. At your service, Captain!

> *They go out together. Camera stays for the moment on the
> door. There is noise from the room and the record of 'Frou-
> Frou' finishes playing. Pan back to the bar covered with the
> squadron flags. Camera holds and closes on the large sign on
> the bar, which has three drawings on it: a hunter, a crocodile,
> and a skull sketched round the following text: SQUADRON M
> F 902—ALCOHOL KILLS—ALCOHOL DRIVES PEOPLE
> MAD—THE SQUADRON LEADER DRINKS IT.*
> [*Captain's Office*]
> *Captain* RINGIS, *followed by* MARECHAL, *comes in through the
> open door of his office. Camera tracks back and pans to the
> 'fellow from the General Staff.' This man wears a monocle and
> seems very haughty. He is waiting for them and examining the
> enlargement of an aerial photograph. He readjusts his monocle
> to have a better look . . . when* RINGIS *and* MARECHAL *come into
> shot.* MARECHAL *gives a military salute.*

---

4. A town on the Marne River in northeastern France that saw heavy fighting during World War
I.   5. Van.

RINGIS *to* MARECHAL. Captain de Bœldieu, of the Divisional Staff.

MARECHAL *saluting:* Maréchal.

BŒLDIEU *icily shaking the photograph.* I say, Monsieur Maréchal, do you know this photograph?

He holds it out to MARECHAL, *who looks at it.*

MARECHAL. Oh, yes, Captain . . . Ricord took it when he was with me.

BŒLDIEU. And is this Monsieur Ricord around?

MARECHAL. He's on leave.

BŒLDIEU. Of course!

BŒLDIEU *goes over to* MARECHAL *and points at the photograph. Behind them, Captain* RINGIS *stands on tip-toe to look at the document.*

BŒLDIEU. It's that grey spot which worries me . . . There, below the road.

RINGIS *interrupting.* It's not a road, it's a canal.

MARECHAL. Is it? I thought it was some railway lines.

BŒLDIEU *ironically.* What touching unanimity! . . . This precise detail gives one a fine idea of the perfection of our photographic equipment.

MARECHAL *shrugging.* Well . . . it was misty that day.

BŒLDIEU. I would like to resolve this enigma.

RINGIS. As you wish. . . . I'll ask for a fighter. *As he speaks, he turns to pick up the telephone.* Hello! Hello! Give me the pursuit squadron.

MARECHAL *looks at the photograph again, then gives it to* BŒLDIEU, *and gets ready to leave.*

MARECHAL. I'll put on my stuff then, Captain.

He goes out. Camera stays on RINGIS *and* BŒLDIEU.

RINGIS. What would you like to put on? A flying suit or a goatskin?[6]

BŒLDIEU *still examining the photograph.* I have no preference. . . . Flying suits smell rather and goatskins shed hairs.

RINGIS *on the telephone again.* Yes. . . . Give me the pursuit squadron, please.

[*German Officers' Canteen*]

Through an open door of a German officers' mess, the German commander enters, followed by a few officers. Camera tracks back to show a part of the room, which is much the same as the officers' mess of Squadron M F 902. There is hardly any difference: a table set for a meal, a bar, bottles. The gramophone is playing a Viennese waltz by Strauss. But there are no drawings on the walls. Commander VON RAUFFENSTEIN, *who has just come in, is still wearing his fighter-pilot's uniform. His back straight,*

6. Leather weatherproof jacket.

his heels together, he takes a glass of spirits[7] and downs it in one gulp, then he scratches his ear. He is small compared with the other officers surrounding him to congratulate him. His type is the Prussian squire: well-bred, strict, hard-faced. He speaks in German, as do the rest.

RAUFFENSTEIN *to his orderly.* Herr Bredow, take a car and go and look in the direction of the sugar plant. . . . I shot down a Caudron.[8] . . . If they are officers, invite them to lunch.

BREDOW. Very good, Commander.

RAUFFENSTEIN *to one of his officers.* Herr Fressler, this is the moment to distinguish yourself. . . . You are going to concoct for us one of your famous fruit punches. . . . *Pause.* We ought to celebrate my second kill.

The other officers raise their glasses and surround him and toast his victory. RAUFFENSTEIN *drinks at one gulp, bending backwards to do so.*

FRESSLER. With pleasure, Commander. *He turns to the barman.* Give me three bottles of Moselle, two of Rhine wine, one of champagne, a half of Martel,[9] one box of pineapple, three lemons . . . and sugar, of course.

During this list spoken partly off shot, pan along the bar to end on photographs of women pinned to the wall. Cut back to the door: BREDOW *comes in again and salutes. The music of the Strauss waltz is loud.*

BREDOW. There's two officers. . . . One of them's got a bullet in his arm; I've just taken him to the ambulance.

Shot of the whole room, taken slightly from above. After a time, BREDOW *enters again, followed by* BŒLDIEU, *then by* MARECHAL, *whose arm is in a sling.* BŒLDIEU *is always pretty immaculate.* MARECHAL *seems tired; he is wearing a jersey, his jacket is over his shoulders, his head is bare, his arm in a sling.* RAUFFENSTEIN *makes a sign to* BŒLDIEU *to come in and clicks his heels together. His officers do the same.* BŒLDIEU *gives them a dignified salute.*

RAUFFENSTEIN *in strongly-accented French.* Captain von Rauffenstein, Commander of Squadron 21. . . . We are very honoured to receive French guests. *Introducing his men.* My officers. . . . Orderly. . . . Their coats.

BŒLDIEU *after saluting.* Captain de Bœldieu.

They shake hands. RAUFFENSTEIN *turns towards* MARECHAL *and bows more formally. He is not very interested in this second Frenchman, immediately guessing that* MARECHAL *is not a career officer.*

[*Long shot.* RAUFFENSTEIN *turns towards the barman. Hubbub.*

---

7. Alcohol.   8. A French fighter plane (made of wood).   9. A French cognac. *Moselle and Rhine:* two German wines.

RAUFFENSTEIN. And your punch?

MULLER. May I serve you some?

RAUFFENSTEIN. Please do.][1]

A German soldier removes BŒLDIEU's *overcoat while* RAUFFEN-STEIN *leads everyone to the table.*

RAUFFENSTEIN *in French.* Gentlemen, please be seated.

RAUFFENSTEIN *seats* BŒLDIEU *on his right and indicates the chair on his left to* MARECHAL. *Everybody sits down. In a medium close-up,* RAUFFENSTEIN *leans over to* BŒLDIEU *and speaks in French to him, putting on his monocle.*

RAUFFENSTEIN. I used to know a de Bœldieu . . . a Count de Bœldieu. . . .

BŒLDIEU *interested.* Ah, yes. . . . That was my cousin Edmond de Bœldieu, military attaché in Berlin. . . .

RAUFFENSTEIN *in English.* He was a marvellous rider. . . .

BŒLDIEU *in English.* Yes, in the good old days. . . .

Slow pan to MARECHAL *and the* GERMAN OFFICER *sitting next to him.* MARECHAL *is looking at his plate.*

GERMAN OFFICER. Aren't you hungry? . . . You're not eating?

MARECHAL. Yes. . . . Yes . . . but . . . *He shows his arm in the sling.* I can't cut the meat. . . .

GERMAN OFFICER. Allow me.

He takes MARECHAL's *knife and fork at once and cuts up his meat for him.*

MARECHAL. You speak French well.

GERMAN OFFICER. I once worked at Gnome,[2] in Lyon.

MARECHAL *joyfully.* No joking! Me too, I'm a mechanic! . . .

All heads turn in the direction of the door which they have heard opening. Cut to a German soldier coming into the room carrying a wreath. Camera tracks before this imposing wreath in close-up to make visible the words written in gilt on the ribbon around it: TO CAPTAIN DE CRUSSOL, FRENCH AIR FORCE, SHOT DOWN IN FLAMES ON MARCH 12TH 1914. . . . FROM THE OFFICERS OF THE GERMAN SQUADRON F S 21. Quick cut back to the group shot at the moment when RAUFFENSTEIN *rises abruptly at the table.*

RAUFFENSTEIN *stiffly.* Gentlemen . . . *To* BŒLDIEU. I apologise for this . . . coincidence.

At a sign from RAUFFENSTEIN, *the music from the gramophone is stopped. All the officers stand to attention in front of the table. Each bows his head.*

RAUFFENSTEIN *after a moment of silence.* May the earth lie lightly on our brave enemy. *All remain still.* Thank you, gentlemen.

---

1. The bracketed section was cut in the final version of the film.   2. A factory that made, among other things, airplane engines.

*Everybody sits down again. The Viennese waltz is replayed on
the gramophone and, while everyone is eating, an old soldier
appears at the door. He salutes, clicking his heels together. He
is a military policeman without flashes,[3] shown in medium close-
up.*

POLICEMAN *in German.* Military police. I have come to take the
officer prisoners into custody.

[*Country*]

*Dissolve on sound of clicking heels becoming sound of train
wheels.*

*Through the windows of a railway carriage, the countryside is
seen as the train passes. There is snow on the ground; the sky is
low and grey. Train sounds and music. The original screenplay
gave the following details: it is the start of captivity, seen through
the windows of a railway carriage: the fields and the forests go
by. Winter landscape, frozen and mournful. Patches of snow
here and there. It is far away, very far away. . . . The train stops
at last. Close on the railway sign:*

---

*KRIEGSGEFANGENEN LAGER Nr 17
HALLBACH
OFFIZIERSLAGER C. K. VII*[4]

Barracks Courtyard

*Very quick shot of a grey, drab, sad building, overlooking a
barracks yard. In the distance, a detachment of some fifty hang-
dog Germans marches by in step.*

*Pan past the prisoners in the camp, who stand in a group wait-
ing for the convoy of new arrivals. Camera stays on the still
group of new prisoners, whose faces show an extreme fatigue.
There are French, English, Russian, and Belgian army officers.
In the middle of this group,* BŒLDIEU *and* MARECHAL *are brought
out by the camera tracking towards them. They stand side by
side, the first looking very haughty, the second tired and yawning in a vulgar way. Seeing* MARECHAL's *'incorrect' behaviour,*
BŒLDIEU *looks at him with a certain contempt from behind his
monocle. . . . Resume long shot: a German officer barks out a
dry and brutal order, an unintelligible yell that makes everybody freeze. This German is the Feldwebel[5]* KRANTZ. *All the*

---

3. Without an officer's stripes.   **4.** "Prisoner of War Camp No. 17, Hallbach, Officer's Camp
C. K. VII."   **5.** German for sergeant-major. A lower rank: often referred to as N.C.O. (noncommissioned officer) in the text.

prisoners turn to look at him curiously, as he produces a piece of paper. Before he reads it, he gives the French officers in particular a hard look. He reads slowly in French with a strong German accent.

KRANTZ. In the name of Camp Commander Krauss, officers will be treated with all due regard to their rank. Commander Krauss, however, reminds you that you are subject here to the authority of the German law. You will therefore, as of to-day, learn German discipline and obey it.

Camera begins on KRANTZ *at the start of his speech, then pans along the German soldiers and the grave faces of the prisoners.*

KRANTZ *off.* Every German soldier working in a camp has the right to give you orders and you will execute these without complaint. You will salute all officers according to German army regulations. In case of attempts at escape, the sentries are ordered to shoot any officer discovered outside the camp boundaries. *Pan continues past* BŒLDIEU's *quizzical look and* MARECHAL's *intrigued one.* It is strictly prohibited to dress in a slovenly manner, to congregate in groups, to speak loudly and disparagingly of the German nation, to quit your quarters after curfew, to communicate either verbally or in writing with civilians outside the camp. *Cut to* KRANTZ *who continues to read aloud from his text.* It is strictly prohibited to talk to the guards. *He folds up the paper he was reading and places it in his pocket; he continues in a jerky French, repeating the words by heart.* Now, gentlemen, we are going to make you proceed to an office for a small formality.

Long shot of the barracks yard. The guards make the prisoners march towards a building. Cut to a group of long-time prisoners who have been watching the scene.

ONE OF THEM. Hey, new boys!

ANOTHER. Hey, look, tip 'em off!

They all begin to sing the tune of 'Ange pur, ange radieux,'[6] *improvising the words in chorus. In the group are certain characters who will be important later,* ROSENTHAL, THE ENGINEER, *and* THE ACTOR.

THE GROUP. Ange pur, ange radieux. . . . Conceal your gold. . . . Hide your watches. . . .

THE ACTOR *advancing.* Oh, yes, hide it well!

Immediately, the German guards jump on these disturbers of the peace and break up the group. Pan towards BŒLDIEU *and* MARECHAL *who are queuing in front of a shed.*

MARECHAL. Hey, what are they getting at?

6. "Pure angel, radiant angel": words sung by Marguerite in the famous final trio of Gounod's opera *Faust.*

BŒLDIEU, *as though it were self-evident.* They are telling us to hide our gold.

> KRANTZ *intervenes and gets rid of the last of the singers. Camera stays on the group containing* BŒLDIEU *and* MARECHAL *as they get ready to enter the control shed.*
> *Inspection Point*
> *Medium close-up of a German soldier searching a struggling English officer rather roughly in the control shed.*

ENGLISH OFFICER *in English:* Keep your hands away! Don't touch me! . . . Do you want my watch?

> *The officer takes his watch out of his pocket and throws it onto the floor. Tilt quickly down to show the watch being smashed under the heel of the officer's boot. The German soldier bends over, and camera follows his gestures as he picks up the broken watch and puts it on a ledger where another soldier examines it and enters it in his book . . . during this, a hubbub of voices:*

VARIOUS VOICES: Ah! Leave me alone! . . . Let me be! Those are mine! . . .

> *The German soldier motions over* MARECHAL *who goes over, followed by* BŒLDIEU.

GERMAN SOLDIER: Look out![7]

> *He feels the arm of* MARECHAL *that is in a sling, then rifles his clothes.*

MARECHAL. Sorry, mate. . . . Got nothing on me. . . . If I'd known I was coming here, I'd have brought along a little cash. . . . Sorry!

GERMAN SOLDIER: Nichts![8]

> *After searching* MARECHAL, *the soldier turns to* BŒLDIEU *and gets ready to rifle the pockets of his fur coat.* BŒLDIEU, *very haughty with his monocle in his eye, stops the soldier and says in a glacial voice.*

BŒLDIEU. But, I say, what is this?

> *The soldier finds a cigarette case, opens it, then lifts his head.*

A GERMAN N.C.O. *in French.* I'm sorry, Captain, but it's our duty to search you. . . . That's war!

BŒLDIEU *very coldly.* I could not agree with you more, but there are polite ways of doing it. . . . Otherwise, I will be obliged to mention the matter to the Commander of the whole army corps.

> [*In a Room*]
> *In their room, the French prisoners surround one of their number,* ROSENTHAL, *who is unpacking a large parcel that he has just received. A German guard watches it all carefully. Pan across the room in which several similar groups of men stand about.*

A GUARD. Open it!

---

7. Literally, "Your turn."   8. "Nothing."

Cut back to ROSENTHAL *who has not finished taking out tin after tin. Behind him,* THE ACTOR *taps him on the shoulder.*

THE ACTOR. How are ya, pal? . . . Keep smilin' . . . ya're happy!

ROSENTHAL *still unwrapping things.* Look, chocolate!

> *Off, an angry soldier begins to argue. Pan onto him: he is facing a sentry and he holds a wrapped tin.*

THE FRENCH SOLDIER. The bastards! You opened my tin of ham. . . . You haven't the right to! . . . No, you don't. . . . It's in the rule book. . . . And now it's gone bad!

> *Angrily and contemptuously, he throws the packet at the German, who does not budge. Cut back to* ROSENTHAL *as he finishes the unwrapping of his parcel.*

ROSENTHAL. Well, as for me, I'm always amazed and delighted every time I get a parcel from my parents. . . . When I think, here we are, in the middle of Germany, separated from our own kind by a line of fire we can't cross . . . and yet, here's a tin of peas for me straight from Paris!

THE TEACHER. What surprises me most is the incredible honesty of our gaolers.[9]

CARTIER, *another prisoner.* Hey . . . that's true!

THE ACTOR *interrupting him in a Paris slang accent.* Our feldwebel, if he really is, Arthur, every day, he gets cabbage. He loathes it. . . . It sits on his stomach. . . . He told me so himself! I bet you he'd rather scoff[1] your peas!

THE ENGINEER. Think it over for a second. If they had a go at our peas, people would stop sending us parcels. Then they'd have to feed us. They've already got enough trouble feeding themselves!

ROSENTHAL. Come. . . . Let's get a move on. Our guests must be hungry. . . .

> [*German Officers' Mess*]
> *Tilt slightly onto a table where three German N.C.O.'s are eating their lean rations. On a wall, a portrait of Kaiser William II.*[2] *They speak in German.*

LEININGER. Ugh! It tastes like old galoshes.

ZINS. What do the Frenchmen get to eat?

ZACH. Cabbage . . . but they don't give a damn, they've got their tins!

ZINS. And the Russians?

ZACH. Cabbage roots . . . minus the tins.

> *They all laugh.*

ZINS. And the English?

ZACH. Plum pudding!

> *All three shrug and continue eating.*

---

9. Jailers.   1. Eat.   2. Emperor of Germany and King of Prussia, 1888–1918.

[In a Room]

In the prisoners' room, MARECHAL *lights a cigarette with a bit of burning paper which* THE ACTOR *is holding out to him. They both smoke as they wait for* CAMILLE, *who serves as* ROSENTHAL's *orderly, to finish setting the table.*

THE ACTOR *to* MARECHAL. In peacetime, I used to act at the Bouffes du Nord.[3] Ever see my turn?

MARECHAL. Well, you know, I never go to the theatre. It's heavy stuff. Are you interested in the Tour de France? Well, I tell you, I've seen Chabert, then Petit-Breton,[4] then those chaps. . . .

He goes on talking while camera pans around the room. Some of the men are moving towards the table. THE ENGINEER *goes over to* BŒLDIEU. *Near them,* ROSENTHAL *takes out food which he puts on the table.*

BŒLDIEU *a little surprised.* Are we allowed to buy everything we want, in town?

THE ENGINEER. Just about anything we want, through the canteen.

BŒLDIEU. Perfect. In that case, I will buy the English sort of arm-chair, some books, playing cards, English cigarettes. . . .

THE ENGINEER *interrupting him.* Oh, those. . . . You won't find that!

BŒLDIEU. No?

In the background, CAMILLE *hands a packet of cigarettes to* ROSENTHAL.

CAMILLE. Here they are, lieutenant . . . I'll try to come back tomorrow. *He salutes him in a friendly way.*

ROSENTHAL. Thanks, Camille. *He turns towards the two groups and waves them over to the table.* And now, my friends, if you'll be so kind, please be seated! *Hubbub; everybody sits down.* ROSENTHAL *continues, partly off shot.* Let me see, what will you have to start with? Cold chicken, pâté de foie gras[5] with truffles from Périgord or, Captain Cook's pickled mackerel?

The dinner sequence is made up of many shots of the various diners, taken slightly from above—only the more important shots are indicated.

BŒLDIEU *sitting down.* You keep a good table, as far as I can see!

MARECHAL. But don't we get fed here?

A NEIGHBOUR. In theory, yes. In practice, no. What they give us isn't eatable. Our parcels are enough . . . *laughing* . . . especially Rosenthal's.

ROSENTHAL. Come off it, it's nothing, really! *To his neighbour* BŒLDIEU. A little brandy, Captain, as an apéritif?

BŒLDIEU *haughtily.* Why not?

3. Theater in Montmartre, in Paris.   4. Well-known cyclists. Tour de France: national bicycle race.   5. Goose liver pâté (Rosenthal has received a package of gourmet delicacies).

Quick dissolve to a few minutes later. Slight tilt onto MARECHAL
and his neighbour at table, THE TEACHER.

THE TEACHER. I've never had such a good meal in my life . . .
holding out a plate to MARECHAL . . . Have a bit more fish.

MARECHAL. Yes, please.

THE TEACHER. And I'm beginning to get used to Rosenthal being
so generous . . . that just shows what adaptable creatures we
are!

Pan to THE ACTOR *sitting opposite* THE TEACHER; *he is listening
and making funny faces. He has a cigarette in his mouth and
brandishes a bottle. He makes broad jokes, always in his strong
Parisian slang.*

THE ACTOR. Needless to say, the lieutenant is a teacher. . . . Sister
Ann . . . anagram . . . grand-daughter . . . Waterloo . . . *laughing at his own joke* . . . Shit! That's a good one!

MARECHAL *ironically, beginning off.*[6] You, you're quite a funny man,
aren't you?

THE ACTOR *stops laughing, as camera shows the whole table.*
BŒLDIEU, *always stiff and unamused, leans towards* THE ACTOR.

BŒLDIEU. Do the rules of the game require that we pretend to find
that funny? *He turns back to* ROSENTHAL. Congratulations, old
boy, the brandy is quite up to scratch.

THE ENGINEER *taking the brandy.* Oh, it's the tip of the top, well
worth it!

Cut back to THE ACTOR *who surreptitiously picks up* BŒLDIEU's
*monocle from the table and tries to screw it in his eye and
mimic* BŒLDIEU *while* ROSENTHAL *answers.*

ROSENTHAL *to* BŒLDIEU. It's the barman at Fouquet's who sent it to
me in a bottle for mouthwash.

THE TEACHER *not understanding.* Fouquet's?

MARECHAL *to* THE TEACHER. Yes . . . a bar on the Champs-Elysées.[7]

THE TEACHER. When I used to go to Paris, I'd eat my meals at my
brother-in-law's. . . . It's much cheaper than a restaurant.

Cut back to BŒLDIEU *and* ROSENTHAL.

ROSENTHAL *whispering to* BŒLDIEU. How long ago were you last in
Paris?

BŒLDIEU. A week.

ROSENTHAL. I envy you. Was everybody there?

BŒLDIEU. The other day, Maxim's[8] was choc-a-bloc.

Cut back to MARECHAL *and* THE TEACHER.

MARECHAL *relaxed.* Oh, me . . . I never go to spots like that . . .
Fouquet's . . . Maxim's . . . I like a good cheap little bistro better
where there's a good line in wine. . . .

---

6. Off-camera.   7. A broad avenue in the center of Paris, famous for its beauty and elegant
stores.   8. An elegant restaurant.

A VOICE *off.* A bit of chicken?

THE TEACHER *in close-up, thoughtfully.* Maxim . . . I don't know him either. . . .

MARECHAL. No loss to you, I can tell you.

THE ACTOR *in a quick close-up.* We know! We know! We all know you scoff at your brother-in-law's . . . *sings* . . . Frère Jacques . . . Frère Jacques. . . . Dormez-vous?[9]

As he sings, he slaps BŒLDIEU *on the shoulder.* BŒLDIEU *puts on his monocle and looks at him rather contemptuously.*
[*Courtyard*]
French prisoners are walking about the camp yard. They are seen from above through the glass of a window in one of the camp buildings. THE ACTOR *goes by and turns towards the window: with the fingers of his left hand raised to his eye, he imitates seeing through a monocle. . . . In the courtyard,* ROSENTHAL *meets him.*

THE ACTOR. Hey, just a sec. . . .

ROSENTHAL. What is it?

THE ACTOR. Is the . . . *continuing to imitate* BŒLDIEU *crudely* . . . monocle around?

ROSENTHAL. No, I haven't seen him.

THE ACTOR. Because I just came from the canteen. You can tell him . . . his English-type chair . . . *gesticulates* . . . pie in the sky. . . .

ROSENTHAL *leaving.* All right, I'll tell him.

Camera tracks back from the window into medium shot of MARECHAL *sitting among the baths and showers of the wash room.*
[*Shower Room*]
He still has his arm in a sling and THE ENGINEER *is washing his feet. He looks out of the window.*

MARECHAL. Must say, he's nice, the chap with the tins . . . *pause* . . . He must be rolling in civvy street.[1]

THE ENGINEER. I'll say. . . . You know the big bankers Rosenthal? MARECHAL *nods.* Well, mate, they're his mum and dad. Cross my throat, they really are.

As he rubs MARECHAL's *feet to dry them,* MARECHAL *shivers.*

MARECHAL. Hey, that tickles . . . *pause* . . . And what does he do?

THE ENGINEER. He owns a big dress designer's.

MARECHAL. That so? Funny. . . . If I had the cash, I wouldn't be in that line. What about you, what do you do outside this lot?[2]

THE ENGINEER. Me, I'm an engineer for the ordnance survey.

MARECHAL *thinking.* Yes . . . on the ordnance survey.

Close-up of THE ENGINEER, *then a series of shots of the two men*

9. A nursery song; literally, "Brother James . . . are you sleeping?"   1. Rolling in money.
2. In civilian life.

as each speaks. Off, the sound of singing German soldiers.

THE ENGINEER *getting up:* Eh, between you and me, your mate with the monocle, can we trust him?

    MARECHAL *is surprised by the question and* THE ENGINEER *looks as if there were a plot in the air.*

MARECHAL. Well . . . he's a bit lah-di-dah . . . but all the same, he's a good bloke! Yes, you can trust him. . . .

THE ENGINEER *speaking softly.* All right, then. . . . *After a pause, he bends over to speak in* MARECHAL's *ear in medium close-up.* Because, you know . . . at night . . . we dig a hole.

MARECHAL *surprised.* A hole? What for?

THE ENGINEER *as if it were obvious.* To escape!

MARECHAL. Impossible! But what do you dig your hole with?

THE ENGINEER. With the coal shovel and old tins.[3] If my plans are right, we should come out at the other end in a garden, behind the buildings you can see over there . . . right out in open country.

MARECHAL. You can't get a move on with that.

THE ENGINEER. We've been working on it for two months. A few weeks more and we'll have it done.

MARECHAL *mocking.* Pooh. . . . The war'll be over by then.

THE ENGINEER. You think? You're under an illusion . . . besides, we like to get it ready just in case.

    Camera tracks back as THE ENGINEER *finishes wiping* MARE-CHAL's *feet.*

MARECHAL, *both interested and sceptical.* And where are you digging this hole of yours?

THE ENGINEER. You'll see this evening, after roll-call.

MARECHAL *wondering at the thought.* A hole? . . . So you're digging a hole! Like Monte Cristo.[4] I think that's very funny.

    THE ENGINEER *finishes his task and gets up.* MARECHAL *also jumps up.*

MARECHAL. Thanks, mate, you've done me a favour.

THE ENGINEER. Come off it, it's only natural, with your arm. *Camera tracks forward into close-up on* MARECHAL.

MARECHAL. Look. . . . If you don't mind, I'd like to ask you something.

THE ENGINEER *off.* Go on.

MARECHAL. In fact . . . what's it mean, the ordnance survey?

    [*The Prisoners' Room*]

    After dinner. Before lights out, the German N.C.O. ZACH *goes by calling the roll. Medium shot of him, in front of the door of*

---

3. Tin cans.   4. The hero of Alexandre Dumas's novel, *The Count of Monte Cristo*, who escaped from prison on Devil's Island.

the prisoners' room. He reads off the list he holds in his hand.
ZACH. Maréchal?
MARECHAL *off.* Present.
ZACH. Bœldieu?
BŒLDIEU *off.* You ought to say, Captain de Bœldieu.
ZACH. Rosenthal?
ROSENTHAL *off.* Hmmm. . . .
ZACH. Rémy?
THE ACTOR *off.* Here . . . we go round the mulberry bush!
ALL *off.* Good night, Arthur.

> ZACH *has folded up the list of prisoners. He scans the room one
> last time and goes out, closing the door behind him. Quick pan
> onto the prisoners who get up quickly from their beds and listen
> to the sound of* ZACH's *footsteps growing fainter. They all have
> solemn and wary looks on their faces. Each one gets ready in
> silence—this is obviously their routine every night at this hour—
> while* MARECHAL *on one side and* BŒLDIEU *on his bed look at
> them with surprise.* THE ACTOR *goes and barricades the door
> with a chair, then the others help him to screen the window
> with a blanket.*

THE ENGINEER. Whose turn is it?
THE ACTOR. It's mine.

> THE ENGINEER *and* THE TEACHER *go to a corner of the room.
> Tilt on them as they pull a bed aside and lift the floorboards,
> revealing a hole.*
> *Cut back to* THE ACTOR *as he gets ready. He ties a string round
> his wrist. Cut to the other end of the string tied round an old
> tin which somebody else is balancing on a shelf.*

MARECHAL *coming closer.* What's that?

> *As he speaks, he points to another empty tin which* THE ACTOR
> *is shoving into his pocket. On the side, there are more tins tied
> together.*

THE ACTOR. It's to get the earth out.
MARECHAL. And this string?
THE ACTOR. If I'm stifling, I pull it . . . and the tin falls over. It's the
    alarm signal. Then the lads pull me out by the feet . . . feet . . .
    feet . . . *sings* . . . marching up and down again! . . . *pause* . . .
    Right. Off I go. . . . To play the mole . . . ecule!

> *Pan to* BŒLDIEU *near* THE ENGINEER. BŒLDIEU *is holding some
> cards and seems to be playing patience.*[5]

BŒLDIEU. Will it hold, your tunnel?
THE ENGINEER. It's got the right props, wood we've borrowed from
    the theatre.

---

5. Solitaire.

BŒLDIEU. What do you do about the earth?

THE ENGINEER. We began by packing it under the floorboards, but now it's full up. You couldn't stick a pin in there. So now we put the earth in bags and take it for a walk with us.

> *Pan to* THE ACTOR *who is ready for his job underground and slides on his belly into the tunnel. He soon vanishes completely, letting the string trail after him. A few seconds later, the string stops moving and lies loosely along the edge of the wall.*
>
> *Cut inside the hole where* THE ACTOR *is face to face with his job. He sighs and attacks the earth.*
>
> *Cut back to the men leaning over the hole. They straighten up again, sighing. Still solemn, they smile as they silently remember* THE ACTOR's *bad jokes.*
>
> *Pan towards* MARECHAL *who is acting as look-out. Suddenly he seems worried and makes a gesture as if he wants the others to be quiet.*

MARECHAL *in a very low voice, troubled.* Didn't you hear anything?

THE TEACHER *coming closer.* No.

MARECHAL. I heard something all right.

> *The others all listen and seem to indicate that* MARECHAL *is dreaming.*

MARECHAL. I tell you, I did. . . . *pause* . . . There, there it is again. . . .

THE ENGINEER *intrigued.* We'll send somebody out to scout around. *To* THE TEACHER. Hey you, with that babyface of yours . . . you go and see what's up.

THE TEACHER: I'll say I'm going to the lavatory.

> THE ENGINEER *pushes* THE TEACHER *towards the door. Cut to* THE ACTOR *underground. He is digging and breathing with difficulty near his candle.*
>
> [*Courtyard: Night*]
>
> *It is night as* THE TEACHER *nervously leaves the barracks and reaches the yard. He meets two German stretcher-bearers carrying a man and watches them in surprise, while the N.C.O.* ZACH *comes up to him on sentry duty with his gun at the ready.* THE TEACHER *pretends to be completely at ease.*

THE TEACHER. Arthur, I mean, what happened just now?

ZACH. It's someone who tried to escape. We caught up with him in the gardens behind the buildings . . . so we shot him down.

THE TEACHER *worried.* Behind the buildings? Is he . . . dead?

ZACH. I think so . . . *He begins to shout at* THE TEACHER . . . You, what are you doing out here?

THE TEACHER *looking stupid.* Me? I'm off to the lavatory.

> *He goes off.*

Cut to THE ACTOR, *who drops his tool and begins to suffocate more and more and pulls the string.*

[*Prisoners' Room*]

Close-up of the tin on the shelf. It falls onto a bed without a sound. Pan onto the group of prisoners at the window, anxiously waiting for THE TEACHER *to come back. They are so absorbed they do not notice the fall of the tin for the alarm.*

Cut to the door as it opens. THE TEACHER *comes in and the others rush over to him.*

THE ENGINEER. Well, what happened?

THE TEACHER *whispering.* Some one tried to escape. I don't now how. . . . They killed him . . . in the gardens . . . behind the buildings!

Dead silence. They are all very upset by the news. Suddenly, THE TEACHER *starts; he has just noticed that the tin for the alarm has fallen on the bed.*

THE TEACHER. The alarm!

Camera shoots from above as they rush over to the hole and struggle to get THE ACTOR *out.*

Cut to MARECHAL *near them, embarrassed not to be able to help because of his arm. Cut back to all who are pulling on the rope. . . .* THE ACTOR'S *feet appear. He is pulled out of the hole and carried over to a bed, where he gasps for breath.*

THE TEACHER. Does it hurt?

THE ACTOR *goes on gasping and shakes his head, while* ROSENTHAL *comes over with a bottle in his hand and puts it to* THE ACTOR'S *lips.*

ROSENTHAL. Drink some of this, old chap . . . drop of brandy!

THE TEACHER. It's the one from Fouquet's!

THE ACTOR *begins to stir on the bed as he feels better. He turns to* ROSENTHAL, *takes the bottle of brandy, has a swig, then sighs.*

THE ACTOR *singing.* I had a little drop about an hour ago. . . . Don't break it!

He drinks some more. Pan to BŒLDIEU, THE ENGINEER, *and* MARECHAL *standing; they sigh and look at each other with relief.*

BŒLDIEU. Whose turn is it tomorrow?

THE ENGINEER. Yours then, Captain, if you'd really care to!

BŒLDIEU. I'd be delighted. People have told me that crawling is simply marvellous as exercise.

[*Courtyard*]

Next morning. Mail is delivered at this time. Slight tilt up at the Feldwebel KRANTZ *guarding the yard. Behind him stands a German soldier.*

KRANTZ. I remind you that it is strictly forbidden to have clothes sent to you which are not military dress.

Cut to the yard. Many prisoners stand in groups, waiting for the mail to be delivered. Medium shot of a group made up from MARECHAL, BŒLDIEU, THE TEACHER *and* THE ENGINEER.

MARECHAL *to* ROSENTHAL. Anything new?

ROSENTHAL *without looking up.* A letter from my aunt in Bordeaux. She says there's an incredible crowd down there.

THE ENGINEER *leafing through the paper.* If I were them, I'd watch it. The Frankfurt Gazette announces a fantastic advance.

MARECHAL *sceptically.* Oh, right! They haven't even run up any flags. . . . They're not ringing the bells. . . . It can't be much!

BŒLDIEU *putting on his monocle.* Gentlemen, shall we proceed to more important matters?

THE OTHERS. Yes . . . yes, of course!

ROSENTHAL. Yes, but not all at the same time.

They split up. A sideways tracking shot follows THE TEACHER *and* MARECHAL. . . . THE ACTOR *catches up with them from behind, whistling between his teeth.*

THE TEACHER. I disapprove of this mania for exaggeration in the German news items.

MARECHAL *gruffly.* Well . . . what about our papers? Remember, right at the start, how the Russian steam-roller was going to crush them?

Shock cut[6] to THE ACTOR *and* THE ENGINEER *reaching a corner of the yard set aside for gardening. They stop in front of a dug patch of earth, but a sudden sound of singing makes them turn their heads. Pan to what they see: a group of young German conscripts marching off to squad drill.*

Cut back to THE ACTOR *and* THE ENGINEER, *as they hold a spade and a shovel and continue their previous conversation.*

THE ENGINEER. And what about famous General Winter, the one who was going to kill off all the bad Jerries[7] with bronchitis and brace up the Allies?

THE ACTOR *bantering.* And what about Turpinite? Remember Turpinite? With a little bottle as . . . big . . . as a radish, we were going to kill off a whole army corps. They even tried it out on a flock of sheep!

THE TEACHER passes near them. As he walks, he shakes out the earth from under his greatcoat.

THE TEACHER. Pity they didn't stop right there with the sheep!

While THE ACTOR *watches out for the sentry who is standing beyond them with his back turned,* THE TEACHER *continues shaking the earth out of his coat, while* THE ENGINEER *conscien-*

---

6. Sudden camera shot.   7. A nickname for Germans. *Turpinite* recalls World War I experiments with poison gas (e.g., mustard gas), which as often as not blew back in the faces of the users.

*tiously pats the fallen earth into place with his shovel. They
sing a little tune. After* THE TEACHER *has finished, he walks off
and his place is taken by the relaxed* MARECHAL, *who also begins
to get rid of the earth in his clothing.*

MARECHAL *pretending to be interested.* Well then? What are you
planting here?

THE ENGINEER *getting up.* Dandelions, my boy. Yes, I dream of making
myself a dandelion salad with lard.

MARECHAL.. Go on! . . . The war'll be over before your dandelions
even poke their heads out.

    BŒLDIEU, *full of dignity, comes up to them. Cautiously, he
takes a bag of earth from below his armpit and empties it. Then
he folds up the bag meticulously, taking care not to get his
gloves too dirty.*

BŒLDIEU *haughtily.* If we go on with this odd business, we'll end up
with hands like navvies.[8]

    As he finishes folding up his bag, ROSENTHAL *comes up and
empties his bag, only more discreetly. Quick pan to a French
prisoner, soldier* DRYANT, *who comes running up to them.*

DRYANT. Oy, oy! Rosenthal! . . . The crates are here.

ROSENTHAL *delighted.* The costumes?

DRYANT. Yes . . . three crates, sent by your firm. We've taken them
to the theatre.

ROSENTHAL *to the others.* Let's go there, boys. There must be one
crate full of women's clothes . . . real ones! . . . *He leads the
others off* . . . Are you coming, Captain?

    THE ACTOR *is already on his way to the buildings: he hums and
he walks waggling his hips and mincing crudely like a woman.*
BŒLDIEU *does not move.*

BŒLDIEU. No thank you. My competence in theatrical matters is
very slight indeed. Besides, I have something else to do. . . .

    They all go off except for MARECHAL *and* BŒLDIEU *who remain
standing face to face.*

MARECHAL *ironically.* A little game of patience, aren't I right?

BŒLDIEU. Exactly . . . I happen to be a realist. . . . *He takes the
opposite direction then turns round.* I'll see you later.

MARECHAL.. See you later! *He laughs mockingly.*

    [*Dance Hall*]

    *Camera begins on English prisoners who are in a line on the
stage of the entertainment hall, dancing and singing together
'Tipperary'.[9] Camera tracks back slightly to show the whole
rehearsal; everyone wears either a soldier's or an officer's uniform. Circular pan round the hall past the orchestra and past*

8. Ditchdiggers.   9. Sentimental song about separation ("It's a long way to Tipperary") popular
during World War I.

*some groups busily making sets; pan ends on a German sentry
who is keeping close watch on* ROSENTHAL *and his friends, as he
undoes the crates which have just arrived. These crates contain
dresses, silk stockings, every sort of feminine finery. The sentry
examines a corset.*

THE ACTOR *to the sentry.* Well, Arthur, found anything?

THE SENTRY *in a strong German accent.* No, I have found nothing.
*The sentry takes a last look, about turns and goes off. Camera
follows him to the door.* [*In the complete version, there is a cut
to the sentry leaving the room and saying good-night in French.*
THE ACTOR *wearing the hat of a marquis replies with the rest,
but he says goodnight in German with a strong Parisian accent.*]

VOICES *off.* Good-bye. . . . Bye for now, Arthur!
Cut back to the group leaning avidly over the crates. ROSENTHAL
waves an evening gown in the air and holds it on himself.

ROSENTHAL. Ah! These things have to be handled with kid gloves
. . . and your eyes shut.
*All are disturbed at the sight of this dress which they look at
with great intensity.*

MARECHAL. Real dresses. . . .

THE TEACHER. Look how short it is. Like a dress for a little girl.

MARECHAL *shrugging.* Eh, didn't you know? All the girls are wearing
short dresses now . . . *looking at the dress again and sighing . . .*
My! . . .

ROSENTHAL *ecstatically.* Just below the knee!

THE ACTOR. My old lady wrote and told me, but I didn't believe it.

MARECHAL. Hey, you! Put one on so we can see what it looks like. . . .
ROSENTHAL *reacts strongly and stops* THE ACTOR.

ROSENTHAL. No, not him. . . . He hasn't shaved properly. What
about you, Maisonneuve, with your angel face? . . .

MAISONNEUVE. If you think that's funny. . . .
MAISONNEUVE *goes off with the dress on his arm.*

MARECHAL. It isn't only their dresses that are short. They've cut off
their hair too!
Cut to concentrate on MARECHAL, THE ACTOR, *and* THE TEACHER.

THE ACTOR *astounded.* You don't say. . . . It must be like going to
bed with a boy!

THE TEACHER. Really, when we aren't around to keep an eye on
them, women go and do such foolish things. When I think of my
wife, all these new-fangled things worry me. . . .

AN N.C.O., AN AGEING PROFESSIONAL SOLDIER. Well, I'm sure my
wife hasn't had her hair cut off. . . . Bah, all that rot's only good
for tarts!
They laugh while ROSENTHAL *takes some women's shoes out of
the crate.*

THE ENGINEER. Oh, shit . . . shoes!

ROSENTHAL *happily.* We'd forgotten how small they were.

> ROSENTHAL *goes on digging into the crate and pulls out some stockings.*

THE ENGINEER *overcome.* Stockings!

THE ACTOR *simultaneously.* Hey . . . stockings! Stockings!

THE TEACHER, *taking a stocking.* Silk! I've never felt silk like that before. . . .

> *Quick cut to another soldier gaping at a pair of black stockings. Slight pan to the soldier* MAISONNEUVE *who appears dressed as a woman—skirt and top—and also wearing a wig. All the men turn to look at him and fall silent, curiously disturbed. How many memories and hopes are there. . . .* MAISONNEUVE *feels uneasy to see their intense looks on him.*

MARECHAL, *with forced laughter.* Don't you think it's funny?

MAISONNEUVE. Funny?

ROSENTHAL. Yes, it's funny. . . .

MARECHAL, *very sane and a little sad.* It's really funny. . . . You look like a real girl.

> *They fall into a heavy silence again. . . . They cannot find anything to say as they look at this soldier in a woman's dress. Very slow pan across the soldier's faces staring at* MAISONNEUVE *in absolute silence. Pan ends on the transvestite who has come forward to the middle of the hall and who cannot help making a few feminine gestures.*

VOICES *off.* Yes. . . . it's funny!

> [*Courtyard*]
>
> *The barracks entrance. The main gate opens and a large cart comes out, pulled by two horses and driven by a German soldier. The cart seems loaded with crudely made coffins. As it goes by, camera stays on the civilians who have followed the cart up to this point. Cut to two old grandmothers dressed in black, seen slightly from below in medium close-up. One of the old women sighs, then speaks in German.*

OLD WOMAN. Poor lads!

> *Cut to the young recruits drilling in the yard. Orders in German are heard off:* Attention! Eyes front! At ease! *The recruits run off in step.*
>
> [*Theater Wing*]
>
> *In an annex of the entertainment hall which* ROSENTHAL *and his friends have converted into a sewing workshop, they are cutting out pieces of cloth and dresses to make stage costumes for the performance. Camera tilts onto the table where they are cutting and sewing. In the background,* MARECHAL *is seen standing*

near the window, not participating in these feverish and femi-
nine activities. At the window, BŒLDIEU *stands and looks out.*
Cut to a close-up of his expression of interest in the scene out-
side—the young recruits at drill. Cut back to the group shot,
then cut back again to the close-up of BŒLDIEU, *as he looks out*
of the window, turns to THE ACTOR *who is singing and the oth-*
ers who are sewing, and then turns back to the window with the
words:

BŒLIEU. On one side, children playing at soldiers. On the other,
   soldiers playing at children. [It doesn't really round things off!]
THE TEACHER *still sewing.* I'd like to know what's going on back home.
THE ENGINEER. Still no news?
THE TEACHER *mournfully.* Nothing.
THE ACTOR *cheerfully.* I couldn't care less what my old lady's up to.
   . . . What makes me want to slope off is, it's such a bloody bore.
   Ah, the Trocadero![1] . . . Cadet Rousselle, and la . . . la . . . la
   . . . *he hums.* . . .
ROSENTHAL *interrupting.* In other words, you want to escape for the
   fun of it. . . .
THE ACTOR *with silly pleasure.* That's it!
THE ENGINEER *in close-up.* With me, it's just being contrary. Ever
   since they've stopped me fighting, I've been dying to get back and
   fight.

   Pan towards BŒLDIEU *and* MARECHAL, *seen in medium shot.*

MARECHAL *as though talking to himself.* I just want to do like everyone else . . . *more loudly.* . . . Besides, it gets me down to be
   here while the others are all getting knocked off!
BŒLDIEU *turning to him.* As far as I'm concerned, the question does
   not come up. *Medium close-up of him.* What is the purpose of a
   golf course? To play golf. A tennis court? To play tennis. Well, a
   prison camp is there to escape from. . . . What do you think,
   Rosenthal? You're a sportsman.
[ROSENTHAL. I want to escape so I can go on fighting for my country.]
THE ACTOR. [Your country?] He's no sportsman! Why, he was born
   in Jerusalem!

   In the medium shot of the group, THE ACTOR *stands between*
   BŒLDIEU *and* ROSENTHAL, *who sits in the foreground with his*
   back to both of them, facing camera with his head apparently
   lowered over his work. He looks down in the mouth, then he
   unenthusiastically puts on the panache[2] of BŒLDIEU *to answer*
   back rather timidly.

1. Well-known Parisian entertainment hall, rebuilt in 1937 as the Palais de Chaillot.
2. Discouraged by the Actor's anti-Semitic implication that—as a Jew—he cannot be a French
patriot, Rosenthal tries to conceal his hurt by imitating Boeldieu's nonchalant self-confidence.

ROSENTHAL. Excuse me, I was born in Vienna, capital of Austria. My mother was Danish, my father Polish, both naturalized citizens of France.

MARECHAL *in a new shot.* Old Breton lords and ladies, eh?

ROSENTHAL *in a new shot.* Perhaps! . . . *still not looking at them* . . . But the rest of you, Frenchmen from way back, you don't own a hundred square metres of your country. Well, the Rosenthals in thirty-five years have found how to get hold of three historic castles with shoots, lakes, fields, orchards, rabbit warrens, fishing rights, pheasants, stud farms . . . and three picture galleries full of ancestors, every one guaranteed! ROSENTHAL *has obviously reached the end of his tether; he turns on the rest of them.* If you think *that* isn't worth escaping for, to go and defend!

BŒLDIEU *lookng surprised.* I must say, I had never thought of patriotism from that angle. How odd!

MARECHAL. Rabbit warrens! Fishing rights! Pheasants! Those flunkies of yours, I bet they scoff a lot of game.

> *Cut to a shot from above of* THE TEACHER; *he has his pipe in his mouth and tries to follow the conversation. A hand pulls off the stage wig which he has been wearing.*

THE TEACHER *chewing his pipe.* I got into action a funny way. Believe it or not, I got into the army because I'm a vegetarian!

> *Cut to the surprised* MARECHAL *and* BŒLDIEU.

MARECHAL. Vegetarian?

THE TEACHER *in close-up.* I'm not joking. My brother and I both had something wrong with our stomachs. So then the doctor told us . . . he told my parents first, of course: 'If you eat meat, you're done for.' *Hands put a clown's ruff round his neck.* Well, I became a vegetarian . . . and I got better. My brother went on eating meat . . . he became very ill . . . He wasn't taken for the army.

> *While he finishes speaking, there is the sound of the boots of German soldiers, marching in step.* BŒLDIEU *bows a little towards* THE TEACHER.

BŒLDIEU. I can see from your decorations . . . being a vegetarian has not stopped you from doing your duty.

THE TEACHER *nodding.* Nor did it stop my wife from sleeping with somebody else!

> *Suddenly a military band starts up: fifes, big drums, trombones. The heavy marching pace of the conscripts blends in with the sound of martial music.* BŒLDIEU *goes back to the window, followed by all the others. Camera tracks back to frame them all as they watch the parade which is invisible.* THE ACTOR, *who is short, lifts himself onto the shoulders of* THE ENGINEER. *Pan in close-up from face to face during the following dialogue, as each watches the march past.*

THE ENGINEER. I must say, it's a good show!

BŒLDIEU *coldly*. I hate fifes.

THE TEACHER: Whatever they say, it really stirs you up!

MARECHAL *with the pan ending on his face*. What stirs you, mate, isn't the music . . . nor the instruments. . . . It's the noise. . . . [The sound of the march, just like in every army.]

> *The sound of marching grows louder. Dissolve to another shot of the group.* THE ACTOR, *still resting on* THE ENGINEER's *shoulders, turns and sees smoke in the room. Camera tracks in front of him as he dashes over to the ironing board.*

THE ACTOR. Blast! Burning. . . . *He picks up the hot iron from his trousers, which now have a hole in them. Furious, he waves the iron in the air.* With all your fancy chat and all, my trousers are done for!

> *Cut to close-up of the ironing board marked by the hot iron.* THE ACTOR *lifts up the burned trousers to show them to everybody and begins to dance and sing. Outside, the young German recruits are marching past. Resume on* THE ACTOR, *who walks backwards as he sings until he bumps into the door which opens. In comes a sentry who takes a look round the room, then turns towards* THE ACTOR. *Seeing them all more or less dressed as women, and* THE ACTOR *now humming to himself, he taps his forehead with his finger and leaves the room.*
> [*Courtyard: Night*]
> *Night in the yard. Start on a close-up of a poster in German and French, which has just been put up by a feldwebel. In French, the headline reads:*

Official Communiqué   General Headquarters
                                              20 February, 1916

DOUAUMONT IS CAPTURED

> *This is followed by a text that is hardly readable. All the bells of the town nearby start pealing wildly.*
> *Pan towards a lighted window and track forwards to show German officers celebrating the victory in their mess. They are drinking, singing, and playing the guitar. One of them rises, singing gaily, and leaves the room. Camera follows him: after a wave to the others, he closes the door. As he walks in the cold night air, he goes on singing, rubbing his hands together. Pan after him briefly in the yard, then tilt up one of the walls of the camp to stop on a window, where the French prisoners are staring in dismay at the joy and the celebrations. Camera tracks*

towards them; the group includes THE ACTOR, BŒLDIEU, MARE-
CHAL, THE ENGINEER, THE TEACHER, *and* ROSENTHAL, *as they*
look down into the yard. Suddenly, THE ACTOR, *speaking gravely,*
breaks the silence.

THE ACTOR. With all that, are we still going to put on our show?

MARECHAL. And how! More so now than ever! I'd even suggest we
invite, for once, the camp commandant and all his officers, just
to show them our morale's all right.

THE TEACHER. Things are going badly, if they've taken Douaumont. . . .

MARECHAL *annoyed.* Who's saying no to that? All the more reason
not to cave in.

BŒLDIEU *turning to* MARECHAL. For once I agree with you, Maréchal. I may not participate in your theatrical ventures, but allow
me to congratulate you all the same. . . . Good show!

[*German Soldiers' Canteen*]
Pan past German soldiers singing and toasting the victory in
their canteen. One of them is playing the guitar very loudly.
[*Dance Hall*]
The wooden barracks hall has been turned into a theatre for the
show. Medium shot of THE ACTOR *on stage. He is wearing tails;*
the suit is a little too large for him, so that the actual tails of the
coat dangle too low. Even though his costume does not fit, he
sings and makes gestures with great gusto.

THE ACTOR *singing.* Si tu veux faire mon bonheur, Marguerite! . . .
Marguerite! . . .[3]

Camera stays on THE ACTOR *singing and moving about on stage,*
as he takes the carnation from his buttonhole sometimes to sniff
it voluptuously, and as he tries to make everybody join in the
chorus. Then camera tracks back on a crane to show the whole
crowded hall. Prisoners from all the camp are there. In the front
row, satisfied German officers. At the back, a few armed sen-
tries stand, as if at the back of a music hall.
Cut back to a close-up of THE ACTOR, *singing and miming another*
verse of the song. A shot of him from the rear shows the audi-
ence laughing. Cut back to him as he makes the audience take
up the refrain. [*The original script added—In the hall, the men*
laugh and temporarily seem to forget their troubles and their
imprisonment. THE ACTOR *is pretty bad and the song he sings is*
vulgar. But he is so much a Parisian that all the Frenchmen are
overcome by the number. As for the German officers, they stay
rather stiff and scornful, hardly open to this little song from
Paris.]

3. Popular song: "If you want to make me happy, Marguerite . . ." and, later, "give me your
heart."

THE ACTOR *still singing.* Si tu veux faire mon bonheur, Margueite, donne-moi ton coeur!

> *Everyone joins in the chorus now, even the Germans, caught up in the enthusiasm of the audience. All laugh out loud, except the German officers, who clap politely. Cut back to* THE ACTOR *on stage, as he wriggles with pleasure while he acknowledges the loud applause.*
>
> *The curtain closes. Cut to the rudimentary orchestra, then cut back to the stage as the curtain rises again.* THE ACTOR *bows once more to a loud crash of music, then goes back-stage to lift a flap and usher in the 'girls.' These come on stage, dancing a sort of can-can. The 'girls' are five English prisoners, dressed in wigs, short dresses, jewels, and feathers. They dance and mince about in a poor imitation of women's airs and graces. They are a huge success! In comes the 'star,' fanning himself with a lace fan and going up to the footlights to dance the finale to 'Tipperary' and then to a song like 'Frou-Frou.' Cut to a pan across the whole audience joining in the chorus, then back to* THE ACTOR *reappearing on stage, sitting on a cardboard motor-car, and also singing.*
>
> *Cut to the wings, where* ROSENTHAL *opens a newspaper; he is very surprised, and makes a sign to* MARECHAL *and* THE ENGINEER.
>
> *Cut back to the stage. Everyone is singing along with the 'girls.' All are having a good time . . . when* MARECHAL, *dressed normally, suddenly bursts onto the scene, pushing the 'girls' aside. He is overcome; he raises his arms to get silence, the newspaper in his hand.*

MARECHAL. Stop! Stop!

> *The orchestra stops playing. Everybody falls silent.* MARECHAL *yells in the total hush.*

MARECHAL. We've recaptured Douaumont! . . . It's the boche[4] news which says it!

> *For a few seconds, everybody in the audience is frozen. Then the orchestra strikes up 'The Marseillaise.' Everyone bursts into song and gets up at the same instant. The English 'girls' pull off their wigs and lead the anthem in French with strong English accents. Pan round the hall at all the prisoners singing in their emotion, while the German officers rise and leave hastily. Pan after the officers as they go out, then return to the men happily chanting in the hall.*
>
> *Dissolve to a shot of German soldiers outside, as they run towards a building.*

---

4. German.

[*Cellar: Night*]

There is the sound of boots advancing in the dark; they seem to be walking down the steps that led to the detention cells.

[*Prison Cell*]

MARECHAL *is sitting on a prison bed, wrapped up in his army greatcoat. He is violently scratching away at the damp slimy wall with a spoon; the cell itself is dark and bare, having a bed, a blanket, and a door with a spy-hole in it that lets in a sparse light. Pan towards the door as it opens. In comes the sentry* ZACH *to investigate the noise that* MARECHAL *is making.* MARECHAL *turns wearily towards* ZACH *and says nothing, but his face is angry.* ZACH *stares at him, surprised and bewildered.*

ZACH *in German.* What are you doing there?

MARECHAL *stupidly.* There? A hole. . . . Yes, yes, yes! I'm digging a hole to escape! *He shouts the last word.*

ZACH *leans further forwards to look, and* MARECHAL *takes the opportunity to leap up, shove* ZACH *onto the ground and run out of the door, which he slams behind him. Camera stays on the door, while the sound of struggling is heard on its far side.*

MARECHAL *yelling off.* Keep your bloody hands off! Let me bloody be! Bloody . . . be!

The door opens again. Three soldiers carry in the half-conscious MARECHAL *and lay him out on the bed. Camera tracks in and tilts down on a close-up of* MARECHAL.

[*Courtyard*]

The shadow of a soldier falls on a poster freshly stuck to a wall in the yard. The poster reads:

DOUAUMONT RECAPTURED BY GERMAN TROOPS

German forces once again occupy the fortress of Douaumont after a battle which caused heavy losses to the enemy. We have taken 3,700 prisoners. The fortress is now safely in German hands.

Camera tracks backwards to show, from the rear, some French prisoners and German sentries or soldiers reading the poster which is in both the languages.

THE TEACHER. There can't be much of it left.

A PRISONER. Oh, you've seen it? It's terrible. Who'd have thought so?

A SENTRY *in German.* They don't say how many got killed taking it. . . .

In fact, the news by now hardly affects anyone. If the Germans

*take Douaumont or the French retake it, the war still goes
on. . . .*
[*Prison Cell*]
Close-up from above of a mess-tin full of soup, then pan up to
MARECHAL *still in his cell. He is sitting down, his back against
the wall, dirty, unshaven, glassy-eyed. Sound of a key in the
lock. He does not move. Pan to the door as it opens and admits
an* OLD GERMAN SOLDIER, *who goes over to* MARECHAL. *A medium
shot shows him looking at the untouched soup, shaking his head
sadly, and slapping* MARECHAL *on the shoulder.*

THE OLD SOLDIER *in German.* Not feeling well today? Not hungry?

MARECHAL, *not understanding and shutting him up by shouting.* Stuff
it, d'you hear?

THE OLD SOLDIER *moves away, but* MARECHAL *overcome by
depression and rage, yells:*

MARECHAL. I'm fed up, d'you hear. . . . Fed up! I want to see daylight, for god's sake! I want to see the light! Shit to this hole! I
want to see the light, hear somebody speaking French . . . French,
d'you get me, speaking French!

THE OLD SOLDIER, *feeling sorry for* MARECHAL *and sensing that
the crisis is nearly over, sits down beside him. He would very
much like to do something for the Frenchman. . . . He looks
about in his pockets and takes out three cigarettes. Without
speaking, he offers them to* MARECHAL *who refuses them. He
puts the cigarettes down next to* MARECHAL *and goes on searching his own pockets, this time pulling out a mouth-organ[5] to
offer to* MARECHAL.

[MARECHAL. You want to make a bloody fool out of me?]

MARECHAL *turns towards the wall.* THE OLD SOLDIER, *very sorry
for him, gets up and leaves behind the cigarettes and the mouth-
organ. Camera follows* THE OLD SOLDIER *as he leaves the cell.*
[*Corridor*]
THE OLD SOLDIER *triple-locks the door of the cell, then noiselessly lifts the hatch over the peep-hole in the door to look inside.*
MARECHAL *picks up the mouth-organ in the end, lifts it to his
lips, plays it.*
Cut back to THE OLD SOLDIER. *He is satisfied and shuts up the
peep-hole and walks down the corridor, humming 'Frou-Frou.'
He meets a guard.*

THE GUARD *in German.* Why did he shout like that?

THE OLD SOLDIER *in German.* Because the war is lasting too long.

[*Prisoner's Room*]
Medium shot of THE ENGINEER, THE TEACHER *and* THE ACTOR

5. Harmonica.

who are smoking and talking softly together in their room.

THE ENGINEER. If I calculated correctly, we'll be under the garden wall in four days' time. . . . Think of all those sacks of earth!

THE TEACHER. Now there's a chance of getting away and back to France, I'm worried about what's waiting for me back home.

THE ACTOR. Ah, there's more than one woman in the world.

THE TEACHER. There's only one for me.

THE ACTOR *as though stating the obvious.* That's why she sleeps around!

Pan towards the seated ROSENTHAL.

ROSENTHAL *sadly.* As for me, I can't bear to think we'll be leaving Maréchal behind.

Pan ends on BŒLDIEU *who is playing patience. He turns his head towards* ROSENTHAL, *takes out his monocle, and still keeps a card in his hand.*

BŒLDIEU. I too find it a bit depressing. It's really too bad, but that's war. . . . Feelings have nothing to do with it.

Quick pan to the door as it opens. MARECHAL *stands in the doorway with a soldier. He has just come out of the detention cell; he needs a shave, a wash, a comb; he is exhausted and dazzled by the daylight.* BŒLDIEU *dashes forward to greet him. Shot of the two men face to face.*

BŒLDIEU. Delighted to see you again, old chap.

All the others surround MARECHAL *to hold him up, for he is about to fall. They make him sit down.*

ROSENTHAL *fussing over* MARECHAL. Do you want to rest? Do you want something to drink?

MARECHAL *in a whisper.* I want to eat. . . . I want to eat. . . . I'm hungry.

Medium close-up of ROSENTHAL *hastily opening a tin and turning his head away to hide the fact that he is wiping a tear off his cheek.*

THE ACTOR *off.* Hey, come and sit here, [you'll be better off.] Rosenthal's getting some grub ready for you!

Dissolve to the same place, a few days later. The prisoners seem nervous and pace up and down the room. Clearly, tonight is the night they are going to try and escape through the tunnel which they have dug with such effort.

MARECHAL. What's the time?

ROSENTHAL. Eleven o'clock.

MARECHAL. Time's pretty fast today.

THE ACTOR *acting.* Yes, but this evening, auf wiedersehen![6]

THE ENGINEER. Rendez-vous in Amsterdam, then!

Medium close-up of THE TEACHER *and* THE ACTOR.

---

6. "Farewell! Till we meet again" (German).

THE TEACHER. I've always wanted to visit Holland because of the tulips.

THE ACTOR. I prefer their cheese. Ah, Dutch cheese! . . . *Pause.* Don't you like Dutch cheese?

THE TEACHER. Yes, but tulips are pretty. They say there are whole fields of them, as far as the eye can see.

Pan to BŒLDIEU *playing patience.*

BŒLDIEU *turning to* THE TEACHER: Really, my dear fellow, you have the taste of a parlour-maid.

MARECHAL, *who is beside the door, sees* ZACH *enter. Shot first shows the two men, then the others clustering around.*

ZACH *in his strongly-accented French.* General roll-call at three o'clock. All officers are changing camps. Get your kits ready.

The prisoners stare at each other, dismayed, as ZACH *leaves the room, closing the door behind him.*

[*Courtyard: Afternoon*]

Pan across English officers grouped in one corner of the yard, then across ranks of French officers looking at them. Among the French are MARECHAL, THE ACTOR, THE ENGINEER, ROSENTHAL *and* BŒLDIEU. *They have just answered roll-call in the afternoon and are standing there with their kits, ready to leave.*

THE GERMAN OFFICER *in his strong accent.* Gentlemen, I wish you a pleasant journey and I hope you will see your wives again soon.

He salutes them, and the little squad of men begin to march away, waving to ZACH *as they pass by.*

THE ACTOR: Bye bye, Arthur!

GERMAN OFFICERS' VOICES *in poor English.* English officers, 'shun! . . . English officers!

BŒLDIEU. Perhaps we ought to warn them.

MARECHAL. What about?

THE ACTOR. 'Bout the tunnel, what else? That it's all ready for them.

When the two squads pass each other, ROSENTHAL *and* THE ACTOR *try to get closer to the English.*

THE GERMAN OFFICER *pushing them back.* Back to your ranks!

Cut to the English marching by. The suitcase of one of them springs open, its contents fall to the ground. Tilt down as the English officer bends, puts down his tennis racket, and begins putting back his things in his case.

Cut to MARECHAL *who profits from this little mix-up to worm his way to the English officer's side, as if to help him repack his case.*

MARECHAL *whispering in French.* Colonel. . . . Dans la chambrée numero sept.[7]

THE ENGLISHMAN. It's really too kind of you. . . .

7. Maréchal's lines: "Colonel . . . In room number seven." "Let me speak . . . We dug a hole . . . Warn your pals." "You don't speak French?" "Hole . . . a hole . . . in the floor . . ."

MARECHAL. Laisse-moi parler. . . . Il y a un trou creusé. . . . Préviens les copains.

THE ENGLISHMAN. I'm sorry, I don't understand French.

MARECHAL. Vous ne comprenez pas le français?

THE ENGLISHMAN. Thank you . . . thank you. . . .

MARECHAL, *annoyed and making signs.* Trou . . . un trou . . . dans le plancher. . . .

THE ENGLISHMAN *straightening up again.* Bon voyage!

A feldwebel comes up and puts an end to this conversation, roughly pushing MARECHAL *back to his squad.*

THE FELDWEBEL. Nicht aus der Reihe treten![8]

(The English and the French are allies in the war, but the English—who are going to be sleeping in the quarters vacated by the French—will never know about the tunnel beneath the floorboards.)

[*German Countryside*]

Through the window of a train compartment, the flat, mournful, desolate countryside moves by. The train speeds through a station without stopping, then rolls on past more countryside. When the train seems to be slowing down, a large sign for a prison camp appears and stays on screen:

KRIEGSGEFANGENEN	LAGER No 2
ALSHEIM	
OFFIZIERSLAGER	C. K. V

Dissolve to more shots of countryside seen from a moving train for a few moments. Then the train slows again and another sign appears and stays on screen:

KRIEGSGEFANGENEN	LAGER No 9
SENTE	
OFFIZIERSLAGER	C. K. XI

Slow dissolve to yet more countryside seen from a moving train. Finally the train begins to slow down, as the officers move from camp to camp.

Night is falling. In the distance, a great fortress perches like an eagle's nest on sheer slopes. The walls are in massive grey stone,

---

8. "Don't step out of line!" (German).

very thick; above them, a fortified keep rises; above it, the impe-
rial German flag.
The train halts in front of yet another sign:

KRIEGSGEFANGENEN   LAGER No 14
            WINTERSBORN
OFFIZIERSLAGER   B.G.K. III

[Commandant's Room]
Camera starts on a huge wooden crucifix, then pans down to its
base to show an altar. On this altar is a framed photograph of
Kaiser William II. Pan in close-up round the room to show the
personal possessions of its occupant—the camp commandant,
who now lives in the old chapel of the fortress. (He is VON
RAUFFENSTEIN, *who shot down* MARECHAL *and* BŒLDIEU *and acted*
as their host in the German officers' mess at the front. The
architecture, stained-glass windows, and carved stone of this
curious room show its original purpose. The camp-bed of the
officer, his collection of riding crops and spurs, his weapons,
his valuable china and silverware look odd in this room where
the mass was once said. . . . VON RAUFFENSTEIN's *plane has*
gone down in flames. He now wears a steel corset and moves
with difficulty. He walks stiffly, like a puppet. He could have
left the army, especially as he is an officer of the old school and
despises the sort of work he now has to do; but he has stayed on
for his country's sake. He continues to serve, mutilated as he is,
in pain, the shadow of the man he was. . . .)
Pan on past the commandant's belongings, including gerani-
ums in a pot, a pair of binoculars and some daggers. There is a
champagne bucket with a bottle in it, a leather-bound copy of
'Casanova'[9] with a pistol lying on it, a framed portrait of a young
woman, all resting on a small table. Pan ends on the comman-
dant's orderly in the act of blowing into his master's white gloves
to open up their fingers. They speak in German to each other.
RAUFFENSTEIN *off.* Open the window. It stinks in here! Enough to
    make you throw up.
ORDERLY *standing to attention.* Yes, sir!
    Camera tracks with the ORDERLY *as he goes over to the window,*
    opens it to the sound of a bugle call, then returns to where he
    was.

---

9. The memoirs of Giovanni Giacomo Casanova de Seingalt (1725–1798), a Venetian adven-
turer especially known as a seducer of women.

ORDERLY. May I bring it to your attention, sir, if you don't mind, sir, that we have only two pairs of white gloves left.

He shows the gloves in question.

RAUFFENSTEIN *off.* Too complicated to have some more come from Paris! Try to make those last out until the end of the war.

ORDERLY *standing at attention.* As you wish, sir. Would you require another cup of coffee, sir?

Tilt down in close-up on RAUFFENSTEIN's *hand setting down a cup on the table where he is being served a large breakfast.*

RAUFFENSTEIN. If you must baptise this slop with the name of coffee. . . . I resign myself. . . . It'll warm my innards.

ORDERLY. As you wish, sir.

The ORDERLY *moves away, then returns, and, as he pours out another cup of coffee, he gives* RAUFFENSTEIN *a dossier.* RAUFFENSTEIN *takes it and begins to read as he drinks his coffee. Front shot of* RAUFFENSTEIN, *putting his monocle in his eye to read. There is a knock at the door. Cut to outside the room where a German soldier is waiting in front of the door which opens.*

ORDERLY. What is it?

SOLDIER. The new ones are there!

Cut back to the room. The orderly leaves the door ajar and walks over to RAUFFENSTEIN.

ORDERLY *clicking his heels.* The new prisoners are in your office.

[*Commandant's Room*]

MARECHAL, BŒLDIEU, *and another French officer, Lieutenant* DEMOLDER, *are standing in the middle of the office. All three are looking at the half-open door. Pan with their gaze: through the doorway,* RAUFFENSTEIN *is seen as he gets up and sprays himself with scent, while his* ORDERLY *fusses over him and tidies his uniform. Finally,* RAUFFENSTEIN *picks up his sabre, his gloves and the dossier he has just been reading, then he walks into his office. He goes directly up to* BŒLDIEU *and bows and speaks in French:*

RAUFFENSTEIN. Delighted to see you again, Bœldieu.

BŒLDIEU *salutes, then shakes* RAUFFENSTEIN's *hand as it is stretched towards him.*

RAUFFENSTEIN. I much regret seeing you again here.

BŒLDIEU. [We share your regrets.] So do we.

MARECHAL *muttering.* Yes, a bit!

RAUFFENSTEIN *glances at* MARECHAL, *then addresses all three men.*

RAUFFENSTEIN. Will you be seated?

MARECHAL. No thanks, sir.

RAUFFENSTEIN: At ease, then.

Very stiffly, RAUFFENSTEIN *walks over to his desk, sits down and*

*opens the dossier. Tilt up on him as he reads aloud: there is a
different shot of each man as he speaks.*

RAUFFENSTEIN. Captain de Bœldieu, four attempts at escape: via the
heating-system, in a refuse cart, through a drain, and in a laundry
basket.

BŒLDIEU *smiling.* There are times when one has to make oneself
rather tiny.

RAUFENSTEIN *with a hint of a smile.* I quite understand. . . . *Returns
to the dossier.* . . . Lieutenant Maréchal, five attempts at escape:
disguised as a chimney-sweep. . . .

MARECHAL. You might say, sir, trying to win the sweepstakes. . . .

RUFFENSTEIN *continuing.* Disguised as a German soldier, disguised
as woman. . . . That is amusing! *His mouth twitches ironically.*
Very amusing!

MARECHAL. Yes, but what was much less amusing, sir, was that an
N.C.O. really took me for a woman . . . and I didn't fancy that
at all!

RAUFFENSTEIN *ironically.* Really?

MARECHAL. Right! Absolutely right!

RAUFFENSTEIN. Lieutenant Demolder three attempts. . . .

RAUFFENSTEIN *gets up and walks in front of the three men as he
speaks, smoking all the time.*

RAUFFENSTEIN. Gentlemen, your courage and patriotism earns my
respect, but here the situation is something else. No one escapes
from this fortress. You understand. . . .

The three officers nod. RAUFFENSTEIN *sits down on the edge of
his desk, facing them.*

RAUFFENSTEIN. So that no one can complain of German brutality, I
have decided to use French rules and regulations here. . . . *He
takes booklets from his desk, distributes them.* . . . Here is a copy
of them. They will make good reading for you when you cannot
go to sleep. And now, gentlemen, would you be so kind as to give
me the pleasure of your company. . . . *He rises and calls his*
ORDERLY. . . . Oswald!

ORDERLY *off.* Zu Befehl, Herr Major!

RAUFFENSTEIN. Mantel![1]

The ORDERLY *hurries to pass* RAUFFENSTEIN *his cape, then his
muff. . . .*

[*Fortress: Different Places*]

Dissolve to RAUFFENSTEIN *as he comes into the fortress, followed by the three French officers whom he is showing around
the place. The little group goes through courtyards and corridors, often patrolled by armed soldiers on guard. They even*

1. "At your service, Major!" "My coat!"

meet soldiers walking some guard-dogs on their leashes, as well as young conscripts at drill. There are various shots of them going up and down stairs until they finally reach an inner court-yard dominated by a watch-tower and mounted machine-guns. Some men present arms.

RAUFFENSTEIN. My men are not young, but they are amused when they play at soldiers.[2]

Various commands in German are heard, off. The group goes down some steps, then halts in front of more soldiers standing at attention near machine-guns and field guns.

RAUFFENSTEIN *showing off the field guns.* I have twenty-five of those.

BŒLDIEU. Hm, really?

RAUFFENSTEIN. I suppose you know Maxims. . . . Excellent machine-guns.

MARECHAL *mimicking* BŒLDIEU. Why, of course, sir. Personally, I prefer the restaurant Maxim's. . . .

BŒLDIEU *tight-lipped.* Touché.

They all smile . . . then continue their tour. BŒLDIEU *and* RAUFFENSTEIN *walk side by side.*

RAUFFENSTEIN *in English.* I used to know a pretty gel[3] at Maxim's . . . back in 1913. Her name was Fifi.

BŒLDIEU *also speaking English.* So did I.

They go by with MARECHAL *and* DEMOLDER *following.* DEMOLDER *stops* MARECHAL *to point out something. Quick pan to the wall to show a niche cut into the stone; it holds a small statue of the Virgin. Return on the two men.*

DEMOLDER *admiringly.* Twelfth century!

MARECHAL *shrugs. They go on until they catch up with the other two just as police dogs pass them again.*

MARECHAL *to* RAUFFENSTEIN. I beg your pardon, sir, but was this little home away from home built just to put up me and Captain de Bœldieu?

RAUFFENSTEIN, *not understanding and adjusting his monocle.* Excuse me?

BŒLDIEU. Are we your only guests?

RAUFFENSTEIN *stretching out his hand.* Of course not! Your comrades are behind there. . . .

Cut to a gigantic wall, then cut back to the group which contin-ues its visit, passing a statue set into the stone.

DEMOLDER *ecstatically.* Thirteenth century!

MARECHAL *bewildered.* Is that so?

But MARECHAL *does not give a damn for these details on the style of the prison. What he notices is the huge height of the*

---

2. "They like to play soldiers."   3. Girl (English accent).

fortress walls. Quick pan up this height. Cut back to the group which has reached the ramparts. RAUFFENSTEIN *leans over the edge of the precipice and shows the perpendicular fall of the walls down to the moat. Quick pan down.*

RAUFFENSTEIN. A drop of one hundred and seventeen feet. No one will escape from here.

[*Commandant's Office*]
The four men are back in the office after their guided tour. The prisoners are waiting to be taken to their quarters.

BŒLDIEU. It was very pleasant of you, sir, to have shown us around your estate.

MARECHAL *joining in ironically* Yes, it's a really pretty castle, sir. . . . *Turning to* DEMOLDER. . . . So ancient! . . . *After a pause.* . . . And so cheery!

[*A Room*]
The door of the prisoners' quarters opens, showing RAUFFENSTIN *and* BŒLDIEU.

BŒLDIEU *going in first.* I beg your pardon.

RAUFFENSTEIN *following him in.* I am sorry I could not have given you a room on your own.

BŒLDIEU. I am very grateful . . . but I could not have accepted in any case, sir.

MARECHAL *and* DEMOLDER *enter in their turn.*

RAUFFENSTEIN. Gentlemen, I hope that our little promenade did not overtire you?

MARECHAL. Not at all, sir . . . not at all.

RAUFFENSTEIN *bows, salutes and leaves the room by another door. Cut back to the three Frenchmen.*

MARECHAL *looking up.* Fourteenth century.

BŒLDIEU *unruffled.* Pure gothic!

At this moment, two German soldiers and an N.C.O. *come over to search them.*

N.C.O. Do you mind? It's the search.

While the soldiers search the pockets of the Frenchmen, the N.C.O. *says to them with a smile:*

N.C.O. You know, your friend, Lieutenant Rosenthal . . . he's here.

MARECHAL *delighted.* I don't believe it! Old Rosenthal!

BŒLDIEU. I see his luck was no better than ours.

N.C.O. The Commandant has given me orders to put you in the same room. . . . He says you'll be better fed that way.

They all laugh . . . but when one of the soldiers grabs MARE-CHAL's *képi to turn it inside out and search it,* MARECHAL *loses his temper and snatches it back.*

MARECHAL. What's that? . . . Enough!

[*Courtyard: Daytime*]

The courtyard of the fortress is covered with snow. DEMOLDER,
*all bundled up, walks towards camera, reading something with
great concentration. A sentry goes over to him and speaks to
him in German, although inaudibly.* DEMOLDER *looks up and
gives a friendly wave before he retraces his steps.*

DEMOLDER. Thank you, my friend. . . . Very kind of you.

[*Room*]

In their new room, Bœldieu *and* MARECHAL *have indeed found*
ROSENTHAL *again, as well provisioned and generous as ever,
sharing everything with his fellow prisoners: a* LOCKSMITH,
DEMOLDER *who is a professor of Greek, a* SENEGALESE NEGRO.[4]
. . . BŒLDIEU *spends most of his days playing patience. . . .
The others read, work, smoke, chat, and feel bored.*

THE LOCKSMITH *is telling the story of one of his 'amours'.*

THE LOCKSMITH. A good-looking blonde . . . big blue eyes. . . . An
angel! Well, three days later I had to go and see the doctor. Don't
trust a blonde!

ROSENTHAL *is seated. Behind him,* THE SENEGALESE, *warmly
dressed, is drawing carefully.*

ROSENTHAL. The same thing happened to me with a brunette.

MARECHAL. You can't trust anyone!

ROSENTHAL. She was a friend of my mother's! Ever so respectable. A
real lady who did good works.

MARECHAL. It's usually clap[5] which gets the posh people. . . . *Turning his head . . .* Isn't that so, BŒLDIEU?

BŒLDIEU. It used to be a question of class . . . as many other things
were [believe you me]. But that, along with so much else, is
becoming democratic. For the time being, the working class does
not suffer from illnesses like gout or cancer . . . but it will some
day, you wait and see. . . .

A group shot of the room shows DEMOLDER *as he comes in.*

THE LOCKSMITH *to* DEMOLDER. And the intellectuals?

DEMOLDER. For us, it's usually tuberculosis!

ROSENTHAL *at the same time.* Here comes Pindar![6]

MARECHAL *getting up and walking around.* And the bourgeois?

ROSENTHAL. Liver complaints. . . Intestinal. . . . They eat too much.
. . . In other words, all the different classes would die of their
various diseases if wars didn't come along to reconcile the mi-
crobes.

DEMOLDER *goes over to the table where* BŒLDIEU *is playing
patience and begins to set out all the books he is studying. As
he does this, he gets in the way of* BŒLDIEU's *game and displaces
the cards with his dictionaries.*

---

4. Senegal, in West Africa, was a French colony from 1895 to 1946 and sent troops to assist
France during World War I.   5. Syphilis, in the French.   6. Demolder is nicknamed Pindar
because he is translating the work of that Greek lyric poet (518–438 B.C.).

BŒLDIEU *coldly.* Excuse me. . . . *He picks up two cards.* . . . Do you mind? Your dictionaries are going to be in my way.

DEMOLDER *rather shyly.* I'm sorry, but it's such difficult work. . . . Pindar has always been so badly translated.

BŒLDIEU *eyeing him through his monocle.* Really? I'm sorry to hear it. Rotten shame!

MARECHAL *coming over to talk to* DEMOLDER. I never asked you before because basically I couldn't care less, but who is this chap of yours, Pindar?

DEMOLDER: You can make fun of it if you like, but to me it's the most important thing in the whole world. . . . No joking, I care about it more than about the war or even my own life. . . . Pindar is the greatest of the Greek poets!

MARECHAL. The greatest Greek poet? Well, I never!

Quick dissolve to a few days later, as MARECHAL *goes off again to join* ROSENTHAL, *who is sitting on his bed consulting a large sheet of paper. The two friends, side by side, look at the map which* ROSENTHAL *has drawn.*

ROSENTHAL. Look . . . *Pointing with his finger.* . . . We're here, above this curve, fifteen miles from the Main.[7] The only way to get to Switzerland without having to cross the Rhine is by Lake Constance. We'll have to walk two hundred miles.

MARECHAL. A nice little stroll.

ROSENTHAL. We'd have to walk for fifteen nights. We could hold out on six lumps of sugar and two biscuits a day.

MARECHAL. Really? *A pause.* . . . Want me to tell you something? You and your map, you're just as loony as him over there with his Pindar! *Nodding his head.* . . . Because, to get out of here. . . .

Behind them, THE SENEGALESE *rises to come and show them his drawing.*

THE SENEGALESE. There, I've finished. It's a picture of Justice hunting down Crime. I think it's pretty good.

MARECHAL *takes a vague look at the drawing, then begins to look at* ROSENTHAL's *map again.*

MARECHAL. No, but, I say, to get to your Constance. . . .

Dissolve to few days later, as MARECHAL's *hands braid a rope in close-up. Pan to his face as he works.* ROSENTHAL *is by his side, examining the rope.*

ROSENTHAL. Do you think it's strong enough?

MARECHAL *pulling at the rope.* Oh, yes. It'll take the weight of ten like you and five like me.

Camera tracks back to show the whole room. THE SENEGALESE *is posted by the door as a look-out. He suddenly turns round.*

THE SENEGALESE. Look out! They're going to search the rooms.

---

7. A river that runs into the Rhine River; *Lake Constance* is bounded by Germany, Austria, and Switzerland.

At once, everybody gets to work concealing everything that is compromising; MARECHAL *and* ROSENTHAL *dash over to a bed with their rope.*

MARECHAL. Under the mattress. . . . Yes. . . . Hurry up!

BŒLDIEU. Come, come, that's no good. It's infantile. . . . Allow me.

As BŒLDIEU *goes over to the window with the rope, cut to the stunned* MARECHAL *and* ROSENTHAL.

MARECHAL. Hey, well, I'd never have thought of that!

BOELDIEU *dusting his fingers.* Out there the gutter's frightfully convenient.

MARECHAL. Look out! Here they come.

Each one goes to his bed. Pan towards the door. Five German soldiers enter. Pan down to MARECHAL *sitting on his mattress, reading a book aloud.*

MARECHAL. 'Louise wrote to Victor: I am as tired as a girl who has made love twenty-two nights running.'

As he reads, MARECHAL *has his belongings searched by a German soldier.* MARECHAL *turns his head towards the man.*

MARECHAL. Twenty-two nights running! Think of that!

Pan to another German soldier searching THE LOCKSMITH'S *pack. The Frenchman, who is stretched out on the bed, lifts his legs to make it easier for the searchers. Pan onto the table where* DEMOLDER *is absorbed in his work on Pindar. A German makes him rise and examines the stool beneath the scholar.*

Cut to the door as RAUFFENSTEIN *suddenly comes in, very dignified and smoking. He had not expected the prisoners to remain indifferent and seated. Quick shots of them all, intercut with medium close-ups of* RAUFFENSTEIN *walking to the centre of the room.*

In medium shot, BŒLDIEU *sits near his bed, while two German soldiers approach him to search his effects. He pays no attention to them and reads a newspaper haughtily. Cut to* RAUFFENSTEIN *as he walks up to* BŒLDIEU.

RAUFFENSTEIN. Do not search that corner.

BŒLDIEU *gets up as* RAUFFENSTEIN *approaches, while the soldiers withdraw.*

RAUFFENSTEIN. Give me your word of honour that there is nothing inside the room which is against regulations.

BŒLDIEU *after a pause.* I give you my word of honour. Thank you. But why . . . *He moves closer to* RAUFFENSTEIN . . . my word of honour rather than any of the others'?

RAUFFENSTEIN *in close-up, ironical.* Hmm! The word of a Rosenthal . . . or a Maréchal?

BŒLDIEU *in reverse close-up.* It is as good as ours.

RAUFFENSTEIN *in a shot with* BŒLDIEU. Perhaps.

They salute each other. Quick pan to DEMOLDER *struggling with a soldier who has grabbed his dictionary.*

DEMOLDER. No, not that one! No! No, it's for Pindar! Don't!

> RAUFFENSTEIN *goes over to the table and picks up the book which* DEMOLDER *is translating. He leafs through it, smiling. Then, with utter contempt, he throws it down on the table, examines with one hand* DEMOLDER's *face, and shrugs condescendingly.*

RAUFFENSTEIN: Pindar. . . . Poor old Pindar!

> *He goes out, followed by the German soldiers. A few seconds later, the door opens to admit a prisoner from a nearby room.*

PRISONER. How did it go with you?

ROSENTHAL. Not too badly.

PRISONER. That's good.

> *The prisoner goes out. Pan to* BŒLDIEU *who is coming back from the window with the rope, which he puts on* MARECHAL's *bed.* MARECHAL *immediately gets to work again.*

> [*Commandant's Room*]

> BŒLDIEU *and* RAUFFENSTEIN, *standing in the commandant's office in front of the crucifix and the altar, are talking rather nostalgically about the days when they were not enemies.*

RAUFFENSTEIN. Any news of your cousin, Edmond de Bœldieu, the military attaché I used to know in Berlin?

BŒLDIEU *walking about.* Yes, he's doing very well. He's happy. He was wounded. He has one arm less and has married a very wealthy woman.

RAUFFENSTEIN. I am so sorry. . . . Such a good horseman!

> *While talking, they have gone over to the window and they sit down next to it. They suddenly talk in English.*

BŒLDIEU *seeing the miniature of a saddle.* Blue Minnie? Of course.

RAUFFENSTEIN. Do you remember?

BŒLDIEU. You were riding her when you won the Grand Military at Liverpool in 1905.

RAUFFENSTEIN. The Prince of Wales Cup![8]

> *They switch back to speaking French. Alternate shots of the two.*

RAUFFENSTEIN *after a pause.* Hmm! . . . De Bœldieu, I would like to tell you something. Believe me, I feel nothing but distaste for my present job, as much as you do.

BŒLDIEU. You are hard on yourself.

RAUFFENSTEIN. I was a fighting man and, now, I am a bureaucrat, a policeman. It is the only way left for me to try and serve my country. . . . *He stresses the last word.* . . . Burned all over—that is

---

8. Horse racing and polo were favorite sports of the international aristocracy, and many races were held at Liverpool. Presumably the "Prince of Wales Cup" was a prize awarded by the Prince, who was an enthusiastic spectator at such events; it is not an established prize.

why I wear these gloves. . . . My backbone fractured in two places, mended with silver plates. Silver strut in my chin, also a silver knee-cap. . . . I owe all this wealth to the misfortune of war.

BŒLDIEU. May I ask you something? Why do you make an exception for me by inviting me to your quarters?

RAUFFENSTEIN *in close-up.* Why? Because your name is Bœldieu, career officer in the French army, and my name is Rauffenstein, career officer in the imperial German army.

BŒLDIEU *in close-up.* But . . . all my friends are officers, too.

RAUFFENSTEIN *disdainfully.* You call Maréchal and Rosenthal . . . officers?

BŒLDIEU. They are very good soldiers.

RAUFFENSTEIN *with contempt.* Yes! . . . [Modern warfare, the nation in arms!] . . . The charming legacy of the French Revolution.[9]

BŒLDIEU *smiling.* I am afraid we can do nothing to turn back the clock.

    RAUFFENSTEIN *rises and puts out his cigarette by the window.*

RAUFFENSTEIN. I do not know who is going to win this war, but I know one thing: the end of it, whatever it may be, will be the end of the Rauffensteins and the Bœldieus.

BŒLDIEU. But perhaps there is no more need for us.

RAUFFENSTEIN. And don't you find that is a pity?

BŒLDIEU. Perhaps!

    RAUFFENSTEIN *seems thoughtful as he looks at the window which opens on a sheer drop of one hundred and thirty feet. The pot of geraniums stands on the inner ledge, next to a small watering-can.*

BŒLDIEU. I do admire the way you look after your geranium.

RAUFFENSTEIN *turning back to him.* Do not think that I have turned into a botanist, but it's the only flower in the castle. . . . *He sits by* BŒLDIEU. . . . Ivy and nettles are the only plants growing here. [*Room*]

    MARECHAL *and* ROSENTHAL *sit side by side, smoking as they talk in the prisoners' room.*

MARECHAL. I'm glad to be escaping with you.

ROSENTHAL. With us both.

MARECHAL. Yes, of course. Mind you, I really like Bœldieu. He's a good bloke, but you can't let yourself go with him, you can't feel free. . . . A different sort of education. . . .

ROSENTHAL. He's a fine chap.

MARECHAL. I agree, but you see, if ever you and I found ourselves in a bad spot, we'd just be a couple of poor down-and-outs, but him,

---

9. The French Revolution of 1789 was seen as the beginning of the modern era and of popular—rather than aristocratic—tastes and rule.

he'd always be Monsieur de Bœldieu. . . . *A pause.* . . . Besides,
you're a fine chap, too! Look at how you've fed us with all those
food parcels from your family!

ROSENTHAL. It was only from vanity. When I fed you, it was my way
of showing you how rich my family is. . . . People think Jews are
mean,[1] but they're wrong. If anything, we're often generous, because
we suffer from the sin of pride.

MARECHAL. That's all rot! What's the sin of pride got to do with it!
All I know is that you've been a good pal.

*A new shot of the room shows a tall shambling man, dressed
almost in rags, as he bursts in. It is a* RUSSIAN OFFICER *also a
prisoner. He speaks French with a strong accent.*

RUSSIAN OFFICER. Comrades! We have been sent a big crate. . . . A
present from the Tsarina.[2] . . . Do us the honour of coming to
share it with us.

MARECHAL. A present from the Tsarina? That means caviar, at least.

*In the great din rising in the room, the words, 'caviar' and 'vodka'
are often heard.*

[*Russians' Room*]

*The Russian prisoners' room is in a distant part of the fortress.
Everybody is over-excited, speaking at once and exulting over
an enormous wooden crate stamped with the letter A. The officer who has invited the Frenchmen ushers in* BŒLDIEU, *who
salutes, then* MARECHAL *and* ROSENTHAL *and* DEMOLDER. *They
all shake hands and congratulate each other on their good luck.*

RUSSIAN OFFICER *cheerfully.* At last we may do something to thank
you for your many kindnesses. The Tsarina . . . *He salutes* . . .
has always been good-hearted.

*Cut back to the crate which three soldiers are trying to open
with hammers and various other tools. Everybody falls silent as
the wood begins to give. Finally, the top of the crate comes off.
Tilt down in close-up on feverish hands pulling off the top layer
of straw. There is a lot of sawdust and straw, which means that
the contents must be fragile.*

VOICE *off.* Hurrah!

*The Tsarina's gifts are finally revealed: the crate is full of books.
The Russians speak in Russian.*

A RUSSIAN *despairingly.* Books . . . books!

ANOTHER. What did you say?

ANOTHER. Books!

ANOTHER. Look underneath. . . . It isn't possible.

Medium close-up of the hands turning over the books.

A RUSSIAN. Nothing but moral treatises, grammars and Bibles!

---

1. Stingy.   2. Queen Alexandra of Russia.

Cut to MARECHAL *and* BŒLDIEU *and* ROSENTHAL, *who examines a book.*

ROSENTHAL. A *cook* book!

MARECHAL. Funny sort of grub!

BŒLDIEU *extremely haughtily.* Jolly poor joke.

A RUSSIAN. Let's set fire to it!

ANOTHER. Yes, fire! Burn the Tsarina's gift.

Quick shots of angry Russians round the crate tossing books and straw about, until the whole place is in chaos. As they do this, they mutter and curse the Tsarina and swear obscenely. DEMOLDER *tries to stop them from destroying the books.*

DEMOLDER. Stop! No, you don't have the right to burn books. For no reason at all!

The furious Russians, not understanding what DEMOLDER *is saying, shove him aside roughly and set fire to the crate. Cut to the Frenchmen.*

MARECHAL. Things are getting hot.

ROSENTHAL. We've got no place here.

ROSENTHAL *pushes his friends* BŒLDIEU *and* MARECHAL *towards the door. They leave just as German guards come running in to see what the racket is about. The guards try vainly to establish order, as flames begin to burst from the pile of straw and books.* [*Corridor*]

Cut to the three Frenchmen in the corridors, as more German sentries rush by to try to put out the fire and the revolt. Soon they are all alone, walking down deserted corridors as they reach the sentries' posts. There is noise in the distance. The three Frenchmen look at the empty walls with envy.
[*Sentry Walk*]

ROSENTHAL. All the sentries have left their posts! They've all gone to tame the Russians. . . . Look over there. . . . What a height, but nobody around!

MARECHAL *sighing.* If only we'd been ready, what a chance! We'd have thrown down the rope and in two secs. . . .

ROSENTHAL. Particularly as it's nearly night. . . .

BŒLDIEU. Well, we can try again another time. They've been good enough to organize a little rehearsal for us. . . . All we have to do would be to put them on a false scent. Now, we know that if one determined man got them to run after him, and if he could hold out for all of five minutes, his friends could escape during that time.

ROSENTHAL. That's a big risk.

BŒLDIEU. Oh, don't exaggerate. . . . *A pause.* . . . It would amuse me. When do you want to leave?

MARECHAL. Why us? You're coming too, old chap.

BŒLDIEU. No, Maréchal.

MARECHAL. Why not? Don't you think we can make it?

BŒLDIEU. Pfft! You know very well, that sort of thing wouldn't stop me going.

MARECHAL. Well, then?

BŒLDIEU. Your plan of escape can only work for two men, no more, and I know your preference as partners.

ROSENTHAL. That isn't fair.

BŒLDIEU. And what is fair in a war?

MARECHAL. Oh, no, no, no and no, old chap. [You'd be risking your life for us.] We can't accept.

BŒLDIEU. I am not asking your advice. I have made up my mind.

[*Room*]

BŒLDIEU *continues talking off, while there is a quick dissolve ending in a close-up of a squirrel in a cage in the prisoners' room.*

BŒLDIEU *continuing off.* I'm not against certain forms of entertainment. . . . In fact, I support them. . . . *A pause.* . . . Do you like music?

Camera tracks back to show MARECHAL *seated on the left of the cage. Standing to the right,* BŒLDIEU *plays with the squirrel through the bars.*

MARECHAL: A bit, quite. A good waltz, yes.

BŒLDIEU: I'm extremely fond of the flute. We'll buy flutes for the whole camp and fix a date for a grand concert. This is the programme: at five o'clock, the full orchestra in all the rooms. That is when night falls. Five minutes later, our guards will confiscate the musical instruments. At quarter past five, there will be a new concert with all the instruments at our disposal—saucepans, animal calls, grinding teeth . . . and all you want. Result? We shall be summoned to a general roll-call.

MARECHAL. And then?

BŒLDIEU. Then? . . . *A pause, as he amuses himself with the squirrel.* . . . That is my affair. You will have five minutes to descend the walls and reach the woods.

MARECHAL. Listen, Bœldieu . . . I don't know how to say this. . . . For the first time in my life, I'm all embarrassed.

BŒLDIEU. Come, come!

MARECHAL. Yes, all embarrassed.

Dissolve to a few days later inside the room. Stay on BŒLDIEU'S *corner of the room, which can be recognised by its neatness and the photographs of horses pinned on the wall.* BŒLDIEU *is by his bed, bending over a basin full of water and washing his white gloves.* MARECHAL *comes and stands in front of him, looking embarrassed and moved, not knowing how to begin.*

MARECHAL. Bœldieu, I'd like to tell you something.

BŒLDIEU *barely raising his eyes.* Could you pour out a little warm water so I can rinse my gloves?

MARECHAL *takes a pitcher of water and does what* BŒLDIEU *asks.*

MARECHAL. Listen, whatever happens, I'd like you to know all the same. . . .

BŒLDIEU *cutting him short.* But I'm not doing . . . I'm not doing anything for you personally. That excuses us from the danger of getting emotional. . . . *He laughs drily.*

MARECHAL. There are certain times in life, all the same. . . .

BŒLDIEU *quite abruptly.* Let's avoid them, if you please.

He has finished rinsing and squeezing out his gloves. He passes in front of MARECHAL *to go and hang them on a line.*

BŒLDIEU. May I?

MARECHAL *follows him and points at the gloves.*

MARECHAL. Are you going to be wearing that stuff?

BŒLDIEU. If you have no objection.

MARECHAL. No, but I must admit that it wouldn't occur to me to put on a pair of white gloves for this sort of job.

BŒLDIEU. Each to his own taste.

MARECHAL. You can't do anything like the rest of us do. I've been with you every day for eighteen months, and you still say *vous*[3] to me . . .

BŒLDIEU *combing his hair.* I say *vous* to my mother and my wife.

MARECHAL. No . . . then. . . .

MARECHAL *admires* BŒLDIEU, *but he is disconcerted because he cannot understand him. He would like, just this once, to get closer to him, to bridge the gap.*

MARECHAL. I'd like to explain it to you.

BŒLDIEU *pretending not to understand.* A cigarette?

MARECHAL *sits on* BŒLDIEU's *bed.*

MARECHAL. English tobacco makes my throat itch. Everything really, your gloves, even your tobacco, comes between us.

These two men, who have faced the same ordeals equally bravely, will never be able to get along.

[*Fortunately,* ROSENTHAL *comes to put an end to their embarrassment.*

ROSENTHAL. I've warned everybody. First concert at five o'clock.

BŒLDIEU. Perfect.]

[*German Officers' Mess*]

In a German mess, start on a close-up of an old ornate clock. The time is one minute to five. Pan to two seated German

---

3. The formal "you" in French, as opposed to the more intimate *tu*. V*ous* implies greater distance or respect.

officers, as they smoke and speak in German. They are, in fact, promoted N.C.O.'s.

GERMAN OFFICER. You can say what you like, but wherever there's a German, there's order. Of course, I grant you the chief is a complete lunatic with his pot of flowers and all. . . . Lucky that I'm here. . . . I know how to keep that gang of devils in their place. Before I joined the army, I was a school-master.

Night is about to fall on the fortress, perched like an eagle's nest on its summit. A flute concert strikes up in the distance. The two officers look up and go over to the window. The one who has not been talking bursts out laughing.

THE FIRST GERMAN *furious.* Lieutenant von Fritzwitz! Get those blasted flutes confiscated immediately!

[*Corridor*]

In the corridors, a succession of quick shots shows the German guards running to the prisoners' rooms. The corridor outside the Frenchmen's room is empty. Suddenly, THE LOCKSMITH, *then* DEMOLDER *and a few others come out of the room dancing and playing the flute. Finally, when they hear the sound of running boots, they go back into their room, still playing. Cut quickly to various rooms as German soldiers storm inside and brutally confiscate the flutes.*

In the room of the main characters, all are sitting around their big table, playing the flute for all they are worth. As soon as the German soldiers come in, they all stop at the same moment and raise their arms as one man to give up their flutes, which the German soldiers snatch away.

A SOLDIER *leaving.* I wouldn't start up again if I were you.

He goes out, slamming the door behind him.

MARECHAL. That's what we're going to do in fifteen minutes.

BŒLDIEU takes another flute out of his pocket and looks at it with an ironical expression.

[*Sentry Post*]

At one of the sentry posts, the German officer, who has been a schoolmaster, walks up and down, looking satisfied because the noise has stopped. He rubs his hands with pleasure. He turns his head as he hears a door open. Soldiers enter and deposit flutes on the table.

A SOLDIER *at attention.* Your orders carried out, Captain!

THE OFFICER. And now, parcels are not to be distributed until further orders. Only dry bread and water to be issued.

At these words, a deafening racket starts up, making the Germans jump. Dissolve on noise to the following shots: In a succession of different rooms, including the Russian one, the prisoners have picked up every object they can—saucepans, metal rods, forks, empty tin cans. All of them are doing their best to make as much noise as possible, while trying to keep time to the tune of 'Petit Navire,' a song they are all bellowing out at the top of their lungs.

Cut to various shots of soldiers, their arms at the ready, rushing down the corridors.

[French Prisoners' Room]

In the room of the Frenchmen, DEMOLDER *is enthusiastically hitting the inside of a metal basin with a big spoon. The others also enjoy the din they are making. Pan to* ROSENTHAL *who is winding the rope for escape round his waist.* THE SENEGALESE *is helping him do this. Pan continues round the room, showing* MARECHAL *also getting ready for the escape, and ends on* BŒLDIEU *in his best uniform putting on his white gloves.*

Cut quickly from corridor to corridor. The Germans are trying to enforce order and push back the milling and shouting prisoners into the rooms.

Cut back to the Frenchmen's room. The door is shoved open by a German.

FELDWEBEL: General roll-call!

All the prisoners drop their noise-making bits and pieces to go out.

DEMOLDER: At last I understand my students. I never had so much fun in my life.

Last to leave is MARECHAL, *followed by* BŒLDIEU. *Camera tracks forward as* MARECHAL *turns to the other man at the door.*

MARECHAL *very embarrassed.* Well. . . . *He does not know what to say.*

BŒLDIEU: What?

MARECHAL: See you soon.

With great dignity, BŒLDIEU *holds out his gloved hand.* MARECHAL *shakes it and goes out.* BŒLDIEU *closes the door and stays in the room. Then he comes towards the camera, does up his gloves, and takes the flute which he fastens to his lapel. He seems to be smiling as he does so.*

[Courtyard: Night]

It is very dark in the courtyard of the fortress, and very cold. From above, all the prisoners are visible standing in rows under the searchlights and hemmed in by sentries. A certain disorder reigns, however, because of what has happened before. Many orders, given and cancelled, show that there is confusion among the Germans as well as the prisoners. RAUFFENSTEIN, *dressed in his long army greatcoat, enters the courtyard. Everybody stands to attention. A* FELDWEBEL *begins to call out the roll. Intercut*

from a close-up of him to shots of prisoners answering 'Present.'
*As he begins to call out the names of the French prisoners, pan
across the faces of* THE LOCKSMITH, DEMOLDER, THE SENE-
GALESE, *and the others. All reply in turn,* 'Present,' *including*
MARECHAL *and* ROSENTHAL.

FELDWEBEL: Bœldieu! *No reply.* Bœldieu! *No reply.* Bœldieu!

Cut to the nervous and surprised RAUFFENSTEIN, *shot from below.
At that moment, in the dimly-lit courtyard, a single flute begins
to play the tune of* 'Petit Navire.' *Everyone, startled by the thin
and shrill sound of the flute, looks upwards. Pan up to locate
this odd music coming from the sky, just as more searchlights
come on and move their beams about in the darkness along the
walls, prying into every hidden recess of the fortress. Everybody
anxiously follows with his gaze the beams of the searchlights as
they locate a flight of steps leading to the sentry posts at the top
of the ramparts. A beam climbs up the steps one by one in
search of the flute-player. Suddenly, a French uniform appears
in the circle of the light. Slowly playing* 'Il était un petit navir
. . .' *over and over again,* BŒLDIEU *is seen from below sitting
on the watch-tower. The soldiers look up. A close-up from below
shows* RAUFFENSTEIN, *also looking upwards. He is trying to
understand. From his angle,* BŒLDIEU *is seen, as he begins to
climb higher.*

Cut to a corridor inside the fortress near a window, where
ROSENTHAL *unrolls the rope with the help of* MARECHAL. *They
finally throw it out of the window, then* ROSENTHAL *lowers himself out while* MARECHAL *remains on the look-out.*

Cut to the exterior wall of the fortress, down which ROSENTHAL
is sliding on the rope.

Cut back to the corridors. Soldiers approach. MARECHAL *closes
the window and hides behind a column. The soldiers pass and,
immediately afterwards,* MARECHAL *opens the window again and
climbs out.*

*Cut back to the exterior wall. The two Frenchmen slide down
their rope, drop from the end of it to the ground and flee towards
the woods.*

*In the courtyard, pan past the sentries all ready to fire by the
searchlight. Everyone is looking up, watching* BŒLDIEU's *antics.
He stops a few times to play* 'Petit Navire.' *Camera cuts quickly
to him as he plays, then cuts back to the yard.*

AN OFFICER *in German.* If he passes the limits of the camp, fire at
will!

Sound of rifles being cocked. Shot of BŒLDIEU, *still climbing.
He has fastened his flute to his jacket so he can use both his
hands to climb. Downward shot of the whole courtyard.*

A GERMAN OFFICER. Fire!

> *Various soldiers fire.* BŒLDIEU *ducks and is not hit; he consults his watch, and goes on climbing higher. After the first volley,* RAUFFENSTEIN *stretches out his arm to halt the fire and walks to the centre of the courtyard to get a better view of* BŒLDIEU.

RAUFFENSTEIN *in medium close-up from above.* Bœldieu! *(Calling in English).* Listen!

> *Cut back to* BŒLDIEU, *who straightens up and plays a few notes, then starts climbing again. There are a series of reverse angles.*

RAUFFENSTEIN *in English.* Bœldieu, have you really gone insane?

BŒLDIEU *in English.* I am perfectly sane.

> RAUFFENSTEIN, *seen in medium close-up, is extremely upset; his voice trembles slightly.*

RAUFFENSTEIN *in English.* Bœldieu, you understand that if you do not obey at once and come down, I shall have to shoot. . . . *A pause, then he takes out his pistol. . . .* I dread to do that. I beg you . . . man to man, come back.

> BŒLDIEU *has almost reached the ramparts and his voice seems to fall from the heights of the citadel.*

BŒLDIEU *in English.* It's damn nice of you, Rauffenstein, but it's impossible.

> *From below,* RAUFFENSTEIN *is seen cocking his pistol, raising his arm, aiming and firing.*
>
> *Cut to* BŒLDIEU *who has been hit. As he falls, he takes a glance at his wrist-watch.*
>
> *Cut back to* RAUFFENSTEIN, *more still than ever. Very slowly, he puts his pistol back in his holster, then he walks about in the courtyard. After a time, a feldwebel goes up to him and comes to attention. Shot of the two speaking in German.*

FELDWEBEL. May I bring to your attention, sir, that Lieutenants Maréchal and Rosenthal have escaped.

RAUFFENSTEIN. Maréchal and Rosenthal! *He glances in the direction of* BŒLDIEU's *fallen body.* So that is why. . . . *Sternly. . . .* Call out the dog patrols, alert the stations, and the military and civilian authorities. Report to me about the progress of the search every quarter of an hour. . . . That is all.

> *Very slowly,* RAUFFENSTEIN *begins walking towards the camera.*
> [*Rauffenstein's Room*]
> *Close-up of a box containing the Extreme Unction, held by a military priest. Camera tracks backward to show* BŒLDIEU, *who is lying in* RAUFFENSTEIN's *room. The military priest, who has just given the wounded man the last sacraments, gets up and leaves on tip-toe, while a nurse takes up her place at* BŒLDIEU's *bedside.* BŒLDIEU *is obviously being looked after with great care, and every effort is being made to nurse the French officer back*

to life. Pan towards the door where the military priest is going.
RAUFFENSTEIN *stands there in silence; he helps the priest to put on his cape and opens the door. As the priest leaves, a German officer comes up to* RAUFFENSTEIN *and they begin to talk very quietly in German.*

THE GERMAN OFFICER. Your orders have been carried out, sir. . . . The patrols have not yet located the escaped prisoners.

RAUFFENSTEIN. Thank you.

The officer leaves. RAUFFENSTEIN *closes the door. Pan with him as he goes over to the bed. The nurse moves away a little to give her place to* RAUFFENSTEIN. *He looks with obvious pain at the man he has fatally wounded, and sits next to the bed. Camera tracks forward to show both men in medium close-up.*

RAUFFENSTEIN. Forgive me.

BŒLDIEU. I would have done the same thing. French or German . . . duty is duty.

RAUFFENSTEIN. Are you in pain?

BŒLDIEU. I would not have believed that a bullet in the stomach could hurt so much.

RAUFFENSTEIN. I was aiming at your leg. . . .

BŒLDIEU. More than fifty yards away, very bad light. . . . And then I was running. . . .

RAUFFENSTEIN. Please, no excuses! I was very clumsy.

BŒLDIEU *speaking with difficulty.* Of us two, it isn't I who should complain the most. I, I'll be finished soon, but you . . . you haven't finished. . . .

RAUFFENSTEIN. Not finished dragging out a useless existence.

BŒLDIEU. For a man of the people, it's terrible to die in the war. For you and me, it was a good solution.

RAUFFENSTEIN. I have missed it.

THE NURSE *interrupting in German.* You are talking too much.

The two men fall silent. Close-up of BŒLDIEU's *face, strained with pain, gradually relaxing.*

RAUFFENSTEIN *rises and goes to a corner of the room, opens a small closet, takes out a flask of spirits, and pours himself out a glass.*

THE NURSE *off.* Sir!

RAUFFENSTEIN *freezes for an instant, downs his drink in one gulp by arching his back, then goes over to the bed.* THE NURSE *is unscrewing the plasma bottle; she looks at her watch and notes the time of* BŒLDIEU's *death in her diary. Pan with* RAUFFENSTEIN's *hand as he closes* BŒLDIEU's *eye-lids gently. . . . After a while,* RAUFFENSTEIN *turns away and paces about the room, moving towards the window. He looks mournfully out of the window. It is snowing. Finally, he looks down at the pot of*

*geraniums standing, as usual, on the sill. He looks at the only
flower in the fortress for a time, then takes a pair of scissors and
lops off the flower.*
[*Countryside: Daytime*]
*Long shot of the countryside beneath the ice and the snow.
Everything seems dead, the trees, the earth, the sky. . . . Not a
sound, not a breath. In the background, coming towards us
along a road, a wrapped-up human figure leads a horse. Slow
pan over the countryside by the roadside.*

ROSENTHAL *off.* God, he gave me a scare. . . . We ought not to have
stayed so close to the road.
   Pan continues down towards the voice. From above, MARECHAL
   and ROSENTHAL *are seen, as they hide in a ditch near the road
   and wait for nightfall. Both men are dressed in shabby civilian
   clothes, dirty and worn out. They both wear felt hats.*
MARECHAL. So? We couldn't sleep in the rushes. They're full of water.
ROSENTHAL *sighing with relief.* He's gone.
MARECHAL *shrugging.* What, couldn't you see it was a woman? *He
   gets up.* Well, are you coming?
ROSENTHAL. Let's wait for night.
   MARECHAL *is standing up, stamping and blowing on his fingers
   to warm himself.*
MARECHAL. Come off it, mate, I'm frozen solid. I've got to get a
   move on.
   He moves off. ROSENTHAL *tries hard to stand up, but he has a
   swollen ankle. He finally gets up, slips, and painfully regains
   his balance again.* MARECHAL, *seen from below, advances towards
   the road. He turns his head towards* ROSENTHAL.
MARECHAL. Come on!
   Cut back to ROSENTHAL, *looking pretty miserable as he finally
   manages to keep upright and reach* MARECHAL. *The two are
   seen slightly from below, as* MARECHAL *takes a tobacco-pouch
   from his pocket.*
MARECHAL. Do you want your sugar?
   ROSENTHAL *takes his sugar lump and looks into the pouch.*
ROSENTHAL. Hey, there isn't much left.
MARECHAL *grumpily.* No . . . and we're not getting on much either!
ROSENTHAL *eating his sugar.* Don't you want some?
   MARECHAL *closes the pouch and hands it to* ROSENTHAL.
MARECHAL. No, I had my share just now. . . . Here, I'd rather you
   took it. . . . Like that, I won't be tempted!
ROSENTHAL *looking at* MARECHAL's *shabby coat.* Have you been eat-
   ing your buttons?
MARECHAL. Can you see they're missing?

He shrugs and starts walking along the road which leads to a
village; its church spire can be seen in the distance.
ROSENTHAL *hesitating.* Are we going on, then? Not waiting till night?
MARECHAL *pointing to the village.* Course not, come along. We'll go
round the dump.
      RROSENTHAL *walks on, limping.*
MARECHAL *further off.* What's wrong? Foot hurting?
ROSENTHAL *in pain.* No, it's nothing . . . just a sprain!
      Dissolve to a new piece of countryside, less flat, but still covered
      with snow. Pan down from the top of a small hill to show from
      above the two Frenchmen sleeping side by side, wrapped in
      their coats. Suddenly, MARECHAL *wakes up and rises, shoving*
      ROSENTHAL *a little.*
MARECHAL. Come along, off we go!
      ROSENTHAL *gets up in his turn and follows* MARECHAL *with dif-*
      ficulty. He walks very slowly, helping himself with an ordinary
      stick which he uses as a crutch.
      Dissolve to a mountain road covered with snow. MARECHAL *is*
      walking about five yards ahead of ROSENTHAL, *who is having*
      more and more trouble keeping up. He no longer even walks
      on his bad foot, but uses the stick to hop along on his other leg.
MARECHAL *annoyed.* Well, are you coming or not?
ROSENTHAL *furious.* I'm doing what I can.
      They walk in silence for a time. MARECHAL *has slowed down.*
      They are side by side.
MARECHAL *exploding.* You and your foot, you're getting on my nerves!
ROSENTHAL *pathetic.* I slipped, it wasn't my fault! *He almost shouts.*
 I slipped!
      The two men stop walking. Pan to show them face to face.
MARECHAL. You slipped! We know you slipped! And when we get
pinched for lagging like this, are you going to explain to them you
slipped? Clumsy oaf! We've got nothing else left to eat, we might
as well give ourselves up straightaway!
      As their tempers rise, the two men look at each other with
      exhaustion and hatred.
ROSENTHAL. Willingly, because I'm fed up, too. *He yells.* Fed up!
Fed up! Fed up! If you only knew how I loathe you!
MARECHAL. Believe me, it's mutual. Shall I tell you what you're for
me? A parcel!⁴ Yes, a parcel, a ball and chain tied to my leg. I
never could stand Jews for a start, get it?
ROSENTHAL *trying to put on a brave show.* A bit late for you to find

---

4. Something that has to be carried; a burden.

that out. . . . *Waving his arms and yelling.* . . . Shove off, will you? What are you waiting for? You're dying to get me off your hands.

MARECHAL. You won't be able to say that twice. . . .

ROSENTHAL *all worked up*. Go on then, shove off! Shove off! Shove off . . . quick! I don't want to see your ugly mug any more.

MARECHAL *shrugging*. Right. Off I go. Try and get by on your own! See you soon.

ROSENTHAL. I'm glad . . . so glad. I could sing. . . .

MARECHAL *turns away and walks off more quickly than before, leaving behind the exhausted* ROSENTHAL. *Stay on* ROSENTHAL, *seen slightly from above; he works at his leg to try to make it better, but he is too far gone. He sinks onto a milestone by the roadside and stretches out his leg. His face is a mask of exhaustion, dirt and despair. His expression remains frozen for a time as he thinks of the awful end of this escape, so carefully prepared with his friend. It is not fair, it is horrible! Full of rage,* ROSENTHAL *begins to sing all by himself, just to show he still has something left in him—and so as not to cry.*

ROSENTHAL *singing*. Il était un petit navire,

Il était un petit navire,

Qui n'avait ja, ja, jamais navigué,

Qui n'avait ja, ja, jamais navigué,[5]

Ohé! Ohé! . . .

Cut to MARECHAL, *quite far away now, and walking with a determined stride. He gives a flick of the head when he hears* ROSENTHAL *begin to sing. Mechanically, he begins humming the song also as he walks. Camera tracks after him in medium close-up, as he sings and drowns out the more distant voice.*

MARECHAL: Au bout de cinq à six semaines,

Au bout de cinq à six semaines,

Les vivres vin, vin, vinrent à manquer,

Les vivres vin, vin, vinrent à manquer,

Ohé! Ohé! . . .[6]

MARECHAL, *still walking, stops singing and can hardly hear* ROSENTHAL's *voice, which still goes on singing stubbornly. But back to* ROSENTHAL, *who is yelling out his song, his face increasingly distorted with sadness and fury.*

ROSENTHAL *yelling*: On tira à la courte paille,

On tira à la courte paille,

Pour savoir qui, qui, qui serait mangé,

---

5. "There was a little boat . . . Which had never sailed."   6. "At the end of five or six weeks . . . The food had just run out."

Pour savoir qui, qui, qui serait mangé,
Ohé! Ohé! . . .[7]

Medium shot from above of ROSENTHAL *who suddenly stops singing, listens carefully, and can no longer hear* MARECHAL. *He is all alone now, abandoned. A pause. Both morally and physically exhausted,* ROSENTHAL *plunges his head in his hands and begins to sob; he does not notice* MARECHAL's *coat which is next to him in shot.* MARECHAL *has, in fact, turned back and is looking at his weeping companion. Camera tracks back to show both men in medium shot.*

ROSENTHAL *finally becomes aware of* MARECHAL's *presence and raises his head, looking like a whipped dog.*

[ROSENTHAL *almost pleading.* Why did you come back?

MARECHAL *does not reply.*]

MARECHAL *bends over and helps* ROSENTHAL *to raise himself up.*

MARECHAL. Come on, mate! Let's go.

Held up by MARECHAL, ROSENTHAL *walks a few steps. New shot of the two men, walking along the road on three legs with great difficulty.* MARECHAL *stops suddenly and looks at his companion. All his hatred and annoyance has gone from him.*

MARECHAL. You can't walk another step, can you?

ROSENTHAL *trying to be brave.* Oh, it's all right. I'm fine!

MARECHAL. Would you like us to stop at that little place over there?

ROSENTHAL. You're mad . . . it's too dangerous!

MARECHAL *trying to convince himself.* It looks deserted. . . . There's no smoke coming out.

ROSENTHAL. That's no reason.

MARECHAL. And when you're on a boat that's caught fire, what d'you do? Chuck yourself into the water, don't you?

ROSENTHAL *crying and laughing with joy.* You're right. Let's chuck ourselves into the water!

[MARECHAL. Let's go then, chum!

And they start walking, step by slow step, towards a farmhouse.]
[*A Stable*]
In a stable, MARECHAL *and* ROSENTHAL *sleep, hidden in the hay. Circular pan shows the stable's small stalls, a feeding trough, a ladder against a wall going up to the loft, an old cart. Suddenly, the sound of footsteps is heard outside. Cut back to a close-up of the two friends, who start up and begin whispering.*

MARECHAL. Did you hear? . . . Somebody. . . .

ROSENTHAL. You get out by the window. You'll have time to get away while they're dealing with me.

---

7. "They drew straws . . . To see who would be eaten."

MARECHAL. Come off it! I'll handle this one! ROSENTHAL *begins to protest.* And keep still!

> MARECHAL *rises. Stay for a few seconds on* ROSENTHAL *who cannot move. Cut to* MARECHAL, *who holds a thick log in his hands. He hides behind the door, waiting to knock out the first entrant. The stable door creaks, then opens to let in a cow. Behind the cow comes a young blonde woman. She looks so fragile that* MARECHAL *does not dare use his log, even though she can see him in the light of the lamp she is holding. When she sees the two men, she does not cry out, but remains quite still in her surprise. In a reverse angle, the men look so filthy and tired that pity comes into her gaze.*
>
> *She is young, dressed very decently in the style of all the local country women, yet slightly more elegantly and tastefully. Her face, framed by a kerchief, is delicate and beautiful. She looks gentle and rather sad. She shows no terror at seeing the two men and, as she closes the door behind her, she talks to them in German, as she knows no other language.*

ELSA. What are you doing here? Prisoners of war? Do you speak German?

> MARECHAL, *who has not understood a word, gathers all the same what the last phrase means.*

MARECHAL. No! *On the defensive.* No! Not bandits! French.

ELSA *in German.* French. Who?

ROSENTHAL *seen from above in medium close-up.* She's asking us who we are. *He shows his ankle, turns towards* ELSA *and speaks in broken German.* . . . I've sprained my ankle. . . . We're terribly tired. . . . We're not robbers.

ELSA. I'm not frightened.

ROSENTHAL *in German.* Call the police! I refuse to go another step. *He shouts in French.* It hurts too much. . . . No, I won't go another step.

ELSA. A sprain.

> *As she says this, she leans over* ROSENTHAL *and feels his ankle. Then she makes a decision and gets up.*

ELSA. Come into my house.

MARECHAL. What is she saying?

ROSENTHAL *to* MARECHAL. She's telling us to go to her house.

> *The two men hesitate and look at each other, not knowing what to do.* ROSENTHAL *is exhausted, but* MARECHAL *shakes his head.*

MARECHAL. I don't trust her.

ELSA. I live alone.

ROSENTHAL. She says she lives all by herself.

> [*Farm: Outdoors, at night*]

ELSA, *carrying her lamp, leads the two men to the door of the farmhouse. They pause before entering.*

ELSA. Come in!

MARECHAL *shrugs and aids* ROSENTHAL. *All three enter.*

[*Kitchen*]

Shot of the door from the inside. The kitchen is lighted. ELSA *turns to the two men and says specifically to* ROSENTHAL, *who understands her language.*

ELSA. Don't make a noise, my child is asleep.

ROSENTHAL *translating.* She says there's a child sleeping. Don't make any noise.

MARECHAL *helps her to seat* ROSENTHAL *carefully in an armchair next to the stove.* MARECHAL *remains standing, a little put out.*

ELSA *to* MARECHAL. Sit down, I'll be back at once.

She goes into the next room. MARECHAL, *who has not understood, remains on the defensive. Shot of* ELSA, *putting down her coat and leaving the room. Cut to* ROSENTHAL, *comfortably seated, and to* MARECHAL, *standing and looking worried. Pan back to* ELSA *who is returning, carrying a basin. She goes and fills the basin with water, and sets it down on the stove; then she puts down a bandage and a towel next to* ROSENTHAL. *While she waits for the water to heat up, she turns to* MARECHAL.

ELSA. Are you hungry?

MARECHAL *trying to understand.* Hmm. . . . Ah, yes! Hungry! . . . Yes. . . . Yes!

Cut to medium close-up of ROSENTHAL, *lying back in the armchair.*

ROSENTHAL. She's asking you if you're hungry.

MARECHAL. Yes. . . . *Impatiently.* . . . I understood.

ELSA *to* ROSENTHAL. What about you?

ROSENTHAL *stretching.* I only want to sleep.

ELSA *pours out some milk into a big glass held by* MARECHAL. *She then gives him a sandwich, which he begins gulping down. They all remain silent. After a moment, the sound of a battalion walking along the road can be heard. The soldiers are singing in the night.*

MARECHAL *looks urgently at* ELSA, *then at* ROSENTHAL. *The sound of marching feet can be heard distinctly over the singing. Suddenly, someone knocks on the shutters. Cut often from* MARECHAL, *alarmed, to* ROSENTHAL, *who gets up, to* ELSA, *who calmly goes over to the window, opens it, and pushes open the shutters. A young feldwebel is standing at the window. Shot of* ELSA *and the feldwebel talking in German.*

FELDWEBEL. Good evening.

ELSA. Good evening.

FELDWEBEL *saluting with one finger.* Sorry to disturb you, but how far is it to Wolfisheim?

ELSA. Seven and a half miles.

FELDWEBEL *sighing.* Seven and a half miles! Well, I'd rather be spending the night with you than on the bloody road to Wolfisheim! Still . . . *He salutes* . . . duty is duty. Thank you and good night.

> *The feldwebel goes off.* ELSA *closes the shutters and the window again with great simplicity, and she turns towards the two Frenchmen, who are standing right by the door and staring at her in bewilderment.* MARECHAL *starts eating again, and* ROSENTHAL *sits down.* ELSA *goes over to the stove, picks up the basin and puts it down next to* ROSENTHAL'S *leg. She picks up his leg and begins pulling at his foot to get the shoe off.* ROSENTHAL *cries out with pain.* ELSA *is very sorry for him, but is also worried about the child.*

ELSA. Hush! My child is asleep!

> *Very slow pan to* MARECHAL. *He is watching the other two and understands their exchange.*

> [*Dining Room*]

> *Close-up of a framed photograph of an N.C.O. Above the frame is the ribbon given for the top German decoration. The photograph is standing on the mantlepiece. It is daylight, and, as* ELSA'S *voice speaks off, pan to show another photograph next to the first one: a group of young men.* ELSA'S *hand can be seen in shot, her finger pointing at various individuals.*

ELSA. My husband, killed at Verdun. My brothers, killed at Liège, Charleroi and Tannenberg.[8] . . . *She sighs.* Our greatest victories! . . . Now the table is too large. . . .

> *Pan to the table in the centre of the dining-room.* ELSA'S *little girl,* LOTTE, *is finishing a slice of bread. She is five years old, brown-haired, blue-eyed, and looks very merry.*

> MARECHAL *is looking after the cow; he is filling up her trough with hay. The fat cow, already used to him, comes to feed from his hand.*

MARECHAL. You're not scared, and you don't mind being fed by a Frenchman. . . . *Slapping the cow's side.* You were born in Wurtemberg and I was born in Paris; well, that doesn't stop us from being pals, does it? You're just a poor cow, and I'm just a poor soldier. And we're both doing our best, aren't we? Go on!

> *He pushes the cow aside and leaves the stable. Stay for a moment*

---

8. Famous battles of World War I; in February 1916 at Verdun 328,500 Germans and 348,000 French were killed.

on the cow, which turns her head towards the door and moos.
[Countryside: Outdoors]
His back to camera, MARECHAL *leaves the stable and goes over*
to take a look at the valley. He yawns and stretches luxuriously.
The bells are ringing in the distance. After a while, MARECHAL
turns away and walks towards camera, humming. He goes off.
MARECHAL *is now seen walking towards the farmhouse and, as*
he passes, he sinks his axe into the chopping block. He goes in.
[Kitchen and Dining Room]
MARECHAL *closes the door behind him and walks over to the*
oven to sniff at what is cooking. In the background, ROSENTHAL
sits in an armchair in the dining-room. LOTTE, *the little girl, is*
next to him, and the two are chattering in German. From a
new angle, MARECHAL, *seen from the front, has stopped at the*
doorway which divides the two rooms. He is looking at ROSEN-
THAL *and* LOTTE, *who have not yet seen him.* MARECHAL *him-*
self has not seen ELSA, *who was scrubbing the floor behind him.*

ROSENTHAL. You're a very clever little girl.

LOTTE *coquettishly.* Mummy and I know everything.

ROSENTHAL. Really? Well then, tell me how much milk the cow
gives every month?

LOTTE. Mummy's the one who knows that. . . . *Counting on her*
fingers. . . . What I know is I've got five fingers. One . . . two
. . . three . . . four . . . five. . . .

Pan towards MARECHAL. ELSA, *behind him, tenderly gazes at her*
daughter. The young woman already seems to have got used to
the presence of the two strangers.

ELSA *in German to* MARECHAL. Could you go and fetch me some
water, please?

MARECHAL *not understanding and turning to* ROSENTHAL. What is
she saying?

ROSENTHAL. She's asking you to go and get some water from the
pump.

MARECHAL. Well, of course. It's a pleasure. . . . *Turning to* ELSA.
. . . Wasser . . . wasser. . . . Ya!

He and ELSA *smile at each other. He cannot speak a word of*
German nor she of French. They enjoy this game which makes
it easy for them to be friendly.

MARECHAL *takes an empty bucket and goes out. Stay for a moment*
on the door, with ROSENTHAL *in the background, stretching in*
his armchair. LOTTE *skips over to her mother, who is smiling at*
her, and throws herself in ELSA's *arms.*
[Dining Room: Night]
It is Christmas eve. MARECHAL *and* ROSENTHAL *have put up a*
Christmas tree on the big table, shown in a long shot slightly

from above. The tree consists of a big pine branch, which they are decorating with paper chains. ROSENTHAL *is cutting out more pink paper, while* MARECHAL *fixes tiny candles onto the branches. At the foot of the tree on the table is a manger which they have constructed out of cardboard and wood. A quick close-up inside the manger shows a rather odd-looking holy family. The baby Jesus and his parents are carved out of potatoes.*

MARECHAL *off.* It's sweet, but it still looks a bit shoddy.

ROSENTHAL. I did my best.

MARECHAL. Of course, you did. I was saying that to Father Christmas.

ELSA *enters on tip-toe and looks moved at the surprise the two foreigners have prepared. It is obviously the very humbleness and oddity of it which touches her.*

ELSA *in German.* Oh! The Virgin Mary!

ROSENTHAL. And baby Jesus . . . *Smiling* . . . my blood brother!

He turns to MARECHAL. *Shot of the three.*

MARECHAL. Touché, as poor Bœldieu would have said.

ROSENTHAL *suddenly sad as he remembers.* What, do you think he got knocked off?

MARECHAL. Better not to talk about it, all right? *He lights the candles on the Christmas tree.* It's ready. Shall we go and fetch Lotte? We ought to hurry, the candles won't last.

MARECHAL *goes over to the bedroom with* ELSA. *Cut to* ROSEN-THAL.

ROSENTHAL. Just a moment!

He goes over to the old-fashioned gramophone and winds it up. Cut back to MARECHAL *and* ELSA *by the door, waiting and looking at each other tenderly. The lights go out.* ELSA *opens the door and goes up to her daughter's bed.* MARECHAL *remains in the foreground by the door, seen from the back.*

ELSA *waking up* LOTTE. Lotte! Hey, Lotte, Father Christmas has come! ELSA *picks up her daughter and carries her into the dining-room.* LOTTE's *eyes begin to shine when she sees the tree and the lights. She slips out of her mother's arms and runs barefoot towards the tree and* ROSENTHAL, *who waits for her with open arms. Shot of* LOTTE's *face above the table, looking ecstatically at the tree and the nativity scene. The faces of* ROSENTHAL, MARECHAL *and* ELSA *appear behind hers.* (German dialogue)

LOTTE *overjoyed.* Is it for me? Oh! I want baby Jesus!

ELSA *leaning towards her daughter.* Do you want to take him to bed with you?

LOTTE. No, I want to eat him.

ELSA. He's not to be eaten.

MARECHAL *smiles.* ROSENTHAL *is in the seventh heaven.*
LOTTE *reaching over to the manger.* I'll eat Joseph then.
ELSA. Eat Joseph, but in bed.
   LOTTE *turns to* ROSENTHAL *and kisses him.*
ROSENTHAL. You're a very nice little girl. . . .
   He kisses the child again, very affectionately. Then MARECHAL
   catches LOTTE *and picks her up to take her back to the bedroom.*
   ROSENTHAL *speaks to* MARECHAL *in German, pronouncing each*
   syllable.
ROSENTHAL. Lotte has blue eyes.
   MARECHAL *is silent for an instant. In the background, leaning*
   against the bedroom door, ELSA *seems to be lost in thought.*
   MARECHAL *repeats the phrase in German with a terrible accent.*
MARECHAL. Lotte—has—blue—eyes. . . .
   A quick close-up of ELSA *shows her smiling and correcting*
   MARECHAL'S *frightful German.*
ELSA. . . . Blue eyes.
MARECHAL. Blue—eyes. . . .
   ELSA *goes into the bedroom, followed by* MARECHAL *carrying*
   LOTTE *over to the little bed.*
ROSENTHAL *in the foreground at the door.* Goodnight, froglet!
   Once the child is in bed, MARECHAL *comes back and looks at*
   the manger. ROSENTHAL *is next to him. They look at each other*
   for a second, but say nothing and turn away as ELSA *comes back*
   after closing the bedroom door. Group shot of the three slightly
   from below.
ELSA *embarrassed.* I . . . don't know how to thank you.
ROSENTHAL *answering in German.* Thank us? When we owe you
  everything!
   All three remain silent for a moment. But the silence is too
   heavy, and ELSA *breaks it.*
ELSA *first to* ROSENTHAL. Well then, goodnight.
   They shake hands affectionately and MARECHAL *gets ready to go*
   to his room.
MARECHAL *to* ROSENTHAL. Goodnight!
   Pan to the gramophone which is still playing. MARECHAL *goes*
   and turns it off. ELSA *is still standing in the middle of the room,*
   her eyes lowered.
MARECHAL *to* ELSA. Goodnight.
ELSA *without raising her head and in French.* Goodnight.
   MARECHAL *walks to the door of* ROSENTHAL'S *room, then returns*
   before opening it. Casually, he goes over to the Christmas tree
   and blows out the lighted candles. He then walks off again. Stay
   on ELSA *for a few seconds, then cut to* MARECHAL *who goes into*

ROSENTHAL's *room with the camera following him.* MARECHAL
*whispers, 'Goodnight,' and leaves by another door to go into his
own room. He closes the door behind him.*
[*Maréchal's Room*]
Medium close-up of MARECHAL, *looking thoughtful. When he
has closed the door, he turns his head towards the dresser. On
the dresser is a tray full of apples set out to dry. He takes one
and begins eating it, as he walks about the room. Follow him
to show at the same time as he notices it, that the door leading
from his room to the dining-room is ajar. In the background,*
ELSA *is still standing where he left her.* MARECHAL, *surprised,
goes up to her very slowly until he is standing right next to her.
She raises her face and he takes her in his arms.*
[*Countryside. Outdoors: Day*]
Cut to the snowy countryside seen by ROSENTHAL *from the window of his room. Camera tracks backward to show* ROSENTHAL,
*seen from the back, leaning against the windowsill. He moves
away.*
[*Rosenthal's Room*]
ROSENTHAL *leaves the window. Follow him to the door which
leads to the dining-room. He opens it and sees* MARECHAL *hold-
ing* ELSA *in his arms.*
Taken by surprise, MARECHAL *and* ELSA *move apart.* ROSENTHAL
goes over to ELSA *and shakes her hand.*
[*Dining Room*]
ROSENTHAL. Hello . . . I'll do the coffee.
MARECHAL *a bit embarrassed.* We were waiting for you. . . . Coffee's
ready. *He turns towards* ELSA *tenderly.* Tell him in French.
  ELSA, *in close-up, shyly pronounces each syllable distinctly in
  French.*
ELSA. Coff . . . ee . . . is . . . read . . . ee. . . .
  *This insignificant little phrase is her declaration of love. . . .
  And all three look at each other, laughing. . . . But* ROSEN-
  THAL's *ankle has already healed. The two men will have to leave
  soon.*
  [*Countryside: Day*]
  *Quick dissolve to medium shot of the two men, seen from the
  back, leaning against the fence, which is the farm's boundary.*
ROSENTHAL. Have you warned her we're leaving?
MARECHAL *without turning round.* No, not yet.
ROSENTHAL. You must, you know. . . .
MARECHAL *embarrassed.* You go and tell her . . . [please . . . I can't
  bring myself to.]
    ROSENTHAL, *extremely put out by the prospect, nonetheless goes*

off in the direction of the farm. MARECHAL, *his back still turned,
lowers his head a little.*

[*Kitchen*]

Medium shot of ELSA: *her expression shows that she is expecting
the news. The door makes a noise as* ROSENTHAL, *looking downcast, comes in.*

ROSENTHAL *in German.* We'll be leaving this evening and. . . .

ELSA *interrupting him in German.* I knew it.

ROSENTHAL. Maréchal is so sad that he didn't dare tell you himself.

ELSA. Why? I always knew he would be leaving one of these days.
She rushes out of the room. ROSENTHAL *opens the window. In
the background is* MARECHAL *leaning against the fence.*

ROSENTHAL. Come in!
MARECHAL, *in the distance, straightens up and walks over to the
farm house.*

MARECHAL. Yes. . . . Coming. . . .
ROSENTHAL, *in the foreground, closes the window.*

[*Dining Room*]

LOTTE *is eating by herself at the big table. Three other bowls
are set on the table.* ELSA, *holding a coffee pot, comes into shot
and pours out the coffee.* MARECHAL, *his head lowered, sits down,
while* ROSENTHAL *goes over to the little girl and strokes her hair.*
ELSA *speaks in German, showing some parcels with a gesture of
her head.*

ELSA. Those parcels are for the. . . . You must eat something hot
before you leave.

ROSENTHAL *to* MARECHAL. Well, we won't start till nightfall then?
Cut to ELSA *in medium close-up. She seems out of breath and
sets down the coffee pot on the table to go quickly over into a
corner. Follow her, as she sits down and starts weeping. Cut
back to* MARECHAL, *who has immediately got up. He goes over
to her. Medium close-up of the two, who remain silent for a
moment.*
Cut back to the table. ROSENTHAL, *wanting to leave the lovers
alone for the last time, begins to make discreetly for the door,
then turns back to go and fetch* LOTTE, *whom he pulls towards
the door.*

ROSENTHAL. Come along, Lotte. Let's go and say goodbye to the
cow.
*They go out. Cut back to the couple, still sitting on the bench
next to the fireplace, holding hands.* ELSA *speaks in German,*
MARECHAL *in French. They speak at random, but they know
that their words are words of love.*

ELSA: I was alone for such a long time. . . . I had stopped waiting.

. . . You will never know the joy it gave me to hear your man's footsteps in this house. . . .

She begins to sob.

MARECHAL. Elsa, listen . . . when the war is over. . . . If I don't get killed, I'll come back. I'll take you and Lotte back to France. . . .

Dissolve to a few hours later:

[*Kitchen*]

The moment of departure has come: the two friends are wearing the same old clothes—now clean and patched—and ROSENTHAL *has put* ELSA'S *small parcels in his pockets.*

ELSA *stands very straight and dry-eyed.* LOTTE *is holding onto her skirt.* ELSA *speaks to* MARECHAL.

ELSA *in German.* Go quickly. . . . It's better that way!

MARECHAL *presses her hand a long time; he would like to say something to soothe her, knowing how upset she is; but what can he say that she will understand? Suddenly, he picks up* LOTTE *and holds her in his arms. He speaks syllable by syllable in German with his execrable accent.*

MARECHAL. Lotte—has—blue—eyes.

MARECHAL *has put all his love, all his gratitude, and more still in this odd farewell. Quick cut to a close-up of* ELSA, *correcting him.*

ELSA. Lotte has blue eyes.

Overwhelmed, MARECHAL *leaves the room, followed by* ROSEN-THAL.

Cut to a night exterior. The two men go forward.

MARECHAL *hesitates to look back.*

Cut back to the room. ELSA *and* LOTTE *are standing at the open door, looking at the two friends walking away. Cut to* MARECHAL *who looks back. In the background is the lighted door and* ELSA, *holding* LOTTE *against her. At that moment:,*

ROSENTHAL. Look back!

MARECHAL *pretends not to have looked back.*

MARECHAL *grumbling.* If I'd looked back, I might not be able to leave. . . .

[*Kitchen*]

Cut back to ELSA *and* LOTTE *still at the door.* ELSA *makes up her mind, closes the door and takes her daughter over to the table, putting her in front of a bowl. She starts moving about busily, removing plates and glasses, then leaves the room. Stay on the little girl.*

[*Frontier*]

Pan to reveal the mountains, covered with snow, then show from above MARECHAL *and* ROSENTHAL *on the look out, in hiding behind some pine-trees. They have been walking for two nights and have reached the Swiss border. Their only problem now is to avoid the German patrols guarding the frontier. So the two men have been hiding at the edge of a wood, as they examine the deserted landscape, all covered in snow.*

ROSENTHAL. Well, aren't we going to wait till night?

MARECHAL. Not a chance. We'd lose our way. Besides, the wood is so thick, when we get to the valley, we can go on our hands and knees. *A pause.* Are you sure, at least, that that's Switzerland over there?

ROSENTHAL *looking at his map.* Absolutely sure.

Quick pan over the valley and come back to the two men.

MARECHAL. It's just that German snow and Swiss snow look pretty much the same!

ROSENTHAL. Don't worry, there's a genuine man-made frontier right there, even though nature doesn't give a damn.

MARECHAL. I don't give a damn either. . . . *A pause.* And when the war's over, I'll come and get Elsa.

ROSENTHAL. Do you love her?

MARECHAL *sighing.* I guess I must!

ROSENTHAL *his hand on his friend's shoulder.* Remember, if we get across, you'll be going back to a squadron, and I back to a battery. We've got to fight again. . . .

MARECHAL *swearing.* We've got to finish this bloody war . . . let's hope it's the last.

ROSENTHAL. That's all an illusion! Come on, back to business. If we're seen by a patrol, what'll we do?

MARECHAL. Well, you run for it in one direction, and I in another . . . and it's each man for himself.

They are standing face to face now, seen from below.

ROSENTHAL. In case that happens, it might be safer to say our good-byes now . . . and see you soon.

They warmly embrace.

MARECHAL. So long, you bloody yid!

ROSENTHAL. Bye bye, old cheese!

Then side by side, they start running across the snow-covered fields towards the frontier. Pan to another area of the mountain to show in long shot from above, a German patrol following the tracks of the two men. Suddenly, a German soldier sees two black shapes in the valley, about one hundred yards away. He makes a gesture to the others, who aim their rifles and fire. Cut to the two black shapes running. Medium close-up of a German soldier starting to raise his rifle again. The sergeant goes over to him and pushes the muzzle of the rifle down. Both are seen from below as they speak in German.

THE SERGEANT. Don't shoot. They're in Switzerland!

The soldier puts the rifle in its sling on his shoulder.
THE SOLDIER. Lucky for them.
  Pan across the valley. Right at the bottom of the valley, the two small shapes strain forward, sinking knee-deep in the snow at every step. Cut to them walking away up the snowy hillside.

WILLIAM FAULKNER
1897–1962

Chronicler of the American South, William Faulkner's inventive imagination and innovative use of language brought him an internatinal reputation and influence on writers as far apart as Europe and Latin America. His account of historical change between the Old and the New South as experienced by a community in mythical Yoknapatawpha County, Mississippi, involved issues that far transcended his regional roots: the clash of generations and ways of life, racial and family tragedies beyond individual comprehension or control, and the opposition of good and evil in almost archetypal terms. Although "Faulknerian" style is best known to many readers for its brilliantly extended narrative sentences, and its adaptation of Joyce's stream of consciousness technique to provide insights into a character's mind, his application of an allegorizing, fantastic imagination to the portrayal of history has also influenced writers like the Colombian Gabriel García Márquez. With Faulkner, the Balzacian tradition of the "human comedy"—the novelist's panorama of society—develops into a new mixture of realism and linguistic innovation.

  William Cuthbert Falkner was born on September 25, 1897, in New Albany, Mississippi, to a prosperous family with many ties to Southern history. The eldest of four sons, Faulkner (he adopted this spelling in 1924 for his first book) was named for a great-grandfather who commanded a Confederate regiment in the Civil War, built railroads, and wrote novels. Faulkner's father worked for the family railroad until it was sold in 1902, afterwards moving the family to Oxford and eventually becoming business manager of the University of Mississippi. Faulkner's close acquaintance with Southern customs and attitudes, his own experience as the descendant of a once-prosperous and influential family, and his attachment to the region of Lafayette County and the town of Oxford (Yoknapatawpha County and Jefferson in the novels) help to shape themes and setting in his fiction.

  Young Faulkner did not like school, although he read widely in his grandfather's library and borrowed books from an older friend, Philip Stone. Leaving high school after two years to work as a bookkeeper in his grandfather's bank, he continued reading and discussing literature with Stone, who introduced him to Balzac's novels and encouraged his writing. In the last six months of 1918 he trained in Canada as a fighter pilot—then a common way of getting more quickly into combat in World War I—but the war ended and he returned to Oxford to enroll at the university as a special student.

While in school, Faulkner published poetry, prose, and drawings in *The Mississippian* and worked on the yearbook, but decided to leave the University in November 1920 to work in a New York bookstore. By December 1921 he had returned to Oxford, where he became postmaster at the university and was dismissed three years later for irresponsibility. During these years he wrote mainly poetry and seems to have been influenced by the French Symbolists: his first published poem, "L'Après-midi d'un faune," takes its title from an earlier poem by Stéphane Mallarmé. With Stone's help, Faulkner published his first book, a collection of lyrics called *The Marble Faun* (also the title of a novel by Nathaniel Hawthorne) in 1924.

In 1925, Faulkner spent six months living in New Orleans where he was attracted to a literary group associated with *The Double Dealer*, a magazine in which he himself published poems, essays, and prose sketches. The group's chief figure was the novelist Sherwood Anderson, author of a series of regional stories published as *Winesburg, Ohio*, who encouraged Faulkner to make fictional use of his Southern background and who recommended his first novel (without having read it) to a publisher. After completing *Soldier's Pay* (published in 1926), Faulkner took a freighter to Europe where he bicycled and hiked through Italy and France and lived for a short while in Paris. He returned to Mississippi at the end of the year, where he wrote his second novel, *Mosquitoes* (1927—a satire on the New Orleans group).

Taking up Anderson's earlier suggestion, Faulkner now embarked on the regional "Yoknapatawpha" (yok-na-pa-TAW-pha) series with *Sartoris* (1929), an account of the return home, marriage, and death of wounded veteran Bayard Sartoris. In Yoknapatawpha County, Faulkner created a whole fictional world with characters who reappear from novel to novel (a technique he would have encountered in Balzac's *Comédie humaine*). Here imaginary families such as the Sartorises, Compsons, Sutpens, McCaslins, and Snopeses rise to prosperity or fall into various kinds of weakness, degradation, and death. Individual characters work out destinies that are already half-shaped by family tradition and invisible community pressures. They are caught in close and often incestuous blood relationships, and make their way in a world where the values, traditions, and privileges of an old plantation society are yielding to the values of a new mercantile class. A network of family dynasties illustrates this picture of a changing society: the decaying and impoverished Compson family (*The Sound and the Fury*, 1929), two generations of Sutpens rising to great wealth and dying in madness and isolation (*Absalom, Absalom!* 1936), the McCaslin family with its history of incest, miscegenation, and guilt (*Go Down, Moses*, 1942), and the viciously grasping and ambitious "poor white" Snopes family (*The Hamlet*, 1940; *The Town*, 1957; *The Mansion*, 1959) who appear in the stories printed here. These are violent works, and the murders, lynchings, and bestialities of all kinds that appear in them account for Faulkner's early American reputation as a lurid local writer. European critics, however, especially the French, who recognized his ability as early as 1931, were quick to recognize mythic overtones and classical and Biblical prototypes in these tales of twisted family relationships. Faulkner's Mississippi countryside is the setting for archetypal conflicts of good and evil, or for local tragedies whose degenerate grandeur is hinted at in the names from Greek tragedy given some of the characters:

Orestes Snopes, Clytemnestra Sutpen.

After *Sartoris*, Faulkner experimented with a new style modeled on the stream of consciousness technique of Joyce's *Ulysses* for his next novel, *The Sound and the Fury*. In this novel, the Compson family's tragedy is told through several different points of view, and the first version the reader encounters is the disconnected and emotionally skewed world of the idiot Benjy. Both novels were rejected several times before finally being published in 1929, and Faulkner supported himself during these years chiefly through odd jobs (working on a shrimp trawler, in a lumber mill, and a power plant and as a carpenter, painter, and paper hanger), and then from his short stories, of which he sold thirty between 1930 and 1932. In 1929 he married Estelle Oldham Franklin, with whom he had one child, Jill, in 1933. Irritated at the difficulty of finding publishers for his serious or experimental works, the novelist set out to write a bestseller—and succeeded. *Sanctuary*, a novel of the Deep South that described the rape and prostitution of a schoolgirl, murder, perjury, and the lynching of an innocent man, was made into a movie and brought Faulkner invitations to work on movie scripts for a variety of Hollywood studios. From 1932 to 1955, the novelist added to his income by working as a "film doctor" revising and collaborating on scripts. Although his works continued to receive critical praise, he did not have any commercial successes after *Sanctuary*; in 1945 when he was, according to the French writer and philosopher Jean-Paul Sartre, the idol of young French readers, almost all his novels were out of print. It took an anthology, *The Portable Faulkner*, to reintroduce Faulkner to a wide audience in 1946. In 1950 he won the Nobel Prize for Literature and used the prize money to establish the William Faulkner Foundation to assist Latin American writers and award educational scholarships to Mississippi blacks. Five years later he received the Pulitzer Prize and the National Book award for *A Fable* (1954). Faulkner's last book was a comedy set in Yoknapatawpha County, *The Reivers* (1962). He died of a heart attack in Oxford, Mississippi, on July 6, 1962.

In Faulkner's world men and women are measured by the breadth of their compassion or the quality of their endurance. Although there are villains, few wholly negative characters appear, and these are seen as grotesque distortions of humanity: the cruel and frustrated Jason Compson, or the impotent rapist Popeye of *Sanctuary*, who "had that vicious depthless quality of stamped tin." Heroes tend to be larger than life, casting their shadow even after death as does Addie Bundren (*As I Lay Dying*, 1930), whose dying wish obliges her family to accompany her coffin across Mississippi in a miniature epic journey through flood and fire. They have the moral endurance of Bayard Sartoris II, who as a boy kills his grandmother's murderer and as a man faces down his father's killer—unarmed—in order to break the pattern of "honorable revenge"; or the physical endurance of the tall convict in *Old Man*, whose "whole purpose," according to Faulkner, was "to prove . . . just how much the human body could bear, stand, endure." Not all characters are heroes. Some are ordinary people whose perseverance and dedication to an idea, a person, or a way of life give them larger significance; some are thoughtful people driven by circumstances to question their own identity and values; some are idiots able only to feel a succession of emotions. Faulkner generally describes such figures from the outside. We see them act, and we may even follow their thoughts in an interior monologue, but these are only traces of an inner personality which has already been decided and to which we have no real access.

The "truth" of the novels comes to us through a variety of perspectives and rhetorical strategies. Three different narrators in *Absalom, Absalom!* tell the story of Thomas Sutpen. The four points of view in *The Sound and the Fury* move from the imagined inner monologue of an idiot to the adult monologues of his nervously suicidal and psychopathic brothers, and finally to a third-person narrative focusing on Dilsey, the black woman who has been in charge of family and household and who "endures." Fifty-nine sections of interior monologue in *As I Lay Dying* express the inner relationships of the Bundren family. The convict in *Old Man* possesses a dogged, wilfully limited view of things modeled on simplistic cops-and-robbers stories and adventure tales. A narrative perspective may change tone, as happens at the end of the epic coffin journey in *As I Lay Dying* when the widowed Anse Bundren returns happily from town with a new set of false teeth, a new wife, and a phonograph. Chronology may be broken, as in the time changes represented by two typefaces in the "Benjy" section of *The Sound and the Fury*; details are exaggerated or distorted; dialect speech emphasizes the presence of the storyteller's art. Throughout, Faulkner's fluid style escapes rigid categories; it is a style of tensions and contradictions, of tragedy and humor, realism and mythic outreach, now short and laconic, now rambling. Like Joyce and Proust, he uses long, involved, and elaborate sentences to draw the reader into a special world of the imagination, sentences that follow the ebb and flow of his characters' thoughts, or meander like a narrative consciousness absorbed in the variety of the world it describes. His tales are rooted in a community of the regional South, itself caught in the large context of historical change, but they are at the same time allegories of human endurance in an often hostile universe. Yet Faulkner's world is by no means unrelievedly somber, and its realism and earthy humor have led to his being called a "comic" writer in the broad sense that implies a universal vision encompassing the pettiness as well as the grandeur of human existence. The two stories paired here, both of which recur in altered form in *The Hamlet*, exhibit the range of Faulkner's art from the dehumanized threat of Abner Snopes in "Barn Burning" to the comic wonder and dismay of V. K. Ratliff in "Spotted Horses," describing how Flem Snopes cheated the whole community into buying wild horses from Texas.

The Snopes family and Snopesism are at the center of both stories. Just as the Sartoris family represents Southern aristocratic tradition in all its romanticism and humanity, the Snopeses originate as the society's shiftless "poor whites" and come to embody the cold, calculating, exploitative side of human nature that is working its way to the fore in a modern, commercially oriented age. Although members of the Snopes family take on individuality and human traits (generally perverse) when described separately, together they become allegorized into "Snopesism," a vision of evil that is openly diabolical and calls up its own counterforce: in Faulkner's view of the eternal battle between good and evil, "There is always someone that will never stop trying to cope with Snopes, that will never stop trying to get rid of Snopes." Abner Snopes, father of Flem (unnamed in this story) and Colonel Sartoris

Snopes, is such a personification of inhuman, two-dimensional evil: "without face or depth—a shape black, flat, and bloodless as though cut from tin . . . a voice harsh like tin and without heat like tin." His human qualities are purely destructive: a ferocious independence and conviction of his own rectitude, linked to deep jealousy and rage against others' prosperity or authority; a vicious paranoia that creates opportunities for revenge; an arsonist's love for the destructive element of fire that speaks to "some deep mainspring" of his being. Young Colonel Sartoris Snopes is torn between two loyalties, as his name implies: dependent on his family and fiercely defensive of his father whenever the "enemy" threatens, he nonetheless dislikes lying, takes joy in imagining Major de Spain's mansion as a sanctuary his father cannot touch, wishes his father would change even as he recognizes he will not, and finally cuts himself off completely from his family by warning Major de Spain of the intended arson. To the psychological realism of individual portraits, and of the struggle between father and son, Faulkner adds the level of a struggle between right and wrong; both sides inextricably related to each other and, at the end, both left with equally open futures.

The picture of pure destruction that plays such a large role in "Barn Burning" returns in comic vein with "Spotted Horses," as the horses bursting out of their pen run wild over the countryside and defy their new owners' best attempts to catch them. Literally an unbridled force of nature (and spotted horses are often demonic in folklore), they invade a house, force one of the inhabitants to jump out the window in his underwear, run over a mule-drawn wagon and its inhabitants, and in general upset the normal order of things. Adding to the ridiculousness of the situation is the fact that the townspeople are caught empty-handed through their own greed, having bought the horses against their better judgment when they knew or suspected that Flem Snopes was behind the sale. V. K. Ratliff, the sewing machine agent who narrates the story, cannot help admiring the monumental craftiness with which Snopes manipulates events to his own profit, although Ratliff is also opposed to everything that Snopes stands for and tries to shame him into returning Mrs. Armstid's money. For this comedy also has somber overtones: Henry Armstid is driven further into madness, and his family pushed further into desperate poverty as Snopes refuses to return the money. Snopes is out of sight for most of the story, and when he appears toward the end and sends Mrs. Armstid on her way with a bag of candy for the children, the comedy turns bitter—an example of Snopesism in all its callous greed. Only a return to the level of storytelling, with Ratliff as a teller of tall tales who can appreciate the scale of Snopes's successful trickery, allows the story to maintain its character as one of Faulkner's most farcical tales.

Suggested studies include Michael Millgate, *The Achievement of William Faulkner* (1963), a critical study of the novels and stories with a brief biography in the first chapter; Cleanth Brooks, *William Faulkner: The Yoknapatawpha Country* (1963), a basic literary analysis and study of Faulkner's mythical South in the Yoknapatawpha stories, with a list of Faulkner's fictional characters; and Linda Wagner, ed., *William Faulkner: Four Decades of Criticism* (1973), a collection of essays. Joseph Blotner is the author of *Faulkner: A Biography*, 2 vols. (1974), the authorized and immensely detailed biography.

Barn Burning

The store in which the Justice of the Peace's court was sitting smelled of cheese. The boy, crouched on his nail keg at the back of the crowded room, knew he smelled cheese, and more: from where he sat he could see the ranked shelves close-packed with the solid, squat, dynamic shapes of tin cans whose labels his stomach read, not from the lettering which meant nothing to his mind but from the scarlet devils and the silver curve of fish—this, the cheese which he knew he smelled and the hermetic[1] meat which his intestines believed he smelled coming in intermittent gusts momentary and brief between the other constant one, the smell and sense just a little of fear because mostly of despair and grief, the old fierce pull of blood. He could not see the table where the Justice sat and before which his father and his father's enemy (*our enemy* he thought in that despair; *ourn! mine and hisn both! He's my father!*) stood, but he could hear them, the two of them that is, because his father had said no word yet:

"But what proof have you, Mr. Harris?"

"I told you. The hog got into my corn. I caught it up and sent it back to him. He had no fence that would hold it. I told him so, warned him. The next time I put the hog in my pen. When he came to get it I gave him enough wire to patch up his pen. The next time I put the hog up and kept it. I rode down to his house and saw the wire I gave him still rolled on to the spool in his yard. I told him he could have the hog when he paid me a dollar pound fee. That evening a nigger came with the dollar and got the hog. He was a strange nigger. He said, 'He say to tell you wood and hay kin burn.' I said, 'What?' 'That whut he say to tell you,' the nigger said. 'Wood and hay kin burn.' That night my barn burned. I got the stock out but I lost the barn."

"Where is the nigger? Have you got him?"

"He was a strange nigger, I tell you. I don't know what became of him."

"But that's not proof. Don't you see that's not proof?"

"Get that boy up here. He knows." For a moment the boy thought too that the man meant his older brother until Harris said, "Not him. The little one. The boy," and, crouching, small for his age, small and wiry like his father, in patched and faded jeans even too small for him, with straight, uncombed, brown hair and eyes gray and wild as storm scud, he saw the men between himself and the table part and become a lane of grim faces, at the end of which he saw the Justice, a shabby, collarless, graying man in spectacles, beckoning him. He felt no floor under his bare feet; he seemed to

1. Sealed-in, canned, in tins whose labels display scarlet devils and the silver curve of fish.

walk beneath the palpable weight of the grim turning faces. His father,
stiff in his black Sunday coat donned not for the trial but for the
moving, did not even look at him. *He aims for me to lie*, he thought,
again with that frantic grief and despair. *And I will have to do hit.*

"What's your name, boy?" the Justice said.

"Colonel Sartoris Snopes,"[2] the boy whispered.

"Hey?" the Justice said. "Talk louder. Colonel Sartoris? I reckon
anybody named for Colonel Sartoris in this country can't help but
tell the truth, can they?" The boy said nothing. *Enemy! Enemy!* he
thought; for a moment he could not even see, could not see that the
Justice's face was kindly nor discern that his voice was troubled when
he spoke to the man named Harris: "Do you want me to question
this boy?" But he could hear, and during those subsequent long seconds while there was absolutely no sound in the crowded little room
save that of quiet and intent breathing it was as if he had swung
outward at the end of a grape vine, over a ravine, and at the top of
the swing had been caught in a prolonged instant of mesmerized
gravity, weightless in time.

"No!" Harris said violently, explosively. "Damnation! Send him
out of here!" Now time, the fluid world, rushed beneath him again,
the voices coming to him again through the smell of cheese and
sealed meat, the fear and despair and the old grief of blood:

"This case is closed. I can't find against you, Snopes, but I can
give you advice. Leave this country and don't come back to it."

His father spoke for the first time, his voice cold and harsh, level,
without emphasis: "I aim to. I don't figure to stay in a country among
people who . . ." he said something unprintable and vile, addressed
to no one.

"That'll do," the Justice said. "Take your wagon and get out of
this country before dark. Case dismissed."

His father turned, and he followed the stiff black coat, the wiry
figure walking a little stiffly from where a Confederate provost's man's[3]
musket ball had taken him in the heel on a stolen horse thirty years
ago, followed the two backs now, since his older brother had appeared
from somewhere in the crowd, no taller than the father but thicker,
chewing tobacco steadily, between the two lines of grim-faced men
and out of the store and across the worn gallery and down the sagging
steps and among the dogs and half-grown boys in the mild May dust,
where as he passed a voice hissed:

"Barn burner!"

Again he could not see, whirling; there was a face in a red haze,
moonlike, bigger than the full moon, the owner of it half again his
size, he leaping in the red haze toward the face, feeling no blow,

2. The Snopes boy is named for Colonel [John] Sartoris, legendary founder of the aristocratic
Sartoris family in Faulkner's Yoknapatawpha County.   3. Military policeman.

feeling no shock when his head struck the earth, scrabbling up and leaping again, feeling no blow this time either and tasting no blood, scrabbling up to see the other boy in full flight and himself already leaping into pursuit as his father's hand jerked him back, the harsh, cold voice speaking above him: "Go get in the wagon."

It stood in a grove of locusts and mulberries across the road. His two hulking sisters in their Sunday dresses and his mother and her sister in calico and sunbonnets were already in it, sitting on and among the sorry residue of the dozen and more movings which even the boy could remember—the battered stove, the broken beds and chairs, the clock inlaid with mother-of-pearl, which would not run, stopped at some fourteen minutes past two o'clock of a dead and forgotten day and time, which had been his mother's dowry. She was crying, though when she saw him she drew her sleeve across her face and began to descend from the wagon. "Get back," the father said.

"He's hurt. I got to get some water and wash his . . ."

"Get back in the wagon," his father said. He got in too, over the tail-gate. His father mounted to the seat where the older brother already sat and struck the gaunt mules two savage blows with the peeled willow, but without heat. It was not even sadistic; it was exactly that same quality which in later years would cause his descendants to over-run the engine before putting a motor car into motion, striking and reining back in the same movement. The wagon went on, the store with its quiet crowd of grimly watching men dropped behind; a curve in the road hid it. *Forever* he thought. *Maybe he's done satisfied now, now that he has* . . . stopping himself, not to say it aloud even to himself. His mother's hand touched his shoulder.

"Does hit hurt?" she said.

"Naw," he said. "Hit don't hurt. Lemme be."

"Can't you wipe some of the blood off before hit dries?"

"I'll wash to-night," he said. "Lemme be, I tell you."

The wagon went on. He did not know where they were going. None of them ever did or ever asked, because it was always somewhere, always a house of sorts waiting for them a day or two days or even three days away. Likely his father had already arranged to make a crop on another farm before he . . . Again he had to stop himself. He (the father) always did. There was something about his wolflike independence and even courage when the advantage was at least neutral which impressed strangers, as if they got from his latent ravening ferocity not so much a sense of dependability as a feeling that his ferocious conviction in the rightness of his own actions would be of advantage to all whose interest lay with his.

That night they camped, in a grove of oaks and beeches where a spring ran. The nights were still cool and they had a fire against it, of a rail lifted from a nearby fence and cut into lengths—a small fire, neat, niggard almost, a shrewd fire; such fires were his father's habit and custom always, even in freezing weather. Older, the boy might have remarked this and wondered why not a big one; why should not a man who had not only seen the waste and extravagance of war, but who had in his blood an inherent voracious prodigality with material not his own, have burned everything in sight? Then he might have gone a step farther and thought that that was the reason: that niggard blaze was the living fruit of nights passed during those four years in the woods hiding from all men, blue or gray,[4] with his strings of horses (captured horses, he called them). And older still, he might have divined the true reason: that the element of fire spoke to some deep mainspring of his father's being, as the element of steel or of powder spoke to other men, as the one weapon for the preservation of integrity, else breath were not worth the breathing, and hence to be regarded with respect and used with discretion.

But he did not think this now and he had seen those same niggard blazes all his life. He merely ate his supper beside it and was already half asleep over his iron plate when his father called him, and once more he followed the stiff back, the stiff and ruthless limp, up the slope and on to the starlit road where, turning, he could see his father against the stars but without face or depth—a shape black, flat, and bloodless as though cut from tin in the iron folds of the frockcoat which had not been made for him, the voice harsh like tin and without heat like tin:

"You were fixing to tell them. You would have told him." He didn't answer. His father struck him with the flat of his hand on the side of the head, hard but without heat, exactly as he had struck the two mules at the store, exactly as he would strike either of them with any stick in order to kill a horse fly, his voice still without heat or anger: "You're getting to be a man. You got to learn. You got to learn to stick to your own blood or you ain't going to have any blood to stick to you. Do you think either of them, any man there this morning, would? Don't you know all they wanted was a chance to get at me because they knew I had them beat? Eh?" Later, twenty years later, he was to tell himself, "If I had said they wanted only truth, justice, he would have hit me again." But now he said nothing. He was not crying. He just stood there. "Answer me," his father said.

"Yes," he whispered. His father turned.

"Get on to bed. We'll be there tomorrow."

To-morrow they were there. In the early afternoon the wagon stopped before a paintless two-room house identical almost with the

---

4. In the Civil War (1861–1865), Union soldiers wore blue and Confederate soldiers gray uniforms.

dozen others it had stopped before even in the boy's ten years, and again, as on the other dozen occasions, his mother and aunt got down and began to unload the wagon, although his two sisters and his father and brother had not moved.

"Likely hit ain't fitten for hawgs," one of the sisters said.

"Nevertheless, fit it will and you'll hog it and like it," his father said. "Get out of them chairs and help your Ma unload."

The two sisters got down, big, bovine, in a flutter of cheap ribbons; one of them drew from the jumbled wagon bed a battered lantern, the other a worn broom. His father handed the reins to the older son and began to climb stiffly over the wheel. "When they get unloaded, take the team to the barn and feed them." Then he said, and at first the boy thought he was still speaking to his brother: "Come with me."

"Me?" he said.

"Yes," his father said. "You."

"Abner," his mother said. His father paused and looked back— the harsh level stare beneath the shaggy, graying, irascible brows.

"I reckon I'll have a word with the man that aims to begin tomorrow owning me body and soul for the next eight months."

They went back up the road. A week ago—or before last night, that is—he would have asked where they were going, but not now. His father had struck him before last night but never before had he paused afterward to explain why; it was as if the blow and the following calm, outrageous voice still rang, repercussed, divulging nothing to him save the terrible handicap of being young, the light weight of his few years, just heavy enough to prevent his soaring free of the world as it seemed to be ordered but not heavy enough to keep him footed solid in it, to resist it and try to change the course of its events.

Presently he could see the grove of oaks and cedars and the other flowering trees and shrubs where the house would be, though not the house yet. They walked beside a fence massed with honeysuckle and Cherokee roses[5] and came to a gate swinging open between two brick pillars, and now, beyond a sweep of drive, he saw the house for the first time and at that instant he forgot his father and the terror and despair both, and even when he remembered his father again (who had not stopped) the terror and despair did not return. Because, for all the twelve movings, they had sojourned until now in a poor country, a land of small farms and fields and houses, and he had never seen a house like this before. *Hit's big as a courthouse* he thought quietly, with a surge of peace and joy whose reason he could not have thought into words, being too young for that: *They are safe from him. People whose lives are a part of this peace and dignity are*

---

5. An evergreen climbing rose with white flowers.

beyond his touch, he no more to them than a buzzing wasp: capable of stinging for a little moment but that's all; the spell of this peace and dignity rendering even the barns and stable and cribs which belong to it impervious to the puny flames he might contrive . . . this, the peace and joy, ebbing for an instant as he looked again at the stiff black back, the stiff and implacable limp of the figure which was not dwarfed by the house, for the reason that it had never looked big anywhere and which now, against the serene columned backdrop, had more than ever that impervious quality of something cut ruthlessly from tin, depthless, as though, sidewise to the sun, it would cast no shadow. Watching him, the boy remarked the absolutely undeviating course which his father held and saw the stiff foot come squarely down in a pile of fresh droppings where a horse had stood in the drive and which his father could have avoided by a simple change of stride. But it ebbed only for a moment, though he could not have thought this into words either, walking on in the spell of the house, which he could even want but without envy, without sorrow, certainly never with that ravening and jealous rage which unknown to him walked in the ironlike black coat before him: *Maybe he will feel it too. Maybe it will even change him now from what maybe he couldn't help but be.*

They crossed the portico. Now he could hear his father's stiff foot as it came down on the boards with clocklike finality, a sound out of all proportion to the displacement of the body it bore and which was not dwarfed either by the white door before it, as though it had attained to a sort of vicious and ravening minimum not to be dwarfed by anything—the flat, wide, black hat, the formal coat of broadcloth which had once been black but which had now that friction-glazed greenish cast of the bodies of old house flies, the lifted sleeve which was too large, the lifted hand like a curled claw. The door opened so promptly that the boy knew the Negro must have been watching them all the time, an old man with neat grizzled hair, in a linen jacket, who stood barring the door with his body, saying, "Wipe you foots, white man, fo you come in here. Major ain't home nohow."

"Get out of my way, nigger," his father said, without heat too, flinging the door back and the Negro also and entering, his hat still on his head. And now the boy saw the prints of the stiff foot on the doorjamb and saw them appear on the pale rug behind the machine-like deliberation of the foot which seemed to bear (or transmit) twice the weight which the body compassed. The Negro was shouting "Miss Lula! Miss Lula!"[6] somewhere behind them, then the boy, deluged as though by a warm wave by a suave turn of carpeted stair and a pendant glitter of chandeliers and a mute gleam of gold frames, heard

6. "Miss" is a traditional Southern form of respectful address used also for married women.

the swift feet and saw her too, a lady—perhaps he had never seen her like before either—in a gray, smooth gown with lace at the throat and an apron tied at the waist and the sleeves turned back, wiping cake or biscuit dough from her hands with a towel as she came up the hall, looking not at his father at all but at the tracks on the blond rug with an expression of incredulous amazement.

"I tried," the Negro cried. "I tole him to . . ."

"Will you please go away?" she said in a shaking voice. "Major de Spain is not at home. Will you please go away?"

His father had not spoken again. He did not speak again. He did not even look at her. He just stood stiff in the center of the rug, in his hat, the shaggy iron-gray brows twitching slightly above the peb-ble-colored eyes as he appeared to examine the house with brief deliberation. Then with the same deliberation he turned; the boy watched him pivot on the good leg and saw the stiff foot drag round the arc of the turning, leaving a final long and fading smear. His father never looked at it, he never once looked down at the rug. The Negro held the door. It closed behind them, upon the hysteric and indistinguishable woman-wail. His father stopped at the top of the steps and scraped his boot clean on the edge of it. At the gate he stopped again. He stood for a moment, planted stiffly on the stiff foot, looking back at the house. "Pretty and white, ain't it?" he said. "That's sweat. Nigger sweat. Maybe it ain't white enough yet to suit him. Maybe he wants to mix some white sweat with it."

Two hours later the boy was chopping wood behind the house within which his mother and aunt and the two sisters (the mother and aunt, not the two girls, he knew that; even at this distance and muffled by walls the flat loud voices of the two girls emanated an incorrigible idle inertia) were setting up the stove to prepare a meal, when he heard the hooves and saw the linen-clad man on a fine sorrel mare, whom he recognized even before he saw the rolled rug in front of the Negro youth following on a fat bay carriage horse—a suffused, angry face vanishing, still at full gallop, beyond the corner of the house where his father and brother were sitting in the two tilted chairs; and a moment later, almost before he could have put the axe down, he heard the hooves again and watched the sorrel mare go back out of the yard, already galloping again. Then his father began to shout one of the sisters' names, who presently emerged backward from the kitchen door dragging the rolled rug along the ground by one end while the other sister walked behind it.

"If you ain't going to tote, go on and set up the wash pot," the first said.

"You, Sarty!" the second shouted. "Set up the wash pot!" His father appeared at the door, framed against that shabbiness, as he had been against that other bland perfection, impervious to either, the mother's anxious face at his shoulder.

"Go on," the father said. "Pick it up." The two sisters stooped, broad, lethargic; stooping, they presented an incredible expanse of pale cloth and a flutter of tawdry ribbons.

"If I thought enough of a rug to have to git hit all the way from France I wouldn't keep hit where folks coming in would have to tromp on hit," the first said. They raised the rug.

"Abner," the mother said. "Let me do it."

"You go back and git dinner," his father said. "I'll tend to this."

From the woodpile through the rest of the afternoon the boy watched them, the rug spread flat in the dust beside the bubbling wash-pot, the two sisters stooping over it with that profound and lethargic reluctance, while the father stood over them in turn, implacable and grim, driving them though never raising his voice again. He could smell the harsh homemade lye[7] they were using; he saw his mother come to the door once and look toward them with an expression not anxious now but very like despair; he saw his father turn, and he fell to with the axe and saw from the corner of his eye his father raise from the ground a flattish fragment of field stone and examine it and return to the pot, and this time his mother actually spoke: "Abner. Abner. Please don't. Please, Abner."

Then he was done too. It was dusk; the whippoorwills had already begun. He could smell coffee from the room where they would presently eat the cold food remaining from the mid-afternoon meal, though when he entered the house he realized they were having coffee again probably because there was a fire on the hearth, before which the rug now lay spread over the backs of the two chairs. The tracks of his father's foot were gone. Where they had been were now long, water-cloudy scoriations resembling the sporadic course of a lilliputian[8] mowing machine.

It still hung there while they ate the cold food and then went to bed, scattered without order or claim up and down the two rooms, his mother in one bed, where his father would later lie, the older brother in the other, himself, the aunt, and the two sisters on pallets on the floor. But his father was not in bed yet. The last thing the boy remembered was the depthless, harsh silhouette of the hat and coat bending over the rug and it seemed to him that he had not even closed his eyes when the silhouette was standing over him, the fire almost dead behind it, the stiff foot prodding him awake. "Catch up the mule," his father said.

When he returned with the mule his father was standing in the

7. A caustic cleanser made from leaching ashes, certain to damage any delicate material.
8. Miniature, after the tiny inhabitants of Lilliput described in Jonathan Swift's *Gulliver's Travels* (1726).

black door, the rolled rug over his shoulder. "Ain't you going to ride?" he said.

"No. Give me your foot."

He bent his knee into his father's hand, the wiry, surprising power flowed smoothly, rising, he rising with it, on to the mule's bare back (they had owned a saddle once; the boy could remember it though not when or where) and with the same effortlessness his father swung the rug up in front of him. Now in the starlight they retraced the afternoon's path, up the dusty road rife with honeysuckle, through the gate and up the black tunnel of the drive to the lightless house, where he sat on the mule and felt the rough warp of the rug drag across his thighs and vanish.

"Don't you want me to help?" he whispered. His father did not answer and now he heard again that stiff foot striking the hollow portico with that wooden and clocklike deliberation, that outrageous overstatement of the weight it carried. The rug, hunched, not flung (the boy could tell that even in the darkness) from his father's shoulder struck the angle of wall and floor with a sound unbelievably loud, thunderous, then the foot again, unhurried and enormous; a light came on in the house and the boy sat, tense, breathing steadily and quietly and just a little fast, though the foot itself did not increase its beat at all, descending the steps now, now the boy could see him.

"Don't you want to ride now?" he whispered. "We kin both ride now," the light within the house altering now, flaring up and sinking. *He's coming down the stairs now*, he thought. He had already ridden the mule up beside the horse block; presently his father was up behind him and he doubled the reins over and slashed the mule across the neck, but before the animal could begin to trot the hard, thin arm came round him, the hard, knotted hand jerking the mule back to a walk.

In the first red rays of the sun they were in the lot, putting plow gear on the mules. This time the sorrel mare was in the lot before he heard it at all, the rider collarless and even bareheaded, trembling, speaking in a shaking voice as the woman in the house had done, his father merely looking up once before stooping again to the hame he was buckling, so that the man on the mare spoke to his stooping back:

"You must realize you have ruined that rug. Wasn't there anybody here, any of your women . . ." he ceased, shaking, the boy watching him, the older brother leaning now in the stable door, chewing, blinking slowly and steadily at nothing apparently. "It cost a hundred dollars. But you never had a hundred dollars. You never will. So I'm going to charge you twenty bushels of corn against your crop. I'll add it in your contract and when you come to the commissary you can sign it. That won't keep Mrs. de Spain quiet but maybe it will teach you to wipe your feet off before you enter her house again."

Then he was gone. The boy looked at his father, who still had not spoken or even looked up again, who was now adjusting the logger-head in the hame.

"Pap," he said. His father looked at him—the inscrutable face, the shaggy brows beneath which the gray eyes glinted coldly. Suddenly the boy went toward him, fast, stopping as suddenly. "You done the best you could!" he cried. "If he wanted hit done different why didn't he wait and tell you how? He won't git no twenty bushels! He won't git none! We'll gether hit and hide hit! I kin watch . . ."

"Did you put the cutter back in that straight stock like I told you?"

"No, sir," he said.

"Then go do it."

That was Wednesday. During the rest of that week he worked steadily, at what was within his scope and some which was beyond it, with an industry that did not need to be driven nor even commanded twice; he had this from his mother, with the difference that some at least of what he did he liked to do, such as splitting wood with the half-size axe which his mother and aunt had earned, or saved money somehow, to present him with at Christmas. In company with the two older women (and on one afternoon, even one of the sisters), he built pens for the shoat and the cow which were a part of his father's contract with the landlord, and one afternoon, his father being absent, gone somewhere on one of the mules, he went to the field.

They were running a middle buster[9] now, his brother holding the plow straight while he handled the reins, and walking beside the straining mule, the rich black soil shearing cool and damp against his bare ankles, he thought *Maybe this is the end of it. Maybe even that twenty bushels that seems hard to have to pay for just a rug will be a cheap price for him to stop forever and always from being what he used to be*; thinking, dreaming now, so that his brother had to speak sharply to him to mind the mule: *Maybe he even won't collect the twenty bushels. Maybe it will all add up and balance and vanish—corn, rug, fire; the terror and grief, the being pulled two ways like between two teams of horses—gone, done with for ever and ever.*

Then it was Saturday; he looked up from beneath the mule he was harnessing and saw his father in the black coat and hat. "Not that," his father said. "The wagon gear." And then, two hours later, sitting in the wagon bed behind his father and brother on the seat, the wagon accomplished a final curve, and he saw the weathered paint-

---

9. A double moldboard plow that throws a ridge of earth both ways.

less store with its tattered tobacco- and patent-medicine posters and
the tethered wagons and saddle animals below the gallery. He mounted
the gnawed steps behind his father and brother, and there again was
the lane of quiet, watching faces for the three of them to walk through.
He saw the man in spectacles sitting at the plank table and he did
not need to be told this was a Justice of the Peace; he sent one glare
of fierce, exultant, partisan defiance at the man in collar and cravat
now, whom he had seen but twice before in his life, and that on a
galloping horse, who now wore on his face an expression not of rage
but of amazed unbelief which the boy could not have known was at
the incredible circumstance of being sued by one of his own tenants,
and came and stood against his father and cried at the Justice: "He
ain't done it! He ain't burnt . . ."

"Go back to the wagon," his father said.

"Burnt?" the Justice said. "Do I understand this rug was burned
too?"

"Does anybody here claim it was?" his father said. "Go back to
the wagon." But he did not, he merely retreated to the rear of the
room, crowded as that other had been, but not to sit down this time,
instead, to stand pressing among the motionless bodies, listening to
the voices:

"And you claim twenty bushels of corn is too high for the damage
you did to the rug?"

"He brought the rug to me and said he wanted the tracks washed
out of it. I washed the tracks out and took the rug back to him."

"But you didn't carry the rug back to him in the same condition
it was in before you made the tracks on it."

His father did not answer, and now for perhaps half a minute there
was no sound at all save that of breathing, the faint, steady suspira-
tion of complete and intent listening.

"You decline to answer that, Mr. Snopes?" Again his father did
not answer. "I'm going to find against you, Mr. Snopes. I'm going
to find that you were responsible for the injury to Major de Spain's
rug and hold you liable for it. But twenty bushels of corn seems a
little high for a man in your circumstances to have to pay. Major de
Spain claims it cost a hundred dollars. October corn will be worth
about fifty cents. I figure that if Major de Spain can stand a ninety-
five dollar loss on something he paid cash for, you can stand a five-
dollar loss you haven't earned yet. I hold you in damages to Major
de Spain to the amount of ten bushels of corn over and above your
contract with him, to be paid to him out of your crop at gathering
time. Court adjourned."

It had taken no time hardly, the morning was but half begun. He
thought they would return home and perhaps back to the field, since
they were late, far behind all other farmers. But instead his father

passed on behind the wagon, merely indicating with his hand for the older brother to follow with it, and crossed the road toward the blacksmith shop opposite, pressing on after his father, overtaking him, speaking, whispering up at the harsh, calm face beneath the weathered hat: "He won't git no ten bushels neither. He won't git one. We'll . . ." until his father glanced for an instant down at him, the face absolutely calm, the grizzled eyebrows tangled above the cold eyes, the voice almost pleasant, almost gentle:

"You think so? Well, we'll wait till October anyway."

The matter of the wagon—the setting of a spoke or two and the tightening of the tires—did not take long either, the business of the tires accomplished by driving the wagon into the spring branch behind the shop and letting it stand there, the mules nuzzling into the water from time to time, and the boy on the seat with the idle reins, looking up the slope and through the sooty tunnel of the shed where the slow hammer rang and where his father sat on an upended cypress bolt, easily, either talking or listening, still sitting there when the boy brought the dripping wagon up out of the branch and halted it before the door.

"Take them on to the shade and hitch," his father said. He did so and returned. His father and the smith and a third man squatting on his heels inside the door were talking, about crops and animals; the boy, squatting too in the ammoniac dust and hoof-parings and scales of rust, heard his father tell a long and unhurried story out of the time before the birth of the older brother even when he had been a professional horsetrader. And then his father came up beside him where he stood before a tattered last year's circus poster on the other side of the store, gazing rapt and quiet at the scarlet horses, the incredible poisings and convolutions of tulle and tights and the painted leers of comedians, and said, "It's time to eat."

But not at home. Squatting beside his brother against the front wall, he watched his father emerge from the store and produce from a paper sack a segment of cheese and divide it carefully and deliberately into three with his pocket knife and produce crackers from the same sack. They all three squatted on the gallery and ate, slowly, without talking; then in the store again, they drank from a tin dipper tepid water smelling of the cedar bucket and of living beech trees. And still they did not go home. It was a horse lot this time, a tall rail fence upon and along which men stood and sat and out of which one by one horses were led, to be walked and trotted and then cantered back and forth along the road while the slow swapping and buying went on and the sun began to slant westward, they—the three of them—watching and listening, the older brother with his muddy eyes and his steady, inevitable tobacco, the father commenting now and then on certain of the animals, to no one in particular.

It was after sundown when they reached home. They ate supper by lamplight, then, sitting on the doorstep, the boy watched the night fully accomplish, listening to the whippoorwills and the frogs, when he heard his mother's voice: "Abner! No! No! Oh, God. Oh, God. Abner!" and he rose, whirled, and saw the altered light through the door where a candle stub now burned in a bottle neck on the table and his father, still in the hat and coat, at once formal and burlesque as though dressed carefully for some shabby and ceremonial violence, emptying the reservoir of the lamp back into the five-gallon kerosene can from which it had been filled, while the mother tugged at his arm until he shifted the lamp to the other hand and flung her back, not savagely or viciously, just hard, into the wall, her hands flung out against the wall for balance, her mouth open and in her face the same quality of hopeless despair as had been in her voice. Then his father saw him standing in the door.

"Go to the barn and get that can of oil we were oiling the wagon with," he said. The boy did not move. Then he could speak.

"What . . ." he cried. "What are you . . ."

"Go get that oil," his father said. "Go."

Then he was moving, running, outside the house, toward the stable: this the old habit, the old blood which he had not been permitted to choose for himself, which had been bequeathed him willy nilly and which had run for so long (and who knew where, battening on what of outrage and savagery and lust) before it came to him. *I could keep on*, he thought. *I could run on and on and never look back, never need to see his face again. Only I can't. I can't*, the rusted can in his hand now, the liquid sploshing in it as he ran back to the house and into it, into the sound of his mother's weeping in the next room, and handed the can to his father.

"Ain't you going to even send a nigger?" he cried. "At least you sent a nigger before!"

This time his father didn't strike him. The hand came even faster than the blow had, the same hand which had set the can on the table with almost excruciating care flashing from the can toward him too quick for him to follow it, gripping him by the back of his shirt and on to tiptoe before he had seen it quit the can, the face stooping at him in breathless and frozen ferocity, the cold, dead voice speaking over him to the older brother, who leaned against the table, chewing with that steady, curious, sidewise motion of cows:

"Empty the can into the big one and go on. I'll catch up with you."

"Better tie him up to the bedpost," the brother said.

"Do like I told you," the father said. Then the boy was moving, his bunched shirt and the hard, bony hand between his shoulder-blades, his toes just touching the floor, across the room and into the other one, past the sisters sitting with spread heavy thighs in the two chairs over the cold hearth, and to where his mother and aunt sat side by side on the bed, the aunt's arms about his mother's shoulders.

"Hold him," the father said. The aunt made a startled movement. "Not you," the father said. "Lennie. Take hold of him. You'll hold him better than that. If he gets loose don't you know what he is going to do? He will go up yonder." He jerked his head toward the road. "Maybe I'd better tie him."

"I'll hold him," his mother whispered.

"See you do then." Then his father was gone, the stiff foot heavy and measured upon the boards, ceasing at last.

Then he began to struggle. His mother caught him in both arms, he jerking and wrenching at them. He would be stronger in the end, he knew that. But he had no time to wait for it. "Lemme go!" he cried. "I don't want to have to hit you!"

"Let him go!" the aunt said. "If he don't go, before God, I am going up there myself!"

"Don't you see I can't?" his mother cried. "Sarty! Sarty! No! No! Help me, Lizzie!"

Then he was free. His aunt grasped at him but it was too late. He whirled, running, his mother stumbled forward on to her knees behind him, crying to the nearer sister: "Catch him, Net! Catch him!" But that was too late too, the sister (the sisters were twins, born at the same time, yet either of them now gave the impression of being, encompassing as much living meat and volume and weight as any other two of the family) not yet having begun to rise from the chair, her head, face, alone merely turned, presenting to him in the flying instant an astonishing expanse of young female features untroubled by any surprise even, wearing only an expression of bovine interest. Then he was out of the room, out of the house, in the mild dust of the starlit road and the heavy rifeness of honeysuckle, the pale ribbon unspooling with terrific slowness under his running feet, reaching the gate at last and turning in, running, his heart and lungs drumming, on up the drive toward the lighted house, the lighted door. He did not knock, he burst in, sobbing for breath, incapable for the moment of speech; he saw the astonished face of the Negro in the linen jacket without knowing when the Negro had appeared.

"De Spain!" he cried, panted. "Where's . . ." then he saw the white man too emerging from a white door down the hall. "Barn!" he cried. "Barn!"

"What?" the white man said. "Barn?"

"Yes!" the boy cried. "Barn!"

"Catch him!" the white man shouted.

But it was too late this time too. The Negro grasped his shirt, but the entire sleeve, rotten with washing, carried away, and he was out that door too and in the drive again, and had actually never ceased to run even while he was screaming into the white man's face.

Behind him the white man was shouting, "My horse! Fetch my horse!" and he thought for an instant of cutting across the park and climbing the fence into the road, but he did not know the park nor how high the vine-massed fence might be and he dared not risk it. So he ran on down the drive, blood and breath roaring; presently he was in the road again though he could not see it. He could not hear either: the galloping mare was almost upon him before he heard her, and even then he held his course, as if the very urgency of his wild grief and need must in a moment more find his wings, waiting until the ultimate instant to hurl himself aside and into the weed-choked roadside ditch as the horse thundered past and on, for an instant in furious silhouette against the stars, the tranquil early summer night sky which, even before the shape of the horse and rider vanished, stained abruptly and violently upward: a long, swirling roar incredible and soundless, blotting the stars, and he springing up and into the road again, running again, knowing it was too late yet still running even after he heard the shot and, an instant later, two shots, pausing now without knowing he had ceased to run, crying "Pap! Pap!", running again before he knew he had begun to run, stumbling, tripping over something and scrabbling up again without ceasing to run, looking backward over his shoulder at the glare as he got up, running on among the invisible trees, panting, sobbing, "Father! Father!"

At midnight he was sitting on the crest of a hill. He did not know it was midnight and he did not know how far he had come. But there was no glare behind him now and he sat now, his back toward what he had called home for four days anyhow, his face toward the dark woods which he would enter when breath was strong again, small, shaking steadily in the chill darkness, hugging himself into the remainder of his thin, rotten shirt, the grief and despair now no longer terror and fear but just grief and despair. *Father. My father,* he thought. "He was brave!" he cried suddenly, aloud but not loud, no more than a whisper: "He was! He was in the war! He was in Colonel Sartoris' cav'ry!" not knowing that his father had gone to that war a private in the fine old European sense, wearing no uniform, admitting the authority of and giving fidelity to no man or army or flag, going to war as Malbrouck[1] himself did: for booty—it meant nothing and less than nothing to him if it were enemy booty or his own.

The slow constellations wheeled on. It would be dawn and then sun-up after a while and he would be hungry. But that would be to-

---

1. The Duke of Marlborough (1650–1722), an English general whose name became distorted as Malbrough and Malbrouck in English and French popular songs celebrating his exploits.

morrow and now he was only cold, and walking would cure that.
His breathing was easier now and he decided to get up and go on,
and then he found that he had been asleep because he knew it was
almost dawn, the night almost over. He could tell that from the
whippoorwills. They were everywhere now among the dark trees below
him, constant and inflectioned and ceaseless, so that, as the instant
for giving over to the day birds drew nearer and nearer, there was no
interval at all between them. He got up. He was a little stiff, but
walking would cure that too as it would the cold, and soon there
would be the sun. He went on down the hill, toward the dark woods
within which the liquid silver voices of the birds called unceasing—
the rapid and urgent beating of the urgent and quiring heart of the
late spring night. He did not look back.

Spotted Horses

Yes, sir. Flem Snopes[1] has filled that whole country full of spotted
horses. You can hear folks running them all day and all night,
whooping and hollering, and the horses running back and forth across
them little wooden bridges ever now and then kind of like thunder.
Here I was this morning pretty near halfway to town, with the team
ambling along and me setting in the buckboard about half asleep,
when all of a sudden something come swurging up outen the bushes
and jumped the road clean, without touching hoof to it. It flew right
over my team, big as a billboard and flying through the air like a
hawk. It taken me thirty minutes to stop my team and untangle the
harness and the buckboard and hitch them up again.

That Flem Snopes. I be dog[2] if he ain't a case, now. One morning
about ten years ago, the boys was just getting settled down on Varner's porch for a little talk and tobacco, when here come Flem out
from behind the counter, with his coat off and his hair all parted like
he might have been clerking for Varner for ten years already. Folks
all knowed him; it was a big family of them about five miles down
the bottom. That year, at least. Share-cropping. They never stayed
on any place over a year. Then they would move on to another
place, with the chap or maybe the twins of that year's litter. It was a
regular nest of them. But Flem. The rest of them stayed tenant farmers, moving ever year, but here come Flem one day, walking out
from behind Jody Varner's counter like he owned it. And he wasn't
there but a year or two before folks knowed that, if him and Jody was
both still in that store in ten years more, it would be Jody clerking
for Flem Snopes. Why, that fellow could make a nickel where it

---

1. The now-grown older brother from "Barn Burning."   2. "I'll be darned."

wasn't but four cents to begin with. He skun me in two trades, myself, and the fellow that can do that, I just hope he'll get rich before I do; that's all.

All right. So here Flem was, clerking at Varner's, making a nickel here and there and not telling nobody about it. No, sir. Folks never knowed when Flem got the better of somebody lessen the fellow he beat told it. He'd just set there in the store-chair, chewing his tobacco and keeping his own business to hisself, until about a week later we'd find out it was somebody else's business he was keeping to hisself— provided the fellow he trimmed was mad enough to tell it. That's Flem.

We give him ten years to own everything Jody Varner had. But he never waited no ten years. I reckon you-all know that gal of Uncle Billy Varner's, the youngest one; Eula. Jody's sister. Ever Sunday ever yellow-wheeled buggy and curried riding horse in that country would be hitched to Bill Varner's fence, and the young bucks setting on the porch, swarming around Eula like bees around a honey pot. One of these here kind of big, soft-looking gals that could giggle richer than plowed newground. Wouldn't none of them leave before the others, and so they would set there on the porch until time to go home, with some of them with nine and ten miles to ride and then get up tomorrow and go back to the field. So they would all leave together and they would ride in a clump down to the creek ford and hitch them curried horses and yellow-wheeled buggies and get out and fight one another. Then they would get in the buggies again and go on home.

Well, one day about a year ago, one of them yellow-wheeled buggies and one of them curried saddle-horses quit this country. We heard they was heading for Texas. The next day Uncle Billy and Eula and Flem come into town in Uncle Bill's surrey, and when they come back, Flem and Eula was married. And on the next day we heard that two more of them yellow-wheeled buggies had left the country. They mought have gone to Texas, too. It's a big place.

Anyway, about a month after the wedding, Flem and Eula went to Texas, too. They was gone pretty near a year. Then one day last month, Eula come back, with a baby. We figgered up, and we decided that it was as well-growed a three-months-old baby as we ever see. It can already pull up on a chair. I reckon Texas makes big men quick, being a big place. Anyway, if it keeps on like it started, it'll be chewing tobacco and voting time it's eight years old.

And so last Friday here come Flem himself. He was on a wagon with another fellow. The other fellow had one of these two-gallon hats and a ivory-handled pistol and a box of gingersnaps sticking out of his hind pocket, and tied to the tailgate of the wagon was about two dozen of them Texas ponies, hitched to one another with barbed wire. They was colored like parrots and they was quiet as doves, and ere[3] a one of them would kill you quick as a rattlesnake. Nere a one of them had two eyes the same color, and nere a one of them had ever see a bridle, I reckon; and when that Texas man got down offen the wagon and walked up to them to show how gentle they was, one of them cut his vest clean offen him, same as with a razor.

Flem had done already disappeared; he had went on to see his wife, I reckon, and to see if that ere baby had done gone on to the field to help Uncle Billy plow, maybe. It was the Texas man that taken the horses on to Mrs. Littlejohn's lot. He had a little trouble at first, when they come to the gate, because they hadn't never see a fence before, and when he finally got them in and taken a pair of wire cutters and unhitched them and got them into the barn and poured some shell corn into the trough, they durn nigh tore down the barn. I reckon they thought that shell corn was bugs, maybe. So he left them in the lot and he announced that the auction would begin at sunup tomorrow.

That night we was setting on Mrs. Littlejohn's porch. You-all mind the moon was nigh full that night, and we would watch them spotted varmints swirling along the fence and back and forth across the lot same as minnows in a pond. And then now and then they would all kind of huddle up against the barn and rest themselves by biting and kicking one another. We would hear a squeal, and then a set of hoofs would go Bam! against the barn, like a pistol. It sounded just like a fellow with a pistol, in a nest of cattymounts,[4] taking his time.

II

It wasn't ere a man knowed yet if Flem owned them things or not. They just knowed one thing: that they wasn't never going to know for sho if Flem did or not, or if maybe he didn't just get on that wagon at the edge of town, for the ride or not. Even Eck Snopes didn't know, Flem's own cousin. But wasn't nobody surprised at that. We knowed that Flem would skin Eck quick as he would ere a one of us.

They was there by sunup next morning, some of them come twelve and sixteen miles, with seed-money tied up in tobacco sacks in their overalls, standing along the fence, when the Texas man come out of Mrs. Littlejohn's after breakfast and clumb onto the gate post with that ere white pistol butt sticking outen his hind pocket. He taken a new box of gingersnaps outen his pocket and bit the end offen it like a cigar and spit out the paper, and said the auction was open. And still they was coming up in wagons and a horse-and-mule-back and hitching the teams across the road and coming to the fence. Flem wasn't nowhere in sight.

But he couldn't get them started. He begun to work on Eck, because Eck holp him last night to get them into the barn and feed them that shell corn. Eck got out jist in time. He come outen that barn like a chip of the crest of a busted dam of water, and clumb into the wagon just in time.

He was working on Eck when Henry Armstid come up in his wagon. Eck was saying he was skeered to bid on one of them, because he might get it, and the Texas man says, "Them ponies? Them little horses?" He clumb down offen the gate post and went toward the horses. They broke and run, and him following them, kind of chirping to them, with his hand out like he was fixing to catch a fly, until he got three or four of them cornered. Then he jumped into them, and then we couldn't see nothing for a while because of the dust. It was a big cloud of it, and them blare-eyed, spotted things swoaring outen it twenty foot to a jump, in forty directions without counting up. Then the dust settled and there they was, that Texas man and the horse. He had its head twisted clean around like a owl's head. Its legs was braced and it was trembling like a new bride and groaning like a saw mill, and him holding its head wrung clean around on its neck so it was snuffing sky. "Look it over," he says, with his heels dug too and that white pistol sticking outen his pocket and his neck swole up like a spreading adder's until you could just tell what he was saying, cussing the horse and talking to us all at once: "Look him over, the fiddle-headed son of fourteen fathers. Try him, buy him; you will get the best—" Then it was all dust again, and we couldn't see nothing but spotted hide and mane, and that ere Texas man's boot-heels like a couple of walnuts on two strings, and after a while that two-gallon hat come sailing out like a fat old hen crossing a fence.

When the dust settled again, he was just getting outen the far fence corner, brushing himself off. He come and got his hat and brushed it off and come and clumb onto the gate post again. He was breathing hard. He taken the gingersnap box outen his pocket and et one, breathing hard. The hammer-head horse was still running round and round the lot like a merry-go-round at a fair. That was when Henry Armstid come shoving up to the gate in them patched overalls and one of them dangle-armed shirts of hisn. Hadn't nobody noticed him until then. We was all watching the Texas man and the horses. Even Mrs. Littlejohn; she had done come out and built a fire under the washpot in her back yard, and she would stand at the fence a while and then go back into the house and come out again with a armful of wash and stand at the fence again. Well, here come Henry shoving up, and then we see Mrs. Armstid right behind him, in that ere faded wrapper and sunbonnet and them tennis shoes. "Git on back to that wagon," Henry says.

"Henry," she says.

"Here, boys," the Texas man says; "make room for missus to git up and see. Come on, Henry," he says; "here's your chance to buy that saddle-horse missus has been wanting. What about ten dollars, Henry?"

"Henry," Mrs. Armstid says. She put her hand on Henry's arm. Henry knocked her hand down.

"Git on back to that wagon, like I told you," he says.

Mrs. Armstid never moved. She stood behind Henry, with her hands rolled into her dress, not looking at nothing. "He hain't no more despair[5] than to buy one of them things," she says. "And us not five dollars ahead of the porehouse, he hain't no more despair." It was the truth, too. They ain't never made more than a bare living offen that place of theirs, and them with four chaps and the very clothes they wears she earns by weaving by the firelight at night while Henry's asleep.

"Shut your mouth and git on back to that wagon," Henry says. "Do you want I taken a wagon stake to you here in the big road?"

Well, that Texas man taken one look at her. Then he begun on Eck again, like Henry wasn't even there. But Eck was skeered. "I can git me a snapping turtle or a water moccasin for nothing. I ain't going to buy none."

So the Texas man said he would give Eck a horse. "To start the auction, and because you holp me last night. If you'll start the bidding on the next horse," he says, "I'll give you that fiddle-head horse."

I wish you could have seen them, standing there with their seed-money in their pockets, watching that Texas man give Eck Snopes a live horse, all fixed to call him a fool if he taken it or not. Finally Eck says he'll take it. "Only I just starts the bidding," he says. "I don't have to buy the next one lessen I ain't overtopped." The Texas man said all right, and Eck bid a dollar on the next one, with Henry Armstid standing there with his mouth already open, watching Eck and the Texas man like a mad dog or something. "A dollar," Eck says.

The Texas man looked at Eck. His mouth was already open too, like he had started to say something and what he was going to say had up and died on him. "A dollar?" he says. "One dollar? You mean, *one* dollar, Eck?"

"Durn it," Eck says; "Two dollars, then."

Well, sir, I wish you could a seen that Texas man. He taken out that gingersnap box and held it up and looked into it, careful, like it

5. To spare.

might have been a diamond ring in it, or a spider. Then he throwed
it away and wiped his face with a bandanna. "Well," he says. "Well.
Two dollars. Two dollars. Is your pulse all right, Eck?" he says. "Do
you have ager-sweats[6] at night, maybe?" he says. "Well," he says, "I
got to take it. But are you boys going to stand there and see Eck get
two horses at a dollar a head?"

That done it. I be dog if he wasn't nigh as smart as Flem Snopes.
He hadn't no more than got the words outen his mouth before here
was Henry Armstid, waving his hand. "Three dollars," Henry says.
Mrs. Armstid tried to hold him again. He knocked her hand off,
shoving up to the gate post.

"Mister," Mrs. Armstid says, "we got chaps in the house and not
corn to feed the stock. We got five dollars I earned my chaps a-
weaving after dark, and him snoring in the bed. And he hain't no
more despair."

"Henry bids three dollars," the Texas man says. "Raise him a dollar, Eck, and the horse is yours."

"Henry," Mrs. Armstid says.

"Raise him, Eck," the Texas man says.

"Four dollars," Eck says.

"Five dollars," Henry says, shaking his fist. He shoved up right
under the gate post. Mrs. Armstid was looking at the Texas man too.

"Mister," she says, "if you take that five dollars I earned my chaps
a-weaving for one of them things, it'll be a curse onto you and yourn
during all the time of man."

But it wasn't no stopping Henry. He had shoved up, waving his
fist at the Texas man. He opened it; the money was in nickels and
quarters, and one dollar bill that looked like a cow's cud. "Five dollars," he says. "And the man that raises it'll have to beat my head
off, or I'll beat hisn."

"All right," the Texas man says. "Five dollars is bid. But don't you
shake your hand at me."

III

It taken till nigh sundown before the last one was sold. He got
them hotted up once and the bidding got up to seven dollars and a
quarter, but most of them went around three or four dollars, him
setting on the gate post and picking the horses out one at a time by
mouthword, and Mrs. Littlejohn pumping up and down at the tub
and stopping and coming to the fence for a while and going back to
the tub again. She had done got done too, and the wash was hung
on the line in the back yard, and we could smell supper cooking.

---

6. Ague; chills and fever with sweating.

Finally they was all sold; he swapped the last two and the wagon for a buckboard.

We was all kind of tired, but Henry Armstid looked more like a mad dog than ever. When he bought, Mrs. Armstid had went back to the wagon, setting in it behind them two rabbit-sized, bone-pore mules, and the wagon itself looking like it would fall all to pieces soon as the mules moved. Henry hadn't even waited to pull it outen the road; it was still in the middle of the road and her setting in it, not looking at nothing, ever since this morning.

Henry was right up against the gate. He went up to the Texas man. "I bought a horse and I paid cash," Henry says. "And yet you expect me to stand around here until they are all sold before I can get my horse. I'm going to take my horse outen that lot."

The Texas man looked at Henry. He talked like he might have been asking for a cup of coffee at the table. "Take your horse," he says.

Then Henry quit looking at the Texas man. He begun to swallow, holding onto the gate. "Ain't you going to help me?" he says.

"It ain't my horse," the Texas man says.

Henry never looked at the Texas man again, he never looked at nobody. "Who'll help me catch my horse?" he says. Never nobody said nothing. "Bring the plowline," Henry says. Mrs. Armstid got outen the wagon and brought the plowline. The Texas man got down offen the post. The woman made to pass him, carrying the rope.

"Don't you go in there, missus," the Texas man says.

Henry opened the gate. He didn't look back. "Come on here," he says.

"Don't you go in there, missus," the Texas man says.

Mrs. Armstid wasn't looking at nobody, neither, with her hands across her middle, holding the rope. "I reckon I better," she says. Her and Henry went into the lot. The horses broke and run. Henry and Mrs. Armstid followed.

"Get him into the corner," Henry says. They got Henry's horse cornered finally, and Henry taken the rope, but Mrs. Armstid let the horse get out. They hemmed it up again, but Mrs. Armstid let it get out again, and Henry turned and hit her with the rope. "Why didn't you head him back?" Henry says. He hit her again. "Why didn't you?" It was about that time I looked around and see Flem Snopes standing there.

It was the Texas man that done something. He moved fast for a big man. He caught the rope before Henry could hit the third time, and Henry whirled and made like he would jump at the Texas man. But he never jumped. The Texas man went and taken Henry's arm and led him outen the lot. Mrs. Armstid come behind them and the Texas man taken some money outen his pocket and he give it into

Mrs. Armstid's hand. "Get him into the wagon and take him on home," the Texas man says, like he might have been telling them he enjoyed his supper.

Then here comes Flem. "What's that for, Buck?" Flem says.

"Thinks he bought one of them ponies," the Texas man says. "Get him on away, missus."

But Henry wouldn't go. "Give him back that money," he says. "I bought that horse and I aim to have him if I have to shoot him."

And there was Flem, standing there with his hands in his pockets, chewing, like he had just happened to be passing.

"You take your money and I take my horse," Henry says. "Give it back to him," he says to Mrs. Armstid.

"You don't own no horse of mine," the Texas man says. "Get him on home, missus."

Then Henry seen Flem. "You got something to do with these horses," he says. "I bought one. Here's the money for it." He taken the bill outen Mrs. Armstid's hand. He offered it to Flem. "I bought one. Ask him. Here. Here's the money," he says, giving the bill to Flem.

When Flem taken the money, the Texas man dropped the rope he had snatched outen Henry's hand. He had done sent Eck Snopes's boy up to the store for another box of gingersnaps, and he taken the box of gingersnaps, and he taken the box outen his pocket and looked into it. It was empty and he dropped it on the ground. "Mr. Snopes will have your money for you tomorrow," he says to Mrs. Armstid. "You can get it from him tomorrow. He don't own no horse. You get him into the wagon and get him on home." Mrs. Armstid went back to the wagon and got in. "Where's that ere buckboard I bought?" the Texas man says. It was after sundown then. And then Mrs. Littlejohn come out on the porch and rung the supper bell.

IV

I come on in and et supper. Mrs. Littlejohn would bring in a pan of bread or something, then she would go out to the porch a minute and come back and tell us. The Texas man had hitched his team to the buckboard he had swapped them last two horses for, and him and Flem had gone, and then she told that the rest of them that never had ropes had went back to the store with I. O. Snopes to get some ropes, and wasn't nobody at the gate but Henry Armstid, and Mrs. Armstid setting in the wagon in the road, and Eck Snopes and that boy of hisn. "I don't care how many of them fool men gets killed by them things," Mrs. Littlejohn says, "but I ain't going to let Eck Snopes take that boy into that lot again." So she went down to the gate, but she come back without the boy or Eck neither.

"It ain't no need to worry about that boy," I says. "He's charmed." He was right behind Eck last night when Eck went to help feed them. The whole drove of them jumped clean over that boy's head and never touched him. It was Eck that touched him. Eck snatched him into the wagon and taken a rope and frailed the tar outen him.

So I had done et and went to my room and was undressing, long as I had a long trip to make next day; I was trying to sell a machine[7] to Mrs. Bundren up past Whiteleaf; when Henry Armstid opened that gate and went in by hisself. They couldn't make him wait for the balance of them to get back with their ropes. Eck Snopes said he tried to make Henry wait, but Henry wouldn't do it. Eck said Henry walked right up to them and that when they broke, they run clean over Henry like a hay-mow breaking down. Eck said he snatched that boy of hisn out of the way just in time and that them things went through that gate like a creek flood and into the wagons and teams hitched side the road, busting wagon tongues and snapping harness like it was fishing line, with Mrs. Armstid still setting in their wagon in the middle of it like something carved outen wood. Then they scattered, wild horses and tame mules with pieces of harness and single trees dangling offen them, both ways up and down the road.

"There goes ourn, paw!" Eck says his boy said. "There it goes, into Mrs. Littlejohn's house." Eck says it run right up the steps and into the house like a boarder late for supper. I reckon so. Anyway, I was in my room, in my underclothes, with one sock on and one sock in my hand, leaning out the window when the commotion busted out, when I heard something run into the melodeon[8] in the hall; it sounded like a railroad engine. Then the door to my room come sailing in like when you throw a tin bucket top into the wind and I looked over my shoulder and see something that looked like a fourteen-foot pinwheel a-blaring its eyes at me. It had to blare them fast, because I was already done jumped out the window.

I reckon it was anxious, too. I reckon it hadn't never seen barbed wire or shell corn before, but I know it hadn't never seen underclothes before, or maybe it was a sewing-machine agent it hadn't never seen. Anyway, it swirled and turned to run back up the hall and outen the house, when it met Eck Snopes and that boy just coming in, carrying a rope. It swirled again and run down the hall and out the back door just in time to meet Mrs. Littlejohn. She had just gathered up the clothes she had washed, and she was coming onto the back porch with a armful of washing on one hand and a scrubbing board in the other, when the horse skidded up to her,

7. The narrator, V. K. Ratliff, is a traveling salesman who sells sewing machines.   8. A small keyboard organ.

trying to stop and swirl again. It never taken Mrs. Littlejohn no time a-tall.

"Git outen here, you son," she says. She hit it across the face with the scrubbing board; that ere scrubbing board split as neat as ere a axe could have done it, and when the horse swirled to run back up the hall, she hit it again with what was left of the scrubbing board, not on the head this time. "And stay out," she says.

Eck and that boy was halfway down the hall by this time. I reckon that horse looked like a pinwheel to Eck too. "Git to hell outen here, Ad!" Eck says. Only there wasn't time. Eck dropped flat on his face, but the boy never moved. The boy was about a yard tall maybe, in overhalls just like Eck's; that horse swoared over his head without touching a hair. I saw that, because I was just coming back up the front steps, still carrying that ere sock and still in my underclothes, when the horse come onto the porch again. It taken one look at me and swirled again and run to the end of the porch and jumped the banisters and the lot fence like a hen-hawk and lit in the lot running and went out the gate again and jumped eight or ten upside-down wagons and went on down the road. It was a full moon then. Mrs. Armstid was still setting in the wagon like she had done been carved outen wood and left there and forgot.

That horse. It ain't never missed a lick. It was going about forty miles a hour when it come to the bridge over the creek. It would have had a clear road, but it so happened that Vernon Tull was already using the bridge when it got there. He was coming back from town; he hadn't heard about the auction; him and his wife and three daughters and Mrs. Tull's aunt, all setting in chairs in the wagon bed, and all asleep, including the mules. They waked up when the horse hit the bridge one time, but Tull said the first he knew was when the mules tried to turn the wagon around in the middle of the bridge and he seen that spotted varmint run right twixt the mules and run up the wagon tongue like a squirrel. He said he just had time to hit it across the face with his whip-stock, because about that time the mules turned the wagon around on that ere one-way bridge and that horse clumb across one of the mules and jumped down onto the bridge again and went on, with Vernon standing up in the wagon and kicking at it.

Tull said the mules turned in the harness and clumb back into the wagon too, with Tull trying to beat them out again, with the reins wrapped around his wrist. After that he says all he seen was overturned chairs and womenfolks' legs and white drawers shining in the moonlight, and his mules and that spotted horse going on up the road like a ghost.

The mules jerked Tull outen the wagon and drug him a spell on the bridge before the reins broke. They thought at first that he was dead, and while they was kneeling around him, picking the bridge splinters outen him, here comes Eck and that boy, still carrying the rope. They was running and breathing a little hard. "Where'd he go?" Eck says.

V

I went back and got my pants and shirt and shoes on just in time to go and help get Henry Armstid outen the trash in the lot. I be dog if he didn't look like he was dead, with his head hanging back and his teeth showing in the moonlight, and a little rim of white under his eyelids. He could still hear them horses, here and there; hadn't none of them got more than four–five miles away yet, not knowing the country, I reckon. So we could hear them and folks yelling now and then: "Whooey. Head him!"

We toted Henry into Mrs. Littlejohn's. She was in the hall; she hadn't put down the armful of clothes. She taken one look at us, and she laid down the busted scrubbing board and taken up the lamp and opened a empty door. "Bring him in here," she says.

We toted him in and laid him on the bed. Mrs. Littlejohn set the lamp on the dresser, still carrying the clothes. "I'll declare, you men," she says. Our shadows was way up the wall, tiptoeing too; we could hear ourselves breathing. "Better get his wife," Mrs. Littlejohn says. She went out, carrying the clothes.

"I reckon we had," Quick says. "Go get her, somebody."

"Whyn't you go?" Winterbottom says.

"Let Ernest git her," Durley says. "He lives neighbors with them."

Ernest went to fetch her. I be dog if Henry didn't look like he was dead. Mrs. Littlejohn come back, with a kettle and some towels. She went to work on Henry, and then Mrs. Armstid and Ernest come in. Mrs. Armstid come to the foot of the bed and stood there, with her hands rolled into her apron, watching what Mrs. Littlejohn was doing, I reckon.

"You men get outen the way," Mrs. Littlejohn says. "Git outside," she says. "See if you can't find something else to play with that will kill some more of you."

"Is he dead?" Winterbottom says.

"It ain't your fault if he ain't," Mrs. Littlejohn says. "Go tell Will Varner to come up here. I reckon a man ain't so different from a mule, come long come short. Except maybe a mule's got more sense."

We went to get Uncle Billy. It was a full moon. We could hear them, now and then, four mile away: "Whooey. Head him." The country was full of them, one on ever wooden bridge in the land, running across it like thunder: "Whooey. There he goes. Head him."

We hadn't got far before Henry begun to scream. I reckon Mrs. Littlejohn's water had brung him to; anyway, he wasn't dead. We went on to Uncle Billy's. The house was dark. We called to him, and after a while the window opened and Uncle Billy put his head out, peart as a peckerwood,[9] listening. "Are they still trying to catch them durn rabbits?" he says.

He come down, with his britches on over his nightshirt, and his suspenders dangling, carrying his horse-doctoring grip. "Yes, sir," he says, cocking his head like a woodpecker; "they're still a-trying."

We could hear Henry before we reached Mrs. Littlejohn's. He was going Ah-Ah-Ah. We stopped in the yard. Uncle Billy went on in. We could hear Henry. We stood in the yard, hearing them on the bridges, this-a-way and that: "Whooey. Whooey."

"Eck Snopes ought to caught hisn," Ernest says.

"Looks like he ought," Winterbottom said.

Henry was going Ah-Ah-Ah steady in the house; then he begun to scream. "Uncle Billy's started," Quick says. We looked into the hall. We could see the light where the door was. Then Mrs. Littlejohn come out.

"Will needs some help," she says. "You, Ernest. You'll do." Ernest went into the house.

"Hear them?" Quick said. "That one was on Four Mile bridge." We could hear them; it sounded like thunder a long way off; it didn't last long:

"Whooey."

We could hear Henry: "Ah-Ah-Ah-Ah-Ah."

"They are both started now," Winterbottom says. "Ernest too."

That was early in the night. Which was a good thing, because it taken a long night for folks to chase them things right and for Henry to lay there and holler, being as Uncle Billy never had none of this here chloryfoam to set Henry's leg with. So it was considerate in Flem to get them started early. And what do you reckon Flem's comment was?

That's right. Nothing. Because he wasn't there. Hadn't nobody see him since that Texas man left.

VI

That was Saturday night. I reckon Mrs. Armstid got home about daylight, to see about the chaps. I don't know where they thought her and Henry was. But lucky the oldest one was a gal, about twelve, big enough to take care of the little ones. Which she did for the next two days. Mrs. Armstid would nurse Henry all night and work in the

9. Pert as a woodpecker.

kitchen for hern and Henry's keep, and in the afternoon she would drive home (it was about four miles) to see to the chaps. She would cook up a pot of victuals and leave it on the stove, and the gal would bar the house and keep the little ones quiet. I would hear Mrs. Littlejohn and Mrs. Armstid talking in the kitchen. "How are the chaps making out?" Mrs. Littlejohn says.

"All right," Mrs. Armstid says.

"Don't they git skeered at night?" Mrs. Littlejohn says.

"Ina May bars the door when I leave," Mrs. Armstid says. "She's got the axe in bed with her. I reckon she can make out."

I reckon they did. And I reckon Mrs. Armstid was waiting for Flem to come back to town; hadn't nobody seen him until this morning; to get her money the Texas man said Flem was keeping for her. Sho. I reckon she was.

Anyway, I heard Mrs. Armstid and Mrs. Littlejohn talking in the kitchen this morning while I was eating breakfast. Mrs. Littlejohn had just told Mrs. Armstid that Flem was in town. "You can ask him for that five dollars," Mrs. Littlejohn says.

"You reckon he'll give it to me?" Mrs. Armstid says.

Mrs. Littlejohn was washing dishes, washing them like a man, like they was made out of iron. "No," she says. "But asking him won't do no hurt. It might shame him. I don't reckon it will, but it might."

"If he wouldn't give it back, it ain't no use to ask," Mrs. Armstid says.

"Suit yourself," Mrs. Littlejohn says. "It's your money."

I could hear the dishes.

"Do you reckon he might give it back to me?" Mrs. Armstid says. "That Texas man said he would. He said I could get it from Mr. Snopes later."

"Then go and ask him for it," Mrs. Littlejohn says.

I could hear the dishes.

"He won't give it back to me," Mrs. Armstid says.

"All right," Mrs. Littlejohn says. "Don't ask him for it, then."

I could hear the dishes; Mrs. Armstid was helping. "You don't reckon he would, do you?" she says. Mrs. Littlejohn never said nothing. It sounded like she was throwing the dishes at one another. "Maybe I better go and talk to Henry about it," Mrs. Armstid says.

"I would," Mrs. Littlejohn says. I be dog if it didn't sound like she had two plates in her hands, beating them together. "Then Henry can buy another five-dollar horse with it. Maybe he'll buy one next time that will out and out kill him. If I thought that, I'd give you back the money, myself."

"I reckon I better talk to him first," Mrs. Armstid said. Then it sounded like Mrs. Littlejohn taken up all the dishes and throwed them at the cookstove, and I come away.

That was this morning. I had been up to Bundren's and back, and I thought that things would have kind of settled down. So after breakfast, I went up to the store. And there was Flem, setting in the store chair and whittling, like he might not have ever moved since he come to clerk for Jody Varner. I. O. was leaning in the door, in his shirt sleeves and with his hair parted too, same as Flem was before he turned the clerking job over to I. O. It's a funny thing about them Snopes: they all looks alike, yet there ain't ere a two of them that claims brothers. They're always just cousins, like Flem and Eck and Flem and I. O. Eck was there too, squatting against the wall, him and that boy, eating cheese and crackers outen a sack; they told me that Eck hadn't been home a-tall. And that Lon Quick hadn't got back to town, even. He followed his horse clean down to Samson's Bridge, with a wagon and a camp outfit. Eck finally caught one of hisn. It run into a blind lane at Freeman's and Eck and the boy taken and tied their rope across the end of the lane, about three foot high. The horse come to the end of the lane and whirled and run back without ever stopping. Eck says it never seen the rope a-tall. He says it looked just like one of these here Christmas pinwheels. "Didn't it try to run again?" I says.

"No," Eck says, eating a bit of cheese offen his knife blade. "Just kicked some."

"Kicked some?" I says.

"It broke its neck," Eck says.

Well, they was squatting there, about six of them, talking, talking at Flem; never nobody knowed yet if Flem had ere a interest in them horses or not. So finally I come right out and asked him. "Flem's done skun all of us so much," I says, "that we're proud of him. Come on, Flem," I says, "how much did you and that Texas man make offen them horses? You can tell us. Ain't nobody here but Eck that bought one of them; the others ain't got back to town yet, and Eck's your own cousin; he'll be proud to hear, too. How much did you-all-make?"

They was all whittling, not looking at Flem, making like they was studying. But you could a heard a pin drop. And I. O. He had been rubbing his back up and down on the door, but he stopped now, watching Flem like a pointing dog. Flem finished cutting the sliver offen his stick. He spit across the porch, into the road. " 'Twarn't none of my horses," he says.

I. O. cackled, like a hen, slapping his legs with both hands. "You boys might just as well quit trying to get ahead of Flem," he said.

Well, about that time I see Mrs. Armstid come outen Mrs. Littlejohn's gate, coming up the road. I never said nothing. I says, "Well, if a man can't take care of himself in a trade, he can't blame the man that trims him."

Flem never said nothing, trimming at the stick. He hadn't seen Mrs. Armstid. "Yes, sir," I says. "A fellow like Henry Armstid ain't got nobody but hisself to blame."

"Course he ain't," I. O. says. He ain't seen her, neither. "Henry Armstid's a born fool. Always is been. If Flem hadn't a got his money, somebody else would."

We looked at Flem. He never moved. Mrs. Armstid come on up the road.

"That's right," I says. "But, come to think of it, Henry never bought no horse." We looked at Flem; you could a heard a match drop. "That Texas man told her to get that five dollars back from Flem next day. I reckon Flem's done already taken that money to Mrs. Littlejohn's and give it to Mrs. Armstid."

We watched Flem. I. O. quit rubbing his back against the door again. After a while Flem raised his head and spit across the porch, into the dust. I. O. cackled, just like a hen. "Ain't he a beating fellow, now?" I. O. says.

Mrs. Armstid was getting closer, so I kept on talking, watching to see if Flem would look up and see her. But he never looked up. I went on talking about Tull, about how he was going to sue Flem, and Flem setting there, whittling his stick, not saying nothing else after he said they wasn't none of his horses.

Then I. O. happened to look around. He seen Mrs. Armstid. "Psssst!" he says. Flem looked up. "Here she comes!" I. O. says. "Go out the back. I'll tell her you done went in to town today."

But Flem never moved. He just set there, whittling, and we watched Mrs. Armstid come up onto the porch, in that ere faded sunbonnet and wrapper and them tennis shoes that made a kind of hissing noise on the porch. She come onto the porch and stopped, her hands rolled into her dress in front, not looking at nothing.

"He said Saturday," she says, "that he wouldn't sell Henry no horse. He said I could get the money from you."

Flem looked up. The knife never stopped. It went on trimming off a sliver same as if he was watching it. "He taken that money off with him when he left," Flem says.

Mrs. Armstid never looked at nothing. We never looked at her, neither, except the boy of Eck's. He had a half-et cracker in his hand, watching her, chewing.

"He said Henry hadn't bought no horse," Mrs. Armstid says. "He said for me to get the money from you today."

"I reckon he forgot about it," Flem said. "He taken that money off with him Saturday." He whittled again. I. O. kept on rubbing his back, slow. He licked his lips. After a while the woman looked up the road, where it went on up the hill, toward the graveyard. She looked up that way for a while, with that boy of Eck's watching her and I. O. rubbing his back slow against the door. Then she turned back toward the steps.

"I reckon it's time to get dinner started," she says.

"How's Henry this morning, Mrs. Armstid?" Winterbottom says.

She looked at Winterbottom; she almost stopped. "He's resting, I thank you kindly," she says.

Flem got up, outen the chair, putting his knife away. He spit across the porch. "Wait a minute, Mrs. Armstid," he says. She stopped again. She didn't look at him. Flem went on into the store, with I. O. done quit rubbing his back now, with his head craned after Flem, and Mrs. Armstid standing there with her hands rolled into her dress, not looking at nothing. A wagon come up the road and passes; it was Freeman, on the way to town. Then Flem come out again, with I. O. still watching him. Flem had one of these little striped sacks of Jody Varner's candy; I bet he still owes Jody that nickel, too. He put the sack into Mrs. Armstid's hand, like he would have put it into a hollow stump. He spit again across the porch. "A little sweetening for the chaps," he says.

"You're right kind," Mrs. Armstid says. She held the sack of candy in her hand, not looking at nothing. Eck's boy was watching the sack, the half-et cracker in his hand; he wasn't chewing now. He watched Mrs. Armstid roll the sack into her apron. "I reckon I better get on back and help with dinner," she says. She turned and went back across the porch. Flem set down in the chair again and opened his knife. He spit across the porch again, past Mrs. Armstid where she hadn't went down the steps yet. Then she went on, in that ere sunbonnet and wrapper all the same color, back down the road toward Mrs. Littlejohn's. You couldn't see her dress move, like a natural woman walking. She looked like a old snag still standing up and moving along on a high water. We watched her turn in at Mrs. Littlejohn's and go outen sight. Flem was whittling. I. O. begun to rub his back on the door. Then he begun to cackle, just like a durn hen.

"You boys might just as well quit trying," I. O. says. "You can't git ahead of Flem. You can't touch him. Ain't he a sight, now?"

I be dog if he ain't. If I had brung a herd of wild cattymounts into town and sold them to my neighbors and kinfolks, they would have lynched me. Yes, sir.

BERTOLT BRECHT
1898–1956

Bertolt Brecht is a dominant figure in modern drama not only as the author of half a dozen plays which rank as modern classics, but as the first master of a powerful new concept of theater. Dissatisfied with the traditional notion, derived from Aristotle's *Poetics*, that drama should draw its spectators into identification with and sympathy for the characters, and with the Realist aesthetic of naturalness and psychological credibility, he saw only harm in such uncritical submission to illusions created on stage. Like Pirandello, Brecht believed that the modern stage should break open the closed world established as a dramatic convention by writers like Ibsen and Chekhov, whose audiences were to look at the action from a distance, as if it were a slice of real life going on behind an invisible "fourth wall." Unlike Pirandello, however, Brecht did not stress the anguish of individuals in society and the difficulty of knowing who we are; his focus was the community at large, and social responsibility. For Brecht, a political activist, the modern audience must not be allowed to indulge in passive emotional identification at a safe distance, or in the subjective whirlpool of existential identity crises. His characters are to be seen as members of society, and his audience must be educated and moved to action. The movement called "epic theater," which was born in the twenties, suited his needs well, and through his plays, theoretical writings, and dramatic productions he developed its basic ideas into one of the most powerful theatrical styles of the century.

Eugen Berthold Brecht was born in the medieval town of Augsburg, Bavaria, on February 10, 1898. His father was a respected town citizen, director of a paper mill, and a Catholic. His mother, the daughter of a civil servant from the Black Forest, was a Protestant who raised young Berthold in her own faith. (The spelling *Bertolt* was adopted later.) Brecht attended local schools until 1917, when he enrolled in Munich University to study natural science and medicine. He continued his studies while acting as drama critic for an Augsburg newspaper and writing his own plays: *Drums in the Night* (1918) won the Kleist Prize in 1922. In 1918, Brecht was mobilized for a year as an orderly in a military hospital, and he pursued medical studies at Munich until 1921. In 1929 he married Helene Weigel, an actress who worked closely with him and for whom he wrote many leading roles. Together, they would direct and make famous the theater group founded for them in 1949 in East Berlin: the Berliner Ensemble.

Moving to Berlin, Brecht worked briefly with the directors Max Reinhardt and Erwin Piscator but was chiefly interested in his own writing. In this pre-Marxist period he is especially concerned with the plight of the individual common man, pushed around by social and economic forces beyond his control until he loses both identity and humanity. In *A Man's a Man* (1924–25), the timid dock worker Galy Gay is transformed by fright and persuasion into another person, the ferociously successful soldier Jeriah Jip. When Jip turns up at the end of the play, he is given Gay's former papers and forced to assume Gay's old identity. The play teaches that human personalities can be broken down and reassembled like a machine; the only weapon against such mindless manipulation is awareness, an awareness that enables people to understand and control their destiny.

Most of Brecht's plays are didactic, either openly or by implication. After he became a fervent Marxist in the mid-twenties, he considered it even more his moral and artistic duty to encourage the audience to remedy social ills. *The Threepenny Opera* (1928), a ballad opera written with composer Kurt Weill (1900–1950) and modeled on John Gay's eighteenth-century *Beggars' Opera*, satirizes capitalist society from the point of view of outcasts and romantic thieves. Brecht also wrote a number of "lesson" plays intended to set forth Communist doctrine and to instruct the workers of Germany in the meaning of social revolution. The lesson was particularly harsh in *The Measures Taken* (1930), which described the necessary execution of a young Party member who had broken discipline and helped the local poor, thus postponing the revolution. Such drama, however doctrinally pure, was not likely to win adherents to the cause, and the lesson plays were condemned as unattractive and "intellectualist" by the Communist press in Berlin and Moscow.

Brecht's unorthodoxy, his pacifism, his enthusiasm for Marx, and his desire to create an activist popular theater that would embody a Marxist view of art all put him at odds with the rising power of Hitler's National Socialism. He fled Germany for Denmark in 1933, before the Nazis could include him in their purge of left-wing intellectuals; in 1935, he was deprived of his German citizenship. Brecht was to flee several more times as the Nazi invasions expanded throughout Europe: in 1939 he went to Sweden, in 1940 to Finland, and in 1941 to America, where he joined a colony of German expatriates in Santa Monica, California, working for the film industry. This was the period of some of his greatest plays: *The Life of Galileo* (1938–39), which attacks society for suppressing Galileo's discovery that the earth revolves around the sun, but also condemns the scientist for not insisting openly on the truth; *Mother Courage and Her Children* (1939), the play reprinted here; *The Good Woman of Setzuan* (1938–40), which shows how an instinctively good and generous person can only survive in this world by putting on a mask of hardness and calculation; and *The Caucasian Chalk Circle* (1944–45), which adapts the legendary choice of Solomon between two mothers who claim the same infant and decides in favor of the servant girl—who cared for the child—over the wealthy mother (the implied comparison is between those who do the work of society and those who merely profit from their possessions). In America, Brecht arranged for the translation of his work into English, and *Galileo*, with Charles Laughton in the title role, was produced in 1947. In the same year, he was questioned by the House Un-American Activities Committee as part of a wide-ranging inquiry into possible Communist activity in the entertainment business. No charges were brought, but he left for Europe the day after being brought before the Committee.

After leaving the United States, Brecht worked for a year in Zurich before going to Berlin with his wife, Helene Weigel, to stage *Mother Courage*. The East Berlin government offered the couple a position as director of their own troupe, the "Berliner Ensemble," and Brecht—who had just finished a theoretical work on the theater, A *Little Organon for the Theater* (1949)—turned his attention to the professional role of director. Although the East Berliners subsidized Brecht's work and advertised the artist's presence among them as a tribute to their own political system, they also obliged him to defend some of his plays against charges of political unorthodoxy and indeed to revise them. After 1934, the prevailing Communist Party view had upheld a style called "socialist realism," whose goal was to offer simple messages and to foster identification with revolutionary heroes. Brecht's mind was too keen and questioning, too attracted by irony and paradox, for him to provide the simplistic drama desired or to have a comfortable relation with authority of the right or of the left. After settling in East Berlin, he wrote no major new plays but only minor propaganda pieces and adaptations of classical works such as Molière's *Don Juan* and Shakespeare's *Coriolanus*. As an additional measure of protection, he took out Austrian citizenship through his wife's nationality. Brecht died in Berlin on August 14, 1956.

The "epic theater" for which Brecht is known derives its name from a famous essay "On Epic and Dramatic Poetry" by Goethe and Schiller, who in 1797 described *dramatic* poetry as pulling the audience into emotional identification, in contrast to *epic* poetry, which by being distanced in the time, place, and nature of the action could be absorbed in calm contemplation. The idea of an epic theater is a paradox: how can a play engage an audience that is still held at a distance? Brecht's solution was to employ many "alienation effects" that were genuinely dramatic, but that prevented total identification with the characters and forced spectators to think critically about what was taking place. These alienation effects have since become standard production techniques in the modern theater. In spite of Brecht's intentions and frequent revisions, however, the characters and situations of his plays remain emotionally engrossing, especially in his best-known works, such as *Mother Courage and Her Children*.

Brecht's concept of an epic theater touches on all aspects: dramatic structure, stage setting, music, and the actor's performance. The structure is to be open, episodic, and broken by dramatic or musical interludes. It is a "chronicle" that recounts events in an epic or distanced perspective. Episodes may also be performed independently as self-contained dramatic parables, instead of being organically tied to a centrally developing plot. Skits appear between scenes: in *A Man's a Man*, there is a fantastic interlude in which an elephant is accused of having murdered its mother. Sometimes a narrator comments on the action (*Three-Penny Opera*, *A Man's a Man*). The alienation effects are also heightened by setting most of the plays in far-away lands (China in *The Good Woman of Setzuan*, India in *A Man's a Man*, England in *The Three-Penny Opera*, Russia in *The Caucasian Chalk Circle*, Chicago in *Saint Joan of the Stockyards* and *The Resistible Rise of Arturo Ui*) or distant times (the seventeenth century in *Mother Courage*, Renaissance Italy in *Galileo*, or an imagined ghostly afterlife in *The Trial of Lucullus*).

Stagecraft and performance further support Brecht's concept of a critical, intellectualized theater. Events on stage are announced beforehand by signs, or are accompanied by projected films and images during the action itself.

Place names are printed on signs and suspended over the actors, and footlights and stage machinery are openly displayed. Songs that interrupt the dramatic action are addressed directly to the audience, and are often heralded by a sign Brecht called a "musical emblem: in *Mother Courage*, 'a trumpet, a drum, a flag, and electric globes that lit up.' " In addition, Brecht described a special kind of acting: actors should "demonstrate" their parts instead of being submerged in them. At rehearsals, Brecht often asked actors to speak their parts in the third person instead of the first. Masks were occasionally used for wicked people, or soldiers' faces chalked white to suggest a stylized fear. Such constant artificiality injected into all aspects of the performance makes it difficult for the audience to identify completely and unselfconsciously with the characters on stage.

Audiences may react emotionally to Brecht's plays and characters, but their reactions are never simple. Brecht's characters are complex and inhabit complex situations. Galileo is both a dedicated scientist who sacrifices his reputation for honesty so as to complete his work, and a weak sensualist who fails to realize how his recantation will affect others' pursuit of scientific knowledge. In *The Good Woman of Setzuan*, the overgenerous Shen Te can survive only by periodically adopting the mask of a harshly practical "cousin," Shui Ta. Mother Courage is both a tragic mother figure and a small-time profiteer who loses her children as she battens on war. Brecht's work teems with such paradoxes at all levels. He is a cynic who deflates religious zeal, militant patriotism, and heroic example as delusions that lead the masses on to futile sacrifice; yet he is also a preacher who makes prominent use of traditional Biblical language and imagery, and themes of individual sacrifice.

Mother Courage, written shortly after Brecht turned forty, combines all these elements. The play is set in Germany, in the middle years of the Thirty Years' War (1618–1648), a conflict involving all Europe and believed at the time of Brecht's writing to have destroyed half the German population. But senseless violence, religious intolerance, artificial patriotism, and cynical opportunism were equally apparent in seventeenth-century Germany and in the Nazi state, and the setting gave Brecht what he needed to write a strongly pacifist play in 1939, the year in which World War II was to begin.

Mother Courage evoked the sympathy of early audiences for her tragic inability to prevent her children's death. Such was not Brecht's intention, and he rewrote several sections of the play to bring out her avarice and blindness, and her belief that she can use the war and profit from others' misery without endangering her own family. To Brecht, the tragedy of her life lay in her failure to relate the general fate of society to that of her own family. In trying to manipulate the system for her personal advantage, she denied the personal rights of others: she called to others to enlist but not to her own children, and she would rather sell shirts to the officers than use them to bind a peasant's wounds. Yet the war that Mother Courage saw as a good provider ended by killing her three children, and even sooner because of their virtues (Eilif's martial zeal, Swiss Cheese's honesty, Kattrin's pity). Mother Courage is ruined, all the more so since she has learned nothing from the war and does not protest it. Instead, her bitter "Song of the Great Capitulation" presents compromise as inevitable, and at the end of the play she is chasing after a new regiment to continue her peddler's career.

Each of the twelve parable-like scenes of *Mother Courage* presents a particular aspect or lesson of the war. Setting and props encourage the audience to see the action as a "demonstration" by drawing attention to the way the play is put on. Signs or titles are projected onto a screen to announce what is about to happen; a revolving stage and projected backgrounds suggest the wagon's travels in a highly stylized way; a group of musicians sits in full view beside the stage to accompany the songs; realistic but sketchy three-dimensional structures represent buildings. The main piece of stage furniture is Mother Courage's canteen wagon, whose increasingly dilapidated appearance reveals her fall from prosperity into lonely poverty. In the first scene, the whole family appears with the wagon: at the end, Mother Courage pulls it alone.

Brecht hoped that *Mother Courage* would show its audiences "that in wartime the big profits are not made by little people. That war, which is a continuation of business by other means, makes the human virtues fatal even to their possessors. That no sacrifice is too great for the struggle against war." This last point is demonstrated by Kattrin's death, for she is the only one of Mother Courage's family whose virtue is not perverted by the war, and whose death is meant to provide a moral example. Drumming frantically to awaken the endangered city of Halle, she sacrifices her life to save the city's threatened children. Religious and secular themes join at this point as they do so often in the course of the play, for Kattrin acts immediately after hearing the peasant family bemoan their helplessness and pray to God for miraculous aid. It is action like hers, not passive prayer, that Brecht hopes to evoke with his epic theater. Both the play itself and its self-conscious, "alienated" staging try to move the audience toward a clearer understanding of forces in society, and to a responsible choice of their own roles.

Martin Esslin provides a basic biography and overview in *Brecht, The Man and His Work* (1974, rev. ed.). *Brecht on Theatre: The Development of an Aesthetic*, edited and translated by John Willett (1964), contains Brecht's own essays and lectures on his theater. Other views of Brecht are found in Peter Demetz, ed., *Brecht: A Collection of Critical Essays* (1962). Ronald Hayman's *Brecht: A Biography* (1983) offers a detailed view of Brecht's life.

Mother Courage and Her Children[1]
A Chronicle of the Thirty Years' War[2]
Characters

MOTHER COURAGE   SWISS CHEESE, *her younger son*
KATTRIN, *her mute daughter*   THE RECRUITER
EILIF, *her elder son*   THE SERGEANT

---

1. Translated by Ralph Manheim.   2. Actually a series of wars fought in central Europe from 1618 to 1648. At the time *Mother Courage* opens, in 1624, a Swedish army has been fighting in Poland for three years. After winning the coastal province of Livonia (now part of the U.S.S.R.),

THE COOK	AN OLDER SOLDIER
THE GENERAL	A PEASANT
THE CHAPLAIN	THE PEASANT'S WIFE
THE ORDNANCE OFFICER	THE YOUNG MAN·
YVETTE POTTIER	THE OLD WOMAN
THE MAN WITH THE PATCH OVER	ANOTHER PEASANT
HIS EYE	THE PEASANT WOMAN
THE OTHER SERGEANT	A YOUNG PEASANT
THE OLD COLONEL	THE LIEUTENANT
A CLERK	SOLDIERS
A YOUNG SOLDIER	A VOICE

1

Spring 1624. General Oxenstjerna recruits troops in Dalarna for the Polish campaign. The canteen woman, Anna Fierling, known as Mother Courage, loses a son.[3]

Highway near a city.

A sergeant and a recruiter stand shivering.

THE RECRUITER. How can anybody get a company together in a place like this? Sergeant, sometimes I feel like committing suicide. The general wants me to recruit four platoons by the twelfth, and the people around here are so depraved I can't sleep at night. I finally get hold of a man, I close my eyes and pretend not to see that he's chicken-breasted and he's got varicose veins, I get him good and drunk and he signs up. While I'm paying for the drinks, he steps out, I follow him to the door because I smell a rat: Sure enough, he's gone, like a fart out of a goose. A man's word doesn't mean a thing, there's no honor, no loyalty. This place has undermined my faith in humanity, sergeant.

THE SERGEANT. It's easy to see these people have gone too long without a war. How can you have morality without a war, I ask you? Peace is a mess, it takes a war to put things in order. In peacetime

it invades Germany in 1630 under the command of King Gustavus Adolphus. The king however fails to relieve the siege of Magdeburg by the imperial general Johan Tserclaes, Count of Tilly, and the Protestant bishopric is burned to the ground. Gustavus Adolphus later defeats Tilly in two major battles, but in 1632 both are killed, and two years later the Swedish force is destroyed by the Imperial army. The ensuing peace is brief, for in 1635 a new Swedish army, joined by troops from Catholic France, renews the fighting. This last phase of the war has just begun at the end of *Mother Courage*, and lasting peace will come only twelve years later.

   Brecht is true to history as he knew it; only recently have historians disputed the traditional belief that the war devastated Germany and halved its population.   **3.** The heading for this and each new scene is projected on a screen on stage; it situates the action and tells what will happen. *General Oxenstjerna:* One of the Swedish generals. *Dalarna:* a rural province in central Sweden. A canteen women sells provisions to soldiers; Mother Courage's wagon is "a cross between a military vehicle and a general store." [Brecht's note.]

the human race goes to the dogs. Man and beast are treated like
so much dirt. Everybody eats what they like, a big piece of cheese
on white bread, with a slice of meat on top of the cheese. Nobody
knows how many young men or good horses there are in that town
up ahead, they've never been counted. I've been in places where
they hadn't had a war in as much as seventy years, the people had
no names, they didn't even know who they were. It takes a war
before you get decent lists and records; then your boots are done
up in bales and your grain in sacks, man and beast are properly
counted and marched away, because people realize that without
order they can't have a war.

THE RECRUITER. How right you are!

THE SERGEANT. Like all good things, a war is hard to get started. But
once it takes root, it's vigorous; then people are as scared of peace
as dice players are of laying off, because they'll have to reckon up
their losses. But at first they're scared of war. It's the novelty.

THE RECRUITER. Say, there comes a wagon. Two women and two
young fellows. Keep the old woman busy, sergeant. If this is another
flop, you won't catch me standing out in this April wind any more.
[*A Jew's harp*[4] *is heard. Drawn by two young men, a covered
wagon approaches. In the wagon sit Mother Courage and her
mute daughter Kattrin*]

MOTHER COURAGE. Good morning, sergeant.

SERGEANT. [*Barring the way*] Good morning, friends. Who are you?

MOTHER COURAGE. Business people. [*Sings*]

Hey, Captains, make the drum stop drumming
And let your soldiers take a seat.
Here's Mother Courage, with boots she's coming
To help along their aching feet.
How can they march off to the slaughter
With baggage, cannon, lice and fleas
Across the rocks and through the water
Unless their boots are in one piece?
    The spring is come. Christian, revive![5]
    The snowdrifts melt. The dead lie dead.
    And if by chance you're still alive
    It's time to rise and shake a leg.

O Captains, don't expect to send them
To death with nothing in their crops.
First you must let Mother Courage mend them
In mind and body with her schnapps.[6]

---

4. A small, twangy instrument held against the teeth, associated with country music.   5. The
phrase in German parodies religious announcements of Easter and Christ's resurrection.
6. Liquor, especially gin. (The original says *wein*, or wine.)

On empty bellies it's distressing
To stand up under shot and shell.
But once they're full, you have my blessing
To lead them to the jaws of hell.
    The spring is come. Christian, revive!
    The snowdrifts melt, the dead lie dead.
    And if by chance you're still alive
    It's time to rise and shake a leg.

THE SERGEANT. Halt, you scum. Where do you belong?

THE ELDER SON. Second Finnish Regiment.

THE SERGEANT. Where are your papers?

MOTHER COURAGE. Papers?

THE YOUNGER SON. But she's Mother Courage!

THE SERGEANT. Never heard of her. Why Courage?

MOTHER COURAGE. They call me Courage, sergeant, because when I saw ruin staring me in the face I drove out of Riga through cannon fire with fifty loaves of bread in my wagon. They were getting moldy, it was high time, I had no choice.

THE SERGEANT. No wisecracks. Where are your papers?

MOTHER COURAGE. [*Fishing a pile of papers out of a tin box and climbing down*] Here are my papers, sergeant. There's a whole missal, picked it up in Alt-Ötting[7] to wrap cucumbers in, and a map of Moravia, God knows if I'll ever get there, if I don't it's total loss. And this here certifies that my horse hasn't got hoof-and-mouth disease, too bad, he croaked on us, he cost fifteen guilders,[8] but not out of my pocket, glory be. Is that enough paper?

THE SERGEANT. Are you trying to pull my leg? I'll teach you to get smart. You know you need a license.

MOTHER COURAGE. You mind your manners and don't go telling my innocent children that I'd go anywhere near your leg, it's indecent. I want no truck with you. My license in the Second Regiment is my honest face, and if you can't read it, that's not my fault. I'm not letting anybody put his seal on it.

THE RECRUITER. Sergeant, I detect a spirit of insubordination in this woman. In our camp we need respect for authority.

MOTHER COURAGE. Wouldn't sausage be better?

THE SERGEANT. Then you're all Fierlings?

MOTHER COURAGE. Anna Fierling.

THE SERGEANT. Then you're all Fierlings?

MOTHER COURAGE. What do you mean? Fierling is my name. Not theirs.

---

7. A place of pilgrimage fifty miles east of Munich in the south German kingdom of Bavaria. *Missal*: Prayer book.   8. The basic unit of Dutch money, also called a *florin*. When Brecht was writing, one guilder was worth about twenty-five cents.

THE SERGEANT. Aren't they all your children?

MOTHER COURAGE. That they are, but why should they all have the same name? [*Pointing at the elder son*] This one, for instance. His name is Eilif Nojocki. How come? Because his father always claimed to be called Kojocki or Mojocki. The boy remembers him well, except the one he remembers was somebody else, a Frenchman with a goatee. But aside from that, he inherited his father's intelligence, that man could strip the pants off a peasant's ass without his knowing it. So, you see, we've each got our own name.

THE SERGEANT. Each different, you mean?

MOTHER COURAGE. Don't act so innocent.

THE SERGEANT. I suppose that one's a Chinaman? [*Indicating the younger son*]

MOTHER COURAGE. Wrong. He's Swiss.

THE SERGEANT. After the Frenchman?

MOTHER COURAGE. What Frenchman? I never heard of any Frenchman. Don't get everything balled up or we'll be here all day. He's Swiss, but his name is Fejos, the name has nothing to do with his father. He had an entirely different name, he was an engineer, built fortifications, but he drank.

[*Swiss Cheese nods, beaming; the mute Kattrin is also tickled*]

THE SERGEANT. Then how can his name be Fejos?

MOTHER COURAGE. I wouldn't want to offend you, but you haven't got much imagination. Naturally his name is Fejos because when he came I was with a Hungarian, it was all the same to him, he was dying of kidney trouble though he never touched a drop, a very decent man. The boy takes after him.

THE SERGEANT. But you said he wasn't his father?

MOTHER COURAGE. He takes after him all the same. I call him Swiss Cheese, how come, because he's good at pulling the wagon. [*Pointing at her daughter*] Her name is Kattrin Haupt, she's half German.

THE SERGEANT. A fine family, I must say.

MOTHER COURAGE. Yes, I've been all over the world with my wagon.

THE SERGEANT. It's all being taken down. [*He takes it down*] You're from Bamberg, Bavaria. What brings you here?

MOTHER COURAGE. I couldn't wait for the war to kindly come to Bamberg.

THE RECRUITER. You wagon pullers ought to be called Jacob Ox and Esau[9] Ox. Do you ever get out of harness?

EILIF. Mother, can I clout him one on the kisser? I'd like to.

MOTHER COURAGE. And I forbid you. You stay put. And now, gentle-

9. Biblical twin brothers (Genesis 25:7).

men, wouldn't you need a nice pistol, or a belt buckle, yours is all worn out, sergeant.

THE SERGEANT. I need something else. I'm not blind. Those young fellows are built like tree trunks, big broad chests, sturdy legs. Why aren't the in the army? That's what I'd like to know.

MOTHER COURAGE. [*Quickly*] Nothing doing, sergeant. My children aren't cut out for soldiers.

THE RECRUITER. Why not? There's profit in it, and glory. Peddling shoes is woman's work. [*To Eilif*] Step up; let's feel if you've got muscles or if you're a sissy.

MOTHER COURAGE. He's a sissy. Give him a mean look and he'll fall flat on his face.

THE RECRUITER. And kill a calf if it happens to be standing in the way. [*Tries to lead him away*]

MOTHER COURAGE. He insulted me. He referred to my face as a kisser. Him and me will now step out in the field and discuss this thing as man to man.

EILIF. Don't worry, mother. I'll take care of him.

MOTHER COURAGE. You stay put. You no-good! I know you, always fighting. He's got a knife in his boot, he's a knifer.

THE RECRUITER. I'll pull it out of him like a milk tooth. Come on, boy.

MOTHER COURAGE. Sergeant, I'll report you to the colonel. He'll throw you in the lock-up. The lieutenant is courting my daughter.

THE SERGEANT. No rough stuff, brother. [*To Mother Courage*] What have you got against the army? Wasn't his father a soldier? Didn't he die fair and square? You said so yourself.

MOTHER COURAGE. He's only a child. You want to lead him off to slaughter, I know you. You'll get five guilders for him.

THE RECRUITER. He'll get a beautiful cap and top boots.

EILIF. Not from you.

MOTHER COURAGE. Oh, won't you come fishing with me? said the fisherman to the worm. [*To Swiss Cheese*] Run and yell that the they're trying to steal your brother. [*She pulls a knife*] Just try to steal him. I'll cut you down, you dogs. I'll teach you to put him in your war! We do an honest business in ham and shirts, we're peaceful folk.

THE SERGEANT. I can see by the knife how peaceful you are. You ought to be ashamed of yourself, put that knife away, you bitch. A minute ago you admitted you lived off war, how else would you live, on what? How can you have a war without soldiers?

MOTHER COURAGE. It doesn't have to be my children.

THE SERGEANT. I see. You'd like the war to eat the core and spit out the apple. You want your brood to batten on war, tax-free. The war can look out for itself, is that it? You call yourself Courage, eh? And you're afraid of the war that feeds you. Your sons aren't afraid of it, I can see that.

EILIF. I'm not afraid of any war.

THE SERGEANT. Why should you be? Look at me: Has the soldier's life disagreed with me? I was seventeen when I joined up.

MOTHER COURAGE. You're not seventy yet.

THE SERGEANT. I can wait.

MOTHER COURAGE. Sure. Under ground.

THE SERGEANT. Are you trying to insult me? Telling me I'm going to die?

MOTHER COURAGE. But suppose it's the truth? I can see the mark on you. You look like a corpse on leave.

SWISS CHEESE. She's got second sight. Everybody says so. She can tell the future.

THE RECRUITER. Then tell the sergeant his future. It might amuse him.

THE SERGEANT. I don't believe in that stuff.

MOTHER COURAGE. Give me your helmet. [*He gives it to her*]

THE SERGEANT. It doesn't mean any more than taking a shit in the grass. But go ahead for the laugh.

MOTHER COURAGE. [*Takes a sheet of parchment and tears it in two*] Eilif, Swiss Cheese, Kattrin: That's how we'd all be torn apart if we got mixed up too deep in the war. [*To the sergeant*] Seeing it's you, I'll do it for nothing. I make a black cross on this piece. Black is death.

SWISS CHEESE. She leaves the other one blank. Get it?

MOTHER COURAGE. Now I fold them, and now I shake them up together. Same as we're all mixed up together from the cradle to the grave. And now you draw, and you'll know the answer.

[*The sergeant hesitates*]

THE RECRUITER. [*To Eilif*] I don't take everybody, I'm known to be picky and choosey, but you've got spirit, I like that.

THE SERGEANT. [*Fishing in the helmet*] Damn foolishness! Hocus-pocus!

SWISS CHEESE. He's pulled a black cross. He's through.

THE RECRUITER. Don't let them scare you, there's not enough bullets for everybody.

THE SERGEANT. [*Hoarsely*] You've fouled me up.

MOTHER COURAGE. You fouled yourself up the day you joined the army. And now we'll be going, there isn't a war every day, I've got to take advantage.

THE SERGEANT. Hell and damnation! Don't try to hornswoggle me. We're taking your bastard to be a soldier.

EILIF. I'd like to be a soldier, mother.

MOTHER COURAGE. You shut your trap, you Finnish devil.

EILIF. Swiss Cheese wants to be a soldier too.

MOTHER COURAGE. That's news to me. I'd better let you draw too, all three of you. [*She goes to the rear to mark crosses on slips of parchment*]

THE RECRUITER. [*To Eilif*] It's been said to our discredit that a lot of religion goes on in the Swedish camp, but that's slander to blacken our reputation. Hymn singing only on Sunday, one verse! And only if you've got a voice.

MOTHER COURAGE. [*Comes back with the slips in the sergeant's helmet*] Want to sneak away from their mother, the devils, and run off to war like calves to a salt lick. But we'll draw lots on it, then they'll see that the world is no vale of smiles[1] with a "Come along, son, we're short on generals." Sergeant, I'm very much afraid they won't come through the war. They've got terrible characters, all three of them. [*She holds out the helmet to Eilif*] There. Pick a slip. [*He picks one and unfolds it. She snatches it away from him*] There you have it. A cross! Oh, unhappy mother that I am, Oh, mother of sorrows. Has he got to die? Doomed to perish in the springtime of his life? If he joins the army, he'll bite the dust, that's sure. He's too brave, just like his father. If he's not smart, he'll go the way of all flesh, the slip proves it. [*She roars at him*] Are you going to be smart?

EILIF. Why not?

MOTHER COURAGE. The smart thing to do is to stay with your mother, and if they make fun of you and call you a sissy, just laugh.

THE RECRUITER. If you're shitting in your pants, we'll take your brother.

MOTHER COURAGE. I told you to laugh. Laugh! And now you pick, Swiss Cheese. I'm not so worried about you, you're honest. [*He picks a slip*] Oh! Why, have you got that strange look? It's got to be blank. There can't be a cross on it. No, I can't lose you. [*She takes the slip*] A cross? Him too? Maybe it's because he's so stupid. Oh, Swiss Cheese, you'll die too, unless you're very honest the whole time, the way I've taught you since you were a baby, always bringing back the change when I sent you to buy bread. That's the only way you can save yourself. Look sergeant, isn't that a black cross?

THE SERGEANT. It's a cross all right. I don't see how I could have pulled one. I always stay in the rear. [*To the recruiter*] It's on the up and up. Her own get it too.

SWISS CHEESE. I get it too. But I can take a hint.

MOTHER COURAGE. [*To Kattrin*] Now you're the only one I'm sure of, you're a cross[2] yourself because you've got a good heart. [*She*

1. Parodying the traditional description of this world as a "vale of tears." 2. I.e., a heavy burden.

holds up the helmet to Kattrin in the wagon, but she herself takes out the slip] It's driving me to despair. It can't be right, maybe I mixed them wrong. Don't be too good-natured, Kattrin, don't, there's a cross on your path too. Always keep very quiet, that ought to be easy seeing you're dumb. Well, now you know. Be careful, all of you, you'll need to be. And now we'll climb up and drive on. [*She returns the sergeant's helmet and climbs up into the wagon*]

THE RECRUITER. [*To the sergeant*] Do something!

THE SERGEANT. I'm not feeling so good.

THE RECRUITER. Maybe you caught cold when you took your helmet off in the wind. Tell her you want to buy something. Keep her busy. [*Aloud*] You could at least take a look at that buckle, sergeant. After all, selling things is these good people's living. Hey, you, the sergeant wants to buy that belt buckle.

MOTHER COURAGE. Half a guilder. A buckle like that is worth two guilders. [*She climbs down*]

THE SERGEANT. It's not new. This wind! I can't examine it here. Let's go where it's quiet. [*He goes behind the wagon with the buckle*]

MOTHER COURAGE. I haven't noticed wind.

THE SERGEANT. Maybe it is worth half a guilder. It's silver.

MOTHER COURAGE. [*Joins him behind the wagon*] Six solid ounces.

THE RECRUITER. [*To Eilif*] And then we'll have a drink, just you and me. I've got your enlistment bonus right here. Come on.

[*Eilif stands undecided*]

MOTHER COURAGE. All right. Half a guilder.

THE SERGEANT. I don't get it. I always stay in the rear. There's no safer place for a sergeant. You can send the men up forward to win glory. You've spoiled my dinner. It won't go down, I know it, not a bite.

MOTHER COURAGE. Don't take it to heart. Don't let it spoil your appetite. Just keep behind the lines. Here, take a drink of schnapps, man. [*She hands him the bottle*]

THE RECRUITER. [*Has taken Eilif's arm and is pulling him away toward the rear*] A bonus of ten guilders, and you'll be a brave man and you'll fight for the king, and the women will tear each other's hair out over you. And you can clout me one on the kisser for insulting you. [*Both go out*]

[*Mute Kattrin jumps down from the wagon and emits raucous sounds*]

MOTHER COURAGE. Just a minute, Kattrin. Just a minute. The sergeant's paying up. [*Bites the half guilder*] I'm always suspicious of money. I'm a burnt child, sergeant. But your coin is good. And now we'll be going. Where's Eilif?

SWISS CHEESE. He's gone with the recruiter.

MOTHER COURAGE. [*Stands motionless, then*] You simple soul. [*To*

Kattrin] I know. You can't talk, you couldn't help it.

THE SERGEANT. You could do with a drink yourself, mother. That's the way it goes. Soldiering isn't the worst thing in the world. You want to live off the war, but you want to keep you and yours out of it. Is that it?

MOTHER COURAGE. Now you'll have to pull with your brother, Kattrin.

[*Brother and sister harness themselves to the wagon and start pulling. Mother Courage walks beside them. The wagon rolls off*]

THE SERGEANT. [*Looking after them*]

If you want the war to work for you
You've got to give the war its due.

2

In 1625 and 1626 Mother Courage crosses Poland in the train[3] of the Swedish armies. Outside the fortress of Wallh of she meets her son again.—A capon is successfully sold, the brave son's fortunes are at their zenith.

The general's tent.

Beside it the kitchen. The thunder of cannon. The cook is arguing with Mother Courage, who is trying to sell him a capon.

THE COOK. Sixty hellers[4] for that pathetic bird?

MOTHER COURAGE. Pathetic bird? You mean this plump beauty? Are you trying to tell me that a general who's the biggest eater for miles around—God help you if you haven't got anything for his dinner—can't afford a measly sixty hellers?

THE COOK. I can get a dozen like it for ten hellers right around the corner.

MOTHER COURAGE. What, you'll find a capon like this right around the corner? With a siege on and everybody so starved you can see right through them. Maybe you'll scare up a rat, maybe, I say, 'cause they've all been eaten, I've seen five men chasing a starved rat for hours. Fifty hellers for a giant capon in the middle of a siege.

THE COOK. We're not besieged; they are. We're the besiegers, can't you get that through your head?

MOTHER COURAGE. But we haven't got anything to eat either, in fact we've got less than the people in the city. They've hauled it all inside. I hear their life is one big orgy. And look at us. I've been

3. I.e., with the supplies and baggage at the end of the line of march. *Wallhof*: Fictional city.
4. A small coin formerly used in Austria and Germany.

around to the peasants, they haven't got a thing.

THE COOK. They've got plenty. They hide it.

MOTHER COURAGE. [*Triumphantly*] Oh, no! They're ruined, that's what they are. They're starving. I've seen them. They're so hungry they're digging up roots. They lick their fingers when they've eaten a boiled strap. That's the situation. And here I've got a capon and I'm supposed to let it go for forty hellers.

THE COOK. Thirty, not forty. Thirty, I said.

MOTHER COURAGE. It's no common capon. They tell me this bird was so talented that he wouldn't eat unless they played music, he had his own favorite march. He could add and subtract, that's how intelligent he was. And you're trying to tell me forty hellers is too much. The general will bite your head off if there's nothing to eat.

THE COOK. You know what I'm going to do? [*He takes a piece of beef and sets his knife to it*] Here I've got a piece of beef. I'll roast it. Think it over. This is your last chance.

MOTHER COURAGE. Roast and be damned. It's a year old.

THE COOK. A day old. That ox was running around only yesterday afternoon, I saw him with my own eyes.

MOTHER COURAGE. Then he must have stunk on the hoof.

THE COOK. I'll cook it five hours if I have to. We'll see if it's still tough. [*He cuts it*]

MOTHER COURAGE. Use plenty of pepper, maybe the general won't notice the stink.

[*The general, a chaplain, and Eilif enter the tent*]

THE GENERAL. [*Slapping Eilif on the back*] All right, son, into your general's tent you go, you'll sit at my right hand. You've done a heroic deed and you're a pious trooper, because this is a war of religion and what you did was done for God, that's what counts with me. I'll reward you with a gold bracelet when I take the city. We come here to save their souls and what do those filthy, shameless peasants do? They drive their cattle away. And they stuff their priests with meat, front and back. But you taught them a lesson. Here's a tankard of red wine for you. [*He pours*] We'll down it on one gulp. [*They do so*] None for the chaplain, he's got his religion. What would you like for dinner, sweetheart?

EILIF. A scrap of meat. Why not?

THE GENERAL. Cook! Meat!

THE COOK. And now he brings company when there's nothing to eat.

[*Wanting to listen, Mother Courage makes him stop talking*]

EILIF. Cutting down peasants whets the appetite.

MOTHER COURAGE. God, it's my Eilif.

THE COOK. Who?

MOTHER COURAGE. My eldest. I haven't seen hide nor hair of him in two years, he was stolen from me on the highway. He must be in good if the general invites him to dinner, and what have you got to offer? Nothing. Did you hear what the general's guest wants for dinner? Meat! Take my advice, snap up this capon. The price is one guilder.

THE GENERAL. [*Has sat down with Eilif. Bellows*] Food, Lamb, you lousy, no-good cook, or I'll kill you.

THE COOK. All right, hand it over. This is extortion.

MOTHER COURAGE. I thought it was a pathetic bird.

THE COOK. Pathetic is the word. Hand it over. Fifty hellers! It's highway robbery.

MOTHER COURAGE. One guilder, I say. For my eldest son, the general's honored guest, I spare no expense.

THE COOK. [*Gives her the money*] Then pluck it at least while I make the fire.

MOTHER COURAGE. [*Sits down to pluck the capon*] Won't he be glad to see me! He's my brave, intelligent son. I've got a stupid one too, but he's honest. The girl's a total loss. But at least she doesn't talk, that's something.

THE GENERAL. Take another drink, son, it's my best Falerno,[5] I've only got another barrel or two at the most, but it's worth it to see that there's still some true faith in my army. The good shepherd here just looks on, all he knows how to do is preach. Can he do anything? No. And now, Eilif my son, tell us all about it, how cleverly you hoodwinked those peasants and captured those twenty head of cattle. I hope they'll be here soon.

EILIF. Tomorrow. Maybe the day after.

MOTHER COURAGE. Isn't my Eilif considerate, not bringing those oxen in until tomorrow, or you wouldn't have even said hello to my capon.

EILIF. Well, it was like this: I heard the peasants were secretly—mostly at night—rounding up the oxen they'd hidden in a certain forest. The city people had arranged to come and get them. I let them round the oxen up, I figured they'd find them easier than I would. I made my men ravenous for meat, put them on short rations for two days until their mouths watered if they even heard a word beginning with *me* . . . like measles.

THE GENERAL. That was clever of you.

EILIF. Maybe. The rest was a pushover. Except the peasants had clubs and there were three times more of them and they fell on us like bloody murder. Four of them drove me into a clump of bushes, they knocked my sword out of my hand and yelled: Surrender! Now what'll I do, I says to myself, they'll make hash out of me.

THE GENERAL. What did you do?

5. A famous wine made from grapes grown in Falerno in Italy.

EILIF. I laughed.

THE GENERAL. You laughed?

EILIF. I laughed. Which led to a conversation. The first thing you know, I'm bargaining. Twenty guilders is too much for that ox, I say, how about fifteen? Like I'm meaning to pay. They're flummoxed, they scratch their heads. Quick, I reach for my sword and mow them down. Necessity knows no law. See what I mean?

THE GENERAL. What do you say to that, shepherd?

CHAPLAIN. Strictly speaking, that maxim is not in the Bible. But our Lord was able to turn five loaves into five hundred.[6] So there was no question of poverty; he could tell people to love their neighbors because their bellies were full. Nowadays it's different.

THE GENERAL. [Laughs] Very different. All right, you Pharisee,[7] take a swig. [To Eilif] You mowed them down, splendid, so my fine troops could have a decent bite to eat. Doesn't the Good Book say: "Whatsoever thou doest for the least of my brethren, thou doest for me"?[8] And what have you done for them? You've got them a good chunk of beef for their dinner. They're not used to moldy crusts; in the old days they had a helmetful of white bread and wine before they went out to fight for God.

EILIF. Yes, I reached for my sword and I mowed them down.

THE GENERAL. You're a young Caesar. You deserve to see the king.

EILIF. I have, in the distance. He shines like a light. He's my ideal.

THE GENERAL. You're a something like him already, Eilif. I know the worth of a brave soldier like you. When I find one, I treat him like my own son. [He leads him to the map] Take a look at the situation, Eilif; we've still got a long way to go.

MOTHER COURAGE. [Who has been listening starts plucking her capon furiously] He must be a rotten general.

THE COOK. Eats like a pig, but why rotten?

MOTHER COURAGE. Because he needs brave soldiers, that's why. If he planned his campaigns right, what would he need brave soldiers for? The run-of-the-mill would do. Take it from me, whenever you find a lot of virtues, it shows that something's wrong.

THE COOK. I'd say it proves that something is all right.

MOTHER COURAGE. No, that something's wrong. See, when a general or a king is real stupid and leads his men up shit creek, his troops need courage, that's a virtue. If he's stingy and doesn't hire enough soldiers, they've all got to be Herculeses. And if he's a slob and lets everything go to pot, they've got to be as sly as serpents or they're done for. And if he's always expecting too much of them,

---

6. Episode in the Gospels when Jesus fed five thousand people with five loaves and two fishes (Matthew 15:33 ff.). 7. Religious hypocrite, quibbler on religious doctrine. 8. Spoken by Jesus in the Gospels (Matthew 25:40 ff.).

they need an extra dose of loyalty. A country that's run right, or a good king or a good general, doesn't need any of these virtues. You don't need virtues in a decent country, the people can all be perfectly ordinary, medium-bright, and cowards too for my money.

THE GENERAL I bet your father was a soldier.

EILIF. A great soldier, I'm told. My mother warned me about it. Makes me think of a song.

THE GENERAL. Sing it! [*Bellowing*] Where's that food!

EILIF. It is called: The Song of the Old Wife and the Soldier.

[*He sings, doing a war dance with his saber*]

A gun or a pike they can kill who they like
And the torrent will swallow a wader
You had better think twice before battling with ice
Said the old wife to the soldier.
Cocking his rifle he leapt to his feet
Laughing for joy as he heard the drum beat
The wars cannot hurt me, he told her.
He shouldered his gun and he picked up his knife
To see the wide world. That's the soldier's life.
Those were the words of the soldier.

Ah, Deep will they lie who wise counsel defy
Learn wisdom from those that are older
Oh, don't venture too high or you'll fall from the sky
Said the old wife to the soldier.
But the young soldier with knife and with gun
Only laughed a cold laugh and stepped into the run.
The water can't hurt me, he told her.
And when the moon on the rooftop shines white
We'll be coming back. You can pray for that night.
Those were the words of the soldier.

MOTHER COURAGE. [*In the kitchen, continues the song, beating a pot with a spoon*]

Like the smoke you'll be gone and no warmth linger on
And your deeds only leave me the colder!
Oh, see the smoke race. Oh, dear God keep him safe!
That's what she said of the soldier.

EILIF. What's that?

MOTHER COURAGE. [*Goes on singing*]

And the young soldier with knife and with gun
Was swept from his feet till he sank in the run
And the torrent swallowed the waders.
Cold shone the moon on the rooftop white
But the soldier was carried away with the ice
And what was it she heard from the soldiers?
Like the smoke he was gone and no warmth lingered on
And his deeds only left her the colder.
Ah, deep will they lie who wise counsel defy!
That's what she said to the soldiers.

THE GENERAL. What do they think they're doing in my kitchen?

EILIF. [*Has gone into the kitchen. He embraces his mother*] Mother!
It's you! Where are the others?

MOTHER COURAGE. [*In his arms*] Snug as a bug in a rug. Swiss Cheese
is paymaster of the Second Regiment; at least he won't be fighting,
I couldn't keep him out altogether.

EILIF. And how about your feet?

MOTHER COURAGE. Well, it's hard getting my shoes on in the morning.

THE GENERAL. [*Has joined them*] Ah, so you're his mother. I hope
you've got more sons for me like this fellow here.

EILIF. Am I lucky! There you're sitting in the kitchen hearing your
son being praised.

MOTHER COURAGE. I heard it all right! [*She gives him a slap in the
face*]

EILIF. [*Holding his cheek*] For capturing the oxen?

MOTHER COURAGE. No. For not surrendering when the four of them
were threatening to make hash out of you! Didn't I teach you to
take care of yourself? You Finnish devil!

[*The general and the chaplain laugh*]

3

Three years later Mother Courage and parts of a Finnish[9] regiment are taken prisoner. She is able to save her daughter and her
wagon, but her honest son dies.

Army camp.

*Afternoon. On a pole the regimental flag. Mother Courage has
stretched a clothesline between her wagon, on which all sorts of
merchandise is hung in display, and a large cannon. She and Kattrin*

9. Finland was under Swedish rule at this time.

are folding washing and piling it on the cannon. At the same time she is negotiating with an ordnance officer[1] over a sack of bullets. Swiss Cheese, now in the uniform of a paymaster, is looking on. A pretty woman, Yvette Pottier, is sitting with a glass of brandy in front of her, sewing a gaudy-colored hat. She is in her stocking feet, her red high-heeled shoes are on the ground beside her.

THE ORDNANCE OFFICER. I'll let you have these bullets for two guilders. It's cheap, I need the money, because the colonel's been drinking with the officers for two days and we're out of liquor.

MOTHER COURAGE. That's ammunition for the troops. If it's found here, I'll be court-martialed. You punks sell their bullets and the men have nothing to shoot at the enemy.

THE ORDNANCE OFFICER. Don't be hard-hearted, you scratch my back, I'll scratch yours.

MOTHER COURAGE. I'm not taking any army property. Not at that price.

THE ORDNANCE OFFICER. You can sell it for five guilders, maybe eight, to the ordnance officer of the Fourth before the day is out, if you're quiet about it and give him a receipt for twelve. He hasn't an ounce of ammunition left.

MOTHER COURAGE. Why don't you do it yourself?

THE ORDNANCE OFFICER. Because I don't trust him, he's a friend of mine.

MOTHER COURAGE. [*Takes the sack*] Hand it over. [*To Kattrin*] Take it back there and pay him one and a half guilders. [*In response to the ordnance officer's protest*] One and a half guilders, I say. [*Kattrin drags the sack behind the wagon, the ordnance officer follows her. Mother Courage to Swiss Cheese*] Here's your underdrawers, take good care of them, this is October, might be coming on fall, I don't say it will be, because I've learned that nothing is sure to happen the way we think, not even the seasons. But whatever happens, your regimental funds have to be in order. Are your funds in order?

SWISS CHEESE. Yes, mother.

MOTHER COURAGE. Never forget that they made you paymaster because you're honest and not brave like your brother, and especially because you're too simple-minded to get the idea of making off with the money. That's a comfort to me. And don't go mislaying your drawers.

SWISS CHEESE. No, mother. I'll put them under my mattress.
   [*Starts to go*]

ORDNANCE OFFICER. I'll go with you, paymaster.

MOTHER COURAGE. Just don't teach him any of your tricks.

---

1. Officer in charge of weapons, particularly explosives.

[*Without saying good-bye the ordnance officer goes out with Swiss Cheese*]

YVETTE. [*Waves her hand after the ordnance officer*] You might say good-bye, officer.

MOTHER COURAGE. [*To Yvette*] I don't like to see those two together. He's not the right kind of company for my Swiss Cheese. But the war's getting along pretty well. More countries are joining in all the time, it can go on for another four, five years, easy. With a little planning ahead, I can do good business if I'm careful. Don't you know you shouldn't drink in the morning with your sickness?

YVETTE. Who says I'm sick, it's slander.

MOTHER COURAGE. Everybody says so.

YVETTE. Because they're all liars. Mother Courage, I'm desperate. They all keep out of my way like I'm a rotten fish on account of those lies. What's the good of fixing my hat? [*She throws it down*] That's why I drink in the morning, I never used to, I'm getting crow's-feet, but it doesn't matter now. In the Second Finnish Regiment they all know me. I should have stayed home when my first love walked out on me. Pride isn't for the likes of us. If we can't put up with shit, we're through.

MOTHER COURAGE. Just don't start in on your Pieter and how it all happened in front of my innocent daughter.

YVETTE. She's just the one to hear it, it'll harden her against love.

MOTHER COURAGE. Nothing can harden them.

YVETTE. Then I'll talk about it because it makes me feel better. It begins with my growing up in fair Flanders, because if I hadn't I'd never have laid eyes on him and I wouldn't be here in Poland now, because he was an army cook, blond, a Dutchman, but skinny. Kattrin, watch out for the skinny ones, but I didn't know that then, and another thing I didn't know is that he had another girl even then, and they all called him Pete the Pipe, because he didn't even take his pipe out of his mouth when he was doing it, that's all it meant to him. [*She sings the Song of Fraternization*]

When I was only sixteen
The foe came into our land.
He laid aside his saber
And with a smile he took my hand.
  After the May parade
  The May light starts to fade.
  The regiment dressed by the right[2]
  Then drums were beaten, that's the drill.[3]

---

2. I.e., each man aligned himself with the man on his right to form straight ranks for the parade.   3. I.e., that's the usual thing.

The foe took us behind the hill
And fraternized all night.

There were so many foes came
And mine worked in the mess.[4]
I loathed him in the daytime.
At night I loved him none the less.
  After the May parade
  The May light starts to fade.
  The regiment dressed by the right
  Then drums were beaten, that's the drill.
  The foe took us behind the hill
  And fraternized all night.

The love which came upon me
Was wished on me by fate.
My friends could never grasp why
I found it hard to share their hate.
  The fields were wet with dew
  When sorrow first I knew.
  The regiment dressed by the right
  Then drums were beaten, that's the drill.
  And then the foe, my lover still
  Went marching from our sight.

Well, I followed him, but I never found him. That was five years
ago. [*She goes behind the wagon with an unsteady gait*]

MOTHER COURAGE. You've left your hat.

YVETTE. Anybody that wants it can have it.

MOTHER COURAGE. Let that be a lesson to you, Kattrin. Have no
truck with soldiers. It's love that makes the world go round, so
you'd better watch out. Even with a civilian it's no picnic. He says
he'd kiss the ground you put your little feet on, talking of feet, did
you wash yours yesterday, and then you're his slave. Be glad you're
dumb, that way you'll never contradict yourself or want to bite
your tongue off because you've told the truth, it's a gift of God to
be dumb. Here comes the general's cook, I wonder what he wants.
  [*The cook and the chaplain enter*]

THE CHAPLAIN. I've got a message for you from your son Eilif. The
cook here thought he'd come along, he's taken a shine to you.

THE COOK. I only came to get a breath of air.

MOTHER COURAGE. You can always do that here if you behave, and

___

4. The kitchen.

if you don't, I can handle you. Well, what does he want? I've got
no money to spare.

THE CHAPLAIN. Actually he wanted me to see his brother, the paymaster.

MOTHER COURAGE. He's not here any more, or anywhere else either.
He's not his brother's paymaster. I don't want him leading him
into temptation and being smart at his expense [*Gives him money
from the bag slung around her waist*] Give him this, it's a sin, he's
speculating on mother love and he ought to be ashamed.

THE COOK. He won't do it much longer, then he'll be marching off
with his regiment, maybe to his death, you never can tell. Better
make it a little more, you'll be sorry later. You women are hard-
hearted, but afterwards you're sorry. A drop of brandy wouldn't
have cost much when it was wanted, but it wasn't given, and later,
for all you know, he'll be lying in the cold ground and you can't
dig him up again.

THE CHAPLAIN. Don't be sentimental, cook. There's nothing wrong
with dying in battle, it's a blessing, and I'll tell you why. This is a
war of religion. Not a common war, but a war for the faith, and
therefore pleasing to God.

THE COOK. That's a fact. In a way you could call it a war, because of
the extortion and killing and looting, not to mention a bit of rape,
but it's a war of religion, which makes it different from all other
wars, that's obvious. But it makes a man thirsty all the same, you've
got to admit that.

THE CHAPLAIN. [*To Mother Courage, pointing at the cook*] I tried to
discourage him, but he says you've turned his head, he sees you
in his dreams.

THE COOK. [*Lights a short-stemmed pipe*] All I want is a glass of
brandy from your fair hand, nothing more sinful. I'm already so
shocked by the jokes the chaplain's been telling me, I bet I'm still
red in the face.

MOTHER COURAGE. And him a clergyman! I'd better give you fellows
something to drink or you'll be making me immoral propositions
just to pass the time.

THE CHAPLAIN. This is temptation, said the deacon, and succumbed
to it. [*Turning toward Kattrin as he leaves*] And who is this delightful
young lady?

MOTHER COURAGE. She's not delightful, she's a respectable young
lady.

[*The chaplain and the cook go behind the wagon with Mother
Courage. Kattrin looks after them, then she walks away from
the washing and approaches the hat. She picks it up, sits down
and puts on the red shoes. From the rear Mother Courage is
heard talking politics with the chaplain and the cook*]

MOTHER COURAGE. The Poles here in Poland shouldn't have butted in. All right, our king marched his army into their country. But instead of keeping the peace, the Poles start butting into their own affairs and attack the king while he's marching quietly through the landscape. That was a breach of the peace and the blood is on their head.

THE CHAPLAIN. Our king had only one thing in mind; freedom. The emperor had everybody under his yoke, the Poles as much as the Germans; the king had to set them free.

THE COOK. I see it this way, your brandy's first-rate, I can see why I liked your face, but we were talking about the king. This freedom he was trying to introduce into Germany cost him a fortune, he had to levy a salt tax in Sweden, which, as I said, cost the poor people a fortune. Then he had to put the Germans in jail and break them on the rack because they liked being the emperor's slaves. Oh yes, the king made short shrift of anybody that didn't want to be free. In the beginning he only wanted to protect Poland against wicked people, especially the emperor, but the more he ate the more he wanted, and pretty soon he was protecting all of Germany.[5] But the Germans didn't take it lying down and the king got nothing but trouble for all his kindness and expense, which he naturally had to defray from taxes, which made for bad blood, but that didn't discourage him. He had one thing in his favor, the word of God, which was lucky, because otherwise people would have said he was doing it all for himself and what he hoped to get out of it. As it was, he always had a clear conscience and that was all he really cared about.

MOTHER COURAGE. It's easy to see you're not a Swede, or you wouldn't talk like that about the Hero-King.

THE CHAPLAIN. You're eating his bread, aren't you?

THE COOK. I don't eat his bread, I bake it.

MOTHER COURAGE. He can't be defeated because his men believe in him. [*Earnestly*] When you listen to the big wheels talk, they're making war for reasons of piety, in the name of everything that's fine and noble. But when you take another look, you see that they're not so dumb; they're making war for profit. If they weren't, the small fry like me wouldn't have anything to do with it.[6]

THE COOK. That's a fact.

THE CHAPLAIN. And it wouldn't hurt you as a Dutchman to take a look at that flag up there before you express opinions in Poland.

MOTHER COURAGE. We're all good Protestants here! Prosit![7]

---

5. Allusion to Hitler's expansion of German territory allegedly to protect German-speaking peoples, first in Bohemia and then, in 1938, through the annexation of Austria.　6. The German expression can also be translated, "Wouldn't be doing the same thing."　7. Cheers!

[*Kattrin has started strutting about with Yvette's hat on, imitating Yvette's gait.*]

[*Suddenly cannon fire and shots are heard. Drums. Mother Courage, the cook, and the chaplain run out from behind the wagon, the two men still with glasses in hand. The ordnance officer and a soldier rush up to the cannon and try to push it away*]

MOTHER COURAGE. What's going on? Let me get my washing first, you lugs. [*She tries to rescue her washing*]

THE ORDNANCE OFFICER. The Catholics. They're attacking. I don't know as we'll get away. [*To the soldier*] Get rid of the gun! [*Runs off*]

THE COOK. Christ, I've got to find the general. Courage, I'll be back for a little chat in a day or two. [*Rushes out*]

MOTHER COURAGE. Stop, you've forgotten your pipe.

THE COOK. [*From the distance*] Keep it for me! I'll need it.

MOTHER COURAGE. Just when we were making a little money!

THE CHAPLAIN. Well, I guess I'll be going too. It might be dangerous though, with the enemy so close. Blessed are the peaceful[8] is the best motto in wartime. If only I had a cloak to cover up with.

MOTHER COURAGE. I'm not lending any cloaks, not on your life. I've had bitter experience in that line.

THE CHAPLAIN. But my religion puts me in special danger.

MOTHER COURAGE. [*Bringing him a cloak*] It's against my better conscience. And now run along.

THE CHAPLAIN. Thank you kindly, you've got a good heart. But maybe I'd better sit here a while. The enemy might get suspicious if they see me running.

MOTHER COURAGE. [*To the soldier*] Leave it lay, you fool, you won't get paid extra. I'll take care of it for you, you'd only get killed.

THE SOLDIER. [*Running away*] I tried. You're my witness.

MOTHER COURAGE. I'll swear it on the Bible. [*Sees her daughter with the hat*] What are you doing with that floozy hat? Take it off, have you gone out of your mind? Now of all times, with the enemy on top of us? [*She tears the hat off Kattrin's head*] You want them to find you and make a whore out of you? And those shoes! Take them off, you woman of Babylon![9] [*She tries to pull them off*] Jesus Christ, chaplain, make her take those shoes off! I'll be right back. [*She runs to the wagon*]

YVETTE. [*Enters, powdering her face*] What's this I hear? The Catholics are coming? Where is my hat? Who's been stamping on it? I

8. A parody of Jesus' Sermon on the Mount: "Blessed are the peacemakers, for they shall be called sons of God" (*Matthew* 5:9). 9. Sinful woman. The ancient Asian city of Babylon is a Biblical locus for sin and decadence: "Babylon the great, mother of harlots and of earth's abominations (*Revelations* 17:5).

can't be seen like this if the Catholics are coming. What'll they think of me? I haven't even got a mirror. [*To the chaplain*] How do I look? Too much powder?

THE CHAPLAIN. Just right.

YVETTE. And where are my red shoes? [*She doesn't see them because Kattrin hides her feet under her skirt*] I left them here. I've got to get back to my tent. In my bare feet. It's disgraceful! [*Goes out*]
[*Swiss Cheese runs in carrying a small box*]

MOTHER COURAGE. [*Comes out with her hands full of ashes. To Kattrin*] Ashes. [*To Swiss Cheese*] What you got there?

SWISS CHEESE. The regimental funds.

MOTHER COURAGE. Throw it away! No more paymastering for you.

SWISS CHEESE. I'm responsible for it. [*He goes rear*]

MOTHER COURAGE. [*To the chaplain*] Take your clergyman's coat off, chaplain, or they'll recognize you, cloak or no cloak. [*She rubs Kattrin's face with ashes*] Hold still! There. With a little dirt you'll be safe. What a mess! The sentries were drunk. Hide your light under a bushel,[1] as the Good Book says. When a soldier, especially a Catholic, sees a clean face, she's a whore before she knows it. Nobody feeds them for weeks. When they finally loot some provisions, the next thing they want is women. That'll do it. Let me look at you. Not bad. Like you'd been wallowing in a pigsty. Stop shaking. You're safe now. [*To Swiss Cheese*] What did you do with the cashbox?

SWISS CHEESE. I thought I'd put it in the wagon.

MOTHER COURAGE. [*Horrified*] What! In my wagon? Of all the sinful stupidity! If my back is turned for half a second! They'll hang us all!

SWISS CHEESE. Then I'll put it somewhere else, or I'll run away with it.

MOTHER COURAGE. You'll stay right here. It's too late.

THE CHAPLAIN. [*Still changing, comes forward*] Heavens, the flag!

MOTHER COURAGE. [*Takes down the regimental flag*] Bozhe moi![2] I'm so used to it I don't see it. Twenty-five years I've had it.
[*The cannon fire grows louder*]

[*Morning, three days later. The cannon is gone. Mother Courage, Kattrin, the chaplain, and Swiss Cheese are sitting dejectedly over a meal*]

SWISS CHEESE. This is the third day I've been sitting here doing nothing; the sergeant has always been easy on me, but now he must be starting to wonder: where can Swiss Cheese be with the cashbox?

---

1. Also parodies the Sermon on the Mount: "Nor do men light a lamp and put it under a bushel [basket] but on a stand, and it gives light to all in the house" (Matthew 5:15).   2. My God! (Polish and Russian expression.)

MOTHER COURAGE. Be glad they haven't tracked you down.

THE CHAPLAIN. What about me? I can't hold a service here either. The Good Book says: "Whosoever hath a full heart, his tongue runneth over."[3] Heaven help me if mine runneth over.

MOTHER COURAGE. That's the way it is. Look what I've got on my hands: one with a religion and one with a cashbox. I don't know which is worse.

THE CHAPLAIN. Tell yourself that we're in the hands of God.

MOTHER COURAGE. I don't think we're that bad off, but all the same I can't sleep at night. If it weren't for you, Swiss Cheese, it'd be easier. I think I've put myself in the clear. I told them I was against the antichrist;[4] he's a Swede with horns, I told them, and I'd noticed the left horn was kind of worn down. I interrupted the questioning to ask where I could buy holy candles cheap. I knew what to say because Swiss Cheese's father was a Catholic and he used to make jokes about it. They didn't really believe me, but their regiment had no provisioner, so they looked the other way. Maybe we stand to gain. We're prisoners, but so are lice on a dog.

THE CHAPLAIN. This milk is good. Though there's not much of it or of anything else. Maybe we'll have to cut down on our Swedish appetites. But such is the lot of the vanquished.

MOTHER COURAGE. Who's vanquished? Victory and defeat don't always mean the same thing to the big wheels up top and the small fry underneath. Not by a long shot. In some cases defeat is a blessing to the small fry. Honor's lost, but nothing else. One time in Livonia[5] our general got such a shellacking from the enemy that in the confusion I laid hands on a beautiful white horse from the baggage train. That horse pulled my wagon for seven months, until we had a victory and they checked up. On the whole, you can say that victory and defeat cost us plain people plenty. The best thing for us is when politics gets bogged down. [*To Swiss Cheese*] Eat!

SWISS CHEESE. I've lost my appetite. How's the sergeant going to pay the men?

MOTHER COURAGE. Troops never get paid when they're running away.

SWISS CHEESE. But they've got it coming to them. If they're not paid, they don't need to run. Not a step.

MOTHER COURAGE. Swiss Cheese, you're too conscientious, it almost frightens me. I brought you up to be honest, because you're not bright, but somewhere it's got to stop. And now me and the chaplain are going to buy a Catholic flag and some meat. Nobody can buy meat like the chaplain, he goes into a trance and heads straight

---

3. "Out of the abundance of the heart the mouth speaketh," Biblical proverb meaning that one's words reflect the good or evil in one's heart. (Jesus to the Pharisees, Matthew 12:34.)   4. Figure of evil, whose appearance on earth is supposed to prefigure the end of the world and the coming of the Last Judgment.   5. Region of the east Baltic, now part of the U.S.S.R.

for the best piece, I guess it makes his mouth water and that shows him the way. At least they let me carry on my business. Nobody cares about a shopkeeper's religion, all they want to know is the price. Protestant pants are as warm as any other kind.

THE CHAPLAIN. Like the friar[6] said when somebody told him the Lutherans were going to stand the whole country on its head. They'll always need beggars, he says. [*Mother Courage disappears into the wagon*] But she's worried about that cashbox. They've taken no notice of us so far, they think we're all part of the wagon, but how long can that go on?

SWISS CHEESE. I can take it away.

THE CHAPLAIN. That would be almost more dangerous. What if somebody sees you? They've got spies. Yesterday morning, just as I'm relieving myself, one of them jumps out of the ditch. I was so scared I almost let out a prayer. That would have given me away. I suppose they think they can tell a Protestant by the smell of his shit. He was a little runt with a patch over one eye.

MOTHER COURAGE. [*Climbing down from the wagon with a basket*] Look what I've found. You shameless slut! [*She hold up the red shoes triumphantly*] Yvette's red shoes! She's swiped them in cold blood. It's your fault. Who told her she was a delightful young lady? [*She puts them into the basket*] I'm giving them back. Stealing Yvette's shoes! She ruins herself for money, that I can understand. But you'd like to do it free of charge, for pleasure. I've told you, you'll have to wait for peace. No soldiers! Just wait for peace with your worldly ways.

THE CHAPLAIN. She doesn't seem very worldly to me.

MOTHER COURAGE. Too worldly for me. In Dalarna she was like a stone, which is all they've got around there. The people used to say: We don't see the cripple. That's the way I like it. That way she's safe. [*To Swiss Cheese*] You leave that box where it is, hear? And keep an eye on your sister, she needs it. The two of you will be the death of me. I'd sooner take care of a bag of fleas. [*She goes off with the chaplain. Kattrin starts clearing away the dishes*]

SWISS CHEESE. Won't be many more days when I can sit in the sun in my shirtsleeves. [*Kattrin points to a tree*] Yes, the leaves are all yellow. [*Kattrin asks him, by means of gestures, whether he wants a drink*] Not now. I'm thinking. [*Pause*] She says she can't sleep. I'd better get the cashbox out of here, I've found a hiding place. All right, get me a drink. [*Kattrin goes behind the wagon*] I'll hide it in the rabbit hole down by the river until I can take it away. Maybe late tonight, I'll go get it and take it to the regiment. I wonder how far they've run in three days? Won't the sergeant be

6. A mendicant or beggar monk.

surprised! Well, Swiss Cheese, this is a pleasant disappointment, that's what he'll say. I trust you with the regimental cashbox and you bring it back.

[*As Kattrin comes out from behind the wagon with a glass of brandy, she comes face to face with two men. One is a sergeant. The other removes his hat and swings it through the air in a ceremonious greeting. He has a patch over one eye*]

THE MAN WITH THE PATCH. Good morning, my dear. Have you by any chance seen a man from the headquarters of the Second Finnish Regiment?

[*Scared out of her wits, Kattrin runs front, spilling the brandy. The two exchange looks and withdraw after seeing Swiss Cheese sitting there*]

SWISS CHEESE. [*Starting up from his thoughts*] You've spilled half of it. What's the fuss about? Poke yourself in the eye? I don't understand you. I'm getting out of here, I've made up my mind, it's best. [*He stands up. She does everything she can think of to call his attention to the danger. He only evades her*] I wish I could understand you. Poor thing, I know you're trying to tell me something, you just can't say it. Don't worry about spilling the brandy, I'll be drinking plenty more. What's one glass? [*He takes the cashbox out of the wagon and hides it under his jacket*] I'll be right back. Let me go, you're making me angry. I know you mean well. If only you could talk.

[*When she tries to hold him back, he kisses her and tears himself away. He goes out. She is desperate, she races back and forth, uttering short inarticulate sounds. The chaplain and Mother Courage come back. Kattrin gesticulates wildly at her mother*]

MOTHER COURAGE. What's the matter? You're all upset. Has somebody hurt you? Where's Swiss Cheese? Tell it to me in order, Kattrin. Your mother understands you. What, the no-good's taken the cashbox? I'll hit him over the head with it, the sneak. Take your time, don't talk nonsense, use your hands, I don't like it when you howl like a dog, what will the chaplain think? It gives him the creeps. A one-eyed man?

THE CHAPLAIN. The one-eyed man is a spy. Did they arrest Swiss Cheese? [*Kattrin shakes her head and shrugs her shoulders*] We're done for.

MOTHER COURAGE. [*Takes a Catholic flag out of her basket. The chaplain fastens it to the flagpole*] Hoist the new flag!

THE CHAPLAIN. [*Bitterly*] All good Catholics here.

[*Voices are heard from the rear. The two men bring in Swiss Cheese*]

SWISS CHEESE. Let me go, I haven't go anything. Stop twisting my shoulder, I'm innocent.

THE SERGEANT. He belongs here. You know each other.

MOTHER COURAGE. What makes you think that?

SWISS CHEESE. I don't know them. I don't even know who they are. I had a meal here, it cost me ten hellers. Maybe you saw me sitting here, it was too salty.

THE SERGEANT. Who are you anyway?

MOTHER COURAGE. We're respectable people. And it's true. He had a meal here. He said it was too salty.

THE SERGEANT. Are you trying to tell me you don't know each other?

MOTHER COURAGE. Why should I know him? I don't know everybody. I don't ask people what their name is or if they're heathens; if they pay, they're not heathens. Are you a heathen?

SWISS CHEESE. Of course not.

THE CHAPLAIN. He ate his meal and he behaved himself. He didn't open his mouth except when he was eating. Then you have to.

THE SERGEANT. And who are you?

MOTHER COURAGE. He's only my bartender. You gentlemen must be thirsty, I'll get you a drink of brandy, you must be hot and tired.

THE SERGEANT. We don't drink on duty. [*To Swiss Cheese*] You were carrying something. You must have hidden it by the river. You had something under your jacket when you left here.

MOTHER COURAGE. Was it really him?

SWISS CHEESE. I think you must have seen somebody else. I saw a man running with something under his jacket. You've got the wrong man.

MOTHER COURAGE. That's what I think too, it's a misunderstanding. These things happen. I'm a good judge of people. I'm Mother Courage, you've heard of me, everybody knows me. Take it from me, this man has an honest face.

THE SERGEANT. We're looking for the cashbox of the Second Finnish Regiment. We know what the man in charge of it looks like. We've been after him for two days. You're him.

SWISS CHEESE. I'm not.

THE SERGEANT. Hand it over. If you don't you're a goner, you know that. Where is it?

MOTHER COURAGE. [*With urgency*] He'd hand it over, wouldn't he, knowing he was a goner if he didn't? I've got it, he'd say, take it, you're stronger. He's not that stupid. Speak up, you stupid idiot, the sergeant's giving you a chance.

SWISS CHEESE. But I haven't got it.

THE SERGEANT. In that case come along. We'll get it out of you.
  [*They lead him away*]

MOTHER COURAGE. [*Shouts after them*] He'd tell you. He's not that stupid. And don't twist his shoulder off! [*Runs after them*]
  [*The same evening. The chaplain and mute Kattrin are wash-*

ing dishes and scouring knives]

THE CHAPLAIN. That boy's in trouble. There are cases like that in the Bible. Take the Passion of our Lord and Savior. There's an old song about it. [*He sings the Song of the Hours*]

In the first hour Jesus mild
Who had prayed since even
Was betrayed and led before
Pontius[7] the heathen.

Pilate found him innocent
Free from fault and error.
Therefore, having washed his hands
Sent him to King Herod.

In the third hour he was scourged
Stripped and clad in scarlet
And a plaited crown of thorns
Set upon his forehead.

On the Son of Man they spat
Mocked him and made merry.
Then the cross of death was brought
Given him to carry.

At the sixth hour with two thieves
To the cross they nailed him
And the people and the thieves
Mocked him and reviled him.

This is Jesus King of Jews
Cried they in derision
Till the sun withdrew its light
From that awful vision.

At the ninth hour Jesus wailed
Why hast thou me forsaken?
Soldiers brought him vinegar
Which he left untaken.

Then he yielded up the ghost
And the earth was shaken.

---

7. Roman judge before whom Jesus was arraigned by the Scribes (Matthew 27:1–24).

Rended was the temple's veil[8]
And the saints were wakened.

Soldiers broke the two thieves' legs
As the night descended
Thrust a spear in Jesus' side
When his life had ended.

Still they mocked, as from his wound
Flowed the blood and water
Thus blasphemed the Son of Man
With their cruel laughter.

MOTHER COURAGE. [*Enters in a state of agitation*] His life's at stake. But they say the sergeant will listen to reason. Only it mustn't come out that he's our Swiss Cheese, or they'll say we've been giving him aid and comfort. All they want is money. But where will we get the money? Hasn't Yvette been here? I met her just now, she's latched onto a colonel, he's thinking of buying her a provisioner's business.

THE CHAPLAIN. Are you really thinking of selling?

MOTHER COURAGE. How else can I get the money for the sergeant?

THE CHAPLAIN. But what will you live on?

MOTHER COURAGE. That's the hitch.

[*Yvette Pottier comes in with a doddering colonel*]

YVETTE. [*Embracing Mother Courage*] My dear Mother Courage. Here we are again! [*Whispering*] He's willing. [*Aloud*] This is my dear friend who advises me on business matters. I just chanced to hear that you wish to sell your wagon, due to circumstances. I might be interested.

MOTHER COURAGE. Mortgage it, not sell it, let's not be hasty. It's not so easy to buy a wagon like this in wartime.

YVETTE. [*Disappointed*] Only mortgage it? I thought you wanted to sell it. In that case, I don't know if I'm interested. [*To the colonel*] What do you think?

THE COLONEL. Just as you say, my dear.

MOTHER COURAGE. It's only being mortgaged.

YVETTE. I thought you needed money.

MOTHER COURAGE. [*Firmly*] I need the money, but I'd rather run myself ragged looking for an offer than sell now. The wagon is our livelihood. It's an opportunity for you, Yvette, God knows when

---

8. Matthew reports that at the moment of Jesus's death, the veil or curtain in the temple which set off the sanctuary was torn from top to bottom; the earth shook, and dead men rose from their graves (Matthew 27:51–3).

you'll find another like it and have such a good friend to advise
you. See what I mean?

YVETTE. My friend thinks I should snap it up, but I don't know. If
it's only being mortgaged . . . Don't you agree that we ought to
buy?

THE COLONEL. Yes, my dear.

MOTHER COURAGE. Then you'll have to look for something that's for
sale, maybe you'll find something if you take your time and your
friend goes around with you. Maybe in a week or two you'll find
the right thing.

YVETTE. Then we'll go looking, I love to go looking for things, and
I love to go around with you, Poldi, it's a real pleasure. Even if it
takes two weeks. When would you pay the money back if you get
it?

MOTHER COURAGE. I can pay it back in two weeks, maybe one.

YVETTE. I can't make up my mind, Poldi, chéri,[9] tell me what to do.
[*She takes the colonel aside*] I know she's got to sell, that's definite.
The lieutenant, you know who I mean, the blond one, he'd be
glad to lend me the money. He's mad about me, he says I remind
him of somebody. What do you think?

THE COLONEL. Keep away from that lieutenant. He's no good. He'll
take advantage. Haven't I told you I'd buy you something, pussy-
kins?

YVETTE. I can't accept it from you. But then if you think the lieutenant might take advantage . . . Poldi, I'll accept it from you.

THE COLONEL. I hope so.

YVETTE. Your advice is to take it?

THE COLONEL. That's my advice.

YVETTE. [*Goes back to Mother Courage*] My friend advises me to do
it. Write me out a receipt, say the wagon belongs to me complete
with stock and furnishings when the two weeks are up. We'll take
the inventory right now, then I'll bring you the two hundred
guilders. [*To the colonel*] You go back to camp, I'll join you in a
little while, I've got to take inventory, I don't want anything missing from my wagon. [*She kisses him. He leaves. She climbs up in
the wagon*] I don't see very many boots.

MOTHER COURAGE. Yvette. This is no time to inspect your wagon if
it is yours. You promised to see the sergeant about my Swiss Cheese,
you've got to hurry. They say he's to be court-martialed in an
hour.

YVETTE. Just let me count the shirts.

MOTHER COURAGE. [*Pulls her down by the skirt*] You hyena, it's Swiss
Cheese, his life's at stake. And don't tell anybody where the offer

9. Darling. *Poldi*: Pet name for Leopold.

comes from, in heaven's name say it's your gentleman friend, or we'll all get it, they'll say we helped him.

YVETTE. I've arranged to meet One-Eye in the woods, he must be there already.

THE CHAPLAIN. And there's no need to start out with the whole two hundred, offer a hundred and fifty, that's plenty.

MOTHER COURAGE. Is it your money? You just keep out of this. Don't worry, you'll get your bread and soup. Go on now and don't haggle. It's his life. [She gives Yvette a push to start her on her way]

THE CHAPLAIN. I didn't mean to butt in, but what are we going to live on? You've got an unemployable daughter on your hands.

MOTHER COURAGE. You muddlehead, I'm counting on the regimental cashbox. They'll allow for his expenses, won't they?

THE CHAPLAIN. But will she handle it right?

MOTHER COURAGE. It's in her own interest. If I spend her two hundred, she gets the wagon. She's mighty keen on it, how long can she expect to hold on to her colonel? Kattrin, you scour the knives, use pumice. And you, don't stand around like Jesus on the Mount of Olives,[1] bestir yourself, wash those glasses, we're expecting at least fifty for dinner, and then it'll be the same old story: "Oh my feet, I'm not used to running around, I don't run around in the pulpit." I think they'll set him free. Thank God they're open to bribery. They're not wolves, they're human and out for money. Bribe-taking in humans is the same as mercy in God. It's our only hope. As long as people take bribes, you'll have mild sentences and even the innocent will get off once in a while.

YVETTE. [Comes in panting] They want two hundred. And we've got to be quick. Or it'll be out of their hands. I'd better take One-Eye to see my colonel right away. He confessed that he'd had the cashbox, they put the thumb screws on him. But he threw it in the river when he saw they were after him. The box is gone. Should I run and get the money from my colonel?

MOTHER COURAGE. The box is gone? How will I get my two hundred back?

YVETTE. Ah, so you thought you could take it out of the cashbox? You thought you'd put one over on me. Forget it. If you want to save Swiss Cheese, you'll just have to pay, or maybe you'd like me to drop the whole thing and let you keep your wagon?

MOTHER COURAGE. This is something I hadn't reckoned with. But don't rush me, you'll get the wagon, I know it's down the drain, I've had it for seventeen years. Just let me think a second, it's all so sudden. What'll I do, I can't give them two hundred, I guess you should have bargained. If I haven't got a few guilders to fall

1. The ridge of hills outside Jerusalem where Jesus waited after the Last Supper to be captured and taken before the high priest.

back on, I'll be at the mercy of the first Tom, Dick, or Harry. Say I'll give them a hundred and twenty, I'll lose my wagon anyway.

YVETTE. They won't go along. One-Eye's in a hurry, he's so keyed-up he keeps looking behind him. Hadn't I better give them the whole two hundred?

MOTHER COURAGE. [*In despair*] I can't do it. Thirty years I've worked. She's twenty-five and no husband. I've got her to keep too. Don't needle me, I know what I'm doing. Say a hundred and twenty or nothing doing.

YVETTE. It's up to you. [*Goes out quickly*]

[*Mother Courage looks neither at the chaplain nor at her daughter. She sits down to help Kattrin scour the knives*]

MOTHER COURAGE. Don't break the glasses. They're not ours any more. Watch what you're doing, you'll cut yourself. Swiss Cheese will be back, I'll pay two hundred if I have to. You'll have your brother. With eighty guilders we can buy a peddler's pack and start all over. Worse things have happened.

THE CHAPLAIN. The Lord will provide.

MOTHER COURAGE. Rub them dry. [*They scour the knives in silence. Suddenly Kattrin runs sobbing behind the wagon*]

YVETTE. [*Comes running*] They won't go along. I warned you. One-Eye wanted to run out on me, he said it was no use. He said we'd hear the drums any minute, meaning he'd been sentenced. I offered a hundred and fifty. He didn't even bother to shrug his shoulders. When I begged and pleaded, he promised to wait till I'd spoken to you again.

MOTHER COURAGE. Say I'll give him the two hundred. Run. [*Yvette runs off. They sit in silence. The chaplain has stopped washing the glasses*]

Maybe I bargained too long. [*Drums are heard in the distance. The chaplain stands up and goes to the rear. Mother Courage remains seated. It grows dark. The drums stop. It grows light again. Mother Courage has not moved*]

YVETTE. [*Enters, very pale*] Now you've done it with your haggling and wanting to keep your wagon. Eleven bullets he got, that's all. I don't know why I bother with you any more, you don't deserve it. But I've picked up a little information. They don't believe the cashbox is really in the river. They suspect it's here and they think you were connected with him. They're going to bring him here, they think maybe you'll give yourself away when you see him. I'm warning you: You don't know him, or you're all dead ducks. I may as well tell you, they're right behind me. Should I keep Kattrin out of the way? [*Mother Courage shakes her head*] Does she know? Maybe she didn't hear the drums or maybe she didn't understand.

MOTHER COURAGE. She knows. Get her.

[*Yvette brings Kattrin, who goes to her mother and stands beside her. Mother Courage takes her by the hand. Two soldiers come in with a stretcher on which something is lying under a sheet. The sergeant walks beside them. They set the stretcher down*]

THE SERGEANT. We've got a man here and we don't know his name. We need it for the records. He had a meal with you. Take a look, see if you know him. [*He removes the sheet*] Do you know him? [*Mother Courage shakes her head*] What? You'd never seen him before he came here for a meal? [*Mother Courage shakes her head*] Pick him up. Throw him on the dump. Nobody knows him. [*They carry him away*]

4

Mother Courage sings the Song of the Great Capitulation.

Outside an officer's tent.

Mother Courage is waiting. A clerk looks out of the tent.

THE CLERK. I know you. You had a Protestant paymaster at your place, he was hiding. I wouldn't put in any complaints if I were you.

MOTHER COURAGE. I'm putting in a complaint. I'm innocent. If I take this lying down, it'll look as if I had a guilty conscience. First they ripped up my whole wagon with their sabers, then they wanted me to pay a fine of five talers[2] for no reason at all.

THE CLERK. I'm advising you for your own good: Keep your trap shut. We haven't got many provisioners and we'll let you keep on with your business, especially if you've got a guilty conscience and pay a fine now and then.

MOTHER COURAGE. I'm putting in a complaint.

THE CLERK. Have it your way. But you'll have to wait till the captain can see you. [*Disappears into the tent*]

A YOUNG SOLDIER. [*Enters in a rage*] Bouque la Madonne![3] Where's that stinking captain? He embezzled my reward and now he's drinking it up with his whores. I'm going to get him!

AN OLDER SOLDIER. [*Comes running after him*] Shut up. They'll put you in the stocks!

THE YOUNG SOLDIER. Come on out, you crook! I'll make chops out of you. Embezzling my reward! Who jumps in the river? Not another man in the whole squad, only me. And I can't even buy

---

2. German silver coins.   3. Screw the Virgin! (French)

myself a beer. I won't stand for it. Come on out and let me cut you to pieces!

THE OLDER SOLDIER. Holy Mary! He'll ruin himself.

MOTHER COURAGE. They didn't give him a reward?

THE YOUNG SOLDIER. Let me go. I'll run you through too, the more the merrier.

THE OLDER SOLDIER. He saved the colonel's horse and they didn't give him a reward. He's young, he hasn't been around long.

MOTHER COURAGE. Let him go, he's not a dog, you don't have to tie him up. Wanting a reward is perfectly reasonable. Why else would he distinguish himself?

THE YOUNG SOLDIER. And him drinking in there! You're all a lot of yellowbellies. I distinguished myself and I want my reward.

MOTHER COURAGE. Young man, don't shout at me. I've got my own worries and besides, go easy on your voice, you may need it. You'll be hoarse when the captain comes out, you won't be able to say boo and he won't be able to put you in the stocks till you're blue in the face. People that yell like that don't last long, maybe half an hour, then they're so exhausted you have to sing them to sleep.

THE YOUNG SOLDIER. I'm not exhausted and who wants to sleep? I'm hungry. They make our bread out of acorns and hemp seed, and they skimp on that. He's whoring away my reward and I'm hungry. I'll murder him.

MOTHER COURAGE. I see. You're hungry. Last year your general made you cut across the fields to trample down the grain. I could have sold a pair of boots for ten guilders if anybody'd had ten guilders and if I'd had any boots. He thought he'd be someplace else this year, but now he's still here and everybody's starving. I can see that you might be good and mad.

THE YOUNG SOLDIER. He can't do this to me, save your breath, I won't put up with injustice.

MOTHER COURAGE. You're right, but for how long? How long won't you put up with injustice? An hour? Two hours? You see, you never thought of that, though it's very important, because it's miserable in the stocks when it suddenly dawns on you that you *can* put up with injustice.

THE YOUNG SOLDIER. I don't know why I listen to you. Bouque la Madonne! Where's the captain?

MOTHER COURAGE. You listen to me because I'm not telling you anything new. You know your temper has gone up in smoke, it was a short temper and you need a long one, but that's a hard thing to come by.

THE YOUNG SOLDIER. Are you trying to say I've no right to claim my reward?

MOTHER COURAGE. Not at all. I'm only saying your temper isn't long enough, it won't get you anywhere. Too bad. If you had a long temper, I'd even egg you on. Chop the bastard up, that's what I'd say, but suppose you don't chop him up, because your tail's drooping and you know it. I'm left standing there like a fool and the captain takes it out on me.

THE OLDER SOLDIER. You're right. He's only blowing off steam.

THE YOUNG SOLDIER. We'll see about that. I'll cut him to pieces. [*He draws his sword*] When he comes, I'll cut him to pieces.

THE CLERK. [*Looks out*] The captain will be here in a moment. Sit down.

[*The young soldier sits down*]

MOTHER COURAGE. There he sits. What did I tell you? Sitting, aren't you? Oh, they know us like a book, they know how to handle us. Sit down! And down we sit. You can't start a riot sitting down. Better not stand up again, you won't be able to stand the way you were standing before. Don't be embarrassed on my account, I'm no better, not a bit of it. We were full of piss and vinegar, but they've bought it off. Look at me. No back talk, it's bad for business. Let me tell you about the great capitulation. [*She sings the Song of the Great Capitulation*][4]

When I was young, no more than a spring chicken
I too thought that I was really quite the cheese
(No common peddler's daughter, not I with my looks and my
      talent and striving for higher things!)
One little hair in the soup would make me sicken
And at me no man would dare to sneeze.
(It's all or nothing, no second best for me. I've got what it takes,
      the rules are for somebody else!)
But a chickadee
Sang wait and see!
   And you go marching with the show
   In step, however fast or slow
   And rattle off your little song:
   It won't be long.
   And then the whole thing slides.
   You think God provides—
   But you've got it wrong.

And before one single year had wasted
I had learned to swallow down the bitter brew
(Two kids on my hands and the price of bread and who do they
      take me for anyway!)

4. Mother Courage punctuates the story of her own gradual disillusionment with proverbs and common sayings that represent a folk wisdom of successful adjustment.

Man, the double-edged shellacking that I tasted
On my ass and knees I was when they were through.
(You've got to get along with people, one good turn deserves another,
     no use trying to ram your head through the wall!)
And the chickadee
Sang wait and see!
    And she goes marching with the show
    In step, however fast or slow
    And rattles off her little song:
    It won't be long.
    And then the whole thing slides
    You think God provides—
    But you've got it wrong.

I've seen many fired by high ambition
No star's big or high enough to reach out for.
(It's ability that counts, where there's a will there's a way, one way
     or another, we'll swing it!)
Then while moving mountains they get a suspicion
That to wear a straw hat is too big a chore.
(No use being too big for your britches!)
And the chickadee
Sings wait and see!
    And they go marching with the show
    In step, however fast or slow
    And rattle off their little song:
    It won't be long.
    And then the whole thing slides!
    You think God provides—
    But you've got it wrong!

MOTHER COURAGE. [*To the young soldier*] So here's what I think:
    Stay here with your sword if your anger's big enough, I know you
    have good reason, but if it's a short quick anger, better make tracks!
THE YOUNG SOLDIER. Kiss my ass! [*He staggers off, the older soldier
    after him*]
THE CLERK. [*Sticking his head out*] The captain is here. You can put
    in your complaint now.
MOTHER COURAGE. I've changed my mind. No complaint. [*She goes
    out*]

5

    Two years have passed. The war has spread far and wide. With
scarcely a pause Mother Courage's little wagon rolls through Poland,

Moravia, Bavaria, Italy, and back again to Bavaria in 1631. Tilly's victory at Magdeburg[5] costs Mother Courage four officers' shirts.

Mother Courage's wagon has stopped in a devastated village.

Thin military music is heard from the distance. Two soldiers at the bar are being waited on by Kattrin and Mother Courage. One of them is wearing a lady's fur coat over his shoulders.

MOTHER COURAGE. What's that? You can't pay? No money, no schnapps. Plenty of victory marches for the Lord but no pay for the men.

THE SOLDIER. I want my schnapps. I came too late for the looting. The general skunked us: permission to loot the city for exactly one hour. Says he's not a monster; the mayor must have paid him.

THE CHAPLAIN. [*Staggers in*] There's still some wounded in the house. The peasant and his family. Help me, somebody, I need linen.

    [*The second soldier goes out with him. Kattrin gets very excited and tries to persuade her mother to hand out linen*

MOTHER COURAGE. I haven't got any. The regiment's bought up all my bandages. You think I'm going to rip up my officers' shirts for the likes of them?

THE CHAPLAIN. [*Calling back*] I need linen, I tell you.

MOTHER COURAGE. [*Sitting down on the wagon steps to keep Kattrin out*] Nothing doing. They don't pay, they got nothing to pay with.

THE CHAPLAIN. [*Bending over a woman whom he has carried out*] Why did you stay here in all that gunfire?

THE PEASANT WOMAN. [*Feebly*] Farm.

MOTHER COURAGE. You won't catch them leaving their property. And I'm expected to foot the bill. I won't do it.

THE FIRST SOLDIER. They're Protestants. Why do they have to be Protestants?

MOTHER COURAGE. Religion is the least of their worries. They've lost their farm.

THE SECOND SOLDIER. They're no Protestants. They're Catholics like us.

THE FIRST SOLDIER. How do we know who we're shooting at?

A PEASANT. [*Whom the Chaplain brings in*] They got my arm.

THE CHAPLAIN. Where's the linen?

    [*All look at Mother Courage, who does not move*]

MOTHER COURAGE. I can't give you a thing. What with all my taxes, duties, fees and bribes! [*Making guttural sounds, Kattrin picks up a board and threatens her mother with it*] Are you crazy? Put that

---

5. City 80 miles west of Berlin, besieged by the Imperial Army in 1630.

board down, you slut, or I'll smack you. I'm not giving anything, you can't make me. I've got to think of myself. [*The chaplain picks her up from the step and puts her down on the ground. Then he fishes out some shirts and tears them into strips*]

My shirts! Half a guilder apiece! I'm ruined!

[*The anguished cry of a baby is heard from the house*]

THE PEASANT. The baby's still in there!

[*Kattrin runs in*]

THE CHAPLAIN. [*To the woman*] Don't move. They're bringing him out.

MOTHER COURAGE. Get her out of there. The roof'll cave in.

THE CHAPLAIN. I'm not going in there again.

MOTHER COURAGE. [*Torn*] Don't run hog-wild with my expensive linen.

[*Kattrin emerges from the ruins carrying an infant*]

MOTHER COURAGE. Oh, so you've found another baby to carry around with you? Give that baby back to its mother this minute, or it'll take me all day to get it away from you. Do you hear me? [*To the second soldier*] Don't stand there gaping, go back and tell them to stop that music, I can see right here that they've won a victory. Your victory's costing me a pretty penny.

[*Kattrin rocks the baby in her arms, humming a lullaby*]

MOTHER COURAGE. There she sits, happy in all this misery; give it back this minute, the mother's coming to. [*She pounces on the first soldier who has been helping himself to the drinks and is now making off with the bottle*] Pshagreff![6] Beast! Haven't you had enough victories for today? Pay up.

FIRST SOLDIER. I'm broke.

MOTHER COURAGE. [*Tears the fur coat off him*] Then leave the coat here, it's stolen anyway.

THE CHAPLAIN. There's still somebody in there.

6

Outside Ingolstadt[7] in Bavaria Mother Courage attends the funeral of Tilly, the imperial field marshal. Conversations about heroes and the longevity of the war. The chaplain deplores the waste of his talents. Mute Kattrin gets the red shoes. 1632.

Inside Mother Courage's tent.

A bar open to the rear. Rain. In the distance drum rolls and funeral music. The chaplain and the regimental clerk are playing a board game. Mother Courage and her daughter are taking inventory.

6. Son of a bitch! (Polish)   7. City 40 miles north of Munich.

THE CHAPLAIN. The procession's starting.

MOTHER COURAGE. It's a shame about the general—socks: twenty-two pairs—I hear he was killed by accident. On account of the fog in the fields. He's up front encouraging the troops. "Fight to the death, boys," he sings out. Then he rides back, but he gets lost in the fog and rides back forward. Before you know it he's in the middle of the battle and stops a bullet—lanterns: we're down to four. [*A whistle from the rear. She goes to the bar*] You men ought to be ashamed, running out on your late general's funeral! [*She pours drinks*]

THE CLERK. They shouldn't have been paid before the funeral. Now they're getting drunk instead.

THE CHAPLAIN. [*To the clerk*] Shouldn't you be at the funeral?

THE CLERK. In this rain?

MOTHER COURAGE. With you it's different, the rain might spoil your uniform. It seems they wanted to ring the bells, naturally, but it turned out the churches had all been shot to pieces by his orders, so the poor general won't hear any bells when they lower him into his grave. They're going to fire a three-gun salute instead, so it won't be too dull—seventeen sword belts.

CRIES. [*From the bar*] Hey! Brandy!

MOTHER COURAGE. Money first! No, you can't come into my tent with your muddy boots! You can drink outside, rain or no rain. [*To the clerk*] I'm only letting officers in. It seems the general had been having his troubles. Mutiny in the Second Regiment because he hadn't paid them. It's a war of religion, he says, should they profit by their faith?

[*Funeral march. All look to the rear*]

THE CHAPLAIN. Now they're marching past the body.

MOTHER COURAGE. I feel sorry when a general or an emperor passes away like this, maybe he thought he'd do something big, that posterity would still be talking about and maybe put up a statue in his honor, conquer the world, for instance, that's a nice ambition for a general, he doesn't know any better. So he knocks himself out, and then the common people come and spoil it all, because what do they care about greatness, all they care about is a mug of beer and maybe a little company. The most beautiful plans have been wrecked by the smallness of the people that are supposed to carry them out. Even an emperor can't do anything by himself, he needs the support of his soldiers and his people. Am I right?

THE CHAPLAIN. [*Laughing*] Courage, you're right, except about the soldiers. They do their best. With those fellows out there, for instance, drinking their brandy in the rain. I'll undertake to carry on one war after another for a hundred years, two at once if I have to, and I'm not a general by trade.

MOTHER COURAGE. Then you don't think the war might stop?

THE CHAPLAIN. Because the general's dead? Don't be childish. They grow by the dozen, there'll always be plenty of heroes.

MOTHER COURAGE. Look here, I'm not asking you for the hell of it. I've been wondering whether to lay in supplies while they're cheap, but if the war stops, I can throw them out the window.

THE CHAPLAIN. I understand. You want a serious answer. There have always been people who say: "The war will be over some day." I say there's no guarantee the war will ever be over. Naturally a brief intermission is conceivable. Maybe the war needs a breather, a war can even break its neck, so to speak. There's always a chance of that, nothing is perfect here below. Maybe there never will be a perfect war, one that lives up to all our expectations. Suddenly, for some unforeseen reason, a war can bog down, you can't think of everything. Some little oversight and your war's in trouble. And then you've got to pull it out of the mud. But the kings and emperors, not to mention the pope, will always come to its help in adversity. On the whole, I'd say this war has very little to worry about, it'll live to a ripe old age.

A SOLDIER. [Sings at the bar]

> A drink, and don't be slow!
> A soldier's got to go
> And fight for his religion.

> Make it double, this is a holiday.

MOTHER COURAGE. If I could only be sure . . .

THE CHAPLAIN. Figure it out for yourself. What's to stop the war?

THE SOLDIER. [Sings]

> Your breasts, girl, don't be slow!
> A soldier's got to go
> And ride away to Pilsen.[8]

THE CLERK. [Suddenly] But why can't we have peace? I'm from Bohemia, I'd like to go home when the time comes.

THE CHAPLAIN. Oh, you'd like to go home? Ah, peace! What becomes of the hole when the cheese has been eaten?

THE SOLDIER. [Sings]

> Play cards, friends, don't be slow!
> A soldier's got to go
> No matter if it's Sunday.

8. City in Bohemia, near the German border.

A prayer, priest, don't be slow!
A soldier's got to go
And die for king and country.

THE CLERK. In the long run nobody can live without peace.

THE CHAPLAIN. The way I see it, war gives you plenty of peace. It has
its peaceful moments. War meets every need, including the peaceful
ones, everything's taken care of, or your war couldn't hold its own.
In a war you can shit the same as in the dead of peace, you can
stop for a beer between battles, and even on the march you can
always lie down on your elbows and take a little nap by the roadside. You can't play cards when you're fighting; but then you can't
when you're plowing in the dead of peace either, but after a victory the sky's the limit. Maybe you've had a leg shot off, at first
you raise a howl; you make a big thing of it. But then you calm
down or they give you schnapps, and in the end you're hopping
around again and the war's no worse off than before. And what's
to prevent you from multiplying in the thick of the slaughter, behind
a barn or someplace, in the long run how can they stop you, and
then the war has your progeny to help it along. Take it from me,
the war will always find an answer. Why would it have to stop?

[*Kattrin has stopped working and is staring at the chaplain*]

MOTHER COURAGE. Then I'll buy the merchandise. You've convinced me. [*Kattrin suddenly throws down a basket full of bottles
and runs out*] Kattrin! [*Laughs*] My goodness, the poor thing's
been hoping for peace. I promised her she'd get a husband when
peace comes. [*She runs after her*]

THE CLERK. [*Getting up*] I win, you've been too busy talking. Pay
up.

MOTHER COURAGE. [*Comes back with Kattrin*] Be reasonable, the
war'll go on a little longer and we'll make a little more money,
then peace will be even better. Run along to town now, it won't
take you ten minutes, and get the stuff from the Golden Lion,
only the expensive things, we'll pick up the rest in the wagon later,
it's all arranged, the regimental clerk here will go with you. They've
almost all gone to the general's funeral, nothing can happen to
you. Look sharp, don't let them take anything away from you,
think of your dowry.

[*Kattrin puts a kerchief over her head and goes with the clerk*]

THE CHAPLAIN. Is it all right letting her go with the clerk?

MOTHER COURAGE. Who'd want to ruin her? She's not pretty enough.

THE CHAPLAIN. I've come to admire the way you handle your business and pull through every time. I can see why they call you
Mother Courage.

MOTHER COURAGE. Poor people need courage. Why? Because they're sunk. In their situation it takes gumption just to get up in the morning. Or to plow a field in the middle of a war. They even show courage by bringing children into the world, because look at the prospects. The way they butcher and execute each other, think of the courage they need to look each other in the face. And putting up with an emperor and a pope takes a whale of a lot of courage, because those two are the death of the poor. [*She sits down, takes a small pipe from her pocket and smokes*] You could be making some kindling.

THE CHAPLAIN. [*Reluctantly takes his jacket off and prepares to chop*] Chopping wood isn't really my trade, you know, I'm a shepherd of souls.

MOTHER COURAGE. Sure. But I have no soul and I need firewood.

THE CHAPLAIN. What's that pipe?

MOTHER COURAGE. Just a pipe.

THE CHAPLAIN. No, it's not "just a pipe," it's a very particular pipe.

MOTHER COURAGE. Really?

THE CHAPLAIN. It's the cook's pipe from the Oxenstjerna regiment.

MOTHER COURAGE. If you know it all, why the mealy-mouthed questions?

THE CHAPLAIN. I didn't know if *you* knew. You could have been rummaging through your belongings and laid hands on some pipe and picked it up without thinking.

MOTHER COURAGE. Yes. Maybe that's how it was.

THE CHAPLAIN. Except it wasn't. You knew who that pipe belongs to.

MOTHER COURAGE. What of it?

THE CHAPLAIN. Courage, I'm warning you. It's my duty. I doubt if you ever lay eyes on the man again, but that's no calamity, in fact you're lucky. If you ask me, he wasn't steady. Not at all.

MOTHER COURAGE. What makes you say that? He was a nice man.

THE CHAPLAIN. Oh, you think he was nice? I differ. Far be it from me to wish him any harm, but I can't say he was nice. I'd say he was a scheming Don Juan.[9] If you don't believe me, take a look at his pipe. You'll have to admit that it shows up his character.

MOTHER COURAGE. I don't see anything. It's beat up.

THE CHAPLAIN. It's half bitten through. A violent man. That is the pipe of a ruthless, violent man, you must see that if you've still got an ounce of good sense.

MOTHER COURAGE. Don't wreck my chopping block.

THE CHAPLAIN. I've told you I wasn't trained to chop wood. I studied theology. My gifts and abilities are being wasted on muscular effort. The talents that God gave me are lying fallow. That's a sin. You've never heard me preach. With one sermon I can whip a regiment

9. Philanderer.

into such a state that they take the enemy for a flock of sheep. Then men care no more about their lives than they would about a smelly old sock that they're ready to throw away in hopes of final victory. God has made me eloquent. You'll swoon when you hear me preach.

MOTHER COURAGE. I don't want to swoon. What good would that do me?

THE CHAPLAIN. Courage, I've often wondered if maybe you didn't conceal a warm heart under that hard-bitten talk of yours. You too are human, you need warmth.

MOTHER COURAGE. The best way to keep this tent warm is with plenty of firewood.

THE CHAPLAIN. Don't try to put me off. Seriously, Courage, I sometimes wonder if we couldn't make our relationship a little closer. I mean, seeing that the whirlwind of war has whirled us so strangely together.

MOTHER COURAGE. Seems to me it's close enough. I cook your meals and you do chores, such as chopping wood, for instance.

THE CHAPLAIN. [*Goes toward her*] You know what I mean by "closer"; it has nothing to do with meals and chopping wood and such mundane needs. Don't harden your heart, let it speak.

MOTHER COURAGE. Don't come at me with that ax. That's too close a relationship.

THE CHAPLAIN. Don't turn it to ridicule. I'm serious. I've given it careful thought.

MOTHER COURAGE. Chaplain, don't be silly. I like you, I don't want to have to scold you. My aim in life is to get through, me and my children and my wagon. I don't think of it as mine and besides I'm not in the mood for private affairs. Right now I'm taking a big risk, buying up merchandise with the general dead and everybody talking peace. What'll you do if I'm ruined? See? You don't know. Chop that wood, then we'll be warm in the evening, which is a good thing in times like these. Now what? [*She stands up*]

[*Enter Kattrin out of breath, with a wound across her forehead and over one eye. She is carrying all sort of things, packages, leather goods, a drum, etc.*]

MOTHER COURAGE. What's this? Assaulted? On the way back? She was assaulted on the way back. Must have been that soldier that got drunk here! I shouldn't have let you go! Throw the stuff down! It's not bad, only a flesh wound. I'll bandage it, it'll heal in a week. They're worse than wild beasts. [*She bandages the wound*]

THE CHAPLAIN. I can't find fault with them. At home they never raped anybody. I blame the people that start wars, they're the ones that dredge up man's lowest instincts.

MOTHER COURAGE. Didn't the clerk bring you back? That's because you're respectable, they don't give a damn. It's not a deep wound, it won't leave a mark. There, all bandaged. Don't fret, I've got something for you. I've been keeping it for you on the sly, it'll be a surprise. [*She fishes Yvette's red shoes out of a sack*] See? You've always wanted them. Now you've got them. Put them on quick before I regret it. It won't leave a mark, though I wouldn't mind if it did. The girls that attract them get the worst of it. They drag them around till there's nothing left of them. If you don't appeal to them, they won't harm you. I've seen girls with pretty faces, a few years later they'd have given a wolf the creeps. They can't step behind a bush without fearing the worst. It's like trees. The straight tall ones get chopped down for ridgepoles, the crooked ones enjoy life. In other words, it's a lucky break. The shoes are still in good condition, I've kept them nicely polished.

[*Kattrin leaves the shoes where they are and crawls into the wagon*]

THE CHAPLAIN. I hope she won't be disfigured.

MOTHER COURAGE. There'll be a scar. She can stop waiting for peace.

THE CHAPLAIN. She didn't let them take anything.

MOTHER COURAGE. Maybe I shouldn't have drummed it into her. If I only knew what went on in her head. One night she stayed out, the only time in all these years. Afterwards she traipsed around as usual, except she worked harder. I never could find out what happened. I racked my brains for quite some time. [*She picks up the articles brought by Kattrin and sorts them angrily*] That's war for you! A fine way to make a living!

[*Cannon salutes are heard*]

THE CHAPLAIN. Now they're burying the general. This is a historic moment.

MOTHER COURAGE. To me it's a historic moment when they hit my daughter over the eye. She's a wreck, she'll never get a husband now, and she's so crazy about children. It's the war that made her dumb too, a soldier stuffed something in her mouth when she was little. I'll never see Swiss Cheese again and where Eilif is, God knows. God damn the war.

7

Mother Courage at the height of her business career.

Highway.

The chaplain, Mother Courage, and her daughter Kattrin are pulling the wagon. New wares are hanging on it. Mother Courage is wearing a necklace of silver talers.

MOTHER COURAGE. Stop running down the war. I won't have it. I
  know it destroys the weak, but the weak haven't a chance in peacetime either. And war is a better provider. [*Sings*]

If you're not strong enough to take it
The victory will find you dead.
A war is only what you make it.
It's business, not with cheese but lead.

And what good is it staying in one place? The stay-at-homes are
  the first to get it. [*Sings*]

Some people think they'd like to ride out
The war, leave danger to the brave
And dig themselves a cozy hideout—
They'll dig themselves an early grave.
I've seen them running from the thunder
To find a refuge from the war
But once they're resting six feet under
They wonder what they hurried for.

> [*They plod on*]

8

In the same year Gustavus Adolphus, King of Sweden, is killed at
the battle of Lützen.[1] Peace threatens to ruin Mother Courage's
business. Her brave son performs one heroic deed too many and dies
an ignominious death.

A camp.

*A summer morning. An old woman and her son are standing by
the wagon. The son is carrying a large sack of bedding.*

MOTHER COURAGE'S VOICE. [*From the wagon*] Does it have to be at
  this unearthly hour?
THE YOUNG MAN. We've walked all night, twenty miles, and we've
  got to go back today.
MOTHER COURAGE'S VOICE. What can I do with bedding? The people
  haven't any houses.
THE YOUNG MAN. Wait till you've seen it.
THE OLD WOMAN. She won't take it either. Come on.
THE YOUNG MAN. They'll sell the roof from over our heads for taxes.
  Maybe she'll give us three guilders if you throw in the cross. [*Bells
  start ringing*] Listen, mother!

---

1. Town a few miles from the great Protestant city of Leipzig.

VOICES. [*From the rear*] Peace! The king of Sweden is dead!

MOTHER COURAGE. [*Sticks her head out of the wagon. She has not yet done her hair*] Why are the bells ringing in the middle of the week?

THE CHAPLAIN. [*Crawls out from under the wagon*] What are they shouting?

MOTHER COURAGE. Don't tell me peace has broken out when I've just taken in more supplies.

THE CHAPLAIN. [*Shouting toward the rear*] Is it true? Peace?

VOICE. Three weeks ago, they say. But we just found out.

THE CHAPLAIN. [*To Mother Courage*] What else would they ring the bells for?

VOICE. There's a whole crowd of Lutherans, they've driven their carts into town. They brought the news.

THE YOUNG MAN. Mother, it's peace. What's the matter?

[*The old woman has collapsed*]

MOTHER COURAGE. [*Going back into the wagon*] Heavenly saints! Kattrin, peace! Put your black dress on! We're going to church. We owe it to Swiss Cheese. Can it be true?

THE YOUNG MAN. The people here say the same thing. They've made peace. Can you get up? [*The old woman stands up, still stunned*] I'll get the saddle shop started again. I promise. Everything will be all right. Father will get his bed back. Can you walk? [*To the chaplain*] She fainted. It was the news. She thought peace would never come again. Father said it would. We'll go straight home. [*Both go out*]

MOTHER COURAGE'S VOICE. Give her some brandy.

THE CHAPLAIN. They're gone.

MOTHER COURAGE'S VOICE. What's going on in camp?

THE CHAPLAIN. A big crowd. I'll go see. Shouldn't I put on my clericals?

MOTHER COURAGE'S VOICE. Better make sure before you step out in your antichrist costume. I'm glad to see peace, even if I'm ruined. At least I've brought two of my children through the war. Now I'll see my Eilif again.

THE CHAPLAIN. Look who's coming down the road. If it isn't the general's cook!

THE COOK. [*Rather bedraggled, carrying a bundle*] Can I believe my eyes? The chaplain!

THE CHAPLAIN. Courage! A visitor!

[*Mother Courage climbs down*]

THE COOK. Didn't I promise to come over for a little chat as soon as I had time? I've never forgotten your brandy, Mrs. Fierling.

MOTHER COURAGE. Mercy, the general's cook! After all these years! Where's Eilif, my eldest?

THE COOK. Isn't he here yet? He left ahead of me, he was coming to see you too.

THE CHAPLAIN. I'll put on my clericals, wait for me. [*Goes out behind the wagon*]

MOTHER COURAGE. Then he'll be here any minute. [*Calls into the wagon*] Kattrin, Eilif's coming! Bring the cook a glass of brandy! [*Kattrin does not appear*] Put a lock of hair over it, and forget it! Mr. Lamb is no stranger. [*Gets the brandy herself*] She won't come out. Peace doesn't mean a thing to her, it's come too late. They hit her over the eye, there's hardly any mark, but she thinks people are staring at her.

THE COOK. Ech, war! [*He and Mother Courage sit down*]

MOTHER COURAGE. Cook, you find me in trouble. I'm ruined.

THE COOK. What? Say, that's a shame.

MOTHER COURAGE. Peace has done me in. Only the other day I stocked up. The chaplain's advice. And now they'll all demobilize and leave me sitting on my merchandise.

THE COOK. How could you listen to the chaplain? If I'd had time, I'd have warned you against him, but the Catholics came too soon. He's a fly-by-night. So now he's the boss here?

MOTHER COURAGE. He washed my dishes and helped me pull the wagon.

THE COOK. Him? Pulling? I guess he's told you a few of his jokes too, I wouldn't put it past him, he has an unsavory attitude toward women, I tried to reform him, it was hopeless. He's not steady.

MOTHER COURAGE. Are you steady?

THE COOK. If nothing else, I'm steady. Prosit!

MOTHER COURAGE. Steady is no good. I've only lived with one steady man, thank the Lord. I never had to work so hard, he sold the children's blankets when spring came, and he thought my harmonica was unchristian. In my opinion you're not doing yourself any good by admitting you're steady.

THE COOK. You've still got your old bite, but I respect you for it.

MOTHER COURAGE. Don't tell me you've been dreaming about my old bite.

THE COOK. Well, here we sit, with the bells of peace and your world-famous brandy, that hasn't its equal.

MOTHER COURAGE. The bells of peace don't strike my fancy right now. I don't see them paying the men, they're behindhand already. Where does that leave me with my famous brandy? Have you been paid?

THE COOK. [*Hesitantly*] Not really. That's why we demobilized ourselves. Under the circumstances, I says to myself, why should I stay on? I'll go see my friends in the meantime. So here we are.

MOTHER COURAGE. You mean you're out of funds?

THE COOK. If only they'd stop those damn bells! I'd be glad to go into some kind of business. I'm sick of being a cook. They give me roots and shoe leather to work with, and then they throw the hot soup in my face. A cook's got a dog's life these days. I'd rather be in combat, but now we've got peace. [*The chaplain appears in his original dress*] We'll discuss it later.

THE CHAPLAIN. It's still in good condition. There were only a few moths in it.

THE COOK. I don't see why you bother. They won't take you back. Who are you going to inspire now to be an honest soldier and earn his pay at the risk of his life? Besides, I've got a bone to pick with you. Advising this lady to buy useless merchandise on the ground that the war would last forever.

THE CHAPLAIN. [*Heatedly*] And why, I'd like to know, is it any of your business?

THE COOK. Because it's unscrupulous. How can you meddle in other people's business and give unsolicited advice?

THE CHAPLAIN. Who's meddling? [*To Mother Courage*] I didn't know you were accountable to this gentleman, I didn't know you were so intimate with him.

MOTHER COURAGE. Don't get excited, the cook is only giving his private opinion. And you can't deny that your war was a dud.

THE CHAPLAIN. Courage, don't blaspheme against peace. You're a battlefield hyena.

MOTHER COURAGE. What am I?

THE COOK. If you insult this lady, you'll hear from me.

THE CHAPLAIN. I'm not talking to you. Your intentions are too obvious. [*To Mother Courage*] But when I see you picking up peace with thumb and forefinger like a snotty handkerchief, it revolts my humanity; you don't want peace, you want war, because you profit by it, but don't forget the old saying: "He hath need of a long spoon that eateth with the devil."

MOTHER COURAGE. I've no use for war and war hasn't much use for me. Anyway, I'm not letting anybody call me a hyena, you and me are through.

THE CHAPLAIN. How can you complain about peace when it's such a relief to everybody else? On account of the old rags in your wagon?

MOTHER COURAGE. My merchandise isn't old rags, it's what I live off, and so did you.

THE CHAPLAIN. Off war, you mean. Aha!

THE COOK. [*To the chaplain*] You're a grown man, you ought to know there's no sense in giving advice. [*To Mother Courage*] The best thing you can do now is to sell off certain articles quick, before the prices hit the floor. Dress yourself and get started, there's no time to lose.

MOTHER COURAGE. That's very sensible advice. I think I'll do it.

THE CHAPLAIN. Because the cook says so!

MOTHER COURAGE. Why didn't *you* say so? He's right, I'd better run over to the market. [*She goes into the wagon*]

THE COOK. My round, chaplain. No presence of mind. Here's what you should have said: me give you advice? All I ever did was talk politics! Don't try to take me on. Cockfighting is undignified in a clergyman.

THE CHAPLAIN. If you don't shut up, I'll murder you, undignified or not.

THE COOK. [*Taking off his shoe and unwinding the wrappings from his feet*] If the war hadn't made a godless bum out of you, you could easily come by a parsonage now that peace is here. They won't need cooks, there's nothing to cook, but people still do a lot of believing, that hasn't changed.

THE CHAPLAIN. See here, Mr. Lamb. Don't try squeeze me out. Being a bum has made me a better man. I couldn't preach to them any more.

[*Yvette Pottier enters, elaborately dressed in black, with a cane. She is much older and fatter and heavily powdered. Behind her a servant*]

YVETTE. Hello there! Is this the residence of Mother Courage?

THE CHAPLAIN. Right you are. With whom have we the pleasure?

YVETTE. The Countess Starhemberg, my good people. Where is Mother Courage.

THE CHAPLAIN. [*Calls into the wagon*] Countess Starhemberg wishes to speak to you!

MOTHER COURAGE. I'm coming.

YVETTE. It's Yvette!

MOTHER COURAGE'S VOICE. My goodness! It's Yvette!

YVETTE. Just dropped in to see how you're doing. [*The cook has turned around in horror*] Pieter!

THE COOK. Yvette!

YVETTE. Blow me down! How did you get here?

THE COOK. In a cart.

THE CHAPLAIN. Oh, you know each other? Intimately?

YVETTE. I should think so. [*She looks the cook over*] Fat!

THE COOK. You're not not exactly willowy yourself.

YVETTE. All the same I'm glad I ran into you, you bum. Now I can tell you what I think of you.

THE CHAPLAIN. Go right ahead, spare no details, but wait until Courage comes out.

MOTHER COURAGE. [*Comes out with all sorts of merchandise*] Yvette! [*They embrace*] But what are you in mourning for?

YVETTE. Isn't it becoming? My husband the colonel died a few years ago.

MOTHER COURAGE. The old geezer that almost bought my wagon?

YVETTE. His elder brother.

MOTHER COURAGE. You must be pretty well fixed. It's nice to find somebody that's made a good thing out of the war.

YVETTE. Oh well, it's been up and down and back up again.

MOTHER COURAGE. Let's not say anything bad about colonels. They make money by the bushel.

THE CHAPLAIN. If I were you, I'd put my shoes back on again. [*To Yvette*] Countess Starhemberg, you promised to tell us what you think of this gentleman.

THE COOK. Don't make a scene here.

MOTHER COURAGE. He's a friend of mine, Yvette.

YVETTE. He's Pete the Pipe, that's who he is.

THE COOK. Forget the nicknames, my name is Lamb.

MOTHER COURAGE. [*Laughs*] Pete the Pipe! That drove the women crazy! Say, I've saved your pipe.

THE CHAPLAIN. And smoked it.

YVETTE. It's lucky I'm here to warn you. He's the worst rotter that ever infested the coast of Flanders. He ruined more girls than he's got fingers.

THE COOK. That was a long time ago. I've changed.

YVETTE. Stand up when a lady draws you into a conversation! How I loved this man! And all the while he was seeing a little bandy-legged brunette, ruined her, too, naturally.

THE COOK. Seems to me I started you off on a prosperous career.

YVETTE. Shut up, you depressing wreck! Watch your step with him, his kind are dangerous even when they've gone to seed.

MOTHER COURAGE. [*To Yvette*] Come along, I've got to sell my stuff before the prices drop. Maybe you can help me, with your army connections. [*Calls into the wagon*] Kattrin, forget about church, I'm running over to the market. When Eilif comes, give him a drink. [*Goes out with Yvette*]

YVETTE. [*In leaving*] To think that such a man could lead me astray! I can thank my lucky stars that I was able to rise in the world after that. I've put a spoke in your wheel, Pete the Pipe, and they'll give me credit for it in heaven when my time comes.

THE CHAPLAIN. Our conversation seems to illustrate the old adage: The mills of God grind slowly.[2] What do you think of my jokes now?

THE COOK. I'm just unlucky. I'll come clean: I was hoping for a hot meal. I'm starving. And now they're talking about me, and she'll get the wrong idea. I think I'll beat it before she comes back.

THE CHAPLAIN. I think so too.

THE COOK. Chaplain, I'm fed up on peace already. Men are sinners

---

2. From a saying by Friedrich von Logan (1605–1655), as translated by Longfellow: "Though the mills of God grind slowly, / Yet they grind exceeding small."

from the cradle, fire and sword are their natural lot. I wish I were cooking for the general again. God knows where he is, I'd roast a fine fat capon, with mustard sauce and a few carrots.

THE CHAPLAIN. Red cabbage. Red cabbage with capon.

THE COOK. That's right, but he wanted carrots.

THE CHAPLAIN. He was ignorant.

THE COOK. That didn't prevent you from gorging yourself.

THE CHAPLAIN. With repugnance.

THE COOK. Anyway you'll have to admit those were good times.

THE CHAPLAIN. I might admit that.

THE COOK. Now you've called her a hyena, your good times here are over. What are you staring at?

THE CHAPLAIN. Eilif? [*Eilif enters, followed by soldiers with pikes. His hands are fettered. He is deathly pale*] What's wrong?

EILIF. Where's mother?

THE CHAPLAIN. Gone to town.

EILIF. I heard she was here. They let me come and see her.

THE COOK. [*To the soldiers*] Where are you taking him?

A SOLDIER. No good place.

THE CHAPLAIN. What has he done?

THE SOLDIER. Broke into a farm. The peasant's wife is dead.

THE CHAPLAIN. How could you do such a thing?

EILIF. It's what I've been doing all along.

THE COOK. But in peacetime!

EILIF. Shut your trap. Can I sit down till she comes?

THE SOLDIER. We haven't time.

THE CHAPLAIN. During the war they honored him for it, he sat at the general's right hand. Then it was bravery. Couldn't we speak to the officer?

THE SOLDIER. No use. What's brave about taking a peasant's cattle?

THE COOK. It was stupid.

EILIF. If I'd been stupid, I'd have starved, wise guy.

THE COOK. And for being smart your head comes off.

THE CHAPLAIN. Let's get Kattrin at least.

EILIF. Leave her be. Get me a drink of schnapps.

THE SOLDIER. No time. Let's go!

THE CHAPLAIN. And what should we tell your mother?

EILIF. Tell her it wasn't any different, tell her it was the same. Or don't tell her anything.

[*The soldiers drive him away*]

THE CHAPLAIN. I'll go with you on your hard journey.

EILIF. I don't need any sky pilot.

THE CHAPLAIN. You don't know yet. [*He follows him*]

THE COOK. [*Calls after them*] I'll have to tell her, she'll want to see him.

THE CHAPLAIN. Better not tell her anything. Or say he was here and
he'll come again, maybe tomorrow. I'll break it to her when I get
back. [*Hurries out*]

    [*The cook looks after them, shaking his head, then he walks,
anxiously about. Finally he approaches the wagon*]

THE COOK. Hey! Come on out! I can see why you'd hide from peace.
I wish I could do it myself. I'm the general's cook, remember?
Wouldn't you have a bite to eat, to do me till your mother gets
back? A slice of ham or just a piece of bread while I'm waiting.
[*He looks in*] She's buried her head in a blanket.

    [*The sound of gunfire in the rear*]

MOTHER COURAGE. [*Runs in. She is out of breath and still has her
merchandise*] Cook, the peace is over, the war started up again
three days ago. I hadn't sold my stuff yet when I found out. Heaven
be praised! They're shooting each other up in town, the Catholics
and Lutherans. We've got to get out of here. Kattrin, start packing. What have *you* got such a long face about? What's wrong?

THE COOK. Nothing.

MOTHER COURAGE. Something's wrong, I can tell by your expression.

THE COOK. Maybe it's the war starting up again. Now I probably
won't get anything hot to eat before tomorrow night.

MOTHER COURAGE. That's a lie, cook.

THE COOK. Eilif was here. He couldn't stay.

MOTHER COURAGE. He was here? Then we'll see him on the march.
I'm going with our troops this time. How does he look?

THE COOK. The same.

MOTHER COURAGE. He'll never change. The war couldn't take him
away from me. He's smart. Could you help me pack? [*She starts
packing*] Did he tell you anything? Is he in good with the general?
Did he say anything about his heroic deeds?

THE COOK. [*Gloomily*] They say he's been at one of them again.

MOTHER COURAGE. Tell me later, we've got to be going. [*Kattrin
emerges*] Kattrin, peace is over. We're moving. [*To the cook*] What's
the matter with you?

THE COOK. I'm going to enlist.

MOTHER COURAGE. I've got a suggestion. Why don't . . . ? Where's
the chaplain?

THE COOK. Gone to town with Eilif.

MOTHER COURAGE. Then come a little way with me, Lamb. I need
help.

THE COOK. That incident with Yvette . . .

MOTHER COURAGE. It hasn't lowered you in my estimation. Far from
it. Where there's smoke there's fire. Coming?

THE COOK. I won't say no.

MOTHER COURAGE. The Twelfth Regiment has shoved off. Take the

shaft. Here's a chunk of bread. We'll have to circle around to meet
the Lutherans. Maybe I'll see Eilif tonight. He's my favorite. It's
been a short peace. And we're on the move again. [*She sings,
while the cook and Kattrin harness themselves to the wagon*]

From Ulm to Metz, from Metz to Pilsen[3]
Courage is right there in the van.
The war both in and out of season
With shot and shell will feed its man.
But lead alone is not sufficient
The war needs soldiers to subsist!
Its diet elseways is deficient.
The war is hungry! So enlist!

9

The great war of religion has been going on for sixteen years.
Germany has lost more than half its population. Those whom the
slaughter has spared have been laid low by epidemics. Once-flour-
ishing countrysides are ravaged by famine. Wolves prowl through
the charred ruins of the cities. In the fall of 1634 we find Mother
Courage in Germany, in the Fichtelgebirge[4] at some distance from
the road followed by the Swedish armies. Winter comes early and is
exceptionally severe. Business is bad, begging is the only resort. The
cook receives a letter from Utrecht[5] and is dismissed.

Outside a half-demolished presbytery.

*Gray morning in early winter. Gusts of wind. Mother Courage
and the cook in shabby sheepskins by the wagon.*

THE COOK. No light. Nobody's up yet.
MOTHER COURAGE. But it's a priest. He'll have to crawl out of bed to
   ring the bells. Then he'll get himself a nice bowl of hot soup.
THE COOK. Go on, you saw the village, everything's been burned to
   a crisp.
MOTHER COURAGE. But somebody's here, I heard a dog bark.
THE COOK. If the priest's got anything, he won't give it away.
MOTHER COURAGE. Maybe if we sing . . .
THE COOK. I've had it up to here. [*Suddenly*] I got a letter from
   Utrecht. My mother's died of cholera and the tavern belongs to
   me. Here's the letter if you don't believe me. It's no business of

---

3. Ulm is about 80 miles west of Munich. Metz, in the province of Lorraine (ceded to France at
the end of the Thirty Years' War), is about 200 miles west of Ulm; to travel from Metz to Pilsen
one must cross the whole of Germany.   4. A range of mountains in Germany near the Bohemian border.   5. City in the south of Holland.

yours what my aunt says about my evil ways, but never mind, read it.

MOTHER COURAGE[6] [*Reads the letter*] Lamb, I'm sick of roaming around, myself. I feel like a butcher's dog that pulls the meat cart but doesn't get any for himself. I've nothing left to sell and the people have no money to pay for it. In Saxony a man in rags tried to foist a cord of books on me for two eggs, and in Württemberg they'd have let their plow go for a little bag of salt. What's the good of plowing? Nothing grows but brambles. In Pomerania[7] they say the villagers have eaten up all the babies, and that nuns have been caught at highway robbery.

THE COOK. It's the end of the world.

MOTHER COURAGE. Sometimes I have visions of myself driving through hell, selling sulfur and brimstone, or through heaven peddling refreshments to the roaming souls. If me and the children I've got left could find a place where there's no shooting, I wouldn't mind a few years of peace and quiet.

THE COOK. We could open up the tavern again. Think it over, Anna. I made up my mind last night; with or without you, I'm going back to Utrecht. In fact I'm leaving today.

MOTHER COURAGE. I'll have to talk to Kattrin. It's kind of sudden, and I don't like to make decisions in the cold with nothing in my stomach. Kattrin! [*Kattrin climbs out of the wagon*] Kattrin, I've got something to tell you. The cook and me are thinking of going to Utrecht. They've left him a tavern there. You'd be living in one place, you'd meet people. A lot of men would be glad to get a nice, well-behaved girl, looks aren't everything. I'm all for it. I get along fine with the cook. I've got to hand it to him: He's got a head for business. We'd eat regular meals, wouldn't that be nice? And you'd have your own bed, wouldn't you like that? It's no life on the road, year in year out. You'll go to rack and ruin. You're crawling with lice already. We've got to decide, you see, we could go north with the Swedes, they must be over there. [*She points to the left*] I think we'll do it, Kattrin.

THE COOK. Anna, could I have a word with you alone?

MOTHER COURAGE. Get back in the wagon, Kattrin.

   [*Kattrin climbs back in*]

THE COOK. I interrupted you because I see there's been a misunderstanding, I thought it was too obvious to need saying. But if it isn't, I'll just have to say it. You can't take her, it's out of the question. Is that plain enough for you?

---

6. In this scene, Mother Courage and the Cook for the first time use *du*, the familiar form of *you* in German. (The familiar form is used between lovers, close friends and family, and young people; the formal *Sie* is used otherwise.)   7. Saxony, Württemberg, and Pomerania are German principalities.

[*Kattrin sticks her head out of the wagon and listens*]

MOTHER COURAGE. You want me to leave Kattrin?

THE COOK. Look at it this way. There's no room in the tavern. It's not one of those places with three taprooms. If the two of us put our shoulder to the wheel, we can make a living, but not three, it can't be done. Kattrin can keep the wagon.

MOTHER COURAGE. I'd been thinking she could find a husband in Utrecht.

THE COOK. Don't make me laugh! How's she going to find a husband? At her age? And dumb! And with that scar!

MOTHER COURAGE. Not so loud.

THE COOK. Shout or whisper, the truth's the truth. And that's another reason why I can't have her in the tavern. The customers won't want a sight like that staring them in the face. Can you blame them?

MOTHER COURAGE. Shut up. Not so loud, I say.

THE COOK. There's a light in the presbytery. Let's sing.

MOTHER COURAGE. How could she pull the wagon by herself? She's afraid of the war. She couldn't stand it. The dreams she must have! I hear her groaning at night. Especially after battles. What she sees in her dreams, God knows. It's pity that makes her suffer so. The other day the wagon hit a hedgehog, I found it hidden in her blanket.

THE COOK. The tavern's too small. [*He calls*] Worthy gentleman and members of the household! We shall now sing the Song of Solomon, Julius Caesar, and other great men, whose greatness didn't help them any. Just to show you that we're God-fearing people ourselves, which makes it hard for us, especially in the winter. [*They sing*]

You saw the wise King Solomon[8]
You know what came of him.
To him all hidden things were plain.
He cursed the hour gave birth to him
And saw that everything was vain.
How great and wise was Solomon!
Now think about his case. Alas
A useful lesson can be won.
It's wisdom that had brought him to that pass!
How happy is the man with none!

Our beautiful song proves that virtues are dangerous things, better steer clear of them, enjoy life, eat a good breakfast, a bowl of hot

8. Old Testament ruler celebrated for his wisdom. In line 4 of the stanza, the cook confuses Solomon with the Biblical Job, who does curse the day he was born. (Job 3:1).

soup, for instance. Take me, I haven't got any soup and wish I had, I'm a soldier, but what has my bravery in all those battles got me, nothing, I'm starving, I'd be better off if I'd stayed home like a yellowbelly. And I'll tell you why.

You saw the daring Caesar[9] next
You know what he became.
They deified him in his life
But then they killed him just the same.
And as they raised the fatal knife
How loud he cried: "You too, my son!"
Now think about his case. Alas
A useful lesson can be won.
It's daring that had brought him to that pass!
How happy is the man with none!

[*In an undertone*] They're not even looking out. Worthy gentleman and members of the household! Maybe you'll say, all right, if bravery won't keep body and soul together, try honesty. That may fill your belly or at least get you a drop to drink. Let's look into it.

You've heard of honest Socrates[1]
Who never told a lie.
They weren't so grateful as you'd think
Instead they sentenced him to die
And handed him the poisoned drink.
How honest was the people's noble son!
Now think about his case. Alas
A useful lesson can be won.
His honesty had brought him to that pass.
How happy is the man with none!

Yes, they tell us to be charitable and to share what we have, but what if we haven't got anything? Maybe philanthropists have a rough time of it too, it stands to reason, they need a little something for themselves. Yes, charity is a rare virtue, because it doesn't pay.

St. Martin[2] couldn't bear to see
His fellows in distress.
He saw a poor man in the snow.

---

9. (100–44 B.C.), Roman general and dictator, assassinated by a republican clique including his young friend Brutus when suspected of imperial ambitions.   1. Greek philosopher, condemned to death in 399 B.C. for teaching the young to question accepted beliefs.   2. (A.D. 330–397) As a young soldier in the Roman army, Martin divided his military cloak with a beggar. He dreamed of Christ that night and was baptized thereafter, later becoming Bishop of Tours.

"Take half my cloak!" He did, and lo!
They both of them froze none the less.
He thought his heavenly reward was won.
Now think about his case. Alas
A useful lesson can be won.
Unselfishness had brought him to that pass.
How happy is the man with none!

That's our situation. We're God-fearing folk, we stick together, we
don't steal, we don't murder, we don't set fire to anything! You
could say that we set an example which bears out the song, we
sink lower and lower, we seldom see any soup, but if we were
different, if we were thieves and murderers, maybe our bellies
would be full. Because virtue isn't rewarded, only wickedness, the
world needn't be like this, but it is.

And here you see God-fearing folk
Observing God's ten laws.
So far He hasn't taken heed.
You people sitting warm indoors
Help to relieve our bitter need!
Our virtue can be counted on.
Now think about our case. Alas
A useful lesson can be won.
The fear of God has brought us to this pass.
How happy is the man with none!

VOICE. [*From above*] Hey, down there! Come on up! We've got some
good thick soup.
MOTHER COURAGE. Lamb, I couldn't get anything down. I know what
you say makes sense, but is it your last word? We've always been
good friends.
THE COOK. My last word. Think it over.
MOTHER COURAGE. I don't need to think it over. I won't leave her.
THE COOK. It wouldn't be wise, but there's nothing I can do. I'm not
inhuman, but it's a small tavern. We'd better go in now, or there
won't be anything left, we'll have been singing in the cold for
nothing.
MOTHER COURAGE. I'll get Kattrin.
THE COOK. Better bring it down for her. They'll get a fright if the
three of us barge in. [*They go out*]
[*Kattrin climbs out of the wagon. She is carrying a bundle. She
looks around to make sure the others are gone. Then she spreads
out an old pair of the cook's trousers and a skirt belonging to
her mother side by side on a wheel of the wagon so they can*

*easily be seen. She is about to leave with her bundle when
Mother Courage comes out of the house]*

MOTHER COURAGE. [*With a dish of soup*] Kattrin! Stop! Kattrin! Where
do you think you're going with that bundle? Have you taken leave
of your wits? [*She examines the bundle*] She's packed her things.
Were you listening? I've told him it's no go with Utrecht and his
lousy tavern, what would we do there? A tavern's no place for you
and me. The war still has a thing or two up its sleeve for us. [*She
sees the trousers and skirt*] You're stupid. Suppose I'd seen that
and you'd been gone? [*Kattrin tries to leave, Mother Courage holds
her back*] And don't go thinking I've given him the gate on your
account. It's the wagon. I won't part with the wagon, I'm used to
it, it's not you, it's the wagon. We'll go in the other direction,
we'll put the cook's stuff out here where he'll find it, the fool. [*She
climbs up and throws down a few odds and ends, to join the trousers*] There. Now we're shut of him, you won't see me taking
anyone else into the business. From now on it's you and me. This
winter will go by like all the rest. Harness up, it looks like snow.

[*They harness themselves to the wagon, turn it around and pull
it away. When the cook comes out he sees his things and stands
dumbfounded*]

10

Throughout 1635 Mother Courage and her daughter Kattrin pull
the wagon over the roads of central Germany in the wake of the
increasingly bedraggled armies.

Highway.

*Mother Courage and Kattrin are pulling the wagon. They come
to a peasant's house. A voice is heard singing from within.*

THE VOICE.
The rose bush is our garden
Rejoiced our hearts in spring
It bore such lovely flowers.
We planted it last season
Before the April showers.
A garden is a blessèd thing
It bore such lovely flowers.

When winter comes a-stalking
And gales great snow storms bring
They trouble us but little.
We've lately finished caulking

The roof with moss and wattle.
A sheltering roof's a blessèd thing
When winter comes a-stalking.

[*Mother Courage and Kattrin have stopped to listen. Then they move on*]

11

January 1636. The imperial troops threaten the Protestant city of Halle.[3] The stone speaks. Mother Courage loses her daughter and goes on alone. The end of the war is not in sight.

The wagon, much the worse for wear, is standing beside a peasant house with an enormous thatch roof. The house is built against the side of a stony hill. Night.

A lieutenant and three soldiers in heavy armor step out of the woods.

THE LIEUTENANT. I don't want any noise. If anybody yells, run him through with your pikes.

FIRST SOLDIER. But we need a guide. We'll have to knock if we want them to come out.

THE LIEUTENANT. Knocking sounds natural. It could be a cow bumping against the barn wall.

[*The soldiers knock on the door. A peasant woman opens. They hold their hands over her mouth. Two soldiers go in*]

A MAN'S VOICE. [*Inside*] Who's there?

[*The soldiers bring out a peasant and his son*]

THE LIEUTENANT. [*Points to the wagon, in which Kattrin has appeared*] There's another one. [*A soldier pulls her out*] Anybody else live here?

THE PEASANT COUPLE. This is our son.—That's a dumb girl.—Her mother's gone into the town on business—Buying up people's belongings, they're selling cheap because they're getting out.— They're provisioners.

THE LIEUTENANT. I'm warning you to keep quiet, one squawk and you'll get a pike over the head. All right. I need somebody who can show us the path to the city. [*Points to the young peasant*] You. Come here!

THE YOUNG PEASANT. I don't know no path.

THE SECOND SOLDIER. [*Grinning*] He don't know no path.

---

3. Protestant city 20 miles northwest of Leipzig.

THE YOUNG PEASANT. I'm not helping the Catholics.

THE LIEUTENANT. [*To the second soldier*] Give him a feel of your pike!

THE YOUNG PEASANT. [*Forced down on his knees and threatened with the pike*] You can kill me. I won't do it.

THE FIRST SOLDIER. I know what'll make him think twice. [*He goes over to the barn*] Two cows and an ox. Get this: If you don't help us, I'll cut them down.

THE YOUNG PEASANT. Not the animals!

THE PEASANT WOMAN. [*In tears*] Captain, spare our animals or we'll starve.

THE LIEUTENANT. If he insists on being stubborn, they're done for.

THE FIRST SOLDIER. I'll start with the ox.

THE YOUNG PEASANT. [*To the old man*] Do I have to? [*The old woman nods*] I'll do it.

THE PEASANT WOMAN. And thank you kindly for your forbearance, Captain, for ever and ever, amen.

[*The peasant stops her from giving further thanks*]

THE FIRST SOLDIER. Didn't I tell you? With them it's the animals that come first.

[*Led by the young peasant, the lieutenant and the soldiers continue on their way*]

THE PEASANT. I wish I knew what they're up to. Nothing good.

THE PEASANT WOMAN. Maybe they're only scouts.—What are you doing?

THE PEASANT. [*Putting a ladder against the roof and climbing up*] See if they're alone. [*On the roof*] Men moving in the woods. All the way to the quarry. Armor in the clearing. And a cannon. It's more than a regiment. God have mercy on the city and everybody in it.

THE PEASANT WOMAN. See any light in the city?

THE PEASANT. No. They're all asleep. [*He climbs down*] If they get in, they'll kill everybody.

THE PEASANT WOMAN. The sentry will see them in time.

THE PEASANT. They must have killed the sentry in the tower on the hill, or he'd have blown his horn.

THE PEASANT WOMAN. If there were more of us . . .

THE PEASANT. All by ourselves up here with a cripple . . .

THE PEASANT WOMAN. We can't do a thing. Do you think . . .

THE PEASANT. Not a thing.

THE PEASANT WOMAN. We couldn't get down there in the dark.

THE PEASANT. The whole hillside is full of them. We can't even give a signal.

THE PEASANT WOMAN. They'd kill us.

THE PEASANT. No, we can't do a thing.

THE PEASANT WOMAN. [*To Kattrin*] Pray, poor thing, pray! We can't stop the bloodshed. If you can't talk, at least you can pray. He'll hear you if nobody else does. I'll help you. [*All kneel, Kattrin behind the peasants*] Our Father which art in heaven, hear our prayer. Don't let the town perish with everybody in it, all asleep and unsuspecting. Wake them, make them get up and climb the walls and see the enemy coming through the night with cannon and pikes, through the fields and down the hillside. [*Back to Kattrin*] Protect our mother and don't let the watchman sleep, wake him before it's too late. And succor our brother-in-law, he's in there with his four children, let them not perish, they're innocent and don't know a thing. [*To Kattrin, who groans*] The littlest is less than two, the oldest is seven. [*Horrified, Kattrin stands up*] Our Father, hear us, for Thou alone canst help, we'll all be killed, we're weak, we haven't any pikes or anything, we are powerless and in Thine hands, we and our animals and the whole farm, and the city too, it's in Thine hands, and the enemy is under the walls with great might.

> [*Kattrin has crept unnoticed to the wagon, taken something out of it, put it under her apron and climbed up the ladder to the roof of the barn*]

THE PEASANT WOMAN. Think upon the children in peril, especially the babes in arms and the old people that can't help themselves and all God's creatures.

THE PEASANT. And forgive us our trespasses as we forgive them that trespass against us. Amen.

> [*Kattrin, sitting on the roof, starts beating the drum that she has taken out from under her apron*]

THE PEASANT WOMAN. Jesus! What's she doing?

THE PEASANT. She's gone crazy.

THE PEASANT WOMAN. Get her down, quick!

> [*The peasant runs toward the ladder, but Kattrin pulls it up on the roof*]

THE PEASANT WOMAN. She'll be the death of us all.

THE PEASANT. Stop that, you cripple!

THE PEASANT WOMAN. She'll have the Catholics down on us.

THE PEASANT. [*Looking around for stones*] I'll throw rocks at you.

THE PEASANT WOMAN. Have you no pity? Have you no heart? We're dead if they find out it's us! They'll run us through!

> [*Kattrin stares in the direction of the city, and goes on drumming*]

THE PEASANT WOMAN. [*To the peasant*] I told you not to let those tramps stop here. What do they care if the soldiers drive our last animals away?

THE LIEUTENANT. [*Rushes in with his soldiers and the young peasant*] I'll cut you to pieces!

THE PEASANT WOMAN. We're innocent, captain. We couldn't help it. She sneaked up there. We don't know her.

THE LIEUTENANT. Where's the ladder?

THE PEASANT. Up top.

THE LIEUTENANT. [*To Kattrin*] Throw down that drum. It's an order!

[*Kattrin goes on drumming*]

THE LIEUTENANT. You're all in this together! This'll be the end of you!

THE PEASANT. They've felled some pine trees in the woods over there. We could get one and knock her down . . .

THE FIRST SOLDIER. [*To the Lieutenant*] Request permission to make a suggestion. [*He whispers something in the lieutenant's ear. He nods*] Listen. We've got a friendly proposition. Come down, we'll take you into town with us. Show us your mother and we won't touch a hair of her head.

[*Kattrin goes on drumming*]

THE LIEUTENANT. [*Pushes him roughly aside*] She doesn't trust you. No wonder with your mug. [*He calls up*] If I give you my word? I'm an officer, you can trust my word of honor.

[*She drums still louder*]

THE LIEUTENANT. Nothing is sacred to her.

THE YOUNG PEASANT. It's not just her mother, lieutenant!

THE FIRST SOLDIER. We can't let this go on. They'll hear it in the city.

THE LIEUTENANT. We'll have to make some kind of noise that's louder than the drums. What could we make noise with?

THE FIRST SOLDIER. But we're not supposed to make noise.

THE LIEUTENANT. An innocent noise, stupid. A peaceable noise.

THE PEASANT. I could chop wood.

THE LIEUTENANT. That's it, chop! [*The peasant gets an ax and chops at a log*] Harder! Harder! You're chopping for your life.

[*Listening, Kattrin has been drumming more softly. Now she looks anxiously around and goes on drumming as before*]

THE LIEUTENANT. [*To the peasant*] Not loud enough. [*To the first soldier*] You chop too.

THE PEASANT. There's only one ax. [*Stops chopping*]

THE LIEUTENANT. We'll have to set the house on fire. Smoke her out.

THE PEASANT. That won't do any good, Captain. If the city people see fire up here, they'll know what's afoot.

[*Still drumming, Kattrin has been listening again. Now she laughs*]

THE LIEUTENANT. Look, she's laughing at us. I'll shoot her down, regardless. Get the musket!

[*Two soldiers run out. Kattrin goes on drumming*]

THE PEASANT WOMAN. I've got it, captain. That's their wagon over there. If we start smashing it up, she'll stop. The wagon's all they've got.

THE LIEUTENANT. [*To the young peasant*] Smash away. [*To Kattrin*]
We'll smash your wagon if you don't stop.
[*The young peasant strikes a few feeble blows at the wagon*]
THE PEASANT WOMAN. Stop it, you beast!
[*Kattrin stares despairingly at the wagon and emits pitiful sounds.
But she goes on drumming*]
THE LIEUTENANT. Where are those stinkers with the musket?
THE FIRST SOLDIER. They haven't heard anything in the city yet, or
we'd hear their guns.
THE LIEUTENANT. [*To Kattrin*] They don't hear you. And now we're
going to shoot you down. For the last time: Drop that drum!
THE YOUNG PEASANT. [*Suddenly throws the plank away*] Keep on
drumming! Or they'll all be killed! Keep on drumming, keep on
drumming . . .
[*The soldier throws him down and hits him with his pike. Kat-
trin starts crying, but goes on drumming*]
THE PEASANT WOMAN. Don't hit him in the back! My God, you're
killing him.
[*The soldiers run in with the musket*]
THE SECOND SOLDIER. The colonel's foaming at the mouth. We'll be
court-martialed.
THE LIEUTENANT. Set it up! Set it up! [*To Kattrin, while the musket
is being set up on its stand*] For the last time: Stop that drumming!
[*Kattrin in tears drums as loud as she can*] Fire!
[*The soldiers fire, Kattrin is hit. She beats the drum for a few
times more and then slowly collapses*]
THE LIEUTENANT. Now we'll have some quiet.
[*But Kattrin's last drumbeats are answered by the city's cannon.
A confused hubbub of alarm bells and cannon is heard in the
distance*]
THE FIRST SOLDIER. She's done it.

12

*Night, toward morning. The fifes and drums of troops marching
away.*

*Outside the wagon Mother Courage sits huddled over her daugh-
ter. The peasant couple are standing beside them.*

THE PEASANT. [*Hostile*] You'll have to be going, woman. There's
only one more regiment to come. You can't go alone.[4]
MOTHER COURAGE. Maybe I can get her to sleep. [*She sings*]

---

4. I.e., for protection and customers, Mother Courage must travel with the army.

Lullaby baby
What stirs in the hay?
The neighbor brats whimper
Mine are happy and gay.
They go in tatters
And you in silk down
Cut from an angel's
Best party gown.
They've nothing to munch on
And you will have pie
Just tell your mother
In case it's too dry.
Lullaby baby
What stirs in the hay?
That one lies in Poland
The other—who can say?

Now she's asleep. You shouldn't have told her about your brother-in-law's children.

THE PEASANT. Maybe it wouldn't have happened if you hadn't gone to town to swindle people.

MOTHER COURAGE. I'm glad she's sleeping now.

THE PEASANT WOMAN. She's not sleeping, you'll have to face it, she's dead.

THE PEASANT. And it's time you got started. There are wolves around here, and what's worse, marauders.

MOTHER COURAGE. Yes. [*She goes to the wagon and takes out a sheet of canvas to cover the body with*]

THE PEASANT WOMAN. Haven't you anybody else? Somebody you can go to?

MOTHER COURAGE. Yes, there's one of them left. Eilif.

THE PEASANT. [*While Mother Courage covers the body*] Go find him. We'll attend to this one, give her a decent burial. Set your mind at rest.

MOTHER COURAGE. Here's money for your expenses. [*She gives the peasant money*]

   [*The peasant and his son shake hands with her and carry Kattrin away*]

THE PEASANT WOMAN. [*On the way out*] Hurry up!

MOTHER COURAGE. [*Harnesses herself to the wagon*] I hope I can pull the wagon alone. I'll manage, there isn't much in it. I've got to get back in business.

   [*Another regiment marches by with fifes and drums in the rear*]

MOTHER COURAGE. Hey, take me with you! [*She starts to pull*]

   [*Singing is heard in the rear:*]

With all the killing and recruiting
The war will worry on a while.
In ninety years they'll still be shooting.
It's hardest on the rank-and-file.
Our food is swill, our pants all patches
The higher-ups steal half our pay
And still we dream of God-sent riches.
Tomorrow is another day!
    The spring is come! Christian, revive!
    The snowdrifts melt, the dead lie dead!
    And if by chance you're still alive
    It's time to rise and shake a leg.

FEDERICO GARCÍA LORCA
1898–1936

Although he died young, the poet and playwright Federico García Lorca is the best-known writer of modern Spain, and perhaps the most famous Spanish writer since Cervantes. A member of the brilliant "Generation of 1927" (along with Jorgé Guillen, Vicente Aleixandre, Pedro Salinas, and Rafael Alberti), known for the striking imagery and lyric musicality of his work, Lorca is both classical and modern, traditional and innovative, difficult and popular, a voice combining regional and universal themes. The poetry and plays that began as (and always were) personal statements took on larger significance first as the expression of tragic conflicts in Spanish culture, and then as poignant laments for humanity—seen especially in the plight of those who are deprived, by society or simply by death, of the fulfillment which could have been theirs. When Lorca was dragged from a friend's house and executed by a Fascist squad on August 19, 1936, his murder outraged the whole European and American literary and artistic community and seemed to symbolize in addition the mindless destruction of humane and cultural values that loomed with the approach of World War II.

Lorca (despite the Spanish practice of using both paternal and maternal last names—correctly "García Lorca"—the author is generally called "Lorca") was born on June 5, 1898, in the small village of Fuentevaqueros, near the Andalusian city of Granada. His parents were well-to-do: his father was a prosperous farmer and his mother, who had been a schoolteacher, encouraged him to read widely and develop his musical talent. The composer Manuel de Falla befriended the young musician, who became an expert pianist and guitar player. Lorca began law studies at the University of Granada where—after several years' absence—he received a degree in 1923. He published a book of *Impressions and Landscapes* (1918) after a trip through Spain, but left Granada in 1919 for Madrid where he entered the Residencia de Estudiantes, a modern college established to provide a cosmopolitan education for Spanish youth. Madrid was not only the capital of Spain but also the center of intellectual and artistic ferment and the Residencia attracted many of those who would be the most influential writers and artists of their generation (among the latter the artist Salvador Dalí and the film director Luis Buñuel). Lorca soon gained the reputation of a rising young poet from poetry readings and the publication of a few poems in magazines, even before the appearance of his first collection of verse, the *Book of Poems* of 1921. Although he lived at the Residencia almost continuously until 1928, he never seriously pursued a degree but spent his time reading, writing, improvising music and poetry in company with his friends, and producing his first plays.

In these early years, before his departure for New York in 1929, Lorca concentrated on writing poetry although he was clearly interested in the theater as well. *The Butterfly's Evil Spell* (1920), a fantasy about a cockroach who is hopelessly enchanted by the beauty of a butterfly, was staged in Barcelona; in 1923 Lorca wrote, designed sets for, and directed a puppet play on a theme from Andalusian folklore, *The Girl Who Waters the Sweet Basil Flower and the Inquisitive Prince,* for which De Falla himself arranged the music. Yet the major achievement of this period is the composition of several books of poetry, not all of which were published right away: the *Book of Poems,* most of the *Songs* (1927), early versions of the poems in the *Poem of the Deep Song,* which was not published as a book until 1931 although several poems were recited at a 1922 Andalusian festival, and the *Gypsy Ballads* (1928) which was an immediate popular success.

The first collection, the *Book of Poems,* introduces themes that will be familiar in later works: death, an innocent or childlike point of view, a closeness to nature which takes the form of animal fables or symbolic meanings attached to images like the pomegranate ("the idea of blood enclosed / In a hard a bitter globe") and overall a certain witty or ironic distance from the situations he describes. The playful tone never quite covers Lorca's constant preoccupation with death, however: death as the common fate that shadows our most vivid experiences. Speaking to a chorus of questioning children in "The Ballad of the Little Square," the poet answers that he feels in his mouth only "the savor of the bones / of my great skull."

The poems of the *Deep Song* marked a return to the gypsy themes and ballads of Lorca's home province of Andalusia, a region known for its mixture of Arab and Spanish culture, and for a tradition of wandering gypsy singers who improvised, to guitar accompaniment, rhythmic laments on themes of love and death. The *cante jondo* ("deep song") was an ancient Andalusian ballad form that centered on repeated notes or phrases, and Lorca took full advantage (as he would in the "Lament for Ignacio Sánchez Mejías") of the haunting quality that could be obtained through this obsessive refrain. The *Songs* written next are noted for their lyricism, and for the capture of particular moments of experience; however, many reach beyond the sensuously precise description of real objects to encompass abstract concepts, psychological states, and clusters of associations—as does the symbolist poetry Lorca knew. Lorca describes how "the ear of grain keeps intact/ its hard yellow laughter," how a little mute boy looks for his voice in a drop of water, and how Narcissus (both youth and flower) is mirrored in a double image where "over your white eyes flicker / shadows and sleeping fish."

Lorca's next collection, the *Gypsy Ballads* of 1928, marks the beginning of his mature verse. Blending classical ballad form with scenes taken directly from contemporary life, the poet expresses, in a mixture of violence and eroticism, the tragic struggle in which innocence, spontaneity, creativity, and freedom are repressed by society and by the inevitable limitations of human nature. In the famous "Ballad of the Spanish Civil Guard," the militia with their "patent-leather souls" and heads filled with "a vague astronomy / of shapeless pistols" cut down the gypsies in their fantastic city with its banners and "cinnamon towers." The unsuspecting populace, caught in the midst of their festival, are helpless to prevent absolute destruction— the tile roofs become "furrows in the soil," and the burned city itself persists only in the sterile "play of moon and sand" on the poet's brow. A hostile, violent world is pictured here, in which even the wind pursues a young girl with lustful breath and "hot sword," and St. Eulalia's martyrdom and mutilation are described with a mixture of eroticism and horror. These themes are not restricted to poetry: they reoccur in a contemporary play, *Mariana Pineda* (1928), where Lorca's heroine is executed for refusing to identify a group of revolutionaries (among them the lover who abandoned her).

Impelled by an emotional crisis, Lorca left Spain for New York in 1929, where he wrote a series of poems later published as *Poet in New York* (1940). The collection does not focus exclusively on the city, however, and moves from the poet's youth in Europe to scenes of rural New York and northern Vermont as Lorca tries to come to terms with his own complex personality against a background of psychological, artistic, and social tensions. Blended with the familiar theme of doomed love and death is a tentative exploration of the homosexuality which Lorca could not admit inside traditional Spanish society, and which he expressed only with hesitation and anxiety in this and later works. A large part of the ten-section *Poet in New York*, however, focuses primarily on the city which is seen as a frightening symbol of the modern industrial West. In a richly varied and densely metaphorical apocalyptic vision, Lorca juxtaposes two ways of life and creates a contrast which, he said, "puts my poetic world in contact with the poetic world of New York." Beginning with a denunciation of the dehumanized commercial city-world of sterile concrete and glass, he moves on to celebrate the only area where the natural world survives: Harlem, with its "garnet violence deaf and dumb in the shadows," and its "great king a prisoner in a janitor's uniform." In the face of this universal despair there are foreshadowings of a coming upheaval where "the Stock Market will be a pyramid of moss" and the oppressed and deprived will unite to proclaim "the reign of the ear of corn." The book's ending sections mark an escape from New York to Havana and (in spite of a continued sense of alienation) to the dancelike harmony of a more primitive life.

From 1930 to his death in 1936, Lorca was extremely active in the theater both as writer and as director (after 1931) of a traveling theatrical group ("La Barraca") subsidized by the Spanish Republic. After a series of farces that mixed romantically tragic and comic themes, he presented the tragedies for which he is best known: *Blood Wedding* (1933) and *Yerma* (1934), and he wrote in 1936 the posthumously published *The House of Bernarda Alba* (1945). All Lorca's theater, from the early fantasy of *The Butterfly's Evil Spell* to the puppet plays, farces, and last tragedies, rejects the conventionally realistic nineteenth-century drama and employs an openly poetic form that suggests musical patterns, includes choruses, songs, and stylized movement, and may even (as in the fragmentary surrealist drama, *The Audience*) attack the audience itself. The tragic themes of Lorca's poetry emerge here in dramatic form, usually centering on the suffering of individual women whose instinctual fulfillment (through love or children) is denied by fate or social circumstance. In *Blood Wedding*, the Mother's last remaining son dies in a moonlit struggle with Leonardo, who has run away with his bride (Leonardo's former betrothed) on their wedding day. Leonardo (who also dies) is a member of the family that has killed the Mother's husband and other sons, and images of approaching death and sensual, frustrated love permeate the whole play. In *Yerma* (the title name also means desert or sterility), the heroine is caught between her own passionate, sensual nature, yearning to love and bear children, and the need—for honor's sake—to remain with a husband who cares only for a well-regulated house. When Yerma realizes the extent of Juan's spiritual as well as sexual sterility, she strangles him and (because she will not remarry) simultaneously kills her only chance to fulfill her natural instincts through bearing children. The posthumously published *House of Bernarda Alba* (subtitled "A Drama About Women in the Villages of Spain") revolves around the same themes of sterility and frustrated love, as the repressed spinster daughters of the stern matriarch Bernarda Alba (and even the mad grandmother) reveal their common desire to marry a young man. Bernarda, however, upholds the proprieties that hedge in Spanish society; she refuses to let her daughters have visitors, ignores their rivalry over young Pepe el Romano (engaged to the wealthy oldest daughter, Angustias), recommends a painful death for an unwed mother being dragged through the streets, and—when the youngest daughter Adela commits suicide over Pepe, who has become her lover—seems chiefly concerned that Adela's body be dressed "as though she were a virgin." The conflict between social custom and individual need takes on mythic proportions in *The House of Bernarda Alba*, where only women appear on a stage that is strangely quarantined and painted white, and where the disturbing male principle represented by Pepe el Romano is reiterated by the noise of a stallion's hooves banging against stable walls.

In 1936, the year of his death, Lorca was revising a series of short lyric poems based on the Arabic forms of *casida* and the *gacela*, a collection eventually published in 1940 as *The Divan at Tamarit* (a "divan" is a poetic collection, and Lorca wrote the poems at a country house called after the ancient place name of Tamarit). In the previous year, he had published a long elegiac poem on the death of his good friend, the famous bullfighter Ignacio Sánchez Mejías, who had been fatally gored by a bull on August 11, 1934, in Manzanares and died two days later in Madrid. Sánchez Mejías was a cultured man, well-known in literary circles and himself the author of a play, and Lorca's "Lament for Ignacio Sánchez Mejías" celebrates both his friend and the value of human grace and courage in a world where everything ends in death.

Lorca's "Lament" is not only cast as an elegy (a medium-length poem that mourns a death), but also recalls one of the most famous poems of Spanish literature: the "Verses on the Death of His Father" written by the medieval poet Jorge Manrique (1440–1479). Manrique's catalogue of his father's noble qualities ("What a friend to his friends!"), and his description of individual lives as flowing into the sea of death, are echoed by passages in the modern elegy. Yet there is a fundamental difference between the two: where Manrique's elegy stresses religious themes and the prospect of eternal life, Lorca—in grim contrast—rejects such consolation and insists that his friend's death is permanent.

The four parts of the "Lament" incorporate a variety of forms and perspectives, all working together to suggest a progression from the report of death in the precise first line—"At five in the afternoon"—to the end where the dead man's nobility and elegance survive in "a sad breeze through the olive trees." The "deep song" technique of an insistent refrain coloring everything else organizes the first section, "Cogida [the bull's toss] and Death," with its throbbing return to the moment of death. The scene in the arena wavers between an objective report—the boy with the shroud, the coffin on wheels—and the shared agony of the bull's bellowing and wounds burning like suns. Lorca moves in the next, ballad section to a personal refusal of Sánchez Mejías' death ("I will not see it!"), and a request that images of whiteness cover up this spilled blood; instead, he imagines Ignacio climbing steps to seek dawn and a mystic meeting with his true self but encountering, bewildered, only his broken body. After a tribute to his princely friend, the poet finally admits what he cannot force himself to see: the finality of physical dissolution as moss and grass invade the buried bullfighter's skull.

In "The Laid Out Body," a series of somber quatrains in regular meter recognizes the inevitability of death and dissolution (Ignacio's "pure shape which had nightingales" is now "filled with depthless holes"), and the fact that the bullfighter will be entombed in unyielding, lifeless stone. In this and the final section with its rhythmic free verse, Lorca accepts physical death ("even the sea dies!") but preserves, in his poetry, a vision of his noble countryman that surpasses such obliteration. For those who exist only on the unthinking, physical level (the bull, fig tree, household ants, the black satin of his funeral suit), Ignacio has indeed "died forever." Yet human beings recognize other qualities beyond the physical and in fact shape their estimate of an individual according to these qualities. In life, Sánchez Mejías was known to his friends for "the signal maturity of your understanding . . . your appetite for death and the taste of its mouth." These qualities survive, for a while, in memory. Lorca, echoing the pride with which the Latin poet Horace claimed to perpetuate his subjects in a "monument of lasting bronze," sings of his friend "for posterity," and captures the life and death of Sánchez Mejías in his "Lament."

Carl W. Cobb, *Federico García Lorca* (1967), is a good general biography; E. Honig's *García Lorca*, rev. ed. (1980), provides a critical introduction to the poet and his work, in literary historical context. *Lorca: A Collection of Critical Essays* (1962), edited by Manuel Durán, is a valuable collection of essays on the poet and his work (mainly the poetry).

Lament for Ignacio Sánchez Mejías[1]

1. Cogida[2] and Death

At five in the afternoon.
It was exactly five in the afternoon.
A boy brought the white sheet
at five in the afternoon.
A frail[3] of lime ready prepared   5
at five in the afternoon.
The rest was death, and death alone
at five in the afternoon.

The wind carried away the cottonwool[4]
at five in the afternoon.   10
And the oxide scattered crystal and nickel
at five in the afternoon.
Now the dove and the leopard[5] wrestle
at five in the afternoon.
And a thigh with a desolate horn   15
at five in the afternoon.
The bass-string struck up
at five in the afternoon.
Arsenic bells[6] and smoke
at five in the afternoon.   20
Groups of silence in the corners
at five in the afternoon.
And the bull alone with a high heart!
At five in the afternoon.
When the sweat of snow was coming   25
at five in the afternoon,
when the bull ring was covered in iodine
at five in the afternoon.
death laid eggs in the wound
at five in the afternoon.   30
At five in the afternoon.
Exactly at five o'clock in the afternoon.

A coffin on wheels is his bed
at five in the afternoon.

1. Translated by Stephen Spender and J. L. Gili.   2. Harvesting; the toss when the bull catches
the bullfighter.   3. A basket. Lime, a disinfectant, was sprinkled on the body after death.
4. To stop the blood; the beginning of a series of medicinal, chemical, and inhuman images that
emphasize the presence of death.   5. Traditional symbols for peace and violence; they wrestle
with one another as the bullfighter's thigh struggles with the bull's horn.   6. Bells were rung to
announce a death; the bass string of the guitar strums a lament.

Bones and flutes resound in his ears[7]   35
at five in the afternoon.
Now the bull was bellowing through his forehead
at five in the afternoon.
The room[8] was iridescent with agony
at five in the afternoon.   40
In the distance the gangrene now comes
at five in the afternoon.
Horn of the lily through green groins[9]
at five in the afternoon.
The wounds were burning like suns   45
at five in the afternoon,
and the crowd was breaking the windows[1]
at five in the afternoon.
At five in the afternoon.
Ah, that fatal five in the afternoon!   50
It was five by all the clocks!
It was five in the shade of the afternoon!

2. *The Spilled Blood*

I will not see it!

Tell the moon to come
for I do not want to see the blood
of Ignacio on the sand.   55

I will not see it!

The moon wide open.
Horse of still clouds,
and the grey bull ring of dreams   60
with willows in the barreras.[2]
I will not see it!

Let my memory kindle![3]
Warn the jasmines
of such minute whiteness!   65

7. A suggestion of the medieval Dance of Death.   8. The room adjoining the arena where
wounded bullfighters were taken for treatment.   9. The shape of the bleeding wound resembles
a lily; gangrene turns flesh a greenish color.   1. A Spanish idiom for the crowd's loud roar.
2. Willows are a symbol of mourning; the barreras are the barriers around the ring within which
the fight takes place and over which a fighter may escape the bull's charge.   3. Literally, "My
memory burns within me." The poet calls on ("warns" as "notify") the small white jasmine flowers
to come and cover the blood.

I will not see it!

The cow of the ancient world
passed her sad tongue
over a snout of blood
spilled on the sand,   70
and the bulls of Guisando,[4]
partly death and partly stone,
bellowed like two centuries
sated with treading the earth.
No.   75
I do not want to see it!
I will not see it!

Ignacio goes up the tiers[5]
with all his death on his shoulders.
He sought for the dawn   80
but the dawn was no more.
He seeks for his confident profile
and the dream bewilders him.
He sought for his beautiful body
and encountered his opened blood.   85
Do not ask me to see it!
I do not want to hear it spurt
each time with less strength:
that spurt that illuminates
the tiers of seats, and spills   90
over the corduroy and the leather
of a thirsty multitude.
Who shouts that I should come near!
Do not ask me to see it!

His eyes did not close   95
when he saw the horns near,
but the terrible mothers[6]
lifted their heads.
And across the ranches,[7]
an air of secret voices rose,   100
shouting to celestial bulls,
herdsmen of pale mist.
There was no prince in Seville[8]

4. Carved stone bulls from the Celtic past; a tourist attraction in the province of Madrid.
5. An imaginary scene in which the bullfighter mounts the stairs of the arena.   6. The three
Fates, who traditionally raised their heads when the thread of life was cut.   7. Fighting bulls
were raised on the ranches of Lorca's home province of Andalusia.   8. Leading city of Andalusia.

who could compare with him,
nor sword like his sword   105
nor heart so true.
Like a river of lions
was his marvellous strength,
and like a marble torso
his firm drawn moderation.   110
The air of Andalusian Rome
gilded his head[9]
where his smile was a spikenard
of wit and intelligence.
What a great torero in the ring!   115
What a good peasant in the sierra![1]
How gentle with the sheaves!
How hard with the spurs!
How tender with the dew!
How dazzling in the fiesta!   120
How tremendous with the final
banderillas[2] of darkness!

But now he sleeps without end.
Now the moss and the grass
open with sure fingers   125
the flower of his skull.
And now his blood comes out singing;
singing along marshes and meadows,
sliding on frozen horns,
faltering soulless in the mist,   130
stumbling over a thousand hoofs
like a long, dark, sad tongue,
to form a pool of agony
close to the starry Guadalquivir.[3]
Oh, white wall of Spain!   135
Oh, black bull of sorrow!
Oh, hard blood of Ignacio!
Oh, nightingale of his veins!
No.
I will not see it!   140
No chalice can contain it,

9. The image suggests a statue from Roman times, when Andalusia was part of the Roman Empire. *Spikenard*: a small, white, fragrant flower common in Andalusia; by extension, the bullfighter's white teeth.   1. Mountainous country; Sánchez Mejías is seen as a good *serrano* or "man of the hills." *Torero*: bullfighter.   2. The multicolored short spears that were thrust in the bull's shoulders to provoke him to attack.   3. A great river that passes through all the major cities of Andalusia. The singing stream of the bullfighter's blood suggests both the river and a nightingale.

no swallows[4] can drink it,
no frost of light can cool it,
nor song nor deluge of white lilies,
no glass can cover it with silver.　　　　　　　　　145
No.
I will not see it!

3. *The Laid Out Body*[5]

Stone is a forehead where dreams grieve
without curving waters and frozen cypresses.
Stone is a shoulder on which to bear Time　　　　150
with trees formed of tears and ribbons and planets.[6]

I have seen grey showers move towards the waves
raising their tender riddled arms,
to avoid being caught by the lying stone
which loosens their limbs without soaking the blood.　　155

For stone gathers seed and clouds,
skeleton larks and wolves of penumbra:
but yields not sounds nor crystals nor fire,
only bull rings and bull rings and more bull rings without walls.

Now Ignacio the well born lies on the stone.　　　　160
All is finished. What is happening? Contemplate his face:
death has covered him with pale sulphur
and has placed on him the head of a dark minotaur.[7]

All is finished. The rain penetrates his mouth.
The air, as if mad, leaves his sunken chest,　　　　165
and Love, soaked through with tears of snow,
warms itself on the peak of the herd.[8]

What are they saying? A stenching silence settles down.
We are here with a body laid out which fades away,
with a pure shape which had nightingales　　　　170
and we see it being filled with depthless holes.

---

4. According to a Spanish legend of the Crucifixion, swallows—a symbol of innocence—drank the blood of Christ on the Cross. The poet is seeking ways of concealing the dead man's blood. 5. Literally, "Present Body," the Spanish expression for a funeral wake, where the body is laid out for public mourning; contrast "Absent Soul." 6. Traditional funeral imagery carved on gravestones. 7. A monster from Greek myth: half man, half bull. 8. Of the ranch, literally.

Who creases the shroud? What he says is not true![9]
Nobody sings here, nobody weeps in the corner,
nobody pricks the spurs, nor terrifies the serpent.
Here I want nothing else but the round eyes   175
to see this body without a chance of rest.

Here I want to see those men of hard voice.
Those that break horses and dominate rivers;
those men of sonorous skeleton who sing
with a mouth full of sun and flint.   180

Here I want to see them. Before the stone.
Before this body with broken reins.
I want to know from them the way out
for this captain strapped down by death.

I want them to show me a lament like a river   185
which will have sweet mists and deep shores,
to take the body of Ignacio where it loses itself
without hearing the double panting of the bulls.

Loses itself in the round bull ring of the moon
which feigns in its youth a sad quiet bull: 190
loses itself in the night without song of fishes
and in the white thicket of frozen smoke.

I don't want them to cover his face with handkerchiefs
that he may get used to the death he carries.
Go, Ignacio; feel not the hot bellowing.   195
Sleep, fly, rest: even the sea dies!

4. Absent Soul

The bull does not know you, nor the fig tree,
nor the horses, nor the ants in your own house.
The child and the afternoon do not know you
because you have died for ever.   200

The back of the stone does not know you,
nor the black satin in which you crumble.
Your silent memory does not know you
because you have died for ever.

9. Lorca criticizes the conventional pieties voiced by someone standing close to the shrouded
body; the poet prefers a clear-eyed, realistic view of death.

The autumn will come with small white snails,[1]   205
misty grapes and with clustered hills,
but no one will look into your eyes
because you have died for ever.

Because you have died for ever,
like all the death of the Earth,   210
like all the dead who are forgotten
in a heap of lifeless dogs.[2]

Nobody knows you. No. But I sing of you.
For posterity I sing of your profile and grace.
Of the signal maturity of your understanding.   215
Of your appetite for death and the taste of its mouth.
Of the sadness of your once valiant gaiety.

It will be a long time, if ever, before there is born
an Andalusian so true, so rich in adventure.
I sing of his elegance with words that groan,   220
and I remember a sad breeze through the olive trees.

4. *Alma ausente*

No te conoce el toro ni la higuera,
ni caballos ni hormigas de tu casa.
No te conoce el niño ni la tarde
porque te has muerto para siempre.

No te conoce el lomo de la piedra,
ni el raso negro donde te destrozas.
No te conoce tu recuerdo mudo
porque te has muerto para siempre.

El otoño vendrá con caracolas,
uva de niebla y montes agrupados,
pero nadie querrá mirar tus ojos
porque te has muerto para siempre.

Porque te has muerto para siempre,
como todos los muertos de la Tierra,
como todos los muertos que se olvidan
en un montón de perros apagados.

1. Actually, conch shell–shaped horns: the shepherds' horns that sounded in the hills each fall
as the sheep were driven to new pastures.   2. Dogs as a (typically Continental) image for undignified, inferior creatures.

No te conoce nadie. No. Pero yo te canto.
Yo canto para luego tu perfil y tu gracia.
La madurez insigne de tu conocimiento.
Tu apetencia de muerte y el gusto de su boca.
La tristeza que tuvo tu valiente alegría.

Tardará mucho tiempo en nacer, si es que nace,
un andaluz tan claro, tan rico de aventura.
Yo canto su elegancia con palabras que gimen
y recuerdo una brisa triste por los olivos.

ALBERT CAMUS

1913–1960

Albert Camus is often linked with the contemporary philosopher Jean-Paul
Sartre as an "existentialist" writer, and indeed—as novelist, playwright, and
essayist—he is widely known for his analysis of two concerns basic to existentialism: its distinctive assessment of the human condition and its search
for authentic values. Yet Camus rejected doctrinaire labels, and Sartre himself suggested that the author was better placed in the tradition of French
"moralist" writers like Montaigne and Pascal, who analyzed human behavior inside an implied ethical context with its own standards of good and evil.
For Camus, "liberty," "justice," "brotherhood," and "happiness" were some
of these standards, along with the terms "revolt" and "absurd" that described
human nonacceptance of a world without meaning or value. From his
childhood among the very poor in Algiers to his later roles as journalist,
Resistance fighter, internationally famous literary figure, and winner of the
Nobel Prize in 1957, Camus never strayed from an intense awareness of the
most basic levels of human existence, or from a sympathy with those—often
poor and oppressed—who lived at that level. "I can understand only in human
terms. I understand the things I touch, things that offer me resistance." He
describes the raw experience of life as it is shared by all human beings, and
provides a bond between them. Camus's reaction to the "absurd," the human
condition stripped bare, is therefore quite different from Samuel Beckett's
retreat into agonized subjectivity; where Beckett is haunted by the fictionality
of experience, Camus asserts human consciousness and human solidarity as
the only values there are.

Camus was born on November 7, 1913, into a "world of poverty and
light" in Mondavi, Algeria (then a colony of France). He was the second
son in a poor family of mixed Alsatian-Spanish descent, and his father died
in one of the first battles of World War I. The two boys lived together with
their mother, uncle, and grandmother in a two-room apartment in the
working-class section of the capital city, Algiers. Camus and his brother,
Lucien, were raised by their strict grandmother while their mother worked
as a cleaning woman to support the family. Images of the Mediterranean

landscape, with its overwhelming, sensual closeness of sea and blazing sun, recur throughout his work, as does a profound compassion for those who— like his mother—labor unrecognized and in silence. (Camus's mother was illiterate, and left deaf and with a speech impediment by an untreated child-hood illness.)

A passionate athlete as well as scholarship student, Camus completed his secondary education and enrolled as a philosophy student at the University of Algiers before contracting, at seventeen, the tuberculosis which under-mined his health and shocked him with its demonstration of the human body's vulnerability to disease and death. Camus later finished his degree, but in the meantime he had gained from his illness a metaphor for every-thing that opposes and puts limits to human fulfillment and happiness: something he was later to term (after Artaud) the "plague" that infects bod-ies, minds, cities, and society (*The Plague* is the title of his second novel).

Camus lived and worked as a journalist in Algeria until 1940. He then moved to France when his political commentary (including a famous report on administrative mismanagement during a famine of Berber tribesmen) embroiled him with the local government so that his paper was suspended and he himself refused a work permit. Now as later, however, his work extended far beyond journalism. He published two collections of essays, *The Wrong Side and the Right Side* (1937) and *Nuptials* (1939), started a novel (*A Happy Death*), and founded a collective theater, "Le Théâtre du Travail" ("The Labor Theater") for which he wrote and adapted a number of plays. The theater always fascinated Camus, possibly because it involved groups of people and live interaction between actors and audience. He not only con-tinued to write plays after leaving Algeria (*Cross Purposes*, 1944; *The Just Assassins*, 1950) but was considering directing a new theater shortly before his death. The "Labor Theater" was a popular theater with performances on the docks in Algiers and was sponsored by the Communist Party which Camus had joined in 1934. Like many intellectuals of his day, Camus found in the Party a promising vehicle for social protest; he was unwilling to abandon either his independence or his convictions, however, and resigned in 1935 when the party line changed and he was asked to give up his support for Algerian nationalism. He left the "Labor Theater" in 1937 and, with a group of young Algerian intellectuals associated with the publishing house of Charlot, founded a similar but politically independent "Team Theater" ("Théâtre de l'Equipe"). During this decade, Camus also began work on his most famous novel, *The Stranger* (1942), the play *Caligula* (1944), and an essay defining his concept of the "absurd" hero, *The Myth of Sisyphus* (1942).

These three works established Camus's reputation as a philosopher of the "absurd": the absurdly grotesque discrepancy between human beings' brief, material existence and their urge to believe in larger meanings—to "make sense" of a world which has no discernible sense. In *The Stranger*, Camus described a thirty-year-old clerk named Meursault who lives a series of "real" events: he attends his mother's funeral, makes love to his mistress, goes swimming, shoots an Arab on the beach, and is tried for murder. All these events are described through Meursault's mind and yet they appear without any connection, as if each one began a new world. They are simply a series of concrete, sensuous *facts* separated from each other and from any kind of human or social meaning. Meursault is finally condemned to death not for murder but for this alienation, and its failure to respond to society's expectations of proper behavior. Just before his execution, when he is infuriated by the prison chaplain's attempt to console him with thoughts of an afterlife, he rises to a new level of existential awareness and an ardent affirmation of life in the here-and-now, the only truly human field of action. Stylistically, much of *The Stranger*'s impact comes from the contrast between the immediacy of the physical experience described, and the objective meaninglessness of that experience. On all levels, the novel reaffirms the importance of life lived moment by moment, in a total awareness that creates whatever meaning exists: the same awareness of his own activity that brings Sisyphus happiness when eternally pushing uphill the rock that will only roll down again or the same search for an absolute honesty free of human pretenses that characterizes the mad emperor Caligula.

During World War II, Camus worked in Paris as a reader for the publishing firm of Gallimard, a post that he kept until his death in 1960. At the same time, he was part of the French Resistance and helped edit the underground journal *Combat*. His friendship with the existentialist philosopher Jean-Paul Sartre began in 1944, and after the war he and Sartre were internationally known as uncompromising analysts of the modern conscience. Camus's second novel, *The Plague* (1947), used a description of plague in a quarantined city, the Algerian Oran, to symbolize the spread of evil during World War II ("the feeling of suffocation from which we all suffered, and the atmosphere of threat and exile") and also to show the human struggle against physical and spiritual death in all its forms. Not content merely to symbolize his views in fiction, he also spoke out in philosophical essays and political statements where his independent mind and refusal of doctrinaire positions brought him attacks from all sides. In the bitter struggle that brought independence to Algeria in 1962, Camus recognized the claims of both French and Arab Algerians to the land in which they were born. In the quest for social reform, he rejected any ideology that subordinated individual freedom and singled out Communism—the doctrine most reformist intellectuals saw as the only active hope—as a particular danger with its emphasis on the de-individualized and inevitable march of history. Camus's open anti-Communism led to a spectacular break with Sartre, whose review *Les Temps Modernes* ("Modern Times") condemned *The Rebel* (1951) in bitter personal attacks. The concept of revolt that Camus outlined in *The Rebel* was more ethical than political: he defined revolt as a basic nonacceptance of preestablished limits (whether by death or by oppression) which was shared by all human beings, and therefore required a reciprocal acceptance and balancing of each person's rights. Such "revolt" was directly opposed to revolutionary nihilism in that it made the rebelious impulse a basis for social tolerance inside the individual's self-assertion; it had no patience for master plans that prescribed patterns of thought or action.

Five years after *The Rebel* was published, Camus produced a very different book in *The Fall* (1956). This book is a rhetorical tour de force spoken by a fallen lawyer who uses all the tricks of language to confess his weaknesses and yet emerge triumphant, the omniscient judge of his fellow creatures. If Camus's *Notebooks* reveal in his early works a cycle of Sisyphus or the "absurd," and his middle ones a Promethean cycle of "revolt," *The Fall* inaugurates a third cycle, that of Nemesis, or judgment. It offers a complex, ironic picture that combines a yearning towards purity with a cynical debunking of all such attempts. The narrator, Clamence, is a composite personality including (among other things) satirized aspects of both Sartre and Camus, but it is impossible to get to the bottom of his character behind the layers of self-consciously manipulated language. The style itself challenges and disorients the reader, who is both included and excluded from a narration that presents Clamence's half of a dialogue where "you," the reader, are presumed to be present as the other half.

Camus was a consummate artist as well as moralist, well aware of the opportunities as well as the illusions of his craft. When he received the Nobel Prize in 1957, his acceptance speech emphasized the artificial but necessary "human" order imposed by art on the chaos of immediate experience. The artist is important as *creator*, because he or she shapes a human perspective, allows understanding in human terms, and therefore provides a basis for action. By stressing the gap between art and reality, Camus in effect provides a bridge between them as two poles of human understanding. His own works illustrate this act of bridging through their juxtaposition of realistic detail and almost mythic allegorization of human destiny. The symbolism of his titles, from *The Stranger* to the last collection of stories, *Exile and the Kingdom* (1957), repeatedly interprets human destiny in terms of a thematic opposition between the individual's sense of alienation and exile in the world, and simultaneous search for the true kingdom of human happiness and action.

With "The Guest," taken from *Exile and the Kingdom*, Camus returns to the landscape of his native Algeria. The colonial context is crucial in this story, not only to explain the real threat of guerrilla reprisal at the end (Camus may be recalling the actual killing of rural schoolteachers in 1954) but to establish the dimensions of a political situation in which the government, police, educational system, and economic welfare of Algeria were all controlled by France. French colonial education reproduced French, not local concerns: the schoolteacher's geography lesson outlines the four main rivers of France. The Arab is led along like an animal behind the gendarme Balducci, who rides a horse: here too, Camus may be recalling a humiliation reported two decades before and used to inspire Algerian nationalists. Inside this political context, however, he concentrates on quite different issues: freedom, brotherhood, responsibility, and the ambiguity of actions along with the inevitability of choice.

The remote desert landscape establishes a total physical and moral isolation for events in the story. "No one, in this desert . . . mattered," and the schoolteacher and his guest must each decide on his own what to do. When Balducci invades Daru's monastic solitude and tells him that he must deliver the Arab to prison, Daru is outraged to be involved and, indeed, to have responsibility for another's fate. Cursing both the system that tries to force him into complicity, and the Arab who has not had enough sense to get away, Daru tries in every way possible to avoid taking a stand. In the morning, however, when the Arab has not in fact run away, the schoolteacher makes up a package of food and money and passes on to the Arab his own freedom of choice. We cannot underestimate the quiet heroism of this act, by which Daru alienates himself from his own people and—unexpectedly—from the Arab's compatriots too; he is, he believes, conveying to a fellow human being the freedom of action which all people require. This level of common humanity is strongly underlined throughout the whole story as a "sort of brotherhood" and "strange alliance" that comes from having shared food and drink, and slept as equals under the same roof. Such hospitality is also the nomadic "law of the desert" that establishes fellowship between guest and host (a law that Daru refers to when he points out the second road at the end). The host's humane hospitality has placed a new burden and reciprocal responsibility on his guest, one that may explain why the Arab chooses—in apparent freedom—the road to prison. Camus considered "Cain" and "The Law" as titles for this story before settling on "The Guest" (and the title word *l'hôte*, is identical for "guest" and "host" in French). Both guest and host are obliged to shoulder the ambiguous, and potentially fatal, burden of freedom.

Germaine Brée is author of *Albert Camus*, rev. ed. (1964), an excellent general study, and editor of *Camus: A Collection of Critical Essays* (1961). Phillip Rhein's *Albert Camus* (1969) is a brief introduction and biography. Herbert Lottman's *Albert Camus: A Biography* (1979) is the fullest and most detailed biography available.

The Guest[1]

The schoolmaster was watching the two men climb toward him. One was on horseback, the other on foot. They had not yet tackled the abrupt rise leading to the schoolhouse built on the hillside. They were toiling onward, making slow progress in the snow, among the stones, on the vast expanse of the high, deserted plateau. From time to time the horse stumbled. Without hearing anything yet, he could see the breath issuing from the horse's nostrils. One of the men, at least, knew the region. They were following the trail although it had disappeared days ago under a layer of dirty white snow. The schoolmaster calculated that it would take them half an hour to get onto the hill. It was cold; he went back into the school to get a sweater.

He crossed the empty, frigid classroom. On the blackboard the four rivers of France,[2] drawn with four different colored chalks, had been flowing toward their estuaries for the past three days. Snow had suddenly fallen in mid-October after eight months of drought without the transition of rain, and the twenty pupils, more or less, who lived in the villages scattered over the plateau had stopped coming. With fair weather they would return. Daru now heated only the single room that was his lodging, adjoining the classroom and giving also onto the plateau to the east. Like the class windows, his window

1. Translated by Justin O'Brien.   2. The Seine, Loire, Rhône, and Gironde rivers; French geography was taught in the French colonies.

looked to the south too. On that side the school was a few kilometers from the point where the plateau began to slope toward the south. In clear weather could be seen the purple mass of the mountain range where the gap opened onto the desert.

Somewhat warmed, Daru returned to the window from which he had first seen the two men. They were no longer visible. Hence they must have tackled the rise. The sky was not so dark, for the snow had stopped falling during the night. The morning had opened with a dirty light which had scarcely become brighter as the ceiling of clouds lifted. At two in the afternoon it seemed as if the day were merely beginning. But still this was better than those three days when the thick snow was falling amidst unbroken darkness with little gusts of wind that rattled the double door of the classroom. Then Daru had spent long hours in his room, leaving it only to go to the shed and feed the chickens or get some coal. Fortunately the delivery truck from Tadjid, the nearest village to the north, had brought his supplies two days before the blizzard. It would return in forty-eight hours.

Besides, he had enough to resist a siege, for the little room was cluttered with bags of wheat that the administration left as a stock to distribute to those of his pupils whose families had suffered from the drought. Actually they had all been victims because they were all poor. Every day Daru would distribute a ration to the children. They had missed it, he knew, during these bad days. Possibly one of the fathers or big brothers would come this afternoon and he could supply them with grain. It was just a matter of carrying them over to the next harvest. Now shiploads of wheat were arriving from France and the worst was over. But it would be hard to forget that poverty, that army of ragged ghosts wandering in the sunlight, the plateaus burned to a cinder month after month, the earth shriveled up little by little, literally scorched, every stone bursting into dust under one's foot. The sheep had died then by thousands and even a few men, here and there, sometimes without anyone's knowing.

In contrast with such poverty, he who lived almost like a monk in his remote schoolhouse, nonetheless satisfied with the little he had and with the rough life, had felt like a lord with his whitewashed walls, his narrow couch, his unpainted shelves, his well, and his weekly provision of water and food. And suddenly this snow, without warning, without the foretaste of rain. This is the way the region was, cruel to live in, even without men—who didn't help matters either. But Daru had been born here. Everywhere else, he felt exiled.

He stepped out onto the terrace in front of the schoolhouse. The two men were now halfway up the slope. He recognized the horseman as Balducci, the old gendarme he had known for a long time. Balducci was holding on the end of a rope an Arab who was walking behind him with hands bound and head lowered. The gendarme waved a greeting to which Daru did not reply, lost as he was in contemplation of the Arab dressed in a faded blue jellaba, his feet in sandals but covered with socks of heavy raw wool, his head surmounted by a narrow, short *chèche*.[3] They were approaching. Balducci was holding back his horse in order not to hurt the Arab, and the group was advancing slowly.

Within earshot, Balducci shouted: "One hour to do the three kilometers from El Ameur!" Daru did not answer. Short and square in his thick sweater, he watched them climb. Not once had the Arab raised his head. "Hello," said Daru when they got up onto the terrace. "Come in and warm up." Balducci painfully got down from his horse without letting go the rope. From under his bristling mustache he smiled at the schoolmaster. His little dark eyes, deep-set under a tanned forehead, and his mouth surrounded with wrinkles made him look attentive and studious. Daru took the bridle, led the horse to the shed, and came back to the two men, who were now waiting for him in the school. He led them into his room. "I am going to heat up the classroom," he said. "We'll be more comfortable there." When he entered the room again, Balducci was on the couch. He had undone the rope tying him to the Arab, who had squatted near the stove. His hands still bound, the *chèche* pushed back on his head, he was looking toward the window. At first Daru noticed only his huge lips, fat, smooth, almost Negroid; yet his nose was straight, his eyes were dark and full of fever. The *chèche* revealed an obstinate forehead and, under the weathered skin now rather discolored by the cold, the whole face had a restless and rebellious look that struck Daru when the Arab, turning his face toward him, looked him straight in the eyes. "Go into the other room," said the schoolmaster, "and I'll make you some mint tea." "Thanks," Balducci said. "What a chore! How I long for retirement." And addressing his prisoner in Arabic: "Come on, you." The Arab got up and, slowly, holding his bound wrists in front of him, went into the classroom.

With the tea, Daru brought a chair. But Balducci was already enthroned on the nearest pupil's desk and the Arab had squatted against the teacher's platform facing the stove, which stood between the desk and the window. When he held out the glass of tea to the prisoner, Daru hesitated at the sight of his bound hands. "He might perhaps be untied." "Sure," said Balducci. "That was for the trip." He started to get to his feet. But Daru, setting the glass on the floor, had knelt beside the Arab. Without saying anything, the Arab watched him with his feverish eyes. Once his hands were free, he rubbed his swollen wrists against each other, took the glass of tea, and sucked up the burning liquid in swift little sips.

3. Scarf; here, wound as a turban around the head. *Jellaba:* a long hooded robe worn by Arabs in North Africa.

"Good," said Daru. "And where are you headed?"

Balducci withdrew his mustache from the tea. "Here, son."

"Odd pupils! And you're spending the night?"

"No. I'm going back to El Ameur. And you will deliver this fellow to Tinguit. He is expected at police headquarters."

Balducci was looking at Daru with a friendly little smile.

"What's this story?" asked the schoolmaster. "Are you pulling my leg?"

"No, son. Those are the orders."

"The orders? I'm not . . ." Daru hesitated, not wanting to hurt the old Corsican.[4] "I mean, that's not my job."

"What! What's the meaning of that? In wartime people do all kinds of jobs."

"Then I'll wait for the declaration of war!"

Balducci nodded.

"O.K. But the orders exist and they concern you too. Things are brewing, it appears. There is talk of a forthcoming revolt. We are mobilized, in a way."

Daru still had his obstinate look.

"Listen, son," Balducci said. "I like you and you must understand. There's only a dozen of us at El Ameur to patrol throughout the whole territory of a small department[5] and I must get back in a hurry. I was told to hand this guy over to you and return without delay. He couldn't be kept there. His village was beginning to stir; they wanted to take him back. You must take him to Tinguit tomorrow before the day is over. Twenty kilometers shouldn't faze a husky fellow like you. After that, all will be over. You'll come back to your pupils and your comfortable life."

Behind the wall the horse could be heard snorting and pawing the earth. Daru was looking out the window. Decidedly, the weather was clearing and the light was increasing over the snowy plateau. When all the snow was melted, the sun would take over again and once more would burn the fields of stone. For days, still, the unchanging sky would shed its dry light on the solitary expanse where nothing had any connection with man.

"After all," he said, turning around toward Balducci, "what did he do?" And, before the gendarme had opened his mouth, he asked: "Does he speak French?"

"No, not a word. We had been looking for him for a month, but they were hiding him. He killed his cousin."

"Is he against us?"[6]

"I don't think so. But you can never be sure."

"Why did he kill?"

---

4. Balducci is a native of Corsica, a French island north of Sardinia.   5. French administrative and territorial division: like a county.   6. Against the French colonial government.

"A family squabble, I think. One owed the other grain, it seems. It's not at all clear. In short, he killed his cousin with a billhook. You know, like a sheep, *kreezk!*"

Balducci made the gesture of drawing a blade across his throat and the Arab, his attention attracted, watched him with a sort of anxiety. Daru felt a sudden wrath against the man, against all men with their rotten spite, their tireless hates, their blood lust.

But the kettle was singing on the stove. He served Balducci more tea, hesitated, then served the Arab again, who, a second time, drank avidly. His raised arms made the jellaba fall open and the schoolmaster saw his thin, muscular chest.

"Thanks, kid," Balducci said. "And now, I'm off."

He got up and went toward the Arab, taking a small rope from his pocket.

"What are you doing?" Daru asked dryly.

Balducci, disconcerted, showed him the rope.

"Don't bother."

The old gendarme hesitated. "It's up to you. Of course, you are armed?"

"I have my shotgun."

"Where?"

"In the trunk."

"You ought to have it near your bed."

"Why? I have nothing to fear."

"You're crazy, son. If there's an uprising, no one is safe, we're all in the same boat."

"I'll defend myself. I'll have time to see them coming."

Balducci began to laugh, then suddenly the mustache covered the white teeth.

"You'll have time? O.K. That's just what I was saying. You have always been a little cracked. That's why I like you, my son was like that."

At the same time he took out his revolver and put it on the desk.

"Keep it; I don't need two weapons from here to El Ameur."

The revolver shone against the black paint of the table. When the gendarme turned toward him, the schoolmaster caught the smell of leather and horseflesh.

"Listen, Balducci," Daru said suddenly, "every bit of this disgusts me, and first of all your fellow here. But I won't hand him over. Fight, yes, if I have to. But not that."

The old gendarme stood in front of him and looked at him severely.

"You're being a fool," he said slowly. "I don't like it either. You don't get used to putting a rope on a man even after years of it, and you're even ashamed—yes, ashamed. But you can't let them have their way."

"I won't hand him over," Daru said again.

"It's an order, son, and I repeat it."

"That's right. Repeat to them what I've said to you: I won't hand him over."

Balducci made a visible effort to reflect. He looked at the Arab and at Daru. At last he decided.

"No, I won't tell them anything. If you want to drop us, go ahead; I'll not denounce you. I have an order to deliver the prisoner and I'm doing so. And now you'll just sign this paper for me."

"There's no need. I'll not deny that you left him with me."

"Don't be mean with me. I know you'll tell the truth. You're from hereabouts and you are a man. But you must sign, that's the rule."

Daru opened his drawer, took out a little square bottle of purple ink, the red wooden penholder with the "sergeant-major" pen he used for making models of penmanship, and signed. The gendarme carefully folded the paper and put it into his wallet. Then he moved toward the door.

"I'll see you off," Daru said.

"No," said Balducci. "There's no use being polite. You insulted me."

He looked at the Arab, motionless in the same spot, sniffed pee-vishly, and turned away toward the door. "Good-by, son," he said. The door shut behind him. Balducci appeared suddenly outside the window and then disappeared. His footsteps were muffled by the snow. The horse stirred on the other side of the wall and several chickens fluttered in fright. A moment later Balducci reappeared outside the window leading the horse by the bridle. He walked toward the little rise without turning around and disappeared from sight with the horse following him. A big stone could be heard bouncing down. Daru walked back toward the prisoner, who, without stirring, never took his eyes off him. "Wait," the schoolmaster said in Arabic and went toward the bedroom. As he was going through the door, he had a second thought, went to the desk, took the revolver, and stuck it in his pocket. Then, without looking back, he went into his room.

For some time he lay on his couch watching the sky gradually close over, listening to the silence. It was this silence that had seemed painful to him during the first days here, after the war. He had requested a post in the little town at the base of the foothills separat-ing the upper plateaus from the desert. There, rocky walls, green and black to the north, pink and lavender to the south, marked the frontier of eternal summer. He had been named to a post farther north, on the plateau itself. In the beginning, the solitude and the silence had been hard for him on these wastelands peopled only by stones. Occasionally, furrows suggested cultivation, but they had been dug to uncover a certain kind of stone good for building. The only plowing here was to harvest rocks. Elsewhere a thin layer of soil accumulated in the hollows would be scraped out to enrich paltry village gardens. This is the way it was: bare rock covered three quarters of the region. Towns sprang up, flourished, then disappeared; men came by, loved one another or fought bitterly, then died. No one in this desert, neither he nor his guest, mattered. And yet, outside this desert neither of them, Daru knew, could have really lived.

When he got up, no noise came from the classroom. He was amazed at the unmixed joy he derived from the mere thought that the Arab might have fled and that he would be alone with no decision to make. But the prisoner was there. He had merely stretched out between the stove and the desk. With eyes open, he was staring at the ceiling. In that position, his thick lips were particularly noticeable, giving him a pouting look. "Come," said Daru. The Arab got up and followed him. In the bedroom, the schoolmaster pointed to a chair near the table under the window. The Arab sat down without taking his eyes off Daru.

"Are you hungry?"

"Yes," the prisoner said.

Daru set the table for two. He took flour and oil, shaped a cake in a frying-pan, and lighted the little stove that functioned on bottled gas. While the cake was cooking, he went out to the shed to get cheese, eggs, dates, and condensed milk. When the cake was done he set it on the window sill to cool, heated some condensed milk diluted with water, and beat up the eggs into an omelette. In one of his motions he knocked against the revolver stuck in his right pocket. He set the bowl down, went into the classroom, and put the revolver in his desk drawer. When he came back to the room, night was falling. He put on the light and served the Arab. "Eat," he said. The Arab took a piece of the cake, lifted it eagerly to his mouth, and stopped short.

"And you?" he asked.

"After you. I'll eat too."

The thick lips opened slightly. The Arab hesitated, then bit into the cake determinedly.

The meal over, the Arab looked at the schoolmaster. "Are you the judge?"

"No, I'm simply keeping you until tomorrow."

"Why do you eat with me?"

"I'm hungry."

The Arab fell silent. Daru got up and went out. He brought back a folding bed from the shed, set it up between the table and the stove, perpendicular to his own bed. From a large suitcase which, upright in a corner, served as a shelf for papers, he took two blankets and arranged them on the camp bed. Then he stopped, felt useless, and sat down on his bed. There was nothing more to do or to get ready. He had to look at this man. He looked at him, therefore, trying to imagine his face bursting with rage. He couldn't do so. He could see nothing but the dark yet shining eyes and the animal mouth.

"Why did you kill him?" he asked in a voice whose hostile tone surprised him.

The Arab looked away.

"He ran away. I ran after him."

He raised his eyes to Daru again and they were full of a sort of woeful interrogation. "Now what will they do to me?"

"Are you afraid?"

He stiffened, turning his eyes away.

"Are you sorry?"

The Arab stared at him openmouthed. Obviously he did not understand. Daru's annoyance was growing. At the same time he felt awkward and self-conscious with his big body wedged between the two beds.

"Lie down there," he said impatiently. "That's your bed."

The Arab didn't move. He called to Daru:

"Tell me!"

The schoolmaster looked at him.

"Is the gendarme coming back tomorrow?"

"I don't know."

"Are you coming with us?"

"I don't know. Why?"

The prisoner got up and stretched out on top of the blankets, his feet toward the window. The light from the electric bulb shone straight into his eyes and he closed them at once.

"Why?" Daru repeated, standing beside the bed.

The Arab opened his eyes under the blinding light and looked at him, trying not to blink.

"Come with us," he said.

In the middle of the night, Daru was still not asleep. He had gone to bed after undressing completely; he generally slept naked. But when he suddenly realized that he had nothing on, he hesitated. He felt vulnerable and the temptation came to him to put his clothes back on. Then he shrugged his shoulders; after all, he wasn't a child and, if need be, he could break his adversary in two. From his bed he could observe him, lying on his back, still motionless with his eyes closed under the harsh light. When Daru turned out the light, the darkness seemed to coagulate all of a sudden. Little by little, the night came back to life in the window where the starless sky was stirring gently. The schoolmaster soon made out the body lying at his feet. The Arab still did not move, but his eyes seemed open. A faint wind was prowling around the schoolhouse. Perhaps it would drive away the clouds and the sun would reappear.

During the night the wind increased. The hens fluttered a little and then were silent. The Arab turned over on his side with his back to Daru, who thought he heard him moan. Then he listened for his guest's breathing, become heavier and more regular. He listened to that breath so close to him and mused without being able to go to sleep. In this room where he had been sleeping alone for a year, this presence bothered him. But it bothered him also by imposing on him a sort of brotherhood he knew well but refused to accept in the present circumstances. Men who share the same rooms, soldiers or prisoners, develop a strange alliance as if, having cast off their armor with their clothing, they fraternized every evening, over and above their differences, in the ancient community of dream and fatigue. But Daru shook himself; he didn't like such musings, and it was essential to sleep.

A little later, however, when the Arab stirred slightly, the schoolmaster was still not asleep. When the prisoner made a second move, he stiffened, on the alert. The Arab was lifting himself slowly on his arms with almost the motion of a sleepwalker. Seated upright in bed, he waited motionless without turning his head toward Daru, as if he were listening attentively. Daru did not stir; it had just occurred to him that the revolver was still in the drawer of his desk. It was better to act at once. Yet he continued to observe the prisoner, who, with the same slithery motion, put his feet on the ground, waited again, then began to stand up slowly. Daru was about to call out to him when the Arab began to walk, in a quite natural but extraordinarily silent way. He was heading toward the door at the end of the room that opened into the shed. He lifted the latch with precaution and went out, pushing the door behind him but without shutting it. Daru had not stirred. "He is running away," he merely thought. "Good riddance!" Yet he listened attentively. The hens were not fluttering; the guest must be on the plateau. A faint sound of water reached him, and he didn't know what it was until the Arab again stood framed in the doorway, closed the door carefully, and came back to bed without a sound. Then Daru turned his back on him and fell asleep. Still later he seemed, from the depths of his sleep, to hear furtive steps around the schoolhouse. "I'm dreaming! I'm dreaming!" he repeated to himself. And he went on sleeping.

When he awoke, the sky was clear; the loose window let in a cold, pure air. The Arab was asleep, hunched up under the blankets now, his mouth open, utterly relaxed. But when Daru shook him, he started dreadfully, staring at Daru with wild eyes as if he had never seen him and such a frightened expression that the schoolmaster stepped back. "Don't be afraid. It's me. You must eat." The Arab nodded his head and said yes. Calm had returned to his face, but his expression was vacant and listless.

The coffee was ready. They drank it seated together on the folding bed as they munched their pieces of the cake. Then Daru led the Arab under the shed and showed him the faucet where he washed. He went back into the room, folded the blankets and the bed, made his own bed and put the room in order. Then he went through the classroom and out onto the terrace. The sun was already rising in the blue sky; a soft, bright light was bathing the deserted plateau. On the ridge the snow was melting in spots. The stones were about to reappear. Crouched on the edge of the plateau, the schoolmaster looked at the deserted expanse. He thought of Balducci. He had hurt him, for he had sent him off in a way as if he didn't want to be associated with him. He could still hear the gendarme's farewell and, without knowing why, he felt strangely empty and vulnerable. At that moment, from the other side of the schoolhouse, the prisoner coughed. Daru listened to him almost despite himself and then, furious, threw a pebble that whistled through the air before sinking into the snow. That man's stupid crime revolted him, but to hand him over was contrary to honor. Merely thinking of it made him smart with humiliation. And he cursed at one and the same time his own people who had sent him this Arab and the Arab too who had dared to kill and not managed to get away. Daru got up, walked in a circle on the terrace, waited motionless, and then went back into the schoolhouse.

The Arab, leaning over the cement floor of the shed, was washing his teeth with two fingers. Daru looked at him and said: "Come." He went back into the room ahead of the prisoner. He slipped a hunting-jacket on over his sweater and put on walking-shoes. Standing, he waited until the Arab had put on his *chèche* and sandals. They went into the classroom and the schoolmaster pointed to the exit, saying: "Go ahead." The fellow didn't budge. "I'm coming," said Daru. The Arab went out. Daru went back into the room and made a package of pieces of rusk, dates, and sugar. In the classroom, before going out, he hesitated a second in front of his desk, then crossed the threshold and locked the door. "That's the way," he said. He started toward the east, followed by the prisoner. But, a short distance from the schoolhouse, he thought he heard a slight sound behind them. He retraced his steps and examined the surroundings of the house, there was no one there. The Arab watched him without seeming to understand. "Come on," said Daru.

They walked for an hour and rested beside a sharp peak of limestone. The snow was melting faster and faster and the sun was drinking up the puddles at once, rapidly cleaning the plateau, which gradually dried and vibrated like the air itself. When they resumed

walking, the ground rang under their feet. From time to time a bird
rent the space in front of them with a joyful cry. Daru breathed in
deeply the fresh morning light. He felt a sort of rapture before the
vast familiar expanse, now almost entirely yellow under its dome of
blue sky. They walked an hour more, descending toward the south.
They reached a level height made up of crumbly rocks. From there
on, the plateau sloped down, eastward, toward a low plain where
there were a few spindly trees and, to the south, toward outcroppings
of rock that gave the landscape a chaotic look.

Daru surveyed the two directions. There was nothing but the sky
on the horizon. Not a man could be seen. He turned toward the
Arab, who was looking at him blankly. Daru held out the package to
him. "Take it," he said. "There are dates, bread, and sugar. You
can hold out for two days. Here are a thousand francs too." The
Arab took the package and the money but kept his full hands at chest
level as if he didn't know what to do with what was being given him.
"Now look," the schoolmaster said as he pointed in the direction of
the east, "there's the way to Tinguit. You have a two-hour walk. At
Tinguit you'll find the administration and the police. They are
expecting you." The Arab looked toward the east, still holding the
package and the money against his chest. Daru took his elbow and
turned him rather roughly toward the south. At the foot of the height
on which they stood could be seen a faint path. "That's the trail
across the plateau. In a day's walk from here you'll find pasturelands
and the first nomads. They'll take you in and shelter you according
to their law." The Arab had now turned toward Daru and a sort of
panic was visible in his expression. "Listen," he said. Daru shook his
head: "No, be quiet. Now I'm leaving you." He turned his back on
him, took two long steps in the direction of the school, looked hesitantly at the motionless Arab, and started off again. For a few minutes he heard nothing but his own step resounding on the cold ground
and did not turn his head. A moment later, however, he turned
around. The Arab was still there on the edge of the hill, his arms
hanging now, and he was looking at the schoolmaster. Daru felt
something rise in his throat. But he swore with impatience, waved
vaguely, and started off again. He had already gone some distance
when he again stopped and looked. There was no longer anyone on
the hill.

Daru hesitated. The sun was now rather high in the sky and was
beginning to beat down on his head. The schoolmaster retraced his
steps, at first somewhat uncertainly, then with decision. When he
reached the little hill, he was bathed in sweat. He climbed it as fast
as he could and stopped, out of breath, at the top. The rock-fields to
the south stood out sharply against the blue sky, but on the plain to
the east a steamy heat was already rising. And in that slight haze,

Daru, with heavy heart, made out the Arab walking slowly on the road to prison.

A little later, standing before the window of the classroom, the schoolmaster was watching the clear light bathing the whole surface of the plateau, but he hardly saw it. Behind him on the blackboard, among the winding French rivers, sprawled the clumsily chalked-up words he had just read: "You handed over our brother. You will pay for this." Daru looked at the sky, the plateau, and, beyond, the invisible lands stretching all the way to the sea. In this vast landscape he had loved so much, he was alone.

Masterpieces of the Twentieth Century: Contemporary Explorations

The closer we come to contemporary times, the more disagreement there is over what is to be called a "masterpiece." Hundreds of works and authors claim to represent the mainstream of modern art and culture, and reviewers frequently inform their readers that they are in the presence of a "contemporary masterpiece." But what does this mean? Is there something radically different about today's literature? Or does modern literary tradition imply instead an evolution of style and content, so that our job is to read with the same care we gave to earlier works, while becoming acquainted with new subject matters, new angles of vision, and new techniques of expression? If the latter is true, as the editors of this anthology believe, we know how to proceed: our experience as readers of literature (*your* experience as a reader of this anthology) provides a basic familiarity with many of the themes, strategies, and cultural contexts that reemerge in contemporary literature.

These authors, from Borges to Soyinka, represent a great range of styles that cannot be subsumed under commonly accepted categories. Our texts move from fragmented visions of ambiguous reality to an almost documentary picture of society, from hallucinations and "magical realism" to medically accurate depictions of death, from insulated drama on an almost bare stage to a multimedia celebration of the clash of cultures. Yet just as the modernists of the first part of the century claimed to discover new modes of perception and literary expression, later writers propose their own even more "accurate" representations of reality, exploit different subject matter, reach out to new audiences, and explore different ways of relating to their readers.

A great deal of contemporary literature prolongs the modernist experiment in certain characteristic ways. Some writers, for example, push to an extreme the modernist refusal of positivist certainty, and create works that are essentially structures of ambiguity (Borges, Beckett, Robbe-Grillet); here, literary language is highly self-reflexive, constantly referring to its own constitution as an act of writing, so that it tends to bring exterior reality into competition with the self-contained play of words. Other writers, extending in their own way the modernist claim to achieve a "truer" reality, ignore modernist emphasis on aesthetic shaping and prefer a more direct representation of historical flow. They may return to the familiar forms of the realistic historical novel or, on the other hand, subvert all sense of traditional genre with works that incorporate actual documents such as personal letters, newspaper clippings, or comments and drawings in the margin to prove their "real" status as a part of contemporary culture. Throughout, they imply that the aesthetic emphasis of earlier modernism proposes an artificially symmetrical picture of human experience which is anchored, moreover, in a single and somewhat solipsistic authorial vision; and that a reality which is basically "jagged" (Ezra Pound's term) needs to be represented with all its rough edges.

This shift of sensibility (which some have unhelpfully labeled "postmodernism") takes to its logical conclusion the modernist emphasis on fragmentation and discontinuity as ways of conveying a sense of reality. When such authors look to the scientific revolution of the early part of the century, it is recognition of randomness and shifting perceptions that is seen as crucial. The essential reference is to Werner Heisenberg's uncertainty principle (see p. 1364) which emphasizes the *approximate* nature of any description of reality, and the fact that the observer's position relative to what is observed changes from moment to moment. A similar emphasis on shifting patterns of perception as constituting identity appears in the later development of Freudian psychoanalysis. Here, attention is displaced from subconscious and instinctual drives to the concept of dialogue and exchange, where individual identity is not so much discovered and adjusted through proper therapy as constantly being defined through interaction with others. Literary predecessors evoked by postmodernist critics include the Joyce of *Finnegans Wake*, who dissolves language into a boundless network of wordplay and allusion; Kafka, who dramatizes unresolvable contradictions as metaphors for reality; or Borges, the master of the verbal labyrinth where historical fact and fiction are indistinguishable. The perfect expression of postmodern consciousness is undoubtedly semiotics, the science of signs, which analyzes networks of cultural, psychoanalytic, and linguistic evidence in its study of the "gamelike" construction of meaning.

Readers will find that there are certain easily identified strategies at work in this literature, strategies whose general aim is to avoid creating any sense of completeness, or any artificially fixed center in which to anchor our understanding. In fiction, this literature replaces the authorial personality (the coordinating core, for example, of Proust's great novel or of Joyce's *Portrait of the Artist*) with an anonymous and even self-contradictory narrative viewpoint (the "unnamable" narrator in Beckett's novel, or the impersonal and contradictory narrative perspective in Robbe-Grillet's "The Secret Room"). Just as there is no unified authorial perspective, so individual characters do not develop a consistent psychological identity. Instead, they must be read in terms of the specific situations in which they appear. Like Hamm and Clov in Beckett's *Endgame*, such characters interact in a meaningless void, reacting moment by moment inside a permanent present, located in an ambiguously allusive situation that cannot be defined in external terms. Nor does the time in which they appear have any solid chronological basis. It leads nowhere: in *Endgame*, we are not even sure whether the action concludes or is simply part of a repetitive pattern. Time in "The Secret Room" moves backward; in Robbe-Grillet's novels and his film *Last Year at Marienbad* it is made up of contradictory scenes so that any settled sense of what happened, or when, is not available. There is no plot, and the narrative line is not patterned by a beginning, middle, and end; overall, there is no sense of action developing toward a logical conclusion. The ambiguity of appearances is heightened by putting history and fantasy on the same level (Borges), or by including impossible "magical" scenes in the midst of apparently realistic narrative (García Márquez).

All these strategies actually serve to engage the reader in a new way, by refusing to provide even the first stage of an interpretation of reality, and offering instead a collection of ambiguously related fragments, strangely emphasized silences, and merely potential themes. The burden, in fact, is placed squarely and openly on the reader to reconstruct a meaning in full awareness of the reading process itself: a tactic foreshadowed two centuries ago by *Tristram Shandy*, and more recently by Bertolt Brecht's "alienation technique" with its refusal of dramatic illusion and insistence on the audience's maintaining a critical distance. It is a form built on a calculated refusal of easy coherence, an "antiform" which requires a great deal of artistic patterning to be convincing. Some of these texts have been called "anti-literature" for their refusal to provide the aesthetic completion suggested by the term "literature." A truly random work, however, would be nothing more than a collection of unrelated words (like Tzara's Dada poem, created from newspaper clippings shaken in a paper bag). In order to impress on the reader the idea of a world which is *not* aesthetically arranged, the authors of "incomplete" literature logically devise artistic forms that continually focus our attention on the artificiality of any totalizing perspective.

Several of the authors included here do not subscribe, however, to the notion of representing contemporary reality by means of structures of incompletion. There are those who—like García Márquez, Mishima, and Soyinka—are brilliant formal experimenters but focus fairly directly on cultural and psychological issues. García Márquez comes the closest to the European "new wave," or radically experimental, techniques, with his manipulation of perspective through magical realism. His focus is clearly the political and cultural reality of Latin America, however, even when he jokes about acquiring a reputation for writing "real literature" by writing impenetrably and imitating Robbe-Grillet. Solzhenitsyn and Narayan are chiefly interested in conveying a picture of their society and the individual and cultural tensions within it; Ellison presents an extraordinary mixture of the harshest social realism framed by a visionary, almost surrealist perspective. Lessing experiments with perspective in several works but characteristically bases her analyses of modern society in a realistic narrative, with deviations explained as images of insanity or (in the interlocking diaries of *The Golden Notebook*) as a conscious technical experiment.

Yet another aspect these writers have in common is an awareness of cultural heterogeneity, shown by the prevalence of multicultural themes and the realistic or direct presentation of social problems that are characteristically *not* seen within the framework of an all-encompassing answer. Without dismissing the presentation of social reality in earlier literature of the twentieth century (of which Mann is a prime example), it is still possible to say that recent years have seen an unprecedented growth in the recognition of different ethnic, sexual, and cultural identities, both as political facts and as the subject matter of literature. Cultural isolation is no longer the norm among nations, and a writer like the Japanese Mishima is fully acquainted with Western literature in addition to his own. Narayan joins other writers who have experienced two types of civilization as he describes the still-unre-solved clash of cultures that defines experience for many today. Emerging African nations have taken visible pride in fostering their own indigenous languages and cultures, and much African literature displays both a native tradition and the coexistence of other (European and Islamic) cultures on the same continent. The "melting pot" of American society no longer rep-resents a blandly homogeneous soup, but requires an understanding of sep-arate ethnic identities inside the whole, and Afro-American, Yiddish, Chicano, Canadian, and Native American literature—as well as regional literatures—have established their own images and value. Since women have been writ-ing literature as long as literature has existed, it would be incorrect to say that literature by women or concerning women is new. Nonetheless, just as women won many legal, political, and economic rights in the modern era, the realistic representation of issues involving women and their position in society emerges particularly strongly toward the middle of this century.

The intricate meetings of cultures, and the difficult integration of com-peting ethnic, sexual, or racial identities in a single culture, have provided the theme of much current writing. Yet there is a larger continuity insofar as these contemporary explorations continue earlier themes (such as cultural and individual identity, or the existence of a meaningful universe) and hold to the notion that style must evolve to reflect current ideas of language and expressive form. The pluralism of twentieth-century society is reflected in its literary styles, and in the place accorded pluralism in the literary canon. In a broad sense, the postmodern decomposition of aesthetic wholes, and its insistent teasing out of contradictory layers of reality, has something in com-mon with a representative pluralism which explores areas beyond the more homogeneous world view of prewar Western society—areas that were earlier seen as marginal to the positivist, European-centered image of Western cul-ture. These contemporary explorations continue the pattern of their prede-cessors, however, by attempting evermore accurate representations of reality through experiments with expressive form, and through increasingly specific historical reference.

FURTHER READING

Ihab Hassan's *The Dismemberment of Orpheus: Toward a Postmodern Lit-erature* (1971) is a good introduction to changes in literary strategy growing out of modernism; it combines theoretical discussion with analyses of Hem-ingway, Kafka, Genet, and Beckett. *Romanticism, Modernism, Postmodern-ism*, ed. Harry R. Garvin (1977), is a useful collection of theoretical essays and practical criticism that describe changing views of the artistic imagina-tion. Essays in *Innovation/Renovation, New Perspectives on the Humanities*, ed. by Ihab and Sally Hassan (1983), explore perspectives on change in contemporary Western culture; drawing on intellectual history, theater, phi-losophy, psychoanalysis and literary theory, they outline an "emergent pat-tern" of interdisciplinary attitudes. H. H. Arnason's *History of Modern Art, Painting, Sculpture, Architecture* (1977), copiously illustrated with plates and photographs, contains many examples of contemporary explorations in the different arts. Abstract Expressionism, concrete art and lettrism, "assem-blage" art, Pop Art and Happenings introduce the reader to different modes of artistic perception at mid-century.

JORGE LUIS BORGES
1899—

Although other modernist writers are known for their formal innovations, it is the Argentine Jorge Luis Borges who represents, above all, the gamelike or playful aspect of literary creation. Historical reality is only one of the possible realities in Borges' idealist universe, which joins the worlds of fantasy and science fiction in considering everything that can be imagined as having equal claim on our attention. His is a world of pure thought, where abstract fictional games are played out when an initial situation or concept is pushed to its elegantly logical extreme. Consequently, there is no room for the artificial constraints imposed by traditional artistic attempts to represent reality: no need for psychological consistency, for a realistic setting, or for a story that unfolds in ordinary time and space. The voice telling the story becomes lost inside the setting it creates just as, in a cartoon by Saul Steinberg or a drawing by M. C. Escher, the hand holding the pen draws the rest of the landscape in which it appears. Not unexpectedly, this thorough immersion in the play of subjective imagination appealed to writers like the French "new novelists," who were experimenting with shifting perspectives and a refusal of "objective" reality. For a long time, Borges' European reputation outstripped his prestige in his native land.

Borges was born in Buenos Aires, Argentina, on August 24, 1899, to a prosperous family whose ancestors were distinguished in Argentine history. The family moved early to a large house whose library and garden were to form an essential part of his literary imagination. His paternal grandmother being English, the young Borges knew English as soon as Spanish, and was educated by an English tutor until age nine. Traveling in Europe, the family was caught in Geneva at the outbreak of World War I; Borges attended secondary school in Switzerland and throughout the war, during which time he learned French and German. After the war they moved to Spain, where he associated with a group of young experimental poets called Ultraists. When Borges returned home in 1921, he founded his own group of Argentine Ultraists (their mural-review, *Prisma*, was printed on sign paper and plastered on walls); became close friends with the philosopher Macedonio Fernandez, whose dedication to pure thought and linguistic intricacies greatly influenced his own attitudes; and contributed regularly to the avant-garde review *Martin Fierro*, at that time associated with an apolitical "art for art's sake" attitude quite at odds with that of the Boedo group of politically committed writers. Although devoted to pure art, Borges consistently opposed the military dictatorship of Juan Perón and made his political views plain in speeches and nonliterary writings even if they were not included in his fiction. His attitude did not go unnoticed: in 1946, the Perón regime removed him from the librarian's post which he had held since 1938 and offered him a job as chicken inspector.

During the thirties, Borges turned to short narrative pieces and in 1935 published a collection of sketches titled *Universal History of Infamy*. His more mature stories—brief, metaphysical fictions whose density and elegance at times approach poetry—came as an experiment after a head injury and operation in 1938. *The Garden of Forking Paths* (1941), his first major collection, introduced him to a wider public as an intellectual and idealist writer, whose short stories subordinated familiar techniques of character, scene, plot, and narrative voice to a central idea, which was often a philosophical concept. This concept was not used as a lesson or dogma, but as the starting point of fantastic elaborations to entertain readers inside the game of literature.

Borges' imaginative world is an immense labyrinth, a "garden of forking paths" in which images of maze and infinite mirroring, cyclical repetition and recall, illustrate the effort of an elusive narrative voice to understand its own significance and that of the world. In "Borges and I," he has commented on the parallel existence of two Borgeses: the one who exists in his work (the one his readers know), and the living, fleshly identity felt by the man who sets pen to paper. "Little by little, I am giving over everything to him . . . I do not know which one of us has written this page." Borges has written on the idea (derived from the British philosophers Hume and Berkeley) of the individual self as a cluster of different perceptions, and he further elaborates this notion in his fictional proliferation of identities and alternate realities. Disdaining the "psychological fakery" of realistic novels (the "draggy novel of characters"), he prefers writing that is openly artful, concerned with technique for its own sake, and invents its own multidimensional reality.

Stories in *The Garden of Forking Paths*, *Fictions* (1944), and *The Aleph* (1949) develop these themes in a variety of styles. Borges is fond of detective stories (and has written a number of them) in which the search for an elusive explanation, given carefully planted clues, matters more than how recognizable the characters may be. In "Death and the Compass," a mysterious murderer leaves tantalizing traces that refer to points of the compass and lead the detective into a fatal trap that closes on him at a fourth compass point symbolized by the architectural lozenges of the house where he dies. The author composes an art of puzzles and discovery, a grand code that treats our universe as a giant library where meaning is locked away in endless hexagonal galleries ("The Library of Babel"), as an enormous lottery whose chances are all the events of our lives ("The Lottery in Babylon"), as a series of dreams within dreams ("The Circular Ruins"), or as a small iridescent sphere containing all of the points in space ("The Aleph"). In "Pierre Menard, Author of the *Quixote*," the narrator is a scholarly reviewer of a certain fictitious Menard, whose masterwork has been to rewrite *Don Quixote* as if it were created today: not revise it, nor yet transcribe it, but actually reinvent it word for word. He has succeeded; the two texts are "verbally identical" although Menard's modern version is "more ambiguous" than Cervantes' and thus "infinitely richer."

The imaginary universe of "Tlön, Uqbar, Orbis Tertius" exemplifies the mixture of fact and fiction with which Borges invites us to speculate on the solidity of our own world. The narrator is engaged in tracking down mysterious references to a country called Tlön, whose language, science, and literature are exactly opposite (and perhaps related to) our own. For example, the Tlönians use verbs or adjectives instead of nouns, since they have no concept of objects in space, and their science consists of an association of ideas in which the most astounding theory becomes the truth. In a post-script, the narrator reveals that the encyclopedia has turned out to be an immense scholarly hoax, yet also mentions that strange and unearthly objects—recognizably from Tlön—have recently been found.

The intricate, riddling, mazelike ambiguity of Borges' stories has given him an international reputation and influence, so that a "style like Borges" is a recognized term. In Argentina, he was given the prestigious post of Director of the National Library after the fall of Perón in 1955 and in 1961 he shared the International Publishers' Prize with Samuel Beckett. Always nearsighted, he grew increasingly blind in the mid-fifties and he was forced to dictate his work. Nonetheless, he continued to travel, teach, and lecture in the company of his wife, Else Astete Milan, whom he married in 1967. Borges now lives in his beloved Buenos Aires, the city he celebrated in his first volume of poetry.

"The Garden of Forking Paths" begins as a simple spy story purporting to reveal the hidden truth about a German bombing raid during World War I. Borges alludes to documented facts: the geographic setting of the town of Albert and the Ancre River; a famous Chinese novel as Ts'ui Pên's proposed model; the *History of the World War (1914–1918)* published by B. H. Liddell Hart in 1934. Official history is undermined on the first page, however, both by the newly discovered confession of Dr. Yu Tsun and by his editor's suspiciously defensive footnote. Ultimately, Yu Tsun will learn from his ancestor's novel that history is a labyrinth of alternate possibilities (much like the "alternate worlds" of science fiction).

Borges executes his detective story with the traditional carefully planted clues. We know from the beginning that Yu Tsun—even though arrested—has successfully outwitted his rival Captain Richard Madden; that his problem was to convey the name of a bombing target to his chief in Berlin; that he went to the telephone book to locate someone capable of transmitting his message; and that he had one bullet in his revolver. The cut-off phone call, the chase at the railroad station, and Madden's hasty arrival at Dr. Albert's house provide the excitement and pressure expected in a straightforward detective plot. Quite different spatial and temporal horizons open up half-way through, however. Coincidences—those chance relationships that might well have happened differently—introduce the idea of forking paths or alter-nate possible routes for history. Both Yu Tsun and Richard Madden are aliens trying to prove their worth inside their respective bureaucracies; the road to Stephen Albert's house turns mazelike always to the left; the only suitable name in the phone book—the man Yu Tsun must kill—is a Sinol-ogist who has reconstructed the labyrinthine text written long ago by Yu Tsun's ancestor. This text, Ts'ui Pên's *The Garden of Forking Paths*, describes the universe as an infinite series of alternate versions of experience. In dif-ferent versions of the story (taking place at different times), Albert and Yu Tsun are enemies—or friends—or not even there. The war and Richard Madden appear diminished (although no less real) in such a kaleidoscopic perspective, for they exist in only one of many possible dimensions. Yet Madden hurries up the walk, and current reality returns to demand Albert's death. It may seem as though the vision of other worlds in which Albert continues to exist (or is Yu Tsun's enemy) would soften the murderer's remorse for his deed. Instead, it makes more poignant the narrator's realization that in this dimension no other way could be found.

George R. McMurray, *Jorge Luis Borges* (1980), is a general introduction to the man and his work. Anna Maria Barrenechea, *Borges The Labyrinth Maker*, rev. ed., translated by R. Lima (1965), introduces Borges' intricate style and includes biographical information. Fernando Sorrentino, *Seven Conversations with Jorge Luis Borges*, translated by Clark M. Zlotchew (1981), is a series of informal, widely ranging interviews from 1972, with a prefaced list of the topics of each conversation and, in appendix, an interview with Borges translator Norman Thomas di Giovanni ("Borges in English") and notes identifying personalities mentioned by Borges.

The Garden of Forking Paths[1]

On page 22 of Liddell Hart's *History of World War I* you will read that an attack against the Serre-Montauban line by thirteen British divisions (supported by 1,400 artillery pieces), planned for the 24th of July, 1916, had to be postponed until the morning of the 29th. The torrential rains, Captain Liddell Hart comments, caused this delay, an insignificant one, to be sure.

The following statement, dictated, reread and signed by Dr. Yu Tsun, former professor of English at the *Hochschule* at Tsingtao,[2] throws an unsuspected light over the whole affair. The first two pages of the document are missing.

". . . and I hung up the receiver. Immediately afterwards, I recognized the voice that had answered in German. It was that of Captain Richard Madden. Madden's presence in Viktor Runeberg's apartment meant the end of our anxieties and and—but this seemed, *or should have seemed*, very secondary to me—also the end of our lives. It meant that Runeberg had been arrested or murdered.[3] Before the sun set on that day, I would encounter the same fate. Madden was implacable. Or rather, he was obliged to be so. An Irishman at the service of England, a man accused of laxity and perhaps of treason, how could he fail to seize and be thankful for such a miraculous opportunity: the discovery, capture, maybe even the death of two agents of the German Reich?[4] I went up to my room; absurdly I locked the door and threw myself on my back on the narrow iron cot. Through the window I saw the familiar roofs and the cloud-shaded six o'clock sun. It seemed incredible to me that that day without premonitions or symbols should be the one of my inexorable

---

1. Translated by Donald A. Yates.   2. Or Ch'ing-tao: a major port in East China, part of territory leased to (and developed by) Germany in 1898. *Hochschule*: university (German).
3. An hypothesis both hateful and odd. The Prussian spy Hans Rabener, alias Viktor Runeberg, attacked with drawn automatic the bearer of the warrant for his arrest, Captain Richard Madden. The latter, in self-defense, inflicted the wound which brought about Runeberg's death. (Editor's note.) [This entire note is by Borges as "Editor."]   4. Empire (German).

death. In spite of my dead father, in spite of having been a child in
a symmetrical garden of Hai Feng, was I—now—going to die? Then
I reflected that everything happens to a man precisely, precisely *now*.
Centuries of centuries and only in the present do things happen;
countless men in the air, on the face of the earth and the sea, and
all that really is happening is happening to me . . . The almost intolerable recollection of Madden's horselike face banished these wanderings. In the midst of my hatred and terror (it means nothing to
me now to speak of terror, now that I have mocked Richard Madden,
now that my throat yearns for the noose) it occurred to me that that
tumultuous and doubtless happy warrior did not suspect that I possessed the Secret. The name of the exact location of the new British
artillery park on the River Ancre. A bird streaked across the gray sky
and blindly I translated it into an airplane and that airplane into
many (against the French sky) annihilating the artillery station with
vertical bombs. If only my mouth, before a bullet shattered it, could
cry out that secret name so it could be heard in Germany . . . My
human voice was very weak. How might I make it carry to the ear of
the Chief? To the ear of that sick and hateful man who knew nothing of Runeberg and me save that we were in Staffordshire[5] and who
was waiting in vain for our report in his arid office in Berlin, endlessly examining newspapers . . . I said out loud: *I must flee.* I sat up
noiselessly, in a useless perfection of silence, as if Madden were already
lying in wait for me. Something—perhaps the mere vain ostentation
of proving my resources were nil—made me look through my pockets. I found what I knew I would find. The American watch, the
nickel chain and the square coin, the key ring with the incriminating
useless keys to Runeberg's apartment, the notebook, a letter which I
resolved to destroy immediately (and which I did not destroy), a crown,
two shillings and a few pence, the red and blue pencil, the handkerchief, the revolver with one bullet. Absurdly, I took it in my hand
and weighed it in order to inspire courage within myself. Vaguely I
thought that a pistol report can be heard at a great distance. In ten
minutes my plan was perfected. The telephone book listed the name
of the only person capable of transmitting the message; he lived in a
suburb of Fenton,[6] less than a half hour's train ride away.

   I am a cowardly man. I say it now, now that I have carried to its
end a plan whose perilous nature no one can deny. I know its execution was terrible. I didn't do it for Germany, no. I care nothing
for a barbarous country which imposed upon me the abjection of
being a spy. Besides, I know of a man from England—a modest
man—who for me is no less great than Goethe.[7] I talked with him

---

5. County in west central England.   6. In Lincolnshire, a county in east England.   7. Johann
Wolfgang von Goethe (1749–1832), German poet, novelist, and dramatist, author of *Faust*; often
taken as representing the peak of German cultural achievement.

for scarcely an hour, but during that hour he was Goethe . . . I did it because I sensed that the Chief somehow feared people of my race—for the innumerable ancestors who merge within me. I wanted to prove to him that a yellow man could save his armies. Besides, I had to flee from Captain Madden. His hands and his voice could call at my door at any moment. I dressed silently, bade farewell to myself in the mirror, went downstairs, scrutinized the peaceful street and went out. The station was not far from my home, but I judged it wise to take a cab. I argued that in this way I ran less risk of being recognized; the fact is that in the deserted street I felt myself visible and vulnerable, infinitely so. I remember that I told the cab driver to stop a short distance before the main entrance. I got out with voluntary, almost painful slowness; I was going to the village of Ashgrove but I bought a ticket for a more distant station. The train left within a very few minutes, at eight-fifty. I hurried; the next one would leave at nine-thirty. There was hardly a soul on the platform. I went through the coaches; I remember a few farmers, a woman dressed in mourning, a young boy who was reading with fervor the *Annals* of Tacitus,[8] a wounded and happy soldier. The coaches jerked forward at last. A man whom I recognized ran in vain to the end of the platform. It was Captain Richard Madden. Shattered, trembling, I shrank into the far corner of the seat, away from the dreaded window.

From this broken state I passed into an almost abject felicity. I told myself that the duel had already begun and that I had won the first encounter by frustrating, even if for forty minutes, even if by a stroke of fate, the attack of my adversary. I argued that this slightest of victories foreshadowed a total victory. I argued (no less fallaciously) that my cowardly felicity proved that I was a man capable of carrying out the adventure successfully. From this weakness I took strength that did not abandon me. I foresee that man will resign himself each day to more atrocious undertakings; soon there will be no one but warriors and brigands; I give them this counsel: *The author of an atrocious undertaking ought to imagine that he has already accomplished it, ought to impose upon himself a future as irrevocable as the past.* Thus I proceeded as my eyes of a man already dead registered the elapsing of that day, which was perhaps the last, and the diffusion of the night. The train ran gently along, amid ash trees. It stopped, almost in the middle of the fields. No one announced the name of the station. "Ashgrove?" I asked a few lads on the platform. "Ashgrove," they replied. I got off.

A lamp enlightened the platform but the faces of the boys were in shadow. One questioned me, "Are you going to Dr. Stephen Albert's

---

8. Cornelius Tacitus (A.D. 55–117), Roman historian whose *Annals* give a vivid picture of the decadence and corruption of the Roman Empire under Tiberius, Claudius, and Nero.

house?" Without waiting for my answer, another said, "The house is a long way from here, but you won't get lost if you take this road to the left and at every crossroads turn again to your left." I tossed them a coin (my last), descended a few stone steps and started down the solitary road. It went downhill, slowly. It was of elemental earth; overhead the branches were tangled; the low, full moon seemed to accompany me.

For an instant, I thought that Richard Madden in some way had penetrated my desperate plan. Very quickly, I understood that that was impossible. The instructions to turn always to the left reminded me that such was the common procedure for discovering the central point of certain labyrinths. I have some understanding of labyrinths: not for nothing am I the great grandson of that Ts'ui Pên who was governor of Yunnan and who renounced worldly power in order to write a novel that might be even more populous than the *Hung Lu Meng*[9] and to construct a labyrinth in which all men would become lost. Thirteen years he dedicated to these heterogeneous tasks, but the hand of a stranger murdered him—and his novel was incoherent and no one found the labyrinth. Beneath English trees I meditated on that lost maze: I imagined it inviolate and perfect at the secret crest of a mountain; I imagined it erased by rice fields or beneath the water; I imagined it infinite, no longer composed of octagonal kiosks and returning paths, but of rivers and provinces and kingdoms . . . I thought of a labyrinth of labyrinths, of one sinuous spreading labyrinth that would encompass the past and the future and in some way involve the stars. Absorbed in these illusory images, I forgot my destiny of one pursued. I felt myself to be, for an unknown period of time, an abstract perceiver of the world. The vague, living countryside, the moon, the remains of the day worked on me, as well as the slope of the road which eliminated any possibility of weariness. The afternoon was intimate, infinite. The road descended and forked among the now confused meadows. A high-pitched, almost syllabic music approached and receded in the shifting of the wind, dimmed by leaves and distance. I thought that a man can be an enemy of other men, of the moments of other men, but not of a country: not of fireflies, words, gardens, streams of water, sunsets. Thus I arrived before a tall, rusty gate. Between the iron bars I made out a poplar grove and a pavilion. I understood suddenly two things, the first trivial, the second almost unbelievable: the music came from the pavilion, and the music was Chinese. For precisely that reason I had openly accepted it without paying it any heed. I do not remember whether there was a bell or whether I knocked with my hand. The sparkling of the music continued.

9. *The Dream of the Red Chamber,* by Ts'ao Hsüeh-ch'in (1791): the most famous Chinese novel, a love story and panorama of Chinese family life involving over 430 separate characters.

From the rear of the house within a lantern approached: a lantern that the trees sometimes striped and sometimes eclipsed, a paper lantern that had the form of a drum and the color of the moon. A tall man bore it. I didn't see his face for the light blinded me. He opened the door and said slowly, in my own language: "I see that the pious Hsi P'êng persists in correcting my solitude. You no doubt wish to see the garden?"

I recognized the name of one of our consuls and I replied, disconcerted, "The garden?"

"The garden of forking paths."

Something stirred in my memory and I uttered with incomprehensible certainty, "The garden of my ancestor Ts'ui Pên."

"Your ancestor? You illustrious ancestor? Come in."

The damp path zigzagged like those of my childhood. We came to a library of Eastern and Western books. I recognized bound in yellow silk several volumes of the Lost Encyclopedia,[1] edited by the Third Emperor of the Luminous Dynasty but never printed. The record on the phonograph revolved next to a bronze phoenix. I also recall a *famille rose* vase[2] and another, many centuries older, of that shade of blue which our craftsmen copied from the potters of Persia . . . .

Stephen Albert observed me with a smile. He was, as I have said, very tall, sharp-featured, with gray eyes and a gray beard. He told me that he had been a missionary in Tientsin "before aspiring to become a Sinologist."

We sat down—I on a long, low divan, he with his back to the window and a tall circular clock. I calculated that my pursuer, Richard Madden, could not arrive for at least an hour. My irrevocable determination could wait.

"An astounding fate, that of Ts'ui Pên," Stephen Albert said. "Governor of his native province, learned in astronomy, in astrology and in the tireless interpretation of the canonical books, chess player, famous poet and calligrapher—he abandoned all this in order to compose a book and a maze. He renounced the pleasures of both tyranny and justice, of his populous couch, of his banquets and even of erudition—all to close himself up for thirteen years in the Pavilion of the Limpid Solitude. When he died, his heirs found nothing save chaotic manuscripts. His family, as you may be aware, wished to condemn them to the fire; but his executor—a Taoist or Buddhist monk—insisted on their publication."

1. The Yung-lo Emperor of the Ming ("bright") Dynasty commissioned a massive encyclopedia between 1403–1408. A single copy of the 11,095 manuscript volumes was made in the mid-1500s; the original was later destroyed and only 370 volumes of the copy remain today.   2. *Famille rose* ("pink family," French) refers to a Chinese decorative enamel ranging in color from an opaque pink to purplish rose; *famille rose* pottery was at its best during the reign of Yung Chên (1723–35).

"We descendants of Ts'ui Pên," I replied, "continue to curse that monk. Their publication was senseless. The book is an indeterminate heap of contradictory drafts. I examined it once: in the third chapter the hero dies, in the fourth he is alive. As for the other undertaking of Ts'ui Pên, his labyrinth . . ."

"Here is Ts'ui Pên's labyrinth," he said, indicating a tall lacquered desk.

"An ivory labyrinth!" I exclaimed. "A minimum labyrinth."

"A labyrinth of symbols," he corrected. "An invisible labyrinth of time. To me, a barbarous Englishman, has been entrusted the revelation of this diaphanous mystery. After more than a hundred years, the details are irretrievable; but it is not hard to conjecture what happened. Ts'ui Pên must have said once: *I am withdrawing to write a book.* And another time: *I am withdrawing to construct a labyrinth.* Every one imagined two works; to no one did it occur that the book and the maze were one and the same thing. The Pavilion of the Limpid Solitude stood in the center of a garden that was perhaps intricate; that circumstance could have suggested to the heirs a physical labyrinth. Ts'ui Pên died; no one in the vast territories that were his came upon the labyrinth; the confusion of the novel suggested to me that *it* was the maze. Two circumstances gave me the correct solution of the problem. One: the curious legend that Ts'ui Pên had planned to create a labyrinth which would be strictly infinite. The other: a fragment of a letter I discovered."

Albert rose. He turned his back on me for a moment; he opened a drawer of the black and gold desk. He faced me and in his hands he held a sheet of paper that had once been crimson, but was now pink and tenuous and cross-sectioned. The fame of Ts'ui Pên as a calligrapher had been justly won. I read, uncomprehendingly and with fervor, these words written with a minute brush by a man of my blood: *I leave to the various futures (not to all) my garden of forking paths.* Wordlessly, I returned the sheet. Albert continued:

"Before unearthing this letter, I had questioned myself about the ways in which a book can be infinite. I could think of nothing other than a cyclic volume, a circular one. A book whose last page was identical with the first, a book which had the possibility of continuing indefinitely. I remembered too that night which is at the middle of the Thousand and One Nights when Scheherazade[3] (through a magical oversight of the copyist) begins to relate word for word the story of the Thousand and One Nights, establishing the risk of coming once again to the night when she must repeat it, and thus on to infinity. I imagined as well a Platonic, hereditary work, transmitted

---

3. The narrator of the collection also known as the *Arabian Nights*, a thousand and one tales supposedly told by Scheherazade to her husband Schariar, king of Samarkand, in order to postpone her execution.

from father to son, in which each new individual adds a chapter or corrects with pious care the pages of his elders. These conjectures diverted me; but none seemed to correspond, not even remotely, to the contradictory chapters of Ts'ui Pên. In the midst of this perplexity, I received from Oxford the manuscript you have examined. I lingered, naturally, on the sentence: *I leave to the various futures (not to all) my garden of forking paths.* Almost instantly, I understood: 'The garden of forking paths' was the chaotic novel; the phrase 'the various futures (not to all)' suggested to me the forking in time, not in space. A broad rereading of the work confirmed the theory. In all fictional works, each time a man is confronted with several alternatives, he chooses one and eliminates the others; in the fiction of Ts'ui Pên, he chooses—simultaneously—all of them. *He creates,* in this way, diverse futures, diverse times which themselves also proliferate and fork. Here, then, is the explanation of the novel's contradictions. Fang, let us say, has a secret; a stranger calls at his door; Fang resolves to kill him. Naturally, there are several possible outcomes: Fang can kill the intruder, the intruder can kill Fang, they both can escape, they both can die, and so forth. In the work of Ts'ui Pên, all possible outcomes occur; each one is the point of departure for other forkings. Sometimes, the paths of this labyrinth converge: for example, you arrive at this house, but in one of the possible pasts you are my enemy, in another, my friend. If you will resign yourself to my incurable pronunciation, we shall read a few pages."

His face, within the vivid circle of the lamplight, was unquestionably that of an old man, but with something unalterable about it, even immortal. He read with slow precision two versions of the same epic chapter. In the first, an army marches to a battle across a lonely mountain; the horror of the rocks and shadows makes the men undervalue their lives and they gain an easy victory. In the second, the same army traverses a palace where a great festival is taking place; the resplendent battle seems to them a continuation of the celebration and they win the victory. I listened with proper veneration to these ancient narratives, perhaps less admirable in themselves than the fact that they had been created by my blood and were being restored to me by a man of a remote empire, in the course of a desperate adventure, on a Western isle. I remember the last words, repeated in each version like a secret commandment: *Thus fought the heroes, tranquil their admirable hearts, violent their swords, resigned to kill and to die.*

From that moment on, I felt about me and within my dark body an invisible, intangible swarming. Not the swarming of the divergent, parallel and finally coalescent armies, but a more inaccessible, more intimate agitation that they in some manner prefigured. Stephen Albert continued:

"I don't believe that your illustrious ancestor played idly with these variations. I don't consider it credible that he would sacrifice thirteen years to the infinite execution of a rhetorical experiment. In your country, the novel is a subsidiary form of literature; in Ts'ui Pên's time it was a despicable form. Ts'ui Pên was a brilliant novelist, but he was also a man of letters who doubtless did not consider himself a mere novelist. The testimony of his contemporaries proclaims— and his life fully confirms—his metaphysical and mystical interests. Philosophic controversy usurps a good part of the novel. I know that of all problems, none disturbed him so greatly nor worked upon him so much as the abysmal problem of time. Now then, the latter is the only problem that does not figure in the pages of the *Garden*. He does not even use the word that signifies *time*. How do you explain this voluntary omission?"

I proposed several solutions—all unsatisfactory. We discussed them. Finally, Stephen Albert said to me:

"In a riddle whose answer is chess, what is the only prohibited word?"

I thought a moment and replied, "The word *chess*."

"Precisely," said Albert. "*The Garden of Forking Paths* is an enormous riddle, or parable, whose theme is time; this recondite cause prohibits its mention. To omit a word always, to resort to inept metaphors and obvious periphrases, is perhaps the most emphatic way of stressing it. That is the tortuous method preferred, in each of the meanderings of his indefatigable novel, by the oblique Ts'ui Pên. I have compared hundreds of manuscripts, I have corrected the errors that the negligence of the copyists has introduced, I have guessed the plan of this chaos, I have re-established—I believe I have re-established—the primordial organization, I have translated the entire work: it is clear to me that not once does he employ the word 'time.' The explanation is obvious: *The Garden of Forking Paths* is an incomplete, but not false, image of the universe as Ts'ui Pên conceived it. In contrast to Newton and Schopenhauer,[4] your ancestor did not believe in a uniform, absolute time. He believed in an infinite series of times, in a growing, dizzying net of divergent, convergent and parallel times. This network of times which approached one another, forked, broke off, or were unaware of one another for centuries, embraces *all* possibilities of time. We do not exist in the majority of these times; in some you exist, and not I; in others I, and not you; in others, both of us. In the present one, which a favorable fate has granted me, you have arrived at my house; in another, while crossing

---

4. *Isaac Newton* (1642–1727), English mathematician and philosopher best known for his formulation of laws of gravitation and motion; *Arthur Schopenhauer*, German philosopher (1788– 1860), whose concept of will proceeded from a concept of the self as enduring through time. In *Seven Conversations with Jorge Luis Borges*, Borges also comments on Schopenhauer's interest in the "oneiric essence of life."

the garden, you found me dead; in still another, I utter these same words, but I am a mistake, a ghost."

"In every one," I pronounced, not without a tremble to my voice, "I am grateful to you and revere you for your re-creation of the garden of Ts'ui Pên."

"Not in all," he murmured with a smile. "Time forks perpetually toward innumerable futures. In one of them I am your enemy."

Once again I felt the swarming sensation of which I have spoken. It seemed to me that the humid garden that surrounded the house was infinitely saturated with invisible persons. Those persons were Albert and I, secret, busy and multiform in other dimensions of time. I raised my eyes and the tenuous nightmare dissolved. In the yellow and black garden there was only one man; but this man was as strong as a statue . . . this man was approaching along the path and he was Captain Richard Madden.

"The future already exists," I replied, "but I am your friend. Could I see the letter again?"

Albert rose. Standing tall, he opened the drawer of the tall desk; for the moment his back was to me. I had readied the revolver. I fired with extreme caution. Albert fell uncomplainingly, immediately. I swear his death was instantaneous—a lightning stroke.

The rest is unreal, insignificant. Madden broke in, arrested me. I have been condemned to the gallows. I have won out abominably; I have communicated to Berlin the secret name of the city they must attack. They bombed it yesterday; I read it in the same papers that offered to England the mystery of the learned Sinologist Stephen Albert who was murdered by a stranger, one Yu Tsun. The Chief had deciphered this mystery. He knew my problem was to indicate (through the uproar of the war) the city called Albert, and that I had found no other means to do so than to kill a man of that name. He does not know (no one can know) my innumerable contrition and weariness.

For Victoria Ocampo

SAMUEL BECKETT

1906—

The sparest, starkest representation of the human condition in all its "absurd" emptiness fills Beckett's novels and plays. Not that other authors do not concern themselves with the problem of representing reality, but where Pirandello plays with allusions to an elusive identity, Joyce with the stream of consciousness, and Proust with layers of the self reconstituted through affective memory, Beckett's world is haunted—like that of Kafka—by an absence of meaning at the core. Whether expressed by the protagonist's ramblings in the early novels *Murphy* (1938), *Molloy* (1951), *Malone Dies* (1951), or *The Unnamable* (1953), by the stripped-down dialogue of the plays *Waiting for Godot* (1952) and *Endgame* (1957), or by the telegraphic style of a late novel, *How It Is* (1961), Beckett's characters engage in a desperate attempt to find or to create meaning for themselves. Born into a world without reason, they live out their lives waiting for an explanation that never comes and whose existence may be only a figment of their imagination. In the meantime, human relationships are reduced to the most elemental tensions of cruelty, hope, frustration, and disillusionment around themes of birth, death, human emotions, material obstacles, and unending consciousness. Beckett's comedy of errors is a bitter one and, even in its puns and parodies, draws heavily on what the author has described as "the power of the text to claw."

Like Joyce and Yeats, Beckett was born in Ireland; like Joyce, he has chosen to live abroad for most of his life. Born outside Dublin on April 13, 1906, he was educated in Ireland and received a B.A. from Trinity College in 1927. From 1928 to 1930, he taught English at the Ecole Normale Supérieure in Paris, where he met James Joyce and was for a while influenced by the older novelist's exuberant and punning use of language. Beckett wrote an essay on the early stages of Joyce's *Finnegans Wake*, and later helped in the French translation of part of the book. In 1930 he entered a competition for a poem about time, and won first prize with a ninety-eight line (and seventeen footnote) monologue, *Whoroscope*, spoken by the seventeenth-century French physicist and philosopher René Descartes. Beckett returned to Trinity College where he took an M.A. in 1931, published an essay on Proust, and stayed on the following year to teach French. It was a brief academic career, for he gave up teaching in 1932 and, after living in London, France, and Germany, made Paris his permanent home in 1937. Although his early novels (*Murphy* and *Watt*, 1953) were written in English, Beckett was already turning to French as his preferred language for original composition; in the years after World War II, he wrote almost exclusively in French and only later translated (often with substantial changes) the same texts into English. He has said that he writes in French because it is easier to write "without style": without the native speaker's temptation to elegance and virtuoso display. Although no generalization holds true for all cases, comparing the French and English versions of the same work often suggests just such a contrast, with the French text closer to basic grammatical forms and therefore possessing a harsher, less nuanced focus.

Whether comic or despairing (often both), Beckett's characters ring changes on the Cartesian image of the Rational Man that has been at the base of Western cultural attitudes ever since Descartes moved from specific questions about the physical sciences to the larger question of human existence. Descartes, like Beckett, went back to zero in order not to be led astray by any preconceived assumptions or doctrines. He doubted everything—except that he doubted, which in itself indicated that he was thinking and that if "I think, therefore I am" ("Cogito, ergo sum"). Upon that certainty Descartes erected a logical system for exploring the natural universe and explaining the human condition. Beckett is not so sure that logic allows us to know what we are looking at, or in fact to match up our terminology with reality at all. In *Watt*, the protagonist is caught in a peculiar hestitation inasmuch as things, "if they consented to be named, did so as it were with reluctance." He looks at a pot, but "it was not a pot, the more he looked, the more he reflected, the more he felt sure of that, that it was not a pot at all. It resembled a pot, it was almost a pot, but it was not a pot of which one could say, Pot, pot and be comforted." The gentle bewilderment that Watt feels turns bitter and more dangerous in later novels such as the famous trilogy *Molloy*, *Malone Dies*, and *The Unnamable*, or in *How It Is*, which refuses to present any image of rational control as it murmurs, free of punctuation, the monologue of an unstructured consciousness inside an accompanying "quaqua [bzzz bzzz] on all sides."

The narrative perspective in Beckett's trilogy moves from a series of related monologue stories in which narrators come more and more to resemble one another, to an "unnamable" speaker who seems to represent them all at the end. In *Molloy*, there are two interlocking points of view as first Molloy tells of setting out on a bicycle to visit his bedridden mother: a search that takes him months and leads him all over (with many echoes of Homer's *Odyssey*). The last we hear of Molloy is that he is crippled and has lost his bicycle, but is determined still to proceed if only by rolling; Moran takes over at that point, and describes a corresponding search for Molloy in the course of which he loses his bicycle, is crippled, and ends up frustrated back home. The next novel, *Malone Dies*, is similarly divided between protagonists, even if in the mind of a single narrator: a dying and bedridden Malone writes the diary of his last days, and also composes the story of Macmann, who is to die at the same moment as Malone and apparently does so as the novel ends. The last in the trilogy, *The Unnamable*, has no fixed authorial perspective or claim to responsibility. "I'm in words, made of words." Someone (unnamed and—by now—clearly unnamable) is seated in an undefined gray space and time, writing a series of stories that may be the tales of Malone, Malloy, and Moran, or of a new Mahood who also becomes Worm, who may in turn be the narrator writing stories about himself; or it may simply evoke the act of story telling as it creates fictions of life in order to establish some mode of reality. In 1949, when the trilogy was just complete, Beckett published a dialogue on modern art which described the artist's disgust with traditional art's "puny exploits . . . doing a little better the same old thing," and his preference for "the expression that there is nothing to express, nothing with which to express, nothing from which to express, no power to express, no desire to express, together with the obligation to express." The disintegration of narrative perspective in Beckett's fiction is one means of denying that there is a knowable "something to express," or an authoritative point of view from which to express "nothing."

How can one possibly make a convincing stage play out of "nothing"? The popularity of Beckett's first performed play, *Waiting for Godot* (French version presented 1953, English 1955), showed that Absurdist theater—with its empty, repetitive dialogue, its grotesquely bare yet apparently symbolic settings, and its refusal to build to a dramatic climax—had meaning even for audiences used to theatrical realism and logically developing plots. These audiences found two clownlike tramps, Vladimir and Estragon (Didi and Gogo), talking, quarreling, falling down, contemplating suicide, and generally filling up time with conversation that ranges from vaudeville patter to metaphysical speculation as they wait under a tree for a Godot who never comes. Instead, the two are joined in the middle of each act by another grotesque pair: the rich Pozzo and his brutally abused servant Lucky, whom he leads around by a rope tied to his neck. The popular interpretation of "Godot" as a diminutive for "God," and of the play as a statement of existential anguish at the inexplicable human condition, is scarcely defused by Beckett's caution that "If by Godot I had meant God, I would have said God." Yet identifying Godot is less important than identifying the ignominious plight on stage as symbolically our own, and identifying *with* the characters as they express the anxious, often repugnant but also comic picture of human relationships in an absurd universe.

After the popular success of *Waiting for Godot*, Beckett wrote *Endgame* (French version performed 1957, English 1958) and a series of stage plays and brief pieces for the radio. The stage plays have the same bare yet striking settings: *Krapp's Last Tape* (1958) presents an old man sitting at a table with his tape recorder, recalling a love affair thirty years past, and *Happy Days* (1961) shows a married couple in which Winnie, the wife, chatters ceaselessly about her possessions although she is buried up to her waist in the first act and to her neck in the second. When Beckett received the Nobel Prize for Literature in 1969, he was recognized as the purest exponent of the twentieth century's chief philosophical dilemma: the notion of the "absurd," or the grotesque contradiction between human attempts to discover meaning in life and the simultaneous conviction that there is no "meaning" available that we have not created ourselves. *Endgame*, often called Beckett's major achievement, is a prime example of this dilemma.

When the curtain rises on *Endgame*, it is as though the world is awaking from sleep. The sheets draping the furniture and central character are taken off, and Hamm sets himself in motion like an actor or chess pawn: "Me . . . to play." Yet we are also near the end for, as the title implies, nothing new will happen: an 'endgame' is the final phase of a chess game, the stage at which the end is predictably in sight although the play must still be completed. Throughout, the theme of "end," "finish," "no more" is sounded, even while Hamm notes the passage of time: "Something is taking its course." But time does not lead anywhere; it is either past or present, and always barren. The past exists as Nagg's and Nell's memories, as Hamm's story which may or may not describe Clov's entry into the home, and as a period in which Clov once loved Hamm. The present shows four characters dwindling away, alone in a dead world, caught between visions of dusty hell and dreams of life reborn. In one of the Biblical echoes that permeate the play, Hamm and Clov repeatedly evoke the last words of the crucified Christ in the Gospel according to Saint John: "It is finished." But this is not a Biblical morality play, and *Endgame* describes a world not of divine but of self-creation. Hamm may be composing and directing the entire performance: a storyteller and playwright with "asides" and "last soliloquy" whose "dialogue" keeps Clov on stage against his will, a mad artist who (when looking out the window onto a flourishing world) can see only dust and ashes, or a magician presiding over an imaginary kingdom who concludes an inner story and unavailing prayer with Prospero's line from *The Tempest* (IV,i,148): "Our revels now are ended." Or he may simply be aware of their lives *as* a performance without any other meaning: Shakespeare's passage continues later: "We are such stuff / As dreams are made on, and our little life / Is rounded with a sleep." The situation at the end of the play is little changed— only barer, as Hamm discards his stick, whistle, and dog, "reckoning closed and story ended." Yet Clov is still waiting to leave as Hamm covers his face, and it is not impossible that the play will resume in precisely the same terms tomorrow.

Endgame, like *Waiting for Godot* (and like Kafka's stories), has been given a number of symbolic interpretations. Some refer to Beckett's love of word play: Hamm as Hamm-actor, Hammlet, Hammer, and Nag and Nell as shortened forms of *Nägel* and *nello*, German and Italian words for *nail*, which are invoked as crucifixion themes suggesting the martyrdom of humanity. The setting of a boxlike room with two windows is seen as a skull, the seat of consciousness, or (emphasizing the bloody handkerchief and the reference to fontanelles—the soft spot in the skull of a newborn child) as a womb. The characters' isolation in a dead world after an unnamed catastrophe (which may be Hamm's fault) suggests the world after atomic holocaust; or, for those who recall Beckett's fascination with the apathetic figure of Belacqua waiting, in the Purgatory of Dante's *Divine Comedy*, for his punishment to begin, it evokes an image of pre-Purgatorial consciousness. The ashcans in which Hamm has "bottled" his parents, and the general cruelty between characters, are to represent the dustbin of modern Western civilized values. Hamm and Clov represent the uneasy adjustment of soul and body, the class struggle of rich and poor, or the master-slave relationship in all senses (including the slave's acceptance of his victimization). Clearly Beckett has created a structure that accommodates all these readings while authorizing none. He himself said to director Alan Schneider that he was less interested in symbolism than in describing a "local situation," an interaction of four characters in a given set of circumstances, and that the audience's interpretation was its own responsibility.

Beckett has both authorized and denied the series of interpretations. He pruned down an earlier, more anecdotal two-act play to achieve *Endgame*'s skeletal plot and almost anonymous characters, and in doing so created a structure that immediately elicits the reader's instinct to "fill in the blanks." His puns and allusions openly point to a further meaning that *may* be contained in the implied reference, but may also be part of an infinite regress of meaning—expressing the "absurd" itself. Working against too heavy an insistence on symbolic meanings is the fact that the play is also funny— especially when performed on stage. The characters popping out of ashcans, the jerky, repetitive motions with which Clov carries out his master's commands, and the often obscene vaudeville patter accompanied by appropriate gestures, all provide a comic perspective that keeps *Endgame* from sinking into tragic despair. The intellectual distance offered by comedy is entirely in keeping with the more somber side of the play, which rejects pathos and constantly drags its characters' escapist fancies down to the minimal facts of survival: food, shelter, sleep, painkiller. Thus it is possible to say that *End-*

game describes—but only among many other things—what it is like to be alive, declining toward death in a world without meaning.

Hugh Kenner, *Samuel Beckett: A Critical Study* (1974), is an excellent general introduction. Deirdre Bair, *Samuel Beckett: A Biography* (1978), provides an extensive view of Beckett. Bell Gale Chevigny, compiler, *Twentieth-Century Interpretations of Endgame* (1969), contains essays on the play.

For Roger Blin

Endgame[1]

The Characters:

NAGG
NELL
HAMM
CLOV

> *Bare interior.*
> *Gray light.*
> *Left and right back, high up, two small windows, curtains drawn.*
> *Front right, a door. Hanging near door, its face to wall, a picture.*
> *Front left, touching each other, covered with an old sheet, two ashbins.*
> *Center, in an armchair on castors, covered with an old sheet,* HAMM.
> *Motionless by the door, his eyes fixed on* HAMM, CLOV. *Very red face.*
> *Brief tableau.*

CLOV *goes and stands under window left. Stiff, staggering walk. He looks up at window left. He turns and looks at window right. He goes and stands under window right. He looks up at window right. He turns and looks at window left. He goes out, comes back immediately with a small step-ladder, carries it over and sets it down under window left, gets up on it, draws back curtain. He gets down, takes six steps (for example) towards window right, goes back for ladder, carries it over and sets it down under window right, gets up on it, draws back curtain. He gets down, takes three steps towards window left, goes back for ladder, carries it over and sets it down under window left, gets up on it, looks out of window. Brief laugh. He gets down, takes one step towards window right, goes back for ladder, carries it over and*

---

1. Translated by the author.

sets it down under window right, gets up on it, looks out of window. Brief laugh. He gets down, goes with ladder towards ashbins, halts, turns, carries back ladder and sets it down under window right, goes to ashbins, removes sheet covering them, folds it over his arm. He raises one lid, stoops and looks into bin. Brief laugh. He closes lid. Same with other bin. He goes to HAMM, *removes sheet covering him, folds it over his arm. In a dressing-gown, a stiff toque[2] on his head, a large blood-stained handkerchief over his face, a whistle hanging from his neck, a rug over his knees, thick socks on his feet,* HAMM *seems to be asleep.* CLOV *looks him over. Brief laugh. He goes to door, halts, turns towards auditorium.*

CLOV [*fixed gaze, tonelessly*]: Finished, it's finished, nearly finished, it must be nearly finished. [*Pause.*] Grain upon grain, one by one, and one day, suddenly, there's a heap, a little heap, the impossible heap. [*Pause.*] I can't be punished any more. [*Pause.*] I'll go now to my kitchen, ten feet by ten feet by ten feet, and wait for him to whistle me. [*Pause.*] Nice dimensions, nice proportions, I'll lean on the table, and look at the wall, and wait for him to whistle me.

[*He remains a moment motionless, then goes out. He comes back immediately, goes to window right, takes up the ladder and carries it out. Pause.* HAMM *stirs. He yawns under the handkerchief. He removes the handkerchief from his face. Very red face. Black glasses.*]

HAMM: Me—[*he yawns*]—to play.[3] [*He holds the handkerchief spread out before him.*] Old Stancher![4] [*He takes off his glasses, wipes his eyes, his face, the glasses, puts them on again, folds the handkerchief and puts it back neatly in the breast-pocket of his dressing-gown. He clears his throat, joins the tips of his fingers.*] Can there be misery—[*he yawns*]—loftier than mine? No doubt. Formerly. But now? [*Pause.*] My father? [*Pause.*] My mother? [*Pause.*] My . . . dog? [*Pause.*] Oh I am willing to believe they suffer as much as such creatures can suffer. But does that mean their sufferings equal mine? No doubt. [*Pause.*] No, all is a—[*he yawns*]—bsolute, [*proudly*] the bigger a man is the fuller he is. [*Pause. Gloomily.*] And the emptier. [*He sniffs.*] Clov! [*Pause.*] No, alone. [*Pause.*] What dreams! Those forests! [*Pause.*] Enough, it's time it ended, in the shelter too. [*Pause.*] And yet I hesitate, I hesitate to . . . to end. Yes, there it is, it's time it ended and yet I hesitate to—[*he yawns*]—to end. [*Yawns.*] God, I'm tired, I'd be better off in bed. [*He whistles. Enter* CLOV *immediately. He halts beside the chair.*]

---

2. A fitted cloth hat with little or no brim, sometimes indicating official status as with a judge's toque.   3. Hamm announces that it is his move at the beginning of *Endgame*; the comparison is with a game of chess, of which the "endgame" is the final stage.   4. The handkerchief that stanches his blood.

You pollute the air! [*Pause.*] Get me ready, I'm going to bed.

CLOV: I've just got you up.

HAMM: And what of it?

CLOV: I can't be getting you up and putting you to bed every five minutes, I have things to do. [*Pause.*]

HAMM: Did you ever see my eyes?

CLOV: No.

HAMM: Did you never have the curiosity, while I was sleeping, to take off my glasses and look at my eyes?

CLOV: Pulling back the lids? [*Pause.*] No.

HAMM: One of these days I'll show them to you. [*Pause.*] It seems they've gone all white. [*Pause.*] What time is it?

CLOV: The same as usual.

HAMM [*gesture towards window right*]: Have you looked?

CLOV: Yes.

HAMM: Well?

CLOV: Zero.

HAMM: It'd need to rain.

CLOV: It won't rain. [*Pause.*]

HAMM: Apart from that, how do you feel?

CLOV: I don't complain.

HAMM: You feel normal?

CLOV [*irritably*]: I tell you I don't complain.

HAMM: I feel a little queer. [*Pause.*] Clov!

CLOV: Yes.

HAMM: Have you not had enough?

CLOV: Yes! [*Pause.*] Of what?

HAMM: Of this . . . this . . . thing.

CLOV: I always had. [*Pause.*] Not you?

HAMM [*gloomily*]: Then there's no reason for it to change.

CLOV: It may end. [*Pause.*] All life long the same questions, the same answers.

HAMM: Get me ready. [CLOV *does not move.*] Go and get the sheet. [CLOV *does not move.*] Clov!

CLOV: Yes.

HAMM: I'll give you nothing more to eat.

CLOV: Then we'll die.

HAMM: I'll give you just enough to keep you from dying. You'll be hungry all the time.

CLOV: Then we won't die. [*Pause.*] I'll go and get the sheet. [*He goes towards the door.*]

HAMM: No! [CLOV *halts.*] I'll give you one biscuit per day. [*Pause.*] One and a half. [*Pause.*] Why do you stay with me?

CLOV: Why do you keep me?

HAMM: There's no one else.

CLOV: There's nowhere else. [*Pause.*]

HAMM: You're leaving me all the same.

CLOV: I'm trying.

HAMM: You don't love me.

CLOV: No.

HAMM: You loved me once.

CLOV: Once!

HAMM: I've made you suffer too much. [*Pause.*] Haven't I?

CLOV: It's not that.

HAMM [*shocked*]: I haven't made you suffer too much?

CLOV: Yes!

HAMM [*relieved*]: Ah you gave me a fright! [*Pause. Coldly.*] Forgive me. [*Pause. Louder.*] I said, Forgive me.

CLOV: I heard you. [*Pause.*] Have you bled?

HAMM: Less. [*Pause.*] Is it not time for my pain-killer?

CLOV: No. [*Pause.*]

HAMM: How are your eyes?

CLOV: Bad.

HAMM: How are your legs?

CLOV: BAD.

HAMM: But you can move.

CLOV: Yes.

HAMM [*violently*]: Then move! [CLOV *goes to back wall, leans against it with his forehead and hands.*] Where are you?

CLOV: Here.

HAMM: Come back! [CLOV *returns to his place beside the chair.*] Where are you?

CLOV: Here.

HAMM: Why don't you kill me?

CLOV: I don't know the combination of the cupboard. [*Pause.*]

HAMM: Go and get two bicycle-wheels.

CLOV: There are no more bicycle-wheels.

HAMM: What have you done with your bicycle?

CLOV: I never had a bicycle.

HAMM: The thing is impossible.

CLOV: When there were still bicycles I wept to have one. I crawled at your feet. You told me to go to hell. Now there are none.

HAMM: And your rounds? When you inspected my paupers. Always on foot?

CLOV: Sometimes on horse. [*The lid of one of the bins lifts and the hands of* NAGG *appear, gripping the rim. Then his head emerges. Nightcap. Very white face.* NAGG *yawns, then listens.*] I'll leave you, I have things to do.

HAMM: In your kitchen?

CLOV: Yes.

HAMM: Outside of here it's death. [*Pause.*] All right, be off. [*Exit* CLOV. *Pause.*] We're getting on.

NAGG: Me Pap![5]

HAMM: Accursed progenitor!

NAGG: Me pap!

HAMM: The old folks at home! No decency left! Guzzle, guzzle, that's all they think of. [*He whistles. Enter* CLOV. *He halts beside the chair.*] Well! I thought you were leaving me.

CLOV: Oh not just yet, not just yet.

NAGG: Me pap!

HAMM: Give him his pap.

CLOV: There's no more pap.

HAMM [*to* NAGG]: Do you hear that? There's no more pap. You'll never get any more pap.

NAGG: I want me pap!

HAMM: Give him a biscuit. [*Exit* CLOV.] Accursed fornicator! How are your stumps?

NAGG: Never mind me stumps. [*Enter* CLOV *with biscuit.*]

CLOV: I'm back again, with the biscuit. [*He gives biscuit to* NAGG *who fingers, it, sniffs it.*]

NAGG [*plaintively*]: What is it?

CLOV: Spratt's medium.[6]

NAGG [*as before*]: It's hard! I can't!

HAMM: Bottle him! [CLOV *pushes* NAGG *back into the bin, closes the lid.*]

CLOV [*returning to his place beside the chair*]: If age but knew!

HAMM: Sit on him!

CLOV: I can't sit.

HAMM: True. And I can't stand.

CLOV: So it is.

HAMM: Every man his speciality. [*Pause.*] No phone calls? [*Pause.*] Don't we laugh?

CLOV [*after reflection*]: I don't feel like it.

HAMM [*after reflection*]: Not I. [*Pause.*] Clov!

CLOV: Yes.

HAMM: Nature has forgotten us.

CLOV: There's no more nature.

HAMM: No more nature! You exaggerate.

CLOV: In the vicinity.

HAMM: But we breathe, we change! We lose our hair, our teeth! Our bloom! Our ideals!

CLOV: Then she hasn't forgotten us.

HAMM: But you say there is none.

5. Food, mush.   6. A common biscuit.

CLOV [*sadly*]: No one that ever lived ever thought so crooked as we.

HAMM: We do what we can.

CLOV: We shouldn't. [*Pause.*]

HAMM: You're a bit of all right, aren't you?[7]

CLOV: A smithereen. [*Pause.*]

HAMM: This is slow work. [*Pause.*] Is it not time for my pain-killer?

CLOV: No. [*Pause.*] I'll leave you, I have things to do.

HAMM: In your kitchen?

CLOV: Yes.

HAMM: What, I'd like to know.

CLOV: I look at the wall.

HAMM: The wall! And what do you see on your wall? Mene, mene?[8] Naked bodies?

CLOV: I see my light dying.

HAMM: Your light dying! Listen to that! Well, it can die just as well here, *your* light. Take a look at me and then come back and tell me what you think of *your* light. [*Pause.*]

CLOV: You shouldn't speak to me like that. [*Pause.*]

HAMM [*coldly*]: Forgive me. [*Pause. Louder.*] I said, Forgive me.

CLOV: I heard you. [*The lid of* NAGG*'s bin lifts. His hands appear, gripping the rim. Then his head emerges. In his mouth the biscuit. He listens.*]

HAMM: Did your seeds come up?

CLOV: No.

HAMM: Did you scratch round them to see if they had sprouted?

CLOV: They haven't sprouted.

HAMM: Perhaps it's still too early.

CLOV: If they were going to sprout they would have sprouted. [*Violently.*] They'll never sprout! [*Pause.* NAGG *takes biscuit in his hand.*]

HAMM: This is not much fun. [*Pause.*] But that's always the way at the end of the day, isn't it, Clov?

CLOV: Always.

HAMM: It's the end of the day like any other day, isn't it, Clov?

CLOV: Looks like it. [*Pause.*]

HAMM: [*anguished*]: What's happening, what's happening?

CLOV: Something is taking its course. [*Pause.*]

HAMM: All right, be off. [*He leans back in his chair, remains motionless.* CLOV *does not move, heaves a great groaning sigh.* HAMM *sits up.*] I thought I told you to be off.

CLOV: I'm trying. [*He goes to door, halts.*] Ever since I was whelped. [*Exit* CLOV.]

---

7. "You're pretty good, aren't you?" (British slang). *Smithereen:* A tiny bit.   8. "Mene, mene, tekel, upharsin": Words written by a divine hand on the wall during the feast of Belshazzar, King of Babylon. They predict doom and tell the king "Thou art weighed in the balances and found wanting." (Daniel 5:25–28)

HAMM: We're getting on.

[*He leans back in his chair, remains motionless.* NAGG *knocks on the lid of the other bin. Pause. He knocks harder. The lid lifts and the hands of* NELL *appear, gripping the rim. Then her head emerges. Lace cap. Very white face.*]

NELL: What is it, my pet? [*Pause.*] Time for love?

NAGG: Were you asleep?

NELL: Oh no!

NAGG: Kiss me.

NELL: We can't.

NAGG: Try. [*Their heads strain towards each other, fail to meet, fall apart again.*]

NELL: Why this farce, day after day? [*Pause.*]

NAGG: I've lost me tooth.

NELL: When?

NAGG: I had it yesterday.

NELL [*elegiac*]: Ah yesterday! [*They turn painfully towards each other.*]

NAGG: Can you see me?

NELL: Hardly. And you?

NAGG: What?

NELL: Can you see me?

NAGG: Hardly.

NELL: So much the better, so much the better.

NAGG: Don't say that. [*Pause.*] Our sight has failed.

NELL: Yes. [*Pause. They turn away from each other.*]

NAGG: Can you hear me?

NELL: Yes. And you?

NAGG: Yes. [*Pause.*] Our hearing hasn't failed.

NELL: Our what?

NAGG: Our hearing.

NELL: No. [*Pause.*] Have you anything else to say to me?

NAGG: Do you remember—

NELL: No.

NAGG: When we crashed on our tandem[9] and lost our shanks. [*They laugh heartily.*]

NELL: It was in the Ardennes.[1] [*They laugh less heartily.*]

NAGG: On the road to Sedan. [*They laugh still less heartily.*] Are you cold?

NELL: Yes, perished. And you?

NAGG: [*Pause.*] I'm freezing. [*Pause.*] Do you want to go in?

NELL: Yes.

NAGG: Then go in. [NELL *does not move*] Why don't you go in?

---

9. A bicycle built for two.   1. A forest in northern France, the scene of bitter fighting in both World Wars. *Sedan:* Town in northern France where the French were defeated in the Franco-Prussian War (1870).

NELL: I don't know. [*Pause.*]

NAGG: Has he changed your sawdust?

NELL: It isn't sawdust. [*Pause. Wearily.*] Can you not be a little accurate, Nagg?

NAGG: Your sand then. It's not important.

NELL: It is important. [*Pause.*]

NAGG: It was sawdust once.

NELL: Once!

NAGG: And now it's sand. [*Pause.*] From the shore. [*Pause. Impatiently.*] Now it's sand he fetches from the shore.

NELL: Now it's sand.

NAGG: Has he changed yours?

NELL: No.

NAGG: Nor mine. [*Pause.*] I won't have it! [*Pause. Holding up the biscuit.*] Do you want a bit?

NELL: No. [*Pause.*] Of what?

NAGG: Biscuit. I've kept you half. [*He looks at the biscuit. Proudly.*] Three quarters. For you. Here. [*He proffers the biscuit.*] No? [*Pause.*] Do you not feel well?

HAMM [*wearily*]: Quiet, quiet, you're keeping me awake. [*Pause.*] Talk softer. [*Pause.*] If I could sleep I might make love. I'd go into the woods. My eyes would see . . . the sky, the earth. I'd run, run, they wouldn't catch me. [*Pause.*] Nature! [*Pause.*] There's something dripping in my head. [*Pause.*] A heart, a heart in my head. [*Pause.*]

NAGG [*soft*]: Do you hear him? A heart in his head! [*He chuckles cautiously.*]

NELL: One mustn't laugh at those things, Nagg. Why must you always laugh at them?

NAGG: Not so loud!

NELL [*Without lowering her voice*]: Nothing is funnier than unhappiness, I grant you that. But—

NAGG [*shocked*]: Oh!

NELL: Yes, yes, it's the most comical thing in the world. And we laugh, we laugh, with a will, in the beginning. But it's always the same thing. Yes, it's like the funny story we have heard too often, we still find it funny, but we don't laugh any more. [*Pause.*] Have you anything else to say to me?

NAGG: No.

NELL: Are you quite sure? [*Pause.*] Then I'll leave you.

NAGG: Do you not want your biscuit? [*Pause.*] I'll keep it for you. [*Pause.*] I thought you were going to leave me.

NELL: I am going to leave you.

NAGG: Could you give me a scratch before you go?

NELL: No. [*Pause.*] Where?

NAGG: In the back.

NELL: No. [*Pause.*] Rub yourself against the rim.

NAGG: It's lower down. In the hollow.

NELL: What hollow?

NAGG: The hollow! [*Pause.*] Could you not? [*Pause.*] Yesterday you scratched me there.

NELL [*elegiac*]: Ah yesterday!

NAGG: Could you not? [*Pause.*] Would you like me to scratch you? [*Pause.*] Are you crying again?

NELL: I was trying. [*Pause.*]

HAMM: Perhaps it's a little vein. [*Pause.*]

NAGG: What was that he said?

NELL: Perhaps it's a little vein.

NAGG: What does that mean? [*Pause.*] That means nothing. [*Pause.*] Will I tell you the story of the tailor?

NELL: No. [*Pause.*] What for?

NAGG: To cheer you up.

NELL: It's not funny.

NAGG: It always made you laugh. [*Pause.*] The first time I thought you'd die.

NELL: It was on Lake Como.[2] [*Pause.*] One April afternoon. [*Pause.*] Can you believe it?

NAGG: What?

NELL: That we once went out rowing on Lake Como. [*Pause.*] One April afternoon.

NAGG: We had got engaged the day before.

NELL: Engaged!

NAGG: You were in such fits that we capsized. By rights we should have been drowned.

NELL: It was because I felt happy.

NAGG [*indignant*]: It was not, it was not, it was my story and nothing else. Happy! Don't you laugh at it still? Every time I tell it. Happy!

NELL: It was deep, deep. And you could see down to the bottom. So white. So clean.

NAGG: Let me tell it again. [*Raconteur's voice.*] An Englishman, needing a pair of striped trousers in a hurry for the New Year festivities, goes to his tailor who takes his measurements. [*Tailor's voice.*] "That's the lot, come back in four days, I'll have it ready." Good. Four days later. [*Tailor's voice.*] "So sorry, come back in a week, I've made a mess of the seat." Good, that's all right, a neat seat can be very ticklish. A week later. [*Tailor's voice.*] "Frightfully sorry, come back in ten days, I've made a hash of the crotch." Good, can't be helped, a snug crotch is always a teaser. Ten days

2. A large lake and tourist resort in northern Italy, near the Swiss border.

later. [*Tailor's voice.*] "Dreadfully sorry, come back in a fortnight, I've made a balls of the fly." Good, at a pinch, a smart fly is a stiff proposition. [*Pause. Normal voice.*] I never told it worse. [*Pause. Gloomy.*] I tell this story worse and worse. [*Pause. Raconteur's voice.*] Well, to make it short, the bluebells are blowing and he ballockses[3] the buttonholes. [*Customer's voice.*] "God damn you to hell, Sir, no, it's indecent, there are limits! In six days, do you hear me, six days, God made the world. Yes Sir, no less Sir, the WORLD! And you are not bloody well capable of making me a pair of trousers in three months!" [*Tailor's voice, scandalized.*] "But my dear Sir, my dear Sir, look—[*disdainful gesture, disgustedly*]—at the world—[*pause*] and look—[*loving gesture, proudly*] —at my TROUSERS!"

> [*Pause. He looks at* NELL *who has remained impassive, her eyes unseeing, breaks into a high forced laugh, cuts it short, pokes his head towards* NELL, *launches his laugh again.*]

HAMM: Silence!

> [NAGG *starts, cuts short his laugh.*]

NELL: You could see down to the bottom.

HAMM [*exasperated*]:

Have you not finished? Will you never finish? [*With sudden fury.*] Will this never finish? [NAGG *disappears into his bin, closes the lid behind him.* NELL *does not move. Frenziedly.*] My kingdom for a nightman![4] [*He whistles. Enter* CLOV.] Clear away this muck! Chuck it in the sea! [CLOV *goes to bins, halts.*]

NELL: So white.

HAMM: What? What's she blathering about? [CLOV *stoops, takes* NELL's *hand, feels her pulse.*]

NELL [*to* CLOV]: Desert! [CLOV *lets go her hand, pushes her back in the bin, closes the lid.*]

CLOV [*returning to his place beside the chair*]: She has no pulse.

HAMM: What was she drivelling about?

CLOV: She told me to go away, into the desert.

HAMM: Damn busybody! Is that all?

CLOV: No.

HAMM: What else?

CLOV: I didn't understand.

HAMM: Have you bottled her?

CLOV: Yes.

HAMM: Are they both bottled?

CLOV: Yes.

HAMM: Screw down the lids. [CLOV *goes towards door.*] Time enough. [CLOV *halts.*] My anger subsides, I'd like to pee.

3. "Bollixes," botches.   4. Parody of Shakespeare's *Richard III*, where the defeated king seeks a horse to escape from the battlefield: "A horse! a horse! My kingdom for a horse!" (Act V, 4, 1. 7)

CLOV [*with alacrity*]: I'll go and get the catheter. [*He goes towards door.*]

HAMM: Time enough. [CLOV *halts.*] Give me my pain-killer.

CLOV: It's too soon. [*Pause.*] It's too soon on top of your tonic, it wouldn't act.

HAMM: In the morning they brace you up and in the evening they calm you down. Unless it's the other way round. [*Pause.*] That old doctor, he's dead naturally?

CLOV: He wasn't old.

HAMM: But he's dead?

CLOV: Naturally. [*Pause.*] *You* ask *me* that? [*Pause.*]

HAMM: Take me for a little turn. [CLOV *goes behind the chair and pushes it forward.*] Not too fast! [CLOV *pushes chair.*] Right round the world! [CLOV *pushes chair.*] Hug the walls, then back to the center again. [CLOV *pushes chair.*] I was right in the center, wasn't I?

CLOV [*pushing*]: Yes.

HAMM: We'd need a proper wheel-chair. With big wheels. Bicycle wheels! [*Pause.*] Are you hugging?

CLOV [*pushing*]: Yes.

HAMM [*groping for wall*]: It's a lie! Why do you lie to me?

CLOV [*bearing closer to wall*]: There! There!

HAMM: Stop! [CLOV *stops chair close to back wall.* HAMM *lays his hand against wall.*] Old wall! [*Pause.*] Beyond is the . . . other hell. [*Pause. Violently.*] Closer! Closer! Up against!

CLOV: Take away your hand. [HAMM *withdraws his hand.* CLOV *rams chair against wall.*] There! [HAMM *leans towards wall, applies his ear to it.*]

HAMM: Do you hear? [*He strikes the wall with his knuckles.*] Do you hear? Hollow bricks! [*He strikes again.*] All that's hollow! [*Pause. He straightens up. Violently.*] That's enough. Back!

CLOV: We haven't done the round.

HAMM: Back to my place! [CLOV *pushes chair back to center.*] Is that my place?

CLOV: Yes, that's your place.

HAMM: Am I right in the center?

CLOV: I'll measure it.

HAMM: More or less! More or less!

CLOV [*moving chair slightly*]: There!

HAMM: I'm more or less in the center?

CLOV: I'd say so.

HAMM: You'd say so! Put me right in the center!

CLOV: I'll go and get the tape.

HAMM: Roughly! Roughly! [CLOV *moves chair slightly.*] Bang in the center!

CLOV: There! [*Pause.*]

HAMM: I feel a little too far to the left. [CLOV *moves chair slightly.*] Now I feel a little too far to the right. [CLOV *moves chair slightly.*] I feel a little too far forward. [CLOV *moves chair slightly.*] Now I feel a little too far back. [CLOV *moves chair slightly.*] Don't stay there, [*i.e., behind the chair*] you give me the shivers. [CLOV *returns to his place beside the chair.*]

CLOV: If I could kill him I'd die happy. [*Pause.*]

HAMM: What's the weather like?

CLOV: As usual.

HAMM: Look at the earth.

CLOV: I've looked.

HAMM: With the glass?

CLOV: No need of the glass.

HAMM: Look at it with the glass.

CLOV: I'll go and get the glass. [*Exit* CLOV.]

HAMM: No need of the glass! [*Enter* CLOV *with telescope.*]

CLOV: I'm back again, with the glass. [*He goes to window right, looks up at it.*] I need the steps.

HAMM: Why? Have you shrunk? [*Exit* CLOV *with telescope.*] I don't like that, I don't like that. [*Enter* CLOV *with ladder, but without telescope.*]

CLOV: I'm back again, with the steps. [*He sets down ladder under window right, gets up on it, realizes he has not the telescope, gets down.*] I need the glass. [*He goes towards door.*]

HAMM [*violently*]: But you have the glass!

CLOV [*halting, violently*]: No, I haven't the glass! [*Exit* CLOV.]

HAMM: This is deadly. [*Enter* CLOV *with telescope. He goes towards ladder.*]

CLOV: Things are livening up. [*He gets up on ladder, raises the telescope, lets it fall.*] I did it on purpose. [*He gets down, picks up the telescope, turns it on auditorium.*] I see . . . a multitude . . . in transports . . . of joy.[5] [*Pause.*] That's what I call a magnifier. [*He lowers the telescope, turns towards* HAMM.] Well? Don't we laugh?

HAMM [*after reflection*]: I don't.

CLOV [*after reflection*]: Nor I. [*He gets up on ladder, turns the telescope on the without.*] Let's see. [*He looks, moving the telescope.*] Zero . . . [*he looks*] . . . zero . . . [*he looks*] . . . and zero.

HAMM: Nothing stirs. All is—

CLOV: Zer—

HAMM [*violently*]: Wait till you're spoke to! [*Normal voice.*] All is . . . all is . . . all is what? [*Violently.*] All is what?

CLOV: What all is? In a word? Is that what you want to know? Just a

---

5. Echo of Revelation 7:9–12: "After this I beheld, and, lo, a great multitude, which . . . cried with a loud voice . . . Salvation. . . ."

moment. [*He turns the telescope on the without, looks, lowers the telescope, turns towards Hamm.*] Corpsed. [*Pause.*] Well? Content?

HAMM: Look at the sea.

CLOV: It's the same.

HAMM: Look at the ocean! [CLOV *gets down, takes a few steps towards window left, goes back for ladder, carries it over and sets it down under window left, gets up on it, turns the telescope on the without, looks at length. He starts, lowers the telescope, examines it, turns it again on the without.*]

CLOV: Never seen anything like that!

HAMM [*anxious*]: What? A sail? A fin? Smoke?

CLOV [*looking*]: The light is sunk.

HAMM [*relieved*]: Pah! We all knew that.

CLOV [*looking*]: There was a bit left.

HAMM: The base.

CLOV [*looking*]: Yes.

HAMM: And now?

CLOV [*looking*]: All gone.

HAMM: No gulls?

CLOV [*looking*]: Gulls!

HAMM: And the horizon? Nothing on the horizon?

CLOV [*lowering the telescope, turning towards Hamm, exasperated*]: What in God's name could there be on the horizon? [*Pause.*]

HAMM: The waves, how are the waves?

CLOV: The waves? [*He turns the telescope on the waves.*] Lead.

HAMM: And the sun?

CLOV [*looking*]: Zero.

HAMM: But it should be sinking. Look again.

CLOV [*looking*]: Damn the sun.

HAMM: Is it night already then?

CLOV [*looking*]: No.

HAMM: Then what is it?

CLOV [*looking*]: Gray. [*Lowering the telescope, turning towards* HAMM, *louder.*] Gray! [*Pause. Still louder.*] GRRAY! [*Pause. He gets down, approaches* HAMM *from behind, whispers in his ear.*]

HAMM [*starting*]: Gray! Did I hear you say gray?

CLOV: Light black. From pole to pole.

HAMM: You exaggerate. [*Pause.*] Don't stay there, you give me the shivers. [CLOV *returns to his place beside the chair.*]

CLOV: Why this farce, day after day?

HAMM: Routine. One never knows. [*Pause.*] Last night I saw inside my breast. There was a big sore.

CLOV: Pah! You saw your heart.

HAMM: No, it was living. [*Pause. Anguished.*] Clov!

CLOV: Yes.

HAMM: What's happening?

CLOV: Something is taking its course. [*Pause.*]

HAMM: Clov!

CLOV [*impatiently*]: What is it?

HAMM: We're not beginning to . . . to . . . mean something?

CLOV: Mean something! You and I, mean something! [*Brief laugh.*] Ah that's a good one!

HAMM: I wonder. [*Pause.*] Imagine if a rational being came back to earth, wouldn't he be liable to get ideas into his head if he observed us long enough. [*Voice of rational being.*] Ah, good, now I see what it is, yes, now I understand what they're at! [CLOV *starts, drops the telescope and begins to scratch his belly with both hands. Normal voice.*] And without going so far as that, we ourselves . . . [*with emotion*] . . . we ourselves . . . at certain moments . . . [*Vehemently.*] To think perhaps it won't all have been for nothing!

CLOV [*anguished, scratching himself*]: I have a flea!

HAMM: A flea! Are there still fleas?

CLOV: On me there's one. [*Scratching.*] Unless it's a crablouse.

HAMM [*very perturbed*]: But humanity might start from there all over again! Catch him, for the love of God!

CLOV: I'll go and get the powder. [*Exit* CLOV.]

HAMM: A flea! This is awful! What a day! [*Enter* CLOV *with a sprinkling-tin.*]

CLOV: I'm back again, with the insecticide.

HAMM: Let him have it! [CLOV *loosens the top of his trousers, pulls it forward and shakes powder into the aperture. He stoops, looks, waits, starts, frenziedly shakes more powder, stoops, looks, waits.*]

CLOV: The bastard!

HAMM: Did you get him?

CLOV: Looks like it. [*He drops the tin and adjusts his trousers.*] Unless he's laying doggo.

HAMM: Laying! Lying you mean. Unless he's *lying* doggo.

CLOV: Ah? One says lying? One doesn't say laying?

HAMM: Use your head, can't you. If he was laying we'd be bitched.

CLOV: Ah. [*Pause.*] What about that pee?

HAMM: I'm having it.

CLOV: Ah that's the spirit, that's the spirit! [*Pause.*]

HAMM: [*with ardour*]: Let's go from here, the two of us! South! You can make a raft and the currents will carry us away, far away, to other . . . mammals!

CLOV: God forbid!

HAMM: Alone, I'll embark alone! Get working on that raft immediately. Tomorrow I'll be gone for ever.

CLOV [*hastening towards door*]: I'll start straight away.

HAMM: Wait! [CLOV *halts.*] Will there be sharks, do you think?

CLOV: Sharks? I don't know. If there are there will be. [*He goes towards door.*]

HAMM: Wait! [CLOV *halts.*] Is it not yet time for my pain-killer?

CLOV [*violently*]: No! [*He goes towards door.*]

HAMM: Wait! [CLOV *halts.*] How are your eyes?

CLOV: Bad.

HAMM: But you can see.

CLOV: All I want.

HAMM: How are your legs?

CLOV: Bad.

HAMM: But you can walk.

CLOV: I come . . . and go.

HAMM: In my house. [*Pause. With prophetic relish.*] One day you'll be blind, like me. You'll be sitting there, a speck in the void, in the dark, for ever, like me. [*Pause.*] One day you'll say to yourself, I'm tired, I'll sit down, and you'll go and sit down. Then you'll say, I'm hungry, I'll get up and get something to eat. But you won't get up. You'll say, I shouldn't have sat down, but since I have I'll sit on a little longer, then I'll get up and get something to eat. But you won't go up and you won't get anything to eat. [*Pause.*] You'll look at the wall a while, then you'll say, I'll close my eyes, perhaps have a little sleep, after that I'll feel better, and you'll close them. And when you open them again there'll be no wall any more. [*Pause.*] Infinite emptiness will be all around you, all the resurrected dead of all the ages wouldn't fill it, and there you'll be like a little bit of grit in the middle of the steppe. [*Pause.*] Yes, one day you'll know what it is, you'll be like me, except that you won't have anyone with you, because you won't have had pity on anyone and because there won't be anyone left to have pity on. [*Pause.*]

CLOV: It's not certain. [*Pause.*] And there's one thing you forget.

HAMM: Ah?

CLOV: I can't sit down.

HAMM [*impatiently*]: Well you'll lie down then, what the hell! Or you'll come to a standstill, simply stop and stand still, the way you are now. One day you'll say, I'm tired, I'll stop. What does the attitude matter? [*Pause.*]

CLOV: So you all want me to leave you.

HAMM: Naturally.

CLOV: Then I'll leave you.

HAMM: You can't leave us.

CLOV: Then I won't leave you. [*Pause.*]

HAMM: Why don't you finish us? [*Pause.*] I'll tell you the combination of the cupboard if you promise to finish me.

CLOV: I couldn't finish you.

HAMM: Then you won't finish me. [*Pause.*]

CLOV: I'll leave you, I have things to do.

HAMM: Do you remember when you came here?

CLOV: No. Too small, you told me.

HAMM: Do you remember your father?

CLOV [*wearily*]: Same answer. [*Pause.*] You've asked me these questions millions of times.

HAMM: I love the old questions. [*With fervor.*] Ah the old questions, the old answers, there's nothing like them! [*Pause.*] It was I was a father to you.

CLOV: Yes. [*He looks at* HAMM *fixedly.*] You were that to me.

HAMM: My house a home for you.

CLOV: Yes. [*He looks about him.*] This was that for me.

HAMM [*proudly*]: But for me, [*gesture towards himself*] no father. But for Hamm, [*gesture towards surroundings*] no home. [*Pause.*]

CLOV: I'll leave you.

HAMM: Did you ever think of one thing?

CLOV: Never.

HAMM: That here we're down in a hole. [*Pause.*] But beyond the hills? Eh? Perhaps it's still green. Eh? [*Pause.*] Flora! Pomona! [*Ecstatically.*] Ceres![6] [*Pause.*] Perhaps you won't need to go very far.

CLOV: I can't go very far. [*Pause.*] I'll leave you.

HAMM: Is my dog ready?

CLOV: He lacks a leg.

HAMM: Is he silky?

CLOV: He's a kind of Pomeranian.

HAMM: Go and get him.

CLOV: He lacks a leg.

HAMM: Go and get him! [*Exit* CLOV.] We're getting on. [*Enter* CLOV *holding by one of its three legs a black toy dog.*]

CLOV: Your dogs are here. [*He hands the dog to* HAMM *who feels it, fondles it.*]

HAMM: He's white, isn't he?

CLOV: Nearly.

HAMM: What do you mean, nearly? Is he white or isn't he?

CLOV: He isn't. [*Pause.*]

HAMM: You've forgotten the sex.

CLOV [*vexed*]: But he isn't finished. The sex goes on at the end. [*Pause.*]

HAMM: You haven't put on his ribbon.

CLOV [*angrily*]: But he isn't finished, I tell you! First you finish your

---

6. In Roman mythology, the goddesses of flowers, fruits, and fertility.

dog and then you put on his ribbon! [*Pause.*]

HAMM: Can he stand?

CLOV: I don't know.

HAMM: Try. [*He hands the dog to* CLOV *who places it on the ground.*] Well?

CLOV: Wait! [*He squats down and tries to get the dog to stand on its three legs, fails, lets it go. The dog falls on its side.*]

HAMM [*impatiently*]: Well?

CLOV: He's standing.

HAMM [*groping for the dog*]: Where? Where is he? [CLOV *holds up the dog in a standing position.*]

CLOV: There. [*He takes* HAMM*'s hand and guides it towards the dog's head.*]

HAMM [*his hand on the dog's head*]: Is he gazing at me?

CLOV: Yes.

HAMM [*proudly*]: As if he were asking me to take him for a walk?

CLOV: If you like.

HAMM [*as before*]: Or as if he were begging me for a bone. [*He withdraws his hand.*] Leave him like that, standing there imploring me. [CLOV *straightens up. The dog falls on its side.*]

CLOV: I'll leave you.

HAMM: Have you had your visions?

CLOV: Less.

HAMM: Is Mother Pegg's light on?

CLOV: Light! How could anyone's light be on?

HAMM: Extinguished!

CLOV: Naturally it's extinguished. If it's not on it's extinguished.

HAMM: No, I mean Mother Pegg.

CLOV: But naturally she's extinguished! [*Pause.*] What's the matter with you today?

HAMM: I'm taking my course. [*Pause.*] Is she buried?

CLOV: Buried! Who would have buried her?

HAMM: You.

CLOV: Me! Haven't I enough to do without burying people?

HAMM: But you'll bury me.

CLOV: No I won't bury you. [*Pause.*]

HAMM: She was bonny once, like a flower of the field. [*With reminiscent leer.*] And a great one for the men!

CLOV: We too were bonny—once. It's a rare thing not to have been bonny—once. [*Pause.*]

HAMM: Go and get the gaff. [CLOV *goes to door, halts.*]

CLOV: Do this, do that, and I do it. I never refuse. Why?

HAMM: You're not able to.

CLOV: Soon I won't do it any more.

HAMM: You won't be able to any more. [*Exit* CLOV.] Ah the creatures, the creatures, everything has to be explained to them. [*Enter* CLOV *with gaff.*]

CLOV: Here's your gaff. Stick it up. [*He gives the gaff to* HAMM *who, wielding it like a puntpole, tries to move his chair.*]

HAMM: Did I move?

CLOV: No. [HAMM *throws down the gaff.*]

HAMM: Go and get the oilcan.

CLOV: What for?

HAMM: To oil the castors.

CLOV: I oiled them yesterday.

HAMM: Yesterday! What does that mean? Yesterday!

CLOV [*violently*]: That means that bloody awful day, long ago, before this bloody awful day. I use the words you taught me. If they don't mean anything any more, teach me others. Or let me be silent. [*Pause.*]

HAMM: I once knew a madman who thought the end of the world had come. He was a painter—and engraver. I had a great fondness for him. I used to go and see him, in the asylum. I'd take him by the hand and drag him to the window. Look! There! All that rising corn! And there! Look! The sails of the herring fleet! All that loveliness! [*Pause.*] He'd snatch away his hand and go back into his corner. Appalled. All he had seen was ashes. [*Pause.*] He alone had been spared. [*Pause.*] Forgotten. [*Pause.*] It appears the case is . . . was not so . . . so unusual.

CLOV: A madman! When was that?

HAMM: Oh way back, way back, you weren't in the land of the living.

CLOV: God be with the days! [*Pause.* HAMM *raises his toque.*]

HAMM: I had a great fondness for him. [*Pause. He puts on his toque again.*] He was a painter—and engraver.

CLOV: There are so many terrible things.

HAMM: No, no, there are not so many now. [*Pause.*] Clov!

CLOV: Yes.

HAMM: Do you not think this has gone on long enough?

CLOV: Yes! [*Pause.*] What?

HAMM: This . . . this . . . thing.

CLOV: I've always thought so. [*Pause.*] You not?

HAMM [*gloomily*]: Then it's a day like any other day.

CLOV: As long as it lasts. [*Pause.*] All life long the same inanities.

HAMM: I can't leave you.

CLOV: I know. And you can't follow me. [*Pause.*]

HAMM: If you leave me how shall I know?

CLOV [*briskly*]: Well you simply whistle me and if I don't come running it means I've left you. [*Pause.*]

HAMM: You won't come and kiss me goodbye?

CLOV: Oh I shouldn't think so. [*Pause.*]

HAMM: But you might be merely dead in your kitchen.

CLOV: The result would be the same.

HAMM: Yes, but how would I know, if you were merely dead in your kitchen?

CLOV: Well . . . sooner or later I'd start to stink.

HAMM: You stink already. The whole place stinks of corpses.

CLOV: The whole universe.

HAMM [*angrily*]: To hell with the universe. [*Pause.*] Think of something.

CLOV: What?

HAMM: An idea, have an idea. [*Angrily.*] A bright idea!

CLOV: Ah good. [*He starts pacing to and fro, his eyes fixed on the ground, his hands behind his back. He halts.*] The pains in my legs! It's unbelievable! Soon I won't be able to think any more.

HAMM: You won't be able to leave me. [CLOV *resumes his pacing.*] What are you doing?

CLOV: Having an idea. [*He paces.*] Ah! [*He halts.*]

HAMM: What a brain! [*Pause.*] Well?

CLOV: Wait! [*He meditates. Not very convinced.*] Yes . . . [*Pause. More convinced.*] Yes! [*He raises his head.*] I have it! I set the alarm. [*Pause.*]

HAMM: This is perhaps not one of my bright days, but frankly—

CLOV: You whistle me. I don't come. The alarm rings. I'm gone. It doesn't ring. I'm dead. [*Pause.*]

HAMM: Is it working? [*Pause. Impatiently.*] The alarm, is it working?

CLOV: Why wouldn't it be working?

HAMM: Because it's worked too much.

CLOV: But it's hardly worked at all.

HAMM [*angrily*]: Then because it's worked too little!

CLOV: I'll go and see. [*Exit* CLOV. *Brief ring of alarm off. Enter* CLOV *with alarm-clock. He holds it against* HAMM'*s ear and releases alarm. They listen to it ringing to the end. Pause.*] Fit to wake the dead! Did you hear it?

HAMM: Vaguely.

CLOV: The end is terrific!

HAMM: I prefer the middle. [*Pause.*] Is it not time for my pain-killer?

CLOV: No! [*He goes to door, turns.*] I'll leave you.

HAMM: It's time for my story. Do you want to listen to my story.

CLOV: No.

HAMM: Ask my father if he wants to listen to my story. [CLOV *goes to bins, raises the lid of* NAGG'*s, stoops, looks into it. Pause. He straightens up.*]

CLOV: He's asleep.

HAMM: Wake him. [CLOV *stoops, wakes* NAGG *with the alarm. Unin-*

telligible words. CLOV *straightens up.*]

CLOV: He doesn't want to listen to your story.

HAMM: I'll give him a bon-bon. [CLOV *stoops. As before.*]

CLOV: He wants a sugar-plum.

HAMM: He'll get a sugar-plum. [CLOV *stoops. As before.*]

CLOV: It's a deal. [*He goes towards door.* NAGG'*s hands appear, gripping the rim. Then the head emerges.* CLOV *reaches door, turns.*] Do you believe in the life to come?

HAMM: Mine was always that. [*Exit* CLOV.] Got him that time!

NAGG: I'm listening.

HAMM: Scoundrel! Why did you engender me?

NAGG: I didn't know.

HAMM: What? What didn't you know?

NAGG: That it'd be you. [*Pause.*] You'll give me a sugar-plum?

HAMM: After the audition.

NAGG: You swear?

HAMM: Yes.

NAGG: On what?

HAMM: My honor. [*Pause. They laugh heartily.*]

NAGG: Two.

HAMM: One.

NAGG: One for me and one for—

HAMM: One! Silence! [*Pause.*] Where was I? [*Pause. Gloomily.*] It's finished, we're finished. [*Pause.*] Nearly finished. [*Pause.*] There'll be no more speech. [*Pause.*] Something dripping in my head, ever since the fontanelles. [*Stifled hilarity of* NAGG.] Splash, splash, always on the same spot. [*Pause.*] Perhaps it's a little vein. [*Pause.*] A little artery. [*Pause. More animated.*] Enough of that, it's story time, where was I? [*Pause. Narrative tone.*] The man came crawling towards me, on his belly. Pale, wonderfully pale and thin, he seemed on the point of—[*Pause. Normal tone.*] No, I've done that bit. [*Pause. Narrative tone.*] I calmly filled my pipe—the meerschaum, lit it with . . . let us say a vesta, drew a few puffs. Aah! [*Pause.*] Well, what is it *you* want? [*Pause.*] It was an extra-ordinarily bitter day, I remember, zero by the thermometer. But considering it was Christmas Eve there was nothing . . . extra-ordinary about that. Seasonable weather, for once in a way. [*Pause.*] Well, what ill wind blows you my way? He raised his face to me, black with mingled dirt and tears. [*Pause. Normal tone.*] That should do it. [*Narrative tone.*] No, no, don't look at me, don't look at me. He dropped his eyes and mumbled something, apologies I presume. [*Pause.*] I'm a busy man, you know, the final touches, before the festivities, you know what it is. [*Pause. Forcibly.*] Come on now, what is the object of this invasion? [*Pause.*] It was a glorious bright day, I remember, fifty by the heliometer,[7] but already the sun was sinking down into the . . . down among the dead. [*Normal tone.*] Nicely put, that. [*Narrative tone.*] Come on now, come on, present your petition and let me resume my labors. [*Pause. Normal tone.*] There's English for you. Ah well . . . [*Narrative tone.*] It was then he took the plunge. It's my little one, he said. T'sstss, a little one, that's bad. My little boy, he said, as if the sex mattered. Where did he come from? He named the hole. A good half-day, on horse. What are you insinuating? That the place is still inhabited? No no, not a soul, except himself and the child— assuming he existed. Good. I enquired about the situation at Kov, beyond the gulf. Not a sinner. Good. And you expect me to believe you have left your little one back there, all alone, and alive into the bargain? Come now! [*Pause.*] It was a howling wild day, I remember, a hundred by the anemometer.[8] The wind was tearing up the dead pines and sweeping them . . . away. [*Pause. Normal tone.*] A bit feeble, that. [*Narrative tone.*] Come on, man, speak up, what is you want from me, I have to put up my holly. [*Pause.*] Well to make it short it finally transpired that what he wanted from me was . . . bread for his brat? Bread? But I have no bread, it doesn't agree with me. Good. Then perhaps a little corn? [*Pause. Normal tone.*] That should do it. [*Narrative tone.*] Corn, yes, I have corn, it's true, in my granaries. But use your head. I give you some corn, a pound, a pound and a half, you bring it back to your child and you make him—if he's still alive—a nice pot of porridge, [NAGG *reacts.*] a nice pot and a half of porridge, full of nourishment. Good. The colors come back into his little cheeks— perhaps. And then? [*Pause.*] I lost patience. [*Violently.*] Use your head, can't you, use your head, you're on earth, there's no cure for that! [*Pause.*] It was an exceedingly dry day, I remember, zero by the hygrometer.[9] Ideal weather, for my lumbago. [*Pause. Violently.*] But what in God's name do you imagine? That the earth will awake in spring? That the rivers and seas will run with fish again? That there's manna in heaven still for imbeciles like you? [*Pause.*] Gradually I cooled down, sufficiently at least to ask him how long he had taken on the way. Three whole days. Good. In what condition he had left the child. Deep in sleep. [*Forcibly.*] But deep in what sleep, deep in what sleep already? [*Pause.*] Well to make it short I finally offered to take him into my service. He had touched a chord. And then I imagined already that I wasn't much longer for this world. [*He laughs. Pause.*] Well? [*Pause.*] Well? Here if you were careful you might die a nice natural death,

---

7. Literally, a "sun meter." Ordinarily, a telescope used to measure distances between celestial bodies.   8. A wind meter.   9. A moisture meter.

in peace and comfort. [*Pause.*] Well? [*Pause.*] In the end he asked me would I consent to take in the child as well—if he were still alive. [*Pause.*] It was the moment I was waiting for. [*Pause.*] Would I consent to take in the child . . . [*Pause.*] I can see him still, down on his knees, his hands flat on the ground, glaring at me with his mad eyes, in defiance of my wishes. [*Pause. Normal tone.*] I'll soon have finished with this story. [*Pause.*] Unless I bring in other characters. [*Pause.*] But where would I find them? [*Pause.*] Where would I look for them? [*Pause. He whistles. Enter* CLOV.] Let us pray to God.

NAGG: Me sugar-plum!

CLOV: There's a rat in the kitchen!

HAMM: A rat! Are there still rats?

CLOV: In the kitchen there's one.

HAMM: And you haven't exterminated him?

CLOV: Half. You disturbed us.

HAMM: He can't get away?

CLOV: No.

HAMM: You'll finish him later. Let us pray to God.

CLOV: Again!

NAGG: Me sugar-plum!

HAMM: God first! [*Pause.*] Are you right?

CLOV [*resigned*]: Off we go.

HAMM [*to* NAGG]: And you?

NAGG [*clasping his hands, closing his eyes, in a gabble*]: Our Father which art—

HAMM: Silence! In silence! Where are your manners? [*Pause.*] Off we go. [*Attitudes of prayer. Silence. Abandoning his attitude, discouraged.*] Well?

CLOV [*abandoning his attitude*]: What a hope! And you?

HAMM: Sweet damn all! [*To* NAGG.] And you?

NAGG: Wait! [*Pause. Abandoning his attitude.*] Nothing doing!

HAMM: The bastard! He doesn't exist!

CLOV: Not yet.

NAGG: Me sugar-plum!

HAMM: There are no more sugar-plums! [*Pause.*]

NAGG: It's natural. After all I'm your father. It's true if it hadn't been me it would have been someone else. But that's no excuse. [*Pause.*] Turkish Delight,[1] for example, which no longer exists, we all know that, there is nothing in the world I love more. And one day I'll ask you for some, in return for a kindness, and you'll promise it to me. One must live with the times. [*Pause.*] Whom did you call when you were a tiny boy, and were frightened, in the dark? Your

---

1. A sticky sweet candy.

mother? No. Me. We let you cry. Then we moved you out of earshot, so that we might sleep in peace. [*Pause.*] I was asleep, as happy as a king, and you woke me up to have me listen to you. It wasn't indispensable, you didn't really need to have me listen to you. [*Pause.*] I hope the day will come when you'll really need to have me listen to you, and need to hear my voice, any voice. [*Pause.*] Yes, I hope I'll live till then, to hear you calling me like when you were a tiny boy, and were frightened, in the dark, and I was your only hope. [*Pause. NAGG knocks on lid of NELL's bin. Pause.*] Nell! [*Pause. He knocks louder. Pause. Louder.*] Nell! [*Pause. NAGG sinks back into his bin, closes the lid behind him. Pause.*]

HAMM: Our revels now are ended.[2] [*He gropes for the dog.*] The dog's gone.

CLOV: He's not a real dog, he can't go.

HAMM [*groping*]: He's not there.

CLOV: He's lain down.

HAMM: Give him up to me. [CLOV *picks up the dog and gives it to* HAMM. HAMM *holds it in his arms. Pause.* HAMM *throws away the dog.*] Dirty brute! [CLOV *begins to pick up the objects lying on the ground.*] What are you doing?

CLOV: Putting things in order. [*He straightens up. Fervently.*] I'm going to clear everything away! [*He starts picking up again.*]

HAMM: Order!

CLOV [*straightening up*]: I love order. It's my dream. A world where all would be silent and still and each thing in its last place, under the last dust. [*He starts picking up again.*]

HAMM [*exasperated*]: What in God's name do you think you are doing?

CLOV [*straightening up*]: I'm doing my best to create a little order.

HAMM: Drop it! [CLOV *drops the objects he has picked up.*]

CLOV: After all, there or elsewhere. [*He goes towards door.*]

HAMM [*irritably*]: What's wrong with your feet?

CLOV: My feet?

HAMM: Tramp! Tramp!

CLOV: I must have put on my boots.

HAMM: Your slippers were hurting you? [*Pause.*]

CLOV: I'll leave you.

HAMM: No!

CLOV: What is there to keep me here?

HAMM: The dialogue. [*Pause.*] I've got on with my story. [*Pause.*] I've got on with it well. [*Pause. Irritably.*] Ask me where I've got to.

CLOV: Oh, by the way, your story?

HAMM [*surprised*]: What story?

---

2. Lines spoken by Prospero in Shakespeare's *The Tempest* (Act IV, 1, l. 148).

CLOV: The one you've been telling yourself all your days.

HAMM: Ah you mean my chronicle?

CLOV: That's the one. [*Pause.*]

HAMM [*angrily*]: Keep going, can't you, keep going!

CLOV: You've got on with it, I hope.

HAMM [*modestly*]: Oh not very far, not very far. [*He sighs.*] There are days like that, one isn't inspired. [*Pause.*] Nothing you can do about it, just wait for it to come. [*Pause.*] No forcing, no forcing, it's fatal. [*Pause.*] I've got on with it a little all the same. [*Pause.*] Technique, you know. [*Pause. Irritably.*] I say I've got on with it a little all the same.

CLOV [*admiringly*]: Well I never! In spite of everything you were able to get on with it!

HAMM [*modestly*]: Oh not very far, you know, not very far, but nevertheless, better than nothing.

CLOV: Better than nothing! Is it possible?

HAMM: I'll tell you how it goes. He comes crawling on his belly—

CLOV: Who?

HAMM: What?

CLOV: Who do you mean, he?

HAMM: Who do I mean! Yet another.

CLOV: Ah him! I wasn't sure.

HAMM: Crawling on his belly, whining for bread for his brat. He's offered a job as gardener. Before—[CLOV *bursts out laughing.*] What is there so funny about that?

CLOV: A job as gardener!

HAMM: Is that what tickles you?

CLOV: It must be that.

HAMM: It wouldn't be the bread?

CLOV: Or the brat. [*Pause.*]

HAMM: The whole thing is comical, I grant you that. What about having a good guffaw the two of us together?

CLOV [*after reflection*]: I couldn't guffaw again today.

HAMM [*after reflection*]: Nor I. [*Pause.*] I continue then. Before accepting with gratitude he asks if he may have his little boy with him.

CLOV: What age?

HAMM: Oh tiny.

CLOV: He would have climbed the trees.

HAMM: All the little odd jobs.

CLOV: And then he would have grown up.

HAMM: Very likely. [*Pause.*]

CLOV: Keep going, can't you, keep going!

HAMM: That's all. I stopped there. [*Pause.*]

CLOV: Do you see how it goes on.

HAMM: More or less.

CLOV: Will it not soon be the end?

HAMM: I'm afraid it will.

CLOV: Pah! You'll make up another.

HAMM: I don't know. [*Pause.*] I feel rather drained. [*Pause.*] The prolonged creative effort. [*Pause.*] If I could drag myself down to the sea! I'd make a pillow of sand for my head and the tide would come.

CLOV: There's no more tide. [*Pause.*]

HAMM: Go and see is she dead. [CLOV *goes to bins, raises the lid of* NELL*'s, stoops, looks into it. Pause.*]

CLOV: Looks like it. [*He closes the lid, straightens up.* HAMM *raises his toque. Pause. He puts it on again.*]

HAMM [*with his hand to his toque*]: And Nagg? [CLOV *raises lid of* NAGG*'s bin, stoops, looks into it. Pause.*]

CLOV: Doesn't look like it. [*He closes the lid, straightens up.*]

HAMM [*letting go his toque*]: What's he doing? [CLOV *raises lid of* NAGG*'s bin, stoops, looks into it. Pause.*]

CLOV: He's crying. [*He closes lid, straightens up.*]

HAMM: Then he's living. [*Pause.*] Did you ever have an instant of happiness?

CLOV: Not to my knowledge. [*Pause.*]

HAMM: Bring me under the window. [CLOV *goes towards chair.*] I want to feel the light on my face. [CLOV *pushes chair.*] Do you remember, in the beginning, when you took me for a turn? You used to hold the chair too high. At every step you nearly tipped me out. [*With senile quaver.*] Ah great fun, we had, the two of us, great fun. [*Gloomily.*] And then we got into the way of it. [CLOV *stops the chair under window right.*] There already? [*Pause. He tilts back his head.*] Is it light?

CLOV: It isn't dark.

HAMM [*angrily*]: I'm asking you is it light.

CLOV: Yes. [*Pause.*]

HAMM: The curtain isn't closed?

CLOV: No.

HAMM: What window is it?

CLOV: The earth.

HAMM: I knew it! [*Angrily.*] But there's no light there! The other! [CLOV *stops the chair under window left.* HAMM *tilts back his head.*] That's what I call light! [*Pause.*] Feels like a ray of sunshine. [*Pause.*] No?

CLOV: No.

HAMM: It isn't a ray of sunshine I feel on my face?

CLOV: No. [*Pause.*]

HAMM: Am I very white? [*Pause. Angrily.*] I'm asking you am I very white!

CLOV: Not more so than usual. [*Pause.*]

HAMM: Open the window.

CLOV: What for?

HAMM: I want to hear the sea.

CLOV: You wouldn't hear it.

HAMM: Even if you opened the window?

CLOV: No.

HAMM: Then it's not worth while opening it?

CLOV: No.

HAMM [*violently*]: Then open it! [CLOV *gets up on the ladder, opens the window. Pause.*] Have you opened it?

CLOV: Yes. [*Pause.*]

HAMM: You swear you've opened it?

CLOV: Yes. [*Pause.*]

HAMM: Well. . . ! [*Pause.*] It must be very calm. [*Pause. Violently.*] I'm asking you is it very calm!

CLOV: Yes.

HAMM: It's because there are no more navigators. [*Pause.*] You haven't much conversation all of a sudden. Do you not feel well?

CLOV: I'm cold.

HAMM: What month are we? [*Pause.*] Close the window, we're going back. [CLOV *closes the window, gets down, pushes the chair back to its place, remains standing behind it, head bowed.*] Don't stay there, you give me the shivers! [CLOV *returns to his place beside the chair.*] Father! [*Pause. Louder.*] Father! [*Pause.*] Go and see did he hear me. [CLOV *goes to* NAGG's *bin, raises the lid, stoops. Unintelligible words.* CLOV *straightens up.*]

CLOV: Yes.

HAMM: Both times? [CLOV *stoops. As before.*]

CLOV: Once only.

HAMM: The first time or the second? [CLOV *stoops. As before.*]

CLOV: He doesn't know.

HAMM: It must have been the second.

CLOV: We'll never know. [*He closes lid.*]

HAMM: Is he still crying?

CLOV: No.

HAMM: The dead go fast. [*Pause.*] What's he doing?

CLOV: Sucking his biscuit.

HAMM: Life goes on. [CLOV *returns to his place beside the chair.*] Give me a rug. I'm freezing.

CLOV: There are no more rugs. [*Pause.*]

HAMM: Kiss me. [*Pause.*] Will you not kiss me?

CLOV: No.

HAMM: On the forehead.

CLOV: I won't kiss you anywhere. [*Pause.*]

HAMM [*holding out his hand*]: Give me your hand at least. [*Pause.*] Will you not give me your hand?

CLOV: I won't touch you. [*Pause.*]

HAMM: Give me the dog. [CLOV *looks round for the dog.*] No!

CLOV: Do you not want your dog?

HAMM: No.

CLOV: Then I'll leave you.

HAMM [*head bowed, absently*]: That's right. [CLOV *goes to door, turns.*]

CLOV: If I don't kill that rat he'll die.

HAMM [*as before*]: That's right. [*Exit* CLOV. *Pause.*] Me to play. [*He takes out his handkerchief, unfolds it, holds it spread out before him.*] We're getting on. [*Pause.*] You weep, and weep, for nothing, so as not to laugh, and little by little . . . you begin to grieve. [*He folds the handkerchief, puts it back in his pocket, raises his head.*] All those I might have helped. [*Pause.*] Helped! [*Pause.*] Saved. [*Pause.*] Saved! [*Pause.*] The place was crawling with them! [*Pause. Violently.*] Use your head, can't you, use your head, you're on earth, there's no cure for that! [*Pause.*] Get out of here and love one another! Lick your neighbor as yourself![3] [*Pause. Calmer.*] When it wasn't bread they wanted it was crumpets. [*Pause. Violently.*] Out of my sight and back to your petting parties! [*Pause.*] All that, all that! [*Pause.*] Not even a real dog! [*Calmer.*] The end is in the beginning and yet you go on. [*Pause.*] Perhaps I could go on with my story, end it and begin another. [*Pause.*] Perhaps I could throw myself out on the floor. [*He pushes himself painfully off his seat, falls back again.*] Dig my nails into the cracks and drag myself forward with my fingers. [*Pause.*] It will be the end and there I'll be, wondering what can have brought it on and wondering what can have . . . [*he hesitates*] . . . why it was so long coming. [*Pause.*] There I'll be, in the old shelter, alone against the silence and . . . [*he hesitates*] . . . the stillness. If I can hold my peace, and sit quiet, it will be all over with sound, and motion, all over and done with. [*Pause.*] I'll have called my father and I'll have called my . . . [*he hesitates*] . . . my son. And even twice, or three times, in case they shouldn't have heard me, the first time, or the second. [*Pause.*] I'll say to myself, He'll come back. [*Pause.*] And then? [*Pause.*] And then? [*Pause.*] He couldn't, he has gone too far. [*Pause.*] And then? [*Pause. Very agitated.*] All kinds of fantasies! That I'm being watched! A rat! Steps! Breath held and then . . . [*He breathes out.*] Then babble, babble, words,

3. Parody of Christ's words in the Bible: "Thou shalt love thy neighbor as thyself" (Matthew 19:19 and elsewhere).

like the solitary child who turns himself into children, two, three,
so as to be together, and whisper together, in the dark. [*Pause.*]
Moment upon moment, pattering down, like the millet grains of
. . . [*he hesitates*] . . . that old Greek,[4] and all life long you wait
for that to mount up to a life. [*Pause. He opens his mouth to
continue, renounces.*] Ah let's get it over! [*He whistles. Enter* CLOV
with alarm-clock. He halts beside the chair.] What? Neither gone
nor dead?

CLOV: In spirit only.

HAMM: Which?

CLOV: Both.

HAMM: Gone from me you'd be dead.

CLOV: And vice versa.

HAMM: Outside of here it's death! [*Pause.*] And the rat?

CLOV: He's got away.

HAMM: He can't go far. [*Pause. Anxious.*] Eh?

CLOV: He doesn't need to go far. [*Pause.*]

HAMM: Is it not time for my pain-killer?

CLOV: Yes.

HAMM: Ah! At last! Give it to me! Quick! [*Pause.*]

CLOV: There's no more pain-killer. [*Pause.*]

HAMM [*appalled*]: Good. . . ! [*Pause.*] No more pain-killer!

CLOV: No more pain-killer. You'll never get any more pain-killer.
   [*Pause.*]

HAMM: But the little round box. It was full!

CLOV: Yes. But now it's empty. [*Pause.* CLOV *starts to move about the
   room. He is looking for a place to put down the alarm-clock.*]

HAMM [*soft*]: What'll I do? [*Pause. In a scream.*] What'll I do? [CLOV
   *sees the picture, takes it down, stands it on the floor with its face
   to the wall, hangs up the alarm-clock in its place.*] What are you
   doing?

CLOV: Winding up.

HAMM: Look at the earth.

CLOV: Again!

HAMM: Since it's calling to you.

CLOV: Is your throat sore? [*Pause.*] Would you like a lozenge? [*Pause.*]
   No. [*Pause.*] Pity. [CLOV *goes, humming, towards window right,
   halts before it, looks up at it.*]

HAMM: Don't sing.

CLOV [*turning towards* HAMM]: One hasn't the right to sing any more?

HAMM: No.

4. Zeno of Elea, a Greek philosopher active around 450 B.C., known for logical paradoxes that
reduce to absurdity various attempts to define Being. Aristotle reports that Zeno's paradox on
sound questioned: If a grain of millet falling makes no sound, how can a bushel of grains make
any sound? (Aristotle, *Physics*, 5:250a,19)

CLOV: Then how can it end?

HAMM: You want it to end?

CLOV: I want to sing.

HAMM: I can't prevent you. [*Pause.* CLOV *turns towards window right.*]

CLOV: What did I do with that steps? [*He looks around for ladder.*] You didn't see that steps? [*He sees it.*] Ah, about time. [*He goes towards window left.*] Sometimes I wonder if I'm in my right mind. Then it passes over and I'm as lucid as before. [*He gets up on ladder, looks out of window.*] Christ, she's under water! [*He looks.*] How can that be? [*He pokes forward his head, his hand above his eyes.*] It hasn't rained. [*He wipes the pane, looks. Pause.*] Ah what a fool I am! I'm on the wrong side! [*He gets down, takes a few steps towards window right.*] Under water! [*He goes back for ladder.*] What a fool I am! [*He carries ladder towards window right.*] Sometimes I wonder if I'm in my right senses. Then it passes off and I'm as intelligent as ever. [*He sets down ladder under window right, gets up on it, looks out of window. He turns towards* HAMM.] Any particular sector you fancy? Or merely the whole thing?

HAMM: Whole thing.

CLOV: The general effect? Just a moment. [*He looks out of window. Pause.*]

HAMM: Clov.

CLOV [*absorbed*]: Mmm.

HAMM: Do you know what it is?

CLOV [*as before*]: Mmm.

HAMM: I was never there. [*Pause.*] Clov!

CLOV [*turning towards* HAMM, *exasperated*]: What is it?

HAMM: I was never there.

CLOV: Lucky for you. [*He looks out of window.*]

HAMM: Absent, always. It all happened without me. I don't know what's happened. [*Pause.*] Do you know what's happened? [*Pause.*] Clov!

CLOV [*turning towards* HAMM, *exasperated*]: Do you want me to look at this muckheap, yes or no?

HAMM: Answer me first.

CLOV: What?

HAMM: Do you know what's happened?

CLOV: When? Where?

HAMM [*violently*]: When! What's happened? Use your head, can't you! What has happened?

CLOV: What for Christ's sake does it matter? [*He looks out of window.*]

HAMM: I don't know. [*Pause.* CLOV *turns towards* HAMM.]

CLOV [*harshly*]: When old Mother Pegg asked you for oil for her lamp and you told her to get out to hell, you knew what was happening then, no? [*Pause.*] You know what she died of, Mother Pegg? Of darkness.

HAMM [*feebly*]: I hadn't any.

CLOV [*as before*]: Yes, you had. [*Pause.*]

HAMM: Have you the glass?

CLOV: No, it's clear enough as it is.

HAMM: Go and get it. [*Pause.* CLOV *casts up his eyes, brandishes his fists. He loses balance, clutches on to the ladder. He starts to get down, halts.*]

CLOV: There's one thing I'll never understand. [*He gets down.*] Why I always obey you. Can you explain that to me?

HAMM: No. . . . Perhaps it's compassion. [*Pause.*] A kind of great compassion. [*Pause.*] Oh you won't find it easy, you won't find it easy. [*Pause.* CLOV *begins to move about the room in search of the telescope.*]

CLOV: I'm tired of our goings on, very tired. [*He searches.*] You're not sitting on it? [*He moves the chair, looks at the place where it stood, resumes his search.*]

HAMM [*anguished*]: Don't leave me there! [*Angrily* CLOV *restores the chair to its place.*] Am I right in the center?

CLOV: You'd need a microscope to find this—[*He sees the telescope.*] Ah, about time. [*He picks up the telescope, gets up on the ladder, turns the telescope on the without.*]

HAMM: Give me the dog.

CLOV [*looking*]: Quiet!

HAMM [*angrily*]: Give me the dog! [CLOV *drops the telescope, clasps his hands to his head. Pause. He gets down precipitately, looks for the dog, sees it, picks it up, hastens towards* HAMM *and strikes him violently on the head with the dog.*]

CLOV: There's your dog for you! [*The dog falls to the ground. Pause.*]

HAMM: He hit me!

CLOV: You drive me mad, I'm mad!

HAMM: If you must hit me, hit me with the axe. [*Pause.*] Or with the gaff, hit me with the gaff. Not with the dog. With the gaff. Or with the axe. [CLOV *picks up the dog and gives it to* HAMM *who takes it in his arms.*]

CLOV [*imploringly*]: Let's stop playing!

HAMM: Never! [*Pause.*] Put me in my coffin.

CLOV: There are no more coffins.

HAMM: Then let it end! [CLOV *goes towards ladder.*] With a bang! [CLOV *gets up on ladder, gets down again, looks for telescope, sees it, picks it up, gets up ladder, raises telescope.*] Of darkness! And me? Did anyone ever have pity on me?

CLOV [*lowering the telescope, turning towards* HAMM]: What? [*Pause.*] Is it me you're referring to?

HAMM [*angrily*]: An aside, ape! Did you never hear an aside before? [*Pause.*] I'm warming up for my last soliloquy.

CLOV: I warn you. I'm going to look at this filth since it's an order. But it's the last time. [*He turns the telescope on the without.*] Let's see. [*He moves the telescope.*] Nothing . . . nothing . . . good . . . good . . . nothing . . . goo—[*He starts, lowers the telescope, examines it, turns it again on the without. Pause.*] Bad luck to it!

HAMM: More complications! [CLOV *gets down.*] Not an underplot, I trust. [CLOV *moves ladder nearer window, gets up on it, turns telescope on the without.*]

CLOV [*dismayed*]: Looks like a small boy!

HAMM [*sarcastic*]: A small . . . boy!

CLOV: I'll go and see. [*He gets down, drops the telescope, goes towards door, turns.*] I'll take the gaff. [*He looks for the gaff, sees it, picks it up, hastens towards door.*]

HAMM: No! [CLOV *halts.*]

CLOV: No? A potential procreator?

HAMM: If he exists he'll die there or he'll come here. And if he doesn't . . . [*Pause.*]

CLOV: You don't believe me? You think I'm inventing? [*Pause.*]

HAMM: It's the end, Clov, we've come to the end. I don't need you any more. [*Pause.*]

CLOV: Lucky for you. [*He goes towards door.*]

HAMM: Leave me the gaff. [CLOV *gives him the gaff, goes towards door, halts, looks at alarm-clock, takes it down, looks round for a better place to put it, goes to bins, puts it on lid of* NAGG's *bin. Pause.*]

CLOV: I'll leave you. [*He goes towards door.*]

HAMM: Before you go . . . [CLOV *halts near door.*] . . . say something.

CLOV: There is nothing to say.

HAMM: A few words . . . to ponder . . . in my heart.

CLOV: Your heart!

HAMM: Yes. [*Pause. Forcibly.*] Yes! [*Pause.*] With the rest, in the end, the shadows, the murmurs, all the trouble, to end up with. [*Pause.*] Clov. . . . He never spoke to me. Then, in the end, before he went, without my having asked him, he spoke to me. He said . . .

CLOV [*despairingly*]: Ah. . . . !

HAMM: Something . . . from your heart.

CLOV: My heart!

HAMM: A few words . . . from your heart. [*Pause.*]

CLOV [*fixed gaze, tonelessly, towards auditorium*]: They said to me, That's love, yes, yes, not a doubt, now you see how—

HAMM: Articulate!

CLOV [*as before*]: How easy it is. They said to me, That's friendship, yes, yes, no question, you've found it. They said to me, Here's the place, stop, raise your head and look at all that beauty. That order! They said to me. Come now, you're not a brute·beast, think upon these things and you'll see how all becomes clear. And simple! They said to me, What skilled attention they get, all these dying of their wounds.

HAMM: Enough!

CLOV [*as before*]: I say to myself—sometimes, Clov, you must learn to suffer better than that if you want them to weary of punishing you—one day. I say to myself—sometimes, Clov, you must be there better than that if you want them to let you go—one day. But I feel too old, and too far, to form new habits. Good, it'll never end, I'll never go. [*Pause.*] Then one day, suddenly, it ends, it changes, I don't understand, it dies, or it's me, I don't understand, that either. I ask the words that remain—sleeping, waking, morning, evening. They have nothing to say. [*Pause.*] I open the door of the cell and go. I am so bowed I only see my feet, if I open my eyes, and between my legs a little trail of black dust. I say to myself that the earth is extinguished, though I never saw it lit. [*Pause.*] It's easy going. [*Pause.*] When I fall I'll weep for happiness. [*Pause. He goes towards door.*]

HAMM: Clov! [CLOV *halts, without turning.*] Nothing. [CLOV *moves on.*] Clov! [CLOV *halts, without turning.*]

CLOV: This is what we call making an exit.

HAMM: I'm obliged to you, Clov. For your services.

CLOV [*turning, sharply*]: Ah pardon, it's I am obliged to you.

HAMM: It's we are obliged to each other. [*Pause.* CLOV *goes towards door.*] One thing more. [CLOV *halts.*] A last favor. [*Exit* CLOV.] Cover me with the sheet. [*Long pause.*] No? Good. [*Pause.*] Me to play. [*Pause. Wearily.*] Old endgame lost of old, play and lose and have done with losing. [*Pause. More animated.*] Let me see. [*Pause.*] Ah yes! [*He tries to move the chair, using the gaff as before. Enter* CLOV, *dressed for the road. Panama hat, tweed coat, raincoat over his arm, umbrella, bag. He halts by the door and stands there, impassive and motionless, his eyes fixed on* HAMM, *till the end.* HAMM *gives up.*] Good. [*Pause.*] Discard. [*He throws away the gaff, makes to throw away the dog, thinks better of it.*] Take it easy. [*Pause.*] And now? [*Pause.*] Raise hat. [*He raises his toque.*] Peace to our . . . arses. [*Pause.*] And put on again. [*He puts on his toque.*] Deuce. [*Pause. He takes off his glasses.*] Wipe. [*He takes out his handkerchief and, without unfolding it, wipes his glasses.*] And put on again. [*He puts on his glasses, puts back the handkerchief in his pocket.*] We're coming. A few more squirms like that and I'll call. [*Pause.*] A little poetry. [*Pause.*] You prayed—

[*Pause. He corrects himself.*] You CRIED for night; it comes—
[*Pause. He corrects himself.*] It FALLS: now cry in darkness. [*He repeats, chanting.*] You cried for night; it falls: now cry in darkness.[5] [*Pause.*] Nicely put, that. [*Pause.*] And now? [*Pause.*] Moments for nothing, now as always, time was never and time is over, reckoning closed and story ended. [*Pause. Narrative tone.*] If he could have his child with him. . . . [*Pause.*] It was the moment I was waiting for. [*Pause.*] You don't want to abandon him? You want him to bloom while you are withering? Be there to solace your last million last moments? [*Pause.*] He doesn't realize, all he knows is hunger, and cold, and death to crown it all. But you! You ought to know what the earth is like, nowadays. Oh I put him before his responsibilities! [*Pause. Normal tone.*] Well, there we are, there I am, that's enough. [*He raises the whistle to his lips, hesitates, drops it. Pause.*] Yes, truly! [*He whistles. Pause. Louder. Pause.*] Good. [*Pause.*] Father! [*Pause. Louder.*] Father! [*Pause.*] Good. [*Pause.*] We're coming. [*Pause.*] And to end up with? [*Pause.*] Discard. [*He throws away the dog. He tears the whistle from his neck.*] With my compliments. [*He throws whistle towards auditorium. Pause. He sniffs. Soft.*] Clov! [*Long pause.*] No? Good. [*He takes out the handkerchief.*] Since that's the way we're playing it . . . [*he unfolds handkerchief*] . . . let's play it that way . . . [*he unfolds*] . . . and speak no more about it . . . [*he finishes unfolding*] . . . speak no more. [*He holds handkerchief spread out before him.*] Old stancher! [*Pause.*] You . . . remain. [*Pause. He covers his face with handkerchief, lowers his arms to armrests, remains motionless.*] [*Brief tableau.*]

Curtain

R. K. NARAYAN
1906—

India's foremost contemporary novelist casts a sympathetic but wryly comic glance on everyday life in his native land. His is a dual, Anglo-Indian sensibility: he uses the fictional techniques of the realistic Western novel, and writes in English for an international audience, but he describes a society where English is only one of fifteen major languages, and where cultural values are quite different from those of the British Isles. Narayan is known for a fictional universe centering in the South Indian town of Malgudi, a town that represents not only his own hometown of Mysore, but also patterns of cultural and generational conflict (and the struggle for identity inside

5. Parody of a line from the poem "Meditation," by Baudelaire: "You were calling for evening; it falls; here it is."

them) whose implications spread far beyond South India: "I can detect Malgudi characters even in New York." Like Faulkner, he is both a regional and a universal writer, and like Faulkner he has reached an international audience, with translations of his work into eight different languages.

A recurrent topic in Narayan's work is the quest for identity, a theme found also in Joyce, Proust, Lessing, or Ellison but whose cultural context is radically different for the Indian novelist. The world he describes is his own middle-class Indian society of the Brahmin caste (the highest level in Hindu religion): a traditional society with rigid expectations according to caste, where marriages are arranged according to horoscopes, men do the marketing and women do not go out alone, and the family structure is not the Western "nuclear family" but a "joint family" in which several related families and generations may live under the same roof sharing duties and expenses. Of course such society is changing: Narayan himself engineered his marriage (including a reinterpreted horoscope) to a woman he fell in love with when he saw her on the street, and much of his fiction depicts tensions between people and generations set apart by social change. At the same time, much has *not* changed in this world. The Hindu religious perspective, stressing the continuity of all life and the cyclical returns of reincarnation, provides a cosmic framework for all events, from the ghostly reappearance of the protagonist's wife in *The English Teacher* (1945) to the possibility of S.'s reincarnation as a dog in "Emden." "Our minds are trained to accept without surprise characters of godly or demoniac proportions with actions and reactions set in limitless worlds and progressing through an incalculable timescale," says Narayan, who maintains a framework of supernatural allusion throughout his work even if events can also be given a realistic or psychological interpretation.

As a result, Narayan's fiction has a characteristically ethical dimension in the midst of its most mundane or comic descriptions. Whether the protagonist is student, English teacher, shady financial expert, printer, tourist guide, vendor of sweets, sign painter, or even tiger, he is seen as a soul in search of spiritual identity. Part of the humor comes from the way in which an impulsive and often greedy hero is alternately thwarted and rewarded by events until he reaches a point where he is able to rise above material circumstances and take a longer view (which in itself may seem either saintly or ridiculous to the surrounding community). Margayya of *The Financial Expert* (1952) moves from poverty to wealth through pyramid schemes to poverty again; Raju of *The Guide* (1958) goes from poverty to wealth as a dancer's impresario to enforced sainthood and death when a village depends on him to fast for rain; Jagan the sweet-vendor becomes prosperous through shrewd business practices, suffers from a corrupt and rebellious son, and retires from the world to help sculpt the statue of a goddess (*The Sweet-Vendor*, 1967); the tiger of *A Tiger for Malgudi* (1983) goes from circus to hermit life and spiritual awareness under the guidance of a Master to whom all beings are equal. In each case, the fictional world is precisely drawn and convincingly real: the streets and shops are those of everyday Mysore in South India; the schools, offices, journals, and even film studios are modeled after Narayan's own experience; the domestic tensions—some of them clearly recalling situations in his own autobiography, *My Days* (1974)—are delicately outlined with careful attention paid both to individual psychology and to the shaping force of cultural context. This blend of closely focused realism and larger ethical vision creates the comic perspective for which Narayan is known: the panorama of a "human comedy" incorporating the most mundane details in the same breath as religious mysticism, in which the variety, sadness, and frustration of human life never appear as ends in themselves but are held somewhat at a distance, parts of a larger picture.

Rasipuram Krishnaswami Narayan was born on October 10, 1906, in a Brahmin family. His father was a headmaster of schools who was often relocated by the government, and his mother was of delicate health, so when the young boy was two years old he went to live with his grandmother and uncle in Madras. The family spoke Tamil (a South Indian language) at home, and Narayan learned English only in school. His grandmother insisted on giving him extra lessons in the evening in which she taught him the multiplication tables, the Tamil alphabet, classical melodies, and prayers in Sanskrit (the ancient language of India). She also told him Indian folk tales and myths, and recited poetry from the Vedas (the sacred writings of the Hindus), so that the young boy was steeped early in Indian language and culture in spite of the very different emphasis of his schools.

In the Lutheran Mission School Narayan attended first, he was the only Brahmin boy in his class and had to attend classes in the Christian Bible in which the Hindu gods were ridiculed and criticized. English was taught as the major language, with examples that were totally unfamiliar to Indian students: "A is for Apple" to students who knew guavas, mangoes, and pomegranates. Echoes of this colonial education (similar to that described by Camus in "The Guest") appear in *The Bachelor of Arts* (1937) and are satirized especially in *The English Teacher*, when Narayan pokes fun at the British headmaster of Albert Mission College for ponderously lecturing the teachers about the disgrace of a student's omitting the British *u* in *honours*. (As the protagonist comments later, Mr. Brown has spent thirty years in India and could not say "The cat chases the rat" in any of the two hundred Indian languages, major and minor.) Narayan attended a series of schools in Madras until his father, who had recently been appointed headmaster of Maharaja's Collegiate High School in Mysore, sent for him to live at home and attend school there. Here he had access to both the school and his father's library, and read voraciously in contemporary literary magazines as well as the English classics, the Indian writer Rabindranath Tagore, and world literature in translation. Nonetheless Narayan—who had always detested examinations and academic discipline—failed the University Entrance Examinations and had to read at home for another year before he finally passed and entered Maharaja's College. Here again his daydreaming habits took hold, and he graduated only in 1930 at the age of twenty-four; as he comments in *My Days*, the temptation to look out the window is so strong that he now blocks off the view with a gray drape when sitting down to write.

Narayan has never really envisaged any career other than writer. He began writing and submitting short pieces during the year spent in preparation for the University Entrance Examinations, and made only a brief and unhappy attempt at teaching after graduation. Living at home and supported as part of the joint-family system, he experimented with different themes and forms to develop his writing style, and expanded an early story about Malgudi into his first novel, *Swami and Friends* (1935). His earnings were small: nine rupees and twelve annas the first year (about $1.25), eighteen rupees the next, and thirty rupees the next. In 1933, however, he took a salaried job as reporter for a Madras paper, *The Justice*, to help support himself and his wife, Rajam, whom he had managed to marry in spite of difference in their horoscopes which seemed to predict an early death for his wife. Narayan spent his mornings gathering the Mysore news to send to Madras: "traffic accidents, suicides, or crimes . . . . Murders were my stand-by." His daily observations of life in the turbulent city would be useful in later work, but payments from *The Justice* were irregular and he was glad to stop working for the paper when a cable from England announced that *Swami and Friends* had been accepted. It was the British novelist Graham Greene who had recommended its publication, and who helped arrange publication of Narayan's next two novels, *The Bachelor of Arts* and *The Dark Room* (1938), with different publishers when sales did not measure up to critical acclaim.

Life became more difficult when Narayan's father died in 1937, and the young writer took to writing weekly humorous articles for the *Merry Magazine* to help support the family. The Mysore government, inspired by rumors of his literary fame in Britain, commissioned him to write a travel book on Mysore but the book—full of factual inaccuracies—was never published. By 1939, he was working on a variety of projects: weekly sketches for *The Hindu*, features for All India Radio, and dialogue or "treatments" for a film studio, and had sold the Tamil rights for serial publication of his third novel. His life changed abruptly, however, when Rajam caught typhoid fever and died in June 1939. Overwhelmed by her death, Narayan temporarily gave up writing and devoted himself to the care of their three-year-old daughter, Hema. The account of this painful period in his life is incorporated into *The English Teacher*, and includes a development in the second half of the novel that will be unexpected for many Western readers: the protagonist's introduction to spiritualist exercises, and his ultimate conviction that he is able to converse with the spirit of his departed wife. Although Narayan does not insist that his reader accept the reality of psychic contact beyond the grave, the autobiographical *My Days* concludes a discussion of Narayan's own psychic experiments at this time with a vision that pervades his later works: "The full view of a personality would extend from the infant curled up in the womb and before it, and beyond it, and ahead of it, into infinity. Our normal view is limited to a physical perception in a condition restricted in time."

With the success of *The English Teacher*, Narayan gained a wide audience. A new series of novels: *Mr. Sampath—The Printer of Malgudi* (1949), *The Financial Expert* (1952), and *The Guide* (1958, receiving the Sahitya Akademi Award in 1960) became famous internationally, and *Mr. Sampath* and *The Guide* were made into films. Narayan's best-known book is probably *The Guide*, a sophisticated interweaving of present and past scenes in the mind of the ex-tourist guide Raju, who has built the talented dancer Rosie into a national star, Nalini, only to be trapped by his own greed into forgery and a two-year jail sentence. Emerging from jail, Raju is taken for a saintly wanderer by local villagers and, when he decides to accept the new role of spiritual guide, he becomes more and more involved in village life until a misunderstanding obliges him to take the final steps of fasting until rains save the countryside. In *The Guide* as in his other works, Narayan evokes a multidimensional picture of domestic and social reality. The family tensions seen in Rosie's broken marriage and Raju's alienation from his disapproving family; the caste attitudes displayed especially in the prejudice against dancers; the amusing public-relations manipulations by which Raju makes Nalini a star, and Raju's less amusing possessive jealousy while he keeps the dancer performing to maintain their new life-style; the quick adjustment he makes to a reassuringly secure life as model prisoner; the religious habits and expectations demonstrated in the village's dependence on their spiritual guide, all allow Narayan ample opportunity to portray modern India as a tapestry of ancient and modern elements interwoven in the lives of specific individuals and contemporary situations.

"Emden" was published in the collection *Malgudi Days* (1982). In the introduction, Narayan defines his stories as moments "when a personality passes through a crisis of spirit or circumstances," or when "a pattern of existence [is] brought to view." Such a pattern emerges in the ambiguous experience of old Rao, called "Emden" after the name of a ruthless German battleship that shelled Madras during World War I. "Emden" is now the patriarch of a large family, twenty-three of whom live at home in a large house partitioned out according to the traditional joint-family system. Master of the household, he keeps to the old customs and insists on sitting on a rosewood plank to eat off a banana leaf instead of using the new dining room table typical of the modern, Westernized Malgudi. He is fond of his family but they have faded into an anonymous blur as his memory grows dim with advancing age. Rao has outlived most of his contemporaries, but a few survive—like the photo framer Jayaraj—who recall his earlier years and the reason for his surname: ruthless, domineering, sexually aggressive, and corrupt, Rao squeezed a fortune out of bribes in his job with the Excise Department until he was finally dismissed from government service. Living at home under the constant and respectful care of his numerous family, he has withdrawn into a private world of regular habits and piecemeal memories.

Rao's favorite column in the daily newspaper is the section on religion and philosophy: the column that deals with reincarnations, with fate or *karma*, with definitions of Good and Evil. It is this preoccupation that provides the tantalizing hint at the end of the story: the possibility that S. has returned as the dog who runs off with Rao's packet of sweets. But the story is also an account of an old man's return into a past which is shifting and impossible to recall: the jasmine he hazily remembers becomes sandalwood later on, and the street whose location he recalls so exactly is not there. Perhaps it is another indication of unconsciousness that he would expect to find S. standing in her doorway, for she is probably dead like most of his contemporaries. Only the diary entry from fifty-one years ago has any hard reality: on that day, March 20, "Emden" slapped and abandoned a woman with whom he had an affair, apparently because she became pregnant and he did not want to accept responsibility for the child. Touched by vague remorse, he sets out excitedly to find the woman and offer her a package of sweets. Just as the reader is certain that the old man is hopelessly lost in the city and his shifting memories, his cane "stabs through a soft surface" and arouses a dusty brown mongrel who races off with the *jilebi* sweets. It may be, as Rao imagines, that he has penetrated the veil of the past and found S's current reincarnation. Or it may be that the old man is simply withdrawing into an inner world of faded reality. In A *Tiger for Malgudi* (1983), the Master describes this gradual deterioration of the senses as "beautiful old age, when faculties are dimmed one by one, so that we may be restful. . . ." What is a move to a higher spiritual realm for the Master and his tiger becomes in this story an ambiguous incident built on unreliable perception, or at most a glimpse into a larger life cycle which "Emden" can perceive but only vaguely comprehend.

The most complete biographical sketch and critical overview is to be found in William Walsh's *R. K. Narayan: A Critical Appreciation* (1982), which should however be read with Narayan's own *My Days* (1974) for fuller descriptions of certain events. *Perspectives on R. K. Narayan*, edited by Atma Ram (1981), is a useful but uneven collection of essays on Narayan's work and themes.

Emden

When he came to be named the oldest man in town, Rao's age was estimated anywhere between ninety and one hundred and five. He had, however, lost count of time long ago and abominated birthdays; especially after his eightieth, when his kinsmen from everywhere came down in a swarm and involved him in elaborate rituals, and with blaring pipes and drums made a public show of his attaining eighty. The religious part of it was so strenuous that he was laid up for fifteen days thereafter with fever. During the ceremony they poured pots of cold water, supposedly fetched from sacred rivers, over his head, and forced him to undergo a fast, while they themselves feasted gluttonously. He was so fatigued at the end of the day that he could hardly pose for the group photo, but flopped down in his chair, much to the annoyance of the photographer, who constantly withdrew his head from under the black hood to plead, "Steady, please." Finally, he threatened to pack up and leave unless they propped up the old gentleman. There were seventy-five heads to be counted in the group— all Rao's descendants one way or another. The photographer insisted upon splitting the group, as otherwise the individuals would be microscopic and indistinguishable on a single plate. That meant that after a little rest Rao had to be propped up a second time in the honoured seat. When he protested against this entire ceremony, they explained, "It's a propitiatory ceremony to give you health and longevity."

"Seems to me rather a device to pack off an old man quickly," he said, at which his first daughter, herself past sixty, admonished him not to utter inauspicious remarks, when everyone was doing so much to help.

By the time he recovered from his birthday celebrations and the group photo in two parts could be hung on the wall, the house had become quiet and returned to its normal strength, which was about twenty in all—three of his sons and their families, an assortment of their children, nephews and nieces. He had his room in the right wing of the house, which he had designed and built in the last century as it looked. He had been the very first to buy a piece of land beyond Vinayak Street; it was considered an act of great daring in those days, being a deserted stretch of land from which thieves could easily slip away into the woods beyond, even in daylight; the place, however, developed into a residential colony and was named Ratnapuri, which meant City of Gems.

Rao's earlier years were spent in Kabir Street. When he came into his own and decided to live in style, he sold off their old house and moved to Ratnapuri. That was after his second wife had borne him four daughters, and the last of them was married off. He had moved along with his first wife's progeny, which numbered eight of varying ages. He seemed to be peculiarly ill-fated in matrimony—his uncle, who cast and read the stars for the whole family, used to say that Rao had Mars in the seventh house, with no other planet to checkmate its fury, and hence was bound to lose every wife.[1] After the third marriage and more children, he was convinced of the malevolence of Mars. He didn't keep a record of the population at home—that was not his concern—his sons were capable of running the family and managing the crowd at home. He detached himself from all transactions and withdrew so completely that a couple of years past the grand ceremony of the eightieth birthday he could not remember the names of most of the children at home or who was who, or how many were living under his roof.

The eightieth birthday had proved a definite landmark in his domestic career. Aided by the dimming of his faculties, he could isolate himself with no effort whatever. He was philosophical enough to accept nature's readjustments: "If I see less or hear less, so much the better. Nothing lost. My legs are still strong enough to take me about, and I can bathe and wash without help. . . . I enjoy my food and digest it." Although they had a dining table, he refused to change his ancient habit of sitting on a rosewood plank on the floor and eating off a banana leaf in a corner of the dining hall. Everything for him went on automatically, and he didn't have to ask for anything, since his needs were anticipated; a daughter-in-law or niece or grand-

---

1. Rao's horoscope, read by his astrologer uncle, shows Mars (the Roman god of War) dominant in the section that concerns marriage, which indicates that Rao is fated to lose his wives.

daughter or a great-grand someone or other was always there to attend him unasked. He did not comment or question, particularly not question, as he feared they would bawl in his left ear and strain their vocal cords, though if they approached his right ear he could guess what they might be saying. But he didn't care either way. His retirement was complete. He had worked hard all his life to establish himself, and provide for his family, each figure in the two-part group photograph owing its existence to him directly or indirectly. Some of the grandchildren had been his favourites at one time or another, but they had all grown out of recognition, and their names—oh, names! they were the greatest impediments to speech—every name remains on the tip of one's tongue but is gone when you want to utter it. This trick of nature reduces one to a state of babbling and stammering without ever completing a sentence. Even such a situation was acceptable, as it seemed to be ordained by nature to keep the mind uncluttered in old age.

He reflected and introspected with clarity in the afternoons—the best part of the day for him, when he had had his siesta; got up and had his large tumbler of coffee (brought to his room exactly at three by one of the ministering angels, and left on a little *teapoy*[2] beside the door). After his coffee he felt revived, reclined in his easy-chair placed to catch the light at the northern window, and unfolded the morning paper, which, after everyone had read it, was brought and placed beside his afternoon coffee. Holding it close enough, he could read, if he wiped his glasses from time to time with a silk rag tied to the arm of his chair; thus comfortably settled, he half-read and half-ruminated. The words and acts of politicians or warmongers sounded stale—they spoke and acted in the same manner since the beginning of time; his eyes travelled down the columns—sometimes an advertisement caught his eye (nothing but an invitation to people to squander their money on all kinds of fanciful things), or reports of deaths (not one recognizable name among the dead). On the last page of the paper, however, half a column invariably gripped his attention—that was a daily report of a religious or philosophical discourse at some meeting at Madras; brief reports, but adequate for him to brush up his thoughts on God, on His incarnations and on definitions of Good and Evil. At this point, he would brood for a while and then fold and put away the paper exactly where he had found it, to be taken away later.

When he heard the hall clock chime four, he stirred himself to go out on a walk. This part of the day's routine was anticipated by him with a great thrill. He washed and put on a long shirt which came down to his knees, changed to a white dhoti,[3] wrapped around his

---

2. A small table.   3. Men's garment, tucked and knotted at the waist.

shoulder an embroidered cotton shawl, seized his staff and an umbrella and sallied out. When he crossed the hall, someone or other always cautioned him by bellowing, "Be careful. Have you got the torch?[4] Usual round? Come back soon." He would just nod and pass on. Once outside, he moved with caution, taking each step only after divining the nature of the ground with the tip of his staff. His whole aim in life was to avoid a fall. One false step and that would be the end. Longevity was guaranteed as long as he maintained his equilibrium and verticality. This restriction forced him to move at snail's pace, and along a well-defined orbit every evening.

Leaving his gate, he kept himself to the extreme left of the street, along Vinayak Street, down Kabir Lane and into Market Road. He loved the bustle, traffic and crowds of Market Road—paused to gaze into shops and marvel at the crowd passing in and out perpetually. He shopped but rarely—the last thing he remembered buying was a crayon set and a drawing book for some child at home. For himself he needed to buy only a particular brand of toothpowder (most of his teeth were still intact), for which he occasionally stopped at Chettiar's at the far end of Market Road, where it branched off to Ellaman Street. When he passed in front of the shop, the shopman would always greet him from his seat, "How are you, sir? Want something to take home today?" Rao would shake his head and cross over to the other side of the road—this was the spot where his orbit curved back, and took him homeward, the whole expedition taking him about two hours. Before 6:30, he would be back at his gate, never having to use his torch, which he carried in his shirt pocket only as a precaution against any sudden eclipse of the sun or an unexpected nightfall.

The passage both ways would always be smooth and uneventful, although he would feel nervous while crossing the Market Gate, where Jayaraj the photo-framer always hailed him from his little shop, "Grand Master, shall I help you across?" Rao would spurn that offer silently and pass on; one had to concentrate on one's steps to avoid bumping into the crowd at the Market Gate, and had no time for people like Jayaraj. After he had passed, Jayaraj, who enjoyed gossiping, would comment to his clients seated on a bench, "At his age! Moves through the crowd as if he were in the prime of youth. Must be at least a hundred and ten! See his recklessness. It's not good to let him out like this. His people are indifferent. Not safe these days. With all these lorries, bicycles and auto-rickshaws, he'll come to grief someday, I'm sure. . . ."

"Who's he?" someone might ask, perhaps a newcomer to the town, waiting for his picture to be framed.

"We used to call him Emden.[5] We were terrified of him when we

---

4. Flashlight (British).   5. A German warship that shelled Madras in 1916; ever since, the term indicates anyone who is formidable and ruthless. (Author's note.)

were boys. He lived somewhere in Kabir Street. Huge, tall and imposing when he went down the road on his bicycle in his khaki uniform and a red turban and all kinds of badges. We took him to be a police inspector from his dress—not knowing that he wore the uniform of the Excise Department. He also behaved like the police—if he noticed anyone doing something he did not like, he'd go thundering at him, chase him down the street and lay the cane on his back. When we were boys, we used to loiter about the market in gangs, and if he saw us he'd scatter us and order us home. Once he caught us urinating against the school wall at Adam's Street, as we always did. He came down on us with a roar, seized four of us and shook us till our bones rattled, pushed us up before the headmaster and demanded, 'What are you doing, Headmaster? Is this the way you train them? Or do you want them to turn out to be guttersnipes? Why don't you keep an eye on them and provide a latrine in your school?' The headmaster rose in his seat, trembling and afraid to come too close to this terrible personality flourishing a cane. Oh, how many such things in his heyday! People were afraid of him. He might well have been a policeman for all his high-and-mighty style, but his business was only to check the taverns selling drinks— And you know how much he collected at the end of the day? Not less than five hundred rupees, that is, fifteen thousand a month, not even a governor could earn so much. No wonder he could build a fancy house at Ratnapuri and bring up his progeny in style. Oh, the airs that family gives themselves! He narrowly escaped being prosecuted—if a national award were given for bribe-taking, it would go to him: when he was dismissed from service, he gave out that he had voluntarily retired! None the worse for it, has enough wealth to last ten generations. Emden! Indeed! He married several wives, seems to have worn them out one after another; that was in addition to countless sideshows, ha! ha! When we were boys, he was the talk of the town: some of us stealthily followed and spied on his movements in the dark lanes at night, and that provided us a lot of fun. He had great appetite for the unattached female tribe, such as nurses and schoolmistresses, and went after them like a bull! Emden, really! . . ." Jayaraj's tongue wagged while his hands were cutting, sawing and nailing a picture frame, and ceased the moment the work was finished, and he would end his narrations with: "That'll be five rupees—special rate for you because you have brought the picture of Krishna, who is my family god. I've not charged for the extra rings for hanging. . . ."

Rao kept his important papers stacked in an *almirah*,[6] which he kept locked, and the key hidden under a lining paper in another

---

6. Cupboard.

cupboard where he kept his clothes and a few odds and ends, and the key of this second cupboard also was hidden somewhere, so that no one could have access to the two cupboards, which contained virtually all the clues to his life. Occasionally on an afternoon, at his hour of clarity and energy, he'd leave his easy-chair, bolt the door and open the first cupboard, take out the key under the paper lining, and then open the other cupboard containing his documents—title-deeds, diaries, papers and a will.

Today he finished reading the newspaper in ten minutes, and had reached his favourite column on the last page—the report of a discourse on reincarnations, to explain why one was born what he was and the working of the law of *karma*.[7] Rao found it boring also: he was familiar with that kind of moralizing and philosophy. It was not four yet; the reading was over too soon. He found an unfilled half-hour between the newspaper reading and his usual time for the evening outing. He rose from the chair, neatly folded the newspaper and put it away on the little stool outside his door, and gently shut and bolted the door—noiselessly, because if they heard him shut the door, they would come up and caution him, "Don't bolt," out of fear that if he fell dead they might have to break the door open. Others were obsessed with the idea of *his* death as if they were all immortals!

He unlocked the cupboard and stood for a moment gazing at the papers tied into neat bundles—all the records of his official career from the start to his "voluntary retirement" were there on the top shelf, in dusty and yellowing paper: he had shut the cupboard doors tight, yet somehow fine dust seeped in and settled on everything. He dared not touch anything for fear of soiling his fingers and catching a cold. He must get someone to destroy them, best to put them in a fire; but whom could he trust? He hated the idea of anyone reading those memos from the government in the latter days of his service— he'd prefer people not to know the official mess and those threats of enquiries before he quit the service. The Secretary to the Government was a demon out to get his blood—inspired by anonymous letters and backbiters. Only one man had stood by him—his first assistant, wished he could remember his name or whereabouts— good fellow; if he were available he'd set him to clean and arrange his *almirah* and burn the papers: he'd be dependable, and would produce the ash if asked. But who was he? He patted his forehead as if to jerk the memory-machine into action. . . . And then his eyes roved down to the next shelf; he ran his fingers over them lovingly— all documents relating to his property and their disposal after his death. No one in the house could have any idea of it or dare come near them. He must get the lawyer-man (what was his name again?)

7. Fate: in Hindu doctrine, the idea that actions in one life continue to have effects in another incarnation.

and closet himself with him someday. He was probably also dead. Not a soul seemed to be left in town. . . . Anyway, must try to send someone to fetch him if he was alive, it was to be done secretly. How? Somehow.

His eyes travelled to a shelf with an assortment of packets containing receipts, bills and several diaries. He had kept a diary regularly for several years, recording a bit of daily observation or event on each page. He always bought the same brand of diary, called "Matchless"—of convenient size, ruled pages, with a flap that would be buttoned so that no one could casually open its pages and read its contents. The Matchless Stationery Mart off the main market manufactured it. On the last day of every December he would stop by for a copy costing four rupees—rather expensive but worth the price . . . more often than not the man would not take money for it, as he'd seek some official favour worth much more. Rao was not the sort to mind dispensing his official favours if it helped some poor soul. There was a stack of thirty old diaries in there (at some point in his life, he had abandoned the practise), which contained the gist of all his day-to-day life and thought: that again was something, an offering for the God of Fire before his death. He stood ruminating at the sight of the diaries. He pulled out one from the stack at random, wiped the thin layer of dust with a towel, went back to his chair and turned over the leaves casually. The diary was fifty-one years old. After glancing through some pages, he found it difficult to read his own close calligraphy in black ink and decided to put it back, as it was time to prepare for his walk. However, he said to himself, "Just a minute. Let me see what I did on this date, on the same day, so long ago. . . ." He looked at the calendar on the wall. The date was the twentieth of March. He opened the diary and leafed through the earlier pages, marvelling at the picture they presented of his early life: what a lot of activities morning till night, connected with the family, office and personal pursuits! His eyes smarted; he skipped longer passages and concentrated on the briefer ones. On the same day fifty-one years ago—the page contained only four lines, which read: "Too lenient with S. She deserves to be taught a lesson. . . ." This triggered a memory, and he could almost hear the echo of his own shouting at somebody, and the next few lines indicated the course of action: "Thrashed her soundly for her own good and left. Will not see her again. . . . How can I accept the responsibility? She must have had an affair—after all a D.G.[8] Wish I had locked her in before leaving." He studied this entry dispassionately. He wondered who it was. The initial was not helpful. He had known no one with a name beginning with S. Among the ladies he had favoured in his days, it

---

8. Dancing Girl, a term denoting a public woman in those days. (Author's note.)

could be anyone . . . but names were elusive anyway.

With great effort, he kept concentrating on this problem. His forehead throbbed with the strain of concentration. Of course, the name eluded him, but the geography was coming back to him in fragments. From Chettiar Stores . . . yes, he remembered going up Market Road . . . and noted the light burning at the shop facing him even at a late hour when returning home; that meant he had gone in that narrow street branching off from Market Road at that point, and that led to a parallel street . . . from there one went on and on and twisted and turned in a maze of by-lanes and reached that house—a few steps up before tapping gently on the rosewood door studded with brass stars, which would open at once as if she was waiting on the other side; he'd slip in and shut the door immediately, lest the neighbours be watching, and retrace his steps at midnight. But he went there only two days in the week, when he had free time. . . . Her name, no, could not get it, but he could recollect her outline rather hazily—fair, plump and loving and jasmine-smelling; he was definite that the note referred to this woman, and not to another one, also plump and jasmine-smelling somewhere not so far away . . . he remembered slapping a face and flouncing out in a rage. The young fellow was impetuous and hot-blooded . . . must have been someone else, not himself in any sense. He could not remember the house, but there used to be a coconut palm and a well in the street in front of the house . . . it suddenly flashed across his mind that the name of the street was Gokulam.

He rose and locked away the diary and secreted the key as usual, washed and dressed, and picked up his staff and umbrella and put on his sandals, with a quiet thrill. He had decided to venture beyond his orbit today, to go up and look for the ancient rosewood, brass-knobbed door, beside the coconut tree in that maze. From Chettiar Stores, his steps were bound to lead him on in the right direction, and if S. was there and happened to stand at the street door, he'd greet her . . . he might not be able to climb the four steps, but he'd offer her a small gift and greeting from the street. She could come down and take it. He should not have slapped her face . . . he had been impetuous and cruel. He should not have acted on jealousy . . . he was filled with remorse. After all, she must have shown him a great deal of kindness and given him pleasure ungrudgingly—otherwise, why would one stay until midnight?

While he tap-tapped his way out of his house now, someone in the hall enquired as usual, "Got your torch? Rather late today. Take care of yourself." He was excited. The shopman on the way, who habitually watched and commented, noted that the old man was moving rather jauntily today. "Oh, Respected One, good day to you, sir," said Mani from his cycle shop. "In such a hurry today? Walk slowly, sir, road is dug up everywhere." Rao looked up and permitted himself a gentle nod of recognition. He did not hear the message, but he could guess what Mani might be saying. He was fond of him—a great-grandson of that fellow who had studied with him at Albert Mission School. Name? As usual Mani's great-grandfather's name kept slipping away . . . he was some Ram or Shankar or something like that. Oh, what a teaser! He gave up and passed on. He kept himself to the edge as usual, slowed down his pace after Mani's advice; after all, his movement should not be noticeable, and it was not good to push oneself in that manner and pant with the effort.

At Jagan's Sweets, he halted. Some unknown fellow at the street counter. Children were crowding in front of the stall holding forth money and asking for this and that. They were blocking the way. He waited impatiently and tapped his staff noisily on the ground till the man at the counter looked up and asked, "Anything, master?" Rao waved away the children with a flourish of his stick and approached the counter and feasted his eyes on the heaped-up sweets in different colours and shapes, and wished for a moment he could eat recklessly as he used to. But perhaps that'd cost him his life today—the secret of his survival being the spartan life he led, rigorously suppressing the cravings of the palate. He asked, "What's fresh today?" The man at the counter said, "We prepare everything fresh every day. Nothing is yesterday's. . . ." Rao could only partly guess what he was saying but, without betraying himself, said, "Pack up *jilebi*[9] for three rupees. . . ." He counted out the cash carefully, received the packet of *jilebi*, held it near his nostrils (the smell of food would not hurt, and there was no medical advice against it), for a moment relishing its rose-scented flavour; and was on his way again. Arriving at the point of Chettiar Stores, he paused and looked up at his right—yes, that street was still there as he had known it. . . .

Noticing him hesitating there, the shopman hailed from his shop, "Oh, grand master, you want anything?" He felt annoyed. Why couldn't they leave him alone? And then a young shop assistant came out to take his order. Rao looked down at him and asked, pointing at the cross street, "Where does it lead?"

"To the next street," the boy said, and that somehow satisfied him. The boy asked, "What can I get you?"

"Oh, will no one leave me alone?" Rao thought with irritation. They seemed to assume that he needed something all the time. He hugged the packet of sweets close to his chest, along with the umbrella slung on the crook of his arm. The boy seemed to be bent on selling him something. And so he said, "Have you sandalwood soap?" He remembered that S., or whoever it was, used to be fond of it. The

9. A sweet.

boy got it for him with alacrity. Its fragrance brought back some old memories. He had thought there was a scent of jasmine about S., but he realized now that it must have been that of sandalwood. He smelt it nostalgically before thrusting it into his pocket. "Anything else, sir?" asked the boy. "No, you may go," and he crossed Market Road over to the other side.

Trusting his instinct to guide him, he proceeded along the cross street ahead of Chettiar Stores. It led to another street running parallel, where he took a turn to his left on an impulse, and then again to his right into a lane, and then left, and then about-turn—but there was no trace of Gokulam Street. As he tap-tapped along, he noticed a cobbler on the roadside, cleared his throat, struck his staff on the ground to attract attention and asked, "Here, which way to Gokulam Street?" At first, the cobbler shook his head, then, to get rid of the enquirer, pointed vaguely in some direction and resumed his stitching. "Is there a coconut tree in this street?" The other once again pointed along the road. Rao felt indignant. "Haughty beggar," he muttered. "In those days I'd have . . . ." He moved on, hoping he'd come across the landmark. He stopped a couple of others to ask the same question, and that did not help. No coconut tree anywhere. He was sure that it was somewhere here that he used to come, but everything was changed. All the generations of men and women who could have known Gokulam Street and the coconut tree were dead—new generations around here, totally oblivious of the past. He was a lone survivor.

He moved cautiously now, as the sun was going down. He became rather nervous and jabbed his staff down at each step, afraid of stumbling in a hole. It was a strain moving in this fashion, so slow and careful, and he began to despair that he'd ever reach the Market Road again. He began to feel anxious, regretted this expedition. The family would blame him if he should have a mishap. Somehow he felt more disturbed at the thought of their resentment than of his own possible suffering. But he kept hobbling along steadily. Some passers-by paused to stare at him and comment on his perambulation. At some point, his staff seemed to stab through a soft surface; at the same moment a brown mongrel, which had lain curled up in dust, in perfect camouflage, sprang up with a piercing howl; Rao instinctively jumped, as he had not done for decades, luckily without falling down, but the packet of *jilebi* flew from his grip and landed in front of the mongrel, who picked it up and trotted away, wagging his tail in gratitude. Rao looked after the dog helplessly and resumed his journey homeward. Brooding over it, he commented to himself, "Who knows, S. is perhaps in this incarnation now. . . ."

RALPH ELLISON

1914—

The prose fiction of Ralph Ellison combines the visionary consciousness and linguistic freedom of modernist writers with a harshly realistic context and stressing of social issues that are often pushed to the background in twentieth-century experimental literature. The "invisible man" of his best-known work is both symbolic and real, a figure whose portrayal is indebted to T. S. Eliot and James Joyce as well as to Richard Wright and Fyodor Dostoevsky. Ellison's world is multidimensional: tragic and comic in the same breath, folkloric yet modern, sordidly real and hallucinatory or surreal, preoccupied with existential questions of individual identity at the same time that it describes the dilemmas of a racist society.

His parents were native Southerners who had moved to Oklahoma City, hoping for a more open society, and when their son was born on March 1, 1914, they named him Ralph Waldo Ellison after the New England poet and philosopher Ralph Waldo Emerson. Ellison's father died when he was three but his mother, working to support her two sons, made sure they had books, records, and chemistry sets, and encouraged them to value learning and social activism. Oklahoma was not as consistently and artificially segregated as the South from which she had come, and although segregation laws crept in later (theaters were segregated in the twenties) Ellison was raised in a generally integrated society. He was especially interested in music, and by the time he attended Tuskegee Institute in 1933 on a music scholarship, he had learned music theory, been first chair trumpeter and student conductor of his high school band, and taken private lessons from the conductor of the Oklahoma City Orchestra.

Tuskegee Institute, in Alabama, was a new experience in many ways. It was Ellison's first encounter with the Deep South and its strict racial divisions; raised in the west, he felt an outsider to the local black as well as the Southern white community. The Institute itself was intended by its founder, Booker T. Washington, to be a broadly useful trade school rather than a college; but Ellison was inspired by Alain Locke's ideal of academic and artistic excellence in *The New Negro* (1925), and by Locke's picture of a "new psychology" and "new spirit" represented in the Harlem Renaissance. Ellison later satirized the accommodating trade-school attitude in Dr. Bledsoe, the college president who achieves power through hypocrisy in *Invisible Man*, but he nonetheless found examples of the new spirit at Tuskegee. During his three years as a music major, he studied with professors who explored both black idiom and traditional "high culture": composer William Dawson, who combined black folk music and classical symphonic forms in his own work, and concert pianist Hazel Harrison, a cosmopolitan figure who encouraged her students to use a range of techniques and introduced them to her friend Alain Locke. Ellison also took up painting and sculpture, read a great deal, and was deeply impressed by *The Waste Land*. T. S. Eliot's poem appealed to him at first for its verbal rhythm and shifts of tone, and for the suggestion of hidden depths in its symbolic organization. Exploring the footnote references, he discovered a buried thematic structure and saw how writers could make use of a common core of anthropological and cultural experience. Ellison's view of black experience would soon reject the "New Negro" definitions of Alain Locke, who suggested that there was a special black artistic sensibility, and he also rebelled against similar racial stereotypes that were proposed in current sociology textbooks as scientific truths. He reached for a larger concept of human (and American, and Afro-American) civilization in which black experience was one important but contributing part. By the time he left Tuskegee for New York in 1936, Ellison had written some poetry although he still saw himself as a potential artist or musician, and worked for a year in New York with the sculptor Richmond Barthé.

New York in 1936 was in the midst of the Depression, and Ellison supported himself by a variety of jobs: barman at the YMCA, file clerk for a psychiatrist (prompting him to study the psychology of dreams), factory worker, and free-lance photographer. He met the poet Langston Hughes and through him Richard Wright, the future novelist and short story writer, who became Ellison's friend and encouraged him to write. It would be several years before Ellison published his own stories, however, and fifteen before the novel *Invisible Man* appeared. His mother's death in February 1937 brought Ellison to Dayton for her funeral, where he made a living during the following months by hunting and selling his catch, and where he practiced writing. Although Ellison read Dostoevsky and the experimental modernists—Joyce, Eliot, and Stein—he took Hemingway as his model when he began to write short stories, the first of which ("Slick Gonna Learn") appeared in September 1939.

In the meantime, Ellison had returned to New York where he worked during 1938–42 with the Federal Writers' Project, a government-sponsored program that supported a number of writers during Depression years. He was one of a group of writers employed to do historical research in libraries and court records for a book called *The Negro in New York*. More important to Ellison's own work, perhaps, was an oral history project for which he conducted hundreds of interviews with children and adults to record the folklore of Harlem culture—stories, songs, boasting, and speech patterns—much of which, he felt, also reflected earlier Southern sources. Ellison had already been struck by the importance given to tradition in Eliot's *The Waste Land* and essay "Tradition and the Individual Talent"; the research into black American tradition that he carried out in New York sharpened his own historical and folkloric perspective. Yet he did not lose sight of the need to blend history and artistic technique; in an early review, "Creative and Cultural Lag" (1937), he criticizes novelist Waters Edward Turpin for ignoring social and political reality, and also for not having "a greater development in technique" that would allow him to achieve "more than one level of writing." In 1941, when many radical writers believed that the direct portrayal of social ills was more important than literary technique, Ellison—himself a radical critic of society—was still proclaiming that black writers should learn from the experimental style of modernists like James Joyce.

Ellison was slow to publish his stories, although he wrote a number of

literary reviews and was editor of the *Negro Quarterly* in 1942 after leaving
the Federal Writers' Project. By 1944 he had published eight stories (while
writing many more) and had turned his back on both the "New Negro"
aestheticism of Langston Hughes and the militant naturalism of his early
mentor, Richard Wright. Wright's heroes, he felt—especially Bigger Thomas,
the protagonist of *Native Son* (1940)—were presented too narrowly as victims of society, and not as full human beings with minds and wills of their
own. Wright's picture of black experience actually imitated the limited stereotypes drawn by white writers: "Wright could imagine Bigger, but Bigger
could not possibly imagine Richard Wright." Ellison's own heroes, even
when they too fall victim to society, are endowed with consciousness and
imagination that lift them beyond any stereotypes. The early stories, set in
the South and emphasizing racial prejudice, imply a response of political
action; the "Buster-Riley" stories weave black folklore and heroic role models
into the games of two young Oklahoma boys outwitting neighbors and family; "Flying Home" (1944) shows how a black pilot, whose plane crashes in
Georgia when it hits a buzzard, copes with threats against his life by understanding a comic folk tale about a black angel thrown out of heaven for
superbly reckless flying; "King of the Bingo Game," printed here, describes
a hallucinatory moment of understanding and self-knowledge in the midst
of ruin.

"Flying Home" was initially part of a novel that Ellison worked on but
never completed during the forties. He had joined the Merchant Marines in
1943 and received a Rosenwald Fellowship in 1945 to write a novel. It was
not the envisoned wartime story of a black pilot shot down on foreign soil
that emerged, however, but a different novel inspired partly by Lord Raglan's
study of archetypal heroic identity in *The Hero* and partly by Ellison's own
concern with Afro-American identity inside modern American history.
Invisible Man (1952) told the story of an unnamed protagonist who was
"invisible," unknown to himself and invisible to a society—black and white—
that could see him only in terms of its own needs and stereotypes: "only by
surroundings, themselves, or figments of their imagination, everything and
anything except me." Prologue and epilogue are spoken from the invisible
man's hideaway, a city manhole where he has retreated after a series of
betrayals and attacks, and whose darkness he illuminates—in a typically grotesque and comic touch—with 1,369 light bulbs burning on electricity drained
from the Monopolated Light and Power company.

The novel is a modern *Bildungsroman*, or novel of education, in which
a naive young protagonist tries to get ahead by living up to the roles held out
to him, but finds in the end that he is always a pawn, exploited for whatever
use can be made of him as the stereotyped "primitive" black. Beginning as
a naive high school senior forced to box blindfolded for the entertainment
of a men's club before repeating his valedictory speech on humility (a chapter often anthologized as the story "Battle Royal"), he experiences expulsion
from college, deception by the business community, patronizing by white
liberals, abusive medical treatment, manipulation by the political Brotherhood, horror at the casual killing of a friend, and enmity from militant black
nationalists. Yet the story of his individual disillusionment is told in a series
of ironically tragicomic, often hallucinatory scenes that are still charged with

some of the beginning's optimistic idealism, with the wounded belief that things can be changed if they are only seen for what they are. The narrator has written in an attempt to articulate mixed motives, to "give pattern to the chaos which lives within the pattern of your certainties." *Invisible Man* has been criticized by those who would prefer a less complicated picture, one that stresses social injustice over psychological complexity, but Ellison protests what he considers a narrow reductionism and upholds instead "a complex double vision, a fluid, ambivalent response to men and events" which alone can represent "the cost of being human in this modern world."

Invisible Man received the National Book Award and the Russwurm Award in 1953, and in 1965 was named by *Book Week*'s poll of artists and critics as "the most significant work of fiction written by an American" between 1945 and 1965. Ellison found himself in demand as lecturer and consultant, and was awarded a fellowship at the American Academy in Rome (1955–57). He began work on a second novel, sections of which have appeared in different journals as stories about the revival circuit evangelist Reverend Alonzo Zuber Hickman and his adopted son Bliss, who takes advantage of his light (possibly white) skin to make a new life in the north as a white politician, the bigoted Senator Sunraider. Ellison has continued writing and teaching at different institutions; since 1970, he has been Albert Schweitzer Professor of Humanities at New York University.

"King of the Bingo Game," published in 1944, combines two levels of narration: the starkly realistic picture of an unemployed black whose anxiety and momentary paralysis keep him from completing his turn at bingo, and the development of an hallucinatory moment of insight in which the dispossessed man achieves a sense of identity by asserting himself against the rigged wheel of fate. The harsh sociological facts of his condition dominate at first: seated in the theater waiting for the movie to end and the bingo game to begin, already light-headed from hunger and anxiety about his sick wife, Laura, the protagonist muses on the difference between the cohesive Southern community he has left (but where births are not always registered for the poor) and the alienated North where a man asking for help is considered crazy (yet, a little farther on, a northerner wakes him from his nightmare and gives him a swallow of whiskey). The sociological facts are then interpreted on a level of dream consciousness: by the nightmare in which the train leaps its tracks to pursue him down the street as white folks laugh; by a similar hallucination at the end, in which the A train subway (through Harlem) chases him and Laura; by the sudden revelation of life as a wheel of fortune on which he is spun helplessly until he intervenes to prevent the game from being completed.

Although the theme of the Wheel of Life, Fate, or Fortune is an old one (updated here by the bingo game), Ellison suggests quite specifically how it is rigged in modern society: the crowd is made up of poor blacks seeking a lucky break, the emcee running the game is white and calls the protagonist "boy" (as does the policeman at the end), and in his moment of insight the protagonist significantly forgets his slave name ("given him by the man who had owned his grandfather a long time ago")—the name that symbolizes the humiliation and lack of self-respect that has been taught to blacks—and is reborn with the name of his own act: "The-man-who-pressed-the-button-who-held-the-prize-who-was-the-King-of-Bingo." Here Ellison combines the existential overtones of achieving identity through personal choice and assertion, and the chantlike rhythm of an older tradition in which tribal heroes earn the names by which they are known. The moment of truth cannot last, however, and with the approach of the policemen the magic circle of the bingo wheel gives way to his own frantic circling on stage at the end of the cord: a grotesque tie to the fateful wheel that ends with a blow on the head, and with the ironic double-zero of a win which will not be honored.

Robert G. O'Meally, *The Craft of Ralph Ellison* (1980), is an excellent study of Ellison's work to date that includes biographical information and a bibliography. John Hersey, ed., *Ralph Ellison: A Collection of Critical Essays* (1974), contains valuable essays on different aspects of Ellison's work, and an interview with Ellison himself. John M. Reilly, ed., *Twentieth-Century Interpretations of Invisible Man* (1970), presents ten interpretations of the novel and five excerpted "viewpoints," several of which criticize Ellison as insufficiently militant.

King of the Bingo Game

The woman in front of him was eating roasted peanuts that smelled so good that he could barely contain his hunger. He could not even sleep and wished they'd hurry and begin the bingo game. There, on his right, two fellows were drinking wine out of a bottle wrapped in a paper bag, and he could hear soft gurgling in the dark. His stomach gave a low, gnawing growl. "If this was down South," he thought, "all I'd have to do is lean over and say, 'Lady, gimme a few of those peanuts, please ma'am,' and she'd pass me the bag and never think nothing of it." Or he could ask the fellows for a drink in the same way. Folks down South stuck together that way; they didn't even have to know you. But up here it was different. Ask somebody for something, and they'd think you were crazy. Well, I ain't crazy. I'm just broke, 'cause I got no birth certificate to get a job, and Laura 'bout to die 'cause we got no money for a doctor. But I ain't crazy. And yet a pinpoint of doubt was focused in his mind as he glanced toward the screen and saw the hero stealthily entering a dark room and sending the beam of a flashlight along a wall of bookcases. This is where he finds the trapdoor, he remembered. The man would pass abruptly through the wall and find the girl tied to a bed, her legs and arms spread wide, and her clothing torn to rags. He laughed softly to himself. He had seen the picture three times, and this was one of the best scenes.

On his right the fellow whispered wide-eyed to his companion, "Man, look a-yonder!"

"Damn!"

"Wouldn't I like to have her tied up like that . . . ."

"Hey! That fool's letting her loose!"

"Aw, man, he loves her."

"Love or no love!"

The man moved impatiently beside him, and he tried to involve himself in the scene. But Laura was on his mind. Tiring quickly of watching the picture he looked back to where the white beam filtered from the projection room above the balcony. It started small and grew large, specks of dust dancing in its whiteness as it reached the screen. It was strange how the beam always landed right on the screen and didn't mess up and fall somewhere else. But they had it all fixed. Everything was fixed. Now suppose when they showed that girl with her dress torn the girl started taking off the rest of her clothes, and when the guy came in he didn't untie her but kept her there and went to taking off his own clothes? *That* would be something to see. If a picture got out of hand like that those guys up there would go nuts. Yeah, and there'd be so many folks in here you couldn't find a seat for nine months! A strange sensation played over his skin. He shuddered. Yesterday he'd seen a bedbug on a woman's neck as they walked out into the bright street. But exploring his thigh through a hole in his pocket he found only goose pimples and old scars.

The bottle gurgled again. He closed his eyes. Now a dreamy music was accompanying the film and train whistles were sounding in the distance, and he was a boy again walking along a railroad trestle down South, and seeing the train coming, and running back as fast as he could go, and hearing the whistle blowing, and getting off the trestle to solid ground just in time, with the earth trembling beneath his feet, and feeling relieved as he ran down the cinder-strewn embankment onto the highway, and looking back and seeing with terror that the train had left the track and was following him right down the middle of the street, and all the white people laughing as he ran screaming . . .

"Wake up there, buddy! What the hell do you mean hollering like that? Can't you see we trying to enjoy this here picture?"

He started at the man with gratitude.

"I'm sorry, old man," he said. "I musta been dreaming."

"Well, here, have a drink. And don't be making no noise like that, damn!"

His hands trembled as he tilted his head. It was not wine, but whiskey. Cold rye whiskey. He took a deep swoller, decided it was better not to take another, and handed the bottle back to its owner.

"Thanks, old man," he said.

Now he felt the cold whiskey breaking a warm path straight through the middle of him, growing hotter and sharper as it moved. He had not eaten all day, and it made him light-headed. The smell of the peanuts stabbed him like a knife, and he got up and found a seat in the middle aisle. But no sooner did he sit than he saw a row of intense-faced young girls, and got up again, thinking, "You chicks musta been Lindy-hopping[1] somewhere." He found a seat several rows ahead as the lights came on, and he saw the screen disappear behind a heavy red and gold curtain; then the curtain rising, and the man with the microphone and a uniformed attendant coming on the stage.

He felt for his bingo cards, smiling. The guy at the door wouldn't like it if he knew about his having *five* cards. Well, not everyone played the bingo game; and even with five cards he didn't have much of a chance. For Laura, though he had to have faith. He studied the cards, each with its different numerals, punching the free center hole in each and spreading them neatly across his lap; and when the lights faded he sat slouched in his seat so that he could look from his cards to the bingo wheel with but a quick shifting of his eyes.

Ahead, at the end of the darkness, the man with the microphone was pressing a button attached to a long cord and spinning the bingo wheel and calling out the number each time the wheel came to rest. And each time the voice rang out his finger raced over the cards for the number. With five cards he had to move fast. He became nervous; there were too many cards, and the man went too fast with his grating voice. Perhaps he should just select one and throw the others away. But he was afraid. He became warm. Wonder how much Laura's doctor would cost? Damn that, watch the cards! And with despair he heard the man call three in a row which he missed on all five cards. This way he'd never win . . .

When he saw the row of holes punched across the third card, he sat paralyzed and heard the man call three more numbers before he stumbled forward, screaming,

"Bingo! Bingo!"

"Let that fool up there," someone called.

"Get up there, man!"

He stumbled down the aisle and up the steps to the stage into a light so sharp and bright that for a moment it blinded him, and he felt that he had moved into the spell of some strange, mysterious power. Yet it was as familiar as the sun, and he knew it was the perfectly familiar bingo.

The man with the microphone was saying something to the audience as he held out his card. A cold light flashed from the man's finger as the card left his hand. His knees trembled. The man stepped closer, checking the card against the numbers chalked on the board. Suppose he had made a mistake? The pomade on the man's hair made him feel faint, and he backed away. But the man was checking

1. The Lindy-hop was a variant of the jitterbug, a lively jazz dance popular in the 1930s and '40s.

the card over the microphone now, and he had to stay. He stood tense, listening.

"Under the O, forty-four," the man chanted. 'Under the I, seven. Under the G, three. Under the B, ninety-six. Under the N, thirteen!"

His breath came easier as the man smiled at the audience.

"Yessir, ladies and gentlemen, he's one of the chosen people!"

The audience rippled with laughter and applause.

"Step right up to the front of the stage."

He moved slowly forward, wishing that the light was not so bright.

"To win tonight's jackpot of $36.90 the wheel must stop between the double zero, understand?"

He nodded, knowing the ritual from the many days and nights he had watched the winners march across the stage to press the button that controlled the spinning wheel and receive the prizes. And now he followed the instructions as though he'd crossed the slippery stage a million prize-winning times.

The man was making some kind of a joke, and he nodded vacantly. So tense had he become that he felt a sudden desire to cry and shook it away. He felt vaguely that his whole life was determined by the bingo wheel; not only that which would happen now that he was at last before it, but all that had gone before, since his birth, and his mother's birth and the birth of his father. It had always been there, even though he had not been aware of it, handing out the unlucky cards and numbers of his days. The feeling persisted, and he started quickly away. I better get down from here before I make a fool of myself, he thought.

"Here, boy," the man called. "You haven't started yet."

Someone laughed as he went hesitantly back.

"Are you all reet?"

He grinned at the man's jive talk, but no words would come, and he knew it was not a convincing grin. For suddenly he knew that he stood on the slippery brink of some terrible embarrassment.

"Where you from, boy?" the man asked.

"Down South."

"He from down South, ladies and gentlemen," the man said. "Where from? Speak right into the mike."

"Rocky Mont," he said. "Rock' Mont, North Car'lina."

"So you decided to come down off that mountain to the U.S.," the man laughed. He felt that the man was making a fool of him, but then something cold was placed in his hand, and the lights were no longer behind him.

Standing before the wheel he felt alone, but that was somehow right, and he remembered his plan. He would give the wheel a short quick twirl. Just a touch of the button. He had watched it many

times, and always it came close to double zero when it was short and
quick. He steeled himself; the fear had left, and he felt a profound
sense of promise, as though he were about to be repaid for all the
things he'd suffered all his life. Trembling, he pressed the button.
There was a whirl of lights, and in a second he realized with finality
that though he wanted to, he could not stop. It was as though he
held a high-powered line in his naked hand. His nerves tightened.
As the wheel increased its speed it seemed to draw him more and
more into its power, as though it held his fate; and with it came a
deep need to submit, to whirl, to lose himself in its swirl of color.
He could not stop it now, he knew. So let it be.

The button rested snugly in his palm where the man had placed
it. And now he became aware of the man beside him, advising him
through the microphone, while behind the shadowy audience
hummed with noisy voices. He shifted his feet. There was still that
feeling of helplessness within him, making part of him desire to turn
back, even now that the jackpot was right in his hand. He squeezed
the button until his fist ached. Then, like the sudden shriek of a
subway whistle, a doubt tore through his head. Suppose he did not
spin the wheel long enough? What could he do, and how could he
tell? And then he knew, even as he wondered, that as long as he
pressed the button, he could control the jackpot. He and only he
could determine whether or not it was to be his. He felt drunk.
Then, as though he had come down from a high hill into a valley of
people, he heard the audience yelling.

"Come down from there, you jerk!"

"Let somebody else have a chance . . ."

"Ole Jack thinks he done found the end of the rainbow . . ."

The last voice was not unfriendly, and he turned and smiled
dreamily into the yelling mouths. Then he turned his back squarely
on them.

"Don't take too long, boy," a voice said.

He nodded. They were yelling behind him. Those folks did not
understand what had happened to him. They had been playing the
bingo game day in and night for years, trying to win rent money or
hamburger change. But not one of those wise guys had discovered
this wonderful thing. He watched the wheel whirling past the numbers and experienced a burst of exaltation: This is God! This is the
really truly God! He said it aloud, "This is God!"

He said it with such absolute conviction that he feared he would
fall fainting into the footlights. But the crowd yelled so loud that
they could not hear. These fools, he thought. I'm here trying to tell
them the most wonderful secret in the world, and they're yelling like
they gone crazy. A hand fell upon his shoulder.

"You'll have to make a choice now, boy. You've taken too long."

He brushed the hand violently away.

"Leave me alone, man. I know what I'm doing!"

The man looked surprised and held on to the microphone for support. And because he did not wish to hurt the man's feelings he smiled, realizing with a sudden pang that there was no way of explaining to the man just why he had to stand there pressing the button forever.

"Come here," he called tiredly.

The man approached, rolling the heavy microphone across the stage.

"Anybody can play this bingo game, right?" he said.

"Sure, but . . ."

He smiled, feeling inclined to be patient with this slick looking white man with his blue sport shirt and his sharp gabardine suit.

"That's what I thought," he said. "Anybody can win the jackpot as long as they get the lucky number, right?"

"That's the rule, but after all . . ."

"That's what I thought," he said. "And the big prize goes to the man who knows how to win it?"

The man nodded speechlessly.

"Well then, go on over there and watch me win like I want to. I ain't going to hurt nobody," he said, "and I'll show you how to win. I mean to show the whole world how it's got to be done."

And because he understood, he smiled again to let the man know that he held nothing against him for being white and impatient. Then he refused to see the man any longer and stood pressing the button, the voices of the crowd reaching him like sounds in distant streets. Let them yell. All the Negroes down there were just ashamed because he was black like them. He smiled inwardly, knowing how it was. Most of the time he was ashamed of what Negroes did himself. Well, let them be ashamed for something this time. Like him. He was like a long thin black wire that was being stretched and wound upon the bingo wheel; wound until he wanted to scream; wound, but this time himself controlling the winding and the sadness and the shame, and because he did, Laura would be all right. Suddenly the lights flickered. He staggered backwards. Had something gone wrong? All this noise. Didn't they know that although he controlled the wheel, it also controlled him, and unless he pressed the button forever and forever and ever it would stop, leaving him high and dry, dry and high on this hard high slippery hill and Laura dead? There was only one chance; he had to do whatever the wheel demanded. And gripping the button in despair, he discovered with surprise that it imparted a nervous energy. His spine tingled. He felt a certain power.

Now he faced the raging crowd with defiance, its screams penetrating his eardrums like trumpets shrieking from a juke-box. The vague faces glowing in the bingo lights gave him a sense of himself that he had never known before. He was running the show, by God! They had to read to him, for he was their luck. This is *me*, he thought. Let the bastards yell. Then someone was laughing inside him, and he realized that somehow he had forgotten his own name. It was a sad, lost feeling to lose your name, and a crazy thing to do. That name had been given him by the white man who had owned his grandfather a long time ago down South. But maybe those wise guys knew his name.

"Who am I?" he screamed.

"Hurry up and bingo, you jerk!"

They didn't know either, he thought sadly. They didn't even know their own names, they were all poor nameless bastards. Well, he didn't need that old name; he was reborn. For as long as he pressed the button he was The-man-who-pressed-the-button-who-held-the-prize-who-was-the-King-of-Bingo. That was the way it was, and he'd have to press the button even if nobody understood, even though Laura did not understand.

"Live!" he shouted.

The audience quieted like the dying of a huge fan.

"Live, Laura, baby. I got holt of it now, sugar. Live!"

He screamed it, tears streaming down his face. "I got nobody but you!"

The screams tore from his very guts. He felt as though the rush of blood to his head would burst out in baseball seams of small red droplets, like a head beaten by police clubs. Bending over he saw a trickle of blood splashing the toe of his shoe. With his free hand he searched his head. It was his nose. God, suppose something has gone wrong? He felt that the whole audience had somehow entered him and was stamping its feet in his stomach and he was unable to throw them out. They wanted the prize, that was it. They wanted the secret for themselves. But they'd never get it; he would keep the bingo wheel whirling forever, and Laura would be safe in the wheel. But would she? It had to be, because if she were not safe the wheel would cease to turn; it could not go on. He had to get away, *vomit* all, and his mind formed an image of himself running with Laura in his arms down the tracks of the subway just ahead of an A train,[2] running desperately *vomit* with people screaming for him to come out but knowing no way of leaving the tracks because to stop would bring the train crushing down upon him and to attempt to leave across the other tracks would mean to run into a hot third rail as high as his

---

2. The subway express train to Harlem.

waist which threw blue sparks that blinded his eyes until he could hardly see.

He heard singing and the audience was clapping its hands.

> Shoot the liquor to him, Jim, boy!
> Clap-clap-clap
> Well a-calla the cop
> He's blowing his top!
> Shoot the liquor to him, Jim, boy!

Bitter anger grew within him at the singing. They think I'm crazy. Well let 'em laugh. I'll do what I got to do.

He was standing in an attitude of intense listening when he saw that they were watching something on the stage behind him. He felt weak. But when he turned he saw no one. If only his thumb did not ache so. Now they were applauding. And for a moment he thought that the wheel had stopped. But that was impossible, his thumb still pressed the button. Then he saw them. Two men in uniform beckoned from the end of the stage. They were coming toward him, walking in step, slowly, like a tap-dance team returning for a third encore. But their shoulders shot forward, and he backed away, looking wildly about. There was nothing to fight them with. He had only the long black cord which led to a plug somewhere back stage, and he couldn't use that because it operated the bingo wheel. He backed slowly, fixing the men with his eyes as his lips stretched over his teeth in a tight, fixed grin; moved toward the end of the stage and realizing that he couldn't go much further, for suddenly the cord became taut and he couldn't afford to break the cord. But he had to do something. The audience was howling. Suddenly he stopped dead, seeing the men halt, their legs lifted as in an interrupted step of a slow-motion dance. There was nothing to do but run in the other direction and he dashed forward, slipping and sliding. The men fell back, surprised. He struck out violently going past.

"Grab him!"

He ran, but all too quickly the cord tightened, resistingly, and he turned and ran back again. This time he slipped them, and discovered by running in a circle before the wheel he could keep the cord from tightening. But this way he had to flail his arms to keep the men away. Why couldn't they leave a man alone? He ran, circling.

"Ring down the curtain," someone yelled. But they couldn't do that. If they did the wheel flashing from the projection room would be cut off. But they had him before he could tell them so, trying to pry open his fist, and he was wrestling and trying to bring his knees into the fight and holding on to the button, for it was his life. And now he was down, seeing a foot coming down, crushing his wrist cruelly, down, as he saw the wheel whirling serenely above.

"I can't give it up," he screamed. Then quietly, in a confidential tone, "Boys, I really can't give it up."

It landed hard against his head. And in the blank moment they had it away from him, completely now. He fought them trying to pull him up from the stage as he watched the wheel spin slowly to a stop. Without surprise he saw it rest at double-zero.

"You see," he pointed bitterly.

"Sure, boy, sure, it's O. K.," one of the men said smiling.

And seeing the man bow his head to someone he could not see, he felt very, very happy; he would receive what all the winners received.

But as he warmed in the justice of the man's tight smile he did not see the man's slow wink, nor see the bow-legged man behind him step clear of the swiftly descending curtain and set himself for a blow. He only felt the dull pain exploding in his skull, and he knew even as it slipped out of him that his luck had run out on the stage.

ALEXANDER SOLZHENITSYN
1918—

The reputation of Russian novelist Alexander Solzhenitsyn is divided almost equally between two complementary aspects: he continues the tradition of the realistic nineteenth-century novel (following the example of his compatriots Tolstoy and Dostoevsky), and he has assumed the role of moral conscience in a modern society where both East and West are fatally flawed. Expelled from the Soviet Union in 1974 and stripped of his citizenship, Solzhenitsyn—who now lives on a farm in Vermont—proclaims the virtues of an older, religious way of life as the only salvation for a civilization that has been dehumanized by political oppression and materialist greed. Art and literature, he feels, are "endowed with the miraculous power to communicate," and thus make it possible for people to experience situations which they have not lived. This basis of common communication erases divisions and allows us to have "a single system of evaluation for evil deeds and for good ones." Solzhenitsyn tries to encompass both the historian's and the moralist's aims when he writes about the history of his own country in the twentieth century and paints a picture of human suffering and moral endurance under oppression. Like Thomas Mann, he includes a range of characters and diverse social types in novels that allude to larger social issues; unlike Mann, his tone is overtly moral and even didactic, especially in his later works. Solzhenitsyn is impelled to testify for all those who cannot speak: for the woman in *Cancer Ward* (1968) who says "Where can I read about us? Will that be only in a hundred years?" His testimony ranges from the more personal account of a day in concentration camp (*One Day in the Life of Ivan Denisovich,* 1963) to broad historical panoramas like *August 1914* (1971), which focuses on the defeat of the Russian Second Army in East Prussia during World War I, and *Gulag Archipelago* (1973–75), a description of the Soviet concentration camp system. Clearly he finds the form of the realistic novel—expanded, in *August 1914,* with documents and imitation film scripts—the most appropriate method for representing the truth of history. Solzhenitsyn has little patience with avant-garde literature which, he says, "has been thought up by empty-headed people"; instead, he tries to render the essence of history by blending documented fact and narrative fiction in his creative works and, in recent years, by editing and publishing (in Russian) historical documents from pre-Revolutionary Russia.

He was born Alexander Isayevich Solzhenitsyn on December 11, 1918, in Kislovodsk, in the northern Caucasus. His father had died six months earlier, and his mother supported them in Rostov-on-Don by working as a typist. The family was extremely poor, and—although Solzhenitsyn would have preferred studying literature in Moscow—he was obliged upon graduation from high school to enroll in the local Department of Mathematics at Rostov University. The choice, he says, was a lucky one, for his double degree in mathematics and physics allowed him to spend four years of his prison camp sentence in a relatively privileged *sharashka,* or research institute, instead of at hard manual labor. During 1939–41 he also took correspondence courses from the Institute of History, Philosophy, and Literature in Moscow. When Solzhenitsyn graduated in 1941 he was immediately inducted into the army, where he drove horse-drawn transport vehicles until he was sent to artillery school in 1942. That November, he was put in charge of an artillery reconnaissance battery at the front, a position he held until his sudden arrest in February 1945.

The military censor had found passages in his letters to a friend that were—even under a pseudonym—visibly disrespectful of Stalin, and Solzhenitsyn was sentenced in July to eight years in the prison camps. During 1946–50 he worked as a mathematician in research institutes staffed by prisoners (such as that described in *The First Circle*) but in 1950 was taken to a new kind of camp for political prisoners only, where he worked as manual laborer. After his sentence was ostensibly over, an administrative order sent him into perpetual exile in southern Kazakhstan. Solzhenitsyn spent the years of exile teaching physics and mathematics in a rural school and wrote prose in secret. The tumor that had developed in his first labor camp grew worse, and in 1954 the author received treatment in a clinic in Tashkent (recalled in the novel *Cancer Ward*). He returned to exile in 1955 (the year he wrote *The First Circle*) and was not released until June 1956. Official rehabilitation came in 1957, and the author moved to Ryazan in European Russia where he continued to teach physics and mathematics, while secretly writing fiction, until 1962. "Matryona's Home" and *One Day in the Life of Ivan Denisovich* were written during this period.

At the age of forty-two, Solzhenitsyn had written a great deal but published nothing. In 1961, however, it looked as though the climate of political censorship might change. Nikita Khrushchev had just publicly attacked the "cult of personality" and hero worship that had surrounded Stalin, and the poet and editor Alexander Tvardovsky called on writers to portray "truth," not the artificial picture of perfect Soviet society that Stalin preferred. Solzhenitsyn was encouraged to submit *One Day in the Life of Ivan Denisovich*, which appeared (with Khrushchev's approval) in the November 1962 issue of Tvardovsky's journal *Novy Mir*. In January 1963 Tvardovsky published the stories "Matryona's Home" and "Incident at Krechetovka Station" but—with the exception of two short stories and an article on style—Solzhenitsyn would not be allowed to publish anything more in his native land. Even the highly praised *One Day in the Life of Ivan Denisovich* was removed from candidacy for the Lenin Prize in 1963. Khrushchev himself was forced into retirement in October 1964, and the temporary loosening of censorship came to an end. The novel *The First Circle* (already accepted by *Novy Mir*) and two plays (*The Lovegirl and the Innocent*, written 1954; *Candle in the Wind*, written 1960) were prohibited during 1964–65, and *Cancer Ward*, after the type was already partially set, was refused publication permission by the Writers' Union in 1966. Solzhenitsyn protested both the censorship and the fact that the Writers' Union did not defend its members before official attacks, but instead he himself was expelled from the Writers' Union in 1969, after *The First Circle* and *Cancer Ward* had appeared in the West. The only means of publishing officially unacceptable works was to convey them abroad to a Western publishing house, or to circulate them in *samizdat* ("self-publishing") form by circulating copies of typewritten manuscripts. Solzhenitsyn made arrangements to have his works published in the West, and continued work on the larger historical novels: the *Gulag Archipelago*, which he had begun earlier, and *August 1914*, which he wrote in 1969–70. In 1970 he was awarded the Nobel Prize for literature, which he accepted in absentia because he was afraid that he would not be permitted to re-enter the Soviet Union once he left. After the publication abroad of the first volume of the *Gulag Archipelago*, however, he was arrested in February 1974 and expelled from the country. During 1974–76 he lived in Zurich, and since 1976 he has lived on a farm in Vermont.

Solzhenitsyn's first three novels have in common the themes of imprisonment, of personal suffering, and of the moral purity to be gained by those who endure and learn from their suffering. *One Day in the Life of Ivan Denisovich* is the story, told at a very basic level of hunger, cold, and brutally demanding work, of one fairly good day in the life of a prison camp inmate, the peasant Ivan Denisovich Shukhov. When the book appeared, it was the first public recognition of Stalin's prison camp system, and Solzhenitsyn's matter-of-fact narration of the prisoners' day-to-day struggle to survive and retain their humanity shocked readers in Russia and in the West. Shukhov is not a heroic figure, or even portrayed as particularly intelligent, but in his deprivation he has found a core of inner spiritual strength that might well be envied, Solzhenitsyn suggests, by those outside prison who compromise their principles, and accede to injustices, for fear of losing what they have.

The worlds of *Cancer Ward* and *The First Circle* are more privileged than that of *One Day in the Life of Ivan Denisovich*, but each retains the atmosphere of imprisonment and imminent death, and each composes a picture of society by juxtaposing characters with different backgrounds and different points of view. Solzhenitsyn calls this technique of juxtaposition "polyphonic" or many-voiced: he writes a "polyphonic novel with concrete details

specifying the time and place of action. A novel without a central hero. . . .
Each character becomes central when the action reverts to him." In *Cancer
Ward*, thirteen patients representing different social and political classes are
brought together in a ward at the cancer clinic in Tashkent; this microcosm
of Soviet society is faced with sickness, suffering, and death, and with an
authoritarian medical system that administers treatment without explaining
it (or its side effects) to the patient. The ward becomes a metaphor for Soviet
society, a metaphor given further dimensions when the inmates articulate
their different values in response to a story by Tolstoy: "What Men Live By."
The ultimate question is not collective but individual, says Kostoglotov: a
man may be a member of a collective, "but only while he's alive . . . he
has to die alone."

The same emphasis on the testing of individual values occurs in *The First
Circle*, a novel whose title refers to the least painful circle of Hell in Dante's
Inferno, and indicates here the *sharashka* or prisoner-staffed reasearch section of the Mavrino Institute. The prisoners working in the *sharashka* are
under pressure from their superiors (who are under pressure from Stalin) to
produce spying devices, including a method for identifying voices on taped
telephone calls, and an impregnable telephone coding system for Stalin. If
they do not produce satisfactory work, they are sent back to almost-certain
death in the labor camps (the lower circles of this Hell); if they do, they
become part of the police state. No one is free, not even the dictator who is
imprisoned by his own suspicions. The whole society of *The First Circle* is
an Inferno, and only by sacrificing everything can one hope to retain spiritual freedom.

Solzhenitsyn turned next to a larger panoramic scope, where the authorial
voice would dominate and interpret a mass of historical information. *August
1914*, written in 1969–70, is the first volume of a planned trilogy inquiring
into the course of modern Russian history: later volumes (of which a few
chapters have appeared in journals and in the fictional portrait, *Lenin in
Zurich*) are titled after revolutionary dates, *October 1916* and *March 1917*.
August 1914 describes the defeat of the Second Russian Army in East Prussia during World War I, and—in a consciously fragmented style that moves
from scene to scene, includes extracts of documents, newspapers, proverbs,
and songs, and provides sections marked "Screen" that imitate film scripts—
attempts to depict a broad social panorama with characters from all classes,
thus recording a moment in history from an epic point of view.

The second broad panorama is the *Gulag Archipelago*, a three-volume,
seven-section account of Stalin's widespread prison camp system. (*Gulag*
stands for "Chief Administration of Corrective Labor Camps," camps which
were scattered across the Soviet Union like islands in a sea [the archipelago.])
Solzhenitsyn describes the horror of these camps in quasi-anecdotal form,
using personal experience, oral testimony, excerpts of documents, written
eyewitness reports, and altogether a massive collection of evidence accumulated inside "An Attempt at Artistic Investigation" (the subtitle). In this
book, perhaps even more than in *August 1914*, there is a tension between
the bare facts which Solzhenitsyn transmits and the spiritual interpretation
of history into which they fit. The author is overtly present, commenting,
guessing intuititively from context when particular facts are missing, and

stressing in his own voice the theme that has pervaded all his work: the purification of the soul through suffering. The title of the fourth section, "The Soul and Barbed Wire," symbolizes the recurrent opposition of soul and imprisoning society that has become familiar to his readers.

Since Solzhenitsyn is such a dedicated anti-Communist and anti-Marxist, many Westerners have jumped to the conclusion that he is in favor of the Western democratic system. Such is not the case. He looks back to an earlier, more nationalist and spiritual authoritarianism represented for him by the image of Holy Russia: "For a thousand years Russia lived with an authoritarian order . . . that authoritarian order possessed a strong moral foundation . . . Christian Orthodoxy." In a speech given at Harvard in 1978, "A World Split Apart," he criticized Western democracy's "herd instinct" and "need to accommodate mass standards," its emphasis on "well-being" and "constant desire to have still more things," its "spiritual exhaustion" in which "mediocrity triumphs under the guise of democratic restraints." Once again, he returns to the theme of purification by suffering which permeates his fiction: "We have been through a spiritual training far in advance of Western experience. The complex and deadly crush of life has produced stronger, deeper, and more interesting personalities than those generated by standardized Western well-being."

One of those strong and deep personalities is surely Matryona in "Matryona's Home." Solzhenistyn's story, which is probably modeled on the old Russian literary form of the saint's life, is a testimony to Matryona's absolute simplicity, her refusal to possess anything more than the basic necessities (and she will not raise a pig to kill for food), her willingness to help others unrewarded, and finally to let her greedy in-laws tear down part of her own home and cart it off. The narrator of the story, like Solzhenitsyn an ex-convict and mathematics teacher, has buried himself deep in the country to avoid signs of modern Soviet society and to find—if it still exists—an image of the Old Russia. The town of Talnovo itself is tainted, not just by the kolkhoz (collective farm) system, which ceases to consider Matryona part of the collective as soon as she becomes ill, but also by the laziness, selfishness, and predatory greed of its inhabitants. Yet there remains Matryona. Her life has been filled with disappointment and deprivation, and she remains an outsider in a materialist society that despises her lack of acquisitive instinct, but she seems to live in a dimension of spiritual contentment and love which is unknown to those around her. Only the narrator, who has learned to value essential qualities from his own experience in the concentration camps, is able finally to recognize her as "the righteous one," one of those whose spiritual merit seems alien to modern society, yet is needed to save society from divine retribution (Genesis 18:23–33).

Andrej Kodjak, *Alexander Solzhenitsyn* (1978), provides a biographical and critical introduction to Solzhenitsyn up to his deportation from the Soviet Union in 1974; includes discussion of Russian terms. Kathryn B. Feuer, ed., *Solzhenitsyn: A Collection of Critical Essays* (1976), contains a range of essays on aspects and particular works, including "Matryona's Home." John Dunlop, Richard Haugh, Alexis Klimoff, eds. *Aleksandr Solzhenitsyn: Critical Essays and Documentary Materials* (1973), is a useful collection with a wide range of essays and reprinted texts, including a short autobiography by Solzhenitsyn and his Nobel Prize lecture.

Matryona's Home[1]

A hundred and fifteen miles from Moscow trains were still slowing down to a crawl a good six months after it happened. Passengers stood glued to the windows or went out to stand by the doors. Was the line under repair, or what? Would the train be late?

It was all right. Past the crossing the train picked up speed again and the passengers went back to their seats.

Only the engine drivers knew what it was all about.

The engine drivers and I.

In the summer of 1953 I was coming back from the hot and dusty desert, just following my nose—so long as it led me back to European Russia. Nobody waited or wanted me at my particular place, because I was a little matter of ten years overdue. I just wanted to get to the central belt, away from the great heats, close to the leafy muttering of forests. I wanted to efface myself, to lose myself in deepest Russia . . . if it was still anywhere to be found.

A year earlier I should have been lucky to get a job carrying a hod this side of the Urals.[2] They wouldn't have taken me as an electrician on a decent construction job. And I had an itch to teach. Those who knew told me that it was a waste of money buying a ticket, that I should have a journey for nothing.

But things were beginning to move. When I went up the stairs of the N—— Regional Education Department and asked for the Personnel Section, I was surprised to find Personnel sitting behind a glass partition, like in a chemist's shop, instead of the usual black leather-padded door. I went timidly up to the window, bowed, and asked, "Please, do you need any mathematicians somewhere where the trains don't run? I should like to settle there for good."

They passed every dot and comma in my documents through a fine comb, went from one room to another, made telephone calls. It was something out of the ordinary for them too—people always wanted the towns, the bigger the better. And lo and behold, they found just the place for me—Vysokoe Polye. The very sound of it gladdened my heart.

Vysokoe Polye[3] did not belie its name. It stood on rising ground, with gentle hollows and other little hills around it. It was enclosed by an unbroken ring of forest. There was a pool behind a weir. Just the place where I wouldn't mind living and dying. I spent a long time sitting on a stump in a coppice and wishing with all my heart that I didn't need breakfast and dinner every day but could just stay

---

1. Translated by H. T. Willetts.   2. Mountain chain separating European Russia from (Asiatic) Siberia.   3. "High Meadow."

here and listen to the branches brushing against the roof in the night, with not a wireless anywhere to be heard and the whole world silent.

Alas, nobody baked bread in Vysokoe Polye. There was nothing edible on sale. The whole village lugged its victuals in sacks from the big town.

I went back to the Personnel Section and raised my voice in prayer at the little window. At first they wouldn't even talk to me. But then they started going from one room to another, made a telephone call, scratched with their pens, and stamped on my orders the word "Torfoprodukt."

Torfoprodukt?[4] Turgenev never knew that you can put words like that together in Russian.

On the station building at Torfoprodukt, an antiquated temporary hut of gray wood, hung a stern notice, BOARD TRAINS ONLY FROM THE PASSENGERS' HALL. A further message had been scratched on the boards with a nail, *And Without Tickets.* And by the booking office, with the same melancholy wit, somebody had carved for all time the words, *No Tickets.* It was only later that I fully appreciated the meaning of these addenda. Getting to Torfoprodukt was easy. But not getting away.

Here too, deep and trackless forests had once stood and were still standing after the Revolution. Then they were chopped down by the peat cutters and the neighboring kolkhoz.[5] Its chairman, Shashkov, had razed quite a few hectares of timber and sold it at a good profit down in the Odessa region.

The workers' settlement sprawled untidily among the peat bogs— monotonous shacks from the thirties, and little houses with carved façades and glass verandas, put up in the fifties. But inside these houses I could see no partitions reaching up to the ceilings, so there was no hope of renting a room with four real walls.

Over the settlement hung smoke from the factory chimney. Little locomotives ran this way and that along narrow-gauge railway lines, giving out more thick smoke and piercing whistles, pulling loads of dirty brown peat in slabs and briquettes. I could safely assume that in the evening a loudspeaker would be crying its heart out over the door of the club and there would be drunks roaming the streets and, sooner or later, sticking knives in each other.

This was what my dream about a quiet corner of Russia had brought me to—when I could have stayed where I was and lived in an adobe hut looking out on the desert, with a fresh breeze at night and only the starry dome of the sky overhead.

---

4. "Peat product." A new word made by combining two words of Germanic origin: "torf" (peat) and "produkt." *Ivan Sergeyevich Turgenev* (1818–83) was a master of Russian prose style best known for the novel *Fathers and Sons* (1861) and for a series of sympathetic sketches of peasant life published as *A Sportsman's Sketches* (1882).   5. Collective farm.

I couldn't sleep on the station bench, and as soon as it started getting light I went for another stroll round the settlement. This time I saw a tiny marketplace. Only one woman stood there at that early hour, selling milk, and I took a bottle and started drinking it on the spot.

I was struck by the way she talked. Instead of a normal speaking voice, she used an ingratiating singsong, and her words were the ones I was longing to hear when I left Asia for this place.

"Drink, and God bless you. You must be a stranger round here?"

"And where are you from?" I asked, feeling more cheerful.

I learnt that the peat workings weren't the only thing, that over the railway lines there was a hill, and over the hill a village, that this village was Talnovo, and it had been there ages ago, when the "gipsy woman" lived in the big house and the wild woods stood all round. And farther on there was a whole countryside full of villages—Chaslitsy, Ovintsy, Spudni, Shevertni, Shestimirovo, deeper and deeper into the woods, farther and farther from the railway, up towards the lakes.

The names were like a soothing breeze to me. They held a promise of backwoods Russia. I asked my new acquaintance to take me to Talnovo after the market was over and find a house for me to lodge in.

It appeared that I was a lodger worth having: in addition to my rent, the school offered a truckload of peat for the winter to whoever took me. The woman's ingratiating smile gave way to a thoughtful frown. She had no room herself, because she and her husband were "keeping" her aged mother, so she took me first to one lot of relatives then to another. But there wasn't a separate room to be had and both places were crowded and noisy.

We had come to a dammed-up stream that was short of water and had a little bridge over it. No other place in all the village took my fancy as this did: there were two or three willows, a lopsided house, ducks swimming on the pond, geese shaking themselves as they stepped out of the water.

"Well, perhaps we might just call on Matryona," said my guide, who was getting tired of me by now. "Only it isn't so neat and cozy-like in her house, neglects things she does. She's unwell."

Matryona's house stood quite near by. Its row of four windows looked out on the cold backs, the two slopes of the roof were covered with shingles, and a little attic window was decorated in the old Russian style. But the shingles were rotting, the beam ends of the house and the once mighty gates had turned gray with age, and there were gaps in the little shelter over the gate.

The small gate was fastened, but instead of knocking my companion just put her hand under and turned the catch, a simple device to prevent animals from straying. The yard was not covered, but there was a lot under the roof of the house. As you went through the outer door a short flight of steps rose to a roomy landing, which was open, to the roof high overhead. To the left, other steps led up to the top room, which was a separate structure with no stove, and yet another flight led down to the basement. To the right lay the house proper, with its attic and its cellar.

It had been built a long time ago, built sturdily, to house a big family, and now one lonely woman of nearly sixty lived in it.

When I went into the cottage she was lying on the Russian stove[6] under a heap of those indeterminate dingy rags which are so precious to a working man or woman.

The spacious room, and especially the big part near the windows, was full of rubber plants in pots and tubs standing on stools and benches. They peopled the householder's loneliness like a speechless but living crowd. They had been allowed to run wild, and they took up all the scanty light on the north side. In what was left of the light, and half-hidden by the stovepipe, the mistress of the house looked yellow and weak. You could see from her clouded eyes that illness had drained all the strength out of her.

While we talked she lay on the stove face downward, without a pillow, her head toward the door, and I stood looking up at her. She showed no pleasure at getting a lodger, just complained about the wicked disease she had. She was just getting over an attack; it didn't come upon her every month, but when it did, "It hangs on two or three days so as I shan't manage to get up and wait on you. I've room and to spare, you can live here if you like."

Then she went over the list of other housewives with whom I should be quieter and cozier and wanted me to make the round of them. But I had already seen that I was destined to settle in this dimly lit house with the tarnished mirror, in which you couldn't see yourself, and the two garish posters (one advertising books, the other about the harvest), bought for a ruble each to brighten up the walls.

Matryona Vasilyevna made me go off round the village again, and when I called on her the second time she kept trying to put me off, "We're not clever, we can't cook, I don't know how we shall suit. . . ." But this time she was on her feet when I got there, and I thought I saw a glimmer of pleasure in her eyes to see me back. We reached an agreement about the rent and the load of peat which the school would deliver.

Later on I found out that, year in year out, it was a long time since Matryona Vasilyevna had earned a single ruble. She didn't get a

---

6. A large stove built of masonry, used both for heating and cooking.

pension. Her relatives gave her very little help. In the kolkhoz she had worked not for money but for credits; the marks recording her labor days in her well-thumbed workbook.

So I moved in with Matryona Vasilyevna. We didn't divide the room. Her bed was in the corner between the door and the stove, and I unfolded my camp bed by one window and pushed Matryona's beloved rubber plants out of the light to make room for a little table by another. The village had electric light, laid on back in the twenties, from Shatury. The newspapers were writing about "Ilyich's little lamps," but the peasants talked wide-eyed about "Tsar Light."[7]

Some of the better-off people in the village might not have thought Matryona's house much of a home, but it kept us snug enough that autumn and winter. The roof still held the rain out, and the freezing winds could not blow the warmth of the stove away all at once, though it was cold by morning, especially when the wind blew on the shabby side.

In addition to Matryona and myself, a cat, some mice, and some cockroaches lived in the house.

The cat was no longer young, and was gammy-legged as well. Matryona had taken her in out of pity, and she had stayed. She walked on all four feet but with a heavy limp: one of her feet was sore and she favored it. When she jumped from the stove she didn't land with the soft sound a cat usually makes, but with a heavy thud as three of her feet struck the floor at once—such a heavy thud that until I got used to it, it gave me a start. This was because she stuck three feet out together to save the fourth.

It wasn't because the cat couldn't deal with them that there were mice in the cottage: she would pounce into the corner like lightning and come back with a mouse between her teeth. But the mice were usually out of reach because somebody, back in the good old days, had stuck embossed wallpaper of a greenish color on Matryona's walls, and not just one layer of it but five. The layers held together all right, but in many places the whole lot had come away from the wall, giving the room a sort of inner skin. Between the timber of the walls and the skin of wallpaper the mice had made themselves runs where they impudently scampered about, running at times right up to the ceiling. The cat followed their scamperings with angry eyes, but couldn't get at them.

Sometimes the cat ate cockroaches as well, but they made her sick. The only thing the cockroaches respected was the partition which screened the mouth of the Russian stove and the kitchen from the best part of the room.

They did not creep into the best room. But the kitchen at night swarmed with them, and if I went in late in the evening for a drink of water and switched on the light the whole floor, the big bench, and even the wall would be one rustling brown mass. From time to time I brought home some borax from the school laboratory and we mixed it with dough to poison them. There would be fewer cockroaches for a while, but Matryona was afraid that we might poison the cat as well. We stopped putting down poison and the cockroaches multiplied anew.

At night, when Matryona was already asleep and I was working at my table, the occasional rapid scamper of mice behind the wallpaper would be drowned in the sustained and ceaseless rustling of cockroaches behind the screen, like the sound of the sea in the distance. But I got used to it because there was nothing evil in it, nothing dishonest. Rustling was life to them.

I even got used to the crude beauty on the poster, forever reaching out from the wall to offer me Belinsky, Panferov,[8] and a pile of other books—but never saying a word. I got used to everything in Matryona's cottage.

Matryona got up at four or five o'clock in the morning. Her wall clock was twenty-seven years old and had been bought in the village shop. It was always fast, but Matryona didn't worry about that—just as long as it didn't lose and make her late in the morning. She switched on the light behind the kitchen screen and moving quietly, considerately, doing her best not to make a noise, she lit the stove, went to milk the goat (all the livestock she had was this one dirty-white goat with twisted horns), fetched water and boiled it in three iron pots: one for me, one for herself, and one for the goat. She fetched potatoes from the cellar, picking out the littlest for the goat, little ones for herself and egg-sized ones for me. There were no big ones, because her garden was sandy, had not been manured since the war, and she always planted with potatoes, potatoes, and potatoes again, so that it wouldn't grow big ones.

I scarcely heard her about her morning tasks. I slept late, woke up in the wintry daylight, stretched a bit, and stuck my head out from under my blanket and my sheepskin. These, together with the prisoner's jerkin round my legs and a sack stuffed with straw underneath me, kept me warm in bed even on nights when the cold wind rattled our wobbly windows from the north. When I heard the discreet noises on the other side of the screen I spoke to her, slowly and deliberately:

"Good morning, Matryona Vasilyevna!"

And every time the same good-natured words came to me from

---

8. Vissarion Grigoryevich Belinsky (1811–48), Russian literary critic who emphasized social and political ideas; Fedor Ivanovich Panferov (1896–1960), socialist-realist writer popular in the 1920s, best known for his novel *The Iron Flood*.

behind the screen. They began with a warm, throaty gurgle, the sort of sound grandmothers make in fairy tales.

"M-m-m . . . same to you too!"

And after a little while, "Your breakfast's ready for you now."

She didn't announce what was for breakfast, but it was easy to guess: taters in their jackets or tatty soup (as everybody in the village called it), or barley gruel (no other grain could be bought in Torfoprodukt that year, and even the barley you had to fight for, because it was the cheapest and people bought it up by the sack to fatten their pigs on it). It wasn't always salted as it should be, it was often slightly burnt, it furred the palate and the gums, and it gave me heartburn.

But Matryona wasn't to blame: there was no butter in Torfoprodukt either, margarine was desperately short, and only mixed cooking fat was plentiful, and when I got to know it, I saw that the Russian stove was not convenient for cooking: the cook cannot see the pots and they are not heated evenly all round. I suppose the stove came down to our ancestors from the Stone Age, because you can stoke it up once before daylight, and food and water, mash and swill will keep warm in it all day long. And it keeps you warm while you sleep.

I ate everything that was cooked for me without demur, patiently putting aside anything uncalled-for that I came across: a hair, a bit of peat, a cockroach's leg. I hadn't the heart to find fault with Matryona. After all, she had warned me herself.

"We aren't clever, we can't cook—I don't know how we shall suit. . . ."

"Thank you," I said quite sincerely.

"What for? For what is your own?" she answered, disarming me with a radiant smile. And, with a guileless look of her faded blue eyes, she would ask, "And what shall I cook you for just now?"

For just now meant for supper. I ate twice a day, like at the front. What could I order for just now? It would have to be one of the same old things, taters or tater soup.

I resigned myself to it, because I had learned by now not to look for the meaning of life in food. More important to me was the smile on her roundish face, which I tried in vain to catch when at last I had earned enough to buy a camera. As soon as she saw the cold eye of the lens upon her, Matryona assumed a strained or else an exaggeratedly severe expression.

Just once I did manage to get a snap of her looking through the window into the street and smiling at something.

Matryona had a lot of worries that winter. Her neighbors put it into her head to try and get a pension. She was all alone in the world, and when she began to be seriously ill she had been dismissed from the kolkhoz as well. Injustices had piled up, one on top of another. She was ill, but was not regarded as a disabled person. She had worked for a quarter of a century in the kolkhoz, but it was a kolkhoz and not a factory, so she was not entitled to a pension for herself. She could only try and get one for her husband, for the loss of her breadwinner. But she had had no husband for twelve years now, not since the beginning of the war, and it wasn't easy to obtain all the particulars from different places about his length of service and how much he had earned. What a bother it was getting those forms through! Getting somebody to certify that he'd earned, say, three hundred rubles a month; that she lived alone and nobody helped her; what year she was born in. Then all this had to be taken to the Pension Office. And taken somewhere else to get all the mistakes corrected. And taken back again. Then you had to find out whether they would give you a pension.

To make it all more difficult the Pension Office was twelve miles east of Talnovo, the Rural Council Offices six miles to the west, the Factory District Council an hour's walk to the north. They made her run around from office to office for two months on end, to get an *i* dotted or a *t* crossed. Every trip took a day. She goes down to the Rural District Council—and the secretary isn't there today. Secretaries of rural councils often aren't here today. So come again tomorrow. Tomorrow the secretary is in, but he hasn't got his rubber stamp. So come again the next day. And the day after that back she goes yet again, because all her papers are pinned together and some cockeyed clerk has signed the wrong one.

"They shove me around, Ignatich," she used to complain to me after these fruitless excursions. "Worn out with it I am."

But she soon brightened up. I found that she had a sure means of putting herself in a good humor. She worked. She would grab a shovel and go off to pull potatoes. Or she would tuck a sack under her arm and go after peat. Or take a wicker basket and look for berries deep in the woods. When she'd been bending her back to bushes instead of office desks for a while, and her shoulders were aching from a heavy load, Matryona would come back cheerful, at peace with the world and smiling her nice smile.

"I'm on to a good thing now, Ignatich. I know where to go for it (peat she meant), a lovely place it is."

"But surely my peat is enough, Matryona Vasilyevna? There's a whole truckload of it."

"Pooh! Your peat! As much again, and then as much again, that might be enough. When the winter gets really stiff and the wind's battling at the windows, it blows the heat out of the house faster than you can make the stove up. Last year we got heaps and heaps of it. I'd have had three loads in by now. But they're out to catch us. They've summoned one woman from our village already."

That's how it was. The frightening breath of winter was already in the air. There were forests all round, and no fuel to be had anywhere. Excavators roared away in the bogs, but there was no peat on sale to the villagers. It was delivered, free, to the bosses and to the people round the bosses, and teachers, doctors, and workers got a load each. The people of Talnovo were not supposed to get any peat, and they weren't supposed to ask about it. The chairman of the kolkhoz walked about the village looking people in the eye while he gave his orders or stood chatting and talked about anything you liked except fuel. He was stocked up. Who said anything about winter coming?

So just as in the old days they used to steal the squire's wood, now they pinched peat from the trust. The women went in parties of five or ten so that they would be less frightened. They went in the daytime. The peat cut during the summer had been stacked up all over the place to dry. That's the good thing about peat, it can't be carted off as soon as it's cut. It lies around drying till autumn, or, if the roads are bad, till the snow starts falling. This was when the women used to come and take it. They could get six peats in a sack if it was damp, or ten if it was dry. A sackful weighed about half a hundredweight and it sometimes had to be carried over two miles. This was enough to make the stove up once. There were two hundred days in the winter. The Russian stove had to be lit in the mornings, and the "Dutch"[9] stove in the evenings.

"Why beat about the bush?" said Matryona angrily to someone invisible. "Since there've been no more horses, what you can't have around yourself you haven't got. My back never heals up. Winter you're pulling sledges, summer it's bundles on your back, it's God's truth I'm telling you."

The women went more than once in a day. On good days Matryona brought six sacks home. She piled my peat up where it could be seen and hid her own under the passageway, boarding up the hole every night.

"If they don't just happen to think of it, the devils will never find it in their born days," said Matryona smiling and wiping the sweat from her brow.

What could the peat trust do? Its establishment didn't run to a watchman for every bog. I suppose they had to show a rich haul in their returns, and then write off so much for crumbling, so much washed away by the rain. Sometimes they would take it into their heads to put out patrols and try to catch the women as they came into the village. The women would drop their sacks and scatter. Or somebody would inform and there would be a house-to-house search. They would draw up a report on the stolen peat and threaten a court

9. Not the real tiled Dutch stove, but a cheap small stove (probably made from an oil barrel) that provided heat with less fuel than the big Russian stove.

action. The women would stop fetching it for a while, but the approach of winter drove them out with sledges in the middle of the night.

When I had seen a little more of Matryona I noticed that, apart from cooking and looking after the house, she had quite a lot of other jobs to do every day. She kept all her jobs, and the proper times for them, in her head and always knew when she woke up in the morning how her day would be occupied. Apart from fetching peat and stumps which the tractors unearthed in the bogs, apart from the cranberries which she put to soak in big jars for the winter ("Give your teeth an edge, Ignatich," she used to say when she offered me some), apart from digging potatoes and all the coming and going to do with her pension, she had to get hay from somewhere for her one and only dirty-white goat.

"Why don't you keep a cow, Matryona?"

Matryona stood there in her grubby apron, by the opening in the kitchen screen, facing my table, and explained to me.

"Oh, Ignatich, there's enough milk from the goat for me. And if I started keeping a cow she'd eat me out of house and home in no time. You can't cut the grass by the railway track, because it belongs to the railway, and you can't cut any in the woods, because it belongs to the foresters, and they won't let me have any at the kolkhoz because I'm not a member any more, they reckon. And those who are members have to work there every day till the white flies swarm and make their own hay when there's snow on the ground—what's the good of grass like that? In the old days they used to be sweating to get the hay in at midsummer, between the end of June and the end of July, while the grass was sweet and juicy."

So it meant a lot of work for Matryona to gather enough hay for one skinny little goat. She took her sickle and a sack and went off early in the morning to places where she knew there was grass growing—round the edges of fields, on the roadside, on hummocks in the bog. When she had stuffed her sack with heavy fresh grass she dragged it home and spread it out in her yard to dry. From a sackfull of grass she got one forkload of dry hay.

The farm had a new chairman, sent down from the town not long ago, and the first thing he did was to cut down the garden plots for those who were not fit to work. He left Matryona a third of an acre of sand—when there was over a thousand square yards just lying idle on the other side of the fence. Yet when they were short of working hands, when the women dug in their heels and wouldn't budge, the chairman's wife would come to see Matryona. She was from the town as well, a determined woman whose short gray coat and intimidating glare gave her a somewhat military appearance. She walked into the house without so much as a good morning and looked sternly at Matryona. Matryona was uneasy.

"Well now, Comrade Vasilyevna," said the chairman's wife, drawing out her words. "You will have to help the kolkhoz! You will have to go and help cart manure out tomorrow!"

A little smile of forgiveness wrinkled Matryona's face—as though she understood the embarrassment which the chairman's wife must feel at not being able to pay her for her work.

"Well—er," she droned. "I'm not well, of course, and I'm not attached to you any more . . . ," then she hurried to correct herself, "What time should I come then?"

"And bring your own fork!" the chairman's wife instructed her. Her stiff skirt crackled as she walked away.

"Think of that!" grumbled Matryona as the door closed. "Bring your own fork! They've got neither forks nor shovels at the kolkhoz. And I don't have a man who'll put a handle on for me!"

She went on thinking about it out loud all evening.

"What's the good of talking, Ignatich. I must help, of course. Only the way they work it's all a waste of time—don't know whether they're coming or going. The women stand propped up on their shovels and waiting for the factory whistle to blow twelve o'clock. Or else they get on to adding up who's earned what and who's turned up for work and who hasn't. Now what I call work, there isn't a sound out of anybody, only—oh dear, dear—dinner time's soon rolled round—what, getting dark already."

In the morning she went off with her fork.

But it wasn't just the kolkhoz—any distant relative, or just a neighbor, could come to Matryona of an evening and say, "Come and give me a hand tomorrow, Matryona. We'll finish pulling the potatoes."

Matryona couldn't say no. She gave up what she should be doing next and went to help her neighbor, and when she came back she would say without a trace of envy, "Ah, you should see the size of her potatoes, Ignatich! It was a joy to dig them up. I didn't want to leave the allotment, God's truth I didn't."

Needless to say, not a garden could be plowed without Matryona's help. The women of Talnovo had got it neatly worked out that it was a longer and harder job for one woman to dig her garden with a spade than for six of them to put themselves in harness and plow six gardens. So they sent for Matryona to help them.

"Well—did you pay her?" I asked sometimes.

"She won't take money. You have to try and hide it on her when she's not looking."

Matryona had yet another troublesome chore when her turn came to feed the herdsmen. One of them was a hefty deaf mute, the other a boy who was never without a cigaret in his drooling mouth. Matryona's turn came round only every six weeks, but it put her to great expense. She went to the shop to buy canned fish and was lavish with sugar and butter, things she never ate herself. It seems that the housewives showed off in this way, trying to outdo one another in feeding the herdsmen.

"You've got to be careful with tailors and herdsmen," Matryona explained. "They'll spread your name all round the village if something doesn't suit them."

And every now and then attacks of serious illness broke in on this life that was already crammed with troubles. Matryona would be off her feet for a day or two, lying flat out on the stove. She didn't complain and didn't groan, but she hardly stirred either. On these days Masha, Matryona's closest friend from her earliest years, would come to look after the goat and light the stove. Matryona herself ate nothing, drank nothing, asked for nothing. To call in the doctor from the clinic at the settlement would have seemed strange in Talnovo and would have given the neighbors something to talk about—what does she think she is, a lady? They did call her in once, and she arrived in a real temper and told Matryona to come down to the clinic when she was on her feet again. Matryona went, although she didn't really want to; they took specimens and sent them off to the district hospital—and that's the last anybody heard about it. Matryona was partly to blame herself.

But there was work waiting to be done, and Matryona soon started getting up again, moving slowly at first and then as briskly as ever.

"You never saw me in the old days, Ignatich. I'd lift any sack you liked, I didn't think a hundredweight was too heavy. My father-in-law used to say, 'Matryona, you'll break your back.' And my brother-in-law didn't have to come and help me lift on the cart. Our horse was a warhorse, a big strong one."

"What do you mean, a warhorse?"

"They took ours for the war and gave us this one instead—he'd been wounded. But he turned out a bit spirited. Once he bolted with the sledge right into the lake, the men folk hopped out of the way, but I grabbed the bridle, as true as I'm here, and stopped him. Full of oats that horse was. They liked to feed their horses well in our village. If a horse feels his oats he doesn't know what heavy means."

But Matryona was a long way from being fearless. She was afraid of fire, afraid of "the lightning," and most of all she was for some reason afraid of trains.

"When I had to go to Cherusti,[1] the train came up from Nechaevka way with its great big eyes popping out and the rails humming away—

---

1. About 100 miles east of Moscow and some 250 miles northwest of Nechaevka.

put me in a regular fever. My knees started knocking. God's truth I'm telling you!" Matryona raised her shoulders as though she surprised herself.

"Maybe it's because they won't give people tickets, Matryona Vasilyevna?"

"At the window? They try to shove only first-class tickets on to you. And the train was starting to move. We dashed about all over the place, 'Give us tickets for pity's sake.' "

"The men folk had climbed on top of the carriages. Then we found a door that wasn't locked and shoved straight in without tickets—and all the carriages were empty, they were all empty, you could stretch out on the seat if you wanted to. Why they wouldn't give us tickets, the hardhearted parasites, I don't know. . . ."

Still, before winter came, Matryona's affairs were in a better state than ever before. They started paying her at last a pension of eighty rubles. Besides this she got just over one hundred from the school and me.

Some of her neighbors began to be envious.

"Hm! Matryona can live forever now! If she had any more money, she wouldn't know what to do with it at her age."

Matryona had some new felt boots made. She bought a new jerkin. And she had an overcoat made out of the worn-out railwayman's greatcoat given to her by the engine driver from Cherusti who had married Kira, her foster daughter. The hump-backed village tailor put a padded lining under the cloth and it made a marvelous coat, such as Matryona had never worn before in all her sixty years.

In the middle of winter Matryona sewed two hundred rubles into the lining of this coat for her funeral. This made her quite cheerful.

"Now my mind's a bit easier, Ignatich."

December went by, January went by—and in those two months Matryona's illness held off. She started going over to Masha's house more often in the evening, to sit chewing sunflower seeds with her. She herself didn't invite guests in the evening out of consideration for my work. Once, on the feast of the Epiphany, I came back from school and found a party going on and was introduced to Matryona's three sisters, who called her "nan-nan" or "nanny" because she was the oldest. Until then not much had been heard of the sisters in our cottage—perhaps they were afraid that Matryona might ask them for help.

But one ominous event cast a shadow on the holiday for Matryona. She went to the church three miles away for the blessing of the water and put her pot down among the others. When the blessing was over, the women went rushing and jostling to get their pots back again. There were a lot of women in front of Matryona and when she got there her pot was missing, and no other vessel had been left behind. The pot had vanished as though the devil had run off with it.

Matryona went round the worshipers asking them, "Have any of you girls accidentally mistook somebody else's holy water? In a pot?"

Nobody owned up. There had been some boys there, and boys got up to mischief sometimes. Matryona came home sad.

No one could say that Matryona was a devout believer. If anything, she was a heathen, and her strongest beliefs were superstitious: you mustn't go into the garden on the fast of St. John or there would be no harvest next year. A blizzard meant that somebody had hanged himself. If you pinched your foot in the door, you could expect a guest. All the time I lived with her I didn't once see her say her prayers or even cross herself. But, whatever job she was doing, she began with a "God bless us," and she never failed to say "God bless you," when I set out for school. Perhaps she did say her prayers, but on the quiet, either because she was shy or because she didn't want to embarrass me. There were icons[2] on the walls. Ordinary days they were left in darkness, but for the vigil of a great feast, or on the morning of a holiday, Matryona would light the little lamp.

She had fewer sins on her conscience than her gammy-legged cat. The cat did kill mice.

Now that her life was running more smoothly, Matryona started listening more carefully to my radio. (I had, of course, installed a speaker, or as Matryona called it, a peeker.)[3]

When they announced on the radio that some new machine had been invented, I heard Matryona grumbling out in the kitchen, "New ones all the time, nothing but new ones. People don't want to work with the old ones any more, where are we going to store them all?"

There was a program about the seeding of clouds from airplanes. Matryona, listening up on the stove, shook her head, "Oh, dear, dear, dear, they'll do away with one of the two—summer or winter."

Once Shalyapin[4] was singing Russian folk songs. Matryona stood listening for a long time before she gave her emphatic verdict, "Queer singing, not our sort of singing."

"You can't mean that, Matryona Vasilyevna—just listen to him."

She listened a bit longer and pursed her lips, "No, it's wrong. It isn't our sort of tune, and he's tricky with his voice."

She made up for this another time. They were broadcasting some

2. Religious images or portraits, usually painted on wood; a small lamp was set in front to illuminate them.   3. The translator is imitating Solzhenitsyn's wordplay. In the original, the narrator calls the speaker *razvedka* (a military term, literally "scout"); Matryona calls it *rozetka* (an electric plug).   4. Feodor Ivanovich Shalyapin (or Chaliapin, 1873–1938), was a Russian operatic bass with an international reputation as a great singer and actor; he included popular Russian music in his song recitals.

of Glinka's[5] songs. After half a dozen of these drawing-room ballads, Matryona suddenly came from behind the screen clutching her apron, with a flush on her face and a film of tears over her dim eyes.

"That's our sort of singing," she said in a whisper.

2

So Matryona and I got used to each other and took each other for granted. She never pestered me with questions about myself. I don't know whether she was lacking in normal female curiosity or just tactful, but she never once asked if I had been married. All the Talnovo women kept at her to find out about me. Her answer was, "You want to know—you ask him. All I know is he's from distant parts."

And when I got round to telling her that I had spent a lot of time in prison, she said nothing but just nodded, as though she had already suspected it.

And I thought of Matryona only as the helpless old woman she was now and didn't try to rake up her past, didn't even suspect that there was anything to be found there.

I knew that Matryona had got married before the Revolution and had come to live in the house I now shared with her, and she had gone "to the stove" immediately. (She had no mother-in-law and no older sister-in-law, so it was her job to put the pots in the oven on the very first morning of her married life.) I knew that she had had six children and that they had all died very young, so that there were never two of them alive at once. Then there was a sort of foster daughter, Kira. Matryona's husband had not come back from the last war. She received no notification of his death. Men from the village who had served in the same company said that he might have been taken prisoner, or he might have been killed and his body not found. In the eight years that had gone by since the war Matryona had decided that he was not alive. It was a good thing that she thought so. If he was still alive he was probably in Brazil or Australia and married again. The village of Talnovo and the Russian language would be fading from his memory.

One day when I got back from school, I found a guest in the house. A tall, dark man, with his hat on his lap, was sitting on a chair which Matryona had moved up to the Dutch stove in the middle of the room. His face was completely surrounded by bushy black hair with hardly a trace of gray in it. His thick black moustache ran into his full black beard, so that his mouth could hardly be seen. Black side-

5. Mikhail Ivanovich Glinka (1804–57), a Russian composer who developed a "Russian" style of music, including the two operas *A Life for the Czar* and *Ruslan and Ludmila*.

whiskers merged with the black locks which hung down from his crown, leaving only the tips of his ears visible; his broad black eyebrows met in a wide double span. But the front of his head as far as the crown was a spacious bald dome. His whole appearance made an impression of wisdom and dignity. He sat squarely on his chair, with his hands folded on his stick, and his stick resting vertically on the floor, in an attitude of patient expectation, and he obviously hadn't much to say to Matryona, who was busy behind the screen.

When I came in, he eased his majestic head round toward me and suddenly addressed me, "Schoolmaster, I can't see you very well. My son goes to your school. Grigoryev, Antoshka."

There was no need for him to say any more. However strongly inclined I felt to help this worthy old man, I knew and dismissed in advance all the pointless things he was going to say. Antoshka Grigoryev was a plump, red-faced lad in 8-D who looked like a cat that's swallowed the cream. He seemed to think that he came to school for a rest and sat at his desk with a lazy smile on his face. Needless to say, he never did his homework. But the worst of it was that he had been put up into the next class from year to year because our district, and indeed the whole region and the neighboring region were famous for the high percentage of passes they obtained; the school had to make an effort to keep its record up. So Antoshka had got it clear in his mind that however much the teachers threatened him they would promote him in the end, and there was no need for him to learn anything. He just laughed at us. There he sat in the eighth class, and he hadn't even mastered his decimals and didn't know one triangle from another. In the first two terms of the school year I had kept him firmly below the passing line and the same treatment awaited him in the third.

But now this half-blind old man, who should have been Antoshka's grandfather rather than his father, had come to humble himself before me—how could I tell him that the school had been deceiving him for years, and that I couldn't go on deceiving him, because I didn't want to ruin the whole class, to become a liar and a fake, to start despising my work and my profession.

For the time being I patiently explained that his son had been very slack, that he told lies at school and at home, that his record book must be checked frequently, and that we must both take him severely in hand.

"Severe as you like, Schoolmaster," he assured me, "I beat him every week now. And I've got a heavy hand."

While we were talking I remembered that Matryona had once interceded for Antoshka Grigoryev, but I hadn't asked what relation of hers he was and I had refused to do what she wanted. Matryona was standing in the kitchen doorway like a mute suppliant on this occasion too. When Faddey Mironovich left, saying that he would call on me to see how things were going, I asked her, "I can't make out what relation this Antoshka is to you, Matryona Vasilyevna."

"My brother-in-law's son," said Matryona shortly, and went out to milk the goat.

When I'd worked it out, I realized that this determined old man with the black hair was the brother of the missing husband.

The long evening went by, and Matryona didn't bring up the subject again. But late at night, when I had stopped thinking about the old man and was working in a silence broken only by the rustling of the cockroaches and the heavy tick of the wall-clock, Matryona suddenly spoke from her dark corner, "You know, Ignatich, I nearly married him once."

I had forgotten that Matryona was in the room. I hadn't heard a sound from her—and suddenly her voice came out of the darkness, as agitated as if the old man were still trying to win her.

I could see that Matryona had been thinking about nothing else all evening.

She got up from her wretched rag bed and walked slowly toward me, as though she were following her own words. I sat back in my chair and caught my first glimpse of a quite different Matryona.

There was no overhead light in our big room with its forest of rubber plants. The table lamp cast a ring of light round my exercise books, and when I tore my eyes from it the rest of the room seemed to be half-dark and faintly tinged with pink. I thought I could see the same pinkish glow in her usually sallow cheeks.

"He was the first one who came courting me, before Efim did— he was his brother—the older one—I was nineteen and Faddey was twenty-three. They lived in this very same house. Their house it was. Their father built it."

I looked round the room automatically. Instead of the old gray house rotting under the faded green skin of wallpaper where the mice had their playground, I suddenly saw new timbers, freshly trimmed, not yet discolored, and caught the cheerful smell of pine tar.

"Well, and what happened then?"

"That summer we went to sit in the woods together," she whispered. "There used to be a woods where the stable yard is now. They chopped it down. I was just going to marry him, Ignatich. Then the German war started. They took Faddey into the army."

She let fall these few words—and suddenly the blue and white and yellow July of the year 1914 burst into flower before my eyes: the sky still peaceful, the floating clouds, the people sweating to get the ripe corn in. I imagined them side by side, the black-haired Hercules with a scythe over his shoulder, and the red-faced girl clasping a sheaf. And there was singing out under the open sky, such songs as nobody can sing nowadays, with all the machines in the fields.

"He went to the war—and vanished. For three years I kept to myself and waited. Never a sign of life did he give."

Matryona's round face looked out at me from an elderly thread-bare headscarf. As she stood there in the gentle reflected light from my lamp, her face seemed to lose its slovenly workday wrinkles, and she was a scared young girl again with a frightening decision to make.

Yes . . . I could see it. The trees shed their leaves, the snow fell and melted. They plowed and sowed and reaped again. Again the trees shed their leaves, and the snow fell. There was a revolution. Then another revolution. And the whole world was turned upside down.

"Their mother died and Efim came to court me. 'You wanted to come to our house,' he says, 'so come.' He was a year younger than me, Efim was. It's a saying with us—sensible girls get married after Michaelmas,[6] and silly ones at midsummer. They were short-handed. I got married. . . . The wedding was on St. Peter's day, and then about St. Nicholas' day in the winter he came back—Faddey, I mean, from being a prisoner in Hungary."

Matryona covered her eyes.

I said nothing.

She turned toward the door as though somebody were standing there. "He stood there at the door. What a scream I let out! I wanted to throw myself at his feet! . . . but I couldn't. 'If it wasn't my own brother,' he says, 'I'd take my ax to the both of you.' "

I shuddered. Matryona's despair, or her terror, conjured up a vivid picture of him standing in the dark doorway and raising his ax to her.

But she quieted down and went on with her story in a sing-song voice, leaning on a chairback, "Oh dear, dear me, the poor dear man! There were so many girls in the village—but he wouldn't marry. I'll look for one with the same name as you, a second Matryona, he said. And that's what he did—fetched himself a Matryona from Lipovka. They built themselves a house of their own and they're still living in it. You pass their place every day on your way to school."

So that was it. I realized that I had seen the other Matryona quite often. I didn't like her. She was always coming to my Matryona to complain about her husband—he beat her, he was stingy, he was working her to death. She would weep and weep, and her voice always had a tearful note in it. As it turned out, my Matryona had nothing to regret, with Faddey beating his Matryona every day of his life and being so tightfisted.

"Mine never beat me once," said Matryona of Efim. "He'd pitch into another man in the street, but me he never hit once. Well,

6. October 12 (September 29, old style). *St. Peter's Day:* Probably July 12 (June 29, old style), Sts. Peter and Paul's Day. *St. Nicholas's Day:* December 19 (December 6, old style).

there was one time—I quarreled with my sister-in-law and he cracked me on the forehead with a spoon. I jumped up from the table and shouted at them, 'Hope it sticks in your gullets, you idle lot of beggars, hope you choke!' I said. And off I went into the woods. He never touched me any more."

Faddey didn't seem to have any cause for regret either. The other Matryona had borne him six children (my Antoshka was one of them, the littlest, the runt) and they had all lived, whereas the children of Matryona and Efim had died, every one of them, before they reached the age of three months, without any illness.

"One daughter, Elena, was born and was alive when they washed her, and then she died right after. . . . My wedding was on St. Peter's day, and it was St. Peter's day I buried my sixth, Alexander."

The whole village decided that there was a curse on Matryona.

Matryona still nodded emphatic belief when she talked about it. "There was a *course*[7] on me. They took me to a woman who used to be a nun to get cured, she set me off coughing and waited for the *course* to jump out of me like a frog. Only nothing jumped out."

And the years had run by like running water. In 1941 they didn't take Faddey into the army because of his poor sight, but they took Efim. And what had happened to the elder brother in the First World War happened to the younger in the Second—he vanished without a trace. Only he never came back at all. The once noisy cottage was deserted, it grew old and rotten, and Matryona, all alone in the world, grew old in it.

So she begged from the other Matryona, the cruelly beaten Matryona, a child of her womb (or was it a drop of Faddey's blood?), the youngest daughter, Kira.

For ten years she brought the girl up in her own house, in place of the children who had not lived. Then, not long before I arrived, she had married her off to a young engine driver from Cherusti. The only help she got from anywhere came in dribs and drabs from Cherusti: a bit of sugar from time to time, or some of the fat when they killed a pig.

Sick and suffering, and feeling that death was not far off, Matryona had made known her will: the top room, which was a separate frame joined by tie beams to the rest of the house, should go to Kira when she died.[8] She said nothing about the house itself. Her three sisters had their eyes on it too.

That evening Matryona opened her heart to me. And, as often happens, no sooner were the hidden springs of her life revealed to me than I saw them in motion.

---

7. *Curse/course* reflects word play in the Russian original, where a similar misuse of language indicates Matryona's lack of formal education.   8. Lumber was scarce and valuable, and old houses well built; moving houses or sections of houses is still common in the country.

Kira arrived from Cherusti. Old Faddey was very worried. To get and keep a plot of land in Cherusti the young couple had to put up some sort of building. Matryona's top room would do. very well. There was nothing else they could put up, because there was no timber to be had anywhere. It wasn't Kira herself so much, and it wasn't her husband, but old Faddey who was consumed with eagerness for them to get their hands on the plot at Cherusti.

He became a frequent visitor, laying down the law to Matryona and insisting that she should hand over the top room right away, before she died. On these occasions I saw a different Faddey. He was no longer an old man propped up by a stick, whom a push or a harsh word would bowl over. Although he was slightly bent by backache, he was still a fine figure; in his sixties he had kept the vigorous black hair of a young man; he was hot and urgent.

Matryona had not slept for two nights. It wasn't easy for her to make up her mind. She didn't grudge them the top room, which was standing there idle, any more than she ever grudged her labor or her belongings. And the top room was willed to Kira in any case. But the thought of breaking up the roof she had lived under for forty years was torture to her. Even I, a mere lodger, found it painful to think of them stripping away boards and wrenching out beams. For Matryona it was the end of everything.

But the people who were so insistent knew that she would let them break up her house before she died.

So Faddey and his sons and sons-in-law came along one February morning, the blows of five axes were heard and boards creaked and cracked as they were wrenched out. Faddey's eyes twinkled busily. Although his back wasn't quite straight yet, he scrambled nimbly up under the rafters and bustled about down below, shouting at his assistants. He and his father had built this house when he was a lad, a long time ago. The top room had been put up for him, the oldest son, to move into with his bride. And now he was furiously taking it apart, board by board, to carry it out of somebody else's yard.

After numbering the beam ends and the ceiling boards, they dismantled the top room and the storeroom underneath it. The living room and what was left of the landing they boarded up with a thin wall of deal. They did nothing about the cracks in the wall. It was plain to see that they were wreckers, not builders, and that they did not expect Matryona to be living there very long.

While the men were busy wrecking, the women were getting the drink ready for moving day—vodka would cost too much. Kira brought forty pounds of sugar from the Moscow region, and Matryona carried the sugar and some bottles to the distiller under cover of night.

The timbers were carried out and stacked in front of the gates, and the engine-driver son-in-law went off to Cherusti for the tractor.

But the very same day a blizzard, or "a blower," as Matryona once called it, began. It howled and whirled for two days and nights and buried the road under enormous drifts. Then, no sooner had they made the road passable and a couple of trucks had gone by, than it got suddenly warmer. Within a day everything was thawing out, damp mist hung in the air and rivulets gurgled as they burrowed into the snow, and you could get stuck up to the top of your jackboots.

Two weeks passed before the tractor could get at the dismantled top room. All this time Matryona went around like someone lost. What particularly upset her was that her three sisters came, with one voice called her a fool for giving the top room away, said they didn't want to see her any more, and went off. At about the same time the lame cat strayed and was seen no more. It was just one thing after another. This was another blow to Matryona.

At last the frost got a grip on the slushy road. A sunny day came along, and everybody felt more cheerful. Matryona had had a lucky dream the night before. In the morning she heard that I wanted to take a photograph of somebody at an old-fashioned handloom. (There were looms still standing in two cottages in the village; they wove coarse rugs on them.) She smiled shyly and said, "You just wait a day or two, Ignatich, I'll just send off the top room there and I'll put my loom up, I've still got it, you know, and then you can snap me. Honest to God!"

She was obviously attracted by the idea of posing in an old-fashioned setting. The red frosty sun tinged the window of the curtailed passageway with a faint pink, and this reflected light warmed Matryona's face. People who are at ease with their consciences always have nice faces.

Coming back from school before dusk I saw some movement near our house. A big new tractor-drawn sledge was already fully loaded, and there was no room for a lot of the timbers, so old Faddey's family and the helpers they had called in had nearly finished knocking together another homemade sledge. They were all working like madmen, in the frenzy that comes upon people when there is a smell of good money in the air or when they are looking forward to some treat. They were shouting at one another and arguing.

They could not agree on whether the sledges should be hauled separately or both together. One of Faddey's sons (the lame one) and the engine-driver son-in-law reasoned that the sledges couldn't both be taken at once because the tractor wouldn't be able to pull them. The man in charge of the tractor, a hefty fat-faced fellow who was very sure of himself, said hoarsely that he knew best, he was the driver, and he would take both at once. His motives were obvious: according to the agreement, the engine driver was paying him for the removal of the upper room, not for the number of trips he had to make. He could never have made two trips in a night—twenty-five kilometers each way, and one return journey. And by morning he had to get the tractor back in the garage from which he had sneaked it out for this job on the side.

Old Faddey was impatient to get the top room moved that day, and at a nod from him his lads gave in. To the stout sledge in front they hitched the one they had knocked together in such a hurry.

Matryona was running about among the men, fussing and helping them to heave the beams on the sledge. Suddenly I noticed that she was wearing my jacket and had dirtied the sleeves on the frozen mud round the beams. I was annoyed and told her so. That jacket held memories for me: it had kept me warm in the bad years.

This was the first time that I was every angry with Matryona Vasilyevna.

Matryona was taken aback. "Oh dear, dear me," she said. "My poor head. I picked it up in a rush, you see, and never thought about it being yours. I'm sorry, Ignatich."

And she took it off and hung it up to dry.

The loading was finished, and all the men who had been working, about ten of them, clattered past my table and dived under the curtain into the kitchen. I could hear the muffled rattle of glasses and, from time to time, the clink of a bottle, the voices got louder and louder, the boasting more reckless. The biggest braggart was the tractor driver. The stink of hooch floated in to me. But they didn't go on drinking long. It was getting dark and they had to hurry. They began to leave. The tractor driver came out first, looking pleased with himself and fierce. The engine-driver son-in-law, Faddey's lame son, and one of his nephews were going to Cherusti. The others went off home. Faddey was flourishing his stick, trying to overtake somebody and put him right about something. The lame son paused at my table to light up and suddenly started telling me how he loved Aunt Matryona, and that he had got married not long ago, and his wife had just had a son. Then they shouted for him and he went out. The tractor set up a roar outside.

After all the others had gone, Matryona dashed out from behind the screen. She looked after them, anxiously shaking her head. She had put on her jacket and her headscarf. As she was going through the door, she said to me, "Why ever couldn't they hire two? If one tractor had cracked up, the other would have pulled them. What'll happen now, God only knows!"

She ran out after the others.

After the boozing and the arguments and all the coming and going, it was quieter than ever in the deserted cottage, and very chilly because the door had been opened so many times. I got into my jacket and sat down to mark exercise books. The noise of the tractor died away in the distance.

An hour went by. And another. And a third. Matryona still hadn't come back, but I wasn't surprised. When she had seen the sledge off, she must have gone round to her friend Masha.

Another hour went by. And yet another. Darkness, and with it a deep silence had descended on the village. I couldn't understand at the time why it was so quiet. Later, I found out that it was because all evening not a single train had gone along the line five hundred yards from the house. No sound was coming from my radio, and I noticed that the mice were wilder than ever. Their scampering and scratching and squeaking behind the wallpaper was getting noisier and more defiant all the time.

I woke up. It was one o'clock in the morning, and Matryona still hadn't come home.

Suddenly I heard several people talking loudly. They were still a long way off, but something told me that they were coming to our house. And sure enough, I heard soon afterward a heavy knock at the gate. A commanding voice, strange to me, yelled out an order to open up. I went out into the pitch darkness with a torch. The whole village was asleep, there was no light in the windows, and the snow had started melting in the last week so that it gave no reflected light. I turned the catch and let them in. Four men in greatcoats went on toward the house. It's a very unpleasant thing to be visited at night by noisy people in greatcoats.

When we got into the light though, I saw that two of them were wearing railway uniforms. The older of the two, a fat man with the same sort of face as the tractor driver, asked, "Where's the woman of the house?"

"I don't know."

"This is the place the tractor with a sledge came from?"

"This is it."

"Had they been drinking before they left?"

All four of them were looking around, screwing up their eyes in the dim light from the table lamp. I realized that they had either made an arrest or wanted to make one.

"What's happened then?"

"Answer the question!"

"But . . ."

"Were they drunk when they went?"

"Were they drinking here?"

Had there been a murder? Or hadn't they been able to move the top room? The men in greatcoats had me off balance. But one thing was certain: Matryona could do time for making hooch.

I stepped back to stand between them and the kitchen door. "I honestly didn't notice. I didn't see anything." (I really hadn't seen anything—only heard.) I made what was supposed to be a helpless gesture, drawing attention to the state of the cottage: a table lamp shining peacefully on books and exercises, a crowd of frightened rubber plants, the austere couch of a recluse, not a sign of debauchery.

They had already seen for themselves, to their annoyance, that there had been no drinking in that room. They turned to leave, telling each other this wasn't where the drinking had been then, but it would be a good thing to put in that it was. I saw them out and tried to discover what had happened. It was only at the gate that one of them growled. "They've all been cut to bits. Can't find all the pieces."

"That's a detail. The nine o'clock express nearly went off the rails. That would have been something." And they walked briskly away.

I went back to the hut in a daze. Who were "they"? What did "all of them" mean? And where was Matryona?

I moved the curtain aside and went into the kitchen. The stink of hooch rose and hit me. It was a deserted battlefield: a huddle of stools and benches, empty bottles lying around, one bottle half-full, glasses, the remains of pickled herring, onion, and sliced fat pork.

Everything was deathly still. Just cockroaches creeping unperturbed about the field of battle.

They had said something about the nine o'clock express. Why? Perhaps I should have shown them all this? I began to wonder whether I had done right. But what a damnable way to behave—keeping their explanations for official persons only.

Suddenly the small gate creaked. I hurried out on to the landing. "Matryona Vasilyevna?"

The yard door opened, and Matryona's friend Masha came in, swaying and wringing her hands. "Matryona—our Matryona, Ignatich—"

I sat her down, and through her tears she told me the story.

The approach to the crossing was a steep rise. There was no barrier. The tractor and the first sledge went over, but the towrope broke and the second sledge, the homemade one, got stuck on the crossing and started falling apart—the wood Faddey had given them to make the second sledge was no good. They towed the first sledge out of the way and went back for the second. They were fixing the towrope—the tractor driver and Faddey's lame son, and Matryona (heaven knows what brought her there) were with them, between the tractor and the sledge. What help did she think she could be to the men? She was forever meddling in men's work. Hadn't a bolting horse nearly tipped her into the lake once, through a hole in the ice? Why did she have to go to the damned crossing? She had handed over the top room and owed nothing to anybody. The engine driver kept a lookout in case the train from Cherusti rushed up on them. Its headlamps would be visible a long way off. But two engines coupled together came from the other direction, from our station, backing without lights. Why they were without lights nobody knows. When an engine is backing, coal dust blows into the driver's eyes from the tender and he can't see very well. The two engines flew into them and crushed the three people between the tractor and the sledge to pulp. The tractor was wrecked, the sledge was matchwood, the rails were buckled, and both engines turned over.

"But how was it they didn't hear the engines coming?"

"The tractor engine was making such a din."

"What about the bodies?"

"They won't let anybody in. They've roped them off."

"What was that somebody was telling me about the express?"

"The nine o'clock express goes through our station at a good clip and on to the crossing. But the two drivers weren't hurt when their engines crashed, they jumped out and ran back along the line waving their hands, and they managed to stop the train. The nephew was hurt by a beam as well. He's hiding at Klavka's now so that they won't know he was at the crossing. If they find out they'll drag him in as a witness. . . . 'Don't know lies up, and do know gets tied up.' Kira's husband didn't get a scratch. He tried to hang himself, they had to cut him down. It's all because of me, he says, my aunty's killed and my brother. Now he's gone and given himself up. But the madhouse is where he'll be going, not prison. Oh, Matryona, my dearest Matryona. . . ."

Matryona was gone. Someone close to me had been killed. And on her last day I had scolded her for wearing my jacket.

The lovingly drawn red and yellow woman in the book advertisement smiled happily on.

Old Masha sat there weeping a little longer. Then she got up to go. And suddenly she asked me, "Ignatich, you remember, Matryona had a gray shawl. She meant it to go to my Tanya when she died, didn't she?"

She looked at me hopefully in the half-darkness—surely I hadn't forgotten?

No, I remembered. "She said so, yes."

"Well, listen, maybe you could let me take it with me now. The family will be swarming in tomorrow and I'll never get it then." And she gave me another hopeful, imploring look. She had been Matryona's friend for half a century, the only one in the village who truly loved her.

No doubt she was right.

"Of course—take it."

She opened the chest, took out the shawl, tucked it under her coat, and went out.

The mice had gone mad. They were running furiously up and down the walls, and you could almost see the green wallpaper rippling and rolling over their backs.

In the morning I had to go to school. The time was three o'clock. The only thing to do was to lock up and go to bed.

Lock up, because Matryona would not be coming.

I lay down, leaving the light on. The mice were squeaking, almost moaning, racing and running. My mind was weary and wandering, and I couldn't rid myself of an uneasy feeling that an invisible Matryona was flitting about and saying good-bye to her home.

And suddenly I imagined Faddey standing there, young and black-haired, in the dark patch by the door, with his ax uplifted. "If it wasn't my own brother, I'd chop the both of you to bits."

The threat had lain around for forty years, like an old broad sword in a corner, and in the end it had struck its blow.

3

When it was light the women went to the crossing and brought back all that was left of Matryona on a hand sledge with a dirty sack over it. They threw off the sack to wash her. There was just a mess . . . no feet, only half a body, no left hand. One woman said, "The Lord has left her her right hand. She'll be able to say her prayers where she's going."

Then the whole crowd of rubber plants were carried out of the cottage—these plants that Matryona had loved so much that once when smoke woke her up in the night she didn't rush to save her house but to tip the plants onto the floor in case they were suffocated. The women swept the floor clean. They hung a wide towel of old homespun over Matryona's dim mirror. They took down the jolly posters. They moved my table out of the way. Under the icons, near the windows, they stood a rough unadorned coffin on a row of stools.

In the coffin lay Matryona. Her body, mangled and lifeless, was covered with a clean sheet. Her head was swathed in a white kerchief. Her face was almost undamaged, peaceful, more alive than dead.

The villagers came to pay their last respects. The women even brought their small children to take a look at the dead. And if anyone raised a lament, all the women, even those who had looked in out of idle curiosity, always joined in, wailing where they stood by the door or the wall, as though they were providing a choral accompaniment. The men stood stiff and silent with their caps off.

The formal lamentation had to be performed by the women of Matryona's family. I observed that the lament followed a coldly calculated, age-old ritual. The more distant relatives went up to the coffin for a short while and made low wailing noises over it. Those who considered themselves closer kin to the dead woman began their lament in the doorway and when they got as far as the coffin, bowed down and roared out their grief right in the face of the departed. Every lamenter made up her own melody. And expressed her own thoughts and feelings.

I realized that a lament for the dead is not just a lament, but a kind of politics. Matryona's three sisters swooped, took possession of the cottage, the goat, and the stove, locked up the chest, ripped the two hundred rubles for the funeral out of the coat lining, and drummed it into everybody who came that only they were near relatives. Their lament over the coffin went like this, "*Oh, nanny, nanny! Oh nan-nan!* All we had in the world was you! You could have lived in peace and quiet, you could. And we should always have been kind and loving to you. Now your top room's been the death of you. Finished you off, it has, the cursed thing! Oh, why did you have to take it down? Why didn't you listen to us?"

Thus the sisters' laments were indictments of Matryona's husband's family: they shouldn't have made her take the top room down. (There was an underlying meaning, too: you've taken the top room, all right, but we won't let you have the house itself!)

Matryona's husband's family, her sisters-in-law, Efim and Faddey's sisters, and the various nieces lamented like this, "*Oh poor auntie, poor auntie!* Why didn't you take better care of yourself! Now they're angry with us for sure. Our own dear Matryona you were, and it's your own fault! The top room is nothing to do with it. Oh why did you go where death was waiting for you? Nobody asked you to go there. And what a way to die! Oh why didn't you listen to us?" (Their answer to the others showed through these laments: we are not to blame for her death, and the house we'll talk about later.)

But the "second" Matryona, a coarse, broad-faced woman, the substitute Matryona whom Faddey had married so long ago for the sake of her name, got out of step with family policy, wailing and sobbing over the coffin in her simplicity, "*Oh my poor dear sister!* You won't be angry with me, will you now? Oh-oh-oh! How we used to talk and talk, you and me! Forgive a poor miserable woman! You've gone to be with your dear mother, and you'll come for me some day, for sure! Oh-oh-oh-oh! . . ."

At every "oh-oh-oh" it was as though she were giving up the ghost. She writhed and gasped, with her breast against the side of the coffin. When her lament went beyond the ritual prescription, the women, as though acknowledging its success, all started saying, "Come away now, come away."

Matryona came away, but back she went again, sobbing with even greater abandon. Then an ancient woman came out of a corner, put her hand on Matryona's shoulder, and said, "There are two riddles in this world: how I was born, I don't remember, how I shall die, I don't know."

And Matryona fell silent at once, and all the others were silent, so that there was an unbroken hush.

But the old woman herself, who was much older than all the other old women there and didn't seem to belong to Matryona at all, after a while started wailing, "Oh, my poor sick Matryona! Oh my poor Vasilyevna! Oh what a weary thing it is to be seeing you into your grave!"

There was one who didn't follow the ritual, but wept straight-forwardly, in the fashion of our age, which has had plenty of practice at it. This was Matryona's unfortunate foster daughter, Kira, from Cherusti, for whom the top room had been taken down and moved. Her ringlets were pitifully out of curl. Her eyes looked red and blood-shot. She didn't notice that her headscarf was slipping off out in the frosty air and that her arm hadn't found the sleeve of her coat. She walked in a stupor from her foster mother's coffin in one house to her brother's in another. They were afraid she would lose her mind, because her husband had to go on trial as well.

It looked as if her husband was doubly at fault: not only had he been moving the top room, but as an engine driver, he knew the regulations about unprotected crossings and should have gone down to the station to warn them about the tractor. There were a thousand people on the Urals express that night, peacefully sleeping in the upper and lower berths of their dimly lit carriages, and all those lives were nearly cut short. All because of a few greedy people, wanting to get their hands on a plot of land, or not wanting to make a second trip with a tractor.

All because of the top room, which had been under a curse ever since Faddey's hands had started itching to take it down.

The tractor driver was already beyond human justice. And the railway authorities were also at fault, both because a busy crossing was unguarded and because the coupled engines were traveling with-out lights. That was why they had tried at first to blame it all on the drink, and then to keep the case out of court.

The rails and the track were so twisted and torn that for three days, while the coffins were still in the house, no trains ran—they were diverted onto another line. All Friday, Saturday, and Sunday, from the end of the investigation until the funeral, the work of repairing the line went on day and night. The repair gang was frozen, and they made fires to warm themselves and to light their work at night, using the boards and beams from the second sledge, which were there for the taking, scattered around the crossing.

The first sledge just stood there, undamaged and still loaded, a little way beyond the crossing.

One sledge, tantalizingly ready to be towed away, and the other perhaps still to be plucked from the flames—that was what harrowed the soul of black-bearded Faddey all day Friday and all day Saturday. His daughter was going out of her mind, his son-in-law had a criminal charge hanging over him, in his own house lay the son he had killed, and along the street the woman he had killed and whom he had once loved. But Faddey stood by the coffins, clutching his beard, only for a short time, and went away again. His high forehead was clouded by painful thoughts, but what he was thinking about was how to save the timbers of the top room from the flames and from Matryona's scheming sisters.

Going over the people of Talnovo in my mind, I realized that Faddey was not the only one like that.

Property, the people's property, or my property, is strangely called our "goods." If you lose your goods, people think you disgrace yourself and make yourself look foolish.

Faddey dashed about, never stopping to sit down, from the settlement to the station, from one official to another, there he stood with his bent back, leaning heavily on his stick, and begged them all to take pity on an old man and give him permission to recover the top room.

Somebody gave permission. And Faddey gathered together his surviving sons, sons-in-law, and nephews, got horses from the kolkhoz and from the other side of the wrecked crossing, by a roundabout way that led through three villages, brought the remnants of the top room home to his yard. He finished the job in the early hours of Sunday morning.

On Sunday afternoon they were buried. The two coffins met in the middle of the village, and the relatives argued about which of them should go first. Then they put them side by side on an open sledge, the aunt and the nephew, and carried the dead over the damp snow, with a gloomy February sky above, to the churchyard two villages away. There was an unkind wind, so the priest and the deacon waited inside the church and didn't come out to Talnovo to meet them.

A crowd of people walked slowly behind the coffins, singing in chorus. Outside the village they fell back.

When Sunday came the women were still fussing around the house. An old woman mumbled psalms by the coffin, Matryona's sisters flitted about, popping things into the oven, and the air round the mouth of the stove trembled with the heat of red-hot peats, those Matryona had carried in a sack from a distant bog. They were making unappetizing pies with poor flour.

When the funeral was over and it was already getting on toward evening, they gathered for the wake. Tables were put together to make a long one, which hid the place where the coffin had stood in the morning. To start with, they all stood round the table, and an old man, the husband of a sister-in-law, said the Lord's Prayer. Then they poured everybody a little honey and warm water,[9] just enough to cover the bottom of the bowl. We spooned it up without bread or anything, in memory of the dead. Then we ate something and drank vodka and the conversation became more animated. Before the jelly they all stood up and sang "Eternal remembrance"[1] (they explained to me that it had to be sung before the jelly). There was more drinking. By now they were talking louder than ever, and not about Matryona at all. The sister-in-law's husband started boasting, "Did you notice, brother Christians, that they took the funeral service slowly today? That's because Father Mikhail noticed me. He knows I know the service. Other times, it's saints defend us, homeward wend us, and that's all."

At last the supper was over. They all rose again. They sang "Worthy Is She." Then again, with a triple repetition of "Eternal Remembrance." But the voices were hoarse and out of tune, their faces drunken, and nobody put any feeling into this "eternal memory."

Then most of the guests went away, and only the near relatives were left. They pulled out their cigarets and lit up, there were jokes and laughter. There was some mention of Matryona's husband and his disappearance. The sister-in-law's husband, striking himself on the chest, assured me and the cobbler who was married to one of Matryona's sisters, "He was dead, Efim was dead! What could stop him coming back if he wasn't? If I knew they were going to hang me when I got to the old place, I'd come back just the same!"

The cobbler nodded in agreement. He was a deserter and had never left the old place. All through the war he was hiding in his mother's cellar.

The stern and silent old woman who was more ancient than all the ancients was staying the night and sat high up on the stove. She looked down in mute disapproval on the indecently animated youngsters of fifty and sixty.

9. Traditionally Russians have *kutiia*, a wheat pudding with honey and almonds, at funerals and memorial gatherings; the villagers are too poor to have the main ingredients and their honey and water are symbolic of the *kutiia*. 1. "Eternal remembrance" and "Worthy Is She" are dirges, religious hymns sung to honor the dead; the village still follows religious rituals in time of crisis and does not use the civil ceremony proposed by the Soviet government.

But the unhappy foster daughter, who had grown up within these walls, went away behind the kitchen screen to cry.

Faddey didn't come to Matryona's wake—perhaps because he was holding a wake for his son. But twice in the next few days he walked angrily into the house for discussions with Matryona's sisters and the deserting cobbler.

The argument was about the house. Should it go to one of the sisters or to the foster daughter? They were on the verge of taking it to court, but they made peace because they realized that the court would hand over the house to neither side, but to the Rural District Council. A bargain was struck. One sister took the goat, the cobbler and his wife got the house, and to make up Faddey's share, since he had "nursed every bit of timber here in his arms," in addition to the top room which had already been carried away, they let him have the shed which had housed the goat and the whole of the inner fence between the yard and the garden.

Once again the insatiable old man got the better of sickness and pain and became young and active. Once again he gathered together his surviving sons and sons-in-law, they dismantled the shed and the fence, he hauled the timbers himself, sledge by sledge, and only toward the end did he have Antoshka of 8-D, who didn't slack this time, to help him.

They boarded Matryona's house up till the spring, and I moved in with one of her sisters-in-law, not far away. This sister-in-law on several occasions came out with some recollection of Matryona and made me see the dead woman in a new light. "Efim didn't love her. He used to say, 'I like to dress in an educated way, but she dresses any old way, like they do in the country.' Well then, he thinks, if she doesn't want anything, he might as well drink whatever's to spare. One time I went with him to the town to work, and he got himself a madam there and never wanted to come back to Matryona."

Everything she said about Matryona was disapproving. She was slovenly, she made no effort to get a few things about her. She wasn't the saving kind. She didn't even keep a pig, because she didn't like fattening them up for some reason. And the silly woman helped other people without pay. (What brought Matryona to mind this time was that the garden needed plowing, and she couldn't find enough helpers to pull the plow.)

Matryona's sister-in-law admitted that she was warmhearted and straightforward, but pitied and despised her for it.

It was only then, after these disapproving comments from her sister-in-law, that a true likeness of Matryona formed before my eyes, and I understood her as I never had when I lived side by side with her.

Of course! Every house in the village kept a pig. But she didn't. What can be easier than fattening a greedy piglet that cares for nothing in the world but food! You warm his swill three times a day, you live for him—then you cut his throat and you have some fat.

But she had none.

She made no effort to get things round her. She didn't struggle and strain to buy things and then care for them more than life itself.

She didn't go all out after fine clothes. Clothes, that beautify what is ugly and evil.

She was misunderstood and abandoned even by her husband. She had lost six children, but not her sociable ways. She was a stranger to her sisters and sisters-in-law, a ridiculous creature who stupidly worked for others without pay. She didn't accumulate property against the day she died. A dirty-white goat, a gammy-legged cat, some rubber plants. . . .

We had all lived side by side with her and had never understood that she was the righteous one without whom, as the proverb says,[2] no village can stand.

Nor any city.

Nor our whole land.

DORIS LESSING
1919—

The clash between cultures, between attitudes within cultures, and between elements of one's own personality, as well as the attempt to integrate opposing elements into a higher level of consciousness, are all fundamental to Doris Lessing's work, and are explored in a style that ranges from the detailed realism of her earliest stories to the fantasies and "inner-space fiction" of her most recent novels. Lessing is very conscious of the conflicts of her era: brought up in Africa, she has written harsh indictments of colonial society and its cruel blindness to black culture and rights; living in London, she has described political and social issues and the way they determine interpersonal relationships; as a woman pursuing independence and the right to shape her own identity, she has investigated the psychology of the self in both sexual and intellectual terms and pondered the relations of the individual to the community. Her style is generally realistic, although she does experiment with descriptions of psychological states (dream or madness) and her most famous work—*The Golden Notebook*—uses a complicated pattern of five interlocking notebooks inside the framework of a sketched-out con-

2. Genesis 18: 23–33, the story of Sodom.

ventional short novel to express the gradual healing of a fragmented personality. Lessing's social realism, her description of the frustrated and incomplete relationships between human beings, and her yearning (especially evident in the last novels) for a higher plane of awareness in which there is perfect understanding, recall to some extent D. H. Lawrence's criticism of society and his vision of perfect harmony in tune with nature. Yet there are important differences, including Lessing's refusal to accept the archetypal roles of the sexes that Lawrence found the key to natural harmony. Her own experience could not be content with such simple answers, and her stories and novels have never ceased to explore the layers of consciousness that make up individual identity and social interaction.

She was born Doris May Tayler in Persia (now Iran), on October 22, 1919, the daughter of a nurse and a British bank clerk crippled in World War I whose horror-filled memories of the "war to end war" punctuate her recollections of childhood. In 1924 the family took up farming in a sparsely settled district of Southern Rhodesia (now Zimbabwe), but the farm never prospered. Lessing attended a convent school in the capital city of Salisbury (now Harare) until fourteen, but considers herself largely self-educated from her avid reading of classics of European and American literature. She especially loved the nineteenth-century novel, and Tolstoy, Dostoevsky, Stendhal, and the other great realists impressed her with their "climate of ethical judgement" in which she felt "the warmth, the compassion, the humanity, the love of people" that are so important in her own works. Gradually Lessing became aware of the problem of racial injustice in her new home, and the fact that she was one of a privileged minority of white immigrants who had displaced the previous owners of the land. Themes of this early awakening, which combines a strong attachment to the land itself with horror at racial inequities and the sterility of white civilization in Rhodesia, run through much of her work: in particular, her first novel *The Grass Is Singing* (1949) and the collected *African Stories* (1964). To Lessing, "literature should be committed" in the face of all forms of tyranny. She herself was politically active in Rhodesia and a member of the British Communist Party from 1952 until 1956, the year of the intervention in Hungary. Much of the *Children of Violence* series and the *Golden Notebook* describes the painful clash of two ideals—individual conscience and collective good—as they were embodied for Lessing in her experience of communism. Her political activism and descriptions of racial injustice made their mark, and in 1956 she was declared a prohibited alien in Southern Rhodesia and South Africa.

While still in Rhodesia, Lessing worked in several office jobs in Salisbury and made two unsuccessful marriages (Lessing is the surname of her second husband). In 1949, she moved to England with the son of her second marriage, and published *The Grass Is Singing*. It was an immediate success, and she was henceforth able to make her living as a writer. She began the five-volume series *Children of Violence* (1952–69), which follows the life of a symbolically-named heroine, Martha Quest, whose career in many instances parallels Lessing's own. *Children of Violence* is the portrait of an age and two cultures, and explores with Lessing's characteristic energy a series of moral and intellectual issues for the time: the (female) protagonist's pursuit of individual freedom and the right to achieve her own identity; parent-child relationships; race relations; the hopes and frustrations of political idealism; reason versus irrationality; the shaping influence of culture and historical events. It follows the form of the nineteenth-century *Bildungsroman*, or "education novel" in which the protagonist progressively learns about life. Martha Quest moves towards greater understanding of the cultural forces acting upon her, but it cannot be said that she controls the process of her development as consciously as will Lessing's later protagonists.

The Golden Notebook (1962), Lessing's most famous novel, makes a sharp break with the linear style of narrative found in *Children of Violence* and in the *Bildungsroman* tradition. Once again, a protagonist (Anna Wulf) is struggling to build a unified identity from the multiple selves that constitute her fragmented personality. Linear narrative, however, cannot do justice to these many dimensions, or to the exploratory process by which Anna finally creates a free, integrated personality. "The point of that book was the relation of its parts to each other," said Lessing, and this relation (although framed by a conventional short novel called *Free Women*) is essentially that of an overlapping series of differently colored notebooks which contain Anna's different versions of her experience: black for Africa, red for politics, yellow for a fictionalized version with herself as a character named Ella, and blue for a factual diary. By analyzing her life from these different perspectives, Anna is able to understand and synthesize their interaction: to write, ultimately, the "Golden Notebook" which is "all of me in one book." A chronological account of the events would start with Anna's breakdown and inability to write, and end with her regained equilibrium after a tangled love affair with a similarly split character, Saul Green. Such an account would miss the core of the book, however, or the process by which it all happens: Lessing's detailed description of a mind healing itself by recalling and assessing its relationships with other people, adjusting earlier views according to new insights, weighing (and sometimes rejecting) the explanations of psychoanalysis, comparing different ways of interpreting experience, and measuring the constantly changing whole against the test of each new encounter.

Although *The Golden Notebook* is now taken as one of the major novels of the twentieth century, it was seen at the time chiefly as a feminist manifesto—a one-sided appraisal that infuriated the author. To accusations of being "unfeminine" and a "man-hater" for putting into print emotions of female aggression, hostility, and resentment, she responded dryly, "apparently what many women were thinking, feeling, experiencing came as a great surprise." Yet, she notes, when recent novels and plays caustically attacked women as underminers and betrayers, "these attitudes in male writers were taken for granted, accepted as sound philosophical bases, as quite normal, certainly not as woman-hating, aggressive, or neurotic." Lessing's feminism is often a matter of establishing balances, and an insistence on honesty of emotions and critical self-awareness in all her protagonists whether male (*The Temptation of Jack Orkney*, 1963) or female (Anna Wulf).

The newly integrated "all of me" at the end of *The Golden Notebook* has broken beyond intellectualized understanding, and reached "beyond the region where words could be made to have sense." In the "inner-space fiction" written during the seventies, Lessing has taken up these themes of quasi-mystical insight: first with a schizophrenic hero whose cosmic imaginings are closer to psychic wholeness than his normal life (*Briefing for a Descent into Hell*, 1971), later in the dream-exploration of other "bizarre" dimensions beyond the "ordinary" living-room wall (*Memoirs of a Survivor*, 1974), and most recently in a science-fiction series, *Canopus in Argos: Archives* (1979–1982 and continuing), which describes the different protagonists' consciousness evolving under pressure to a higher plane of existence. These later books, as Lessing states, are influenced by Sufi mysticism with its vision of the evolution of consciousness and the need to learn by discovering the right questions. The wordless moment of understanding that comes when the right question is asked may seem a long way from Lessing's first novels about race relations in Southern Rhodesia, or Martha Quest's awakening to emotional, intellectual, and political maturity. But in each case it is a process of listening to experience that is required to formulate the question, or recognize the crucial issue. The focus has not changed when she writes in the "Afterword" to the fourth Canopus novel: "It seems to me that we do not know nearly enough about ourselves." The attempt to know about ourselves, to grow through such knowledge, and finally to achieve harmony inside society and "even, in worlds or dimensions elsewhere" pervades her entire work. Sometimes the attempt reaches transcendental success; sometimes it ends in failure, as in the following story.

"To Room Nineteen" is the story of a "failure in intelligence": a failure with monstrous consequences, since it leads to the death of a woman who prided herself on being half of a consciously "intelligent marriage." And yet if Susan Rawlings commits suicide after becoming totally alienated from her family, the failure is not so much lack of intelligence as too much of it. Planning ahead, being sensible, not overreacting, keeping things under control, doing the right thing and always being reasonable: in other words, believing that life can be arranged, emotions kept on leash, and traumatic experiences avoided by rationality, falls short of the full experience of living. Lessing stresses the emptiness and aridity of this attempt to control events and inconvenient emotions, in which a center is lacking or a "wellspring to live from." Matthew and Susan are unable to deal with strong emotions except by fitting them into acceptable patterns of thought. When she seeks a place to herself, "Mother's Room" has to be explained and ultimately is rationalized as the children's lesson in respect for other people's rights. Her rented room in town is most easily understood as a lovers' tryst. Susan is slowly driven into silence or self-blame when Matthew cannot or (terrified) will not understand her irrational sense of being caged.

As Susan becomes more and more alienated, to the point that her very "soul" seems to reside in the tawdry room of Fred's Hotel, she focuses more and more on the physical, sensuous, even hallucinatory aspect of things. Lessing illustrates the conflict between reason and irrationality in Susan's mind by showing her escape into a world of wordless physicality at moments of crisis. She is repeatedly fascinated by the dark river, consoled by Matthew's "big solid body," terrified by the personified "demon" of restlessness, and above all attracted by the restfully anonymous physical space of Room Nineteen, to which she escapes from home. The texture and feel of surrounding space have powerful significance throughout the story, which shares with Virginia Woolf's *A Room of One's Own* and Charlotte Perkins Gilman's "The Yellow Room" the image of a woman's room as personal space that can be either prison or sanctuary, maddening cage or restorative source of strength.

The Rawlings' "intelligence" has failed them because it is a superficial rationality based on borrowed experience, not the real intelligence that would let them recognize the causes of Susan's gradual alienation from her world and Matthew's suffering inability to cope. The rulebook which tells them how to cope with problems is based on an imprisoning series of assumptions defined by a particular middle-class society for both men and women. It leaves little room for individual development outside that frame, and almost none for women. Biology defines Susan's primary career, the focus of her adult individuality, and Matthew and Susan reasonably adjust to her inescapable domestic role by considering that the "essential Susan" will only be in abeyance or "cold storage" for the child-raising years. She will take up at fifty the development interrupted at twenty-eight. Small wonder that she finds it difficult to decide who the "essential Susan" is whom she must preserve, or that she is unable to keep a focused sense of individuality when separated into so many roles at home. Lessing gives a devastating description of the numerous ways in which Susan is unable to have time to herself, either at home or outside, without upsetting social expectations and the smooth running of the domestic machine. Only at Fred's sleazy hotel is privacy easily purchased, and there because it is assumed to be for prostitution. When Susan's retreat is tracked down by her husband's detective, the easiest explanation for everyone is that she has a lover; once more, she cooperates with expectations and provides a name—"Michael Plant"—and identity. Matthew reveals that he too has a lover and proposes that they all meet for lunch: a "reasonable" suggestion that will push Susan to increasingly artificial layers of explanation. The effort is too great and, faced with this final loss of her privacy, she seeks the ultimate privacy in death.

Michael Thorpe, *Doris Lessing* (1973), provides an introduction. A good critical study is Roberta Rubenstein, *The Novelistic Vision of Doris Lessing* (1979). Annis Pratt and L. S. Dembo, eds., *Doris Lessing: Critical Studies* (1974), is a useful collection with bibliography. Betsy Draine, *Substance Under Pressure: Artistic Coherence and Evolving Form in the Novels of Doris Lessing* (1983), analyzes the evolution of Lessing's literary form as evolving modes of perception.

To Room Nineteen

This is a story, I suppose, about a failure in intelligence: the Rawlings' marriage was grounded in intelligence.

They were older when they married than most of their married friends: in their well-seasoned late twenties. Both had had a number of affairs, sweet rather than bitter; and when they fell in love—for they did fall in love—had known each other for some time. They joked that they had saved each other "for the real thing." That they had waited so long (but not too long) for this real thing was to them a proof of their sensible discrimination. A good many of their friends had married young, and now (they felt) probably regretted lost opportunities; while others, still unmarried, seemed to them arid, self-doubting, and likely to make desperate or romantic marriages.

Not only they, but others, felt they were well-matched: their friends' delight was an additional proof of their happiness. They had played the same roles, male and female, in this group or set, if such a wide, loosely connected, constantly changing constellation of people could be called a set. They had both become, by virtue of their moderation, their humour, and their abstinence from painful experience, people to whom others came for advice. They could be, and were, relied on. It was one of those cases of a man and a woman linking themselves whom no one else had ever thought of linking, probably because of their similarities. But then everyone exclaimed: Of course! How right! How was it we never thought of it before!

And so they married amid general rejoicing, and because of their foresight and their sense for what was probable, nothing was a surprise to them.

Both had well-paid jobs. Matthew was a subeditor on a large London newspaper, and Susan worked in an advertising firm. He was not the stuff of which editors or publicised journalists are made, but he was much more than "a subeditor," being one of the essential background people who in fact steady, inspire and make possible the people in the limelight. He was content with this position. Susan had a talent for commercial drawing. She was humorous about the advertisements she was responsible for, but she did not feel strongly about them one way or the other.

Both, before they married, had had pleasant flats, but they felt it unwise to base a marriage on either flat, because it might seem like a submission of personality on the part of the one whose flat it was not. They moved into a new flat in South Kensington[1] on the clear understanding that when their marriage had settled down (a process they knew would not take long, and was in fact more a humorous concession to popular wisdom than what was due to themselves) they would buy a house and start a family.

And this is what happened. They lived in their charming flat for two years, giving parties and going to them, being a popular young married couple, and then Susan became pregnant, she gave up her job, and they bought a house in Richmond.[2] It was typical of this couple that they had a son first, then a daughter, then twins, son and daughter. Everything right, appropriate, and what everyone would wish for, if they could choose. But people did feel these two had

---

1. A pleasant district on the outskirts of Central London. *Flat*: Apartment. 2. Richmond-on-Thames is a prosperous outer borough, less crowded than the inner city and with more green space.

chosen; this balanced and sensible family was no more than what was due to them because of their infallible sense for *choosing* right.

And so they lived with their four children in their gardened house in Richmond and were happy. They had everything they had wanted and had planned for.

And yet . . .

Well, even this was expected, that there must be a certain flatness. . . .

Yes, yes, of course, it was natural they sometimes felt like this. Like what?

Their life seemed to be like a snake biting its tail. Matthew's job for the sake of Susan, children, house, and garden—which caravan-serai needed a well-paid job to maintain it. And Susan's practical intelligence for the sake of Matthew, the children, the house and the garden—which unit would have collapsed in a week without her.

But there was no point about which either could say: "For the sake of *this* is all the rest." Children? But children can't be a centre of life and a reason for being. They can be a thousand things that are delightful, interesting, satisfying, but they can't be a wellspring to live from. Or they shouldn't be. Susan and Matthew knew that well enough.

Matthew's job? Ridiculous. It was an interesting job, but scarcely a reason for living. Matthew took pride in doing it well, but he could hardly be expected to be proud of the newspaper; the newspaper he read, *his* newspaper, was not the one he worked for.

Their love for each other? Well, that was nearest it. If this wasn't a centre, what was? Yes, it was around this point, their love, that the whole extraordinary structure revolved. For extraordinary it certainly was. Both Susan and Matthew had moments of thinking so, of looking in secret disbelief at this thing they had created: marriage, four children, big house, garden, charwomen, friends, cars . . . and this *thing*, this entity, all of it had come into existence, been blown into being out of nowhere, because Susan loved Matthew and Matthew loved Susan. Extraordinary. So that was the central point, the wellspring.

And if one felt that it simply was not strong enough, important enough, to support it all, well whose fault was that? Certainly neither Susan's nor Matthew's. It was in the nature of things. And they sensibly blamed neither themselves nor each other.

On the contrary, they used their intelligence to preserve what they had created from a painful and explosive world: they looked around them, and took lessons. All around them, marriages collapsing, or breaking, or rubbing along (even worse, they felt). They must not make the same mistakes, they must not.

They had avoided the pitfall so many of their friends had fallen into—of buying a house in the country *for the sake of the children*, so that the husband became a weekend husband, a weekend father, and the wife always careful not to ask what went on in the town flat which they called (in joke) a bachelor flat. No, Matthew was a full-time husband, a full-time father, and at night, in the big married bed in the big married bedroom (which had an attractive view of the river), they lay beside each other talking and he told her about his day, and what he had done, and whom he had met; and she told him about her day (not as interesting, but that was not her fault), for both knew of the hidden resentments and deprivations of the woman who has lived her own life—and above all, has earned her own living—and is now dependent on a husband for outside interests and money.

Nor did Susan make the mistake of taking a job for the sake of her independence, which she might very well have done, since her old firm, missing her qualities of humour, balance, and sense, invited her often to go back. Children needed their mother to a certain age, that both parents knew and agreed on; and when these four healthy wisely brought up children were of the right age, Susan would work again, because she knew, and so did he, what happened to women of fifty at the height of their energy and ability, with grownup children who no longer needed their full devotion.

So here was this couple, testing their marriage, looking after it, treating it like a small boat full of helpless people in a very stormy sea. Well, of course, so it was. . . . The storms of the world were bad, but not too close—which is not to say they were selfishly felt: Susan and Matthew were both well-informed and responsible people. And the inner storms and quicksands were understood and charted. So everything was all right. Everything was in order. Yes, things were under control.

So what did it matter if they felt dry, flat? People like themselves, fed on a hundred books (psychological, anthropological, sociological), could scarcely be unprepared for the dry, controlled wistfulness which is the distinguishing mark of the intelligent marriage. Two people, endowed with education, with discrimination, with judgement, linked together voluntarily from their will to be happy together and to be of use to others—one sees them everywhere, one knows them, one even is that thing oneself: sadness because so much is after all so little. These two, unsurprised, turned towards each other with even more courtesy and gentle love: this was life, that two people, no matter how carefully chosen, could not be everything to each other. In fact, even to say so, to think in such a way, was banal; they were ashamed to do it.

It was banal, too, when one night Matthew came home late and confessed he had been to a party, taken a girl home and slept with her. Susan forgave him, of course. Except that forgiveness is hardly the word. Understanding, yes. But if you understand something, you don't forgive it, you are the thing itself: forgiveness is for what you *don't* understand. Nor had he *confessed*—what sort of word is that?

The whole thing was not important. After all, years ago they had joked: Of course I'm not going to be faithful to you, no one can be faithful to one other person for a whole lifetime. (And there was the word "faithful"—stupid, all these words, stupid, belonging to a savage old world.) But the incident left both of them irritable. Strange, but they were both bad-tempered, annoyed. There was something unassimilable about it.

Making love splendidly after he had come home that night, both had felt that the idea that Myra Jenkins, a pretty girl met at a party, could be even relevant was ridiculous. They had loved each other for over a decade, would love each other for years more. Who, then, was Myra Jenkins?

Except, thought Susan, unaccountably bad-tempered, she was (is?) the first. In ten years. So either the ten years' fidelity was not important, or she isn't. (No, no, there is something wrong with this way of thinking, there must be.) But if she isn't important, presumably it wasn't important either when Matthew and I first went to bed with each other that afternoon whose delight even now (like a very long shadow at sundown) lays a long, wandlike finger over us. (Why did I say sundown?) Well, if what we felt that afternoon was not important, nothing is important, because if it hadn't been for what we felt, we wouldn't be Mr. and Mrs. Rawlings with four children, et cetera, et cetera. The whole thing is *absurd*—for him to have come home and told me was absurd. For him not to have told me was absurd. For me to care or, for that matter, not to care, is absurd . . . and who is Myra Jenkins? Why, no one at all.

There was only one thing to do, and of course these sensible people did it; they put the thing behind them, and consciously, knowing what they were doing, moved forward into a different phase of their marriage, giving thanks for past good fortune as they did so.

For it was inevitable that the handsome, blond, attractive, manly man, Matthew Rawlings, should be at times tempted (oh, what a word!) by the attractive girls at parties she could not attend because of the four children; and that sometimes he would succumb (a word even more repulsive, if possible) and that she, a good-looking woman in the big well-tended garden at Richmond, would sometimes be pierced as by an arrow from the sky with bitterness. Except that bitterness was not in order, it was out of court. Did the casual girls touch the marriage? They did not. Rather it was they who knew defeat because of the handsome Matthew Rawlings' marriage body and soul to Susan Rawlings.

In that case why did Susan feel (though luckily not for longer than a few seconds at a time) as if life had become a desert, and that nothing mattered, and that her children were not her own?

Meanwhile her intelligence continued to assert that all was well. What if her Matthew did have an occasional sweet afternoon, the odd affair? For she knew quite well, except in her moments of aridity, that they were very happy, that the affairs were not important.

Perhaps that was the trouble? It was in the nature of things that the adventures and delights could no longer be hers, because of the four children and the big house that needed so much attention. But perhaps she was secretly wishing, and even knowing that she did, that the wildness and the beauty could be his. But he was married to her. She was married to him. They were married inextricably. And therefore the gods could not strike him with the real magic, not really. Well, was it Susan's fault that after he came home from an adventure he looked harassed rather than fulfilled? (In fact, that was how she knew he had been *unfaithful*, because of his sullen air, and his glances at her, similar to hers at him: What is it that I share with this person that shields all delight from me?) But none of it by anybody's fault. (But what did they feel ought to be somebody's fault?) Nobody's fault, nothing to be at fault, no one to blame, no one to offer or to take it . . . and nothing wrong, either, except that Matthew never was really struck, as he wanted to be, by joy; and that Susan was more and more often threatened by emptiness. (It was usually in the garden that she was invaded by this feeling: she was coming to avoid the garden, unless the children or Matthew were with her.) There was no need to use the dramatic words "unfaithful," "forgive," and the rest: intelligence forbade them. Intelligence barred, too, quarrelling, sulking, anger, silences of withdrawal, accusations and tears. Above all, intelligence forbids tears.

A high price has to be paid for the happy marriage with the four healthy children in the large white gardened house.

And they were paying it, willingly, knowing what they were doing. When they lay side by side or breast to breast in the big civilised bedroom overlooking the wild sullied river, they laughed, often, for no particular reason; but they knew it was really because of these two small people, Susan and Matthew, supporting such an edifice on their intelligent love. The laugh comforted them; it saved them both, though from what, they did not know.

They were now both fortyish. The older children, boy and girl, were ten and eight, at school. The twins, six, were still at home. Susan did not have nurses[3] or girls to help her: childhood is short; and she did not regret the hard work. Often enough she was bored,

---

3. Nursemaids, women hired to take charge of the children.

since small children can be boring; she was often very tired; but she regretted nothing. In another decade, she would turn herself back into being a woman with a life of her own.

Soon the twins would go to school, and they would be away from home from nine until four. These hours, so Susan saw it, would be the preparation for her own slow emancipation away from the role of hub-of-the-family into woman-with-her-own-life. She was already planning for the hours of freedom when all the children would be "off her hands." That was the phrase used by Matthew and by Susan and by their friends, for the moment when the youngest child went off to school. "They'll be off your hands, darling Susan, and you'll have time to yourself." So said Matthew, the intelligent husband, who had often enough commended and consoled Susan, standing by her in spirit during the years when her soul was not her own, as she said, but her children's.

What it amounted to was that Susan saw herself as she had been at twenty-eight, unmarried; and then again somewhere about fifty, blossoming from the root of what she had been twenty years before. As if the essential Susan were in abeyance, as if she were in cold storage. Matthew said something like this to Susan one night: and she agreed that it was true—she did feel something like that. What, then, was this essential Susan? She did not know. Put like that it sounded ridiculous, and she did not really feel it. Anyway, they had a long discussion about the whole thing before going off to sleep in each other's arms.

So the twins went off to their school, two bright affectionate children who had no problems about it, since their older brother and sister had trodden this path so successfully before them. And now Susan was going to be alone in the big house, every day of the school term, except for the daily woman who came in to clean.

It was now, for the first time in this marriage, that something happened which neither of them had foreseen.

This is what happened. She returned, at nine-thirty, from taking the twins to the school by car, looking forward to seven blissful hours of freedom. On the first morning she was simply restless, worrying about the twins "naturally enough" since this was their first day away at school. She was hardly able to contain herself until they came back. Which they did happily, excited by the world of school, looking forward to the next day. And the next day Susan took them, dropped them, came back, and found herself reluctant to enter her big and beautiful home because it was as if something was waiting for her there that she did not wish to confront. Sensibly, however, she parked the car in the garage, entered the house, spoke to Mrs. Parkes, the daily woman,[4] about her duties, and went up to her

---

4. Woman who came in each day to clean and cook.

bedroom. She was possessed by a fever which drove her out again, downstairs, into the kitchen, where Mrs. Parkes was making a cake and did not need her, and into the garden. There she sat on a bench and tried to calm herself looking at trees, at a brown glimpse of the river. But she was filled with tension, like a panic: as if an enemy was in the garden with her. She spoke to herself severely, thus: All this is quite natural. First, I spent twelve years of my adult life working, *living my own life*. Then I married, and from the moment I became pregnant for the first time I signed myself over, so to speak, to other people. To the children. Not for one moment in twelve years have I been alone, had time to myself. So now I have to learn to be myself again. That's all.

And she went indoors to help Mrs. Parkes cook and clean, and found some sewing to do for the children. She kept herself occupied every day. At the end of the first term she understood she felt two contrary emotions. First: secret astonishment and dismay that during those weeks when the house was empty of children she had in fact been more occupied (had been careful to keep herself occupied) than ever she had been when the children were around her needing her continual attention. Second: that now she knew the house would be full of them, and for five weeks, she resented the fact she would never be alone. She was already looking back at those hours of sewing, cooking (but by herself) as at a lost freedom which would not be hers for five long weeks. And the two months of term which would succeed the five weeks stretched alluringly open to her—freedom. But what freedom—when in fact she had been so careful *not* to be free of small duties during the last weeks? She looked at herself, Susan Rawlings, sitting in a big chair by the window in the bedroom, sewing shirts or dresses, which she might just as well have bought. She saw herself making cakes for hours at a time in the big family kitchen: yet usually she bought cakes. What she saw was a woman alone, that was true, but she had not felt alone. And she did not like being in the garden at all, because of the closeness there of the enemy—irritation, restlessness, emptiness, whatever it was—which keeping her hands occupied made less dangerous for some reason.

Susan did not tell Matthew of these thoughts. They were not sensible. She did not recognise herself in them. What should she say to her dear friend and husband Matthew? "When I go into the garden, that is, if the children are not there, I feel as if there is an enemy there waiting to invade me." "What enemy, Susan darling?" "Well I don't know, really. . . ." "Perhaps you should see a doctor?"

No, clearly this conversation should not take place. The holidays began and Susan welcomed them. Four children, lively, energetic, intelligent, demanding: she was never, not for a moment of her day, alone. If she was in a room they would be in the next room, or waiting for her to do something for them; or it would soon be time for lunch or tea, or to take one of them to the dentist. Something to do: five weeks of it, thank goodness.

On the fourth day of these so welcome holidays, she found she was storming with anger at the twins; two shrinking beautiful children who (and this is what checked her) stood hand in hand looking at her with sheer dismayed disbelief. This was their calm mother, shouting at them. And for what? They had come to her with some game, some bit of nonsense. They looked at each other, moved closer for support, and went off hand in hand, leaving Susan holding on to the windowsill of the livingroom, breathing deep, feeling sick. She went to lie down, telling the older children she had a headache. She heard the boy Harry telling the little ones: "It's all right, Mother's got a headache." She heard that *It's all right* with pain.

That night she said to her husband: "Today I shouted at the twins, quite unfairly." She sounded miserable, and he said gently: "Well, what of it?"

"It's more of an adjustment than I thought, their going to school."

"But Susie, Susie darling. . . ." For she was crouched weeping on the bed. He comforted her: "Susan, what is all this about? You shouted at them? What of it? If you shouted at them fifty times a day it would be more than the little devils deserve." But she wouldn't laugh. She wept. Soon he comforted her with his body. She became calm. Calm, she wondered what was wrong with her, and why she should mind so much that she might, just once have behaved unjustly with the children. What did it matter? They had forgotten it all long ago: Mother had a headache and everything was all right.

It was a long time later that Susan understood that that night, when she had wept and Matthew had driven the misery out of her with his big solid body, was the last time, ever in their married life, that they had been—to use their mutual language—with each other. And even that was a lie, because she had not told him of her real fears at all.

The five weeks passed, and Susan was in control of herself, and good and kind, and she looked forward to the holidays with a mixture of fear and longing. She did not know what to expect. She took the twins off to school (the elder children took themselves to school) and she returned to the house determined to face the enemy wherever he was, in the house, or the garden or—where?

She was again restless, she was possessed by restlessness. She cooked and sewed and worked as before, day after day, while Mrs. Parkes remonstrated: "Mrs. Rawlings, what's the need for it? I can do that, it's what you pay me for."

And it was so irrational that she checked herself. She would put the car into the garage, go up to her bedroom, and sit, hands in her lap, forcing herself to be quiet. She listened to Mrs. Parkes moving around the house. She looked out into the garden and saw the branches shake the trees. She sat defeating the enemy, restlessness. Emptiness. She ought to be thinking about her life, about herself. But she did not. Or perhaps she could not. As soon as she forced her mind to think about Susan (for what else did she want to be alone for?), it skipped off to thoughts of butter or school clothes. Or it thought of Mrs. Parkes. She realised that she sat listening for the movements of the cleaning woman, following her every turn, bend, thought. She followed her in her mind from kitchen to bathroom, from table to oven, and it was as if the duster, the cleaning cloth, the saucepan, were in her own hand. She would hear herself saying: No, not like that, don't put that there. . . . Yet she did not give a damn what Mrs. Parkes did, or if she did it at all. Yet she could not prevent herself from being conscious of her, every minute. Yes, this was what was wrong with her: she needed, when she was alone, to be really alone, with no one near. She could not endure the knowledge that in ten minutes or in half an hour Mrs. Parkes would call up the stairs: "Mrs. Rawlings, there's no silver polish. Madam, we're out of flour."

So she left the house and went to sit in the garden where she was screened from the house by trees. She waited for the demon to appear and claim her, but he did not.

She was keeping him off, because she had not, after all, come to an end of arranging herself.

She was planning how to be somewhere where Mrs. Parkes would not come after her with a cup of tea, or a demand to be allowed to telephone (always irritating, since Susan did not care who she telephoned or how often), or just a nice talk about something. Yes, she needed a place, or a state of affairs, where it would not be necessary to keep reminding herself: In ten minutes I must telephone Matthew about . . . and at half past three I must leave early for the children because the car needs cleaning. And at ten o'clock tomorrow I must remember. . . . She was possessed with resentment that the seven hours of freedom in every day (during weekdays in the school term) were not free, that never, not for one second, ever, was she free from the pressure of time, from having to remember this or that. She could never forget herself; never really let herself go into forgetfulness.

Resentment. It was poisoning her. (She looked at this emotion and thought it was absurd. Yet she felt it.) She was a prisoner. (She looked at this thought too, and it was no good telling herself it was a ridiculous one.) She must tell Matthew—but what? She was filled with emotions that were utterly ridiculous, that she despised, yet that nevertheless she was feeling so strongly she could not shake them off.

The school holidays came round, and this time they were for nearly two months, and she behaved with a conscious controlled decency that nearly drove her crazy. She would lock herself in the bathroom, and sit on the edge of the bath, breathing deep, trying to let go into some kind of calm. Or she went up into the spare room, usually empty, where no one would expect her to be. She heard the children calling "Mother, Mother," and kept silent, feeling guilty. Or she went to the very end of the garden, by herself, and looked at the slow-moving brown river; she looked at the river and closed her eyes and breathed slow and deep, taking it into her being, into her veins.

Then she returned to the family, wife and mother, smiling and responsible, feeling as if the pressure of these people—four lively children and her husband—were a painful pressure on the surface of her skin, a hand pressing on her brain. She did not once break down into irritation during these holidays, but it was like living out a prison sentence, and when the children went back to school, she sat on a white stone near the flowing river, and she thought: It is not even a year since the twins went to school, since *they were off my hands* (what on earth did I think I meant when I used that stupid phrase?), and yet I'm a different person. I'm simply not myself. I don't understand it.

Yet she had to understand it. For she knew that this structure—big white house, on which the mortgage still cost four hundred a year, a husband, so good and kind and insightful; four children, all doing so nicely; and the garden where she sat; and Mrs. Parkes, the cleaning woman—all this depended on her, and yet she could not understand why, or even what it was she contributed to it.

She said to Matthew in their bedroom: "I think there must be something wrong with me."

And he said: "Surely not, Susan? You look marvellous—you're as lovely as ever."

She looked at the handsome blond man, with his clear, intelligent, blue-eyed face, and thought: Why is it I can't tell him? Why not? And she said: "I need to be alone more than I am."

At which he swung his slow blue gaze at her, and she saw what she had been dreading: Incredulity. Disbelief. And fear. An incredulous blue stare from a stranger who was her husband, as close to her as her own breath.

He said: "But the children are at school and off your hands."

She said to herself: I've got to force myself to say: Yes, but do you realize that I never feel free? There's never a moment I can say to myself: There's nothing I have to remind myself about, nothing I have to do in half an hour, or an hour, or two hours. . . .

But she said: "I don't feel well."

He said: "Perhaps you need a holiday."

She said, appalled: "But not without you, surely?" For she could not imagine herself going off without him. Yet that was what he meant. Seeing her face, he laughed, and opened his arms, and she went into them, thinking: Yes, yes, but why can't I say it? And what it is I have to say?

She tried to tell him, about never being free. And he listened and said: "But Susan, what sort of freedom can you possibly want—short of being dead! Am I ever free? I go to the office, and I have to be there at ten—all right, half past ten, sometimes. And I have to do this or that, don't I? Then I've got to come home at a certain time—I don't mean it, you know I don't—but if I'm not going to be back home at six I telephone you. When can I ever say to myself: I have nothing to be responsible for in the next six hours?"

Susan, hearing this, was remorseful. Because it was true. The good marriage, the house, the children depended just as much on his voluntary bondage as it did on hers. But why did he not feel bound? Why didn't he chafe and become restless? No, there was something really wrong with her and this proved it.

And that word "bondage"—why had she used it? She had never felt marriage, or the children, as bondage. Neither had he, or surely they wouldn't be together lying in each other's arms content after twelve years of marriage.

No, her state (whatever it was) was irrelevant, nothing to do with her real good life with her family. She had to accept the fact that, after all, she was an irrational person and to live with it. Some people had to live with crippled arms, or stammers, or being deaf. She would have to live knowing she was subject to a state of mind she could not own.

Nevertheless, as a result of this conversation with her husband, there was a new regime next holidays.

The spare room at the top of the house now had a cardboard sign saying: PRIVATE! DO NOT DISTURB! on it. (This sign had been drawn in coloured chalks by the children, after a discussion between the parents in which it was decided this was psychologically the right thing.) The family and Mrs. Parkes knew this was "Mother's Room" and that she was entitled to her privacy. Many serious conversations took place between Matthew and the children about not taking Mother for granted. Susan overheard the first, between father and Harry, the older boy, and was surprised at her irritation over it. Surely she could have a room somewhere in that big house and retire into it without such a fuss being made? Without it being so solemnly discussed? Why couldn't she simply have announced: "I'm going to fit out the little top room for myself, and when I'm in it I'm not to be disturbed for anything short of fire"? Just that, and finished; instead of long earnest discussions. When she heard Harry and Matthew explaining it to the twins with Mrs. Parkes coming in—"Yes, well, a family sometimes gets on top of a woman"—she had to go right away to the bottom of the garden until the devils of exasperation had finished their dance in her blood.

But now there was a room, and she could go there when she liked, she used it seldom: she felt even more caged there than in her bedroom. One day she had gone up there after a lunch for ten children she had cooked and served because Mrs. Parkes was not there, and had sat alone for a while looking into the garden. She saw the children stream out from the kitchen and stand looking up at the window where she sat behind the curtains. They were all—her children and their friends—discussing Mother's Room. A few minutes later, the chase of children in some game came pounding up the stairs, but ended as abruptly as if they had fallen over a ravine, so sudden was the silence. They had remembered she was there, and had gone silent in a great gale of "Hush! Shhhhhh! Quiet, you'll disturb her. . . ." And they went tiptoeing downstairs like criminal conspirators. When she came down to make tea for them, they all apologised. The twins put their arms around her, from front and back, making a human cage of loving limbs, and promised it would never occur again. "We forgot, Mummy, we forgot all about it!"

What it amounted to was that Mother's Room, and her need for privacy, had become a valuable lesson in respect for other people's rights. Quite soon Susan was going up to the room only because it was a lesson it was a pity to drop. Then she took sewing up there, and the children and Mrs. Parkes came in and out: it had become another family room.

She sighed, and smiled, and resigned herself—she made jokes at her own expense with Matthew over the room. That is, she did from the self she liked, she respected. But at the same time, something inside her howled with impatience, with rage. . . . And she was frightened. One day she found herself kneeling by her bed and praying: "Dear God, keep it away from me, keep him away from me." She meant the devil, for she now thought of it, not caring if she was irrational, as some sort of demon. She imagined him, or it, as a youngish man, or perhaps a middle-aged man pretending to be young. Or a man young-looking from immaturity? At any rate, she saw the young-looking face which, when she drew closer, had dry lines about mouth and eyes. He was thinnish, meagre in build. And he had a reddish complexion, and ginger hair. That was he—a gingery, energetic man, and he wore a reddish hairy jacket, unpleasant to the touch.

Well, one day she saw him. She was standing at the bottom of the garden, watching the river ebb past, when she raised her eyes and saw this person, or being, sitting on the white stone bench. He was looking at her, and grinning. In his hand was a long crooked stick, which he had picked off the ground, or broken off the tree above him. He was absent-mindedly, out of an absent-minded or freakish impulse of spite, using the stick to stir around in the coils of a blindworm[5] or a grass snake (or some kind of snakelike creature: it was whitish and unhealthy to look at, unpleasant). The snake was twisting about, flinging its coils from side to side in a kind of dance of protest against the teasing prodding stick.

Susan looked at him, thinking: Who is the stranger? What is he doing in our garden? Then she recognised the man around whom her terrors had crystallised. As she did so, he vanished. She made herself walk over to the bench. A shadow from a branch lay across thin emerald grass, moving jerkily over its roughness, and she could see why she had taken it for a snake, lashing and twisting. She went back to the house thinking: Right, then, so I've seen him with my own eyes, so I'm not crazy after all—there *is* a danger because I've seen him. He is lurking in the garden and sometimes even in the house, and he wants to *get into me and to take me over.*

She dreamed of having a room or a place, anywhere, where she could go and sit, by herself, no one knowing where she was.

Once, near Victoria,[6] she found herself outside a news agent that had Rooms to Let advertised. She decided to rent a room, telling no one. Sometimes she could take the train in from Richmond and sit alone in it for an hour or two. Yet how could she? A room would cost three or four pounds a week, and she earned no money, and how could she explain to Matthew that she needed such a sum? What for? It did not occur to her that she was taking it for granted she wasn't going to tell him about the room.

Well, it was out of the question, having a room; yet she knew she must.

One day, when a school term was well established, and none of the children had measles or other ailments, and everything seemed in order, she did the shopping early, explained to Mrs. Parkes she was meeting an old school friend, took the train to Victoria, searched until she found a small quiet hotel, and asked for a room for the day. They did not let rooms by the day, the manageress said, looking doubtful, since Susan so obviously was not the kind of woman who needed a room for unrespectable reasons. Susan made a long explanation about not being well, being unable to shop without frequent rests for lying down. At last she was allowed to rent the room provided she paid a full night's price for it. She was taken up by the manageress and a maid, both concerned over the state of her health . . . which must be pretty bad if, living at Richmond (she had signed

5. A limbless European lizard that looks like a snake.   6. Victoria Station, a main terminus of the Underground or subway system.

her name and address in the register), she needed a shelter at Victoria.

The room was ordinary and anonymous, and was just what Susan needed. She put a shilling in the gas fire, and sat, eyes shut, in a dingy armchair with her back to a dingy window. She was alone. She was alone. She was alone. She could feel pressures lifting off her. First the sounds of traffic came very loud; then they seemed to vanish; she might even have slept a little. A knock on the door: it was Miss Townsend, the manageress, bringing her a cup of tea with her own hands, so concerned was she over Susan's long silence and possible illness.

Miss Townsend was a lonely woman of fifty, running this hotel with all the rectitude expected of her, and she sensed in Susan the possibility of understanding companionship. She stayed to talk. Susan found herself in the middle of a fantastic story about her illness, which got more and more impossible as she tried to make it tally with the large house at Richmond, well-off husband, and four children. Suppose she said instead: Miss Townsend, I'm here in your hotel because I need to be alone for a few hours, above all *alone and with no one knowing where I am*. She said it mentally, and saw, mentally, the look that would inevitably come on Miss Townsend's elderly maiden's face. "Miss Townsend, my four children and my husband are driving me insane, do you understand that? Yes, I can see from the gleam of hysteria in your eyes that comes from loneliness controlled but only just contained that I've got everything in the world you've ever longed for. Well, Miss Townsend, I don't want any of it. You can have it, Miss Townsend. I wish I was absolutely alone in the world, like you. Miss Townsend, I'm besieged by seven devils, Miss Townsend, Miss Townsend, I'm besieged by seven devils, Miss Townsend, Miss Townsend, let me stay here in your hotel where the devils can't get me. . . ." Instead of saying all this, she described her anaemia, agreed to try Miss Townsend's remedy for it, which was raw liver, minced, between whole-meal bread, and said yes, perhaps it would be better if she stayed at home and let a friend do shopping for her. She paid her bill and left the hotel, defeated.

At home Mrs. Parkes said she didn't really like it, no, not really, when Mrs. Rawlings was away from nine in the morning until five. The teacher had telephoned from school to say Joan's teeth were paining her, and she hadn't known what to say; and what was she to make for the children's tea, Mrs. Rawlings hadn't said.

All this was nonsense, of course, Mrs. Parkes's complaint was that Susan had withdrawn herself spiritually, leaving the burden of the big house on her.

Susan looked back at her day of "freedom" which had resulted in her becoming a friend of the lonely Miss Townsend, and in Mrs.

Parkes's remonstrances. Yet she remembered the short blissful hour of being alone, really alone. She was determined to arrange her life, no matter what it cost, so that she could have that solitude more often. An absolute solitude, where no one knew her or cared about her.

But how? She thought of saying to her old employer: I want you to back me up in a story with Matthew that I am doing part-time work for you. The truth is that . . . But she would have to tell him a lie too, and which lie? She could not say: I want to sit by myself three or four times a week in a rented room. And besides, he knew Matthew, and she could not really ask him to tell lies on her behalf, apart from being bound to think it meant a lover.

Suppose she really took a part-time job, which she could get through fast and efficiently, leaving time for herself. What job? Addressing envelopes? Canvassing?

And there was Mrs. Parkes, working widow, who knew exactly what she was prepared to give to the house, who knew by instinct when her mistress withdrew in spirit from her responsibilities. Mrs. Parkes was one of the servers of this world, but she needed someone to serve. She had to have Mrs. Rawlings, her madam, at the top of the house or in the garden, so that she could come and get support from her: "Yes, the bread's not what it was when I was a girl. . . . Yes, Harry's got a wonderful appetite, I wonder where he puts it all. . . . Yes, it's lucky the twins are so much of a size, they can wear each other's shoes, that's a saving in these hard times. . . . Yes, the cherry jam from Switzerland is not a patch on the jam from Poland, and three times the price . . ." And so on. That sort of talk Mrs. Parkes must have, every day, or she would leave, not knowing herself why she left.

Susan Rawlings thinking these thoughts, found that she was prowling through the great thicketed garden like a wild cat: she was walking up the stairs, down the stairs, through the rooms into the garden, along the brown running river, back, up through the house, down again. . . . It was a wonder Mrs. Parkes did not think it strange. But on the contrary, Mrs. Rawlings could do what she liked, she could stand on her head if she wanted, provided she was *there*. Susan Rawlings prowled and muttered through her house, hating poor Miss Townsend, dreaming of her hour of solitude in the dingy respectability of Miss Townsend's hotel bedroom, and she knew quite well she was mad. Yes, she was mad.

She said to Matthew that she must have a holiday. Matthew agreed with her. This was not as things had been once—how they had talked in each other's arms in the marriage bed. He had, she knew, diagnosed her finally as *unreasonable*. She had become someone outside himself that he had to manage. They were living side by side in this house like two tolerably friendly strangers.

Having told Mrs. Parkes—or rather, asked for her permission—she went off on a walking holiday in Wales. She chose the remotest place she knew of. Every morning the children telephoned her before they went off to school, to encourage and support her, just as they had over Mother's Room. Every evening she telephoned them, spoke to each child in turn, and then to Matthew. Mrs. Parkes, given permission to telephone for instructions or advice, did so every day at lunchtime. When, as happened three times, Mrs. Rawlings was out on the mountainside, Mrs. Parkes asked that she should ring back at such-and-such a time, for she would not be happy in what she was doing without Mrs. Rawlings' blessing.

Susan prowled over wild country with the telephone wire holding her to her duty like a leash. The next time she must telephone, or wait to be telephoned, nailed her to her cross. The mountains themselves seemed trammelled by her unfreedom. Everywhere on the mountains, where she met no one at all, from breakfast time to dusk, excepting sheep, or a shepherd, she came face to face with her own craziness, which might attack her in the broadest valleys, so that they seemed too small, or on a mountain top from which she could see a hundred other mountains and valleys, so that they seemed too low, too small, with the sky pressing down too close. She would stand gazing at a hillside brilliant with ferns and bracken, jewelled with running water, and see nothing but her devil, who lifted inhuman eyes at her from where he leaned negligently on a rock, switching at his ugly yellow boots with a leafy twig.

She returned to her home and family, with the Welsh emptiness at the back of her mind like a promise of freedom.

She told her husband she wanted to have an *au pair* girl.[7]

They were in their bedroom, it was late at night, the children slept. He sat, shirted and slippered, in a chair by the window, looking out. She sat brushing her hair and watching him in the mirror. A time-hallowed scene in the connubial bedroom. He said nothing, while she heard the arguments coming into his mind, only to be rejected because every one was *reasonable*.

"It seems strange to get one now; after all, the children are in school most of the day. Surely the time for you to have help was when you were stuck with them day and night. Why don't you ask Mrs. Parkes to cook for you? She's even offered to—I can understand if you are tired of cooking for six people. But you know that an *au pair* girl means all kinds of problems; it's not like having an ordinary char in during the day. . . ."

---

7. A girl who received room and board in return for household duties; it was a way for young foreigners to travel abroad and practice speaking a foreign language. Au pair, equal exchange (French).

Finally he said carefully: "Are you thinking of going back to work?"

"No," she said, "no, not really." She made herself sound vague, rather stupid. She went on brushing her black hair and peering at herself so as to be oblivious of the short uneasy glances her Matthew kept giving her. "Do you think we can't afford it?" she went on vaguely, not at all the old efficient Susan who knew exactly what they could afford.

"It's not that," he said, looking out of the window at dark trees, so as not to look at her. Meanwhile she examined a round, candid, pleasant face with clear dark brows and clear grey eyes. A sensible face. She brushed thick healthy black hair and thought: Yet that's the reflection of a madwoman. How very strange! Much more to the point of what looked back at me was the gingery green-eyed demon with his dry meagre smile. . . . Why wasn't Matthew agreeing? After all, what else could he do? She was breaking her part of the bargain and there was no way of forcing her to keep it: that her spirit, her soul, should live in this house, so that the people in it could grow like plants in water, and Mrs. Parkes remain content in their service. In return for this, he would be a good loving husband, and responsible towards the children. Well, nothing like this had been true of either of them for a long time. He did his duty, perfunctorily; she did not even pretend to do hers. And he had become like other husbands, with his real life in his work and the people he met there, and very likely a serious affair. All this was her fault.

At last he drew heavy curtains, blotting out the trees, and turned to force her attention: "Susan, are you really sure we need a girl?" But she would not meet his appeal at all. She was running the brush over her hair again and again, lifting fine black clouds in a small hiss of electricity. She was peering in and smiling as if she were amused at the clinging hissing hair that followed the brush.

"Yes, I think it would be a good idea, on the whole," she said, with the cunning of a madwoman evading the real point.

In the mirror she could see her Matthew lying on his back, his hands behind his head, staring upwards, his face sad and hard. She felt her heart (the old heart of Susan Rawlings) soften and call out to him. But she set it to be indifferent.

He said: "Susan, the children?" It was an appeal that *almost* reached her. He opened his arms, lifting them palms up, empty. She had only to run across and fling herself into them, onto his hard, warm chest, and melt into herself, into Susan. But she could not. She would not see his lifted arms. She said vaguely: "Well, surely it'll be even better for them? We'll get a French or a German girl and they'll learn the language."

In the dark she lay beside him, feeling frozen, a stranger. She felt as if Susan had been spirited away. She disliked very much this woman who lay here, cold and indifferent beside a suffering man, but she could not change her.

Next morning she set about getting a girl, and very soon came Sophie Traub from Hamburg, a girl of twenty, laughing, healthy, blue-eyed, intending to learn English. Indeed, she already spoke a good deal. In return for a room—"Mother's Room"—and her food, she undertook to do some light cooking, and to be with the children when Mrs. Rawlings asked. She was an intelligent girl and understood perfectly what was needed. Susan said: "I go off sometimes, for the morning or for the day—well, sometimes the children run home from school, or they ring up, or a teacher rings up. I should be here, really. And there's the daily woman. . . ." And Sophie laughed her deep fruity *Fräulein's*[8] laugh, showed her fine white teeth and her dimples, and said: "You want some person to play mistress of the house sometimes, not so?"

"Yes, that is just so," said Susan, a bit dry, despite herself, thinking in secret fear how easy it was, how much nearer to the end she was than she thought. Healthy Fräulein Traub's instant understanding of their position proved this to be true.

The *au pair* girl, because of her own common sense, or (as Susan said to herself, with her new inward shudder) because she had been *chosen* so well by Susan, was a success with everyone, the children liking her, Mrs. Parkes forgetting almost at once that she was German, and Matthew finding her "nice to have around the house." For he was now taking things as they came, from the surface of life, withdrawn both as a husband and a father from the household.

One day Susan saw how Sophie and Mrs. Parkes were talking and laughing in the kitchen, and she announced that she would be away until tea time. She knew exactly where to go and what she must look for. She took the District Line to South Kensington, changed to the Circle, got off at Paddington,[9] and walked around looking at the smaller hotels until she was satisfied with one which had FRED'S HOTEL painted on windowpanes that needed cleaning. The facade was a faded shiny yellow, like unhealthy skin. A door at the end of a passage said she must knock; she did, and Fred appeared. He was not at all attractive, not in any way, being fattish, and run-down, and wearing a tasteless striped suit. He had small sharp eyes in a white creased face, and was quite prepared to let Mrs. Jones (she chose the farcical name deliberately, staring him out) have a room three days a week from ten until six. Provided of course that she paid in advance each time she came? Susan produced fifteen shillings (no price had been set by him) and held it out, still fixing him with a bold unblinking challenge she had not known until then she could

8. German for girl, or Miss.   9. Stops on the rail service in and around Central London.

use at will. Looking at her still, he took up a ten-shilling note from her palm between thumb and forefinger, fingered it; then shuffled up two half-crowns, held out his own palm with these bits of money displayed thereon, and let his gaze lower broodingly at them. They were standing in the passage, a red-shaded light above, bare boards beneath, and a strong smell of floor polish rising about them. He shot his gaze up at her over the still-extended palm, and smiled as if to say: What do you take me for? "I shan't," said Susan, "be using this room for the purposes of making money." He still waited. She added another five shillings, at which he nodded and said: "You pay, and I ask no questions." "Good," said Susan. He now went past her to the stairs, and there waited a moment: the light from the street door being in her eyes, she lost sight of him momentarily. Then she saw a sober-suited, white-faced, white-balding little man trotting up the stairs like a waiter, and she went after him. They proceeded in utter silence up the stairs of this house where no questions were asked—Fred's Hotel, which could afford the freedom for its visitors that poor Miss Townsend's hotel could not. The room was hideous. It had a single window, with thin green brocade curtains, a three-quarter bed that had a cheap green satin bedspread on it, a fireplace with a gas fire and a shilling meter[1] by it, a chest of drawers, and a green wicker armchair.

"Thank you," said Susan, knowing that Fred (if this was Fred, and not George, or Herbert or Charlie) was looking at her, not so much with curiosity, an emotion he would not own to, for professional reasons, but with a philosophical sense of what was appropriate. Having taken her money and shown her up and agreed to everything, he was clearly disapproving of her for coming here. She did not belong here at all, so his look said. (But she knew, already, how very much she did belong: the room had been waiting for her to join it.) "Would you have me called at five o'clock, please?" and he nodded and went downstairs.

It was twelve in the morning. She was free. She sat in the armchair, she simply sat, she closed her eyes and sat and let herself be alone. She was alone and no one knew where she was. When a knock came on the door she was annoyed, and prepared to show it: but it was Fred himself; it was five o'clock and he was calling her as ordered. He flicked his sharp little eyes over the room—bed, first. It was undisturbed. She might never have been in the room at all. She thanked him, said she would be returning the day after tomorrow, and left. She was back home in time to cook supper, to put the children to bed, to cook a second supper for her husband and herself later. And to welcome Sophie back from the pictures where she had

---

1. To pay for the gas.

gone with a friend. All these things she did cheerfully, willingly. But she was thinking all the time of the hotel room; she was longing for it with her whole being.

Three times a week. She arrived promptly at ten, looked Fred in the eyes, gave him twenty shillings, followed him up the stairs, went into the room, and shut the door on him with gentle firmness. For Fred, disapproving of her being here at all, was quite ready to let friendship, or at least acquaintanceship, follow his disapproval, if only she would let him. But he was content to go off on her dismissing nod, with the twenty shillings in his hand.

She sat in the armchair and shut her eyes.

What did she *do* in the room? Why, nothing at all. From the chair, when it had rested her, she went to the window, stretching her arms, smiling, treasuring her anonymity, to look out. She was no longer Susan Rawlings, mother of four, wife of Matthew, employer of Mrs. Parkes and of Sophie Traub, with these and those relations with friends, school-teachers, tradesmen. She no longer was mistress of the big white house and garden, owning clothes suitable for this and that activity or occasion. She was Mrs. Jones, and she was alone, and she had no past and no future. Here I am, she thought, after all these years of being married and having children and playing those roles of responsibility—and I'm just the same. Yet there have been times I thought that nothing existed of me except the roles that went with being Mrs. Matthew Rawlings. Yes, here I am, and if I never saw any of my family again, here I would still be . . . how very strange that is! And she leaned on the sill, and looked into the street, loving the men and women who passed, because she did not know them. She looked at the down-trodden buildings over the street, and at the sky, wet and dingy, or sometimes blue, and she felt she had never seen buildings or sky before. And then she went back to the chair, empty, her mind a blank. Sometimes she talked aloud, saying nothing—an exclamation, meaningless, followed by a comment about the floral pattern on the thin rug, or a stain on the green satin coverlet. For the most part, she wool-gathered—what word is there for it?—brooded, wandered, simply went dark, feeling emptiness run deliciously through her veins like the movement of her blood.

This room had become more her own than the house she lived in. One morning she found Fred taking her a flight higher than usual. She stopped, refusing to go up, and demanded her usual room, Number 19. "Well, you'll have to wait half an hour, then," he said. Willingly she descended to the dark disinfectant-smelling hall, and sat waiting until the two, man and woman, came down the stairs, giving her swift indifferent glances before they hurried out into the street, separating at the door. She went up to the room, *her* room, which they had just vacated. It was no less hers, though the windows were set wide open, and a maid was straightening the bed as she came in.

After these days of solitude, it was both easy to play her part as mother and wife, and difficult—because it was so easy: she felt an imposter. She felt as if her shell moved here, with her family, answering to Mummy, Mother, Susan, Mrs. Rawlings. She was surprised no one saw through her, that she wasn't turned out of doors, as a fake. On the contrary, it seemed the children loved her more; Matthew and she "got on" pleasantly, and Mrs. Parkes was happy in her work under (for the most part, it must be confessed) Sophie Traub. At night she lay beside her husband, and they made love again, apparently just as they used to, when they were really married. But she, Susan, or the being who answered so readily and improbably to the name of Susan, was not there: she was in Fred's Hotel, in Paddington, waiting for the easing hours of solitude to begin.

Soon she made a new arrangement with Fred and with Sophie. It was for five days a week. As for the money, five pounds, she simply asked Matthew for it. She saw that she was not even frightened he might ask what for: he would give it to her, she knew that, and yet it was terrifying it could be so, for this close couple, these partners, had once known the destination of every shilling they must spend. He agreed to give her five pounds a week. She asked for just so much, not a penny more. He sounded indifferent about it. It was as if he were paying her, she thought: *paying her off*—yes, that was it. Terror came back for a moment when she understood this, but she stilled it: things had gone too far for that. Now, every week, on Sunday nights, he gave her five pounds, turning away from her before their eyes could meet on the transaction. As for Sophie Traub, she was to be somewhere in or near the house until six at night, after which she was free. She was not to cook, or to clean; she was simply to be there. So she gardened or sewed, and asked friends in, being a person who was bound to have a lot of friends. If the children were sick, she nursed them. If teachers telephoned, she answered them sensibly. For the five daytimes in the school week, she was altogether the mistress of the house.

One night in the bedroom, Matthew asked: "Susan, I don't want to interfere—don't think that, please—but are you sure you are well?"

She was brushing her hair at the mirror. She made two more strokes on either side of her head, before she replied: "Yes, dear, I am sure I am well."

He was again lying on his back, his blond head on his hands, his elbows angled up and part-concealing his face. He said: "Then Susan, I have to ask you this question, though you must understand, I'm not putting any sort of pressure on you." (Susan heard the word "pressure" with dismay, because this was inevitable; of course she could not go on like this.) "Are things going to go on like this?"

"Well," she said, going vague and bright and idiotic again, so as to escape: "Well, I don't see why not."

He was jerking his elbows up and down, in annoyance or in pain, and, looking at him, she saw he had got thin, even gaunt; and restless angry movements were not what she remembered of him. He said: "Do you want a divorce, is that it?"

At this, Susan only with the greatest difficulty stopped herself from laughing: she could hear the bright bubbling laughter she *would* have emitted, had she let herself. He could only mean one thing: she had a lover, and that was why she spent her days in London, as lost to him as if she had vanished to another continent.

Then the small panic set in again: she understood that he hoped she did have a lover, he was begging her to say so, because otherwise it would be too terrifying.

She thought this out as she brushed her hair, watching the fine black stuff fly up to make its little clouds of electricity, hiss, hiss, hiss. Behind her head, across the room, was a blue wall. She realised she was absorbed in watching the black hair making shapes against the blue. She should be answering him. "Do *you* want a divorce, Matthew?"

He said: "That surely isn't the point, is it?"

"You brought it up, I didn't," she said, brightly, suppressing meaningless tinkling laughter.

Next day she asked Fred: "Have enquiries been made for me?"

He hesitated, and she said: "I've been coming here a year now. I've made no trouble, and you've been paid every day. I have a right to be told."

"As a matter of fact, Mrs. Jones, a man did come asking."

"A man from a detective agency?"

"Well, he could have been, couldn't he?"

"I was asking you. . . . Well, what did you tell him?"

"I told him a Mrs. Jones came every weekday from ten until five or six and stayed in Number 19 by herself."

"Describing me?"

"Well, Mrs. Jones, I had no alternative. Put yourself in my place."

"By rights I should deduct what that man gave you for the information."

He raised shocked eyes: she was not the sort of person to make jokes like this! Then he chose to laugh: a pinkish wet slit appeared across his white crinkled face; his eyes positively begged her to laugh, otherwise he might lose some money. She remained grave, looking at him.

He stopped laughing and said: "You want to go up now?"—returning to the familiarity, the comradeship, of the country where no questions are asked, on which (and he knew it) she depended completely.

She went up to sit in her wicker chair. But it was not the same. Her husband had searched her out. (The world had searched her out.) The pressures were on her. She was here with his connivance. He might walk in at any moment, here, into Room 19. She imagined the report from the detective agency: "A woman calling herself Mrs. Jones, fitting the description of your wife (et cetera, et cetera, et cetera), stays alone all day in Room No. 19. She insists on this room, waits for it if it is engaged. As far as the proprietor knows, she receives no visitors there, male or female." A report something on these lines Matthew must have received.

Well, of course he was right: things couldn't go on like this. He had put an end to it all simply by sending the detective after her.

She tried to shrink herself back into the shelter of the room, a snail pecked out of its shell and trying to squirm back. But the peace of the room had gone. She was trying consciously to revive it, trying to let go into the dark creative trance (or whatever it was) that she had found there. It was no use, yet she craved for it, she was as ill as a suddenly deprived addict.

Several times she returned to the room, to look for herself there, but instead she found the unnamed spirit of restlessness, a pricking fevered hunger for movement, an irritable self-consciousness that made her brain feel as if it had coloured lights going on and off inside it. Instead of the soft dark that had been the room's air, were now waiting for her demons that made her dash blindly about, muttering words of hate; she was impelling herself from point to point like a moth dashing itself against a windowpane, sliding to the bottom, fluttering off on broken wings, then crashing into the invisible barrier again. And again and again. Soon she was exhausted, and she told Fred that for a while she would not be needing the room, she was going on holiday. Home she went, to the big white house by the river. The middle of a weekday, and she felt guilty at returning to her own home when not expected. She stood unseen, looking in at the kitchen window. Mrs. Parkes, wearing a discarded floral overall of Susan's, was stooping to slide something into the oven. Sophie, arms folded, was leaning her back against a cupboard and laughing at some joke made by a girl not seen before by Susan—a dark foreign girl, Sophie's visitor. In an armchair Molly, one of the twins, lay curled, sucking her thumb and watching the grownups. She must have some sickness, to be kept from school. The child's listless face, the dark circles under her eyes, hurt Susan: Molly was looking at the three grownups working and talking in exactly the same way Susan looked at the four through the kitchen window: she was remote, shut off from them.

But then, just as Susan imagined herself going in, picking up the little girl, and sitting in an armchair with her, stroking her probably heated forehead, Sophie did just that: she had been standing on one leg, the other knee flexed, its foot set against the wall. Now she let her foot in its ribbon-tied red shoe slide down the wall, stood solid on two feet, clapping her hands before and behind her, and sang a couple of lines in German, so that the child lifted her heavy eyes at her and began to smile. Then she walked, or rather skipped, over to the child, swung her up, and let her fall into her lap at the same moment she sat herself. She said "Hopla! Hopla! Molly . . ." and began stroking the dark untidy young head that Molly laid on her shoulder for comfort.

Well. . . . Susan blinked the tears of farewell out of her eyes, and went quietly up through the house to her bedroom. There she sat looking at the river through the trees. She felt at peace, but in a way that was new to her. She had no desire to move, to talk, to do anything at all. The devils that had haunted the house, the garden, were not there; but she knew it was because her soul was in Room 19 in Fred's Hotel; she was not really here at all. It was a sensation that should have been frightening: to sit at her own bedroom window, listening to Sophie's rich young voice sing German nursery songs to her child, listening to Mrs. Parkes clatter and move below, and to know that all this had nothing to do with her: she was already out of it.

Later, she made herself go down and say she was home: it was unfair to be here unannounced. She took lunch with Mrs. Parkes, Sophie, Sophie's Italian friend Maria, and her daughter Molly, and felt like a visitor.

A few days later, at bedtime, Matthew said: "Here's your five pounds," and pushed them over at her. Yet he must have known she had not been leaving the house at all.

She shook her head, give it back to him, and said, in explanation, not in accusation: "As soon as you knew where I was, there was no point."

He nodded, not looking at her. He was turned away from her: thinking, she knew, how best to handle this wife who terrified him.

He said: "I wasn't trying to . . . It's just that I was worried."

"Yes, I know."

"I must confess that I was beginning to wonder . . ."

"You thought I had a lover?"

"Yes, I am afraid I did."

She knew that he wished she had. She sat wondering how to say: "For a year now I've been spending all my days in a very sordid hotel room. It's the place where I'm happy. In fact, without it I don't exist." She heard herself saying this, and understood how terrified he was that she might. So instead she said: "Well, perhaps you're not far wrong."

Probably Matthew would think the hotel proprietor lied: he would want to think so.

"Well," he said, and she could hear his voice spring up, so to speak, with relief, "in that case I must confess I've got a bit of an affair on myself."

She said, detached and interested: "Really? Who is she?" and saw Matthew's startled look because of this reaction.

"It's Phil. Phil Hunt."

She had known Phil Hunt well in the old unmarried days. She was thinking: No, she won't do, she's too neurotic and difficult. She's never been happy yet. Sophie's much better. Well, Matthew will see that himself, as sensible as he is.

This line of thought went on in silence, while she said aloud: "It's no point telling you about mine, because you don't know him."

Quick, quick, invent, she thought. Remember how you invented all that nonsense for Miss Townsend.

She began slowly, careful not to contradict herself: "His name is Michael" (*Michael What?*)—"Michael Plant." (What a silly name!)" He's rather like you—in looks, I mean." And indeed, she could imagine herself being touched by no one but Matthew himself. "He's a publisher." (Really? Why?) "He's got a wife already and two children."

She brought out this fantasy, proud of herself.

Matthew said: "Are you two thinking of marrying?"

She said, before she could stop herself: "Good God, *no!*"

She realised, if Matthew wanted to marry Phil Hunt, that this was too emphatic, but apparently it was all right, for his voice sounded relieved as he said: "It is a bit impossible to imagine oneself married to anyone else, isn't it?" With which he pulled her to him, so that her head lay on his shoulder. She turned her face into the dark of his flesh, and listened to the blood pounding through her ears saying: I am alone, I am alone, I am alone.

In the morning Susan lay in bed while he dressed.

He had been thinking things out in the night, because now he said: "Susan, why don't we make a foursome?"

Of course, she said to herself, of course he would be bound to say that. If one is sensible, if one is reasonable, if one never allows oneself a base thought or an envious emotion, naturally one says: Let's make a foursome!

"Why not?" she said.

"We could all meet for lunch. I mean, it's ridiculous, you sneaking off to filthy hotels, and me staying late at the office, and all the lies everyone has to tell."

What on earth did I say his name was?—she panicked, then said: "I think it's a good idea, but Michael is away at the moment. When he comes back, though—and I'm sure you two would like each other."

"He's away, is he? So that's why you've been . . ." Her husband put his hand to the knot of his tie in a gesture of male coquetry she would not before have associated with him; and he bent to kiss her cheek with the expression that goes with the words: Oh you naughty little puss! And she felt its answering look, naughty and coy, come onto her face.

Inside she was dissolving in horror at them both, at how far they had both sunk from honesty of emotion.

So now she was saddled with a lover, and he had a mistress! How ordinary, how reassuring, how jolly! And now they would make a foursome of it, and go about to theatres and restaurants. After all, the Rawlings could well afford that sort of thing, and presumably the publisher Michael Plant could afford to do himself and his mistress quite well. No, there was nothing to stop the four of them developing the most intricate relationship of civilised tolerance, all enveloped in a charming afterglow of autumnal passion. Perhaps they would all go off on holidays together? She had known people who did. Or perhaps Matthew would draw the line there? Why should he, though, if he was capable of talking about "foursomes" at all?

She lay in the empty bedroom, listening to the car drive off with Matthew in it, off to work. Then she heard the children clattering off to school to the accompaniment of Sophie's cheerfully ringing voice. She slid down into the hollow of the bed, for shelter against her own irrelevance. And she stretched out her hand to the hollow where her husband's body had lain, but found no comfort there: he was not her husband. She curled herself up in a small tight ball under the clothes: she could stay here all day, all week, indeed, all her life.

But in a few days she must produce Michael Plant, and—but how? She must presumably find some agreeable man prepared to impersonate a publisher called Michael Plant. And in return for which she would—what? Well, for one thing they would make love. The idea made her want to cry with sheer exhaustion. Oh no, she had finished with all that—the proof of it was that the words "make love," or even imagining it, trying hard to revive no more than the pleasures of sensuality, let alone affection, or love, made her want to run away and hide from the sheer effort of the thing. . . . Good Lord, why make love at all? Why make love with anyone? Or if you are going to make love, what does it matter who with? Why shouldn't she simply walk into the street, pick up a man and have a roaring sexual affair with him? Why not? Or even with Fred? What difference did it make?

But she had let herself in for it—an interminable stretch of time with a lover, called Michael, as part of a gallant civilised foursome. Well, she could not, and she would not.

She got up, dressed, went down to find Mrs. Parkes, and asked her for the loan of a pound, since Matthew, she said, had forgotten to leave her money. She exchanged with Mrs. Parkes variations on the theme that husbands are all the same, they don't think, and without saying a word to Sophie, whose voice could be heard upstairs from the telephone, walked to the underground, travelled to South Kensington, changed to the Inner Circle, got out at Paddington, and walked to Fred's Hotel. There she told Fred that she wasn't going on holiday after all, she needed the room. She would have to wait an hour, Fred said. She went to a busy tearoom-cum-restaurant around the corner, and sat watching the people flow in and out the door that kept swinging open and shut, watched them mingle and merge, and separate, felt her being flow into them, into their movement. When the hour was up, she left a half-crown for her pot of tea, and left the place without looking back at it, just as she had left her house, the big, beautiful white house, without another look, but silently dedicating it to Sophie. She returned to Fred, received the key of Number 19, now free, and ascended the grimy stairs slowly, letting floor after floor fall away below her, keeping her eyes lifted, so that floor after floor descended jerkily to her level of vision, and fell away out of sight.

Number 19 was the same. She saw everything with an acute, narrow, checking glance: the cheap shine of the satin spread, which had been replaced carelessly after the two bodies had finished their convulsions under it; a trace of powder on the glass that topped the chest of drawers; an intense green shade in a fold of the curtain. She stood at the window, looking down, watching people pass and pass and pass until her mind went dark from the constant movement. Then she sat in the wicker chair, letting herself go slack. But she had to be careful, because she did not want, today, to be surprised by Fred's knock at five o'clock.

The demons were not here. They had gone forever, because she was buying her freedom from them. She was slipping already into the dark fructifying dream that seemed to caress her inwardly, like the movement of her blood . . . but she had to think about Matthew first. Should she write a letter for the coroner? But what should she say? She would like to leave him with the look on his face she had seen this morning—banal, admittedly, but at least confidently healthy. Well, that was impossible, one did not look like that with a wife dead from suicide. But how to leave him believing she was dying because of a man—because of the fascinating publisher Michael Plant? Oh, how ridiculous! How absurd! How humiliating! But she decided not to trouble about it, simply not to think about the living. If he wanted to believe she had a lover, he would believe it. And he *did* want to believe it. Even when he had found out that there was no publisher in London called Michael Plant, he would think: Oh poor Susan, she was afraid to give me his real name.

And what did it matter whether he married Phil Hunt or Sophie? Though it ought to be Sophie, who was already the mother of those children . . . and what hypocrisy to sit here worrying about the children, when she was going to leave them because she had not got the energy to stay.

She had about four hours. She spent them delightfully, darkly, sweetly, letting herself slide gently, gently, to the edge of the river. Then, with hardly a break in her consciousness, she got up, pushed the thin rug against the door, made sure the windows were tight shut, put two shillings in the meter, and turned on the gas. For the first time since she had been in the room she lay on the hard bed that smelled stale, that smelled of sweat and sex.

She lay on her back on the green satin cover, but her legs were chilly. She got up, found a blanket folded in the bottom of the chest of drawers, and carefully covered her legs with it. She was quite content lying there, listening to the faint soft hiss of the gas that poured into the room, into her lungs, into her brain, as she drifted off into the dark river.

ALAIN ROBBE-GRILLET
1922—

More than anyone else, Alain Robbe-Grillet represents in his novels, *ciné-romans* (film-novels), and theoretical statements the rejection of the nineteenth-century realistic tradition and the exploration of a new "mental realism." Terms like "antinovel" and "new novel," early applied to his works, reflect both the turning away from older models (like Balzac and Flaubert), and the notion that a new experiment with form is under way. Not that it is completely new: clearly there are links to other twentieth-century works in the modernist tradition (and experiments with novel form as early as *Tristram Shandy*, 1760–1767). Robbe-Grillet himself mentions the influence of Kafka, Camus, and Faulkner (as well as *Alice in Wonderland*), and other readers will note parallel experimentation in Pirandello, Woolf, Beckett, and Joyce. Moreover, Robbe-Grillet calls on some of the same sources of fascination as his nineteenth-century predecessors. He may not use a linear plot, but he writes ambiguous, circular detective stories where erotic and violent crimes seem to have been committed; he may refuse to portray a consistently developing character, but his minutely detailed descriptions of objects and gestures lead the reader to guess at the psychology of the observer, and to speculate on the meaning of repetition and distortion in details.

Nonetheless, with Robbe-Grillet, we move to a particular phenomenon of mid-twentieth-century literature and a prime example of the "postmodernist" tradition. To the breakdown of conventional storytelling models familiar from literary modernism, he adds an insistence on the artificiality of all writing and representation until the reader is finally faced with total uncertainty: a self-contained "text" where a single voice and authorized meaning are impossible to ascertain. This literature has become a "game"—not because it is foolish or insignificant, but because it expresses the notion that human beings, with their capacity to adapt and to look at things in different ways, are essentially game-playing animals. The game-playing element is a strong part of Robbe-Grillet's fascination for his readers. At the same time that he reminds us that reality is opaque, and that we share the world with a host of objects different from ourselves, he entices the reader to try to figure out meanings and then reestablishes, at every turn, the absolute subjectivity of our most "objective" perceptions. Throughout his career, Robbe-Grillet is constantly exploring the limits of a collagelike technique of assembly and juxtaposition that he finds more true to life than the artistic coherence of the conventionally "realistic" novel.

Robbe-Grillet was born in Brittany, in northwestern France, to a family of scientists and engineers. His early training was not at all literary: in 1939 and 1941 the future writer took baccalaureate degrees in mathematics and natural science, and in 1946 (his career interrupted by forced labor in a German factory) a further degree from the National Agronomy Institute. He began work with the National Institute of Statistics and published an article on "Livestock Possibilities" before deciding to work part-time in his sister's biology laboratory and write a novel. This novel, A *Regicide*, was completed in 1949 but not published until 1978, well after Robbe-Grillet had become a successful novelist. In the meantime he took a position with an agricultural institute that sent him to Martinique, in the West Indies, to supervise banana plantations. Falling ill in 1951, Robbe-Grillet took advantage of the leisure time in the hospital and on the voyage home to write his second novel, *The Erasers*, which was immediately accepted and appeared in 1953.

The Erasers is a puzzling detective story involving confused identities, an abortive assassination carried out exactly twenty-four hours later by the muddled detective sent to investigate the original attempt, repeated allusions to the Oedipus myth, changing perspectives, and an overwhelming copiousness of detail about the most mundane natural objects. The novel became famous for its meticulous description of a tomato wedge catalogued with such scientific precision that it took on an objective existence of its own, and implicitly challenged the human-centered orientation of a perspective that would see it only as part of a salad. "The flesh on the periphery, compact and uniform, of a fine chemical red, is evenly thick between a strip of shiny skin and the compartment where the seeds are lined up, yellow, well sized, held in place by a thin layer of greenish jelly alongside a swelling of the heart. This latter, of a faded and slightly grainy pink, begins, on the side of the depression below, in a cluster of white veins, one of which extends up to the seeds—in, perhaps, a somewhat uncertain manner." While minutely detailed descriptions are not new in literature, this catalogue of physical properties had additional significance for its readers because it correlated so well with the notion, in contemporary phenomenological or existential philosophy, that we should recognize that things have their own existence separate from ourselves, their own "being-in-the-world."

The Erasers received the Fénéon Prize in 1954, but was not widely known; it was not until the scandal caused by *The Voyeur* (1955) that Robbe-Grillet reached a wide audience. Although *The Voyeur* was awarded the Critics' Prize in 1955, the jury was split between those who felt that it was not a "novel" at all (and was immoral and insane to boot), and those who admired its formal innovations. Mathias, the "voyeur" of the title, is a traveling watch salesman who may or may not have murdered a young girl during a sales trip on an island. The reader must piece together a version of what happened from a fragmented time span during which Mathias neglects to describe certain crucial hours, from actions and anxieties that suggest a guilty conscience, from a schizophrenic crisis when the crime is described in a café, and from obsessive erotic imaginings which may be just that—imaginings— or may be traces of the crime. Whether or not Mathias committed the crime (and he departs with his mind at rest), the scenes recorded as real or imaginary show him sexually obsessed and surely psychotic. Although the weight of evidence suggests that he is the murderer, there is no authorized conclusion and the text leaves its readers with a peculiar combination of objectivity and subjectivity: a world of objects described in great detail, and a series of events whose objective "truth" remains hidden inside the unreliability of its deranged observer.

With the controversy over *The Voyeur*, Robbe-Grillet and his new mode of writing became the focus of critical debate in France. In "Objective Literature," the influential critic Roland Barthes proposed that Robbe-Grillet had discovered a truer "neutral" writing by focusing on objects instead of repeating traditional socially inspired interpretations of reality. In 1955, the author began a series of articles on modern literature which he collected in 1963 as *For a New Novel*. The term "new novel" became popular, and although not all those described as "new novelists" wrote in the same way, they all rejected the traditional novel's assumption of a core of meaning— with a logically developing plot and psychologically consistent characters— that claimed to reflect a similar core of meaning in society. In their assertion that the traditional novel upheld unity and profundity only because these values presupposed the coherence and validity of contemporary society, the "new novelists" put forth a metaphysical and social argument as well as a revolutionary aesthetic strategy. They would prepare the citizen of the future (Robbe-Grillet titled a 1961 essay "New Novel, New Man") by clarifying that most basic level of social relationships: literally, how we "look at things."

Robbe-Grillet's next two novels, *Jealousy* (1957) and *In the Labyrinth* (1959), as well as the separate short pieces collected in *Snapshots* (1962), exploit the same patterns of potential meaning behind extended, "objective" description. In 1959, Robbe-Grillet temporarily abandoned novels to experiment with films, writing the script for *Last Year at Marienbad* (1961, filmed by Alain Resnais), and writing and direction *The Immortal One* (1963), in collaboration with producer Samy Halfon and composer Michel Fano. Films, like novels, allowed Robbe-Grillet to manipulate visions of reality as he insistently focused on surfaces and shapes, presented different versions of the same scene, composed a sound track that contradicted or commented on photographed action and—in recent works—challenged his own imagination by including unexpected incidents that occurred on location. Robbe-Grillet published the scenarios of *Last Year at Marienbad* and *The Immortal One*, and a more documentary account of *The Progressing Slippages of Pleasure* (1974) as *ciné-romans*, or film-novels that represent his pluralistic, decentered view of reality in audiovisual as well as verbal form.

Novels up to and including *In the Labyrinth* could still be interpreted as the subterranean story of a single protagonist. Later novels eliminated that anchoring center to display the presence of many centers—each a competing version of reality. Here emphasis is on the writer's freedom to create different and even mutually contradictory worlds, and on the readers' freedom to choose and arrange their own version of events. Some passages do not really fit into any of the story lines; the action progresses according to the suggestions of word-play or verbal echoes; the same narrative persona may appear grammatically as "he" or "she"; or books are composed in collage fashion. Robbe-Grillet has been taught in the classroom for many years as a master of formal experimentation, and only recently challenged on the quarantined atmosphere and obsessive sadism of his work. Uncomfortable, perhaps, at this change in critical perspective, he has justified sadistic fantasies in his work partly as reflecting popular themes in a correspondingly sadistic and dehumanized world, and partly as the therapeutic expression of his own obsessions (therapeutic because they are brought to a conscious level and thereby subject to change).

Therapeutic or not, there is no mistaking the basic images of Robbe-Grillet's world, or the familiar angles from which they are presented. "The Secret Room," reprinted here from *Snapshots*, arranges in an artistic homage to the Symbolist painter Gustave Moreau many of Robbe-Grillet's most obsessive images: the spreading bloodstain; the young woman stretched out erotically in chains and stabbed under the left breast; the ascending staircase; the different points of view directed down upon the victim; the mysterious, anonymous criminal; and even the figure eight of smoke coiling upward from the incense burner. Taken "realistically," the scene is bound to shock for its artistic savoring of human sacrifice, and the erotic pleasure it suggests in female victimization. It is at the same time a technical triumph in which verbal art emulates a painterly style. Robbe-Grillet imitates the Oriental luxury and morbid eroticism of a famous painter so convincingly that one could almost name the artist even without the dedication. Yet this verbal art goes beyond its painterly model when the author's manipulation of "surface" impressions brings a strange life to his subject, seen paradoxically both as a finished canvas and as recreated stages of the same murderous event.

"The Secret Room" begins as a painterly description from which human characteristics are absent; the stain is a "rosette" and not blood, and it stands out against a "smooth pale surface," not a body. It is a theatrical setting, and "space is filled" with colonnades, ascending staircase, and a mysterious silhouette fleeing in the distance. The body itself—when finally recognized—is described with excessive surface detail as if the painter's eye registered only the shapes and textures of flesh, hair, velvet, and stone. If there is any psychological involvement in the narration, it too exists as a compositional element: the opposition of murderer and victim, with her mouth open "as if screaming," and his face revealing a "violent exaltation." Thus far, the scene is an exotic tableau remarkable only for its precise description, but Robbe-Grillet also invests it with puzzling movement and life when he describes the caped figure in four different, incompatible poses. First seen near the top of the stair and facing away, he has next moved several steps back and appears on the first steps, turning to look at the body. Later he appears standing a yard away from her, looking down, and finally he is kneeling close to the woman as she breathes convulsively and dies. It is as though time has moved backwards, reviewing the stages of the murder and flight before they become fixed on the artist's canvas. Beginning and ending as a painted scene, "The Secret Room" extends the reality it describes by attributing movement and difference to figures on the canvas. One of Robbe-Grillet's earlier works, it already demonstrates the artist's ability to create separate, fictional realities inside the given frames of art or literature.

Ilona Leki, *Alain Robbe-Grillet* (1983), is a good biography and survey of Robbe-Grillet's work in historical context. It includes the most recent work and proceeds work by work, with a last chapter on the films. Bruce Morrissette, *The Novels of Robbe-Grillet* (1975; rev. ed.), provides a valuable critical study that takes the works and films in chronological order; preface by Roland Barthes. Ben Stoltzfus, *Alain Robbe-Grillet and the New French Novel* (1964), is an earlier introduction to Robbe-Grillet in the context of the emerging "new novel" form.

The Secret Room[1]

To Gustave Moreau[2]

The first thing to be seen is a red stain, of a deep, dark, shiny red, with almost black shadows. It is in the form of an irregular rosette, sharply outlined, extending in several directions in wide outflows of unequal length, dividing and dwindling afterward into single sinuous streaks. The whole stands out against a smooth, pale surface, round in shape, at once dull and pearly, a hemisphere joined by gentle curves to an expanse of the same pale color—white darkened by the shadowy quality of the place: a dungeon, a sunken room, or a cathedral—glowing with a diffused brilliance in the semidarkness.

Farther back, the space is filled with the cylindrical trunks of columns, repeated with progressive vagueness in their retreat toward the beginning of a vast stone stairway, turning slightly as it rises, growing narrower and narrower as it approaches the high vaults where it disappears.

The whole setting is empty, stairway and colonnades. Alone, in the foreground, the stretched-out body gleams feebly, marked with the red stain—a white body whose full, supple flesh can be sensed,

1. Translated by Bruce Morissette.   2. French Symbolist painter (1826–98) known for exotic, luminous scenes with subtly erotic and morbid overtones, such as *The Death of Darius* and *Dance of Salome*.

fragile, no doubt, and vulnerable. Alongside the bloody hemisphere another identical round form, this one intact, is seen at almost the same angle of view; but the haloed point at its summit, of darker tint, is in this case quite recognizable, whereas the other one is entirely destroyed, or at least covered by the wound.

In the background, near the top of the stairway, a black silhouette is seen fleeing, a man wrapped in a long, floating cape, ascending the last steps without turning around, his deed accomplished. A thin smoke rises in twisting scrolls from a sort of incense burner placed on a high stand of ironwork with a silvery glint. Nearby lies the milkwhite body, with wide streaks of blood running from the left breast, along the flank and on the hip.

It is a fully rounded woman's body, but not heavy, completely nude, lying on its back, the bust raised up somewhat by thick cushions thrown down on the floor, which is covered with Oriental rugs. The waist is very narrow, the neck long and thin, curved to one side, the head thrown back into a darker area where, even so, the facial features may be discerned, the partly opened mouth, the wide-staring eyes, shining with a fixed brilliance, and the mass of long, black hair spread out in a complicated wavy disorder over a heavily folded cloth, of velvet perhaps, on which also rest the arm and shoulder.

It is a uniformly colored velvet of dark purple, or which seems so in this lighting. But purple, brown, blue also seem to dominate in the colors of the cushions—only a small portion of which is hidden beneath the velvet cloth, and which protrude noticeably, lower down, beneath the bust and waist—as well as in the Oriental patterns of the rugs on the floor. Farther on, these same colors are picked up again in the stone of the paving and the columns, and vaulted archways, the stairs, and the less discernible surfaces that disappear into the farthest reaches of the room.

The dimensions of this room are difficult to determine exactly; the body of the young sacrificial victim seems at first glance to occupy a substantial portion of it, but the vast size of the stairway leading down to it would imply rather that this is not the whole room, whose considerable space must in reality extend all around, right and left, as it does toward the faraway browns and blues among the columns standing in line, in every direction, perhaps toward other sofas, thick carpets, piles of cushions and fabrics, other tortured bodies, other incense burners.

It is also difficult to say where the light comes from. No clue, on the columns or on the floor, suggests the direction of the rays. Nor is any window or torch visible. The milkwhite body itself seems to light the scene, with its full breasts, the curve of its thighs, the rounded belly, the full buttocks, the stretched-out legs, widely spread, and the black tuft of the exposed sex, provocative, proffered, useless now.

The man has already moved several steps back. He is now on the first steps of the stairs, ready to go up. The bottom steps are wide and deep, like the steps leading up to some great building, a temple or theater; they grow smaller as they ascend, and at the same time describe a wide, helical curve, so gradually that the stairway has not yet made a half-turn by the time it disappears near the top of the vaults, reduced them to a steep, narrow flight of steps without handrail, vaguely outlined, moreover, in the thickening darkness beyond.

But the man does not look in this direction, where his movement nonetheless carries him; his left foot on the second step and his right foot already touching the third, with his knee bent, he has turned around to look at the spectacle for one last time. The long, floating cape thrown hastily over his shoulders, clasped in one hand at his waist, has been whirled around by the rapid circular motion that has just caused his head and chest to turn in the opposite direction, and a corner of the cloth remains suspended in the air as if blown by a gust of wind; this corner, twisting around upon itself in the form of a loose S, reveals the red silk lining with its gold embroidery.

The man's features are impassive, but tense, as if in expectation— or perhaps fear—of some sudden event, or surveying with one last glance the total immobility of the scene. Though he is looking backward, his whole body is turned slightly forward, as if he were continuing up the stairs. His right arm—not the one holding the edge of the cape—is bent sharply toward the left, toward a point in space where the balustrade should be, if this stairway had one, an interrupted gesture, almost incomprehensible, unless it arose from an instinctive movement to grasp the absent support.

As to the direction of his glance, it is certainly aimed at the body of the victim lying on the cushions, its extended members stretched out in the form of a cross, its bust raised up, its head thrown back. But the face is perhaps hidden from the man's eyes by one of the columns, standing at the foot of the stairs. The young woman's right hand touches the floor just at the foot of this column. The fragile wrist is encircled by an iron bracelet. The arm is almost in darkness, only the hand receiving enough light to make the thin, outspread fingers clearly visible against the circular protrusion at the base of the stone column. A black metal chain running around the column passes through a ring affixed to the bracelet, binding the wrist tightly to the column.

At the top of the arm a rounded shoulder, raised up by the cushions, also stands out well lighted, as well as the neck, the throat, and the other shoulder, the armpit with its soft hair, the left arm likewise pulled back with its wrist bound in the same manner to the base of another column, in the extreme foreground; here the iron bracelet and the chain are fully displayed, represented with perfect clarity down to the slightest details.

The same is true, still in the foreground but at the other side, for a similar chain, but not quite as thick, wound directly around the ankle, running twice around the column and terminating in a heavy iron embedded in the floor. About a yard farther back, or perhaps slightly farther, the right foot is identically chained. But it is the left foot, and its chain, that are the most minutely depicted.

The foot is small, delicate, finely modeled. In several places the chain has broken the skin, causing noticeable if not extensive depressions in the flesh. The chain links are oval, thick, the size of an eye. The ring in the floor resembles those used to attach horses; it lies almost touching the stone pavement to which it is riveted by a massive iron peg. A few inches away is the edge of a rug; it is grossly wrinkled at this point, doubtless as a result of the convulsive, but necessarily very restricted, movements of the victim attempting to struggle.

The man is still standing about a yard away, half leaning over her. He looks at her face, seen upside down, her dark eyes made larger by their surrounding eyeshadow, her mouth wide open as if screaming. The man's posture allows his face to be seen only in a vague profile, but one senses in it a violent exaltation, despite the rigid attitude, the silence, the immobility. His back is slightly arched. His left hand, the only one visible, holds up at some distance from the body a piece of cloth, some dark-colored piece of clothing, which drags on the carpet, and which must be the long cape with its gold-embroidered lining.

This immense silhouette hides most of the bare flesh over which the red stain, spreading from the globe of the breast, runs in long rivulets that branch out, growing narrower, upon the pale background of the bust and the flank. One thread has reached the armpit and runs in an almost straight, thin line along the arm; others have run down toward the waist and traced out, along one side of the belly, the hip, the top of the thigh, a more random network already starting to congeal. Three or four tiny veins have reached the hollow between the legs, meeting in a sinuous line, touching the point of the V formed by the outspread legs, and disappearing into the black tuft.

Look, now the flesh is still intact: the black tuft and the white belly, the soft curve of the hips, the narrow waist, and, higher up, the pearly breasts rising and falling in time with the rapid breathing, whose rhythm grows more accelerated. The man, close to her, one knee on the floor, leans farther over. The head, with its long, curly hair, which alone is free to move somewhat, turns from side to side, struggling; finally the woman's mouth twists open, while the flesh is torn open, the blood spurts out over the tender skin, stretched tight, the carefully shadowed eyes grow abnormally large, the mouth opens wider, the head twists violently, one last time, from right to left, then more gently, to fall back finally and become still, amid the mass of black hair spread out on the velvet.

Afterward, the whole setting is empty, the enormous room with its purple shadows and its stone columns proliferating in all directions, the monumental staircase with no handrail that twists upward, growing narrower and vaguer as it rises into the darkness, toward the top of the vaults where it disappears.

Near the body, whose wound has stiffened, whose brilliance is already growing dim, the thin smoke from the incense burner traces complicated scrolls in the still air: first a coil turned horizontally to the left, which then straightens out and rises slightly, then returns to the axis of its point of origin, which it crosses as it moves to the right, then turns back in the first direction, only to wind back again, thus forming an irregular sinusoidal[3] curve, more and more flattened out, and rising, vertically, toward the top of the canvas.

YUKIO MISHIMA
1925–1970

Japan's most famous modern novelist was at home in both Eastern and Western literary traditions. Spokesman for an "essentially Japanese" culture toward the end of his life, Yukio Mishima was at the same time better acquainted with Western civilization and literature than any of his contemporaries. A master stylist who revived the fourteenth-century No theater in modern form, and whose knowledge of classical Japanese language allowed him to write convincing Kabuki plays, he had also read widely in European and American literature from the ancient Greeks to Thomas Mann and Tennessee Williams. One of his novels, he said, blended the styles of Thomas Mann and the Japanese stoic writer Ogai Mori (1862–1922): Mishima found especially congenial the "unique character of tragedy in German literature," a tragedy whose full expression he sought to embody in his own work. Like the modern Japanese society he portrayed, Mishima was truly international and absorbed influences from East and West, from the traditional Japanese past and a newly Westernized present. Along with his society, he experienced the radical change from prewar Imperial culture to postwar constitutional democracy, with its emphasis on popular values: a change that was all the more unsettling because it was associated with the trauma of World War II and Japan's defeat and occupation by Western forces. Mishima's harshly

3. S-shaped.

realistic portrayals, the ironic introspection and often philosophic discourse of his novels, the rich vocabulary and calculated balance and order of all his writing, became vehicles for the expression of a lost purity of Japanese culture that the author wished to revive in a vulgarized modern society.

Mishima's notion of the "essence of Japanese culture" was not shared by most of his contemporaries, who found it a highly idiosyncratic combination of elements in the national tradition. The ultimate beauty that he sought in a blend of art and physical perfection, and its self-destructive end in "Death and Night and Blood," was the goal of a personal quest appearing throughout his works from the youthful story "A Forest in Full Bloom" to his final tetralogy, *The Sea of Fertility.* Beyond individual frustrations and the betrayal of society, Mishima's heroes seek mystic completion in a moment of transcendent beauty and death. His ideal, expressed more and more fully in the last years of his life, was to unite the "way of the warrior" *(bushido)* and aesthetic elegance *(yuga)* in a revival of the samurai (warrior) code expressing the dual values of art and martial courage, themselves given larger authenticity through the social framework of shared loyalty to the god-Emperor of Japan. This complex ethic of total devotion was put forth, however, by a man who had an unparalleled sense of irony and masks. The description of the split between social masks and inner identity given in Mishima's semiautobiographical novel, *Confessions of a Mask* (1949), visibly prevents any definition of the protagonist's "true" motivations, and illustrates the impossibility—perhaps even for the author—of knowing which was the "real" personality and which the masquerade. It has been suggested by those who met him that Mishima adopted a new mask for each person he encountered, and indeed the author's work explores a series of identities or masks in an attempt to realize, through the illuminating forms of art, the reality that lies within but ultimately transcends the power of words.

Mishima's extraordinary childhood already set him apart from others, and established the pattern of living different roles for different people. He was born Kimitake Hiraoka on January 14, 1925, the eldest of three children born to an authoritarian civil servant, Azusa Hiraoka, and his wife Shizue, a scholar's daughter. (He adopted the pen name Mishima—taken from a town close to Mount Fuji—in 1941.) Living with the family were Azusa's parents: the somewhat irresponsible grandfather, Jotaro, and his aristocratic and unbalanced wife, Natsuko. Natsuko was in constant pain and bitterness from attacks of sciatic neuralgia, but fifty days after her first grandchild was born she took him away from his mother and raised him in her darkened sickroom until he was twelve years old. Little Kimitake was rarely allowed to go outside; instead, he read fairy tales or played quietly with three older girls in Natsuko's room. A frail child when he went to the aristocratic Peers School in 1931, he was not permitted to eat in the school cafeteria, take physical education, or go on class excursions.

Kimitake's early school years were unhappy, but in 1937 he entered middle school (seventh grade) where he not only performed better academically but gained acceptance into the school's literary group, contributed to their magazine, and became editor in 1941. One of his teachers, Fumio Shimizu, took an interest in the talented youth and invited him to publish a story in the literary magazine *Art and Culture.* "A Forest in Full Bloom" was serialized in late 1941 under the pen name Yukio Mishima, and already presented several themes for which the author would later be known: the young hero's intuitive continuation of his noble ancestors and samurai past, his quest for Beauty as a "gorgeous, runaway horse" (the second volume of *The Sea of Fertility* is titled *Runaway Horses*), his unspecified "longing . . . like a river" that empties into a distant sea, and the linkage of death and eroticism in a supreme moment. Unfortunately, Azusa strongly disapproved of his son's "girlishness" and desire to write: a strict Confucian (follower of the Chinese philosopher Confucius), he considered fiction a lie and a sign of moral degeneracy, and he tore up any manuscripts found in his son's room. Shizue was not able to help, and during 1942–44 Mishima preserved his work (eight novellas, three long essays, and a volume of poetry) at school, where he had friends and admirers.

In this early period, Mishima's chief supporters were academics who followed the "Nippon Roman-ha," or Japanese Romantic School, a movement created in direct and conscious emulation of the "German Romantic School" sponsored by the Nazis, and whose emphasis on national tradition, Emperor worship, beauty and pure emotions, and the exaltation of death and destruction already coincided with the young writer's tastes. Mishima also read the Japanese classics, the modern psychological writer Junichiro Tanizaki (1886–1965), a number of European authors including Rilke, Proust, Cocteau, Oscar Wilde, and *The Ball of Count Orgel* by the Frenchman Raymond Radiguet, whose death in 1923 at twenty fascinated him as much as his novel. In 1944 he graduated at the head of his class, and received the traditional award of a silver watch presented by the Emperor. In the same year— despite wartime shortages, and the fact that Tokyo was already burning under bombing raids—the young writer petitioned for paper and found a publisher for his first book, *The Forest in Full Bloom*, which sold out immediately.

It was a success in a vacuum, however, for the war had reached a crisis point in which literary achievements received scant notice. Mishima entered the Imperial University to study German law, obeying his father's wishes and expressed intention to "tear him away from literature once and for all," but before long his entire class was mobilized and sent to work in an airplane factory outside Tokyo. Drafted in February 1945, he was rejected for medical reasons, and moved with his class in May 1945 to work at a navy arsenal. Mishima commented later on the influence of these years when every Japanese male of military age expected shortly to die for the Emperor: it was a situation that both liberated the mind from petty concerns and—more ominously—separated it from any sense of reality. "Seventeen years after the end of the war, I cannot be sure of reality; it is temporary and fleeting. Perhaps I have an inherent inclination to think that way, but it may be that the war, during which things were there one day and gone the next, influenced me a great deal." When the war ended, Mishima had to adjust to a world whose former center, the Emperor, had renounced his divine status, and where the author's obsessional themes of beauty and death no longer found an echo in everyday events.

Mishima graduated from law school in 1947, briefly filled a position in the Finance Ministry, and devoted himself completely to writing after September 1948. He became an overnight success with the publication of an autobiographical novel, *Confessions of a Mask*, in 1949. In *Confessions*, the author claimed that he would "dissect myself alive," and "analyze comprehensively the root source of this desperate, nihilistic aestheticism of mine." This fictional account of Mishima's childhood, recounting the protagonist's gradual awareness of his latent homosexuality, his sadomasochistic tendencies, and the simultaneous and half-unconscious masquerade of his real personality, is in many ways an ambiguous portrait because it is so obviously a piece of aesthetic fiction: the protagonist claims to remember his first bath (including an image of reflected light that foreshadows a similar image at the end of the book), and the whole picture is governed by the artist's drive to establish precisely the masklike personality of the title. Yet the themes dear to Mishima are all here, starting with the erotic obsession with gory and heroic death which he discovered in Guido Reni's picture of St. Sebastian pierced with arrows. (Shortly before his death, Mishima posed as St. Sebastian for one of a series of photographs showing his death by various means: the book, which was never published, was to be called *Death of a Man*.) The success of *Confessions of a Mask* launched him on an extraordinarily prolific writing career which was actually divided between the "serious" novels and plays, and a number of simplified popular novels he wrote in about ten days purely for income and termed "minor works." His idea of the novel was much more structured and plot-oriented than were prevailing Japanese models, which stressed loose, episodic construction and the development of a mood: for Mishima, "the story would progress with all the predictability of a railway train running on schedule. . . . A fastidious sense of balance should pervade the novel as it does the balance sheet of a commercial firm."

A series of novels, plays, and short stories established Mishima in the 1950s as a best-selling and critically acclaimed author. Novels included *Thirst for Love* (1950), the story of a widow who becomes her father-in-law's mistress before seducing and murdering a young peasant, and *The Temple of the Golden Pavilion* (1957), a psychological analysis of a stuttering Zen Buddhist acolyte who grew to hate—and burn down—the famous pavilion representing a beauty he could not attain. Starting in 1950, Mishima wrote modern No Plays that were not only praised at home but, translated, were even more popular abroad as expressions of Japanese culture. In 1953 his first Kabuki play appeared, and in 1955 he received an award for a full-length modern play, *The Nest of the White Ant*, a story of adultery and suicide among Japanese emigrés in Brazil. Displaying his virtuoso talents, he wrote plays in a variety of styles and traditions: German expressionism, No, Kabuki, and even the "Shimpa" style of melodrama in *Madame de Sade*. After 1953 Mishima wrote at least one full-length play a year for the rest of his life, and considered novels and plays the two "magnetic poles" of his literary work. He married Yoko Sugiyama in 1958, became a father, and had an imposing Western-style house built with an annex for his parents. Yet the stability was only apparent.

Mishima had traveled to the West in 1952 and 1957, visiting America, Brazil, France, and especially Greece, where he was overwhelmed by the harmony of body and intellect represented by ancient Greek art. The artist ashamed of his weak body found in 1952 that "Greece cured my self-hatred and my loneliness and awoke in me a *will to health* in the Nietzschean sense" where "beauty and ethics were one and the same." He took up body building at the age of thirty, adding to his literary powers a "language of the flesh" with which he would create another kind of artwork that would be the "ultimate verification of existence." According to the autobiographical essay published in 1968 as *Sun and Steel*, "a powerful, tragic frame and sculpturesque muscles were indispensable in a romantically noble death." Throughout the sixties, Mishima moved imperceptibly towards the romantic death he had envisaged in his earliest fantasies. His newly muscular body (celebrated in numerous publicity photographs) was a suitable vehicle for heroic death, and the discovery of right-wing political values with their "samurai" devotion to the Emperor would provide him with a cause for which to die. He took up kendo (fencing), followed basic training with the Self-Defense Forces in 1967 (according to the postwar treaty, Japan could not have a national army), and organized and financed a small private army, the "Shield Society," dedicated to the defense of the Emperor.

Mishima's new emphasis on the body did not interfere with his writing; his popularity in Japan, however, fell off slightly in the sixties and especially after the publication of a long novel, *Kyoko's House* (1959), which was called his "first big failure." *Kyoko's House* followed the careers of four different heroes (businessman, boxer, artist, and actor) seen as four aspects of Mishima himself, and suggesting all together that a real sense of existence is found only in the moment of death. *The Sailor Who Fell From Grace With the Sea* (1963), a novel about a sailor who gives up his seagoing life to live with a widow on shore, and is vivisected by a youth gang that includes her son, had respectable sales but only mild critical praise. In 1965 Mishima began the tetralogy that would be his last work, *The Sea of Fertility* (named ironically after an arid region on the moon, and referring in parallel fashion to what Mishima saw as the spiritually sterility of modern Japan). The novel comprised four episodes in Japanese society over seventy years in the twentieth century, and was linked by the protagonist Honda who, over a long life, sought out his schoolboy friend's reincarnated spirit in three different bodies. Mishima's ambivalence about reality appears again at the end, which he called a "catastrophe": although the tetralogy is based on a theory of reincarnation which is given as fact in the third volume, at the very end the abbess Satoko, to whom Honda has come for confirmation of his tale, denies that the schoolboy ever existed and leaves the protagonist in an empty garden, bereft even of his memories.

Mishima handed in the last chapters of *The Sea of Fertility* on the same day—November 25, 1970—that he went with members of his Shield Society to take hostage a general of the Self-Defense Forces in a vain attempt to launch a coup that would reestablish the Emperor's military supremacy. Jeered by the men he hoped to inspire, he retired to the general's office and proceeded—with a young friend from the Society—to commit *seppuku*, or ritual suicide. Given the complexity of the author's personality, and the visible hopelessness of his attempt, it has seemed to many that he was in fact seeking a way to achieve the warrior's death that he had long envisaged as the blazing consummation of individual existence.

"Patriotism" (1960), one of Mishima's many explorations of heroic death, is based on an actual uprising, the Ni Ni Roku Incident of February 26,

1936 ("Ni Ni Roku" is literally "two two six," the date of the event). On that day, twenty-one officers and over a thousand men occupied a section of Tokyo and assassinated three ministers in the civil government headed by Emperor Hirohito. Paradoxically, they were inspired by devotion to the emperor: they wished to overthrow the civil government and strengthen imperial power by giving Hirohito supreme command over the armed forces. The emperor, however, considered them mutineers and refused even to order them to surrender. Imperial forces surrounded the rebels and arrested them; two rebels committed ritual suicide. Mishima was fascinated by this tale of soldierly devotion and death, and felt that the emperor had broken the bond of samurai loyalty by not recognizing the rebels' dedication. He was struck, in addition, by the difficult position of Imperial soldiers ordered to attack their colleagues, a dilemma which the young lieutenant of "Patriotism" resolves by committing *seppuku*. In 1965 Mishima produced a film version of "Patriotism" under the English title of *Rite of Love and Death*. The action took place on a No stage, bringing out the mythic quality of the sacrifice; the only sound was the "Liebestod" ("Love-death") theme from Wagner's opera *Tristan and Isolde*; and Mishima himself starred in the role of the lieutenant who commits ritual suicide.

The first sentence of "Patriotism" already states the outcome, and the short initial paragraph making up the first section reads like a newspaper account of events to be examined more fully, and with increasing tension, in succeeding sections. The "rite of love and death" which Mishima stressed in his foreign title is everywhere subordinate to the concept of patriotism; the flawless, newly married couple are defined by their shared dedication to patriotic values, and to the worship of the emperor who—as semidivine—is represented by his photograph in their household shrine. In the midst of passionate love, their hearts are "sober and serious," and they find confirmation of their love and respect for each other in their mutual understanding of the necessary "honorable death." If it is clear that the lieutenant chooses ritual suicide as protest against an untenable situation (it is dishonorable to disobey an imperial order, but there is also dishonor in attacking his colleagues), and that his wife chooses to accompany him out of love and loyalty, it may still be puzzling that the author could refer to "Patriotism" as a "story of happiness" rather than as a tragedy. For Mishima, however, both husband and wife have been granted a great gift. At the peak of their love and physical perfection, they are given an opportunity to freeze things as they are: to transcend the compromises and ambiguities of ordinary life, and the physical decline in which one ages and grows infirm, by honorably sacrificing themselves to a communal ideal. The extremely painful ritual of *seppuku*, or cutting open the stomach, is proof of the husband's commitment (hence the detailed description), and the couple's *shinju* or double "lovers' suicide" is further ennobled because it is not gratuitous but takes place in order to avoid dishonor. Mishima wrote on many occasions about the importance of seizing such an appropriate moment if it came, and about the regret that comes from having missed the right opportunity. It is a peculiar version of the romantic ideal of seizing life at a peak of unquestioned perfection; in this case, of stopping life before it can fall back into mundane reality.

John Nathan's *Mishima, A Biography* (1974) is an interesting and informative biography written by a translator who knew Mishima; it is based on extensive interviews with Mishima's family and friends. Donald Keene's chapter on Mishima in *Landscapes and Portraits* (1971) is an excellent brief account of Mishima's work. The British journalist Henry Scott-Stokes, who met Mishima in 1966, gives a more personal account in *The Life and Death of Yukio Mishima* (1974); the book includes many passages from Mishima's works and a discussion of *Sea of Fertility*. Masao Miyoshi's "Mute's Rage," in *Accomplices of Silence* (1974), is an excellent study of Mishima's sense of self, centering on *Confessions of a Mask* and *The Temple of the Golden Pavilion*. A chapter in Makuoto Ueda's *Modern Japanese Writers* (1976) discusses Mishima as thinker and novelist.

Patriotism[1]

On the twenty-eighth of February, 1936 (on the third day, that is, of the February 26 Incident),[2] Lieutenant Shinji Takeyama of the Konoe Transport Battalion—profoundly disturbed by the knowledge that his closest colleagues had been with the mutineers from the beginning, and indignant at the imminent prospect of Imperial troops attacking Imperial troops—took his officer's sword and ceremonially disemboweled himself in the eight-mat room of his private residence in the sixth block of Aoba-chō, in Yotsuya Ward. His wife, Reiko, followed him, stabbing herself to death. The lieutenant's farewell note consisted of one sentence: "Long live the Imperial Forces." His wife's, after apologies for her unfilial conduct in thus preceding her parents to the grave,[3] concluded: "The day which, for a soldier's wife, had to come, has come. . . ." The last moments of this heroic and dedicated couple were such as to make the gods themselves weep. The lieutenant's age, it should be noted, was thirty-one, his wife's twenty-three; and it was not half a year since the celebration of their marriage.

2

Those who saw the bride and bridegroom in the commemorative photograph—perhaps no less than those actually present at the lieutenant's wedding—had exclaimed in wonder at the bearing of this handsome couple. The lieutenant, majestic in military uniform, stood protectively beside his bride, his right hand resting upon his sword, his officer's cap held at his left side. His expression was severe, and

1. Translated by Geoffrey W. Sargent.   2. An abortive rebellion (the Ni Ni Roku Incident) against the civil government by junior officers who wished to restore military power to the Emperor, and eventually to conquer Asia.   3. Children were expected to support their parents in their old age, and to honor their memory.

his dark brows and wide-gazing eyes well conveyed the clear integrity of youth. For the beauty of the bride in her white over-robe no comparisons were adequate. In the eyes, round beneath soft brows, in the slender, finely shaped nose, and in the full lips, there was both sensuousness and refinement. One hand, emerging shyly from a sleeve of the over-robe, held a fan, and the tips of the fingers, clustering delicately, were like the bud of a moonflower.

After the suicide, people would take out this photograph and examine it, and sadly reflect that too often there was a curse on these seemingly flawless unions. Perhaps it was no more than imagination, but looking at the picture after the tragedy it almost seemed as if the two young people before the gold-lacquered screen were gazing, each with equal clarity, at the deaths which lay before them.

Thanks to the good offices of their go-between,[4] Lieutenant General Ozeki, they had been able to set themselves up in a new home at Aoba-chō in Yotsuya. "New home" is perhaps misleading. It was an old three-room rented house backing onto a small garden. As neither the six- nor the four-and-a-half-mat room downstairs was favored by the sun, they used the upstairs eight-mat room[5] as both bedroom and guest room. There was no maid, so Reiko was left alone to guard the house in her husband's absence.

The honeymoon trip was dispensed with on the grounds that these were times of national emergency.[6] The two of them had spent the first night of their marriage at this house. Before going to bed, Shinji, sitting erect on the floor with his sword laid before him, had bestowed upon his wife a soldierly lecture. A woman who had become the wife of a soldier should know and resolutely accept that her husband's death might come at any moment. It could be tomorrow. It could be the day after. But, no matter when it came—he asked—was she steadfast in her resolve to accept it? Reiko rose to her feet, pulled open a drawer of the cabinet, and took out what was the most prized of her new possessions, the dagger her mother had given her.[7] Returning to her place, she laid the dagger without a word on the mat before her, just as her husband had laid his sword. A silent understanding was achieved at once, and the lieutenant never again sought to test his wife's resolve.

In the first few months of her marriage Reiko's beauty grew daily more radiant, shining serene like the moon after rain.

As both were possessed of young, vigorous bodies, their relationship was passionate. Nor was this merely a matter of the night. On more than one occasion, returning home straight from maneuvers,

---

4. The person chosen to mediate between the two families in arranging a marriage.   5. The size of the room was measured by the number of mats (each three by six feet) that could be used in it.   6. After 1931, Japan was at war with Manchuria.   7. The traditional gift of the dagger to the new bride symbolized the fact that she was to endure whatever came without complaining, and not to return alive to her parents' house.

and begrudging even the time it took to remove his mud-splashed uniform, the lieutenant had pushed his wife to the floor almost as soon as he had entered the house. Reiko was equally ardent in her response. For a little more or a little less than a month, from the first night of their marriage Reiko knew happiness, and the lieutenant, seeing this, was happy too.

Reiko's body was white and pure, and her swelling breasts conveyed a firm and chaste refusal; but, upon consent, those breasts were lavish with their intimate, welcoming warmth. Even in bed these two were frighteningly and awesomely serious. In the very midst of wild, intoxicating passions, their hearts were sober and serious.

By day the lieutenant would think of his wife in the brief rest periods between training; and all day long, at home, Reiko would recall the image of her husband. Even when apart, however, they had only to look at the wedding photograph for their happiness to be once more confirmed. Reiko felt not the slightest surprise that a man who had been a complete stranger until a few months ago should now have become the sun about which her whole world revolved.

All these things had a moral basis, and were in accordance with the Education Rescript's[8] injunction that "husband and wife should be harmonious." Not once did Reiko contradict her husband, nor did the lieutenant ever find reason to scold his wife. On the god shelf below the stairway, alongside the tablet from the Great Ise Shrine, were set photographs of their Imperial Majesties,[9] and regularly every morning, before leaving for duty, the lieutenant would stand with his wife at this hallowed place and together they would bow their heads low. The offering water was renewed each morning, and the sacred sprig of *sasaki* was always green and fresh. Their lives were lived beneath the solemn protection of the gods and were filled with an intense happiness which set every fiber in their bodies trembling.

3

Although Lord Privy Seal Saitō's[1] house was in their neighborhood, neither of them heard any noise of gunfire on the morning of February 26. It was a bugle, sounding muster in the dim, snowy dawn, when the ten-minute tragedy had already ended, which first disrupted the lieutenant's slumbers. Leaping at once from his bed, and without speaking a word, the lieutenant donned his uniform,

8. The Imperial Rescript on Education, a code of ethics based on Confucian principles that was issued on October 30, 1890, by the Emperor Meiji and taught in the schools until 1945. It prescribed a system of social and family relationships that included at its peak absolute loyalty to the Emperor as source of all moral authority.   9. The Inner Shrine at Ise (a city on Ise Bay) was dedicated to Amaterasu Omikami, the Sun Goddess and "divine ancestress" of the Imperial family. Pictures of the semidivine Emperor and Empress occupy the household shrine. *Sasaki:* An evergreen plant used in Shinto ceremonies.   1. Admiral Saitō Makoto, a minister assassinated in the Ni Ni Roku Incident.

buckled on the sword held ready for him by his wife, and hurried swiftly out into the snow-covered streets of the still darkened morning. He did not return until the evening of the twenty-eighth.

Later, from the radio news, Reiko learned the full extent of this sudden eruption of violence. Her life throughout the subsequent two days was lived alone, in complete tranquillity, and behind locked doors.

In the lieutenant's face, as he hurried silently out into the snowy morning, Reiko had read the determination to die. If her husband did not return, her own decision was made: she too would die. Quietly she attended to the disposition of her personal possessions. She chose her sets of visiting kimonos as keepsakes for friends of her schooldays, and she wrote a name and address on the stiff paper wrapping in which each was folded. Constantly admonished by her husband never to think of the morrow, Reiko had not even kept a diary and was now denied the pleasure of assiduously rereading her record of the happiness of the past few months and consigning each page to the fire as she did so. Ranged across the top of the radio were a small china dog, a rabbit, a squirrel, a bear, and a fox. There were also a small vase and a water pitcher. These comprised Reiko's one and only collection. But it would hardly do, she imagined, to give such things as keepsakes. Nor again would it be quite proper to ask specifically for them to be included in the coffin. It seemed to Reiko, as these thoughts passed through her mind, that the expressions on the small animals' faces grew even more lost and forlorn.

Reiko took the squirrel in her hand and looked at it. And then, her thoughts turning to a realm far beyond these childlike affections, she gazed up into the distance at the great sunlike principle which her husband embodied. She was ready, and happy, to be hurtled along to her destruction in that gleaming sun chariot—but now, for these few moments of solitude, she allowed herself to luxuriate in this innocent attachment to trifles. The time when she had genuinely loved these things, however, was long past. Now she merely loved the memory of having once loved them, and their place in her heart had been filled by more intense passions, by a more frenzied happiness. . . . For Reiko had never, even to herself, thought of those soaring joys of the flesh as a mere pleasure. The February cold, and the icy touch of the china squirrel, had numbed Reiko's slender fingers; yet, even so, in her lower limbs, beneath the ordered repetition of the pattern which crossed the skirt of her trim *meisen*[2] kimono, she could feel now, as she thought of the lieutenant's powerful arms reaching out toward her, a hot moistness of the flesh which defied the snows.

2. A common silk kimono.

She was not in the least afraid of the death hovering in her mind. Waiting alone at home, Reiko firmly believed that everything her husband was feeling or thinking now, his anguish and distress, was leading her—just as surely as the power in his flesh—to a welcome death. She felt as if her body could melt away with ease and be transformed to the merest fraction of her husband's thought.

Listening to the frequent announcements on the radio, she heard the names of several of her husband's colleagues mentioned among those of the insurgents. This was news of death. She followed the developments closely, wondering anxiously, as the situation became daily more irrevocable, why no Imperial ordinance was sent down, and watching what had at first been taken as a movement to restore the nation's honor come gradually to be branded with the infamous name of mutiny. There was no communication from the regiment. At any moment, it seemed, fighting might commence in the city streets, where the remains of the snow still lay.

Toward sundown on the twenty-eighth Reiko was startled by a furious pounding on the front door. She hurried downstairs. As she pulled with fumbling fingers at the bolt, the shape dimly outlined beyond the frosted-glass panel made no sound, but she knew it was her husband. Reiko had never known the bolt on the sliding door to be so stiff. Still it resisted. The door just would not open.

In a moment, almost before she knew she had succeeded, the lieutenant was standing before her on the cement floor inside the porch, muffled in a khaki greatcoat, his top boots heavy with slush from the street. Closing the door behind him, he returned the bolt once more to its socket. With what significance, Reiko did not understand.

"Welcome home."

Reiko bowed deeply, but her husband made no response. As he had already unfastened his sword and was about to remove his greatcoat, Reiko moved around behind to assist. The coat, which was cold and damp and had lost the odor of horse dung it normally exuded when exposed to the sun, weighed heavily upon her arm. Draping it across a hanger, and cradling the sword and leather belt in her sleeves, she waited while her husband removed his top boots and then followed behind him into the "living room." This was the six-mat room downstairs.

Seen in the clear light from the lamp, her husband's face, covered with a heavy growth of bristle, was almost unrecognizably wasted and thin. The cheeks were hollow, their luster and resilience gone. In his normal good spirits he would have changed into old clothes as soon as he was home and have pressed her to get supper at once, but now he sat before the table still in his uniform, his head drooping dejectedly. Reiko refrained from asking whether she should prepare the supper.

After an interval the lieutenant spoke.

"I knew nothing. They hadn't asked me to join. Perhaps out of consideration, because I was newly married. Kanō, and Homma too, and Yamaguchi."

Reiko recalled momentarily the faces of high-spirited young officers, friends of her husband, who had come to the house occasionally as guests.

"There may be an Imperial ordinance sent down tomorrow. They'll be posted as rebels, I imagine. I shall be in command of a unit with orders to attack them. . . . I can't do it. It's impossible to do a thing like that."

He spoke again.

"They've taken me off guard duty, and I have permission to return home for one night. Tomorrow morning, without question, I must leave to join the attack. I can't do it, Reiko."

Reiko sat erect with lowered eyes. She understood clearly that her husband had spoken of his death. The lieutenant was resolved. Each word, being rooted in death, emerged sharply and with powerful significance against this dark, unmovable background. Although the lieutenant was speaking of his dilemma, already there was no room in his mind for vacillation.

However, there was a clarity, like the clarity of a stream fed from melting snows, in the silence which rested between them. Sitting in his own home after the long two-day ordeal, and looking across at the face of his beautiful wife, the lieutenant was for the first time experiencing true peace of mind. For he had at once known, though she said nothing, that his wife divined the resolve which lay beneath his words.

"Well, then . . ." The lieutenant's eyes opened wide. Despite his exhaustion they were strong and clear, and now for the first time they looked straight into the eyes of his wife. "Tonight I shall cut my stomach."[3]

Reiko did not flinch.

Her round eyes showed tension, as taut as the clang of a bell.

"I am ready," she said. "I ask permission to accompany you."

The lieutenant felt almost mesmerized by the strength in those eyes. His words flowed swiftly and easily, like the utterances of a man in delirium, and it was beyond his understanding how permission in a matter of such weight could be expressed so casually.

"Good. We'll go together. But I want you as a witness, first, for my own suicide. Agreed?"

When this was said a sudden release of abundant happiness welled up in both their hearts. Reiko was deeply affected by the greatness of her husband's trust in her. It was vital for the lieutenant, whatever

---

3. Commit ritual suicide, *seppuku* (often called *hara-kiri*).

else might happen, that there should be no irregularity in his death. For that reason there had to be a witness. The fact that he had chosen his wife for this was the first mark of his trust. The second, and even greater mark, was that though he had pledged that they should die together he did not intend to kill his wife first—he had deferred her death to a time when he would no longer be there to verify it. If the lieutenant had been a suspicious husband, he would doubtless, as in the usual suicide pact, have chosen to kill his wife first.

When Reiko said, "I ask permission to accompany you," the lieutenant felt these words to be the final fruit of the education which he had himself given his wife, starting on the first night of their marriage, and which had schooled her, when the moment came, to say what had to be said without a shadow of hesitation. This flattered the lieutenant's opinion of himself as a self-reliant man. He was not so romantic or conceited as to imagine that the words were spoken spontaneously, out of love for her husband.

With happiness welling almost too abundantly in their hearts, they could not help smiling at each other. Reiko felt as if she had returned to her wedding night.

Before her eyes was neither pain nor death. She seemed to see only a free and limitless expanse opening out into vast distances.

"The water is hot. Will you take your bath now?"

"Ah yes, of course."

"And supper . . . ?"

The words were delivered in such level, domestic tones that the lieutenant came near to thinking, for the fraction of a second, that everything had been a hallucination.

"I don't think we'll need supper. But perhaps you could warm some sake?"[4]

"As you wish."

As Reiko rose and took a *tanzen*[5] gown from the cabinet for after the bath, she purposely directed her husband's attention to the opened drawer. The lieutenant rose, crossed to the cabinet, and looked inside. From the ordered array of paper wrappings he read, one by one, the addresses of the keepsakes. There was no grief in the lieutenant's response to this demonstration of heroic resolve. His heart was filled with tenderness. Like a husband who is proudly shown the childish purchases of a young wife, the lieutenant, overhelmed by affection, lovingly embraced his wife from behind and implanted a kiss upon her neck.

Reiko felt the roughness of the lieutenant's unshaven skin against her neck. This sensation, more than being just a thing of this world, was for Reiko almost the world itself, but now—with the feeling that

---

4. Rice wine; pronounced SA-keh.   5. A padded kimono.

it was soon to be lost forever—it had freshness beyond all her experience. Each moment had its own vital strength, and the senses in
every corner of her body were reawakened. Accepting her husband's
caresses from behind, Reiko raised herself on the tips of her toes,
letting the vitality seep through her entire body.

"First the bath, and then, after some sake . . . lay out the bedding
upstairs, will you?"

The lieutenant whispered the words into his wife's ear. Reiko silently
nodded.

Flinging off his uniform, the lieutenant went to the bath. To faint
background noises of slopping water Reiko tended the charcoal brazier in the living room and began the preparations for warming the
sake.

Taking the *tanzen*, a sash, and some underclothes, she went to
the bathroom to ask how the water was. In the midst of a coiling
cloud of steam the lieutenant was sitting cross-legged on the floor,
shaving, and she could dimly discern the rippling movements of the
muscles on his damp, powerful back as they responded to the movement of his arms.

There was nothing to suggest a time of any special significance.
Reiko, going busily about her tasks, was preparing side dishes from
odds and ends in stock. Her hands did not tremble. If anything, she
managed even more efficiently and smoothly than usual. From time
to time, it is true, there was a strange throbbing deep within her
breast. Like distant lightning, it had a moment of sharp intensity and
then vanished without trace. Apart from that, nothing was in any
way out of the ordinary.

The lieutenant, shaving in the bathroom, felt his warmed body
miraculously healed at last of the desperate tiredness of the days of
indecision and filled—in spite of the death which lay ahead—with
pleasurable anticipation. The sound of his wife going about her work
came to him faintly. A healthy physical craving, submerged for two
days, reasserted itself.

The lieutenant was confident there had been no impurity in that
joy they had experienced when resolving upon death. They had both
sensed at that moment—though not, of course, in any clear and
conscious way—that those permissible pleasures which they shared
in private were once more beneath the protection of Righteousness
and Divine Power, and of a complete and unassailable morality. On
looking into each other's eyes and discovering there an honorable
death, they had felt themselves safe once more behind steel walls
which none could destroy, encased in an impenetrable armor of Beauty
and Truth. Thus, so far from seeing any inconsistency or conflict
between the urges of his flesh and the sincerity of his patriotism, the
lieutenant was even able to regard the two as parts of the same thing.

Thrusting his face close to the dark, cracked, misted wall mirror, the lieutenant shaved himself with great care. This would be his death face. There must be no unsightly blemishes. The clean-shaven face gleamed once more with a youthful luster, seeming to brighten the darkness of the mirror. There was a certain elegance, he even felt, in the association of death with this radiantly healthy face.

Just as it looked now, this would become his death face! Already, in fact, it had half departed from the lieutenant's personal possession and had become the bust above a dead soldier's memorial. As an experiment he closed his eyes tight. Everything was wrapped in blackness, and he was no longer a living, seeing creature.

Returning from the bath, the traces of the shave glowing faintly blue beneath his smooth cheeks, he seated himself beside the now well-kindled charcoal brazier. Busy though Reiko was, he noticed, she had found time lightly to touch up her face. Her cheeks were gay and her lips moist. There was no shadow of sadness to be seen. Truly, the lieutenant felt, as he saw this mark of his young wife's passionate nature, he had chosen the wife he ought to have chosen.

As soon as the lieutenant had drained his sake cup he offered it to Reiko. Reiko had never before tasted sake, but she accepted without hesitation and sipped timidly.

"Come here," the lieutenant said.

Reiko moved to her husband's side and was embraced as she leaned backward across his lap. Her breast was in violent commotion, as if sadness, joy, and the potent sake were mingling and reacting within her. The lieutenant looked down into his wife's face. It was the last face he would see in this world, the last face he would see of his wife. The lieutenant scrutinized the face minutely, with the eyes of a traveler bidding farewell to splendid vistas which he will never revisit. It was a face he could not tire of looking at—the features regular yet not cold, the lips lightly closed with a soft strength. The lieutenant kissed those lips, unthinkingly. And suddenly, though there was not the slightest distortion of the face into the unsightliness of sobbing, he noticed that tears were welling slowly from beneath the long lashes of the closed eyes and brimming over into a glistening stream.

When, a little later, the lieutenant urged that they should move to the upstairs bedroom, his wife replied that she would follow after taking a bath. Climbing the stairs alone to the bedroom, where the air was already warmed by the gas heater, the lieutenant lay down on the bedding with arms outstretched and legs apart. Even the time at which he lay waiting for his wife to join him was no later and no earlier than usual.

He folded his hands beneath his head and gazed at the dark boards of the ceiling in the dimness beyond the range of the standard lamp. Was it death he was now waiting for? Or a wild ecstasy of the senses? The two seemed to overlap, almost as if the object of this bodily desire was death itself. But, however that might be, it was certain that never before had the lieutenant tasted such total freedom.

There was the sound of a car outside the window. He could hear the screech of its tires skidding in the snow piled at the side of the street. The sound of its horn re-echoed from nearby walls. . . . Listening to these noises he had the feeling that this house rose like a solitary island in the ocean of a society going as restlessly about its business as ever. All around, vastly and untidily, stretched the country for which he grieved. He was to give his life for it. But would that great country, with which he was prepared to remonstrate to the extent of destroying himself, take the slightest heed of his death? He did not know; and it did not matter. His was a battlefield without glory, a battlefield where none could display deeds of valor: it was the front line of the spirit.

Reiko's footsteps sounded on the stairway. The steep stairs in this old house creaked badly. There were fond memories in that creaking, and many a time, while waiting in bed, the lieutenant had listened to its welcome sound. At the thought that he would hear it no more he listened with intense concentration, striving for every corner of every moment of this precious time to be filled with the sound of those soft footfalls on the creaking stairway. The moments seemed transformed to jewels, sparkling with inner light.

Reiko wore a Nagoya sash about the waist of her *yukata*,[6] but as the lieutenant reached toward it, its redness sobered by the dimness of the light, Reiko's hand moved to his assistance and the sash fell away, slithering swiftly to the floor. As she stood before him, still in her *yukata*, the lieutenant inserted his hands through the side slits beneath each sleeve, intending to embrace her as she was; but at the touch of his finger tips upon the warm naked flesh, and as the armpits closed gently about his hands, his whole body was suddenly aflame.

In a few moments the two lay naked before the glowing gas heater.

Neither spoke the thought, but their hearts, their bodies, and their pounding breasts blazed with the knowledge that this was the very last time. It was as if the words "The Last Time" were spelled out, in invisible brushstrokes, across every inch of their bodies.

The lieutenant drew his wife close and kissed her vehemently. As their tongues explored each other's mouths, reaching out into the smooth, moist interior, they felt as if the still-unknown agonies of death had tempered their senses to the keenness of red-hot steel. The

6. A light cotton kimono. *Nagoya:* A style of formal sash developed in the city of Nagoya (on Ise Bay) early in this century, fashionable in the 1920s and '30s.

agonies they could not yet feel, the distant pains of death, had refined their awareness of pleasure.

"This is the last time I shall see your body," said the lieutenant. "Let me look at it closely." And, tilting the shade on the lampstand to one side, he directed the rays along the full length of Reiko's outstretched form.

Reiko lay still with her eyes closed. The light from the low lamp clearly revealed the majestic sweep of her white flesh. The lieutenant, not without a touch of egocentricity, rejoiced that he would never see this beauty crumble in death.

At his leisure, the lieutenant allowed the unforgettable spectacle to engrave itself upon his mind. With one hand he fondled the hair, with the other he softly stroked the magnificent face, implanting kisses here and there where his eyes lingered. The quiet coldness of the high, tapering forehead, the closed eyes with their long lashes beneath faintly etched brows, the set of the finely shaped nose, the gleam of teeth glimpsed between full, regular lips, the soft cheeks and the small, wise chin . . . these things conjured up in the lieutenant's mind the vision of a truly radiant death face, and again and again he pressed his lips tight against the white throat—where Reiko's own hand was soon to strike—and the throat reddened faintly beneath his kisses. Returning to the mouth he laid his lips against it with the gentlest of pressures, and moved them rhythmically over Reiko's with the light rolling motion of a small boat. If he closed his eyes, the world became a rocking cradle.

Wherever the lieutenant's eyes moved his lips faithfully followed. The high, swelling breasts, surmounted by nipples like the buds of a wild cherry, hardened as the lieutenant's lips closed about them. The arms flowed smoothly downward from each side of the breast, tapering toward the wrists, yet losing nothing of their roundness or symmetry, and at their tips were those delicate fingers which had held the fan at the wedding ceremony. One by one, as the lieutenant kissed them, the fingers withdrew behind their neighbor as if in shame. . . . The natural hollow curving between the bosom and the stomach carried in its lines a suggestion not only of softness but of resilient strength, and while it gave forewarning of the rich curves spreading outward from here to the hips it had, in itself, an appearance only of restraint and proper discipline. The whiteness and richness of the stomach and hips was like milk brimming in a great bowl, and the sharply shadowed dip of the navel could have been the fresh impress of a raindrop, fallen there that very moment. Where the shadows gathered more thickly, hair clustered, gentle and sensitive, and as the agitation mounted in the now no longer passive body there hung over this region a scent like the smoldering of fragrant blossoms, growing steadily more pervasive.

At length, in a tremulous voice, Reiko spoke.

"Show me. . . . Let me look too, for the last time."

Never before had he heard from his wife's lips so strong and une-quivocal a request. It was as if something which her modesty had wished to keep hidden to the end had suddenly burst its bonds of constraint. The lieutenant obediently lay back and surrendered him-self to his wife. Lithely she raised her white, trembling body, and—burning with an innocent desire to return to her husband what he had done for her—placed two white fingers on the lieutenant's eyes, which gazed fixedly up at her, and gently stroked them shut.

Suddenly overwhelmed by tenderness, her cheeks flushed by a dizzying uprush of emotion, Reiko threw her arms about the lieuten-ant's close-cropped head. The bristly hairs rubbed painfully against her breast, the prominent nose was cold as it dug into her flesh, and his breath was hot. Relaxing her embrace, she gazed down at her husband's masculine face. The severe brows, the closed eyes, the splendid bridge of the nose, the shapely lips drawn firmly together . . . the blue, clean-shaven cheeks reflecting the light and gleaming smoothly. Reiko kissed each of these. She kissed the broad nape of the neck, the strong, erect shoulders, the powerful chest with its twin circles like shields and its russet nipples. In the armpits, deeply shad-owed by the ample flesh of the shoulders and chest, a sweet and melancholy odor emanated from the growth of hair, and in the sweetness of this odor was contained, somehow, the essence of young death. The lieutenant's naked skin glowed like a field of barley, and everywhere the muscles showed in sharp relief, converging on the lower abdomen about the small, unassuming navel. Gazing at the youthful, firm stomach, modestly covered by a vigorous growth of hair, Reiko thought of it as it was soon to be, cruelly cut by the sword, and she laid her head upon it, sobbing in pity, and bathed it with kisses.

At the touch of his wife's tears upon his stomach the lieutenant felt ready to endure with courage the cruelest agonies of his suicide.

What ecstasies they experienced after these tender exchanges may well be imagined. The lieutenant raised himself and enfolded his wife in a powerful embrace, her body now limp with exhaustion after her grief and tears. Passionately they held their faces close, rubbing cheek against cheek. Reiko's body was trembling. Their breasts, moist with sweat, were tightly joined, and every inch of the young and beautiful bodies had become so much one with the other that it seemed impossible there should ever again be a separation. Reiko cried out. From the heights they plunged into the abyss, and from the abyss they took wing and soared once more to dizzying heights. The lieutenant panted like the regimental standard-bearer on a route march. . . . As one cycle ended, almost immediately a new wave of passion would be generated, and together—with no trace of fatigue—they would climb again in a single breathless movement to the very summit.

4

When the lieutenant at last turned away, it was not from weariness. For one thing, he was anxious not to undermine the considerable strength he would need in carrying out his suicide. For another, he would have been sorry to mar the sweetness of these last memories by overindulgence.

Since the lieutenant had clearly desisted, Reiko too, with her usual compliance, followed his example. The two lay naked on their backs, with fingers interlaced, staring fixedly at the dark ceiling. The room was warm from the heater, and even when the sweat had ceased to pour from their bodies they felt no cold. Outside, in the hushed night, the sounds of passing traffic had ceased. Even the noises of the trains and streetcars around Yotsuya station did not penetrate this far. After echoing through the region bounded by the moat, they were lost in the heavily wooded park fronting the broad driveway before Akasaka Palace. It was hard to believe in the tension gripping this whole quarter, where the two factions of the bitterly divided Imperial Army now confronted each other, poised for battle.

Savoring the warmth glowing within themselves, they lay still and recalled the ecstasies they had just known. Each moment of the experience was relived. They remembered the taste of kisses which had never wearied, the touch of naked flesh, episode after episode of dizzying bliss. But already, from the dark boards of the ceiling, the face of death was peering down. These joys had been final, and their bodies would never know them again. Not that joy of this intensity—and the same thought had occurred to them both—was ever likely to be reexperienced, even if they should live on to old age.

The feel of their fingers intertwined—this too would soon be lost. Even the wood-grain patterns they now gazed at on the dark ceiling boards would be taken from them. They could feel death edging in, nearer and nearer. There could be no hesitation now. They must have the courage to reach out to death themselves, and to seize it.

"Well, let's make our preparations," said the lieutenant. The note of determination in the words was unmistakable, but at the same time Reiko had never heard her husband's voice so warm and tender.

After they had risen, a variety of tasks awaited them.

The lieutenant, who had never once before helped with the bedding, now cheerfully slid back the door of the closet, lifted the mattress across the room by himself, and stowed it away inside.

Reiko turned off the gas heater and put away the lamp standard.

During the lieutenant's absence she had arranged this room carefully, sweeping and dusting it to a fresh cleanness, and now—if one
overlooked the rosewood table drawn into one corner—the eight-mat
room gave all the appearance of a reception room ready to welcome
an important guest.

"We've seen some drinking here, haven't we? With Kanō and
Homma and Noguchi . . ."

"Yes, they were great drinkers, all of them."

"We'll be meeting them before long, in the other world. They'll
tease us, I imagine, when they find I've brought you with me."

Descending the stairs, the lieutenant turned to look back into this
calm, clean room, now brightly illuminated by the ceiling lamp.
There floated across his mind the faces of the young officers who had
drunk there, and laughed, and innocently bragged. He had never
dreamed then that he would one day cut open his stomach in this
room.

In the two rooms downstairs husband and wife busied themselves
smoothly and serenely with their respective preparations. The lieutenant went to the toilet, and then to the bathroom to wash. Meanwhile Reiko folded away her husband's padded robe, placed his
uniform tunic, his trousers, and a newly cut bleached loincloth in
the bathroom, and set out sheets of paper on the living-room table
for the farewell notes. Then she removed the lid from the writing
box and began rubbing ink from the ink tablet.[7] She had already
decided upon the wording of her own note.

Reiko's fingers pressed hard upon the cold gilt letters of the ink
tablet, and the water in the shallow well at once darkened, as if a
black cloud had spread across it. She stopped thinking that this repeated
action, this pressure from her fingers, this rise and fall of faint sound,
was all and solely for death. It was a routine domestic task, a simple
paring away of time until death should finally stand before her. But
somehow, in the increasingly smooth motion of the tablet rubbing
on the stone, and in the scent from the thickening ink, there was
unspeakable darkness.

Neat in his uniform, which he now wore next to his skin, the
lieutenant emerged from the bathroom. Without a word he seated
himself at the table, bolt upright, took a brush in his hand, and
stared undecidedly at the paper before him.

Reiko took a white silk kimono with her and entered the bathroom. When she reappeared in the living room, clad in the white
kimono and with her face lightly made up, the farewell note lay
completed on the table beneath the lamp. The thick black brushstrokes said simply:

7. Ink was made by rubbing particles of dye from an ink block into water; the brand name was
often written in gilt letters on the block's surface.

"Long Live the Imperial Forces—Army Lieutenant Takeyama Shinji."

While Reiko sat opposite him writing her own note, the lieutenant gazed in silence, intensely serious, at the controlled movement of his wife's pale fingers as they manipulated the brush.

With their respective notes in their hands—the lieutenant's sword strapped to his side, Reiko's small dagger thrust into the sash of her white kimono—the two of them stood before the god shelf and silently prayed. Then they put out all the downstairs lights. As he mounted the stairs the lieutenant turned his head and gazed back at the striking, white-clad figure of his wife, climbing behind him, with lowered eyes, from the darkness beneath.

The farewell notes were laid side by side in the alcove of the upstairs room. They wondered whether they ought not to remove the hanging scroll, but since it had been written by their go-between, Lieutenant General Ozeki, and consisted, moreover, of two Chinese characters signifying "Sincerity,"[8] they left it where it was. Even if it were to become stained with splashes of blood, they felt that the lieutenant general would understand.

The lieutenant, sitting erect with his back to the alcove, laid his sword on the floor before him.

Reiko sat facing him, a mat's width away. With the rest of her so severely white the touch of rouge on her lips seemed remarkably seductive.

Across the dividing mat they gazed intently into each other's eyes. The lieutenant's sword lay before his knees. Seeing it, Reiko recalled their first night and was overwhelmed with sadness. The lieutenant spoke, in a hoarse voice:

"As I have no second to help me I shall cut deep.[9] It may look unpleasant, but please do not panic. Death of any sort is a fearful thing to watch. You must not be discouraged by what you see. Is that all right?"

"Yes."

Reiko nodded deeply.

Looking at the slender white figure of his wife the lieutenant experienced a bizarre excitement. What he was about to perform was an act in his public capacity as a soldier, something he had never previously shown his wife. It called for a resolution equal to the courage to enter battle; it was a death of no less degree and quality than death in the front line. It was his conduct on the battlefield that he was now to display.

8. The Japanese language employs many loan-words from Chinese: these particular characters imply the samurai's absolute loyalty to his lord.   9. Traditionally, a second would behead the suicide at the first sign of faltering or extreme pain. Since Reiko cannot fill this role, the lieutenant must be sure to kill himself.

Momentarily the thought led the lieutenant to a strange fantasy. A lonely death on the battlefield, a death beneath the eyes of his beautiful wife . . . in the sensation that he was now to die in these two dimensions, realizing an impossible union of them both, there was sweetness beyond words. This must be the very pinnacle of good fortune, he thought. To have every moment of his death observed by those beautiful eyes—it was like being borne to death on a gentle, fragrant breeze. There was some special favor here. He did not understand precisely what it was, but it was a domain unknown to others: a dispensation granted to no one else had been permitted to himself. In the radiant, bridelike figure of his white-robed wife the lieutenant seemed to see a vision of all those things he had loved and for which he was to lay down his life—the Imperial Household, the Nation, the Army Flag. All these, no less than the wife who sat before him, were presences observing him closely with clear and never-faltering eyes.

Reiko too was gazing intently at her husband, so soon to die, and she thought that never in this world had she seen anything so beautiful. The lieutenant always looked well in uniform, but now, as he contemplated death with severe brows and firmly closed lips, he revealed what was perhaps masculine beauty at its most superb.

"It's time to go," the lieutenant said at last.

Reiko bent her body low to the mat in a deep bow. She could not raise her face. She did not wish to spoil her make-up with tears, but the tears could not be held back.

When at length she looked up she saw hazily through the tears that her husband had wound a white bandage around the blade of his now unsheathed sword, leaving five or six inches of naked steel showing at the point.

Resting the sword in its cloth wrapping on the mat before him, the lieutenant rose from his knees, resettled himself crosslegged, and unfastened the hooks of his uniform collar. His eyes no longer saw his wife. Slowly, one by one, he undid the flat brass buttons. The dusky brown chest was revealed, and then the stomach. He unclasped his belt and undid the buttons of his trousers. The pure whiteness of the thickly coiled loincloth showed itself. The lieutenant pushed the cloth down with both hands, further to ease his stomach, and then reached for the white-bandaged blade of his sword. With his left hand he massaged his abdomen, glancing doward as he did so.

To reassure himself on the sharpness of his sword's cutting edge the lieutenant folded back the left trouser flap, exposing a little of his thigh, and lightly drew the blade across the skin. Blood welled up in the wound at once, and several streaks of red trickled downward, glistening in the strong light.

It was the first time Reiko had ever seen her husband's blood, and she felt a violent throbbing in her chest. She looked at her husband's face. The lieutenant was looking at the blood with calm appraisal. For a moment—though thinking at the same time that it was hollow comfort—Reiko experienced a sense of relief.

The lieutenant's eyes fixed his wife with an intense, hawklike stare. Moving the sword around to his front, he raised himself slightly on his hips and let the upper half of his body lean over the sword point. That he was mustering his whole strength was apparent from the angry tension of the uniform at his shoulders. The lieutenant aimed to strike deep into the left of his stomach. His sharp cry pierced the silence of the room.

Despite the effort he had himself put into the blow, the lieutenant had the impression that someone else had struck the side of his stomach agonizingly with a thick rod of iron. For a second or so his head reeled and he had no idea what had happened. The five or six inches of naked point had vanished completely into his flesh, and the white bandage, gripped in his clenched fist, pressed directly against his stomach.

He returned to consciousness. The blade had certainly pierced the wall of the stomach, he thought. His breathing was difficult, his chest thumped violently, and in some far deep region, which he could hardly believe was a part of himself, a fearful and excruciating pain came welling up as if the ground had split open to disgorge a boiling stream of molten rock. The pain came suddenly nearer, with terrifying speed. The lieutenant bit his lower lip and stifled an instinctive moan.

Was this *seppuku?*—he was thinking. It was a sensation of utter chaos, as if the sky had fallen on his head and the world was reeling drunkenly. His will power and courage, which had seemed so robust before he made the incision, had now dwindled to something like a single hairlike thread of steel, and he was assailed by the uneasy feeling that he must advance along this thread, clinging to it with desperation. His clenched fist had grown moist. Looking down, he saw that both his hand and the cloth about the blade were drenched in blood. His loincloth too was dyed a deep red. It struck him as incredible that, amidst this terrible agony, things which could be seen could still be seen, and existing things existed still.

The moment the lieutenant thrust the sword into his left side and she saw the deathly pallor fall across his face, like an abruptly lowered curtain, Reiko had to struggle to prevent herself from rushing to his side. Whatever happened, she must watch. She must be a witness. That was the duty her husband had laid upon her. Opposite her, a mat's space away, she could clearly see her husband biting his lip to stifle the pain. The pain was there, with absolute certainty, before her eyes. And Reiko had no means of rescuing him from it.

The sweat glistened on her husband's forehead. The lieutenant closed his eyes, and then opened them again, as if experimenting. The eyes had lost their luster, and seemed innocent and empty like the eyes of a small animal.

The agony before Reiko's eyes burned as strong as the summer sun, utterly remote from the grief which seemed to be tearing herself apart within. The pain grew steadily in stature, stretching upward. Reiko felt that her husband had already become a man in a separate world, a man whose whole being had been resolved into pain, a prisoner in a cage of pain where no hand could reach out to him. But Reiko felt no pain at all. Her grief was not pain. As she thought about this, Reiko began to feel as if someone had raised a cruel wall of glass high between herself and her husband.

Ever since her marriage her husband's existence had been her own existence, and every breath of his had been a breath drawn by herself. But now, while her husband's existence in pain was a vivid reality, Reiko could find in this grief of hers no certain proof at all of her own existence.

With only his right hand on the sword the lieutenant began to cut sideways across his stomach. But as the blade became entangled with the entrails it was pushed constantly outward by their soft resilience; and the lieutenant realized that it would be necessary, as he cut, to use both hands to keep the point pressed deep into his stomach. He pulled the blade across. It did not cut as easily as he had expected. He directed the strength of his whole body into his right hand and pulled again. There was a cut of three or four inches.

The pain spread slowly outward from the inner depths until the whole stomach reverberated. It was like the wild clanging of a bell. Or like a thousand bells which jangled simultaneously at every breath he breathed and every throb of his pulse, rocking his whole being. The lieutenant could no longer stop himself from moaning. But by now the blade had cut its way through to below the navel, and when he noticed this he felt a sense of satisfaction, and a renewal of courage.

The volume of blood had steadily increased, and now it spurted from the wound as if propelled by the beat of the pulse. The mat before the lieutenant was drenched red with splattered blood, and more blood overflowed onto it from pools which gathered in the folds of the lieutenant's khaki trousers. A spot, like a bird, came flying across to Reiko and settled on the lap of her white silk kimono.

By the time the lieutenant had at last drawn the sword across to the right side of his stomach, the blade was already cutting shallow and had revealed its naked tip, slippery with blood and grease. But, suddenly stricken by a fit of vomiting, the lieutenant cried out hoarsely. The vomiting made the fierce pain fiercer still, and the stomach, which had thus far remained firm and compact, now abruptly heaved, opening wide its wound, and the entrails burst through, as if the wound too were vomiting. Seemingly ignorant of their master's suffering, the entrails gave an impression of robust health and almost disagreeable vitality as they slipped smoothly out and spilled over into the crotch. The lieutenant's head drooped, his shoulders heaved, his eyes opened to narrow slits, and a thin trickle of saliva dribbled from his mouth. The gold markings on his epaulettes caught the light and glinted.

Blood was scattered everywhere. The lieutenant was soaked in it to his knees, and he sat now in a crumpled and listless posture, one hand on the floor. A raw smell filled the room. The lieutenant, his head drooping, retched repeatedly, and the movement showed vividly in his shoulders. The blade of the sword, now pushed back by the entrails and exposed to its tip, was still in the lieutenant's right hand.

It would be difficult to imagine a more heroic sight than that of the lieutenant at this moment, as he mustered his strength and flung back his head. The movement was performed with sudden violence, and the back of his head struck with a sharp crack against the alcove pillar. Reiko had been sitting until now with her face lowered, gazing in fascination at the tide of blood advancing toward her knees, but the sound took her by surprise and she looked up.

The lieutenant's face was not the face of a living man. The eyes were hollow, the skin parched, the once so lustrous cheeks and lips the color of dried mud. The right hand alone was moving. Laboriously gripping the sword, it hovered shakily in the air like the hand of a marionette and strove to direct the point at the base of the lieutenant's throat. Reiko watched her husband make this last, most heart-rendering, futile exertion. Glistening with blood and grease, the point was thrust at the throat again and again. And each time it missed its aim. The strength to guide it was no longer there. The straying point struck the collar and the collar badges. Although its hooks had been unfastened, the stiff military collar had closed together again and was protecting the throat.

Reiko could bear the sight no longer. She tried to go to her husband's help, but she could not stand. She moved through the blood on her knees, and her white skirts grew deep red. Moving to the rear of her husband, she helped no more than by loosening the collar. The quivering blade at last contacted the naked flesh of the throat. At that moment Reiko's impression was that she herself had propelled her husband forward; but that was not the case. It was a movement planned by the lieutenant himself, his last exertion of strength. Abruptly he threw his body at the blade, and the blade pierced his neck, emerging at the nape. There was a tremendous spurt of blood and the lieutenant lay still, cold blue-tinged steel protruding from his neck at the back.

5

Slowly, her socks slippery with blood, Reiko descended the stairway. The upstairs room was now completely still.

Switching on the ground-floor lights, she checked the gas jet and the main gas plug and poured water over the smoldering, half-buried charcoal in the brazier. She stood before the upright mirror in the four-and-a-half-mat room and held up her skirts. The bloodstains made it seem as if a bold, vivid pattern was printed across the lower half of her white kimono. When she sat down before the mirror, she was conscious of the dampness and coldness of her husband's blood in the region of her thighs, and she shivered. Then, for a long while, she lingered over her toilet preparations. She applied the rouge generously to her cheeks, and her lips too she painted heavily. This was no longer make-up to please her husband. It was make-up for the world which she would leave behind, and there was a touch of the magnificent and the spectacular in her brushwork. When she rose, the mat before the mirror was wet with blood. Reiko was not concerned about this.

Returning from the toilet, Reiko stood finally on the cement floor of the porchway. When her husband had bolted the door here last night it had been in preparation for death. For a while she stood immersed in the consideration of a simple problem. Should she now leave the bolt drawn? If she were to lock the door, it could be that the neighbors might not notice their suicide for several days. Reiko did not relish the thought of their two corpses putrifying before discovery. After all, it seemed, it would be best to leave it open. . . . She released the bolt, and also drew open the frosted-glass door a fraction. . . . At once a chill wind blew in. There was no sign of anyone in the midnight streets, and stars glittered ice-cold through the trees in the large house opposite.

Leaving the door as it was, Reiko mounted the stairs. She had walked here and there for some time and her socks were no longer slippery. About halfway up, her nostrils were already assailed by a peculiar smell.

The lieutenant was lying on his face in a sea of blood. The point protruding from his neck seemed to have grown even more prominent than before. Reiko walked heedlessly across the blood. Sitting beside the lieutenant's corpse, she stared intently at the face, which lay on one cheek on the mat. The eyes were opened wide, as if the lieutenant's attention had been attracted by something. She raised the head, folding it in her sleeve, wiped the blood from the lips, and bestowed a last kiss.

Then she rose and took from the closet a new white blanket and a waist cord. To prevent any derangement of her skirts, she wrapped the blanket about her waist and bound it there firmly with the cord.

Reiko sat herself on a spot about one foot distant from the lieutenant's body. Drawing the dagger from her sash, she examined its dully gleaming blade intently, and held it to her tongue. The taste of the polished steel was slightly sweet.

Reiko did not linger. When she thought how the pain which had previously opened such a gulf between herself and her dying husband was now to become a part of her own experience, she saw before her only the joy of herself entering a realm her husband had already made his own. In her husband's agonized face there had been something inexplicable which she was seeing for the first time. Now she would solve that riddle. Reiko sensed that at last she too would be able to taste the true bitterness and sweetness of that great moral principle in which her husband believed. What had until now been tasted only faintly through her husband's example she was about to savor directly with her own tongue.

Reiko rested the point of the blade against the base of her throat. She thrust hard. The wound was only shallow. Her head blazed, and her hands shook uncontrollably. She gave the blade a strong pull sideways. A warm substance flooded into her mouth, and everything before her eyes reddened, in a vision of spouting blood. She gathered her strength and plunged the point of the blade deep into her throat.

GABRIEL GARCÍA MÁRQUEZ
1928—

A Colombian whom the whole continent claims as a "Latin American writer," one of the great novelists and prose stylists of the twentieth century, Gabriel García Márquez possesses both the technical virtuosity of the French "new novelists" and the breadth and historical scope of the traditional realistic writer. His most famous work, *One Hundred Years of Solitude* (1967), is the best-known novel from the amazing literary explosion of the sixties and seventies called the Latin American "Boom," and embodies the mixture of fantasy and realism called "magical realism." In this novel and related stories, he follows the rise and fall of the Buendía family fortunes in a mythical town called Macondo, and sketches at the same time an echoing, intricate pattern of social, cultural, and psychological themes that become a symbolic picture of Latin American society. Not all of García Márquez's works are about Macondo, but the same themes and images reappear throughout: the contrast of dreamlike and everyday reality and the "magical" aspect of fictional creation, mythic overtones often rooted in local folklore, the representation of broader social and psychological conflicts through regional tales, the essential solitude of individuals facing love and death in a society of which they never quite seem a part. García Márquez is a political novelist in that many of his fictional situations are openly drawn from conditions in Latin American history, so that local readers will recognize current history in the change from prosperity to misery in Macondo that accompanies the presence and withdrawal of the banana company, the massacre of striking banana workers by government forces in 1928, the general extreme separation of rich and poor, and the grotesquely oppressive power of political dictators pictured most recently in *The Autumn of the Patriarch* (1975). Yet his fiction achieves its impact not because of its base in real events but because these events are transformed and interpreted inside an artistic vision and language which—experimenting with many forms—creates a fictional universe all its own.

García Márquez was born in the small town of Aracataca in the "banana zone" of Colombia on March 6, 1928, to Gabriel Eligio García and Maria Márquez Iguarán. The first of twelve children, he was raised by his maternal grandparents until his grandfather died in 1936. He attributes his love of fantasy to his grandmother, who would tell him fantastic tales whenever she did not want to answer his questions. The recurring image of an old military man battered by circumstances (the grandfather of *Leaf Storm*, 1955; the protagonist of *No One Writes to the Colonel*, 1958; and in his younger days, Colonel Aureliano Buendía of *One Hundred Years of Solitude*) likewise recalls his grandfather, a retired colonel who had served on the Liberal side of a civil war at the beginning of the century. A scholarship student at the National Colegio in Zipaquirá, he received his bachelor's degree in 1946 and studied law at universities in Bogotá and Cartagena from 1947 to 1950. In 1947 he published his first story, "The Third Resignation," a Kafkaesque tale of a dead man who continued to grow and retain consciousness in his coffin for seventeen years after his death. García Márquez had worked as a journalist while studying law, and in 1950 he abandoned his legal studies for journalism in order to have more time as a writer. His first novel, *Leaf Storm*, was published in 1955, and—in its use of interior monologue and juxtaposition of different perspectives—shows the strong influence of Faulkner. He would soon abandon the more subjective Faulknerian style for an objective manner derived both from journalism and from Hemingway. In *Leaf Storm*, we may perceive reality through the mind of a ten-year-old boy: "The heat won't let you breathe in the closed room. You can hear the sun buzzing in the streets, but that's all. The air is stagnant, like concrete; you get the feeling that it could get all twisted like a sheet of steel." In his next novel, *No One Writes to the Colonel*, an impersonal narrator catalogues the actions of the colonel about to make coffee: "He removed the pot from the fire, poured half the water onto the earthen floor, and scraped the inside of the can with a knife until the last scrapings of the ground coffee, mixed with bits of rust, fell into the pot."

In 1954 García Márquez had joined *El Espectador* (The Spectator) in Bogotá; a report he wrote in 1955 that indirectly revealed corruption in the navy irritated the Rojas Pinilla dictatorship and his newspaper was shut down. Working in Paris as *El Espectador*'s foreign correspondent when he learned that his job had been abolished, he lived in extreme poverty for the next year while beginning *The Evil Hour* (1962) and *No One Writes to the Colonel*. In 1957, after traveling in Eastern Europe, he came back to Latin America. Here he worked for several different newspapers in Venezuela, and later for the international press agency, Prensa Latina, in Cuba and New York, and for the Mexican periodicals *La Familia* and *Sucesos* (a sensationalist magazine) before beginning to write film scripts in 1963. A collection of short stories, *Big Mama's Funeral*, was published in 1962, along with the first edition of *The Evil Hour* which, printed in Spain, was later repudiated by the author because of tampering by proofreaders. In 1965 the various themes and characters he had been developing throughout his earlier novels and short stories came together as the fully developed concept of a new book, and García Márquez shut himself up in his study for a year and a half to write *One Hundred Years of Solitude*. Published in 1967, the novel was a best seller immediately translated into numerous (now twenty-five) languages; it received prizes in Italy and France in 1969, and—when published in English in 1970—was chosen by American critics as one of the twelve best books of the year.

Layers of meaning accumulate around a core story in *One Hundred Years*, as the history of the doomed Buendía family takes on different and intertwined shades of significance. The family is cursed from the moment that its founder, José Arcadio Buendía, kills a friend who had insulted him and consummates an incestuous marriage; he then sets out in search of the sea and stops to settle in Macondo. Throughout a hundred years of family history in the nineteenth and twentieth centuries, the Buendías are soldiers, scholars, merchants, explorers, revolutionaries, inventors, lovers, ascetics, labor organizers, and above all stubborn individuals. Yet these individuals are caught up in, and defined by, a larger family history of which they sometimes appear only interrelated, component parts: names echo one another, and parallel situations evoke a feeling of half-recognition inside a mirrorlike pattern of structural oppositions. The Buendía story is set in history but also exists on a mythic level: Remedios the Beauty is lifted up into heaven clutching her sheets when she dies, and when José Arcadio is killed, blood runs from his ear down the street all the way to his mother in her kitchen. The last Buendía, the son of Aureliano Babilonia and Amaranta Ursula, is born with the sign of the curse—a pig's tail—and dies eaten by ants at the end. Yet this is not really the end, for in the very last pages, after his son's death and as the whirlwind gathers to destroy Macondo, Aureliano Babilonia reads the manuscript left by the dead magician Melquíades. At last able to decipher a text that could not be read until one hundred years had passed, Aureliano Babilonia finds that this text is the story of his own family; thus he is learning about his own existence, predicted and described a century ago. "It was the history of the family, written by Melquíades, down to the most trivial details, one hundred years ahead of time. He had written it in Sanskrit, which was his mother tongue, and he had encoded the even lines in the private cipher of the Emperor Augustus and the odd ones in a Lacedemonian military code." Behind García Márquez there is yet another author— Melquíades—who has written *One Hundred Years of Solitude*, a novel whose complexity and self-contained referentiality recall the circular fictions of Borges.

The "magical realism" of *One Hundred Years of Solitude* reposes on the juxtaposition of real and fantastic worlds, and it elicits a series of interpretations whose variety can be only emulated by interpretations of Kafka. For some readers, the novel is an allegory of the human condition and its fall from innocence; for others, it recounts the destructive, alienating influence on Latin American society of the aggressive individualism in Western culture; for others, it depicts essential human loneliness and the failure to communicate—even in love; for still others, it is a "total fiction" peculiarly valid for intricate repetitive patterns that refer to folklore and real life but finally create only a fictional universe. Each interpretation draws on the novel's blurring of real and unreal worlds, so that historical facts become the basis for fiction and fictional manipulation liberates our perspective on reality—a typically modernist method of using the imagination to encourage historical change.

After *One Hundred Years of Solitude*, García Márquez found new ways to combine magical-realist techniques and social commentary. In 1972, he published a collection of seven stories: *The Incredible and Sad Story of Innocent Eréndira and Her Heartless Grandmother*, which contains the story printed here, "Death Constant Beyond Love." From the title story, in which Eréndira's monstrously fat, tattooed, green-blooded grandmother is finally murdered after prostituting her grandchild to the entire countryside to repay a debt, to symbolic fantasies like "A Very Old Man with Enormous Wings" (where a castaway angel is exhibited in a chicken coop until his feathers grow back and he can fly away, and a woman has been turned into a gigantic spider for disobeying her parents), the author presents tales in which the substance is incredible but the details themselves are highly realistic. The winged man smells bad and his wings are infested with parasites; the farm truck in which Eréndira tries to escape with her lover Ulises has an old motor and can't outrun the military patrol summoned by her grandmother. The mixture of fantasy and realism is not easily interpretable in a single symbolic sense: Eréndira's prostitution may be political and cultural as well as personal, and larger social relationships may be symbolized in the town's attitude towards the angel and the spider woman. Throughout, the narrative line can easily be followed but also interpreted in several ways.

Increasingly preoccupied with contemporary political events, he next published *The Autumn of the Patriarch*, an intricate study of the idea of dictatorship embodied in reactions to a first, false death of the patriarch (his double was assassinated instead), and a second, apparently real death upon which new authorities are already gathering to divide up the power. García Márquez is aiming at more than a specific political situation: he points to a habit of mind, a social lethargy in which there is no apparent connection between the passive acceptance of life as it always has been and the manipulation of society by a succession of dictators. In his next novel, *Chronicle of a Death Foretold* (1981), he describes the same inertia in a small town where everyday life continues its ordinary gossipy routine around two life-shattering events: the rejection of Angela Vicario by her new husband when he finds she is not a virgin, and her brothers' murder of the local dandy whom she names (probably falsely) as her seducer. Against the background of a whole society's passive complicity in a murder that everyone knows will happen, it is death and love that are the two overriding realities: the often foretold death of Santiago Nasar, and the strange passion of the abandoned bride, who writes letter after letter to her husband until he finally returns to her years later, the unopened letters in his hand.

In recent years—questioning the effectiveness of literature to remedy the social ills he so often describes—García Márquez has been more and more active politically, speaking out for revolutionary governments in Latin America and organizing assistance for political prisoners. Living in Mexico City, he nonetheless continues to write, including a number of stories that are still unpublished and an account of Cuba under the US blockade. He received the Nobel Prize for Literature in 1982.

The story printed here, "Death Constant Beyond Love" (1970), also has a political background although its protagonist, Senator Onésimo Sánchez, is seen chiefly as he struggles with his elemental problem of death. He is no hero: in "Innocent Eréndira" he writes a letter vouching for the grandmother's morality, and in this story he is clearly a corrupt politician who accepts bribes and stays in power by helping the local property owners avoid reform. His electoral train is a traveling circus with carnival wagons, fireworks, a ready made audience of hired Indians, and a cardboard village with imitation brick houses and a painted ocean liner to offer the illusion of future prosperity; he uses carefully placed gifts to encourage support and a feeling of dependence; he is, as one onlooker says, a real political huckster.

Yet the background of poverty and corruption, the entertaining spectacle of the senator's "fictional world," and the political campaign itself fade into insignificance before broader themes of life and death: the senator has exactly six months and eleven days to live. Forty-two, happily married, in full control of his own and others' lives as a successful politician in midcareer, he is made to feel suddenly helpless, vulnerable, and alone when told that all this will stop and he will be dead "forever" by next Christmas. Theoretically, he knows that death is inevitable and nature cannot be defeated. He has read the Stoic philosopher Marcus Aurelius (A.D. 121–180) and even refers to the fourth book of the *Meditations*, which recommends the cheerful acceptance of natural order (including death and oblivion), criticizes the delusions of those "who have tenaciously stuck to life," and stresses both the tranquil "ordering of the mind" and the idea that human beings are all "fellow-citizens" of a shared "political community." The example of the philosopher is not mere chance: Marcus Aurelius was also a political figure, a Roman emperor who wrote his *Meditations* as personal guidelines in a time of plague and political unrest, so that the figure of the philosopher-king becomes a shadowy contrast to the modern politician and potential dictator.

The senator does gain some Stoic insight into the illusions of his career: he notices how similar are the dusty village and the worn cardboard façade that represents its hopes, and he is fed up with what he recognizes to be background maneuverings that keep him in power by prolonging the exploitation of the poor. But he also loses sympathy for the barefoot Indians standing in the square, and his newly alienated perspective is not accompanied by the Stoic injunction to maintain a just and ordered mind, and to accept everything that happens as necessary and good. In this crisis, the senator is reduced to a basic and instinctual existence, expressed in García Márquez's recurrent themes of solitude, love, and death. "No one loves us," he sighs while caressing Nelson Farina's beautiful "woods-animal" daughter. Laura provides an opportunity for him to sublimate his fear of death in erotic passion (inextricably intertwined, according to Freud). His choice means scandal and the destruction of his political career, but by now Onésimo Sánchez has felt the emptiness of his earlier activities and is engaged in a struggle to cheat death.

He does not succeed, of course, and dies weeping with rage that death separates him from Laura Farina. "Death Constant Beyond Love" has reversed the ambitious claim of a famous sonnet by the Spanish Golden Age writer Quevedo (1580–1645), according to which there is "Love Constant Beyond Death." Such love is an illusion, for it is death that awaits us beyond everything else. García Márquez repeatedly plays on these oppositions and inversions when he describes the real village and the cardboard version created by false political promises, the paper birds that magically take on life and fly out to sea, the paper butterfly that seems to fly and lands on the wall, the bribery money that flaps around like butterflies, the grotesquely padlocked chastity belt that Laura Farina wears, and even the initial opposition between the senator's living rose (symbol of womanhood and love) and the roseless town (named "The Viceroy's Rosebush") where he encounters his destiny. His destiny is to be liberated from some illusions but not all: his final delusion is to try to hide from death in erotic love. The senator's defeat at the end, which is clearly emphasized as a defeat, suggests that his response was a futile retreat, and—at the same time that it evokes pity for his loneliness, terror, and rage—puts in question what that response should be.

Regina Janes, *Gabriel García Márquez, Revolutions in Wonderland* (1981), is an excellent general study on García Márquez in a Latin American context. An introduction to the writer and his work is found in George P. McMurray, *Gabriel García Márquez* (1977). The Summer 1972 issue of *Books Abroad* is dedicated to García Márquez.

Death Constant Beyond Love[1]

Senator Onésimo Sánchez had six months and eleven days to go before his death when he found the woman of his life. He met her in Rosal del Virrey,[2] an illusory village which by night was the furtive wharf for smugglers' ships, and on the other hand, in broad daylight looked like the most useless inlet on the desert, facing a sea that was arid and without direction and so far from everything no one would have suspected that someone capable of changing the

---

1. Translated by Gregory Rabassa.   2. "The rosebush of the Viceroy (governor)."

destiny of anyone lived there. Even its name was a kind of joke, because the only rose in that village was being worn by Senator Onésimo Sánchez himself on the same afternoon when he met Laura Farina.

It was an unavoidable stop in the electoral campaign he made every four years. The carnival wagons had arrived in the morning. Then came the trucks with the rented Indians[3] who were carried into the towns in order to enlarge the crowds at public ceremonies. A short time before eleven o'clock, along with the music and rockets and jeeps of the retinue, the ministerial automobile, the color of strawberry soda, arrived. Senator Onésimo Sánchez was placid and weatherless inside the air-conditioned car, but as soon as he opened the door he was shaken by a gust of fire and his shirt of pure silk was soaked in a kind of light-colored soup and he felt many years older and more alone than ever. In real life he had just turned forty-two, had been graduated from Göttingen[4] with honors as a metallurgical engineer, and was an avid reader, although without much reward, of badly translated Latin classics. He was married to a radiant German woman who had given him five children and they were all happy in their home, he the happiest of all until they told him, three months before, that he would be dead forever by next Christmas.

While the preparations for the public rally were being completed, the senator managed to have an hour alone in the house they had set aside for him to rest in. Before he lay down he put in a glass of drinking water the rose he had kept alive all across the desert, lunched on the diet cereals that he took with him so as to avoid the repeated portions of fried goat that were waiting for him during the rest of the day, and he took several analgesic pills before the time prescribed so that he would have the remedy ahead of the pain. Then he put the electric fan close to the hammock and stretched out naked for fifteen minutes in the shadow of the rose, making a great effort at mental distraction so as not to think about death while he dozed. Except for the doctors, no one knew that he had been sentenced to a fixed term, for he had decided to endure his secret all alone, with no change in his life, not because of pride but out of shame.[5]

He felt in full control of his will when he appeared in public again at three in the afternoon, rested and clean, wearing a pair of coarse linen slacks and a floral shirt, and with his soul sustained by the anti-pain pills. Nevertheless, the erosion of death was much more pernicious than he had supposed, for as he went up onto the platform he felt a strange disdain for those who were fighting for the good luck

---

3. People descended from the original inhabitants of the continent; generally poorer and less privileged than those descended from Spanish or Portuguese colonists.   4. A well-known German university.   5. "Death is such as generation is, a mystery of nature . . . altogether not a thing of which any man should be ashamed." [Marcus Aurelius, *Meditations*, IV,5.]

to shake his hand, and he didn't feel sorry as he had at other times for the groups of barefoot Indians who could scarcely bear the hot saltpeter coals of the sterile little square. He silenced the applause with a wave of his hand, almost with rage, and he began to speak without gestures, his eyes fixed on the sea, which was sighing with heat. His measured, deep voice had the quality of calm water, but the speech that had been memorized and ground out so many times had not occurred to him in the nature of telling the truth, but, rather, as the opposite of a fatalistic pronouncement by Marcus Aurelius in the fourth book of his *Meditations*.

"We are here for the purpose of defeating nature," he began, against all his convictions. "We will no longer be foundlings in our own country, orphans of God in a realm of thirst and bad climate, exiles in our own land. We will be different people, ladies and gentlemen, we will be a great and happy people."

There was a pattern to his circus. As he spoke his aides threw clusters of paper birds into the air and the artificial creatures took on life, flew about the platform of planks, and went out to sea. At the same time, other men took some prop trees with felt leaves out of the wagons and planted them in the saltpeter soil behind the crowd. They finished by setting up a cardboard façade with make-believe houses of red brick that had glass windows, and with it they covered the miserable real-life shacks.

The senator prolonged his speech with two quotations in Latin in order to give the farce more time. He promised rainmaking machines, portable breeders for table animals, the oils of happiness which would make vegetables grow in the saltpeter and clumps of pansies in the window boxes. When he saw that his fictional world was all set up, he pointed to it. "That's the way it will be for us, ladies and gentlemen," he shouted. "Look! That's the way it will be for us."

The audience turned around. An ocean liner made of painted paper was passing behind the houses and it was taller than the tallest houses in the artificial city. Only the senator himself noticed that since it had been set up and taken down and carried from one place to another the superimposed cardboard town had been eaten away by the terrible climate and that it was almost as poor and dusty as Rosal del Virrey.

For the first time in twelve years, Nelson Farina didn't go to greet the senator. He listened to the speech from his hammock amidst the remains of his siesta, under the cool bower of a house of unplaned boards which he had built with the same pharmacist's hands with which he had drawn and quartered his first wife. He had escaped from Devil's Island[6] and appeared in Rosal del Virrey on a ship loaded

---

6. A former French penal colony off the coast of French Guiana in northern South America.

with innocent macaws, with a beautiful and blasphemous black woman he had found in Paramaribo[7] and by whom he had a daughter. The woman died of natural causes a short while later and she didn't suffer the fate of the other, whose pieces had fertilized her own cauliflower patch, but was buried whole and with her Dutch name in the local cemetery. The daughter had inherited her color and her figure along with her father's yellow and astonished eyes, and he had good reason to imagine that he was rearing the most beautiful woman in the world.

Ever since he had met Senator Onésimo Sánchez during his first electoral campaign, Nelson Farina had begged for his help in getting a false identity card which would place him beyond the reach of the law. The senator, in a friendly but firm way, had refused. Nelson Farina never gave up, and for several years, every time he found the chance, he would repeat his request with a different recourse. But this time he stayed in his hammock, condemned to rot alive in that burning den of buccaneers. When he heard the final applause, he lifted his head, and looking over the boards of the fence, he saw the back side of the farce: the props for the buildings, the framework of the trees, the hidden illusionists who were pushing the ocean liner along. He spat without rancor.

"*Merde,*" he said. "*C'est le Blacamán de la politique.*"[8]

After the speech, as was customary, the senator took a walk through the streets of the town in the midst of the music and the rockets and was besieged by the townspeople, who told him their troubles. The senator listened to them good-naturedly and he always found some way to console everybody without having to do them any difficult favors. A woman up on the roof of a house with her six youngest children managed to make herself heard over the uproar and the fireworks.

"I'm not asking for much, Senator," she said. "Just a donkey to haul water from Hanged Man's Well."

The senator noticed the six thin children. "What became of your husband?" he asked.

"He went to find his fortune on the island of Aruba,"[9] the woman answered good-humoredly, "and what he found was a foreign woman, the kind that put diamonds on their teeth."

The answer brought on a roar of laughter.

"All right," the senator decided, "you'll get your donkey."

A short while later an aide of his brought a good pack donkey to the woman's house and on the rump it had a campaign slogan writ-

---

7. Capital of Surinam (formerly Dutch Guiana) and a large port.   8. "Shit. He's the Blacamán of politics." (French Blacamán is a charlatan and huckster who appears in several stories, including "Blacamán the Good, Vendor of Miracles.")   9. An island off the coast of Venezuela, famous as a tourist resort.

ten in indelible paint so that no one would ever forget that it was a gift from the senator.

Along the short stretch of street he made other, smaller gestures, and he even gave a spoonful of medicine to a sick man who had had his bed brought to the door of his house so he could see him pass. At the last corner, through the boards of the fence, he saw Nelson Farina in his hammock, looking ashen and gloomy, but nonetheless the senator greeted him, with no show of affection.

"Hello, how are you?"

Nelson Farina turned in his hammock and soaked him in the sad amber of his look.

"*Moi, vous savez,*"[1] he said.

His daughter came out into the yard when she heard the greeting. She was wearing a cheap, faded Guajiro Indian[2] robe, her head was decorated with colored bows, and her face was painted as protection against the sun, but even in that state of disrepair it was possible to imagine that there had never been another so beautiful in the whole world. The senator was left breathless. "I'll be damned!" he breathed in surprise. "The Lord does the craziest things!"

That night Nelson Farina dressed his daughter up in her best clothes and sent her to the senator. Two guards armed with rifles who were nodding from the heat in the borrowed house ordered her to wait on the only chair in the vestibule.

The senator was in the next room meeting with the important people of Rosal del Virrey, whom he had gathered together in order to sing for them the truths he had left out of his speeches. They looked so much like all the ones he always met in all the towns in the desert that even the senator himself was sick and tired of that perpetual nightly session. His shirt was soaked with sweat and he was trying to dry it on his body with the hot breeze from an electric fan that was buzzing like a horse fly in the heavy heat of the room.

"We, of course, can't eat paper birds," he said. "You and I know that the day there are trees and flowers in this heap of goat dung, the day there are shad instead of worms in the water holes, that day neither you nor I will have anything to do here, do I make myself clear?"

No one answered. While he was speaking, the senator had torn a sheet off the calendar and fashioned a paper butterfly out of it with his hands. He tossed it with no particular aim into the air current coming from the fan and the butterfly flew about the room and then went out through the half-open door. The senator went on speaking

---

1. "Oh well, as for me, you know . . ."   2. Inhabitants of the rural Guajira Peninsula of northern Colombia; the figure of Laura Farina is thus connected with the rustic poor, with earthy reality (*farina* means flour), and with erotic inspiration (*Laura* was the beloved celebrated by the Italian poet Petrarch, 1304–74).

with a control aided by the complicity of death.

"Therefore," he said, "I don't have to repeat to you what you already know too well: that my reelection is a better piece of business for you than it is for me, because I'm fed up with stagnant water and Indian sweat, while you people, on the other hand, make your living from it."

Laura Farina saw the paper butterfly come out. Only she saw it because the guards in the vestibule had fallen asleep on the steps, hugging their rifles. After a few turns, the large lithographed butterfly unfolded completely, flattened against the wall, and remained stuck there. Laura Farina tried to pull it off with her nails. One of the guards, who woke up with the applause from the next room, noticed her vain attempt.

"It won't come off," he said sleepily. "It's painted on the wall."

Laura Farina sat down again when the men began to come out of the meeting. The senator stood in the doorway of the room with his hand on the latch, and he only noticed Laura Farina when the vestibule was empty.

"What are you doing here?"

"*C'est de la part de mon père*,"[3] she said.

The senator understood. He scrutinized the sleeping guards, then he scrutinized Laura Farina, whose unusual beauty was even more demanding than his pain, and he resolved then that death had made his decision for him.

"Come in," he told her.

Laura Farina was struck dumb standing in the doorway to the room: thousands of bank notes were floating in the air, flapping like the butterfly. But the senator turned off the fan and the bills were left without air and alighted on the objects in the room.

"You see," he said, smiling, "even shit can fly."

Laura Farina sat down on a schoolboy's stool. Her skin was smooth and firm, with the same color and the same solar density as crude oil, her hair was the mane of a young mare, and her huge eyes were brighter than the light. The senator followed the thread of her look and finally found the rose, which had been tarnished by the saltpeter.

"It's a rose," he said.

"Yes," she said with a trace of perplexity. "I learned what they were in Riohacha."[4]

The senator sat down on an army cot, talking about roses as he unbuttoned his shirt. On the side where he imagined his heart to be inside his chest he had a corsair's tattoo of a heart pierced by an

---

3. "My father sent me."   4. A port on the Guajira Peninsula.

arrow. He threw the soaked shirt to the floor and asked Laura Farina to help him off with his boots.

She knelt down facing the cot. The senator continued to scrutinize her, thoughtfully, and while he was untying the laces he wondered which one of them would end up with the bad luck of that encounter.

"You're just a child," he said.

"Don't you believe it," she said. "I'll be nineteen in April."

The senator became interested.

"What day?"

"The eleventh," she said.

The senator felt better. "We're both Aries,"[5] he said. And smiling, he added:

"It's the sign of solitude."

Laura Farina wasn't paying attention because she didn't know what to do with the boots. The senator, for his part, didn't know what to do with Laura Farina, because he wasn't used to sudden love affairs and, besides, he knew that the one at hand had its origins in indignity. Just to have some time to think, he held Laura Farina tightly between his knees, embraced her about the waist, and lay down on his back on the cot. Then he realized that she was naked under her dress, for her body gave off the dark fragrance of an animal of the woods, but her heart was frightened and her skin disturbed by a glacial sweat.

"No one loves us," he sighed.

Laura Farina tried to say something, but there was only enough air for her to breathe. He laid her down beside him to help her, he put out the light and the room was in the shadow of the rose. She abandoned herself to the mercies of her fate. The senator caressed her slowly, seeking her with his hand, barely touching her, but where he expected to find her, he came across something iron that was in the way.

"What have you got there?"

"A padlock,"[6] she said.

"What in hell!" the senator said furiously and asked what he knew only too well. "Where's the key?"

Laura Farina gave a breath of relief.

"My papa has it," she answered. "He told me to tell you to send one of your people to get it and to send along with him a written promise that you'll straighten out his situation."

The senator grew tense. "Frog[7] bastard," he murmured indig-

---

5. The first sign in the zodiac; people born from March 21 to April 19 are said to be under the sign of Aries.   6. She is wearing a chastity belt, a medieval device worn by women to prevent intercourse.   7. Epithet for "French."

nantly. Then he closed his eyes in order to relax and he met himself in the darkness. *Remember,* he remembered, *that whether it's you or someone else, it won't be long before you'll be dead and it won't be long before your name won't even be left.*[8]

He waited for the shudder to pass.

"Tell me one thing," he asked then. "What have you heard about me?"

"Do you want the honest-to-God truth?"

"The honest-to-God truth."

"Well," Laura Farina ventured, "they say you're worse than the rest because you're different."

The senator didn't get upset. He remained silent for a long time with his eyes closed, and when he opened them again he seemed to have returned from his most hidden instincts.

"Oh, what the hell," he decided. "Tell your son of a bitch of a father that I'll straighten out his situation."

"If you want, I can go get the key myself," Laura Farina said.

The senator held her back.

"Forget about the key," he said, "and sleep awhile with me. It's good to be with someone when you're so alone."

Then she laid his head on her shoulder with her eyes fixed on the rose. The senator held her about the waist, sank his face into woods-animal armpit, and gave in to terror. Six months and eleven days later he would die in that same position, debased and repudiated because of the public scandal with Laura Farina and weeping with rage at dying without her.

WOLE SOYINKA

1934—

Realism and fantasy, mythology and politics, verbal brilliance with mime and spectacle characterize the drama of Africa's best-known modern play-wright. A Nigerian whose works have been translated into French and Japanese, a novelist, poet, essayist, and translator, Wole Soyinka is a complex figure who draws consciously upon both African and European traditions. Like many modern African intellectuals, he received his college education in Europe and is thus steeped in classical European literature as well as in the traditions of his native land. When these European-educated intellectuals returned home, they became part of a new political climate in which the emerging African nations sought to develop (or recapture) an indigenous culture separate from the colonial example, and to assert—in different ways—

8. A direct translation of a sentence from Marcus Aurelius in the fourth book of the *Meditations* (IV, 6).

their African roots. Some espoused the movement known as Negritude, a militant assertion of exclusively black identity; Soyinka, in contrast, proposed what became known as the "Nigerian view" with its dry assurance that "a tiger does not need to proclaim his tigritude." Soyinka's plays are full of themes and dramatic strategies derived from the culture of his own Yoruba people (Western Nigeria), and he has translated Yoruba texts into English to enable them to find a wider audience. However, he proclaims "selective eclecticism as the right of every productive being, scientist or artist" and refuses to limit his own work to any one ideological model.

Non-African readers need some acquaintance with Yoruba culture to grasp several aspects of Soyinka's work. The seasonal rhythms of farming life patterns everyday existence, and the major Yoruba festivals (themselves dramatic spectacles) come at harvest time. Images of fertility or destruction underlie many of Soyinka's plays, and in *The Swamp Dwellers* (staged 1958) and *Kongi's Harvest* (1965) both moral and political well-being are suggested by the success or failure of the harvest. (In the latter play, the symbolic first yam which the dictator Kongi expects to be offered to him is replaced by the political "harvest" of a bloody head upon a platter.) Yoruba religion is dominated by a pantheon of major and minor gods representing absolute concepts, specific powers, and regional spirits (like ancient Greece), and even the ghosts of ancestors. The supreme creator is Olodumare; there is also Sango, the god of electricity, Esu, the spirit of disorder, and Soyinka's favorite figure, Ogun—patron of craftsmen, god of creation and destruction, the god so pained by the separation between gods and humans that he launched himself into the dividing abyss to create a path toward humanity. Menacing as well as protective, Ogun is the deity most closely involved with humanity because he combines the creative and destructive impulses found in human nature. He is also a daring god, "the god that ventures first" into the realm of nothingness to seek completion, and represents for Soyinka the very essence of Yoruba tragic consciousness ("The Fourth Stage: Through the Mysteries of Ogun to the Origin of Yoruba Tragedy"). All these figures are seen as interacting with human beings in everyday life, thus establishing a broad continuum of existence in a natural order that includes but transcends mortal experience.

It is this longer perspective, beginning before birth and reaching beyond the grave, that is so important in Yoruba religious ritual and also—as a cultural ethic—in Soyinka's plays, which often describe a tragic clash of values. When the colonial authorities prevent a ritual suicide in *Death and the King's Horseman* (1976; based on an actual event in 1946), they are asserting the exclusive value of earthly existence and contradicting a different cultural ethic in which loyalty to the departed king mandates following him into the next stage of his life. Worse, the colonial district officer and his wife wear *egungun* masks (improved with modern gadgets for convenient manipulation of parts) to a costume ball, hoping to receive a prize. Although they are impatient with the superstitious disapproval of the local inhabitants (the masks are used as part of a ritual death ceremony and are inhabited by the spirits of ancestors welcoming the recently dead into their midst), the couple paradoxically do represent death not just for the protagonist but for his son; they also mean death for an older way of life that cannot be comprehended by their mechanical, "commonsense" priorities. In Soyinka's work, the hero—whether he embodies or falls short of community values—is directly connected to them. Although some critics have referred to Beckett and Absurdist theater in connection with grotesque and apparently meaningless images in later plays (e.g., *Madmen and Specialists*, 1970), the comparison falls short because Soyinka keeps an implied reference point in communal values, and because his heroes—even if isolated—fill a significant role that represents the core and perhaps salvation of their society.

He was born Oluwole Akinwande Soyinka (pronounced Shoy-ING-ka) on July 13, 1934, at Abeokuta, a city on the Ogun River in Western Nigeria, the son of a school inspector. Soyinka went to primary school in Abeokuta and secondary school at Government College in Ibadan, then the capital of Western Nigeria. His Nigerian education already reflected English academic tradition, including the Christian and classical heritage which—linked to Yoruba mythology—permeates his imagery. Nigeria is one of the Anglophone (English-speaking) countries of Africa; most of the early colonists of Africa spoke either English or French, and the two languages have become the major languages of the continent. (There are so many different tribal languages that no single "African" language has been accepted, although Swahili has been proposed.) In 1952 Soyinka entered the new University College in Ibadan, but after two years moved to Leeds University in England where he took an honors degree in English in 1957.

While at Leeds, Soyinka wrote poetry and short stories, studied with the influential dramatic critic G. Wilson Knight, and had an opportunity to attend a wide variety of classical and modern plays performed in the extremely active university theater. Upon graduating, he taught in various schools and worked as a script reader for the Royal Court Theatre in London. Here he not only observed the actual mechanics of direction and stage production, but also saw the early work of gifted dramatists like Samuel Beckett, John Osborne, Arnold Wesker, and John Arden, and himself joined the writers' group and participated in dramatic improvisations. His first play, *The Swamp Dwellers*, a somber story whose protagonist is caught between the poisonous old order of the rotten swamp and the soulless new order of the cities, was produced as part of the annual University of London Drama Festival in 1958. Another play, *The Invention*, a satire in which an accidental missile explosion eliminates dark pigment (and thus racial barriers) in Africa, was put on as part of a Sunday night production at the Royal Court Theatre in November 1959.

Soyinka's reputation was not limited to London, however; in February 1959 *The Swamp Dwellers* and *The Lion and the Jewel* were both produced at the Arts Theatre in Ibadan to enthusiastic audiences. He received a research grant from the Rockefeller Foundation to study African traditional drama in 1960–62, during which time he was attached to the English Department of the University of Ibadan. Traveling around the country, Soyinka was able to study the extended dramatic structure of the religious rituals and festival performances that embody so much of Nigerian folklore. Harvest festivals, initiation ceremonies, rites for the dead: all involved community participation in highly structured rituals that extended over days or weeks at a time, and used music, dance, masquerade, and symbolic acts to link the living with unseen forces. Not only the themes but also the dramatic structure of these ceremonial spectacles reappears in Soyinka's plays: his use of masquerade, of the symbolic ceremonial gesture, of the play within a play, of song and dance conveying mood and meaning in addition to words. Even more than usual, these plays require performance: in Soyinka's term, they represent a "total artwork" employing many media and ultimately involve the whole community as they act out issues important to all.

In Ibadan, a student group performed a one-act farce which would become one of Soyinka's most popular plays: *The Trials of Brother Jero*, a satire on the Bar Beach sects at Lagos and the story of a religious charlatan whose survival instincts and ingenious imagination enable him to outwit inconvenient disciples and creditors at the same time. The playwright also formed an acting company, "The 1960 Masks," which presented *A Dance of the Forests* in 1960 with the author taking the role of the Forest Father. *A Dance of the Forests*, a complex spectacle interweaving singing, dancing, and masquerade, was staged during the celebration of Nigerian independence, and in some ways may be seen as a lesson to the country in the confrontation of past with present. Answering the bidding of the contemporary Gathering of the Tribes, which wishes to establish links with its glorious past, a dead soldier and his wife come forward to meet four mortals who—in a previous life—were tied to the dead couple in violence and blood. The action takes place in the depths of the forest (recalling Shakespeare's *As You Like It* or *Midsummer Night's Dream*), presided over by the deities Osanyin, Ogun, and Eshuoro, and it ends with two of the mortals shaken and recognizing their crimes.

Soyinka became Lecturer in English at the University of Ife in 1962, but he resigned with other faculty in 1963 in protest against a proclaimed State of Emergency that imprisoned the Western Nigerian Chief Awolowo. Until taking up a position as Senior Lecturer at the University of Lagos in 1965, he devoted himself to social protest and to developing a Nigerian theater. He wrote for and acted in a highly popular satirical revue, *The Republican*, had part of a new play, *The Strong Breed*, performed on the radio, and founded the Orisun Theatre (a professional acting company, as opposed to the largely-amateur "1960 Masks") in 1964. In 1965, after a disputed election, Soyinka was briefly arrested for having substituted a satirical tape for the broadcast of Chief Akintola's victory speech; he was acquitted for lack of evidence. The same year brought his first novel *(The Interpreters)*, the production of two major plays *(Kongi's Harvest* and *The Road)*, and a new position as Senior Lecturer at the University of Lagos. Two years later, shortly before he was to take up the position of Chairman of the Drama Department at the University of Ibadan, he was arrested and imprisoned on suspicion of aiding Biafran rebels. From August 1967 to October 1969 (with fifteen months in solitary confinement), Soyinka was kept incommunicado by a government that hoped to repress his rebellious voice; the record of this imprisonment appears in the autobiographical *The Man Died* (1972).

Both before and after his imprisonment, Soyinka's work portrays the efforts of individuals to find their way inside an often-corrupt society caught by the clash of old and new values. Death (and the hope of rebirth) is a central reference point throughout, whether the death of a visionary, sacrificial figure (like Eman the scapegoat in *The Strong Breed*), death in political upheaval (the victims of the dictator Kongi in *Kongi's Harvest*), or the many versions of death in *The Road*.

Death accompanies thinly veiled references to corrupt power struggles on the contemporary political scene. In *Kongi's Harvest*, the old order of king Oba Danlola and his heir Daodu struggle against the new order of dictator Kongi. In *Madmen and Specialists* (1970), society is governed by Dr. Bero, a cannibal specialist in blood and destruction who worships the incomprehensible god As. Soyinka adapted Euripides' *Bacchae* (1973) to include a society of chained slaves who are ritual scapegoats until the ruler Pentheus accepts that role for himself. In *Death and the King's Horseman*, the lonely protagonist Elesin fails to achieve the ritual death that would guarantee traditional values. *Opera Wonyosi* (1977), a murderous comedy modeled on Bertolt Brecht and Kurt Weill's *Three-Penny Opera*, attacks the "oil-booming society of the seventies" with its institutionalized corruption and public executions, and ends with a satire of the gaudy coronation of Jean-Bedel Bokassa as Emperor of the Central African Empire.

Yet all is not death and seriousness. A recent autobiography of his childhood, *Ake* (1981) is filled with humor, and there is a rich vein of fantastic comedy stretching from the earliest farces to the absurdist scenes of social folly in later, more bitter plays. Soyinka's early comedy, *The Lion and the Jewel*, prefigures in a lighthearted manner the cultural themes developed more somberly later on, and employs at the same time the whole range of verbal play, dramatic tension, spectacle and masquerade that typifies the author's dramatic art.

A farcical tone is set from the beginning, as the schoolteacher Lakunle whacks the schoolboys admiring Sidi and spills water on himself when he tries to carry her bucket. Lakunle's imitation of European manners does not fit him any better than his too-small suit, and he is a figure of fun for Sidi and the others as he tries to persuade this "race of savages" to renounce barbarism for a "civilized" life with ballroom dancing, cocktail parties, "breakable plates," and above all no bride-price for the groom to pay. It is impossible to take the schoolteacher seriously, for the snobbery and self-interest of his zeal for "European" culture are perennially evident, and only emphasized by the incongruous examples and flowery rhetoric that he employs when trying to impress Sidi.

Opposed to Lakunle's mania for European progress are the old customs and values represented by Sidi, the village beauty, and the Bale (Chief) Baroka. Within this framework of old and new values, traditional comic themes are set in motion: the competition of two tricksters as to who will outsmart the other, the battle of the sexes, and the competition of two suitors, two generations, and two rivals for power. In this sense, *The Lion and the Jewel* recalls medieval European farce with its joyful manipulation of trickery, seduction, and a combative opposition of the sexes. It is the game that is important, rather than psychological depth or individual characters, and the Old Fox Baroka—the Lion of Ilujinle—wins in the end because he is more clever and foresighted than his opponents. Baroka is the master trickster, able not only to set traps and predict the reaction of his opponents, but also to use his opponent's weapons better than anyone else. The chief wins, in fact, because he can handle language much better than Lakunle.

In contrast to the schoolteacher's mixed metaphors and choppy logic, he overwhelms Sidi with a gradually developing argument and sequence of poetic images calculated to appeal on many levels: to Sidi's vanity and her fascination with modernity (the stamp machine), and to her respect for the traditional values of the village. When Baroka innocently pictures a meeting of souls, and then an abstract union of youth and experience, or beauty and wisdom, Sidi's own project of tricking and tantalizing him is forgotten and the Bale's seductive rhetoric accomplishes its aim.

Stage play and "body language" play an important part in *The Lion and the Jewel*. Dialogue pauses for song and dance on several occasions, or for a mime such as the one reconstructing the photographer's arrival in the village. These are not artificial interruptions; the photographer's mime, for example, is part of an ebullient celebration of Sidi's joy at her newfound fame. It also displays Lakunle's two sides (his initial civilized scorn and subsequent enthusiasm, pinching the girls), and is fused again with the "real" plot when the Bale arrives coincidentally to play his own part in the play-within-a-play. The wrestling match enacts a preliminary seduction through body language as the Bale displays his physical strength while simultaneously sparring verbally with Sidi. Staging *The Lion and the Jewel* requires visual, musical, and choreographic imagination; like all Soyinka's theater, it is spectacle as well as drama, and here an expression of true carnival spirit.

Eldred D. Jones's *The Writing of Wole Soyinka* (1973) is a good study of Soyinka's work through *Madmen and Specialists*, with a brief section on cultural background. James Gibbs's *Critical Perspectives on Wole Soyinka* (1980) is a valuable collection of essays on work through *Death and the King's Horseman*; included are discussions of Yoruba traditions, of Soyinka's early writings, contemporary reviews, and a brief general introduction offering biographical information. Gerald Moore's *Wole Soyinka* (1971) is an early biography covering the time up to Soyinka's arrest.

The Lion and the Jewel

Characters

SIDI, *the Village Belle*	A WRESTLER
LAKUNLE, *Schoolteacher*	A SURVEYOR
BAROKA, *the "Bale" of Ilujinle*	SCHOOLBOYS
SADIKU, *his head wife*	ATTENDANTS ON THE "BALE"
THE FAVOURITE	*Musicians, Dancers, Mummers,*
VILLAGE GIRLS	*Prisoners, Traders, the* VILLAGE.

Morning

A clearing on the edge of the market, dominated by an immense "odan"[1] tree. It is the village centre. The wall of the bush school

---

1. A variety of fig planted as a shade tree.

*flanks the stage on the right, and a rude window opens on to
the stage from the wall. There is a chant of the "Arithmetic
Times" issuing from this window. It begins a short while before
the action begins. Sidi enters from left, carrying a small pail of
water on her head. She is a slim girl with plaited hair. A true
village belle. She balances the pail on her head with accustomed ease. Around her is wrapped the familiar broad cloth
which is folded just above her breasts, leaving the shoulders
bare.*

*Almost as soon as she appears on the stage, the schoolmaster's
face also appears at the window. (The chanting continues—
"Three times two are six," "Three times three are nine," etc.)
The teacher Lakunle disappears. He is replaced by two of his
pupils, aged roughly eleven, who make a buzzing noise at Sidi,
repeatedly clapping their hands across the mouth. Lakunle now
reappears below the window and makes for Sidi, stopping only
to give the boys admonitory whacks on the head before they can
duck. They vanish with a howl and he shuts the window on
them. The chanting dies away. The schoolmaster is nearly twenty-
three. He is dressed in an old-style English suit, threadbare but
not ragged, clean but not ironed, obviously a size or two too
small. His tie is done in a very small knot, disappearing beneath
a shiny black waistcoat. He wears twenty-three-inch-bottom
trousers, and blanco-white tennis shoes.*

LAKUNLE: Let me take it.

SIDI: No.

LAKUNLE: Let me. [*Seizes the pail. Some water spills on him.*]

SIDI: [*delighted.*]
    There. Wet for your pains.
    Have you no shame?

LAKUNLE: That is what the stewpot said to the fire.
    Have you no shame—at your age
    Licking my bottom? But she was tickled
    Just the same.

SIDI: The school teacher is full of stories
    This morning. And now, if the lesson
    Is over, may I have the pail?

LAKUNLE: No. I have told you not to carry loads
    On your head. But you are as stubborn
    As an illiterate goat. It is bad for the spine.
    And it shortens your neck, so that very soon
    You will have no neck at all. Do you wish to look
    Squashed like my pupils' drawings?

SIDI: Why should that worry me? Haven't you sworn
    That my looks do not affect your love?

Yesterday, dragging your knees in the dust
You said, Sidi, if you were crooked or fat,
And your skin was scaly like a . . .

LAKUNLE: Stop!

SIDI: I only repeat what you said.

LAKUNLE: Yes, and I will stand by every word I spoke.
But must you throw away your neck on that account?
Sidi, it is so unwomanly. Only spiders
Carry loads the way you do.

SIDI: [*huffily, exposing the neck to advantage.*]
Well, it is my neck, not your spider.

LAKUNLE: [*looks, and gets suddenly agitated.*]
And look at that! Look, look at that!
[*Makes a general sweep in the direction of her breasts.*]
Who was it talked of shame just now?
How often must I tell you, Sidi, that
A grown-up girl must cover up her . . .
Her . . . shoulders? I can see quite . . . quite
A good portion of—that! And so I imagine
Can every man in the village. Idlers
All of them, good-for-nothing shameless men
Casting their lustful eyes where
They have no business . . .

SIDI: Are you at that again? Why, I've done the fold
So high and so tight, I can hardly breathe.
And all because you keep at me so much.
I have to leave my arms so I can use them . . .
Or don't you know that?

LAKUNLE: You could wear something.
Most modest women do. But you, no.
You must run about naked in the streets.
Does it not worry you . . . the bad names,
The lewd jokes, the tongue-licking noises
Which girls, uncovered like you,
Draw after them?

SIDI: This is too much. Is it you, Lakunle,
Telling me that I make myself common talk?
When the whole world knows of the madman
Of Ilujinle, who calls himself a teacher!
Is it Sidi who makes the men choke
In their cups, or you, with your big loud words
And no meaning? You and your ragged books
Dragging your feet to every threshold
And rushing them out again as curses
Greet you instead of welcome. Is it Sidi

They call a fool—even the children—
Or you with your fine airs and little sense!

LAKUNLE: [*first indignant, then recovers composure.*]
For that, what is a jewel to pigs?
If now I am misunderstood by you
And your race of savages, I rise above taunts
And remain unruffled.

SIDI: [*furious, shakes both fists at him.*]
O . . . oh, you make me want to pulp your brain.

LAKUNLE: [*retreats a little, but puts her aside with a very lofty gesture.*]
A natural feeling, arising out of envy;
For, as a woman, you have a smaller brain
Than mine.

SIDI: [*madder still.*]
Again! I'd like to know
Just what gives you these thoughts
Of manly conceit.

LAKUNLE: [*very very, patronizing.*]
No, no. I have fallen for that trick before.
You can no longer draw me into arguments
Which go above your head.

SIDI: [*can't find the right words, chokes back.*]
Give me the pail now. And if you ever dare
To stop me in the streets again . . .

LAKUNLE: Now, now, Sidi . . .

SIDI: Give it or I'll . . .

LAKUNLE: [*holds on to her.*]
Please, don't be angry with me.
I didn't mean you in particular.
And anyway, it isn't what I say.
The scientists have proved it. It's in my books.
Women have a smaller brain than men
That's why they are called the weaker sex.

SIDI: [*throws him off.*]
The weaker sex, is it?
Is it a weaker breed who pounds the yam
Or bends all day to plant the millet
With a child strapped to her back?

LAKUNLE: That is all part of what I say.
But don't you worry. In a year or two
You will have machines which will do
Your pounding, which will grind your pepper
Without it getting in your eyes.

SIDI: O-oh. You really mean to turn

The whole world upside down.

LAKUNLE: The world? Oh, that. Well, maybe later.
　　Charity, they say, begins at home.
　　For now, it is this village I shall turn
　　Inside out. Beginning with that crafty rogue,
　　Your past master of self-indulgence—Baroka.

SIDI: Are you still on about the Bale?[2]
　　What has he done to you?

LAKUNLE: He'll find out. Soon enough, I'll let him know.

SIDI: These thoughts of future wonders—do you buy them
　　Or merely go mad and dream of them?

LAKUNLE: A prophet has honour except
　　In his own home. Wise men have been called mad
　　Before me and after, many more shall be
　　So abused. But to answer you, the measure
　　Is not entirely of my own coinage.
　　What I boast is known in Lagos,[3] that city
　　Of magic, in Badagry where Saro women bathe
　　In gold, even in smaller towns less than
　　Twelve miles from here . . .

SIDI: Well go there. Go to these places where
　　Women would understand you
　　If you told them of your plans with which
　　You oppress me daily. Do you not know
　　What name they give you here?
　　Have you lost shame completely that jeers
　　Pass you over.

LAKUNLE: No. I have told you no. Shame belongs
　　Only to the ignorant.

SIDI: Well, I am going.
　　Shall I take the pail or not?

LAKUNLE: Not till you swear to marry me.
　　　[*Takes her hand, instantly soulful.*]
　　Sidi, a man must prepare to fight alone.
　　But it helps if he has a woman
　　To stand by him, a woman who . . .
　　Can understand . . . like you.

SIDI: I do?

LAKUNLE: Sidi, my love will open your mind
　　Like the chaste leaf in the morning, when
　　The sun first touches it.

SIDI: If you start that I will run away.

---

2. Chief of a town.　　3. Capital city of Nigeria. *Badagry* is a large town in southwest Nigeria. The *Saro* are a population group (originally emancipated slaves returned from Sierra Leone) close to Europeans in education and life-style.

I had enough of that nonsense yesterday.

LAKUNLE: Nonsense? Nonsense? Do you hear?
Does anybody listen? Can the stones
Bear to listen to this? Do you call it
Nonsense that I poured the waters of my soul
To wash your feet?

SIDI: You did what!

LAKUNLE: Wasted! Wasted! Sidi, my heart
Bursts into flowers with my love.
But you, you and the dead of this village
Trample it with feet of ignorance.

SIDI: [shakes her head in bafflement.]
If the snail finds splinters in his shell
He changes house. Why do you stay?

LAKUNLE: Faith. Because I have faith.
Oh Sidi, vow to me your own undying love
And I will scorn the jibes of these bush minds
Who know no better. Swear, Sidi,
Swear you will be my wife and I will
Stand against earth, heaven, and the nine
Hells . . .

SIDI: Now there you go again.
One little thing
And you must chirrup like a cockatoo.
You talk and talk and deafen me
With words which always sound the same
And make no meaning.
I've told you, and I say it again
I shall marry you today, next week
Or any day you name.
But my bride-price[4] must first be paid.
Aha, now you turn away.
But I tell you, Lakunle, I must have
The full bride-price. Will you make me
A laughing-stock? Well, do as you please.
But Sidi will not make herself
A cheap bowl for the village spit.

LAKUNLE: On my head let fall their scorn.

SIDI: They will say I was no virgin
That I was forced to sell my shame
And marry you without a price.

LAKUNLE: A savage custom, barbaric, out-dated,
Rejected, denounced, accursed,

---

4. The amount paid to her family for the bride; a large bride-price is a symbol of status.

Excommunicated, archaic, degrading,
Humiliating, unspeakable, redundant.
Retrogressive, remarkable, unpalatable.

SIDI: Is the bag empty? Why did you stop?

LAKUNLE: I own only the Shorter Companion
Dictionary, but I have ordered
The Longer One—you wait!

SIDI: Just pay the price.

LAKUNLE: [*with a sudden shout.*]
An ignoble custom, infamous, ignominious
Shaming our heritage before the world.
Sidi, I do not seek a wife
To fetch and carry,
To cook and scrub,
To bring forth children by the gross . . .

SIDI: Heaven forgive you! Do you now scorn
Child-bearing in a wife?

LAKUNLE: Of course I do not. I only mean . . .
Oh Sidi, I want to wed
Because I love,
I seek a life-companion . . .
[*pulpit-declamatory.*]
"And the man shall take the woman
And the two shall be together
As one flesh."[5]
Sidi, I seek a friend in need.
An equal partner in my race of life.

SIDI: [*attentive no more. Deeply engrossed in counting the beads on
her neck.*]
Then pay the price.

LAKUNLE: Ignorant girl, can you not understand?
To pay the price would be
To buy a heifer off the market stall.
You'd be my chattel, my mere property.
No, Sidi! [*very tenderly.*]
When we are wed, you shall not walk or sit
Tethered, as it were, to my dirtied heels.
Together we shall sit at table
—Not on the floor—and eat,
Not with fingers, but with knives
And forks, and breakable plates
Like civilized beings.
I will not have you wait on me

5. Genesis 2:24.

Till I have dined my fill.
No wife of mine, no lawful wedded wife
Shall eat the leavings off my plate—
That is for the children.
I want to walk beside you in the street,
Side by side and arm in arm
Just like the Lagos couples I have seen
High-heeled shoes for the lady, red paint
On her lips. And her hair is stretched
Like a magazine photo. I will teach you
The waltz and we'll both learn the foxtrot
And we'll spend the week-end in night-clubs at Ibadan.[6]
Oh I must show you the grandeur of towns
We'll live there if you like or merely pay visits.
So choose. Be a modern wife, look me in the eye
And give me a little kiss—like this.
  [*Kisses her.*]

SIDI: [*backs away.*]
No, don't! I tell you I dislike
This strange unhealthy mouthing you perform.
Every time, your action deceives me
Making me think that you merely wish
To whisper something in my ear.
Then comes this licking of my lips with yours.
It's so unclean. And then,
The sound you make—'Pyout!'
Are you being rude to me?

LAKUNLE: [*wearily.*] It's nevery any use.
Bush-girl you are, bush-girl you'll always be;
Uncivilized and primitive—bush-girl!
I kissed you as all educated men—
And Christians—kiss their wives.
It is the way of civilized romance.

SIDI: [*lightly.*] A way you mean, to avoid
Payment of lawful bride-price
A cheating way, mean and miserly.

LAKUNLE: [*violently.*] It is not.
  [SIDI *bursts out laughing.* LAKUNLE *changes his tone to a soulful one, both eyes dreamily shut.*]
Romance is the sweetening of the soul
With fragrance offered by the stricken heart.

SIDI: [*looks at him in wonder for a while.*]
Away with you. The village says you're mad,

---

6. A cosmopolitan city, the second largest in Nigeria and a major trade center.

And I begin to understand.
I wonder that they let you run the school.
You and your talk. You'll ruin your pupils too
And then they'll utter madness just like you.
    [*Noise off-stage.*]
There are people coming
Give me the bucket or they'll jeer.
    [*Enter a crowd of youths and drummers, the girls being in various stages of excitement.*]

FIRST GIRL: Sidi, he has returned. He came back just as he said he would.

SIDI: Who has?

FIRST GIRL: The stranger. The man from the outside world. The clown who fell in the river for you.
    [*They all burst out laughing.*]

SIDI: The one who rode on the devil's own horse?

SECOND GIRL: Yes, the same. The stranger with the one-eyed box.
    [*She demonstrates the action of a camera amidst admiring titters.*]

THIRD GIRL: And he brought his new horse right into the village square this time. This one has only two feet. You should have seen him. B-r-r-r-r.
    [*Runs around the platform driving an imaginary motor-bike.*]

SIDI: And has he brought . . . ?

FIRST GIRL: The images? He brought them all. There was hardly any part of the village which does not show in the book.
    [*Clicks the imaginary shutter.*]

SIDI: The book? Did you see the book?
Had he the precious book
That would bestow upon me
Beauty beyond the dreams of a goddess?
For so he said.
The book which would announce
This beauty to the world—
Have you seen it?

THIRD GIRL: Yes, yes, he did. But the Bale is still feasting his eyes on the images. Oh, Sidi, he was right. You *are* beautiful. On the cover of the book is an image of you from here [*touches the top of her head*] to here [*her stomach*]. And in the middle leaves, from the beginning of one leaf right across to the end of another, is one of you from head to toe. Do you remember it? It was the one for which he made you stretch your arms towards the sun. [*Rapturously.*] Oh, Sidi, you looked as if, at that moment, the sun himself had been your lover. [*They all gasp with pretended shock at this blasphemy and one slaps her playfully on the buttocks.*]

FIRST GIRL: The Bale is jealous, but he pretends to be proud of you.
And when this man tells him how famous you are in the capital,
he pretends to be pleased, saying how much honour and fame you
have brought to the village.

SIDI: [*with amazement.*] Is not Baroka's image in the book at all?

SECOND GIRL: [*contemptuous.*] Oh yes, it is. But it would have been
much better for the Bale if the stranger had omitted him altogether. His image is in a little corner somewhere in the book, and
even that corner he shares with one of the village latrines.

SIDI: Is that the truth? Swear! Ask Ogun[7] to
Strike you dead.

GIRL: Ogun strike me dead if I lie.

SIDI: If that is true, then I am more esteemed
Than Bale Baroka,
The Lion of Ilujinle.
This means that I am greater than
The Fox of the Undergrowth,
The living god among men . . .

LAKUNLE: [*peevishly.*] And devil among women.

SIDI: Be silent, you.
You are merely filled with spite.

LAKUNLE: I know him what he is. This is
Divine justice that a mere woman
Should outstrip him in the end.

SIDI: Be quiet;
Or I swear I'll never speak to you again.
    [*Affects sudden coyness.*]
In fact, I am not so sure I'll want to wed you now.

LAKUNLE: Sidi!

SIDI: Well, why should I?
Known as I am to the whole wide world,
I would demean my worth to wed
A mere village school teacher.

LAKUNLE: [*in agony.*] Sidi!

SIDI: And one who is too mean
To pay the bride-price like a man.

LAKUNLE: Oh, Sidi, don't!

SIDI: [*plunging into an enjoyment of* LAKUNLE'S *misery.*]
Well, don't you know?
Sidi is more important even than the Bale.
More famous than that panther of the trees.
He is beneath me now—
Your fearless rake, the scourge of womanhood!

7. God of iron, war, and craftsmanship.

But now,
He shares the corner of the leaf
With the lowest of the low—
With the dug-out village latrine!
While I—How many leaves did my own image take?
FIRST GIRL: Two in the middle and . . .
SIDI: No, no. Let the school teacher count!
How many were there, teacher-man?
LAKUNLE: Three leaves.
SIDI: [*threateningly.*] One leaf for every heart that I shall break.
Beware!
[*Leaps suddenly into the air.*]
Hurray! I'm beautiful!
Hurray for the wandering stranger!
CROWD: Hurray for the Lagos man!
SIDI: [*wildly excited.*] I know. Let us dance the dance of the lost
Traveller.
SHOUTS: Yes, let's.
SIDI: Who will dance the devil-horse?
You, you, you and you.
[*The four girls fall out.*]
A python. Who will dance the snake?
Ha ha! Your eyes are shifty and your ways are sly.
[*The selected youth is pushed out amidst jeers.*]
The stranger. We've got to have the being
From the mad outer world . . . You there,
No, you have never felt the surge
Of burning liquor in your milky veins.
Who can we pick that knows the walk of drunks?
You? . . . No, the thought itself
Would knock you out as sure as wine . . . Ah!
[*Turns round slowly to where* LAKUNLE *is standing with a kindly, fatherly smile for the children at play.*]
Come on book-worm, you'll play his part.
LAKUNLE: No, no. I've never been drunk in all my life.
SIDI: We know. But your father drank so much,
He must have drunk your share, and that
Of his great grandsons.
LAKUNLE: [*tries to escape.*] I won't take part.
SIDI: You must.
LAKUNLE: I cannot stay. It's nearly time to take
Primary four in Geography.
SIDI: [*goes over to the window and throws it open.*]
Did you think your pupils would remain in school
Now that the stranger has returned?

The village is on holiday, you fool.

LAKUNLE: [*as they drag him towards the platform.*]

No, no. I won't. This foolery bores me.

It is a game of idiots. I have work of more importance.

SIDI: [*bending down over* LAKUNLE *who has been seated forcibly on the platform.*]

You are dressed like him
You look like him
You speak his tongue
You think like him
You're just as clumsy
In your Lagos ways—
You'll do for him!

[*This chant is taken up by all and they begin to dance round* LAKUNLE, *speaking the words in a fast rhythm. The drummers join in after the first time, keeping up a steady beat as the others whirl round their victim. They go faster and faster and chant faster and faster with each round. By the sixth or seventh,* LAKUNLE *has obviously had enough.*]

LAKUNLE: [*raising his voice above the din.*] All right! I'll do it.

Come now, let's get it over with.

[*A terrific shout and a clap of drums.* LAKUNLE *enters into the spirit of the dance with enthusiasm. He takes over from* SIDI, *stations his cast all over the stage as the jungle, leaves the right top-stage clear for the four girls who are to dance the motor-car. A mime follows of the visitor's entry into Ilujinle, and his short stay among the villagers. The four girls crouch on the floor, as four wheels of a car.* LAKUNLE *directs their spacing, then takes his place in the middle, and sits on air. He alone does not dance. He does realistic miming. Soft throbbing drums, gradually swelling in volume, and the four "wheels" begin to rotate the upper halves of their bodies in perpendicular circles.* LAKUNLE *clowning the driving motions, obviously enjoying this fully. The drums gain tempo, faster, faster, faster. A sudden crash of drums and the girls quiver and dance the stall. Another effort at rhythm fails, and the "stalling wheels" give a corresponding shudder, finally, and let their faces fall on to their laps.* LAKUNLE *tampers with a number of controls, climbs out of the car and looks underneath it. His lips indicate that he is swearing violently. Examines the wheels, pressing them to test the pressure, betrays the devil in him by seizing his chance to pinch the girls' bottoms. One yells and bites him on the ankle. He climbs hurriedly back into the car, makes a final attempt to re-start it, gives it up and decides to abandon it. Picks up his camera and his helmet, pockets a flask of whisky from which he takes a swig,*

*before beginning the trek. The drums resume beating, a differ-
ent, darker tone and rhythm, varying with the journey. Full use
of "gangan" and "iya ilu."*[8] *The "trees" perform a subdued and
unobtrusive dance on the same spot. Details as a snake slithering out of the branches and poising over* LAKUNLE*'s head when
he leans against a tree for a rest. He flees, restoring his nerves
shortly after by a swig. A monkey drops suddenly in his path
and gibbers at him before scampering off. A roar comes from
somewhere, etc. His nerves go rapidly and he recuperates himself by copious draughts. He is soon tipsy, battles violently with
the undergrowth and curses silently as he swats the flies off his
tortured body.
Suddenly, from somewhere in the bush comes the sound of a
girl singing. The Traveller shakes his head but the sound persists. Convinced he is suffering from sun-stroke, he drinks again.
His last drop, so he tosses the bottle in the direction of the
sound, only to be rewarded by a splash, a scream and a torrent
of abuse, and finally, silence again. He tip-toes, clears away the
obstructing growth, blinks hard and rubs his eyes. Whatever he
has seen still remains. He whistles softly, unhitches his camera
and begins to jockey himself into a good position for a take.
Backwards and forwards, and his eyes are so closely glued to the
lens that he puts forward a careless foot and disappears completely. There is a loud splash and the invisible singer alters her
next tone to a sustained scream. Quickened rhythm and shortly
afterwards, amidst sounds of splashes,* SIDI *appears on the stage,
with a piece of cloth only partially covering her.* LAKUNLE *follows a little later, more slowly, trying to wring out the water
from his clothes. He has lost all his appendages except the camera.*
SIDI *has run right across the stage, and returns a short while
later, accompanied by the Villagers. The same cast has disappeared and re-forms behind* SIDI *as the Villagers. They are in
an ugly mood, and in spite of his protests, haul him off to the
town centre, in front of the "Odan" tree.
Everything comes to a sudden stop as* BAROKA *the Bale, wiry,
goateed, tougher than his sixty-two years, himself emerges at
this point from behind the tree. All go down, prostrate or kneeling with the greetings of "Kabiyesi" "Baba,"*[9] *etc. All except*
LAKUNLE *who begins to sneak off.*]

BAROKA: Akowe.[1] Teacher wa. Misita Lakunle.

[*As the others take up the cry "Misita Lakunle" he is forced to*

---

8. Different types of drum.   9. "Kabiyesi," "Your highness," is used in addressing the ruler;
"Baba" is a term of respect for an older man. Both are customary greetings to the Bale, who
responds by calling his people "my children."   1. "Akowe," contraction of "Alakowe," teacher
or (literally) "person who can write." Baroka comments that the teacher replaces the customary
offer of a drink with "Good morning," which won't wet anyone's throat.

stop. He returns and bows deeply from the waist.]

LAKUNLE: A good morning to you sir.

BAROKA: Guru morin guru morin, ngh-hn! That is
  All we get from "alakowe." You call at his house
  Hoping he sends for beer, but all you get is
  Guru morin. Will guru morin wet my throat?
  Well, well our man of knowledge, I hope you have no
  Query for an old man today.

LAKUNLE: No complaints.

BAROKA: And we are not feuding in something
  I have forgotten.

LAKUNLE: Feuding sir? I see no cause at all.

BAROKA: Well, the play was much alive until I came.
  And now everything stops, and you were leaving
  Us. After all, I knew the story and I came in
  Right on cue. It makes me feel as if I was
  Chief Baseje.[2]

LAKUNLE: One hardly thinks the Bale would have the time
  For such childish nonsense.

BAROKA: A-ah Mister Lakunle. Without these things you call
  Nonsense, a Bale's life would be pretty dull.
  Well, now that you say I am welcome, shall we
  Resume your play?
    [*Turns suddenly to his attendants.*]
  Seize him!

LAKUNLE: [*momentarily baffled.*] What for? What have I done?

BAROKA: You tried to steal our village maidenhead
  Have you forgotten: If he has, serve him a slap
  To wake his brain.
    [*An uplifted arm being proffered,* LAKUNLE *quickly recollects
    and nods his head vigorously. So the play is back in perfor-
    mance. The Villagers gather round threatening, clamouring for
    his blood.* LAKUNLE *tries bluff, indignation, appeasement in turn.
    At a sudden signal from the Bale, they throw him down pros-
    trate on his face. Only then does the Chief begin to show him
    sympathy, appear to understand the Stranger's plight, and pacify
    the villagers on his behalf. He orders dry clothes for him, seats
    him on his right and orders a feast in his honour. The Stranger
    springs up every second to take photographs of the party, but
    most of the time his attention is fixed on* SIDI *dancing with
    abandon. Eventually he whispers to the Chief, who nods in
    consent, and* SIDI *is sent for. The Stranger arranges* SIDI *in all
    sorts of magazine postures and takes innumerable photographs*]

2. *Baseje* means someone who upsets a party or feast; a chief is expected to be a good organizer of feasts but "Chief Baseje" spoils the party.

of her. Drinks are pressed upon him; he refuses at first, even-
tually tries the local brew with skepticism, appears to relish it,
and drinks profusely. Before long, however, he leaves the party
to be sick. They clap him on the back as he goes out, and two
drummers who insist on dancing round him nearly cause the
calamity to happen on the spot. However, he rushes out with
his hand held to the mouth. LAKUNLE*'s exit seems to signify the*
end of the mime. He returns almost at once and the others
discard their roles.]

SIDI: [*delightedly.*] What did I say? You played him to the bone,
A court jester would have been the life for you,
Instead of school.
　[*Points contemptuously to the school.*]

BAROKA: And where would the village be, robbed of
Such wisdom as Mister Lakunle dispenses
Daily? Who would tell us where we go wrong?
Eh, Mister Lakunle?

SIDI: [*hardly listening, still in the full grip of her excitement.*]
Who comes with me to find the man?
But Lakunle, you'll have to come and find sense
In his clipping tongue. You see book-man
We cannot really do
Without your head.
　[LAKUNLE *begins to protest, but they crowd him and try to bear*
　him down. Suddenly he breaks free and takes to his heels with
　all the women in full pursuit. BAROKA *is left sitting by himself—*
　his wrestler, who accompanied him on his entry, stands a
　respectful distance away—staring at the flock of women in flight.
　From the folds of his agbada[3] he brings out his copy of the
　magazine and admires the heroine of the publication. Nods
　slowly to himself.]

BAROKA: Yes, yes . . . it is five full months since last
I took a wife . . . five full months . . .

　　　　　　　　　　Noon

A road by the market. Enter SIDI, *happily engrossed in the pic-*
tures of herself in the magazine. LAKUNLE *follows one or two*
paces behind carrying a bundle of firewood which SIDI *has set*
out to obtain. They are met in the centre by SADIKU, *who has*
entered from the opposite side. SADIKU *is an old woman, with a*
shawl over her head.

---

3. A long robe.

SADIKU: Fortune is with me. I was going to your house to see you.

SIDI: [*startled out of her occupation.*] What! Oh, it is you, Sadiku.

SADIKU: The Lion sent me. He wishes you well.

SIDI: Thank him for me.

    [*Then excitedly.*]

  Have you seen these?

  Have you seen these images of me

  Wrought by the man from the capital city?

  Have you felt the gloss? [*Caresses the page.*]

  Smoother by far than the parrot's breast.

SADIKU: I have. I have. I saw them as soon as the city man came . . .

  Sidi, I bring a message from my lord. [*Jerks her head at* LAKUNLE.]

  Shall we draw aside a little?

SIDI: Him? Pay no more heed to that

  Than you would a eunuch.

SADIKU: Then, in as few words as it takes to tell, Baroka wants you

  for a wife.

LAKUNLE: [*bounds forward, dropping the wood.*]

  What! The greedy dog!

  Insatiate camel of a foolish, doting race;

  Is he at his tricks again?

SIDI: Be quiet, 'Kunle. You get so tiresome.

  The message is for me, not you.

LAKUNLE: [*down on his knees at once. Covers* SIDI's *hands with kisses.*]

  My Ruth, my Rachel, Esther, Bathsheba[4]

  Thou sum of fabled perfections

  From Genesis to the Revelations

  Listen not to the voice of this infidel . . .

SIDI: [*snatches her head away.*]

  Now that's your other game;

  Giving me funny names you pick up

  In your wretched books.

  My name is Sidi. And now, let me be.

  My name is Sidi, and I am beautiful.

  The stranger took my beauty

  And placed it in my hands.

  Here, here it is. I need no funny names

  To tell me of my fame.

  Loveliness beyond the jewels of a throne—

  That is what he said.

SADIKU: [*gleefully.*] Well, will you be Baroka's own jewel? Will you

  be his sweetest princess, soothing him on weary nights? What answer

  shall I give my lord?

SIDI: [*wags her finger playfully at the woman.*]

---

4. Fabled wives from the Old Testament.

Ha ha. Sadiku of the honey tongue.
Sadiku, head of the Lion's wives.
You'll make no prey of Sidi with your wooing tongue
Not this Sidi whose fame has spread to Lagos
And beyond the seas.

[LAKUNLE *beams with satisfaction and rises.*]

SADIKU: Sidi, have you considered what a life of bliss awaits you? Baroka swears to take no other wife after you. Do you know what it is to be the Bale's last wife? I'll tell you. When he dies—and that should not be long; even the Lion has to die sometime—well, when he does, it means that you will have the honour of being the senior wife of the new Bale. And just think, until Baroka dies, you shall be his favourite. No living in the outhouses for you, my girl. Your place will always be in the palace; first as the latest bride, and afterwards, as the head of the new harem . . . It is a rich life, Sidi. I know. I have been in that position for forty-one years.

SIDI: You waste your breath.
Why did Baroka not request my hand
Before the stranger
Brought his book of images?
Why did the Lion not bestow his gift
Before my face was lauded to the world?
Can you not see? Because he sees my worth
Increased and multiplied above his own;
Because he can already hear
The ballad-makers and their songs
In praise of Sidi, the incomparable,
While the Lion is forgotten.
He seeks to have me as his property
Where I must fade beneath his jealous hold.
Ah, Sadiku,
The school-man here has taught me certain things
And my images have taught me all the rest.
Baroka merely seeks to raise his manhood
Above my beauty
He seeks new fame
As the one man who has possessed
The jewel of Ilujinle!

SADIKU: [*shocked, bewildered, incapable of making any sense of* SIDI's *words.*] But Sidi, are you well? Such nonsense never passed your lips before. Did you not sound strange, even in your own hearing? [*Rushes suddenly at* LAKUNLE.] Is this your doing, you popinjay? Have you driven the poor girl mad at last? Such rubbish . . . I will beat your head for this!

LAKUNLE: [*retreating in panic.*] Keep away from me, old hag.

SIDI: Sadiku, let him be.
  Tell your lord that I can read his mind,
  That I will none of him.
  Look—judge for yourself.
      [*Opens the magazine and points out the pictures.*]
  He's old. I never knew till now,
  He was that old . . .
      [*During the rest of her speech,* SIDI *runs her hand over the*
      surface of the relevant part of the photographs, tracing the con-
      tours with her fingers.
      . . . To think I took
  No notice of my velvet skin.
  How smooth it is!
  And no man ever thought
  To praise the fullness of my breasts . . .
LAKUNLE: [*laden with guilt and full of apology.*]
  Well, Sidi, I did think . . .
  But somehow it was not the proper thing.
SIDI: [*ignores the interruption.*]
  See I hold them to the warm caress
      [*unconsciously pushes out her chest.*]
  Of a desire-filled sun.
      [*Smiles mischievously.*]
  There's a deceitful message in my eyes
  Beckoning insatiate men to certain doom.
  And teeth that flash the sign of happiness,
  Strong and evenly, beaming full of life.
  Be just, Sadiku,
  Compare my image and your lord's—
  An age of difference!
  See how the water glistens on my face
  Like the dew-moistened leaves on a Harmattan[5] morning
  But he—his face is like a leather piece
  Torn rudely from the saddle of his horse,
      [SADIKU *gasps.*]
  Sprinkled with the musty ashes
  From a pipe that is long over-smoked.
  And this goat-like tuft
  Which I once thought was manly;
  It is like scattered twists of grass—
  Not even green—
  But charred and lifeless, as after a forest fire!
  Sadiku, I am young and brimming; he is spent.

---

5. A dry, dusty wind that blows seasonally in Africa.

I am the twinkle of a jewel
But he is the hind-quarters of a lion!

SADIKU: [*recovering at last from helpless amazement.*] May Sango[6] restore your wits. For most surely some angry god has taken possession of you. [*Turns around and walks away. Stops again as she remembers something else.*] Your ranting put this clean out of my head. My lord says that if you would not be his wife, would you at least come to supper at his house tonight. There is a small feast in your honour. He wishes to tell you how happy he is that the great capital city has done so much honour to a daughter of Ilujinle. You have brought great fame to your people.

SIDI: Ho ho! Do you think that I was only born
Yesterday?
The tales of Baroka's little suppers,
I know all.
Tell your lord that Sidi does not sup with
Married men.

SADIKU: They are lies, lies. You must not believe everything you hear, Sidi, would I deceive you? I swear to you . . .

SIDI: Can you deny that
Every woman who has supped with him one night,
Becomes his wife or concubine the next.

LAKUNLE: Is it for nothing he is called the Fox?

SADIKU: [*advancing on him.*] You keep out of this, or so Sango be my witness . . .

LAKUNLE: [*retreats just a little, but continues to talk.*]
His wiliness is known even in the larger towns.
Did you never hear
Of how he foiled the Public Works attempt
To build the railway through Ilujinle.

SADIKU: Nobody knows the truth of that. It is all hearsay.

SIDI: I love hearsays. Lakunle, tell me all.

LAKUNLE: Did you not know it? Well sit down and listen.
My father told me, before he died. And few men
Know of this trick—oh he's a die-hard rogue
Sworn against our progress . . . yes . . . it was . . . somewhere here
The track should have been laid just along
The outskirts. Well, the workers came, in fact
It was prisoners who were brought to do
The harder part . . . to break the jungle's back . . .
[*Enter the prisoners, guarded by two warders. A white surveyor examines his map (khaki helmet, spats, etc.). The foreman runs*]

---

6. God of thunder and lightning.

up with his camp stool, table etc., erects the umbrella over him
and unpacks the usual box of bush comforts—soda siphon, whisky
bottle and geometric sandwiches. His map consulted, he directs
the sweat team where to work. They begin felling, hatchet
swinging, log dragging, all to the rhythm of the work gang's
metal percussion (rod on gong or rude triangle, etc.). The two
performers are also the song leaders and the others fill the chorus. "N'ijo itoro," "Amunda el'ebe l'aiya," "Gbe je on'ipa,"
etc.][7]

LAKUNLE: They marked the route with stakes, ate
   Through the jungle and began the tracks. Trade,
   Progress, adventure, success, civilization,
   Fame, international conspicuousity . . . it was
   All within the grasp of Ilujinle . . .
   [The wrestler enters, stands horrified at the sight and flees. Returns
   later with the Bale himself who soon assesses the situation. They
   disappear. The work continues, the surveyor occupies himself
   with the fly-whisk and whisky. Shortly after, a bull-roarer[8] is
   heard. The prisoners falter a little, pick up again. The bull-
   roarer continues on its way, nearer and farther, moving in circles, so that it appears to come from all round them. The foreman is the first to break and then the rest is chaos. Sole survivor
   of the rout is the surveyor who is too surprised to move.
   BAROKA enters a few minutes later accompanied by some attendants and preceded by a young girl bearing a calabash[9] bowl.
   The surveyor, angry and threatening, is prevailed upon to open
   his gift. From it he reveals a wad of pound notes and kola nuts.
   Mutual understanding is established. The surveyor frowns heavily,
   rubs his chin and consults his map. Re-examines the contents
   of the bowl, shakes his head. BAROKA adds more money, and a
   coop of hens. A goat follows, and more money. This time "truth"
   dawns on him at last, he has made a mistake. The track really
   should go the other way. What an unfortunate error, discovered
   just in time! No, no, no possibility of a mistake this time, the
   track should be much further away. In fact (scooping up the
   soil) the earth is most unsuitable, couldn't possibly support the
   weight of a railway engine. A gourd of palm wine is brought to
   seal the agreement and a kola nut is broken. Baroka's men help
   the surveyor pack and they leave with their arms round each
   other followed by the surveyor's booty.]

7. Fragments of a prisoners' song; such songs were usually sung during hard labor to ease the
work—"In the dance of itoro" (itoro is the name of a neighborhood); "Amuda [name] is a big
man"; "Keep the strong one cool."   8. A noisemaker made of a small wooden slat whirled on
a string.   9. A hard-shelled gourd dried, often carved, and used as a utensil. Kola nuts are the
seeds of the kola (cola) tree, containing caffeine oil and chewed as a stimulant; they are offered in
sign of hospitality.

LAKUNLE: [*as the last of the procession disappears, shakes his fist at them, stamping on the ground.*]
　Voluptuous beast! He loves this life too well
　To bear to part from it. And motor roads
　And railways would do just that, forcing
　Civilization at his door. He foresaw it
　And he barred the gates, securing fast
　His dogs and horses, his wives and all his
　Concubines . . . ah, yes . . . all those concubines
　Baroka has such a selective eye, none suits him
　But the best . . .
　　[*His eyes truly light up.* SIDI *and* SADIKU *snigger, tip-toe off stage.*]
　　. . . Yes, one must grant him that.
　Ah, I sometimes wish I led his kind of life.
　Such luscious bosoms make his nightly pillow.
　I am sure he keeps a time-table just as
　I do at school. Only way to ensure fair play.
　He must be healthy to keep going as he does.
　I don't know what the women see in him. His eyes
　Are small and always red with wine. He must
　Possess some secret . . . No! I do not envy him!
　Just the one woman for me. Alone I stand
　For progress, with Sidi my chosen soul-mate, the one
　Woman of my life . . . Sidi! Sidi where are you?
　　[*Rushes out after them, returns to fetch the discarded firewood and runs out again.*]

*

[BAROKA *in bed, naked except for baggy trousers, calf-length. It is a rich bedroom covered in animal skins and rugs. Weapons round the wall. Also a strange machine, a most peculiar contraption with a long lever. Kneeling beside the bed is Baroka's current Favourite, engaged in plucking the hairs from his armpit. She does this by first massaging the spot around the selected hair very gently with her forefinger. Then, with hardly a break, she pulls out the hair between her finger and the thumb with a sudden sharp movement.* BAROKA *twitches slightly with each pull. Then an aspirated "A-ah," and a look of complete beatitude spreads all over his face.*]

FAVOURITE: Do I improve my lord?
BAROKA: You are still somewhat over-gentle with the pull
　As if you feared to hurt the panther of the trees.
　Be sharp and sweet
　Like the swift sting of a vicious wasp

For there the pleasure lies—the cooling aftermath.

FAVOURITE: I'll learn, my lord.

BAROKA: You have not time, my dear.
Tonight I hope to take another wife.
And the honour of this task, you know,
Belongs by right to my latest choice.
But—A-ah—Now that was sharp.
It had in it the scorpion's sudden sting
Without its poison.
It was an angry pull; you tried to hurt
For I had made you wrathful with my boast.
But now your anger flows in my blood-stream.
How sweet it is! A-ah! That was sweeter still.
I think perhaps that I shall let you stay,
The sole out-puller of my sweat-bathed hairs.
Ach!
　　[*Sits up suddenly and rubs the sore point angrily.*]
　　　Now that had far more pain than pleasure
Vengeful creature, you did not caress
The area of extraction long enough!
　　[*Enter* SADIKU. *She goes down on her knees at once and bows
　　her head into her lap.*]
Aha! Here comes Sadiku.
Do you bring some balm,
To soothe the smart of my misused armpit?
Away, you enemy!
　　[*Exit the Favourite.*]

SADIKU: My lord . . .

BAROKA: You have my leave to speak.
What did she say?

SADIKU: She will not, my lord. I did my best, but she will have none
　of you.

BAROKA: It follows the pattern—a firm refusal
At the start. Why will she not?

SADIKU: That is the strange part of it. She says you're much too old.
　If you ask me, I think that she is really off her head. All this
　excitement of the books has been too much for her.

BAROKA: [*springs to his feet.*]
　She says . . . That I am old
　That I am much too old? Did a slight
　Unripened girl say this of me?

SADIKU: My lord, I heard the incredible words with my ears, and I
　thought the world was mad.

BAROKA: But is it possible, Sadiku? Is this right?
　Did I not, at the festival of Rain,

Defeat the men in the log-tossing match?
Do I not still with the most fearless ones,
Hunt the leopard and the boa at night
And save the farmers' goats from further harm?
And does she say I'm old?
Did I not, to announce the Harmattan,
Climb to the top of the silk-cotton tree,
Break the first pod, and scatter tasselled seeds
To the four winds—and this but yesterday?
Do any of my wives report
A failing in my manliness?
The strongest of them all
Still wearies long before the Lion does!
And so would she, had I the briefest chance
To teach this unfledged birdling
That lacks the wisdom to embrace
The rich mustiness of age . . . if I could once . . .
Come hither, soothe me, Sadiku
For I am wroth at heart.

> [*Lies back on the bed, staring up as before.* SADIKU *takes her place at the foot of the bed and begins to tickle the soles of his feet.* BAROKA *turns to the left suddenly, reaches down the side, and comes up with a copy of the magazine. Opens it and begins to study the pictures. He heaves a long sigh.*]

That is good, Sadiku, very good.

> [*He begins to compare some pictures in the book, obviously his own and Sidi's. Flings the book away suddenly and stares at the ceiling for a second or two. Then, unsmiling.*]

Perhaps it is as well, Sadiku.

SADIKU: My lord, what did you say?

BAROKA: Yes, faithful one, I say it is as well.
The scorn, the laughter and the jeers
Would have been bitter.
Had she consented and my purpose failed,
I would have sunk with shame.

SADIKU: My lord, I do not understand.

BAROKA: The time has come when I can fool myself
No more. I am no man, Sadiku. My manhood
Ended near a week ago.

SADIKU: The gods forbid.

BAROKA: I wanted Sidi because I still hoped—
A foolish thought I know, but still—I hoped
That, with a virgin young and hot within,
My failing strength would rise and save my pride.

> [SADIKU *begins to moan.*]

A waste of hope. I knew it even then.
But it's a human failing never to accept
The worst; and so I pandered to my vanity.
When manhood must, it ends.
The well of living, tapped beyond its depth,
Dries up, and mocks the wastrel in the end.
I am withered and unsapped, the joy
Of ballad-mongers, the aged butt
Of youth's ribaldry.

SADIKU: [*tearfully.*] The Gods must have mercy yet.

BAROKA: [*as if suddenly aware of her presence, starts up.*]
I have told this to no one but you,
Who are my eldest, my most faithful wife.
But if you dare parade my shame before the world . . .

> [SADIKU *shakes her head in protest and begins to stroke the soles
> of his feet with renewed tenderness.* BAROKA *sighs and falls back
> slowly.*]

How irritable I have grown of late
Such doubts to harbour of your loyalty . . .
But this disaster is too much for one
Checked thus as I upon the prime of youth.
That rains that blessed me from my birth
Number a meagre sixty-two;
While my grandfather, that man of teak,
Fathered two sons, late on sixty-five.
But Okiki, my father beat them all
Producing female twins at sixty-seven.
Why then must I, descendant of these lions
Forswear my wives at a youthful sixty-two
My veins of life run dry, my manhood gone!

> [*His voice goes drowsy;* SADIKU *sighs and moans and caresses his
> feet. His face lights up suddenly with rapture.*]

Sango bear witness! These weary feet
Have felt the loving hands of much design
In women.
My soles have felt the scratch of harsh,
Gravelled hands.
They have borne the heaviness of clumsy,
Gorilla paws.
And I have known the tease of tiny,
Dainty hands,
Toy-like hands that tantalized
My eager senses,
Promised of thrills to come
Remaining

Unfulfilled because the fingers
Were too frail
The touch too light and faint to pierce
The incredible thickness of my soles.
But thou Sadiku, thy plain unadorned hands
Encase a sweet sensuality which age
Will not destroy. A-ah,
Oyayi! Beyond a doubt Sadiku,
Thou art the queen of them all.
    [*Falls asleep.*]

Night

The village centre. SIDI *stands by the Schoolroom window, admiring her photos as before. Enter* SADIKU *with a longish bundle. She is very furtive. Unveils the object which turns out to be a carved figure of the Bale, naked and in full detail. She takes a good look at it, bursts suddenly into derisive laughter, sets the figure standing in front of the tree.* SIDI *stares in utter amazement.*

SADIKU: So we did for you too did we? We did for you in the end. Oh high and mighty lion, have we really scotched you? A—ya-ya-ya . . . we women undid you in the end. I was there when it happened to your father, the great Okiki. I did for him, I, the youngest and freshest of the wives. I killed him with my strength. I called him and he came at me, but no, for him, this was not like other times. I, Sadiku, was I not flame itself and he the flax on old women's spindles? I ate him up! Race of mighty lions, we always consume you, at our pleasure we spin you, at our whim we make you dance; like the foolish top you think the world revolves around you . . . fools! fools! . . . it is you who run giddy while we stand still and watch, and draw your frail thread from you, slowly, till nothing is left but a runty old stick. I scotched Okiki, Sadiku's unopened treasure-house demanded sacrifice, and Okiki came with his rusted key. Like a snake he came at me, like a rag he went back, a limp rag, smeared in shame. . . . [*Her ghoulish laugh re-possesses her.*] Ah, take warning my masters, we'll scotch you in the end . . . [*With a yell she leaps up, begins to dance round the tree, chanting.*]
Take warning, my masters
We'll scotch you in the end.
    [SIDI *shuts the window gently, comes out,* SADIKU *as she comes round again, gasps and is checked in mid-song.*]
SADIKU: Oh it is you my daughter. You should have chosen a better

time to scare me to death. The hour of victory is no time for any
woman to die.

SIDI: Why? What battle have you won?

SADIKU: Not me alone girl. You too. Every woman. Oh my daughter, that I have lived to see this day . . . To see him fizzle with
the drabbest puff of a mis-primed "sakabula."[1]

    [*Resumes her dance.*]

Take warning, my masters
We'll scotch you in the end.

SIDI: Wait Sadiku. I cannot understand.

SADIKU: You will my girl. You will.

Take warning my masters . . .

SIDI: Sadiku, are you well?

SADIKU: Ask no questions my girl. Just join my victory dance. Oh
Sango my lord, who of us possessed your lightning and ran like
fire through that lion's tail . . .

SIDI: [*holds her firmly as she is about to go off again.*]

Stop your loose ranting. You will not
Move from here until you make some sense.

SADIKU: Oh you are troublesome. Do you promise to tell no one?

SIDI: I swear it. Now tell me quickly.

    [*As* SADIKU *whispers, her eyes widen.*]

O-ho-o-o-o-!
But Sadiku, if he knew the truth, why
Did he ask me to . . .

    [*Again* SADIKU *whispers.*]

Ha ha! Some hope indeed. Oh Sadiku
I suddenly am glad to be a woman.

    [*Leaps in the air.*]

We won! We won! Hurray for womankind!

    [*Falls in behind* SADIKU.]

Take warning, my masters
We'll scotch you in the end. [LAKUNLE *enters unobserved.*]

LAKUNLE: The full moon is not yet, but
The women cannot wait.
They must go mad without it.

    [*The dancing stops.* SADIKU *frowns.*]

SADIKU: The scarecrow is here. Begone fop! This is the world of women.
At this moment our star sits in the centre of the sky. We are supreme.
What is more, we are about to perform a ritual. If you remain, we
will chop you up, we will make you the sacrifice.

LAKUNLE: What is the hag gibbering?

SADIKU: [*advances menacingly.*] You less than man, you less than

---

1. A gun locally made by a blacksmith, not very effective.

the littlest woman, I say begone!

LAKUNLE: [*nettled.*] I will have you know that I am a man
As you will find out if you dare
To lay a hand on me.

SADIKU: [*throws back her head in laughter.*] You a man? Is Baroka
not more of a man than you? And if he is no longer a man, then
what are you? [LAKUNLE, *understanding the meaning, stands rooted,
shocked.*] Come on, dear girl, let him look on if he will. After all,
only *men* are barred from watching this ceremony.
Take warning, my masters
We'll . . .

SIDI: Stop. Sadiku stop. Oh such an idea
Is running in my head. Let me to the palace for
This supper he promised me. Sadiku, what a way
To mock the devil. I shall ask forgiveness
For my hasty words . . . No need to change
My answer and consent to be his bride—he might
Suspect you've told me. But I shall ask a month
To think on it.

SADIKU: [*somewhat doubtful.*] Baroka is no child you know, he will
know I have betrayed him.

SIDI: No, he will not. Oh Sadiku let me go.
I long to see him thwarted, to watch his longing
His twitching hands which this time cannot
Rush to loosen his trouser cords.

SADIKU: You will have to match the Fox's cunning. Use your bashful
looks and be truly repentant. Goad him my child, torment him
until he weeps for shame.

SIDI: Leave it to me. He will never suspect you of decit.

SADIKU: [*with another of her energetic leaps.*] Yo-roooo o! Yo-rororo
o!
Shall I come with you?

SIDI: Will that be wise? You forget
We have not seen each other.

SADIKU: Away then. Away woman. I shall bide here.
Haste back and tell Sadiku how the no-man is.
Away, my lovely child.

LAKUNLE: [*he has listened with increasing horror.*]
No, Sidi, don't. If you care
One little bit for what I feel,
Do not go to torment the man.
Suppose he knows that you have come to jeer—
And he will know, if he is not a fool—
He is a savage thing, degenerate
He would beat a helpless woman if he could . . .

SIDI: [*running off gleefully.*] Ta-raa school teacher. Wait here for me.

LAKUNLE: [*stamps his foot helplessly.*]

Foolish girl! . . . And this is all your work.
Could you not keep a secret?
Must every word leak out of you
As surely as the final drops
Of mother's milk
Oozed from your flattened breast
Generations ago?

SADIKU: Watch your wagging tongue, unformed creature!

LAKUNLE: If any harm befalls her . . .

SADIKU: Woman though she is, she can take better care of herself than you can of her. Fancy a thing like you actually wanting a girl like that, all to your little self. [*Walks round him and looks him up and down.*] Ah! Oba Ala[2] is an accommodating god. What a poor figure you cut!

LAKUNLE: I wouldn't demean myself to bandy words
With a woman of the bush.

SADIKU: At this moment, your betrothed is supping with the Lion.

LAKUNLE: [*pleased at the use of the word "Betrothed."*]

Well, we are not really betrothed as yet,
I mean, she is not promised yet.
But it will come in time, I'm sure.

SADIKU: [*bursts into her cackling laughter,*] The bride-price, is that paid?

LAKUNLE: Mind your own business.

SADIKU: Why don't you do what other men have done. Take a farm for a season. One harvest will be enough to pay the price, even for a girl like Sidi. Or will the smell of the wet soil be too much for your delicate nostrils?

LAKUNLE: I said mind your own business.

SADIKU: A—a—ah. It is true what they say then. You are going to convert the whole village so that no one will ever pay the bride-price again. Ah, you're a clever man. I must admit that it is a good way for getting out of it, but don't you think you'd use more time and energy that way than you would if . . .

LAKUNLE: [*with conviction.*] Within a year or two, I swear,
This town shall see a transformation
Bride-price will be a thing forgotten
And wives shall take their place by men.
A motor road will pass this spot.

---

2. Contraction of Obatala, the god who fashioned the human body.

And bring the city ways to us.
We'll buy saucepans for all the women
Clay pots are crude and unhygienic.
No man shall take more wives than one
That's why they're impotent too soon.
The ruler shall ride cars, not horses
Or a bicycle at the very least.
We'll burn the forest, cut the trees
Then plant a modern park for lovers
We'll print newspapers every day
With pictures of seductive girls.
The world will judge our progress by
The girls that win beauty contests.
While Lagos builds new factories daily
We only play "ayo"[3] and gossip.
Where is our school of Ballroom dancing?
Who here can throw a cocktail party?
We must be modern with the rest
Or live forgotten by the world.
We must reject the palm wine habit
And take to tea, with milk and sugar.

> [*Turns on* SADIKU *who has been staring at him in terror. She retreats, and he continues to talk down at her as they go round, then down and off-stage,* LAKUNLE's *hectoring voice trailing away in the distance.*]

This is my plan, you withered face
And I shall start by teaching you.
From now you shall attend my school
And take your place with twelve-year olds.
For though you're nearly seventy,
Your mind is simple and unformed.
Have you no shame that at your age,
You neither read nor write nor think?
You spend your days as senior wife,
Collecting brides for Baroka.
And now because you've sucked him dry,
You send my Sidi to his shame. . . .

> [*The scene changes to Baroka's bedroom. On the left in a one-knee-on-floor posture, two men are engaged in a kind of wrestling, their arms clasped round each other's waist, testing the right moment to leave. One is* BAROKA, *the other a short squat figure of apparent muscular power. The contest is still in the*

---

3. A widely played board game.

balanced stage. *In some distant part of the house,* SIDI's *voice is heard lifted in the familiar general greeting, addressed to no one in particular.*]

SIDI: A good day to the head and people
Of this house.

[BAROKA *lifts his head, frowns as if he is trying to place the voice.*]

A good day to the head and people
Of this house.

[BAROKA *now decides to ignore it and to concentrate on the contest.* SIDI's *voice draws progressively nearer. She enters nearly backwards, as she is still busy admiring the room through which she has just passed. Gasps on turning round to see the two men.*]

BAROKA: [*without looking up.*] Is Sadiku not at home then?

SIDI: [*absent-mindedly.*] Hm?

BAROKA: I asked, is Sadiku not at home?

SIDI: [*recollecting herself, she curtsys quickly.*] I saw no one, Baroka.

BAROKA: No one? Do you mean there was no one
To bar unwanted strangers from my privacy?

SIDI [*retreating.*] The house . . . seemed . . . empty.

BAROKA: Ah, I forget. This is the price I pay
Once every week, for being progressive.
Prompted by the school teacher, my servants
Were prevailed upon to form something they call
The Palace Workers' Union. And in keeping
With the habits—I am told—of modern towns,
This is their day off.

SIDI: [*seeing that* BAROKA *seems to be in a better mood, she becomes somewhat bolder. Moves forward—saucily.*]
Is this also a day off
For Baroka's wives?

BAROKA: [*looks up sharply, relaxes and speaks with a casual voice.*]
No, the madness had not gripped them—yet.
Did you not meet with one of them?

SIDI: No, Baroka. There was no one about.

BAROKA: Not even Ailatu, my favourite?
Was she not at her usual place,
Beside my door?

SIDI: [*absently. She is deeply engrossed in watching the contest.*]
Her stool is there. And I saw
The slippers she was embroidering.

BAROKA: Hm. Hm. I think I know
Where she'll be found. In a dark corner
Sulking like a slighted cockroach.
By the way, look and tell me

If she left her shawl behind.
    [*So as not to miss any part of the tussle, she moves backwards,
    darts a quick look round the door and back again.*]
SIDI: There is a black shawl on the stool.
BAROKA: [*a regretful sigh.*]
    Then she'll be back tonight. I had hoped
    My words were harsh enough
    To free me from her spite for a week or more.
SIDI: Did Ailatu offend her husband?
BAROKA: Offend? My armpit still weeps blood
    For the gross abuse I suffered from one
    I called my favourite.
SIDI: [*in a disappointed voice.*]
    Oh. Is that all?
BAROKA: Is that not enough? Why child?
    What more could the woman do?
SIDI: Nothing. Nothing, Baroka. I thought perhaps—
    Well—young wives are known to be—
    Forward—sometimes—to their husbands.
BAROKA: In an ill-kept household perhaps. But not
    Under Baroka's roof. And yet,
    Such are the sudden spites of women
    That even I cannot foresee them all.
    And child—if I lose this little match
    Remember that my armpit
    Burns and itches turn by turn.
    [SIDI *continues watching for some time, then clasps her hand
    over her mouth as she remembers what she should have done
    to begin with. Doubtful how to proceed, she hesitates for some
    moments, then comes to a decision and kneels.*]
SIDI: I have come, Bale, as a repentant child.
BAROKA: What?
SIDI: [*very hesitantly, eyes to the floor, but she darts a quick look up
    when she thinks the Bale isn't looking.*]
    The answer which I sent to the Bale
    Was given in a thoughtless moment . . .
BAROKA: Answer, child? To what?
SIDI: A message brought by . . .
BAROKA: [*groans and strains in a muscular effort.*]   Will you say that
    again? It is true that for supper
    I did require your company. But up till now
    Sadiku has brought no reply.
SIDI: [*amazed.*] But the other matter! Did not the Bale
    Send . . . did Baroka not send . . . ?
BAROKA: [*with sinister encouragement.*]

What did Baroka not, my child?

SIDI: [*cowed, but angry, rises.*]
  It is nothing, Bale. I only hope
  That I am here at the Bale's invitation.

BAROKA: [*as if trying to understand, he frowns as he looks at her.*]
  A-ah, at last I understand. You think
  I took offence because you entered
  Unannounced?

SIDI: I remember that the Bale called me
  An unwanted stranger.

BAROKA: That could be expected. Is a man's bedroom
  To be made naked to any flea
  That chances to wander through?
      [SIDI *turns away, very hurt.*]
  Come, come, my child. You are too quick
  To feel aggrieved. Of course you are
  More than welcome. But I expected Ailatu
  To tell me you were here.
      [SIDI *curtsys briefly with her back to* BAROKA. *After a while, she
      turns round. The mischief returns to her face. Baroka's attitude
      of denial has been a setback but she is now ready to pursue her
      mission.*]

SIDI: I hope the Bale will not think me
  Forward. But, like everyone, I had thought
  The Favourite was a gentle woman.

BAROKA: And so had I.

SIDI: [*slyly.*] One would hardly think that *she*
  Would give offence without a cause
  Was the Favourite . . . in some way . . .
  Dissatisfied . . . with her lord and husband?
      [*With a mock curtsy, quickly executed as* BAROKA *begins to look
      up.*]

BAROKA: [*slowly turns towards her.*]
        Now that
  Is a question which I never thought to hear
  Except from a school teacher. Do you think
  The Lion has such leisure that he asks
  The whys and wherefores of a woman's
  Squint?
      [SIDI *steps back and curtsys. As before, and throughout this scene,
      she is easily cowed by Baroka's change of mood, all the more
      easily as she is, in any case, frightened by her own boldness.*]

SIDI: I meant no disrespect . . .

BAROKA: [*gently.*] I know. [*Breaks off.*] Christians on my
  Father's shrines, child!

Do you think I took offence? A—aw
Come in and seat yourself. Since you broke in
Unawares, and appear resolved to stay,
Try, if you can, not to make me feel
A humourless old ram. I allow no one
To watch my daily exercise, but as we say,
The woman gets lost in the woods one day
And every wood deity dies the next.

> [SIDI *curtsys, watches and moves forward warily, as if expecting
> the two men to spring apart too suddenly.*]

SIDI: I think he will win.
BAROKA: Is that a wish, my daughter?
SIDI: No, but—[*Hesitates, but boldness wins.*]
>   If the tortoise cannot tumble
> It does not mean that he can stand.

> [BAROKA *looks at her, seemingly puzzled.* SIDI *turns away, hum-
> ming.*]

BAROKA: When the child is full of riddles, the mother
    Has one water-pot the less.

> [SIDI *tiptoes to Baroka's back and pulls asses' ears at him.*]

SIDI: I think he will win.
BAROKA: He knows he must. Would it profit me
    To pit my strength against a weakling?
    Only yesterday, this son of—I suspect—
    A python for a mother, and fathered beyond doubt
    By a blubber-bottomed baboon,

> [*The complimented man grins.*]

    Only yesterday, he nearly
    Ploughed my tongue with my front teeth
    In a friendly wrestling bout.

WRESTLER: [*encouraged, makes an effort.*] Ugh. Ugh.
SIDI: [*bent almost over them. Genuinely worried.*]
    Oh! Does it hurt?
BAROKA: Not yet . . . but, as I was saying
    I change my wrestlers when I have learnt
    To throw them. I also change my wives
    When I have learnt to tire them.
SIDI: And is this another . . . changing time
    For the Bale?
BAROKA: Who knows? Until the finger nails
    Have scraped the dust, no one can tell
    Which insect released his bowels.

> [SIDI *grimaces in disgust and walks away. Returns as she thinks
> up a new idea.*]

SIDI: A woman spoke to me this afternoon.

BAROKA: Indeed. And does Sidi find this unusual—
    That a woman speak with her in the afternoon?
SIDI: [*stamping.*] No. She had the message of a go-between.
BAROKA: Did she? Then I rejoice with you.
    [SIDI *stands biting her lips.* BAROKA *looks at her, this time with*
      deliberate appreciation.]
    And now I think of it, why not?
    There must be many men who
    Build their loft to fit your height.
SIDI: [*unmoving, pointedly.*] Her message came from one
    With many lofts.
BAROKA: Ah! Such is the greed of men.
SIDI: If Baroka were my father
[*aside*]—which many would take him to be—
    [*Makes a rude sign.*]
    Would he pay my dowry to this man
    And give his blessings?
BAROKA: Well, I must know his character.
    For instance, is the man rich?
SIDI: Rumour has it so.
BAROKA: Is he repulsive?
SIDI: He is old. [BAROKA *winces.*]
BAROKA: Is he mean and miserly?
SIDI: To strangers—no. There are tales
    Of his open-handedness, which are never
    Quite without a motive. But his wives report
    —to take one little story—
    How he grew the taste for ground corn
    And pepper—because he would not pay
    The price of snuff!
    [*With a sudden burst of angry energy,* BAROKA *lifts his opponent*
    and throws him over his shoulder.]
BAROKA: A lie! The price of snuff
    Had nothing to do with it.
SIDI: [*too excited to listen.*] You won!
BAROKA: By the years on my beard, I swear
    They slander me!
SIDI: [*excitedly.*] You won. You won!
    [*She breaks into a kind of shoulder dance and sings.*]
    Yokolu Yokolu. Ko ha tan bi
    Iyawo gb'oko san'le
    Oko yo 'ke . . .[4]

---

4. Not completely translatable: sung or drummed as a message to announce a huge disgrace, or
to provoke an opponent after a defeat. *Ko ha tan bi* means "it is finished," and the implied
reference is to a wife's throwing her husband so heavily that he develops a hunchback. *Ako*, bench:
a strong bench.

[*She repeats this throughout Baroka's protests.* BAROKA *is pacing angrily up and down. The defeated man, nursing a hip, goes to the corner of the room and lifts out a low "ako" bench. He sits on the floor, and soon,* BAROKA *joins him; using only their arms now, they place their elbows on the bench and grip hands.* BAROKA *takes his off again, replaces it, takes it off again and so on during the rest of his outburst.*]

BAROKA: This means nothing to me of course. Nothing!
But I know the ways of women, and I know
Their ruinous tongues.
Suppose that, as a child—only suppose—
Suppose then, that as a child, I—
And remember, I only use myself
To illustrate the plight of many men . . .
So, once again, suppose that as a child
I grew to love "tanfiri"[5]—with a good dose of pepper
And growing old, I found that—
Sooner than die away, my passion only
Bred itself upon each mouthful of
Ground corn and pepper I consumed.
Now, think child, would it be seemly
At my age, and the father of children,
To be discovered, in public
Thrusting fistfuls of corn and pepper
In my mouth? Is it not wise to indulge
In the little masquerade of a dignified
Snuff-box?—But remember, I only make
A pleading for this prey of women's
Malice. I feel his own injustice,
Being myself, a daily fellow-sufferer!
    [BAROKA *seems to realize for the first time that* SIDI *has paid no attention to his explanation. She is, in fact, still humming and shaking her shoulders. He stares questioningly at her.* SIDI *stops, somewhat confused and embarrassed, points sheepishly to the wrestler.*]

SIDI: I think this time he will win.
    [BAROKA's *grumbling subsides slowly. He is now attentive to the present bout.*]

BAROKA: Now let us once again take up
The questioning. [*Almost timidly.*] Is this man
Good and kindly.

SIDI: They say he uses well
His dogs and horses.

BAROKA: [*desperately.*]

---

5. A local food.

Well is he fierce then? Reckless!
Does the bush cow run to hole
When he hears his beaters' Hei-ei-wo-rah!

SIDI: There are heads and skins of leopards
Hung around his council room.
But the market is also
Full of them.

BAROKA: Is he not wise? Is he not sagely?
Do the young and old not seek
His counsel?

SIDI: The Fox is said to be wise
So cunning that he stalks and dines on
New-hatched chickens.

BAROKA: [*more and more desperate.*]
Does he not beget strength on wombs?
Are his children not tall and stout-limbed?

SIDI: Once upon a time.

BAROKA: Once upon a time?
What do you mean, girl?

SIDI: Just once upon a time
Perhaps his children have of late
Been plagued with shyness and refuse
To come into the world. Or else
He is so tired with the day's affairs
That at night, he turns his buttocks
To his wives. But there have been
No new reeds cut by his servants,
No new cots woven.
And his household gods are starved
For want of child-naming festivities
Since the last two rains went by.

BAROKA: Perhaps he is a frugal man.
Mindful of years to come,
Planning for a final burst of life, he
Husbands his strength.

SIDI: [*giggling. She is actually stopped, half-way, by giggling at the cleverness of her remark.*]
To husband his wives surely ought to be
A man's first duties—at all times.

BAROKA: My beard tells me you've been a pupil,
A most diligent pupil of Sadiku.
Among all shameless women,
The sharpest tongues grow from that one
Peeling bark—Sadiku, my faithful lizard!
[*Growing steadily warmer during this speech, he again slaps*

down his opponent's arm as he shouts "Sadiku."]

SIDI: [*backing away, aware that she has perhaps gone too far and betrayed knowledge of the "secret."*]

I have learnt nothing of anyone.

BAROKA: No more. No more.
Already I have lost a wrestler
On your account. This town-bred daring
Of little girls, awakes in me
A seven-horned devil of strength.
Let one woman speak a careless word
And I can pin a wriggling—Bah!
[*Lets go the man's arm. He has risen during the last speech but held on to the man's arm, who is forced to rise with him.*]
The tappers should have called by now.
See if we have a fresh gourd by the door.
[*The wrestler goes out.* BAROKA *goes to sit on the bed,* SIDI *eyeing him, doubtfully.*]
What an ill-tempered man I daily grow
Towards. Soon my voice will be
The sand between two grinding stones.
But I have my scattered kindliness
Though few occasions serve to herald it.
And Sidi, my daughter, you do not know
The thoughts which prompted me
To ask the pleasure that I be your host
This evening, I would not tell Sadiku,
Meaning to give delight
With the surprise of it. Now, tell me, child
Can you guess a little at this thing?

SIDI: Sadiku told me nothing.

BAROKA: You are hasty with denial. For how indeed
Could Sadiku, since I told her
Nothing of my mind, But, my daughter,
Did she not, perhaps . . . invent some tale?
For I know Sadiku loves to be
All-knowing.

SIDI: She said no more, except the Bale
Begged my presence.

BAROKA: [*rises quickly to the bait.*]
Begged? Bale Baroka begged?
[*Wrestler enters with gourd and calabash-cups.* BAROKA *relapses.*]
Ah! I see you love to bait your elders.
One way the world remains the same,
The child still thinks she is wiser than
The cotton head of age.

Do you think Baroka deaf or blind
To little signs? But let that pass.
Only, lest you fall victim to the schemes
Of busy women, I will tell you this—
I know Sadiku plays the match-maker
Without the prompting. If I look
On any maid, or call her name
Even in the course of harmless, neighbourly
Well-wishing—How fares your daughter?
—Is your sister now recovered from her
Whooping cough?—How fast your ward
Approaches womanhood! Have the village lads
Begun to gather at your door?—
Or any word at all which shows I am
The thoughtful guardian of the village health,
If it concerns a woman, Sadiku straightway
Flings herself into the role of go-between
And before I even don a cap, I find
Yet another stranger in my bed!

SIDI: It seems a Bale's life
   Is full of great unhappiness.

BAROKA: I do not complain. No, my child
   I accept the sweet and sour with
   A ruler's grace. I lose my patience
   Only when I meet with
   The new immodesty with women.
   Now, my Sidi, you have not caught
   This new and strange disease, I hope.

SIDI: [curtsying.] The threading of my smock—
   Does Baroka not know the marking
   Of the village loom?

BAROKA: But will Sidi, the pride of mothers,
   Will she always wear it?

SIDI: Will Sidi, the proud daughter of Baroka,
   Will she step out naked?
      [A pause. BAROKA surveys SIDI in an almost fatherly manner and
      she bashfully drops her eyes.]

BAROKA: To think that once I thought,
   Sidi is the eye's delight, but
   She is vain, and her head
   Is feather-light, and always giddy
   With a trivial thought. And now
   I find her deep and wise beyond her years.
      [Reaches under his pillow, brings out the now familiar maga-

*zine, and also an addressed envelope. Retains the former and
gives her the envelope.*]

Do you know what this means?
The trim red piece of paper
In the corner?

SIDI: I know it. A stamp. Lakunle receives
Letters from Lagos marked with it.

BAROKA: [*obviously disappointed.*]
Hm. Lakunle. But more about him
Later. Do you know what it means—
This little frippery?

SIDI: [*very proudly.*]
Yes. I know that too. Is it not a tax on
The habit of talking with paper?

BAROKA: Oh. Oh. I see you dip your hand
Into the pockets of the school teacher
And retrieve it bulging with knowledge.
    [*Goes to the strange machine, and pulls the lever up and down.*]
Now this, not even the school teacher can tell
What magic this performs. Come nearer,
It will not bite.

SIDI: I have never seen the like.

BAROKA: The work dear child, of the palace blacksmiths
    Built in full secrecy. All is not well with it—
    But I will find the cause and then Ilujinle
    Will boast its own tax on paper, made with
    Stamps like this. For long I dreamt it
    And here it stands, child of my thoughts.

SIDI: [*wonder-struck.*] You mean . . . this will work some day?

BAROKA: Ogun has said the word. And now my girl
    What think you of that image on the stamp
    This spiderwork of iron, wood and mortar?

SIDI: Is it not a bridge?

BAROKA: It is a bridge. The longest—so they say—
    In the whole country. When not a bridge,
    You'll find a print of groundnuts
    Stacked like pyramids,
    Or palm trees, or cocoa-trees, and farmers
    Hacking pods, and workmen
    Felling trees and tying skinned logs
    Into rafts. A thousand thousand letters
    By road, by rail, by air,
    From one end of the world to another,
    And not one human head among them;

Not one head of beauty on the stamp?

SIDI: But I once saw Lakunle's letter
With a head of bronze.

BAROKA: A figurehead, my child, a lifeless work
Of craft, with holes for eyes, and coldness
For the warmth of life and love
In youthful cheeks like yours,
My daughter . . .
[*Pauses to watch the effect on* SIDI.]
. . . Can you see it, Sidi?
Tens of thousands of these dainty prints
And each one with this legend of Sidi.
[*Flourishes the magazine, open in the middle.*]
The village goddess, reaching out
Towards the sun, her lover.
Can you see it, my daughter!
[SIDI *drowns herself totally in the contemplation, takes the magazine but does not even look at it. Sits on the bed.*]

BAROKA: [*very gently.*]
I hope you will not think it too great
A burden, to carry the country's mail
All on your comeliness.
[*Walks away, an almost business-like tone.*]
Our beginnings will
Of course be modest. We shall begin
By cutting stamps for our own village alone.
As the schoolmaster himself would say—
Charity begins at home.
[*Pause. Faces* SIDI *from nearly the distance of the room.*]
For a long time now,
The town-dwellers have made up tales
Of the backwardness of Ilujinle
Until it hurts Baroka, who holds
The welfare of his people deep at heart.
Now, if we do this thing, it will prove more
Than any single town has done!
[*The wrestler, who has been listening open-mouthed, drops his cup in admiration.* BAROKA, *annoyed, realizing only now in fact that he is still in the room, waves him impatiently out.*]
I do not hate progress, only its nature
Which makes all roofs and faces look the same.
And the wish of one old man is
That here and there,
[*Goes progressively towards* SIDI, *until he bends over her, then sits beside her on the bed.*]

Among the bridges and the murderous roads,
Below the humming birds which
Smoke the face of Sango, dispenser of
The snake-tongue lightning; between this moment
And the reckless broom that will be wielded
In these years to come, we must leave
Virgin plots of lives, rich decay
And the tang of vapour rising from
Forgotten heaps of compost, lying
Undisturbed . . . But the skin of progress
Masks, unknown, the spotted wolf of sameness . . .
Does sameness not revolt your being,
My daughter?
   [SIDI *is capable only of a bewildered nod, slowly.*]
BAROKA: [*sighs, hands folded piously on his lap.*]
  I find my soul is sensitive, like yours,
  Indeed, although there is one—no more think I—
  One generation between yours and mine,
  Our thoughts fly crisply through the air
  And meet, purified, as one.
  And our first union
  Is the making of this stamp.
  The one redeeming grace on any paper-tax
  Shall be your face. And mine,
  The soul behind it all, worshipful
  Of Nature for her gift of youth
  And beauty to our earth. Does this
  Please you, my daughter?
SIDI: I can no longer see the meaning, Baroka.
  Now that you speak
  Almost like the school teacher, except
  Your words fly on a different path,
  I find . . .
BAROKA: It is a bad thing, then, to sound
  Like your school teacher?
SIDI: No Bale, but words are like beetles
  Boring at my ears, and my head
  Becomes a jumping bean. Perhaps after all,
  As the school teacher tells me often,
    [*Very miserably.*]
  I have a simple mind.
BAROKA: [*pats her kindly on the head.*]
  No, Sidi, not simple, only straight and truthful
  Like a fresh-water reed. But I do find
  Your school teacher and I are much alike.

The proof of wisdom is the wish to learn
Even from children. And the haste of youth
Must learn its temper from the gloss
Of ancient leather, from a strength
Knit close along the grain. The school teacher
And I, must learn one from the other.
Is this not right?
    [*A tearful nod.*]

BAROKA: The old must flow into the new, Sidi,
Not blind itself or stand foolishly
Apart. A girl like you must inherit
Miracles which age alone reveals
Is this not so?

SIDI: Everything you say, Bale,
Seems wise to me.

BAROKA: Yesterday's wine alone is strong and blooded, child,
And though the Christians' holy book denies
The truth of this, old wine thrives best
Within a new bottle. The coarseness
Is mellowed down, and the rugged wine
Acquires a full and rounded body . . .
Is this not so—my child?
    [*Quite overcome,* SIDI *nods.*]

BAROKA: Those who know little of Baroka think
His life one pleasure-living course.
But the monkey sweats, my child,
The monkey sweats,
It is only the hair upon his back
Which still deceives the world . . .
    [SIDI's *head falls slowly on the Bale's shoulder. The Bale remains
in his final body-weighed-down-by-burdens-of-State attitude.
Even before the scene is completely shut off a crowd of dancers
burst in at the front and dance off at the opposite side without
slackening pace. In their brief appearance it should be apparent
that they comprise a group of female dancers pursuing a masked
male. Drumming and shouts continue quite audibly and shortly
afterwards. They enter and re-cross the stage in the same manner.*

    *The shouts fade away and they next appear at the market clear-
ing. It is now full evening.* LAKUNLE *and* SADIKU *are still waiting
for Sidi's return. The traders are beginning to assemble one by
one, ready for the evening market. Hawkers pass through with
oil-lamps beside their ware. Food sellers enter with cooking-
pots and foodstuffs, set up their "adogan," or stone hearth and
build a fire.*]

All this while, LAKUNLE *is pacing wretchedly,* SADIKU *looks on placidly.*]

LAKUNLE: [*he is pacing furiously.*]

He's killed her.

I warned you. You know him,

And I warned you.

   [*Goes up all the approaches to look.*]

She's been gone half the day. It will soon

Be daylight. And still no news.

Women have disappeared before.

No trace. Vanished. Now we know how.

   [*Checks, turns round.*]

And why!

Mock an old man, will you? So?

You can laugh? Ha ha! You wait.

I'll come and see you

Whipped like a dog. Baroka's head wife

Driven out of the house for plotting

With a girl.

   [*Each approaching footstep brings* LAKUNLE *to attention, but it is only a hawker or a passer-by. The wrestler passes.* SADIKU *greets him familiarly. Then, after he has passed, some significance of this breaks on* SADIKU *and she begins to look a little puzzled.*]

LAKUNLE: I know he has dungeons. Secret holes

Where a helpless girl will lie

And rot for ever. But not for nothing

Was I born a man. I'll find my way

To rescue her. She little deserves it, but

I shall risk my life for her.

   [*The mummers can now be heard again, distantly.* SADIKU *and* LAKUNLE *become attentive as the noise approaches,* LAKUNLE *increasingly uneasy. A little, but not too much notice is paid by the market people.*]

What is that?

SADIKU: If my guess is right, it will be mummers. [*Adds slyly.*] Somebody must have told them the news.

LAKUNLE: What news?

   [SADIKU *chuckles darkly and comprehension breaks on the School teacher.*]

Baroka! You dared . . . ?

Woman, is there no mercy in your veins?

He gave you children, and he stood

Faithfully by you and them.

He risked his life that you may boast

A warrior-hunter for your lord . . . But you—
You sell him to the rhyming rabble
Gloating in your disloyalty . . .

SADIKU: [*calmly dips her hand in his pocket.*]
Have you any money?

LAKUNLE: [*snatching out her hand.*]
Why? What? . . . Keep away, witch! Have you
Turned pickpocket in your dotage?

SADIKU: Don't be a miser. Will you let them go without giving you a special performance?

LAKUNLE: If you think I care for their obscenity . . .

SADIKU: [*wheedling.*] Come on, school teacher. They'll expect it of you . . . The man of learning . . . the young sprig of foreign wisdom . . . You must not demean yourself in their eyes . . . you must give them money to perform for your lordship . . .

[*Re-enter the mummers, dancing straight through (more centrally this time) as before. Male dancer enters first, pursued by a number of young women and other choral idlers. The man dances in tortured movements. He and about half of his pursuers have already danced off-stage on the opposite side when* SADIKU *dips her hand briskly in Lakunle's pocket, this time with greater success. Before* LAKUNLE *can stop her, she has darted to the drummers and pressed a coin apiece on their foreheads, waving them to possession of the floor. Tilting their heads backwards, they drum her praises.* SADIKU *denies the credit, points to* LAKUNLE *as the generous benefactor. They transfer their attention to him where he stands biting his lips at the trick. The other dancers have now been brought back and the drummers resume the beat of thei interrupted dance. The treasurer removes the coins from their foreheads and placed them in a pouch. Now begins the dance of virility which is of course none other than the Baroka story. Very athletic movements. Even in his prime, "Baroka" is made a comic figure, held in a kind of tolerant respect by his women. At his decline and final downfall, they are most unsparing in their taunts and tantalizing motions.* SADIKU *has never stopped bouncing on her toes through the dance, now she is done the honour of being invited to join at the kill. A dumb show of bashful refusals, then she joins them, reveals surprising agility for her age, to the wild enthusiasm of the rest who surround and spur her on. With "Baroka" finally scotched, the crowd dances away to their incoming movement, leaving* SADIKU *to dance on oblivious of their departure. The drumming becomes more distant and she unwraps her eyelids. Sighs, looks around her and walks contentedly towards* LAKUNLE. *As usual he has enjoyed the specta-*

*cle in spite of himself, showing especial relish where "Baroka"
gets the worst of it from his women.* SADIKU *looks at him for a
moment while he tries to replace his obvious enjoyment with
disdain. She shouts "Boo" at him, and breaks into a dance
movement, shakes a sudden leg at* LAKUNLE.]

SADIKU: Sadiku of the duiker's feet . . . that's what the men used to
call me. I could twist and untwist my waist with the smoothness
of a water snake . . .

LAKUNLE: No doubt. And you are still just as slippery.
I hope Baroka kills you for this.
When he finds out what your wagging tongue
Has done to him, I hope he beats you
Till you choke on your own breath . . .
[SIDI *bursts in, she has been running all the way. She throws
herself on the ground against the tree and sobs violently, beat-
ing herself on the ground.*]

SADIKU: [*on her knees beside her.*] Why, child. What is the matter?

SIDI: [*pushes her off.*]
Get away from me. Do not touch me.

LAKUNLE: [*with a triumphant smile, he pulls* SADIKU *away and takes
her place.*]
Oh, Sidi, let me kiss your tears . . .

SIDI: [*pushes him so hard that he sits down abruptly.*]
Don't touch me.

LAKUNLE: [*dusting himself.*]
He must have beaten her.
Did I not warn you both?
Baroka is a creature of the wilds,
Untutored, mannerless, devoid of grace.
[SIDI *only cries all the more, beats on the ground with clenched
fists and stubs her toes in the ground.*]
Chief though he is,
I shall kill him for this . . .
No. Better still, I shall demand
Redress from the central courts.
I shall make him spend
The remainder of his wretched life
In prison—with hard labour.
I'll teach him
To beat defenceless women . . .

SIDI: [*lifting her head.*]
Fool! You little fools! It was a lie.
The frog. The cunning frog!
He lied to you, Sadiku.

SADIKU: Sango forbid!

SIDI: He told me . . . afterwards, crowing.
    It was a trick.
    He knew Sadiku would not keep it to herself,
    That I, or maybe other maids would hear of it
    And go to mock his plight.
    And how he laughed!
    How his frog-face croaked and croaked
    And called me little fool!
    Oh how I hate him! How I loathe
    And long to kill the man!
LAKUNLE: [retreating.] But Sidi, did he . . . ? I mean . . .
    Did you escape?
        [Louder sobs from SIDI.]
    Speak, Sidi, this is agony.
    Tell me the worst; I'll take it like a man.
    Is it the fright which effects you so,
    Or did he . . . ? Sidi, I cannot bear the thought.
    The words refuse to form.
    Do not unman me, Sidi. Speak
    Before I burst in tears.
SADIKU: [raises SIDI's chin in her hand.]
    Sidi, are you a maid or not?
        [SIDI shakes her head violently and bursts afresh in tears.]
LAKUNLE: The Lord forbid!
SADIKU: Too late for prayers. Cheer up. It happens to the best of us.
LAKUNLE: Oh heavens, strike me dead!
    Earth, open up and swallow Lakunle.
    For he no longer has the wish to live.
    Let the lightning fall and shrivel me
    To dust and ashes . . .
        [Recoils.]
    No, that wish is cowardly. This trial is my own.
    Let Sango and his lightning keep out of this. It
    Is my cross, and let it not be spoken that
    In the hour of need, Lakunle stood
    Upon the scales and was proved wanting.
    My love is selfless—the love of spirit
    Not of flesh.
        [Stands over SIDI.]
    Dear Sidi, we shall forget the past.
    This great misfortune touches not
    The treasury of my love.
    But you will agree, it is only fair
    That we forget the bride-price totally

Since you no longer can be called a maid.
Here is my hand; if on these terms,
You'll be my cherished wife.
We'll take an oath, between us three
That this shall stay
A secret to our dying days . . .
    [*Takes a look at* SADIKU *and adds quickly.*]
Oh no, a secret even after we're dead and gone.
And if Baroka dares to boast of it,
I'll swear he is a liar—and swear by Sango too!
    [SIDI *raises herself slowly, staring at* LAKUNLE *with unbelieving
    eyes. She is unsmiling, her face a puzzle.*]

SIDI: You would? You would marry me?
LAKUNLE: [*puffs out his chest.*] Yes.
    [*Without a change of expression,* SIDI *dashes suddenly off the
    stage.*]
SADIKU: What on earth has got into her?
LAKUNLE: I wish I knew
    She took off suddenly
    Like a hunted buck.
      [*Looks off-stage.*]
    I think—yes, she is,
    She is going home.
    Sadiku, will you go?
    Find out if you can
    What she plans to do.
      [SADIKU *nods and goes.* LAKUNLE *walks up and down.*]
    And now I know I am the biggest fool
    That ever walked this earth.
    There are women to be found
    In every town or village in these parts,
    And every one a virgin.
    But I obey my books.
      [*Distant music. Light drums, flutes, box-guitars, "sekere."*[6]]
    "Man takes the fallen woman by the hand"
    And ever after they live happily.
    Moreover, I will admit,
    It solves the problem of her bride-price too.
    A man must live or fall by his true
    Principles. That, I had sworn,
    Never to pay.
      [*Enter* SADIKU.]

---

6. A musical instrument made of a calabash netted with strings of cowrie shells, and shaken.

SADIKU: She is packing her things. She is gathering her clothes and
   trinkets together, and oiling herself as a bride does before her wed-
   ding.
LAKUNLE: Heaven help us! I am not impatient.
   Surely she can wait a day or two at least.
   There is the asking to be done,
   And then I have to hire a praise-singer,
   And such a number of ceremonies
   Must firstly be performed.
SADIKU: Just what I said but she only laughed at me and called me a
   . . . a . . . what was it now . . . a bra . . . braba . . . brabararian.
   It serves you right. It all comes of your teaching. I said what about
   the asking and the other ceremonies. And she looked at me and
   said, leave all that nonsense to savages and brabararians.
LAKUNLE: But I must prepare myself.
   I cannot be
   A single man one day and a married one the next.
   It must come gradually.
   I will not wed in haste.
   A man must have time to prepare,
   To learn to like the thought.
   I must think of my pupils too:
   Would they be pleased if I were married
   Not asking their consent . . . ?
      [*The singing group is now audible even to him.*]
   What is that? The musicians?
   Could they have learnt so soon?
SADIKU: The news of a festivity travels fast. You ought to know that.
LAKUNLE: The goddess of malicious gossip
   Herself must have a hand in my undoing.
   The very spirits of the partial air
   Have all conspired to blow me, willy-nilly
   Down the slippery slope of grim matrimony.
   What evil have I done . . . ? Ah, here they come!
      [*Enter crowd and musicians.*]
   Go back. You are not needed yet. Nor ever.
   Hence parasites, you've made a big mistake.
   There is no one getting wedded; get you home.
      [SIDI *now enters. In one hand she holds a bundle, done up in a
      richly embroidered cloth: in the other the magazine. She is
      radiant, jewelled, lightly clothed, and wears light leather-thong
      sandals. They all go suddenly silent except for the long-drawn
      O-Ohs of admiration. She goes up to* LAKUNLE *and hands him
      the book.*]
SIDI: A present from Sidi.

I tried to tear it up
But my fingers were too frail.
[*To the crowd.*]
Let us go.
[*To* LAKUNLE.]
You may come too if you wish,
You are invited.
LAKUNLE: [*lost in the miracle of transformation.*]
Well I should hope so indeed
Since I am to marry you.
SIDI: [*turns round in surprise.*]
Marry who . . . ? You thought . . .
Did you really think that you, and I . . .
Why, did you think that after him,
I could endure the touch of another man?
I who have felt the strength,
The perpetual youthful zest
Of the panther of the trees?
And would I choose a watered-down,
A beardless version of unripened man?
LAKUNLE: [*bars her way.*]
I shall not let you.
I shall protect you from yourself.
SIDI: [*gives him a shove that sits him down again, hard against the
tree base.*]
Out of my way, book-nourished shrimp.
Do you see what strength he has given me?
That was not bad. For a man of sixty,
It was the secret of God's own draught
A deed for drums and ballads.
But you, at sixty, you'll be ten years dead!
In fact, you'll not survive your honeymoon . . .
Come to my wedding if you will. If not . . .
[*She shrugs her shoulders. Kneels down at Sadiku's feet.*]
Mother of brides, your blessing . . .
SADIKU: [*lays her hand on Sidi's head.*] I invoke the fertile gods. They
will stay with you. May the time come soon when you shall be as
round-bellied as a full moon in a low sky.
SIDI: [*hands her the bundle.*]
Now bless my wordly goods.
[*Turns to the musicians.*]
Come, sing to me of seeds
Of children, sired of the lion stock.
[*The Musicians resume their tune.* SIDI *sings and dances.*]
Mo te'ni. Mo te'ni.

Mo te'ni. Mo te'ni.
Sun mo mi, we mo mi
Sun mo mi, fa mo mi
Yarabi lo m'eyi t'o le d'omo . . .

[*Festive air, fully pervasive. Oil lamps from the market mulitply
as traders desert their stalls to join them. A young girl flaunts
her dancing buttocks at* LAKUNLE *and he rises to the bait.* SADIKU
*gets in his way as he gives chase. Tries to make him dance with
her.* LAKUNLE *last seen, having freed himself of* SADIKU, *clearing
a space in the crowd for the young girl.*

The crowd repeat the song after SIDI.]

Tolani Tolani
T'emi ni T'emi ni
Sun mo mi, we mo mi
Sun mo mi, fa mo mi
Yarabi lo m'eyi t'o le d'omo.[7]

7. "My net is spread, my net is spread
Come close to me, wrap yourself around me
Only God knows which moment makes the child . . .

Tolani Tolani
She belongs to me, belongs to me
Come close to me, wrap yourself around me
Only god knows which moment makes the child."

A Note on Translation

Reading literature in translation is a pleasure on which it is fruitless to frown. The purist may insist that we ought always read in the original languages, and we know ideally that this is true. But it is a counsel of perfection, quite impractical even for the purist, since no one in a lifetime can master all the languages whose literatures it would be a joy to explore. Master languages as fast as we may, we shall always have to read to some extent in translation, and this means we must be alert to what we are about: if in reading a work of literature in translation we are not reading the "original," what preciely are we reading? This is a question of great complexity, to which justice cannot be done in a brief note, but the following sketch of some of the considerations may be helpful.

One of the memorable scenes of ancient literature is the meeting of Hector and Andromache in Book VI of Homer's *Iliad*. Hector, leader and mainstay of the armies defending Troy, is implored by his wife Andromache to withdraw within the city walls and carry on the defense from there, where his life will not be constantly at hazard. In Homer's text her opening words to him are these: δαιμόνιε, φθίσει σε τὸ σὸν μένος (daimonie, phthisei se to son menos). How should they be translated into English?

Here is how they have actually been translated into English by capable translators, at various periods, in verse and prose.

1. George Chapman, 1598

> O noblest in desire,
> Thy mind, inflamed with others' good, will set thy self on fire.

2. John Dryden, 1693

> Thy dauntless heart (which I foresee too late),
> Too daring man, will urge thee to thy fate.

3. Alexander Pope, 1715

> Too daring Prince! . . .
> For sure such courage length of life denies,
> And thou must fall, thy virtue's sacrifice.

4. William Cowper, 1791

> Thy own great courage will cut short thy days,
> My noble Hector. . . .

5. Lang, Leaf, and Myers, 1883 (prose)

> Dear my lord, this thy hardihood will undo thee. . . .

6. A. T. Murray, 1924 (prose, Loeb Library)

> Ah, my husband, this prowess of thine will be thy doom. . . .

7. E. V. Rieu, 1950 (prose)

> "Hector," she said, "you are possessed. This bravery of yours will be your end."

8. I. A. Richards, 1950 (prose)

> "Strange man," she said, "your courage will be your destruction."

9. Richmond Lattimore, 1951

> Dearest,
> Your own great strength will be your death. . . .

From these strikingly different renderings of the same six words, certain facts about the nature of translation begin to emerge. We notice, for one thing, that Homer's word μένος (menos) is diversified by the translators into "mind," "dauntless heart," "such courage," "great courage," "hardihood," "prowess," "bravery," "courage," and "great strength." The word has in fact all these possibilities. Used of things, it normally means "force"; of animals, "fierceness" or "brute strength" or (in the case of horses) "mettle"; of men, "passion" or "spirit" or even "purpose." Homer's application of it in the present case points our attention equally—whatever particular sense we may imagine Andromache to have uppermost—to Hector's force, strength, fierceness in battle, spirited heart and mind. But since English has no matching term of like inclusiveness, the passage as the translators give it to us reflects this lack and we find one attribute singled out to the exclusion of the rest.

Here then is the first and most crucial fact about any work of literature read in translation. It cannot escape the linguistic characteristics of the language into which it is turned: the grammatical, syntactical, lexical, and phonetic boundaries which constitute collectively the individuality or "genius" of that language. A Greek play or a Russian novel in English will be governed first of all by the resources of the English language, resources which are certain to be in every instance very different, as the efforts with μένος show, from those of the original.

Turning from μένος to δαιμόνιε (daimonie) in Homer's clause, we encounter a second crucial fact about translations. Nobody knows exactly what shade of meaning δαιμόνιε had for Homer. In later writers the word normally suggests divinity, something miraculous, wondrous; but in Homer it appears as a vocative of address for both chieftain and commoner, man and wife. The coloring one gives it must therefore be determined either by the way one thinks a Greek wife of Homer's era might actually address her husband (a subject on which we have no information whatever), or in the way one thinks it suitable for a hero's wife to address her husband in an epic poem, that is to say, a highly stylized and formal work. In general, the translators of our century will be seen to have abandoned formality in order to stress the intimacy, the wifeliness, and, especially in Lattimore's case, a certain chiding tenderness, in Andromache's appeal: (6) "Ah, my husband," (7) "Hector" (with perhaps a hint, in "you are possessed," of the alarmed distaste with which wives have so often viewed their husbands' bellicose moods), (8) "Strange man," (9) "Dearest." On the other hand, the older translators have obviously removed Andromache to an epic or heroic distance from her beloved, whence she sees and kindles to his selfless courage, acknowledging, even in the moment of pleading with him to be otherwise, his moral grandeur and the tragic destiny this too certainly implies: (1) "O noblest in desire, . . . inflamed by others' good"; (2) "Thy dauntless heart (which I foresee too late), / Too daring man"; (3) "Too daring Prince! . . . / And thou must fall, thy virtue's sacrifice"; (4) "My noble Hector." Even the less specific "Dear my lord" of Lang, Leaf, and Myers looks in the same direction because of its echo of the speech of countless Shakespearean men and women who have shared this powerful moral sense: "Dear my lord, make me acquainted with your cause of grief"; "Perseverance, dear my lord, keeps honor bright"; etc.

The fact about translation which emerges from all this is that just as the translated work reflects the individuality of the language it is turned into, so it reflects the individuality of the age in which it is made, and the age will permeate it everywhere like yeast in dough. We think of one kind of permeation when we think of the governing verse forms and attitudes toward verse at a given epoch. In Chapman's time, experiments seeking an "heroic" verse form for English were widespread, and accordingly he tries a "fourteener" couplet (two rhymed lines of seven stresses each) in his *Iliad* and a pentameter couplet in his *Odyssey*. When Dryden and Pope wrote, a closed pentameter couplet had become established as the heroic form *par excellence*. By Cowper's day, thanks largely to the prestige of *Paradise Lost*, the couplet had gone out of fashion for narrative poetry in favor of blank verse. Our age, inclining to prose and in verse to proselike informalities and relaxations, has, predictably, produced half a dozen excellent prose translations of the *Iliad*, but only two in verse (Lattimore's and that of Robert Fitzgerald), both relying on rhythms that are much of the time closer to the verse of William Carlos Williams and some of the prose of novelists like Faulkner than to the swift firm tread of Homer's Greek. For if it is true that what we translate from a given work is what, wearing the spectacles of our time, we see in it, it is also true that we see in it what we have the power to translate.

Of course there are other effects of the translator's epoch on his translation besides those exercised by contemporary taste in verse and verse forms. Chapman writes in a great age of poetic metaphor and therefore almost instinctively translates his understanding of Homer's verb φθίσει (phthisei, "to cause to wane, consume, waste, pine") into metaphorical terms of flame, presenting his Hector to us as a man of burning generosity who will be consumed by his very ardor. This is a conception rooted in large part in the psychology of the Elizabethans, who had the habit of speaking of the soul as

"fire," of one of the four temperaments as "fiery," of even the more material
bodily processes, like digestion, as if they were carried on by the heat of fire
("concoction," "decoction"). It is rooted too in that characteristic Renaissance élan so unforgettably expressed in characters like Tamburlaine and
Dr. Faustus, the former of whom exclaims to the stars above:

> . . . I, the chiefest lamp of all the earth,
> First rising in the East with mild aspect,
> But fixèd now in the meridian line,
> Will send up fire to your turning spheres,
> And cause the sun to borrow light of you. . . .

Pope and Dryden, by contrast, write to audiences for whom strong metaphor has become suspect. They therefore reject the fire image (which we
must recall is not present in the Greek) in favor of a form of speech more
congenial to their age, the *sententia* or aphorism, and give it extra vitality
by making it the scene of a miniature drama: in Dryden's case, the hero's
dauntless heart "urges" him (in the double sense of physical as well as moral
pressure) to his fate; in Pope's, the hero's courage, like a judge, "denies"
continuance of life, with the consequence that he "falls"—and here Pope's
second line suggests analogy to the sacrificial animal—the victim of his own
essential nature, of what he is.

To pose even more graphically the pressures that a translator's period brings,
consider the following lines from Hector's reply to Andromache's appeal that
he withdraw, first in Chapman's Elizabethan version, then in Lattimore's
twentieth-century one:

Chapman, 1598:

>   The spirit I did first breathe
> Did never teach   me that—much less since the contempt of death
> Was settled in me, and my mind knew what a Worthy was,
> Whose office is to lead in fight and give no danger pass
> Without improvement. In this fire must Hector's trial shine.
> Here must his country, father, friends be in him made divine.

Lattimore, 1951:

> and the spirit will not let me, since I have learned to be valiant and
> to fight always among the foremost ranks of the Trojans, winning for
> my own self great glory, and for my father.

If one may exaggerate to make a necessary point, the world of Henry V and
Othello suddenly gives way here to our own, a world whose discomfort with
any form of heroic self-assertion is remarkably mirrored in the burial of
Homer's key terms (*spirit, valiant, fight, foremost, glory*)—five out of twenty-
two words in the original, five out of thirty-six in the translation—in a cush-
ioning huddle of harmless sounds.

Besides the two factors so far mentioned, language and period, as affecting
the character of a translation, there is inevitably a third—the translator, with
a particular degree of talent, a personal way of regarding the work to be
translated, a special hierarchy of values, moral, esthetic, metaphysical (which
may or may not be summed up in a "world view"), and a unique style or

lack of it. But this influence all readers are likely to bear in mind, and it needs no laboring here. That, for example, two translators of Hamlet, one a Freudian, the other a Jungian, will produce impressively different translations is obvious from the fact that when Freudian and Jungian argue about the play in English they often seem to have different plays in mind.

We can now return to the question from which we started. After all allowances have been made for language, age, and individual translator, is anything of the original left? What, in short, does the reader of translations read? Let it be said at once that in utility prose—prose whose function is mainly referential—the reader who reads a translation reads everything that matters. "*Nicht Rauchen,*" "*Défense de Fumer,*" and "*No Smoking,*" posted in a railway car, make their point, and the differences between them in sound and form have no significance for us in that context. Since the prose of a treatise and of most fiction is preponderantly referential, we rightly feel, when we have paid close attention to Cervantes or Montaigne or Machiavelli or Tolstoy in a good English translation, that we have had roughly the same experience as a native Spaniard, Frenchman, Italian, or Russian. But "roughly" is the correct word; for good prose points iconically *to* itself as well as referentially beyond itself, and everything that it points to in itself in the original (rhythms, sounds, idioms, word play, etc.) must alter radically in being translated. The best analogy is to imagine a Van Gogh painting reproduced in the medium of tempera, etching, or engraving: the "picture" remains, but the intricate interanimation of volumes with colorings with brushstrokes has disappeared.

When we move on to poetry, even in its longer narrative and dramatic forms—plays like *Oedipus*, poems like the *Iliad* or the *Divine Comedy*—our situation as English readers worsens appreciably, as the many unlike versions of Andromache's appeal to Hector make very clear. But, again, only appreciably. True, this is the point at which the fact that a translation is *always* an interpretation explodes irresistibly on our attention; but if it is the best translation of its time, like John Ciardi's translation of the *Divine Comedy* for our time, the result will be not only a sensitive interpretation but also a work with intrinsic interest in its own right—at very best, a true work of art, a new poem. It is only when the shorter, primarily lyrical forms of poetry are presented that the reader of translations faces insuperable disadvantage. In these forms, the referential aspect of language has a tendency to disappear into, or, more often, draw its real meaning and accreditation from, the iconic aspect. Let us look for just a moment at a brief poem by Federico García Lorca and its English translation (by Stephen Spender and J. L. Gili):

> *Alto pinar!*
> *Cuatro palomas por el aire van.*
>
> *Cuatro palomas*
> *vuelan y tornan.*
> *Llevan heridas*
> *sus cuatro sombras.*
>
> *Bajo pinar!*
> *Cuatro palomas en la tierra están.*

Above the pine trees:
Four pigeons go through the air.

Four pigeons
fly and turn round.
They carry wounded
their four shadows.

Below the pine trees:
Four pigeons lie on the earth.

In this translation the referential sense of the English words follows with remarkable exactness the referential sense of the Spanish words they replace. But the life of Lorca's poem does not lie in that sense. It lies in such matters as the abruptness, like an intake of breath at a sudden revelation, of the two exclamatory lines (1 and 7), which then exhale musically in images of flight and death; or as the echoings of *palomas* in *heridas* and *sombras*, bringing together (as in fact the hunter's gun has done) these unrelated nouns and the unrelated experiences they stand for in a sequence that seems, momentarily, to have all the logic of a tragic action, in which *doves* become *wounds* become *shadows*; or as the external and internal rhyming among the five verbs, as though all motion must (as in fact it must) end with *están*.

Since none of this can be brought over into another tongue (least of all Lorca's rhythms), the translator must decide between leaving a reader to wonder why Lorca is a poet to be bothered about at all, and making a new but true poem, whose merit will almost certainly be in inverse ratio to its likeness to the original. Samuel Johnson made such a poem in translating Horace's famous *Diffugere nives*, and so did A. E. Housman. If we juxtapose the last two stanzas of each translation, and the corresponding Latin, we can see at a glance that each has the consistency and inner life of a genuine poem, and that neither of them (even if we consider only what is obvious to the eye, the line-lengths) is very close to Horace.

Cum semel occideris, et de te splendida Minos
        fecerit arbitria,
non, Torquate, genus, non te facundia, non te
        restituet pietas.

Infernis neque enim tenebris Diana pudicum
        liberat Hippolytum
nec Lethaea valet Theseus abrumpere caro
        vincula Pirithoo.

Johnson:

Not you, Torquatus, boast of Rome,
When Minos once has fixed your doom,
Or eloquence, or splendid birth,
Or virtue, shall restore to earth.
Hippolytus, unjustly slain,
Diana calls to life in vain;

Nor can the might of Theseus rend
The chains of hell that hold his friend.

Housman:

When thou descendest once the shades among,
   The stern assize and equal judgment o'er,
Not thy long lineage nor thy golden tongue,
   No, nor thy righteousness, shall friend thee more.

Night holds Hippolytus the pure of stain,
   Diana steads him nothing, he must stay;
And Theseus leaves Pirithous in the chain
   The love of comrades cannot take away.

The truth of the matter is that when the translator of short poems chooses to be literal, most or all of the poetry is lost; and when the translator succeeds in forging a new poetry, most or all of the original author is lost. Since there is no way out of this dilemma, we have always been sparing, in this anthology, in our use of short poems in translation, the sole exceptions at the present time being a modest selection from one lyric poet of each of the four major European languages: Petrarch, Baudelaire, Rilke, and Lorca.

We may assure ourselves, then, that the reading of literature in translation is not the disaster it has sometimes been represented. It is true that, however good the translation, we remain at a remove from the original, the remove becoming closest to impassable in the genre of the lyric poem. But with this exception, it is obvious that translation brings us closer by far to the work than we could be if we did not read it at all, or read it with a defective knowledge of the language. "To a thousand cavils," said Samuel Johnson, "one answer is sufficient; the purpose of a writer is to be read, and the criticism which would destroy the power of pleasing must be blown aside." Johnson was defending Pope's Homer for those marks of its own time and place that make it the great interpretation it is; but Johnson's exhilarating common sense applies equally to the problem we are considering here. Literature is to be read, and the criticism that would destroy the reader's power to make some form of contact with much of the world's great writing must indeed be blown aside.

MAYNARD MACK

Index